WEBSTER'S NEW WORLD®

Children's Dictionary

Second Edition, Revised

Editor in Chief
Michael Agnes

WILEY
Wiley Publishing, Inc.

Published simultaneously in Canada

For general information on our other products and services please contact our Customer Care Department within the U.S. at 800-762-2974, outside the U.S. at 317-572-3993 or fax 317-572-4002.

Wiley also publishes its books in a variety of electronic formats. Some content that appears in print may not be available in electronic books. For more information about Wiley products, visit our web site at www.wiley.com.

Library of Congress Cataloging-in-Publication Data:
Webster's New World children's dictionary / editor in chief, Michael Agnes.-- 2nd ed., rev.
p. cm.
ISBN-13: 978-0-471-78688-7
ISBN-10: 0-471-78688-8
1.English language--Dictionaries, Juvenile. I. Title: Children's dictionary. II. Agnes, Michael.
PE1628.5.W3877 2006
423--dc22

2005053750

Manufactured in the United States of America

10 9 8 7 6

Pronunciation Key

Symbol	Key Words
a	c**a**t
ā	**a**pe
ä	c**o**t, c**a**r
e	t**e**n, b**e**rry
ē	m**e**
i	f**i**t, h**e**re
ī	**i**ce, f**i**re
ō	g**o**
ô	l**aw**, f**o**r
oi	**oi**l
oo	l**oo**k, p**u**ll
o͞o	t**oo**l, r**u**le
ou	**ou**t, cr**ow**d
u	**u**p
ʉ	f**u**r, sh**i**rt
ə	**a** in **a**go **e** in ag**e**nt **i** in penc**i**l **o** in at**o**m **u** in circ**u**s

Symbol	Key Words
b	**b**ed
d	**d**og
f	**f**all
g	**g**et
h	**h**elp
j	**j**ump
k	**k**iss, **c**all
l	**l**eg
m	**m**eat
n	**n**ose
p	**p**ut
r	**r**ed
s	**s**ee
t	**t**op
v	**v**at
w	**w**ish
y	**y**ard
z	**z**ebra
ch	**ch**in, ar**ch**
ŋ	ri**ng**, dri**n**k
sh	**sh**e, pu**sh**
th	**th**in, tru**th**
th	**th**en, fa**th**er
zh	mea**s**ure

A heavy stress mark ′ is placed after a syllable that gets a heavy, or primary, stress, as in **picture** (pik′chər).

A light stress mark ʹ is placed after a syllable that gets a weaker, or secondary, stress, as in **dictionary** (dik′shə nerʹē).

See also the explanation of how to use the Pronunciation Key, beginning on page FM 12.

Contents

Contents

Webster's New World Children's Dictionary

Foreword

One of the most important skills students can learn in school is the ability to use language in an effective way. Having this skill allows them to achieve many essential goals both inside and outside of school. The single most important tool in the educational process of acquiring language skills is a dictionary that meets the needs of the student. Such a dictionary must be prepared specifically with children in mind. It must excite their interest and be able to answer their questions about words in a clear and inviting way.

Webster's New World Children's Dictionary is this kind of dictionary. It is the first in a series of carefully prepared dictionaries for students of all ages, from those in the early grades to those at the college level. This new edition of the *Children's Dictionary* responds to the changing needs of children with a new design, an expanded vocabulary, fresh illustrations and photographs, and updated information in the front and back of the book for inquiring young minds. It was prepared in collaboration with skilled teachers, educators, and consultants.

Students in the third through sixth grades, for whom this dictionary is intended, will find a carefully selected vocabulary. The dictionary staff has used its many years of experience to make certain that the most useful and appropriate words are covered with clear and easily understood definitions, accompanied by complementary illustrations, photographs, and maps that broaden understanding of the concepts involved.

A new feature of this second edition is a unique *Thesaurus* in the back of the book. It is designed to stretch children's language skills and provide a bridge to the next highest level of dictionary, *Webster's New World Student's Dictionary*.

A number of other features found in the first edition have been continued and expanded. The many *Word Histories* help students grasp the meanings of words more confidently by pointing out the connection between the origins of the words and their current use. The *Word Makers* help students understand the use of prefixes and suffixes. *Spelling Tips* help students avoid making common spelling mistakes. *Word Choices* show the shades of meaning of synonyms and other closely related words. All of these features are set off from the definitions in colorful insert sections, and all of them provide useful material for classroom units of study.

We are confident that students who use this dictionary will find that it satisfies their current needs and provides a sound basis for their future explorations in American English.

Michael Agnes
Editor in Chief

Jonathan L. Goldman
James E. Naso
Project Editors,
Second Edition, Revised

September 2010

Foreword

How To Use This Dictionary

A dictionary is a book about words. It tells you what words mean. It tells you how to spell and pronounce words. A dictionary tells you other interesting facts about words, too.

Knowing about words is important. It helps you understand the things you hear and read. It also helps you say and write things that other people can understand.

The words we use make up our language. Our language is English. It is hundreds of years old, but it changes all the time. People make up new words when they invent or discover new things. People also find new ways to use old words. Many words have more than one meaning. It's fun to see the different ways you can use a single word.

The English language has many words. Not all of them are in this dictionary. We hope you find all the words you need in it. If you cannot find a word, look in a bigger dictionary. Ask for help if you cannot understand the bigger dictionary.

The next few pages tell you what is in the dictionary and explain how to use it. Reading them first will make using the dictionary easier.

HOW DOES THE DICTIONARY WORK?

A dictionary is made up of entries. At the right is an example of an *entry*.

An entry starts with the ● *entry word*. The entry word is the word you are looking up. It is in heavy black letters, so it is easy to find. The entry word in the example is **lighthouse**.

The ● *pronunciation* comes next. A word may not sound the way it looks. The pronunciation tells you how the word sounds. The pronunciation in the example is (līt′hous).

The main part of the entry is the ● *definition*. The definition tells you what the word means. The definition in the example is "a tower with a bright light on top to guide ships at night or in fog."

An entry has other parts too. You will learn about them later.

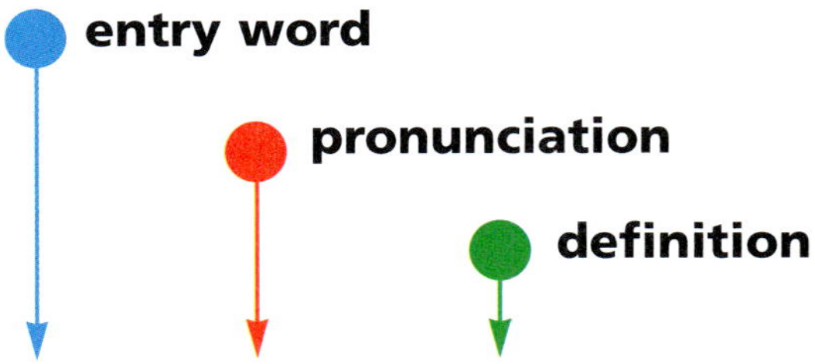

lighthouse (līt′hous) *noun* a tower with a bright light on top to guide ships at night or in fog.
light·house • *noun, plural* **lighthouses**

HOW YOU FIND A WORD IN THE DICTIONARY

The entries in this dictionary are in *alphabetical order*. That is the same order as the letters of the alphabet. All the entry words that begin with the letter *A* are together at the beginning of the dictionary. All the entry words that begin with the letter *B* are next. Then come entry words that begin with *C*, and so on, through *Z*.

All the *A* words also follow alphabetical order. A word that starts with *aa* comes before a word that starts with *ab*. A word that starts with *abd* comes before a word that starts with *abi*. Here are some words in alphabetical order:

aground	aid
ah	aide
aha	AIDS
ahead	ail
ahoy	

Finding a Word If You Can't Spell It

Sometimes you may not know the right way to spell a word. Many English words contain *silent* letters. Some words even start with silent letters. For example, people once pronounced the word *knee* as ke-nee. No one says the *k* sound any more, but *k* is still in the spelling.

Another problem is that some letters stand for more than one sound. The letter *c* can sound like *k* or *s*. And some sounds have several different spellings.

The *Word Finder Table* inside the back cover of the dictionary can help. Look up the first sound in a word. The Word Finder Table shows different letters that can spell that sound.

Try spelling the word with each different letter until you find the entry word.

Using Color Tabs To Help Find a Word

Pages of the dictionary are marked with color tabs. They are rounded, colored shapes that lie along the right edge of the right-hand pages. These colored shapes help you find different parts of the alphabet quickly. Each color is used with a different group of letters.

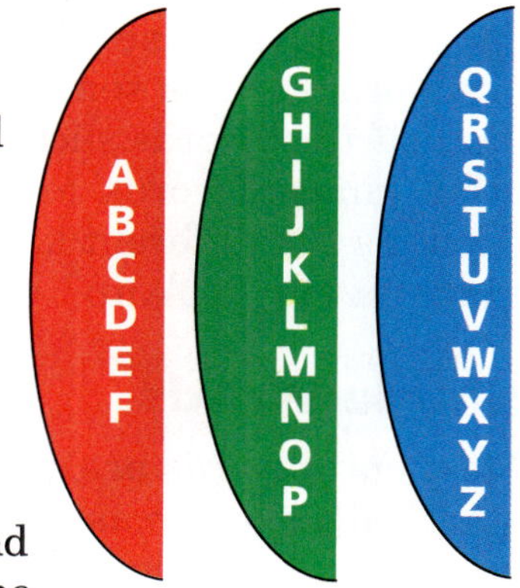

Red shapes are always near the top of the page. Green shapes are always in the middle. Blue shapes are always at the bottom. You can see the edges of the shapes even when the dictionary is closed.

Using Guide Words To Help Find a Word

Look at the top of each page. You will see a thin striped bar across the top of the page. Above this bar are two words called *guide words*. Guide words tell you the first and last entry words on a page. They look like this:

abbreviate ▶ abolitionist

This tells you that **abbreviate** is the first entry word on the page and **abolitionist** is the last entry. Any word that comes after **abbreviate** and before **abolitionist** will be on this page.

DIFFERENT KINDS OF WORDS YOU CAN LOOK UP

You can look up many kinds of words in this dictionary. Many are single words, such as **lighthouse**. Others are more than one word, such as **sea horse**. Some are only parts of words such as **un-**. There are other kinds of words, as well. This section explains the different kinds of entry words that you may look up.

Single Words

Most entry words are single words that start with a lowercase letter. Many single words have only one spelling and only one meaning. Other words are not that simple.

Some words have more than one spelling. If the two spellings look and sound almost the same, then both spellings appear together at the beginning of the entry. Here is an example.

ax or **axe** (aks) *noun* a tool for chopping or splitting wood. It has a long handle and a metal head with a sharp cutting edge.
ax or **axe** • *noun, plural* **axes**

If the two spellings look or sound very different, each spelling has its own entry. The two entries may not be together in the dictionary. Look at the entries **ameba** on page 24 and **amoeba** on page 25. The spelling that most people use has all the information in its entry. The other spelling has a note that tells you to look up the common spelling. This note is called a *cross-reference*.

Sometimes different words have the same spelling. They may even sound the same. But they have very different meanings and histories. These words are called *homographs*. A good example is **bit** on page 75. There are four different entry words spelled *b-i-t*. The dictionary tells you they are homographs by putting a small number next to each one. The first homograph entry word is **bit**^{1} and the last is **bit**^{4}.

Compound Words

A *compound word* contains more than one word. The words together have a special meaning. You cannot always understand this meaning just from the meanings of the separate words. The compound word **sea horse** is a good example. Each of the single words **sea** and **horse** has many meanings. It would be hard to use those meanings to get the right meaning of **sea horse**. So **sea horse** has its own entry. This kind of entry is called a *compound entry word*.

Abbreviations

An *abbreviation* is a short form of a word or phrase. Here are two examples.

in. *abbreviation for* **1** inch. **2** inches.

U.S.A. or **USA** *abbreviation for* United States of America.

An abbreviation entry gives the abbreviation, then the complete word or phrase. To find the meaning, you must look up the complete word or phrase.

Contractions

A *contraction* is another kind of shortened word or phrase. It leaves out certain letters and replaces them with an apostrophe ('). **Can't** is a contraction for **cannot**.

A contraction entry shows the contraction, then the complete word or phrase. To find the meaning, you must look up the complete word or phrase.

can't (kant) cannot.

DIFFERENT KINDS OF WORDS YOU CAN LOOK UP

Names of Places

The dictionary has entries for many cities and countries.There are entries for all the States of the United States and for all the provinces of Canada. There are also entries for rivers, lakes, oceans, and continents. These are all part of our world's geography. Entries that describe them are called *geographical entries*.

Some place names start with words that name the kind of place, such as "Lake" or "Mount" (for mountain). The word telling what special lake or mountain it is comes second. To find these names, look for the word that tells what special place it is. For example, you will find Mount Everest under *E* for Everest. You will find Lake Superior under *S* for Superior.

Prefixes and Suffixes

A *prefix* is a group of letters that can be joined to the beginning of a word to change its meaning. A *suffix* is a group of letters that can be joined to the end of a word to change its meaning. A prefix or suffix is never used alone.

An entry for a prefix or suffix gives its meaning and shows how it changes the meaning of other words. A hyphen shows where the prefix or suffix would join a word. Here are the entries for the prefix **ultra-** and the suffix **-free**.

ultra- *a prefix meaning:* **1** beyond [*Ultraviolet* rays lie beyond the violet end of the spectrum.] **2** beyond what is usual; very [An *ultramodern* house is a very modern house.]

-free *a suffix meaning* free of or free from; without [Our principal wants a drug-*free* school.]

Learning the meanings of prefixes and suffixes can help you figure out the meaning of other words that use them.

Names of People

The dictionary has entries for many famous people. The story of a person's life is called a *biography*. Entries that describe people are called *biographical entries*.

To find a person's name, look for his or her last name. You will Jane Addams under *A* for Addams. You will find Abraham Lincoln under *L* for Lincoln.

Here is the entry for Jane Addams. It shows that she was born in 1860 and died in 1935.

Addams (ad′əmz), **Jane** (jān) 1860-1935; U.S. social worker and writer. In 1889 she opened a place in Chicago called Hull House to offer services to the poor.
Ad·dams, Jane

Special Forms of Words

If you want to find the word **insects** or **walked**, you have to find **insect** or **walk** first. **Insect** is the *simple form* of the word. Entries are listed by the simple form of words. Special forms of a word are at the end of the entry. One special form is the plural of nouns, such as **insects**. Another is the past tense of verbs, such as **walked**. There are other special forms also. These special forms are called *inflected forms*. You will learn more about them on page FM 11, in the "End Lines: Parts of Speech" section.

Some words have inflected forms that are not made in the usual way. These forms have their own, separate entries. They are also part of the entry for the simple form of the word. Here are two examples.

went (went) *verb past tense of* **go**.

wives (wīvz) *noun plural of* **wife**.

WHAT CAN YOU LEARN FROM AN ENTRY?

Ways To Use a Word

The ways that a word can be used are called *parts of speech*. Here are the eight parts of speech:

noun	*adverb*
verb	*preposition*
pronoun	*conjunction*
adjective	*interjection*

The same word may be used as more than one part of speech. A dictionary entry tells which parts of speech a word can be used as, and sorts the meanings according to these parts of speech.

The first part of speech comes after the pronunciation. Other parts of speech come after the definition for the first part of speech.

age (āj) *noun* **1** the time that a person or a thing has existed from birth or beginning [She graduated at the *age* of eighteen.] **2** a part of life [Adolescence is often called an awkward *age*.] **3** the fact of being old [The pages of the book were yellow with *age*.] **4** a period of time in history [the Stone *Age;* the Space *Age*] —Look for the WORD CHOICES box at the entry **period**. **5** *usually* **ages** [*an informal use*] a long time [It's been *ages* since I've seen her.]
verb **1** to grow old [Our dog is *aging* quickly.] **2** to make old [Hard work has *aged* him.]
age • *noun, plural* **ages** • *verb* **aged, aging**

What a Word Means

The *definition* tells you what the entry word means. Some words have more than one definition. The first definition tells you the most common meaning of the word. This is what most people mean when they use the word. Less common meanings come next.

If a word has different parts of speech, each part of speech has its own definition or definitions. The entry for **age** has five definitions for the noun **age** and two definitions for the verb **age**.

Usage Labels: When To Use a Word

Some words or meanings are *informal* or *slang*. They are fine to use in everyday talk but not for a school paper. Informal words or meanings often stay around for a long time. Slang words or meanings come and go more quickly.

When there are limits to the situations in which you can use a word, a dictionary warns you with a *usage label*. A usage label tells you if certain words or meanings are informal or slang. For example, in the entry **age**, look at the last definition for the noun part of speech. It has a label in brackets: [*an informal use*].

In some entries, the phrase [*a slang use*] appears in brackets. When all the meanings of a word are informal or slang, a usage label with the phrase [*an informal word*] or [*a slang word*] is used.

Sample Sentences: How To Use a Word

Many entries give examples that show how to use a word. Some examples are whole sentences. Some are just phrases. All examples are in brackets. The entry word in the example is in slanted letters (*italics*).

A *cross-reference* is a note that sends you to another entry. Here are some examples:

Amsterdam (am′stər dam) a seaport in the Netherlands. It is the official capital. *See also* The **Hague**.
Am·ster·dam

capital (kap′i təl) *noun* **1** *the same as* **capital letter**. **2** a city where the government…

CD (sē′ dē′) *noun a short form of* **compact disc**.
CD • *noun, plural* **CDs**

puma (pyo͞o′mə *or* po͞o′mə) *noun another name for* **cougar**.
pu·ma • *noun, plural* **pumas**

Idioms: Special Phrases with Special Meanings

An *idiom* is a phrase that has a special meaning. You cannot tell the meaning of an idiom from the meanings of the words that form it. The two idioms in this example are part of the entry **between**.

—**between you and me** as a secret that you and I share. —**in between** in a middle position.

Idioms in an entry come after all the parts of speech. An idiom has a long dash (—) before it. Idioms in an entry are listed in alphabetical order.

To find an idiom, look at the entry for the word that seems most important. It might not be the first word in the idiom.

Homonyms

Homonyms are words that sound the same but have different meanings. Often they have different spellings. Entries for homonyms with different spellings end with special help for telling the different homonyms apart. Each homonym is used in a sentence or phrase. The sentence or phrase helps you understand the meaning of each homonym.

This example shows the difference between **carrot** and its homonyms **carat**, **caret**, and **karat**. It appears after each of the four entries.

- The words **carat, caret, carrot,** and **karat** sound alike.
  A *carat* is less than a gram.
  The *caret* is a common editor's mark.
  Our rabbit enjoys a *carrot* each day.
  Her ring is 14-*karat* gold.

End Lines

How To Divide a Word—Most entries end with a line or section that gives two kinds of information. First, it shows how to divide the entry word into syllables. Small dots mark the syllables.

el·e·phant **his·to·ry**

You may divide a word wherever a dot appears. Always put a hyphen at the end of the syllable where you divide a word.

On our trip to Africa, we saw many ele-phants.

To see how to divide a compound word, look up its individual words.

Parts of Speech—The other kind of information in the end line is about the parts of speech in the entry. This section shows all the *inflected forms* of each part of speech. (Reread "Special Forms of Words" on FM 9 if you don't remember what an inflected form is.) Look at the end lines from **fancy**.

fan·cy • *adjective* **fancier, fanciest** • *noun, plural* **fancies** • *verb* **fancied, fancying, fancies**

adjective tells you that **fancy** can be used as an adjective. There are two inflected forms. First is the *comparative* form, made with the suffix *-er* (**fancier**). Next is the *superlative* form, made with the suffix *-est* (**fanciest**). Some adverb parts of speech also show comparative and superlative forms. If these forms are not shown, then there is no *-er* or *-est* form for that word.

noun tells you that **fancy** can be used as a noun. It has a special plural form (**fancies**).

verb tells you that **fancy** can be used as a verb. It has several inflected forms called *principal parts*. First is the *past-tense* form (**fancied**). Then comes the *-ing* form (**fancy-ing**). Then, because **fancy** ends in *y*, the special *present-tense* form is shown (**fancies**). It is used with *he, she,* and *it*.

HOW TO PRONOUNCE A WORD

Your dictionary helps you say words the right way by giving a pronunciation at each entry. The pronunciation is shown in parentheses right after the entry word.

demonstration (dem ən strā′shən) ***noun*** **1**...

The pronunciation uses both regular letters of the alphabet and special symbols. We use the special symbols because many letters of the alphabet have several different sounds. For example, the *a* in *cat* sounds different from the *a* in *ape* or the *a* in *father*.

The letters and symbols that show pronunciation are listed in the *Pronunciation Key*. You will find the Pronunciation Key inside the front cover of this book. Below is a shorter form of the Key found at the bottom of each left-hand page of the dictionary. Both forms of the Pronunciation Key will help you say correctly all the words in this dictionary.

Using the Pronunciation Key

Look at the full Pronunciation Key at the front of the book or the small one on this page. Each letter or symbol is followed by one or two *key words*. Key words are short, simple words that you already know. These words help you know how to say the sound of the letter or symbol next to them. As you use your dictionary more, you will need the Pronunciation Key less. You will come to learn the different symbols and the sounds that they stand for.

The Pronunciation Keys list the vowel sounds and the consonant sounds. On the vowels, special marks have been added. We could not use only *a*, *e*, *i*, *o*, and *u* because there are more than five vowel sounds. The special marks show you the difference of the sound of *i* in *lit* and in *light*, or the difference of the sound of *oo* in *blood*, *hood*, and *mood*. This is why the key words are so important. They help you learn all the different vowel sounds.

a	cat	ō	go	ʉ	fur	ə =	a *in* ago
ā	ape	ô	law, for	ch	chin		e *in* agent
ä	cot, car	oo	look	sh	she		i *in* pencil
e	ten	o͞o	tool	th	thin		o *in* atom
ē	me	oi	oil	*th*	then		u *in* circus
i	fit	ou	out	zh	measure		
ī	ice	u	up	ŋ	ring		

Special Symbols

ə This symbol [ə] is called the *schwa*. It stands for an *uh* sound that can be heard in the first syllable of **about** (ə bout′) or in the last syllable of **comma** (käm′ə).

ŋ This symbol [ŋ] stands for the sound that comes at the end of **sing** and **thing**. It also stands for the sound which comes before the *k* sound in **drink** and **think**.

Some pronunciation symbols are made up of two letters joined together. The joined letters make a single sound.

sh The symbol [sh] stands for the sound at the beginning of **she** or at the end of **push**. It is also the sound you hear in the last syllable of **demonstration** (dem ən strā′shən).

ch [ch] stands for the sound at the beginning of **chin** and at the beginning and end of **church**. It is also the sound that is heard in the last syllable of **adventure** (ad ven′chər).

Use the Pronunciation Key to find the sounds of the other two-letter symbols.

HOW TO PRONOUNCE A WORD

Putting Stress on the Right Syllable

There are two additional marks that help you pronounce words correctly. These marks are called *stress marks*. They are sometimes called *accents*. They are listed at the bottom of the Pronunciation Key inside the front cover of this book.

When you speak, you say some syllables with more force than you say others. Say the word **picture**. Notice that the first syllable is said with more force than the second syllable. Now say the word **about**. Notice that the second syllable is said with more force than the first syllable.

The dictionary shows that a syllable should be spoken with more force by placing a stress mark [ʹ] after the syllable. The pronunciation of **picture** (pikʹchər) has a stress mark after the first syllable. The pronunciation of **about** (ə boutʹ) has a stress mark after the second syllable.

Some words have stress marks on more than one syllable. The syllable that is said with the most force is marked with a heavy, or *primary*, stress mark [ʹ]. The syllable that is said with less force is marked with a light, or *secondary*, stress mark [ˊ].

dictionary (dikʹshə nerˊē)

The first syllable of **dictionary** is said with the most force. The third syllable is said with slightly less force. The second and fourth syllables are spoken with the least force.

Words with More Than One Pronunciation

Sometimes, two people will say the same word differently. Many words in English have two or more pronunciations.

aunt (ant *or* änt)
grandpa (granʹpä *or* gramʹpä)

When two or more pronunciations are shown for a word, any of them may be used. Because one is listed first does not mean that it is better or more correct. It simply means that the first one is used by more people.

Sometimes, the pronunciation of a word depends on how the word is used in a sentence. For example, a word may be said one way if it is used as a noun and said another way if it is used as a verb. Read the following sentences aloud. Listen to the way in which you say *excuse* in each sentence.

Please *excuse* me.

There was no *excuse* for his unkind remarks.

Excuse is a verb in the first sentence. It is a noun in the second sentence. When *excuse* is used as a verb, the final sound is a *z* sound (ek skyo͞ozʹ). When it is used as a noun, the final sound is an *s* sound (ek skyo͞osʹ). The pronunciation of this word is shown in your dictionary like this:

excuse (ek skyo͞ozʹ *for verb;* ek skyo͞osʹ *for noun*)

Spelling and Pronunciation

Some words are spelled very differently but they have pronunciations that are nearly alike, for example, **boar** (bôr), **door** (dôr), **four** (fôr), and **more** (môr). On the other hand, some words are spelled very much alike but they have very different pronunciations. Think, for example, of **four** (fôr), **hour** (our), and **tour** (to͝or).

This dictionary has other special information. This information is not in the entries. Some is in special boxes. Some is in the back of the book.

Word Makers

Some words are made up of parts that may look familiar to you. If you know the meanings of the parts, you can often figure out the meaning of the new word. A good example is a new word that comes from adding a prefix or suffix to a word you already know. The word you already know is called the *base word*.

This dictionary helps you make new words out of base words and prefixes or suffixes. It does this with WORD MAKER boxes. These boxes usually come after the entry for a common prefix or suffix. Here is the Word Maker box for **ex-**.

WORD MAKER

The prefix **ex-**

Many words contain the prefix **ex-** plus a word that you already know. You can understand these words if you add the idea "earlier or former" to the meaning of the base word.

prefix + base word	⇨	*new word*
ex- + Senator	⇨	**ex-Senator** *(a former Senator)*
chairperson		ex-chairperson
diplomat		ex-diplomat
husband		ex-husband
mayor		ex-mayor
owner		ex-owner
partner		ex-partner
president		ex-president

Word Choices

Synonyms are words that mean nearly the same thing. You will find information about synonyms in WORD CHOICES boxes. Look at the Word Choices box for **fit**.

This box shows two synonyms for **fit**. Each synonym has an example phrase. The example phrases show the differences in meaning and use. They help you make the best choice when you are writing.

WORD CHOICES

Synonyms of **fit**

The words **fit**, **proper**, and **suitable** share the meaning "right for the purpose."

a meal *fit* for a king
the *proper* tool for the job
a car *suitable* for mountain driving

The box for **fast** does not show examples, but it has more word choices.

WORD CHOICES

Synonyms of **fast**

Many words share the meaning "moving or acting at high speed."

brisk	quick	speedy
fleet	rapid	swift

All the word choices are entry words in the dictionary. Each of these entry words has a cross-reference. The cross-reference sends you to the Word Choices box.

suitable (so͞ot′ə bəl) *adjective* right for the purpose; proper [a *suitable* gift] —Look for the WORD CHOICES box at the entry **fit**[1].
suit·a·ble • *adjective*

SPECIAL FEATURES IN THE DICTIONARY

Word Histories

Remember we said that English is an old language, but it changes all the time. Many words started out meaning something very different from what they mean today. Many words came from other languages. This dictionary has many WORD HISTORY boxes. These boxes tell you where certain words came from. They tell you how certain words got their meanings.

WORD HISTORY

elbow

Long ago, people who wove cloth measured it by holding it along the arm from the bending joint to the end of the finger. That distance was called an *ell*, and the bend in the arm was the *ell bow*, which we now write **elbow**.

Illustrations

You will find many pictures in this dictionary. The pictures help you understand some of the definitions. They show how things look or how they are used. Below each picture is a *caption* telling the name of what is in the picture.

cockatoo

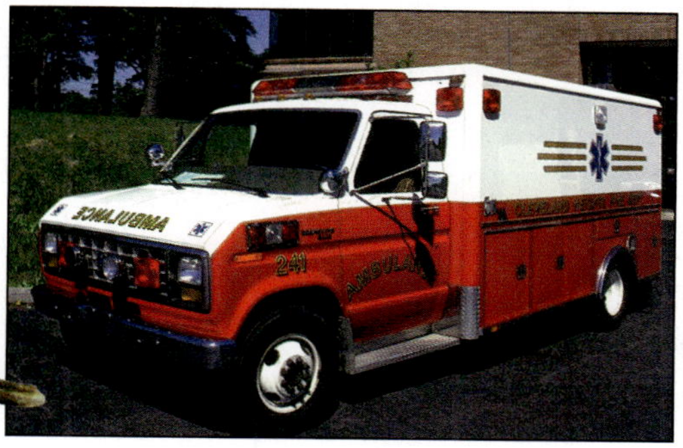

ambulance

Maps

There are two kinds of maps in this dictionary. There are small maps next to the entry for each of the fifty States of the United States. These maps show the location of the State.

You will also find maps in the back of this dictionary. These larger maps show the United States, Canada, Mexico, Central and South America, Europe, Africa, Asia, and Australia.

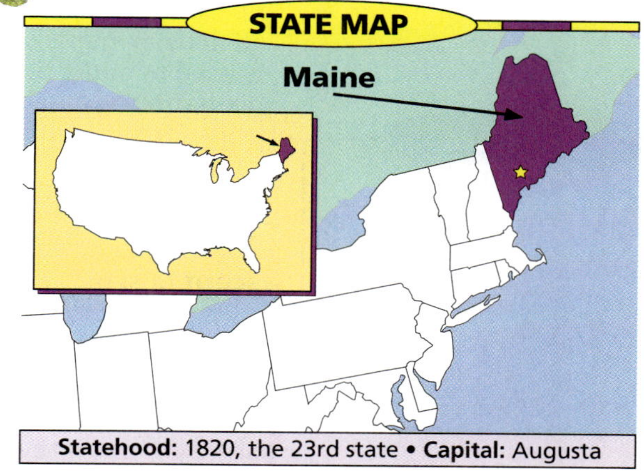

Spelling Tips

Some words are hard to spell. They may contain a letter that is not pronounced. Or the order of certain letters may be hard to remember. Sometimes there is an easy clue that can help you remember how to spell a word. This dictionary gives you many spelling clues, in SPELLING TIP boxes.

SPELLING TIP

Use this memory aid to spell **believe**. Don't be***lie***ve a ***lie***.

THE PARTS OF A DICTIONARY ENTRY

Entry Word FM 8/9
Pronunciation FM 12/13
Definition FM 10
Sample Sentence FM 10
Parts of Speech FM 10
Idioms FM 11
Usage Label FM 10
Syllable Division FM 11
End Lines FM 11
Inflected Forms FM 11
Plural Form FM 11
Homographs FM 8

as (az) ***adverb*** **1** to the same amount or degree; equally [Are you *as* tall as your cousin?] **2** for instance; for example [Some plants, *as* corn and potatoes, are native to America.]
conjunction **1** to the same amount or degree that [I'm as hungry *as* you are.] **2** in the way that [Do *as* I tell you.] **3** at the same time that; while [She laughed *as* she spoke.] **4** because; since [*As* I am tired, I'll stay home.]
preposition in the role or manner of [He poses *as* a friend. That table can serve *as* a desk.]
—as if or **as though** as it would if; as a person would if [They acted *as if* they were tired. It looks *as though* it will rain.] **—as is** [*an informal use*] just as it is [This used car costs $800 *as is*.] **—as of** up to, on, or from a certain time [You can reach me here *as of* next Friday.]

asbestos (as bes′təs *or* az bes′təs) ***noun*** a grayish mineral that separates into long fibers like thread. It can be made into a kind of cloth or paper. Asbestos will not burn and is used to make fireproof curtains and electric insulation.
as·bes·tos • ***noun***

ascend (ə send′) ***verb*** to go up; move upward; climb [The balloon *ascended* into the air.]
as·cend • ***verb*** **ascended, ascending**

ascent (ə sent′) ***noun*** **1** the act of moving up, rising, or climbing [Our *ascent* up the hill was very difficult.] **2** a way leading up; slope [We looked for a better *ascent*.]
as·cent • ***noun,*** *plural* **ascents**

ash[1] (ash) ***noun*** the grayish powder and flakes that are left after something has been burned.
ash • ***noun,*** *plural* **ashes**

ash[2] (ash) ***noun*** a shade tree whose tough wood is used for timber and to make furniture.
ash • ***noun,*** *plural* **ashes**

A a

Aa Aa Aa Aa

*"**A** is for **apple**" is a very old phrase that beginning readers use to remind themselves of how to say the letter **a** in a word. But we know that letters of the alphabet and the sounds they stand for are not as simple as that saying makes it seem. The letter **a** in a word can stand for several different sounds. Try to think beyond the word **apple**. Think of **able**, **about**, **airplane**, and **ah**.*

a[1] or **A** (ā) ***noun*** the first letter of the English alphabet.
a or **A** • ***noun,*** *plural* **a's** or **A's**

a[2] (ə *or* ā) ***indefinite article*** **1** one; one kind of [I'll bake *a* peach pie.] **2** any one [Pick *a* peach from the tree.] **3** for each [Pears cost a dollar *a* bag.] Use *a* before a word that begins with a consonant sound. Use *an* before a word that begins with a vowel sound.

A (ā) ***noun*** **1** in some schools, the highest grade, meaning "excellent" or "best." **2** in music, the sixth tone in the scale of C major.
A • ***noun,*** *plural* **A's**

aardvark (ärd′värk) ***noun*** a southern African animal with a long snout. It eats ants and termites and is active at night.
aard·vark • ***noun,*** *plural* **aardvarks**

AB *abbreviation for* Alberta.

aback (ə bak′) ***adverb*** *used mainly in the phrase* **taken aback,** surprised and confused [She was *taken aback* by the change of plans.]
a·back • ***adverb***

abacus (ab′ə kəs) ***noun*** a frame with groups of beads that slide back and forth on wires. The abacus is used for doing arithmetic quickly without writing.
ab·a·cus • ***noun,*** *plural* **abacuses**

abacus

abalone (ab′ə lō′nē) ***noun*** a shellfish with a soft body and a single oval shell lined with mother-of-pearl. The body is used as food and the shell is used in jewelry.
ab·a·lo·ne • ***noun,*** *plural* **abalones**

abandon (ə ban′dən) ***verb*** **1** to give up completely [Don't *abandon* hope.] **2** to leave;

desert [The crew *abandoned* the ship.]
a·ban·don • *verb* **abandoned, abandoning**

WORD CHOICES

Synonyms of **abandon**

The words **abandon**, **desert**, and **forsake** share the meaning "to go away from."

She *abandoned* her car and began walking.

The sentry *deserted* his post.

Don't *forsake* a friend in need.

abbreviate (ə brē′vē āt′) *verb* to make shorter by leaving out letters [The word "Street" can be *abbreviated* to "St."]
ab·bre·vi·ate • *verb* **abbreviated, abbreviating**

abbreviation (ə brē′vē ā′shən) *noun* a shortened form of a word or phrase ["U.S.A." is the *abbreviation* for "United States of America."]
ab·bre·vi·a·tion • *noun, plural* **abbreviations**

ABC's (ā′bē′sēz′) *plural noun* **1** the alphabet. **2** the simplest facts of a subject or the simplest ways of doing something [We learned the *ABC's* of tennis at camp.]

abdomen (ab′də mən *or* ab dō′mən) *noun* **1** the part of the body between the chest and hips; belly. It contains the stomach, intestines, and liver. **2** the rear part of an insect's body.
ab·do·men • *noun, plural* **abdomens**

abdominal (ab däm′ə nəl) *adjective* having to do with the abdomen [*abdominal* pains].
ab·dom·i·nal • *adjective*

ability (ə bil′ə tē) *noun* **1** the power to do something [Does he have the *ability* to pay?] **2** a skill or talent [You have musical *ability*.]
a·bil·i·ty • *noun, plural* **abilities**

ablaze (ə blāz′) *adjective* burning with flames [The barn was *ablaze*.]
a·blaze • *adjective*

able (ā′bəl) *adjective* **1** having the means or power to do something [She is *able* to take care of herself.] **2** having the skill or talent that is needed [an *able* teacher].
a·ble • *adjective* **abler, ablest**

-able *a suffix meaning:* **1** capable of being [A *usable* object is capable of being used.] **2** likely to [Food that is *perishable* is likely to perish, or spoil, easily.]

WORD MAKER

The suffix **-able**

Many words contain the suffix **-able** plus a word that you already know. You can understand these words if you add the idea "capable of being" to the meaning of the base word.

base word	*+ suffix*	⇨	*new word*
believe	+ **-able**	⇨	**believable** *(capable of being believed)*

base word	*+ suffix* ⇨	*new word*
break		breakable
excuse		excusable
explain		explainable
forgive		forgivable
identify		identifiable
inflate		inflatable
measure		measurable
predict		predictable
prevent		preventable
recognize		recognizable
understand		understandable
wash		washable

abnormal (ab nôr′məl) *adjective* not normal; not usual [Snow in July is *abnormal* in Iowa.]
ab·nor·mal • *adjective*

aboard (ə bôrd′) *adverb* on, in, or into a ship, airplane, bus, or train [When all the passengers were *aboard*, the airplane took off.] *preposition* on or in; on board [We went *aboard* the ship.]
a·board • *adverb* • *preposition*

abolish (ə bäl′ish *or* ə bôl′ish) *verb* to get rid of completely [Congress may *abolish* a law.]
a·bol·ish • *verb* **abolished, abolishing**

abolition (ab′ə lish′ən) *noun* the act of getting rid of completely [the *abolition* of slavery].
ab·o·li·tion • *noun*

abolitionist or **Abolitionist** (ab′ə lish′ən ist)

a cat	ō go	ʉ fur	ə = a *in* ago
ā ape	ô law, for	ch chin	e *in* agent
ä cot, car	oo look	sh she	i *in* pencil
e ten	o͞o tool	th thin	o *in* atom
ē me	oi oil	*th* then	u *in* circus
i fit	ou out	zh measure	
ī ice	u up	ŋ ring	

noun one of the people who wanted to put an end to slavery in the U.S. before the Civil War.
ab·o·li·tion·ist or **Ab·o·li·tion·ist**
• *noun, plural* **abolitionists** or **Abolitionists**

abominable (ə bäm′ə nə bəl) *adjective* very unpleasant; very bad [an *abominable* movie].
a·bom·i·na·ble • *adjective*

Abominable Snowman *noun* a large, hairy, manlike animal that is said to live in the Himalayas.

aborigine (ab′ə rij′ə nē) *noun* one of the first people known to have lived in a certain place; native person.
ab·o·rig·i·ne • *noun, plural* **aborigines**

abound (ə bound′) *verb* to be found in large numbers or amounts [Insects *abound* in the jungle.]
a·bound • *verb* **abounded, abounding**

about (ə bout′) *adverb* **1** on every side; all around [Look *about*.] **2** here and there; in all directions [Birds fly *about*.] **3** in or to the opposite direction [Turn yourself *about*.] **4** more or less [She's *about* ten years old.] **5** almost ready [I was *about* to cry.] **6** [*an informal use*] almost [I'm just *about* ready.]
adjective active; awake or well again [At dawn I was up and *about*.]
preposition **1** around; on all sides of [Waves rose *about* the boat.] **2** here and there in; everywhere in [Stop running *about* the house.] **3** near to [He was born *about* 1920.] **4** taking care of [Go *about* your business.] **5** having to do with [Here is a book *about* ships.]
a·bout • *adverb* • *adjective* • *preposition*

above (ə buv′) *adverb* in or at a higher place; up [Birds are flying *above*.]
preposition **1** higher than; over [We flew *above* the clouds.] **2** better than [*above* average].
—**above all** mostly; mainly.
a·bove • *adverb* • *preposition*

abracadabra (ab′rə kə dab′rə) *noun* a word thought to have magic powers and used in casting spells.
ab·ra·ca·dab·ra • *noun, plural* **abracadabras**

Abraham (ā′brə ham) in the Bible, the ancestor and first leader of the Hebrews.
A·bra·ham

abrasive (ə brā′siv) *adjective* causing a wearing away by scraping or rubbing [Sandpaper is very *abrasive*.]
ab·ra·sive • *adjective*

abreast (ə brest′) *adverb* side by side and going or facing forward; in line [The band members marched three *abreast*.]
adjective at the side of; beside [The two ships were *abreast* of one another.]
a·breast • *adverb* • *adjective*

abridge (ə brij′) *verb* to shorten [Her story was *abridged* for publication in the magazine.]
a·bridge • *verb* **abridged, abridging**

abroad (ə brôd′) *adverb* outside a person's own country [They were going *abroad* to Europe.]
a·broad • *adverb*

abrupt (ə brupt′) *adjective* coming or happening suddenly, without warning [an *abrupt* stop].
a·brupt • *adjective*

abscess (ab′ses) *noun* a sore, swollen, sick place in the body, that is filled with pus.
ab·scess • *noun, plural* **abscesses**

absence (ab′səns) *noun* **1** the fact of being absent [During their *absence*, I fed their cats.] **2** the fact of being without; lack [The *absence* of food causes hunger.]
ab·sence
• *noun, plural for sense 1 only* **absences**

absent (ab′sənt) *adjective* **1** not present; away [No one in the class was *absent* that day.] **2** lacking or missing [If calcium is *absent* from the diet, the bones will become soft.]
ab·sent • *adjective*

absent-minded (ab′sənt mīn′did) *adjective* **1** thinking or dreaming of something else and not paying attention. **2** always forgetting things.
ab·sent-mind·ed • *adjective*

absolute (ab′sə lo͞ot) *adjective* perfect; complete [It's hard to have *absolute* silence.]
ab·so·lute • *adjective*

absolutely (ab′sə lo͞ot′lē) *adverb* perfectly; completely [*absolutely* clean].
ab·so·lute·ly • *adverb*

absorb (ab sôrb′ *or* ab zôrb′) *verb* **1** to suck up [A sponge *absorbs* water.] **2** to take up the full attention of [I was so *absorbed* in studying I forgot to eat.] **3** to take in and not reflect or throw back [Black walls *absorb* light.]
ab·sorb • *verb* **absorbed, absorbing**

A

absorbent (ab sôr′bənt *or* ab zôr′bənt) ***adjective*** able to absorb something [*absorbent* cotton].
ab·sorb·ent • ***adjective***

absorption (ab sôrp′shən *or* ab zôrp′shən) ***noun*** the act or way of absorbing [A plant gets food from the soil by the *absorption* of water and minerals through its roots.]
ab·sorp·tion • ***noun,*** *plural* **absorptions**

abstract (ab strakt′ *or* ab′strakt) ***adjective*** **1** formed in the mind and considered separate from a real act or thing [An apple is something real, but your idea about how it will taste is *abstract*.] **2** formed with designs taken from real things, but not actually like any real object or being [an *abstract* painting].
ab·stract • ***adjective***

absurd (ab surd′ *or* ab zurd′) ***adjective*** so untrue or without good sense as to be something to make fun of; silly or foolish [It is *absurd* to eat peas with a knife.]
ab·surd • ***adjective***

abundance (ə bun′dəns) ***noun*** a great supply [Alaska has an *abundance* of natural resources.]
a·bun·dance • ***noun***

abundant (ə bun′dənt) ***adjective*** very plentiful; more than enough [an *abundant* crop].
a·bun·dant • ***adjective***

abuse (ə byo͞oz′ *for v.;* ə byo͞os′ *for n.*) ***verb*** **1** to use in a wrong or improper way [We never *abuse* the privilege of lunching outside by leaving litter about.] **2** to hurt by treating badly; mistreat [It is wrong to *abuse* animals.]
noun unkind, cruel, or wrong ways of dealing with someone or something.
a·buse • ***verb*** **abused, abusing** • ***noun,*** *plural* **abuses**

academic (ak′ə dem′ik) ***adjective*** having to do with schools, colleges, or teaching [*academic* life].
ac·a·dem·ic • ***adjective***

academy (ə kad′ə mē) ***noun*** **1** a private high school. **2** a school for special training in something such as music or art.
a·cad·e·my • ***noun,*** *plural* **academies**

accelerate (ak sel′ər āt) ***verb*** to make run or work faster; to increase the speed of [The driver *accelerated* the engine.]
ac·cel·er·ate • ***verb*** **accelerated, accelerating**

acceleration (ak sel′ər ā′shən) ***noun*** the act of accelerating; an increase in speed.
ac·cel·er·a·tion • ***noun,*** *plural* **accelerations**

accelerator (ak sel′ər āt′ər) ***noun*** the foot pedal that can make an automobile go faster by feeding the engine more gasoline.
ac·cel·er·a·tor • ***noun,*** *plural* **accelerators**

accent (ak′sent) ***noun*** **1** extra force, or stress, given to some syllables or words in speaking [The *accent* in "accident" is on the first syllable.] **2** a kind of mark (′ or ′) that is used to show such extra force. The heavier mark (′) is placed after the syllable with the strongest accent. **3** the special way of pronouncing words and phrases that is used by people from a certain area or country [My grandmother speaks English with a French *accent*.]
verb **1** to pronounce with special force [*Accent* the first syllable of "Washington."] **2** to mark with an accent mark.
ac·cent • ***noun,*** *plural* **accents**
• ***verb*** **accented, accenting**

accept (ak sept′) ***verb*** **1** to take what is offered or given [She *accepted* his apology.] **2** to answer "yes" to [We *accept* your invitation to the party.] **3** to allow to become a member of a group [The team quickly *accepted* the new player.] **4** to think of as true; believe [The teacher *accepted* his excuse for being late.]
ac·cept • ***verb*** **accepted, accepting**

acceptable (ak sep′tə bəl) ***adjective*** good enough to be accepted; proper [*acceptable* behavior].
ac·cept·a·ble • ***adjective***

acceptance (ak sep′təns) ***noun*** **1** the act of accepting [the *acceptance* of an award]. **2** the condition of being accepted; approval or belief [The theory has the *acceptance* of scientists.]
ac·cept·ance • ***noun,*** *plural for sense 1 only* **acceptances**

access (ak′ses) ***noun*** **1** a way of approach [The *access* to the park is by this road.] **2** the right or ability to approach, enter, or use [Do the students have *access* to a good library?]
ac·cess • ***noun,*** *plural* **accesses**

accessory (ak ses′ər ē) ***noun*** **1** a thing added for comfort or decoration; something extra [An air conditioner is an *accessory* on a car. A scarf

a	cat	ō	go	u̇r	fur	ə =	a *in* ago
ā	ape	ô	law, for	ch	chin		e *in* agent
ä	cot, car	o͝o	look	sh	she		i *in* pencil
e	ten	o͞o	tool	th	thin		o *in* atom
ē	me	oi	oil	*th*	then		u *in* circus
i	fit	ou	out	zh	measure		
ī	ice	u	up	ŋ	ring		

is an *accessory* to an outfit.] **2** a person who helps another to break the law.
ac·ces·so·ry • ***noun,*** *plural* **accessories**

accident (ak′sə dənt) ***noun*** **1** something that happens without being planned and that is not expected [Our meeting was a happy *accident.*] **2** an unfortunate happening or event that is not expected [I've had three *accidents* driving a car.] **3** luck; chance [His lost watch was found by *accident.*]
ac·ci·dent • ***noun,*** *plural* **accidents**

accidental (ak′sə dent′l) ***adjective*** happening by luck or chance [an *accidental* meeting].
ac·ci·den·tal • ***adjective***

accommodate (ə käm′ə dāt) ***verb*** **1** to make fit; adjust [She *accommodated* her walk to the slow steps of her grandfather.] **2** to have room or lodging for [This motel will *accommodate* 250 people.]
ac·com·mo·date • ***verb*** **accommodated, accommodating**

accommodations (ə käm′ə dā′shənz) ***plural noun*** rented rooms or space for travelers in a hotel, ship, or similar place.
ac·com·mo·da·tions • ***plural noun***

accompaniment (ə kum′pə nə mənt) ***noun*** music played along with a solo part.
ac·com·pa·ni·ment • ***noun,*** *plural* **accompaniments**

accompany (ə kum′pə nē) ***verb*** **1** to go along with; be together with [Adults must *accompany* children to this movie.] **2** to play a musical accompaniment for or to [Will you *accompany* my singing on your guitar?]
ac·com·pa·ny • ***verb*** **accompanied, accompanying, accompanies**

WORD CHOICES

Synonyms of **accompany**

The words **accompany**, **attend**, and **escort** share the meaning "to go or be with."

I *accompanied* her to the theater.

The king was *attended* by three knights.

An usher *escorted* us down the aisle.

accomplice (ə käm′plis) ***noun*** a person who helps another break the law.
ac·com·plice • ***noun,*** *plural* **accomplices**

accomplish (ə käm′plish) ***verb*** to do; carry out [The task was *accomplished* in one day.]
ac·com·plish • ***verb*** **accomplished, accomplishing**

accomplishment (ə käm′plish mənt) ***noun*** **1** a task that has been successfully completed; achievement [Building the first skyscraper was a great *accomplishment.*] **2** an art or skill that has been learned [One of my cousin's *accomplishments* is cooking.]
ac·com·plish·ment • ***noun,*** *plural* **accomplishments**

accord (ə kôrd′) ***verb*** **1** to give or grant [The poet was *accorded* many honors.] **2** to be in agreement or harmony [The story you tell does not *accord* with the facts.]
noun agreement; harmony [The three judges were in *accord* concerning the winner.]
—of one's own accord willingly, without being asked [Jane and Don washed the dishes *of their own accord.*]
ac·cord • ***verb*** **accorded, according** • ***noun***

according (ə kôrd′iŋ) ***adjective*** *used mainly in the phrase* **according to, 1** in agreement with [The bus left *according to* schedule.] **2** in the order of [The plants were arranged *according to* height.] **3** as stated or reported by [*According to* the newspaper, there was a fire.]
ac·cord·ing • ***adjective***

accordion

accordion (ə kôr′dē ən) ***noun*** a musical instrument with keys, metal reeds, and a bellows. It is played by pulling out and pressing together the bellows to force air through the reeds. The reeds are opened by fingering the keys.

A

ac·cor·di·on • *noun, plural* **accordions**

account (ə kount′) *verb* **1** to give a complete record of money handled [Our treasurer can *account* for every penny we spent.] **2** to give a satisfactory reason; explain [How do you *account* for your absence from school?] **3** to be the reason or cause [Carelessness *accounts* for many accidents.]
noun **1** *often* **accounts** a list of money received, paid, or owed. **2** an explanation [There is no satisfactory *account* of the cause of the sickness.] **3** a report or story [The book is an *account* of their trip.]
—on account of because of. **—take into account** to allow for; keep in mind [*Take* my feelings *into account* when you decide.]
ac·count • *verb* **accounted, accounting** • *noun, plural* **accounts**

accountant (ə kount′nt) *noun* a person whose work is keeping or checking accounts, or business records.
ac·count·ant • *noun, plural* **accountants**

accumulate (ə kyo͞om′yo͞o lāt) *verb* to pile up, collect, or gather over a period of time [Junk has *accumulated* in the garage. Our school has *accumulated* a large library.]
ac·cu·mu·late • *verb* **accumulated, accumulating**

accumulation (ə kyo͞om′yo͞o lā′shən) *noun* **1** the condition or process of being accumulated [The *accumulation* of water on the road made driving difficult.] **2** something accumulated; a collection of things [an *accumulation* of books].
ac·cu·mu·la·tion • *noun, plural for sense 2 only* **accumulations**

accuracy (ak′yoor ə sē) *noun* the fact of being accurate, or without mistakes [His reports are known for their *accuracy*.]
ac·cu·ra·cy • *noun*

accurate (ak′yoor it) *adjective* exact or correct; without mistakes or errors [an *accurate* clock; an *accurate* weather forecast] —Look for the WORD CHOICES box at the entry **correct**.
ac·cu·rate • *adjective*

accusation (ak′yo͞o zā′shən) *noun* a claim or charge that a person is guilty of doing wrong or of breaking the law.
ac·cu·sa·tion • *noun, plural* **accusations**

accuse (ə kyo͞oz′) *verb* to blame someone for doing something wrong or for breaking the law [He is *accused* of robbing the store.]
ac·cuse • *verb* **accused, accusing**

accustom (ə kus′təm) *verb* to make used to [I'll try to *accustom* myself to the new schedule.]
ac·cus·tom • *verb* **accustomed, accustoming**

accustomed (ə kus′təmd) *adjective* usual; expected [She greeted us with her *accustomed* charm.]
—accustomed to used to; in the habit of [He is *accustomed to* staying up late.]
ac·cus·tomed • *adjective*

ace (ās) *noun* **1** a playing card marked with one spot. **2** a person who is an expert at something.
ace • *noun, plural* **aces**

ache (āk) *verb* **1** to have or give a dull, steady pain [My head *aches*.] **2** [*an informal use*] to want very much; long for [She is *aching* to take a trip.]
noun a dull, steady pain.
ache • *verb* **ached, aching** • *noun, plural* **aches**

achieve (ə chēv′) *verb* **1** to do; succeed in doing; accomplish [He *achieved* very little while he was mayor.] —Look for the WORD CHOICES box at the entry **reach**. **2** to get or reach by trying hard; gain [She *achieved* her goal.]
a·chieve • *verb* **achieved, achieving**

achievement (ə chēv′mənt) *noun* something achieved by skill, work, or courage [Landing on the moon was a remarkable *achievement*.]
a·chieve·ment • *noun, plural* **achievements**

acid (as′id) *noun* a chemical compound that dissolves in water, tastes sour, and makes blue litmus paper turn red.
adjective **1** containing or like an acid [an *acid* mixture]. **2** sour; sharp and biting to the taste [Lemons and limes are *acid* fruits.] —Look for the WORD CHOICES box at the entry **sour**.
ac·id • *noun, plural* **acids** • *adjective*

acid rain *noun* rain or snow that is full of acids formed in the air when fuels such as coal and petroleum are burned. Acid rain is harmful to crops, lakes, and buildings.

acknowledge (ak näl′ij) *verb* **1** to admit to be true [I *acknowledge* that you are right.] **2** to take notice of and answer [She *acknowl-*

a	cat	ō	go	ʉ	fur	ə =	a *in* ago
ā	ape	ô	law, for	ch	chin		e *in* agent
ä	cot, car	o͝o	look	sh	she		i *in* pencil
e	ten	o͞o	tool	th	thin		o *in* atom
ē	me	oi	oil	*th*	then		u *in* circus
i	fit	ou	out	zh	measure		
ī	ice	u	up	ŋ	ring		

edged my greeting with a smile.] **3** to give thanks for [Have you written to your uncle to *acknowledge* his gift?]
ac·knowl·edge • *verb* **acknowledged, acknowledging**

acknowledgment or **acknowledgement** (ak näl′ij mənt) *noun* something given or done in acknowledging [The hug she gave me was an *acknowledgment* of my apology.]
ac·knowl·edg·ment or **ac·knowl·edge·ment** • *noun, plural* **acknowledgments** or **acknowledgements**

acne (ak′nē) *noun* a common skin disease of young people in which pimples keep appearing on the face, back, and chest. It happens when oil glands in the skin become blocked and swollen.
ac·ne • *noun*

acorn

acorn (ā′kôrn) *noun* the nut, or fruit, of the oak.
a·corn • *noun, plural* **acorns**

acoustic (ə ko͞os′tik) or **acoustical** (ə ko͞os′ti kəl) *adjective* **1** having to do with hearing or with sound [*Acoustic* tile is used to deaden sound.] **2** referring to a musical instrument that is not electronically amplified [an *acoustic* guitar].
a·cous·tic or **a·cous·ti·cal** • *adjective*

acquaint (ə kwānt′) *verb* to make familiar [*Acquaint* yourself with the facts. Are you *acquainted* with my sister?]
ac·quaint • *verb* **acquainted, acquainting**

acquaintance (ə kwānt′ns) *noun* a person one knows but not as a close friend.
ac·quaint·ance • *noun, plural* **acquaintances**

acquire (ə kwīr′) *verb* to get as one's own; become the owner of [The museum *acquired* a very old vase.] —Look for the WORD CHOICES box at the entry **get**.
ac·quire • *verb* **acquired, acquiring**

acquit (ə kwit′) *verb* to make an official statement that a person accused of something is not guilty [The judge *acquitted* the suspect.]
ac·quit • *verb* **acquitted, acquitting**

acre (ā′kər) *noun* a measure of land equal to 43,560 square feet. The playing area of a football field is a little larger than an acre.
a·cre • *noun, plural* **acres**

acreage (ā′kər ij) *noun* the number of acres in a piece of land.
a·cre·age • *noun, plural* **acreages**

acrobat (ak′rə bat) *noun* a person who does tricks in tumbling or on the trapeze, tightrope, or other equipment.
ac·ro·bat • *noun, plural* **acrobats**

Acropolis (ə kräp′ə lis) the hill in Athens on top of which the Parthenon was built.
A·crop·o·lis

across (ə kräs′ *or* ə krôs′) *adverb* from one side to the other [The new bridge makes it easy to get *across* in a car.]
preposition **1** from one side to the other of [We swam *across* the river.] **2** on the other side of [They live *across* the street.] **3** into contact with [I came *across* an old friend today.]
a·cross • *adverb* • *preposition*

acrylic (ə kril′ik) *noun* a kind of plastic. It is made either in sheets that look like glass, used to make boxes and other things, or in fibers that are made into yarns and fabrics for clothing.
a·cryl·ic • *noun, plural* **acrylics**

act (akt) *noun* **1** a thing done; deed [Rescuing the cat from the roof was an *act* of bravery.] **2** the doing of something; an action [He was caught in the *act* of stealing.] **3** a law; official decision [an *act* of Congress]. **4** one of the main parts of a play, opera, or similar program [The first *act* takes place in a palace.] **5** a showing of some emotion that is not real or true [Bill's anger was just an *act*.]
verb **1** to perform in a play or movie; play a role [She *acts* very well.] **2** to behave; conduct oneself [Don't *act* like a fool.] **3** to seem or pretend to be [He *acted* worried.] **4** to do something [*Act* now if you want tickets.]
—**act up** [*an informal use*] to behave in a joking or bad way.
act • *noun, plural* **acts** • *verb* **acted, acting**

action (ak′shən) *noun* **1** the doing of something [An emergency calls for quick *action*.] **2** an act or thing done [The decision to stop the program was an unpopular *action*.] **3** fighting in war; battle [He was wounded in *action*.]
ac·tion • *noun, plural* **actions**

active (ak′tiv) *adjective* **1** doing something; functioning; working [an *active* volcano]. **2** full of action; lively [She's an *active* child.]
ac·tive • *adjective*

WORD CHOICES

Synonyms of active

Many words share the meaning "full of energy or activity."

brisk	energetic	lively
busy	forceful	vigorous

activity (ak tiv′ə tē) ***noun*** **1** the condition of being active; action; motion [There was not much *activity* in the store.] **2** something that one does besides one's regular work [I take part in many *activities* after school.]
ac·tiv·i·ty ◦ ***noun,*** *plural* **activities**

actor (ak′tər) ***noun*** a person who acts in plays, movies, or television shows. This word can be used for a male or a female actor.
ac·tor ◦ ***noun,*** *plural* **actors**

actress (ak′tris) ***noun*** a woman or girl who acts in plays, movies, or television shows.
ac·tress ◦ ***noun,*** *plural* **actresses**

actual (ak′cho͞o əl) ***adjective*** as it really is; real; true [Sue's *actual* name is Susan.]
ac·tu·al ◦ ***adjective***

actually (ak′cho͞o əl ē) ***adverb*** really; in fact [At what time did we *actually* start?] —Look for the WORD CHOICES box at the entry **really**.
ac·tu·al·ly ◦ ***adverb***

acute (ə kyo͞ot′) ***adjective*** **1** sharp and quick; very sensitive [*acute* eyesight or hearing]. **2** very strong and deep [*acute* pain].
a·cute ◦ ***adjective***

acute angle ***noun*** an angle that is less than 90 degrees.
acute angle ◦ ***noun,*** *plural* **acute angles**

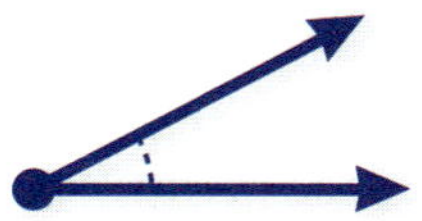

acute angle

ad (ad) ***noun*** *a short form of* **advertisement**.
ad ◦ ***noun,*** *plural* **ads**

● The words **ad** and **add** sound alike.
He placed an *ad* in the newspaper.
Can you *add* a column of numbers?

A.D. the abbreviation for *Anno Domini*, Latin words that mean "in the year of the Lord." It is used in giving dates after the year in which Jesus Christ is believed to have been born. [The ancient Roman Empire lasted from 27 B.C. to A.D. 395.]

Adam (ad′əm) in the Bible, the first man and the husband of Eve.
Ad·am

Adams (ad′əmz), **John** (jän) 1735-1826; the second president of the U.S., from 1797 to 1801.
Ad·ams, John

Adams (ad′əmz), **John Quincy** (jän kwin′sē) 1767-1848; the sixth president of the U.S., from 1825 to 1829. He was the son of John Adams.
Ad·ams, John Quin·cy

adapt (ə dapt′) ***verb*** **1** to change so as to make fit or usable [The size of the cap can be *adapted* to fit a smaller head.] **2** to change in order to fit new conditions [The colonists had to *adapt* to the new land.]
a·dapt ◦ ***verb*** **adapted, adapting**

add (ad) ***verb*** **1** to join something to another thing so that there will be more [We *added* some books to our library.] **2** to join numbers so as to get a total, or sum [*Add* 3 and 5 to get 8.] **3** to say more [Jane agreed to go but *added* that she would be late.]
—add up **1** to equal the sum that is expected [These numbers don't *add up*.] **2** to seem right [His excuse just doesn't *add up*.]
add ◦ ***verb*** **added, adding**

● The words **add** and **ad** sound alike.
Tom will *add* sugar to the lemonade.
She hopes an *ad* will help sell her car.

Addams (ad′əmz), **Jane** (jān) 1860-1935; U.S. social worker and writer. In 1889 she opened a place in Chicago called Hull House to offer services to the poor.
Ad·dams, Jane

addend (ad′end *or* ə dend′) ***noun*** a number that is added to another number. In *3 + 5 = 8, 3* and *5* are addends.
ad·dend ◦ ***noun,*** *plural* **addends**

adder (ad′ər) ***noun*** **1** a small, poisonous snake of Europe. **2** a harmless snake of North America.
ad·der ◦ ***noun,*** *plural* **adders**

addict (ad′ikt *for n.;* ə dikt′ *for v.*) ***noun*** a person who has a habit so strong that it cannot easily be given up [a drug *addict*].

a	cat	ō	go	ʉ	fur	ə = a *in* ago
ā	ape	ô	law, for	ch	chin	e *in* agent
ä	cot, car	o͝o	look	sh	she	i *in* pencil
e	ten	o͞o	tool	th	thin	o *in* atom
ē	me	oi	oil	*th*	then	u *in* circus
i	fit	ou	out	zh	measure	
ī	ice	u	up	ŋ	ring	

verb to give oneself up to some strong habit [Some people are *addicted* to watching TV.]
ad·dict • *noun, plural* **addicts**
• *verb* **addicted, addicting**

addiction (ə dik′shən) *noun* the condition of being addicted to something, especially a harmful drug.
ad·dic·tion • *noun, plural* **addictions**

addition (ə dish′ən) *noun* **1** the adding of two or more numbers to get a sum or total. **2** the act of adding one thing to another thing [The lemonade tasted better with the *addition* of sugar.] **3** a person, thing, or part added [The twins were a new *addition* to the family.]
—in addition besides; as well [And, *in addition*, we visited relatives while we were in town.] **—in addition to** besides [*In addition to* playing the flute, Sue is on the swim team.]
ad·di·tion • *noun, plural* **additions**

additional (ə dish′ən əl) *adjective* more; extra; added [We ordered *additional* pencils.]
ad·di·tion·al • *adjective*

additive (ad′i tiv) *noun* a substance added to something else in small amounts to produce a particular result. Many foods contain additives that keep the food from spoiling quickly.
ad·di·tive • *noun, plural* **additives**

address (ə dres′; *for n. sense 1 also* a′dres) *noun* **1** the place to which mail or packages can be sent to someone; place where someone lives or works. **2** a formal speech [The President's *address* was broadcast on television.]
verb **1** to write on a letter or package the name, street name and number, city, State, and Zip Code of the person to whom it is being sent. **2** to speak or write to [The principal will *address* our first assembly.]
ad·dress • *noun, plural* **addresses**
• *verb* **addressed, addressing**

adenoids (ad′n oidz *or* ad′noidz) *plural noun* growths of tissue in the upper part of the throat, behind the nose. Adenoids sometimes swell up and make it hard to breathe and speak.
ad·e·noids • *plural noun*

adept (ə dept′) *adjective* highly skilled; expert [He's quite *adept* at skating.]
a·dept • *adjective*

adequate (ad′ə kwət) *adjective* enough or good enough for what is needed; suitable [an *adequate* supply of food].
ad·e·quate • *adjective*

adhesive (ad hē′siv) *adjective* having a sticky surface [*Adhesive* tape holds bandages in place.]
noun a sticky substance [Glue is an *adhesive*.]
ad·he·sive • *adjective* • *noun, plural* **adhesives**

adios (a′dē ōs′ *or* ä′dē ōs′) *interjection* a word used to say goodbye. This is a Spanish word.
a·di·os • *interjection*

Adirondacks (ad′ə rän′daks) a mountain range in northeastern New York State. It is also called the **Adirondack Mountains**.
Ad·i·ron·dacks

adj. *abbreviation for* adjective.

adjacent (ə jā′sənt) *adjective* near or next [The playground is *adjacent* to the school.]
ad·ja·cent • *adjective*

adjective (aj′ik tiv) *noun* a word that is used with a noun or pronoun to describe it. Adjectives can tell what kind (a *red* house, the *tallest* mountain) or which one (*this* dog, *those* boys). They can also tell how many or how much (*six* cows, *less* money) or whose (*my* family).
ad·jec·tive • *noun, plural* **adjectives**

adjourn (ə jurn′) *verb* to end a meeting for the day or for a time [Congress had *adjourned* for two weeks.]
ad·journ • *verb* **adjourned, adjourning**

adjust (ə just′) *verb* **1** to change or move in order to make fit [You can *adjust* the piano stool to suit your size.] **2** to arrange the parts of something in order to make it work the right way; set [He *adjusted* his watch to the correct time.] **3** to get used to; adapt [He could not *adjust* to the cold climate.]
ad·just • *verb* **adjusted, adjusting**

adjustable (ə jus′tə bəl) *adjective* capable of being adjusted [The *adjustable* seat can be raised.]
ad·just·a·ble • *adjective*

adjustment (ə just′mənt) *noun* the act or process of adjusting something so that it works the right way [The TV needed only a small *adjustment* to make the picture clear.]
ad·just·ment • *noun, plural* **adjustments**

administer (ad min′is tər) *verb* **1** to be in charge of; to manage or direct the work of [The principal *administers* the school.] **2** to give or dispense [The courts *administer* jus-

A

tice. She *administered* first aid to the injured man.]
ad·min·is·ter • *verb* **administered, administering**

administration (ad min′is trā′shən) *noun* **1** the people who administer, or direct the work of, a company, school, or other organization. **2** *often* **Administration** the president and the other members of the executive branch of a government.
ad·min·is·tra·tion • *noun, plural* **administrations**

admirable (ad′mər ə bəl) *adjective* deserving to be admired or praised [an *admirable* essay].
ad·mi·ra·ble • *adjective*

admiral (ad′mər əl) *noun* **1** the commanding officer of a navy or of a fleet of ships. **2** an officer in the U.S. Navy of the highest rank.
ad·mi·ral • *noun, plural* **admirals**

admiration (ad′mər ā′shən) *noun* a feeling of delight and approval for someone or something having beauty, skill, or other pleasing quality.
ad·mi·ra·tion • *noun*

admire (ad mīr′) *verb* **1** to show delight and approval for [We *admire* his music.] **2** to have much respect for [I *admire* her for her courage.]
ad·mire • *verb* **admired, admiring**

admission (ad mish′ən) *noun* **1** permission to enter [The reporter was refused *admission* to the meeting.] **2** the price charged for entering [*Admission* to the movie is $5.] **3** the act of admitting the truth; confession [His silence seems to be an *admission* of guilt.]
ad·mis·sion • *noun, plural* **admissions**

admit (ad mit′) *verb* **1** to let enter; permit to come or go in [One ticket *admits* two persons to the dance.] **2** to accept as being true; confess [He finally *admitted* his mistake.]
ad·mit • *verb* **admitted, admitting**

admittance (ad mit′ns) *noun* the right to enter ["No *Admittance*" read the sign on the gate.]
ad·mit·tance • *noun*

admonish (ad män′ish) *verb* **1** to warn a person to correct some fault or mistake [The judge *admonished* her to drive more slowly.] **2** to criticize in a mild way [We were *admonished* for coming home late.]
ad·mon·ish • *verb* **admonished, admonishing**

adobe (ə dō′bē) *noun* **1** brick made with clay that has dried in the sun. **2** a house or other building made of adobe bricks.
a·do·be • *noun, plural* **adobes**

adolescence (ad′ə les′ns) *noun* the time of growing up when a person is changing from a child into an adult.
ad·o·les·cence • *noun*

adolescent (ad′ə les′nt) *noun* a boy or girl who is changing from a child into an adult; a teenager.
ad·o·les·cent • *noun, plural* **adolescents**

adopt (ə däpt′) *verb* **1** to take into one's own family according to the law and raise as a son or daughter [They *adopted* a son.] **2** to take and use as one's own [He *adopted* her teaching methods for his own classroom.]
a·dopt • *verb* **adopted, adopting**

adoption (ə däp′shən) *noun* the act of adopting [They discussed the *adoption* of a child.]
a·dop·tion • *noun, plural* **adoptions**

adorable (ə dôr′ə bəl) [*an informal word*] *adjective* very attractive and likable; delightful [What an *adorable* baby!]
a·dor·a·ble • *adjective*

adore (ə dôr′) *verb* **1** to love greatly or to honor highly [He *adores* his wife.] **2** [*an informal use*] to like very much [I *adore* your new hat.]
a·dore • *verb* **adored, adoring**

adorn (ə dôrn′) *verb* to add beauty to; decorate [A gold vase *adorned* the table.]
a·dorn • *verb* **adorned, adorning**

adrift (ə drift′) *adjective* drifting or floating freely without being steered [The boat is *adrift* on the ocean.] This word can also be used as an adverb [The boat was set *adrift*.]
a·drift • *adjective*

adult (ə dult′ *or* ad′ult) *noun* **1** a person who is fully grown up [The *adults* sat and talked while the children played.] **2** a plant or animal that is fully developed.
adjective **1** fully grown up or developed [At one time, only *adult* males were permitted to

a	cat	ō	go	ʉ	fur	ə =	a *in* ago
ā	ape	ô	law, for	ch	chin		e *in* agent
ä	cot, car	oo	look	sh	she		i *in* pencil
e	ten	ōō	tool	th	thin		o *in* atom
ē	me	oi	oil	*th*	then		u *in* circus
i	fit	ou	out	zh	measure		
ī	ice	u	up	ŋ	ring		

vote.] **2** for adults [Our school offers *adult* classes.]
a·dult • *noun, plural* **adults** • *adjective*

adulthood (ə dult′hood) *noun* the time of being an adult.
a·dult·hood • *noun*

adv. *abbreviation for* **adverb**.

advance (ad vans′) *verb* **1** to go or bring forward; move ahead [The runner *advanced* the football two yards.] —Look for the WORD CHOICES boxes at the entries **go** and **progress**. **2** to get a higher or more important job [She *advanced* to manager in six months.]
noun **1** a move forward or ahead [This book is about the latest *advances* in science.] **2** a payment of salary or wages made before it is owed [Mom gave me a $.50 *advance* on my allowance today.]
adjective ahead of time [We received *advance* information about the concert.]
—**in advance 1** in front [The dog walked *in advance* of its owner.] **2** ahead of time [Let us know *in advance* when you will visit us.]
ad·vance • *verb* **advanced, advancing** • *noun, plural* **advances** • *adjective*

advanced (ad vanst′) *adjective* **1** far on in life; old [She started a new career at an *advanced* age.] **2** at a higher or more difficult level [We enrolled in the *advanced* swimming class.]
ad·vanced • *adjective*

advancement (ad vans′mənt) *noun* **1** the act of moving forward or ahead. **2** the act of getting or making better [Education helps the *advancement* of humanity.]
ad·vance·ment • *noun, plural* **advancements**

advantage (ad vant′ij) *noun* **1** a better chance; more favorable position [His long legs gave him an *advantage* in the race.] **2** something that helps or gives a better chance; a benefit [The cheering of the fans can be an *advantage* for the home team.]
—**take advantage of** to make use of and benefit by [*Take advantage of* her offer to drive you home.]
ad·van·tage • *noun, plural* **advantages**

adventure (ad ven′chər) *noun* **1** an exciting and dangerous event [We read about his *adventures* in the jungle.] **2** an unusual experience that will be remembered [Going to the circus is an *adventure* for a child.]
ad·ven·ture • *noun, plural* **adventures**

adventurous (ad ven′chər əs) *adjective* **1** liking adventure; willing to take risks [an *adventurous* explorer]. **2** full of danger; risky [an *adventurous* voyage].
ad·ven·tur·ous • *adjective*

adverb (ad′vurb) *noun* a word that is used to say something about a verb, an adjective, or another adverb. Adverbs can tell when (*always* sad) or where (Come *here*. Go *home*.) They can also tell how (going *fast*, running *swiftly*) or how much (*very* quickly, *slightly* angry).
ad·verb • *noun, plural* **adverbs**

adversary (ad′vər ser′ē) *noun* a person who is against another; enemy or opponent.
ad·ver·sar·y • *noun, plural* **adversaries**

advertise (ad′vər tīz) *verb* **1** to tell many people about a product in a way that makes them want to buy it [The company *advertises* on TV.] **2** to tell people about or ask them for [She *advertised* in the paper for a baby sitter.]
ad·ver·tise • *verb* **advertised, advertising**

advertisement (ad′vər tīz′mənt *or* ad vur′tiz mənt) *noun* a public announcement that advertises something.
ad·ver·tise·ment • *noun, plural* **advertisements**

advertising (ad′vər tīz′iŋ) *noun* **1** an advertisement or advertisements [Their *advertising* calls attention to their low prices.] **2** the work of preparing advertisements and getting them printed or on radio and TV.
ad·ver·tis·ing • *noun*

advice (ad vīs′) *noun* opinion given as to what to do or how to do something.
ad·vice • *noun*

advisable (ad vīz′ə bəl) *adjective* being good advice; wise; sensible [It is *advisable* to use the seat belts in a car.]
ad·vis·a·ble • *adjective*

advise (ad vīz′) *verb* **1** to give advice to [The doctor *advised* him to get enough sleep.] **2** to offer something as advice [The doctor *advised* a long vacation.] **3** to let know; notify [The telegram *advised* us that we had won the contest.] —Look for the WORD CHOICES box at the entry **inform**.
ad·vise • *verb* **advised, advising**

advisor or **adviser** (ad vī′zər) *noun* a person who offers advice [A pastor is a spiritual *advisor*.]

A

ad·vi·sor or **ad·vi·ser** • *noun, plural* **advisors** or **advisers**

advisory (ad vī′zər ē) ***noun*** a warning that bad weather is on the way [The thunderstorm *advisory* will remain in effect until midnight.]
ad·vi·so·ry • ***noun,*** *plural* **advisories**

advocate (ad′və kāt *for v.;* ad′və kit *for n.*) ***verb*** to speak or write in favor of [The senator *advocated* the new housing law.]
noun a person who advocates something.
ad·vo·cate • ***verb*** **advocated, advocating** • ***noun,*** *plural* **advocates**

aerial (er′ē əl) ***adjective*** having to do with aircraft or flying [*aerial* photographs of the city].
noun a radio or television antenna.
aer·i·al ***adjective*** • ***noun,*** *plural* **aerials**

aerie or **aery** (er′ē *or* ir′ē) ***noun*** the nest of an eagle, falcon, or other bird of prey. It is built near the top of a cliff or in some other high place.
aer·ie or **aer·y** • ***noun,*** *plural* **aeries**
● The words **aerie** (or **aery**) and **airy** sound alike.
We saw a hawk's *aerie* on the cliff.
The melody is light and *airy*.

aero- *a prefix meaning* air or flying [*Aerobatics* are done by an airplane in the air.]

aerobatics (er′ə bat′iks) ***plural noun*** spectacular feats done with an airplane. Aerobatics may include loops and rolls and flying upside down.
aer·o·bat·ics • ***plural noun***

aerobic (er ō′bik) ***adjective*** making the body able to take in more oxygen and use it better [Running and swimming are *aerobic* exercises.]
aer·o·bic • ***adjective***

aerobics (er ō′biks) ***plural noun*** [*used with a singular or plural verb*] **1** aerobic exercises. **2** an exercise program that combines various stretching movements with dance steps. It is usually done along with music. [The group does *aerobics* three times a week.]
aer·o·bics • ***plural noun***

aeronautics (er′ə nôt′iks *or* er′ə nät′iks) ***plural noun*** [*used with a singular verb*] the science or work of making and flying aircraft.
aer·o·nau·tics • ***plural noun***

aerosol (er′ə säl *or* er′ə sôl) ***adjective*** using a gas under pressure to produce a fine spray of liquid [an *aerosol* can; an *aerosol* deodorant].
aer·o·sol • ***adjective***

aerospace (er′ō spās) ***noun*** the earth's atmosphere and all the space outside it.
aer·o·space • ***noun***

Aesop (ē′säp) a Greek writer of fables, who is thought to have lived in the sixth century B.C.
Ae·sop

afar (ə fär′) ***adverb*** *used mainly in the phrase* **from afar**, from a distance [The news *from afar* arrived after a long time.]
a·far • ***adverb***

affair (ə fer′) ***noun*** **1** any event or happening [This meeting is a boring *affair*.] **2 affairs** matters of business [Who will take care of your *affairs* while you are away?]
af·fair • ***noun,*** *plural* **affairs**

affect (ə fekt′) ***verb*** **1** to bring about a change in; have an effect on [Bright light *affects* the eyes.] **2** to make feel sad or sorry [The story's unhappy ending *affects* most readers.]
af·fect • ***verb*** **affected, affecting**

affection (ə fek′shən) ***noun*** a warm liking; loving feeling [He sent her flowers as a sign of his *affection*.] —Look for the WORD CHOICES box at the entry **love**.
af·fec·tion • ***noun,*** *plural* **affections**

affectionate (ə fek′shən it) ***adjective*** full of affection [an *affectionate* look].
af·fec·tion·ate • ***adjective***

affirm (ə fʉrm′) ***verb*** to say something and say that it is true [She *affirmed* that the danger was great.]
af·firm • ***verb*** **affirmed, affirming**

affirmative (ə fʉrm′ə tiv) ***adjective*** saying that something is true; answering "yes" [an *affirmative* reply].
af·firm·a·tive • ***adjective***

afflict (ə flikt′) ***verb*** to cause pain or suffering to; trouble [He is *afflicted* with a skin rash.]
af·flict • ***verb*** **afflicted, afflicting**

affliction (ə flik′shən) ***noun*** suffering or the cause of suffering; pain; trouble.
af·flic·tion • ***noun,*** *plural* **afflictions**

afford (ə fôrd′) ***verb*** **1** to have money enough to spare for [Can we *afford* a new car? We are able to *afford* it.] **2** to be able to do something

a cat	ō go	ʉ fur	ə = a *in* ago
ā ape	ô law, for	ch chin	e *in* agent
ä cot, car	oo look	sh she	i *in* pencil
e ten	ōō tool	th thin	o *in* atom
ē me	oi oil	*th* then	u *in* circus
i fit	ou out	zh measure	
ī ice	u up	ŋ ring	

without taking a great risk [She can't *afford* to miss any more days of school.]
af·ford • *verb* **afforded, affording**

affront (ə frunt′) *noun* speech or behavior that is meant to be rude or to hurt someone; an insult made on purpose.
af·front • *noun, plural* **affronts**

afghan

afghan (af′gan) *noun* a soft, crocheted or knitted blanket or shawl.
af·ghan • *noun, plural* **afghans**

Afghanistan (af gan′i stan) a country in southwestern Asia, between Iran and Pakistan.
Af·ghan·i·stan

afield (ə fēld′) *adverb* away from home or off the right path [He wandered far *afield*.]
a·field • *adverb*

afloat (ə flōt′) *adjective* floating on the surface [Several toy boats are *afloat* on the pond.] This word can also be used as an adverb [The boat stayed *afloat* throughout the storm.]
a·float • *adjective*

afoot (ə foot′) *adverb* **1** on foot; walking [We set out *afoot* while the others waited for the bus.] **2** going on or being made; in progress [There is trouble *afoot*.]
a·foot • *adverb*

afraid (ə frād′) *adjective* **1** feeling fear; frightened [There is no reason to be *afraid* of the dark.] **2** [*an informal use*] feeling sorry; full of regret [I'm *afraid* that I can't go with you.]
a·fraid • *adjective*

Africa (af′ri kə) the second largest continent. It is south of Europe, between the Atlantic and Indian oceans.
Af·ri·ca

African (af′ri kən) *adjective* of or having to do with Africa, its peoples, or their cultures [an *African* language; *African* art].
noun a person born or living in Africa.
Af·ri·can • *adjective* • *noun, plural* **Africans**

African-American (af′ri kən ə mer′i kən) *noun* an American whose ancestors came from Africa south of the Sahara desert.
Af·ri·can-A·mer·i·can • *noun, plural* **African-Americans**

after (af′tər) *adverb* **1** behind in place or time; coming next [You go on ahead, and we'll follow *after*.] **2** following in time; later [They came at noon and left three hours *after*.]
preposition **1** behind in place or time [The soldiers marched one *after* the other.] **2** with the purpose of catching, following, or finding [The dog ran *after* the rabbit.] **3** later than [It's ten minutes *after* four.] **4** because of [*After* what has happened, he won't go.] **5** in honor of [named *after* her aunt].
conjunction following the time when [They left the party *after* we did.]
af·ter • *adverb* • *preposition* • *conjunction*

afternoon (af tər no͞on′) *noun* the time of day from noon to evening.
af·ter·noon • *noun, plural* **afternoons**

afterward (af′tər wərd) *adverb* at a later time [We ate and went for a walk *afterward*.]
af·ter·ward • *adverb*

afterwards (af′tər wərdz) *adverb the same as the adverb* **afterward**.
af·ter·wards • *adverb*

again (ə gen′) *adverb* **1** once more; a second time [I enjoyed the book so much that I may read it *again*.] **2** back into a former place or condition; as before [She is home *again*.]
a·gain • *adverb*

against (ə genst′) *preposition* **1** opposed or contrary to [The council is *against* the proposal.] **2** toward in order to strike [She threw the ball *against* the wall.] **3** opposite to the direction of [It was hard to walk *against* the wind.]
a·gainst • *preposition*

agate (ag′ət) *noun* **1** a hard stone with striped or clouded coloring, used in jewelry. **2** a small glass ball that looks like this, used in playing marbles.
ag·ate • *noun, plural* **agates**

age (āj) *noun* **1** the time that a person or a thing has existed from birth or beginning [She graduated at the *age* of eighteen.] **2** a part of life [Adolescence is often called an awkward *age*.] **3** the fact of being old [The pages of the book were yellow with *age*.] **4** a period of time in history [the Stone *Age;* the Space *Age*]

A

—Look for the WORD CHOICES box at the entry **period**. **5** *usually* **ages** [*an informal use*] a long time [It's been *ages* since I've seen her.]
verb **1** to grow old [Our dog is *aging* quickly.] **2** to make old [Hard work has *aged* him.]
age • ***noun,*** *plural* **ages** • ***verb*** **aged, aging**

aged (ā′jid *for sense 1;* ājd *for sense 2*) ***adjective*** **1** grown old [my *aged* grandmother]. **2** of the age of [a pupil *aged* ten].
a·ged • ***adjective***

agency (ā′jən sē) ***noun*** **1** the work or office of a person or company that acts for someone else [An employment *agency* helps people find jobs.] **2** a part of government or some other organization that gives a special kind of help [The social *agency* gives food and clothing to people in need.]
a·gen·cy • ***noun,*** *plural* **agencies**

agent (ā′jənt) ***noun*** **1** something that brings about a certain result [Education is an *agent* for changing society.] **2** a person or company that does something for another [Most actors hire *agents* to handle their business.]
a·gent • ***noun,*** *plural* **agents**

aggravate (ag′rə vāt) ***verb*** **1** to make worse; make more troublesome [Walking will *aggravate* your sprained ankle.] **2** [*an informal use*] to make angry; annoy; bother [The talking in the audience began to *aggravate* us.]
ag·gra·vate • ***verb*** **aggravated, aggravating**

WORD HISTORY

aggravate

The word **aggravate** comes from a Latin verb that means "to make heavier" and is related to the word **gravity**. When a problem is **aggravated,** it is made heavier or greater than it was before.

aggression (ə gresh′ən) ***noun*** the actions of starting a fight or war by a person or nation.
ag·gres·sion • ***noun,*** *plural* **aggressions**

aggressive (ə gres′iv) ***adjective*** **1** ready to start fights or quarrels [an *aggressive* bully]. **2** bold and active [an *aggressive* leader].
ag·gres·sive • ***adjective***

aghast (ə gast′) ***adjective*** feeling shock or horror; horrified [*aghast* at the sight of blood].
a·ghast • ***adjective***

agile (aj′əl) ***adjective*** moving with quickness and ease; active; nimble [an *agile* jumper] —Look for the WORD CHOICES box at the entry **nimble**.
ag·ile • ***adjective***

agility (ə jil′ə tē) ***noun*** the ability to move with quickness and ease [Tennis requires *agility*.]
a·gil·i·ty • ***noun***

agitate (aj′ə tāt) ***verb*** **1** to stir up or shake up [A washing machine *agitates* the clothes.] **2** to excite or disturb the feelings of [News of the accident *agitated* them.]
ag·i·tate • ***verb*** **agitated, agitating**

aglow (ə glō′) ***adjective*** filled with color; glowing [Her face was *aglow* with anger.]
a·glow • ***adjective***

ago (ə gō′) ***adjective*** gone by; before now [They were married ten years *ago*.]
adverb in the past [That happened long *ago*.]
a·go • ***adjective*** • ***adverb***

agony (ag′ə nē) ***noun*** very great pain in the body or mind [The injured man is in *agony*.] —Look for the WORD CHOICES boxes at the entries **distress** and **torment**.
ag·o·ny • ***noun,*** *plural* **agonies**

agree (ə grē′) ***verb*** **1** to say "yes"; consent [The detective *agreed* to investigate the case.] **2** to have the same opinion [The waiter *agreed* that the steak was overdone.] **3** to be alike or similar [Our tastes in art *agree*.] —Look for the WORD CHOICES box at the entry **coincide**. **4** in grammar, to match with another word in certain ways. In "We are here," the subject "We" and the verb "are" agree in number.
a·gree • ***verb*** **agreed, agreeing**

agreeable (ə grē′ə bəl) ***adjective*** **1** pleasing or pleasant [an *agreeable* odor] —Look for the WORD CHOICES box at the entry **pleasant**. **2** willing or ready to say "yes" [The principal was *agreeable* to our plan.]
a·gree·a·ble • ***adjective***

agreement (ə grē′mənt) ***noun*** **1** the fact or condition of agreeing [The news report was not in *agreement* with the facts.] **2** an understanding between two or more people, groups,

a	cat	ō	go	ʉ	fur	ə = a *in* ago	
ā	ape	ô	law, for	ch	chin	e *in* agent	
ä	cot, car	oo	look	sh	she	i *in* pencil	
e	ten	ōō	tool	th	thin	o *in* atom	
ē	me	oi	oil	*th*	then	u *in* circus	
i	fit	ou	out	zh	measure		
ī	ice	u	up	ŋ	ring		

or nations [The U.S. and Japan signed a new trade *agreement*.]
a·gree·ment • *noun,*
plural for sense 2 only **agreements**

agricultural (ag′ri kul′chər əl) *adjective* working in or having to do with farming [Where are the main *agricultural* regions of the country?]
ag·ri·cul·tur·al • *adjective*

agriculture (ag′ri kul′chər) *noun* the work of growing crops and raising farm animals; science of farming.
ag·ri·cul·ture • *noun*

aground (ə ground′) *adverb* on or onto the shore, the water's bottom, or a reef [The ship ran *aground* in the shallow bay.]
a·ground • *adverb*

ah (ä) *interjection* a sound made to show pain, surprise, delight, or various other feelings.

aha (ä hä′) *interjection* a sound made to show satisfaction, success, joy, or other similar feelings.
a·ha • *interjection*

ahead (ə hed′) *adjective* in or to the front; forward [Her desk is directly *ahead* of mine.] This word can also be used as an adverb [Our horse moved *ahead* halfway through the race.]
—ahead of before [I arrived at the theater *ahead of* him.]
a·head • *adjective*

ahoy (ə hoi′) *interjection* a word shouted by sailors on one ship to get the attention of sailors on another ship [Ship *ahoy!*]
a·hoy • *interjection*

aid (ād) *verb* to give help to; assist [The cane *aided* the patient in walking.]
noun **1** help or assistance given to persons in need [*Aid* was sent to the area destroyed by the flood.] **2** a helpful device [The globe is an *aid* to learning geography.] **3** a helper; assistant [She worked as a nurse's *aid*.]
aid • *verb* **aided, aiding** • *noun, plural* **aids**
● The words **aid** and **aide** sound alike.
I will *aid* the committee any way
that I possibly can.
The senator's *aide* wrote the speech.

aide (ād) *noun* an assistant [She is an *aide* to the senator.]
aide • *noun, plural* **aides**
● The words **aide** and **aid** sound alike.
She was hired as *aide* to the diplomat.
The crutch will *aid* you till you heal.

AIDS (ādz) *noun* a condition caused by a virus that leads to a dangerous illness and, usually, death. AIDS stands for *Acquired Immune Deficiency Syndrome*.

ail (āl) *verb* **1** to cause pain to; trouble; distress [What is *ailing* our grandfather today?] **2** to be ill; feel sick [Grandfather is *ailing* today.]
ail • *verb* **ailed, ailing**
● The words **ail** and **ale** sound alike.
To *ail* is to feel sick.
She prefers *ale* that is not so sweet.

ailment (āl′mənt) *noun* an illness; sickness [The school nurse treats our minor *ailments*.]
ail·ment • *noun, plural* **ailments**

aim (ām) *verb* **1** to point a gun or other weapon in order to hit [It is hard to *aim* at a moving target.] **2** to direct the path of something, such as a punch or a thrown ball [He *aimed* the plane toward the runway.] **3** to have as a goal or purpose [We *aim* to please our guests.]
noun **1** the ability to hit a target [Your *aim* will improve with practice.] **2** a goal or purpose [Her chief *aim* is to become a doctor.]
aim • *verb* **aimed, aiming** • *noun,*
plural **aims**

aimless (ām′lis) *adjective* having no aim or purpose [an *aimless* stroll through the park].
aim·less • *adjective*

ain't (ānt) [*an informal word*] *a short form of* am not, is not, are not, has not, or have not.
■ Most people do not now think of **ain't** as correct English. But it once was considered acceptable to use *ain't* instead of *am not* in questions [I'm going too, *ain't* I?]

air (er) *noun* **1** the mixture of gases that is all around the earth. Air cannot be seen, but it can spread to fill a space and it can move in currents. It is made up mainly of nitrogen and oxygen. **2** space above the earth; sky [The lark flew into the *air*.] **3** a feeling or mood gotten from someone or something [An *air* of mystery surrounds the old house.]
verb **1** to let air into or through in order to dry, cool, or freshen [We *aired* the room to let out the smoke.] **2** to make widely known [They shouldn't *air* private quarrels at the meeting.]
—on the air being broadcast on radio or TV [The news is *on the air* at six o'clock.]
air • *noun, plural for sense 3 only* **airs**
• *verb* **aired, airing**

A

● The words **air, heir,** and often **err** sound alike.
  Open the window to let in fresh *air*.
  He was *heir* to his mother's estate.
  To *err* is human, to forgive divine.

air bag

air bag *noun* a large bag that fills with air at once inside a car at the moment of a crash. Air bags protect the riders from being thrown forward.
air bag ◦ *noun, plural* **air bags**

air conditioner *noun* a machine for cleaning and cooling the air.
air conditioner ◦ *noun, plural* **air conditioners**

air conditioning *noun* a system for cleaning and cooling the air in a building, car, or other enclosed space.

aircraft (er′kraft) *noun* any machine for flying [Jets and helicopters are *aircraft*.]
air·craft ◦ *noun, plural* **aircraft**

air force *noun* the part of a nation's armed forces that fights with aircraft.
air force ◦ *noun, plural* **air forces**

airless (er′lis) *adjective* without fresh air [a smelly, *airless* attic].
air·less ◦ *adjective*

airline (er′līn) *noun* a company that carries passengers or freight by aircraft [Which *airlines* fly to Mexico?]
air·line ◦ *noun, plural* **airlines**

airliner (er′līn′ər) *noun* a large passenger airplane.
air·lin·er ◦ *noun, plural* **airliners**

airmail (er′māl) *noun* mail carried overseas by aircraft. It is charged higher postage rates than regular mail.
adjective having to do with airmail [An *airmail* envelope is usually made of very thin paper.]
air·mail ◦ *noun* ◦ *adjective*

airman (er′mən) *noun* **1** a pilot or crew member of an aircraft. **2** an enlisted man or enlisted woman in the U.S. Air Force.
air·man ◦ *noun, plural* **airmen**

air mass *noun* a huge body of air of a particular kind, spread over hundreds of miles. Warm air masses form in tropical areas and cold air masses form in polar areas.
air mass ◦ *noun, plural* **air masses**

airplane (er′plān) *noun* an aircraft that is kept up by the force of air upon its wings. Airplanes are driven forward by jet engines or propellers.
air·plane ◦ *noun, plural* **airplanes**

airport (er′pôrt) *noun* a place where aircraft can take off and land.
air·port ◦ *noun, plural* **airports**

airs (erz) *noun used mainly in the phrase* **put on airs**, to act as if one is better than others [You will lose friends if you *put on airs*.]

airship (er′ship) *noun* any aircraft that is filled with a gas lighter than air and that can be steered. Blimps and dirigibles are airships.
air·ship ◦ *noun, plural* **airships**

airsick (er′sik) *adjective* feeling sick or throwing up from traveling in an aircraft.
air·sick ◦ *adjective*

airstrip (er′strip) *noun* an area of hard, flat ground for planes to take off and land. It is usually for temporary use.
air·strip ◦ *noun, plural* **airstrips**

airtight (er′tīt) *adjective* **1** closed so tightly that air cannot get in or out [an *airtight* thermos of soup]. **2** having no weak points that could be easily attacked or proved to be false [an *airtight* excuse].
air·tight ◦ *adjective*

airy (er′ē) *adjective* **1** open to the air [an *airy* room]. **2** light as air; delicate [*airy* music].
air·y ◦ *adjective* **airier, airiest**

● The words **airy** and **aerie** (or **aery**) sound alike.
  The melody is light and *airy*.
  We saw a hawk's *aerie* on the cliff.

a	cat	ō	go	ʉ	fur	ə = a *in* ago	
ā	ape	ô	law, for	ch	chin	e *in* agent	
ä	cot, car	oo	look	sh	she	i *in* pencil	
e	ten	ōō	tool	th	thin	o *in* atom	
ē	me	oi	oil	*th*	then	u *in* circus	
i	fit	ou	out	zh	measure		
ī	ice	u	up	ŋ	ring		

aisle (īl) ***noun*** an open way for passing between sections of seats in such a place as a church or theater.
aisle • ***noun,*** *plural* **aisles**
- The words **aisle, I'll,** and **isle** sound alike.
  We took the side *aisle* to our seats.
  I'll be seeing you in the fall.
  The tiny *isle* had a sandy beach.

ajar (ə jär′) ***adverb*** slightly open [Leave the door *ajar* for the cat.] This word can also be used as an adjective [The door is *ajar.*]
a·jar • ***adverb***

AK *abbreviation for* Alaska.

akimbo

akimbo (ə kim′bō) ***adjective*** with the hands on the hips and the elbows bent outward [The referee stood with his arms *akimbo.*]
a·kim·bo • ***adjective***

akin (ə kin′) ***adjective*** alike in some ways; similar [Lemons and limes are *akin* in taste.]
a·kin • ***adjective***

-al *a suffix meaning:* **1** of or like [*Musical* sounds are sounds of or like music.] **2** the act or process of [*Denial* is the act of denying.]

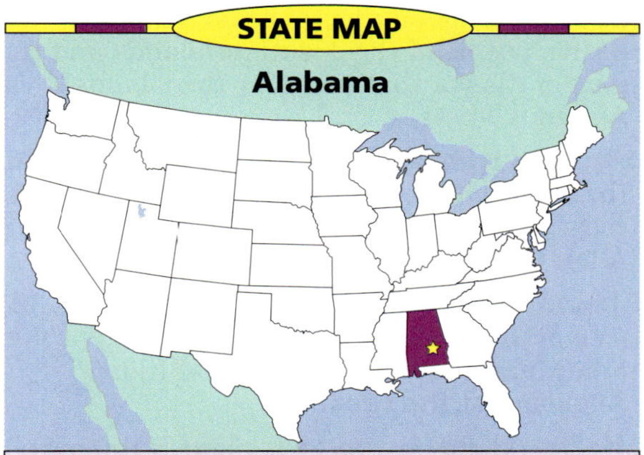

Statehood: 1819, the 22nd state • **Capital:** Montgomery

Alabama (al′ə bam′ə) a State in the southeastern part of the U.S. Its capital is Montgomery. Abbreviated **AL** or **Ala.**
Al·a·bam·a

alabaster (al′ə bas′tər) ***noun*** a smooth, white stone that is used for statues.
al·a·bas·ter • ***noun***

Aladdin (ə lad′n) a boy in *The Arabian Nights* who finds a magic lamp and a magic ring. Whenever he rubs these, a genie appears to do whatever he asks.
A·lad·din

Alamo (al′ə mō) a mission, later a fort, at San Antonio, Texas. Mexican troops captured it in 1836.
Al·a·mo

a la mode (ä′lə mōd′) ***adjective*** served with ice cream [pie *a la mode*].

alarm (ə lärm′) ***noun*** **1** a bell, siren, or other signal that warns of danger or an emergency [a fire *alarm*]. **2** the bell or buzzer on an alarm clock. **3** sudden fear caused by possible danger [The rapidly rising river filled the town with *alarm.*] —Look for the WORD CHOICES box at the entry **panic**.
verb to make suddenly afraid [News of the flood *alarmed* us.]
a·larm • ***noun,*** *plural* **alarms**
• ***verb*** **alarmed, alarming**

alarm clock ***noun*** a clock that can be set to ring or buzz at the time that a person wants to wake up.
alarm clock • ***noun,*** *plural* **alarm clocks**

alas (ə las′) ***interjection*** a word used to show regret, sadness, pity, or worry.
a·las • ***interjection***

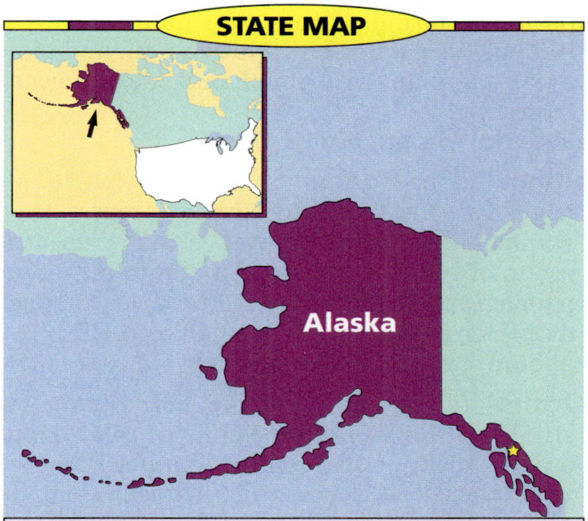

Statehood: 1959, the 49th state • **Capital:** Juneau

Alaska (ə las′kə) a State of the U.S. in northwestern North America, separated by a narrow strait from Asia. Its capital is Juneau. Abbreviated **AK** or **Alas.**
A·las·ka

Albania (al bā′nē ə) a country in southern Europe.
Al·ba·ni·a

Albany (ôl′bə nē) the capital of New York State, on the Hudson River.
Al·ba·ny

albatross

albatross (al′bə träs *or* al′bə trôs) ***noun*** a large sea bird with long, narrow wings, webbed feet, and a large hooked beak.
al·ba·tross • ***noun,*** *plural* **albatrosses**

Alberta (al bʉrt′ə) a province of western Canada. Abbreviated **AB** or **Alta.**
Al·ber·ta

albino (al bī′nō) ***noun*** **1** a person who lacks normal coloring of the skin, hair, and eyes. Albinos have pale skin, whitish hair, and pink eyes. **2** a plant or animal that lacks normal coloring.
al·bi·no • ***noun,*** *plural* **albinos**

album (al′bəm) ***noun*** **1** a book with blank pages for collecting things like photographs or stamps. **2** a recording that is made up of a group of songs or stories. An album may be a phonograph record, cassette tape, or compact disc [Her new *album* is available on CD.]
al·bum • ***noun,*** *plural* **albums**

alcohol (al′kə häl *or* al′kə hôl) ***noun*** **1** a strong-smelling liquid that has no color, evaporates quickly, and burns with a hot flame. It is produced by fermenting things, such as grain or fruit, and is used in industry and medicine. **2** any drink or beverage that has alcohol in it.
al·co·hol • ***noun,*** *plural* **alcohols**

alcoholic (al′kə häl′ik *or* al′kə hôl′ik) ***adjective*** containing alcohol [an *alcoholic* beverage].
noun a person who suffers from alcoholism.
al·co·hol·ic • ***adjective*** • ***noun,*** *plural* **alcoholics**

alcoholism (al′kə häl′iz əm *or* al′kə hôl′ iz əm) ***noun*** a condition in which there is a strong need or desire to drink a large amount of alcohol.
al·co·hol·ism • ***noun***

alder (ôl′dər) ***noun*** a small tree like the birch. It grows in cool, wet soil.
al·der • ***noun,*** *plural* **alders**

ale (āl) ***noun*** an alcoholic drink made from malt and hops. It is very much like beer.
ale • ***noun,*** *plural* **ales**
● The words **ale** and **ail** sound alike.
She prefers *ale* that is not so sweet.
To *ail* is to feel sick.

alert (ə lʉrt′) ***adjective*** **1** watching closely and ready [an *alert* guard]. **2** quick in thought or action; active [an *alert* mind].
noun **1** a warning signal; alarm [The tornado *alert* was sounded.] **2** the time from such a warning signal until the danger is over [The storm *alert* was ended at midnight.]
verb **1** to warn to be ready [The captain *alerted* the troops.] **2** to make aware [The warden *alerted* the police that a convict had escaped.]
a·lert • ***adjective*** • ***noun,*** *plural* **alerts** • ***verb*** **alerted, alerting**

Aleut (al′ē o͞ot *or* ə lo͞ot′) ***noun*** a member of a native people of the Aleutian Islands and the part of Alaska that lies near the islands.
Al·e·ut • ***noun***

Aleutian Islands (ə lo͞o′shən) a part of Alaska that is a chain of islands off the southwest coast.
A·leu·tian Islands

Alexander the Great (al′ig zan′dər) 356-323 B.C.; a Greek king who conquered Egypt and other lands between Turkey and India.
Al·ex·an·der the Great

alfalfa (al fal′fə) ***noun*** a plant with purple flowers and long, deep roots. It is grown as food for animals such as cattle or horses.
al·fal·fa • ***noun***

algae (al′jē) ***plural noun*** a group of simple

a	cat	ō	go	ʉ	fur	ə =	a *in* ago
ā	ape	ô	law, for	ch	chin		e *in* agent
ä	cot, car	o͝o	look	sh	she		i *in* pencil
e	ten	o͞o	tool	th	thin		o *in* atom
ē	me	oi	oil	*th*	then		u *in* circus
i	fit	ou	out	zh	measure		
ī	ice	u	up	ŋ	ring		

plants that have no leaves, stems, or roots. They grow in water or on wet surfaces. Most seaweeds are algae.
al·gae • ***plural noun***

Algeria (al jir′ē ə) a country in northern Africa.
Al·ge·ri·a

Algonquian (al gäŋ′kē ən *or* al gäŋ′kwē ən) ***noun*** **1** a large group of North American Indian languages. **2** a member of a people speaking any of these languages.
Al·gon·qui·an • ***noun***

alias (ā′lē əs) ***noun*** a name that a person uses to hide who he or she really is [The man who cheated us used an *alias.*]
adverb also named [He is Robin Smith, *alias* Robert Jones.]
a·li·as • ***noun,*** *plural* **aliases** • ***adverb***

Ali Baba (ä′lē bä′bə *or* al′ē bab′ə) in *The Arabian Nights*, a poor woodcutter who finds the treasure of forty thieves in a cave. He makes the door of the cave open by saying, "Open sesame!"
A·li Ba·ba

alibi (al′ə bī) ***noun*** the claim or proof that a person blamed for committing a crime was not at the scene of the crime when it took place.
al·i·bi • ***noun,*** *plural* **alibis**

WORD HISTORY

alibi

The Latin word *alibi* was formed from a phrase meaning "somewhere else." A person who gives an **alibi** often says, "I was somewhere else when the crime was committed."

alien (āl′ē ən *or* āl′yən) ***adjective*** belonging to another country or people; foreign [*alien* customs].
noun **1** a person from another country. **2** a person living in a country but not a citizen of it. **3** an imaginary being from outer space.
al·ien • ***adjective*** • ***noun,*** *plural* **aliens**

alight (ə līt′) ***verb*** **1** to get down or off; dismount [Kit *alighted* from the horse.] **2** to come down after flight; settle [The crow *alighted* on the fence.]
a·light • ***verb*** **alighted** or **alit, alighting**

align (ə līn′) ***verb*** **1** to put into a straight line [*Align* the chairs along the wall.] **2** to adjust the parts of something so that they work well together [The car steered easily after she *aligned* the front wheels.]
a·lign • ***verb*** **aligned, aligning**

alike (ə līk′) ***adjective*** like one another; similar [He and his father look *alike.*]
adverb in the same way; similarly [They were dressed *alike.*]
a·like • ***adjective*** • ***adverb***

alit (ə lit′) ***verb*** *a past tense and past participle of* **alight**.
a·lit • ***verb***

alive (ə līv′) ***adjective*** **1** having life; living [He was badly hurt but still *alive.*] **2** going on; in action; not ended or destroyed [The memory of those times is still *alive.*]
—alive with full of living or moving things [The garden is *alive with* insects.]
a·live • ***adjective***

all (ôl) ***adjective*** **1** the whole of or the whole amount of [I never heard such talk in *all* my life. He gave her *all* the money.] **2** every one of [*All* the people are here.] **3** without anything else; only [Life is not *all* fun.]
pronoun **1** [*used with a plural verb*] every one [*All* of us are here.] **2** every part or bit; everything [*All* of the candy is gone.]
noun **1** everything that a person has [He gave his *all* but still lost the game.] **2** the whole amount [That's *all* you are going to get.]
adverb **1** completely; entirely [The food is *all* gone.] **2** each; apiece [The score is ten *all.*]
—all over **1** ended; finished [The game was *all over* by one o'clock.] **2** everywhere [We looked *all over* for the cat.] **—at all** in the smallest amount; in any way [I don't understand this *at all.*]

- The words **all** and **awl** sound alike.
  All the lettuce went into the salad.
  I used the *awl* with the broken handle.

Allah (al′ä *or* ä′lä) the Muslim name for God.
Al·lah

all-American (ôl′ə mer′i kən) ***adjective*** **1** made up entirely of Americans [an *all-American* group of scientists]. **2** chosen as one of the best college athletes of the year in the U.S. [an *all-American* football player].
all-A·mer·i·can • ***adjective***

all-around (ôl′ə round′) ***adjective*** able to do

many things or be used for many purposes [A tractor is an *all-around* farm machine.]
all·a·round • *adjective*

allege (ə lej′) ***verb*** to say firmly but usually without having proof [The pilot *alleged* that she saw a flying saucer.]
al·lege • ***verb*** **alleged, alleging**

Allegheny Mountains (al′ə gā′nē) a mountain range in central Pennsylvania, Maryland, West Virginia, and Virginia. It is also called **the Alleghenies**.
Al·le·ghe·ny Mountains

allegiance (ə lē′jəns) ***noun*** loyalty or devotion that a person has to his or her country or leader or to family or friends.
al·le·giance • ***noun***

WORD CHOICES

Synonyms of **allegiance**

The words **allegiance**, **faithfulness**, and **loyalty** share the meaning "support and respect for something or someone."

pledging *allegiance* to the flag

our old dog's *faithfulness*

his *loyalty* to his friend

alleluia (al′ə lo͞o′yə) ***interjection*** *the same as* **hallelujah**.
al·le·lu·ia • ***interjection***

Allen (al′ən), **Ethan** (ē′thən) 1738-1789; American soldier in the American Revolution.
Al·len, E·than

allergic (ə lʉr′jik) ***adjective*** **1** caused by an allergy [He had an *allergic* reaction to the medicine.] **2** having an allergy [I am *allergic* to milk.]
al·ler·gic • ***adjective***

allergy (al′ər jē) ***noun*** a condition in which coughing, sneezing, or a rash develops when a person comes in contact with certain things. The things that can cause an allergy in one person usually do not affect most people.
al·ler·gy • ***noun,*** *plural* **allergies**

alley (al′ē) ***noun*** **1** a narrow street or path behind or between buildings [Garbage cans are kept in the *alley*.] **2** one of the long, narrow lanes of polished wood used for bowling.
al·ley • ***noun,*** *plural* **alleys**

alliance (ə lī′əns) ***noun*** the agreement made to join or come together for some purpose. An alliance may be made by joining two families by marriage or two nations by a treaty.
al·li·ance • ***noun,*** *plural* **alliances**

allied (ə līd′ *or* al′īd) ***adjective*** united by treaty, agreement, or other alliance [The U.S. and Great Britain are *allied* countries.]
al·lied • ***adjective***

alligator

alligator (al′ə gāt′ər) ***noun*** a large animal with a long body and tail, four short legs, and a long, blunt snout. Alligators are reptiles and live in rivers and swamps in the southeastern U.S. and in China.
al·li·ga·tor • ***noun,*** *plural* **alligators** or **alligator**

allot (ə lät′) ***verb*** **1** to divide or give out in shares [The land was *allotted* equally to the two farmers.] **2** to give to a person as a share [The rules *allotted* each speaker five minutes.]
al·lot • ***verb*** **allotted, allotting**

allow (ə lou′) ***verb*** **1** to let be done; permit [No swimming is *allowed* in the river.] —Look for the WORD CHOICES box at the entry **let**. **2** to let have [Dad *allowed* Mary $10 for expenses.] **3** to let enter or stay [Dogs are not *allowed* on buses.] **4** to give or keep an extra amount in order to have enough [*Allow* an extra ten minutes to get to her house.]
—allow for to keep in mind [*Allow for* the difference in their ages.]
al·low • ***verb*** **allowed, allowing**

allowance (ə lou′əns) ***noun*** an amount of money or of something else that is given at

a cat	ō go	ʉ fur	ə = a *in* ago
ā ape	ô law, for	ch chin	e *in* agent
ä cot, car	oo look	sh she	i *in* pencil
e ten	o͞o tool	th thin	o *in* atom
ē me	oi oil	*th* then	u *in* circus
i fit	ou out	zh measure	
ī ice	u up	ŋ ring	

regular times or for a special purpose [His parents give him an *allowance* of $5 a week.]
al·low·ance • *noun, plural* **allowances**

alloy (al′oi) ***noun*** a metal that is a mixture of other metals, or of a metal and something else. Bronze is an alloy of copper and tin.
al·loy • ***noun****, plural* **alloys**

all right ***adjective*** **1** good enough for what is needed; satisfactory [Your work is *all right*.] **2** not hurt; safe [Are you *all right?*]
adverb yes; very well [*All right*, I'll do it.]

all-round (ôl′round′) ***adjective*** *the same as* **all-around.**

all-star (ôl′stär) ***adjective*** made up of outstanding or star athletes or performers [an *all-star* team].
noun a member of an all-star team or group.
all-star • ***adjective*** • ***noun****, plural* **all-stars**

ally (ə lī′ *for v.;* al′ī *for n.*) ***verb*** to join together or unite for a special purpose [The two nations *allied* themselves to fight the common enemy.]
noun a country or person that has joined with another for a special purpose.
al·ly • ***verb*** **allied, allying, allies**
• ***noun****, plural* **allies**

almanac (ôl′mə nak) ***noun*** **1** a book published each year containing a calendar, forecasts of the weather, the tides, sunsets and sunrises, and other information. **2** a book published each year with facts and figures, charts, and other information on many subjects.
al·ma·nac • ***noun****, plural* **almanacs**

almighty (ôl mīt′ē) ***adjective*** having power that has no limits.
—the Almighty God.
al·might·y • ***adjective***

almond (ä′mənd *or* äl′mənd) ***noun*** **1** an oval nut that is good to eat. An almond is the seed of a fruit that looks like a small peach. **2** the small tree that this fruit grows on.
al·mond • ***noun****, plural* **almonds**

almost (ôl′mōst) ***adverb*** very nearly but not completely [Sue is *almost* ten.]
al·most • ***adverb***

aloft (ə lôft′ *or* ə läft′) ***adverb*** **1** far above the ground; high up [The ape swung *aloft* into the upper branches of the tree.] **2** near the top of a ship's mast [The sailor climbed *aloft* to fix the sail.]
a·loft • ***adverb***

aloha (ä lō′hä) ***interjection*** a word that is used to say "hello" or "goodbye." This is a Hawaiian word that means *love*.
a·lo·ha • ***interjection***

alone (ə lōn′) ***adjective*** **1** away from anything or anyone else [I was *alone* on the beach.] **2** without anything else; only [The carton *alone* weighs two pounds.]
adverb without any other person [She lives *alone*.]
—leave alone or **let alone** not to bother [*Leave* her *alone* until she finishes her work.]
a·lone • ***adjective*** • ***adverb***

WORD CHOICES

Synonyms of **alone**

The words **alone, lonely,** and **solitary** share the meaning "with no others around."

a tiny hut *alone* on the prairie
a *lonely* little town in the woods
a *solitary* mountain peak

along (ə lôŋ′) ***preposition*** on or beside the length of [We walked *along* the beach.]
adverb **1** forward or onward [The police officer told us to move *along*.] **2** as a companion [Come *along* with us.] **3** with one [Take your camera *along*.]
—get along to be on friendly terms; agree [We can't *get along* with the new neighbors.]
a·long • ***preposition*** • ***adverb***

alongside (ə lôŋ′sīd′) ***preposition*** at the side of; side by side with [The car is *alongside* the house.]
adverb at or by the side [Her car pulled up *alongside* and she waved at us.]
a·long·side • ***preposition*** • ***adverb***

aloof (ə lo͞of′) ***adjective*** showing no interest or sympathy [We did not like him because of his *aloof* manner.]
adverb keeping oneself apart or at a distance [They stood *aloof* from their classmates.]
a·loof • ***adjective*** • ***adverb***

aloud (ə loud′) ***adverb*** with the normal voice [Read the letter *aloud*.]
a·loud • ***adverb***

alpaca

alpaca (al pak′ə) ***noun*** an animal that has long, silky brown or black wool. The alpaca is related to the llama and lives in the mountains of South America.
al·pac·a • ***noun,*** *plural* **alpacas** or **alpaca**

alphabet (al′fə bet) ***noun*** the letters used to write a language, given in the regular order.
al·pha·bet • ***noun,*** *plural* **alphabets**

alphabetical (al′fə bet′i kəl) ***adjective*** arranged in the regular order of the alphabet [Entries in a dictionary are in *alphabetical* order.]
al·pha·bet·i·cal • ***adjective***

alphabetize (al′fə bə tīz) ***verb*** to arrange in alphabetical order [The computer *alphabetized* all the names on the list.]
al·pha·bet·ize • ***verb*** **alphabetized, alphabetizing**

Alps (alps) a mountain system in Europe, with ranges in France, Switzerland, Germany, Italy, Austria, Slovenia, Croatia, Bosnia and Herzegovina, and Serbia and Montenegro.

already (ôl red′ē) ***adverb*** **1** by or before this time [When we arrived, the show had *already* begun.] **2** even now [I am *already* late.]
al·read·y • ***adverb***

also (ôl′sō) ***adverb*** in addition; too; besides [She sang and *also* played the piano.]
al·so • ***adverb***

Alta. *abbreviation for* Alberta.

altar (ôl′tər) ***noun*** a table, stand, or other raised place that is used for certain religious services.
al·tar • ***noun,*** *plural* **altars**
● The words **altar** and **alter** sound alike.
Candles lighted the *altar.*
Use of the cane will *alter* her posture.

alter (ôl′tər) ***verb*** to make or become different in part; change [The tailor *altered* the sleeves.] —Look for the WORD CHOICES box at the entry **transform**.
al·ter • ***verb*** **altered, altering**
● The words **alter** and **altar** sound alike.
We *alter* cuffs at no extra charge.
The priest knelt in front of the *altar.*

alternate (ôl′tər nit *for adj. and n.;* ôl′tər nāt *for v.*) ***adjective*** **1** happening or appearing in turns; first one and then the other [The banner had *alternate* stripes of blue and yellow.] **2** every other; every second [We take piano lessons on *alternate* Tuesdays.] **3** being or giving a choice between two or more things [He took an *alternate* route to avoid traffic.]
verb **1** to do, use, or happen by turns [Good times *alternate* with bad.] **2** to take turns [The classes *alternate* in using the gym in the morning.]
noun a person or thing that is ready to take the place of another if needed; substitute.
al·ter·nate • ***adjective*** • ***verb*** **alternated, alternating** • ***noun,*** *plural* **alternates**

alternating current ***noun*** an electric current that changes to the opposite direction at regular time periods.

alternative (ôl tʉr′nə tiv) ***adjective*** allowing a choice between two or more things [There are *alternative* routes to our farm.]
noun **1** a choice between two or more things [You have the *alternative* of singing or playing the piano.] —Look for the WORD CHOICES box at the entry **choice**. **2** one of two or more things that can be chosen [The *alternative* to singing was playing the piano.]
al·ter·na·tive • ***adjective***
• ***noun,*** *plural* **alternatives**

although (ôl *th*ō′) ***conjunction*** **1** in spite of the fact that; though [*Although* the sun is shining, it may rain later.] **2** and yet; however [They will probably lose, *although* no one

a	cat	ō	go	ʉ	fur	ə = a *in* ago	
ā	ape	ô	law, for	ch	chin	e *in* agent	
ä	cot, car	oo	look	sh	she	i *in* pencil	
e	ten	o͞o	tool	th	thin	o *in* atom	
ē	me	oi	oil	*th*	then	u *in* circus	
i	fit	ou	out	zh	measure		
ī	ice	u	up	ŋ	ring		

else thinks so.] **3** even if [*Although* you may fail, you will have tried.]
al·though • *conjunction*

altitude (al′tə to͞od) *noun* the height of a thing above the earth's surface or above sea level [The airplane flew at an *altitude* of 15,000 feet.]
al·ti·tude • *noun, plural* **altitudes**

alto (al′tō) *noun* **1** the lowest kind of singing voice of women, girls, and young boys. **2** a singer with such a voice.
al·to • *noun, plural* **altos**

altogether (ôl′to͞o geth′ər) *adverb* **1** to the full extent; completely [You're not *altogether* wrong.] **2** all being counted; in all [They read six books *altogether*.] **3** when everything is kept in mind; on the whole [The concert was *altogether* a success.]
al·to·geth·er • *adverb*

aluminum (ə lo͞o′mə nəm) *noun* a silvery, lightweight metal that is a chemical element. It does not rust.
adjective of or containing aluminum [*aluminum* foil; *aluminum* cans].
a·lu·mi·num • *noun* • *adjective*

always (ôl′wāz) *adverb* **1** at all times; at every time [He is *always* polite.] **2** all the time [Oxygen is *always* present in the air.] **3** forever [I will *always* love her.]
al·ways • *adverb*

am (am) *verb* the form of the verb **be** that is used to show the present time with *I* [I *am* happy.]

AM or **am** in the time from midnight to noon. *AM* is the abbreviation of *ante meridiem*, a Latin phrase that means *before noon* [Be here at 8:30 *AM*.] This abbreviation is also written **A.M.** or **a.m.**

amaryllis (am′ə ril′is) *noun* a plant that has several large flowers that look like lilies, growing on a single stem. It grows from a bulb.
am·a·ryl·lis • *noun*

amateur (am′ə chər *or* am′ə tʉr) *noun* **1** a person who is not a professional; a person who does something for the pleasure of it rather than for money. **2** a person who does something without much skill.
am·a·teur • *noun, plural* **amateurs**

amaze (ə māz′) *verb* to cause to feel great surprise or wonder; astonish [The height of the waterfall *amazed* the tourists.]
a·maze • *verb* **amazed, amazing**

amazement (ə māz′mənt) *noun* great surprise or wonder —Look for the WORD CHOICES box at the entry **wonder**.
a·maze·ment • *noun*

amazing (ə māz′iŋ) *adjective* causing great surprise or wonder [The telephone was an *amazing* invention.]
a·maz·ing • *adjective*

Amazon (am′ə zän) a river in South America, flowing across Brazil into the Atlantic. It is over 3,000 miles long and is the longest river in South America.
Am·a·zon

WORD HISTORY

Amazon

In Greek myths, an *Amazon* was a member of a tribe of women warriors. The **Amazon** River was given its name by Spanish explorers, who thought that women warriors like the ones in the myths lived along the river's banks.

ambassador (am bas′ə dər) *noun* **1** an official of the highest rank sent by a country to represent it in another country. **2** a person sent as a representative or messenger [Our dancers tour as cultural *ambassadors*.]
am·bas·sa·dor • *noun, plural* **ambassadors**

amber (am′bər) *noun* **1** a brownish-yellow substance that is the hardened resin of ancient pine trees. It is used for making jewelry or ornaments. **2** the color of amber; brownish yellow.
am·ber • *noun, plural* **ambers**

ambiguous (am big′yo͞o əs) *adjective* **1** having two or more possible meanings. The sentence "Joe is a funny person" is ambiguous because it can mean that Joe is either comical or strange. **2** not clear; not definite [Don't be so *ambiguous* in your answers.]
am·big·u·ous • *adjective*

ambition (am bish′ən) *noun* **1** strong desire to be successful or to gain power, fame, or wealth. **2** the thing that is so strongly desired [Her *ambition* is to be a lawyer.]
am·bi·tion • *noun, plural* **ambitions**

ambitious (am bish′əs) *adjective* **1** having a

A

strong desire to be successful or to gain power, fame, or wealth [a senator *ambitious* to be president]. **2** needing great effort, skill, or ability [an *ambitious* plan].
am·bi·tious • *adjective*

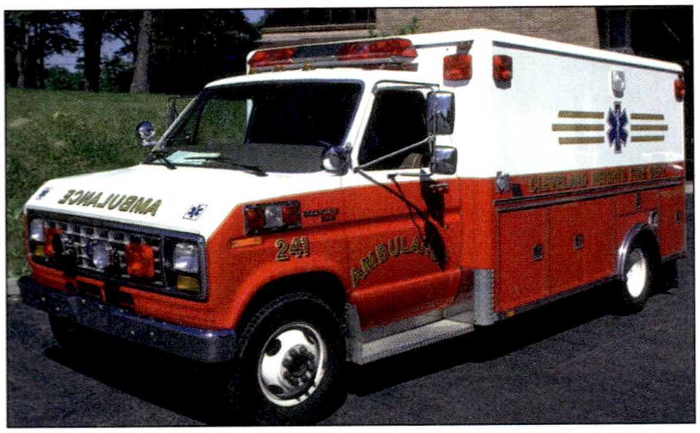

ambulance

ambulance (am′byə ləns *or* am′byo͞o ləns) ***noun*** a large automobile that is used to carry sick or injured people to a hospital.
am·bu·lance • ***noun,*** *plural* **ambulances**

ambush (am′bo͝osh) ***noun*** **1** a surprise attack made from a place of hiding [The soldiers were caught in an *ambush* when they crossed the river.] **2** the place of hiding from which a surprise attack is made [The enemy troops waited in *ambush* near the river.]
verb to attack from a place of hiding [The enemy troops *ambushed* our soldiers in the jungle.]
am·bush • ***noun,*** *plural* **ambushes**
• ***verb*** **ambushed, ambushing**

ameba (ə mē′bə) ***noun*** *another spelling of* **amoeba**.
a·me·ba • ***noun,*** *plural* **amebas** or **a·me·bae** (ə mē′bē)

amen (ā′men′ *or* ä′men′) ***interjection*** **1** a word used at the end of a prayer. **2** a word used after a statement to express agreement. This is a Hebrew word that means *may it be so!*
a·men • ***interjection***

amend (ə mend′) ***verb*** to change in order to correct or make better [Helen *amended* the spelling and grammar of our compositions.]
a·mend • ***verb*** **amended, amending**

amendment (ə mend′mənt) ***noun*** a change in or addition to something, such as a bill or law [an *amendment* to the Constitution].
a·mend·ment • ***noun,*** *plural* **amendments**

amends (ə mendz′) ***plural noun*** *used mainly in the phrase* **make amends**, to make up for a wrong or mistake [She tried to *make amends* for her rudeness by apologizing to him.]
a·mends • ***plural noun***

America (ə mer′i kə) **1** *another name for* the **United States of America**. **2** the Western Hemisphere, including North, Central, and South America and the West Indies.
A·mer·i·ca

American (ə mer′i kən) ***adjective*** **1** of or having to do with the U.S. [She has a course in *American* history this semester.] **2** of or having to do with North America, Central America, or South America [the *American* Indians].
noun a person who was born in or is a citizen of the U.S.
A·mer·i·can • ***adjective*** • ***noun,*** *plural* **Americans**

American Indian ***noun*** **1** a member of any of the native peoples living in North America, especially south of the Arctic, or in South America or the West Indies, when Europeans first arrived. **2** a descendant of any of these peoples.
American Indian • ***noun,*** *plural* **American Indians**

American Revolution the revolution from 1763 to 1783 by which the American colonies won their independence from England. It became the Revolutionary War in 1775.

amethyst (am′ə thist) ***noun*** a kind of quartz that has a purple or violet color. Amethyst is used as a gem.
am·e·thyst • ***noun,*** *plural* **amethysts**

amid (ə mid′) ***preposition*** in the middle of; among [Weeds grew *amid* the flowers.]
a·mid • ***preposition***

amidships (ə mid′ships) ***adverb*** in or in the direction of the middle of the ship [The other vessel struck us *amidships*.]
a·mid·ships • ***adverb***

amidst (ə midst′) ***preposition*** *the same as* **amid**.
a·midst • ***preposition***

a	cat	ō	go	ʉ	fur	ə = a *in* ago
ā	ape	ô	law, for	ch	chin	e *in* agent
ä	cot, car	o͝o	look	sh	she	i *in* pencil
e	ten	o͞o	tool	th	thin	o *in* atom
ē	me	oi	oil	*th*	then	u *in* circus
i	fit	ou	out	zh	measure	
ī	ice	u	up	ŋ	ring	

amigo (ə mē′gō) *noun* friend. This is a Spanish word.
a·mi·go • *noun, plural* **amigos**

amiss (ə mis′) *adjective* wrong; not right or proper [If nothing goes *amiss*, he will return soon.]
a·miss • *adjective*

ammo (am′ō) [*a slang word*] *noun a short form of* **ammunition.**
am·mo • *noun*

ammonia (ə mōn′yə) *noun* **1** a gas that has a very strong smell and no color. It is made up of nitrogen and hydrogen and is used in making fertilizers. **2** a liquid made by putting this gas in water. The liquid is used in cleaning.
am·mo·nia • *noun*

ammunition (am′yoo nish′ən) *noun* bullets, bombs, rockets, or anything else that can be fired from a gun or can be exploded to cause harm or damage.
am·mu·ni·tion • *noun*

amnesia (am nē′zhə) *noun* the condition of suddenly forgetting all or some of the past. It is caused by injury to the brain or by shock.
am·ne·sia • *noun*

amoeba (ə mē′bə) *noun* a tiny animal made up of just one cell, found in the ground and in water. It can be seen only through a microscope and it moves by changing its shape.
a·moe·ba • *noun, plural* **amoebas** or **a·moe·bae** (ə mē′bē)

among (ə muŋ′) *preposition* **1** in the middle of or included with [There were some daffodils *among* the tulips.] **2** in the company of; together with [You are *among* friends.] **3** in the number or class of [Shopping and sightseeing are *among* the things we do on a vacation.] **4** with a share for each of [The pie was divided *among* the four guests.] **5** from place to place in [They passed *among* the crowd.]
a·mong • *preposition*

amount (ə mount′) *verb* **1** to be equal in number or quantity; add up [The bill *amounts* to $24.] **2** to be equal in meaning or effect [Her failure to reply to the invitation *amounts* to a refusal.]
noun **1** the sum of two or more quantities; total [The bill was $50, but he paid only half that *amount*.] **2** quantity [a small *amount* of rain].
a·mount • *verb* **amounted, amounting** • *noun, plural* **amounts**

ampersand (am′pər sand) *noun* a sign or symbol (&) that represents the word *and*.
am·per·sand • *noun, plural* **ampersands**

amphibian
Above Center: Animal *Below: Vehicle*

amphibian (am fib′ē ən) *noun* **1** a coldblooded animal that lives both on land and in the water. Adult amphibians have lungs, but they begin life in the water as tadpoles with gills. Frogs are amphibians. **2** an airplane that can take off from or come down on either land or water. **3** a tank, truck, or other vehicle that can travel on either land or water.
am·phib·i·an • *noun, plural* **amphibians**

amphibious (am fib′ē əs) *adjective* **1** able to live both on land and in water [*amphibious* animals]. **2** able to operate or travel on both land and water [an *amphibious* truck].
am·phib·i·ous • *adjective*

amphitheater (am′fə thē′ət ər) *noun* a round or oval building that has rows of seats gradually rising around an open space. An amphitheater can be used to present such things as sports, theater, or music.
am·phi·the·a·ter • *noun, plural* **amphitheaters**

ample (am′pəl) *adjective* **1** having plenty of space; roomy; large [an *ample* kitchen for a large family]. **2** more than enough; abundant [The farm has an *ample* supply of water.]
am·ple • *adjective* **ampler, amplest**

amplifier (am′plə fī′ər) *noun* a device used to make electric signals stronger before they are changed into sounds in a speaker of a radio or other system for reproducing sound.
am·pli·fi·er • *noun, plural* **amplifiers**

amplify (am′plə fī) *verb* **1** to make larger, stronger, or louder [The electric system will

A

amplify the rock singer's voice.] **2** to give more details about; expand [The audience asked the speaker to *amplify* his remarks.]
am·pli·fy • *verb* **amplified, amplifying, amplifies**

amputate (am′pyoo tāt) *verb* to cut off, especially by surgery [The doctor *amputated* the leg of the wounded soldier.]
am·pu·tate • *verb* **amputated, amputating**

Amsterdam (am′stər dam) a seaport in the Netherlands. It is the official capital. *See also* The **Hague**.
Am·ster·dam

amulet (am′yoo lit) *noun* a small object that is worn on the body because it is supposed to have magic to protect against harm or evil.
am·u·let • *noun, plural* **amulets**

Amundsen (ä′moon sən), **Roald** (rō′äl) 1872-1928; Norwegian explorer. He was the first person to reach the South Pole, in 1911.
A·mund·sen, Ro·ald

amuse (ə myōōz′) *verb* **1** to keep busy or interested with something pleasant [We *amused* ourselves with games.] —Look for the WORD CHOICES box at the entry **entertain**. **2** to cause to smile or laugh [Her jokes *amuse* me.]
a·muse • *verb* **amused, amusing**

amusement (ə myōōz′mənt) *noun* **1** the condition of being amused or entertained [The students played word games for their own *amusement*.] **2** something that amuses or entertains [Have you planned any *amusements* for Jane's birthday party?]
a·muse·ment • *noun, plural* **amusements**

amusement park *noun* an outdoor park with rides and other things to entertain people.
amusement park • *noun, plural* **amusement parks**

amusing (ə myōō′ziŋ) *adjective* causing laughter or smiles [The puppy's attempts to catch the ball were *amusing*.] —Look for the WORD CHOICES box at the entry **funny**.
a·mus·ing • *adjective*

an (an *or* ən) *indefinite article* **1** one; one kind of [Will you bake *an* apple pie?] **2** any one [Pick *an* apple for me.] **3** for each [The perfume cost fifty dollars *an* ounce.] Use *a* before a word that begins with a consonant sound. Use *an* before a word that begins with a vowel sound.

-an *a suffix meaning:* **1** in or having to do with [A *suburban* home is in a suburb.] **2** born in or living in [An *Asian* is a person born or living in Asia.]

anaconda (an′ə kän′də) *noun* a very long, heavy snake found in South America. The anaconda kills another animal by crushing it in its coils.
an·a·con·da • *noun, plural* **anacondas**

analysis (ə nal′ə sis) *noun* **1** the separation of something into its parts in order to examine them [A chemical *analysis* of a substance will tell what elements are in it.] **2** a careful study or examination of something [The *analysis* of a problem will help tell what caused it.]
a·nal·y·sis • *noun, plural* **analyses** (ə nal′ə sēz)

analyze (an′ə līz) *verb* **1** to separate something into its parts in order to examine them [The chemists *analyzed* the water and found many harmful chemicals in it.] **2** to study or examine carefully [He *analyzed* the problem hoping to find out what caused it.]
an·a·lyze • *verb* **analyzed, analyzing**

anarchy (an′ər kē) *noun* the complete lack of government and law.
an·arch·y • *noun*

anatomy (ə nat′ə mē) *noun* **1** the science that studies the different parts that make up an animal or plant. Anatomy deals with the tissues, organs, and systems of a body or plant. **2** the way a body is put together [The *anatomy* of a frog is much like that of a person.]
a·nat·o·my • *noun, plural* **anatomies**

ancestor (an′ses′tər) *noun* someone who comes earlier in a family, especially someone earlier than a grandparent; forefather [Their *ancestors* came from Italy.]
an·ces·tor • *noun, plural* **ancestors**

ancestry (an′ses′trē) *noun* all of a person's ancestors [She is of Italian *ancestry*.]
an·ces·try • *noun, plural* **ancestries**

anchor (aŋ′kər) *noun* **1** a heavy object that is let down into the water by a chain to keep a ship or boat from drifting. An anchor is usually a metal piece with hooks that grip the ground at the bottom of the water. **2** anything

a cat	ō go	ʉ fur	ə = a *in* ago
ā ape	ô law, for	ch chin	e *in* agent
ä cot, car	oo look	sh she	i *in* pencil
e ten	ōō tool	th thin	o *in* atom
ē me	oi oil	*th* then	u *in* circus
i fit	ou out	zh measure	
ī ice	u up	ŋ ring	

that keeps something else firm, steady, or in place [Hope was his *anchor*.]
verb **1** to keep in one place by using an anchor [We *anchored* the boat near the beach.] **2** to attach firmly; fasten [The shelves were *anchored* to the wall.]
an·chor • ***noun,*** *plural* **anchors**
• ***verb*** **anchored, anchoring**

anchovy (an′chō′vē) ***noun*** a very small fish with a large mouth, found mostly in warm seas. Anchovies are usually canned in oil or made into a salty paste.
an·cho·vy • ***noun,*** *plural* **anchovies**

ancient (ān′chənt *or* ān′shənt) ***adjective*** **1** having to do with times long past [The *ancient* Egyptians built the pyramids.] **2** having lasted a long time; very old [He told us an *ancient* tale of knights and dragons.] —Look for the WORD CHOICES box at the entry **old**.
an·cient • ***adjective***

and (and) ***conjunction*** **1** also; in addition; as well as [They preserved plums *and* pears.] **2** added to; plus [6 *and* 2 equals 8.] **3** as a result [Help me *and* I'll be grateful.] **4** [*an informal use*] to; in order to [Try *and* get it.]

Andersen (an′dər sən), **Hans Christian** (hans′ kris′chən) 1805-1875; Danish writer of fairy stories.
An·der·sen, Hans Chris·tian

Andes (an′dēz) a mountain system along the length of western South America.
An·des

andiron

andiron (and′ī′ərn) ***noun*** one of a pair of metal supports that are used for holding logs in a fireplace.
and·i·ron • ***noun,*** *plural* **andirons**

Andorra (an dôr′ə) a tiny republic in the mountains between France and Spain.
An·dor·ra

android (an′droid) ***noun*** a robot that is made to look like a human being.
an·droid • ***noun,*** *plural* **androids**

anecdote (an′ək dōt) ***noun*** a short, interesting or amusing story about something that has happened or about some person.
an·ec·dote • ***noun,*** *plural* **anecdotes**

anemia (ə nē′mē ə) ***noun*** an unhealthy condition in which a person's blood does not have enough red cells. A person with anemia often becomes pale and tired.
a·ne·mi·a • ***noun***

anemone (ə nem′ə nē) ***noun*** a plant with white, pink, red, or purple flowers shaped like small cups.
a·nem·o·ne • ***noun,*** *plural* **anemones**

anesthesia (an′es thē′zhə) ***noun*** a condition in which there is a loss of feeling or of consciousness. The loss of feeling may be in all or part of the body.
an·es·the·sia • ***noun***

anesthetic (an′es thet′ik) ***noun*** a drug, gas, or other substance that causes a numb feeling in just a part of the body or a complete loss of consciousness.
an·es·thet·ic • ***noun,*** *plural* **anesthetics**

anew (ə nōō′ *or* ə nyōō′) ***adverb*** once more; again [After the earthquake, we built *anew*.]
a·new • ***adverb***

angel (ān′jəl) ***noun*** **1** a heavenly being that has more power and goodness than human beings. Angels are often mentioned in the Bible as messengers of God. **2** a person who is beautiful, good, or helpful like an angel.
an·gel • ***noun,*** *plural* **angels**

anger (aŋ′gər) ***noun*** a strong feeling of being very annoyed at someone or something and wanting to fight back.
verb to make or become angry [Jim's rudeness *angered* his sister. The coach *angers* easily.]
an·ger • ***noun*** • ***verb*** **angered, angering**

angle (aŋ′gəl) ***noun*** **1** the shape made by two straight lines meeting in a point, or by two flat surfaces meeting along a line. **2** the space between these lines or surfaces. It is measured in degrees. **3** a way of looking at something [Consider the problem from all *angles*.]
verb to turn sharply in a different direction [The road *angles* to the left.]

an·gle • *noun, plural* **angles** • *verb* **angled, angling**

Angola (aŋ gō′lə) a country on the southwestern coast of Africa.
An·go·la

Angora (aŋ gôr′ə) ***noun*** a soft yarn or cloth made from the long, silky hair of a kind of goat or rabbit. Angora is used to make sweaters, scarves, or other clothing. This word is also written **angora**.
An·go·ra • *noun, plural* **Angoras**

angry (aŋ′grē) ***adjective*** feeling or showing anger [She was *angry* with her friend for ruining her dress. They exchanged *angry* words.]
an·gry • *adjective* **angrier, angriest**

anguish (aŋ′gwish) ***noun*** great suffering caused by worry, grief, or pain; agony.
an·guish • *noun*

animal (an′ə məl) ***noun*** **1** any living being that can move about by itself, has sense organs, and does not make its own food as a plant does. Insects, worms, frogs, fish, and lizards are animals. Bears, seals, birds, and people are also animals. **2** an animal other than a human being, especially one with four feet.
an·i·mal • *noun, plural* **animals**

animated cartoon (an′ə māt′id) ***noun*** a film made by photographing a series of drawings. Each of these drawings is slightly changed from the one before. The drawn figures seem to move when the drawings are shown on a screen, one quickly after the other.
an·i·mat·ed car·toon • *noun, plural* **animated cartoons**

anise (an′is) ***noun*** **1** a plant that has seeds with a strong, pleasant smell. **2** the seed of this plant. These seeds are used for flavoring.
an·ise • *noun, plural* **anises**

ankle (aŋ′kəl) ***noun*** the joint that connects the foot and the leg.
an·kle • *noun, plural* **ankles**

anklet (aŋk′lit) ***noun*** a short sock that reaches just above the ankle.
an·klet • *noun, plural* **anklets**

annals (an′əlz) ***plural noun*** a record of events year by year. The events are put down in the order in which they happened.
an·nals • *plural noun*

Annapolis (ə nap′ə lis) the capital of Maryland. The U.S. Naval Academy is there.
An·nap·o·lis

annex (ə neks′ *for v.;* an′eks *for n.*) ***verb*** to add or attach a smaller thing to a larger one [The U.S. *annexed* Texas in 1845.]
noun an extra part added to a building or a separate building near a bigger building.
an·nex • *verb* **annexed, annexing** • *noun, plural* **annexes**

annihilate (ə nī′ə lāt) ***verb*** to destroy completely [A tornado can *annihilate* a small town.]
an·ni·hi·late • *verb* **annihilated, annihilating**

anniversary (an′ə vʉr′sə rē) ***noun*** **1** the date on which something happened in the past [June 14 will be the tenth *anniversary* of their wedding.] **2** the celebration of this date [We attended their *anniversary*.]
an·ni·ver·sa·ry • *noun, plural* **anniversaries**

announce (ə nouns′) ***verb*** **1** to make something known [Ads in the paper *announced* the opening of the new store.] **2** to say; tell [Mother *announced* she was going with us.] —Look for the WORD CHOICES box at the entry **say**. **3** to say that someone has arrived [Will you please *announce* me to Mrs. Lopez?]
an·nounce • *verb* **announced, announcing**

announcement (ə nouns′mənt) ***noun*** **1** the act of making something known [The *announcement* of the score drew cheers from the students.] **2** a written or printed notice that makes something known [The wedding *announcements* were mailed.]
an·nounce·ment • *noun, plural* **announcements**

announcer (ə noun′sər) ***noun*** a person on radio or TV who introduces programs, reads the news, and presents commercials.
an·nounc·er • *noun, plural* **announcers**

annoy (ə noi′) ***verb*** to irritate, bother, or make slightly angry [Their loud talk *annoyed* me.]
an·noy • *verb* **annoyed, annoying**

annoyance (ə noi′əns) ***noun*** **1** the act of annoying [He apologized to the librarian for his brother's constant *annoyance*.] **2** the fact of being annoyed [He showed his *annoyance* by frowning.] **3** a thing or person that annoys [A barking dog is an *annoyance* to neighbors.]
an·noy·ance • *noun, plural* **annoyances**

a	cat	ō	go	ʉ	fur	ə =	a *in* ago
ā	ape	ô	law, for	ch	chin		e *in* agent
ä	cot, car	oo	look	sh	she		i *in* pencil
e	ten	ōō	tool	th	thin		o *in* atom
ē	me	oi	oil	*th*	then		u *in* circus
i	fit	ou	out	zh	measure		
ī	ice	u	up	ŋ	ring		

annual (an′yo͞o əl) ***adjective*** **1** happening or coming once a year; yearly [They went to California on their *annual* summer vacation.] **2** for a period of a year [She receives an *annual* salary of $25,000.] **3** living or lasting for only one growing season [Corn is an *annual* plant.]
an·nu·al • ***adjective***

annually (an′yo͞o əl ē) ***adverb*** each year; every year.
an·nu·al·ly • ***adverb***

anoint (ə noint′) ***verb*** to put oil on as part of a religious ceremony [The minister prayed over the ill woman and *anointed* her.]
a·noint • ***verb*** **anointed, anointing**

anonymous (ə nän′ə məs) ***adjective*** **1** with a name that is not known or not given [an *anonymous* writer]. **2** from or by a person whose name is not known or not given [The library received an *anonymous* gift of $100.]
a·non·y·mous • ***adjective***

another (ə nu*th*′ər) ***adjective*** **1** one more [Have *another* cup of tea.] **2** a different; not the same [Exchange the book for *another* one.] ***pronoun*** **1** one more [I've had two cookies, but I'd like *another*.] **2** a different one [If one store doesn't have the book, try *another*.]
an·oth·er • ***adjective*** • ***pronoun***

answer (an′sər) ***noun*** **1** anything said, written, or done in return to something, such as a question, letter, request, or statement; reply [She didn't get an *answer* to her letter. The only *answers* required for the test were "true" or "false."] **2** any act done in response to something else [The phone rang, but there was no *answer*.] **3** a solution to a problem [The right *answer* to the problem is 150.] ***verb*** **1** to give an answer; reply or react to something, such as a question or action [I *answered* his letter. Mary stopped reading to *answer* the telephone.] **2** to be responsible [You must *answer* for the child's behavior.] **3** to match or agree with [That house *answers* to the description given in the newspaper.]
an·swer • ***noun,*** *plural* **answers** • ***verb*** **answered, answering**

answering machine ***noun*** a machine that can record or play telephone messages.
answering machine • ***noun,*** *plural* **answering machines**

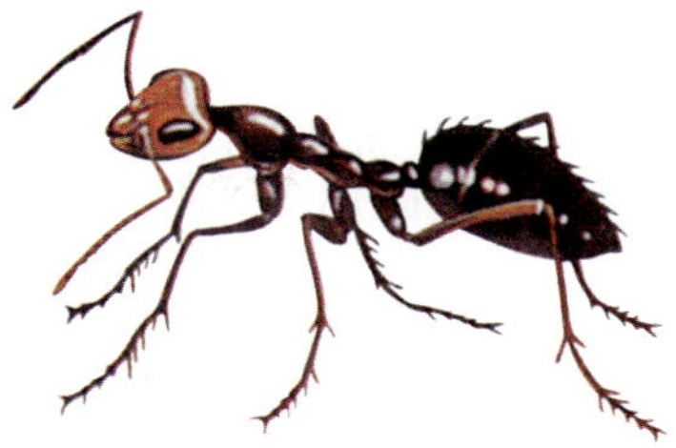
ant

ant (ant) ***noun*** a small insect that lives in large, organized groups called colonies. Ants usually do not have wings. They live in or on the ground, in holes in dead wood, or in other places.
ant • ***noun,*** *plural* **ants**

- The words **ant** and **aunt** sound alike.
  An *ant* crawled on our picnic basket.
  My *aunt* and uncle live in Ohio.

antacid (ant′as′id) ***noun*** a substance that makes an acid lose its power [Baking soda is an *antacid*.]
ant·ac·id • ***noun,*** *plural* **antacids**

antagonism (an tag′ə niz′əm) ***noun*** a strong feeling of being against a person or thing [There was *antagonism* between the teams.]
an·tag·o·nism • ***noun***

antagonize (an tag′ə nīz) ***verb*** to cause dislike in; make an enemy of [Rudeness will *antagonize* store customers.]
an·tag·o·nize • ***verb*** **antagonized, antagonizing**

antarctic (ant ärk′tik *or* ant är′tik) ***adjective*** of or having to do with the South Pole or the area around it [Penguins live in *antarctic* waters.]
—the Antarctic *another name for* **Antarctica**.
ant·arc·tic • ***adjective***

WORD HISTORY

antarctic

We get **antarctic** from a Greek prefix that means "opposite" and a Greek word for "north." The **antarctic** region is opposite the **arctic**, or northern, region on the globe of the earth.

Antarctica (ant ärk′ti kə *or* ant är′ti kə) a continent around the South Pole. Antarctica is almost completely covered with ice all year long.
Ant·arc·ti·ca

Antarctic Ocean the ocean around Antarctica.

anteater (ant′ēt′ər) ***noun*** an animal with a long snout and a long, sticky tongue. An anteater uses its sticky tongue to catch ants, termites, or other small insects. Anteaters live in Central and South America.
ant·eat·er • ***noun,*** *plural* **anteaters**

antelope

antelope (an′tə lōp) ***noun*** **1** a swift, graceful animal that is a little like a deer but has long horns without branches. Antelopes are related to goats and are found in Africa and Asia. **2** *another name for* **pronghorn**.
an·te·lope • ***noun,*** *plural* **antelope** or **antelopes**

antenna (an ten′ə) ***noun*** **1** one of a pair of long, thin, movable body parts on the head of an insect, crab, lobster, or other similar animal. Antennae are used for touching and smelling. **2** a wire or set of wires that is used to send out or receive radio or TV signals; aerial.
an·ten·na • ***noun,*** *plural for sense 1* **an·ten·nae** (an ten′ē) or **antennas**, *plural for sense 2* **antennas**

anthem (an′thəm) ***noun*** **1** the official song of a country, school, or other institution [The national anthem of the U.S. is *The Star-Spangled Banner*.] **2** a religious song or hymn, usually with words from the Bible.
an·them • ***noun,*** *plural* **anthems**

anther (an′thər) ***noun*** the part of a flower that holds the pollen. Anthers are the small heads on the slender stems that grow at the center of a flower.

anther

an·ther • ***noun,*** *plural* **anthers**

anthill (ant′hil) ***noun*** a heap of dirt carried by ants in digging their underground nest. The dirt is piled around the entrance of the nest.
ant·hill • ***noun,*** *plural* **anthills**

anthology (an thäl′ə jē) ***noun*** a collection of poems, stories, or other writings.
an·thol·o·gy • ***noun,*** *plural* **anthologies**

Anthony (an′thə nē), **Susan B.** (so͞o′zən) 1820-1906; American teacher who was a leader in the movement to gain women the right to vote.
An·tho·ny, Su·san B.

anthropology (an′thrə päl′ə jē) ***noun*** the science that studies human beings. Anthropology deals with the beginning, development, groups, and customs of human beings.
an·thro·pol·o·gy • ***noun***

anti- *a prefix meaning* against; opposed to.

antibiotic (an′ti bī ät′ik) ***noun*** a chemical substance that can kill or stop the growth of germs that cause disease. Antibiotics are produced by certain bacteria or fungi.
an·ti·bi·ot·ic • ***noun,*** *plural* **antibiotics**

antibody (an′ti bäd′ē) ***noun*** a substance made in the body that can act against a virus or other foreign substance. In this way the body becomes protected against certain diseases.
an·ti·bod·y • ***noun,*** *plural* **antibodies**

antic (an′tik) ***noun*** a playful or silly act; a prank [The child laughed at the clown's *antics*.]
an·tic • ***noun,*** *plural* **antics**

anticipate (an tis′ə pāt) ***verb*** **1** to look forward to; expect [We *anticipate* a pleasant trip.] **2** to think of or take care of ahead of time [Our hosts *anticipated* our every wish.]
an·tic·i·pate • ***verb*** **anticipated, anticipating**

anticipation (an tis′ə pā′shən) ***noun*** the act of looking forward to [The principal met with teachers in *anticipation* of fall classes.]
an·tic·i·pa·tion • ***noun***

antidote (ant′ə dōt) ***noun*** a substance that is taken to work against the effect of a poison.

a	cat	ō	go	ʉ	fur	ə = a *in* ago
ā	ape	ô	law, for	ch	chin	e *in* agent
ä	cot, car	o͝o	look	sh	she	i *in* pencil
e	ten	o͞o	tool	th	thin	o *in* atom
ē	me	oi	oil	*th*	then	u *in* circus
i	fit	ou	out	zh	measure	
ī	ice	u	up	ŋ	ring	

an·ti·dote • *noun, plural* **antidotes**

antifreeze (an′ti frēz) ***noun*** a liquid that is added to the water in the radiator of a car, truck, or other vehicle to prevent freezing. Antifreeze is often a kind of alcohol.
an·ti·freeze • ***noun***

Antigua and Barbuda (an tē′gwə and bär bo͞o′də) a country in the eastern West Indies. It consists of three islands, including Antigua and Barbuda.
An·ti·gua and Bar·bu·da

Antilles (an til′ēz) the main group of islands of the West Indies.
An·til·les

antique (an tēk′) ***adjective*** made a long time ago; very old [The museum has a large collection of *antique* furniture.] —Look for the WORD CHOICES box at the entry **old**.
noun something made a long time ago. An antique can be a piece of furniture or silverware, a tool, or some other object.
an·tique • ***adjective*** • ***noun,*** *plural* **antiques**

antiseptic (an′tə sep′tik) ***noun*** a substance that kills germs or stops their growth. Iodine and alcohol are antiseptics.
an·ti·sep·tic • ***noun,*** *plural* **antiseptics**

antler

antler (ant′lər) ***noun*** one of the two horns on the head of a deer or other related animal. Antlers usually have branches and are grown and shed every year, usually by males.
ant·ler • ***noun,*** *plural* **antlers**

Antony (an′tə nē), **Mark** (märk) 83-30 B.C.; Roman general and statesman, who was a follower of Julius Caesar.
An·to·ny, Mark

antonym (an′tə nim) ***noun*** a word that means the opposite of a certain other word ["Sad" is an *antonym* of "happy."]
an·to·nym • ***noun,*** *plural* **antonyms**

anvil (an′vəl) ***noun*** a heavy block of iron or steel with a smooth, flat top. Horseshoes and other metal objects are hammered into shape on an anvil.
an·vil • ***noun,*** *plural* **anvils**

anvil

anxiety (aŋ zī′ə tē) ***noun*** the condition of feeling uneasy or worried about what may happen; concern [She waited with *anxiety* to hear what the doctor would say.] —Look for the WORD CHOICES box at the entry **care**.
anx·i·e·ty • ***noun,*** *plural* **anxieties**

anxious (aŋk′shəs) ***adjective*** **1** feeling uneasy or worried about what may happen; worried [Were you *anxious* during the flight?] **2** having a strong desire; eager [He was *anxious* to do well in the test.]
anx·ious • ***adjective***

any (en′ē) ***adjective*** **1** one, no matter which one, out of three or more [Take *any* book you want.] **2** some, no matter how many or what kind [Do you have *any* apples?] **3** every [*Any* person knows this song.]
pronoun **1** any one or ones [I lost my pencils; do you have *any?* She plays tennis better than *any* before her.] **2** any amount or number [Did you eat *any* of your dinner?]
adverb to any degree; at all [Do you feel *any* better today?]
an·y • ***adjective*** • ***pronoun*** • ***adverb***

anybody (en′ē bud′ē *or* en′ē bäd′ē) ***pronoun*** any person; anyone [Is *anybody* home?]
an·y·bod·y • ***pronoun***

anyhow (en′ē hou) ***adverb*** no matter what else is true; just the same; anyway [You may know these words, but study them *anyhow*.]
an·y·how • ***adverb***

anymore (en′ē môr′) ***adverb*** now; nowadays

[They don't live here *anymore*.] This word is also written **any more**.
an·y·more • *adverb*

anyone (en′ē wun) ***pronoun*** any person; anybody [Does *anyone* know where the house is?]
an·y·one • ***pronoun***

any one ***pronoun*** any single person or thing [Take *any one* of those cakes that you want.]

anything (en′ē thiŋ) ***pronoun*** any thing; something, no matter what [Is there *anything* left on the table?]
adverb in any way; at all [That car isn't *anything* like yours.]
an·y·thing • ***pronoun*** • ***adverb***

anyway (en′ē wā) ***adverb*** no matter what happens; in any case [I'm going *anyway*.]
an·y·way • ***adverb***

anywhere (en′ē hwer) ***adverb*** in, at, or to any place [Leave it *anywhere* in the room.]
an·y·where • ***adverb***

aorta (ā ôr′tə) ***noun*** the main artery of the body. It carries blood from the heart to all parts of the body except the lungs.
a·or·ta • ***noun,*** *plural* **aortas**

Apache (ə pach′ē) ***noun*** **1** a member of a North American Indian people of northern Mexico and the southwestern U.S. **2** any of several languages spoken by these peoples.
A·pach·e • ***noun,*** *plural* **Apaches** or **Apache**

apart (ə pärt′) ***adverb*** **1** separately or away from each other in place or time [I cannot get these two pages *apart*. We were born two years *apart*.] **2** in or into pieces or parts [The ship was blown *apart* by a bomb. She took the motor *apart*.]
adjective separated from one another; not together [We were *apart* for a month last summer.]
a·part • ***adverb*** • ***adjective***

apartment (ə pärt′mənt) ***noun*** a single large room or a group of rooms used to live in.
a·part·ment • ***noun,*** *plural* **apartments**

apatosaurus (ə pat′ə sôr′əs) ***noun*** *another name for* **brontosaur**.
a·pat·o·saur·us • ***noun,*** *plural* **apatosauruses**

ape (āp) ***noun*** a large animal that has no tail and is related to the monkeys. Most apes can walk in an almost upright position. Gorillas, chimpanzees, orangutans, and gibbons are apes.
verb to copy the actions of; imitate [The children *aped* the clown they had seen in the circus.]
ape • ***noun,*** *plural* **apes** • ***verb*** **aped, aping**

apex (ā′peks) ***noun*** the highest point of anything; peak [Playing in the Super Bowl was the *apex* of his career.]
a·pex • ***noun,*** *plural* **apexes**

aphid (ā′fid *or* af′id) ***noun*** a small insect that sucks juices from plants.
a·phid • ***noun,*** *plural* **aphids**

apiece (ə pēs′) ***adverb*** for each one; each [These apples are 20 cents *apiece*.]
a·piece • ***adverb***

Apollo (ə päl′ō *or* ə pôl′ō) the Greek and Roman god of music, poetry, medicine, and of the sun.
A·pol·lo

apologize (ə päl′ə jīz *or* ə pôl′ə jīz) ***verb*** to make an apology; say that one is sorry about something [They *apologized* for being late.]
a·pol·o·gize • ***verb*** **apologized, apologizing**

apology (ə päl′ə jē *or* ə pôl′ə jē) ***noun*** a statement that one is sorry for something wrong, such as an offense or mistake.
a·pol·o·gy • ***noun,*** *plural* **apologies**

Apostle (ə päs′əl *or* ə pôs′əl) ***noun*** one of the twelve disciples chosen to spread the teachings of Jesus.
A·pos·tle • ***noun,*** *plural* **Apostles**

apostrophe (ə päs′trə fē *or* ə pôs′trə fē) ***noun*** a mark of punctuation ('). It is used in a shortened word to show that one or more letters have been left out (*I'm*, shortened from *I am*). This mark is also used to show the possessive form of a word (*Peter's* jacket) and to form some plurals (five *6's*; dotting the *i's*).
a·pos·tro·phe • ***noun,*** *plural* **apostrophes**

apothecary (ə päth′ə ker′ē) ***noun*** a person who makes and sells medicines; pharmacist.
a·poth·e·car·y • ***noun,*** *plural* **apothecaries**

Appalachian Mountains (ap′ə lā′chən *or* ap′ə lā′chē ən *or* ap′ə lach′ən) a mountain system of eastern North America. It reaches from Canada to Alabama. It is also called **the Appalachians**.
Ap·pa·la·chi·an Mountains

a	cat	ō	go	ʉ	fur	ə =	a *in* ago
ā	ape	ô	law, for	ch	chin		e *in* agent
ä	cot, car	ꝏ	look	sh	she		i *in* pencil
e	ten	ꝏ̄	tool	th	thin		o *in* atom
ē	me	oi	oil	*th*	then		u *in* circus
i	fit	ou	out	zh	measure		
ī	ice	u	up	ŋ	ring		

appall (ə pôl′) *verb* to cause to feel shock or horror; be greatly upset [We were *appalled* by the destruction caused by the hurricane.]
ap·pall • *verb* **appalled, appalling**

appaloosa

appaloosa (ap′ə lo͞o′sə) *noun* a riding horse with dark or white spotted markings.
ap·pa·loo·sa • *noun, plural* **appaloosas**

apparatus (ap′ə rat′əs *or* ap′ə rāt′əs) *noun* the tools, instruments, or equipment needed for a particular job or purpose [Test tubes and gas burners are the *apparatus* of the chemist.]
ap·pa·ra·tus • *noun, plural* **apparatus** or **apparatuses**

apparel (ə per′əl) *noun* clothing; garments [The store sells only children's *apparel*.]
ap·par·el • *noun*

apparent (ə per′ənt) *adjective* **1** easy to see or understand; obvious; clear [It was *apparent* he was ill.] **2** appearing to be true or real, but perhaps not really so; seeming [an *apparent* lack of interest].
ap·par·ent • *adjective*

appeal (ə pēl′) *verb* **1** to ask in a strong way for help, support, or something else that is needed [He *appealed* to the bank for a loan.] **2** to be interesting or attractive [This is a movie that *appeals* to everyone.]
noun **1** a strong request for help, support, or something else that is needed [The earthquake victims made an *appeal* to the President for help.] **2** a quality that makes something or someone interesting or attractive [Mystery stories have a great *appeal* to many people.]
ap·peal • *verb* **appealed, appealing**
• *noun, plural* **appeals**

WORD CHOICES

Synonyms of **appeal**

The words **appeal, plead,** and **pray** share the meaning "to ask seriously."

She *appealed* to the bank for a loan.

He *pleaded* for help for his sick child.

The farmers *prayed* for rain.

appear (ə pir′) *verb* **1** to come into sight; become visible [A ship *appeared* on the horizon.] **2** to come into being [Leaves *appear* on the tree every spring.] **3** to have the look of being; seem [He *appears* to be in good health.] **4** to come before the public [The actor will *appear* on TV this week.]
ap·pear • *verb* **appeared, appearing**

appearance (ə pir′əns) *noun* **1** the act of appearing, or coming into sight [the sudden *appearance* of a pirate ship in the harbor]. **2** the way a person or thing looks [From his *appearance*, we knew he was angry.] **3** a false or wrong impression [She gave the *appearance* of being busy.] **4** the act of coming before the public [her last *appearance* on TV].
ap·pear·ance • *noun, plural* **appearances**

appendices (ə pen′də sēz) *noun a plural of* **appendix**.
ap·pen·di·ces • *noun*

appendicitis (ə pen′də sīt′is) *noun* a condition in which a person's appendix becomes red and swollen. The appendix usually is removed by surgery.
ap·pen·di·ci·tis • *noun*

appendix (ə pen′diks) *noun* **1** an extra section added at the end of a book that gives more information about the subject of the book. An appendix may contain charts, lists, tables, or other materials. **2** a small closed tube that grows out of the large intestine. It has no known function.
ap·pen·dix • *noun, plural* **appendixes** or **appendices**

appetite (ap′ə tīt) *noun* **1** a desire for food [Exercise gave her a strong *appetite*.] **2** any strong desire [an *appetite* for good books].
ap·pe·tite • *noun, plural* **appetites**

appetizer (ap′ə tī′zər) *noun* a small bit of a tasty food or a drink served before a meal.

A

Olives or shrimp are often served as appetizers.
ap·pe·tiz·er • *noun, plural* **appetizers**

appetizing (ap**′**ə tī′ziŋ) ***adjective*** giving a person a bigger appetite [What an *appetizing* smell!]
ap·pe·tiz·ing • ***adjective***

applaud (ə plôd**′** *or* ə pläd**′**) ***verb*** to show approval or enjoyment of something, especially by clapping the hands [The audience *applauded* loudly. We *applauded* the speaker.]
ap·plaud • ***verb*** **applauded, applauding**

applause (ə plôz**′** *or* ə pläz**′**) ***noun*** the act of showing approval or enjoyment of something, especially by clapping the hands.
ap·plause • ***noun***

apple

apple (ap**′**əl) ***noun*** **1** a round, firm fruit with red, yellow, or green skin. Apples have juicy, white flesh and small seeds. **2** the tree this fruit grows on.
ap·ple • *noun, plural* **apples**

applesauce (ap**′**əl sôs) ***noun*** a food made by cooking pieces of apple in water until they become a soft, pulpy mass.
ap·ple·sauce • ***noun***

Appleseed (ap**′**əl sēd), **Johnny** (jän**′**ē) 1775-1845; American pioneer who planted apple trees throughout the Midwest. His real name was *John Chapman*.
Ap·ple·seed, John·ny

appliance (ə plī**′**əns) ***noun*** a machine or device that is used to do a special job around the house more easily. Toasters, vacuum cleaners, and refrigerators are appliances.
ap·pli·ance • *noun, plural* **appliances**

applicable (ap**′**li kə bəl) ***adjective*** capable of being applied or used; suitable [Your solution is not *applicable* to the problem.]
ap·pli·ca·ble • ***adjective***

applicant (ap**′**li kənt) ***noun*** a person who applies, or asks for something [There were many *applicants* for the job.]
ap·pli·cant • *noun, plural* **applicants**

application (ap′li kā**′**shən) ***noun*** **1** the act of applying, or putting something on [This brush is designed for the smooth *application* of paint to the walls.] **2** the act of putting something to use [This job calls for the *application* of many technical skills.] **3** a medicine, ointment, or something similar that is applied. **4** a way of being used [Plastics have many *applications* in industry.] **5** the act of asking for something; a request [an *application* for a job].
ap·pli·ca·tion • *noun, plural* **applications**

apply (ə plī**′**) ***verb*** **1** to put or spread on [*Apply* glue to the surface.] **2** to put into use [*Apply* your knowledge to this problem. She *applied* the brakes to stop the car.] **3** to work hard at [He *applied* himself to his studies.] **4** to make a request; ask [I *applied* for permission to leave early. He *applied* for a job at the plant.] **5** to have to do with [This rule *applies* to all of us.]
ap·ply • ***verb*** **applied, applying, applies**

appoint (ə point**′**) ***verb*** **1** to name or choose for an office or position [The mayor *appointed* her to be the new police chief.] **2** to decide upon; set [Let's *appoint* a time to meet.]
ap·point • ***verb*** **appointed, appointing**

appointment (ə point**′**mənt) ***noun*** **1** the act of appointing to an office or position [The *appointment* of Mr. Smith as chief of police was praised by the press.] **2** the office or position to which a person has been appointed. **3** an arrangement to meet with someone at a particular time and place [You have a two o'clock *appointment*.]
ap·point·ment • *noun, plural* **appointments**

appraise (ə prāz**′**) ***verb*** **1** to decide how much something is worth; set a price for [The agent *appraised* the house at $90,000.] **2** to judge

a	cat	ō	go	ʉ	fur	ə =	a *in* ago
ā	ape	ô	law, for	ch	chin		e *in* agent
ä	cot, car	oo	look	sh	she		i *in* pencil
e	ten	ōō	tool	th	thin		o *in* atom
ē	me	oi	oil	*th*	then		u *in* circus
i	fit	ou	out	zh	measure		
ī	ice	u	up	ŋ	ring		

how good or useful something is [A literary critic *appraises* books.]
ap·praise • *verb* **appraised, appraising**

appreciate (ə prē′shē āt) ***verb*** **1** to understand and enjoy [Her father *appreciates* classical music.] —Look for the WORD CHOICES box at the entry **value**. **2** to recognize and be grateful for [We *appreciate* all you have done for us.] **3** to be fully aware of [I can *appreciate* your problems.] **4** to become more valuable [Gold *appreciates* in value over time.]
ap·pre·ci·ate • *verb* **appreciated, appreciating**

appreciation (ə prē′shē ā′shən) ***noun*** **1** an understanding of the worth or importance of things [After reading his book, I had a better *appreciation* of his paintings.] **2** a feeling of being grateful [He showed his *appreciation* for our help by sending flowers.]
ap·pre·ci·a·tion • *noun*

apprehend (ap′rē hend′) ***verb*** **1** to capture and arrest [The police *apprehended* the burglar.] **2** to catch the meaning of; understand [I don't quite *apprehend* your last remark.]
ap·pre·hend • *verb* **apprehended, apprehending**

apprehension (ap′rē hen′shən) ***noun*** **1** the act of capturing and arresting [The *apprehension* of the burglar made everyone feel safer.] **2** an anxious feeling that something bad may happen [I answered the telephone with *apprehension*.]
ap·pre·hen·sion • *noun*

apprentice (ə pren′tis) ***noun*** a person who is learning a trade or craft by helping a skilled worker.
ap·pren·tice • *noun, plural* **apprentices**

approach (ə prōch′) ***verb*** **1** to come near or nearer [A storm is *approaching*.] **2** to go to someone with a plan or request [Have you *approached* the coach about missing the game tonight?] **3** to begin to work on [How should I *approach* this new task?]
noun **1** the act of approaching, or coming near [The first flowers mark the *approach* of spring.] **2** a way of doing something [Did you find a new *approach* to solving the puzzle?] **3** a path or road that leads to some place [The *approaches* to the city are clogged with traffic every morning.]
ap·proach • *verb* **approached, approaching** • *noun, plural* **approaches**

appropriate (ə prō′prē āt *for v.;* ə prō′prē it *for adj.*) ***verb*** to set aside for a special use [Congress *appropriated* money for highways.] ***adjective*** just right for the purpose; suitable [the *appropriate* uniforms for the parade.]
ap·pro·pri·ate • *verb* **appropriated, appropriating** • *adjective*

approval (ə prōō′vəl) ***noun*** **1** a favorable opinion [The audience showed its *approval* by applauding.] **2** permission; consent [The invitation was sent with my *approval*.]
ap·prov·al • *noun, plural* **approvals**

approve (ə prōōv′) ***verb*** **1** to have a favorable opinion of [My parents *approved* my idea of getting a part-time job. The teacher does not *approve* of listening to earphones in the classroom.] **2** to give one's consent to [The mayor *approved* the plans for the new school.]
ap·prove • *verb* **approved, approving**

approximate (ə präk′sə mit) ***adjective*** more or less correct or exact [The *approximate* distance is 300 miles.]
ap·prox·i·mate • *adjective*

approximately (ə präk′sə mit lē) ***adverb*** almost exactly; nearly; about [The whole trip will take *approximately* three hours.]
ap·prox·i·mate·ly • *adverb*

Apr. *abbreviation for* April.

apricot

apricot (ap′rə kät *or* ā′prə kät) ***noun*** **1** a pale orange fruit that looks like a small peach. **2** the tree it grows on.
ap·ri·cot • *noun, plural* **apricots**

April (ā′prəl) ***noun*** the fourth month of the year. April has 30 days. Abbreviated **Apr.**
A·pril • *noun*

April Fools' Day ***noun*** April 1. On this day it is a custom to play harmless tricks on people.

A

apron (ā′prən) ***noun*** a garment that is worn over the front part of the body, to cover and protect the clothes. Aprons are made of cloth, leather, or a similar material.
a·pron • ***noun,*** *plural* **aprons**

WORD HISTORY

apron

The word **apron** was once written *napron* (it comes from the same word as **napkin**). Over the centuries, though, some people thought they were hearing "an apron" when someone said "a napron," and the word's spelling gradually changed.

apt (apt) ***adjective*** **1** likely or almost certain; inclined [It is *apt* to rain today.] **2** just right for what is being done or said; appropriate [She made an *apt* remark that showed she had done her homework.] **3** quick to learn or understand [an *apt* student].

apt. *abbreviation for* apartment.

aptitude (ap′tə to͞od *or* ap′tə tyo͞od) ***noun*** **1** a natural ability; talent [Mary has an *aptitude* for mathematics.] —Look for the WORD CHOICES box at the entry **talent**. **2** quickness to learn or understand [Bill showed great *aptitude* in Mr. Smith's fifth grade class.]
ap·ti·tude • ***noun,*** *plural* **aptitudes**

aqua (ak′wə *or* äk′wə) ***noun*** light bluish green.
adjective bluish-green.
aq·ua • ***noun*** • ***adjective***

aquamarine (ak′wə mə rēn′) ***noun*** a clear, pale bluish-green mineral that is used in jewelry.
adjective bluish-green.
aq·ua·ma·rine • ***noun,*** *plural* **aquamarines** • ***adjective***

aquarium (ə kwer′ē əm) ***noun*** **1** a tank, bowl, or other container in which living fishes, water animals, or water plants are kept. An aquarium is made of glass or some other clear material. **2** a building where collections of living fishes, water animals, and water plants are kept so the public may see them.
a·quar·i·um • ***noun,*** *plural* **aquariums**

aquatic (ə kwät′ik *or* ə kwat′ik) ***adjective*** **1** growing or living in water [an *aquatic* plant]. **2** taking place in or on water [an *aquatic* sport].
a·quat·ic • ***adjective***

aqueduct

aqueduct (ak′wə dukt) ***noun*** **1** a large pipe or channel that brings water from a distant place. **2** a high structure like a bridge that holds up this pipe across low ground or a river.
aq·ue·duct • ***noun,*** *plural* **aqueducts**

AR *abbreviation for* Arkansas.

Arab (er′əb *or* ar′əb) ***noun*** a member of a people that began in Arabia and who now also live in many nearby countries and in northern Africa. Many groups of Arabs are nomads who roam the deserts.
adjective of or having to do with the Arabs or Arabia.
Ar·ab • ***noun,*** *plural* **Arabs** • ***adjective***

Arabia (ə rā′bē ə) a large peninsula in southwestern Asia. It is mostly a desert region.
A·ra·bi·a

Arabian (ə rā′bē ən) ***noun*** a person born or living in Arabia.
adjective of or having to do with the Arabs or Arabia.
A·ra·bi·an • ***noun,*** *plural* **Arabians** • ***adjective***

Arabic (er′ə bik *or* ar′ə bik) ***noun*** the language of the Arabs. It is related to Hebrew.
adjective of or having to do with the Arabs or their language.
Ar·a·bic • ***noun*** • ***adjective***

a	cat	ō	go	ʉ	fur	ə =	a *in* ago
ā	ape	ô	law, for	ch	chin		e *in* agent
ä	cot, car	oo	look	sh	she		i *in* pencil
e	ten	o͞o	tool	th	thin		o *in* atom
ē	me	oi	oil	*th*	then		u *in* circus
i	fit	ou	out	zh	measure		
ī	ice	u	up	ŋ	ring		

Arabic numerals ***plural noun*** the figures 1, 2, 3, 4, 5, 6, 7, 8, 9, and 0 (zero). They were first taught to Europeans by the Arabs.

arbitrary (är′bə trer′ē) ***adjective*** based only on personal feelings, opinions, or wishes and not on law or good judgment [The coach made an *arbitrary* decision to cancel the practice.]
ar·bi·trar·y • ***adjective***

arbitrate (är′bə trāt) ***verb*** **1** to make a decision that settles an argument [Michael had to *arbitrate* the fight between his sisters over who would borrow his bike.] **2** to submit to or settle by arbitration [The court will *arbitrate* in the property dispute between the two farmers.]
ar·bi·trate • ***verb*** **arbitrated, arbitrating**

arbitration (är′bə trā′shən) ***noun*** the act or process of settling an argument by letting an outside person or group listen to both sides and make a decision.
ar·bi·tra·tion • ***noun,*** *plural* **arbitrations**

arbor

arbor (är′bər) ***noun*** a place that is shaded by trees or bushes or by vines growing on frames.
ar·bor • ***noun,*** *plural* **arbors**

arc (ärk) ***noun*** a part of the line that forms a circle or any curve.
arc • ***noun,*** *plural* **arcs**

● The words **arc** and **ark** sound alike.
Measure the *arc* of the round window.
Noah took his family into the *ark*.

arcade (är kād′) ***noun*** **1** a passageway that is covered by an arched roof. An arcade often has small shops on both sides. **2** a place with machines that play video games. A person can play these games by paying a fee.
ar·cade • ***noun,*** *plural* **arcades**

arch (ärch) ***noun*** **1** a curved structure that extends across an open space. An arch serves as a support for the weight of the building material on top of it. Arches are often used to hold up bridges and form doorways and windows in many buildings. **2** anything shaped like an arch [the *arch* of the foot].
verb **1** to curve into an arch [The cat *arched* its back.] **2** to form an arch [The bridge *arches* over the river.]
arch • ***noun,*** *plural* **arches** • ***verb*** **arched, arching**

archaeology (är′kē äl′ə jē) ***noun*** the study of ancient times and ancient peoples by examining what is left of their buildings, tools, dishes, weapons, and other things.
ar·chae·ol·o·gy • ***noun***

archbishop (ärch′bish′əp) ***noun*** a bishop of the highest rank.
arch·bish·op • ***noun,*** *plural* **archbishops**

archeology (är′kē äl′ə jē) ***noun*** *another spelling of* **archaeology**.
ar·che·ol·o·gy • ***noun***

archer (är′chər) ***noun*** a person who shoots with bow and arrow.
arch·er • ***noun,*** *plural* **archers**

archery (är′chər ē) ***noun*** the skill or sport of shooting with bow and arrow.
arch·er·y • ***noun***

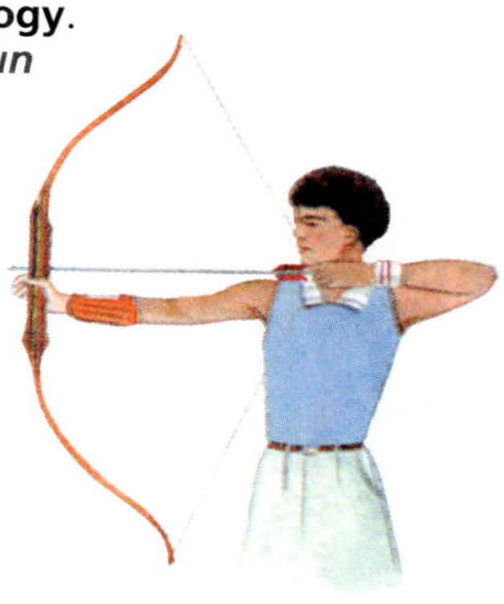

archer

archipelago (är′kə pel′ə gō) ***noun*** a group or chain of many islands in a sea.
ar·chi·pel·a·go • ***noun,*** *plural* **archipelagoes** or **archipelagos**

architect (är′kə tekt) ***noun*** a person who designs buildings, bridges, and other large structures. An architect also works with builders to make sure that the buildings are constructed the way they were designed.
ar·chi·tect • ***noun,*** *plural* **architects**

architecture (är′kə tek′chər) ***noun*** **1** the science or work of designing and planning buildings. **2** a style or special way of building [The temple is a fine example of Greek *architecture*.]
ar·chi·tec·ture • ***noun***

arctic (ärk′tik *or* är′tik) ***adjective*** of or having to do with the North Pole or the region around it [Seals are found in *arctic* waters.]

A

—**the Arctic** the region around the North Pole.
arc·tic • *adjective*

SPELLING TIP

Use this memory aid to spell **arctic**. There is an ***arc*** in ***arc***tic.

Arctic Ocean the ocean around the North Pole.

are (är) *verb* the form of the verb **be** that is used to show the present time with *you*, *we*, and *they*. This form is also used with plural nouns. [*Are* we late? These trees *are* maples.]

area (er′ē ə) *noun* **1** the amount or size of a surface. If a floor is 10 feet wide and 20 feet long, its area is 200 square feet. **2** a section or region of land [an industrial *area*]. **3** a space that is used for a special purpose [a shaded picnic *area*]. **4** a field of activity, study, or interest [What is her *area* of study?]
ar·e·a • *noun, plural* **areas**

area code *noun* a set or series of three numbers given to each telephone service area in the U.S. and Canada. Area codes are used in calling a telephone number outside one's own area.
area code • *noun, plural* **area codes**

arena (ə rē′nə) *noun* **1** an enclosed space for sports events and for circuses, concerts, and other large shows. **2** a building that has an arena. **3** an area or place of conflict or activity [The senator loved the political *arena*.]
a·re·na • *noun, plural* **arenas**

aren't (ärnt) are not.
are·n't

Argentina (är′jən tē′nə) a country in southern South America.
Ar·gen·ti·na

argue (är′gyo͞o) *verb* **1** to have a disagreement; to quarrel [Frank and Larry *argued* about who was going to drive the car.] **2** to give reasons for or against something [The lawyer *argued* the case in court.]
ar·gue • *verb* **argued, arguing**

argument (är′gyo͞o mənt) *noun* **1** an angry disagreement; a quarrel [The two friends had an *argument* and yelled at each other.] **2** a discussion of something by people with different opinions [They were deeply involved in an *argument* about yesterday's football game.] **3** a reason given for or against something [What are your *arguments* for not voting?]
ar·gu·ment • *noun, plural* **arguments**

WORD CHOICES

Synonyms of **argument**

The words **argument, controversy,** and **dispute** share the meaning "a discussion in which people disagree."

an *argument* among friends
the *controversy* about raising taxes
a *dispute* over a boundary line

arid (er′id *or* ar′id) *adjective* not having enough water for things to grow; dry and barren [A desert is an *arid* region.]
ar·id • *adjective*

arise (ə rīz′) *verb* **1** to get up from sitting, lying, or kneeling [He *arose* and bowed to his visitor.] **2** to move upward; rise [Clouds of dust *arose* from the plains.] **3** to come into being; appear [When the chance to go to the zoo *arose*, she took it.]
a·rise • *verb* **arose, arisen, arising**

arisen (ə riz′ən) *verb past participle of* **arise**.
a·ris·en • *verb*

aristocracy (er′ə stäk′rə sē *or* ar′ə stäk′rə sē) *noun* **1** a class of people who have a high position in society because they are born into families with great wealth and sometimes titles. **2** a group of people thought to be the best in some way [The university created an *aristocracy* of scientists and scholars.]
ar·is·toc·ra·cy • *noun, plural* **aristocracies**

aristocrat (ə ris′tə krat) *noun* a person who belongs to an aristocracy.
a·ris·to·crat • *noun, plural* **aristocrats**

Aristotle (er′is tät′l *or* ar′is tät′l) 384-322 B.C.; Greek philosopher, who was a student of Plato.
Ar·is·tot·le

a	cat	ō	go	ʉ	fur	ə =	a *in* ago
ā	ape	ô	law, for	ch	chin		e *in* agent
ä	cot, car	o͝o	look	sh	she		i *in* pencil
e	ten	o͞o	tool	th	thin		o *in* atom
ē	me	oi	oil	*th*	then		u *in* circus
i	fit	ou	out	zh	measure		
ī	ice	u	up	ŋ	ring		

arithmetic (ə rith′mə tik) ***noun*** the science or skill of using numbers in adding, subtracting, multiplying, or dividing.
a·rith·me·tic • ***noun***

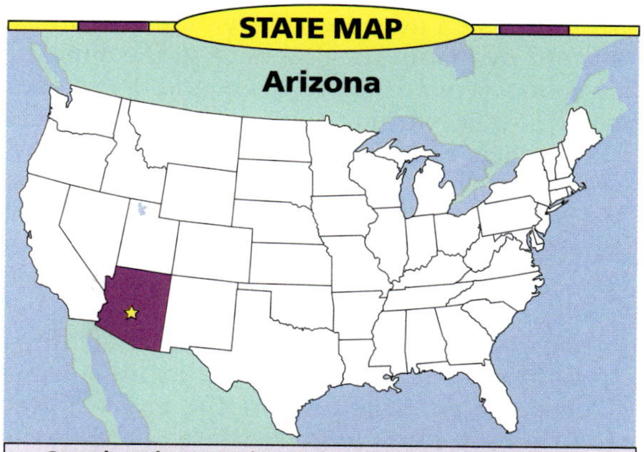

Statehood: 1912, the 48th state • **Capital:** Phoenix

Arizona (er′i zō′nə *or* ar′i zō′nə) a State in the southwestern part of the U.S. Its capital is Phoenix. Abbreviated **AZ** or **Ariz.**
Ar·i·zo·na

ark (ärk) in the Bible, the ship in which Noah, his family, and two of every kind of animal lived during the great flood.
- The words **ark** and **arc** sound alike.
  Noah took his family into the *ark*.
  Measure the *arc* of the round window.

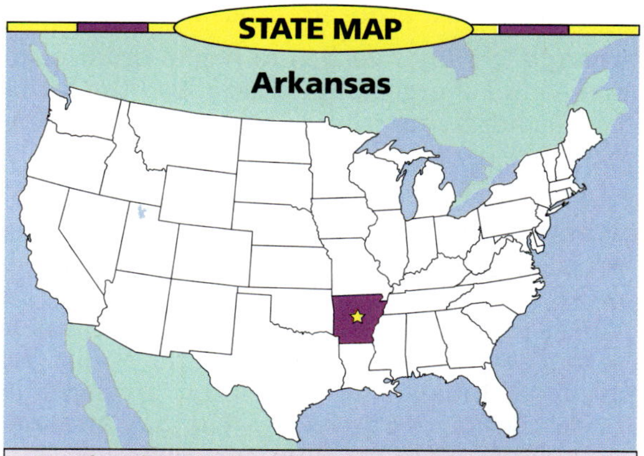

Statehood: 1836, the 25th state • **Capital:** Little Rock

Arkansas (är′kən sô) a State in the south central part of the U.S. Its capital is Little Rock. Abbreviated **AR** or **Ark.**
Ar·kan·sas

arm[1] (ärm) ***noun*** **1** the part of the body between the shoulder and the hand. **2** anything that is like an arm, in shape, use, or position. **3** the ability to pitch or throw a ball [Our catcher has a good *arm*.]
arm • ***noun, plural*** **arms**

arm[2] (ärm) ***noun*** **1 arms** weapons of all kinds that are used in war or for defense. Guns, tanks, bombs, and missiles are all arms. **2 arms** the designs and figures on a coat of arms of a nation, family, or institution.
verb **1** to supply with weapons or a means of defense [The villagers *armed* themselves with sticks.] **2** to furnish with protection [I was *armed* against the cold with a coat.]
arm • ***noun, plural*** **arms** • ***verb*** **armed, arming**

armada (är mä′də) ***noun*** a large fleet of warships.
ar·ma·da • ***noun, plural*** **armadas**

armadillo

armadillo (är′mə dil′ō) ***noun*** a burrowing animal that has an armor of bony plates around its back and head. Armadillos are found in Texas, Central America, and South America.
ar·ma·dil·lo • ***noun, plural*** **armadillos**

armament (är′mə mənt) ***noun*** *often* **armaments** all the guns, ships, bombs, planes, troops, or other military equipment of a country.
ar·ma·ment • ***noun, plural*** **armaments**

armchair (ärm′cher) ***noun*** a chair that has supports at the sides for the arms or elbows.
arm·chair • ***noun, plural*** **armchairs**

armed forces ***plural noun*** all the military, naval, and air forces of a country.

Armenia (är mēn′yə) a country in southwestern Asia. It was a part of the Soviet Union.
Ar·me·ni·a

Armenian (är mēn′yən) ***noun*** **1** a person born or living in Armenia. **2** the language of the people of Armenia.

Ar·me·ni·an • *noun, plural for sense 1 only* **Armenians**

armistice (är′mə stis) ***noun*** an agreement by both sides in a war to a temporary stop in fighting; a truce.
ar·mis·tice • ***noun,*** *plural* **armistices**

armor (är′mər) ***noun*** **1** a covering worn to protect the body against weapons. Armor was usually made of metal. **2** any protective covering. The shell of a turtle or the metal plates on a warship are armor.
ar·mor • ***noun,*** *plural* **armors**

armor

armored (är′mərd) ***adjective*** covered with armor [The money was carried in an *armored* truck.]
ar·mored • ***adjective***

armory (är′mər ē) ***noun*** **1** a place where weapons are stored. **2** a building where a military unit is trained.
ar·mor·y • ***noun,*** *plural* **armories**

armpit (ärm′pit) ***noun*** the curved, hollow part under the arm at the shoulder.
arm·pit • ***noun,*** *plural* **armpits**

Armstrong (ärm′strôŋ), **Louis** (lo͞o′is) 1901-1971; American jazz musician.
Arm·strong, Lou·is

Armstrong (ärm′strôŋ), **Neil** (nēl) 1930- ; American astronaut. He was the first person to step on the moon.
Arm·strong, Neil

army (är′mē) ***noun*** **1** a large group of soldiers organized and trained to fight on land. **2** *often* **Army** all the soldiers of a country [the U.S. *Army*]. **3** *often* **Army** a large group of persons organized to work for some cause [the Salvation *Army*]. **4** a large group of persons or animals [an *army* of construction workers].
ar·my • ***noun,*** *plural* **armies**

Arnold (är′nəld), **Benedict** (ben′ə dikt) 1741-1801; American general in the Revolutionary War who became a traitor.
Ar·nold, Ben·e·dict

aroma (ə rō′mə) ***noun*** a pleasant smell; fragrance [the delicious *aroma* of an apple pie].
a·ro·ma • ***noun,*** *plural* **aromas**

arose (ə rōz′) ***verb*** *past tense of* **arise**.
a·rose • ***verb***

around (ə round′) ***adverb*** **1** in a circle [The wheel turned *around*.] **2** in circumference [A baseball measures about nine inches *around*.] **3** on all sides [The valley is hemmed *around* by mountains.] **4** in or to the opposite direction [We turned *around* and went back home.] **5** in various places; here and there [The coach is looking *around* for new players.] **6** in every part of; throughout [We swim the year *around*.] **7** for everyone [There's not enough cake to go *around*.] **8** [*an informal use*] near by [Stay *around* in case we need you.]
preposition **1** in a circle that surrounds [Pine trees grew *around* the lake.] **2** on all sides of [There are suburbs *around* the city.] **3** here and there in [Toys were scattered *around* the room.] **4** close to; about [It cost *around* four dollars.] **5** on the other side of [The store is *around* the corner.] In Great Britain the word *round* is used for the meanings of *around* as an adverb and preposition.
adjective active; about [She's up and *around* now.]
a·round • ***adverb*** • ***preposition*** • ***adjective***

arouse (ə rouz′) ***verb*** **1** to awaken from sleep [The noise of the trucks *arouses* me every morning.] **2** to work up; excite [His speech *aroused* the crowd.] **3** to bring into being; stir up [Her suffering *aroused* our pity.]
a·rouse • ***verb*** **aroused, arousing**

arrange (ə rānj′) ***verb*** **1** to put in order or in some kind of order [Maria *arranged* the furniture in her living room.] **2** to make plans; prepare [We *arranged* to meet at the theater.]
ar·range • ***verb*** **arranged, arranging**

arrangement (ə rānj′mənt) ***noun*** **1** the act of arranging, or putting in order [The *arrangement* of furniture took hours.] **2** the way in which persons or things are arranged [a new *arrangement* of the pictures on the wall]. **3** a group of things that have been arranged [a bride's flower *arrangement*]. **4** *usually* **arrangements** plans or preparations [*Arrangements* have been made for the party.]
ar·range·ment • ***noun,*** *plural* **arrangements**

a	cat	ō	go	ʉ	fur	ə =	a *in* ago
ā	ape	ô	law, for	ch	chin		e *in* agent
ä	cot, car	oo	look	sh	she		i *in* pencil
e	ten	o͞o	tool	th	thin		o *in* atom
ē	me	oi	oil	*th*	then		u *in* circus
i	fit	ou	out	zh	measure		
ī	ice	u	up	ŋ	ring		

array (ə rā′) *verb* **1** to put in the proper order [The troops were *arrayed* for battle.] **2** to dress in fine clothes [*arrayed* in velvet].
noun **1** arrangement in the proper order [The captain positioned the soldiers in battle *array*.] **2** a large or impressive display [The table was set with an *array* of fine china.] **3** fine clothes; finery [in royal *array*].
ar·ray • *verb* **arrayed, arraying**
• *noun, plural* **arrays**

arrest (ə rest′) *verb* **1** to seize or take to jail on a charge of breaking the law [The police officer *arrested* him for careless driving.] **2** to stop from growing or spreading [A coat of paint will *arrest* the rust.] **3** to catch and hold [The large sign *arrested* her attention.]
noun the act of arresting by authority of the law [The *arrest* was announced last night.]
ar·rest • *verb* **arrested, arresting**
• *noun, plural* **arrests**

arrival (ə rī′vəl) *noun* **1** the act of arriving [Birds and squirrels welcomed the *arrival* of spring.] **2** a person or thing that has arrived [There are many new *arrivals* at the hotel every week.]
ar·riv·al • *noun, plural* **arrivals**

arrive (ə rīv′) *verb* **1** to come to a place [They *arrived* in the city at night.] **2** to come [The time has *arrived* to say goodbye.]
—**arrive at** to reach by work, thinking, discussing, or some other means [Have you *arrived at* a decision yet?]
ar·rive • *verb* **arrived, arriving**

arrogant (er′ə gənt *or* ar′ə gənt) *adjective* having too much pride and acting more important than everyone else [Jane was very *arrogant* after she won the science prize.] —Look for the WORD CHOICES box at the entry **proud**.
ar·ro·gant • *adjective*

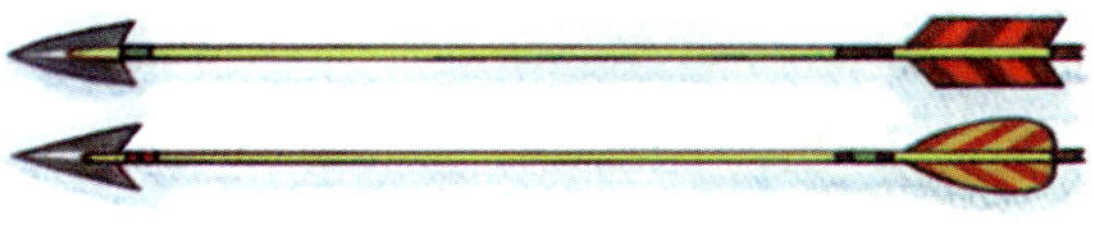

arrow

arrow (er′ō *or* ar′ō) *noun* **1** a slender rod that is shot from a bow. Arrows usually have a point at the front end and feathers at the back end. **2** anything that looks or is used like an arrow [The *arrow* on the road sign tells you to turn right.]
ar·row • *noun, plural* **arrows**

arrowhead (er′ō hed *or* ar′ō hed) *noun* the pointed tip of an arrow.
ar·row·head • *noun, plural* **arrowheads**

arroyo (ə roi′ō) *noun* a small channel with steep sides and with a nearly flat floor, formed by the force of running water. Arroyos are usually dry except after heavy rains. This word is used in the Southwest.
ar·roy·o • *noun, plural* **arroyos**

arsenal (är′sə nəl) *noun* a place where guns and ammunition are made or stored.
ar·se·nal • *noun, plural* **arsenals**

arsenic (är′sə nik) *noun* a silvery-white metal that is a chemical element. Arsenic is very poisonous and is used in powders and sprays for killing insects, rats, and mice.
ar·se·nic • *noun*

arson (är′sən) *noun* the crime of setting fire to a building or other property on purpose.
ar·son • *noun*

art (ärt) *noun* **1** any activity in which a person makes or does something that is beautiful. Painting, sculpture, music, and literature are forms of art. **2** a painting, statue, poem, symphony, or other thing made or created by an artist [The museum has a fine *art* collection.] **3** a practical craft or skill [the *art* of cooking]. **4** a special ability to do something easily [He has mastered the *art* of making friends.]
art • *noun, plural* **arts**

WORD CHOICES

Synonyms of **art**

The words **art**, **craft**, and **skill** share the meaning "the ability to make or do something."

Painting portraits is an *art*.
Weaving baskets is a *craft*.
Repairing plumbing is a *skill*.

artery (ärt′ər ē) *noun* **1** one of the blood vessels that carry blood away from the heart to all parts of the body. **2** a main road or channel.
ar·ter·y • *noun, plural* **arteries**

arthritis (är thrīt′is) *noun* a disease in which the joints of the body swell up and become sore and stiff.
ar·thri·tis • *noun*

arthropod (är′thrə päd′) ***noun*** one of a large group of animals that have legs with several joints and a body divided into two or more parts. Insects, spiders, crabs, and lobsters are all arthropods.
ar·thro·pod • ***noun,*** *plural* **arthropods**

Arthur (är′thər) a king of Britain in legends, who led the knights of the Round Table.
Ar·thur

Arthur (är′thər), **Chester Alan** (ches′tər al′ən) 1829-1886; the twenty-first president of the U.S., from 1881 to 1885.
Ar·thur, Ches·ter Al·an

artichoke

artichoke (ärt′i chōk) ***noun*** **1** a plant that looks like a large thistle. **2** the flower head of this plant. It is cooked and eaten as a vegetable.
ar·ti·choke • ***noun,*** *plural* **artichokes**

article (ärt′i kəl) ***noun*** **1** a complete piece of writing on a single subject that is part of a newspaper, magazine, or book [Did you read the *article* on air pollution in Sunday's newspaper?] **2** a separate section of a contract, treaty, or other formal document [an *article* of the Constitution]. **3** a thing of a certain kind; a separate thing; item [A shirt is an *article* of clothing.] **4** any one of the words *a*, *an*, or *the*.
ar·ti·cle • ***noun,*** *plural* **articles**

articulate (är tik′yo͞o lit *for adj.;* är tik′yo͞o lāt *for v.*) ***adjective*** able to speak or express oneself in a clear and effective way [The senator is a very *articulate* speaker.]
verb to say in a clear, distinct way [You must *articulate* all the syllables of this word.]
ar·tic·u·late • ***adjective*** • ***verb*** **articulated, articulating**

artificial (ärt′ə fish′əl) ***adjective*** **1** made by a human being, not by nature; not natural [*artificial* flowers made of plastic]. **2** put on just for an effect; not sincere; false [an *artificial* smile].
ar·ti·fi·cial • ***adjective***

artificial respiration ***noun*** the act of forcing air into and out of the lungs of a person who has stopped breathing. It is used in cases of drowning, shock, and other emergencies.

artillery (är til′ər ē) ***noun*** large guns that are too heavy to carry. These guns may be mounted on wheels or on vehicles with wheels or tracks. They may also be set up on stationary bases.
ar·til·ler·y • ***noun,*** *plural* **artilleries**

artisan (är′tə zən) ***noun*** a person who works at a craft that requires manual or artistic skill. Persons who make quilts or silk flowers or who weave rugs are artisans.
ar·ti·san • ***noun,*** *plural* **artisans**

artist (ärt′ist) ***noun*** **1** a person who works in painting, sculpture, music, or any other form of art. **2** a person who does something very well [That baker is a true *artist*.]
art·ist • ***noun,*** *plural* **artists**

artistic (är tis′tik) ***adjective*** **1** of or having to do with art or artists [All the members of his family have *artistic* interests.] **2** done with skill and a good sense of color, form, or design [She did an *artistic* job of decorating the office.]
ar·tis·tic • ***adjective***

-ary *a suffix meaning:* **1** having to do with [*Planetary* means "having to do with a planet."] **2** a person or thing that is connected with [A *revolutionary* is a person who takes part in a revolution.]

as (az) ***adverb*** **1** to the same amount or degree; equally [Are you *as* tall as your cousin?] **2** for instance; for example [Some plants, *as* corn and potatoes, are native to America.]
conjunction **1** to the same amount or degree that [I'm as hungry *as* you are.] **2** in the way that [Do *as* I tell you.] **3** at the same time that; while [She laughed *as* she spoke.] **4** because; since [*As* I am tired, I'll stay home.]
preposition in the role or manner of [He poses *as* a friend. That table can serve *as* a desk.]

a	cat	ō	go	ʉ	fur	ə = a *in* ago	
ā	ape	ô	law, for	ch	chin	e *in* agent	
ä	cot, car	o͝o	look	sh	she	i *in* pencil	
e	ten	o͞o	tool	th	thin	o *in* atom	
ē	me	oi	oil	*th*	then	u *in* circus	
i	fit	ou	out	zh	measure		
ī	ice	u	up	ŋ	ring		

—as if or **as though** as it would if; as a person would if [They acted *as if* they were tired. It looks *as though* it will rain.] **—as is** [*an informal use*] just as it is [This used car costs $800 *as is*.] **—as of** up to, on, or from a certain time [You can reach me here *as of* next Friday.]

asbestos (as bes′təs *or* az bes′təs) ***noun*** a grayish mineral that separates into long fibers like thread. It can be made into a kind of cloth or paper. Asbestos will not burn and is used to make fireproof curtains and electric insulation.
as·bes·tos • ***noun***

ascend (ə send′) ***verb*** to go up; move upward; climb [The balloon *ascended* into the air.]
as·cend • ***verb*** **ascended, ascending**

ascent (ə sent′) ***noun*** **1** the act of moving up, rising, or climbing [Our *ascent* up the hill was very difficult.] **2** a way leading up; slope [We looked for a better *ascent*.]
as·cent • ***noun, plural*** **ascents**

ash[1] (ash) ***noun*** the grayish powder and flakes that are left after something has been burned.
ash • ***noun, plural*** **ashes**

ash[2] (ash) ***noun*** a shade tree whose tough wood is used for timber and to make furniture.
ash • ***noun, plural*** **ashes**

ashamed (ə shāmd′) ***adjective*** **1** feeling shame because something bad, wrong, or foolish was done [They were *ashamed* because they broke the window.] **2** not ready to do something because of a fear that one will feel shame or be embarrassed [I am *ashamed* to ask for help.]
a·shamed • ***adjective***

ashore (ə shôr′) ***adverb*** to or on the shore [They jumped overboard and swam *ashore*.]
a·shore • ***adverb***

Asia (ā′zhə) the largest continent. Asia lies between the Pacific Ocean on one side and Europe and Africa on the other.
A·sia

Asian (ā′zhən) ***adjective*** of or having to do with Asia, its people, or their cultures [an *Asian* language; *Asian* art].
noun a person born or living in Asia.
A·sian • ***adjective*** • ***noun***

aside (ə sīd′) ***adverb*** **1** on or to one side [Pull the curtain *aside*.] **2** away; for use later [Put a cookie *aside* for me.] **3** apart; out of consideration [All joking *aside*, I mean what I said.]
—aside from except for [*Aside from* math class, she likes school.]
a·side • ***adverb***

ask (ask) ***verb*** **1** to use words in order to find out; seek the answer to [We *asked* for directions to your house. She *asked* how old he was.] **2** to put a question to; seek information from [*Ask* her where she's going.] **3** to make a request of [I *asked* my brother for a loan. John *asked* to be excused from school.] **4** to invite [We weren't *asked* to the party.]
ask • ***verb*** **asked, asking**

askew (ə skyo͞o′) ***adjective*** on or to one side; not straight [His hat was knocked *askew*.]
a·skew • ***adjective***

asleep (ə slēp′) ***adjective*** **1** in a condition of sleep; sleeping [The baby is *asleep*.] **2** numb except for a prickly feeling [My foot is *asleep*.]
adverb into a sleeping condition [She fell *asleep* at the movies.]
a·sleep • ***adjective*** • ***adverb***

asparagus (ə sper′ə gəs *or* ə spar′ə gəs) ***noun*** a plant with small leaves. Its young shoots are cooked and eaten as a vegetable.
as·par·a·gus • ***noun***

asparagus

A.S.P.C.A. or **ASPCA** *abbreviation for* American Society for the Prevention of Cruelty to Animals.

aspect (as′pekt) ***noun*** **1** a way that one may think about something [Have you thought about all *aspects* of the problem?] **2** the way something looks from a particular place; view [This *aspect* of the city is very beautiful.]
as·pect • ***noun, plural*** **aspects**

aspen (as′pən) ***noun*** a kind of poplar tree whose leaves flutter in the slightest breeze.
as·pen • ***noun, plural*** **aspens**

asphalt (as′fôlt) ***noun*** **1** a dark, sticky substance like tar that is found in the ground. **2** a mixture of this with sand or gravel, that is used mainly to pave roads.

aspen

A

as·phalt • *noun*

aspiration (as′pə rā′shən) ***noun*** a strong wish, hope, or ambition [Her *aspiration* is to become a doctor.]
as·pi·ra·tion • ***noun,*** *plural* **aspirations**

aspire (ə spīr′) ***verb*** to have a strong desire to get or do something [He *aspires* to be a dancer.]
as·pire • ***verb*** **aspired, aspiring**

aspirin (as′pə rin) ***noun*** **1** a medicine that is used to lessen pain and bring down fever. It is a white powder that is usually pressed into tablets. **2** a tablet of this powder.
as·pi·rin • ***noun,*** *plural for sense 2 only* **aspirins**

ass (as) ***noun*** **1** a donkey. **2** a stupid or silly person; fool.
ass • ***noun,*** *plural* **asses**

assassin (ə sas′ən) ***noun*** a person who murders a government leader, usually for political reasons.
as·sas·sin • ***noun,*** *plural* **assassins**

assassinate (ə sas′ən āt) ***verb*** to murder a government leader, usually for political reasons.
as·sas·si·nate • ***verb*** **assassinated, assassinating**

assassination (ə sas′ə nā′shən) ***noun*** the act of assassinating.
as·sas·si·na·tion • ***noun,*** *plural* **assassinations**

assault (ə sôlt′ *or* ə sält′) ***noun*** a violent attack [The soldiers made an *assault* on the fortress.]
verb to make a violent attack upon.
as·sault • ***noun,*** *plural* **assaults**
• ***verb*** **assaulted, assaulting**

assemble (ə sem′bəl) ***verb*** **1** to gather together into a group; collect [Members of our family *assembled* for a reunion.] —Look for the WORD CHOICES box at the entry **gather**. **2** to put together the parts of [Pat quickly *assembled* the bicycle because he had done it before.]
as·sem·ble • ***verb*** **assembled, assembling**

assembly (ə sem′blē) ***noun*** **1** a group of people gathered together; meeting [Our school has an *assembly* in the auditorium every Friday afternoon.] **2 Assembly** the lower branch of the legislature in some States. **3** the act of putting together parts or pieces [The instructions made the *assembly* of the swing set easy.] **4** a number of parts that fit or work together [the tail *assembly* of an airplane].
as·sem·bly • ***noun,*** *plural* **assemblies**

assembly line ***noun*** a process in which the job of making a product is divided into many smaller jobs. Each worker assembles the same part on every item made. The workers stay in the same place while the individual items pass slowly by on a moving belt or track.
assembly line • ***noun,*** *plural* **assembly lines**

assert (ə surt′) ***verb*** to say in a clear, sure way; declare [The doctors *asserted* that his health was good.] —Look for the WORD CHOICES box at the entry **say**.
—assert oneself to insist on one's rights [You must *assert yourself* if you want respect.]
as·sert • ***verb*** **asserted, asserting**

assess (ə ses′) ***verb*** to decide or try to find out the importance or value of something; evaluate; estimate [The city officials *assessed* the damage done by the earthquake.]
as·sess • ***verb*** **assessed, assessing**

asset (as′et) ***noun*** a fine or valuable thing to have [Good health can be your greatest *asset*.]
as·set • ***noun,*** *plural* **assets**

assign (ə sīn′) ***verb*** **1** to place at some work or task [The teacher *assigned* Louise to write the report.] **2** to give out as work or as a task [The teacher *assigned* homework to our class.] **3** to set apart for a special purpose [The coach *assigned* a date for the game.]
as·sign • ***verb*** **assigned, assigning**

assignment (ə sīn′mənt) ***noun*** a lesson, task, or something else that is assigned [Our weekly *assignment* was to collect assorted rocks for the experiment.]
as·sign·ment • ***noun,*** *plural* **assignments**

assist (ə sist′) ***verb*** to help; aid [He *assisted* by holding the door open.]
noun **1** a throw or other play in baseball that helps another player make a putout. **2** a pass in basketball or hockey that helps another player score.
as·sist • ***verb*** **assisted, assisting**
• ***noun,*** *plural* **assists**

assistance (ə sis′təns) ***noun*** help; aid [We got out with the *assistance* of a snowplow.]

a	cat	ō	go	ʉ	fur	ə =	a *in* ago
ā	ape	ô	law, for	ch	chin		e *in* agent
ä	cot, car	oo	look	sh	she		i *in* pencil
e	ten	ōō	tool	th	thin		o *in* atom
ē	me	oi	oil	*th*	then		u *in* circus
i	fit	ou	out	zh	measure		
ī	ice	u	up	ŋ	ring		

as·sist·ance • *noun*

assistant (ə sis′tənt) ***noun*** a person who assists or helps another; helper.
as·sist·ant • ***noun,*** *plural* **assistants**

associate (ə sō′shē āt *or* ə sō′sē āt) ***verb*** **1** to bring or come together as friends or partners [Don't *associate* with people who gossip.] **2** to connect with something else in one's mind; think of together [We *associate* the taste of something with its smell.]
as·so·ci·ate • ***verb*** **associated, associating**

association (ə sō′sē ā′shən *or* ə sō′shē ā′shən) ***noun*** **1** a group of people joined in some way for some purpose; society ["NAACP" stands for the National *Association* for the Advancement of Colored People.] **2** a partnership or friendship [Their close *association* started during their school days.] **3** a connection of one idea or feeling with another [the *association* of the color blue with coolness].
as·so·ci·a·tion • ***noun,*** *plural* **associations**

associative property (ə sō′shē ā′tiv *or* ə sō′shə tiv) ***noun*** in mathematics, the property that states that the way the elements are grouped does not change the result. For example, in addition, 3 + (5 + 2) = 10 and (3 + 5) + 2 = 10. In multiplication, 1 x (2 x 4) = 8 and (1 x 2) x 4 = 8.
as·so·ci·a·tive property • ***noun,*** *plural* **associative properties**

assorted (ə sôrt′id) ***adjective*** of different sorts; of various kinds [a box of *assorted* candies].
as·sort·ed • ***adjective***

assortment (ə sôrt′mənt) ***noun*** a collection of various sorts; variety [A library carries a wide *assortment* of books.]
as·sort·ment • ***noun,*** *plural* **assortments**

assume (ə so͞om′ *or* ə syo͞om′) ***verb*** **1** to suppose something to be a fact; take for granted [Let's *assume* our guests will be on time.] **2** to take over; seize [He *assumed* control of the situation.] **3** to pretend to have; put on [Although she was afraid, she *assumed* a brave air.]
as·sume • ***verb*** **assumed, assuming**

assumption (ə sump′shən) ***noun*** something that is believed to be true; anything that is taken for granted [We made the *assumption* that he would want to go with us.]
as·sump·tion • ***noun,*** *plural* **assumptions**

assurance (ə sho͝or′əns) ***noun*** **1** the fact of being sure about something; confidence [I have no *assurance* that we will win.] **2** something said or done to make one feel confident [I felt better after hearing the manager's *assurance* that there were plenty of tickets.] **3** self-confidence; belief in one's own abilities [He walked gracefully with the *assurance* of a dancer.]
as·sur·ance • ***noun,*** *plural for sense 2 only* **assurances**

assure (ə sho͝or′) ***verb*** **1** to tell or promise in a positive way [I *assure* you that I'll be there.] **2** to make a person sure of something; convince [I want to *assure* you that our friendship is important to me.]
as·sure • ***verb*** **assured, assuring**

aster (as′tər) ***noun*** a plant with purple, pink, or white flowers. The simple kinds look like daisies, but some asters are large and have many petals.
as·ter • ***noun,*** *plural* **asters**

aster

asterisk (as′tər isk) ***noun*** a mark or sign in the shape of a star (*). It is used in printing to call attention to a note of explanation somewhere else on a page or to show that something has been left out.
as·ter·isk • ***noun,*** *plural* **asterisks**

asteroid (as′tər oid) ***noun*** one of the many small planets that move in orbits around the sun. The asteroids orbit in an area between Mars and Jupiter.
as·ter·oid • ***noun,*** *plural* **asteroids**

asthma (az′mə) ***noun*** an illness in which there are attacks of wheezing, coughing, and hard breathing. Asthma is usually caused by an allergy.
asth·ma • ***noun***

astir (ə stur′) ***adjective*** moving about; in motion; active [The town is *astir* with visitors.]
a·stir • ***adjective***

astonish (ə stän′ish) ***verb*** to surprise greatly; fill with wonder; amaze [Her new behavior *astonished* me.]
as·ton·ish • ***verb*** **astonished, astonishing**

astonishment (ə stän′ish mənt) ***noun*** the condition of being astonished; great amaze-

A

ment or surprise [To my *astonishment*, he was fired.]
as·ton·ish·ment • *noun*

astound (ə stound′) ***verb*** to surprise so greatly as to make confused or unable to speak [Their praise *astounded* her.]
as·tound • ***verb*** **astounded, astounding**

astray (ə strā′) ***adverb*** off the right path [The cows went *astray* and trampled the garden.]
a·stray • ***adverb***

astride (ə strīd′) ***preposition*** with one leg on each side of [He sat *astride* the bench.]
a·stride • ***preposition***

astro- *a prefix meaning* star or stars [*Astrophysics* is the science that investigates the properties of stars and planets that can be studied by physics and chemistry.]

astrology (ə sträl′ə jē *or* ə strôl′ə jē) ***noun*** a false science that is based on a belief that the stars, planets, and moon affect people's lives. Some people believe that astrology can be used to tell what the future will be.
as·trol·o·gy • ***noun***

astronaut

astronaut (as′trə nôt *or* as′trə nät) ***noun*** a person trained to make rocket flights in outer space.
as·tro·naut • ***noun,*** *plural* **astronauts**

WORD HISTORY

astronaut

We can think of an **astronaut** as a sailor among the stars. The word **astronaut** comes from two Greek words that mean "star" and "sailor."

astronomer (ə strän′ə mər) ***noun*** a scientist who practices astronomy.
as·tron·o·mer • ***noun,*** *plural* **astronomers**

astronomical (as′trə näm′i kəl) ***adjective*** **1** having to do with astronomy [*Astronomical* research has been made easier by computers.] **2** very great [The number of people living in New York City is *astronomical*.]
as·tro·nom·i·cal • ***adjective***

astronomy (ə strän′ə mē) ***noun*** the science that studies the motion, size, and makeup of the stars, planets, comets, and other things found in space.
as·tron·o·my • ***noun***

asylum (ə sī′ləm) ***noun*** **1** a place where one is safe and secure; refuge. **2** a place that is home for large groups of helpless people. Orphans, people who are mentally ill, and those who are very old once lived in asylums.
a·sy·lum • ***noun,*** *plural* **asylums**

at (at) ***preposition*** **1** on, in, near, or by [Are they *at* home?] **2** to or toward [Look *at* her. Aim *at* the target.] **3** attending [Virginia was *at* the party.] **4** busy with [Everyone was *at* work.] **5** in a condition of [England and France were *at* war.] **6** in the amount, rate, or price of [Apples sold *at* 20 cents each.] **7** on or close to the time or age of [We eat *at* six o'clock.]

ate (āt) ***verb*** *past tense of* **eat**.
• The words **ate** and **eight** sound alike.
We *ate* lunch at noon.
Dinner is at *eight* o'clock.

-ate *a suffix meaning:* **1** to make, become, or form. **2** to treat with [To *vaccinate* is to treat with vaccine.] **3** of or like.

Athena (ə thē′nə) the Greek goddess of wisdom and skills. The Romans called this goddess *Minerva*.
A·the·na

Athens (ath′ənz) the capital of Greece.
Ath·ens

athlete (ath′lēt) ***noun*** a person who is skilled at games, sports, or exercises in which one usually needs strength, skill, or speed.
ath·lete • ***noun,*** *plural* **athletes**

a cat	ō go	ʉ fur	ə = a *in* ago
ā ape	ô law, for	ch chin	e *in* agent
ä cot, car	oo look	sh she	i *in* pencil
e ten	ōō tool	th thin	o *in* atom
ē me	oi oil	*th* then	u *in* circus
i fit	ou out	zh measure	
ī ice	u up	ŋ ring	

athlete's foot ***noun*** a skin disease of the feet in which small blisters form and there is itching. It is caused by a fungus.

athletic (ath let′ik) ***adjective*** **1** of or for athletes or their sports [*athletic* shoes]. **2** like an athlete; physically strong and active [Dancers must be both graceful and *athletic*.]
ath·let·ic • ***adjective***

athletics (ath let′iks) ***plural noun*** [*sometimes used with a singular verb*] athletic activities; games and sports.
ath·let·ics • ***plural noun***

-ation *a suffix meaning:* **1** the act of [*Multiplication* is the act of multiplying.] **2** the condition of being [*Frustration* is the condition of being frustrated.] **3** the result of [A *complication* is the result of complicating.]

Atlanta (at lan′tə) the capital of Georgia.
At·lan·ta

Atlantic (at lan′tik) the ocean that lies between North and South America to the west and Europe and Africa to the east.
adjective of, having to do with, or in this ocean.
At·lan·tic

Atlantis (at lan′tis) an island or continent told about in legends. It was supposed to have sunk into the Atlantic Ocean.
At·lan·tis

atlas (at′ləs) ***noun*** a book of maps.
at·las • ***noun, plural*** **atlases**

WORD HISTORY

atlas

In Greek myths, *Atlas* was a giant who held up the sky on his shoulders. A book of maps came to be called an **atlas** because in earlier times this kind of book often had a drawing on its first page showing Atlas holding up a globe of the earth.

ATM (ā′tē′em′) ***noun*** a machine which a bank customer may use to deposit or withdraw money. ATM stands for *Automated Teller Machine*.
ATM • ***noun, plural*** **ATMs**

atmosphere (at′məs fir) ***noun*** **1** all the air around the earth. **2** the gases around any planet. **3** the general feeling of a place or thing [a cheerful *atmosphere*].
at·mos·phere • ***noun, plural for senses 2 and 3 only*** **atmospheres**

atoll (a′täl *or* a′tôl) ***noun*** an island made of coral and shaped like a ring around a lagoon.
at·oll • ***noun, plural*** **atolls**

atom (at′əm) ***noun*** one of the tiny particles of which all things are made. Each atom is made up of protons and neutrons in a nucleus, and electrons which revolve around the nucleus.
at·om • ***noun, plural*** **atoms**

atom bomb ***noun*** *the same as* **atomic bomb**.
atom bomb • ***noun, plural*** **atom bombs**

atomic (ə täm′ik) ***adjective*** **1** using atomic energy [an *atomic* submarine]. **2** using atomic bombs [*atomic* warfare].
a·tom·ic • ***adjective***

atomic bomb ***noun*** a very destructive type of bomb in which atoms of plutonium or uranium are split apart, causing energy to be released in a very powerful, hot explosion.
atomic bomb • ***noun, plural*** **atomic bombs**

atomic energy ***noun*** the energy that is released when atoms are forced to join together or to split apart.

atop (ə täp′) ***preposition*** on the top of [He has a red feather *atop* his hat.]
a·top • ***preposition***

atrocious (ə trō′shəs) ***adjective*** **1** very cruel or evil [To mistreat animals is *atrocious*.] **2** very bad or unpleasant [Ten days of rain is *atrocious*.]
a·tro·cious • ***adjective***

attach (ə tach′) ***verb*** **1** to fasten or join together by sticking, tying, or using some other means [She *attached* a stamp to the envelope.] **2** to be connected to someone or something by feelings of love or affection [Most people are *attached* to their pets.] **3** to think of as properly belonging to [I *attach* great importance to this bit of news.]
at·tach • ***verb*** **attached, attaching**

attachment (ə tach′mənt) ***noun*** **1** a strong liking or love; friendship; affection [The *attachment* between the friends is easy to see.] —Look for the WORD CHOICES box at the entry **love**. **2** anything attached or added [Vacuum cleaners come with *attachments*.]
at·tach·ment • ***noun, plural*** **attachments**

A

attack (ə tak′) *verb* **1** to start a fight with; strike out at [The prisoner *attacked* the guard. The troops will *attack* at dawn.] **2** to speak or write against; criticize; oppose [The newspaper article *attacked* the mayor.] **3** to begin working on with energy [It is best to *attack* a problem right away.]
noun **1** the act of attacking [The enemy made a surprise *attack* that morning.] **2** a sudden beginning of a disease [an *attack* of the flu].
at·tack • *verb* **attacked, attacking** • *noun, plural* **attacks**

attempt (ə tempt′) *verb* to try to do or get [He will *attempt* a dangerous dive.] —Look for the WORD CHOICES box at the entry **try**.
noun **1** a try [Their *attempt* to reach the top of the mountain was successful.] **2** an attack [An *attempt* was made on his life.]
at·tempt • *verb* **attempted, attempting** • *noun, plural* **attempts**

attend (ə tend′) *verb* **1** to be present at [We *attend* school five days a week.] —Look for the WORD CHOICES box at the entry **accompany**. **2** to give care or attention [I'll *attend* to the matter soon.]
at·tend • *verb* **attended, attending**

attendance (ə ten′dəns) *noun* **1** the act of attending [*Attendance* by all grades is required at the assembly.] **2** the number of people present [*Attendance* at the ballgame was 36,000.]
at·tend·ance • *noun*

attendant (ə ten′dənt) *noun* a person who attends or serves; a servant, keeper, or similar person.
at·tend·ant • *noun, plural* **attendants**

attention (ə ten′shən) *noun* **1** the act of keeping one's mind on a particular thing [The speaker had everyone's *attention*.] **2** the act of noticing; observation [Your smile caught my *attention*.] **3** careful thought; consideration [This matter will receive the principal's immediate *attention*.] **4** thoughtful care; kindness and affection [The mother gave the baby much *attention*.] **5** *usually* **attentions** a kind act or thoughtful behavior; courtesy [We were grateful for our hosts' *attentions*.] **6** a position of standing straight and still, waiting for a command. [The soldiers stood at *attention*.]
at·ten·tion • *noun, plural* **attentions**

attic (at′ik) *noun* the room or space just below the roof of a house.
at·tic • *noun, plural* **attics**

Attila (ə til′ə) A.D. 406?-453; king of an Asian people who invaded Europe, from about A.D. 433 to 453.
At·ti·la

attire (ə tīr′) *noun* clothes [formal *attire*].
verb to dress [She was *attired* in riding clothes.]
at·tire • *noun* • *verb* **attired, attiring**

attitude (at′ə to͞od *or* at′ə tyo͞od) *noun* **1** a way of acting or behaving that shows what one is feeling or thinking; state of mind; disposition [Even when unpleasant things happen, he keeps his positive *attitude*.] **2** The position of the body in doing a particular thing [She assumed a relaxed *attitude*.]
at·ti·tude • *noun, plural* **attitudes**

attorney (ə tʉr′nē) *noun the same as* **lawyer**.
at·tor·ney • *noun, plural* **attorneys**

attorney general *noun* the chief law officer of a nation or State.
attorney general • *noun, plural* **attorneys general** or **attorney generals**

attract (ə trakt′) *verb* **1** to make come closer; pull toward oneself [A magnet *attracts* iron.] **2** to be admired or noticed by [Our beautiful park *attracts* many people.]
at·tract • *verb* **attracted, attracting**

attraction (ə trak′shən) *noun* **1** the act or power of attracting [Sports have a great *attraction* for some people.] **2** anything that attracts [The roller coaster is a big *attraction*.]
at·trac·tion • *noun, plural* **attractions**

attractive (ə trak′tiv) *adjective* having the power to attract; pretty or handsome; charming or pleasing [an *attractive* dress].
at·trac·tive • *adjective*

attribute (a′trə byo͞ot) *noun* a quality that is thought of as a natural part of some person or thing; characteristic [A friendly manner is an *attribute* of a good neighbor.]
at·trib·ute • *noun, plural* **attributes**

auburn (ô′bərn *or* ä′bərn) *adjective* reddish-brown.
noun a reddish brown color.
au·burn • *adjective* • *noun*

a cat	ō go	ʉ fur	ə = a *in* ago
ā ape	ô law, for	ch chin	e *in* agent
ä cot, car	oo look	sh she	i *in* pencil
e ten	o͞o tool	th thin	o *in* atom
ē me	oi oil	*th* then	u *in* circus
i fit	ou out	zh measure	
ī ice	u up	ŋ ring	

auction (ôk′shən *or* äk′shən) ***noun*** a public sale at which each thing is sold to the person offering to pay the highest price.
verb to sell at an auction [They *auctioned* their furniture instead of taking it with them.]
auc·tion • ***noun,*** *plural* **auctions**
• ***verb*** **auctioned, auctioning**

audience (ô′dē əns *or* ä′dē əns) ***noun*** **1** a group of people gathered together to hear and see a speaker, a play, or any similar kind of program. **2** all those people who are tuned in to a radio or TV program. **3** an interview with an important person [The prime minister has an *audience* with the queen.]
au·di·ence • ***noun,*** *plural* **audiences**

audio (ô′dē ō *or* ä′dē ō) ***adjective*** having to do with the part that is heard on a TV broadcast [We lost the *audio* portion of the program.]
au·di·o • ***adjective***

audiobook (ô′dē ō book′ *or* ä′dē ō book′) ***noun*** a recording of all or some of the words of a book, read by the author or by an actor. Most audiobooks are recorded on cassette tapes.
au·di·o·book • ***noun,*** *plural* **audiobooks**

audio-visual (ô′dē ō vizh′ōō əl *or* ä′dē ō vizh′ōō əl) ***adjective*** involving both hearing and sight [Filmstrips are *audio-visual* aids used in teaching.]
au·di·o-vis·u·al • ***adjective***

audition (ô dish′ən *or* ä dish′ən) ***noun*** an opportunity for an actor, singer, or musician to be tested for a job. In an audition the person or group gives a short performance.
verb **1** to give an audition to [The director *auditioned* many students for each role.] **2** to perform in an audition [An actor often *auditions* many times before getting a part.]
au·di·tion • ***noun,*** *plural* **auditions**
• ***verb*** **auditioned, auditioning**

auditorium (ô′də tôr′ē əm *or* ä′də tôr′ē əm) ***noun*** a building or room where an audience can gather for a school assembly, concert, or other event.
au·di·to·ri·um • ***noun,*** *plural* **auditoriums**

Audubon (ôd′ə bän), **John James** (jän′ jāmz′) 1785-1851; American naturalist, famous for his paintings of birds.
Au·du·bon, John James

Aug. *abbreviation for* August.

auger (ô′gər *or* ä′gər) ***noun*** a tool for making holes in wood or other materials, or in the earth.
au·ger • ***noun,*** *plural* **augers**

August (ô′gəst *or* ä′gəst) ***noun*** the eighth month of the year. August has 31 days. Abbreviated **Aug.**
Au·gust • ***noun***

Augusta (ô gus′tə) the capital of Maine.
Au·gus·ta

auk (ôk *or* äk) ***noun*** a bird of the northern seas, with short wings and webbed feet. It dives into the water for its food.
auk • ***noun,*** *plural* **auks**

aunt (ant *or* änt) ***noun*** **1** a sister of one's mother or father. **2** the wife of one's uncle.
aunt • ***noun,*** *plural* **aunts**

auk

● The words **aunt** and **ant** sound alike in most people's speech.
My *aunt* and uncle live in Ohio.
An *ant* crawled on our picnic basket.

austere (ô stir′ *or* ä stir′) ***adjective*** **1** very strict or stern in the way one looks or acts. **2** very simple and plain; without decoration; not fancy [Pioneers usually led an *austere* life.]
aus·tere • ***adjective***

Austin (ôs′tən), **Stephen** (stē′vən) 1793-1836; American pioneer. He founded the first American colony in Texas.
Aus·tin, Ste·phen

Austin (ôs′tən) the capital of Texas.
Aus·tin

Australia (ô stral′yə) **1** an island continent in the Southern Hemisphere, southeast of Asia. **2** a country made up of this continent and nearby islands.
Aus·tral·ia

Austria (ôs′trē ə) a country in central Europe.
Aus·tri·a

authentic (ô then′tik *or* ä then′tik) ***adjective*** genuine; real [an *authentic* antique].
au·then·tic • ***adjective***

author (ô′thər *or* ä′thər) ***noun*** a person who writes a book, story, or other similar work.

A

au·thor • *noun, plural* **authors**

authoritative (ə thôr′ə tāt′iv) *adjective* **1** having or showing authority; official [She spoke in an *authoritative* manner.] **2** capable of being trusted because it comes from an authority, or expert [The scientist gave his *authoritative* opinion about the new theory.]
au·thor·i·ta·tive • *adjective*

authority (ə thôr′ə tē) *noun* **1** the right to give orders, make decisions, or take action [The Constitution gives Congress the *authority* to make laws.] —Look for the WORD CHOICES box at the entry **power**. **2 authorities** people in government who have the right to enforce laws [We handed the prisoner over to the *authorities*.] **3** a person, book, or other source that can be trusted to give the right information or advice [He is an *authority* on cooking.]
au·thor·i·ty • *noun, plural* **authorities**

authorize (ô′thər īz *or* ä′thər īz) *verb* to give permission for [Their boss *authorized* a day off.]
au·thor·ize • *verb* **authorized, authorizing**

auto (ôt′ō *or* ä′tō) *noun a short form of* **automobile**.
au·to • *noun, plural* **autos**

auto- *a prefix meaning:* **1** of or for oneself. **2** by oneself or itself [*automobile*].

autobiography (ôt′ō bī ä′grə fē *or* ät′ō bī ä′grə fē) *noun* the story of a person's life written by that person.
au·to·bi·og·ra·phy • *noun, plural* **autobiographies**

autograph (ôt′ə graf *or* ät′ə graf) *noun* the name of a person, especially a famous person, written in his or her own handwriting.
verb to write one's name on [Please *autograph* this baseball!]
au·to·graph • *noun, plural* **autographs** • *verb* **autographed, autographing**

automatic (ôt′ə mat′ik *or* ät′ə mat′ik) *adjective* **1** done without thinking about it; unconscious [Breathing is usually *automatic*.] **2** moving or working by itself [*automatic* machinery].
au·to·mat·ic • *adjective*

automation (ôt ə mā′shən *or* ät ə mā′shən) *noun* a system of manufacturing in which some jobs are done by machines instead of people.
au·to·ma·tion • *noun*

automobile

automobile (ôt′ə mə bēl *or* ät′ə mə bēl) *noun* a car that is moved by an engine that is part of it. It is used for traveling on streets and roads.
au·to·mo·bile • *noun, plural* **automobiles**

automotive (ôt′ə mōt′iv *or* ät′ə mōt′iv) *adjective* **1** having to do with automobiles [the *automotive* industry]. **2** able to move by its own power [Cars and trucks are *automotive* vehicles.]
au·to·mo·tive • *adjective*

autopsy (ô′täp′sē *or* ä′täp′sē) *noun* an examination of a dead body to find the cause of death or the damage done by a disease.
au·top·sy • *noun, plural* **autopsies**

autumn (ôt′əm *or* ät′əm) *noun* the season of the year between summer and winter; fall.
au·tumn • *noun, plural* **autumns**

auxiliary (ôg zil′yə rē *or* äg zil′yə rē) *adjective* acting as a help for a main body or group [*auxiliary* police].
aux·il·ia·ry • *adjective*

auxiliary verb *noun the same as* **helping verb**.
auxiliary verb • *noun, plural* **auxiliary verbs**

available (ə vāl′ə bəl) *adjective* **1** ready for use or service; at hand [He's not *available* for baby-sitting tonight.] **2** possible to get or obtain [This style is *available* in three colors.]
a·vail·a·ble • *adjective*

avalanche (av′ə lanch) *noun* **1** a large mass of snow, ice, and rocks sliding swiftly down a mountain. **2** anything that comes suddenly or in large numbers [an *avalanche* of mail].
av·a·lanche • *noun, plural* **avalanches**

a	cat	ō	go	ʉ	fur	ə =	a *in* ago
ā	ape	ô	law, for	ch	chin		e *in* agent
ä	cot, car	oo	look	sh	she		i *in* pencil
e	ten	ōō	tool	th	thin		o *in* atom
ē	me	oi	oil	*th*	then		u *in* circus
i	fit	ou	out	zh	measure		
ī	ice	u	up	ŋ	ring		

Ave. *abbreviation for* Avenue.

avenge (ə venj′) ***verb*** to get revenge for [The knight *avenged* the insult to his king.]
a·venge • ***verb*** **avenged, avenging**

avenue (av′ə no͞o *or* av′ə nyo͞o) ***noun*** a wide main street.
av·e·nue • ***noun,*** *plural* **avenues**

average (av′ər ij *or* av′rij) ***noun*** **1** the number gotten by dividing the sum of two or more quantities by the number of quantities added [The *average* of 1, 2, and 6 is 3 (1 + 2 + 6 = 9; 9 ÷ 3 = 3).] **2** the usual kind or amount; something that is found most often [Her time in this race is far above the *average*.]
adjective **1** being the average [The *average* test score was 82.] **2** of the usual kind; normal; ordinary [The *average* pet is a cat or a dog.]
verb **1** to figure the average of [He *averaged* the grocery bills for each month.] **2** to be, do, or have as an average [The children *average* about eight hours of sleep each night.]
av·er·age • ***noun,*** *plural* **averages**
• ***adjective*** • ***verb*** **averaged, averaging**

aviation (ā′vē ā′shən) ***noun*** the science, skill, or work of flying airplanes.
a·vi·a·tion • ***noun***

aviator (ā′vē āt′ər) ***noun*** a person who flies an airplane; pilot.
a·vi·a·tor • ***noun,*** *plural* **aviators**

avid (av′id) ***adjective*** very eager or full of enthusiasm [I am an *avid* reader of books.] —Look for the WORD CHOICES box at the entry **eager**.
av·id • ***adjective***

avocado (av′ə kä′dō *or* äv′ə kä′dō) ***noun*** a tropical fruit that is shaped like a pear. It has a tough green or purple skin, buttery flesh, and a large seed in the middle. It grows on a tree.
av·o·ca·do • ***noun,*** *plural* **avocados**

avoid (ə void′) ***verb*** **1** to keep away from [I *avoid* crowds.] **2** to keep from happening [*Avoid* spilling the milk.]
a·void • ***verb*** **avoided, avoiding**

await (ə wāt′) ***verb*** **1** to wait for; expect [We *await* your arrival.] **2** to be ready for; be in store for [A surprise *awaits* you.]
a·wait • ***verb*** **awaited, awaiting**

awake (ə wāk′) ***verb*** **1** to bring or come out of sleep; wake [I *awoke* from a deep sleep.] **2** to make or become active; stir up [A familiar smell sometimes *awakes* old memories.]
adjective not asleep [I was *awake* all night.]
a·wake • ***verb*** **awoke** or **awaked, awaked** or **awoken, awaking** • ***adjective***

awaken (ə wā′kən) ***verb*** to awake; wake up [The loud noise *awakened* me.]
a·wak·en • ***verb*** **awakened, awakening**

award (ə wôrd′) ***noun*** something given as a prize for special quality or performance.
verb to give an award [The judges *awarded* Sue first prize for her essay.]
a·ward • ***noun,*** *plural* **awards**
• ***verb*** **awarded, awarding**

aware (ə wer′) ***adjective*** knowing or understanding something [Are you *aware* it's snowing?]
a·ware • ***adjective***

away (ə wā′) ***adverb*** **1** from one place to another [Tom Sawyer ran *away* from home.] **2** in the right place [Put the tools *away*.] **3** in another direction [Turn *away*.] **4** off; aside [Please clear the snow *away*.] **5** out of one's keeping [Don't give *away* the secret.] **6** out of hearing or out of sight [The sound faded *away*.] **7** without stopping [He worked *away* all night.]
adjective **1** not here; absent [*away* for the day]. **2** at a distance [The lake is ten miles *away*.]
—do away with to get rid of; put an end to [They have *done away with* the old rules.]
a·way • ***adverb*** • ***adjective***

awe (ô *or* ä) ***noun*** deep respect mixed with fear and wonder [The waterfall filled them with *awe*.] —Look for the WORD CHOICES boxes at the entries **panic** and **wonder**.
verb to make have a feeling of awe [We were *awed* by the Grand Canyon.]
awe • ***noun*** • ***verb*** **awed, awing**

awesome (ô′səm *or* ä′səm) ***adjective*** causing a person to feel awe [The burning building was an *awesome* sight.]
awe·some • ***adjective***

awful (ô′fəl *or* ä′fəl) ***adjective*** **1** making a person feel awe or dread [I had an *awful* feeling that this was the end.] **2** very bad, ugly, or unpleasant [an *awful* joke; *awful* shoes].
aw·ful • ***adjective***

awfully (ô′fə lē *or* ä′fə lē) ***adverb*** **1** in a bad or unpleasant way [She behaved *awfully*.] **2** [*an informal use*] very [He's *awfully* nice.]
aw·ful·ly • ***adverb***

A

awhile (ə hwīl′ *or* ə wīl′) ***adverb*** for a while; for a short time [Sit down and rest *awhile.*]
a·while • ***adverb***

awkward (ôk′wərd *or* äk′wərd) ***adjective*** **1** not having grace or skill; clumsy [an *awkward* dancer]. **2** hard to use or manage [an *awkward* bundle; an *awkward* tool]. **3** uncomfortable [sitting in an *awkward* position]. **4** embarrassed or embarrassing [an *awkward* smile; an *awkward* excuse].
awk·ward • ***adjective***

WORD CHOICES

Synonyms of **awkward**

Many words share the meaning "not having grace or skill."

clumsy	rusty
gawky	unskilled

awl (ôl *or* äl) ***noun*** a small, pointed tool for making holes in wood or leather.
awl • ***noun,*** *plural* **awls**
• The words **awl** and **all** sound alike.
I used the *awl* with the broken handle.
All the lettuce went into the salad.

awning (ôn′iŋ *or* än′iŋ) ***noun*** a covering made of canvas, metal, or wood fixed to a frame over a window or door, or on a porch. Awnings are used to keep out the sun and rain.
awn·ing • ***noun,*** *plural* **awnings**

awoke (ə wōk′) ***verb*** *a past tense of* **awake**.
a·woke • ***verb***

awoken (ə wō′kən) ***verb*** *a past participle of* **awake**.
a·wok·en • ***verb***

ax or **axe** (aks) ***noun*** a tool for chopping or splitting wood. It has a long handle and a metal head with a sharp cutting edge.
ax or **axe** • ***noun,*** *plural* **axes**

axis (ak′sis) ***noun*** a real or imaginary straight line about which something turns. The imaginary axis of the earth passes through the North and South poles.
ax·is • ***noun,*** *plural* **axes** (ak′sēz)

axle (ak′səl) ***noun*** **1** the rod on which a wheel turns by itself. **2** a rod that is connected to a wheel and turns with the wheel. **3** the bar or rod that connects two opposite wheels on an automobile, wagon, or other similar vehicle.
ax·le • ***noun,*** *plural* **axles**

ayatollah (ī′yə tō′lə) ***noun*** a leader of one of the two main branches of Islam.
a·ya·tol·lah • ***noun,*** *plural* **ayatollahs**

aye (ī) ***adverb*** yes.
noun a vote of "yes." [The vote was 20 *ayes* and 10 nays.]
aye • ***adverb*** • ***noun,*** *plural* **ayes**
• The words **aye, eye,** and **I** sound alike.
Only three members voted *aye*.
The doorknob poked him in the *eye*.
I have four years till high school.

AZ *abbreviation for* **Arizona**.

azalea (ə zāl′yə) ***noun*** a shrub that has small, narrow leaves that are shed in the fall and funnel-shaped flowers of various colors.
a·zal·ea • ***noun,*** *plural* **azaleas**

azalea

Azerbaijan (äz′ər bī jän′) a country in southwestern Asia. It was a part of the Soviet Union.
Az·er·bai·jan

Aztec (az′tek) ***noun*** a member of a native people of Mexico. The Aztecs had a highly developed civilization at the time of the discovery of America by explorers from Spain.
Az·tec • ***noun,*** *plural* **Aztecs**

azure (azh′ər) ***noun*** the blue color of a clear sky.
adjective of this color [a gown of *azure* silk].
az·ure • ***noun*** • ***adjective***

a	cat	ō	go	ʉ	fur	ə =	a *in* ago
ā	ape	ô	law, for	ch	chin		e *in* agent
ä	cot, car	oo	look	sh	she		i *in* pencil
e	ten	o͞o	tool	th	thin		o *in* atom
ē	me	oi	oil	*th*	then		u *in* circus
i	fit	ou	out	zh	measure		
ī	ice	u	up	ŋ	ring		

B b

Bb Bb Bb Bb

The sound heard at the beginning of **bear** *is the only sound represented by* **b**. *However, in some words, such as* **lamb** *and* **debt**, **b** *is silent. Our letter* **B** *comes from a letter first used by the Egyptians and Greeks. You hear its Greek name in the word* **alphabet** *itself—the first two letters in the Greek alphabet were* **alpha** *and* **beta**, *now our* **A** *and* **B**.

b or **B** (bē) ***noun*** the second letter of the English alphabet.
b or **B** • ***noun,*** *plural* **b's** or **B's**

B (bē) ***noun*** **1** in some schools, a grade meaning "good" or "better than average." **2** in music, the seventh tone in the scale of C major.
B • ***noun,*** *plural* **B's**

baa (bä) ***noun*** the sound that a sheep makes.
verb to make this sound; to bleat.
baa • ***noun,*** *plural* **baas** • ***verb*** **baaed, baaing**

babble (bab′əl) ***verb*** **1** to make sounds like a baby trying to talk. **2** to talk or say fast or foolishly. **3** to make a low, bubbling sound.
bab·ble • ***verb*** **babbled, babbling**

babe (bāb) ***noun*** a baby; an infant.
babe • ***noun,*** *plural* **babes**

baboon (ba bo͞on′) ***noun*** a large, fierce monkey of Africa and Arabia with a snout like a dog's.
ba·boon • ***noun,*** *plural* **baboons**

baby (bā′bē) ***noun*** **1** a very young child. **2** a childish person, or one who cries easily.
adjective **1** of or for a baby [*baby* food]. **2** very young or small [a *baby* fox]. **3** like a baby; childish [*baby* talk].
verb to treat like a baby; to pamper.
ba·by • ***noun,*** *plural* **babies** • ***adjective*** • ***verb*** **babied, babying, babies**

baby-sit (bā′bē sit′) ***verb*** to act as a baby sitter.
ba·by-sit • ***verb*** **baby-sat, baby-sitting**

baby sitter ***noun*** a person who is hired to take care of a child when the parents are away.
baby sitter • ***noun,*** *plural* **baby sitters**

Bach (bäk), **Johann Sebastian** (yō′hän sə bas′ chən) 1685-1750; German composer.
Bach, Jo·hann Se·bas·tian

bachelor (bach′ə lər) ***noun*** a man who has not married.
bach·e·lor • ***noun,*** *plural* **bachelors**

back (bak) ***noun*** **1** the part of the body that is opposite the chest and stomach. In most animals other than human beings, it is the part opposite the underside. **2** the backbone. **3** the part of something that is behind or opposite the front [the *back* of the room]. **4** a football player who has a position behind the line.
adjective **1** at the rear or back [the *back* wheel of a bicycle]. **2** of or for a time in the past; past; old [a *back* copy of a magazine].
adverb **1** at or to the back; backward [Please move *back* in the elevator.] **2** to the place that it came from [Throw the ball *back*.] **3** to an earlier condition or time [Think *back* to your

earliest memories.] **4** in return [I paid *back* the money I had borrowed.]
verb **1** to move backward or to the rear [The truck *backed* up to the platform.] **2** to help or support [We all *backed* the plan.] —Look for the WORD CHOICES box at the entry **support**.
—**back and forth** to the rear and then to the front, or from side to side [The cradle rocked *back and forth*.] —**back out** to refuse to do something that one has promised to do [He's *backing out* of the agreement.] —**back up** to support or help [Will you *back* me *up* when I talk to the coach?] —**behind someone's back** without someone's knowing or allowing it. —**in back of** at or to the rear of; behind.
back • ***noun**, plural* **backs** • ***adjective*** • ***adverb*** • ***verb*** **backed, backing**

backboard (bak′bôrd) ***noun*** in basketball, a flat, hard, usually rectangular board to which the basket is attached. It is often made of glass.
back·board • ***noun**, plural* **backboards**

backbone (bak′bōn) ***noun*** **1** the long row of connected bones in the back of human beings and many animals; the spine. **2** willpower, courage, and similar qualities.
back·bone • ***noun**, plural* **backbones**

backfire (bak′fīr) ***noun*** an explosion of gases at the wrong time or in the wrong place in the kind of engine that is used in a car or truck.
verb **1** to have a backfire. **2** to have a bad or unexpected result [The plan *backfired*.]
back·fire • ***noun**, plural* **backfires** • ***verb*** **backfired, backfiring**

backgammon (bak′gam ən) ***noun*** a game that is played on a board by two persons. The players throw dice to see how to move the pieces.
back·gam·mon • ***noun***

background (bak′ground) ***noun*** **1** the part of a scene or picture that is or seems to be toward the back. **2** a surface behind something that is shown or seen [The flag has white stars on a blue *background*.] **3** a person's training and experience [She has a *background* in law.]
back·ground • ***noun**, plural* **backgrounds**

backhand (bak′hand) ***noun*** a stroke that is made with the back of the hand swinging away from the body. It is used in tennis and other games.
back·hand • ***noun**, plural* **backhands**

backpack (bak′pak) ***noun*** a leather or canvas bag that has straps for the shoulders. It is worn on the back by campers and hikers for carrying supplies. Many backpacks have a lightweight metal frame attached.
verb to hike wearing a backpack.
back·pack • ***noun**, plural* **backpacks** • ***verb*** **backpacked, backpacking**

backpack

backslash (bak′slash) ***noun*** a slanted line (\ ) that is used as a mark of punctuation in some commands entered into a computer.
back·slash • ***noun**, plural* **backslashes**

backup or **back-up** (bak′up) ***noun*** **1** an amount that has piled up because the flow has stopped [The accident created a huge *backup* on the freeway.] **2** a support or help [The pilot had a *backup* for the flight.]
back·up or **back-up** • ***noun**, plural* **backups** or **back-ups**

backward (bak′wərd) ***adverb*** **1** toward the back [A car can move forward or *backward*.] **2** with the back facing toward the front [If we walk *backward*, we may trip.] **3** in a way opposite to the usual way ["Saw" spelled *backward* is "was."]
adjective turned toward the back or in an opposite way [a *backward* glance].
back·ward • ***adverb*** • ***adjective***

backwards (bak′wərdz) ***adverb*** *the same as the adverb* **backward**.
back·wards • ***adverb***

backyard (bak′yärd′) ***noun*** a yard at the back of a house or other building. This word is also written **back yard**.
back·yard • ***noun**, plural* **backyards**

bacon (bā′kən) ***noun*** salted and smoked meat from the sides and back of a hog.
ba·con • ***noun***

bacteria (bak tir′ē ə) ***plural noun*** living things

a	cat	ō	go	ʉ	fur	ə =	a *in* ago
ā	ape	ô	law, for	ch	chin		e *in* agent
ä	cot, car	o͝o	look	sh	she		i *in* pencil
e	ten	o͞o	tool	th	thin		o *in* atom
ē	me	oi	oil	*th*	then		u *in* circus
i	fit	ou	out	zh	measure		
ī	ice	u	up	ŋ	ring		

that have one cell and can be seen only with a microscope. Some bacteria cause diseases.
bac·te·ri·a • ***plural noun,*** *singular* **bac·te·ri·um** (bak tir′ē əm)

bad (bad) ***adjective*** **1** not good; not what it should be [*bad* lighting; *bad* workmanship]. **2** not pleasant; not what is hoped for [*bad* news]. **3** rotten; spoiled [a *bad* apple]. **4** in error; wrong [*bad* spelling]. **5** wicked; evil [a *bad* man]. **6** not behaving properly; mischievous ["*Bad* dog!" yelled John.] **7** harmful; causing injury [Reading in poor light is *bad* for the eyes.] **8** serious; severe [a *bad* mistake; a *bad* storm]. **9** disgusting; offensive [a *bad* smell]. **10** in poor health; ill [She felt *bad* from eating too much chocolate.] **11** sorry; unhappy [Pat felt *bad* about losing the money.]
—not bad [*an informal use*] fairly good.
bad • ***adjective*** **worse, worst**

WORD CHOICES

Synonyms of **bad**

Many words share the meaning "doing what is wrong."

dishonest	naughty	wicked
evil	unjust	

bade (bad) ***verb*** *a past tense of* **bid**.

badge (baj) ***noun*** a pin, emblem, or ribbon that people wear to show that they belong to a certain group or have done something special [a police *badge;* a girl scout *badge*].
badge • ***noun,*** *plural* **badges**

badger (baj′ər) ***noun*** an animal that has a broad back, thick fur, and short legs. It lives in holes that it digs in the ground.
verb to annoy; pester [Some people in the audience *badgered* the speaker with silly questions.]
badg·er • ***noun,*** *plural* **badgers** • ***verb*** **badgered, badgering**

badly (bad′lē) ***adverb*** **1** in a bad way; not well [She played *badly* and lost]. **2** [*an informal use*] very much [We *badly* need a new car.]
bad·ly • ***adverb***

badminton (bad′mint′n) ***noun*** a game that is like tennis but is played with a cork with feathers in one end. Players use light rackets to bat this cork back and forth across a high net.
bad·min·ton • ***noun***

baffle (baf′əl) ***verb*** to confuse in order to keep from understanding or solving; to puzzle [The crime *baffled* the police.]
baf·fle • ***verb*** **baffled, baffling**

bag (bag) ***noun*** **1** a container made of paper, cloth, or other soft material, for holding or carrying things. It has a closed bottom and sides and an open top. **2** a woman's purse. **3** a suitcase [Pack your *bags* for the trip.]
verb to put into a bag [*Bag* the groceries for her.]
bag • ***noun,*** *plural* **bags** • ***verb*** **bagged, bagging**

bagel (bā′gəl) ***noun*** a hard, chewy bread roll shaped like a doughnut. Bagels are cooked in simmering water before they are baked.
ba·gel • ***noun,*** *plural* **bagels**

baggage (bag′ij) ***noun*** the suitcases and other belongings that a person takes on a trip; luggage.
bag·gage • ***noun***

baggy (bag′ē) ***adjective*** hanging loosely and bulging in places [*baggy* pants].
bag·gy • ***adjective*** **baggier, baggiest**

bagpipe (bag′pīp) ***noun*** a musical instrument with a leather bag into which the player blows air. The air is then forced with the arm through several pipes to make shrill tones. Bagpipes are now mainly played in Scotland.
bag·pipe • ***noun,*** *plural* **bagpipes**

Bahamas (bə hä′məz) a country on a group of islands in the West Indies, southeast of Florida.
Ba·ha·mas

Bahrain or **Bahrein** (bä rān′) a country on a group of islands in the Persian Gulf.
Bah·rain or **Bah·rein**

bail[1] (bāl) ***noun*** money that is left with a law court to obtain the temporary release of an arrested person from jail. When the person appears for trial, the court returns the money.
verb **1** to have an arrested person set free by giving bail [They *bailed* me out of jail.] **2** to set free from some difficulty [My friends *bailed* me out when I was in debt.]
bail • ***noun,*** *plural* **bails** • ***verb*** **bailed, bailing**
• The words **bail** and **bale** sound alike.
Will you *bail* him out if he is caught?

B

Bail the boat with those buckets.
A *bale* of hay is too heavy to lift.

bail[2] (bāl) ***verb*** to dip out water from a boat with a bucket or other container.
—**bail out** to parachute from an aircraft in an emergency.
bail • ***verb*** **bailed, bailing**
● The words **bail** and **bale** sound alike.

bait (bāt) ***noun*** **1** food put on a hook or in a trap to attract and catch fish or animals. **2** anything used to tempt or attract a person.
verb **1** to put bait on or in [*Bait* the hook with a worm.] **2** to tease again and again in a cruel way [They *baited* me by calling me names.]
bait • ***noun,*** *plural* **baits** • ***verb*** **baited, baiting**

bake (bāk) ***verb*** **1** to cook in an oven, with little or no liquid [I *baked* a cake. The potatoes *baked* too long.] **2** to make or become dry and hard by heat [The land *baked* in the hot sun.]
bake • ***verb*** **baked, baking**

baker (bā′kər) ***noun*** a person whose work or business is baking bread, cakes, and pastry.
bak·er • ***noun,*** *plural* **bakers**

bakery (bā′kər ē) ***noun*** a place where bread, cakes, and other foods are baked or sold.
bak·er·y • ***noun,*** *plural* **bakeries**

baking powder ***noun*** a white powder containing baking soda that is used in cooking and baking to make dough or batter rise.

baking soda ***noun*** a white powder that neutralizes acids. It is used in cooking.

balance

balance (bal′əns) ***noun*** **1** equality between two things or between the parts of a single thing. They may be equal in amount, weight, value, or importance [The two children were in *balance* on the seesaw.] **2** the ability to keep the body steady without falling down [She lost her *balance* when she looked down from the ladder.] **3** the amount of money that a person has in a bank account [Your account has a *balance* of $20.50.] **4** the part that is left over; remainder [If you carry some of these bags, I'll carry the *balance*.] **5** a device for weighing. It has two shallow pans hanging from the ends of a bar that is supported in the middle.
verb **1** to keep from falling by holding steady [Try to *balance* this box on your head.] **2** to make two things or parts equal in weight, value, or importance [If I sit in the front and you in the back, we can *balance* the boat.]
bal·ance • ***noun,*** *plural* **balances**
• ***verb*** **balanced, balancing**

Balboa (bal bō′ə), **Vasco de** (väs′kō de) 1475?-1519?; Spanish explorer. In 1513, he became the first European to see the Pacific Ocean.
Bal·bo·a, Vas·co de

balcony (bal′kə nē) ***noun*** **1** a platform with a low wall or railing that juts out from the side of an upper floor of a building. **2** an upper floor of rows of seats in a theater or auditorium.
bal·co·ny • ***noun,*** *plural* **balconies**

bald (bôld) ***adjective*** **1** having no hair on all or part of the scalp [a *bald* man]. **2** not covered by natural growth [a *bald*, rocky hill].

bald eagle

bald eagle ***noun*** a large, strong eagle of North America. It has a white-feathered head and neck when it is fully grown.
bald eagle • ***noun,*** *plural* **bald eagles**

bale (bāl) ***noun*** a large bundle of tightly

a	cat	ō	go	ʉ	fur	ə =	a *in* ago
ā	ape	ô	law, for	ch	chin		e *in* agent
ä	cot, car	oo	look	sh	she		i *in* pencil
e	ten	ōō	tool	th	thin		o *in* atom
ē	me	oi	oil	*th*	then		u *in* circus
i	fit	ou	out	zh	measure		
ī	ice	u	up	ŋ	ring		

packed cotton, hay, straw, or other material that is bound or wrapped up for shipping.
bale • *noun, plural* **bales**
- The words **bale** and **bail** sound alike.
  Will a *bale* fit in your truck?
  Bail was set at $5,000.
  You can't *bail* out without a parachute.

balk (bôk) ***verb*** to stop and refuse in a stubborn way to move or act.
balk • *verb* **balked, balking**

ball[1] (bôl) ***noun*** **1** any round object; sphere [a *snowball;* a *ball* of yarn]. **2** a round or egg-shaped object that is used in playing a game [a golf *ball;* a *football*]. **3** a game that is played with a ball, especially baseball [Let's play *ball*.] **4** in baseball, a pitch that is not a strike and is not swung at by the batter. Four balls allow the batter to go to first base.
ball • *noun, plural* **balls**
- The words **ball** and **bawl** sound alike.
  She caught the *ball* without a mitt.
  Refreshments were served at the *ball*.
  Will she *bawl* us out for being late?

ball[2] (bôl) ***noun*** a large, formal dancing party.
ball • *noun, plural* **balls**
- The words **ball** and **bawl** sound alike.

ballad (bal′əd) ***noun*** a song or poem that tells a story in short verses.
bal·lad • *noun, plural* **ballads**

ballast (bal′əst) ***noun*** heavy material, such as sand, that is carried in a ship, balloon, or vehicle to keep it steady or balanced.
bal·last • *noun, plural* **ballasts**

ball bearing ***noun*** **1** a part of a machine in which moving parts turn or slide on rolling metal balls to reduce friction. **2** one of these balls.
ball bearing • *noun, plural* **ball bearings**

ballerina (bal′ə rē′nə) ***noun*** a woman ballet dancer.
bal·le·ri·na • *noun, plural* **ballerinas**

ballet (ba lā′) ***noun*** a kind of dance that is performed on a stage, usually by a group of dancers in costumes. It often tells a story by means of its system of graceful movements.
bal·let • *noun, plural* **ballets**

ballgame (bôl′gām) ***noun*** a game played with a ball, especially a baseball game.
ball·game • *noun, plural* **ballgames**

balloon

balloon (bə lo͞on′) ***noun*** **1** a large bag that floats high above the ground when it is filled with hot air or a special gas. Balloons are now often used to carry instruments for studying the upper air. **2** a small, brightly colored rubber bag that is blown up with air or gas and used as a toy or for decoration.
verb to swell out like a balloon.
bal·loon • *noun, plural* **balloons**
• *verb* **ballooned, ballooning**

SPELLING TIP

Use this memory aid to spell **balloon**. Remember the ***ball*** in **ball**oon.

ballot (bal′ət) ***noun*** **1** a piece of paper on which a person marks a choice in voting. **2** the act or a way of voting [The council's decisions are made by secret *ballot*.] **3** the right to vote.
bal·lot • *noun, plural* **ballots**

ballpoint pen (bôl′point) ***noun*** a kind of pen whose writing point is a tiny ball that rolls the ink onto the paper.
ball·point pen • *noun, plural* **ballpoint pens**

ballroom (bôl′ro͞om) ***noun*** a large room or hall for dancing.
ball·room • *noun, plural* **ballrooms**

baloney (bə lō′nē) ***noun*** **1** *another spelling of* **bologna**. **2** [*a slang use*] nonsense.
ba·lo·ney • *noun*

balsa (bôl′sə) ***noun*** **1** a tree that grows in tropical North and South America and has very lightweight wood. **2** this wood.
bal·sa • *noun, plural* **balsas**

Baltimore (bôl′tə môr) a seaport in northern Maryland.
Bal·ti·more

bamboo (bam bo͞o′) *noun* a tropical plant with woody stems that are hollow and jointed. It is a kind of grass that grows as tall as trees. Its stems are used in making furniture.
bam·boo • *noun, plural* **bamboos**

ban (ban) *verb* to have a rule against certain actions or things [The principal *banned* talking in the halls.] —Look for the WORD CHOICES box at the entry **forbid**.
ban • *verb* **banned, banning**

banana

banana (bə nan′ə) *noun* **1** a large tropical plant with long, broad leaves. It has a large bunch of fruit growing on a single stalk. **2** its narrow, slightly curved fruit. It has a sweet, creamy flesh covered by a yellow or reddish skin.
ba·nan·a • *noun, plural* **bananas**

band[1] (band) *noun* **1** a cord or wire, or a strip of some material, that is used to encircle something or bind something together [Iron *bands* hold the parts of a barrel together.] **2** a stripe of some different color or material [a *band* of shiny metal along the side of the car].
verb to mark with a band [The scientists *banded* the pigeons on the leg to identify them.]
band • *noun, plural* **bands** • *verb* **banded, banding**

band[2] (band) *noun* **1** a group of people who are joined together to do something [a *band* of explorers]. **2** a group of musicians playing together.
verb to join together or unite [The neighbors *banded* together to build a barn.]
band • *noun, plural* **bands** • *verb* **banded, banding**

bandage (ban′dij) *noun* a strip of cloth or gauze for covering a sore or wound or for binding up an injured body part.
verb to bind or cover with a bandage.
band·age • *noun, plural* **bandages** • *verb* **bandaged, bandaging**

Band-Aid (band′ād) *trademark* a small bandage of gauze and adhesive tape.

bandanna (ban dan′ə) *noun* a large, colored handkerchief. Bandannas are often worn around the neck or head.
ban·dan·na • *noun, plural* **bandannas**

bandit (ban′dit) *noun* a robber, especially one who is a member of a gang.
ban·dit • *noun, plural* **bandits**

bang (baŋ) *verb* **1** to hit hard and make a noise [She *banged* her fist on the table.] **2** to shut hard and make a noise [Don't *bang* the door!]
noun **1** a hard, noisy blow or knock [We heard a *bang* on the door.] **2** a sudden loud noise [Bombs go off with a *bang*.]
bang • *verb* **banged, banging** • *noun, plural* **bangs**

Bangladesh (bäŋ′glə desh) a country in southern Asia, northeast of India.
Ban·gla·desh

bangle (baŋ′gəl) *noun* a bracelet or a band around the ankle that is worn as an ornament.
ban·gle • *noun, plural* **bangles**

bangs (baŋz) *plural noun* hair cut short and straight across the forehead.

banish (ban′ish) *verb* **1** to force a person to leave his or her country as a punishment; to exile. **2** to put away; get rid of [*Banish* all thoughts of your troubles.]
ban·ish • *verb* **banished, banishing**

a cat	ō go	ʉ fur	ə = a *in* ago
ā ape	ô law, for	ch chin	e *in* agent
ä cot, car	oo look	sh she	i *in* pencil
e ten	o͞o tool	th thin	o *in* atom
ē me	oi oil	*th* then	u *in* circus
i fit	ou out	zh measure	
ī ice	u up	ŋ ring	

WORD CHOICES

Synonyms of **banish**

The words **banish, deport**, and **exile** share the meaning "to force to leave a country."

The dictator *banished* his enemies.

Should illegal aliens be *deported*?

Napoleon was *exiled* to a small island.

banister (ban′is tər) *noun* a handrail along a staircase. It is held up by a row of small posts.
ban·is·ter • *noun, plural* **banisters**

banjo

banjo (ban′jō) *noun* a stringed musical instrument with a long neck and a round body covered on top with tightly stretched skins. It has, usually, four or five strings that are plucked with the fingers or a pick.
ban·jo • *noun, plural* **banjos** or **banjoes**

bank[1] (baŋk) *noun* **1** a small container that is used for saving coins and other money. **2** a place of business for keeping, exchanging, or lending money. **3** a place for keeping a reserve supply of something [a blood *bank*].
verb to do business with a bank [My father *banks* at the savings bank near our house.]
bank • *noun, plural* **banks** • *verb* **banked, banking**

bank[2] (baŋk) *noun* **1** a large or long mound or pile [a *bank* of earth; a *bank* of clouds]. **2** the land along the sides of a river or stream.
verb to pile up to form a bank or mound.
bank • *noun, plural* **banks** • *verb* **banked, banking**

banker (baŋk′ər) *noun* a person who owns or runs a bank where money is kept.
bank·er • *noun, plural* **bankers**

bankrupt (baŋk′rupt) *adjective* not able to pay debts and freed by law from the need to pay.
verb to make bankrupt [The very bad weather *bankrupted* many farmers.]
bank·rupt • *adjective* • *verb* **bankrupted, bankrupting**

banner (ban′ər) *noun* a flag or other piece of cloth with a special design or words on it.
adjective top; outstanding [The company had a *banner* year in sales.]
ban·ner • *noun, plural* **banners** • *adjective*

banquet (baŋ′kwət) *noun* a formal dinner or feast for many people.
ban·quet • *noun, plural* **banquets**

banter (ban′tər) *noun* playful teasing or joking.
verb to make jokes or tease in a playful way.
ban·ter • *noun, plural* **banters** • *verb* **bantered, bantering**

baptism (bap′tiz əm) *noun* the religious ceremony of taking persons into a Christian church by dipping them in water or sprinkling water on them.
bap·tism • *noun, plural* **baptisms**

baptize (bap′tīz) *verb* **1** to take a person into a Christian church by baptism. **2** to give a name to during baptism; christen.
bap·tize • *verb* **baptized, baptizing**

bar (bär) *noun* **1** a long, fairly narrow piece of wood, metal, or other rigid material. Bars are often used to block the way, to fasten something, or as a lever to pry or lift something. **2** a solid piece of something, with an oblong, even shape [a *bar* of soap]. **3** something that prevents or stands in the way [Being a woman should be no *bar* to becoming President.] **4** a stripe or band of color or light [*Bars* of sunlight came through the clouds.] **5** the profession of a lawyer [She is studying for the *bar*.] **6** a counter or place where drinks are served. **7** one of the lines that run from top to bottom on a musical staff. Bars divide the staff into equal groups of beats, called measures.
verb **1** to fasten with a bar [The door was *barred* and bolted.] **2** to block; shut off [A fallen tree *bars* the way.] **3** to keep out [The dog was *barred* from the house.]
bar • *noun, plural* **bars** • *verb* **barred, barring**

B

- The words **bar** and **barre** sound alike.
  A candy *bar* will spoil your appetite.
  Ballet dancers practice with a *barre*.

barb (bärb) ***noun*** a sharp point that sticks out in an opposite direction from the main point [the *barb* on a fishhook].
barb • ***noun,*** *plural* **barbs**

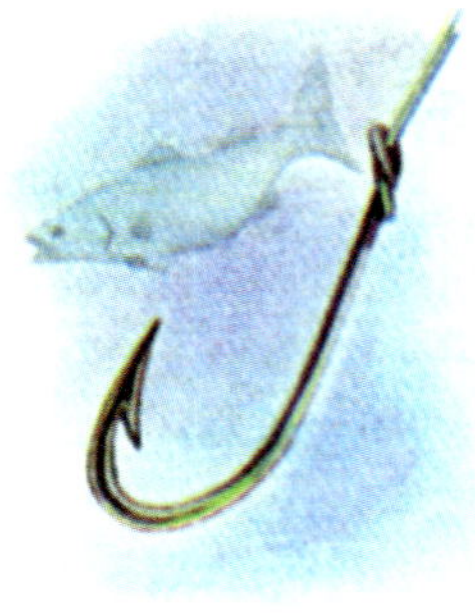
barb

Barbados (bär bā′dōs) a country on an island of the West Indies.
Bar·ba·dos

barbarian (bär ber′ē ən) ***noun*** **1** a person living in a society that others see as savage or not civilized. **2** a crude or cruel person.
bar·bar·i·an • ***noun,*** *plural* **barbarians**

barbecue (bär′bə kyo͞o) ***noun*** **1** a picnic or party where roasted meat is served. **2** a special stove or pit for cooking outdoors.
verb to roast over an open fire.
bar·be·cue • ***noun,*** *plural* **barbecues**
• ***verb*** **barbecued, barbecuing**

barbed wire (bärbd) ***noun*** wire with very sharp points fastened on it at even distances. Barbed wire is used for cattle fences.

barber (bär′bər) ***noun*** a person whose work is cutting hair and trimming or shaving beards.
bar·ber • ***noun,*** *plural* **barbers**

bare (ber) ***adjective*** **1** not covered or clothed; naked; stripped [*bare* legs; a *bare* spot in the lawn]. **2** not furnished; empty [a *bare* room]. **3** simple; plain [Give me just the *bare* facts about the robbery.] **4** no more than; mere [He stood a *bare* ten feet away.]
verb to make bare; uncover; expose.
bare • ***adjective*** • ***verb*** **bared, baring**

- The words **bare** and **bear** sound alike.
  Her *bare* arms became chilly.
  Some trees *bear* fruit.
  A polar *bear* blends in with the snow.

bareback (ber′bak) ***adjective*** on a horse with no saddle [a *bareback* rider]. This word can also be used as an adverb [He rode *bareback* across the field.]
bare·back • ***adjective***

barefoot (ber′fo͝ot) ***adjective*** with bare feet; without shoes and socks or stockings [The *barefoot* child played on the beach.] This word can also be used as an adverb [We walked *barefoot*.]
bare·foot • ***adjective***

barely (ber′lē) ***adverb*** only just; scarcely; hardly [The dog is *barely* a year old.]
bare·ly • ***adverb***

bargain (bär′gən) ***noun*** **1** an agreement to give or do something in return for something else. **2** something that is being sold or is bought for less than the usual cost.
verb to talk over a sale or trade, trying to get the best possible deal.
bar·gain • ***noun,*** *plural* **bargains**
• ***verb*** **bargained, bargaining**

barge (bärj) ***noun*** a large boat with a flat bottom, for carrying goods on rivers or canals.
barge • ***noun,*** *plural* **barges**

baritone (ber′ə tōn) ***noun*** **1** a man's voice that is lower than a tenor but higher than a bass. **2** a singer with such a voice.
bar·i·tone • ***noun,*** *plural* **baritones**

bark[1] (bärk) ***noun*** the outside covering of the trunk and branches of a tree.
verb to scrape some skin off [Don't *bark* your shins on that low table.]
bark • ***noun,*** *plural* **barks** • ***verb*** **barked, barking**

bark[2] (bärk) ***verb*** **1** to make the short cry of a dog or certain other animals. **2** to speak or shout sharply [The coach *barked* out orders.]
noun the sound made in barking.
bark • ***verb*** **barked, barking** • ***noun,*** *plural* **barks**

barley (bär′lē) ***noun*** **1** a kind of grass that farmers grow for its seeds. **2** the seeds, which are used as food.
bar·ley • ***noun***

barn (bärn) ***noun*** a farm building for sheltering cows and other animals and for storing farm machines and crops.
barn • ***noun,*** *plural* **barns**

barnacle (bär′nə kəl) ***noun*** a small sea animal with a shell. Barnacles fasten themselves to rocks, to the bottoms of ships, and even to whales.
bar·na·cle • ***noun,*** *plural* **barnacles**

a	cat	ō	go	ʉ	fur	ə =	a *in* ago
ā	ape	ô	law, for	ch	chin		e *in* agent
ä	cot, car	o͝o	look	sh	she		i *in* pencil
e	ten	o͞o	tool	th	thin		o *in* atom
ē	me	oi	oil	*th*	then		u *in* circus
i	fit	ou	out	zh	measure		
ī	ice	u	up	ŋ	ring		

barnyard (bärn′yärd) ***noun*** the yard or ground near a barn. It often has a fence around it.
barn·yard • ***noun,*** *plural* **barnyards**

barometer (bə räm′ət ər) ***noun*** an instrument that measures the pressure of the air around us. It is used in forecasting the weather.
ba·rom·e·ter • ***noun,*** *plural* **barometers**

baron (ber′ən) ***noun*** a nobleman in some countries.
bar·on • ***noun,*** *plural* **barons**
● The words **baron** and **barren** sound alike.
A *baron* ranks below an earl.
A desert is a *barren* place.

baroness (ber′ən is) ***noun*** **1** a baron's wife or widow. **2** a woman with a baron's rank.
bar·on·ess • ***noun,*** *plural* **baronesses**

barracks (ber′əks) ***plural noun*** [*used with a singular or plural verb*] a building or group of buildings where soldiers live.
bar·racks • ***plural noun***

barracuda (ber ə ko͞o′də) ***noun*** a large, fierce fish that lives in warm seas.
bar·ra·cu·da • ***noun,*** *plural* **barracuda** or **barracudas**

barrage (bə räzh′) ***noun*** the continued shooting of artillery against an area.
bar·rage • ***noun,*** *plural* **barrages**

barre

barre (bär) ***noun*** a handrail fastened to a wall at waist level. Dancers hold onto it while they practice their ballet exercises.
barre • ***noun,*** *plural* **barres**
● The words **barre** and **bar** sound alike.
The ballerina lightly touched the *barre*.
Wash with a *bar* of soap.

barrel (ber′əl) ***noun*** **1** a large, round container that has bulging sides and a flat top and bottom. It is usually made of wooden slats bound together by metal hoops. **2** the amount that a barrel holds. **3** the straight tube that is part of a gun. The bullet or shell is shot through it.
bar·rel • ***noun,*** *plural* **barrels**

barren (ber′ən) ***adjective*** not producing crops or fruit [*barren* soil; a *barren* tree].
bar·ren • ***adjective***
● The words **barren** and **baron** sound alike.
The apple tree is *barren* this year.
The Red *Baron* was a pilot for Germany.

barrette (bə ret′) ***noun*** a clasp for holding a girl's or woman's hair in place.
bar·rette • ***noun,*** *plural* **barrettes**

barricade (ber′ə kād) ***noun*** a pile of things that is built up quickly to block a road or entrance.
verb to put up barricades in; to block.
bar·ri·cade • ***noun,*** *plural* **barricades** • ***verb*** **barricaded, barricading**

barrier (ber′ē ər) ***noun*** a fence, wall, or other thing that blocks the way.
bar·ri·er • ***noun,*** *plural* **barriers**

barter (bärt′ər) ***verb*** to pay for things with other things instead of money; to trade [I'll *barter* my hamster for your turtle.] —Look for the WORD CHOICES box at the entry **sell**.
noun the act or process of bartering.
bar·ter • ***verb*** **bartered, bartering** • ***noun***

Barton (bärt′n), **Clara** (klar′ə) 1821-1912; American nurse. She organized the American Red Cross in 1881.
Bar·ton, Clar·a

base[1] (bās) ***noun*** **1** the thing or part on which something rests; the lowest part or bottom [A cement slab forms the *base* of the statue.] **2** the main part, on which everything else depends; basis [Arithmetic is the *base* for more advanced kinds of math.] **3** one of the four goals that a baseball player must safely reach, one after the other, to score a run. **4** the place where soldiers, planes, ships, or explorers start out, or the place that provides their supplies [There are military *bases* in all parts of the world.] **5** a chemical compound that feels slippery in water, tastes bitter, and makes red litmus paper turn blue. Household ammonia is a base.
verb to use as a base for [We *based* our grocery list on the number of guests who were coming.]

B

base • *noun, plural* **bases** • *verb* **based, basing**
● The words **base** and **bass** sound alike.
Is the compound an acid or a *base*?
Her actions were cowardly and *base*.
The tenor and *bass* left the stage.

WORD CHOICES

Synonyms of **base**

The words **base, basis,** and **foundation** share the meaning "a part on which something else rests for support."

the *base* of a lamp
a story with no *basis* in fact
the *foundation* of a building

base[2] (bās) *adjective* **1** not having or showing much courage, decency, or honor; not noble [a *base* coward]. **2** low in value as compared to others [Iron is a *base* metal.]
base • *adjective* **baser, basest**
● The words **base** and **bass** sound alike.

baseball (bās′bôl) *noun* **1** a game played by two teams on a field with four bases that form the corners of a diamond-shaped path. A player tries to hit a thrown ball with a bat in order to get on base. A team scores when one of its players reaches safely all four bases. **2** the ball that is used in this game.
base·ball • *noun, plural* **baseballs**

baseman (bās′mən) *noun* a baseball player who has a position at first, second, or third base.
base·man • *noun, plural* **basemen**

basement (bās′mənt) *noun* the lowest floor of a building, below or partly below the surface of the ground.
base·ment • *noun, plural* **basements**

base word *noun* the simplest form of a word, without prefixes or suffixes [From the *base word* "place," we can make the plural "places" and the verb forms "placed" and "placing."]
base word • *noun, plural* **base words**

bashful (bash′fəl) *adjective* timid, shy, and easily embarrassed.
bash·ful • *adjective*

basic (bā′sik) *adjective* at the base or serving as a basis; fundamental or main [These are the *basic* rules of the game.]
bas·ic • *adjective*

BASIC (bā′sik) *noun* a simple computer language that is often used to teach beginners.

basin (bās′ən) *noun* **1** a wide, shallow bowl for holding a liquid. **2** a sink. **3** all the land that is drained by a river and by all the streams flowing into the river.
ba·sin • *noun, plural* **basins**

basis (bā′sis) *noun* the main thing or part on which something depends [The ideas in the U.S. Constitution are the *basis* of our government.] —Look for the WORD CHOICES box at the entry **base**[1].
ba·sis • *noun, plural* **bases** (bā′sēz)

bask (bask) *verb* to stay in a warm, pleasant place and get warm [The cat *basked* in the sun.]
bask • *verb* **basked, basking**

basket (bas′kət) *noun* **1** a container that is made by weaving together wood strips or various kinds of grasslike material. It often has a handle or handles [a bushel *basket*]. **2** the amount that a basket holds. **3** a thing that looks like a basket or is used in the same way as a basket [a wastepaper *basket;* a clothes *basket*]. **4** an open net hanging from a metal hoop that is used as a goal in basketball. **5** an act of scoring by putting the basketball through this net.
bas·ket • *noun, plural* **baskets**

basket

basketball (bas′kət bôl′) *noun* **1** a game for two teams of five players each that is played on a court with a raised basket at each end. A player scores by putting a large ball through the basket at the other team's end of the court. **2** the air-filled ball that is used in this game.
bas·ket·ball • *noun, plural* **basketballs**

a cat	ō go	ʉ fur	ə = a *in* ago
ā ape	ô law, for	ch chin	e *in* agent
ä cot, car	oo look	sh she	i *in* pencil
e ten	ōō tool	th thin	o *in* atom
ē me	oi oil	*th* then	u *in* circus
i fit	ou out	zh measure	
ī ice	u up	ŋ ring	

WORD HISTORY

basketball

The nets with hoops that we use in **basketball** do not look much like baskets. But when Dr. James Naismith invented the game in 1891, he used real peach baskets with their bottoms cut out. He had wanted to use boxes, but their school custodian had only baskets. Can you imagine playing "boxball"?

bass[1] (bās) ***noun*** **1** the lowest kind of man's singing voice. **2** a singer with such a voice. ***adjective*** having low, deep tones [a *bass* drum].
bass • ***noun,*** *plural* **basses** • ***adjective***
● The words **bass** and **base** sound alike.
The tenor and *bass* left the stage.
She slid into first *base*.
The opposite of "noble" is "*base*."

bass[2] (bas) ***noun*** one of several freshwater or saltwater North American fishes that are caught for food or sport.
bass • ***noun,*** *plural* **bass** or **basses**

bassoon (bə so͞on′) ***noun*** a woodwind musical instrument with deep, low tones. It has a long, curved mouthpiece with two reeds.
bas·soon • ***noun,*** *plural* **bassoons**

bassoon

baste[1] (bāst) ***verb*** to sew with long, loose stitches so as to hold the parts together until the final sewing is done.
baste • ***verb*** **basted, basting**

baste[2] (bāst) ***verb*** to keep meat moist during roasting by pouring the meat juices or melted fat on it [to *baste* chicken].
baste • ***verb*** **basted, basting**

bat[1] (bat) ***noun*** a wooden club used to hit the ball in games such as baseball or softball. ***verb*** to hit with a bat or with something like a bat [The cat *batted* the ball with his paw.]
—**at bat** having a turn to hit the ball in baseball or softball.
bat • ***noun,*** *plural* **bats** • ***verb*** **batted, batting**

bat[2] (bat) ***noun*** a furry animal that looks like a mouse but has wings of stretched skin. Bats usually fly at night.
bat • ***noun,*** *plural* **bats**

batch (bach) ***noun*** the amount of something made at one time [a *batch* of cookies].
batch • ***noun,*** *plural* **batches**

bath (bath) ***noun*** **1** the act of washing something in water [He takes a *bath* every day. Give the dog a *bath*.] **2** the water used for a bath [The *bath* is too hot.] **3** a bathroom.
bath • ***noun,*** *plural* **baths** (ba*th*z *or* baths)

bathe (bā*th*) ***verb*** **1** to take a bath or give a bath to; to wash [He *bathes* every day. Mary is going to *bathe* the baby.] **2** to go swimming [Do you like to *bathe* in the sea?] **3** to seem to come pouring in and cover [Moonlight *bathed* the trees.]
bathe • ***verb*** **bathed, bathing**

bathing suit ***noun*** a garment worn for swimming.
bathing suit • ***noun,*** *plural* **bathing suits**

bathrobe (bath′rōb) ***noun*** a loose garment that is similar to a coat and has a belt of the same material. A bathrobe is used before and after a bath or while relaxing.
bath·robe • ***noun,*** *plural* **bathrobes**

bathroom (bath′ro͞om) ***noun*** **1** a room with a bathtub or shower, a toilet, and a sink. **2** a room with a sink and a toilet.
bath·room • ***noun,*** *plural* **bathrooms**

bathtub (bath′tub) ***noun*** a large tub in which a person takes a bath.
bath·tub • ***noun,*** *plural* **bathtubs**

baton (bə tän′) ***noun*** **1** a thin stick used by a conductor to direct an orchestra. **2** a metal rod twirled in a showy way by the person who leads a marching band.
ba·ton • ***noun,*** *plural* **batons**

Baton Rouge (bat′n ro͞ozh′) the capital of Louisiana, on the Mississippi River.
Bat·on Rouge

battalion (bə tal′yən) ***noun*** a large group of soldiers from an army. A battalion is the basic unit of a division and is made up of several companies.
bat·tal·ion • ***noun,*** *plural* **battalions**

B

batter[1] (bat′ər) ***verb*** to beat or hit with blow after blow; pound in a noisy way [The waves *battered* the rocks on the shore.]
bat·ter • ***verb*** **battered, battering**

batter[2] (bat′ər) ***noun*** the player whose turn it is to bat in games such as baseball.
bat·ter • ***noun,*** *plural* **batters**

batter[3] (bat′ər) ***noun*** a mixture of eggs, flour, and milk or water beaten together. Batter is fried or baked to make cakes, waffles, or cookies.
bat·ter • ***noun,*** *plural* **batters**

battering ram ***noun*** a heavy, wooden beam that was used to batter down gates and walls.
battering ram • ***noun,*** *plural* **battering rams**

battery (bat′ər ē) ***noun*** **1** a device that uses chemicals to produce electric current. It is usually made up of a number of smaller parts called cells. A battery provides electrical power for things such as cars, flashlights, and toys. **2** a group of people or things that are alike or do something together [A *battery* of microphones surrounded the mayor.]
bat·ter·y • ***noun,*** *plural* **batteries**

battle (bat′l) ***noun*** **1** a fight between armed forces during a war [The naval *battle* lasted two days.] **2** armed fighting; warfare [a wound received in *battle*]. **3** a long or hard struggle [Rowing upstream was a *battle*.]
verb to fight or struggle [The ship *battled* against the storm.]
bat·tle • ***noun,*** *plural* **battles** • ***verb*** **battled, battling**

battlefield (bat′l fēld) ***noun*** the place where a battle is fought or was fought.
bat·tle·field • ***noun,*** *plural* **battlefields**

battleground (bat′l ground) ***noun*** a battlefield.
bat·tle·ground • ***noun,*** *plural* **battlegrounds**

battlement (bat′l mənt) ***noun*** a low wall built along the top of a tower, castle, or fort. Battlements had a series of openings for soldiers to shoot through.
bat·tle·ment • ***noun,*** *plural* **battlements**

battleship (bat′l ship) ***noun*** a large warship with big guns and very heavy armor.
bat·tle·ship • ***noun,*** *plural* **battleships**

batty (bat′ē) [*a slang word*] ***adjective*** crazy; strange or eccentric [a *batty* neighbor].
bat·ty • ***adjective*** **battier, battiest**

bawl (bôl *or* bäl) ***verb*** **1** to call out in a loud, rough voice; bellow ["Forward march!" *bawled* the sergeant.] **2** to weep and cry loudly [The child *bawled* in the other room.]
—bawl out [*a slang use*] to scold angrily [I was *bawled out* for not cleaning my plate.]
bawl • ***verb*** **bawled, bawling**

● The words **bawl** and **ball** sound alike.
Will she *bawl* us out for being late?
She caught the *ball* without a mitt.
What will you wear to the *ball*?

bay[1] (bā) ***noun*** a part of a sea or lake that cuts into a coastline to form a hollow curve.
bay • ***noun,*** *plural* **bays**

bay[2] (bā) ***verb*** to bark or howl with long, deep sounds [The hound *bayed* at the moon.]
noun the sound of baying.
bay • ***verb*** **bayed, baying** • ***noun,*** *plural* **bays**

bayonet (bā ə net′) ***noun*** a large knife attached to the front end of a rifle. A bayonet is used in close fighting.
bay·o·net • ***noun,*** *plural* **bayonets**

bayou (bī′o͞o) ***noun*** a stream that moves slowly through a low, wet area of land and into or out of a lake or river. Bayous are found in some parts of the southern U.S.
bay·ou • ***noun,*** *plural* **bayous**

bazaar (bə zär′) ***noun*** **1** a sale of many different things. Bazaars are usually held to raise money for a church or charity. **2** a market made up of a street lined with small shops or stalls.
ba·zaar • ***noun,*** *plural* **bazaars**

B.C. *abbreviation for* **1** before Christ; before the year in which Jesus Christ is believed to have been born [Rome was founded in 753 *B.C.*] **2** British Columbia. This abbreviation is also written **BC** when it is used in writing addresses.

B.C.E. *abbreviation for* before (the) Common Era. This abbreviation is sometimes used instead of **B.C.**

be (bē) ***verb*** *Be* can join a subject with a word or words that tell something about it. *Be* can also tell that something exists or takes place. *Be* can also be a linking verb and a helping

a	cat	ō	go	ʉ	fur	ə = a *in* ago	
ā	ape	ô	law, for	ch	chin	e *in* agent	
ä	cot, car	o͝o	look	sh	she	i *in* pencil	
e	ten	o͞o	tool	th	thin	o *in* atom	
ē	me	oi	oil	*th*	then	u *in* circus	
i	fit	ou	out	zh	measure		
ī	ice	u	up	ŋ	ring		

verb. **I.** *Be* may mean: **1** to live [Lincoln *is* no more.] **2** to happen or take place [The wedding will *be* next Sunday.] **3** to stay or continue [I will *be* here until Monday.] **4** to have a place or position [The door *is* on your left.] **II.** When *be* is a linking verb, it joins a subject with: **1** a noun [He *is* a student.] **2** an adjective [Ingrid *is* tall.] **3** a pronoun [Who *is* he?] **III.** When *be* is a helping verb, it is used with: **1** a past participle [The diamonds *are* gone!] **2** a present participle [I *am* going.] **3** an infinitive [We *are* to see the movie later.]

INFLECTED FORMS OF THE VERB **be**

	First Person	Second Person	Third Person
Present Tense			
singular	**am**	**are**	**is**
plural	**are**	**are**	**are**
Present Participle	**being**	**being**	**being**
Past Tense			
singular	**was**	**were**	**was**
plural	**were**	**were**	**were**
Past Participle	**been**	**been**	**been**

● The words **be** and **bee** sound alike.
To *be* or not to be.
The ant and the *bee* are social insects.

beach (bēch) ***noun*** a smooth, sloping stretch of sand and pebbles at the edge of a sea, lake, or other body of water.
verb to run onto a beach [The storm winds *beached* several boats on the island.]
beach • ***noun,*** *plural* **beaches** • ***verb*** **beached, beaching**
● The words **beach** and **beech** sound alike.
I like to walk on the *beach* at dawn.
Beech trees line our street.

beacon (bē′kən) ***noun*** a fire, light, or other signal used to guide or warn ships or aircraft.
bea·con • ***noun,*** *plural* **beacons**

bead (bēd) ***noun*** **1** a small, round piece of glass, metal, wood, or other material. A bead has a small hole in it so that it can be put on a string. **2** any small, round object [*beads* of sweat].
verb to decorate or cover with beads.
bead • ***noun,*** *plural* **beads** • ***verb*** **beaded, beading**

beady (bēd′ē) ***adjective*** small, round, and sparkling [the *beady* eyes of a snake].
bead·y • ***adjective*** **beadier, beadiest**

beagle (bē′gəl) ***noun*** a small dog with a smooth coat, short legs, and drooping ears. Beagles are often used as hunting dogs.
bea·gle • ***noun,*** *plural* **beagles**

beak (bēk) ***noun*** the sharp, hard, curved and pointed mouth part of a bird; a bill.
beak • ***noun,*** *plural* **beaks**

beaker (bēk′ər) ***noun*** a wide glass that has a lip for pouring. Beakers are used by chemists.
beak·er • ***noun,*** *plural* **beakers**

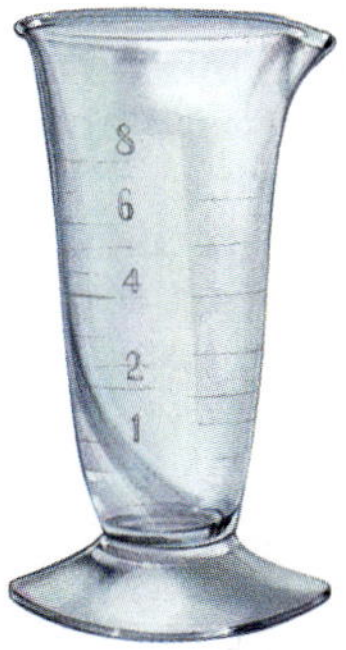

beaker

beam (bēm) ***noun*** **1** a long, thick piece of wood or metal. Beams are used in buildings and ships as horizontal supports for roofs, floors, and decks. **2** a narrow ray or stream of light.
verb **1** to shine brightly [A light *beamed* from the window.] **2** to smile happily or widely.
beam • ***noun,*** *plural* **beams** • ***verb*** **beamed, beaming**

bean

bean (bēn) ***noun*** **1** a smooth, hard seed that is eaten as a vegetable. Kidney beans are seeds of this kind. **2** a long, narrow pod with such seeds. String beans are cooked and eaten as a vegetable, pod and all. **3** any seed or fruit that looks like a bean [a coffee *bean*].
bean • ***noun,*** *plural* **beans**

beanstalk (bēn′stôk) ***noun*** the main stem of a bean plant.
bean·stalk ◦ ***noun,*** *plural* **beanstalks**

bear[1] (ber) ***verb*** **1** to hold up; support [The walls *bear* the weight of the roof.] **2** to take from one place to another [The guests arrived *bearing* gifts.] —Look for the WORD CHOICES box at the entry **carry**. **3** to have or show [She *bears* a resemblance to her mother.] **4** to give birth to [She has *borne* two children.] **5** to come into being [He was *born* in June.] **6** to produce or yield [Our pear tree *bore* no fruit.] **7** to be able to stand something painful or annoying; put up with [I can't *bear* the heat.] —**bear down** to press or push down. —**bear with** to put up with; endure.
bear ◦ ***verb*** **bore, borne** or **born** *(for sense 5),* **bearing**
● The words **bear** and **bare** sound alike.
I can't *bear* to see her cry.
A polar *bear* blends in with the snow.
The room looked *bare* without furniture.

bear

bear[2] (ber) ***noun*** a large, heavy animal with shaggy fur and a very short tail. There are many kinds of bears, such as brown bears and polar bears.
bear ◦ ***noun,*** *plural* **bears** or **bear**
● The words **bear** and **bare** sound alike.

beard (bird) ***noun*** **1** the hair that grows on the lower part of a man's face. **2** something that looks like a beard [The hair on a goat's chin is called a *beard*.]
beard ◦ ***noun,*** *plural* **beards**

bearing (ber′iŋ) ***noun*** **1** the way that a person stands, moves, walks, or acts [He has the upright *bearing* of a soldier.] **2** the fact of having something to do with; connection [Homework has a *bearing* on grades.] **3 bearings** direction or position in relation to something else [The sailboat lost its *bearings* in the fog.] **4** a part of a machine on which another part turns or slides. The bearing helps the part to move with little friction.
bear·ing ◦ ***noun,*** *plural* **bearings**

beast (bēst) ***noun*** any large, four-footed animal.
beast ◦ ***noun,*** *plural* **beasts**

beat (bēt) ***verb*** **1** to hit or strike again and again; pound [Rain was *beating* on the roof. The school bully *beat* him with his fists.] **2** to mix by stirring strongly [*Beat* the whites of two eggs.] **3** to move up and down; flap [The bird *beat* its wings against the window.] **4** to move or sound in an even, regular way; throb [He could feel his heart *beat*.] **5** to win over; defeat [Our team *beat* theirs.]
noun **1** a blow, sound, or stroke made again and again [We could hear the *beat* of the hail on the window.] **2** a throbbing or pounding sound, sensation, or rhythm [the *beat* of a heart]. **3** the unit of rhythm in music [Waltz rhythm has three *beats* in each measure.]
beat ◦ ***verb*** **beat, beaten** or **beat, beating** ◦ ***noun,*** *plural* **beats**
● The words **beat** and **beet** sound alike.
She *beat* the big bass drum.
The *beet* is not my favorite vegetable.

WORD CHOICES

Synonyms of **beat**

Many words share the meaning "to hit again and again."

hammer	pound
lash	thrash

beaten (bēt′'n) ***verb*** *a past participle of* **beat**.
beat·en ◦ ***verb***

beautiful (byo͞ot′ə fəl) ***adjective*** delightful to look at, listen to, or think about; pleasing to the mind or senses [a *beautiful* scene; *beautiful* music].
beau·ti·ful ◦ ***adjective***

a	cat	ō	go	ʉ	fur	ə =	a *in* ago
ā	ape	ô	law, for	ch	chin		e *in* agent
ä	cot, car	o͝o	look	sh	she		i *in* pencil
e	ten	o͞o	tool	th	thin		o *in* atom
ē	me	oi	oil	*th*	then		u *in* circus
i	fit	ou	out	zh	measure		
ī	ice	u	up	ŋ	ring		

beautify (byo͞ot′ə fī) ***verb*** to make beautiful [Parks and trees *beautify* the city.]
beau·ti·fy • ***verb*** **beautified, beautifying, beautifies**

beauty (byo͞ot′ē) ***noun*** **1** the quality in a person or thing that makes it pleasant to look at, listen to, or think about [The violin produced a sound of great *beauty*.] **2** a person or thing that is beautiful [That car is a *beauty*.]
beau·ty • ***noun,*** *plural* **beauties**

beaver (bē′vər) ***noun*** an animal that has soft, brown fur, a flat, broad tail, and webbed hind feet to help it swim. Beavers can live on land and in water. They cut down trees with their strong teeth and build dams across rivers.
bea·ver • ***noun,*** *plural* **beavers** or **beaver**

became (bē kām′) ***verb*** *past tense of* **become**.
be·came • ***verb***

because (bē kôz′ *or* bē käz′) ***conjunction*** for the reason that; since [I'm late *because* I overslept.]
—because of on account of; as a result of [He was absent from school *because of* illness.]
be·cause • ***conjunction***

beckon (bek′n) ***verb*** to signal to someone by moving the head or hand [The waitress *beckoned* to us when she found an empty table.]
beck·on • ***verb*** **beckoned, beckoning**

become (bē kum′) ***verb*** **1** to come to be [She *became* ill last week. My baby brother had *become* a young man.] **2** to be right or suitable for [That dress *becomes* you.]
—become of to happen to [What *became of* that movie star?]
be·come • ***verb*** **became, become, becoming**

becoming (bē kum′iŋ) ***adjective*** right or suitable; attractive [a *becoming* dress].
be·com·ing • ***adjective***

bed (bed) ***noun*** **1** a piece of furniture for sleeping or resting on. **2** a piece of ground where plants are grown [a flower *bed*]. **3** the ground at the bottom of a river, lake, or other body of water. **4** a flat base or foundation [The masons set the columns on a *bed* of concrete.] ***verb*** to go to sleep; rest ["You may *bed* here for the night," he said.]
—bed and board a place to sleep and meals.
bed • ***noun,*** *plural* **beds** • ***verb*** **bedded, bedding**

bedding (bed′iŋ) ***noun*** mattresses, sheets, blankets, and other coverings for a bed.
bed·ding • ***noun,*** *plural* **beddings**

bedraggled (bē drag′əld) ***adjective*** looking like something that has been dragged through mud; wet and dirty; messy.
be·drag·gled • ***adjective***

bedrock (bed′räk) ***noun*** the solid layer of rock that lies beneath the soil and other loose rocks.
bed·rock • ***noun***

bedroom (bed′ro͞om) ***noun*** a room with a bed, for sleeping in.
bed·room • ***noun,*** *plural* **bedrooms**

bedside (bed′sīd) ***noun*** the space beside a bed [A nurse was at her *bedside*.]
bed·side • ***noun,*** *plural* **bedsides**

bedspread (bed′spred) ***noun*** a cover for a bed. It goes on over the sheets and blanket.
bed·spread • ***noun,*** *plural* **bedspreads**

bedtime (bed′tīm) ***noun*** the time when a person usually goes to bed.
bed·time • ***noun,*** *plural* **bedtimes**

bee (bē) ***noun*** **1** an insect that has four wings, a hairy body and, sometimes, a stinger. Bees feed on the nectar of flowers. Some bees live together in colonies, or hives, and make honey and wax. **2** a meeting of people in a contest or for working at something together [a spelling *bee;* a sewing *bee*].

bee

bee • ***noun,*** *plural* **bees**
● The words **bee** and **be** sound alike.
The queen *bee* lays eggs for the hive.
Be friendly when I introduce you.

beech (bēch) ***noun*** a tree with smooth, light-gray bark. It has nuts that may be eaten.
beech • ***noun,*** *plural* **beeches**
● The words **beech** and **beach** sound alike.
Beech trees line our street.
I like to walk on the *beach* at dawn.

beef (bēf) ***noun*** the meat from a steer, cow, or bull.
beef • ***noun,*** *plural* **beeves** or **beefs**

beefsteak (bēf′stāk) ***noun*** a thick slice of beef to be broiled or fried.
beef·steak • ***noun,*** *plural* **beefsteaks**

beehive (bē′hīv) *noun* **1** a box or other place for a colony of bees. **2** a very busy place.
bee·hive • *noun, plural* **beehives**

been (bin) *verb past participle of* **be**.
● The words **been** and **bin** sound alike.
How have you *been?*
Grain can be stored in the *bin*.

beep (bēp) *noun* the short, high-pitched sound made by an electronic device or by some automobile horns.
verb to make or cause to make this sound [The oven timer *beeped* after five minutes.]
beep • *noun, plural* **beeps** • *verb* **beeped, beeping**

beeper (bēp′ər) *noun* **1** an electronic device that sends or receives a beep. **2** a pocket-sized, portable receiver that is used to tell a person that an important message is waiting.
beep·er • *noun, plural* **beepers**

beer (bir) *noun* an alcoholic drink made of malt and water, and flavored with hops.
beer • *noun, plural* **beers**

beeswax (bēz′waks) *noun* the wax that some bees make for building their honeycomb. It is used to make candles and furniture polish.
bees·wax • *noun*

beet (bēt) *noun* a plant with a thick, heavy root. One kind of beet has a round, red root that is eaten as a vegetable. Another kind has a long, white root that is used to make sugar.
beet • *noun, plural* **beets**
● The words **beet** and **beat** sound alike.
His face turned *beet* red.
We could hear the baby's heart *beat*.

beet

Beethoven (bā′tō vən), **Ludwig van** (lo͞ot′vik vän) 1770-1827; German composer.
Bee·tho·ven, Lud·wig van

beetle (bēt′l) *noun* an insect that has two pairs of wings. The hard front wings cover the thin back wings when the back wings are folded.
bee·tle • *noun, plural* **beetles**

before (bē fôr′) *preposition* **1** ahead of [The valley stretched *before* us.] **2** in front of [We paused *before* the door.] **3** earlier than; previous to [Will you finish *before* noon?]
adverb **1** in the past; earlier [I've heard that song *before*.] **2** at an earlier time; sooner [Come to see me at ten, not *before*.]
conjunction **1** earlier than the time that [Think *before* you speak.] **2** sooner than [I'd die *before* I'd tell anyone your secret.]
be·fore • *preposition* • *adverb* • *conjunction*

beforehand (bē fôr′hand′) *adverb* ahead of time [Let's check the bus schedule *beforehand*.]
be·fore·hand • *adverb*

befriend (bē frend′) *verb* to act as a friend to [Jim and Maria *befriended* the new student.]
be·friend • *verb* **befriended, befriending**

beg (beg) *verb* **1** to ask for as charity or as a gift [He *begged* a dollar from me.] **2** to ask for in a humble or polite way [She *begged* for mercy.] **3** to ask as a favor or in a serious or insisting way [She *begged* us not to tell.]
beg • *verb* **begged, begging**

began (bē gan′) *verb past tense of* **begin**.
be·gan • *verb*

beggar (beg′ər) *noun* a person who lives by asking others for money, clothes, or food.
beg·gar • *noun, plural* **beggars**

begin (bē gin′) *verb* **1** to start to do, act, or go; get under way [Work *begins* at 8:00 A.M.] **2** to come into being; start [The football season *begins* in the fall.]
be·gin • *verb* **began, begun, beginning**

beginner (bē gin′ər) *noun* a person who is just beginning to learn or to do something.
be·gin·ner • *noun, plural* **beginners**

beginning (bē gin′iŋ) *noun* **1** the first part [the *beginning* of the movie]. **2** the time when or the place where something begins [Today is the *beginning* of our vacation.]
be·gin·ning • *noun, plural* **beginnings**

begun (bē gun′) *verb past participle of* **begin**.
be·gun • *verb*

a	cat	ō	go	ʉ	fur	ə =	a *in* ago
ā	ape	ô	law, for	ch	chin		e *in* agent
ä	cot, car	o͝o	look	sh	she		i *in* pencil
e	ten	o͞o	tool	th	thin		o *in* atom
ē	me	oi	oil	*th*	then		u *in* circus
i	fit	ou	out	zh	measure		
ī	ice	u	up	ŋ	ring		

behalf (bē haf′) *noun used only in the phrases*: **1 in** or **on behalf of**, speaking or acting for [She accepted the trophy *on behalf of* her team.] **2 in someone's behalf**, in someone's interest [His friends spoke *in his behalf*.]
be·half • *noun*

behave (bē hāv′) *verb* **1** to act or work in a certain way [The children *behaved* badly at the picnic.] **2** to act in a proper way; do the right things [Try to *behave* yourself in public.]
be·have • *verb* **behaved, behaving**

behavior (bē hāv′yər) *noun* the way a person or thing behaves, or acts; conduct or action [His *behavior* at the dance was rude. In physics, scientists study the *behavior* of atoms.]
be·hav·ior • *noun, plural* **behaviors**

behead (bē hed′) *verb* to cut off the head of [The rebels captured and *beheaded* the king.]
be·head • *verb* **beheaded, beheading**

beheld (bē held′) *verb past tense and past participle of* **behold**.
be·held • *verb*

behind (bē hīnd′) *adverb* **1** in or to the rear or back [The children trailed *behind*.] **2** in an earlier time or condition [My happy days lie *behind*.] **3** late or slow in action or progress [We fell *behind* in our work.]
preposition **1** in the rear of; in back of [Sit *behind* me.] **2** lower in position than [They are two grades *behind* me in school.] **3** later than [The train was *behind* schedule.] **4** supporting; in favor of [The mayor is *behind* the plan.]
be·hind • *adverb* • *preposition*

behold (bē hōld′) *verb* to look at; see [There was never a sadder sight to *behold*.]
be·hold • *verb* **beheld, beholding**

beige (bāzh) *noun* the color of sand; grayish tan.
adjective having this color [a *beige* rug].

beige • *noun, plural* **beiges** • *adjective*

being (bē′iŋ) *verb present participle of* **be**.
noun **1** the state or fact of existing; existence or life [Our club came into *being* last year.] **2** a living creature [a human *being*].
be·ing • *verb* • *noun, plural* **beings**

Belarus (bel ə ro͞os′) a country in central Europe. It was a part of the Soviet Union.
Bel·a·rus

belated (bē lāt′əd) *adjective* too late; not on time [a card with *belated* birthday greetings].
be·lat·ed • *adjective*

belch (belch) *verb* **1** to let gas from the stomach out through the mouth, usually with a noise; burp. **2** to throw out with force [The volcano *belched* smoke and flames.]
noun the act of belching; a burp.
belch • *verb* **belched, belching**
• *noun, plural* **belches**

belfry (bel′frē) *noun* a tower or a room in a tower in which a bell or bells are hung.
bel·fry • *noun, plural* **belfries**

belfry

Belgium (bel′jəm) a country in western Europe.
Bel·gium

belief (bə lēf′) *noun* **1** a feeling that something is true or real; faith [You cannot destroy his *belief* in the honesty of most people.] **2** something that is believed to be true [Early peoples held the *belief* that the earth is flat.]
be·lief • *noun, plural* **beliefs**

WORD CHOICES

Synonyms of **belief**

The words **belief, confidence, faith,** and **trust** share the meaning "certainty about someone or something."

My *belief* in his innocence is firm.
They have *confidence* in my skill.
She has *faith* that she will be cured.
Put your *trust* in me.

believe (bə lēv′) *verb* **1** to accept as true or real [Can we *believe* his story?] **2** to have religious faith [We *believe* in life after death.] **3** to have trust or confidence [I know you will win; I *believe* in you.] **4** to suppose; guess [I *believe* it will rain tonight.]
be·lieve • *verb* **believed, believing**

B

SPELLING TIP

Use this memory aid to spell **believe**. Don t be*lie*ve a ***lie***.

Belize (bə lēz′) a country in Central America, on the Caribbean Sea.
Be·lize

bell (bel) ***noun*** **1** a hollow, metal object that makes a ringing sound when it is struck. Usually the bell is shaped like an upside-down cup, with a clapper hanging inside. **2** something that is shaped like a bell [the *bell* of a trumpet].
bell • ***noun,*** *plural* **bells**

Bell (bel), **Alexander Graham** (al′ig zan′dər grā′əm) 1847-1922; American scientist who invented the telephone.
Bell, Al·ex·an·der Gra·ham

belligerent (bə lij′ər ənt) ***adjective*** **1** taking part in a war; at war [The two *belligerent* nations agreed to sign a peace treaty.] **2** showing a condition of being ready to fight or quarrel; hostile [the *belligerent* actions of the bully].
bel·lig·er·ent • ***adjective***

bellow (bel′ō) ***verb*** **1** to roar loudly [The bull *bellowed* at the cows.] **2** to shout out [The sergeant *bellowed* commands.]
bel·low • ***verb*** **bellowed, bellowing**

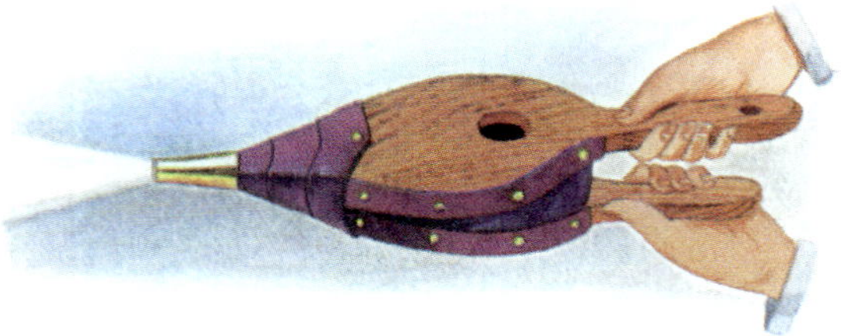

bellows

bellows (bel′ōz) ***noun*** [*used with a singular or plural verb*] a device that blows out air when its sides are squeezed together. It is used especially to make fires burn strongly.
bel·lows • ***noun,*** *plural* **bellows**

belly (bel′ē) ***noun*** **1** the front part of the human body below the chest and above the thighs; abdomen. **2** the stomach. **3** the underside of an animal's body.
bel·ly • ***noun,*** *plural* **bellies**

bellybutton (bel′ē but′n) [*an informal word*] ***noun*** *another name for* **navel**.
bel·ly·but·ton • ***noun,*** *plural* **bellybuttons**

belong (bē lôŋ′) ***verb*** to have its proper place [This chair *belongs* in the corner.]
—belong to **1** to be owned by someone [This book *belongs to* me.] **2** to be a member of [She *belongs to* the fencing team.]
be·long • ***verb*** **belonged, belonging**

belongings (bē lôŋ′iŋz) ***plural noun*** the things that belong to a person; possessions.
be·long·ings • ***plural noun***

beloved (bē luv′əd *or* bē luvd′) ***adjective*** much loved [Molly is my *beloved* cousin.]
be·lov·ed • ***adjective***

below (bē lō′) ***adverb*** in or to a lower place; beneath [See the picture *below*.]
preposition **1** lower than in place, location, position, or rank [the floor *below* us]. **2** lower in amount or number [a price *below* $25].
be·low • ***adverb*** • ***preposition***

belt (belt) ***noun*** **1** a strip of leather, cloth, or any other material. Belts are worn around the waist to hold up clothing or as an ornament. **2** an area or zone that is different in some way from others [The corn *belt* is the area where corn is grown.] **3** a strap looped around two or more wheels. When one wheel turns, it moves the belt, which turns the other wheel.
belt • ***noun,*** *plural* **belts**

bench (bench) ***noun*** **1** a long, hard seat for several people. A bench may or may not have a back. **2** a strong table on which work with tools is done [a carpenter's *bench*].
bench • ***noun,*** *plural* **benches**

bend (bend) ***verb*** **1** to pull or press something hard or stiff into a curve or angle [*Bend* the branches down so we can reach the apples.] **2** to be curved in this way [The trees *bent* under the weight of the snow.] **3** to turn in a certain direction [The road *bends* to the left.] **4** to stoop [*Bend* over and touch your toes.]
noun something that is bent or curved [The farmhouse is just around the *bend* in the road.]
bend • ***verb*** **bent, bending** • ***noun,*** *plural* **bends**

a	cat	ō	go	ʉ	fur	ə =	a *in* ago
ā	ape	ô	law, for	ch	chin		e *in* agent
ä	cot, car	oo	look	sh	she		i *in* pencil
e	ten	ōō	tool	th	thin		o *in* atom
ē	me	oi	oil	*th*	then		u *in* circus
i	fit	ou	out	zh	measure		
ī	ice	u	up	ŋ	ring		

beneath (bē nēth′) *adverb* in a lower place; below or just below [Look *beneath* the table.]
preposition **1** lower than; below; under [*beneath* sunny skies]. **2** not worthy of [She felt it was *beneath* her to cheat.]
be·neath • *adverb* • *preposition*

benefit (ben′ə fət) *noun* **1** help; advantage [Speak louder for the *benefit* of those in the rear.] **2** something that is good or helpful [Good health is one of the *benefits* of exercising.]
verb • **1** to do good for; help [A vacation will *benefit* the whole family.] **2** to be helped; profit [You'll *benefit* from exercise.]
ben·e·fit • *noun, plural* **benefits**
• *verb* **benefited, benefiting**

Benin (be nēn′) a country in western Africa, on the Atlantic Ocean.
Be·nin

bent (bent) *verb past tense and past participle of* **bend**.
adjective **1** curved and crooked [a *bent* pin for a fishhook.] **2** wanting very much; determined [She is *bent* on going to the circus.]

beret (bə rā′) *noun* a flat, round cap of wool, felt, or other soft material.
be·ret • *noun, plural* **berets**

Berlin (bər lin′) the capital of Germany.
Ber·lin

berry (ber′ē) *noun* a small, juicy fruit that has many seeds. Strawberries and blueberries are berries.
ber·ry • *noun, plural* **berries**
● The words **berry** and **bury** sound alike.
The holly bush has a red *berry*.
Pirates were known to *bury* treasure.

berth (burth) *noun* **1** a bed or bunk along a wall on a ship, aircraft, or train. **2** a place where a ship ties up to a dock.
berth • *noun, plural* **berths**
● The words **berth** and **birth** sound alike.
I paid for an upper *berth* on the train.
She gave *birth* to twins.

beside (bē sīd′) *preposition* **1** by the side of; close to [The garage is *beside* the house.] **2** compared with [My share seems small *beside* yours.]
be·side • *preposition*

besides (bē sīdz′) *adverb* in addition; as well [We'll have games and dancing *besides*.]
preposition in addition to; as well as [Will anyone be there *besides* you?]
be·sides • *adverb* • *preposition*

besiege (bē sēj′) *verb* to surround a place with troops in order to capture [The rebels *besieged* the fort for two weeks.]
be·siege • *verb* **besieged, besieging**

best (best) *adjective* **1** *superlative of* **good**. **2** better than all others; most excellent, most fit, or most desirable [the *best* player on the team; the *best* time to plant corn]. **3** being the most; almost all [the *best* part of an hour].
adverb • **1** *superlative of* **well**[2]. **2** in a way that is best or most excellent [Which team played *best?*] **3** more than any other; most [Of all your books, I like that one *best*.]
noun **1** a person or thing that is most excellent, most fit, or most suitable [When I buy shoes, I buy the *best*.] **2** the finest effort or appearance; the most that can be done [looking his *best*. We did our *best* to win.]
verb to defeat [We *bested* them at tennis.]
—at best as the most that can be expected; at most [With all their injuries, the team may win second place, *at best*.]
best • *adjective* • *adverb* • *noun*
• *verb* **bested, besting**

bestow (bē stō′) *verb* to give as a gift or an honor [The king *bestowed* gifts on the explorers.]
be·stow • *verb* **bestowed, bestowing**

bet (bet) *noun* **1** an agreement between two persons that the person who is wrong about something will pay or do something to the person who is right [She lost the *bet* and had to pay one dollar.] **2** the money to be paid or thing to be done [Her *bet* was one dollar.]
verb **1** to risk something in a bet [I'll *bet* one candy bar that I finish first.] **2** to say with certainty [I *bet* he doesn't go.]
bet • *noun, plural* **bets** • *verb* **bet** or **betted, betting**

betray (bē trā′) *verb* **1** to help the enemy of; be a traitor to [The spy *betrayed* his country by selling secrets to the enemy.] **2** to fail to keep a promise, secret, or agreement [My cousin *betrayed* my trust by telling my secret.]
be·tray • *verb* **betrayed, betraying**

better (bet′ər) *adjective* **1** *comparative of* **good**. **2** more excellent, more fit, or more desirable than another [Grace is a *better* player than Chris. I have a *better* idea.] **3** being more than half; greater [It takes the *better* part of a day to get there.] **4** not so sick; more healthy than before [She is *better* today.]

B

adverb **1** *comparative of* **well**[2]. **2** in a way that is better or more excellent [They will sing *better* with more practice.] **3** more [I like the orange drink *better* than the lime.]
noun a person or thing that is more excellent, more fit, or more suitable [Who is the *better* of these two players?]
verb **1** to make better; improve [*Better* your chances of winning by practicing more.] —Look for the WORD CHOICES box at the entry **improve**. **2** to do better than [The runner has *bettered* the record by two seconds.]
—**better off** in a better or improved condition [You would be *better off* if you studied more.]
—**had better** ought to; should [You *had better* mind your own business.]
bet·ter • *adjective* • *adverb* • *noun, plural* **betters** • *verb* **bettered, bettering**

between (bē twēn′) *preposition* **1** in the space that separates [a lake *between* the U.S. and Canada]. **2** in the time that separates [The doctor has office hours *between* one and five o'clock.] **3** in the amount that separates or in one of the steps that separate [a number *between* three and eight; a color *between* blue and green]. **4** having to do with; involving [the war *between* the North and the South]. **5** connecting [a road *between* Boston and New York]. **6** with a part for or from each of [We split the money *between* us.] **7** from one or the other of [You must choose *between* chocolate and caramels.]
—**between you and me** as a secret that you and I share. —**in between** in a middle position.
be·tween • *preposition*

beverage (bev′ər ij *or* bev′rij) *noun* any kind of liquid for drinking except water.
bev·er·age • *noun, plural* **beverages**

beware (bē wer′) *verb* to be careful [*Beware* of the dog.]
be·ware • *verb*

bewilder (bē wil′dər) *verb* to make confused; to puzzle [The winding streets *bewildered* me.]
be·wil·der • *verb* **bewildered, bewildering**

bewitch (bē wich′) *verb* **1** to use magic on; put a spell on [In the fairy tale, the sorcerer *bewitches* the prince and turns him into a toad.] **2** to charm and delight; fascinate.
be·witch • *verb* **bewitched, bewitching**

beyond (bē änd′) *preposition* **1** on the far side of [The town is just *beyond* the hill.] **2** later than [I stayed up *beyond* midnight.]
be·yond • *preposition*

Bhutan (bo͞o tän′) a country in the Himalayas, northeast of India.
Bhu·tan

bi- *a prefix meaning:* **1** having two [A *bicuspid* tooth has two points.] **2** happening every two [A *biennial* election takes place every two years.]

bias (bī′əs) *noun* **1** a slanting line that is cut or sewn across the weave of cloth. **2** a leaning in favor of or against something or someone; prejudice [a *bias* against foreigners].
verb to cause to have a bias in thinking; to influence [The jury was *biased* by news stories.] —Look for the WORD CHOICES box at the entry **sway**.
bi·as • *noun, plural* **biases** • *verb* **biased** or **biassed, biasing** or **biassing**

bib (bib) *noun* **1** a cloth that is tied around a child's neck and hangs down in front to protect clothing during meals. **2** the part of an apron or a pair of overalls that is above the waist.
bib • *noun, plural* **bibs**

bib

Bible (bī bəl) **1** the collection of writings that became the sacred book of the Christian religion; the Old Testament and New Testament. **2** the collection of writings that became the sacred book of the Jewish religion; the Old Testament.
Bi·ble

biblical or **Biblical** (bib′li kəl) *adjective* in or having to do with the Bible [*Biblical* language].
bib·li·cal or **Bib·li·cal** • *adjective*

bibliography (bib′lē äg′rə fē) *noun* a list of

a	cat	ō	go	ʉ	fur	ə =	a *in* ago
ā	ape	ô	law, for	ch	chin		e *in* agent
ä	cot, car	oo	look	sh	she		i *in* pencil
e	ten	o͞o	tool	th	thin		o *in* atom
ē	me	oi	oil	*th*	then		u *in* circus
i	fit	ou	out	zh	measure		
ī	ice	u	up	ŋ	ring		

books and other writings about a certain subject or by a certain author.
bib·li·og·ra·phy • *noun,* *plural* **bibliographies**

biceps (bī′seps) *noun* the large muscle in the front of the upper arm.
bi·ceps • *noun, plural* **biceps**

bicker (bik′ər) *verb* to have a small quarrel over an unimportant matter [Those two brothers are always *bickering* about something.] —Look for the WORD CHOICES box at the entry **quarrel**.
bick·er • *verb* **bickered, bickering**

bicuspid (bī kus′pəd) *noun* a tooth with two points on its top. An adult has eight bicuspids.
bi·cus·pid • *noun,* *plural* **bicuspids**

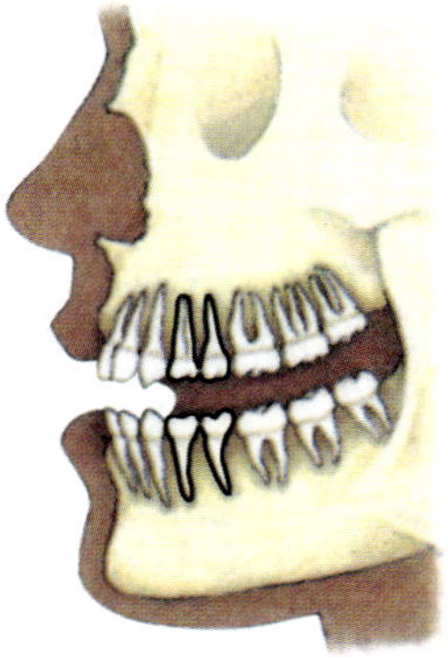
bicuspid

bicycle (bī′si kəl) *noun* a vehicle that has two wheels, one behind the other. It is moved by foot pedals and steered by a handlebar.
verb to ride a bicycle [I *bicycled* to the store.]
bi·cy·cle • *noun, plural* **bicycles** • *verb* **bicycled, bicycling**

bid (bid) *verb* **1** to command or ask [Do as you are *bidden*.] **2** to offer as the price of something [I *bid* $10 for a vase at the auction.]
noun **1** the act of offering an amount as the price of something [They are still making *bids* on the painting.] **2** the amount that is offered [My *bid* for the vase is $10.]
bid • *verb* **bade** or **bid** *(for sense 2)*, **bidden** or **bid** *(for sense 2)*, **bidding** • *noun,* *plural* **bids**

bidden (bid′n) *verb a past participle of* **bid**.
bid·den • *verb*

bifocals (bī′fō kəlz) *plural noun* eyeglasses in which each lens has two parts. One part is used for reading and seeing nearby objects. The other part is for seeing things that are far away.
bi·fo·cals • *plural noun*

big (big) *adjective* **1** of great size; large [a *big* cake; a *big* city] —Look for the WORD CHOICES box at the entry **large**. **2** great in force [a *big* wind]. **3** older [My *big* sister is 20 years old.] **4** important; outstanding [a *big* day in her life].
big • *adjective* **bigger, biggest**

bighorn (big′hôrn) *noun* a wild sheep with long, curved horns. Bighorns are found in western mountains of North America.
big·horn • *noun, plural* **bighorns** or **bighorn**

bike
A bicycle

bike (bīk) *noun* a bicycle or motorcycle.
verb to ride a bicycle or motorcycle [We *biked* down to the park.]
bike • *noun, plural* **bikes** • *verb* **biked, biking**

biker (bīk′ər) *noun* a person who rides a bicycle or motorcycle.
bik·er • *noun, plural* **bikers**

bikini (bi kē′nē) *noun* a very small two-piece bathing suit for women.
bi·ki·ni • *noun, plural* **bikinis**

bile (bīl) *noun* the bitter, yellowish or greenish fluid that the liver produces. It helps in digestion and is stored in the gallbladder.

bilingual (bī liŋ′gwəl) *adjective* using or able to use two languages [a *bilingual* secretary].
bi·lin·gual • *adjective*

bill[1] (bil) *noun* **1** a listing of the money that a person owes for goods or services [a grocery *bill*]. **2** a piece of paper money [a dollar *bill*]. **3** a proposed law that a group of lawmakers is to vote on [A *bill* to provide health insurance is before Congress.]
verb to send a bill to [That store *bills* us on the first of the month.]
bill • *noun, plural* **bills** • *verb* **billed, billing**

bill[2] (bil) *noun* the hard, pointed jaws of a bird; beak.
bill • *noun, plural* **bills**

B

billboard

billboard (bil′bôrd) *noun* a large outdoor board, on which advertisements are posted.
bill·board • *noun, plural* **billboards**

billfold (bil′fōld) *noun* a thin, flat case for carrying paper money in the pocket; wallet.
bill·fold • *noun, plural* **billfolds**

billiards (bil′yərdz) *noun* a game played with three hard balls that are hit with a long stick across a special table that has a felt surface and cushioned edges.
bil·liards • *noun*

billion (bil′yən) *noun* a thousand millions (1,000,000,000).
adjective adding up to one billion.
bil·lion • *noun, plural* **billions** • *adjective*

billionaire (bil yə ner′) *noun* a person who has at least a billion dollars.
bil·lion·aire • *noun, plural* **billionaires**

billow (bil′ō) *noun* **1** a large wave on the ocean or another body of water. **2** anything that sweeps along and swells like a wave [Great *billows* of smoke rose from the chimney.]
verb to swell out in billows.
bil·low • *noun, plural* **billows**
• *verb* **billowed, billowing**

bin (bin) *noun* a box for storing things. Coal, flour, and tools can be stored in bins.
bin • *noun, plural* **bins**
● The words **bin** and **been** sound alike.
Grain can be stored in the *bin*.
How have you *been?*

binary system (bī′nər ē) *noun* a system of numbers in which each number is shown by using only the digits 0 and 1. The binary system is used in computers.
bi·na·ry system • *noun*

bind (bīnd) *verb* **1** to tie together with rope or something similar; tie tightly [*Bind* logs together to make a raft.] **2** to force to do something because of a promise or law [The witness is *bound* by an oath to tell the truth.] **3** to put a bandage on [The nurse will *bind* up your wounds.]
bind • *verb* **bound, binding**

WORD CHOICES

Synonyms of **bind**

The words **bind, fasten,** and **tie** share the meaning "to join one thing to another."

The pirates *bound* his legs together.

He *fastened* the poster to the wall.

Tie the boat to the dock.

bingo (biŋ′gō) *noun* a game that is played with cards having rows of numbered squares. No two cards are numbered alike. Someone draws numbers from a box and calls them out. Players cover the squares that have these numbers. The first player to cover a row of squares wins.
bin·go • *noun*

binoculars (bī näk′yə lərz) *plural noun* a pair of small telescopes that are fastened together for use with both eyes.
bin·oc·u·lars • *plural noun*

bio- *a prefix meaning:* **1** life or living [A *biography* tells the story of a person's life.] **2** having to do with living things [*Biochemistry* is the science that studies the chemical processes in living things.]

biodegradable (bī′ō dē grā′də bəl) *adjective* capable of easily breaking down into its basic parts when bacteria act on it [a *biodegradable* detergent].
bi·o·de·grad·a·ble • *adjective*

biography (bī äg′rə fē) *noun* the story of a person's life, written by another person.
bi·og·ra·phy • *noun, plural* **biographies**

biological (bī′ə läj′i kəl) *adjective* having to do with biology.
bi·o·log·i·cal • *adjective*

a cat	ō go	ʉ fur	ə = a *in* ago
ā ape	ô law, for	ch chin	e *in* agent
ä cot, car	oo look	sh she	i *in* pencil
e ten	ōō tool	th thin	o *in* atom
ē me	oi oil	*th* then	u *in* circus
i fit	ou out	zh measure	
ī ice	u up	ŋ ring	

biology (bī äl′ə jē) *noun* the science that studies living things; the study of plants and animals and the way they live and grow.
bi·ol·o·gy • *noun*

biomass (bī′ō mas) *noun* all the living things in a particular area, thought of as a group or mass.
bi·o·mass • *noun*

bionic (bī än′ik) *adjective* **1** of or having to do with an artificial replacement for a part of the body. **2** having a part or parts like this so that strength and ability are much greater [a *bionic* man]. This extra strength and ability is only an imaginary power in science-fiction stories.
bi·on·ic • *adjective*

birch (burch) *noun* **1** a tree that has a thin, smooth bark that is easily peeled off in thin strips from the trunk. **2** the hard wood of this tree. It is used for making furniture.
birch • *noun, plural* **birches**

bird (burd) *noun* a warmblooded animal that has a backbone, two feet, and two wings and is covered with feathers. Birds lay eggs, and most birds can fly.
bird • *noun, plural* **birds**

bird of prey *noun* a bird that kills other animals for food [The eagle is a *bird of prey*.]
bird of prey • *noun, plural* **birds of prey**

Birmingham (bur′miŋ ham) a city in north central Alabama.
Bir·ming·ham

birth (burth) *noun* **1** the act of coming into life or being born [the *birth* of twins]. **2** the beginning of something new [The year 1957 marks the *birth* of the Space Age.]
—give birth to to bring into being [The cow *gave birth to* a calf. The invention of the automobile *gave birth to* a new way of life.]
birth • *noun, plural* **births**

● The words **birth** and **berth** sound alike.
She gave *birth* to twins.
I paid for an upper *berth* on the train.

birthday (burth′dā) *noun* **1** the day on which a person is born or something begins. **2** the anniversary of this day.
birth·day • *noun, plural* **birthdays**

birthmark (burth′märk) *noun* a mark or spot on a person's skin that is present at birth.
birth·mark • *noun, plural* **birthmarks**

birthplace (burth′plās) *noun* the place where a person was born or where something began.
birth·place • *noun, plural* **birthplaces**

biscuit (bis′kit) *noun* a small bread roll that is made of dough that contains baking powder.
bis·cuit • *noun, plural* **biscuits**

bisect (bī sekt′ *or* bī′sekt) *verb* **1** to cut into two parts [Our city is *bisected* by a busy freeway.] **2** to divide into two equal parts [A diameter *bisects* a circle.]
bi·sect • *verb* **bisected, bisecting**

bishop (bish′əp) *noun* **1** a minister or priest of high rank who is the head of a church district. **2** a chess piece that can move in a diagonal, or slanting, path.
bish·op • *noun, plural* **bishops**

Bismarck (biz′märk) the capital of North Dakota.
Bis·marck

bison

bison (bī′sən) *noun* a wild animal that is related to the ox. It has a shaggy mane, short, curved horns, and a humped back. The American bison is often called a *buffalo*.
bi·son • *noun, plural* **bison**

bit[1] (bit) *noun* **1** the metal piece of a bridle that fits into the horse's mouth. **2** the cutting part of a tool for drilling or boring.
bit • *noun, plural* **bits**

bit[2] (bit) *noun* **1** a small piece or amount [She tore the note to *bits*.] **2** a short time; moment [Wait a *bit*.]
—a bit a little; slightly [I'm *a bit* bored with that TV show.] **—bit by bit** a little at a time; in a gradual way.
bit • *noun, plural* **bits**

bit[3] (bit) *verb* **1** *past tense of* **bite**. **2** *a past participle of* **bite**.

bit[4] (bit) *noun* the smallest piece of information in a computer.
bit • *noun, plural* **bits**

B

bite (bīt) ***verb*** **1** to seize, snap at, or cut with the teeth or with parts like jaws [The dog *bit* the mail carrier's leg. The trap *bit* into the rabbit's foot.] **2** to sting, in the way that a mosquito or bee does. **3** to be tricked into swallowing bait [The fish aren't *biting* today.]
noun **1** the act of biting [A dog's *bite* can be dangerous.] **2** a wound or sting from biting [a mosquito *bite*]. **3** a mouthful [Don't take such big *bites*.] **4** a light meal or snack.
bite • ***verb*** **bit, bitten** or **bit, biting** • ***noun,*** *plural* **bites**

- The words **bite** and **byte** sound alike.
  Does your dog *bite?*
  One computer *byte* equals eight bits.

bitten (bit′n) ***verb*** *a past participle of* **bite**.
bit·ten • ***verb***

bitter (bit′ər) ***adjective*** **1** having a strong, often unpleasant taste [The seed in a peach pit is *bitter*.] **2** full of sorrow or pain [Poor people often suffer *bitter* hardships.] **3** with strong feelings of hatred [*bitter* enemies].
bit·ter • ***adjective***

bivalve (bī′valv) ***noun*** a shellfish whose soft body is inside a shell that is made up of two parts that are hinged together. Clams and oysters are bivalves.
bi·valve • ***noun,*** *plural* **bivalves**

bizarre (bi zär′) ***adjective*** **1** very odd; looking very strange [a *bizarre* expression on the clown's face]. **2** fantastic; not able to be believed [a *bizarre* story about spaceships].
bi·zarre • ***adjective***

black (blak) ***adjective*** **1** opposite of white; of the color of coal or pitch. **2** without any light [a *black* night without a moon]. **3** very dark. **4** having to do with or belonging to a large group of people in Africa or from Africa. Its members generally have dark skin and black hair. **5** by, for, or about black people [We read some *black* literature in school this year.] **6** without milk or cream, and sometimes without sugar [*black* coffee]. **7** sad or gloomy [*black* thoughts].
noun **1** the color black. **2** *sometimes* **Black** a black person.
—black out **1** to put out all lights. **2** to lose consciousness.
black • ***adjective*** **blacker, blackest** • ***noun,*** *plural* **blacks**

black belt ***noun*** **1** a black-colored belt that a person earns by reaching the highest level of skill in judo or karate. **2** a person who has earned a black belt.
black belt • ***noun,*** *plural* **black belts**

blackberry (blak′ber′ē) ***noun*** **1** the small, black or dark-purple fruit of a prickly bush or vine. **2** this bush or vine.
black·ber·ry • ***noun,*** *plural* **blackberries**

blackbird (blak′burd) ***noun*** one of several kinds of bird whose males have black feathers.
black·bird • ***noun,*** *plural* **blackbirds**

blackboard (blak′bôrd) ***noun*** a chalkboard. Many blackboards are made of black slate.
black·board • ***noun,*** *plural* **blackboards**

blacken (blak′ən) ***verb*** to make or become black or dark; darken [Rain clouds *blackened* the sky. The sky *blackened* as the storm came closer.]
black·en • ***verb*** **blackened, blackening**

black eye ***noun*** a bruise on the skin around or near the eye.
black eye • ***noun,*** *plural* **black eyes**

Blackfoot (blak′foot) ***noun*** **1** a member of a North American Indian people living in Montana in the U.S. and in Saskatchewan and Alberta in Canada. **2** their language.
Black·foot • ***noun,*** *plural* **Black·feet** (blak′fēt) or **Blackfoot**

black hole ***noun*** an object that scientists believe exists in space. It is formed when a star collapses from its own gravity. Nothing, not even light, can escape from it.
black hole • ***noun,*** *plural* **black holes**

blackmail (blak′māl) ***noun*** **1** the crime of threatening to tell something harmful about someone unless the person pays some money. **2** money that is obtained in this way.
verb to get or try to get money in this way.
black·mail • ***noun*** • ***verb*** **blackmailed, blackmailing**

blackout (blak′out) ***noun*** **1** the act of turning off or hiding all lights that an enemy might see at night. **2** a loss of electric power for a time in an area [The storm caused a *blackout*

a	cat	ō	go	ʉ	fur	ə = a *in* ago		
ā	ape	ô	law, for	ch	chin	e *in* agent		
ä	cot, car	oo	look	sh	she	i *in* pencil		
e	ten	ōō	tool	th	thin	o *in* atom		
ē	me	oi	oil	*th*	then	u *in* circus		
i	fit	ou	out	zh	measure			
ī	ice	u	up	ŋ	ring			

in our neighborhood.] **3** the condition of being unconscious or not remembering for a time.
black·out • ***noun,*** *plural* **blackouts**

Black Sea a sea between southeastern Europe and Asia, north of Turkey.

blacksmith (blak′smith) ***noun*** a person who makes or fixes iron objects by heating them and then hammering them on an anvil. A blacksmith often makes and fits horseshoes.
black·smith • ***noun,*** *plural* **blacksmiths**

WORD HISTORY

blacksmith

The *black* in **blacksmith** comes from *black metal*, an old way of saying "iron." A *smith* is a person who works with metal.

blacktop (blak′täp) ***noun*** an asphalt mixture for paving roads.
verb to cover with blacktop.
black·top • ***noun*** • ***verb*** **blacktopped, blacktopping**

black widow ***noun*** a black spider that has red marks on its underside. The female has a poisonous bite and often eats its mate.
black widow • ***noun,*** *plural* **black widows**

bladder (blad′ər) ***noun*** **1** an organ inside the body that is like a bag and collects the urine coming from the kidneys. **2** any other similar organ [the *gallbladder*].
blad·der • ***noun,*** *plural* **bladders**

blade (blād) ***noun*** **1** the sharp, cutting part of a knife, sword, or saw. **2** a broad, flat part of something [the *blade* of an oar]. **3** the runner of an ice skate. **4** the leaf of a grass plant.
blade • ***noun,*** *plural* **blades**

blame (blām) ***verb*** **1** to say or think that someone or something is the cause of something wrong or bad [Don't *blame* others for your own mistakes.] **2** to find fault with; criticize [I can't *blame* you for being angry.] —Look for the WORD CHOICES box at the entry **criticize**.
noun the fact of being the cause of what is wrong or bad [I will take the *blame* for the broken window.]
blame • ***verb*** **blamed, blaming** • ***noun***

bland (bland) ***adjective*** mild and plain in flavor [Cottage cheese is a *bland* food.]
bland • ***adjective*** **blander, blandest**

blank (blaŋk) ***adjective*** **1** not marked or written on [a *blank* sheet of paper]. **2** showing no expression or interest [a *blank* look on my face]. **3** empty of thoughts [a *blank* mind].
noun **1** a printed piece of paper with empty spaces for a person to write in [Fill out the application *blank*.] **2** an empty space on a paper like this [Fill in all the *blanks*.] **3** a gun cartridge that has powder but no bullet. It is fired only to make a noise.
blank • ***adjective*** **blanker, blankest** • ***noun,*** *plural* **blanks**

blanket (blaŋk′it) ***noun*** **1** a large, soft piece of thick cloth that is used as a covering for warmth. **2** any covering that is spread out [a *blanket* of snow].
verb to cover with a blanket [Brown leaves *blanketed* the lawn.]
blan·ket • ***noun,*** *plural* **blankets** • ***verb*** **blanketed, blanketing**

blare (bler) ***verb*** to sound out with loud, harsh tones [Car horns *blared* in the traffic jam.]
blare • ***verb*** **blared, blaring**

blast (blast) ***noun*** **1** a strong rush of air or gust of wind. **2** the sound of a rush of air through an instrument or whistle [a trumpet *blast*]. **3** an explosion [a dynamite *blast*].
verb to blow up with an explosive [They're *blasting* rock to make a road.]
—**blast off** to take off with an explosion and begin its flight [The rocket *blasted off*.]
blast • ***noun,*** *plural* **blasts** • ***verb*** **blasted, blasting**

blastoff

blastoff (blast′ôf) ***noun*** the launching of a rocket, missile, or spacecraft.

blast·off • *noun, plural* **blastoffs**

blaze[1] (blāz) ***noun*** **1** a bright flame or fire. **2** a very bright light [The *blaze* of TV lights nearly blinded him.] **3** a bright display [The garden was a *blaze* of color.]
verb to burn or shine brightly.
blaze • *noun, plural* **blazes** • *verb* **blazed, blazing**

WORD CHOICES

Synonyms of **blaze**

The words **blaze, flash,** and **glare** share the meaning "a bright light."

the *blaze* of the sun at noon

a *flash* of lightning

the *glare* of the headlights

blaze[2] (blāz) ***noun*** **1** a white spot on an animal's face. **2** a mark on a tree that is made by cutting off a piece of bark.
verb to mark with blazes [*Blaze* a trail by marking trees as you go along.]
blaze • *noun, plural* **blazes** • *verb* **blazed, blazing**

blazer (blā′zər) ***noun*** a lightweight sports jacket in a solid, often bright color or with stripes. Blazers often have metal buttons.
blaz·er • *noun, plural* **blazers**

bldg. *abbreviation for* building.

bleach (blēch) ***verb*** to make white or pale by the use of chemicals or by putting out in sunlight.
noun a chemical or a mixture of substances that is used for bleaching something.
bleach • *verb* **bleached, bleaching** • *noun, plural* **bleaches**

bleachers (blēch′ərz) ***plural noun*** **1** a section of seats that are benches set in rows, one above another, without a roof, for watching outdoor sports. **2** benches in rows like this in a gymnasium or other indoor arena.
bleach·ers • *plural noun*

bleak (blēk) ***adjective*** not cheerful; dark or gloomy [The castle's rooms were *bleak* and empty.]
bleak • *adjective* **bleaker, bleakest**

bleat (blēt) ***verb*** to make the sound of a sheep, goat, or calf.
noun this sound.
bleat • *verb* **bleated, bleating** • *noun, plural* **bleats**

bled (bled) ***verb*** *past tense and past participle of* **bleed**.

bleed (blēd) ***verb*** **1** to give off or lose blood [My cut finger *bled* for a long time. The man was *bleeding* from his nose.] **2** to feel pain, grief, or sympathy [My heart *bleeds* for the widow.]
bleed • *verb* **bled, bleeding**

blemish (blem′ish) ***noun*** **1** a mark or scar that spoils or damages; a spot [*blemishes* on the skin]. **2** a flaw or weakness [That mistake is the only *blemish* in her record.] —Look for the WORD CHOICES box at the entry **defect**.
verb to make a blemish on or in.
blem·ish • *noun, plural* **blemishes** • *verb* **blemished, blemishing**

blend (blend) ***verb*** **1** to mix different kinds together in order to get a certain color or flavor [The artist *blended* her paints.] **2** to come together or mix so that the separate parts cannot be seen [Sky *blended* with sea at the horizon.] **3** to go well together [His blue sweater *blends* well with his gray pants.]
noun a mixture [a *blend* of coffee].
blend • *verb* **blended, blending** • *noun, plural* **blends**

blended family ***noun*** a family made up of two parents who once were married to other people and all the children from the parents' earlier marriages.
blended family • *noun, plural* **blended families**

blender (blen′dər) ***noun*** an electrical appliance that can mix, chop, or whip foods or turn them to liquid.
blend·er • *noun, plural* **blenders**

bless (bles) ***verb*** **1** to make holy [Please *bless* this food that we are about to eat.] **2** to ask God's good will and care for [The rabbi *blessed* the congregation.] **3** to bring happiness or good fortune to [God *bless* you!]
bless • *verb* **blessed** (blest) or **blest, blessing**

blessing (bles′iŋ) ***noun*** **1** a prayer that asks God's good will and care for someone or something. **2** good wishes or approval [The parents

a cat	ō go	ʉ fur	ə = a *in* ago
ā ape	ô law, for	ch chin	e *in* agent
ä cot, car	oo look	sh she	i *in* pencil
e ten	ōō tool	th thin	o *in* atom
ē me	oi oil	*th* then	u *in* circus
i fit	ou out	zh measure	
ī ice	u up	ŋ ring	

gave the engaged couple their *blessing*.] **3** anything that brings joy or comfort [Rain would be a *blessing* in this dry summer.]
bless·ing • *noun, plural* **blessings**

blest (blest) ***verb*** *a past tense and past participle of* **bless**.

blew (blo͞o) ***verb*** *past tense of* **blow**[1].
• The words **blew** and **blue** sound alike.
She *blew* the trumpet loudly.
The U.S. flag is red, white, and *blue*.

blight (blīt) ***noun*** **1** one of a number of diseases that hurt or kill plants. **2** something that hurts or destroys [The garbage dump was a *blight* on the city.]
blight • *noun, plural* **blights**

blimp (blimp) [*an informal word*] ***noun*** an airship shaped somewhat like an egg.
blimp • *noun, plural* **blimps**

blind (blīnd) ***adjective*** **1** not able to see; having no sight. **2** not able to notice, understand, or judge [Her parents were *blind* to her faults.] **3** closed at one end [a *blind* alley].
verb **1** to make blind; make unable to see [The TV lights *blinded* her for a moment.] **2** to make unable to understand or judge well [Love *blinded* him to her faults.]
noun a window shade that is made of stiffened cloth, metal slats, or another material.
blind • ***adjective*** • ***verb*** **blinded, blinding** • *noun, plural* **blinds**

blindfold (blīnd′fōld) ***verb*** to cover the eyes of with a cloth tied around the head.
noun a thing that is used to cover the eyes.
blind·fold • ***verb*** **blindfolded, blindfolding** • *noun, plural* **blindfolds**

blindman's buff or **blindman's bluff** (blīnd′manz buf *or* blīnd′manz bluf) ***noun*** a game in which a blindfolded player has to catch another player and then tell who it is.
blind·man's buff or **blindman's bluff** • ***noun***

blindness (blīnd′nis) ***noun*** the condition of being blind.
blind·ness • ***noun***

blink (bliŋk) ***verb*** **1** to keep closing and opening the eyes rapidly. **2** to flash off and on [The yellow light at the corner *blinked* all day.]
noun a brief flash of light.
—on the blink [*a slang use*] not working right.
blink • ***verb*** **blinked, blinking** • *noun, plural* **blinks**

blinker (bliŋ′kər) ***noun*** **1** a flashing signal that warns. **2 blinkers** two leather flaps on a bridle that keep a horse from seeing to the sides.
blink·er • *noun, plural* **blinkers**

bliss (blis) ***noun*** great joy or happiness.

blister (blis′tər) ***noun*** **1** a small, swollen place on the skin that is filled with a watery substance. It can be caused by a burn or by rubbing. **2** a part that swells like a blister [There are *blisters* on the new coat of paint.]
verb **1** to make blisters on [The sun *blistered* my nose.] **2** to form blisters.
blis·ter • *noun, plural* **blisters** • ***verb*** **blistered, blistering**

blizzard (bliz′ərd) ***noun*** a heavy snowstorm with very strong, cold winds.
bliz·zard • *noun, plural* **blizzards**

bloat (blōt) ***verb*** to puff up in the way that something swells when it is full of air or water.
bloat • ***verb*** **bloated, bloating**

blob (bläb) ***noun*** a small lump of something that is soft and wet [a *blob* of jelly on my toast].
blob • *noun, plural* **blobs**

block (bläk) ***noun*** **1** a thick piece of wood, stone, metal, or other material that usually has flat sides. **2** a wooden or plastic toy brick or cube. **3** something that prevents movement or progress [Lazy habits are a *block* to success.] **4** a number of things that are thought of as a single unit [We have a *block* of seats in the auditorium.] **5** the square or rectangle that is formed by four streets [The city hall takes up the whole *block*.] **6** the area along one of these streets [They live on our *block*.] **7** a pulley in a frame. **8** in sports, a stopping of an opponent's play or movement.
verb **1** to stop movement or progress; stand in the way of —Look for the WORD CHOICES box at the entry **hinder**. **2** in sports, to stop an opponent or a play.
block • *noun, plural* **blocks** • ***verb*** **blocked, blocking**

block

B

blockade (blä kād′) *noun* a situation in which enemy troops or warships shut off a port or other place. This is done to keep people and supplies from moving in or out.
verb to put under a blockade.
block·ade • *noun, plural* **blockades**
• *verb* **blockaded, blockading**

blond (bländ) *adjective* **1** having light-colored or yellow hair. **2** light-colored [*blond* hair].
noun a blond person.
blond • *adjective* **blonder, blondest** • *noun, plural* **blonds**

blonde (bländ) *adjective another spelling of* **blond**.
noun a blond woman or girl.
blonde • *adjective* **blonder, blondest**
• *noun, plural* **blondes**

blood (blud) *noun* **1** the red liquid that the heart pumps through the arteries and veins. The blood carries oxygen and material for building cells to the body's tissues. It carries away carbon dioxide and waste material. **2** family line or ancestors [They are of the same *blood*.]

blood bank *noun* a place where blood is stored, separated according to its type. The blood can then be used to replace a person's blood during an operation or after an accident.
blood bank • *noun, plural* **blood banks**

bloodhound (blud′hound) *noun* a large dog that has a wrinkled face and long, drooping ears. Bloodhounds have a keen sense of smell.
blood·hound • *noun, plural* **bloodhounds**

blood pressure *noun* the pressure of the blood against the walls of the arteries and other blood vessels.

bloodshed (blud′shed) *noun* the act of shedding blood; killing [War brings much *bloodshed*.]
blood·shed • *noun*

bloodshot (blud′shät) *adjective* red because the small blood vessels are swollen or broken [*bloodshot* eyes from too little sleep].
blood·shot • *adjective*

blood vessel *noun* one of the many tubes in the body that carry the blood; an artery, vein, or capillary.
blood vessel • *noun, plural* **blood vessels**

bloody (blud′ē) *adjective* **1** full of or covered with blood [He had a *bloody* nose.] **2** with much killing or wounding [a *bloody* battle].
verb to cover with blood.
blood·y • *adjective* **bloodier, bloodiest**
• *verb* **bloodied, bloodying, bloodies**

bloom (bloom) *noun* **1** a flower or blossom. **2** the time or condition of bearing blossoms [The lilies are in *bloom*.]
verb to bear blossoms [Tulips *bloom* in the spring.]
bloom • *noun, plural* **blooms**
• *verb* **bloomed, blooming**

blooper (bloop′ər) *noun* [*a slang word*] **1** a foolish or stupid mistake. **2** in baseball, a softly hit ball that falls just beyond the infield.
bloop·er • *noun, plural* **bloopers**

blossom (bläs′əm) *noun* **1** a flower, especially of a plant that bears fruit. **2** the time or condition of flowering [The pear trees are in *blossom*.]
verb **1** to bear blossoms; to bloom. **2** to unfold or develop [Her musical talent has *blossomed*.]
blos·som • *noun, plural* **blossoms**
• *verb* **blossomed, blossoming**

blot (blät) *noun* **1** a spot or stain of ink or some other liquid. **2** something that spoils or damages [The shack was a *blot* on the landscape.]
verb **1** to spot or stain [The pen leaked and *blotted* his shirt.] **2** to dry by soaking up the wet liquid [You can *blot* ink with paper.]
blot • *noun, plural* **blots** • *verb* **blotted, blotting**

blotch (bläch) *noun* a large spot or stain.
verb to mark with blotches.
blotch • *noun, plural* **blotches**
• *verb* **blotched, blotching**

blotter (blät′ər) *noun* a piece of thick, soft paper for blotting extra ink from something that has just been written.
blot·ter • *noun, plural* **blotters**

blouse (blous) *noun* a loose piece of clothing that is like a shirt and is worn by women and girls.
blouse • *noun, plural* **blouses**

blow[1] (blō) *verb* **1** to move with some force [There is a wind *blowing* today.] **2** to force air

a	cat	ō	go	ʉ	fur	ə =	a *in* ago
ā	ape	ô	law, for	ch	chin		e *in* agent
ä	cot, car	oo	look	sh	she		i *in* pencil
e	ten	ōō	tool	th	thin		o *in* atom
ē	me	oi	oil	*th*	then		u *in* circus
i	fit	ou	out	zh	measure		
ī	ice	u	up	ŋ	ring		

out through the mouth [*Blow* on your hands to warm them.] **3** to make sound by blowing or being blown [The noon whistle is *blowing*. *Blow* your trumpet.] **4** to force air through in order to clear [Please *blow* your nose more quietly.] **5** to be carried by the wind [The paper *blew* away.] **6** to drive by blowing [The fan *blew* the paper out the window.] **7** to form or cause to swell by blowing in air or gas [The children are *blowing* bubbles.] **8** to burst suddenly [My tire *blew* on the highway.] **9** to melt [The overloaded circuit *blew* a fuse.]
—**blow out** to put out by blowing [*Blow out* all the candles on your cake.] —**blow up** **1** to fill with air or gas [We *blew up* balloons for the party.] **2** to burst or explode [They *blew up* the building with dynamite.] **3** [*an informal use*] to get very angry.
blow • *verb* **blew, blown, blowing**

blow[2] (blō) *noun* **1** a hard hit. **2** a sudden misfortune [His death was a great *blow* to us.]
blow • *noun, plural* **blows**

blow-dry (blō′drī) *verb* to dry with a blow-dryer.
blow-dry • *verb* **blow-dried, blow-drying, blow-dries**

blow-dryer (blō′drī ər) *noun* an electric device for drying hair. It is held in the hand and sends out a strong stream of heated air.
blow-dry·er • *noun, plural* **blow-dryers**

blown (blōn) *verb past participle of* **blow**[1].

blowout (blō′out) *noun* the bursting of a tire.
blow·out • *noun, plural* **blowouts**

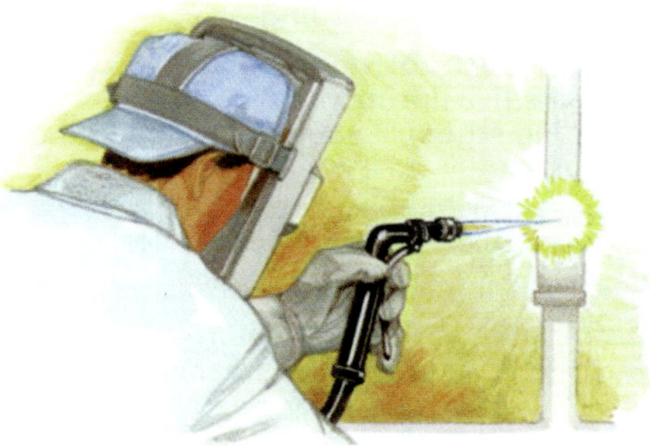

blowtorch

blowtorch (blō′tôrch) *noun* a small device that shoots out a hot flame. It is used to melt metal or burn off old paint.
blow·torch • *noun, plural* **blowtorches**

blubber (blub′ər) *noun* the fat of whales and other sea mammals. It can be processed to produce a certain type of oil.
blub·ber • *noun*

blue (blo͞o) *adjective* **1** having the color of the clear sky or the deep sea. **2** sad or gloomy [I've been feeling *blue* since my dog died.]
noun the color of the clear sky or the deep sea.
—**out of the blue** suddenly and without being expected. —**the blues** **1** [*an informal use*] a sad, gloomy feeling; low spirits. **2** a type of folk song that has a slow tempo and sad words.
blue • *adjective* **bluer, bluest** • *noun, plural* **blues**

• The words **blue** and **blew** sound alike.
The U.S. flag is red, white, and *blue*.
She *blew* the trumpet loudly.

blueberry (blo͞o′ber′ē) *noun* **1** a small, round, dark-blue berry that can be eaten. **2** the shrub on which it grows.
blue·ber·ry • *noun, plural* **blueberries**

blueberry

bluebird (blo͞o′burd) *noun* a songbird of North America that has a blue back and blue wings.
blue·bird • *noun, plural* **bluebirds**

bluegrass (blo͞o′gras) *noun* a kind of grass that has bluish-green stems.
blue·grass • *noun, plural* **bluegrasses**

blue jay

blue jay *noun* a bird that has a blue back and a crest of feathers on its head.
blue jay • *noun, plural* **blue jays**

bluejeans (blo͞o′jēnz) ***plural noun*** pants made of blue denim.
blue·jeans • ***plural noun***

blueprint (blo͞o′print) ***noun*** **1** a photograph that is a copy of the plans for a building, bridge, or other structure. It has white lines and white print on a blue background. **2** a plan for something that has many details.
blue·print • ***noun,*** *plural* **blueprints**

bluff[1] (bluf) ***verb*** to fool or try to fool a person by acting very sure of oneself.
noun the act or an example of bluffing.
bluff • ***verb*** **bluffed, bluffing** • ***noun,*** *plural* **bluffs**

bluff[2] (bluf) ***noun*** a high, steep cliff or bank.
bluff • ***noun,*** *plural* **bluffs**

bluish (blo͞o′ish) ***adjective*** somewhat blue.
blu·ish • ***adjective***

blunder (blun′dər) ***noun*** a foolish or stupid mistake —Look for the WORD CHOICES box at the entry **error**.
verb to make a foolish or stupid mistake.
blun·der • ***noun,*** *plural* **blunders** • ***verb*** **blundered, blundering**

blunt (blunt) ***adjective*** **1** having a dull edge or point; not sharp [a *blunt* ax or knife]. **2** speaking in a plain and honest way, without trying to be polite [His *blunt* reply was, "I don't like you."]
verb to make dull [Much use had *blunted* the knife.]
blunt • ***adjective*** **blunter, bluntest** • ***verb*** **blunted, blunting**

blur (blʉr) ***verb*** **1** to make or become less clear and sharp [Bad photography *blurred* the face in the picture.] **2** to smear or smudge [Greasy fingerprints *blurred* the car window.]
noun **1** the condition of being blurred or not clear [The events happened in a *blur.*] **2** something that is not clear to the eyes or the mind [The countryside was only a *blur* to the passengers of the high-speed train.]
blur • ***verb*** **blurred, blurring** • ***noun,*** *plural* **blurs**

blush (blush) ***verb*** to become red in the face because of shyness, shame, or confusion [He *blushed* at the compliment.]
noun **1** redness in the face because of shyness, shame, or confusion. **2** a pink color.
blush • ***verb*** **blushed, blushing** • ***noun,*** *plural* **blushes**

bluster (blus′tər) ***verb*** **1** to blow in a stormy way [Winds *blustered* over the sea.] **2** to speak or act in a noisy or boasting way.
noun **1** stormy noise. **2** noisy or boasting talk.
blus·ter • ***verb*** **blustered, blustering** • ***noun,*** *plural* **blusters**

Blvd. *abbreviation for* Boulevard.

boa (bō′ə) ***noun*** one of several very large snakes that live in the tropics. The boa winds itself around its prey and crushes it to death.
bo·a • ***noun,*** *plural* **boas**

boar (bôr) ***noun*** **1** a male pig. **2** a wild pig of Europe, Africa, and Asia.
boar • ***noun,*** *plural* **boars** or **boar**
• The words **boar** and **bore** sound alike.
They hunted the *boar* with spears.
Miners will *bore* through the rock wall.
The waves *bore* us up.

board (bôrd) ***noun*** **1** a long, flat, broad piece of sawed wood. Boards are used in building. **2** a flat piece of wood or other hard material that is made for a special use [a bulletin *board;* an ironing *board;* a *checkerboard*]. **3** the meals that a person can pay for to eat each day, usually in another person's home. **4** a group of people who manage or control a business, school, or other organization [the *board* of education].
verb **1** to cover up with boards [The windows of the old house were *boarded* up by its owners.] **2** to give or get meals, or a room and meals, in a regular way by paying. **3** to get on a ship, airplane, or train.
—on board on a ship, airplane, or train.
board • ***noun,*** *plural* **boards** • ***verb*** **boarded, boarding**

boarding school ***noun*** a school where the students live during the school year.
boarding school • ***noun,*** *plural* **boarding schools**

boardsailing (bôrd′sāl iŋ) ***noun*** *the same as* **windsurfing.**
board·sail·ing • ***noun***

boardwalk (bôrd′wôk) ***noun*** a sidewalk or path, often along a beach, that is made of thick boards.
board·walk • ***noun,*** *plural* **boardwalks**

a	cat	ō	go	ʉ	fur	ə =	a *in* ago
ā	ape	ô	law, for	ch	chin		e *in* agent
ä	cot, car	oo	look	sh	she		i *in* pencil
e	ten	o͞o	tool	th	thin		o *in* atom
ē	me	oi	oil	*th*	then		u *in* circus
i	fit	ou	out	zh	measure		
ī	ice	u	up	ŋ	ring		

boast (bōst) ***verb*** **1** to talk about with too much pride and pleasure; brag [They *boasted* about their team's success.] —Look for the WORD CHOICES box at the entry **brag**. **2** to be proud of having [Our city *boasts* a fine new zoo.]
noun the act of boasting or bragging.
boast • ***verb*** **boasted, boasting** • ***noun,*** *plural* **boasts**

boat (bōt) ***noun*** **1** a small, open structure that is used for traveling on water. It can be moved by oars, by wind on its sails, or by a motor. **2** a ship of any size: this sense of the word is used by many people, but not by sailors. **3** a dish that is shaped like a boat [a gravy *boat*].
verb to row or sail in a boat; go in a boat [We went *boating* on the river.]
boat • ***noun,*** *plural* **boats** • ***verb*** **boated, boating**

bob[1] (bäb) ***verb*** to move with short, jerky motions [Our heads *bobbed* up and down in the boat.]
noun a short, jerky movement.
bob • ***verb*** **bobbed, bobbing** • ***noun,*** *plural* **bobs**

bob[2] (bäb) ***noun*** **1** a style of short haircut for women or children. **2** a float or cork on a fishing line.
verb to cut off short [She had her hair *bobbed*.]
bob • ***noun,*** *plural* **bobs** • ***verb*** **bobbed, bobbing**

bobbin (bäb′ən) ***noun*** a kind of spool around which thread or yarn is wound. Some kinds of bobbin are used in sewing machines. Other kinds are used for making lace.
bob·bin • ***noun,*** *plural* **bobbins**

bobby pin (bäb′ē) ***noun*** a small metal hairpin with the sides pressing close together.
bob·by pin • ***noun,*** *plural* **bobby pins**

bobcat (bäb′kat) ***noun*** a small lynx of North America.
bob·cat • ***noun,*** *plural* **bobcats** or **bobcat**

bobolink (bäb′ə liŋk) ***noun*** a North American blackbird. Its name is meant to suggest the sound of its song.
bob·o·link • ***noun,*** *plural* **bobolinks**

bobsled (bäb′sled) ***noun*** a long sled for racing. A team of two or four persons rides it down a slide. It has a steering wheel and a brake.
bob·sled • ***noun,*** *plural* **bobsleds**

bobsled

bobwhite (bäb hwīt′ *or* bäb wīt′) ***noun*** a small North American bird that is a kind of quail. It has brown and white markings on a gray body.
bob·white • ***noun,*** *plural* **bobwhites** or **bobwhite**

bodice (bäd′is) ***noun*** the upper part of a woman's or girl's dress.
bod·ice • ***noun,*** *plural* **bodices**

bodily (bäd′l ē) ***adjective*** **1** of or by the body [*bodily* labor]. **2** in or to the body [*bodily* harm].
bod·i·ly • ***adjective***

body (bäd′ē) ***noun*** **1** the whole physical part of a person or animal [Athletes have strong *bodies*.] **2** the main part of a person or animal, not including the head, legs, and arms [The boxer received many blows to the *body*.] **3** the main or central part of anything [Sound vibrates through the *body* of a violin.] **4** a separate portion of matter; a mass [An ocean is a *body* of water.] **5** a group of persons or things that form a unit [the student *body* at a university].
bod·y • ***noun,*** *plural* **bodies**

bodyguard (bäd′ē gärd′) ***noun*** a person or group of people whose work is to protect someone.
bod·y·guard • ***noun,*** *plural* **bodyguards**

bog (bôg) ***noun*** an area of soft, wet ground; a small marsh or swamp.
verb to sink or become stuck in the way that a person would become stuck in a bog. Often used with *down* [We got *bogged down* in our homework.]
bog • ***noun,*** *plural* **bogs** • ***verb*** **bogged, bogging**

bogyman (bʊog′ē man′) ***noun*** an imaginary being that is very frightening.

B

bo·gy·man • *noun, plural* **bogymen**

boil[1] (boil) ***verb*** **1** to heat a liquid until it bubbles up and becomes steam [She *boiled* water for tea.] **2** to bubble up and turn to steam by being heated [Water will *boil* at 212° Fahrenheit.] **3** to cook in a boiling liquid [He *boiled* the potatoes.]
noun the condition of boiling [Heat the water to a *boil*.]
boil • ***verb*** **boiled, boiling** • ***noun***

WORD HISTORY

boil

The word **boil** comes from the Latin word for "bubble." We know a liquid is **boiling** when we see many bubbles rising to the top of it.

boil[2] (boil) ***noun*** a painful, red swelling on the skin. Boils are filled with a thick yellowish matter and are caused by infection.
boil • ***noun, plural*** **boils**

boiler (boil′ər) ***noun*** a tank in which water is heated until it turns to steam. The steam can be used to heat a building or run a machine.
boil·er • ***noun, plural*** **boilers**

boiling point ***noun*** the temperature at which a liquid boils [The *boiling point* of water at sea level is 212° Fahrenheit.]

Boise (boi′sē *or* boi′zē) the capital of Idaho.
Boi·se

bold (bōld) ***adjective*** **1** ready to take a risk or to do something that may be dangerous; brave [The *bold* explorer climbed the mountain.] **2** not polite or respectful [a *bold* remark]. **3** very sharp and clear so that it stands out [*bold* handwriting].
bold • ***adjective*** **bolder, boldest**

Bolivia (bə liv′ē ə) a country in western South America.
Bo·liv·i·a

boll (bōl) ***noun*** the rounded pod that holds seeds in the cotton plant and certain other plants.
boll • ***noun, plural*** **bolls**
● The words **boll** and **bowl** sound alike.
The *boll* weevil is a kind of beetle.
He served us each a *bowl* of chili.
If you like to *bowl*, join our league.

bologna (bə lō′nē) ***noun*** a large sausage made of beef or pork or veal, or made of a mixture of these meats.
bo·lo·gna • ***noun***

boloney (bə lō′nē) ***noun*** *another spelling of* **baloney**.
bo·lo·ney • ***noun***

bolster (bōl′stər) ***noun*** a pillow or cushion that is long and narrow.
verb to support or prop up with something that seems like a bolster [The coach's talk *bolstered* our spirits.]
bol·ster • ***noun, plural*** **bolsters** • ***verb*** **bolstered, bolstering**

bolt (bōlt) ***noun*** **1** a piece of metal like a nail that has a spiral groove cut around it. It looks a bit like a screw but is usually heavier and not pointed. It is used with a nut to fasten things together. **2** a metal bar that slides into a part and can be used to keep a door shut. **3** the part of a lock that is moved by the key. **4** a flash of lightning. **5** a large roll of cloth. **6** a quick dash, run, or escape.
verb **1** to fasten with a bolt [*Bolt* the door.] **2** to run out or run away suddenly [The horse *bolted* through the gate.] **3** to eat quickly or without chewing [She *bolted* her dinner.]
bolt • ***noun, plural*** **bolts** • ***verb*** **bolted, bolting**

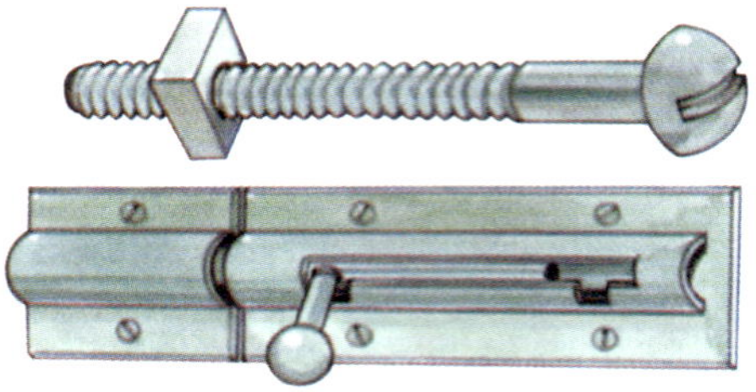

bolt

bomb (bäm) ***noun*** **1** a hollow case filled with an explosive, a poisonous gas, or something else that is harmful. A bomb blows up when it is set off by a fuse or a timing device, or when it strikes something. **2** [*a slang use*] a complete failure.
verb **1** to attack or destroy with bombs [The enemy *bombed* the city for days.] **2** [*a slang use*] to fail completely.

a cat	ō go	ʉ fur	ə = a *in* ago
ā ape	ô law, for	ch chin	e *in* agent
ä cot, car	oo look	sh she	i *in* pencil
e ten	ōō tool	th thin	o *in* atom
ē me	oi oil	*th* then	u *in* circus
i fit	ou out	zh measure	
ī ice	u up	ŋ ring	

bomb • *noun, plural* **bombs** • *verb* **bombed, bombing**

bombard (bäm bärd′) *verb* **1** to attack with bombs or heavy gunfire; to shell. **2** to keep on directing questions or requests at [The reporters *bombarded* her with questions.]
bom·bard • *verb* **bombarded, bombarding**

bomber (bäm′ər) *noun* **1** an airplane made for dropping bombs during a war. **2** a person who bombs places and things.
bomb·er • *noun, plural* **bombers**

Bonaparte (bō′nə pärt), **Napoleon** (nə pō′lē ən) 1769-1821; French general; emperor of France from 1804-1815. In full **Napoleon I**.
Bo·na·parte, Na·po·le·on

bonbon (bän′bän) *noun* a small piece of candy. Bonbons often contain a creamy filling.
bon·bon • *noun, plural* **bonbons**

bond (bänd) *noun* **1** something that binds or ties. **2** a force that connects or ties [the *bond* of friendship]. **3** a certificate that a government or business sells to raise money. It promises that the seller will pay back the money at a certain time, along with interest.
bond • *noun, plural* **bonds**

bondage (bän′dij) *noun* the condition of being a slave; slavery.
bond·age • *noun*

bone (bōn) *noun* **1** any one of the hard pieces that are joined together in the skeleton of a person or animal. **2** the material that makes up these pieces.
verb to take the bones out of [*Bone* the fish.]
bone • *noun, plural* **bones** • *verb* **boned, boning**

bonfire (bän′fīr) *noun* a large outdoor fire. A bonfire may be built for celebration or warmth.
bon·fire • *noun, plural* **bonfires**

bongo (bäŋ′gō) *noun* a small drum that is played with the hands. Bongos are fastened together in pairs. Each one has a different sound because one drum is a bit larger than the other.
bon·go • *noun, plural* **bongos**

bonnet (bän′it) *noun* a hat for women and children, with ribbons that are tied under the chin.
bon·net • *noun, plural* **bonnets**

bonobo (bə nō′bō) *noun* a kind of small chimpanzee.
bo·no·bo • *noun, plural* **bonobos**

bonus (bō′nəs) *noun* an extra amount or thing that is paid or given in addition to what is owed or expected.
bo·nus • *noun, plural* **bonuses**

bony (bō′nē) *adjective* **1** made of bone or like bone [The skull is a *bony* structure.] **2** full of bones [a *bony* piece of fish]. **3** with bones sticking out; thin [a *bony* hand].
bon·y • *adjective* **bonier, boniest**

boo (bo͞o) *noun* **1** a long, low sound that is made to show dislike [The pitcher was greeted with *boos* from the crowd.] **2** a sudden, short sound like this, made to startle a person.
verb to shout "boo" at to show dislike.
interjection **1** a word that is used to show dislike. **2** a word that is used to startle or frighten.
boo • *noun, plural* **boos** • *verb* **booed, booing** • *interjection*

book (bo͝ok) *noun* **1** a group of sheets of paper that are fastened together at one side, between protective covers. Books usually have writing or printing in them. **2** a long piece of writing [He wrote a *book* about dinosaurs.] **3** one of the main parts of a long piece of writing ["Genesis" is the first *book* of the Bible.]
verb **1** to write down in a book or record [The police *booked* the suspect.] **2** to arrange for ahead of time [I *booked* a seat on the bus.]
book • *noun, plural* **books** • *verb* **booked, booking**

bookcase (bo͝ok′kās) *noun* a cabinet or set of shelves for holding books.
book·case • *noun, plural* **bookcases**

bookkeeping (bo͝ok′kēp iŋ) *noun* the work of keeping records of the money a business receives and spends.
book·keep·ing • *noun*

booklet (bo͝ok′lit) *noun* a little book with paper covers.
book·let • *noun, plural* **booklets**

bookmark (bo͝ok′märk) *noun* a strip of paper, a ribbon, or another object that is put between the pages of a book to mark a special place.
book·mark • *noun, plural* **bookmarks**

boom[1] (bo͞om) *noun* a deep, hollow sound [the *boom* of the jet].
verb to make a deep, hollow sound [Thunder *boomed* through the air.]
boom • *noun, plural* **booms** • *verb* **boomed, booming**

B

boom[2] (bo͞om) ***noun*** a pole that comes out from the mast of a boat to keep the bottom of a sail stretched out.
boom • ***noun,*** *plural* **booms**

boom[3] (bo͞om) ***verb*** to grow suddenly or rapidly [The city's population *boomed* after the war.]
noun growth that is sudden and rapid.
boom • ***verb*** **boomed, booming** • ***noun,*** *plural* **booms**

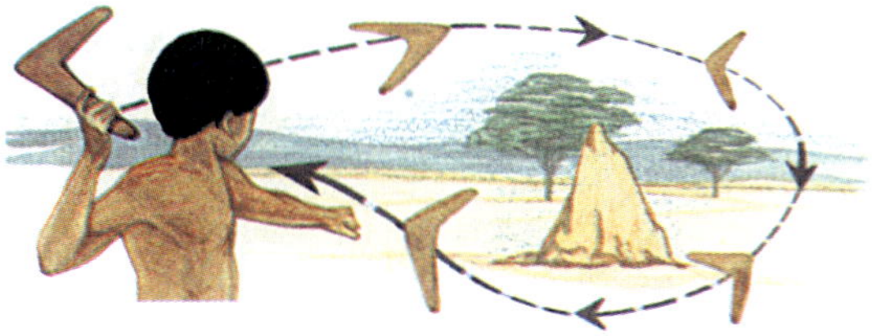

boomerang

boomerang (bo͞om′ər aŋ) ***noun*** a flat and curved stick that is made for throwing. It can be thrown so that it will return to the thrower.
boom·er·ang • ***noun,*** *plural* **boomerangs**

Boone (bo͞on), **Daniel** (dan′yəl) 1734-1820; American pioneer and explorer.
Boone, Dan·iel

boost (bo͞ost) ***verb*** **1** to push up from below [*Boost* the child into the tree.] **2** to make higher or greater [The government *boosted* taxes.] **3** to urge other people to support [a club to *boost* the baseball team].
noun a push upward; a raise [Our new ads gave a big *boost* to sales of our cookies.]
boost • ***verb*** **boosted, boosting** • ***noun,*** *plural* **boosts**

booster shot (bo͞ost′ər) ***noun*** an injection of a vaccine that is given some time after the first injection. It keeps a person protected by adding to the power of the earlier injection.
boost·er shot • ***noun,*** *plural* **booster shots**

boot (bo͞ot) ***noun*** a covering for the foot and part of the leg. It is usually made of leather or rubber.
verb to kick [He *booted* the ball.]
boot • ***noun,*** *plural* **boots** • ***verb*** **booted, booting**

boot

bootee (bo͞ot′ē) ***noun*** a soft shoe for a baby. It is knitted or made of cloth.
boot·ee • ***noun,*** *plural* **bootees**

- The words **bootee** and **booty** sound alike.
  She was knitting a red *bootee*.
  The pirates divided up the *booty*.

booth (bo͞oth) ***noun*** **1** a small space with sides or walls around it. Booths can be used for selling or displaying things or for privacy [the ticket *booth* at a fair; a telephone *booth;* a voting *booth*]. **2** a table and seats with low walls around them. Some restaurants have booths.
booth • ***noun,*** *plural* **booths**

booty (bo͞ot′ē) ***noun*** **1** things taken from the enemy in war. **2** anything taken by force or in a robbery; plunder.
boo·ty • ***noun***

- The words **booty** and **bootee** sound alike.

border (bôr′dər) ***noun*** **1** a line that divides one country or State from another [We crossed the *border* into Mexico.] **2** the place where one area ends and another begins; an edge [Ducks nest at the *border* of the marsh.] **3** a narrow strip along the edge of something [a *border* of flowers around the garden].
verb to lie along the edge of.
bor·der • ***noun,*** *plural* **borders** • ***verb*** **bordered, bordering**

WORD CHOICES

Synonyms of border

Many words share the meaning "the line or part where something begins or ends."

boundary	brink	margin
brim	edge	rim

bore[1] (bôr) ***verb*** **1** to make by digging or drilling [They *bored* a tunnel through the mountain.] **2** to make tired by being dull or uninteresting [The speaker *bored* the audience.]
noun a dull or uninteresting person or thing.

a	cat	ō	go	ʉ	fur	ə =	a *in* ago
ā	ape	ô	law, for	ch	chin		e *in* agent
ä	cot, car	o͝o	look	sh	she		i *in* pencil
e	ten	o͞o	tool	th	thin		o *in* atom
ē	me	oi	oil	*th*	then		u *in* circus
i	fit	ou	out	zh	measure		
ī	ice	u	up	ŋ	ring		

bore • *verb* **bored, boring** • *noun, plural* **bores**
● The words **bore** and **boar** sound alike.
Talking to him is a real *bore*.
They hunted the *boar* with spears.
She *bore* three sons.

bore[2] (bôr) *verb past tense of* **bear**[1].
● The words **bore** and **boar** sound alike.

boredom (bôr′dəm) *noun* the condition of being bored by something that is uninteresting.
bore·dom • *noun*

boring (bôr′iŋ) *adjective* not interesting or lively.
bor·ing • *adjective*

born (bôrn) *verb a past participle of* **bear**[1].
adjective **1** brought into life or being [a newly *born* idea]. **2** having certain abilities or qualities that seem to have been part of the person from birth; natural [She's a *born* leader.]
● The words **born** and **borne** sound alike.
I was *born* in March.
The shell was *borne* away by the tide.

borne (bôrn) *verb a past participle of* **bear**[1].
● The words **borne** and **born** sound alike.

borough (bur′ō) *noun* **1** a town that has the right to govern itself. **2** one of the five main divisions of New York City.
bor·ough • *noun, plural* **boroughs**
● The words **borough, burro,** and **burrow** sound alike.
Manhattan is a *borough* of New York.
The *burro* was brown with dark ears.
Our dog can *burrow* under the snow.

borrow (bär′ō *or* bôr′ō) *verb* **1** to take or receive something by promising to return or replace it later [I *borrowed* Bill's bike for a week. May I *borrow* a piece of gum?] **2** to take something and use it as one's own [English has *borrowed* many words from French.]
bor·row • *verb* **borrowed, borrowing**

Bosnia and Herzegovina (bäz′nē ə and hert′sə gō vē′nə) a country in southeastern Europe. It was a part of Yugoslavia.
Bos·ni·a and Her·ze·go·vi·na

bosom (booz′əm) *noun* a person's breast or chest.
adjective very close and dear [a *bosom* friend].
bos·om • *noun, plural* **bosoms** • *adjective*

boss (bôs) *noun* a person who is in charge of workers; supervisor.
boss • *noun, plural* **bosses**

bossy (bôs′ē) [*an informal word*] *adjective* acting like a boss and trying to tell people what to do.
boss·y • *adjective* **bossier, bossiest**

Boston (bôs′tən) a seaport that is the capital of Massachusetts.
Bos·ton

botanical (bə tan′i kəl) *adjective* having to do with botany [a *botanical* garden].
bo·tan·i·cal • *adjective*

botany (bät′n ē) *noun* the science that studies plants and how they grow.
bot·a·ny • *noun*

both (bōth) *adjective* the two [*Both* birds are small.]
pronoun **1** the two [*Both* of the birds are small.] **2** the two of them [*Both* are small.]
conjunction in an equal way: used in phrases with *and* [I am *both* tired and hungry.]

bother (bäth′ər) *verb* **1** to annoy [Does the noise *bother* you?] **2** to take the time or trouble [Don't *bother* to answer this letter.]
noun something that annoys or causes worry or trouble [Mosquitoes are a *bother*.]
both·er • *verb* **bothered, bothering** • *noun, plural* **bothers**

Botswana (bät swä′nə) country in southern Africa, north of the country of South Africa.
Bot·swa·na

bottle (bät′l) *noun* **1** a container that is used mostly for liquids. It is usually made of glass or plastic and is narrow at the top [a *bottle* of root beer; a baby's *bottle*]. **2** the amount that a bottle holds [I drank a whole *bottle* of soda.]
verb to put into a bottle or several bottles [This company *bottles* spring water.]
bot·tle • *noun, plural* **bottles**
• *verb* **bottled, bottling**

bottom (bät′əm) *noun* **1** the lowest part [the *bottom* of the page]. **2** the part on which a thing rests [the *bottom* of the lamp]. **3** the ground under a body of water [the *bottom* of the sea]. **4** the main reason; the cause [Get to the *bottom* of the problem.]
adjective of or at the bottom; lowest [the *bottom* shelf].
bot·tom • *noun, plural* **bottoms** • *adjective*

bough (bou) *noun* a large branch of a tree.
bough • *noun, plural* **boughs**
● The words **bough** and **bow** sound alike.
Saw off that broken *bough*.
The dancer made a deep *bow*.
The sailor stood in the ship's *bow*.

B

bought (bôt *or* bät) ***verb*** *past tense and past participle of* **buy**.

boulder (bōl′dər) ***noun*** a large rock that running water and harsh weather have made round.
boul·der • ***noun,*** *plural* **boulders**

boulevard (bool′ə värd) ***noun*** a wide street. Many boulevards have rows of trees at their sides.
boul·e·vard • ***noun,*** *plural* **boulevards**

bounce (bouns) ***verb*** **1** to hit against a surface so as to spring back [She *bounced* the ball against the wall. He *bounced* up and down on the sofa.] **2** to jump [I *bounced* out of bed.]
bounce • ***verb*** **bounced, bouncing**

bound[1] (bound) ***verb*** to move with a leap or leaps [The dog *bounded* into the room.]
noun a jump or leap.
bound • ***verb*** **bounded, bounding** • ***noun,*** *plural* **bounds**

bound[2] (bound) ***verb*** *past tense and past participle of* **bind**.
adjective sure; certain [She's *bound* to win.]

bound[3] (bound) ***adjective*** going or ready to go; headed [The train is *bound* for Chicago.] This word is sometimes used as a suffix [He left on a *northbound* train.]

bound[4] (bound) ***noun*** a boundary line or limit.
verb to form a boundary of [Ohio is *bounded* on the south by the Ohio River.]
—out of bounds **1** outside the playing limits. **2** not to be used; forbidden.
bound • ***noun,*** *plural* **bounds** • ***verb*** **bounded, bounding**

boundary (boun′də rē *or* boun′drē) ***noun*** a line or thing that marks the outside edge or limit [the southern *boundary* of Kansas] —Look for the WORD CHOICES box at the entry **border**.
bound·a·ry • ***noun,*** *plural* **boundaries**

bountiful (boun′tə fəl) ***adjective*** giving or providing more than enough [a *bountiful* harvest].
boun·ti·ful • ***adjective***

bounty (boun′tē) ***noun*** **1** the quality of being generous; willingness to give much [The hungry people were saved through the good king's *bounty*.] **2** a reward for capturing criminals or killing harmful animals.
boun·ty • ***noun,*** *plural for sense 2 only* **bounties**

bouquet (boo kā′ *or* bō kā′) ***noun*** a bunch of flowers.
bou·quet • ***noun,*** *plural* **bouquets**

bout (bout) ***noun*** **1** a contest or a fight [a boxing *bout*]. **2** a period of time when one is ill or one is doing something [a *bout* of the flu].
bout • ***noun,*** *plural* **bouts**

boutique (boo tēk′ *or* bō tēk′) ***noun*** a small shop that sells fancy or expensive articles or clothes.
bou·tique • ***noun,*** *plural* **boutiques**

bow[1] (bou) ***verb*** **1** to bend down the head or body in order to show respect or greet someone [He *bowed* to the queen.] **2** to give in [She *bowed* to her parents' wishes.]
noun the act of bending down the head or body to show respect or greet someone.
bow • ***verb*** **bowed, bowing** • ***noun,*** *plural* **bows**
• The words **bow** and **bough** sound alike.
The dancer made a deep *bow*.
Saw off that broken *bough*.
The sailor stood in the ship's *bow*.

bow
Of cello

bow[2] (bō) ***noun*** **1** a weapon for shooting arrows. It is made of a curved strip of wood with a cord tied to both ends. **2** a slender stick with strands of horsehair tied to both ends. A musician draws it across the strings of a violin or other similar instrument to make musical tones. **3** a knot that is tied with loops in it [shoelaces tied in a *bow*].
bow • ***noun,*** *plural* **bows**

bow[3] (bou) ***noun*** the front part of a boat or ship.
bow • ***noun,*** *plural* **bows**
• The words **bow** and **bough** sound alike.

a	cat	ō	go	ʉ	fur	ə =	a *in* ago
ā	ape	ô	law, for	ch	chin		e *in* agent
ä	cot, car	oo	look	sh	she		i *in* pencil
e	ten	ōō	tool	th	thin		o *in* atom
ē	me	oi	oil	*th*	then		u *in* circus
i	fit	ou	out	zh	measure		
ī	ice	u	up	ŋ	ring		

bowel movement (bou′əl) ***noun*** the passing of waste matter from the intestines.
bow·el move·ment • ***noun, plural*** **bowel movements**

bowels (bou′əlz) ***plural noun*** **1** the intestines, especially the human intestines. **2** the part deep inside [The coal mine is deep within the *bowels* of the earth.]
bow·els • ***plural noun***

bowl[1] (bōl) ***noun*** **1** a dish that is deep and rounded. **2** the amount of something that a bowl holds [He ate a *bowl* of soup.] **3** something that is shaped like a bowl [She washed her hands in the *bowl* of the sink.]
bowl • ***noun, plural*** **bowls**
● The words **bowl** and **boll** sound alike.
He served us each a *bowl* of chili.
There are seeds in a cotton *boll*.
If you like to *bowl*, join our league.

bowl[2] (bōl) ***verb*** **1** to play at bowling [They *bowl* once a week.] **2** to take a turn at bowling.
—bowl over [*an informal use*] to surprise or shock [I was *bowled over* by my "A" in math.]
bowl • ***verb*** **bowled, bowling**
● The words **bowl** and **boll** sound alike.

bowlegged (bō′leg′əd *or* bō′legd) ***adjective*** having legs that are bowed, or curved, outward.
bow·leg·ged • ***adjective***

bowling (bōl′iŋ) ***noun*** a game with a heavy ball and ten wooden pins. Each player rolls the ball along a wooden lane and tries to knock down the pins at the other end.
bowl·ing • ***noun***

box[1] (bäks) ***noun*** **1** a container for holding or carrying things. It is made of cardboard or wood or some other stiff material. A box usually has four sides, a bottom, and a lid on top. **2** the amount that a box holds [I ate a whole *box* of cereal.] **3** an area or place that is closed in or shaped like a box [a jury *box*].
verb to put into a box.
box • ***noun, plural*** **boxes** • ***verb*** **boxed, boxing**

box[2] (bäks) ***verb*** **1** to fight with the fists. **2** to hit with the hand or fist.
box • ***verb*** **boxed, boxing**

boxer (bäk′sər) ***noun*** **1** a man who fights with his fists as a sport. **2** a large dog that has a sturdy body and short ears.
box·er • ***noun, plural*** **boxers**

boxing (bäk′siŋ) ***noun*** the skill or sport of fighting with the fists.
box·ing • ***noun***

box office ***noun*** an area where tickets are sold in a theater, concert hall, or other similar place.
box office • ***noun, plural*** **box offices**

boy (boi) ***noun*** a male child.
boy • ***noun, plural*** **boys**
● The words **boy** and **buoy** sound alike.
A young *boy* delivers our newspaper.
A red *buoy* marked the shallow water.

boycott (boi′kät) ***verb*** to join with others and refuse to buy or sell something or to deal with someone.
noun the act of refusing in this way.
boy·cott • ***verb*** **boycotted, boycotting** • ***noun, plural*** **boycotts**

boyfriend (boi′frend) [*an informal word*] ***noun*** a sweetheart or escort of a girl or woman.
boy·friend • ***noun, plural*** **boyfriends**

boyhood (boi′hood) ***noun*** the time of being a boy.
boy·hood • ***noun***

boyish (boi′ish) ***adjective*** like or having to do with a boy [*boyish* pranks; a *boyish* face].
boy·ish • ***adjective***

Boy Scout ***noun*** a member of the Boy Scouts.
Boy Scout • ***noun, plural*** **Boy Scouts**

Boy Scouts ***noun*** a club for boys. It teaches camping, hiking, and other outdoor skills.

bozo (bō′zō) [*a slang word*] ***noun*** someone that people think is foolish or not smart.
bo·zo • ***noun, plural*** **bozos**

bra (brä) ***noun*** an undergarment that women wear to support the breasts.
bra • ***noun, plural*** **bras**

brace (brās) ***verb*** **1** to make stronger by propping up [*Brace* the shelf with a support.] **2** to make ready for a jolt or shock [*Brace* yourself for trouble.]
noun **1** a thing that supports a weak part or keeps parts in place [After the operation, he had to wear a *brace* on his back and neck.] **2 braces** metal bands or wires on the

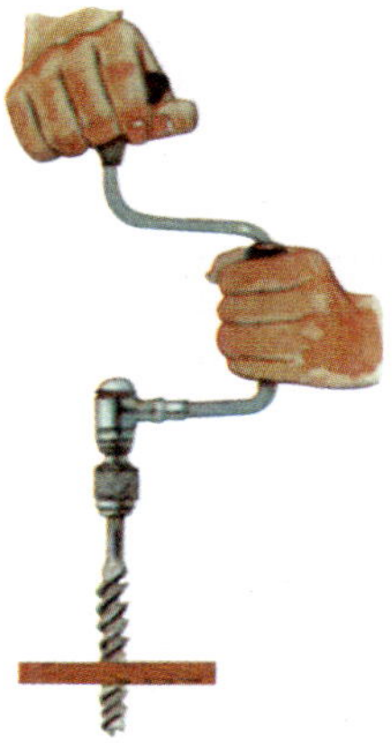

brace and bit

B

teeth for straightening them. **3** either of the signs { }, used in pairs to group words together. **4** a tool for boring holes. This tool is also called **brace and bit**.
brace • *verb* **braced, bracing** • *noun, plural* **braces**

bracelet (brās′lit) *noun* a chain or band that a person wears around the wrist or arm for decoration or for identification.
brace·let • *noun, plural* **bracelets**

bracket (brak′it) *noun* **1** a support that is fastened to a wall to hold up a shelf or other object. **2** either of the signs [ ], used mainly in pairs in writing. Brackets are put around words, numbers, and symbols that are added to explain something or make a comment.
brack·et • *noun, plural* **brackets**

brag (brag) *verb* to talk about with too much pride and pleasure; boast.
brag • *verb* **bragged, bragging**

WORD CHOICES

Synonyms of **brag**

The words **brag, boast,** and **crow** share the meaning "to talk about with too much pride."

Margo *bragged* about her skill as a skater.

Dad *boasted* about my grades.

Good sports don't *crow* over their victories.

Brahma (brä′mə) in Hinduism, the god who created the universe.
Brah·ma

Brahms (brämz), **Johannes** (yō hän′əs) 1833-1897; German composer.
Brahms, Jo·han·nes

braid (brād) *verb* **1** to weave together three or more strands [Ann is *braiding* her hair. We are *braiding* ribbon for a decoration.] **2** to make by weaving strands [They *braided* a colorful rug.]
noun **1** a section of hair that has been braided. **2** a band of cloth or braided material that is used for decoration.
braid • *verb* **braided, braiding** • *noun, plural* **braids**

Braille or **braille** (brāl) *noun* a system of writing and printing for blind people. Patterns of tiny raised dots or bumps on the paper represent the letters. The reader runs the fingers over them and feels the patterns.

brain (brān) *noun* **1** the gray and white tissue inside the skull of a person or of any animal that has a backbone. The brain controls many of the body's actions and processes. In human beings, the brain is the center of thought, memory, and feelings. **2** *often* **brains** intelligence; understanding. **3** [*an informal use*] a very intelligent person.
verb [*a slang use*] to hit hard on the head.
brain • *noun, plural* **brains** • *verb* **brained, braining**

brainstorm (brān′stôrm) [*an informal word*] *noun* a sudden, clever or intelligent idea.
brain·storm • *noun, plural* **brainstorms**

brake (brāk) *noun* a device that is used to slow down or stop a vehicle or a machine.
verb to slow down or stop with a brake [The engineer *braked* the locomotive.]
brake • *noun* • *verb* **braked, braking**
• The words **brake** and **break** sound alike.
Use your *brake* at the bottom of the hill.
Did you see the window *break?*

bramble (bram′bəl) *noun* a prickly shrub or vine. Raspberry and blackberry bushes are examples.
bram·ble • *noun, plural* **brambles**

bran (bran) *noun* the husks of ground wheat, rye, or other grains. Bran is used in some baked goods and in breakfast cereals.

branch (branch) *noun* **1** a main limb growing from the trunk of a tree, or a part growing from a main limb. **2** something that comes out like this from a main part [the *branch* of a river]. **3** a division or part [Chemistry is a *branch* of science.] **4** a part that is away from the main unit [library *branches* in the suburbs].
verb to divide into branches [The road *branches* ahead.]
branch • *noun, plural* **branches** • *verb* **branched, branching**

brand (brand) *noun* **1** a mark or name that a company puts on the things it makes or sells;

a cat	ō go	ʉ fur	ə = a *in* ago
ā ape	ô law, for	ch chin	e *in* agent
ä cot, car	oo look	sh she	i *in* pencil
e ten	ōō tool	th thin	o *in* atom
ē me	oi oil	*th* then	u *in* circus
i fit	ou out	zh measure	
ī ice	u up	ŋ ring	

trademark. **2** a certain type or kind [We tried a new *brand* of toothpaste.] **3** a mark on the skin that is burned in with a hot iron.
verb **1** to mark with a hot iron [Cowboys were *branding* the cattle.] **2** to set apart and think of as something shameful [His enemies *branded* him a coward.]
brand • *noun, plural* **brands**
• *verb* **branded, branding**

brand-new (brand′no͞o′ *or* brand′nyo͞o′) *adjective* completely new; never used before [a *brand-new* dollar bill].

brandy (bran′dē) *noun* a strong alcoholic beverage that is made from wine or sometimes made from fruit juice.
bran·dy • *noun, plural* **brandies**

brass (bras) *noun* a yellow metal that is a mixture of copper and zinc.

brass instrument *noun* a musical instrument made of brass or a similar kind of metal. Brass instruments have mouthpieces shaped like cups. Tubas, trombones, and trumpets are all brass instruments.
brass instrument • *noun, plural* **brass instruments**

brat (brat) *noun* a child who does not behave or who is hard to control.
brat • *noun, plural* **brats**

bratty (brat′ē) *adjective* like or having to do with a child who does not behave [*bratty* remarks].
brat·ty • *adjective* **brattier, brattiest**

brave (brāv) *adjective* **1** willing to face danger, pain, or trouble; not afraid [We had a *brave* leader on our canoeing trip.] **2** full of courage [*brave* actions of the firefighters].
noun a Native American warrior.
verb to face without fear [We *braved* the storm to get to school.]
brave • *adjective* **braver, bravest** • *noun, plural* **braves** • *verb* **braved, braving**

bravery (brā′vər ē) *noun* the quality of being brave; courage.
brav·er·y • *noun*

bray (brā) *noun* the loud, harsh cry that a donkey makes.
verb to make this sound.
bray • *noun, plural* **brays** • *verb* **brayed, braying**

Brazil (brə zil′) a country in central and northeastern South America.
Bra·zil

Brazil nut *noun* a three-sided nut that is used for food. It is the seed of a tree that grows in South America.
Brazil nut • *noun, plural* **Brazil nuts**

breach (brēch) *noun* an opening that is made by breaking through [Soldiers forced a *breach* in the enemy's lines.]
breach • *noun, plural* **breaches**

bread (bred) *noun* **1** a food that is baked from a dough made with flour, water, yeast, sugar, and other ingredients. **2** food and other things that a person needs in order to live [We earned our *bread* working a long day.]
bread • *noun, plural for sense 1 only* **breads**
● The words **bread** and **bred** sound alike.
A sandwich is made with *bread.*
The horse was *bred* to race.

breadth (bredth) *noun* the distance from one side to another of a thing; width.
breadth • *noun, plural* **breadths**

break (brāk) *verb* **1** to come or make come apart by force; split or crack sharply into pieces [The rusty hinge *broke* when the door slammed. She *broke* a glass in the sink.] **2** to crack a bone of; to fracture [She *broke* her arm.] **3** to force one's way [The firefighters *broke* through the door.] **4** to get out of working order; make or become useless [My flashlight *broke*. You can *break* your watch if you wind it too tightly.] **5** to cut open the surface of [They are *breaking* ground for a new gym.] **6** to tame by using force [The cowboy *broke* the wild pony.] **7** to do better than [He *broke* the record for home runs.] **8** to fail to follow [They *broke* the law.] **9** to end, stop, or interrupt [The net *broke* the acrobat's fall. The melted fuse *broke* the electric circuit.] **10** to fill with sorrow [The sad story *broke* my heart.] **11** to begin or come suddenly [Dawn was *breaking*.] **12** to become known or make known [The news story *broke* today. Who will *break* the sad news to her?] **13** to curve suddenly near the plate: in this sense, this word applies to a pitched baseball.
noun **1** a broken place [The X-ray showed a *break* in the bone.] **2** an interruption; a sudden change [a *break* in the weather]. **3** a sudden move [We made a *break* for the door.] **4** a short period of rest [a five-minute *break*]. **5** a piece of good fortune [a lucky *break*].
—break down **1** to lose control of oneself; begin to cry. **2** to go out of working order [The TV set *broke down* again.] **3** to separate into parts for study [Let's *break down* this math

B

problem into smaller steps.] **—break in** **1** to enter by force [The burglar *broke in* and ransacked the house.] **2** to interrupt [Ann and I were talking, and John *broke in*.] **3** to prepare for use; to train [He *broke in* his new shoes.] **—break into** **1** to enter by force [The burglar *broke into* the house.] **2** to interrupt [John *broke into* our conversation.] **—break off** to stop suddenly [The conversation *broke off* abruptly.] **—break out** **1** to develop a rash on the skin [I *broke out* in measles.] **2** to begin suddenly [A riot *broke out*.] **3** to escape suddenly [They *broke out* of prison.] **—break up** **1** to come or bring to an end [The meeting *breaks up* at noon. The teacher *broke up* the argument.] **2** [*an informal use*] to end a friendship [Jane *broke up* with John.]
break • *verb* **broke, broken, breaking**
• *noun, plural* **breaks**

● The words **break** and **brake** sound alike.
Did you see the window *break?*
You must *brake* at a red light.

WORD CHOICES

Synonyms of break

The words **break, shatter,** and **smash** share the meaning "to separate into pieces as the result of a blow."

The bat *broke* in two.

The windshield *shattered* when the stone struck it.

The plate fell to the floor and *smashed*.

breakdown (brāk′doun) *noun* **1** a failure to work properly [the *breakdown* of a machine.] **2** a failure of physical or mental health [He had a nervous *breakdown*.]
break·down • *noun, plural* **breakdowns**

breaker (brāk′ər) *noun* a wave that breaks into foam against the shore.
break·er • *noun, plural* **breakers**

breakfast (brek′fəst) *noun* the first meal of the day. It is eaten in the morning.
verb to eat this meal.
break·fast • *noun, plural* **breakfasts**
• *verb* **breakfasted, breakfasting**

breakthrough (brāk′thro͞o) *noun* a very important discovery or step in the progress of something [a *breakthrough* in medicine].
break·through • *noun, plural* **breakthroughs**

breast (brest) *noun* **1** the upper, front part of the body, between the neck and the stomach; the chest. **2** either one of the two glands on this part of a woman's body. Babies get milk from these glands.
breast • *noun, plural* **breasts**

breastbone (brest′bōn) *noun* the thin, flat bone in the front of the chest. Most ribs are joined to this bone.
breast·bone • *noun, plural* **breastbones**

breath (breth) *noun* **1** air that a person takes into the lungs and then lets back out. **2** easy or natural breathing [Wait till I get my *breath* back.] **3** the act of breathing [Hold your *breath*.] **4** a slight breeze.
breath • *noun, plural* **breaths**

breathe (brē*th*) *verb* to take air into the lungs and then let it out.
—breathe a word of something to say or reveal something secret.
breathe • *verb* **breathed, breathing**

breathless (breth′lis) *adjective* **1** breathing hard; panting [She was *breathless* after the race.] **2** not breathing for a moment because of excitement or fear [The movie left us *breathless*.]
breath·less • *adjective*

breathtaking (breth′tāk′iŋ) *adjective* exciting or thrilling [a *breathtaking* view of the canyon].
breath·tak·ing • *adjective*

bred (bred) *verb past tense and past participle of* **breed**.
● The words **bred** and **bread** sound alike.
Flies *bred* near the house.
Do you prefer rye or wheat *bread?*

breeches (brich′iz) *plural noun* **1** short trousers reaching just below the knees. **2** [*an informal use*] any trousers.
breech·es • *plural noun*

breed (brēd) *verb* **1** to give birth to or hatch offspring [Mosquitoes *breed* in swamps.] **2** to keep and raise animals or plants [They *breed*

a	cat	ō	go	ʉ	fur	ə =	a *in* ago
ā	ape	ô	law, for	ch	chin		e *in* agent
ä	cot, car	o͝o	look	sh	she		i *in* pencil
e	ten	o͞o	tool	th	thin		o *in* atom
ē	me	oi	oil	*th*	then		u *in* circus
i	fit	ou	out	zh	measure		
ī	ice	u	up	ŋ	ring		

cattle on their farm.] **3** to produce or cause [Idle hands *breed* trouble.]
noun a special type of some animal or plant.
breed • *verb* **bred, breeding** • *noun, plural* **breeds**

breeze (brēz) *noun* a light and gentle wind.
breeze • *noun, plural* **breezes**

brew (bro͞o) *verb* **1** to make by soaking something in very hot water [We *brew* coffee from ground coffee beans.] **2** to make from malt and hops [That company *brews* beer.] **3** to plan or scheme [They are *brewing* mischief.] **4** to begin to form [A storm is *brewing*.]
brew • *verb* **brewed, brewing**

briar (brī′ər) *noun another spelling of* **brier**.
bri·ar • *noun, plural* **briars**

bribe (brīb) *noun* a thing that is given or promised in order to get a person to do what that person does not want to do.
verb to offer or give a bribe to.
bribe • *noun, plural* **bribes** • *verb* **bribed, bribing**

brick (brik) *noun* **1** a block of baked clay that is used to build things. **2** bricks as material for building things [a house built of *brick*]. **3** something that is shaped like a brick.
brick • *noun, plural for senses 1 and 3 only* **bricks**

bridal (brīd′l) *adjective* having to do with a bride or a wedding [a *bridal* gown].
brid·al • *adjective*
- The words **bridal** and **bridle** sound alike.
  Not every tailor can sew a *bridal* gown.
  To turn a horse, pull on the *bridle*.

bride (brīd) *noun* a woman who has just been married or is about to be married.
bride • *noun, plural* **brides**

bridegroom (brīd′gro͞om) *noun* a man who has just been married or is about to be married.
bride·groom • *noun, plural* **bridegrooms**

bridge (brij) *noun* **1** a structure that is built over a river, railroad, or other obstacle. It provides a path across. **2** the upper, bony part of the nose. **3** the thin piece of wood that supports the strings on a violin, cello, or other similar instrument. **4** the high platform on a ship where the person in charge stands.
verb to make or build a bridge over [The workers brought logs to *bridge* the river.]
bridge • *noun, plural* **bridges** • *verb* **bridged, bridging**

bridge
Left: Over river Right: Over violin

bridle (brīd′l) *noun* the part of a horse's harness that fits the head. The bridle is used to control and guide the horse.
verb **1** to put a bridle on. **2** to hold back or control [You must *bridle* your anger.]
bri·dle • *noun, plural* **bridles** • *verb* **bridled, bridling**
- The words **bridle** and **bridal** sound alike.
  Put the *bridle* on the horse.
  Gifts are given at a *bridal* shower.

bridle

brief (brēf) *adjective* **1** not lasting very long; short in time [a *brief* visit; a *brief* spell of dizziness]. **2** using just a few words; not wordy [a *brief* speech]. **3** short in length [a *brief* bathing suit].
noun **briefs** underpants without legs that fit in a snug way.
verb to give instructions or information to [They *briefed* the soldiers before battle.]

brief *adjective* • *noun, plural* **briefs**
• *verb* **briefed, briefing**

briefcase (brēf′kās) *noun* a flat case that is used for carrying papers, books, and other items.
brief·case • *noun, plural* **briefcases**

brier (brī′ər) *noun* a prickly or thorny bush. The wild rose is a brier.
bri·er • *noun, plural* **briers**

bright (brīt) *adjective* **1** full of light; shining [a *bright* star; a *bright* day]. **2** very strong or clear in color or sound [a *bright* red; the *bright* tones of a trumpet]. **3** lively or cheerful [a *bright* smile]. **4** having a quick mind; intelligent [a *bright* student] —Look for the WORD CHOICES box at the entry **intelligent**.
bright • *adjective* **brighter, brightest**

brighten (brīt′n) *verb* to make or become bright or brighter.
bright·en • *verb* **brightened, brightening**

brilliant (bril′yənt) *adjective* **1** very bright; glittering or sparkling [the *brilliant* sun on the water]. **2** extraordinary or outstanding [a *brilliant* performance]. **3** very clever or intelligent [a *brilliant* student] —Look for the WORD CHOICES box at the entry **intelligent**.
bril·liant • *adjective*

brim

brim (brim) *noun* **1** the top rim of a cup, bowl, or other container that holds liquids. **2** a rim or edge that sticks out [the *brim* of a hat] —Look for the WORD CHOICES box at the entry **border**.
verb to fill or be filled to the brim [Her eyes *brimmed* over with tears.]
brim • *noun, plural* **brims** • *verb* **brimmed, brimming**

brine (brīn) *noun* **1** water full of salt that is used for pickling meat or other foods. **2** salt water.

bring (briŋ) *verb* **1** to carry or lead here or to the place where the speaker will be [*Bring* the book to my house. Please *bring* your brother with you tomorrow.] **2** to cause to happen or come [War *brings* death and hunger.] **3** to persuade or influence [I can't *bring* myself to sell my old desk.] **4** to cause to reach a certain condition, state, or position [*Bring* the water to a boil. She *brought* the car to a stop.] **5** to sell for [Coffee *brings* a high price.]
—**bring about** to be the cause of; to cause [Lying *brings about* unpleasant consequences.] —**bring out** to make known or make clear [He *brings out* the best in people. Injustice should be *brought out* into the open.] —**bring up 1** to take care of during childhood [He was *brought up* by his grandfather.] **2** to mention or suggest in a discussion [Please stop *bringing up* that subject!]
bring • *verb* **brought, bringing**

brink (briŋk) *noun* **1** the edge at the top of a steep place [at the *brink* of the cliff] —Look for the WORD CHOICES box at the entry **border**. **2** the point just short of [at the *brink* of war].
brink • *noun, plural* **brinks**

brisk (brisk) *adjective* **1** quick and full of energy [a *brisk* pace] —Look for the WORD CHOICES boxes at the entries **active** and **fast**[1]. **2** cool, dry, and refreshing [a *brisk* October morning].
brisk • *adjective* **brisker, briskest**

bristle (bris′əl) *noun* **1** any short, stiff, prickly hair, especially of a hog. **2** such a hair, or an artificial hair like it, used for brushes.
verb **1** to stand up in a stiff way, like bristles [The hair on the cat's back *bristled* as the dog came near.] **2** to become tense with anger; be ready to fight back [She *bristled* at the insult.]
bris·tle • *noun, plural* **bristles**
• *verb* **bristled, bristling**

Brit. *abbreviation for* **1** Britain. **2** British.

Britain (brit′n) *the same as* **Great Britain**.
Brit·ain

British (brit′ish) *adjective* of Great Britain or its people.
—**the British** the people of Great Britain.
Brit·ish • *adjective*

British Columbia (kə lum′bē ə) a province of

a	cat	ō	go	ʉ	fur	ə =	a *in* ago
ā	ape	ô	law, for	ch	chin		e *in* agent
ä	cot, car	oo	look	sh	she		i *in* pencil
e	ten	ōō	tool	th	thin		o *in* atom
ē	me	oi	oil	*th*	then		u *in* circus
i	fit	ou	out	zh	measure		
ī	ice	u	up	ŋ	ring		

Canada, on the Pacific. Abbreviated **BC** or **B.C.**
British Co·lum·bi·a

British Isles a group of islands northwest of France, including Great Britain, Ireland, and several smaller islands.

brittle (brit′l) *adjective* easily broken because it is hard and not flexible.
noun a brittle, crunchy candy with nuts in it.
brit·tle • *adjective* • *noun*

broad (brôd) *adjective* **1** large from side to side; wide [a *broad* highway]. **2** clear and open [*broad* daylight]. **3** allowing many possibilities; having few limits [a *broad* selection].
broad • *adjective* **broader, broadest**

broadcast (brôd′kast) *verb* **1** to send through the air by means of radio or television [This station *broadcasts* his favorite radio program on Friday evenings.] **2** to spread widely [They *broadcast* the gossip quickly.] —Look for the WORD CHOICES box at the entry **sprinkle**.
noun **1** the act of broadcasting. **2** a radio or television program.
broad·cast • *verb* **broadcast** or **broadcasted, broadcasting** • *noun, plural* **broadcasts**

broaden (brôd′n) *verb* to make or become broad or broader; widen [Last year the city *broadened* the road from two lanes to four.]
broad·en • *verb* **broadened, broadening**

brocade (brō kād′) *noun* a fine cloth with a complicated raised design woven into it.
bro·cade • *noun, plural* **brocades**

broccoli (bräk′ə lē) *noun* a vegetable with tender shoots and loose heads of tiny green buds that are cooked for eating.
broc·co·li • *noun*

brochure (brō shoor′) *noun* a thin booklet with a paper cover that advertises something.
bro·chure • *noun, plural* **brochures**

broil (broil) *verb* **1** to cook or be cooked close to a flame or other high heat [We *broiled* the meat on the grill. The meat *broiled* slowly.] **2** to make or be very hot [I'm *broiling* under this summer sun.]
broil • *verb* **broiled, broiling**

broiler (broil′ər) *noun* **1** a pan or grill for broiling. **2** the part of a stove used for broiling.
broil·er • *noun, plural* **broilers**

broke (brōk) *verb past tense of* **break**.
adjective [*an informal use*] having no money.

broken (brō′kən) *verb past participle of* **break**.
adjective **1** split or cracked into pieces [a *broken* dish; a *broken* leg]. **2** not in working condition [a *broken* watch]. **3** not kept or carried out [a *broken* promise]. **4** not following the usual rules of grammar and word order [They speak *broken* English.]
bro·ken • *verb* • *adjective*

bronchial (bräŋ′kē əl) *adjective* having to do with the tubes of the windpipe.
bron·chi·al • *adjective*

bronchial tubes *plural noun* the two main branches of the windpipe. The air we breathe passes through the bronchial tubes to the lungs.

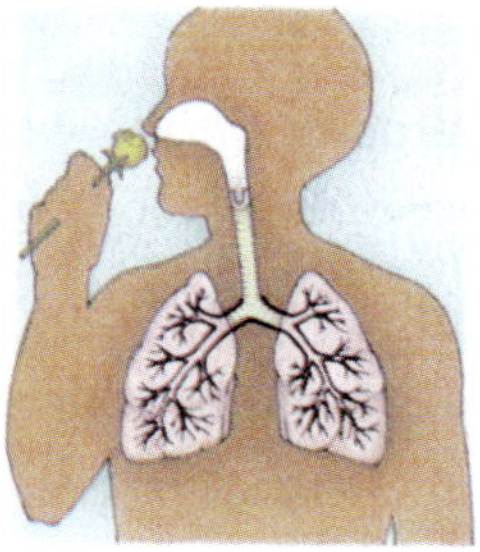

bronchial tubes

bronchitis (bräŋ kī′tis) *noun* an illness in which the bronchial tubes are sore and irritated and cause painful coughing.
bron·chi·tis • *noun*

bronco (bräŋ′kō) *noun* a wild or only partly tamed horse or pony of the western U.S.
bron·co • *noun, plural* **broncos**

brontosaur

brontosaur (brän′tə sôr′) *noun* a huge dinosaur that ate plants. It had a long, slender neck.
bron·to·saur • *noun, plural* **brontosaurs**

bronze (bränz) *noun* **1** a metal that is a mixture of copper and tin. **2** a reddish-brown color like the color of bronze.
adjective made of or similar to bronze [a *bronze* statue; *bronze* hair].

brooch (brōch *or* broōch) *noun* a large pin with a clasp that is worn as an ornament.

brooch • *noun, plural* **brooches**

brood (bro͞od) ***noun*** **1** a group of birds hatched at one time and cared for together. **2** all the children in a family.
verb **1** to sit on and hatch eggs. **2** to keep thinking in a worried or troubled way [She *brooded* over the loss of her money.]
brood • *noun, plural* **broods**
• *verb* **brooded, brooding**

brook (bro͝ok) ***noun*** a small stream.
brook • *noun, plural* **brooks**

broom (bro͞om) ***noun*** a bundle of long, stiff fibers or straws, or a brush, fastened to a long handle. It is used for sweeping.
broom • *noun, plural* **brooms**

broomstick (bro͞om′stik) ***noun*** the handle of a broom.
broom·stick • *noun, plural* **broomsticks**

broth (brôth) ***noun*** a clear soup made with water in which meat or a vegetable has been boiled.
broth • *noun, plural* **broths**

brother (bru*th*′ər) ***noun*** a boy or man as he is related to the other children of his parents.
broth·er • *noun, plural* **brothers**

brotherhood (bru*th*′ər ho͝od) ***noun*** **1** the tie between brothers or between people who feel they all belong to one big family. **2** a group of men joined together in the same interest, work, or belief.
broth·er·hood • *noun, plural* **brotherhoods**

brother-in-law (bru*th*′ər in lô′) ***noun*** **1** the brother of one's husband or wife. **2** the husband of one's sister.
broth·er-in-law • *noun, plural* **brothers-in-law**

brotherly (bru*th*′ər lē) ***adjective*** like a brother; friendly, loyal, or kind [*brotherly* advice].
broth·er·ly • *adjective*

brought (brôt *or* brät) ***verb*** *past tense and past participle of* **bring**.

brow (brou) ***noun*** **1** an eyebrow. **2** the forehead.
brow • *noun, plural* **brows**

brown (broun) ***noun*** the color of chocolate or coffee, a mixture of red, black, and yellow.
adjective having this color [*brown* shoes].
verb to make or become brown [The turkey is *browning* in the oven.]
brown • *noun, plural* **browns** • *adjective* **browner, brownest** • *verb* **browned, browning**

Brown (broun), **John** (jän) 1800-1859; an American who fought slavery. He led a raid on a U.S. arsenal and was hanged for treason.

brownie (broun′ē) ***noun*** **1** a small elf in folk tales who does good deeds for people at night. **2 Brownie** a member of the Girl Scouts in the youngest group, six, seven, and eight years old. **3** a small, flat bar of chocolate cake that has nuts.
brown·ie • *noun, plural* **brownies**

brownish (broun′ish) ***adjective*** somewhat brown.
brown·ish • *adjective*

browse (brouz) ***verb*** **1** to nibble at leaves, twigs, shoots of grass, or other plants [We could see deer *browsing* in the forest.] **2** to look through something in a casual way [She *browsed* through the books. He *browsed* in the shops while waiting for his friend.]
browse • *verb* **browsed, browsing**

bruise (bro͞oz) ***noun*** an injury to the outer part or flesh that does not break the skin but darkens it in color.
verb **1** to cause bruises to appear on a part of the body by a bump or blow or in some other way [He *bruised* his knee on the corner of the table.] **2** to hurt the outside of [They dropped and *bruised* the peaches.]
bruise • *noun, plural* **bruises**
• *verb* **bruised, bruising**

brunch (brunch) ***noun*** breakfast and lunch eaten as one meal late in the morning.
brunch • *noun, plural* **brunches**

WORD HISTORY

brunch

You can hear the sources of the word **brunch** when you say it. Part of the word *breakfast* is combined with part of the word *lunch*, just as foods from both meals are put together in one meal.

a	cat	ō	go	u̇	fur	ə =	a *in* ago
ā	ape	ô	law, for	ch	chin		e *in* agent
ä	cot, car	o͝o	look	sh	she		i *in* pencil
e	ten	o͞o	tool	th	thin		o *in* atom
ē	me	oi	oil	*th*	then		u *in* circus
i	fit	ou	out	zh	measure		
ī	ice	u	up	ŋ	ring		

Brunei (broo nī′) a country on an island in the western Pacific.
Bru·nei

brunet (bro͞o net′) ***adjective*** having black or dark brown hair, and often dark eyes and dark skin.
noun a brunet person.
bru·net • ***adjective*** • ***noun,*** *plural* **brunets**

brunette (bro͞o net′) ***adjective*** *another spelling of* **brunet**.
noun a brunette woman or girl.
bru·nette • ***adjective*** • ***noun,*** *plural* **brunettes**

brush

brush (brush) ***noun*** **1** a bunch of bristles, hairs, or wires fastened into a hard back or handle. Brushes are used for cleaning, polishing, grooming, painting, and many other things. **2** the act of rubbing with a brush [He gave his coat one last *brush.*] **3** a light, grazing stroke [She removed the lint from her jacket with a *brush* of her hand.] **4** a thick growth of small trees and shrubs; underbrush.
verb **1** to use a brush on; clean, polish, paint, smooth, or do some other work with a brush [*Brush* your shoes. *Brush* the paint on evenly.] **2** to remove with a stroking motion as if holding a brush [*Brush* the flies away from the cake.] **3** to touch or graze when passing [The tire of the car *brushed* against the curb.]
brush • ***noun,*** *plural* **brushes** • ***verb*** **brushed, brushing**

Brussels sprout (brus′əl sprout′) ***noun*** **1** *often* **Brussels sprouts** a vegetable with green buds like tiny cabbage heads growing on its stem. **2** one of these buds.
Brus·sels sprout • ***noun,*** *plural* **Brussels sprouts**

brutal (bro͞ot′l) ***adjective*** cruel and without feeling; savage [a *brutal* storm].
bru·tal • ***adjective***

brutality (bro͞o tal′ə tē) ***noun*** the fact or condition of being brutal.
bru·tal·i·ty • ***noun,*** *plural* **brutalities**

brute (bro͞ot) ***noun*** **1** an animal. **2** a person who is brutal or very stupid, coarse, and crude.
brute • ***noun,*** *plural* **brutes**

bubble (bub′əl) ***noun*** **1** a very thin layer of liquid forming a ball around air or gas [We love to blow soap *bubbles* outside.] **2** a tiny ball of air or gas in a liquid [the *bubbles* in soda water].
verb **1** to make bubbles; foam [Boiling water *bubbles.*] **2** to make a boiling or gurgling sound [The soup is *bubbling* on the stove.]
bub·ble • ***noun,*** *plural* **bubbles** • ***verb*** **bubbled, bubbling**

Buchanan (byo͞o kan′ən), **James** (jāmz) 1791-1868; the fifteenth president of the U.S., from 1857 to 1861.
Bu·chan·an, James

buck (buk) ***noun*** **1** the male of certain animals, especially of the deer, goat, or rabbit. **2** [*a slang use*] a dollar.
verb **1** to jump upward quickly, with the head down and the back curved. A horse moves in this way when it tries to throw a rider off its back. **2** to force a way through; plunge against [The sailboat *bucked* strong winds.]
buck • ***noun,*** *plural* **bucks** • ***verb*** **bucked, bucking**

bucket (buk′it) ***noun*** **1** a round container with a flat bottom and a curved handle, used to hold or carry water, sand, and other things; pail. **2** the amount a bucket can hold.
buck·et • ***noun,*** *plural* **buckets**

buckle

buckle[1] (buk′əl) ***noun*** a clasp at one end of a strap or belt for fastening the other end in place.
verb to fasten with a buckle.
—**buckle down** to set to work with great concentration [On such a beautiful day he found it hard to *buckle down.*]
buck·le • ***noun,*** *plural* **buckles** • ***verb*** **buckled, buckling**

buckle[2] (buk′əl) ***verb*** to bend, warp, or crumple [The bridge *buckled* under the truck's weight.]
buck·le • ***verb*** **buckled, buckling**

B

buckskin (buk′skin) ***noun*** a soft, strong, tan leather made from the skins of deer or sheep.
buck·skin • ***noun,*** *plural* **buckskins**

bucktoothed (buk′to͞otht′) ***adjective*** having large upper front teeth that stick out.
buck·toothed • ***adjective***

buckwheat (buk′hwēt *or* buk′wēt) ***noun*** **1** a plant grown for its seeds that look like small black triangles. **2** the seeds of this plant, often ground into flour or used as food for farm animals. **3** flour made from these seeds.
buck·wheat • ***noun***

bud (bud) ***noun*** **1** a small swelling on a plant from which a shoot, a flower, or leaves will grow. **2** a partly opened flower.
verb to begin to show buds [The cherry trees are beginning to *bud*.]
bud • ***noun,*** *plural* **buds** • ***verb*** **budded, budding**

Buddha (bo͝od′ə *or* bo͞od′ə) 563?-483? B.C.; a religious leader of India.
Bud·dha

Buddhism (bo͝od′iz′əm *or* bo͞od′iz′əm) ***noun*** a religion of Asia. It was founded by Buddha. It teaches that by right living and right thinking the soul is freed from pain, sorrow, and desire.
Bud·dhism • ***noun***

buddy (bud′ē) [*an informal word*] ***noun*** a close friend; companion.
bud·dy • ***noun,*** *plural* **buddies**

budge (buj) ***verb*** to move even a little [Two strong people could not *budge* the boulder.]
budge • ***verb*** **budged, budging**

budget (buj′it) ***noun*** a careful plan for spending a certain amount of money in a period of time.
verb to plan carefully how to spend [I *budgeted* my allowance.]
budg·et • ***noun,*** *plural* **budgets** • ***verb*** **budgeted, budgeting**

buff (buf) ***noun*** **1** a soft, dark-yellow leather made from the skin of a buffalo or ox. **2** a stick or wheel covered with leather, used for cleaning and shining. **3** a dark-yellow color.
verb to clean or shine with a buff or similar tool [He repaired my shoes and then *buffed* them.]
buff • ***noun,*** *plural* **buffs** • ***verb*** **buffed, buffing**

buffalo (buf′ə lō) ***noun*** **1** one of several wild oxen of Africa and Asia. **2** *another name for* the North American **bison**.
buf·fa·lo • ***noun,*** *plural* **buffaloes** or **buffalos** or **buffalo**

Buffalo (buf′ə lō) a city in western New York State, on Lake Erie.
Buf·fa·lo

Buffalo Bill *name for* **Cody**, William Frederick.

buffet (bə fā′ *or* bo͞o fā′) ***noun*** **1** a piece of furniture with drawers and cupboards in which silverware, linens, and dishes are stored. **2** a meal at which people serve themselves from platters of food set out on a buffet or table.
buf·fet • ***noun,*** *plural* **buffets**

bug (bug) ***noun*** **1** a crawling insect with sucking mouthparts. The bedbug is a bug. **2** any insect or crawling animal. Ants and spiders are also called bugs. **3** [*an informal use*] a germ that causes sickness [I caught the flu *bug* last week.] **4** [*a slang use*] a tiny microphone hidden in order to record conversation secretly. **5** [*a slang use*] a flaw or defect in a machine, computer program, or plan.
verb **1** [*an informal use*] to hide a microphone in order to record conversation secretly. **2** [*a slang use*] to annoy, bother, or pester [Stop *bugging* me!]
bug • ***noun,*** *plural* **bugs** • ***verb*** **bugged, bugging**

buggy (bug′ē) ***noun*** **1** a light carriage with one seat, pulled by one horse. **2** a baby carriage.
bug·gy • ***noun,*** *plural* **buggies**

bugle

bugle (byo͞o′gəl) ***noun*** a type of small trumpet, usually without keys or valves.

a cat	ō go	ʉ fur	ə = a *in* ago
ā ape	ô law, for	ch chin	e *in* agent
ä cot, car	o͝o look	sh she	i *in* pencil
e ten	o͞o tool	th thin	o *in* atom
ē me	oi oil	*th* then	u *in* circus
i fit	ou out	zh measure	
ī ice	u up	ŋ ring	

bu·gle • ***noun,*** *plural* **bugles**

build (bild) ***verb*** **1** to make by putting together materials or parts; construct [Some American pioneers *built* their houses out of sod.] **2** to bring into being; create or develop [Love and trust *build* strong friendships.]
noun the way something is built or shaped; form or figure [He has a stocky *build.*]
build • ***verb*** **built, building** • ***noun,*** *plural* **builds**

builder (bil′dər) ***noun*** a person or animal that builds.
build·er • ***noun,*** *plural* **builders**

building (bil′diŋ) ***noun*** **1** anything that is built with walls and a roof; a house, factory, school, or any other permanent structure. **2** the act or work of one who builds [a contract for the *building* of a bridge].
build·ing • ***noun,*** *plural* **buildings**

built (bilt) ***verb*** *past tense and past participle of* **build.**

built-in (bilt′in′) ***adjective*** made as part of the building; not movable [*built-in* cabinets].

bulb (bulb) ***noun*** **1** the round, firm, underground part of the onion, daffodil, and other plants, made up of many layers. **2** anything shaped like a bulb [an electric light *bulb*].
bulb • ***noun,*** *plural* **bulbs**

bulb

Bulgaria (bəl ger′ē ə *or* bo͞ol ger′ē ə) a country in southeastern Europe, on the Black Sea.
Bul·gar·i·a

bulge (bulj) ***noun*** a part that swells out [The marbles make a *bulge* in your pocket.]
verb to swell outward [The mail carrier's bag *bulged* with mail.]
bulge • ***noun,*** *plural* **bulges** • ***verb*** **bulged, bulging**

bulk (bulk) ***noun*** **1** a great size or mass [The empty cardboard box was hard to carry because of its *bulk.*] **2** the largest or main part [He spends the *bulk* of his allowance.]
bulk • ***noun,*** *plural* **bulks**

bulky (bul′kē) ***adjective*** having great bulk; so big as to be awkward to handle [a *bulky* sofa].
bulk·y • ***adjective*** **bulkier, bulkiest**

bull (bo͝ol) ***noun*** **1** the fully grown male of cattle, buffalo, or other similar animals. **2** the fully grown male of the elephant, moose, whale, or some other large animals.
bull • ***noun,*** *plural* **bulls**

bulldog (bo͝ol′dôg *or* bo͝ol′däg) ***noun*** a stocky dog with short hair and a square jaw. It has a stubborn grip with its teeth.
bull·dog • ***noun,*** *plural* **bulldogs**

bulldozer (bo͝ol′dō zər) ***noun*** a tractor with a large blade like a shovel on the front for pushing earth or rough, broken pieces of buildings.
bull·doz·er • ***noun,*** *plural* **bulldozers**

bullet (bo͝ol′it) ***noun*** a small ball or cone of metal for shooting from a firearm.
bul·let • ***noun,*** *plural* **bullets**

bulletin (bo͝ol′ə tin) ***noun*** a short, up-to-date report [a news *bulletin* on the radio].
bul·le·tin • ***noun,*** *plural* **bulletins**

bulletin board ***noun*** a board or wall space on which bulletins or announcements are put up.
bulletin board • ***noun,*** *plural* **bulletin boards**

bullfight (bo͝ol′fīt) ***noun*** a public show in an arena in which a person with assistants challenges and, usually, kills a bull with a sword. Bullfights are popular in Spain and Mexico.
bull·fight • ***noun,*** *plural* **bullfights**

bullfrog (bo͝ol′frôg *or* bo͝ol′fräg) ***noun*** a large frog that has a deep, loud croak.
bull·frog • ***noun,*** *plural* **bullfrogs**

bull's-eye (bo͝olz′ī) ***noun*** **1** the round center of a target. **2** the shot that hits this mark.
bull's-eye • ***noun,*** *plural* **bull's-eyes**

bull's-eye

bully (bo͝ol′ē) ***noun*** a person who likes to hurt or frighten those who are smaller or weaker.
verb to hurt or frighten as a bully does.
bul·ly • ***noun,*** *plural* **bullies** • ***verb*** **bullied, bullying, bullies**

bulrush (bo͝ol′rush) ***noun*** a tall plant that grows in shallow water and marshes.

bul·rush • *noun, plural* **bulrushes**

bum (bum) [*an informal word*] ***noun*** **1** a person who wanders from place to place, doing odd jobs or begging. **2** a person who does little work and spends much time loafing.
bum • *noun, plural* **bums**

bumble (bum′bəl) ***verb*** to make foolish mistakes; act in a confused way [She *bumbled* through her speech.]
bum·ble • ***verb*** **bumbled, bumbling**

bumblebee (bum′bəl bē) ***noun*** a large, hairy, yellow-and-black bee that buzzes loudly.
bum·ble·bee • *noun, plural* **bumblebees**

bump (bump) ***verb*** **1** to knock against something; hit with a jolt [The bus *bumped* the car ahead of it. Don't *bump* into the wall.] **2** to move with jerks or jumps; jolt [The car *bumped* over the tracks.]
noun **1** a light blow or jolt. **2** a part that bulges out, causing an uneven surface. **3** a swelling caused by a blow.
bump • ***verb*** **bumped, bumping** • *noun, plural* **bumps**

bumper[1] (bump′ər) ***noun*** a bar across the front or back of a car or truck to give the vehicle protection if it bumps into something.
bump·er • *noun, plural* **bumpers**

bumper[2] (bump′ər) ***adjective*** very large or full [a *bumper* crop].
bump·er • ***adjective***

bumpy (bump′ē) ***adjective*** full of bumps; rough [a *bumpy* road].
bump·y • ***adjective*** **bumpier, bumpiest**

bun (bun) ***noun*** **1** a small roll made of bread dough, often sweetened. **2** hair worn twisted into a round, soft mass like a bun or roll.
bun • *noun, plural* **buns**

bunch (bunch) ***noun*** **1** a group of things of the same kind growing or placed together [a *bunch* of keys]. **2** [*an informal use*] a group of people [A *bunch* of us went out.]
verb to gather into a bunch [Passengers *bunched* up at the front of the bus.]
bunch • *noun, plural* **bunches** • ***verb*** **bunched, bunching**

bunch

bundle (bun′dəl) ***noun*** **1** a group of things tied up or wrapped up together [a *bundle* of old clothes]. **2** any package or parcel.
verb to wrap or tie together into a bundle.
—**bundle up** to put on plenty of warm clothing.
bun·dle • *noun, plural* **bundles** • ***verb*** **bundled, bundling**

bungalow (buŋ′gə lō) ***noun*** a small house with one story and an attic.
bun·ga·low • *noun, plural* **bungalows**

bungee cord (bun′jē) ***noun*** a special kind of elastic cord that is used to hold objects in place, such as luggage on a rack. It is also used in a sport in which it is attached to a person who jumps from a high place, falls, and comes close to the ground without hitting it.
bun·gee cord • *noun, plural* **bungee cords**

bungle (buŋ′gəl) ***verb*** to spoil by clumsy work.
bun·gle • ***verb*** **bungled, bungling**

bunk (buŋk) ***noun*** **1** a bed that sticks out from the wall like a shelf. **2** any narrow bed.
bunk • *noun, plural* **bunks**

bunny (bun′ē) ***noun*** a rabbit.
bun·ny • *noun, plural* **bunnies**

bunt (bunt) ***verb*** to bat a pitched baseball lightly without swinging [He *bunted* the ball toward third base.]
noun **1** the act of bunting [The batter attempted a *bunt*.] **2** a bunted ball [The *bunt* rolled toward the pitcher.]
bunt • ***verb*** **bunted, bunting** • *noun, plural* **bunts**

bunting (bun′tiŋ) ***noun*** flags or pieces of cloth in the colors of the flag, used as decorations.
bun·ting • ***noun***

buoy (bɔi *or* bo͞o′ē) ***noun*** an object floating in water and held in place by an anchor to warn of danger or to mark a channel. It often has a light or bell.
buoy • *noun, plural* **buoys**
● The words **buoy** and **boy** sound alike.
A red *buoy* marked the shallow water.
A young *boy* delivers our newspaper.

bur (bʉr) ***noun*** **1** the rough, prickly outer covering of some seeds. It often sticks to clothing and animal fur. **2** a plant with burs.

a cat	ō go	ʉ fur	ə = a *in* ago
ā ape	ô law, for	ch chin	e *in* agent
ä cot, car	oo look	sh she	i *in* pencil
e ten	o͞o tool	th thin	o *in* atom
ē me	ɔi oil	*th* then	u *in* circus
i fit	ɔu out	zh measure	
ī ice	u up	ŋ ring	

bur • *noun, plural* **burs**

burden (bʉrd′n) ***noun*** **1** anything that is carried; load [a light *burden* of pillows]. **2** anything that is very hard to bear; heavy load.
verb to put a burden on; load; weigh down [Don't *burden* me with your troubles.]
bur·den • ***noun,*** *plural* **burdens**
• ***verb*** **burdened, burdening**

bureau (byoor′ō) ***noun*** **1** a chest of drawers for holding clothes. It usually has a mirror. **2** a department of the government [the Federal *Bureau* of Investigation].
bu·reau • ***noun,*** *plural* **bureaus** or **bureaux**

burger (bʉr′gər) [*an informal word*] ***noun*** *a short form of* **hamburger, cheeseburger,** or the names of other similar sandwiches.
bur·ger • ***noun,*** *plural* **burgers**

burglar (bʉr′glər) ***noun*** a person who breaks into a building in order to steal.
bur·glar • ***noun,*** *plural* **burglars**

burial (ber′ē əl) ***noun*** the act of burying a dead body in a grave, a tomb, or the sea.
bur·i·al • ***noun,*** *plural* **burials**

Burkina Faso (boor kē′nə fä′sō) a country in western Africa, north of Ghana.
Bur·ki·na Fa·so

burlap (bʉr′lap) ***noun*** a coarse cloth made of the fibers of the jute or hemp plants, used for making sacks, bags, and other things.
bur·lap • ***noun,*** *plural* **burlaps**

burly (bʉr′lē) ***adjective*** big and strong; husky.
bur·ly • ***adjective*** **burlier, burliest**

Burma (bʉr′mə) *old name for* **Myanmar**.
Bur·ma

burn (bʉrn) ***verb*** **1** to be on fire; blaze [The campfire *burned* for a long time.] **2** to set on fire in order to give heat or light [They *burn* natural gas in their furnace.] **3** to destroy or be destroyed by fire [Forest fires *burn* many trees each year.] **4** to injure or be injured by fire, heat, or friction; scorch, singe, or scald [I slid down the rope too quickly and *burned* my hands.] **5** to make by fire, heat, or acid [A spark from the bonfire *burned* a hole in his coat.] **6** to feel or make feel hot [His head *burned* with fever. Pepper *burns* the throat.]
noun hurt or harm caused by fire, heat, wind, acid, or friction.
burn • ***verb*** **burned** or **burnt, burning**
• ***noun,*** *plural* **burns**

WORD CHOICES

Synonyms of burn

The words **burn, scorch,** and **singe** share the meaning "to destroy or damage by fire or heat."

She *burned* her old letters.

The iron was too hot and *scorched* the shirt.

I bent over the fire and *singed* my eyebrows.

burner (bʉrn′ər) ***noun*** the part of a stove or furnace from which the flame comes.
burn·er • ***noun,*** *plural* **burners**

burnt (bʉrnt) ***verb*** *a past tense and past participle of* **burn**.

burp (bʉrp) ***noun*** [*an informal use*] a belch.
verb **1** [*an informal use*] to belch. **2** to help a baby get rid of stomach gas by patting its back.
burp • ***noun,*** *plural* **burps** • ***verb*** **burped, burping**

burr (bʉr) ***noun*** *another spelling of* **bur**.
burr • ***noun,*** *plural* **burrs**

burrito (boo rē′tō) ***noun*** a Mexican dish made of a soft tortilla wrapped around a filling of meat, cheese, beans, and other foods.
bur·ri·to • ***noun,*** *plural* **burritos**

burro (bʉr′ō *or* boor′ō) ***noun*** in the southwestern U.S., a donkey that is used for carrying loads.
bur·ro • ***noun,*** *plural* **burros**

• The words **burro, borough,** and **burrow** sound alike.
Have you ever ridden a *burro?*
Manhattan is a *borough* of New York.
Groundhogs *burrow* in our garden.

burrow (bʉr′ō) ***noun*** a hole or tunnel dug in the ground by an animal.
verb **1** to dig a burrow. **2** to crawl into or hide in a place like a burrow [I *burrowed* into the blankets to get warm.]
bur·row • ***noun,*** *plural* **burrows**
• ***verb*** **burrowed, burrowing**

• The words **burrow, borough,** and **burro** sound alike.

burst (bʉrst) ***verb*** **1** to break open suddenly with force, especially because of pressure from

the inside; explode [A balloon will *burst* if you blow too much air into it.] **2** to go, come, start, or appear suddenly and with force [She *burst* into the room.] **3** to be as full or as crowded as possible [His sack was *bursting* with toys.]
noun **1** a sudden outbreak; explosion [a *burst* of cheers]. **2** a sudden, forceful effort or action [a *burst* of speed].
burst • ***verb*** **burst, bursting** • ***noun,*** *plural* **bursts**

Burundi (bo͝o ro͝on′dē) a country in east central Africa.
Bu·run·di

bury (ber′ē) ***verb*** **1** to put a dead body into the earth, a tomb, or the sea [They *buried* him in Iowa.] **2** to hide something in the ground [The pirates *buried* the treasure on an island.] **3** to cover up in order to hide [She *buried* her face in her hands.] —Look for the WORD CHOICES box at the entry **hide**[1].
bur·y • ***verb*** **buried, burying, buries**
● The words **bury** and **berry** sound alike.
Pirates were known to *bury* treasure.
The holly bush has a red *berry*.

bus (bus) ***noun*** a large motor vehicle for carrying many passengers along a regular route.
verb to go or carry by bus [They *bused* the children to school every day.]
bus • ***noun,*** *plural* **buses** or **busses**
• ***verb*** **bused** or **bussed, busing** or **bussing**

WORD HISTORY

bus

The word **bus** is shortened from *omnibus*, the original name for this kind of motor coach. *Omnibus* is a Latin word meaning "for everybody." So a **bus** is a coach on which everyone can ride.

bush (bo͝osh) ***noun*** a plant with a woody stem, smaller than a tree; shrub. A bush has many stems branching out from top to bottom instead of one main stem or trunk.
—beat around the bush to talk around a subject without getting to the point.
bush • ***noun,*** *plural* **bushes**

Bush (bo͝osh), **George** (jôrj) 1924- ; the forty-first president of the U.S., from 1989 to 1993.

Bush (bo͝osh), **George W.** (jôrj) 1946- ; the forty-third president of the U.S., from 2001 to 2009. He is the son of George Bush.

bushel (bo͝osh′əl) ***noun*** a unit of volume for grain, fruit, and vegetables. It is equal to 4 pecks or 32 quarts.
bush·el • ***noun,*** *plural* **bushels**

bushy (bo͝osh′ē) ***adjective*** thick and spreading out like a bush [a *bushy* tail; *bushy* eyebrows].
bush·y • ***adjective*** **bushier, bushiest**

busily (biz′ə lē) ***adverb*** in a busy way.
bus·i·ly • ***adverb***

business (biz′nis) ***noun*** **1** a person's work or occupation [My *business* is plumbing.] **2** a place where things are made or sold; a store or factory [Pat owns three *businesses*.] **3** the buying and selling of goods and services [the grocery *business;* the *business* of banking]. **4** something that a person has a right or duty to know, do, or be concerned with [You had no *business* telling her.] **5** a matter, project, or affair [I'm disgusted with the whole *business*.]
busi·ness • ***noun,*** *plural* **businesses**

businessman (biz′nis man′) ***noun*** a man who works in a business, especially as an owner or manager.
busi·ness·man • ***noun,*** *plural* **businessmen**

businessperson (biz′nis pʉr′sən) ***noun*** a businessman or businesswoman. Many people prefer this word.
busi·ness·per·son • ***noun,*** *plural* **businesspersons**

businesswoman (biz′nis wo͝om′ən) ***noun*** a woman who works in a business, especially as an owner or manager.
busi·ness·wom·an • ***noun,*** *plural* **businesswomen**

busing or **bussing** (bus′iŋ) ***noun*** the practice of carrying children by bus to schools outside of their neighborhoods, so that classes will be made up of various ethnic groups.
bus·ing or **bus·sing** • ***noun***

busses (bus′iz) ***noun a plural of*** **bus**.
bus·ses • ***noun***

bust[1] (bust) ***noun*** a piece of sculpture showing the head and upper chest of a person.
bust • ***noun,*** *plural* **busts**

bust[2] (bust) [*an informal word*] ***verb*** **1** to burst

a	cat	ō	go	ʉ	fur	ə =	a *in* ago
ā	ape	ô	law, for	ch	chin		e *in* agent
ä	cot, car	o͝o	look	sh	she		i *in* pencil
e	ten	o͞o	tool	th	thin		o *in* atom
ē	me	oi	oil	*th*	then		u *in* circus
i	fit	ou	out	zh	measure		
ī	ice	u	up	ŋ	ring		

or break [Mary *busted* her new bicycle.] **2** to hit. **3** to arrest [The police *busted* the gang.]
bust • ***verb*** **busted, busting**

bustle[1] (bus′əl) ***verb*** to hurry busily or with a great deal of fuss [We *bustled* about getting ready for the party.]
noun busy and noisy activity; commotion [the *bustle* of traffic at rush hour].
bus·tle • ***verb*** **bustled, bustling**
• ***noun***

bustle

bustle[2] (bus′əl) ***noun*** a padding or frame worn at the back by women in former times to puff out the skirt.
bus·tle • ***noun,*** *plural* **bustles**

busy (biz′ē) ***adjective*** **1** at work; doing something; active [The students are *busy* at their desks.] **2** with much action or motion; full of activity [a *busy* day; a *busy* store] —Look for the WORD CHOICES box at the entry **active**. **3** being used [a *busy* telephone line].
verb to make or keep busy [The cooks *busied* themselves in the kitchen.]
bus·y • ***adjective*** **busier, busiest**
• ***verb*** **busied, busying, busies**

busybody (biz′ē bäd′ē) ***noun*** a person who mixes into other people's business.
bus·y·bod·y • ***noun,*** *plural* **busybodies**

but (but) ***preposition*** except; other than [Nobody came *but* me.]
conjunction **1** yet; however [The story is long, *but* it is never dull.] **2** as opposed to what has been said [I am old, *but* you are young.] **3** unless; if not [It never rains *but* it pours.]
adverb **1** only [If I had *but* known, I would've gone.] **2** no more than [He is *but* a child.]
● The words **but** and **butt** sound alike.
Listen, *but* don't say anything.
Rest the rifle *butt* on your arm.
Rams will *butt* heads when they fight.

butcher (booch′ər) ***noun*** a person who cuts up meat for sale.
butch·er • ***noun,*** *plural* **butchers**

butler (but′lər) ***noun*** a male servant, usually in charge of the other servants.
but·ler • ***noun,*** *plural* **butlers**

butt[1] (but) ***noun*** **1** the thick end of anything [a rifle *butt*]. **2** the end left after something is used [a cigarette *butt*].
butt • ***noun,*** *plural* **butts**
● The words **butt** and **but** sound alike.

butt[2] (but) ***verb*** to strike or push with the head; to ram [The goat *butted* the fence.]
—**butt in** or **butt into** [*an informal use*] to mix into someone else's business.
butt • ***verb*** **butted, butting**
● The words **butt** and **but** sound alike.

butter (but′ər) ***noun*** **1** the yellow fat gotten by churning cream. It is used as a spread on bread and in cooking. **2** a spread or other substance somewhat like butter [peanut *butter*].
verb to spread with butter [*Butter* the toast.]
but·ter • ***noun,*** *plural* **butters**
• ***verb*** **buttered, buttering**

buttercup (but′ər kup) ***noun*** a plant with yellow flowers shaped like cups, growing in fields.
but·ter·cup • ***noun,*** *plural* **buttercups**

butterfly

butterfly (but′ər flī) ***noun*** an insect with a slender body and four broad wings, usually brightly colored.
but·ter·fly • ***noun,*** *plural* **butterflies**

buttermilk (but′ər milk) ***noun*** **1** the sour liquid that is left after churning butter from milk. **2** a kind of milk made by adding bacteria to skim milk.
but·ter·milk • ***noun***

butterscotch (but′ər skäch) ***noun*** a hard, sticky candy made from brown sugar and butter.
but·ter·scotch • ***noun***

buttery (but′ər ē) ***adjective*** **1** like butter [a *buttery* yellow color]. **2** having butter spread on it [*buttery* toast].

but·ter·y • *adjective*

buttocks (but′əks) ***plural noun*** the fleshy parts at the back of the hips; rump.
but·tocks • *plural noun*

button (but′n) ***noun*** **1** a small disk or knob sewn to a garment. It is pushed through a buttonhole to fasten parts together or is just used for decoration. **2** a small knob that is pushed or turned to work a bell, light, or machine.
verb to fasten or close with a button or buttons.
but·ton • *noun, plural* **buttons**
• *verb* **buttoned, buttoning**

buttonhole (but′n hōl) ***noun*** a slit in a garment through which a button can be fastened.
but·ton·hole • *noun, plural* **buttonholes**

buy (bī) ***verb*** to get by paying money or something else [We *bought* our house last year.]
noun the value of a thing compared with its price [Potatoes are a good *buy* this week.]
buy • *verb* **bought, buying** • *noun, plural* **buys**
• The words **buy** and **by** sound alike.
Buy now, pay later.
We are paid *by* the hour.

buyer (bī′ər) ***noun*** a person who buys; customer.
buy·er • *noun, plural* **buyers**

buzz (buz) ***verb*** **1** to make a humming sound like a long, steady *z* [Bees *buzz* as they fly.] **2** to talk in or be full of low, excited tones [The town *buzzed* with the news.] **3** to signal with a buzzer.
noun a humming sound like a long, steady *z*.
buzz • *verb* **buzzed, buzzing** • *noun, plural* **buzzes**

buzzard (buz′ərd) ***noun*** *another name for* **turkey vulture**.
buz·zard • *noun, plural* **buzzards**

buzzer (buz′ər) ***noun*** an electrical device that makes a buzzing sound used as a signal.
buzz·er • *noun, plural* **buzzers**

by (bī) ***preposition*** **1** near or beside [Sit *by* the fire.] **2** in or during [We traveled *by* night.] **3** for a fixed time [Bill is paid *by* the hour.] **4** no later than [Be back *by* ten o'clock.] **5** going through; by way of [We drove to New Jersey *by* the Holland Tunnel.] **6** past; beyond [He walked right *by* me.] **7** through the means or work of [I like to travel *by* car. We've read books *by* famous authors.] **8** according to [Mother learned to play piano *by* ear.] **9** in the measure or amount of; in units of [Do you sell apples *by* the pound?] **10** to the extent of [She's older than Mary *by* three months.] **11** and in another dimension [a room that is 15 feet *by* 20 feet].
adverb **1** near; close at hand [Stand *by!*] **2** away; aside [Put some money *by* for an emergency.] **3** past [We watched the bus go *by*.]
—by and by after a while. **—by oneself** **1** without any other person; alone. **2** without any help.
• The words **by** and **buy** sound alike.
It's midnight *by* my watch.
Are grapes a good *buy* this week?

by-and-by (bī′n bī′) ***noun*** a future time that is not known [I'll be home *by-and-by*.]

bye-bye (bī′bī *or* bī bī′) ***noun, interjection*** *the same as* **goodbye**.
bye-bye • *noun, plural* **bye-byes**
• *interjection*

bygone (bī′gôn) ***adjective*** gone by [*bygone* days].
noun *used mainly in the phrase* **let bygones be bygones**, let the past be forgotten.
by·gone • *adjective* • *noun, plural* **bygones**

bypass (bī′pas) ***noun*** a road that leaves the main route in order to go around something that is in the way.
verb to go around instead of through [We *bypassed* the busy city streets.]
by·pass • *noun, plural* **bypasses**
• *verb* **bypassed, bypassing**

Byron (bī′rən), **Lord** (lôrd) 1788-1824; English poet. His full name was *George Gordon Byron*.
By·ron, Lord

bystander (bī′stan dər) ***noun*** a person who stands by or near but does not take part in what is happening; onlooker.
by·stand·er • *noun, plural* **bystanders**

byte (bīt) ***noun*** a group of eight bits. A basic unit in a computer memory.
byte • *noun, plural* **bytes**
• The words **byte** and **bite** sound alike.
One computer *byte* equals eight bits.
Does your dog *bite?*

a	cat	ō	go	ʉ	fur	ə =	a *in* ago
ā	ape	ô	law, for	ch	chin		e *in* agent
ä	cot, car	oo	look	sh	she		i *in* pencil
e	ten	ōō	tool	th	thin		o *in* atom
ē	me	oi	oil	*th*	then		u *in* circus
i	fit	ou	out	zh	measure		
ī	ice	u	up	ŋ	ring		

C c

Cc Cc Cc Cc

The letter **c** *stands for a variety of sounds. Followed by* **a, o,** *or* **u, c** *sounds like* **k (cake, corn)***; this is called its "hard" sound. Followed by* **e, i,** *or* **y,** *it sounds like* **s (cent, circle, cyclone)***; this is its "soft" sound. Followed by* **h, c** *usually stands for the sound you hear at the beginning of* **chair***, but it can also stand for the* **k** *sound, as in* **character**.

c or **C** (sē) ***noun*** the third letter of the English alphabet.
c or **C** • ***noun,*** *plural* **c's** or **C's**

C (sē) ***noun*** **1** the Roman numeral for 100. **2** in some schools, a grade meaning "fair" or "average." **3** in music, the first tone in the scale of C major.
C • ***noun,*** *plural* **C's**

c or **c.** *abbreviation for* **1** centimeter. **2** cup.

C or **C.** *abbreviation for* **1** Celsius *or* centigrade [The temperature at which water freezes is 0° Celsius.] **2** cup.

CA *abbreviation for* California.

cab (kab) ***noun*** **1** a car or van that can be hired to carry persons in need of a ride. The riders pay the driver a fare for this. **2** the place in a truck, crane, or other big machine where the driver or operator sits.
cab • ***noun,*** *plural* **cabs**

cabbage (kab′ij) ***noun*** a plant with layers of broad, thick leaves forming a hard, round head. The leaves are eaten as a vegetable.
cab·bage • ***noun,*** *plural* **cabbages**

cabin (kab′in) ***noun*** **1** a small house that is built in a simple, rough way, usually out of wood. **2** a room on a ship with berths for sleeping. **3** the part of an airplane where the passengers ride.
cab·in • ***noun,*** *plural* **cabins**

cabinet (kab′i nət) ***noun*** **1** a case or cupboard with drawers or shelves. Cabinets are used for holding or storing things [a china *cabinet*]. **2** *often* **Cabinet** a group of officials who act as advisors to the head of a nation.
cab·i·net • ***noun,*** *plural* **cabinets**

cable (kā′bəl) ***noun*** **1** a thick, heavy, strong line made of strands of wire twisted together. **2** a bundle of insulated wires that carry electric current [Telephone *cables* run along the ocean floor.]
ca·ble • ***noun,*** *plural* **cables**

cable TV ***noun*** a TV system that uses large antennas to pick up signals from distant stations or satellites. The signals are then sent by cable to the homes of people who pay for them.
cable TV • ***noun,*** *plural* **cable TVs**

caboose

caboose (kə bo͞os′) ***noun*** a rail car for the crew on a freight train. It is usually the last car.

ca·boose • *noun, plural* **cabooses**

Cabot (kab′ət), **John** (jän) 1450?-1498?; Italian explorer who discovered the coast of North America in 1497 while sailing for England.
Cab·ot, John

cacao (kə kā′ō) *noun* a small tropical tree that bears seeds that are used to make chocolate and cocoa.
ca·ca·o • *noun, plural* **cacaos**

cackle (kak′əl) *verb* **1** to make the shrill, broken sounds of a hen. **2** to laugh or talk in a shrill way [They *cackled* at the comedian's jokes.]
noun the act or sound of cackling.
cack·le • *verb* **cackled, cackling** • *noun, plural* **cackles**

cactus (kak′təs) *noun* a plant with large, thick stems that bear spines or scales instead of leaves. Cactuses grow in hot, dry places.
cac·tus • *noun, plural* **cactuses** or **cacti** (kak′tī)

cadence (kād′ns) *noun* **1** a rhythm with a regular beat [The band marched in fast *cadence*.] **2** a flow of sound with a regular beat [the easy *cadence* of the waves breaking upon the shore].
ca·dence • *noun, plural* **cadences**

cadet (kə det′) *noun* **1** a student in training to become an officer in the army, navy, or air force. **2** a student at any military school.
ca·det • *noun, plural* **cadets**

Cadette (kə det′) *noun* a member of a division of the Girl Scouts for girls aged 12 through 14.
Ca·dette • *noun, plural* **Cadettes**

Caesar (sē′zər), **Julius** (jo͞ol′yəs) 100?-44 B.C.; Roman general and dictator who built up the Roman Empire. The name *Caesar* was later used as the title of Roman emperors.
Cae·sar, Jul·ius

café or **cafe** (ka fā′) *noun* a small restaurant.
ca·fé or **ca·fe** • *noun, plural* **cafés** or **cafes**

cafeteria (kaf′ə tir′ē ə) *noun* a restaurant where people go to a counter to buy their meals. They then carry their meals on trays to tables.
caf·e·te·ri·a • *noun, plural* **cafeterias**

caffeine (kaf′ēn) *noun* a substance that is found in coffee, tea, and cola drinks. It stimulates the heart and nervous system.
caf·feine • *noun*

cage (kāj) *noun* **1** a box or closed-off space with the sides made of wires or bars. Cages are used to keep birds or animals. **2** a screen that is used in baseball batting practice to keep missed and foul balls from getting away.
verb to shut up in a cage [The zoo *cages* the birds indoors during the winter.]
cage • *noun, plural* **cages** • *verb* **caged, caging**

Cain (kān) in the Bible, the oldest son of Adam and Eve. He killed his brother Abel.

cake (kāk) *noun* **1** a baked food that is made from a sweetened and flavored batter. It is often covered with icing. **2** a small, flat mass of batter or of chopped food that is fried or baked [a *pancake;* a fish *cake*]. **3** a solid mass with a definite shape [a *cake* of soap].
cake • *noun, plural* **cakes**

Cal. *abbreviation for* California.

calamity (kə lam′i tē) *noun* a terrible thing that happens, causing great sorrow; disaster.
ca·lam·i·ty • *noun, plural* **calamities**

calcium (kal′sē əm) *noun* a soft, silvery-white metal that is a chemical element. It is found in bones and teeth and in marble, limestone, and other rocks.
cal·ci·um • *noun*

calculate (kal′kyo͞o lāt) *verb* **1** to find out by using arithmetic; compute [We *calculate* the batting averages after each game.] **2** to find out by reasoning; estimate.
cal·cu·late • *verb* **calculated, calculating**

calculation (kal′kyo͞o lā′shən) *noun* **1** the act of calculating [By my *calculation*, the total cost of the car repairs will be $400.] **2** the answer found by calculating [precise *calculations*].
cal·cu·la·tion • *noun, plural* **calculations**

calculator (kal′kyo͞o lāt′ər) *noun* a small electronic or mechanical device that can solve mathematical problems.
cal·cu·la·tor • *noun, plural* **calculators**

calendar (kal′ən dər) *noun* **1** a chart or table that shows the months, weeks, and days of the year. **2** a list or schedule [a *calendar* of events].
cal·en·dar • *noun, plural* **calendars**

a cat	ō go	ʉ fur	ə = a *in* ago
ā ape	ô law, for	ch chin	e *in* agent
ä cot, car	o͝o look	sh she	i *in* pencil
e ten	o͞o tool	th thin	o *in* atom
ē me	oi oil	*th* then	u *in* circus
i fit	ou out	zh measure	
ī ice	u up	ŋ ring	

calf

calf[1] (kaf) ***noun*** **1** a young cow or bull. **2** the young of the elephant, whale, seal, hippopotamus, or other large animal. **3** a soft, flexible leather made from the hide of a calf.
calf • ***noun,*** *plural* **calves**

calf[2] (kaf) ***noun*** the rounded back part of the leg between the knee and the ankle.
calf • ***noun,*** *plural* **calves**

caliber (kal′i bər) ***noun*** **1** the diameter, or thickness, of a bullet or shell or the size of the inside of a gun barrel. **2** quality or ability [a musician of high *caliber*].
cal·i·ber • ***noun,*** *plural* **calibers**

calico (kal′i kō) ***noun*** a printed cotton cloth.
adjective **1** made of calico [a *calico* dress]. **2** spotted like calico [a *calico* cat].
cal·i·co • ***noun,*** *plural* **calicoes** or **calicos** • ***adjective***

STATE MAP

California

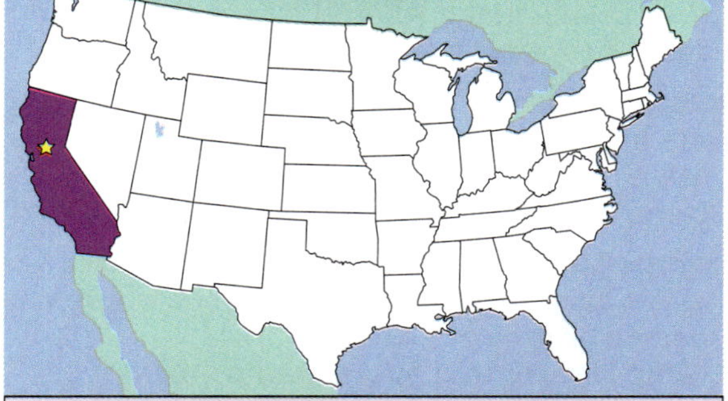

Statehood: 1850, the 31st state • **Capital:** Sacramento

California (kal′i fôr′nyə) a State in the southwestern part of the U.S., on the Pacific Coast. Its capital is Sacramento. Abbreviated **CA, Cal.,** or **Calif.**
Cal·i·for·nia

call (kôl) ***verb*** **1** to say in a loud voice [Please answer when I *call* your name.] **2** to ask or order to come [Please *call* a taxi. *Call* me when you're ready.] **3** to telephone [Please *call* me on Friday.] **4** to give a name to [Let's *call* the cat Molly.] **5** to make a short visit [We can *call* there on our way home.] **6** to stop [They *called* the game because of rain.] **7** to declare to be [The umpire *called* him out.]
noun **1** the act of calling; a shout or cry [a *call* for help]. **2** the special cry or sound of an animal, especially a bird. **3** the act of telephoning [a long-distance *call*]. **4** a short visit. **5** a ruling by an official [a good *call* by the referee].
—call for **1** to come and get [I will *call for* you at eight.] **2** to require [This job *calls for* special skills.] **—call up** to telephone. **—on call** ready when called for [The nurse is *on call* all night.]
call • ***verb*** **called, calling** • ***noun,*** *plural* **calls**

caller (kôl′ər) ***noun*** **1** a person who calls on the telephone [a long-distance *caller*]. **2** a person who makes a short visit [Several *callers* came to the house .]
call·er • ***noun,*** *plural* **callers**

callus (kal′əs) ***noun*** a place on the skin that becomes hard and thick. Calluses usually form on the hands and feet.
cal·lus • ***noun,*** *plural* **calluses**

calm (käm) ***adjective*** not disturbed, excited, or stirred up; still; quiet [a *calm* sea; a *calm* discussion] —Look for the WORD CHOICES box at the entry **cool**.
noun lack of wind or motion [an eerie *calm*].
verb to make or become calm [She *calmed* the baby by holding him.]
calm • ***adjective*** **calmer, calmest** • ***noun,*** *plural* **calms** • ***verb*** **calmed, calming**

WORD CHOICES

Synonyms of **calm**

The words **calm, placid,** and **tranquil** share the meaning "quiet or peaceful."

a *calm* sea

as *placid* as a cow

a *tranquil* summer day

calorie (kal′ər ē) ***noun*** a unit for measuring the energy that food supplies to the body [One large egg has about 100 *calories*.]
cal·o·rie • ***noun,*** *plural* **calories**

calves (kavz) ***noun plural of*** **calf**[1] and **calf**[2].

Calvin (kal′vin), **John** (jän) 1509-1564; French Protestant leader.
Cal·vin, John

Cambodia (kam bō′dē ə) a country in a large peninsula south of central China.
Cam·bo·di·a

camcorder (kam′kôrd′ər) ***noun*** a small, portable videotape recorder and TV camera.
cam·cord·er • ***noun,*** *plural* **camcorders**

came (kām) ***verb*** *past tense of* **come**.

camel

camel (kam′əl) ***noun*** a large animal with one or two humps on its back. Camels are commonly used for riding and carrying loads in Asian and northern African deserts. They are able to keep going for days without food or water.
cam·el • ***noun,*** *plural* **camels** or **camel**

Camelot (kam′ə lät) in British legend, the city where King Arthur lived.
Cam·e·lot

camera (kam′ər ə *or* kam′rə) ***noun*** **1** a closed box with space for film inside, for taking photographs. **2** the part of a TV transmitter that picks up the picture and changes it to electrical signals so that it can be sent.
cam·er·a • ***noun,*** *plural* **cameras**

WORD HISTORY

camera

The source of **camera** is a Latin word that means "room" or "chamber." The full name of the box for taking pictures was once *camera obscura*, meaning "dark chamber." This described the closed part in which the image is formed on the film by the lens. Today, this name has been shortened to **camera**.

Cameroon (kam ə ro͞on′) a country in Western Africa, on the Atlantic Ocean.
Ca·me·roon

camouflage (kam′ə fläzh) ***noun*** **1** the hiding of soldiers, weapons, and equipment from the enemy by dressing, painting, or covering them to look like part of the landscape. **2** color, shape, or other quality that acts like a disguise in nature.
verb to disguise in order to hide [The soldiers *camouflaged* the planes with green paint.]
cam·ou·flage • ***noun,*** *plural* **camouflages** • ***verb*** **camouflaged, camouflaging**

camp (kamp) ***noun*** **1** a group of tents, huts, or other rough shelters to live in for a time. **2** a place in the country where children can have an outdoor vacation [summer *camp*].
verb to set up or live in a camp [Let's *camp* by the river tonight.]
camp • ***noun,*** *plural* **camps** • ***verb*** **camped, camping**

campaign (kam pān′) ***noun*** a series of planned actions that are taken to reach a goal [an election *campaign;* a military *campaign*].
verb to take part in a campaign [We *campaigned* for her election.]
cam·paign • ***noun,*** *plural* **campaigns** • ***verb*** **campaigned, campaigning**

camper (kamp′ər) ***noun*** **1** a person who vacations at a camp. **2** a special vehicle or trailer that is used for camping.
camp·er • ***noun,*** *plural* **campers**

campfire (kamp′fīr) ***noun*** a small outdoor fire that people make when they are camping.
camp·fire • ***noun,*** *plural* **campfires**

camping (kamp′iŋ) ***noun*** the activity of living in the outdoors for a time, usually for recreation.
camp·ing • ***noun***

campsite (kamp′sīt) ***noun*** **1** a park area set aside for people to camp. **2** a spot where one person or group is camping.
camp·site • ***noun,*** *plural* **campsites**

campus (kam′pəs) ***noun*** the grounds and buildings of a school or college.
cam·pus • ***noun,*** *plural* **campuses**

a	cat	ō	go	ʉ	fur	ə =	a *in* ago
ā	ape	ô	law, for	ch	chin		e *in* agent
ä	cot, car	oo	look	sh	she		i *in* pencil
e	ten	o͞o	tool	th	thin		o *in* atom
ē	me	oi	oil	*th*	then		u *in* circus
i	fit	ou	out	zh	measure		
ī	ice	u	up	ŋ	ring		

can[1] (kan) ***verb*** (*helping verb*) This verb is used with other verbs to show that the subject: **1** knows how to [I *can* speak Russian.] **2** is able to [The baby *can* walk.] **3** is likely to [*Can* that be true?] **4** has the right to [You *can* vote when you are eighteen years old.] **5** has permission to; may [*Can* I go out to play?] The word "to" is not used between *can* and the verb that follows it.
can • ***verb*** *past tense* **could**; *he / she / it* **can**

can[2] (kan) ***noun*** **1** a metal or plastic container of various kinds, usually with a separate cover [a garbage *can;* a *can* of shoe polish]. **2** a metal container for food, that can be sealed. Food is sealed in cans to keep it from spoiling. **3** the amount that a can holds [The recipe calls for one *can* of tomato sauce.]
verb to put in sealed cans [The vegetables are *canned* at a large plant in California.]
can • ***noun,*** *plural* **cans** • ***verb*** **canned, canning**

Can. *abbreviation for* Canada.

Canada (kan′ə də) a country in the northern part of North America. Abbreviated **Can.**
Can·a·da

Canadian (kə nā′dē ən) ***noun*** a person born or living in Canada.
Ca·na·di·an • ***noun,*** *plural* **Canadians**

canal

canal (kə nal′) ***noun*** a channel dug and filled with water so that ships may cross a stretch of land. Canals are also used to carry water for crops.
ca·nal • ***noun,*** *plural* **canals**

canary (kə ner′ē) ***noun*** a small, yellow songbird that is commonly kept as a pet.
ca·nar·y • ***noun,*** *plural* **canaries**

cancel (kan′səl) ***verb*** **1** to do away with; say that it will no longer be [She *canceled* the order.] **2** to cross out with lines or mark in some other way [Postage stamps are *canceled* to show that they have been used.]
can·cel • ***verb*** **canceled** or **cancelled, canceling** or **cancelling**

cancellation (kan sə lā′shən) ***noun*** **1** the act of canceling [Heavy snow caused the *cancellation* of school classes.] **2** a mark that cancels [the *cancellation* of a postage stamp].
can·cel·la·tion • ***noun,*** *plural* **cancellations**

cancer (kan′sər) ***noun*** a disease in which certain cells grow out of control and spread to other parts of the body.
can·cer • ***noun,*** *plural* **cancers**

candidate (kan′di dāt *or* kan′di dət) ***noun*** a person who seeks, or who has been recommended for, a political office or an honor.
can·di·date • ***noun,*** *plural* **candidates**

candied (kan′dēd) ***adjective*** cooked in or glazed with sugar [*candied* apples].
can·died • ***adjective***

candle (kan′dəl) ***noun*** a piece of wax with a wick through its center. A candle is burned to give light.
can·dle • ***noun,*** *plural* **candles**

candlestick (kan′dəl stik) ***noun*** a stand or support for a candle.
can·dle·stick • ***noun,*** *plural* **candlesticks**

candlestick

candy (kan′dē) ***noun*** **1** a sweet food that is made from sugar or syrup, with flavoring, coloring, fruits, nuts, or other ingredients added. **2** a piece of this kind of food.
verb to cook with sugar or syrup in order to preserve or glaze [Mother was *candying* apples.]
can·dy • ***noun,*** *plural* **candies** • ***verb*** **candied, candying, candies**

cane (kān) ***noun*** **1** a stick that a person may carry for help in walking. **2** the thin, tough stem of bamboo and certain other plants.
cane • ***noun,*** *plural* **canes**

canine (kā′nīn) ***adjective*** of or having to do with the group of animals that includes dogs,

foxes, and wolves.
noun **1** an animal that belongs to this group. **2** one of the four sharp-pointed teeth on either side of the upper and lower front teeth; cuspid.
ca·nine • *adjective*
• *noun, plural* **canines**

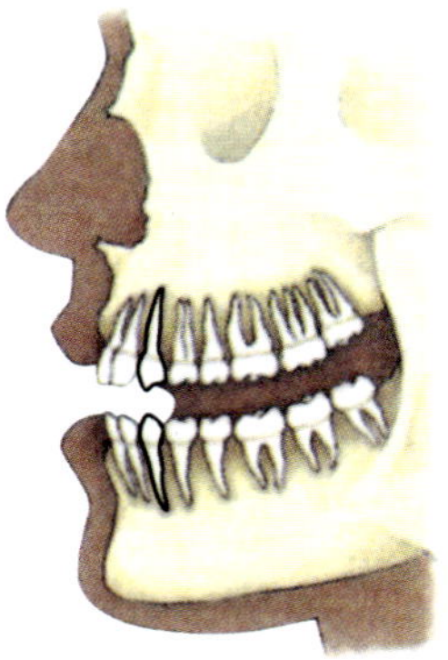

canine teeth

cannery (kan′ər ē) *noun* a place where foods are canned.
can·ner·y • *noun, plural* **canneries**

cannibal (kan′i bəl) *noun* a person who eats human flesh.
can·ni·bal • *noun, plural* **cannibals**

cannon (kan′ən) *noun* a large gun mounted on a base; a piece of artillery.
can·non • *noun, plural* **cannons** or **cannon**

cannot (kan′ät *or* kə nät′) can not.
can·not

canoe (kə n͞oo′) *noun* a narrow, light boat with its sides coming together in a sharp edge at each end. It is moved by using paddles.
ca·noe • *noun, plural* **canoes**

canola oil (kə nō′lə) *noun* an oil that comes from certain plant seeds. It is used in cooking and in salads.
ca·no·la oil • *noun*

canopy (kan′ə pē) *noun* a cloth or other covering that is like a roof or awning.
can·o·py • *noun, plural* **canopies**

can't (kant) cannot.

cantaloupe

cantaloupe or **cantaloup** (kant′ə lōp) *noun* a round melon with hard, rough skin and sweet, juicy, orange-colored flesh.
can·ta·loupe or **can·ta·loup** • *noun, plural* **cantaloupes** or **cantaloups**

canteen (kan tēn′) *noun* **1** a small container for carrying drinking water on a hike or march. **2** a store in a factory or at a military base.
can·teen • *noun, plural* **canteens**

canter (kan′tər) *noun* a slow, easy gallop.
verb to ride or go at a canter.
can·ter • *noun, plural* **canters**
• *verb* **cantered, cantering**
• The words **canter** and **cantor** sound alike.
Make the horse *canter* around the track.
Our synagogue just hired a new *cantor*.

cantor (kan′tər) *noun* a singer who leads the congregation in prayer in a synagogue.
can·tor • *noun, plural* **cantors**

canvas (kan′vəs) *noun* a strong, heavy cloth of hemp, cotton, or linen. It is used for things such as sails, tents, and oil paintings.
can·vas • *noun, plural* **canvases**

canyon (kan′yən) *noun* a long, narrow valley with high cliffs on each side.
can·yon • *noun, plural* **canyons**

cap (kap) *noun* **1** a close-fitting covering for the head that has no brim but often has a visor. **2** a lid, top, or other thing that is like a cap [a bottle *cap;* a *cap* of snow]. **3** a dot of gunpowder set in paper for firing in a toy gun.
verb **1** to put a cap on [She *capped* the bottle.] **2** to cover the top of [Snow *capped* the hill.]
cap • *noun, plural* **caps** • *verb* **capped, capping**

capability (kā′pə bil′i tē) *noun* the power to do something; ability [She has the *capability* to become a lawyer.]
ca·pa·bil·i·ty • *noun, plural* **capabilities**

capable (kā′pə bəl) *adjective* able to do things well; fit or skilled [a *capable* mechanic].
—capable of 1 able or ready to [*capable of* telling a lie]. **2** having what is necessary for [*capable of* being a great doctor].
ca·pa·ble • *adjective*

capacity (kə pas′i tē) *noun* **1** the amount of space that can be filled; room for holding [The

a	cat	ō	go	ʉ	fur	ə = a *in* ago
ā	ape	ô	law, for	ch	chin	e *in* agent
ä	cot, car	oo	look	sh	she	i *in* pencil
e	ten	ōō	tool	th	thin	o *in* atom
ē	me	oi	oil	*th*	then	u *in* circus
i	fit	ou	out	zh	measure	
ī	ice	u	up	ŋ	ring	

stadium has a seating *capacity* of 50,000.] **2** the ability to be or become; fitness or skill [He has the *capacity* to be a great actor.] **3** position or office [She set the rules in her *capacity* as school principal.]
ca·pac·i·ty • *noun, plural* **capacities**

cape[1] (kāp) *noun* an outer garment without sleeves that closes at the neck and hangs over the back and shoulders.
cape • *noun, plural* **capes**

cape

cape[2] (kāp) *noun* a piece of land that sticks out into a lake or sea.
cape • *noun, plural* **capes**

caper (kā′pər) *verb* to skip about in a playful way; frolic [The children *capered* in the yard.] *noun* **1** a playful skipping or dancing. **2** a playful or silly trick; prank.
ca·per • *verb* **capered, capering** • *noun, plural* **capers**

Cape Verde (kāp vurd) a country on a group of islands in the Atlantic, west of Africa.

capillary (kap′i ler′ē) *noun* one of the tiny blood vessels that join the arteries and the veins.
cap·il·lar·y • *noun, plural* **capillaries**

capital (kap′i təl) *noun* **1** *the same as* **capital letter**. **2** a city where the government of a nation or state is located [Washington, D.C. is the *capital* of the U.S.] **3** money or property that is put into a business or that is used to produce more money [His *capital* was just $100 in cash when he opened his repair shop.] *adjective* **1** very fine; excellent [a *capital* idea]. **2** that can be punished by death [a *capital* crime].
cap·i·tal • *noun, plural* **capitals** • *adjective*
● The words **capital** and **Capitol** sound alike.
Juneau is the *capital* of Alaska.
We took a tour inside the *Capitol*.

capitalism (kap′i təl iz′əm) *noun* an economic system in which the land, factories, and other resources used in producing goods are private property. Goods are sold to the public with the hope of making a profit.
cap·i·tal·ism • *noun*

capitalize (kap′i təl īz′) *verb* to begin with a capital letter or write all in capital letters [We usually *capitalize* the name of a person.]
cap·i·tal·ize • *verb* **capitalized, capitalizing**

capital letter *noun* a letter that is not a small letter. It is used to begin a sentence or a name [B is a *capital letter*.]
capital letter • *noun, plural* **capital letters**

capital punishment *noun* the killing of a person by law as punishment for a crime.
capital punishment • *noun, plural* **capital punishments**

Capitol

Capitol (kap′i təl) *noun* **1** the building in which the U.S. Congress meets, in Washington, D.C. **2** *usually* **capitol** the building in which a State legislature meets.
Cap·i·tol • *noun, plural* **Capitols**
● The words **Capitol** and **capital** sound alike.
The *Capitol* is in Washington, D.C.
Cheyenne is the *capital* of Wyoming.

SPELLING TIP

Use this memory aid to spell **capitol**.
See the d**o**me on the capit**o**l.

capsize (kap′sīz) *verb* to turn over or upset [The storm *capsized* the small boat. The boat *capsized* in the storm.]
cap·size • *verb* **capsized, capsizing**

capsule (kap′səl) *noun* **1** a small, rounded container that holds a dose of medicine. A capsule is made of gelatin that dissolves quickly

after it is swallowed. **2** the enclosed part of a spacecraft that holds the crew.
cap·sule • *noun, plural* **capsules**

Capt. *abbreviation for* Captain.

captain (kap′tən) ***noun*** **1** a chief or leader of some group or activity [a police *captain;* the *captain* of a football team]. **2** the person in charge of a ship. **3** a military officer.
verb to be captain of [She *captains* the team.]
cap·tain • *noun, plural* **captains**
• ***verb*** **captained, captaining**

caption (kap′shən) ***noun*** the words that describe a picture in a book, magazine, or newspaper. The caption is usually just below the picture.
cap·tion • *noun, plural* **captions**

captive (kap′tiv) ***noun*** a person caught and held a prisoner.
cap·tive • *noun, plural* **captives**

captivity (kap tiv′i tē) ***noun*** the condition of being held a captive [At the zoo we saw the largest lion in *captivity*.]
cap·tiv·i·ty • *noun, plural* **captivities**

capture (kap′chər) ***verb*** to catch and hold by force or skill [The police *captured* the thief. The new song *captured* her attention.]
noun the act of capturing or of being captured [The fugitive avoided *capture*.]
cap·ture • ***verb*** **captured, capturing** • *noun, plural* **captures**

car (kär) ***noun*** **1** an automobile. **2** a vehicle that moves on rails [a freight *car*]. **3** the part of an elevator that people ride in.
car • *noun, plural* **cars**

caramel (kär′məl *or* ker′ə məl) ***noun*** **1** burnt sugar that is used to flavor or color food or drink. **2** a smooth, chewy candy.
car·a·mel • *noun, plural* **caramels**

carat (ker′ət) ***noun*** the unit that is used for weighing gems. It is equal to ⅕ of a gram.
car·at • *noun, plural* **carats**

- The words **carat, caret, carrot,** and **karat** sound alike.
  A *carat* is less than a gram.
  The *caret* is a common editor's mark.
  Our rabbit enjoys a *carrot* each day.
  Her ring is 14-*karat* gold.

caravan (ker′ə van) ***noun*** a group of people traveling together, especially for safety when crossing a desert or in the Arctic.
car·a·van • *noun, plural* **caravans**

carbon (kär′bən) ***noun*** a chemical element that is found in all plants and animals. Carbon is also found in rocks, coal, petroleum, and many other nonliving things. Diamonds are a pure form of carbon.
car·bon • ***noun***

carbonated (kär′bə nāt′əd) ***adjective*** of or describing a drink containing carbon dioxide, which makes bubbles when exposed to the air.
car·bon·at·ed • ***adjective***

carbon dioxide (dī äks′īd′) ***noun*** a gas made up of carbon and oxygen. It has no color and no smell. We breathe it out of our lungs.
carbon di·ox·ide • ***noun***

carbon monoxide (mə näks′īd) ***noun*** a very poisonous gas that has no color and no smell. It is formed when carbon is not fully burned.
carbon mon·ox·ide • ***noun***

carburetor (kär′bər āt ər) ***noun*** the part of a gasoline engine that mixes air and gasoline spray. This mixture is burned by the engine when it runs.
car·bu·ret·or • *noun, plural* **carburetors**

carcass (kär′kəs) ***noun*** the body of a dead animal.
car·cass • *noun, plural* **carcasses**

card (kärd) ***noun*** a flat piece of cardboard or stiff paper, often having something printed on it [Greeting *cards* are sent on holidays. He used a score *card* to keep track of the game.]
card • *noun, plural* **cards**

cardboard (kärd′bôrd) ***noun*** a thick, stiff kind of paper. It is used to make cards and boxes.
card·board • *noun, plural* **cardboards**

cardinal

cardinal (kärd′n əl) ***adjective*** of most importance; chief [The *cardinal* points of a compass

a cat	ō go	ʉ fur	ə = a *in* ago
ā ape	ô law, for	ch chin	e *in* agent
ä cot, car	oo look	sh she	i *in* pencil
e ten	ōō tool	th thin	o *in* atom
ē me	oi oil	*th* then	u *in* circus
i fit	ou out	zh measure	
ī ice	u up	ŋ ring	

are north, south, east, and west.]
noun **1** a bright-red American songbird. **2** a high official of the Roman Catholic Church.
car·di·nal • ***adjective*** • ***noun,*** *plural* **cardinals**

cardinal number ***noun*** a number used in counting or in showing how many [Three, sixty, and 169 are *cardinal numbers.*]
cardinal number • ***noun,*** *plural* **cardinal numbers**

care (ker) ***noun*** **1** worry or concern [a mind filled with *care.* She didn't have a *care* in the world.] **2** the act of watching over or tending; protection [The books were left in my *care.*] **3** serious attention or interest; regard [She did her homework with *care.*]
verb **1** to feel an interest, worry, or regret [Do you *care* if I go? I didn't *care* that I lost.] **2** to wish or want [Do you *care* to come along?] **3** to watch over or take charge of something [She *cared* for my cat while I was gone.] **4** to feel a liking [I don't *care* for dancing.]
—take care to be careful; watch out. **—take care of** **1** to watch over; protect [*Take care of* the baby.] **2** to look after; do what needs to be done about [He will *take care of* the problem.]
care • ***noun,*** *plural* **cares** • ***verb*** **cared, caring**

WORD CHOICES

Synonyms of **care**

The words **care, anxiety,** and **concern** share the meaning "worry or fear."

without a *care*
feeling *anxiety* about his missing pet
showing little *concern* for our safety

career (kə rir′) ***noun*** what a person does to make a living; occupation or profession [a baseball *career;* a *career* in teaching].
ca·reer • ***noun,*** *plural* **careers**

carefree (ker′frē) ***adjective*** without care or worry [He spends money in a *carefree* way.]
care·free • ***adjective***

careful (ker′fəl) ***adjective*** **1** taking care so that there are no mistakes or accidents; cautious [a *careful* driver]. **2** done or made with care [a *careful* inspection].
care·ful • ***adjective***

careless (ker′lis) ***adjective*** **1** not paying enough attention; not concerned enough [He dropped it because he was *careless.*] **2** done or made without attention or interest [a *careless* wave of the hand].
care·less • ***adjective***

caress (kə res′) ***verb*** to stroke or touch in a loving or gentle way [He *caressed* the cat.]
noun a loving or gentle touch.
ca·ress • ***verb*** **caressed, caressing** • ***noun,*** *plural* **caresses**

caret (ker′ət) ***noun*** the mark ʌ. It shows where something is to be added in a written or printed line.
car·et • ***noun,*** *plural* **carets**

- The words **caret, carat, carrot,** and **karat** sound alike.
  He drew a *caret* where the word goes.
  A *carat* is less than a gram.
  The *carrot* is a source of vitamin A.
  Her ring is 14-*karat* gold.

caretaker (ker′tāk ər) ***noun*** a person who takes care of some thing or place; custodian.
care·tak·er • ***noun,*** *plural* **caretakers**

cargo (kär′gō) ***noun*** the load of goods carried by a ship, airplane, truck, or other vehicle.
car·go • ***noun,*** *plural* **cargoes** or **cargos**

Caribbean Sea (ker′i bē′ən *or* kə rib′ē ən) a sea bounded by the West Indies, Central America, and South America. It is a part of the Atlantic Ocean.
Car·ib·be·an Sea

caribou

caribou (ker′i bo͞o) ***noun*** a large North American deer that is a kind of reindeer.
car·i·bou • ***noun,*** *plural* **caribous** or **caribou**

carnation (kär nā′shən) ***noun*** **1** a plant with white, pink, or red flowers. **2** one of these flowers.
car·na·tion • ***noun,*** *plural* **carnations**

Carnegie (kär′nə gē), **Andrew** (an′dro͞o) 1835-1919; U.S. businessman in the steel industry. He was born in Scotland. He gave much money to public institutions.
Car·ne·gie, An·drew

carnival (kär′ni vəl) ***noun*** an entertainment that travels from place to place, with sideshows, rides, and games.
car·ni·val • ***noun,*** *plural* **carnivals**

carnivore (kär′ni vôr′) ***noun*** a carnivorous animal.
car·ni·vore • ***noun,*** *plural* **carnivores**

carnivorous (kär niv′ər əs) ***adjective*** describing animals that feed on other animals; flesh-eating [Lions are *carnivorous* animals.]
car·niv·o·rous • ***adjective***

carol (ker′əl) ***noun*** a song of joy or praise, especially a Christmas song.
car·ol • ***noun,*** *plural* **carols**

carousel (ker ə sel′) ***noun*** a merry-go-round.
car·ou·sel • ***noun,*** *plural* **carousels**

carp[1] (kärp) ***noun*** a freshwater fish with soft fins and large scales that is used for food.
carp • ***noun,*** *plural* **carp** or **carps**

carp[2] (kärp) ***verb*** to complain or find fault in a nagging way [She *carped* about the homework assignment during the entire ride home.]
carp • ***verb*** **carped, carping**

carpenter (kär′pən tər) ***noun*** a person whose work is building and repairing things made of wood.
car·pen·ter • ***noun,*** *plural* **carpenters**

carpentry (kär′pən trē) ***noun*** the work or trade of a carpenter.
car·pen·try • ***noun***

carpet (kär′pət) ***noun*** **1** a thick, heavy fabric used to cover floors. **2** anything that covers like a carpet [a *carpet* of snow].
verb to cover with a carpet or with something like a carpet [We *carpeted* the upstairs bedrooms.]
car·pet • ***noun,*** *plural* **carpets**
• ***verb*** **carpeted, carpeting**

car pool ***noun*** an arrangement in which the members of a group take turns driving the group to or from a certain place.
car pool • ***noun,*** *plural* **car pools**

carriage (ker′ij) ***noun*** **1** a vehicle with wheels that is used for carrying people. It is usually drawn by horses. **2** a light vehicle for wheeling a baby about; buggy. **3** a moving part of a machine for carrying something along [The *carriage* of a typewriter holds the paper.] **4** the way a person stands or walks; posture.
car·riage • ***noun,*** *plural* **carriages**

carrier (ker′ē ər) ***noun*** **1** a person or thing that carries [a mail *carrier;* an aircraft *carrier*]. **2** a company that is in the business of moving goods or passengers. **3** a person or animal that can pass on a disease germ, but does not seem to be sick with the disease.
car·ri·er • ***noun,*** *plural* **carriers**

Carroll (ker′əl), **Lewis** (lo͞o′is) 1832-1898; the English author who wrote *Alice's Adventures in Wonderland*. His real name was *Charles L. Dodgson*.
Car·roll, Lew·is

carrot (ker′ət) ***noun*** a plant with a long, thick, orange-red root that is eaten as a vegetable.
car·rot • ***noun,*** *plural* **carrots**

carrot

● The words **carrot, carat, caret,** and **karat** sound alike.
The *carrot* is a source of vitamin A.
A *carat* is less than a gram.
The *caret* is a common editor's mark.
Her ring is 14-*karat* gold.

carry (ker′ē) ***verb*** **1** to take from one place to another; to transport or conduct [I will *carry* the groceries. This pipe *carries* hot water. Air *carries* sound.] **2** to bring over a figure from one column to the next in adding a row of figures. **3** to hold or support; to bear [These beams *carry* the weight of the roof.] **4** to have for sale [This store does not *carry* school supplies.] **5** to be able to reach over a distance [Her voice *carries* well.] **6** to be able to sing a song correctly [I can't *carry* a tune.]

a	cat	ō	go	ʉ	fur	ə =	a *in* ago
ā	ape	ô	law, for	ch	chin		e *in* agent
ä	cot, car	o͝o	look	sh	she		i *in* pencil
e	ten	o͞o	tool	th	thin		o *in* atom
ē	me	oi	oil	*th*	then		u *in* circus
i	fit	ou	out	zh	measure		
ī	ice	u	up	ŋ	ring		

noun the act of carrying something [The half-back gained five yards on that *carry*.]
—carry on **1** to do or manage [They *carry on* business with several Japanese companies.] **2** to go on as before [We *carried on* in spite of the rain.] **—carry out** to get done; bring to a finish; accomplish [Will they *carry out* their threat?] **—get carried away** to be filled with such strong feelings that one does not think clearly [She *got carried away* at the auction and spent too much money.]
car·ry • ***verb*** **carried, carrying, carries**
• ***noun,*** *plural* **carries**

WORD CHOICES

Synonyms of **carry**

The words **carry, bear,** and **transport** share the meaning "to take from one place to another."

Air *carries* sound.

The kings came *bearing* gifts.

We *transported* the supplies by truck.

Carson (kär′sən), **Kit** (kit) 1809-1868; American frontiersman who served as a scout in the West. His real name was *Christopher Carson*.
Car·son, Kit

Carson City (kär′sən sit′ē) the capital of Nevada.
Car·son Cit·y

cart (kärt) ***noun*** a small wagon, often with only two wheels, moved by hand or drawn by an animal [a grocery *cart*].
cart • ***noun,*** *plural* **carts**

Carter (kärt′ər), **Jimmy** (jim′ē) 1924- ; thirty-ninth president of the U.S., from 1977 to 1981. His full legal name is *James Earl Carter, Jr.*
Car·ter, Jim·my

Cartier (kär tyā′), **Jacques** (zhäk) 1491-1557; French explorer in northeastern North America.
Car·tier, Jacques

cartilage (kärt′l ij) ***noun*** a tough but flexible tissue that is connected to the bones and forms part of the skeleton; gristle. The outside part of the ear is made of cartilage.
car·ti·lage • ***noun***

carton (kärt′n) ***noun*** a box or other container usually made of cardboard or plastic.
car·ton • ***noun,*** *plural* **cartons**

cartoon (kär to͞on′) ***noun*** **1** a drawing in a newspaper or magazine that shows how the editor or artist feels about some person or thing in the news. It is often drawn in a joking or mocking way. **2** *the same as* **comic strip**. **3** *the same as* **animated cartoon**.
car·toon • ***noun,*** *plural* **cartoons**

cartridge (kär′trij) ***noun*** **1** the metal or card-board tube that holds the gunpowder and the bullet or shot for use in a firearm. **2** a small container that is put into a larger device or machine. It holds material that is needed to operate the device [the *cartridge* of an ink pen; a film *cartridge* for a camera]. **3** a unit holding the needle for a phonograph.
car·tridge • ***noun,*** *plural* **cartridges**

cartwheel (kärt′hwēl *or* kärt′wēl) ***noun*** a kind of handspring done sideways.
cart·wheel • ***noun,*** *plural* **cartwheels**

carve (kärv) ***verb*** **1** to make or shape by cutting or chipping [She *carved* a statue in wood.] **2** to cut into pieces or slices [*Carve* the turkey.]
carve • ***verb*** **carved, carving**

Carver (kär′vər), **George Washington** (jôrj′ wôsh′iŋ tən) 1864-1943; American scientist who developed many products from peanuts, soybeans, and other plants.
Car·ver, George Wash·ing·ton

carving (kär′viŋ) ***noun*** **1** the work or art of someone who carves. **2** a carved form or design.
carv·ing • ***noun,*** *plural for sense 2 only* **carvings**

cascade (kas kād′) ***noun*** a small, steep waterfall.
verb to fall in a cascade or like a cascade [Sparks *cascaded* from the broken power lines.]
cas·cade • ***noun,*** *plural* **cascades**
• ***verb*** **cascaded, cascading**

cascade

case[1] (kās) ***noun*** **1** a single happening or example [a *case* of mistaken identity; four *cases* of measles]. **2** any matter that needs to be or is being watched, studied, or

investigated [It was a *case* for the police.] **3** a matter to be decided by a court of law [Two lawyers will handle this *case*.] **4** the real facts or condition [I'm sorry, but that's not the *case*.]
—in case if it should be that; if [Remind me *in case* I forget.] **—in case of** if there should happen to be [*In case of* a fire, use the stairs.]
case • ***noun,*** *plural* **cases**

case[2] (kās) ***noun*** a container for holding and protecting something [a violin *case;* a display *case* in a museum].
case • ***noun,*** *plural* **cases**

cash (kash) ***noun*** **1** money that one actually has, in coins or bills [I'm short on *cash*.] **2** money or a check paid at the time of buying something [I always pay *cash* and never charge.]
verb to give or get cash for [I *cashed* my check at the bank.]
cash • ***noun*** • ***verb*** **cashed, cashing**

cashew (kash′o͞o) ***noun*** **1** a curved nut that is the seed of a tropical evergreen tree. **2** this tree.
cash·ew • ***noun,*** *plural* **cashews**

cashier (ka shir′) ***noun*** a person who handles the money in a store, bank, or other business where money passes from one person to another.
cash·ier • ***noun,*** *plural* **cashiers**

cash register ***noun*** a machine used in business, that shows the amount of each sale and records it on a strip of paper. It usually has a drawer for money.
cash register • ***noun,*** *plural* **cash registers**

cash register

cask (kask) ***noun*** a barrel for holding liquids.
cask • ***noun,*** *plural* **casks**

casket (kas′kət) ***noun*** a coffin.
cas·ket • ***noun,*** *plural* **caskets**

casserole (kas′ər ōl) ***noun*** **1** a covered baking dish in which food can be cooked and then served. **2** the food baked in such a dish.
cas·se·role • ***noun,*** *plural* **casseroles**

cassette (kə set′) ***noun*** **1** a case with a roll of film in it, for loading a camera quickly and easily. **2** a case with recording tape in it, for use in a tape recorder, VCR, or other similar machine.
cas·sette • ***noun,*** *plural* **cassettes**

cast (kast) ***verb*** **1** to throw out or down; toss; fling [The boy *cast* a stone. She *cast* a line in fishing.] **2** to cause to turn; direct [Mary *cast* her eyes at them.] **3** to give forth; project [The light from the lamp *cast* shadows on the wall.] **4** to choose actors for a play or movie [The director began to *cast* the play today.] **5** to deposit a ballot or vote [Each council member *cast* a vote.] **6** to form or shape a liquid or soft material by pouring or pressing into a mold and letting it harden [The sculptor *cast* a bronze statue.]
noun **1** the act of casting; a throw. **2** something formed in a mold. **3** a stiff, plaster form for keeping a broken body part in place while it is healing. **4** the set of actors in a play.
—cast off **1** to get rid of; discard [to *cast off* one's old clothes]. **2** to free a ship from a dock by untying a line or lines [We *cast off* and headed out onto the lake.]
cast • ***verb*** **cast, casting** • ***noun,*** *plural* **casts**

castanets (kas tə nets′) ***plural noun*** a pair of small, hollowed pieces of hard wood or ivory that are held in the hand and clicked together to beat time to music. They are used especially in Spanish dances.
cas·ta·nets • ***plural noun***

castaway (kas′tə wā) ***noun*** a shipwrecked person.
cast·a·way • ***noun,*** *plural* **castaways**

castle (kas′əl) ***noun*** **1** a large building or group of buildings that was the home of a king or noble in the Middle Ages. **2** a rook used in chess.
cas·tle • ***noun,*** *plural* **castles**

casual (kazh′o͞o əl) ***adjective*** **1** happening by chance; not planned [a *casual* visit]. **2** not having any particular purpose [a *casual* glance]. **3** for wear at times when dressy clothes are not needed [*casual* sports clothes].
cas·u·al • ***adjective***

casualty (kazh′o͞o əl tē) ***noun*** **1** a person in

a	cat	ō	go	ʉ	fur	ə = a *in* ago	
ā	ape	ô	law, for	ch	chin	e *in* agent	
ä	cot, car	o͝o	look	sh	she	i *in* pencil	
e	ten	o͞o	tool	th	thin	o *in* atom	
ē	me	oi	oil	*th*	then	u *in* circus	
i	fit	ou	out	zh	measure		
ī	ice	u	up	ŋ	ring		

the armed forces who has been killed, wounded, or captured or who is missing. **2** anyone who is hurt or killed in an accident.
cas·u·al·ty • *noun, plural* **casualties**

cat (kat) *noun* **1** a small animal with soft fur, often kept as a pet or for killing mice. **2** a lion, tiger, leopard, or any other larger animal that is related to and resembles a cat.
cat • *noun, plural* **cats**

catalog or **catalogue** (kat′ə lôg) *noun* **1** a file giving a complete list of things in a collection. A library catalog, for example, can be stored in a computer. **2** a book or paper listing all the things for sale or on display [a department store's *catalog*].
cat·a·log or **cat·a·logue** • *noun, plural* **catalogs** or **catalogues**

catamaran

catamaran (kat ə mər an′) *noun* a boat with two hulls side by side.
cat·a·ma·ran • *noun, plural* **catamarans**

catapult (kat′ə pult) *noun* **1** a large weapon that worked like a slingshot. It was used in olden times to throw spears, arrows, rocks, or other things at the enemy. **2** a modern machine for launching an airplane from the deck of a ship.
verb to throw from or as if from a catapult [The soldiers *catapulted* large rocks over the walls.]
cat·a·pult • *noun, plural* **catapults** • *verb* **catapulted, catapulting**

cataract (kat′ər akt) *noun* **1** a large waterfall. **2** a clouding of the lens of the eye, which can result in a gradual loss of sight.
cat·a·ract • *noun, plural* **cataracts**

catastrophe (kə tas′trə fē) *noun* a sudden happening that causes great loss, suffering, or damage; a terrible disaster.
ca·tas·tro·phe • *noun, plural* **catastrophes**

catbird (kat′burd) *noun* a gray North American songbird whose calls sound like the mewing of a cat.
cat·bird • *noun, plural* **catbirds**

catch (kach) *verb* **1** to take hold of, especially after a chase; capture [The police *caught* the thief.] **2** to get by a hook, trap, or other tool [to *catch* fish; a trap to *catch* mice]. **3** to stop the motion of something by grasping it with the hands or arms [She *caught* the ball.] **4** to become or cause to become held or entangled [My sleeve *caught* on a nail.] **5** to get to in time; be in time for [I *catch* the 8 o'clock bus each morning.] **6** to become sick or infected with [He *caught* a cold.] **7** to get by seeing, hearing, or thinking [I *caught* sight of her red jacket in the crowd. I didn't *catch* what you said.] **8** [*an informal use*] to manage to see, hear, or watch [I want to *catch* that TV program tonight.] **9** to come upon or see by surprise; discover [They were *caught* reading comic books in study hall.] **10** to hit one's mind or feelings suddenly [The toss *caught* him by surprise. Her poem *caught* my attention.] **11** to act as a catcher in baseball [I'm *catching* this game.]
noun **1** the act of catching something, especially a ball [The outfielder made a running *catch*.] **2** anything that is caught [We brought home a *catch* of 14 fish.] **3** a thing that catches or fastens [Fix the *catch* on the cupboard door.] **4** a game in which two or more players throw and catch a ball. **5** [*an informal use*] a hidden or tricky part [What's the *catch?*]
—catch fire to begin to burn. **—catch on** **1** to become popular [It was a good song, but it didn't *catch on*.] **2** to understand [She *caught on* right away that I was joking.] **—catch up** to come up even from behind [I stopped and waited for him to *catch up*.]
catch • *verb* **caught, catching** • *noun, plural* **catches**

catcher (kach′ər) *noun* **1** someone or something that catches. **2** the baseball player whose position is behind home plate. The catcher catches pitched balls that are not hit away by the batter.
catch·er • *noun, plural* **catchers**

C

catching (kach′iŋ) ***adjective*** easily passed on to another; contagious [Measles are *catching*.]
catch·ing • ***adjective***

catchup (kach′əp) ***noun*** *another spelling of* **ketchup**.
catch·up • ***noun,*** *plural* **catchups**

catchy (kach′ē) ***adjective*** pleasing and easy to remember [a *catchy* tune].
catch·y • ***adjective*** **catchier, catchiest**

category (kat′ə gôr′ē) ***noun*** a division of a main subject or group; class [Biology is divided into two *categories*, zoology and botany.]
cat·e·go·ry • ***noun,*** *plural* **categories**

cater (kāt′ər) ***verb*** **1** to provide food and service, especially for parties [My father's company *catered* the wedding.] **2** to try to please by doing or giving what is wanted [This store *caters* to young people.]
ca·ter • ***verb*** **catered, catering**

caterpillar

caterpillar (kat′ər pil ər) ***noun*** the larva of the moth or butterfly. It looks like a worm.
cat·er·pil·lar • ***noun,*** *plural* **caterpillars**

WORD HISTORY

caterpillar

The source of **caterpillar** is two Latin words that mean "cat" and "hairy." Some **caterpillars** look a little like hairy cats.

catfish (kat′fish) ***noun*** a fish without scales, and with feelers around the mouth that are a little like a cat's whiskers.
cat·fish • ***noun,*** *plural* **catfish** or **catfishes**

cathedral (kə thē′drəl) ***noun*** **1** the main church of a bishop's district. **2** any large, important church.
ca·the·dral • ***noun,*** *plural* **cathedrals**

Catholic (kath′ə lik *or* kath′lik) ***adjective*** having to do with the Christian church whose head is the pope; Roman Catholic.
noun a member of the Roman Catholic Church.
Cath·o·lic • ***adjective*** • ***noun,*** *plural* **Catholics**

catnap (kat′nap) ***noun*** a short, light sleep.
cat·nap • ***noun,*** *plural* **catnaps**

catnip (kat′nip) ***noun*** a plant of the mint family, with downy leaves. Cats like its smell.
cat·nip • ***noun***

cat's cradle

cat's cradle ***noun*** a game in which a string is looped over the fingers and passed back and forth between the players. Each time a different design is made.
cat's cradle • ***noun,*** *plural* **cat's cradles**

catsup (kat′səp) ***noun*** *another spelling of* **ketchup**.
cat·sup • ***noun,*** *plural* **catsups**

cattail (kat′tāl) ***noun*** a plant that grows in wet places. It has long, flat leaves and long, fuzzy flower spikes that look a little like cats' tails.
cat·tail • ***noun,*** *plural* **cattails**

cattle (kat′l) ***plural noun*** cows, bulls, steers,

a	cat	ō	go	ʉ	fur	ə =	a *in* ago
ā	ape	ô	law, for	ch	chin		e *in* agent
ä	cot, car	oo	look	sh	she		i *in* pencil
e	ten	ōō	tool	th	thin		o *in* atom
ē	me	oi	oil	*th*	then		u *in* circus
i	fit	ou	out	zh	measure		
ī	ice	u	up	ŋ	ring		

and oxen. Cattle are raised on farms and ranches.
cat·tle • *plural noun*

Caucasian (kô kā′zhən *or* kä kā′zhən) ***adjective*** *another name for* **Caucasoid**.
Cau·ca·sian • ***adjective***

Caucasoid (kôk′ə soid *or* käk′ə soid) ***adjective*** belonging to one of the major geographical varieties of human beings that includes peoples from Europe, northern Africa, India, and other regions. This group is loosely called the *white race*, although it includes many people with dark skin.
Cau·ca·soid • ***adjective***

caught (kôt *or* kät) ***verb*** *past tense and past participle of* **catch**.

cauliflower (kôl′i flou′ər *or* käl′i flou′ər) ***noun*** a kind of cabbage with a head of white, firm flower clusters growing tightly together.
cau·li·flow·er • ***noun***

caulk (kôk *or* käk) ***verb*** to fill up cracks or seams with putty, tar, or something else that seals [Sal *caulked* the boat so it would not leak.]
caulk • ***verb*** **caulked, caulking**

cause (kôz *or* käz) ***noun*** **1** a person or thing that brings about some action or happening [A spark from a wire was the *cause* of the fire.] **2** a goal or movement that many are interested in [The group works for the *cause* of peace.]
verb to be the cause of; make happen [The wet road *caused* some accidents.]
cause • ***noun,*** *plural* **causes** • ***verb*** **caused, causing**

caution (kô′shən *or* kä′shən) ***noun*** **1** the act of being careful not to get into danger or make mistakes [Use *caution* when crossing a street.] **2** a warning [a word of *caution*].
verb to tell of danger; warn [The highway sign *cautioned* us to slow down.]
cau·tion • ***noun,*** *plural* **cautions** • ***verb*** **cautioned, cautioning**

cautious (kô′shəs *or* kä′shəs) ***adjective*** careful not to get into danger or make mistakes [Construction workers must be *cautious* on the job.]
cau·tious • ***adjective***

cavalry (kav′əl rē) ***noun*** soldiers who fight on horseback. Nowadays the cavalry usually uses armored vehicles.
cav·al·ry • ***noun,*** *plural* **cavalries**

cave (kāv) ***noun*** a hollow place inside the earth. A cave is often an opening in the side of a hill.
verb *used mainly in the phrase* **cave in,** to fall in or sink in; collapse [The heavy rain made the tunnel *cave in.*]
cave • ***noun,*** *plural* **caves** • ***verb*** **caved, caving**

cave man ***noun*** a human being of many thousands of years ago who lived in caves.
cave man • ***noun,*** *plural* **cave men**

cavern (kav′ərn) ***noun*** a cave, especially a large one.
cav·ern • ***noun,*** *plural* **caverns**

caviar (kav′ē är′) ***noun*** the salted eggs of certain fish. Caviar is eaten as an appetizer.
cav·i·ar • ***noun,*** *plural* **caviars**

cavity (kav′i tē) ***noun*** **1** a hole in a tooth caused by decay. **2** a natural hollow space in the body [The chest *cavity* holds the heart and lungs.]
cav·i·ty • ***noun,*** *plural* **cavities**

caw (kô *or* kä) ***noun*** the loud, harsh cry of a crow or raven.
verb to make this sound.
caw • ***noun,*** *plural* **caws** • ***verb*** **cawed, cawing**

CB (sē′bē′) ***noun*** a radio that uses radio waves that are set aside by the government for the use of private citizens. *CB* is taken from the first letters of the words *citizen's band*.
CB • ***noun,*** *plural* **CBs**

CD (sē′dē′) ***noun*** *a short form of* **compact disc**.
CD • ***noun,*** *plural* **CDs**

CD-ROM (sē′dē′räm′) ***noun*** a kind of compact disc for storing computer information.
CD-ROM • ***noun,*** *plural* **CD-ROMs**

C.E. *abbreviation for* Common Era. This abbreviation is sometimes used instead of **A.D.**

cease (sēs) ***verb*** to bring or come to an end; stop [The rain finally *ceased*.]
cease • ***verb*** **ceased, ceasing**

cedar (sē′dər) ***noun*** **1** an evergreen tree that has small cones and sweet-smelling, reddish wood. **2** this wood, which is used to make chests for storing clothes.
ce·dar • ***noun,*** *plural for sense 1 only* **cedars**

cedilla (sə dil′ə) ***noun*** a mark that looks a bit like a comma. It is put under the letter *c* (ç) in the spelling of some French words to show that *c* represents the sound (s).

C

ce·dil·la • ***noun,*** *plural* **cedillas**

ceiling (sēl′iŋ) ***noun*** the inside top part of a room, opposite the floor.
—hit the ceiling [*a slang use*] to lose one's temper.
ceil·ing • ***noun,*** *plural* **ceilings**

celebrate (sel′ə brāt) ***verb*** **1** to honor a special day or event with a party, ceremony, or other such activity [Most people *celebrate* their birthday every year.] **2** to perform a ceremony in worshiping [The priest *celebrated* Mass.] **3** [*an informal use*] to have a good time [Let's *celebrate* when we finish work.]
cel·e·brate • ***verb*** **celebrated, celebrating**

celebration (sel ə brā′shən) ***noun*** the act or an instance of celebrating.
cel·e·bra·tion • ***noun,*** *plural* **celebrations**

celebrity (sə leb′ri tē) ***noun*** a famous person.
ce·leb·ri·ty • ***noun,*** *plural* **celebrities**

celery (sel′ər ē) ***noun*** a pale green plant with long, crisp stalks that are eaten as a vegetable.
cel·e·ry • ***noun***

celery

cell (sel) ***noun*** **1** a small, plain room in a prison, convent, or monastery. **2** any one of a connected group of small, hollow spaces [The hollows in a honeycomb are called *cells*.] **3** the basic unit of all plants and animals. A cell is very small. It is made up of protoplasm and is surrounded by a cell wall or membrane. **4** a container holding metal or carbon pieces in a liquid or paste, for making electricity by chemical action. A battery is made up of one or more cells.
cell • ***noun,*** *plural* **cells**
● The words **cell** and **sell** sound alike.
The prison *cell* was without windows.
A salesman's job is to *sell* things.

cellar (sel′ər) ***noun*** a room or group of rooms underground, usually beneath a building.
cel·lar • ***noun,*** *plural* **cellars**
● The words **cellar** and **seller** sound alike.
Go into the *cellar* if there's a storm.
That ticket *seller* is always friendly.

cello (chel′ō) ***noun*** a musical instrument shaped like a violin but larger and having a deeper tone.
cel·lo • ***noun,*** *plural* **cellos**

cello

cellophane (sel′ə fān) ***noun*** a material made from cellulose into thin, clear, waterproof sheets. It is used for wrapping food and other things.
cel·lo·phane • ***noun***

cellular phone (sel′yo͞o lər) ***noun*** a portable telephone that uses a system of many small radio transmitters and receivers to send and receive sound. It is also called a **cell phone**.
cel·lu·lar phone • ***noun,*** *plural* **cellular phones**

cellulose (sel′yo͞o lōs) ***noun*** the substance that makes up the walls of plant cells. The woody part of trees is mostly made up of cellulose.
cel·lu·lose • ***noun***

Celsius (sel′sē əs) ***adjective*** of or describing a thermometer on which the freezing point of pure water is 0° and the boiling point is 100°.
Cel·si·us • ***adjective***

Celtic (sel′tik *or* kel′tik) ***noun*** a family of languages including modern Welsh, Irish, and Scottish.
Cel·tic • ***noun***

cement (sə ment′) ***noun*** **1** a powder made of lime and clay. When cement is mixed with water, sand, and gravel it makes concrete, a mixture that becomes hard when it dries. **2** paste, glue, or any other soft substance that fastens things together when it hardens.
verb to fasten together or cover with cement.
ce·ment • ***noun,*** *plural* **cements**
• ***verb*** **cemented, cementing**

cemetery (sem′ə ter′ē) ***noun*** a place for burying the dead; graveyard.
cem·e·ter·y • ***noun,*** *plural* **cemeteries**

a	cat	ō	go	ʉ	fur	ə =	a *in* ago
ā	ape	ô	law, for	ch	chin		e *in* agent
ä	cot, car	o͝o	look	sh	she		i *in* pencil
e	ten	o͞o	tool	th	thin		o *in* atom
ē	me	oi	oil	*th*	then		u *in* circus
i	fit	ou	out	zh	measure		
ī	ice	u	up	ŋ	ring		

WORD HISTORY

cemetery

The word **cemetery** comes from an ancient Greek word that means "a place for sleeping." Poets sometimes write about death as "slumber," or sleep. A person's grave, in a **cemetery**, is sometimes called that person's "final resting place."

census (sen′səs) ***noun*** an official counting to find out how many people there are in a country or area. A census also makes a record of the sex of the people counted and their ages, jobs, and other information.
cen·sus • ***noun,*** *plural* **censuses**

cent (sent) ***noun*** a coin that is a 100th part of a dollar; penny.
cent • ***noun,*** *plural* **cents**
● The words **cent, scent,** and **sent** sound alike.
A penny is worth one *cent.*
The perfume has a lovely *scent.*
We *sent* her a birthday card.

centennial (sen ten′ē əl) ***noun*** a 100th anniversary or its celebration [Our nation's *centennial* was in 1876.]
cen·ten·ni·al • ***noun,*** *plural* **centennials**

center (sen′tər) ***noun*** **1** a point inside a circle or sphere that is the same distance from all points on the outside line or surface. **2** the middle point or part; the place at the middle [the *center* of the table] —Look for the WORD CHOICES box at the entry **middle**. **3** a main point, place, or person [a shopping *center*. She was the *center* of attention at the party.] **4** a player whose position is at the middle of the playing line or area [Josh is the *center* on our basketball team.]
verb **1** to place in or at the center [Try to *center* the design on the page.] **2** to focus on something; concentrate [We *centered* all our attention on the baby.]
cen·ter • ***noun,*** *plural* **centers**
• ***verb*** **centered, centering**

centi- *a prefix meaning* **1** one hundred [Not all *centipedes* have a hundred feet.] **2** a hundredth part of [How many *centimeters* are there in a meter?]

centigrade (sen′ti grād) ***adjective*** *the same as* **Celsius**.
cen·ti·grade • ***adjective***

centigram (sen′ti gram) ***noun*** a unit of weight that is equal to 1/100 gram.
cen·ti·gram • ***noun,*** *plural* **centigrams**

centimeter (sen′ti mēt′ər) ***noun*** a unit of measure that is equal to 1/100 meter.
cen·ti·me·ter • ***noun,*** *plural* **centimeters**

centipede (sen′ti pēd′) ***noun*** a small animal like a worm with many pairs of legs along its body. The two front legs are poison claws.
cen·ti·pede • ***noun,*** *plural* **centipedes**

central (sen′trəl) ***adjective*** **1** in, at, or near the center [The sun is the *central* point in our solar system.] **2** most important; main [the *central* idea in a story].
cen·tral • ***adjective***

Central African Republic a country in central Africa.

Central America the narrow part of America between Mexico and South America. It includes Guatemala, Belize, Honduras, El Salvador, Nicaragua, Costa Rica, and Panama.

century (sen′chər ē) ***noun*** a period of 100 years. From 1901 to 2000 is the twentieth century.
cen·tu·ry • ***noun,*** *plural* **centuries**

ceramic (sə ram′ik) ***adjective*** made of baked clay [a *ceramic* pot].
ce·ram·ic • ***adjective***

ceramics (sə ram′iks) ***plural noun*** [*used with a singular verb*] the art or work of making objects of baked clay.
ce·ram·ics • ***plural noun***

cereal (sir′ē əl) ***noun*** **1** any grass that bears seeds that are used for food. Rice, wheat, and oats are common cereals. **2** food made from grain and eaten for breakfast.
ce·re·al • ***noun,*** *plural* **cereals**
● The words **cereal** and **serial** sound alike.
I eat cold *cereal* in the morning.
What is the *serial* number on that dollar bill?

cerebral palsy (ser′ə brəl pôl′zē) ***noun*** a condition in which there is some difficulty in moving or speaking. It is caused by an injury to the brain before or during birth.
cer·e·bral pal·sy • ***noun***

ceremonial (ser′ə mō′nē əl) ***adjective*** having

to do with or for a ceremony [*ceremonial* robes].
cer·e·mo·ni·al • ***adjective***

ceremony (ser′ə mō′nē) ***noun*** an act or set of acts done in a particular way to celebrate a special occasion [a wedding *ceremony*].
cer·e·mo·ny • ***noun,*** *plural* **ceremonies**

WORD CHOICES

Synonyms of **ceremony**

The words **ceremony, rite,** and **ritual** share the meaning "a formal act done according to fixed rules."

a graduation *ceremony*
marriage *rites*
making a *ritual* of doing housework

certain (sʉrt′n) ***adjective*** **1** without any doubt or question; sure; positive [Are you *certain* of your facts?] **2** not named or described, though perhaps known [It happened in a *certain* town out west.] **3** some, but not very much [I agree, but only to a *certain* extent.]
cer·tain • ***adjective***

certainly (sʉrt′n lē) ***adverb*** without any doubt; surely [I shall *certainly* be there.]
cer·tain·ly • ***adverb***

certainty (sʉrt′n tē) ***noun*** the condition of being certain or sure [The weather cannot be predicted with absolute *certainty.*]
cer·tain·ty • ***noun***

certificate (sʉr tif′i kət) ***noun*** an official written or printed statement that says that a particular fact is true [A birth *certificate* proves where and when someone was born.]
cer·tif·i·cate • ***noun,*** *plural* **certificates**

Cervantes (sər van′tēz), **Miguel de** (mē gel′ dā) 1547-1616; Spanish writer who wrote *Don Quixote*.
Cer·van·tes, Mi·guel de

Ceylon (sə län′) *old name of* **Sri Lanka**.
Cey·lon

cg or **cg.** *abbreviation for* centigram.

ch. *abbreviation for* chapter.

Chad (chad) a country in north-central Africa.

chain (chān) ***noun*** **1** a number of links or loops joined together in a line that can be easily bent [a necklace made of gold *chain*]. **2 chains** anything that binds or holds someone prisoner [The prisoners' *chains* kept them from escaping.] **3** a series of things joined together [a mountain *chain;* a *chain* of events]. **4** a number of stores, restaurants, or other businesses owned by one company.

chain

verb to fasten or bind with a chain or with something that is like a chain [The dog is *chained* inside the yard.]
chain • ***noun,*** *plural* **chains** • ***verb*** **chained, chaining**

chair (cher) ***noun*** **1** a piece of furniture that is a seat for one person and has a back and usually four legs. **2** a chairman; chairperson.
chair • ***noun,*** *plural* **chairs**

chairlift

chairlift (cher′lift) ***noun*** a line of seats hanging from a cable moved by a motor. It is used in ski resorts to carry people up a slope.
chair·lift • ***noun,*** *plural* **chairlifts**

chairman (cher′mən) ***noun*** a person who is in charge of a meeting or is the head of a committee or some other group.
chair·man • ***noun,*** *plural* **chairmen**

chairperson (cher′pʉr sən) ***noun*** *the same as* **chairman**. Many people prefer this word.

a	cat	ō	go	ʉ	fur	ə =	a *in* ago
ā	ape	ô	law, for	ch	chin		e *in* agent
ä	cot, car	oo	look	sh	she		i *in* pencil
e	ten	ōō	tool	th	thin		o *in* atom
ē	me	oi	oil	*th*	then		u *in* circus
i	fit	ou	out	zh	measure		
ī	ice	u	up	ŋ	ring		

chair·per·son • *noun, plural* **chairpersons**

chalk (chôk) ***noun*** **1** a whitish limestone that is soft and easily crushed. It is made up of tiny fossil sea shells. **2** a piece of chalk or of material like it, for writing on blackboards.
***verb** used mainly in the phrase* **chalk up**, **1** to score points in a game [Their team *chalked up* several more points.] **2** to give credit to someone or something [*Chalk* it *up* to experience.]
chalk • ***noun**, plural* **chalks** • ***verb*** **chalked, chalking**

chalkboard (chôk′bôrd) ***noun*** a large piece of smooth, dark material used to write or draw on with chalk.
chalk·board • ***noun**, plural* **chalkboards**

challenge (chal′ənj) ***verb*** **1** to call to take part in a contest or fight; dare [She *challenged* him to a game of chess.] **2** to question the right or rightness of; refuse to believe unless proof is given [They *challenged* his right to tell them what to do.] **3** to refuse to let pass until a certain sign is given [The sentry *challenged* the soldier.] **4** to call for skill, effort, or imagination [That puzzle will really *challenge* you.]
noun **1** the act of challenging [I accepted his *challenge* to a race.] **2** something that calls for much effort; hard task [Climbing Mt. Everest is a real *challenge*.]
chal·lenge • ***verb*** **challenged, challenging** • ***noun**, plural* **challenges**

challenged (chal′ənjd) ***adjective*** not able to move, work, or do certain things in the usual way [The boy who is in a wheelchair is physically *challenged*.]
chal·lenged • ***adjective***

chamber (chām′bər) ***noun*** **1** a room in a house, especially a bedroom. **2** a number of people working together as a group for some purpose [A *chamber* of commerce works to help the businesses of a city or region.] **3** an enclosed space in the body of a plant or animal [The human heart has four *chambers*.]
cham·ber • ***noun**, plural* **chambers**

chameleon (kə mē′lē ən *or* kə mēl′yən) ***noun*** a small lizard that can change the color of its skin to match its background.
cha·me·le·on • ***noun**, plural* **chameleons**

champagne (sham pān′) ***noun*** a pale yellow wine that bubbles like soda water.
cham·pagne • ***noun**, plural* **champagnes**

champion (cham′pē ən) ***noun*** **1** a person, animal, or thing that wins first place or is judged to be best in a contest or sport [a spelling *champion;* a racing *champion*]. **2** a person who fights for another or for a cause; defender [a *champion* of the poor].
cham·pi·on • ***noun**, plural* **champions**

championship (cham′pē ən ship′) ***noun*** the position or title of a champion; first place.
cham·pi·on·ship • ***noun**, plural* **championships**

chance (chans) ***noun*** **1** the way things turn out; the happening of events by accident; luck [They didn't plan when they would meet again, but left it to *chance*.] **2** the fact of being possible or likely [There is little *chance* that it will rain.] **3** a time to take advantage; opportunity [This is your last *chance*.] **4** a risk; a gamble [I'll take a *chance* that tickets will still be available tomorrow.]
verb to risk; to gamble [This plan may fail, but let's *chance* it.]
chance • ***noun**, plural* **chances** • ***verb*** **chanced, chancing**

chancellor (chan′sə lər) ***noun*** a very high official in government or education. In some European countries the prime minister is called a chancellor.
chan·cel·lor • ***noun**, plural* **chancellors**

chandelier (shan də lir′) ***noun*** a large set of lights that hangs from a ceiling, with several branches for candles or light bulbs.
chan·de·lier • ***noun**, plural* **chandeliers**

chandelier

change (chānj) ***verb*** **1** to make or become different in some way [In the fall, the leaves of many trees *change* color. People often *change* as they grow older.] **2** to put or take something in place of something else; to substitute [I *changed* into clean clothes. I had to *change* schools when we moved.]
noun **1** the act of changing in some way [There will be a *change* in the weather.] **2** something put or taken in place of something else [I brought along a *change* of clothing.] **3** the money returned when one has paid more than the amount that is owed. **4** small, loose coins [Do you have any *change?*]
—**change off** to take turns [My brother and I *change off* washing dishes every other week.]

change • *verb* **changed, changing** • *noun, plural for senses 1 and 2 only* **changes**

changeable (chān′jə bəl) *adjective* changing often or likely to change [*changeable* weather].
change·a·ble • *adjective*

channel (chan′əl) *noun* **1** the bottom part of a river or stream. **2** a body of water joining two larger bodies of water [the English *Channel*]. **3** the small group of radio or television waves a station is allowed to use to send out its programs.
chan·nel • *noun, plural* **channels**

chant (chant) *noun* **1** a song, especially one in which strings of words or syllables are sung in the same tone [*Chants* are used in some church services.] **2** a phrase, slogan, or other words that are repeated over and over [the *chant* of the crowd at the stadium].
verb to sing or say in a chant.
chant • *noun, plural* **chants** • *verb* **chanted, chanting**

Chanukah (hä′noo kä′) *noun another spelling for* **Hanuka**.
Cha·nu·kah • *noun, plural* **Chanukahs**

chaos (kā′äs) *noun* the greatest confusion and lack of order [The locker room was in a state of *chaos* after the game.] —Look for the WORD CHOICES box at the entry **confusion**.
cha·os • *noun*

chap[1] (chap) [*an informal word*] *noun* a man or boy; fellow.
chap • *noun, plural* **chaps**

chap[2] (chap) *verb* to crack open or make or become rough [The cold wind *chapped* my skin.]
chap • *verb* **chapped, chapping**

chap. *abbreviation for* chapter.

chapel (chap′əl) *noun* a room or building for holding religious services.
chap·el • *noun, plural* **chapels**

chaperon or **chaperone** (shap′ər ōn) *noun* an older person who accompanies young, unmarried people to a party or dance. A chaperon makes sure that they behave properly.
verb to be a chaperon to [The teachers *chaperon* all of the school dances.]
chap·er·on or **chap·er·one** • *noun, plural* **chaperons** or **chaperones** • *verb* **chaperoned, chaperoning**

chaplain (chap′lən) *noun* a minister, priest, or rabbi serving in the armed forces or in a hospital or prison.
chap·lain • *noun, plural* **chaplains**

chaps (chaps) *plural noun* heavy leather leg coverings without a seat that are worn over trousers. Chaps are worn by cowboys to protect their legs from thorny bushes.

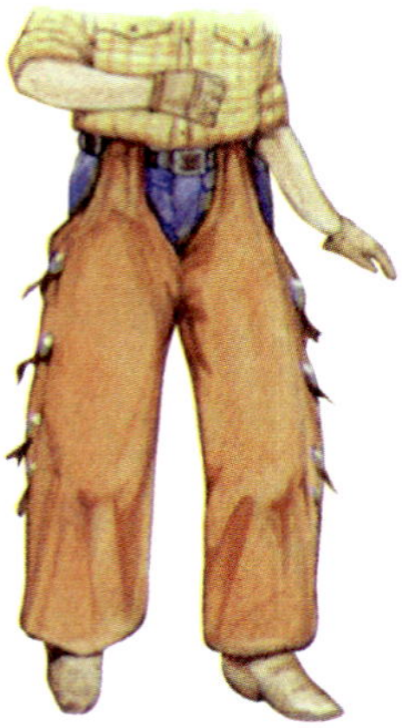
chaps

chapter (chap′tər) *noun* **1** one of the main parts into which a book, such as a story or text, is divided. **2** a local branch of a club or society.
chap·ter • *noun, plural* **chapters**

character (ker′ək tər) *noun* **1** all the things that a person does, feels, and says, by which the person is judged as being good or bad, or strong or weak [That unkind remark showed her true *character*.] **2** all these things when thought of as being especially good or strong [People of *character* are needed in high positions.] **3** all those things that make one person or thing different from others; special quality; nature [The countryside around the farm has a peaceful *character*.] **4** any letter, figure, or symbol used in writing or printing. **5** a person in a story, book, play, or film. **6** [*an informal use*] a person who is unusual, funny, or strange [She's a real *character*.]
char·ac·ter • *noun, plural* **characters**

characteristic (ker′ək tər is′tik) *adjective* having to do with or showing the character or special quality of a person or thing; typical [A peacock has *characteristic* tail feathers.]
noun something that makes a person or thing different from others; special part or quality [Fast action is a *characteristic* of the game of basketball.]
char·ac·ter·is·tic • *adjective* • *noun, plural* **characteristics**

a	cat	ō	go	ʉ	fur	ə =	a *in* ago
ā	ape	ô	law, for	ch	chin		e *in* agent
ä	cot, car	oo	look	sh	she		i *in* pencil
e	ten	ōō	tool	th	thin		o *in* atom
ē	me	oi	oil	*th*	then		u *in* circus
i	fit	ou	out	zh	measure		
ī	ice	u	up	ŋ	ring		

WORD CHOICES

Synonyms of **characteristic**

The words **characteristic, distinctive**, and **individual** share the meaning "different from others."

the *characteristic* taste of honey
the *distinctive* call of the wren
her *individual* writing style

characterize (ker′ək tər īz) ***verb*** **1** to describe or show the character or qualities of [He *characterized* life on a farm as calm and peaceful.] **2** to be characteristic or typical of [Bright colors *characterized* her paintings.]
char·ac·ter·ize • ***verb*** **characterized, characterizing**

charcoal (chär′kōl) ***noun*** a black material that is a form of carbon. It is produced by heating wood or other plant or animal matter to a high temperature in the absence of air. Charcoal is used as a fuel, in filters, and as pencils for drawing.
char·coal • ***noun***

charge (chärj) ***verb*** **1** to set as a price [Barbers once *charged* a quarter for a haircut.] **2** to ask for payment [We do not *charge* for gift wrapping.] **3** to write down as an amount that is owed, to be paid for later [He asked the clerk to *charge* his purchase.] **4** to accuse of doing wrong; blame [She was *charged* with theft.] **5** to make responsible for [The parents *charged* the nurse with the care of the child.] **6** to rush with force; attack [Our troops *charged* the enemy.] **7** to fill or load [The soldiers *charged* the cannon with powder.] **8** to supply with electrical energy [The mechanic will *charge* the car battery.]
noun **1** the amount that is asked or made as payment; price or cost [The *charge* for the haircut was $9.] **2** care; responsibility [The children were placed in the nurse's *charge*.] **3** a claim that someone has done wrong; accusation [He was arrested on a *charge* of speeding.] **4** an attack [The hunters escaped the *charge* of the wild elephant.] **5** the amount of electrical energy that is or can be stored in a battery.
—in charge having the power to supervise, give orders, and make decisions; in command [I would like to speak to the person *in charge*.]
—in charge of having the supervision of [He is *in charge of* the football team.]
charge • ***verb*** **charged, charging** • ***noun***, *plural* **charges**

chariot

chariot (cher′ē ət) ***noun*** an open cart with two wheels that is drawn by horses. It was used in ancient times.
char·i·ot • ***noun***, *plural* **chariots**

charity (cher′i tē) ***noun*** **1** the giving of money or help to people in need [He devoted his life to *charity*.] **2** an institution, fund, or other group for giving help to people in need [We will contribute $500 to the *charity* of your choice.] **3** kindness or understanding in judging other people [He always looked at our selfish behavior with *charity*.]
char·i·ty • ***noun***, *plural for sense 2 only* **charities**

Charleston (chärls′tən) the capital of West Virginia.
Charles·ton

charm (chärm) ***noun*** **1** a quality or feature in a person or thing that attracts or pleases greatly [His greatest *charm* is his smile.] **2** an act, thing, word, or phrase that is supposed to have magic power to help or hurt [Some people think that a rabbit's foot is a lucky *charm*.] **3** a small object that is worn as a decoration on a bracelet or necklace.
verb to attract or please greatly; delight [The dancers *charmed* the audience.]
charm • ***noun***, *plural* **charms**
• ***verb*** **charmed, charming**

charming (chärm′iŋ) ***adjective*** full of charm; very pleasing; attractive [a *charming* smile].
charm·ing • ***adjective***

chart (chärt) ***noun*** **1** a sheet that gives information about something in the form of a table,

C

graph, or list. **2** a map that is used for steering a ship or guiding an aircraft [A sailor's *chart* shows coastlines and currents.]
verb **1** to make a map of [Ancient explorers *charted* the coast of Africa.] **2** to show on a chart [We learned how to *chart* the weather.]
chart • ***noun,*** *plural* **charts** • ***verb*** **charted, charting**

charter (chärt′ər) ***noun*** **1** an official paper in which certain rights are given by a government to a person or business [The explorers were granted a royal *charter* to settle the colony.] **2** an official paper telling the aims or principles of a group [the *Charter* of the United Nations].
verb **1** to give a charter to [The city *chartered* the company to operate a bus line.] **2** to hire or lease for the special use of a group [The school *chartered* a bus for the picnic.]
char·ter • ***noun,*** *plural* **charters** • ***verb*** **chartered, chartering**

chase (chās) ***verb*** **1** to go after or keep following in order to catch or harm [The fox *chased* the rabbit across the field.] **2** to drive away [She waved her hand to *chase* the flies away.]
noun the act of chasing; pursuit.
chase • ***verb*** **chased, chasing** • ***noun,*** *plural* **chases**

chasm (kaz′əm) ***noun*** a deep, wide crack in the earth's surface.
chasm • ***noun,*** *plural* **chasms**

chat (chat) ***verb*** to talk in an easy, relaxed way.
noun an easy, relaxed talk or conversation.
chat • ***verb*** **chatted, chatting** • ***noun,*** *plural* **chats**

chatter (chat′ər) ***verb*** **1** to make short, quick sounds that seem almost like talk [Birds and monkeys *chatter.*] **2** to talk fast and in a foolish way, without stopping [The children *chattered* all through class.]
noun **1** the noise of chattering [The *chatter* of squirrels filled the air.] **2** fast, foolish talk.
chat·ter • ***verb*** **chattered, chattering** • ***noun,*** *plural* **chatters**

Chaucer (chô′sər), **Geoffrey** (jef′rē) 1340?-1400; English poet.
Chau·cer, Geof·frey

chauffeur (shō′fər *or* shō fur′) ***noun*** a person whose work is driving an automobile.
chauf·feur • ***noun,*** *plural* **chauffeurs**

cheap (chēp) ***adjective*** **1** low in price [Vegetables are *cheap* this week.] **2** charging low prices [a good, *cheap* hotel]. **3** of low value or of poor quality [*cheap* jewelry]. **4** [*an informal use*] stingy.
cheap • ***adjective*** **cheaper, cheapest**

cheat (chēt) ***verb*** **1** to act in a dishonest or unfair way [He was caught *cheating* on the test.] **2** to take something away from dishonestly; swindle [They *cheated* her out of her money.]
noun a person who cheats.
cheat • ***verb*** **cheated, cheating** • ***noun,*** *plural* **cheats**

WORD CHOICES

Synonyms of cheat

Many words share the meaning "to fool someone in a way that is not fair or honest."

deceive	swindle
mislead	trick

check (chek) ***verb*** **1** to test, compare, or examine to find out if something is right or as it should be [*Check* your answers on the test.] **2** to seek information by questioning; ask [*Check* with the librarian for that book.] **3** to search through [We *checked* the files, but did not find the letter.] **4** to mark with a sign (✓) to show that something is right, has been noted, or has been chosen [Please *check* the right answer.] **5** to leave something to be kept for a time [We *checked* our coats during the concert.] **6** to leave something to be shipped [We *checked* our bags through to Seattle.] **7** to stop suddenly or hold back [The guard *checked* the prisoner's escape.]
noun **1** a mark (✓) that is used to show that something is right, has been noted, or has been chosen. **2** a written order to a bank to pay a certain amount of money from a person's account. **3** a piece of paper telling how much is owed for food or drink in a restaurant or bar [Ask the waiter for the *check*.] **4** a ticket, tag, or other token given to a person in return for something that has been left to be kept, to be shipped, or for repairs [a coat

check; a baggage *check*]. **5** a test to find out if something is right or as it should be. **6** an examination or search. **7** a pattern of small squares.
—check in to write one's name on a list as a guest at a hotel or motel. **—check out** **1** to pay one's bill and leave a hotel or motel. **2** to add up prices and collect the amount owed [She *checks out* groceries at the supermarket.]
check • *verb* **checked, checking** • *noun, plural* **checks**

checkerboard (chek′ər bôrd) *noun* a board divided into 64 squares of two alternating colors. It is used in checkers and chess.
check·er·board • *noun, plural* **checkerboards**

checkers (chek′ərz) *plural noun* [*used with a singular verb*] a game that is played on a checkerboard by two players. Each player tries to capture all 12 flat, round pieces of the other player.
check·ers • *plural noun*

checkout (chek′out) *noun* the place where purchases are paid for in a supermarket or discount store.
check·out • *noun, plural* **checkouts**

checkup (chek′up) *noun* **1** a complete medical examination of a person. **2** a complete inspection of something to find out its condition.
check·up • *noun, plural* **checkups**

cheek (chēk) *noun* the side of the face between the nose and the ear and below the eye.
cheek • *noun, plural* **cheeks**

cheer (chir) *noun* **1** a glad, excited shout of welcome, joy, or approval [The crowd gave the team three *cheers*.] **2** good or glad feelings; happiness [good *cheer* for the holidays].
verb **1** to urge on or applaud with cheers [We *cheered* the runners across the finish line. When our team won, we *cheered*.] **2** to make or become glad or hopeful [*Cheer* up!]
cheer • *noun, plural for sense 1 only* **cheers** • *verb* **cheered, cheering**

cheerful (chir′fəl) *adjective* **1** full of cheer; glad; joyful [a *cheerful* smile]. **2** bright and lively; pleasant [a *cheerful* room].
cheer·ful • *adjective*

cheerleader (chir′lēd ər) *noun* a person who leads others in cheering at sports events.
cheer·lead·er • *noun, plural* **cheerleaders**

cheery (chir′ē) *adjective* cheerful; lively and happy [They gave us a *cheery* welcome.]
cheer·y • *adjective* **cheerier, cheeriest**

cheese (chēz) *noun* a solid food made by pressing together the less watery part of curdled milk.
cheese • *noun, plural* **cheeses**

cheeseburger (chēz′bur gər) *noun* a hamburger with melted cheese on top.
cheese·burg·er • *noun, plural* **cheeseburgers**

cheetah

cheetah (chēt′ə) *noun* a spotted wildcat that is like a leopard but smaller. Cheetahs live in Africa and southern Asia. They can run very fast and are often trained to hunt.
chee·tah • *noun, plural* **cheetahs**

chef (shef) *noun* a cook, especially the head cook of a restaurant or hotel.
chef • *noun, plural* **chefs**

chemical (kem′i kəl) *adjective* **1** of or having to do with chemistry [*chemical* engineering]. **2** made by or used in chemistry [a *chemical* compound].
noun a substance that is produced by or used in a chemical process.
chem·i·cal • *adjective* • *noun, plural* **chemicals**

chemist (kem′ist) *noun* a person who is an expert in chemistry.
chem·ist • *noun, plural* **chemists**

chemistry (kem′is trē) *noun* the science that deals with chemical elements and compounds. It studies the special qualities of each element and compound, and examines how each changes when heated or cooled, or when combined with something else.
chem·is·try • *noun*

cherish (cher′ish) *verb* to treat with love and care; hold dear [We *cherish* our rights.]
cher·ish • *verb* **cherished, cherishing**

C

Cherokee (cher′ə kē) *noun* **1** a member of a North American Indian people that formerly inhabited a large area of the southeastern U.S. They now live in Oklahoma and North Carolina. **2** the language of this people.
Cher·o·kee • *noun, plural for sense 1 only* **Cherokees** or **Cherokee**

cherry (cher′ē) *noun* **1** a smooth, round fruit with a sweet, juicy part covering a hard stone. Cherries are bright red, dark red, or yellow. **2** the tree that this fruit grows on.
cher·ry • *noun, plural* **cherries**

chess (ches) *noun* a game played on a checkerboard by two players. Each player tries to capture the other's king.

chest (chest) *noun* **1** the part of the body inside the ribs [a cold in the *chest*]. **2** the outside front part of this. **3** a piece of furniture with several drawers, used mostly for holding clothing; bureau: this piece of furniture is also called a **chest of drawers**.
chest • *noun, plural* **chests**

chestnut (ches′nut) *noun* **1** a sweet-tasting, dark-brown nut that has a smooth shell. Chestnuts grow inside a prickly bur. **2** the tree that this nut grows on.
chest·nut • *noun, plural* **chestnuts**

chew (cho͞o) *verb* to bite and grind up with the teeth [*Chew* your food slowly and thoroughly.] **—chew out** [*a slang use*] to scold sharply.
chew • *verb* **chewed, chewing**

chewing gum *noun* gum for chewing. It is usually sweet and flavored with mint, fruit, or spices.
chewing gum • *noun, plural* **chewing gums**

chewy (cho͞o′ē) *adjective* needing much chewing [*chewy* taffy].
chew·y • *adjective* **chewier, chewiest**

Cheyenne[1] (shī an′ *or* shī en′) *noun* **1** a member of a North American Indian people from the area of Minnesota. They now live mainly in Oklahoma. **2** the language of this people.
Chey·enne • *noun, plural for sense 1 only* **Cheyennes** or **Cheyenne**

Cheyenne[2] (shī an′ *or* shī en′) the capital of Wyoming.
Chey·enne

chic (shēk) *adjective* having the newest style in a pleasing or attractive way [a *chic* new dress].
• The words **chic** and **sheik** sound alike.
Her clothes are always very *chic*.
A *sheik* is an Arab leader.

Chicago (shə kä′gō) a city in northeastern Illinois, on Lake Michigan.
Chi·ca·go

Chicana (chi kä′nə) *noun* an American woman or girl who was born in Mexico or whose parents or ancestors were from Mexico.
Chi·ca·na • *noun, plural* **Chicanas**

Chicano (chi kä′nō) *noun* an American man or boy who was born in Mexico or whose parents or ancestors were from Mexico.
Chi·ca·no • *noun, plural* **Chicanos**

chick (chik) *noun* **1** a young chicken. **2** any young bird.
chick • *noun, plural* **chicks**

chickadee (chik′ə dē) *noun* a small, plump bird that is mostly gray with a black head and throat. It has a call that sounds like its name.
chick·a·dee • *noun, plural* **chickadees**

chicken (chik′ən) *noun* **1** a common farm bird that is raised for its eggs and meat; hen or rooster. **2** the meat of a chicken used for food. **3** [*a slang use*] a person who is afraid to do something.
chick·en • *noun, plural* **chickens**

chickenpox (chik′ən päks′) *noun* a children's disease caused by a virus that spreads to others easily. Chickenpox causes fever and small blisters.
chick·en·pox • *noun*

chief (chēf) *noun* a person with the highest position or rank [the *chief* of the hospital staff].
adjective **1** having the highest position or rank [*chief* foreman at the factory]. **2** most important; main [Her *chief* interest is golf.] —Look for the WORD CHOICES box at the entry **principal**.
chief • *noun, plural* **chiefs** • *adjective*

chiefly (chēf′lē) *adverb* most of all; mainly [A watermelon is *chiefly* water.]
chief·ly • *adverb*

chieftain (chēf′tən) *noun* a leader or chief of a tribe or clan.
chief·tain • *noun, plural* **chieftains**

a cat	ō go	ʉ fur	ə = a *in* ago
ā ape	ô law, for	ch chin	e *in* agent
ä cot, car	oo look	sh she	i *in* pencil
e ten	o͞o tool	th thin	o *in* atom
ē me	oi oil	*th* then	u *in* circus
i fit	ou out	zh measure	
ī ice	u up	ŋ ring	

Chihuahua (chi wä′wä) ***noun*** a very small dog with large, pointed ears.
Chi·hua·hua • ***noun,*** *plural* **Chihuahuas**

child (chīld) ***noun*** **1** a baby; infant. **2** a young boy or girl. **3** a son or daughter [Their *children* are all grown up.]
child • ***noun,*** *plural* **children**

childhood (chīld′hood) ***noun*** the time when a person is a child [He has known her since his *childhood.*]
child·hood • ***noun,*** *plural* **childhoods**

childish (chīld′ish) ***adjective*** **1** of or fit for a child [*childish* laughter; *childish* games]. **2** not fit for a grown-up; not mature enough [a *childish* reason for leaving].
child·ish • ***adjective***

childlike (chīld′līk) ***adjective*** like a child; innocent and trusting [a *childlike* faith].
child·like • ***adjective***

children (chil′drən) ***noun*** *plural of* **child**.
chil·dren • ***noun***

Chile (chil′ē) a country on the southwestern coast of South America.
Chil·e

chili (chil′ē) ***noun*** **1** the dried pod of a kind of red pepper. It is used to make a very hot seasoning. **2** a spicy Mexican food made with ground beef, chilies, and often beans.
chil·i • ***noun,*** *plural* **chilies**

chili

• The words **chili** and **chilly** sound alike.
The restaurant served *chili* with beans.
The morning was *chilly* and damp.

chill (chil) ***noun*** **1** a feeling of coldness that makes a person shiver [She went home with *chills* and fever.] **2** a coolness that is uncomfortable [There is a *chill* in the air.]
adjective unpleasantly cold; chilly [A *chill* wind blew from the lake.]
verb **1** to make or become cool or cold [*Chill* the drinks in the refrigerator.] **2** to cause a chill in [The evening breeze *chilled* us.]
chill • ***noun,*** *plural* **chills** • ***adjective*** • ***verb*** **chilled, chilling**

chilly (chil′ē) ***adjective*** **1** cool enough to cause a feeling of unpleasant coldness; producing a chill [a *chilly* morning]. **2** not friendly [a *chilly* smile].
chil·ly • ***adjective*** **chillier, chilliest**
• The words **chilly** and **chili** sound alike.

WORD CHOICES

Synonyms of **chilly**

The words **chilly, cold,** and **frigid** share the meaning "cool enough to be uncomfortable."

a *chilly* evening in June
a *cold* January day
the *frigid* waters of the icy lake

chime (chīm) ***noun*** **1** one of a set of bells or metal tubes that are tuned to make musical sounds. **2** *usually* **chimes** the sounds made by these bells or tubes.
verb to ring or make a musical sound by ringing [The clock *chimed* in the hallway.]
chime • ***noun,*** *plural* **chimes** • ***verb*** **chimed, chiming**

chimney (chim′nē) ***noun*** a pipe or shaft going up above a roof to carry off smoke from a furnace, fireplace, or stove.
chim·ney • ***noun,*** *plural* **chimneys**

chimp (chimp) ***noun*** *a short form of* **chimpanzee**.
chimp • ***noun,*** *plural* **chimps**

chimpanzee (chim′pan zē′ *or* chim pan′zē) ***noun*** an African ape that is smaller than a gorilla.
chim·pan·zee • ***noun,*** *plural* **chimpanzees**

chin (chin) ***noun*** the part of the face below the lower lip; front part of the lower jaw.
verb to pull oneself up, while hanging by the hands from a bar, until the chin is just above the bar. This is done as an exercise.
chin • ***noun,*** *plural* **chins** • ***verb*** **chinned, chinning**

china (chī′nə) ***noun*** **1** a fine, hard pottery. It is usually white and often decorated with designs in bright colors. This kind of pottery was first made in China. **2** dishes and other things made of this pottery.
chi·na • ***noun***

China (chī′nə) a country in eastern Asia.
Chi·na

chinchilla (chin chil′ə) ***noun*** a small animal that looks like a squirrel. It has soft, gray fur and lives in the high mountains of South America.
chin·chil·la • ***noun,*** *plural* **chinchillas**

Chinese (chī nēz′) ***noun*** **1** a member of a people whose native country is China. **2** the language of China.
—**the Chinese** the people of China.
Chi·nese • ***noun,*** *plural for sense 1 only* **Chinese**

chink (chiŋk) ***noun*** a narrow opening; a crack [*chinks* in the walls of the old house].
chink • ***noun,*** *plural* **chinks**

chip (chip) ***noun*** **1** a small, thin piece broken or cut off [Wood *chips* covered the floor of the carpenter's shop.] **2** a place where a small piece has been broken or cut off [There is a *chip* on the edge of the plate.] **3** a tiny electronic device [a computer *chip*].
verb **1** to break or cut a small piece or thin slice from [Who *chipped* that cup?] **2** to break off into small pieces [This glass *chips* easily.]
—**chip in** [*an informal use*] to share in giving money or help [We all *chipped in* to buy her a birthday gift.]
chip • ***noun,*** *plural* **chips** • ***verb*** **chipped, chipping**

Chipewyan (chip′ə wī′ən) ***noun*** **1** a member of a North American Indian people of northwestern Canada. **2** the language of this people.
Chip·e·wyan • ***noun,*** *plural for sense 1 only* **Chipewyans** or **Chipewyan**

chipmunk

chipmunk (chip′muŋk) ***noun*** a small North American squirrel that has brown fur with striped markings on its head and back. Chipmunks live in holes in the ground.
chip·munk • ***noun,*** *plural* **chipmunks**

chirp (chʉrp) ***verb*** to make the short, shrill sound of some birds or insects [The birds start *chirping* early in the morning.]
noun this sound [The *chirp* of the crickets kept me awake.]
chirp • ***verb*** **chirped, chirping** • ***noun,*** *plural* **chirps**

chisel (chiz′əl) ***noun*** a tool that has a strong blade with a sharp edge for cutting or shaping wood, stone, or metal.
verb to cut or shape with a chisel [The sculptor *chiseled* his likeness in the stone.]
chis·el • ***noun,*** *plural* **chisels** • ***verb*** **chiseled** or **chiselled, chiseling** or **chiselling**

chisel

chivalry (shiv′əl rē) ***noun*** **1** the way of life followed by the knights of the Middle Ages. **2** the noble qualities that a knight was supposed to have. They included courage, politeness, honor, and being ready to help the weak.
chiv·al·ry • ***noun***

chlorine (klôr′ēn) ***noun*** a greenish-yellow, poisonous gas that is a chemical element. It is used in bleaches and for making water pure.
chlo·rine • ***noun***

chlorophyll or **chlorophyl** (klôr′ə fil) ***noun*** the green coloring matter in plants. Sunlight causes it to change carbon dioxide and water into food for the plant.
chlo·ro·phyll or **chlo·ro·phyl** • ***noun***

chocolate (chôk′ə lət *or* chäk′ə lət) ***noun*** **1** a dark-brown food made from the roasted and ground seeds of the cacao tree. Chocolate comes in the form of a paste, liquid, or solid bar. **2** a drink made from chocolate or cocoa, sugar, and milk or water. **3** a candy made of chocolate or covered with chocolate.
choc·o·late • ***noun,*** *plural* **chocolates**

choice (chois) ***noun*** **1** the act of choosing; selection [You must make a *choice* between

a	cat	ō	go	ʉ	fur	ə =	a *in* ago
ā	ape	ô	law, for	ch	chin		e *in* agent
ä	cot, car	oo	look	sh	she		i *in* pencil
e	ten	o͞o	tool	th	thin		o *in* atom
ē	me	oi	oil	*th*	then		u *in* circus
i	fit	ou	out	zh	measure		
ī	ice	u	up	ŋ	ring		

the two books.] **2** the right or chance to choose [Mom gave us a *choice* between chicken or pork chops for dinner.] **3** a person or thing chosen [Jeff was the coach's *choice* for quarterback.] **4** a group of things from which to choose [What are the *choices?*]
adjective of the best kind; of fine quality; very good [a *choice* location for a house; *choice* meat].
choice • ***noun,*** *plural* **choices**
• ***adjective*** **choicer, choicest**

WORD CHOICES

Synonyms of choice

The words **choice, alternative,** and **option** share the meaning "a chance to pick what is wanted."

There was no *choice*; I had to eat it.

We have the *alternative* of going by train or bus.

The court gave her the *option* of paying a fine or going to jail.

choir (kwīr) ***noun*** a group of people trained to sing together, especially in a church.
choir • ***noun,*** *plural* **choirs**

choke (chōk) ***verb*** **1** to keep from breathing by blocking the windpipe or squeezing the throat; strangle; suffocate. **2** to be unable to breathe, swallow, or speak normally because the throat is blocked [The thick smoke made me *choke*. He *choked* on a piece of steak.] **3** to block up a passage; clog [Heavy traffic *choked* the main roads.] **4** to hold back the growth or progress of; smother [Weeds are *choking* the lawn.]
choke • ***verb*** **choked, choking**

choose (cho͞oz) ***verb*** **1** to pick out one or more from a number or group [*Choose* a book from this list.] **2** to make up one's mind; decide or prefer [She *chose* to stay home.]
choose • ***verb*** **chose, chosen, choosing**

chop (chäp) ***verb*** **1** to cut by strokes with an ax or other sharp tool [The gardener *chopped* down a tree.] **2** to cut into small bits [He *chopped* up an onion for the salad.]
noun **1** a short, quick stroke or blow [a *chop* of the hand]. **2** a slice of pork, veal, or lamb that is cut with a piece of bone in it.
chop • ***verb*** **chopped, chopping** • ***noun,*** *plural* **chops**

chopper (chäp′ər) ***noun*** **1** a person or thing that chops. **2** [*an informal use*] a helicopter.
chop·per • ***noun,*** *plural* **choppers**

chopsticks

chopsticks (chäp′stiks) ***plural noun*** a pair of small sticks used to lift food to the mouth, especially in some Asian countries.
chop·sticks • ***plural noun***

WORD HISTORY

chopsticks

The Chinese word for these eating utensils sounded a little like "chopsticks" to the English sailors who first saw them. The word means "the quick ones." If you have tried to use **chopsticks** and not picked up much food with them the first time, you may not think that this way of eating is quick or easy. But if you practice, you will see that using **chopsticks** can be as quick and easy as using a fork. Millions of people use them every day.

chord (kôrd) ***noun*** a combination of three or more musical tones that make harmony when played together.
chord • ***noun,*** *plural* **chords**
• The words **chord** and **cord** sound alike.
So far, I can play only one *chord* on the guitar.
Tie the package with strong *cord*.

chore (chôr) ***noun*** **1** a small job that has to be

done regularly [One of her *chores* is mowing the lawn.] —Look for the WORD CHOICES box at the entry **task**. **2** any hard or boring task [Writing letters is a real *chore* for him.]
chore • ***noun,*** *plural* **chores**

chortle (chôrt′l) ***verb*** to laugh in a loud, gleeful way —Look for the WORD CHOICES box at the entry **laugh**.
chor·tle • ***verb*** **chortled, chortling**

chorus (kôr′əs) ***noun*** **1** a group of people trained to sing or speak together. **2** the part of a song that is repeated after each verse; refrain [The *chorus* of "The Battle Hymn of the Republic" begins "Glory, glory, hallelujah!"] **3** singers or dancers who work together as a group and not as soloists.
chor·us • ***noun,*** *plural* **choruses**

chose (chōz) ***verb*** *past tense of* **choose**.

chosen (chō′zən) ***verb*** *past participle of* **choose**.
cho·sen • ***verb***

chowder (chou′dər) ***noun*** a thick soup made with seafood or vegetables, usually with potatoes and milk [clam *chowder;* corn *chowder*].
chow·der • ***noun,*** *plural* **chowders**

Christ (krīst) Jesus, the founder of the Christian religion.

christen (kris′ən) ***verb*** **1** to give a name to at baptism [The baby was *christened* Jessica.] **2** to give a name to [We *christened* the boat "Star of the Sea."]
chris·ten • ***verb*** **christened, christening**

Christian (kris′chən) ***noun*** a person who believes in Jesus or follows the religion based on the teachings of Jesus.
adjective **1** having to do with Jesus or the religion based on his teachings. **2** following the example of Jesus; showing a kind, gentle, and loving nature.
Chris·tian • ***noun,*** *plural* **Christians**
• ***adjective***

Christianity (kris′chē an′i tē) ***noun*** **1** the religion based on the teachings of Jesus. **2** all the Christian people.
Chris·ti·an·i·ty • ***noun***

Christmas (kris′məs) ***noun*** December 25, a holiday that celebrates the birth of Jesus Christ.
Christ·mas • ***noun***

Christmastime (kris′məs tīm) ***noun*** the Christmas season.
Christ·mas·time • ***noun***

Christmas tree ***noun*** an evergreen tree that is decorated at Christmastime.
Christmas tree • ***noun,***
plural **Christmas trees**

chrome (krōm) ***noun*** chromium, when it is used as a coating over steel or another metal.

chromium (krō′mē əm) ***noun*** a hard, steel-gray metal that is a chemical element. Chromium is added to other metals because it is strong and does not rust easily.
chro·mi·um • ***noun***

chromosome (krō′mə sōm) ***noun*** one of certain tiny particles in the nucleus of cells. Chromosomes carry the genes that pass on inherited characteristics such as eye and hair color.
chro·mo·some • ***noun,*** *plural* **chromosomes**

chronic (krän′ik) ***adjective*** **1** going on for a long time [a *chronic* disease]. **2** doing something by habit; constant [a *chronic* complainer].
chron·ic • ***adjective***

chronological (krän′ə läj′i kəl) ***adjective*** arranged in the order in which things happened [a *chronological* chart of American history].
chron·o·log·i·cal • ***adjective***

chrysanthemum (kri san′thə məm) ***noun*** **1** a garden plant with flowers that bloom in late summer and fall. **2** one of these flowers.
chrys·an·the·mum
• ***noun,*** *plural* **chrysanthemums**

chubby (chub′ē) ***adjective*** round and plump [a *chubby* face].
chub·by • ***adjective*** **chubbier, chubbiest**

chuckle (chuk′əl) ***verb*** to laugh softly [She *chuckled* when she read the comics.] —Look for the WORD CHOICES box at the entry **laugh**.
noun a soft laugh.
chuck·le • ***verb*** **chuckled, chuckling** • ***noun,*** *plural* **chuckles**

chug (chug) ***noun*** a short, puffing sound that is like the sound made by steam escaping from a steam engine [the steady *chug* of the engine].

a	cat	ō	go	ʉ	fur	ə =	a *in* ago
ā	ape	ô	law, for	ch	chin		e *in* agent
ä	cot, car	oo	look	sh	she		i *in* pencil
e	ten	ōō	tool	th	thin		o *in* atom
ē	me	oi	oil	*th*	then		u *in* circus
i	fit	ou	out	zh	measure		
ī	ice	u	up	ŋ	ring		

verb to move while making such sounds [The train *chugged* up the hill.]
chug • *noun, plural* **chugs** • *verb* **chugged, chugging**

chum (chum) [*an informal word*] *noun* a close friend; pal.
chum • *noun, plural* **chums**

chunk (chuŋk) *noun* a short, thick piece [a *chunk* of meat].
chunk • *noun, plural* **chunks**

chunky (chuŋ′kē) *adjective* **1** short and heavy; stout [a *chunky* person]. **2** full of chunks; coarse [Do you like *chunky* peanut butter?]
chunk·y • *adjective* **chunkier, chunkiest**

church (church) *noun* **1** a building for public Christian religious services. **2** religious services [*Church* will be at 11 on Sunday.] **3** a group of Christians who have the same beliefs and forms of worship [the *Church* of England].
church • *noun, plural* **churches**

Churchill (chur′chil), **Winston** (win′stən) 1874-1965; the British prime minister from 1940 to 1945 and from 1951 to 1955.
Church·ill, Win·ston

churchyard (church′yärd) *noun* the yard around a church. It is often used as a cemetery.
church·yard • *noun, plural* **churchyards**

churn (churn) *noun* a container in which milk or cream is stirred and shaken to make butter.
verb **1** to stir and shake milk or cream in a churn to make butter. **2** to stir or move about with much force [The motorboats *churned* up the water of the lake.]
churn • *noun, plural* **churns**
• *verb* **churned, churning**

chute (sho͞ot) *noun* a long tube or slide in which things can be dropped or slid down to a lower place [a mail *chute;* a laundry *chute*].
chute • *noun, plural* **chutes**
● The words **chute** and **shoot** sound alike.
Dirty laundry goes down the *chute*.
The hunter will only *shoot* birds.

-cide *a suffix meaning* killer or killing [An *insecticide* kills insects.]

cider (sī′dər) *noun* a drink made from apple juice.
ci·der • *noun, plural* **ciders**

cigar (si gär′) *noun* a tight roll of tobacco leaves that is used for smoking.
ci·gar • *noun, plural* **cigars**

cigarette (sig ər et′ *or* sig′ər et) *noun* a small roll of finely cut tobacco wrapped in thin paper for smoking.
cig·a·rette • *noun, plural* **cigarettes**

cilia (sil′ē ə) *plural noun* fine hairlike parts that grow out from the surface of some plant and animal cells. Certain one-celled animals move by waving their cilia.
cil·i·a • *plural noun, singular* **cil·i·um** (sil′ē əm)

cinch (sinch) *noun* **1** a band that is put around the belly of a horse or other animal to keep a saddle or pack in place on the animal's back. **2** [*a slang use*] something that is easy or is sure to happen [It's a *cinch* our team will win.]
cinch • *noun, plural* **cinches**

Cincinnati (sin′si nat′ē) a city in southwestern Ohio.
Cin·cin·nat·i

cinder (sin′dər) *noun* **1** a tiny bit of partly burned wood, coal, or other material. **2 cinders** the ashes from coal or wood.
cin·der • *noun, plural* **cinders**

Cinderella (sin dər el′ə) a girl in a fairy tale who works hard in the house of her stepmother until her fairy godmother helps her to meet a prince, who marries her.
Cin·der·el·la

cinema (sin′ə mə) *noun* a movie theater. This sense is used mainly in Britain.
cin·e·ma • *noun, plural* **cinemas**

cinnamon (sin′ə mən) *noun* a brown spice made from the dried bark of a tropical tree.
cin·na·mon • *noun*

circle (sur′kəl) *noun* **1** an unbroken line that has no angles and is drawn around a real or imaginary center point. Each point on the line is the same distance from the center point. **2** the figure formed by this line and the space inside it. **3** something round like a circle or ring [We found a *circle* of mushrooms in the lawn.] **4** a group of people having the same interests [He has a wide *circle* of friends.]
verb **1** to form a circle around [The soldiers *circled* the flagpole.] **2** to move around in a circle [The planets *circle* the sun.]
cir·cle • *noun, plural* **circles** • *verb* **circled, circling**

circuit (sur′kət) *noun* **1** the act of going around something; a course or journey in a circle [The moon's *circuit* of the earth takes

C

about 28 days.] **2** a regular route followed by a judge who travels from town to town in order to hear legal cases in each of them. **3** the complete path of an electric current.
cir·cuit • *noun, plural* **circuits**

circuit breaker *noun* a device that automatically stops the flow of an electric current in its circuit when the current is too high.
circuit breaker • *noun, plural* **circuit breakers**

circular (sur′kyə lər) *adjective* **1** having the shape of a circle; round [a *circular* path]. **2** moving in a circle [a *circular* dance].
noun a letter or advertisement that is prepared in many copies for sending to many people.
cir·cu·lar • *adjective* • *noun, plural* **circulars**

circulate (sur′kyə lāt) *verb* **1** to move in a regular course and return to the same point [Blood *circulates* through the body from the heart.] **2** to move or send about from person to person or place to place [That rumor has been *circulating* through the town.]
cir·cu·late • *verb* **circulated, circulating**

circulation (sur′kyə lā′shən) *noun* **1** free movement around from place to place [The fan kept the air in *circulation*.] **2** the movement of blood through the veins and arteries. **3** the passing of something from person to person or place to place [Gold money is not in *circulation* in the U.S.]
cir·cu·la·tion • *noun, plural* **circulations**

circulatory (sur′kyə lə tôr′ē) *adjective* having to do with circulation of the blood [the *circulatory* system].
cir·cu·la·to·ry • *adjective*

circumflex (sur′kəm fleks′) *noun* a mark that looks like a tiny roof or tent (^). It is put over certain vowel letters to show a certain sound. In this dictionary it is placed over the letter *o* to show the sound of this vowel in *or* (ôr).
cir·cum·flex • *noun, plural* **circumflexes**

circumstance (sur′kəm stans) *noun* a fact or event connected in some way with a situation [Do you know what the *circumstances* were that led to his arrest?]
cir·cum·stance • *noun, plural* **circumstances**

circus (sur′kəs) *noun* a traveling show with clowns, trained animals, acrobats, and other entertainers.
cir·cus • *noun, plural* **circuses**

WORD HISTORY

circus

When we speak of the center ring of a **circus**, we are repeating ourselves. The Greek word from which we got **circus** means "ring" or "circle." The words **circle** and **circulate** come from the same Greek word, and have to do with the idea expressed by "round" or "around."

citizen (sit′i zən) *noun* **1** a person who is a member of a country either because of being born there or having been made a member by law. Citizens of the U.S. are given certain rights and have certain duties to the country. **2** a person who lives in a particular city or town [the *citizens* of Atlanta].
cit·i·zen • *noun, plural* **citizens**

citizenship (sit′i zən ship′) *noun* the condition of being a citizen [*Citizenship* is required before a person may vote in an election.]
cit·i·zen·ship • *noun*

citrus (sit′rəs) *noun* **1** any fruit of the group that includes oranges, grapefruits, limes, and lemons. **2** a tree on which such a fruit grows.
cit·rus • *noun, plural* **citruses**

city (sit′ē) *noun* **1** a large, important town, usually with many thousands or millions of people. **2** all the people of a city [The *city* will vote on the issue next Tuesday.]
cit·y • *noun, plural* **cities**

city hall *noun* a building in which the offices of the city government are located.
city hall • *noun, plural* **city halls**

civic (siv′ik) *adjective* **1** of a city [The professor had a plan for *civic* development.] **2** of citizens or citizenship [Voting is a *civic* duty.]
civ·ic • *adjective*

civics (siv′iks) *plural noun* the study of how the government works and of the duties and rights of citizens.
civ·ics • *plural noun*

civil (siv′əl) *adjective* **1** of a citizen or citizens

a	cat	ō	go	ʉr	fur	ə =	a *in* ago
ā	ape	ô	law, for	ch	chin		e *in* agent
ä	cot, car	oo	look	sh	she		i *in* pencil
e	ten	o͞o	tool	th	thin		o *in* atom
ē	me	oi	oil	*th*	then		u *in* circus
i	fit	ou	out	zh	measure		
ī	ice	u	up	ŋ	ring		

[*civil* rights]. **2** not rude; polite [Stop shouting and give me a *civil* answer.] **3** not having to do with religion or the military [a *civil* marriage].
civ·il • *adjective*

WORD CHOICES

Synonyms of **civil**

The words **civil, courteous,** and **polite** share the meaning "showing kindness or thoughtfulness."

Give me a *civil* answer.

Always be *courteous* to strangers.

It isn't *polite* to interrupt.

civilian (si vil′yən) ***noun*** a person who is not a member of the armed forces.
ci·vil·ian • ***noun,*** *plural* **civilians**

civilization (siv′i li zā′shən) ***noun*** **1** the stage in the progress of human beings when they have developed a written language, arts, sciences, and government. **2** the countries and peoples that are civilized. **3** the way of life of a people, nation, or period [She is interested in ancient Egyptian *civilization*.]
civ·i·li·za·tion • ***noun,*** *plural* **civilizations**

civilize (siv′i līz′) ***verb*** to bring out of an ignorant or primitive condition and give training in the arts, sciences, or government.
civ·i·lize • ***verb*** **civilized, civilizing**

civil liberties ***plural noun*** the freedom that a person has by law to think, speak, and act so long as other people are not harmed.

civil rights ***plural noun*** the rights of all citizens regardless of race, religion, sex, or place of birth. In the U.S., these rights are guaranteed by the Constitution.

civil war ***noun*** war between sections or groups of the same nation.
—**the Civil War** the war from 1861 to 1865 between the northern and southern States of the U.S.
civil war • ***noun,*** *plural* **civil wars**

clack (klak) ***verb*** to make a sudden, sharp sound or to cause to make this sound [The dancers *clack* their heels on the floor.]
noun a sudden, sharp sound [The door closed with a *clack*.]
clack • ***verb*** **clacked, clacking** • ***noun,*** *plural* **clacks**

clad (klad) ***verb*** *a past tense and past participle of* **clothe**.

claim (klām) ***verb*** **1** to demand or ask for something that one thinks one has a right to [He *claimed* the package at the post office.] —Look for the WORD CHOICES box at the entry **demand**. **2** to state as a fact something that may or may not be true [They *claimed* they were robbed.]
noun **1** a demand that one thinks one has a right to [She made a *claim* for the damage done to her car.] **2** something said as a fact that may or may not be true [False *claims* are sometimes made by dishonest salespersons.]
claim • ***verb*** **claimed, claiming** • ***noun,*** *plural* **claims**

clam (klam) ***noun*** a shellfish with a soft body enclosed in two hard shells that are joined by a hinge. Some kinds are used as food.
clam • ***noun,*** *plural* **clams**

clambake (klam′bāk) ***noun*** a picnic at which clams are steamed or baked with chicken, lobster, corn, and other foods.
clam·bake • ***noun,*** *plural* **clambakes**

clamber (klam′bər) ***verb*** to climb with effort by using both the hands and feet [We *clambered* up the steep hill.]
clam·ber • ***verb*** **clambered, clambering**

clammy (klam′ē) ***adjective*** slightly wet and cold [His hands are *clammy* when he is afraid.]
clam·my • ***adjective*** **clammier, clammiest**

clamp (klamp) ***noun*** a device with two parts that are brought together by a screw so that they grip something.
verb to grip or fasten with a clamp.
clamp • ***noun,*** *plural* **clamps** • ***verb*** **clamped, clamping**

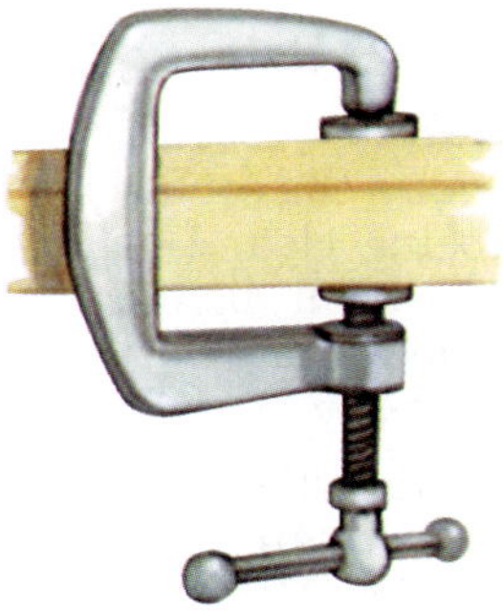
clamp

clan (klan) ***noun*** a group of families who claim to be descended from the same ancestor.
clan • ***noun,*** *plural* **clans**

clang (klaŋ) ***noun*** a loud, ringing sound [the *clang* of a bell].
verb to make such a sound [The bells *clanged*.]

C

clang • *noun, plural* **clangs** • *verb* **clanged, clanging**

clank (klaŋk) ***noun*** a sound like a clang but not so ringing.
verb to make such a sound.
clank • ***noun**, plural* **clanks** • ***verb*** **clanked, clanking**

clap (klap) ***verb*** **1** to make the sudden, loud sound of two flat surfaces being struck together. **2** to strike the palms of the hands together to show approval. **3** to strike with the palm of the hand in a friendly way [He *clapped* me on the shoulder.]
noun **1** a sudden loud sound of clapping [a *clap* of thunder]. **2** a sharp blow; slap.
clap • ***verb*** **clapped, clapping** • ***noun**, plural* **claps**

clapper (klap′ər) ***noun*** the moving part inside a bell that strikes the sides of the bell.
clap·per • ***noun**, plural* **clappers**

clarify (kler′i fī′) ***verb*** to make or become easier to understand [She *clarified* the problem by drawing a diagram.]
clar·i·fy • ***verb*** **clarified, clarifying, clarifies**

clarinet (kler′i net′) ***noun*** a woodwind musical instrument that is shaped like a tube. It has a mouthpiece with one reed and is played by opening and closing holes with the fingers or keys.
clar·i·net • ***noun**, plural* **clarinets**

clarinet

clarity (kler′i tē) ***noun*** the condition of being clear [We saw the fish because of the water's *clarity*.]
clar·i·ty • ***noun***

Clark (klärk), **William** (wil′yəm) 1770-1838; American explorer. *See also the entry for* **Lewis**, Meriwether
Clark, Wil·liam

clash (klash) ***noun*** **1** the sound of metal striking against metal with great force or a similar loud, harsh noise [the *clash* of a sword on a shield]. **2** a sharp disagreement; conflict [a *clash* between friends].
verb **1** to strike together with a loud, harsh noise [The cymbals *clashed*.] **2** to disagree sharply [Our ideas *clash*.] **3** to not match or go together [The dog mask *clashed* with the cat costume.]
clash • ***noun**, plural* **clashes** • ***verb*** **clashed, clashing**

clasp (klasp) ***noun*** **1** a hook, catch, or other fastening for holding two things or parts together. **2** the act of holding with the hand or in the arms [He gave my hand a firm *clasp*.]
verb **1** to fasten with a clasp. **2** to hold tightly in the arms [The baby *clasped* a doll while she slept.] **3** to grip with the hand [I *clasped* her hand in greeting.]
clasp • ***noun**, plural* **clasps** • ***verb*** **clasped, clasping**

class (klas) ***noun*** **1** a number of people, animals, or things that are thought of as a group because they are alike in certain ways [We are members of the working *class*.] **2** a group of students that meet together to be taught [Half the *class* missed school today.] **3** a meeting of these students [My English *class* is held at 9 o'clock.] **4** all the students who graduate together [the *class* of 1995]. **5** a rank or division according to such things as quality [a better *class* of cars].
verb to put in a class; classify [My teacher *classes* me with her best students.]
class • ***noun**, plural* **classes** • ***verb*** **classed, classing**

classic (klas′ik) ***adjective*** **1** of the highest quality or rank [Her story is a *classic* example of good writing.] **2** famous because it is typical and has become a tradition [Turkey is the *classic* dish for Thanksgiving dinner.]
noun a book, painting, or other work of the highest excellence ["The Wizard of Oz" is a *classic* among American movies.]
clas·sic • ***adjective*** • ***noun**, plural* **classics**

classical (klas′i kəl) ***adjective*** **1** describing a kind of music that is not simple in form and requires much study and training to compose and perform. This music is based on traditional forms of European origin [The music of Mozart and Beethoven is called *classical* music.] **2** of the art, literature, and culture of the ancient Greeks and Romans.
clas·si·cal • ***adjective***

a	cat	ō	go	ʉ	fur	ə =	a *in* ago
ā	ape	ô	law, for	ch	chin		e *in* agent
ä	cot, car	oo	look	sh	she		i *in* pencil
e	ten	ōō	tool	th	thin		o *in* atom
ē	me	oi	oil	*th*	then		u *in* circus
i	fit	ou	out	zh	measure		
ī	ice	u	up	ŋ	ring		

classification (klas′i fi kā′shən) ***noun*** the arrangement of things into classes or groups according to some system.
clas·si·fi·ca·tion • ***noun,*** *plural* **classifications**

classify (klas′i fī′) ***verb*** to arrange by putting into classes or groups according to some system [The library *classifies* books by author, title, and subject.]
clas·si·fy • ***verb*** **classified, classifying, classifies**

classmate (klas′māt) ***noun*** a member of the same class at a school or college.
class·mate • ***noun,*** *plural* **classmates**

classroom (klas′ro͞om) ***noun*** a room in a school or college where classes meet.
class·room • ***noun,*** *plural* **classrooms**

clatter (klat′ər) ***noun*** a series of sharp, clashing sounds [I heard the *clatter* of feet running through the halls.] —Look for the WORD CHOICES box at the entry **noise**.
verb to make a clatter.
clat·ter • ***noun*** • ***verb*** **clattered, clattering**

clause (klôz *or* kläz) ***noun*** **1** a group of words that includes a subject and a verb, but that forms only part of a sentence. The sentence "She will visit us if she can," has two clauses: "she will visit us" and "if she can". **2** a separate point or article in a law, contract, or other document.
clause • ***noun,*** *plural* **clauses**

claw (klô *or* klä) ***noun*** **1** a sharp, curved nail on the foot of an animal or bird. **2** the grasping part on each front leg of a lobster, crab, or scorpion.
verb to scratch, pull, dig, or tear with claws or as if with claws [The cat *clawed* her arm.]
claw • ***noun,*** *plural* **claws** • ***verb*** **clawed, clawing**

claw
Above: Of eagle
Below: Of tiger

clay (klā) ***noun*** a stiff, sticky earth that becomes hard when it is baked. It is used in making bricks, pottery, tile, and china.
clay • ***noun,*** *plural* **clays**

clean (klēn) ***adjective*** **1** not dirty or soiled [*clean* water; *clean* clothes]. **2** neat and tidy [He keeps a *clean* desk.] **3** complete or thorough [a *clean* shave; a *clean* sweep].
adverb **1** so as to be clean [The room was swept *clean*.] **2** completely; entirely [She has gone *clean* out of her mind.]
verb to make clean [The dentist *cleans* my teeth twice each year.]
clean • ***adjective*** **cleaner, cleanest** • ***adverb*** • ***verb*** **cleaned, cleaning**

cleaner (klēn′ər) ***noun*** **1** a person or thing that cleans. **2 cleaners** a business that does dry cleaning.
clean·er • ***noun,*** *plural* **cleaners**

cleanse (klenz) ***verb*** to make clean or pure.
cleanse • ***verb*** **cleansed, cleansing**

cleanser (klen′zər) ***noun*** a scouring powder or other substance used for cleaning.
cleans·er • ***noun,*** *plural* **cleansers**

clear (klir) ***adjective*** **1** bright or sunny; without clouds or mist [a *clear* day]. **2** capable of being seen through; transparent [*clear* glass]. **3** seen or heard with ease; not faint or blurred [a *clear* outline; a *clear* tone]. **4** easy to understand; not confusing [a *clear* explanation]. **5** not guilty; innocent [a *clear* conscience]. **6** without anything in the way; not blocked; open [a *clear* view; a *clear* passage].
adverb **1** in a clear manner; clearly [The bells rang out loud and *clear*.] **2** all the way [It sank *clear* to the bottom of the lake.]
verb **1** to make or become clear [The sun *cleared* the mist from the sky. The sky *cleared* after the storm.] **2** to empty or remove [We *cleared* the snow from the driveway.] **3** to open [We *cleared* a path through the snow.] **4** to free from guilt or blame [The suspect was *cleared* by the police.] **5** to pass over, under, or by without touching [The leaping horse *cleared* the fence by a few inches.]
—**clear up** **1** to explain [She tried to *clear up* the confusion.] **2** to cure or become cured [The medicine *cleared up* the infection. The infection *cleared up* in a few days.]
clear • ***adjective*** **clearer, clearest** • ***adverb*** • ***verb*** **cleared, clearing**

clearance (klir′əns) ***noun*** **1** the act of clearing [He ordered more trucks to help in the *clearance* of snow from the streets.] **2** the clear space between two objects, such as between the top of a truck and the bottom of a bridge.
clear·ance • ***noun,*** *plural* **clearances**

clearing (klir′iŋ) ***noun*** a piece of land that has been cleared of trees [A log cabin stood in the middle of the *clearing*.]
clear·ing • ***noun,*** *plural* **clearings**

clearly (klir′lē) ***adverb*** in a clear manner [She spoke slowly and *clearly*.]
clear·ly • ***adverb***

cleat (klēt) ***noun*** a piece of metal or wood fastened to something to make it stronger or to prevent slipping.
cleat • ***noun,*** *plural* **cleats**

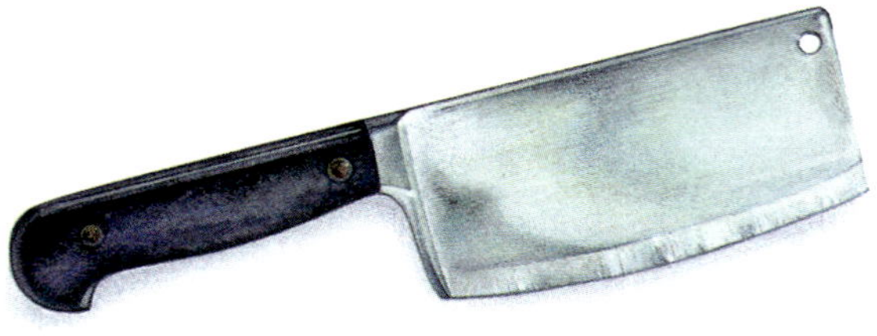

cleaver

cleaver (klēv′ər) ***noun*** a heavy cutting tool with a broad blade, used by butchers.
cleav·er • ***noun,*** *plural* **cleavers**

clef

clef (klef) ***noun*** a sign at the beginning of a musical staff that shows how high or low the notes are. The treble or G clef shows that the notes that follow it are mainly above middle C. The bass or F clef shows that the notes that follow it are mainly below middle C.
clef • ***noun,*** *plural* **clefs**

cleft (kleft) ***adjective*** split open; divided [A *cleft* palate is a split in the roof of the mouth.] ***noun*** an opening or hollow made by splitting [He entered the cave through a *cleft* in the rocks.]
cleft • ***adjective*** • ***noun,*** *plural* **clefts**

Clemens (klem′ənz), **Samuel Langhorne** (sam′yo͞o əl laŋ′hôrn) *the real name of* Mark **Twain**.
Clem·ens, Sam·u·el Lang·horne

clench (klench) ***verb*** **1** to close or press tightly together [He *clenched* his fists. She is *clenching* her teeth.] **2** to grip firmly [She *clenched* her purse with both hands.]
noun a firm grip.
clench • ***verb*** **clenched, clenching** • ***noun,*** *plural* **clenches**

Cleopatra (klē ə pat′rə) 69?-30 B.C.; queen of Egypt who was loved by Julius Caesar and by Mark Antony.
Cle·o·pa·tra

clergy (klʉr′jē) ***noun*** ministers, priests, rabbis, and other ordained persons as a group.
cler·gy • ***noun,*** *plural* **clergies**

clergyman (klʉr′jē mən) ***noun*** a minister, priest, rabbi, or other ordained person.
cler·gy·man • ***noun,*** *plural* **clergymen**

clerical (kler′i kəl) ***adjective*** **1** having to do with a clergyman or the clergy [Some priests and ministers wear a *clerical* collar.] **2** having to do with office clerks or their work [She has a *clerical* job at the bank.]
cler·i·cal • ***adjective***

clerk (klʉrk) ***noun*** **1** a person who keeps records, types letters, or does other similar work in an office. **2** a salesperson.
clerk • ***noun,*** *plural* **clerks**

Cleveland (klēv′lənd), **Grover** (grō′vər) 1837-1908; twenty-second president of the U.S., from 1885 to 1889, and twenty-fourth president, from 1893 to 1897.
Cleve·land, Gro·ver

Cleveland (klēv′lənd) a city in northeastern Ohio.
Cleve·land

clever (klev′ər) ***adjective*** **1** quick in thinking or learning; smart; intelligent [She is a *clever* student.] **2** showing skill or good thinking [He won the chess game with several *clever* moves.] —Look for the WORD CHOICES box at the entry **intelligent**.
clev·er • ***adjective***

a	cat	ō	go	ʉ	fur	ə =	a *in* ago
ā	ape	ô	law, for	ch	chin		e *in* agent
ä	cot, car	o͝o	look	sh	she		i *in* pencil
e	ten	o͞o	tool	th	thin		o *in* atom
ē	me	oi	oil	*th*	then		u *in* circus
i	fit	ou	out	zh	measure		
ī	ice	u	up	ŋ	ring		

click (klik) ***noun*** a slight, sharp sound like the sound of a lock snapping shut.
verb to make or cause to make a click [His boots *clicked* as he walked across the tile floor.]
click • ***noun,*** *plural* **clicks** • ***verb*** **clicked, clicking**

client (klī′ənt) ***noun*** **1** a person or company that is being represented by a professional person, such as a lawyer or accountant. **2** a customer.
cli·ent • ***noun,*** *plural* **clients**

cliff (klif) ***noun*** a high, steep face of rock that goes down sharply without a slope.
cliff • ***noun,*** *plural* **cliffs**

climate (klī′mət) ***noun*** the usual weather conditions of a place over a long period of time [Arizona has a mild, dry *climate*.]
cli·mate • ***noun,*** *plural* **climates**

climax (klī′maks) ***noun*** the point of greatest interest or excitement at or near the end of a story or series of events [the *climax* of a movie].
cli·max • ***noun,*** *plural* **climaxes**

WORD CHOICES

Synonyms of **climax**

The words **climax, peak,** and **summit** share the meaning "the highest point."

the *climax* of excitement in the game
the *peak* of factory production
the *summit* of her career

climb (klīm) ***verb*** **1** to go up by using the feet and often the hands [He *climbed* the stairs.] **2** to move up, down, over, or across by using the feet and often the hands [The cat *climbed* down the tree.] **3** to rise to a higher level or position [The airplane *climbed* to 30,000 feet.] **4** to grow upward on some support [The ivy *climbed* the wall.]
noun **1** the act of climbing [We made several *climbs* up the mountain.] **2** a thing to be climbed [The steep stairs are a difficult *climb*.]
climb • ***verb*** **climbed, climbing** • ***noun,*** *plural* **climbs**

clinch (klinch) ***verb*** to settle definitely; fix [His run in the ninth inning *clinched* the victory.]
clinch • ***verb*** **clinched, clinching**

cling (kliŋ) ***verb*** **1** to hold on tightly [The child *clung* to her father's hand.] **2** to hold in place; stick [The vine *clings* to the wall.]
cling • ***verb*** **clung, clinging**

clinic (klin′ik) ***noun*** a place that gives medical treatment to patients who do not need to stay in a hospital. It is usually a department of a hospital or medical school.
clin·ic • ***noun,*** *plural* **clinics**

clink (kliŋk) ***noun*** a short, tinkling sound.
clink • ***noun,*** *plural* **clinks**

Clinton (klint′n), **Bill** (bil) 1946- ; the forty-second president of the U.S., from 1993 to 2001. His full name is *William Jefferson Clinton*.
Clin·ton, Bill

clip[1] (klip) ***verb*** **1** to cut off or cut out with shears or scissors [He *clipped* the picture from a magazine.] **2** to cut the hair or wool of [We *clipped* the dog.]
noun **1** the act of clipping. **2** a high rate of speed [The traffic moved at a dangerous *clip*.]
clip • ***verb*** **clipped, clipping** • ***noun,*** *plural* **clips**

clip[2] (klip) ***noun*** anything that is used to hold two or more things together [a paper *clip*].
verb to fasten with a clip [I *clipped* the pages together with a staple.]
clip • ***noun,*** *plural* **clips** • ***verb*** **clipped, clipping**

clipper

clipper (klip′ər) ***noun*** **1** *often* **clippers** a tool for clipping or shearing [a *clipper* for trimming hedges; a barber's *clippers*]. **2** a swift, narrow sailing ship with a sharp bow.
clip·per • ***noun,*** *plural* **clippers**

clipping (klip′iŋ) ***noun*** **1** a piece cut off or out of something [hair *clippings*]. **2** an item cut out from a newspaper or magazine.
clip·ping • ***noun,*** *plural* **clippings**

cloak (klōk) ***noun*** **1** a loose outer garment, usually without sleeves. **2** something that

C

covers or hides [The prisoner escaped under the *cloak* of darkness.]
verb **1** to cover with a cloak. **2** to conceal; hide [She *cloaked* her anger by telling jokes.]
cloak • ***noun****, plural* **cloaks** • ***verb*** **cloaked, cloaking**

clobber (kläb′ər) [*a slang word*] ***verb*** to hit very hard or many times.
clob·ber • ***verb*** **clobbered, clobbering**

clock (kläk) ***noun*** a device for measuring and showing the time. A clock shows time either by pointers moving around a dial or by showing a changing series of numbers. A clock is not meant to be worn or carried like a watch.
verb to measure the time of a race or runner [He was *clocked* at three minutes.]
clock • ***noun****, plural* **clocks** • ***verb*** **clocked, clocking**

clockwise (kläk′wīz) ***adverb*** in the direction in which the hands of a clock move [Turn the knob *clockwise* to turn on the radio.] This word can also be used as an adjective [A *clockwise* turn will decrease the water flow.]
clock·wise • ***adverb***

clog (kläg *or* klôg) ***noun*** a heavy shoe, usually with a wooden sole.
verb to slow up or block up; jam [Traffic *clogs* the streets at rush hour.]
clog • ***noun****, plural* **clogs** • ***verb*** **clogged, clogging**

cloister (kloi̇s′tər) ***noun*** **1** a place where monks or nuns live; monastery or convent. **2** a covered walk along the inside wall of a monastery or convent. The cloister borders on a courtyard.
clois·ter • ***noun****, plural* **cloisters**

close[1] (klōs) ***adjective*** **1** with not much space between; near [The boat is *close* to the shore.] **2** near in relationship [a *close* relative of mine]. **3** much liked or loved [a *close* friend]. **4** complete or careful [Pay *close* attention.] **5** nearly equal or even [a *close* game].
adverb in a close position [Park *close* to our car.]
close • ***adjective*** **closer, closest** • ***adverb***

close[2] (klōz) ***verb*** **1** to make no longer open; shut [*Close* the door.] **2** to fill up or stop up [The doctor *closed* the wound.] **3** to bring or come to a finish; end [She *closed* her speech with words of thanks.] **4** to stop the working or operation of [The store will be *closed* at 9 o'clock.]
close • ***verb*** **closed, closing**

• The words **close** and **clothes** sound alike.
Close the door when you leave.
Pack the *clothes* in the suitcase.

closed circuit ***noun*** a system of sending television signals by cable to just a certain number of receiving sets for some special purpose.

closet (kläz′ət *or* klôz′ət) ***noun*** a small room or cupboard for things such as clothes, linens, or supplies.
clos·et • ***noun****, plural* **closets**

close-up (klōs′up) ***noun*** a photograph taken with the camera very close to the subject.
close-up • ***noun****, plural* **close-ups**

close-up

clot (klät) ***noun*** a soft, thickened area or lump that forms in a liquid [a blood *clot*].
verb to form a clot or clots [The blood *clotted* around the wound after a few minutes.]
clot • ***noun****, plural* **clots** • ***verb*** **clotted, clotting**

cloth (klôth *or* kläth) ***noun*** **1** a material made from threads of cotton, wool, silk, or some other fiber, by weaving or knitting. **2** a piece of such a material for a particular use [a *tablecloth*].
cloth • ***noun****, plural* **cloths**

clothe (klōth) ***verb*** to put clothes on; dress [The child is still too young to *clothe* herself.]
clothe • ***verb*** **clothed** or **clad, clothing**

clothes (klōz *or* klōthz) ***plural noun*** cloth or other material made up in different shapes and styles to wear on the body; garments. Shirts, slacks, dresses, and hats are kinds of clothes.
• The words **clothes** and **close** sound alike.
She bought new *clothes* for the trip.
What time does the store *close?*

a cat	ō go	ʉ fur	ə = a *in* ago
ā ape	ô law, for	ch chin	e *in* agent
ä cot, car	oo look	sh she	i *in* pencil
e ten	ōō tool	th thin	o *in* atom
ē me	oi oil	*th* then	u *in* circus
i fit	ou out	zh measure	
ī ice	u up	ŋ ring	

clothing (klō′*th*iŋ) ***noun*** clothes; garments.
cloth·ing • ***noun***

cloud (kloud) ***noun*** **1** a mass of tiny water drops or ice crystals that float in the air above the earth. **2** a mass of smoke, dust, or steam. **3** anything that threatens or makes gloomy [They are under a *cloud* of suspicion.]
verb **1** to cover or make dark with a cloud or clouds [The sun is *clouded* over by the smoke.] **2** to make or become cloudy [Soap *clouded* the water.]
cloud • ***noun,*** *plural* **clouds** • ***verb*** **clouded, clouding**

cloudburst (kloud′burst) ***noun*** a sudden, very heavy rain.
cloud·burst • ***noun,*** *plural* **cloudbursts**

cloudy (kloud′ē) ***adjective*** **1** covered with clouds; overcast. **2** not clear; muddy, foggy, vague, or dim [*cloudy* water; a *cloudy* memory].
cloud·y • ***adjective*** **cloudier, cloudiest**

clover (klō′vər) ***noun*** a plant that grows low to the ground, with leaves in three parts and small, sweet-smelling flowers.
clo·ver • ***noun,*** *plural* **clovers**

clown (kloun) ***noun*** **1** a person who entertains by doing comical tricks and silly stunts [a circus *clown*]. **2** a person who likes to make jokes or do funny things [Joe is the family *clown*.]
verb to play practical jokes or act silly [Sit down and stop *clowning* around!]
clown • ***noun,*** *plural* **clowns** • ***verb*** **clowned, clowning**

clown

club (klub) ***noun*** **1** a heavy wooden stick that is used as a weapon. **2** one of the sticks with a wooden or metal head that is used in golf. **3** a group of people who meet together for pleasure or for some special purpose [an athletic *club;* a social *club*]. **4** the mark ♣, used on a black suit of playing cards. **5** one of the playing cards of this suit [She dealt me all *clubs*.]
verb to hit with a club or with something like a club [He *clubbed* three home runs today.]
club • ***noun,*** *plural* **clubs** • ***verb*** **clubbed, clubbing**

club soda ***noun*** *another name for* **soda water**.

cluck (kluk) ***verb*** to make the low, clicking sound of a hen calling her chicks.
noun this sound or a sound like it.
cluck • ***verb*** **clucked, clucking** • ***noun,*** *plural* **clucks**

clue (klo͞o) ***noun*** a fact or thing that helps to solve a puzzle or mystery [The fingerprints are the only *clue* that the police have.]
clue • ***noun,*** *plural* **clues**

clump (klump) ***noun*** **1** a group of things close together; cluster [a *clump* of trees]. **2** a mass or lump [a *clump* of dirt]. **3** the sound of heavy footsteps.
verb to walk with heavy footsteps [She *clumped* loudly up the stairs.]
clump • ***noun,*** *plural* **clumps** • ***verb*** **clumped, clumping**

clumsy (klum′zē) ***adjective*** **1** not having good control in moving the hands or feet; awkward [The *clumsy* waiter dropped the dish.] —Look for the WORD CHOICES box at the entry **awkward**. **2** done or made badly; crude [a *clumsy* shelter].
clum·sy • ***adjective*** **clumsier, clumsiest**

WORD HISTORY

clumsy

The original meaning of **clumsy** 600 years ago was "numb with cold." The modern meaning of **clumsy** has developed from its original meaning. A person whose feet and hands are numb with cold will move in an awkward, or **clumsy**, way.

clung (kluŋ) ***verb*** *past tense and past participle of* **cling**.

clunk (kluŋk) ***noun*** a dull, heavy, hollow sound [The bowling ball landed with a loud *clunk*.]
clunk • ***noun,*** *plural* **clunks**

cluster (klus′tər) ***noun*** a number of things growing together or seen together [a *cluster* of grapes].
verb to grow or gather together [Pigeons *clustered* around her.]

clus·ter • *noun, plural* **clusters** • *verb* **clustered, clustering**

clutch (kluch) *verb* **1** to grasp or hold tightly [She *clutched* his hand as they walked across the icy street.] —Look for the WORD CHOICES box at the entry **grasp**. **2** to reach or grab for; snatch [As he stumbled he *clutched* at the railing.]
noun **1** the grasp of a hand or claw; an act of clutching [The thief made a *clutch* at her handbag.] **2 clutches** power or control [The villain has the heroine in his *clutches*.] **3** a device that puts the transmission of a car in gear or out of gear. When the car is in gear, the engine can give power to the wheels.
clutch • *verb* **clutched, clutching** • *noun, plural* **clutches**

clutter (klut′ər) *noun* a number of things scattered in a messy way; disorder [The *clutter* in his office was amazing.]
verb to make messy [Papers *clutter* his desk.]
clut·ter • *noun* • *verb* **cluttered, cluttering**

cm or **cm.** *abbreviation for* **1** centimeter. **2** centimeters.

co- *a prefix meaning:* **1** together with [A *co-worker* is a person who works together with another.] **2** equally; to the same extent [A *co-owner* is a person who owns something equally with another.]

c/o or **c.o.** *abbreviation for* care of. This is used in an address when a letter or package is sent to one person at another person's address.

CO *abbreviation for* Colorado.

Co. *abbreviation for* Company [Brown, Jones, and *Co.* is a new firm.]

coach (kōch) *noun* **1** a large, closed carriage drawn by horses, with the driver's seat outside. **2** a railroad car with seats for passengers. **3** a bus. **4** the regular class of seats on an airplane. They are less expensive than first-class seats. **5** a person who teaches and trains students, athletes, or performers. **6** a person in charge of a sports team.
verb **1** to teach, train, or tutor [My sister *coached* me before the spelling contest.] **2** to lead or be in charge of a sports team.
coach • *noun, plural* **coaches** • *verb* **coached, coaching**

coachman (kōch′mən) *noun* the driver of a coach or carriage.
coach·man • *noun, plural* **coachmen**

coal (kōl) *noun* **1** a black, solid substance that is dug up from the ground. It is used as a fuel. Coal is mostly carbon, formed from decaying plant matter that has been pressed together for millions of years. **2** a piece of glowing coal, wood, or other substance; ember [He threw a log on the hot *coals*.]
coal • *noun, plural* **coals**

coarse (kôrs) *adjective* **1** made up of rather large particles; not fine [*coarse* sand]. **2** rough or harsh to the touch [Burlap is a *coarse* cloth.] **3** not polite; vulgar; crude [a *coarse* joke].
coarse • *adjective* **coarser, coarsest**
● The words **coarse** and **course** sound alike.
The salt is *coarse*, not fine.
The ship changed *course*.

WORD CHOICES

Synonyms of **coarse**

The words **coarse, gross,** and **vulgar** share the meaning "not polite or in good taste."

loud, *coarse* laughter
gross table manners
a cruel and *vulgar* joke

coast (kōst) *noun* land along the sea; seashore.
verb **1** to ride or slide downhill. **2** to keep on moving after the driving power is cut off [The car ran out of gas, but we were able to *coast* into a gas station.]
coast • *noun, plural* **coasts** • *verb* **coasted, coasting**

coastal (kōs′təl) *adjective* of, near, or along the coast [a *coastal* city].
coast·al • *adjective*

Coast Guard a branch of the U.S. armed forces. Its work is to protect the coasts, stop smuggling, and help ships in trouble.

coastline (kōst′līn) *noun* the outline or shape of a coast.
coast·line • *noun, plural* **coastlines**

coat (kōt) *noun* **1** an outer garment with sleeves, that opens down the front [a winter *coat;* a suit *coat*]. **2** the fur, skin, or other nat-

a	cat	ō	go	ʉ	fur	ə =	a *in* ago
ā	ape	ô	law, for	ch	chin		e *in* agent
ä	cot, car	oo	look	sh	she		i *in* pencil
e	ten	ōō	tool	th	thin		o *in* atom
ē	me	oi	oil	*th*	then		u *in* circus
i	fit	ou	out	zh	measure		
ī	ice	u	up	ŋ	ring		

ural covering of an animal [Our dog has a shiny, black *coat*.] **3** a layer of some substance on a surface [The wall has a fresh *coat* of paint.]
verb to cover with a layer of something [Ice *coated* the streets.]
coat • ***noun,*** *plural* **coats** • ***verb*** **coated, coating**

coating (kōt′iŋ) ***noun*** a layer of something covering a surface [The car had a *coating* of snow.]
coat·ing • ***noun,*** *plural* **coatings**

coat of arms ***noun*** a group of designs and figures that serves as the special mark of a person, family, or institution. It is usually displayed on a shield.
coat of arms • ***noun,*** *plural* **coats of arms**

coauthor (kō′ô thər *or* kō′ä thər) ***noun*** an author who works with another author in writing something.
co·au·thor • ***noun,*** *plural* **coauthors**

coax (kōks) ***verb*** to keep on asking for something in a pleasant and gentle way [She *coaxed* her parents to let her go swimming.]
coax • ***verb*** **coaxed, coaxing**

cob (käb) ***noun*** *a short form of* **corncob**.
cob • ***noun,*** *plural* **cobs**

cobalt (kō′bôlt) ***noun*** a hard, shiny, gray metal that is a chemical element. It is mixed with other metals to make them harder. Cobalt is also used to make blue-colored paints.
co·balt • ***noun***

cobbler (käb′lər) ***noun*** a person whose work is mending or patching shoes and boots.
cob·bler • ***noun,*** *plural* **cobblers**

cobblestone (käb′əl stōn) ***noun*** a rounded stone, used at one time for paving streets.
cob·ble·stone • ***noun,*** *plural* **cobblestones**

cobra (kō′brə) ***noun*** a very poisonous snake of Asia and Africa. The skin around its head swells into a hood when it gets excited.
co·bra • ***noun,*** *plural* **cobras**

cobra

cobweb (käb′web) ***noun*** a web spun by a spider.
cob·web • ***noun,*** *plural* **cobwebs**

cocaine (kō kān′) ***noun*** an illegal drug that is habit-forming.
co·caine • ***noun***

cock (käk) ***noun*** **1** a rooster; male chicken. **2** a faucet or valve that controls the flow of a liquid or gas.
verb **1** to tilt or turn the eyes, ears, or head toward something [The dog *cocked* its head in the direction of the sound.] **2** to set the hammer of a gun in firing position.
cock • ***noun,*** *plural* **cocks** • ***verb*** **cocked, cocking**

cock-a-doodle-doo (käk′ə do͞od′əl do͞o′) ***noun*** a word that imitates the sound made by a rooster.
cock-a-doo·dle-doo • ***noun,*** *plural* **cock-a-doodle-doos**

cockatoo (käk′ə to͞o) ***noun*** a parrot that has a high crest of mostly white feathers.
cock·a·too • ***noun,*** *plural* **cockatoos**

cockatoo

cocker spaniel (käk′ər) ***noun*** a small dog with long, silky hair and long, drooping ears.
cock·er spaniel • ***noun,*** *plural* **cocker spaniels**

cockpit (käk′pit) ***noun*** **1** the part of an airplane where the pilot sits. In a large plane, the pilot's crew also sits in the cockpit. **2** the driver's seat in a racing car.
cock·pit • ***noun,*** *plural* **cockpits**

cockroach (käk′rōch) ***noun*** an insect with long feelers and a flat, soft, brown or black body. It is a common household pest in some places.
cock·roach • ***noun,*** *plural* **cockroaches**

cocktail (käk′tāl) ***noun*** **1** a small bit of food or a drink served at the beginning of a meal [The shrimp *cocktail* had a spicy sauce.] **2** an alcoholic drink made by mixing liquor with other beverages such as fruit juice.
cock·tail • ***noun,*** *plural* **cocktails**

cocky (käk′ē) [*an informal word*] ***adjective*** sure of oneself in a rude and bold way; conceited.

C

cock·y • *adjective* **cockier, cockiest**

cocoa (kō′kō) *noun* **1** a reddish-brown powder made from liquid chocolate by pressing out most of the fat. **2** a hot drink made from this powder, with sugar and hot water or milk.
co·coa • *noun*

coconut or **cocoanut** (kō′kə nut) *noun* the large, round fruit of a tropical palm tree. Coconuts have a hard, brown shell and an inside layer of sweet, white matter used as food. The hollow center is filled with a sweet liquid.
co·co·nut or **co·coa·nut** • *noun, plural* **coconuts** or **cocoanuts**

cocoon (kə ko͞on′) *noun* a silky case spun by a caterpillar to use as a shelter while it changes into a butterfly or moth.
co·coon • *noun, plural* **cocoons**

cod (käd) *noun* a large fish found in northern seas, used for food.
cod • *noun, plural* **cod** or **cods**

Cod (käd), **Cape** a peninsula in southeastern Massachusetts.

C.O.D. or **c.o.d.** *abbreviation for* collect on delivery. When goods are sent C.O.D., the person who orders the goods must pay for them when they are delivered.

code (kōd) *noun* **1** a body of laws set down in a clear and orderly way [Builders must obey the city's building *code*.] **2** any set of rules for proper behavior [His moral *code* does not allow revenge.] **3** a set of signals for sending messages [Telegraph messages are sent by *code*.] **4** a system of secret writing in which words, letters, or figures are given special meanings [The captain's secret order was written in *code* so that the enemy could not read it.]
verb to put a message into the signals or secret writing of a code.
code • *noun, plural* **codes** • *verb* **coded, coding**

codfish (käd′fish) *noun the same as* **cod**.
cod·fish • *noun, plural* **codfish** or **codfishes**

Cody (kō′dē), **William Frederick** (wil′yəm fred′ər ik) 1846-1917; American army scout, who was famous for his shooting and riding skills. He performed in shows under the name *Buffalo Bill*.
Co·dy, Wil·liam Fred·er·ick

coffee (kôf′ē) *noun* **1** a dark-brown drink made by passing boiling water through the ground and roasted seeds of a tropical plant. **2** the seeds, or beans, used to make this drink. **3** the tropical plant that produces these seeds.
cof·fee • *noun, plural* **coffees**

coffin (kôf′in) *noun* a case or box for burying a dead person.
cof·fin • *noun, plural* **coffins**

coil (koil) *verb* to wind around and around in circles [The sailors *coil* the ropes. The vines *coil* around the trunk of the tree.]
noun **1** something wound in circles or in a spiral [a *coil* of wire]. **2** one circle of something that is wound in this way [the *coils* of a spring].
coil • *verb* **coiled, coiling** • *noun, plural* **coils**

coin (koin) *noun* a piece of metal money.
verb **1** to make coins from [The government no longer *coins* gold.] **2** to make up or invent [A 17th-century chemist from Belgium *coined* the word "gas."]
coin • *noun, plural* **coins** • *verb* **coined, coining**

coincide (kō′in sīd′) *verb* **1** to happen at the same time [My birthday *coincides* with hers.] **2** to be the same; agree [Our interests *coincide*.]
co·in·cide • *verb* **coincided, coinciding**

WORD CHOICES

Synonyms of **coincide**

The words **coincide, agree,** and **correspond** share the meaning "to be the same or similar."

Our tastes in art *coincide*.

The stories of the witnesses don't *agree*.

Their opinions *correspond* with mine.

coincidence (kō in′si dəns) *noun* the happening of two or more events that seem to be

a	cat	ō	go	ʉ	fur	ə = a *in* ago	
ā	ape	ô	law, for	ch	chin	e *in* agent	
ä	cot, car	o͝o	look	sh	she	i *in* pencil	
e	ten	o͞o	tool	th	thin	o *in* atom	
ē	me	oi	oil	*th*	then	u *in* circus	
i	fit	ou	out	zh	measure		
ī	ice	u	up	ŋ	ring		

connected but are not [It is just a *coincidence* that we both missed school yesterday.]
co·in·ci·dence • *noun, plural* **coincidences**

coke (kōk) ***noun*** coal that has been heated to remove the gases. It burns with great heat and little smoke.

Col. *abbreviation for* Colonel.

cola (kō′lə) ***noun*** a soft drink with a flavoring that comes from the nut of an African tree.
co·la • *noun, plural* **colas**

colander (kul′ən dər *or* käl′ən dər) ***noun*** a bowl with holes in the bottom and sides for draining liquids.
col·an·der • *noun, plural* **colanders**

cold (kōld) ***adjective*** **1** having a temperature much lower than the temperature of the body [a *cold* day; a *cold* drink] —Look for the WORD CHOICES box at the entry **chilly**. **2** without the right heat or warmth [The soup had gotten *cold.*] **3** feeling chilled [Put on a sweater if you are *cold.*] **4** not friendly or kind [a *cold* stare]. **5** [*an informal use*] unconscious [The last punch knocked him *cold.*]
noun **1** a lack of heat or warmth [the *cold* of northern winters]. **2** a common illness that causes coughing, sneezing, and a runny nose.
—catch cold to become ill with a cold.
cold • ***adjective*** **colder, coldest** • ***noun,*** *plural for sense 2 only* **colds**

coldblooded (kōld′blud əd) ***adjective*** **1** having a body temperature that becomes colder or warmer as the temperature of the air or water becomes colder or warmer. Fishes and snakes are coldblooded animals. **2** cruel or without pity [a *coldblooded* murderer].
cold·blood·ed • ***adjective***

coldhearted (kōld′härt əd) ***adjective*** not feeling sympathy or kindness [a *coldhearted* person].
cold·heart·ed • ***adjective***

coleslaw (kōl′slô *or* kōl′slä) ***noun*** a salad made with shredded raw cabbage. This word is also written **cole slaw**.
cole·slaw • ***noun***

coliseum (käl′i sē′əm) ***noun*** a large building or stadium for sports and entertainment events.
col·i·se·um • *noun, plural* **coliseums**

collaborate (kə lab′ə rāt) ***verb*** to work together in producing something [The teachers *collaborated* on our new textbook.]
col·lab·o·rate • ***verb*** **collaborated, collaborating**

collage (kə läzh′) ***noun*** a work of art in which a picture is made by attaching photographs, pieces of newspaper or cloth, and other objects to a surface.
col·lage • *noun, plural* **collages**

WORD HISTORY

collage

The name of this kind of art comes from a French word for "paste," which comes from an ancient Greek word for "glue." When you make a **collage**, you may put together all sorts of things, but the one thing you must always have is paste or glue.

collapse (kə laps′) ***verb*** **1** to fall down or fall to pieces [The pier *collapsed* into the raging river.] **2** to break down or lose strength suddenly [The wounded soldier *collapsed* from loss of blood.] **3** to fold together neatly in a small space [The beach chair *collapses.*]
noun the act of collapsing [The wind caused the *collapse* of the old barn.]
col·lapse • ***verb*** **collapsed, collapsing** • *noun, plural* **collapses**

collapsible (kə lap′si bəl) ***adjective*** capable of being folded together into a small space [a *collapsible* table].
col·laps·i·ble • ***adjective***

collar

collar (käl′ər) ***noun*** **1** the part of a garment that fits around the neck. It is sometimes fold-

ed over. **2** a band of leather or metal for the neck of a dog or cat. **3** the part of a harness that fits around the neck of a horse.
col·lar • *noun, plural* **collars**

collarbone (käl′ər bōn) *noun* a narrow bone that joins the breastbone and the shoulder blade.
col·lar·bone • *noun, plural* **collarbones**

colleague (käl′ēg) *noun* a fellow worker [The doctor asked a *colleague* for advice.]
col·league • *noun, plural* **colleagues**

collect (kə lekt′) *verb* **1** to gather in one place [The city *collects* the rubbish on Monday. Water *collects* in the barrel when it rains.] —Look for the WORD CHOICES box at the entry **gather**. **2** to gather things as a hobby [He *collects* stamps.] **3** to call for and get money owed [The building manager *collects* the rent.]
col·lect • *verb* **collected, collecting**

collection (kə lek′shən) *noun* **1** the act of gathering [Rubbish *collection* is on Friday.] **2** things collected [Her rare coin *collection* is kept in a safe.] **3** money collected [Last Sunday's *collection* was small for our parish.]
col·lec·tion • *noun, plural* **collections**

collector (kə lek′tər) *noun* **1** a person who collects things as a hobby [a stamp *collector*]. **2** a person who collects money that is owed [A bill *collector* will call if you do not pay on time.]
col·lec·tor • *noun, plural* **collectors**

college (käl′ij) *noun* a school that a person can go to after high school. Colleges give degrees to students when they graduate.
col·lege • *noun, plural* **colleges**

collide (kə līd′) *verb* to come together with force; bump into [The car *collided* with the bus.]
col·lide • *verb* **collided, colliding**

collie (käl′ē) *noun* a large dog that has long hair and a narrow head. Collies were first used to herd sheep.
col·lie • *noun, plural* **collies**

collision (kə lizh′ən) *noun* the act of coming together with force; a crash.
col·li·sion • *noun, plural* **collisions**

Colo. *abbreviation for* Colorado.

cologne (kə lōn′) *noun* a liquid with a pleasing smell. It is like perfume, but not so strong.
co·logne • *noun, plural* **colognes**

Colombia (kə lum′bē ə) a country in northwestern South America.
Co·lom·bi·a

colon[1] (kō′lən) *noun* a mark of punctuation (:). It is used after a word that introduces a quotation, explanation, or series.
co·lon • *noun, plural* **colons**

colon[2] (kō′lən) *noun* the main part of the large intestine.
co·lon • *noun, plural* **colons**

colonel (kʉr′nəl) *noun* a military officer.
colo·nel • *noun, plural* **colonels**
• The words **colonel** and **kernel** sound alike.
She was a *colonel* in the army.
The baker uses the whole wheat *kernel*.

colonial (kə lō′nē əl) *adjective* **1** having to do with a colony or colonies [England once ruled a large *colonial* empire.] **2 Colonial** having to do with the thirteen British colonies in North America that became the United States.
co·lo·ni·al • *adjective*

colonist (käl′ə nist) *noun* a person who helps start a colony or lives in one.
col·o·nist • *noun, plural* **colonists**

colonize (käl′ə nīz) *verb* to start a colony in [Spain was the first country to *colonize* America.]
col·o·nize • *verb* **colonized, colonizing**

colonnade

colonnade (käl′ə nād′) *noun* a row of columns holding up a roof or a series of arches.
col·on·nade • *noun, plural* **colonnades**

a	cat	ō	go	ʉ	fur	ə =	a *in* ago
ā	ape	ô	law, for	ch	chin		e *in* agent
ä	cot, car	oo	look	sh	she		i *in* pencil
e	ten	o͞o	tool	th	thin		o *in* atom
ē	me	oi	oil	*th*	then		u *in* circus
i	fit	ou	out	zh	measure		
ī	ice	u	up	ŋ	ring		

colony (käl′ə nē) ***noun*** **1** a group of people who settle in a distant land but are still under the rule of the country from which they came. **2** the place where they settle [the Pilgrim *colony* in Massachusetts]. **3** a land that is ruled by a distant country [This island was once a Dutch *colony*.] **4** a group of animals or plants living or growing together [an ant *colony*].
—the Colonies the thirteen British colonies in North America that won their independence and became the United States.
col·o·ny • ***noun,*** *plural* **colonies**

color (kul′ər) ***noun*** **1** what we see as a result of light waves being reflected from objects. The white light from the sun or a light bulb is made up of many parts like waves. These waves are reflected differently by different objects, producing the colors we see. The basic color names are red, orange, yellow, green, blue, indigo, and violet. **2** a paint or dye or anything used to give or add color [His crayon set has 64 *colors*.] **3 colors** a flag or banner [The ship hoisted its *colors*.]
verb to give a color or colors to [*Color* the drawing with these crayons.]
col·or • ***noun,*** *plural* **colors** • ***verb*** **colored, coloring**

STATE MAP

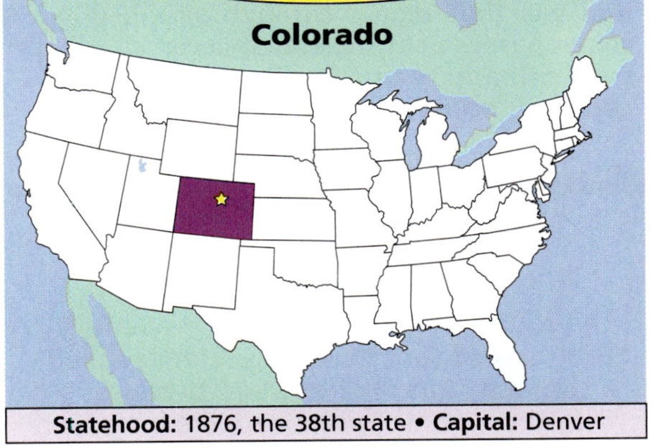

Statehood: 1876, the 38th state • **Capital:** Denver

Colorado (käl′ə rä′dō *or* käl′ə rad′ō) a State in the southwestern part of the U.S. Its capital is Denver. Abbreviated **CO** or **Colo.**
Col·o·rad·o

colorful (kul′ər fəl) ***adjective*** **1** having bright colors or many colors [a *colorful* tie]. **2** lively and interesting [a *colorful* story].
col·or·ful • ***adjective***

coloring (kul′ər iŋ) ***noun*** **1** the act of adding colors [*Coloring* can be done with crayons.] **2** something used to add color [Lipstick is a *coloring* for the lips.] **3** the way something is colored [a bird with bright *coloring*].
col·or·ing • ***noun,*** *plural* **colorings**

colossal (kə läs′əl) ***adjective*** very large or very great [a *colossal* elephant; a *colossal* mistake] —Look for the WORD CHOICES box at the entry **enormous.**
co·los·sal • ***adjective***

colt (kōlt) ***noun*** a young male horse or similar animal, such as a donkey or zebra.
colt • ***noun,*** *plural* **colts**

Columbia (kə lum′bē ə) the capital of South Carolina.
Co·lum·bi·a

Columbus (kə lum′bəs), **Christopher** (kris′ tə fər) 1451-1506; the Italian explorer who discovered America in 1492 while sailing in the service of Spain.
Co·lum·bus, Chris·to·pher

Columbus (kə lum′bəs) the capital of Ohio.
Co·lum·bus

column (käl′əm) ***noun*** **1** a long, upright structure that is usually round; pillar. Columns usually stand in groups to hold up a roof or other part of a building, but they are sometimes used just for decoration. **2** something long and upright like a column [A *column* of smoke rose from the volcano.] **3** one of the long sections of printed words lying side by side on a page [Each page of this book has two *columns*.] **4** an article that is one of a regular series in a newspaper or magazine [She writes a weekly sports *column* for the paper.] **5** a long, straight line of people or things placed one behind or below another.
col·umn • ***noun,*** *plural* **columns**

column

com- *a prefix meaning* with or together [*Compressing* a mass of something means pressing it together.]

Comanche (kə man′chē) ***noun*** **1** a member of a North American Indian people who used to

live in the Western plains but now live mainly in Oklahoma. **2** the language of this people.
Co·man·che • *noun, plural for sense 1 only* **Comanches** or **Comanche**

comb (kōm) ***noun*** **1** a thin strip of plastic or other material that has teeth along one edge. A comb may be passed through the hair to make it neat, or it may be placed in the hair to hold it in place. **2** any tool used like a comb for the hair. **3** the red, fleshy growth on the head of a rooster and some other birds.
verb **1** to smooth or arrange with a comb [She *combed* her hair.] **2** to search thoroughly [They *combed* the woods for the lost child.]
comb • ***noun***, *plural* **combs** • ***verb*** **combed, combing**

combat (kəm bat′ *for v.;* käm′bat *for n.*) ***verb*** to fight or struggle against [Scientists are developing new drugs to *combat* disease.]
noun **1** battle [He was wounded in *combat*.] **2** a fight or struggle [hand-to-hand *combat*].
com·bat • ***verb*** **combated** or **combatted, combating** or **combatting** • ***noun***, *plural* **combats**

combination (käm′bi nā′shən) ***noun*** **1** something made by combining other things [The green paint is a *combination* of blue and yellow paints.] **2** the series of numbers or letters that must be turned to in the right order to open certain locks [the *combination* to a safe].
com·bi·na·tion • ***noun***, *plural* **combinations**

combine (kəm bīn′ *for v. sense 1;* käm′bīn *for v. sense 2 and n.*) ***verb*** **1** to bring together; unite [*Combine* flour and water to make a paste.] **2** to harvest with a combine.
noun a machine that gathers grain and threshes it at the same time.
com·bine • ***verb*** **combined, combining** • ***noun***, *plural* **combines**

combustible (kəm bus′tə bəl) ***adjective*** capable of catching fire and burning easily [Gasoline is a *combustible* liquid.]
com·bus·ti·ble • ***adjective***

combustion (kəm bus′chən) ***noun*** the process of burning [*Combustion* of fuel takes place inside the engine of a car.]
com·bus·tion • ***noun***, *plural* **combustions**

come (kum) ***verb*** **1** to move from "there" to "here" [The dogs *come* to me quickly when I whistle.] **2** to reach a certain place or result; arrive or appear [She *came* home late.] **3** to be descended or be a native; originate [Her family *comes* from Colorado.] **4** to be in a certain order [After 9 *comes* 10.] **5** to be caused [Poor grades may *come* from lack of study.] **6** to get to be; become [My shoelaces have *come* untied.] **7** to be made or sold [This shoe *comes* in brown or black.]
—come across to meet or find by accident [I *came across* some old pictures in the drawer.] **—come back** to return [I will *come back* after lunch.] **—come in** **1** to enter [The burglar *came in* through the window.] **2** to arrive [Their plane *comes in* at noon.] **3** to finish in a contest [I *came in* third.] **—come to** **1** to add up to [The bill *came to* $9.75.] **2** to become conscious again [The wounded soldier finally *came to*.] **—come up with** to find or produce [Can you *come up with* the answer?] **—how come?** [*an informal use*] why?
come • ***verb*** **came, come, coming**

comedian (kə mē′dē ən) ***noun*** **1** a performer who plays comic parts or who tells jokes and does funny things. **2** a person who is often very funny [She's quite a *comedian*.]
co·me·di·an • ***noun***, *plural* **comedians**

comedienne (kə mē′dē en′) ***noun*** a woman who performs as a comedian.
co·me·di·enne • ***noun***, *plural* **comediennes**

comedy (käm′ə dē) ***noun*** a play, film, or TV show that is funny and has a happy ending.
com·e·dy • ***noun***, *plural* **comedies**

comet (käm′ət) ***noun*** a frozen mass of dust and gas that moves through space. When a comet passes near the sun, it becomes a bright ball with a fiery tail.
com·et • ***noun***, *plural* **comets**

WORD HISTORY

comet

The source of this word is the ancient Greek word for "hair." The Greeks called a **comet** a "long-haired star" because they thought its tail looked like long hair floating behind the bright main part.

comfort (kum′fərt) ***noun*** **1** a pleasant condition that is the result of not having hardships,

a cat	ō go	ʉ fur	ə = a *in* ago
ā ape	ô law, for	ch chin	e *in* agent
ä cot, car	ꝏ look	sh she	i *in* pencil
e ten	ōō tool	th thin	o *in* atom
ē me	oi oil	*th* then	u *in* circus
i fit	ou out	zh measure	
ī ice	u up	ŋ ring	

worry, pain, or other unpleasant sensations [Her family's wealth has enabled them to live in great *comfort*.] **2** a person or thing that gives a feeling of comfort [A book is a great *comfort* when a person is sick in bed.]
verb to make feel less sad; soothe [How can we *comfort* the boy who lost his dog?]
com·fort • ***noun,*** *plural for sense 2 only* **comforts** • ***verb*** **comforted, comforting**

WORD CHOICES

Synonyms of **comfort**

The words **comfort, console,** and **soothe** share the meaning "to make feel less sad or troubled."

Your kind words *comforted* me.

We *consoled* the lost child with candy.

The father *soothed* the crying baby by rocking him.

comfortable (kum′fər tə bəl *or* kumf′tər bəl) ***adjective*** **1** giving comfort or ease [*comfortable* shoes]. **2** feeling comfort; at ease [Are you *comfortable* in that chair?]
com·fort·a·ble • ***adjective***

comic (käm′ik) ***adjective*** funny or amusing [a *comic* story] —Look for the WORD CHOICES box at the entry **funny**.
noun **1** *another word for* **comedian**. **2 comics** a part of a newspaper with comic strips.
com·ic • ***adjective*** • ***noun,*** *plural* **comics**

comical (käm′i kəl) ***adjective*** funny or amusing [The clown performed many *comical* acts.] —Look for the WORD CHOICES box at the entry **funny**.
com·i·cal • ***adjective***

comic book ***noun*** a magazine or booklet containing comic strips.
comic book • ***noun,*** *plural* **comic books**

comic strip ***noun*** a series of drawings that tell a comical or exciting story.
comic strip • ***noun,*** *plural* **comic strips**

comma (käm′ə) ***noun*** a mark of punctuation (,). It is used to show a pause that is shorter than the pause at the end of a sentence. A comma is used to separate words, phrases, or clauses in a sentence.
com·ma • ***noun,*** *plural* **commas**

command (kə mand′) ***verb*** **1** to give an order to; direct [I *command* you to halt!] **2** to be in control of; have power over [Captain Stone *commands* Company B.] **3** to deserve to have [Her courage *commands* our respect.]
noun **1** an order or direction [He obeyed the queen's *command*.] **2** an instruction entered into a computer to make it do some task. **3** the power or ability to command or control [He has no *command* of his temper.]
com·mand • ***verb*** **commanded, commanding** • ***noun,*** *plural for senses 1 & 2 only* **commands**

commander (kə man′dər) ***noun*** **1** a person who is in command; leader. **2** an officer in the navy.
com·mand·er • ***noun,*** *plural* **commanders**

commandment (kə mand′mənt) ***noun*** a law; especially, any of the Ten Commandments.
com·mand·ment • ***noun,*** *plural* **commandments**

commence (kə mens′) ***verb*** to begin or start [The judge *commenced* the trial at noon.]
com·mence • ***verb*** **commenced, commencing**

commencement (kə mens′mənt) ***noun*** the ceremony of a school or college, when graduates receive their degrees or diplomas.
com·mence·ment • ***noun,*** *plural* **commencements**

comment (käm′ent) ***noun*** **1** a note or remark that explains or gives an opinion [Our teacher writes *comments* on our report cards.] **2** talk or gossip [His blue hair caused much *comment*.]
verb to make comments; remark [The teacher *commented* about our grades.]
com·ment • ***noun,*** *plural for sense 1 only* **comments** • ***verb*** **commented, commenting**

commerce (käm′ərs) ***noun*** the buying and selling of goods; trade [There is active *commerce* between the U.S. and Europe.]
com·merce • ***noun***

commercial (kə mur′shəl) ***adjective*** **1** having to do with commerce or trade [There is much *commercial* activity between the U.S. and Japan.] **2** concerned with making a profit [a *commercial* radio station].
noun a paid advertisement on TV or radio [I ran to the kitchen during the *commercial*.]
com·mer·cial • ***adjective*** • ***noun,*** *plural* **commercials**

commission (kə mish′ən) ***noun*** **1** a group of people who are chosen to do a certain thing [A

C

commission was appointed to study the schools.] **2** something that a person or group is authorized to do [The artist received a *commission* to do the queen's portrait.] **3** the act of doing something bad [the *commission* of a crime]. **4** money that is given to a person for making a sale [She received 10% of the sale price as her *commission*.]
verb **1** to give the power, right, or duty to do something [The actor *commissioned* him to write a book about his life.] **2** to put a ship into active service.
—out of commission not in working order [My television is *out of commission*.]
com·mis·sion • ***noun,*** *plural* **commissions** • ***verb*** **commissioned, commissioning**

commissioner (kə mish′ə nər) ***noun*** **1** a member of a commission. **2** a person who is in charge of a government commission or department.
com·mis·sion·er • ***noun,*** *plural* **commissioners**

commit (kə mit′) ***verb*** **1** to place in the care of; put under the charge of [The thief was *committed* to prison.] **2** to do something wrong or bad [Who would *commit* such a crime?] **3** to do or say something that has one making a pledge or promise [If you join that book club, you *commit* yourself to buying four books.]
com·mit • ***verb*** **committed, committing**

commitment (kə mit′mənt) ***noun*** a pledge or promise [a *commitment* to finish on time].
com·mit·ment • ***noun,*** *plural* **commitments**

committee (kə mit′ē) ***noun*** a group of people who are chosen to do something [I'm on the *committee* that's in charge of planning the party.]
com·mit·tee • ***noun,*** *plural* **committees**

commodity (kə mäd′i tē) ***noun*** something that can be bought or sold. A commodity is usually a basic product of farming or mining [Cotton is an important *commodity* from the South.]
com·mod·i·ty • ***noun,*** *plural* **commodities**

common (käm′ən) ***adjective*** **1** belonging equally to each one or everyone [The U.S. and Canada share a *common* language.] **2** often seen or heard; widespread [Squirrels are *common* in these woods.] **3** ordinary or average; not special [*common* courtesy].
noun *often* **commons** all the land that is owned or used by all the people of a town or village.
com·mon • ***adjective*** **commoner, commonest** • ***noun,*** *plural* **commons**

WORD CHOICES

Synonyms of common

The words **common, familiar,** and **ordinary** share the meaning "not special in any way."

music for the *common* man
such a *familiar* feeling
a person of *ordinary* talent

common noun ***noun*** a noun that names any one of a group of persons, places, or things. A common noun does not begin with a capital letter. For example, the nouns *woman, country, cup,* and *idea* are common nouns.
common noun • ***noun,*** *plural* **common nouns**

commonplace (käm′ən plās) ***adjective*** not new or interesting; ordinary [The robin is a *commonplace* bird in this part of the country.]
com·mon·place • ***adjective***

common sense ***noun*** ordinary good judgment in everyday matters [It is *common sense* to look both ways before crossing a street.]

commonwealth (käm′ən welth) ***noun*** **1** the people of a nation or state. **2** a nation or state that is governed by the people. Some States of the U.S., such as Kentucky and Massachusetts, call themselves commonwealths.
com·mon·wealth • ***noun,*** *plural* **commonwealths**

commotion (kə mō′shən) ***noun*** a noisy rushing about; confusion [There was a *commotion* on the bus when someone spotted a mouse.]
com·mo·tion • ***noun,*** *plural* **commotions**

communicate (kə myo͞o′ni kāt) ***verb*** **1** to pass along; transmit [to *communicate* a disease]. **2** to tell, show, or make known [Tears can *communicate* sorrow or joy.] **3** to exchange information [We *communicate* by mail.]

a cat	ō go	ʉ fur	ə = a *in* ago
ā ape	ô law, for	ch chin	e *in* agent
ä cot, car	oo look	sh she	i *in* pencil
e ten	o͞o tool	th thin	o *in* atom
ē me	oi oil	*th* then	u *in* circus
i fit	ou out	zh measure	
ī ice	u up	ŋ ring	

com·mu·ni·cate • *verb* **communicated, communicating**

communication (kə myo͞o′ni kā′shən) *noun* **1** the act of communicating [the *communication* of disease; the *communication* of news]. **2** a way or means of communicating [The storm broke down all *communication*.]
com·mu·ni·ca·tion • *noun, plural* **communications**

communion (kə myo͞on′yən) *noun* **1** a close relationship with deep understanding [Camping outdoors gave us a feeling of *communion* with nature.] **2 Communion** the part of a religious service in Christian churches that commemorates the last supper of Jesus and his Apostles.
com·mun·ion • *noun, plural for sense 1 only* **communions**

communism (käm′yə niz əm) *noun also* **Communism** the political and economic system in which there is one party and the government owns all the factories and natural resources and controls the production of goods.
com·mu·nism • *noun*

communist (käm′yə nist) *noun also* **Communist** a person who favors or supports communism.
com·mu·nist • *noun, plural* **communists**

community (kə myo͞o′ni tē) *noun* **1** all the people who live in a particular area [The pool is for use by the whole *community*.] **2** a group of persons who have similar qualities or interests [the business *community*].
com·mu·ni·ty • *noun, plural* **communities**

commutative property (kə myo͞ot′ə tiv *or* käm′yə tāt′iv) *noun* in mathematics, the property that states that the order of the elements does not change the result. For example, in addition, 3 + 5 = 8 and 5 + 3 = 8. In multiplication, 4 x 3 = 12 and 3 x 4 = 12.
com·mu·ta·tive property • *noun, plural* **commutative properties**

commute (kə myo͞ot′) *verb* to travel as a commuter [He *commutes* to work by bus.]
com·mute • *verb* **commuted, commuting**

commuter (kə myo͞ot′ər) *noun* a person who travels quite a long distance between home and work or between home and school every day.
com·mut·er • *noun, plural* **commuters**

Comoros (käm′ə rōz) a country on a group of islands in the Indian Ocean, east of the southeastern coast of Africa.
Com·o·ros

compact (kəm pakt′ *or* käm′pakt *for adj. and v.;* käm′pakt *for n.*) *adjective* **1** closely and firmly packed together [Stack the bricks in a neat, *compact* pile.] **2** having parts fitted together so as not to waste space [a *compact* kitchen].
noun **1** a small case that contains a mirror and face powder. **2** an agreement between persons or groups [The nations joined in a *compact* to increase trade with one another.] **3** a model of automobile smaller than the full size.
verb to pack closely and firmly together [This machine *compacts* trash into neat bundles.]
com·pact • *adjective* • *noun, plural* **compacts** • *verb* **compacted, compacting**

compact disc *noun* a disc something like a small phonograph record. It is played on a machine that uses a laser beam to read the music or other information on it.
compact disc • *noun, plural* **compact discs**

compactor (kəm pak′tər *or* käm′pak′tər) *noun* a machine for pressing trash tightly into small bundles.
com·pac·tor • *noun, plural* **compactors**

companion (kəm pan′yən) *noun* a person who goes along with or spends time with another; comrade.
com·pan·ion • *noun, plural* **companions**

companionship (kəm pan′yən ship) *noun* the relationship between companions; friendship.
com·pan·ion·ship • *noun*

company (kum′pə nē) *noun* **1** a group of people joined together in some kind of work or activity [a *company* of actors]. **2** the state of being companions; companionship [We enjoy each other's *company*.] **3** friends or companions [You may be judged by the *company* you keep.] **4** guests in someone's home.
com·pa·ny • *noun, plural for senses 1, 2, and 3 only* **companies**

comparable (käm′pər ə bəl) *adjective* nearly the same; close for purposes of comparison [*comparable* test scores].
com·pa·ra·ble • *adjective*

comparative (kəm per′ə tiv) *adjective* **1** having to do with the comparing of one thing with another [Our class made a *comparative* study of lions and tigers.] **2** measured or judged by comparing with others [Our book sale was a *comparative* success.] **3** describing the form of

C

an adjective or adverb that shows a greater degree in meaning, but not the greatest degree. The comparative degree is usually made with the suffix *-er* or the word *more*. For example, *warmer*, *more beautiful*, and *worse* are the comparatives of *warm, beautiful*, and *bad*.
noun the comparative degree or the comparative form of a word.
com·par·a·tive • ***adjective*** • ***noun,*** *plural* **comparatives**

compare (kəm per′) ***verb*** **1** to describe as being the same [He *compared* the sound of thunder to the roll of a drum.] **2** to look at two or more things in order to find out how they are alike or different [*Compare* the various cameras before buying one.] **3** to equal or come close to by comparison [Nothing can *compare* with my mom's cooking.]
com·pare • ***verb*** **compared, comparing**

comparison (kəm per′i sən) ***noun*** **1** the act of comparing two or more things [a *comparison* of various cameras]. **2** enough similarity between things to make it worthwhile to compare them [There is no *comparison* between them when it comes to batting.]
com·par·i·son • ***noun,*** *plural* **comparisons**

compartment (kəm pärt′mənt) ***noun*** a part or section of something that is separated from the rest by walls or sides. It often has a specific use [the passenger *compartment* of a plane].
com·part·ment • ***noun,*** *plural* **compartments**

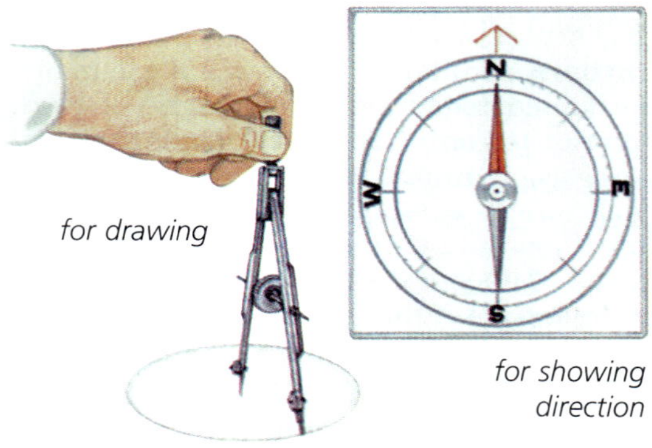

compass

compass (kum′pəs) ***noun*** **1** an instrument for showing direction. A typical compass has a moving needle that always points to magnetic north. **2** an instrument with two hinged legs that is used for drawing circles or measuring distances.
com·pass • ***noun,*** *plural* **compasses**

compassion (kəm pash′ən) ***noun*** a feeling of being sorry for others and wanting to help them; pity —Look for the WORD CHOICES box at the entry **pity**.
com·pas·sion • ***noun***

compatible (kəm pat′i bəl) ***adjective*** **1** capable of getting along well together [The two girls are *compatible* roommates.] **2** that look or sound good together; in harmony. **3** capable of working in a specified computer or electronic system [*compatible* software].
com·pat·i·ble • ***adjective***

compel (kəm pel′) ***verb*** to make do something; to force [Fear of failing *compelled* him to study.]
com·pel • ***verb*** **compelled, compelling**

compensate (käm′pən sāt) ***verb*** to make up for; take the place of; pay or repay [He worked late to *compensate* for time off.]
com·pen·sate • ***verb*** **compensated, compensating**

compensation (käm pən sā′shən) ***noun*** something given or done to make up for something else [She received a large sum of money as *compensation* for her injuries.]
com·pen·sa·tion • ***noun,*** *plural* **compensations**

compete (kəm pēt′) ***verb*** **1** to take part in a contest [Ten runners will *compete* in the 100-yard dash.] **2** to be a rival for something [The companies are *competing* for new customers.]
com·pete • ***verb*** **competed, competing**

competence (käm′pə təns) ***noun*** skill or ability to do something [These problems will test your *competence* in math.]
com·pe·tence • ***noun***

competent (käm′pə tənt) ***adjective*** having enough ability to do what is needed; capable [A *competent* plumber can do the job quickly.]
com·pe·tent • ***adjective***

competition (käm pə tish′ən) ***noun*** the act of competing; a contest or rivalry [Students are in *competition* for the scholarship.]
com·pe·ti·tion • ***noun,*** *plural* **competitions**

competitive (kəm pet′i tiv) ***adjective*** having

a	cat	ō	go	ʉ	fur	ə = a *in* ago	
ā	ape	ô	law, for	ch	chin	e *in* agent	
ä	cot, car	oo	look	sh	she	i *in* pencil	
e	ten	ōō	tool	th	thin	o *in* atom	
ē	me	oi	oil	*th*	then	u *in* circus	
i	fit	ou	out	zh	measure		
ī	ice	u	up	ŋ	ring		

to do with competition or based on competition [Football is a *competitive* sport.]
com·pet·i·tive • ***adjective***

competitor (kəm pet′ət ər) ***noun*** a person or group that competes [The two friends were *competitors* for the prize. Japan is a major *competitor* in the auto industry.]
com·pet·i·tor • ***noun,*** *plural* **competitors**

compile (kəm pīl′) ***verb*** to bring together in an orderly way [He *compiled* a book of his favorite stories.]
com·pile • ***verb*** **compiled, compiling**

complain (kəm plān′) ***verb*** **1** to find fault with something [We *complained* about the food.] —Look for the WORD CHOICES box at the entry **criticize**. **2** to make a formal report about something bad [We *complained* to the police about the barking dogs.]
com·plain • ***verb*** **complained, complaining**

complaint (kəm plānt′) ***noun*** **1** something to complain about [Too much homework is a common *complaint* of students.] **2** a statement that something is bad or wrong [They made a *complaint* about the food.]
com·plaint • ***noun,*** *plural* **complaints**

complement (käm′plə mənt *for n.;* käm′plə ment *for v.*) ***noun*** something that completes a whole or makes something perfect [The ice cream was a delicious *complement* to the apple pie.]
verb to make complete or perfect by supplying what is needed.
com·ple·ment • ***noun,*** *plural* **complements** • ***verb*** **complemented, complementing**

• The words **complement** and **compliment** sound alike.
A red tie will *complement* that suit.
I *compliment* you on your performance.

complete (kəm plēt′) ***adjective*** **1** having no part missing; full; whole [a *complete* set of dishes]. **2** thorough; perfect [I have *complete* confidence in my doctor.]
verb to make complete; finish or make whole, or full, or perfect [Did you *complete* your homework?]
com·plete • ***adjective*** • ***verb*** **completed, completing**

completion (kəm plē′shən) ***noun*** **1** the act of completing, or finishing something [*Completion* of the bridge will take six months.] **2** the condition of being completed [Payment for the work will be made upon *completion*.]
com·ple·tion • ***noun,*** *plural* **completions**

complex (käm pleks′ *or* käm′pleks *for adj.;* käm′pleks *for n.*) ***adjective*** made up of different parts connected in a way that is hard to understand; not simple [Computers are *complex* machines.]
noun **1** a group of connected things that form a whole [stores in a shopping *complex*]. **2** a mixed-up feeling about something that makes a person afraid or unhappy [He has a *complex* about traveling in a plane.]
com·plex • ***adjective*** • ***noun,*** *plural* **complexes**

WORD CHOICES

Synonyms of **complex**

The words **complex, complicated,** and **intricate** share the meaning "hard to understand because made up of many parts."

a *complex* electronic device
a *complicated* problem
the *intricate* plot of the novel

complexion (kəm plek′shən) ***noun*** the color or condition of the skin, especially the skin of the face [a pale *complexion*, a dry *complexion*].
com·plex·ion • ***noun,*** *plural* **complexions**

complicate (käm′pli kāt) ***verb*** to make hard to solve, understand, or do [Bad weather *complicated* the repair work.]
com·pli·cate • ***verb*** **complicated, complicating**

complicated (käm′pli kāt′əd) ***adjective*** hard to solve, understand, or do [a *complicated* jigsaw puzzle] —Look for the WORD CHOICES box at the entry **complex**.
com·pli·cat·ed • ***adjective***

complication (käm′pli kā′shən) ***noun*** something that happens which makes a situation more complicated [Long delays are a possible *complication* when you travel by plane.]
com·pli·ca·tion • ***noun,*** *plural* **complications**

compliment (käm′pli mənt *for n.;* käm′ pli ment *for v.*) ***noun*** **1** something said when a person wants to praise, approve, or admire [He accepted the *compliment* with a smile.] **2 compliments** polite greetings [Give your parents my *compliments*.]

C

verb to pay a compliment to; congratulate [We *complimented* her fine performance.]
com·pli·ment • ***noun,*** *plural* **compliments** • ***verb*** **complimented, complimenting**

- The words **compliment** and **complement** sound alike.
  He didn't receive a single *compliment*.
  Milk is a tasty *complement* to cookies.

SPELLING TIP

Use this memory aid to spell **compliment**.
I ***li**ke* compl***i**ments.*

complimentary (käm′pli men′tər ē) ***adjective*** **1** giving praise or admiring [He made a *complimentary* remark about her new dress.] **2** given free [We won *complimentary* tickets.]
com·pli·men·ta·ry • ***adjective***

comply (kəm plī′) ***verb*** to do what is asked or demanded; submit to [He refuses to *comply* with the rules of the game.]
com·ply • ***verb*** **complied, complying, complies**

component (kəm pō′nənt) ***noun*** one of the main parts making up a whole [My stereo system has five *components*.] —Look for the WORD CHOICES box at the entry **part**.
com·po·nent • ***noun,*** *plural* **components**

compose (kəm pōz′) ***verb*** **1** to be the members or components of [That is a picture of the six people who *compose* the team. Mortar is *composed* of lime, sand, and water.] **2** to create or write [She *composed* a song.] **3** to make calm in the mind [Try to *compose* yourself.]
com·pose • ***verb*** **composed, composing**

composed (kəm pōzd′) ***adjective*** calm; peaceful; not excited or confused [He is *composed* even when under pressure.] —Look for the WORD CHOICES box at the entry **cool**.
com·posed • ***adjective***

composer (kəm pō′zər) ***noun*** a person who composes music.
com·pos·er • ***noun,*** *plural* **composers**

composition (käm′pə zish′ən) ***noun*** **1** the act or work of composing something [The *composition* of his symphony took years.] **2** a poem, song, or something else that has been composed. **3** the parts or materials of a thing and the way that they are put together [the *composition* of the atmosphere].
com·po·si·tion • ***noun,*** *plural* **compositions**

compound (käm′pound *for n. and adj.;* käm pound′ *or* kəm pound′ *for v.*) ***noun*** **1** anything made up of two or more parts or materials; mixture. **2** a substance formed by combining two or more chemical elements [Water is a *compound* formed of hydrogen and oxygen.]
adjective made up of two or more parts ["Airplane" and "blackbird" are *compound* words.]
verb to make greater by adding something extra [Crying *compounds* the problem.]
com·pound • ***noun,*** *plural* **compounds** • ***adjective*** • ***verb*** **compounded, compounding**

comprehend (käm′prē hend′) ***verb*** to understand [I could not *comprehend* that science book.]
com·pre·hend • ***verb*** **comprehended, comprehending**

comprehension (käm′prē hen′shən) ***noun*** the power to understand.
com·pre·hen·sion • ***noun***

comprehensive (käm′prē hen′siv) ***adjective*** including all or most of the details [A *comprehensive* story of World War II requires hundreds of pages.]
com·pre·hen·sive • ***adjective***

compress (käm′pres *for n.;* kəm pres′ *for v.*) ***noun*** a folded cloth or pad for putting heat, cold, or pressure on a part of the body. It is often wet.
verb to press or squeeze closely together [Air is *compressed* in a tire.]
com·press • ***noun,*** *plural* **compresses** • ***verb*** **compressed, compressing**

compromise (käm′prə mīz) ***noun*** an ending of an argument brought about by each side giving up something [The *compromise* between labor and management avoided a strike.]
verb to end an argument by compromise [We *compromised* by agreeing to take turns washing the dishes.]
com·pro·mise • ***noun,*** *plural* **compromises** • ***verb*** **compromised, compromising**

a	cat	ō	go	ʉ	fur	ə =	a *in* ago
ā	ape	ô	law, for	ch	chin		e *in* agent
ä	cot, car	ʊ	look	sh	she		i *in* pencil
e	ten	ū	tool	th	thin		o *in* atom
ē	me	oi	oil	*th*	then		u *in* circus
i	fit	ou	out	zh	measure		
ī	ice	u	up	ŋ	ring		

compulsion (kəm pul′shən) ***noun*** a feeling of being compelled or forced to do something [a *compulsion* to eat ice cream].
com·pul·sion • ***noun,*** *plural* **compulsions**

compute (kəm pyo͞ot′) ***verb*** **1** to figure something by using arithmetic; calculate [Do you know how to *compute* your batting average?] **2** to figure or calculate by using a computer.
com·pute • ***verb*** **computed, computing**

computer

computer (kəm pyo͞ot′ər) ***noun*** an electronic machine for storing large amounts of information, performing difficult calculations at very high speed, or controlling the operation of other machines.
com·put·er • ***noun,*** *plural* **computers**

computerize (kəm pyo͞ot′ər īz) ***verb*** to equip with or operate by computers [The company has *computerized* its billing system.]
com·put·er·ize • ***verb*** **computerized, computerizing**

comrade (käm′rad) ***noun*** a friend; companion or fellow worker.
com·rade • ***noun,*** *plural* **comrades**

con- *a prefix meaning* with or together. This is the form of the prefix **com-** that is used before *c, d, g, j, n, q, s, t,* and *v* [A *condominium* is property that people own together.]

concave (kän kāv′ *or* kän′kāv) ***adjective*** hollow and rounded like the inside of a bowl [a *concave* lens].
con·cave • ***adjective***

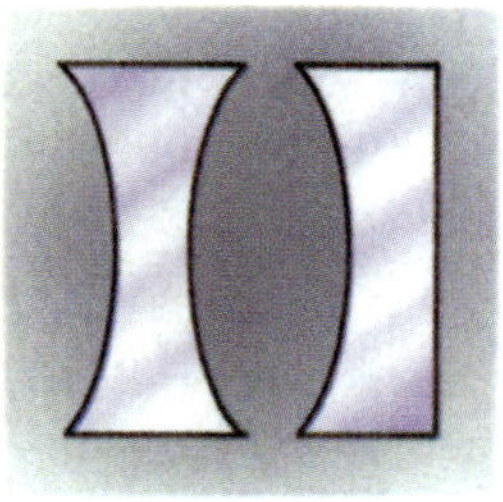

concave

conceal (kən sēl′) ***verb*** to hide or keep secret; to put or keep out of sight [I *concealed* my anger. The thief *concealed* the jewel in a pocket.] —Look for the WORD CHOICES box at the entry **hide**[1].
con·ceal • ***verb*** **concealed, concealing**

concede (kən sēd′) ***verb*** to admit to be true [They *conceded* that we had won.]
con·cede • ***verb*** **conceded, conceding**

conceited (kən sēt′əd) ***adjective*** having too high an opinion of oneself [a *conceited* actor].
con·ceit·ed • ***adjective***

concentrate (kän′sən trāt) ***verb*** **1** to gather all of one's thoughts or efforts [*Concentrate* on the problem.] **2** to bring or come close together in one place [The population of the State is *concentrated* in a few cities.]
con·cen·trate • ***verb*** **concentrated, concentrating**

concentration (kän′sən trā′shən) ***noun*** **1** careful, close attention [Math problems require *concentration.*] **2** the state of being concentrated; a gathering together in one place [the *concentration* of the population in the cities].
con·cen·tra·tion • ***noun***

concept (kän′sept) ***noun*** a general idea of what a thing or a class of things is [My mother's *concept* of good manners is a bit strict.] —Look for the WORD CHOICES box at the entry **idea**.
con·cept • ***noun,*** *plural* **concepts**

conception (kən sep′shən) ***noun*** a general idea; concept [A baby has little *conception* of time.] —Look for the WORD CHOICES box at the entry **idea**.
con·cep·tion • ***noun,*** *plural* **conceptions**

concern (kən surn′) ***verb*** **1** to be important to; to involve [This matter *concerns* all of us.] **2** to make anxious; to worry [Don't let their rudeness *concern* you.]
noun **1** something that is important to a person [What I eat is my *concern.*] **2** worry or anxiety [She shows *concern* for the hungry people.] —Look for the WORD CHOICES box at the entry **care**.
con·cern • ***verb*** **concerned, concerning**
• ***noun,*** *plural for sense 1 only* **concerns**

concert (kän′sərt) ***noun*** a musical performance given by a musician or a number of musicians.
con·cert • ***noun,*** *plural* **concerts**

concerto (kən cher′tō) ***noun*** a piece of music for one or more solo instruments and an orchestra.

C

con·cer·to • *noun, plural* **concertos**

concession (kən sesh′ən) ***noun*** **1** an act of conceding, or giving in [The mayor makes no *concession* to threats of a strike.] **2** a thing conceded [As a *concession* to the students' protest, the principal allowed them to attend the basketball game.] **3** a right or lease given by a government, company, or other authority [a food *concession* at the ballpark].
con·ces·sion • *noun, plural* **concessions**

conch (käŋk *or* känch) ***noun*** **1** a shellfish with a large spiral shell. **2** this shell.
conch • *noun, plural* **conchs** or **conches**

concise (kən sīs′) ***adjective*** telling much in few words; short and to the point [a *concise* letter].
con·cise • ***adjective***

conclude (kən klōōd′) ***verb*** **1** to bring or come to an end [I *concluded* my speech with a question.] **2** to form an opinion about something after careful thinking [I *concluded* that they were right.]
con·clude • ***verb*** **concluded, concluding**

conclusion (kən klōō′zhən) ***noun*** **1** the end; the last part [the *conclusion* of the film]. **2** an opinion formed after careful thinking [My *conclusion* is that you are wrong.]
con·clu·sion • *noun, plural* **conclusions**

Concord (käŋ′kərd) capital of New Hampshire.
Con·cord

concrete (kän′krēt *for n.;* kän′krēt *or* kän krēt′ *for adj.*) ***noun*** a hard substance that is made from cement, sand, gravel, and water. It is used for making roads, bridges, and buildings.
adjective **1** real or exact; not imaginary or vague [a *concrete* example]. **2** made of concrete [a *concrete* block].
con·crete • ***noun*** • ***adjective***

concussion (kən kush′ən) ***noun*** an injury to the brain from being hit on the head.
con·cus·sion • *noun, plural* **concussions**

condemn (kən dem′) ***verb*** **1** to disapprove of or criticize strongly; call wrong or bad [We *condemn* cruelty to animals.] **2** to declare to be guilty and give punishment to [The judge *condemned* the man to life in prison.] **3** to declare to be unsafe for use [The city *condemned* the old building.]
con·demn • ***verb*** **condemned, condemning**

condensation (kän dən sā′shən) ***noun*** **1** something that has been condensed [This is a *condensation* of the long novel.] **2** droplets of water that have condensed from the air onto a window or other surface.
con·den·sa·tion • *noun, plural* **condensations**

condense (kən dens′) ***verb*** **1** to make or become thicker or more closely packed together [Steam *condenses* to water when it touches a cold surface.] **2** to put into fewer words [I *condensed* my essay down from six pages to three.]
con·dense • ***verb*** **condensed, condensing**

condition (kən dish′ən) ***noun*** **1** the particular way a person or thing is [Weather *conditions* made us cancel the picnic.] **2** the right or healthy way to be [The whole team is in *condition*.] **3** [*an informal use*] an illness [a lung *condition*]. **4** anything that must be or must happen before something else can take place; a requirement [They made it a *condition* that I have to do my chores first.]
verb **1** to develop a habit in [He has been *conditioned* to expect the worst.] **2** to bring into fit condition [Exercise *conditions* our athletes.]
con·di·tion • *noun, plural for senses 1, 3, and 4 only* **conditions** • ***verb*** **conditioned, conditioning**

conditioner (kən dish′ən ər) ***noun*** something that helps to bring a person or thing into fit condition [hair *conditioner;* soil *conditioner*].
con·di·tion·er • *noun, plural* **conditioners**

condo (kän′dō) ***noun*** *a short form of* **condominium**.
con·do • *noun, plural* **condos**

condominium (kän′də min′ē əm) ***noun*** an apartment building or a group of small, connected houses. People who live there own their own units separately and together own the land and common parts of the building or houses.
con·do·min·i·um • *noun, plural* **condominiums**

condor (kän′dər) ***noun*** a large bird that is related to eagles and hawks but has a bare

a	cat	ō	go	ʉ	fur	ə =	a *in* ago
ā	ape	ô	law, for	ch	chin		e *in* agent
ä	cot, car	oo	look	sh	she		i *in* pencil
e	ten	ōō	tool	th	thin		o *in* atom
ē	me	oi	oil	*th*	then		u *in* circus
i	fit	ou	out	zh	measure		
ī	ice	u	up	ŋ	ring		

head and neck. Condors live in the mountains of California and South America.
con·dor • ***noun,*** *plural* **condors**

conduct (kän′dukt *for n.;* kən dukt′ *for v.*) ***noun*** the way a person acts or behaves [The teacher warned Anne about her *conduct* in class.]
verb **1** to lead or guide [She *conducts* the student orchestra.] **2** to be a means for carrying [Copper *conducts* electricity.]
con·duct • ***noun*** • ***verb*** **conducted, conducting**

conductor (kən duk′tər) ***noun*** **1** a person who conducts or directs [an orchestra *conductor*]. **2** the person in charge who collects fares [a railroad *conductor*]. **3** something that conducts electricity, heat, or sound [Metals are good *conductors* of heat.]
con·duc·tor • ***noun,*** *plural* **conductors**

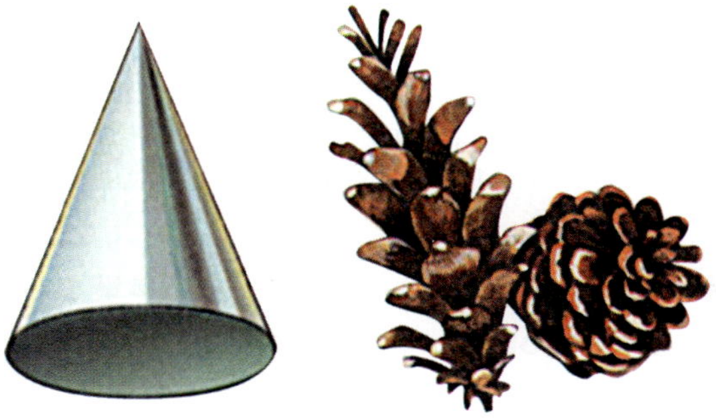

cone
Left: Geometric solid   Right: Of pine tree

cone (kōn) ***noun*** **1** a solid object that narrows evenly from a flat circle at one end to a point at the other. **2** anything shaped like this [an ice-cream *cone*]. **3** the fruit of some evergreen trees, with the seeds in it [a pine *cone*].
cone • ***noun,*** *plural* **cones**

confederacy (kən fed′ər ə sē) ***noun*** a union of people, groups, or states for a certain purpose.
—the Confederacy the eleven Southern States that separated from the U.S. in 1860 and 1861.
con·fed·er·a·cy • ***noun,*** *plural* **confederacies**

confederate (kən fed′ər ət) ***adjective*** **1** joined in or belonging to a confederacy. **2 Confederate** of or having to do with the Confederacy.
noun **Confederate** a person who supported the Confederacy.
con·fed·er·ate • ***adjective*** • ***noun,*** *plural* **confederates**

confederation (kən fed′ər ā′shən) ***noun*** a group of nations or states joined for some purpose; an alliance.
con·fed·er·a·tion • ***noun,*** *plural* **confederations**

conference (kän′fər əns) ***noun*** a meeting of people to discuss something [A *conference* on education was held in Washington.]
con·fer·ence • ***noun,*** *plural* **conferences**

confess (kən fes′) ***verb*** **1** to tell what one has done that is bad; to admit a fault or crime [He *confessed* to the theft.] **2** to admit [She *confessed* that she hated spinach.]
con·fess • ***verb*** **confessed, confessing**

confession (kən fesh′ən) ***noun*** the act of confessing; the telling of one's faults or sins.
con·fes·sion • ***noun,*** *plural* **confessions**

confetti (kən fet′ē) ***noun*** [*used with a singular verb*] colored paper in tiny pieces. It is thrown about at parades and other celebrations.
con·fet·ti • ***noun***

confide (kən fīd′) ***verb*** to share a secret or personal information with someone [She *confided* her troubles to me. I *confide* in my older brother.]
con·fide • ***verb*** **confided, confiding**

confidence (kän′fi dəns) ***noun*** **1** strong belief or trust in someone or something [I have *confidence* in you.] —Look for the WORD CHOICES box at the entry **belief**. **2** belief or trust in oneself [I have *confidence* that I will pass the test.] **3** the belief that another person will keep a secret [I told him my story in strict *confidence*.]
con·fi·dence • ***noun***

confident (kän′fi dənt) ***adjective*** full of confidence; sure or certain [He was *confident* of success in his new business.]
con·fi·dent • ***adjective***

confidential (kän′fi den′shəl) ***adjective*** told in confidence; secret [a *confidential* report].
con·fi·den·tial • ***adjective***

confine (kən fīn′) ***verb*** **1** to keep within limits [Please *confine* your speech to five minutes.] **2** to keep shut up in some place [The guards *confined* the prisoner in the dungeon.]
con·fine • ***verb*** **confined, confining**

confirm (kən furm′) ***verb*** **1** to make sure or firm by agreeing or approving [The Senate *confirmed* the treaty.] **2** to make definite [I will call the hotel to *confirm* our reserva-

tions.] **3** to prove to be true [He *confirmed* the rumor.]
—be confirmed to take part in the religious ceremony of confirmation.
con·firm • *verb* **confirmed, confirming**

confirmation (kän′fər mā′shən) *noun* **1** the act of confirming, or making sure [Did you get *confirmation* of our reservations?] **2** something that confirms or proves. **3** a ceremony in which a person becomes a full member in a church or synagogue.
con·fir·ma·tion • *noun, plural* **confirmations**

conflict (kän′flikt *for n.;* kən flikt′ *for v.*) *noun* **1** a fight or battle. **2** a sharp disagreement [Their ideas were in *conflict*.] —Look for the WORD CHOICES box at the entry **discord**.
verb to act against; be opposed to [Their wishes *conflict* with mine.]
con·flict • *noun, plural* **conflicts**
• *verb* **conflicted, conflicting**

conform (kən fôrm′) *verb* to be or act in the required way [Jim didn't like to *conform* to rules.]
con·form • *verb* **conformed, conforming**

confront (kən frunt′) *verb* to meet face to face, in a bold way; stand up against [Our troops *confronted* the enemy soldiers.]
con·front • *verb* **confronted, confronting**

confuse (kən fyo͞oz′) *verb* **1** to mix up in the mind; bewilder [You will *confuse* me with all these different instructions.] **2** to fail to see the difference between [You're *confusing* him with his twin brother.]
con·fuse • *verb* **confused, confusing**

confusion (kən fyo͞o′zhən) *noun* the act of confusing or the condition of being confused [There was *confusion* when fire broke out.]
con·fu·sion • *noun, plural* **confusions**

WORD CHOICES

Synonyms of **confusion**

The words **confusion, chaos,** and **jumble** share the meaning "a mixed-up condition."

the *confusion* caused by the alarm

a locker room in *chaos* after the big win

papers in a *jumble* in the drawer

Congo (käŋ′gō) **1 Democratic Republic of the Congo** a country in central Africa, on the equator. Its old name was *Zaire*. **2 Republic of the Congo** a country in west central Africa, west of Democratic Republic of the Congo.
Con·go

congratulate (kən grach′ə lāt *or* kən graj′ ə lāt) *verb* to express happiness to another person because of that person's success or good luck [Let's *congratulate* José on winning the election.]
con·grat·u·late • *verb* **congratulated, congratulating**

congratulation (kən grach′ə lā′shən *or* kən graj′ə lā′shən) *noun* **1** the act of congratulating [The coach sent words of *congratulation* to the team.] **2** *usually* **congratulations** words that tell of one's happiness at another person's success or good luck [Let's send *congratulations* to the winner.]
con·grat·u·la·tion • *noun, plural* **congratulations**

congregate (käŋ′grə gāt) *verb* to come together; assemble [We *congregated* around the piano.]
con·gre·gate • *verb* **congregated, congregating**

congregation (käŋ′grə gā′shən) *noun* **1** a group of people meeting for a religious service. **2** the members of a particular church, synagogue, or other place of worship.
con·gre·ga·tion • *noun, plural* **congregations**

congress (käŋ′grəs) *noun* **1** a meeting or convention. **2 Congress** the group of people in the U.S. government who are elected to make the laws. Congress is made up of the Senate and the House of Representatives.
con·gress • *noun, plural for sense 1 only* **congresses**

congressman (käŋ′grəs mən) *noun* a member of Congress, especially of the House of Representatives.
con·gress·man • *noun, plural* **congressmen**

congressperson (käŋ′grəs pʉr sən) *noun* *another name for* **congressman**.

a	cat	ō	go	ʉ	fur	ə = a *in* ago	
ā	ape	ô	law, for	ch	chin	e *in* agent	
ä	cot, car	oo	look	sh	she	i *in* pencil	
e	ten	o͞o	tool	th	thin	o *in* atom	
ē	me	oi	oil	*th*	then	u *in* circus	
i	fit	ou	out	zh	measure		
ī	ice	u	up	ŋ	ring		

con·gress·per·son • ***noun,*** *plural* **congresspersons**

congresswoman (käŋ′grəs woom ən) ***noun*** a woman who is a member of Congress, especially of the House of Representatives.
con·gress·wom·an • ***noun,*** *plural* **congresswomen**

conical (kän′i kəl) ***adjective*** shaped like a cone [The wizard wore a *conical* hat.]
con·i·cal • ***adjective***

conj. *abbreviation for* conjunction.

conjunction (kən juŋk′shən) ***noun*** a word that is used to join other single words or groups of words. In the sentence "Burt and Selma will go to the beach if it doesn't rain," the words *and* and *if* are conjunctions.
con·junc·tion • ***noun,*** *plural* **conjunctions**

Conn. *abbreviation for* Connecticut.

connect (kə nekt′) ***verb*** **1** to join together; unite [The bridge *connects* the two freeways.] —Look for the WORD CHOICES box at the entry **join.** **2** to think of together [Do you *connect* ice cream with birthdays?] **3** to plug into an electrical circuit [We *connected* the Christmas tree lights.]
con·nect • ***verb*** **connected, connecting**

STATE MAP

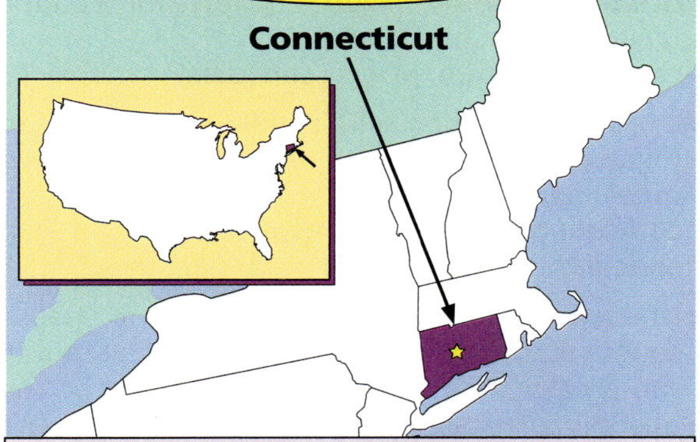

Statehood: 1788, the 5th state • **Capital:** Hartford

Connecticut (kə net′i kət) a New England State of the U.S. Its capital is Hartford. Abbreviated **CT, Ct.,** or **Conn.**
Con·nect·i·cut

connection (kə nek′shən) ***noun*** **1** the act of joining or the condition of being joined [*connection* of the engine to the passenger cars]. **2** a part or thing that connects [A bad *connection* makes the lamp flicker.] **3** the fact of being related in some way [a *connection* between Easter and rabbits].
con·nec·tion • ***noun,*** *plural* **connections**

conquer (käŋ′kər) ***verb*** **1** to get or gain by the use of force [The Spaniards *conquered* Mexico.] **2** to overcome by trying hard; get the better of [She *conquered* her bad habits.]
con·quer • ***verb*** **conquered, conquering**

conqueror (käŋ′kər ər) ***noun*** a person, group, or nation that conquers or defeats another.
con·quer·or • ***noun,*** *plural* **conquerors**

conquest (käŋ′kwest) ***noun*** **1** the act of conquering. **2** something that has been conquered.
con·quest • ***noun,*** *plural* **conquests**

conscience (kän′shəns) ***noun*** the sense of right and wrong; a feeling that keeps a person from doing bad things.
con·science • ***noun,*** *plural* **consciences**

conscious (kän′shəs) ***adjective*** **1** aware of one's own feelings or of things in the surrounding area [We were suddenly *conscious* of a slight noise on the stair.] **2** able to feel and think; in the normal waking state [I was *conscious* again soon after the operation.]
con·scious • ***adjective***

consciousness (kän′shəs nis) ***noun*** **1** the condition of being conscious [She lost *consciousness* when she broke her arm.] **2** all the thoughts and feelings that a person has when awake [Memory of the accident was gone from the driver's *consciousness*.]
con·scious·ness • ***noun***

consecutive (kən sek′yə tiv) ***adjective*** coming in regular order without a break [I have exams on three *consecutive* days.]
con·sec·u·tive • ***adjective***

consent (kən sent′) ***verb*** to agree or give approval.
noun permission or approval [May I have your *consent* to go?]
con·sent • ***verb*** **consented, consenting**
• ***noun***

consequence (kän′sə kwens) ***noun*** a result or outcome [the *consequences* of an action].
con·se·quence • ***noun,*** *plural* **consequences**

consequently (kän′sə kwent lē) ***adverb*** as a result; therefore [I broke my arm and *consequently* wore a cast for a while.]
con·se·quent·ly • ***adverb***

conservation (kän sər vā′shən) ***noun*** **1** the

act of conserving. **2** the care and protection of forests, water, and other natural resources.
con·ser·va·tion • ***noun***

conservative (kən sʉr′və tiv) ***adjective*** **1** wanting to keep things as they are and being against change [My father is a very *conservative* person.] **2** cautious or safe; not risky [a *conservative* estimate of costs].
noun a conservative person.
con·ser·va·tive • ***adjective*** • ***noun,*** *plural* **conservatives**

conserve (kən sʉrv′) ***verb*** to keep from being lost or wasted [*Conserve* your energy.]
con·serve • ***verb*** **conserved, conserving**

consider (kən sid′ər) ***verb*** **1** to think about in order to make a decision [We are *considering* moving to a new apartment.] **2** to be thoughtful about [*Consider* other people's feelings.] **3** to keep in mind; take into account [He plays the piano well, if you *consider* his youth.]
con·sid·er • ***verb*** **considered, considering**

WORD CHOICES

Synonyms of **consider**

The words **consider, reflect,** and **weigh** share the meaning "to think about something carefully or seriously."

You must *consider* the possible results.

I must *reflect* on the matter before deciding.

The jury *weighed* the evidence.

considerable (kən sid′ər ə bəl) ***adjective*** much or large [a *considerable* distance from home].
con·sid·er·a·ble • ***adjective***

considerate (kən sid′ər ət) ***adjective*** thoughtful of other people's feelings; kind [It was *considerate* of him to offer to fix the window.] —Look for the WORD CHOICES box at the entry **kind**[2].
con·sid·er·ate • ***adjective***

consideration (kən sid ər ā′shən) ***noun*** **1** the act of considering; careful thought [The President gave the matter serious *consideration*.] **2** thoughtfulness or kindness to other people.
—under consideration in the process of being thought over.
con·sid·er·a·tion • ***noun,*** *plural* **considerations**

considering (kən sid′ər iŋ) ***preposition*** keeping in mind; taking into account [This tastes good, *considering* that you cooked it.]
con·sid·er·ing • ***preposition***

consist (kən sist′) ***verb*** to be made up of [Bronze *consists* of copper and tin.]
con·sist • ***verb*** **consisted, consisting**

consistency (kən sis′tən sē) ***noun*** **1** the degree of thickness or firmness of something [The gravy had a watery *consistency*.] **2** the quality of being consistent; a way of acting that is always the same [You cannot tell what she is going to do because she lacks *consistency*.]
con·sis·ten·cy • ***noun,*** *plural* **consistencies**

consistent (kən sis′tənt) ***adjective*** **1** acting or thinking always in the same way [They are *consistent* in the way they treat their children.] **2** in agreement [What she does is not *consistent* with what she says.]
con·sis·tent • ***adjective***

console[1] (kən sōl′) ***verb*** to make less sad or troubled; to comfort [An ice cream cone *consoled* the lost child.] —Look for the WORD CHOICES box at the entry **comfort**.
con·sole • ***verb*** **consoled, consoling**

console[2] (kän′sôl) ***noun*** a cabinet for a radio, record player, or TV set.
con·sole • ***noun,*** *plural* **consoles**

consolidate (kən säl′i dāt) ***verb*** to join together into one [The merger *consolidated* many companies.]
con·sol·i·date • ***verb*** **consolidated, consolidating**

consonant (kän′sə nənt) ***noun*** **1** a speech sound made by stopping or partly stopping the breath with the tongue, the teeth, or the lips. Some consonants are the sounds (p), (n), (s), and (r). **2** a letter that represents a sound like this [Two of the *consonants* in the word "night" are not pronounced.]
con·so·nant • ***noun,*** *plural* **consonants**

conspicuous (kən spik′yo͞o əs) ***adjective*** easy

a	cat	ō	go	ʉ	fur	ə =	a *in* ago
ā	ape	ô	law, for	ch	chin		e *in* agent
ä	cot, car	oo	look	sh	she		i *in* pencil
e	ten	o͞o	tool	th	thin		o *in* atom
ē	me	oi	oil	*th*	then		u *in* circus
i	fit	ou	out	zh	measure		
ī	ice	u	up	ŋ	ring		

to see or notice; obvious [There is a *conspicuous* mistake in the book.]
con·spic·u·ous • *adjective*

conspiracy (kən spir′ə sē) *noun* a secret plan by two or more people to do something that is bad or unlawful; a plot.
con·spir·a·cy • *noun, plural* **conspiracies**

conspire (kən spīr′) *verb* to plan together secretly to do something bad or unlawful [They *conspired* to kill the king.]
con·spire • *verb* **conspired, conspiring**

constable (kän′stə bəl) *noun* a police officer in a town or village.
con·sta·ble • *noun, plural* **constables**

constant (kän′stənt) *adjective* **1** not changing; staying the same [driving at a *constant* speed]. **2** going on all the time without a pause [their *constant* complaints].
con·stant • *adjective*

constellation (kän stə lā′shən) *noun* a particular group of stars in the sky. It is usually named after something that it seems to picture in outline.
con·stel·la·tion • *noun, plural* **constellations**

WORD HISTORY

constellation

The word **constellation** comes from a Latin adjective that means "set with stars" or "having stars scattered on it." This Latin word comes from a Latin prefix that means "with" and the Latin word for "star."

constituent (kən stich′o͞o ənt) *adjective* needed to form a whole thing [a *constituent* part]. *noun* **1** one of the parts that make up a whole thing [Oxygen is a *constituent* of air.] **2** a voter who is represented by a particular official [I am a *constituent* of Senator Jones.]
con·stit·u·ent • *adjective* • *noun, plural* **constituents**

constitute (kän′sti to͞ot′ *or* kän′sti tyo͞ot′) *verb* to make up; to form [Eleven votes of the total of twenty would *constitute* a majority.]
con·sti·tute • *verb* **constituted, constituting**

constitution (kän′sti to͞o′shən *or* kän′sti tyo͞o′shən) *noun* **1** the way a person or thing is made or formed [He has a strong *constitution*.] **2** the system of basic laws of a nation or state. **3 Constitution** the document that contains the basic laws of the U.S. It sets forth the structure and powers of the government and the rights of the individual.
con·sti·tu·tion • *noun, plural* **constitutions**

constitutional (kän′sti to͞o′shə nəl *or* kän′sti tyo͞o′shə nəl) *adjective* **1** having to do with a constitution [a *constitutional* right; a *constitutional* convention]. **2** in agreement with a constitution [The court ruled the law *constitutional*.]
con·sti·tu·tion·al • *adjective*

construct (kən strukt′) *verb* to make or build according to a plan [They *constructed* the house from bricks.]
con·struct • *verb* **constructed, constructing**

construction (kən struk′shən) *noun* the act of constructing or building [*Construction* of the new city hall began last month.]
con·struc·tion • *noun, plural* **constructions**

construction paper *noun* heavy paper in various colors. It is used for making drawings or for cutting out figures.

constructive (kən struk′tiv) *adjective* serving or helping to improve; useful [*Constructive* criticism helps us to correct our mistakes.]
con·struc·tive • *adjective*

consul (kän′səl) *noun* an official who is appointed by the government of a country to look after the interests of its citizens in a foreign city.
con·sul • *noun, plural* **consuls**

consult (kən sult′) *verb* to go to for information or advice [*Consult* the encyclopedia. *Consult* a doctor.]
con·sult • *verb* **consulted, consulting**

consultant (kən sult′nt) *noun* an expert who is called on for special advice or services [a financial *consultant*].
con·sult·ant • *noun, plural* **consultants**

consultation (kän səl tā′shən) *noun* a meeting to talk over some problem [a *consultation* with a lawyer].
con·sul·ta·tion • *noun, plural* **consultations**

consume (kən so͞om′ *or* kən syo͞om′) *verb* **1** to destroy [The fire *consumed* the building.] **2** to use up [The meeting *consumed* most of the day.] **3** to drink up or eat up [She *consumed* four hot dogs in record time.]
con·sume • *verb* **consumed, consuming**

consumer (kən so͞o′mər) *noun* a person who buys products or services for his own use and not for resale.

C

con·sum·er • *noun, plural* **consumers**

consumption (kən sump′shən) ***noun*** **1** the process of consuming or using up. **2** the amount that is used up.
con·sump·tion • ***noun,*** *plural* **consumptions**

contact (kän′takt) ***noun*** **1** the fact of touching or meeting [The light is turned on by the *contact* of an electrical switch with a wire.] **2** communication [The pilot made *contact* with the airport.]
verb to get in touch with; communicate with [*Contact* your doctor if you have pain.]
con·tact • ***noun,*** *plural* **contacts**
• ***verb*** **contacted, contacting**

contact lens ***noun*** a tiny, thin lens worn on the front of the eye to correct vision. The lens floats on a film of tears.
contact lens • ***noun,*** *plural* **contact lenses**

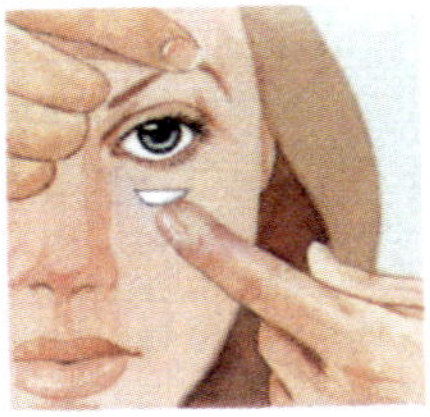

contact lens

contagious (kən tā′jəs) ***adjective*** capable of being spread by contact [a *contagious* disease].
con·ta·gious • ***adjective***

contain (kən tān′) ***verb*** **1** to hold within itself; enclose or include [The garden *contains* many rare flowers.] **2** to be able to hold; be equal to [A gallon *contains* four quarts.]
con·tain • ***verb*** **contained, containing**

container (kən tān′ər) ***noun*** a box, bottle, or something else used for containing something.
con·tain·er • ***noun,*** *plural* **containers**

contaminate (kən tam′ə nāt) ***verb*** to make dirty, impure, or infected by touching or mixing with.
con·tam·i·nate • ***verb*** **contaminated, contaminating**

WORD CHOICES

Synonyms of **contaminate**

The words **contaminate**, **infect**, and **pollute** share the meaning "to make unfit for use."

canned goods *contaminated* by chemicals

water *infected* by bacteria

air *polluted* by exhaust fumes

contd. *abbreviation for* continued.

contemporary (kən tem′pər er′ē) ***adjective*** happening or living in the same period of time.
noun a person living in the same period as another [George Washington and Benjamin Franklin were *contemporaries*.]
con·tem·po·rar·y • ***adjective*** • ***noun,*** *plural* **contemporaries**

contempt (kən tempt′) ***noun*** **1** feelings toward someone or something that a person thinks of as low, worthless, or evil; scorn [Many people feel *contempt* for a liar.] **2** the state of being despised or scorned [He was held in *contempt* by everyone.]
con·tempt • ***noun***

contemptible (kən tempt′i bəl) ***adjective*** deserving contempt or scorn [a *contemptible* act].
con·tempt·i·ble • ***adjective***

content[1] (kən tent′) ***adjective*** happy with what one has or is; not wanting anything else [Juanita is *content* with her family life.]
con·tent • ***adjective***

content[2] (kän′tent) ***noun*** **1** the amount that something holds or contains [The *content* of this bottle is one quart.] **2 contents** all that is contained [the *contents* of a trunk]. **3 contents** the things that are included in a piece of writing [the book's table of *contents*].
con·tent • ***noun,*** *plural* **contents**

contented (kən tent′əd) ***adjective*** satisfied [We are *contented* with our roles in the play.]
con·tent·ed • ***adjective***

contest (kän′test) ***noun*** a race or other event that involves a struggle to become the winner.
con·test • ***noun,*** *plural* **contests**

contestant (kən test′ənt) ***noun*** a person who takes part in a contest.
con·test·ant • ***noun,*** *plural* **contestants**

context (kän′tekst) ***noun*** the words in a piece of writing that come just before and after a certain word or sentence. They help to make clear what the word or sentence means [It was clear from the *context* that the word "mad" meant "angry."]

a	cat	ō	go	ʉ	fur	ə =	a *in* ago
ā	ape	ô	law, for	ch	chin		e *in* agent
ä	cot, car	oo	look	sh	she		i *in* pencil
e	ten	ōō	tool	th	thin		o *in* atom
ē	me	oi	oil	*th*	then		u *in* circus
i	fit	ou	out	zh	measure		
ī	ice	u	up	ŋ	ring		

con·text • *noun, plural* **contexts**

continent (kän′ti nənt) ***noun*** one of the seven main land areas on earth. The continents are Africa, Antarctica, Asia, Australia, Europe, North America, and South America.
con·ti·nent • *noun, plural* **continents**

continental (kän′ti nent′l) ***adjective*** like or having to do with a continent.
con·ti·nen·tal • ***adjective***

continual (kən tin′yo͞o əl) ***adjective*** **1** happening over and over again; repeated often [the *continual* banging of the door]. **2** going on without stopping; continuous [the *continual* roar of the waterfall].
con·tin·u·al • ***adjective***

continue (kən tin′yo͞o) ***verb*** **1** to keep on being or doing [The rain *continued* to fall.] **2** to start again after a stop [Classes will *continue* after lunch.]
con·tin·ue • ***verb*** **continued, continuing**

continuity (kän′tə no͞o′ə tē) ***noun*** the condition of being continuous [The speech moved from point to point with clearness and *continuity*.]
con·ti·nu·i·ty • ***noun***

continuous (kən tin′yo͞o əs) ***adjective*** going on without a stop or break [the *continuous* flowing of the waterfall].
con·tin·u·ous • ***adjective***

contortion (kən tôr′shən) ***noun*** a twisted or distorted position or shape, especially of the face or body.
con·tor·tion • *noun, plural* **contortions**

contour (kän′to͝or) ***noun*** the outline of something.
con·tour • *noun, plural* **contours**

contract (kän′trakt *for n.;* kən trakt′ *for v.*) ***noun*** **1** an agreement that is supported by the law. **2** a document that shows such an agreement.
verb **1** to get; come to have [They *contracted* measles.] **2** to make or become smaller; draw together [Cold *contracts* metals. The judge's eyebrows *contracted* in a frown.]
con·tract • *noun, plural* **contracts**
• ***verb*** **contracted, contracting**

contraction (kən trak′shən) ***noun*** **1** the act or process of contracting [A cramp is a sudden *contraction* of a muscle.] **2** a shortened form of a word or phrase. *I'm* is a contraction of *I am*.
con·trac·tion • *noun, plural* **contractions**

contradict (kän trə dikt′) ***verb*** to say the opposite of [Karla just *contradicted* what she said earlier.]
con·tra·dict • ***verb*** **contradicted, contradicting**

contradiction (kän trə dik′shən) ***noun*** the act of contradicting [He was surprised by the child's *contradiction* of what he had said.]
con·tra·dic·tion • *noun, plural* **contradictions**

contrary (kän′trer ē; *for sense 2 often* kən trer′ē) ***adjective*** **1** going or being against; opposed [That play was *contrary* to the rules.] **2** stubborn [a *contrary* child].
noun the opposite [Just the *contrary* of what you say is true.]
—on the contrary as opposed to what has been said.
con·trar·y • ***adjective*** • *noun, plural* **contraries**

contrast (kən trast′ *for v.;* kän′trast *for n.*) ***verb*** **1** to compare in a way that shows the differences [Her book *contrasts* life in the U.S. and life in Japan.] **2** to show differences when compared [Basketball *contrasts* with baseball as a sport.]
noun a difference between things being compared [a *contrast* between air and rail travel].
con·trast • ***verb*** **contrasted, contrasting**
• *noun, plural* **contrasts**

contribute (kən trib′yo͞ot) ***verb*** to give together with others [We *contributed* books to the sale. We *contribute* to several charities.]
—contribute to to have a part in bringing about [Good luck *contributed* to our success.]
con·trib·ute • ***verb*** **contributed, contributing**

contribution (kän′tri byo͞o′shən) ***noun*** **1** the act of contributing [Please help in the *contribution* of money for the homeless.] **2** something that is contributed; a donation.
con·tri·bu·tion • *noun, plural* **contributions**

control (kən trōl′) ***verb*** **1** to be in charge of; direct [The coach *controls* the actions of the football players on the field.] **2** to have the power of guiding or operating [A thermostat *controls* the heat in the house.] **3** to hold back; curb [*Control* your temper!]
noun **1** power to direct or manage [He's a poor coach, with little *control* over the team.] —Look for the WORD CHOICES box at the entry **power**. **2** the condition of being directed or restrained [The car went out of *control*.]

3 *often* **controls** a part or thing that controls a machine [the *controls* of the helicopter].
con·trol • *verb* **controlled, controlling**
• *noun, plural* **controls**

control tower

control tower *noun* a high tower at an airport. Workers in a control tower direct all aircraft landings and takeoffs.
control tower • *noun, plural* **control towers**

controversial (kän trə vʉr′shəl) *adjective* causing or able to cause arguments [Politics and religion are *controversial* subjects.]
con·tro·ver·sial • *adjective*

controversy (kän′trə vʉr′sē) *noun* argument or debate; disagreement [The new traffic rules at rush hour caused a lot of *controversy*.] —Look for the WORD CHOICES boxes at the entries **argument** and **discord**.
con·tro·ver·sy • *noun, plural* **controversies**

convalescent (kän və les′ənt) *noun* a person who is getting back health and strength after an illness.
con·va·les·cent • *noun, plural* **convalescents**

convene (kən vēn′) *verb* to come or call together for a meeting; assemble [Congress regularly *convenes* in January.]
con·vene • *verb* **convened, convening**

convenience (kən vēn′yəns) *noun* **1** the quality of being suitable, handy, or useful [the *convenience* of living near a mall]. **2** personal comfort or advantage [The store has a telephone for the *convenience* of customers.] **3** something that saves time and work [Her kitchen was equipped with all the latest *conveniences*.]
con·ven·ience • *noun, plural* **conveniences**

convenient (kən vēn′yənt) *adjective* **1** easy to reach; handy [She picked a *convenient* place for their meeting.] **2** making things easier; suited to one's comfort [We'll set a time for the meeting that is *convenient* for you.]
con·ven·ient • *adjective*

convent (kän′vənt) *noun* the place where a group of nuns live.
con·vent • *noun, plural* **convents**

convention (kən ven′shən) *noun* **1** a formal meeting of people who have something in common [a political *convention;* a national *convention* of English teachers]. **2** a custom or way of behaving that most people follow [It is a *convention* to say "How do you do?" on being introduced to someone.]
con·ven·tion • *noun, plural* **conventions**

conventional (kən ven′shə nəl) *adjective* following accepted custom; usual ["Yours truly" is a *conventional* way to end a letter.]
con·ven·tion·al • *adjective*

conversation (kän vər sā′shən) *noun* a friendly and informal talk between persons.
con·ver·sa·tion • *noun, plural* **conversations**

converse (kən vʉrs′) *verb* to talk; have a conversation —Look for the WORD CHOICES box at the entry **speak**.
con·verse • *verb* **conversed, conversing**

conversion (kən vʉr′zhən) *noun* **1** the act or process of converting, or changing; change [the *conversion* of electricity to heat]. **2** a change from one belief or religion to another.
con·ver·sion • *noun, plural* **conversions**

convert (kən vʉrt′ *for v.;* kän′vərt *for n.*) *verb* **1** to change from one form or use to another [The mill *converts* grain into flour.] —Look for the WORD CHOICES box at the entry **transform**. **2** to change from one belief or religion to another.
noun a person who has changed from one religion or belief to another.
con·vert • *verb* **converted, converting**
• *noun, plural* **converts**

convertible (kən vʉrt′i bəl) *adjective* able to be changed into something else [A savings bond is easily *convertible* into cash.]
noun an automobile with a top that can be folded back.

a cat	ō go	ʉ fur	ə = a *in* ago
ā ape	ô law, for	ch chin	e *in* agent
ä cot, car	oo look	sh she	i *in* pencil
e ten	ōō tool	th thin	o *in* atom
ē me	oi oil	*th* then	u *in* circus
i fit	ou out	zh measure	
ī ice	u up	ŋ ring	

C

con·vert·i·ble • *adjective* • *noun, plural* **convertibles**

convex (kän veks′ *or* kän′veks) *adjective* curving outward like the outside of a ball [a *convex* lens].
con·vex • *adjective*

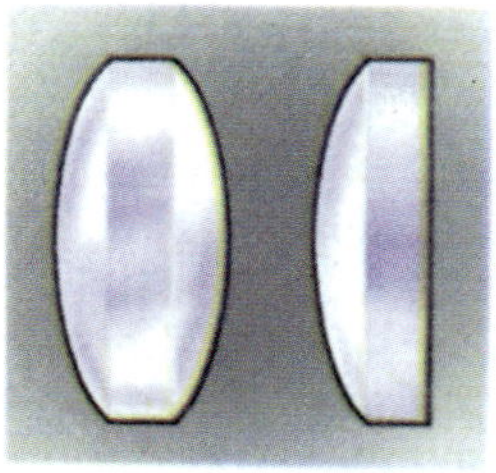
convex

convey (kən vā′) *verb* **1** to take from one place to another; to carry [The helicopter *conveyed* us from the airport to the city.] **2** to make known; to express [Please *convey* my thanks.]
con·vey • *verb* **conveyed, conveying**

conveyance (kən vā′əns) *noun* a car, bus, truck, or any other vehicle that is used to carry passengers or goods.
con·vey·ance • *noun, plural* **conveyances**

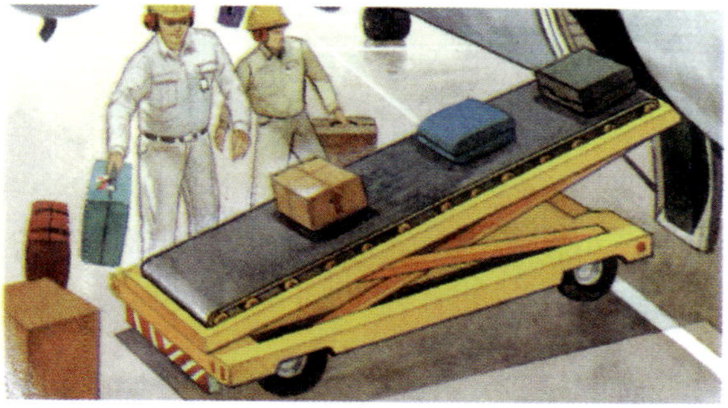
conveyor

conveyor or **conveyer** (kən vā′ər) *noun* an endless chain or belt that is used to carry things from one place to another. Conveyors are used in factories or in airports to carry luggage. This is also called **conveyor belt**.
con·vey·or or **con·vey·er** • *noun, plural* **conveyors** or **conveyers**

convict (kən vikt′ *for v.;* kän′vikt *for n.*) *verb* to judge and find guilty [The jury *convicted* her of robbery.]
noun a person who is serving a sentence in prison.
con·vict • *verb* **convicted, convicting** • *noun, plural* **convicts**

conviction (kən vik′shən) *noun* **1** the act or process of judging that someone is guilty [evidence resulting in the *conviction* of the thief]. **2** a strong feeling or belief about something [It is my *conviction* that democracy is the best form of government.]
con·vic·tion • *noun, plural* **convictions**

convince (kən vins′) *verb* to cause to believe something [I finally *convinced* her that her brother was telling the truth.]
con·vince • *verb* **convinced, convincing**

convulsion (kən vul′shən) *noun* a sudden, sharp drawing together or twitching of the muscles.
con·vul·sion • *noun, plural* **convulsions**

coo (ko͞o) *noun* the soft, murmuring sound made by doves and pigeons.
verb to make this sound.
coo • *noun, plural* **coos** • *verb* **cooed, cooing**

cook (ko͝ok) *verb* **1** to prepare food for eating by using heat [You can *cook* carrots or eat them raw.] **2** to be cooked [The roast should *cook* longer.]
noun a person who prepares food for eating.
cook • *verb* **cooked, cooking** • *noun, plural* **cooks**

cookie or **cooky** (ko͝ok′ē) *noun* a small, flat, sweet cake that is crisp or chewy.
cook·ie or **cook·y** • *noun, plural* **cookies**

cookout (ko͝ok′out) *noun* a meal cooked and eaten outdoors.
cook·out • *noun, plural* **cookouts**

cool (ko͞ol) *adjective* **1** not warm but not very cold [*cool* weather; a *cool* glass of lemonade]. **2** not easily excited; calm [She always keeps *cool* in an emergency.] **3** not friendly or interested; showing dislike [He greeted me with a *cool* "hello."] **4** [*a slang use*] very good.
noun **1** a place, time, or something else that is cool [She likes to walk to the beach in the *cool* of the evening.] **2** [*a slang use*] calm or controlled manner or behavior.
verb to make or become cool [Let the cake *cool* before you slice it.]
cool • *adjective* **cooler, coolest** • *noun* • *verb* **cooled, cooling**

WORD CHOICES

Synonyms of **cool**

The words **cool, calm,** and **composed** share the meaning "not excited."

keeping *cool* in an emergency
staying *calm* during a fire
remaining *composed* during the storm

cooler (ko͞ol′ər) *noun* a container or room in which things are cooled or kept cool.
cool·er • *noun, plural* **coolers**

Coolidge (ko͞o′lij), **Calvin** (kal′vin) 1872-1933; the thirtieth president of the U.S., from 1923 to 1929.
Coo·lidge, Cal·vin

coop (ko͞op) *noun* a cage or pen for chickens, ducks, or other small animals.
verb to shut up in a small space [She was *cooped* up in her room all day.]
coop • *noun, plural* **coops** • *verb* **cooped, cooping**

Cooper (ko͞op′ər), **James Fenimore** (jāmz′ fen′ i môr) 1789-1851; U.S. novelist.
Coop·er, James Fen·i·more

cooperate (kō äp′ər āt) *verb* to work together to get something done [If we all *cooperate*, we can finish painting this room today.]
co·op·er·ate • *verb* **cooperated, cooperating**

cooperation (kō äp′ər ā′shən) *noun* the act of cooperating, or working together [To finish on time will require the *cooperation* of all.]
co·op·e·ra·tion • *noun*

coordinate (kō ôr′di nāt′) *verb* to work or cause to work well together [The brain *coordinates* the body's movements.]
co·or·di·nate • *verb* **coordinated, coordinating**

coordination (kō ôr′di nā′shən) *noun* **1** the act or condition of working together smoothly. **2** the ability of body parts to work together well [Athletes need good muscular *coordination*.]
co·or·di·na·tion • *noun*

cope (kōp) *verb* to deal with successfully [The police were able to *cope* with the crowd.]
cope • *verb* **coped, coping**

copper (käp′ər) *noun* a reddish-brown metal that is a chemical element. Copper is soft and easy to shape. It is also a good conductor of heat and electricity.
cop·per • *noun*

copperhead (käp′ər hed) *noun* a poisonous snake of eastern North America. It has a copper-colored head.
cop·per·head • *noun, plural* **copperheads**

copter (käp′tər) *noun a short form of* **helicopter**.
cop·ter • *noun, plural* **copters**

copy (käp′ē) *noun* **1** a thing that is made to look exactly like another; imitation or reproduction [a *copy* of a famous painting]. **2** one of a number of books, magazines, or newspapers that have been printed at the same time [The store has six *copies* of *Tom Sawyer*.]
verb **1** to make a copy or copies of [*Copy* this drawing.] **2** to follow as a model or example [Mary *copied* the way Jane wore her hair.] —Look for the WORD CHOICES box at the entry **imitate**.
cop·y • *noun, plural* **copies** • *verb* **copied, copying, copies**

coral

coral (kôr′əl) *noun* **1** a hard, stony substance that is made up of the skeletons of many tiny sea animals. Reefs of coral are found in tropical seas. Coral is often white, pink, or reddish. **2** yellowish red.
cor·al • *noun, plural* **corals**

coral snake *noun* a poisonous snake that has a narrow head and red, yellow, and black bands around its body.
coral snake • *noun, plural* **coral snakes**

cord (kôrd) *noun* **1** a thick string or thin rope. **2** a wire or wires covered with insulation and fitted with a plug. A cord is used to carry electricity from an outlet to a lamp or an appliance. **3** a part of the body that is like a cord [the spinal *cord;* the vocal *cords*]. **4** a measure of cut firewood. A cord is a pile of wood that is 8 feet long, 4 feet wide, and 4 feet high.
cord • *noun, plural* **cords**
• The words **cord** and **chord** sound alike.
The lamp's *cord* has a plug on the end.

a cat	ō go	ʉ fur	ə = a *in* ago
ā ape	ô law, for	ch chin	e *in* agent
ä cot, car	oo look	sh she	i *in* pencil
e ten	o͞o tool	th thin	o *in* atom
ē me	oi oil	*th* then	u *in* circus
i fit	ou out	zh measure	
ī ice	u up	ŋ ring	

So far, I can play only one *chord* on the guitar.

cordial (kôr′jəl) ***adjective*** warm and friendly; hearty; sincere [a *cordial* welcome].
cor·dial • ***adjective***

corduroy (kôr′də roi) ***noun*** **1** a heavy cotton cloth that has a soft surface with raised ridges. **2 corduroys** trousers made of this cloth.
cor·du·roy • ***noun,*** *plural* **corduroys**

core (kôr) ***noun*** **1** the hard center of an apple, pear, and some other fruits. It contains the seeds. **2** the central or most important part of anything [The *core* of a friendship is respect.] ***verb*** to cut out the core of [*Core* the apples.]
core • ***noun,*** *plural* **cores** • ***verb*** **cored, coring**

● The words **core** and **corps** sound alike.
I threw the apple *core* away.
My cousin joined the Marine *Corps*.

cork (kôrk) ***noun*** **1** the thick outer bark of a kind of oak tree. Cork is very light and tough. It is used to make bottle stoppers, rafts, and floor covering. **2** a stopper for a bottle or jar, made from cork or other soft material.
cork • ***noun,*** *plural* **corks**

corkscrew (kôrk′skro͞o) ***noun*** a tool that is used for pulling cork stoppers out of bottles.
cork·screw • ***noun,*** *plural* **corkscrews**

corkscrew

cormorant (kôr′mər ənt) ***noun*** a large sea bird with webbed toes and a long, hooked beak.
cor·mo·rant • ***noun,*** *plural* **cormorants**

corn (kôrn) ***noun*** **1** a kind of grain that grows in kernels on the large ears of a tall plant. Corn is grown as food for people and animals. **2** the plant that corn grows on. **3** the ears and kernels of the corn plant.

corncob (kôrn′käb) ***noun*** the hard, woody part of an ear of corn on which the kernels grow.
corn·cob • ***noun,*** *plural* **corncobs**

cornea (kôr′nē ə) ***noun*** the clear outer layer of the eyeball that covers the iris and the pupil.
cor·ne·a • ***noun,*** *plural* **corneas**

corner (kôr′nər) ***noun*** **1** the place where two lines or surfaces come together to form an angle. **2** the space between such lines or surfaces [a lamp in the *corner* of the room]. **3** a place where two roads or streets meet [a traffic light on the *corner*]. **4** a place or region [They came from every *corner* of America.] ***verb*** to force or drive into a difficult position from which it is hard to escape [The dogs *cornered* the fox at the edge of the forest.] ***adjective*** in, at, or on a corner [She went to the *corner* drugstore to buy a book.]
cor·ner • ***noun,*** *plural* **corners** • ***verb*** **cornered, cornering** • ***adjective***

cornet

cornet (kôr net′) ***noun*** a musical instrument like the trumpet, but shorter.
cor·net • ***noun,*** *plural* **cornets**

cornmeal (kôrn′mēl) ***noun*** meal that is made from coarsely ground kernels of corn.
corn·meal • ***noun***

corny (kôrn′ē) [*an informal word*] ***adjective*** **1** having lost its freshness or interest; old-fashioned [a *corny* joke]. **2** sentimental in a foolish way [She loves to watch *corny* soap operas.]
corn·y • ***adjective*** **cornier, corniest**

coronation (kôr ə nā′shən) ***noun*** the act or ceremony of crowning a king or queen.
cor·o·na·tion • ***noun,*** *plural* **coronations**

coronet (kôr′ə net) ***noun*** a small crown worn by princes and other noble persons.
cor·o·net • ***noun,*** *plural* **coronets**

Corp. *abbreviation for* Corporation.

corporal (kôr′pər əl) ***noun*** a military noncommissioned officer.
cor·po·ral • ***noun,*** *plural* **corporals**

corporation (kôr pər ā′shən) ***noun*** a business or other organization that is allowed by law to

act as a single person. Cities and colleges, as well as businesses, can be organized as corporations.
cor·po·ra·tion • *noun, plural* **corporations**

corps (kôr) *noun* **1** a section or special branch of the armed forces [the Marine *Corps*]. **2** a group of people who act or work together [A reporter is a member of the press *corps*.]
corps • *noun, plural* **corps** (kôrz)
• The words **corps** and **core** sound alike.
My cousin joined the Marine *Corps*.
I threw the apple *core* away.

corpse (kôrps) *noun* the dead body of a person.
corpse • *noun, plural* **corpses**

corpuscle (kôr′pus əl) *noun* one of the red or white cells that float in the blood.
cor·pus·cle • *noun, plural* **corpuscles**

corral (kər al′) *noun* a place fenced in for holding horses or cattle.
verb **1** to round up or shut up in a corral [They *corralled* the wild horses.] **2** [*a slang use*] to get hold of; round up; seize [The teacher *corralled* students to hand out programs.]
cor·ral • *noun, plural* **corrals**
• *verb* **corralled, corralling**

correct (kər ekt′) *verb* **1** to get rid of mistakes in; make right [*Correct* your spelling before turning in your papers.] **2** to mark the mistakes in [The teacher *corrected* our papers.] **3** to make right by changing or adjusting [These new glasses will *correct* her eyesight.] **4** to scold or punish [They *corrected* their child for rudeness.] —Look for the WORD CHOICES box at the entry **punish**.
adjective **1** without a mistake; right [a *correct* answer] —Look for the WORD CHOICES box at the entry **true**. **2** proper [A written note is the *correct* way to thank people for a gift.]
cor·rect • *verb* **corrected, correcting**
• *adjective*

WORD CHOICES

Synonyms of **correct**

The words **correct, accurate,** and **exact** share the meaning "without mistakes."

a *correct* answer
an *accurate* report of the meeting
an *exact* quotation

correction (kər ek′shən) *noun* a change that corrects a mistake; a change from wrong to right [Write your *corrections* in the margin.]
cor·rec·tion • *noun, plural* **corrections**

correspond (kôr ə spänd′) *verb* **1** to be in agreement with; match [His opinions *correspond* with mine.] —Look for the WORD CHOICES box at the entry **coincide**. **2** to be the same or equal to [A general in the army *corresponds* to an admiral in the navy.] **3** to write letters to and receive letters from someone [Susan *corresponds* with her friends in California.]
cor·re·spond • *verb* **corresponded, corresponding**

correspondence (kôr ə spän′dəns) *noun* **1** the fact of corresponding; agreement [There is not much *correspondence* between his opinions and mine.] **2** the writing and receiving of letters. **3** the letters written or received [She is not allowed to read my *correspondence*.]
cor·re·spond·ence • *noun, plural* **correspondences**

correspondent (kôr ə spän′dənt) *noun* **1** a person who writes letters to another regularly. **2** a person who reports news, especially from a distant city or country.
cor·re·spond·ent • *noun, plural* **correspondents**

corridor (kôr′i dər) *noun* a long hall or passageway in a building, with rooms opening onto it.
cor·ri·dor • *noun, plural* **corridors**

corrode (kər ōd′) *verb* to eat into or wear away slowly [The strong acid *corroded* the metal.]
cor·rode • *verb* **corroded, corroding**

corrupt (kər upt′) *adjective* **1** capable of being bribed or of engaging in other dishonest behavior; crooked [The *corrupt* judge was forced to resign.] **2** having no morals; evil; wicked [the *corrupt* court of the Roman emperors].
verb to make or become corrupt [The lawyer tried to *corrupt* the judge.]
cor·rupt • *adjective* • *verb* **corrupted, corrupting**

corruption (kər up′shən) *noun* **1** the act of

a cat	ō go	ʉ fur	ə = a *in* ago
ā ape	ô law, for	ch chin	e *in* agent
ä cot, car	oo look	sh she	i *in* pencil
e ten	ōō tool	th thin	o *in* atom
ē me	oi oil	*th* then	u *in* circus
i fit	ou out	zh measure	
ī ice	u up	ŋ ring	

accepting a bribe or of engaging in other dishonest dealings [*corruption* in city government]. **2** evil or wicked ways.
cor·rup·tion • *noun*

corsage (kôr säzh′ *or* kôr säj′) ***noun*** a small bunch of flowers to be worn by a woman, usually at the shoulder.
cor·sage • ***noun,*** *plural* **corsages**

corsage

Cortés or **Cortez** (kôr tez′), **Hernando** (hər nan′dō) 1485-1547; Spanish soldier. He and his men conquered Mexico.
Cor·tés, Her·nan·do or **Cor·tez, Her·nan·do**

cosmetic (käz met′ik) ***noun*** any substance that is used to make the skin or hair beautiful. Lipstick and powder are cosmetics.
cos·met·ic • ***noun,*** *plural* **cosmetics**

cosmic (käz′mik) ***adjective*** having to do with the universe [*cosmic* rays from outer space].
cos·mic • ***adjective***

cost (kôst *or* käst) ***noun*** the amount of money asked and paid for something; price [The *cost* of meat is going up.]
verb **1** to be priced at [The book *costs* $15.] **2** to cause the loss of [The flood *cost* many lives.]
cost • ***noun,*** *plural* **costs** • ***verb*** **cost, costing**

Costa Rica (käs′tə rē′kə) a country in Central America.
Cos·ta Ri·ca

costly (kôst′lē *or* käst′lē) ***adjective*** costing much; expensive.
cost·ly • ***adjective*** **costlier, costliest**

WORD CHOICES

Synonyms of **costly**

The words **costly, expensive,** and **precious** share the meaning "high in price."

a *costly* dinner
an *expensive* coat
precious jewels

costume (käs′to͞om *or* käs′tyo͞om) ***noun*** **1** clothing worn at a certain time or place [an eighteenth-century *costume;* a Japanese *costume*]. **2** clothing worn by a person playing a part or by a person trying to look like someone else [pirate *costumes* for the school play].
cos·tume • ***noun,*** *plural* **costumes**

cot (kät) ***noun*** a narrow bed. A cot is usually made of canvas stretched on a frame that can be folded up.
cot • ***noun,*** *plural* **cots**

cottage (kät′ij) ***noun*** a small house [a peasant's *cottage;* a summer *cottage* at the beach].
cot·tage • ***noun,*** *plural* **cottages**

cottage cheese ***noun*** a soft, white cheese with a mild flavor. Cottage cheese is made from the curds of sour skim milk.

cotton (kät′n) ***noun*** **1** the fluffy white fibers around the seeds of a tall plant. These fibers are used to make thread or cloth. **2** this plant. **3** thread or cloth made of these fibers.
cot·ton • ***noun***

cotton

cottontail (kät′n tāl) ***noun*** an American rabbit that has brown or grayish fur and a short, white, fluffy tail.
cot·ton·tail • ***noun,*** *plural* **cottontails**

couch (kouch) ***noun*** a piece of furniture for seating two or more persons. A couch is usually upholstered and has a back.
couch • ***noun,*** *plural* **couches**

cougar (ko͞o′gər) ***noun*** a large wild cat that has a long, slender, tan body and a long tail. The cougar is found from Canada to southern South America.
cou·gar • ***noun,*** *plural* **cougars** or **cougar**

cough (kôf) ***verb*** **1** to force air from the lungs with a sudden, loud noise. **2** to get out of the throat by coughing.
noun **1** the act or sound of coughing. **2** an illness that causes a person to cough [She stayed home today with a bad *cough.*]
cough • ***verb*** **coughed, coughing** • ***noun,*** *plural* **coughs**

could (kood) ***verb*** (*helping verb*) **1** *past tense* *of* **can**[1]. **2** a helping verb with about the same meaning as **can**[1], but showing less force or sureness [You *could* be right. I *could* do it tomorrow.] The word "to" is not used between *could* and the verb that follows it.

couldn't (koo͝d′nt) could not.
could·n't

council (koun′səl) ***noun*** **1** a group of people meeting together to plan or decide something or to give advice. **2** a group of people elected to make the laws for a city or town.
coun·cil • ***noun,*** *plural* **councils**
• The words **council** and **counsel** sound alike.
Six *council* members showed up.
She refused to accept Mom's *counsel*.

counsel (koun′səl) ***noun*** **1** ideas or opinions about what to do; advice. **2** a lawyer or group of lawyers that are handling a case.
verb to give advice to; advise.
coun·sel • ***noun*** • ***verb*** **counseled** or **counselled, counseling** or **counselling**
• The words **counsel** and **council** sound alike.

counselor (koun′sə lər) ***noun*** **1** a person who gives counsel; advisor. **2** a lawyer. **3** a person who is in charge of children at a summer camp.
coun·se·lor • ***noun,*** *plural* **counselors**

count[1] (kount) ***verb*** **1** to name numbers in a regular order [I'll *count* to five.] **2** to add up so as to get a total [*Count* the people here.] **3** to take account of; include [There are ten here, *counting* you.] **4** to be taken into account; have importance, value, etc. [Every bit of help *counts*.] **5** to believe to be; consider [I *count* myself lucky.] **6** to depend on: used with *on* [You can *count* on us to help.] —Look for the WORD CHOICES box at the entry **rely**.
noun **1** the act of counting or adding up [By my *count*, you have already bought three dresses.] **2** the number reached by counting.
count • ***verb*** **counted, counting** • ***noun,*** *plural* **counts**

count[2] (kount) ***noun*** a nobleman in some European countries.
count • ***noun,*** *plural* **counts**

countdown (kount′doun) ***noun*** **1** the schedule of things or operations that have to be done in order just before the launching of a rocket or the start of an event. **2** the act of counting backward to zero to show how much time is left until the start of an event [The *countdown* for the launch has just started.]
count·down • ***noun,*** *plural* **countdowns**

counter[1] (kount′ər) ***noun*** **1** a long, flat surface on which things are sold or food is prepared, served, or eaten. Counters are found in some restaurants and in most kitchens and stores. **2** a small disk or other object that is used in counting or in games to keep score.
count·er • ***noun,*** *plural* **counters**

counter[2] (kount′ər) ***adverb*** in the opposite direction or way; contrary [The vote of the council went *counter* to the mayor's wishes.]
adjective opposing or opposite; contrary [Their political views are *counter* to mine.]
verb to go or act against; oppose [They *countered* my plans for the school pageant with suggestions of their own.]
coun·ter • ***adverb*** • ***adjective*** • ***verb*** **countered, countering**

counter- *a prefix meaning:* **1** opposite; against [When a medicine *counteracts* an illness, it acts against it.] **2** in return [A *counterattack* is an attack against another attack.]

counterclockwise (kount′ər kläk′wīz) ***adverb*** in a direction opposite to that in which the hands of a clock move [Turn the lid of the jar *counterclockwise* to open it.]
adjective moving in a counterclockwise direction [skating in a *counterclockwise* circle].
coun·ter·clock·wise • ***adverb*** • ***adjective***

counterfeit (kount′ər fit) ***adjective*** made in imitation of the real thing in order to fool or cheat people [*counterfeit* money] —Look for the WORD CHOICES box at the entry **false**.
noun a thing that is counterfeit.
verb to make a copy or imitation of in order to fool or cheat people.
coun·ter·feit • ***adjective*** • ***noun,*** *plural* **counterfeits** • ***verb*** **counterfeited, counterfeiting**

counterpart (kount′ər pärt) ***noun*** a person or thing that is like another [Their prime minister is the *counterpart* of our President.]
coun·ter·part • ***noun,*** *plural* **counterparts**

countess (kount′is) ***noun*** **1** the wife or widow of a count or earl. **2** a woman with the rank of a count or earl.
coun·tess • ***noun,*** *plural* **countesses**

a	cat	ō	go	ʉ	fur	ə =	a *in* ago
ā	ape	ô	law, for	ch	chin		e *in* agent
ä	cot, car	oo	look	sh	she		i *in* pencil
e	ten	o͞o	tool	th	thin		o *in* atom
ē	me	oi	oil	*th*	then		u *in* circus
i	fit	ou	out	zh	measure		
ī	ice	u	up	ŋ	ring		

countless (kount′lis) ***adjective*** too many to be counted [There are *countless* stars in the sky.]
count·less • ***adjective***

country (kun′trē) ***noun*** **1** an area of land in which a group of people live together under the same government; nation [The *country* of Japan is made up of islands.] **2** the people of a nation [The speech was broadcast to the whole *country*.] **3** the nation a person was born in or belongs to ["I miss my *country*," said the refugee.] **4** an area of land; region [the mountain *country* of Vermont]. **5** land with farms and small towns; land outside of cities [Let's drive out to the *country*.]
adjective of or having to do with the land outside of cities; rural [winding *country* roads] —Look for the WORD CHOICES box at the entry **rural**.
coun·try • ***noun**, plural* **countries** • ***adjective***

countryman (kun′trē mən) ***noun*** a man from one's own country.
coun·try·man • ***noun**, plural* **countrymen**

countryside (kun′trē sīd′) ***noun*** the land outside of cities; country; rural area.
coun·try·side • ***noun**, plural* **countrysides**

countrywoman (kun′trē woom′ən) ***noun*** a woman from one's own country.
coun·try·wom·an • ***noun**, plural* **countrywomen**

county (kount′ē) ***noun*** **1** in the U.S., one of the sections into which a State is divided. **2** one of the units into which some countries are divided for local government.
coun·ty • ***noun**, plural* **counties**

couple (kup′əl) ***noun*** **1** two things of the same kind that go together; pair. **2** a man and woman who are married, engaged, or partners in a dance, game, or other activity. **3** [*an informal use*] a few; several [I've got only a *couple* of dollars left after paying for dinner.]
verb to join together; unite [The workers *coupled* the railroad cars to the engine.]
cou·ple • ***noun**, plural* **couples** • ***verb*** **coupled, coupling**

coupon (ko͞o′pän *or* kyo͞o′pän) ***noun*** a ticket or part of a ticket or advertisement. A coupon can be exchanged for a gift, for money, or for a discount on the price of merchandise.
cou·pon • ***noun**, plural* **coupons**

courage (kur′ij) ***noun*** the quality of mind or character that makes a person able to face danger, pain, or trouble without fear; bravery.
cour·age • ***noun***

courageous (kər ā′jəs) ***adjective*** having or showing courage; brave [a *courageous* soldier].
cou·ra·geous • ***adjective***

course (kôrs) ***noun*** **1** forward or onward movement from one point to the next; progress in space or time [We travel to New York several times in the *course* of a year.] **2** a way or path along which something moves; channel; track [We followed the *course* of the river.] **3** the direction taken by something that moves [The captain set the ship's *course* for the islands.] **4** an area of land or water used for certain sports or games [a golf *course*]. **5** a complete series of studies [I took a business *course* in high school.] **6** a part of a meal served at one time [The main *course* was ham.]
—of course **1** as one expects; naturally [Room service is available, *of course*.] **2** without doubt; certainly [*Of course* we'll go.]
course • ***noun**, plural* **courses**

• The words **course** and **coarse** sound alike.
The ship changed *course*.
The salt is *coarse*, not fine.

court

court (kôrt) ***noun*** **1** an open space that is surrounded by buildings or enclosed by walls; courtyard. **2** a space that is marked out for playing certain games [a *basketball* court; a tennis *court*]. **3** the palace of a king or other ruler. **4** the family, advisors, and other followers of a king or other ruler. **5** a person or persons who examine and decide cases of law; judge or judges [the Supreme *Court*]. **6** a place where law trials are held.
verb **1** to pay attention to or try to please in order to get something [Politicians usually *court* the voters before an election.] **2** to try to get the love of in order to marry; woo [He's been *courting* her for five years.]

C

court • *noun, plural* **courts** • *verb* **courted, courting**

courteous (kʉr′tē əs) *adjective* polite and kind —Look for the WORD CHOICES box at the entry **civil**.
cour·te·ous • *adjective*

courtesy (kʉr′tə sē) *noun* **1** courteous or polite behavior [Thank you for your *courtesy* in replying to my letter.] **2** a polite act or remark.
cour·te·sy • *noun, plural for sense 2 only* **courtesies**

courthouse (kôrt′hous) *noun* **1** a building in which law trials are held. **2** a building that contains the offices of a county government.
court·house • *noun, plural* **courthouses**

courtier (kôr′tē ər) *noun* a member of the court of a king or other ruler.
cour·ti·er • *noun, plural* **courtiers**

courtyard

courtyard (kôrt′yärd) *noun* an open space that has buildings or walls around it.
court·yard • *noun, plural* **courtyards**

cousin (kuz′ən) *noun* the son or daughter of one's uncle or aunt.
cous·in • *noun, plural* **cousins**

cove (kōv) *noun* a small bay or inlet.
cove • *noun, plural* **coves**

cover (kuv′ər) *verb* **1** to place one thing over another [*Cover* the bird cage at night. *Cover* the wall with white paint.] **2** to spread over the surface of [Flood waters *covered* the fields.] **3** to keep from being seen or known; hide [He tried to *cover* up the scandal.] **4** to go; travel [The bus *covered* 300 miles that day.] **5** to get the news or pictures of [Many reporters *covered* the airplane crash.]
noun **1** something that covers something else. The lid of a jar, a blanket, and the stiff surface of a book are all covers. **2** anything that hides or protects [The prisoners escaped under *cover* of darkness.]
cov·er • *verb* **covered, covering** • *noun, plural* **covers**

covered wagon

covered wagon *noun* a large wagon with an arched cover of canvas. American pioneers traveled westward in covered wagons.
covered wagon • *noun, plural* **covered wagons**

covering (kuv′ər iŋ) *noun* anything that covers [A blanket is a *covering* for a bed.]
cov·er·ing • *noun, plural* **coverings**

covet (kuv′ət) *verb* to want something very much, especially something that belongs to another person [Mary *coveted* her sister's bike.]
cov·et • *verb* **coveted, coveting**

cow (kou) *noun* **1** the full-grown female of cattle. **2** the female of some other large animal such as seal, elephant, or whale.
cow • *noun, plural* **cows**

coward (kou′ərd) *noun* a person who has no courage or is easily frightened.
cow·ard • *noun, plural* **cowards**

cowardice (kou′ər dis) *noun* lack of courage; the way a coward acts or feels.
cow·ar·dice • *noun*

cowardly (kou′ərd lē) *adjective* of or like a coward [a *cowardly* action].
cow·ard·ly • *adjective*

a	cat	ō	go	ʉ	fur	ə =	a *in* ago
ā	ape	ô	law, for	ch	chin		e *in* agent
ä	cot, car	oo	look	sh	she		i *in* pencil
e	ten	ōō	tool	th	thin		o *in* atom
ē	me	oi	oil	*th*	then		u *in* circus
i	fit	ou	out	zh	measure		
ī	ice	u	up	ŋ	ring		

cowboy (kou′boi) ***noun*** a male ranch worker who herds and takes care of cattle.
cow·boy • ***noun,*** *plural* **cowboys**

cowgirl (kou′gurl) ***noun*** a female ranch worker who herds and takes care of cattle.
cow·girl • ***noun,*** *plural* **cowgirls**

coyote (kī ōt′ē *or* kī′ōt) ***noun*** an animal that looks like a small wolf and lives in the western prairies of North America.
coy·o·te • ***noun,*** *plural* **coyotes** or **coyote**

cozy (kō′zē) ***adjective*** warm and comfortable; snug [We were *cozy* in our sleeping bags.]
co·zy • ***adjective*** **cozier, coziest**

CPU (sē′pē′yoo′) ***noun*** the part of a computer that controls what the computer does. *CPU* is taken from the first letters of the words *central processing unit*.
CPU • ***noun,*** *plural* **CPUs**

crab (krab) ***noun*** a broad, flat shellfish with four pairs of legs and a pair of claws. Some kinds are used as food.
crab • ***noun,*** *plural* **crabs**

crab apple ***noun*** **1** a small, very sour apple that is used for making jelly and preserves. **2** the tree it grows on.
crab apple • ***noun,*** *plural* **crab apples**

crack (krak) ***verb*** **1** to make or cause to make a sudden, sharp noise like the sound of something breaking [The lion tamer *cracked* his whip.] **2** to break or split, with or without the pieces falling apart [The snowball *cracked* the window.] **3** [*an informal use*] to hit with a sudden, sharp blow [I *cracked* my knee against the desk.]
noun **1** a break that usually leaves the parts holding together [a *crack* in the window]. **2** a narrow opening [a *crack* in the fence]. **3** a sudden, sharp noise like the sound of something breaking [The rock hit the sidewalk with a loud *crack*.] **4** [*an informal use*] a sudden, sharp blow [a *crack* on the head].
—**crack down on** to become strict or stricter with [The police will *crack down on* gangs.]
crack • ***verb*** **cracked, cracking** • ***noun,*** *plural* **cracks**

cracker (krak′ər) ***noun*** a thin, crisp biscuit.
crack·er • ***noun,*** *plural* **crackers**

crackle (krak′əl) ***verb*** to make sharp, snapping sounds [The dry wood *crackled* as it burned.]
noun a series of such sounds.
crack·le • ***verb*** **crackled, crackling** • ***noun,*** *plural* **crackles**

cradle (krād′l) ***noun*** **1** a baby's small bed. It usually has rockers. **2** the place where something began [Boston is often called the *cradle* of the American Revolution.]
verb to rock or hold in a cradle or in a similar way [He gently *cradled* the baby in his arms.]
cra·dle • ***noun,*** *plural* **cradles**
• ***verb*** **cradled, cradling**

craft (kraft) ***noun*** **1** work that requires special skill in using the hands [the *craft* of weaving]. **2** skill in fooling or tricking people. **3** a boat, ship, or airplane.
craft • ***noun,*** *plural* **crafts** or *for sense 3* **craft**

craftsman (krafts′mən) ***noun*** a person with special skill in making things from wood, clay, yarn, paper, metal, or other material.
crafts·man • ***noun,*** *plural* **craftsmen**

crafty (kraf′tē) ***adjective*** skillful in fooling or tricking others; sly [a *crafty* person] —Look for the WORD CHOICES box at the entry **wily**.
craft·y • ***adjective*** **craftier, craftiest**

crag (krag) ***noun*** a steep, rugged rock that rises above other rocks or juts out from them.
crag • ***noun,*** *plural* **crags**

cram (kram) ***verb*** **1** to pack full or pack too full [My suitcase is *crammed* with clothes.] **2** to stuff or force [She *crammed* the papers into a drawer.] **3** to study many facts in a hurry [He *crammed* for the test the night before.]
cram • ***verb*** **crammed, cramming**

cramp (kramp) ***noun*** **1** a sharp, painful tightness in a muscle. It can be caused by the cold or by using the muscle too hard or too much. **2 cramps** sharp pains in the belly.
verb to cause a cramp in.
cramp • ***noun,*** *plural* **cramps**
• ***verb*** **cramped, cramping**

cranberry (kran′ber′ē) ***noun*** **1** a hard and sour red berry that is made into sauces, jelly, and juice. **2** the plant that it grows on. It is found in marshes and bogs.
cran·ber·ry • ***noun,*** *plural* **cranberries**

crane (krān) ***noun*** **1** a large wading bird that has very long legs and neck, and a long, straight bill. **2** a machine for lifting or moving heavy weights. One kind has a long, movable arm.
verb to stretch up or forward in trying to see better [I *craned* my neck to see the parade.]

C

crane • *noun, plural* **cranes** • *verb* **craned, craning**

crank (kraŋk) ***noun*** **1** a handle that is bent at right angles and connected to a shaft of a machine in order to turn the machine. The handle of a pencil sharpener and the bar that is attached to a bicycle's pedal are cranks. **2** [*an informal use*] a person who has odd, stubborn ideas about something.
verb to start or work by turning a crank.
crank • *noun, plural* **cranks** • *verb* **cranked, cranking**

cranky (kraŋʹkē) ***adjective*** cross or complaining [The *cranky* baby is probably hungry.]
crank·y • *adjective* **crankier, crankiest**

crash (krash) ***verb*** **1** to fall, hit, or break with force and with a loud, smashing noise. **2** to move forward or go with a loud noise [The tanks *crashed* through the rubble of the buildings.] **3** to fall to the earth and be damaged or smashed [The airplane *crashed*.] **4** to get into without an invitation or a ticket [Don't *crash* their party.] **5** to fail suddenly [The stock market *crashed*.]
noun **1** a loud, smashing noise. **2** the act of crashing [an airplane *crash*]. **3** a sudden failure or ruin [a *crash* in the stock market].
crash • *verb* **crashed, crashing** • *noun, plural* **crashes**

crate (krāt) ***noun*** a box that is made of wooden slats, for packing things [an orange *crate*].
crate • *noun, plural* **crates**

crater

crater (krātʹər) ***noun*** a hollow area that is shaped like a bowl [the *crater* of a volcano].
cra·ter • *noun, plural* **craters**

crave (krāv) ***verb*** to long for very much; want badly [He *craved* a big bowl of hot soup.] —Look for the WORD CHOICES box at the entry **desire**.
crave • *verb* **craved, craving**

craving (krāʹviŋ) ***noun*** a strong longing or appetite.
crav·ing • *noun, plural* **cravings**

crawfish (krôʹfish *or* kräʹfish) ***noun*** *the same as* **crayfish**.
craw·fish • *noun, plural* **crawfish** or **crawfishes**

crawl (krôl) ***verb*** **1** to move along the ground on the hands and knees in the way that a baby does. **2** to move slowly [The bus *crawled* up the hill.] **3** to be full of crawling things [The rotten log was *crawling* with worms.]
noun **1** a slow, gradual movement. **2** a swimming stroke. The swimmer keeps his face in the water, except for breathing, and kicks his feet without stopping.
crawl • *verb* **crawled, crawling** • *noun, plural* **crawls**

crayfish (krāʹfish) ***noun*** a small, freshwater shellfish that looks like a small lobster.
cray·fish • *noun, plural* **crayfish** or **crayfishes**

crayon (krāʹən *or* krāʹän) ***noun*** a small stick of colored wax, chalk, or charcoal that is used for drawing or writing.
verb to draw or color with crayons.
cray·on • *noun, plural* **crayons** • *verb* **crayoned, crayoning**

craze (krāz) ***noun*** a temporary fashion; fad.
craze • *noun, plural* **crazes**

crazy (krāʹzē) ***adjective*** **1** mentally ill; insane. **2** very foolish or unwise [a *crazy* idea]. **3** [*an informal use*] very eager or enthusiastic [I'm *crazy* about sports.]
cra·zy • *adjective* **crazier, craziest**

creak (krēk) ***verb*** to make a harsh, squeaking sound [The rusty hinges *creaked*.]
noun this kind of sound.
creak • *verb* **creaked, creaking** • *noun, plural* **creaks**
● The words **creak** and **creek** sound alike.
When he sat down, the chair gave a *creak*.
She fishes in the *creek*.

cream (krēm) ***noun*** **1** the oily, yellowish part

a cat	ō go	ʉ fur	ə = a *in* ago
ā ape	ô law, for	ch chin	e *in* agent
ä cot, car	oo look	sh she	i *in* pencil
e ten	ōō tool	th thin	o *in* atom
ē me	oi oil	*th* then	u *in* circus
i fit	ou out	zh measure	
ī ice	u up	ŋ ring	

of milk that rises to the top and contains the fat that is made into butter. **2** a food that is made of cream or is like cream [ice *cream*]. **3** a smooth, oily substance that is used to clean and soften the skin. **4** the best part [the *cream* of the crop].
cream • *noun, plural* **creams**

creamy (krēm′ē) ***adjective*** of, like, or full of cream; smooth and rich.
cream·y • ***adjective*** **creamier, creamiest**

crease (krēs) ***noun*** a line or ridge that is made by folding or pressing [The *creases* in a pair of trousers must be straight.]
verb to make a crease or creases in.
crease • *noun, plural* **creases**
• ***verb*** **creased, creasing**

create (krē āt′) ***verb*** **1** to bring into being; make [That artist has *created* many fine paintings.] **2** to bring about; give rise to; cause [New industries can *create* new jobs.]
cre·ate • ***verb*** **created, creating**

WORD CHOICES

Synonyms of **create**

The words **create, invent,** and **originate** share the meaning "to bring into being."

Shakespeare *created* interesting characters.

Alexander Graham Bell *invented* the telephone.

The English *originated* government postage stamps.

creation (krē ā′shən) ***noun*** **1** the act or process of creating something [The *creation* of a work of art takes time and effort.] **2** the whole universe and everything in it. **3** something that is created or brought into being.
cre·a·tion • *noun, plural* **creations**

creative (krē āt′iv) ***adjective*** creating or able to create things; having imagination and ability.
cre·a·tive • ***adjective***

creator (krē āt′ər) ***noun*** a person who creates.
—**the Creator** God; the Supreme Being.
cre·a·tor • *noun, plural* **creators**

creature (krē′chər) ***noun*** a living being; any person or animal.
crea·ture • *noun, plural* **creatures**

credit (kred′it) ***noun*** **1** belief; trust [I don't give much *credit* to what he says.] **2** praise or approval [I give her *credit* for trying to do it.] **3** a person or thing that brings praise [She's a *credit* to the team.] **4** trust that a person will pay later [This store doesn't give *credit*, so you have to pay cash.]
verb to add to a person's account [*Credit* her with $10.00.]
cred·it • *noun, plural* **credits**
• ***verb*** **credited, crediting**

credit card ***noun*** a card that entitles its owner to charge bills at stores, hotels, restaurants, and other businesses.
credit card • *noun, plural* **credit cards**

creed (krēd) ***noun*** **1** a statement of the main beliefs of a religion. **2** a belief or set of beliefs that guides a person.
creed • *noun, plural* **creeds**

creek (krēk *or* krik) ***noun*** a small stream, a little larger than a brook.
creek • *noun, plural* **creeks**
• The words **creek** and **creak** sound alike.
The *creek* runs past our house.
The floors *creak* in the old house.

creep (krēp) ***verb*** **1** to move along with the body close to the ground, in the way that a baby does. **2** to move slowly [The heavy traffic *crept* along.] **3** to grow along the ground or a wall [Ivy *crept* up the side of the house.]
noun the act of creeping.
—**the creeps** [*an informal use*] a feeling of fear or disgust, like the feeling of insects crawling on the skin.
creep • ***verb*** **crept, creeping** • ***noun,*** *plural* **creeps**

creepy (krē′pē) ***adjective*** **1** causing a feeling of disgust, as if insects were crawling on the skin. **2** having this kind of feeling [That scary movie makes me feel *creepy*.]
creep·y • ***adjective*** **creepier, creepiest**

Creole (krē′ōl) ***noun*** **1** a person who is a descendant of the first French settlers in Louisiana. **2** the kind of French that these people speak.
Cre·ole • *noun, plural* **Creoles**

crepe (krāp; *for sense 2 also* krep) ***noun*** **1** a thin, crinkled type of cloth. **2** a very thin pancake that is rolled up or folded with a filling.
crepe • *noun, plural* **crepes**

crepe paper ***noun*** thin paper that is crinkled like crepe.

crept (krept) *verb past tense and past participle of* **creep**.

crescent (kres′ənt) *noun* the slim, curved shape that the moon has twice a month.
cres·cent • *noun, plural* **crescents**

crest (krest) *noun* **1** a tuft of feathers or fur on the head of some birds and animals. **2** the top of anything [the *crest* of a wave].
crest • *noun, plural* **crests**

crevice (krev′is) *noun* a narrow opening that is caused by a crack or split.
crev·ice • *noun, plural* **crevices**

crew (kro͞o) *noun* **1** all the people who work on a ship or aircraft. **2** any group of people who work together [a road *crew*].
crew • *noun, plural* **crews**

crew cut *noun* a style of haircut for men and boys. The hair is cut very close to the head.
crew cut • *noun, plural* **crew cuts**

crib (krib) *noun* **1** a small bed with high sides, for a baby. **2** a structure that is made of slats and used for storing grain [a corn *crib*]. **3** a box or trough for feeding animals.
crib • *noun, plural* **cribs**

cricket

cricket (krik′ət) *noun* a leaping insect that is related to the grasshopper. The male cricket makes a chirping sound by rubbing its front wings together.
crick·et • *noun, plural* **crickets**

crime (krīm) *noun* **1** an act or a kind of behavior that breaks the law. **2** actions like this, thought of as a group [She fights *crime*.] **3** an evil or foolish act; a sin [It would be a *crime* to waste this food.]
crime • *noun, plural* **crimes**

criminal (krim′i nəl) *adjective* **1** having the qualities of crime [a *criminal* act]. **2** having to do with crime [*criminal* law].
noun a person who is guilty of a crime.
crim·i·nal • *adjective* • *noun, plural* **criminals**

crimson (krim′zən *or* krim′sən) *adjective* deep red [Blood is *crimson*.]
noun a deep-red color.
crim·son • *adjective* • *noun*

cringe (krinj) *verb* to draw back or tremble with fear [The dog *cringed* and slunk away.]
cringe • *verb* **cringed, cringing**

crinkle (kriŋ′kəl) *verb* **1** to make or become full of wrinkles or creases [He *crinkled* the ribbons on the birthday present.] **2** to make a sound like the sound of paper being crushed.
crin·kle • *verb* **crinkled, crinkling**

cripple (krip′əl) *verb* **1** to hurt or injure in a way that makes movement difficult or impossible —Look for the WORD CHOICES box at the entry **maim**. **2** to hurt or weaken [The quake *crippled* the city.]
noun a person or animal that is hurt and cannot move in a normal way. Some people think it is unkind to use this word about a person.
crip·ple • *verb* **crippled, crippling** • *noun, plural* **cripples**

crisis (krī′sis) *noun* a time of great danger, difficulty, or anxiety about the future.
cri·sis • *noun, plural* **crises** (krī′sēz)

crisp (krisp) *adjective* **1** hard or firm, but easy to break or snap [*crisp* bacon; *crisp* lettuce]. **2** fresh and tingling [cold, *crisp* air]. **3** sharp, clear, and to the point ["No comment" was his *crisp* reply.]
crisp • *adjective* **crisper, crispest**

crisscross (kris′krôs) *adjective* **1** marked with crossing lines [a *crisscross* pattern]. **2** moving in crossing lines.
verb **1** to move in crossing lines or back and forth across [Patrols *crisscrossed* the valley.] **2** to form a pattern of crossing lines [Railroad tracks *crisscross* the valley.]
criss·cross • *adjective* • *verb* **crisscrossed, crisscrossing**

critic (krit′ik) *noun* **1** a person whose work is judging things. A critic may write about books, plays, music, or restaurants. **2** a person who is quick to find fault.
crit·ic • *noun, plural* **critics**

critical (krit′i kəl) *adjective* **1** tending to find fault or disapprove [You're too *critical* of other people.] **2** having to do with critics or criticism. **3** dangerous or risky; causing worry [The school's budget is in a *critical* condition.]
crit·i·cal • *adjective*

criticism (krit′i siz′əm) *noun* **1** the act of forming judgments about things. **2** the act of

a	cat	ō	go	ʉ	fur	ə =	a *in* ago
ā	ape	ô	law, for	ch	chin		e *in* agent
ä	cot, car	oo	look	sh	she		i *in* pencil
e	ten	o͞o	tool	th	thin		o *in* atom
ē	me	oi	oil	*th*	then		u *in* circus
i	fit	ou	out	zh	measure		
ī	ice	u	up	ŋ	ring		

finding fault; disapproval [Your blunt *criticism* of his behavior annoyed him greatly.]
crit·i·cism • *noun, plural* **criticisms**

criticize (krit′i sīz′) *verb* **1** to judge as a critic [She *criticized* the artist's work for the daily newspaper.] **2** to find fault with; disapprove of [The boss *criticizes* everything I do.]
crit·i·cize • *verb* **criticized, criticizing**

WORD CHOICES

Synonyms of **criticize**

The words **criticize, blame,** and **complain** share the meaning "to find fault with."

Drivers *criticized* the way the road was built.

I don't *blame* you for being angry.

The students *complained* about the food in the cafeteria.

critter (krit′ər) *noun* a creature; an animal. This word is mainly a dialect word.
crit·ter • *noun, plural* **critters**

croak (krōk) *verb* to make a deep, hoarse sound in the throat [Frogs and ravens *croak*.]
noun a deep, hoarse sound.
croak • *verb* **croaked, croaking** • *noun, plural* **croaks**

Croatia (krō ā′shə) a country in southeastern Europe. It was a part of Yugoslavia.
Cro·a·tia

crochet (krō shā′) *noun* a kind of needlework done with yarn or thread and one hooked needle.
verb **1** to do this kind of needlework by pulling loops of yarn through one another with a hooked needle. **2** to make by doing this.
cro·chet • *noun* • *verb* **crocheted, crocheting**

crocodile

crocodile (kräk′ə dīl) *noun* a large reptile with a long body and tail, tough skin, a long, pointed snout, and four short legs. Crocodiles live in rivers and swamps in many warm areas of the earth. They are related to alligators.
croc·o·dile • *noun, plural* **crocodiles**

crocus (krō′kəs) *noun* a small plant that grows from an underground stem like a bulb. It has a yellow, purple, or white flower and is one of the first plants to bloom in spring.
cro·cus • *noun, plural* **crocuses**

crook (kro͝ok) *noun* **1** a thing or part that is bent [a *crook* in the road]. **2** a shepherd's staff with a hook at the end. **3** [*an informal use*] a person who steals or cheats.
verb to bend or curve.
crook • *noun, plural* **crooks** • *verb* **crooked** (kro͝okt), **crooking**

crooked (kro͝ok′əd) *adjective* **1** not straight; bent, curved, or twisted [a *crooked* road]. **2** not honest; tending to cheat or steal.
crook·ed • *adjective*

crop (kräp) *noun* **1** a farm product that is grown in the soil [Their main *crop* is wheat.] **2** the amount of a farm product that is grown or produced at one time [This year's apple *crop* is rather small.] **3** a group of things or persons [We have a new *crop* of students every fall.] **4** a pouch in the tube between a bird's mouth and its stomach. Food is stored in this pouch before digestion. **5** a short whip with a loop at the end. It is used in horseback riding.
verb **1** to cut or bite off the tops or ends of [The sheep *cropped* the grass.] **2** to cut short; to trim [He *cropped* the boy's hair.]
—**crop up** to come up or appear in a way that is not expected.
crop • *noun, plural* **crops** • *verb* **cropped, cropping**

croquet (krō kā′) *noun* an outdoor game that is usually played on a lawn. Each player uses a wooden hammer with a long handle to hit a wooden ball through hoops on the ground.
cro·quet • *noun*

cross (krôs) *noun* **1** an upright post with a bar across it near the top. **2** the figure of a cross that is used as a symbol of the Christian religion because Jesus died on a cross. **3** any trouble that a person has to deal with [A sick child had been Mrs. Brown's *cross* to bear.] **4** a design or mark that is made by crossing lines. **5** the result of mixing different breeds of animals or plants [A bull terrier is a *cross* between a bulldog and a terrier.]

verb **1** to place across, or one over the other [I sat back and *crossed* my legs.] **2** to draw a line or lines across [*Cross* your *t*'s.] **3** to lie or cut across; intersect [The two roads *cross* in Greenville.] **4** to go from one side to the other of [The bridge *crosses* the river.] **5** to pass each other while moving in opposite directions [Our letters *crossed* in the mail.] **6** to oppose or hinder [No one likes to be *crossed*.] **7** to mix different breeds of [They *crossed* a donkey with a horse.]
adjective **1** lying or passing across; crossing [a *cross* street]. **2** cranky or irritable; having a bad temper [My cat is always *cross*.] —Look for the WORD CHOICES box at the entry **irritable**.
—**cross off** to cancel by drawing lines across [The coach *crossed* my name *off* the list.]
cross • ***noun,*** *plural* **crosses** • ***verb*** **crossed, crossing** • ***adjective*** **crosser, crossest**

crossbow

crossbow (krôs′bō) ***noun*** a weapon that was used in the Middle Ages and is now sometimes used for hunting. It is a bow that lies across a long, thin wooden body.
cross·bow • ***noun,*** *plural* **crossbows**

cross-eyed (krôs′īd) ***adjective*** having the eyes turned toward each other.

crossing (krôs′iŋ) ***noun*** **1** a place where lines or streets cross one another. **2** a place where it is possible to cross a street, river, or railroad.
cross·ing • ***noun,*** *plural* **crossings**

cross-reference (krôs′ref ər əns) ***noun*** a note telling a reader to look in another place in a book, list, dictionary, or other publication for more information.
cross-ref·er·ence • ***noun,*** *plural* **cross-references**

crossroad (krôs′rōd) ***noun*** **1** a road that crosses another road. **2** *usually* **crossroads** [*often used with a singular verb*] the place where roads cross each other [We turned left at the *crossroads*.]
cross·road • ***noun,*** *plural* **crossroads**

cross section ***noun*** **1** a piece that is taken from an object with a single cut straight through it. A cross section shows how the inside or hidden part of something is put together [a *cross section* of an apple]. **2** a sample that has enough of each kind in it to show what the whole is like [a *cross section* of the city's voters].
cross section • ***noun,*** *plural* **cross sections**

crosswalk (krôs′wôk) ***noun*** a lane that is marked off for people to use in walking across a street.
cross·walk • ***noun,*** *plural* **crosswalks**

crossword puzzle (krôs′wurd) ***noun*** a puzzle that consists of a large square that is made up of blank spaces. These spaces are to be filled with letters that form certain words. Clues to these words are given with the square.
cross·word puzzle • ***noun,*** *plural* **crossword puzzles**

crotch (kräch) ***noun*** **1** the place where branches fork from a tree. **2** the place where the legs fork from the human body. **3** the place where the legs of a pair of pants meet.
crotch • ***noun,*** *plural* **crotches**

crouch (krouch) ***verb*** to stoop with the legs bent close to the ground [The tiger *crouched*.]
noun the act or position of crouching.
crouch • ***verb*** **crouched, crouching** • ***noun,*** *plural* **crouches**

crow

a cat	ō go	ur fur	ə = a *in* ago
ā ape	ô law, for	ch chin	e *in* agent
ä cot, car	oo look	sh she	i *in* pencil
e ten	ōō tool	th thin	o *in* atom
ē me	oi oil	*th* then	u *in* circus
i fit	ou out	zh measure	
ī ice	u up	ŋ ring	

crow[1] (krō) *noun* a large black bird that is known for its harsh cry, or caw.
—as the crow flies in a straight line between two places.
crow • *noun, plural* **crows**

crow[2] (krō) *verb* **1** to make the shrill cry of a rooster. **2** to boast with glee; gloat [Stop *crowing* over your victory.] —Look for the WORD CHOICES box at the entry **brag**.
noun the shrill cry of a rooster.
crow • *verb* **crowed, crowing** • *noun, plural* **crows**

Crow (krō) *noun* **1** a member of a North American Indian people of eastern Montana. **2** the language of this people.
Crow • *noun, plural for sense 1 only* **Crows** or **Crow**

crowbar (krō′bär) *noun* a long metal bar that has one end that is like a chisel. It is used for prying objects.
crow·bar • *noun, plural* **crowbars**

crowd (kroud) *noun* **1** a large group of people gathered together [a *crowd* of football fans]. **2** people in general [Don't just follow the *crowd* in everything. Be yourself.]
verb **1** to push or squeeze [Can we all *crowd* into one car?] **2** to come together in a large group [People *crowded* to see the show.] **3** to pack or fill too full [Don't *crowd* the room with furniture.]
crowd • *noun, plural* **crowds**
• *verb* **crowded, crowding**

crown (kroun) *noun* **1** a covering or decoration for the head that is made of gold, silver, and jewels. It is worn by a king or queen. **2** often **Crown** the power, position, or government of a king or queen. **3** a wreath that is worn on the head as a sign of honor or victory. **4** the top part of something [the *crown* of a hat]. **5** the part of a tooth that sticks out from the gum.
verb **1** to make a king or queen by putting a crown on [Elizabeth II was *crowned* queen in 1952.] **2** to honor or reward [The winner was *crowned* with glory.] **3** to be at the top of [Woods *crowned* the hill.]
crown • *noun, plural* **crowns**
• *verb* **crowned, crowning**

crow's-nest (krōz′nest) *noun* a small box or platform near the top of a ship's mast.
crow's-nest • *noun, plural* **crow's-nests**

crucial (kro͞o′shəl) *adjective* of the greatest importance; needed in order to decide something [The final exam is *crucial* to your grade.]
cru·cial • *adjective*

crude (kro͞od) *adjective* **1** in its natural or raw condition, before it has been prepared for use [*crude* oil]. **2** lacking finish, grace, tact, or manners [a *crude* remark]. **3** not carefully made or done; rough [a *crude* drawing].
crude • *adjective* **cruder, crudest**

cruel (kro͞o′əl) *adjective* **1** having no mercy or pity; liking to make others suffer [The *cruel* king made slaves of the enemy.] **2** causing pain and suffering [*cruel* insults; a *cruel* winter].
cru·el • *adjective*

cruelty (kro͞o′əl tē) *noun* the quality of being cruel [a dictator famous for his *cruelty*].
cru·el·ty • *noun, plural* **cruelties**

cruise (kro͞oz) *verb* **1** to sail or drive about from place to place, for pleasure or in search of something. **2** to move smoothly at an efficient speed [The airplane *cruised* at 300 mph.]
noun a ship voyage for pleasure.
cruise • *verb* **cruised, cruising** • *noun, plural* **cruises**

cruiser (kro͞oz′ər) *noun* **1** a fast ship for use in war. A cruiser is smaller than a battleship and has less powerful guns. **2** a police car. **3** a large motorboat with a cabin equipped with facilities for living on board.
cruis·er • *noun, plural* **cruisers**

crumb (krum) *noun* a tiny piece that is broken off from bread, cake, or something similar.
crumb • *noun, plural* **crumbs**

SPELLING TIP

Use this memory aid to spell **crumb**.
When you spell ***crumb***, think of the ***b*** in crum**b**le.

crumble (krum′bəl) *verb* to break into crumbs or small pieces [Don't *crumble* the crackers into your soup. The old plaster walls *crumbled*.]
crum·ble • *verb* **crumbled, crumbling**

crumple (krum′pəl) *verb* to crush or become crushed together into creases; to wrinkle [*Crumple* the paper in your hand.]

crum·ple • *verb* **crumpled, crumpling**

crunch (krunch) ***verb*** **1** to chew with a noisy, crackling sound [The children *crunched* their raw carrots.] **2** to grind or move over with a noisy, crushing sound [The wheels *crunched* the pebbles in the driveway.]
noun **1** the act or sound of crunching [My arm broke with a *crunch*.] **2** [*a slang use*] a tight or difficult situation.
crunch • *verb* **crunched, crunching** • *noun, plural* **crunches**

crunchy (krunch′ē) ***adjective*** making a crunching sound when it is chewed or broken.
crunch·y • *adjective* **crunchier, crunchiest**

crusade (kro͞o sād′) ***noun*** **1** *sometimes* **Crusade** any one of the wars that Christians from Western Europe fought in the years between 1000 and 1300. Their goal was to capture the Holy Land from the Muslims. **2** a fight for a cause that is thought to be good or against something that is thought to be bad [a *crusade* for better housing; a *crusade* against cancer].
verb to take part in a crusade [The citizens *crusaded* against crime.]
cru·sade • *noun, plural* **crusades** • *verb* **crusaded, crusading**

crush (krush) ***verb*** **1** to press or squeeze with force so that something is broken, hurt, or put out of shape [He *crushed* his hat when he sat on it.] **2** to bring to an end by force [The government *crushed* the revolt.] **3** to become crumpled or wrinkled [That cotton scarf *crushes* easily.]
noun **1** a large group of people or things that are crowded together [We were caught in a *crush* of people leaving the stadium.] **2** [*an informal use*] a strong attraction toward someone [She has a *crush* on Brian.]
crush • *verb* **crushed, crushing** • *noun, plural* **crushes**

Crusoe (kro͞o′sō), **Robinson** (räb′in sən) the hero of a famous novel, *Robinson Crusoe*, who is shipwrecked on a desert island. The novel was first published in 1719.
Cru·soe, Rob·in·son

crust (krust) ***noun*** **1** the hard, crisp outer part of bread. **2** the shell or cover of a pie. It is made of flour and shortening. **3** a hard covering or top layer [a *crust* of snow].
verb to cover or become covered with a crust [The storm *crusted* the roofs with ice.]
crust • *noun, plural* **crusts** • *verb* **crusted, crusting**

crustacean (krus tā′shən) ***noun*** an animal that has a hard outer shell and usually lives in water. Shrimps, crabs, and lobsters are crustaceans.
crus·ta·cean • *noun, plural* **crustaceans**

WORD HISTORY

crustacean

The word **crustacean** comes from a modern scientific Latin word that means "having a crust or shell," which was made from the Latin word for "crust."

crusty (krus′tē) ***adjective*** having a crust or like a crust [warm, *crusty* bread; *crusty* snow].
crust·y • *adjective* **crustier, crustiest**

crutch (kruch) ***noun*** a wooden or metal support for a person who cannot walk or stand alone easily. The padded top of a crutch fits under the armpit. Crutches are often used in pairs.
crutch • *noun, plural* **crutches**

crutch

cry (krī) ***verb*** **1** to show sorrow, pain, or other strong feelings by sobbing or shedding tears. **2** to say loudly; to shout ["Help! Help!" the victim *cried*.] **3** to bring into a certain condition by crying [I *cried* myself to sleep.]
noun **1** a shout or call [I heard a *cry* for help.] **2** a fit of sobbing and weeping [I had a good *cry* and fell asleep.] **3** the special sound that an animal makes [the *cry* of a lost sheep].
cry • *verb* **cried, crying, cries** • *noun, plural* **cries**

a cat	ō go	ʉ fur	ə = a *in* ago
ā ape	ô law, for	ch chin	e *in* agent
ä cot, car	oo look	sh she	i *in* pencil
e ten	o͞o tool	th thin	o *in* atom
ē me	oi oil	*th* then	u *in* circus
i fit	ou out	zh measure	
ī ice	u up	ŋ ring	

WORD CHOICES

Synonyms of **cry**

Many words share the meaning "to make sounds of sorrow or pain."

groan	sob	whimper
moan	wail	

crystal (kris′təl) ***noun*** **1** a clear, transparent quartz that looks like glass. **2** a very clear, sparkling glass. **3** the glass or plastic cover over the face of a watch or clock. **4** any of the regularly shaped pieces into which many substances are formed when they become solids. A crystal has a number of flat surfaces and an orderly arrangement. Salt, sugar, and snow are made up of crystals.
crys·tal • ***noun,*** *plural* **crystals**

CT or **Ct.** *abbreviation for* Connecticut.

cub (kub) ***noun*** the young offspring of the lion, bear, whale, or certain other mammals.
cub • ***noun,*** *plural* **cubs**

Cuba (kyo͞o′bə) a country on an island in the West Indies.
Cu·ba

cube (kyo͞ob) ***noun*** **1** a solid object with six square sides that are the same size. **2** a thing that has this shape. **3** the result of multiplying a number by itself and then multiplying the product by the same number. The cube of 2 is 8 because 2 x 2 x 2 = 8.
verb to cut into cubes [I *cubed* apples.]
cube • ***noun,*** *plural* **cubes** • ***verb*** **cubed, cubing**

cubic (kyo͞o′bik) ***adjective*** **1** shaped like a cube. **2** having a length, a width, and a height [A *cubic* foot is the volume of a cube that is one foot long, one foot wide, and one foot high.]
cu·bic • ***adjective***

cubicle (kyo͞o′bi kəl) ***noun*** a small, separate room or compartment that is used for studying, sleeping, or some other purpose.
cu·bi·cle • ***noun,*** *plural* **cubicles**

Cub Scout ***noun*** a member of a division of the Boy Scouts for boys eight to ten years old.
Cub Scout • ***noun,*** *plural* **Cub Scouts**

cuckoo (ko͞o′ko͞o) ***noun*** a dull-brown bird with a long, slender body. The bird's name is an imitation of this sound.
adjective [*a slang use*] crazy or silly.
cuck·oo • ***noun,*** *plural* **cuckoos** • ***adjective***

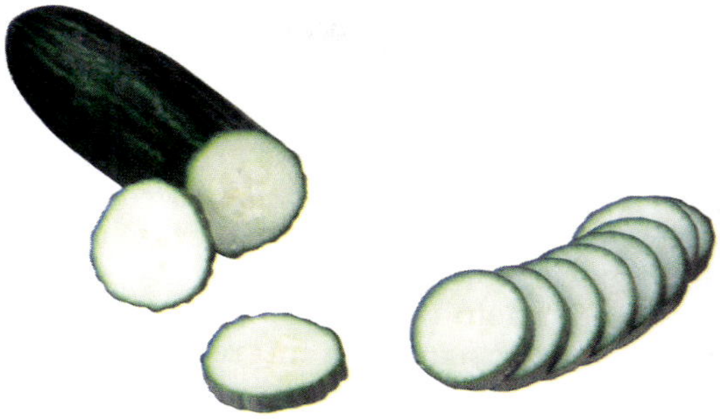

cucumber

cucumber (kyo͞o′kum bər) ***noun*** **1** a long vegetable with a green skin and firm, white flesh. It is used in salads and made into pickles. **2** the vine that it grows on.
cu·cum·ber • ***noun,*** *plural* **cucumbers**

cud (kud) ***noun*** a mouthful of swallowed food from the stomach of a cow, sheep, goat, or other similar mammal. The animal brings the food back up to chew it again a second time.
cud • ***noun,*** *plural* **cuds**

cuddle (kud′l) ***verb*** **1** to hold in a loving and gentle way in the arms [They *cuddled* the baby.] **2** to lie close and snug; nestle.
cud·dle • ***verb*** **cuddled, cuddling**

cuddly (kud′lē) ***adjective*** lovable and cute, or soft and furry, in a way that makes people want to cuddle it [a *cuddly* baby; a *cuddly* puppy].
cud·dly • ***adjective*** **cuddlier, cuddliest**

cue (kyo͞o) ***noun*** **1** the last few words in an actor's speech that are a signal to another actor to enter or to speak. **2** a signal, hint, or suggestion [Give me a *cue* when you want to go.]
verb to give a cue to [*Cue* me when it's time.]
cue • ***noun,*** *plural* **cues** • ***verb*** **cued, cuing** or **cueing**

cuff[1] (kuf) ***noun*** **1** a band at the wrist of a sleeve. **2** a fold that is turned up at the bottom of either leg on a pair of trousers.
cuff • ***noun,*** *plural* **cuffs**

cuff[2] (kuf) ***verb*** to hit with the open hand; to slap [*Cuff* the dog if it tries to jump up.]
noun a slap.
cuff • ***verb*** **cuffed, cuffing** • ***noun,*** *plural* **cuffs**

cult (kult) ***noun*** **1** a way of worshiping; system

C

of religious rites. **2** a group of people, often living in a colony, with a very strong leader and very strong, extreme religious beliefs. **3** very great enthusiasm for something that is popular for a time.
cult • *noun, plural* **cults**

cultivate (kul′ti vāt) *verb* **1** to prepare and use for growing crops [He *cultivated* his land with care.] **2** to grow from seeds or other plant parts [She *cultivates* many types of roses.] **3** to help to grow by care, training, or study [She *cultivated* an interest in music.]
cul·ti·vate • *verb* **cultivated, cultivating**

cultivator (kul′ti vāt′ər) *noun* a tool or machine for loosening the soil and killing weeds around plants.
cul·ti·va·tor • *noun, plural* **cultivators**

cultural (kul′chər əl) *adjective* having to do with culture [concerts and other *cultural* events].
cul·tu·ral • *adjective*

culture (kul′chər) *noun* **1** the ideas, skills, arts, tools, and way of life of a certain people at a certain time; civilization [the *culture* of the Aztecs]. **2** the quality in a person or group that is the result of a love for the arts, knowledge, and good taste. **3** the process of raising or improving a certain plant or animal [rose *culture*]. **4** a growth of bacteria that is made for medical or scientific research.
cul·ture • *noun, plural* **cultures**

cumbersome (kum′bər səm) *adjective* hard to handle because of size, weight, or number of parts; clumsy [a *cumbersome* package].
cum·ber·some • *adjective*

cunning (kun′iŋ) *adjective* skillful in cheating or tricking; crafty or sly.
noun skill in cheating or tricking.
cun·ning • *adjective* • *noun*

cup (kup) *noun* **1** a small container for drinking from, in the shape of a bowl and usually with a handle. **2** the amount that a cup holds; cupful [We need a *cup* of flour.] **3** a cup and what it holds [Order me a *cup* of cocoa, please.] **4** something that is shaped like a cup or bowl [The winner of the race received a silver *cup*.]
verb to shape like a cup [*Cup* your hands to hold these little candies.]
cup • *noun, plural* **cups** • *verb* **cupped, cupping**

cupboard (kub′ərd) *noun* a cabinet or closet with shelves for holding dishes or food.
cup·board • *noun, plural* **cupboards**

cupcake (kup′kāk) *noun* a little cake for one person. It is baked in a small, cup-shaped mold.
cup·cake • *noun, plural* **cupcakes**

cupful (kup′fo͝ol) *noun* the amount a cup will hold.
cup·ful • *noun, plural* **cupfuls**

cupola (kyo͞o′pə lə) *noun* **1** a rounded roof or ceiling. **2** a small dome on a roof.
cu·po·la • *noun, plural* **cupolas**

cupola

curb (kʉrb) *noun* **1** the stone or concrete border at either side of a street. **2** something that checks or holds back [Fear of being punished can be a *curb* to bad behavior.] **3** a chain or strap that is attached to a horse's bit. It holds the horse back when the reins are pulled.
verb to hold back; restrain [Try to *curb* your appetite.]
curb • *noun, plural* **curbs** • *verb* **curbed, curbing**

curd (kʉrd) *noun often* **curds** the thick, clotted part of milk that has been made sour. It is used for making cheese.
curd • *noun, plural* **curds**

curdle (kʉrd′l) *verb* to form into curd or clots; form little lumps [Milk *curdles* when you add lemon juice to it.]
cur·dle • *verb* **curdled, curdling**

cure (kyoor) *noun* **1** something that makes a sick person well; a treatment or remedy [Penicillin is a *cure* for pneumonia.] **2** the fact or process of healing or being healed [The child's *cure* was long and difficult.]
verb **1** to make well; heal [The doctor has *cured* me.] **2** to keep from spoiling by drying or by using salt or smoke [He *cured* pork to make bacon.]

a cat	ō go	ʉ fur	ə = a *in* ago
ā ape	ô law, for	ch chin	e *in* agent
ä cot, car	oo look	sh she	i *in* pencil
e ten	o͞o tool	th thin	o *in* atom
ē me	oi oil	*th* then	u *in* circus
i fit	ou out	zh measure	
ī ice	u up	ŋ ring	

cure • *noun, plural* **cures** • *verb* **cured, curing**

curfew (kʉr′fyo͞o) *noun* a time in the evening after which certain persons or all people are not allowed to be on the streets.
cur·few • *noun, plural* **curfews**

Curie (kyo͞o rē′), **Marie** (mə rē′) 1867-1934; Polish scientist living in France. She and her husband discovered radium.
Cu·rie, Ma·rie

curiosity (kyoor′ē äs′i tē) *noun* **1** a strong feeling of wanting to know or learn [*Curiosity* is a great teacher.] **2** a strange or unusual thing [A gold coin is now a *curiosity*.]
cu·ri·os·i·ty • *noun, plural* **curiosities**

curious (kyoor′ē əs) *adjective* **1** wanting very much to learn or know [*curious* about the origin of the sun]. **2** strange or unusual [some *curious* names on the old map].
cu·ri·ous • *adjective*

curl (kʉrl) *verb* **1** to twist into coils [She *curled* her hair.] **2** to move in circles or rings [The fog *curled* around our feet.] **3** to curve or bend around; roll up [I *curled* up on the sofa.]
noun **1** a little coil of hair. **2** anything curled [A *curl* of smoke rose from the chimney.]
curl • *verb* **curled, curling** • *noun, plural* **curls**

curly (kʉr′lē) *adjective* tending to curl or full of curls [She has long, *curly* hair.]
curl·y • *adjective* **curlier, curliest**

currant (kʉr′ənt) *noun* **1** a small, sour, red, white, or black berry. Currants are used for making jams and jellies. **2** a small, sweet, black raisin that is used in baking.
cur·rant • *noun, plural* **currants**
• The words **currant** and **current** sound alike.
He served homemade *currant* jam.
The *current* is too strong for swimming.

currency (kʉr′ən sē) *noun* the money that is used in a country [Cents, dimes, quarters, and dollar bills are different kinds of U.S. *currency*.]
cur·ren·cy • *noun, plural* **currencies**

current (kʉr′ənt) *adjective* **1** of the present time; most recent [She bought the *current* issue of the magazine. We keep track of *current* events.] **2** widely accepted or used [Many slang words are no longer *current*.]
noun **1** a flow of water or air in a certain direction [The canoe was caught in the river *current* and thrown against the rocks.] **2** the flow of electricity in a wire or through something.
cur·rent • *adjective* • *noun, plural* **currents**
• The words **current** and **currant** sound alike.

curse (kʉrs) *noun* **1** an appeal to heaven to bring evil on some person or thing. **2** a word or words used in swearing at someone. **3** a cause of evil or trouble [Raccoons are a *curse* in this part of the country.]
verb **1** to appeal to heaven to harm or punish; damn [The old witch *cursed* the princess and put her to sleep.] **2** to cause evil, harm, or trouble to; harm [He was *cursed* with seasickness.] **3** to use bad language; swear at.
curse • *noun, plural* **curses** • *verb* **cursed, cursing**

cursor (kʉr′sər) *noun* a movable marker on a computer screen. It marks the place to put in or to take out a letter, number, or symbol. Some cursors are small lights that flash on and off.
cur·sor • *noun, plural* **cursors**

curt (kʉrt) *adjective* rudely short and abrupt in speech or manner ["Go away" was his *curt* reply to the child.]

curtain (kʉrt′n) *noun* **1** a piece of cloth or other material hung across an opening. Curtains are hung at a window, in a doorway, or in front of a stage. They are used to decorate or to cover, hide, or shut off something. **2** anything that covers, hides, or shuts off [A *curtain* of fog helped the ships make their escape.]
cur·tain • *noun, plural* **curtains**

curtsy (kʉrt′sē) *noun* a bow of greeting or respect made by women and girls. In making a curtsy one foot is kept forward and the knees are bent to lower the body a little.
verb to make a curtsy.
curt·sy • *noun, plural* **curtsies** • *verb* **curtsied, curtsying, curtsies**

curve (kʉrv) *noun* **1** a line that has no straight part. A curve keeps bending in one direction without sharp angles. **2** anything that has the shape of a curve [a *curve* in the road].
verb **1** to turn or bend; take the shape of a curve [The trail *curves* to the left.] **2** to move in a curve [The pitch *curved* in to the batter.]
curve • *noun, plural* **curves** • *verb* **curved, curving**

cushion (ko͝osh′ən) *noun* **1** a pillow or soft pad that is used to sit on or lean against.

C

2 anything that is used to soften a blow, reduce shock, or protect against harm.
verb **1** to make a cushion for [Mother *cushioned* the seats of the dining room chairs.] **2** to protect from shock by means of a cushion [Grass *cushioned* his fall.]
cush·ion • ***noun,*** *plural* **cushions**
• ***verb*** **cushioned, cushioning**

custard (kus′tərd) ***noun*** a soft food that is a mixture of eggs, milk, sugar, and flavoring, either baked or boiled.
cus·tard • ***noun,*** *plural* **custards**

Custer (kus′tər), **George Armstrong** (jôrj′ ärm′strôŋ) 1839-1876; U.S. army officer. He was killed in a battle with the Sioux Indians.
Cus·ter, George Arm·strong

custodian (kəs tō′dē ən) ***noun*** **1** a person whose work is to take care of something; a caretaker. **2** a person whose work is to take care of a building; janitor.
cus·to·di·an • ***noun,*** *plural* **custodians**

custody (kus′tə dē) ***noun*** the right or duty to take care of someone or something [The court gave the mother the *custody* of the children.] **—in custody** in the keeping of the police; in jail or prison. **—take into custody** to arrest.
cus·to·dy • ***noun***

custom (kus′təm) ***noun*** **1** something that a person usually does; habit [It is her *custom* to have tea after dinner.] **2** something that has been done for a long time and is widely accepted or has become a tradition [It is the *custom* to eat turkey on Thanksgiving.]
adjective made or done to order [*custom* shoes].
cus·tom • ***noun,*** *plural* **customs** • ***adjective***

customary (kus′tə mer′ē) ***adjective*** according to custom; usual [It is *customary* to leave a tip here.] —Look for the WORD CHOICES box at the entry **usual**.
cus·tom·ar·y • ***adjective***

customer (kus′tə mər) ***noun*** a person who buys something, especially a person who buys regularly at a particular store.
cus·tom·er • ***noun,*** *plural* **customers**

cut (kut) ***verb*** **1** to make an opening in with a knife or other sharp tool; pierce [He *cut* his chin while shaving.] **2** to divide into parts with a sharp tool [Will you *cut* the cake?] **3** to be capable of being cut [This wood *cuts* easily.] **4** to be able to penetrate, divide, or make an opening [This knife *cuts* well]. **5** to make by cutting [They *cut* a path through the jungle.] **6** to go through or across [The tunnel *cuts* through the mountain.] **7** to make less; reduce; decrease [Prices were *cut* during the sale.] **8** to get rid of; remove [The director *cut* the scene from the play.] **9** to stop or interrupt [During the strike, electric power was *cut*.] **10** to grow a new tooth that makes it way through the gum [The baby *cut* two new front teeth.] **11** [*an informal use*] to stay away from a school class without being excused.
noun **1** an opening made by a knife or other sharp tool; a slit, wound, or gash. **2** a reduction; a decrease [The workers were asked to take a *cut* in pay.] **3** a piece that has been cut off [She always buys the most expensive *cuts* of beef.] **4** the style in which a thing is cut [I like the *cut* of his new suit.]
cut • ***verb*** **cut, cutting** • ***noun,*** *plural* **cuts**

cute (kyo͞ot) [*an informal word*] ***adjective*** very pretty or pleasing; charming; adorable [a *cute* puppy].
cute • ***adjective*** **cuter, cutest**

cutlass

cutlass (kut′ləs) ***noun*** a short, curved sword that has a sharp edge on one side.
cut·lass • ***noun,*** *plural* **cutlasses**

cutter (kut′ər) ***noun*** **1** a person who cuts something, such as glass or cloth. **2** a tool or machine that is used for cutting [cookie *cutters* of different shapes]. **3** a small, fast, armed ship used by the Coast Guard.
cut·ter • ***noun,*** *plural* **cutters**

cutting (kut′iŋ) ***noun*** a small part cut off from a plant that is used for starting a new plant.
adjective **1** able to cut; sharp [the *cutting*

a	cat	ō	go	ʉ	fur	ə = a *in* ago	
ā	ape	ô	law, for	ch	chin	e *in* agent	
ä	cot, car	oo	look	sh	she	i *in* pencil	
e	ten	o͞o	tool	th	thin	o *in* atom	
ē	me	oi	oil	*th*	then	u *in* circus	
i	fit	ou	out	zh	measure		
ī	ice	u	up	ŋ	ring		

edge of a knife]. **2** hurting the feelings; mean and insulting [*cutting* remarks].
cut·ting • *noun, plural* **cuttings** • *adjective*

cyborg (sī′bôrg) *noun* a person with mechanical or electronic devices functioning as organs or body parts. This being exists in science fiction only.
cy·borg • *noun, plural* **cyborgs**

cycle (sī′kəl) *noun* **1** a complete set of events that keep coming back in the same order [the life *cycle* of a frog; the yearly *cycle* of the seasons]. **2** a series of operations that make up a complete process [Our washer has eight *cycles*.]
verb to ride a bicycle or motorcycle [Last Sunday we *cycled* through the park.]
cy·cle • *noun, plural* **cycles** • *verb* **cycled, cycling**

cyclist (sīk′list *or* sīk′əl ist) *noun* a person who rides a bicycle or motorcycle.
cy·clist • *noun, plural* **cyclists**

cyclone (sī′klōn) *noun* a storm with strong winds that move around a center of low pressure.
cy·clone • *noun, plural* **cyclones**

WORD HISTORY

cyclone

The word **cyclone** comes from a Greek verb that means "to circle around" or "to whirl." The winds during a **cyclone** move around a center in either a clockwise or a counterclockwise direction.

cylinder (sil′in dər) *noun* a hollow or solid object that is shaped like a soup can or a tree trunk. The flat ends of a cylinder are parallel circles of the same size.
cyl·in·der • *noun, plural* **cylinders**

cymbal (sim′bəl) *noun* one of a pair of brass plates that are used in orchestras and bands. Cymbals make a sharp, ringing sound when they are struck together.
cym·bal • *noun, plural* **cymbals**

cymbal

- The words **cymbal** and **symbol** sound alike.
  Cymbals are used in bands.
  The lion is a *symbol* of royalty.

cypress (sī′prəs) *noun* an evergreen tree that has small, dark-green leaves that look like scales. It bears cones and has a hard wood.
cy·press • *noun, plural* **cypresses**

Cyprus (sī′prəs) a country on an island in the Mediterranean, south of Turkey.
Cy·prus

czar (zär) *noun* the title of any of the emperors who ruled Russia before 1917.
czar • *noun, plural* **czars**

czarina (zä rē′nə) *noun* the wife of a czar.
cza·ri·na • *noun, plural* **czarinas**

Czech (chek) *noun* **1** a person born or living in the Czech Republic. **2** the language of the Czechs.
Czech • *noun, plural for sense 1 only* **Czechs**

Czechoslovakia (chek′ə slō vä′kē ə) a former country in central Europe. In 1993 it was divided into the **Czech Republic** and **Slovakia.**
Czech·o·slo·va·ki·a

Czech Republic a country in central Europe. It was the western part of Czechoslovakia.

Dd

Dd Dd *Dd* Dd

D, *the fourth letter of the alphabet, has only one sound, the one heard at the beginning of* **dog**. *About 3,500 years ago, when it was first used by the Phoenicians, this letter was shaped like a triangle. The Greeks called the triangular letter* **delta**, *which today means a piece of land shaped like a triangle.*

d or **D** (dē) ***noun*** the fourth letter of the English alphabet.
d or **D** • ***noun,*** *plural* **d's** or **D's**

D (dē) ***noun*** **1** the Roman numeral for 500. **2** in some schools, a grade meaning "poor" or "below average." **3** in music, the second tone in the scale of C major.
D • ***noun,*** *plural* **D's**

dab (dab) ***verb*** **1** to pat lightly and quickly [She *dabbed* her face with cotton.] **2** to put on with soft, gentle strokes.
noun **1** a light, quick stroke. **2** a small bit of something soft or moist [a *dab* of butter].
dab • ***verb*** **dabbed, dabbing** • ***noun,*** *plural* **dabs**

dabble (dab′əl) ***verb*** **1** to dip in and out of water in a light and playful way [The children sat and *dabbled* their feet in the pool.] **2** to do or work on something, but not in a serious or thorough way [He *dabbles* at gardening in his spare time.]
dab·ble • ***verb*** **dabbled, dabbling**

dachshund (däks′ənd *or* däks′hoont) ***noun*** a small dog with a long body, long, drooping ears, and very short legs.
dachs·hund • ***noun,*** *plural* **dachshunds**

dad (dad) [*an informal word*] ***noun*** father.
dad • ***noun,*** *plural* **dads**

daddy (dad′ē) [*an informal word*] ***noun*** father.
dad·dy • ***noun,*** *plural* **daddies**

daddy-longlegs (dad′ē lôŋ′legz) ***noun*** an animal like a spider with very long and slender legs.
dad·dy-long·legs • ***noun,*** *plural* **daddy-longlegs**

daffodil (daf′ə dil) ***noun*** a plant that has long, narrow leaves and usually yellow flowers with a center part that is shaped like a trumpet.
daf·fo·dil • ***noun,*** *plural* **daffodils**

daffodil

daffy (daf′ē) [*an informal word*] ***adjective*** crazy; silly.
daf·fy • ***adjective*** **daffier, daffiest**

dagger (dag′ər) ***noun*** a weapon with a short, pointed blade that is used for stabbing.
dag·ger • ***noun,*** *plural* **daggers**

dahlia (dal′yə) ***noun*** a garden plant that has large, showy flowers in various bright colors.
dahl·ia • ***noun,*** *plural* **dahlias**

daily (dā′lē) ***adjective*** done, happening, or published every day or every weekday [*daily* exercises].
adverb every day [Feed the cat *daily*.]
noun a daily newspaper.
dai·ly • ***adjective*** • ***adverb*** • ***noun,*** *plural* **dailies**

dainty (dān′tē) ***adjective*** pretty or lovely in a delicate way [a *dainty* lace handkerchief].
dain·ty • ***adjective*** **daintier, daintiest**

dairy (der′ē) ***noun*** **1** a place where milk and cream are stored and butter and cheese are made. **2** a business or store that sells milk, cream, butter, and cheese. **3** a farm where cows are raised and milk, cream, butter, and cheese are produced.
dair·y • ***noun,*** *plural* **dairies**

dais (dā′is) ***noun*** a platform at one end of a room [The royal throne stood on a *dais*.]
da·is • ***noun,*** *plural* **daises**

daisy (dā′zē) ***noun*** a common plant with flowers that have white, yellow, or pink petals around a yellow center.
dai·sy • ***noun,*** *plural* **daisies**

WORD HISTORY

daisy

The source of **daisy** is two English words from about a thousand years ago that mean "day's eye." In the evening, the petals of this flower close around the yellow disk in the center. In the morning, the petals open up again. The daisy is the eye of the day, closed at night and open during the day.

Dakota (də kō′tə) ***noun*** **1** a member of a group of North American Indian peoples of the northern plains of the U.S. and nearby southern Canada. These peoples are also called *Sioux*. **2** their language.
—the Dakotas North Dakota and South Dakota.
Da·ko·ta • ***noun,*** *plural for sense 1 only* **Dakotas** or **Dakota**

dale (dāl) ***noun*** a valley.
dale • ***noun,*** *plural* **dales**

Dallas (dal′əs) a city in northeastern Texas.
Dal·las

Dalmatian (dal mā′shən) ***noun*** a large dog that has a short, smooth white coat covered with small black or brown spots.
Dal·ma·tian • ***noun,*** *plural* **Dalmatians**

dam
Hoover Dam, on the Colorado River

dam (dam) ***noun*** a wall built across a stream or river to hold back and control the flow of water.
verb to hold back with a dam or with something that functions like a dam [Beavers *dammed* the river that flows through our farm.]
dam • ***noun,*** *plural* **dams** • ***verb*** **dammed, damming**

damage (dam′ij) ***noun*** injury or harm that causes something to lose its value or causes a loss [The storm caused some *damage* to the barn.]
verb to do damage to —Look for the WORD CHOICES box at the entry **injure**.
dam·age • ***noun,*** *plural* **damages** • ***verb*** **damaged, damaging**

damp (damp) ***adjective*** slightly wet; moist [*damp* clothes; *damp* weather] —Look for the WORD CHOICES box at the entry **wet**.
noun a slightly wet quality or condition; moisture [Rains caused *damp* in the basement.]
damp • ***adjective*** **damper, dampest** • ***noun***

dampen (dam′pən) ***verb*** **1** to make or become slightly wet or moist [*Dampen* the clothes before ironing them.] **2** to lessen; deaden [Lou's cold reply *dampened* our enthusiasm.]
damp·en • ***verb*** **dampened, dampening**

dance (dans) ***verb*** **1** to move the body and feet in some kind of rhythm, usually to music. **2** to move about or up and down lightly and quick-

D

ly [The waves *danced* in the moonlight.]
noun **1** the act of dancing or one round of dancing [May I have the next *dance* with you?] **2** the special steps of a particular kind of dancing [Her favorite *dance* is the polka.] **3** a party where people dance. **4** the art of dancing [He is studying *dance*.]
dance • ***verb*** **danced, dancing** • ***noun,*** *plural* **dances**

dancer (dan′sər) ***noun*** a person who dances.
danc·er • ***noun,*** *plural* **dancers**

dandelion

dandelion (dan′də lī′ən) ***noun*** a common plant that has bright yellow flowers and leaves with jagged edges.
dan·de·li·on • ***noun,*** *plural* **dandelions**

WORD HISTORY

dandelion

The name of the **dandelion** came into English hundreds of years ago from French words meaning "tooth of the lion." It is called this because the plant's jagged leaves have the outline of sharp teeth.

dandruff (dan′drəf) ***noun*** small, light flakes of dead skin that fall from the scalp.
dan·druff • ***noun***

Dane (dān) ***noun*** a person born or living in Denmark.
Dane • ***noun,*** *plural* **Danes**

danger (dān′jər) ***noun*** **1** a condition in which something bad or harmful could happen; risk; peril [The acrobats lived in constant *danger* of falling.] **2** something that may cause harm [Jungle explorers face many *dangers*.]
dan·ger • ***noun,*** *plural for sense 2 only* **dangers**

dangerous (dān′jər əs) ***adjective*** likely to cause harm, pain, or injury; full of danger; unsafe.
dan·ger·ous • ***adjective***

dangle (daŋ′gəl) ***verb*** to hang loosely with a swaying motion [The keys *dangled* from his waist.]
dan·gle • ***verb*** **dangled, dangling**

Danish (dān′ish) ***noun*** **1** the language spoken in Denmark. **2** a pastry or raised dough filled with fruit and covered with icing: the full name of this pastry is **Danish pastry** or **danish pastry**.
Dan·ish • ***noun***

dare (der) ***verb*** **1** to be brave or bold enough to do a certain thing [He wouldn't *dare* to disobey orders.] **2** to challenge someone to do a certain thing in order to show courage [She *dared* me to swim across the lake.]
noun a challenge [I accepted her *dare*.]
dare • ***verb*** **dared, daring** • ***noun,*** *plural* **dares**

daredevil (der′dev əl) ***noun*** a bold, reckless person.
dare·dev·il • ***noun,*** *plural* **daredevils**

daring (der′iŋ) ***adjective*** bold enough to take risks.
noun bold courage.
dar·ing • ***adjective*** • ***noun***

dark (därk) ***adjective*** **1** having little or no light [a *dark* room; a *dark* night]. **2** closer to black or brown than to white; deep in shade; not light [She has *dark* hair. I bought a *dark* green tie.]
noun **1** lack of light [My little brother is afraid of the *dark*.] **2** night or nightfall ["Be home before *dark*," she told him.]
—in the dark not knowing or informed; not aware [I'm *in the dark* about your plans.]
dark • ***adjective*** **darker, darkest** • ***noun***

a	cat	ō	go	ʉ	fur	ə =	a *in* ago
ā	ape	ô	law, for	ch	chin		e *in* agent
ä	cot, car	oo	look	sh	she		i *in* pencil
e	ten	ōō	tool	th	thin		o *in* atom
ē	me	oi	oil	*th*	then		u *in* circus
i	fit	ou	out	zh	measure		
ī	ice	u	up	ŋ	ring		

D

WORD CHOICES

Synonyms of **dark**

Many words share the meaning "having little or no light."

dim
gloomy
murky
somber

darken (där′kən) *verb* to make or become dark [Storm clouds *darkened* the afternoon sky.]
dark·en • *verb* **darkened, darkening**

darkness (därk′nəs) *noun* the condition of being dark [The power failure left us in *darkness*.]
dark·ness • *noun*

darling (där′liŋ) *noun* a person who is loved very much.
dar·ling • *noun, plural* **darlings**

darn (därn) *verb* to mend by sewing stitches back and forth across a hole or tear in [He *darned* the heels of his socks.]
darn • *verb* **darned, darning**

dart

dart (därt) *noun* a short arrow with a sharp point. Darts are usually thrown by hand as a weapon, or at a target in games.
verb **1** to move suddenly and fast [They *darted* across the clearing.] **2** to send out or throw suddenly [She *darted* a look at the window.]
dart • *noun, plural* **darts** • *verb* **darted, darting**

Darwin (där′win), **Charles** (chärlz) 1809-1882; English scientist and writer. He is known for his theory on the origin of plants and animals.
Dar·win, Charles

dash (dash) *verb* **1** to throw with force; smash [He *dashed* the bottle to the floor.] **2** to hit roughly [The storm *dashed* the boat on the rocks.] **3** to put an end to; destroy [Losing the game *dashed* her hopes of winning the trophy.] **4** to do or write something quickly [I'll *dash* off a note to Liza.]
noun **1** a sudden, quick move or run [At the school bell, they made a *dash* for the door.] **2** a short, fast race [a 100-yard *dash*]. **3** a little bit; a pinch [Put a *dash* of salt in the salad.] **4** a mark that is a long straight line (—). It is used in printing and writing to show a break in thought in a sentence, or to show that something has been left out.
dash • *verb* **dashed, dashing** • *noun, plural* **dashes**

dashboard (dash′bôrd) *noun* the panel below the windshield in an automobile or other vehicle. The dashboard has gauges and controls on it.
dash·board • *noun, plural* **dashboards**

data (dāt′ə *or* dat′ə) *plural noun* [*now usually used with a singular verb*] facts and figures from which something can be learned; information [This *data* was taken from the appendix.]
da·ta • *plural noun, singular* **datum**

database (dāt′ə bās *or* dat′ə bās) *noun* a large collection of information stored in a computer. The information is put together in a way that makes it available for various uses.
da·ta·base • *noun, plural* **databases**

data processing *noun* the recording or handling of information by mechanical or electronic equipment.

date[1] (dāt) *noun* **1** the time at which a thing happens or is done [The *date* of Lincoln's birth was February 12, 1809.] **2** the day of the month [What's the *date* today?] **3** an agreement to meet someone or be somewhere at a certain time [I have a *date* with her for dinner on Tuesday.] **4** a person with whom one goes to a social event [He still does not have a *date* to take to the party.]
verb **1** to mark with a date [He *dated* the letter before mailing it.] **2** to find out or give the date or age of [They *dated* the tree by counting the rings on its trunk.] **3** to belong to a particular time [The museum's new paintings *date* from the late 18th century.] **4** to have dates with [Sarah is *dating* Joe.]
—out of date no longer in use; old-fashioned.
—up to date keeping up with the latest ideas, facts, or styles; modern.
date • *noun, plural* **dates** • *verb* **dated, dating**

date[2] (dāt) *noun* the sweet, fleshy fruit of a tall

palm tree. The fruit has a long, hard seed.
date • *noun, plural* **dates**

datum (dāt′əm *or* dat′əm) *noun singular of* **data**.
da·tum • *noun*

daughter (dôt′ər *or* dät′ər) *noun* a girl or woman as she is related to a parent or to both parents.
daugh·ter • *noun, plural* **daughters**

daughter-in-law (dôt′ər in lô *or* dät′ər in lä′) *noun* the wife of one's son.
daugh·ter-in-law • *noun, plural* **daughters-in-law**

David (dā′vid) the second king of Israel, whose story is told in the Bible. He killed Goliath.
Da·vid

da Vinci (də vin′chē), **Leonardo** (lē′ə när′dō) 1452-1519; Italian artist and scientist.
da Vin·ci, Le·o·nar·do

Davis (dā′vis), **Jefferson** (jef′ər sən) 1808-1889; the president of the Confederacy from 1861 to 1865.
Da·vis, Jef·fer·son

dawn (dôn *or* dän) *noun* **1** the first light that appears in the morning as the sun rises. **2** the beginning of anything [the *dawn* of the Space Age].
verb **1** to begin to grow light as the sun rises [Day is *dawning*.] **2** to begin to be understood [His meaning suddenly *dawned* on me.]
dawn • *noun, plural* **dawns** • *verb* **dawned, dawning**

day (dā) *noun* **1** the time of light between sunrise and sunset. **2** the period that includes one day and one night. A day has 24 hours. **3** the part of the day spent in work or other activity [She works an eight-hour *day*.] **4** a period or time [She was the best writer of her *day*.]
day • *noun, plural* **days**

daybreak (dā′brāk) *noun* the time in the morning when light begins to show; dawn.
day·break • *noun*

day-care (dā′ker) *adjective* of or describing a place where very young children not yet in school may be cared for and taught during the day while their parents are working. A place like this is often called a **day-care center** or **day nursery**.

daydream (dā′drēm) *noun* a pleasant, dreamy thinking or wishing.
verb to have daydreams.
day·dream • *noun, plural* **daydreams** • *verb* **daydreamed, daydreaming**

daylight (dā′līt) *noun* **1** the light of day; sunlight [He likes to paint by *daylight*.] **2** dawn; daybreak [We were up at *daylight*.]
day·light • *noun*

daylight saving time *noun* time that is one hour later than the standard time for a given place. Daylight saving time is used from late spring to early fall.

daytime (dā′tīm) *noun* the time of daylight between sunrise and sunset.
day·time • *noun*

daze (dāz) *verb* to stun or confuse [The loud explosion *dazed* us for a few seconds.]
noun a stunned or confused condition [She walked around in a *daze* after hearing the news of the plane crash.]
daze • *verb* **dazed, dazing** • *noun, plural* **dazes**

dazzle (daz′əl) *verb* **1** to make nearly blind with too much bright light [He was *dazzled* by the headlights of the approaching car.] **2** to overcome, amaze, or impress with something brilliant or showy [The magician's tricks *dazzled* the audience.]
daz·zle • *verb* **dazzled, dazzling**

D.C. *abbreviation for* District of Columbia [Washington, *D.C.*]

de- *a prefix meaning:* **1** away from; off [*Debriefing* a pilot means getting information from the pilot after a flight.] **2** down [*Descending* means moving down.] **3** to do in reverse; undo [*Defrosting* food means making it not frozen.]

DE *abbreviation for* Delaware.

deacon (dē′kən) *noun* **1** a church officer who helps the minister. **2** a member of the clergy who ranks just below a priest.
dea·con • *noun, plural* **deacons**

dead (ded) *adjective* **1** no longer living; without life [Throw out those *dead* flowers.] **2** without life or living things [Is Mars a *dead* planet?] **3** not active; not working [I can't call her because her telephone is *dead*.] **4** without activity or excitement [The village is *dead* after 8 p.m.] **5** sure; exact [The bullet hit the

a cat	ō go	ʉ fur	ə = a *in* ago
ā ape	ô law, for	ch chin	e *in* agent
ä cot, car	oo look	sh she	i *in* pencil
e ten	ōō tool	th thin	o *in* atom
ē me	oi oil	*th* then	u *in* circus
i fit	ou out	zh measure	
ī ice	u up	ŋ ring	

target at *dead* center.] **6** complete [Please bring the car to a *dead* stop.]
adverb **1** completely; entirely [I am *dead* tired.] **2** directly; straight [Steer *dead* ahead.]
noun the time of most cold, most dark, or most silence [They escaped in the *dead* of night.]
—the dead those who have died.

WORD CHOICES

Synonyms of **dead**

The words **dead, deceased,** and **late** share the meaning "no longer living."

a *dead* wasp

the *deceased* wife of the owner

our *late* president

deaden (ded′n) ***verb*** **1** to take away feeling; make numb [The dentist *deadens* the nerve before drilling a tooth.] **2** to make less strong or sharp; dull; weaken [Heavy curtains will *deaden* street noise.]
dead·en • ***verb*** **deadened, deadening**

dead end ***noun*** a street, alley, or other passage that is closed at one end.
dead end • ***noun,*** *plural* **dead ends**

deadline (ded′līn) ***noun*** the latest time by which something must be done or finished.
dead·line • ***noun,*** *plural* **deadlines**

deadly (ded′lē) ***adjective*** **1** causing death; able to kill [a *deadly* weapon]. **2** full of hate or violence [*deadly* enemies].
dead·ly • ***adjective*** **deadlier, deadliest**

deaf (def) ***adjective*** **1** not able to hear or not able to hear well. **2** not willing to hear; not paying attention [The boss was *deaf* to his complaints.]
deaf • ***adjective*** **deafer, deafest**

deafen (def′ən) ***verb*** **1** to make deaf. **2** to overwhelm with too much noise [The sound of the jet *deafened* us.]
deaf·en • ***verb*** **deafened, deafening**

deal (dēl) ***verb*** **1** to have to do; be about [Science *deals* with facts.] **2** to act or behave [The principal *dealt* fairly with the tardy student.] **3** to do business; trade [He *deals* in rare books. They prefer to *deal* with the store owner herself.] **4** to give; deliver [The police officer *dealt* the thief a blow on the head.]
noun **1** an agreement [They made a *deal* to rent the house.] **2** a bargain [She got a *deal* on a used car.]
—a good deal or **a great deal** very much [I have *a good deal* of time. You must walk *a great deal* faster.]
deal • ***verb*** **dealt, dealing** • ***noun,*** *plural* **deals**

dealer (dēl′ər) ***noun*** a person who buys and sells something as a business [a car *dealer*].
deal·er • ***noun,*** *plural* **dealers**

dealt (delt) ***verb*** *past tense and past participle of* **deal**.

dear (dir) ***adjective*** **1** much loved; beloved [a *dear* friend]. **2** respected; well-liked: this is a word used before a person's name when writing a letter ["*Dear* Janet," she wrote at the top of the paper.]
noun a much loved person; darling.
interjection a word used to show disappointment, surprise, or worry [Oh *dear!* What shall I do?]
dear • ***adjective*** **dearer, dearest** • ***noun,*** *plural* **dears** • ***interjection***
• The words **dear** and **deer** sound alike.
Our baby is very *dear* to us.
My uncle hunts *deer* in the fall.

dearly (dir′lē) ***adverb*** very much; greatly [Susan *dearly* loves her cat.]
dear·ly • ***adverb***

death (deth) ***noun*** **1** the act or fact of dying; the end of life. **2** the condition of being dead [His eyes were closed in *death*.] **3** any end that is like dying [The loss was the *death* of our hopes for the championship.]
death • ***noun,*** *plural* **deaths**

debate (dē bāt′) ***verb*** **1** to give reasons for or against; argue about in a somewhat formal way [The Senate *debated* the question of aid to foreign countries.] **2** to consider reasons for and against; think about [I *debated* the problem in my own mind.]
noun the act of debating something; a discussion or formal argument [The *debate* between the two candidates will be on TV tonight.]
de·bate • ***verb*** **debated, debating** • ***noun,*** *plural* **debates**

debris or **débris** (də brē′) ***noun*** the scattered remains of something that has been broken, destroyed, or thrown away; rubbish [The picnic area was covered with the *debris* of yesterday's celebration.]
de·bris or **dé·bris** • ***noun***

debt (det) ***noun*** **1** something that is owed to another [a *debt* of gratitude. I promised to pay

D

all my *debts* before the end of the year.] **2** the condition of owing [I am in *debt* to you for all your help.]
debt • *noun, plural* **debts**

debtor (det′ər) *noun* a person who owes something to another.
debt·or • *noun, plural* **debtors**

Dec. *abbreviation for* December.

deca- *a prefix meaning* ten [A *decathlon* is an athletic contest with ten parts.]

decade (dek′ād) *noun* a period of ten years.
dec·ade • *noun, plural* **decades**

decal (dē′kal) *noun* a picture or design on specially prepared paper. Decals can be transferred to glass or other hard, flat surfaces.
de·cal • *noun, plural* **decals**

decay (dē kā′) *verb* **1** to become rotten by the action of bacteria [Fallen apples *decay* on the ground.] —Look for the WORD CHOICES box at the entry **rot**. **2** to decline slowly in strength or quality; fall into ruins [Many civilizations have developed and *decayed*.]
noun **1** the slow rotting of plant or animal matter by the action of bacteria [tooth *decay*]. **2** a slow decline in strength or quality [the *decay* of ancient civilizations].
de·cay • *verb* **decayed, decaying** • *noun*

deceased (dē sēst′) *adjective* dead [a ceremony in honor of a *deceased* governor] —Look for the WORD CHOICES box at the entry **dead**.
—**the deceased** the dead person or dead persons.
de·ceased • *adjective*

deceit (dē sēt′) *noun* **1** the act or practice of lying or cheating [The lawyer exposed their *deceit* to the jury.] **2** the quality of being deceitful [He was a man full of *deceit*.]
de·ceit • *noun, plural for sense 1 only* **deceits**

deceitful (dē sēt′fəl) *adjective* **1** practicing lying and cheating [a *deceitful* person]. **2** intended to deceive; misleading [*deceitful* actions].
de·ceit·ful • *adjective*

deceive (dē sēv′) *verb* to make someone believe what is not true; fool or trick; mislead [The wicked queen *deceived* Snow White.] —Look for the WORD CHOICES box at the entry **cheat**.
de·ceive • *verb* **deceived, deceiving**

WORD CHOICES

Synonyms of **deceive**

The words **deceive, fool,** and **mislead** share the meaning "to make someone believe what is not true."

She was *deceived* by the salesman.

He *fooled* her by pretending to be asleep.

The students were *misled* by information in the old book.

December (dē sem′bər) *noun* the last month of the year. December has 31 days. Abbreviated **Dec.**
De·cem·ber • *noun*

decency (dē′sən sē) *noun* the quality of being decent; proper behavior [He didn't have the *decency* to thank her for all her help.]
de·cen·cy • *noun, plural* **decencies**

decent (dē′sənt) *adjective* **1** proper and fitting; suitable [*decent* manners; *decent* language] —Look for the WORD CHOICES box at the entry **good**. **2** fairly good; adequate [He is not rich, but he earns a *decent* salary.] **3** kind; generous; fair [It was *decent* of you to help.]
de·cent • *adjective*

deception (dē sep′shən) *noun* **1** the act of deceiving or lying [practicing *deception* on innocent people]. **2** a trick or lie intended to deceive [His claim of being a magician was a *deception*.]
de·cep·tion • *noun, plural* **deceptions**

deci- *a prefix meaning* a tenth part of [A *decimeter* is a tenth of a meter.]

decide (dē sīd′) *verb* **1** to make up one's mind [I can't *decide* what to wear.] **2** to end a contest or argument by giving one side the victory; settle [A jury will *decide* the case.]
de·cide • *verb* **decided, deciding**

decimal (des′i məl) *adjective* of or based on the number 10. The numbers we count with make up a decimal system.
noun a fraction with a denominator of 10 or

a	cat	ō	go	ʉ	fur	ə =	a *in* ago
ā	ape	ô	law, for	ch	chin		e *in* agent
ä	cot, car	oo	look	sh	she		i *in* pencil
e	ten	ōō	tool	th	thin		o *in* atom
ē	me	oi	oil	*th*	then		u *in* circus
i	fit	ou	out	zh	measure		
ī	ice	u	up	ŋ	ring		

some power of 10 that is written without the denominator. Instead of the denominator, it has a point, called a **decimal point**, in front of the numerator. For example, the fraction 5⁄10 can be written as the decimal .5.
dec·i·mal • *adjective* • *noun, plural* **decimals**

decision (dē sizh′ən) *noun* **1** the act or result of deciding [His *decision* to quit the team surprised all of us.] **2** a determined, firm way of thinking or acting [a man of *decision*].
de·ci·sion • *noun, plural for sense 1 only* **decisions**

decisive (dē sī′siv) *adjective* **1** having the power to settle a question, dispute, or argument; most important [a *decisive* battle in a war]. **2** showing a firm mind or character [The company's president is a *decisive* businesswoman.]
de·ci·sive • *adjective*

deck (dek) *noun* **1** one of the floors on a ship or boat, reaching from side to side. **2** a platform or floor that is like this [The house has a wooden *deck* at the back.] **3** a pack of playing cards.
deck • *noun, plural* **decks**

declaration (dek lər ā′shən) *noun* **1** the act of declaring. **2** something that is declared; a public statement [a touching *declaration* of affection].
dec·la·ra·tion • *noun, plural* **declarations**

Declaration of Independence the document that declared the thirteen American colonies independent of Great Britain. It was written by Thomas Jefferson and was adopted July 4, 1776, by the Second Continental Congress.

declarative (dē kler′ə tiv) *adjective* of or describing a sentence such as "I have a pet canary" or "Our team won the game," that makes a statement about something.
de·clar·a·tive • *adjective*

declare (dē kler′) *verb* to say or announce openly; make known [Let us *declare* war on cancer. "I'm leaving forever!" he *declared*.] —Look for the WORD CHOICES box at the entry **say**.
de·clare • *verb* **declared, declaring**

declaw (dē klô′ *or* dē klä′) *verb* to remove the claws from the feet of by surgery. This is sometimes done to pet cats that are to be kept in the house.
de·claw • *verb* **declawed, declawing**

decline (dē klīn′) *verb* **1** to become less in health, power, or value [A person's strength usually *declines* in old age.] —Look for the WORD CHOICES box at the entry **wane**. **2** to refuse something, most often in a polite way. *noun* the process or result of becoming less, smaller, or weaker [a *decline* in prices; a serious *decline* in Mr. Brown's health].
de·cline • *verb* **declined, declining** • *noun, plural* **declines**

WORD CHOICES

Synonyms of **decline**

The words **decline, refuse,** and **reject** share the meaning "to say no to something."

He *declined* the invitation.

I *refused* her request for a loan.

She *rejected* the offer.

decode (dē kōd′) *verb* to figure out the meaning of by translating from a code into everyday language [The spy *decoded* the secret message.]
de·code • *verb* **decoded, decoding**

decompose (dē kəm pōz′) *verb* to rot or decay [Meat *decomposes* quickly on a hot day.]
de·com·pose • *verb* **decomposed, decomposing**

decorate (dek′ər āt) *verb* **1** to add something in order to make prettier or more pleasing; to ornament [I *decorated* the room for the party.] **2** to give a medal to [The mayor *decorated* the brave firefighter.]
dec·o·rate • *verb* **decorated, decorating**

decoration

decoration (dek ər ā′shən) *noun* **1** the act of decorating. **2** something that is used for decorating; an ornament [We made all the *decorations* for our Christmas tree.] **3** a medal, ribbon, or other sign of honor.

D

dec·o·ra·tion • *noun, plural* **decorations**

decorator (dek′ər ā tər) *noun* a person whose work is decorating and furnishing rooms.
dec·o·ra·tor • *noun, plural* **decorators**

decoy (dē′koi *or* dē koi′) *noun* **1** a model of a bird or other animal, usually made of wood, that is used by hunters to attract game. **2** a thing or person that is used to lure someone into a trap.
verb to lure into a trap or danger.
de·coy • *noun, plural* **decoys**
• *verb* **decoyed, decoying**

decrease (dē krēs′ *or* dē′krēs) *verb* to make or become less or smaller [He *decreased* his weight by dieting. My pain is *decreasing*.] —Look for the WORD CHOICES box at the entry **wane**.
noun **1** the process of growing less [They feared a *decrease* in sales.] **2** the amount of decreasing [a sales *decrease* of $400].
de·crease • *verb* **decreased, decreasing**
• *noun, plural* **decreases**

decree (dē krē′) *noun* an official order or decision.
verb to order or decide by decree [The governor *decreed* a special holiday.]
de·cree • *noun, plural* **decrees**
• *verb* **decreed, decreeing**

dedicate (ded′i kāt) *verb* to set aside for or devote to a special purpose [She *dedicated* her life to caring for the poor.]
ded·i·cate • *verb* **dedicated, dedicating**

deduct (dē dukt′) *verb* to take away; subtract [*Deduct* 10% to get the sale price.]
de·duct • *verb* **deducted, deducting**

deduction (dē duk′shən) *noun* **1** the act of deducting. **2** the amount that is deducted [a *deduction* of $20 from the regular price].
de·duc·tion • *noun, plural* **deductions**

deed (dēd) *noun* **1** a thing that is done; an act or action [She is to be rewarded for her good *deeds*.] **2** a paper that is written according to law to transfer the ownership of a piece of land with its buildings from one person to another.
deed • *noun, plural* **deeds**

deep (dēp) *adjective* **1** reaching far down, far in, or far back [a *deep* lake; a *deep* wound; a *deep* closet]. **2** reaching a certain distance down, in, or back [This pot is only five inches *deep*.] **3** having a low tone or tones [a *deep* groan; a *deep* voice]. **4** hard to understand [This novel is too *deep* for me.] **5** great in degree; intense; heavy [a *deep* sleep]. **6** dark and rich [*deep* colors]. **7** very much taken up; greatly involved [*deep* in thought].
adverb far down, far in, or far back [Miners dug *deep* into the ground.]
deep • *adjective* & • *adverb* **deeper, deepest**

deepen (dē′pən) *verb* to make or become deeper.
deep·en • *verb* **deepened, deepening**

deer (dir) *noun* an animal that has long, slender legs with hoofs, and that chews its cud and can run very fast. Usually only the male has antlers, that it sheds every year.
deer • *noun, plural* **deer** or **deers**
● The words **deer** and **dear** sound alike.
My uncle hunts *deer* in the fall.
Our baby is very *dear* to us.

deface (dē fās′) *verb* to spoil the looks of; mar [He *defaced* the statue with paint.]
de·face • *verb* **defaced, defacing**

defeat (dē fēt′) *verb* **1** to win victory over; beat [They *defeated* their opponent.] **2** to cause to fail; bring to nothing [His hopes were *defeated* by a stroke of bad luck.]
noun **1** the fact of being defeated; failure to win [Our team has not yet suffered *defeat*.] **2** the act or fact of defeating; victory [We cheered our team's *defeat* of the visitors.]
de·feat • *verb* **defeated, defeating** • *noun, plural* **defeats**

defect (dē′fekt) *noun* a fault or flaw in something; an imperfect part [a *defect* in a diamond].
de·fect • *noun, plural* **defects**

WORD CHOICES

Synonyms of **defect**

The words **defect, blemish,** and **flaw** share the meaning "an imperfect part that spoils something."

a *defect* in the fabric
skin without a *blemish*
a *flaw* in a diamond

a cat	ō go	ʉ fur	ə = a *in* ago
ā ape	ô law, for	ch chin	e *in* agent
ä cot, car	oo look	sh she	i *in* pencil
e ten	ōō tool	th thin	o *in* atom
ē me	oi oil	*th* then	u *in* circus
i fit	ou out	zh measure	
ī ice	u up	ŋ ring	

defective (dē fek′tiv) ***adjective*** having a defect or defects; imperfect [a *defective* toaster].
de·fec·tive • ***adjective***

defend (dē fend′) ***verb*** **1** to keep safe from harm or danger; guard or protect [She learned karate to *defend* herself.] **2** to act, speak, or write in support of [The accused man will be *defended* by a lawyer.]
de·fend • ***verb*** **defended, defending**

defense (dē fens′ *for sense 1;* dē′fens *for sense 2*) ***noun*** **1** something that defends; a means of protecting [Forts were built as *defenses* along the frontier in pioneer days.] **2** the side in a game that defends a goal against scoring by an opponent.
de·fense • ***noun, plural*** **defenses**

defenseless (dē fens′ləs) ***adjective*** having no defense; helpless or unprotected.
de·fense·less • ***adjective***

defensive (dē fen′siv) ***adjective*** protecting from attack [Soldiers set up *defensive* barricades.]
de·fen·sive • ***adjective***

defiance (dē fī′əns) ***noun*** the act of defying or opposing a powerful person or thing [Colonists showed their *defiance* of King George.]
de·fi·ance • ***noun***

defiant (dē fī′ənt) ***adjective*** full of defiance; bold in opposing someone or something [The *defiant* knight did not obey the king.]
de·fi·ant • ***adjective***

deficiency (dē fish′ən sē) ***noun*** a lack in the amount that is needed or expected; shortage [A vitamin *deficiency* can make a person ill.]
de·fi·cien·cy • ***noun, plural*** **deficiencies**

define (dē fīn′) ***verb*** **1** to tell the meaning or meanings of; explain [This dictionary *defines* "double" as "twice as much or as many."] **2** to describe in detail; make clear [Can you *define* your duties as a secretary?]
de·fine • ***verb*** **defined, defining**

definite (def′i nit) ***adjective*** **1** clear and exact [The doctor gave *definite* orders.] **2** certain; sure [It's *definite* that she has a broken arm.]
def·i·nite • ***adjective***

definite article ***noun*** the word **the**. The phrase "the dog" talks about a definite, particular dog, one that has been mentioned before or is already known.
definite article • ***noun, plural*** **definite articles**

definition (def′i nish′ən) ***noun*** a statement that tells what a thing is or what a word means.
def·i·ni·tion • ***noun, plural*** **definitions**

deform (dē fôrm′) ***verb*** to spoil the form or appearance of [The hot oven had *deformed* the plastic dish.]
de·form • ***verb*** **deformed, deforming**

defrost (dē frôst′) ***verb*** **1** to get rid of frost or ice from [Dad *defrosted* the refrigerator.] **2** to cause to be no longer frozen [We *defrosted* the turkey and cooked it.]
de·frost • ***verb*** **defrosted, defrosting**

deft (deft) ***adjective*** quick but sure; skillful [*deft* hands. She painted with *deft* strokes.] —Look for the WORD CHOICES box at the entry **nimble**.
deft • ***adjective*** **defter, deftest**

defy (dē fī′) ***verb*** **1** to oppose boldly and openly [They *defied* their leader.] **2** to resist completely in a puzzling way [This problem *defies* solution.] **3** to dare or challenge [I *defy* you to prove I'm wrong.]
de·fy • ***verb*** **defied, defying, defies**

degrade (dē grād′) ***verb*** to cause to be less deserving of respect; disgrace [Politicians who take bribes *degrade* themselves.]
de·grade • ***verb*** **degraded, degrading**

degree (də grē′) ***noun*** **1** a step in a series; a stage in the progress of something [He advanced by *degrees* from a rookie to a star basketball player.] **2** a unit that is used in measuring temperature. It is shown by the symbol ° [The boiling point of water is 212° Fahrenheit.] **3** a unit that is used in measuring angles and parts of circles. It is shown by the symbol ° [There are 360° in a circle.] **4** a rank that a college or university gives to a student who has been successful in finishing a course of study [a B.A. *degree*]. **5** amount or extent [He knows how to play the piano to some *degree*.]
de·gree • ***noun, plural*** **degrees**

deity (dē′i tē) ***noun*** a god or goddess [temples to honor Greek and Roman *deities*].
—**the Deity** God.
de·i·ty • ***noun, plural*** **deities**

dejected (dē jek′təd) ***adjective*** discouraged; in low spirits [The team was *dejected* after los-

D

ing.] —Look for the WORD CHOICES box at the entry **sad**.
de·ject·ed • *adjective*

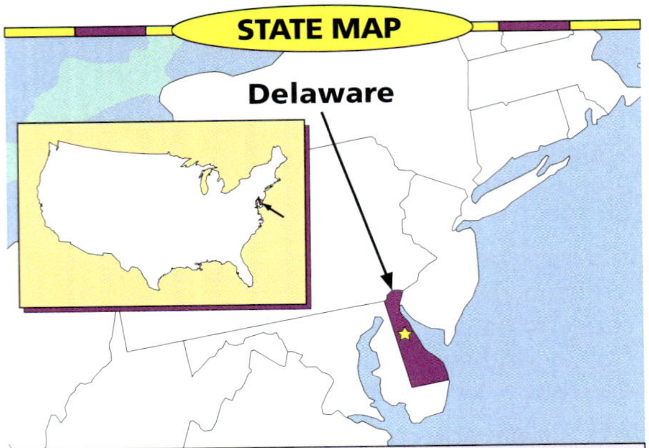

Statehood: 1787, the 1st state • **Capital:** Dover

Delaware (del′ə wer) a State on the eastern coast of the U.S. Its capital is Dover. Abbreviated **DE** or **Del.**
Del·a·ware

delay (dē lā′) *verb* **1** to put off to a later time; postpone [They had to *delay* the wedding because of the bride's illness.] **2** to make late or hold back [We were *delayed* by the storm.]
noun **1** the act of delaying or the fact of being delayed [You must return my call without *delay*.] **2** the period of time during which something is delayed [Engine trouble caused a *delay* of two hours.]
de·lay • *verb* **delayed, delaying** • *noun, plural* **delays**

delegate (del′ə gət *for n.;* del′ə gāt *for v.*) *noun* a person that another person or a group sends to speak and act for it; a representative [our *delegate* to the convention].
verb **1** to give a right or duty to another [The people *delegate* the power to make laws to a legislature.] **2** to choose or appoint to perform a duty or do a task [I'm *delegating* you to grade the students' exams.]
del·e·gate • *noun, plural* **delegates** • *verb* **delegated, delegating**

delegation (del ə gā′shən) *noun* a group of delegates [the *delegation* from Utah].
del·e·ga·tion • *noun, plural* **delegations**

deli (del′ē) *noun a short form of* **delicatessen**.
del·i • *noun, plural* **delis**

deliberate (dē lib′ər ət *for adj.;* dē lib′ər āt′ *for v.*) *adjective* carefully thought out and made or done on purpose [a *deliberate* choice; a *deliberate* insult].
verb to think or discuss carefully in order to decide [The jury *deliberated* for six hours before declaring him guilty.]
de·lib·er·ate • *adjective* • *verb* **deliberated, deliberating**

delicate (del′i kət) *adjective* **1** pleasing in being light, fine, or soft [a *delicate* flavor; *delicate* workmanship; a *delicate* color]. **2** requiring great care or skill [a *delicate* operation]. **3** easily hurt or spoiled; not strong [*delicate* china; *delicate* health] —Look for the WORD CHOICES box at the entry **fragile**. **4** needing careful handling [a *delicate* problem].
del·i·cate • *adjective*

delicatessen (del′i kə tes′ən) *noun* a store that sells prepared foods. Cooked meats, cheeses, salads, and sandwiches are sold in a delicatessen.
del·i·ca·tes·sen • *noun, plural* **delicatessens**

delicious (dē lish′əs) *adjective* very pleasing to the sense of taste.
de·li·cious • *adjective*

delight (dē līt′) *verb* **1** to give great pleasure to [The party *delighted* us all.] **2** to rejoice [We *delighted* in her good fortune.]
noun **1** great joy or pleasure [The new toy gave the baby great *delight*.] **2** something that gives great joy or pleasure [The beautiful garden is a *delight* to us all.]
de·light • *verb* **delighted, delighting** • *noun, plural* **delights**

delightful (dē līt′fəl) *adjective* giving delight or pleasure; very pleasing [We've had a *delightful* afternoon at your party.]
de·light·ful • *adjective*

deliver (dē liv′ər) *verb* **1** to take or carry and hand over; to transfer [*Deliver* the groceries to my house.] **2** to take something around and leave it at the right places; distribute [The postal service *delivers* packages.] **3** to speak or read aloud [She *delivered* the speech to a large crowd.] **4** to strike [He *delivered* the blow with great force.] **5** to set free or rescue [*Deliver* us from evil.]
de·liv·er • *verb* **delivered, delivering**

a	cat	ō	go	ʉ	fur	ə =	a *in* ago
ā	ape	ô	law, for	ch	chin		e *in* agent
ä	cot, car	oo	look	sh	she		i *in* pencil
e	ten	ōō	tool	th	thin		o *in* atom
ē	me	oi	oil	*th*	then		u *in* circus
i	fit	ou	out	zh	measure		
ī	ice	u	up	ŋ	ring		

delivery (dē liv′ər ē) *noun* **1** the act of transferring or distributing something [They made *deliveries* to customers every day.] **2** the way that a person speaks, strikes, or throws [the fast *delivery* of a TV announcer. That pitcher has a good *delivery*.]
de·liv·er·y • *noun, plural* **deliveries**

delphinium (del fin′ē əm) *noun* a plant with spikes of tube-shaped flowers on tall stalks. The flowers are usually blue.
del·phin·i·um • *noun, plural* **delphiniums**

delta (del′tə) *noun* a triangle-shaped piece of land at the mouth of a large river. It is formed by deposits of soil and sand at the mouth.
del·ta • *noun, plural* **deltas**

Dem. *abbreviation for* Democrat.

demand (dē mand′) *verb* **1** to ask for as a right, or in a way that suggests that one has the right to ask; ask for with authority [We *demanded* the money that they had promised us.] **2** to call for; to need [This work *demands* great care.]
noun **1** something that is demanded [Higher wages were one of the *demands* of the workers.] **2** a claim or need [This job makes great *demands* on my time.] **3** the desire for a product by buyers who are ready to buy at the price that is asked [There is great *demand* for new cars now.]
de·mand • *verb* **demanded, demanding** • *noun, plural* **demands**

WORD CHOICES

Synonyms of **demand**

The words **demand, claim,** and **require** share the meaning "to insist on having or getting something."

The king *demanded* obedience.

He *claimed* the right to speak openly.

The coach *requires* us to attend practice.

democracy (də mäk′rə sē) *noun* **1** government in which the people hold the ruling power. This power is usually held by representatives elected to make the laws and run the government. **2** a country with this kind of government.
de·moc·ra·cy • *noun, plural* **democracies**

WORD HISTORY

democracy

The word **democracy** comes to us from an ancient Greek word with a similar meaning. That word was made up of two Greek words that mean "the people" and "to rule."

democrat (dem′ə krat) *noun* **1** a person who believes in and supports democracy. **2 Democrat** a member of the Democratic Party.
dem·o·crat • *noun, plural* **democrats**

democratic (dem′ə krat′ik) *adjective* **1** having to do with democracy; practicing or supporting democracy [*democratic* values]. **2** treating everyone in a fair and equal way [a *democratic* solution to the problem]. **3 Democratic** of or belonging to the Democratic Party [the *Democratic* candidate].
dem·o·crat·ic • *adjective*

Democratic Party one of the two major political parties in the U.S.

demolish (dē mäl′ish) *verb* to tear down; to smash [The tornado *demolished* the barn.]
de·mol·ish • *verb* **demolished, demolishing**

demon (dē′mən) *noun* **1** a devil; evil spirit. **2** a very evil or cruel person or thing.
de·mon • *noun, plural* **demons**

demonstrate (dem′ən strāt) *verb* **1** to show or prove by facts, actions, or feelings [I *demonstrate* my love for my puppy by taking good care of it.] **2** to explain by the use of examples or experiments [We *demonstrate* basic laws of chemistry in the lab.] **3** to show how something works or is used [She will *demonstrate* the new coffee maker.] **4** to take part in a public meeting, parade, or other activity to show feelings about a matter.
dem·on·strate • *verb* **demonstrated, demonstrating**

demonstration (dem ən strā′shən) *noun* **1** the act of demonstrating something; the process of showing or explaining [the *demonstration* of a car; a public *demonstration* of affection]. **2** a meeting or parade of many people to show in public how they feel about something.
dem·on·stra·tion • *noun, plural* **demonstrations**

D

den (den) ***noun*** **1** a cave or other place where a wild animal makes its home. **2** a cozy room where a person can read or work.
den • ***noun,*** *plural* **dens**

denial (dē nī′əl) ***noun*** **1** the act of saying "no" to a request. **2** a statement that something is not true or right.
de·ni·al • ***noun,*** *plural* **denials**

denim (den′im) ***noun*** a coarse cotton cloth that is very strong and does not wear out easily. It is used for work clothes or play clothes.
den·im • ***noun***

Denmark (den′märk) a country in northern Europe, on a peninsula and on several islands.
Den·mark

denomination (dē näm′i nā′shən) ***noun*** **1** a class or kind of thing with a particular name or value [coins and stamps of various *denominations*]. **2** a religious group or division [There are many Protestant *denominations*.]
de·nom·i·na·tion • ***noun,*** *plural* **denominations**

denominator (dē näm′i nāt′ər) ***noun*** the number that is below or to the right of the line in a fraction. In the fraction ⅖, 5 is the denominator.
de·nom·i·na·tor • ***noun,*** *plural* **denominators**

denote (dē nōt′) ***verb*** to stand for or be the name of; to mean [The word "comic" *denotes* "very funny."]
de·note • ***verb*** **denoted, denoting**

denounce (dē nouns′) ***verb*** to speak out against in some way; call bad [We must *denounce* lack of honesty in government.]
de·nounce • ***verb*** **denounced, denouncing**

dense (dens) ***adjective*** having the parts or particles very close together; thick [a *dense* forest; a *dense* fog].
dense • ***adjective*** **denser, densest**

density (den′si tē) ***noun*** the condition of being dense, thick, or crowded.
den·si·ty • ***noun,*** *plural* **densities**

dent (dent) ***noun*** a slight hollow that is made in a hard surface by a hit or by pressure [a *dent* in the side of the car].
verb to make a dent in.
dent • ***noun,*** *plural* **dents** • ***verb*** **dented, denting**

dental (dent′l) ***adjective*** having to do with teeth or with a dentist's work [*dental* surgery].
den·tal • ***adjective***

dentin (den′tin) ***noun*** the hard, bony material that forms the main part of a tooth. It lies just under the enamel.
den·tin • ***noun***

dentist (den′tist) ***noun*** a doctor whose work is taking care of people's teeth. Dentists work to prevent disease in teeth, and they repair, treat, or replace damaged teeth.
den·tist • ***noun,*** *plural* **dentists**

Denver (den′vər) the capital of Colorado.
Den·ver

deny (dē nī′) ***verb*** **1** to say that something is not true or right [They *denied* that they had broken the window.] **2** to refuse to grant or give [She *denied* them permission to go.]
de·ny • ***verb*** **denied, denying, denies**

deodorant (dē ō′dər ənt) ***noun*** a cream, liquid, spray, or other substance that is used on the body to stop or cover up unwanted odors.
de·o·dor·ant • ***noun,*** *plural* **deodorants**

depart (dē pärt′) ***verb*** to go away; leave [The train will *depart* on time.]
de·part • ***verb*** **departed, departing**

department (dē pärt′mənt) ***noun*** a separate part of a government, business, or other organization [the police *department;* the *department* of history at a college].
de·part·ment • ***noun,*** *plural* **departments**

department store ***noun*** a large store with separate departments for selling many different products.
department store • ***noun,*** *plural* **department stores**

departure (dē pär′chər) ***noun*** the act of departing or going away [The train's *departure* is scheduled for ten o'clock.]
de·par·ture • ***noun,*** *plural* **departures**

depend (dē pend′) ***verb*** **1** to be controlled or decided by [The number of people attending will *depend* on the weather.] **2** to have trust; be sure; rely [You can't *depend* on the weather in March. They *depend* on their parents

a	cat	ō	go	u	fur	ə = a *in* ago		
ā	ape	ô	law, for	ch	chin	e *in* agent		
ä	cot, car	oo	look	sh	she	i *in* pencil		
e	ten	ōō	tool	th	thin	o *in* atom		
ē	me	oi	oil	*th*	then	u *in* circus		
i	fit	ou	out	zh	measure			
ī	ice	u	up	ŋ	ring			

for good advice.] —Look for the WORD CHOICES box at the entry **rely**.
de·pend • *verb* **depended, depending**

dependable (dē pen′də bəl) *adjective* capable of being trusted or depended on; reliable.
de·pend·a·ble • *adjective*

dependence (dē pen′dəns) *noun* the condition of being dependent on someone or something else.
de·pend·ence • *noun*

dependent (dē pen′dənt) *adjective* **1** controlled or decided by something else [The size of my allowance was *dependent* on our family income.] **2** relying on someone else for help or support. **3** in grammar, describing a clause with a structure that does not allow it to stand alone as a complete sentence. In the sentence "She will visit us if she can," the words "if she can" form a dependent clause.
noun a person who depends on someone else for help or support.
de·pend·ent • *adjective* • *noun, plural* **dependents**

depict (dē pikt′) *verb* **1** to be a picture of [This painting *depicts* a street in Pittsburgh.] **2** to describe [The story *depicts* life on a farm.]
de·pict • *verb* **depicted, depicting**

deport (dē pôrt′) *verb* to force to leave a country by an official order [They were *deported* after entering the country illegally.] —Look for the WORD CHOICES box at the entry **banish**.
de·port • *verb* **deported, deporting**

deposit (dē päz′it) *verb* **1** to put into a bank account [We *deposited* $15 yesterday.] **2** to lay down [I *deposited* my books on the chair.]
noun **1** an amount of money that is put into a bank account [I made a *deposit* of $15.] **2** the condition of being deposited [I have $200 on *deposit*.] **3** money that is given as a pledge or a partial payment [We made a *deposit* on the car and arranged to pay the rest in installments.] **4** sand, clay, minerals, or other materials that are left by water, wind, or other forces of nature.
de·pos·it • *verb* **deposited, depositing** • *noun, plural* **deposits**

depot

depot (dē′pō) *noun* a railroad or bus station.
de·pot • *noun, plural* **depots**

depress (dē pres′) *verb* to make sad or gloomy; discourage [A long, cold, dark winter always *depresses* me.]
de·press • *verb* **depressed, depressing**

depression (dē presh′ən) *noun* **1** sadness; a gloomy feeling. **2** a hollow or low place [*depressions* in the rock's surface]. **3** a time when business is bad and many people lose their jobs.
de·pres·sion • *noun, plural* **depressions**

deprive (dē prīv′) *verb* to keep from having or enjoying [A bad cold *deprived* her of a good night's rest.]
de·prive • *verb* **deprived, depriving**

dept. *abbreviation for* department.

depth (depth) *noun* **1** the distance from the top downward or from front to back [The *depth* of the pool is 7 feet. We built a closet 5 feet in *depth*.] **2** *usually* **depths** the deep or deepest part [the *depths* of the ocean]. **3** the quality of being deep [the *depth* of her love for her children].
—in depth in a thorough way [She reported *in depth* on the problem.]
depth • *noun, plural* **depths**

deputy (dep′yo͞o tē) *noun* a person who is chosen to help or take the place of another person [a sheriff's *deputy*].
dep·u·ty • *noun, plural* **deputies**

derby (dur′bē) *noun* a stiff felt hat with a round top.
der·by • *noun, plural* **derbies**

derive (dē rīv′) *verb* to get or receive from a source [Many English words are *derived* from French.]

D

de·rive • *verb* **derived, deriving**

derrick (der′ik) *noun* **1** a large machine for lifting and moving heavy things. It has a long beam that is supported and moved by ropes and pulleys. **2** a tall framework that holds machinery for drilling or pumping [an oil *derrick*].
der·rick • *noun, plural* **derricks**

derrick

descend (dē send′) *verb* **1** to move down to a lower place [The skier *descended* from the top of the hill.] **2** to come from a certain source [They are *descended* from pioneers.]
de·scend • *verb* **descended, descending**

descendant (dē sen′dənt) *noun* a person who is descended from a certain ancestor.
de·scend·ant • *noun, plural* **descendants**

descent (dē sent′) *noun* **1** the act or process of descending, or moving downward. **2** a way or slope downward [the steep *descent* of the mountain road]. **3** the ancestors that a person has descended from [a man of French *descent*].
de·scent • *noun, plural* **descents**

describe (də skrīb′) *verb* to tell or write about in some detail [He *described* his vacation.]
de·scribe • *verb* **described, describing**

description (də skrip′shən) *noun* **1** the act of describing or the words that describe something [The ad in the newspaper had a clear *description* of the lost dog.] **2** kind or sort [The library has books of every *description*.]
de·scrip·tion • *noun, plural* **descriptions**

descriptive (də skrip′tiv) *adjective* having to do with or giving a description [We had a lesson on *descriptive* writing.]
de·scrip·tive • *adjective*

desegregate (dē seg′rə gāt′) *verb* to stop the practice of keeping people of different races apart [They worked to *desegregate* the public schools.]
de·seg·re·gate • *verb* **desegregated, desegregating**

desert[1] (dē zʉrt′) *verb* to go away and leave someone or something that should not be left; abandon [She *deserted* her husband.] —Look for the WORD CHOICES box at the entry **abandon**.
de·sert • *verb* **deserted, deserting**

● The words **desert** and **dessert** sound alike.
A guard shouldn't *desert* his post.
Dessert is eaten at the end of the meal.

desert[2] (dez′ərt) *noun* **1** a dry, sandy region with few plants or no plants in it. **2** a wild region; wilderness.
des·ert • *noun, plural* **deserts**

deserve (dē zʉrv′) *verb* to have a right to; be one that ought to get [This question *deserves* more discussion. You *deserve* a scolding.]
de·serve • *verb* **deserved, deserving**

design (dē zīn′) *verb* **1** to think up and draw plans for [They *designed* a new model of the car.] **2** to arrange the parts, colors, or patterns of [Who *designed* this rug?] **3** to intend or set apart for a certain use [This chair was *designed* for use outside.]
noun **1** a drawing or plan that must be followed in order to make something [a *design* for a house] —Look for the WORD CHOICES box at the entry **plan**. **2** the arrangement of parts, colors, patterns; decoration [the *design* in a rug].
de·sign • *verb* **designed, designing** • *noun, plural* **designs**

designate (dez′ig nāt) *verb* **1** to point out; mark [A dot on this map *designates* a city.] **2** to choose or appoint [We have *designated* José to chair our committee.] **3** to give a name to; call [The geyser erupts every hour and so was *designated* "Old Faithful."]
des·ig·nate • *verb* **designated, designating**

designer (dē zīn′ər) *noun* a person who designs [a dress *designer*].
de·sign·er • *noun, plural* **designers**

desirable (dē zīr′ə bəl) *adjective* worth wanting or having; pleasing, excellent, or attractive [a highly *desirable* job].
de·sir·a·ble • *adjective*

desire (dē zīr′) *verb* to wish or long for; want strongly [She *desires* fame and fortune.]
noun **1** a strong wish or want [a *desire* for

a	cat	ō	go	ʉ	fur	ə =	a *in* ago
ā	ape	ô	law, for	ch	chin		e *in* agent
ä	cot, car	oo	look	sh	she		i *in* pencil
e	ten	ōō	tool	th	thin		o *in* atom
ē	me	oi	oil	*th*	then		u *in* circus
i	fit	ou	out	zh	measure		
ī	ice	u	up	ŋ	ring		

praise]. **2** the thing that a person wishes for [My fondest *desire* is a trip to Hawaii.]
de·sire • *verb* **desired, desiring** • *noun, plural* **desires**

WORD CHOICES

Synonyms of **desire**

The words **desire, crave,** and **want** share the meaning "to long for."

Ted *desires* greater success.

I sometimes *crave* peanut brittle.

Do you *want* a new car?

desk (desk) *noun* a piece of furniture that has a broad, smooth top, and usually drawers. A desk is used for reading or writing.
desk • *noun, plural* **desks**

Des Moines (də moin′) the capital of Iowa.

desolate (des′ə lət) *adjective* **1** not lived in; deserted [a *desolate* plain.] **2** very unhappy; miserable [They were *desolate* when their friend died.]
des·o·late • *adjective*

De Soto (dē sōt′ō), **Hernando** (hər nan′dō) 1500?-1542; Spanish explorer who discovered the Mississippi River.
De So·to, Her·nan·do

despair (də sper′) *noun* the condition of being without hope; loss of hope [He could not find his cat and his *despair* showed on his face.] *verb* to lose or give up hope [The prisoner *despaired* that she would be free again.]
de·spair • *noun* • *verb* **despaired, despairing**

desperate (des′pər ət) *adjective* **1** reckless or careless because one has lost hope [The *desperate* criminals escaped from the jail.] **2** making one lose hope; very dangerous or serious [a *desperate* situation.]
des·per·ate • *adjective*

desperation (des pər ā′shən) *noun* reckless or careless behavior that comes from despair [In *desperation* he jumped into the river to escape.]
des·per·a·tion • *noun*

despise (də spīz′) *verb* to dislike very much [I *despise* him for being a hypocrite.]
de·spise • *verb* **despised, despising**

dessert (dē zʉrt′) *noun* something sweet served at the end of a meal. Fruit, pie, and cake are desserts.
des·sert • *noun, plural* **desserts**

destination (des′ti nā′shən) *noun* the place that a person or thing is going to [The final *destination* of this bus is Chicago.]
des·ti·na·tion • *noun, plural* **destinations**

destiny (des′ti nē) *noun* something that is bound to happen to a person; fate.
des·tin·y • *noun, plural* **destinies**

destroy (dē stroi′) *verb* to put an end to by breaking up, tearing down, ruining, or spoiling.
de·stroy • *verb* **destroyed, destroying**

destroyer

destroyer (dē stroi′ər) *noun* a small, fast warship.
de·stroy·er • *noun, plural* **destroyers**

destruction (dē struk′shən) *noun* **1** the act of destroying. **2** the condition of being destroyed [The forest fire caused much *destruction*.]
de·struc·tion • *noun*

destructive (dē struk′tiv) *adjective* destroying or likely to destroy [a *destructive* thunderstorm].
de·struc·tive • *adjective*

detach (dē tach′) *verb* to unfasten or separate and take away [The railroad workers *detached* five cars from the train.]
de·tach • *verb* **detached, detaching**

detail (dē′tāl *or* dē tāl′) *noun* **1** any one of the small parts that go to make up something; item [Tell us the *details* of your plans.] **2** the process of dealing with things item by item [I

D

hate *detail*. Tell us the general story; don't go into *detail*.]
de·tail • *noun, plural* **details**

detain (dē tān′) *verb* **1** to keep from going on; hold back [A traffic jam *detained* us.] **2** to keep for a while in custody; confine [The police *detained* them for questioning.]
de·tain • *verb* **detained, detaining**

detect (dē tekt′) *verb* to discover something hidden or not easily noticed [I *detected* a slight flaw in one of the glasses my mother bought.]
de·tect • *verb* **detected, detecting**

detective (dē tek′tiv) *noun* a person, often a police officer, whose work is trying to solve crimes or getting secret information.
de·tec·tive • *noun, plural* **detectives**

detector (dē tek′tər) *noun* a device that is used to show that something is present [Every house should have a smoke *detector*.]
de·tec·tor • *noun, plural* **detectors**

detention (dē ten′shən) *noun* **1** the act of detaining, or keeping confined. **2** a kind of punishment in which a student must stay after school.
de·ten·tion • *noun, plural* **detentions**

detergent (dē tʉr′jənt) *noun* a substance that is used for cleaning. It looks and acts like soap but is made of chemicals.
de·ter·gent • *noun, plural* **detergents**

determination (dē tʉr′mi nā′shən) *noun* the condition of having one's mind set on achieving a particular goal and not changing from this course [Our team's *determination* helped us win.]
de·ter·mi·na·tion • *noun*

determine (dē tʉr′min) *verb* **1** to reach a decision about something after thinking about it and investigating it [I need to *determine* whether to go to college.] **2** to set one's mind on something; resolve [She's *determined* to be a lawyer.] **3** to find out exactly [*Determine* your size before you try on a sweater.] **4** to have a decisive effect on [Rainfall often *determines* how well farm crops will do.]
de·ter·mine • *verb* **determined, determining**

detest (dē test′) *verb* to dislike very much; hate [I *detest* liars.]
de·test • *verb* **detested, detesting**

detour (dē′to͝or) *noun* a route used when another route is blocked or closed to traffic [We took a *detour* in order to avoid the traffic jam.]
verb to go by a detour.
de·tour • *noun, plural* **detours**
• *verb* **detoured, detouring**

detract (dē trakt′) *verb* to take away something worthwhile or attractive [Weeds *detract* from the beauty of a lawn.]
de·tract • *verb* **detracted, detracting**

Detroit (dē troit′) a city in southeastern Michigan.
De·troit

devastate (dev′əs tāt) *verb* to ruin or destroy [A nuclear war could *devastate* the earth.]
dev·as·tate • *verb* **devastated, devastating**

develop (dē vel′əp) *verb* **1** to make or become larger, fuller, or better in some way; grow or expand [The seedling *developed* into a tree.] **2** to bring or come into being; evolve [Scientists *developed* a vaccine for polio. Mold *developed* on the cheese.] **3** to treat film used for photographs with chemicals in order to bring the pictures to view.
de·vel·op • *verb* **developed, developing**

development (dē vel′əp mənt) *noun* **1** the act or process of developing; the act of causing to grow, expand, or improve in some other way [The *development* of a quarterback's passing style takes many years.] **2** an area of land that is built with new homes.
de·vel·op·ment • *noun, plural* **developments**

device (dē vīs′) *noun* **1** something made or invented for some special use; a tool, machine, or other piece of equipment. **2** a plan or scheme [Sending him on an errand was a *device* to get him out of the house.]
de·vice • *noun, plural* **devices**

devil (dev′əl) *noun* **1** any one of various evil spirits in religious beliefs and folk tales; demon. **2** a very wicked, cruel, or evil person. **3** a person who is very lively, playful, or daring.
—**the Devil** the chief evil spirit in some religions, who is also called Satan.
dev·il • *noun, plural* **devils**

devise (dē vīz′) *verb* to work out; think up;

a cat	ō go	ʉ fur	ə = a *in* ago
ā ape	ô law, for	ch chin	e *in* agent
ä cot, car	o͝o look	sh she	i *in* pencil
e ten	o͞o tool	th thin	o *in* atom
ē me	oi oil	*th* then	u *in* circus
i fit	ou out	zh measure	
ī ice	u up	ŋ ring	

plan or invent something [She *devised* a new way of washing the car.]
de·vise • ***verb*** **devised, devising**

devote (dē vōt′) ***verb*** to give up oneself or one's time to some goal, activity, or person [They *devote* many hours to helping others.]
de·vote • ***verb*** **devoted, devoting**

devoted (dē vōt′əd) ***adjective*** very loving or loyal [a *devoted* son; *devoted* fans].
de·vot·ed • ***adjective***

devotion (dē vō′shən) ***noun*** loyalty or deep affection [His *devotion* to his wife is obvious.]
de·vo·tion • ***noun***

devour (dē vour′) ***verb*** **1** to eat up in a hungry or greedy way [The cat *devoured* the piece of meat.] **2** to take in with the eyes and ears in a greedy way [My cousin *devours* comic books.]
de·vour • ***verb*** **devoured, devouring**

devout (dē vout′) ***adjective*** **1** very religious. **2** having or showing deep feeling; serious and sincere [a *devout* fan].
de·vout • ***adjective***

dew (do͞o *or* dyo͞o) ***noun*** water that forms in little drops on grass, plants, and other things during the night. Dew forms when warm air meets a cool surface.

- The words **dew, do,** and **due** sound alike.
  There was *dew* on the grass.
  What do you want to *do*?
  I was *due* to arrive before her.

dewlap

dewlap (do͞o′lap *or* dyo͞o′lap) ***noun*** a fold of skin hanging under the throat of cattle and some other animals.
dew·lap • ***noun, plural*** **dewlaps**

di- *a prefix meaning* two or double.

diabetes (dī′ə bēt′ēz *or* dī′ə bēt′əs) ***noun*** a sickness in which the body produces little or no insulin. Insulin is the substance that helps the body use any sugar that is eaten.
di·a·be·tes • ***noun***

diagnosis (dī′əg nō′sis) ***noun*** a decision or opinion about a patient's disease that is formed after examining the patient and studying the symptoms.
di·ag·no·sis • ***noun,***
plural **di·ag·no·ses** (dī′əg nō′sēz)

diagonal (dī ag′ə nəl) ***adjective*** **1** slanting from one corner to the opposite corner of a square or another figure with four sides. **2** going in a slanting direction [a tie with *diagonal* stripes].
noun a diagonal line, plane, course, or part.
di·ag·o·nal • ***adjective*** • ***noun,***
plural **diagonals**

diagram (dī′ə gram) ***noun*** a drawing or plan that helps to explain something by showing all its parts, how it is put together, or how it works.
di·a·gram • ***noun, plural*** **diagrams**

dial (dī′əl) ***noun*** **1** the face of an instrument such as a clock or a water meter. A dial is marked with lines, letters, or numbers. A pointer points to these markings to show time, an amount, or some other kind of information. **2** a control on a radio or TV set that can be turned to choose the station or channel. **3** a disk that can be turned or a set of push buttons on a telephone for making a connection with another telephone.
verb to call on a telephone by using a dial [I *dialed* his number.]
di·al • ***noun, plural*** **dials** • ***verb*** **dialed** or **dialled, dialing** or **dialling**

dialect (dī′ə lekt) ***noun*** a form of a language that is used only in a certain region or by a certain group of people. A dialect does not usually have a written form.
di·a·lect • ***noun, plural*** **dialects**

dialogue or **dialog** (dī′ə lôg) ***noun*** the part of a play, novel, or radio or TV program that is conversation.
di·a·logue or **di·a·log** • ***noun,***
plural **dialogues** or **dialogs**

dial tone ***noun*** a buzzing or humming sound on a telephone. A dial tone tells the user of the telephone that the line is free and that a number may be dialed.

dial tone • *noun, plural* **dial tones**

diameter (dī am′ət ər) ***noun*** **1** a straight line that passes through the center of a circle or sphere from one side to the other. **2** the length of such a line [The *diameter* of the moon is about 2,160 miles.]
di·am·e·ter • ***noun,*** *plural* **diameters**

diamond (dī′ə mənd *or* dī′mənd) ***noun*** **1** a mineral that is a crystal form of nearly pure carbon. It often has no color. Diamond is the hardest natural substance known. It is used in jewelry and to make cutting edges for some tools. **2** a jewel cut from this mineral. Diamonds are very valuable. **3** a figure shaped like this: ♦. **4** a playing card of a suit marked with this figure in red. **5** the infield of a baseball field or the whole playing field.
di·a·mond • ***noun,*** *plural for senses 2, 3, 4, and 5 only* **diamonds**

diaper (dī′ə pər *or* dī′pər) ***noun*** a pad of soft cloth or other material that is worn like panties by a baby, to absorb and contain urine and stool.
di·a·per • ***noun,*** *plural* **diapers**

diaphragm (dī′ə fram) ***noun*** the wall of muscles and tendons between the chest and the abdomen.
di·a·phragm • ***noun,*** *plural* **diaphragms**

diarrhea or **diarrhoea** (dī ər ē′ə) ***noun*** a condition in which bowel movements come too often.
di·ar·rhe·a or **di·ar·rhoe·a** • ***noun***

diary (dī′ər ē) ***noun*** **1** a record written day by day of the things done, seen, or thought by the writer. **2** a book for keeping such a record.
di·a·ry • ***noun,*** *plural* **diaries**

dice (dīs) ***plural noun*** small cubes marked on each side with one to six dots. Dice are used in various games and are usually used in pairs.
verb to cut into small cubes [I *diced* the potatoes for the hash.]
dice • ***plural noun,*** *singular* **die** (dī) or **dice** • ***verb*** **diced, dicing**

dice

Dickens (dik′ənz), **Charles** (chärlz) 1812-1870; English novelist.
Dick·ens, Charles

Dickinson (dik′in sən), **Emily** (em′ə lē) 1830-1886; U.S. poet.
Dick·in·son, Em·i·ly

dictate (dik′tāt) ***verb*** **1** to speak or read something aloud for someone else to write down [The lawyer *dictated* a letter to her secretary.] **2** to command or order [The school *dictates* what clothes students are allowed to wear.]
dic·tate • ***verb*** **dictated, dictating**

dictator (dik′tāt ər) ***noun*** a ruler who has complete power over a country.
dic·ta·tor • ***noun,*** *plural* **dictators**

dictionary (dik′shə ner′ē) ***noun*** a book in which words are listed alphabetically with their meanings, pronunciations, and other information.
dic·tion·ar·y • ***noun,*** *plural* **dictionaries**

did (did) ***verb*** *past tense of* **do**[1].

didn't (did′nt) did not.
did·n't

die[1] (dī) ***verb*** **1** to stop living; become dead. **2** to stop going, moving, acting, etc. [The motor sputtered and *died.*] **3** to lose force; become weak or faint [The storm passed and the wind slowly *died.*] **4** [*an informal use*] to want very much [She's *dying* to know my secret.]
die • ***verb*** **died, dying**

● The words **die** and **dye** sound alike.
Without sunlight, the plant will *die.*
You may roll one *die* or two dice.
Does Grandfather *dye* his hair?

die[2] (dī) ***noun*** **1** either of a pair of dice [Some games are played with one *die.*] **2** a tool or device that is used to give a certain form to some object. Dies are used to punch holes in metal, cut threads in screws, or stamp the design on coins.
die • ***noun,*** *plural for sense 1 only* **dice** *or, for sense 2 only,* **dies**

● The words **die** and **dye** sound alike.
Dad is a tool and *die* maker.
The bugs will *die* off in the fall.
The icing was colored with food *dye.*

dieresis (dī er′ə sis) ***noun*** a mark that is made up of two dots (¨). It is put over certain vowel letters to show a certain sound. In this

a	cat	ō	go	ʉ	fur	ə =	a *in* ago
ā	ape	ô	law, for	ch	chin		e *in* agent
ä	cot, car	oo	look	sh	she		i *in* pencil
e	ten	ōō	tool	th	thin		o *in* atom
ē	me	oi	oil	*th*	then		u *in* circus
i	fit	ou	out	zh	measure		
ī	ice	u	up	ŋ	ring		

dictionary, it is placed over the letter *a* in pronunciations to show the sound of the vowel in *car* (kär) and *lot* (lät).
di·er·e·sis • ***noun,*** *plural* **di·er·e·ses** (dī er′ə sēz′)

diesel (dē′zəl *or* dē′səl) ***noun*** **1** a type of engine that burns fuel by using the heat that comes from air put under high pressure: this type of engine is also called **diesel engine** or **diesel motor**. **2** a train, automobile, or truck that has a diesel engine or motor.
die·sel • ***noun,*** *plural* **diesels**

diet (dī′ət) ***noun*** **1** what a person or animal usually eats or drinks; usual food. **2** a group of foods or an amount of food chosen and eaten for a special reason. A person can go on a diet in order to become healthier or in order to gain or lose weight.
verb to eat certain kinds and amounts of food, especially in order to lose weight.
di·et • ***noun,*** *plural* **diets** • ***verb*** **dieted, dieting**

differ (dif′ər) ***verb*** **1** to be not the same; be unlike [My hobbies *differ* from yours.] **2** to have different or opposite opinions or ideas; disagree [We *differed* about how to spend the money.]
dif·fer • ***verb*** **differed, differing**

difference (dif′ər əns *or* dif′rəns) ***noun*** **1** the condition of being not alike or the way in which people or things are not alike [A new rug made a big *difference*. One of the *differences* between the twins was the color of their hair.] **2** disagreement or argument [They are friends in spite of their *differences* over sports.] **3** the amount that is left after one number is subtracted from another. In the problem 11 - 7 = 4, 4 is the difference.
dif·fer·ence • ***noun,*** *plural* **differences**

different (dif′ər ənt *or* dif′rənt) ***adjective*** **1** not alike; unlike [Cottage cheese is *different* from Swiss cheese.] **2** not the same; separate [There are three *different* colleges in the city.]
dif·fer·ent • ***adjective***

difficult (dif′i kult′) ***adjective*** **1** hard to do, make, or understand; needing much trouble, thought, or skill [This arithmetic problem is *difficult*.] **2** hard to deal with or get along with [In our family we have several *difficult* relatives.]
dif·fi·cult • ***adjective***

difficulty (dif′i kul′tē) ***noun*** **1** the condition of being difficult [These lessons are arranged in order of their *difficulty*.] **2** something that is difficult [The astronauts overcame many *difficulties* in order to land on the moon.]
dif·fi·cul·ty • ***noun,*** *plural* **difficulties**

dig (dig) ***verb*** **1** to turn up or remove ground with a spade, the hands, claws, or in some other way [The children are *digging* in the sand.] **2** to make by digging [Prairie dogs *dig* burrows.] **3** to get out by digging [Mary *digs* potatoes from her garden.] **4** to find out, especially by careful study [The police *dug* out the truth about the robberies.]
dig • ***verb*** **dug, digging**

digest (di jest′ *or* dī jest′ *for v.;* dī′jest *for n.*) ***verb*** **1** to change food in the stomach and intestines into a form that can be used by the body [Small babies cannot *digest* solid food.] **2** to be digested [Some foods do not *digest* easily.]
noun a short version of an article, story, or other written work —Look for the WORD CHOICES box at the entry **summary**.
di·gest • ***verb*** **digested, digesting** • ***noun,*** *plural* **digests**

digestion (di jes′chən *or* dī jes′chən) ***noun*** **1** the act or process of digesting foods. **2** the ability to digest food [His *digestion* is good.]
di·ges·tion • ***noun,*** *plural* **digestions**

digestive (di jes′tiv *or* dī jes′tiv) ***adjective*** having to do with digestion [the *digestive* juices].
di·ges·tive • ***adjective***

digestive system
noun the tube through which food passes, is digested, and leaves as waste. In humans, the digestive system includes the mouth, the esophagus, the stomach, the intestines, and certain other organs.
digestive system • ***noun,*** *plural* **digestive systems**

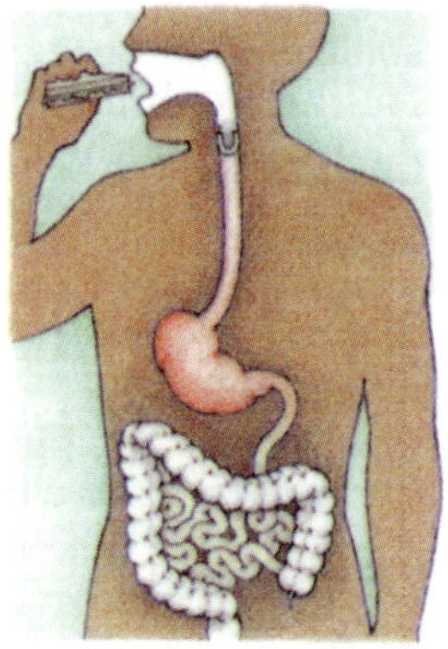
digestive system

digit (dij′it) ***noun*** **1** any number from 0 through 9. **2** a finger or toe.
dig·it • ***noun,*** *plural* **digits**

digital (dij′i təl) ***adjective*** **1** showing the time, temperature, or some other information by a row of digits rather than by numbers on

a dial [a *digital* clock]. **2** using a way of recording sound that has been changed into electronic bits and stored on a compact disc or a tape [a *digital* recording].
dig·it·al • *adjective*

dignified (dig′ni fīd) *adjective* having or showing dignity; stately or imposing [a *dignified* way of walking. He gave a *dignified* answer to the rude question.]
dig·ni·fied • *adjective*

dignity (dig′ni tē) *noun* **1** the quality of being worthy of honor or respect [We should respect the *dignity* of all persons.] **2** stately appearance or manner [Swans move through the water with graceful *dignity*.]
dig·ni·ty • *noun*

dike (dīk) *noun* a wall or dam that is built to keep a sea or river from flooding over land.
dike • *noun, plural* **dikes**

dilapidated (di lap′i dāt′əd) *adjective* falling to pieces; broken down; shabby and neglected [a *dilapidated* building].
di·lap·i·dat·ed • *adjective*

diligent (dil′i jənt) *adjective* doing one's work in a careful, steady way; working hard; industrious [Sue is a *diligent* worker.]
dil·i·gent • *adjective*

dilute (di lo͞ot′ *or* dī lo͞ot′) *verb* to thin out or weaken by adding water [As the ice cubes melted, they *diluted* the juice.]
di·lute • *verb* **diluted, diluting**

dim (dim) *adjective* **1** not bright or clear; somewhat dark [a *dim* star in the sky] —Look for the WORD CHOICES box at the entry **dark**. **2** not clear to the eyes, the ears, or the mind; faint [a *dim* sound; a *dim* memory of an event].
verb to make or grow dim [When cars approach each other they should *dim* their headlights.]
dim • *adjective* **dimmer, dimmest**
• *verb* **dimmed, dimming**

DiMaggio (di mä′jē ō′), **Joseph (Paul)** (jō′zəf) 1914-1999; U.S. baseball player.
Di·Mag·gi·o, Jo·seph (Paul)

dime (dīm) *noun* a coin of the U.S. and Canada that is equal to ten cents. A dime is one-tenth of a dollar.
dime • *noun, plural* **dimes**

dimension (di men′shən) *noun* a measurement of something in length, width, or height.
di·men·sion • *noun, plural* **dimensions**

diminish (di min′ish) *verb* to make or become smaller in force, importance, size, or some other way [The drought *diminished* the size of the crops. Danger of frost *diminishes* in April.] —Look for the WORD CHOICES box at the entry **wane**.
di·min·ish • *verb* **diminished, diminishing**

dimple (dim′pəl) *noun* a small hollow on the skin, usually on the cheek or chin.
dim·ple • *noun, plural* **dimples**

din (din) *noun* a loud, steady noise or confused uproar [the *din* of the crowd] —Look for the WORD CHOICES box at the entry **noise**.
din • *noun, plural* **dins**

dine (dīn) *verb* to eat dinner [We *dine* at 8:00.]
dine • *verb* **dined, dining**

diner (dī′nər) *noun* **1** a person eating dinner. **2** a railroad car in which meals are served. **3** a small restaurant with a counter.
din·er • *noun, plural* **diners**

dinette (dī net′) *noun* **1** a small room or area used as a dining room. **2** a set of table and chairs used in this space.
din·ette • *noun, plural* **dinettes**

dinghy

dinghy (diŋ′gē) *noun* a small boat.
din·ghy • *noun, plural* **dinghies**

dingy (din′jē) *adjective* having a dull, dirty look; not bright or clean [a *dingy* room].
din·gy • *adjective* **dingier, dingiest**

dining room *noun* a room where meals are eaten.
dining room • *noun, plural* **dining rooms**

a cat	ō go	ʉ fur	ə = a *in* ago
ā ape	ô law, for	ch chin	e *in* agent
ä cot, car	o͝o look	sh she	i *in* pencil
e ten	o͞o tool	th thin	o *in* atom
ē me	oi oil	*th* then	u *in* circus
i fit	ou out	zh measure	
ī ice	u up	ŋ ring	

dinner (din′ər) ***noun*** **1** the main meal of the day. **2** a formal meal in honor of some person or event [Thanksgiving *dinner*].
din·ner • ***noun,*** *plural* **dinners**

dinosaur (dī′nə sôr) ***noun*** one of a group of reptiles that lived millions of years ago. Dinosaurs had four legs and a long, tapering tail. Some dinosaurs were much bigger than elephants and others were as small as cats.
di·no·saur • ***noun,*** *plural* **dinosaurs**

diocese (dī′ə sis *or* dī′ə sēz) ***noun*** the church district under the control of a bishop.
di·o·cese • ***noun,*** *plural* **dioceses**

dip (dip) ***verb*** **1** to put into a liquid and quickly pull out again [He *dipped* the brush into the paint.] **2** to go down into a liquid and quickly come out again [The canoe paddles *dipped* gently through the water.] **3** to lower and quickly raise or rise again [The airplane *dipped* its right wing.] **4** to slope downward [Signs show where the road *dips*.] **5** to take out by scooping with a dipper, the hand, or by some other means [She *dipped* water from a bucket.]
noun **1** something dipped or scooped out [a *dip* of ice cream]. **2** a short swim [We have time for a quick *dip* before dinner.] **3** a downward slope [a *dip* in the road]. **4** a thick, creamy sauce in which potato chips, vegetables, or crackers are dipped to be eaten as appetizers or snacks.
dip • ***verb*** **dipped, dipping** • ***noun,*** *plural* **dips**

diphthong (dif′thôŋ *or* dip′thôŋ) ***noun*** a sound that is made by pronouncing two vowels one right after the other. Listen carefully to the diphthong (oi) in "boy," and you will hear sounds much like (ō) and (ē) that have been run together.
diph·thong • ***noun,*** *plural* **diphthongs**

diploma (di plō′mə) ***noun*** an official paper given to a student by a school or college. It shows that the student has finished the required courses.
di·plo·ma • ***noun,*** *plural* **diplomas**

diplomat (dip′lə mat) ***noun*** **1** a person in a government whose work is dealing with the governments of other nations. **2** a person who has tact in dealing with others.
dip·lo·mat • ***noun,*** *plural* **diplomats**

dipper (dip′ər) ***noun*** **1** a cup with a long handle, used for scooping up liquids. **2** either of two groups of stars in the shape of a dipper. One is called the *Big Dipper*, and the other is called the *Little Dipper*.
dip·per • ***noun,*** *plural* **dippers**

direct (dər ekt′) ***adjective*** **1** by the shortest way; without turning or stopping; straight [a *direct* route home]. **2** honest and to the point; frank [He gave me a *direct* answer to my question.]
verb **1** to be in charge of; manage; control [We have no one to *direct* the play.] **2** to command or order [The king *directed* his subjects to pay higher taxes.] **3** to tell someone the way to a place [Can you *direct* me to the office?] **4** to aim or steer; point [He *directed* his remark to me.]
adverb directly [This bus runs *direct* to Miami.]
di·rect • ***adjective*** • ***verb*** **directed, directing** • ***adverb***

direct current ***noun*** an electric current that flows in one direction only. This is the type of power that is produced by batteries.

direction (dər ek′shən) ***noun*** **1** the act of directing or managing; control [The choir is under the *direction* of Ms. Jones.] **2** *usually* **directions** instructions on how to get some place or how to do something [I need *directions* for driving to your house.] **3** the point toward which something faces; the line along which something lies or moves [We drove in the *direction* of the lake.]
di·rec·tion • ***noun,*** *plural* **directions**

directly (dər ekt′lē) ***adverb*** **1** in a direct line or way; straight [Come *directly* home after school.] **2** with nothing coming between [The books were given *directly* to me.]
di·rect·ly • ***adverb***

direct object ***noun*** the word or words in a sentence, such as "apples" in "We picked apples," that tell who or what receives the action of the verb.
direct object • ***noun,*** *plural* **direct objects**

director (dər ek′tər) ***noun*** a person who directs or manages the work of others [the *director* of a play; a band *director*].
di·rec·tor • ***noun,*** *plural* **directors**

directory (dər ek′tər ē) ***noun*** a book or list of names and addresses [a telephone *directory*].
di·rec·to·ry • ***noun,*** *plural* **directories**

dirigible (dər ij′i bəl) ***noun*** a large, long airship that can be steered.
dir·i·gi·ble • ***noun,*** *plural* **dirigibles**

D

dirt (durt) *noun* **1** matter such as mud or soot that makes things unclean. **2** earth or soil.

dirty (durt′ē) *adjective* **1** not clean; needing to be washed [a *dirty* face; *dirty* clothes]. **2** unfair; dishonest [a *dirty* player]. **3** not nice; mean; nasty [a *dirty* trick].
verb to make or become dirty [How did you *dirty* yourself so quickly?]
dirt·y • *adjective* **dirtier, dirtiest**
• *verb* **dirtied, dirtying, dirties**

WORD CHOICES

Synonyms of **dirty**

Many words share the meaning "covered or filled with dirt."

filthy	grimy
foul	unclean

dis- *a prefix meaning:* **1** away from or out of [The police officer *disarmed* the robber by taking away his gun.] **2** the opposite of [Being *dishonest* is the opposite of being honest.] **3** to fail, stop, or refuse [A person who *disobeys* is refusing to obey.]

WORD MAKER

The prefix **dis-**

Many words contain the prefix **dis-** plus a word that you already know. You can understand these words if you add the idea "not" or "the opposite of" to the meaning of the base word.

prefix	*+ base word*	⇨	*new word*
dis-	**+ prove**	⇨	**disprove** *(the opposite of "prove")*
	believe		disbelieve
	comfort		discomfort
	courteous		discourteous
	entangle		disentangle
	respectful		disrespectful
	satisfaction		dissatisfaction
	similar		dissimilar
	unite		disunite

disability (dis′ə bil′i tē) *noun* **1** the condition of not being able or fit to do something [His *disability* prevented him from joining the sports program.] **2** something that disables [A broken leg may be a long-term *disability*.]
dis·a·bil·i·ty • *noun, plural* **disabilities**

disable (dis ā′bəl) *verb* to make unable to move, act, or work in a normal way [The accident *disabled* her for weeks.]
dis·a·ble • *verb* **disabled, disabling**

disadvantage (dis′əd vant′ij) *noun* **1** anything that stands in the way of success; handicap [A weak knee is a *disadvantage* to a baseball player.] **2** loss or harm [This decision will work to your *disadvantage*.]
dis·ad·van·tage • *noun, plural* **disadvantages**

disagree (dis ə grē′) *verb* **1** to differ in opinion [My mother and her sister strongly *disagree* on politics.] **2** to be different; differ [The facts in these two book reports *disagree*.] **3** to be harmful or give discomfort: followed by *with* [Raw vegetables *disagree* with me.]
dis·a·gree • *verb* **disagreed, disagreeing**

disagreeable (dis ə grē′ə bəl) *adjective* **1** unpleasant; offensive [a *disagreeable* odor]. **2** hard to get along with [a *disagreeable* person].
dis·a·gree·a·ble • *adjective*

disagreement (dis ə grē′mənt) *noun* a difference of opinion or an argument [We had a *disagreement* about which movie to see.]
dis·a·gree·ment • *noun, plural* **disagreements**

disappear (dis ə pir′) *verb* to stop being seen or to stop existing; vanish [The car *disappeared* around a curve. Dinosaurs *disappeared* millions of years ago.] —Look for the WORD CHOICES box at the entry **vanish**.
dis·ap·pear • *verb* **disappeared, disappearing**

disappearance (dis ə pir′əns) *noun* the act or fact of disappearing [The *disappearance* of my bicycle is still a mystery.]
dis·ap·pear·ance • *noun, plural* **disappearances**

disappoint (dis ə point′) *verb* to fail to give or

a cat	ō go	ʉ fur	ə = a *in* ago
ā ape	ô law, for	ch chin	e *in* agent
ä cot, car	oo look	sh she	i *in* pencil
e ten	ōō tool	th thin	o *in* atom
ē me	oi oil	*th* then	u *in* circus
i fit	ou out	zh measure	
ī ice	u up	ŋ ring	

do something wanted, expected, or promised [You promised to come, but you *disappointed* us.]
dis·ap·point • *verb* **disappointed, disappointing**

disappointment (dis ə point′mənt) *noun* **1** the feeling of being disappointed [Their *disappointment* over not winning showed in their faces.] **2** a person or thing that disappoints [Our team is a *disappointment* this year.]
dis·ap·point·ment • *noun, plural* **disappointments**

disapproval (dis ə pro͞o′vəl) *noun* an opinion or feeling against someone or something [The crowd showed its *disapproval* by booing.]
dis·ap·prov·al • *noun*

disapprove (dis ə pro͞ov′) *verb* to have an opinion or feeling against; think to be wrong [The Puritans *disapproved* of dancing.]
dis·ap·prove • *verb* **disapproved, disapproving**

disaster (di zas′tər) *noun* a happening that causes much damage or suffering. An earthquake is a disaster.
dis·as·ter • *noun, plural* **disasters**

disbelief (dis bə lēf′) *noun* the condition of not believing [The man stared at me in *disbelief*.]
dis·be·lief • *noun*

disc (disk) *noun* **1** *another spelling of* **disk**. **2** a phonograph record.
disc • *noun, plural* **discs**

discard (dis kärd′) *verb* to throw away or get rid of something that is no longer wanted [Many people *discard* clothes when they tear.]
dis·card • *verb* **discarded, discarding**

discharge (dis chärj′ *for v.;* dis′chärj *for n.*) *verb* **1** to release from something that controls or holds in [The doctor *discharged* the patient from the hospital.] **2** to remove a burden or load; unload [The boat *discharged* its cargo.] **3** to fire or go off [The gun accidentally *discharged*.]
noun **1** the act of discharging or an instance of being discharged [The soldier received an honorable *discharge* from the army.] **2** something discharged [A watery *discharge* flowed from his eye.]
dis·charge • *verb* **discharged, discharging** • *noun, plural* **discharges**

disciple (di sī′pəl) *noun* a pupil or follower of a teacher or leader.
dis·ci·ple • *noun, plural* **disciples**

discipline (dis′i plin) *noun* **1** training that teaches one to obey rules and control one's behavior [the strict *discipline* of the army]. **2** the result of such training; self-control; orderly behavior [The pupils showed perfect *discipline*.] **3** punishment [harsh *discipline*].
verb **1** to train in discipline [Regular chores help to *discipline* children.] **2** to punish —Look for the WORD CHOICES box at the entry **punish**.
dis·ci·pline • *noun* • *verb* **disciplined, disciplining**

disc jockey *noun* **1** a person who broadcasts a radio program of recorded popular music. **2** a person who plays recorded music in a nightclub or at a social function.
disc jockey • *noun, plural* **disc jockeys**

disconnect (dis kə nekt′) *verb* to break or undo the connection of or between [The repairman *disconnected* the plug from the wall socket.]
dis·con·nect • *verb* **disconnected, disconnecting**

discontent (dis kən tent′) *noun* a feeling of not being satisfied and wanting something different.
dis·con·tent • *noun*

discontented (dis kən tent′əd) *adjective* wanting things to be different from what they are; not satisfied.
dis·con·tent·ed • *adjective*

discontinue (dis′kən tin′yo͞o) *verb* to stop doing, using, or making; give up.
dis·con·tin·ue • *verb* **discontinued, discontinuing**

discord (dis′kôrd) *noun* the fact of failing to get along well together; lack of agreement; conflict.
dis·cord • *noun*

WORD CHOICES

Synonyms of **discord**

The words **discord**, **conflict**, and **controversy** share the meaning "a failure to agree or get along well together."

There was much *discord* among the nations of Africa.

They tried to settle a *conflict* within the labor union.

The new tax caused much *controversy*.

D

discount (dis′kount *for n.;* dis kount′ *for v.*) ***noun*** an amount that is subtracted from a price, bill, or debt [She got a 10% *discount* on the $100 radio, so it cost only $90.]
verb **1** to subtract a certain amount from a price, bill, or debt. **2** to tend not to believe [You'd better *discount* that rumor.]
dis·count • ***noun,*** *plural* **discounts** • ***verb*** **discounted, discounting**

discourage (di skʉr′ij) ***verb*** **1** to try to prevent by disapproving or interfering [We *discouraged* her from buying the bike.] **2** to cause to lose hope or confidence [The lack of applause *discouraged* the singer.]
dis·cour·age • ***verb*** **discouraged, discouraging**

discover (di skuv′ər) ***verb*** **1** to be the first person to find, see, or learn about [An astronomer in Arizona *discovered* the planet Pluto in 1930.] **2** to come upon or find out about [I *discovered* my name on the list.]
dis·cov·er • ***verb*** **discovered, discovering**

discovery (di skuv′ər ē) ***noun*** **1** the act or process of discovering. **2** something that is discovered [Radium was a great scientific *discovery*.]
dis·cov·er·y • ***noun,*** *plural* **discoveries**

discreet (di skrēt′) ***adjective*** prudent or careful in saying or doing things; able to keep secrets.
dis·creet • ***adjective***

discriminate (di skrim′i nāt′) ***verb*** **1** to see the difference; make a distinction [Some people cannot *discriminate* between red and green.] **2** to show prejudice by treating someone in a less kind or fair way.
dis·crim·i·nate • ***verb*** **discriminated, discriminating**

discrimination (di skrim′i nā′shən) ***noun*** **1** the act of discriminating or distinguishing [Learn *discrimination* between right and wrong.] **2** the practice of treating persons in a less kind or fair way because of prejudice [*Discrimination* against minority groups is wrong.]
dis·crim·i·na·tion • ***noun,*** *plural* **discriminations**

discus (dis′kəs) ***noun*** a heavy disk of metal and wood. Athletes throw this disk as far as they can in a contest of strength and skill.
dis·cus • ***noun,*** *plural* **discuses**

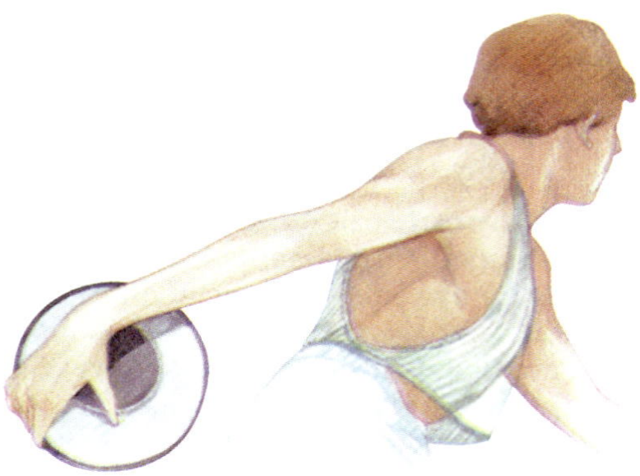

discus

discuss (di skus′) ***verb*** to talk or write about, giving various ideas and opinions.
dis·cuss • ***verb*** **discussed, discussing**

discussion (di skush′ən) ***noun*** talk or writing about something in depth.
dis·cus·sion • ***noun,*** *plural* **discussions**

disease (di zēz′) ***noun*** a condition of not being healthy; sickness or illness.
dis·ease • ***noun,*** *plural* **diseases**

disgrace (dis grās′) ***noun*** **1** loss of respect or honor; shame [She is in *disgrace* for cheating on the test.] **2** a person or thing that brings shame [Dirty streets are a *disgrace*.]
verb to bring shame or dishonor upon [My cousin's crime has *disgraced* our family.]
dis·grace • ***noun,*** *plural* **disgraces** • ***verb*** **disgraced, disgracing**

disgraceful (dis grās′fəl) ***adjective*** causing disgrace; shameful [His behavior was *disgraceful*.]
dis·grace·ful • ***adjective***

disguise (dis gīz′) ***verb*** to make seem so different as to be not recognizable [He *disguised* himself with a false beard.]
noun **1** clothes, makeup, ways of acting, and other things that are used to hide a person's identity. **2** the act of disguising or the condition of being disguised [Come to the Halloween party in *disguise*.]
dis·guise • ***verb*** **disguised, disguising** • ***noun,*** *plural* **disguises**

a cat	ō go	ʉ fur	ə = a *in* ago
ā ape	ô law, for	ch chin	e *in* agent
ä cot, car	oo look	sh she	i *in* pencil
e ten	ōō tool	th thin	o *in* atom
ē me	oi oil	*th* then	u *in* circus
i fit	ou out	zh measure	
ī ice	u up	ŋ ring	

disgust (dis gust′) ***noun*** strong dislike that makes a person feel almost sick [The smell of garbage filled me with *disgust*.]
verb to cause this kind of dislike in [His table manners always *disgust* me.]
dis·gust • ***noun*** • ***verb*** **disgusted, disgusting**

dish (dish) ***noun*** **1** a plate, bowl, saucer, or other container that is used to serve food at the table. **2** an amount of food that is served in a dish [a *dish* of ice cream]. **3** a type of food [Spaghetti is my favorite *dish*.]
dish • ***noun,*** *plural* **dishes**

dishonest (dis än′əst) ***adjective*** not honest; tending to lie, cheat, or steal —Look for the WORD CHOICES box at the entry **bad**.
dis·hon·est • ***adjective***

dishonor (dis än′ər) ***noun*** loss of honor or respect; shame.
verb to bring shame upon.
dis·hon·or • ***noun*** • ***verb*** **dishonored, dishonoring**

dishwasher (dish′wôsh ər) ***noun*** **1** a machine for washing dishes, pots, pans, and other cooking utensils. **2** a person who washes dishes in a restaurant.
dish·wash·er • ***noun,*** *plural* **dishwashers**

disinfect (dis′in fekt′) ***verb*** to kill disease germs in or on; sterilize [The nurse *disinfected* the thermometer.]
dis·in·fect • ***verb*** **disinfected, disinfecting**

disinfectant (dis′in fek′tənt) ***noun*** something that disinfects. Iodine is a disinfectant.
dis·in·fect·ant • ***noun,*** *plural* **disinfectants**

disintegrate (dis in′tə grāt′) ***verb*** to break up into parts or pieces [The old books *disintegrated* in the library.]
dis·in·te·grate • ***verb*** **disintegrated, disintegrating**

disinterested (dis in′trəs təd) ***adjective*** not having a personal interest in something [A *disinterested* judge chose the winner.]
dis·in·ter·est·ed • ***adjective***

disk (disk) ***noun*** **1** something that is round, thin, and flat. **2** a thin, flat, round plate with a special coating that is used for storing information in a computer.
disk • ***noun,*** *plural* **disks**

diskette (di sket′) ***noun*** *the same as* **floppy disk**.
disk·ette • ***noun,*** *plural* **diskettes**

dislike (dis līk′) ***verb*** to have a feeling of not liking; be opposed to [I *dislike* people who lie.]
noun a feeling of not liking [The gardener felt a strong *dislike* for toads and slugs.]
dis·like • ***verb*** **disliked, disliking** • ***noun,*** *plural* **dislikes**

dislocate (dis′lō kāt′) ***verb*** to put out of proper position [I *dislocated* my shoulder.]
dis·lo·cate • ***verb*** **dislocated, dislocating**

dislodge (dis läj′) ***verb*** to force from a resting or hiding place [The landslide *dislodged* a huge rock and sent it crashing down the hill.]
dis·lodge • ***verb*** **dislodged, dislodging**

disloyal (dis loi′əl) ***adjective*** not loyal or faithful.
dis·loy·al • ***adjective***

dismal (diz′məl) ***adjective*** **1** causing gloom or misery; sad [a *dismal* story]. **2** dark and gloomy [a *dismal* room].
dis·mal • ***adjective***

WORD HISTORY

dismal

The word **dismal** comes from two Latin words that mean "evil days." People who lived about 600 years ago believed that certain days of the year were unlucky or evil. These "evil days" tended to make people worry or feel unhappy. After a while, anything that made people unhappy could be called **dismal**.

dismay (dis mā′) ***verb*** to fill with fear, concern, or dread so that one is not sure of what to do [We were *dismayed* at the news of her accident.]
noun loss of courage or confidence in the face of trouble or danger [The doctor's report filled her with *dismay*.]
dis·may • ***verb*** **dismayed, dismaying** • ***noun***

dismiss (dis mis′) ***verb*** **1** to send away; tell or allow to leave [The teacher *dismissed* the class.] **2** to remove from a job or position; to fire [The boss *dismissed* two employees.]
dis·miss • ***verb*** **dismissed, dismissing**

dismissal (dis mis′əl) ***noun*** **1** the act of dismissing [The boss ordered the *dismissal* of several workers.] **2** the condition of being dismissed [He took a job after his *dismissal* from school.]

dis·miss·al • *noun, plural* **dismissals**

dismount (dis mount′) *verb* to get off a horse, bicycle, or motorcycle.
dis·mount • *verb* **dismounted, dismounting**

disobedience (dis′ō bē′dē əns) *noun* the act of refusing to obey; a lack of obedience.
dis·o·be·di·ence • *noun*

disobey (dis′ō bā′) *verb* to refuse to obey.
dis·o·bey • *verb* **disobeyed, disobeying**

disorder (dis ôr′dər) *noun* **1** lack of order; confusion [His room is in complete *disorder*.] **2** a sickness; ailment [a stomach *disorder*].
dis·or·der • *noun, plural* **disorders**

disorderly (dis ôr′dər lē) *adjective* **1** not orderly or neat; messy [a *disorderly* desk]. **2** disturbing the peace and quiet [*disorderly* conduct].
dis·or·der·ly • *adjective*

dispatch (di spach′ *for v.;* dis′pach *for n.*) *verb* to send out quickly to a certain place or for a certain job [We've *dispatched* a person to repair the telephones.]
noun **1** an official message [A *dispatch* was sent from the government to the ambassador.] **2** a news story that is sent to a newspaper or a TV or radio station.
dis·patch • *verb* **dispatched, dispatching** • *noun, plural* **dispatches**

dispel (di spel′) *verb* to scatter and drive away; make disappear [Wind *dispelled* the fog.]
dis·pel • *verb* **dispelled, dispelling**

dispense (di spens′) *verb* **1** to give out; distribute [The agency *dispenses* clothing to refugees.] **2** to prepare and give out [A pharmacist *dispenses* medicines.]
dis·pense • *verb* **dispensed, dispensing**

WORD CHOICES

Synonyms of **dispense**

The words **dispense, distribute,** and **ration** share the meaning "to give out."

A doctor *dispenses* drugs to patients.

The politician *distributed* leaflets to the crowd.

Supplies were *rationed* to the flood victims.

dispenser (di spen′sər) *noun* a container that dispenses what is in it in handy amounts.
dis·pens·er • *noun, plural* **dispensers**

displace (dis plās′) *verb* **1** to move from the usual or proper place [The storm *displaced* people along the coast.] **2** to take the place of; replace [Computers have *displaced* many office workers.]
dis·place • *verb* **displaced, displacing**

display (di splā′) *verb* **1** to put or spread out so as to be seen; to exhibit [I *displayed* my stamp collection for the whole class to see.] —Look for the WORD CHOICES box at the entry **show**. **2** to do something that is a sign or example of; to show or reveal [She *displayed* great courage.]
noun **1** the act of displaying or showing [a *display* of courage]. **2** something that is displayed [a *display* of toys in the store window].
dis·play • *verb* **displayed, displaying** • *noun, plural* **displays**

displease (dis plēz′) *verb* to make angry or not satisfied; annoy.
dis·please • *verb* **displeased, displeasing**

disposable (di spō′zə bəl) *adjective* meant to be thrown away after use [*disposable* soft-drink bottles; *disposable* syringes].
dis·pos·a·ble • *adjective*

disposal (di spō′zəl) *noun* **1** the act of disposing [The city provides for *disposal* of rubbish.] **2** a machine in the drain of a kitchen sink that grinds garbage so it can be washed down the drain.
dis·pos·al • *noun, plural* **disposals**

dispose (di spōz′) *verb used mainly in the phrase* **dispose of**, to get rid of by giving or throwing away, using up, or selling [*Dispose of* those apples before they rot.]
dis·pose • *verb* **disposed, disposing**

disposition (dis pə zish′ən) *noun* **1** a person's usual or general mood; nature [He has a cheerful *disposition*.] **2** a particular tendency; inclination [a *disposition* to be helpful].
dis·po·si·tion • *noun, plural* **dispositions**

dispute (di spyo͞ot′) *verb* **1** to argue or debate [The crowd *disputed* with the police over the right to demonstrate.] **2** to question or deny

a	cat	ō	go	ʉ	fur	ə =	a *in* ago
ā	ape	ô	law, for	ch	chin		e *in* agent
ä	cot, car	o͝o	look	sh	she		i *in* pencil
e	ten	o͞o	tool	th	thin		o *in* atom
ē	me	oi	oil	*th*	then		u *in* circus
i	fit	ou	out	zh	measure		
ī	ice	u	up	ŋ	ring		

the truth of [The U.S. *disputed* Spain's claim to Cuba.]
noun an argument or debate [a *dispute* over the meaning of the new law.] —Look for the WORD CHOICES box at the entry **argument**.
dis·pute • ***verb*** **disputed, disputing** • ***noun,*** *plural* **disputes**

disqualify (dis kwôl′i fī′) ***verb*** to make unfit for or say that someone is unfit for a position or action [Being born in a foreign country *disqualifies* a person from being President.]
dis·qual·i·fy • ***verb*** **disqualified, disqualifying, disqualifies**

disregard (dis′ri gärd′) ***verb*** to pay no attention to; ignore [They *disregarded* our warning.]
noun lack of attention; the fact of ignoring [He acted with total *disregard* for his own safety.]
dis·re·gard • ***verb*** **disregarded, disregarding** • ***noun***

disrespect (dis′ri spekt′) ***noun*** lack of respect or courtesy; rude behavior.
dis·re·spect • ***noun***

disrupt (dis rupt′) ***verb*** to disturb or interrupt the orderly progress of [A few noisy members *disrupted* the club meeting.]
dis·rupt • ***verb*** **disrupted, disrupting**

dissatisfy (dis sat′is fī′) ***verb*** to fail to satisfy; leave wanting more or wanting something different [She is *dissatisfied* with her salary.]
dis·sat·is·fy • ***verb*** **dissatisfied, dissatisfying, dissatisfies**

dissent (di sent′) ***verb*** to differ in opinion; disagree [Several of us *dissented* from the vote of the majority.]
noun a difference of opinion; disagreement.
dis·sent • ***verb*** **dissented, dissenting** • ***noun,*** *plural* **dissents**

dissolve (di zôlv′) ***verb*** to mix thoroughly with a liquid [I *dissolved* the sugar in my coffee.] —Look for the WORD CHOICES box at the entry **melt**.
dis·solve • ***verb*** **dissolved, dissolving**

dissuade (di swād′) ***verb*** to persuade not to do something [Try to *dissuade* them from going.]
dis·suade • ***verb*** **dissuaded, dissuading**

distance (dis′təns) ***noun*** **1** the length of a line between two points [The *distance* between New York and Chicago is about 700 miles.] **2** a place far away [We saw the mountain from a *distance*.]
dis·tance • ***noun,*** *plural* **distances**

distant (dis′tənt) ***adjective*** **1** far away in space or time; remote [a *distant* country; a *distant* century]. **2** unfriendly or cool toward someone. **3** not closely related [*distant* relatives].
dis·tant • ***adjective***

distaste (dis tāst′) ***noun*** dislike [She had a great *distaste* for worms and slugs.]
dis·taste • ***noun***

distasteful (dis tāst′fəl) ***adjective*** not to a person's liking; unpleasant or disagreeable.
dis·taste·ful • ***adjective***

distinct (di stiŋkt′) ***adjective*** **1** not alike; different [My twin sisters have *distinct* personalities.] **2** separate [four *distinct* parts]. **3** clearly seen, heard, felt, or perceived in some other way [a *distinct* smell of smoke in the hall].
dis·tinct • ***adjective***

distinction (di stiŋk′shən) ***noun*** **1** the act of keeping distinct or separate [This school is open to everyone, without *distinction* of race or religion.] **2** the way in which things differ [We can see the *distinctions* between two breeds of dog.] **3** a quality, mark, or feature that makes someone or something different [Captain Smith had the *distinction* of receiving a medal.]
dis·tinc·tion • ***noun,*** *plural* **distinctions**

distinctive (di stiŋk′tiv) ***adjective*** making or being distinct or different from others; characteristic [the *distinctive* markings of a skunk] —Look for the WORD CHOICES box at the entry **characteristic**.
dis·tinc·tive • ***adjective***

distinguish (di stiŋ′gwish) ***verb*** **1** to make different; be the difference in [What *distinguishes* human beings from the apes?] **2** to see the difference in [I can *distinguish* right from wrong.] **3** to make famous or outstanding [She certainly has *distinguished* herself as an athlete.]
dis·tin·guish • ***verb*** **distinguished, distinguishing**

distort (di stôrt′) ***verb*** **1** to twist out of a usual shape or look [The old mirror *distorted* my reflection.] **2** to change in a way that gives a false idea [The newspaper *distorted* the facts to fit its own opinion.]
dis·tort • ***verb*** **distorted, distorting**

distract (di strakt′) ***verb*** **1** to draw the mind or attention away to something else [The movie *distracted* him from his worries.] **2** to

D

make unable to think clearly; confuse [I get *distracted* when two people try to talk to me at the same time.]
dis·tract • *verb* **distracted, distracting**

distress (di stres′) *verb* to cause pain, sorrow, or worry to; to trouble [The bad news *distressed* us.]
noun **1** pain, sorrow, or worry. **2** a condition of danger or trouble [a ship in *distress*].
dis·tress • *verb* **distressed, distressing** • *noun*

WORD CHOICES

Synonyms of **distress**

The words **distress, agony,** and **suffering** share the meaning "pain, sorrow, or worry."

distress caused by the famine
the *agony* of the fire victims
the *suffering* of the homeless

distribute (dis trib′yo͞ot) *verb* **1** to give out in portions; deal out [They *distributed* food to the hungry people.] —Look for the WORD CHOICES box at the entry **dispense**. **2** to spread out or scatter [*Distribute* the paint evenly over the wall.]
dis·trib·ute • *verb* **distributed, distributing**

distribution (dis′tri byo͞o′shən) *noun* **1** the act of distributing something [She supervised the *distribution* of food among the needy people.] **2** the way that something is distributed [They demanded a fair *distribution* of the money.]
dis·tri·bu·tion • *noun, plural* **distributions**

district (dis′trikt) *noun* **1** any one of the parts into which an area, such as a city, is divided for some special purpose [a school *district*]. **2** a part of a country, city, or other larger area [the business *district* of Cleveland].
dis·trict • *noun, plural* **districts**

District of Columbia (kə lum′bē ə) a Federal district in the eastern U.S. on the Potomac River, occupied entirely by Washington, the capital. Abbreviated **D.C.**
District of Co·lum·bia

distrust (dis trust′) *noun* a lack of trust; doubt or suspicion [She has a *distrust* of strangers.]
verb to have no trust in; to doubt [He *distrusts* even his friends.]
dis·trust • *noun* • *verb* **distrusted, distrusting**

disturb (di sturb′) *verb* **1** to break up the quiet or calm of [The roar of motorcycles *disturbed* the neighborhood.] **2** to upset [They are *disturbed* by their parents' divorce.] **3** to put into disorder [Someone *disturbed* the papers on my desk.] **4** to bother or interrupt [Don't *disturb* me while I'm working.]
dis·turb • *verb* **disturbed, disturbing**

disturbance (di stur′bəns) *noun* **1** the act of disturbing or the condition of being disturbed. **2** something that disturbs [His coughing was a *disturbance* to the rest of the audience.]
dis·turb·ance • *noun, plural* **disturbances**

ditch (dich) *noun* a long, narrow opening that is dug in the earth [an irrigation *ditch*].
ditch • *noun, plural* **ditches**

dive (dīv) *verb* **1** to plunge headfirst into water [He likes to *dive* in the pool.] **2** to plunge into anything [The fox *dived* into its hole as the hounds got closer.] **3** to make a sudden, steep drop [The airplane *dived* into the clouds.]
noun **1** the act of diving into water. **2** a sudden drop of any kind [The airplane's *dive* scared all the passengers, but no one was hurt.]
dive • *verb* **dived** or **dove, dived, diving** • *noun, plural* **dives**

diver (dī′vər) *noun* **1** a person who dives. **2** a person who works under water wearing a special suit and a helmet with an air supply.
div·er • *noun, plural* **divers**

diverse (di vurs′ *or* dī′vurs) *adjective* different [The school's craft exhibit showed the *diverse* interests of the students.]
di·verse • *adjective*

diversion (di vur′zhən *or* dī vur′zhən) *noun* **1** the act or an example of diverting or turning aside [The dam caused a *diversion* of the stream.] **2** something that a person turns to for fun or in order to relax; a pastime.
di·ver·sion • *noun, plural* **diversions**

a	cat	ō	go	ʉ	fur	ə =	a *in* ago
ā	ape	ô	law, for	ch	chin		e *in* agent
ä	cot, car	o͝o	look	sh	she		i *in* pencil
e	ten	o͞o	tool	th	thin		o *in* atom
ē	me	oi	oil	*th*	then		u *in* circus
i	fit	ou	out	zh	measure		
ī	ice	u	up	ŋ	ring		

diversity (di vur′si tē *or* dī vur′si tē) ***noun*** the condition of being different or varied; difference or variety [There was a great *diversity* of opinion.]
di·ver·si·ty • ***noun,*** *plural* **diversities**

divert (di vurt′ *or* dī vurt′) ***verb*** **1** to turn aside [The dam *diverts* the stream. The thief *diverted* my attention and stole my purse.] **2** to amuse; entertain —Look for the WORD CHOICES box at the entry **entertain**.
di·vert • ***verb*** **diverted, diverting**

divide (di vīd′) ***verb*** **1** to separate into parts; split up [A stream *divides* the valley. An orange *divides* into sections.] **2** to find out how many times one number is contained in another [If you *divide* 12 by 3, you get 4.] **3** to make separate or keep apart [A stone wall *divides* one farm from the other. A quarrel *divided* the family.] **4** to give out in shares [*Divide* the cake among the guests.]
noun a ridge that separates two regions that are drained by rivers.
di·vide • ***verb*** **divided, dividing** • ***noun,*** *plural* **divides**

dividend (div′i dend′) ***noun*** **1** a number that is divided by another number. In 6 ÷ 3 = 2, the number 6 is the dividend. **2** a share of the money that a company makes that it divides among those owning stock in the company.
div·i·dend • ***noun,*** *plural* **dividends**

divine (di vīn′) ***adjective*** **1** of or like God or a god [*divine* power]. **2** coming from God; holy [*divine* scripture].
di·vine • ***adjective***

divisible (di viz′i bəl) ***adjective*** capable of being divided without having anything left over [The number 6 is *divisible* by either 2 or 3.]
di·vis·i·ble • ***adjective***

division (di vizh′ən) ***noun*** **1** the act of dividing or the condition of being divided [the *division* of the year into months, weeks, and days]. **2** the process in arithmetic of finding out how many times one number is contained in another. **3** the act of sharing or giving out in portions [The *division* of the pie among the children was fair.] **4** a section, department, or part [the sales *division* of a company] —Look for the WORD CHOICES box at the entry **part**. **5** a large unit of an army.
di·vi·sion • ***noun,*** *plural* **divisions**

divisor (di vī′zər) ***noun*** a number by which another number is divided. In 6 ÷ 3 = 2, the number 3 is the divisor.
di·vi·sor • ***noun,*** *plural* **divisors**

divorce (di vôrs′) ***noun*** the legal ending of a marriage.
verb to end a marriage legally [The Smiths *divorced* last year. Mrs. Brown has *divorced* Mr. Brown.]
di·vorce • ***noun,*** *plural* **divorces**
• ***verb*** **divorced, divorcing**

dizzy (diz′ē) ***adjective*** **1** having a whirling or spinning feeling; unsteady [Riding the merry-go-round made us *dizzy*.] **2** capable of making a person feel this way [We looked down from a *dizzy* height.]
diz·zy • ***adjective*** **dizzier, dizziest**

DJ (dē′jā) ***noun*** *the same as* **disc jockey**.
DJ • ***noun,*** *plural* **DJs**

Djibouti (ji bo͞ot′ē) a country in eastern Africa, south of the Red Sea.
Dji·bou·ti

do[1] (do͞o) ***verb*** *Do* can be both a main verb and a helping verb. **I.** When *do* is a main verb, it means: **1** to carry out or perform [*Do* what I tell you.] **2** to work at; have as an occupation [What does he *do* for a living?] **3** to bring about; to cause [The storm *did* a lot of damage.] **4** to put forth; put into use [She *did* her best.] **5** to take care of; see to [I'll *do* the dishes tonight.] **6** to work out; solve [He *did* the math problem in no time at all.] **7** to get along [The patient is *doing* well.] **8** to be right for a purpose; to suit [Will this dress *do* for the party?] **II.** When *do* is a helping verb, it is used to: **1** ask a question [*Do* you want some candy?] **2** give force to what is being said [I *do* have to go.] **3** make a negative command or statement [I *do* not know the answer.] The word "to" is not used between the helping verb *do* and the verb that follows it.
—do without to get along without. **—have to do with** to be related to or connected with.
do • ***verb*** **did, done, doing, does**
• The words **do, dew,** and **due** sound alike.
What *do* you want to be?
There was *dew* on the grass.
I was *due* to arrive before her.

do[2] (dō) ***noun*** the first or last note of a musical scale.
• The words **do, doe,** and **dough** sound alike.
Do is the note between ti and re.
The *doe* stayed near the other deer.
He tossed the pizza *dough* into the air.

D

Doberman pinscher (dō′bər mən pin′chər) ***noun*** a large dog with smooth, dark hair and tan markings.
Do·ber·man pin·scher • ***noun,*** *plural* **Doberman pinschers**

docile (däs′əl) ***adjective*** easy to handle or train; obedient or tame [a *docile* horse].
doc·ile • ***adjective***

dock (däk) ***noun*** **1** a long platform that is built over water as a landing place for ships or boats; a pier or wharf —Look for the WORD CHOICES box at the entry **pier**. **2** the water in the area between two of these platforms. **3** a platform where trucks or railroad cars are loaded and unloaded.
verb **1** to bring or come to a dock [Tugboats help to *dock* ships. The ship *docks* at Pier 9.] **2** to join with another space vehicle in outer space [The space capsules *docked* in flight.]
dock • ***noun,*** *plural* **docks** • ***verb*** **docked, docking**

doctor (däk′tər) ***noun*** **1** a person who has been trained to heal sick people; a physician or surgeon. **2** a person who has received the highest degree that a university gives.
doc·tor • ***noun,*** *plural* **doctors**

doctrine (däk′trin) ***noun*** something that is taught as a belief or principle of a religion or of a political party or other group.
doc·trine • ***noun,*** *plural* **doctrines**

WORD CHOICES

Synonyms of **doctrine**

The words **doctrine, law,** and **principle** share the meaning "a general idea believed in by many people."

the political *doctrines* of democracy
the *laws* of physics
the *principles* of modern biology

document (däk′yo͞o mənt *for n.;* däk′ yo͞o ment′ *for v.*) ***noun*** a printed or written record that is used to prove something [A birth certificate is a very important *document.*]
verb to prove with documents [The scientist *documented* his claims with reports and graphs.]
doc·u·ment • ***noun,*** *plural* **documents** • ***verb*** **documented, documenting**

dodge (däj) ***verb*** **1** to move quickly to one side in order to get out of the way of a person or thing [We *dodged* into an alley when we saw them coming.] **2** to get away from or avoid in this way [They *dodged* the runaway horse and wagon.] **3** to avoid by tricks or cleverness [The senator just *dodged* another question from the reporter.]
dodge • ***verb*** **dodged, dodging**

dodo (dō′dō) ***noun*** a large, extinct bird that had small wings and could not fly. Dodos lived on an island in the Indian Ocean.
do·do • ***noun,*** *plural* **dodos** or **dodoes**

doe (dō) ***noun*** the female of certain animals, such as the deer, antelope, and rabbit.
doe • ***noun,*** *plural* **does** or **doe**
● The words **doe, do,** and **dough** sound alike.
The *doe* watched her fawn as he fed.
Do, re, mi, fa, sol, la, ti, do.
Add chocolate chips to the cookie *dough*.

does (duz) ***verb*** the form of the verb **do**[1] that is used to show the present time with *he, she*, or *it*. This form is also used with singular nouns.

doesn't (duz′ənt) does not.
does·n't

dog (dôg) ***noun*** a meat-eating animal that is related to the fox and the wolf. Dogs are raised to be pets or to work in hunting and herding.
verb to follow or hunt like a dog [The child *dogged* his father's footsteps.]
dog • ***noun,*** *plural* **dogs** • ***verb*** **dogged, dogging**

dogwood (dôg′wo͝od) ***noun*** a tree with small blossoms that are surrounded by four white or pink leaves that look like petals.
dog·wood • ***noun,*** *plural* **dogwoods**

doings (do͞o′iŋz) ***plural noun*** things that are done or being done; actions or activities [Thanksgiving *doings* at our house this year include a party and weekend guests.]
do·ings • ***plural noun***

doll (däl) ***noun*** a toy made to look like a person. Children's dolls usually look like babies or children.
doll • ***noun,*** *plural* **dolls**

a	cat	ō	go	ʉ	fur	ə =	a *in* ago
ā	ape	ô	law, for	ch	chin		e *in* agent
ä	cot, car	o͝o	look	sh	she		i *in* pencil
e	ten	o͞o	tool	th	thin		o *in* atom
ē	me	oi	oil	*th*	then		u *in* circus
i	fit	ou	out	zh	measure		
ī	ice	u	up	ŋ	ring		

dollar (däl′ər) ***noun*** **1** the basic unit of money in the U.S. It is equal to 100 cents, and its symbol is $. **2** a unit of money in some other countries, including Canada.
dol·lar • ***noun,*** *plural* **dollars**

dolphin

dolphin (dôl′fin) ***noun*** a sea animal that lives in the water and is related to the whale but smaller. It has a long snout. Although a dolphin looks like a fish, it is a mammal.
dol·phin • ***noun,*** *plural* **dolphins**

-dom *a suffix meaning:* **1** the position or domain of [A *kingdom* is the domain of a king or queen.] **2** the condition of being [*Wisdom* is the condition of being wise.]

domain (dō mān′) ***noun*** all the land that a government or ruler controls [the queen's *domain*].
do·main • ***noun,*** *plural* **domains**

dome (dōm) ***noun*** a round roof that is shaped more or less like half a globe.
dome • ***noun,*** *plural* **domes**

domestic (dō mes′tik) ***adjective*** **1** having to do with the home or family [*domestic* chores]. **2** not wild; used to living with people [Dogs, cows, and horses are *domestic* animals.]
noun a maid, cook, butler, or other house servant.
do·mes·tic • ***adjective*** • ***noun,*** *plural* **domestics**

dominant (däm′i nənt) ***adjective*** most important or most powerful; ruling or controlling [Great Britain once was *dominant* in the world.]
dom·i·nant • ***adjective***

dominate (däm′i nāt) ***verb*** **1** to control or rule; be most important or powerful [In the soccer league, our team *dominates*.] **2** to tower over; rise high above [These tall buildings *dominate* the skyline.]
dom·i·nate • ***verb*** **dominated, dominating**

Dominica (də min′i kə) a country that is an island of the West Indies.
Do·min·i·ca

Dominican Republic (də min′i kən) a country occupying part of an island in the West Indies. The other part of the island is *Haiti*.
Do·min·i·can Republic

dominion (də min′yən) ***noun*** **1** a territory or a country that is controlled by a ruler or government. **2** the power of governing.
do·min·ion • ***noun,*** *plural* **dominions**

domino

domino (däm′i nō) ***noun*** **1** a small, oblong piece of wood or plastic that is marked with two patterns of dots on one of its flat sides. **2 dominoes** [*used with a singular verb*] a game in which players try to match the patterns on the halves of these pieces.
dom·i·no • ***noun,*** *plural* **dominoes** or **dominos**

donate (dō′nāt) ***verb*** to give to a charity, fund, campaign, or other cause; contribute [They *donated* money to feed homeless people.]
do·nate • ***verb*** **donated, donating**

donation (dō nā′shən) ***noun*** a gift; contribution.
do·na·tion • ***noun,*** *plural* **donations**

done (dun) ***verb*** *past participle of* **do**[1].
adjective cooked long enough [The roast is *done*.]

donkey (däŋ′kē) ***noun*** an animal that is like a horse but smaller and with longer ears.
don·key • ***noun,*** *plural* **donkeys**

donor (dō′nər) ***noun*** a person who donates, or gives, something [a blood *donor;* the *donors* to the school's athletic program].
do·nor • ***noun,*** *plural* **donors**

don't (dōnt) do not.

donut (dō′nut) ***noun*** *an informal spelling of* **doughnut**.
do·nut • ***noun,*** *plural* **donuts**

doom (do͞om) ***noun*** the bad or tragic things that are to happen; ruin or death [The wicked witch tried to lure the hero to his *doom*.]
verb to sentence or direct to some bad or tragic end [The bank robber was *doomed* to spend the rest of her life in prison.]
doom • ***noun*** • ***verb*** **doomed, dooming**

door (dôr) ***noun*** **1** a movable panel for opening or closing an entrance to something such as a building or room. **2** an opening with a door in it; doorway.
—out of doors outside a house or building; outdoors.
door • ***noun, plural*** **doors**

doorbell (dôr′bel) ***noun*** a bell or buzzer at an entrance that is used to let people inside know that someone is at the door.
door·bell • ***noun, plural*** **doorbells**

doorknob (dôr′näb) ***noun*** a knob or lever that operates the latch for opening a door.
door·knob • ***noun, plural*** **doorknobs**

doorman (dôr′man) ***noun*** a person whose work is mainly opening the door of a building for people who enter or leave.
door·man • ***noun, plural*** **doormen**

doormat (dôr′mat) ***noun*** a mat for people to wipe their shoes on before they enter a building or a room.
door·mat • ***noun, plural*** **doormats**

doorstep (dôr′step) ***noun*** the step or steps in front of an outside door.
door·step • ***noun, plural*** **doorsteps**

doorway (dôr′wā) ***noun*** an opening in a wall that can be closed by a door.
door·way • ***noun, plural*** **doorways**

dope (dōp) [*an informal word*] ***noun*** **1** any drug or narcotic. **2** a stupid person.
verb to give a narcotic drug to.
dope • ***noun, plural for sense 2 only*** **dopes** • ***verb*** **doped, doping**

dormant (dôr′mənt) ***adjective*** not active; quiet [a *dormant* volcano].
dor·mant • ***adjective***

dormitory (dôr′mi tôr′ē) ***noun*** a building at a college or a boarding school with many rooms for many people to live and sleep in.
dor·mi·to·ry • ***noun, plural*** **dormitories**

dormouse (dôr′mous) ***noun*** a European animal that is like a small squirrel.
dor·mouse • ***noun, plural*** **dormice** (dôr′mīs)

dorsal (dôr′səl) ***adjective*** on or having to do with the back [The *dorsal* fin of a shark in the water signals danger.]
dor·sal • ***adjective***

dose (dōs) ***noun*** an amount of medicine that is to be taken at one time.
dose • ***noun, plural*** **doses**

dot (dät) ***noun*** **1** a tiny mark or spot like one made with a pencil [Put a *dot* over every "i" and "j."] **2** a small, round spot [polka *dots*].
verb **1** to mark with a dot or dots [*Dot* the "i."] **2** to cover with things that seem like dots [Islands *dotted* the bay.]
—on the dot [*an informal use*] at the exact time.
dot • ***noun, plural*** **dots** • ***verb*** **dotted, dotting**

dote (dōt) ***verb*** to show too much affection or love [The kids are spoiled because their grandparents *dote* on them.]
dote • ***verb*** **doted, doting**

double (dub′əl) ***adjective*** **1** twice as much or as many; two times as much in amount, number, size, extent, or strength [a garage *double* the size of the neighbor's]. **2** having two parts that are alike [*double* doors leading to the garden]. **3** made for two [a *double* bed]. **4** acting two parts or in two ways [a *double* life as a spy and as a dancer].
adverb two at one time; in a pair [Jane and Bill rode *double* on the bicycle.]
noun **1** an amount twice as great [Six is the *double* of three.] **2** a person or thing that looks very much like another [The girl is her mother's *double*.] **3** a hit in baseball that lets the batter get to second base safely.
verb **1** to make or become twice as much or as many [*Double* the recipe. The population of the city has *doubled*.] **2** to fold over or up [The tailor made a hem by *doubling* over the edge of the cloth.] **3** to make a sharp turn and go back [The prisoners *doubled* back on their tracks to escape the dogs.] **4** to be used for more than one purpose [The bedroom *doubles* as a study.] **5** to do two jobs at the same time [She *doubles* as a lawyer and a housewife.] **6** to hit a double in baseball.

a	cat	ō	go	ʉ	fur	ə = a *in* ago	
ā	ape	ô	law, for	ch	chin	e *in* agent	
ä	cot, car	oo	look	sh	she	i *in* pencil	
e	ten	o͞o	tool	th	thin	o *in* atom	
ē	me	oi	oil	*th*	then	u *in* circus	
i	fit	ou	out	zh	measure		
ī	ice	u	up	ŋ	ring		

dou·ble • *adjective* • *adverb* • *noun, plural* **doubles** • *verb* **doubled, doubling**

double bass

double bass *noun* a musical instrument that looks like a huge violin. Its strings are plucked or played with a bow and it has deep tones.
double bass • *noun, plural* **double basses**

double-cross (dub′əl krôs′) [*an informal word*] *verb* to cheat or betray by doing the opposite of what one has promised.
dou·ble-cross • *verb* **double-crossed, double-crossing**

double-header (dub′əl hed′ər) *noun* two games that are played one right after the other on the same day, usually by the same two teams.
dou·ble-head·er • *noun, plural* **double-headers**

double-park (dub′əl pärk′) *verb* to park a car, truck, or other vehicle right beside another one that is parked alongside a curb.
dou·ble-park • *verb* **double-parked, double-parking**

doubly (dub′lē) *adverb* twice or twice as much [You must be *doubly* careful when driving in the rain.]
dou·bly • *adverb*

doubt (dout) *verb* **1** to think that something may not be true or right; be unsure of [I *doubt* that this is the correct answer.] **2** to consider unlikely [I *doubt* that it will snow today.] *noun* **1** a feeling of not being sure or certain [I have no *doubt* that he will win today.] **2** a condition of being uncertain or not yet decided [The result of the election is still in *doubt*.]
doubt • *verb* **doubted, doubting** • *noun, plural* **doubts**

doubtful (dout′fəl) *adjective* feeling or causing doubt; not sure; not decided [I'm *doubtful* about our chances of winning.]
doubt·ful • *adjective*

doubtless (dout′ləs) *adverb* without doubt; certainly [She will *doubtless* win the election.]
doubt·less • *adverb*

dough (dō) *noun* a mixture of flour, water or milk, and other ingredients that is worked into a soft, thick mass. Dough is used to make bread, cookies, pies, and other baked goods.
dough • *noun, plural* **doughs**

• The words **dough, do,** and **doe** sound alike.
He tossed the pizza *dough* into the air.
Do, re, mi, fa, sol, la, ti, *do*.
The *doe* strayed from the other deer.

doughnut (dō′nut) *noun* a small, sweet cake that is usually shaped like a ring. Doughnuts are fried in deep fat.
dough·nut • *noun, plural* **doughnuts**

Douglass (dug′ləs), **Frederick** (fred′rick) 1817-1895; U.S. black leader and writer.
Doug·lass, Fred·er·ick

dove[1] (duv) *noun* a pigeon, especially any of the smaller kinds. The dove is often used as a symbol of peace.
dove • *noun, plural* **doves**

dove[2] (dōv) *verb a past tense of* **dive**.

Dover (dō′vər) the capital of Delaware.
Do·ver

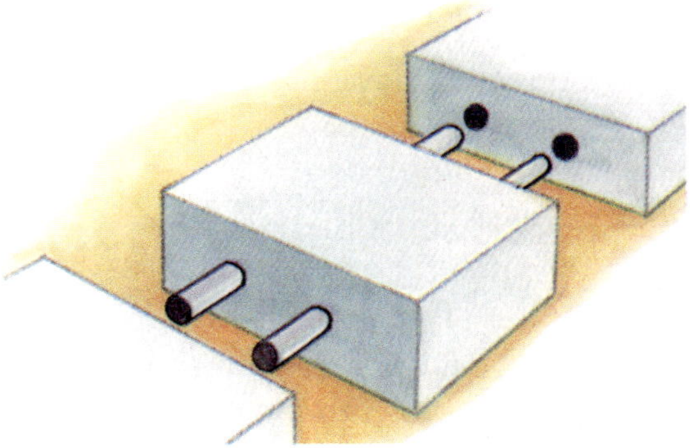

dowel

dowel (dou′əl) *noun* a round peg of wood, metal, or other material that fits into holes in two pieces to join them together.
dow·el • *noun, plural* **dowels**

down[1] (doun) *adverb* **1** from a higher to a lower place [If you can't jump *down*, climb *down*. Pull *down* the shades.] **2** to or in a lower position, level, or condition [He told the children to sit *down*. The train has slowed *down*.] **3** to or on the floor or ground [He fell *down*.] **4** from an earlier to a later time [The wedding gown was passed *down* from mother to daughter.] **5** in or to a worse condition [She came *down* with a cold.] **6** from a greater to a smaller amount, size, or strength [The price of oil has gone *down*.] **7** to a more quiet or serious condition [The children settled *down* to study.] **8** as partial payment at the time of purchase [Pay $50 *down* and $10 a week.] **9** in writing [Take *down* his name.]

adjective **1** moving or going downward [the *down* escalator]. **2** being in a low position or on the ground, floor, or bottom; not up [The shades are *down*. The sun is *down*.] **3** not feeling well; ill [She is *down* with the flu.] **4** out of order [The bank's computer has been *down* all morning.]

preposition **1** from a higher to a lower place or position on, over, or along [The bus rolled *down* the hill. Tears ran *down* her face.] **2** along [He walked *down* the street to the store.]

verb **1** to bring, put, or knock down [The boxer *downed* his opponent.] **2** to swallow quickly [She *downed* a glass of milk.]

noun **1** in football, one of the four plays in a row during which a team must either score or move the ball forward by at least ten yards. If the team fails, it must give up the ball to the other team. **2** a turn for the worse or a piece of bad luck [Her career has had its ups and *downs*.]

down • ***adverb*** • ***adjective*** • ***preposition*** • ***verb*** **downed, downing** • ***noun,*** *plural* **downs**

WORD HISTORY

down

The source of **down** is a thousand-year-old English word with the meaning "from the hill." When we come from a hill, we go to a lower place.

down[2] (doun) ***noun*** soft, fluffy feathers [The newly hatched chick was covered with *down*.]

downcast (doun′kast) ***adjective*** **1** looking downward [The photograph showed her with *downcast* eyes.] **2** very unhappy; sad [We were *downcast* at losing the game.] —Look for the WORD CHOICES box at the entry **sad**.
down·cast • ***adjective***

downhill (doun′hil′) ***adverb*** **1** toward the bottom of a hill. **2** into a worse, weaker, or inferior condition [His health has been going *downhill* since the operation.]
down·hill • ***adverb***

downpour (doun′pôr) ***noun*** a very heavy rain.
down·pour • ***noun***

downright (doun′rīt) ***adverb*** very; really; extremely [She was *downright* rude.]
adjective absolute; complete ["It's a *downright* lie," he shouted.]
down·right • ***adverb*** • ***adjective***

downstairs (doun′sterz′) ***adverb*** **1** down the stairs [He fell *downstairs*.] **2** to or on a lower floor [She went *downstairs* to get milk.]
adjective on a lower floor [a *downstairs* bedroom].
noun [*used with a singular verb*] a lower floor or floors [The *downstairs* is being painted.]
down·stairs • ***adverb*** • ***adjective*** • ***noun***

downstream (doun′strēm) ***adverb*** in the direction in which a stream is flowing [He rowed the boat *downstream*.] This word can also be used as an adjective [a *downstream* current].
down·stream • ***adverb***

downtown (doun′toun) ***adverb*** in or toward the main business section of a city or town [She works *downtown*.] This word can also be used as an adjective [*downtown* traffic; a *downtown* shopping mall].
down·town • ***adverb***

downward (doun′wərd) ***adverb*** from a higher to a lower place or position [The kite glided *downward* and hit the tree.] This word can also be used as an adjective [a *downward* slope].
down·ward • ***adverb***

downwards (doun′wərdz) ***adverb*** *the same as the adverb* **downward**.
down·wards • ***adverb***

downy (doun′ē) ***adjective*** **1** of or like down; soft and fluffy [a *downy* blanket] —Look for the WORD CHOICES box at the entry **soft**. **2** covered with down [The baby chicks were all *downy*.]
down·y • ***adjective*** **downier, downiest**

dowry (dou′rē) ***noun*** money or property that

a	cat	ō	go	ʉ	fur	ə =	a *in* ago
ā	ape	ô	law, for	ch	chin		e *in* agent
ä	cot, car	oo	look	sh	she		i *in* pencil
e	ten	ōō	tool	th	thin		o *in* atom
ē	me	oi	oil	*th*	then		u *in* circus
i	fit	ou	out	zh	measure		
ī	ice	u	up	ŋ	ring		

a bride brings to her husband when she is married.
dow·ry • *noun, plural* **dowries**

Doyle (doil), Sir **Arthur Conan** (är′thər kō′nən) 1859-1930; English novelist. He wrote the *Sherlock Holmes* stories.
Doyle, Sir **Ar·thur Co·nan**

doz. *abbreviation for* dozen.

doze (dōz) *verb* to sleep lightly; nap [The kittens *dozed* in the sun.]
—**doze off** to fall into a light sleep.
doze • *verb* **dozed, dozing**

dozen (duz′ən) *noun* a group of twelve.
doz·en • *noun, plural* **dozens** or **dozen**

Dr. *abbreviation for* **1** Doctor. **2** Drive.

drab (drab) *adjective* not bright or cheerful; dull [She lived in a *drab* old house.]
drab • *adjective* **drabber, drabbest**

draft (draft) *noun* **1** a current of air in a room or other enclosed space [You'll catch cold if you sit in a *draft*.] **2** a part that controls the flow of air in a furnace, fireplace, or some stoves. **3** a plan, sketch, or drawing of something to be built [the architect's *draft* for the new building]. **4** an outline or rough copy of a piece of writing [the first *draft* of a speech]. **5** the choosing of a person or persons for service in the armed forces or for some special purpose [In times of war most young men are eligible for the *draft*.]
verb **1** to make a sketch, outline, or rough copy of [She *drafted* a letter to her congressman.] **2** to choose or take for service in the armed forces or for some special purpose [The new coach *drafted* a fine quarterback.]
adjective used for pulling loads [*draft* animals].
draft • *noun, plural* **drafts** • *verb* **drafted, drafting** • *adjective*

drag (drag) *verb* **1** to pull in a slow, hard way, especially along the ground; haul [She *dragged* the sled up the hill.] **2** to be pulled along the ground, floor, or other surface [Her coat was so long that it *dragged* in the mud.] **3** to move, go, or pass too slowly [He *dragged* behind the other boys. The performance *dragged* on and on.] **4** to search for something in a river, lake, or other body of water by dragging a net or hooks along the bottom [The police *dragged* the lake for the missing child.]
drag • *verb* **dragged, dragging**

WORD CHOICES

Synonyms of drag

The words **drag, haul,** and **tow** share the meaning "to move by pulling."

She *dragged* the desk across the floor.

The campers *hauled* the boat out of the water.

The mechanic *towed* the stalled car.

dragon (drag′ən) *noun* a make-believe monster in stories that looks like a giant lizard, usually with wings and claws. Dragons are supposed to breathe out fire and smoke.
drag·on • *noun, plural* **dragons**

dragonfly (drag′ən flī) *noun* an insect that has a long, slender body and four delicate wings. Dragonflies live near fresh water.
drag·on·fly • *noun, plural* **dragonflies**

drain (drān) *verb* **1** to take out or remove slowly [*Drain* the water from the swimming pool.] **2** to take out or remove liquid from; make empty or dry [Workmen *drained* the swimming pool.] **3** to make or become empty or dry as water flows away [Wash the dishes and leave them on the counter to *drain*.] **4** to flow off [Water won't *drain* from a flat roof.] **5** to use up slowly; exhaust [Stress *drained* her energy.]
noun **1** a pipe or channel for carrying off water, sewage, and other liquids that are not wanted [a bathtub *drain*]. **2** something that drains or uses up slowly [The big medical bills have been a *drain* on his resources.]
drain • *verb* **drained, draining** • *noun, plural* **drains**

drainage (drān′ij) *noun* the act or process of draining off water or other liquid [These plants need soil with good *drainage*.]
drain·age • *noun*

drake (drāk) *noun* a male duck.
drake • *noun, plural* **drakes**

drama (drä′mə *or* dram′ə) *noun* **1** a story that is written to be performed by actors on a stage; play. **2** a series of events or a situation in real life that is as exciting or interesting as a play [The people in the court enjoyed the *drama* of the trial.]
dra·ma • *noun, plural* **dramas**

dramatic (drə mat′ik) ***adjective*** **1** of or having to do with drama or the theater [a course in the *dramatic* arts]. **2** like a drama or play; interesting and exciting [a *dramatic* baseball game].
dra·mat·ic • ***adjective***

dramatize (dram′ə tīz) ***verb*** **1** to make into a drama or play [The life of Lincoln was *dramatized* in a TV series.] **2** to be very dramatic about; make seem very exciting [He likes to *dramatize* the troubles he has with his boss.]
dram·a·tize • ***verb*** **dramatized, dramatizing**

drank (draŋk) ***verb*** *past tense of* **drink**.

drape (drāp) ***verb*** **1** to cover or decorate with cloth that hangs in loose folds [She *draped* the windows with red velvet.] **2** to arrange or hang in graceful folds [She *draped* a shawl about her shoulders.]
noun *usually* **drapes** cloth hanging in loose folds, especially curtains.
drape • ***verb*** **draped, draping** • ***noun,*** *plural* **drapes**

drapery (drā′pər ē) ***noun*** a curtain or other cloth hanging in loose folds.
drap·er·y • ***noun,*** *plural* **draperies**

drastic (dras′tik) ***adjective*** extremely severe or harsh; having a strong effect [The governor adopted *drastic* measures to fight crime.]
dras·tic • ***adjective***

draw (drô *or* drä) ***verb*** **1** to make a picture or design with a pencil, pen, chalk, or other writing tool [Pedro *drew* a ship in his notebook. Sheila *draws* well.] **2** to cause to move by pulling [The mules *drew* the wagon.] **3** to pull out or take out; remove [The waiter *drew* the cork from the bottle.] **4** to withdraw [I need to *draw* money from the bank.] **5** to pull across or move in order to close; shut [She *drew* the curtains in the bedroom.] **6** to get the attention of; attract [The new movie is *drawing* a large audience.] **7** to come or move [The train *drew* away from the station.] **8** to bring about; result in [The reporter's questions *drew* no reply.] **9** to inhale [*Draw* a deep breath.]
noun **1** the act of drawing, or taking out a weapon [The sheriff was quick on the *draw*.] **2** a game or contest in which the final scores are the same; tie [Our team has had two wins and one *draw* this season.]
—draw out to cause to become longer; stretch [Grandpa *draws out* his fishing stories.] **—draw up** **1** to put in the proper written form [The lawyer *drew up* a contract.] **2** to stop [The car *drew up* next to ours.]
draw • ***verb*** **drew, drawn, drawing** • ***noun,*** *plural* **draws**

drawbridge

drawbridge (drô′brij *or* drä′brij) ***noun*** a bridge that can be raised or turned to allow ships to pass through or to prevent someone from crossing.
draw·bridge • ***noun,*** *plural* **drawbridges**

drawer (drôr) ***noun*** a box that slides in and out of a table, chest, desk, or other piece of furniture.
draw·er • ***noun,*** *plural* **drawers**

drawing (drô′iŋ *or* drä′iŋ) ***noun*** **1** a picture, design, or likeness made using a pencil, pen, chalk, or other writing tool. **2** the art or process of making such pictures [She studied *drawing* at school.]
draw·ing • ***noun,*** *plural for sense 1 only* **drawings**

drawl (drôl) ***verb*** to speak in a slow way, drawing out the syllables.
noun speech that is drawled.
drawl • ***verb*** **drawled, drawling** • ***noun,*** *plural* **drawls**

drawn (drôn *or* drän) ***verb*** *past participle of* **draw**.

dread (dred) ***verb*** to look forward to with great fear or worry [I *dread* taking exams.]
noun great fear and anxiety [He lives in *dread* of the future. Cats have a *dread* of water.] —Look for the WORD CHOICES box at the entry **panic**.

a cat	ō go	ʉ fur	ə = a *in* ago
ā ape	ô law, for	ch chin	e *in* agent
ä cot, car	oo look	sh she	i *in* pencil
e ten	ōō tool	th thin	o *in* atom
ē me	oi oil	*th* then	u *in* circus
i fit	ou out	zh measure	
ī ice	u up	ŋ ring	

adjective causing great fear [a *dread* disease].
dread • *verb* **dreaded, dreading** • *noun* • *adjective*

dreadful (dred′fəl) *adjective* **1** causing dread; fearful; terrible [a *dreadful* storm]. **2** [*an informal use*] very bad or unpleasant; awful [a *dreadful* movie].
dread·ful • *adjective*

dream (drēm) *noun* **1** a series of thoughts, pictures, or feelings that passes through the mind of a sleeping person. **2** a hope or aim for the future [Her *dream* is to become a lawyer.]
verb **1** to have a dream or dreams [She *dreams* often. I *dreamed* I was sailing in Hawaii.] **2** to imagine as possible; have any idea [I wouldn't *dream* of going without you.]
dream • *noun, plural* **dreams** • *verb* **dreamed** or **dreamt, dreaming**

dreamt (dremt) *verb a past tense and past participle of* **dream**.

dreamy (drēm′ē) *adjective* **1** fond of daydreaming or of imagining things; not practical [a *dreamy* person]. **2** like something in a dream; soft, misty, or vague [listening to *dreamy* music].
dream·y • *adjective* **dreamier, dreamiest**

dreary (drir′ē) *adjective* without happiness or cheer; gloomy, sad, or dull [a long, *dreary* novel].
drear·y • *adjective* **drearier, dreariest**

dredge (drej) *noun* a large machine that scoops or sucks up mud, sand, or other material from the bottom of a harbor, lake, or other body of water.
verb to clean out or deepen with a dredge.
dredge • *noun, plural* **dredges** • *verb* **dredged, dredging**

dregs (dregz) *plural noun* solid bits that settle to the bottom in a liquid; sediment.

drench (drench) *verb* to wet completely; soak [They were *drenched* by the storm.] —Look for the WORD CHOICES box at the entry **soak**.
drench • *verb* **drenched, drenching**

dress (dres) *noun* **1** an outer garment worn by girls and women, consisting of a top and skirt, usually forming one piece. **2** clothes in general [The Japanese girls came in native *dress*. He wore formal *dress* to the ball.]
verb **1** to put clothes on [The nurse was *dressing* the baby. I *dressed* in a hurry this morning.] **2** to choose and wear clothes [Mrs. Smith has to *dress* well in her new position.] **3** to arrange the hair in a certain way [She had her hair *dressed* at the beauty shop.] **4** to put medicine or bandages on a wound or sore [The nurse *dressed* the soldier's wounds.] **5** to make ready for use; prepare [You have to *dress* the turkey before you roast it.]
dress • *noun, plural* **dresses** • *verb* **dressed, dressing**

dresser (dres′ər) *noun* a chest of drawers for a bedroom, often with a mirror.
dress·er • *noun, plural* **dressers**

dressing (dres′iŋ) *noun* **1** a sauce that is often made with oil, vinegar, and seasoning. It is added to salads and some other foods. **2** a mixture of bread crumbs and seasoning that is used to stuff roast chicken, turkey, and some other foods. **3** a bandage or medicine for a wound or sore.
dress·ing • *noun, plural* **dressings**

dressy (dres′ē) *adjective* fancy or showy in dress or looks [Those shoes are too *dressy* for school.]
dress·y • *adjective* **dressier, dressiest**

drew (dro͞o) *verb past tense of* **draw**.

dribble (drib′əl) *verb* **1** to flow or let flow in drops or in a trickle [Water *dribbled* from the pipe.] **2** in basketball or soccer, to move a ball along by using short bounces or short, light kicks.
noun a small drop or a trickle [A *dribble* of milk ran down the baby's chin.]
drib·ble • *verb* **dribbled, dribbling** • *noun, plural* **dribbles**

drier (drī′ər) *adjective comparative of* **dry**.
noun another spelling of **dryer**.
dri·er • *adjective* • *noun, plural* **driers**

driest (drī′əst) *adjective superlative of* **dry**.
dri·est • *adjective*

drift (drift) *verb* **1** to be carried along by a current of water or air [The raft *drifted* downstream. The leaves *drifted* to the ground.] **2** to go from place to place without a purpose or aim [The young man *drifted* from job to job.] **3** to pile up in heaps by the force of wind [The snow *drifted* against the door.]
noun **1** the movement or direction of something being driven or carried along [The general *drift* of the ocean current is easterly.] **2** a pile formed by the force of wind or water [A dune is a sand *drift*.] **3** general meaning [I got the *drift* of her speech.]
drift • *verb* **drifted, drifting** • *noun, plural for senses 1 and 2 only* **drifts**

D

driftwood (drift′wood) ***noun*** wood that is floating on water or that has been washed ashore.
drift·wood • ***noun***

drill (dril) ***noun*** **1** a tool that is used to make holes in wood, plastic, metal, or other hard materials. A drill has a long, sharp point that is turned by a crank or by an electric motor. **2** training or teaching by having someone practice the same thing over and over —Look for the WORD CHOICES box at the entry **practice**.

drill

verb **1** to make a hole with a drill or drills. **2** to teach or train by having someone practice the same thing over and over [Will you help *drill* the class in spelling?]
drill • ***noun,*** *plural* **drills** • ***verb*** **drilled, drilling**

drink (driŋk) ***verb*** **1** to swallow a liquid [She *drank* water.] **2** to soak up or draw in [The dry soil quickly *drank* up the rain.] **3** to drink alcohol [Don't *drink* and drive.]
noun **1** a liquid for drinking [Orange juice is a *drink* full of vitamins.] **2** an amount of liquid to be swallowed [May I have a *drink* of water, please?] **3** an alcoholic beverage [They went out for a *drink*.]
drink • ***verb*** **drank, drunk, drinking** • ***noun,*** *plural* **drinks**

drip (drip) ***verb*** **1** to fall in drops [Sweat *dripped* from his brow.] **2** to let drops of liquid fall [That faucet *drips*.]
noun **1** the process of falling in drops. **2** liquid falling in drops [Try to fix the *drip* of the faucet.]
drip • ***verb*** **dripped, dripping** • ***noun,*** *plural* **drips**

drive (drīv) ***verb*** **1** to control the movement of a car, horse and wagon, bus, or other vehicle [She *drives* a school bus. Please *drive* carefully.] **2** to move or go [The truck *drove* slowly up the hill.] **3** to go or take in a car, bus, or other vehicle [Shall we *drive* to Phoenix? Our neighbor *drives* us to school.] **4** to cause to move or go [They *drove* the cattle along the trail. This engine is *driven* by steam.] **5** to cause to go or move with a powerful blow [He *drove* the nail into the board.] **6** to force into a certain condition or act [Their constant talking *drives* me crazy.]
noun **1** a short trip in a car or other vehicle [We went for a *drive* in the country.] **2** a street, road, or driveway. **3** a hard, swift blow [The golfer hit a 200-yard *drive*.] **4** a group effort to get something done; campaign [She organized a *drive* to collect money for charity.]
drive • ***verb*** **drove, driven, driving** • ***noun,*** *plural* **drives**

drive-in (drīv′in) ***noun*** a restaurant, movie theater, bank, or other establishment designed to serve people who drive up and remain seated in their cars.
drive-in • ***noun,*** *plural* **drive-ins**

driven (driv′ən) ***verb*** *past participle of* **drive**.
driv·en • ***verb***

driver (drī′vər) ***noun*** a person who drives a car, truck, or other vehicle.
driv·er • ***noun,*** *plural* **drivers**

driveway (drīv′wā) ***noun*** a private road that leads from a street or road to a garage, house, or other building.
drive·way • ***noun,*** *plural* **driveways**

drizzle (driz′əl) ***verb*** to rain in fine drops like mist.
noun a light rain like mist.
driz·zle • ***verb*** **drizzled, drizzling** • ***noun,*** *plural* **drizzles**

dromedary (dräm′ə der′ē) ***noun*** a camel with one hump.
drom·e·dar·y • ***noun,*** *plural* **dromedaries**

drone[1] (drōn) ***noun*** a male honeybee. It has no sting and does no work.
drone • ***noun,*** *plural* **drones**

drone[2] (drōn) ***verb*** **1** to make a humming or buzzing sound [The planes *droned* overhead.] **2** to talk on and on in a dull way [The speaker *droned* on for hours on his favorite subject.]
noun a low humming or buzzing sound.
drone • ***verb*** **droned, droning** • ***noun,*** *plural* **drones**

drool (dro͞ol) ***verb*** to let saliva flow from the mouth.
drool • ***verb*** **drooled, drooling**

droop (dro͞op) ***verb*** **1** to sink, hang, or bend

a	cat	ō	go	ʉ	fur	ə =	a *in* ago
ā	ape	ô	law, for	ch	chin		e *in* agent
ä	cot, car	oo	look	sh	she		i *in* pencil
e	ten	o͞o	tool	th	thin		o *in* atom
ē	me	oi	oil	*th*	then		u *in* circus
i	fit	ou	out	zh	measure		
ī	ice	u	up	ŋ	ring		

down [The heavy snow made the branches *droop*.] **2** to become sad or depressed.
droop • *verb* **drooped, drooping**

drop (dräp) ***noun*** **1** a very small amount of liquid, especially when it has a rounded shape, as when it is falling [*drops* of rain]. **2** anything like this in shape [She ate a whole box of lemon *drops*.] **3** a very small amount [He hasn't a *drop* of courage.] **4 drops** liquid medicine taken or applied in drops [nose *drops*]. **5** a sudden fall or decrease [a *drop* in the price of gasoline]. **6** the distance between a higher and lower level [a *drop* of 6 feet from the window to the ground].
verb **1** to fall or let fall in drops [Tears *dropped* from the actor's eyes.] **2** to fall or let fall [Ripe fruit *dropped* from the trees. He *dropped* his lunch on the floor.] **3** to make or become lower or less [The store *dropped* the prices of all clothing. Gasoline prices *dropped* overnight.] **4** to make less loud [They *dropped* their voices as they went into the library.] **5** to pass into a certain condition [She was tired and *dropped* off to sleep.] **6** to cause to come to an end; to stop or end [Let's *drop* this argument.] **7** to send or say in a casual way [I'll *drop* her a note to thank her. Johnny *dropped* a hint that he wanted a puppy as a gift.] **8** [*an informal use*] to leave at a certain place [The taxi *dropped* us at our hotel.]
—drop in or **drop by** to make an unexpected or informal visit. **—drop out** to stop taking part; stop being a member.
drop • *noun, plural* **drops** • *verb* **dropped, dropping**

droplet (dräp′lət) ***noun*** a very small drop.
drop·let • *noun, plural* **droplets**

dropper (dräp′ər) ***noun*** a small hollow tube with a hollow rubber bulb at one end. A dropper is used to draw in a liquid and release it in drops.
drop·per • *noun, plural* **droppers**

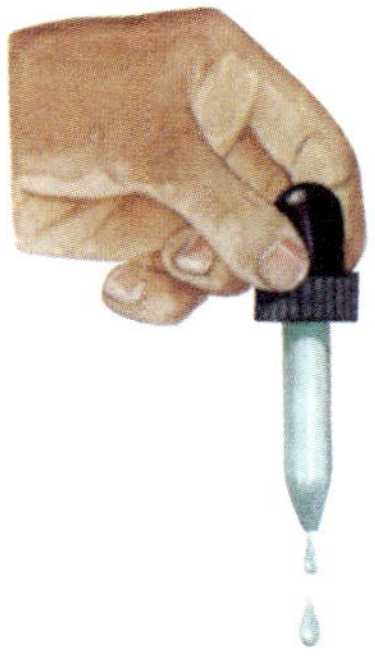
dropper

drought (drout) ***noun*** a long period of dry weather, with little or no rain.
drought • *noun, plural* **droughts**

drove[1] (drōv) ***noun*** **1** a group of cattle, sheep, or other animals that move or are being driven along together; herd; flock. **2** a large number of people; crowd [*droves* of tourists].
drove • *noun, plural* **droves**

drove[2] (drōv) ***verb*** *past tense of* **drive**.

drown (droun) ***verb*** **1** to die from being under water [The man fell overboard and *drowned*.] **2** to kill in this way [The flood waters *drowned* many farm animals near the river.] **3** to be so loud as to overcome some other sound [Cheers *drowned* out the speaker.]
drown • *verb* **drowned, drowning**

drowsy (drou′zē) ***adjective*** half asleep or sleepy [Do you feel *drowsy* after dinner?]
drow·sy • *adjective* **drowsier, drowsiest**

drug (drug) ***noun*** **1** a substance that is used to prevent or cure disease or to relieve pain; medicine. A drug may be used by itself as a medicine or in a mixture used to make medicine. **2** a substance that dulls the senses, causes sleep, eases pain, or can cause a person to become addicted to it.
verb to give a drug to, especially in order to put to sleep or make unconscious.
drug • *noun, plural* **drugs** • *verb* **drugged, drugging**

druggist (drug′ist) ***noun*** **1** a person who has a license to prepare and sell medicine; pharmacist. **2** a person who runs a drugstore.
drug·gist • *noun, plural* **druggists**

drugstore (drug′stôr) ***noun*** a store where medicines are sold and often prepared. Most drugstores today also sell magazines, cosmetics, and a variety of other things.
drug·store • *noun, plural* **drugstores**

drum (drum) ***noun*** **1** a percussion instrument that is a hollow cylinder with skin stretched tightly over one or both ends. It is played by beating the ends with sticks or the hands. **2** a container or other object that is shaped like a drum [an oil *drum*].
verb **1** to beat or play on a drum. **2** to keep on beating or tapping [He kept *drumming* on the counter with his fingers.] **3** to cause to remember by repeating again and again [The teacher *drummed* the multiplication table into us.]
drum • *noun, plural* **drums** • *verb* **drummed, drumming**

drum major ***noun*** a person who twirls a baton at the head of a marching band.
drum major • *noun, plural* **drum majors**

drum majorette ***noun*** a girl or young woman who twirls a baton at the head of a marching band.
drum majorette • *noun, plural* **drum majorettes**

D

drummer (drum′ər) ***noun*** a person who plays a drum.
drum·mer • ***noun,*** *plural* **drummers**

drumstick (drum′stik) ***noun*** **1** a stick used in playing a drum. **2** the lower half of the leg of a cooked chicken, turkey, or other fowl.
drum·stick • ***noun,*** *plural* **drumsticks**

drunk (druŋk) ***verb*** *past participle of* **drink.**
adjective having had too much alcohol to drink; intoxicated.
noun a person who drinks too much alcohol.
drunk • ***verb*** • ***adjective*** **drunker, drunkest** • ***noun,*** *plural* **drunks**

dry (drī) ***adjective*** **1** not in or under water [*dry* land]. **2** not wet or damp; without moisture [*dry* wood; *dry* clothes]. **3** having little or no rain or water [a *dry* summer; a *dry* climate]. **4** no longer containing water or other liquid [a *dry* well; a *dry* river bed]. **5** thirsty [I felt very *dry* after the tennis game.]
verb to make or become dry [*Dry* the dishes with this towel. Our clothes soon *dried* out.]
dry • ***adjective*** **drier, driest** • ***verb*** **dried, drying, dries**

dry cell ***noun*** an electric battery cell with its chemicals stored in paste form so that they cannot spill. The batteries used in toys, flashlights, and portable radios are dry cells.
dry cell • ***noun,*** *plural* **dry cells**

dry-clean (drī′klēn) ***verb*** to clean by using chemicals instead of water.
dry-clean • ***verb*** **dry-cleaned, dry-cleaning**

dryer (drī′ər) ***noun*** a machine for drying things by heating or blowing air [a clothes *dryer*].
dry·er • ***noun,*** *plural* **dryers**

DST or **D.S.T.** *abbreviation for* daylight saving time.

dual (do͞o′əl *or* dyo͞o′əl) ***adjective*** having or made up of two parts [a *dual* role in the movie; a car with *dual* controls].
du·al • ***adjective***
● The words **dual** and **duel** sound alike.
Good and evil make up his *dual* nature.
They intended to *duel* with swords.

Du Bois (do͞o bois′), **W(illiam) E(dward) B(urghardt)** 1868-1963; U.S. historian and black leader.

duchess (duch′əs) ***noun*** **1** the wife or widow of a duke. **2** a woman with the rank of a duke.
duch·ess • ***noun,*** *plural* **duchesses**

duck

duck[1] (duk) ***noun*** **1** a swimming bird that has a flat bill, short legs, and webbed feet. **2** a female duck. The male is called a *drake.*
duck • ***noun,*** *plural* **ducks**

duck[2] (duk) ***verb*** **1** to push quickly under water for a very short time [The bully *ducked* the little boy in the swimming pool.] **2** to lower the head or body quickly [She *ducked* as she walked through the low entrance.] **3** [*an informal use*] to avoid; evade [He was very good at *ducking* the reporters' questions.]
duck • ***verb*** **ducked, ducking**

duckling (duk′liŋ) ***noun*** a young duck.
duck·ling • ***noun,*** *plural* **ducklings**

duct (dukt) ***noun*** a tube or channel through which a gas or liquid moves [an air *duct;* the tear *ducts* of the eyes].
duct • ***noun,*** *plural* **ducts**

WORD HISTORY

duct

The words **duct** and **duke** come from the same Latin word, the verb that means "to lead." A **duct** leads a fluid from one place to another; **dukes** used to lead men into battle.

dud (dud) [*an informal word*] ***noun*** **1** a bomb or shell that fails to explode. **2** a person or thing that fails to do what is expected.
dud • ***noun,*** *plural* **duds**

a	cat	ō	go	ʉ	fur	ə =	a *in* ago
ā	ape	ô	law, for	ch	chin		e *in* agent
ä	cot, car	o͝o	look	sh	she		i *in* pencil
e	ten	o͞o	tool	th	thin		o *in* atom
ē	me	oi	oil	*th*	then		u *in* circus
i	fit	ou	out	zh	measure		
ī	ice	u	up	ŋ	ring		

D

due (do͞o *or* dyo͞o) ***adjective*** **1** owed or owing as a debt; payable [Our telephone bill is *due* today.] **2** proper; suitable [They treated the old woman with *due* respect.] **3** expected to come or to be done at a certain time [The plane is *due* at noon.]
adverb in a straight line; directly [Their farm is *due* west of the town.]
noun **dues** money that is paid regularly for being a member of a club or institution.
—due to **1** caused by [Her absence was *due to* illness.] **2** [*an informal use*] because of [The bus was late *due to* the storm.]
due • ***adjective*** • ***adverb*** • ***noun,*** *plural* **dues**
- The words **due, dew,** and **do** sound alike.
  I was *due* to arrive before her.
  There was *dew* on the grass.
  Why *do* you act that way?

duel (do͞o′əl *or* dyo͞o′əl) ***noun*** a formal fight between two people armed with weapons. A duel is fought according to set rules and is watched by witnesses.
verb to fight a duel [The rivals *dueled* at dawn.]
du·el • ***noun,*** *plural* **duels** • ***verb*** **dueled** or **duelled, dueling** or **duelling**
- The words **duel** and **dual** sound alike.
  Hamilton was wounded in a *duel.*
  Dual exhaust involves two tailpipes.

duet (do͞o et′ *or* dyo͞o et′) ***noun*** a piece of music for two voices or two instruments.
du·et • ***noun,*** *plural* **duets**

dug (dug) ***verb*** *past tense and past participle of* **dig.**

dugout

dugout (dug′out) ***noun*** **1** a boat or canoe that is made by hollowing out a large log. **2** a shelter dug in the ground or in a hillside. **3** a covered shelter near a baseball diamond where the players of a team sit when not at bat or in the field.
dug·out • ***noun,*** *plural* **dugouts**

duke (do͞ok *or* dyo͞ok) ***noun*** a nobleman of the highest rank below that of a prince.
duke • ***noun,*** *plural* **dukes**

dull (dul) ***adjective*** **1** not having a sharp edge or point; blunt [a *dull* knife]. **2** not interesting; boring [a *dull* book]. **3** not feeling or felt in a sharp way; weak [a *dull* ache]. **4** not bright; dim [a *dull* color; a *dull* glow].
verb to make or become dull [Chopping the wood *dulled* the ax. Cheap scissors *dull* easily.]
dull • ***adjective*** **duller, dullest** • ***verb*** **dulled, dulling**

dumb (dum) ***adjective*** **1** not having the power to speak; mute [a *dumb* beast]. **2** not speaking for a time; speechless [*dumb* with fear]. **3** [*an informal use*] stupid.
dumb • ***adjective*** **dumber, dumbest**

dumbbell (dum′bel) ***noun*** a short bar with round weights at the ends. Dumbbells are used to exercise the muscles of the arms and back.
dumb·bell • ***noun,*** *plural* **dumbbells**

dummy (dum′ē) ***noun*** **1** a figure made to look like a person and used to display clothing. **2** something that is made to look like and serve the purpose of something else [wooden *dummies* instead of rifles]. **3** [*a slang use*] a stupid person.
dum·my • ***noun,*** *plural* **dummies**

dump (dump) ***verb*** **1** to unload in a pile or heap [The truck *dumped* the firewood outside the barn.] **2** to throw away or get rid of [He *dumped* the rotten bananas in the garbage.]
noun a place where garbage, trash, or rubbish is dumped.
dump • ***verb*** **dumped, dumping** • ***noun,*** *plural* **dumps**

dunce (duns) ***noun*** a stupid person.
dunce • ***noun,*** *plural* **dunces**

dune

dune (do͞on *or* dyo͞on) ***noun*** a rounded hill or ridge of sand that has been heaped up by the wind.
dune • ***noun,*** *plural* **dunes**

dungaree (duŋ gər ē′) ***noun*** **1** a heavy cotton cloth, especially blue denim. **2 dungarees** pants or overalls made of this cloth.
dun·ga·ree • ***noun, plural*** **dungarees**

dungeon (dun′jən) ***noun*** a dark underground room that is used as a prison.
dun·geon • ***noun, plural*** **dungeons**

duplicate (do͞o′pli kət *or* dyo͞o′pli kət *for adj. & n.;* do͞o′pli kāt *or* dyo͞o′pli kāt *for v.*) ***adjective*** exactly like another or like each other [*duplicate* keys].
noun something that is exactly like another; an exact copy [I have a *duplicate* of the original letter in my files.]
verb to make an exact copy or copies of.
du·pli·cate • ***adjective*** • ***noun, plural*** **duplicates** • ***verb*** **duplicated, duplicating**

durable (do͝or′ə bəl *or* dʉr′ə bəl) ***adjective*** capable of lasting a long time in spite of hard wear or much use [*durable* shoes].
du·ra·ble • ***adjective***

duration (do͝or ā′shən *or* dʉr ā′shən) ***noun*** the period of time during which something goes on or continues [They stayed in the country for the *duration* of the holidays.]
du·ra·tion • ***noun***

during (do͝or′iŋ *or* dʉr′iŋ) ***preposition*** **1** throughout the whole time of; all through [Her grandparents live in Florida *during* the winter.] **2** at some time in the course of [We left *during* the night.]
dur·ing • ***preposition***

dusk (dusk) ***noun*** the time of evening when it is beginning to get dark.
dusk • ***noun, plural*** **dusks**

dust (dust) ***noun*** tiny, dry particles of earth, dirt, or other material that float in the air and settle on surfaces.
verb **1** to wipe the dust from [*Dust* the table with this cloth.] **2** to sprinkle with a fine powder [*Dust* the cake with powdered sugar.]
dust • ***noun*** • ***verb*** **dusted, dusting**

dusty (dus′tē) ***adjective*** **1** covered or filled with dust [*dusty* books; *dusty* tables]. **2** like dust or powder [poor, *dusty* soil].
dust·y • ***adjective*** **dustier, dustiest**

Dutch (duch) ***noun*** the language spoken in the Netherlands.
—go Dutch to have each person pay his or her own expenses. **—the Dutch** the people of the Netherlands.

Dutchman (duch′mən) ***noun*** a person born or living in the Netherlands.
Dutch·man • ***noun, plural*** **Dutchmen**

dutiful (do͞ot′i fəl *or* dyo͞ot′i fəl) ***adjective*** doing or ready to do one's duty; having a proper sense of duty [a *dutiful* son].
du·ti·ful • ***adjective***

duty (do͞ot′ē *or* dyo͞ot′ē) ***noun*** **1** something that a person should do because it is thought to be right, fair, or moral [It is the *duty* of every citizen to vote.] **2** any of the things that are supposed to be done as part of a person's work [household *duties;* the *duties* of a teacher]. **3** a tax paid to a government, especially on goods brought in from another country.
du·ty • ***noun, plural*** **duties**

DVD (dē′vē′dē′) ***noun*** a disc that stores video, sound, or other information through digital recording. It is played by a machine connected to a TV or computer that uses a laser beam to read the information on it.
DVD • ***noun, plural*** **DVDs**

DVD

dwarf (dwôrf) ***noun*** **1** a person, animal, or plant that is much smaller than most of its kind. **2** a little man in fairy tales who is supposed to have magic powers.
verb to make something seem small in comparison; tower over [The redwood *dwarfs* other trees.]
dwarf • ***noun, plural*** **dwarfs** or **dwarves** • ***verb*** **dwarfed, dwarfing**

a cat	ō go	ʉr fur	ə = a *in* ago
ā ape	ô law, for	ch chin	e *in* agent
ä cot, car	o͝o look	sh she	i *in* pencil
e ten	o͞o tool	th thin	o *in* atom
ē me	oi oil	*th* then	u *in* circus
i fit	ou out	zh measure	
ī ice	u up	ŋ ring	

dwarves (dwôrvz) ***noun*** *a plural of* **dwarf**.

dwell (dwel) ***verb*** to live; reside [The President of the U.S. *dwells* in the White House.]
—dwell on or **dwell upon** to go on thinking or talking about for a long time [He *dwells* too much *on* his past football career.]
dwell • ***verb*** **dwelt** (dwelt) or **dwelled, dwelling**

dwelling (dwel′iŋ) ***noun*** a house, home, apartment, or other place to live in.
dwell·ing • ***noun,*** *plural* **dwellings**

dwelt (dwelt) ***verb*** *a past tense and past participle of* **dwell**.

dwindle (dwin′dəl) ***verb*** to keep on becoming smaller or less; diminish [Her savings *dwindled* away.] —Look for the WORD CHOICES box at the entry **wane**.
dwin·dle • ***verb*** **dwindled, dwindling**

dye (dī) ***noun*** a substance that is dissolved in water and is used to color hair, cloth, leather, or other material.
verb to color with a dye [She *dyed* her white dress blue. This material does not *dye* well.]
dye • ***noun,*** *plural* **dyes** • ***verb*** **dyed, dyeing**
● The words **dye** and **die** sound alike.
Does Grandmother *dye* her hair?
You can roll one *die* or two dice.
Without sunlight, the plant will *die*.

dying (dī′iŋ) ***verb*** *present participle of* **die**[1].
dy·ing • ***verb***

dynamic (dī nam′ik) ***adjective*** full of energy or power; active; vigorous [Her father is a very *dynamic* person.]
dy·nam·ic • ***adjective***

dynamite (dī′nə mīt) ***noun*** a powerful explosive. Dynamite is used to blow up buildings or rocks or to make tunnels.
verb to blow up with dynamite.
dy·na·mite • ***noun*** • ***verb*** **dynamited, dynamiting**

WORD HISTORY

dynamite

The Swedish inventor who invented this powerful explosive in the 1860's also made up the word for its name, **dynamite**. He used the Greek word for "power" as the root of the new word.

dynamo (dī′nə mō) ***noun*** **1** *another name for* **generator**. **2** a very energetic person.
dy·na·mo • ***noun,*** *plural* **dynamos**

dynasty (dī′nəs tē) ***noun*** a series of kings or rulers who belong to the same family.
dy·nas·ty • ***noun,*** *plural* **dynasties**

D

Ee

Ee Ee Ee Ee

Although it may not look as impressive as an elephant, **e** *is a powerful letter: it is used more frequently than all other letters. By itself, this vowel has a "long" sound, as in* **be**, *and a "short" sound, as in* **bed**. *Like other vowels,* **e** *can stand for the schwa sound, as in* **harden**. *Even when it is silent,* **e** *can affect the sound of vowels that come before it; compare, for example, the* **a** *sounds in* **mad** *and* **made**.

e or **E** (ē) ***noun*** the fifth letter of the English alphabet.
e or **E** • ***noun,*** *plural* **e's** or **E's**

E ***noun*** in music, the third tone in the scale of C major.
E • ***noun,*** *plural* **E's**

E or **E.** *abbreviation for* east.

ea. *abbreviation for* each.

each (ēch) ***pronoun*** every one of two or more things, thought of separately [*Each* of these books is special. *Each* is special.]
adjective every one of two or more, thought of separately [*Each* book has something special to teach us.]
adverb for every one of two or more things, thought of separately; apiece [Tickets are a dollar *each*.]
—each other one another [We love *each other*. They gave presents to *each other*.]

WORD CHOICES

Synonyms of **eager**

The words **eager, avid,** and **keen** share the meaning "enthusiastic."

in *eager* pursuit of fame
an *avid* baseball fan
not very *keen* about traveling

eager (ē′gər) ***adjective*** wanting very much; anxious to do or get [He is *eager* for praise.]
ea·ger • ***adjective***

eagle (ē′gəl) ***noun*** a large, strong bird of prey that has sharp eyesight.
ea·gle • ***noun,*** *plural* **eagles**

ear[1] (ir) ***noun*** **1** either one of the two organs in the head with which a human being or an animal hears sounds. **2** the part of the ear that sticks out from the head. **3** the sense of hearing [She has a good *ear* for music.]
ear • ***noun,*** *plural* **ears**

ear[2] (ir) ***noun*** the part of a cereal plant on which the seeds grow [an *ear* of corn].
ear • ***noun,*** *plural* **ears**

eardrum (ir′drum) ***noun*** the thin, tight skin that is stretched inside the ear. It vibrates when sound waves strike it.
ear·drum • ***noun,*** *plural* **eardrums**

Earhart (er′härt), **Amelia** (ə mēl′yə) 1898-1937; early U.S. airplane pilot who set records for long-distance flying.
Ear·hart, A·mel·i·a

a	cat	ō	go	ʉ	fur	ə =	a *in* ago
ā	ape	ô	law, for	ch	chin		e *in* agent
ä	cot, car	oo	look	sh	she		i *in* pencil
e	ten	ōō	tool	th	thin		o *in* atom
ē	me	oi	oil	*th*	then		u *in* circus
i	fit	ou	out	zh	measure		
ī	ice	u	up	ŋ	ring		

earl (ʉrl) ***noun*** a British nobleman.
earl • ***noun,*** *plural* **earls**

early (ʉr′lē) ***adverb*** **1** near the beginning of something; soon after the start [He won great fame *early* in his career.] **2** before the usual or expected time [The bus arrived *early*.]
adjective **1** near the beginning of something; soon after the start [We ate in the *early* afternoon.] **2** happening, coming, or appearing before the usual or expected time [an *early* spring].
ear·ly • ***adverb*** • ***adjective*** **earlier, earliest**

earmuffs (ir′mufs) ***plural noun*** a pair of cloth or fur coverings that are worn over the ears to keep them warm.
ear·muffs • ***plural noun***

earn (ʉrn) ***verb*** **1** to get as pay for work that has been done [She *earns* $10 an hour.] **2** to get or deserve because of something done [He *earned* a medal for swimming.]
earn • ***verb*** **earned, earning**
- The words **earn** and **urn** sound alike.
  How much money do you *earn* in a year?
  The museum has a Greek *urn* collection.

earnest (ʉr′nəst) ***adjective*** serious or sincere; not light or joking [It is my *earnest* wish that you will go to college.]
ear·nest • ***adjective***

earring

earnings (ʉrn′iŋz) ***plural noun*** money that has been earned; wages, salary, or profits.
earn·ings • ***plural noun***

earphone (ir′fōn) ***noun*** a device for sending sounds to the ear from a radio, telephone, hearing aid, or other apparatus. An earphone is held to the ear or placed in the ear.
ear·phone • ***noun,*** *plural* **earphones**

earring (ir′iŋ) ***noun*** a piece of jewelry that is a decoration for the lobe of the ear.
ear·ring • ***noun,*** *plural* **earrings**

earth (ʉrth) ***noun*** **1** the planet that we live on. It is the fifth largest planet and the third in distance away from the sun. **2** the dry part of this planet's surface, which is not the sea. **3** the soft, crumbly layer of the land's surface; soil or ground [The clay pot is filled with good, rich *earth*.]
—down to earth practical or sincere.

earthen (ʉrth′ən) ***adjective*** **1** made of earth [The hut had a hard *earthen* floor.] **2** made of baked clay [He carried water from the well in an *earthen* jar.]
earth·en • ***adjective***

earthly (ʉrth′lē) ***adjective*** **1** having to do with the earth, or life in this world, and not with the idea of a future life in heaven [She left all her *earthly* possessions to her children.] **2** possible [Your advice is of no *earthly* use.]
earth·ly • ***adjective***

earthquake (ʉrth′kwāk) ***noun*** a movement of the ground that feels like strong shaking or trembling. It is caused by shifts in rock underground or by the action of a volcano.
earth·quake • ***noun,*** *plural* **earthquakes**

earthworm (ʉrth′wʉrm) ***noun*** a worm that lives in the ground and helps to keep the soil loose.
earth·worm • ***noun,*** *plural* **earthworms**

ease (ēz) ***noun*** **1** the condition of not having to try too hard [She swam a mile with *ease*.] **2** a calm or relaxed condition [She quickly put us at *ease*.] **3** the condition of being without worry, trouble, or need [They lived a life of *ease*.]
verb **1** to make less hard to bear; relieve [The pills *eased* my headache.] **2** to take away some of the strain or pressure [*Ease* up on that rope.]
ease • ***noun*** • ***verb*** **eased, easing**

easel

easel (ē′zəl) ***noun*** a standing framework for holding a painter's canvas, a picture, or a display.
ea·sel • ***noun,*** *plural* **easels**

easily (ē′zi lē) ***adverb*** without trying too hard; without trouble or difficulty.
eas·i·ly • ***adverb***

east (ēst) ***noun*** **1** the direction a person faces to see the sun rise. **2** a place or region in this direction [He lives in the *east*.]
adjective **1** in, of, or to the east [the *east* side of town]. **2** from the east [an *east* wind].
adverb in the direction of the east; to the east [Go *east* one mile.]
—the East the eastern part of the U.S., especially the part along the Atlantic Ocean.

Easter (ēs′tər) ***noun*** a Christian festival held on a Sunday early in spring to celebrate Jesus's rising from the grave.
East·er • ***noun***

easterly (ēs′tər lē) ***adjective*** **1** in or toward the east [an *easterly* course across the bay]. **2** from the east [an *easterly* breeze]. This word can also be used as an adverb [He sailed *easterly* across the bay.]
east·er·ly • ***adjective***

eastern (ēs′tərn) ***adjective*** **1** in, of, or to the east [an *eastern* city]. **2** from the east [an *eastern* wind].
east·ern • ***adjective***

Eastern Hemisphere the half of the earth that includes Europe, Africa, Asia, and Australia.

East Germany the name of a former country consisting of the eastern part of Germany. It existed from 1949 to 1990.

East Timor (ēst′ tē′môr) a country on the eastern side of an island north of Australia. The western side of the island is part of Indonesia.
East Ti·mor

eastward (ēst′wərd) ***adjective*** in the direction of the east [an *eastward* journey]. This word can also be used as an adverb [We journeyed *eastward*.]
east·ward • ***adjective***

eastwards (ēst′wərdz) ***adverb*** *the same as the adverb* **eastward**.
east·wards • ***adverb***

easy (ē′zē) ***adjective*** **1** not hard to do, learn, or get; not difficult [an *easy* job]. **2** without worry, pain, or trouble [an *easy* life]. **3** not hard to put up with; not too strict [an *easy* boss]. **4** not rushed; not too fast [an *easy* pace].
—easy does it! [*an informal use*] be careful!
—take it easy [*an informal use*] **1** to keep from being rushed, hasty, or angry. **2** to keep from doing hard work; relax or rest.
eas·y • ***adjective*** **easier, easiest**

eat (ēt) ***verb*** **1** to put into the mouth, chew, and swallow [We *ate* pizza for lunch.] **2** to have a meal [We *eat* at six o'clock.] **3** to destroy by wearing away [Rust has been *eating* away our car's fenders.]
eat • ***verb*** **ate, eaten, eating**

eaten (ēt′n) ***verb*** *past participle of* **eat**.
eat·en • ***verb***

eaves (ēvz) ***plural noun*** the under part of a roof that sticks out past the side of a building.

eavesdrop (ēvz′dräp) ***verb*** to listen to other people talking when they do not know that they are being overheard.
eaves·drop • ***verb*** **eavesdropped, eavesdropping**

ebb (eb) ***noun*** the flow of water back toward the sea as the tide falls.
verb **1** to fall back, in the way that the tide does. **2** to become weaker or less [Our hopes for victory *ebbed*.] —Look for the WORD CHOICES box at the entry **wane**.
ebb • ***noun,*** *plural* **ebbs** • ***verb*** **ebbed, ebbing**

ebony (eb′ə nē) ***noun*** the hard, very dark wood of certain trees of warm regions.
eb·on·y • ***noun***

eccentric (ek sen′trik) ***adjective*** not usual or normal in behavior; odd.
noun a person who is odd in behavior.
ec·cen·tric • ***adjective*** • ***noun,*** *plural* **eccentrics**

echo (ek′ō) ***noun*** a sound that is heard again

a	cat	ō	go	ʉ	fur	ə =	a *in* ago
ā	ape	ô	law, for	ch	chin		e *in* agent
ä	cot, car	oo	look	sh	she		i *in* pencil
e	ten	o͞o	tool	th	thin		o *in* atom
ē	me	oi	oil	*th*	then		u *in* circus
i	fit	ou	out	zh	measure		
ī	ice	u	up	ŋ	ring		

when sound waves bounce back from a surface.
verb **1** to be filled with echoes [The long hall *echoed* with our footsteps.] **2** to be repeated as an echo [Her shout *echoed* in the empty theater.] **3** to repeat the words or actions of another person ["It's a pity, " he said. "It's a pity," she *echoed*.]
ech·o • *noun, plural* **echoes** • *verb* **echoed, echoing, echoes**

eclipse
Of the sun

eclipse (ē klips′) *noun* a partial or complete darkening or hiding of a heavenly body by another. In an eclipse of the sun, the sun is hidden because the moon is passing between it and the earth. In an eclipse of the moon, the moon is hidden because the earth is passing between it and the sun.
e·clipse • *noun, plural* **eclipses**

ecological (ek′ə läj′i kəl *or* ē′kə läj′i kəl) *adjective* having to do with ecology.
ec·o·log·i·cal • *adjective*

ecology (ē käl′ə jē) *noun* the science that studies the relations between living things and all of the things and conditions that surround and affect them.
e·col·o·gy • *noun*

economic (ek′ə näm′ik *or* ē′kə näm′ik) *adjective* having to do with economics [a new *economic* program].
e·co·nom·ic • *adjective*

economical (ek′ə näm′i kəl *or* ē′kə näm′ i kəl) *adjective* not wasting money, time, or material; thrifty [an *economical* person].
e·co·nom·i·cal • *adjective*

economics (ek′ə näm′iks *or* ē′kə näm′iks) *plural noun* [*used with a singular verb*] the study of the way that goods and wealth are produced, distributed, and used.
e·co·nom·ics • *plural noun*

economy (ē kän′ə mē) *noun* **1** the control of money that is earned and spent in a home, business, or government. **2** careful use of money and other things, in order to avoid waste [He writes with great *economy*.]
e·con·o·my • *noun, plural* **economies**

WORD HISTORY

economy

We get **economy** from the Greek word for "manager," which comes from the Greek word for "house." To run a home well, a person must carefully balance money and other resources that come in with those that go out. The Greek word for "house" also forms part of the word **ecology**. We might say that **ecology** studies the way living things live together on their home, the earth.

ecosystem (ek′ō sis′təm *or* ē′kō sis′təm) *noun* all the animals, plants, and bacteria that make up a particular community living in a certain environment. The parts of an ecosystem depend on one another to live.
e·co·sys·tem • *noun, plural* **ecosystems**

Ecuador (ek′wə dôr) a country on the northwestern coast of South America.
Ec·ua·dor

-ed *a suffix:* **1** used to form the past tense of many verbs [I *hated* practicing piano, but now I love it.] **2** used to form the past participle of many verbs [I have always *loved* chocolate ice cream.] **3** *used to form adjectives from nouns and meaning* having [The *moneyed* class is the group of people who have much money.]

ed. *abbreviation for* education.

Eden (ēd′n) in the Bible, the garden where Adam and Eve first lived.
E·den

edge (ej) *noun* **1** a thin, sharp part for cutting [the *edge* of a knife]. **2** the line or part where something begins or ends; a border or margin [the *edge* of a plate; the *edge* of the forest] —Look for the WORD CHOICES box at the entry **border**.
verb **1** to form or put an edge on [Please *edge* the apron with braid.] **2** to move in a slow or careful way [He *edged* his way through the crowd.]—**on edge** very tense or nervous.
edge • *noun, plural* **edges** • *verb* **edged, edging**

E

edible (ed′i bəl) ***adjective*** fit to be eaten; safe to eat [Are these berries *edible* or poisonous?]
ed·i·ble • ***adjective***

Edison (ed′i sən), **Thomas A.** (täm′əs) 1847-1931; U.S. inventor. Among his chief inventions are the incandescent lamp, the phonograph, and the microphone.
Ed·i·son, Thom·as A.

edit (ed′it) ***verb*** **1** to get a piece of writing ready for printing, by arranging, correcting, or changing what has been written. **2** to get a film, tape, or recording ready by cutting and rearranging parts and then putting it all back together. **3** to be in charge of a newspaper or magazine and decide what is to be printed in it [Mr. Wong *edits* the newspaper.]
ed·it • ***verb*** **edited, editing**

edition (e dish′ən) ***noun*** **1** the size or form in which a book is published [I bought a paperback *edition* of the novel.] **2** all of the copies of a book, newspaper, or other publication that are printed at about the same time [the final *edition* of the newspaper].
e·di·tion • ***noun,*** *plural* **editions**

editor (ed′it ər) ***noun*** **1** a person who edits. **2** the head of a department of a newspaper, magazine, or similar publication.
ed·i·tor • ***noun,*** *plural* **editors**

editorial (ed′i tôr′ē əl) ***adjective*** of or by an editor [*editorial* opinion].
noun a newspaper or magazine article, or a talk on radio or TV, that openly gives the opinion of the editor, publisher, or owner.
ed·i·to·ri·al • ***adjective*** • ***noun,*** *plural* **editorials**

Edmonton (ed′mən tən) the capital of Alberta, Canada.
Ed·mon·ton

educate (ej′o͞o kāt′) ***verb*** to teach or train, especially in a school or college; develop the mind of.
ed·u·cate • ***verb*** **educated, educating**

education (ej′o͞o kā′shən) ***noun*** **1** the act or work of educating or training people; teaching [She made a career in *education*.] **2** the things that a person learns by being taught [He has a high-school *education*.]
ed·u·ca·tion • ***noun***

educational (ej′o͞o kā′shə nəl) ***adjective*** **1** having to do with education. **2** used for teaching or giving information [an *educational* film].
ed·u·ca·tion·al • ***adjective***

educator (ej′o͞o kāt′ər) ***noun*** a teacher.
ed·u·ca·tor • ***noun,*** *plural* **educators**

eek (ēk) ***interjection*** an exclamation of surprise, fright, or disgust.

eel

eel (ēl) ***noun*** a fish that has a long, slippery body and looks like a snake.
eel • ***noun,*** *plural* **eels** or **eel**

eerie (ir′ē) ***adjective*** giving a person a feeling of fear or mystery; weird [an *eerie* story] —Look for the WORD CHOICES box at the entry **uncanny**.
ee·rie • ***adjective*** **eerier, eeriest**

effect (e fekt′) ***noun*** **1** something that is caused by some other thing; a result [Candy can have a bad *effect* on your teeth.] **2** the power to bring about results [Scolding has no *effect* on them.] **3 effects** goods or belongings [They piled all their household *effects* into the trailer.]
verb to make happen; bring about [The new medicine *effected* a cure.]
—**in effect** in force or operation [The new law is *in effect* today.]
ef·fect • ***noun,*** *plural* **effects** • ***verb*** **effected, effecting**

effective (e fek′tiv) ***adjective*** **1** making the thing that is wanted happen [an *effective* remedy for a headache]. **2** making a strong impression on the mind [an *effective* speaker].
ef·fec·tive • ***adjective***

efficient (ə fish′ənt) ***adjective*** bringing about the result that is wanted, with the least waste of time, effort, or materials [The assembly line is an *efficient* way of producing cars.]
ef·fi·cient • ***adjective***

a cat	ō go	ʉ fur	ə = a *in* ago
ā ape	ô law, for	ch chin	e *in* agent
ä cot, car	oo look	sh she	i *in* pencil
e ten	o͞o tool	th thin	o *in* atom
ē me	oi oil	*th* then	u *in* circus
i fit	ou out	zh measure	
ī ice	u up	ŋ ring	

effort (ef′ərt) ***noun*** **1** a strong attempt to do something, using the mind or the body [It took great *effort* to resist eating a third piece of cake.] **2** a try or attempt [They made no *effort* to be friendly.]
ef·fort • ***noun,*** *plural* **efforts**

effortless (ef′ərt ləs) ***adjective*** using or seeming to use very little effort [an *effortless* golf swing].
ef·fort·less • ***adjective***

egg[1] (eg) ***noun*** **1** the oval or round object that is laid by a female bird, fish, reptile, insect, or other animal. A young animal of the same kind hatches from it at a later time. The egg has a brittle shell or a tough outer skin. **2** the cell formed by a female, which will make a new plant or animal of the same kind if it is fertilized. **3** the raw or cooked egg of a hen [scrambled *eggs*].
egg • ***noun,*** *plural* **eggs**

egg[2] (eg) ***verb*** *used only in the phrase* **egg on,** to urge to do something [Jill didn't want to climb the tree, but the other children *egged* her *on.*]
egg • ***verb*** **egged, egging**

eggplant (eg′plant) ***noun*** a large vegetable that is shaped like a pear and has purple skin. It is eaten cooked.
egg·plant • ***noun,*** *plural* **eggplants**

egotism (ē′gə tiz əm) ***noun*** a thinking or talking about oneself too much.
e·go·tism • ***noun***

egret (ē′gret) ***noun*** a wading bird that is a kind of heron. Most egrets have white feathers. These feathers were once used in women's hats.
e·gret • ***noun,*** *plural* **egrets** or **egret**

egret

Egypt (ē′jipt) a country in northeastern Africa on the Mediterranean and Red seas.
E·gypt

Egyptian (ē jip′shən) ***noun*** **1** a person born or living in Egypt. **2** the language of the ancient Egyptians. Egyptians now speak Arabic.
E·gyp·tian • ***noun,*** *plural for sense 1 only* **Egyptians**

eight (āt) ***noun*** the cardinal number between seven and nine; 8.
adjective being one more than seven [*eight* hours of work].
eight • ***noun,*** *plural* **eights** • ***adjective***

- The words **eight** and **ate** sound alike.
  Breakfast is at *eight* o'clock.
  We *ate* lunch at noon.

eighteen (ā′tēn′) ***noun*** the cardinal number between seventeen and nineteen; 18.
adjective being one more than seventeen [a truck with *eighteen* wheels].
eight·een • ***noun,*** *plural* **eighteens** • ***adjective***

eighteenth (ā′tēnth′) ***adjective*** coming after seventeen others in a series; 18th in order.
noun **1** the number, person, or thing that is eighteenth. **2** one of eighteen equal parts of something; 1/18.
eight·eenth • ***adjective*** • ***noun,*** *plural* **eighteenths**

eighth (āth) ***adjective*** coming after seven others in a series; 8th in order.
noun **1** the number, person, or thing that is eighth. **2** one of eight equal parts of something; 1/8.
eighth • ***adjective*** • ***noun,*** *plural* **eighths**

eighth note ***noun*** a note in music that is held for one eighth as long as a whole note.
eighth note • ***noun,*** *plural* **eighth notes**

eightieth (āt′ē əth) ***adjective*** being ten more than seventy others in a series; 80th in order.
noun **1** the number, person, or thing that is eightieth. **2** one of eighty equal parts of something; 1/80.
eight·i·eth • ***adjective*** • ***noun,*** *plural* **eightieths**

eighty (āt′ē) ***noun*** the cardinal number that is equal to eight times ten; 80.
adjective being eight times ten [*eighty* hours].
eight·y • ***noun,*** *plural* **eighties** • ***adjective***

Einstein (īn′stīn), **Albert** (al′bərt) 1879-1955; a famous scientist who was born in Germany and became a U.S. citizen. He developed a theory of the universe that deals with the relationship of matter, energy, space, and time.
Ein·stein, Al·bert

Eisenhower (ī′zən hou ər), **Dwight D.** (dwīt) 1890-1969; the thirty-fourth president of the U.S., from 1953 to 1961.
Ei·sen·how·er, Dwight D.

either (ē′thər *or* ī′thər) ***adjective*** **1** one or the other of two [You may use *either* door.] **2** both

one and the other; each [She had a tool in *either* hand.]
pronoun one or the other of two persons or things [*Either* of these recipes will work.]
conjunction taking the first of two choices. Used in phrases with *or* [I'll buy *either* roses or daisies.]
adverb any more than the other; also [If you don't go, I won't go *either*.]
ei·ther • ***adjective*** • ***pronoun*** • ***conjunction*** • ***adverb***

eject (ē jekt′) ***verb*** to force out; throw out or expel.
e·ject • ***verb*** **ejected, ejecting**

WORD CHOICES

Synonyms of eject

The words **eject**, **expel**, and **oust** share the meaning "to force out."

The policemen *ejected* the rowdy fans.

The principal *expelled* him from school.

The council *ousted* the dishonest mayor.

elaborate (ē lab′ər ət *for adj.;* ē lab′ər āt′ *for v.*) ***adjective*** worked out in a very careful way, with many details; complicated [an *elaborate* plan; an *elaborate* outfit].
verb to give more details [Please *elaborate* on your answer.]
e·lab·o·rate • ***adjective*** • ***verb*** **elaborated, elaborating**

WORD HISTORY

elaborate

This word comes from a Latin verb that means "to work out" or "to labor very hard." An **elaborate** design on a piece of jewelry, for example, is a complicated design that someone has worked on for a long time.

elastic (ē las′tik) ***adjective*** capable of springing back into shape or position after being stretched or squeezed; springy [Rubber is *elastic*.]
noun a cloth or tape with rubber threads or threads that are like rubber running through it to make it elastic.
e·las·tic • ***adjective*** • ***noun***

elbow (el′bō) ***noun*** **1** the joint where the forearm and upper arm meet. The elbow allows the arm to bend. **2** anything that is bent like an elbow [The plumber replaced an *elbow* connecting two water pipes.]
verb to push or shove with the elbows [He *elbowed* his way through the crowd.]
el·bow • ***noun,*** *plural* **elbows** • ***verb*** **elbowed, elbowing**

WORD HISTORY

elbow

Long ago, people who wove cloth measured it by holding it along the arm from the bending joint to the end of the finger. That distance was called an *ell*, and the bend in the arm was the *ell bow*, which we now write **elbow**.

elder (el′dər) ***adjective*** older [the *elder* son].
noun an older person [We can learn a lot from our *elders*.]
eld·er • ***adjective*** • ***noun,*** *plural* **elders**

elderly (el′dər lē) ***adjective*** somewhat old; past middle age.
eld·er·ly • ***adjective***

eldest (el′dəst) ***adjective*** oldest [Carlos is the *eldest* son.]
eld·est • ***adjective***

elect (ē lekt′) ***verb*** **1** to choose for an office by voting [We *elected* a new student council in September.] **2** to choose or decide [We *elected* to stay.]
e·lect • ***verb*** **elected, electing**

election (ē lek′shən) ***noun*** **1** the fact of being chosen [Her *election* surprised many people.] **2** the process of choosing among candidates or issues by voting [The *election* will be held in November.]
e·lec·tion • ***noun,*** *plural* **elections**

a cat	ō go	ʉ fur	ə = a *in* ago
ā ape	ô law, for	ch chin	e *in* agent
ä cot, car	oo look	sh she	i *in* pencil
e ten	ōō tool	th thin	o *in* atom
ē me	oi oil	*th* then	u *in* circus
i fit	ou out	zh measure	
ī ice	u up	ŋ ring	

electric (ē lek′trik) ***adjective*** **1** of or having to do with electricity [*electric* current; an *electric* wire]. **2** making or made by electricity [an *electric* generator]. **3** worked by electricity [an *electric* toothbrush].
e·lec·tric • ***adjective***

electrical (ē lek′tri kəl) ***adjective*** **1** *the same as* **electric** [an *electrical* outlet in the wall]. **2** having to do with the science or use of electricity [an *electrical* engineer].
e·lec·tri·cal • ***adjective***

electric guitar

electric guitar ***noun*** a guitar whose tones are changed into electrical signals. These signals are changed back to louder tones by an amplifier and are then sent out through a loudspeaker.
electric guitar • ***noun,*** *plural* **electric guitars**

electrician (ē lek′trish′ən) ***noun*** a person whose work is setting up or fixing electrical equipment.
e·lec·tri·cian • ***noun,*** *plural* **electricians**

electricity (ē lek′tris′i tē) ***noun*** a form of energy that comes from the movement of the positive and negative charges that are in everything. Electricity is the power that lights lamps, heats houses, and makes appliances work.
e·lec·tric·i·ty • ***noun***

electro- *a prefix meaning* electric or electricity [An *electromagnet* is an electric magnet.]

electron (ē lek′trän′) ***noun*** any one of the tiny particles that move around the nucleus of an atom. An electron has a negative electrical charge.
e·lec·tron • ***noun,*** *plural* **electrons**

electronic (ē lek′trän′ik *or* el′ek trän′ik) ***adjective*** **1** having to do with electrons. **2** having to do with electronics [*electronic* equipment].
e·lec·tron·ic • ***adjective***

electronics (ē lek′trän′iks *or* el′ek trän′iks) ***plural noun*** [*used with a singular verb*] the science that deals with the action of electrons and their use in radios, TVs, computers, and other devices or systems.
e·lec·tron·ics • ***plural noun***

elegant (el′ə gənt) ***adjective*** **1** rich-looking and attractive in a dignified or refined way [an *elegant* silk dress]. **2** showing good taste and politeness [*elegant* manners].
el·e·gant • ***adjective***

element (el′ə mənt) ***noun*** **1** any one of the parts or qualities of a thing, especially a necessary or basic part [the *elements* of arithmetic; a story with an *element* of suspense]. **2** any substance that cannot be broken down into different substances. All living and nonliving things are made up of such elements. There are more than 100 chemical elements. Examples are oxygen, iron, and carbon.
—the elements wind, rain, and the other forces of nature that make the weather.
el·e·ment • ***noun,*** *plural* **elements**

elementary (el′ə ment′ər ē) ***adjective*** having to do with the first or simplest things to be learned about something; basic [*elementary* arithmetic].
el·e·men·ta·ry • ***adjective***

elementary school ***noun*** a school where basic subjects are taught. It consists of the first five or six, or sometimes the first eight, grades.
elementary school • ***noun,*** *plural* **elementary schools**

elephant

elephant (el′ə fənt) ***noun*** a huge animal that has a thick grayish skin, two ivory tusks, and a long trunk. It is found in Africa and India, and it is the largest of the four-legged animals.
el·e·phant • ***noun,*** *plural* **elephants**

elevate (el′ə vāt′) ***verb*** to lift up; raise [We *elevated* the counter because it was too low.]
el·e·vate • ***verb*** **elevated, elevating**

E

elevation (el′ə vā′shən) ***noun*** **1** a high place or position [The house is on a slight *elevation.*] **2** height above sea level [The mountain has an *elevation* of 20,000 feet.]
el·e·va·tion • ***noun,*** *plural* **elevations**

elevator (el′ə vāt′ər) ***noun*** **1** a platform or box for carrying people and things up and down, in a building, mine, or other place. It is attached by cables to a machine that moves it. **2** a building for storing grain.
el·e·va·tor • ***noun,*** *plural* **elevators**

eleven (ē lev′ən) ***noun*** the cardinal number between ten and twelve; 11.
adjective being one more than ten [*eleven* football players on each side].
e·lev·en • ***noun,*** *plural* **elevens** • ***adjective***

eleventh (ē lev′ənth) ***adjective*** coming after ten others in a series; 11th in order.
noun **1** the number, person, or thing that is eleventh. **2** one of eleven equal parts of something; $\frac{1}{11}$.
e·lev·enth • ***adjective*** • ***noun,*** *plural* **elevenths**

elf (elf) ***noun*** in folk and fairy tales, a tiny imaginary being that looks like a human being and has magic powers.
elf • ***noun,*** *plural* **elves**

eligible (el′i ji bəl) ***adjective*** having the qualities or conditions that are required; qualified [She is *eligible* to be in the race.]
el·i·gi·ble • ***adjective***

eliminate (ē lim′i nāt) ***verb*** to get rid of; take out or leave out [Each day we *eliminate* waste matter from our bodies.]
e·lim·i·nate • ***verb*** **eliminated, eliminating**

WORD HISTORY

eliminate

The word **eliminate** comes from a Latin verb that means "to turn out of doors." That word is made up of two Latin words that mean "out" and "threshold." When you **eliminate** something from a group, it is as though you throw it out over your threshold.

Elizabeth I (ē liz′ə bəth) 1533-1603; the queen of England from 1558 to 1603.
E·liz·a·beth I

Elizabeth II (ē liz′ə bəth) 1926- ; the queen of Britain, Canada, and some other countries since 1952.
E·liz·a·beth II

elk

elk (elk) ***noun*** a large deer of North America with branching antlers.
elk • ***noun,*** *plural* **elk** or **elks**

ellipse

ellipse (e lips′) ***noun*** a curved shape that is made by an unbroken line. An ellipse is shaped like an egg, but with equal ends. It is a perfect oval.
el·lipse • ***noun,*** *plural* **ellipses**

elm (elm) ***noun*** **1** a tall shade tree with spreading branches. **2** its hard wood.
elm • ***noun,*** *plural* **elms**

elope (ē lōp′) ***verb*** to run away secretly in order to get married.
e·lope • ***verb*** **eloped, eloping**

eloquent (el′ə kwənt) ***adjective*** using words that are put together in a strong and graceful way and that can excite or convince people.
el·o·quent • ***adjective***

El Salvador (el sal′və dôr) a country in western Central America.
El Sal·va·dor

else (els) ***adjective*** **1** not the same; different or other [I thought you were someone *else.*] **2** in addition; more [Do you want anything *else?*]

a cat	ō go	ʉ fur	ə = a *in* ago
ā ape	ô law, for	ch chin	e *in* agent
ä cot, car	oo look	sh she	i *in* pencil
e ten	ōō tool	th thin	o *in* atom
ē me	oi oil	*th* then	u *in* circus
i fit	ou out	zh measure	
ī ice	u up	ŋ ring	

adverb **1** in a different time, place, or way [Where *else* did you go?] **2** if not; otherwise [Study or *else* you will fail.]

elsewhere (els′hwer *or* els′wer) *adverb* in or to some other place [Look for it *elsewhere*.]
else·where • *adverb*

elude (ē lo͞od′) *verb* to keep away from by being quick or clever [The thief *eluded* the police.]
e·lude • *verb* **eluded, eluding**

elves (elvz) *noun plural of* **elf**.

'em (əm) [*an informal word*] *pronoun* them.

e-mail (ē′māl) *noun* messages that are typed on computer keyboards and sent over the telephone lines to other computers. E-mail stands for *electronic mail*.

emancipate (ē man′si pāt′) *verb* to set free from slavery or from strict control [Lincoln *emancipated* the slaves.]
e·man·ci·pate • *verb* **emancipated, emancipating**

Emancipation Proclamation (ē man′si pā′ shən) the proclamation by President Lincoln stating that the slaves in the Confederacy would be free as of January 1, 1863.
E·man·ci·pa·tion Proclamation

embankment (em baŋk′mənt) *noun* a long mound or wall that is used to hold back water or hold up a roadway.
em·bank·ment • *noun, plural* **embankments**

embark (em bärk′) *verb* to start out; begin [We *embarked* on our great adventure.]
em·bark • *verb* **embarked, embarking**

embarrass (em ber′əs) *verb* to make feel uncomfortable or self-conscious [The politician was *embarrassed* by the reporters' questions.]
em·bar·rass • *verb* **embarrassed, embarrassing**

embassy (em′bə sē) *noun* the building where an ambassador lives and works.
em·bas·sy • *noun, plural* **embassies**

embed (em bed′) *verb* to set firmly in something [We *embedded* the tiles in cement.]
em·bed • *verb* **embedded, embedding**

ember (em′bər) *noun* a piece of coal or wood that is still glowing in the ashes of a fire.
em·ber • *noun, plural* **embers**

emblem (em′bləm) *noun* a thing that stands for another thing or for an idea; a sign or symbol [The cardinal is the *emblem* of our team.]
em·blem • *noun, plural* **emblems**

embody (em bäd′ē) *verb* to put into a definite form that can be seen or recognized; make real in some way [The Constitution *embodies* Thomas Jefferson's ideas about government.]
em·bod·y • *verb* **embodied, embodying, embodies**

emboss (em bôs′) *verb* to decorate with patterns that stand out from the surface [The wallpaper is *embossed* with a leaf design.]
em·boss • *verb* **embossed, embossing**

embrace (em brās′) *verb* **1** to hold closely in the arms in showing fond feeling or love [The mother *embraced* her child.] **2** to hug each other [The mother and child *embraced*.] **3** to take up in an eager or serious way [They *embraced* the customs of their ancestors.] *noun* the act of embracing; a hug.
em·brace • *verb* **embraced, embracing** • *noun, plural* **embraces**

embroider (em broi′dər) *verb* **1** to stitch designs on cloth with a needle and thread [We *embroidered* letters on the aprons.] **2** to add imaginary details in order to make something more interesting [He *embroidered* the story of how he caught the fish.]
em·broi·der • *verb* **embroidered, embroidering**

embroidery

embroidery (em broi′dər ē) *noun* **1** the art or work of embroidering. **2** an embroidered decoration.
em·broi·der·y • *noun, plural* **embroideries**

embryo (em′brē ō) *noun* **1** an animal in the first stages of its growth, just after its development from an egg cell. **2** the part of a seed from which a plant develops.
em·bry·o • *noun, plural* **embryos**

emcee (em′sē′) [*an informal word*] ***noun*** a master of ceremonies.
verb to act as a master of ceremonies.
em·cee • ***noun,*** *plural* **emcees**
• ***verb*** **emceed, emceeing**

WORD HISTORY

emcee

This is just a way of writing the pronunciation of *M.C.*, the initials of the phrase "Master of Ceremonies."

emerald (em′ər əld *or* em′rəld) ***noun*** **1** a clear, bright-green jewel. **2** a bright green.
em·er·ald • ***noun,*** *plural* **emeralds**

emerald

emerge (ē murj′) ***verb*** **1** to come out so that it can be seen; appear [A bear *emerged* from the woods.] **2** to become known [Slowly the true story *emerged*.]
e·merge • ***verb*** **emerged, emerging**

emergency (ē mur′jən sē) ***noun*** a situation that develops suddenly and calls for action or attention right away [The hurricane created an *emergency* along the coast.]
e·mer·gen·cy • ***noun,*** *plural* **emergencies**

Emerson (em′ər sən), **Ralph Waldo** (ralf′ wôl′dō) 1803-1882; a U.S. writer and philosopher.
Em·er·son, Ralph Wal·do

emigrant (em′i grənt) ***noun*** a person who leaves one country or region to settle in another.
em·i·grant • ***noun,*** *plural* **emigrants**

emigrate (em′i grāt′) ***verb*** to leave one country or region in order to settle in another [Many people have *emigrated* from Ireland to the U.S.]
em·i·grate • ***verb*** **emigrated, emigrating**

eminent (em′i nənt) ***adjective*** standing above most others in rank or fame; very famous [an *eminent* scientist].
em·i·nent • ***adjective***

emit (ē mit′) ***verb*** to send out or give forth [The owl *emitted* a screech. A volcano *emits* lava.]
e·mit • ***verb*** **emitted, emitting**

emotion (ē mō′shən) ***noun*** strong feeling. Love, hate, anger, joy, and fear are emotions.
e·mo·tion • ***noun,*** *plural* **emotions**

emotional (ē mō′shə nəl) ***adjective*** **1** having to do with the emotions or feelings [Everyone has *emotional* needs that must be fulfilled.] **2** full of emotion or strong feeling [an *emotional* speech]. **3** having feelings that are easily stirred; quick to cry or be angry [They're very *emotional* people.]
e·mo·tion·al • ***adjective***

emperor (em′pər ər) ***noun*** a person who rules an empire.
em·per·or • ***noun,*** *plural* **emperors**

emphasis (em′fə sis) ***noun*** **1** special attention that is given to something in order to make it stand out; importance [That school puts too much *emphasis* on sports.] **2** special force that is given to certain words or syllables by a person who is speaking.
em·pha·sis • ***noun,*** *plural* **em·pha·ses** (em′fə sēz)

emphasize (em′fə sīz) ***verb*** to give special force or attention to; to stress [I want to *emphasize* the importance of honesty.]
em·pha·size • ***verb*** **emphasized, emphasizing**

empire (em′pīr) ***noun*** **1** a group of countries or territories under the control of one government or ruler [Much of Europe was once a part of the Roman *Empire*.] **2** a country ruled by an emperor or empress.
em·pire • ***noun,*** *plural* **empires**

employ (em ploi′) ***verb*** **1** to hire and pay for the work or services of [The company *employs* 50 people.] **2** to use [The workmen *employed* all their skills to build the church.]
noun the condition of being employed [Phil is no longer in their *employ*.]
em·ploy • ***verb*** **employed, employing**
• ***noun***

employee (em ploi′ē *or* em′ploi ē′) ***noun*** a person who works for another in return for pay.

a cat	ō go	ʉ fur	ə = a *in* ago
ā ape	ô law, for	ch chin	e *in* agent
ä cot, car	oo look	sh she	i *in* pencil
e ten	ōō tool	th thin	o *in* atom
ē me	oi oil	*th* then	u *in* circus
i fit	ou out	zh measure	
ī ice	u up	ŋ ring	

em·ploy·ee • *noun, plural* **employees**

employer (em ploi′ər) ***noun*** a person or business for whom other people work for pay.
em·ploy·er • *noun, plural* **employers**

employment (em ploi′mənt) ***noun*** **1** the act of employing [The company had a policy regarding the *employment* of alien workers.] **2** the condition of being employed [He left the company after ten years of *employment*.] **3** a person's work, trade, or profession; job [She found *employment* in a department store.]
em·ploy·ment • *noun, plural* **employments**

empress (em′prəs) ***noun*** **1** a woman who rules an empire. **2** the wife or widow of an emperor.
em·press • *noun, plural* **empresses**

empty (emp′tē) ***adjective*** **1** having nothing or no one in it; not occupied; vacant [an *empty* bottle; an *empty* house]. **2** without real meaning or worth [*empty* promises].
verb **1** to make or become empty [He *emptied* his glass. The auditorium *emptied* quickly after the show.] **2** to take out or pour out [*Empty* the dirty water from the pail into the sink.] **3** to flow out [The river *empties* into the Atlantic Ocean.]
emp·ty • ***adjective*** **emptier, emptiest**
• ***verb*** **emptied, emptying, empties**

emu (ē′myo͞o) ***noun*** a large bird of Australia that looks like an ostrich. Emus cannot fly.
e·mu • ***noun,*** *plural* **emus**

emu

-en *a suffix meaning:* **1** to make or become [The gray walls *darken* the room.] **2** to get or give [Something that *strengthens* us gives us strength.] **3** made of [*Wooden* toys are made of wood.]

enable (en ā′bəl) ***verb*** to make able; give the means or power to [Mrs. Garcia's large gift will *enable* the school to build a new gym.]
en·a·ble • ***verb*** **enabled, enabling**

enact (en akt′) ***verb*** to make into law [Congress *enacted* a bill raising taxes.]
en·act • ***verb*** **enacted, enacting**

enamel (e nam′əl) ***noun*** **1** a substance that is baked onto metal, pottery, porcelain, glass, or some other surface. Enamel forms a coating like glass that protects or decorates. **2** the hard, glossy outer layer of the teeth. **3** a paint that leaves a hard, glossy coating when it dries.
verb to coat or decorate with enamel.
en·am·el • *noun, plural* **enamels**
• ***verb*** **enameled** or **enamelled, enameling** or **enamelling**

-ence *a suffix meaning* act, condition, or quality [*Excellence* is the condition of being excellent.]

enchant (en chant′) ***verb*** **1** to cast a magic spell over; bewitch [The evil magician *enchanted* the princess and turned her into a swan.] **2** to charm greatly; delight [She was *enchanted* by the flowers she received.]
en·chant • ***verb*** **enchanted, enchanting**

enchantment (en chant′mənt) ***noun*** **1** the condition of being enchanted by a magic spell [The *enchantment* of the princess was broken by a kiss.] **2** something that charms or delights [the *enchantments* of the tropical islands].
en·chant·ment • *noun, plural* **enchantments**

enchilada (en′chi lä′də) ***noun*** a tortilla rolled with meat inside and served with a chili sauce.
en·chi·la·da • *noun, plural* **enchiladas**

encircle (en sur′kəl) ***verb*** to form a circle around; surround [High hills *encircle* the valley.]
en·cir·cle • ***verb*** **encircled, encircling**

enclose (en klōz′) ***verb*** **1** to shut in all around; surround [High walls *enclose* the prison.] **2** to put in the same envelope, package, or other container [*Enclose* a check with your order.]
en·close • ***verb*** **enclosed, enclosing**

enclosure (en klō′zhər) ***noun*** **1** a space that is enclosed [We keep our dog in an *enclosure* in the backyard.] **2** anything that is put into an envelope along with a letter.
en·clo·sure • *noun, plural* **enclosures**

encompass (en kum′pəs) ***verb*** **1** to surround on all sides; enclose or encircle [A low wooden fence *encompasses* the churchyard.] **2** to have in it; contain or include [A dictionary *encompasses* much information.]
en·com·pass • ***verb*** **encompassed, encompassing**

encore (än′kôr) ***interjection*** a word that is used by an audience in calling out for a performer to repeat a song or piece or do an extra one. This is a French word that means *again*.
noun **1** a request that is made by an audience to a performer for an extra performance. It is

E

now usually expressed by clapping or cheering for a long time. **2** an extra performance in answer to such a request.
en·core • ***interjection*** • ***noun,*** *plural* **encores**

encounter (en koun′tər) ***verb*** **1** to meet by chance or unexpectedly [I *encountered* an old friend on my vacation.] **2** to come up against; be faced with [She *encountered* many problems in her new job.]
noun a sudden or unexpected meeting with a person or thing.
en·coun·ter • ***verb*** **encountered, encountering** • ***noun,*** *plural* **encounters**

encourage (en kʉr′ij) ***verb*** **1** to give courage or hope to; make feel more confident [Praise *encouraged* her to do better in school.] **2** to give help to; to aid; promote [Rain *encourages* the growth of plants.]
en·cour·age • ***verb*** **encouraged, encouraging**

encouragement (en kʉr′ij mənt) ***noun*** **1** the act of encouraging [The players were received with shouts of *encouragement* from the fans.] **2** something that encourages [Praise acts as an *encouragement* to many young students.]
en·cour·age·ment • ***noun,*** *plural* **encouragements**

-ency *a suffix meaning the same as* **-ence** [*efficiency*].

encyclopedia (en sī′klə pē′dē ə) ***noun*** a book or set of books that gives information on a wide variety of subjects or, sometimes, on just one subject. It is made up of articles that are usually arranged in alphabetical order.
en·cy·clo·pe·di·a • ***noun,*** *plural* **encyclopedias**

WORD HISTORY

encyclopedia

The Greek word from which we get **encyclopedia** is made up of three words that mean "in," "a circle," and "education." So an **encyclopedia** is a collection of writings that deals with all subjects that lie within the circle, or boundaries, of education.

end (end) ***noun*** **1** the last part; finish; conclusion [the *end* of the day; the *end* of a story]. **2** the place where something begins or stops [the west *end* of town. His vacation is coming to an *end*.] **3** something that a person hopes to get or do; aim; goal [He will stop at nothing to achieve his *ends*.]
verb to bring or come to an end; to finish; to stop [What a sad way to *end* a story! When will the movie *end?*]
—on end **1** standing straight up [The ghost story made her hair stand *on end*.] **2** with no interruption [They traveled for days *on end*.]
end • ***noun,*** *plural* **ends** • ***verb*** **ended, ending**

endanger (en dān′jər) ***verb*** to put in danger or peril [The explosion *endangered* their lives.]
en·dan·ger • ***verb*** **endangered, endangering**

endangered species ***noun*** a species of animal or plant that is in danger of becoming extinct, or dying off [The whooping crane is an *endangered species*.]
endangered species • ***noun,*** *plural* **endangered species**

endeavor (en dev′ər) ***verb*** to make an effort; try hard [He *endeavored* to please his parents.]
noun a serious effort or attempt [The explorer failed in his *endeavor* to reach the North Pole.]
en·deav·or • ***verb*** **endeavored, endeavoring** • ***noun,*** *plural* **endeavors**

ending (en′diŋ) ***noun*** the last part; end; finish [The story had a happy *ending*.]
end·ing • ***noun,*** *plural* **endings**

endless (end′ləs) ***adjective*** **1** having no end; going on, or seeming to go on, forever [*endless* space; his sister's *endless* arguments; customers' *endless* complaints]. **2** with the ends joined to form a closed ring [an *endless* belt].
end·less • ***adjective***

endorse (en dôrs′) ***verb*** **1** to sign one's name on the back of a check in order to cash it or pass it on to another person. **2** to give support to; approve of [We *endorse* Jones for mayor.]
en·dorse • ***verb*** **endorsed, endorsing**

endow (en dou′) ***verb*** **1** to give money or property to [The city's wealthy families

a	cat	ō	go	ʉ	fur	ə =	a *in* ago
ā	ape	ô	law, for	ch	chin		e *in* agent
ä	cot, car	oo	look	sh	she		i *in* pencil
e	ten	ōō	tool	th	thin		o *in* atom
ē	me	oi	oil	*th*	then		u *in* circus
i	fit	ou	out	zh	measure		
ī	ice	u	up	ŋ	ring		

endowed the museum.] **2** to provide with some quality or thing [She is *endowed* with musical talent.]
en·dow • *verb* **endowed, endowing**

endurance (en door′əns *or* en dyoor′əns) *noun* the ability to hold up or last under hardship, strain, or pain [Boxing takes *endurance*.]
en·dur·ance • *noun*

endure (en door′ *or* en dyoor′) *verb* **1** to hold up under strain, pain, fatigue, or hardship; put up with; bear [Many pioneers *endured* hunger and cold.] **2** to go on for a long time; last [His fame will *endure* forever.]
en·dure • *verb* **endured, enduring**

enemy (en′ə mē) *noun* **1** a person, group, or country that hates another or fights against another; foe. **2** a person who hates or fights against an idea, cause, or condition [Abraham Lincoln was an *enemy* of slavery.] **3** anything that harms or injures [Drought is one of a farmer's worst *enemies*.]
en·e·my • *noun, plural* **enemies**

energetic (en′ər jet′ik) *adjective* full of energy; active or ready to act; forceful [an *energetic* child] —Look for the WORD CHOICES box at the entry **active**.
en·er·get·ic • *adjective*

energy (en′ər jē) *noun* **1** strength or power to work or be active; force; vigor [Our mother was a woman of great *energy*.] **2** the power of certain forces in nature to do work [Electricity and heat are forms of *energy*.]
en·er·gy • *noun, plural* **energies**

enforce (en fôrs′) *verb* to force people to pay attention to; make people obey [The police *enforce* traffic laws.]
en·force • *verb* **enforced, enforcing**

Eng. *abbreviation for* **1** England. **2** English.

engage (en gāj′) *verb* **1** to promise to marry [Harry is *engaged* to Grace.] **2** to get the right to use something or the services of someone [He *engaged* a hotel room for Friday evening. Mrs. Smith *engaged* a new lawyer.] **3** to get and hold [I'm trying to *engage* Lou's attention.] **4** to take part; be active [I have no time to *engage* in school politics.] **5** to meet in battle with [Our troops *engaged* the enemy.]
en·gage • *verb* **engaged, engaging**

engagement (en gāj′mənt) *noun* **1** a promise to marry [Their *engagement* was announced last night at the party.] **2** an appointment to meet someone or go somewhere [Sorry, I have an earlier *engagement* for lunch.] **3** the condition of being hired for some job [The band's *engagement* at the club will last three weeks.]
en·gage·ment • *noun, plural* **engagements**

engine (en′jən) *noun* **1** a machine that uses energy of some kind to make something run or move [an automobile *engine*]. **2** a railroad locomotive.
en·gine • *noun, plural* **engines**

engineer (en jə nir′) *noun* **1** a person who is trained in some branch of engineering. **2** a person who drives a railroad locomotive.
en·gi·neer • *noun, plural* **engineers**

engineering (en jə nir′iŋ) *noun* the science or work of applying scientific knowledge for practical purposes, such as planning and building machinery, roads, bridges, or buildings, or producing plastics.
en·gi·neer·ing • *noun*

England (iŋ′glənd) the largest part of Great Britain, south of Scotland. It is a division of the United Kingdom.
Eng·land

English (iŋ′glish) *noun* the language spoken in England, the U.S., Canada, Australia, New Zealand, and many other countries.
—the English the people of England.
Eng·lish • *noun*

English Channel the part of the Atlantic Ocean between England and France.

English horn *noun* a woodwind instrument with two reeds. It is like an oboe but a little larger and lower in pitch.
English horn • *noun, plural* **English horns**

English horn

Englishman (iŋ′glish mən) *noun* a person born or living in England.
Eng·lish·man • *noun, plural* **Englishmen**

English muffin *noun* a flat, round roll that is usually split and toasted for serving.
English muffin • *noun, plural* **English muffins**

E

Englishwoman (iŋ′glish woom′ən) ***noun*** a woman born or living in England.
Eng·lish·wom·an • ***noun,*** *plural* **Englishwomen**

engrave (en grāv′) ***verb*** **1** to carve or cut letters, figures, or designs into wood, metal, or another hard surface [She had the jeweler *engrave* her initials on the bracelet.] **2** to print from an engraved surface [The printer *engraved* the invitations for the White House ball.]
en·grave • ***verb*** **engraved, engraving**

engraving (en grāv′iŋ) ***noun*** **1** the art or work of carving or cutting letters, figures, or designs into a hard surface. **2** a picture or design printed from an engraved surface.
en·grav·ing • ***noun,*** *plural* **engravings**

engulf (en gulf′) ***verb*** to cover completely; swallow up [A huge wave *engulfed* the swimmer.]
en·gulf • ***verb*** **engulfed, engulfing**

enhance (en hans′) ***verb*** to make greater or better [A new patio *enhanced* our home's value.] —Look for the WORD CHOICES box at the entry **improve**.
en·hance • ***verb*** **enhanced, enhancing**

enjoy (en joi′) ***verb*** **1** to get joy or pleasure from [We *enjoyed* the baseball game.] —Look for the WORD CHOICES box at the entry **like**[2]. **2** to have as an advantage or benefit [I *enjoy* good health.]
—enjoy oneself to have a good time; have fun [We *enjoyed ourselves* at the baseball game.]
en·joy • ***verb*** **enjoyed, enjoying**

enjoyable (en joi′ə bəl) ***adjective*** giving joy or pleasure; delightful [an *enjoyable* time at the zoo].
en·joy·a·ble • ***adjective***

enjoyment (en joi′mənt) ***noun*** pleasure; joy [Gardening is her greatest *enjoyment*.]
en·joy·ment • ***noun,*** *plural* **enjoyments**

enlarge (en lärj′) ***verb*** to make or become larger [She has *enlarged* her stamp collection.]
en·large • ***verb*** **enlarged, enlarging**

enlargement (en lärj′mənt) ***noun*** **1** the act of enlarging [They were planning the *enlargement* of their kitchen.] **2** something such as a photograph or picture that has been made larger than the original.
en·large·ment • ***noun,*** *plural* **enlargements**

enlighten (en līt′n) ***verb*** to give knowledge or understanding to [The teacher *enlightened* him on the subject of drug abuse.]
en·light·en • ***verb*** **enlightened, enlightening**

enlist (en list′) ***verb*** **1** to join or get someone to join some branch of the armed forces [She *enlisted* in the Navy.] **2** to get the support of [He *enlisted* his parents to serve as umpires.]
en·list • ***verb*** **enlisted, enlisting**

enormous (ē nôr′məs) ***adjective*** much larger than usual; huge [an *enormous* building; an *enormous* sum of money].
e·nor·mous • ***adjective***

WORD CHOICES

Synonyms of **enormous**

Many words share the meaning "very large."

colossal	immense	massive
gigantic	mammoth	vast
huge		

enough (ē nuf′) ***adjective*** as much or as many as needed or wanted; sufficient [There is *enough* food for all.]
noun the amount needed or wanted [I have heard *enough* of that music.]
adverb to an amount or degree that is wanted or needed [Are you warm *enough?*]
e·nough • ***adjective*** • ***noun*** • ***adverb***

enrage (en rāj′) ***verb*** to make very angry; put into a rage [Tim's older brother *enraged* him by his constant teasing.]
en·rage • ***verb*** **enraged, enraging**

enrich (en rich′) ***verb*** **1** to make rich or richer [Large oil deposits will *enrich* the nation.] **2** to improve by adding something; make better [This bread is *enriched* with vitamins.]
en·rich • ***verb*** **enriched, enriching**

enroll (en rōl′) ***verb*** to make or become a member [We want to *enroll* you in our swim club.]
en·roll • ***verb*** **enrolled, enrolling**

enrollment (en rōl′mənt) ***noun*** **1** the act of enrolling [College *enrollment* starts next

a cat	ō go	ʉ fur	ə = a *in* ago
ā ape	ô law, for	ch chin	e *in* agent
ä cot, car	oo look	sh she	i *in* pencil
e ten	o͞o tool	th thin	o *in* atom
ē me	oi oil	*th* then	u *in* circus
i fit	ou out	zh measure	
ī ice	u up	ŋ ring	

week.] **2** the number of people enrolled [a school with an *enrollment* of 800].
en·roll·ment • ***noun,*** *plural* **enrollments**

en route (en ro͞ot′) ***adverb*** on the way [The plane stops in Chicago *en route* to Los Angeles.]

ensign (en′sīn *for sense 1;* en′sən *for sense 2*) ***noun*** **1** a flag or banner. **2** an officer in the navy.
en·sign • ***noun,*** *plural* **ensigns**

ensure (en shoor′) ***verb*** to make sure or certain [Good weather will *ensure* a large attendance.]
en·sure • ***verb*** **ensured, ensuring**

entangle (en taŋ′gəl) ***verb*** to catch or trap in a tangle [Her fishing line was *entangled* with ours.]
en·tan·gle • ***verb*** **entangled, entangling**

enter (ent′ər) ***verb*** **1** to come or go in or into [The teacher *entered* the room.] **2** to force a way into; pierce [The bullet *entered* his leg.] **3** to become a member of; join [Jack *entered* the Navy.] **4** to cause to join or be let in; register [She *entered* her horse in the Kentucky Derby.] **5** to write down on a list [Her name was *entered* on the honor roll.]
en·ter • ***verb*** **entered, entering**

enterprise (ent′ər prīz) ***noun*** an important project or undertaking. An enterprise is often difficult or complicated, or involves a great amount of risk.
en·ter·prise • ***noun,*** *plural* **enterprises**

entertain (ent ər tān′) ***verb*** **1** to keep interested and give pleasure to [She *entertained* the guests by playing the piano.] **2** to have as a guest; be a host to [His parents *entertained* friends for dinner.]
en·ter·tain • ***verb*** **entertained, entertaining**

WORD CHOICES

Synonyms of **entertain**

The words **entertain, amuse,** and **divert** share the meaning "to keep interested with something enjoyable."

A magician *entertained* the crowd.

The monkey's tricks *amused* us.

The traveler *diverted* herself with a novel.

entertainer (ent ər tān′ər) ***noun*** a person who performs for an audience. Singers, dancers, and comedians are entertainers.
en·ter·tain·er • ***noun,*** *plural* **entertainers**

entertainment (ent ər tān′mənt) ***noun*** **1** a show, concert, or other performance that entertains [There will be some *entertainment* at the dinner for the mayor.] **2** the pleasure or fun that comes from being entertained; amusement [The clown fell into the water, much to the *entertainment* of the audience.]
en·ter·tain·ment • ***noun,*** *plural* **entertainments**

enthusiasm (en tho͞o′zē az′əm) ***noun*** a strong liking or interest [an *enthusiasm* for baseball].
en·thu·si·asm • ***noun***

enthusiastic (en tho͞o′zē as′tik) ***adjective*** full of enthusiasm; showing great interest or liking [an *enthusiastic* follower of baseball; *enthusiastic* applause].
en·thu·si·as·tic • ***adjective***

entire (en tīr′) ***adjective*** including all the parts; whole; complete [I've read the *entire* book.]
en·tire • ***adjective***

entitle (en tīt′l) ***verb*** **1** to give a right or claim to [The coupon *entitled* me to a free seat for the game.] **2** to give a name or title to; call [Mark Twain *entitled* his book "The Adventures of Tom Sawyer."]
en·ti·tle • ***verb*** **entitled, entitling**

entrance[1] (en′trəns) ***noun*** **1** the act of entering [Everyone stood up at the Queen's *entrance*.] **2** a door, gate, or other opening for entering [the *entrance* to a building]. **3** the right to enter [The sign at the drive read, "No *entrance*."]
en·trance • ***noun,*** *plural* **entrances**

entrance[2] (en trans′) ***verb*** to fill with joy and delight; enchant [The hikers were *entranced* by the sunset on the lake.]
en·trance • ***verb*** **entranced, entrancing**

entrust (en trust′) ***verb*** **1** to put in charge of [She *entrusted* her secretary with opening her mail.] **2** to give over to another for care or protection [He *entrusted* his car keys to her.]
en·trust • ***verb*** **entrusted, entrusting**

entry (en′trē) ***noun*** **1** the act of entering [The Queen's *entry* into the palace was preceded by a military parade.] **2** a door, gate, or other passage for entering [The *entry* to the

building was blocked by a truck.] **3** each separate thing put down in a list, diary, book, or other type of record [In this dictionary, an *entry* is printed in heavy type.] **4** a person or thing that is entered in a contest [There were over 600 *entries* in the marathon.]
en·try • *noun, plural* **entries**

envelop (en vel′əp) ***verb*** to cover on all sides; wrap up or wrap in [Darkness *enveloped* the camp.]
en·vel·op • ***verb*** **enveloped, enveloping**

envelope (än′və lōp *or* en′və lōp) ***noun*** a folded paper cover in which letters are sealed for mailing.
en·ve·lope • *noun, plural* **envelopes**

envious (en′vē əs) ***adjective*** full of envy or showing envy [He's *envious* of her success.]
en·vi·ous • ***adjective***

environment (en vī′rən mənt) ***noun*** all the things and conditions that surround a person, animal, or plant and affect the health, growth, development, and character of such living things [an *environment* of poverty. Cleaning our air will improve the *environment*.]
en·vi·ron·ment • *noun, plural* **environments**

envy (en′vē) ***noun*** **1** a feeling of jealousy or dislike toward someone who has what one would like to have [He glared at the winner with *envy*.] **2** the person or thing that causes such feeling [His new car is the *envy* of the neighborhood.]
verb to feel envy toward or because of [They *envy* her for her wealth.]
en·vy • *noun, plural for sense 2 only* **envies** • ***verb*** **envied, envying, envies**

epic (ep′ik) ***noun*** a long, serious poem that tells the story of a hero or heroes.
adjective **1** of or like an epic [an *epic* poem about medieval knights]. **2** fit to be celebrated as heroic; impressive or tremendous [the *epic* western march of the pioneers].
ep·ic • *noun, plural* **epics** • ***adjective***

epidemic (ep′i dem′ik) ***noun*** the rapid spreading of a disease to many people at the same time [an *epidemic* of flu in the city].
ep·i·dem·ic • *noun, plural* **epidemics**

episode (ep′i sōd) ***noun*** **1** an event in the course of a series of events in a person's life [She told us of an *episode* in her childhood.] **2** a part of a whole story, or a separate part of a story that continues from week to week or day to day [the latest *episode* of my favorite TV series].
ep·i·sode • *noun, plural* **episodes**

epoch (ep′ək) ***noun*** a period of time that is marked by important happenings, changes, or events [The first earth satellite marked a new *epoch* in the study of the universe.]
ep·och • *noun, plural* **epochs**

equal (ē′kwəl) ***adjective*** **1** being the same in amount, size, value, or other quality [The horses were of *equal* height.] **2** having the same rights, ability, or position [All persons are *equal* in a court of law.]
noun a person or thing that is equal to another [As a sculptor, he has few *equals*.]
verb to be equal to; match [Six minus four *equals* two.]
e·qual • ***adjective*** • *noun, plural* **equals** • ***verb*** **equaled** or **equalled, equaling** or **equalling**

equality (ē kwôl′i tē) ***noun*** the quality or condition of being equal, especially in political, social, and economic rights and duties.
e·qual·i·ty • ***noun***

equation (ē kwā′zhən) ***noun*** a statement in arithmetic that shows that amounts or figures are equal. For example, 2 - 2 = 0 is an equation.
e·qua·tion • *noun, plural* **equations**

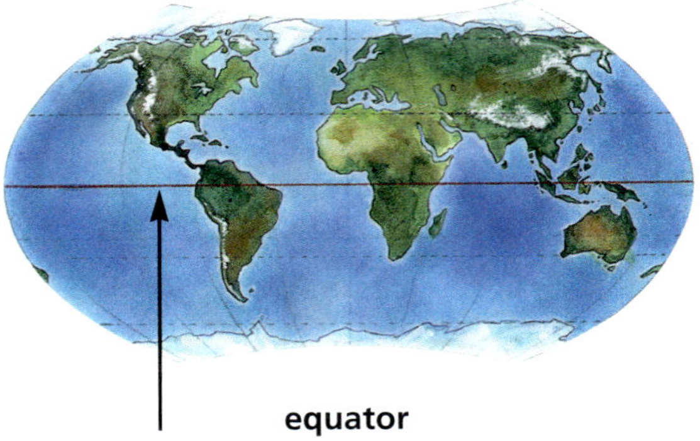
equator

equator (ē kwāt′ər) ***noun*** an imaginary line around the middle of the earth, at an equal distance from the North Pole and South Pole.
e·qua·tor • *noun, plural* **equators**

equatorial (ē′kwə tôr′ē əl) ***adjective*** having to do with or near the equator [*equatorial* regions].

a cat	ō go	ʉ fur	ə = a *in* ago
ā ape	ô law, for	ch chin	e *in* agent
ä cot, car	ᴏᴏ look	sh she	i *in* pencil
e ten	ᴏ͞ᴏ tool	th thin	o *in* atom
ē me	ᴏi oil	*th* then	u *in* circus
i fit	ᴏu out	zh measure	
ī ice	u up	ŋ ring	

e·qua·to·ri·al • *adjective*

Equatorial Guinea (ē′kwə tôr′ē əl gin′ē) a country on the west coast of Africa.
E·qua·to·ri·al Guin·ea

equilateral (ē′kwi lat′ər əl) *adjective* having all sides equal in length [an *equilateral* triangle].
e·qui·lat·er·al • *adjective*

equilateral
triangle

equilibrium (ē′kwi lib′rē əm) *noun* the condition in which opposite weights or forces are in balance.
e·qui·lib·ri·um • *noun*

equinox (ē′kwi näks) *noun* either one of the two times of the year when the sun is exactly above the equator, about March 21 and September 22. At these times night and day are both 12 hours long all over the earth.
e·qui·nox • *noun, plural* **equinoxes**

WORD HISTORY

equinox

The word **equinox** comes from the Latin words for "equal" and "night."

equip (ē kwip′) *verb* to provide with what is needed; outfit [The car is *equipped* with power brakes.]
e·quip • *verb* **equipped, equipping**

equipment (ē kwip′mənt) *noun* all the special things that are needed for some purpose; supplies [fishing *equipment*].
e·quip·ment • *noun*

equivalent (ē kwiv′ə lənt) *adjective* equal or the same in amount, value, or meaning [A foot is *equivalent* to 12 inches.]
noun something that is equal or the same [A foot is the *equivalent* of 12 inches.]
e·quiv·a·lent • *adjective* • *noun, plural* **equivalents**

-er[1] *a suffix* used to make the form of an adjective or adverb that expresses the idea "more" [*Greater* means "more great."]

-er[2] *a suffix meaning:* **1** a person or thing that does something [A *catcher* is a person or thing that catches.] **2** a person who lives in [A *New Yorker* lives in New York.]

era (er′ə) *noun* a period of time. An era usually starts or ends with an important event [The Christian *Era* is dated from the birth of Jesus.] —Look for the WORD CHOICES box at the entry **period**.
e·ra • *noun, plural* **eras**

erase (ē rās′) *verb* **1** to remove by rubbing or wiping off [Paula *erased* the wrong answer and corrected it.] **2** to remove writing or a recording from [The teacher *erased* the chalkboard. I *erased* the message from the tape.]
e·rase • *verb* **erased, erasing**

eraser (ē rā′sər) *noun* a thing that erases, such as a piece of rubber that is used to rub out pencil marks.
e·ras·er • *noun, plural* **erasers**

erect (ē rekt′) *adjective* straight up; not bending or leaning; upright [The guard stood *erect*.]
verb **1** to put up or put together; build; construct [A new house is being *erected* next to the old barn.] **2** to set in an upright position [Five men struggled to *erect* the flagpole.]
e·rect • *adjective* • *verb* **erected, erecting**

Erie (ir′ē), **Lake** one of the Great Lakes, between Lake Huron and Lake Ontario.
Er·ie, Lake

Eritrea (er′ə trē′ə) a country in eastern Africa on the Red Sea.
Er·i·tre·a

ermine (ʉr′min) *noun* a kind of weasel that lives in northern regions. Its fur is brown in summer, but turns white in winter.
er·mine • *noun, plural* **ermines** or **ermine**

erode (ē rōd′) *verb* to wear away; eat away [Rust *erodes* iron. Heavy rains *eroded* the hillside.]
e·rode • *verb* **eroded, eroding**

erosion (ē rō′zhən) *noun* the process of being worn away slowly, especially by wind or water.
e·ro·sion • *noun*

err (ʉr *or* er) *verb* to be wrong; make a mistake [It's better to *err* on the side of caution.]
err • *verb* **erred, erring**

- Sometimes the words **err, air,** and **heir** sound alike.
  To *err* is human, to forgive divine.
  Open the window to let in fresh *air*.
  She was *heir* to her father's estate.

errand (er′ənd) *noun* **1** a short trip to do a thing, often for someone else. **2** the thing to

be done on such a trip [My *errand* is to pick up a letter at the post office.]
er·rand • *noun, plural* **errands**

error (er′ər) ***noun*** **1** something that is untrue, incorrect, or wrong; mistake [a spelling *error;* an *error* in multiplication]. **2** a poor play by a baseball fielder that allows a runner to be safe.
er·ror • ***noun,*** *plural* **errors**

WORD CHOICES

Synonyms of **error**

The words **error**, **blunder**, and **mistake** share the meaning "something said, done, or believed that is not accurate or true."

an *error* in reporting the facts

an accident caused by the driver's *blunder*

a *mistake* in spelling

erupt (ē rupt′) ***verb*** **1** to break out or burst forth suddenly and violently [Lava *erupted* from the volcano.] **2** to throw forth lava, water, gases, or other material [The volcano *erupted* and covered the ground with ashes.]
e·rupt • ***verb*** **erupted, erupting**

escalator

escalator (es′kə lāt ər) ***noun*** a moving staircase in a store, subway station, or other public place. It carries people up or down.
es·ca·la·tor • ***noun,*** *plural* **escalators**

escape (e skāp′) ***verb*** **1** to break loose; get free [Many have *escaped* from that prison.] **2** to keep from getting hurt, killed, or injured [Very few people *escaped* the dreaded disease.]
noun **1** the act of escaping [The prisoners made plans for an *escape*.] **2** a way of escaping [There seemed to be no *escape* from the fire.]
es·cape • ***verb*** **escaped, escaping** • ***noun,*** *plural* **escapes**

WORD HISTORY

escape

We get **escape** from two Latin words that mean "out" and "cape." When a thief was caught and held, he might try to **escape** by slipping out of his cape, or cloak, and running away.

escort (es′kôrt *for n.;* es kôrt′ *for v.*) ***noun*** **1** one or more persons, ships, automobiles, or airplanes that go along with another or others to give protection, show respect, or honor [The President was accompanied by a large police *escort*. The merchant ships had an *escort* of four destroyers.] **2** a man who goes along with a woman to a party or other social event.
verb to go along with as an escort [Police motorcycles *escorted* the presidential limousine. My brother will *escort* Jane to the dance.] —Look for the WORD CHOICES box at the entry **accompany**.
es·cort • ***noun,*** *plural* **escorts**
• ***verb*** **escorted, escorting**

-ese *a suffix meaning:* **1** having to do with the country of [*Japanese* food is very different from *Chinese* food.] **2** the language of [*Portuguese* is the language of Portugal.]

Eskimo (es′ki mō) ***noun*** **1** a member of a group of peoples who live mainly in Alaska, northern Canada, and other arctic regions of North America and Asia. **2** the language of the Eskimos.
Es·ki·mo • ***noun,*** *plural for sense 1 only* **Eskimos** or **Eskimo**

a	cat	ō	go	ʉr	fur	ə =	a *in* ago
ā	ape	ô	law, for	ch	chin		e *in* agent
ä	cot, car	oo	look	sh	she		i *in* pencil
e	ten	o͞o	tool	th	thin		o *in* atom
ē	me	oi	oil	*th*	then		u *in* circus
i	fit	ou	out	zh	measure		
ī	ice	u	up	ŋ	ring		

esophagus (e säf′ə gəs) ***noun*** the tube through which food passes from the throat to the stomach.
e·soph·a·gus • ***noun***

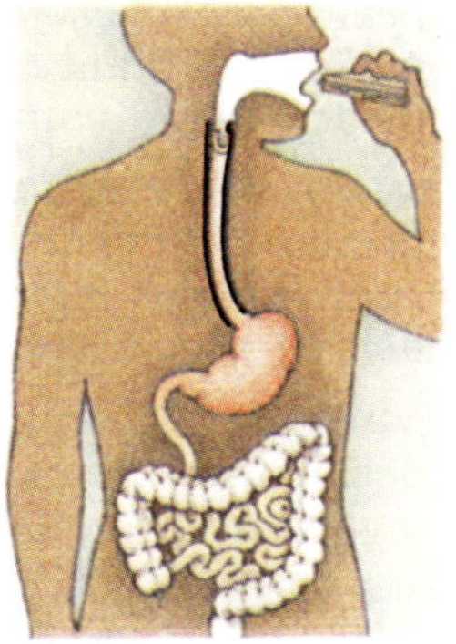

esophagus

esp. *abbreviation for* especially.

especially (e spesh′əl ē) ***adverb*** **1** mainly; in particular; specially [I like all fruit, but I am *especially* fond of pears.] **2** more than usually; very [She has been *especially* nice to us.]
es·pe·cial·ly • ***adverb***

espionage (es′pē ə näzh′) ***noun*** the use of spies by a government to learn the military secrets of other countries.
es·pi·o·nage • ***noun***

-ess *a suffix meaning* female [A *lioness* is a female lion.]

essay (es′ā) ***noun*** a short piece of writing on some subject, giving the author's personal opinions.
es·say • ***noun,*** *plural* **essays**

essence (es′əns) ***noun*** something that makes a thing what it is; most important or basic quality of a thing [The *essence* of friendship is mutual trust.]
es·sence • ***noun,*** *plural* **essences**

essential (e sen′shəl) ***adjective*** **1** most typical or basic [His friendly manner is an *essential* part of his character.] **2** most important or necessary; vital [A good diet and exercise are *essential* to health.]
noun something that is most important or necessary [We had time to pack only a few clothes and other *essentials*.]
es·sen·tial • ***adjective*** • ***noun,*** *plural* **essentials**

-est *a suffix* used to make the form of an adjective or adverb that expresses the idea "most" [*Greatest* means "most great."]

establish (e stab′lish) ***verb*** **1** to begin or start; found; create [The town settlers *established* the college in 1860.] **2** to show to be true; prove [The report *established* our town as the safest in the nation.]
es·tab·lish • ***verb*** **established, establishing**

establishment (e stab′lish mənt) ***noun*** **1** the act of establishing [A large bank loan helped in the *establishment* of the new college.] **2** something established. A business, a household, an army, and a church are establishments.
es·tab·lish·ment • ***noun,*** *plural* **establishments**

estate (e stāt′) ***noun*** **1** everything that a person owns, including money, land, and other property [She left her entire *estate* to her nephew.] **2** a large piece of land with a large home on it [an *estate* in the country].
es·tate • ***noun,*** *plural* **estates**

esteem (e stēm′) ***noun*** good opinion; high regard; respect [She holds her boss in high *esteem*.]
es·teem • ***noun***

estimate (es′ti māt′ *for v.;* es′ti mət *for n.*) ***verb*** to make a general but careful guess about the size, quality, value, or cost of.
noun a general guess about the size, quality, value, or cost of something [We received an *estimate* of $250 to repair the car.]
es·ti·mate • ***verb*** **estimated, estimating** • ***noun,*** *plural* **estimates**

Estonia (es tō′nē ə) a country in northeastern Europe.
Es·to·ni·a

estuary (es′tyoo er ē *or* es′choo er ē) ***noun*** the wide mouth of a river where the tide flows in.
es·tu·ar·y • ***noun,*** *plural* **estuaries**

etc. *abbreviation for* the Latin words *et cetera*, which mean "and others" or "and so forth" [Apples, pears, *etc.*, are called fruits.]

etch (ech) ***verb*** to engrave a design on a metal or glass plate by the use of an acid. A design is scratched into a coating on the surface of the plate. Acid is then used to cut into the plate where the coating has been scratched away.
etch • ***verb*** **etched, etching**

etching (ech′iŋ) ***noun*** a picture or design that is printed from an etched plate.
etch·ing • ***noun,*** *plural* **etchings**

eternal (ē tur′nəl) ***adjective*** **1** lasting forever; without a beginning or end [the *eternal* motion of the planets around the sun]. **2** seeming to have no end; going on and on [Stop your *eternal* arguments.]
e·ter·nal • ***adjective***

eternity (ē tur′ni tē′) ***noun*** **1** all time, without beginning or end; endless time. **2** a long

E

period of time that seems to have no end [It seemed an *eternity* before they arrived.]
e·ter·ni·ty • *noun, plural for sense 2 only* **eternities**

ether (ē′thər) ***noun*** a liquid that makes a person not able to think, feel, or move. Ether was formerly used in hospitals during operations.
e·ther • ***noun***

ethical (eth′i kəl) ***adjective*** of or having to do with moral standards —Look for the WORD CHOICES box at the entry **moral**.
eth·i·cal • ***adjective***

Ethiopia (ē′thē ō′pē ə) a country in eastern Africa, south of Egypt.
E·thi·o·pi·a

ethnic (eth′nik) ***adjective*** having to do with a group of people who have the same language and culture and share a way of life [Our city has many *ethnic* restaurants.]
eth·nic • ***adjective***

-ette *a suffix meaning:* **1** small [A *kitchenette* is a small kitchen.] **2** a girl or woman [A drum *majorette* is a drum major who is a girl or young woman.] **3** a substitute for [*Leatherette* is a substitute for leather.]

etymology (et′ə mäl′ə jē) ***noun*** the history of a word, which shows where it came from and how it has changed to its present form and meaning. In this dictionary, etymologies are given for some words. They are printed in boxes with the heading "Word History."
et·y·mol·o·gy • ***noun***, *plural* **etymologies**

eucalyptus (yo͞o kə lip′təs) ***noun*** an evergreen tree that grows in hot, moist regions. An oil with a strong smell is made from its leaves.
eu·ca·lyp·tus • ***noun***, *plural* **eucalyptuses**

Eurasia (yoo rā′zhə) a land mass made up of the continents of Europe and Asia.
Eur·a·sia

euro (yoor′ō) ***noun*** the basic unit of money in a group of European countries that includes France, Germany, Italy, Spain, the Netherlands, and certain other countries.
eu·ro • ***noun***, *plural* **euros**

Europe (yoor′əp) the continent between Asia and the Atlantic Ocean.
Eu·rope

European (yoor ə pē′ən) ***adjective*** of or having to do with Europe or its people.
noun a person born or living in Europe.
Eu·ro·pe·an • ***adjective*** • ***noun***, *plural* **Europeans**

evacuate (ē vak′yo͞o āt′) ***verb*** to leave or cause to leave a place for reasons of safety [The police *evacuated* the people from the burning building.]
e·vac·u·ate • ***verb*** **evacuated, evacuating**

evade (ē vād′) ***verb*** to keep away from or avoid by using tricks or clever planning [The running back *evaded* the tackle by dodging.]
e·vade • ***verb*** **evaded, evading**

evaluate (ē val′yo͞o āt′) ***verb*** to find out or decide the value or worth of; judge; appraise.
e·val·u·ate • ***verb*** **evaluated, evaluating**

evaporate (ē vap′ər āt′) ***verb*** **1** to change into a vapor or gas [Heat *evaporates* water. Water *evaporates* when it is boiled.] **2** to disappear like vapor; vanish [Our courage *evaporated* when we saw the lion.]
e·vap·o·rate • ***verb*** **evaporated, evaporating**

eve (ēv) ***noun*** *often* **Eve** the evening or day before a holiday or other special day [New Year's *Eve*.]
eve • ***noun***, *plural* **eves**

Eve (ēv) in the Bible, the first woman and the wife of Adam.

even (ē′vən) ***adjective*** **1** flat, level, or smooth [an *even* surface]. **2** regular or steady; not changing [an *even* flow of air; an *even* temper]. **3** on the same level [The water was *even* with the brim.] **4** capable of being divided by two without leaving a remainder [2, 4, 6, and 8 are *even* numbers.] **5** equal [*even* shares]. **6** exact [an *even* mile]. **7** just; fair [an *even* contest]. **8** having the same score; tied [The teams were *even* at half time.]
adverb **1** though it may seem unlikely; indeed [*Even* a child could do it.] **2** by comparison [She knows *even* less about music than I do.] **3** at the same time; while [*Even* as she spoke, the bell rang.]
verb to make or become even [*Even* off the ends of the logs. A goal *evened* the score.]
e·ven • ***adjective*** • ***adverb*** • ***verb*** **evened, evening**

evening (ēv′niŋ) ***noun*** the close of the day and the early part of the night; the time from sunset to bedtime.
eve·ning • ***noun***, *plural* **evenings**

a cat	ō go	ʉ fur	ə = a *in* ago
ā ape	ô law, for	ch chin	e *in* agent
ä cot, car	oo look	sh she	i *in* pencil
e ten	o͞o tool	th thin	o *in* atom
ē me	oi oil	*th* then	u *in* circus
i fit	ou out	zh measure	
ī ice	u up	ŋ ring	

event (ē vent′) *noun* **1** something that happens, especially something that is important [The annual circus was a great *event*.] **2** one of the contests in a sports program [The final *event* in the track meet was the pole vault.]
—in any event no matter what happens; in any case [It may snow tonight, but *in any event* we'll go to the theater.] **—in the event of** in case of [*In the event of* rain we'll hold the party indoors.]
e·vent • *noun, plural* **events**

WORD CHOICES

Synonyms of **event**

The words **event, incident,** and **occurrence** share the meaning " a happening."

a historic *event*

a minor *incident* in the war

a daily *occurrence*

eventful (ē vent′fəl) *adjective* full of important happenings [an *eventful* career].
e·vent·ful • *adjective*

eventual (ē ven′chōō əl) *adjective* coming at the end or as a result [Quarrels between nations can lead to *eventual* war.]
e·ven·tu·al • *adjective*

eventually (ē ven′chōō əl ē) *adverb* in the end; finally [We *eventually* became friends.]
e·ven·tu·al·ly • *adverb*

ever (ev′ər) *adverb* **1** at any time [Have you *ever* seen a movie star?] **2** at all times; always [They lived happily *ever* after.] **3** in any way; at all [How can I *ever* repay you?]
ev·er • *adverb*

Everest (ev′ər əst), **Mount** a mountain in southeastern Asia, between India and China. It is the highest mountain in the world, a little over 29,000 feet (or 8,845 meters).
Ev·er·est, Mount

evergreen (ev′ər grēn) *adjective* having green leaves or needles all through the year.
noun an evergreen tree or bush. Pines and spruces are evergreens.
ev·er·green • *adjective* • *noun, plural* **evergreens**

everlasting (ev′ər las′tiŋ) *adjective* lasting forever; eternal [dreams of *everlasting* fame].
ev·er·last·ing • *adjective*

every (ev′rē) *adjective* **1** all or each one of the people or things that are part of a group; each with no exceptions [*Every* student must take the test.] **2** all that there could be [You've been given *every* chance.]
ev·er·y • *adjective*

everybody (ev′rē bäd′ē *or* ev′rē bud′ē) *pronoun* every person; everyone [*Everybody* loves a good story.]
ev·er·y·bod·y • *pronoun*

everyday (ev′rē dā) *adjective* **1** happening each day; daily [Car accidents have become an *everyday* occurrence.] **2** fit for usual or common use [*everyday* clothes] —Look for the WORD CHOICES box at the entry **usual**.
ev·er·y·day • *adjective*

everyone (ev′rē wun) *pronoun* every person [In a small town *everyone* knows *everyone* else.]
ev·er·y·one • *pronoun*

everything (ev′rē thiŋ) *pronoun* **1** every thing that there is [Did you remember to bring *everything* for the picnic?] **2** the most important thing [His daughter is *everything* to him.]
ev·er·y·thing • *pronoun*

everywhere (ev′rē hwer *or* ev′rē wer) *adverb* in every place; in all places [We looked *everywhere* for him.]
ev·er·y·where • *adverb*

evidence (ev′i dəns) *noun* anything that makes clear or proves something; facts that give reason for believing something [The footprints are *evidence* that someone has been here.]
—in evidence easily seen; in plain sight.
ev·i·dence • *noun*

evident (ev′i dənt) *adjective* easy to see or understand; clear; plain [It was *evident* from her smile that she had won the game.]
ev·i·dent • *adjective*

evil (ē′vəl) *adjective* bad or wrong on purpose; wicked [*evil* thoughts. He led an *evil* life.] —Look for the WORD CHOICES box at the entry **bad**.
noun **1** something bad or wrong done on purpose; sin ["Deliver us from *evil*."] **2** anything that causes harm, pain, or suffering [War is a great *evil*.]

E

e·vil • *adjective* • *noun, plural for sense 2 only* **evils**

evolution (ev ə lo͞o′shən) ***noun*** **1** the gradual change that takes place as something develops into a different or more complicated form [the *evolution* of the frog from a tadpole]. **2** the scientific theory that all plants and animals have developed from earlier forms by changes that took place over many years and were passed on from one generation to the next.
ev·o·lu·tion • *noun, plural* **evolutions**

evolve (ē vôlv′) ***verb*** to develop by gradual changes [The scientists *evolved* a new theory. Our game plan *evolved* as we talked.]
e·volve • ***verb*** **evolved, evolving**

ewe (yo͞o) ***noun*** a female sheep.
ewe • *noun, plural* **ewes**

- The words **ewe, yew,** and **you** sound alike.
  The *ewe* strayed from the other sheep.
  A row of *yew* trees lined the drive.
  Where are *you* going?

ex- *a prefix meaning:* **1** out, from, or beyond. This use of this prefix is found in many words that come from Greek and Latin [*Exhaling* is breathing out. When we *exceed* a limit, we go beyond it.] **2** earlier or former. This use of this prefix is followed by a hyphen [An *ex-judge* is a former judge, meaning a person who is no longer a judge.]

WORD MAKER

The prefix **ex-**

Many words contain the prefix **ex-** plus a word that you already know. You can understand these words if you add the idea "earlier or former" to the meaning of the base word.

prefix	+ *base word*	⇨	*new word*
ex-	+ **Senator**	⇨	**ex-Senator** *(a former Senator)*
	chairperson		ex-chairperson
	convict		ex-convict
	diplomat		ex-diplomat
	husband		ex-husband
	mayor		ex-mayor
	member		ex-member
	officer		ex-officer
	opponent		ex-opponent
	owner		ex-owner
	partner		ex-partner
	president		ex-president
	pupil		ex-pupil
	soldier		ex-soldier
	wife		ex-wife

ex. *abbreviation for* example.

exact (eg zakt′) ***adjective*** correct and precise; accurate [*exact* measurements; the *exact* time; her *exact* words] —Look for the WORD CHOICES box at the entry **correct**.
ex·act • ***adjective***

exactly (eg zakt′lē) ***adverb*** **1** in an exact way; precisely [That's *exactly* the bike I want.] **2** in every respect; just [She always does *exactly* as she pleases.] **3** quite true; I agree: used as an answer to something said by another.
ex·act·ly • ***adverb***

exaggerate (eg zaj′ər āt) ***verb*** to make seem larger or greater than it really is [He always *exaggerates* the difficulties of a problem.]
ex·ag·ger·ate • ***verb*** **exaggerated, exaggerating**

WORD HISTORY

exaggerate

The word **exaggerate** comes from a Latin word meaning "to heap up." Heaping something up into a tall pile tends to make it look larger.

exam (eg zam′) [*an informal word*] ***noun*** an examination.
ex·am • *noun, plural* **exams**

examination (eg zam′i nā′shən) ***noun*** **1** the act or process of examining; inspection [an *examination* by a doctor]. **2** a test to find out how much someone knows [Did you pass the math *examination*?]
ex·am·i·na·tion • *noun, plural* **examinations**

examine (eg zam′in) ***verb*** **1** to look at closely

a	cat	ō	go	ʉ	fur	ə =	a *in* ago
ā	ape	ô	law, for	ch	chin		e *in* agent
ä	cot, car	o͝o	look	sh	she		i *in* pencil
e	ten	o͞o	tool	th	thin		o *in* atom
ē	me	oi	oil	*th*	then		u *in* circus
i	fit	ou	out	zh	measure		
ī	ice	u	up	ŋ	ring		

E

in order to find out the facts about or the condition of; inspect [The farmer *examines* the sky for signs of rain. The doctor *examined* her eyes.] **2** to ask questions in order to find out how much someone knows [The lawyer *examined* the witness in court.]
ex·am·ine • *verb* **examined, examining**

example (eg zam′pəl) ***noun*** **1** something chosen to show what the rest are like or to explain a general rule [This essay is an *example* of her work.] **2** a model or pattern that is to be copied [Dr. King's courage is an *example* to us all.] —Look for the WORD CHOICES box at the entry **model**.
ex·am·ple • ***noun,*** *plural* **examples**

excavate (eks′kə vāt) ***verb*** **1** to dig or dig out [The workmen *excavated* a hill to build the tunnel.] **2** to uncover by digging [The explorers *excavated* the ruins of an ancient temple.]
ex·ca·vate • ***verb*** **excavated, excavating**

excavation (eks kə vā′shən) ***noun*** **1** the act or process of excavating. **2** a hole or hollow made by excavating.
ex·ca·va·tion • ***noun,*** *plural* **excavations**

exceed (ek sēd′) ***verb*** **1** to go beyond what is allowed [She *exceeded* the speed limit.] **2** to be more or better than [The success of the school play *exceeded* our hopes.]
ex·ceed • ***verb*** **exceeded, exceeding**

exceedingly (ek sēd′iŋ lē) ***adverb*** very; extremely [His family is *exceedingly* rich.]
ex·ceed·ing·ly • ***adverb***

excel (ek sel′) ***verb*** to be better or greater than others [She *excels* in tennis and swimming.]
ex·cel • ***verb*** **excelled, excelling**

excellence (ek′sə ləns) ***noun*** the fact of being better or greater [We all praised the *excellence* of their singing.]
ex·cel·lence • ***noun***

excellent (ek′sə lənt) ***adjective*** much better than others of its kind; very good [Their cakes are fairly good, but their pies are *excellent*.]
ex·cel·lent • ***adjective***

except (ek sept′) ***preposition*** with the exception of; but [Everyone *except* you liked the movie.]
conjunction [*an informal use*] if it were not for the fact that; but [I'd go *except* I'm tired.]
ex·cept • ***preposition*** • ***conjunction***

exception (ek sep′shən) ***noun*** **1** the fact or condition of being left out [Everyone was there, with the *exception* of Don.] **2** a person or thing that is different from others of its kind [Most mammals do not lay eggs, but the platypus is an *exception*.]
ex·cep·tion • ***noun,*** *plural* **exceptions**

exceptional (ek sep′shə nəl) ***adjective*** not ordinary; outstanding [an *exceptional* pianist].
ex·cep·tion·al • ***adjective***

excess (ek′ses) ***adjective*** more than the usual limit; extra [Airlines charge for *excess* baggage.]
ex·cess • ***adjective***

excessive (ek ses′iv) ***adjective*** being too much or too great; more than is necessary or proper [*excessive* fees; his *excessive* smoking].
ex·ces·sive • ***adjective***

exchange (eks chānj′) ***verb*** **1** to give in return for something else; to trade [She *exchanged* the bicycle for a larger one.] **2** to give each other similar things [The bride and groom *exchanged* rings during the ceremony.]
noun **1** the act of giving something in return for another; a trade [I'll give you my pen in *exchange* for that book.] **2** a place where things are bought and sold [a stock *exchange*]. **3** a central system for connecting telephones that serve a certain area.
ex·change • ***verb*** **exchanged, exchanging** • ***noun,*** *plural* **exchanges**

excite (ek sīt′) ***verb*** to cause strong feeling in; stir up; arouse [The sight of men landing on the moon *excited* the whole world.]
ex·cite • ***verb*** **excited, exciting**

excitement (ek sīt′mənt) ***noun*** **1** the condition of being excited [The hotel fire caused great *excitement*.] **2** anything that excites [In all the *excitement* of the fair he lost his keys.]
ex·cite·ment • ***noun***

exciting (ek sīt′iŋ) ***adjective*** causing excitement; thrilling [an *exciting* basketball game].
ex·cit·ing • ***adjective***

exclaim (ek sklām′) ***verb*** to speak out suddenly and with anger, surprise, or other strong feeling ["I won't go!" she *exclaimed*.]
ex·claim • ***verb*** **exclaimed, exclaiming**

exclamation (ek sklə mā′shən) ***noun*** **1** the act of exclaiming; a sudden outcry [His speech was often interrupted by angry *exclamations* from the crowd.] **2** a word or phrase that is exclaimed to show strong feeling; interjection ["Oh!" and "Help!" are *exclamations*.]
ex·cla·ma·tion • ***noun,*** *plural* **exclamations**

exclamation mark ***noun*** *the same as* **exclamation point**.
exclamation mark • ***noun,*** *plural* **exclamation marks**

exclamation point ***noun*** a mark of punctuation (!). It is used after a word or a sentence to show surprise, anger, or other strong feeling.
exclamation point • ***noun,*** *plural* **exclamation points**

exclude (eks klo͞od′) ***verb*** to keep out or shut out [They *excluded* John from their club.]
ex·clude • ***verb*** **excluded, excluding**

exclusive (eks klo͞o′siv) ***adjective*** **1** given or belonging to no other; not shared; sole [That gallery has the *exclusive* right to sell his paintings.] **2** keeping out certain people, especially those who are not wealthy or against whom there is prejudice; not open to the public [an *exclusive* club].
ex·clu·sive • ***adjective***

excursion (eks kʉr′zhən) ***noun*** a short trip taken for pleasure.
ex·cur·sion • ***noun,*** *plural* **excursions**

excuse (ek skyo͞oz′ *for v.;* ek skyo͞os′ *for n.*) ***verb*** **1** to think of a fault or wrongdoing as not important; forgive [Please *excuse* this interruption.] **2** to release from a duty or promise [The sick student was *excused* from classes.] **3** to serve as a proper reason or explanation for [Nothing can *excuse* such a cruel act.]
noun **1** a reason given to explain some action or behavior; apology [She's always making *excuses* for being late.] **2** anything that serves as an excuse [Her sprained ankle was Jane's *excuse* for staying home.]
ex·cuse • ***verb*** **excused, excusing** • ***noun,*** *plural* **excuses**

execute (ek′sə kyo͞ot) ***verb*** **1** to carry out; put into effect [The President promises to *execute* the law passed by Congress.] **2** to perform; do [He *executed* a perfect somersault.] **3** to put to death in a way that is ordered by law.
ex·e·cute • ***verb*** **executed, executing**

execution (ek sə kyo͞o′shən) ***noun*** **1** the act of executing, or carrying out something [The plan was a good one, and her *execution* of it was perfect.] **2** the act of putting someone to death as ordered by law.
ex·e·cu·tion • ***noun,*** *plural* **executions**

executive (eg zek′yo͞o tiv) ***noun*** **1** one of the persons who help manage the affairs of a business, corporation, or other institution. **2** one of the persons who see that the laws of a nation or state are carried out [The Constitution makes the President our chief *executive*.]
adjective **1** having to do with managing; of or like an executive [A mayor should have *executive* ability.] **2** having the power to see that the laws of a nation or state are carried out [the *executive* branch of a government].
ex·ec·u·tive • ***noun,*** *plural* **executives** • ***adjective***

exempt (eg zempt′) ***verb*** to free from a rule or duty that others must follow [He was *exempted* from gym class because of his health.]
adjective free from a usual rule or duty [Charities are often *exempt* from taxes.]
ex·empt • ***verb*** **exempted, exempting** • ***adjective***

exercise (ek′sər sīz) ***noun*** **1** active use of the body in order to make it stronger or healthier [Long walks are good outdoor *exercise*.] **2** an activity or drill done regularly to make some part of the body stronger or to develop some skill [These *exercises* will strengthen your legs.] —Look for the WORD CHOICES box at the entry **practice**. **3** a problem or lesson to be worked on by a student in order to get more skill [piano *exercises*].
verb **1** to do certain regular movements, in order to develop or train [I *exercise* every morning. *Exercise* your weak ankle.] **2** to put into action; to use [*Exercise* caution in crossing the street.]
ex·er·cise • ***noun,*** *plural* **exercises** • ***verb*** **exercised, exercising**

exert (eg zʉrt′) ***verb*** to put into use; to use [He *exerted* all his strength to open the gate.]
ex·ert • ***verb*** **exerted, exerting**

exhale (eks hāl′) ***verb*** to breathe out [Take a deep breath, then *exhale*.]
ex·hale • ***verb*** **exhaled, exhaling**

exhaust (eg zôst′ *or* eg zäst′) ***verb*** **1** to make very tired; tire out; weaken [That long walk *exhausted* them.] **2** to use up completely [The bikers nearly *exhausted* their supply of drinking water.]
noun **1** the used steam or gas that is released from a running engine. The fumes from a car's engine are a kind of exhaust. **2** a pipe through which such steam or gas is forced out.
ex·haust • ***verb*** **exhausted, exhausting** • ***noun,*** *plural* **exhausts**

exhaustion (eg zôs′chən *or* eg zäs′chən) ***noun*** **1** the act of exhausting, or using up a

a cat	ō go	ʉ fur	ə = a *in* ago
ā ape	ô law, for	ch chin	e *in* agent
ä cot, car	o͝o look	sh she	i *in* pencil
e ten	o͞o tool	th thin	o *in* atom
ē me	oi oil	*th* then	u *in* circus
i fit	ou out	zh measure	
ī ice	u up	ŋ ring	

supply. **2** extreme or great fatigue [They were in a state of *exhaustion* after the long run.]
ex·haus·tion • ***noun***

exhibit (eg zib′it) ***verb*** **1** to display to the public [A museum *exhibits* its paintings.] —Look for the WORD CHOICES box at the entry **show**. **2** to show or reveal [He *exhibited* great courage.]
noun something exhibited to the public [an art *exhibit*].
ex·hib·it • ***verb*** **exhibited, exhibiting** • ***noun, plural*** **exhibits**

exhibition (ek′si bish′ən) ***noun*** **1** the act of exhibiting or showing [an *exhibition* of bad manners]. **2** a public showing [an *exhibition* of new cars].
ex·hi·bi·tion • ***noun, plural*** **exhibitions**

exhilarate (eg zil′ər āt′) ***verb*** to make feel cheerful and lively [The fresh air *exhilarated* us.]
ex·hil·a·rate • ***verb*** **exhilarated, exhilarating**

exile (eg′zīl *or* eks′īl) ***verb*** to force a person to leave his or her own country and live somewhere else; banish —Look for the WORD CHOICES box at the entry **banish**.
noun **1** the condition of being exiled [He lived in *exile* in France.] **2** a person who is exiled.
ex·ile • ***verb*** **exiled, exiling** • ***noun, plural*** **exiles**

exist (eg zist′) ***verb*** **1** to be; have actual being [The unicorn never really *existed*.] **2** to occur or be found [Tigers do not *exist* in Africa.] **3** to live [Fish cannot *exist* long out of water.]
ex·ist • ***verb*** **existed, existing**

existence (eg zis′təns) ***noun*** **1** the condition of being [There are a few steam locomotives still in *existence*.] **2** the fact of being present; occurrence [He believes in the *existence* of other life forms in the universe.] **3** life or way of life [The pioneers led a difficult *existence*.]
ex·ist·ence • ***noun, plural for sense 3 only*** **existences**

exit (eg′zit *or* eks′it) ***noun*** **1** a place for going out; door or passage out [The *exits* are marked with red signs.] **2** the act of going out; departure [We made a quick *exit*.]
verb to go out; leave.
ex·it • ***noun, plural*** **exits** • ***verb*** **exited, exiting**

exotic (eg zät′ik) ***adjective*** strange, different, or foreign [These *exotic* plants come from Hawaii.]
ex·ot·ic • ***adjective***

expand (ek spand′) ***verb*** to make or grow bigger or wider [A deep breath *expands* one's chest.]
ex·pand • ***verb*** **expanded, expanding**

WORD CHOICES

Synonyms of expand

The words **expand, inflate,** and **swell** share the meaning "to make or become larger or wider."

Breathe deeply to *expand* your chest.

They used helium to *inflate* the balloon.

Her sprained ankle *swelled* up.

expanse (ek spans′) ***noun*** a large, open area [a great *expanse* of the ocean].
ex·panse • ***noun, plural*** **expanses**

expansion (ek span′shən) ***noun*** **1** the act of expanding or the fact of being expanded [the *expansion* of the town into a large city]. **2** the amount or part that is expanded [Plans for the school include a six-room *expansion*.]
ex·pan·sion • ***noun, plural*** **expansions**

expect (ek spekt′) ***verb*** **1** to think that something will happen or come; look forward to [I *expect* to hear from Jane soon.] **2** to look for as proper or due [He *expected* a reward for finding her watch.] **3** [*an informal use*] to guess or suppose [I *expect* you'll be wanting dinner.]
ex·pect • ***verb*** **expected, expecting**

expectation (ek′spek tā′shən) ***noun*** **1** the act of expecting, or looking forward to something [She sat on the edge of her seat in *expectation* of a crash.] **2** also **expectations** a reason for looking forward to something good [She has *expectations* of being promoted.]
ex·pec·ta·tion • ***noun, plural*** **expectations**

expedition (eks pə dish′ən) ***noun*** **1** a long journey or voyage by a group of people to explore a region or for some other purpose [The Navy sent a party of men on an *expedition* to Antarctica.] **2** the people, ships, or equipment making such a journey [The *expedition* had to wait for spring to land on Antarctica.]
ex·pe·di·tion • ***noun, plural*** **expeditions**

expel (ek spel′) ***verb*** **1** to drive out or force out [He coughed hard, and *expelled* the piece of food from his windpipe.] —Look for the WORD CHOICES box at the entry **eject**. **2** to send away; dismiss [The principal *expelled* the boys from school.]

E

ex·pel • *verb* **expelled, expelling**

expenditure (ek spen′di chər) *noun* **1** the act of spending [The new school gym will require the *expenditure* of a great deal of money.] **2** the amount used up or spent [an *expenditure* of $250 on new furniture].
ex·pend·i·ture • *noun, plural* **expenditures**

expense (ek spens′) *noun* **1** money spent for something; cost [We can't afford the *expense* of a trip to Europe.] **2** something that causes spending [Owning a car is a great *expense*.]
ex·pense • *noun, plural* **expenses**

expensive (ek spen′siv) *adjective* having a high price; costing much [an *expensive* car] —Look for the WORD CHOICES box at the entry **costly**.
ex·pen·sive • *adjective*

experience (ek spir′ē əns) *noun* **1** something that a person has done or lived through [The trip was an *experience* that I will never forget.] **2** skill or knowledge that a person acquires by training, practice, or work [We need a lawyer with much *experience*.]
verb to have the experience of; live through [The pioneers *experienced* many hardships.]
ex·pe·ri·ence • *noun, plural* **experiences** • *verb* **experienced, experiencing**

experiment (ek sper′i mənt) *noun* a test or tests that are used to find out or prove something or to see whether a theory is correct.
verb to make experiments [The doctors *experimented* with a new medication.]
ex·per·i·ment • *noun, plural* **experiments** • *verb* **experimented, experimenting**

experimental (ek sper′i ment′l) *adjective* **1** based on or having to do with experiments [an *experimental* science]. **2** being an experiment; trial [a project still in the *experimental* stage].
ex·per·i·men·tal • *adjective*

expert (eks′pərt) *adjective* **1** having much special knowledge and experience; very skillful [an *expert* golfer]. **2** of or from an expert [*expert* advice].
noun a person who has great knowledge or skill in a special area; authority [Her father is an *expert* in American colonial art.]
ex·pert • *adjective* • *noun, plural* **experts**

expiration (ek spər ā′shən) *noun* the act or fact of coming to an end [the *expiration* of a lease].
ex·pi·ra·tion • *noun, plural* **expirations**

expire (ek spīr′) *verb* **1** to come to an end; stop [The magazine subscription *expires* next month.] **2** to die. **3** to breathe out; exhale.
ex·pire • *verb* **expired, expiring**

explain (ek splān′) *verb* **1** to make clear or plain; give details of [He *explained* how the engine works.] **2** to show the meaning of [The teacher *explained* the story to the class.] **3** to give reasons for [*Explain* your absence.]
ex·plain • *verb* **explained, explaining**

explanation (eks′plə nā′shən) *noun* **1** the act or process of explaining [He gave a lengthy *explanation* of his new plan to improve the team.] **2** something that explains; reason [This long nail is the *explanation* for the flat tire.]
ex·pla·na·tion • *noun, plural* **explanations**

explicit (eks plis′it) *adjective* clearly stated so that there can be no doubt as to the meaning; definite [The doctors gave her *explicit* orders to stay in bed and rest.]
ex·plic·it • *adjective*

explode (ek splōd′) *verb* **1** to blow up or burst with a loud noise and force [The firecracker *exploded*.] **2** to burst forth in a noisy or sudden way [The audience *exploded* with laughter.]
ex·plode • *verb* **exploded, exploding**

WORD HISTORY

explode

This word first meant "to chase an unpopular actor off the stage by clapping and hooting." Later **explode** came to mean "to make any loud noise," including the noise that a bomb makes when it goes off.

exploit (eks′ploit *for n.;* eks ploit′ *for v.*) *noun* a daring act or bold deed [the *exploits* of Robin Hood].
verb **1** to use to the greatest advantage [They founded a company to *exploit* the water power of the river.] **2** to take unfair advantage of; use in a selfish way [They *exploited* children by making them work in the factories.]

a cat	ō go	ʉ fur	ə = a *in* ago
ā ape	ô law, for	ch chin	e *in* agent
ä cot, car	oo look	sh she	i *in* pencil
e ten	o͞o tool	th thin	o *in* atom
ē me	oi oil	*th* then	u *in* circus
i fit	ou out	zh measure	
ī ice	u up	ŋ ring	

ex·ploit • *noun, plural* **exploits** • *verb* **exploited, exploiting**

exploration (eks plər ā′shən) *noun* the act of exploring [the *exploration* of the sea].
ex·plo·ra·tion • *noun, plural* **explorations**

explore (ek splôr′) *verb* **1** to travel in a region that is unknown or not well known, in order to find out more about it [The hunters *explored* the wild jungle.] **2** to look into or examine carefully [The scientists *explored* new methods of growing wheat.]
ex·plore • *verb* **explored, exploring**

explorer (ek splôr′ər) *noun* a person who explores an unknown or little-known region.
ex·plor·er • *noun, plural* **explorers**

explosion (ek splō′zhən) *noun* **1** the act of exploding, or blowing up with a loud noise [the *explosion* of a bomb]. **2** a sudden or noisy outburst [an *explosion* of laughter].
ex·plo·sion • *noun, plural* **explosions**

explosive (ek splō′siv) *adjective* capable of exploding or causing an explosion [*explosive* gases].
noun a substance that can explode.
ex·plo·sive • *adjective* • *noun, plural* **explosives**

export (eks pôrt′ *for v.;* eks′pôrt *for n.*) *verb* to send goods from one country for sale in another [Japan *exports* many cars.]
noun **1** the act of exporting [Brazil raises coffee for *export*.] **2** something exported [Oil is the country's chief *export*.]
ex·port • *verb* **exported, exporting** • *noun, plural* **exports**

expose (eks pōz′) *verb* **1** to be or leave without cover or protection [People on a golf course during a thunderstorm are *exposed* to lightning.] **2** to bring under an influence; cause to know about [She was *exposed* to classical music at an early age.] **3** to make known; reveal [The police *exposed* a plot to rob a bank.] **4** to let light fall on the film or plate in a camera, and in this way cause a picture to be recorded.
ex·pose • *verb* **exposed, exposing**

exposure (eks pō′zhər) *noun* **1** the act of exposing [the *exposure* of the gangsters' plot]. **2** the fact of being exposed [His face was tanned by *exposure* to the sun.] **3** the position of a room or a building, in relation to how it is exposed to sun and wind [Our kitchen has a pleasant southern *exposure*.] **4** the act of exposing a photographic film to light or the length of time that the film is exposed to light.
ex·po·sure • *noun, plural* **exposures**

express (eks pres′) *verb* **1** to put into words; state [It is hard to *express* my feelings.] **2** to give or be a sign of; show [Her smile *expressed* her happiness at the news.]
adjective **1** clearly said or meant; definite [I came for the *express* purpose of seeing you.] **2** making the fastest trip; not making many stops [an *express* train or bus]. **3** for fast driving [an *express* highway].
noun **1** a train, bus, or elevator that makes the fastest trip, not making many stops. **2** a way of sending goods, packages, or mail that is faster than the ordinary ways.
ex·press • *verb* **expressed, expressing** • *adjective* • *noun, plural* **expresses**

expression (eks presh′ən) *noun* **1** the act of expressing or putting into words [This note is an *expression* of my gratitude.] **2** the act of showing how one feels or what one means [Laughter is an *expression* of joy.] **3** a look that shows how one feels or what one means [a sad *expression* on her face]. **4** a common word, phrase, or saying ["You bet" is an everyday *expression* meaning "certainly."]
ex·pres·sion • *noun, plural* **expressions**

expressway

expressway (eks pres′wā) *noun* a wide highway that is built for fast traffic.
ex·press·way • *noun, plural* **expressways**

exquisite (eks′kwi zit *or* eks′kwiz′it) *adjective* **1** very beautiful [an *exquisite* sunset]. **2** of the best quality; excellent [She gave an *exquisite* performance in the play.]
ex·qui·site • *adjective*

extend (ek stend′) *verb* **1** to make longer; stretch out [Careful cleaning *extends* the life of a rug.] **2** to lie or stretch [The fence *extends* along the meadow.] **3** to offer or give [May I *extend* congratulations to the winner?]
ex·tend • *verb* **extended, extending**

E

WORD CHOICES

Synonyms of **extend**

The words **extend, lengthen,** and **prolong** share the meaning "to make longer".

The city plans to *extend* the road.

A tailor can *lengthen* the pants.

They *prolonged* their visit.

extension (ek sten′shən) ***noun*** **1** the act of extending or the condition of being extended [the *extension* of a deadline for another week]. **2** something that extends, or makes larger; addition [We are building an *extension* to the library.] **3** an extra telephone on the same line as the main telephone.
ex·ten·sion • ***noun,*** *plural* **extensions**

extensive (ek sten′siv) ***adjective*** large, great, or widespread [the *extensive* jungles and deserts of Africa].
ex·ten·sive • ***adjective***

extent (ek stent′) ***noun*** **1** the amount or length to which something extends [the full *extent* of the park]. **2** the scope or range of something [The *extent* of our knowledge has increased over the centuries.]
ex·tent • ***noun***

exterior (ek stir′ē ər) ***adjective*** of or on the outside; outer [the *exterior* walls of a building].
noun the outside or outer part [The *exterior* of the house was painted white.]
ex·te·ri·or • ***adjective*** • ***noun,*** *plural* **exteriors**

exterminate (ek stur′mi nāt′) ***verb*** to kill or destroy completely; wipe out [They hired a company to *exterminate* the rats.]
ex·ter·mi·nate • ***verb*** **exterminated, exterminating**

external (eks tur′nəl) ***adjective*** **1** on the outside; outer [Red spots are an *external* sign of an allergy.] **2** on the outside of the body [This medicine is for *external* use only.]
ex·ter·nal • ***adjective***

extinct (ek stiŋkt′) ***adjective*** **1** no longer living; having died out [Dinosaurs are *extinct*.] **2** no longer burning or active [an *extinct* volcano].
ex·tinct • ***adjective***

extinction (ek stiŋk′shən) ***noun*** **1** the fact of becoming extinct, or dying out [The California condor faces *extinction*.] **2** the act of putting an end to or wiping out [working for the cure and eventual *extinction* of diseases]. **3** the act of extinguishing, or putting out [the *extinction* of a fire].
ex·tinc·tion • ***noun,*** *plural for sense 3 only* **extinctions**

extinguish (ek stiŋ′gwish) ***verb*** **1** to put out; quench [The campers *extinguished* their fire.] **2** to destroy [The loss of the game on Sunday *extinguished* all hope of a championship.]
ex·tin·guish • ***verb*** **extinguished, extinguishing**

extinguisher (ek stiŋ′ gwish ər) ***noun*** a device that is used to put out a fire by spraying a liquid or gas on it.
ex·tin·guish·er • ***noun,*** *plural* **extinguishers**

extra (eks′trə) ***adjective*** more than is usual, expected, or necessary [Remember to carry *extra* water.]
noun **1** something added to what is usual, expected, or necessary [a new car with all the *extras*]. **2** a special edition of a newspaper to tell an important news story. Such editions are now seldom published.
adverb more than it usually is; especially [We saw an *extra* long movie on television.]
ex·tra • ***adjective*** • ***noun,*** *plural* **extras** • ***adverb***

extract (eks trakt′ *for v.;* eks′trakt *for n.*) ***verb*** to pull out by using great effort [The dentist *extracted* three of my teeth.]
noun a strong substance that has been extracted from something, for use as a flavoring or food [We flavor cookies with vanilla *extract*.]
ex·tract • ***verb*** **extracted, extracting** • ***noun,*** *plural* **extracts**

extraordinary (ek strôr′di ner′e) ***adjective*** far from the ordinary; remarkable or unusual [The pianist played with *extraordinary* skill.]
ex·traor·di·nar·y • ***adjective***

extraterrestrial (eks′trə tər es′trē əl) ***adjective*** happening, existing, or coming from a place beyond the earth [an *extraterrestrial* being].

a	cat	ō	go	u̶	fur	ə =	a *in* ago
ā	ape	ô	law, for	ch	chin		e *in* agent
ä	cot, car	oo	look	sh	she		i *in* pencil
e	ten	o͞o	tool	th	thin		o *in* atom
ē	me	oi	oil	*th*	then		u *in* circus
i	fit	ou	out	zh	measure		
ī	ice	u	up	ŋ	ring		

noun a being from a place away from the earth.
ex·tra·ter·res·tri·al • *adjective* • *noun, plural* **extraterrestrials**

extravagant (ek strav′ə gənt) *adjective* going beyond what is proper [*extravagant* praise].
ex·trav·a·gant • *adjective*

extreme (ek strēm′) *adjective* **1** to the greatest degree; very great [He was in *extreme* pain after the accident.] **2** farthest away [the *extreme* end of the room]. **3** far from what is usual [*extreme* political views].
noun either one of two things that are as far apart or as different as they can be [He went through the *extremes* of laughter and tears.]
ex·treme • *adjective* • *noun, plural* **extremes**

extremely (ek strēm′lē) *adverb* very [I was *extremely* worried when they were late.]
ex·treme·ly • *adverb*

extremity (ek strem′i tē) *noun* the farthest point or part; an end [We walked to the eastern *extremity* of the island.]
ex·trem·i·ty • *noun, plural* **extremities**

eye (ī) *noun* **1** the part of the body that a human being or an animal uses to see. **2** the iris of the eye [brown *eyes*]. **3** the ability to judge by looking [She has a good *eye* for distances.] **4** *often* **eyes** judgment; opinion [In his mother's *eyes*, Bill is perfect.] **5** something, such as the bud on a potato or the hole in a needle, that seems like an eye in some way. **6** a loop of metal or thread [a hook and *eye*].
verb to look at; observe [We *eyed* the stranger with suspicion.]
—have an eye for to be able to notice and appreciate [She *has an eye for* modern art.] **—keep an eye on** to take care of; watch with care. **—see eye to eye** to agree completely [We don't *see eye to eye* on this.]
eye • *noun, plural* **eyes** • *verb* **eyed, eyeing** or **eying**

● The words **eye, aye,** and **I** sound alike.
The pencil poked him in the *eye*.
Only three members voted *aye*.
She and *I* walked to the theater.

eyeball (ī′bôl) *noun* the ball-shaped part of the eye inside the socket and eyelids.
eye·ball • *noun, plural* **eyeballs**

eyebrow (ī′brou) *noun* **1** the curved, bony part of the face above each eye. **2** the hair growing on this part of the face.
eye·brow • *noun, plural* **eyebrows**

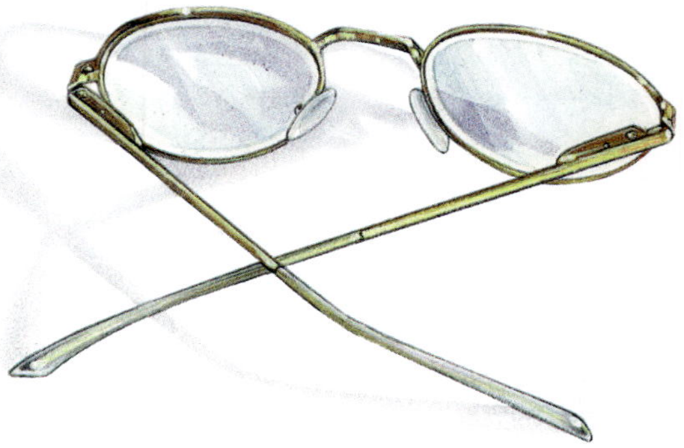
eyeglasses

eyeglasses (ī′glas əz) *plural noun* a pair of lenses for helping a person see better. They are fitted into a plastic or metal frame.
eye·glass·es • *plural noun*

eyelash (ī′lash) *noun* any one of the hairs that grow along the edge of the eyelid.
eye·lash • *noun, plural* **eyelashes**

eyelet (ī′lət) *noun* **1** a small hole for a cord, lace, or hook to go through. **2** a metal ring that is placed in this kind of hole to make it stronger.
eye·let • *noun, plural* **eyelets**
● The words **eyelet** and **islet** sound alike.
Each *eyelet* in the boot was sewn.
We rowed to the tiny *islet* in the bay.

eyelid (ī′lid) *noun* either one of the two folds of skin that cover and uncover the eyeball.
eye·lid • *noun, plural* **eyelids**

eyesight (ī′sīt) *noun* the ability to see; sight or vision [I have very keen *eyesight*.]
eye·sight • *noun*

eyesore (ī′sôr) *noun* a thing that is unpleasant to look at [A lawn full of weeds is an *eyesore*.]
eye·sore • *noun, plural* **eyesores**

eyetooth (ī′to͞oth) *noun* either one of the two canine teeth in the upper jaw.
eye·tooth • *noun, plural* **eyeteeth**

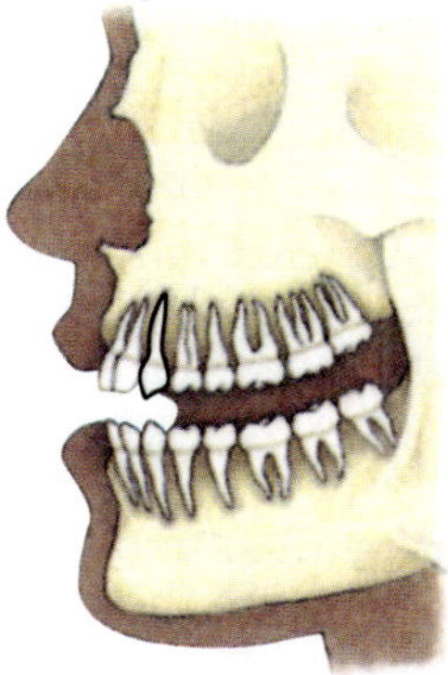
eyetooth

eyewitness (ī′wit′nəs) *noun* a person who saw something happen, and did not just hear about it from someone else.
eye·wit·ness • *noun, plural* **eyewitnesses**

F f

Ff Ff *Ff* **Ff**

F, the sixth letter of the alphabet, has only one sound, which is heard at the beginning of the words **fox** *and* **frog**.

f or **F** (ef) ***noun*** the sixth letter of the English alphabet.
f or **F** • ***noun,*** *plural* **f's** or **F's**

F (ef) ***noun*** **1** in some schools, the lowest grade, meaning "failing." **2** in music, the fourth tone in the scale of C major.
F • ***noun,*** *plural* **F's**

F or **F.** *abbreviation for* Fahrenheit [Water freezes into ice at 32°*F*.]

fa (fä) ***noun*** the fourth note of a musical scale.

fable (fā′bəl) ***noun*** a very short story that teaches a lesson. It is usually about animals that talk.
fa·ble • ***noun,*** *plural* **fables**

fabric (fab′rik) ***noun*** a material that is made from fibers or threads by weaving, knitting, or some other similar method.
fab·ric • ***noun,*** *plural* **fabrics**

fabulous (fab′yo͞o ləs) ***adjective*** **1** hard to believe; amazing or very unusual [They spent a *fabulous* amount of money.] **2** [*an informal use*] very good; wonderful [a *fabulous* vacation].
fab·u·lous • ***adjective***

face (fās) ***noun*** **1** the front part of the head, including the eyes, nose, and mouth. **2** a look that shows meaning or feeling [a sad *face*]. **3** the main side of something [the clock's *face*]. ***verb*** **1** to turn toward or have the face turned toward [Our house *faces* a park.] **2** to meet with courage [Firefighters often *face* danger.]
face • ***noun,*** *plural* **faces** • ***verb*** **faced, facing**

facility (fə sil′i tē) ***noun*** **1** ease or skill [She reads French with great *facility*.] **2** *usually* **facilities** a thing that helps a person do something [an apartment with no laundry *facilities*].
fa·cil·i·ty • ***noun,*** *plural* **facilities**

fact (fakt) ***noun*** **1** something that has actually happened or that is really true [I can't deny the *fact* that I was late.] **2** something that is said to have happened or is supposed to be true [Check to see if your *facts* are correct.]
fact • ***noun,*** *plural* **facts**

factor (fak′tər) ***noun*** **1** any one of the causes or events that bring about a result [The warm weather was a *factor* in my decision to move south.] **2** any one of the numbers or symbols that are multiplied together to form a product [2, 5, and 10 are *factors* of 100.]
fac·tor • ***noun,*** *plural* **factors**

factory (fak′tər ē) ***noun*** a building or group of buildings where products are made, especially by machinery.
fac·to·ry • ***noun,*** *plural* **factories**

factual (fak′cho͞o əl) ***adjective*** based on or containing facts; real or true [a *factual* report].
fac·tu·al • ***adjective***

faculty (fak′əl tē) ***noun*** **1** a natural power of

a	cat	ō	go	ʉ	fur	ə =	a *in* ago
ā	ape	ô	law, for	ch	chin		e *in* agent
ä	cot, car	o͝o	look	sh	she		i *in* pencil
e	ten	o͞o	tool	th	thin		o *in* atom
ē	me	oi	oil	*th*	then		u *in* circus
i	fit	ou	out	zh	measure		
ī	ice	u	up	ŋ	ring		

the body or mind [the *faculty* of speech]. **2** a special skill; knack [the *faculty* of remembering names]. **3** all of the teachers of a school or college or of one of its departments [the biology *faculty*].
fac·ul·ty • *noun, plural* **faculties**

fad (fad) *noun* a custom or style that many people become interested in for a short time.
fad • *noun, plural* **fads**

fade (fād) *verb* **1** to make or become less bright [The painting *faded* with age.] **2** to become less fresh or strong; wither [The roses *faded* and their petals fell.] **3** to disappear slowly; die out [The music *faded* away.] —Look for the WORD CHOICES box at the entry **vanish**.
fade • *verb* **faded, fading**

WORD HISTORY

fade

The word **fade** came into English at least 600 years ago from a French word that means "pale." When things **fade** in color, they become pale or less bright.

Fahrenheit (fer′ən hīt) *adjective* having to do with a thermometer that measures the freezing point of water as 32 degrees above zero and the boiling point of water as 212 degrees above zero.
Fahr·en·heit • *adjective*

fail (fāl) *verb* **1** to not do what one tried to do; not succeed [She *failed* as a singer.] **2** to not do what one should have done; to neglect [He *failed* to keep his promise.] **3** to give or get a grade that shows one has not passed a test or a school course [Ms. Martin *failed* me on the math exam. I *failed* math that year.] **4** to not be present when needed [Our courage *failed* us when we saw the shark.] **5** to lose strength; weaken [His health was *failing*.] **6** to stop working [The brakes *failed*.] **7** to become bankrupt [Many banks *failed* in 1933.]
fail • *verb* **failed, failing**

failure (fāl′yər) *noun* **1** the act of failing, or not succeeding [the *failure* of the plan]. **2** the fact of becoming weak [the *failure* of eyesight in old age]. **3** the fact of not doing [His *failure* to answer my letter worried me.] **4** a person or thing that fails [The play I wrote was a *failure*.]
fail·ure • *noun, plural* **failures**

faint (fānt) *adjective* **1** weak; not strong or clear [a *faint* whisper; a *faint* odor]. **2** weak and dizzy, as if about to become unconscious.
noun a condition in which a person becomes unconscious.
verb to fall into a faint.
faint • *adjective* **fainter, faintest** • *noun, plural* **faints** • *verb* **fainted, fainting**

fair[1] (fer) *adjective* **1** beautiful [the *fair* young maiden]. **2** light in color; blond [*fair* hair; *fair* skin]. **3** clear and sunny [*fair* weather]. **4** just and honest; according to what is right [a *fair* price; *fair* play] —Look for the WORD CHOICES box at the entry **just**. **5** neither very bad nor very good; average [only a *fair* chance of winning].
adverb in a fair manner [Play *fair*.]
fair • *adjective* & • *adverb* **fairer, fairest**
• The words **fair** and **fare** sound alike.
It's not *fair* to punish only one of us.
Our rabbit won a prize at the *fair*.
The bus *fare* is one dollar.

fair[2] (fer) *noun* **1** an event that is held from time to time, where people buy and sell things and display their crops and animals. There may also be entertainment and games at a fair [a county *fair*]. **2** any large display of products [a book *fair*]. **3** an event where there is entertainment and things are sold to raise money for a charity [a church *fair*].
fair • *noun, plural* **fairs**
• The words **fair** and **fare** sound alike.

fairly (fer′lē) *adverb* **1** in a just and honest way. **2** to a fair degree; neither too much nor too little [It is *fairly* certain that we will go.]
fair·ly • *adverb*

fairy (fer′ē) *noun* a tiny, graceful being in folk tales and legends. Fairies were believed to look like little people and to have magic powers.
fair·y • *noun, plural* **fairies**

fairy tale *noun* a story about fairies, giants, or other imaginary creatures.
fairy tale • *noun, plural* **fairy tales**

faith (fāth) *noun* **1** belief or trust that does not question or ask for proof [They have *faith* in their doctor.] —Look for the WORD CHOICES box at the entry **belief**. **2** belief in God and religion. **3** a particular religion [the Jewish *faith*]. **4** the condition of being loyal [The knights pledged their *faith* to the king.]
faith • *noun, plural* **faiths**

faithful (fāth′fəl) *adjective* continuing to believe in, stay with, or care for someone or

F

something; loyal [She is a *faithful* friend to all of us.]
faith·ful • ***adjective***

WORD CHOICES

Synonyms of **faithful**

The words **faithful**, **loyal**, and **steadfast** share the meaning "staying true to a person, group, or ideal."

a *faithful* friend

a *loyal* follower

a *steadfast* defender of freedom

faithfulness (fāth′fəl nəs) ***noun*** the quality or state of being faithful —Look for the WORD CHOICES box at the entry **allegiance**.
faith·ful·ness • ***noun***

fake (fāk) ***verb*** to make something seem real in order to fool or deceive [I *faked* an illness.]
noun a person or thing that is not really what he, she, or it is supposed to be.
adjective not real or true; false [*fake* tears] —Look for the WORD CHOICES box at the entry **false**.
fake • ***verb*** **faked, faking** • ***noun,*** *plural* **fakes** • ***adjective***

falcon (fal′kən *or* fôl′kən) ***noun*** a hawk with long, pointed wings and a short, curved beak. People sometimes use falcons to hunt.
fal·con • ***noun,*** *plural* **falcons**

falcon

fall (fôl) ***verb*** **1** to drop to a lower place; come down [Rain is *falling*.] **2** to come down suddenly from an upright position; to tumble or collapse [The runner stumbled and *fell*.] **3** to be killed in battle [Thousands *fell* on the first day of the war.] **4** to hang down [Her hair *fell* to her shoulders.] **5** to become lower, less, or weaker [Prices are *falling*.] **6** to lose power [The government *fell*.] **7** to be conquered [The city *fell* to the enemy.] **8** to become; to pass into a certain condition [I *fell* asleep. He *fell* into a rage.] **9** to happen; take place [The holiday *falls* on a Friday.]
noun **1** the act of dropping or coming down [I took a *fall* on the ice.] **2** *usually* **falls** a waterfall. **3** something that has fallen [a heavy *fall* of snow]. **4** the amount that has fallen [a six-inch *fall* of snow]. **5** the distance that something falls [a *fall* of 50 feet]. **6** the time of year when leaves fall from the trees, between summer and winter; autumn. **7** a sudden loss of power [the *fall* of the government]. **8** a decrease; the fact of becoming less [a *fall* in the temperature].
—fall back on to turn to for help when others fail. **—fall behind** **1** to drop back [I *fell behind* in the race.] **2** to not pay in time [I *fell behind* in my rent payments.] **—fall for** [*an informal use*] **1** to fall in love with [They *fell for* each other.] **2** to be fooled by [I sure *fell for* that trick!] **—fall off** to become smaller, less, or worse [Car sales have *fallen off*.]
fall • ***verb*** **fell, fallen, falling** • ***noun,*** *plural* **falls**

fallen (fôl′ən) ***verb*** *past participle of* **fall**.
fall·en • ***verb***

fallout (fôl′out) ***noun*** the tiny radioactive particles that fall to the earth after a nuclear explosion.
fall·out • ***noun***

fallow (fal′ō) ***adjective*** plowed but not planted during the growing season [Farmers let land lie *fallow* to make the soil richer.]
fal·low • ***adjective***

false (fôls) ***adjective*** **1** not true; wrong [a *false* idea]. **2** not honest; lying [*false* advertising]. **3** not real or genuine [*false* teeth].
false • ***adjective*** **falser, falsest**

WORD CHOICES

Synonyms of **false**

The words **false**, **counterfeit**, and **fake** share the meaning "not real or genuine."

false teeth

counterfeit money

fake pearls

a cat	ō go	ʉ fur	ə = a *in* ago
ā ape	ô law, for	ch chin	e *in* agent
ä cot, car	oo look	sh she	i *in* pencil
e ten	ōō tool	th thin	o *in* atom
ē me	oi oil	*th* then	u *in* circus
i fit	ou out	zh measure	
ī ice	u up	ŋ ring	

falsehood (fôls′hood) ***noun*** a lie.
false·hood • ***noun,*** *plural* **falsehoods**

falter (fôl′tər) ***verb*** **1** to move in a shaky or unsteady way [The car *faltered* and then stopped.] **2** to speak in a broken or stumbling way [She *faltered* as she talked about the accident.] **3** to act in an unsure way; hesitate [I *faltered* when the dog growled.]
fal·ter • ***verb*** **faltered, faltering**

fame (fām) ***noun*** the condition of being well-known or talked about a great deal.

famed (fāmd) ***adjective*** well-known; famous.

familiar (fə mil′yər) ***adjective*** **1** knowing about; acquainted with [Are you *familiar* with this book?] **2** well-known; common [Car accidents are a *familiar* sight here.] —Look for the WORD CHOICES box at the entry **common**.
fa·mil·iar • ***adjective***

familiarity (fə mil′ē er′i tē) ***noun*** the fact of having knowledge of or experience with something [the hunter's long *familiarity* with guns].
fa·mil·i·ar·i·ty • ***noun,*** *plural* **familiarities**

family (fam′ə lē) ***noun*** **1** a group that is made up of one or two parents and all their children. **2** the children only [The widow raised a large *family* all by herself.] **3** a group of people who are related by marriage or through an ancestor that they share; relatives. **4** a large group of related plants or animals [The robin is a member of the thrush *family*.] **5** a group of related things [a *family* of languages].
fam·i·ly • ***noun,*** *plural* **families**

famine (fam′in) ***noun*** a great lack of food that causes people to starve throughout a wide area.
fam·ine • ***noun,*** *plural* **famines**

famous (fā′məs) ***adjective*** talked about or known by a great many people [a *famous* politician].
fa·mous • ***adjective***

fan
Left: Paper fan Above: Ceiling fan Right: Portable fan

fan[1] (fan) ***noun*** a thing that is used to stir up the air to make it cool or fresh. Simple fans are waved with the hand and some can be folded together when they are not being used. Electric fans have blades that are turned by a motor.
verb **1** to stir or move with a fan or in a similar way [We *fanned* the air to cool ourselves.] **2** to blow air toward, in a way similar to using a fan [She *fanned* herself with the book.]
fan • ***noun,*** *plural* **fans** • ***verb*** **fanned, fanning**

fan[2] (fan) ***noun*** a person who is very interested in some sport, or who very much admires some famous performer [a baseball *fan*].
fan • ***noun,*** *plural* **fans**

WORD HISTORY

fan

The word **fan** is a shortened form of the word *fanatic*. The **fans** of a famous baseball player or rock star sometimes seem to act like fanatics when they see the person they admire so much.

fanatic (fə nat′ik) ***noun*** a person who takes an interest in something to a point that is not reasonable or sensible [a sports *fanatic*].
fa·nat·ic • ***noun,*** *plural* **fanatics**

fanciful (fan′si fəl) ***adjective*** **1** having or showing a quick and playful imagination [*fanciful* costumes for Halloween]. **2** not real; imaginary [the *fanciful* idea that horseshoes bring luck].
fan·ci·ful • ***adjective***

fancy (fan′sē) ***adjective*** **1** having much decoration; not plain [a *fancy* blouse]. **2** of higher quality than usual; special [a *fancy* grade of jam].
noun a feeling of liking [The cat took a *fancy* to me right away.]
verb to have a liking for [He *fancies* Swiss chocolate.]
fan·cy • ***adjective*** **fancier, fanciest** • ***noun,*** *plural* **fancies** • ***verb*** **fancied, fancying, fancies**

fang (faŋ) ***noun*** **1** any one of the long, pointed teeth that meat-eating animals use to seize and

fang

tear the animals that they catch. **2** either one of the long, hollow teeth that certain snakes use to shoot poison into their victims.
fang • *noun, plural* **fangs**

fantastic (fan tas′tik) *adjective* **1** very strange; not seeming real; weird [*fantastic* Halloween costumes]. **2** seeming to be beyond belief [We saw *fantastic* trips to the moon on TV.]
fan·tas·tic • *adjective*

fantasy (fant′ə sē) *noun* something created by the mind, such as a story or idea, that is full of imagination but does not seem very real.
fan·ta·sy • *noun, plural* **fantasies**

far (fär) *adjective* **1** not near or close; distant in place or time [a *far* land; the *far* past]. **2** more distant [Go to the *far* side of the room.]
adverb **1** to or from a great distance [She has traveled *far*.] **2** to a certain distance or degree [How *far* have you read in this book?] **3** a great deal; very much [She is a *far* better player than I am.]
—by far very much [He is *by far* the best speller.] **—so far** up to this place, time, or degree.
far • *adjective* & • *adverb* **farther, farthest**

faraway (fär′ə wā) *adjective* **1** distant; far [a *faraway* place]. **2** seeming to be distant or away [He had a *faraway* look on his face.]
far·a·way • *adjective*

fare (fer) *verb* to get along; do or be [We *fared* well on our trip.]
noun money that is paid for a ride on a vehicle such as a bus or plane [How much is the *fare* on the subway?]
fare • *verb* **fared, faring** • *noun, plural* **fares**

● The words **fare** and **fair** sound alike.
The bus *fare* is one dollar.
It's not *fair* to punish only one of us.
Our hen won a prize at the *fair*.

Far East the countries of eastern Asia, including China, Japan, and Korea.

farewell (fer wel′) *interjection* goodbye.
noun good wishes that a person says when leaving [We said our *farewells* as the train left.]
fare·well • *interjection* • *noun, plural* **farewells**

far-fetched (fär′fecht′) *adjective* not based on plain, clear thinking [a *far-fetched* explanation].

farm (färm) *noun* **1** a piece of land, with the house and other buildings on it, that is used for raising crops or animals. **2** a place where certain kinds of things are raised [a catfish *farm*].
verb to use land to raise crops or animals [He *farms* ten acres of land.]
farm • *noun, plural* **farms** • *verb* **farmed, farming**

farmer (fär′mər) *noun* a person who owns or works on a farm.
farm·er • *noun, plural* **farmers**

farmhouse (färm′hous) *noun* a house on a farm.
farm·house • *noun, plural* **farmhouses**

farming (färm′iŋ) *noun* the work of running a farm; the process of raising crops and animals.
farm·ing • *noun*

farmyard (färm′yärd) *noun* the yard that is around the buildings of a farm.
farm·yard • *noun, plural* **farmyards**

far-off (fär′ôf′) *adjective* distant; faraway.

farsighted (fär′sīt əd) *adjective* able to see things that are far away more clearly than near things.
far·sight·ed • *adjective*

farther (fär′*th*ər) *adjective comparative of* **far** [My home is *farther* from school than hers is.]
adverb comparative of **far** [Tim swam *farther* than Ralph.]
far·ther • *adjective* • *adverb*

farthest (fär′*th*əst) *adjective superlative of* **far** [Eating was the *farthest* thing from my mind!]
adverb superlative of **far** [Who threw the ball *farthest?*]
far·thest • *adjective* • *adverb*

fascinate (fas′i nāt′) *verb* to hold the attention of by being interesting or delightful [Working on old watches *fascinates* him.]
fas·ci·nate • *verb* **fascinated, fascinating**

fashion (fash′ən) *noun* **1** the popular or up-to-date way of dressing, speaking, or behaving; the style [the *fashion* in jeans this year]. **2** the way that something is done or made [serving tea in the Japanese *fashion*].
verb to make, form, or shape [Bees *fashion*

a	cat	ō	go	ʉ	fur	ə =	a *in* ago
ā	ape	ô	law, for	ch	chin		e *in* agent
ä	cot, car	oo	look	sh	she		i *in* pencil
e	ten	ōō	tool	th	thin		o *in* atom
ē	me	oi	oil	*th*	then		u *in* circus
i	fit	ou	out	zh	measure		
ī	ice	u	up	ŋ	ring		

honeycombs out of wax.]
fash·ion • *noun, plural* **fashions** • *verb* **fashioned, fashioning**

fashionable (fash′ən ə bəl) *adjective* following the newest fashions or styles; in style.
fash·ion·a·ble • *adjective*

fast[1] (fast) *adjective* **1** moving or doing something at high speed; rapid [a *fast* train]. **2** making high speed possible [a *fast* highway]. **3** taking little time [a *fast* lunch]. **4** showing a time that is ahead of the real time [Your watch is *fast*.] **5** close and true; loyal [They are *fast* friends.] **6** not fading [*fast* colors].
adverb **1** at high speed [She was arrested for driving too *fast*.] **2** in a firm way [The boat was stuck *fast* on the sandbar.] **3** in a complete way [The baby is *fast* asleep.]
fast • *adjective* & • *adverb* **faster, fastest**

WORD CHOICES

Synonyms of **fast**

Many words share the meaning "moving or acting at high speed."

brisk	quick	speedy
fleet	rapid	swift

fast[2] (fast) *verb* to go without any food or certain foods, sometimes for religious reasons.
noun a time of going without food in this way.
fast • *verb* **fasted, fasting** • *noun, plural* **fasts**

fasten (fas′ən) *verb* **1** to join or become joined; attach [The collar is *fastened* to the shirt.] —Look for the WORD CHOICES box at the entry **bind**. **2** to make stay closed or in place [*Fasten* the door.]
fas·ten • *verb* **fastened, fastening**

fastener (fas′ən ər) *noun* a device that is used for fastening, or holding, things together [A zipper is a very strong *fastener* for clothing.]
fas·ten·er • *noun, plural* **fasteners**

fast-food (fast′fo͞od′) *adjective* describing a business that sells food that is cooked and served quickly.

fat (fat) *noun* an oily, yellow or white substance that is found in animal bodies and in plant seeds. Some fats are used in cooking and frying.
adjective **1** covered with much fat or flesh; plump or too plump [the baby's *fat* cheeks]. **2** full of fat; oily or greasy [Butter is a *fat* food.]
fat • *noun, plural* **fats** • *adjective* **fatter, fattest**

fatal (fāt′l) *adjective* **1** causing death [a *fatal* disease]. **2** causing ruin or disaster [The storm dealt a *fatal* blow to their hopes.]
fa·tal • *adjective*

fatality (fə tal′i tē) *noun* a death that is caused by an accident, war, or some other disaster.
fa·tal·i·ty • *noun, plural* **fatalities**

fate (fāt) *noun* **1** a power that is supposed to settle, ahead of time, the way things will happen [She believed that *fate* had chosen her to be a famous actress.] **2** the things that happen in a way that might seem to be controlled by this power [Was it his *fate* to be President?]
fate • *noun, plural* **fates**

fateful (fāt′fəl) *adjective* having very important results [a *fateful* decision].
fate·ful • *adjective*

father (fä′*th*ər) *noun* **1** a man as he is related to his child or children; a male parent. **2 Father** God. **3** a person who is or was important at the beginning of something; founder [George Washington is called the *father* of his country.] **4** *often* **Father** a priest.
fa·ther • *noun, plural* **fathers**

father-in-law (fä′*th*ər in lô′ *or* fä′*th*ər in lä′) *noun* the father of a person's wife or husband.
fa·ther-in-law • *noun, plural* **fathers-in-law**

fatherly (fä′*th*ər lē) *adjective* like or having to do with a father [*fatherly* advice; a *fatherly* hug].
fa·ther·ly • *adjective*

fathom (fa*th*′əm) *noun* a length of six feet. It is used as a measure for the depth of water.
verb to understand [I can't *fathom* the mystery.]
fath·om • *noun, plural* **fathoms** • *verb* **fathomed, fathoming**

fatigue (fə tēg′) *noun* the condition of being tired from hard work or not enough rest.
verb to tire out; make weary.
fa·tigue • *noun* • *verb* **fatigued, fatiguing**

fatten (fat′n) *verb* to make fat [The farmer is *fattening* his cattle for market.]
fat·ten • *verb* **fattened, fattening**

fatty (fat′ē) *adjective* **1** containing or made of

F

fat [*fatty* body tissue]. **2** like fat; oily [There was a *fatty* substance smeared on the fork.]
fat·ty • *adjective* **fattier, fattiest**

faucet (fô′sət *or* fä′sət) *noun* a device with a valve that can be turned on or off to control the flow of a liquid; a tap or spigot.
fau·cet • *noun, plural* **faucets**

fault (fôlt) *noun* **1** a thing that keeps something from being perfect; a defect or flaw [We all have our *faults*.] **2** the blame or responsibility for something [It's my *fault* that we're late.]
fault • *noun, plural* **faults**

faulty (fôlt′ē) *adjective* having one or more faults; imperfect [*Faulty* wiring started the fire.]
fault·y • *adjective* **faultier, faultiest**

faun (fôn *or* fän) *noun* in Roman myths, a being who had the body of a man, and the horns, tail, and hind legs of a goat.
faun • *noun, plural* **fauns**
• The words **faun** and **fawn** sound alike.
The *faun* exists only in myth.
The doe watched her *fawn* as he fed.

fauna (fô′nə *or* fä′nə) *noun* all the animals of a particular place or time [the *fauna* of Alaska].
fau·na • *noun, plural* **faunas**

favor (fā′vər) *noun* **1** a helpful and kind action [I did a *favor* for my grandmother.] **2** the condition of being liked; approval [She tried to win the teacher's *favor*.] **3** a small gift.
verb **1** to like or approve of [We *favor* any plan for better schools.] **2** to prefer or help in an unfair way [The umpire seemed to *favor* the other team.] **3** to use carefully in order to keep from hurting [He *favors* his sore leg.]
—in favor of 1 supporting or approving of [I'm *in favor of* the project.] **2** to the advantage of [ten to five *in favor of* our team].
fa·vor • *noun, plural* **favors** • *verb* **favored, favoring**

favorable (fā′vər ə bəl) *adjective* **1** helpful [*favorable* winds for our boat trip]. **2** approving [a *favorable* opinion]. **3** pleasing [a *favorable* impression on the crowd].
fa·vor·a·ble • *adjective*

favorite (fā′vər it) *adjective* liked best of all; preferred [Spaghetti is my *favorite* food.]
noun **1** the person or thing that is liked best of all. **2** the one thought most likely to win.
fa·vor·ite • *adjective* • *noun, plural* **favorites**

fawn (fôn *or* fän) *noun* a deer less than one year old.
fawn • *noun, plural* **fawns**
• The words **fawn** and **faun** sound alike.
The *fawn* is watched by the other deer.
The *faun* is half man and half goat.

fawn

faze (fāz) [*an informal word*] *verb* to disturb or upset [Nothing *fazes* our teacher.]
faze • *verb* **fazed, fazing**
• The words **faze** and **phase** sound alike.
His best pitch didn't *faze* the batter.
The baby went through a bashful *phase*.

FBI or **F.B.I.** *abbreviation for* **Federal Bureau of Investigation.** The FBI is an agency of the U.S. government. The FBI investigates crimes against U.S. law.

fear (fir) *noun* the emotion felt when danger, pain, or trouble is near; a feeling of being worried or excited or of wanting to run and hide [Jungle animals have a *fear* of lions.]
verb **1** to feel fear of; be afraid of [Even brave people can *fear* real danger.] **2** to be uneasy or anxious [I *fear* that I'll miss the bus.]
fear • *noun, plural* **fears** • *verb* **feared, fearing**

fearful (fir′fəl) *adjective* **1** causing fear; terrifying [We faced a *fearful* danger.] **2** feeling fear; afraid [The child was *fearful* of the dark.]
fear·ful • *adjective*

fearless (fir′ləs) *adjective* having no fear; brave.
fear·less • *adjective*

fearsome (fir′səm) *adjective* frightening.
fear·some • *adjective*

feast (fēst) *noun* **1** a large meal with many courses; banquet. **2** a religious festival.

a	cat	ō	go	ʉ	fur	ə =	a *in* ago
ā	ape	ô	law, for	ch	chin		e *in* agent
ä	cot, car	oo	look	sh	she		i *in* pencil
e	ten	ōō	tool	th	thin		o *in* atom
ē	me	oi	oil	*th*	then		u *in* circus
i	fit	ou	out	zh	measure		
ī	ice	u	up	ŋ	ring		

verb to eat a big or rich meal [We *feasted* on chicken and chocolate cake.]
—feast one's eyes on to look at with pleasure.
feast • *noun, plural* **feasts** • *verb* **feasted, feasting**

feat (fēt) *noun* an action or deed that shows great courage, skill, or strength.
feat • *noun, plural* **feats**
• The words **feat** and **feet** sound alike.
Their canoe trip was a real *feat*.
I have sore *feet* from the hike.

feather (fe*th*′ər) *noun* one of the soft, light parts that grow out of the skin of birds, covering the body and filling out the wings and tail.
feath·er • *noun, plural* **feathers**

feature (fē′chər) *noun* **1** a part of the face. The nose and the eyes are features. **2** a separate or special part or quality [A path for bicycles is a *feature* of the city park.] **3** a full-length movie.
verb to make a feature of [The program *features* a magician.]
fea·ture • *noun, plural* **features**
• *verb* **featured, featuring**

February (feb′ro͞o er′ē *or* feb′yo͞o er′ē) *noun* the second month of the year. February usually has 28 days, but in leap year it has 29 days. Abbreviated **Feb.**
Feb·ru·ar·y • *noun*

fed (fed) *verb past tense and past participle of* **feed**.
—fed up [*an informal use*] disgusted or bored.

federal (fed′ər əl) *adjective* **1** of or describing a union of states having a central government. **2 Federal** of the central government of the U.S. [*Federal* courts].
fed·er·al • *adjective*

federation (fed ər ā′shən) *noun* a union of groups or states under a central power.
fed·er·a·tion • *noun, plural* **federations**

fee (fē) *noun* a payment that is asked or given for services, admission to an event, tuition, or something else.
fee • *noun, plural* **fees**

feeble (fē′bəl) *adjective* not strong; weak [a *feeble* old horse; a *feeble* excuse for being late]
—Look for the WORD CHOICES box at the entry **weak**.
fee·ble • *adjective* **feebler, feeblest**

feed (fēd) *verb* **1** to give food to [Sue *fed* the cat.] **2** to offer as food [Farmers *feed* oats to horses.] **3** to eat [The cattle are *feeding*.]
noun food for animals; fodder.
feed • *verb* **fed, feeding** • *noun, plural* **feeds**

feedback (fēd′bak) *noun* **1** a response. **2** a process in which factors that produce a result are changed or corrected by that result.
feed·back • *noun*

feel (fēl) *verb* **1** to touch in order to find out something [*Feel* the baby's bottle to see if the milk is warm.] **2** to be aware of through the senses or the mind [He *felt* rain on his face.] **3** to be aware of being; be [I *feel* sad.] **4** to have grief, pity, or another painful emotion because of [He *felt* his mother's death very deeply.] **5** to be or seem to the sense of touch [The water *feels* cold.] **6** to think or believe [She *feels* that we should go.]
noun the way a thing feels to the touch [The shirt seems to be all wool by the *feel* of it.]
—feel up to [*an informal use*] to feel capable of [I don't *feel up to* playing softball today.]
feel • *verb* **felt, feeling** • *noun*

feeler (fēl′ər) *noun* a slender part growing out from an animal or insect. The animal or insect uses this part to touch and feel things.
feel·er • *noun, plural* **feelers**

feeling (fēl′iŋ) *noun* **1** the sense of touch. It helps a person find out things such as whether something is rough or smooth, or hot or cold. **2** the condition of being aware of something [a *feeling* of pain]. **3** what a person feels deeply inside; love, hate, joy, or some other emotion [He must learn to control his *feelings*.] **4** pity or sympathy [She spoke with *feeling* about their suffering.] **5** an opinion or belief [I have a *feeling* that you are right.]
—hurt someone's feelings to make someone feel unhappy or hurt inside.
feel·ing • *noun, plural* **feelings**

feet (fēt) *noun plural of* **foot**.
• The words **feet** and **feat** sound alike.
She has blisters on her hands and *feet*.
The rescue was a *feat* of courage.

feline (fē′līn) *adjective* like or having to do with a cat or related animal.
fe·line • *adjective*

fell[1] (fel) *verb past tense of* **fall**.

fell[2] (fel) *verb* to cause to fall down [The boxer *felled* his opponent.]
fell • *verb* **felled, felling**

fellow (fel′ō *or* fel′ə) *noun* **1** [*an informal use*] a man or boy. **2** a partner or companion [They were *fellows* in crime.]

F

adjective in the same situation [*fellow* workers].
fel·low • *noun, plural* **fellows** • *adjective*

fellowship (fel′ō ship) *noun* **1** friendship; the condition of being companions. **2** a group of people who share the same activities.
fel·low·ship • *noun, plural* **fellowships**

felt[1] (felt) *noun* a heavy material that is mostly wool. It is made by heating or pressing together the fibers.
felt • *noun, plural* **felts**

felt[2] (felt) *verb past tense and past participle of* **feel**.

female (fē′māl) *adjective* **1** belonging to the sex that bears the young or produces eggs. **2** having to do with women or girls.
noun a female person, animal, or plant.
fe·male • *adjective* • *noun, plural* **females**

feminine (fem′i nin) *adjective* of or having to do with women or girls; female [a *feminine* voice].
fem·i·nine • *adjective*

feminism (fem′i niz′əm) *noun* the principle that women should have political, economic, and social rights that are equal to those of men.
fem·i·nism • *noun*

feminist (fem′i nist) *noun* a person who believes in and supports feminism.
fem·i·nist • *noun, plural* **feminists**

femur (fē′mər) *noun* the thighbone.
fe·mur • *noun, plural* **femurs**

fence (fens) *noun* a barrier of posts, rails, or wire, put around a field or yard, usually to keep something in or out.
verb **1** to close in with a fence. **2** to take part in the sport of fencing.
fence • *noun, plural* **fences** • *verb* **fenced, fencing**

fencing

fencing (fen′siŋ) *noun* **1** the sport of fighting with swords. **2** material for making fences.
fenc·ing • *noun*

fender (fen′dər) *noun* a metal part over the wheel of a car, bicycle, or other vehicle, that protects against splashing water or mud.
fend·er • *noun, plural* **fenders**

ferment (fər ment′) *verb* to undergo a slow chemical change that takes place in certain substances. Yeast and bacteria can cause this change. [Apple juice *ferments* into vinegar.]
fer·ment • *verb* **fermented, fermenting**

fern (fʉrn) *noun* a plant with small leaves that grows in shady and moist places. It has no flowers but instead has special seeds, called spores, that grow on the back of its leaves.
fern • *noun, plural* **ferns**

ferocious (fər ō′shəs) *adjective* fierce; savage.
fe·ro·cious • *adjective*

ferret (fer′ət) *noun* a small animal like a weasel that has been tamed for use in hunting rabbits, rats, or other small animals.
fer·ret • *noun, plural* **ferrets**

Ferris wheel

Ferris wheel (fer′is) *noun* a very large wheel that turns in an upright position. It has seats hanging from its rim. It is used as an amusement park ride.
Fer·ris wheel • *noun, plural* **Ferris wheels**

a	cat	ō	go	ʉ	fur	ə =	a *in* ago
ā	ape	ô	law, for	ch	chin		e *in* agent
ä	cot, car	o͝o	look	sh	she		i *in* pencil
e	ten	o͞o	tool	th	thin		o *in* atom
ē	me	oi	oil	*th*	then		u *in* circus
i	fit	ou	out	zh	measure		
ī	ice	u	up	ŋ	ring		

WORD HISTORY

Ferris wheel

The first **Ferris wheel** was made by George Washington Gale *Ferris* for a World's Fair in Chicago in 1893. It was very large, with 36 cars, and each car could hold 40 to 60 persons. Most **Ferris wheels** today have swinging seats that hold just two or three persons.

ferry

ferry (fer′ē) ***verb*** to take across a stretch of water in a boat or raft [They *ferried* our cars to the island.]
noun a boat used for taking people or cars across a stretch of water.
fer·ry • ***verb*** **ferried, ferrying, ferries** • ***noun, plural*** **ferries**

ferryboat (fer′ē bōt) ***noun*** *the same as* **ferry**.
fer·ry·boat • ***noun, plural*** **ferryboats**

fertile (fʉrt′l) ***adjective*** **1** producing much; rich in things such as crops or ideas [*fertile* soil; a *fertile* imagination]. **2** able to produce seeds, fruit, or young [*fertile* cattle]. **3** able to grow into a new plant or animal [*fertile* eggs].
fer·tile • ***adjective***

fertilize (fʉrt′l īz) ***verb*** **1** to put fertilizer on. **2** to bring a male germ cell to a female egg cell so that a new plant or animal can develop [Bees *fertilize* flowers by carrying pollen from one to another.]
fer·til·ize • ***verb*** **fertilized, fertilizing**

fertilizer (fʉrt′l ī zər) ***noun*** manure or chemicals put on or in the soil as a food for plants.
fer·til·iz·er • ***noun, plural*** **fertilizers**

fervent (fʉr′vənt) ***adjective*** showing very strong feeling; intense [a *fervent* desire to win].
fer·vent • ***adjective***

fester (fes′tər) ***verb*** to become filled with pus [The cut on his leg *festered*.]
fes·ter • ***verb*** **festered, festering**

festival (fes′ti vəl) ***noun*** **1** a day or time of special celebration; happy holiday [Our town holds a maple sugar *festival* each year.] **2** a planned series of concerts, films, or other cultural events [a film *festival*].
fes·ti·val • ***noun, plural*** **festivals**

festive (fes′tiv) ***adjective*** merry; joyous [in a *festive* mood].
fes·tive • ***adjective***

festivity (fes tiv′i tē) ***noun*** **1** joyful celebration [a time of *festivity*]. **2 festivities** things done as part of a celebration [The *festivities* included dining and dancing.]
fes·tiv·i·ty • ***noun, plural*** **festivities**

fetch (fech) ***verb*** **1** to go after and bring back; get [The dog *fetched* the stick.] **2** to sell for [The sofa should *fetch* $50.]
fetch • ***verb*** **fetched, fetching**

fetching (fech′iŋ) ***adjective*** attractive or charming [Molly has a *fetching* smile.]
fetch·ing • ***adjective***

fetter (fet′ər) ***noun*** a chain or metal fastening for the feet of a prisoner.
fet·ter • ***noun, plural*** **fetters**

feud (fyo͞od) ***noun*** a bitter quarrel usually between two families.
verb to carry on a feud.
feud • ***noun, plural*** **feuds** • ***verb*** **feuded, feuding**

fever (fē′vər) ***noun*** **1** a body temperature that is higher than normal. **2** a sickness in which there is a high fever [yellow *fever*].
fe·ver • ***noun, plural*** **fevers**

feverish (fē′vər ish) ***adjective*** **1** having a fever [She is *feverish* and has a sore throat.] **2** excited or nervous [the *feverish* state of the crowd].
fe·ver·ish • ***adjective***

few (fyo͞o) ***adjective*** not many; a small number of [just a *few* minutes more].
pronoun not many; a small number [*Few* stayed until the end of his speech.]
few • ***adjective*** **fewer, fewest** • ***pronoun***

fiancé (fē′än sā′) ***noun*** the man who is engaged to marry a certain woman.
fi·an·cé • ***noun, plural*** **fiancés**

fiancée (fē′än sā′) ***noun*** the woman who is engaged to marry a certain man.
fi·an·cée • ***noun,*** *plural* **fiancées**

fib (fib) ***noun*** a lie about something not very important.
verb to tell a fib.
fib • ***noun,*** *plural* **fibs** • ***verb*** **fibbed, fibbing**

fiber (fī′bər) ***noun*** **1** any of the parts like threads that form the tissue of animals and plants [Cotton *fibers* are spun into yarn.] **2** the part of food that cannot be digested. Fiber aids digestion by helping move food through the intestines. Bran, fruits, and vegetables have a high content of fiber.
fi·ber • ***noun,*** *plural* **fibers**

Fiberglas (fī′bər glas) ***trademark*** very fine fibers of glass that are spun into yarn. Fiberglas is used as insulation.
Fi·ber·glas • ***trademark***

fickle (fik′əl) ***adjective*** changing often in feelings or interests [The *fickle* fans began to boo.]
fick·le • ***adjective***

fiction (fik′shən) ***noun*** **1** something made up, such as a statement or a story [Truth is stranger than *fiction*.] **2** novels and short stories [She reads only *fiction*.]
fic·tion • ***noun***

fictional (fik′shən əl) ***adjective*** made up or imagined.
fic·tion·al • ***adjective***

fiddle (fid′əl) ***noun*** a violin.
verb to move the fingers in a restless or nervous way [Stop *fiddling* with your pen.]
fid·dle • ***noun,*** *plural* **fiddles** • ***verb*** **fiddled, fiddling**

fiddler (fid′lər) ***noun*** a person who plays a fiddle.
fid·dler • ***noun,*** *plural* **fiddlers**

fidelity (fi del′i tē) ***noun*** the quality of being true to a duty or cause; loyalty.
fi·del·i·ty • ***noun,*** *plural* **fidelities**

fidget (fij′ət) ***verb*** to move about in a restless or nervous way [He *fidgeted* in his seat.]
fidg·et • ***verb*** **fidgeted, fidgeting**

field (fēld) ***noun*** **1** a wide piece of open land without many trees. **2** a piece of land for raising crops or grazing animals. **3** a piece of open land having a special use [a landing *field*]. **4** an area where athletic events are held. **5** a branch of learning or of special work [the *field* of science].
verb to stop or catch a batted baseball.
field • ***noun,*** *plural* **fields** • ***verb*** **fielded, fielding**

fielder (fēl′dər) ***noun*** a player in the field in a baseball game or in certain other games.
field·er • ***noun,*** *plural* **fielders**

field glasses ***plural noun*** powerful binoculars.

field goal ***noun*** **1** a goal kicked from the field in football, scoring three points. **2** a basket made from play in basketball, scoring either two or three points.
field goal • ***noun,*** *plural* **field goals**

fiend (fēnd) ***noun*** **1** an evil spirit; devil; demon. **2** a very evil or cruel person.
fiend • ***noun,*** *plural* **fiends**

fierce (firs) ***adjective*** **1** wild or cruel; savage [a *fierce* dog]. **2** violent; raging [a *fierce* storm].
fierce • ***adjective*** **fiercer, fiercest**

fiery (fī′ər ē *or* fī′rē) ***adjective*** **1** filled with fire; flaming [a *fiery* crash]. **2** very hot [Pepper has a *fiery* taste.] **3** full of strong feeling or emotion; excited [a *fiery* temper].
fi·er·y • ***adjective*** **fierier, fieriest**

fiesta (fē es′tə) ***noun*** a holiday or festival.
fi·es·ta • ***noun,*** *plural* **fiestas**

fife

fife (fīf) ***noun*** a small flute that has a shrill tone.
fife • ***noun,*** *plural* **fifes**

fifteen (fif′tēn′) ***noun*** the cardinal number between fourteen and sixteen; 15.
adjective being five more than ten [*fifteen* years].
fif·teen • ***noun,*** *plural* **fifteens** • ***adjective***

a cat	ō go	ʉ fur	ə = a *in* ago
ā ape	ô law, for	ch chin	e *in* agent
ä cot, car	oo look	sh she	i *in* pencil
e ten	ōō tool	th thin	o *in* atom
ē me	oi oil	*th* then	u *in* circus
i fit	ou out	zh measure	
ī ice	u up	ŋ ring	

fifteenth (fif′tēnth′) ***adjective*** coming after fourteen others in a series; 15th in order.
noun **1** the number, person, or thing that is fifteenth. **2** one of fifteen equal parts of something; $\frac{1}{15}$.
fif·teenth • ***adjective*** • ***noun,*** *plural* **fifteenths**

fifth (fifth) ***adjective*** coming after four others in a series; 5th in order.
noun **1** the number, person, or thing that is fifth. **2** one of five equal parts of something; $\frac{1}{5}$.
fifth • ***adjective*** • ***noun,*** *plural* **fifths**

fiftieth (fif′tē əth) ***adjective*** being ten more than forty others in a series; 50th in order.
noun **1** the number, person, or thing that is fiftieth. **2** one of fifty equal parts of something; $\frac{1}{50}$.
fif·ti·eth • ***adjective*** • ***noun,*** *plural* **fiftieths**

fifty (fif′tē) ***noun*** the cardinal number that is equal to five times ten; 50.
adjective being five times ten [*fifty* States].
fif·ty • ***noun,*** *plural* **fifties** • ***adjective***

fifty-fifty (fif′tē fif′tē) [*an informal word*] ***adverb*** in two equal parts [John and I split the reward money *fifty-fifty*.]
fif·ty-fif·ty • ***adverb***

fig (fig) ***noun*** a sweet fruit that is filled with a soft pulp containing many seeds. Figs are often dried for eating.
fig • ***noun,*** *plural* **figs**

fight (fīt) ***verb*** **1** to use fists, weapons, or other force in trying to beat or overcome someone or something; to struggle [The soldiers *fought* hand to hand.] **2** to work hard in trying to overcome [Let's *fight* pollution.] **3** to quarrel; argue [Lisa and her brother always *fight*.]
noun **1** the use of force to try to overcome someone or something; battle. **2** any struggle [the *fight* against poverty]. **3** an angry quarrel.
fight • ***verb*** **fought, fighting** • ***noun,*** *plural* **fights**

figure (fig′yər) ***noun*** **1** shape, outline, or form [a *figure* with four equal sides; her slim *figure*]. **2** a drawing or diagram [The *figure* on page 12 shows how to tie a slipknot.] **3** a person thought of in a certain way [an important *figure* in history]. **4** the symbol for a number [The *figure* for five is "5."]
verb to find out by using arithmetic [He *figured* the cost of building a new garage.]
—figure out to find the answer to; understand [I couldn't *figure out* how the dog got out.]
fig·ure • ***noun,*** *plural* **figures** • ***verb*** **figured, figuring**

figurehead (fig′yər hed) ***noun*** **1** a carved figure on the bow of a ship. **2** a person who holds a high position but has no real power.
fig·ure·head • ***noun,*** *plural* **figureheads**

figurehead

figurine (fig yər ēn′) ***noun*** a small statue made of china or other material.
fig·u·rine • ***noun,*** *plural* **figurines**

Fiji (fē′jē) a country on a group of islands in the South Pacific.
Fi·ji

filament (fil′ə mənt) ***noun*** a very thin wire, thread, or fiber.
fil·a·ment • ***noun,*** *plural* **filaments**

file[1] (fīl) ***noun*** **1** a folder, box, or cabinet for keeping papers in order. **2** a number of cards, letters, or other groups of papers, kept in an orderly way. **3** information about one subject that is stored in a computer. **4** a number of persons or things arranged in a line.
verb **1** to arrange cards, letters, or other papers in order [*File* these letters according to date.] **2** to put into official records [He *filed* a claim for his missing luggage.] **3** to move in a line [The audience *filed* out of the room.]
—on file kept in a file so that it can be looked at or referred to later.
file • ***noun,*** *plural* **files** • ***verb*** **filed, filing**

WORD HISTORY

file

The word **file** came into English from an older verb that means "to string papers on a thread." One way to **file** or arrange papers in order would be to string them on a thread. The French word goes back to the Latin word for "thread."

file[2] (fīl) ***noun*** a steel tool with a surface of rough ridges for smoothing or grinding down something.

verb to smooth or grind down with a file or similar tool [She *filed* her fingernails.]
file • *noun, plural* **files** • *verb* **filed, filing**

fill (fil) *verb* **1** to put as much as possible into; make full [She *filled* the pail with water.] **2** to become full [My eyes *filled* with tears.] **3** to take up all the space in; occupy all of [The crowd *filled* the hall.] **4** to put someone into a certain job or office [The Mayor *filled* the position of treasurer.] **5** to supply the things needed in [The clerk *filled* our order.]
noun all that is needed to make full or to satisfy [I had my *fill* of ice cream at the party.]
—**fill out** to write the information that is asked for [She *filled out* the order form.]
fill • *verb* **filled, filling** • *noun*

fillet (fi lā′ *or* fil′ā) *noun* a piece of fish or meat without bones.
fil·let • *noun, plural* **fillets**

filling (fil′iŋ) *noun* **1** the material that a dentist puts into a tooth cavity. **2** any material used to fill something [a fruit *filling* for pies].
fill·ing • *noun, plural* **fillings**

Fillmore (fil′môr), **Millard** (mil′ərd) 1800-1874; the thirteenth president of the U.S., from 1850 to 1853.
Fill·more, Mill·ard

filly (fil′ē) *noun* a young female horse.
fil·ly • *noun, plural* **fillies**

film (film) *noun* **1** a sheet or roll of material covered with a chemical substance that is changed by light. Film is used for taking photographs and making movies. **2** a series of pictures that are projected on a screen quickly, one after another, so that persons and things in them seem to move. **3** a thin coating [a *film* of ice on the roads].
verb to make a film of [Father *filmed* my sister's wedding.]
film • *noun, plural* **films** • *verb* **filmed, filming**

filmstrip (film′strip) *noun* a strip of film made up of still photographs that are shown one at a time on a screen. Filmstrips are used in schools as an aid in teaching.
film·strip • *noun, plural* **filmstrips**

filmy (fil′mē) *adjective* **1** like a film [a *filmy* layer of dust]. **2** covered with a film [a *filmy* lens].
film·y • *adjective* **filmier, filmiest**

filter (fil′tər) *noun* **1** a device that makes air, water, or other fluid clean or pure. The fluid is passed through sand, charcoal, or some other material that keeps back dirt or other unwanted substances. **2** a colored disk placed over the lens of a camera that does not let through a certain color or colors.
verb **1** to pass or put through a filter [We have to *filter* our drinking water.] **2** to remove with a filter [She *filtered* out the chemicals.] **3** to pass slowly [The news *filtered* through town.]
fil·ter • *noun, plural* **filters** • *verb* **filtered, filtering**

filth (filth) *noun* sewage, garbage, or other matter that is sickening or disgusting.

filthy (filth′ē) *adjective* full of filth; disgusting —Look for the WORD CHOICES box at the entry **dirty**.
filth·y • *adjective* **filthier, filthiest**

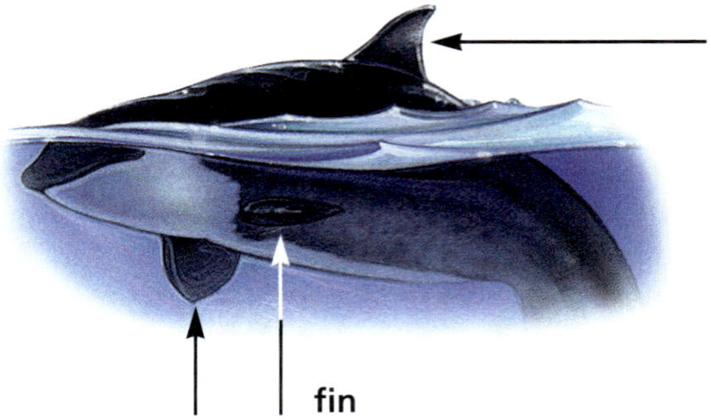
fin

fin (fin) *noun* **1** one of the parts like a blade or fan that stick out from the body of a water animal. Fins are used in swimming and balancing. **2** anything that looks or works like a fin.
fin • *noun, plural* **fins**

final (fī′nəl) *adjective* **1** coming at the end; last [the *final* chapter]. **2** allowing no further change [The decision of the judges is *final*.]
noun **1** anything final. **2 finals** the last of a series of tests or games [Our team lost in the *finals*.]
fi·nal • *adjective* • *noun, plural* **finals**

finance (fi nans′ *or* fī′nans) *noun* **1** the business of taking care of money matters [Bankers are experts in *finance*.] **2 finances** all the money or income of a person, company,

a	cat	ō	go	ʉ	fur	ə = a *in* ago	
ā	ape	ô	law, for	ch	chin	e *in* agent	
ä	cot, car	oo	look	sh	she	i *in* pencil	
e	ten	ōō	tool	th	thin	o *in* atom	
ē	me	oi	oil	*th*	then	u *in* circus	
i	fit	ou	out	zh	measure		
ī	ice	u	up	ŋ	ring		

or government [in charge of our family *finances*].
fi·nance • *noun, plural* **finances**

financial (fi nan′shəl *or* fī nan′shəl) ***adjective*** having to do with money matters [in *financial* difficulty].
fi·nan·cial • ***adjective***

finch (finch) ***noun*** a songbird that has a short beak and eats seeds, such as the sparrow.
finch • *noun, plural* **finches**

find (fīnd) ***verb*** **1** to come upon by chance; discover [I sometimes *find* violets in the woods.] **2** to get by searching [I finally *found* my lost book.] **3** to learn about; come to know [I *find* that I was wrong.] **4** to declare after careful thought [The jury *found* her guilty.] **5** to think to be [He *finds* TV boring.]
noun something of value that is found [The sunken treasure was a great *find*.]
—**find out** to learn [He *found out* the truth.]
find • ***verb*** **found, finding** • ***noun***, *plural* **finds**

finding (fīn′diŋ) ***noun*** *often* **findings** a conclusion reached after thinking carefully about the facts [The scientist published his *findings*.]
find·ing • *noun, plural* **findings**

fine[1] (fīn) ***adjective*** **1** very good or excellent [a *fine* report card]. **2** clear and bright [a *fine* day]. **3** having small grains or particles [*fine* sand]. **4** very thin or small [*fine* thread]. **5** in good health [Do you feel *fine* now?]
adverb [*an informal use*] very well [We did just *fine* on the test.]
fine • ***adjective*** **finer, finest** • ***adverb***

fine[2] (fīn) ***noun*** money paid as punishment for breaking a law or rule [a *fine* for speeding].
verb to order to pay a fine [The librarian *fined* her fifty cents for returning the books late.]
fine • *noun, plural* **fines** • ***verb*** **fined, fining**

fine arts ***plural noun*** drawing, painting, sculpture, and other arts in which beautiful things are made.

finery (fīn′ər ē) ***noun*** fine or fancy clothes and jewelry.
fin·er·y • *noun, plural* **fineries**

finger (fiŋ′gər) ***noun*** **1** one of the five parts at the end of each hand. **2** the part of a glove that covers a finger.
fin·ger • *noun, plural* **fingers**

fingernail (fiŋ′gər nāl) ***noun*** the hard, growing part that covers the top of each fingertip.
fin·ger·nail • *noun, plural* **fingernails**

finger painting ***noun*** a kind of painting in which the fingers or hands are used to spread the paints on the paper.

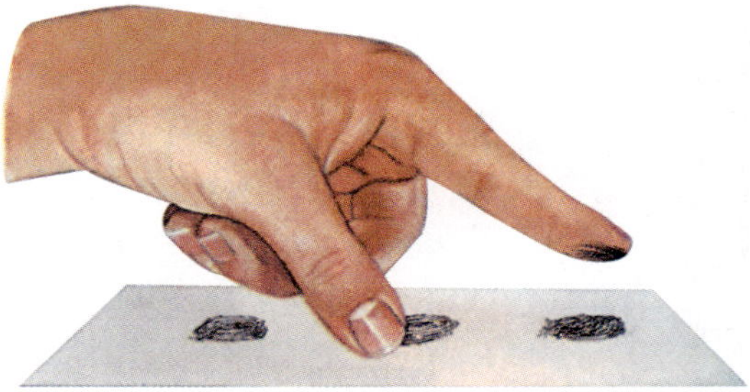

fingerprint

fingerprint (fiŋ′gər print) ***noun*** the mark made by pressing the tip of a finger against a flat surface. The fine lines and circles form a pattern that can be used to identify a person.
verb to take the fingerprints of a person by pressing the tips of the fingers on an inked surface and then on paper.
fin·ger·print • *noun, plural* **fingerprints** • ***verb*** **fingerprinted, fingerprinting**

fingertip (fiŋ′gər tip) ***noun*** the tip of a finger.
fin·ger·tip • *noun, plural* **fingertips**

finicky (fin′ik ē) ***adjective*** too hard to please; fussy.
fin·ick·y • ***adjective*** **finickier, finickiest**

finish (fin′ish) ***verb*** **1** to bring or come to an end; complete [He *finished* his work.] **2** to use up; consume completely [*Finish* your milk.] **3** to give a certain surface to something by applying paint, polish, or other substance [She sanded and *finished* the old table.]
noun **1** the last part; end [We stayed to the *finish*.] **2** the kind of surface that a thing has [a smooth wax *finish*].
fin·ish • ***verb*** **finished, finishing** • ***noun***, *plural* **finishes**

fink (fiŋk) [*a slang word*] ***noun*** a person who secretly tells things about another; informer.
fink • *noun, plural* **finks**

Finland (fin′lənd) a country in northern Europe, east of Sweden.
Fin·land

Finn (fin) ***noun*** a person born or living in Finland.
Finn • *noun, plural* **Finns**

F

Finnish (fin′ish) ***noun*** the language of the Finns.
Finn·ish • ***noun***

fiord

fiord (fyôrd) ***noun*** a narrow inlet of the sea between steep cliffs.
fiord • ***noun,*** *plural* **fiords**

fir (fur) ***noun*** a pine tree with flat needles and hard, woody cones.
fir • ***noun,*** *plural* **firs**
● The words **fir** and **fur** sound alike.
A row of *fir* trees lines our street.
She wore a brand-new *fur* coat last week.

fire (fīr) ***noun*** **1** the heat and light of something burning. **2** something burning in a furnace, stove, or fireplace. **3** an instance of burning that destroys or kills [a forest *fire*]. **4** strong feeling; excitement [a team full of *fire*]. **5** the shooting of guns [enemy *fire*].
verb **1** to stir up; excite [The story *fired* her imagination.] **2** to shoot [He *fired* the gun.] **3** to shoot a gun or bullet [The soldiers *fired* on the enemy.] **4** to bake in a kiln [Do you know how to *fire* bricks?] **5** to throw or direct with great force [The reporter *fired* a question at the mayor.] —Look for the WORD CHOICES box at the entry **throw**. **6** to send away from a job or position; dismiss.
—**on fire** burning [The house is *on fire!*] —**open fire** to begin to shoot. —**play with fire** to do something risky. —**set fire to** to make burn [He *set fire to* the pile of dry leaves.]
fire • ***noun,*** *plural* **fires** • ***verb*** **fired, firing**

firearm (fīr′ärm) ***noun*** a rifle, pistol, or other weapon that shoots bullets or shells and that is small enough to carry.
fire·arm • ***noun,*** *plural* **firearms**

firebomb (fīr′bäm) ***noun*** a bomb that is intended to start a fire.
fire·bomb • ***noun,*** *plural* **firebombs**

firecracker (fīr′krak ər) ***noun*** a roll of paper with gunpowder inside and a fuse. It explodes with a loud noise when the fuse is lighted.
fire·crack·er • ***noun,*** *plural* **firecrackers**

fire engine ***noun*** a motor truck for carrying firefighters and equipment to put out fires.
fire engine • ***noun,*** *plural* **fire engines**

fire escape ***noun*** a metal ladder or stairway on an outside wall of a building. It is used to get out of the building during a fire.
fire escape • ***noun,*** *plural* **fire escapes**

fire extinguisher ***noun*** a device for spraying chemicals on a fire to put it out.
fire extinguisher • ***noun,*** *plural* **fire extinguishers**

firefighter (fīr′fīt ər) ***noun*** a person whose work is putting out fires.
fire·fight·er • ***noun,*** *plural* **firefighters**

firefly (fīr′flī) ***noun*** a small, flying beetle whose lower body glows with a light that goes on and off at night.
fire·fly • ***noun,*** *plural* **fireflies**

firehouse (fīr′hous) ***noun*** *the same as* **fire station**.
fire·house • ***noun,*** *plural* **firehouses**

fireman (fīr′mən) ***noun*** a firefighter.
fire·man • ***noun,*** *plural* **firemen**

fireplace (fīr′plās) ***noun*** a place built to hold a fire. Most inside fireplaces are open structures in a wall, at the base of a chimney.
fire·place • ***noun,*** *plural* **fireplaces**

fireproof (fīr′proof) ***adjective*** made in such a way that it does not burn or is not easily destroyed by fire [a *fireproof* carpet].
fire·proof • ***adjective***

fireside (fīr′sīd) ***noun*** the part of a room near a fireplace.
fire·side • ***noun,*** *plural* **firesides**

fire station ***noun*** a building where fire engines are kept and where firefighters stay when on duty.
fire station • ***noun,*** *plural* **fire stations**

a	cat	ō	go	ʉ	fur	ə =	a *in* ago
ā	ape	ô	law, for	ch	chin		e *in* agent
ä	cot, car	oo	look	sh	she		i *in* pencil
e	ten	ōō	tool	th	thin		o *in* atom
ē	me	oi	oil	*th*	then		u *in* circus
i	fit	ou	out	zh	measure		
ī	ice	u	up	ŋ	ring		

firetrap (fīr′trap) ***noun*** a building that would be dangerous if it caught on fire.
fire·trap • ***noun,*** *plural* **firetraps**

firewood (fīr′wood) ***noun*** wood used as fuel.
fire·wood • ***noun***

fireworks (fīr′wʉrks) ***plural noun*** things made with gunpowder or other explosive matter that make loud noises or a fancy show of lights.
fire·works • ***plural noun***

firm[1] (fʉrm) ***adjective*** **1** not giving way easily when pressed; solid [a *firm* bed]. **2** not moved easily; fixed; stable [a *firm* foundation]. **3** not changing; staying the same [a *firm* friendship].
firm • ***adjective*** **firmer, firmest**

> **WORD CHOICES**
>
> Synonyms of **firm**
>
> The words **firm, hard,** and **solid** share the meaning "not easy to crush, bend, or cut."
>
> a *firm* mattress
>
> as *hard* as a rock
>
> *solid* muscle

firm[2] (fʉrm) ***noun*** a business company.
firm • ***noun,*** *plural* **firms**

first (fʉrst) ***adjective*** before all others in time, order, or quality [the *first* snow of winter; *first* prize; *first* class].
adverb **1** before anyone or anything else [The guests are served *first*.] **2** for the first time [When did you *first* meet them?]
noun **1** the number, person, or thing that is first [She was the *first* to finish the test.] **2** the beginning; start [At *first*, I believed him.] **3** the first day of the month.
first • ***adjective*** • ***adverb*** • ***noun,*** *plural* **firsts**

first aid ***noun*** help given to a sick or injured person while waiting for regular medical help.

first-class (fʉrst′klas′) ***adjective*** best of its kind; of the highest quality [a *first-class* hotel].
adverb in a first-class way [He travels *first-class*.]

first cousin ***noun*** the son or daughter of one's aunt or uncle.
first cousin • ***noun,*** *plural* **first cousins**

firsthand (fʉrst′hand′) ***adjective*** straight from the source; not from a second person or thing; direct [a *firsthand* account of the accident]. This word can also be used as an adverb [We received the information *firsthand*.]
first·hand • ***adjective***

first person ***noun*** **1** the form of a pronoun, such as *I, me, we, us,* that refers to the person who is speaking or the persons who are speaking. **2** the form of a verb, such as *I am* or *we are*, that belongs with this kind of pronoun.

first-rate (fʉrst′rāt′) ***adjective*** of the highest class or quality; excellent [a *first-rate* movie].

fish (fish) ***noun*** **1** an animal with a backbone, fins, and gills that lives in water. Most fish are covered with scales. **2** the flesh of a fish used as food.
verb **1** to catch or try to catch fish. **2** to search or feel about for, find, and pull out [He *fished* a dime out of his pocket.]
fish • ***noun,*** *plural* **fish** or **fishes**
• ***verb*** **fished, fishing**

fisherman (fish′ər mən) ***noun*** a person who fishes either for sport or for a living.
fish·er·man • ***noun,*** *plural* **fishermen**

fishhook (fish′hook) ***noun*** a hook with a barb or barbs for catching fish.
fish·hook • ***noun,*** *plural* **fishhooks**

fishing (fish′iŋ) ***noun*** the work or sport of catching fish.
fish·ing • ***noun***

fishing rod ***noun*** a long pole with a line, hook, and sometimes a reel, used to catch fish.
fishing rod • ***noun,*** *plural* **fishing rods**

fishy (fish′ē) ***adjective*** **1** tasting or smelling of fish. **2** dull or without expression [a *fishy* stare]. **3** [*an informal use*] causing doubt; not likely [a *fishy* story].
fish·y • ***adjective*** **fishier, fishiest**

fission (fish′ən) ***noun*** *the same as* **nuclear fission.**
fis·sion • ***noun***

fist (fist) ***noun*** a hand with the fingers closed tightly into the palm.
fist • ***noun,*** *plural* **fists**

fit[1] (fit) ***verb*** **1** to be the right size or shape for [The coat *fits* me well.] **2** to make or change

so that something is the right size or shape [The tailor *fitted* the suit.] **3** to be right for; to suit [Let the punishment *fit* the crime.] **4** to put one thing into another thing; insert [He *fitted* the key into the lock.]
adjective **1** suitable or suited to someone or something [a meal *fit* for a king]. **2** in good physical condition; healthy.
noun the way something fits [a tight *fit*].
fit • ***verb*** **fitted** or **fit, fitted, fitting** • ***adjective*** **fitter, fittest** • ***noun***

WORD CHOICES

Synonyms of fit

The words **fit**, **proper**, and **suitable** share the meaning "right for the purpose."

a meal *fit* for a king
the *proper* tool for the job
a car *suitable* for mountain driving

fit[2] (fit) ***noun*** a sudden attack or outburst that is hard to control [a *fit* of coughing].
fit • ***noun,*** *plural* **fits**

fitness (fit′nəs) ***noun*** the condition of being fit [physical *fitness*].
fit·ness • ***noun***

five (fīv) ***noun*** the cardinal number between four and six; 5.
adjective being one more than four [*five* hours].
five • ***noun,*** *plural* **fives** • ***adjective***

fix (fiks) ***verb*** **1** to fasten firmly [We *fixed* the flagpole in concrete.] **2** to direct and hold [She *fixed* her eyes on the target.] **3** to decide on; settle [The couple *fixed* the date of the wedding.] **4** to set right or set in order; adjust [She is *fixing* her hair.] **5** to make whole again; repair [Can you *fix* this radio?] **6** to get ready; prepare [I will *fix* dinner.]
—fix up [*an informal use*] **1** to repair [He will *fix up* that old car.] **2** to set in order [*Fix up* the house before the guests arrive.]
fix • ***verb*** **fixed, fixing**

fixings (fiks′iŋz) ***plural noun*** [*an informal word*] all the things that go with the main food in a meal [turkey with all the *fixings*].
fix·ings • ***plural noun***

fixture (fiks′chər) ***noun*** wiring, plumbing, or furniture that is attached to a building and is considered part of it [bathroom *fixtures*].
fix·ture • ***noun,*** *plural* **fixtures**

fizz (fiz) ***noun*** a hissing or sputtering sound.
verb to make this sound [The soda water *fizzed* when she opened the bottle.]
fizz • ***noun,*** *plural* **fizzes** • ***verb*** **fizzed, fizzing**

fizzle (fiz′əl) ***verb*** **1** to make a hissing or sputtering sound. **2** [*an informal use*] to fail after a good start.
fiz·zle • ***verb*** **fizzled, fizzling**

FL or **Fla.** *abbreviation for* Florida.

flabby (flab′ē) ***adjective*** soft and limp; not firm and strong [*flabby* muscles].
flab·by • ***adjective*** **flabbier, flabbiest**

WORD HISTORY

flabby

The word **flabby** is related to the adjective *flappy*, which comes from *flap*. If your arm muscles are **flabby**, they can seem to move in a flapping way when you move your arm.

flag

flag (flag) ***noun*** a piece of cloth with certain colors and designs. It is used as a symbol of a country or State or as a signal.

a	cat	ō	go	ʉ	fur	ə = a *in* ago	
ā	ape	ô	law, for	ch	chin	e *in* agent	
ä	cot, car	oo	look	sh	she	i *in* pencil	
e	ten	ōō	tool	th	thin	o *in* atom	
ē	me	oi	oil	*th*	then	u *in* circus	
i	fit	ou	out	zh	measure		
ī	ice	u	up	ŋ	ring		

verb **1** to signal with a flag. **2** to signal to stop [The man *flagged* down a taxi.]
flag • ***noun,*** *plural* **flags** • ***verb*** **flagged, flagging**

flagpole (flag′pōl) ***noun*** a pole on which a flag is raised and flown.
flag·pole • ***noun,*** *plural* **flagpoles**

flair (fler) ***noun*** a natural skill; talent [She has a *flair* for acting.]
● The words **flair** and **flare** sound alike.
He has a real *flair* for math.
My back pain will *flare* up now and then.

flake (flāk) ***noun*** **1** a small, thin piece or chip [a *flake* of snow]. **2** [*a slang use*] a person who behaves in a strange or odd way.
verb to come off in small, thin pieces [The paint is *flaking* off the walls.]
flake • ***noun,*** *plural* **flakes** • ***verb*** **flaked, flaking**

flaky (flāk′ē) ***adjective*** **1** made up of flakes. **2** breaking easily into flakes [a *flaky* pie crust]. **3** [*a slang use*] strange or odd [*flaky* ideas].
flak·y • ***adjective*** **flakier, flakiest**

flamboyant (flam boi′ənt) ***adjective*** too showy or fancy [a *flamboyant* costume].
flam·boy·ant • ***adjective***

flame (flām) ***noun*** **1** the burning gas of a fire seen as a flickering light; blaze. **2** the condition of burning with a blaze [to burst into *flame*].
verb to burn with a flame; blaze.
flame • ***noun,*** *plural* **flames** • ***verb*** **flamed, flaming**

flamingo (flə miŋ′gō) ***noun*** a tropical bird that has pink or red feathers, a very long neck, and long legs.
fla·min·go • ***noun,*** *plural* **flamingos** or **flamingoes**

flamingo

flammable (flam′ə bəl) ***adjective*** easily set on fire [Gasoline is *flammable.*]
flam·ma·ble • ***adjective***

flank (flaŋk) ***noun*** **1** the side of an animal between the ribs and the hip. **2** the side of anything [the army's right *flank*].
verb to be at the side of [Bodyguards *flanked* the actress as she moved through the crowd.]
flank • ***noun,*** *plural* **flanks** • ***verb*** **flanked, flanking**

flannel (flan′əl) ***noun*** a soft cloth made usually of cotton or wool.
flan·nel • ***noun***

flap (flap) ***noun*** anything flat and broad that hangs loose or covers an opening [a pocket *flap;* the *flap* of an envelope].
verb **1** to move with a slapping sound [The flag *flapped* in the wind.] **2** to move up and down or back and forth [The bird *flapped* its wings.]
flap • ***noun,*** *plural* **flaps** • ***verb*** **flapped, flapping**

flare (fler) ***verb*** **1** to blaze up with a bright flame or burn with a flame that is whipped about [The torch *flared* in the wind.] **2** to spread outward [The front end of a clarinet *flares.*]
noun **1** a short burst of bright light. **2** a bright light that is used as a distress signal.
flare • ***verb*** **flared, flaring** • ***noun,*** *plural* **flares**
● The words **flare** and **flair** sound alike.
The driver lit a *flare* by her car.
She has a real *flair* for running.

flare-up (fler′up) ***noun*** **1** an outburst of flame. **2** a sudden, brief outburst of anger or trouble.
flare-up • ***noun,*** *plural* **flare-ups**

flash (flash) ***verb*** **1** to send out short and bright bursts of light [Neon signs *flashed.*] **2** to gleam or sparkle [Her eyes *flashed* with anger.] **3** to come, move, or send in a swift or sudden manner [The train *flashed* by.]
noun **1** a short burst of light [a lightning *flash*] —Look for the WORD CHOICES box at the entry **blaze**[1]. **2** a very short time; moment [I'll be there in a *flash.*]
flash • ***verb*** **flashed, flashing** • ***noun,*** *plural* **flashes**

flashbulb (flash′bulb) ***noun*** a light bulb that gives a short, bright light. It is used for taking photographs, especially indoors.
flash·bulb • ***noun,*** *plural* **flashbulbs**

flashlight (flash′līt) ***noun*** an electric light that gets its power from batteries and that is small enough to carry.
flash·light • ***noun,*** *plural* **flashlights**

flashy (flash′ē) ***adjective*** too showy [*flashy* clothes].

F

flash·y • *adjective* **flashier, flashiest**

flask (flask) ***noun*** a small bottle with a narrow neck, usually used by chemists in a laboratory.
flask • ***noun,*** *plural* **flasks**

flat (flat) ***adjective*** **1** smooth and level [a *flat* field]. **2** not very thick or deep [*flat* as a pancake]. **3** definite [a *flat* denial of the charges]. **4** not changing; staying the same [a *flat* rate of 50 cents per rider]. **5** without much sparkle or taste [*flat* ginger ale]. **6** without air [a *flat* tire]. **7** not shiny [*flat* paint].
adverb **1** in a definite or positive way [She turned him down *flat*.] **2** exactly [She ran the course in three minutes *flat*.] **3** spread out at full length; horizontal [We lay *flat* in the grass.]
noun **1** *often* **flats** an area of flat land. **2** a musical note or tone one half step below another [B *flat* is the only *flat* in the key of F.] **3** the sign (♭) used to mark such a note.
flat • ***adjective*** **flatter, flattest** • ***adverb*** • ***noun,*** *plural* **flats**

flatcar (flat′kär) ***noun*** a railroad car without sides, for carrying certain kinds of freight.
flat·car • ***noun,*** *plural* **flatcars**

flatfish (flat′fish) ***noun*** a fish with both eyes on the same side of a very flat body. The flounder, halibut, and sole are all flatfishes.
flat·fish • ***noun,*** *plural* **flatfish** or **flatfishes**

flatten (flat′n) ***verb*** to make flat [The car ran over the can and *flattened* it.]
flat·ten • ***verb*** **flattened, flattening**

flatter (flat′ər) ***verb*** **1** to praise too much or without meaning it [He *flattered* her with many compliments.] **2** to make seem more attractive than is really so [This photo *flatters* me.] **3** to make feel pleased or honored [I was *flattered* that they remembered me.]
flat·ter • ***verb*** **flattered, flattering**

flattery (flat′ər ē) ***noun*** too much praise or praise that is not really meant.
flat·ter·y • ***noun***

flavor (flā′vər) ***noun*** **1** the special quality of something that is a mixing of its taste and smell [the *flavor* of chocolate]. **2** taste in general [a soup lacking *flavor*].
verb to give flavor to [Spices will *flavor* the stew.]
fla·vor • ***noun,*** *plural* **flavors** • ***verb*** **flavored, flavoring**

flavoring (flā′vər iŋ) ***noun*** something added in order to give flavor [vanilla *flavoring*].
fla·vor·ing • ***noun,*** *plural* **flavorings**

flaw (flô *or* flä) ***noun*** a break, crack, or other defect that spoils something; blemish —Look for the WORD CHOICES box at the entry **defect**.
flaw • ***noun,*** *plural* **flaws**

flax (flaks) ***noun*** **1** a plant with blue flowers and narrow leaves. The fibers from its stem are spun into linen thread and its seeds are used to make linseed oil. **2** the fibers of this plant.

flea (flē) ***noun*** a small insect that cannot fly but can jump very far. It bites animals and people and feeds on their blood.
flea • ***noun,*** *plural* **fleas**
● The words **flea** and **flee** sound alike.
The dog scratched at a *flea*.
The police told them to *flee* the area.

fleck (flek) ***noun*** a small spot or patch; speck [*flecks* of color on a bird's feathers].
fleck • ***noun,*** *plural* **flecks**

fled (fled) ***verb*** *past tense and past participle of* **flee**.

flee (flē) ***verb*** to run away from danger or from something unpleasant; escape.
flee • ***verb*** **fled, fleeing**
● The words **flee** and **flea** sound alike.

fleece (flēs) ***noun*** the coat of wool on a sheep, goat, or other similar animal.
fleece • ***noun,*** *plural* **fleeces**

fleet[1] (flēt) ***noun*** **1** a group of warships under one command [our Pacific *fleet*]. **2** the entire navy of a country [the British *fleet*]. **3** a large group of ships, cars, trucks, or other vehicles moving together or under one management [a fishing *fleet;* a *fleet* of taxicabs].
fleet • ***noun,*** *plural* **fleets**

fleet[2] (flēt) ***adjective*** swift; quick [*fleet* of foot] —Look for the WORD CHOICES box at the entry **fast**[1].
fleet • ***adjective*** **fleeter, fleetest**

Fleming (flem′iŋ), Sir **Alexander** (al′ig zan′ dər) 1881-1955; British scientist. He and a colleague discovered penicillin.
Flem·ing, Sir **Al·ex·an·der**

flesh (flesh) ***noun*** **1** the soft parts of the body, especially the parts between the skin and the

a	cat	ō	go	ʉ	fur	ə =	a *in* ago
ā	ape	ô	law, for	ch	chin		e *in* agent
ä	cot, car	oo	look	sh	she		i *in* pencil
e	ten	ōō	tool	th	thin		o *in* atom
ē	me	oi	oil	*th*	then		u *in* circus
i	fit	ou	out	zh	measure		
ī	ice	u	up	ŋ	ring		

bones. **2** these parts of an animal used as food; meat.

fleshy (flesh′ē) ***adjective*** having too much flesh; plump.
flesh·y • ***adjective*** **fleshier, fleshiest**

flew (flo͞o) ***verb*** *past tense of* **fly**[1].
- The words **flew, flu,** and **flue** sound alike.
  The jet *flew* for eight hours.
  Half our class was sick with the *flu*.
  The stove has a *flue* for smoke.

flex (fleks) ***verb*** **1** to bend [*Flex* your arm.] **2** to make tighter and harder; contract [The athlete *flexed* her muscles.]
flex • ***verb*** **flexed, flexing**

flexible (flek′si bəl) ***adjective*** **1** capable of being bent easily without breaking [a *flexible* rubber hose]. **2** easily changed or controlled [Our doctor has *flexible* office hours.]
flex·i·ble • ***adjective***

flick (flik) ***noun*** a light, quick snap or stroke with something, such as the tip of a finger.
verb to strike with a light, quick stroke [I *flicked* the ant off the table.]
flick • ***noun, plural*** **flicks** • ***verb*** **flicked, flicking**

flicker[1] (flik′ər) ***verb*** **1** to burn or shine in a way that is not clear or steady; waver [The candle *flickered* in the wind.] **2** to move in a quick, unsteady way [Shadows *flickered* on the wall.]
noun **1** a flickering light or flame. **2** a quick, back-and-forth movement [the *flicker* of a snake's tongue].
flick·er • ***verb*** **flickered, flickering** • ***noun, plural*** **flickers**

flicker[2] (flik′ər) ***noun*** a large woodpecker of North America. It is mostly brown and white with a red mark on the head.
flick·er • ***noun, plural*** **flickers**

flied (flīd) ***verb*** *a past tense and past participle of* **fly**[1] (sense 7).

flier (flī′ər) ***noun*** **1** something that flies. **2** a person who flies an airplane. **3** a small printed piece of paper that is handed out. A flier usually announces or advertises something.
fli·er • ***noun, plural*** **fliers**

flies (flīz) ***verb*** the form of the verb **fly**[1] that is used to show the present time with *he, she,* or *it*. This form is also used with singular nouns.
noun *plural of* **fly**[1] and **fly**[2].

flight[1] (flīt) ***noun*** **1** the act or way of flying or moving through space [the swift *flight* of hummingbirds]. **2** a trip through the air [It's a long *flight* between Los Angeles and New York.] **3** the distance covered by such a trip [a 500-mile *flight*]. **4** a set of stairs between two landings or floors.
flight • ***noun, plural*** **flights**

flight[2] (flīt) ***noun*** the act of fleeing; escape.
flight • ***noun, plural*** **flights**

flight attendant ***noun*** a person who looks after the passengers' comfort and safety on an airplane.
flight attendant • ***noun, plural*** **flight attendants**

flimsy (flim′zē) ***adjective*** easily damaged; not solid and strong; weak [a *flimsy* box].
flim·sy • ***adjective*** **flimsier, flimsiest**

flinch (flinch) ***verb*** to draw back from a blow or from anything painful or difficult [He *flinched* when the dentist touched his tooth.]
flinch • ***verb*** **flinched, flinching**

fling (fliŋ) ***verb*** to throw hard; hurl; cast [The hunter *flung* the spear at the tiger.] —Look for the WORD CHOICES box at the entry **throw**.
noun **1** a hard throw. **2** a short period of carefree enjoyment of a life of fun and pleasure [I had one last *fling* before getting a job.]
fling • ***verb*** **flung, flinging** • ***noun, plural*** **flings**

flint (flint) ***noun*** a very hard stone that makes sparks when it is struck against steel. Flint is a kind of quartz.
flint • ***noun, plural*** **flints**

flip (flip) ***verb*** **1** to toss or move with a quick jerk [*Flip* the switch to turn the lights on.] **2** to throw so as to cause to turn over in the air [*Flip* a coin to decide who gets the window seat.]
noun **1** an act of flipping; a toss [a *flip* of a coin]. **2** a somersault in the air.
flip • ***verb*** **flipped, flipping** • ***noun, plural*** **flips**

flipper (flip′ər) ***noun*** a broad, flat limb on a seal, whale, or other similar animal. Flippers are used for swimming.
flip·per • ***noun, plural*** **flippers**

flirt (flurt) ***verb*** to act in a playful or bold way in trying to get someone's interest [He *flirts* with every pretty girl he sees.]
noun a person who flirts with others.
flirt • ***verb*** **flirted, flirting** • ***noun, plural*** **flirts**

flit (flit) ***verb*** to move in a quick and light way; dart [Butterflies *flitted* about the garden.]
flit • ***verb*** **flitted, flitting**

float

float (flōt) ***verb*** **1** to rest on top of water or other liquid and not sink [Ice *floats*.] **2** to move or drift slowly on a liquid or through the air [A raft of logs *floated* down the river.]
noun **1** something that floats on a liquid or keeps something else afloat. An anchored raft used by swimmers and a cork on a fishing line are common types of float. **2** a platform on wheels that carries a display in a parade.
float • ***verb*** **floated, floating** • ***noun**, plural* **floats**

flock (fläk) ***noun*** **1** a group of animals or birds that live, feed, and travel together [a *flock* of sheep; a *flock* of geese]. **2** a large group of people or things [*flocks* of tourists].
verb to come or travel together in a group ["Birds of a feather *flock* together."]
flock • ***noun**, plural* **flocks** • ***verb*** **flocked, flocking**

floe (flō) ***noun*** a large sheet of floating ice.
floe • ***noun**, plural* **floes**
● The words **floe** and **flow** sound alike.
An ice *floe* is not safe for skating.
The *flow* of traffic is heavy at noon.

flood (flud) ***noun*** **1** a great overflow of water onto a place that is usually dry. **2** a great flow of anything [a *flood* of tears; a *flood* of tourists].
verb **1** to flow over its banks onto nearby land [The river *floods* every spring.] **2** to cover or fill with water [The heavy rains *flooded* the basement.] **3** to flow, cover, or fill like a flood [The sound of music *flooded* the room.]
flood • ***noun**, plural* **floods** • ***verb*** **flooded, flooding**

floodlight (flud′līt) ***noun*** a lamp that sends out a broad beam of bright light.
flood·light • ***noun**, plural* **floodlights**

floor (flôr) ***noun*** **1** the surface of a room that a person stands or walks on. **2** the bottom surface of anything [the ocean *floor*]. **3** a story of a building [an office on the fifth *floor*].
verb **1** to cover with a floor [They *floored* the room with tile.] **2** to knock down [The boxer *floored* his opponent.] **3** [*an informal use*] to puzzle or confuse [Her answer *floored* me.]
floor • ***noun**, plural* **floors** • ***verb*** **floored, flooring**

flop (fläp) ***verb*** **1** to move or flap about in a loose or clumsy way [The fish *flopped* about in the bottom of the boat.] **2** to fall or drop in this way [She *flopped* into a chair.] **3** [*an informal use*] to fail [Our school play *flopped*.]
noun **1** the act or sound of flopping. **2** [*an informal use*] a failure.
flop • ***verb*** **flopped, flopping** • ***noun**, plural* **flops**

floppy (fläp′ē) [*an informal use*] ***adjective*** flopping or tending to flop [a *floppy* hat].
flop·py • ***adjective*** **floppier, floppiest**

floppy disk ***noun*** a small, flexible computer disk that stores data for small computers.
floppy disk • ***noun**, plural* **floppy disks**

flora (flôr′ə) ***noun*** all the plants of a particular place or time [the *flora* of Alaska].
flo·ra • ***noun**, plural* **floras**

floral (flôr′əl) ***adjective*** having to do with, made up of, or like flowers [a *floral* arrangement].
flo·ral • ***adjective***

STATE MAP

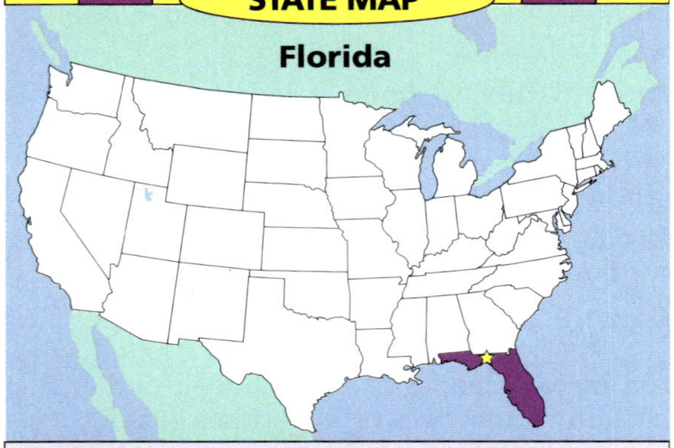

Statehood: 1845, the 27th state • **Capital:** Tallahassee

a cat	ō go	ʉ fur	ə = a *in* ago
ā ape	ô law, for	ch chin	e *in* agent
ä cot, car	oo look	sh she	i *in* pencil
e ten	ōō tool	th thin	o *in* atom
ē me	oi oil	*th* then	u *in* circus
i fit	ou out	zh measure	
ī ice	u up	ŋ ring	

Florida (flôr′i də) a State in the southeastern part of the U.S. Its capital is Tallahassee. Abbreviated **FL** or **Fla.**
Flor·i·da

florist (flôr′ist) ***noun*** a person whose business is selling flowers and house plants.
flo·rist • ***noun,*** *plural* **florists**

floss (flôs) ***noun*** thin, strong thread used for cleaning between the teeth. The full name of this thread is **dental floss**.
verb to clean between the teeth with dental floss.
floss • ***noun,*** *plural* **flosses** • ***verb*** **flossed, flossing**

flounder[1] (floun′dər) ***verb*** **1** to move in a clumsy way [He *floundered* about in the mud.] **2** to speak or act in a clumsy or confused way.
floun·der • ***verb*** **floundered, floundering**

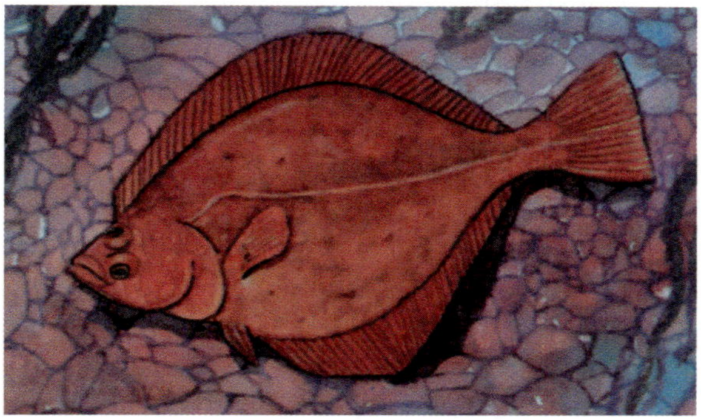

flounder

flounder[2] (floun′dər) ***noun*** a kind of flatfish that is caught for food.
floun·der • ***noun,*** *plural* **flounders** or **flounder**

flour (flour) ***noun*** a fine powder that is made by grinding wheat or other grain. Flour is used to make bread, spaghetti, and other foods.
flour • ***noun,*** *plural* **flours**

flourish (flur′ish) ***verb*** **1** to grow well and in a strong way; be successful or healthy; prosper [These plants will *flourish* in full sun. The arts *flourished* in ancient Greece.] **2** to wave in the air [The pirate *flourished* his sword.]
noun a sweeping movement [The actress entered the room with a *flourish*.]
flour·ish • ***verb*** **flourished, flourishing** • ***noun,*** *plural* **flourishes**

flow (flō) ***verb*** **1** to move in a stream as water does [Oil *flows* through the pipeline. The crowds *flowed* by.] **2** to move in a smooth and easy way [The talk *flowed* on for hours.] **3** to hang loose [Her hair *flowed* down her back.]
noun **1** the act, way, or amount of flowing [trying to stop the *flow* of lava]. **2** anything that moves along in a steady way; a stream or current [a steady *flow* of traffic].
flow • ***verb*** **flowed, flowing** • ***noun,*** *plural* **flows**

● The words **flow** and **floe** sound alike.
Don't try to swim against the *flow*.
The bear was trapped on the ice *floe*.

flower (flou′ər) ***noun*** **1** the part of a plant that bears the seeds and usually has brightly colored petals; a blossom or bloom. **2** a plant grown for its blossoms.
verb to come into bloom; bear flowers [Daffodils and tulips *flower* in the early spring.]
flow·er • ***noun,*** *plural* **flowers** • ***verb*** **flowered, flowering**

flown (flōn) ***verb*** *past participle of* **fly**[1].

flu (flo͞o) ***noun*** *a short form of* **influenza**.
flu • ***noun,*** *plural* **flus**

● The words **flu, flew,** and **flue** sound alike.
I was in bed with the *flu* for a week.
The birds *flew* off.
The *flue* in our chimney needs cleaning.

flue (flo͞o) ***noun*** a pipe, tube, or passage through which smoke, steam, or hot air can escape. A flue is usually found inside a chimney.
flue • ***noun,*** *plural* **flues**

● The words **flue, flew,** and **flu** sound alike.

fluffy (fluf′ē) ***adjective*** **1** soft and light like feathers or cotton [*fluffy* pillows] —Look for the WORD CHOICES box at the entry **soft**. **2** covered with downy material [*fluffy* slippers].
fluff·y • ***adjective*** **fluffier, fluffiest**

fluid (flo͞o′id) ***noun*** a substance that flows; any liquid or gas. Air, water, and molten metal are fluids.
adjective capable of flowing [Water remains *fluid* at temperatures above 32°F.]
flu·id • ***noun,*** *plural* **fluids** • ***adjective***

flung (fluŋ) ***verb*** *past tense and past participle of* **fling**.

flunk (fluŋk) [*an informal word*] ***verb*** to fail in schoolwork, such as a test.
flunk • ***verb*** **flunked, flunking**

fluorescent (flôr es′ənt) ***adjective*** capable of producing a cool light when acted on by some

form of energy, such as an electric current [*fluorescent* lights].
flu·o·res·cent • ***adjective***

fluoride (flôr′īd) ***noun*** a chemical made up of fluorine combined with some other element or elements. Various kinds of fluoride are put into drinking water and toothpaste to help prevent tooth decay.
flu·o·ride • ***noun,*** *plural* **fluorides**

fluorine (flôr′ēn) ***noun*** a greenish-yellow poisonous gas that is a chemical element. It combines very easily with most other elements, and many of these compounds are not poisonous.
flu·o·rine • ***noun***

flurry (flʉr′ē) ***noun*** **1** a sudden, light fall of rain or snow. **2** a sudden state of confusion [a *flurry* of excitement].
flur·ry • ***noun,*** *plural* **flurries**

flush (flush) ***verb*** **1** to become red in the face; blush [He *flushed* with anger.] **2** to empty out with a sudden flow of water [*Flush* the toilet.]
noun a blush or reddish glow [a healthy *flush* on their cheeks].
adjective being even or on the same line or plane with [a door that is *flush* with the wall].
flush • ***verb*** **flushed, flushing** • ***noun,*** *plural* **flushes** • ***adjective***

fluster (flus′tər) ***verb*** to make or become excited and confused.
flus·ter • ***verb*** **flustered, flustering**

flute

flute (flo͞ot) ***noun*** a woodwind instrument with a high pitch. It is a long, thin tube that is played by blowing across a hole at one end. The tones are changed by opening or closing holes along the side with the fingers or with keys.
flute • ***noun,*** *plural* **flutes**

flutist (flo͞ot′ist) ***noun*** a flute player.
flut·ist • ***noun,*** *plural* **flutists**

flutter (flut′ər) ***verb*** **1** to flap the wings quickly in flying or without flying at all [Butterflies *fluttered* by. The sick bird *fluttered* helplessly.] **2** to wave rapidly [The flag *fluttered* in the breeze.]
noun **1** a quick, light flapping motion. **2** a state of excitement or confusion [Her parents were in a *flutter* over the wedding.]
flut·ter • ***verb*** **fluttered, fluttering** • ***noun,*** *plural* **flutters**

fly[1] (flī) ***verb*** **1** to move through the air by using wings [An ostrich is a bird that cannot *fly*.] **2** to be carried through the air [Bits of paper were *flying* about in the wind.] **3** to travel or carry through the air in an aircraft or spacecraft [We *flew* in supplies for the survivors.] **4** to pilot an aircraft or spacecraft [She is learning to *fly*.] **5** to display, wave, or float in the air [A flag *flew* from the top of the monument.] **6** to move swiftly [The door *flew* open. Time *flies*.] **7** to hit a fly in baseball.
noun **1** a flap of cloth that covers a set of buttons or a zipper in a garment, especially on the front of trousers. **2** a baseball that is batted high in the air inside the foul lines.
—**fly out** to be put out in baseball by hitting a fly that is caught.
fly • ***verb*** **flew** *or* **flied** (*for sense 7*), **flown** *or* **flied** (*for sense 7*), **flying, flies** • ***noun,*** *plural* **flies**

fly[2] (flī) ***noun*** **1** *a short form of* **housefly. 2** a flying insect that has one pair of wings. Houseflies and gnats are flies.
fly • ***noun,*** *plural* **flies**

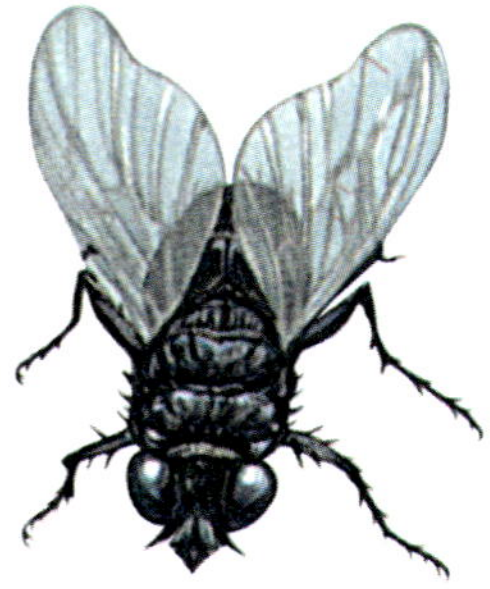
fly

flycatcher (flī′kach ər) ***noun*** a small bird that catches flying insects. There are many different kinds of flycatcher.
fly·catch·er • ***noun,*** *plural* **flycatchers**

flyer (flī′ər) ***noun*** *another spelling of* **flier.**
fly·er • ***noun,*** *plural* **flyers**

flying fish ***noun*** a fish of warm seas that has

a cat	ō go	ʉr fur	ə = a *in* ago
ā ape	ô law, for	ch chin	e *in* agent
ä cot, car	o͝o look	sh she	i *in* pencil
e ten	o͞o tool	th thin	o *in* atom
ē me	oi oil	*th* then	u *in* circus
i fit	ou out	zh measure	
ī ice	u up	ŋ ring	

a pair of fins like wings. It can leap out of the water and use its fins to glide through the air.
flying fish • *noun, plural* **flying fishes**

flying saucer *noun another name for* **UFO**.
flying saucer • *noun, plural* **flying saucers**

foal (fōl) *noun* a very young horse, mule, zebra, or similar animal.
foal • *noun, plural* **foals**

foam (fōm) *noun* **1** a mass of tiny bubbles that is formed on liquids. Foam is whitish and can be formed when the liquid is shaken. **2** saliva or something else that looks like foam.
verb to form or collect foam [The mad dog *foamed* at the mouth.]
foam • *noun, plural* **foams**
• *verb* **foamed, foaming**

foam rubber *noun* rubber that is made in the form of firm sponge. Foam rubber is used for seats, mattresses, and pillows.

focus
Out of focus

focus (fō′kəs) *noun* **1** a point where rays of light or heat, for example, come together or from which they spread. **2** an adjustment made to a lens in order to make clear the thing being viewed. [By turning a knob, one can change the *focus* of a microscope and see a slide more clearly.] **3** a center of activity or interest [A baby is a *focus* of attention.]
verb **1** to bring to a focus [*Focus* the sun's rays on a piece of paper and burn a hole.] **2** to adjust the eye or a lens in order to make a clear image [Glasses help him to *focus* his eyes on small print.] **3** to fix on something; direct [When the TV is off, I can *focus* on homework.]
fo·cus • *noun, plural* **focuses** • *verb* **focused** or **focussed, focusing** or **focussing**

fodder (fäd′ər) *noun* hay, straw, stalks of corn, or other dry food for farm animals.
fod·der • *noun*

foe (fō) *noun* an enemy or opponent.
foe • *noun, plural* **foes**

fog (fôg) *noun* **1** a large mass of tiny drops of water floating near the ground. Fog is a thick mist that is hard to see through —Look for the WORD CHOICES box at the entry **mist**. **2** a condition of being confused and bewildered [After taking the medicine, I was in a *fog*.]
verb to cover or become covered with fog or with something like fog [The bathroom mirror *fogged* up.]
fog • *noun, plural* **fogs** • *verb* **fogged, fogging**

foggy (fôg′ē) *adjective* **1** full of fog [a *foggy* day]. **2** mixed up; confused [a *foggy* idea].
fog·gy • *adjective* **foggier, foggiest**

foghorn (fôg′hôrn) *noun* a horn that is blown during a fog to warn ships of danger.
fog·horn • *noun, plural* **foghorns**

foil[1] (foil) *verb* to keep from being successful; stop [The police *foiled* the robbery.]
foil • *verb* **foiled, foiling**

foil[2] (foil) *noun* a very thin sheet of metal [aluminum *foil*].
foil • *noun, plural* **foils**

fold (fōld) *verb* **1** to bend something over upon itself so that one part is on top of another [*Fold* the letter twice.] **2** to bring together and twist around one another [She *folded* her arms.] **3** to clasp or embrace [He *folded* his baby in his arms.] **4** [*an informal use*] to fail [Their new business *folded*.]
noun **1** a layer made in folding [The handkerchief has six *folds*.] **2** a mark or crease made by folding [Cut the sheet along the *fold*.]
fold • *verb* **folded, folding** • *noun, plural* **folds**

folder (fōl′dər) *noun* **1** a folded piece of heavy paper or cardboard that is used to hold loose papers. **2** a booklet that is made of folded sheets [a travel *folder*].
fold·er • *noun, plural* **folders**

foliage (fō′lē ij) *noun* the leaves of a tree or plant, or of many trees or plants.
fo·li·age • *noun*

folk (fōk) *noun* **1** people or persons in general [The farmer disliked city *folk*. *Folks* differ in their tastes.] **2 folks** parents or other relatives [Her *folks* live in Virginia.]
adjective of or having to do with the common people [*folk* medicine; a *folk* hero].

F

folk • *noun, plural* **folk** or **folks** • *adjective*

folk dance *noun* a dance that the common people of a region or country have danced over a long period of time.
folk dance • *noun, plural* **folk dances**

folklore (fōk′lôr) *noun* the beliefs, stories, and customs that have been handed down among the common people of a region or country for a long time.
folk·lore • *noun*

folk music *noun* the traditional music of the common people of a region or country. It is usually handed down from one generation to the next and its composers are often unknown.

folk singer *noun* a person who sings folk songs.
folk singer • *noun, plural* **folk singers**

folk song *noun* **1** a song that has been handed down among the common people of a region or country for a long time. **2** a song composed in the style of a traditional folk song.
folk song • *noun, plural* **folk songs**

folk tale *noun* a story that has been handed down among the common people of a region or country for a long time.
folk tale • *noun, plural* **folk tales**

follow (fä′lō) *verb* **1** to come or go after [A dog *followed* him home. Who *followed* Washington as President?] **2** to travel along [*Follow* this road for two miles.] **3** to come as a result [Sal worked hard, and success *followed*.] **4** to watch or listen to closely [She *follows* the news on TV.] **5** to understand [I can't *follow* your explanation.] **6** to be guided or led by [Just *follow* the instructions.]
fol·low • *verb* **followed, following**

follower (fä′lō ər) *noun* **1** a person or thing that follows. **2** a person who follows another's teachings or supports certain beliefs [*followers* of Islam]. **3** an attendant or servant [The king and his *followers* went hunting.]
fol·low·er • *noun, plural* **followers**

following (fä′lō iŋ) *adjective* going or coming after [She went home the *following* day.]
noun a group of fans or disciples [The baseball team has a large *following*.]
—**the following** the persons or things to be mentioned next [She bought *the following*: shoes, hats, dresses, and handbags.]
fol·low·ing • *adjective* • *noun, plural* **followings**

folly (fä′lē) *noun* a lack of good sense [the *folly* of dropping out of school].
fol·ly • *noun, plural* **follies**

fond (fänd) *adjective* loving and tender [*fond* parents; a *fond* kiss].
—**fond of** having a liking for [*fond of* cats].
fond • *adjective* **fonder, fondest**

food (fo͞od) *noun* anything that is taken in by a plant or animal to keep up its life and growth; what is eaten or drunk by an animal or absorbed by a plant.
food • *noun, plural* **foods**

food processor (präs′es ər) *noun* an electrical appliance for mixing, slicing, grating, or chopping foods.
food proc·ess·or • *noun, plural* **food processors**

fool (fo͞ol) *noun* **1** a person who lacks judgment or good sense; a silly or stupid person. **2** a man kept by a nobleman or king of earlier times to entertain people.
verb **1** to get someone to believe something that is not true; deceive; trick [He *fooled* her by pretending to be asleep.] —Look for the WORD CHOICES box at the entry **deceive**. **2** to speak or act in a playful way [I was only *fooling*.]
—**fool around** [*an informal use*] to spend time in a useless way; to waste time. —**fool with** [*an informal use*] to use in a foolish way.
fool • *noun, plural* **fools** • *verb* **fooled, fooling**

foolish (fo͞ol′ish) *adjective* without good sense; silly [a *foolish* remark; *foolish* behavior].
fool·ish • *adjective*

foot (foot) *noun* **1** the end part of the leg of a person or animal, on which it stands or moves. **2** the lowest part; base [the *foot* of a page; the *foot* of a mountain]. **3** the part that is farthest from the head or beginning [the *foot* of the bed]. **4** the part that covers the foot [the *foot* of a stocking]. **5** a unit of length that is equal to 12 inches or 0.3048 meter.
—**on foot** walking or running rather than riding. —**put one's foot down** [*an informal use*] to be firm [The coach *put his foot down* and told the players that they could not miss prac-

a cat	ō go	ʉ fur	ə = a *in* ago
ā ape	ô law, for	ch chin	e *in* agent
ä cot, car	oo look	sh she	i *in* pencil
e ten	o͞o tool	th thin	o *in* atom
ē me	oi oil	*th* then	u *in* circus
i fit	ou out	zh measure	
ī ice	u up	ŋ ring	

tice.] —**under foot** in the way [The dog is always *under foot* when we're cooking.]
foot • *noun, plural* **feet**

football (foot′bôl) *noun* **1** a game played with an oval, inflated leather ball by two teams of 11 players each. It is played on a long field with a goal at each end. **2** the ball used in this game.
foot·ball • *noun, plural* **footballs**

foothill (foot′hil) *noun* a low hill at or near the bottom of a mountain or mountain range.
foot·hill • *noun, plural* **foothills**

footing (foot′iŋ) *noun* **1** a firm placing of the feet [She lost her *footing* on the icy bridge and fell.] **2** a place to put the foot down safely [There's no *footing* on that icy surface.] **3** the way things are arranged; condition or relationship [We are on a friendly *footing* with our neighbors.]
foot·ing • *noun, plural* **footings**

footlights (foot′līts) *plural noun* a row of lights along the front of a stage floor.
foot·lights • *plural noun*

footnote (foot′nōt) *noun* a note at the bottom of a page that explains something on the page.
foot·note • *noun, plural* **footnotes**

footprint (foot′print) *noun* a mark made by a foot or shoe.
foot·print • *noun, plural* **footprints**

footstep (foot′step) *noun* **1** a step taken in walking. **2** the sound of a step. **3** a footprint.
foot·step • *noun, plural* **footsteps**

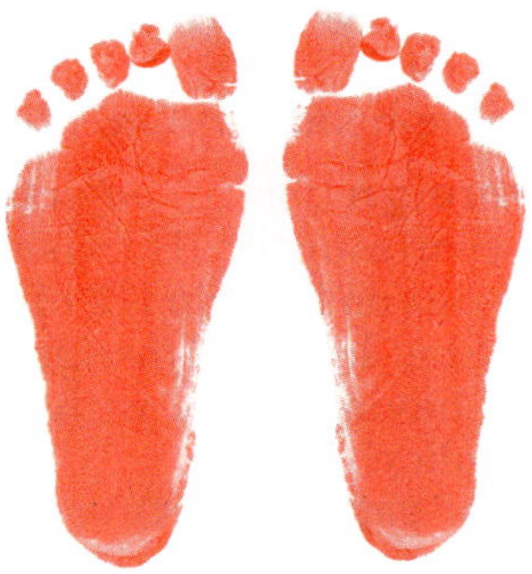

footprint

footstool

footstool (foot′stōōl) *noun* a low stool that is used as a rest for the feet while sitting.
foot·stool • *noun, plural* **footstools**

for (fôr *or* fər) *preposition* **1** meant to be received by or used in [a present *for* you; money *for* paying bills]. **2** because of [He was praised *for* his honesty.] **3** in search of [hunting *for* berries]. **4** in place of; instead of [Let's use our coats *for* blankets.] **5** on the side of; in support of [I will vote *for* the new tax for the library.] **6** in honor of [The baby was named *for* her aunt.] **7** in order to be, have, or get [We left *for* home. I asked *for* Mae.] **8** with regard to; concerning [a need *for* understanding]. **9** if a person considers; considering [She's tall *for* her age.] **10** as compared with [Try to save a dime *for* every dollar you earn.] **11** in the amount of; equal to [a bill *for* $20]. **12** at the price of [He's selling them *for* ten cents each.] **13** to the distance of; as far as [Every day we walk *for* two miles.] **14** as long as; through the time of [The movie runs *for* an hour.] **15** at a certain time [I have an appointment *for* one o'clock.]
conjunction because; since [Help her, *for* she is in pain.]
• The words **for** and **four** sound alike.
The recipe calls *for* one cup of sugar.
The recipe calls for *four* eggs.

forage (fôr′ij) *verb* **1** to go about looking for food [The sheep were *foraging* in the meadow.] **2** to look about for what one needs or wants; search [I *foraged* in the attic for some old magazines.]
for·age • *verb* **foraged, foraging**

forbade or **forbad** (fər bad′) *verb past tense of* **forbid**.
for·bade or **for·bad** • *verb*

forbid (fər bid′) *verb* to order not to do something; prohibit [Loud talking is *forbidden*.]
for·bid • *verb* **forbade** or **forbad, forbidden, forbidding**

WORD CHOICES

Synonyms of **forbid**

The words **forbid**, **ban**, and **prohibit** share the meaning "to have a rule against doing something."

Most libraries *forbid* loud talking.
Our town *bans* the sale of guns.
They *prohibit* smoking in this building.

forbidden (fər bid′n) ***verb*** *past participle of* **forbid**.
for·bid·den • ***verb***

force (fôrs) ***noun*** **1** power or energy that can do or make something [Electricity is a powerful natural *force*. The *force* of the high winds broke the windows.] **2** power or strength used against a person or thing [The police used *force* to scatter the crowd.] **3** the power to cause motion or to stop or change motion [the *force* of gravity]. **4** a group of people working together for some special purpose [a sales *force;* a military *force*].
verb **1** to make do something by using strength or power of some kind [You shouldn't *force* him to go.] **2** to break open or through by using strength [He *forced* the lock.] **3** to get or put by using strength [Can you *force* the lid off this jar?]
force • ***noun,*** *plural* **forces** • ***verb*** **forced, forcing**

forceful (fôrs′fəl) ***adjective*** having much force; strong; powerful; vigorous [a *forceful* speech] —Look for the WORD CHOICES box at the entry **active**.
force·ful • ***adjective***

forceps (fôr′seps) ***noun*** a tool that looks like a pair of small tongs or pincers. It is used for holding and pulling by dentists and surgeons.
for·ceps • ***noun,*** *plural* **forceps**

ford (fôrd) ***noun*** a shallow place in a river or stream where a person can walk or ride across.
verb to cross a river or stream at a shallow place.
ford • ***noun,*** *plural* **fords** • ***verb*** **forded, fording**

Ford (fôrd), **Gerald R., Jr.** (jer′əld) 1913-2006; the thirty-eighth president of the U.S., from 1974 to 1977.
Ford, Ger·ald R., Jr.

Ford (fôrd), **Henry** (hen′rē) 1863-1947; U.S. businessman and maker of automobiles.
Ford, Hen·ry

fore- *a prefix meaning:* **1** before [When the witch in the story was *foretelling* the king's future, she was telling what would happen before it did happen.] **2** the front part of [The *forehead* is on the front of the head.]

forearm (fôr′ärm) ***noun*** the part of the arm between the elbow and the wrist.
fore·arm • ***noun,*** *plural* **forearms**

forecast (fôr′kast) ***verb*** to tell or try to tell what will happen ahead of time; predict [The weather report *forecasts* rain for tomorrow.] —Look for the WORD CHOICES box at the entry **foretell**.
noun a statement of what will happen; prediction [a weather *forecast*].
fore·cast • ***verb*** **forecast** or **forecasted, forecasting** • ***noun,*** *plural* **forecasts**

forefather (fôr′fä *th*ər) ***noun*** an ancestor.
fore·fa·ther • ***noun,*** *plural* **forefathers**

forefinger (fôr′fiŋ gər) ***noun*** the finger nearest the thumb; index finger.
fore·fin·ger • ***noun,*** *plural* **forefingers**

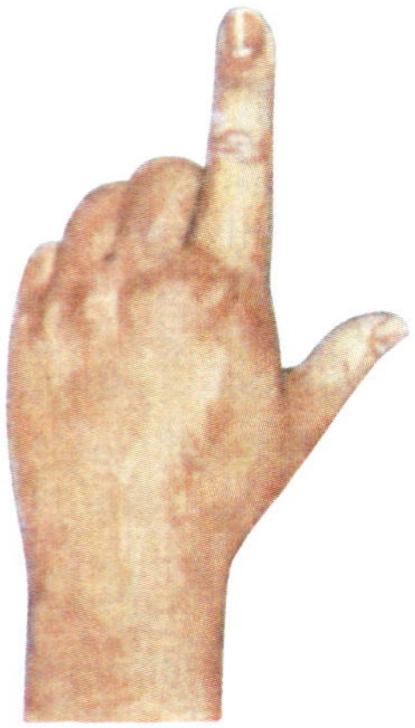
forefinger

foregone (fôr gôn′) ***adjective*** decided in advance; already known or done [Our defeat Sunday seemed a *foregone* conclusion.]
fore·gone • ***adjective***

forehead (fôr′hed *or* fôr′ed) ***noun*** the part of the face above the eyebrows.
fore·head • ***noun,*** *plural* **foreheads**

foreign (fôr′in) ***adjective*** **1** outside a person's own country [He visited many *foreign* countries on his trip.] **2** of or from another country [She learned *foreign* languages in school.] **3** having to do with other countries [*foreign* policy].
for·eign • ***adjective***

foreigner (fôr′in ər) ***noun*** a person who is from another country.
for·eign·er • ***noun,*** *plural* **foreigners**

foreleg (fôr′leg) ***noun*** one of the front legs of an animal that has four legs.
fore·leg • ***noun,*** *plural* **forelegs**

foreman (fôr′mən) ***noun*** **1** a person who is in charge of a group of workers [a *foreman* in a factory]. **2** the person on a jury who serves as its leader and speaks for the jury in court.
fore·man • ***noun,*** *plural* **foremen**

a	cat	ō	go	ʉ	fur	ə =	a *in* ago
ā	ape	ô	law, for	ch	chin		e *in* agent
ä	cot, car	oo	look	sh	she		i *in* pencil
e	ten	ōō	tool	th	thin		o *in* atom
ē	me	oi	oil	*th*	then		u *in* circus
i	fit	ou	out	zh	measure		
ī	ice	u	up	ŋ	ring		

foremost (fôr′mōst) ***adjective*** first in position or importance [today's *foremost* scientists].
fore·most • ***adjective***

forerunner (fôr′run ər) ***noun*** something that comes before another thing [Adding machines were the *forerunners* of modern calculators.]
fore·run·ner • ***noun,*** *plural* **forerunners**

foresaw (fôr sô′ *or* fôr sä′) ***verb*** *past tense of* **foresee**.
fore·saw • ***verb***

foresee (fôr sē′) ***verb*** to see or know ahead of time [Can you *foresee* the future?]
fore·see • ***verb*** **foresaw, foreseen, foreseeing**

foreseen (fôr sēn′) ***verb*** *past participle of* **foresee**.
fore·seen • ***verb***

foresight (fôr′sīt) ***noun*** the ability to look ahead and plan for the future [I'm glad you had the *foresight* to bring along a snack.]
fore·sight • ***noun***

forest (fôr′əst) ***noun*** a thick growth of trees covering a large piece of land; large woods.
for·est • ***noun,*** *plural* **forests**

forestry (fôr′əs trē) ***noun*** the science and work of planting and taking care of forests.
for·est·ry • ***noun***

foretell (fôr tel′) ***verb*** to tell or show what will take place in the future; predict [The witches *foretold* that he would kill the dragon.]
fore·tell • ***verb*** **foretold, foretelling**

WORD CHOICES

Synonyms of **foretell**

The words **foretell, forecast,** and **predict** share the meaning "to tell what one thinks will happen."

The generals could not *foretell* the outcome of the war.

Can you *forecast* the weather?

He *predicted* which team would win.

foretold (fôr tōld′) ***verb*** *past tense and past participle of* **foretell**.
fore·told • ***verb***

forever (fôr ev′ər) ***adverb*** **1** for all time; without ever coming to an end [Nothing lasts *forever*.] **2** always; at all times; constantly [The phone was *forever* ringing.]
for·ev·er • ***adverb***

foreword (fôr′wurd) ***noun*** a piece of writing at the beginning of a book that tells something about it; introduction.
fore·word • ***noun,*** *plural* **forewords**

forfeit (fôr′fit) ***verb*** to have to give up or lose something because of a mistake or a failure to do something [Because our team was late in arriving, we had to *forfeit* the game.]
noun the act of forfeiting [The loss of the rented tape resulted in the *forfeit* of her deposit.]
for·feit • ***verb*** **forfeited, forfeiting** • ***noun,*** *plural* **forfeits**

forgave (fər gāv′) ***verb*** *past tense of* **forgive**.
for·gave • ***verb***

forge[1] (fôrj) ***noun*** **1** a furnace or fire where metal is heated. The fire softens the metal so that it can be hammered or bent into shape. **2** a place where such work with metal is done.
verb **1** to shape by heating and pounding [He *forged* iron into a pair of horseshoes.] **2** to form or make by steady work or effort [The sergeant *forged* the recruits into real soldiers.] **3** to make a copy of something in order to trick or deceive [He *forged* the paintings and tried to sell them to the art museum.] **4** to commit the crime of copying someone else's signature on a bank check.
forge • ***noun,*** *plural* **forges** • ***verb*** **forged, forging**

forge[2] (fôrj) ***verb*** to move ahead with difficulty in a steady way or move with sudden speed and energy [Julia *forged* ahead and won the race.]
forge • ***verb*** **forged, forging**

forget (fər get′) ***verb*** **1** to be unable to remember; fail to keep in the memory [I *forgot* her address.] **2** to fail to do, bring, take, or act because one is careless [I *forgot* my books again.]
for·get • ***verb*** **forgot, forgotten** or **forgot, forgetting**

forgetful (fər get′fəl) ***adjective*** always forgetting things; having a poor memory [She's so *forgetful* she can't remember her own address.]
for·get·ful • ***adjective***

forget-me-not (fər get′mē nät′) ***noun*** a low-growing plant that has clusters of small blue, white, or pink flowers.
for·get-me-not • ***noun,*** *plural* **forget-me-nots**

F

forgive (fər giv′) ***verb*** to stop being angry at or wanting to punish; excuse or pardon [She *forgave* him for his rudeness to her.]
for·give • ***verb*** **forgave, forgiven, forgiving**

forgiven (fər giv′ən) ***verb*** *past participle of* **forgive**.
for·giv·en • ***verb***

forgiveness (fər giv′nəs) ***noun*** the act of forgiving [He asked for her *forgiveness* for his being rude.]
for·give·ness • ***noun***

forgot (fər gät′) ***verb*** *past tense and a past participle of* **forget**.
for·got • ***verb***

forgotten (fər gät′n) ***verb*** *a past participle of* **forget**.
for·got·ten • ***verb***

fork (fôrk) ***noun*** **1** a tool with a handle at one end and two or more points or prongs at the other. Forks are used to pick up things. Small forks are used in eating and large forks are used for pitching hay on a farm. **2** the point where something divides into two or more branches [the *fork* of a road; the *fork* of a tree].
verb to divide into branches [Go left where the road *forks*.]
fork • ***noun,*** *plural* **forks** • ***verb*** **forked, forking**

forlorn (fôr lôrn′) ***adjective*** lonely and sad; unhappy.
for·lorn • ***adjective***

form (fôrm) ***noun*** **1** a shape or outline; figure [I saw a dark *form* against the sky.] **2** the way something is put together to make it what it is; kind [Ice and snow are *forms* of water.] **3** a way of doing something; style [She is working to improve her *form* in golf.] **4** the ability to perform with skill [The boxer was in good *form* for the fight.] **5** a printed sheet of paper that has blank spaces to be filled in [an order *form*]. **6** any of the ways in which a word is changed for different uses ["Am" is a *form* of "be."]
verb **1** to give a particular shape to; make [She *formed* the wet sand into a castle.] **2** to take shape [An idea *formed* in his mind.] **3** to come together in order to make [Let's *form* a hiking club.] **4** to make up out of separate parts [The U.S. is *formed* of 50 States.]
form • ***noun,*** *plural* **forms** • ***verb*** **formed, forming**

formal (fôr′məl) ***adjective*** **1** following the usual rules or customs in an exact way [The ambassador paid a *formal* visit to the President.] **2** made for wear at ceremonies or fancy parties [*formal* clothing].
noun **1** a dance at which people are expected to wear formal clothes. **2** a woman's long evening dress.
for·mal • ***adjective*** • ***noun,*** *plural* **formals**

formation (fôr mā′shən) ***noun*** **1** the act or process of forming [The *formation* of a new island is a rare event.] **2** something that has been formed [Scientists studied the rock *formations* of the canyon.] **3** the way something is formed or put together; arrangement [The geese flew in a V *formation*.]
for·ma·tion • ***noun,*** *plural* **formations**

former (fôr′mər) ***adjective*** **1** coming before; earlier; past [in *former* times; a *former* senator]. **2** being the first of two just mentioned [In the contest between Kennedy and Nixon, the *former* was elected.]
for·mer • ***adjective***

formerly (fôr′mər lē) ***adverb*** at an earlier time; in the past [Mexico *formerly* belonged to Spain.]
for·mer·ly • ***adverb***

formula (fôr′myoo lə) ***noun*** **1** a group of symbols and figures that show the elements in a chemical compound [The *formula* for water is H_2O.] **2** a set of directions for doing or making something; a recipe or set of ingredients [a *formula* for a new perfume]. **3** a special food that is made for a baby to drink from a bottle. **4** a fixed way of doing something [a TV show written according to the same old *formula*].
for·mu·la • ***noun,*** *plural* **formulas**

formulate (fôr′myoo lāt) ***verb*** to put into words in a clear and exact way [The scientist *formulated* a new theory.]
for·mu·late • ***verb*** **formulated, formulating**

forsake (fôr sāk′) ***verb*** to go away from or give up; leave; abandon [She will never *forsake* a friend in trouble.] —Look for the WORD CHOICES box at the entry **abandon**.
for·sake • ***verb*** **forsook, forsaken, forsaking**

forsaken (fôr sā′kən) ***verb*** *past participle of* **forsake**.
for·sak·en • ***verb***

forsook (fôr sook′) ***verb*** *past tense of* **forsake**.
for·sook • ***verb***

a	cat	ō	go	ʉ	fur	ə = a *in* ago	
ā	ape	ô	law, for	ch	chin	e *in* agent	
ä	cot, car	oo	look	sh	she	i *in* pencil	
e	ten	o͞o	tool	th	thin	o *in* atom	
ē	me	oi	oil	*th*	then	u *in* circus	
i	fit	ou	out	zh	measure		
ī	ice	u	up	ŋ	ring		

forsythia (fôr sith′ē ə) ***noun*** a shrub that has yellow flowers that bloom in the early spring.
for·syth·i·a • ***noun,*** *plural* **forsythias**

fort (fôrt) ***noun*** a building with strong walls, guns, and other equipment for defending against attacks by an enemy.
fort • ***noun,*** *plural* **forts**

forth (fôrth) ***adverb*** **1** forward or onward [I never left the house from that day *forth*.] **2** into view; out [The bears came *forth* from their den.]

- The words **forth** and **fourth** sound alike.
  A rocking chair moves back and *forth*.
  She enters the *fourth* grade this fall.

fortieth (fôrt′ē əth) ***adjective*** being ten more than thirty others in a series; 40th in order.
noun **1** the number, person, or thing that is fortieth. **2** one of forty equal parts of something; 1/40.
for·ti·eth • ***adjective*** • ***noun,*** *plural* **fortieths**

fortification (fôrt′i fi kā′shən) ***noun*** **1** the act of fortifying [the *fortification* of the castle]. **2** a structure that is used to fortify or defend.
for·ti·fi·ca·tion • ***noun,*** *plural* **fortifications**

fortify (fôrt′i fī) ***verb*** **1** to make stronger; strengthen [They *fortified* the city by building walls.] **2** to add vitamins and minerals to [This milk is *fortified* with vitamin D.]
for·ti·fy • ***verb*** **fortified, fortifying, fortifies**

fortress (fôr′trəs) ***noun*** a fort or other strong place.
for·tress • ***noun,*** *plural* **fortresses**

fortunate (fôr′chə nət) ***adjective*** having or bringing good luck; lucky [a *fortunate* man].
for·tu·nate • ***adjective***

fortune (fôr′chən) ***noun*** **1** the supposed power that brings good or bad to people; luck [I have the good *fortune* to have loving parents.] **2** what is going to happen to a person in the future [The gypsy told me my *fortune*.] **3** a large sum of money; wealth [She inherited a *fortune*.]
for·tune • ***noun,*** *plural* **fortunes**

fortuneteller (fôr′chən tel ər) ***noun*** a person who claims to be able to tell what is going to happen in people's lives.
for·tune·tell·er • ***noun,*** *plural* **fortunetellers**

forty (fôrt′ē) ***noun*** the cardinal number that is equal to four times ten; 40.
adjective being four times ten [*forty* acres].
for·ty • ***noun,*** *plural* **forties** • ***adjective***

forum (fôr′əm) ***noun*** **1** the main public square of an ancient Roman city. The forum was the place where people gathered for business and meetings. **2** a meeting of people to discuss public matters.
fo·rum • ***noun,*** *plural* **forums**

forward (fôr′wərd) ***adjective*** **1** at, toward, or of the front [the *forward* part of the airplane]. **2** too bold or free in manners ["Don't be *forward!*" she scolded the boy.]
adverb **1** to the front; ahead [We moved *forward* slowly in the ticket line.] **2** toward the future [He looks *forward* to seeing her.]
noun a player in or near the front of the team in basketball, hockey, or certain other games.
verb to send on, especially to a new address [*Forward* his mail to California.]
for·ward • ***adjective*** • ***adverb*** • ***noun,*** *plural* **forwards** • ***verb*** **forwarded, forwarding**

forwards (fôr′wərdz) ***adverb*** *the same as the adverb* **forward**.
for·wards • ***adverb***

fossil (fäs′əl) ***noun*** the remains, prints, or traces of plants and animals that lived long ago. Fossils are found embedded in rocks or in other materials that form the earth's crust.
fos·sil • ***noun,*** *plural* **fossils**

WORD HISTORY

fossil

We get **fossil** from a Latin verb that means "to dig up." The English noun that developed from it started out with the meaning "a rock or mineral that has been dug out of the earth." Petrified wood and other **fossils** are usually found buried in the ground and must be dug up.

fossil fuel ***noun*** fuel that was formed from the remains of plants and animals from long ago. Coal, petroleum, and natural gas are fossil fuels.
fossil fuel • ***noun,*** *plural* **fossil fuels**

foster (fôs′tər) ***verb*** to help grow or develop;

encourage; promote [The piano teacher *fostered* his musical ability.]
adjective giving or receiving care in a family that is not related by birth or adoption [*foster* parents; a *foster* child].
fos·ter • ***verb*** **fostered, fostering** • ***adjective***

Foster (fôs′tər), **Stephen Collins** (stē′vən käl′inz) 1826-1864; U.S. composer of songs.
Fos·ter, Ste·phen Col·lins

fought (fôt *or* fät) ***verb*** *past tense and past participle of* **fight**.

foul (foul) ***adjective*** **1** having a bad taste, smell, or appearance; disgusting [a *foul* pigsty; a *foul* odor] —Look for the WORD CHOICES box at the entry **dirty**. **2** not clear; stormy [*foul* weather]. **3** very wicked; evil [a *foul* crime]. **4** not according to the rules; not fair [The boxer struck a *foul* blow below the belt.] **5** outside the foul lines in a baseball game [The batter hit a *foul* ball.]
noun **1** an act that is against the rules of a game [Pushing is a *foul* in basketball.] **2** a ball that is hit outside the foul lines in baseball.
verb **1** to make or become foul [Factory smoke *fouled* the air.] **2** to make a foul against in a game [The football player *fouled* an opponent by grabbing his uniform.] **3** to hit a baseball outside the foul lines.
foul • ***adjective*** **fouler, foulest** • ***noun,*** *plural* **fouls** • ***verb*** **fouled, fouling**
● The words **foul** and **fowl** sound alike.
Was the ball hit fair or *foul?*
The turkey is a *fowl.*

foul line ***noun*** in baseball, either of the two straight lines that run from home plate through the outside corners of first and third base to the end of the playing field.
foul line • ***noun,*** *plural* **foul lines**

found[1] (found) ***verb*** *past tense and past participle of* **find**.

found[2] (found) ***verb*** to set up; establish [They *founded* a new college.]
found • ***verb*** **founded, founding**

foundation (foun dā′shən) ***noun*** **1** the part at the bottom that supports a wall, house, or other structure; base [The *foundation* of the house was made of concrete.] **2** the basis on which something rests [A good education gives a person a good *foundation* for life. His story has no *foundation* in fact.] —Look for the WORD CHOICES box at the entry **base**[1]. **3** the act of founding [the *foundation* of a new college]. **4** an organization that controls a fund set up by gifts of money. The money is used for helping others or paying for research, for example.
foun·da·tion • ***noun,*** *plural* **foundations**

founder (foun′dər) ***noun*** a person who founds, or establishes [the *founder* of a city].
found·er • ***noun,*** *plural* **founders**

foundry (foun′drē) ***noun*** a place where metal is melted and cast into different shapes.
found·ry • ***noun,*** *plural* **foundries**

fountain (fount′n) ***noun*** **1** a structure that is built for a stream of water to rise and fall in [three large *fountains* in the park; a drinking *fountain*]. **2** a source [A library is a *fountain* of knowledge.]
foun·tain • ***noun,*** *plural* **fountains**

fountain

four (fôr) ***noun*** the cardinal number between three and five; 4.
adjective being one more than three [*four* seasons].
—on all fours on hands and knees [We were *on all fours*, looking for the lost pin.]
four • ***noun,*** *plural* **fours** • ***adjective***
● The words **four** and **for** sound alike.
She is *four* years old today.
He works *for* five dollars an hour.

four-footed (fôr′fo͝ot əd) ***adjective*** having four feet [The bear is a *four-footed* animal.]
four-foot·ed • ***adjective***

Four-H club or **4-H club** (fôr′āch′) ***noun*** a national club for young people living in farm areas. It gives training in farming and home economics.
Four-H club or **4-H club** • ***noun,*** *plural* **Four-H clubs** or **4-H clubs**

fourscore (fôr′skôr′) ***adjective*** four times twenty; 80 ["*Fourscore* and seven years ago..."]
four·score • ***adjective***

fourteen (fôr′tēn′) ***noun*** the cardinal number between thirteen and fifteen; 14.

a	cat	ō	go	ʉ	fur	ə = a	*in* ago
ā	ape	ô	law, for	ch	chin	e	*in* agent
ä	cot, car	o͝o	look	sh	she	i	*in* pencil
e	ten	o͞o	tool	th	thin	o	*in* atom
ē	me	oi	oil	*th*	then	u	*in* circus
i	fit	ou	out	zh	measure		
ī	ice	u	up	ŋ	ring		

adjective being one more than thirteen [*fourteen* pupils].
four·teen • *noun, plural* **fourteens**
• *adjective*

fourteenth (fôr′tēnth′) *adjective* coming after thirteen others in a series; 14th in order.
noun **1** the number, person, or thing that is fourteenth. **2** one of fourteen equal parts of something; $\frac{1}{14}$.
four·teenth • *adjective* • *noun, plural* **fourteenths**

fourth (fôrth) *adjective* coming after three others in a series; 4th in order.
noun **1** the number, person, or thing that is fourth. **2** one of four equal parts of something; $\frac{1}{4}$.
fourth • *adjective* • *noun, plural* **fourths**
● The words **fourth** and **forth** sound alike.
She enters the *fourth* grade this fall.
A rocking chair moves back and *forth*.

Fourth of July *noun another name for* **Independence Day**.

fowl (foul) *noun* a chicken, turkey, duck, or other large bird that is raised for food.
fowl • *noun, plural* **fowls** or **fowl**
● The words **fowl** and **foul** sound alike.
I prefer beef to fish or *fowl*.
Do not *foul* their best shooter.

fox

fox (fäks) *noun* a wild animal that has a pointed nose, a bushy tail, and, usually, reddish-brown fur. The fox is closely related to the dog.
fox • *noun, plural* **foxes** or **fox**

fraction (frak′shən) *noun* **1** an amount or quantity that is written with a numerator and a denominator [$\frac{1}{2}$, $\frac{19}{25}$, and $\frac{8}{7}$ are all *fractions*.] **2** a small part or amount [He saves only a *fraction* of what he earns.] —Look for the WORD CHOICES box at the entry **part**.
frac·tion • *noun, plural* **fractions**

WORD HISTORY

fraction

This word comes from a Latin verb that means "to break." A **fraction** is one of the parts that are broken from a whole amount. The words **fracture, fragile,** and **fragment** also come from this Latin verb, and all three have to do with the idea of breaking.

fracture (frak′chər) *noun* a break or crack, especially in a bone [an arm *fracture*].
verb to break or crack [She *fractured* an arm.]
frac·ture • *noun, plural* **fractures**
• *verb* **fractured, fracturing**

fragile (fraj′əl) *adjective* easily broken or damaged; delicate [a *fragile* china plate].
frag·ile • *adjective*

WORD CHOICES

Synonyms of **fragile**

The words **fragile, delicate,** and **frail** share the meaning "easily broken or damaged."

a *fragile* crystal goblet
a rose with a *delicate* stem
a small, *frail* boat

fragment (frag′mənt) *noun* **1** a piece of something that has broken; a part broken away [*fragments* of a broken cup]. **2** a part taken from a whole [The composer played *fragments* of her latest composition.] —Look for the WORD CHOICES box at the entry **part**.
frag·ment • *noun, plural* **fragments**

fragrance (frā′grəns) *noun* a sweet or pleasant smell; odor [the *fragrance* of roses] —Look for the WORD CHOICES box at the entry **scent**.
fra·grance • *noun, plural* **fragrances**

fragrant (frā′grənt) *adjective* having a sweet or pleasant smell [*fragrant* flowers].
fra·grant • *adjective*

frail (frāl) ***adjective*** lacking strength; slender and delicate; weak [a sickly, *frail* child].
frail • ***adjective*** **frailer, frailest**

frame (frām) ***noun*** **1** the support or skeleton around which a thing is built. A frame is what gives the thing its shape [the *frame* of a house]. **2** the build of a body [He is a man with a large *frame*.] **3** the border or case into which a window, door, or picture is set.
verb **1** to put a frame, or border, around [Judy *framed* the picture.] **2** to put together carefully; shape [They were assembled to *frame* a new constitution for the country.]
—frame of mind the way a person thinks or feels; mood.
frame • ***noun,*** *plural* **frames** • ***verb*** **framed, framing**

framework (frām′wʉrk) ***noun*** a structure that holds together or supports the thing built around it [the *framework* of a house].
frame·work • ***noun,*** *plural* **frameworks**

France (frans) a country in western Europe.

frank (fraŋk) ***adjective*** open and honest about what one is thinking and feeling; speaking one's mind freely.
frank • ***adjective*** **franker, frankest**

WORD CHOICES

Synonyms of **frank**

The words **frank, open,** and **outspoken** share the meaning "saying what one thinks in a blunt, open way."

a *frank* criticism of the movie
her *open* admiration for him
an *outspoken* attack on his friends

Frankenstein (fraŋk′ən stīn) **1** the man in a famous novel who builds a monster that destroys him. **2** the monster itself: this sense is not entirely correct, but many people use it.
Frank·en·stein

Frankfort (fraŋk′fərt) the capital of Kentucky.
Frank·fort

frankfurter (fraŋk′fʉrt ər) ***noun*** a smoked sausage of beef or of beef and pork; wiener.
frank·furt·er • ***noun,*** *plural* **frankfurters**

WORD HISTORY

frankfurter

The sausage in a hot dog gets one of its names from the city of *Frankfurt* am Main in Germany, where one type of small sausage was first made. Many other foods have been named for places throughout the world.

Franklin (fraŋk′lin), **Benjamin** (ben′jə min) 1706-1790; American statesman, inventor, and writer.
Frank·lin, Ben·ja·min

frantic (fran′tik) ***adjective*** very excited with worry or fear [They heard *frantic* cries for help.]
fran·tic • ***adjective***

fraud (frôd *or* fräd) ***noun*** **1** the act or practice of deceiving someone in order to profit or to get an unfair advantage [The jeweler was accused of *fraud* when he sold cut glass as diamonds.] **2** something used to cheat or trick. **3** a person who cheats or is not what he or she pretends to be.
fraud • ***noun,*** *plural* **frauds**

fray (frā) ***verb*** to wear down so as to have loose threads showing [a coat *frayed* at the elbows].
fray • ***verb*** **frayed, fraying**

freak (frēk) ***noun*** **1** an animal or plant that is very much different from what is normal [A two-headed calf is a *freak*.] **2** anything odd.
freak • ***noun,*** *plural* **freaks**

freckle (frek′əl) ***noun*** a small brownish spot on the skin. Freckles are brought out on the face or arms, for example, by exposure to the sun.
freck·le • ***noun,*** *plural* **freckles**

free (frē) ***adjective*** **1** having or enjoying personal rights or liberty; not a slave or not in prison [The prisoners were set *free*. This is a land of *free* people.] **2** existing under or having political and civil liberties [The U.S. is among the *free* nations of the world.] **3** not

a	cat	ō	go	ʉ	fur	ə =	a *in* ago
ā	ape	ô	law, for	ch	chin		e *in* agent
ä	cot, car	oo	look	sh	she		i *in* pencil
e	ten	ōō	tool	th	thin		o *in* atom
ē	me	oi	oil	*th*	then		u *in* circus
i	fit	ou	out	zh	measure		
ī	ice	u	up	ŋ	ring		

under the control of another; independent [a *free* press]. **4** able to do something at will; at liberty [You are perfectly *free* to disagree with me.] **5** not tied up, fastened, or shut in; loose [As soon as the bird was *free*, it flew away. Grab the *free* end of the rope.] **6** not bothered, troubled, or held down by something [*free* from pain; *free* of debt]. **7** not busy or not in use [The phone booth is *free* now.] **8** with no charge; without cost [two *free* tickets to the game]. **9** with no blocking; open or clear [The harbor was *free* of ice all winter.]
adverb with no charge; without cost [We were let in *free*.]
verb to make or set free [She *freed* the raccoon from the trap.]
free • ***adjective*** **freer, freest** • ***adverb*** • ***verb*** **freed, freeing**

-free *a suffix meaning* free of or free from; without [Our principal wants a drug-*free* school.]

freedom (frēʹdəm) ***noun*** **1** the condition of being free; liberty; independence [The Emancipation Proclamation gave the slaves their *freedom*.] **2** the condition of being able to use or move about in as one wishes [Has your dog been given *freedom* of the house?] **3** ease of action or movement [The tight coat hindered his *freedom* of movement.]
free·dom • ***noun,*** *plural* **freedoms**

freeway (frēʹwā) ***noun*** a highway with many lanes and few, if any, traffic lights, stop signs, or intersections. On a freeway traffic can move at high speeds.
free·way • ***noun,*** *plural* **freeways**

freeze (frēz) ***verb*** **1** to make or become solid because of cold; harden into ice [Water *freezes* at 0°C or 32°F.] **2** to make or become filled or covered with ice [The river *froze* over.] **3** to make or become very cold [I *froze* when the blanket slipped off the bed.] **4** to damage, kill, or die with cold [The cold spell *froze* the oranges in the groves.] **5** to make or become motionless or stunned [The fox *froze* in its tracks.]
noun a period of very cold weather.
freeze • ***verb*** **froze, frozen, freezing** • ***noun,*** *plural* **freezes**

freezer (frēʹzər) ***noun*** a refrigerator or part of a refrigerator that is used to freeze foods or to store frozen foods.
freez·er • ***noun,*** *plural* **freezers**

freezing point ***noun*** the temperature at which a liquid becomes a solid. The freezing point of water, for example, is 32°F.
freezing point • ***noun,*** *plural* **freezing points**

freight (frāt) ***noun*** **1** goods shipped by train, truck, ship, or airplane. **2** the act or business of shipping goods in this way [Box the books and send them by *freight*.]

freighter (frātʹər) ***noun*** a ship that is used to carry freight.
freight·er • ***noun,*** *plural* **freighters**

French (french) ***noun*** the language of France.
—the French the people of France.

French fries ***plural noun*** *often* **french fries** thin strips of potato that have been fried in deep fat until crisp.

French horn ***noun*** a brass musical instrument with a long, coiled tube ending in a wide bell. It has a soft, mellow tone.
French horn • ***noun,*** *plural* **French horns**

French horn

Frenchman (frenchʹ mən) ***noun*** a person born or living in France.
French·man • ***noun,*** *plural* **Frenchmen**

Frenchwoman (frenchʹwoom ən) ***noun*** a woman born or living in France.
French·wom·an • ***noun,*** *plural* **Frenchwomen**

frenzy (frenʹzē) ***noun*** a wild or mad outburst of feeling or action [a *frenzy* of work; in a *frenzy* to catch the last bus].
fren·zy • ***noun,*** *plural* **frenzies**

frequency (frēʹkwən sē) ***noun*** **1** the fact of being frequent, or happening often. **2** the number of times something is repeated in a certain period of time.
fre·quen·cy • ***noun,*** *plural* **frequencies**

frequent (frēʹkwənt) ***adjective*** happening often or time after time [We take *frequent* trips to the beach during the summer.]
fre·quent • ***adjective***

fresh[1] (fresh) ***adjective*** **1** newly made, gotten, or grown; not spoiled or stale [*fresh* coffee; *fresh* eggs]. **2** not preserved by pickling, canning, or smoking [*fresh* meat; *fresh*

vegetables]. **3** further; additional [The expedition needed *fresh* supplies.] **4** new or different [a *fresh* approach to the problem]. **5** cool and clean [*fresh* air]. **6** not worn or dirty [*fresh* clothes; *fresh* towels]. **7** not tired; lively [I feel *fresh* after a nap.] **8** looking youthful or healthy [a *fresh* complexion].
fresh • *adjective* **fresher, freshest**

fresh[2] (fresh) [*a slang word*] *adjective* acting too bold; rude.
fresh • *adjective* **fresher, freshest**

freshen (fresh′ən) *verb* to make or become fresh [We need rain to *freshen* the garden.]
fresh·en • *verb* **freshened, freshening**

freshener (fresh′ən ər) *noun* anything that freshens or refreshes [Spray the air *freshener* to clear the room of cooking odors.]
fresh·en·er • *noun, plural* **fresheners**

freshman (fresh′mən) *noun* a student in the ninth grade in high school, or one in the first year of college.
fresh·man • *noun, plural* **freshmen**

freshwater (fresh′wôt ər) *adjective* of or living in water that is not salty [The pike is a *freshwater* fish.]
fresh·wa·ter • *adjective*

fret (fret) *verb* to become annoyed or worried [Don't *fret* about your sister's problems.]
fret • *verb* **fretted, fretting**

Fri. *abbreviation for* Friday.

friar (frī′ər) *noun* a man who belongs to any of certain religious orders of the Roman Catholic Church.
fri·ar • *noun, plural* **friars**

friction (frik′shən) *noun* **1** the rubbing of one thing against another [*Friction* wore holes in the elbows of my sweater.] **2** the force that slows the motion of two surfaces that touch each other [Oiling a bicycle reduces the *friction* that makes it hard to pedal.] **3** arguments or quarrels caused by differences of opinion [There is *friction* in his family over politics.]
fric·tion • *noun, plural for sense 3 only* **frictions**

Friday (frī′dā) *noun* the sixth day of the week. Abbreviated **Fri.**
Fri·day • *noun, plural* **Fridays**

fried (frīd) *verb past tense and past participle of* **fry**.
adjective cooked by frying [*fried* chicken].

friend (frend) *noun* **1** a person whom one knows well and likes. **2** a person who helps or supports something [a *friend* of school sports].
friend • *noun, plural* **friends**

friendly (frend′lē) *adjective* **1** of, like, or from a friend; kindly [*friendly* advice]. **2** showing good and peaceful feelings [a *friendly* nation].
friend·ly • *adjective* **friendlier, friendliest**

friendship (frend′ship) *noun* the close feeling or relationship between friends.
friend·ship • *noun, plural* **friendships**

fries (frīz) *verb* the form of the verb **fry** that is used to show the present time with *he, she,* or *it*. This form is also used with singular nouns.
plural noun a short form of **French fries**.

fright (frīt) *noun* sudden fear; alarm; terror —Look for the WORD CHOICES box at the entry **panic**.

frighten (frīt′n) *verb* **1** to make or become suddenly afraid; scare [Did the noise frighten you? Birds *frighten* easily.] **2** to force to do something by making afraid [The hunters *frightened* away the deer.]
fright·en • *verb* **frightened, frightening**

WORD CHOICES

Synonyms of **frighten**

The words **frighten, scare,** and **terrify** share the meaning "to cause to feel fear."

The smell of smoke *frightened* us.
Even the thought of mice *scares* me.
Earthquakes *terrified* the city.

frightful (frīt′fəl) *adjective* causing fright; making afraid [a *frightful* dream].
fright·ful • *adjective*

frigid (frij′id) *adjective* **1** very cold; freezing [a *frigid* day in January] —Look for the WORD CHOICES box at the entry **chilly**. **2** not warm or

a cat	ō go	ʉ fur	ə = a *in* ago
ā ape	ô law, for	ch chin	e *in* agent
ä cot, car	oo look	sh she	i *in* pencil
e ten	o͞o tool	th thin	o *in* atom
ē me	oi oil	*th* then	u *in* circus
i fit	ou out	zh measure	
ī ice	u up	ŋ ring	

friendly; stiff [She received a *frigid* welcome from her classmates.]
frig·id • *adjective*

frill (fril) ***noun*** **1** a piece of cloth or lace that is used as a trimming; ruffle. **2** something of little or no value that is added just for show [a simple meal without *frills*].
frill • ***noun**, plural* **frills**

fringe (frinj) ***noun*** **1** a border of hanging threads or strips. Fringes are used for decoration on curtains, bedspreads, or clothing. **2** an outside edge or border [We stood on the *fringe* of the crowd.]
fringe • ***noun**, plural* **fringes**

Frisbee (friz′bē) ***trademark*** a plastic, saucer-shaped disk that is tossed back and forth in various games.
Fris·bee • ***trademark**, plural* **Frisbees**

frisky (fris′kē) ***adjective*** lively or playful [*frisky* kittens] —Look for the WORD CHOICES box at the entry **nimble**.
frisk·y • ***adjective*** **friskier, friskiest**

fritter (frit′ər) ***noun*** a small cake of fried batter filled with fruit, corn, or some other ingredient.
frit·ter • ***noun**, plural* **fritters**

frivolous (friv′ə ləs) ***adjective*** not at all serious or important [a *frivolous* remark].
friv·o·lous • ***adjective***

fro (frō) ***adverb** used only in the phrase* **to and fro,** back and forth [pacing *to and fro*].

frog

frog (frôg) ***noun*** a small, coldblooded animal that can live on land and in water. It has long, strong hind legs with which it leaps.
frog • ***noun**, plural* **frogs**

frolic (frä′lik) ***verb*** to play about in a happy and carefree way.
frol·ic • ***verb*** **frolicked, frolicking, frolics**

from (frum *or* främ) ***preposition*** **1** beginning at [*from* Boston to New York]. **2** starting with [*from* noon to midnight]. **3** out of [The prisoner was released *from* jail.] **4** out of the chance of [They kept the baby *from* danger.] **5** made, sent, or said by [I got a letter *from* my friend in Spain.] **6** at a place that is not near to [Stay away *from* the dog.] **7** out of the whole of [Subtract 2 *from* 4.] **8** as not being like [I can't tell one car *from* another.] **9** because of [We trembled *from* fear.]

frond (fränd) ***noun*** the leaf of a fern or a palm tree.
frond • ***noun**, plural* **fronds**

front (frunt) ***noun*** **1** the part that faces forward; most important side [The *front* of the house usually faces the street.] **2** the first part; beginning [That chapter is toward the *front* of the book.] **3** the place or position directly before a person or thing [There was a crowd in *front* of the theater.] **4** a forward or leading position [Is our team still in *front?*] **5** land that lies next to a road, street, or body of water [There are docks on the lake *front*.] **6** the part where the actual fighting is going on during a war [The general sent more troops to the *front*.] **7** the boundary between two large masses of air [a cold *front*].
adjective in, on, near, or facing the front [the *front* door; the *front* page of a newspaper].
front • ***noun**, plural* **fronts** • ***adjective***

frontier (frun tir′) ***noun*** **1** the line or border between two countries. **2** the part of a settled country that lies next to a region that is still a wild area [the steady westward movement of the American *frontier*]. **3** any new subject or area of activity not yet completely studied [new *frontiers* in medicine].
fron·tier • ***noun**, plural* **frontiers**

frontiersman (frun tirz′mən) ***noun*** a man who lives on the frontier.
fron·tiers·man • ***noun**, plural* **frontiersmen**

frost (frôst) ***noun*** **1** a covering of tiny ice crystals that forms on a surface when dew or water vapor freezes [The windshield of the car was covered with *frost* in the morning.] **2** cold weather that can freeze things [*Frost* in the spring may damage fruit trees.]
verb **1** to cover with frost or with frosting. **2** to give a surface like frost to [The workmen *frosted* the glass by a special process.]

F

frost • *noun, plural* **frosts** • *verb* **frosted, frosting**

frostbite (frôst′bīt) *noun* damage to the ears, toes, or other parts of the body caused by exposure to very cold temperatures.
frost·bite • *noun*

frostbitten (frôst′bit′n) *adjective* damaged by having been exposed to very cold temperatures.
frost·bit·ten • *adjective*

frosting (frôs′tiŋ) *noun* a mixture of sugar, butter, and flavoring used to cover and decorate cakes and cookies; icing.
frost·ing • *noun, plural* **frostings**

frosty (frôs′tē) *adjective* **1** cold enough to have frost [a *frosty* day]. **2** covered with frost [a *frosty* window]. **3** not warm and friendly [a *frosty* greeting].
frost·y • *adjective* **frostier, frostiest**

froth (frôth *or* fräth) *noun* a white mass of bubbles in or on a liquid; foam.
verb to foam or make foam [The dog *frothed* at the mouth.]
froth • *noun, plural* **froths** • *verb* **frothed, frothing**

frown (froun) *verb* **1** to wrinkle the forehead and draw the eyebrows together in anger, worry, or deep thought. **2** to show that one dislikes or does not approve [The cook *frowned* upon any waste of food.]
noun the act of frowning or the look a person has in frowning [a *frown* of disapproval].
frown • *verb* **frowned, frowning** • *noun, plural* **frowns**

froze (frōz) *verb past tense of* **freeze**.

frozen (frō′zən) *verb past participle of* **freeze**.
fro·zen • *verb*

frozen custard *noun* a food that is like ice cream, but not so thick.
frozen custard • *noun, plural* **frozen custards**

frugal (fro͞o′gəl) *adjective* **1** careful in using or spending; not wasteful [a *frugal* manager]. **2** costing little and very plain [a *frugal* meal].
fru·gal • *adjective*

fruit (fro͞ot) *noun* **1** the part of a flowering plant that contains the seeds. Nuts, berries, and pods are fruit. **2** a plant part that can be eaten and contains the seeds inside a sweet and juicy pulp. Apples, pears, and grapes are fruits. Many fruits that are not sweet, as tomatoes or green peppers, are called vegetables by most people.
fruit • *noun, plural* **fruit** or **fruits**

frustrate (frus′trāt) *verb* **1** to keep a person from getting or doing what that person wants [He wants to play basketball, but his lack of skill *frustrates* him.] **2** to keep something from being carried out [The rain *frustrated* our plans for a picnic.]
frus·trate • *verb* **frustrated, frustrating**

fry (frī) *verb* to cook in hot fat over direct heat.
fry • *verb* **fried, frying, fries**

ft. *abbreviation for* **1** foot. **2** feet.

fudge (fuj) *noun* a soft candy made of butter, sugar, milk, and chocolate or other flavoring.

fuel (fyo͞o′əl) *noun* something that is burned to give heat or power. Coal, gas, oil, and wood are fuels.
fu·el • *noun, plural* **fuels**

fugitive (fyo͞o′ji tiv) *noun* a person who is running away, especially from the police.
fu·gi·tive • *noun, plural* **fugitives**

-ful *a suffix meaning:* **1** full of [*Joyful* means "full of joy."] **2** able or likely to [A *forgetful* person is likely to forget things.] **3** the amount that will fill [Two *teaspoonfuls* is the amount that will fill two teaspoons.]

fulcrum

fulcrum (fo͝ol′krəm) *noun* the support or point on which a lever rests when it is lifting something.
ful·crum • *noun, plural* **fulcrums**

a	cat	ō	go	ʉ	fur	ə = a *in* ago	
ā	ape	ô	law, for	ch	chin	e *in* agent	
ä	cot, car	o͝o	look	sh	she	i *in* pencil	
e	ten	o͞o	tool	th	thin	o *in* atom	
ē	me	oi	oil	*th*	then	u *in* circus	
i	fit	ou	out	zh	measure		
ī	ice	u	up	ŋ	ring		

fulfill (fool fil′) ***verb*** **1** to carry out; do or perform what is called for [The knight *fulfilled* his promise to the king by rescuing the princess.] **2** to satisfy; meet [She *fulfilled* all requirements to enter the tournament.] —Look for the WORD CHOICES box at the entry **satisfy**.
ful·fill • ***verb*** **fulfilled, fulfilling**

full (fool) ***adjective*** **1** holding or containing as much as possible; filled [a *full* jar]. **2** having much or many in it [a pond *full* of fish]. **3** having eaten all that one wants ["I'm *full*," he said after eating his dinner.] **4** whole or complete [a *full* dozen; a *full* set of teeth]. **5** filled out; plump [She has a round, *full* face.] **6** with loose, wide folds [a *full* skirt].
adverb **1** completely [a *full*-grown animal]. **2** straight; directly [The ball struck her *full* in the face.] **3** very [You know *full* well that you should have called her.]
—in full **1** to the complete amount [The bill was paid *in full*.] **2** not abbreviated [Write your name *in full*.]
full • ***adjective*** **fuller, fullest** • ***adverb***

fullback (fool′bak) ***noun*** a player on a football or soccer team who has the position farthest behind the front line.
full·back • ***noun,*** *plural* **fullbacks**

full moon ***noun*** the moon seen as a full circle.
full moon • ***noun,*** *plural* **full moons**

fully (fool′lē) ***adverb*** in a way that is complete, exact, or thorough [I didn't *fully* understand the lesson. The apple is *fully* ripe.]
full·y • ***adverb***

Fulton (fool′tən), **Robert** (räb′ərt) 1765-1815; U.S. engineer. He invented the steamboat.
Ful·ton, Rob·ert

fumble (fum′bəl) ***verb*** **1** to handle or search for in a clumsy way [She *fumbled* for the keys in her purse.] **2** to lose one's grip on something while trying to catch or hold it; drop [The quarterback *fumbled* the ball.]
noun the act of fumbling [Our team lost the game because of two *fumbles* in the second half.]
fum·ble • ***verb*** **fumbled, fumbling** • ***noun,*** *plural* **fumbles**

fume (fyoom) ***noun*** *often* **fumes** a gas, smoke, or vapor that is harmful or has a bad smell.
verb to be very angry or irritated [He *fumed* at the long delay.]
fume • ***noun,*** *plural* **fumes** • ***verb*** **fumed, fuming**

fun (fun) ***noun*** **1** a happy or joyful time [What *fun* we had at the party!] **2** something that gives this [A trip to the beach would be *fun*.]

function (fuŋk′shən) ***noun*** **1** normal or special work of a person or thing; purpose; role [A teacher's *function* is to educate. The *function* of the brakes is to stop the car.] **2** a formal party or an important ceremony [There are many *functions* that the mayor must attend.]
verb **1** to do its work; act [The motor is not *functioning* properly.] **2** to be used; serve [That table can *function* as a desk.]
func·tion • ***noun,*** *plural* **functions** • ***verb*** **functioned, functioning**

fund (fund) ***noun*** **1** an amount of money set aside for a particular purpose [a scholarship *fund* for gifted students]. **2** a supply; stock [The library is a *fund* of information.] **3 funds** money on hand, ready for use.
fund • ***noun,*** *plural* **funds**

fundamental (fun də ment′l) ***adjective*** of or forming a basis or foundation; basic [Freedom of the press is *fundamental* to democracy.]
noun a basic principle or rule; a very necessary part [Mathematics is one of the *fundamentals* of science.]
fun·da·men·tal • ***adjective*** • ***noun,*** *plural* **fundamentals**

funeral (fyoo′nər əl) ***noun*** the service held for a dead person.
adjective of or for a funeral [a *funeral* march].
fu·ner·al • ***noun,*** *plural* **funerals** • ***adjective***

fungi (fun′jī *or* fuŋ′gī) ***noun*** *a plural of* **fungus**.
fun·gi • ***noun***

fungous (fuŋ′gəs) ***adjective*** of, having to do with, or caused by a fungus.
fun·gous • ***adjective***

fungus (fuŋ′gəs) ***noun*** one of a group of plants that has no leaves, flowers, or green color. Mildews, molds, mushrooms, and toadstools are forms of fungus.
fun·gus • ***noun,*** *plural* **fungi** or **funguses**

WORD HISTORY

fungus

In Latin, the word *fungus* means "mushroom." The Latin word comes from a Greek word for "sponge." Some types of **fungus**, including mushrooms, look or feel somewhat like a sponge.

funnel (fun′əl) *noun* **1** a utensil that is shaped like a wide cone that narrows to a slender, open tube at the bottom. A funnel is used to pour a liquid, powder, or other substance into a container with a small opening. **2** a smokestack on a steamship or locomotive.
fun·nel • *noun, plural* **funnels**

funnel

funny (fun′ē) *adjective* **1** causing smiles or laughter; amusing [a *funny* joke]. **2** [*an informal use*] odd or unusual [It's *funny* that he's late.]
fun·ny • *adjective* **funnier, funniest**

WORD CHOICES

Synonyms of **funny**

Many words share the meaning "causing laughter or smiles."

amusing	comical	humorous
comic	hilarious	laughable

fur (fur) *noun* **1** the soft, thick hair that covers many animals. Cats, foxes, rabbits, and raccoons have fur. **2** an animal's skin with such hair on it. **3** a coat, scarf, or other piece of clothing made of fur.
fur • *noun, plural* **furs**
• The words **fur** and **fir** sound alike.
She wore a *fur* coat last winter.
A row of *fir* trees lines our street.

furious (fyoor′ē əs) *adjective* **1** full of or showing wild anger [She was *furious* over the theft of her car.] **2** very fierce, strong, or wild; violent; intense [a *furious* battle; a *furious* storm].
fu·ri·ous • *adjective*

furlough (fur′lō) *noun* a vacation given to a soldier or sailor.
fur·lough • *noun, plural* **furloughs**

furnace (fur′nəs) *noun* a large enclosed place in which heat is produced by burning fuel. A furnace is used to heat a building or to melt ores and metals.
fur·nace • *noun, plural* **furnaces**

furnish (fur′nish) *verb* **1** to put furniture in [My parents are *furnishing* our new home.] **2** to give whatever is needed; supply [That company *furnishes* the paper to print our books.]
fur·nish • *verb* **furnished, furnishing**

furnishings (fur′nish iŋz) *plural noun* **1** furniture, carpets, and other equipment for a home or office. **2** things to wear; clothing [a store for men's *furnishings*].
fur·nish·ings • *plural noun*

furniture (fur′ni chər) *noun* all the movable things that are needed to make a home or office fit for living or working. Tables, chairs, beds, and desks are pieces of furniture.
fur·ni·ture • *noun*

furrow

furrow (fur′ō) *noun* a long groove made in the ground by a plow or other tool. Farmers plant seeds in the furrows they dig.
fur·row • *noun, plural* **furrows**

furry (fur′ē) *adjective* **1** covered with fur [a *furry* kitten]. **2** of or like fur [cloth with a *furry* surface].
fur·ry • *adjective* **furrier, furriest**

further (fur′*th*ər) *adjective* **1** *a comparative of* **far**. **2** more distant; farther. **3** additional; more [I have no *further* news.]
adverb **1** *a comparative of* **far**. **2** to a greater extent; more [I'll study your request *further*.] **3** in addition; moreover; besides [*Further*, I

a	cat	ō	go	u	fur	ə =	a *in* ago
ā	ape	ô	law, for	ch	chin		e *in* agent
ä	cot, car	oo	look	sh	she		i *in* pencil
e	ten	o͞o	tool	th	thin		o *in* atom
ē	me	oi	oil	*th*	then		u *in* circus
i	fit	ou	out	zh	measure		
ī	ice	u	up	ŋ	ring		

want you to leave at once.] **4** at or to a greater distance; farther [Let's swim a little *further*.]
verb to help onward; promote; support [The committee was formed to *further* the cause of public education in the State.]
fur·ther • ***adjective*** • ***adverb*** • ***verb*** **furthered, furthering**

furthermore (fur′*th*ər môr) ***adverb*** besides; also; moreover [Mr. Smith is at a meeting; *furthermore*, he left orders not to be interrupted.]
fur·ther·more • ***adverb***

furthest (fur′*th*əst) ***adjective*** **1** *a superlative of* **far**. **2** most distant; farthest [He swam to the *furthest* corner of the pool.]
adverb **1** *a superlative of* **far**. **2** at or to the most distant point [Of all her family, Jane traveled *furthest* from home.] **3** to the greatest degree or extent; most [The doctor went *furthest* toward finding a cure for the disease.]
fur·thest • ***adjective*** • ***adverb***

fury (fyoor′ē) ***noun*** **1** wild anger; great rage [She is in a *fury* over her wrecked car.] **2** rough or wild force; violent action [The *fury* of the storm blew down the tall tree.]
fu·ry • ***noun**, plural* **furies**

fuse[1] (fyo͞oz) ***verb*** **1** to melt or join by melting [The electrician *fused* the two pieces of wire together.] **2** to join together completely; unite [The two companies *fused*.]
fuse • ***verb*** **fused, fusing**

fuse[2] (fyo͞oz) ***noun*** **1** a wick on a bomb, firecracker, or other explosive device. The fuse is lighted to set off the explosion. **2** a strip of metal that melts easily. It is a part of a safety device for some electrical systems. Sometimes an electric current flowing through a circuit can become too strong. When this happens, the fuse melts and breaks the circuit.
fuse • ***noun**, plural* **fuses**

fuselage (fyo͞o′sə läzh) ***noun*** the body of an airplane, not including the wings, tail, and engines.
fu·se·lage • ***noun**, plural* **fuselages**

fusion (fyo͞o′zhən) ***noun*** **1** the act or process of melting or joining together [The *fusion* of copper and zinc makes brass.] **2** anything made by fusing; a mix or blend [Bronze is a *fusion* of copper and tin.] **3** *the same as* **nuclear fusion**.
fu·sion • ***noun**, plural* **fusions**

fuss (fus) ***noun*** **1** too much bother or worry; nervous or excited action over a small thing [All this *fuss* over spilled water!] **2** a display of emotion, such as pleasure or worry [They made a big *fuss* over the baby.]
verb to get excited over or bother with small things [He *fussed* over every detail of the trip.]
fuss • ***noun**, plural* **fusses** • ***verb*** **fussed, fussing**

fussy (fus′ē) ***adjective*** always fussing; too particular about things; hard to please [*fussy* parents; a *fussy* eater].
fuss·y • ***adjective*** **fussier, fussiest**

futile (fyo͞ot′l) ***adjective*** not capable of producing any result; useless [He made a *futile* attempt to climb the wall.]
fu·tile • ***adjective***

future (fyo͞o′chər) ***adjective*** **1** in the time to come; after the present time [We will meet at a *future* date.] **2** showing time to come [the *future* tense of a verb].
noun **1** the time that is to come [We'll buy a new car sometime in the *future*.] **2** chance to succeed [She has a great *future* as a lawyer.]
fu·ture • ***adjective*** • ***noun**, plural* **futures**

future tense ***noun*** a form of a verb that shows that the verb's action will take place in the future. This tense is formed with the helping verbs *will* and *shall*. In the sentence "They will get a surprise," "will get" is in the future tense.

fuzz (fuz) ***noun*** soft, light hairs or fibers; loose, light particles of wool or a similar material [the *fuzz* on a sweater; the *fuzz* on a peach].

fuzzy (fuz′ē) ***adjective*** **1** like or covered with tiny, fine hairs or particles [a *fuzzy* sweater]. **2** not clear; blurred [The TV picture is *fuzzy*.]
fuzz·y • ***adjective*** **fuzzier, fuzziest**

F

Gg Gg Gg Gg

The letter **g** *has several different sounds. It may have the sound you hear in the words* **game**, **go**, **gum**, *and* **guitar**, *or it may have the sound you hear in the words* **gem**, **giraffe**, *and* **gym**. *When* **g** *appears after the letter* **n** *at the very end of a word, the two letters together have the combination sound you hear in the words* **sing** *and* **hang**. *The letter combination* **gh** *may have the sound of* **f**, *as in* **laugh** *and* **rough**, *or it may even not be pronounced at all, as in* **though**. *In a very few words,* **g** *can appear with* **n** *at the very beginning of a word, as in* **gnat** *and* **gnaw**; *in these cases only the* **n** *is pronounced.*

g or **G** (jē) ***noun*** the seventh letter of the English alphabet.
g or **G** • ***noun,*** *plural* **g's** or **G's**

G (jē) ***noun*** in music, the fifth tone in the scale of C major.
G • ***noun,*** *plural* **G's**

g or **g.** *abbreviation for* **1** gram. **2** grams.

GA or **Ga.** *abbreviation for* Georgia.

gable (gā′bəl) ***noun*** the triangle-shaped part that is formed in a wall of a building by the sloping ends of a roof.
ga·ble • ***noun,*** *plural* **gables**

gable

Gabon (gä bōn′) a country in western Africa, on the Atlantic Ocean.
Ga·bon

gadget (gaj′ət) ***noun*** a small mechanical device that has a special use [a new *gadget* for peeling apples].
gadg·et • ***noun,*** *plural* **gadgets**

Gaelic (gāl′ik) ***noun*** the language of Ireland and parts of northern Scotland.
Gael·ic • ***noun***

gag (gag) ***verb*** **1** to strain or choke in the way that a person does in vomiting. **2** to keep from talking or calling out, especially by putting something into or over the mouth [The robbers tied and *gagged* their victims.]
noun **1** something that gags a person or keeps a person from talking. **2** a joke.
gag • ***verb*** **gagged, gagging** • ***noun,*** *plural* **gags**

gaily (gā′lē) ***adverb*** **1** in a merry or cheerful way [The children sang *gaily*.] **2** in a colorful or bright way [a *gaily* decorated room].
gai·ly • ***adverb***

gain (gān) ***noun*** a thing or amount that is added; an increase [a slight *gain* in weight].
verb **1** to get by trying hard or as a reward [He

a	cat	ō	go	ʉ	fur	ə = a *in* ago	
ā	ape	ô	law, for	ch	chin	e *in* agent	
ä	cot, car	oo	look	sh	she	i *in* pencil	
e	ten	ōō	tool	th	thin	o *in* atom	
ē	me	oi	oil	*th*	then	u *in* circus	
i	fit	ou	out	zh	measure		
ī	ice	u	up	ŋ	ring		

gained experience by working at his father's store.] **2** to get as an increase or an advantage [I've *gained* five pounds.] **3** to be fast or go faster by [My watch *gained* two minutes today.]
gain • ***noun,*** *plural* **gains** • ***verb*** **gained, gaining**

gait (gāt) ***noun*** a way of walking or running.
gait • ***noun,*** *plural* **gaits**
• The words **gait** and **gate** sound alike.
A horse's gallop is a fast *gait.*
Shut the *gate* to keep in the cows.

gal (gal) [*an informal word*] ***noun*** a girl.
gal • ***noun,*** *plural* **gals**

gal. *abbreviation for* **1** gallon. **2** gallons.

gala (gā′lə *or* gal′ə) ***adjective*** like or having to do with a happy celebration [The first night of the play was a *gala* occasion.]
noun a happy celebration.
ga·la • ***adjective*** • ***noun,*** *plural* **galas**

Galahad (gal′ə had) the purest knight of King Arthur's Round Table.
Gal·a·had

galaxy (gal′ək sē) ***noun*** a very large group of stars. The earth and sun are part of the Milky Way galaxy.
gal·ax·y • ***noun,*** *plural* **galaxies**

WORD HISTORY

galaxy

We get **galaxy** from a Greek word that means "milk." The Milky Way **galaxy** gets its name from the cloudy or milky appearance it has in the sky.

gale (gāl) ***noun*** **1** a strong wind. **2** a loud outburst [We broke into *gales* of laughter.]
gale • ***noun,*** *plural* **gales**

gall[1] (gôl) ***noun*** **1** the bitter liquid that the liver produces; bile. **2** [*an informal use*] bold and rude behavior; lack of respect [How can he have the *gall* to call me that?]

gall[2] (gôl) ***verb*** to annoy or irritate [The insult *galled* her.]
gall • ***verb*** **galled, galling**

gallant (gal′ənt) ***adjective*** **1** brave and noble; daring [a *gallant* knight]. **2** very polite and respectful to women.
gal·lant • ***adjective***

gallbladder (gôl′blad ər) ***noun*** a small sac that is attached to the liver. The gall, or bile, is stored in it.
gall·blad·der • ***noun,*** *plural* **gallbladders**

galleon (gal′ē ən *or* gal′yən) ***noun*** a large Spanish sailing ship that was first used five hundred years ago.
gal·le·on • ***noun,*** *plural* **galleons**

gallery (gal′ər ē) ***noun*** **1** a room, building, or other place for showing or selling works of art. **2** a long hall or corridor that has windows or is open along one side. **3** a balcony.
gal·ler·y • ***noun,*** *plural* **galleries**

galley (gal′ē) ***noun*** **1** a large, low ship that was used long ago. It had sails and many oars. **2** the kitchen of a boat or ship.
gal·ley • ***noun,*** *plural* **galleys**

gallon (gal′ən) ***noun*** a unit of measure for liquids that is equal to four quarts or eight pints. One gallon equals 3.785 liters.
gal·lon • ***noun,*** *plural* **gallons**

gallop (gal′əp) ***noun*** the fastest gait of a horse. In a gallop, all four feet are off the ground at the same time in each stride.
verb to go or ride at a gallop [The horse *galloped* up to the fence.]
gal·lop • ***noun,*** *plural* **gallops** • ***verb*** **galloped, galloping**

gallows (gal′ōz) ***noun*** a wooden framework with a rope that is used for executing a person by hanging.
gal·lows • ***noun,*** *plural* **gallows** or **gallowses** (gal′ō zəz)

galore (gə lôr′) ***adverb*** in a large amount or number [The circus attracted crowds *galore.*]
ga·lore • ***adverb***

galosh (gə läsh′) ***noun*** a kind of waterproof shoe worn over the regular shoe in wet weather or snow.
ga·losh • ***noun,*** *plural* **galoshes**

Gambia (gam′bē ə) a country in western Africa, on the Atlantic Ocean.
Gam·bi·a

gamble (gam′bəl) ***verb*** **1** to take part in games such as poker, in which the players make bets. **2** to make a bet. **3** to take a risk [We *gambled* that it wouldn't rain until after the picnic.]
noun an act in which a person risks something [Starting a new business is usually a *gamble.*]
gam·ble • ***verb*** **gambled, gambling** • ***noun,*** *plural* **gambles**

G

game (gām) ***noun*** **1** a sport or contest that is carried on according to rules by persons or teams playing against one another. Baseball and chess are games. **2** a single contest of this kind [a baseball *game;* a *game* of chess]. **3** the set of things that are used in playing a game [I was given some books and *games* for my birthday.] **4** wild animals and birds that are hunted for sport or food.
adjective **1** full of spirit and courage [a *game* fighter]. **2** ready and willing: used with *for* [Are you *game* for a swim?]
game • ***noun,*** *plural* **games** • ***adjective*** **gamer, gamest**

game show ***noun*** a TV program in which people from the audience play against each other in games to try to win prizes.
game show • ***noun,*** *plural* **game shows**

gander (gan′dər) ***noun*** a male goose.
gan·der • ***noun,*** *plural* **ganders**

gang (gaŋ) ***noun*** a group of people who work together or spend much time together [a railroad *gang;* a neighborhood *gang*].
gang • ***noun,*** *plural* **gangs**

gangster (gaŋ′stər) ***noun*** a member of a gang of criminals.
gang·ster • ***noun,*** *plural* **gangsters**

gantry (gan′trē) ***noun*** a framework on wheels with a crane and several platforms. It is used for putting a rocket into position at its launching site.
gan·try • ***noun,*** *plural* **gantries**

gap (gap) ***noun*** **1** an opening that is made by breaking, tearing, or doing something similar [a *gap* in the fence]. **2** a mountain pass. **3** an empty space [a *gap* in my memory].
gap • ***noun,*** *plural* **gaps**

gape (gāp) ***verb*** to stare with the mouth open [We *gaped* at the huge models of dinosaurs.]
gape • ***verb*** **gaped, gaping**

garage (gər äzh′ *or* gər äj′) ***noun*** **1** a building where motor vehicles are kept. **2** a place of business where motor vehicles are repaired or serviced.
ga·rage • ***noun,*** *plural* **garages**

garb (gärb) ***noun*** clothing; style or kind of clothes [The ushers were in formal *garb*.]

garbage (gär′bij) ***noun*** spoiled or useless food that is thrown away.
gar·bage • ***noun***

garden (gärd′n) ***noun*** a piece of ground where flowers or vegetables are grown.
verb to take care of a garden.
gar·den • ***noun,*** *plural* **gardens** • ***verb*** **gardened, gardening**

gardenia (gär dēn′yə) ***noun*** a flower with white petals that feel like wax and a very sweet odor.
gar·de·nia • ***noun,*** *plural* **gardenias**

Garfield (gär′fēld), **James A(bram)** (jāmz′ ā′brəm) 1831-1881; became the twentieth president of the U.S. in 1881. He was assassinated.
Gar·field, James A(bram)

gargle (gär′gəl) ***verb*** to rinse the throat with a liquid that is moved around without swallowing, by forcing the breath out with the head held back.
noun a liquid that is used for gargling.
gar·gle • ***verb*** **gargled, gargling** • ***noun,*** *plural* **gargles**

gargoyle

gargoyle (gär′goil) ***noun*** a decoration on a building in the form of a strange, imaginary creature. It usually has a hollow place inside to carry off water after a rainfall.
gar·goyle • ***noun,*** *plural* **gargoyles**

garish (ger′ish) ***adjective*** gaudy or showy in a glaring way.
gar·ish • ***adjective***

garland (gär′lənd) ***noun*** a wreath or string of leaves or flowers.
gar·land • ***noun,*** *plural* **garlands**

garlic (gär′lik) ***noun*** the strong-smelling bulb of a plant that is related to the onion. It is used as a seasoning in foods.
gar·lic • ***noun***

garlic

a	cat	ō	go	ʉ	fur	ə =	a *in* ago
ā	ape	ô	law, for	ch	chin		e *in* agent
ä	cot, car	oo	look	sh	she		i *in* pencil
e	ten	ōō	tool	th	thin		o *in* atom
ē	me	oi	oil	*th*	then		u *in* circus
i	fit	ou	out	zh	measure		
ī	ice	u	up	ŋ	ring		

garment (gär′mənt) ***noun*** a piece of clothing.
gar·ment • ***noun,*** *plural* **garments**

garnet (gär′nət) ***noun*** a clear, deep-red stone that is used in jewelry.
gar·net • ***noun,*** *plural* **garnets**

garnish (gär′nish) ***verb*** to decorate food to make it look or taste better [The cook *garnished* the ham with slices of pineapple.]
noun something, such as parsley, that is used for decorating food.
gar·nish • ***verb*** **garnished, garnishing** • ***noun,*** *plural* **garnishes**

garrison (ger′i sən) ***noun*** a fort and the soldiers and equipment that are located in it; a military post.
verb to put soldiers into a fort or town to protect it.
gar·ri·son • ***noun,*** *plural* **garrisons** • ***verb*** **garrisoned, garrisoning**

garter (gärt′ər) ***noun*** an elastic band or strap that is worn to hold up a stocking or sock.
gar·ter • ***noun,*** *plural* **garters**

garter snake ***noun*** a small striped snake of North America that is not poisonous.
garter snake • ***noun,*** *plural* **garter snakes**

Garvey (gär′vē), **Marcus** (mär′kəs) 1880-1940; black political leader in the U.S., born in Jamaica.
Gar·vey, Mar·cus

gas (gas) ***noun*** **1** a form of matter that is neither a liquid nor a solid. Gas is the form of a substance that can spread out and take up all the space that is open to it. The air around us is a combination of several different gases such as oxygen and nitrogen. **2** a mixture of gases that will burn easily, used for heating and lighting. **3** [*an informal use*] *a short form of* **gasoline**.
gas • ***noun,*** *plural* **gases** or **gasses**

gash (gash) ***verb*** to make a long, deep cut in [I *gashed* my finger when I was peeling potatoes.]
noun a long, deep cut.
gash • ***verb*** **gashed, gashing** • ***noun,*** *plural* **gashes**

gas mask

gas mask ***noun*** a mask for the face that has a chemical filter. A person wears it to keep from breathing in dangerous gases.
gas mask • ***noun,*** *plural* **gas masks**

gasoline (gas′ə lēn) ***noun*** a clear liquid that burns very easily and is used mainly as a motor fuel. It is made from petroleum.
gas·o·line • ***noun***

gasp (gasp) ***verb*** **1** to breathe in suddenly in surprise. **2** to breathe with effort [I *gasped* as I ran.] **3** to say or tell while doing this [She *gasped* out the story.]
noun the act of gasping [a *gasp* of horror].
gasp • ***verb*** **gasped, gasping** • ***noun,*** *plural* **gasps**

gas station ***noun*** *another name for* **service station**.
gas station • ***noun,*** *plural* **gas stations**

gate (gāt) ***noun*** a door in a fence or an outside wall. A gate usually swings on hinges.
gate • ***noun,*** *plural* **gates**
• The words **gate** and **gait** sound alike.
Shut the *gate* to keep in the cows.
A horse's gallop is a fast *gait*.

gateway (gāt′wā) ***noun*** **1** an opening in a fence or wall that has a gate in it. **2** a way of getting to [Education can be the *gateway* to a good job.]
gate·way • ***noun,*** *plural* **gateways**

gather (ga*th*′ər) ***verb*** **1** to bring or come together in one place or group [The child *gathered* her toys together. The families *gathered* for a picnic.] **2** to get or collect a little at a time [We are *gathering* news for the school paper.] **3** to get as an idea; conclude [I *gather* that he is rich.] **4** to gain a little at a time [The train *gathered* speed.]
gath·er • ***verb*** **gathered, gathering**

WORD CHOICES

Synonyms of gather

The words **gather, assemble,** and **collect** share the meaning "to bring or come together."

He is *gathering* shells on the beach.
Students *assembled* in the gym.
Terry *collects* stamps.

gathering (ga*th*′ər iŋ) ***noun*** a group of people who have come together; a meeting.
gath·er·ing • ***noun,*** *plural* **gatherings**

G

gaudy (gôd′ē *or* gäd′ē) ***adjective*** too bright and decorated too much; not in good taste [He wore a *gaudy* shirt to the party.]
gaud·y • ***adjective*** **gaudier, gaudiest**

gauge (gāj) ***noun*** **1** a measure of size according to a standard. The gauge of a railroad is the distance between the rails. The gauge of a wire is its thickness. The gauge of machine-knitted fabric tells how fine it is. **2** a device for measuring something. The gauge on a boiler tells the pressure of the steam inside. **3** a means of estimating or judging [Polls are a *gauge* of public opinion.]
verb **1** to measure the size or amount of carefully and exactly. **2** to judge or estimate [How do we *gauge* the judge's honesty?]
gauge • ***noun,*** *plural* **gauges** • ***verb*** **gauged, gauging**

gaunt (gônt *or* gänt) ***adjective*** so thin that the bones show; lean and worn, especially from hunger or illness [His *gaunt* face shocked all of us.] —Look for the WORD CHOICES box at the entry **lean**[2].
gaunt • ***adjective*** **gaunter, gauntest**

gauntlet (gônt′lət *or* gänt′lət) ***noun*** a glove that knights in armor wore. It was usually made of leather covered with metal plates.
gaunt·let • ***noun,*** *plural* **gauntlets**

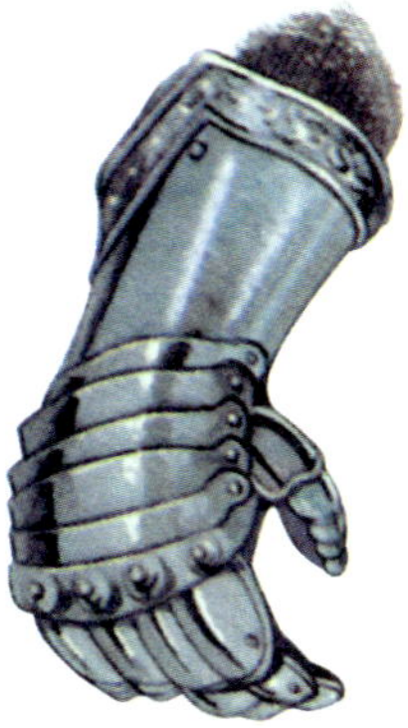
gauntlet

gauze (gôz *or* gäz) ***noun*** a light, thin cloth that is woven so loosely that a person can see through it. Cotton gauze is used for bandages.

gave (gāv) ***verb*** *past tense of* **give**.

gavel (gav′əl) ***noun*** a small wooden hammer. A judge or a person who runs a meeting raps on the table with it to call for attention or quiet.
gav·el • ***noun,*** *plural* **gavels**

gawk (gôk *or* gäk) ***verb*** to stare in a stupid way [The crowd *gawked* at the overturned truck.]
gawk • ***verb*** **gawked, gawking**

gawky (gô′kē *or* gä′kē) ***adjective*** awkward or clumsy [a *gawky* fellow] —Look for the WORD CHOICES box at the entry **awkward**.
gawk·y • ***adjective*** **gawkier, gawkiest**

gay (gā) ***adjective*** **1** lively and full of joy; merry. **2** bright and lively to the eye [*gay* colors].
gay • ***adjective*** **gayer, gayest**

gaze (gāz) ***verb*** to look in a steady way [They *gazed* into each other's eyes.] —Look for the WORD CHOICES box at the entry **look**.
noun a steady look.
gaze • ***verb*** **gazed, gazing** • ***noun,*** *plural* **gazes**

gazelle

gazelle (gə zel′) ***noun*** a small, graceful antelope of Africa and Asia. It has horns that twist back in a spiral and large, shining eyes.
ga·zelle • ***noun,*** *plural* **gazelles** or **gazelle**

gear (gir) ***noun*** **1** *often* **gears** a part of a machine that is made up of two or more wheels that have teeth. The teeth of one wheel fit together with the teeth of another wheel. When one wheel moves, it makes the other wheel move also [In a car, the *gears* pass on the motion of the engine to the wheels.] **2** a certain arrangement of the gears [Shift into first *gear* if you want more power.] **3** equipment and tools needed for doing something [fishing *gear*].
verb to adjust or make fit [Our new cafeteria is *geared* to feed more students.]
gear • ***noun,*** *plural* **gears** • ***verb*** **geared, gearing**

gearshift (gir′shift) ***noun*** a lever or handle for connecting a set of gears to a motor.
gear·shift • ***noun,*** *plural* **gearshifts**

a cat	ō go	ʉ fur	ə = a *in* ago
ā ape	ô law, for	ch chin	e *in* agent
ä cot, car	oo look	sh she	i *in* pencil
e ten	ōō tool	th thin	o *in* atom
ē me	oi oil	*th* then	u *in* circus
i fit	ou out	zh measure	
ī ice	u up	ŋ ring	

gearwheel (gir′hwēl *or* gir′wēl) ***noun*** any one of the wheels with teeth in a system of gears.
gear·wheel • ***noun,*** *plural* **gearwheels**

gearwheel

gee (jē) [*a slang word*] ***interjection*** a word expressing surprise or wonder [*Gee!* I didn't know that!]

geese (gēs) ***noun*** *plural of* **goose**.

Geiger counter (gī′gər) ***noun*** a device that is used to measure amounts of radioactivity.
Gei·ger counter • ***noun,*** *plural* **Geiger counters**

Geisel (gī′zəl), **Theodor Seuss** (thē′ə dôr so͞os) *the real name of* Dr. **Seuss**.
Gei·sel, The·o·dor Seuss

geisha (gā′shə) ***noun*** a Japanese woman whose work is to entertain by singing and dancing.
gei·sha • ***noun,*** *plural* **geisha** or **geishas**

gelatin (jel′ə tin) ***noun*** a substance that is made by boiling the bones and other parts of animals. Gelatin dissolves in hot water and forms a sort of jelly when it cools. It is used in food, medicine capsules, and other things.
gel·a·tin • ***noun***

gem (jem) ***noun*** **1** a cut and polished stone or a pearl for use in jewelry. **2** a person or thing that is of great value [What a *gem* that student of hers is!]
gem • ***noun,*** *plural* **gems**

Gen. *abbreviation for* general.

gene (jēn) ***noun*** any one of the tiny units that make up a section of a chromosome. Genes carry qualities that are passed on to a person's children. Genes pass on characteristics such as hair color and eye color.
gene • ***noun,*** *plural* **genes**

general (jen′ər əl) ***adjective*** **1** of, for, or from all or the whole, not just a part [*General* anesthesia keeps all of the body from feeling pain.] **2** common or widespread [The *general* opinion of him is rather low.] **3** having to do with the main parts but not with details [Here are the *general* features of my plan.] **4** highest in rank; most important [the *general* manager of a factory].
noun a military officer of the highest rank.
—in general usually; in most cases.
gen·er·al • ***adjective*** • ***noun,*** *plural* **generals**

generally (jen′ər əl ē) ***adverb*** in most cases; usually [Her speeches are *generally* quite long.]
gen·er·al·ly • ***adverb***

general store ***noun*** a store where many different kinds of things are sold, but not in separate departments.
general store • ***noun,*** *plural* **general stores**

generate (jen′ər āt) ***verb*** to bring into being; produce [A special mechanism in a power dam *generates* electricity.]
gen·er·ate • ***verb*** **generated, generating**

generation (jen′ər ā′shən) ***noun*** **1** a single stage in the history of a family [A grandmother, mother, and son are three *generations*.] **2** all the people who are born at about the same time [Many teenagers in this *generation* want to go to college.] **3** the average time between the birth of the parents and the births of their children, about 25 years. **4** the act or process of bringing into being or producing [the *generation* of electricity by water power.]
gen·er·a·tion • ***noun,*** *plural* **generations**

generator (jen′ər āt′ər) ***noun*** a machine that changes the power or energy from a natural source, such as water or wind, into electricity.
gen·er·a·tor • ***noun,*** *plural* **generators**

generous (jen′ər əs) ***adjective*** **1** willing to give or share; not selfish. **2** large; great in amount [She served *generous* helpings of ice cream.]
gen·er·ous • ***adjective***

WORD HISTORY

generous

The word **generous** comes from a Latin word that means "born into a noble family." People once expected that members of noble families would be kind, unselfish, and forgiving. Any person who has these qualities is seen as being **generous**.

Genesis (jen′ə sis) the first book of the Bible. It tells how God created the world.
Gen·e·sis

genial (jē′nē əl) ***adjective*** **1** friendly and cheerful. **2** pleasant and healthful [a *genial* climate].
gen·i·al • ***adjective***

G

genie (jē′nē) ***noun*** in Muslim legends, an imaginary being that can take the shape of a person or animal and can harm or help people.
ge·nie • ***noun,*** *plural* **genies**

genius (jēn′yəs) ***noun*** **1** the special power of mind or the special ability that shows itself in the greatest artists, writers, and scientists. **2** a person who has this kind of ability [Leonardo da Vinci was a *genius* in both science and art.] **3** a person who is very intelligent. **4** a special ability [She has a *genius* for making friends].
gen·i·us • ***noun,*** *plural for senses 2, 3, and 4* **geniuses**

gentile or **Gentile** (jen′tīl) ***noun*** a person who is not Jewish.
gen·tile or **Gen·tile** • ***noun,*** *plural* **gentiles** or **Gentiles**

gentle (jent′l) ***adjective*** **1** mild, soft, or easy; not rough [a *gentle* touch; a *gentle* scolding]. **2** tame and easy to handle [a *gentle* horse]. **3** polite, kind, or patient [a *gentle* manner]. **4** gradual; not sudden [a *gentle* slope].
gen·tle • ***adjective*** **gentler, gentlest**

WORD CHOICES

Synonyms of **gentle**

The words **gentle, mild,** and **soft** share the meaning "not harsh or severe."

a *gentle* breeze
a *mild* winter
a *soft* voice

gentleman (jent′l mən) ***noun*** **1** a man who is polite and kind and can be relied upon. **2** any man ["Ladies and *gentlemen*," the speaker began.]
gen·tle·man • ***noun,*** *plural* **gentlemen**

gently (jent′lē) ***adverb*** in a gentle way.
gen·tly • ***adverb***

genuine (jen′yoo͞ in) ***adjective*** really being what it seems to be; not false [a *genuine* diamond].
gen·u·ine • ***adjective***

genus (jē′nəs) ***noun*** a large group of plants or animals that are closely related. A genus is divided into individual kinds, called species. Dogs and wolves are different species that belong to the same genus.
ge·nus • ***noun,*** *plural* **genuses**

geo- *a prefix meaning* having to do with the earth [*Geography* is the study of the surface of the earth.]

geodesic dome

geodesic dome (jē′ō des′ik) ***noun*** a dome that is made of many short straight bars that form a grid of polygons. It is strong, light in weight, and needs no supports inside to hold it up.
ge·o·des·ic dome • ***noun,*** *plural* **geodesic domes**

geographical (jē′ə graf′i kəl) or **geographic** (jē′ə graf′ik) ***adjective*** having to do with geography.
ge·o·graph·i·cal or **ge·o·graph·ic** • ***adjective***

geography (jē ôg′rə fē *or* jē ä′grə fē) ***noun*** **1** the study of the surface of the earth and how it is divided into continents, countries, seas, and other parts. Geography also deals with the climates, plants, animals, and resources of the earth. **2** the natural features of a certain part of the earth [the varied *geography* of China].
ge·og·ra·phy • ***noun***

geologic (jē′ə läj′ik) or **geological** (jē′ə läj′i kəl) ***adjective*** having to do with geology [*Geologic* time is measured in millions of years.]
ge·o·log·ic or **ge·o·log·i·cal** • ***adjective***

geology (jē ä′lə jē) ***noun*** the study of the earth's crust and the way in which its layers were formed. It includes the study of rocks.
ge·ol·o·gy • ***noun***

geometric (jē′ə me′trik) or **geometrical** (jē′ə me′tri kəl) ***adjective*** **1** having to do with geometry [A square is a *geometric* figure.]

a cat	ō go	ʉ fur	ə = a *in* ago
ā ape	ô law, for	ch chin	e *in* agent
ä cot, car	oo look	sh she	i *in* pencil
e ten	o͞o tool	th thin	o *in* atom
ē me	oi oil	*th* then	u *in* circus
i fit	ou out	zh measure	
ī ice	u up	ŋ ring	

2 having straight lines, circles, triangles, or other regular shapes [a *geometric* pattern in the cloth].
ge·o·met·ric or **ge·o·met·ri·cal** • *adjective*

geometry (jē äm′ə trē) ***noun*** the branch of mathematics that deals with lines, angles, planes, and figures and with measuring them.
ge·om·e·try • ***noun***

George III (jôrj) 1738-1820; the king of England from 1760 to 1820. He ruled at the time of the American Revolution.

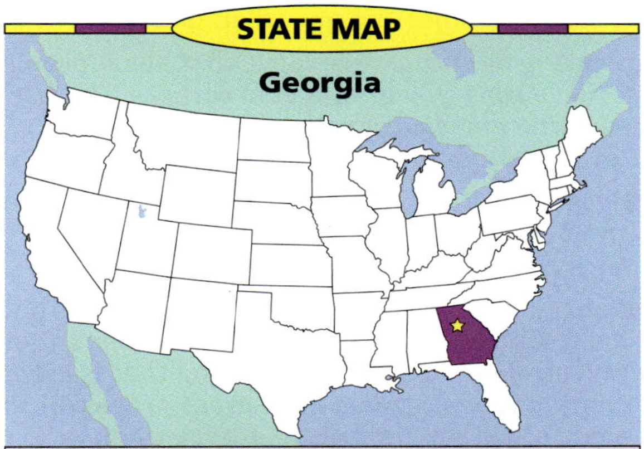

Statehood: 1788, the 4th state • **Capital:** Atlanta

Georgia (jôr′jə) **1** a State in the southeastern part of the U.S. Its capital is Atlanta. Abbreviated **GA** or **Ga.** **2** a country on the Black Sea, south of Russia. It was a part of the Soviet Union.
Geor·gia

geranium (jər ā′nē əm) ***noun*** a plant with large, bright pink, red, or white flowers.
ge·ra·ni·um • ***noun,*** *plural* **geraniums**

gerbil (jʉr′bəl) ***noun*** an animal that is like a mouse but has very long hind legs. It is found in Africa and Asia. In the U.S., it is often a pet.
ger·bil • ***noun,*** *plural* **gerbils**

germ (jʉrm) ***noun*** **1** a living thing that can cause disease. Germs are too small to be seen unless a person uses a microscope. Bacteria are germs. **2** a seed, bud, or tiny beginning part from which a plant or animal develops.
germ • ***noun,*** *plural* **germs**

German (jʉr′mən) ***noun*** **1** a person born or living in Germany. **2** the language of the Germans.
Ger·man • ***noun,*** *plural for sense 1 only* **Germans**

Germanic (jər man′ik) ***adjective*** **1** having to do with Germany or the Germans; German. **2** of or describing any of a group of languages that are related to German. Norwegian, Danish, Dutch, and English are Germanic languages.
Ger·man·ic • ***adjective***

German shepherd ***noun*** a large dog that looks somewhat like a wolf. It is often used to help the police or to guide blind persons.
German shepherd • ***noun,*** *plural* **German shepherds**

Germany (jʉr′mə nē) a country in north central Europe: in 1949 it was divided into **East Germany** and **West Germany**, each with its own government. In 1990 the two Germanys became one country again.
Ger·ma·ny

Gershwin (gʉrsh′win), **George** (jôrj) 1898-1937; U.S. composer.
Gersh·win, George

gesture (jes′chər) ***noun*** **1** a movement of the hands or arms, or of another part of the body, to help express an idea or feeling. **2** something that a person does to express a feeling [Our neighbor's gift was a *gesture* of friendship.]
verb to make a gesture or gestures [The policeman *gestured* to us to cross the street.]
ges·ture • ***noun,*** *plural* **gestures**
• ***verb*** **gestured, gesturing**

Gesundheit (gə zo͝ont′hīt) ***interjection*** a word used to wish good health to someone who has just sneezed. This is a German word that means "health."
Ge·sund·heit • ***interjection***

get (get) ***verb*** **1** to become the owner of by receiving, buying, or earning; to gain or obtain [We *got* a new car.] **2** to arrive at; reach [They *got* home early.] **3** to reach or receive by telephone, radio, or TV [I *got* John the first time I dialed.] **4** to go and bring [*Get* your books.] **5** to catch; gain hold of [*Get* her attention.] **6** to persuade; make willing [I can't *get* him to leave.] **7** to cause to be [We couldn't *get* the door open. He *got* his hands dirty.] **8** to be or become [She *got* caught in the rain. Don't *get* angry.] **9** to prepare; make ready [I'll *get* dinner tonight.] **10** to become ill with [I *got* a cold over the weekend.] **11** [*an informal use*] to be forced or required: used with *have* or *has* [I've *got* to pass the test.] **12** [*an informal use*] to own or possess: used with *have* or *has* [He's *got* a hundred dollars.] **13** [*an informal use*] to understand [Did you *get* the joke?]
—get along **1** to manage [Can they *get along*

on $110 a week?] **2** to be on friendly terms; agree [We can't *get along* with the new neighbors.] **—get away with** [*a slang use*] to manage to do without being found out or punished [They *got away with* the prank.] **—get in** **1** to enter. **2** to arrive. **—get out** **1** to go out. **2** to go away. **3** to become known. **—get out of** to escape or avoid. **—get over** to recover from [I've just *gotten over* the mumps. You'll *get over* our quarrel.] **—get up** to rise from bed [He *gets up* early every day.]
get • ***verb*** **got, gotten** or **got, getting**

WORD CHOICES

Synonyms of **get**

The words **get, acquire,** and **obtain** share the meaning "to come to have or own."

You must *get* a job.
She worked to *acquire* an education.
How do you *obtain* a passport?

getaway (get′ə wā) ***noun*** the act of escaping, especially from the police.
get·a·way • ***noun,*** *plural* **getaways**

geyser (gī′zər) ***noun*** a spring that shoots streams of boiling water and steam up into the air from time to time.
gey·ser • ***noun,*** *plural* **geysers**

geyser

Ghana (gä′nə) a country in western Africa, on the Atlantic Ocean.
Gha·na

ghastly (gast′lē) ***adjective*** **1** horrible or frightening [a *ghastly* crime; a *ghastly* smell of blood]. **2** pale like a ghost [Forgive me, but you're looking *ghastly* today. Are you ill?]
ghast·ly • ***adjective*** **ghastlier, ghastliest**

ghetto (get′ō) ***noun*** a section of a city where many members of some group live or where they must live because of poverty or prejudice.
ghet·to • ***noun,*** *plural* **ghettos** or **ghettoes**

ghost (gōst) ***noun*** **1** a pale, unclear figure that some people think they can see and that is supposed to be the spirit of a dead person. **2** a tiny amount [a *ghost* of a chance].
ghost • ***noun,*** *plural* **ghosts**

SPELLING TIP

Use this memory aid to spell **ghost**.
There is a ***host*** in g***host***.

ghostly (gōst′lē) ***adjective*** like or having to do with a ghost.
ghost·ly • ***adjective*** **ghostlier, ghostliest**

ghoul (go͞ol) ***noun*** **1** a spirit that some people believe robs graves and eats corpses. **2** a person who enjoys disgusting things.
ghoul • ***noun,*** *plural* **ghouls**

GI (jē′ī′) [*an informal word*] ***noun*** a person in the U.S. Army who is not an officer.
GI • ***noun,*** *plural* **GIs**

giant (jī′ənt) ***noun*** **1** an imaginary being that looks like a person but is many times larger and stronger. **2** a person or thing that is especially large or strong, or is great or special in some other way [a mental *giant*].
adjective very great in size or power [We took *giant* steps in the snow.]
gi·ant • ***noun,*** *plural* **giants** • ***adjective***

gibberish (jib′ər ish) ***noun*** confused talk or chatter, or talk that does not mean anything.
gib·ber·ish • ***noun***

gibbon

gibbon (gib′ən) ***noun*** a small, slender ape with long arms. It lives in southern Asia.

a	cat	ō	go	ʉ	fur	ə =	a *in* ago
ā	ape	ô	law, for	ch	chin		e *in* agent
ä	cot, car	o͝o	look	sh	she		i *in* pencil
e	ten	o͞o	tool	th	thin		o *in* atom
ē	me	oi	oil	*th*	then		u *in* circus
i	fit	ou	out	zh	measure		
ī	ice	u	up	ŋ	ring		

gib·bon • *noun, plural* **gibbons**

giblets (jib′ləts) ***plural noun*** the parts inside a chicken, turkey, or other bird that can be used as food. They include the heart and liver.
gib·lets • ***plural noun***

giddy (gid′ē) ***adjective*** having a feeling that things are whirling about; dizzy [Climbing ladders makes me *giddy*.]
gid·dy • ***adjective*** **giddier, giddiest**

gift (gift) ***noun*** **1** something that a person gives because of friendship, thanks, or love or for other reasons; a present [Christmas *gifts;* a *gift* of $100 to the hospital fund] —Look for the WORD CHOICES box at the entry **present**. **2** a natural ability; talent [She has a *gift* for music.] —Look for the WORD CHOICES box at the entry **talent**.
gift • *noun, plural* **gifts**

gifted (gift′əd) ***adjective*** **1** having great natural ability [He's a *gifted* pianist.] **2** very intelligent [a *gifted* child].
gift·ed • ***adjective***

gigantic (jī gan′tik) ***adjective*** like a giant in size; very big or huge [a *gigantic* dinosaur] —Look for the WORD CHOICES box at the entry **enormous**.
gi·gan·tic • ***adjective***

giggle (gig′əl) ***verb*** to laugh with high, quick sounds in a silly or nervous way, often through trying to hold back the laughter —Look for the WORD CHOICES box at the entry **laugh**.
noun the act or sound of laughing in this way.
gig·gle • ***verb*** **giggled, giggling** • *noun, plural* **giggles**

Gila monster

Gila monster (hē′lə) ***noun*** a poisonous lizard of the southwestern U.S. and Mexico. Its thick body is covered with black and orange scales that are like beads.
Gi·la monster • *noun, plural* **Gila monsters**

gild (gild) ***verb*** to cover with a thin layer of gold [The jewelry maker *gilded* the earrings.]
gild • ***verb*** **gilded** or **gilt, gilding**
● The words **gild** and **guild** sound alike.
Melt the gold to *gild* the bracelet.
They joined a *guild* to raise money.

gill (gil) ***noun*** the organ for breathing of most animals living in water. As water passes through the gills, they remove oxygen from it. Fish, lobsters, and clams have gills.
gill • *noun, plural* **gills**

gilt (gilt) ***verb*** *a past tense and past participle of* **gild**.
noun a thin layer of gold or a gold-colored paint that is used to cover a surface.
adjective covered with gilt.
● The words **gilt** and **guilt** sound alike.
They specialize in *gilt* jewelry.
The jury was to decide on her *guilt*.

gimmick (gim′ik) [*an informal word*] ***noun*** a clever gadget, trick, or idea.
gim·mick • *noun, plural* **gimmicks**

gin (jin) ***noun*** a strong liquor that is flavored with the berries of the juniper shrub.

ginger (jin′jər) ***noun*** **1** a spice that is made from the root of a tropical plant. **2** this plant.
gin·ger • ***noun***

ginger ale ***noun*** a sweet drink that is made of soda water flavored with ginger.

gingerbread (jin′jər bred) ***noun*** a dark cake that is flavored with ginger and molasses.
gin·ger·bread • *noun, plural* **gingerbreads**

Gipsy (jip′sē) ***noun*** *another spelling of* **Gypsy**.
Gip·sy • *noun, plural* **Gipsies**

giraffe

giraffe (ji raf′) ***noun*** a large animal of Africa that chews its cud. It has a very long neck, long legs, and a spotted coat.

G

gi·raffe • *noun, plural* **giraffes** or **giraffe**

girder (gur′dər) ***noun*** a long beam of steel or wood that is used to support some part in a building, bridge, or other structure.
gird·er • ***noun,*** *plural* **girders**

girl (gurl) ***noun*** a female child or a young, unmarried woman.
girl • ***noun,*** *plural* **girls**

girlfriend (gurl′frend) [*an informal word*] ***noun*** **1** a sweetheart of a boy or man. **2** a girl who is one's friend.
girl·friend • ***noun,*** *plural* **girlfriends**

girlhood (gurl′hood) ***noun*** the time of being a girl.
girl·hood • ***noun,*** *plural* **girlhoods**

girlish (gurl′ish) ***adjective*** of, like, or having to do with a girl [my aunt's *girlish* face].
girl·ish • ***adjective***

girl scout ***noun*** a member of the Girl Scouts.
girl scout • ***noun,*** *plural* **girl scouts**

Girl Scouts ***noun*** a club for girls. It teaches camping, hiking, and other outdoor skills, and it encourages its members to help other people.

girth (gurth) ***noun*** the distance around something, such as a tree trunk or a person's waist.
girth • ***noun,*** *plural* **girths**

give (giv) ***verb*** **1** to pass or hand over to another [*Give* your coat to me and I'll hang it up.] **2** to make a gift of [My uncle *gave* a book to me for my birthday.] **3** to cause a person to have [Music *gives* me great pleasure.] **4** to be the source of [Cows *give* milk.] **5** to pay in order to buy something [I'll *give* you $20 for that bike.] **6** to show [She *gave* signs of waking up.] **7** to cause to take place [He *gives* good parties. She *gave* a concert.] **8** to bend or move because of force or pressure [The boards in the floor *gave* under our weight.]
noun the quality or condition of being elastic [This mattress doesn't have much *give*.]
—give away **1** to make a gift of. **2** [*an informal use*] to make known [He *gave away* the secret plan.] **—give back** to return [*Give back* the book you borrowed.] **—give in** to stop fighting or working against a person or thing. **—give off** to send out; emit [The burning dinner *gave off* smoke and a horrid smell.] **—give out** **1** to hand out; distribute. **2** to become worn out or used up [Our supply of chalk is *giving out*.] **—give up** **1** to stop doing something [My mother *gave up* smoking.] **2** to stop trying; admit failure.
give • ***verb*** **gave, given, giving** • ***noun***

WORD CHOICES

Synonyms of **give**

The words **give, grant,** and **present** share the meaning "to hand over or award to someone."

She *gave* me her old bike.

The fairy queen *granted* his wish.

They *presented* a watch to him.

given (giv′ən) ***verb*** *past participle of* **give**.
giv·en • ***verb***

given name ***noun*** a person's first name ["Donald" is a *given name*.]
given name • ***noun,*** *plural* **given names**

gizmo (giz′mō) [*a slang word*] ***noun*** any sort of gadget or device.
giz·mo • ***noun,*** *plural* **gizmos**

glacial (glā′shəl) ***adjective*** like or having to do with ice or glaciers.
gla·cial • ***adjective***

glacier (glā′shər) ***noun*** a large mass of ice and snow that moves very slowly down a mountain or across land until it melts. Icebergs are pieces of a glacier that have broken away into the sea.
gla·cier • ***noun,*** *plural* **glaciers**

glad (glad) ***adjective*** **1** feeling or showing joy; happy or pleased [I'm *glad* to be here.] **2** very willing [I'll be *glad* to help you.]
glad • ***adjective*** **gladder, gladdest**

gladden (glad′n) ***verb*** to make glad [The news *gladdens* my heart.]
glad·den • ***verb*** **gladdened, gladdening**

glade (glād) ***noun*** an open space in a forest.
glade • ***noun,*** *plural* **glades**

gladiator (glad′ē āt′ər) ***noun*** a man who fought against animals or other men in the arenas of ancient Rome to entertain people.

a cat	ō go	ʉ fur	ə = a *in* ago
ā ape	ô law, for	ch chin	e *in* agent
ä cot, car	oo look	sh she	i *in* pencil
e ten	ōō tool	th thin	o *in* atom
ē me	oi oil	*th* then	u *in* circus
i fit	ou out	zh measure	
ī ice	u up	ŋ ring	

Gladiators were usually slaves or prisoners.
glad·i·a·tor • *noun, plural* **gladiators**

gladioli (glad′ē ō′lī) *noun a plural of* **gladiolus**.
glad·i·o·li • *noun*

gladiolus (glad′ē ō′ləs) *noun* **1** a plant with long, sword-shaped leaves and tall stems with flowers of various colors. **2** the flower of this plant.
glad·i·o·lus • *noun, plural* **gladioluses** or **gladioli**

glamorous or **glamourous** (glam′ər əs) *adjective* full of glamour; fascinating [a *glamorous* movie star].
glam·or·ous or **glam·our·ous** • *adjective*

glamour or **glamor** (glam′ər) *noun* mysterious beauty or charm; exotic attraction [the *glamour* of faraway islands].
glam·our or **glam·or** • *noun*

glance (glans) *verb* **1** to take a quick look [She *glanced* at her watch.] **2** to hit at a slant and go off at an angle [Hail *glanced* off the roof.]
noun a quick look.
glance • *verb* **glanced, glancing** • *noun, plural* **glances**

gland (gland) *noun* a part of the body that produces a fluid that the body can use or give off as waste. The liver, kidneys, and thyroid are glands. Bile, milk, and sweat are produced by glands.
gland • *noun, plural* **glands**

glare (gler) *verb* **1** to shine with a light so bright that it hurts the eyes [The tropical sun *glared* down on us at the beach.] **2** to stare in an angry way [She stood *glaring* at the police officer who had given her the ticket.]
noun **1** a strong, blinding light [the *glare* of headlights; the *glare* of the sun on the snow] —Look for the WORD CHOICES box at the entry **blaze**[1]. **2** an angry look or stare.
glare • *verb* **glared, glaring** • *noun, plural* **glares**

glaring (gler′iŋ) *adjective* **1** shining so brightly as to hurt the eyes [*glaring* headlights]. **2** staring in an angry way [*glaring* eyes]. **3** too easily noticed to be missed [a *glaring* error].
glar·ing • *adjective*

glass (glas) *noun* **1** a hard substance that breaks easily and that lets light through. Glass is used to make containers, windowpanes, camera lenses, and many other things. **2** a container made of glass and used for drinking. **3** the amount a drinking glass holds [He drank two *glasses* of milk.] **4 glasses** a pair of lenses made of glass and set into a frame, used to help a person see better; eyeglasses.
glass • *noun, plural* **glasses**

glassy (glas′ē) *adjective* **1** like glass; smooth and clear [the *glassy* surface of a lake]. **2** having a dull or lifeless look [a *glassy* stare].
glass·y • *adjective* **glassier, glassiest**

glaze (glāz) *verb* **1** to give a hard, shiny finish to [She learned how to *glaze* pottery.] **2** to fit with glass [The workman *glazed* the window.]
noun **1** a glassy coating [the *glaze* on pottery]. **2** a thin coating of ice.
glaze • *verb* **glazed, glazing** • *noun, plural* **glazes**

gleam (glēm) *noun* **1** a flash or beam of light [the *gleam* of the sun on the snow]. **2** a faint light or one that lasts only a short time [the *gleam* of a dying fire]. **3** a faint show or sign [a *gleam* of hope in her eyes].
verb to shine with a gleam [Polish the silver until it *gleams*.]
gleam • *noun, plural* **gleams** • *verb* **gleamed, gleaming**

glee (glē) *noun* a feeling of joy; delight [He looked forward to his vacation with *glee*.]

gleeful (glē′fəl) *adjective* full of glee; merry; joyous [the *gleeful* shouts of the cheerleaders].
glee·ful • *adjective*

glen (glen) *noun* a small, narrow valley.
glen • *noun, plural* **glens**

glide (glīd) *verb* to move along in a smooth and easy way [Skaters *glided* across the ice.]
noun the act or process of gliding; a smooth, easy movement.
glide • *verb* **glided, gliding** • *noun, plural* **glides**

glider (glīd′ər) *noun* an aircraft that is like an airplane except that it has no engine and is carried along by air currents.
glid·er • *noun, plural* **gliders**

glimmer (glim′ər) *verb* to give a faint and unsteady light [Stars *glimmered* in the sky.]
noun **1** a faint, unsteady light. **2** a faint show or sign [He saw a *glimmer* of fear in her eyes.]
glim·mer • *verb* **glimmered, glimmering** • *noun, plural* **glimmers**

glimpse (glimps) *verb* to get a quick look at [I *glimpsed* a fox as it ran across the trail.]
noun a quick look [We caught a *glimpse* of her boyfriend as we drove by the school.]

G

glimpse • *verb* **glimpsed, glimpsing** • *noun, plural* **glimpses**

glint (glint) *noun* a gleam or flash [There was a *glint* of mischief in his eyes.]
verb to gleam or flash [We could see pieces of glass *glinting* in the sunlight.]
glint • *noun, plural* **glints** • *verb* **glinted, glinting**

glisten (glis′ən) *verb* to shine or sparkle with reflected light [The snow *glistened* in the sunshine. Her eyes *glistened* with tears.]
glis·ten • *verb* **glistened, glistening**

glitter (glit′ər) *verb* to shine with a sparkling light [The Christmas tree *glittered* with tinsel.]
noun **1** a sparkling light or brightness [the *glitter* of gold]. **2** small bits of brightly colored or sparkling material that are used in decoration.
glit·ter • *verb* **glittered, glittering** • *noun, plural for sense 1 only* **glitters**

gloat (glōt) *verb* to feel a mean or selfish kind of pleasure [He *gloated* over their loss.]
gloat • *verb* **gloated, gloating**

glob (gläb) *noun* a rounded mass or lump [a *glob* of dough].
glob • *noun, plural* **globs**

global (glō′bəl) *adjective* **1** having the shape of a globe. **2** of or involving the whole world; worldwide [Air pollution is a *global* problem.]
glob·al • *adjective*

global warming *noun* the recent slight but steady warming of the earth's lower atmosphere. Many scientists believe that pollution in the air traps heat from the sun and causes the atmosphere to get warmer.

globe (glōb) *noun* **1** anything shaped like a ball; sphere. **2** a round model of the earth showing the continents, oceans, countries, and other important features. **3** the earth.
globe • *noun, plural* **globes**

glockenspiel

glockenspiel (gläk′ən spēl *or* gläk′ən shpēl) *noun* a percussion instrument that has flat, metal bars in a frame. Small hammers strike the bars to produce bell-like tones.
glock·en·spiel • *noun, plural* **glockenspiels**

gloom (glo͞om) *noun* **1** dimness of light; partial darkness [We couldn't read our map in the *gloom* of the cave.] **2** a feeling of deep sadness; low spirits [The news of the factory's closing cast a *gloom* over the small town.]

gloomy (glo͞om′ē) *adjective* **1** dark or dim [a *gloomy* dungeon] —Look for the WORD CHOICES box at the entry **dark**. **2** having or causing a feeling of deep sadness [a *gloomy* mood; a *gloomy* novel] —Look for the WORD CHOICES box at the entry **sad**.
gloom·y • *adjective* **gloomier, gloomiest**

glop (gläp) [*an informal word*] *noun* any soft, messy substance or thick liquid.

glorify (glôr′i fī) *verb* **1** to give glory to; cause to be famous and respected [The citizens *glorified* the war heroes by building a monument.] **2** to make seem better than is really the case [Some older people *glorify* their school days.]
glo·ri·fy • *verb* **glorified, glorifying, glorifies**

glorious (glôr′ē əs) *adjective* **1** giving, having, or deserving glory or honor [a *glorious* act of bravery]. **2** beautiful in a splendid way; magnificent [a *glorious* poem; a *glorious* sunset].
glo·ri·ous • *adjective*

glory (glôr′ē) *noun* **1** great honor or fame [The scientist's discovery brought *glory* to his profession.] **2** a person or thing that brings great honor, fame, or admiration; an object of pride [The Capitol is one of the *glories* of Washington.] **3** great beauty or splendor [the *glory* of the woods in the fall].
verb to be very proud or happy [The football team *gloried* in their victory.]
glo·ry • *noun, plural* **glories** • *verb* **gloried, glorying, glories**

gloss (glôs *or* gläs) *noun* a polish or shine on a smooth surface.
gloss • *noun, plural* **glosses**

glossary (glôs′ə rē) *noun* a list of hard words

a	cat	ō	go	ʉ	fur	ə =	a *in* ago
ā	ape	ô	law, for	ch	chin		e *in* agent
ä	cot, car	o͝o	look	sh	she		i *in* pencil
e	ten	o͞o	tool	th	thin		o *in* atom
ē	me	oi	oil	*th*	then		u *in* circus
i	fit	ou	out	zh	measure		
ī	ice	u	up	ŋ	ring		

with their meanings. Glossaries are often printed at the end of a book.
glos·sa·ry • ***noun,*** *plural* **glossaries**

WORD HISTORY

glossary

We get **glossary** from a Greek word that means "tongue." The tongue is one of the main organs that we use in forming words. In some languages, the word for "tongue" is also the word for "language."

glossy (glôs′ē) ***adjective*** smooth and shiny [*glossy* paper; a *glossy* fabric].
gloss·y • ***adjective*** **glossier, glossiest**

glove (gluv) ***noun*** **1** a covering to protect the hand, with a separate section for each finger and the thumb. **2** a padded mitt worn to protect the hand in certain sports like baseball and boxing.
glove • ***noun,*** *plural* **gloves**

glow (glō) ***verb*** **1** to give off light because of great heat [There were embers *glowing* in the fire.] **2** to give out light without flame or heat [Fireflies *glowed* in the dark.] **3** to show a warm rosy color [Their faces *glowed* with health.] **4** to show emotion or excitement [His parents *glowed* with pride at his graduation.]
noun **1** light given off as a result of great heat [the *glow* of a furnace]. **2** light without flame or heat [the orange *glow* of the sky at sunset]. **3** warm or rosy look of the skin that suggests a good or pleasant feeling.
glow • ***verb*** **glowed, glowing** • ***noun,*** *plural* **glows**

glowworm (glō′wurm) ***noun*** an insect without wings or an insect larva that glows in the dark.
glow·worm • ***noun,*** *plural* **glowworms**

glue (gloo) ***noun*** a thick, sticky substance that is used to stick things together.
verb **1** to stick with glue [The carpenter *glued* the corners of the drawer together.] **2** to cause to stay without moving [The exciting movie kept us *glued* to our seats.]
glue • ***noun,*** *plural* **glues** • ***verb*** **glued, gluing**

gnarled (närld) ***adjective*** having a twisted and knotty look [a *gnarled* oak tree; the *gnarled* hands of the old woman].

gnat (nat) ***noun*** a small biting insect with two wings.
gnat • ***noun,*** *plural* **gnats**

gnaw (nô *or* nä) ***verb*** to bite and wear away bit by bit [The rat *gnawed* the rope in two. The dog *gnawed* on the bone.]
gnaw • ***verb*** **gnawed, gnawing**

gnome (nōm) ***noun*** a dwarf in folk tales who lives inside the earth and guards treasures.
gnome • ***noun,*** *plural* **gnomes**

gnu

gnu (noo *or* nyoo) ***noun*** a large African antelope with a head like an ox and a long tail.
gnu • ***noun,*** *plural* **gnus** or **gnu**

- The words **gnu, knew,** and **new** sound alike.
  Lions hunt the zebra and the *gnu*.
  I *knew* him when he was a baby.
  Don't you know any *new* jokes?

go (gō) ***verb*** **1** to move along or pass from one place, point, or person to another [I must *go* to the store today. He *went* to New York last night. The rumor *went* all over town.] **2** to move away; leave [I must *go* now or I'll be late.] **3** to slip by; pass [Time *goes* fast.] **4** to be spent, lost, or used up [Her money is all *gone* now.] **5** to be given [The prize *goes* to you. Most of her allowance *goes* to buy books.] **6** to be sold [The chair *went* for $30.] **7** to turn out; to result [Our plans *went* wrong.] **8** to work, run, or operate [His car wouldn't *go*.] **9** to be or become [The explorers *went* hungry for days. She's *gone* mad.] **10** to begin or take part in a certain activity [Will you *go* to college? Let's *go* swimming.] **11** to belong in a certain place [The brooms *go* in that closet.] **12** to fit or suit [Does this tie *go* well with my shirt?] **13** to extend; reach [The road *goes* from one

G

end of town to the other.] **14** to come to an end; cease [Has the pain *gone?*] **15** to make a certain sound [The gun *went* "bang!"]
—go into to be contained in [5 *goes into* 10 twice.] **—go off** to be fired; explode [The gun *went off* by accident.] **—go on** **1** to continue [The movie *went on* past my bedtime.] **2** to happen ["What's *going on*?" she asked.] **—go out** to go to a party, the theater, or another place for entertainment [Her parents *go out* almost every night.] **—go through** to undergo; to experience [The early settlers of America *went through* many hardships.] **—let go** **1** to stop holding; release ["*Let go* of my arm!" he said angrily.] **2** to dismiss from a job; fire [Business was bad and many workers were *let go*.]
go • ***verb*** **went, gone, going, goes**

WORD CHOICES

Synonyms of **go**

Many words share the meaning "to move along from one place to another."

advance   proceed   travel
pass   progress

goal (gōl) ***noun*** **1** something that a person wants or works for; aim; purpose [His *goal* was to become a teacher.] **2** the place at which a race or trip is ended. **3** the line, net, or any other similar area over or into which a ball or puck must go to score in certain games. **4** a score made by driving a ball or puck into a goal.
goal • ***noun,*** *plural* **goals**

goalie (gōl′ē) ***noun*** *a short form of* **goalkeeper**.
goal·ie • ***noun,*** *plural* **goalies**

goalkeeper

goalkeeper (gōl′kēp ər) ***noun*** a player who stays at a goal to keep a ball or puck from crossing or entering it.
goal·keep·er • ***noun,*** *plural* **goalkeepers**

goat (gōt) ***noun*** an animal that chews its cud and is related to the sheep. Goats have hollow horns, hoofs, and a growth of hair under their chins like a beard. Goats are raised in many parts of the world for their milk and wool.
goat • ***noun,*** *plural* **goats** or **goat**

gob (gäb) ***noun*** a soft lump or mass.
gob • ***noun,*** *plural* **gobs**

gobble[1] (gäb′əl) ***noun*** the sound made by a male turkey.
verb to make this sound.
gob·ble • ***noun,*** *plural* **gobbles**
• ***verb*** **gobbled, gobbling**

gobble[2] (gäb′əl) ***verb*** to eat quickly without chewing properly.
gob·ble • ***verb*** **gobbled, gobbling**

gobbler (gäb′lər) ***noun*** a male turkey.
gob·bler • ***noun,*** *plural* **gobblers**

goblet (gäb′lət) ***noun*** a drinking glass with a base and stem.
gob·let • ***noun,*** *plural* **goblets**

goblin (gäb′lin) ***noun*** a mischievous, ugly little elf or spirit in folk tales.
gob·lin • ***noun,*** *plural* **goblins**

god (gäd) ***noun*** **1** a being that is thought of as having power over people and nature. Ancient peoples believed in many gods and goddesses. **2** a person or thing that is considered most important [Money is their *god*.]
god • ***noun,*** *plural* **gods**

God (gäd) in the Christian, Jewish, and Muslim religions, the all-powerful being who made and rules the universe and is perfectly good and just.

godchild (gäd′chīld) ***noun*** a child for whom a man or woman acts as godparent.
god·child • ***noun,*** *plural* **godchildren**

goddess (gäd′əs) ***noun*** a female god.
god·dess • ***noun,*** *plural* **goddesses**

godfather (gäd′fä *th*ər) ***noun*** a man who pledges, usually at the baptism of a child, that he will be responsible for its religious training.

a	cat	ō	go	ʉ	fur	ə =	a *in* ago
ā	ape	ô	law, for	ch	chin		e *in* agent
ä	cot, car	oo	look	sh	she		i *in* pencil
e	ten	ōō	tool	th	thin		o *in* atom
ē	me	oi	oil	*th*	then		u *in* circus
i	fit	ou	out	zh	measure		
ī	ice	u	up	ŋ	ring		

god·fa·ther • *noun, plural* **godfathers**

godmother (gäd′mu*th* ər) ***noun*** a woman who pledges, usually at the baptism of a child, that she will be responsible for its religious training.
god·moth·er • *noun, plural* **godmothers**

godparent (gäd′per ənt) ***noun*** a godfather or godmother.
god·par·ent • *noun, plural* **godparents**

goer (gō′ər) ***noun*** a person who goes very often to a particular place [a church*goer;* a movie*goer*].
go·er • *noun, plural* **goers**

goes (gōz) ***verb*** the form of the verb **go** that is used to show the present time with *he, she,* or *it*. This form is also used with singular nouns.

goggles (gäg′əlz) ***plural noun*** large eyeglasses that fit tightly around the eyes to protect them from dust, wind, sparks, or glare.
gog·gles • *plural noun*

gold (gōld) ***noun*** **1** a heavy, yellow metal that is a chemical element. Gold is very valuable and is used in coins and jewelry. **2** a bright or shining yellow.
adjective **1** of or made of gold [*gold* coins; a *gold* watch]. **2** having the color of gold.

golden (gōld′n) ***adjective*** **1** made of or containing gold [*golden* earrings]. **2** having the color of gold; bright-yellow. **3** very good or favorable; excellent [If you go to the party, you will have a *golden* opportunity to meet her parents.]
gold·en • *adjective*

goldenrod (gōld′n räd) ***noun*** a common wild plant that has small, yellow flowers on long stalks. It blooms at the end of summer.
gold·en·rod • *noun, plural* **goldenrods**

goldfinch (gōld′finch) ***noun*** a small American finch. The male has a yellow body with black markings on the wings.
gold·finch • *noun, plural* **goldfinches**

goldfish (gōld′fish) ***noun*** a small, yellow or orange fish that is often kept in ponds or fish bowls.
gold·fish • *noun, plural* **goldfish**

goldsmith (gōld′smith) ***noun*** a skilled worker who makes things of gold.
gold·smith • *noun, plural* **goldsmiths**

golf (gôlf) ***noun*** a game played outdoors on a special course with 9 or 18 holes. It is played with a small, hard ball and a set of long, thin clubs with steel or wooden heads. The player tries to hit the ball into each of a series of holes, using as few strokes as possible.
verb to play this game.
golf • *noun* • *verb* **golfed, golfing**

Goliath (gə lī′əth) in the Bible, a giant killed by David with a stone from a sling.
Go·li·ath

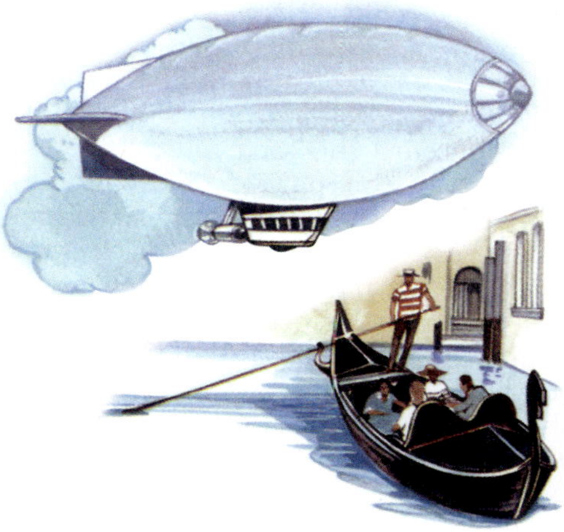

gondola
Above: Of airship Below: On canal

gondola (gän′də lə *or* gän dō′lə) ***noun*** **1** a long, narrow boat with high, pointed ends. It is rowed with an oar or pole by a person standing at one of the ends. Gondolas carry passengers on the canals of Venice, a city in Italy. **2** a railroad freight car with no top. **3** a cabin that is suspended from a balloon or dirigible.
gon·do·la • *noun, plural* **gondolas**

gone (gôn *or* gän) ***verb*** *past participle of* **go**.

gong

gong (gôŋ) ***noun*** a big metal disk that gives a loud, booming sound when struck.
gong • *noun, plural* **gongs**

G

goo (go͞o) [*a slang word*] ***noun*** something that is sticky or both sticky and sweet.
goo • ***noun, plural*** **goos**

good (go͝od) ***adjective*** **1** having the right or desirable qualities; not bad or poor [*good* work; *good* food; a *good* book; a *good* writer]. **2** better than the usual or average [She is a *good* student who always gets *good* grades.] **3** not for everyday use; best [Let's use our *good* china.] **4** right for the purpose; suitable [This cloth is *good* for polishing silver.] **5** pleasing or satisfying; enjoyable or happy [Have you heard the *good* news? They had a *good* time at the party.] **6** having a good effect; tending to help [Exercise is *good* for the health.] **7** favorable [*good* luck]. **8** doing what is right or proper; well-behaved [a *good* child]. **9** proper; correct [*good* manners; *good* grammar]. **10** in good condition; sound, strong, or fresh [*good* health; *good* eggs]. **11** thorough; complete [Do a *good* job.]
noun **1** something that is good [As a child she didn't know *good* from evil.] **2** benefit [He resigned the Presidency for the *good* of the country.]
—as good as nearly; almost [With new paint, your old car looks *as good as* new.] **—for good** forever; for all time [She says she's leaving the country *for good*.] **—no good** useless or worthless [It's *no good* arguing with him. She gave him a check that was *no good*.]
good • ***adjective*** **better, best** • ***noun***

WORD CHOICES

Synonyms of **good**

Many words share the meaning "doing what is right."

decent	just	respectable
honest	proper	

goodby or **good-by** (go͝od bī′) ***interjection, noun*** *other spellings of* **goodbye**.
good·by or **good-by** • ***interjection*** • ***noun, plural*** **goodbys** or **good-bys**

goodbye or **good-bye** (go͝od bī′) ***interjection*** a word that is used as an expression of farewell [She called out "*Goodbye*" and drove away.]
noun an expression of farewell [They said their *goodbyes* to their host and left the house.]
good·bye or **good-bye** • ***interjection*** • ***noun, plural*** **goodbyes** or **good-byes**

Good Friday ***noun*** the Friday before Easter. It is a Christian holiday marking the anniversary of the day Jesus died.

good-looking (go͝od′lo͝ok′iŋ) ***adjective*** pleasing to look at; handsome or beautiful [a *good-looking* man; a *good-looking* car].
good-look·ing • ***adjective***

good-natured (go͝od′nā′chərd) ***adjective*** easy to get along with; pleasant and friendly.
good-na·tured • ***adjective***

goodness (go͝od′nəs) ***noun*** the quality or condition of being good.
interjection a word that is used to express surprise.
good·ness • ***noun*** • ***interjection***

goods (go͝odz) ***plural noun*** **1** things that can be bought and sold; wares [All leather *goods* are on sale today.] **2** personal property that can be moved; belongings [household *goods*].

goodwill (go͝od′wil′) ***noun*** a kindly or friendly feeling. This word is also written **good will**.
good·will • ***noun***

goody (go͝od′ē) ***noun*** [*an informal use*] something, such as a candy, that is good to eat.
interjection a word that is used especially by a child to express approval or delight.
good·y • ***noun, plural*** **goodies** • ***interjection***

gooey (go͞o′ē) [*a slang word*] ***adjective*** sticky or both sticky and sweet.
goo·ey • ***adjective*** **gooier, gooiest**

goof (go͞of) [*a slang word*] ***noun*** **1** a foolish or stupid person. **2** a mistake; blunder.
verb **1** to make a mistake; blunder. **2** to waste or kill time; avoid work or responsibility [Stop *goofing* around and do your homework!]
goof • ***noun, plural*** **goofs** • ***verb*** **goofed, goofing**

goofy (go͞of′ē) [*a slang word*] ***adjective*** a little crazy or ridiculous; silly.
goof·y • ***adjective*** **goofier, goofiest**

goop (go͞op) [*a slang word*] ***noun*** a sticky, somewhat liquid substance; goo.
goop • ***noun, plural*** **goops**

a cat	ō go	ʉ fur	ə = a *in* ago
ā ape	ô law, for	ch chin	e *in* agent
ä cot, car	o͝o look	sh she	i *in* pencil
e ten	o͞o tool	th thin	o *in* atom
ē me	oi oil	*th* then	u *in* circus
i fit	ou out	zh measure	
ī ice	u up	ŋ ring	

goose (go͞os) ***noun*** **1** a swimming bird that is like a duck but has a larger body and a longer neck. Some geese are raised for food. **2** a female bird of this kind. The male is called a *gander*. **3** the flesh of the goose used as food.
goose • ***noun,*** *plural* **geese**

goose flesh, goose bumps, or **goose pimples** ***noun*** a rough condition of the skin that is caused by cold or fear.

gopher (gō′fər) ***noun*** a furry animal with pouches like pockets in its cheeks. Gophers are rodents and live in tunnels that they dig underground.
go·pher • ***noun,*** *plural* **gophers**

Gorbachev (gôr′bə chôf′ *or* gôr′bə chôf′), **Mikhail** (mē′kä ēl′) 1931- ; leader of the Communist Party of the Soviet Union, from 1985 to 1991.
Gor·ba·chev, Mi·kha·il

gorge (gôrj) ***noun*** a narrow pass or valley between steep heights.
verb to stuff with food in a greedy way [She *gorged* herself with cake.]
gorge • ***noun,*** *plural* **gorges** • ***verb*** **gorged, gorging**

gorgeous (gôr′jəs) ***adjective*** **1** having brilliant, rich colors; splendid [the *gorgeous* tail of the peacock]. **2** [*an informal use*] extremely beautiful [a *gorgeous* day; a *gorgeous* dress].
gor·geous • ***adjective***

gorilla

gorilla (gə ril′ə) ***noun*** the largest and strongest of the apes. Gorillas have broad, heavy bodies and dark hair. They live in Africa.
go·ril·la • ***noun,*** *plural* **gorillas**

- The words **gorilla** and **guerrilla** sound alike.
  The *gorilla* and the chimp are related.
  The sniper was a *guerrilla*.

gosh (gäsh) ***interjection*** a word that is used to express an emotion such as surprise or wonder.

gosling (gäz′liŋ) ***noun*** a young goose.
gos·ling • ***noun,*** *plural* **goslings**

gospel (gäs′pəl) ***noun*** **1** *often* **Gospel** the teachings of Jesus and the Apostles. **2 Gospel** any of the first four books of the New Testament: *Matthew, Mark, Luke*, or *John*. **3** anything that is believed to be absolutely true [We accepted the story as *gospel*.]
gos·pel • ***noun,*** *plural* **gospels**

gossip (gäs′ip) ***noun*** **1** small talk about someone, often about things heard from others but not known to be facts; idle talk; rumors. **2** a person who spends much time in such talk.
verb to spread gossip.
gos·sip • ***noun,*** *plural for sense 2 only* **gossips** • ***verb*** **gossiped, gossiping**

got (gät) ***verb*** *past tense and a past participle of* **get**.

gotten (gät′n) ***verb*** *a past participle of* **get**.
got·ten • ***verb***

gouge (gouj) ***noun*** **1** a chisel that has a curved, hollow blade for cutting grooves in wood. **2** a groove or hole made with a sharp object.
verb to make grooves in, dig, or force out with a gouge [She *gouged* the leather desk top.]
gouge • ***noun,*** *plural* **gouges** • ***verb*** **gouged, gouging**

gourd (gôrd *or* goord) ***noun*** a large fruit that has many seeds and is related to the squash or pumpkin. Gourds grow on vines and have a hard outer rind. Gourds cannot be eaten but are often dried and used to make cups, bowls, dippers, and other objects.
gourd • ***noun,*** *plural* **gourds**

gov. or **govt.** *abbreviation for* government.

Gov. *abbreviation for* Governor.

govern (guv′ərn) ***verb*** to have control over; rule; manage [Who *governs* the nation? You must learn how to *govern* your emotions.]
gov·ern • ***verb*** **governed, governing**

government (guv′ərn mənt) ***noun*** **1** the direction of the affairs of a country, state, city, or other political unit [What that country needs is strong *government*.] **2** the form or system of rule by which a country, state, city, or other political unit is governed [The U.S.

G

has a democratic *government*.] **3** all the people who control the affairs of a country, state, city, or other political unit.
gov·ern·ment • *noun, plural* **governments**

governor (guv′ər nər) *noun* **1** a person elected to be the head of a State of the United States. **2** a person who is appointed to govern a province, territory, or other large political unit.
gov·er·nor • *noun, plural* **governors**

gown (goun) *noun* **1** a woman's dress, especially one that is elegant or formal. **2** a long, flowing robe like that worn by judges, ministers, or students at graduation ceremonies.
gown • *noun, plural* **gowns**

grab (grab) *verb* to seize or snatch suddenly [I *grabbed* him by the collar.] —Look for the WORD CHOICES box at the entry **grasp**.
noun the act of grabbing [He made a *grab* for the ball as it flew by.]
grab • *verb* **grabbed, grabbing** • *noun, plural* **grabs**

grace (grās) *noun* **1** beauty or charm of form, design, movement, or style [the *grace* of a statue; the *grace* of the ballerina's movements]. **2** a pleasing quality or manner [She has learned all the social *graces*.] **3** a sense of what is right and proper; courtesy or kindness to others [They could have had the *grace* to make their visit brief.] **4** a short prayer asking a blessing or giving thanks for a meal.
verb **1** to bring honor to [The mayor *graced* our banquet with her presence.] **2** to add beauty or charm to; adorn [Valuable paintings *graced* the walls of the castle.]
—in someone's good graces liked or approved by [I'm not *in* her parents' *good graces* because I didn't send them a Christmas card.]
grace • *noun, plural* **graces** • *verb* **graced, gracing**

graceful (grās′fəl) *adjective* having grace, or beauty of form or movement [a *graceful* dancer; the *graceful* leap of a deer].
grace·ful • *adjective*

gracious (grā′shəs) *adjective* kind, polite, and charming [a *gracious* host and hostess].
gra·cious • *adjective*

grackle (grak′əl) *noun* a kind of blackbird that is a little smaller than a crow.
grack·le • *noun, plural* **grackles**

grad (grad) [*an informal word*] *noun a short form of* **graduate**.
grad • *noun, plural* **grads**

grade (grād) *noun* **1** a division of a school course, usually equal to one year [Jim is in the seventh *grade*.] **2** a mark or score on a test or in a school course [Her *grades* are mostly B's.] **3** a degree or position in a scale of rank, quality, or value [The rank of captain is one *grade* higher than that of lieutenant.] **4** a group of people or class of things that are of the same rank, quality, or value [*grade* A eggs]. **5** the amount of slope in a road or surface [The train went up a steep *grade*.]
verb **1** to arrange in grades; sort [The farmer *graded* the eggs by size.] **2** to give a grade to; mark [The teacher *graded* the science tests.] **3** to make ground level or less steep [The bulldozer *graded* the land for the new road.]
grade • *noun, plural* **grades** • *verb* **graded, grading**

grader (grād′ər) *noun* **1** a pupil in a certain grade at a school [a fifth *grader*]. **2** a person or thing that grades [The new math teacher is a hard *grader*.]
grad·er • *noun, plural* **graders**

grade school *noun another name for* **elementary school**.
grade school • *noun, plural* **grade schools**

gradual (gra′jo͞o əl) *adjective* taking place by degrees or changes that are often so small that they can hardly be noticed [her *gradual* return to health].
grad·u·al • *adjective*

SPELLING TIP

Use this memory aid to spell **gradual**. Think of a ***grad***ual ***grad***e.

graduate (gra′jo͞o ət *for n.;* gra′jo͞o āt′ *for v.*) *noun* a person who has finished a course of study at a school or college and has been given a diploma or degree.
verb **1** to make or become a graduate of a school or college [He *graduated* last month. The college *graduated* 250 students this

a cat	ō go	ʉ fur	ə = a *in* ago
ā ape	ô law, for	ch chin	e *in* agent
ä cot, car	oo look	sh she	i *in* pencil
e ten	o͞o tool	th thin	o *in* atom
ē me	oi oil	*th* then	u *in* circus
i fit	ou out	zh measure	
ī ice	u up	ŋ ring	

year.] **2** to mark off with small lines for measuring [A thermometer is *graduated* in degrees.]
grad·u·ate • *noun, plural* **graduates** • *verb* **graduated, graduating**

graduation (gra′jo͞o ā′shən) *noun* **1** the act or process of graduating; the completion of a course of study. **2** the ceremony for giving out diplomas to graduating students [Are you going to attend her *graduation* on Monday?]
grad·u·a·tion • *noun, plural* **graduations**

graffiti

graffiti (grə fēt′ē) *plural noun* words, slogans, or drawings scratched or scribbled on a wall in some public place.
graf·fi·ti • *plural noun, singular* **graf·fi·to** (grə fēt′ō)

graft (graft) *noun* **1** a shoot or bud of one plant or tree that is set into a cut made in another so that the two grow together as a single plant. **2** a piece of skin, bone, or other living tissue that is taken from one body or from a part of a body and set into another so as to grow there and become a permanent part.

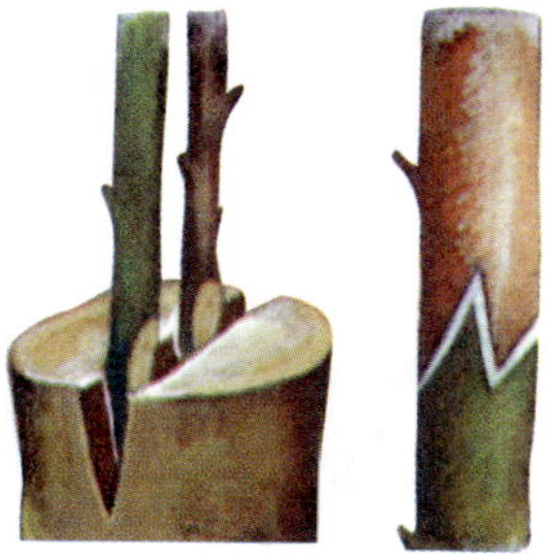

graft

verb to set a graft into a plant or animal [The surgeon *grafted* skin from the patient's thigh over the burn on his chest.]
graft • *noun, plural* **grafts** • *verb* **grafted, grafting**

Grail (grāl) in medieval legend, the lost cup from which Jesus drank at the Last Supper.

grain (grān) *noun* **1** the small, hard seed of wheat, corn, rye, or other cereal plants. **2** cereal plants or the seeds of such plants in general [The farmers planted fields of *grain*. The warehouse was full of bags of *grain*.] **3** a single particle of salt, sugar, or something similar [*grains* of sand]. **4** the markings or pattern formed by the way the layers or fibers are arranged in a piece of wood, stone, marble, or other material.
grain • *noun, plural for senses 1, 3, and 4 only* **grains**

gram (gram) *noun* the basic unit of weight in the metric system. One gram equals .035 of an ounce; one ounce is equal to about 28 grams.
gram • *noun, plural* **grams**

grammar (gram′ər) *noun* **1** the study of the forms of words and of the way they are arranged in sentences. **2** a system of rules for speaking and writing a certain language. **3** a book that contains these rules [a Spanish *grammar*]. **4** the way that a person speaks or writes, judged by these rules [I was amazed at her poor *grammar*.]
gram·mar • *noun, plural* **grammars**

grammatical (grə mat′i kəl) *adjective* of or according to the rules of grammar ["Between you and I" is a *grammatical* mistake.]
gram·mat·i·cal • *adjective*

granary (grān′ər ē) *noun* a building or place for storing grain.
gran·a·ry • *noun, plural* **granaries**

grand (grand) *adjective* **1** impressive because of great size or beauty; magnificent; splendid [*grand* scenery]. **2** most important; main [the *grand* ballroom of the hotel]. **3** including everything; complete [a *grand* total of $200]. **4** [*an informal use*] very pleasing; wonderful; excellent [We had a *grand* time at the circus.]
grand • *adjective* **grander, grandest**

WORD CHOICES

Synonyms of **grand**

The words **grand, magnificent,** and **stately** share the meaning "impressive because of great size, beauty, or splendor."

the *Grand* Canyon
a *magnificent* landscape
a *stately* mansion

G

grandchild (grand′chīld) ***noun*** a child of one's son or daughter.
grand·child • ***noun**, plural* **grandchildren**

granddaughter (gran′dät ər) ***noun*** a daughter of one's son or daughter.
grand·daugh·ter • ***noun**, plural* **granddaughters**

grandfather (grand′fä′*th*ər) ***noun*** the father of one's father or mother.
grand·fa·ther • ***noun**, plural* **grandfathers**

grandfather clock or **grandfather's clock** ***noun*** a large clock with a pendulum. It is contained in a tall cabinet that stands on the floor.

grandfather clock

grandma (gran′mä *or* gra′mä) [*an informal word*] ***noun*** grandmother.
grand·ma • ***noun**, plural* **grandmas**

grandmother (grand′mu*th* ər) ***noun*** the mother of one's father or mother.
grand·moth·er • ***noun**, plural* **grandmothers**

grandpa (gran′pä *or* gram′pä) [*an informal word*] ***noun*** grandfather.
grand·pa • ***noun**, plural* **grandpas**

grandparent (grand′per ənt) ***noun*** a grandfather or grandmother.
grand·par·ent • ***noun**, plural* **grandparents**

grand piano ***noun*** a large piano with its strings set flat in a case that is shaped like a harp.
grand piano • ***noun**, plural* **grand pianos**

grandson (grand′sun) ***noun*** a son of one's son or daughter.
grand·son • ***noun**, plural* **grandsons**

grandstand (grand′stand) ***noun*** the main seating area for people watching a parade or an outdoor sports event. A grandstand has raised rows of seats and is sometimes covered with a roof.
grand·stand • ***noun**, plural* **grandstands**

granite (gran′it) ***noun*** a very hard rock that is used for buildings and monuments. It is usually gray or pink and can be polished like marble.
gran·ite • ***noun***

granny or **grannie** (gran′ē) [*an informal word*] ***noun*** **1** a grandmother. **2** an old woman.
gran·ny or **gran·nie** • ***noun**, plural* **grannies**

granola (grə nōl′ə) ***noun*** a breakfast cereal made of oats, wheat germ, honey, bits of dried fruit and nuts, and other ingredients.
gran·o·la • ***noun***

grant (grant) ***verb*** **1** to give what is asked or wanted; let have; allow [Her parents *granted* her request.] —Look for the WORD CHOICES box at the entry **give**. **2** to admit that something is true; agree [I *grant* that you have reason to be angry.]
noun something that is granted or given [The school received a *grant* of $5,000 for the library.] —Look for the WORD CHOICES box at the entry **present**.
—take for granted to believe to be true or probable; assume [The coach always *takes for granted* that the players will be on time for the game.]
grant • ***verb*** **granted, granting** • ***noun**, plural* **grants**

Grant (grant), **Ulysses S.** (yo͞o lis′ēz) 1822-1885; the eighteenth president of the U.S., from 1869 to 1877. He was commander of the Union forces in the Civil War.
Grant, U·lys·ses S.

grape (grāp) ***noun*** a small, round, juicy fruit that grows in bunches on a woody vine. Grapes have a smooth skin that is usually purple, red, or green. They are eaten raw and are used to make wine, raisins, juice, jelly, and jam.
grape • ***noun**, plural* **grapes**

grapefruit (grāp′fro͞ot) ***noun*** a large, round fruit that has a yellow rind and a juicy, somewhat sour pulp. The grapefruit is related to the orange and the lemon.
grape·fruit • ***noun**, plural* **grapefruit** or **grapefruits**

grapefruit

a cat	ō go	ʉ fur	ə = a *in* ago
ā ape	ô law, for	ch chin	e *in* agent
ä cot, car	oo look	sh she	i *in* pencil
e ten	o͞o tool	th thin	o *in* atom
ē me	oi oil	*th* then	u *in* circus
i fit	ou out	zh measure	
ī ice	u up	ŋ ring	

WORD HISTORY

grapefruit

The **grapefruit** got its name from the fact that it grows in clusters on the tree, in much the way that *grapes* grow in bunches.

WORD CHOICES

Synonyms of **grasp**

Many words share the meaning "to take hold of."

clutch, grip, snatch, grab, seize

grapevine (grāp′vīn) ***noun*** **1** a woody vine that grapes grow on. **2** an informal way of spreading news or gossip from one person to another [I heard through the *grapevine* he was fired.]
grape·vine • ***noun,*** *plural* **grapevines**

graph (graf) ***noun*** a chart or diagram that shows the relationships or connections between two or more changing things. Connected lines, curves, pie shapes, or bars can be used in graphs to show these relationships.
graph • ***noun,*** *plural* **graphs**

-graph *a suffix meaning:* **1** something that is written or recorded [A *photograph* is a picture that is recorded by light on the film inside a camera.] **2** something that writes or records [A *seismograph* records earthquakes.]

graphics (graf′iks) ***plural noun*** the pictures, designs, and charts that are made by a computer and displayed on its screen.
graph·ics • ***plural noun***

graphite (graf′īt) ***noun*** a soft, black form of carbon that is used as the writing part in pencils.
graph·ite • ***noun***

grasp (grasp) ***verb*** **1** to seize firmly with the hand; grip [The pirate *grasped* the hilt of his sword and cut the rope with one blow.] **2** to take hold of with the mind; understand [Did you *grasp* what the story is about?]
noun **1** the act of grasping; grip of the hand [The fish squirmed from his *grasp* and fell into the water.] **2** control or possession [These towns were in the *grasp* of the enemy.] **3** the ability to seize or reach [It is on the top shelf, beyond the baby's *grasp*.] **4** understanding or knowledge [She has a good *grasp* of the subject.]
grasp • ***verb*** **grasped, grasping** • ***noun,*** *plural* **grasps**

grass (gras) ***noun*** **1** the common green plants with narrow, pointed leaves that cover lawns and meadows. **2** a plant with narrow leaves, pointed stems, and clusters of seeds. Wheat, oats, bamboo, and sugar cane are grasses.
grass • ***noun,*** *plural* **grasses**

grasshopper

grasshopper (gras′häp ər) ***noun*** a leaping insect that has two pairs of wings and strong hind legs. It feeds on leafy plants.
grass·hop·per • ***noun,*** *plural* **grasshoppers**

grassland (gras′land) ***noun*** open land with grass growing on it. Meadows and prairies are grasslands.
grass·land • ***noun,*** *plural* **grasslands**

grate[1] (grāt) ***verb*** **1** to grind into small bits or shreds by rubbing against a rough surface [The waiter *grated* some cheese on top of my plate of spaghetti.] **2** to make a harsh or rasping sound by rubbing or scraping [The door *grated* on its rusty hinges.] **3** to annoy or irritate [His boasting *grated* on us all.]
grate • ***verb*** **grated, grating**

• The words **grate** and **great** sound alike.
His voice can *grate* on my nerves.
A *grate* covers the basement window.
Emily Dickinson is a *great* American poet.

grate[2] (grāt) ***noun*** **1** a frame of metal bars for holding burning fuel in a fireplace or furnace. **2** a framework of metal bars or wires set in a window or door; grating.

G

grate • *noun, plural* **grates**
• The words **grate** and **great** sound alike.
Lay some logs on the fireplace *grate*.
If the hinges *grate*, apply some oil.
The party came as a *great* surprise.

grateful (grāt′fəl) ***adjective*** feeling thankful or showing thanks [I am *grateful* for her help.]
grate·ful • *adjective*

gratify (grat′i fī) ***verb*** to cause to feel pleased or satisfied [Actors are *gratified* by applause.]
grat·i·fy • *verb* **gratified, gratifying, gratifies**

grating (grāt′iŋ) ***noun*** a framework of parallel or crossed bars set over a window, door, or other opening. Windows on the ground floor often have gratings as protection.
grat·ing • *noun, plural* **gratings**

gratitude (grat′i to͞od *or* grat′i tyo͞od) ***noun*** a feeling of being grateful for some gift, favor, or kindness; appreciation.
grat·i·tude • *noun*

grave[1] (grāv) ***adjective*** **1** extremely serious; important [*grave* doubts; a *grave* responsibility]. **2** full of danger; threatening [a *grave* illness]. **3** dignified; solemn [a *grave* manner].
grave • *adjective* **graver, gravest**

grave[2] (grāv) ***noun*** **1** a place in the ground where a dead body is buried. **2** any place where a dead body is laid or comes to rest [The sea becomes the *grave* for many sailors.]
grave • *noun, plural* **graves**

gravel (grav′əl) ***noun*** a loose mixture of small stones and pebbles, used for paving roads or covering paths.
grav·el • *noun*

graveyard (grāv′yärd) ***noun*** a place where the dead are buried; cemetery.
grave·yard • *noun, plural* **graveyards**

gravitation (grav′i tā′shən) ***noun*** the force that causes all objects to be pulled toward one another. Gravitation keeps all the planets revolving around the sun and keeps them from moving off into space.
grav·i·ta·tion • *noun*

gravity (grav′i tē) ***noun*** **1** the condition of being grave, or serious; serious nature; importance [the *gravity* of a situation]. **2** the natural force that draws objects toward the center of the earth. Things fall to the ground because of gravity.
grav·i·ty • *noun*

gravy (grā′vē) ***noun*** **1** the juices given off by meat in cooking. **2** a sauce made by mixing these juices with flour and seasoning.
gra·vy • *noun, plural* **gravies**

gray (grā) ***noun*** a color made by mixing black and white.
adjective **1** of the color gray. **2** somewhat dark; dull or dismal [a *gray*, rainy day].
gray • *noun, plural* **grays**
• *adjective* **grayer, grayest**

grayish (grā′ish) ***adjective*** somewhat gray.
gray·ish • *adjective*

graze[1] (grāz) ***verb*** **1** to feed on growing grass or other plants in pastures [Cows are *grazing* in the meadow.] **2** to put into a pasture to feed [The farmer *grazes* livestock for a small fee.]
graze • *verb* **grazed, grazing**

WORD HISTORY

graze

The word **graze** comes from the old English word that means "grass." When sheep or cattle **graze,** they feed on grass.

graze[2] (grāz) ***verb*** to rub lightly or scrape in passing [The car swerved and *grazed* the tree.]
noun a scratch or scrape caused by grazing.
graze • *verb* **grazed, grazing** • *noun, plural* **grazes**

grease (grēs) ***noun*** **1** melted animal fat. **2** a soft, oily substance that is put on the moving parts of machines to make them run smoothly.
verb to smear with grease [He *greased* the cake pan before pouring in the batter.]
grease • *noun, plural* **greases**
• *verb* **greased, greasing**

greasy (grē′sē) ***adjective*** **1** smeared or soiled with grease [*greasy* hands]. **2** full of grease [*greasy* food]. **3** like grease; oily [a *greasy* hair lotion].
greas·y • *adjective* **greasier, greasiest**

a	cat	ō	go	ʉ	fur	ə =	a *in* ago
ā	ape	ô	law, for	ch	chin		e *in* agent
ä	cot, car	o͝o	look	sh	she		i *in* pencil
e	ten	o͞o	tool	th	thin		o *in* atom
ē	me	oi	oil	*th*	then		u *in* circus
i	fit	ou	out	zh	measure		
ī	ice	u	up	ŋ	ring		

great (grāt) ***adjective*** **1** much above the average in size, number, or amount [a *great* distance; *great* herds of buffalo] —Look for the WORD CHOICES box at the entry **large**. **2** very eager; enthusiastic [She's a *great* reader.] **3** very important; noted; remarkable [a *great* composer; a *great* discovery]. **4** more than usual in degree, power, or intensity; considerable [a *great* surprise; a *great* beauty; a *great* pain]. **5** [*an informal use*] fine or excellent [a *great* party].
great • ***adjective*** **greater, greatest**
• The words **great** and **grate** sound alike.
We swam a *great* distance that day.
Grate some cheese on the pizza.
She repaired the fireplace *grate*.

Great Britain (brit′n) the largest of the British Isles. It is divided into England, Wales, and Scotland.
Great Brit·ain

Great Dane ***noun*** a very large dog with short, smooth hair.
Great Dane • ***noun,*** *plural* **Great Danes**

great-grandchild (grāt′ grand′ chīld) ***noun*** a child of one's grandchild.
great-grand·child • ***noun,*** *plural* **great-grandchildren**

great-grandfather (grāt′ grand′ fä′ *th*ər) ***noun*** the father of one's grandparent.
great-grand·fa·ther • ***noun,*** *plural* **great-grandfathers**

great-grandmother (grāt′ grand′ mu*th*′ ər) ***noun*** the mother of one's grandparent.
great-grand·moth·er • ***noun,*** *plural* **great-grandmothers**

great-grandparent (grāt′ grand′ per′ ənt) ***noun*** the mother or father of one's grandparent.
great-grand·par·ent • ***noun,*** *plural* **great-grandparents**

Great Lakes a chain of lakes in Canada and the United States. They are Lakes Superior, Michigan, Huron, Erie, and Ontario.

Great Plains the broad, level land that stretches eastward from the base of the Rocky Mountains for about 400 miles in the U.S. and Canada.

Great Salt Lake a shallow salt lake in northern Utah.

Greece (grēs) a country in southeastern Europe, on the Mediterranean.

greed (grēd) ***noun*** the condition of being greedy [the miser's *greed* for money].

greedy (grēd′ē) ***adjective*** wanting or taking all that one can get with no thought of what others need [He was *greedy* for power and money.]
greed·y • ***adjective*** **greedier, greediest**

Greek (grēk) ***noun*** **1** a person born or living in Greece. **2** the language of the Greeks.
Greek • ***noun,*** *plural for sense 1 only* **Greeks**

green (grēn) ***adjective*** **1** having the color of growing grass [*green* peas; *green* leaves]. **2** covered with grass, trees, or other growing plants [*green* pastures; a *green* meadow]. **3** not ripe [*green* bananas]. **4** not having had training or experience [He is still *green* at his job.]
noun **1** the color of growing grass. **2** an area of land covered with grass that is in the center of a town [the village *green*]. **3** an area covered with short grass around each of the holes on a golf course. **4 greens** green leaves and stems of plants that are eaten as vegetables [salad *greens;* turnip *greens*].
green • ***adjective*** **greener, greenest** • ***noun,*** *plural* **greens**

greenhouse

greenhouse (grēn′hous) ***noun*** a heated building with a glass roof and sides that is used for growing plants.
green·house • ***noun,*** *plural* **greenhouses**

greenhouse effect ***noun*** the warm effect produced on the earth when heat from the sun is trapped by the atmosphere. A greenhouse works in the same way, trapping in heat from the sun.

greenish (grēn′ish) ***adjective*** somewhat green [a *greenish* yellow].
green·ish • ***adjective***

Greenland (grēn′lənd) a Danish island north-

east of North America. It is the largest island in the world.
Green·land

WORD HISTORY

Greenland

More than 85 percent of this island is covered with ice, and only a small part of the land is ever green. But the Scandinavian people who discovered it about 1,000 years ago wanted to attract settlers to it, and they knew that people would not want to live in ice and snow. They gave the island a very pretty, but false, name in their own language that was translated into English as **Greenland**.

green thumb *noun* a skill that a person seems to have for growing plants easily.

greet (grēt) *verb* **1** to meet and speak to with polite and friendly words; hail or welcome [Our host *greeted* us with a warm "Hello!"] **2** to meet or receive in a particular way [The speech was *greeted* with cheers.]
greet • *verb* **greeted, greeting**

greeting (grēt′iŋ) *noun* **1** the act or words of a person who greets others [Our hostess received us with a warm *greeting*.] **2 greetings** a message of friendly wishes [My parents send you *greetings*.]
greet·ing • *noun, plural* **greetings**

gremlin (grem′lin) *noun* a mischievous invisible being said to cause trouble. Gremlins are blamed in a humorous way for engine trouble in airplanes or for any sort of mechanical difficulty.
grem·lin • *noun, plural* **gremlins**

Grenada (grə nā′də) a country on an island in the West Indies. It includes a nearby chain of small islands.
Gre·na·da

grenade (grə nād′) *noun* a small bomb that is set off by a fuse and is usually thrown by hand.
gre·nade • *noun, plural* **grenades**

grew (gro͞o) *verb past tense of* **grow**.

greyhound (grā′hound) *noun* a tall, slender, swift dog with a smooth coat and a narrow head.
grey·hound • *noun, plural* **greyhounds**

grid (grid) *noun* **1** a framework of parallel or crossed bars; grating or gridiron. **2** a pattern of evenly spaced horizontal and vertical lines that form squares. Grids are used for locating points on a map or chart.
grid • *noun, plural* **grids**

griddle (grid′əl) *noun* a heavy, flat metal plate with a handle or a special flat, heated surface on the top of a stove, used for cooking pancakes and other foods.
grid·dle • *noun, plural* **griddles**

gridiron (grid′ī ərn) *noun* **1** a framework of metal bars or wires for broiling meat or fish; grill. **2** a football field.
grid·i·ron • *noun, plural* **gridirons**

gridlock (grid′läk) *noun* a traffic condition in which no vehicle can move in any direction. Gridlock can happen at an intersection or over a large urban area.
grid·lock • *noun*

grief (grēf) *noun* deep and painful sorrow.

grieve (grēv) *verb* **1** to fill with grief; sadden deeply [His death *grieved* us all.] **2** to feel grief; be sad [She is *grieving* over a lost cat.]
grieve • *verb* **grieved, grieving**

grill (gril) *noun* a framework of metal bars or wires for broiling meat or fish.
verb **1** to cook on a grill. **2** to question closely and for a long time [The police *grilled* the suspect.]
grill • *noun, plural* **grills** • *verb* **grilled, grilling**

grim (grim) *adjective* **1** not giving up; firm [The players had a *grim* determination to win the game.] **2** looking stern or harsh [a woman with a *grim* face]. **3** frightful; ghastly; sinister [*grim* jokes about death].
grim • *adjective* **grimmer, grimmest**

grimace (gri mās′ *or* grim′əs) *noun* a twisting of the muscles of the face. People often make a grimace when they are in pain or not happy about something.
verb to make a grimace [She *grimaced* when the doctor touched her bruised arm.]

a cat	ō go	ʉ fur	ə = a *in* ago
ā ape	ô law, for	ch chin	e *in* agent
ä cot, car	oo look	sh she	i *in* pencil
e ten	o͞o tool	th thin	o *in* atom
ē me	oi oil	*th* then	u *in* circus
i fit	ou out	zh measure	
ī ice	u up	ŋ ring	

grim·ace • *noun, plural* **grimaces** • *verb* **grimaced, grimacing**

grime (grīm) *noun* dirt or soot rubbed into a surface [faces covered with *grime* and sweat].

grimy (grīm′ē) *adjective* covered with grime; very dirty [*grimy* hands] —Look for the WORD CHOICES box at the entry **dirty**.
grim·y • *adjective* **grimier, grimiest**

grin (grin) *verb* to draw back the lips and show the teeth in a big happy or foolish smile [Jane was *grinning* with delight at the compliment.]
noun a big happy or foolish smile.
grin • *verb* **grinned, grinning** • *noun, plural* **grins**

grind (grīnd) *verb* **1** to crush or chop into small pieces or into powder [a machine that *grinds* coffee beans]. **2** to sharpen, smooth, or shape by rubbing against a rough surface [He *ground* the knives and scissors on the grindstone.] **3** to press down and rub together in a harsh and noisy way [She *ground* her teeth in anger.]
grind • *verb* **ground, grinding**

grindstone (grīnd′stōn) *noun* a flat, round stone that is turned on an axle for sharpening or polishing things.
grind·stone • *noun, plural* **grindstones**

grip (grip) *verb* to grasp and hold fast [The frightened girl *gripped* her father's hand.] —Look for the WORD CHOICES box at the entry **grasp**.
noun **1** the act of grasping and holding fast; a tight hold [Get a good *grip* on the baseball bat and swing it.] **2** firm control; full hold; power [Keep a *grip* on your emotions.] **3** a part that is designed to be gripped; a handle [a hammer with a wooden *grip*].
grip • *verb* **gripped, gripping** • *noun, plural* **grips**

grit (grit) *noun* small bits of stone or sand.
verb to clench or grind together [He *gritted* his teeth in anger.]
grit • *noun* • *verb* **gritted, gritting**

grits (grits) *plural noun* coarsely ground hominy.

gritty (grit′ē) *adjective* **1** full of or like grit; sandy. **2** full of courage; brave.
grit·ty • *adjective* **grittier, grittiest**

grizzled (griz′əld) *adjective* mixed or streaked with gray [a *grizzled* beard].
griz·zled • *adjective*

grizzly (griz′lē) *adjective* grayish; grizzled.
noun a short form of **grizzly bear**.
griz·zly • *adjective* **grizzlier, grizzliest** • *noun, plural* **grizzlies**

grizzly bear

grizzly bear *noun* a very large, ferocious bear. It has coarse brownish or grayish fur and lives in western North America.
grizzly bear • *noun, plural* **grizzly bears**

groan (grōn) *verb* to make a deep sound showing sorrow, pain, annoyance, or disapproval —Look for the WORD CHOICES box at the entry **cry**.
noun a groaning sound.
groan • *verb* **groaned, groaning** • *noun, plural* **groans**
• The words **groan** and **grown** sound alike.
His jokes usually get a *groan*.
Our dog is now fully *grown*.

grocer (grō′sər) *noun* a person who sells food and household supplies.
gro·cer • *noun, plural* **grocers**

grocery (grō′sər ē) *noun* **1** a store that sells food and household supplies. **2** **groceries** the goods sold by a grocer.
gro·cer·y • *noun, plural* **groceries**

groggy (grä′gē) *adjective* weak and unsteady as the result of something such as illness or lack of sleep; shaky and dizzy.
grog·gy • *adjective* **groggier, groggiest**

groom (gro͞om) *noun* **1** a person whose work is taking care of horses. **2** *a short form of* **bridegroom**.
verb **1** to brush, clean, and take care of horses. **2** to make neat and tidy in appearance [He *groomed* his hair.]
groom • *noun, plural* **grooms** • *verb* **groomed, grooming**

groove (gro͞ov) *noun* **1** a long and narrow hollow that is cut in or worn on a surface [The wheels of the truck left *grooves* in the driveway of our house.] **2** the track cut in a phonograph record for the needle to follow.
groove • *noun, plural* **grooves**

G

grope (grōp) ***verb*** **1** to feel or search about in a blind or fumbling way [She *groped* for her car keys in her coat pocket. He *groped* for an answer.] **2** to seek or find by feeling about [She *groped* her way in the dark.]
grope • ***verb*** **groped, groping**

gross (grōs) ***adjective*** **1** very bad or very easily noticed; extreme [a *gross* error; a *gross* lie]. **2** not refined; vulgar; coarse [*gross* language; *gross* manners] —Look for the WORD CHOICES box at the entry **coarse**. **3** with nothing taken away; total; entire [What is your *gross* income before you pay taxes?]
noun **1** a whole amount received; total [We earned a *gross* of $30, but we owed $10 for supplies.] **2** twelve dozen; 144 [He ordered a *gross* of pencils.]
gross • ***adjective*** **grosser, grossest** • ***noun,*** *plural for sense 1* **grosses** *or for sense 2* **gross**

grotesque (grō tesk′) ***adjective*** very ugly, strange, and unreal in a wild way; fantastic [*grotesque* drawings of imaginary sea creatures].
gro·tesque • ***adjective***

grouch (grouch) ***verb*** to be in a bad mood and keep finding fault with everything.
noun a person who grouches.
grouch • ***verb*** **grouched, grouching** • ***noun,*** *plural* **grouches**

grouchy (grouch′ē) ***adjective*** cross and complaining; in a bad mood —Look for the WORD CHOICES box at the entry **irritable**.
grouch·y • ***adjective*** **grouchier, grouchiest**

ground[1] (ground) ***noun*** **1** the solid part of the earth's surface; land; earth. **2** a piece of land used for a particular purpose [The students put up their tents on the *campground*.] **3 grounds** the lawns, garden, and other lands attached to a house or other building. **4** *often* **grounds** a reason, cause, or basis [On what *grounds* are you refusing?] **5 grounds** solid bits that settle to the bottom of a liquid [coffee *grounds*].
verb **1** to cause to run aground [The ship was *grounded* on the reef by the storm.] **2** to base or establish [On what do you *ground* your argument?] **3** to keep from flying [The storm *grounded* all airplanes.] **4** [*an informal use*] to punish by not allowing to leave home to meet with friends [Jenny's parents *grounded* her for a week.] **5** to connect a wire from an electrical circuit to the ground.
—get off the ground to get started [The science project *got off the ground* with the help of the students.] **—lose ground** to drop back; fall behind.
ground • ***noun,*** *plural* **grounds** • ***verb*** **grounded, grounding**

ground[2] (ground) ***verb*** *past tense and past participle of* **grind**.

grounder (groun′dər) ***noun*** a batted ball in baseball that rolls or bounces along the ground. This is also called a **ground ball**.
ground·er • ***noun,*** *plural* **grounders**

groundhog (ground′hôg) ***noun*** *another name for* **woodchuck**.
ground·hog • ***noun,*** *plural* **groundhogs**

group (gro͞op) ***noun*** **1** a number of persons or things gathered together [a *group* of students playing basketball]. **2** a number of related persons or things that form a class [the four food *groups*].
verb to gather into a group [*Group* yourselves in a circle.]
group • ***noun,*** *plural* **groups** • ***verb*** **grouped, grouping**

grouse (grous) ***noun*** a wild bird that looks like a plump chicken. Grouse are hunted as game.
grouse • ***noun,*** *plural* **grouse** or **grouses**

grove (grōv) ***noun*** a small group of trees.
grove • ***noun,*** *plural* **groves**

grow (grō) ***verb*** **1** to increase in size by natural development; develop; mature [She *grew* very fast until she was fifteen.] **2** to become larger; increase [The company has *grown* rapidly.] **3** to be found; exist [Oranges *grow* in warm regions.] **4** to cause to grow; raise [They *grow* wheat on their farm.] **5** to come to be; become [We *grew* tired during the long drive.]
—grow up to become an adult.
grow • ***verb*** **grew, grown, growing**

growl (groul) ***verb*** **1** to make a low, rumbling sound in the throat, such as the one made by an angry dog. **2** to grumble or complain ["I can't take any more work," he *growled*.]
noun the act or sound of growling.
growl • ***verb*** **growled, growling** • ***noun,*** *plural* **growls**

grown (grōn) ***verb*** *past participle of* **grow**.
● The words **grown** and **groan** sound alike.

a	cat	ō	go	ʉ	fur	ə = a *in* ago	
ā	ape	ô	law, for	ch	chin	e *in* agent	
ä	cot, car	o͝o	look	sh	she	i *in* pencil	
e	ten	o͞o	tool	th	thin	o *in* atom	
ē	me	oi	oil	*th*	then	u *in* circus	
i	fit	ou	out	zh	measure		
ī	ice	u	up	ŋ	ring		

The twins have *grown* up together.
I heard him *groan* with pain.

grown-up (grōn′up′) ***adjective*** of or for an adult [Running a bank is a *grown-up* activity. She has a very *grown-up* manner for her age.]
noun a fully grown person; adult. This noun is also spelled **grownup**.
grown-up • ***adjective*** • ***noun,*** *plural* **grown-ups** or **grownups**

growth (grōth) ***noun*** **1** the act or process of growing; development [Sunlight is necessary for the *growth* of most plants.] **2** an amount grown; increase [The tree showed a *growth* of two inches.] **3** something that grows or has grown [He shaved off two weeks' *growth* of beard. A tumor is a *growth* in the body that is not normal.]
growth • ***noun,*** *plural* **growths**

grub (grub) ***verb*** to dig in the ground; dig up; uproot [The boys went *grubbing* for potatoes in the vegetable garden.]
noun the larva of certain beetles and other insects. It looks like a short, fat worm.
grub • ***verb*** **grubbed, grubbing** • ***noun,*** *plural* **grubs**

grubby (grub′ē) ***adjective*** dirty or untidy [The mechanic had *grubby* hands.]
grub·by • ***adjective*** **grubbier, grubbiest**

grudge (gruj) ***verb*** to envy or resent something that a person has or has done [All the students *grudged* her success.]
noun bad feeling against a person who has or is supposed to have done something wrong [He bore a *grudge* against me all his life.]
grudge • ***verb*** **grudged, grudging** • ***noun,*** *plural* **grudges**

grueling or **gruelling** (gro͞o′əl iŋ) ***adjective*** very tiring; exhausting [a *grueling* race].
gru·el·ing or **gru·el·ling** • ***adjective***

gruesome (gro͞o′səm) ***adjective*** causing fear and disgust; horrible [a *gruesome* murder].
grue·some • ***adjective***

WORD HISTORY

gruesome

We get **gruesome** from a 600-year-old English word that means "to shudder." Something **gruesome** or horrible often makes us shudder.

gruff (gruf) ***adjective*** **1** rough and unfriendly; rude [a *gruff* reply; a *gruff* manner]. **2** harsh in sound; hoarse [*gruff* voices].
gruff • ***adjective*** **gruffer, gruffest**

grumble (grum′bəl) ***verb*** **1** to make a low growling or rumbling sound [We could hear thunder *grumbling* in the distance.] **2** to complain in an angry or sullen way [The students *grumbled* about the food in the cafeteria.]
noun an angry or sullen complaint [I don't want to hear any more *grumbles* about homework.]
grum·ble • ***verb*** **grumbled, grumbling** • ***noun,*** *plural* **grumbles**

grump (grump) ***noun*** a person who is constantly complaining.
grump • ***noun,*** *plural* **grumps**

grumpy (grum′pē) ***adjective*** in a bad or sullen mood; grouchy [Grandfather is *grumpy* today.]
grump·y • ***adjective*** **grumpier, grumpiest**

grunt (grunt) ***verb*** **1** to make the short, deep, hoarse sound of a hog. **2** to make a sound like this [Joe *grunted* as he lifted the chair.] **3** to say by grunting [She *grunted* a reply.]
noun the sound made in grunting.
grunt • ***verb*** **grunted, grunting** • ***noun,*** *plural* **grunts**

guarantee (gər′ən tē′) ***noun*** **1** a promise to replace something sold if it does not work or last as it should [a one-year *guarantee* on the clock]. **2** a promise or assurance that something will be done [You have my *guarantee* that we'll be on time for the game.]
verb **1** to give a guarantee for [The store will *guarantee* the refrigerator for two years.] **2** to promise or assure [I cannot *guarantee* that she will be there.]
guar·an·tee • ***noun,*** *plural* **guarantees** • ***verb*** **guaranteed, guaranteeing**

guard (gärd) ***verb*** **1** to watch over; protect; defend [A dog *guards* the house.] **2** to keep from escaping [Two police officers *guarded* the prisoners.] **3** to be watchful; take care [Lock the doors to *guard* against burglars.]
noun **1** a person or group that guards or protects [a museum *guard*. The palace *guard* left by the front gate.] **2** the act of guarding; careful watch; protection [The bank is under *guard*.] **3** something that protects against injury or loss [The hilt of a sword usually has a *guard* for the hand.] **4** either of two basketball players who set up offensive plays.

G

5 either of two football players on offense, left and right of the center.
—on one's guard careful and watchful [She's always *on her guard* in public.]
guard • *verb* **guarded, guarding** • *noun, plural* **guards**

guardian (gär′dē ən) *noun* **1** a person chosen by a court to take care of a child or of someone else who cannot take care of his or her own affairs. **2** a person who guards or protects; custodian.
guard·i·an • *noun, plural* **guardians**

guardsman (gärdz′mən) *noun* a member of a military guard.
guards·man • *noun, plural* **guardsmen**

Guatemala (gwä tə mä′lə) a country in Central America, south and east of Mexico.
Gua·te·ma·la

guava (gwä′və) *noun* the yellowish, pear-shaped fruit of a tropical American tree or shrub. It is used for making jelly.
gua·va • *noun, plural* **guavas**

guerrilla (gə ril′ə) *noun* a member of a small group of soldiers who are not part of a regular army. Guerrillas usually make surprise attacks behind the enemy's lines. This word is also spelled **gue·ril·la**.
guer·ril·la • *noun, plural* **guerrillas**

• The words **guerrilla** and **gorilla** sound alike.
The sniper was a *guerrilla*.
The *gorilla* and the chimp are related.

guess (ges) *verb* **1** to judge or decide about something without having enough facts to know for certain [Can you *guess* how old he is?] **2** to judge correctly by doing this [She *guessed* the exact number of beans in the jar.] **3** to think or suppose [I *guess* you're right.]
noun a judgment formed by guessing [Your *guess* is as good as mine.]
guess • *verb* **guessed, guessing** • *noun, plural* **guesses**

guest (gest) *noun* **1** a person who is visiting another's home. **2** a person who is being treated to something such as a meal or a concert [We were his *guests* tonight and didn't have to pay for anything.] **3** a paying customer of a hotel or restaurant. **4** a person who is invited to appear on a program [a TV show *guest*].
guest • *noun, plural* **guests**

guidance (gīd′ns) *noun* **1** the act of guiding, or directing; leadership [Our school clubs are under the *guidance* of teachers.] **2** advice or counsel; help [Mr. Smith will provide *guidance* to students in choosing their school courses.]
guid·ance • *noun*

guide (gīd) *verb* **1** to show the way to; lead [Can you *guide* me through the museum?] **2** to manage or control; steer [The President and Congress *guide* the affairs of the nation.]
noun **1** a person who leads others on a trip or tour. **2** something that controls, directs, or instructs [A dictionary is a *guide* to the meaning and use of words.]
guide • *verb* **guided, guiding** • *noun, plural* **guides**

guided missile *noun* a war missile or rocket that is guided to its target by electronic devices.
guided missile • *noun, plural* **guided missiles**

guide word *noun* a word that is printed at the top of the page of a dictionary or other reference book. It is usually the first or last entry on the page.
guide word • *noun, plural* **guide words**

guild (gild) *noun* **1** a group of people joined together in some work or for some purpose [The Ladies' *Guild* of our church is planning a supper.] **2** a union of men in the same trade in the Middle Ages. A guild set standards of work and protected the interests of its members.
guild • *noun, plural* **guilds**

• The words **guild** and **gild** sound alike.
They joined a *guild* to raise money.
Melt the gold to *gild* the bracelet.

guillotine (gil′ə tēn) *noun* an instrument for cutting off a person's head. It consists of two tall posts with grooves in them and a heavy blade that drops down between them along the grooves.
guil·lo·tine • *noun, plural* **guillotines**

guilt (gilt) *noun* **1** the condition or fact of having done wrong or committed a crime [Is there proof of his *guilt*?] **2** a feeling that one has done wrong or is to blame [She is filled with *guilt* but isn't sure why.]
• The words **guilt** and **gilt** sound alike.

a cat	ō go	ʉ fur	ə = a *in* ago
ā ape	ô law, for	ch chin	e *in* agent
ä cot, car	oo look	sh she	i *in* pencil
e ten	ōō tool	th thin	o *in* atom
ē me	oi oil	*th* then	u *in* circus
i fit	ou out	zh measure	
ī ice	u up	ŋ ring	

The jury was to decide on her *guilt*.
They specialize in *gilt* jewelry.

guilty (gil′tē) *adjective* **1** having done something wrong; being to blame for something [She is *guilty* of telling lies.] **2** judged in court to have done something against the law [The jury found him *guilty*.] **3** caused by a feeling of guilt [He had a *guilty* look on his face.]
guilt·y • *adjective* **guiltier, guiltiest**

Guinea (gin′ē) a country on the western coast of Africa.
Guin·ea

Guinea-Bissau (gin′ē bi sou′) a country in western Africa, on the Atlantic coast between Senegal and Guinea.
Guin·ea-Bis·sau

guinea pig

guinea pig (gin′ē) *noun* **1** a small, fat animal that has short ears and a short tail. It is related to the rat and is used in biology experiments. **2** any person or thing that is used in an experiment.
guin·ea pig • *noun, plural* **guinea pigs**

Guinevere (gwin′ə vir) the wife of King Arthur.
Guin·e·vere

guitar (gi tär′) *noun* a musical instrument with six strings. It is played by plucking the strings with the fingers or with a pick.
gui·tar • *noun, plural* **guitars**

guitarist (gi tär′ist) *noun* a guitar player.
gui·tar·ist • *noun, plural* **guitarists**

gulch (gulch) *noun* a narrow valley that has steep walls and is often cut by a swift stream.
gulch • *noun, plural* **gulches**

gulf (gulf) *noun* **1** a large area of ocean that reaches into land. It is larger than a bay. **2** a wide gap [a *gulf* between the two cultures].
gulf • *noun, plural* **gulfs**

Gulf Stream a warm ocean current, about 50 miles wide, that flows from the Gulf of Mexico along the U.S. coast and across the Atlantic.

gull (gul) *noun* a water bird that has large wings, webbed feet, and gray and white feathers.
gull • *noun, plural* **gulls** or **gull**

gullible (gul′i bəl) *adjective* capable of being easily cheated or tricked [a *gullible* person].
gul·li·ble • *adjective*

gully (gul′ē) *noun* a channel that has been worn away by running water; a small, narrow ravine.
gul·ly • *noun, plural* **gullies**

gulp (gulp) *verb* **1** to swallow in a hurried or greedy way [She *gulped* her breakfast and ran to school.] **2** to catch one's breath; gasp [The diver came up *gulping* for air.]
noun **1** the act of gulping [He drank the whole glass of milk in one *gulp*.] **2** the amount swallowed at one time [a big *gulp* of milk].
gulp • *verb* **gulped, gulping** • *noun, plural* **gulps**

gum[1] (gum) *noun* **1** a sticky substance that is given off by certain trees and plants. It is used in pastes, jellies, varnishes, and other products. **2** *a short form of* **chewing gum**.
verb **1** to stick together or cover with gum [She *gummed* the two pieces of paper together.] **2** to become sticky or clogged [The drain in the sink is always *gumming* up.]
gum • *noun, plural* **gums** • *verb* **gummed, gumming**

gum[2] (gum) *noun often* **gums** the firm flesh around the teeth.
gum • *noun, plural* **gums**

gumdrop (gum′dräp) *noun* a small candy that is like firm and chewy jelly.
gum·drop • *noun, plural* **gumdrops**

gun (gun) *noun* **1** a weapon that has a metal tube through which a bullet or shell is shot by exploding gunpowder. Rifles, pistols, machine guns, and cannons are guns. **2** anything like this that shoots or squirts something [The painter used a spray *gun* to paint the house.]
verb to shoot or hunt with a gun [The police officers *gunned down* the escaping criminals.]
gun • *noun, plural* **guns** • *verb* **gunned, gunning**

gunfire (gun′fīr) *noun* the shooting of a gun or guns.
gun·fire • *noun*

G

gunner (gun′ər) ***noun*** a person who operates a large gun or cannon.
gun·ner • ***noun,*** *plural* **gunners**

gunpowder (gun′pou dər) ***noun*** an explosive powder that is used in firing guns, in fireworks, or for blasting.
gun·pow·der • ***noun,*** *plural* **gunpowders**

guppy (gup′ē) ***noun*** a tiny tropical fish that lives in fresh water and is kept in home aquariums.
gup·py • ***noun,*** *plural* **guppies**

WORD HISTORY

guppy

The **guppy** was named after R. J. L. *Guppy*, a clergyman in the West Indies who sent the first samples of this kind of fish to England to be studied (around 1865).

gurgle (gʉr′gəl) ***verb*** **1** to flow with a bubbling sound [The water *gurgled* down the drain.] **2** to make a bubbling sound in the throat [Babies *gurgle* when they are pleased.]
noun the act or noise of gurgling.
gur·gle • ***verb*** **gurgled, gurgling** • ***noun,*** *plural* **gurgles**

gush (gush) ***verb*** **1** to flow out with force and in large amounts; spout [Water *gushed* from the broken pipe.] **2** to talk with too much feeling or enthusiasm and in a silly way [Paul and Janet *gushed* over their new grandson.]
noun the act or result of gushing; a sudden, heavy flow [a *gush* of water].
gush • ***verb*** **gushed, gushing** • ***noun,*** *plural* **gushes**

gust (gust) ***noun*** a strong and sudden rush of air or of something carried by the air [a *gust* of wind].
gust • ***noun,*** *plural* **gusts**

gut (gut) ***noun*** **1 guts** the intestines or bowels: this sense is now thought by some people to be not a polite use. **2** tough cord made from the intestines of sheep, goats, or other animals. It is used for violin strings, fishing lines, or in tennis rackets. **3 guts** [*a slang use*] courage or daring.
verb to destroy the inside of [The fire *gutted* the building, causing heavy damage.]
gut • ***noun,*** *plural* **guts** • ***verb*** **gutted, gutting**

Gutenberg (go͞ot′n bʉrg), **Johann** (yō′hän) 1400?-1468; German printer thought to be the first European to use separate pieces of type.
Gu·ten·berg, Jo·hann

gutter (gut′ər) ***noun*** **1** a narrow channel along the edge of a road or street to carry surface water. **2** a narrow channel of metal or tile along the edge of a roof for carrying rain water.
gut·ter • ***noun,*** *plural* **gutters**

guy (gī) [*a slang word*] ***noun*** **1** a boy or man. **2** any person [She's a good *guy*.]
guy • ***noun,*** *plural* **guys**

Guyana (gī an′ə *or* gī än′ə) a country in northeastern South America.
Guy·a·na

gym (jim) [*an informal word*] ***noun*** **1** *a short form of* **gymnasium**. **2** *another name for* **physical education**.
gym • ***noun,*** *plural* **gyms**

gymnasium (jim nā′zē əm) ***noun*** a building or room with equipment for doing exercises and playing games.
gym·na·si·um • ***noun,*** *plural* **gymnasiums**

gymnast (jim′nəst) ***noun*** a person who is trained in doing gymnastics.
gym·nast • ***noun,*** *plural* **gymnasts**

gymnastics (jim nas′tiks) ***plural noun*** exercises that develop and train the body.
gym·nas·tics • ***plural noun***

Gypsy (jip′sē) ***noun*** **1** *also* **gypsy** a member of a wandering people with dark skin and black hair. Gypsies are found throughout the world. They are thought to have come from India many centuries ago. **2 gypsy** a person who lives a wandering life.
Gyp·sy • ***noun,*** *plural* **Gypsies**

gyro (yir′ō *or* gir′ō) ***noun*** a sandwich of roasted lamb, or lamb and beef, in pita bread.
gy·ro • ***noun,*** *plural* **gyros**

gyroscope (jī′rə skōp) ***noun*** an instrument that consists of a heavy, spinning wheel mounted inside a set of movable rings. Its axis remains steady as the outer rings are shifted. It is used to keep ships, planes, and guided missiles steady and on course.
gy·ro·scope • ***noun,*** *plural* **gyroscopes**

a	cat	ō	go	ʉ	fur	ə =	a *in* ago
ā	ape	ô	law, for	ch	chin		e *in* agent
ä	cot, car	o͝o	look	sh	she		i *in* pencil
e	ten	o͞o	tool	th	thin		o *in* atom
ē	me	oi	oil	*th*	then		u *in* circus
i	fit	ou	out	zh	measure		
ī	ice	u	up	ŋ	ring		

H h

Hh Hh Hh Hh

The letter **h** *usually has the quiet sound you hear at the beginning of the words* **hello** *and* **haystack**. *In a few words, like* **honest** *and* **hour**, *it is not pronounced at all.* **H** *combines with some other letters to form combinations that have special sounds all their own: try pronouncing the words* **ch***air,* **ph***one,* **sh***ow,* **th***ick, and* **th***at.*

h or **H** (āch) ***noun*** the eighth letter of the English alphabet.
h or **H** • ***noun,*** *plural* **h's** or **H's**

H. or **h.** *abbreviation for* height.

ha (hä) ***interjection*** a word that is used to express a feeling such as surprise, triumph, scorn, or wonder.

habit (hab′it) ***noun*** **1** something that a person has done so often without thinking about it that it becomes hard to stop [He has the *habit* of biting his nails.] **2** special clothing such as a religious costume or an outfit for a particular use [a nun's *habit;* a riding *habit*].
hab·it • ***noun,*** *plural* **habits**

habitat (hab′i tat) ***noun*** the place where an animal or plant is normally found [Woodland streams are the *habitat* of beavers.]
hab·i·tat • ***noun,*** *plural* **habitats**

habitual (hə bich′o͞o əl) ***adjective*** **1** doing something by habit [He's a *habitual* smoker.] **2** resulting from habit; done or happening again and again [*habitual* rudeness] —Look for the WORD CHOICES box at the entry **usual**.
ha·bit·u·al • ***adjective***

hacienda (hä′sē en′də) ***noun*** a large ranch or country home in Spanish-speaking countries of the Americas.
ha·ci·en·da • ***noun,*** *plural* **haciendas**

hack (hak) ***verb*** to chop or cut with heavy blows [The explorers *hacked* their way through the underbrush.]
hack • ***verb*** **hacked, hacking**

hackle (hak′əl) ***noun*** **1** any of the feathers at the neck of a bird such as a rooster, a pigeon, or a peacock. **2 hackles** the hairs on a dog's neck and back that become stiff and stand up when the dog is ready to fight.
hack·le • ***noun,*** *plural* **hackles**

had (had) ***verb*** *past tense and past participle of* **have**.

haddock (had′ək) ***noun*** a small ocean fish used as food. It is related to the cod.
had·dock • ***noun,*** *plural* **haddock** or **haddocks**

hadn't (had′nt) had not.
had·n't

haggard (hag′ərd) ***adjective*** having a gaunt and tired look from illness, hunger, worry, or grief [the *haggard* survivors of a shipwreck].
hag·gard • ***adjective***

Hague (hāg), **The** one of the two capitals of the Netherlands. It is the seat of the government.

Haida (hī′də′) ***noun*** **1** a member of a North American Indian people who live in British Columbia and Alaska. **2** their language.
Hai·da • ***noun,*** *plural for sense 1 only* **Haidas** or **Haida**

hail[1] (hāl) ***verb*** **1** to welcome or greet with a shout; to cheer [The students *hailed* the ath-

letes as they walked into the stadium.] **2** to get the attention of by shouting or calling out [She *hailed* a cab.]
hail • *verb* **hailed, hailing**
● The words **hail** and **hale** sound alike.
I tried to *hail* the hiker from my car.
Sleet and *hail* make driving difficult.
A year after his operation, he was *hale*.

hail[2] (hāl) *noun* small round pieces of ice that sometimes fall during a thunderstorm.
verb to pour down hail [It *hailed* last night.]
hail • *noun* • *verb* **hailed, hailing**
● The words **hail** and **hale** sound alike.

hailstone (hāl′stōn) *noun* a piece of hail.
hail·stone • *noun, plural* **hailstones**

hair (her) *noun* **1** one of the thin growths, like threads, from the skin of animals and human beings. **2** the mass of these growths that cover a person's head or the skin of an animal. **3** a growth like a fine thread on the leaves or stems of some plants or on some insects.
hair • *noun, plural for senses 1 and 3* **hairs**
● The words **hair** and **hare** sound alike.
Uncle Mike was losing his *hair*.
The dog chased the *hare* down its hole.

haircut (her′kut) *noun* the act or a style of cutting the hair of the head.
hair·cut • *noun, plural* **haircuts**

hairdo (her′do͞o) *noun* the style in which a person's hair is arranged.
hair·do • *noun, plural* **hairdos**

hairdresser (her′dres ər) *noun* a person whose work is cutting and arranging hair.
hair·dress·er • *noun, plural* **hairdressers**

hairless (her′ləs) *adjective* having no hair; bald.
hair·less • *adjective*

hairpin (her′pin) *noun* a piece of flexible material such as wire or plastic that is shaped like a U. It is used to keep the hair in place.
hair·pin • *noun, plural* **hairpins**

hairstyle (her′stīl) *noun* a special way in which a person's hair is cut and arranged.
hair·style • *noun, plural* **hairstyles**

hairstylist (her′stīl ist) *noun* a person whose work is cutting and arranging hair.
hair·styl·ist • *noun, plural* **hairstylists**

hairy (her′ē) *adjective* covered with hair or having much hair [a *hairy* animal; *hairy* arms].
hair·y • *adjective* **hairier, hairiest**

Haiti (hāt′ē) a country on the western part of an island in the West Indies. The eastern part of the island is the Dominican Republic.
Hai·ti

hale (hāl) *adjective* healthy and strong.
hale • *adjective* **haler, halest**
● The words **hale** and **hail** sound alike.
The elderly man was fairly *hale*.
Shall I *hail* a cab for you?
Rain and *hail* interrupted our picnic.

Hale (hāl), **Nathan** (nā′thən) 1755-1776; an American soldier in the Revolutionary War who was hanged by the British as a spy.
Hale, Na·than

half (haf) *noun* **1** either of two equal parts of something [Five is *half* of ten.] **2** a half hour [It is *half* past two.] **3** either of the two main time periods of a game such as football or basketball.
adjective being either of two equal parts [a *half* gallon].
adverb **1** to half or about half of a whole amount [The bottle was *half* full.] **2** to some degree; partly [I was *half* convinced of her innocence.] **—in half** into halves [She sliced the apple *in half*.]
half • *noun, plural* **halves** • *adjective* • *adverb*

halfback (haf′bak) *noun* a football player whose position is behind the quarterback.
half·back • *noun, plural* **halfbacks**

half brother *noun* a person who is one's brother through one parent only.
half brother • *noun, plural* **half brothers**

halfhearted (haf′härt əd) *adjective* lacking enthusiasm or interest [He made a *half-hearted* attempt at grabbing the ball.]
half·heart·ed • *adjective*

half-mast (haf′mast) *noun* the position of a flag that is lowered

half-mast

a cat	ō go	ʉ fur	ə = a *in* ago
ā ape	ô law, for	ch chin	e *in* agent
ä cot, car	o͞o look	sh she	i *in* pencil
e ten	o͞o tool	th thin	o *in* atom
ē me	oi oil	*th* then	u *in* circus
i fit	ou out	zh measure	
ī ice	u up	ŋ ring	

about halfway down its staff. It is usually a sign of respect for someone who has died.

half note *noun* a note in music that is held half as long as a whole note.
half note • *noun, plural* **half notes**

half sister *noun* a person who is one's sister through one parent only.
half sister • *noun, plural* **half sisters**

half time *noun* the rest period between the halves of a game such as football or basketball.
half time • *noun, plural* **half times**

halfway (haf′wā) *adjective* **1** at the middle between two points or limits [The movie has reached the *halfway* mark.] **2** not complete; partial [*Halfway* measures will not solve the problem.]
adverb **1** to the midway point; half the distance [They had gone *halfway* home.] **2** not completely; partly [The house is *halfway* built.]
half·way • *adjective* • *adverb*

halibut (hal′i bət) *noun* a large flatfish of the northern seas, used as food.
hal·i·but • *noun, plural* **halibut** or **halibuts**

Halifax (hal′i faks) the capital of Nova Scotia, Canada.
Hal·i·fax

hall (hôl) *noun* **1** a passageway from which doors open into various rooms. **2** a room or passageway at the entrance of a building. **3** a large room that is used for meetings, dances, or other public gatherings. **4** one of the buildings of a college.
hall • *noun, plural* **halls**
● The words **hall** and **haul** sound alike.
There's a mirror at the end of the *hall*.
Will you help me *haul* out the sofa?

hallelujah or **halleluiah** (hal ə lo͞o′yə) *interjection* a word used to express praise to God.
hal·le·lu·jah or **hal·le·lu·iah** • *interjection*

Halloween or **Hallowe'en** (hal ə wēn′ *or* häl ə wēn′) *noun* the evening of October 31, celebrated by children in costumes asking for treats.
Hal·low·een or **Hal·low·e'en** • *noun*

hallway (hôl′wā) *noun* a passageway in a building; corridor.
hall·way • *noun, plural* **hallways**

halo (hā′lō) *noun* **1** a ring of light around a light source such as the sun, the moon, or a street light. **2** a ring of light showing that someone or something is holy. It appears in paintings around the heads of holy figures.
ha·lo • *noun, plural* **halos** or **haloes**

halo

halt (hôlt) *noun* a stop [I worked all morning without a *halt*.]
verb to stop [We *halted* often during our walk to enjoy the scenery. Rain *halted* the game.]
—call a halt to order a stop.
halt • *noun, plual* **halts** • *verb* **halted, halting**

halter (hôl′tər) *noun* **1** an upper garment without a back that is worn by a woman or girl. It is held up by a strap around the neck. **2** a rope or strap for leading or tying an animal.
hal·ter • *noun, plural* **halters**

halve (hav) *verb* **1** to divide into two equal parts [She *halved* the melon.] **2** to make only half as large, half as much, or half as many.
halve • *verb* **halved, halving**
● The words **halve** and **have** sound alike.
He will *halve* prices during the sale.
I *have* a red and white house.

halves (havz) *noun plural of* **half**.

ham (ham) *noun* **1** the meat from the upper part of a hog's hind leg that has been salted or smoked. **2** [*an informal use*] an amateur radio operator. **3** [*a slang use*] an actor who performs in an exaggerated way.
ham • *noun, plural* **hams**

hamburger (ham′bʉrg ər) *noun* **1** ground beef. **2** a small, flat patty of ground beef that has been fried or broiled. **3** a sandwich that is made of a patty of cooked ground beef, usually in a round bun.
ham·burg·er • *noun, plural for senses 2 and 3 only* **hamburgers**

WORD HISTORY

hamburger

The **hamburger**, or "Hamburg steak," as it was once called, gets its name from the city of *Hamburg* in Germany. At first, the name meant only the ground beef. By the 1930's in the U.S., **hamburger** was also a word for the sandwich. Now we also call the sandwich just a **burger**, and we even name other sandwiches by using this shortened name as a suffix. So a **cheeseburger** does have *cheese* in it, but remember that the **hamburger** was not named after *ham*.

Hamilton (ham′əl tən), **Alexander** (al′ig zan′ dər) 1755?-1804; the first secretary of the U.S. treasury, from 1789 to 1795.
Ham·il·ton, Al·ex·an·der

hamlet (ham′lət) ***noun*** a very small village.
ham·let • ***noun, plural*** **hamlets**

hammer (ham′ər) ***noun*** **1** a hand tool that is used for driving in nails, breaking stones, shaping metal, and other kinds of pounding. It usually has a metal head and a handle. **2** a thing that is like this in shape or use [The *hammers* in a piano strike the strings to produce tones.] ***verb*** **1** to hit with many blows [He *hammered* on the door with his fists.] —Look for the WORD CHOICES box at the entry **beat**. **2** to make or shape with a hammer [*Hammer* the silver into a plate.] **3** to drive or force [Quit trying to *hammer* your ideas into my head!]
ham·mer • ***noun, plural*** **hammers** • ***verb*** **hammered, hammering**

hammock (ham′ək) ***noun*** a long piece of canvas that hangs from ropes at each end and is used as a bed or couch.
ham·mock • ***noun, plural*** **hammocks**

hamper[1] (ham′pər) ***verb*** to get in the way of [Rains *hampered* the repairs.] —Look for the WORD CHOICES box at the entry **hinder**.
ham·per • ***verb*** **hampered, hampering**

hamper[2] (ham′pər) ***noun*** a large basket that usually has a cover [a picnic *hamper;* a *hamper* for dirty clothes].
ham·per • ***noun, plural*** **hampers**

hamster (ham′stər) ***noun*** a small animal like a mouse, with large pouches in its cheeks. It is often used in scientific experiments or kept as a pet.
ham·ster • ***noun, plural*** **hamsters**

Hancock (han′käk), **John** (jän) 1737-1793; a leader in the American Revolution. He was the first to sign the Declaration of Independence.
Han·cock, John

hand (hand) ***noun*** **1** the part of the body that is at the end of the arm. It includes the palm, fingers, and thumb. **2** a pointer on a clock or watch. **3** a side [The guest of honor will sit at your right *hand*.] **4** a person who is hired to work with the hands [a farm *hand*]. **5** control or power [The matter is now in the *hands* of our lawyer.] **6** a part or share in some action [Take a *hand* in the work.] **7** help [Give me a *hand* with this job.] **8** an outburst of applause [They gave the dancer a big *hand*.] **9** handwriting [I recognize your clear *hand*.] **10** a promise to marry [He asked for her *hand* in marriage.] **11** the width of the hand, about four inches [This horse is 15 *hands* high.] ***verb*** to give with the hand; pass [Please *hand* me that book.] **—by hand** with the hands, not with the use of machines [This purse was made *by hand*.] **—hand down** to pass along [This ring has been *handed down* from mother to daughter.] **—hand out** to give out; distribute.
hand • ***noun, plural*** **hands** • ***verb*** **handed, handing**

handbag (hand′bag) ***noun*** a woman's purse.
hand·bag • ***noun, plural*** **handbags**

handbook (hand′bo͝ok) ***noun*** a small book that contains facts or instructions on some subject; a manual [a scouting *handbook*].
hand·book • ***noun, plural*** **handbooks**

handcuff (hand′kuf) ***noun*** one of a pair of connected metal rings that are locked around a prisoner's wrists.
verb to put handcuffs on.
hand·cuff • ***noun, plural*** **handcuffs** • ***verb*** **handcuffed, handcuffing**

handcuff

a	cat	ō	go	ʉ	fur	ə =	a *in* ago
ā	ape	ô	law, for	ch	chin		e *in* agent
ä	cot, car	o͝o	look	sh	she		i *in* pencil
e	ten	o͞o	tool	th	thin		o *in* atom
ē	me	oi	oil	*th*	then		u *in* circus
i	fit	ou	out	zh	measure		
ī	ice	u	up	ŋ	ring		

handful (hand′fo͝ol) *noun* **1** as much or as many as the hand can hold [a *handful* of popcorn]. **2** a small number; a few [Only a *handful* of people attended the play.]
hand·ful • *noun, plural* **handfuls**

handicap (han′dē kap′) *noun* **1** a difficulty or advantage that is given to a player or contestant in a game or race. This is done so that everyone will have an equal chance to win. **2** something that holds a person back or makes things harder [Lack of education can be a great *handicap*.] **3** a physical or mental disability.
verb to be or give a handicap to; make things harder for [The fact that she couldn't speak Spanish *handicapped* Sue in Mexico.]
hand·i·cap • *noun, plural* **handicaps**
• *verb* **handicapped, handicapping**

handicraft (han′dē kraft) *noun* **1** an art or kind of work that calls for great skill in using the hands [carving, weaving, and other *handicrafts*]. **2** something that is made with the hands [Woven skirts, silver jewelry, and other *handicrafts* were on display.]
hand·i·craft • *noun, plural* **handicrafts**

handkerchief (haŋ′kər chif) *noun* a small, square piece of cloth that is used for wiping the nose, eyes, or face or for decoration.
hand·ker·chief • *noun, plural* **handkerchiefs**

handle (han′dəl) *noun* the part of a thing that can be held, lifted, pulled, or turned with the hand [the *handle* of a screwdriver; the *handle* of a mug].
verb **1** to hold or touch with the hand [*Handle* that glass vase with care.] **2** to take care of, manage, or control [Police *handled* the traffic well.] **3** to deal with [There are many ways to *handle* that problem.]
han·dle • *noun, plural* **handles**
• *verb* **handled, handling**

handlebar (han′dəl bär) *noun* *often* **handlebars** a curved metal bar on a bicycle or motorcycle that is used for steering.
han·dle·bar • *noun, plural* **handlebars**

handmade (hand′mād) *adjective* made by hand and not by machine [*handmade* boots].
hand·made • *adjective*

handout (hand′out) *noun* **1** a gift of something such as food or clothing to a person who asks for or needs it. **2** anything that is handed out, such as a homework assignment.
hand·out • *noun, plural* **handouts**

handrail (hand′rāl) *noun* a narrow rail that can be grasped by the hand for support. Stairways usually have handrails.
hand·rail • *noun, plural* **handrails**

handshake (hand′shāk) *noun* the act of holding another person's hand and shaking it up and down. People do this as a greeting or as a sign that they have come to agree on something.
hand·shake • *noun, plural* **handshakes**

handsome (han′səm) *adjective* **1** pleasant to look at; good-looking, especially in a masculine or dignified way [a *handsome* man; a *handsome* house]. **2** large in amount or size [a *handsome* sum of money].
hand·some • *adjective* **handsomer, handsomest**

handspring

handspring (hand′spriŋ) *noun* a kind of somersault that a person does while letting just the hands or one hand touch the ground.
hand·spring • *noun, plural* **handsprings**

handwork (hand′wurk) *noun* work that is done or made by hand.
hand·work • *noun*

handwriting (hand′rīt iŋ) *noun* **1** writing that a person does by hand with a pen or pencil. **2** a person's own way of forming letters and words in writing [Your *handwriting* is very clear.]
hand·writ·ing • *noun*

handy (han′dē) *adjective* **1** nearby; easy to reach [The bus stop is *handy*.] **2** easy to use; saving time or work [This is a *handy* device for opening cans.] **3** clever in using the hands; deft [She is *handy* with tools.]
hand·y • *adjective* **handier, handiest**

hang (haŋ) *verb* **1** to fasten or be fastened to

H

something above without being held up from below [We used a hook to *hang* the picture. The laundry *hung* on the line all day.] **2** to put to death or to die by hanging from a rope tied around the neck. **3** to fasten or be fastened in order to swing freely [The shutters are *hung* on hinges.] **4** to fasten to walls with paste [We *hung* the wallpaper upside down.]
—hang on **1** to keep hold. **2** to listen closely to [We were *hanging on* his every word.]
—hang up **1** to put a telephone receiver back in place at the end of a call. **2** to delay [We were *hung up* in heavy traffic.]
hang • *verb* **hung** or **hanged** (*for sense 2*), **hanging**

hangar (haŋ′ər) *noun* a shed that is used for repairing or storing airplanes.
hang·ar • *noun, plural* **hangars**
● The words **hangar** and **hanger** sound alike.
Planes are repaired in the *hangar*.
The suit is on a *hanger* in the closet.

hanger (haŋ′ər) *noun* a frame that is made of wood, wire, or plastic and is used for hanging clothes. A hanger usually has three corners and a hook at the top.
hang·er • *noun, plural* **hangers**
● The words **hanger** and **hangar** sound alike.

hang glider *noun* a large plastic sail or kite on a metal frame, with a harness underneath from which a person hangs and steers the sail in the sport of gliding through the air.
hang glider • *noun, plural* **hang gliders**

hangnail (haŋ′nāl) *noun* a bit of torn skin at the side or base of a fingernail.
hang·nail • *noun, plural* **hangnails**

hangout (haŋ′out) [*a slang word*] *noun* a place where some person or group spends much time.
hang·out • *noun, plural* **hangouts**

hanker (haŋ′kər) *verb* to have a strong wish or longing; crave [Her brother always *hankered* after fame and wealth.]
han·ker • *verb* **hankered, hankering**

Hanuka (hä′no͞o kä′ *or* hä′nə kə) *noun* a Jewish festival celebrating the restoring of a holy temple in Jerusalem in 165 B.C.
Ha·nu·ka • *noun*

haphazard (hap haz′ərd) *adjective* marked by lack of order or planning [a *haphazard* collection of books].
adverb by chance; in a random way [The toys were scattered *haphazard* on the floor.]
hap·haz·ard • *adjective* • *adverb*

happen (hap′ən) *verb* **1** to take place; occur [What *happened* at the party?] **2** to take place by chance [It *happened* to rain that day.]
hap·pen • *verb* **happened, happening**

happening (hap′ən iŋ) *noun* something that happens; an event [The *happenings* of the past week made exciting news.]
hap·pen·ing • *noun, plural* **happenings**

happily (hap′ə lē) *adverb* in a happy way or manner; with joy.
hap·pi·ly • *adverb*

happiness (hap′ē nəs) *noun* the fact or condition of being happy; joy.
hap·pi·ness • *noun*

happy (hap′ē) *adjective* **1** feeling or showing pleasure or joy; glad or content [a *happy* person; a *happy* song]. **2** lucky; fortunate [The story has a *happy* ending.]
hap·py • *adjective* **happier, happiest**

harbor (här′bər) *noun* **1** a place where ships can be safe from storms; a port. **2** a place where a person is safe; a shelter.
verb to shelter or hide [They were *harboring* a prisoner who had run away.]
har·bor • *noun, plural* **harbors**
• *verb* **harbored, harboring**

hard (härd) *adjective* **1** not easy to cut, bend, or crush; not soft [a *hard* rock] —Look for the WORD CHOICES box at the entry **firm**[1]. **2** not easy to do, understand, or deal with; difficult [a *hard* job; a *hard* problem]. **3** strong or powerful; violent [a *hard* punch]. **4** very cold and stormy [a *hard* winter]. **5** not showing love or being kind; not friendly [a *hard* heart; *hard* feelings]. **6** harsh or severe [a *hard* life]. **7** using energy and steady effort [a *hard* worker].
adverb **1** with effort and energy [We work *hard*.] **2** with strength or power [She hits *hard*.] **3** with pain or trouble [He took the bad news *hard*.]
—hard of hearing not able to hear well.
—hard up [*an informal use*] in great need of money.
hard • *adjective* **harder, hardest**
• *adverb* **harder, hardest**

hard-boiled (härd′boild′) *adjective* cooked in

a	cat	ō	go	ʉ	fur	ə = a *in* ago	
ā	ape	ô	law, for	ch	chin	e *in* agent	
ä	cot, car	o͝o	look	sh	she	i *in* pencil	
e	ten	o͞o	tool	th	thin	o *in* atom	
ē	me	oi	oil	*th*	then	u *in* circus	
i	fit	ou	out	zh	measure		
ī	ice	u	up	ŋ	ring		

hot water until all of the inside is solid [*hard-boiled* eggs].

hard copy ***noun*** a computer printout.
hard copy • ***noun,*** *plural* **hard copies**

hard drive ***noun*** the part of a computer that stores information on a rigid metal disk.
hard drive • ***noun,*** *plural* **hard drives**

harden (härdʹn) ***verb*** to make or become hard [We *hardened* the clay pots by leaving them out to dry. The pots *hardened* quickly.]
hard·en • ***verb*** **hardened, hardening**

hard hat ***noun*** **1** a helmet that is worn by construction workers and miners to protect the head. **2** [*a slang use*] a worker of this kind.
hard hat • ***noun,*** *plural* **hard hats**

hard hat

hardheaded (härdʹhed əd) ***adjective*** stubborn.
hard·head·ed • ***adjective***

hardhearted (härdʹhärt əd) ***adjective*** without pity or sympathy; cruel.
hard·heart·ed • ***adjective***

Harding (härʹdiŋ), **Warren G.** (wôrʹən) 1865-1923; the twenty-ninth president of the U.S., from 1921 to 1923.
Har·ding, War·ren G.

hardly (härdʹlē) ***adverb*** **1** only just; almost not [I can *hardly* tell them apart. There is *hardly* any time left.] **2** probably not [This can *hardly* be the best way.]
hard·ly • ***adverb***

hardship (härdʹship) ***noun*** something, such as pain or poverty, that is hard to bear and often causes suffering.
hard·ship • ***noun,*** *plural* **hardships**

hardware (härdʹwer) ***noun*** **1** tools, nails, hinges, and other things that are made of metal. **2** the mechanical and electronic part of a computer.
hard·ware • ***noun***

hardwood (härdʹwood) ***noun*** a type of wood that is hard and not easy to cut. The fibers of its grain are very close together. Oak, walnut, and maple are kinds of hardwood.
hard·wood • ***noun,*** *plural* **hardwoods**

hardy (härʹdē) ***adjective*** capable of surviving under bad conditions; strong [*Hardy* plants can live through frost.]
har·dy • ***adjective*** **hardier, hardiest**

hare (her) ***noun*** a swift, furry animal that has long ears, a split upper lip, and large, powerful hind legs for leaping. Hares are related to rabbits but usually are larger and have longer ears.
hare • ***noun,*** *plural* **hares** or **hare**

● The words **hare** and **hair** sound alike.
The dog chased the *hare* down its hole.
Uncle Mike was losing his *hair*.

harm (härm) ***noun*** **1** damage or hurt [Too much rain can do *harm* to crops.] **2** wrong; evil [I meant no *harm* by my remark.]
verb to hurt or damage; do harm to [Too much rain will *harm* the crops.] —Look for the WORD CHOICES box at the entry **injure**.
harm • ***noun*** • ***verb*** **harmed, harming**

harmful (härmʹfəl) ***adjective*** doing or capable of doing damage or harm [Sugar is *harmful* to teeth.]
harm·ful • ***adjective***

harmless (härmʹləs) ***adjective*** doing no damage or harm; not harmful [Most snakes are *harmless* to people.]
harm·less • ***adjective***

harmonica (här mänʹi kə) ***noun*** a small musical instrument with a row of reeds that sound tones when the breath is blown out or sucked in across them; mouth organ.
har·mon·i·ca • ***noun,*** *plural* **harmonicas**

harmonize (härʹmə nīz) ***verb*** **1** to sing or play in harmony [The four friends like to *harmonize* when they get together.] **2** to be in or bring into harmony [Those colors *harmonize* well.]
har·mo·nize • ***verb*** **harmonized, harmonizing**

harmony (härʹmə nē) ***noun*** **1** a pleasing arrangement of the parts that make something up [The *harmony* of the painting comes from the pleasant use of color.] **2** peace and friendship; friendly relations. **3** the sounding together of musical tones in a chord.
har·mo·ny • ***noun,*** *plural* **harmonies**

harness (härʹnəs) ***noun*** **1** an arrangement of leather straps and metal pieces that connects a horse or other animal to a wagon, plow, or load. **2** an arrangement of straps somewhat like this for another purpose [The *harness* under a parachute must be very strong.]
verb **1** to put a harness on. **2** to control in

order to use the power of [We've *harnessed* the energy of waterfalls to produce electricity.]
har·ness • *noun, plural* **harnesses**
• *verb* **harnessed, harnessing**

harp (härp) *noun* a musical instrument that has many tuned strings stretched on a large, upright frame. The harp strings are plucked by the fingers.
harp • *noun, plural* **harps**

harp

harpist (här′pist) *noun* a person who plays the harp.
harp·ist • *noun, plural* **harpists**

harpoon (här po͞on′) *noun* a spear with a barb at one end and a cord attached to theshaft. It is used for spearing whales or other sea animals.
verb to strike or catch with a harpoon.
har·poon • *noun, plural* **harpoons**
• *verb* **harpooned, harpooning**

harpsichord

harpsichord (härp′si kôrd) *noun* a musical instrument like a piano, that has a keyboard and strings that are plucked.
harp·si·chord • *noun, plural* **harpsichords**

Harrisburg (her′is burg) the capital of Pennsylvania.
Har·ris·burg

Harrison (her′i sən), **Benjamin** (ben′jə mən) 1833-1901; the twenty-third president of the U.S., from 1889 to 1893.
Har·ri·son, Ben·ja·min

Harrison (her′i sən), **William Henry** (wil′yəm hen′rē) 1773-1841; the ninth president of the U.S., in 1841. He was the grandfather of Benjamin Harrison.
Har·ri·son, Wil·liam Hen·ry

harrow (her′ō) *noun* a heavy frame with metal spikes or sharp disks that is pulled over plowed ground to break up the soil and to cover seeds.
verb to pull a harrow over.
har·row • *noun, plural* **harrows**
• *verb* **harrowed, harrowing**

harsh (härsh) *adjective* **1** cruel and severe [*harsh* punishment] —Look for the WORD CHOICES box at the entry **severe**. **2** rough or not pleasing [*harsh* rock music; *harsh* cloth].
harsh • *adjective* **harsher, harshest**

Hartford (härt′fərd) the capital of Connecticut.
Hart·ford

harvest (här′vəst) *noun* **1** the act or process of gathering a crop when it becomes ripe. **2** the time of the year when a crop is gathered. **3** all the grain, fruit, or other plant products that are gathered in one season; crop [They had a large *harvest* in 1989.]
verb **1** to gather in a crop [We're *harvesting* peaches.] **2** to gather a crop from [The farmers *harvested* the fields near the house.]
har·vest • *noun, plural* **harvests**
• *verb* **harvested, harvesting**

has (haz) *verb* the form of the verb **have** that is used to show the present time with *he, she,* and *it*. This form is also used with singular nouns [She *has* a new bike.]

hash (hash) *noun* a dish that is made of meat and vegetables that are chopped into small pieces, mixed together, and baked or fried.
hash • *noun, plural* **hashes**

hasn't (haz′ənt) has not.
has·n't

hassle (has′əl) *noun* [*an informal use*] something that troubles or bothers a person.
verb [*a slang use*] to bother or trouble.
has·sle • *noun, plural* **hassles**
• *verb* **hassled, hassling**

haste (hāst) *noun* **1** the act of hurrying [She left in *haste*.] **2** the act of hurrying in a careless way [*Haste* makes waste.]

a	cat	ō	go	ʉ	fur	ə =	a *in* ago
ā	ape	ô	law, for	ch	chin		e *in* agent
ä	cot, car	o͝o	look	sh	she		i *in* pencil
e	ten	o͞o	tool	th	thin		o *in* atom
ē	me	oi	oil	*th*	then		u *in* circus
i	fit	ou	out	zh	measure		
ī	ice	u	up	ŋ	ring		

hasten (hās′ən) ***verb*** **1** to go or act quickly; hurry [I *hastened* to call the doctor.] **2** to bring about faster; speed up [Bad weather *hastened* their departure from the beach.]
has·ten • ***verb*** **hastened, hastening**

hasty (hās′tē) ***adjective*** **1** done or made with haste [a *hasty* lunch]. **2** done or made too quickly, without enough thought [a *hasty* decision].
hast·y • ***adjective*** **hastier, hastiest**

hat (hat) ***noun*** a covering for the head that usually has a brim and a crown.
hat • ***noun,*** *plural* **hats**

hatch[1] (hach) ***verb*** **1** to bring forth offspring, such as young birds or fish, from an egg [Birds *hatch* their eggs by keeping them warm. The eggs began to *hatch* this morning.] **2** to come forth from an egg [All the ducklings have *hatched*.] **3** to think up or plan, especially in a secret or bad way [They *hatched* a plot to rob the bank.]
hatch • ***verb*** **hatched, hatching**

hatch[2] (hach) ***noun*** **1** *a short form of* **hatchway**. **2** a covering for a hatchway.
hatch • ***noun,*** *plural* **hatches**

hatchback (hach′bak) ***noun*** a car body with a rear panel that swings up to make a wide opening into an area in which things can be stored.
hatch·back • ***noun,*** *plural* **hatchbacks**

hatchery (hach′ər ē) ***noun*** a place for hatching eggs [a fish *hatchery*].
hatch·er·y • ***noun,*** *plural* **hatcheries**

hatchet (hach′ət) ***noun*** a small ax with a short handle.
hatch·et • ***noun,*** *plural* **hatchets**

hatchway (hach′wā) ***noun*** **1** an opening with a cover in the deck of a ship. Cargo is moved through it into and out of the place below, where it is stored. **2** an opening like this in the floor or roof of a building.
hatch·way • ***noun,*** *plural* **hatchways**

hate (hāt) ***verb*** to have very strong dislike for; to dislike very much [They *hate* their enemies. I *hate* to clean house.]
noun very strong dislike; hatred.
hate • ***verb*** **hated, hating** • ***noun,*** *plural* **hates**

hateful (hāt′fəl) ***adjective*** deserving to be hated [a *hateful* crime; a *hateful* bully].
hate·ful • ***adjective***

hatred (hā′trəd) ***noun*** very strong dislike; a feeling of hate.
ha·tred • ***noun***

hatter (hat′ər) ***noun*** a person who makes or sells men's hats.
hat·ter • ***noun,*** *plural* **hatters**

haughty (hôt′ē *or* hät′ē) ***adjective*** having or showing too much pride while looking down on others —Look for the WORD CHOICES box at the entry **proud**.
haugh·ty • ***adjective*** **haughtier, haughtiest**

haul (hôl *or* häl) ***verb*** **1** to move by pulling; drag or tug [We *hauled* the boat up onto the beach.] —Look for the WORD CHOICES box at the entry **drag**. **2** to carry by wagon, truck, or other vehicle [He *hauls* steel for a large company.]
noun **1** the act of hauling; a pull [Give a *haul* on the rope.] **2** an amount that is caught, taken, or won at one time [a large *haul* of fish]. **3** the distance over which something is hauled or someone travels [It's a long *haul* to town.]
haul • ***verb*** **hauled, hauling** • ***noun,*** *plural* **hauls**

● The words **haul** and **hall** sound alike.
Will you help me *haul* out the sofa?
There's a mirror at the end of the *hall*.

haunch (hônch *or* hänch) ***noun*** the part of the body that includes the hip, the buttock, and the upper part of the thigh.
haunch • ***noun,*** *plural* **haunches**

haunt (hônt *or* hänt) ***verb*** **1** to stay at or visit often [Some people believe ghosts *haunt* houses.] **2** to keep coming back to the mind of [Memories *haunted* him.]
noun a place that is visited often [After we moved away, I still went back to my old *haunts*.]
haunt • ***verb*** **haunted, haunting** • ***noun,*** *plural* **haunts**

have (hav) ***verb*** *Have* can be both a main verb and a helping verb. **I.** When *have* is a main verb, it means: **1** to be the owner of; possess [She *has* a car.] **2** to contain; include [A week *has* seven days.] **3** to hold in the mind [I *have* an idea.] **4** to go through; undergo [I *have* the measles.] **5** to get or take [The mechanic will *have* a look at our car.] **6** to take or accept to eat or drink [*Have* some cookies and milk.] **7** to be the parent of [Mrs. Moore *has* twins.] **8** to cause to do, be, or go [*Have* the plumber fix the leak. He *had* his shoes shined.] **9** to put up with; allow ["I won't *have* any more arguing," said the teacher.] **II.** *Have* as a helping verb is used with: **1** a past participle showing that an action has been completed [They *have* gone. They left before we *had* talked to them.] **2** a verb form preceded by the word *to* showing

H

that something is required or needed [We *have* to go. You will *have* to do it.]
—**have on** to be wearing [The teacher *has on* a red tie today.]
have • *verb* **had, having, has**

● The words **have** and **halve** sound alike.
I *have* a red and white house.
He will *halve* prices during the sale.

WORD CHOICES

Synonyms of **have**

The words **have, own,** and **possess** share the meaning "to be the one that something belongs to."

Mike *has* just one pair of shoes.

My dad *owns* a sailboat.

Einstein *possessed* great intelligence.

haven (hā′vən) *noun* **1** a place where a person can be safe [My home is my *haven* from the pressures and noises of the city.] —Look for the WORD CHOICES box at the entry **shelter**. **2** a port or harbor.
ha·ven • *noun, plural* **havens**

have-not (hav′nät′) *noun* a person or country that is poor or that has few resources.
have-not • *noun, plural* **have-nots**

haven't (hav′ənt) have not.
have·n't

STATE MAP

Statehood: 1959, the 50th state • **Capital:** Honolulu

Hawaii (hə wä′ē *or* hə wī′ē) a State of the U.S., consisting of a group of islands (**Hawaiian Islands**) in the northern Pacific Ocean. Its capital is Honolulu. Abbreviated **HI**.
Ha·wai·i

Hawaiian (hə wä′yən) *noun* **1** a person born or living in Hawaii. **2** the original language of Hawaii.
Ha·wai·ian • *noun, plural for sense 1 only* **Hawaiians**

hawk (hôk *or* häk) *noun* a large bird that has a strong, hooked beak and claws and has keen eyesight. It captures and eats smaller birds and animals.
hawk • *noun, plural* **hawks**

hawthorn (hô′thôrn *or* hä′thôrn) *noun* a shrub or small tree that has sweet-smelling white or pink flowers, small red berries, and thorns.
haw·thorn • *noun, plural* **hawthorns**

Hawthorne (hô′thôrn *or* hä′thôrn), **Nathaniel** (nə than′yəl) 1804-1864; a U.S. writer of novels and stories.
Haw·thorne, Na·than·iel

hay (hā) *noun* grass, clover, and other similar plants that have been cut and dried for feeding animals.
verb to cut down grass, clover, and similar plants and spread them out to dry.
hay • *noun* • *verb* **hayed, haying**
● The words **hay** and **hey** sound alike.
The farmer stores *hay* in her barn.
Hey! Look what I've got!

Hayes (hāz), **Rutherford B.** (ruth′ər fərd) 1822-1893; the nineteenth president of the U.S., from 1877 to 1881.
Hayes, Ruth·er·ford B.

hay fever *noun* an illness like a cold that makes the eyes water and causes sneezing and coughing. It develops in people who are sensitive to the pollen of ragweed and other plants.

hayloft (hā′lôft) *noun* a loft in a barn or stable that is used for storing hay.
hay·loft • *noun, plural* **haylofts**

haystack (hā′stak) *noun* a large heap of hay that is piled up outdoors.
hay·stack • *noun, plural* **haystacks**

hazard (haz′ərd) *noun* danger or something that is dangerous; risk [the *hazards* of icy roads].

a	cat	ō	go	ʉ	fur	ə =	a *in* ago
ā	ape	ô	law, for	ch	chin		e *in* agent
ä	cot, car	oo	look	sh	she		i *in* pencil
e	ten	ōō	tool	th	thin		o *in* atom
ē	me	oi	oil	*th*	then		u *in* circus
i	fit	ou	out	zh	measure		
ī	ice	u	up	ŋ	ring		

verb to take a chance on; to risk [He *hazarded* a guess.]
haz·ard • ***noun,*** *plural* **hazards** • ***verb*** **hazarded, hazarding**

hazardous (haz′ər dəs) ***adjective*** dangerous [Some factories give out *hazardous* waste.]
haz·ard·ous • ***adjective***

haze (hāz) ***noun*** fine mist, smoke, or dust in the air. It can make things hard to see —Look for the WORD CHOICES box at the entry **mist**.

hazel (hā′zəl) ***noun*** a shrub or small tree that is related to the birch. It produces edible nuts.
adjective light-brown.
ha·zel • ***noun,*** *plural* **hazels** • ***adjective***

hazel

hazelnut (hā′zəl nut) ***noun*** the small, round nut of the hazel. It is used as food.
haz·el·nut • ***noun,*** *plural* **hazelnuts**

hazy (hā′zē) ***adjective*** **1** covered by or full of haze [a *hazy* day in the fall]. **2** not certain; vague [Her future plans are *hazy*.]
ha·zy • ***adjective*** **hazier, haziest**

H-bomb (āch′bäm) ***noun*** *another name for* **hydrogen bomb**.
H-bomb • ***noun,*** *plural* **H-bombs**

he (hē) ***pronoun*** the man, boy, or male animal that is being talked about [Jim thought *he* was right.]
noun a man, boy, or male animal [This dog is a *he*.]
he • ***pronoun,*** *plural* **they** • ***noun,*** *plural* **hes**

head (hed) ***noun*** **1** the part of the body that contains the brain, eyes, ears, nose, and mouth. **2** a person's mind, intelligence, or common sense [Use your *head*.] **3** a single person of a group [Dinner is six dollars a *head*.] **4** a single animal of a group [fifty *head* of cattle]. **5** *often* **heads** the main side of a coin. It often shows a person's head. **6** the top part of a something [the *head* of a nail]. **7** the front part of something [She stood at the *head* of the line.] **8** the part of a thing that is opposite the foot [the *head* of a bed]. **9** the part of a thing that is used to hit other things [the *head* of a hammer]. **10** the part of a tape recorder that records or plays back the magnetic signals on the tape. **11** a large bud or a round, tight cluster of leaves [a *head* of cabbage]. **12** the person who is in charge; leader or ruler [the *head* of a committee]. **13** the highest position or rank [She's at the *head* of the class.]
adjective most important; of highest rank [the *head* coach].
verb **1** to be in charge of; direct [Who will *head* the new school?] **2** to be at the front or top of; lead [Maria *heads* the class in spelling.] **3** to turn in a certain direction [*Head* the horses home.] **4** to go in a certain direction [Are you *heading* toward town?]
—come to a head to reach a point at which something decisive happens. **—keep one's head** to keep control over oneself in a confusing or dangerous situation. **—lose one's head** to lose control over one's feelings or common sense. **—over one's head** beyond one's ability [These math problems are *over my head*.]
head • ***noun,*** *plural* **heads** *or for sense 4 only* **head** • ***adjective*** • ***verb*** **headed, heading**

headache (hed′āk) ***noun*** **1** a pain in the head. **2** [*an informal use*] a cause of worry or trouble [This old car has really been a *headache*.]
head·ache • ***noun,*** *plural* **headaches**

headband (hed′band) ***noun*** a strip of cloth that is worn around the head.
head·band • ***noun,*** *plural* **headbands**

headdress (hed′dres) ***noun*** a covering or decoration for the head.
head·dress • ***noun,*** *plural* **headdresses**

headfirst (hed′furst′) ***adverb*** with the head in front; headlong [He dived *headfirst* into the water.]
head·first • ***adverb***

heading (hed′iŋ) ***noun*** a title at the top of a paragraph, chapter, or other division of a piece of writing.
head·ing • ***noun,*** *plural* **headings**

headlight

headlight (hed′līt) ***noun*** a light at the front of a car, train, or other vehicle. It throws a bright light on the road ahead.
head·light • ***noun,*** *plural* **headlights**

headline (hed′līn) ***noun*** a line or lines of words in large letters at the top of a newspaper article. They tell about the article in a few words.
head·line • ***noun,*** *plural* **headlines**

headlong (hed′lôŋ) ***adverb*** **1** with the head first [He fell *headlong* into the pond.] **2** with wild speed or force; in a reckless way [She rushed *headlong* into a fight.]
head·long • ***adverb***

headmaster (hed′mas tər) ***noun*** a man who is principal of a school, especially a private school.
head·mas·ter • ***noun,*** *plural* **headmasters**

headmistress (hed′mis trəs) ***noun*** a woman who is principal of a school, especially a private school.
head·mis·tress • ***noun,*** *plural* **headmistresses**

head-on (hed′än′) ***adjective*** made or done with the head or front first [a *head-on* crash]. ***adverb*** with the head or front first [The two cars hit *head-on*.]

headphone (hed′fōn) ***noun*** a device for listening to a telephone, radio, or stereo. It has tiny speakers that are held to the ears by a band worn over the head.
head·phone • ***noun,*** *plural* **headphones**

headquarters (hed′kwôrt ərz) ***plural noun*** [*often used with a singular verb*] **1** the main office or center of work for the people in charge of an army or a police force. **2** a main office of any kind.
head·quar·ters • ***plural noun***

headrest (hed′rest) ***noun*** a support for the head such as the one on a dentist's chair.
head·rest • ***noun,*** *plural* **headrests**

headstand (hed′stand) ***noun*** the act of holding the body upright while it is resting on the head and both hands.
head·stand • ***noun,*** *plural* **headstands**

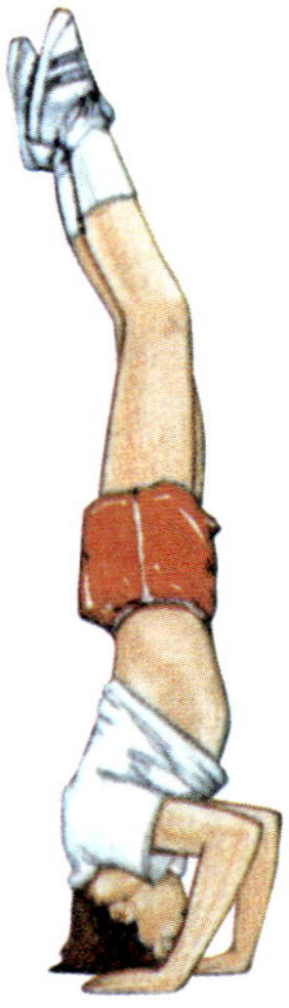
headstand

head start ***noun*** an advantage such as an early start given to someone taking part in a race.

headstone (hed′stōn) ***noun*** a stone marker that is placed at the head of a grave.
head·stone • ***noun,*** *plural* **headstones**

headstrong (hed′strôŋ) ***adjective*** doing just as one pleases, without listening to others; stubborn.
head·strong • ***adjective***

headway (hed′wā) ***noun*** **1** motion forward or ahead [The boat made slow *headway* against the current.] **2** advance or progress [The club has made *headway* in raising money.]
head·way • ***noun***

heal (hēl) ***verb*** to come or bring back to good health or sound condition; to cure or mend [The wound *healed* slowly. Time *heals* grief.]
heal • ***verb*** **healed, healing**

• The words **heal, heel,** and **he'll** sound alike.
Her broken heart began to *heal*.
There's a hole in the *heel* of my sock.
He'll never be the same again.

health (helth) ***noun*** **1** the condition of being well in body or mind; freedom from sickness. **2** a certain condition of body or mind [good *health;* bad *health*].

healthcare (helth′ker) ***noun*** **1** the work of preventing and treating people's illnesses and injuries that is done by doctors, nurses, dentists, and others. **2** a system or program that provides this kind of care.
health·care • ***noun***

health food ***noun*** food that is grown without chemical fertilizers and that is prepared without using additives or preservatives.

healthful (helth′fəl) ***adjective*** good for a person's health [*healthful* food].
health·ful • ***adjective***

healthy (hel′thē) ***adjective*** **1** having good health; well [a *healthy* baby]. **2** showing good health [a *healthy* appetite]. **3** good for a person's health; healthful [a *healthy* climate].
health·y • ***adjective*** **healthier, healthiest**

heap (hēp) ***noun*** a group of things lying together in a pile [The leaves were raked into *heaps*.]
verb **1** to pile up in a heap [She *heaped* her toys in the corner.] **2** to fill very full; load up [The plate was *heaped* with food by the cook.]
heap • ***noun,*** *plural* **heaps** • ***verb*** **heaped, heaping**

a	cat	ō	go	ʉ	fur	ə = a *in* ago	
ā	ape	ô	law, for	ch	chin	e *in* agent	
ä	cot, car	oo	look	sh	she	i *in* pencil	
e	ten	o͞o	tool	th	thin	o *in* atom	
ē	me	oi	oil	*th*	then	u *in* circus	
i	fit	ou	out	zh	measure		
ī	ice	u	up	ŋ	ring		

hear (hir) ***verb*** **1** to receive sound through the ears [I *hear* music. Pat doesn't *hear* well.] **2** to listen to; pay attention to [*Hear* what I have to say.] **3** to learn about; be told [I *hear* that prices are going up.] **—hear from** to get a letter, phone call, or other message from.
hear • ***verb*** **heard, hearing**
- The words **hear** and **here** sound alike.
  I can't *hear* you when the water is on.
  Plant the flowers *here*, under the tree.

SPELLING TIP

Use this memory aid to spell **hear**.
You h***ear*** with your ***ear***s.

heard (hʉrd) ***verb*** *past tense and past participle of* **hear**.
- The words **heard** and **herd** sound alike.
  Have you *heard* the bad news?
  A *herd* of elephants charged our camp.

hearing (hir′iŋ) ***noun*** **1** the power to hear; the sense that receives sound [His *hearing* is poor.] **2** a chance to be heard [The city council granted them a *hearing*.] **3** the distance over which sound can be heard [Are you within *hearing* of my voice?]
hear·ing • ***noun, plural*** **hearings**

hearing aid ***noun*** a small electronic device that makes it easier to hear sounds. It is worn by a person whose hearing is poor.
hearing aid • ***noun, plural*** **hearing aids**

hearsay (hir′sā) ***noun*** something that a person has heard but does not know to be true; rumor or gossip.
hear·say • ***noun***

heart (härt) ***noun*** **1** the hollow muscle that pumps blood from the veins through the arteries by contracting and expanding. **2** the part at the center [*hearts* of celery; the *heart* of the jungle]. **3** the main or most important part [Get to the *heart* of the problem.] **4** the human heart thought of as the part that feels love, pity, sorrow, and other emotions [a kind *heart*]. **5** courage or spirit [Don't lose *heart!*] **6** a figure that is shaped a little like the heart: ♥. **7** a playing card of a suit that is marked with this figure in red. **—by heart** **1** by memorizing [I learned the poem *by heart*.] **2** from memory [He knew the song *by heart*.]
heart • ***noun, plural*** **hearts**

heartbeat (härt′bēt) ***noun*** a single instance of contracting and expanding of the heart muscle.
heart·beat • ***noun, plural*** **heartbeats**

heartbroken (härt′brō kən) ***adjective*** very unhappy; filled with grief or sorrow [We were *heartbroken* when our dog died.]
heart·bro·ken • ***adjective***

hearth (härth) ***noun*** **1** the stone or brick floor of a fireplace. **2** home or life in the home.
hearth • ***noun, plural*** **hearths**

heartless (härt′ləs) ***adjective*** unkind or cruel [That was a *heartless* thing to do!]
heart·less • ***adjective***

hearty (härt′ē) ***adjective*** **1** warm and friendly [They gave us a *hearty* welcome.] **2** healthy, lively, or strong [a *hearty* laugh; a *hearty* appetite]. **3** large and satisfying [a *hearty* meal].
heart·y • ***adjective*** **heartier, heartiest**

heat (hēt) ***noun*** **1** the condition of being hot; great warmth [the *heat* of the sun]. **2** hot weather or climate [the *heat* of summer in the southern U.S.] **3** warmth for a room or house [We get our *heat* from a gas furnace.] **4** a single round or trial in a contest, especially a race.
verb to make or become warm or hot [We *heat* our water with electric power. The food *heated* slowly on the stove.]
heat • ***noun, plural for sense 4 only*** **heats**
• ***verb*** **heated, heating**

heater (hēt′ər) ***noun*** a stove, furnace, or appliance for providing heat.
heat·er • ***noun, plural*** **heaters**

heath (hēth) ***noun*** an open area of land that is covered with heather and low shrubs.
heath • ***noun, plural*** **heaths**

heathen (hē′*th*ən) ***noun*** a person who does not believe in the God of the Bible; someone who is not a Jew, Christian, or Muslim.
hea·then • ***noun, plural*** **heathens** or **heathen**

heather (he*th*′ər) ***noun*** a low plant that has tiny purple flowers.
heath·er • ***noun***

heave (hēv) ***verb*** **1** to lift or pull with much effort [We *heaved* the sofa onto the truck.] **2** to lift and throw with much effort [He *heaved* a skillet at me!] **3** to give out or say in a way that suggests effort or pain [She *heaved* a big sigh.] **4** to rise and fall in a regular rhythm [His chest *heaved* with sobs.]

noun the act or strain of pulling hard.
heave • ***verb*** **heaved** or **hove, heaving** • ***noun,*** *plural* **heaves**

heaven (hev′ən) ***noun*** **1** *usually* **heavens** the space that surrounds the earth and seems to arch over it, where the sun, moon, and stars appear; sky. **2** *often* **Heaven** in the Christian religion, the place where God and the angels are thought to be. **3** a place or condition of great happiness [It's *heaven* to be home again!]
heav·en • ***noun,*** *plural* **heavens**

heavenly (hev′ən lē) ***adjective*** **1** in or having to do with the heavens or the sky [The sun is a *heavenly* body.] **2** [*an informal use*] giving delight [This dessert is just *heavenly!*]
heav·en·ly • ***adjective***

heavily (hev′ə lē) ***adverb*** in a heavy way [It snowed *heavily* all day.]
heav·i·ly • ***adverb***

heavy (hev′ē) ***adjective*** **1** weighing a great deal; hard to lift or move because of weight [a *heavy* load]. **2** weighing more than others of the same type [Lead is a *heavy* metal.] **3** larger, deeper, or greater than usual [*heavy* sleep; *heavy* traffic]. **4** very serious or important [a *heavy* responsibility]. **5** full of sorrow; sad [a *heavy* heart]. **6** hard to do or deal with; difficult [*heavy* work; *heavy* sorrow]. **7** hard to digest [a *heavy* meal].
heav·y • ***adjective*** **heavier, heaviest**

WORD CHOICES

Synonyms of **heavy**

The words **heavy, massive,** and **stout** share the meaning "weighing very much."

a *heavy* load

a *massive* statue

a *stout* gentleman

Hebrew (hē′broo) ***noun*** **1** a member of the ancient people of the Bible who settled in a region that is now part of modern Israel. The Hebrews were the ancestors of the Jews. **2** the ancient language of this people. **3** the modern form of this language used in Israel today. Hebrew is written in a different alphabet from English.
He·brew • ***noun,*** *plural for sense 1 only* **Hebrews**

heckle (hek′əl) ***verb*** to annoy again and again by breaking in with many questions, shouting insults, and voicing opposing ideas or feelings [Some people in the audience *heckled* the speaker.]
heck·le • ***verb*** **heckled, heckling**

hectic (hek′tik) ***adjective*** full of rush, confusion, and excitement [a *hectic* day at work].
hec·tic • ***adjective***

he'd (hēd) **1** he had. **2** he would.
• The words **he'd** and **heed** sound alike.
He'd like to eat with us.
I paid no *heed* to her warning.

hedge

hedge (hej) ***noun*** a row of shrubs or bushes that are planted close together to form a kind of fence.
hedge • ***noun,*** *plural* **hedges**

hedgehog (hej′hôg) ***noun*** a small animal that has sharp spines on its back. They stand up when the animal curls up to protect itself. Hedgehogs live in Europe, Asia, and Africa.
hedge·hog • ***noun,*** *plural* **hedgehogs**

heed (hēd) ***verb*** to pay careful attention to [*Heed* my advice.]
noun careful attention.
heed • ***verb*** **heeded, heeding** • ***noun***
• The words **heed** and **he'd** sound alike.
You are wise to *heed* her advice.
He'd been in Paris during the war.

heel (hēl) ***noun*** **1** the back part of the foot, below the ankle and behind the arch. **2** the part of a stocking or sock that covers the heel. **3** the part of a shoe that is built up to support the heel. **4** something that seems like a heel

a	cat	ō	go	ʉ	fur	ə =	a *in* ago
ā	ape	ô	law, for	ch	chin		e *in* agent
ä	cot, car	oo	look	sh	she		i *in* pencil
e	ten	ōō	tool	th	thin		o *in* atom
ē	me	oi	oil	*th*	then		u *in* circus
i	fit	ou	out	zh	measure		
ī	ice	u	up	ŋ	ring		

in shape, position, or some other way. The end of a loaf of bread is called the heel.
verb to follow someone closely [Have you taught your dog to *heel?*]
heel • ***noun,*** *plural* **heels** • ***verb*** **heeled, heeling**

- The words **heel, heal,** and **he'll** sound alike.
  Teaching a dog to *heel* takes time.
  My leg took two months to *heal.*
  He'll be arriving in London tonight.

heifer (hef′ər) ***noun*** a young cow that has not given birth to a calf.
heif·er • ***noun,*** *plural* **heifers**

height (hīt) ***noun*** **1** the distance from the bottom to the top [The *height* of the building is 120 feet. She is four feet in *height.*] **2** the distance above the surface of the earth; altitude [The plane flew at a *height* of 20,000 feet.] **3** the highest point or degree [The painter had reached the *height* of fame.] **4** *often* **heights** a high place or point [Are you afraid of *heights?*]
height • ***noun,*** *plural* **heights**

heighten (hīt′n) ***verb*** to make or become higher, greater, or stronger; to increase [Music helps *heighten* the excitement of a movie.]
height·en • ***verb*** **heightened, heightening**

Heimlich maneuver (hīm′lik) ***noun*** an emergency treatment used to help a person who is choking on food or another object. Air is forced upward from the lungs by applying sudden pressure to the upper abdomen, just below the ribs. This forces the object out.
Heim·lich maneuver • ***noun***

heir (er) ***noun*** a person who gets or has the legal right to get another person's property or title when the other person dies.
heir • ***noun,*** *plural* **heirs**

- The words **heir, air,** and sometimes **err** sound alike.
  He was *heir* to his aunt's estate.
  Open the window to let in fresh *air.*
  To *err* is human, to forgive divine.

heiress (er′əs) ***noun*** a female heir.
heir·ess • ***noun,*** *plural* **heiresses**

heirloom (er′lo͞om) ***noun*** a valuable or valued article that is handed down in a family over the years.
heir·loom • ***noun,*** *plural* **heirlooms**

held (held) ***verb*** *past tense and past participle of* **hold**[1].

Helena (hel′ə nə) the capital of Montana.
Hel·e·na

helicopter

helicopter (hel′i käp′tər) ***noun*** a kind of aircraft that has no wings and has a large, horizontal propeller fixed above. It can be flown backward, forward, or straight up and down.
hel·i·cop·ter • ***noun,*** *plural* **helicopters**

WORD HISTORY

helicopter

The word **helicopter** comes to us through French, from the Greek words for "a spiral" and "a wing." The propeller, the part that acts as a wing, turns around and around in a way that suggests a turning spiral.

helium (hē′lē əm) ***noun*** a very light gas that is a chemical element. It is used to inflate large and small balloons because it is lighter than air and because it will not burn or explode.
he·li·um • ***noun***

hell (hel) ***noun*** *often* **Hell** the place where Christians believe that devils live and wicked people go to be punished after they die.

he'll (hēl) he will.

- The words **he'll, heal,** and **heel** sound alike.
  He'll go if you do.
  When will this cut *heal?*
  The *heel* of my shoe broke off.

hello (he lō′) ***interjection*** a word used to greet someone or to answer the telephone.
noun the act of saying or calling "hello."
hel·lo • ***interjection*** • ***noun,*** *plural* **hellos**

helm (helm) ***noun*** the wheel or tiller by which a ship is steered.
helm • ***noun,*** *plural* **helms**

H

helmet (hel′mət) ***noun*** a hard covering to protect the head. Helmets are worn by soldiers, football players, and bicycle riders.
hel·met • ***noun,*** *plural* **helmets**

helmet

help (help) ***verb*** **1** to give or do something that is needed or useful; make things easier for; aid; assist [We *helped* the homeless in our neighborhood. *Help* me lift this box.] **2** to make better; give relief to [This medicine will *help* your cold.] **3** to keep oneself from; to stop [He can't *help* coughing.] **4** to prevent from happening; avoid [an accident that couldn't be *helped*]. **5** to serve or wait on ["May I *help* you," asked the clerk at the store.]
noun **1** the act of helping; aid; assistance [Thank you for your *help*.] **2** someone or something that helps [Your advice was a great *help*.] **3** a person or persons hired to help, especially in housework or farming [The manager tries to find student *help* for the store.]
—help oneself to **1** to serve oneself with [*Help yourself to* some ice cream.] **2** to take without asking [He *helped himself to* some of my pudding.] **—help out** to help in getting or doing something [He does most of the cooking, but she likes to *help out*.]
help • ***verb*** **helped, helping** • ***noun***

helpful (help′fəl) ***adjective*** giving help; useful [a *helpful* person; *helpful* advice; *helpful* hints].
help·ful • ***adjective***

helping (help′iŋ) ***noun*** an amount of food for one person.
help·ing • ***noun,*** *plural* **helpings**

helping verb ***noun*** a verb that is used to help other verbs show special features, including: **1** time [I *have* gone there. He *is* going today. We *will* go tomorrow.] **2** possibility [Sue *can* swim.] **3** a want or desire [I wish they *would* stop talking.] **4** emphasis [I *do* hope we will win!]
helping verb • ***noun,*** *plural* **helping verbs**

helpless (help′ləs) ***adjective*** **1** not able to help oneself or take care of one's own needs [a *helpless* invalid]. **2** without help or protection [They were left *helpless* on the desert island.]
help·less • ***adjective***

hem (hem) ***noun*** the finished border or edge of a piece of cloth or of a skirt or other garment. A hem is made by folding the edge over and sewing it down.
verb to fold back the edge of and sew down [The seamstress *hemmed* the skirt.]
hem • ***noun,*** *plural* **hems** • ***verb*** **hemmed, hemming**

hemisphere (hem′i sfir) ***noun*** **1** one half of a sphere or globe. **2 Hemisphere** any of the halves into which the earth's surface is divided in geography. The earth is divided by the equator into the *Northern* and *Southern Hemispheres* or by a meridian into the *Eastern* and *Western Hemispheres*. The Western Hemisphere contains North and South America.
hem·i·sphere • ***noun,*** *plural* **hemispheres**

hemlock (hem′läk) ***noun*** **1** an evergreen tree with drooping branches, short needles, and small cones. The hemlock is related to the pine. **2** a poisonous weed that is related to parsley. A strong poison is made from this weed.
hem·lock • ***noun,*** *plural* **hemlocks**

hemp (hemp) ***noun*** a tall plant that has tough fibers in its stalk. This fiber is used for making rope or heavy cloth.

hen (hen) ***noun*** **1** an adult female chicken. **2** the female of the turkey, pheasant, or various other birds.
hen • ***noun,*** *plural* **hens**

hence (hens) ***adverb*** for this reason; as a result; therefore [He eats too much and is, *hence*, overweight.]

Henry (hen′rē), **Patrick** (pa′trik) 1736-1799; one of the leaders of the American Revolution.
Hen·ry, Pa·trick

her (hʉr) ***pronoun*** the form of **she** that is used: **1** after certain verbs [The dog bit *her*. I saw *her*. We have known *her* for many years.] **2** after prepositions [Tell the story to *her*. The song was written by *her*. Without *her* we would not have a team.]
adjective done by her or having to do with her [*her* work; *her* shoes].

herald (her′əld) ***noun*** an official in earlier

a	cat	ō	go	ʉ	fur	ə = a *in* ago	
ā	ape	ô	law, for	ch	chin	e *in* agent	
ä	cot, car	oo	look	sh	she	i *in* pencil	
e	ten	ōō	tool	th	thin	o *in* atom	
ē	me	oi	oil	*th*	then	u *in* circus	
i	fit	ou	out	zh	measure		
ī	ice	u	up	ŋ	ring		

times who made public announcements or carried messages, especially for kings and lords.
her·ald • *noun, plural* **heralds**

herb (ʉrb *or* hʉrb) ***noun*** a plant with leaves, roots, or other parts that are used to flavor food or as medicine. Mint, parsley, and sage are herbs.
herb • *noun, plural* **herbs**

herbivore (hʉr′bi vôr′) ***noun*** a herbivorous animal.
her·bi·vore • *noun, plural* **herbivores**

herbivorous (hər biv′ər əs) ***adjective*** feeding mainly on grass or other plants. Cows and deer are herbivorous.
her·biv·o·rous • *adjective*

Hercules (hʉr′kyo͞o lēz) a very strong and powerful hero in Greek and Roman myths.
Her·cu·les

herd (hʉrd) ***noun*** a number of cattle or other large animals that live and feed together.
verb to gather or keep together in a herd, group, or crowd [The cowboys *herded* the cattle. The teacher *herded* us through the museum.]
herd • *noun, plural* **herds** • *verb* **herded, herding**
• The words **herd** and **heard** sound alike.
A *herd* of elephants charged our camp.
Have you *heard* the bad news?

here (hir) ***adverb*** **1** at or in this place [Who lives *here*?] **2** to or into this place [Come *here*.] **3** at this point; now [The speaker paused *here*, and everybody applauded.]
interjection a word that is used to get attention, call an animal, or answer a roll call.
noun this place [Let's get out of *here*.]
• The words **here** and **hear** sound alike.
Plant the flowers *here*, under the tree.
I can't *hear* you when the water is on.

hereafter (hir af′tər) ***adverb*** after this; from now on [*Hereafter* I'll be careful.]
here·af·ter • *adverb*

hereby (hir′bī) ***adverb*** by means of this [He received a letter that said, "You are *hereby* ordered to appear in court."]
here·by • *adverb*

hereditary (hər ed′i ter′ē) ***adjective*** passing or capable of passing from a parent to offspring [Red hair is *hereditary*.]
he·red·i·tar·y • *adjective*

heredity (hər ed′i tē) ***noun*** the passing on of certain characteristics from parent to offspring [The color of a person's hair is determined by *heredity*.]
he·red·i·ty • *noun*

here's (hirz) here is.

heritage (her′i tij) ***noun*** something that is handed down from one's ancestors or from the past [Free speech is part of our *heritage*.]
her·it·age • *noun, plural* **heritages**

hermit (hʉr′mit) ***noun*** a person who lives alone, away from others. A hermit often chooses this way of life for religious reasons.
her·mit • *noun, plural* **hermits**

hero (hir′ō *or* hē′rō) ***noun*** **1** a person who is looked up to for having done something brave or noble [She became a *hero* when she saved the family from a burning house. Washington was the *hero* of the American Revolution.] **2** the most important male character in a story, poem, or play.
he·ro • *noun, plural* **heroes**

heroic (hi rō′ik) ***adjective*** **1** of or like a hero [She had a *heroic* life.] **2** showing great bravery or daring [the *heroic* deeds of the medieval knights]. **3** of or about heroes and their deeds [a *heroic* poem].
he·ro·ic • *adjective*

heroin (her′ō in) ***noun*** an illegal drug that is habit-forming.
her·o·in • *noun*
• The words **heroin** and **heroine** sound alike.
He was arrested for possessing *heroin*.
The *heroine* of the novel is a little girl.

heroine (her′ō in) ***noun*** **1** a woman or girl who is looked up to for having done something brave or noble [She became a *heroine* when she saved her brother from drowning.] **2** the most important female character in a story, poem, or play.
her·o·ine • *noun, plural* **heroines**
• The words **heroine** and **heroin** sound alike.

heron (her′ən) ***noun*** a bird that has long, thin legs, a long neck, and a long, pointed bill. Herons live in marshes

heron

or along river banks.
her·on • *noun, plural* **herons**

herring (her′iŋ) ***noun*** a small fish of the northern Atlantic Ocean. The full-grown fish are eaten cooked, dried, salted, or smoked. The young of some kinds of herring are canned as sardines.
her·ring • *noun, plural* **herrings** or **herring**

hers (hʉrz) ***pronoun*** the one or the ones that belong to her [I know that this book is *hers*. We all planted flowers, but *hers* haven't come up.]

herself (hər self′) ***pronoun*** **1** her own self. This form of **she** is used when the person who does the action of the verb is the same as the person who is affected by the action [She cut *herself*.] **2** her usual or true self [She's not *herself* today. She's being very mean.] This word is also used to give more force to what is being said [She *herself* told me.]
her·self • *pronoun*

he's (hēz) **1** he is. **2** he has.

hesitant (hez′i tənt) ***adjective*** stopping or waiting because one is not sure; having doubt [I am *hesitant* to lend them money.]
hes·i·tant • *adjective*

hesitate (hez′i tāt) ***verb*** **1** to stop or wait for a moment because one is not sure [He *hesitated* at the door before entering. Never *hesitate* to speak the truth.] **2** to feel unwilling [I *hesitate* to ask you for money.]
hes·i·tate • *verb* **hesitated, hesitating**

hexagon (hek′sə gän) ***noun*** a flat figure with six angles and six sides.
hex·a·gon • *noun, plural* **hexagons**

hexagon

hey (hā) ***interjection*** a word that is used to call out to get attention or to show surprise, pleasure, or wonder [*Hey*, watch out! *Hey*, I won!]
- The words **hey** and **hay** sound alike.
  Hey! Look what I've got!
  The farmer stores *hay* in his barn.

hi (hī) ***interjection*** a word that is used to say "hello." This is an informal word of greeting.
- The words **hi** and **high** sound alike.
  Say "*hi*" when you see her.
  How *high* will the price of oil go?

HI *abbreviation for* Hawaii.

hibernate (hī′bər nāt) ***verb*** to spend the winter in a kind of sleep. Bears, woodchucks, and snakes are some of the animals that hibernate.
hi·ber·nate • *verb* **hibernated, hibernating**

hiccup (hik′əp) ***noun*** a sudden stopping of the breath with a sharp gulping sound. Hiccups are caused by tightening of the muscles used in breathing and are hard to stop.
verb to have hiccups.
hic·cup • *noun, plural* **hiccups**
• *verb* **hiccuped** or **hiccupped, hiccuping** or **hiccupping**

hickory (hik′ər ē) ***noun*** a tall North American tree that has strong, hard wood. The hickory has smooth-shelled nuts that can be eaten.
hick·o·ry • *noun, plural* **hickories**

hid (hid) ***verb*** *past tense and a past participle of* **hide**[1].

hidden (hid′n) ***verb*** *a past participle of* **hide**[1].
hid·den • *verb*

hide[1] (hīd) ***verb*** **1** to put or keep out of sight; conceal [He *hid* the present in the closet. I *hid* behind the large tree.] **2** to keep others from knowing about; keep secret [She tried to *hide* her joy at the good news.] **3** to keep from being seen; cover up [The billboard *hides* the view.]
hide • *verb* **hid, hidden** or **hid, hiding**

WORD CHOICES

Synonyms of **hide**

The words **hide, bury,** and **conceal** share the meaning "to put something where it cannot easily be seen."

The toy was *hidden* deep in the chest.

The book was *buried* beneath a pile of clothes.

The key is *concealed* under the doormat.

hide[2] (hīd) ***noun*** the skin of an animal.
hide • *noun, plural* **hides**

hide-and-seek (hīd′n sēk′) ***noun*** a children's game in which one player tries to find the other players, who have hidden.

a cat	ō go	ʉ fur	ə = a *in* ago
ā ape	ô law, for	ch chin	e *in* agent
ä cot, car	oo look	sh she	i *in* pencil
e ten	ōō tool	th thin	o *in* atom
ē me	oi oil	*th* then	u *in* circus
i fit	ou out	zh measure	
ī ice	u up	ŋ ring	

hideaway (hīd′ə wā) [*an informal word*] ***noun*** a place where a person can hide.
hide·a·way • ***noun,*** *plural* **hideaways**

hideous (hid′ē əs) ***adjective*** horrible to see, hear, or think about; very ugly or disgusting [a *hideous* plane crash; a *hideous* sound].
hid·e·ous • ***adjective***

hide-out (hīd′out) [*an informal word*] ***noun*** a hiding place [The escaped prisoners used the empty house as their *hide-out.*]
hide-out • ***noun,*** *plural* **hide-outs**

high (hī) ***adjective*** **1** reaching a long distance up; tall; lofty [a *high* mountain]. **2** having a particular height as measured from top to bottom [The fence is four feet *high.*] **3** far above the ground [The plane was *high* in the clouds.] **4** upward to or downward from a height [a *high* jump; a *high* dive]. **5** above others in rank or position; more important; superior [She has a *high* position in city government.] **6** greater than usual in amount, cost, power, size, or degree [These are *high* prices for food. Yesterday the *high* temperature was 80°F. *High* winds damaged the sailboats in the harbor.] **7** raised in pitch [The soprano hit a *high* note.]
adverb in or to a high place, level, or degree [Throw the ball *high.*]
noun **1** a high place, level, or degree [Prices reached a new *high.*] **2** an arrangement of gears that gives the greatest speed [I shifted into *high.*]
—**high and dry** alone and helpless; abandoned [She missed the train and was left *high and dry* in the little country depot.]
high • ***adjective*** **higher, highest** • ***adverb*** **higher, highest** • ***noun,*** *plural* **highs**
• The words **high** and **hi** sound alike.
The kite flew *high* in the air.
Hi! How are you?

highchair (hī′cher) ***noun*** a baby's chair that is set on long legs and has a tray for food.
high·chair • ***noun,*** *plural* **highchairs**

high jump ***noun*** an athletic contest to see who can jump the highest over a bar that is raised higher after each jump.

highland (hī′lənd) ***noun*** a part of a country that is higher or more hilly than the region around it.
high·land • ***noun,*** *plural* **highlands**

highlight (hī′līt) ***noun*** the most important or interesting part or event [The trip down the canyon was the *highlight* of our vacation.]
high·light • ***noun,*** *plural* **highlights**

highly (hī′lē) ***adverb*** **1** to a high degree; very much [We were *highly* pleased with his work.] **2** in a kind or friendly way [They speak *highly* of you.] **3** in a high position or rank [a *highly* placed official]. **4** at a high rate [a *highly* paid executive].
high·ly • ***adverb***

Highness (hī′nəs) ***noun*** a title of respect used when speaking to or about a member of a royal family.
High·ness • ***noun,*** *plural* **Highnesses**

high-rise (hī′rīz) ***noun*** a very tall apartment house or office building.
high-rise • ***noun,*** *plural* **high-rises**

high school ***noun*** a school that includes grades 10, 11, and 12 and sometimes grade 9. It prepares students for college or trains them for a business or a trade.
high school • ***noun,*** *plural* **high schools**

high seas ***plural noun*** the open parts of the ocean that do not belong to any country.

high-strung (hī′struŋ′) ***adjective*** very nervous or tense [Some dogs are very *high-strung.*]

high-tech (hī′tek) ***adjective*** of or using very complex, electronic devices [Computers were an important part of the *high-tech* revolution.]

high-technology (hī′tek näl′ə jē) ***adjective*** *the same as* **high-tech**.
high-tech·nol·o·gy • ***adjective***

high tide ***noun*** the time when the tide reaches its highest level on the shore.
high tide • ***noun,*** *plural* **high tides**

highway (hī′wā) ***noun*** a main road.
high·way • ***noun,*** *plural* **highways**

hijack (hī′jak) ***verb*** to seize control of by force and take to a place that is not the original destination [The gangsters *hijacked* a truck full of goods.]
hi·jack • ***verb*** **hijacked, hijacking**

hike (hīk) ***noun*** a long walk, especially in the country or in woods.
verb to take a long walk.
hike • ***noun,*** *plural* **hikes** • ***verb*** **hiked, hiking**

hilarious (hi ler′ē əs) ***adjective*** very funny [a *hilarious* comedy] —Look for the WORD CHOICES box at the entry **funny**.
hi·lar·i·ous • ***adjective***

hill (hil) ***noun*** **1** a rounded area of the earth that is higher than the land around it. A hill is not as high as a mountain. **2** a small heap

H

or mound [an *anthill*].
hill • *noun, plural* **hills**

hillside (hil′sīd) ***noun*** the slope of a hill.
hill·side • *noun, plural* **hillsides**

hilltop (hil′täp) ***noun*** the top of a hill.
hill·top • *noun, plural* **hilltops**

hilly (hil′ē) ***adjective*** full of hills [the *hilly* countryside; a *hilly* city].
hill·y • ***adjective*** **hillier, hilliest**

hilt (hilt) ***noun*** the handle of a sword or dagger.
hilt • *noun, plural* **hilts**

him (him) ***pronoun*** The form of **he** that is used: **1** after certain verbs [The dog bit *him*. I saw *him*. We knew *him* for many years.] **2** after prepositions [Tell the story to *him*. The song was written by *him*. Without *him*, we would not have a team.]
● The words **him** and **hymn** sound alike.
Tell *him* to wash the car today.
We will now sing *Hymn* number 40.

Himalayas (him ə lā′əz) a group of very high mountains between India and China.
Hi·ma·la·yas

himself (him self′) ***pronoun*** **1** his own self. This form of **he** is used when the person who does the action of the verb is the same as the person who is affected by the action [He cut *himself*.] **2** his usual or true self [He's not *himself* today. He's being very mean.] This word is also used to give more force to what is being said. [He *himself* told me.]
him·self • ***pronoun***

hind (hīnd) ***adjective*** back; rear [a *hind* leg].

hinder (hin′dər) ***verb*** to hold back; get in the way of [Heavy snows *hindered* us on our trip.]
hin·der • ***verb*** **hindered, hindering**

WORD CHOICES

Synonyms of **hinder**

Many words share the meaning "to get in the way and slow down or hold back."

bar	hamper
block	obstruct

Hindi (hin′dē) ***noun*** the main language of India. It is now the official language.
Hin·di • ***noun***

hindrance (hin′drəns) ***noun*** a person or thing that gets in the way of progress; obstacle [A poor education can be a *hindrance* to success.]
hin·drance • *noun, plural* **hindrances**

Hinduism (hin′do͞o iz′əm) ***noun*** the main religion of India.
Hin·du·ism • ***noun***

hinge (hinj) ***noun*** a joint on which a door, gate, or lid swings open and shut or up and down.
verb **1** to put a hinge or hinges on. **2** to depend on in an important way [Our chances of winning *hinge* on whether or not you play.]
hinge • *noun, plural* **hinges** • ***verb*** **hinged, hinging**

hint (hint) ***noun*** a slight suggestion that is not made in an open or direct way [When she began reading again, we took the *hint* and left.]
verb to suggest in a way that is not open or direct [He *hinted* that he would like to go with us.]
hint • *noun, plural* **hints** • ***verb*** **hinted, hinting**

hip (hip) ***noun*** the part between the upper thigh and the waist on either side of the body.
hip • *noun, plural* **hips**

hippo (hip′ō) [*an informal word*] ***noun*** *a short form of* **hippopotamus**.
hip·po • *noun, plural* **hippos**

hippopotamus

hippopotamus (hip ə pät′ə məs) ***noun*** a large animal with a thick skin and short legs. It feeds on plants and lives in or near rivers in Africa.
hip·po·pot·a·mus • ***noun***, *plural* **hippopotamuses**

a cat	ō go	ʉ fur	ə = a *in* ago
ā ape	ô law, for	ch chin	e *in* agent
ä cot, car	oo look	sh she	i *in* pencil
e ten	o͞o tool	th thin	o *in* atom
ē me	oi oil	*th* then	u *in* circus
i fit	ou out	zh measure	
ī ice	u up	ŋ ring	

WORD HISTORY

hippopotamus

To people living in ancient Greece, the **hippopotamus** looked like a large horse. Since it also spent so much time in water, they took their word for "horse" and put it together with their word for "river" to form a name for the animal that means "river horse."

hire (hīr) ***verb*** **1** to agree to pay wages to in return for work; employ [She has *hired* a new secretary.] **2** to pay money for the use of; rent [Let's *hire* bicycles for the picnic.]
noun an amount of money that is paid for the services of a person or the use of a thing.
—for hire available for work or use in return for pay [Are these bikes *for hire?*]
hire • ***verb*** **hired, hiring** • ***noun***

his (hiz) ***pronoun*** the one or the ones that belong to him [I know that this book is *his.* We all planted flowers, but *his* haven't come up.]
adjective done by him or having to do with him [*his* work; *his* shoes].

Hispanic (hi span′ik) ***noun*** a person of Latin American origin who lives in the U.S. and usually speaks Spanish.
adjective **1** of or having to do with Hispanics. **2** having to do with Spain or Latin America, their people, or their culture.
His·pan·ic • ***noun,*** *plural* **Hispanics** • ***adjective***

hiss (his) ***verb*** **1** to make a sound like the sound of an *S* that is held for a long time [The snake *hissed.* Gas *hissed* from the stove burner.] **2** to make such a sound in showing dislike [The students *hissed* the speaker.]
noun the act or sound of hissing.
hiss • ***verb*** **hissed, hissing** • ***noun,*** *plural* **hisses**

historian (his tôr′ē ən) ***noun*** a person who writes or knows a great deal about history.
his·to·ri·an • ***noun,*** *plural* **historians**

historic (his tôr′ik) ***adjective*** famous in history; historical [a *historic* building].
his·tor·ic • ***adjective***

historical (his tôr′i kəl) ***adjective*** **1** of or having to do with history [*historical* facts; *historical* records]. **2** based on real people or events of the past [a *historical* novel].
his·tor·i·cal • ***adjective***

history (his′tər ē) ***noun*** **1** all that has happened in the life of something or someone such as a people, country, science, art, or person [the *history* of Maine; the *history* of medicine]. **2** the record of everything that has happened in the past [one of the most famous generals in *history*]. **3** the study that keeps a record of past events. History is a special field of knowledge [How will *history* treat his presidency?] **4** a story or tale [This hat has a strange *history.*]
his·to·ry • ***noun,*** *plural* **histories**

hit (hit) ***verb*** **1** to come against with force; strike [The car *hit* the tree.] **2** to cause to knock, bump, or strike [He *hit* his head on the door.] **3** to strike by throwing or shooting something at [She *hit* the target with her next shot.] **4** to drive or propel by striking with something such as a bat or racket [He grabbed the bat and *hit* the ball as far as he could.] **5** to have a great effect or influence on; affect [Floods *hit* the small towns by the river hard.] **6** to get a hit in baseball [She *hit* a home run.]
noun **1** a blow or stroke that strikes its mark. **2** something such as a song, play, record, or book that is a great success. **3** the successful hitting of a baseball, which lets the batter get on base safely. This play is also called a **base hit.**
—hit it off to get along well together.
hit • ***verb*** **hit, hitting** • ***noun,*** *plural* **hits**

hitch (hich) ***verb*** **1** to fasten with something such as a hook, knot, or strap [She *hitched* her horse to the fence.] **2** to raise with a quick pull [He *hitched* up his pants.]
noun **1** a quick pull; tug or jerk [She gave her skirt a *hitch.*] **2** something that gets in the way [The parade went on without a *hitch.*]
hitch • ***verb*** **hitched, hitching** • ***noun,*** *plural* **hitches**

hitchhike (hich′hīk) ***verb*** to travel by asking for rides from drivers along the way.
hitch·hike • ***verb*** **hitchhiked, hitchhiking**

Hitler (hit′lər), **Adolf** (ad′ôlf *or* ā′dôlf) 1889-1945; the dictator of Germany from 1933 to 1945.
Hit·ler, Ad·olf

H

hive

hive (hīv) ***noun*** **1** a box or other shelter for a colony of bees; beehive. **2** a colony of bees living in a hive.
hive • ***noun,*** *plural* **hives**

hives (hīvz) ***plural noun*** a skin disease caused by an allergy. Raised, itchy, red patches form on the skin.

hoard (hôrd) ***verb*** to collect and store away, often secretly [A squirrel *hoards* acorns.]
noun anything that is hoarded [He found the squirrel's *hoard* of acorns.]
hoard • ***verb*** **hoarded, hoarding** • ***noun,*** *plural* **hoards**

- The words **hoard** and **horde** sound alike.
  Misers *hoard* money.
  A *horde* of barbarians sacked Rome.

hoarse (hôrs) ***adjective*** sounding rough and husky [She became *hoarse* from shouting during the basketball game.]
hoarse • ***adjective*** **hoarser, hoarsest**

- The words **hoarse** and **horse** sound alike.
  I am too *hoarse* to sing.
  Have you ever ridden a *horse?*

hoax (hōks) ***noun*** something that is meant to trick or fool others.
hoax • ***noun,*** *plural* **hoaxes**

hobble (häb′əl) ***verb*** to walk in a lame or clumsy way; limp.
hob·ble • ***verb*** **hobbled, hobbling**

hobby (häb′ē) ***noun*** something that one likes to do for pleasure in one's spare time [Her *hobby* is collecting stamps.]
hob·by • ***noun,*** *plural* **hobbies**

hobo (hō′bō) ***noun*** a person who wanders from place to place, often doing odd jobs.
ho·bo • ***noun,*** *plural* **hobos** or **hoboes**

hockey (häk′ē) ***noun*** **1** a game played on ice in which the players wear ice skates and use curved sticks to try to drive a puck into the other team's goal. This game is also called **ice hockey**. **2** a game like this played on a dry field with a small ball. This game is also called **field hockey**.
hock·ey • ***noun***

hoe

hoe (hō) ***noun*** a garden tool with a thin, flat blade on a long handle. It is used for removing weeds and for loosening the soil.
verb to dig, loosen the soil, or remove weeds with a hoe.
hoe • ***noun,*** *plural* **hoes** • ***verb*** **hoed, hoeing**

hog (hôg) ***noun*** a pig, especially a full-grown pig raised for its meat.
verb [*a slang use*] to take all or too much of [Don't *hog* all the room on the bench.]
hog • ***noun,*** *plural* **hogs** • ***verb*** **hogged, hogging**

hogan (hō′gən) ***noun*** a house made of logs or branches covered with mud or sod. Some Navajo Indians live in hogans.
ho·gan • ***noun,*** *plural* **hogans**

hoist (hoist) ***verb*** to lift or pull up; to raise, with a crane, pulley, or rope [They *hoisted* the clock into place on top of the building.]
hoist • ***verb*** **hoisted, hoisting**

hold[1] (hōld) ***verb*** **1** to take and keep in the hands or arms [Please *hold* the baby for a

a	cat	ō	go	ʉ	fur	ə = a *in* ago	
ā	ape	ô	law, for	ch	chin	e *in* agent	
ä	cot, car	ŏŏ	look	sh	she	i *in* pencil	
e	ten	o͞o	tool	th	thin	o *in* atom	
ē	me	oi	oil	*th*	then	u *in* circus	
i	fit	ou	out	zh	measure		
ī	ice	u	up	ŋ	ring		

while.] **2** to keep in a certain place or position [*Hold* your head up. They were *held* in jail.] **3** to keep from falling; bear the weight of; support [This hook won't *hold* such a heavy picture.] **4** to keep from acting, moving, or doing; keep back [It took four of us to *hold* the dog at the vet's.] **5** to get and keep control of [The speaker *held* our attention.] **6** to keep and reserve for use later [They will *hold* the motel room for us.] **7** to have or keep as one's own; occupy [She *holds* the office of mayor.] **8** to have or carry on; conduct [Our club *held* a meeting on Friday.] **9** to have room for; contain [This bottle *holds* a liter.] **10** to stay together or in one piece; remain firm or fast [Will this knot *hold?*] **11** to stay the same or be true [Years ago the company put together a set of rules that still *holds* today.]

noun **1** the act or a way of holding or grasping [Take a firm *hold* on the rope. I learned a new *hold* in wrestling.] **2** influence or power [She has a strong *hold* over her brother.] **—get hold of** **1** to take; seize or grasp [*Get hold of* that railing.] **2** to talk to, especially by telephone; reach [I can't *get hold of* her at her office.] **—hold back** **1** to restrain; control [The police *held back* the crowd at the parade.] **2** to withhold [I know he's *holding back* important information from you.] **—hold out** **1** to go on; last [Do you think our supplies will *hold out* until next week?] **2** to continue to resist without giving in [How long can the troops *hold out* against these enemy attacks?] **—hold up** **1** to continue or last [This coat should *hold up* for a few years.] **2** to stop or delay [Heavy snow *held* us *up* on the highway.] **3** to rob by using force [Three men *held up* the bank.]

hold • ***verb*** **held, holding** • ***noun,*** *plural* **holds**

hold[2] (hōld) ***noun*** the inside of a ship below the deck. Cargo is put in the hold.

hold • ***noun,*** *plural* **holds**

holdup (hōld′up) ***noun*** **1** a delay [There was a *holdup* in the building of the new school gym.] **2** a robbery by someone who is armed [There was a *holdup* at the bank this morning.]

hold·up • ***noun,*** *plural* **holdups**

hole (hōl) ***noun*** **1** an opening in or through something; a break or tear [*holes* in the roof of the building; a *hole* in of my sweater]. **2** a hollow place; cavity [a *hole* in the ground]. **3** the burrow or den of an animal. **4** one of the small cups sunk into the green of a golf course. The ball is to be hit into the hole.

hole • ***noun,*** *plural* **holes**

● The words **hole** and **whole** sound alike.

That *hole* was dug by a chipmunk.

They ate the *whole* pizza in one night.

holiday (häl′i dā) ***noun*** **1** a day on which most people do not have to work [Thanksgiving is a *holiday* in all States.] **2** a vacation: this sense is used mainly in Great Britain and Canada.

hol·i·day • ***noun,*** *plural* **holidays**

Holland (häl′ənd) *another name for* **Netherlands**.

Hol·land

holler (häl′ər) [*an informal word*] ***verb*** to yell.

hol·ler • ***verb*** **hollered, hollering**

hollow (häl′ō) ***adjective*** **1** having an empty space on the inside; not solid [a *hollow* log; a *hollow* pipe]. **2** shaped like a bowl; concave [a *hollow* surface]. **3** sunken in [The sick man had *hollow* cheeks.] **4** sounding deep and dull; echoing as if coming out of a large, empty space [a *hollow* voice; a *hollow* sound].

noun **1** a hollow place; hole or cavity [The cart hit a *hollow* in the driveway.] **2** a small valley.

verb to make or become hollow [She *hollowed* the log to make a pot for flowers.] **—hollow out** **1** to make a hollow in [The gardener *hollowed out* a tree trunk.] **2** to make by hollowing [The moles *hollowed out* tunnels under the lawn.]

hol·low • ***adjective*** **hollower, hollowest** • ***noun,*** *plural* **hollows** • ***verb*** **hollowed, hollowing**

holly (häl′ē) ***noun*** a small tree or shrub with shiny leaves and red berries. Its branches are used as Christmas decorations.

hol·ly • ***noun,*** *plural* **hollies**

hollyhock (häl′ē häk) ***noun*** a tall plant that has a hairy stem and large, brightly colored flowers.

hol·ly·hock • ***noun,*** *plural* **hollyhocks**

Hollywood (häl′ē wood) a part of Los Angeles where many movie studios were once located.

Hol·ly·wood

Holmes (hōmz), **Oliver Wendell** (äl′i vər wen′ dəl) 1841-1935; U.S. lawyer. He was a Supreme Court justice from 1902 to 1932.

Holmes, Ol·i·ver Wen·dell

holocaust (hôl′ə kôst *or* hôl′ə käst) ***noun*** great destruction of life, especially by fire.

hol·o·caust • ***noun,*** *plural* **holocausts**

holster (hōl′stər) ***noun*** a leather case for

H

holding a pistol. A holster is usually fastened to a belt.
hol·ster • *noun, plural* **holsters**

holy (hō′lē) ***adjective*** **1** set apart for religious use; having to do with God or religion; sacred [a *holy* festival; the *Holy* Bible]. **2** very good or very religious; like a saint [a *holy* person].
ho·ly • ***adjective*** **holier, holiest**
• The words **holy** and **wholly** sound alike.
For many, Sunday is a *holy* day.
The mistake is *wholly* my fault.

Holy Land a historical region in southwestern Asia at the eastern end of the Mediterranean. It includes parts of modern Israel, Jordan, and Egypt.

Holy Scripture or **Holy Scriptures** *another name for* **Bible**.

Holy Spirit or **Holy Ghost** the third person of the Trinity; spirit of God.

homage (häm′ij *or* äm′ij) ***noun*** anything done to show honor or respect [Lincoln's speech paid *homage* to the men who fought at Gettysburg.]
hom·age • ***noun***

home (hōm) ***noun*** **1** the place where one lives; one's house or apartment. **2** the city, country, or other place where one was born or brought up [California was her *home*.] **3** a family or family life [They came from a *home* broken up by divorce.] **4** a place where orphans or people who are old or helpless are taken care of. **5** the place where a certain plant or animal is normally found [Australia is the *home* of the kangaroo.] **6** the base or goal in baseball and certain other games.
adjective **1** of or having to do with one's home [my *home* town]. **2** having to do with the home or family [*home* cooking].
adverb **1** at or to home [Go *home!*] **2** to the point aimed at [With a blow of the hammer she hit the nail *home*.]
—at home **1** in one's home [He's *at home* now.] **2** at ease; comfortable [She always makes us feel *at home* when we visit her.]
home • ***noun, plural*** **homes** • ***adjective*** • ***adverb***

homeland (hōm′land) ***noun*** the country in which a person was born or has lived for a long time.
home·land • ***noun, plural*** **homelands**

homeless (hōm′ləs) ***adjective*** having no home [a *homeless* child; *homeless* persons].
—the homeless the group of poor or mentally ill people who do not have money to have a home and are found sleeping in the streets, parks, and other places of large cities.
home·less • ***adjective***

homely (hōm′lē) ***adjective*** not very pretty or handsome; plain [a *homely* face].
home·ly • ***adjective*** **homelier, homeliest**

homemade (hōm′mād′) ***adjective*** made at home [*homemade* bread].
home·made • ***adjective***

home plate ***noun*** in baseball, the slab that a player stands beside when batting. It is the last base that a player must touch to score a run.

homer (hō′mər) [*an informal word*] ***noun*** *another name for* **home run**.
hom·er • ***noun, plural*** **homers**

Homer (hō′mər) a Greek poet who is thought to have lived in the 8th century B.C. and to have written the *Iliad* and the *Odyssey*.
Ho·mer

homeroom (hōm′ro͞om) ***noun*** the room where students meet for a short time each day to have attendance checked and to hear announcements.
home·room • ***noun, plural*** **homerooms**

home run ***noun*** in baseball, a hit that allows the batter to touch all bases and score a run.
home run • ***noun, plural*** **home runs**

homesick (hōm′sik) ***adjective*** longing to be home again.
home·sick • ***adjective***

homespun (hōm′spun) ***noun*** **1** cloth that is made of yarn that was spun at home. **2** a coarse cloth like this.
adjective plain or simple [*homespun* humor].
home·spun • ***noun*** • ***adjective***

homestead (hōm′sted) ***noun*** **1** the place where a family makes its home, including the house and the land around it. **2** a piece of public land that was given by the U.S. government to a settler to develop into a farm.
home·stead • ***noun, plural*** **homesteads**

homework (hōm′wʉrk) ***noun*** schoolwork that a student is to do outside the classroom.
home·work • ***noun***

a cat	ō go	ʉ fur	ə = a *in* ago
ā ape	ô law, for	ch chin	e *in* agent
ä cot, car	o͝o look	sh she	i *in* pencil
e ten	o͞o tool	th thin	o *in* atom
ē me	oi oil	*th* then	u *in* circus
i fit	ou out	zh measure	
ī ice	u up	ŋ ring	

homey (hōm′ē) ***adjective*** like a home; cozy.
home·y • ***adjective*** **homier, homiest**

hominy (häm′i nē) ***noun*** dry corn kernels that have had the hulls removed and have been broken into coarse bits. Hominy is mixed with water and boiled to make a soft, mushy food.
hom·i·ny • ***noun***

homogenize (hə mäj′ə nīz) ***verb*** to put milk through a process that breaks up and blends in the fat particles. This keeps the cream from separating and rising to the top.
ho·mog·e·nize • ***verb*** **homogenized, homogenizing**

homograph (häm′ə graf) ***noun*** a word that has the same spelling as another word but has a different meaning and source. Homographs are sometimes pronounced differently. The *bow* (bō) on a birthday present, and the *bow* (bou) of a ship are homographs.
hom·o·graph • ***noun,*** *plural* **homographs**

homonym (häm′ə nim) ***noun*** a word that is pronounced in the same way as another word but has a different meaning and source. Homonyms are usually spelled differently, for example, *for* and *four*.
hom·o·nym • ***noun,*** *plural* **homonyms**

Honduras (hän door′əs) a country in Central America.
Hon·du·ras

hone (hōn) ***verb*** to sharpen by rubbing on a hard stone that has a fine grain [We *honed* the knife before we carved the turkey.]
hone • ***verb*** **honed, honing**

honest (än′əst) ***adjective*** **1** capable of being trusted; not stealing, cheating, or lying [an *honest* person] —Look for the WORD CHOICES box at the entry **good**. **2** earned in a fair way, not by stealing, cheating, or lying [He makes an *honest* living as a bus driver.] **3** sincere or real [She made an *honest* effort to learn the subject.]
adverb [*an informal use*] really; in fact; honestly [*Honest*, I didn't do it!]
hon·est • ***adjective*** • ***adverb***

honestly (än′əst lē) ***adverb*** **1** in an honest way. **2** really; in fact [*Honestly*, I meant no harm.]
hon·est·ly • ***adverb***

honesty (än′əs tē) ***noun*** the condition or fact of being honest —Look for the WORD CHOICES box at the entry **honor**.
hon·es·ty • ***noun***

honey (hun′ē) ***noun*** a thick, sweet syrup that bees make from the nectar of flowers and store in honeycombs.
hon·ey • ***noun,*** *plural* **honeys**

honeybee (hun′ē bē) ***noun*** a bee that makes honey.
hon·ey·bee • ***noun,*** *plural* **honeybees**

honeycomb (hun′ ē kōm) ***noun*** a cluster of wax cells that bees make to hold their honey or eggs. Each cell has six sides.
verb to cause to be filled with holes like a honeycomb [The hill is *honeycombed* with caves.]
hon·ey·comb • ***noun,*** *plural* **honeycombs**
• ***verb*** **honeycombed, honeycombing**

honeycomb

honeydew melon (hun′ē dōō *or* hun′ē dyōō) ***noun*** a melon with a smooth, whitish skin and sweet, greenish flesh.
hon·ey·dew melon • ***noun,*** *plural* **honeydew melons**

honeydew melon

honeymoon (hun′ē mōōn) ***noun*** the vacation that a couple spends together just after their wedding.
verb to have a honeymoon [They will *honeymoon* in Florida.]
hon·ey·moon • ***noun,*** *plural* **honeymoons**
• ***verb*** **honeymooned, honeymooning**

honeysuckle (hun′ē suk′əl) ***noun*** a climbing vine with small flowers that have a sweet smell.
hon·ey·suck·le • ***noun***

Hong Kong (hôŋ′kôŋ′) **1** a region of southeastern China. **2** the chief city of this region.

honk (hôŋk) ***noun*** **1** the sound that a wild goose makes. **2** the sound of a car's horn or any other similar, loud sound.
verb to make or cause to make this sound [I *honked* at the man in the road. I *honked* the horn at the man in the road.]
honk • ***noun,*** *plural* **honks** • ***verb*** **honked, honking**

Honolulu (hän′ə lōō′lōō) the capital of Hawaii.
Hon·o·lu·lu

honor (än′ər) ***noun*** **1** great respect such as

that given to recognize great worth or noble deeds. **2** glory or credit [the *honor* of winning a blue ribbon at the county fair]. **3** a person or thing that brings glory to others [Our teacher is an *honor* to her profession.] **4** something that is done or given as a sign of respect [The astronaut received many *honors* for his work.] **5 Honor** a title of respect for a high official such as a judge [His *Honor*, the mayor]. **6** good name or reputation [You must uphold the *honor* of the family.] **7** the act or fact of being true to what is right, honest, or decent [Her sense of *honor* kept her from cheating.]
verb **1** to have or show great respect for [America *honors* the memory of Abraham Lincoln.] **2** to do something in order to give respect or glory to [We *honored* the team with a banquet.] **3** to accept as payment [That store *honors* most credit cards.]
hon·or • *noun, plural* **honors**
• *verb* **honored, honoring**

WORD CHOICES

Synonyms of **honor**

The words **honor, honesty,** and **integrity** share the meaning "the condition or fact of being truthful or reliable."

Can there be *honor* among thieves?

Honesty is the best policy.

We must elect people of *integrity*.

honorable (än′ər ə bəl) *adjective* worthy of being honored or respected [an *honorable* career].
hon·or·a·ble • *adjective*

honorable mention *noun* a notice of honor that a person or thing in a contest receives but not the very highest honor [Audrey's quilt received an *honorable mention* at the county fair.]

honorary (än′ər er′ē) *adjective* given as an honor, without the usual classes and tests [an *honorary* degree from a college].
hon·or·ar·y • *adjective*

hood (hood) *noun* **1** a covering for the head and neck that is often part of a coat or cloak. **2** something that is like this. The fold of skin around the neck of a cobra is called a hood. **3** the metal cover over a car's engine.
hood • *noun, plural* **hoods**

-hood *a suffix meaning:* **1** the condition or time of being [*Childhood* is the time of being a child.] **2** the whole group of [The *priesthood* is the whole group of priests.]

hoodlum (hood′ləm *or* hōōd′ləm) *noun* a rough person who does not respect the law.
hood·lum • *noun, plural* **hoodlums**

hoof (hōōf *or* hoof) *noun* **1** the hard, tough covering on the feet of cows, horses, deer, pigs, and certain other animals. **2** the whole foot of an animal of this kind.
hoof • *noun, plural* **hoofs** or **hooves**

hook (hook) *noun* **1** a piece of metal, plastic, or other material that is curved or bent so that it will catch or hold something [a *fishhook;* a coat *hook*]. **2** something that is shaped like a hook. A bend in a river is sometimes called a hook. **3** in sports, the act of hooking a ball.
verb **1** to curve in the way that a hook does [The river *hooked* around the hills.] **2** to catch or fasten with a hook [I *hooked* a fish. Please *hook* the screen door.] **3** in sports, to hit a ball so that it curves [When a right-handed golfer *hooks* a ball, it curves to the left.]
—**hook up** to set up and connect the parts of [We *hooked up* our new radio.]
hook • *noun, plural* **hooks** • *verb* **hooked, hooking**

hooked (hookt) *adjective* **1** curved like a hook [The witch had a *hooked* nose.] **2** [*a slang use*] depending so much on something that it is not easy to do without it [Mom says that my brother and I are *hooked* on TV.]

hooky (hook′ē) *noun used mainly in the phrase* **play hooky**, to stay away from school without permission.
hook·y • *noun*

hoop (hōōp) *noun* **1** a round band of metal that holds the wooden pieces in a barrel together. **2** something that is round like this. The metal rim of the basket in basketball is called a hoop. **3** one of the small wire arches through which the balls must be hit in certain games such as croquet.
hoop • *noun, plural* **hoops**

a cat	ō go	ʉ fur	ə = a *in* ago
ā ape	ô law, for	ch chin	e *in* agent
ä cot, car	oo look	sh she	i *in* pencil
e ten	ōō tool	th thin	o *in* atom
ē me	oi oil	*th* then	u *in* circus
i fit	ou out	zh measure	
ī ice	u up	ŋ ring	

hooray (hoo rā′) *interjection another spelling of* **hurray**.
hoo·ray • *interjection*

hoot (ho͞ot) *noun* **1** the sound that an owl makes. **2** a shout of anger or scorn.
verb **1** to make an owl's sound or a sound like it. **2** to show scorn with this kind of sound.
hoot • *noun, plural* **hoots** • *verb* **hooted, hooting**

Hoover (ho͞o′vər), **Herbert** (hur′bərt) 1874-1964; the thirty-first president of the U.S., from 1929 to 1933.
Hoo·ver, Her·bert

hooves (ho͞ovz *or* hoovz) *noun a plural of* **hoof**.

hop[1] (häp) *verb* **1** to make a short leap or leaps on one foot. **2** to jump over [They *hopped* the fence.] **3** to move by jumps in the way that a frog or bird does.
noun **1** a short leap or jump. **2** a bounce such as the one a baseball makes.
hop • *verb* **hopped, hopping** • *noun, plural* **hops**

hop[2] (häp) *noun* **1** a climbing vine with small yellow flowers. **2 hops** these flowers, which are dried and used to flavor beer.
hop • *noun, plural* **hops**

hope (hōp) *noun* **1** a feeling that what is wanted will happen [We gave up *hope* of being found.] **2** the thing that a person wants [It is my *hope* to go to college.] **3** a person or thing on which a person can base some hope [A cab was our only *hope* of going.]
verb **1** to have hope; to want and expect [I *hope* to see you soon.] **2** to want to believe [I *hope* I didn't overlook anybody.]
hope • *noun, plural* **hopes** • *verb* **hoped, hoping**

hopeful (hōp′fəl) *adjective* **1** feeling or showing hope [a *hopeful* smile]. **2** causing or giving hope [The warmer weather is a *hopeful* sign.]
hope·ful • *adjective*

hopefully (hōp′fəl ē) *adverb* **1** in a hopeful way [She smiled *hopefully*.] **2** it is to be hoped [We'll leave early, *hopefully* by noon.]
hope·ful·ly • *adverb*

hopeless (hōp′ləs) *adjective* **1** without hope [We were feeling *hopeless* about the exam.] **2** causing a person to lose hope; discouraging [a *hopeless* situation].
hope·less • *adjective*

hopper (häp′ər) *noun* **1** a person or animal that hops. **2** a container from which the contents can be emptied in a slow and even way. It is often shaped like a funnel.
hop·per • *noun, plural* **hoppers**

hopscotch

hopscotch (häp′skäch) *noun* a children's game in which players take turns hopping through a diagram they draw on the ground.
hop·scotch • *noun*

horde (hôrd) *noun* a large crowd [a *horde* of campers].
horde • *noun, plural* **hordes**
• The words **horde** and **hoard** sound alike.
A *horde* of barbarians sacked Rome.
Misers *hoard* money.

horizon (hər ī′zən) *noun* **1** a line where the sky seems to meet the earth. **2** the limit of a person's experience, ability, or knowledge [Travel widens our *horizons*.]
ho·ri·zon • *noun, plural* **horizons**

horizontal (hôr′i zänt′l) *adjective* parallel to the horizon; level or flat [The top of a table is *horizontal;* its legs are vertical.]
noun a horizontal line or plane.
hor·i·zon·tal • *adjective* • *noun, plural* **horizontals**

hormone (hôr′mōn) *noun* a substance that is produced by a gland or organ to control various body processes, such as growth. A hormone is usually carried through the body in the blood.
hor·mone • *noun, plural* **hormones**

horn (hôrn) *noun* **1** a hard, pointed growth on the head of cattle, rhinoceroses, and certain other animals. The horns of cattle and goats usually grow in pairs. **2** the substance that

H

horns are made of. **3** something that sticks out or is curved like a horn. The tentacles on the head of a snail or the tuft of feather on certain owls are called horns. **4** a container that is made by hollowing out an animal's horn [People once kept the powder for their guns in a powder *horn*.] **5** a musical instrument of the brass family. **6** a device that makes a loud noise as a warning or a signal [The fire truck blew its *horn*.]
horn • ***noun**, plural* **horns**

horned (hôrnd) ***adjective*** having one or more horns.

horned toad ***noun*** a small reptile with a short tail and spines that look like horns on its head.
horned toad • ***noun**, plural* **horned toads**

hornet (hôr′nət) ***noun*** a large wasp that lives in colonies and can give a painful sting.
hor·net • ***noun**, plural* **hornets**

horrible (hôr′i bəl) ***adjective*** **1** causing a feeling of horror; very frightening [a *horrible* accident]. **2** [*an informal use*] very bad, ugly, or unpleasant [What a *horrible* dinner!]
hor·ri·ble • ***adjective***

horrid (hôr′id) ***adjective*** **1** causing a feeling of horror; very frightening [the *horrid* face of the monster]. **2** very bad or unpleasant [What a *horrid* thing to say!]
hor·rid • ***adjective***

horrify (hôr′i fī′) ***verb*** **1** to fill with horror [He was *horrified* by the sight of the accident.] **2** [*an informal use*] to shock or disgust [His bad manners *horrified* her.]
hor·ri·fy • ***verb*** **horrified, horrifying, horrifies**

horror (hôr′ər) ***noun*** **1** a feeling of great fear or disgust that makes a person shudder —Look for the WORD CHOICES box at the entry **panic**. **2** strong dislike [She had a *horror* of being photographed.] **3** something that causes great fear or disgust [the *horrors* of war].
hor·ror • ***noun**, plural* **horrors**

horse (hôrs) ***noun*** **1** a large, strong animal with four legs, solid hoofs, and a flowing mane and tail. Human beings have ridden horses and used them to pull loads since ancient times. **2** a padded block on legs that is used in gymnastics for doing certain exercises.
horse • ***noun**, plural* **horses**

● The words **horse** and **hoarse** sound alike.
Have you ever ridden a *horse?*
I am too *hoarse* to sing.

horseback (hôrs′bak) ***noun*** the back of a horse. ***adverb*** on the back of a horse [We rode *horseback* on our vacation.]
horse·back • ***noun*** • ***adverb***

horsehair (hôrs′her) ***noun*** hair from the mane or tail of a horse.
horse·hair • ***noun***

horseman (hôrs′mən) ***noun*** a man who is skilled in riding or caring for horses.
horse·man • ***noun**, plural* **horsemen**

horseplay (hôrs′plā) ***noun*** rough play.
horse·play • ***noun***

horsepower (hôrs′pou ər) ***noun*** a unit for measuring the power of motors or engines.
horse·pow·er • ***noun***

horseradish (hôrs′rad ish) ***noun*** **1** a plant with a long white root that has a sharp, burning taste. **2** a paste that is made by grating this root. It is served with certain foods to add flavor.
horse·rad·ish • ***noun***

horseshoe (hôrs′shōō) ***noun*** **1** a flat metal plate that is shaped like a U. It is nailed to the bottom of a horse's hoof to protect it. **2** anything shaped like a horseshoe. **3 horseshoes** [*used with a singular verb*] a game in which the players toss horseshoes at a stake.
horse·shoe • ***noun**, plural* **horseshoes**

horseshoe crab

horseshoe crab ***noun*** a sea animal that is shaped somewhat like a horseshoe and has a long, narrow, pointed tail.
horseshoe crab • ***noun**, plural* **horseshoe crabs**

a	cat	ō	go	ʉ	fur	ə =	a *in* ago
ā	ape	ô	law, for	ch	chin		e *in* agent
ä	cot, car	oo	look	sh	she		i *in* pencil
e	ten	ōō	tool	th	thin		o *in* atom
ē	me	oi	oil	*th*	then		u *in* circus
i	fit	ou	out	zh	measure		
ī	ice	u	up	ŋ	ring		

horsewoman (hôrs′woom ən) ***noun*** a woman who is skilled in riding or caring for horses.
horse·wom·an • ***noun,*** *plural* **horsewomen**

hose (hōz) ***noun*** a tube of flexible material such as rubber or plastic through which water or other fluids can pass.
plural noun stockings or socks [These *hose* are torn.]
verb to put water on with a hose [We *hosed* down the sidewalk after the storm.]
hose • ***noun,*** *plural* **hoses** • ***plural noun*** • ***verb*** **hosed, hosing**

hospital (häs′pi təl) ***noun*** a place where doctors, nurses, and others take care of people who are sick or hurt.
hos·pi·tal • ***noun,*** *plural* **hospitals**

hospitality (häs′pi tal′i tē) ***noun*** a friendly and generous way of treating guests.
hos·pi·tal·i·ty • ***noun***

host (hōst) ***noun*** **1** a person who has guests in the home or who pays for entertaining them away from home. **2** a person who talks with guests on a radio or TV show.
verb to act as host of [They *hosted* a wonderful party. He *hosts* a TV show.]
host • ***noun,*** *plural* **hosts** • ***verb*** **hosted, hosting**

hostage (häs′tij) ***noun*** a person who is given to or taken by an enemy and is held prisoner until certain demands are met.
hos·tage • ***noun,*** *plural* **hostages**

hostel (häs′təl) ***noun*** a kind of inn or other place that provides cheap lodging, especially for young people on bicycle tours or hikes.
hos·tel • ***noun,*** *plural* **hostels**
● The words **hostel** and **hostile** sound alike.
Will you stay at the student *hostel?*
Their fans were *hostile* to our team.

hostess (hōs′təs) ***noun*** **1** a woman who has guests in the home or who pays for entertaining them away from home. **2** a woman whose work is welcoming people to a restaurant and taking them to their tables.
host·ess • ***noun,*** *plural* **hostesses**

hostile (häs′təl) ***adjective*** **1** like or having to do with an enemy [*hostile* tribes]. **2** having or showing hate or dislike; not friendly [He gave me a *hostile* look.]
hos·tile • ***adjective***
● The words **hostile** and **hostel** sound alike.

hostility (häs til′i tē) ***noun*** **1** a feeling of hate or dislike. **2 hostilities** acts of war; warfare [*hostilities* between the two countries].
hos·til·i·ty • ***noun,*** *plural* **hostilities**

hot (hät) ***adjective*** **1** having a temperature that is usually much higher than the temperature of the human body; very warm [a *hot* day; a *hot* oven]. **2** causing a burning feeling in the mouth [This chili has a lot of *hot* pepper in it.] **3** full of strong feeling; angry or violent [a *hot* temper; a *hot* argument].
hot • ***adjective*** **hotter, hottest**

hot dog [*an informal word*] ***noun*** a wiener or frankfurter, especially one that is served in a long roll.
hot dog • ***noun,*** *plural* **hot dogs**

hotel (hō tel′) ***noun*** a building where travelers can rent rooms, buy meals, hold meetings, and have other needs looked after.
ho·tel • ***noun,*** *plural* **hotels**

hot line ***noun*** a direct telephone line, like one between heads of governments, for use in an emergency.
hot line • ***noun,*** *plural* **hot lines**

hound (hound) ***noun*** **1** a hunting dog with long, drooping ears and short hair. **2** any dog.
verb to chase or follow all the time; pester [Reporters *hounded* the movie star.]
hound • ***noun,*** *plural* **hounds** • ***verb*** **hounded, hounding**

hour (our) ***noun*** **1** any one of the 24 equal parts of a day; 60 minutes. **2** a particular time of day [At what *hour* shall we meet?] **3** a usual time for doing something [the dinner *hour*]. **4** *often* **hours** a time set aside for activity such as work [The doctor's office *hours* are from 2 to 5.]
hour • ***noun,*** *plural* **hours**
● The words **hour** and **our** sound alike.
It is now five minutes past the *hour.*
Our mayor was reelected.

hourglass (our′glas) ***noun*** a device for measuring time with sand that trickles from one glass bulb through a small opening to another bulb below it. It takes exactly one hour to empty the top bulb.
hour·glass • ***noun,*** *plural* **hourglasses**

hourglass

hourly (our′lē) ***adjective*** **1** done, taken, or happening every hour [an *hourly* dose

H

of medicine]. **2** for every hour [an *hourly* wage of $5.00].
adverb every hour [The bells ring *hourly*.]
hour·ly • *adjective* • *adverb*

house (hous *for n.;* houz *for v.*) *noun* **1** a building for people to live in. **2** the people who live in a house; family [The fire alarm had the whole *house* in an uproar.] **3** a building that is used for storing or sheltering something or for another specific purpose [the elephant *house* at the zoo; a *house* of worship]. **4** an audience [The actors played to a full *house*.] **5** a group of persons who make laws [the *House* of Representatives].
verb to give shelter or lodging to [The cottage *houses* a family of five.]
—**keep house** to take care of a home; do housework. —**on the house** given free by the owner of a business [You pay for the meal, but coffee is *on the house*.]
house • *noun, plural* **houses** (hou′ziz) • *verb* **housed, housing**

houseboat (hous′bōt) *noun* a large boat that is made to be lived in as a home.
house·boat • *noun, plural* **houseboats**

housefly (hous′flī) *noun* a common fly with two wings that is found in and around houses. It feeds on garbage and food.
house·fly • *noun, plural* **houseflies**

household (hous′hōld) *noun* **1** the family or the whole group of persons that live in one house. **2** the home and matters having to do with it [It is a big job to manage a *household*.]
house·hold • *noun, plural* **households**

housekeeper (hous′kēp ər) *noun* a person who is hired to manage a home.
house·keep·er • *noun, plural* **housekeepers**

House of Representatives *noun* **1** the lower house of the U.S. Congress. The number of representatives from a State depends upon the number of people living in that State. Representatives are elected for a period of two years. **2** the lower house of most State legislatures.

house-raising (hous′rā ziŋ) *noun* a gathering of neighbors in a rural area to help build someone's house or the framework for it.
house-rais·ing • *noun, plural* **house-raisings**

housewife (hous′wīf) *noun* a married woman whose main work is taking care of her household.
house·wife • *noun, plural* **housewives**

housework (hous′wʉrk) *noun* the work that a person does in keeping house, including cleaning and cooking.
house·work • *noun*

housing (houz′iŋ) *noun* **1** houses or other buildings where people live [There is some new *housing* in our area.] **2** a frame or box in which something is protected [the *housing* of an engine].
hous·ing • *noun, plural for sense 2 only* **housings**

Houston (hyōō s′tən), **Samuel** (sam′yōō əl) 1793-1863; U.S. statesman who was president of the Republic of Texas before it became a State.
Hous·ton, Sam·u·el

Houston (hyōōs′tən) a city in southeastern Texas.
Hous·ton

hove (hōv) *verb a past tense and past participle of* **heave**.

hovel (huv′əl *or* häv′əl) *noun* a small house or hut that is old and broken down.
hov·el • *noun, plural* **hovels**

hover (huv′ər) *verb* **1** to stay fluttering or hanging in the air near one place [The butterfly *hovered* over the flower.] **2** to stay or wait very close by [The fans *hovered* about the TV star.]
hov·er • *verb* **hovered, hovering**

how (hou) *adverb* **1** in what way [*How* do you start the motor? She taught him *how* to dance.] **2** in what condition [*How* is your mother today?] **3** for what reason; why [*How* is it that you don't know?] **4** to what degree [*How* high will it fly?] **5** it is very: used to make an exclamation stronger [*How* nice!]
—**how about** how do you think or feel about? [*How about* going to the zoo?] —**how come?** [*an informal use*] why?

how'd (houd) **1** how did. **2** how had. **3** how would.

howdy (hou′dē) [*an informal word*] *interjection* hello; how do you do?
how·dy • *interjection*

a cat	ō go	ʉ fur	ə = a *in* ago
ā ape	ô law, for	ch chin	e *in* agent
ä cot, car	oo look	sh she	i *in* pencil
e ten	ōō tool	th thin	o *in* atom
ē me	oi oil	*th* then	u *in* circus
i fit	ou out	zh measure	
ī ice	u up	ŋ ring	

Howe (hou), **Elias** (ē lī′əs) 1819-1867; the U.S. inventor of a sewing machine.
Howe, E·li·as

however (hou ev′ər) ***adverb*** **1** in whatever way; by whatever means [We'll get there *however* we can.] **2** no matter how [*However* hard the task, he did it.]
conjunction in spite of that; but [We try to do the right thing; *however*, we sometimes fail.]
how·ev·er • ***adverb*** • ***conjunction***

howl (houl) ***verb*** **1** to make the long, wailing cry that wolves and dogs make. **2** to make a sound like this [The boy *howled* in pain.] **3** to shout or laugh in scorn or glee.
noun **1** the wailing cry of dogs and wolves. **2** a sound like this [*howls* of laughter].
howl • ***verb*** **howled, howling** • ***noun,*** *plural* **howls**

how's (houz) **1** how is. **2** how has. **3** how does.

HQ, H.Q., hq, or **h.q.** *abbreviation for* headquarters.

hr. *abbreviation for* hour.

hrs. *abbreviation for* hours.

ht. *abbreviation for* height.

hub (hub) ***noun*** **1** the center part of a wheel. It is fastened to an axle or it turns on an axle. **2** a center of activity or interest [Detroit is the *hub* of the auto industry.]
hub • ***noun,*** *plural* **hubs**

huckleberry (huk′əl ber′ē) ***noun*** **1** a dark-blue berry that looks like a blueberry. **2** the shrub that it grows on.
huck·le·ber·ry • ***noun,*** *plural* **huckleberries**

huddle (hud′əl) ***verb*** to crowd or push close together [Cows often *huddle* in a storm. We were *huddled* under the tent during the shower.]
noun **1** a group of people or things crowded close together [A *huddle* of customers waited for the store to open.] **2** a meeting of football players crowded close together to get the signals for the next play.
hud·dle • ***verb*** **huddled, huddling** • ***noun,*** *plural* **huddles**

Hudson (hud′sən) a river in eastern New York. Its mouth is at New York City.
Hud·son

hue (hyo͞o) ***noun*** color, especially a particular shade of a color [a reddish *hue*].
hue • ***noun,*** *plural* **hues**

huff (huf) ***noun*** a fit of anger [I don't blame you for being in a *huff*—she insulted you.]
verb to blow or puff ["The wolf *huffed* and puffed and blew the house down!"]
huff • ***noun,*** *plural* **huffs** • ***verb*** **huffed, huffing**

hug (hug) ***verb*** to clasp in the arms and hold close in a loving way.
noun a close embrace.
hug • ***verb*** **hugged, hugging** • ***noun,*** *plural* **hugs**

huge (hyo͞oj) ***adjective*** very large; immense [The redwood tree has a *huge* trunk.] —Look for the WORD CHOICES box at the entry **enormous**.
huge • ***adjective*** **huger, hugest**

huh (hu) ***interjection*** a sound that is made to show surprise or scorn or to ask a question.

hula (ho͞o′lə) ***noun*** a Hawaiian dance that uses flowing movements of the hands and arms to tell a story.
hu·la • ***noun***

hulk (hulk) ***noun*** **1** an old ship that no longer sails on voyages. **2** a person or thing that is clumsy or hard to handle.
hulk • ***noun,*** *plural* **hulks**

hull (hul) ***noun*** **1** the outer covering of a seed or fruit. The shell of a nut, the pod in which peas grow, and the outside of a grain of wheat are hulls. **2** the sides and bottom of a boat or ship. **3** the tiny leaves at the base of a strawberry and some other berries.
verb to take the hulls from [The children *hulled* peanuts.]
hull • ***noun,*** *plural* **hulls** • ***verb*** **hulled, hulling**

hum (hum) ***verb*** **1** to make a low, even buzzing sound in the way that a bee or a motor does. **2** to sing with the lips closed, not saying any words. **3** [*an informal use*] to be very busy or active [The office is *humming* with activity.]
noun the act or sound of humming.
hum • ***verb*** **hummed, humming** • ***noun***

human (hyo͞o′mən) ***adjective*** **1** belonging to the group that includes all people [a *human* being]. **2** having to do with people in general [*human* feelings].
noun a person.
hu·man • ***adjective*** • ***noun,*** *plural* **humans**

human being ***noun*** a person; a member of the group of all people: some people prefer this phrase to the noun **human**.
human being • ***noun,*** *plural* **human beings**

humane (hyo͞o mān′) ***adjective*** kind, gentle, and showing mercy [She works for *humane*

H

treatment of people who are in prison.] —Look for the WORD CHOICES box at the entry **kind**[2].
hu·mane • *adjective*

humanity (hyo͞o man′i tē) *noun* **1** the human race; all people [Could *humanity* survive a nuclear war?] **2** kindness or sympathy [She showed her *humanity* by caring for the sick.]
—the humanities studies that deal with human relations and human thought. They include subjects such as literature, philosophy, music, and art but not the sciences.
hu·man·i·ty • *noun*

humankind (hyo͞o′mən kīnd) *noun* the human race; all people.
hu·man·kind • *noun*

humanoid (hyo͞o′mə noid) *noun* in science fiction, an alien or robot that looks much like a human being.
hu·man·oid • *noun, plural* **humanoids**

humble (hum′bəl) *adjective* **1** knowing one's own faults; modest; not proud [That *humble* man is really a great scientist.] **2** low in rank or position; plain and simple ["Be it ever so *humble*, there's no place like home."]
verb to make humble; take away the pride, fame, or power of [Our team *humbled* theirs in the big game.]
hum·ble • *adjective* **humbler, humblest** • *verb* **humbled, humbling**

humid (hyo͞o′mid) *adjective* full of water vapor; damp or moist [a *humid* summer day].
hu·mid • *adjective*

humidity (hyo͞o mid′i tē) *noun* the amount of moisture, or water, in the air [The *humidity* is high today.]
hu·mid·i·ty • *noun*

humiliate (hyo͞o mil′ē āt′) *verb* to take away the pride or dignity of; cause to feel ashamed [I was *humiliated* when he laughed at my painting.]
hu·mil·i·ate • *verb* **humiliated, humiliating**

hummingbird

humility (hyo͞o mil′i tē) *noun* the condition or quality of being humble.
hu·mil·i·ty • *noun*

hummingbird (hum′iŋ burd) *noun* a tiny bird with a long, thin bill that it uses to suck nectar from flowers. Its wings move very fast, with a humming sound.
hum·ming·bird • *noun, plural* **hummingbirds**

humongous (hyo͞o mäŋ′ gəs) [*a slang word*] *adjective* very large or great; huge.
hu·mon·gous • *adjective*

humor (hyo͞o′mər) *noun* **1** the feature that makes something seem funny or amusing [The story was full of *humor*.] **2** the ability to see or express what is funny or amusing [She has no sense of *humor*.] **3** a state of mind; mood [He was in a bad *humor* and yelled at us.]
verb to give in to; give what is wanted to [If you don't *humor* him, he starts to complain.]
hu·mor • *noun, plural for sense 3 only* **humors** • *verb* **humored, humoring**

humorous (hyo͞o′mər əs) *adjective* funny or amusing —Look for the WORD CHOICES box at the entry **funny**.
hu·mor·ous • *adjective*

hump (hump) *noun* a rounded lump on the back. Camels have humps.
hump • *noun, plural* **humps**

humph (humf) *interjection* a snorting sound that is made to show doubt, surprise, or disgust.

humus (hyo͞o′məs) *noun* a brown or black substance that is made up of decayed leaves, plants, and animals. It is a part of the soil.
hu·mus • *noun*

hunch (hunch) *verb* to draw up the body, especially the shoulders or back, so as to form a hump [She *hunched* herself over her desk. We *hunched* over the table to read the menu.]
noun **1** a hump. **2** [*an informal use*] a feeling about something that is not based on known facts [I have a *hunch* you'll win.]
hunch • *verb* **hunched, hunching** • *noun, plural* **hunches**

hundred (hun′drəd) *noun* the cardinal number that is equal to ten times ten; 100.
adjective being ten times ten [a *hundred* cars].
hun·dred • *noun, plural* **hundreds** • *adjective*

a cat	ō go	ʉ fur	ə = a *in* ago
ā ape	ô law, for	ch chin	e *in* agent
ä cot, car	oo look	sh she	i *in* pencil
e ten	o͞o tool	th thin	o *in* atom
ē me	oi oil	*th* then	u *in* circus
i fit	ou out	zh measure	
ī ice	u up	ŋ ring	

hundredth (hun′drədth) ***adjective*** being ten more than ninety others in a series; 100th in order.
noun **1** the number in a series that is ten more than the ninetieth. **2** one of a hundred equal parts of something; 1/100.
hun·dredth • ***adjective*** • ***noun,*** *plural* **hundredths**

hung (huŋ) ***verb*** *a past tense and a past participle of* **hang**.

Hungarian (huŋ ger′ē ən) ***noun*** **1** a person born or living in Hungary. **2** the language of the Hungarians.
Hun·gar·i·an • ***noun,*** *plural for sense 1 only* **Hungarians**

Hungary (huŋ′gər ē) a country in central Europe.
Hun·ga·ry

hunger (huŋ′gər) ***noun*** **1** the discomfort or weakness that is caused by having little or nothing to eat. **2** an appetite for food [The meal satisfied their *hunger*.] **3** a strong desire or want [a *hunger* for knowledge].
verb **1** to be hungry; need food. **2** to have a strong desire; crave [The children *hungered* for love that they did not get from their cruel parents.]
hun·ger • ***noun,*** *plural* **hungers** • ***verb*** **hungered, hungering**

hungry (huŋ′grē) ***adjective*** **1** wanting or needing food [Exercise makes me *hungry*.] **2** having a strong desire; eager [*hungry* for praise].
hun·gry • ***adjective*** **hungrier, hungriest**

hunk (huŋk) [*an informal word*] ***noun*** a large piece or lump [a *hunk* of meat].
hunk • ***noun,*** *plural* **hunks**

hunt (hunt) ***verb*** **1** to set out to kill or capture wild animals or birds for food or as a sport. **2** to try to find; search for or seek [The sailors helped them *hunt* for buried treasure.] —Look for the WORD CHOICES box at the entry **seek**.
noun the act of hunting; a search.
hunt • ***verb*** **hunted, hunting** • ***noun,*** *plural* **hunts**

hunter (hunt′ər) ***noun*** a person or animal that hunts.
hunt·er • ***noun,*** *plural* **hunters**

hurdle (hʉr′dəl) ***noun*** **1** any one of the small fences or frames that runners or horses must jump over in a certain kind of race. **2** something difficult that has to be overcome [Passing the final exams is our last *hurdle*.]
verb to jump over [She *hurdled* the fence.]
hur·dle • ***noun,*** *plural* **hurdles** • ***verb*** **hurdled, hurdling**

hurl (hʉrl) ***verb*** to throw with great force [He *hurled* a rock at the tree.] —Look for the WORD CHOICES box at the entry **throw**.
hurl • ***verb*** **hurled, hurling**

Huron (hyoor′än), **Lake** one of the Great Lakes, between Lake Michigan and Lake Erie.
Hu·ron, Lake

hurrah (hə rä′) ***interjection*** *the same as* **hurray**.
hur·rah • ***interjection***

hurray (hə rā′) ***interjection*** a word that is called out to show joy, approval, or praise [*Hurray* for our team!]
hur·ray • ***interjection***

hurricane (hʉr′i kān) ***noun*** a very strong windstorm, often with heavy rain, in which the wind blows in a circle at 73 or more miles per hour. Hurricanes usually start in the Caribbean Sea and move northward.
hur·ri·cane • ***noun,*** *plural* **hurricanes**

hurried (hʉr′ēd) ***adjective*** in a hurry; rushed or rushing [We ate a *hurried* lunch.]
hur·ried • ***adjective***

hurry (hʉr′ē) ***verb*** **1** to move or act quickly or too quickly [I *hurried* down the street. You fell because you *hurried*.] **2** to carry or send quickly or too quickly [A taxi *hurried* us to the airport.]
noun **1** the act of hurrying [In my *hurry* I left the door open.] **2** the need for hurrying [There's no *hurry* about paying me back.]
hur·ry • ***verb*** **hurried, hurrying, hurries** • ***noun,*** *plural* **hurries**

hurt (hʉrt) ***verb*** **1** to cause pain or harm to; to wound [I *hurt* my leg when I fell.] **2** to have pain [My head *hurts*.] **3** to harm or damage in some way [Water won't *hurt* the top of this table.] **4** to make angry or unhappy [She was *hurt* by the unkind remarks.]
noun pain, damage, or harm [Time will take away the *hurt*.]
hurt • ***verb*** **hurt, hurting** • ***noun,*** *plural* **hurts**

hurtle (hʉrt′əl) ***verb*** to move or throw with great speed or much force [The rocket *hurtled* through space.]
hur·tle • ***verb*** **hurtled, hurtling**

husband (huz′bənd) ***noun*** the man to whom a woman is married.
verb to use carefully so that nothing is wasted

H

[The farmer *husbanded* water so the well wouldn't run dry.]
hus·band • *noun, plural* **husbands**
• *verb* **husbanded, husbanding**

hush (hush) *verb* to make or become quiet [I *hushed* the baby.]
noun the fact or condition of being quiet; silence [A sudden *hush* fell over the room.]
interjection a word that is used to make someone be quiet [*Hush!* You'll scare away the rabbits!]
—**hush up** **1** to keep quiet. **2** to keep people from talking about; keep secret [They *hushed up* the embarrassing news.]
hush • *verb* **hushed, hushing** • *noun, plural* **hushes** • *interjection*

hush puppy *noun* a small ball of fried cornmeal dough.
hush puppy • *noun, plural* **hush puppies**

husk (husk) *noun* the dry covering of certain kinds of fruits and seeds.
verb to remove the husk from [We *husked* 30 ears of corn for the picnic.]
husk • *noun, plural* **husks** • *verb* **husked, husking**

husky[1] or **Husky** (hus′kē) *noun* a strong dog with a thick coat. Huskies are used for pulling sleds in the far northern parts of the earth.
hus·ky or **Hus·ky** • *noun, plural* **huskies** or **Huskies**

husky[2] (hus′kē) *adjective* **1** sounding deep and hoarse; rough [a *husky* voice]. **2** big and strong [a *husky* farmer].
husk·y • *adjective* **huskier, huskiest**

hustle (hus′əl) *verb* **1** to push or make a path quickly [We *hustled* through the crowd.] **2** to force in a rough and hurried way [The waiter *hustled* the rude customer out the door.] **3** [*an informal use*] to go or do something quickly or with much enthusiasm [You'll have to *hustle* to catch the bus.]
noun the act of moving fast or with force.
hus·tle • *verb* **hustled, hustling** • *noun*

hut (hut) *noun* a little house or cabin of the plainest kind.
hut • *noun, plural* **huts**

hutch (huch) *noun* **1** a pen or coop for small animals. **2** a cabinet for dishes that has open shelves on top.
hutch • *noun, plural* **hutches**

hyacinth (hī′ə sinth) *noun* a plant that has long, narrow leaves and a spike of sweet-smelling flowers. The flowers are shaped like bells and may be blue, white, yellow, purple, or red.
hy·a·cinth • *noun, plural* **hyacinths**

hybrid (hī′brid) *noun* the offspring of two animals or plants of different species or varieties. The mule is a hybrid whose male parent is a donkey and whose female parent is a horse.
hy·brid • *noun, plural* **hybrids**

hydrant (hī′drənt) *noun* a closed pipe with a spout, located at a street curb. It can be opened in order to draw water for putting out fires or cleaning the street gutters.
hy·drant • *noun, plural* **hydrants**

hydrant

hydro- *a prefix meaning* water [The river in our city has a dam with a *hydroelectric* power plant.]

hydroelectric (hī′drō ē lek′ trik) *adjective* having to do with electricity that is produced by water power. A hydroelectric dam uses the force of flowing water to produce electricity.
hy·dro·e·lec·tric • *adjective*

hydrogen (hī′drə jən) *noun* a gas that has no color or smell and burns very easily. It is a chemical element and the lightest of all substances.
hy·dro·gen • *noun*

hydrogen bomb *noun* a very destructive type of bomb in which atoms of a special kind of hydrogen are forced to join together, releasing energy in a very powerful and very hot explosion.
hydrogen bomb • *noun, plural* **hydrogen bombs**

hydrogen peroxide (pər äks′īd) *noun* a chemical compound that is made up of hydrogen and oxygen. It is usually used by combining it with water. It is used as a bleach and to kill germs.
hydrogen per·ox·ide • *noun*

a cat	ō go	ʉ fur	ə = a *in* ago
ā ape	ô law, for	ch chin	e *in* agent
ä cot, car	oo look	sh she	i *in* pencil
e ten	ōō tool	th thin	o *in* atom
ē me	oi oil	*th* then	u *in* circus
i fit	ou out	zh measure	
ī ice	u up	ŋ ring	

hydroponics (hī′drə pän′iks) ***plural noun*** [*used with a singular verb*] the science or practice of growing plants in water that has minerals added, rather than in soil.
hy·dro·pon·ics • ***plural noun***

hyena

hyena (hī ē′nə) ***noun*** a wild animal of Africa and Asia that looks like a large dog. It eats the remains of dead animals and has a shrill cry.
hy·e·na • ***noun, plural*** **hyenas**

hygiene (hī′jēn) ***noun*** **1** the practice of keeping clean [good personal *hygiene*]. **2** rules for keeping healthy and preventing disease.
hy·giene • ***noun***

hymn (him) ***noun*** a song that praises God.
hymn • ***noun, plural*** **hymns**
• The words **him** and **hymn** sound alike.
We will now sing *Hymn* number 40.
Tell *him* to wash the car today.

hymnal (him′nəl) ***noun*** a book of hymns.
hym·nal • ***noun, plural*** **hymnals**

hyper- *a prefix meaning* over; more than normal; too much [*Hypertension* is blood pressure that is so high that it is abnormal.]

hyphen (hī′fən) ***noun*** a mark that is a short line (-). It is used between the parts of some compound words, such as *well-known*. This mark is also used after a part of a word that is divided at the end of a line.
hy·phen • ***noun, plural*** **hyphens**

hyphenate (hī′fə nāt) ***verb*** to write with a hyphen.
hy·phen·ate • ***verb*** **hyphenated, hyphenating**

hypnosis (hip nō′sis) ***noun*** a relaxed condition that is a little like sleep. A person usually enters this condition through the direction of another person and will do or say the things that the other person suggests, within certain limits. Hypnosis is used in medical and psychological treatment.
hyp·no·sis • ***noun***

hypnotize (hip′nə tīz) ***verb*** to put into the condition of hypnosis.
hyp·no·tize • ***verb*** **hypnotized, hypnotizing**

hypo- *a prefix meaning:* **1** under [A *hypodermic* syringe places a substance under the skin.] **2** less than.

hypocrite (hip′ə krit) ***noun*** a person who pretends to be good, religious, kind, honest, or loyal without really being so.
hyp·o·crite • ***noun, plural*** **hypocrites**

hysteria (hi ster′ē ə) ***noun*** a wild fit of laughing or crying that gets out of control.
hys·te·ri·a • ***noun***

hysterical (hi ster′i kəl) ***adjective*** having or likely to have wild fits of laughing or crying that are out of control.
hys·ter·i·cal • ***adjective***

hysterics (hi ster′iks) ***plural noun*** [*used with a singular verb*] a wild fit of laughing or crying that is out of control.
hys·ter·ics • ***plural noun***

H

Ii Ii *Ii* Ii

The letter **i** *has a long vowel sound, as in* **iceberg**, *and a short vowel sound, as in* **it**.

You will also notice some words where the **i** *is pronounced like a long* **e** *vowel, as in* **police**.

i or **I** (ī) ***noun*** the ninth letter of the English alphabet.
i or **I** • ***noun,*** *plural* **i's** or **I's**

I[1] (ī) ***noun*** the Roman numeral for the figure 1.
I • ***noun,*** *plural* **I's**

I[2] (ī) ***pronoun*** the person who is speaking [*I* like candy. It is *I* who will go.]
I • ***pronoun,*** *plural* **we**
• The words **I, aye,** and **eye** sound alike.
She and *I* walked to the movies.
Only three members voted *aye*.
The baby poked him in the *eye*.

IA or **Ia.** *abbreviation for* Iowa.

-ible *a suffix the same as* **-able**.

-ic *a suffix meaning:* **1** like or having to do with [An *angelic* voice is a voice like an angel's.] **2** made by or caused by [A *photographic* copy is made by taking a photograph.] **3** made up of or containing [A *metallic* substance contains metal.]

-ical *a suffix the same as* **-ic**. Some words have a different meaning if the suffix is **-ical** instead of **-ic** [*Economical* means "thrifty," but *economic* refers to economics.]

ice (īs) ***noun*** **1** water that is frozen solid by cold. Water turns to ice at 32°F. **2** a frozen dessert, usually made of water, fruit juice, egg white, and sugar.
verb **1** to change into ice; freeze [The lake *iced* over.] **2** to cover or decorate with icing or frosting [She *iced* the birthday cake.]
ice • ***noun,*** *plural* **ices** • ***verb*** **iced, icing**

ice age ***noun*** a period of time when a large part of the earth was covered with glaciers. This has happened many times in the history of the earth. The last ice age ended 10,000 years ago.
ice age • ***noun,*** *plural* **ice ages**

iceberg (īs′bʉrg) ***noun*** a very large mass of ice that has broken off from a glacier and is floating in the sea.
ice·berg • ***noun,*** *plural* **icebergs**

icebox (īs′bäks) ***noun*** **1** a box or cabinet with ice in it for keeping food cold. **2** a refrigerator.
ice·box • ***noun,*** *plural* **iceboxes**

icebreaker (īs′brāk ər) ***noun*** a sturdy ship that is designed to break a passage through ice.
ice·break·er • ***noun,*** *plural* **icebreakers**

ice cap ***noun*** a thick mass of ice and snow over an area. An ice cap spreads out slowly in all directions from a center.
ice cap • ***noun,*** *plural* **ice caps**

ice cream ***noun*** a frozen food made of cream or milk with sugar and flavorings.
ice cream • ***noun,*** *plural* **ice creams**

ice hockey ***noun*** *another name for* **hockey** (sense 1).

a	cat	ō	go	ʉ	fur	ə =	a *in* ago
ā	ape	ô	law, for	ch	chin		e *in* agent
ä	cot, car	o͝o	look	sh	she		i *in* pencil
e	ten	o͞o	tool	th	thin		o *in* atom
ē	me	oi	oil	*th*	then		u *in* circus
i	fit	ou	out	zh	measure		
ī	ice	u	up	ŋ	ring		

Iceland (īs′lənd) a country on a large island in the North Atlantic, east of Greenland.
Ice·land

Icelandic (īs lan′dik) ***noun*** the language of Iceland.
Ice·land·ic • ***noun***

ice skate ***noun*** a boot or shoe with a metal blade or runner attached to the bottom. It is worn for skating on ice.
ice skate • ***noun,*** *plural* **ice skates**

ice-skate (īs′skāt) ***verb*** to skate on ice.
ice-skate • ***verb*** **ice-skated, ice-skating**

icicle (ī′sik əl) ***noun*** a hanging stick of ice. It is formed by water that freezes as it drips down.
i·ci·cle • ***noun,*** *plural* **icicles**

icing (īs′iŋ) ***noun*** a mixture of sugar, butter, flavoring, and sometimes egg whites; frosting. It is put on cakes and cookies.
ic·ing • ***noun,*** *plural* **icings**

icky (ik′ē) [*a slang word*] ***adjective*** **1** sticky or sweet in an unpleasant way [an *icky* dessert]. **2** sickening or disgusting [Jim and Billy think that broccoli is *icky*.]
ick·y • ***adjective*** **ickier, ickiest**

icy (ī′sē) ***adjective*** **1** full of or covered with ice [*icy* streets]. **2** very cold like ice [*icy* winds; the *icy* waters of the lake]. **3** cold in feeling; not friendly [She gave him an *icy* look and left.]
i·cy • ***adjective*** **icier, iciest**

ID (ī′dē′) ***noun*** [*an informal word*] a card or printed record that shows or proves something about a person.
ID • ***noun,*** *plural* **IDs**

I'd (īd) **1** I had. **2** I would.

STATE MAP

Idaho

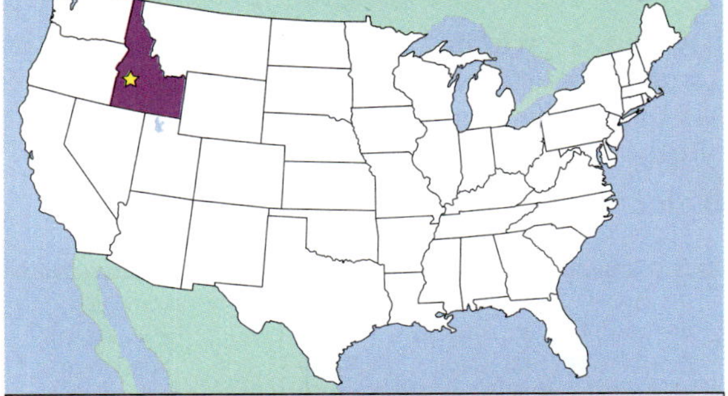

Statehood: 1890, the 43rd state • **Capital:** Boise

Idaho (ī′də hō) a State in the northwestern part of the U.S. Its capital is Boise. Abbreviated **ID** or **Ida.**
I·da·ho

idea (ī dē′ə) ***noun*** **1** something that a person thinks, imagines, or knows; a picture in the mind [Her book gives a good *idea* of life in the American Colonies.] **2** an opinion or belief [She has strong *ideas* about fighting crime.] **3** a plan or purpose [He was always full of new *ideas* for making money.]
i·de·a • ***noun,*** *plural* **ideas**

WORD CHOICES

Synonyms of idea

Many words share the meaning "anything that may be in the mind as an object of knowledge or thought."

concept	impression	thought
conception	notion	

ideal (ī dē′əl) ***adjective*** being exactly as one would wish; perfect [an *ideal* vacation spot]. ***noun*** a person or thing that is thought of as perfect [Mary says that her older sister is her *ideal* of the perfect lawyer.]
i·de·al • ***adjective*** • ***noun,*** *plural* **ideals**

identical (ī den′ti kəl) ***adjective*** exactly alike [These two photos are *identical*.]
i·den·ti·cal • ***adjective***

identification (ī den′ti fi kā′shən) ***noun*** anything that is used to show or prove who a person is or what something is [A driver's license is often used as *identification*.]
i·den·ti·fi·ca·tion • ***noun,*** *plural* **identifications**

identify (ī den′ti fī) ***verb*** to show or prove to be a certain person or thing [Fingerprints are sometimes used to *identify* a person.]
i·den·ti·fy • ***verb*** **identified, identifying, identifies**

identity (ī den′ti tē) ***noun*** **1** the condition of being the same or exactly alike [The *identity* of the fingerprints proved that Jim Smith and John Doe were the same person.] **2** who or what a person or thing is [The *identity* of the thief was unknown.]
i·den·ti·ty • ***noun,*** *plural for sense 2 only* **identities**

I

idiom (id′ē əm) ***noun*** a phrase or expression that has a different meaning from the regular meanings of the separate words in it. "To catch someone's eye," meaning "to get someone's attention," is an idiom.
id·i·om • ***noun,*** *plural* **idioms**

idiot (id′ē ət) ***noun*** a very foolish or stupid person.
id·i·ot • ***noun,*** *plural* **idiots**

idle (ī′dəl) ***adjective*** **1** not working or being used [The closed factory had rows of *idle* machines.] **2** not wanting to work; lazy [*Idle* students seldom finish their homework on time.] **3** having no use or value [*idle* talk]. **4** having no basis or reason; not true [*idle* gossip].
verb **1** to spend time doing useless things or nothing [We *idled* away the summer.] —Look for the WORD CHOICES box at the entry **loiter**. **2** to run while not in gear [Let the engine *idle*.]
i·dle • ***adjective*** **idler, idlest** • ***verb*** **idled, idling**
● The words **idle** and **idol** sound alike.
I don't listen to *idle* gossip.
That quarterback is his *idol*.

idol (ī′dəl) ***noun*** **1** a statue, picture, or other object that is worshiped as a god. **2** a person or thing that is greatly admired or loved [Baseball players are *idols* to many young people.]
i·dol • ***noun,*** *plural* **idols**
● The words **idol** and **idle** sound alike.
The islanders worship a stone *idol*.
Let the car *idle* till I get back.

if (if) ***conjunction*** **1** in case that; supposing that [*If* I were you, I would quit.] **2** whether [I wonder *if* it will rain.] **3** allowing that [*If* he was there, I didn't see him.] **4** I wish that [*If* only I had known!]

igloo (ig′lo͞o) ***noun*** a dome-shaped hut built from blocks of snow. Igloos were used as winter homes by the Eskimos.
ig·loo • ***noun,*** *plural* **igloos**

WORD HISTORY

igloo

We get **igloo** from a word meaning "snow house" in the Eskimo language.

igneous (ig′nē əs) ***adjective*** formed by fire or great heat, under the earth's surface or in volcanoes [Granite is an *igneous* rock.]
ig·ne·ous • ***adjective***

ignite (ig nīt′) ***verb*** **1** to set fire to; make burn [The glowing coals *ignited* the dry leaves.] **2** to catch fire; burn [Dry paper *ignites* easily.]
ig·nite • ***verb*** **ignited, igniting**

ignition (ig nish′ən) ***noun*** an electrical system that starts the engine of a car, boat, or other vehicle. The ignition sets fire to the mixture of gases in a gasoline engine.
ig·ni·tion • ***noun,*** *plural* **ignitions**

ignorance (ig′nər əns) ***noun*** lack of knowledge or education [Prejudice against people who are different often comes from *ignorance*.]
ig·no·rance • ***noun***

ignorant (ig′nər ənt) ***adjective*** **1** having or showing little or no knowledge or education [an *ignorant* person; an *ignorant* statement]. **2** not knowing about; not aware of [She made the mistake because she was *ignorant* of the rules.]
ig·no·rant • ***adjective***

ignore (ig nôr′) ***verb*** to pay no attention to; take no notice of [The phone rang, but he *ignored* it.]
ig·nore • ***verb*** **ignored, ignoring**

iguana

iguana (i gwä′nə) ***noun*** a large lizard of the tropical parts of Central and South America. It has a row of spines from neck to tail.
i·gua·na • ***noun,*** *plural* **iguanas**

IL *abbreviation for* Illinois.

a	cat	ō	go	ʉ	fur	ə =	a *in* ago
ā	ape	ô	law, for	ch	chin		e *in* agent
ä	cot, car	oo	look	sh	she		i *in* pencil
e	ten	o͞o	tool	th	thin		o *in* atom
ē	me	oi	oil	*th*	then		u *in* circus
i	fit	ou	out	zh	measure		
ī	ice	u	up	ŋ	ring		

ill (il) ***adjective*** **1** not healthy; having a disease; sick. **2** harmful or evil; bad [the *ill* effects of not eating properly].
adverb in an unkind way; badly [Don't speak *ill* of someone you don't know.]
noun something that causes trouble or suffering [Sickness is one of the *ills* of old age.]
ill • ***adjective*** **&** • ***adverb*** **worse, worst**
• ***noun,*** *plural* **ills**

I'll (īl) **1** I will. **2** I shall.
● The words **I'll, aisle,** and **isle** sound alike.
I'll be seeing you in the fall.
We took the side *aisle* to our seats.
I rowed our boat over to the tiny *isle*.

Ill. *abbreviation for* Illinois.

illegal (i lē′gəl) ***adjective*** not legal; against the law or rules [It is *illegal* to park here in the morning.]
il·le·gal • ***adjective***

illegible (il ej′i bəl) ***adjective*** hard to read or impossible to read [Her handwriting is *illegible*.]
il·leg·i·ble • ***adjective***

STATE MAP

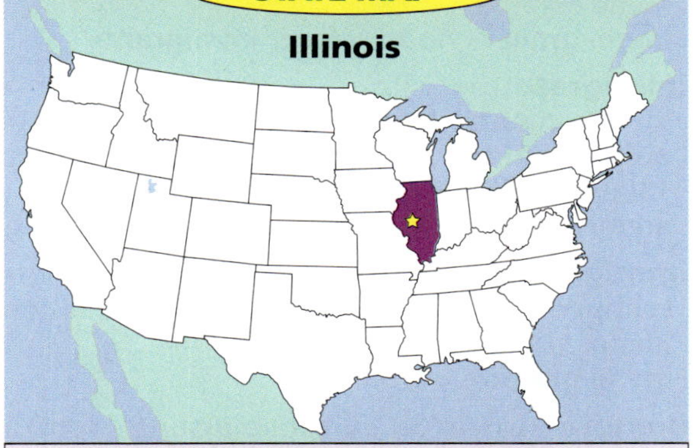

Statehood: 1818, the 21st state • **Capital:** Springfield

Illinois (il′i noi′) a State in the north central part of the U.S. Its capital is Springfield. Abbreviated **IL** or **Ill.**
Il·li·nois

illiterate (i lit′ər ət) ***adjective*** not knowing how to read or write [an *illiterate* person].
il·lit·er·ate • ***adjective***

illness (il′nəs) ***noun*** the condition of being ill or in poor health; sickness; disease [His *illness* lasted many weeks.]
ill·ness • ***noun,*** *plural* **illnesses**

illuminate (i lo͞o′mi nāt′) ***verb*** to give light to; light up [Candles *illuminated* the room.]
il·lu·mi·nate • ***verb*** **illuminated, illuminating**

illusion (i lo͞o′zhən) ***noun*** **1** a false idea or mistaken belief [She is under the *illusion* that the party is tomorrow night.] **2** something that fools the eye, the ear, or any of the other senses by producing a false impression of reality [A large mirror can create an *illusion* of more space in the room.]
il·lu·sion • ***noun,*** *plural* **illusions**

illustrate (il′əs trāt) ***verb*** **1** to make clear by giving examples, making comparisons, or showing pictures [He *illustrated* how gravity works by dropping a baseball and a pingpong ball at the same time.] **2** to add pictures or drawings that decorate or explain [She wants to *illustrate* children's books.]
il·lus·trate • ***verb*** **illustrated, illustrating**

illustration (il′əs trā′shən) ***noun*** **1** a picture used to explain or decorate something [This book has hundreds of *illustrations*.] **2** an example or comparison that helps explain [The teacher gave several *illustrations* of the way sound travels through space.]
il·lus·tra·tion • ***noun,*** *plural* **illustrations**

illustrator (il′əs trāt ər) ***noun*** an artist who makes illustrations for books and magazines.
il·lus·tra·tor • ***noun,*** *plural* **illustrators**

ill will ***noun*** unfriendly feeling; dislike [She felt no *ill will* toward the child who broke her watch.]

I'm (īm) I am.

image (im′ij) ***noun*** **1** a picture or other likeness of some person or thing [Whose *image* is on a dollar bill?] **2** a picture of a real object formed by a mirror or other similar surface [He saw his own *image* reflected in the pool.] **3** a person or thing that looks very much like another [Meg is the *image* of her aunt.]
im·age • ***noun,*** *plural* **images**

imaginary (i maj′i ner′ē) ***adjective*** existing only in the imagination; not real [Unicorns are *imaginary* beasts.]
i·mag·i·nar·y • ***adjective***

imagination (i maj′i nā′shən) ***noun*** **1** the act or power of the mind of forming pictures of things that are not actually present or are not real [The flying saucer you thought you saw is just in your *imagination*.] **2** the ability to create new images or ideas; creative power [It takes great *imagination* to write a play.]
i·mag·i·na·tion • ***noun***

imaginative (i maj′i nə tiv *or* i maj′i nāt′iv) ***adjective*** having or showing imagination

[The *imaginative* child is always making up stories.]
i·mag·i·na·tive • *adjective*

imagine (i maj′in) *verb* **1** to make up a picture or idea in the mind; form an idea [*Imagine* that you are on the planet Mars.] **2** to suppose; guess [I *imagine* Terry will be there.]
i·mag·ine • *verb* **imagined, imagining**

imitate (im′i tāt) *verb* **1** to copy the way someone looks, acts, or sounds [Some birds *imitate* human speech.] **2** to look like; resemble [The glass pieces were cut to *imitate* diamonds.]
im·i·tate • *verb* **imitated, imitating**

WORD CHOICES

Synonyms of **imitate**

The words **imitate, copy,** and **mimic** share the meaning "to use something as a model."

The baby *imitated* my movements.

The student *copied* the writer's style.

The comedian *mimicked* the politician's accent.

imitation (im′ə tā′shən) *noun* **1** the act or process of imitating or copying [She does a great *imitation* of a rock singer. The children danced in *imitation* of flying bees.] **2** a copy or likeness [These are clever *imitations* of gems.] *adjective* made to look like something better; not real [He bought a belt of *imitation* leather.]
im·i·ta·tion • *noun, plural* **imitations** • *adjective*

immaculate (i mak′yoo͞ lət) *adjective* perfectly clean; spotless [Their kitchen is always *immaculate*.]
im·mac·u·late • *adjective*

immature (im ə to͝or′ *or* im ə cho͝or′) *adjective* **1** not mature; not fully grown or developed [*Immature* fruit is not ready to be eaten.] **2** not in keeping with one's age; behaving in a foolish or childish way [It was *immature* of him to refuse to admit he was wrong.]
im·ma·ture • *adjective*

immediate (i mē′dē ət) *adjective* **1** without delay; happening at once [The medicine had an *immediate* effect on the sick child.] **2** with nothing coming between; nearest; closest [Mr. and Mrs. Smith are our *immediate* neighbors.]
im·me·di·ate • *adjective*

immediately (i mē′dē ət lē) *adverb* **1** without delay; at once; right away [Please call home *immediately*.] **2** right after; next [Go to the gym *immediately* after lunch.]
im·me·di·ate·ly • *adverb*

immense (i mens′) *adjective* very large; huge; vast [There are *immense* deserts in Africa.] —Look for the WORD CHOICES box at the entry **enormous**.
im·mense • *adjective*

immerse (i murs′) *verb* **1** to cover completely by plunging or dipping into a liquid [He *immersed* himself in the clear water of the pool.] **2** to get or be deeply in; absorb [She was *immersed* in her studies and didn't hear the phone.]
im·merse • *verb* **immersed, immersing**

immigrant (im′i grənt) *noun* a person who comes into a foreign country to make a new home.
im·mi·grant • *noun, plural* **immigrants**

immigrate (im′i grāt′) *verb* to come into a foreign country to make a new home [Over 15 million persons *immigrated* into the U.S. from 1900 to 1955.]
im·mi·grate • *verb* **immigrated, immigrating**

immigration (im′i grā′shən) *noun* the act of coming into a foreign country to make a new home.
im·mi·gra·tion • *noun*

immoral (i môr′əl) *adjective* against what is right or moral; not good or decent.
im·mor·al • *adjective*

immortal (i môrt′l) *adjective* **1** never dying; living forever [There are many tales of *immortal* beings in science fiction.] **2** never to be forgotten; lasting forever [Abraham Lincoln wrote the *immortal* "Gettysburg Address."]
im·mor·tal • *adjective*

immune (i myoo͞n′) *adjective* **1** protected from a disease [A vaccine can make a person

a	cat	ō	go	ʉr	fur	ə =	a *in* ago
ā	ape	ô	law, for	ch	chin		e *in* agent
ä	cot, car	o͝o	look	sh	she		i *in* pencil
e	ten	o͞o	tool	th	thin		o *in* atom
ē	me	oi	oil	*th*	then		u *in* circus
i	fit	ou	out	zh	measure		
ī	ice	u	up	ŋ	ring		

immune to smallpox.] **2** protected against something bad or unpleasant [Don't think you are *immune* from punishment.]
im·mune • *adjective*

immune system *noun* the system that protects the body from disease. White blood cells and antibodies are part of the human immune system.
immune system • *noun, plural* **immune systems**

immunity (i myo͞on′i tē) *noun* the power of the body to resist disease.
im·mu·ni·ty • *noun, plural* **immunities**

immunize (im′yo͞o nīz′) *verb* to make immune, especially by vaccination.
im·mu·nize • *verb* **immunized, immunizing**

imp (imp) *noun* a naughty, mischievous child.
imp • *noun, plural* **imps**

impact (im′pakt) *noun* **1** the action of one object hitting another with force; violent collision [The *impact* of the car hitting the tree broke the windshield.] **2** the power of something such as an event or idea to cause changes or strong feelings [the *impact* of high prices on our daily lives].
im·pact • *noun, plural* **impacts**

impair (im per′) *verb* to make less or weaker; weaken or damage [The disease *impaired* her sense of hearing.]
im·pair • *verb* **impaired, impairing**

impartial (im pär′shəl) *adjective* not favoring one side over another; fair [an *impartial* referee] —Look for the WORD CHOICES box at the entry **just**.
im·par·tial • *adjective*

impatience (im pā′shəns) *noun* the condition of being impatient; lack of patience.
im·pa·tience • *noun*

impatient (im pā′shənt) *adjective* not patient; not willing to put up with something such as delay, pain, annoyance, or resistance [Some parents become *impatient* when their children cry.]
im·pa·tient • *adjective*

impeach (im pēch′) *verb* to charge a public official with wrongdoing in office [President Andrew Johnson was *impeached* in the U.S. Senate, but was found innocent.]
im·peach • *verb* **impeached, impeaching**

imperative (im per′ə tiv) *adjective* **1** absolutely necessary; urgent [It is *imperative* that I call her today.] **2** of or describing a sentence such as "Please be seated" or "Throw me the ball!" that makes a request or command.
im·per·a·tive • *adjective*

imperfect (im pur′fikt) *adjective* not perfect; having some fault or flaw [They did not buy the diamond because it was *imperfect*.]
im·per·fect • *adjective*

imperial (im pir′ē əl) *adjective* of or having to do with an empire, emperor, or empress [the *imperial* army; an *imperial* court].
im·pe·ri·al • *adjective*

impersonate (im pur′sə nāt′) *verb* **1** to imitate or mimic in fun [The students *impersonated* their teachers in the school play.] **2** to pretend to be in order to cheat or trick [They were arrested for *impersonating* police officers.]
im·per·son·ate • *verb* **impersonated, impersonating**

impetuous (im pech′o͞o əs) *adjective* acting or done suddenly with little thought; rash [an *impetuous* person; an *impetuous* decision].
im·pet·u·ous • *adjective*

implement (im′plə mənt) *noun* something used in doing some work; tool or instrument.
im·ple·ment • *noun, plural* **implements**

implore (im plôr′) *verb* to plead for or beg with much feeling [We *implore* you to let us leave.]
im·plore • *verb* **implored, imploring**

imply (im plī′) *verb* to mean without actually saying [Her frown *implied* disapproval of the students' plans for the picnic.]
im·ply • *verb* **implied, implying, implies**

import (im pôrt′ *for v.;* im′pôrt *for n.*) *verb* to bring goods into one country from another [The U.S. *imports* much of its oil.]
noun something imported from another country [Automobiles are one of the United States' chief *imports*.]
im·port • *verb* **imported, importing** • *noun, plural* **imports**

importance (im pôrt′ns) *noun* the condition or fact of being important [Nowadays we realize the *importance* of conservation.]
im·por·tance • *noun*

important (im pôrt′nt) *adjective* **1** having much meaning or value [His wedding anniversary is an *important* day in his life.] **2** having power, authority, or influence [an *important* government official].
im·por·tant • *adjective*

I

impose (im pōz′) *verb* to set as something that has to be paid, obeyed, or fulfilled [The city *imposes* a tax on beer.]
—impose on (or **upon**) to make demands that are not fair or polite; take advantage of [Can I *impose on* you to drive me home?]
im·pose • *verb* **imposed, imposing**

imposing (im pō′ziŋ) *adjective* grand in size, manner, or looks [an *imposing* building; an *imposing* leader].
im·pos·ing • *adjective*

impossible (im päs′i bəl) *adjective* **1** not possible; not capable of being done or happening [It is *impossible* for a horse to fly.] **2** very unpleasant or hard to put up with [an *impossible* situation].
im·pos·si·ble • *adjective*

impostor (im päs′tər) *noun* a person who cheats or tricks people by pretending to be someone else.
im·pos·tor • *noun, plural* **impostors**

impress (im pres′) *verb* **1** to have a strong effect on the mind or feelings of [Your quick answers *impressed* the teacher greatly.] **2** to fix firmly in the mind [Let me *impress* on you the importance of a good diet.]
im·press • *verb* **impressed, impressing**

impression (im presh′ən) *noun* **1** an effect produced on the mind [The book made a great *impression* on us.] —Look for the WORD CHOICES box at the entry **idea**. **2** a vague feeling [I have the *impression* that someone was here.] **3** a mark made on a surface by pressing [The police took an *impression* of his fingerprints.]
im·pres·sion • *noun, plural* **impressions**

impressive (im pres′iv) *adjective* having a strong effect on the mind; making a strong impression [New York is an *impressive* city.]
im·pres·sive • *adjective*

imprint (im print′ *for v.;* im′print *for n.*) *verb* **1** to mark by pressing or stamping [The paper was *imprinted* with his initials.] **2** to fix firmly [Her face is *imprinted* in my memory.]
noun **1** a mark made by pressing; a print [the *imprint* of a dirty hand on the wall]. **2** a strong effect [Thomas Jefferson's *imprint* on American political life.]

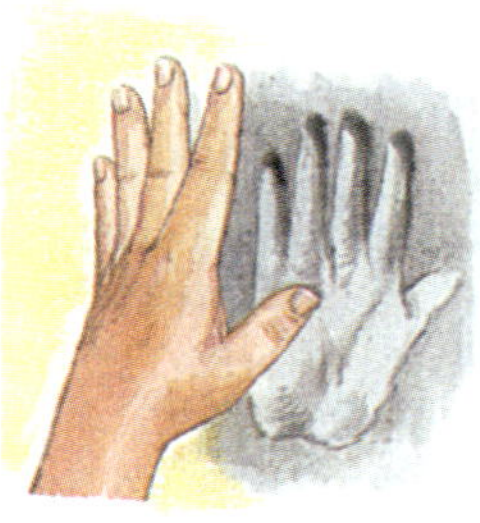
imprint

im·print • *verb* **imprinted, imprinting**
• *noun, plural* **imprints**

imprison (im priz′ən) *verb* to put or keep in prison.
im·pris·on • *verb* **imprisoned, imprisoning**

improbable (im präb′ə bəl) *adjective* not probable; not likely to happen or be true [It is *improbable* that we will win again.]
im·prob·a·ble • *adjective*

improper (im präp′ər) *adjective* **1** not proper or suitable; not right [Sandals are *improper* shoes for tennis.] **2** not according to good taste or good manners [*improper* behavior].
im·prop·er • *adjective*

improper fraction *noun* a fraction in which the denominator is less than the numerator. For example, $8/5$ and $19/7$ are improper fractions.
improper fraction • *noun, plural* **improper fractions**

improve (im pr$\overline{oo}$v′) *verb* to make or become better [His handwriting has *improved*.] —Look for the WORD CHOICES box at the entry **progress**.
im·prove • *verb* **improved, improving**

WORD CHOICES

Synonyms of **improve**

The words **improve**, **better**, and **enhance** share the meaning "to make better."

> The chef worked to *improve* the recipe.
>
> She hopes to *better* her grades.
>
> The new haircut *enhances* his appearance.

improvement (im pr$\overline{oo}$v′mənt) *noun* **1** the act or process of making or becoming better [Your playing shows *improvement*.] **2** an addition or change that makes something better or worth more [A new roof is one of the *improvements* we made to the house.] **3** a person or thing that is better than another

a cat	ō go	ʉ fur	ə = a *in* ago
ā ape	ô law, for	ch chin	e *in* agent
ä cot, car	oo look	sh she	i *in* pencil
e ten	$\overline{oo}$ tool	th thin	o *in* atom
ē me	oi oil	*th* then	u *in* circus
i fit	ou out	zh measure	
ī ice	u up	ŋ ring	

[The new car is an *improvement* over the old one.]
im·prove·ment • *noun, plural* **improvements**

improvise (im′prə vīz) *verb* **1** to make up and perform at the same time, without preparation [He often *improvises* lyrics as he sings.] **2** to make quickly with whatever is available [We *improvised* a bed by putting some chairs together.]
im·pro·vise • *verb* **improvised, improvising**

impulse (im′puls) *noun* **1** a sudden feeling that makes a person want to do something [She had an *impulse* to phone her sister.] **2** a force that starts some action; push or thrust [The *impulse* of the propeller drives the boat.]
im·pulse • *noun, plural* **impulses**

impulsive (im pul′siv) *adjective* **1** acting or likely to act suddenly and without thinking [Johnny is an *impulsive* child who spends his allowance as soon as he gets it.] **2** done or made on a sudden impulse [an *impulsive* remark].
im·pul·sive • *adjective*

impure (im pyoor′) *adjective* not clean; dirty [Smoke made the air *impure*.]
im·pure • *adjective*

in (in) *preposition* **1** contained by [There are five fish *in* the bowl.] **2** covered by [dressed *in* fine clothes]. **3** surrounded by [We were caught *in* a storm.] **4** during [It was done *in* a day.] **5** after [Let's leave *in* an hour.] **6** working at or involved with [She's *in* business.] **7** having or showing [*in* trouble; *in* tears]. **8** having to do with; with regard to [*in* my opinion]. **9** using; by means of [written *in* ink]. **10** because of [He cried out *in* pain.] **11** living or located at [They are *in* Chicago.] **12** into ["Get *in* the house now," she said.]
adverb **1** inside or toward the inside [Walk *in* slowly.] **2** to or toward a certain place or direction [We flew *in* today.] **3** within a certain place [Keep the cat *in*.]
adjective **1** having power or control [the *in* group]. **2** [*an informal use*] now popular or in fashion [Is that hairdo still *in*?] —**in on** having a share or part of [George was *in on* the secret.]
● The words **in** and **inn** sound alike.
Put the money *in* the drawer.
We stayed overnight at the *inn*.

in. *abbreviation for* **1** inch. **2** inches.

IN *abbreviation for* Indiana.

inability (in′ə bil′i tē) *noun* the condition of being unable; lack of ability or power [his *inability* to get his team to win].
in·a·bil·i·ty • *noun, plural* **inabilities**

inaccurate (in ak′yər ət) *adjective* not accurate or exact [That old clock is very *inaccurate*.]
in·ac·cu·rate • *adjective*

inappropriate (in′ə prō′prē ət) *adjective* not appropriate; not suitable or proper [His tennis shoes were *inappropriate* for such a formal occasion.]
in·ap·pro·pri·ate • *adjective*

inaugurate (in ô′gyoo rāt′ *or* in ä′gyoo rāt′) *verb* **1** to place in office with a ceremony; install [The new President will be *inaugurated* on January 20.] **2** to mark the first public use of with a ceremony [The mayor *inaugurated* the new bridge.]
in·au·gu·rate • *verb* **inaugurated, inaugurating**

inauguration (in ô′gyoo rā′shən *or* in ä′gyoo rā′shən) *noun* the public and formal ceremony of inaugurating.
in·au·gu·ra·tion • *noun, plural* **inaugurations**

inborn (in′bôrn) *adjective* being with a person from birth; not acquired; natural [She has an *inborn* talent for playing basketball.]
in·born • *adjective*

Inc. *abbreviation for* Incorporated.

Inca (iŋ′kə) *noun* a member of a highly civilized South American Indian people of ancient Peru.
In·ca • *noun, plural* **Incas**

incandescent lamp (in kən des′ənt) *noun* a lamp that is incandescent, or glowing with heat. It contains a thin metal wire that becomes hot and gives off light when an electric current passes through it. Many of the light bulbs that we use in our homes are incandescent lamps.
in·can·des·cent lamp • *noun, plural* **incandescent lamps**

incandescent lamp

I

incapable (in kā′pə bəl) ***adjective*** not capable; not having the ability or power that is needed [This car is *incapable* of very high speeds. He seems to be *incapable* of working with other people.]
in·ca·pa·ble • ***adjective***

incense (in′sens) ***noun*** a substance that gives off a sweet smell when it is burned.
in·cense • ***noun,*** *plural* **incenses**

incentive (in sen′tiv) ***noun*** the thing that makes a person want to work, try, or do something [Praise was the *incentive* that made him study.]
in·cen·tive • ***noun,*** *plural* **incentives**

inch (inch) ***noun*** a unit of length. It is equal to $\frac{1}{12}$ foot or 2.54 centimeters.
verb to move a little at a time [I *inched* along the diving board because I was scared.]
—inch by inch in a slow or gradual way.
inch • ***noun,*** *plural* **inches** • ***verb*** **inched, inching**

incident (in′si dənt) ***noun*** something that happens in real life or in a story —Look for the WORD CHOICES box at the entry **event**.
in·ci·dent • ***noun,*** *plural* **incidents**

incinerator (in sin′ər āt′ər) ***noun*** a furnace that burns garbage or other waste materials.
in·cin·er·a·tor • ***noun,*** *plural* **incinerators**

incisor (in sī′zər) ***noun*** any one of the front teeth that have a cutting edge. They are located between the canine teeth. A human being has eight incisors.
in·ci·sor • ***noun,*** *plural* **incisors**

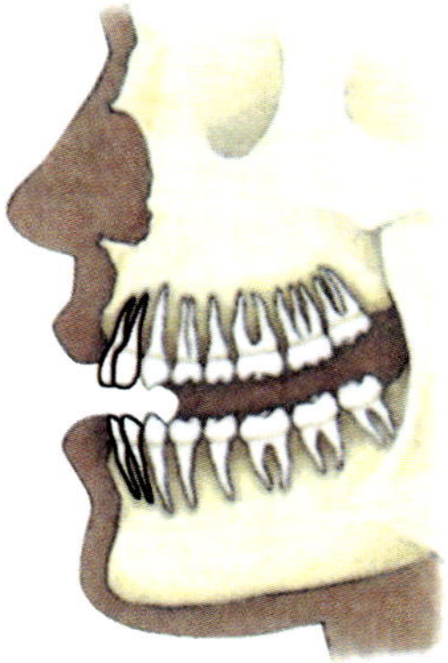
incisor

inclination (in′kli nā′shən) ***noun*** a natural liking for or leaning toward something; tendency [an *inclination* to talk too much].
in·cli·na·tion • ***noun,*** *plural* **inclinations**

incline (in klīn′ *for v.;* in′klīn *for n.*) ***verb*** to lean, slope, or slant [The flagpole *inclines* toward the east.]
noun a sloping surface; a slope or slant [a road with a steep *incline*].
in·cline • ***verb*** **inclined, inclining** • ***noun,*** *plural* **inclines**

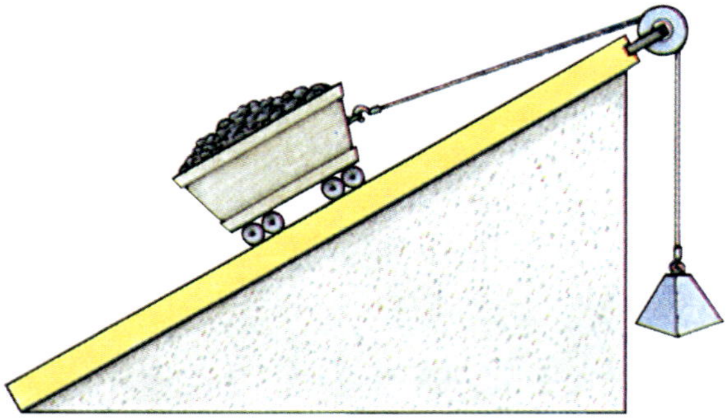
inclined plane

inclined plane ***noun*** a flat surface that is set between two horizontal surfaces, at an angle that is less than 90 degrees. It is a simple machine that makes doing certain kinds of work easier.
inclined plane • ***noun,*** *plural* **inclined planes**

include (in klo͞od′) ***verb*** to have or take in as part of a whole; contain [The prices on this list *include* taxes.]
in·clude • ***verb*** **included, including**

income (in′kum) ***noun*** money that is received in the form of wages, salary, rent, interest, profit, or gifts.
in·come • ***noun,*** *plural* **incomes**

incoming (in′kum iŋ) ***adjective*** moving in or about to move in [*Incoming* traffic is heavy today.]
in·com·ing • ***adjective***

incompetent (in käm′pə tənt) ***adjective*** not able to do what is needed; without enough skill or knowledge [an *incompetent* painter].
in·com·pe·tent • ***adjective***

incomplete (in kəm plēt′) ***adjective*** not complete or whole or finished; without all of its parts.
in·com·plete • ***adjective***

inconsiderate (in kən sid′er ət) ***adjective*** not thinking about the feelings of other people.
in·con·sid·er·ate • ***adjective***

inconvenient (in kən vēn′yənt) ***adjective*** not convenient; causing trouble or bother.
in·con·ven·ient • ***adjective***

a cat	ō go	ʉ fur	ə = a *in* ago
ā ape	ô law, for	ch chin	e *in* agent
ä cot, car	oo look	sh she	i *in* pencil
e ten	o͞o tool	th thin	o *in* atom
ē me	oi oil	*th* then	u *in* circus
i fit	ou out	zh measure	
ī ice	u up	ŋ ring	

incorporate (in kôr′pər āt′) ***verb*** **1** to make part of another thing; combine with something else [*Incorporate* these new facts into your report.] **2** to form into a legal corporation [The owner of a store may *incorporate* his business.]
in·cor·po·rate • ***verb*** **incorporated, incorporating**

incorrect (in kər ekt′) ***adjective*** not correct or true; wrong [The address we have is *incorrect*.]
in·cor·rect • ***adjective***

increase (in krēs′ *for v.;* in′krēs *for n.*) ***verb*** to make or become greater or larger; add to or grow [Please *increase* my allowance.]
noun **1** the act of increasing or the fact of being increased; growth [The State had a large *increase* in population.] **2** the amount by which something increases [an *increase* of 10% over last year's crop].
in·crease • ***verb*** **increased, increasing** • ***noun, plural*** **increases**

incredible (in kred′ə bəl) ***adjective*** very great, unusual, or special in a way that makes it hard or impossible to believe [an *incredible* story; *incredible* speed].
in·cred·i·ble • ***adjective***

incubate (iŋ′kyoo bāt′) ***verb*** to keep warm and protected in order to hatch. Hens incubate their eggs by sitting on them.
in·cu·bate • ***verb*** **incubated, incubating**

incubator (iŋ′kyoo bāt′ər) ***noun*** **1** a container that is kept warm for hatching eggs. **2** a container for protecting babies that are born too early and keeping them warm.
in·cu·ba·tor • ***noun, plural*** **incubators**

incurable (in kyoor′ə bəl) ***adjective*** not having a cure; incapable of being cured [an *incurable* disease].
in·cur·a·ble • ***adjective***

Ind. *abbreviation for* Indiana.

indebted (in det′əd) ***adjective*** owing money, thanks, or something else; in debt [I am *indebted* to you for the help you've given me.]
in·debt·ed • ***adjective***

indeed (in dēd′) ***adverb*** in fact; really [It is *indeed* a great shame.]
interjection a word that is used to show surprise, doubt, or scorn.
in·deed • ***adverb*** • ***interjection***

indefinite (in def′i nit) ***adjective*** **1** not having exact limits [an *indefinite* area]. **2** not clear or exact in meaning; vague [*indefinite* instructions]. **3** not sure or certain [We have somewhat *indefinite* plans for our vacation.]
in·def·i·nite • ***adjective***

indefinite article ***noun*** the word **a** or **an**. The phrase "a dog" does not mean any particular or definite dog.
indefinite article • ***noun, plural*** **indefinite articles**

indelible (in del′i bəl) ***adjective*** permanent; not capable of being erased or rubbed out [*indelible* ink; an *indelible* incident in her memory].
in·del·i·ble • ***adjective***

indent (in dent′) ***verb*** to begin a line of written or printed words farther in from the left edge than other lines on the page [We usually *indent* the beginning of a paragraph.]
in·dent • ***verb*** **indented, indenting**

independence (in′dē pen′dəns) ***noun*** the condition of being independent; freedom from being controlled by other people or governments.
in·de·pend·ence • ***noun***

Independence Day ***noun*** the Fourth of July, a legal holiday. The Declaration of Independence was adopted on July 4, 1776.

independent (in′dē pen′dənt) ***adjective*** **1** not ruled or controlled by another; governing oneself or itself [Many colonies became *independent* countries after World War II.] **2** not influenced by others; thinking as an individual [Sally is very *independent*.] **3** not depending on another person for money to live on. **4** of or describing a clause in grammar with a structure that allows it to stand alone as a complete sentence. In the sentence "She will visit us if she can," the words "she will visit us" form an independent clause.
in·de·pend·ent • ***adjective***

indestructible (in′dē struk′ti bəl) ***adjective*** incapable of being destroyed; very strong [an *indestructible* toy].
in·de·struct·i·ble • ***adjective***

index (in′deks) ***noun*** **1** a list of names, subjects, and other items in alphabetical order at the end of a book. An index shows the numbers of the pages where such names, subjects, and other items appear. **2** a thing that points out, or indicates, something else [Low wages can be an *index* of problems in the economy.]
verb to make an index for [*Indexing* books is a very special skill.]

I

in·dex • *noun, plural* **indexes** • *verb* **indexed, indexing**

index finger *noun* the finger next to the thumb; forefinger.
index finger • *noun, plural* **index fingers**

India (in′dē ə) a country in the central and southern part of a large peninsula of southern Asia.
In·di·a

Indian (in′dē ən) *noun* **1** a member of any of the peoples who were living in the Western Hemisphere long before Europeans arrived. A member of any of these peoples is also called an **American Indian** or **Native American**. **2** a person born or living in India.
In·di·an • *noun, plural* **Indians**

STATE MAP

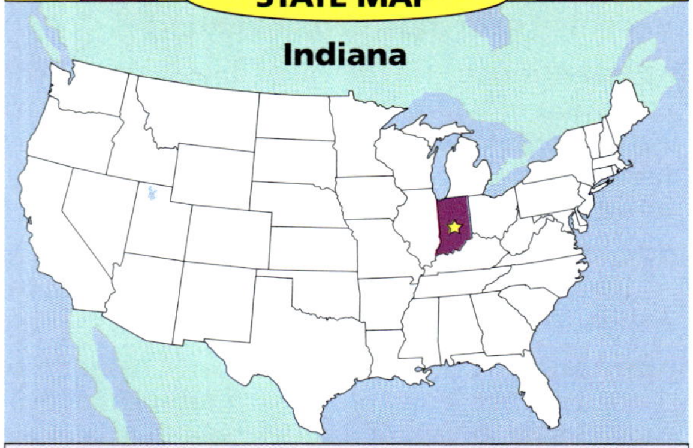

Statehood: 1816, the 19th state • **Capital:** Indianapolis

Indiana (in′dē an′ə) a State in the north central part of the U.S. Its capital is Indianapolis. Abbreviated **IN** or **Ind.**
In·di·an·a

Indianapolis (in′dē ə nap′ə lis) the capital of Indiana.
In·di·an·ap·o·lis

Indian Ocean an ocean south of Asia, between Africa and Australia.

Indian summer *noun* a short time of warm weather after the first frosts of fall.
Indian summer • *noun, plural* **Indian summers**

indicate (in′di kāt′) *verb* **1** to point out or point to; make known or show [*Indicate* where our city is on this map.] **2** to give or be a sign of [Smoke *indicates* fire.]
in·di·cate • *verb* **indicated, indicating**

indicator (in′di kāt′ər) *noun* a pointer, dial, gauge, or other device that measures or shows something [The *indicator* on the dashboard shows that the car is almost out of gas.]
in·di·ca·tor • *noun, plural* **indicators**

indict (in dīt′) *verb* to charge with a crime according to law [The court *indicted* the suspect on robbery charges.]
in·dict • *verb* **indicted, indicting**

indifference (in dif′ər əns *or* in dif′rəns) *noun* lack of interest or concern [people's *indifference* toward poverty].
in·dif·fer·ence • *noun*

indifferent (in dif′ər ənt *or* in dif′rənt) *adjective* having or showing no interest or concern [They were *indifferent* to our pleas for help.]
in·dif·fer·ent • *adjective*

indigent (in′di jənt) *adjective* very poor or needy.
in·di·gent • *adjective*

indigestion (in′di jes′chən) *noun* **1** difficulty in digesting food. **2** the unpleasant condition and feeling that this causes.
in·di·ges·tion • *noun*

indignant (in dig′nənt) *adjective* angry about something that seems not to be fair [He was *indignant* when she called him a liar.]
in·dig·nant • *adjective*

indigo (in′di gō) *noun* **1** a blue dye that is made from a plant or by artificial means. **2** a deep violet blue.
in·di·go • *noun, plural* **indigos**

WORD HISTORY

indigo

We get the word **indigo** from Spanish from two Greek words that mean "Indian dye." The plant from which the dye was first made came from India.

indirect (in′də rekt′) *adjective* **1** not direct or straight; by a longer way [We took an *indirect* route and arrived late.] **2** not the main one [an *indirect* result]. **3** not straight to the point [She gave an *indirect* reply.] —Look for the

a	cat	ō	go	ʉ	fur	ə =	a *in* ago
ā	ape	ô	law, for	ch	chin		e *in* agent
ä	cot, car	oo	look	sh	she		i *in* pencil
e	ten	ōō	tool	th	thin		o *in* atom
ē	me	oi	oil	*th*	then		u *in* circus
i	fit	ou	out	zh	measure		
ī	ice	u	up	ŋ	ring		

WORD CHOICES box at the entry **subtle**.
in·di·rect • *adjective*

indirect object *noun* the word or words in a sentence that name the person that something is given to or done for. In the sentences "They gave us gifts" and "I did him a favor" the words "us" and "him" are indirect objects.
indirect object • *noun, plural* **indirect objects**

indistinct (in′di stiŋkt′) *adjective* not clearly heard, seen, or understood; dim or confused [an *indistinct* murmur of voices].
in·dis·tinct • *adjective*

individual (in′di vij′o͞o əl) *adjective* **1** existing as one separate being or thing [We talked to each *individual* guest. They studied each *individual* painting.] **2** for or from each person or thing [We made *individual* reports on our trip.] **3** different from others; personal or unusual [your own *individual* way of signing your name]. —Look for the WORD CHOICES box at the entry **characteristic**.
noun a single being or thing.
in·di·vid·u·al • *adjective* • *noun, plural* **individuals**

individually (in′di vij′o͞o əl ē) *adverb* as individuals; one at a time [I'll answer each of you *individually*.]
in·di·vid·u·al·ly • *adverb*

indivisible (in′di viz′i bəl) *adjective* **1** not capable of being divided or broken up [This nation is an *indivisible* union of States.] **2** not able to be divided by another number without leaving a remainder [The number 17 is *indivisible*.]
in·di·vis·i·ble • *adjective*

Indochina (in′dō chī′nə) **1** a large peninsula in Asia, south of China. **2** a part of this peninsula, consisting of Laos, Cambodia, and Vietnam.
In·do·chi·na

Indonesia (in′də nē′zhə) a country made up of a large group of islands between southeast Asia and Australia.
In·do·ne·sia

Indonesian (in′də nē′zhən) *noun* **1** a person born or living in Indonesia. **2** the official language of Indonesia.
In·do·ne·sian • *noun, plural for sense 1 only* **Indonesians**

indoor (in′dôr) *adjective* done or located in, or having to do with, the inside of a house or building [*indoor* sports; an *indoor* rink].
in·door • *adjective*

indoors (in dôrz′ *or* in′dôrz) *adverb* in or into a building [Let's go *indoors* to avoid the rain.]
in·doors • *adverb*

indulge (in dulj′) *verb* **1** to give in to something that one wants to do; let oneself have some pleasure [We *indulge* in sleeping late on weekends.] **2** to give in to the wishes of; to humor [They *indulge* their children far too much.]
in·dulge • *verb* **indulged, indulging**

industrial (in dus′trē əl) *adjective* having to do with industries or with the people working in industries [an *industrial* district; *industrial* unions].
in·dus·tri·al • *adjective*

industrious (in dus′trē əs) *adjective* working hard and in a steady way.
in·dus·tri·ous • *adjective*

industry (in′dəs trē) *noun* **1** a branch of business, especially manufacturing [the steel *industry;* the movie *industry*]. **2** all kinds of businesses, thought of together [Leaders of *industry* met in Chicago.]
in·dus·try • *noun, plural* **industries**

inedible (in ed′i bəl) *adjective* not good or safe to eat [an *inedible* plant].
in·ed·i·ble • *adjective*

inefficient (in ə fish′ənt) *adjective* not capable of doing what is needed without wasting time, effort, or materials [an *inefficient* worker].
in·ef·fi·cient • *adjective*

ineligible (in el′i ji bəl) *adjective* not able to be chosen for something according to the rules; not qualified [Low grades can make a student *ineligible* for sports teams.]
in·el·i·gi·ble • *adjective*

inertia (in ʉr′shə) *noun* the tendency of an object to remain at rest if it is at rest, or to remain in motion if it is moving. For example, a cup on a table will remain motionless on the table until someone or something moves it.
in·er·tia • *noun*

inevitable (in ev′i tə bəl) *adjective* sure to happen; unavoidable.
in·ev·i·ta·ble • *adjective*

inexcusable (in′ek skyo͞o′zə bəl) *adjective* so rude, wicked, or bad in some other way that it cannot be excused or forgiven.

I

in·ex·cus·a·ble • *adjective*

inexpensive (in′ek spen′siv) *adjective* not expensive; low in price.
in·ex·pen·sive • *adjective*

inexperienced (in′ek spir′ē ənst) *adjective* not having experience in something or the skill that experience brings [an *inexperienced* teacher].
in·ex·pe·ri·enced • *adjective*

infancy (in′fən sē) *noun* **1** the time of being an infant or baby. **2** the earliest stage of something [The space program was in its *infancy* in the 1960's.]
in·fan·cy • *noun*

infant (in′fənt) *noun* a very young child; a baby.
in·fant • *noun, plural* **infants**

WORD HISTORY

infant

The word **infant** comes from a Latin word that means "not yet speaking." During the first year after they are born, **infants** usually are "not yet speaking," except for a word or two.

infantry (in′fən trē) *noun* the part of an army that is made up of soldiers who have been trained for fighting mainly on foot.
in·fan·try • *noun, plural* **infantries**

infect (in fekt′) *verb* **1** to make full of bacteria, viruses, or other living things that can enter the body and cause a disease [Rotting garbage can *infect* well water with all kinds of germs.] —Look for the WORD CHOICES box at the entry **contaminate**. **2** to cause disease in [Germs had *infected* the wound on her leg.]
in·fect • *verb* **infected, infecting**

infection (in fek′shən) *noun* **1** a disease that is caused by bacteria, viruses, or other living things that can enter the body [an eye *infection;* a measles *infection*]. **2** the act or process of giving or getting a disease of this kind [Washing hands helps to prevent *infection*.]
in·fec·tion • *noun, plural* **infections**

infectious (in fek′shəs) *adjective* caused by infection [Measles is an *infectious* disease.]
in·fec·tious • *adjective*

inferior (in fir′ē ər) *adjective* **1** not very good; below average [*inferior* products]. **2** lower in position or rank [A private is *inferior* to a general.]
in·fe·ri·or • *adjective*

infest (in fest′) *verb* to swarm in or over in a way that harms or bothers [Rats *infested* the old, empty house.]
in·fest • *verb* **infested, infesting**

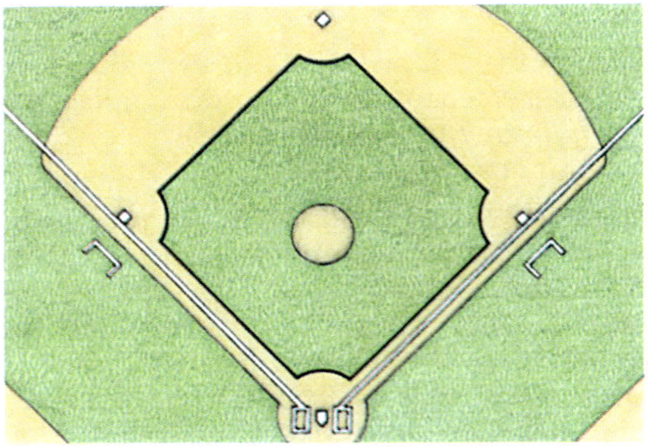

infield

infield (in′fēld) *noun* **1** the part of a baseball field that is inside the four lines connecting the bases. **2** all of the infielders.
in·field • *noun, plural* **infields**

infielder (in′fēl dər) *noun* a baseball player with a position in the infield; the shortstop or any of the three basemen.
in·field·er • *noun, plural* **infielders**

infiltrate (in′fil trāt′) *verb* to pass through or into, in the way that water passes through a filter; penetrate [Our troops *infiltrated* the enemy lines.]
in·fil·trate • *verb* **infiltrated, infiltrating**

infinite (in′fi nit) *adjective* having no limits; without beginning or end [The universe is *infinite*.]
in·fi·nite • *adjective*

infinitive (in fin′i tiv) *noun* a form of a verb that is not limited by having a subject or showing past, present, or future time. It is usually made with the word *to* plus the base form of the verb. In the sentence "I need to eat," "to eat" is an infinitive.
in·fin·i·tive • *noun, plural* **infinitives**

a	cat	ō	go	ʉ	fur	ə =	a *in* ago
ā	ape	ô	law, for	ch	chin		e *in* agent
ä	cot, car	oo	look	sh	she		i *in* pencil
e	ten	ōō	tool	th	thin		o *in* atom
ē	me	oi	oil	*th*	then		u *in* circus
i	fit	ou	out	zh	measure		
ī	ice	u	up	ŋ	ring		

inflamed (in flāmd′) *adjective* hot, swollen, red, or sore [an *inflamed* wound].
in·flamed • *adjective*

inflammation (in flə mā′shən) *noun* a swollen area in some part of the body that is hot, red, and sore. It can be caused by disease or injury.
in·flam·ma·tion • *noun, plural* **inflammations**

inflate (in flāt′) *verb* to cause to swell out by putting in air or gas; expand [We *inflated* balloons for the party.] —Look for the WORD CHOICES box at the entry **expand**.
in·flate • *verb* **inflated, inflating**

inflation (in flā′shən) *noun* **1** the act of inflating something or the fact of being inflated. **2** a general increase in the prices of goods and services.
in·fla·tion • *noun*

inflect (in flekt′) *verb* to change the form of a word to show certain characteristics.
in·flect • *verb* **inflected, inflecting**

inflection (in flek′shən) *noun* a change in the form of a word to show its use in the sentence. An inflection shows whether a noun is singular or plural, whether an adjective is a comparative or superlative, or whether a verb shows present or past time. For example, the ending **-est** is added to the adjective *calm* to make *calmest*, meaning "most calm."
in·flec·tion • *noun, plural* **inflections**

inflict (in flikt′) *verb* **1** to cause by hitting or in a way that seems like hitting [The explosion *inflicted* severe wounds on the enemy soldiers.] **2** to impose, or put on [The judge *inflicted* a harsh penalty on the criminals.]
in·flict • *verb* **inflicted, inflicting**

influence (in′flo͞o əns) *noun* **1** the power to act on or affect persons or things in ways that are either good or bad [A person under the *influence* of a drug may suffer great harm.] **2** a person or thing that has this power [He's a good *influence* on the children.]
verb to have influence or power over [Her advice *influenced* my decision.] —Look for the WORD CHOICES box at the entry **sway**.
in·flu·ence • *noun, plural* **influences**
• *verb* **influenced, influencing**

influential (in′flo͞o en′shəl) *adjective* having or using great influence; powerful [an *influential* news program].
in·flu·en·tial • *adjective*

influenza (in′flo͞o en′zə) *noun* a disease that is caused by a virus. It is like a bad cold but more serious.
in·flu·en·za • *noun, plural* **influenzas**

info (in′fō) [*a slang word*] *noun a short form of* **information**.
in·fo • *noun*

inform (in fôrm′) *verb* **1** to give facts to; tell [*Inform* us when you change your address.] **2** to give information or tell secrets that harm another person or thing [He *informed* against his boss.]
in·form • *verb* **informed, informing**

WORD CHOICES

Synonyms of **inform**

The words **inform, advise,** and **notify** share the meaning "to let know about something."

He *informed* me of his decision to leave.

The letter *advised* them of the change in schedule.

Please *notify* us when they arrive.

informal (in fôr′məl) *adjective* **1** not following fixed rules or forms; relaxed or familiar [an *informal* letter; an *informal* dinner]. **2** of, used, or worn in everyday situations [*informal* writing; *informal* clothes].
in·for·mal • *adjective*

information (in fər mā′shən) *noun* **1** the fact of informing or being informed [This is for your *information*.] **2** something that is told or facts that are learned; news or knowledge [An encyclopedia gives *information* on many topics.] **3** a service that answers certain questions [Ask *Information* for the phone number of the doctor.]
in·for·ma·tion • *noun*

infrared (in frə red′) *adjective* describing rays of light that are just beyond red in the color spectrum. Infrared light rays cannot be seen, but they produce heat that can be felt and measured.
in·fra·red • *adjective*

infuriate (in fyo͝or′ē āt′) *verb* to make very angry; enrage [The injustice *infuriated* her.]
in·fu·ri·ate • *verb* **infuriated, infuriating**

I

-ing *a suffix:* **1** used to form the present participle of verbs [We were *walking* in the park.] **2** used to form nouns from verbs [A *painting* is something made by a person who paints.]

ingenious (in jēn′yəs) ***adjective*** clever or skillful [an *ingenious* architect; an *ingenious* plan].
in·gen·ious • ***adjective***

ingredient (in grē′dē ənt) ***noun*** any one of the things that a mixture is made of [Sugar is a basic *ingredient* of candy.]
in·gre·di·ent • ***noun,*** *plural* **ingredients**

ingrown (in′grōn) ***adjective*** having grown into the flesh [An *ingrown* toenail is one that curves in and under at the sides.]
in·grown • ***adjective***

inhabit (in hab′it) ***verb*** to live in or on; occupy [The island is *inhabited* by exotic birds and animals.]
in·hab·it • ***verb*** **inhabited, inhabiting**

inhabitant (in hab′i tənt) ***noun*** a person or animal that lives in a certain place.
in·hab·it·ant • ***noun,*** *plural* **inhabitants**

inhale (in hāl′) ***verb*** to draw into the lungs; breathe in [She *inhaled* the fresh sea air. "*Inhale* deeply," said the doctor.]
in·hale • ***verb*** **inhaled, inhaling**

inherit (in her′it) ***verb*** **1** to receive from someone when that person dies; to get as an heir [She *inherited* her aunt's fine dishes.] **2** to have or get from parents by the biological process of heredity [He *inherited* his father's blue eyes.]
in·her·it • ***verb*** **inherited, inheriting**

inhuman (in hyoo͞′mən) ***adjective*** cruel or heartless; seeming to have no feelings.
in·hu·man • ***adjective***

initial (i nish′əl) ***adjective*** at or having to do with the beginning; first [the *initial* stage of a disease].
noun the first letter of a name [George Washington's *initials* are G.W.]
verb to mark with one's initials [Her teacher *initialed* the hall pass.]
in·i·tial • ***adjective*** • ***noun,*** *plural* **initials**
• ***verb*** **initialed** or **initialled, initialing** or **initialling**

initiate (i nish′ē āt′) ***verb*** **1** to start; begin to do, make, or use [Our school has *initiated* a new program to improve math skills.] **2** to take in as a club member, often with a ceremony.
in·i·ti·ate • ***verb*** **initiated, initiating**

initiative (i nish′ē ə tiv *or* i nish′ə tiv) ***noun*** the ability to get things started or done without needing to be told what to do [Carlos is a person with *initiative*.]
in·i·ti·a·tive • ***noun***

inject (in jekt′) ***verb*** **1** to force a fluid into some part of the body with a syringe and needle [The doctor *injected* the vaccine into the baby's arm.] **2** to bring in a missing quality or feature [She *injected* a note of humor into the story.]
in·ject • ***verb*** **injected, injecting**

injection (in jek′shən) ***noun*** a fluid that is injected into the body [an *injection* to stop the pain].
in·jec·tion • ***noun,*** *plural* **injections**

injure (in′jər) ***verb*** to do harm to; to hurt or damage [I *injured* my leg in the fall. The teacher's comments *injured* her pride.]
in·jure • ***verb*** **injured, injuring**

WORD CHOICES

Synonyms of injure

The words **injure, damage,** and **harm** share the meaning "to hurt the appearance, condition, or value of."

Rumors *injured* his reputation.

The cargo was *damaged* during the storm.

She wouldn't *harm* a fly.

injury (in′jər ē) ***noun*** harm or damage that is done to a person or thing [She received serious *injuries* in the accident.]
in·ju·ry • ***noun,*** *plural* **injuries**

injustice (in jus′tis) ***noun*** **1** lack of justice or fairness. **2** an act that is not just [It was an *injustice* to imprison them without a trial.]
in·jus·tice • ***noun,*** *plural for sense 2 only* **injustices**

ink (iŋk) ***noun*** a black or colored liquid or paste for writing, printing, or drawing.

a cat	ō go	ʉ fur	ə = a *in* ago
ā ape	ô law, for	ch chin	e *in* agent
ä cot, car	oo look	sh she	i *in* pencil
e ten	o͞o tool	th thin	o *in* atom
ē me	oi oil	*th* then	u *in* circus
i fit	ou out	zh measure	
ī ice	u up	ŋ ring	

verb to color, mark, or cover with ink.
ink • *noun, plural* **inks** • *verb* **inked, inking**

inkling (iŋk′liŋ) *noun* a vague idea [I had no *inkling* that he was a thief.]
ink·ling • *noun, plural* **inklings**

inland (in′lənd) *adjective* not on or near the coast or border; inside a country or region [The Ohio River is an *inland* waterway.]
adverb into or toward this kind of area.
in·land • *adjective* • *adverb*

in-law (in′lô *or* in′lä) [*an informal word*] *noun* a relative by marriage [Her *in-laws* live in Little Rock.]
in-law • *noun, plural* **in-laws**

inlet (in′lət) *noun* a narrow strip of water that runs into a piece of land from a river, lake, or ocean.
in·let • *noun, plural* **inlets**

in-line skate (in′līn) *noun* a roller skate with the wheels set in a line from toe to heel like the blade of an ice skate.
in-line skate • *noun, plural* **in-line skates**

in-line skate

inn (in) *noun* a hotel or motel that has a tavern or restaurant, especially one in the country or along a highway.
inn • *noun, plural* **inns**
- The words **inn** and **in** sound alike.
  We stayed overnight at the *inn*.
  Put the money *in* the drawer.

WORD HISTORY

inn

The word **inn** is really just a thousand-year-old spelling of the adverb *in*. In earlier times, the owner of a place with rooms to rent would put up a sign that said "INN," which meant "Come in if you need a place to stay." Today, in much the same way, some small restaurants put up a sign that says "EAT."

inner (in′ər) *adjective* farther in; interior [the *inner* rooms of the palace].
in·ner • *adjective*

inner city *noun* an older part in or near the center of a large city that usually is too crowded and in bad condition.
inner city • *noun, plural* **inner cities**

inning (in′iŋ) *noun* a part of a baseball game in which both teams have a turn at bat. There are usually nine innings in a game.
in·ning • *noun, plural* **innings**

innkeeper (in′kē pər) *noun* a person who owns or manages an inn.
inn·keep·er • *noun, plural* **innkeepers**

innocence (in′ə səns) *noun* the condition or fact of being innocent; freedom from guilt for moral or legal wrong [The lawyer proved the *innocence* of his client.]
in·no·cence • *noun*

innocent (in′ə sənt) *adjective* not guilty of a crime, sin, or fault [If he is telling the truth, he is *innocent* of the theft.]
in·no·cent • *adjective*

innovation (in ə vā′shən) *noun* a new device or a new way of doing something; a change [Lighting by electricity was an *innovation* 100 years ago.]
in·no·va·tion • *noun, plural* **innovations**

inoculate (i näk′yoo lāt′) *verb* to inject into the body a vaccine that will cause a mild form of a disease. In this way the body is able to build up its ability to fight off that disease later.
in·oc·u·late • *verb* **inoculated, inoculating**

input (in′poot) *noun* **1** information that is put into a computer to be stored in its memory. **2** advice or an opinion [They asked for our *input* before making their decision.]
verb to put information into a computer [She *input* the names of all the children in class.]
in·put • *noun* • *verb* **input, inputting**

inquire (in kwīr′) *verb* to ask in order to learn [The students *inquired* about their grades.]
in·quire • *verb* **inquired, inquiring**

inquiry (in′kwi rē *or* in kwīr′ē) *noun* the act or process of inquiring; a request for information [All *inquiries* should be sent to the main office.]
in·quir·y • *noun, plural* **inquiries**

inquisitive (in kwiz′i tiv) ***adjective*** asking many questions; eager to learn; curious [Joe was an *inquisitive* child. He had an *inquisitive* mind.]
in·quis·i·tive • ***adjective***

insane (in sān′) ***adjective*** **1** having a mental illness; not sane. **2** very foolish; without clear thinking [This is an *insane* idea.]
in·sane • ***adjective***

insanity (in san′i tē) ***noun*** the condition of being insane.
in·san·i·ty • ***noun***

inscribe (in skrīb′) ***verb*** to write, print, engrave, or carve something on or in [The jeweler will *inscribe* all their names on the trophy.]
in·scribe • ***verb*** **inscribed, inscribing**

inscription (in skrip′shən) ***noun*** **1** the act of inscribing [The *inscription* of the names on the trophy took hours.] **2** something that is inscribed on a coin or other hard surface, or in a book.
in·scrip·tion • ***noun,*** *plural* **inscriptions**

insect

insect (in′sekt) ***noun*** **1** a tiny animal with six legs, usually two pairs of wings, and a body divided into three parts. Bees, wasps, flies, and mosquitoes are insects. **2** any tiny animal somewhat like this, such as a spider or a centipede.
in·sect • ***noun,*** *plural* **insects**

WORD HISTORY

insect

An **insect's** body is made up of three parts that are very clearly marked off, almost as if the body had been cut into. The Latin word from which **insect** comes means "to cut into."

insecticide (in sek′ti sīd′) ***noun*** any poison used to kill insects.
in·sec·ti·cide • ***noun,*** *plural* **insecticides**

insecure (in sə kyoor′) ***adjective*** **1** not secure or safe; not providing good support [an *insecure* balcony]. **2** not feeling safe or confident [A person can feel *insecure* in a new job.]
in·se·cure • ***adjective***

insert (in surt′) ***verb*** to put or fit into [She *inserted* the key into the lock and tried to open the door.]
in·sert • ***verb*** **inserted, inserting**

inside (in′sīd′) ***noun*** the side or part that is within [Wash the windows on the *inside*.]
adjective **1** on or in the inside; internal; indoor [The workmen are doing *inside* work on the house.] **2** secret or private [The coach tried to get *inside* information about the other team's strategy].
adverb on or in the inside; within [They played *inside*.]
preposition within; in [What's *inside* the box?]
—inside out with the inside where the outside should be [Turn the sweater *inside out* before washing it.]
in·side • ***noun*** • ***adjective*** • ***adverb*** • ***preposition***

insignia (in sig′nē ə) ***noun*** a special mark or badge that shows rank, membership in an organization, or a position of some honor [He wore the *insignia* of commander of the U.S. Navy.]
in·sig·ni·a • ***noun,*** *plural* **insignia** or **insignias**

insignificant (in′sig nif′ i kənt) ***adjective*** not important; of little value [Don't worry about *insignificant* details.]
in·sig·nif·i·cant • ***adjective***

insignia

a	cat	ō	go	ur	fur	ə =	a *in* ago
ā	ape	ô	law, for	ch	chin		e *in* agent
ä	cot, car	oo	look	sh	she		i *in* pencil
e	ten	ōō	tool	th	thin		o *in* atom
ē	me	oi	oil	*th*	then		u *in* circus
i	fit	ou	out	zh	measure		
ī	ice	u	up	ŋ	ring		

WORD CHOICES

Synonyms of **insignificant**

The words **insignificant, petty,** and **trivial** share the meaning "small and unimportant."

an *insignificant* matter

a *petty* grudge

a *trivial* remark

insincere (in′sin sir′) *adjective* not sincere; not meaning what one says or does [I don't trust him; he's very *insincere*.]
in·sin·cere • *adjective*

insist (in sist′) *verb* **1** to stick strongly to a belief [I *insist* that I saw her in the theater Monday night.] **2** to demand strongly [She *insisted* that we stay for dinner.]
in·sist • *verb* **insisted, insisting**

insolent (in′sə lənt) *adjective* not having or showing the proper respect; rude [He was punished for his *insolent* behavior in class.]
in·so·lent • *adjective*

inspect (in spekt′) *verb* **1** to look at carefully; examine [*Inspect* the bicycle before you buy it.] **2** to examine or review in an official way [The general *inspects* the troops today.]
in·spect • *verb* **inspected, inspecting**

inspection (in spek′shən) *noun* **1** the act or process of inspecting [a careful *inspection* of the bicycle]. **2** an official examination or review [The general's *inspection* of the troops was delayed by rain.]
in·spec·tion • *noun, plural* **inspections**

inspector (in spek′tər) *noun* **1** a person who inspects [She has a job as an *inspector* at the toy factory.] **2** a police officer of high rank.
in·spec·tor • *noun, plural* **inspectors**

inspiration (in′spər ā′shən) *noun* **1** the power to cause, urge, or influence to do something [Our cheers gave *inspiration* to the team to win.] **2** something or someone that inspires thought or action [The ocean was the painter's *inspiration* for his masterpiece.] **3** a sudden bright idea [Having the birthday party at the zoo was an *inspiration*.]
in·spi·ra·tion • *noun, plural* **inspirations**

inspire (in spīr′) *verb* **1** to cause, urge, or influence to do something [The sunset *inspired* her to write a poem.] **2** to bring about, cause, or be the source of [Your kindness *inspired* his love. The book about President Kennedy *inspired* a TV program.]
in·spire • *verb* **inspired, inspiring**

install (in stôl′) *verb* to fix in a position for use [The telephone company sent two workers to *install* the telephones in our house.]
in·stall • *verb* **installed, installing**

installment (in stôl′mənt) *noun* a sum of money that a person pays at regular times as part of a series of payments [The car will be paid for in nine monthly *installments*.]
in·stall·ment • *noun, plural* **installments**

instance (in′stəns) *noun* something that shows or proves; an example [This gift is another *instance* of their generosity.]
in·stance • *noun, plural* **instances**

instant (in′stənt) *noun* **1** a very short time; moment [Wait just an *instant*.] **2** a particular moment [At that *instant* I fell.]
adjective **1** with no delay; immediate [His *instant* reply was that they were wrong.] **2** capable of being prepared quickly [*instant* coffee].
in·stant • *noun, plural* **instants** • *adjective*

instantly (in′stənt lē) *adverb* with no delay; immediately [Bill recognized her *instantly*.]
in·stant·ly • *adverb*

instant replay *noun* the act of showing a videotaped action again, often in slow motion, immediately after it has been recorded [an *instant replay* of a touchdown].
instant replay • *noun, plural* **instant replays**

instead (in sted′) *adverb* in place of the other; as a substitute [If you have no cream, use milk *instead*.] **—instead of** in place of [Use cream *instead of* milk.]
in·stead • *adverb*

instep (in′step) *noun* **1** the upper part of the foot that is above the arch. **2** the part of a shoe or stocking that covers this.
in·step • *noun, plural* **insteps**

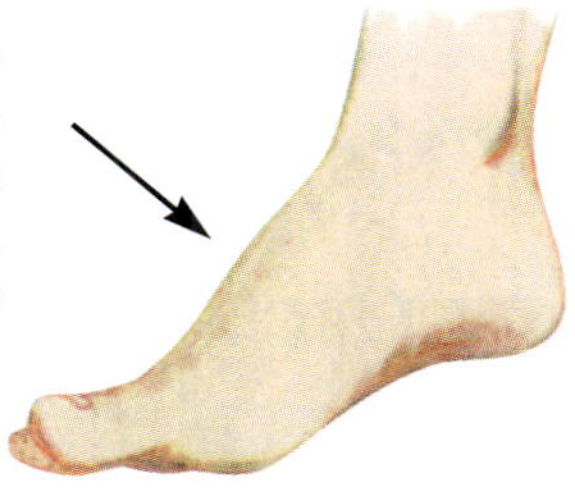

instep

instill (in stil′) *verb* to put an idea or feeling into someone's mind in a slow but sure way [Grandpa *instilled* the

principle of honesty in the minds of all his children.]
in·still • *verb* **instilled, instilling**

instinct (in′stiŋkt) *noun* **1** a way of behaving that is natural to an animal or person from birth [the *instinct* of birds for building nests]. **2** a natural ability; talent [She has an *instinct* for saying the right thing.]
in·stinct • *noun, plural* **instincts**

instinctive (in stiŋk′tiv) *adjective* caused or done by instinct [Most animals have an *instinctive* fear of fire.]
in·stinc·tive • *adjective*

institute (in′sti to͞ot′ *or* in′sti tyo͞ot′) *verb* **1** to set up; bring into being [The modern Olympic games were *instituted* in 1896.] **2** to start [The police *instituted* a search for the child.]
noun a school or organization for some special study or work in education, art, science, or some other field of knowledge.
in·sti·tute • *verb* **instituted, instituting** • *noun, plural* **institutes**

institution (in′sti to͞o′shən *or* in′sti tyo͞o′shən) *noun* **1** an established law, custom, practice, or pattern of behavior [the *institution* of marriage]. **2** a church, school, prison, or other organization with a special purpose.
in·sti·tu·tion • *noun, plural* **institutions**

instruct (in strukt′) *verb* **1** to teach or train [She *instructed* me in physics.] **2** to order; direct [I was *instructed* to wait outside.]
in·struct • *verb* **instructed, instructing**

instruction (in struk′shən) *noun* **1** the act of teaching; education [The teacher spent a lifetime in the *instruction* of children.] **2 instructions** orders or directions [The *instructions* for the test are on a separate sheet.]
in·struc·tion • *noun, plural* **instructions**

instructor (in struk′tər) *noun* a person who instructs; a teacher.
in·struc·tor • *noun, plural* **instructors**

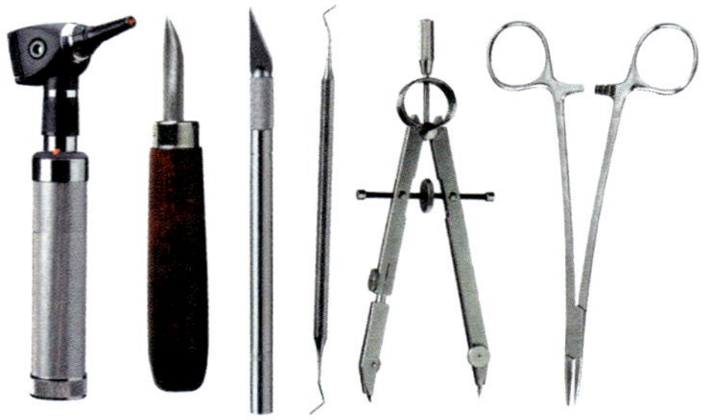

instrument

instrument (in′strə mənt) *noun* **1** a tool, implement, or other device for doing very precise work [The surgeon asked the nurse to hand over another *instrument*.] **2** a flute, violin, piano, or other device used in making music.
in·stru·ment • *noun, plural* **instruments**

insulate (in′sə lāt) *verb* to cover or separate with a material that keeps electricity, heat, or sound from escaping [Electric wires are always *insulated*. They *insulated* their old house.]
in·su·late • *verb* **insulated, insulating**

insulation (in sə lā′shən) *noun* **1** the act or process of insulating [The *insulation* of the house took longer than expected.] **2** any material used to insulate.
in·su·la·tion • *noun*

insulin (in′sə lin) *noun* a hormone that is made in the body by the pancreas. It helps the body use sugars and starches. Insulin taken from animals is used to treat diabetes.
in·su·lin • *noun*

insult (in sult′ *for v.;* in′sult *for n.*) *verb* to say or do something that hurts a person's feelings or pride [He *insulted* me by calling me a liar.] —Look for the WORD CHOICES box at the entry **offend**.
noun an insulting act or remark.
in·sult • *verb* **insulted, insulting** • *noun, plural* **insults**

insurance (in sho͝or′əns) *noun* **1** a contract by which a company guarantees a person that a certain sum of money will be paid in case the person has a loss by fire, death, accident, theft, or another similar event. The insured person makes regular payments to buy this guarantee. **2** the amount for which something is insured [How much *insurance* does she have on her car?] **3** the business of insuring against loss.
in·sur·ance • *noun*

insure (in sho͝or′) *verb* **1** to get or give insurance on [We *insured* our car against theft.] **2** *another spelling of* **ensure**.
in·sure • *verb* **insured, insuring**

intact (in takt′) *adjective* kept or left whole;

a cat	ō go	ʉ fur	ə = a *in* ago
ā ape	ô law, for	ch chin	e *in* agent
ä cot, car	o͝o look	sh she	i *in* pencil
e ten	o͞o tool	th thin	o *in* atom
ē me	oi oil	*th* then	u *in* circus
i fit	ou out	zh measure	
ī ice	u up	ŋ ring	

with nothing missing, broken, or injured; in one piece [When we moved, all our mirrors and other breakable objects arrived *intact*.]
in·tact • *adjective*

intake (in′tāk) *noun* **1** the act or process of taking in [A gasp is a sharp *intake* of breath.] **2** the place in a pipe or channel where water, air, or gas is taken in.
in·take • *noun, plural* **intakes**

integer (in′tə jər) *noun* a number that is not a fraction; a whole number. The numbers 2, -3, 0, and 195 are integers.
in·te·ger • *noun, plural* **integers**

integrate (in′tə grāt) *verb* **1** to bring together into a whole; unite or unify [The teacher tried to *integrate* the study of art with the study of history.] **2** to open to people of all races [The city *integrated* all its schools.]
in·te·grate • *verb* **integrated, integrating**

integration (in′tə grā′shən) *noun* the act or process of integrating [They supported the *integration* of the city schools.]
in·te·gra·tion • *noun*

integrity (in teg′ri tē) *noun* the quality of being honest and trustworthy; honesty [A judge is expected to be a person of *integrity*.] —Look for the WORD CHOICES box at the entry **honor**.
in·teg·ri·ty • *noun*

intellect (in′tə lekt) *noun* the ability to understand ideas and to think [a person of great *intellect*.]
in·tel·lect • *noun*

intellectual (in′tə lek′cho͞o əl) *adjective* **1** of or having to do with the intellect or its use [The scientist was a man of great *intellectual* powers.] **2** needing intelligence and much thought [Chess is an *intellectual* game.]
noun **1** a very smart person. **2** a person who does work or has interests that require intelligence and much thought.
in·tel·lec·tu·al • *adjective* • *noun, plural* **intellectuals**

intelligence (in tel′i jəns) *noun* the ability to learn and understand, or to solve problems [Dogs have greater *intelligence* than birds.]
in·tel·li·gence • *noun*

intelligent (in tel′i jənt) *adjective* having or showing intelligence; being able to learn, think, and understand.
in·tel·li·gent • *adjective*

WORD CHOICES

Synonyms of **intelligent**

Many words share the meaning "having or showing a keen mind and the ability to learn easily."

bright	quick	sharp
brilliant	perceptive	smart
clever		

intend (in tend′) *verb* to have in mind; to plan [I *intend* to leave for California tomorrow.]
in·tend • *verb* **intended, intending**

intense (in tens′) *adjective* **1** very strong or deep; very great; extreme [The lighthouse sent out a beam of *intense* light. His reply was marked by *intense* anger.] **2** having very deep or strong feelings [Jane is an *intense* person.]
in·tense • *adjective*

intensity (in ten′si tē) *noun* the quality of being intense; great strength or force [The *intensity* of the game left the players exhausted. He spoke with *intensity* on the issue.]
in·ten·si·ty • *noun, plural* **intensities**

intensive (in ten′siv) *adjective* complete and in great detail; deep and thorough [They conducted an *intensive* search for the missing books.]
in·ten·sive • *adjective*

intent (in tent′ *for adj.;* in tent′ *or* in′tent *for n.*) *adjective* **1** having the mind or attention fixed; concentrating [They were *intent* on their studies.] **2** firmly decided; determined [She is *intent* on saving money.]
noun something intended; purpose; intention [It was not my *intent* to hurt you.]
in·tent • *adjective* • *noun, plural* **intents**

intention (in ten′shən) *noun* something intended or planned; purpose [He went to see his boss with the *intention* of asking for a raise.]
in·ten·tion • *noun, plural* **intentions**

intentional (in ten′shə nəl) *adjective* done on purpose; intended [It was not a mistake but an *intentional* hiding of the truth. The basketball player committed an *intentional* foul.]
in·ten·tion·al • *adjective*

inter- *a prefix meaning:* **1** between or among [An *interstate* highway can be used for travel-

I

ing between States.] **2** with or on each other; together [Parts that *interconnect* are parts that connect with each other.]

intercept

intercept (in tər septʹ) ***verb*** to stop or take hold of on the way; cut off [Mother *intercepted* a message from Julie to her boyfriend.]
in·ter·cept • ***verb*** **intercepted, intercepting**

interchangeable (in tər chānʹjə bəl) ***adjective*** capable of being put or used in place of another [A car's tires are *interchangeable*.]
in·ter·change·a·ble • ***adjective***

intercom (inʹtər käm) ***noun*** a system for communicating by radio or telephone between sections of an airplane or ship, or between different rooms in a house or other building.
in·ter·com • ***noun, plural*** **intercoms**

interest (inʹtrist *or* inʹtər ist) ***noun*** **1** a feeling of wanting to know, learn, see, or take part in something; curiosity or concern [She had shown a great *interest* in mathematics from her childhood. The movie captures the audience's *interest* from the first scenes.] **2** the power of causing this feeling [The library had many books of *interest* to children.] **3** something that causes this feeling [My main *interest* is dancing.] **4** anything that helps or is good for a person or group; benefit; advantage [When you make your decision, please keep our best *interests* in mind.] **5** money paid for the use of someone else's money [Add up all the *interest* you paid on your loans.] **6** the rate at which this money is paid [We had to pay 15% *interest* on the loan.]
verb **1** to stir up the interest of [That new movie *interests* me.] **2** to cause to take part in; involve [Can I *interest* you in a game of tennis?]
in·ter·est • ***noun, plural*** **interests**
• ***verb*** **interested, interesting**

interesting (inʹtrist iŋ *or* inʹtər est iŋ) ***adjective*** arousing one's interest; engaging and holding one's attention [an *interesting* book].
in·ter·est·ing • ***adjective***

interfere (in tər firʹ) ***verb*** **1** to get involved in another's business or activities without being asked [My parents seldom *interfere* in my plans.] **2** to get in the way so as to hinder; disturb [Noise *interferes* with our work.]
in·ter·fere • ***verb*** **interfered, interfering**

interference (in tər firʹəns) ***noun*** the act or process of interfering.
in·ter·fer·ence • ***noun***

interior (in tirʹē ər) ***noun*** **1** the inside or inner part [The *interior* of the house was painted white.] **2** the part of a country or region that is not on or near the coast or border [The *interior* of Alaska is largely uninhabited.]
adjective of or having to do with the interior; inside; inner [The *interior* walls of the building needed to be plastered.]
in·te·ri·or • ***noun, plural*** **interiors**
• ***adjective***

interj. *abbreviation for* interjection.

interjection (in tər jekʹshən) ***noun*** **1** a word or words that show strong feeling. "Oh" and "ouch" are interjections. **2** a group of words that is used in a similar way ["*Good grief*, I failed the test!"]
in·ter·jec·tion • ***noun, plural*** **interjections**

intermediate (in tər mēʹdē ət) ***adjective*** being or coming between two things or happenings; in the middle [A teenager is in an *intermediate* stage between childhood and adulthood.]
in·ter·me·di·ate • ***adjective***

intermission (in tər mishʹən) ***noun*** a rest or pause between periods of activity [a ten-minute *intermission* at the theater].
in·ter·mis·sion • ***noun, plural*** **intermissions**

intern (inʹtərn) ***noun*** a doctor who has just

a	cat	ō	go	ʉ	fur	ə = a *in* ago	
ā	ape	ô	law, for	ch	chin	e *in* agent	
ä	cot, car	oo	look	sh	she	i *in* pencil	
e	ten	ōō	tool	th	thin	o *in* atom	
ē	me	oi	oil	*th*	then	u *in* circus	
i	fit	ou	out	zh	measure		
ī	ice	u	up	ŋ	ring		

graduated from medical school and is getting more training by assisting other doctors in a hospital.
in·tern • *noun, plural* **interns**

internal (in tʉr′nəl) ***adjective*** having to do with or on the inside; inner [He suffered *internal* bleeding after the accident.]
in·ter·nal • ***adjective***

international (in tər nash′ə nəl) ***adjective*** **1** between or among nations [*international* trade]. **2** for or by people in several nations [an *international* organization].
in·ter·na·tion·al • ***adjective***

Internet (in′tər net) the very large system for obtaining all kinds of information by using a computer. The information comes from many different sources, including schools and businesses.
In·ter·net

interplanetary (in tər plan′ə ter′ē) ***adjective*** between planets [*interplanetary* travel].
in·ter·plan·e·tar·y • ***adjective***

interpret (in tʉr′prət) ***verb*** **1** to explain the meaning of [The teacher *interpreted* the poem to the students.] **2** to put into the words of another language; translate [Mr. Smith will *interpret* the speech given by the Japanese diplomat.] **3** to understand in one's own way [I *interpret* his silence as a sign of approval.]
in·ter·pret • ***verb*** **interpreted, interpreting**

interpretation (in tʉr′prə tā′shən) ***noun*** the act or a way of interpreting; explanation.
in·ter·pre·ta·tion • ***noun,*** *plural* **interpretations**

interrogative (in tər äg′ə tiv) ***adjective*** having to do with or asking a question ["Who are you?" is an *interrogative* sentence.]
in·ter·rog·a·tive • ***adjective***

interrupt (in tər upt′) ***verb*** **1** to break in on [We *interrupt* this program with a news bulletin. She rudely *interrupted* their conversation.] **2** to make a break in; put a temporary stop to [A strike *interrupted* steel production.]
in·ter·rupt • ***verb*** **interrupted, interrupting**

interruption (in tər up′shən) ***noun*** the act of interrupting or the condition of being interrupted ["No more *interruptions*," said the teacher.]
in·ter·rup·tion • ***noun,*** *plural* **interruptions**

intersect (in tər sekt′) ***verb*** to divide into two parts by passing through or across [A river *intersects* the plain.]
in·ter·sect • ***verb*** **intersected, intersecting**

intersection (in′tər sek shən) ***noun*** the place where two or more things, such as lines or streets, meet or cross [There is a new traffic light at that busy *intersection*.]
in·ter·sec·tion • ***noun,*** *plural* **intersections**

intersection

interstate (in′tər stāt) ***adjective*** having to do with, between, or connecting two or more States [an *interstate* highway].
in·ter·state • ***adjective***

interval (in′tər vəl) ***noun*** space or time between things [an *interval* of five feet between bookcases; an *interval* of twenty years between appearances of the comet].
in·ter·val • ***noun,*** *plural* **intervals**

interview (in′tər vyo͞o) ***noun*** a meeting with a person to answer questions or talk about something [an *interview* with a reporter; an *interview* with a boss about a job].
verb to have an interview with [The actress was *interviewed* about her new film role.]
in·ter·view • ***noun,*** *plural* **interviews**
• ***verb*** **interviewed, interviewing**

intestinal (in tes′ti nəl) ***adjective*** having to do with or in the intestines [an *intestinal* infection].
in·tes·ti·nal • ***adjective***

intestine (in tes′tin) ***noun*** *usually* **intestines** the tube through which food passes from the stomach. It is part of the digestive system and it is divided into the *small intestine* and the *large intestine*. Food is digested in the intestines as well as in the stomach.
in·tes·tine • ***noun,*** *plural* **intestines**

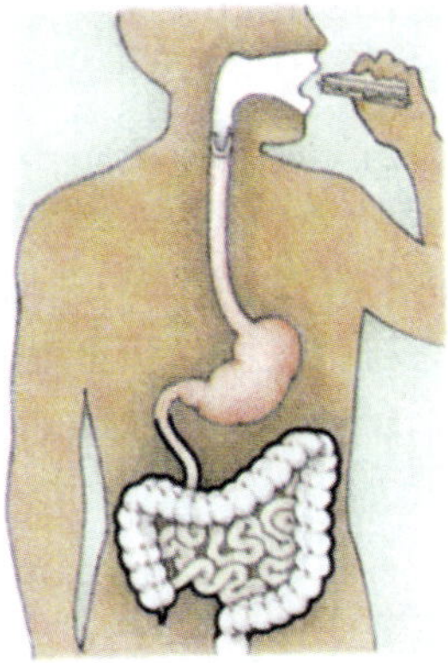
intestine

intimate (in′ti mət) ***adjective*** **1** very close or familiar [I have very few *intimate* friends.] **2** most private or personal [She didn't want to share her *intimate* thoughts with her sister.]
in·ti·mate • ***adjective***

I

into (in′to͞o *or* in′tə) ***preposition*** **1** to the inside of [Let's go *into* the house.] **2** to the form or condition of [They turned the empty lot *into* a park. I got *into* trouble.] **3** in such a way as to strike; against [The car skidded *into* a tree.] **4** This word is used to show division in arithmetic [Two *into* ten equals five.]
in·to • ***preposition***

intolerant (in tä′lər ənt) ***adjective*** not willing to accept or put up with different ideas or beliefs or with people of other races or ethnic backgrounds.
in·tol·er·ant • ***adjective***

intoxicate (in täks′i kāt′) ***verb*** **1** to make lose control of oneself in the way that alcohol does; make drunk [They were obviously *intoxicated*.] **2** to make very excited or happy [The fans were *intoxicated* by the team's victory.]
in·tox·i·cate • ***verb*** **intoxicated, intoxicating**

intransitive (in tran′si tiv) ***adjective*** describing a verb that does not have a noun following it as an object. In the sentence "The door opened wide," "opened" is an intransitive verb.
in·tran·si·tive • ***adjective***

intravenous (in trə vē′nəs) ***adjective*** directly into a vein [an *intravenous* injection].
in·tra·ve·nous • ***adjective***

intricate (in′tri kət) ***adjective*** hard to follow or grasp because complicated and full of details [The Oriental rug has an *intricate* pattern of lines and squares.] —Look for the WORD CHOICES box at the entry **complex**.
in·tri·cate • ***adjective***

intrigue (in trēg′ *for v.;* in′trēg *or* in trēg′ *for n.*) ***verb*** to stir up the interest of; make curious; fascinate [His stories about faraway places always *intrigue* us.]
noun secret plotting [*intrigue* against the queen].
in·trigue • ***verb*** **intrigued, intriguing**
• ***noun,*** *plural* **intrigues**

introduce (in trə do͞os′ *or* in trə dyo͞os′) ***verb*** **1** to make known; make acquainted; present [Please *introduce* me to your parents.] **2** to bring into use; make popular or common [Science has *introduced* many new words into the language.] **3** to make familiar with something [My friends *introduced* me to rock-and-roll music.] **4** to add or put in [We must *introduce* some humor into this play.]
in·tro·duce • ***verb*** **introduced, introducing**

introduction (in trə duk′shən) ***noun*** **1** the act of introducing [John made the *introductions* at the party. The *introduction* of the potato to Europe changed the diet of the general population.] **2** the part at the beginning of something, such as a book or speech, that leads into or explains what follows.
in·tro·duc·tion • ***noun,*** *plural* **introductions**

introductory (in trə duk′tər ē) ***adjective*** used to introduce or begin something; preliminary [an *introductory* course in drawing; the speaker's *introductory* remarks].
in·tro·duc·to·ry • ***adjective***

invade (in vād′) ***verb*** **1** to enter with an army in order to conquer [Germany *invaded* the Soviet Union during World War II.] **2** to break in on; to force oneself upon [Our nosy questions *invaded* her privacy.]
in·vade • ***verb*** **invaded, invading**

invalid (in′və lid) ***noun*** a person who is sick or disabled, especially for a long time.
in·va·lid • ***noun,*** *plural* **invalids**

invaluable (in val′yo͞o ə bəl) ***adjective*** having a value that is too great to measure; priceless [The museum has many *invaluable* objects in its rooms.]
in·val·u·a·ble • ***adjective***

invasion (in vā′zhən) ***noun*** **1** the act of entering with an army in order to conquer [the *invasion* of France by Germany in 1940]. **2** the act of breaking in on someone or something without being asked [Listening in on others' conversations is an *invasion* of privacy.]
in·va·sion • ***noun,*** *plural* **invasions**

invent (in vent′) ***verb*** **1** to make or think of something that did not exist before; be the first to do or make —Look for the WORD CHOICES box at the entry **create**. **2** to think up; make up [She's always *inventing* excuses for being late.]
in·vent • ***verb*** **invented, inventing**

invention (in ven′shən) ***noun*** **1** the act of inventing [The *invention* of television changed the way people spend their hours at home.] **2** something that is invented [The computer is an important *invention*.]
in·ven·tion • ***noun,*** *plural* **inventions**

inventive (in ven′tiv) ***adjective*** good at

a	cat	ō	go	ʉ	fur	ə =	a *in* ago
ā	ape	ô	law, for	ch	chin		e *in* agent
ä	cot, car	o͝o	look	sh	she		i *in* pencil
e	ten	o͞o	tool	th	thin		o *in* atom
ē	me	oi	oil	*th*	then		u *in* circus
i	fit	ou	out	zh	measure		
ī	ice	u	up	ŋ	ring		

inventing; having the ability to think up new things.
in·ven·tive • *adjective*

inventor (in ven′tər) *noun* a person who invents [Thomas Edison was the *inventor* of the microphone.]
in·ven·tor • *noun, plural* **inventors**

inventory (in′vən tôr′ē) *noun* **1** a complete list of goods, supplies, possessions, or other things [The store makes an *inventory* of its stock every year.] **2** the articles or food on hand [The store has a large *inventory* of shoes.]
in·ven·to·ry • *noun, plural* **inventories**

invert (in vurt′) *verb* **1** to turn upside down [If you *invert* the jar, the cookies will fall out.] **2** to reverse the order, position, or direction of [If you *invert* the phrase "she said," you get the phrase "said she."]
in·vert • *verb* **inverted, inverting**

invertebrate (in vur′tə brət *or* in vur′tə brāt′) *adjective* having no backbone, or spinal column.
noun an animal that has no backbone. Worms, insects, clams, and crabs are invertebrates.
in·ver·te·brate • *adjective* • *noun, plural* **invertebrates**

invest (in vest′) *verb* **1** to use or lend money to buy something in order to make more money [He *invested* in a company that makes plastic.] **2** to spend in order to get something in return [The doctors *invested* years in their search of a cure.]
in·vest • *verb* **invested, investing**

investigate (in ves′ti gāt′) *verb* to look into so as to learn the facts [The police are *investigating* the accident.]
in·ves·ti·gate • *verb* **investigated, investigating**

investigation (in ves′ti gā′shən) *noun* the act of investigating [The *investigation* of the crime kept the detectives busy for many weeks.]
in·ves·ti·ga·tion • *noun, plural* **investigations**

investment (in vest′mənt) *noun* **1** the act of investing money, time, or effort in order to get something in return. **2** the amount of money that is invested [She made an *investment* of ten thousand dollars in her sister's new company.] **3** something in which money is invested [A house is usually a good *investment*.]
in·vest·ment • *noun, plural* **investments**

investor (in vest′ər) *noun* a person, company, or other institution that invests money.
in·ves·tor • *noun, plural* **investors**

invisible (in viz′i bəl) *adjective* not visible; not able to be seen [The moon was *invisible* behind the clouds. Oxygen is *invisible*.]
in·vis·i·ble • *adjective*

invitation (in′vi tā′shən) *noun* **1** the act of inviting to come somewhere or do something [The host extended an *invitation* to us to come for another visit.] **2** the written or spoken form used in inviting a person [Have you mailed the wedding *invitations* yet?]
in·vi·ta·tion • *noun, plural* **invitations**

invite (in vīt′) *verb* **1** to ask in a polite way to come somewhere or do something; ask to be one's guest [They *invited* me to dine with them after the performance.] **2** to ask for; request [After her talk she *invited* questions from the audience.] **3** to bring on; give the chance for [You're *inviting* trouble if you don't drive more carefully.]
in·vite • *verb* **invited, inviting**

involuntary (in vä′lən ter′ē) *adjective* not done consciously or on purpose; not voluntary; accidental or automatic [Sneezing is *involuntary*.]
in·vol·un·tar·y • *adjective*

involve (in välv′ *or* in vôlv′) *verb* **1** to have as a part; include or require [Becoming a doctor *involves* years of study.] **2** to make busy; occupy [She's *involved* in her homework.] **3** to draw in; include [His teammates *involved* him in their dispute with the coach.]
in·volve • *verb* **involved, involving**

invulnerable (in vul′nər ə bəl) *adjective* not able to be hurt, destroyed, or damaged [an *invulnerable* fort; an *invulnerable* reputation for honesty].
in·vul·ner·a·ble • *adjective*

inward (in′wərd) *adjective* of or toward the inside [Give the door an *inward* push.]
adverb toward the inside or center [The door swung *inward*. The explorers found a passage heading *inward*.]
in·ward • *adjective* • *adverb*

iodine (ī′ə dīn *or* ī′ə din) *noun* **1** a chemical element that is found in the form of very dark crystals. **2** a liquid made up of a small amount of iodine mixed with alcohol. It is used to stop infection in cuts on the skin.
i·o·dine • *noun*

I

ion (ī′ən *or* ī′än) *noun* an atom or a group of atoms that has a positive or negative electrical charge.
i·on • *noun, plural* **ions**

IOU or **I.O.U.** *noun* **1** I owe you. **2** a paper with these letters on it that is signed by someone who owes money to someone else [I gave her my *IOU* for $20.]
IOU or **I.O.U.** • *noun, plural* **IOUs** or **I.O.U.'s**

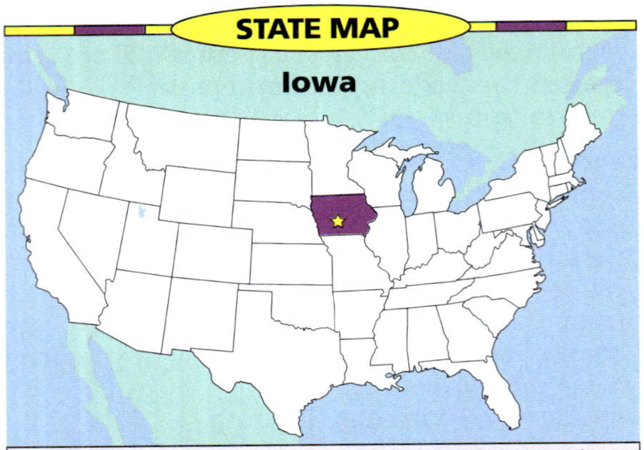

Statehood: 1846, the 29th state • **Capital:** Des Moines

Iowa (ī′ə wə) a State in the north central part of the U.S. Its capital is Des Moines. Abbreviated **IA** or **Ia.**
I·o·wa

IQ or **I.Q.** a number that is supposed to tell whether a person's intelligence is average, below average, or above average. The IQ score is based on the answers to an IQ test. IQ stands for intelligence quotient.

Iran (i ran′ *or* i rän′) a country in southwestern Asia. Its older name is *Persia*.
I·ran

Iraq (i räk′ *or* i rak′) a country in southwestern Asia.
I·raq

Ireland (īr′lənd) a large island west of Great Britain. An independent country, the Republic of Ireland, takes up most of the island, but a small part in the north (*Northern Ireland*) is in the United Kingdom.
Ire·land

iris (ī′ris) *noun* **1** the colored part of the eye, around the pupil. **2** a plant that has long, sword-shaped leaves and large flowers. The flowers come in a wide variety of colors.
i·ris • *noun, plural* **irises**

Irish (ī′rish) *noun* a language spoken in Ireland.
—the Irish the people of Ireland.
I·rish • *noun*

iron (ī′ərn) *noun* **1** a strong metal that is a chemical element. It can be molded and stretched into various shapes when it is hot or melted. It is used to make steel. **2** an appliance with a handle and a flat, smooth bottom that is used when heated to smooth wrinkles in cloth or clothing. Irons used to be made of iron. **3 irons** chains that are used to keep a prisoner from moving.
adjective **1** of or made of iron [*iron* bars]. **2** like iron; strong and hard [an *iron* will].
verb to press or smooth with a hot iron [I will *iron* your shirts tonight.]
i·ron • *noun, plural* **irons** • *adjective* • *verb* **ironed, ironing**

irony (ī′rən ē) *noun* an event or result that is the opposite of what might be expected [It was an *irony* that the fire station burned down.]
i·ro·ny • *noun, plural* **ironies**

Iroquois (ir′ə kwoi) *noun* **1** a member of a large group of North American Indian peoples that lived in northern New York. They now live in New York State and Oklahoma in the U.S. and in Ontario and Quebec, Canada. **2** the languages of these peoples.
Ir·o·quois • *noun, plural for sense 1 only* **Ir·o·quois** (ir′ə kwoi *or* ir′ə kwoiz)

irrational (ir rash′ə nəl) *adjective* not making sense; absurd [I have an *irrational* fear of the dark.]
ir·ra·tion·al • *adjective*

irregular (ir reg′yoo lər) *adjective* **1** not regular; not like the usual way, rule, or custom [an *irregular* sleeping schedule. The noun "child" has an *irregular* plural form.] **2** not straight, even, or the same all the way through [an *irregular* pattern of dots in different sizes].
ir·reg·u·lar • *adjective*

irrelevant (ir rel′ə vənt) *adjective* not to the point; not having anything to do with the subject [The remark about the candidate's height was *irrelevant* to the issues of the election.]
ir·rel·e·vant • *adjective*

a	cat	ō	go	ʉ	fur	ə =	a *in* ago
ā	ape	ô	law, for	ch	chin		e *in* agent
ä	cot, car	oo	look	sh	she		i *in* pencil
e	ten	ōō	tool	th	thin		o *in* atom
ē	me	oi	oil	*th*	then		u *in* circus
i	fit	ou	out	zh	measure		
ī	ice	u	up	ŋ	ring		

irreplaceable (ir′rē plās′ə bəl) *adjective* not capable of being replaced; without a replacement [Aunt Edna says the vase we broke is *irreplaceable*.]
ir·re·place·a·ble • *adjective*

irresistible (ir rē zis′ti bəl) *adjective* too strong to resist or fight against [an *irresistible* force].
ir·re·sist·i·ble • *adjective*

irresponsible (ir′rē spän′si bəl) *adjective* not responsible; not showing a sense of duty [Leaving your books out in the rain was an *irresponsible* thing to do.]
ir·re·spon·si·ble • *adjective*

irreversible (ir′i vʉr′sə bəl) *adjective* not able to be reversed or changed [the *irreversible* decision of the judge].
ir·re·vers·i·ble • *adjective*

irrigate (ir′ə gāt) *verb* to water by means of ditches, canals, or pipes [They *irrigated* the desert land so that it could produce crops.]
ir·ri·gate • *verb* **irrigated, irrigating**

irrigation

irrigation (ir ə gā′shən) *noun* the practice of supplying land with water by irrigating.
ir·ri·ga·tion • *noun*

irritable (ir′i tə bəl) *adjective* easy to annoy or make angry.
ir·ri·ta·ble • *adjective*

WORD CHOICES

Synonyms of **irritable**

Many words share the meaning "easily annoyed or made angry."

cross	peevish
grouchy	touchy

irritate (ir′ə tāt) *verb* **1** to bother or annoy; make impatient or angry [Your bragging *irritates* most of the other students.] **2** to make red, raw, or sore [Harsh soap can *irritate* the skin.]
ir·ri·tate • *verb* **irritated, irritating**

Irving (ʉr′viŋ), **Washington** (wôsh′iŋ tən *or* wäsh′iŋ tən) 1783-1859; U.S. writer.
Ir·ving, Wash·ing·ton

is (iz) *verb* the form of the verb **be** that is used to show the present time with *he*, *she*, or *it*. This form is also used with singular nouns [The sky *is* blue. She *is* friendly. It *is* raining.]

-ish *a suffix meaning:* **1** of or belonging to [A *Swedish* citizen is a citizen of Sweden.] **2** like [A *devilish* person is like a devil.] **3** like something that belongs to [A *devilish* grin is like the grin of a devil.] **4** somewhat [*Warmish* weather is somewhat warm.]

Islam (is′läm *or* iz′läm) *noun* **1** the Muslim religion, founded by Mohammed, in which God is called Allah. **2** all the Muslims, or all the countries in which most of the people are Muslim.
Is·lam • *noun*

island (ī′lənd) *noun* **1** a piece of land that is smaller than a continent and is surrounded by water. **2** a place that is set apart from what is around it [The oasis was an *island* of green in the desert.]
is·land • *noun, plural* **islands**

islander (ī′lənd ər) *noun* a person who was born on an island or lives on an island.
is·land·er • *noun, plural* **islanders**

isle (īl) *noun* an island, usually a small one.
isle • *noun, plural* **isles**
• The words **isle, aisle,** and **I'll** sound alike.
I rowed our boat over to the tiny *isle*.
We took the side *aisle* to our seats.
I'll be seeing you in the fall.

islet (ī′lət) *noun* a very small island.
is·let • *noun, plural* **islets**
• The words **islet** and **eyelet** sound alike.
We sailed to the tiny *islet* in the bay.
Pass the shoelace through each *eyelet*.

-ism *a suffix meaning:* **1** belief or theory [*Liberalism* is a belief in liberal ideas.] **2** the act or result of [*Criticism* is the act or result of criticizing.] **3** the condition, behavior, or qualities of [*Patriotism* is the behavior of a patriot.]

isn't (iz′ənt) is not.
is·n't

I

isolate (ī′sə lāt) *verb* to set apart from others [The snowstorm *isolated* the village.]
i·so·late • *verb* **isolated, isolating**

isosceles triangle (ī säs′ə lēz) *noun* a triangle with two sides that are the same length and two equal angles.
i·sos·ce·les triangle • *noun, plural* **isosceles triangles**

isosceles triangle

Israel (iz′rē əl) **1** a country between the Mediterranean Sea and Jordan. **2** the ancient land of the Hebrews, at the southeastern end of the Mediterranean. **3** the Jewish people.
Is·ra·el

Israeli (iz rā′lē) *noun* a person born or living in Israel.
Is·rae·li • *noun, plural* **Israelis**

issue (ish′o͞o *or* ish′yo͞o) *noun* **1** a thing that is sent or given out [the July *issue* of a magazine]. **2** something that needs to be talked over or decided [The candidates will debate the *issues*.]
verb **1** to put forth or send out [A city *issues* bonds. A general *issues* orders.] **2** to give out; distribute [The teacher *issued* new books.]
is·sue • *noun, plural* **issues** • *verb* **issued, issuing**

-ist *a suffix meaning:* **1** a person who does or makes [An *accompanist* is a musician who accompanies another musician's solo.] **2** a person who is skilled in or who works at [An *artist* is a person who makes works of art.] **3** a person who believes in [A *socialist* is a person who believes in socialism.]

isthmus (is′məs) *noun* a narrow strip of land with water on each side, that joins two larger pieces of land [the *Isthmus* of Panama].
isth·mus • *noun, plural* **isthmuses**

it (it) *pronoun* the thing or animal that is being talked about [I read that book and *it* taught me something new. The driver didn't see the deer, and the car hit *it*.]. This pronoun has many other uses in certain kinds of phrases and sentences [*It* is snowing. *It* is warm in this room. *It's* all right; I'm not hurt.]
it • *pronoun, plural* **they**

Italian (i tal′yən) *noun* **1** a person born or living in Italy. **2** the language of the Italians.
I·tal·ian • *noun, plural for sense 1 only* **Italians**

italic (i tal′ik) *adjective* describing type for printing that has letters slanting upward and to the right. This kind of type is used to call attention to words [*This is printed in italic type.*]
noun usually **italics** italic type [A book's title is printed in *italics*.]
i·tal·ic • *adjective* • *noun, plural* **italics**

italicize (i tal′i sīz′ *or* ī tal′i sīz′) *verb* **1** to print in italic type [The last word in this sentence has been *italicized*.] **2** to underline something that has been written, in order to show that it is to be printed in italic type.
i·tal·i·cize • *verb* **italicized, italicizing**

Italy (it′l ē) a country in southern Europe, including two large nearby islands.
It·a·ly

itch (ich) *verb* **1** to have a tickling feeling on the skin that makes a person want to scratch [This mosquito bite *itches*.] **2** to cause to have this feeling [This wool shirt *itches* my skin.] **3** to have a restless desire [I'm *itching* to be on my way to the mountains.]
noun **1** a tickling feeling on the skin that makes a person want to scratch. **2** a restless desire [I have an *itch* to travel.]
itch • *verb* **itched, itching** • *noun, plural* **itches**

itchy (ich′ē) *adjective* feeling or causing an itch.
itch·y • *adjective* **itchier, itchiest**

it'd (it′əd) **1** it would. **2** it had.

item (īt′əm) *noun* **1** a separate thing; one in a group or series of things [Check each *item* on this list.] **2** a piece of news or information.
i·tem • *noun, plural* **items**

it'll (it′l) it will.

its (its) *pronoun* the one or the ones that belong to it.
adjective done by it or having to do with it [Every plant has *its* particular needs for soil, light, water, and food.]
● The words **its** and **it's** sound alike.
The hamster has *its* own cage.
It's been a good summer.

it's (its) **1** it is. **2** it has.
● The words **it's** and **its** sound alike.

itself (it self′) *pronoun* **1** its own self. This

a	cat	ō	go	ʉ	fur	ə =	a *in* ago
ā	ape	ô	law, for	ch	chin		e *in* agent
ä	cot, car	o͝o	look	sh	she		i *in* pencil
e	ten	o͞o	tool	th	thin		o *in* atom
ē	me	oi	oil	*th*	then		u *in* circus
i	fit	ou	out	zh	measure		
ī	ice	u	up	ŋ	ring		

form of **it** is used when the one that does the action of the verb is the same as the one that is affected by the action [The dog scratched *itself.*] **2** its usual or true self [The cat is not *itself* today.]
it·self • ***pronoun***

-ity *a suffix meaning* the condition of or an example of [*Simplicity* is the condition of being simple. A *possibility* is an example of something that is possible.]

IV (ī′vē′) ***noun*** a device for holding a needle in place in a person's vein and providing a steady supply of liquid medicine or food through a tube to the needle.
IV • ***noun,*** *plural* **IVs**

I've (īv) I have.

Ives (īvz), **Charles** (charlz) 1874-1954; U.S. composer.

ivory (ī′vər ē *or* ī′vrē) ***noun*** **1** the hard, white substance that forms the tusks of the elephant, the walrus, and certain other animals. **2** a substance that is like this. A white plastic that looks like ivory is used to cover piano keys. **3** the color of ivory; creamy white.
i·vo·ry • ***noun,*** *plural* **ivories**

Ivory Coast a country on the western coast of Africa.

ivy

ivy (ī′vē) ***noun*** **1** a climbing vine with a woody stem and shiny evergreen leaves. **2** a plant that is similar in some way [poison *ivy*].
i·vy • ***noun,*** *plural* **ivies**

-ize *a suffix meaning:* **1** to make or become [When doctors' instruments are *sterilized*, they are made sterile, or free from germs.] **2** to act in a certain way [A person who *sympathizes* acts with sympathy, or concern, for another person.] **3** to treat or unite with [When a substance *oxidizes*, it unites with oxygen.]

I

J j

Jj Jj Jj Jj

The letter **j** *most often has the sound you hear in the names* **Jane**, **Jim**, *and* **John** *and in the words* **jack-o'-lantern** *and* **just**. *Be sure to write the letter carefully so readers will see clearly that it is not the letter* **i**.

j or **J** (jā) ***noun*** the tenth letter of the English alphabet.
j or **J** • ***noun,*** *plural* **j's** or **J's**

jab (jab) ***verb*** **1** to poke with something hard or sharp [Your elbow is *jabbing* me in the ribs.] **2** to punch with short blows.
noun a poke or punch.
jab • ***verb*** **jabbed, jabbing** • ***noun,*** *plural* **jabs**

jabber (jab′ər) ***verb*** to talk fast in a way that is silly or makes no sense; to chatter.
noun talk of this kind.
jab·ber • ***verb*** **jabbered, jabbering** • ***noun***

jack (jak) ***noun*** **1** a machine or tool that is used to lift or move something heavy, such as an automobile, for a short distance. **2** a playing card with a picture of a servant from a royal court on it. **3** a small metal piece with six points or prongs that is used in playing the game of jacks. **4** an electrical device that a plug is put into in order to make an electrical connection [a phone *jack*].
verb **1** to lift with or as if with a jack. **2** [*an informal use*] to raise [They're *jacking up* the price of gasoline again.]
jack • ***noun,*** *plural* **jacks** • ***verb*** **jacked, jacking**

jackal (jak′əl) ***noun*** a wild dog of Asia and Africa that is smaller than a wolf. Jackals hunt in packs and often eat meat that other animals have left behind.
jack·al • ***noun,*** *plural* **jackals** or **jackal**

jacket (jak′ət) ***noun*** **1** a short coat. **2** an outer covering for something such as a book or record.
jack·et • ***noun,*** *plural* **jackets**

jack-in-the-box (jak′in *th*ə bäks′) ***noun*** a toy that is made up of a box with a little doll on a spring in it. The doll jumps up when the lid is lifted.
jack-in-the-box • ***noun,*** *plural* **jack-in-the-boxes**

jack-in-the-box

jack-in-the-pulpit (jak′in *th*ə po͞ol′pit) ***noun*** a wildflower that grows in the woods. Its flower spike is covered by a kind of hood.
jack-in-the-pul·pit • ***noun,*** *plural* **jack-in-the-pulpits**

jackknife (jak′nīf) ***noun*** a large pocketknife.
jack·knife • ***noun,*** *plural* **jackknives**

jack-o'-lantern (jak′ə lant ərn) ***noun*** a hollowed out pumpkin with a face cut into its side

a cat	ō go	ʉ fur	ə = a *in* ago
ā ape	ô law, for	ch chin	e *in* agent
ä cot, car	oo look	sh she	i *in* pencil
e ten	o͞o tool	th thin	o *in* atom
ē me	oi oil	*th* then	u *in* circus
i fit	ou out	zh measure	
ī ice	u up	ŋ ring	

and a source of light inside it. It is used as a decoration at Halloween.
jack-o'-lan·tern • ***noun,*** *plural* **jack-o'-lanterns**

jackpot (jak′pät) ***noun*** the highest prize that can be won.
—hit the jackpot [*a slang use*] to get the highest prize or have the greatest success.
jack·pot • ***noun,*** *plural* **jackpots**

jack rabbit ***noun*** a large hare of western North America, with long ears and strong hind legs.
jack rabbit • ***noun,*** *plural* **jack rabbits**

jacks (jaks) ***plural noun*** a children's game in which a player tosses and picks up small, six-pointed metal pieces while bouncing a ball.

Jackson (jak′sən), **Andrew** (an′dro͞o) 1767-1845; the seventh president of the U.S., from 1829 to 1837.
Jack·son, An·drew

Jackson (jak′sən), **Thomas J.** (täm′əs) 1824-1863; Confederate general in the Civil War. He was also called *Stonewall Jackson*.
Jack·son, Tho·mas J.

Jackson (jak′sən) the capital of Mississippi.
Jack·son

Jacksonville (jak′sən vil) a city in northeastern Florida.
Jack·son·ville

jade (jād) ***noun*** a hard, green stone that is made into jewelry and carved into works of art.
jade • ***noun,*** *plural* **jades**

jagged (jag′əd) ***adjective*** having sharp points and notches [A saw has a *jagged* edge.]
jag·ged • ***adjective***

jaguar

jaguar (jag′wär) ***noun*** a large wildcat that looks like a large leopard. It is yellowish with black spots. It is found in South America and the southwestern U.S.
jag·uar • ***noun,*** *plural* **jaguars** or **jaguar**

jail (jāl) ***noun*** a building where people are locked up while they are waiting for a trial. People also are put in jail to serve short sentences for breaking the law.
verb to put into jail or keep in jail.
jail • ***noun,*** *plural* **jails** • ***verb*** **jailed, jailing**

jam[1] (jam) ***verb*** **1** to squeeze or force tightly [He *jammed* his hands into his pockets.] **2** to injure or crush by squeezing [His hand was *jammed* in the car door.] **3** to fill or block up by crowding in [Cars *jammed* the parking lot.] **4** to push or shove hard [She *jammed* on the brakes.]
noun **1** many things that are jammed all together [a traffic *jam*]. **2** [*an informal use*] a difficult situation [She was in a real *jam* when she lost her car keys.]
jam • ***verb*** **jammed, jamming** • ***noun,*** *plural* **jams**

jam[2] (jam) ***noun*** a sweet food that is made by boiling fruit and sugar to form a thick mixture.
jam • ***noun,*** *plural* **jams**

Jamaica (jə mā′kə) a country on an island in the West Indies.
Ja·mai·ca

Jan. *abbreviation for* January.

jangle (jaŋ′gəl) ***verb*** to make or cause to make a harsh, clashing sound [The old church bells *jangled* together madly.]
noun a harsh sound.
jan·gle • ***verb*** **jangled, jangling** • ***noun,*** *plural* **jangles**

janitor (jan′i tər) ***noun*** a person whose work is cleaning and taking care of a building.
jan·i·tor • ***noun,*** *plural* **janitors**

January (jan′yo͞o er′ē) ***noun*** the first month of the year. January has 31 days. Abbreviated **Jan.**
Jan·u·ar·y • ***noun***

WORD HISTORY

January

January gets its name from the Roman god *Janus*, who had a face in front and another at the back of his head. He was supposed to watch over the beginnings and ends of things. **January** marks the beginning of the new year and the end of the old one.

Japan (jə pan′) a country in eastern Asia, east of Korea, made up of many islands.
Ja·pan

J

Japanese (jap ə nēz′) *noun* **1** a member of a people whose native country is Japan. **2** the language of Japan.
Jap·a·nese • *noun, plural for sense 1 only* **Japanese**

jar[1] (jär) *verb* to shake up or rattle; to jolt [The explosion *jarred* our windows.]
noun a jolt or shock.
jar • *verb* **jarred, jarring** • *noun*

jar[2] (jär) *noun* **1** a container that is made from glass, pottery, or stone and has a wide mouth. **2** the amount that a jar will hold.
jar • *noun, plural* **jars**

jasmine (jaz′min) *noun* a plant of warm regions with sweet-smelling red, yellow, or white flowers.
jas·mine • *noun, plural* **jasmines**

javelin (jav′lin *or* jav′ə lin) *noun* a light spear. It is now used in athletic contests to see who can throw it farthest.
jav·e·lin • *noun, plural* **javelins**

jaw (jô *or* jä) *noun* **1** either one of the two bony parts that form the frame of the mouth and that hold the teeth. **2** one of two parts of a device, such as a tool, that close to grip or crush something [Pliers have *jaws*.]
jaw • *noun, plural* **jaws**

jay (jā) *noun* any of several noisy, brightly colored birds that are related to the crow but smaller.
jay • *noun, plural* **jays**

jaywalk (jā′wôk) *verb* to walk across a street, in a careless way, without obeying traffic rules and signals.
jay·walk • *verb* **jaywalked, jaywalking**

jazz (jaz) *noun* a kind of music that started with Southern black Americans in the 19th century. It has strong, often very complex rhythms and the players or singers often make up parts as they go along.

jealous (jel′əs) *adjective* **1** worried or afraid that someone is taking the love or attention that one has or wants. **2** having a bad feeling toward another person who has something regarded as valuable or desirable; filled with envy [Are you *jealous* of Tom because he has a new bike?]
jeal·ous • *adjective*

jealousy (jel′əs ē) *noun* **1** the condition of being jealous. **2** a jealous feeling.
jeal·ous·y • *noun, plural* **jealousies**

jeans (jēnz) *plural noun* trousers or overalls that are made of a heavy cotton cloth, usually blue.

jeep (jēp) *noun* a small, powerful automobile that was first made during World War II for use by the armed forces.
jeep • *noun, plural* **jeeps**

jeer (jir) *verb* to make fun of in a rude or mean way; to mock or taunt [The crowd *jeered* the baseball player who missed the ball.]
noun a mocking cry or rude remark [The football players did their best in spite of the crowd's *jeers*.]
jeer • *verb* **jeered, jeering** • *noun, plural* **jeers**

Jefferson (jef′ər sən), **Thomas** (täm′əs) 1743-1826; the third president of the U.S., from 1801 to 1809.
Jef·fer·son, Thom·as

Jefferson City the capital of Missouri.

Jehovah (jə hō′və) God; the Lord.
Je·ho·vah

Jell-O (jel′ō) *trademark* a kind of flavored gelatin that is eaten as a dessert or used in molded salads.

jelly (jel′ē) *noun* a soft, firm food that looks smooth and is somewhat clear. Jellies are made from fruit juice cooked with sugar or from meat juices that are cooked for a long time.
jel·ly • *noun, plural* **jellies**

jelly bean *noun* a small, soft candy that is shaped like a bean.
jelly bean • *noun, plural* **jelly beans**

jellyfish

jellyfish (jel′ē fish′) *noun* a sea animal with a body that is shaped like a bag and made of a substance that feels like jelly.
jel·ly·fish • *noun, plural* **jellyfish** or **jellyfishes**

a cat	ō go	ʉ fur	ə = a *in* ago
ā ape	ô law, for	ch chin	e *in* agent
ä cot, car	oo look	sh she	i *in* pencil
e ten	ōō tool	th thin	o *in* atom
ē me	oi oil	*th* then	u *in* circus
i fit	ou out	zh measure	
ī ice	u up	ŋ ring	

jeopardy (jep′ər dē) ***noun*** great danger or risk [A firefighter's life is often in *jeopardy*.]
jeop·ard·y • ***noun***

jerk (jʉrk) ***noun*** **1** a pull, lift, push, or other sudden, sharp movement [One *jerk* of the rope will ring the bell.] **2** [*a slang use*] a person who is thought of as stupid or foolish.
verb to move or pull with a jerk or jerks [She *jerked* the book from my hands.]
jerk • ***noun,*** *plural* **jerks** • ***verb*** **jerked, jerking**

jerky (jʉrk′ē) ***adjective*** making sudden, sharp movements; moving by jerks.
jerk·y • ***adjective*** **jerkier, jerkiest**

jersey (jʉr′zē) ***noun*** **1** a soft, machine-made knitted cloth. **2** a blouse or shirt that is made of this cloth.
jer·sey • ***noun,*** *plural* **jerseys**

Jerusalem (jə ro͞oz′ə ləm *or* jə ro͞o′sə ləm) the capital of Israel.
Je·ru·sa·lem

jester (jes′tər) ***noun*** a clown who was hired to do tricks and tell jokes in royal courts in Europe hundreds of years ago.
jest·er • ***noun,*** *plural* **jesters**

Jesus (jē′zəz *or* jē′zəs) the founder of the Christian religion. He is also called **Jesus Christ**.
Je·sus

jet (jet) ***noun*** **1** a stream of liquid or gas that is forced from a nozzle or spout. **2** an airplane that moves by jet propulsion.
jet • ***noun,*** *plural* **jets**

jet airplane ***noun*** a jet-propelled airplane. This plane is also called a **jet plane**.
jet airplane • ***noun,*** *plural* **jet airplanes**

jet-black (jet′blak′) ***adjective*** having a deep black color and a shiny surface.

jet-propelled (jet′prō peld′) ***adjective*** given the power to move forward by jet propulsion [a *jet-propelled* rocket].
jet-pro·pelled • ***adjective***

jet propulsion ***noun*** a way of giving an airplane, boat, spacecraft, or rocket the power to move forward. Jet propulsion forces a jet or stream of hot gases under high pressure to go through a rear opening.

jetty (jet′ē) ***noun*** a pier where boats can land.
jet·ty • ***noun,*** *plural* **jetties**

Jew (jo͞o) ***noun*** **1** a person whose ancestors were the ancient Hebrews. **2** a person whose religion is Judaism.
Jew • ***noun,*** *plural* **Jews**

jewel (jo͞o′əl) ***noun*** **1** a precious stone; gem. A diamond or a ruby is a jewel. **2** a valuable ring, pin, necklace, or other ornament, especially one with precious stones.
jew·el • ***noun,*** *plural* **jewels**

jeweler (jo͞ol′ər) ***noun*** a person who makes, sells, or repairs jewelry and watches.
jew·el·er • ***noun,*** *plural* **jewelers**

jewelry (jo͞ol′rē) ***noun*** rings, bracelets, and other ornaments made with jewels.
jew·el·ry • ***noun***

Jewish (jo͞o′ish) ***adjective*** of or having to do with Jews [*Jewish* traditions].
Jew·ish • ***adjective***

jib (jib) ***noun*** a triangular sail that is set in front of the mast and is attached to the bow.
jib • ***noun,*** *plural* **jibs**

jiffy (jif′ē) [*an informal word*] ***noun*** a very short time [I'll do it in a *jiffy*.]
jif·fy • ***noun,*** *plural* **jiffies**

jig (jig) ***noun*** **1** a fast, lively dance. **2** the music for this dance.
verb to dance a jig.
jig • ***noun,*** *plural* **jigs** • ***verb*** **jigged, jigging**

jiggle (jig′əl) ***verb*** to move quickly up and down or back and forth [We had to *jiggle* the key in the lock to make it work.]
noun a movement like this.
jig·gle • ***verb*** **jiggled, jiggling** • ***noun,*** *plural* **jiggles**

jigsaw (jig′sô *or* jig′sä) ***noun*** a saw with a narrow blade that is set in a frame. The blade moves up and down and is used for cutting curved lines.
jig·saw • ***noun,*** *plural* **jigsaws**

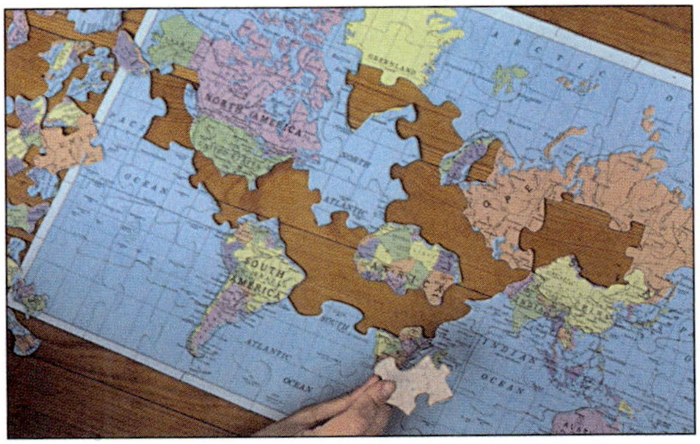

jigsaw puzzle

jigsaw puzzle ***noun*** a puzzle that is made by cutting up a picture into pieces with uneven

shapes. The pieces must be put together to form the picture again.
jigsaw puzzle • *noun, plural* **jigsaw puzzles**

jingle (jiŋ′gəl) ***verb*** to make or cause to make ringing, tinkling sounds, like the sound of bits of metal striking together.
noun **1** a ringing, tinkling sound. **2** a poem or song that has simple rhymes and is easy to remember [He was tired of listening to advertising *jingles* on the radio.]
jin·gle • ***verb*** **jingled, jingling** • ***noun,*** *plural* **jingles**

jinx (jiŋks) [*an informal word*] ***verb*** to cause bad luck to.
noun a person or thing that is felt to bring bad luck.
jinx • ***verb*** **jinxed, jinxing** • ***noun,*** *plural* **jinxes**

Joan of Arc (jōn əv ärk) 1412-1431; French heroine who led the French army to victory over the English. She was burned as a witch.

job (jäb) ***noun*** **1** a piece of work that a person does for pay [We gave her the *job* of painting our house.] **2** something that a person has to do; task or duty [This week it is my *job* to do the dishes.] —Look for the WORD CHOICES box at the entry **task**. **3** a kind of work; employment [I'm looking for a new *job*.]
job • ***noun,*** *plural* **jobs**

jock (jäk) [*a slang word*] ***noun*** an athlete.
jock • ***noun,*** *plural* **jocks**

jockey

jockey (jäk′ē) ***noun*** a person whose work is riding horses in races.
jock·ey • ***noun,*** *plural* **jockeys**

jodhpurs (jäd′pərz) ***plural noun*** trousers with loose upper legs, worn for horseback riding.
jodh·purs • ***plural noun***

jog (jäg) ***verb*** **1** to give a little shake to; to nudge [*Jog* her to wake her up. I need something to *jog* my memory.] **2** to run or move along at a slow, steady pace [I *jog* two miles every morning.]
noun **1** a little shake or nudge. **2** a jogging pace; a trot.
jog • ***verb*** **jogged, jogging** • ***noun,*** *plural* **jogs**

jogging (jäg′iŋ) ***noun*** a form of exercise in which a person trots at a slow, steady pace for a certain distance.
jog·ging • ***noun***

joggle (jäg′əl) ***verb*** to shake or jolt slightly.
noun a slight jolt.
jog·gle • ***verb*** **joggled, joggling** • ***noun***

Johnson (jän′sən), **Andrew** (an′dro͞o) 1808-1875; the seventeenth president of the U.S., from 1865 to 1869.
John·son, An·drew

Johnson (jän′sən), **Lyndon B.** (lin′dən) 1908-1973; the thirty-sixth president of the U.S., from 1963 to 1969.
John·son, Lyn·don B.

join (join) ***verb*** **1** to bring together; connect or fasten [We *joined* hands and danced.] **2** to come together; meet [Where do the Ohio and Mississippi rivers *join?*] **3** to become a part or member of [Paula *joined* our club.] **4** to go along with [*Join* us in a walk.] **5** to take part along with others [*Join* in the game.]
join • ***verb*** **joined, joining**

WORD CHOICES

Synonyms of **join**

The words **join, connect,** and **unite** share the meaning "to bring and put together."

We all *joined* hands.

A bridge *connects* the two islands.

A judge *united* the couple in marriage.

joint (joint) ***noun*** **1** a place where two things or parts are joined [Water leaked from the

a	cat	ō	go	ʉ	fur	ə =	a *in* ago
ā	ape	ô	law, for	ch	chin		e *in* agent
ä	cot, car	oo	look	sh	she		i *in* pencil
e	ten	o͞o	tool	th	thin		o *in* atom
ē	me	oi	oil	*th*	then		u *in* circus
i	fit	ou	out	zh	measure		
ī	ice	u	up	ŋ	ring		

joint in the pipe.] **2** a place or part where two bones are joined, usually in a way that allows them to move [the elbow *joint*].
adjective **1** done by two or more persons or groups [The charities made a *joint* request for money.] **2** owned by two or more persons or groups [The house is the *joint* property of the wife and the husband.]
—out of joint not in order; not organized.
joint • ***noun,*** *plural* **joints** • ***adjective***

joist

joist (joist) ***noun*** any one of the parallel pieces that hold up the boards of a floor or the supports of a ceiling.
joist • ***noun,*** *plural* **joists**

joke (jōk) ***noun*** something that a person says or does to get a laugh.
verb **1** to tell or play jokes. **2** to say or do something as a joke [Don't get mad; I was only *joking*.]
joke • ***noun,*** *plural* **jokes** • ***verb*** **joked, joking**

jolly (jäl′ē) ***adjective*** full of fun; cheerful and playful [We think of Santa Claus as a *jolly* old man.]
jol·ly • ***adjective*** **jollier, jolliest**

jolt (jōlt) ***verb*** **1** to shake up; to jar [The explosion *jolted* the house.] **2** to move along in a bumpy, jerky way [The cart *jolted* down the rough road.]
noun **1** a sudden bump or jerk. **2** a shock or surprise [The bad news gave us quite a *jolt*.]
jolt • ***verb*** **jolted, jolting** • ***noun,*** *plural* **jolts**

Jones (jōnz), **John Paul** (jän′ pôl′) 1747-1792; American naval officer in the Revolutionary War.

Jordan (jôr′dən) a country in the Middle East, east of Israel.
Jor·dan

Joseph (jō′zəf *or* jō′səf) the husband of Mary, the mother of Jesus.
Jo·seph

jostle (jäs′əl) ***verb*** to shove or push in a rough way.
jos·tle • ***verb*** **jostled, jostling**

jot (jät) ***verb*** to make a brief note of [She *jotted* down their phone number.]
jot • ***verb*** **jotted, jotting**

journal (jʉr′nəl) ***noun*** **1** a diary or other record of what happens each day [She kept a *journal* of her trip.] **2** a newspaper or magazine.
jour·nal • ***noun,*** *plural* **journals**

WORD HISTORY

journal

The source of **journal** is the Latin word for "day." It was first used in English for a book of prayers and worship that was to be used in the daytime. The word **journey** also comes from the same Latin word. An early meaning of **journey** was "the distance that a person can travel in one day."

journalism (jʉr′nəl iz əm) ***noun*** the work of gathering and preparing news for sending it out in newspapers or magazines or on radio or TV.
jour·nal·ism • ***noun***

journalist (jʉr′nəl ist) ***noun*** a reporter or other person whose work is gathering, preparing, and sending out the news.
jour·nal·ist • ***noun,*** *plural* **journalists**

journey (jʉr′nē) ***noun*** a trip; an act of traveling from one place to another —Look for the WORD CHOICES box at the entry **trip**.
verb to go on a trip; to travel.
jour·ney • ***noun,*** *plural* **journeys** • ***verb*** **journeyed, journeying**

joust (joust *or* just) ***noun*** a fight between two knights on horseback using lances.
verb to take part in a joust. This was done as a sport hundreds of years ago.
joust • ***noun,*** *plural* **jousts** • ***verb*** **jousted, jousting**

jowl (joul) ***noun*** *often* **jowls** the plump parts of the face hanging under the lower jaw.
jowl • ***noun,*** *plural* **jowls**

joy (joi) ***noun*** **1** a very happy feeling; great pleasure or delight [The new baby brought us *joy*.] **2** something that causes this feeling [This book is a *joy* to read.]
joy • ***noun,*** *plural* **joys**

joyful (joi′fəl) *adjective* feeling, showing, or causing joy; glad or happy.
joy·ful • *adjective*

joyous (joi′əs) *adjective* full of joy; happy.
joy·ous • *adjective*

joystick

joystick (joi′stik) *noun* a device that has a control lever and is connected to a computer terminal. The lever can be tilted in various directions to move the cursor on the video screen.
joy·stick • *noun, plural* **joysticks**

Jr. or **jr.** *abbreviation for* junior [John Smith, *Jr.*]

jubilant (jo͞o′bi lənt) *adjective* joyful and proud; glad [*Jubilant* crowds cheered the winning team.]
ju·bi·lant • *adjective*

jubilee (jo͞o′bi lē) *noun* **1** a celebration of an anniversary, especially a fiftieth or twenty-fifth anniversary. **2** a time of great joy.
ju·bi·lee • *noun, plural* **jubilees**

Judaism (jo͞o′dā iz′əm *or* jo͞o′dē iz′əm) *noun* the religion of the Jewish people, which is based on a belief in one God and on the teachings of the Holy Scriptures.
Ju·da·ism • *noun*

Judas Iscariot (jo͞o′dəs is ker′ē ət) the disciple who betrayed Jesus for money.
Ju·das Is·car·i·ot

judge (juj) *noun* **1** a public official who has power to hear cases and make decisions about them in a court of law. **2** a person who is chosen to decide the winner in a contest or to settle an argument. **3** a person who knows enough about something to give a useful opinion on it [She's a good *judge* of music.]
verb **1** to hear cases and make decisions in a court of law. **2** to decide the winner of [She *judged* the knitting contest.] **3** to form an opinion on [Don't *judge* spinach by your first taste of it.]
judge • *noun, plural* **judges**
• *verb* **judged, judging**

judgment (juj′mənt) *noun* **1** a decision that is given by a judge or a law court [The *judgment* was against the person accused of stealing.] **2** an opinion; the way a person thinks or feels about something [In my *judgment*, she will win the election.] **3** the ability to decide what is right, good, or valuable; good sense [a person of clear *judgment*].
judg·ment • *noun, plural* **judgments**

judicial (jo͞o dish′əl) *adjective* having to do with judges, law courts, or what they do [*judicial* robes; *judicial* duties].
ju·di·cial • *adjective*

judo (jo͞o′dō) *noun* a sport and a method of self-defense without the use of weapons.
ju·do • *noun*

jug (jug) *noun* **1** a container for liquids, with a small opening and a handle. **2** the amount that a jug will hold.
jug • *noun, plural* **jugs**

juggle (jug′əl) *verb* to do skillful tricks with the hands. A person who is juggling tosses a number of things up into the air one by one and keeps them all moving.
jug·gle • *verb* **juggled, juggling**

juice (jo͞os) *noun* the liquid from vegetables, fruits, or meats.
juice • *noun, plural* **juices**

SPELLING TIP

Use this memory aid to spell **juice**.
June likes ju***ice ice***-cold.

juicy (jo͞o′sē) *adjective* full of juice [a *juicy* plum].
juic·y • *adjective* **juicier, juiciest**

a	cat	ō	go	ʉ	fur	ə =	a *in* ago
ā	ape	ô	law, for	ch	chin		e *in* agent
ä	cot, car	o͝o	look	sh	she		i *in* pencil
e	ten	o͞o	tool	th	thin		o *in* atom
ē	me	oi	oil	*th*	then		u *in* circus
i	fit	ou	out	zh	measure		
ī	ice	u	up	ŋ	ring		

jukebox (jo͝ok′bäks) *noun* a large record player that works when a person drops a coin into a slot and presses a button to get a song to play.
juke·box • *noun, plural* **jukeboxes**

jukebox

July (jo͞o lī′) *noun* the seventh month of the year. July has 31 days. Abbreviated **Jul.**
Ju·ly • *noun*

jumble (jum′bəl) *verb* to mix up or put into a confused condition [The papers were *jumbled* together on the desk.]
noun a confused heap or condition —Look for the WORD CHOICES box at the entry **confusion**.
jum·ble • *verb* **jumbled, jumbling** • *noun, plural* **jumbles**

jumbo (jum′bō) *adjective* larger than usual [a *jumbo* strawberry sundae].
jum·bo • *adjective*

WORD HISTORY

jumbo

The word **jumbo** came into American English when it was used as the name for an enormous circus elephant in the 1880's. It comes from a word that means "elephant" in a language of western Africa.

jump (jump) *verb* **1** to move suddenly from the ground or floor by using the leg muscles; to spring or leap [He *jumped* up to catch the ball. I *jumped* on the bus.] **2** to leap over [The child *jumped* the creek.] **3** to move suddenly [He *jumped* in surprise as the door slammed.] **4** to rise suddenly [The price of milk *jumped* ten cents last week.]
noun **1** a leap or bound. **2** the distance that is covered in a leap or bound [a *jump* of ten feet]. **3** a fall from an airplane by parachute.
—jump at to take quickly and gladly [I'd *jump at* the chance to go there.]
jump • *verb* **jumped, jumping** • *noun, plural* **jumps**

jumper (jump′ər) *noun* a dress without sleeves that is worn over a blouse or sweater.
jump·er • *noun, plural* **jumpers**

jumpsuit (jump′so͞ot) *noun* a garment that covers the body, arms, and legs and opens down the front.
jump·suit • *noun, plural* **jumpsuits**

jumpsuit

jumpy (jum′pē) *adjective* easily startled; nervous [Ghost stories make me *jumpy*.]
jump·y • *adjective* **jumpier, jumpiest**

junction (juŋk′shən) *noun* a place where two roads cross or come together [the *junction* of Main Street and Route 10].
junc·tion • *noun, plural* **junctions**

June (jo͞on) *noun* the sixth month of the year. June has 30 days. Abbreviated **Jun.**

Juneau (jo͞o′nō) the capital of Alaska.
Ju·neau

jungle (juŋ′gəl) *noun* land in tropical regions that is thickly covered with trees and vines.
jun·gle • *noun, plural* **jungles**

junior (jo͞on′yər) *adjective* **1** the younger: this word is written after the name of a son who has exactly the same name as his father. **2** lower in position or rank [a *junior* member of the club]. **3** having to do with juniors in a high school or college [the *junior* class].
noun **1** a person who is younger or has a lower rank than another [She is my *junior* by two years.] **2** a student in the second last year of high school or college.
jun·ior • *adjective* • *noun, plural* **juniors**

junior high school *noun* a school between elementary school and senior high school. It usually includes grades seven, eight, and nine.
junior high school • *noun, plural* **junior high schools**

juniper (jo͞o′ni pər) *noun* a small evergreen shrub or tree with cones that look like berries.
ju·ni·per • *noun, plural* **junipers**

junk[1] (juŋk) *noun* **1** old metal parts, pieces of glass, or other things that are thrown away but may be cleaned up or fixed up and used again in some way. **2** [*an informal use*] things of no use or value; trash.

J

junk

junk[2] (juŋk) ***noun*** a sailing ship with a flat bottom usually found in China and southeastern Asia.
junk • ***noun,*** *plural* **junks**

junk food ***noun*** potato chips, candy bars, soda pop, or other snacks that are high in sugar or fat but low in vitamins or protein.

junk mail ***noun*** advertisements, requests for money, and similar material people often receive without their asking for it.

Jupiter (jo͞o′pit ər) **1** the chief Roman god. He rules over all other gods. **2** the largest planet. It is the fifth in distance away from the sun.
Ju·pi·ter

jurisdiction (jo͝or′is dik′shən) ***noun*** **1** the power of a court, a judge, or the police [Juvenile court has *jurisdiction* in cases involving children.] **2** the area or limits of this power [The matter is outside the *jurisdiction* of the local police.]
ju·ris·dic·tion • ***noun,*** *plural for sense 2 only* **jurisdictions**

juror (jo͝or′ər *or* jʉr′ər) ***noun*** a member of a jury.
ju·ror • ***noun,*** *plural* **jurors**

jury (jo͝or′ē *or* jʉr′ē) ***noun*** a group of people who are chosen to listen to the facts and evidence in a law trial. The jury reaches a decision based on the facts it hears and on the law.
ju·ry • ***noun,*** *plural* **juries**

just (just) ***adjective*** **1** right or fair [a *just* decision]. **2** doing what is right or honest [a *just* person] —Look for the WORD CHOICES box at the entry **good**.
adverb **1** neither more nor less than; exactly [It's *just* two o'clock now.] **2** almost at the point of; nearly [I was *just* leaving.] **3** no more than; only [I'm *just* teasing you.] **4** by a very small amount; barely [I *just* missed the bus.] **5** a very short time ago [The plane *just* took off.] **6** [*an informal use*] quite; really [You look *just* fine.]

WORD CHOICES

Synonyms of **just**

The words **just**, **fair**, and **impartial** share the meaning "treating both sides or all sides in the same honest way."

a *just* decision

a *fair* trial

an *impartial* judge

justice (jus′tis) ***noun*** **1** the quality of being just or fair [The coach treated all his players with *justice*.] **2** the use of authority to uphold what is just or lawful [We went to court seeking *justice*.] **3** a judge, such as one who is a member of the U.S. Supreme Court.
jus·tice • ***noun,*** *plural for sense 3 only* **justices**

justice of the peace ***noun*** a public official with power to marry people and decide law cases that involve minor offenses.
justice of the peace • ***noun,*** *plural* **justices of the peace**

justification (jus′tə fi kā′shən) ***noun*** a fact that gives a good reason for something [There is no *justification* for such a crime.]
jus·ti·fi·ca·tion • ***noun***

justify (jus′ti fī′) ***verb*** **1** to show to be right or fair [Her special skills *justified* her higher salary.] **2** to give good reasons for [Can you *justify* your decision?]
jus·ti·fy • ***verb*** **justified, justifying, justifies**

jut (jut) ***verb*** to stick out; project [A thin strip of land *juts* into the lake.]
jut • ***verb*** **jutted, jutting**

jute (jo͞ot) ***noun*** a strong fiber that comes from a tropical plant and is used for making rope.
jute • ***noun,*** *plural* **jutes**

juvenile (jo͞o′və nəl *or* jo͞o′və nīl) ***adjective*** **1** of or having to do with children or young people [*juvenile* books]. **2** childish or foolish.
noun a young person.
ju·ven·ile • ***adjective*** • ***noun,*** *plural* **juveniles**

a	cat	ō	go	ʉ	fur	ə =	a *in* ago
ā	ape	ô	law, for	ch	chin		e *in* agent
ä	cot, car	o͝o	look	sh	she		i *in* pencil
e	ten	o͞o	tool	th	thin		o *in* atom
ē	me	oi	oil	*th*	then		u *in* circus
i	fit	ou	out	zh	measure		
ī	ice	u	up	ŋ	ring		

K k

Kk Kk Kk Kk

The letter **k** *has the sound you hear at the beginning of the word* **kite**. *This is the same sound that you often hear in words that are spelled with the letter* **c**. *Although the sound is the same, it is important to remember which letter to write in words that have either of these two letters.*

When you see the combination of letters **kn** *at the beginning of a word, such as* **knife** *and* **knock**, *you can be sure that the* **k** *is not pronounced.*

k or **K** (kā) ***noun*** the eleventh letter of the English alphabet.
k or **K** • ***noun,*** *plural* **k's** or **K's**

K or **k** *abbreviation for* **1** karat. **2** karats. **3** kilobyte. **4** kilobytes. **5** kilogram. **6** kilograms. **7** kilometer. **8** kilometers.

kaleidoscope

kaleidoscope (kə lī′də skōp) ***noun*** a small tube with mirrors and loose bits of colored glass or plastic in it. When the tube is held to the eye and turned, the mirrors cause the bits to form one pattern after another.
ka·lei·do·scope • ***noun,*** *plural* **kaleidoscopes**

kangaroo (kaŋ gər o͞o′) ***noun*** an animal of Australia with short forelegs and strong, large hind legs with which it makes long leaps. The female carries her young in a pouch on her belly.
kan·ga·roo • ***noun,*** *plural* **kangaroos** or **kangaroo**

STATE MAP

Kansas

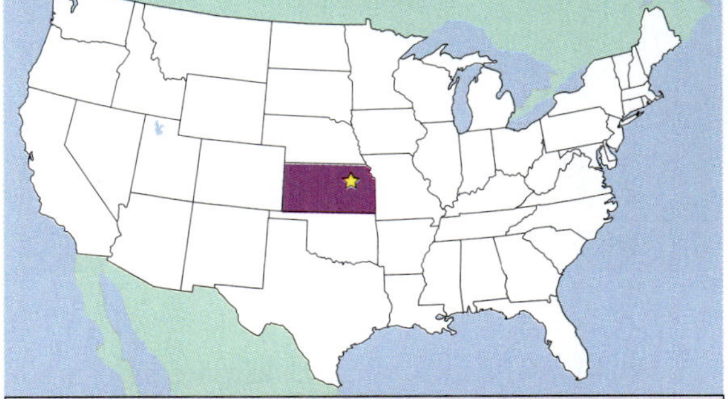

Statehood: 1861, the 34th state • **Capital:** Topeka

Kansas (kan′zəs) a State in the central part of the U.S. Its capital is Topeka. Abbreviated **KS** or **Kans.**
Kan·sas

Kansas City **1** a city in western Missouri. **2** a city next to it in eastern Kansas.

karat (ker′ət) ***noun*** one 24th part of pure gold. A gold necklace of 14 karats is 14 parts pure gold and 10 parts other metal.
kar·at • ***noun,*** *plural* **karats**

- The words **karat, carat, caret,** and **carrot** sound alike.
  Her ring is 14-*karat* gold.
  A *carat* is less than a gram.
  The *caret* is a common editor's mark.
  Our rabbit enjoys a *carrot* each day.

karate (kə rät′ē) ***noun*** a Japanese form of self-defense in which sharp, quick blows are struck with the hands and feet.
ka·ra·te • ***noun***

WORD HISTORY

karate

We get **karate** from Japanese words that mean "open" and "hand." In **karate**, a person uses the side of the hand, held open and stiff, to strike blows to the opponent.

katydid (kāt′ē did′) ***noun*** a large, green insect that looks like a grasshopper. The male katydid makes a sharp, high sound with its wings.
ka·ty·did • ***noun,*** *plural* **katydids**

kayak

kayak (kī′ak) ***noun*** **1** an Eskimo canoe made of a wooden frame covered with skins all around, except for an opening for the person who paddles. **2** a light canoe that looks like this, usually covered with canvas.
kay·ak • ***noun,*** *plural* **kayaks**

Kazakhstan (kä′zäk stan′) a country in southwestern Asia. It was a part of the Soviet Union.
Ka·zakh·stan

Keats (kēts), **John** (jän) 1795-1821; English poet.

keel (kēl) ***noun*** the center timber or steel plate that runs the length of the bottom of a ship.
keel • ***noun,*** *plural* **keels**

keen (kēn) ***adjective*** **1** sharp and quick in seeing, hearing, or thinking [*keen* eyesight; a *keen* mind]. **2** eager or enthusiastic [Are you *keen* about going?] —Look for the WORD CHOICES box at the entry **eager**.
keen • ***adjective*** **keener, keenest**

keep (kēp) ***verb*** **1** to have or hold and not let go [The teacher *kept* us after school. Can you *keep* a secret?] **2** to hold for a later time; save [*Keep* the sandwich until I get back.] **3** to stop; prevent [I could not *keep* the dog from barking.] **4** to take care of; look after [One *keeps* house while the other takes care of the yard.] **5** to write down on a daily or regular basis in [I *keep* a diary during my vacations.] **6** to stay or make stay as is; continue [The fish will *keep* if you pack it in ice. *Keep* the engine running. *Keep* walking.] **7** to carry out; fulfill [You should always *keep* a promise.]
noun **1** food and shelter; support [The cat earns its *keep* by catching mice.] **2** a castle or the inner tower of a castle.
—for keeps [*an informal use*] forever [We are friends *for keeps*.] **—keep up** to continue; go on [This weather can't *keep up* much longer.] **—keep up with** to go or do as fast as; stay even with [I *kept up with* the leaders until the last lap.]
keep • ***verb*** **kept, keeping** • ***noun,*** *plural* **keeps**

keeper (kēp′ər) ***noun*** a person or thing that keeps, guards, or takes care of something.
keep·er • ***noun,*** *plural* **keepers**

keeping (kēp′iŋ) ***noun*** care or protection [He left the money in her *keeping*.]
keep·ing • ***noun***

keepsake (kēp′sāk) ***noun*** an object kept in memory of some person or event.
keep·sake • ***noun,*** *plural* **keepsakes**

keg (keg) ***noun*** a small barrel.
keg • ***noun,*** *plural* **kegs**

Keller (kel′ər), **Helen Adams** (hel′ən ad′əmz) 1880-1968; U.S. writer. She was blind and deaf from the time she was an infant, but she was taught to speak and read.
Kel·ler, Hel·en Ad·ams

kelp (kelp) ***noun*** **1** a large, coarse, brown seaweed. **2** ashes of burned seaweed, from which iodine is obtained.

Kennedy (ken′ə dē), **John F.** (jän) 1917-1963;

a cat	ō go	ʉ fur	ə = a *in* ago
ā ape	ô law, for	ch chin	e *in* agent
ä cot, car	oo look	sh she	i *in* pencil
e ten	o͞o tool	th thin	o *in* atom
ē me	oi oil	*th* then	u *in* circus
i fit	ou out	zh measure	
ī ice	u up	ŋ ring	

the thirty-fifth president of the U.S., from 1961-1963. He was assassinated.
Ken·ne·dy, John F.

kennel (ken′əl) ***noun*** *often* **kennels** a place where dogs are raised or kept.
ken·nel • ***noun,*** *plural* **kennels**

STATE MAP

Statehood: 1792, the 15th state • **Capital:** Frankfort

Kentucky (kən tuk′ē) a State in the eastern central part of the U.S. Its capital is Frankfort. Abbreviated **KY** or **Ky.**
Ken·tuck·y

Kenya (ken′yə *or* kēn′yə) a country in east central Africa, on the Indian Ocean.
Ken·ya

kept (kept) ***verb*** *past tense and past participle of* **keep**.

kerchief (kur′chif) ***noun*** a piece of cloth, usually square, that is worn over the head or around the neck.
ker·chief • ***noun,*** *plural* **kerchiefs**

kernel (kur′nəl) ***noun*** **1** a grain or seed, especially of corn, wheat, or some other cereal plant. **2** the soft inner part of a nut or fruit pit.
ker·nel • ***noun,*** *plural* **kernels**
● The words **kernel** and **colonel** sound alike.
The baker uses the whole wheat *kernel*.
She was a *colonel* in the army.

kerosene (ker′ə sēn) ***noun*** a thin oil made mainly from petroleum. It is used as a fuel.
ker·o·sene • ***noun***

ketchup (kech′əp) ***noun*** a thick sauce made of tomatoes, onions, salt, sugar, and spices.
ketch·up • ***noun***

kettle (ket′l) ***noun*** a metal container for boiling or cooking.
ket·tle • ***noun,*** *plural* **kettles**

kettledrum

kettledrum (ket′l drum) ***noun*** a large drum that is half a hollow, metal globe with a membrane of calf skin or plastic stretched across the top. It can be made tighter or looser to change the pitch.
ket·tle·drum • ***noun,*** *plural* **kettledrums**

key[1] (kē) ***noun*** **1** a small piece of metal that is cut in a special way so that it can open or close a lock. **2** such a piece used to open or close an electric circuit. **3** anything that looks or works like a key [a *key* to wind up a clock or music box]. **4** one of the buttons or other devices on a keyboard that is pressed down with the fingers [piano *keys*]. **5** a chart or list that has the correct answers to problems or that helps explain something [The *key* at the bottom of the page will help you pronounce words.] **6** the most important or necessary thing [I believe that education is the *key* to success.] **7** a group of musical notes that form a musical scale based on a keynote. These notes form a musical scale whose lowest tone is the keynote. A key is always named after its keynote [The *key* of C major has no sharps or flats.]
adjective most important or necessary [He is the *key* player on their team.]
verb to type into a computer using a keyboard [She *keyed* in the data.]
key • ***noun,*** *plural* **keys** • ***adjective*** • ***verb*** **keyed, keying**
● The words **key** and **quay** sound alike.
Play the song in the *key* of G.
A *key* is a kind of low island.
The ship unloaded at the *quay*.

key[2] (kē) ***noun*** a reef or an island just above the surface of the water.
key • ***noun,*** *plural* **keys**
● The words **key** and **quay** sound alike.

K

We went to a *key* off Florida's coast.
I lost the *key* to my car.
The *quay* was built on the left bank.

Key (kē), **Francis Scott** (fran′sis skät) 1779-1843; U.S. lawyer. He wrote the words for "The Star-Spangled Banner."
Key, Fran·cis Scott

keyboard (kē′bôrd) ***noun*** the row or rows of keys on a piano, organ, typewriter, or computer.
key·board • ***noun,*** *plural* **keyboards**

keyhole (kē′hōl) ***noun*** the opening in a lock in which the key is put.
key·hole • ***noun,*** *plural* **keyholes**

keynote (kē′nōt) ***noun*** the lowest and basic tone or note of a musical scale or key. Every musical scale or key is named after its keynote. F is the keynote of the key of F.
key·note • ***noun,*** *plural* **keynotes**

key ring ***noun*** a metal ring for holding keys.
key ring • ***noun,*** *plural* **key rings**

keystone

keystone (kē′stōn) ***noun*** the central stone of an arch. It is at the very top of the arch and is thought of as holding the other stones in place.
key·stone • ***noun,*** *plural* **keystones**

kg or **kg.** *abbreviation for* **1** kilogram. **2** kilograms.

khaki (kak′ē) ***noun*** **1** yellowish brown. **2** a strong, heavy cotton cloth of this color. It is used most often for military uniforms. **3** *often* **khakis** a uniform made of this cloth.
kha·ki • ***noun,*** *plural* **khakis**

kick (kik) ***verb*** **1** to strike with the foot [She *kicked* him in the shin.] **2** to move by striking with the foot [He *kicked* the football.] **3** to score by kicking a ball in this way [He *kicked* a field goal.] **4** to strike outward with the foot or feet in dancing, swimming, or other activity.
noun **1** a blow with the foot [He gave the ball a *kick*.] **2** a kicking motion of the foot or feet [The swimmer has a strong *kick*.] —**kick off** to put a football into play by kicking it.
kick • ***verb*** **kicked, kicking** • ***noun,*** *plural* **kicks**

kickoff (kik′ôf) ***noun*** a kick in football that begins play at the beginning of each half or after one of the teams scores a touchdown or field goal.
kick·off • ***noun,*** *plural* **kickoffs**

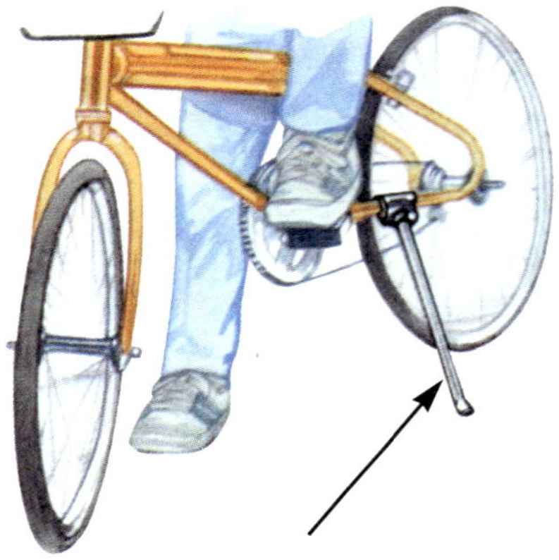

kickstand

kickstand (kik′stand) ***noun*** a short metal bar attached to a bicycle. When it is kicked down, it holds the bicycle in an upright position.
kick·stand • ***noun,*** *plural* **kickstands**

kid (kid) ***noun*** **1** a young goat. **2** leather from the skin of young goats, used for gloves or shoes. **3** [*an informal use*] a child.
verb [*an informal use*] to tease or fool [He was *kidding* me about my funny-looking socks.]
kid • ***noun,*** *plural* **kids** • ***verb*** **kidded, kidding**

Kidd (kid), Captain 1645?-1701; Scottish pirate. His full name was *William Kidd*.

kiddie or **kiddy** (kid′ē) [*an informal word*] ***noun*** a child.
kid·die or **kid·dy** • ***noun,*** *plural* **kiddies**

kidnap (kid′nap) ***verb*** to carry a person off by force, often in order to get a ransom.

a	cat	ō	go	ʉ	fur	ə = a *in* ago	
ā	ape	ô	law, for	ch	chin	e *in* agent	
ä	cot, car	oo	look	sh	she	i *in* pencil	
e	ten	o͞o	tool	th	thin	o *in* atom	
ē	me	oi	oil	*th*	then	u *in* circus	
i	fit	ou	out	zh	measure		
ī	ice	u	up	ŋ	ring		

kid·nap • *verb* **kidnapped** or **kidnaped, kidnapping** or **kidnaping**

kidney (kid′nē) ***noun*** **1** one of a pair of organs in the central part of the body that removes water and waste matter from the blood and passes them to the bladder in the form of urine. **2** the kidney of an animal, used as food.
kid·ney • *noun, plural* **kidneys**

kidney bean ***noun*** the seed of the bean plant, used as food. It is shaped like a kidney.
kidney bean • *noun, plural* **kidney beans**

kill (kil) ***verb*** **1** to cause the death of; make die. **2** to put an end to; destroy or ruin [That last touchdown *killed* our hopes of winning the game.] **3** to stop or turn off [*Kill* the engine.] **4** to use up [We *killed* two hours watching the animals in the zoo.] **5** [*an informal use*] to make feel great pain [This headache is *killing* me.]
noun **1** the act of killing. **2** an animal or animals killed [Hunters in our State are allowed one *kill* a season.]
kill • *verb* **killed, killing** • *noun, plural* **kills**
● The words **kill** and **kiln** often sound alike.
The senator's speech can *kill* the bill.
The vase was baked in the *kiln*.

killdeer (kil′dir) ***noun*** a small wading bird that has a shrill cry.
kill·deer • *noun, plural* **killdeers** or **killdeer**

kiln (kil *or* kiln) ***noun*** a furnace or oven for drying or baking bricks or pottery.
kiln • *noun, plural* **kilns**
● The words **kiln** and **kill** often sound alike.
How many bowls are now in the *kiln?*
Our cat tried to *kill* the robin.

kilo (kē′lō *or* kil′ō) ***noun*** *a short form of* **kilogram**.
ki·lo • *noun, plural* **kilos**

kilo- *a prefix meaning* one thousand [A *kilometer* is one thousand meters in length.]

kilobyte (kil′ə bīt) ***noun*** an amount equal to 1,024 bytes.
kil·o·byte • *noun, plural* **kilobytes**

kilogram (kil′ə gram) ***noun*** a unit of weight in the metric system. A kilogram is equal to 1,000 grams or about two pounds and three ounces.
kil·o·gram • *noun, plural* **kilograms**

kilometer (ki läm′ət ər *or* kil′ə mēt ər) ***noun*** a unit of length in the metric system. The kilometer is equal to 1,000 meters or about 5⁄8 mile.
ki·lo·me·ter • *noun, plural* **kilometers**

kilowatt (kil′ə wät) ***noun*** a unit of electrical power, equal to 1,000 watts.
kil·o·watt • *noun, plural* **kilowatts**

kilt (kilt) ***noun*** a short skirt with pleats, especially the tartan skirt sometimes worn by men in Scotland.
kilt • *noun, plural* **kilts**

kilt

kimono (ki mō′nō) ***noun*** **1** a loose robe with wide sleeves and a sash. It used to be the common outer garment of Japanese men and women. **2** a woman's dressing gown like this.
ki·mo·no • *noun, plural* **kimonos**

kin (kin) ***noun*** relatives or family.
—next of kin a person's nearest relative or relatives.

kind[1] (kīnd) ***noun*** sort or variety [What *kinds* of books do you enjoy?] —Look for the WORD CHOICES box at the entry **type**.
—kind of [*an informal use*] somewhat; rather [It's *kind of* cold in here.]
kind • *noun, plural* **kinds**

kind[2] (kīnd) ***adjective*** **1** always ready to help others and do good; friendly, gentle, generous, or sympathetic. **2** showing kindness [*kind* deeds].
kind • *adjective* **kinder, kindest**

WORD CHOICES

Synonyms of kind

The words **kind, considerate,** and **humane** share the meaning "having or showing a wish to help others and do good."

your *kind* letter

their *considerate* request that my sister come too

working for a more *humane* treatment of prisoners

kindergarten (kin′dər gärt′n) ***noun*** a school or class for young children about five years old. It gets them ready for regular school.
kin·der·gar·ten • ***noun,*** *plural* **kindergartens**

WORD HISTORY

kindergarten

A German man who developed a special system for teaching young children in the mid-1800's also invented the name for this system. He combined the words for "child" and "garden" to make *Kindergarten*, or "children's garden," and we have taken the word into English, as **kindergarten**, to describe any school or class for young children.

kindle (kin′dəl) ***verb*** **1** to set on fire; light [We *kindled* the logs in the fireplace.] **2** to catch fire; start burning [The logs *kindled* quickly.] **3** to stir up; arouse [His speech *kindled* my interest in politics.]
kin·dle • ***verb*** **kindled, kindling**

kindling (kind′liŋ) ***noun*** bits of dry wood or of other materials that catch fire easily, used for starting a fire.
kin·dling • ***noun***

kindly (kīnd′lē) ***adjective*** showing kindness [a *kindly* act of charity].
adverb **1** in a kind way [He spoke to us *kindly*.] **2** please [*Kindly* shut the door.]
kind·ly • ***adjective*** **kindlier, kindliest**
• ***adverb***

kindness (kīnd′nəs) ***noun*** **1** the condition or habit of being kind. **2** a kind act or kind treatment.
kind·ness • ***noun,*** *plural for sense 2 only* **kindnesses**

king (kiŋ) ***noun*** **1** a man who rules a country and whose position is usually handed down from parent to child. Kings today usually have little power to rule. **2** a playing card with a picture of a king on it. **3** the chief piece in chess. **4** a piece in checkers that has moved the length of the board.
king • ***noun,*** *plural* **kings**

King (kiŋ), **Martin Luther, Jr.** (märt′n lo͞o′thər) 1929-1968; U.S. clergyman and leader in the civil rights movement. He was assassinated.
King, Mar·tin Lu·ther, Jr.

kingdom (kiŋ′dəm) ***noun*** **1** a country ruled by a king or queen; monarchy. **2** one of the three groups into which all things are placed [the animal, vegetable, and mineral *kingdoms*].
king·dom • ***noun,*** *plural* **kingdoms**

kingfisher

kingfisher (kiŋ′fish ər) ***noun*** a bright-colored bird with a short tail, a large head, and a strong beak. It usually eats fish.
king·fish·er • ***noun,*** *plural* **kingfishers**

king-size (kiŋ′sīz) ***adjective*** larger than the regular size; extra large [a *king-size* bed].

king-sized (kiŋ′sīzd′) ***adjective*** *the same as* **king-size**.

kink (kiŋk) ***noun*** **1** a short twist or curl in something such as a hair, wire, or rope. **2** a painful cramp in a muscle.
kink • ***noun,*** *plural* **kinks**

Kiowa (kī′ə wä) ***noun*** **1** a member of a North American Indian people who formerly lived in Colorado, Oklahoma, and other nearby States and now live in Oklahoma. **2** the language of this people.
Ki·o·wa • ***noun,*** *plural for sense 1 only* **Kiowas** or **Kiowa**

Kipling (kip′liŋ), **Rudyard** (rud′yərd) 1865-1936; English writer and poet, born in India.
Kip·ling, Rud·yard

Kiribati (kir ə bas′) a country made up of three groups of atolls in the west central Pacific, east of Papua New Guinea.
Kir·i·bati

kiss (kis) ***verb*** to touch with the lips as a way of showing love or respect or as a greeting.
noun **1** a touch with the lips. **2** a small piece of chocolate or other candy.

a	cat	ō	go	ʉ	fur	ə =	a *in* ago
ā	ape	ô	law, for	ch	chin		e *in* agent
ä	cot, car	oo	look	sh	she		i *in* pencil
e	ten	o͞o	tool	th	thin		o *in* atom
ē	me	oi	oil	*th*	then		u *in* circus
i	fit	ou	out	zh	measure		
ī	ice	u	up	ŋ	ring		

kiss • *verb* **kissed, kissing** • *noun, plural* **kisses**

kit (kit) *noun* **1** a set of tools or other things having a special use [a repair *kit;* an art *kit*]. **2** a set of parts that must be put together [a radio *kit*]. **3** a box or bag for carrying a set of tools or other items.
kit • *noun, plural* **kits**

kitchen (kich′ən) *noun* a room for preparing and cooking food.
kitch·en • *noun, plural* **kitchens**

kitchenette (kich ən et′) *noun* a very small kitchen.
kitch·en·ette • *noun, plural* **kitchenettes**

kite (kīt) *noun* a light frame of wood or other material that is covered with paper or cloth. It is tied to a string and flown in the air when the wind is blowing.
kite • *noun, plural* **kites**

kite

kitten (kit′n) *noun* a young cat.
kit·ten • *noun, plural* **kittens**

kitty (kit′ē) *noun* a pet name for a cat or kitten.
kit·ty • *noun, plural* **kitties**

Kleenex (klē′neks) *trademark* soft paper tissue used as a handkerchief.
Klee·nex • *trademark*

km or **km.** *abbreviation for* **1** kilometer. **2** kilometers.

knack (nak) *noun* a special ability or skill [He has a *knack* for making friends.]
knack • *noun, plural* **knacks**

knapsack (nap′sak) *noun* a bag for carrying supplies, made of canvas or other material. It is usually worn on the back when hiking.
knap·sack • *noun, plural* **knapsacks**

knead (nēd) *verb* **1** to press and squeeze over and over until ready for use [We *kneaded* the bread dough.] **2** to rub or press with the hands in order to soothe or relax; massage [The trainer *kneaded* the player's cramped leg muscle.]
knead • *verb* **kneaded, kneading**
● The words **knead** and **need** sound alike.
You must *knead* the dough before baking.
Do I really *need* another subscription?

knee (nē) *noun* **1** the joint between the upper and lower parts of the leg. **2** something shaped like a bent knee.
knee • *noun, plural* **knees**

kneecap (nē′kap) *noun* the flat bone that forms the front of a person's knee.
knee·cap • *noun, plural* **kneecaps**

kneel (nēl) *verb* to rest on a knee or the knees [Some people *kneel* when they pray.]
kneel • *verb* **knelt** or **kneeled, kneeling**

knelt (nelt) *verb a past tense and past participle of* **kneel**.

knew (no͞o *or* nyo͞o) *verb past tense of* **know**.
● The words **knew, gnu,** and **new** sound alike.
I *knew* her when she was in school.
Lions hunt the zebra and the *gnu*.
We're getting a *new* car this year.

knickers (nik′ərz) *plural noun* short, loose trousers with legs that are gathered in just below the knees.
knick·ers • *plural noun*

knickknack (nik′nak) *noun* a small, showy thing having no great value, used as an ornament or decoration.
knick·knack • *noun, plural* **knickknacks**

knife (nīf) *noun* a tool having a flat, sharp blade set in a handle, used for cutting or stabbing.
verb to cut or stab with a knife.
knife • *noun, plural* **knives** • *verb* **knifed, knifing, knifes**

knight (nīt) *noun* **1** a man in the Middle Ages who was given a military rank of honor after training. A knight pledged loyalty to a monarch or lord and in return was given the right to hold land. **2** a man in Great Britain who has been honored with this title for service to his country. He is allowed to use *Sir* before his first name. **3** a chess piece, usually shaped like the head of a horse.
verb to give the rank of knight to [The queen *knighted* him for his great deeds.]
knight • *noun, plural* **knights** • *verb* **knighted, knighting**
● The words **knight** and **night** sound alike.
The *knight* wore a suit of armor.
The stars and moon light up the *night*.

K

knit (nit) ***verb*** **1** to make by looping yarn or thread together with special needles [She *knitted* a scarf.] **2** to join or grow together in a close or firm way [Father's illness *knit* our family even more closely.] **3** to draw together in wrinkles [She *knits* her brows when she thinks hard.]
noun cloth or a garment made by knitting.
knit • ***verb*** **knitted** or **knit, knitting** • ***noun,*** *plural* **knits**

knives (nīvz) ***noun*** *plural of* **knife**.

knob (näb) ***noun*** **1** a round or nearly round handle, used for opening or closing a door or drawer. **2** a device that is turned to control something on a radio, TV, or some other appliance or machine [This *knob* is for changing channels.]
knob • ***noun,*** *plural* **knobs**

knock (näk) ***verb*** **1** to hit or rap with the fist or some hard object [We *knocked* on the window.] **2** to hit and cause to fall [She *knocked* over the vase. He *knocked* down the quarterback.] **3** to make a pounding or tapping noise [The engine *knocked* when he used the wrong gasoline.] **4** [*an informal use*] to find fault with; criticize [Don't *knock* it until you've tried it.]
noun **1** a sharp blow [The *knock* on the door startled me.] **2** a pounding or tapping noise [That *knock* in the engine means that something is wrong.]
—**knock out 1** to hit so as to make unconscious [That last punch *knocked* him *out*.] **2** to cause to lose consciousness or become very tired [That medicine *knocks* me *out*.]
knock • ***verb*** **knocked, knocking** • ***noun,*** *plural* **knocks**

knocker (näk′ər) ***noun*** a metal ring or hammer that swings on a hinge. It is fastened to a door and is used for knocking.
knock·er • ***noun,*** *plural* **knockers**

knockout (näk′out) ***noun*** a blow that knocks a boxer down so that he cannot get up and go on fighting. It ends a boxing match.
knock·out • ***noun,*** *plural* **knockouts**

knoll (nōl) ***noun*** a little, rounded hill; mound.
knoll • ***noun,*** *plural* **knolls**

knot (nät) ***noun*** **1** a fastening made by tying together parts or pieces of something such as string, wire, or rope [The sailor knew how to tie many different *knots*.] **2** a tightly twisted lump or tangle [The dog's coat was full of *knots*.] **3** a small group [A *knot* of people gathered near the accident.] **4** a unit used to measure the speed of a boat or ship. It is equal to about 1.15 miles per hour. **5** a hard lump on a tree trunk where a branch grows out, or a section of such a lump in a board.
verb to tie or fasten with a knot; make a knot in.
knot • ***noun,*** *plural* **knots** • ***verb*** **knotted, knotting**
● The words **knot** and **not** sound alike.
The child has a *knot* in her shoelace.
I will *not* be coming to dinner.

knot

knothole (nät′hōl) ***noun*** a hole in a tree trunk or a board where a knot has fallen out.
knot·hole • ***noun,*** *plural* **knotholes**

knotty (nät′ē) ***adjective*** **1** full of knots [*knotty* pine]. **2** hard to deal with [a *knotty* problem].
knot·ty • ***adjective*** **knottier, knottiest**

know (nō) ***verb*** **1** to be sure of or have the facts about [Do you *know* why grass is green?] **2** to be aware of; realize [He suddenly *knew* he would be late.] **3** to have in the mind or memory [The actress *knows* her lines.] **4** to be acquainted with [I *know* your brother well.] **5** to recognize [I'd *know* that face anywhere.] **6** to have skill in or understanding of as a result of study or experience [Her sister *knows* how to play the piano.]
know • ***verb*** **knew, known, knowing**
● The words **know** and **no** sound alike.
Do you *know* how to dance?
There are *no* sandwiches left.

know-how (nō′hou) [*an informal word*] ***noun*** knowledge of how to do something well [Her *know-how* came in handy for fixing the flat tire.]

a cat	ō go	ʉ fur	ə = a *in* ago
ā ape	ô law, for	ch chin	e *in* agent
ä cot, car	oo look	sh she	i *in* pencil
e ten	o͞o tool	th thin	o *in* atom
ē me	oi oil	*th* then	u *in* circus
i fit	ou out	zh measure	
ī ice	u up	ŋ ring	

know-it-all (nō′it ôl′) [*an informal word*] ***noun*** a person who pretends or claims to know much about almost everything.
know-it-all • ***noun,*** *plural* **know-it-alls**

knowledge (nä′lij) ***noun*** **1** the fact or condition of knowing [*Knowledge* of the crime spread quickly through town.] **2** what is known or learned [His *knowledge* of history comes from reading many books.]
knowl·edge • ***noun***

knowledgeable (nä′lij ə bəl) ***adjective*** having or showing knowledge or intelligence [Her mother is a very *knowledgeable* person.]
knowl·edge·a·ble • ***adjective***

known (nōn) ***verb*** *past participle of* **know**.

knuckle (nuk′əl) ***noun*** **1** a joint of the finger [He rapped sharply on the door with his *knuckles*.] **2** the knee or ankle joint of a pig or calf, used as food.
knuck·le • ***noun,*** *plural* **knuckles**

koala

koala (kō ä′lə) ***noun*** an animal of Australia that looks like a small bear and lives in trees. The mother carries her young in a pouch on her belly.
ko·a·la • ***noun,*** *plural* **koalas** or **koala**

kook (ko͞ok) [*a slang word*] ***noun*** a person who is thought of as silly or crazy.
kook • ***noun,*** *plural* **kooks**

kooky (ko͞o′kē) [*a slang word*] ***adjective*** of or like a kook; silly or crazy [*kooky* ideas].
kook·y • ***adjective*** **kookier, kookiest**

Koran (kər an′ *or* kôr′an) the sacred book of Islam.
Ko·ran

Korea (kə rē′ə *or* kô rē′ə) a country in eastern Asia, divided into two republics, **North Korea** and **South Korea**.
Ko·re·a

Korean (kô rē′ən) ***noun*** **1** a person born or living in Korea. **2** the language of the Koreans.
Kor·e·an • ***noun,*** *plural for sense 1 only* **Koreans**

kosher (kō′shər) ***adjective*** fit to eat according to the Jewish laws of diet.
ko·sher • ***adjective***

WORD HISTORY

kosher

The word **kosher** comes from a Hebrew word that means "fit" or "proper," which comes from a root word that means "to be appropriate." Jewish people who follow these rules for preparing and serving food make sure that the food is pure and fit to eat according to their beliefs.

Kremlin (krem′lin) a large fortress in the center of Moscow. It contains some of the government offices of Russia.
Krem·lin

krypton (krip′tän) ***noun*** a rare gas that is a chemical element. It has no color, odor, or taste.
kryp·ton • ***noun***

KS *abbreviation for* Kansas.

kung fu (ko͝oŋ′fo͞o′ *or* kuŋ′fo͞o′) ***noun*** a Chinese form of self-defense. It is similar to karate.

Kuwait (ko͞o wāt′) a country in eastern Arabia.
Ku·wait

Kwanzaa (kwän′zä) ***noun*** a cultural festival that African Americans celebrate from December 26 through January 1. This is also spelled **Kwan·za**.
Kwan·zaa • ***noun***

KY or **Ky.** *abbreviation for* Kentucky.

Kyrgyzstan (kir′gi stan′) a country in southwestern Asia. It was a part of the Soviet Union.
Kyr·gyz·stan

K

L l

Ll Ll *Ll* Ll

The letter **l** *has the sound you hear at the beginning of the words* **lip**, **lobster**, *and* **luck**. *In some words, like* **talk** *and* **calm**, *you do not hear a separate sound for the* **l**. *Be careful with words that have the* **l** *sound at the end: many of them are spelled not with one* **l** *but with two, as in* **all**, **doll**, **fell**, **pill**, *and* **pull**.

l or **L** (el) ***noun*** **1** the twelfth letter of the English alphabet. **2** something shaped like an L.
l or **L** • ***noun**, plural* **l's** or **L's**

L (el) ***noun*** the Roman numeral for 50.
L • ***noun**, plural* **L's**

l or **L** *abbreviation for* **1** liter. **2** liters.

L. or **l.** *abbreviation for* **1** length. **2** liter. **3** liters.

la (lä) ***noun*** the sixth note of a musical scale.

LA or **La.** *abbreviation for* Louisiana.

L.A. or **LA** *abbreviation for* Los Angeles.

lab (lab) [*an informal word*] ***noun*** a laboratory.
lab • ***noun**, plural* **labs**

label (lā′bəl) ***noun*** a piece of paper, cloth, or other material that is marked and attached to an object. The label shows what the object is, what it contains, or who owns it [a *label* on a can; a mailing *label* on a package].
verb **1** to attach a label to [We *labeled* the package.] **2** to name or describe as; call [No one wants to be *labeled* a coward.]
la·bel • ***noun**, plural* **labels** • ***verb*** **labeled** or **labelled, labeling** or **labelling**

labor (lā′bər) ***noun*** **1** physical work; toil —Look for the WORD CHOICES box at the entry **work**. **2** workers as a group [an agreement between *labor* and management].
verb **1** to work or toil [Coal miners *labor* underground.] **2** to move slowly and with effort [The old car *labored* up the steep hill.]
la·bor • ***noun**, plural* **labors** • ***verb*** **labored, laboring**

laboratory (lab′rə tôr′ē) ***noun*** a room or building where scientific work is carried on or where chemicals, drugs, or other substances are prepared.
lab·o·ra·to·ry • ***noun**, plural* **laboratories**

Labor Day ***noun*** the first Monday in September. It is a legal holiday that honors working people.

lace (lās) ***noun*** **1** a piece of string that is put through the holes or around the hooks of a shoe or boot. The lace is pulled and tied so that the shoe or boot stays on the foot. **2** a delicate fabric of fine thread woven into fancy designs with many open spaces.
verb to pull together and fasten with a lace [He *laced* his boots.]
lace • ***noun**, plural* **laces** • ***verb*** **laced, lacing**

lack (lak) ***noun*** a need for something that is missing; shortage [A *lack* of money forced him to skip lunch.]
verb **1** to be without or have too little of; need [The soil *lacked* nitrogen.] **2** to be missing

a	cat	ō	go	ʉ	fur	ə =	a *in* ago
ā	ape	ô	law, for	ch	chin		e *in* agent
ä	cot, car	oo	look	sh	she		i *in* pencil
e	ten	ōō	tool	th	thin		o *in* atom
ē	me	oi	oil	*th*	then		u *in* circus
i	fit	ou	out	zh	measure		
ī	ice	u	up	ŋ	ring		

[The book *lacks* several pages.]
lack • *noun, plural* **lacks** • *verb* **lacked, lacking**

lacquer (lak′ər) *noun* a liquid that is put on wood or metal to give it a glossy finish.
verb to put lacquer on [She *lacquered* the chair.]
lac·quer • *noun, plural* **lacquers** • *verb* **lacquered, lacquering**

lacrosse (lə krôs′) *noun* a game played by two teams on a field with a goal at each end. The players use webbed rackets on long handles to throw, catch, and carry a ball.
la·crosse • *noun*

lad (lad) *noun* a boy or young man.
lad • *noun, plural* **lads**

ladder (lad′ər) *noun* a wooden or metal framework for climbing up to high places. It has two long pieces like rails that are connected by a series of rungs or steps.
lad·der • *noun, plural* **ladders**

ladder

laden (lād′n) *adjective* having or carrying a load; burdened [shoppers *laden* with packages].
lad·en • *adjective*

ladle (lād′əl) *noun* a spoon that is like a cup with a long handle. It is used for dipping out liquids from a pot or other container.
la·dle • *noun, plural* **ladles**

lady (lād′ē) *noun* **1** a woman, especially a woman who is polite and refined. **2 Lady** in Britain, a title given to some women of high rank.
la·dy • *noun, plural* **ladies**

WORD HISTORY

lady

We get **lady** from a thousand-year-old English word that means "one who makes the bread." This was a way of saying that a woman was in charge of a household. As you can see, the meaning of **lady** is now very different.

ladybug (lād′ē bug′) *noun* a small, round, flying beetle. Its back is brightly colored with dark spots.
la·dy·bug • *noun, plural* **ladybugs**

ladybug

Lafayette (lä′fē et′), Marquis **de** (də) 1757-1834; French general who served in the American Revolutionary army.
La·fa·yette, Marquis **de**

lag (lag) *verb* to move so slowly as to fall behind [If you *lag* behind, you might get lost.]
noun **1** the act of falling behind. **2** the amount by which someone or something falls behind or comes in late [There will be a two-week *lag* in filling these orders.]
lag • *verb* **lagged, lagging** • *noun, plural* **lags**

lagoon (lə gōōn′) *noun* a pond or shallow lake that joins a larger body of water.
la·goon • *noun, plural* **lagoons**

laid (lād) *verb past tense and past participle of* **lay**[1].

lain (lān) *verb past participle of* **lie**[1].
● The words **lain** and **lane** sound alike.
The book had *lain* there on the table.
Avoid driving in the passing *lane*.

lair (ler) *noun* the resting place of a wild animal; den.
lair • *noun, plural* **lairs**

lake (lāk) *noun* a large body of water surrounded by land.
lake • *noun, plural* **lakes**

lamb (lam) *noun* **1** a young sheep. **2** its meat, used as food.
lamb • *noun, plural* **lambs** or **lamb**

lame (lām) *adjective* **1** having a hurt leg or foot that causes a limp [The old man is *lame*.] **2** stiff and very painful [a *lame* back]. **3** not good enough; poor or weak [a *lame* excuse].
lame • *adjective* **lamer, lamest**

lamp (lamp) *noun* a device that gives off light. Some lamps work by electricity and hold light bulbs. Other lamps burn a fuel, such as gas or oil.
lamp • *noun, plural* **lamps**

lance (lans) *noun* a weapon that is like a long spear with a handle at the end. It was used for fighting on horseback.
lance • *noun, plural* **lances**

L

Lancelot (lan′sə lät) the bravest knight of King Arthur's Round Table.
Lan·ce·lot

land (land) ***noun*** **1** the solid part of the earth's surface [by *land* or by sea]. **2** a country or region [one's native *land*]. **3** ground or soil [fertile *land*].
verb **1** to put or go on shore from a ship [The ship *landed* its cargo. The Marines *landed*.] **2** to bring an aircraft down to the ground. **3** to come down after flying, jumping, or falling [The cat *landed* on its feet.] **4** to catch [We *landed* three fish.]
land • ***noun**, plural for sense 2 only* **lands** • ***verb*** **landed, landing**

landing (lan′diŋ) ***noun*** **1** the act of coming to shore or putting on shore [The *landing* of the troops took all morning.] **2** a place where a ship or boat can land; pier or dock. **3** a platform at the end of a flight of stairs. **4** the act of coming down after flying, jumping, or falling [The damaged plane made a safe *landing*.]
land·ing • ***noun**, plural* **landings**

landing field ***noun*** a field with a smooth surface, used by airplanes for landing and taking off.
landing field • ***noun**, plural* **landing fields**

landing gear ***noun*** something, such as wheels or pontoons, underneath an aircraft that supports it for landing.

landlady (land′lād′ē) ***noun*** a woman who owns land, a house, an apartment, or other property that she rents to others.
land·la·dy • ***noun**, plural* **landladies**

landlocked (land′läkt) ***adjective*** shut in on all sides or nearly all sides by land [Switzerland is a *landlocked* country.]
land·locked • ***adjective***

landlord (land′lôrd) ***noun*** a person, especially a man, who owns land, a house, an apartment, or other property and rents it to others.
land·lord • ***noun**, plural* **landlords**

landmark (land′märk) ***noun*** **1** a building, hill, tree, or other feature that is familiar and serves as a guide. **2** an important building or place [The Statue of Liberty is a New York *landmark*.]
land·mark • ***noun**, plural* **landmarks**

landscape (land′skāp) ***noun*** **1** a large area of natural scenery that can be seen in one view [the striking *landscape* of the desert]. **2** a picture of such scenery [She painted a mountain *landscape*.]
verb to make a piece of ground more attractive by adding trees, shrubs, grass, or other plants.
land·scape • ***noun**, plural* **landscapes** • ***verb*** **landscaped, landscaping**

landslide (land′slīd) ***noun*** **1** a great mass of rocks and earth sliding down the side of a hill. **2** the winning of an election by a great majority of the votes.
land·slide • ***noun**, plural* **landslides**

lane (lān) ***noun*** **1** a narrow path between hedges, walls, or buildings; a narrow country road or city street. **2** a route for cars going in the same direction [a two-*lane* highway]. **3** the long stretch of polished wood down which the balls are rolled in bowling; alley.
lane • ***noun**, plural* **lanes**
● The words **lane** and **lain** sound alike.
Avoid driving in the passing *lane*.
The book had *lain* there on the table.

language (laŋ′gwij) ***noun*** **1** human speech [People communicate by means of *language*.] **2** writing that stands for human speech. **3** the speech of a certain nation, group, or people [the English *language*]. **4** anything that a person can use to express thoughts or feelings to others [sign *language*]. **5** a system of symbols, numbers, and letters for use in working with information in a computer.
lan·guage • ***noun**, plural* **languages**

lanky (laŋk′ē) ***adjective*** tall and slender in an awkward way [a *lanky* cowboy] —Look for the WORD CHOICES box at the entry **lean**[2].
lank·y • ***adjective*** **lankier, lankiest**

Lansing (lan′siŋ) the capital of Michigan.
Lan·sing

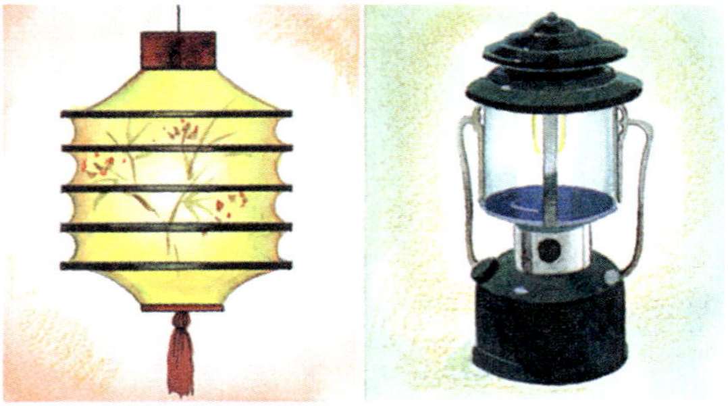

lantern
Two kinds of lantern

a cat	ō go	ʉ fur	ə = a *in* ago
ā ape	ô law, for	ch chin	e *in* agent
ä cot, car	oo look	sh she	i *in* pencil
e ten	ōō tool	th thin	o *in* atom
ē me	oi oil	*th* then	u *in* circus
i fit	ou out	zh measure	
ī ice	u up	ŋ ring	

lantern (lan′tərn) ***noun*** a case of glass, paper, or other material that holds a light and protects it from wind and rain.
lan·tern • ***noun,*** *plural* **lanterns**

Laos (lous *or* lä′ōs) a country south of central China.
La·os

lap[1] (lap) ***noun*** **1** the front part of a person sitting down, from the waist to the knees. **2** one complete trip around a track [They fell behind in the third *lap* of the race.]
verb to put something so that it lies partly on something else [*Lap* each row of shingles over the row before.]
lap • ***noun,*** *plural* **laps** • ***verb*** **lapped, lapping**

lap[2] (lap) ***verb*** **1** to drink by dipping up with the tip of the tongue as a dog or cat does. **2** to hit against with a gentle splash [Waves *lapped* the shore.]
noun the act or sound of lapping.
lap • ***verb*** **lapped, lapping** • ***noun,*** *plural* **laps**

lapel (lə pel′) ***noun*** either of the front parts of a coat or jacket that are folded back.
la·pel • ***noun,*** *plural* **lapels**

lapse (laps) ***noun*** **1** a small mistake or slip; fault [a *lapse* of memory]. **2** a period of time between events; interval [a *lapse* of five years].
verb to fall or slip into some condition [He *lapsed* into his old, lazy habits.]
lapse • ***noun,*** *plural* **lapses** • ***verb*** **lapsed, lapsing**

laptop

laptop (lap′täp) ***noun*** a computer that is small and light enough to rest on a person's lap. Laptops can run on power from batteries.
lap·top • ***noun,*** *plural* **laptops**

larch (lärch) ***noun*** a kind of pine tree that has leaves shaped like needles that are shed every year.
larch • ***noun,*** *plural* **larches**

lard (lärd) ***noun*** the fat of pigs or hogs, melted down for use in cooking.

larder (lärd′ər) ***noun*** a place in a home where food is kept.
lard·er • ***noun,*** *plural* **larders**

large (lärj) ***adjective*** being of great size or amount [a *large* house; a *large* sum of money].
adverb in a large way [Don't write so *large*.]
large • ***adjective*** & • ***adverb*** **larger, largest**

WORD CHOICES

Synonyms of **large**

The words **large, big,** and **great** share the meaning "of more than usual size."

a *large* room
a *big* boulder
a *great* river

large intestine ***noun*** the thicker and lower section of the intestine. It absorbs water from digested food.
large intestine • ***noun,*** *plural* **large intestines**

largely (lärj′lē) ***adverb*** for the most part; mostly; mainly [Pat is *largely* to blame for the fight.]
large·ly • ***adverb***

lariat (ler′ē ət) ***noun*** *another name for* **lasso**.
lar·i·at • ***noun,*** *plural* **lariats**

lark[1] (lärk) ***noun*** any of a group of birds of Europe. The lark often sings as it flies high in the air.
lark • ***noun,*** *plural* **larks**

lark[2] (lärk) ***noun*** something, such as a prank, done for fun.
lark • ***noun,*** *plural* **larks**

lariat

L

larva (lär′və) *noun* the young form of an insect or some animals without a backbone. A larva looks like a worm and has no wings. A caterpillar is the larva of a butterfly.
lar·va • *noun, plural* **larvae** (lär′vē) or **larvas**

laryngitis (ler′in jīt′is) *noun* a condition in which the larynx is sore and swollen. In this condition the voice is often lost for a while.
lar·yn·gi·tis • *noun*

larynx (ler′iŋks) *noun* the upper end of the windpipe. It contains the vocal cords.
lar·ynx • *noun, plural* **larynxes**

La Salle (lə sal′), **Robert** (räb′ərt) 1643-1687; French explorer in North America.
La Salle, Rob·ert

laser (lā′zər) *noun* a device that sends out a very narrow and strong beam of light. Laser beams can drill holes in diamonds and perform delicate eye surgery.
la·ser • *noun, plural* **lasers**

lash[1] (lash) *noun* **1** a whip, especially the part that strikes the blow [The prisoner felt the sting of the *lash*.] **2** a blow or stroke with a whip [The prisoner was given ten *lashes*.] **3** an eyelash.
verb **1** to strike or make move with a whip [The cruel driver *lashed* the horses.] **2** to strike with force; beat [Waves *lash* against the rocks.] —Look for the WORD CHOICES box at the entry **beat**.
lash • *noun, plural* **lashes** • *verb* **lashed, lashing**

lash[2] (lash) *verb* to fasten or tie with a rope, cord, string, or some similar material [During the storm, the sail was *lashed* to the mast.]
lash • *verb* **lashed, lashing**

lass (las) *noun* a girl or young woman.
lass • *noun, plural* **lasses**

lasso (las′ō *for n.;* la sōō′ *for v.*) *noun* a long rope with a sliding loop at one end. It is used to catch horses or cattle.
verb to catch with a lasso [She *lassoed* the cow.]
las·so • *noun, plural* **lassos** or **lassoes** • *verb* **lassoed, lassoing, lassoes**

last[1] (last) *adjective* **1** being or coming after all others [the *last* month of the year; the *last* word in an argument]. **2** being the only one left [the *last* cookie]. **3** being the one just before this one in time [I was ill *last* week.] **4** being the least likely or expected [He's the *last* person I would invite.]
adverb **1** after all others [Our team came in *last*.] **2** most recently [When did you see them *last?*]
noun **1** someone or something which comes last [The *last* of the guests has left.] **2** the end [They were friends to the *last*.]
—**at last** after a long time [*At last* we reached the top of the hill.]

last[2] (last) *verb* **1** to go on; continue [The play *lasts* only an hour.] **2** to stay in good condition; wear well [Stone *lasts* longer than wood.]
last • *verb* **lasted, lasting**

lasting (las′tiŋ) *adjective* continuing a long time [a *lasting* peace].
last·ing • *adjective*

Last Supper the last meal eaten by Jesus with the Apostles before his death on the cross.

Las Vegas (läs vā′gəs) a city in southeastern Nevada.
Las Ve·gas

latch (lach) *noun* a simple fastening for a door, window, or gate. It usually is a bar that falls into a notch. Modern locks on doors are now often called latches.
verb to fasten with a latch [*Latch* the door.]
latch • *noun, plural* **latches** • *verb* **latched, latching**

late (lāt) *adjective* **1** happening or coming after the usual or expected time; tardy [*late* for school; a *late* bus]. **2** being near or toward the end of some period [He arrived in the *late* afternoon.] **3** happening or appearing just before now; recent [His *latest* book sold well.] **4** having recently died [my *late* grandmother] —Look for the WORD CHOICES box at the entry **dead**.
adverb **1** after the usual or expected time [Last year the roses bloomed *late*.] **2** toward the end of some period [The game will take place *late* in the day.] **3** recently [I saw them as *late* as yesterday.]
late • *adjective* & • *adverb* **later, latest**

lately (lāt′lē) *adverb* just before this time; not long ago; recently [She has been cheerful *lately*.]
late·ly • *adverb*

lateral (lat′ər əl) *adjective* of, at, from, or toward the side; sideways [a *lateral* movement].

a	cat	ō	go	ʉ	fur	ə =	a *in* ago
ā	ape	ô	law, for	ch	chin		e *in* agent
ä	cot, car	oo	look	sh	she		i *in* pencil
e	ten	ōō	tool	th	thin		o *in* atom
ē	me	oi	oil	*th*	then		u *in* circus
i	fit	ou	out	zh	measure		
ī	ice	u	up	ŋ	ring		

noun a short pass in football that goes to the side or in a slightly backward direction.
lat·er·al • ***adjective*** • ***noun,*** *plural* **laterals**

lathe

lathe (lā*th*) ***noun*** a machine for shaping a piece of wood, metal, or other material. A lathe both holds the material and turns it rapidly against a sharp cutting tool.
lathe • ***noun,*** *plural* **lathes**

lather (la*th*′ər) ***noun*** **1** foam made by mixing soap and water. **2** sweat that is like foam, especially on a horse after a race.
verb **1** to cover with lather [He *lathered* his face and shaved.] **2** to form lather [Few soaps *lather* in salt water.]
lath·er • ***noun,*** *plural* **lathers**
• ***verb*** **lathered, lathering**

Latin (lat′n) ***noun*** **1** the language of the ancient Romans. **2** a person who speaks a language developed from Latin. Spaniards, Italians, Portuguese, and the French are Latins.
adjective **1** of or having to do with the language of the ancient Romans [a *Latin* inscription]. **2** having to do with the languages that developed from Latin or with the peoples who speak them or their cultures [*Latin* America].
Lat·in • ***noun*** • ***adjective***

Latin America all the countries in the Western Hemisphere that are south of the U.S., where Spanish, Portuguese, and French are spoken.

latitude (lat′i to͞od *or* lat′i tyo͞od) ***noun*** distance north or south from the equator. Latitude is measured in degrees [Minneapolis is at 45 degrees north *latitude*.]
lat·i·tude • ***noun,*** *plural* **latitudes**

latter (lat′ər) ***adjective*** **1** nearer the end or last part; later [the *latter* part of June]. **2** being the second of the two just mentioned [I'd like the *latter* book.] This word is also often used as a noun with *the* [I like both football and baseball but I prefer the *latter*.]
lat·ter • ***adjective***

Latvia (lat′vē ə) a country in northeastern Europe, south of Estonia.
Lat·vi·a

laugh (laf) ***verb*** to make a series of quick sounds with the voice that show amusement or scorn.
noun the act or sound of laughing.
—laugh at **1** to be amused by something or someone. **2** to make fun of.
laugh • ***verb*** **laughed, laughing** • ***noun,*** *plural* **laughs**

WORD CHOICES

Synonyms of **laugh**

Many words share the meaning "to make sounds showing that one is happy or amused."

chortle — giggle — titter
chuckle — snicker

laughable (laf′ə bəl) ***adjective*** causing laughter —Look for the WORD CHOICES box at the entry **funny**.
laugh·a·ble • ***adjective***

laughter (laf′tər) ***noun*** the act or sound of laughing.
laugh·ter • ***noun***

launch[1] (lônch *or* länch) ***verb*** **1** to throw, hurl, or send off with some kind of force [We *launched* a rocket into space.] **2** to cause to slide into the water; set afloat [A new ship was *launched* yesterday.] **3** to start or begin [They *launched* a campaign against drugs.]
noun the act of launching something [The rocket *launch* is scheduled for tomorrow.]
launch • ***verb*** **launched, launching** • ***noun,*** *plural* **launches**

launch[2] (lônch *or* länch) ***noun*** an open or partly enclosed motorboat.
launch • ***noun,*** *plural* **launches**

launch pad or **launching pad** ***noun*** the platform from which a rocket or missile is launched.

launch pad or **launching pad** • *noun, plural* **launch pads** or **launching pads**

laundromat (lôn′drə mat *or* län′drə mat) *noun* a laundry where a person pays to use machines for washing and drying clothes.
laun·dro·mat • *noun, plural* **laundromats**

laundry (lôn′drē *or* län′drē) *noun* **1** a place where clothes are washed and ironed. **2** clothes, linens, and other items that have been, or are about to be, washed and ironed.
laun·dry • *noun, plural for sense 1 only* **laundries**

laurel (lôr′əl) *noun* **1** an evergreen tree or shrub with large, glossy leaves. The ancient Greeks crowned winners of contests with wreaths of laurel leaves. **2 laurels** honor or victory.
lau·rel • *noun, plural* **laurels**

lava (lä′və *or* lav′ə) *noun* **1** hot, melted rock pouring out of a volcano. **2** the rock formed when this substance has cooled and is solid.
la·va • *noun*

lavatory (lav′ə tôr′ē) *noun* a room with a toilet and a basin for washing the hands and face.
lav·a·to·ry • *noun, plural* **lavatories**

lavender (lav′ən dər) *noun* **1** a sweet-smelling plant of the mint family, with pale-purple flowers. **2** pale purple.
lav·en·der • *noun, plural* **lavenders**

lavender

lavish (lav′ish) *adjective* much more than enough; very generous in amount [*lavish* decorations; a *lavish* allowance].
verb to give or spend in a generous way [They *lavished* attention on their children.]
lav·ish • *adjective* • *verb* **lavished, lavishing**

law (lô *or* lä) *noun* **1** a body of rules that tells people what they must or must not do [The Constitution is the supreme *law* of the land.] **2** any one of these rules. **3** the profession of lawyers and judges.
law • *noun, plural* **laws**

lawful (lô′fəl *or* lä′fəl) *adjective* permitted or recognized by law [a *lawful* act; a *lawful* claim].
law·ful • *adjective*

lawn (lôn *or* län) *noun* ground covered with grass that is cut short. Houses and parks have lawns.
lawn • *noun, plural* **lawns**

lawn mower

lawn mower *noun* a machine with steel blades that turn for cutting the grass of a lawn.
lawn mower • *noun, plural* **lawn mowers**

lawsuit (lô′so͞ot *or* lä′so͞ot) *noun* a case brought before a law court by one person or group against another to settle a dispute between them.
law·suit • *noun, plural* **lawsuits**

lawyer (lô′yər *or* lä′yər) *noun* a person whose profession is giving others advice on law or representing them in a law court.
law·yer • *noun, plural* **lawyers**

lay[1] (lā) *verb* **1** to put down so as to rest on, in, or against something [*Lay* your books on the shelf.] **2** to knock down [One blow *laid* me low.] **3** to put down in a special way; set in place [They hired two workers to *lay* the carpet.] **4** to bring forth an egg.
—**lay aside** or **lay by** to put away for future use; save. —**lay away** **1** to lay aside; save. **2** to set merchandise aside until it is paid for.
—**lay off** to put a person out of work especially for a short time.
lay • *verb* **laid, laying**
● The words **lay** and **lei** sound alike.
Lay the tools down on the ground.
The mummy *lay* in the tomb for centuries.
The *lei* is a Hawaiian wreath.

lay[2] (lā) *verb past tense of* **lie**[1].
● The words **lay** and **lei** sound alike.

layer (lā′ər) *noun* a single thickness, fold, coating, or section [a cake with two *layers*].
lay·er • *noun, plural* **layers**

a	cat	ō	go	ʉ	fur	ə =	a *in* ago
ā	ape	ô	law, for	ch	chin		e *in* agent
ä	cot, car	o͝o	look	sh	she		i *in* pencil
e	ten	o͞o	tool	th	thin		o *in* atom
ē	me	oi	oil	*th*	then		u *in* circus
i	fit	ou	out	zh	measure		
ī	ice	u	up	ŋ	ring		

layoff (lā′ôf) ***noun*** **1** the act of putting a person or a group of people out of work. A layoff is usually only for a short time. **2** this period of time.
lay·off • ***noun,*** *plural* **layoffs**

lazy (lā′zē) ***adjective*** not eager or willing to work or try hard [a *lazy* person].
la·zy • ***adjective*** **lazier, laziest**

lb. *abbreviation for* **1** pound. **2** pounds.

lead[1] (lēd) ***verb*** **1** to show the way for; guide [*Lead* us to the path. The lights *led* me through the house.] **2** to go or cause to go in some direction [This path *leads* to the lake. Pipes *lead* the water to a ditch.] **3** to be at the head of or be first [She *leads* the band. Their team was *leading* at the half.] **4** to live [The homeless *lead* a hard life.]
noun **1** the first place or position [The gray horse took the *lead*.] **2** example [Let's follow her *lead*.] **3** the amount or distance that one is ahead [Our team has a six-point *lead*.] **4** a clue [The police followed every *lead*.] **5** the most important role in a play or movie.
lead • ***verb*** **led, leading** • ***noun,*** *plural* **leads**

lead[2] (led) ***noun*** **1** a heavy, silvery-gray metal that is a chemical element. It is soft and easily shaped and is used to make pipes and solder. **2** a thin stick of graphite or other substance, used in pencils.
lead • ***noun,*** *plural for sense 2 only* **leads**
● The words **lead** and **led** sound alike.
The *lead* in my pencil is broken.
He *led* the soldiers into battle.

leaden (led′n) ***adjective*** **1** made of lead. **2** having a dull gray color [a *leaden* sky].
lead·en • ***adjective***

leader (lēd′ər) ***noun*** a person or thing that leads or guides.
lead·er • ***noun,*** *plural* **leaders**

leadership (lēd′ər ship) ***noun*** ability or skill as a leader.
lead·er·ship • ***noun***

leaf (lēf) ***noun*** **1** any of the flat, green parts growing from the stem of a plant or tree. **2** a sheet of paper in a book [Each side of a *leaf* is a page.] **3** a board hinged to a table or put into a table top, to make it larger.
verb **1** to grow leaves. **2** to turn the pages of [She *leafed* casually through her book.]
leaf • ***noun,*** *plural* **leaves** • ***verb*** **leafed, leafing**

leaf
Of a table

leaflet (lēf′lət) ***noun*** **1** a sheet of printed matter that is folded once or twice; a booklet or pamphlet. **2** a small or young leaf.
leaf·let • ***noun,*** *plural* **leaflets**

leafy (lēf′ē) ***adjective*** made up of many leaves or having many leaves [a *leafy* vegetable].
leaf·y • ***adjective*** **leafier, leafiest**

league[1] (lēg) ***noun*** a number of persons, groups, or nations joined together to help one another, or for some other purpose [a bowling *league*].
league • ***noun,*** *plural* **leagues**

league[2] (lēg) ***noun*** an old measure of distance, usually equal to about three miles.
league • ***noun,*** *plural* **leagues**

leak (lēk) ***verb*** **1** to let water, air, gas, or some other fluid substance in or out by accident [The roof *leaks* when it rains. The oven is *leaking* gas.] **2** to go in or come out by accident [The air in the tire *leaked* out through the valve.] **3** to become known little by little or by accident [The truth *leaked* out.]
noun a hole, crack, or other opening that lets something in or out by accident.
leak • ***verb*** **leaked, leaking** • ***noun,*** *plural* **leaks**
● The words **leak** and **leek** sound alike.
Can you fix the *leak* in the boat?
She cooked *leek* and potato soup.

lean[1] (lēn) ***verb*** **1** to bend or slant so as to rest upon something [Pedro *leaned* against the desk. *Lean* the ladder against the house.] **2** to bend to one side; stand at a slant [The tree *leans* over the creek.] **3** to depend on for advice, comfort, or some other kind of help

L

[She *leans* on her brother when she feels down.]
lean • *verb* **leaned, leaning**

lean[2] (lēn) ***adjective*** **1** with little flesh or fat; thin [a *lean* athlete]. **2** containing little or no fat [*lean* meat].
lean • ***adjective*** **leaner, leanest**

WORD CHOICES

Synonyms of lean

The words **lean, gaunt,** and **lanky** share the meaning "having little or no fat."

a *lean*, healthy athlete
the invalid's *gaunt* body
an awkward, *lanky* teenager

leap (lēp) ***verb*** to jump; spring [The cat *leaped* into my lap.]
noun the act of leaping; a jump.
leap • ***verb*** **leaped** or **leapt, leaping** • ***noun,*** *plural* **leaps**

leapfrog (lēp′frôg) ***noun*** a game in which each player takes a turn jumping over the backs of the other players. The other players are all bending over, one in front of the other.
leap·frog • ***noun***

leapfrog

leapt (lept *or* lēpt) ***verb*** *a past tense and a past participle of* **leap**.

leap year ***noun*** a year of 366 days. The extra day falls in February, which has 29 days in a leap year. The next five leap years will be 2000, 2004, 2008, 2012, and 2016.
leap year • ***noun,*** *plural* **leap years**

learn (lʉrn) ***verb*** **1** to get some knowledge or skill by studying or by being taught [I have *learned* to knit.] **2** to find out about something; come to know [I just *learned* about his accident.] **3** to fix in the mind; memorize [*Learn* this poem by tomorrow.]
learn • ***verb*** **learned** or **learnt, learning**

learned (lʉrn′əd) ***adjective*** full of knowledge or learning [a *learned* professor; a *learned* book].
learn·ed • ***adjective***

learning (lʉrn′iŋ) ***noun*** knowledge that is gained by careful study.
learn·ing • ***noun***

learnt (lʉrnt) ***verb*** *a past tense and a past participle of* **learn**.

lease (lēs) ***noun*** **1** an agreement by which an owner rents a house, a car, or other property to someone else. A lease lasts for a certain period of time and is set at a certain price. **2** the period of time a lease agreement lasts [a three-year *lease*].
verb to give or get by means of a lease; rent [I *leased* this car for a week.]
lease • ***noun,*** *plural* **leases** • ***verb*** **leased, leasing**

leash (lēsh) ***noun*** a strap or chain by which a dog or other animal is led or held.
verb to put a leash on [*Leash* the dog before opening the door.]
leash • ***noun,*** *plural* **leashes** • ***verb*** **leashed, leashing**

least (lēst) ***adjective*** **1** *a superlative of* **little**. **2** smallest in size, amount, or importance [He didn't show the *least* interest in going.]
adverb **1** *superlative of* **little**. **2** in the smallest way or amount [the *least* attractive fabric].
noun the smallest in amount, size, or importance [The *least* you can do is apologize.]
—at least in any case [*At least* I tried.]

leather (le*th*′ər) ***noun*** a material made from the skin of cows, horses, goats, or other animals by cleaning and tanning it.
leath·er • ***noun,*** *plural* **leathers**

leathery (le*th*′ər ē) ***adjective*** like leather; tough or tan-colored [*leathery* skin].
leath·er·y • ***adjective*** **leatherier, leatheriest**

leave[1] (lēv) ***verb*** **1** to go away or go from [Rosa *left* early. Anthony *leaves* the house at 8 p.m.] **2** to stop living in, working at, or belonging to [He *left* his job at the grocery store.] **3** to let stay or be [*Leave* the door open.] **4** to cause to remain behind [He *left* his name with the receptionist. They *left* footprints on the floor.] **5** to let another do something; entrust: used

a	cat	ō	go	ʉ	fur	ə =	a *in* ago
ā	ape	ô	law, for	ch	chin		e *in* agent
ä	cot, car	oo	look	sh	she		i *in* pencil
e	ten	ōō	tool	th	thin		o *in* atom
ē	me	oi	oil	*th*	then		u *in* circus
i	fit	ou	out	zh	measure		
ī	ice	u	up	ŋ	ring		

with *to* or *up to* [They *leave* such decisions to me.] **6** to give as a remainder in subtraction [Five minus two *leaves* three.] **7** to give at one's death; to give by a will [She *left* her money to charity.]
—**leave off** to stop [We started the lecture where we had *left off* the day before.]
—**leave out** to fail to include [Whoever made the list *left out* my name.]
leave • *verb* **left, leaving**

leave[2] (lēv) *noun* **1** permission [May I have your *leave* to go?] **2** permission to be absent [She was granted *leave* by the lieutenant.]
leave • *noun, plural* **leaves**

leaves (lēvz) *noun plural of* **leaf**.

Lebanon (leb′ə nän) a country at the eastern end of the Mediterranean, north of Israel.
Leb·a·non

lecture (lek′chər) *noun* **1** a talk on some subject to an audience or class. **2** a long or tiresome scolding.
verb **1** to give a lecture [College professors often *lecture* to their classes.] **2** to scold [My parents *lectured* me about jaywalking.]
lec·ture • *noun, plural* **lectures**
• *verb* **lectured, lecturing**

led (led) *verb past tense and past participle of* **lead**[1].
● The words **led** and **lead** sound alike.
He *led* the soldiers into battle.
The *lead* in my pencil is broken.

ledge (lej) *noun* a flat part like a narrow shelf that comes out from a cliff or wall [a *ledge* of rock; a window *ledge*].
ledge • *noun, plural* **ledges**

lee (lē) *noun* the side of anything away from the wind [The cows stood in the *lee* of the barn.]

Lee (lē), **Robert E.** (räb′ərt) 1807-1870; commander in chief of the Confederate army in the Civil War.
Lee, Rob·ert E.

leech (lēch) *noun* a worm that lives in water or wet earth and sucks blood from animals. Leeches were once used in medicine to draw blood from people.
leech • *noun, plural* **leeches**

leek (lēk) *noun* a vegetable like a thick green onion, but with a milder taste.
leek • *noun, plural* **leeks**
● The words **leek** and **leak** sound alike.
He cooked *leek* and potato soup.
Can you fix the *leak* in the boat?

left

left[1] (left) *adjective* on or to the side that is toward the west when a person faces north [the *left* hand; a *left* turn].
noun **1** the left side [Forks are placed to the *left* of the plate.] **2** a turn toward the left side [Take a *left* at the next intersection.]
adverb on or toward the left hand or side [Turn *left* here.]

left[2] (left) *verb past tense and past participle of* **leave**[1].

left-hand (left′hand′) *adjective* **1** on or to the left [the *left-hand* side of the street]. **2** of, for, or with the left hand [a *left-hand* pitch].

left-handed (left′han′dəd) *adjective* **1** using the left hand more easily than the right [Some people are *left-handed*.] **2** done with the left hand [a *left-handed* throw]. **3** made for people who are left-handed [*left-handed* scissors].
left-hand·ed • *adjective*

leftover (left′ō vər) *noun* **1** something left over. **2** *usually* **leftovers** food left over from a meal and, often, eaten at a later meal.
left·o·ver • *noun, plural* **leftovers**

leg (leg) *noun* **1** one of the parts of the body that is used for standing and walking. **2** one of the parts of a pair of slacks, trousers, pants, or stockings that cover the legs. **3** anything like a leg in looks or use [the *legs* of a chair]. **4** a stage in a trip, race, or some other course [the last *leg* of a race].
leg • *noun, plural* **legs**

legacy (leg′ə sē) *noun* **1** money or property left to someone by a will. **2** anything handed down from an ancestor.
leg·a·cy • *noun, plural* **legacies**

legal (lē′gəl) *adjective* **1** based on or allowed by law; lawful [Is it *legal* to park here?] **2** of

L

or having to do with lawyers or the law [the *legal* profession; *legal* advice].
le·gal • *adjective*

legend (lej′ənd) *noun* **1** a story that is handed down through the years. A legend is connected with some real events but it probably is not true in itself. **2** a title or description under a picture or map in a book.
leg·end • *noun, plural* **legends**

legendary (lej′ən der′ē) *adjective* having to do with a legend or legends [a *legendary* castle].
leg·end·ar·y • *adjective*

legible (lej′i bəl) *adjective* clear enough to be read easily [*legible* handwriting].
leg·i·ble • *adjective*

legion (lē′jən) *noun* **1** any large group of soldiers; army. **2** a large number [A *legion* of fans waited for the star in front of the theater.]
le·gion • *noun, plural* **legions**

legislation (lej′is lā′shən) *noun* **1** the act or process of making laws. **2** the law or laws made [*Legislation* to clean polluted rivers was passed by the Congress.]
leg·is·la·tion • *noun*

legislative (lej′is lāt′iv) *adjective* having to do with making laws [Congress is the *legislative* branch of the U.S. government.]
leg·is·la·tive • *adjective*

legislator (lej′is lāt′ər) *noun* a member of a congress, parliament, or other group that makes laws.
leg·is·la·tor • *noun, plural* **legislators**

legislature (lej′is lā′chər) *noun* a congress, parliament, or other group of people with the power to make and change laws.
leg·is·la·ture • *noun, plural* **legislatures**

legitimate (lə jit′i mət) *adjective* **1** according to or allowed by law; lawful [Mr. Smith is the *legitimate* owner of the farm, not his cousin.] **2** according to what is right; reasonable [a *legitimate* complaint].
le·git·i·mate • *adjective*

legume (leg′yo͞om *or* li gyo͞om′) *noun* any plant of a large family with seeds growing in pods. Peas, beans, and lentils are legumes.
leg·ume • *noun, plural* **legumes**

lei (lā *or* lā′ē) *noun* a wreath of flowers, often worn around the neck in Hawaii.
lei • *noun, plural* **leis**

● The words **lei** and **lay** sound alike.
The *lei* contained pink flowers.
Lay the tools down on the ground.
I *lay* on the bed but could not sleep.

leisure (lē′zhər) *noun* free time that is not taken up with work, study, or other duties. Leisure may be used by a person for rest or recreation.
lei·sure • *noun*

lemon

lemon (lem′ən) *noun* **1** a small citrus fruit that has a yellow skin and a juicy, sour pulp. **2** the tree that this fruit grows on.
lem·on • *noun, plural* **lemons**

lemonade (lem ən ād′) *noun* a drink made of lemon juice, sugar, and water.
lem·on·ade • *noun, plural* **lemonades**

lend (lend) *verb* **1** to let someone use something for a while [Will you *lend* me your umbrella?] **2** to let someone have a sum of money that must be paid back with interest [The bank *lent* her money to buy a car.]
lend • *verb* **lent, lending**

length (leŋkth) *noun* **1** the measure of how long a thing is; distance from one end to the other end [a rope 20 feet in *length*]. **2** a piece of a certain length [a *length* of pipe]. **3** the amount or extent measured from beginning to end [a class 30 minutes in *length*].
length • *noun, plural* **lengths**

lengthen (leŋk′thən) *verb* to make or become longer —Look for the WORD CHOICES box at the entry **extend**.
length·en • *verb* **lengthened, lengthening**

lengthwise (leŋkth′wīz) *adverb* in the direction of the length [Carry the box in *lengthwise*.] This word can also be used as an adjective [Please give me the precise *lengthwise* measurement.]
length·wise • *adverb*

lengthy (leŋk′thē) *adjective* long or too long [a *lengthy* speech; a *lengthy* trip].
length·y • *adjective* **lengthier, lengthiest**

lens (lenz) *noun* **1** a piece of clear glass or plastic that is curved on one or both sides to make light rays move apart or come together.

a cat	ō go	ʉ fur	ə = a *in* ago
ā ape	ô law, for	ch chin	e *in* agent
ä cot, car	oo look	sh she	i *in* pencil
e ten	o͞o tool	th thin	o *in* atom
ē me	oi oil	*th* then	u *in* circus
i fit	ou out	zh measure	
ī ice	u up	ŋ ring	

Something looked at through a lens can become smaller or larger. Lenses are used in eyeglasses, cameras, microscopes, and magnifying glasses. **2** a clear part of the eye that helps the eye see things clearly.
lens • *noun, plural* **lenses**

WORD HISTORY

lens

This word comes without change from the Latin word *lens*, which means "lentil." A **lens** that has both of its sides curved slightly outward looks very much like a lentil seed.

lent (lent) ***verb*** *past tense and past participle of* **lend**.

Lent (lent) ***noun*** the forty weekdays that come before Easter. Lent is a time of fasting, praying, and repenting for sins.

lentil (lent′'l) ***noun*** a small, nearly flat seed that grows in pods and is used for food.
len·til • *noun, plural* **lentils**

leopard

leopard (lep′ərd) ***noun*** **1** a large wildcat that has a tan coat with black spots. It is found in Africa and Asia. **2** *another name for* **jaguar**.
leop·ard • *noun, plural* **leopards**

leotard (lē′ə tärd) ***noun*** a one-piece garment that fits close to the body. It is worn by dancers and gymnasts.
le·o·tard • *noun, plural* **leotards**

Lesotho (le sōō′tōō) a country in southern Africa, surrounded by South Africa.
Le·sot·ho

less (les) ***adjective*** **1** *a comparative of* **little**. **2** not so much; smaller in size or amount [drink *less* soda; take *less* time]. **3** fewer [6 is *less* than 8.]
adverb **1** *comparative of* **little**. **2** not so much; to a smaller or lower amount or extent [Please talk *less* and work more.]
noun a smaller amount [He ate *less* because he was not hungry.]
preposition minus [5 *less* 1 equals 4.]
—less and less to an ever smaller amount or extent [I like TV *less and less*.]

-less *a suffix meaning:* **1** without [A *worthless* thing is without worth, or value.] **2** not able or likely to [A *ceaseless* effort is not likely to cease.] **3** not capable of being or not likely to be [*Measureless* wealth is wealth that is so great that it cannot be measured.]

lessen (les′ən) ***verb*** to make or become less [Your help *lessens* my work. The rain *lessened*.]
less·en • ***verb*** **lessened, lessening**
- The words **lessen** and **lesson** sound alike.
  Remove the top box to *lessen* the load.
  Today's *lesson* was on the infinitive.

lesser (les′ər) ***adjective*** **1** *a comparative of* **little**. **2** smaller, less, or less important [a *lesser* evil].
less·er • ***adjective***

lesson (les′ən) ***noun*** **1** something to be learned, taught, or studied. **2** the teaching done during one class period [Our spelling *lesson* lasted only 15 minutes today.]
les·son • *noun, plural* **lessons**
- The words **lesson** and **lessen** sound alike.
  She learned her *lesson* about lying.
  Do you think the snow will *lessen* any?

SPELLING TIP

Use this memory aid to spell **lesson**.
Dad taught his ***son*** a les***son***.

let (let) ***verb*** *Let* can be both a main verb and a helping verb. **I.** When *let* is a main verb, it means: **1** to give permission to; allow [They *let* me help.] **2** to allow to pass, come, or go [*Let* them in.] **3** to cause to; make: usually used with *know* or *hear* [*Let* me know when you're ready. *Let* me hear from you when you get back.] **II.** When *let* is a helping verb, it is used to: **1** give commands [*Let* us give all that we can. *Let's* go now!] **2** make suggestions or dares [Just *let* them try to stop us!] The word

L

"to" is not used between the helping verb *let* and the verb that follows.
—let down to disappoint [She *let* me *down* by not phoning.] **—let off** to treat in a mild or gentle way [The noisy group was *let off* with a warning.] **—let on** [*an informal use*] to show that one is aware of something [Kim didn't *let on* that he was part of the joke.] **—let out** **1** to give forth; utter [She *let out* a scream.] **2** to make a garment larger [He *let out* the sleeves.] **—let up** to slow down or stop [After three days the rain *let up*.]
let • ***verb*** **let, letting**

WORD CHOICES

Synonyms of let

The words **let, allow,** and **permit** share the meaning "to give someone permission to do something."

Will you *let* us go to the zoo?

Honor students are *allowed* to miss exams.

I was *permitted* to see the prisoner.

-let *a suffix meaning* a small one of a certain kind of thing [A *booklet* is a small book.]

let's (lets) let us.

letter (let′ər) ***noun*** **1** a mark used in writing or printing that stands for a speech sound. There are 26 letters in the English alphabet. **2** a written message, usually sent by mail. **3** an emblem bearing the initials of a school or college that is given as a prize to students who have done well in sports.
verb to print letters of the alphabet by hand [She *lettered* a sign with bright red paint.]
let·ter • ***noun, plural*** **letters** • ***verb*** **lettered, lettering**

letter carrier ***noun*** a person who picks up and delivers mail.
letter carrier • ***noun, plural*** **letter carriers**

lettuce (let′əs) ***noun*** a plant with crisp, green leaves that are much used in salads.
let·tuce • ***noun, plural*** **lettuces**

lettuce

WORD HISTORY

lettuce

Our word **lettuce** comes from the Latin word for "milk." The root and stems of the lettuce plant contain a milky juice.

leukemia (lo͞o kē′mē ə) ***noun*** a disease that causes the body to form too many white blood cells.
leu·ke·mi·a • ***noun, plural*** **leukemias**

levee (lev′ē) ***noun*** **1** a bank built along a river to keep it from overflowing. **2** a landing place for ships, built along a river.
lev·ee • ***noun, plural*** **levees**

level (lev′əl) ***adjective*** **1** with no part higher than any other part; flat and even [a *level* piece of ground]. **2** as high as something else; even [The top of my head is *level* with his chin.]
noun **1** a tool for finding out if a surface is level. It is a frame with a small tube of liquid. A bubble in the liquid moves to the center of the tube when the frame is level. **2** height [The water rose to a *level* of five feet.] **3** a stage, degree, or rank [the reading *level* of sixth graders].
verb **1** to make level or flat [The worker *leveled* the ground with a bulldozer.] **2** to knock to the ground [The storm *leveled* many trees.]
—on the level [*a slang use*] honest and fair.
lev·el • ***adjective*** • ***noun, plural*** **levels** • ***verb*** **leveled** or **levelled, leveling** or **levelling**

lever (lev′ər *or* lē′vər) ***noun*** **1** a bar resting on a fulcrum, or support, that is pushed down at one end in order to lift a weight at the other end. A lever is a simple machine. **2** a bar that can be turned or moved to work something [This *lever* controls the speed of the machine.]
lev·er • ***noun, plural*** **levers**

Lewis (lo͞o′is), **Meriwether** (mer′i weth′ər) 1774-1809; U.S. explorer and leader, along with **William Clark**, of the Lewis and Clark expedition (1804-1806) to the northwestern part of the U.S.
Lew·is, Mer·i·weth·er

a	cat	ō	go	ʉ	fur	ə = a *in* ago		
ā	ape	ô	law, for	ch	chin	e *in* agent		
ä	cot, car	oo	look	sh	she	i *in* pencil		
e	ten	o͞o	tool	th	thin	o *in* atom		
ē	me	oi	oil	*th*	then	u *in* circus		
i	fit	ou	out	zh	measure			
ī	ice	u	up	ŋ	ring			

liable (lī′ə bəl) ***adjective*** **1** obliged by law to pay; responsible [The person who caused the accident is *liable* for the damage done.] **2** likely [Stray animals are *liable* to have fleas.]
li·a·ble • ***adjective***

liar (lī′ər) ***noun*** a person who tells lies.
li·ar • ***noun,*** *plural* **liars**

liberal (lib′ər əl) ***adjective*** **1** generous or plentiful [a *liberal* gift]. **2** open to new ideas; tolerant.
noun a person who is liberal.
lib·er·al • ***adjective*** • ***noun,*** *plural* **liberals**

liberate (lib′ər āt) ***verb*** to set free [They *liberated* all prisoners.]
lib·er·ate • ***verb*** **liberated, liberating**

Liberia (lī bir′ē ə) a country on the western coast of Africa.
Li·ber·i·a

liberty (lib′ər tē) ***noun*** **1** the condition of being free from the control of others; independence. **2** the right or power to believe and act in the way that one thinks is right [The Constitution guarantees the *liberty* of American citizens.]
—at liberty allowed; permitted [I am not *at liberty* to tell you.]
lib·er·ty • ***noun,*** *plural* **liberties**

librarian (lī brer′ē ən) ***noun*** a person who is in charge of or works in a library.
li·brar·i·an • ***noun,*** *plural* **librarians**

library (lī′brer′ē) ***noun*** **1** a place where books, magazines, newspapers, records, and other materials are kept for reading or borrowing. **2** a collection of books, records, or other items.
li·brar·y • ***noun,*** *plural* **libraries**

Libya (lib′ē ə) a country in northern Africa.
Lib·y·a

lice (līs) ***noun*** *plural of* **louse**.

license (lī′səns) ***noun*** a paper, card, or other document showing that someone is permitted by law to do something [a marriage *license;* a driver's *license*].
verb to give a license to; permit by law [Are they *licensed* to fish?]
li·cense • ***noun,*** *plural* **licenses**
• ***verb*** **licensed, licensing**

lichen (lī′kən) ***noun*** a plant that looks like dry moss and grows in patches on rocks and trees.
li·chen • ***noun,*** *plural* **lichens**

lick (lik) ***verb*** **1** to rub the tongue over [He *licked* his lips.] **2** to pass lightly over like a tongue [Flames *licked* the roof of the house.] **3** [*an informal use*] to defeat [Our team can *lick* theirs.]
noun **1** the act of licking with the tongue [The dog gave my hand a *lick*.] **2** a small amount; bit [I haven't done a *lick* of work today.]
lick • ***verb*** **licked, licking** • ***noun,*** *plural* **licks**

licorice (lik′ər ish) ***noun*** **1** a black, sweet flavoring made from the root of a plant. **2** candy that is flavored with this.
lic·o·rice • ***noun***

lid (lid) ***noun*** **1** a cover for something, such as a pot or box, that can be opened or removed. **2** *a short form of* **eyelid**.
lid • ***noun,*** *plural* **lids**

lie[1] (lī) ***verb*** **1** to stretch the body in a flat position [She *lay* down on the sofa to read.] **2** to be in a flat position; rest [Don't let the books *lie* on the floor.] **3** to be placed or located [Georgia *lies* east of Alabama.] **4** to be or stay in some condition [The building *lay* empty for two years.]
lie • ***verb*** **lay, lain, lying**
● The words **lie** and **lye** sound alike.
The dog likes to *lie* by the door.
How can you *lie* to your best friend?
Strong soap contains *lye*.

lie[2] (lī) ***noun*** something that is not true, said on purpose to fool or trick someone.
verb to tell a lie; say what is not true.
lie • ***noun,*** *plural* **lies** • ***verb*** **lied, lying**
● The words **lie** and **lye** sound alike.

Liechtenstein (lik′tən stīn) a small country in Europe, west of Austria.
Liech·ten·stein

lieutenant (lo͞o ten′ənt) ***noun*** a military officer of low rank.
lieu·ten·ant • ***noun,*** *plural* **lieutenants**

life (līf) ***noun*** **1** the quality of plants and animals that makes it possible for them to take in food, grow, and make others of their kind. This quality makes plants and animals different from rocks, water, and other matter that is not alive. **2** the state or fact of having this quality [Firefighters risk their *lives* to save others.] **3** a human being [Three *lives* were lost in the crash.] **4** living things as a group [the plant *life* in a pond]. **5** the time that a person is alive [He wished us a long and happy *life*.] **6** the time that a thing lasts [What is the *life* of this battery?] **7** the story

L

of a person's life; biography [She is writing a *life* of Thomas Jefferson.] **8** the way that a person or group lives [a *life* of luxury; military *life*]. **9** energy; spirit [She is full of *life*.]
life • ***noun,*** *plural for senses 2, 3, 5, and 7 only* **lives**

lifeboat (līf′bōt) ***noun*** a sturdy boat used for saving lives at sea or along the shore. A lifeboat is often carried on a larger ship.
life·boat • ***noun,*** *plural* **lifeboats**

life buoy ***noun*** a ring-shaped life preserver.
life buoy • ***noun,*** *plural* **life buoys**

life cycle ***noun*** the set of stages and changes in the development of an animal or a plant, beginning with the earliest stage of one generation and ending with that same stage in the next generation. The life cycle of a frog begins with the egg and continues through the stage of the tadpole and then the stage of the adult. It ends with the egg from the new adult.
life cycle • ***noun,*** *plural* **life cycles**

lifeguard (līf′gärd) ***noun*** an expert swimmer hired to protect and help people at a beach or pool.
life·guard • ***noun,*** *plural* **lifeguards**

life jacket ***noun*** a life preserver that looks like a jacket without sleeves.
life jacket • ***noun,*** *plural* **life jackets**

life jacket

lifeless (līf′ləs) ***adjective*** **1** no longer living; dead [a *lifeless* body]. **2** having no living beings [a *lifeless* planet]. **3** dull; not lively [a *lifeless* expression].
life·less • ***adjective***

lifelike (līf′līk) ***adjective*** like real life; looking alive [a *lifelike* drawing].
life·like • ***adjective***

lifelong (līf′lôŋ′) ***adjective*** lasting or not changing during a person's life [His *lifelong* dream was to become an astronaut.]
life·long • ***adjective***

life preserver (prē zʉrv′ər) ***noun*** a belt, jacket, or large ring that keeps a person afloat in water.
life pre·serv·er • ***noun,*** *plural* **life preservers**

lifesaver (līf′sāv′ər) ***noun*** a person or thing that saves people from drowning.
life·sav·er • ***noun,*** *plural* **lifesavers**

lifetime (līf′tīm) ***noun*** the length of time that someone lives or something lasts.
life·time • ***noun,*** *plural* **lifetimes**

lift (lift) ***verb*** **1** to bring up to a higher place, level, or condition; raise [Please *lift* this box onto the truck. The good news *lifted* her spirits.] **2** to raise or direct upward [She *lifted* her arm and waved at us.] **3** to rise or go up [The helicopter *lifted* from the roof of the building.] **4** to rise and vanish [The fog *lifted*.]
noun **1** the act of lifting. **2** a rise in spirits [Today's victory gave the entire team a *lift*.] **3** a ride to the place or in the direction that one is going [His father gave us a *lift* to the ballgame.] **4** a device for carrying people up or down a slope [a ski *lift*].
lift • ***verb*** **lifted, lifting** • ***noun,*** *plural* **lifts**

liftoff (lift′ôf) ***noun*** the sudden, upward movement of a rocket when it is launched.
lift·off • ***noun,*** *plural* **liftoffs**

liftoff

ligament (lig′ə mənt) ***noun*** a band of strong, tough tissue that joins bones or holds organs of the body in place.
lig·a·ment • ***noun,*** *plural* **ligaments**

light[1] (līt) ***noun*** **1** the form of energy that acts on the eye so a person can see. **2** a lamp or other thing that gives off light [Please turn on the *lights*.] **3** a traffic light [Stop at the red *light*.] **4** a flame or spark to start something burning [the pilot *light* of a stove]. **5** helpful information or knowledge [She shed *light* on the problem.] **6** public attention or notice [The investiga-

a cat	ō go	ʉ fur	ə = a *in* ago	
ā ape	ô law, for	ch chin	e *in* agent	
ä cot, car	oo look	sh she	i *in* pencil	
e ten	ōō tool	th thin	o *in* atom	
ē me	oi oil	*th* then	u *in* circus	
i fit	ou out	zh measure		
ī ice	u up	ŋ ring		

tion brought to *light* new evidence.] **7** a way in which something appears or is seen [The article presented him in a good *light*.]
adjective **1** not dark; bright [Let's play while it's still *light* outside.] **2** having a pale color; fair [*light* skin and hair].
verb **1** to set on fire or catch fire [He *lit* a match. The match *lighted* when struck.] **2** to cause to give off light [She *lighted* the lamp.] **3** to cast light on or in [A lantern *lighted* the cave.] **4** to become bright or lively [Her face *lighted* with joy.] **5** to guide with or by a light [He *lighted* our way with a candle.]
light • ***noun**, plural for senses 2, 3, and 4 only* **lights** • ***adjective*** **lighter, lightest** • ***verb*** **lighted** or **lit, lighting**

light[2] (līt) ***adjective*** **1** having little weight for its size; not heavy [a *light* suitcase]. **2** little or less than usual [a *light* rain; a *light* meal]. **3** not serious or important; amusing or entertaining [*light* reading]. **4** not sad; happy [*light* spirits]. **5** easy to do or put up with; not hard or severe [*light* work; a *light* punishment]. **6** moving in a quick, easy way; nimble [The ballerina was *light* on her feet.]
verb to come to rest after flying [Birds *lighted* on the branches of the tree.]
light • ***adjective*** **lighter, lightest** • ***verb*** **lighted** or **lit, lighting**

lighten[1] (līt′n) ***verb*** to make or become light or brighter; brighten [The white walls *lighten* the room. The sky *lightened*.]
light·en • ***verb*** **lightened, lightening**

lighten[2] (līt′n) ***verb*** **1** to make or become less heavy [He *lightened* the load by removing the large box.] **2** to make or become more cheerful [Her spirits *lightened* when she heard the good news.]
light·en • ***verb*** **lightened, lightening**

light-footed (līt′foot əd) ***adjective*** moving lightly and gracefully on the feet; nimble.
light-foot·ed • ***adjective***

lightheaded (līt′hed əd) ***adjective*** feeling dizzy [The medicine makes me *lightheaded*.]
light·head·ed • ***adjective***

lighthearted (līt′härt əd) ***adjective*** free from care; cheerful [a *lighthearted* person].
light·heart·ed • ***adjective***

lighthouse (līt′hous) ***noun*** a tower with a bright light on top to guide ships at night or in fog.
light·house • ***noun**, plural* **lighthouses**

lighthouse

lighting (līt′iŋ) ***noun*** the lights in a place such as a building or room.
light·ing • ***noun***

lightning (līt′niŋ) ***noun*** a flash of light in the sky. It is produced when electricity passes from one cloud to another or between a cloud and the earth.
light·ning • ***noun***

lightning rod ***noun*** a metal rod placed on the roof of a building and connected to the ground by a cable. It protects the building from fire by carrying off the electricity in lightning.
lightning rod • ***noun**, plural* **lightning rods**

light pen ***noun*** an electronic device shaped like a pen that is used to make or change drawings on a computer screen or to give commands to the computer.
light pen • ***noun**, plural* **light pens**

light-year (līt′yir) ***noun*** the distance that light travels through space in one year. This distance is about six trillion miles. The distance between stars is very great, so it is measured in light-years.
light-year • ***noun**, plural* **light-years**

likable or **likeable** (līk′ə bəl) ***adjective*** easy to like because friendly or pleasing [a *likable* person].
lik·a·ble or **like·a·ble** • ***adjective***

like[1] (līk) ***preposition*** **1** similar to; somewhat the same as [hands *like* claws]. **2** in the same way as [crying *like* a baby]. **3** typical of; to be expected of [It isn't *like* her to be late.] **4** in the mood for [He felt *like* eating.] **5** as if there will be [It looks *like* rain.] **6** as for example [We had fruit, *like* pears and peaches, for dessert.]
conjunction [*an informal use*] **1** the same as [It was just *like* you said.] **2** as if [It looks *like* you'll win.]

L

like[2] (līk) *verb* to be fond of or pleased with; enjoy [She *likes* dogs. I *like* to read.]
—likes and dislikes things that a person enjoys together with things that a person does not enjoy [I can give a long list of her *likes and dislikes*.]
like • *verb* **liked, liking**

WORD CHOICES

Synonyms of like

The words **like, enjoy,** and **love** share the meaning "to get joy or pleasure from."

I *like* the sound of a marching band.

My parents *enjoy* gardening.

Don't you just *love* to walk in the rain?

-like *a suffix meaning* like; like what belongs to [A *ducklike* waddle is like the waddle of a duck.]

likelihood (līk′lē hood′) *noun* the fact of being likely to happen [There is a strong *likelihood* that it will rain today.]
like·li·hood • *noun*

likely (līk′lē) *adjective* **1** apt to happen; to be expected [A storm is *likely* before noon.] **2** seeming to be true; able to be believed [a *likely* story].
adverb probably [It will *likely* snow tomorrow.]
like·ly • *adjective* **likelier, likeliest** • *adverb*

likeness (līk′nəs) *noun* **1** the fact of being like or similar [Her *likeness* to him can be seen in this photograph.] —Look for the WORD CHOICES box at the entry **resemblance**. **2** a portrait or picture of a person.
like·ness • *noun, plural for sense 2 only* **likenesses**

likewise (līk′wīz) *adverb* **1** also; too [He has to leave and I *likewise*.] **2** in the same way [I watched her cook so that I could do *likewise*.]
like·wise • *adverb*

liking (līk′iŋ) *noun* the fact of enjoying or being fond of something [a *liking* for bright colors].
lik·ing • *noun*

lilac (lī′lak) *noun* a shrub that has clusters of tiny, sweet-smelling flowers. The flowers range in color from white to purple.
li·lac • *noun, plural* **lilacs**

lilt (lilt) *noun* a light, swaying rhythm or movement [She talks with a *lilt*.]

lily (lil′ē) *noun* a plant that grows from a bulb and has white or colored flowers shaped like trumpets.
lil·y • *noun, plural* **lilies**

lily

lily of the valley *noun* a low plant with tiny, sweet-smelling, white flowers that grow along a single stem.
lily of the valley • *noun, plural* **lilies of the valley**

lima bean (lī′mə) *noun* a broad, flat bean that grows in pods and is used for food.
li·ma bean • *noun, plural* **lima beans**

WORD HISTORY

lima bean

The **lima bean** is named after *Lima*, the capital of Peru. It is a native of the tropical regions of North and South America.

limb (lim) *noun* **1** an arm, leg, or wing. **2** any large part of a tree growing from the trunk or from a main branch.
limb • *noun, plural* **limbs**

lime[1] (līm) *noun* a white substance that is gotten by burning limestone or shells. It is used in making cement, mortar, and fertilizers.

lime[2] (līm) *noun* a fruit like a lemon, with a greenish-yellow skin and a sour, juicy pulp.
lime • *noun, plural* **limes**

lime

limerick (lim′ər ik) *noun* a funny poem of five lines, with this kind of rhyme and rhythm:

a	cat	ō	go	ʉ	fur	ə = a *in* ago	
ā	ape	ô	law, for	ch	chin	e *in* agent	
ä	cot, car	oo	look	sh	she	i *in* pencil	
e	ten	ōō	tool	th	thin	o *in* atom	
ē	me	oi	oil	*th*	then	u *in* circus	
i	fit	ou	out	zh	measure		
ī	ice	u	up	ŋ	ring		

"There was a small maiden named Maggie,
Whose dog was enormous and shaggy,
The front end of him
Looked vicious and grim—
But the tail end was friendly and waggy."

lim·er·ick • *noun, plural* **limericks**

limestone (līm′stōn) ***noun*** a rock containing large amounts of calcium. It is easily cut and shaped and is often used for building. Marble is a kind of limestone.
lime·stone • ***noun***

limit (lim′it) ***noun*** **1** the point or line where something ends or must end [There is a *limit* to my patience.] **2** **limits** boundary lines; bounds [the city *limits*]. **3** the greatest amount allowed [What is the speed *limit* here?]
verb to set a limit to; restrict [Please *limit* your phone call to ten minutes.]
lim·it • ***noun,*** *plural* **limits** • ***verb*** **limited, limiting**

limo (lim′ō) [*an informal word*] ***noun*** *a short form of* **limousine**.
lim·o • ***noun,*** *plural* **limos**

limousine (lim ə zēn′) ***noun*** **1** a large, luxurious automobile with a driver, usually used to carry important or wealthy persons. **2** a small bus or van used to carry passengers to or from an airport, train station, or hotel.
lim·ou·sine • ***noun,*** *plural* **limousines**

limp[1] (limp) ***verb*** to walk in an uneven way because of a lame leg [The dog *limped* down the road.]
noun a lame or uneven step [He walks with a *limp*.]
limp • ***verb*** **limped, limping** • ***noun,*** *plural* **limps**

limp[2] (limp) ***adjective*** not stiff, or firm, or crisp [a *limp*, wet rag].
limp • ***adjective*** **limper, limpest**

Lincoln (liŋ′kən), **Abraham** (ā′brə ham) 1809-1865; the sixteenth president of the U.S., from 1861 to 1865. He was assassinated.
Lin·coln, A·bra·ham

Lincoln (liŋ′kən) the capital of Nebraska.
Lin·coln

Lindbergh (lind′bərg), **Charles Augustus** (chärlz ô gus′təs) 1902-1974; U.S. aviator. He made the first nonstop solo flight from New York to Paris, in 1927.
Lind·bergh, Charles Au·gus·tus

linden (lin′dən) ***noun*** a tree that has yellowish, sweet-smelling flowers and leaves shaped like hearts.
lin·den • ***noun,*** *plural* **lindens**

line[1] (līn) ***noun*** **1** a long, thin mark [pencil *lines*]. **2** a border or boundary [the county *line*]. **3** a row of persons or things [There are long *lines* at the ticket windows. A column of the newspaper has 40 *lines*.] —Look for the WORD CHOICES box at the entry **row**[1]. **4** a company that carries people or goods [a bus *line*]. **5** the path of a moving object [the *line* of flight of a flock of birds]. **6** a supply of goods of a certain kind [This store carries a fine *line* of shoes.] **7** a short letter [Drop me a *line*.] **8** **lines** all the speeches of an actor in a play [The actor rehearsed his *lines*.] **9** a cord, rope, or string [a fishing *line*]. **10** a wire or pipe that carries electricity, water, or some other fluid. **11** the football players on a team arranged in a row even with the ball at the start of each play. **12** in geometry, a straight path that extends in both directions without ending.
verb **1** to mark with lines [Age *lined* her face.] **2** to form a line along [Trees *line* our street.]
—hold the line to stand firm; not allow anyone or anything through. **—in line** in a straight row [We stood *in line*.] **—line up** to bring or come into a line, or row. **—out of line** lacking proper respect; rude [Your behavior is *out of line*.]
line • ***noun,*** *plural* **lines** • ***verb*** **lined, lining**

line[2] (līn) ***verb*** to cover on the inside with a lining [The tailor *lined* the jacket with silk.]
line • ***verb*** **lined, lining**

linebacker (līn′bak ər) ***noun*** one of the football players in a defensive formation who takes a position directly behind the line.
line·back·er • ***noun,*** *plural* **linebackers**

line drive ***noun*** a baseball that has been hit hard and moves in a line not far above the ground.
line drive • ***noun,*** *plural* **line drives**

lineman (līn′mən) ***noun*** **1** a person whose work is putting up and repairing telephone, telegraph, or power lines. **2** a football player who takes a position in the line.
line·man • ***noun,*** *plural* **linemen**

linen (lin′ən) ***noun*** **1** thread or cloth made of flax. **2** *often* **linens** tablecloths, sheets, and similar things for the house.
lin·en • ***noun,*** *plural* **linens**

liner (līn′ər) ***noun*** **1** a ship or airplane in regular service for a transportation line [an

L

ocean *liner*]. **2** something that fits inside something else [a plastic *liner* for the wastebasket].
lin·er • ***noun,*** *plural* **liners**

linesman (līnz′mən) ***noun*** **1** *another name for* **lineman. 2** a football official who keeps track of the yards gained or lost.
lines·man • ***noun,*** *plural* **linesmen**

lineup (līn′up) ***noun*** **1** a group of persons lined up [a long *lineup* at the ticket window]. **2** a list of players on a team who play in a game [Our best batter is not in the *lineup* for today's game.]
line·up • ***noun,*** *plural* **lineups**

linger (liŋ′gər) ***verb*** to keep on staying [The crowd of fans *lingered* outside hoping to meet the actors.] —Look for the WORD CHOICES box at the entry **stay**.
lin·ger • ***verb*** **lingered, lingering**

lining (līn′iŋ) ***noun*** material that covers the inside of a surface [a coat with a heavy wool *lining*].
lin·ing • ***noun,*** *plural* **linings**

link (liŋk) ***noun*** **1** one of the rings or loops that form a chain. **2** anything that joins or connects [Books are a *link* to the past.]
verb to join or connect [We *linked* arms.]
link • ***noun,*** *plural* **links** • ***verb*** **linked, linking**

linking verb ***noun*** a verb that connects the subject of a sentence with the word or words that tell about the subject. In the sentence "She feels ill," the word "feels" is a linking verb.
linking verb • ***noun,*** *plural* **linking verbs**

linoleum (li nō′lē əm) ***noun*** a hard, smooth floor covering.
li·no·le·um • ***noun***

lint (lint) ***noun*** fine bits of thread or fluff from cloth or yarn.

lion

lion (lī′ən) ***noun*** a large, strong animal that is related to the cat and lives in Africa and Asia. Lions have a brownish-yellow coat and the males have a heavy mane.
li·on • ***noun,*** *plural* **lions**

lioness (lī′ən əs) ***noun*** a female lion.
li·on·ess • ***noun,*** *plural* **lionesses**

lip (lip) ***noun*** **1** the upper or lower edge of the mouth. **2** the rim of a cup or any other edge that is like a lip.
lip • ***noun,*** *plural* **lips**

lip-read (lip′rēd) ***verb*** to understand a person's speech by lip reading.
lip-read • ***verb*** **lip-read, lip-reading**

lip reading ***noun*** the act or skill of understanding what a person is saying by watching the movements of the person's mouth, without hearing the words.

lipstick (lip′stik) ***noun*** small stick of paste set in a case, used for coloring the lips.
lip·stick • ***noun,*** *plural* **lipsticks**

liquid (lik′wid) ***noun*** a substance that flows easily; matter that is neither a solid nor a gas. Water is a liquid when it is not ice or steam.
adjective flowing easily; fluid [Gasoline is a *liquid* fuel.]
liq·uid • ***noun,*** *plural* **liquids** • ***adjective***

liquor (lik′ər) ***noun*** a strong alcoholic drink. Whiskey is a liquor.
liq·uor • ***noun,*** *plural* **liquors**

lisp (lisp) ***noun*** a speech problem in which a person uses the sounds (th) and (*th*) in place of the sounds (s) and (z).
verb to say with a lisp.
lisp • ***noun,*** *plural* **lisps** • ***verb*** **lisped, lisping**

list[1] (list) ***noun*** a series of names, words, or numbers set down one after the other [a grocery *list*].
verb **1** to make a list of [She *listed* her ten favorite books.] **2** to put into a list [Is your name *listed* in the telephone book?]
list • ***noun,*** *plural* **lists** • ***verb*** **listed, listing**

list[2] (list) ***verb*** to tilt to one side [The ship *listed* in the stormy waters.]

a	cat	ō	go	ʉ	fur	ə =	a *in* ago
ā	ape	ô	law, for	ch	chin		e *in* agent
ä	cot, car	oo	look	sh	she		i *in* pencil
e	ten	ōō	tool	th	thin		o *in* atom
ē	me	oi	oil	*th*	then		u *in* circus
i	fit	ou	out	zh	measure		
ī	ice	u	up	ŋ	ring		

noun a tilt to one side.
list • *verb* **listed, listing** • *noun*

listen (lis′ən) *verb* **1** to pay attention in order to hear; try to hear [She *listened* to the radio. He is *listening* for the phone to ring.] **2** to heed and obey [*Listen* to your parents.]
lis·ten • *verb* **listened, listening**

lit (lit) *verb a past tense and a past participle of* **light**[1] and **light**[2].

liter (lēt′ər) *noun* a unit of capacity for liquids in the metric system. A liter is equal to a little more than a quart of liquid.
li·ter • *noun, plural* **liters**

literacy (lit′ər ə sē) *noun* the ability to read and write.
lit·er·a·cy • *noun*

literal (lit′ər əl) *adjective* based on the actual words in their usual meanings [A person who obeys the *literal* meaning of "Go jump in a lake" will end up all wet.]
lit·er·al • *adjective*

literally (lit′ər əl ē) *adverb* **1** word for word [He translated the poem from French into English *literally*.] **2** actually; in fact [The house *literally* burned to the ground.]
lit·er·al·ly • *adverb*

literate (lit′ər ət) *adjective* able to read and write.
lit·er·ate • *adjective*

literature (lit′ər ə chər) *noun* **1** writing that has lasting value because of its beauty, imagination, and excellence. **2** [*an informal use*] printed matter of any kind [Did you get any *literature* with your new TV set?]
lit·er·a·ture • *noun*

Lithuania (lith′o͞o ā′nē ə) a country in northeastern Europe.
Lith·u·a·ni·a

litmus paper (lit′məs) *noun* a specially treated paper that turns red in an acid and blue in a base.
lit·mus paper • *noun*

litter (lit′ər) *noun* **1** odd bits or scraps scattered about [*Litter* filled the park after the parade.] **2** all the young born at one time to an animal [a *litter* of kittens]. **3** a stretcher for carrying an injured person.
verb to make messy or untidy with things scattered about [Bottles and cans *littered* the picnic area.]
lit·ter • *noun, plural* **litters** • *verb* **littered, littering**

litterbug (lit′ər bug) *noun* a person who litters public places with bits of paper, empty cans, or other rubbish.
lit·ter·bug • *noun, plural* **litterbugs**

little (lit′l) *adjective* **1** small in size; not large or big [a *little* dog] —Look for the WORD CHOICES box at the entry **small**. **2** small in amount or degree; not much [a *little* sugar; a *little* danger]. **3** short or brief [Let's rest a *little* while.]
adverb to a small degree; not very much [She feels a *little* better today. I know *little* about his past.]
noun **1** a small amount [I'll have a *little*.] **2** a short time or distance [Stay a *little*.]
—little by little in a slow way or in small amounts; gradually.
lit·tle • *adjective* **littler** or **less** or **lesser, littlest** or **least** • *adverb* **less, least** • *noun*

Little Rock (lit′l räk′) the capital of Arkansas.

livable (liv′ə bəl) *adjective* fit or pleasant to live in [a *livable* house].
liv·a·ble • *adjective*

live[1] (liv) *verb* **1** to have life; be alive [No one *lives* forever.] **2** to stay alive; last or endure [Our cat *lived* to be 20 years old.] **3** to pass through life in a certain way [He *lived* well.] **4** to support oneself [She *lives* on a small income.] **5** to feed [Bats *live* on insects and fruit.] **6** to dwell; reside [He *lives* on a farm.]
live • *verb* **lived, living**

live[2] (līv) *adjective* **1** having life; not dead [He keeps a *live* snake as a pet.] **2** still burning or glowing [*live* coals]. **3** not fired or blown up [a *live* bomb]. **4** carrying an electric current [a *live* wire]. **5** being broadcast while it is taking place; not photographed, taped, filmed, or recorded [a *live* TV or radio program].

livelihood (līv′lē ho͝od′) *noun* the means of staying alive, or of supporting oneself [She earns her *livelihood* as a writer.]
live·li·hood • *noun*

lively (līv′lē) *adjective* **1** full of life or energy; active [a *lively* puppy] —Look for the WORD CHOICES boxes at the entries **active** and **nimble**. **2** full of excitement [a *lively* meeting]. **3** cheerful or bright [*lively* colors].
adverb in a lively way [Step *lively*.]
live·ly • *adjective* & • *adverb* **livelier, liveliest**

liven (līv′ən) *verb* to make or become lively [Games *liven* up a party.]
liv·en • *verb* **livened, livening**

L

liver (liv′ər) ***noun*** **1** a large organ of the body that is near the stomach. It makes bile and helps break down food into substances that the body can absorb. **2** the liver of some animals, used as food.
liv·er • ***noun,*** *plural* **livers**

livery (liv′ər ē) ***noun*** **1** a uniform worn by a servant or by a person doing a certain kind of work. **2** the work of keeping and feeding horses for pay.
liv·er·y • ***noun,*** *plural* **liveries**

lives (līvz) ***noun*** *plural of* **life**.

livestock (līv′stäk) ***noun*** cattle, horses, pigs, sheep, or other animals kept and raised on a farm.
live·stock • ***noun***

living (liv′iŋ) ***adjective*** **1** having life; alive; not dead [all *living* creatures]. **2** still active or in common use among people [a *living* tradition]. **3** of or having to do with the place or way that a person lives [poor *living* conditions].
noun **1** the fact of being alive [*Living* has its joys and sorrows.] **2** the way in which one earns money [He makes a *living* selling shoes.] **3** the way in which a person lives [She enjoys a high standard of *living*.]
—the living all who are still alive.
liv·ing • ***adjective*** • ***noun***

living room ***noun*** a room in a house with furniture such as a sofa and chairs, used by the entire family. It is also used for entertaining guests.
living room • ***noun,*** *plural* **living rooms**

lizard (liz′ərd) ***noun*** an animal that has a long, slender body and tail, four legs, and scales. Lizards are reptiles. The chameleon and the iguana are lizards.
liz·ard • ***noun,*** *plural* **lizards**

llama

llama (lä′mə) ***noun*** a South American animal that is related to the camel but is smaller and has no hump. The llama is used for carrying loads and its wool is used for making cloth.
lla·ma • ***noun,*** *plural* **llamas**

load (lōd) ***noun*** **1** something that is carried or to be carried at one time or in one trip [He has a heavy *load* on his back.] **2** an amount carried or held at one time [The truck delivered a *load* of bricks to the building site.] **3** something that makes one worried or anxious [Her safe arrival took a *load* off my mind.] **4** *often* **loads** [*an informal use*] a great amount or number [He has *loads* of friends.]
verb **1** to put something to be carried into or upon a carrier [They *loaded* the boxes into the truck. They *loaded* the truck with furniture.] **2** to fill with something that is needed to make an apparatus work [*Load* the camera with film.]
load • ***noun,*** *plural* **loads** • ***verb*** **loaded, loading**

loaf[1] (lōf) ***noun*** **1** a portion of bread baked in one piece, usually oblong in shape. **2** any food baked in this shape [a meat *loaf*].
loaf • ***noun,*** *plural* **loaves**

loaf[2] (lōf) ***verb*** to spend time doing little or nothing [Don't *loaf* on the job.] —Look for the WORD CHOICES box at the entry **loiter**.
loaf • ***verb*** **loafed, loafing**

loafer (lōf′ər) ***noun*** a person who loafs; lazy person.
loaf·er • ***noun,*** *plural* **loafers**

Loafer

Loafer (lōf′ər) ***trademark*** a shoe that looks somewhat like a moccasin.
Loaf·er • ***trademark,*** *plural* **Loafers**

loan (lōn) ***noun*** **1** the act of lending [Thanks for the *loan* of your pen.] **2** something, such as a sum of money, that is lent [The bank gave him a *loan*.]
verb to lend money or some other thing that must be repaid or returned [I *loaned* him $20.]

a	cat	ō	go	ʉ	fur	ə =	a *in* ago
ā	ape	ô	law, for	ch	chin		e *in* agent
ä	cot, car	oo	look	sh	she		i *in* pencil
e	ten	ōō	tool	th	thin		o *in* atom
ē	me	oi	oil	*th*	then		u *in* circus
i	fit	ou	out	zh	measure		
ī	ice	u	up	ŋ	ring		

loan • *noun, plural* **loans** • *verb* **loaned, loaning**

● The words **loan** and **lone** sound alike.
They took out a bank *loan*.
I watched the *lone* bird in the sky.

loathe (lōth) *verb* to feel hate or disgust for.
loathe • *verb* **loathed, loathing**

loathsome (lōth′səm) *adjective* very disgusting [A cockroach is a *loathsome* bug.]
loath·some • *adjective*

loaves (lōvz) *noun plural of* **loaf**[1].

lobby (läb′ē) *noun* an entrance hall or waiting room [We met in the hotel *lobby*.]
lob·by • *noun, plural* **lobbies**

lobe (lōb) *noun* the rounded, fleshy lower end of the human ear.
lobe • *noun, plural* **lobes**

lobster

lobster (läb′stər) *noun* **1** a large shellfish that has five pairs of legs. The front pair of legs ends in large pincers. **2** the flesh of this animal, used as food.
lob·ster • *noun, plural* **lobsters**

local (lō′kəl) *adjective* **1** having to do with a particular place; not general [*local* events]. **2** having an effect on just one area of the body [a *local* anesthetic]. **3** making all stops along its run [a *local* bus].
noun **1** a local bus or train. **2** [*an informal use*] a local resident.
lo·cal • *adjective* • *noun, plural* **locals**

locate (lō′kāt) *verb* **1** to set up or place; situate [He *located* his shop in the mall.] **2** to find out where something is [I *located* the missing glove under the sofa.]
lo·cate • *verb* **located, locating**

location (lō kā′shən) *noun* **1** the act of locating. **2** the place where something is or will be [We will build a house on this *location*.]
lo·ca·tion • *noun, plural for sense 2 only* **locations**

lock[1] (läk) *noun* **1** a mechanical device with a bolt for keeping shut something such as a door, gate, or safe. A lock can be opened only by someone who has a key or knows the combination. **2** an enclosed section of a canal or river with gates at each end. Water can be let in or out of the lock to raise or lower ships from one level to another.
verb **1** to fasten or become fastened with a lock [She *locked* the door. The door *locked* safely behind her.] **2** to shut in or out [He *locked* the money in the safe. She *locked* the cat out of the house.] **3** to join together firmly [The elks *locked* horns while fighting.]
lock • *noun, plural* **locks** • *verb* **locked, locking**

lock[2] (läk) *noun* a curl or other small piece of hair.
lock • *noun, plural* **locks**

locker (läk′ər) *noun* a closet or chest that is usually made of metal and can be locked. It is used for storing things securely.
lock·er • *noun, plural* **lockers**

locker room *noun* a room that has many lockers, which are used for storing clothing or equipment. Schools, factories, and stadiums have locker rooms.
locker room • *noun, plural* **locker rooms**

locket (läk′ət) *noun* a small metal case for holding a picture, a lock of hair, or some other souvenir. It is usually worn around the neck on a chain or ribbon.
lock·et • *noun, plural* **lockets**

lockjaw (läk′jô *or* läk′jä) *noun another name for* **tetanus**.
lock·jaw • *noun*

locksmith (läk′smith) *noun* a person whose work is making or repairing locks and making keys.
lock·smith • *noun, plural* **locksmiths**

locomotive

locomotive (lō′kə mōt′iv) *noun* an engine on wheels designed to run on rails, that is used to

L

pull or push railroad cars.
lo·co·mo·tive • *noun, plural* **locomotives**

locust (lō′kəst) *noun* **1** a large insect like a grasshopper. It often travels in great swarms and destroys crops. **2** a tree that has leaves made up of many smaller leaves. It has clusters of white, sweet-smelling flowers.
lo·cust • *noun, plural* **locusts**

lodge (läj) *noun* **1** a small house or cabin that is used for some special purpose [a hunting *lodge*]. **2** a local branch or meeting place of certain societies or clubs.
verb **1** to provide a place to live or sleep in for a time [We *lodged* them.] **2** to live in a place for a time [Dan *lodged* with us for two years.] **3** to come to rest and stick firmly [The kite *lodged* in the tree.]
lodge • *noun, plural* **lodges** • *verb* **lodged, lodging**

lodging (läj′iŋ) *noun* **1** a place to live in, especially for a short time. **2 lodgings** a room or rooms rented in someone's house.
lodg·ing • *noun, plural* **lodgings**

loft (lôft) *noun* **1** the space just below the roof of a house or barn [a *hayloft*]. **2** a gallery or balcony [a choir *loft*]. **3** a large, open floor in a former warehouse or factory, used as an apartment or an artist's studio.
loft • *noun, plural* **lofts**

lofty (lôf′tē) *adjective* **1** very high [a *lofty* tree]. **2** too proud; haughty [The king's *lofty* manner angered the people.]
loft·y • *adjective* **loftier, loftiest**

log (lôg) *noun* **1** a part of a tree that has been cut down [a stack of *logs* for firewood]. **2** the record of the voyage of a ship or the flight of an airplane. A log keeps a record of speed, position, weather, and any happenings.
verb **1** to cut down trees and take the logs to a sawmill. **2** to record in a log [The captain *logged* the ship's position.]
—log off to give directions to a computer terminal to stop working. **—log on** to give directions to a computer terminal to start working.
log • *noun, plural* **logs** • *verb* **logged, logging**

loganberry (lō′gən ber′ē) *noun* a purple-red berry that is a cross between the blackberry and the red raspberry.
lo·gan·ber·ry • *noun, plural* **loganberries**

logger (lôg′ər) *noun* a person who logs trees; lumberjack.
log·ger • *noun, plural* **loggers**

logic (läj′ik) *noun* **1** correct reasoning; sound thinking [He based his decision on his feelings rather than on *logic*.] **2** any way of reasoning, whether it is correct or incorrect [I can't follow her *logic* at all.] **3** the study of the rules of correct reasoning.
log·ic • *noun*

logical (läj′i kəl) *adjective* **1** based on correct reasoning [He gave a *logical* explanation.] **2** using correct reasoning [She is a *logical* person.] **3** that is to be expected because of what goes on before [If you didn't do yesterday's homework, then it is *logical* that you would have trouble with today's lesson.]
log·i·cal • *adjective*

LOGO (lō′gō) *noun* a computer language for use by young people. This language can be used to draw pictures.

-logy *a suffix meaning* the science or study of [*Biology* is the science or study of living things.]

loin (loin) *noun* **1** *usually* **loins** the part of an animal or person between the hip and the ribs; lower back. **2** a cut of meat from this part of an animal.
loin • *noun, plural* **loins**

loiter (loit′ər) *verb* to spend time in an idle way; linger [Do not *loiter* in the halls.]
loi·ter • *verb* **loitered, loitering**

WORD CHOICES

Synonyms of **loiter**

The words **loiter**, **idle**, and **loaf** share the meaning "to spend time in a lazy or pointless way."

youngsters *loitering* around street corners

a team *idling* through a practice

a factory worker *loafing* on the job

loll (läl) *verb* to sit or lean back in a lazy way [She *lolled* in the big, comfortable chair.]
loll • *verb* **lolled, lolling**

a cat	ō go	ʉ fur	ə = a *in* ago
ā ape	ô law, for	ch chin	e *in* agent
ä cot, car	oo look	sh she	i *in* pencil
e ten	ōō tool	th thin	o *in* atom
ē me	oi oil	*th* then	u *in* circus
i fit	ou out	zh measure	
ī ice	u up	ŋ ring	

lollipop (läl′ē päp) ***noun*** a piece of hard candy on a small stick.
lol·li·pop • ***noun,*** *plural* **lollipops**

London (lun′dən) the capital of the United Kingdom, in southeastern England.
Lon·don

lone (lōn) ***adjective*** by itself or oneself; solitary [A *lone* tree on a prairie can be seen for miles.]
● The words **lone** and **loan** sound alike.
I watched the *lone* bird in the sky.
They took out a bank *loan*.

lonely (lōn′lē) ***adjective*** **1** unhappy because one is alone or away from friends or family [Billy was *lonely* his first day at camp.] **2** without others nearby; alone [a *lonely* cottage] —Look for the WORD CHOICES box at the entry **alone**. **3** with few or no people [a *lonely* island].
lone·ly • ***adjective*** **lonelier, loneliest**

lonesome (lōn′səm) ***adjective*** **1** having a lonely feeling [a *lonesome* newcomer]. **2** seldom used; remote [a *lonesome* mountain road].
lone·some • ***adjective***

long[1] (lôŋ) ***adjective*** **1** measuring much from end to end or from beginning to end; not short [a *long* board; a *long* trip; a *long* wait]. **2** having a certain extent or duration; in length [The TV program was two hours *long*. This rope is six feet *long*.] **3** describing a vowel sound that takes a little longer to say than other vowel sounds. In this dictionary, long sounds are marked with a macron.
adverb **1** for a long time [Don't be gone *long*.] **2** from the beginning to the end [We went to the beach all summer *long*.] **3** at a time in the far past [They lived *long* ago.]
long • ***adjective*** & • ***adverb*** **longer, longest**

long[2] (lôŋ) ***verb*** to want very much; feel a strong desire for [We *long* to go home.]
long • ***verb*** **longed, longing**

long distance ***noun*** a system by which telephone calls can be made between distant places.

Longfellow (lôŋ′fel′ō), **Henry Wadsworth** (hen′rē wädz′wurth) 1807-1882; U.S. poet.
Long·fel·low, Hen·ry Wads·worth

longhand (lôŋ′hand) ***noun*** ordinary handwriting, with the words written out in full.
long·hand • ***noun***

longhorn (lôŋ′hôrn) ***noun*** a breed of cattle with long horns, raised in the Southwest.
long·horn • ***noun,*** *plural* **longhorns** or **longhorn**

longhorn

Long Island a large island in southeast New York State, on the Atlantic.

longitude (län′jə to͞od *or* län′jə tyo͞od) ***noun*** distance that is measured in degrees east or west of an imaginary line running north and south through the town of Greenwich, England [Chicago is at 87 degrees west *longitude*.]
lon·gi·tude • ***noun,*** *plural* **longitudes**

look (lo͝ok) ***verb*** **1** to turn or aim one's eyes in order to see [Don't *look* back.] **2** to keep one's eyes fixed on [*Look* me in the face.] **3** to bring one's attention to [Just *look* at the trouble you've caused.] **4** to search or hunt [Did you *look* everywhere for it?] **5** to seem or appear [Maria *looks* happy today.] **6** to face in a certain direction [The new hotel *looks* toward the lake.]
noun **1** the act of looking; a glance or inspection [She gave him an angry *look*. Take a good *look* at the car before you buy it.] **2** the way someone or something seems; appearance [This racing horse has the *look* of a winner.] **3 looks** [*an informal use*] appearance [The actress was famous for her good *looks*. I don't like the *looks* of this place.]
—look after to take care of [Will you *look after* the baby?] **—look down on** to think of as bad or worthless [Don't *look down on* the homeless.] **—look forward to** to wait eagerly for [We *look forward to* seeing you again.] **—look out** to be careful. **—look up** **1** to search for, especially in a dictionary [*Look up* the meaning of this word in the dictionary.] **2** [*an informal use*] to pay a visit to [When you get to Miami, *look up* my friend Bill.] **—look up to** to respect; admire [He *looks up to* his uncle.]
look • ***verb*** **looked, looking** • ***noun,*** *plural* **looks**

L

WORD CHOICES

Synonyms of **look**

The words **look, gaze,** and **stare** share the meaning "to direct one's eyes at something."

I *looked* up at the steeple.

He *gazed* into my eyes.

They *stared* at the huge snake.

looking glass ***noun*** a mirror made of glass.
look·ing glass • ***noun,*** *plural* **looking glasses**

lookout (lo͝ok′out) ***noun*** **1** the action of careful watching for someone or something [She's on the *lookout* for a new job.] **2** a person who is supposed to keep watch; guard; sentry. **3** a place, especially a high place with a good view, from which to watch.
look·out • ***noun,*** *plural for senses 2 and 3 only* **lookouts**

loom

loom[1] (lo͞om) ***noun*** a machine for weaving thread or yarn into cloth.
loom • ***noun,*** *plural* **looms**

loom[2] (lo͞om) ***verb*** to come into sight in a sudden or frightening way [A ship *loomed* out of the fog.]
loom • ***verb*** **loomed, looming**

loon (lo͞on) ***noun*** a diving bird that looks like a duck but has a pointed bill and a weird cry.
loon • ***noun,*** *plural* **loons**

loony (lo͞on′ē) [*a slang word*] ***adjective*** crazy.
noun a loony person.
loon·y • ***adjective*** **loonier, looniest** • ***noun,*** *plural* **loonies**

loop (lo͞op) ***noun*** **1** a figure made by a line, string, wire, or other flexible material that curves back to cross itself [a *loop* in the garden hose]. **2** anything having or forming a figure like this or like a ring [The letter *g* has a *loop*. The belt goes through the *loops* at the waistband.]
verb **1** to make a loop of or in [He *looped* the rope when he tied a knot.] **2** to form a loop or loops [The airplane *looped* several times.]
loop • ***noun,*** *plural* **loops** • ***verb*** **looped, looping**

loose (lo͞os) ***adjective*** **1** not tied up or held back; free [The dog is *loose!*] **2** not firmly fastened on or in something [a *loose* tooth; *loose* pages]. **3** not tight [*loose* pants]. **4** not packed down or pressed tightly together [*loose* soil; cloth with a *loose* weave]. **5** not put up in a special package or box [*loose* salt; a bin of *loose* potatoes]. **6** not bound, tied, or joined together [I always carry *loose* change.]
adverb in a loose way [My coat hangs *loose*.]
verb **1** to make loose or set free; release [Don't *loose* the chickens in the yard.] **2** to make less tight; loosen [She *loosed* her shoelaces.]
loose • ***adjective*** & • ***adverb*** **looser, loosest** • ***verb*** **loosed, loosing**

loosen (lo͞os′ən) ***verb*** to make or become loose or looser [He *loosened* his belt.]
loos·en • ***verb*** **loosened, loosening**

loot (lo͞ot) ***noun*** something stolen or taken by force; booty.
verb to rob or take by force [Stores were *looted* during the riot.]
loot • ***noun*** • ***verb*** **looted, looting**

WORD HISTORY

loot

Our word **loot** comes from a noun in a modern language of India. This noun comes from a verb that means "to rob" in an ancient Indian language.

lop (läp) ***verb*** to cut off or chop off [The gardener *lopped* a branch from a tree.]
lop • ***verb*** **lopped, lopping**

a	cat	ō	go	ʉ	fur	ə =	a *in* ago
ā	ape	ô	law, for	ch	chin		e *in* agent
ä	cot, car	o͝o	look	sh	she		i *in* pencil
e	ten	o͞o	tool	th	thin		o *in* atom
ē	me	oi	oil	*th*	then		u *in* circus
i	fit	ou	out	zh	measure		
ī	ice	u	up	ŋ	ring		

lope (lōp) ***verb*** to move along easily, with long, swinging steps [She *loped* home.]
lope • ***verb*** **loped, loping**

lopsided (läp′sīd əd) ***adjective*** larger, heavier, or lower on one side than the other [a *lopsided* circle; a *lopsided* cake].
lop·sid·ed • ***adjective***

lord (lôrd) ***noun*** **1** a person with much power or authority; ruler or master [the *lord* of these lands]. **2** the owner of an estate in the Middle Ages. **3 Lord** God. **4 Lord** Jesus Christ. **5 Lord** in Britain, a title given to some men of high rank.
lord • ***noun,*** *plural* **lords**

WORD HISTORY

lord

We get **lord** from a thousand-year-old English word that means "loaf keeper," or "a person who feeds the people who depend on him." In the Middle Ages, a **lord** had many servants and knights who depended on him. Compare this word's history to the history of **lady**.

Los Angeles (lôs an′jə ləs) a city on the southwestern coast of California.
Los An·gel·es

lose (lo͞oz) ***verb*** **1** to be unable to find; have no longer [She *lost* her keys.] **2** to fail to keep or control [I *lost* my temper.] **3** to fail to win; be defeated in [We *lost* the contest.] **4** to fail to have or take advantage of; miss [I *lost* my chance.] **5** to fail to make use of; waste [Don't *lose* any time.] **6** to get rid of [I *lost* four pounds.]
lose • ***verb*** **lost, losing**

loss (lôs) ***noun*** **1** the act of losing something or the condition of being lost [Diet caused her *loss* of weight. The *loss* of his watch upset him.] **2** the amount, person, or thing lost [The store's yearly *loss* to theft is a serious problem.] **3** damage, trouble, or pain caused by losing something [The death of both her parents was a great *loss*.]
loss • ***noun,*** *plural* **losses**

lost (lôst) ***verb*** *past tense and past participle of* **lose**.
adjective **1** not to be found; missing or misplaced [a *lost* glove]. **2** not won or likely to be won [The king knew that the war was *lost*.] **3** having wandered from the way; not certain about one's location [a *lost* puppy]. **4** not spent in a useful way; wasted [*lost* time]. **5** destroyed; ruined [a ship *lost* at sea].
—lost in very much interested in; absorbed by [*lost in* thought]. **—lost on** having no effect on [My advice was *lost on* them.]

lot (lät) ***noun*** **1** *often* **lots** [*an informal use*] a great amount or number [a *lot* of cars; *lots* of money]. **2** a number of persons or things thought of as a group [This horse is the best of the *lot*.] **3** a small piece of land [a *lot* to build a house on]. **4** any object used in deciding something by chance. The lots are placed in a container and then people draw them out one by one without looking. **5** the fate of a person in life [his unhappy *lot*].
adverb very much [I'm a *lot* better.]
lot • ***noun,*** *plural* **lots** • ***adverb***

lotion (lō′shən) ***noun*** a liquid rubbed on the skin to keep it soft or to heal it.
lo·tion • ***noun,*** *plural* **lotions**

lottery (lät′ər ē) ***noun*** a form of gambling in which people buy numbered tickets. Prizes are given to those whose numbers are picked by chance.
lot·ter·y • ***noun,*** *plural* **lotteries**

loud (loud) ***adjective*** **1** strong in sound; not soft or quiet [a *loud* cry]. **2** noisy [a *loud* party]. **3** [*an informal use*] gaudy [a *loud* tie].
adverb in a loud manner [Don't talk so *loud*.]
loud • ***adjective*** & • ***adverb*** **louder, loudest**

loudspeaker (loud′spēk ər) ***noun*** a device that changes electric current into sound. It makes the sound loud enough to be heard in an auditorium or other large area.
loud·speak·er • ***noun,*** *plural* **loudspeakers**

STATE MAP

Louisiana

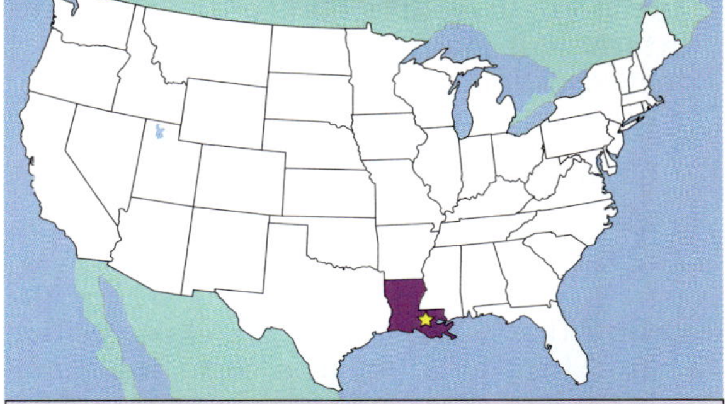

Statehood: 1812, the 18th state • **Capital:** Baton Rouge

Louisiana (lo͞o ē′zē an′ə) a State in the south central part of the U.S. Its capital is Baton

Rouge. Abbreviated **LA** or **La.**
Lou·i·si·an·a

lounge (lounj) ***verb*** to move, sit, or lie in an easy or lazy way; loll.
noun **1** a room with comfortable furniture where people can lounge. **2** a couch; sofa.
lounge • ***verb*** **lounged, lounging** • ***noun,*** *plural* **lounges**

louse (lous) ***noun*** a small insect pest that lives in the hair or on the skin of human beings and other animals. It gets food by sucking blood.
louse • ***noun,*** *plural* **lice**

lousy (lou′zē) [*a slang word*] ***adjective*** dirty, disgusting, poor, bad, or having some other negative characteristic [a *lousy* golfer; a *lousy* trick; a *lousy* day].
lous·y • ***adjective*** **lousier, lousiest**

lovable or **loveable** (luv′ə bəl) ***adjective*** easy to love or like [a *lovable* teddy bear].
lov·a·ble or **love·a·ble** • ***adjective***

love (luv) ***noun*** **1** a deep and tender feeling of fondness and loyalty [parents' *love* for their children]. **2** a strong liking [a *love* of books]. **3** a person that is loved very much [Mary was his own true *love*.]
verb **1** to feel love for [We *love* our parents.] **2** to have a strong liking for; take great pleasure in [I *love* to eat. He *loves* animals.] —Look for the WORD CHOICES box at the entry **like**[2].
—**fall in love** to begin to love. —**in love** feeling love.
love • ***noun,*** *plural* **loves** • ***verb*** **loved, loving**

WORD CHOICES

Synonyms of **love**

The words **love, affection,** and **attachment** share the meaning "a feeling of fondness and devotion."

her *love* for her country

his mild *affection* for cats

Mom's *attachment* to her fuzzy sweater

lovebird (luv′burd) ***noun*** a small parrot that is often kept as a pet in a cage. The mates seem to show great fondness for each other.
love·bird • ***noun,*** *plural* **lovebirds**

lovely (luv′lē) ***adjective*** **1** very pleasing in looks or character; beautiful [a *lovely* person]. **2** [*an informal use*] very enjoyable [We had a *lovely* time.]
love·ly • ***adjective*** **lovelier, loveliest**

loving (luv′iŋ) ***adjective*** feeling or showing love.
lov·ing • ***adjective***

low[1] (lō) ***adjective*** **1** reaching only a short distance up; not high or tall [a *low* building]. **2** close to the earth; not high above the ground [*low* clouds]. **3** below the usual surface or level [*low* land]. **4** not very deep; shallow [The river is *low* in summer.] **5** below what is considered as average; below others [*low* grades in school]. **6** less than usual in amount, cost, power, strength, or some other way [*low* wages]. **7** having only a little of [*low* on gas; *low* in calories]. **8** not good or positive; poor [a *low* opinion of someone]. **9** sad or gloomy [*low* spirits]. **10** not loud; soft [a *low* voice]. **11** deep in pitch [the *low* notes of the tuba].
adverb in or to a low level, place, point, or degree [Pitch the ball *low*. Speak *low*.]
noun **1** a low level, place, point, or degree [Prices hit a record *low*.] **2** an arrangement of gears in a car that gives the lowest speed and greatest power [Shift into *low* on hills.]
low • ***adjective &*** • ***adverb*** **lower, lowest** • ***noun,*** *plural for sense 1 only* **lows**

low[2] (lō) ***noun*** the sound that a cow makes; moo.
verb to make this sound.
low • ***noun,*** *plural* **lows** • ***verb*** **lowed, lowing**

Low Countries the Netherlands, Belgium, and Luxembourg.

lower (lō′ər) ***adjective*** *comparative of* **low**[1].
verb **1** to let or put down [*lower* the window]. **2** to make or become less in height, amount, value, or pitch [They will *lower* the price. He *lowered* his voice to a whisper.]
low·er • ***adjective*** • ***verb*** **lowered, lowering**

lowland (lō′lənd) ***noun*** land that is lower than the land around it.
low·land • ***noun,*** *plural* **lowlands**

low tide ***noun*** the time when the tide sinks lowest.
low tide • ***noun,*** *plural* **low tides**

a	cat	ō	go	ʉ	fur	ə =	a *in* ago
ā	ape	ô	law, for	ch	chin		e *in* agent
ä	cot, car	oo	look	sh	she		i *in* pencil
e	ten	ōō	tool	th	thin		o *in* atom
ē	me	oi	oil	*th*	then		u *in* circus
i	fit	ou	out	zh	measure		
ī	ice	u	up	ŋ	ring		

loyal (loi′əl) ***adjective*** faithful to one's country, family, duty, or beliefs [a *loyal* citizen; a loyal friend; a *loyal* member of the group] —Look for the WORD CHOICES box at the entry **faithful**.
loy·al • ***adjective***

loyalty (loi′əl tē) ***noun*** the condition or an example of being loyal —Look for the WORD CHOICES box at the entry **allegiance**.
loy·al·ty • ***noun,*** *plural* **loyalties**

lozenge (läz′ənj) ***noun*** a cough drop or a hard piece of candy shaped somewhat like a diamond.
loz·enge • ***noun,*** *plural* **lozenges**

Lt. *abbreviation for* lieutenant.

lubricant (lo͞o′bri kənt) ***noun*** oil, grease, or other slippery material put on the parts of a machine. It helps the parts move more smoothly against each other.
lu·bri·cant • ***noun,*** *plural* **lubricants**

lubricate (lo͞o′bri kāt) ***verb*** to put a lubricant in or on in order to make the parts more slippery [The mechanic *lubricated* the motor.]
lu·bri·cate • ***verb*** **lubricated, lubricating**

Lucifer (lo͞o′si fər) Satan; the Devil.
Lu·ci·fer

luck (luk) ***noun*** **1** the things that seem to happen to a person by chance, good or bad; fortune [My *luck* took a turn for the worse.] **2** good fortune [I had the *luck* to be first.]

luckily (luk′i lē) ***adverb*** by good fortune [*Luckily* we brought enough food.]
luck·i·ly • ***adverb***

lucky (luk′ē) ***adjective*** **1** having good luck [*lucky* at cards]. **2** having a good result by chance [A *lucky* accident led to the discovery.] **3** thought to bring good luck [a *lucky* rabbit's foot].
luck·y • ***adjective*** **luckier, luckiest**

lug (lug) ***verb*** to carry or drag with effort [We *lugged* the heavy box upstairs.]
lug • ***verb*** **lugged, lugging**

luggage (lug′ij) ***noun*** the suitcases, trunks, or boxes of a traveler; baggage.
lug·gage • ***noun***

Luke (lo͝ok) **1** an early Christian who was a companion of Paul the Apostle. **2** the third book of the New Testament. Luke is believed to have written this book.

lukewarm (lo͝ok′wôrm) ***adjective*** **1** just barely warm [*lukewarm* water]. **2** not very eager or enthusiastic [a *lukewarm* compliment].
luke·warm • ***adjective***

lull (lul) ***verb*** to make or become calm [She *lulled* the baby to sleep in a cradle.]
noun a short period when things are quiet or less active [a *lull* in the day's activities].
lull • ***verb*** **lulled, lulling** • ***noun,*** *plural* **lulls**

lullaby (lul′ə bī) ***noun*** a song for lulling a baby to sleep.
lull·a·by • ***noun,*** *plural* **lullabies**

lumber (lum′bər) ***noun*** wood that has been sawed into beams, planks, and boards.
lum·ber • ***noun***

lumberjack (lum′bər jak) ***noun*** *another name for* **logger**.
lum·ber·jack • ***noun,*** *plural* **lumberjacks**

luminous (lo͞o′mi nəs) ***adjective*** **1** giving off light; shining; bright [the *luminous* rays of the sun; *luminous* eyes]. **2** glowing in the dark [*luminous* paint].
lu·mi·nous • ***adjective***

lump (lump) ***noun*** **1** a small, solid mass, with no special shape; hunk [a *lump* of clay]. **2** a raised place; swelling [a *lump* from a bee sting].
adjective in a lump or lumps [*lump* sugar].
verb **1** to form into a lump or lumps. **2** to put or group together [They *lumped* all their money together to buy a TV.]
—lump in one's throat a tight feeling in the throat when one tries to keep from crying.
lump • ***noun,*** *plural* **lumps** • ***adjective*** • ***verb*** **lumped, lumping**

lumpy (lump′ē) ***adjective*** full of lumps [*lumpy* pudding; a *lumpy* old couch].
lump·y • ***adjective*** **lumpier, lumpiest**

lunar (lo͞o′nər) ***adjective*** having to do with the moon [a *lunar* spacecraft; a *lunar* crater].
lu·nar • ***adjective***

lunch (lunch) ***noun*** a meal eaten in the middle of the day, between breakfast and dinner.
verb to eat lunch.
lunch • ***noun,*** *plural* **lunches** • ***verb*** **lunched, lunching**

luncheon (lun′chən) ***noun*** a lunch that is a formal meal with other people.
lunch·eon • ***noun,*** *plural* **luncheons**

lung (luŋ) ***noun*** either of the two organs in the chest that are used in breathing. The lungs

put oxygen into the blood and take carbon dioxide from it.
lung • *noun, plural* **lungs**

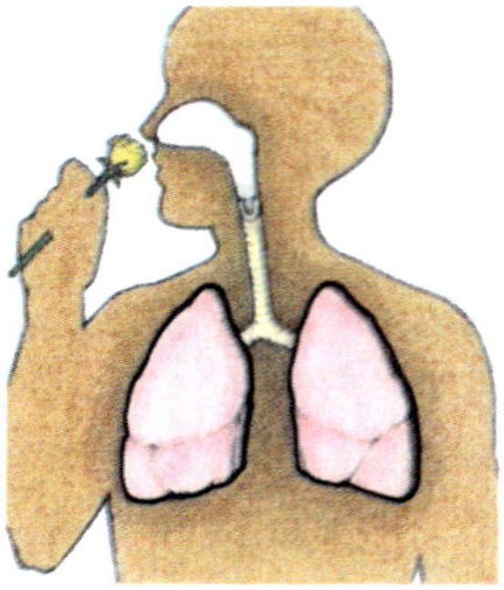

lung

lunge (lunj) ***noun*** a sudden, sharp move forward [He made a *lunge* for the basketball.]
verb to make a lunge [She *lunged* to catch the ball.]
lunge • ***noun****, plural* **lunges** • ***verb*** **lunged, lunging**

lurch[1] (lʉrch) ***verb*** to lean or roll suddenly forward or to one side.
noun a lurching movement [The bus started with a *lurch*.]
lurch • ***verb*** **lurched, lurching** • ***noun****, plural* **lurches**

lurch[2] (lʉrch) ***noun*** *used only in the phrase* **leave in the lurch**, to leave in trouble and needing help.

lure (loor) ***verb*** to attract or lead by offering something that seems pleasant.
noun **1** anything that lures [the *lure* of delicious smells from the kitchen]. **2** an artificial bait that is used in fishing.
lure • ***verb*** **lured, luring** • ***noun****, plural* **lures**

lurk (lʉrk) ***verb*** to stay hidden, ready to spring out and attack; lie in wait.
lurk • ***verb*** **lurked, lurking**

luscious (lush′əs) ***adjective*** **1** having a delicious taste or smell; full of flavor [a *luscious* peach]. **2** very pleasing to see, hear, feel, or experience [the *luscious* sound of the violins].
lus·cious • ***adjective***

lush (lush) ***adjective*** **1** growing thick and healthy [*lush* jungle plants]. **2** covered with thick, healthy growth [*lush* fields].

lust (lust) ***noun*** a strong desire [a *lust* for success].
verb to feel a strong desire [The dictator *lusted* for more power.]
lust • ***noun****, plural* **lusts** • ***verb*** **lusted, lusting**

luster (lus′tər) ***noun*** the brightness of things that reflect light; gloss [the *luster* of silver].
lus·ter • ***noun***

lustrous (lus′trəs) ***adjective*** having luster; shining; bright [the *lustrous* moon].
lus·trous • ***adjective***

Luther (lo͞o′thər), **Martin** (märt′n) 1483-1546; German Protestant leader.
Lu·ther, Mar·tin

Luxembourg (luk′səm bʉrg) a small country in western Europe surrounded by Belgium, Germany, and France.
Lux·em·bourg

luxurious (lug zhoor′ē əs) ***adjective*** giving a feeling of comfort and pleasure [a big, soft, *luxurious* chair].
lux·u·ri·ous • ***adjective***

luxury (luk′shər ē *or* lug′zhər ē) ***noun*** something that gives great comfort and pleasure. It is usually something that is not really needed.
lux·u·ry • ***noun****, plural* **luxuries**

-ly *a suffix meaning:* **1** in a certain way [Thinking *seriously* is thinking in a serious way.] **2** to a certain degree [We are *equally* excited about the trip; we are excited to an equal degree.] **3** at a certain time [We were in Chicago *recently*, just two weeks ago.] **4** in a certain order [*Secondly* means second in order.]

WORD MAKER

The suffix -ly

Many words contain the suffix **-ly** plus a word that you already know. You can understand these words if you add the idea "in a certain way," "to a certain extent," or "at a certain time or place" to the meaning of the base word.

I. *in a certain way (how):*

base word	*+ suffix*	⇨	*new word*
brave	**+ -ly**	⇨	**bravely** *(in a brave way)*

badly	clearly	fairly
blindly	completely	falsely
bravely	constantly	firmly
brightly	correctly	freely
calmly	cruelly	gladly
carefully	eagerly	gradually
carelessly	easily	gratefully
cheerfully	evenly	honestly

a	cat	ō	go	ʉ	fur	ə =	a *in* ago
ā	ape	ô	law, for	ch	chin		e *in* agent
ä	cot, car	oo	look	sh	she		i *in* pencil
e	ten	o͞o	tool	th	thin		o *in* atom
ē	me	oi	oil	*th*	then		u *in* circus
i	fit	ou	out	zh	measure		
ī	ice	u	up	ŋ	ring		

incorrectly	quickly	smoothly
joyfully	quietly	strongly
loudly	rapidly	suddenly
neatly	regularly	swiftly
nicely	sadly	tightly
normally	safely	truthfully
painfully	seriously	unfairly
patiently	sharply	weakly
poorly	shyly	wildly
promptly	silently	willingly
properly	sincerely	wisely
proudly	slowly	wrongly

Note: Sometimes there is a spelling change in the base word when the suffix is added.

base word	*+ suffix*	⇨	*new word*
angry			angrily
comfortable			comfortably
dizzy			dizzily
dull			dully
energetic			energetically
gay			gaily
greedy			greedily
happy			happily
horrible			horribly
lazy			lazily
merry			merrily
noisy			noisily
simple			simply
sleepy			sleepily

II. *to a certain degree (how much):*

base word	*+ suffix*	⇨	*new word*
great	+ -ly	⇨	**greatly** *(to a great extent)*
full	+ -ly	⇨	**fully** *(to the full extent)*
definite			definitely
entire			entirely
equal			equally
perfect			perfectly
rare			rarely
slight			slightly
wide			widely

III. *at a certain time or at certain times (when):*

base word	*+ suffix*	⇨	*new word*
recent	+ -ly	⇨	**recently** *(at a recent time)*
final			finally
frequent			frequently
occasional			occasionally

lye (lī) ***noun*** a strong, harsh substance, used in cleaning and in making soap. In earlier times lye was made from wood ashes.
● The words **lye** and **lie** sound alike.
Household *lye* is poisonous.
Lie down for a while and rest.
Don't *lie*—tell the truth!

lynch (linch) ***verb*** to murder someone by the decision of a mob, without a lawful trial. A person who is lynched is usually hanged.
lynch • ***verb*** **lynched, lynching**

lynx

lynx (liŋks) ***noun*** a wildcat of North America that has long legs, a short tail, and long, silky, yellow fur.
lynx • ***noun,*** *plural* **lynxes**

lyre (līr) ***noun*** an old instrument like a small harp. It was used by the ancient Greeks to accompany singers or poets.
lyre • ***noun,*** *plural* **lyres**

lyre

lyric (lir′ik) ***noun*** *usually* **lyrics** the words of a song [She writes her own music and *lyrics*.]
lyr·ic • ***noun,*** *plural* **lyrics**

M m

Mm Mm *Mm* Mm

The letter **m** *has the sound you hear at the beginning of the words* **me, miss,** *and* **moth**. *The letter* **m** *is also used as an abbreviation for the units of measure* **mile** *and* **meter**. *Abbreviations do not have a pronunciation of their own; instead, you pronounce the words that they stand for.*

m or **M** (em) ***noun*** the thirteenth letter of the English alphabet.
m or **M** • ***noun,*** *plural* **m's** or **M's**

M (em) ***noun*** the Roman numeral for 1,000.

m or **m.** *abbreviation for* **1** meter. **2** meters. **3** mile. **4** miles.

ma (mä) [*an informal word*] ***noun*** mother.

MA *abbreviation for* Massachusetts.

ma'am (mam) ***noun*** [*an informal word*] madam.

macaroni (mak′ə rō′nē) ***noun*** small, hollow, curved tubes of pasta, often baked with cheese.
mac·a·ro·ni • ***noun***

macaw (mə kô′ *or* mə kä′) ***noun*** a large, bright-colored parrot of Central and South America. It has a long tail and a harsh cry.
ma·caw • ***noun,*** *plural* **macaws**

Macedonia (mas′ə dō′nē ə) a country in southeastern Europe. It was a part of Yugoslavia.
Mac·e·do·ni·a

machine (mə shēn′) ***noun*** **1** a thing made up of fixed and moving parts, for doing some kind of work [a sewing *machine*]. **2** *the same as* **simple machine**.
ma·chine • ***noun,*** *plural* **machines**

machine gun ***noun*** an automatic gun that fires many bullets, one right after the other.
machine gun • ***noun,*** *plural* **machine guns**

machinery (mə shēn′ər ē) ***noun*** **1** machines in general [the *machinery* of a factory]. **2** the working parts of a machine [the *machinery* of a printing press].
ma·chin·er·y • ***noun***

machinist (mə shēn′ist) ***noun*** a worker who is skilled in using the heavy, motor-powered tools that are used to make machines and machine parts.
ma·chin·ist • ***noun,*** *plural* **machinists**

mackerel (mak′ər əl) ***noun*** a fish of the northern Atlantic ocean, used for food.
mack·er·el • ***noun,*** *plural* **mackerel** or **mackerels**

macron (mā′krən *or* mā′krän) ***noun*** a short, straight mark (¯). It is placed over certain vowel letters to show a certain pronunciation. In this dictionary, it is placed over vowels to show long vowel sounds, like "a" in "late" (lāt).
ma·cron • ***noun,*** *plural* **macrons**

mad (mad) ***adjective*** **1** angry [Don't be *mad* at us for leaving.] **2** crazy; insane. **3** fond or enthusiastic in a way that is foolish [*mad* about hats]. **4** having rabies [a *mad* dog].
mad • ***adjective*** **madder, maddest**

a	cat	ō	go	ʉ	fur	ə =	a *in* ago
ā	ape	ô	law, for	ch	chin		e *in* agent
ä	cot, car	o͝o	look	sh	she		i *in* pencil
e	ten	o͞o	tool	th	thin		o *in* atom
ē	me	oi	oil	*th*	then		u *in* circus
i	fit	ou	out	zh	measure		
ī	ice	u	up	ŋ	ring		

Madagascar (mad ə gas′kər) a country on a large island off the southeastern coast of Africa.
Mad·a·gas·car

madam (mad′əm) ***noun*** a polite form used in speaking to or of a woman [May I help you, *madam?*]
mad·am • ***noun***

madame (mə däm′ *or* mad′əm) ***noun*** a French word used, like "Mrs.," as a title for a married woman.
mad·ame • ***noun,*** *plural* **mesdames** (mā däm′)

made (mād) ***verb*** *past tense and past participle of* **make**.
- The words **made** and **maid** sound alike.
  He *made* breakfast for us.
  She hired a butler and a *maid.*

madhouse (mad′hous′) ***noun*** a place of noise and confusion [The playground is a *madhouse* at the lunch hour.]
mad·house • ***noun,*** *plural* **madhouses**

Madison (mad′i sən), **James** (jāmz) 1751-1836; the fourth president of the U.S., from 1809 to 1817.
Mad·i·son, James

Madison (mad′i sən) the capital of Wisconsin.
Mad·i·son

madly (mad′lē) ***adverb*** in a way that is insane, wild, or foolish [*madly* in love].
mad·ly • ***adverb***

madness (mad′nəs) ***noun*** **1** the condition of being mad or insane. **2** great foolishness.
mad·ness • ***noun***

magazine (mag ə zēn′) ***noun*** **1** a printed collection of writing that comes out weekly, monthly, or at some other regular time. It contains articles, stories, pictures, and various other kinds of information. **2** the space in a gun that holds the cartridges.
mag·a·zine • ***noun,*** *plural* **magazines**

WORD HISTORY

magazine

The source of the word **magazine** is an Arabic verb that means "to store up." We can think of a **magazine** as something that holds information or news that has been stored up.

Magellan (mə jel′ən), **Ferdinand** (furd′n and) 1480?-1521; Portuguese explorer who led a voyage that became the first around the world. He died on the way.
Ma·gel·lan, Fer·di·nand

maggot (mag′ət) ***noun*** an insect, especially a housefly, in an early stage, when it looks like a worm. Some maggots are found in rotting matter.
mag·got • ***noun,*** *plural* **maggots**

magic (maj′ik) ***noun*** **1** the use of charms, spells, and special ceremonies that are supposed to control forces of nature and events. **2** the skill of doing tricks that fool people. It is done by moving the hands very quickly and by using strings, mirrors, and other devices. **3** any power or force that seems mysterious or hard to explain [the *magic* of love].
adjective **1** of or relating to the practice of magic. **2** of or as if by magic [*magic* tricks].
mag·ic • ***noun*** • ***adjective***

magical (maj′i kəl) ***adjective*** of or like magic [a *magical* day; a *magical* spell].
mag·i·cal • ***adjective***

magician (mə jish′ən) ***noun*** **1** a person who works magic in fairy tales. **2** a person who does magic tricks.
ma·gi·cian • ***noun,*** *plural* **magicians**

magnesium (mag nē′zē əm) ***noun*** a silvery, very light metal that is a chemical element. Magnesium is mixed with other metals to make light, strong parts for aircraft and spacecraft.
mag·ne·si·um • ***noun***

magnet (mag′nət) ***noun*** any piece of iron, steel, or iron ore that has the natural power to draw iron and steel to it.
mag·net • ***noun,*** *plural* **magnets**

magnet

magnetic (mag net′ ik) ***adjective*** working like a magnet [a *magnetic* needle in a compass].
mag·net·ic • ***adjective***

magnetic field ***noun*** the area around a magnetic pole in which magnetism exists.

M

magnetic field • *noun, plural* **magnetic fields**

magnetic north *noun* the direction toward which the needle of a compass points. In most places it is not true north.

magnetic pole *noun* **1** either pole of a magnet from which the magnetism seems to originate. **2** either of the regions on the earth's surface that behave like the poles of a magnet. They are located near the North and South Poles.
magnetic pole • *noun, plural* **magnetic poles**

magnetic tape *noun* a thin plastic ribbon that has a special coating that is magnetic. It is used for recording sound or images or computer data.

magnetism (mag′nə tiz əm) *noun* the power of a magnet to draw things toward it.
mag·net·ism • *noun*

magnificence (mag nif′i səns) *noun* great and impressive beauty; splendor [the *magnificence* of the emperor's palace].
mag·nif·i·cence • *noun*

magnificent (mag nif′i sənt) *adjective* rich, fine, noble, or beautiful in a great way; splendid [a *magnificent* palace; a singer with a *magnificent* voice] —Look for the WORD CHOICES box at the entry **grand**.
mag·nif·i·cent • *adjective*

magnify (mag′ni fī′) *verb* **1** to make something look or seem larger or greater than it really is [This lens *magnifies* an object to ten times its size.] **2** to make something appear more important than is really so; exaggerate [He *magnified* the importance of his discovery.]
mag·ni·fy • *verb* **magnified, magnifying, magnifies**

magnifying glass

magnifying glass *noun* a lens that makes the things seen through it look larger.
magnifying glass • *noun, plural* **magnifying glasses**

magnitude (mag′ni to͞od *or* mag′ni tyo͞od) *noun* great importance [At the time, people did not realize the *magnitude* of the American Revolution.]
mag·ni·tude • *noun*

magnolia (mag nō′lē ə *or* mag nōl′yə) *noun* a tree or shrub that has large, sweet-smelling, white, pink, or purple flowers.
mag·no·li·a • *noun, plural* **magnolias**

magpie (mag′pī) *noun* a black-and-white bird with a long tail. Magpies have the habit of chattering noisily. They are related to crows.
mag·pie • *noun, plural* **magpies**

Mahican (mə hē′kən) *noun* **1** a member of a North American Indian people who lived chiefly in upper New York State. **2** the language of this people.
Ma·hi·can • *noun, plural for sense 1 only* **Mahicans** or **Mahican**

mahogany (mə häg′ə nē *or* mə hôg′ə nē) *noun* **1** a tropical, evergreen American tree that has hard, reddish-brown wood. **2** the wood of this tree that is often used in furniture.
ma·hog·a·ny • *noun*

Mahomet (mə häm′ət) *another name for* **Mohammed**.
Ma·hom·et

maid (mād) *noun* **1** a girl or young woman who is not married. **2** a girl or woman who is paid to do housework.
maid • *noun, plural* **maids**

● The words **maid** and **made** sound alike.
Our *maid* has keys to the house.
The trade was *made* with Boston's team.

maiden (mād′n) *noun* a girl or young woman who is not married.
adjective **1** not married [a *maiden* aunt]. **2** first or earliest [The ship's *maiden* voyage was delayed by a great ocean storm.]

a cat	ō go	ʉ fur	ə = a *in* ago
ā ape	ô law, for	ch chin	e *in* agent
ä cot, car	oo look	sh she	i *in* pencil
e ten	o͞o tool	th thin	o *in* atom
ē me	oi oil	*th* then	u *in* circus
i fit	ou out	zh measure	
ī ice	u up	ŋ ring	

maid·en • *noun, plural* **maidens** • *adjective*

maiden name *noun* the family name that a woman had before she was married.
maiden name • *noun, plural* **maiden names**

mail (māl) *noun* **1** letters, packages, or other items that are carried and delivered by the post office. **2** a delivery of mail at a certain time ["Has the morning *mail* arrived yet?"] **3** the system of picking up and delivering letters, packages, and other items. It is usually run by a department of a country's government. [We sent all the packages by *mail*.]
verb to send by mail [Have you *mailed* the wedding invitations?]
mail • *noun, plural* **mails** • *verb* **mailed, mailing**

- The words **mail** and **male** sound alike.
  We have afternoon *mail* delivery.
  "*Male*" is the opposite of "female."

WORD HISTORY

mail

We get **mail** from a 600-year-old English word that came from a German word. That word at first meant "wallet" and then came to mean "traveling bag." Letter carriers today still carry **mail** in bags that resemble those early traveling bags.

mailbox (māl′bäks) *noun* **1** a box for mail delivery at a home. **2** a special box for the public into which mail is put so that it can be picked up for delivery.
mail·box • *noun, plural* **mailboxes**

mail carrier *noun* a person whose work is carrying and delivering mail.
mail carrier • *noun, plural* **mail carriers**

mailman (māl′man) *noun* a person whose work is carrying and delivering mail; mail carrier.
mail·man • *noun, plural* **mailmen**

maim (mām) *verb* to hurt a person so that an arm, eye, or other body part loses its use or is lost; cripple.
maim • *verb* **maimed, maiming**

WORD CHOICES

Synonyms of **maim**

The words **maim, cripple,** and **mutilate** share the meaning "to remove or badly damage a part of a person or thing."

He was *maimed* in an auto accident.
Arthritis has *crippled* my grandmother.
Vandals *mutilated* the statue.

main (mān) *adjective* first in size or importance; chief; principal [the *main* office of a company; the *main* characters in a movie; the *main* clause in a sentence] —Look for the WORD CHOICES box at the entry **principal**.
noun a large pipe or duct that is used to carry water, gas, or electricity to homes or other buildings.
main • *adjective* • *noun, plural* **mains**

- The words **main** and **mane** sound alike.
  The water *main* runs under the street.
  A lion's *mane* can grow quite long.

STATE MAP

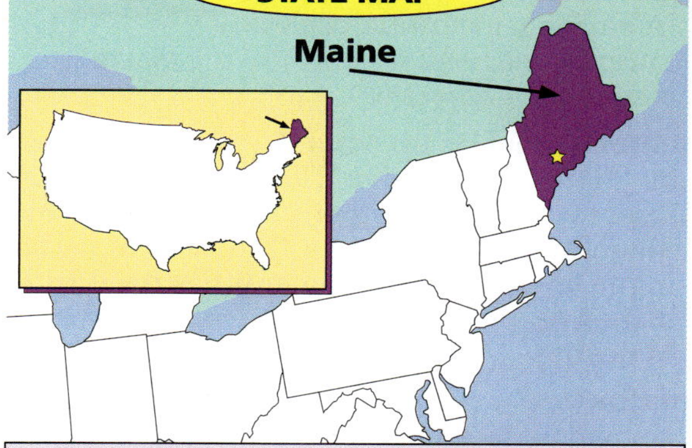

Statehood: 1820, the 23rd state • **Capital:** Augusta

Maine (mān) a New England State of the U.S. Its capital is Augusta. Abbreviated **ME** or **Me.**

mainland (mān′land *or* mān′lənd) *noun* the main land mass of a country or largest part of a continent, as distinguished from nearby islands.
main·land • *noun*

mainly (mān′lē) *adverb* most of all; chiefly [Her paintings are *mainly* of country landscapes.]
main·ly • *adverb*

maintain (mān tān′) ***verb*** **1** to keep or keep up; continue in the same condition [*Maintain* an even speed.] **2** to keep in good condition; take care of [The city *maintains* the parks and beaches.] **3** to take care of by supplying what is needed; support [He *maintains* a large family.] **4** to say in a positive way; declare [He still *maintains* that he's innocent.]
main·tain • ***verb*** **maintained, maintaining**

maintenance (mān′tə nəns) ***noun*** the act or process of maintaining; support [Taxes pay for the *maintenance* of schools.]
main·te·nance • ***noun***

maize (māz) ***noun*** the corn plant or its ears and kernels.
• The words **maize** and **maze** sound alike.
The Indians served *maize* and beans.
The rats moved through the *maze*.

maize

Maj. *an abbreviation for* Major.

majestic (mə jes′tik) ***adjective*** having majesty; grand or stately; dignified [A *majestic* mountain peak towered above all others.]
ma·jes·tic • ***adjective***

majesty (maj′əs tē) ***noun*** **1** great size, beauty, or dignity; splendor [The travelers were impressed by the *majesty* of the Rocky Mountains.] **2 Majesty** a title used in speaking to or of a king, queen, or other royal ruler.
maj·es·ty • ***noun****, plural for sense 2 only* **Majesties**

major (mā′jər) ***adjective*** greater in size, number, amount, or importance [The *major* part of her allowance went to buy tapes. Shakespeare is one of the *major* English writers.]
noun a military officer.
ma·jor • ***adjective*** • ***noun****, plural* **majors**

majorette (mā jər et′) ***noun*** *a short form of* **drum majorette**.
ma·jor·ette • ***noun****, plural* **majorettes**

majority (mə jôr′i tē) ***noun*** **1** the greater part or number of something; more than half [A *majority* of the students went to the football game.] **2** the difference between a larger number and a smaller number of votes cast [The mayor got 50,000 votes and her opponent got 30,000, so the mayor won with a *majority* of 20,000 votes.]
ma·jor·i·ty • ***noun****, plural for sense 2 only* **majorities**

make (māk) ***verb*** **1** to bring into being; build, create, produce, or put together [She *made* a new dress. Let's *make* a fire. He *made* plans to go to New Mexico.] **2** to bring about; cause to exist, happen, or appear [Please don't *make* trouble for us. The children *made* a lot of noise last night.] **3** to cause to be or become [His giggling *makes* me nervous.] **4** to turn out to be [Her book will *make* a great movie.] **5** to do, perform, or carry on [*Make* a right turn at the next traffic light. The principal *made* a speech at the party.] **6** to get or gain for oneself; earn [She *made* a lot of money in real estate. How does he *make* so many friends?] **7** to prepare for use; arrange [He *made* the bed.] **8** to amount to; total [Two pints *make* a quart.] **9** to cause or force to [Don't *make* me laugh. *Make* them put their toys away.] **10** [*an informal use*] to succeed in becoming a member of or being mentioned in [Ten of us *made* the honor roll. The earthquake *made* the headlines.]
noun **1** the way something is made or put together [a machine of a very simple *make*]. **2** a brand or type of product [What's the *make* of your new car?]
—make believe to pretend [She likes to *make believe* she's a ballerina.] **—make it** [*an informal use*] **1** to achieve a certain thing [She *made it* to the train on time.] **2** to succeed [He'll never *make it* in business.] **—make out** **1** to see or hear clearly enough to understand [I can barely *make out* the numbers on the license plate.] **2** to fill out [*Make* the check *out* to Mrs. Jones, please.] **3** to understand [Can you *make out* what she means by that?] **4** to get along; succeed [How did he *make out* in his new job?] **—make up** **1** to form; be the parts of [Twelve students *make up* the debating team in our school.] **2** to invent [She *made up* a story about meeting a famous movie star.] **3** to become friendly again after a quarrel [They shook hands and *made up*.] **4** to supply what is missing [Dad will *make up* the difference between the cost of the bicycle and the

a	cat	ō	go	ʉ	fur	ə =	a *in* ago
ā	ape	ô	law, for	ch	chin		e *in* agent
ä	cot, car	oo	look	sh	she		i *in* pencil
e	ten	o͞o	tool	th	thin		o *in* atom
ē	me	oi	oil	*th*	then		u *in* circus
i	fit	ou	out	zh	measure		
ī	ice	u	up	ŋ	ring		

money you have.] **5** to decide [He *made up* his mind to go to the movie.]
make • *verb* **made, making** • *noun, plural for sense 2 only* **makes**

make-believe (māk′bə lēv) *noun* the act of pretending or imagining [Toys coming to life are part of a child's world of *make-believe*.] *adjective* imagined [a *make-believe* playmate].
make-be·lieve • *noun* • *adjective*

maker (māk′ər) *noun* a person or thing that makes something [He is a good pastry *maker*. We bought an electric coffee *maker*.]
mak·er • *noun, plural* **makers**

makeshift (māk′shift) *adjective* used for a time in place of the usual thing [a *makeshift* table].
make·shift • *adjective*

makeup or **make-up** (māk′up) *noun* **1** lipstick, mascara, and other cosmetics. **2** the way a thing is put together; composition [Do you know the *makeup* of the atom?]
make·up or **make-up** • *noun*

malaria (mə ler′ē ə) *noun* a disease in which a person keeps having chills and fever. Malaria is carried by the bite of certain mosquitoes.
ma·lar·i·a • *noun*

Malawi (mä′lä wē) a country in southeastern Africa.
Ma·la·wi

Malaysia (mə lā′zhə) a country in southeastern Asia, mainly on a peninsula.
Ma·lay·sia

Maldives (mal′dīvz) a country on a group of islands in the Indian Ocean, southwest of Sri Lanka.
Mal·dives

male (māl) *adjective* **1** of or belonging to the sex that can make the egg of the female fertile. **2** of or for men or boys [a *male* chorus]. *noun* a male person, animal, or plant.
male • *adjective* • *noun, plural* **males**
• The words **male** and **mail** sound alike.
We bought two hamsters, both *male*.
The *mail* carrier left two letters.

Mali (mä′lē) a country in western Africa.
Ma·li

malice (mal′is) *noun* a feeling of wanting to hurt or harm someone; ill will; spite.
mal·ice • *noun*

malicious (mə lish′əs) *adjective* having or showing malice; spiteful [*malicious* rumors].
ma·li·cious • *adjective*

malignant (mə lig′nənt) *adjective* causing or likely to cause death; very dangerous [A cancer is a *malignant* growth.]
ma·lig·nant • *adjective*

mall (môl) *noun* **1** an enclosed, air-conditioned shopping center with a broad passageway through it and shops on each side of the passageway. **2** a street closed to motor vehicles, with shops on each side. **3** a broad, often shaded place for the public to walk.
mall • *noun, plural* **malls**
• The words **mall** and **maul** sound alike.
We're going to shop up at the *mall*.
Some bears do *maul* their trainers.

mallard

mallard (mal′ərd) *noun* a common wild duck. The male has a dark-green head and a white ring around the neck.
mal·lard • *noun, plural* **mallards**

mallet (mal′ət) *noun* **1** a kind of hammer with a wooden head and a short handle. It is used as a tool. **2** a long-handled hammer with a wooden head that is used for playing croquet or polo.
mal·let • *noun, plural* **mallets**

malnutrition (mal′no͞o trish′ən) *noun* an unhealthy condition of the body that is caused by not getting enough food or enough of the right foods.
mal·nu·tri·tion • *noun*

malt (môlt) *noun* barley or other grain that is soaked in water until it sprouts, and then is dried. Malt is used especially in making beer, ale, and other alcoholic drinks.

Malta (môl′tə) a country on a group of islands in the Mediterranean Sea, between Italy and northern Africa.
Mal·ta

M

malted milk (môl′təd) ***noun*** a drink made by mixing milk with a powder made of malt and dried milk. It often contains ice cream and flavoring.
malt·ed milk • ***noun***

mama or **mamma** (mä′mə) ***noun*** mother. This is a word used mainly by children.
ma·ma or **mam·ma** • ***noun,*** *plural* **mamas** or **mammas**

mammal (mam′əl) ***noun*** a warmblooded animal that has a backbone. A female mammal has glands that produce milk for feeding its young. Dogs, lions, whales, mice, and human beings are mammals.
mam·mal • ***noun,*** *plural* **mammals**

mammoth (mam′əth) ***noun*** a type of large elephant that lived long ago. Mammoths had shaggy, brown hair and long, curved tusks.
adjective very big; gigantic; huge —Look for the WORD CHOICES box at the entry **enormous**.
mam·moth • ***noun,*** *plural* **mammoths**
• ***adjective***

man (man) ***noun*** **1** an adult male human being. **2** any human being; person ["All *men* are created equal."] **3** the human race; mankind [*Man's* conquest of space began in the 20th century.] **4** one of the pieces used in playing chess, checkers, or other games.
verb to supply with people for work or defense [Thirty sailors *manned* the ship.]
man • ***noun,*** *plural for senses 1, 2, and 4 only* **men** • ***verb*** **manned, manning**

-man *a suffix meaning:* **1** a man or person of a certain kind [a *Frenchman*]. **2** a man or person in a certain job or activity [A *mailman* delivers mail. A *sportsman* takes part in sports.]

Man. *abbreviation for* Manitoba.

manage (man′ij) ***verb*** **1** to have control of; direct the work of [Rachel's mother *manages* a store.] **2** to control the movement or behavior of [Grandma *manages* the children easily.] **3** to succeed in getting something done [I *managed* to pass the test.]
man·age • ***verb*** **managed, managing**

management (man′ij mənt) ***noun*** **1** the act or skill of managing [A successful business needs careful *management*.] **2** the persons who manage a certain business [*Management* declared there would be no layoffs.]
man·age·ment • ***noun***

manager (man′ij ər) ***noun*** a person who manages a business, baseball team, or other institution.
man·ag·er • ***noun,*** *plural* **managers**

manatee

manatee (man′ə tē) ***noun*** a large animal that lives in shallow tropical waters and feeds on plants. It has flippers and a broad, flat tail.
man·a·tee • ***noun,*** *plural* **manatees**

mandarin (man′dər in) ***noun*** **1** a high public official of imperial China, before 1911. **2 Mandarin** the main form of the Chinese language. It is the official language of China.
man·da·rin • ***noun,*** *plural for sense 1 only* **mandarins**

mandate (man′dāt) ***noun*** **1** the will of the people as made known to their representatives in government through votes cast in an election [The President received a *mandate* to end the war.] **2** an official order or command.
man·date • ***noun,*** *plural* **mandates**

mandolin

mandolin (man də lin′) ***noun*** a musical instrument with four or five pairs of strings. It is played with a pick.
man·do·lin • ***noun,*** *plural* **mandolins**

a	cat	ō	go	ʉ	fur	ə =	a *in* ago
ā	ape	ô	law, for	ch	chin		e *in* agent
ä	cot, car	ŏŏ	look	sh	she		i *in* pencil
e	ten	ōō	tool	th	thin		o *in* atom
ē	me	oi	oil	*th*	then		u *in* circus
i	fit	ou	out	zh	measure		
ī	ice	u	up	ŋ	ring		

mane (mān) ***noun*** the long hair growing along or around the neck of a horse, male lion, or certain other animals.
mane • ***noun,*** *plural* **manes**
• The words **mane** and **main** sound alike.
She tied ribbons in the horse's *mane*.
He works at the *main* library.

maneuver (mə no͞o′vər *or* mə nyo͞o′vər) ***noun*** **1** a carefully planned movement of troops, ships, or aircraft [The army scheduled *maneuvers* to train the new troops.] **2** a skillful move or clever trick [an unexpected *maneuver* to get control of the business].
verb **1** to move or guide in a careful, planned way [He *maneuvered* his ship to avoid the shallow waters.] **2** to use or get by using clever tricks [I *maneuvered* Dad into raising my allowance.]
ma·neu·ver • ***noun,*** *plural* **maneuvers**
• ***verb*** **maneuvered, maneuvering**

manger (mān′jər) ***noun*** a large box or trough in a barn that holds food for horses or cattle.
man·ger • ***noun,*** *plural* **mangers**

mangle (maŋ′gəl) ***verb*** to tear, cut, or crush badly [The lawn mower *mangled* her toy.]
man·gle • ***verb*** **mangled, mangling**

mango (maŋ′gō) ***noun*** a yellowish-red tropical fruit that has a thick rind and a hard stone. The mango has a sweet and juicy pulp.
man·go • ***noun,*** *plural* **mangoes** or **mangos**

mangrove (maŋ′grōv) ***noun*** a tropical tree with branches that spread and send down roots. These branches then form new trunks.
man·grove • ***noun,*** *plural* **mangroves**

manhandle (man′han dəl) ***verb*** to handle in a rough way.
man·han·dle • ***verb*** **manhandled, manhandling**

Manhattan (man hat′n) an island at the mouth of the Hudson River. It is a borough of New York City.
Man·hat·tan

manhole (man′hōl) ***noun*** an opening or hole in a street with a cover that can be removed. Workers go down manholes to build, repair, and inspect things such as sewers, pipes, or electrical lines.
man·hole • ***noun,*** *plural* **manholes**

manhood (man′ho͝od) ***noun*** **1** the condition or time of being a grown man. **2** men as a group [the *manhood* of the nation].
man·hood • ***noun***

mania (mā′nē ə) ***noun*** too great an enthusiasm or liking for something [a *mania* for dancing].
ma·ni·a • ***noun,*** *plural* **manias**

maniac (mā′nē ak) ***noun*** an insane or violent person.
ma·ni·ac • ***noun,*** *plural* **maniacs**

manicure (man′i kyo͝or) ***noun*** a treatment for the fingernails that includes trimming, cleaning, and sometimes polishing.
verb to give a manicure to.
man·i·cure • ***noun,*** *plural* **manicures**
• ***verb*** **manicured, manicuring**

Manitoba (man′i tō′bə) a province of south central Canada. Abbreviated **MB** or **Man.**
Man·i·to·ba

mankind (man kīnd′) ***noun*** all human beings; the human race ["That's one small step for a man, one giant leap for *mankind*."]
man·kind • ***noun***

manlike (man′līk) ***adjective*** resembling or having the qualities of a human being.
man·like • ***adjective***

man-made (man′mād′) ***adjective*** made by people, not by nature; artificial [Nylon is a *man-made* fiber.]

manner (man′ər) ***noun*** **1** a way in which something happens or is done; style [He washed his hands in the usual *manner*, but could not remove the stains. He dresses in a casual *manner*.] **2** a way of acting; behavior [Her friendly *manner* made people like her right away.] **3 manners** polite ways of behaving or acting [It's good *manners* to say "Thank you."]
man·ner • ***noun***
• The words **manner** and **manor** sound alike.
He had a funny *manner* of speaking.
They moved into an old country *manor*.

man-of-war (man əv wôr′) ***noun*** a warship used in earlier times.
man-of-war • ***noun,*** *plural* **men-of-war**

manor (man′ər) ***noun*** **1** a district under the authority of a lord in the Middle Ages. Part of the land was divided among peasants who worked on small farms and paid the lord by doing jobs or giving him part of their crops. The lord lived in a large house in another part of the district. **2** a large estate.
man·or • ***noun,*** *plural* **manors**
• The words **manor** and **manner** sound alike.
The Lord and Lady lived at the *manor*.
She behaved in a rough *manner*.

M

mansion (man′shən) ***noun*** a very large, stately house.
man·sion • ***noun,*** *plural* **mansions**

manslaughter (man′slôt ər *or* man′slät ər) ***noun*** the unlawful act of killing someone without having planned to do so.
man·slaugh·ter • ***noun***

mantel (man′təl) ***noun*** **1** the structure of stone, marble, bricks, or other material that surrounds the opening of a fireplace. **2** a mantelpiece.
man·tel • ***noun,*** *plural* **mantels**

mantelpiece (man′təl pēs) ***noun*** the shelf above a fireplace.
man·tel·piece • ***noun,*** *plural* **mantelpieces**

mantis (man′tis) ***noun*** a large insect that eats other insects. It holds its front pair of legs as if praying; praying mantis.
man·tis • ***noun,*** *plural* **mantises**

mantle (man′təl) ***noun*** a loose cloak without sleeves; cape.
man·tle • ***noun,*** *plural* **mantles**

manual (man′yo͞o əl) ***adjective*** made, done, or worked with the hands [*manual* labor; *manual* controls].
noun a small book that gives instruction or information about something; handbook [a car owner's *manual*].
man·u·al • ***adjective*** • ***noun,*** *plural* **manuals**

manufacture (man′yo͞o fak′chər) ***noun*** the act or process of making goods and articles, especially in large amounts and with the use of machinery.
verb **1** to make goods, especially in large amounts. **2** to make up; invent [She *manufactured* an excuse for being late.]
man·u·fac·ture • ***noun***
• ***verb*** **manufactured, manufacturing**

manure (mə no͝or′ *or* mə nyo͝or′) ***noun*** waste matter of animals that is used to fertilize soil.
ma·nure • ***noun***

manuscript (man′yo͞o skript) ***noun*** a book, magazine article, or other written material that is typed or written by hand.
man·u·script • ***noun,*** *plural* **manuscripts**

many (men′ē) ***adjective*** a large number of; not few [*many* boxes; *many* times].
noun a large number [*Many* of us plan to go.]
pronoun a large number of persons or things [*Many* came to see our play.]
man·y • ***adjective*** **more, most** • ***noun***
• ***pronoun***

WORD CHOICES

Synonyms of **many**

The words **many, multiple,** and **numerous** share the meaning "a large number of."

many pets

multiple cuts and bruises

numerous complaints

Maori (mou′rē) ***noun*** **1** a member of a people native to New Zealand. **2** the language of these people.
Ma·o·ri • ***noun,*** *plural for sense 1 only* **Maoris** or **Maori**

map (map) ***noun*** a drawing or chart of all or part of the earth's surface, showing where countries, oceans, rivers, cities, and other features are.
verb **1** to make a map of [Explorers in the 19th century *mapped* western North America.] **2** to plan in a careful way step by step [The students *mapped* out a plan to raise money.]
map • ***noun,*** *plural* **maps** • ***verb*** **mapped, mapping**

maple (mā′pəl) ***noun*** **1** a tree that has broad leaves with deep notches. The seeds grow in pairs and have narrow, thin parts that look like wings. The sweet sap of one kind of maple is used to make syrup and sugar. **2** the hard, light-colored wood of this tree. It is often used to make furniture.
ma·ple • ***noun,*** *plural* **maples**

mar (mär) ***verb*** to hurt or spoil the looks, value, or appearance of [The kitten's claws *marred* the table top.]
mar • ***verb*** **marred, marring**

Mar. *abbreviation for* March.

marathon (mer′ə thän) ***noun*** **1** a race for runners covering a distance of 26 miles, 385 yards. **2** any contest or competition to test how long a person can keep on doing some-

a	cat	ō	go	ʉ	fur	ə =	a *in* ago
ā	ape	ô	law, for	ch	chin		e *in* agent
ä	cot, car	o͝o	look	sh	she		i *in* pencil
e	ten	o͞o	tool	th	thin		o *in* atom
ē	me	oi	oil	*th*	then		u *in* circus
i	fit	ou	out	zh	measure		
ī	ice	u	up	ŋ	ring		

thing [a dance *marathon*].
mar·a·thon • *noun, plural* **marathons**

marble (mär′bəl) *noun* **1** a hard kind of limestone that is white or colored and sometimes streaked with different colors. Marble takes a high polish and is used as a building material and in statues. **2** a little ball of stone, glass, or clay that is used in a children's game.
mar·ble • *noun, plural for sense 2 only* **marbles**

march (märch) *verb* **1** to walk with regular, steady steps as soldiers do [The school band *marched* in today's parade.] **2** to move or go in a steady way [Time *marches* on.]
noun **1** the act of marching [The army's *march* to the sea took eleven days.] **2** a piece of music with a steady rhythm. It is usually played while people march.
march • *verb* **marched, marching** • *noun, plural* **marches**

March (märch) *noun* the third month of the year. March has 31 days. Abbreviated **Mar.**

Marconi (mär kō′nē), **Guglielmo** (gōō lyel′mō) 1874-1937; Italian inventor who developed the telegraph operated by radio transmission.
Mar·co·ni, Gu·gliel·mo

mare (mer) *noun* the female of the horse, donkey, or certain other animals.
mare • *noun, plural* **mares**

margarine (mär′jər in) *noun* a spread or cooking fat that looks like butter. It is made mostly of vegetable oils.
mar·ga·rine • *noun*

margin (mär′jin) *noun* **1** the blank space around the printing on a page [He wrote notes in the *margins* of his textbook.] **2** a border or edge [the *margin* of a pond] —Look for the WORD CHOICES box at the entry **border**. **3** an extra amount that can be used if needed [A budget must allow a *margin* for an emergency.]
mar·gin • *noun, plural* **margins**

marigold (mer′i gōld) *noun* a plant that bears yellow, red, or orange flowers in summer.
mar·i·gold • *noun, plural* **marigolds**

marina (mə rē′nə) *noun* a small harbor where boats can dock or pick up supplies.
ma·ri·na • *noun, plural* **marinas**

marine (mə rēn′) *adjective* **1** of the sea [Seaweeds are *marine* plants.] **2** having to do with sailing or shipping [*marine* insurance].
noun often **Marine** a member of the Marine Corps.
ma·rine • *adjective* • *noun, plural* **marines** or **Marines**

Marine Corps *noun* a branch of the U.S. armed forces that is trained to fight on land, at sea, or in the air.

marionette (mer′ē ə net′) *noun* a puppet or small jointed doll that is moved by means of strings or wires. Marionettes are used to put on shows on a small stage.
mar·i·o·nette • *noun, plural* **marionettes**

marionette

maritime (mer′i tīm) *adjective* **1** on, near, or living near the sea [California is a *maritime* state.] **2** having to do with sailing or shipping on the sea [*maritime* laws].
mar·i·time • *adjective*

Maritime Provinces the Canadian provinces of Nova Scotia, New Brunswick, and Prince Edward Island.

mark (märk) *noun* **1** a spot, stain, scratch, or dent made on a surface. **2** a printed or written sign or label [The period and the comma are punctuation *marks*.] **3** a sign of some quality [Politeness is the *mark* of good training.] **4** a grade or rating that shows how good a person's work is [She received high *marks* in spelling.] **5** a line or notch that shows a certain position [Fill the cup to this *mark*.] **6** something aimed at; target [The arrow fell short of the *mark*.]
verb **1** to make a mark or marks on [The wet glass *marked* the surface of the table.] **2** to make clear; show clearly [The fence *marks* the end of our property.] **3** to show by a mark or marks [*Mark* the state capitals on the map.] **4** to pay attention; note [*Mark* what I say.] **5** to give a grade to [The teacher spent hours *marking* the test papers.]
—**mark down** to mark for sale at a lower price.
—**mark up** to mark for sale at a higher price.
mark • *noun, plural* **marks** • *verb* **marked, marking**

Mark (märk) **1** an early follower of Jesus. **2** the second book of the New Testament. Mark is believed to have written this book.

market (mär′kət) *noun* **1** an open place, or a building, with stalls where goods are sold.

M

2 any store where food is sold [a meat *market*]. **3** a region where goods can be sold [The U.S. needs foreign *markets* for its products.] **4** a desire by many people to buy; demand [The *market* for used cars is good now.]
verb to sell or offer to sell [He *markets* his paintings through an agent.]
mar·ket • ***noun,*** *plural for senses 1, 2, and 3 only* **markets** • ***verb*** **marketed, marketing**

marketplace (mär′kət plās) ***noun*** an open place where food and other goods are offered for sale.
mar·ket·place • ***noun,*** *plural* **marketplaces**

marking (märk′iŋ) ***noun*** a mark or marks [a bird with black and white *markings* on its back].
mark·ing • ***noun,*** *plural* **markings**

marmalade (mär′mə lād) ***noun*** a sweet food like jam that is made from oranges or other fruit.
mar·ma·lade • ***noun,*** *plural* **marmalades**

maroon[1] (mə ro͞on′) ***noun*** a dark brownish red.
ma·roon • ***noun***

maroon[2] (mə ro͞on′) ***verb*** to put on the shore and leave in a lonely place [The shipwreck left them *marooned* on an island.]
ma·roon • ***verb*** **marooned, marooning**

marquee

marquee (mär kē′) ***noun*** a small roof built out over an entrance to a theater, store, hotel, or other public place.
mar·quee • ***noun,*** *plural* **marquees**

Marquette (mär ket′), **Jacques** (zhäk) 1637-1675; French missionary who explored part of the Mississippi River. He was called *Pere Marquette.*
Mar·quette, Jacques

marriage (mer′ij) ***noun*** **1** the state of being married; married life [Their *marriage* was not a happy one.] **2** the act of marrying; wedding [They set the date for their *marriage.*]
mar·riage • ***noun,*** *plural* **marriages**

married (mer′ēd) ***adjective*** **1** being husband and wife [a *married* couple]. **2** of marriage [*married* life].
mar·ried • ***adjective***

marrow (mer′ō) ***noun*** the soft, fatty substance that fills the hollow centers of most bones.
mar·row • ***noun***

marry (mer′ē) ***verb*** **1** to join as husband and wife [The ship's captain *married* us at sea.] **2** to take as one's husband or wife [Jane *married* Paul last June.]
mar·ry • ***verb*** **married, marrying, marries**

Mars (märz) **1** the Roman god of war. **2** the seventh largest planet, known for its reddish color. Mars is the fourth planet in distance away from the Sun.

marsh (märsh) ***noun*** low land that is wet and soft; swamp; bog.
marsh • ***noun,*** *plural* **marshes**

marshal (mär′shəl) ***noun*** **1** an officer of a U.S. Federal Court. A marshal has duties like those of a sheriff. **2** a person in charge of a parade or certain ceremonies.
verb to place in proper order; arrange [She *marshaled* her ideas before delivering her speech to the audience.]
mar·shal • ***noun,*** *plural* **marshals**
• ***verb*** **marshaled** or **marshalled, marshaling** or **marshalling**

● The words **marshal** and **martial** sound alike.
The cowboy later became a U.S. *marshal.*
The ex-soldier had a *martial* stride.

Marshall (mär′shəl), **John** (jän) 1755-1835; the chief justice of the U.S. from 1801 to 1835.
Mar·shall, John

Marshall Islands (mär′shəl) a country on a group of islands in the western Pacific.
Mar·shall Islands

marshmallow (märsh′mel′ō *or* märsh′mal′ō) ***noun*** a soft, spongy candy coated with powdered sugar.
marsh·mal·low • ***noun,*** *plural* **marshmallows**

a cat	ō go	ʉ fur	ə = a *in* ago
ā ape	ô law, for	ch chin	e *in* agent
ä cot, car	o͝o look	sh she	i *in* pencil
e ten	o͞o tool	th thin	o *in* atom
ē me	oi oil	*th* then	u *in* circus
i fit	ou out	zh measure	
ī ice	u up	ŋ ring	

marsupial (mär so͞o′pē əl) ***noun*** an animal whose newly born young are carried by the female in a pouch on the front of her body. Kangaroos and opossums are marsupials.
mar·su·pi·al • ***noun,*** *plural* **marsupials**

martial (mär′shəl) ***adjective*** having to do with war, armies, or military life [*martial* music].
mar·tial • ***adjective***
- The words **martial** and **marshal** sound alike.
  A "court-*martial*" is a military court.
  The *marshal* arrested all six bandits.

martin (märt′n) ***noun*** a bird that is related to the swallows. It has a deeply forked tail and dark feathers.
mar·tin • ***noun,*** *plural* **martins**

martyr (märt′ər) ***noun*** a person who chooses to suffer or die rather than give up his or her religion or beliefs.
mar·tyr • ***noun,*** *plural* **martyrs**

marvel (mär′vəl) ***noun*** a wonderful or astonishing thing [Geysers and volcanoes are some of the many *marvels* of nature.]
verb to wonder; be amazed [We *marveled* at the skill of the pianist.]
mar·vel • ***noun,*** *plural* **marvels**
• ***verb*** **marveled** or **marvelled, marveling** or **marvelling**

marvelous (mär′və ləs) ***adjective*** **1** causing wonder or astonishment [His book tells the story of *marvelous* journeys to other lands.] **2** [*an informal use*] very good; excellent [We had a *marvelous* dinner at the restaurant.]
mar·vel·ous • ***adjective***

Mary (mer′ē) the mother of Jesus. She is often called the **Virgin Mary**.
Mar·y

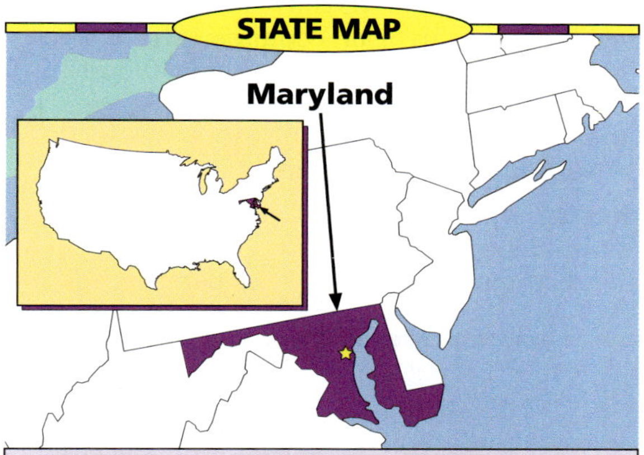

Statehood: 1788, the 7th state • **Capital:** Annapolis

Maryland (mer′ə lənd) a State on the eastern coast of the U.S. Its capital is Annapolis. Abbreviated **MD** or **Md.**
Mar·y·land

mascara (mas ker′ə) ***noun*** a paste put on the eyelashes and eyebrows to darken or color them.
mas·ca·ra • ***noun,*** *plural* **mascaras**

mascot (mas′kät) ***noun*** a person, animal, or thing that is supposed to bring good luck by being present [A goat is the *mascot* of their school's football team.]
mas·cot • ***noun,*** *plural* **mascots**

masculine (mas′kyo͞o lin) ***adjective*** of or having to do with men or boys; male [Robert and Julio are *masculine* names.]
mas·cu·line • ***adjective***

mash (mash) ***noun*** **1** a mixture of bran, meal, and other cereals that is fed to horses, cattle, or poultry. **2** a soft mass or mixture.
verb to beat or crush into a soft mash [She *mashed* the potatoes.]
mash • ***noun*** • ***verb*** **mashed, mashing**

mask
Three types of mask

mask (mask) ***noun*** **1** something worn over the face to hide or protect it [a Halloween *mask;* a baseball catcher's *mask*]. **2** anything that hides, covers up, or disguises something [His smile was a *mask* to hide his disappointment.]
verb **1** to cover or hide with a mask [The bank robbers *masked* their faces to avoid identification.] **2** to hide or disguise [Her nervous giggling *masked* her fear of the empty house.]
mask • ***noun,*** *plural* **masks** • ***verb*** **masked, masking**

mason (mā′sən) ***noun*** a person whose work is building with brick, stone, or concrete.
ma·son • ***noun,*** *plural* **masons**

masonry (mā′sən rē) ***noun*** something that is built of stone, brick, or other material by a mason.
ma·son·ry • ***noun***

masquerade (mas kər ād′) ***noun*** a party or dance where people wear masks and fancy costumes.
verb to pretend to be someone else [The spy spent years *masquerading* as a taxi driver.]
mas·quer·ade • ***noun,*** *plural* **masquerades** • ***verb*** **masqueraded, masquerading**

mass (mas) ***noun*** **1** a piece or amount that has no definite shape or size [a *mass* of clay; a *mass* of cold air]. **2** a large amount or number [a *mass* of freckles].
adjective having to do with a large number of persons or things [a *mass* meeting; *mass* production].
verb to gather or form into a mass [Crowds were *massing* at the front gate.]
—the masses **1** the great mass of common people. **2** the working people as a class.
mass • ***noun,*** *plural* **masses** • ***adjective*** • ***verb*** **massed, massing**

Mass or **mass** (mas) ***noun*** the service in the Roman Catholic Church and some other churches at which Communion takes place.
Mass or **mass** • ***noun,*** *plural* **Masses** or **masses**

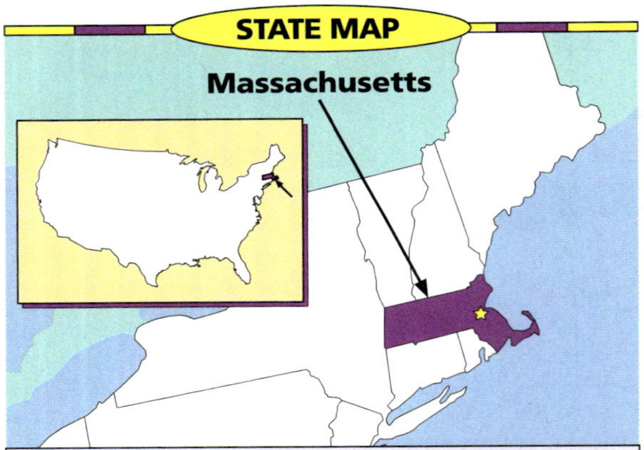

Statehood: 1788, the 6th state • **Capital:** Boston

Massachusetts (mas ə cho͞o′səts) a New England State of the U.S. Its capital is Boston. Abbreviated **MA** or **Mass.**
Mas·sa·chu·setts

massacre (mas′ə kər) ***noun*** the act or fact of killing a large number of people in a cruel and violent way.
verb to kill in large numbers.
mas·sa·cre • ***noun,*** *plural* **massacres** • ***verb*** **massacred, massacring**

massage (mə säzh′ *or* mə säj′) ***noun*** the process of rubbing and kneading part of the body to loosen up muscles and help the blood circulate better.
verb to give a massage to.
mas·sage • ***noun,*** *plural* **massages** • ***verb*** **massaged, massaging**

massive (mas′iv) ***adjective*** large, solid, and heavy [a *massive* statue] —Look for the WORD CHOICES boxes at the entries **enormous** and **heavy**.
mas·sive • ***adjective***

mass media ***plural noun*** all of the ways of giving information to large numbers of people and trying to affect their opinions. These ways include newspapers, magazines, TV, and radio.

mass production ***noun*** the process of making products in large quantities, especially by using machines and dividing work into simpler tasks to be performed by individual persons.

mass transit ***noun*** a large system for providing transportation to the people in a city or region. It may include buses, subways, streetcars, and trains.

mast (mast) ***noun*** a tall pole that stands upright on a ship or boat, for supporting sails and other parts.
mast • ***noun,*** *plural* **masts**

master (mas′tər) ***noun*** **1** a man who rules others or has control over something. A master may be the owner of an animal or the winner in a contest. **2** a person who has great skill or knowledge [She is a *master* at painting portraits.] **3 Master** a title that is used with the name of a boy who is too young to be called *Mr.* [*Master* John].
adjective main or controlling [This *master* switch controls all of those other switches.]
verb **1** to control or conquer [She *mastered* her fear of heights.] **2** to become expert in [It took him years to *master* the piano.]
mas·ter • ***noun,*** *plural* **masters** • ***adjective*** • ***verb*** **mastered, mastering**

master of ceremonies ***noun*** a person who is in charge of a program, banquet, or other kind of entertainment. This person performs

a	cat	ō	go	ʉ	fur	ə =	a *in* ago
ā	ape	ô	law, for	ch	chin		e *in* agent
ä	cot, car	o͝o	look	sh	she		i *in* pencil
e	ten	o͞o	tool	th	thin		o *in* atom
ē	me	oi	oil	*th*	then		u *in* circus
i	fit	ou	out	zh	measure		
ī	ice	u	up	ŋ	ring		

several duties, such as introducing speakers and performers.
master of ceremonies • *noun, plural* **masters of ceremonies**

masterpiece (mas′tər pēs) ***noun*** **1** a thing that is made or done with very great skill; a great work of art. **2** the best thing that a person has ever made or done.
mas·ter·piece • *noun, plural* **masterpieces**

mastery (mas′tər ē) ***noun*** the kind of skill or knowledge that an expert has [He was happy to show off his *mastery* of the trumpet.]
mas·ter·y • *noun*

mastiff (mas′tif) ***noun*** a large, strong dog with a smooth coat and powerful jaws.
mas·tiff • *noun, plural* **mastiffs**

mastodon (mas′tə dän) ***noun*** an animal that was like the elephant, but much larger. It lived a very long time ago and is now extinct.
mas·to·don • *noun, plural* **mastodons**

mat (mat) ***noun*** **1** a flat piece of rough material that covers a floor or other surface, for protection or for wiping off shoes. It may be made of rubber or woven from hemp or another material. **2** a flat piece of cloth, woven straw, or other material placed under a vase, a hot dish, or something else that could mar a surface. **3** a thick, padded floor covering for use in a gym for wrestling, tumbling, or other activities. **4** something that is tangled or woven together [The roots in the lawn formed a thick, tight *mat*.]
verb to weave together or tangle into a thick mass.
mat • *noun, plural* **mats** • *verb* **matted, matting**

match[1] (mach) ***noun*** a slender piece of wood or cardboard used to start a fire. It has a tip that is coated with chemicals. The tip catches fire when it is rubbed on a certain kind of rough surface.
match • *noun, plural* **matches**

match[2] (mach) ***noun*** **1** a person or thing that is like or equal to another person or thing in some way [This blue skirt is a good *match* for the blue dots on this blouse. Sally met her *match* in chess when she played José.] **2** two or more people or things that go well together [That suit and tie are a good *match*.] **3** a game or contest between two persons or teams [a tennis *match*].
verb **1** to go well together [Do your shirt and tie *match*?] **2** to make or get something that is like or equal to [Can you *match* this cloth?] **3** to be equal to [I could never *match* that swimmer in a race.] **4** to pit against one another [I don't think they've *matched* those two tennis players very well.]
match • *noun, plural* **matches** • *verb* **matched, matching**

mate (māt) ***noun*** **1** one of a pair of things [Where is the *mate* to this sock?] **2** a husband or wife. **3** the male or female of a pair of animals. **4** a friend or companion [a *schoolmate*]. **5** an officer of a merchant ship.
verb to join or be joined as a pair, especially in order to produce offspring.
mate • *noun, plural* **mates** • *verb* **mated, mating**

material (mə tir′ē əl) ***adjective*** **1** having to do with matter; physical [An idea is not a *material* object.] **2** having to do with the body and its needs [*material* comforts].
noun **1** what a thing is made up of [Clay is a raw *material*.] **2** cloth; fabric. **3 materials** the things or tools that are needed to do something [writing *materials*].
ma·te·ri·al • *adjective* • *noun, plural* **materials**

maternal (mə tur′nəl) ***adjective*** **1** like or having to do with a mother. **2** related to a person on the person's mother's side [My *maternal* aunt is my mother's sister.]
ma·ter·nal • *adjective*

math (math) [*an informal word*] ***noun*** *a short form of* **mathematics**.

mathematical (math′ə mat′i kəl) ***adjective*** having to do with mathematics.
math·e·mat·i·cal • *adjective*

mathematician (math′ə mə tish′ən) ***noun*** an expert in mathematics.
math·e·ma·ti·cian • *noun, plural* **mathematicians**

mathematics (math′ə mat′iks) ***plural noun*** [*used with a singular verb*] the group of sciences that uses numbers and symbols to study amounts and forms. Mathematics includes arithmetic and geometry.
math·e·mat·ics • *plural noun*

matinee (mat′n ā′) ***noun*** a performance, such as a play or concert, that takes place in the afternoon.
mat·i·nee • *noun, plural* **matinees**

matrimony (ma′tri mō′nē) ***noun*** the condition of being married; marriage.
mat·ri·mo·ny • *noun*

M

matron (mā′trən) *noun* **1** a wife or a widow, especially one who is not young. **2** a woman who is in charge of other people in a prison.
ma·tron ▪ *noun, plural* **matrons**

matter (mat′ər) *noun* **1** what all things are made of; anything that takes up space. Solids, liquids, and gases are all matter. **2** what a thing is made of; material [The red *matter* in blood is an iron compound.] **3** something that must be talked about or decided [business *matters*]. **4** the contents or meaning of something that has been written or spoken, apart from its style or form [the subject *matter* of the poem]. **5** an amount or number [It is a *matter* of seconds before the race starts.] **6** trouble; something bad that happens [What's the *matter?*]
verb to be important [My health *matters* to me.]
—as a matter of fact to tell the truth; really.
—no matter in spite of [*No matter* what happens, we'll still be friends.]
mat·ter ▪ *noun, plural for sense 3 only* **matters** ▪ *verb* **mattered, mattering**

matter-of-fact (mat′ər əv fakt′) *adjective* keeping to the facts; not showing imagination or strong feelings [Today's newspaper gave a *matter-of-fact* description of the accident.]
mat·ter-of-fact ▪ *adjective*

Matthew (math′yo͞o) **1** one of the twelve Apostles of Jesus. **2** the first book of the New Testament. Matthew is believed to have written this book.
Mat·thew

mattress (ma′trəs) *noun* a pad made of a strong cloth case filled with cotton or foam rubber, and often coiled springs. It is used on a bed.
mat·tress ▪ *noun, plural* **mattresses**

mature (mə to͝or′ *or* mə cho͝or′) *adjective* **1** fully grown [a *mature* pine tree]. **2** developed fully [a *mature* person; a *mature* mind].
verb to become mature.
ma·ture ▪ *adjective* ▪ *verb* **matured, maturing**

maturity (mə to͝or′i tē *or* mə cho͝or′i tē) *noun* the condition of being fully grown or developed.
ma·tu·ri·ty ▪ *noun*

matzo (mät′sə) *noun* **1** a type of thin, crisp bread that does not contain yeast or anything else that makes bread rise. It is eaten during Passover. **2** a piece of this bread.
mat·zo ▪ *noun, plural* **mat·zot** (mät′sōt) or **matzos**

maul (môl *or* mäl) *verb* to handle in a rough way or injure by being rough.
maul ▪ *verb* **mauled, mauling**
● The words **maul** and **mall** sound alike.
Some bears do *maul* their trainers.
We're going to shop up at the *mall*.

Mauritania (môr′i tā′nē ə) a country in western Africa, on the Atlantic Ocean.
Mau·ri·ta·ni·a

Mauritius (mô rish′ē əs) a country on an island and several nearby islands in the Indian Ocean, east of Madagascar.
Mau·ri·ti·us

maximum (maks′i məm) *noun* **1** the greatest amount or number that is possible or allowed [Forty pounds of luggage is the *maximum* that you can take.] **2** the highest degree or point that has been reached or recorded [It was hot today but not nearly up to the *maximum* for July.]
adjective greatest possible or allowed [*maximum* speed].
max·i·mum ▪ *noun, plural* **maximums** ▪ *adjective*

may (mā) *verb* (*helping verb*) **I.** The verb *may* is used with other verbs to show that the subject: **1** can or is likely to [I *may* stay home. It *may* rain.] **2** is allowed or has permission to [You *may* go now.] **3** is able to as a result [Be silent so that we *may* hear.] **II.** *May* is used in exclamations to express a wish or hope [*May* you win!] The word "to" is not used between *may* and the verb that follows it.
may ▪ *verb past tense* **might**; *he/she/it* **may**

May (mā) *noun* the fifth month of the year. May has 31 days.

Maya (mä′yə *or* mī′ə) *noun* **1** a member of an American Indian people of southern Mexico, Belize, and northern Guatemala. The Mayas had a highly developed civilization long before the arrival of Europeans early in the 16th century. **2** their language.
Ma·ya ▪ *noun, plural for sense 1 only* **Mayas** or **Maya**

maybe (mā′bē) *adverb* it may be; perhaps.
may·be ▪ *adverb*

a cat	ō go	ʉ fur	ə = a *in* ago
ā ape	ô law, for	ch chin	e *in* agent
ä cot, car	oo look	sh she	i *in* pencil
e ten	o͞o tool	th thin	o *in* atom
ē me	oi oil	*th* then	u *in* circus
i fit	ou out	zh measure	
ī ice	u up	ŋ ring	

Mayflower (mā′flou ər) the ship that carried the Pilgrims to America in 1620.
May·flow·er

mayo (mā′ō) [*an informal word*] ***noun*** *a short form of* **mayonnaise**.
may·o • ***noun***

mayonnaise (mā ə nāz′) ***noun*** a thick, creamy sauce that is made of egg yolks, oil, seasonings, and lemon juice or vinegar.
may·on·naise • ***noun***

mayor (mā′ər) ***noun*** the head of the government of a city or town.
may·or • ***noun,*** *plural* **mayors**

maze

maze (māz) ***noun*** a series of twisting paths or passages, some of which do not lead anywhere, through which people may have trouble finding their way.
maze • ***noun,*** *plural* **mazes**
- The words **maze** and **maize** sound alike.
  The park has a *maze* of tall hedges.
  "*Maize*" is another name for "corn."

MB *abbreviation for* Manitoba.

MC or **M.C.** *abbreviation for* Master of Ceremonies.

McKinley (mə kin′lē), **William** (wil′yəm) 1843-1901; the twenty-fifth president of the U.S., from 1897 to 1901. He was assassinated.
Mc·Kin·ley, Wil·liam

MD or **M.D.** *abbreviation for* Doctor of Medicine [Marta Cruz, *MD*].

MD or **Md.** *abbreviation for* Maryland.

me (mē) ***pronoun*** the form of **I**[1] that is used: **1** as the object of a verb [The dog bit *me*. He saw *me*.] **2** as the object of a preposition [Tell the story to *me*.]
- The words **me** and **mi** sound alike.
  Mom gave *me* a kiss on the cheek.
  Do, re, *mi*, fa, sol, la, ti, do.

ME or **Me.** *abbreviation for* Maine.

meadow (med′ō) ***noun*** a piece of land where grass is grown for hay.
mead·ow • ***noun,*** *plural* **meadows**

meadowlark

meadowlark (med′ō lärk′) ***noun*** a North American bird with a yellow breast and a black, V-shaped mark at the front of its neck.
mead·ow·lark • ***noun,*** *plural* **meadowlarks**

meager (mē′gər) ***adjective*** of poor quality or small amount [a *meager* lunch].
mea·ger • ***adjective***

WORD CHOICES

Synonyms of **meager**

The words **meager**, **scanty**, and **sparse** share the meaning "made up of less or fewer than needed or wanted."

a *meager* diet
a *scanty* income
a *sparse* crowd

meal[1] (mēl) ***noun*** **1** one of the regular times when food is eaten; breakfast, lunch, or dinner [Our evening *meal* is at six.] **2** the food that is eaten at one of these times [a delicious *meal*].
meal • ***noun,*** *plural* **meals**

meal[2] (mēl) ***noun*** grain that is ground up, but not so fine as flour.

mean[1] (mēn) ***verb*** **1** to express or be a sign of; indicate [What does this word *mean*? Falling leaves *mean* that winter is near.] **2** to want to make known or understood [He always says just what he *means*.] **3** to have a certain kind of effect or be important in a certain way [Your friendship *means* very much to me.]

M

4 to have in mind as a purpose; intend [She *meant* to go, but changed her mind.]
—mean well to have a good purpose in mind [He *means well*, but he always says the wrong thing.]
mean • *verb* **meant, meaning**

mean[2] (mēn) *adjective* **1** selfish, unkind, rude, or nasty [Our neighbors were *mean* to their dog, so it ran away.] **2** dangerous or bad-tempered; hard to control [a *mean* bull]. **3** poor in looks or quality; shabby [a *mean*, run-down part of town]. **4** [*a slang use*] hard to deal with; difficult [That pitcher throws a *mean* curve ball.]
mean • *adjective* **meaner, meanest**

mean[3] (mēn) *adjective* halfway between two extremes [The *mean* temperature is the temperature halfway between the highest and the lowest.]
noun **1** the number that is obtained by dividing a sum by the number of items that have been added together; average [The *mean* of 2, 3, and 7 is 4 (2 + 3 + 7 = 12; 12 ÷ 3 = 4)]. **2** something that is in the middle, between extremes [Her way of life was a happy *mean* between working too hard and doing nothing.]
mean • *adjective* • *noun, plural for sense 1 only* **means**

meander (mē an′dər) *verb* to go winding back and forth [a stream that *meanders* through the valley].
me·an·der • *verb* **meandered, meandering**

meaning (mēn′iŋ) *noun* what is supposed to be understood; what is meant [She repeated the words to make her *meaning* clear.]
mean·ing • *noun, plural* **meanings**

meaningful (mēn′iŋ fəl) *adjective* filled with meaning; having a purpose [He gave me a *meaningful* look.]
mean·ing·ful • *adjective*

meaningless (mēn′iŋ ləs) *adjective* having no meaning; without sense or purpose [This letter is a *meaningless* collection of words.]
mean·ing·less • *adjective*

means (mēnz) *plural noun* **1** a way of getting or doing something [Flying is the fastest *means* of travel.] **2** wealth; riches [He is a man of *means*.]
—by all means of course; certainly. **—by means of** by using [They won the game *by means of* hard work.] **—by no means** certainly not.

meant (ment) *verb past tense and past participle of* **mean**[1].

meantime (mēn′tīm) *noun* the time in between [Dinner won't be ready for an hour. In the *meantime*, let's set the table.]
adverb the same as **meanwhile**.
mean·time • *noun* • *adverb*

meanwhile (mēn′hwīl *or* mēn′wīl) *adverb* **1** during the time between [They were gone an hour. *Meanwhile*, I had washed the dishes.] **2** at the same time [We watched TV. *Meanwhile*, he read.]
mean·while • *adverb*

measles (mē′zəlz) *plural noun* [*used with a singular verb*] a disease that causes a fever and red spots on the skin. It is more common in children than in adults.
mea·sles • *plural noun*

measure (mezh′ər) *verb* **1** to find out the size, amount, or extent of, by comparing with something else [*Measure* the young child's height with a yardstick. How do you *measure* a person's worth?] **2** to find out the size, amount, or extent of something [Please *measure* carefully.] **3** to set apart or mark off a certain amount or length of [*Measure* out three pounds of sugar.] **4** to be of a certain size, amount, or extent [The table *measures* five feet on each side.]
noun **1** a unit or a standard for use in measuring something [The yard is a *measure* of length.] **2** a certain amount, extent, or degree [His success is due in some *measure* to his charm.] **3** an action that is meant to bring something about [The mayor promised to take new *measures* to stop crime.] **4** the notes or rests between two bars on a staff of music.
meas·ure • *verb* **measured, measuring** • *noun, plural for senses 1, 3, and 4 only* **measures**

measurement (mezh′ər mənt) *noun* **1** the act or process of measuring. **2** the size, amount, or extent that is found by measuring [His waist *measurement* is 36 inches.]
meas·ure·ment • *noun, plural for sense 2 only* **measurements**

a cat	ō go	ʉ fur	ə = a *in* ago
ā ape	ô law, for	ch chin	e *in* agent
ä cot, car	oo look	sh she	i *in* pencil
e ten	ōō tool	th thin	o *in* atom
ē me	oi oil	*th* then	u *in* circus
i fit	ou out	zh measure	
ī ice	u up	ŋ ring	

meat (mēt) ***noun*** **1** the flesh of animals that is used as food. This word is used especially for the flesh of cattle, hogs, and other four-footed animals, but sometimes also chickens and other birds. **2** the part of something that can be eaten [the *meat* of a nut]. **3** the main part [the *meat* of a book].
● The words **meat** and **meet** sound alike.
Do you prefer white *meat* or dark?
They hold the track *meet* across town.

mechanic (mə kan′ik) ***noun*** a worker who is skilled in using tools or in making, repairing, and using machines [an automobile and truck *mechanic*].
me·chan·ic • ***noun,*** *plural* **mechanics**

mechanical (mə kan′i kəl) ***adjective*** **1** using or having to do with machines [*mechanical* skill]. **2** made by or run by a machine [a *mechanical* toy]. **3** acting like a machine or done as if by a machine [She greeted him in a *mechanical* way.]
me·chan·i·cal • ***adjective***

mechanism (mek′ə niz əm) ***noun*** **1** the system of working parts of a machine. **2** a system of any kind with parts that work together like the parts of a machine [The human body is a very complicated *mechanism*.]
mech·a·nism • ***noun,*** *plural* **mechanisms**

medal (med′əl) ***noun*** a small, flat piece of metal that has a design or some words on it. Medals are given as an honor or reward for some great action or service.
med·al • ***noun,*** *plural* **medals**
● The words **medal** and **meddle** sound alike.
You deserve a *medal* for your hard work.
Don't *meddle* with my things when I go.

medal

medallion (mə dal′yən) ***noun*** a round decoration that looks like a medal.
me·dal·lion • ***noun,*** *plural* **medallions**

meddle (med′əl) ***verb*** to touch someone else's belongings or take part in someone else's activities or interests without being asked or wanted; interfere [Don't *meddle* in my life! Don't *meddle* with my stamp collection.]
med·dle • ***verb*** **meddled, meddling**
● The words **meddle** and **medal** sound alike.
Must you *meddle* in my affairs?
She won a gold *medal* in the Olympics.

media (mē′dē ə) ***noun*** *a plural of* **medium** *usually used with a singular verb in the phrase* **the media**, all the ways of communicating that give the public news and entertainment, usually along with advertising. Newspapers, radio, and TV are the most important media.
me·di·a • ***noun***

median (mē′dē ən) ***adjective*** in the middle; halfway between two ends. For example, 7 is the median number in the series 1, 4, 7, 25, 48. ***noun*** **1** a median number, point, or line. **2** a strip of land in the middle of a divided highway. It separates the lanes of traffic that are going in opposite directions.
me·di·an • ***adjective*** • ***noun,*** *plural* **medians**

medical (med′i kəl) ***adjective*** having to do with the practice or study of medicine [*medical* care; *medical* school].
med·i·cal • ***adjective***

medicated (med′i kāt′əd) ***adjective*** having medicine in or on it [a *medicated* cough drop].
med·i·cat·ed • ***adjective***

medication (med′i kā′shən) ***noun*** a medicine.
med·i·ca·tion • ***noun,*** *plural* **medications**

medicine (med′i sin) ***noun*** **1** a substance that is used in or on the body to treat disease, take away pain, or heal a wound. **2** the science of treating and preventing disease.
med·i·cine • ***noun,*** *plural* **medicines**

SPELLING TIP

Use this memory aid to spell **medicine.** Both ***medic***ine and ***medic***al are spelled with **c.**

medicine man ***noun*** among Native Americans and some other peoples, a man who is thought to have magic powers to cure illness or keep evil away.
medicine man • ***noun,*** *plural* **medicine men**

medieval (mē′dē ē′vəl *or* med ē′vəl) ***adjective*** having to do with or like the Middle Ages.
me·di·e·val • ***adjective***

M

Mediterranean Sea (med′i tər ā′nē ən) a large sea surrounded by Europe, Africa, and Asia.
Med·i·ter·ra·ne·an Sea

medium (mē′dē əm) *adjective* in the middle in amount, degree, or some other quantity or quality; average [a *medium* price].
noun **1** a thing or condition in the middle; something that is not an extreme [A temperature of 70°F. is a happy *medium*.] **2** a thing through which a force acts or an effect is produced [Copper is a good *medium* for conducting electricity.] **3** any way or thing by which something is done. **4** a way of communicating with the public [TV is a good advertising *medium*.]
me·di·um • *adjective* • *noun, plural* **mediums** or **media** (*usually for sense 4*)

medley (med′lē) *noun* **1** a mixture of things that are not alike. **2** a group of songs or tunes that are played together as a single musical piece.
med·ley • *noun, plural* **medleys**

meek (mēk) *adjective* **1** patient and mild; not showing anger. **2** very humble or too humble in actions or feelings; not showing spirit.
meek • *adjective* **meeker, meekest**

meet (mēt) *verb* **1** to come face to face with [We *met* two friends walking down the street.] **2** to come together [We *met* as we walked down the street.] **3** to be introduced to [I *met* you at a party.] **4** to become acquainted [Have you two *met*?] **5** to be present at the arrival of [Please *meet* the bus.] **6** to keep an appointment with [I'll *meet* you at noon.] **7** to come together in a group; gather [The school board *meets* today.] **8** to be joined [The rivers *meet* beyond the bridge.] **9** to satisfy [The store did not have enough books to *meet* the demand.] —Look for the WORD CHOICES box at the entry **satisfy**. **10** to pay [I will *meet* all my debts.]
noun a gathering for a sporting event [a track *meet*].
meet • *verb* **met, meeting** • *noun, plural* **meets**

● The words **meet** and **meat** sound alike.
Would you like to *meet* my best friend?
Beef and pork are kinds of *meat*.

meeting (mēt′iŋ) *noun* **1** the act of coming together [Our unexpected *meeting* on the sidewalk gave me an idea for a new story.] **2** a gathering of people for some purpose; assembly [a *meeting* of the city council].
meet·ing • *noun, plural* **meetings**

megabyte (meg′ə bīt) *noun* an amount equal to 1,048,576 bytes.
meg·a·byte • *noun, plural* **megabytes**

megaphone

megaphone (meg′ə fōn) *noun* a large tube that is shaped like a cone. When a person speaks or shouts through it, the megaphone sends the voice farther and makes it sound louder.
meg·a·phone • *noun, plural* **megaphones**

melancholy (mel′ən käl′ē) *noun* a sad feeling; low spirits.
adjective **1** sad and filled with gloom —Look for the WORD CHOICES box at the entry **sad**. **2** causing a sad feeling or gloom [a *melancholy* song].
mel·an·chol·y • *noun* • *adjective*

mellow (mel′ō) *adjective* **1** soft, sweet, and juicy because of being ripe [a *mellow* apple]. **2** having a good flavor from being aged long enough [a *mellow* cheese]. **3** rich, soft, and pure in sound; not harsh [the *mellow* tone of a cello]. **4** made gentle and kind by age and experience [a *mellow* personality].
verb to make or become mellow [His strong feelings have *mellowed* over the years.]
mel·low • *adjective* **mellower, mellowest** • *verb* **mellowed, mellowing**

melody (mel′ə dē) *noun* **1** a series of musical tones that make up a tune [He was whistling a cheerful *melody*.] **2** the main tune in a musical piece that has more than one part [In a choir, the sopranos often sing the *melody*.]
mel·o·dy • *noun, plural* **melodies**

melon (mel′ən) *noun* a large, juicy fruit that grows on a vine and is full of seeds. Watermelons and cantaloupes are melons.
mel·on • *noun, plural* **melons**

melt (melt) *verb* **1** to change from a solid to a liquid by heat [The snow *melted* in the spring

a	cat	ō	go	ʉ	fur	ə =	a *in* ago
ā	ape	ô	law, for	ch	chin		e *in* agent
ä	cot, car	ʊ	look	sh	she		i *in* pencil
e	ten	ū	tool	th	thin		o *in* atom
ē	me	ɔi	oil	*th*	then		u *in* circus
i	fit	ʊu	out	zh	measure		
ī	ice	u	up	ŋ	ring		

sunshine. We *melted* butter to make the sauce.] **2** to dissolve [The sugar *melted* in the hot tea.] **3** to disappear or go away [Our fear *melted* away.]
melt • *verb* **melted, melting**

WORD CHOICES

Synonyms of **melt**

The words **melt, dissolve,** and **thaw** share the meaning "to change into a liquid."

Butter *melts* when heated.

Sugar *dissolves* in water.

The ice on the roof *thawed* in the sun.

melting point *noun* the temperature at which a solid becomes a liquid [The *melting point* of ice, the solid form of water, is 32°F.]
melting point • *noun, plural* **melting points**

Melville (mel′vil), **Herman** (hur′mən) 1819-1891; U.S. writer of novels.
Mel·ville, Her·man

member (mem′bər) *noun* **1** any one of the persons who make up a club, church, political party, or other group. **2** a leg, arm, or other part of the body.
mem·ber • *noun, plural* **members**

membership (mem′bər ship) *noun* **1** the condition of being a member [She applied for *membership* in the club.] **2** all of the members of a group. **3** the number of members of a group.
mem·ber·ship • *noun*

membrane (mem′brān) *noun* a thin, soft layer of tissue that covers a part of an animal or plant. The eardrum is a membrane.
mem·brane • *noun, plural* **membranes**

memo (mem′ō) *noun a short form of* **memorandum**.
mem·o • *noun, plural* **memos**

memoirs (mem′wärz *or* mem′wôrz) *plural noun* a story of a person's life that is written by that person; autobiography.
mem·oirs • *plural noun*

memorable (mem′ər ə bəl) *adjective* worth remembering; not easy to forget.
mem·o·ra·ble • *adjective*

memorandum (mem ə ran′dəm) *noun* a short, informal note. It may be written to help remember something or to give information to someone in another office.
mem·o·ran·dum • *noun, plural* **memorandums** or **mem·o·ran·da** (mem ə ran′də)

memorial (mə môr′ē əl) *adjective* held or done to remember and honor some person or event [a *memorial* service for the dead sailors].
noun something that is meant to remind people of some event or person. A holiday or a statue can be a memorial.
me·mo·ri·al • *adjective* • *noun, plural* **memorials**

memorize (mem′ə rīz) *verb* to place firmly in the memory word for word or exactly; learn by heart [*Memorize* the spelling of these words.]
mem·o·rize • *verb* **memorized, memorizing**

memory (mem′ər ē) *noun* **1** the power to remember [a good *memory* for faces]. **2** all that a person remembers. **3** something remembered [The song brought back *memories*.] **4** the part of a computer that stores information.
mem·o·ry • *noun, plural* **memories**

Memphis (mem′fis) a city in southwestern Tennessee.
Mem·phis

men (men) *noun plural of* **man**.

menace (men′əs) *noun* a threat or danger.
men·ace • *noun, plural* **menaces**

mend (mend) *verb* **1** to repair or fix [Mother *mended* the broken lamp.] **2** to make or become better; to improve [You must *mend* your ways. Her health *mended*.]
noun a part that has been mended.
—on the mend becoming better [Her health is *on the mend*.]
mend • *verb* **mended, mending** • *noun*

menorah

menorah (mə nō′rə *or* mə nôr′ə) *noun* a candlestick with seven branches. It is a symbol of

M

Judaism. Menorahs for use during Hanuka have nine branches.
me·no·rah • *noun, plural* **menorahs**

-ment *a suffix meaning:* **1** the act or result of [*Improvement* is the act of improving. *Improvements* are the results of improving.] **2** the condition or fact of being [*Disappointment* is the condition of being disappointed.]

WORD MAKER

The suffix -ment

Many words contain the suffix **-ment** plus a word that you already know. You can understand these words if you add the idea "the condition or fact of being" to the meaning of the base word.

base word	*+ suffix*	⇨	*new word*
embarrass	**+ -ment**	⇨	**embarrassment** *(the condition or fact of being embarrassed)*
bewilder			bewilderment
confine			confinement
content			contentment
discourage			discouragement
entangle			entanglement
imprison			imprisonment
involve			involvement
merry			merriment

mental (ment′l) *adjective* **1** for or having to do with the mind [*mental* ability]. **2** having an illness in the mind [a *mental* patient]. **3** for or having to do with persons having an illness in the mind [a *mental* hospital].
men·tal • *adjective*

mention (men′shən) *verb* to speak or write about in just a few words [They *mentioned* your name in their report.]
noun something that is said or written in just a few words, without details.
men·tion • *verb* **mentioned, mentioning** • *noun, plural* **mentions**

menu (men′yo͞o) *noun* **1** a list of the foods that are served at a meal or the foods offered by a restaurant. **2** a list that is displayed on a computer video screen. It shows the commands that a computer user can choose.
men·u • *noun, plural* **menus**

meow (mē ou′) *noun* the sound that a cat makes.
verb to make this sound.
me·ow • *noun, plural* **meows**
• *verb* **meowed, meowing**

mercenary (mʉr′sə ner′ē) *noun* a soldier who is hired to fight for a foreign country's army.
mer·ce·nar·y • *noun, plural* **mercenaries**

merchandise (mʉr′chən dīs) *noun* things that are bought and sold; goods.
mer·chan·dise • *noun*

merchant (mʉr′chənt) *noun* a person who buys and sells things to make a profit.
adjective having to do with or used for buying and selling goods [a *merchant* ship].
mer·chant • *noun, plural* **merchants**
• *adjective*

merciful (mʉr′si fəl) *adjective* having or showing mercy; kind or forgiving [a *merciful* act].
mer·ci·ful • *adjective*

merciless (mʉr′si ləs) *adjective* not having or showing mercy; cruel [a *merciless* tyrant].
mer·ci·less • *adjective*

mercury (mʉr′kyo͝o rē) *noun* a heavy, silver-white metal that is a chemical element. It is usually a liquid. It is used in thermometers and barometers.
mer·cu·ry • *noun*

Mercury (mʉr′kyo͝o rē) **1** the Roman god of trade and cleverness. He was also the messenger of the gods. **2** the planet that is closest to the sun. Mercury is the second smallest planet.
Mer·cu·ry

mercy (mʉr′sē) *noun* **1** kindness to an enemy or a guilty person, that is greater than might be expected. **2** the power to forgive or be kind [He threw himself on the *mercy* of the court.]
—at the mercy of in the power of, with no way to escape.
mer·cy • *noun, plural* **mercies**

mere (mir) *adjective* nothing more than; only [a *mere* child].
mere • *adjective* **merest**

a	cat	ō	go	ʉ	fur	ə =	a *in* ago
ā	ape	ô	law, for	ch	chin		e *in* agent
ä	cot, car	o͝o	look	sh	she		i *in* pencil
e	ten	o͞o	tool	th	thin		o *in* atom
ē	me	oi	oil	*th*	then		u *in* circus
i	fit	ou	out	zh	measure		
ī	ice	u	up	ŋ	ring		

merely (mir′lē) ***adverb*** no more than; only [What I'm saying to you is *merely* a suggestion.]
mere·ly • ***adverb***

merge (mʉrj) ***verb*** to combine or unite into one larger thing and lose separate qualities [The two roads *merge* farther ahead.]
merge • ***verb*** **merged, merging**

merger (mʉr′jər) ***noun*** the combining of two or more companies into one.
merg·er • ***noun,*** *plural* **mergers**

meridian (mə rid′ē ən) ***noun*** an imaginary line that passes north and south across the surface of the earth between the poles. The lines of longitude on a map are a series of such lines.
me·rid·i·an • ***noun,*** *plural* **meridians**

merit (mer′it) ***noun*** **1** good quality; worth [Your suggestion has great *merit.*] **2 merits** the actual fact of being right or wrong, apart from people's feelings [The judge must decide the question only on its *merits.*]
verb to deserve; be worthy of [Her work *merits* praise.]
mer·it • ***noun*** • ***verb*** **merited, meriting**

mermaid (mʉr′mād) ***noun*** an imaginary sea creature with the head and upper body of a woman and the tail of a fish.
mer·maid • ***noun,*** *plural* **mermaids**

merry (mer′ē) ***adjective*** filled with fun and laughter; lively and cheerful [a *merry* party].
mer·ry • ***adjective*** **merrier, merriest**

merry-go-round

merry-go-round (mer′ē gō round′) ***noun*** a round platform that is turned around and around by a machine. It has wooden animals and seats on which people ride for fun.
mer·ry-go-round • ***noun,*** *plural* **merry-go-rounds**

mesa (mā′sə) ***noun*** a large, high rock with steep sides and a flat top.
me·sa • ***noun,*** *plural* **mesas**

WORD HISTORY

mesa

This is a Spanish word that means "table." Some **mesas** looked like huge tables to the Spaniards who explored what is now the southwestern U.S. several hundred years ago.

mesh (mesh) ***noun*** a woven material that has open spaces between its cords, threads, or wires [A screen door has panels of wire or nylon *mesh.*]
verb **1** to fit or lock together [The gears *meshed* perfectly.] **2** to fit together closely [Our plans and schedules *meshed.*]
mesh • ***noun*** • ***verb*** **meshed, meshing**

mesquite (mes kēt′) ***noun*** a tree or shrub with thorns that grows in the southwestern U.S. and in Mexico. It has pods that look like beans and are fed to cattle.
mes·quite • ***noun,*** *plural* **mesquites**

mess (mes) ***noun*** **1** a heap or mass of things that have been thrown together or mixed up; a jumble [Your clothes are lying in a *mess* on the bed.] **2** the condition of being dirty, untidy, or confused [The house is in a *mess.*] **3** a condition of trouble; a difficult situation [He's in a real *mess* for not doing his homework.]
verb **1** to make a mess of; make dirty, confused, or untidy [You've *messed* up your room for the last time!] **2** to spoil or ruin [She *messed up* her chance to get a promotion.]
mess • ***noun,*** *plural for sense 1 only* **messes** • ***verb*** **messed, messing**

message (mes′ij) ***noun*** **1** something, such as information or a request, sent from one person or group to another. **2** a formal speech or other official communication [the President's *message* to Congress].
mes·sage • ***noun,*** *plural* **messages**

messenger (mes′ən jər) ***noun*** a person who carries a message or is sent on an errand.
mes·sen·ger • ***noun,*** *plural* **messengers**

Messiah (mə sī′ə) **1** in Jewish belief, the person that God will send to save the Jewish

M

people. **2** in Christian belief, Jesus.
Mes·si·ah

messy (mes′ē) ***adjective*** in a mess; dirty or not tidy.
mess·y • ***adjective*** **messier, messiest**

met (met) ***verb*** *past tense and past participle of* **meet**.

metabolism (mə tab′ə liz əm) ***noun*** the set of processes in all plants and animals by which food is changed into energy, new cells, and waste materials.
me·tab·o·lism • ***noun,*** *plural* **metabolisms**

metal (met′l) ***noun*** **1** a chemical element that is more or less shiny and can be hammered or stretched. Heat and electricity pass through a metal easily. Iron, gold, aluminum, lead, and copper are metals. **2** a combination of more than one metal or of a metal and other substances. Brass, bronze, and steel are metals.
met·al • ***noun,*** *plural* **metals**

metallic (mə tal′ik) ***adjective*** **1** containing metal [*metallic* ore]. **2** of or like metal [a *metallic* sound].
me·tal·lic • ***adjective***

metamorphosis

metamorphosis (met′ə môr′fə sis) ***noun*** **1** the change in form that some animals go through in developing. The change from caterpillar to butterfly and the change from tadpole to frog are examples of metamorphosis. **2** any complete change.
met·a·mor·pho·sis • ***noun,*** *plural* **met·a·mor·pho·ses** (met′ə môr′fə sēz)

meteor (mēt′ē ər) ***noun*** a small, solid body that moves with great speed from outer space into the earth's atmosphere. In the atmosphere it becomes visible as it is made white-hot by friction. Meteors usually burn up.
me·te·or • ***noun,*** *plural* **meteors**

WORD HISTORY

meteor

The word **meteor** comes from a Greek word that means "things up in the air."

meteorite (mēt′ē ər īt′) ***noun*** a mass of metal or stone remaining from a meteor that has fallen upon the earth.
me·te·or·ite • ***noun,*** *plural* **meteorites**

meteorologist (mēt′ē ər äl′ə jist) ***noun*** an expert in meteorology.
me·te·or·ol·o·gist • ***noun,*** *plural* **meteorologists**

meteorology (mēt′ē ər äl′ə jē) ***noun*** the science that studies weather, climate, and the earth's atmosphere.
me·te·or·ol·o·gy • ***noun***

meter[1] (mēt′ər) ***noun*** **1** the basic unit of length in the metric system. One meter is equal to 39.37 inches. **2** rhythm in music; the arrangement of beats in each measure [Marches are often in 4/4 *meter*, with four beats in each measure.]
me·ter • ***noun,*** *plural* **meters**

meter[2] (mēt′ər) ***noun*** an instrument that measures how much of something passes through it [a gas *meter;* postage *meter*].
me·ter • ***noun,*** *plural* **meters**

-meter *a suffix meaning* a device for measuring [A *thermometer* measures temperatures.]

method (meth′əd) ***noun*** a way of doing something; process [Frying is one *method* of cooking fish.]
meth·od • ***noun,*** *plural* **methods**

metric (me′trik) ***adjective*** of or in the metric system.
met·ric • ***adjective***

metric system ***noun*** a system of weights and measures in which units go up or down by tens, hundreds, or thousands. The basic unit of length in this system is the meter.

a	cat	ō	go	ʉ	fur	ə =	a *in* ago
ā	ape	ô	law, for	ch	chin		e *in* agent
ä	cot, car	oo	look	sh	she		i *in* pencil
e	ten	ōō	tool	th	thin		o *in* atom
ē	me	oi	oil	*th*	then		u *in* circus
i	fit	ou	out	zh	measure		
ī	ice	u	up	ŋ	ring		

metronome (me′trə nōm) ***noun*** a device that makes a regular clicking noise, used to set the tempo for playing a piece of music. It can be set to click at different speeds.
met·ro·nome • ***noun,*** *plural* **metronomes**

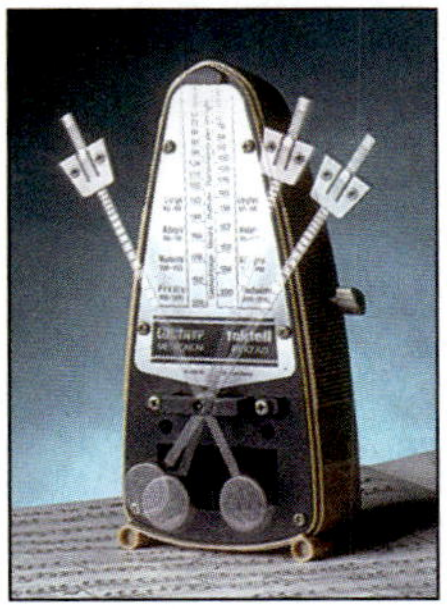
metronome

metropolis (mə träp′ə lis) ***noun*** a large, important city.
me·trop·o·lis • ***noun,*** *plural* **metropolises**

metropolitan (me′trə päl′i tən) ***adjective*** of or having to do with a large city, its suburbs, and other surrounding communities [The *metropolitan* area of Cleveland has nearly two million people.]
met·ro·pol·i·tan • ***adjective***

mew (myo͞o) ***noun*** the sound that a cat makes. ***verb*** to make this sound.
mew • ***noun,*** *plural* **mews** • ***verb*** **mewed, mewing**

Mexican (meks′i kən) ***noun*** a person born or living in Mexico.
Mex·i·can • ***noun,*** *plural* **Mexicans**

Mexico (mek′si kō) a country in North America, south of the U.S.
Mex·i·co

Mexico, Gulf of a gulf of the Atlantic, east of Mexico and south of the U.S.

Mexico City the capital of Mexico.

mg or **mg.** *abbreviation for* **1** milligram. **2** milligrams.

mi (mē) ***noun*** the third note of a musical scale.
● The words **mi** and **me** sound alike.
Do, re, *mi*, fa, sol, la, ti, do.
Mom gave *me* a kiss on the cheek.

mi. *abbreviation for* **1** mile. **2** miles.

MI *abbreviation for* Michigan.

Miami (mī am′ē) a city on the southeastern coast of Florida.
Mi·am·i

mica (mī′kə) ***noun*** a mineral that forms in thin layers that can be separated easily. It is not affected by heat or electricity.
mi·ca • ***noun***

mice (mīs) ***noun*** *plural of* **mouse**.

Michelangelo (mī′kəl an′jə lō) 1475-1564; Italian artist, architect, and poet.
Mi·chel·an·ge·lo

STATE MAP

Michigan

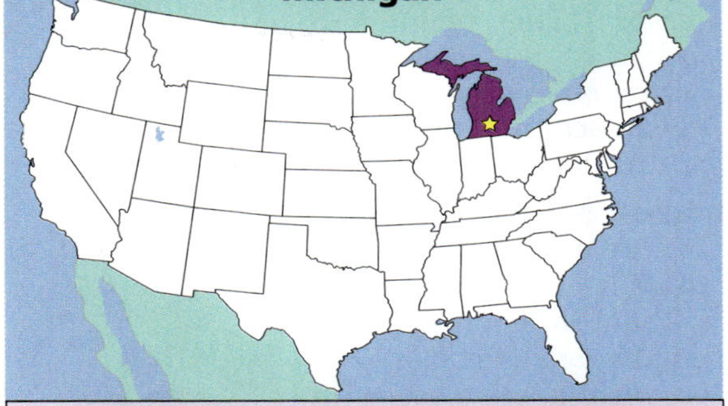

Statehood: 1837, the 26th state • **Capital:** Lansing

Michigan (mish′i gən) a State in the north central part of the U.S. Its capital is Lansing. Abbreviated **MI** or **Mich.**
Mich·i·gan

Michigan, Lake one of the Great Lakes, west of Lake Huron.

micro- *a prefix meaning:* **1** little, small, or tiny. **2** making small things look larger [A *microscope* makes very small things look larger.]

microbe (mī′krōb) ***noun*** **1** a germ. **2** any living thing so small that it can be seen only with a microscope.
mi·crobe • ***noun,*** *plural* **microbes**

WORD HISTORY

microbe

A **microbe** can be thought of as "a tiny bit of life," for it comes from the Greek words for "tiny" and "life."

microfilm (mī′krō film) ***noun*** film for taking tiny pictures of printed pages or documents. It is used for storing a large amount of information in a small space.
mi·cro·film • ***noun,*** *plural* **microfilms**

Micronesia (mī′krō nē′zhə) a country on a group of islands in the western Pacific Ocean.
Mi·cro·ne·sia

microphone (mī′krə fōn) ***noun*** a device that picks up sounds and changes them into electric waves. Microphones are used with devices that make sounds louder or that broadcast or record them.
mi·cro·phone • ***noun,*** *plural* **microphones**

M

microscope (mī′krə skōp) ***noun*** an instrument with a group of lenses for making tiny things look larger [The technician looked at the blood cells with a *microscope*.]
mi·cro·scope • ***noun,*** *plural* **microscopes**

microscope

microscopic (mī′krə skäp′ ik) ***adjective*** **1** so tiny that it cannot be seen without a microscope [a *microscopic* particle]. **2** of or with a microscope [a *microscopic* study of a strand of hair].
mi·cro·scop·ic • ***adjective***

microwave (mī′krō wāv) ***noun*** **1** a kind of radio wave. Some microwaves create great heat when they pass through food and are used in microwave ovens. Other microwaves are used to transmit signals to and from satellites. **2** a microwave oven.
mi·cro·wave • ***noun,*** *plural* **microwaves**

microwave oven ***noun*** an oven that uses microwaves to cook food very quickly.
microwave oven • ***noun,*** *plural* **microwave ovens**

mid (mid) ***adjective*** *a short form of* **middle**.

mid- *a prefix meaning* middle or middle part of [*Mid-June* is the middle part of June.]

midday (mid′dā) ***noun*** the middle of the day; noon.
mid·day • ***noun***

WORD CHOICES

Synonyms of **middle**

The words **middle, center,** and **midst** share the meaning "the part that is equally far away from all sides or boundaries."

in the *middle* of the field
in the *center* of the ring
in the *midst* of the crowd

middle (mid′əl) ***noun*** the point or part that is halfway between the ends or that is in the center [the *middle* of the night; the *middle* of a lake]. ***adjective*** being in the middle [the *middle* toe].
mid·dle • ***noun,*** *plural* **middles** • ***adjective***

middle age ***noun*** the time of life when a person is neither young nor old; the years from about 40 to about 65.

Middle Ages the period of history in Europe between ancient and modern times: the time from about A.D. 500 to about A.D. 1450.

middle class ***noun*** all the people who are not rich or poor.
middle class • ***noun,*** *plural* **middle classes**

Middle East a region of southwestern Asia and northeastern Africa. It includes Israel, Egypt, Jordan, Syria, Lebanon, Iran, Iraq, Arabia, Cyprus, and the part of Turkey that is in Asia.

middle school ***noun*** a school between elementary school and high school, having three or four grades, between the fifth and eighth grades.

Middle West the part of the U.S. between the Rocky Mountains and the eastern border of Ohio, north of the Ohio River and the southern borders of Kansas and Missouri.

Middle Western ***adjective*** of or having to do with the Middle West [a *Middle Western* town; *Middle Western* traditions].

midget (mij′ət) ***noun*** a very small person.
midg·et • ***noun,*** *plural* **midgets**

midnight (mid′nīt) ***noun*** twelve o'clock at night. This is the time when one day ends and the next day begins.
mid·night • ***noun,*** *plural* **midnights**

midst (midst) ***noun*** *used mainly in the phrase* **in the midst of,** in the course of; during [The phone rang when she was *in the midst of* washing her hair.] —Look for the WORD CHOICES box at the entry **middle**.

midsummer (mid′sum′ər) ***noun*** the middle of summer.
mid·sum·mer • ***noun***

midway (mid′wā) ***adjective*** in the middle; halfway [The ship's captain set a *midway* course between the islands.] This word can also be used as an adverb [The ship sailed *midway* between the islands.]

a	cat	ō	go	ʉ	fur	ə =	a *in* ago
ā	ape	ô	law, for	ch	chin		e *in* agent
ä	cot, car	ꝏ	look	sh	she		i *in* pencil
e	ten	ꝏ̄	tool	th	thin		o *in* atom
ē	me	oi	oil	*th*	then		u *in* circus
i	fit	ou	out	zh	measure		
ī	ice	u	up	ŋ	ring		

noun the part of a carnival or fair where sideshows and other amusements are located.
mid·way • ***adjective*** • ***noun,*** *plural* **midways**

Midwest (mid west′) *another name for* **Middle West**.
Mid·west

Midwestern (mid wes′tərn) ***adjective*** of or having to do with the Middle West.
Mid·west·ern • ***adjective***

might[1] (mīt) ***verb (helping verb)*** **I.** *past tense of* **may**. **II.** a helping verb with about the same meaning as **may**, but often showing a bit of doubt [It *might* be raining there. I *might* go.] The word "to" is not used between *might* and the verb that follows it.
might • ***verb*** *he / she / it* **might**
● The words **might** and **mite** sound alike.
I *might* have visited Vermont once.
She swung the bat with all her *might*.
A *mite* is a tiny parasite.

might[2] (mīt) ***noun*** great strength, force, or power [Pull with all your *might*.]
● The words **might** and **mite** sound alike.

mighty (mīt′ē) ***adjective*** **1** very strong; powerful [a *mighty* blow]. **2** very large [a *mighty* tree; a *mighty* ship].
adverb [*an informal use*] very; extremely [I'm *mighty* tired.]
might·y • ***adjective*** **mightier, mightiest** • ***adverb***

migrant (mī′grənt) ***noun*** a person or animal that migrates, especially a farm worker who moves from place to place to pick crops.
mi·grant • ***noun,*** *plural* **migrants**

migrate (mī′grāt) ***verb*** **1** to move from one country to another [People from Norway *migrated* to Iceland in the Middle Ages.] **2** to move from one country or region to another when the season changes [Many birds *migrate* south for the winter.]
mi·grate • ***verb*** **migrated, migrating**

migration (mī grā′shən) ***noun*** the act of migrating [the *migration* of birds].
mi·gra·tion • ***noun,*** *plural* **migrations**

mike (mīk) [*an informal word*] ***noun*** a microphone.
mike • ***noun,*** *plural* **mikes**

mild (mīld) ***adjective*** **1** not harsh or severe; gentle [a *mild* winter; a *mild* punishment] —Look for the WORD CHOICES box at the entry **gentle**. **2** not strong or sharp in taste [*mild* cheese].
mild • ***adjective*** **milder, mildest**

mildew (mil′do͞o *or* mil′dyo͞o) ***noun*** a fungus that usually appears as a furry, white coating or a brown spot. It attacks plants and also forms on cloth, paper, or other things that are kept damp.
mil·dew • ***noun***

mile (mīl) ***noun*** a measure of length, equal to 5,280 feet or 1.6093 kilometers.
mile • ***noun,*** *plural* **miles**

mileage (mīl′ij) ***noun*** **1** total number of miles [What is the *mileage* between Denver and Chicago?] **2** the average number of miles a vehicle will go on a gallon of fuel [Small cars usually get better gas *mileage* than large ones.]
mile·age • ***noun***

milestone (mīl′stōn) ***noun*** **1** something, such as a stone or pillar, that shows the distance in miles to a certain place. **2** an important event [Landing on the moon was a *milestone* in the history of space travel.]
mile·stone • ***noun,*** *plural* **milestones**

military (mil′i ter′ē) ***adjective*** of or having to do with soldiers or the armed forces [*military* ranks].
—the military soldiers as a group; armed forces [The *military* is in a state of alert.]
mil·i·tar·y • ***adjective***

militia (mə lish′ə) ***noun*** a group of citizens who are not regular soldiers, but who may be called to serve in an emergency.
mi·li·tia • ***noun,*** *plural* **militias**

milk (milk) ***noun*** **1** a white liquid formed in special glands of female mammals for feeding their young. **2** the milk of cows, commonly used as food by humans. **3** any liquid or juice that looks like milk.
verb to squeeze out milk from a cow, goat, or other animal.
milk • ***noun*** • ***verb*** **milked, milking**

milkman (milk′man) ***noun*** a man who sells or delivers milk.
milk·man • ***noun,*** *plural* **milkmen**

milkshake (milk′shāk) ***noun*** a drink made with milk, ice cream, and flavoring, shaken up or mixed.
milk·shake • ***noun,*** *plural* **milkshakes**

milky (mil′kē) ***adjective*** **1** like milk [The walls were *milky* white.] **2** of or containing milk.
milk·y • ***adjective*** **milkier, milkiest**

Milky Way a broad band of cloudy light seen across the sky at night. It is what we see of the galaxy that includes the sun, the earth, and the rest of our solar system.

mill

mill (mil) ***noun*** **1** a building with machines that grind grain into flour or meal. **2** a machine that grinds, crushes, or cuts up [A coffee *mill* grinds coffee beans.] **3** a factory [a steel *mill*].
verb **1** to grind, form, or make in a mill. **2** to move slowly without direction or purpose [The crowd *milled* around outside the stadium.]
mill • ***noun,*** *plural* **mills** • ***verb*** **milled, milling**

millennium (mi len′ē əm) ***noun*** a thousand years.
mil·len·ni·um • ***noun,*** *plural* **millenniums** or **mil·len·ni·a** (mi len′ē ə)

miller (mil′ər) ***noun*** a person who owns or works in a mill where grain is ground.
mill·er • ***noun,*** *plural* **millers**

milli- *a prefix meaning* a thousandth part of [How many *millimeters* are there in a meter?]

milligram (mil′i gram) ***noun*** a unit of weight in the metric system, equal to 1⁄1000 gram.
mil·li·gram • ***noun,*** *plural* **milligrams**

milliliter (mil′i lēt′ər) ***noun*** a unit of volume in the metric system, equal to 1⁄1000 liter.
mil·li·li·ter • ***noun,*** *plural* **milliliters**

millimeter (mil′i mēt′ər) ***noun*** a unit of length in the metric system, equal to 1⁄1000 meter.
mil·li·me·ter • ***noun,*** *plural* **millimeters**

million (mil′yən) ***noun*** the cardinal number that is equal to a thousand times a thousand; 1,000,000.
adjective adding up to one million.
mil·lion • ***noun,*** *plural* **millions** • ***adjective***

millionaire (mil yə ner′) ***noun*** a person who has at least a million dollars.
mil·lion·aire • ***noun,*** *plural* **millionaires**

millionth (mil′yənth) ***adjective*** last of a million things in a series.
noun **1** the millionth one. **2** one of a million equal parts of something; 1⁄1,000,000.
mil·lionth • ***adjective*** • ***noun,*** *plural* **millionths**

Milwaukee (mil wô′kē *or* mil wä′kē) a city in southeastern Wisconsin, on Lake Michigan.
Mil·wau·kee

mimic (mim′ik) ***verb*** to imitate, often in order to make fun of —Look for the WORD CHOICES box at the entry **imitate**.
noun a performer who mimics.
mim·ic • ***verb*** **mimicked, mimicking, mimics** • ***noun,*** *plural* **mimics**

min. *abbreviation for* **1** minute. **2** minutes.

mince (mins) ***verb*** to cut into small pieces [I will *mince* the onions.]
mince • ***verb*** **minced, mincing**

mind (mīnd) ***noun*** **1** the part of a person that thinks, understands, decides, and feels. **2** what a person thinks or intends; opinion, desire, or purpose [He changed his *mind* about going.] **3** the ability to think or reason; intelligence [Have you lost your *mind?*] **4** attention [Your *mind* is not on your work.] **5** memory [That brings your story to *mind*.]
verb **1** to pay attention to; heed [*Mind* your manners.] **2** to take care of; look after [*Mind* the store while I'm gone.] **3** to care about; object to [I don't *mind* the heat.]
—**bear in mind** or **keep in mind** to remember [Here are a few rules to *keep in mind*.] —**make up one's mind** to decide. —**never mind** do not be concerned. —**out of one's mind** **1** crazy or foolish. **2** very excited or upset [I was *out of my mind* with worry.]
mind • ***noun,*** *plural for senses 1, 2, 3, and 4 only* **minds** • ***verb*** **minded, minding**

mindless (mīnd′ləs) ***adjective*** thoughtless or careless [a *mindless* act of violence].
mind·less • ***adjective***

mine[1] (mīn) ***pronoun*** the one or the ones that belong to me [I know this book is *mine*. We all planted flowers, but *mine* haven't bloomed.]

mine[2] (mīn) ***noun*** **1** a large hole made in the earth so that minerals or other matter may be removed [a coal *mine*]. **2** a large supply; a good source [The library is a *mine* of information.] **3** an explosive hidden in the ground or under the water to blow up an enemy.

a	cat	ō	go	ʉ	fur	ə =	a *in* ago
ā	ape	ô	law, for	ch	chin		e *in* agent
ä	cot, car	oo	look	sh	she		i *in* pencil
e	ten	o͞o	tool	th	thin		o *in* atom
ē	me	oi	oil	*th*	then		u *in* circus
i	fit	ou	out	zh	measure		
ī	ice	u	up	ŋ	ring		

verb **1** to get from a mine [The company *mines* copper in Arizona.] **2** to put explosive mines in or under [The navy *mined* the harbor.]
mine ◦ *noun, plural* **mines** ◦ *verb* **mined, mining**

miner (mī′nər) *noun* a person whose work is digging out minerals or other matter in a mine.
min·er ◦ *noun, plural* **miners**
● The words **miner** and **minor** sound alike.
The *miner* was trapped in the tunnel.
I had only a few *minor* bruises.

mineral (min′ər əl) *noun* **1** a solid substance that was never an animal or a plant and that was formed in the earth by nature. Iron, granite, and salt are minerals. Coal is sometimes called a mineral, too. **2** one of the chemical elements needed by plants and animals [A good diet should supply the *minerals* you need.]
adjective of or full of minerals [*mineral* water].
min·er·al ◦ *noun, plural* **minerals** ◦ *adjective*

mingle (miŋ′gəl) *verb* to join with others [We *mingled* with the crowd.] —Look for the WORD CHOICES box at the entry **mix**.
min·gle ◦ *verb* **mingled, mingling**

mini- *a prefix meaning:* **1** miniature; very small. **2** smaller than usual [A *minibus* is smaller than a regular bus.]

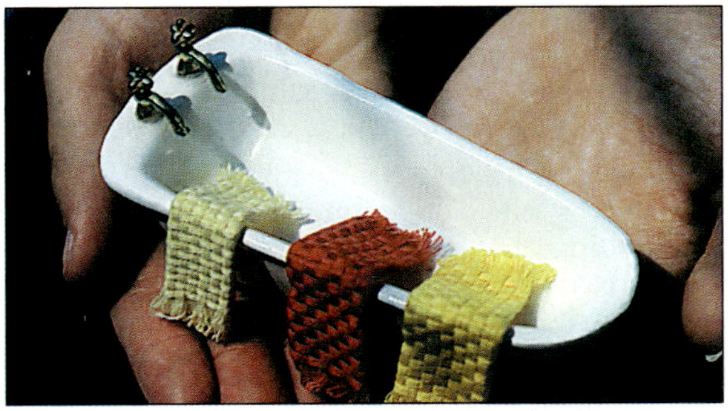

miniature

miniature (min′ē ə chər *or* min′i chər) *noun* a very small copy, model, or version [a *miniature* of the Statue of Liberty].
adjective very small in size or scale [a *miniature* poodle].
min·i·a·ture ◦ *noun, plural* **miniatures** ◦ *adjective*

minibus (min′ē bus′) *noun* a small bus.
min·i·bus ◦ *noun, plural* **minibuses**

minicam (min′ē kam′) *noun* a small TV camera that can be carried easily on the shoulder.
min·i·cam ◦ *noun, plural* **minicams**

minimize (min′ə mīz) *verb* **1** to make as small as possible [Safe storage of gas will *minimize* the danger of fire.] **2** to make seem small or not important [The firefighters *minimized* the dangers they faced.]
min·i·mize ◦ *verb* **minimized, minimizing**

minimum (min′i məm) *noun* **1** the smallest amount or number that is possible or allowed [In football, a *minimum* of seven players must be in the line.] **2** the lowest degree or point that has been reached or recorded [Today's temperature reached a *minimum* of 0°F.]
adjective smallest or least that is possible or allowed [Congress raised the *minimum* wage.]
min·i·mum ◦ *noun, plural* **minimums** ◦ *adjective*

mining (mīn′iŋ) *noun* the work of digging minerals or ores from mines.
min·ing ◦ *noun*

minister (min′is tər) *noun* a person who is the head of a church, especially a Protestant church.
verb to give help; serve or attend [The volunteers *ministered* to the sick.]
min·is·ter ◦ *noun, plural* **ministers** ◦ *verb* **ministered, ministering**

mink (miŋk) *noun* **1** an animal like a weasel that lives on land and in water. **2** its costly, thick, brown fur [a coat made of *mink*].
mink ◦ *noun, plural* **minks** or **mink**

Minneapolis (min′ē ap′ə lis) a city in eastern Minnesota.
Min·ne·ap·o·lis

STATE MAP

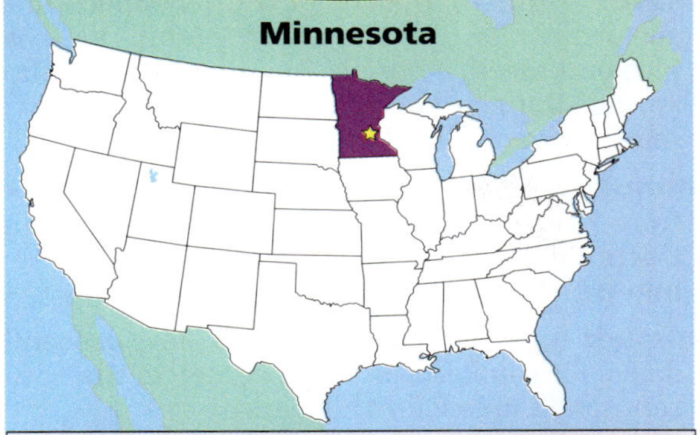

Statehood: 1858, the 32nd state • **Capital:** St. Paul

Minnesota (min ə sōt′ə) a State in the north central part of the U.S. Its capital is St. Paul. Abbreviated **MN** or **Minn.**
Min·ne·so·ta

M

minnow (min′ō) ***noun*** a very small fish that lives in fresh water. It is commonly used as bait in fishing.
min·now • ***noun,*** *plural* **minnows**

minor (mī′nər) ***adjective*** lesser in size, importance, or amount [a *minor* accident; *minor* leagues].
noun a person who is under the age for being an adult according to the law [In our State, a *minor* becomes an adult at age 18.]
mi·nor • ***adjective*** • ***noun,*** *plural* **minors**
● The words **minor** and **miner** sound alike.
You cannot sell beer to a *minor*.
My grandfather was a coal *miner*.

minority (mī nôr′i tē *or* mi nôr′i tē) ***noun*** **1** the smaller part or number; less than half [A *minority* of the Senate voted for the law.] **2** a small group of people whose race, religion, or culture is quite different from those of the main groups in a society.
mi·nor·i·ty • ***noun,*** *plural* **minorities**

minstrel (min′strəl) ***noun*** a person in the Middle Ages who traveled from place to place and entertained with songs and poems.
min·strel • ***noun,*** *plural* **minstrels**

mint[1] (mint) ***noun*** **1** a place where the government makes coins. **2** a large amount [That piece of jewelry must have cost a *mint*.]
adjective never used; new or like new [a coin in *mint* condition].
verb to make coins by stamping metal [The government *mints* millions of pennies every year.]
mint • ***noun,*** *plural for sense 1 only* **mints**
• ***adjective*** • ***verb*** **minted, minting**

mint[2] (mint) ***noun*** **1** the peppermint, spearmint, or certain other plants with a pleasant smell, whose leaves are used as a flavoring. **2** a piece of candy flavored with mint.
mint • ***noun,*** *plural* **mints**

minuend (min′yo͞o end′) ***noun*** the number from which another number is subtracted. In the problem 9 - 5 = 4, 9 is the minuend.
min·u·end • ***noun,*** *plural* **minuends**

minuet (min′yo͞o et′) ***noun*** **1** a slow, graceful dance for couples that was popular in the 18th century. **2** music for this dance.
min·u·et • ***noun,*** *plural* **minuets**

minus (mī′nəs) ***preposition*** **1** less; made smaller by subtracting [Four *minus* two equals two.] **2** [*an informal use*] without [Thanks to the wind, I arrived *minus* my hat.]
adjective **1** less than zero; negative [The temperature is *minus* 5°, or five degrees below zero.] **2** a little less than [a grade of A *minus*].
noun *a short form of* **minus sign**.
mi·nus • ***preposition*** • ***adjective*** • ***noun,*** *plural* **minuses**

minus sign ***noun*** a sign (-) in arithmetic put before a number to show that the number is to be subtracted. The minus sign can also show that a number is less than zero.
minus sign • ***noun,*** *plural* **minus signs**

minute[1] (min′ət) ***noun*** **1** one of the sixty equal parts of an hour; 60 seconds. **2** a short period of time more or less equal to 60 seconds; moment [I'll be there in a *minute*.] **3** a particular time [I'll call you the *minute* I get home.] **4 minutes** a written record of what happened during a meeting.
min·ute • ***noun,*** *plural for senses 1, 2, and 4 only* **minutes**

minute[2] (mī no͞ot′ *or* mī nyo͞ot′) ***adjective*** very small; tiny [*minute* particles of dust].
mi·nute • ***adjective*** **minuter, minutest**

miracle (mir′ə kəl) ***noun*** **1** a thing that happens which seems to go against the known laws of nature or science [the *miracles* in the Bible]. **2** an amazing or unusual thing [It was a *miracle* that we won the game.]
mir·a·cle • ***noun,*** *plural* **miracles**

miraculous (mi rak′yo͞o ləs) ***adjective*** very amazing or unusual [It seems *miraculous* that no one was hurt in the crash.]
mi·rac·u·lous • ***adjective***

mirage (mi räzh′) ***noun*** an illusion that is caused by the reflection of light. It may be something that is unreal or it may be something real that appears much closer than it is.
mi·rage • ***noun,*** *plural* **mirages**

mire (mīr) ***noun*** **1** an area of wet, soft ground; bog. **2** deep mud.

mirror (mir′ər) ***noun*** a smooth surface that reflects the image of a person or thing placed in front of it. Most mirrors are made of glass with a coating of silver or aluminum on the back.
verb to reflect in a mirror or in something that acts like a mirror [The moon was *mirrored* in the lake.]

a cat	ō go	ʉ fur	ə = a *in* ago
ā ape	ô law, for	ch chin	e *in* agent
ä cot, car	o͞o look	sh she	i *in* pencil
e ten	o͞o tool	th thin	o *in* atom
ē me	oi oil	*th* then	u *in* circus
i fit	ou out	zh measure	
ī ice	u up	ŋ ring	

mir·ror • *noun, plural* **mirrors**
• *verb* **mirrored, mirroring**

mis- *a prefix meaning:* **1** wrong or wrongly [*Misplacing* something means putting it in the wrong place.] **2** bad or badly [*Misconduct* is bad conduct or behavior.]

misbehave (mis′bē hāv′) *verb* to behave in a bad way; do what should not be done.
mis·be·have • *verb* **misbehaved, misbehaving**

miscellaneous (mis′ə lā′nē əs) *adjective* of many different kinds; mixed; varied [A *miscellaneous* collection of objects filled the shelf.]
mis·cel·la·ne·ous • *adjective*

mischief (mis′chif) *noun* **1** a playful trick; prank [Who is responsible for this *mischief?*] **2** playful, harmless spirits [The children are full of *mischief.*]
mis·chief • *noun*

mischievous (mis′chə vəs) *adjective* **1** causing some slight harm or bother, often in a playful way [a *mischievous* act]. **2** full of playful tricks; teasing [a *mischievous* child].
mis·chie·vous • *adjective*

misconduct (mis kän′dukt) *noun* bad or wrong conduct or behavior.
mis·con·duct • *noun*

miser (mī′zər) *noun* a greedy, stingy person who saves up money without ever spending it.
mi·ser • *noun, plural* **misers**

miserable (miz′ər ə bəl) *adjective* **1** very unhappy; sad [The bad news made us *miserable.*] —Look for the WORD CHOICES box at the entry **sad**. **2** causing unhappiness, discomfort, or pain [*miserable* weather]. **3** bad, poor, or unpleasant [a *miserable* movie].
mis·er·a·ble • *adjective*

misery (miz′ər ē) *noun* a condition in which one suffers very much or is very unhappy [a life full of *misery*].
mis·er·y • *noun*

misfit (mis′fit) *noun* a person who does not get along well with other people.
mis·fit • *noun, plural* **misfits**

misfortune (mis fôr′chən) *noun* **1** bad luck; trouble [He took advantage of their *misfortune.*] **2** an accident that brings trouble; mishap.
mis·for·tune • *noun, plural for sense 2 only* **misfortunes**

misgiving (mis giv′iŋ) *noun often* **misgivings** a feeling of doubt, fear, or worry [I had *misgivings* about taking the old car on a long trip.]
mis·giv·ing • *noun, plural* **misgivings**

misguided (mis gīd′əd) *adjective* led into making mistakes or doing wrong [The *misguided* youth ran away from home.]
mis·guid·ed • *adjective*

mishap (mis′hap) *noun* an accident that brings trouble; misfortune.
mis·hap • *noun, plural* **mishaps**

misinterpret (mis′in tur′prət) *verb* to give a wrong meaning to; explain or understand in a wrong way [She *misinterpreted* the instructions.]
mis·in·ter·pret • *verb* **misinterpreted, misinterpreting**

mislaid (mis lād′) *verb past tense and past participle of* **mislay**.
mis·laid • *verb*

mislay (mis lā′) *verb* to put something in a place and then forget where it is [I *mislaid* my keys.]
mis·lay • *verb* **mislaid, mislaying**

mislead (mis lēd′) *verb* to cause to believe what is not true; deceive [She *misled* us into thinking she would help.] —Look for the WORD CHOICES boxes at the entries **cheat** and **deceive**.
mis·lead • *verb* **misled, misleading**

misled (mis led′) *verb past tense and past participle of* **mislead**.
mis·led • *verb*

misplace (mis plās′) *verb* to put in a wrong place [I *misplaced* my pen.]
mis·place • *verb* **misplaced, misplacing**

misprint (mis′print) *noun* a mistake in something printed [That book is full of *misprints.*]
mis·print • *noun, plural* **misprints**

mispronounce (mis prə nouns′) *verb* to pronounce in a wrong way [Teachers almost always *mispronounce* my last name.]
mis·pro·nounce • *verb* **mispronounced, mispronouncing**

miss (mis) *verb* **1** to fail to hit, meet, reach, get, catch, see, or hear [She *missed* the ball. I *missed* my bus.] **2** to escape; avoid [He just *missed* being hit.] **3** to fail to do, keep, have, or attend [I *missed* work today.] **4** to let go by; fail to take [You *missed* your turn.] **5** to notice or feel the absence or loss of [I suddenly *missed* my wallet. I *miss* my friends in Kentucky.]

M

noun a failure to hit [My first shot at the target was a *miss*.]
miss • *verb* **missed, missing** • *noun, plural* **misses**

Miss (mis) *noun* a title used before the name of a girl or unmarried woman.
Miss • *noun, plural* **Misses**

Miss. *abbreviation for* Mississippi.

missile (mis′əl) *noun* a weapon or other object that is thrown or shot at a target.
mis·sile • *noun, plural* **missiles**

missing (mis′iŋ) *adjective* absent, lost, gone, or lacking [The children found the *missing* cat.]
miss·ing • *adjective*

mission (mish′ən) *noun* **1** a special duty or piece of work that a person or a group is sent out to do [a space *mission;* a bombing *mission*]. **2** a group of missionaries or the place where they live and work [the old *missions* in California].
mis·sion • *noun, plural* **missions**

missionary (mish′ən er′ē) *noun* a person sent out by a church to spread its religion in a foreign country.
mis·sion·ar·y • *noun, plural* **missionaries**

STATE MAP

Mississippi

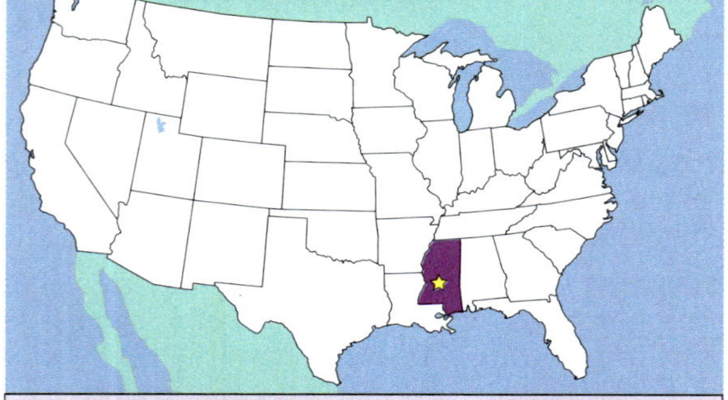

Statehood: 1817, the 20th state • **Capital:** Jackson

Mississippi (mis′i sip′ē) **1** a river in the U.S., flowing from Minnesota to the Gulf of Mexico. **2** a State in the southeastern part of the U.S. Its capital is Jackson. Abbreviated **MS** or **Miss.**
Mis·sis·sip·pi

Missouri (mi zoor′ē) **1** a river in the U.S., flowing from Montana into the Mississippi River. **2** a State in the central part of the U.S. Its capital is Jefferson City. Abbreviated **MO** or **Mo.**
Mis·sou·ri

STATE MAP

Missouri

Statehood: 1821, the 24th state • **Capital:** Jefferson City

misspell (mis spel′) *verb* to spell incorrectly [She *misspelled* only one word.]
mis·spell • *verb* **misspelled** or **misspelt** (mis spelt′), **misspelling**

misspelling (mis spel′iŋ) *noun* an incorrect spelling [Please correct your *misspellings*.]
mis·spell·ing • *noun, plural* **misspellings**

mist (mist) *noun* a large mass of tiny drops of water in the air, like a light fog [There is *mist* along the banks of the river at dawn.]
verb to make or become slightly wet with mist, or something like mist [My breath *misted* the window. His eyes *misted* with tears.]
mist • *noun, plural* **mists** • *verb* **misted, misting**

WORD CHOICES

Synonyms of **mist**

The words **mist**, **fog**, and **haze** share the meaning "a mass of water vapor, or of smoke or dust, floating in the air."

The sun burned away the *mist* over the lake.

Our headlights cut through the *fog*.

We drove into an urban *haze* of fumes and dust.

mistake (mi stāk′) *noun* an idea, answer, or act that is wrong; error or blunder —Look for

a cat	ō go	ʉ fur	ə = a *in* ago
ā ape	ô law, for	ch chin	e *in* agent
ä cot, car	oo look	sh she	i *in* pencil
e ten	o͞o tool	th thin	o *in* atom
ē me	oi oil	*th* then	u *in* circus
i fit	ou out	zh measure	
ī ice	u up	ŋ ring	

the WORD CHOICES box at the entry **error**.
verb **1** to get a wrong idea of; misunderstand [She *mistook* the meaning of my remarks.] **2** to think that one person is someone else or that one thing is something else [I am always *mistaking* you for your twin brother.]
mis·take • ***noun,*** *plural* **mistakes**
• ***verb*** **mistook, mistaken, mistaking**

mistaken (mi stāk′ən) ***adjective*** making or showing a mistake; wrong [a *mistaken* idea].
verb *past participle of* **mistake.**
mis·tak·en • ***adjective*** • ***verb***

Mister (mis′tər) ***noun*** a title used before the name of a man or the position he holds. It is usually written *Mr.* [*Mr.* Green; *Mr.* President].
Mis·ter • ***noun***

mistletoe (mis′əl tō) ***noun*** an evergreen plant with shiny white berries that grows as a parasite on trees. It is used as a Christmas decoration.
mis·tle·toe • ***noun***

mistook (mis to͝ok′) ***verb*** *past tense of* **mistake.**
mis·took • ***verb***

mistreat (mis trēt′) ***verb*** to treat badly; abuse.
mis·treat • ***verb*** **mistreated, mistreating**

mistress (mis′trəs) ***noun*** **1** a woman who has control over something [the *mistress* of the household]. **2 Mistress** a title used in earlier times before the name of a woman. It is now replaced by *Mrs., Miss,* or *Ms.*
mis·tress • ***noun,*** *plural* **mistresses**

mistrust (mis trust′) ***noun*** a lack of trust or confidence; doubt; suspicion.
verb to have no trust or confidence in; doubt [I *mistrust* all strangers.]
mis·trust • ***noun*** • ***verb*** **mistrusted, mistrusting**

misty (mis′tē) ***adjective*** **1** having to do with or like mist [*misty* air]. **2** covered by mist [*misty* mountains].
mist·y • ***adjective*** **mistier, mistiest**

misunderstand (mis′un dər stand′) ***verb*** to understand in a wrong way; give a wrong meaning to [I *misunderstood* the teacher's directions.]
mis·un·der·stand • ***verb*** **misunderstood, misunderstanding**

misunderstanding (mis′un dər stand′iŋ) ***noun*** **1** a failure to understand correctly [My *misunderstanding* of the rules caused the confusion.] **2** a quarrel or disagreement [My brother and I settled our little *misunderstanding*.]
mis·un·der·stand·ing • ***noun,*** *plural for sense 2 only* **misunderstandings**

misunderstood (mis′un dər sto͝od′) ***verb*** *past tense and past participle of* **misunderstand.**
mis·un·der·stood • ***verb***

misuse (mis yo͞oz′ *for v.;* mis yo͞os′ *for n.*)
verb **1** to use in a wrong way [Don't *misuse* your time.] **2** to treat badly; abuse [He *misused* the toy and it broke.]
noun wrong or incorrect use [*misuse* of funds by the treasurer].
mis·use • ***verb*** **misused, misusing** • ***noun***

Mitchell (mich′əl), **Maria** (mə rē′ə) 1818-1889; U.S. astronomer and teacher.
Mitch·ell, Ma·ri·a

mite (mīt) ***noun*** a tiny animal related to the spider that lives as a parasite on plants and animals.
mite • ***noun,*** *plural* **mites**
● The words **mite** and **might** sound alike.
My dog has a tick and *mite* problem.
We still *might* go to the show.
She swung the bat with all her *might*.

mitt

mitt (mit) ***noun*** **1** a large padded glove, with a thumb but usually without separate fingers, worn by baseball players [a catcher's *mitt*]. **2** *the same as* **mitten.**
mitt • ***noun,*** *plural* **mitts**

mitten (mit′n) ***noun*** a glove with one pouch for the thumb and a larger pouch for the four fingers.
mit·ten • ***noun,*** *plural* **mittens**

mix (miks) ***verb*** **1** to put, stir, or come together to form a single blended thing [He *mixed* red and yellow paint to get orange. Oil and

M

water will not *mix*.] **2** to join or combine [She *mixed* work and play during her trip.]
noun a mixture or a group of things that are to be mixed together.
—mix up **1** to mix completely. **2** to confuse [I was a little *mixed up* about where to meet you.] **3** to involve [The mayor is *mixed up* in the scandal].
mix • ***verb*** **mixed, mixing** • ***noun,*** *plural* **mixes**

WORD CHOICES

Synonyms of **mix**

The words **mix**, **blend**, and **mingle** share the meaning "to bring together to form a single mass or substance."

You can't *mix* oil and water.

Blend the butter and flour into a smooth paste.

Fans of both teams *mingled* on the sidelines.

mixed (mikst) ***adjective*** **1** put or stirred together in a single blend. **2** of different kinds [*mixed* nuts]. **3** made up of men and women [*mixed* company]. **4** confused [*mixed* feelings].

mixed number ***noun*** a number, such as $6\frac{7}{8}$, that is made up of a whole number and a fraction.
mixed number • ***noun,*** *plural* **mixed numbers**

mixer (miks′ər) ***noun*** a device for mixing things [a *mixer* for the cake batter; a cement *mixer*].
mix·er • ***noun,*** *plural* **mixers**

mixture (miks′chər) ***noun*** something made by mixing [Punch is a *mixture* of fruit juices.]
mix·ture • ***noun,*** *plural* **mixtures**

ml or **ml.** *abbreviation for* **1** milliliter. **2** milliliters.

mm or **mm.** *abbreviation for* **1** millimeter. **2** millimeters.

MN *abbreviation for* Minnesota.

MO or **Mo.** *abbreviation for* Missouri.

moan (mōn) ***noun*** a low, long sound of sorrow or of pain.
verb **1** to make a moan or moans [She *moaned* when the dentist touched her sore tooth.] —Look for the WORD CHOICES box at the entry **cry**. **2** to say with a moan [He *moaned* his answer to the doctor's question.]
moan • ***noun,*** *plural* **moans** • ***verb*** **moaned, moaning**

● The words **moan** and **mown** sound alike.
A *moan* came from the hospital room.
I had *mown* the lawn before it rained.

moat

moat (mōt) ***noun*** a deep, wide ditch dug around a castle to keep enemies out. Moats were often filled with water.
moat • ***noun,*** *plural* **moats**

mob (mäb) ***noun*** **1** a large group of people; a crowd [There was a *mob* at the airport waiting for the football players.] **2** a large, angry, unruly crowd.
verb to crowd around in anger or excitement [The rock star was *mobbed* by the teenagers.]
mob • ***noun,*** *plural* **mobs** • ***verb*** **mobbed, mobbing**

mobile (mō′bəl *or* mō′bīl *for adj.;* mō′bēl *for n.*) ***adjective*** able to move or be moved from place to place quickly and easily [a *mobile* military force].
noun a kind of movable sculpture consisting of parts that are usually hung from rods or thin wires. A mobile can be easily moved by air currents.
mo·bile • ***adjective*** • ***noun,*** *plural* **mobiles**

mobile home ***noun*** a large trailer that is furnished as a home. It is usually parked for a

a	cat	ō	go	ʉ	fur	ə = a *in* ago	
ā	ape	ô	law, for	ch	chin		e *in* agent
ä	cot, car	oo	look	sh	she		i *in* pencil
e	ten	o͞o	tool	th	thin		o *in* atom
ē	me	oi	oil	*th*	then		u *in* circus
i	fit	ou	out	zh	measure		
ī	ice	u	up	ŋ	ring		

long time in one location.
mobile home • *noun, plural* **mobile homes**

moccasin (mäk′ə sən) *noun* a slipper made of soft leather, without a heel.
moc·ca·sin • *noun, plural* **moccasins**

moccasin

mock (mäk) *verb* **1** to make fun of in a rude or mean way; to ridicule [Many scientists *mocked* his theories.] **2** to make fun of by imitating or mimicking.
adjective not real; pretended [The troops were engaged in a *mock* battle.]
mock • *verb* **mocked, mocking** • *adjective*

mockingbird (mäk′iŋ burd) *noun* a small, gray and white American bird. It often imitates the calls of other birds.
mock·ing·bird • *noun, plural* **mockingbirds**

mode (mōd) *noun* a way or style of acting or doing something; method [Airplanes, trains, and automobiles are some of the many *modes* of transportation available.]
mode • *noun, plural* **modes**

model (mäd′əl) *noun* **1** a small copy of something [a *model* of a ship]. **2** a person or thing that is considered a good example of something and ought to be imitated or copied [He is a *model* of honesty.] **3** a style or design [Our new car is a two-door *model*.] **4** a person who poses for an artist or photographer. **5** a person whose work is wearing new clothes that are for sale, so that customers can see how they look.
adjective **1** being or serving as a model [a *model* airplane]. **2** worthy to serve as an example; excellent [a *model* student].
verb **1** to plan, form, or make using a model as a guide [The architect *modeled* our city hall after a famous building in Washington.] **2** to make a piece of sculpture [Linda *models* animals in clay.] **3** to show how an article of clothing looks by wearing it [Will you *model* this coat for me?] **4** to pose for an artist or wear new clothes to show them to customers [He *models* for a photographer in town.]
mod·el • *noun, plural* **models** • *adjective* • *verb* **modeled** or **modelled, modeling** or **modelling**

WORD CHOICES

Synonyms of **model**

The words **model, example,** and **pattern** share the meaning "someone or something to be copied or imitated."

He is a perfect *model* of good manners.

Her cheating offers a poor *example* for others.

You can use a *pattern* when making a dress.

moderate (mäd′ər ət *for adj.;* mäd′ər āt *for v.*) *adjective* neither too much nor too little; reasonable or average [The doctor charged a *moderate* fee. We have *moderate* temperatures all year.]
verb **1** to make or become less strong or extreme [The temperature *moderated* during the day.] **2** to serve as chairman of a discussion or debate.
mod·er·ate • *adjective* • *verb* **moderated, moderating**

modern (mäd′ərn) *adjective* **1** of or having to do with the present time or the period we live in [a *modern* painter; a *modern* invention]. **2** of or having to do with the latest styles, methods, or ideas; up-to-date [*modern* technology].
mod·ern • *adjective*

modernize (mäd′ərn īz) *verb* to make or become modern; bring up to date in style or design [We need to *modernize* our kitchen.]
mod·ern·ize • *verb* **modernized, modernizing**

modest (mäd′əst) *adjective* **1** not bragging or valuing too much one's own ability, talents, or deeds; humble [The scientist was a famous but *modest* person.] **2** within reason; not extreme [a *modest* salary].
mod·est • *adjective*

modify (mäd′i fī′) *verb* **1** to make a small change in [The architect *modified* the plans for the new house.] **2** in grammar, to limit the meaning of; describe or qualify [In the phrase "old man" the adjective "old" *modifies* the noun "man."]
mod·i·fy • *verb* **modified, modifying, modifies**

M

module (mäj′o͞ol) *noun* a section of a machine or device that can be separated and taken off for some special use [the landing *module* of a spacecraft].
mod·ule • *noun, plural* **modules**

Mohammed (mō ham′əd) A.D. 570?-632; Arab prophet. He was the founder of Islam.
Mo·ham·med

Mohawk (mō′hôk *or* mō′häk) *noun* **1** a member of a North American Indian people who lived in New York State and now live in Ontario, Quebec, and New York. **2** the language of this people.
Mo·hawk • *noun, plural for sense 1 only* **Mohawks** or **Mohawk**

Mohican (mō hē′kən) *noun the same as* **Mahican**.
Mo·hi·can • *noun, plural* **Mohicans** or **Mohican**

moist (moist) *adjective* damp or a little wet [a *moist* towel] —Look for the WORD CHOICES box at the entry **wet**.
moist • *adjective* **moister, moistest**

moisten (mois′ən) *verb* to make or become moist [*Moisten* the cloth and wipe the mirror.]
mois·ten • *verb* **moistened, moistening**

moisture (mois′chər) *noun* water or other liquid that is in the air or in the ground or that forms tiny drops on a surface.
mois·ture • *noun*

molar (mō′lər) *noun* one of the large back teeth, used for grinding food. An adult usually has twelve molars, including the wisdom teeth.
mo·lar • *noun, plural* **molars**

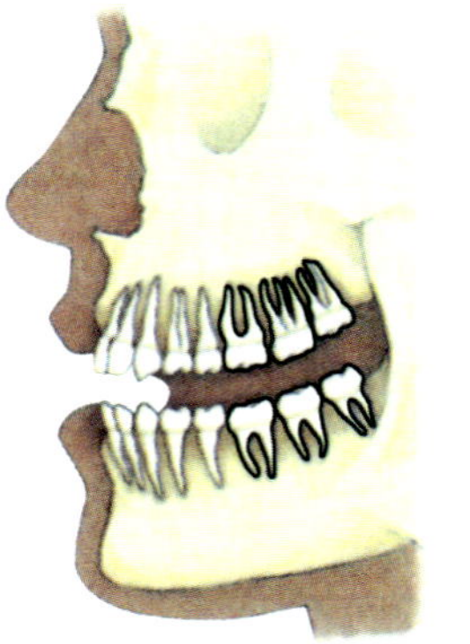
molar

molasses (mə las′əz *or* mə las′əs) *noun* a sweet, thick, dark-brown syrup that is made from sugar cane.
mo·las·ses • *noun*

mold[1] (mōld) *noun* a hollow container that is made in a particular shape and used to form things. Wax, gelatin, plaster, or other material is put into a mold when it is soft or liquid. The material hardens in the shape of the mold.
verb **1** to give a certain shape or form to, by placing in a mold or by using the hands [She *molded* the clay into a vase.] **2** to have a strong influence on [The newspapers try to *mold* public opinion.]
mold • *noun, plural* **molds** • *verb* **molded, molding**

mold[2] (mōld) *noun* a fuzzy growth that is caused by a fungus. It forms a coating on food and damp surfaces.
mold • *noun, plural* **molds**

molding (mōl′diŋ) *noun* a strip of wood, plastic, or other material that is fastened around or along the edge of a surface such as the frame of a door or window or the upper part of a wall. Moldings are often used for decoration.
mold·ing • *noun, plural* **moldings**

Moldova (môl dō′və) a country in southeastern Europe. It was a part of the Soviet Union.
Mol·do·va

moldy (mōl′dē) *adjective* like or covered with mold [*moldy* bread].
mold·y • *adjective* **moldier, moldiest**

mole[1] (mōl) *noun* a small, dark-colored and slightly raised spot on the skin.
mole • *noun, plural* **moles**

mole

mole[2] (mōl) *noun* a small animal with long claws, small eyes and ears, and soft fur. Moles burrow holes and live mainly underground.
mole • *noun, plural* **moles**

molecule (mäl′ə kyo͞ol) *noun* the smallest unit of a substance that still is that substance. A molecule is made up of one or more atoms. The kinds of atoms that make up a molecule determine what kind of substance it will be.
mol·e·cule • *noun, plural* **molecules**

a	cat	ō	go	ʉ	fur	ə =	a *in* ago
ā	ape	ô	law, for	ch	chin		e *in* agent
ä	cot, car	o͝o	look	sh	she		i *in* pencil
e	ten	o͞o	tool	th	thin		o *in* atom
ē	me	oi	oil	*th*	then		u *in* circus
i	fit	ou	out	zh	measure		
ī	ice	u	up	ŋ	ring		

mollusk (mäl′əsk) ***noun*** one of a large group of animals, such as oysters, clams, and snails, that have a soft body that is usually protected by a hard shell.
mol·lusk • ***noun,*** *plural* **mollusks**

molt (mōlt) ***verb*** to shed skin, feathers, hair, or a shell before getting a new covering. Snakes and birds molt.
molt • ***verb*** **molted, molting**

molten (mōl′tən) ***adjective*** made liquid by heat [He poured *molten* lead into molds to make toy soldiers.]
mol·ten • ***adjective***

mom (mäm) [*an informal word*] ***noun*** mother.
mom • ***noun,*** *plural* **moms**

moment (mō′mənt) ***noun*** **1** a very short period of time; an instant [We stopped working and rested for a *moment*.] **2** a particular time [At that *moment* the bell rang.]
mo·ment • ***noun,*** *plural* **moments**

momentary (mō′mən ter′ē) ***adjective*** lasting for only a moment [a *momentary* pain].
mo·men·tar·y • ***adjective***

momentous (mō men′təs) ***adjective*** very important [a *momentous* occasion].
mo·men·tous • ***adjective***

momentum (mō men′təm) ***noun*** the amount of force a moving body has because of its weight and the speed at which it is moving [His sled gained *momentum* as it coasted downhill.]
mo·men·tum • ***noun***

Mon. *abbreviation for* Monday.

Monaco (män′ə kō) a small country on the Mediterranean, mostly surrounded by France.
Mon·a·co

monarch (män′ərk *or* män′ärk) ***noun*** **1** a king, queen, emperor, or other ruler of a state or country. **2** a large North American butterfly that has reddish-brown wings with black edges.
mon·arch • ***noun,*** *plural* **monarchs**

monarchy (män′ər kē *or* män′är kē) ***noun*** a state or country that is ruled by a monarch.
mon·ar·chy • ***noun,*** *plural* **monarchies**

monastery (män′ə ster′ē) ***noun*** a place where a group of monks live and work together.
mon·as·ter·y • ***noun,*** *plural* **monasteries**

Monday (mun′dā) ***noun*** the second day of the week. Abbreviated **Mon.**
Mon·day • ***noun,*** *plural* **Mondays**

WORD HISTORY

Monday

Monday comes from a thousand-year-old English word that means "the moon's day." The English name was a translation of this day's name in Latin. In many modern languages that are related to English as well as modern languages that developed from Latin, the source of the name for this day of the week is this same idea: "the moon's day."

monetary (män′ə ter′ē) ***adjective*** in, of, or having to do with money [That old car has little *monetary* value.]
mon·e·tar·y • ***adjective***

money (mun′ē) ***noun*** the coins and paper bills printed by the government of a country; currency. Money is used to buy or pay for things and services. Pennies, nickels, dimes, quarters, and dollar bills are U.S. money.
mon·ey • ***noun***

Mongolia (mäŋ gō′lē ə) a country in east central Asia, north of China.
Mon·go·li·a

mongoose

mongoose (mäŋ′gōōs) ***noun*** an animal that has a pointed face, a long, narrow body, and a long tail. Mongooses live in Africa and Asia and are good at killing poisonous snakes. They also kill rats and birds.
mon·goose • ***noun,*** *plural* **mongooses**

mongrel (mäŋ′grəl *or* muŋ′grəl) ***noun*** a dog that is not of any particular breed. This word is also sometimes used for other animals or

M

plants produced by accidental crossing of different kinds.
mon·grel • *noun, plural* **mongrels**

monitor (män′i tər) *noun* **1** a student chosen to take attendance, help keep order, or perform any other special duty. **2** a speaker or a TV screen used in a radio or TV studio for checking on how a program is coming through. **3** a video screen used with computers for showing pictures or information.
verb to listen or watch in order to check on.
mon·i·tor • *noun, plural* **monitors**
• *verb* **monitored, monitoring**

monk (muŋk) *noun* a man who has joined a religious order whose members live and work together in a monastery.
monk • *noun, plural* **monks**

monkey (muŋ′kē) *noun* **1** any of a group of furry animals that usually have a flat, hairless face and a long tail. Monkeys are primates and have hands and feet that can grasp things. **2** any similar animal, such as the chimpanzee. **3** a playful child who is full of mischief.
verb [*an informal use*] to play or fool around in an idle way; meddle [Don't *monkey* around with my model train.]
mon·key • *noun, plural* **monkeys**
• *verb* **monkeyed, monkeying**

monkey wrench *noun* a wrench with one movable jaw that can be adjusted to fit various sizes of nuts and bolts or pipes.
monkey wrench • *noun, plural* **monkey wrenches**

monkey wrench

mono- *a prefix meaning* one, alone, or single [A *monologue* is spoken by one person.]

monogram (män′ə gram) *noun* initials of a person's name put together in a design and used on clothing, stationery, and other articles.
mon·o·gram • *noun, plural* **monograms**

monologue (män′ə lôg) *noun* **1** a long speech made by one person during a conversation. **2** a long dramatic or comic speech made by a performer.
mon·o·logue • *noun, plural* **monologues**

monopolize (mə näp′ə līz) *verb* to get or take up all of; dominate completely [He had the bad habit of *monopolizing* the conversation when they had guests.]
mo·nop·o·lize • *verb* **monopolized, monopolizing**

monopoly (mə näp′ə lē) *noun* **1** complete control of a product or service in some place by a single person or company. A company with a monopoly has no competition. **2** a person or company that has a monopoly.
mo·nop·o·ly • *noun, plural for sense 2 only* **monopolies**

monorail (män′ə rāl) *noun* **1** a single rail that serves as a track for train cars that are suspended from it or balanced on it. **2** a railway that runs on a monorail.
mon·o·rail • *noun, plural* **monorails**

monotone (män′ə tōn) *noun* **1** a series of sounds made with little or no change in pitch or tone of voice. **2** a person who cannot carry a tune.
mon·o·tone • *noun, plural for sense 2 only* **monotones**

monotonous (mə nät′n əs) *adjective* having little or no change; boring or tiresome [a *monotonous* voice; a *monotonous* trip; *monotonous* work].
mo·not·o·nous • *adjective*

Monroe (mən rō′), **James** (jāmz) 1758-1831; the fifth president of the U.S., from 1817 to 1825.
Mon·roe, James

monsieur (mə syʉr′) *noun* a French word used, like "Mr.," as a title for a man.
mon·sieur • *noun, plural* **mes·sieurs** (mes′ərz)

monsoon (män so͞on′) *noun* a strong wind of the Indian Ocean and southern Asia. From April to October, it blows from the ocean toward the land, bringing very heavy rains. It blows from the land toward the ocean the rest of the year.
mon·soon • *noun, plural* **monsoons**

monster (män′stər) *noun* **1** a dragon or other imaginary creature that is huge and frightening. **2** a huge animal, plant, or thing. **3** a very cruel or wicked person. **4** a plant or animal

a	cat	ō	go	ʉ	fur	ə = a *in* ago	
ā	ape	ô	law, for	ch	chin	e *in* agent	
ä	cot, car	oo	look	sh	she	i *in* pencil	
e	ten	o͞o	tool	th	thin	o *in* atom	
ē	me	oi	oil	*th*	then	u *in* circus	
i	fit	ou	out	zh	measure		
ī	ice	u	up	ŋ	ring		

that is not normal in shape or form. A fish with two heads is a monster.
mon·ster • ***noun,*** *plural* **monsters**

monstrous (män′strəs) ***adjective*** **1** very large; huge; enormous [The ship hit a *monstrous* iceberg.] **2** very ugly in shape or form [The accident left him with *monstrous* scars on his face.] **3** very wicked; horrible [a *monstrous* crime].
mon·strous • ***adjective***

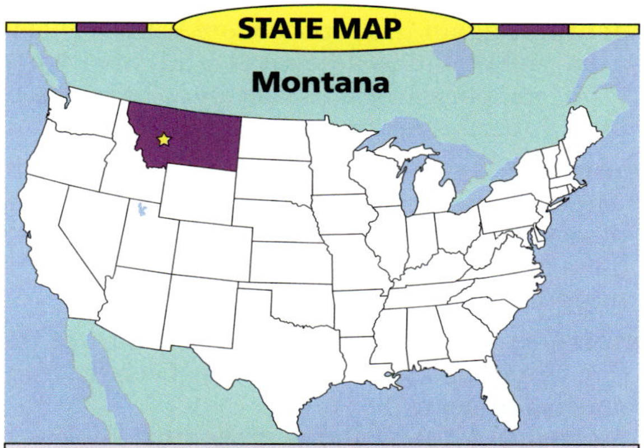

Statehood: 1889, the 41st state • **Capital:** Helena

Montana (män tan′ə) a State in the northwestern part of the U.S. Its capital is Helena. Abbreviated **MT** or **Mont.**
Mon·tan·a

Montenegro (mänt′ə nē′grō) a country in southeastern Europe.
Mon·te·ne·gro

Montessori (mänt′ə sôr′ē), **Maria** (mə rē′ə) 1870-1952; Italian educator.
Mon·tes·so·ri, Ma·ri·a

Montgomery (mänt gum′ər ē) the capital of Alabama.
Mont·gom·er·y

month (munth) ***noun*** one of the twelve parts into which the year is divided.
month • ***noun,*** *plural* **months**

monthly (munth′lē) ***adjective*** **1** happening, done, or being due once a month [*monthly* meetings; a *monthly* magazine; *monthly* payments]. **2** for a period of one month [the *monthly* sales figures for the company].
adverb once a month; every month [The rent for the apartment must be paid *monthly*.]
noun a magazine that comes out once a month.
month·ly • ***adjective*** • ***adverb*** • ***noun,*** *plural* **monthlies**

Montpelier (mänt pēl′yər) the capital of Vermont.
Mont·pel·ier

Montreal (män′trē ôl′) a city in Quebec, Canada, on an island in the St. Lawrence River.
Mon·tre·al

monument (män′yo͞o mənt) ***noun*** **1** a statue, building, or other structure that is put up in memory of a person or happening. **2** something kept or admired for its beauty or importance.
mon·u·ment • ***noun,*** *plural* **monuments**

moo (mo͞o) ***noun*** the sound that a cow makes.
verb to make this sound.
moo • ***noun,*** *plural* **moos** • ***verb*** **mooed, mooing**

mood (mo͞od) ***noun*** the way that a person feels [I'm in no *mood* for joking.]
mood • ***noun,*** *plural* **moods**

moody (mo͞o′dē) ***adjective*** **1** having changes of mood often [a *moody* person]. **2** having or showing sad, gloomy moods [He's *moody* today because he's sick.]
mood·y • ***adjective*** **moodier, moodiest**

moon (mo͞on) ***noun*** **1** the heavenly body that revolves around the earth from west to east once in about every 29½ days. The moon shines at night by reflecting sunlight. **2** any natural, small body that revolves around a planet.
moon • ***noun,*** *plural for sense 2 only* **moons**

moonbeam (mo͞on′bēm) ***noun*** a ray of moonlight.
moon·beam • ***noun,*** *plural* **moonbeams**

moonlight (mo͞on′līt) ***noun*** the light of the moon.
moon·light • ***noun***

moor[1] (mo͝or) ***noun*** a broad stretch of land with few trees in England and Scotland. Moors are often swampy and covered with heather.
moor • ***noun,*** *plural* **moors**

moor[2] (mo͝or) ***verb*** to hold a boat or ship in place by means of cables to the shore or by anchors.
moor • ***verb*** **moored, mooring**

moose

moose (mo͞os) ***noun*** a large animal that is related to the deer. The male has broad

antlers with many points. Moose live in northern forests.
moose • ***noun,*** *plural* **moose**

mop (mäp) ***noun*** **1** a bundle of rags or yarn, or a sponge, attached to the end of a stick for dusting or washing floors. **2** a thick head of hair or anything else that looks like a mop.
verb to wipe, wash, or dry with a mop [*Mop* the bathroom floor.]
mop • ***noun,*** *plural* **mops** • ***verb*** **mopped, mopping**

mope (mōp) ***verb*** to be gloomy and depressed [She *moped* about the house all day.]
mope • ***verb*** **moped, moping**

moped (mō′ped) ***noun*** a bicycle with a small motor to make it go.
mo·ped • ***noun,*** *plural* **mopeds**

moral (môr′əl) ***adjective*** **1** having to do with right and wrong in conduct [Cheating is a *moral* issue.] **2** good and honest; just, decent, or virtuous [A *moral* person does not lie or steal.]
noun **1** a lesson about what is right and wrong, taught by a story or event. **2 morals** standards of behavior that have to do with right and wrong.
mor·al • ***adjective*** • ***noun,*** *plural* **morals**

WORD CHOICES

Synonyms of **moral**

The words **moral, ethical,** and **virtuous** share the meaning "having to do with what is right or good in the way people live."

our *moral* duty to care for the aged

ethical standards which most doctors accept

a *virtuous* wish to help the poor

morale (môr al′) ***noun*** the spirit, enthusiasm, or other state of mind of a person or group working toward some goal.
mo·rale • ***noun***

morality (môr al′i tē) ***noun*** **1** the quality of being right or wrong [We discussed the *morality* of getting help on our homework.] **2** good or proper conduct; virtue.
mo·ral·i·ty • ***noun***

more (môr) ***adjective*** **1** *comparative of* **much** or **many**. **2** greater in amount or degree or in number [He has *more* free time than I do. We need *more* helpers.] **3** further; added [We'll have *more* news later.]
noun **1** a greater amount or degree [She spends *more* of her time playing than studying.] **2** [*used with a plural verb*] a greater number [*More* of us are going this time. *More* are going this time.] **3** something extra or further [I'll have *more* to say later.]
adverb **1** in or to a greater degree or extent [Judy laughs *more* than she used to.] **2** in addition; again [Do it once *more*.] *More* is also used before many adjectives and adverbs to form comparatives, just as *most* is used to form superlatives [*more* quickly].

moreover (môr ō′vər) ***adverb*** in addition to what has been said; besides; also [I don't want to go because it's raining, and *moreover* I don't have an umbrella.]
more·o·ver • ***adverb***

morning (môrn′iŋ) ***noun*** the early part of the day, from midnight to noon or, especially, from sunrise to noon.
morn·ing • ***noun,*** *plural* **mornings**

- The words **morning** and **mourning** sound alike.

  It rained this *morning*.
  They were in *mourning* for their aunt.

morning glory ***noun*** a climbing plant with white, pink, lavender, or blue flowers that are shaped like trumpets.
morning glory • ***noun,*** *plural* **morning glories**

Morocco (mə rä′kō) a country in northwestern Africa.
Mo·roc·co

Morse (môrs), **Samuel F. B.** (sam′yo͞o əl) 1791-1872; U.S. inventor of the telegraph.
Morse, Sam·u·el F. B.

morsel (môr′səl) ***noun*** a small bite or bit of food [I cannot eat another *morsel*.]
mor·sel • ***noun,*** *plural* **morsels**

mortal (môrt′l) ***adjective*** **1** certain to die at some time [All human beings are *mortal*.] **2** causing death of the body or soul [a *mortal* wound; *mortal* sin]. **3** lasting until death

a	cat	ō	go	ʉ	fur	ə = a *in* ago
ā	ape	ô	law, for	ch	chin	e *in* agent
ä	cot, car	o͝o	look	sh	she	i *in* pencil
e	ten	o͞o	tool	th	thin	o *in* atom
ē	me	oi	oil	*th*	then	u *in* circus
i	fit	ou	out	zh	measure	
ī	ice	u	up	ŋ	ring	

[*mortal* combat; *mortal* enemies]. **4** very great; extreme [She has a *mortal* fear of snakes.]
noun a human being.
mor·tal • ***adjective*** • ***noun,*** *plural* **mortals**

mortar (mort′ər) ***noun*** **1** a building material that is a mixture of cement or lime with sand and water. Mortar is used to hold bricks or stones together. **2** a hard bowl in which things are crushed or ground to a powder with a pestle.
mor·tar • ***noun,*** *plural for sense 2 only* **mortars**

mosaic (mō zā′ik) ***noun*** a picture or design made by putting together small bits of colored stone, glass, or tile. The pieces are held in place by mortar.
mo·sa·ic • ***noun,*** *plural* **mosaics**

Moscow (mäs′kō *or* mäs′kou) the capital of Russia, located in the western part.
Mos·cow

Moses (mō′zəz) in the Bible, the man who led the people of ancient Israel out of slavery in Egypt and passed on to them laws from God.
Mo·ses

Moslem (mäz′ləm) ***noun, adjective*** *another spelling of* **Muslim**.
Mos·lem • ***noun,*** *plural* **Moslems** • ***adjective***

mosque (mäsk) ***noun*** a Muslim place of worship.
mosque • ***noun,*** *plural* **mosques**

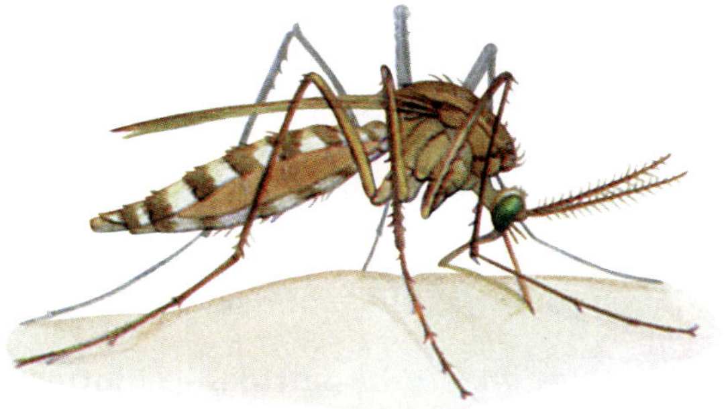

mosquito

mosquito (mə skēt′ō) ***noun*** a small insect with two wings. The female bites animals to suck their blood. Some mosquitoes spread diseases.
mos·qui·to • ***noun,*** *plural* **mosquitoes** or **mosquitos**

moss (môs) ***noun*** tiny green plants growing in clumps like velvet, on rocks, trees, or on moist ground. Mosses grow in damp, shady places.
moss • ***noun,*** *plural* **mosses**

most (mōst) ***adjective*** **1** *superlative of* **much** or **many**. **2** greatest in amount or degree or in number [Who won the *most* money? *Most* people like summer.]
noun **1** the greatest amount or degree [We spent *most* of our money.] **2** [*used with a plural verb*] the greatest number [*Most* of us are going this time. *Most* are going this time.]
adverb **1** in or to the greatest degree or extent [The music pleased me *most*.] **2** very [a *most* beautiful dress]. *Most* is also used before many adjectives and adverbs to form superlatives, just as *more* is used to form comparatives [*most* horrible; *most* quickly].

mostly (mōst′lē) ***adverb*** for the most part; mainly; chiefly [The dog is *mostly* brown with black and white spots.]
most·ly • ***adverb***

motel (mō tel′) ***noun*** a hotel for people traveling by car. It is usually built near a main road and has a parking area that is easy to reach from each room.
mo·tel • ***noun,*** *plural* **motels**

WORD HISTORY

motel

An architect invented the word **motel** around 1925 to describe a new hotel of this kind in California. He combined parts of the words *motor* and *hotel*.

moth

moth (môth) ***noun*** an insect that is like a butterfly, but usually smaller and less brightly

M

colored. Moths fly mostly at night. One kind of moth has larvae that eat holes in fur and wool.
moth • ***noun,*** *plural* **moths** (môt*h*z *or* môths)

mother (mu*th*′ər) ***noun*** **1** a woman as she is related to her child or children; a female parent. **2** the origin, source, or cause of something [Virginia is the State known as the *mother* of Presidents.]
adjective **1** of, like, or being a mother [*mother* love; a *mother* hen]. **2** having a relationship like that of a mother [All the branches report to the *mother* company in Detroit.]
verb to care for as a mother does [We *mothered* the abandoned kittens.]
moth·er • ***noun,*** *plural* **mothers** • ***adjective*** • ***verb*** **mothered, mothering**

mother-in-law (mu*th*′ər in lô *or* mu*th*′ər in lä) ***noun*** the mother of one's wife or husband.
moth·er-in-law • ***noun,*** *plural* **mothers-in-law**

motherly (mu*th*′ər lē) ***adjective*** of or like a mother [a *motherly* hug; *motherly* concern for the orphan].
moth·er·ly • ***adjective***

mother-of-pearl (mu*th*′ər əv pʉrl′) ***noun*** the hard, shiny layer on the inside of some seashells. Mother-of-pearl shines with different soft colors and is used in making buttons and in jewelry.
moth·er-of-pearl • ***noun***

motion (mō′shən) ***noun*** **1** the act or process of moving from one place to another; movement [The sea is always in *motion*.] **2** a movement of the head, arm, or other part of the body in a way that has meaning; gesture [The waiter made a beckoning *motion* to tell us that our table was ready.] **3** a formal suggestion or request made during a meeting or trial [He made a *motion* to end the meeting at 5 p.m.]
verb to move the head, hand, or other part of the body so as to show what one means or wants [The police officer *motioned* us to stop.]
mo·tion • ***noun,*** *plural for senses 2 and 3 only* **motions** • ***verb*** **motioned, motioning**

motionless (mō′shən ləs) ***adjective*** not moving [He stood *motionless* at the top of the stairs.]
mo·tion·less • ***adjective***

motion picture ***noun*** *the same as* **movie**.
motion picture • ***noun,*** *plural* **motion pictures**

motive (mōt′iv) ***noun*** a reason that makes a person do something [What was their *motive* for inviting us to their house?]
mo·tive • ***noun,*** *plural* **motives**

motor (mōt′ər) ***noun*** a device or machine that provides the power to make something move or work [The fan has an electric *motor*.]
adjective **1** driven by a motor or engine [a *motor* bicycle]. **2** having to do with or for motors [*motor* oil; *motor* parts]. **3** of or having to do with nerves or muscles that control movement [The long illness left her with poor *motor* control.]
verb to travel by car [We *motored* through Mississippi.]
mo·tor • ***noun,*** *plural* **motors** • ***adjective*** • ***verb*** **motored, motoring**

motorboat (mōt′ər bōt) ***noun*** a boat that is run by a motor.
mo·tor·boat • ***noun,*** *plural* **motorboats**

motorcycle (mōt′ər sī kəl) ***noun*** a kind of very heavy bicycle that is run by a gasoline engine.
mo·tor·cy·cle • ***noun,*** *plural* **motorcycles**

motor vehicle ***noun*** a vehicle on wheels, having its own motor, and not running on rails or tracks. Cars, trucks, buses, and motorcycles are motor vehicles.
motor vehicle • ***noun,*** *plural* **motor vehicles**

Mott (mät), **Lucretia** (lo͞o krē′shə) 1793-1880; U.S. abolitionist and leader in the women's rights movement.
Mott, Lu·cre·ti·a

motto (mät′ō) ***noun*** **1** a brief saying that is used as a rule to live by ["Honesty is the best policy" was his *motto*.] **2** a word or phrase chosen to show the goals or ideals of a nation, club, or other organization. A motto is usually inscribed on a coin, seal, or flag ["Don't tread on me!" was the *motto* on an early U.S. flag.]
mot·to • ***noun,*** *plural* **mottoes** or **mottos**

mound (mound) ***noun*** **1** a heap or hill of earth, sand, or other material [There are *mounds* of stones all over the fields.] **2** the slightly raised place from which a baseball

a cat	ō go	ʉ fur	ə = a *in* ago
ā ape	ô law, for	ch chin	e *in* agent
ä cot, car	o͝o look	sh she	i *in* pencil
e ten	o͞o tool	th thin	o *in* atom
ē me	oi oil	*th* then	u *in* circus
i fit	ou out	zh measure	
ī ice	u up	ŋ ring	

pitcher throws. The mound is more or less in the center of a baseball diamond.
mound • *noun, plural* **mounds**

mount[1] (mount) ***noun*** a mountain or hill. This word is now used mainly as part of a name [*Mount* Everest].

mount[2] (mount) ***verb*** **1** to climb or go up [He *mounted* the stairs in a big hurry.] **2** to get up on [The knights *mounted* their horses and rode off to battle.] **3** to rise or increase [The flood waters are *mounting*. Profits *mounted* slowly this year.] **4** to attach to or fix on something that supports or strengthens [He *mounted* the new photographs of the family in his album.]
noun **1** a horse for riding. **2** a support, frame, or stand that is used to hold or display something [a gold *mount* for a gem].
mount • *verb* **mounted, mounting** • *noun, plural* **mounts**

mountain (mount′'n) ***noun*** **1** a part of the earth's surface that rises high above the surrounding area. A mountain is higher than a hill. **2** a large heap or amount of something [a *mountain* of trash].
moun·tain • *noun, plural* **mountains**

mountaineer (mount'n ir′) ***noun*** **1** a person who lives in a region of mountains. **2** a person who climbs mountains as a sport.
moun·tain·eer • *noun, plural* **mountaineers**

mountain lion ***noun*** *another name for* **cougar.**
mountain lion • *noun, plural* **mountain lions**

mountainous (mount′'n əs) ***adjective*** full of mountains [Vermont is a *mountainous* State.]
moun·tain·ous • *adjective*

mourn (môrn) ***verb*** to be sad or show sorrow or grief [They *mourned* for their son, who was killed in a car accident.]
mourn • *verb* **mourned, mourning**

mourning (môrn′iŋ) ***noun*** **1** the act of showing sorrow or grief [She was in *mourning* for her husband, who died in an accident.] **2** black clothes or some other symbol to show sorrow at someone's death.
mourn·ing • *noun*

- The words **mourning** and **morning** sound alike.

  They were in *mourning* for their aunt.
  There was dew on the grass this *morning*.

mouse

mouse (mous) ***noun*** **1** a small, furry animal that has small ears, a long, thin, almost hairless tail, and a pointed nose. Mice are rodents. Some kinds of mice live in or near people's houses. **2** a small device attached to a computer terminal. It is moved by the hand across a flat surface in order to make the cursor move on a computer screen.
mouse • *noun, plural* **mice**

mousetrap (mous′trap) ***noun*** a trap for catching mice.
mouse·trap • *noun, plural* **mousetraps**

mouth (mouth) ***noun*** **1** the opening in an animal's head through which food is taken in and sounds are made. The human mouth contains the tongue, teeth, and lips. **2** any opening that is like a mouth [the *mouth* of a river; the *mouth* of a cave].
mouth • *noun, plural* **mouths** (mou*th*z)

mouthful (mouth′fool) ***noun*** the amount of food or drink that is put into the mouth at one time.
mouth·ful • *noun, plural* **mouthfuls**

mouth organ ***noun*** *another name for* **harmonica.**
mouth organ • *noun, plural* **mouth organs**

mouthpiece (mouth′pēs) ***noun*** the part of a telephone, musical instrument, or other object that is held in or near the mouth.
mouth·piece • *noun, plural* **mouthpieces**

mouthwash (mouth′wôsh) ***noun*** a liquid that is used for rinsing the mouth or for gargling.
mouth·wash • *noun*

movable (mo͞ov′ə bəl) ***adjective*** capable of being moved; not fixed or fastened [*movable* shelves].
mov·a·ble • *adjective*

M

move (mo͞ov) ***verb*** **1** to change or cause to change place or position [*Move* the lamp closer. Can you *move* your legs? Please *move* to the left.] **2** to put or keep in motion [The steering wheel *moves* the front wheels of the car.] **3** to change the place where one lives [We *moved* to New York.] **4** to cause; give a reason for [What *moved* you to get a cat?] **5** to cause to have strong feelings [Your song *moved* me deeply.] **6** to suggest or propose in a meeting [I *move* that we accept their offer.]
noun **1** the act of moving; movement [Don't make a *move!*] **2** the act of moving a piece in chess or another game. **3** a player's turn to move a piece.
move • ***verb*** **moved, moving** • ***noun,*** *plural* **moves**

movement (mo͞ov′mənt) ***noun*** **1** the act of moving [the graceful *movements* of the dancer's hands]. **2** the actions of a group of people who are working together to bring about a certain result [the *movement* for world peace]. **3** the moving parts of a watch or clock. **4** a section of a long musical piece such as a symphony.
move·ment • ***noun,*** *plural* **movements**

mover (mo͞ov′ər) ***noun*** a person or company whose work is moving people's belongings from one home or office to another.
mov·er • ***noun,*** *plural* **movers**

movie (mo͞ov′ē) ***noun*** *the same as* **film** (see sense 2 of the noun).
—the movies a performance of a movie at a theater [We went to *the movies* last night.]
mov·ie • ***noun,*** *plural* **movies**

moving (mo͞ov′iŋ) ***adjective*** **1** being in motion or causing movement [a *moving* car; the *moving* force that changed history]. **2** capable of making a person feel sad or full of pity [It was a *moving* story, that made me cry.]
mov·ing • ***adjective***

WORD CHOICES

Synonyms of **moving**

The words **moving, pathetic,** and **touching** share the meaning "causing feelings of pity or sympathy."

a *moving* story about the flood victims

the lost child's *pathetic* plea for help

a *touching* gift of food to a poor family

mow (mō) ***verb*** to cut grass or grain with a lawn mower, sickle, or other device [It's your turn to *mow* the grass.]
mow • ***verb*** **mowed, mowed** or **mown, mowing**

mower (mō′ər) ***noun*** a person or machine that mows [a lawn *mower*].
mow·er • ***noun,*** *plural* **mowers**

mown (mōn) ***verb*** *a past participle of* **mow.**
● The words **mown** and **moan** sound alike.
I had *mown* the lawn before it rained.
A *moan* came from the hospital room.

Mozambique (mō zam bēk′) a country in southeastern Africa.
Mo·zam·bique

Mozart (mō′tsärt), **Wolfgang Amadeus** (wôlf gäŋ ä mə dā′əs) 1756-1791; composer of classical music. He was born in Austria.
Mo·zart, Wolf·gang A·ma·de·us

mph or **m.p.h.** *abbreviation for* miles per hour.

Mr. (mis′tər) Mister. Used before the name of a man or his title [*Mr.* Shapiro; *Mr.* President].

Mrs. (mis′əz) Mistress. Used before the name of a woman who is or has been married [*Mrs.* Rodriguez. *Mrs.* Jones is a widow.]

MS *abbreviation for* Mississippi.

Ms. (miz) a title used before the name of a woman instead of either *Miss* or *Mrs.* [*Ms.* Bell].

MT *abbreviation for* Montana.

Mt. *abbreviation for* mount [*Mt.* Rushmore].

much (much) ***adjective*** great in amount or degree [*much* applause; *much* joy].
adverb **1** to a great degree or extent [I feel *much* happier.] **2** just about; almost [The patient is *much* the same.] **3** often [Do you go out *much* in the evenings?]
noun **1** a great amount [We learned *much* from the teacher.] **2** something great or important [Our car is not *much* to look at.]
—not much of a not so good as a [I'm *not much of a* pitcher.]
much • ***adjective*** & • ***adverb*** **more, most** • ***noun***

mucilage (myo͞o′si lij) ***noun*** a kind of thick glue for holding paper and other materials.
mu·ci·lage • ***noun***

a	cat	ō	go	ʉ	fur	ə =	a *in* ago
ā	ape	ô	law, for	ch	chin		e *in* agent
ä	cot, car	o͝o	look	sh	she		i *in* pencil
e	ten	o͞o	tool	th	thin		o *in* atom
ē	me	oi	oil	*th*	then		u *in* circus
i	fit	ou	out	zh	measure		
ī	ice	u	up	ŋ	ring		

muck (muk) ***noun*** mud, manure, or any other dirty, moist substance.

mucus (myo͞o′kəs) ***noun*** the thick, slimy substance that coats and protects the inside of the mouth, nose, throat, and other parts of the body.
mu·cus • ***noun***

mud (mud) ***noun*** wet earth that is soft and sticky.

muddle (mud′əl) ***verb*** **1** to mix up; confuse [They *muddled* the discussion of the new rules.] **2** to act or think in a confused way [I *muddled* through another long, hard day at work.]
noun a confused or mixed-up condition; a mess.
mud·dle • ***verb*** **muddled, muddling**
• ***noun,*** *plural* **muddles**

muddy (mud′ē) ***adjective*** full of mud or smeared with mud [a *muddy* yard; *muddy* boots].
verb to make or become muddy.
mud·dy • ***adjective*** **muddier, muddiest**
• ***verb*** **muddied, muddying, muddies**

muff (muf) ***noun*** a thick, tube-shaped covering for the hands that is used to keep them warm. It is usually made of fur or other soft material. A person puts one hand into each end.
muff • ***noun,*** *plural* **muffs**

muffin (muf′in) ***noun*** a kind of bread that is baked in a small, cup-shaped mold.
muf·fin • ***noun,*** *plural* **muffins**

muffle (muf′əl) ***verb*** **1** to wrap up or cover in order to keep warm or protect, or to deaden sound [I *muffled* myself in a scarf against the cold.] **2** to make less loud or less clear [Heavy curtains *muffled* the traffic noise.]
muf·fle • ***verb*** **muffled, muffling**

muffler (muf′lər) ***noun*** **1** a scarf that a person wears around the throat for warmth. **2** a part that is attached to the exhaust pipe of a car to lessen the noise from the engine.
muf·fler • ***noun,*** *plural* **mufflers**

mug (mug) ***noun*** **1** a heavy drinking cup with a handle. **2** the amount that a mug will hold.
verb to attack and rob someone.
mug • ***noun,*** *plural* **mugs** • ***verb*** **mugged, mugging**

muggy (mug′ē) ***adjective*** hot and damp, with little movement of the air [*muggy* weather].
mug·gy • ***adjective*** **muggier, muggiest**

Muhammad (mo͝o ham′əd) *the same as* **Mohammed.**
Mu·ham·mad

mulberry (mul′ber′ē) ***noun*** a tree that bears fruit that looks like a raspberry. The fruit can be eaten.
mul·ber·ry • ***noun,*** *plural* **mulberries**

mulch (mulch) ***noun*** straw, leaves, or other material that is spread on the ground around plants. It helps to keep moisture in the soil and prevent weeds from growing.

mule (myo͞ol) ***noun*** the offspring of a male donkey and a female horse.
mule • ***noun,*** *plural* **mules**

multi- *a prefix meaning:* **1** having many [A *multicolored* scarf has many colors in it.] **2** many times more than [A *multimillionaire* has many times more than one million dollars.]

multicultural (mul′tē kul′chər əl) ***adjective*** made up of or including many different cultures [a *multicultural* school].
mul·ti·cul·tur·al • ***adjective***

multiple (mul′ti pəl) ***adjective*** having to do with or made up of many parts or elements [a person of *multiple* interests] —Look for the WORD CHOICES box at the entry **many.**
noun a number that contains another number an exact number of times, with no remainder. For example, 18 is a multiple of 9 and 2 ($2 \times 9 = 18$; $18 \div 9 = 2$).
mul·ti·ple • ***adjective*** • ***noun,*** *plural* **multiples**

multiple sclerosis (sklə rō′sis) ***noun*** a disease which can cause speech problems or loss of control of the muscles.
multiple scle·ro·sis • ***noun***

multiplicand (mul′ti pli kand′) ***noun*** a number that is multiplied by another. In the equation $2 \times 3 = 6$, 2 is the multiplicand.
mul·ti·pli·cand • ***noun,*** *plural* **multiplicands**

multiplication (mul′ti pli kā′shən) ***noun*** the act or process of multiplying or being multiplied; the adding of a certain figure to itself a certain number of times and finding the result.
mul·ti·pli·ca·tion • ***noun***

multiplier (mul′ti plī′ər) ***noun*** the number by which a number is multiplied. In the equation $2 \times 3 = 6$, 3 is the multiplier.
mul·ti·pli·er • ***noun,*** *plural* **multipliers**

M

multiply (mul′ti plī′) ***verb*** **1** to become greater or cause to become greater; to increase [Our wealth was *multiplying* month by month.] **2** to repeat a certain figure a certain number of times. If 10 is multiplied by 4, this means 10 is repeated 4 times to get a product of 40 (10 x 4 = 40).
mul·ti·ply • ***verb*** **multiplied, multiplying, multiplies**

multitude (mul′ti to͞od *or* mul′ti tyo͞od) ***noun*** a large number of persons or things; a crowd.
mul·ti·tude • ***noun, plural*** **multitudes**

mum (mum) ***noun*** *a short form of* **chrysanthemum**.
mum • ***noun, plural*** **mums**

mumble (mum′bəl) ***verb*** to speak or say with the mouth partly closed or in any other way that makes it hard to hear —Look for the WORD CHOICES box at the entry **murmur**.
noun talk or sound that is produced in this way.
mum·ble • ***verb*** **mumbled, mumbling** • ***noun***

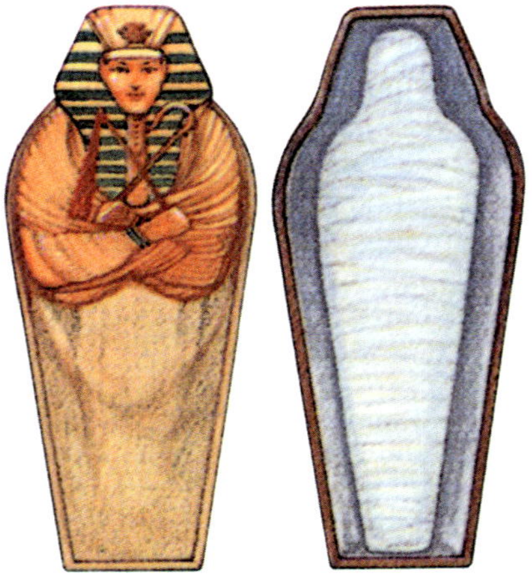

mummy

mummy (mum′ē) ***noun*** a dead body that is kept from rotting in various ways. The ancient Egyptians made mummies by treating dead bodies with chemicals.
mum·my • ***noun, plural*** **mummies**

mumps (mumps) ***plural noun*** [*used with a singular verb*] a disease that causes the swelling of certain glands, usually the ones in the jaw below each ear.

munch (munch) ***verb*** to chew in a noisy, steady way [Rabbits *munch* carrots.]
munch • ***verb*** **munched, munching**

municipal (myo͞o nis′i pəl) ***adjective*** having to do with a city or town, or with its government [a *municipal* election].
mu·nic·i·pal • ***adjective***

mural (myoor′əl) ***noun*** a large picture or photograph that is painted or put on a wall.
mu·ral • ***noun, plural*** **murals**

murder (mʉr′dər) ***noun*** the unlawful killing of one person by another.
verb to kill a person in an unlawful way.
mur·der • ***noun, plural*** **murders** • ***verb*** **murdered, murdering**

murderer (mʉr′dər ər) ***noun*** a person who is guilty of murder.
mur·der·er • ***noun, plural*** **murderers**

murderous (mʉr′dər əs) ***adjective*** **1** like or having to do with murder; brutal [a *murderous* act; *murderous* rage]. **2** guilty of murder or ready to murder [a *murderous* beast].
mur·der·ous • ***adjective***

murky (mʉrk′ē) ***adjective*** dark or full of gloom [a *murky* cave] —Look for the WORD CHOICES box at the entry **dark**.
murk·y • ***adjective*** **murkier, murkiest**

murmur (mʉr′mər) ***noun*** a low, steady sound [the *murmur* of voices in the distance].
verb to make a low, steady sound [The wind *murmured* through the trees.]
mur·mur • ***noun, plural*** **murmurs** • ***verb*** **murmured, murmuring**

WORD CHOICES

Synonyms of **murmur**

The words **murmur, mumble,** and **mutter** share the meaning "to say something in a way that is hard to hear or understand."

The dying man *murmured* a prayer.

She *mumbled* a farewell and fell asleep.

The hungry beggar *muttered* a curse.

muscle (mus′əl) ***noun*** **1** the tissue in an animal's body that is made up of bundles of long

a cat	ō go	ʉ fur	ə = a *in* ago
ā ape	ô law, for	ch chin	e *in* agent
ä cot, car	oo look	sh she	i *in* pencil
e ten	o͞o tool	th thin	o *in* atom
ē me	oi oil	*th* then	u *in* circus
i fit	ou out	zh measure	
ī ice	u up	ŋ ring	

cells or fibers that can be stretched or squeezed together to move parts of the body. **2** a mass of this tissue that moves a particular part of the body [He has strong arm *muscles*.]
mus·cle • ***noun,*** *plural for sense 2 only* **muscles**

- The words **muscle** and **mussel** sound alike.
  It takes a lot of *muscle* to be a mover.
  The *mussel* is related to the clam.

SPELLING TIP

Use this memory aid to spell **muscle**. When you spell ***muscle***, think of the ***c*** in mus**c**ular.

muscular (mus′kyoo lər) ***adjective*** **1** made up of or having to do with muscles [*muscular* tissue]. **2** with muscles that are well developed; strong [*muscular* legs].
mus·cu·lar • ***adjective***

muscular dystrophy (dis′trə fē) ***noun*** a disease in which the muscles waste away little by little.
muscular dys·tro·phy • ***noun***

muse (myooz) ***verb*** to think about various things in a quiet, careful way.
muse • ***verb*** **mused, musing**

museum (myoo zē′əm) ***noun*** a building for keeping and showing objects that are important in history, art, or science.
mu·se·um • ***noun,*** *plural* **museums**

mush (mush) ***noun*** **1** a food that is made by boiling cornmeal in water or milk. **2** a thick, soft mass of something.

mushroom

mushroom (mush′room) ***noun*** a small, firm fungus that grows very fast. It has a stalk that is topped with a cap that may be flat, knob-shaped, or umbrella-shaped. Some kinds of mushrooms can be eaten, but others are poisonous.
verb to grow and spread out fast like a mushroom [The city *mushroomed* quickly when the freeway was finished.]
mush·room • ***noun,*** *plural* **mushrooms** • ***verb*** **mushroomed, mushrooming**

mushy (mush′ē) ***adjective*** thick and soft like mush —Look for the WORD CHOICES box at the entry **soft**.
mush·y • ***adjective*** **mushier, mushiest**

music (myoo′zik) ***noun*** **1** the art of putting tones together in various melodies, rhythms, and harmonies in a pleasing or meaningful way. **2** a musical composition [Do you know the *music* to this song?] **3** the written or printed form of a musical composition [Can you read *music*?]
mu·sic • ***noun***

musical (myoo′zi kəl) ***adjective*** **1** of music or for making music [a *musical* instrument; a *musical* career]. **2** like music; full of melody or pleasing sounds [Wind can have a *musical* sound.] **3** fond of or skilled in music [She comes from a *musical* family.]
noun a play or movie in which singing and dancing are used to help tell the story.
mu·si·cal • ***adjective*** • ***noun,*** *plural* **musicals**

music box ***noun*** a box or case that contains a mechanism that plays a song.
music box • ***noun,*** *plural* **music boxes**

musician (myoo zish′ən) ***noun*** a person who is skilled in music, especially a professional composer or performer.
mu·si·cian • ***noun,*** *plural* **musicians**

musk (musk) ***noun*** a substance with a strong smell that is gotten from a gland in certain animals. It is used in making perfume.

musket (mus′kət) ***noun*** a gun with a long barrel that was used before the rifle was invented.
mus·ket • ***noun,*** *plural* **muskets**

musketeer (mus kə tir′) ***noun*** in earlier times, a soldier who was armed with a musket.
mus·ket·eer • ***noun,*** *plural* **musketeers**

musk ox ***noun*** a sturdy animal that is related to cattle and buffaloes and lives in arctic regions. It has long hair and long, curved horns.
musk ox • ***noun,*** *plural* **musk oxen**

M

muskrat (musk′rat) ***noun*** a North American animal that is like a large rat. It lives in water and has glossy brown fur.
musk·rat • ***noun,*** *plural* **muskrats**

Muslim (muz′lim *or* mo͝os′lim) ***noun*** a person who believes in the religion of Islam.
adjective of or having to do with Islam or the Muslims [*Muslim* traditions].
Mus·lim • ***noun,*** *plural* **Muslims** • ***adjective***

muss (mus) ***verb*** to make untidy or messy [The wind *mussed* her hair.]
muss • ***verb*** **mussed, mussing**

mussel (mus′əl) ***noun*** a shellfish with a soft body enclosed in two shells that are hinged together. Some kinds of saltwater mussels are used as food, and the shells of freshwater mussels are used to make buttons.
mus·sel • ***noun,*** *plural* **mussels**
● The words **mussel** and **muscle** sound alike.
Mussel is served at the restaurant.
She pulled a *muscle* while running.

must (must) ***verb*** (*helping verb*) **1** to be required or obliged to; to have to [I *must* pay the bill. They told him that he *must* do the job.] **2** to be likely or certain to [It *must* be five o'clock. I thought it *must* be midnight.] The word "to" is not used between *must* and the verb that follows.
must • ***verb*** *past tense* **must**; *he / she / it* **must**

mustache (mus′tash *or* məs tash′) ***noun*** the hair that a man has let grow out on his upper lip.
mus·tache • ***noun,*** *plural* **mustaches**

mustache

mustang (mus′taŋ) ***noun*** a small wild horse living on the plains of the southwestern U.S.
mus·tang • ***noun,*** *plural* **mustangs**

mustard (mus′tərd) ***noun*** a dark yellow powder or paste that is made from the hot-tasting seeds of a plant. It is used as a seasoning.
mus·tard • ***noun***

mustn't (mus′ənt) must not.
must·n't

musty (mus′tē) ***adjective*** having a stale smell or taste like that of mold [a *musty* attic; *musty* bread].
mus·ty • ***adjective*** **mustier, mustiest**

mutant (myo͞ot′nt) ***noun*** an animal or plant that has a characteristic that neither of its parents has, and that can pass on this characteristic to the next generation.
mu·tant • ***noun,*** *plural* **mutants**

mutation (myo͞o tā′shən) ***noun*** the appearance in some plant or animal of a characteristic that its parents do not have and that can be inherited.
mu·ta·tion • ***noun,*** *plural* **mutations**

mute
Of trombone

mute (myo͞ot) ***adjective*** **1** not able to speak. **2** not speaking or making any sounds; silent [He sat there *mute* and still.] —Look for the WORD CHOICES box at the entry **still**.
noun **1** a person who cannot speak. **2** a device that is used to soften or muffle the sound of a musical instrument.
verb to soften or muffle the sound of.
mute • ***adjective*** • ***noun,*** *plural* **mutes** • ***verb*** **muted, muting**

mutilate (myo͞ot′l āt) ***verb*** to hurt or damage badly by cutting or breaking off a needed part or an important part [He *mutilated* the book by tearing out the pictures.] —Look for the WORD CHOICES box at the entry **maim**.
mu·ti·late • ***verb*** **mutilated, mutilating**

mutiny (myo͞ot′n ē) ***noun*** the act of rebelling or fighting against the leaders of a group. A mutiny is usually a rebellion by sailors or soldiers against their officers.
verb to rebel or fight in this way [The sailors *mutinied* and took over the ship.]

a cat	ō go	ʉ fur	ə = a *in* ago
ā ape	ô law, for	ch chin	e *in* agent
ä cot, car	o͝o look	sh she	i *in* pencil
e ten	o͞o tool	th thin	o *in* atom
ē me	oi oil	*th* then	u *in* circus
i fit	ou out	zh measure	
ī ice	u up	ŋ ring	

mu·ti·ny • ***noun,*** *plural* **mutinies**
• ***verb*** **mutinied, mutinying, mutinies**

mutt (mut) [*a slang word*] ***noun*** a dog that is a mongrel.
mutt • ***noun,*** *plural* **mutts**

mutter (mut′ər) ***verb*** **1** to speak or say in low tones with the lips almost closed, in the way of a person talking to himself or herself —Look for the WORD CHOICES box at the entry **murmur**. **2** to complain or grumble [People always *mutter* about higher taxes.]
mut·ter • ***verb*** **muttered, muttering**

mutton (mut′n) ***noun*** the flesh of an adult sheep, used as food.
mut·ton • ***noun***

mutual (myo͞o′cho͞o əl) ***adjective*** **1** given or received in an equal manner [*mutual* admiration]. **2** of each other [Those two kinds of animals are *mutual* enemies.] **3** shared together [We have a *mutual* interest in sports.]
mu·tu·al • ***adjective***

muzzle (muz′əl) ***noun*** **1** the mouth, nose, and jaws of a dog, horse, or other animal; snout. **2** a device that is made of wire, leather, or other material and is fastened over an animal's mouth to keep it from biting. **3** the front end of the barrel of a gun. ***verb*** to put a muzzle on [*Muzzle* your dog!]

muzzle

muz·zle • ***noun,*** *plural* **muzzles**
• ***verb*** **muzzled, muzzling**

MVP or **M.V.P.** *abbreviation for* most valuable player.

my (mī) ***adjective*** done by me or having to do with me [*my* work; *my* shoes].

Myanmar (myun′mär) a country in southeast Asia. Its old name was *Burma*.
Myan·mar

myrtle (murt′l) ***noun*** **1** an evergreen shrub with white or pink flowers and dark berries. **2** an evergreen plant that grows along the ground and has blue flowers.
myr·tle • ***noun***

myself (mī self′) ***pronoun*** **1** my own self. This form of *I* is used when the person who does the action of the verb is the same as the person who is affected by the action [I cut *myself*.] **2** my usual or true self [I'm not *myself* today.] This word is also used to give more force to what is being said [I *myself* am telling you this; believe it.]
my·self • ***pronoun***

mysterious (mis tir′ē əs) ***adjective*** full of or suggesting mystery; hard to explain or solve [*mysterious* crimes].
mys·te·ri·ous • ***adjective***

mystery (mis′tər ē) ***noun*** **1** something that is not known or explained, or that is kept secret [That murder is still a *mystery*.] **2** a story or play about a crime or other event that is puzzling [She reads five murder *mysteries* a week.]
mys·ter·y • ***noun,*** *plural* **mysteries**

WORD HISTORY

mystery

The source of **mystery** is a Greek word that means "to close the eyes or mouth." A person who was shown secrets of ancient religious ceremonies was not supposed to tell what had been seen and heard.

mystify (mis′ti fī) ***verb*** to puzzle or bewilder [I was *mystified* by her answer.]
mys·ti·fy • ***verb*** **mystified, mystifying, mystifies**

myth (mith) ***noun*** **1** an old story that is handed down through the years and is usually meant to explain how something came to be [The ancient Greeks had a *myth* explaining how human beings received fire for their use.] **2** an imaginary or made-up person, thing, or story [That home run he bragged about was just a *myth*.]
myth • ***noun,*** *plural* **myths**

mythical (mith′i kəl) ***adjective*** **1** in, having to do with, or like a myth [*mythical* creatures; a *mythical* tale]. **2** imaginary; not real [his *mythical* friend].
myth·i·cal • ***adjective***

mythology (mi thäl′ə jē) ***noun*** **1** myths as a group. **2** all the myths of a certain people [Roman *mythology*].
my·thol·o·gy • ***noun***

M

N n

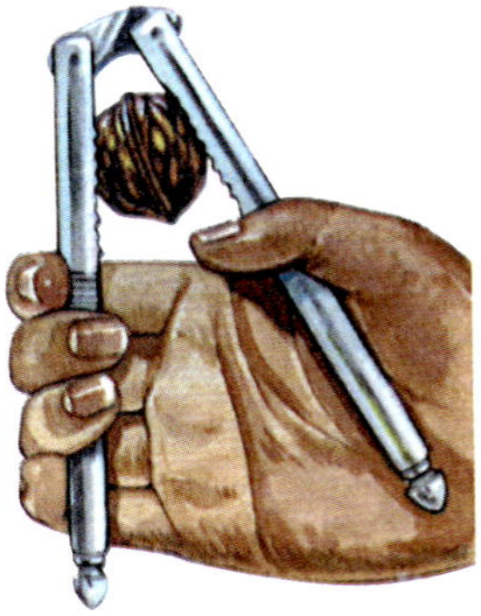

Nn Nn *Nn* **Nn**

The letter **n** *usually has the sound that you hear at the beginning of the words* **nap**, **not**, *and* **nutcracker**. *When* **n** *appears before the letter* **g** *at the very end of a word, the two letters together have the combination sound that you hear in the words* **hang** *and* **sing**.

n or **N** (en) ***noun*** the fourteenth letter of the English alphabet.
n or **N** • ***noun,*** *plural* **n's** or **N's**

n. *abbreviation for* noun.

N or **N.** *abbreviation for* **1** north. **2** northern.

nacho (nä′chō) ***noun*** a tortilla chip spread with beef, hot sauce, or other mixture, then covered with cheese and broiled.
na·cho • ***noun,*** *plural* **nachos**

nag[1] (nag) ***verb*** to annoy by scolding, urging, or complaining all the time.
noun a person who nags.
nag • ***verb*** **nagged, nagging** • ***noun,*** *plural* **nags**

nag[2] (nag) ***noun*** an old, worn-out horse.
nag • ***noun,*** *plural* **nags**

nail (nāl) ***noun*** **1** a narrow, pointed piece of metal with a flat head. It is hammered into pieces of wood or other material to hold them together. **2** a thin layer of a hard substance that grows out from the end of a finger or toe.
verb to fasten with nails [*Nail* the box shut. *Nail* the sign to the fence.]
nail • ***noun,*** *plural* **nails** • ***verb*** **nailed, nailing**

naked (nā′kəd) ***adjective*** **1** without any clothes on; bare or nude. **2** without its usual covering [a *naked* sword]. **3** not helped by any device [You can see the moon with the *naked* eye.]
na·ked • ***adjective***

name (nām) ***noun*** **1** the word or words by which a person, animal, thing, or place is known. **2** a bad or insulting word or words that are used to refer to someone or something [They were mean and called him "liar" and other nasty *names*.] **3** reputation [Guard your good *name* from harm.]
verb **1** to give a name to [They *named* the baby after her grandmother.] **2** to tell the name or names of [Can you *name* all the Presidents?] **3** to choose for a certain job or position; appoint [She was *named* president.]
name • ***noun,*** *plural* **names** • ***verb*** **named, naming**

nameless (nām′ləs) ***adjective*** **1** not having a name [a *nameless* puppy]. **2** not capable of being described [a *nameless* horror].
name·less • ***adjective***

namely (nām′lē) ***adverb*** that is to say; in other words [You have a choice of two desserts, *namely*, cake or pie.]
name·ly • ***adverb***

namesake (nām′sāk) ***noun*** a person who is named after another [Cousin Sarah is Grandma Sarah's *namesake*.]
name·sake • ***noun,*** *plural* **namesakes**

a	cat	ō	go	ʉ	fur	ə =	a *in* ago
ā	ape	ô	law, for	ch	chin		e *in* agent
ä	cot, car	oo	look	sh	she		i *in* pencil
e	ten	ōō	tool	th	thin		o *in* atom
ē	me	oi	oil	*th*	then		u *in* circus
i	fit	ou	out	zh	measure		
ī	ice	u	up	ŋ	ring		

Namibia (nə mib′ē ə) a country in southern Africa, on the Atlantic Ocean.
Na·mib·i·a

nap[1] (nap) ***verb*** to sleep for a short time; doze.
noun a short sleep; a period of dozing.
nap • ***verb*** **napped, napping** • ***noun,*** *plural* **naps**

nap[2] (nap) ***noun*** the fuzzy or hairy surface of certain kinds of cloth.
nap • ***noun,*** *plural* **naps**

nape (nāp) ***noun*** the back of the neck.
nape • ***noun,*** *plural* **napes**

napkin (nap′kin) ***noun*** a piece of cloth or paper that a person uses while eating to protect clothing or to wipe the fingers and lips.
nap·kin • ***noun,*** *plural* **napkins**

Napoleon *see* **Bonaparte,** Napoleon
Na·po·le·on

narcissus (när sis′əs) ***noun*** a plant that grows from a bulb and has yellow or white flowers.
nar·cis·sus • ***noun,*** *plural* **narcissus** or **narcissuses**

narcotic (när kät′ik) ***noun*** a drug that makes a person feel dull or sleepy and that can lessen pain.
nar·cot·ic • ***noun,*** *plural* **narcotics**

narrate (ner′āt) ***verb*** to give the story of in writing or in speech; tell what has happened.
nar·rate • ***verb*** **narrated, narrating**

narrative (ner′ə tiv) ***noun*** a story; a report of what has happened.
nar·ra·tive • ***noun,*** *plural* **narratives**

narrow (ner′ō) ***adjective*** **1** small in width compared to length or less wide than usual [a *narrow* board; a *narrow* road]. **2** small or limited in size, amount, or degree [We won the election by a *narrow* majority.] **3** with barely enough space, time, or help; very close [a *narrow* escape].
verb to lessen in size, width, or degree [The road *narrows* after this corner.]
noun *usually* **narrows** a strait or channel between two large bodies of water.
nar·row • ***adjective*** **narrower, narrowest** • ***verb*** **narrowed, narrowing** • ***noun,*** *plural* **narrows**

NASA (nas′ə) National Aeronautics and Space Administration.

nasal (nā′zəl) ***adjective*** in or having to do with the nose [*nasal* congestion; the *nasal* cavity].
na·sal • ***adjective***

Nashville (nash′vil) the capital of Tennessee.
Nash·ville

nasturtium (nə stur′shəm) ***noun*** a garden plant that has brilliant red, yellow, or orange flowers.
na·stur·tium • ***noun,*** *plural* **nasturtiums**

nasturtium

nasty (nas′tē) ***adjective*** **1** full of or resulting from spite; mean [a *nasty* person; *nasty* rumors]. **2** very unpleasant [some *nasty* weather]. **3** painful or harmful [a *nasty* bruise; a *nasty* fall]. **4** very dirty; filthy [a pair of *nasty* old sneakers].
nas·ty • ***adjective*** **nastier, nastiest**

nation (nā′shən) ***noun*** a group of people living together in a certain area under the same government; country [the American *nation*].
na·tion • ***noun,*** *plural* **nations**

national (nash′ə nəl) ***adjective*** **1** having to do with a nation as a whole [a *national* election; *national* pride]. **2** made, kept, or owned by a country's government [a *national* park].
noun a citizen of a certain country.
na·tion·al • ***adjective*** • ***noun,*** *plural* **nationals**

nationalism (nash′ə nəl iz əm) ***noun*** devotion and loyalty to one's own nation, or country.
na·tion·al·ism • ***noun***

nationality (nash′ə nal′i tē) ***noun*** **1** identity as belonging to a certain nation by being born in it or by becoming a citizen of that nation [What is your *nationality?*] **2** a nation [Many *nationalities* are represented in the United Nations.]
na·tion·al·i·ty • ***noun,*** *plural* **nationalities**

nationwide (nā′shən wīd) ***adjective*** by or through the whole nation [A *nationwide* effort must be made to curb pollution.]
na·tion·wide • ***adjective***

native (nāt′iv) ***adjective*** **1** belonging to a person because of the place where the person was born [Chinese is her *native* language. Poland is his *native* land.] **2** born in or belonging in a natural way in a certain place

or country [a *native* Canadian; a plant that is *native* to Japan]. **3** belonging to a person by nature; not learned [a *native* ability to make friends].
noun **1** a person who was born in a certain place or region [a *native* of California]. **2** a member of the original people living in a place where many people from other places and cultures have settled. The natives of North America are the Eskimos and North American Indians. **3** an animal or plant that lives or grows naturally in a certain region [The dandelion is a *native* of Europe and Asia.]
na·tive • ***adjective*** • ***noun,*** *plural* **natives**

Native American ***noun*** *another name for* **American Indian**.
Native American • ***noun,*** *plural* **Native Americans**

natural (nach′ər əl) ***adjective*** **1** produced by nature; not made by human beings [*natural* resources; hair that has *natural* curls]. **2** dealing with or studying nature [Biology and chemistry are *natural* sciences.] **3** belonging to a person by birth [a *natural* ability in music]. **4** true to nature; lifelike [a very *natural* portrait]. **5** normal or usual; being what is expected [It is *natural* for rivers to flood in the spring.] **6** in music, being neither sharp nor flat [B *natural*].
noun **1** a musical note that is neither a sharp nor a flat. **2** the sign (♮) used to show that a particular note should not be played as a sharp or flat. **3** [*an informal use*] a person who seems just right for something [She's a *natural* for the job.]
nat·u·ral • ***adjective*** • ***noun,*** *plural* **naturals**

natural gas ***noun*** a mixture of gases that is found naturally in the earth. It is taken out through pipes and is used as fuel.

natural history ***noun*** the study of physical things in nature, including animals, plants, rocks, and minerals.

naturalist (nach′ər əl ist) ***noun*** a person who studies things in nature, especially plants and animals.
nat·u·ral·ist • ***noun,*** *plural* **naturalists**

naturalize (nach′ər əl īz) ***verb*** to make a citizen of someone who was born in another country.
nat·u·ral·ize • ***verb*** **naturalized, naturalizing**

naturally (nach′ər əl ē) ***adverb*** **1** in a natural way [Act *naturally* when you shake the speaker's hand.] **2** by nature [He is *naturally* shy.] **3** as might be expected; of course [*Naturally* you will be fined for the overdue book.]
nat·u·ral·ly • ***adverb***

natural resources ***plural noun*** things that are supplied by nature and are useful to human beings in various ways. Coal, oil, water, forests, and mineral deposits are natural resources.

nature (nā′chər) ***noun*** **1** the physical world and everything in it that is not made by human beings; all things in the universe. **2** scenery that is not artificial, and the plants and animals in it [Are you a *nature* lover?] **3** the basic quality or character of a person or thing [the *nature* of light; a child with a happy *nature*]. **4** kind or type [books, magazines, and other things of that *nature*].
—by nature in a way that seems to be part of the basic qualities of a person or thing.
na·ture • ***noun,*** *plural* **natures**

naughty (nôt′ē *or* nät′ē) ***adjective*** not behaving in the right way; not obedient; bad [a *naughty* child] —Look for the WORD CHOICES box at the entry **bad**.
naugh·ty • ***adjective*** **naughtier, naughtiest**

Nauru (nä o͞o′ro͞o) a country on an island in the western Pacific Ocean, just south of the equator.
Na·u·ru

nausea (nô′zhə *or* nä′zhə *or* nô′zē ə) ***noun*** a feeling of sickness in the stomach that makes a person want to vomit.
nau·se·a • ***noun***

nautical (nôt′i kəl *or* nät′i kəl) ***adjective*** having to do with sailors or ships, or with travel by boat or ship.
nau·ti·cal • ***adjective***

Navajo (nav′ə hō) ***noun*** **1** a member of a North American Indian people who live in Arizona, New Mexico, and Utah. **2** the language of this people.
Nav·a·jo • ***noun,*** *plural for sense 1 only* **Navajos** or **Navajoes**

a	cat	ō	go	ʉ	fur	ə =	a *in* ago
ā	ape	ô	law, for	ch	chin		e *in* agent
ä	cot, car	oo	look	sh	she		i *in* pencil
e	ten	o͞o	tool	th	thin		o *in* atom
ē	me	oi	oil	*th*	then		u *in* circus
i	fit	ou	out	zh	measure		
ī	ice	u	up	ŋ	ring		

naval (nā′vəl) ***adjective*** **1** for or having to do with a navy or its ships and crews [*naval* vessels]. **2** having a navy [a great *naval* power].
na·val • ***adjective***
● The words **naval** and **navel** sound alike.
He was a *naval* officer in the war.
A *navel* is also called a "bellybutton."

nave (nāv) ***noun*** the main part of a church building, in the middle, where the seats are located.
nave • ***noun,*** *plural* **naves**

navel (nā′vəl) ***noun*** the small scar in the middle of the belly that is left when the umbilical cord is separated from a baby after birth.
na·vel • ***noun,*** *plural* **navels**
● The words **navel** and **naval** sound alike.

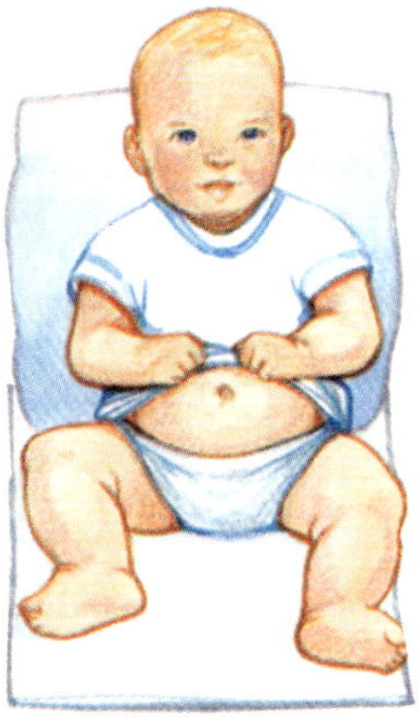
navel

navigate (nav′i gāt) ***verb*** **1** to steer, or control the course of [She *navigated* the plane through the storm.] **2** to travel through, on, or over [They were the first to *navigate* that river.]
nav·i·gate • ***verb*** **navigated, navigating**

navigation (nav′i gā′shən) ***noun*** **1** the act or skill of navigating. **2** the science of figuring the path of a ship or aircraft.
nav·i·ga·tion • ***noun***

navigator (nav′i gāt′ər) ***noun*** a person who is trained to figure the path of a ship or aircraft.
nav·i·ga·tor • ***noun,*** *plural* **navigators**

navy (nā′vē) ***noun*** **1** *often* **Navy** all of a country's warships together with their crews, officers, supplies, and bases. **2** *a short form of* **navy blue**.
adjective dark blue [a *navy* sweater].
na·vy • ***noun,*** *plural* **navies** • ***adjective***

navy blue ***noun*** a very dark blue.

nay (nā) ***noun*** a vote of "no" [The count was 57 *nays* and 43 yeas.]
nay • ***noun,*** *plural* **nays**
● The words **nay** and **neigh** sound alike.
Only three members voted *nay.*
Some horses will *neigh* at strangers.

NB or **N.B.** *abbreviation for* New Brunswick.

NC or **N.C.** *abbreviation for* North Carolina.

ND, N.D., or **N.Dak.** *abbreviation for* North Dakota.

NE *abbreviation for* Nebraska.

NE or **N.E.** *abbreviation for* **1** northeast. **2** northeastern.

near (nir) ***adverb*** **1** at or to a short distance in space or time [They live quite *near.* Spring is drawing *near.*] **2** almost [I was *near* frozen.]
adjective **1** not far in space or time; close [It happened in the *near* past.] **2** close in relationship or affection [his *nearest* friend]. **3** by a small degree; narrow [a *near* escape]. **4** almost happening [a *near* accident].
preposition close to; not far from [Stay *near* me.]
verb to come near to; to approach [Slow down as you *near* the curve.]
near • ***adverb*** & • ***adjective*** **nearer, nearest** • ***preposition*** • ***verb*** **neared, nearing**

nearby (nir′bī′) ***adjective*** near; close at hand [We often have lunch at a *nearby* restaurant.] This word can also be used as an adverb [Linda stood *nearby* with a bucket of water.]
near·by • ***adjective***

nearly (nir′lē) ***adverb*** almost; not quite [We are *nearly* ready.]
—**not nearly** not at all; far from [That's *not nearly* enough.]
near·ly • ***adverb***

nearsighted (nir′sīt′əd) ***adjective*** able to see things that are near more clearly than things that are far away.
near·sight·ed • ***adjective***

neat (nēt) ***adjective*** **1** clean and tidy [Keep your desk *neat.*] **2** careful and exact [He's a very *neat* worker.] **3** done or said in a clever way [That's a *neat* trick.]
neat • ***adjective*** **neater, neatest**

WORD CHOICES

Synonyms of **neat**

The words **neat, tidy,** and **trim** share the meaning "orderly and without excess."

a *neat* pattern
a *tidy* closet
a *trim* ship

N

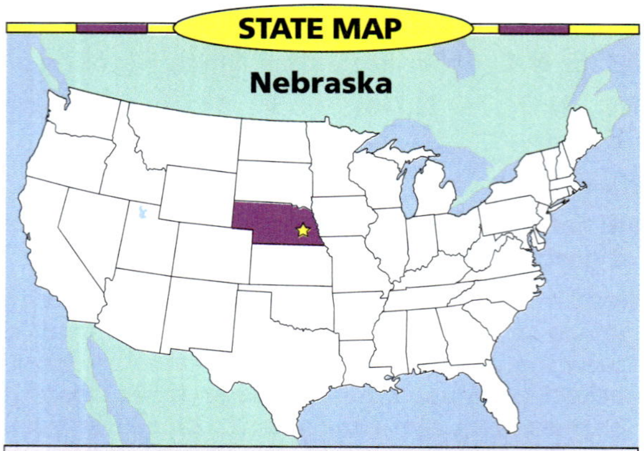

Statehood: 1867, the 37th state • Capital: Lincoln

Nebraska (nə bras′kə) a State in the north central part of the U.S. Its capital is Lincoln. Abbreviated **NE, Neb.,** or **Nebr.**
Ne·bras·ka

necessarily (nes′ə ser′i lē) ***adverb*** as a necessary result; always [Clouds in the sky do not *necessarily* mean rain.]
nec·es·sar·i·ly • ***adverb***

necessary (nes′ə ser′ē) ***adjective*** needed or having to be done; required [Do only the *necessary* repairs.]
nec·es·sar·y • ***adjective***

necessity (nə ses′i tē) ***noun*** **1** something that is necessary or needed or that cannot be done without [Food and a place to live are *necessities*.] **2** great need [Call the doctor only in case of *necessity*.]
ne·ces·si·ty • ***noun,*** *plural for sense 1 only* **necessities**

neck (nek) ***noun*** **1** the part of a human being or animal that joins the head to the body. **2** the part of a piece of clothing that goes around the neck. **3** the narrowest part of something [the *neck* of a bottle].
—neck and neck very close or even in a race or contest.
neck • ***noun,*** *plural* **necks**

necklace (nek′ləs) ***noun*** a gold or silver chain or a string of beads, pearls, or jewels that is worn around the neck as an ornament.
neck·lace • ***noun,*** *plural* **necklaces**

necktie (nek′tī) ***noun*** a cloth band that is worn around the neck, usually under the collar of a shirt, and tied in a knot or bow in front.
neck·tie • ***noun,*** *plural* **neckties**

nectar (nek′tər) ***noun*** the sweet liquid in many flowers, made into honey by bees.
nec·tar • ***noun,*** *plural* **nectars**

nectarine (nek tə rēn′) ***noun*** a kind of peach that has a smooth skin.
nec·tar·ine • ***noun,*** *plural* **nectarines**

need (nēd) ***noun*** **1** something that one wants or must have; a lack [His greatest *need* now is for rest.] **2** a condition that makes something necessary [There is no *need* to worry.] **3** a time or condition when help is wanted [A friend in *need* is a friend indeed.] **4** a condition of being very poor [Give to those in *need*.]
verb *Need* can be both a main verb and a helping verb. **I.** When *need* is a main verb, it means: to have need of; want; require [She *needs* a car.] **II.** When *need* is a helping verb, it means: **1** should: in this use, *need* is followed by *to* [She *needs* to rest.] **2** to be required to: in this use, the form of *need* does not change, and it is not followed by *to* [*Need* I tell you? He *need* not go.]
need • ***noun,*** *plural for sense 1 only* **needs**
• ***verb*** **needed, needing**

● The words **need** and **knead** sound alike.
Do I really *need* another pet?
You must *knead* the dough.

needle (nēd′əl) ***noun*** **1** a small, very slender piece of steel with a sharp point and a hole for a thread, used for sewing. **2** the thin, pointed leaf of a pine, spruce, or similar tree or bush. **3** a slender rod of steel or plastic used in knitting or crocheting. **4** the pointer of a compass, gauge, or meter. **5** the sharp, thin, hollow metal tube at the end of the kind of syringe that is used to give shots.
verb [*an informal use*] to tease or annoy [Don't *needle* your brother.]
nee·dle • ***noun,*** *plural* **needles**
• ***verb*** **needled, needling**

needlepoint
Left: Finished pillow
Right: Enlargement to show detail

a	cat	ō	go	ʉ	fur	ə =	a *in* ago
ā	ape	ô	law, for	ch	chin		e *in* agent
ä	cot, car	ŏŏ	look	sh	she		i *in* pencil
e	ten	ōō	tool	th	thin		o *in* atom
ē	me	oi	oil	*th*	then		u *in* circus
i	fit	ou	out	zh	measure		
ī	ice	u	up	ŋ	ring		

needlepoint (nēd′əl point) ***noun*** embroidery done on canvas, used for upholstery, tapestries, and other decorations.
nee·dle·point • ***noun***

needless (nēd′ləs) ***adjective*** not needed; not necessary [The new car was a *needless* expense.]
need·less • ***adjective***

needlework (nēd′əl wurk) ***noun*** work such as embroidery or sewing that is done with a needle.

needn't (nēd′nt) need not.
need·n't

needy (nēd′ē) ***adjective*** very poor.
need·y • ***adjective*** **needier, neediest**

negative (neg′ə tiv) ***adjective*** **1** saying that something is not so or refusing; answering "no" [a *negative* reply]. **2** not offering help or improvement [a *negative* comment]. **3** opposite to or lacking something that is positive [He always takes a *negative* attitude and expects the worst.] **4** showing that a certain disease or condition is not present [The reaction to her allergy test was *negative*.] **5** describing an amount or number that is less than zero [-4 is a *negative* number.] **6** describing or having to do with a kind of electrical charge associated with too many electrons. When a piece of silk is rubbed on a glass rod the silk captures electrons and takes on a negative charge.
noun **1** a word or phrase that shows that a person does not agree or approve ["No" and "not" are *negatives*.] **2** the film or plate from which a finished photograph is printed. The negative shows the light areas of the original subject as dark and the dark areas as light.
neg·a·tive • ***adjective*** • ***noun***, *plural* **negatives**

neglect (ni glekt′) ***verb*** **1** to fail to do what one should do [In her hurry, Sharon *neglected* to lock the door.] **2** to fail to take care of as one should; give too little attention to [He was so busy with work that he *neglected* his family.]
noun the condition of being neglected [The old house fell into *neglect*.]
neg·lect • ***verb*** **neglected, neglecting** • ***noun***

negotiate (ni gō′shē āt) ***verb*** **1** to talk over a question, quarrel, or business deal in the hope of reaching an agreement [The buyer and the seller of the house are still *negotiating*.] **2** to arrange by talking about [He *negotiated* a contract with the team's owners.]
ne·go·ti·ate • ***verb*** **negotiated, negotiating**

negotiation (ni gō′shē ā′shən) ***noun*** *often* **negotiations** the act of discussing and bargaining to reach an agreement [*Negotiations* between the two countries have gone on for months.]
ne·go·ti·a·tion • ***noun***, *plural* **negotiations**

Negro (nē′grō) ***noun*** **1** a member of any of the native, dark-skinned peoples of Africa that live chiefly south of the Sahara. **2** a person having some African ancestors; a black person.
adjective of or having to do with Negroes.
Ne·gro • ***noun***, *plural* **Negroes** • ***adjective***

Negroid (nē′groid) ***adjective*** belonging to one of the major geographical varieties of human beings that includes the majority of the peoples of Africa south of the Sahara.
Ne·groid • ***adjective***

neigh (nā) ***noun*** the loud cry that a horse makes; whinny.
verb to make this cry.
neigh • ***noun***, *plural* **neighs** • ***verb*** **neighed, neighing**
• The words **neigh** and **nay** sound alike.
Some horses will *neigh* at strangers.
Only three members voted *nay*.

neighbor (nā′bər) ***noun*** **1** a person who lives near another. **2** a person or thing that is near another [France and Spain are *neighbors*.] **3** another human being; fellow person [love your *neighbor*].
neigh·bor • ***noun***, *plural* **neighbors**

neighborhood (nā′bər hood) ***noun*** **1** a small part or district of a city or town [an old *neighborhood*]. **2** the people in such a district [The whole *neighborhood* helped.]
neigh·bor·hood • ***noun***, *plural* **neighborhoods**

neighboring (nā′bər iŋ) ***adjective*** near or next to each other [*neighboring* farms].
neigh·bor·ing • ***adjective***

neighborly (nā′bər lē) ***adjective*** friendly, kind, and helpful, like a neighbor.
neigh·bor·ly • ***adjective***

neither (nē′*th*ər *or* nī′*th*ər) ***adjective*** not one or the other of two; not either [*Neither* boy went to the park.]
pronoun not one or the other of two persons or things [*Neither* of them was invited.]

N

conjunction not either: used in phrases with *nor* [I'll buy *neither* roses nor daisies.]
nei·ther • *adjective* • *pronoun* • *conjunction*

neon

neon (nē′än) ***noun*** a chemical element that is a gas. Neon has no color and no smell and it glows when an electric current is sent through it. Tubes filled with neon are often used in advertising signs.
ne·on • ***noun***

Nepal (nə pôl′) a country in the Himalayas, between India and China.
Ne·pal

nephew (nef′yo͞o) ***noun*** **1** the son of one's brother or sister. **2** the son of one's brother-in-law or sister-in-law.
neph·ew • ***noun, plural*** **nephews**

Neptune (nep′to͞on *or* nep′tyo͞on) **1** the Roman god of the sea. **2** the fourth largest planet. It is the eighth in distance from the sun.
Nep·tune

nerve (nʉrv) ***noun*** **1** any one of the fibers that connect the muscles, organs, and other parts of the body with the brain and spinal cord. Nerves carry messages to and from the brain. These messages control all activity in the body. **2** the power to control one's feelings in facing danger or risk [The tightrope walker is a person with *nerve*.] **3** [*an informal use*] boldness that is without shame or that shows a lack of respect [She had a lot of *nerve* taking my bicycle without asking.] **—get on someone's nerves** to make someone annoyed or angry.
nerve • ***noun, plural*** **nerves**

nervous (nʉr′vəs) ***adjective*** **1** having to do with the nerves [the *nervous* system]. **2** feeling fear or expecting trouble [He is *nervous* about seeing a doctor.] **3** restless and easily annoyed or upset [Fire makes horses *nervous*.]
nerv·ous • ***adjective***

-ness *a suffix meaning:* **1** the condition of being [*Sadness* is the condition of being sad.] **2** an example of being; an act or thing that is [A *kindness* is an act or example of being kind.]

WORD MAKER

The suffix -ness

Many words contain the suffix **-ness** plus a word that you already know. You can understand these words if you add the idea "the condition of being" to the meaning of the base word.

base word	*+ suffix*	⇨ *new word*
cheerful	**+ -ness**	⇨ **cheerfulness** *(the condition of being cheerful)*
gloomy	**+ -ness**	⇨ **gloominess** *(the condition of being gloomy)*

awkwardness	emptiness	laziness
baldness	exactness	lightness
bitterness	fairness	liveliness
blackness	falseness	loneliness
boldness	fierceness	loudness
brightness	firmness	loveliness
calmness	fondness	meanness
carelessness	foolishness	messiness
cheapness	freshness	mildness
cleanness	friendliness	narrowness
cleverness	gentleness	naughtiness
clumsiness	gladness	neatness
coldness	gracefulness	nervousness
colorfulness	grayness	newness
coolness	greatness	numbness
correctness	greediness	paleness
craftiness	hardness	peacefulness
craziness	harshness	politeness
deafness	heaviness	prettiness
dimness	helpfulness	quickness
dizziness	helplessness	redness
drowsiness	hoarseness	rightness
dryness	hopelessness	ripeness
dullness	idleness	roughness
eagerness	joyousness	rudeness
effectiveness	lateness	sadness

a	cat	ō	go	ʉ	fur	ə =	a *in* ago
ā	ape	ô	law, for	ch	chin		e *in* agent
ä	cot, car	o͝o	look	sh	she		i *in* pencil
e	ten	o͞o	tool	th	thin		o *in* atom
ē	me	oi	oil	*th*	then		u *in* circus
i	fit	ou	out	zh	measure		
ī	ice	u	up	ŋ	ring		

selfishness	smugness	tidiness
seriousness	softness	tiredness
shallowness	soreness	ugliness
shamefulness	stiffness	unfairness
sharpness	stillness	unhappiness
shyness	strangeness	uniqueness
silliness	stubbornness	usefulness
sleepiness	sturdiness	uselessness
slimness	suddenness	vagueness
sloppiness	sureness	weariness
slowness	sweetness	whiteness
slyness	swiftness	wickedness
smallness	tardiness	wildness
smoothness	thoughtfulness	worthlessness

nest (nest) ***noun*** **1** the place built by a bird for laying its eggs and caring for its young. **2** a place where hornets, ants, fish, mice, and various other animals live and breed. **3** a group of birds, insects, or animals in such a place [There is a *nest* of squirrels inside the tree trunk.] **4** a cozy or snug place [The cat made a *nest* in the sheets.]
verb to build or live in a nest [Swallows often *nest* in chimneys.]
nest • ***noun,*** *plural* **nests** • ***verb*** **nested, nesting**

nest egg ***noun*** money saved for the future; savings.
nest egg • ***noun,*** *plural* **nest eggs**

nestle (nes′əl) ***verb*** **1** to lie or settle down in a comfortable or snug way [The baby *nestled* in his mother's arms.] **2** to press or hold close for comfort or in fondness; cuddle [She *nestled* the puppy in her lap.]
nes·tle • ***verb*** **nestled, nestling**

net[1] (net) ***noun*** **1** a fabric of thread, cord, or similar material that is woven or knotted together so that open spaces are left between the strands. **2** something made of net [a *net* to catch butterflies; a hair *net;* a tennis *net*].
verb to catch with a net [I *netted* three fish.]
net • ***noun,*** *plural* **nets** • ***verb*** **netted, netting**

net[2] (net) ***adjective*** describing what is left after certain amounts have been subtracted [*Net* weight is the weight of an article without the weight of its container.]
verb to get or gain [The sale of the house will *net* him a good profit.]
net • ***adjective*** • ***verb*** **netted, netting**

Netherlands (ne*th*′ər ləndz) a country in western Europe, on the North Sea; Holland.
Neth·er·lands

nettle (net′l) ***noun*** a weed with hairs on its leaves that sting the skin when they are touched.
verb to annoy or make angry [His unkind remarks don't *nettle* her.]
net·tle • ***noun,*** *plural* **nettles**
• ***verb*** **nettled, nettling**

network (net′wʉrk) ***noun*** **1** any system of things that cross or are connected more or less like the strands in a net [a *network* of city streets]. **2** a chain of radio or television stations that usually broadcast many of the same programs.
net·work • ***noun,*** *plural* **networks**

neutral (no͞o′trəl *or* nyo͞o′trəl) ***adjective*** **1** not taking either side in a quarrel or war [a *neutral* country]. **2** neither an acid nor a base [Water is a *neutral* substance.] **3** not strong or definite [Gray and tan are *neutral* colors.]
noun **1** a person or nation not taking part in a quarrel or war. **2** the position of the gears in a car when they are not meshed together. When the gears are in neutral, the engine cannot pass on power to the wheels.
neu·tral • ***adjective*** • ***noun,*** *plural for sense 1 only* **neutrals**

neutralize (no͞o′trə līz *or* nyo͞o′trə līz) ***verb*** to make neutral.
neu·tral·ize • ***verb*** **neutralized, neutralizing**

neutron (no͞o′trän *or* nyo͞o′trän) ***noun*** one of the tiny particles that make up the nucleus of an atom. A neutron has no electrical charge.
neu·tron • ***noun,*** *plural* **neutrons**

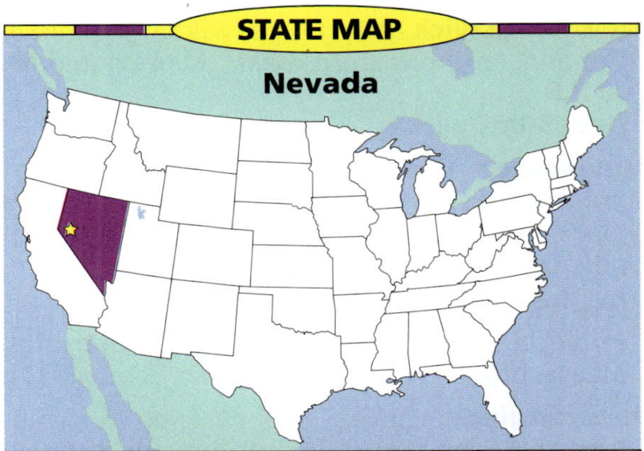

Statehood: 1864, the 36th state • **Capital:** Carson City

Nevada (nə vad′ə *or* nə väd′ə) a State in the southwestern part of the U.S. Its capital is Carson City. Abbreviated **NV** or **Nev.**
Ne·va·da

N

never (nev′ər) ***adverb*** **1** at no time; not ever [I *never* saw her again.] **2** not at all; under no conditions [*Never* mind what he says.]
nev·er • ***adverb***

nevermore (nev′ ər môr′) ***adverb*** never again.
nev·er·more • ***adverb***

nevertheless (nev′ ər *th*ə les′) ***adverb*** in spite of that; however [They were losing the game. *Nevertheless*, they kept on trying.]
nev·er·the·less • ***adverb***

new (no͞o *or* nyo͞o) ***adjective*** **1** seen, made, thought of, or discovered for the first time [a *new* song; a *new* plan; a *new* star]. **2** different from the earlier one [She has a *new* haircut.] **3** that is the more recent or the most recent one [This is the *new* library.] **4** having just come recently [the *new* kid on the block]. **5** that has not been worn or used [*new* and used cars]. **6** recently grown or made; fresh [*new* potatoes; *new* pennies]. **7** beginning again; starting once more [the *new* year].
new • ***adjective*** **newer, newest**
● The words **new, gnu,** and **knew** sound alike.
Don't you know any *new* jokes?
Lions hunt the zebra and the *gnu*.
I *knew* him when he was a baby.

Newark (no͞o′ərk *or* nyo͞o′ərk) a city in northeastern New Jersey.
New·ark

newborn (no͞o′bôrn′ *or* nyo͞o′bôrn′) ***adjective*** **1** just born [a *newborn* calf; a *newborn* baby]. **2** born again; fresh or made stronger [Her *newborn* courage made her daring.]
new·born • ***adjective***

New Brunswick (no͞o′ brunz′wik) a province of Canada, on the eastern coast. Abbreviated **NB** or **N.B.**
New Bruns·wick

newcomer (no͞o′kum′ ər *or* nyo͞o′kum′ ər) ***noun*** a person who has recently arrived in a place; new arrival.
new·com·er • ***noun,*** *plural* **newcomers**

New England the six northeastern States of the U.S.: Maine, Vermont, New Hampshire, Massachusetts, Rhode Island, and Connecticut.

newfangled (no͞o′faŋ′gəld *or* nyo͞o′faŋ′gəld) ***adjective*** new and different, but not of much use [It's some kind of *newfangled* gadget.]
new·fan·gled • ***adjective***

Newfoundland and Labrador (no͞o′fənd lənd and lab′rə dôr) **1** an island off the eastern coast of Canada. **2** a province of Canada made up of this island and a large peninsula in northeastern Canada: abbreviated **NL** or **Nfld. & Lab.**
New·found·land and Lab·ra·dor

New Guinea (no͞o′ gin′ē) a large island north of Australia. The western half is part of Indonesia; the eastern half is a country called **Papua New Guinea**.
New Guin·ea

STATE MAP

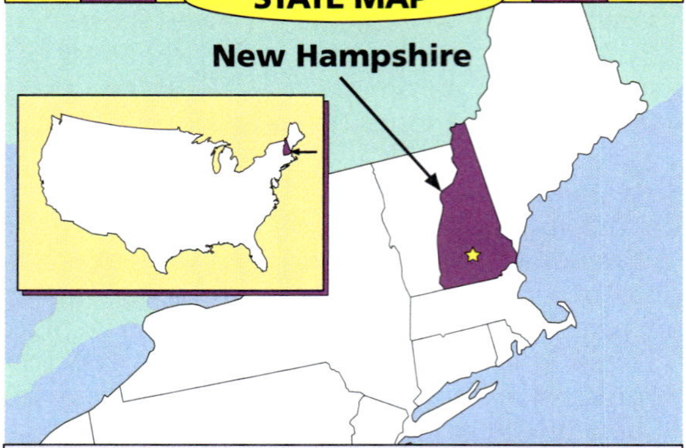

Statehood: 1788, the 9th state • **Capital:** Concord

New Hampshire (no͞o′ hamp′shir) a New England State of the U.S. Its capital is Concord. Abbreviated **NH** or **N.H.**
New Hamp·shire

STATE MAP

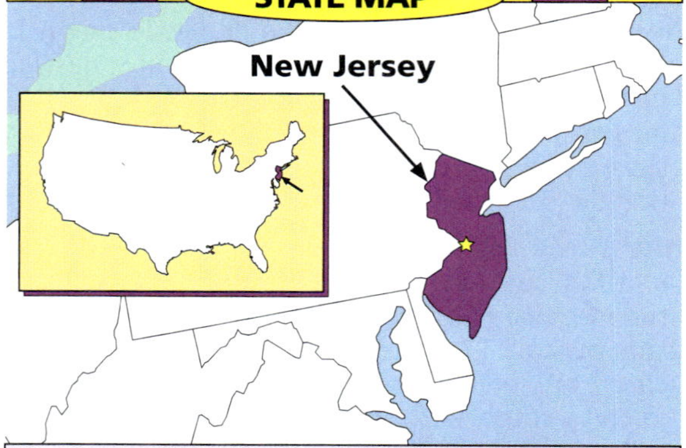

Statehood: 1787, the 3rd state • **Capital:** Trenton

New Jersey (no͞o′ jʉr′zē) a State in the northeastern part of the U.S. Its capital is Trenton. Abbreviated **NJ** or **N.J.**
New Jer·sey

a cat	ō go	ʉ fur	ə = a *in* ago
ā ape	ô law, for	ch chin	e *in* agent
ä cot, car	o͝o look	sh she	i *in* pencil
e ten	o͞o tool	th thin	o *in* atom
ē me	oi oil	*th* then	u *in* circus
i fit	ou out	zh measure	
ī ice	u up	ŋ ring	

newly (nōō′lē *or* nyōō′lē) ***adverb*** a short time ago; recently [a *newly* paved road].
new·ly • ***adverb***

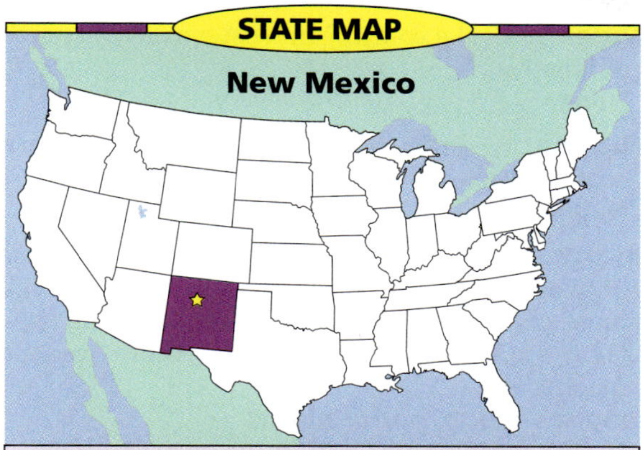

Statehood: 1912, the 47th state • **Capital:** Santa Fe

New Mexico a State in the southwestern part of the U.S. Its capital is Santa Fe. Abbreviated **NM, N.M.,** or **N.Mex.**

new moon ***noun*** the moon when it cannot be seen at all.
new moon • ***noun,*** *plural* **new moons**

New Orleans (nōō ôr′lē ənz *or* nōō ôr′lənz *or* nōō′ ôr lēnz′) a city in southeastern Louisiana, on the Mississippi.
New Or·le·ans

news (nōōz *or* nyōōz) ***plural noun*** [*used with a singular verb*] **1** happenings that have just taken place and are told about in a newspaper or magazine or over radio or TV. **2** something that a person has not known before [That story about the fire is *news* to me.]

newscast (nōōz′kast *or* nyōōz′kast) ***noun*** a program of news broadcast over radio or TV.
news·cast • ***noun,*** *plural* **newscasts**

newspaper (nōōz′pā′pər *or* nyōōz′pā′pər) ***noun*** a number of large, folded sheets of paper printed with news, opinions, advertising, and other information. Most newspapers are brought out every day or once a week.
news·pa·per • ***noun,*** *plural* **newspapers**

newsstand (nōōz′stand *or* nyōōz′stand) ***noun*** a stand where newspapers and magazines are sold.
news·stand • ***noun,*** *plural* **newsstands**

newt (nōōt *or* nyōōt) ***noun*** a small salamander that lives both on land and in water.
newt • ***noun,*** *plural* **newts**

New Testament the part of the Christian Bible that tells of the life and teachings of Jesus and his followers.

Newton (nōōt′n *or* nyōōt′n), Sir **Isaac** (ī′zək) 1642-1727; English scientist and philosopher. He developed important laws dealing with motion and gravity.
New·ton, Sir **I·saac**

New World the Western Hemisphere; the Americas.

New Year's Day or **New Year's** ***noun*** January 1, a legal holiday in the U.S.

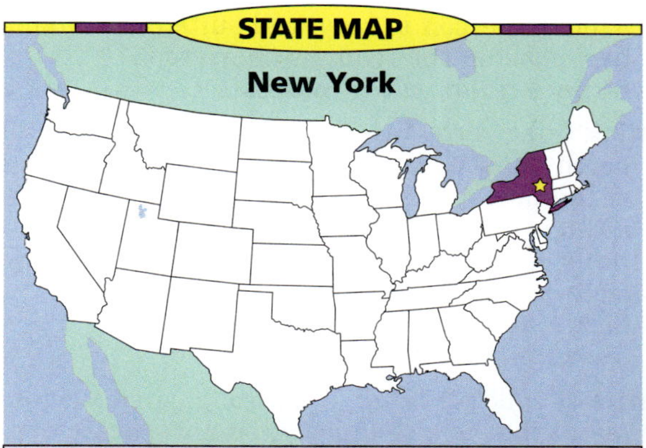

Statehood: 1788, the 11th state • **Capital:** Albany

New York (nōō yôrk) **1** a State in the northeastern part of the U.S. Its capital is Albany. Abbreviated **NY** or **N.Y.** **2** a seaport in southeastern New York State, on the Atlantic Ocean. It is the largest city in the U.S. This city is often called **New York City**.

New Zealand (nōō zē′lənd) a country in the southern Pacific, made up of two large islands and some smaller ones.
New Zea·land

next (nekst) ***adjective*** coming just before or just after; nearest or closest [the *next* person in line; the *next* room; *next* Monday].
adverb **1** in the nearest place or time [She sits *next* to me in school. Arithmetic class is *next*.] **2** at the first chance after this [Please wait on me *next*. What should I do *next?*]

next-door (nekst′dôr′) ***adjective*** in or at the next house, building, or apartment.

NH or **N.H.** *abbreviation for* New Hampshire.

nibble (nib′əl) ***verb*** **1** to eat with quick, small bites, taking only a small amount at a time [The mouse *nibbled* the cheese.] **2** to take small bites [He *nibbled* at the cookie.]
noun a small bite.

nib·ble • *verb* **nibbled, nibbling** • *noun, plural* **nibbles**

Nicaragua (nik ə rä′gwə) a country in Central America.
Nic·a·ra·gua

nice (nīs) *adjective* **1** pleasant; delightful [a *nice* time; a *nice* day]. **2** pretty; attractive [a *nice* dress]. **3** polite and considerate [*nice* manners; a *nice* neighbor].
nice • *adjective* **nicer, nicest**

niche (nich) *noun* **1** a hollow place in a wall, for a statue or vase. **2** a place or position for which a person is very well suited [She found her *niche* on the team as shortstop.]
niche • *noun, plural* **niches**

nick (nik) *verb* **1** to make a small cut, chip, or notch on or in [I *nicked* the glass on the edge of the faucet.] **2** to barely touch [The bat just *nicked* the ball.]
noun a small cut, chip, or notch made in an edge or surface.
nick • *verb* **nicked, nicking** • *noun, plural* **nicks**

nickel (nik′əl) *noun* **1** a strong, silvery-white metal that is a chemical element. Nickel does not rust easily and is used to coat and protect other metals. **2** a coin of the U.S. and Canada, worth five cents.
nick·el • *noun, plural for sense 2 only* **nickels**

nickname (nik′nām) *noun* **1** a name given to a person or thing in fun or affection. It often describes some trait ["Shorty" and "Slim" are common *nicknames*.] **2** a familiar, often shorter, form of a person's name ["Tony" is a *nickname* for "Anthony."]
verb to give a nickname to.
nick·name • *noun, plural* **nicknames** • *verb* **nicknamed, nicknaming**

WORD HISTORY

nickname

The source of this word is the 600-year-old English word *ekename*, which means "an added name," often a last name that was added to identify a certain person. As time passed, when people said "an ekename," some people thought they were hearing "a nekename." Today we spell this word **nickname**.

niece (nēs) *noun* **1** the daughter of one's brother or sister. **2** the daughter of one's brother-in-law or sister-in-law.
niece • *noun, plural* **nieces**

Niger (nī′jər) a country in western Africa, north of Nigeria.
Ni·ger

Nigeria (nī jir′ē ə) a country on the western coast of Africa.
Ni·ger·i·a

night (nīt) *noun* **1** the time of darkness between sunset and sunrise [We sleep through most of the *night*.] **2** the darkness of this time [The *night* was very black for there was no moon.]
night • *noun, plural* **nights**

• The words **night** and **knight** sound alike.
The moon and stars light up the *night*.
The *knight* wore a suit of armor.

night crawler (krôl′ər *or* kräl′ər) *noun* any large earthworm that crawls on the ground at night. It is often used as fish bait.
night crawl·er • *noun, plural* **night crawlers**

nightfall (nīt′fôl) *noun* the day's end; dusk.
night·fall • *noun*

nightgown (nīt′goun) *noun* a loose garment worn in bed by women or girls.
night·gown • *noun, plural* **nightgowns**

nightingale (nīt′n gāl) *noun* a small European bird related to the robin. The male is known for its sweet singing, especially at night.
night·in·gale • *noun, plural* **nightingales**

Nightingale (nīt′n gāl), **Florence** (flôr′əns) 1820-1910; an English nurse who is thought of as the founder of modern nursing.
Night·in·gale, Flor·ence

nightly (nīt′lē) *adjective* done or happening every night [their *nightly* game of chess].
adverb at night or every night [I read a chapter *nightly*.]
night·ly • *adjective* • *adverb*

nightmare (nīt′mer) *noun* **1** a frightening dream. **2** any very frightening experience [The trip through the blizzard was a *nightmare*.]
night·mare • *noun, plural* **nightmares**

a cat	ō go	ʉ fur	ə = a *in* ago
ā ape	ô law, for	ch chin	e *in* agent
ä cot, car	oo look	sh she	i *in* pencil
e ten	ōō tool	th thin	o *in* atom
ē me	oi oil	*th* then	u *in* circus
i fit	ou out	zh measure	
ī ice	u up	ŋ ring	

nighttime (nīt′tīm) ***noun*** the time of darkness between sunset and sunrise; night.
night·time • ***noun***

Nile (nīl) a river in eastern Africa, flowing through Egypt into the Mediterranean.

nimble (nim′bəl) ***adjective*** **1** moving quickly and lightly. **2** clever or alert [a *nimble* mind].
nim·ble • ***adjective*** **nimbler, nimblest**

WORD CHOICES

Synonyms of **nimble**

Many words share the meaning "moving rapidly and easily."

agile	frisky	spry
deft	lively	

nine (nīn) ***noun*** the cardinal number between eight and ten; 9.
adjective being one more than eight [the *nine* lives of a cat].
nine • ***noun,*** *plural* **nines** • ***adjective***

nineteen (nīn′tēn′) ***noun*** the cardinal number between eighteen and twenty; 19.
adjective being one more than eighteen [*nineteen* miles to go].
nine·teen • ***noun,*** *plural* **nineteens** • ***adjective***

nineteenth (nīn′tēnth′) ***adjective*** coming after eighteen others in a series; 19th in order.
noun **1** the number, person, or thing that is nineteenth. **2** one of nineteen equal parts of something; 1⁄19.
nine·teenth • ***adjective*** • ***noun,*** *plural* **nineteenths**

ninetieth (nīn′tē əth) ***adjective*** being ten more than eighty others in a series; 90th in order.
noun **1** the number, person, or thing that is ninetieth. **2** one of ninety equal parts of something; 1⁄90.
nine·ti·eth • ***adjective*** • ***noun,*** *plural* **ninetieths**

ninety (nīn′tē) ***noun*** the cardinal number that is equal to nine times ten; 90.
adjective being nine times ten [*ninety* days].
nine·ty • ***noun,*** *plural* **nineties** • ***adjective***

ninja (nin′jə) ***noun*** one of a group of warriors in medieval Japan, trained to be spies and assassins.
nin·ja • ***noun,*** *plural* **ninja** or **ninjas**

ninth (nīnth) ***adjective*** coming after eight others in a series; 9th in order.
noun **1** the number, person, or thing that is ninth. **2** one of nine equal parts of something; 1⁄9.
ninth • ***adjective*** • ***noun,*** *plural* **ninths**

nip (nip) ***verb*** **1** to pinch, squeeze, or bite [He *nipped* his finger in the door.] **2** to cut or pinch off; clip [She *nipped* the dead leaves from the plant.] **3** to hurt or spoil because of cold [Frost *nipped* the buds.]
noun **1** a pinch, squeeze, or bite. **2** stinging cold; chill [There's a *nip* in the air.]
nip • ***verb*** **nipped, nipping** • ***noun,*** *plural* **nips**

nipple (nip′əl) ***noun*** **1** the part of a breast or udder through which a baby or young animal sucks milk. **2** a rubber cap on a baby's bottle.
nip·ple • ***noun,*** *plural* **nipples**

nitrogen (nī′trə jən) ***noun*** a chemical element that is a gas. It has no odor, taste, or smell. It makes up almost four fifths of the air around the earth and is found in all living things.
ni·tro·gen • ***noun***

Nixon (nik′sən), **Richard M.** (rich′ərd) 1913-1994; the thirty-seventh president of the U.S., from 1969-1974. He resigned after a scandal.
Nix·on, Rich·ard M.

NJ or **N.J.** *abbreviation for* New Jersey.

NL *abbreviation for* Newfoundland and Labrador.

NM, N.M., or **N.Mex.** *abbreviation for* New Mexico.

no (nō) ***adverb*** **1** not so; the opposite of *yes*. It can mean things like "I won't," "I can't," "I refuse," or "it isn't." **2** not at all [He is *no* worse today.]
adjective not a; not any or not one [He is *no* dancer. There are *no* errors in this letter.]
noun **1** the act of saying "no"; the act of refusing or denying. **2** a vote against something.
no • ***adverb*** • ***adjective*** • ***noun,*** *plural* **noes**
● The words **no** and **know** sound alike.
There are *no* sandwiches left.
Do you *know* how to read music?

No. or **no.** *abbreviation for* number.

Noah (nō′ə) a man in the Bible who was told by God to build an ark, so that he and his family and a pair of every kind of creature would be saved during a great flood.
No·ah

N

noble (nō′bəl) ***adjective*** **1** having or showing a very high character or morals [Wanting to help other people is a *noble* idea.] **2** of or having a high rank or title [a *noble* family]. **3** grand; splendid [a *noble* oak].
noun a person who has noble rank or title.
no·ble • ***adjective*** **nobler, noblest** • ***noun,*** *plural* **nobles**

nobleman (nō′bəl mən) ***noun*** a man who has a noble rank or title.
no·ble·man • ***noun,*** *plural* **noblemen**

noblewoman (nō′bəl woom′ən) ***noun*** a woman who has a noble rank or title.
no·ble·wom·an • ***noun,*** *plural* **noblewomen**

nobody (nō′bud′ē *or* nō′bäd′ē) ***pronoun*** no person; not anybody; no one [*Nobody* lives there.]
noun a person of no importance.
no·bod·y • ***pronoun*** • ***noun,*** *plural* **nobodies**

nocturnal (näk tur′nəl) ***adjective*** active at night [The bat is a *nocturnal* animal.]
noc·tur·nal • ***adjective***

nod (näd) ***verb*** **1** to bend the head forward quickly as a sign of agreement or as a greeting [We all *nodded* "yes."] **2** to show by bending the head forward quickly [The teacher *nodded* his approval to my request.] **3** to let the head fall forward in falling asleep [Halfway through the program the children started to *nod*.] **4** to sway back and forth [The daffodils *nodded* in the breeze.]
noun the act of nodding.
nod • ***verb*** **nodded, nodding** • ***noun,*** *plural* **nods**

Noel or **Noël** (nō el′) ***noun*** *another name for* **Christmas**.
No·el or **No·ël** • ***noun,*** *plural* **Noels** or **Noëls**

noise (noiz) ***noun*** **1** a loud, harsh, or confused sound [the *noise* of fireworks]. **2** a sound of any kind [the *noise* of the rain].
noise • ***noun,*** *plural* **noises**

WORD CHOICES

Synonyms of **noise**

Many words share the meaning "a loud, unpleasant sound."

clatter	racket
din	uproar

noisy (noi′zē) ***adjective*** **1** making much noise [The children were *noisy* and happy.] **2** full of noise [a *noisy* street; a *noisy* playground].
nois·y • ***adjective*** **noisier, noisiest**

nomad (nō′mad) ***noun*** a member of a people that has no permanent home. Nomads keep moving about looking for food or for places where their animals can graze.
no·mad • ***noun,*** *plural* **nomads**

nominate (näm′i nāt′) ***verb*** **1** to name as a candidate for an election [Each party *nominated* a candidate for president.] **2** to appoint to a position [The President *nominated* a new ambassador.]
nom·i·nate • ***verb*** **nominated, nominating**

nomination (näm′i nā′shən) ***noun*** **1** the act of nominating; choice of a person as a candidate [The *nomination* for governor took place during the convention.] **2** appointment of a person to a position, office, or honor.
nom·i·na·tion • ***noun,*** *plural* **nominations**

nominee (näm′i nē′) ***noun*** a person who is nominated, especially as a candidate for an election.
nom·i·nee • ***noun,*** *plural* **nominees**

non- *a prefix meaning* not [A *nondairy* food is one that does not contain milk or other dairy products.]

WORD MAKER

The prefix **non-**

Many words contain the prefix **non-** plus a word that you already know. You can understand these words if you add the idea "not" to the meaning of the base word.

I. *when added to adjectives:*

prefix	*+ base word*	⇨	*new word*
non-	**+ poisonous**	⇨	**nonpoisonous** *(not capable of poisoning)*
	Catholic		non-Catholic

a cat	ō go	ur fur	ə = a *in* ago
ā ape	ô law, for	ch chin	e *in* agent
ä cot, car	oo look	sh she	i *in* pencil
e ten	o͞o tool	th thin	o *in* atom
ē me	oi oil	*th* then	u *in* circus
i fit	ou out	zh measure	
ī ice	u up	ŋ ring	

contagious	noncontagious
democratic	nondemocratic
essential	nonessential
Jewish	non-Jewish
magnetic	nonmagnetic
medical	nonmedical
religious	nonreligious
scientific	nonscientific
technical	nontechnical
toxic	nontoxic

II. *when added to nouns:*

prefix	*+ base word* ➪	*new word*
non-	**+ driver** ➪	**nondriver** *(a person who does not drive)*
	Catholic	non-Catholic
	citizen	non-citizen
	member	nonmember
	reader	nonreader
	smoker	nonsmoker

noncommissioned officer (nän′kə mish′ənd) ***noun*** a member of the armed forces, such as a corporal or sergeant, who holds a rank higher than the lowest enlisted person, but does not have the full rank of an officer.
non·com·mis·sioned officer • ***noun,*** *plural* **noncommissioned officers**

none (nun) ***pronoun*** **1** not one or not any [*None* of these books is new. *None* of the cake was eaten.] **2** no one [*None* but the brave will try.]
adverb in no way; not at all [We arrived *none* too soon.]
● The words **none** and **nun** sound alike.
None of us wanted to go home.
Our fifth-grade teacher was a *nun*.

nonsense (nän′sens) ***noun*** **1** speech or writing that is foolish or has no meaning. **2** silly or annoying behavior [I won't put up with any *nonsense*.]
non·sense • ***noun***

nonstop (nän′stäp′) ***adverb*** without making a stop [He was talking *nonstop*.]
adjective without a stop [a *nonstop* flight from Miami to Chicago].
non·stop • ***adverb*** • ***adjective***

noodle (nōōd′əl) ***noun*** a flat, narrow strip of dough, usually made with egg. Noodles are used especially in soups and casseroles.
noo·dle • ***noun***

nook (nook) ***noun*** **1** a corner of a room, or a part cut off from a main part [Next to the kitchen is a breakfast *nook*.] **2** a small, sheltered spot [When I'm hiking on a hot day, I tend to walk slowly through any shady *nook* I come across.]
nook • ***noun,*** *plural* **nooks**

noon (nōōn) ***noun*** twelve o'clock in the daytime.

noonday (nōōn′dā) ***noun*** noon.
noon·day • ***noun***

no one ***pronoun*** no person; not anybody; nobody.

noontime (nōōn′tīm) ***noun*** noon.
noon·time • ***noun***

noose (nōōs) ***noun*** a loop made by putting one end of a rope or cord through a knot. When the rope is pulled, the knot slides along the rope and the loop becomes smaller.
noose • ***noun,*** *plural* **nooses**

nor (nôr) ***conjunction*** and not; and not either [I know neither José *nor* Frank.]

normal (nôr′məl) ***adjective*** **1** agreeing with a standard; usual; regular [It is *normal* to make a mistake sometimes.] —Look for the WORD CHOICES box at the entry **usual**. **2** usual according to the laws of nature or science [The *normal* temperature of the human body is 98.6°F.]
noun what is normal; the usual condition, amount, level, or degree.
nor·mal • ***adjective*** • ***noun***

north (nôrth) ***noun*** **1** the direction to the right of a person who is facing the sunset [At night, sailors used stars to find *north*.] **2** a place or region in this direction [Most of my relatives live in the *north*.]
adjective **1** in, of, or to the north [the *north* side of town]. **2** from the north [a *north* wind].
adverb in the direction of the north; to the north [Go *north* five miles.]
—the North the northern part of the U.S., especially the part that formed the Union in the Civil War.

North America the northern continent in the Western Hemisphere. Canada, the U.S., and Mexico are in North America.
North A·mer·i·ca

North Carolina (nôrth′ kar′ə lī′nə) a State in the southeastern part of the U.S. Its capital is Raleigh. Abbreviated **NC** or **N.C.**
North Car·o·li·na

N

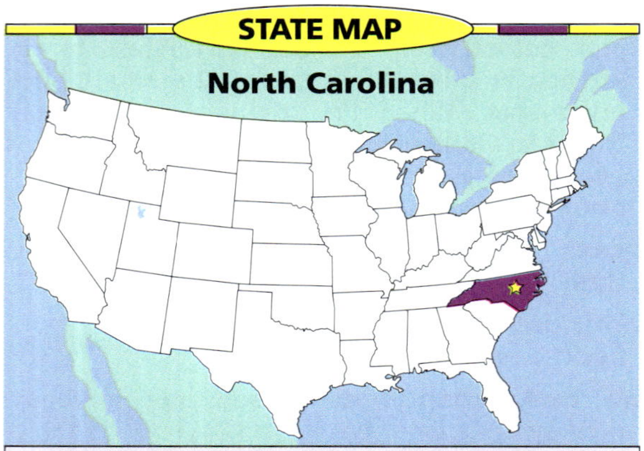

Statehood: 1789, the 12th state • **Capital:** Raleigh

North Dakota (nôrth′ də kō′tə) a State in the north central part of the U.S. Its capital is Bismarck. Abbreviated **ND, N.D.,** or **N.Dak.**
North Da·ko·ta

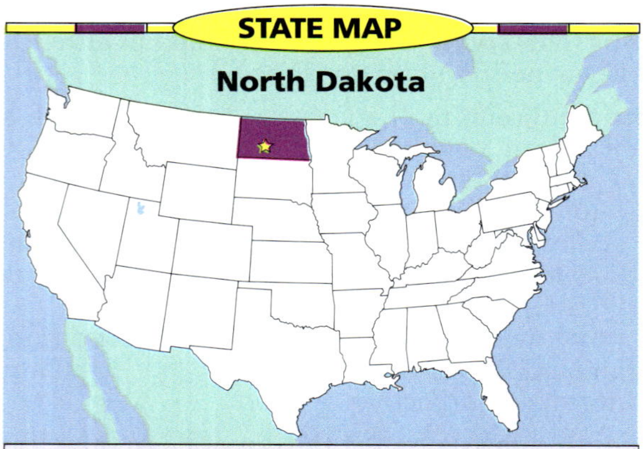

Statehood: 1889, the 39th state • **Capital:** Bismarck

northeast (nôrth ēst′) ***noun*** **1** the direction halfway between north and east [Look to the *northeast.*] **2** a place or region in this direction [His sister lives in the *northeast.*]
adjective **1** in, of, or to the northeast [the *northeast* part of the country; a *northeast* route]. **2** from the northeast [*northeast* winds].
adverb in the direction of the northeast; to the northeast [They sailed *northeast.*]
north·east • ***noun*** • ***adjective*** • ***adverb***

northeastern (nôrth ēs′tərn) ***adjective*** **1** in, of, or to the northeast [*northeastern* towns]. **2** from the northeast [*northeastern* winds].
north·east·ern • ***adjective***

northerly (nôr′*th*ər lē) ***adjective*** **1** in or toward the north [a *northerly* path through the woods]. **2** from the north [*northerly* winds]. This word can also be used as an adverb [They hiked *northerly* through the woods.]
north·er·ly • ***adjective***

northern (nôr′*th*ərn) ***adjective*** **1** in, of, or to the north [a *northern* climate]. **2** from the north [a *northern* wind].
north·ern • ***adjective***

Northerner (nôr′*th*ərn ər) ***noun*** a person born or living in the North.
North·ern·er • ***noun,*** *plural* **Northerners**

Northern Hemisphere the half of the earth that is north of the equator.
North·ern Hem·i·sphere

Northern Ireland a part of the United Kingdom, in the northeastern part of the island of Ireland.
North·ern Ire·land

North Pole the spot that is farthest north on the earth; northern end of the earth's axis.

North Sea a part of the Atlantic Ocean, east of Great Britain and west of Norway and Denmark.

northward (nôrth′wərd) ***adjective*** in the direction of the north [a *northward* journey]. This word can also be used as an adverb [We journeyed *northward.*]
north·ward • ***adjective***

northwards (nôrth′wərdz) ***adverb*** *the same as the adverb* **northward**.
north·wards • ***adverb***

northwest (nôrth west′) ***noun*** **1** the direction halfway between north and west [Look to the *northwest.*] **2** a place or region in this direction [Her brother lives in the *northwest.*]
adjective **1** in, of, or to the northwest [the *northwest* part of the country; a *northwest* passage]. **2** from the northwest [*northwest* winds].
adverb in the direction of the northwest; to the northwest [They traveled *northwest.*]
north·west • ***noun*** • ***adjective*** • ***adverb***

northwestern (nôrth wes′tərn) ***adjective*** **1** in, of, or to the northwest [*northwestern*

a	cat	ō	go	ʉ	fur	ə =	a *in* ago
ā	ape	ô	law, for	ch	chin		e *in* agent
ä	cot, car	o͝o	look	sh	she		i *in* pencil
e	ten	o͞o	tool	th	thin		o *in* atom
ē	me	oi	oil	*th*	then		u *in* circus
i	fit	ou	out	zh	measure		
ī	ice	u	up	ŋ	ring		

mountains]. **2** from the northwest [*northwestern* winds].
north·west·ern • *adjective*

Northwest Territories a large division of northern Canada, on the Arctic Ocean. Abbreviated **NT** or **N.W.T.**
North·west Ter·ri·to·ries

Norway (nôr′wā) a country in northern Europe, west of Sweden.
Nor·way

Norwegian (nôr wē′jən) *noun* **1** a person born or living in Norway. **2** the language of Norway.
Nor·we·gian • *noun, plural for sense 1 only* **Norwegians**

nose (nōz) *noun* **1** the part of the face above the mouth that has the two openings for smelling and breathing. **2** an animal's snout. **3** the sense of smell [a dog with a good *nose*]. **4** something, such as the front of an aiplane, that is like a nose in shape or position.
verb **1** to move cautiously with the front end forward [The ship *nosed* into the harbor.] **2** to meddle in another's affairs [Stop *nosing* in my business!] **3** to smell with the nose [The hounds *nosed* the deer in the woods.] **4** to rub, push, or check with the nose.
—under one's nose in plain view.
nose • *noun, plural* **noses** • *verb* **nosed, nosing**

nosebleed (nōz′blēd) *noun* the condition of bleeding from the nose.
nose·bleed • *noun, plural* **nosebleeds**

nostril (näs′trəl) *noun* either of the two openings in the nose through which a person smells and breathes.
nos·tril • *noun, plural* **nostrils**

nosy (nō′zē) [*an informal word*] *adjective* too curious about others' affairs; prying.
nos·y • *adjective* **nosier, nosiest**

not (nät) *adverb* in no way; to no degree [Do *not* talk. They are *not* happy.]
● The words **not** and **knot** sound alike.
I will *not* be coming to dinner.
The child has a *knot* in her shoelace.

notable (nōt′ə bəl) *adjective* worth noticing or paying attention to; remarkable [a *notable* success].
no·ta·ble • *adjective*

notation (nō tā′shən) *noun* **1** a brief note jotted down to remind a person of something [She made a *notation* to send a letter.] **2** a system of signs or symbols used to stand for various things such as words, numbers, or musical notes.
no·ta·tion • *noun, plural* **notations**

notch (näch) *noun* a cut in the form of a V, made in an edge or across a surface.
verb to cut a notch in.
notch • *noun, plural* **notches** • *verb* **notched, notching**

note (nōt) *noun* **1** a word, phrase, or sentence written down to help a person remember something [In some classes, students take *notes*.] **2** a short letter [She sent a *note* to invite them to the party.] **3** a printed explanation or comment added to a book. **4** a piece of paper with a written promise to pay back a sum of money. **5** close attention; notice [Take *note* of what I say.] **6** a musical tone. **7** the symbol for such a tone, showing how long it is to be sounded [a quarter *note*]. **8** a sign or hint [a *note* of sadness in her voice]. **9** importance or fame [a person of *note*].
verb **1** to notice; observe [I *noted* that you left early.] **2** to set down in writing; make a note of [His teacher *noted* on his report card that he was hard-working.]
note • *noun, plural* **notes** • *verb* **noted, noting**

notebook (nōt′bo͝ok) *noun* a book with blank pages to keep notes.
note·book • *noun, plural* **notebooks**

notebook computer *noun* a small laptop computer.
notebook computer • *noun, plural* **notebook computers**

noted (nōt′əd) *adjective* famous; well-known [a *noted* poet].
not·ed • *adjective*

nothing (nuth′iŋ) *noun* **1** not anything; no thing [We saw *nothing* to frighten us.] **2** a person or thing not important in any way [A few falls are *nothing* to a gymnast.] **3** zero [The score is still *nothing* to *nothing*.]
adverb in no way; not at all [It's *nothing* like I thought it would be.]
—for nothing **1** free [No one gives something *for nothing*.] **2** with no effect; pointless [I'm afraid that all our work was *for nothing*.]
noth·ing • *noun, plural for sense 2 only* **nothings** • *adverb*

notice (nōt′is) *noun* **1** the fact of being seen or observed; observation [He escaped *notice* by hiding behind a door.] **2** attention; heed;

N

regard [Pay them no *notice*.] **3** the act of seeing or observing; interested or favorable attention [She took *notice* of his kindness.] **4** an announcement or warning [Did you give your landlord *notice* that you were moving?] **5** a written or printed announcement in a public place or publication [a *notice* of a change in the schedule].
verb to pay attention to; take note of; observe [I didn't *notice* when she walked into the room.]
no·tice • ***noun**, plural for senses 4 and 5 only* **notices** • ***verb*** **noticed, noticing**

noticeable (nōt′is ə bəl) ***adjective*** easily seen; likely to be noticed [a *noticeable* improvement].
no·tice·a·ble • ***adjective***

WORD CHOICES

Synonyms of **noticeable**

The words **noticeable**, **prominent**, and **remarkable** share the meaning "likely to be noticed."

a *noticeable* change in the weather

a *prominent* nose

a *remarkable* sense of smell

notify (nōt′i fī′) ***verb*** to let know; give notice to; inform [Please *notify* me when they arrive.] —Look for the WORD CHOICES box at the entry **inform**.
no·ti·fy • ***verb*** **notified, notifying, notifies**

notion (nō′shən) ***noun*** **1** a general idea [Do you have any *notion* of what he meant?] —Look for the WORD CHOICES box at the entry **idea**. **2** a sudden fancy; a desire or whim [She had a *notion* to sing and play the piano at the party.] **3 notions** needles, thread, pins, and other small, useful things that are sold in a store.
no·tion • ***noun**, plural* **notions**

notorious (nō tôr′ē əs) ***adjective*** well-known, especially for something bad [She is *notorious* for telling dull stories.]
no·to·ri·ous • ***adjective***

noun (noun) ***noun*** a word that is the name of something. A noun can name a thing (*truth*, the *dog*, an *apple*), a person (a *girl, Tom*, the *teacher*), or a place (a *state, Ohio*).
noun • ***noun**, plural* **nouns**

nourish (nʉr′ish) ***verb*** **1** to provide with what is needed for life and growth; feed [Water and sunlight *nourish* plants.] **2** to make grow; foster; promote [Patience and encouragement *nourish* learning.]
nour·ish • ***verb*** **nourished, nourishing**

nourishment (nʉr′ish mənt) ***noun*** something that is needed for life and growth; food.
nour·ish·ment • ***noun***

Nov. *abbreviation for* November.

Nova Scotia (nō′və skō′shə) a province of Canada, on the eastern coast. Abbreviated **NS** or **N.S.**
No·va Sco·tia

novel (näv′əl) ***adjective*** new and unusual [In 1895, the automobile was still a *novel* invention.]
noun a long story about imaginary people and events. A novel is usually a complete book.
nov·el • ***adjective*** • ***noun**, plural* **novels**

novelist (näv′əl ist) ***noun*** a person who writes novels.
nov·el·ist • ***noun**, plural* **novelists**

novelty (näv′əl tē) ***noun*** **1** the quality of being new or unusual [the *novelty* of rain in the desert]. **2** something that is new, fresh, or unusual; change [Flying was a *novelty* in 1920.] **3** *usually* **novelties** small, often cheap toys, decorations, or similar objects.
nov·el·ty • ***noun**, plural for senses 2 and 3 only* **novelties**

November (nō vem′bər) ***noun*** the eleventh month of the year. November has 30 days. Abbreviated **Nov.**
No·vem·ber • ***noun***

WORD HISTORY

November

The name of this month comes from the Latin word for "nine." **November** was the ninth month of the ancient Roman year, which began with March, not January.

a	cat	ō	go	ʉ	fur	ə = a *in* ago	
ā	ape	ô	law, for	ch	chin	e *in* agent	
ä	cot, car	oo	look	sh	she	i *in* pencil	
e	ten	ōō	tool	th	thin	o *in* atom	
ē	me	oi	oil	*th*	then	u *in* circus	
i	fit	ou	out	zh	measure		
ī	ice	u	up	ŋ	ring		

now (nou) ***adverb*** **1** at this moment; at the present time [They are eating *now*.] **2** at once; immediately [We'd better leave *now* before it starts to rain.] **3** at that time; then [*Now* their happiness was complete.] **4** with things the way they are [*Now* we'll never know what happened.] *Now* is also used without a definite meaning at the beginning of a sentence, to emphasize a thought or feeling [*Now* see here! *Now* stop that!]
conjunction since; seeing that [*Now* that you're here, we can start.]
noun the present time [That's all for *now*.]
—just now only a short while ago [They left *just now*.] **—now and again** sometimes; once in a while. **—now and then** sometimes; once in a while.

nowadays (nou′ə dāz) ***adverb*** in these days; at the present time [News travels fast *nowadays*.]
now·a·days • ***adverb***

nowhere (nō′hwer *or* nō′wər) ***adverb*** not in, at, or to any place [His wallet was *nowhere* to be found.]
noun a place that does not exist or is not well-known [lost in the middle of *nowhere*].
no·where • ***adverb*** • ***noun***

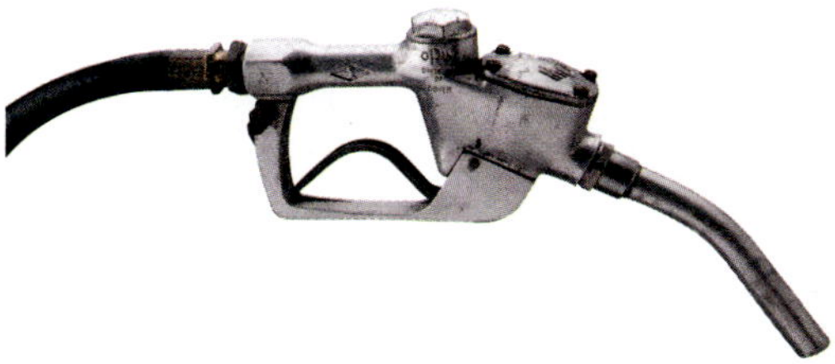

nozzle

nozzle (näz′əl) ***noun*** a spout at the end of a hose or pipe.
noz·zle • ***noun,*** *plural* **nozzles**

NS or **N.S.** *abbreviation for* Nova Scotia.

NT *abbreviation for* Northwest Territories.

NU *abbreviation for* Nunavut.

nuclear (no͞o′klē ər *or* nyo͞o′klē ər) ***adjective*** **1** involving or using the nuclei of atoms [*nuclear* energy]. **2** of or involving atomic bombs or similar weapons.
nu·cle·ar • ***adjective***

nuclear energy ***noun*** the energy released from a radioactive substance or in nuclear fission or nuclear fusion.

nuclear fission ***noun*** the process of splitting the nuclei of atoms. Nuclear fission is used in the atomic bomb and in nuclear reactors.

nuclear fusion ***noun*** the process of forcing together the nuclei of atoms. Nuclear fusion is used in the hydrogen bomb.

nuclear reactor ***noun*** a device that starts nuclear fission in a special material and then keeps it going. Nuclear reactors are used to produce energy for electricity or radioactive substances for weapons and research.
nuclear reactor • ***noun,*** *plural* **nuclear reactors**

nuclei (no͞o′klē ī′ *or* nyo͞o′klē ī′) ***noun*** *a plural of* **nucleus**.

nucleus (no͞o′klē əs *or* nyo͞o′klē əs) ***noun*** **1** the central part around which other things are grouped or gathered [His few books from childhood became the *nucleus* of a large library.] **2** the small mass at the center of most living cells. It is needed for the plant or animal to grow, reproduce itself, or perform any other cell activity. **3** the central part of an atom. It is made up of protons and neutrons. The electrons revolve around the nucleus.
nu·cle·us • ***noun,*** *plural* **nu·cle·i** (no͞o′klē ī *or* nyo͞o′klē ī) or **nucleuses**

nude (no͞od *or* nyo͞od) ***adjective*** completely without covering or clothing; naked.

nudge (nuj) ***verb*** to push or poke gently in order to get the attention of.
noun a gentle push, especially with the elbow.
nudge • ***verb*** **nudged, nudging** • ***noun,*** *plural* **nudges**

nugget (nug′ət) ***noun*** a lump or rough piece [a gold *nugget*].
nug·get • ***noun,*** *plural* **nuggets**

nuisance (no͞o′səns *or* nyo͞o′səns) ***noun*** an act, thing, or person that causes trouble or bother.
nui·sance • ***noun,*** *plural* **nuisances**

numb (num) ***adjective*** not able to feel or feeling very little [*numb* with cold; *numb* with grief].
verb to make numb [The cold *numbed* his toes.]
numb • ***adjective*** **number, numbest** • ***verb*** **numbed, numbing**

number (num′bər) ***noun*** **1** a symbol or word that is used in counting or that tells how many or which one in a series. Two, tenth, 7, and 237 are all numbers. **2** the sum or total of persons or things [Can you guess the *number* of pennies in the jar?] **3** quantity or amount that is not counted exactly [She made a

N

number of errors in her test. A small *number* of people waited outside.]
verb **1** to give a number or numbers to [Please *number* the pages.] **2** to amount to in number; total [The guests *numbered* almost eighty.] **3** to include as one of a group or class [He is *numbered* among our friends.] **4** to limit the number of [The old horse's days were *numbered*.]
num·ber • ***noun,*** *plural* **numbers** • ***verb*** **numbered, numbering**

numberless (num′bər ləs) ***adjective*** too many to be counted [the *numberless* stars in the sky].
num·ber·less • ***adjective***

numeral (no͞o′mər əl *or* nyo͞o′mər əl) ***noun*** a figure or letter, or a group of these that stands for a number [Roman *numerals*. The *numeral* for nine is 9.]
nu·mer·al • ***noun,*** *plural* **numerals**

numerator (no͞o′mə rāt′ər *or* nyo͞o′mə rāt′ər) ***noun*** the number above or to the left of the line in a fraction. In the fraction $^2/_5$, 2 is the numerator.
nu·mer·a·tor • ***noun,*** *plural* **numerators**

numerical (no͞o mer′i kəl *or* nyo͞o mer′i kəl) ***adjective*** having to do with a number or numbers; by numbers [Put the pages in *numerical* order.]
nu·mer·i·cal • ***adjective***

numerous (no͞o′mər əs *or* nyo͞o′mər əs) ***adjective*** very many [She has *numerous* friends.] —Look for the WORD CHOICES box at the entry **many**.
nu·mer·ous • ***adjective***

nun (nun) ***noun*** a woman who has joined a religious order.
nun • ***noun,*** *plural* **nuns**
● The words **nun** and **none** sound alike.
A *nun* was our fifth-grade teacher.
None of us wanted to go home.

Nunavut (no͞o′nə vo͞ot) a territory of northern Canada. Abbreviated **NU**.
Nu·na·vut

nurse (nʉrs) ***noun*** **1** a person who has been trained to take care of sick people, help doctors, and perform many other related activities. **2** a person hired to take care of a child or children.
verb **1** to take care of [She *nursed* her sick brother.] **2** to treat; try to cure [I'm *nursing* a cold.] **3** to give milk to from a breast [The mother *nursed* her baby.] **4** to feed at the breast [We watched the puppies *nursing*.]
nurse • ***noun,*** *plural* **nurses** • ***verb*** **nursed, nursing**

nursery (nʉrs′ər ē) ***noun*** **1** a baby's bedroom. **2** a room set aside for the special use of children or infants. **3** a place where very young children, not yet in school, may be cared for during the day while their parents are working. **4** a place where young trees or plants are raised and sold.
nurs·er·y • ***noun,*** *plural* **nurseries**

nursery school ***noun*** a school for children who are too young for kindergarten.
nursery school • ***noun,*** *plural* **nursery schools**

nut (nut) ***noun*** **1** the dry fruit of certain kinds of trees or shrubs. Nuts have a hard or leathery shell and a kernel inside that is often good to eat. Walnuts, pecans, and acorns are nuts. **2** the kernel of a nut. **3** a small metal piece with a hole in the center. The nut screws onto a bolt to hold the bolt in place. **4** [*a slang use*] a person who does silly or crazy things.
nut • ***noun,*** *plural* **nuts**

nutcracker (nut′krak ər) ***noun*** a tool that is used to crack the shells of nuts.
nut·crack·er • ***noun,*** *plural* **nutcrackers**

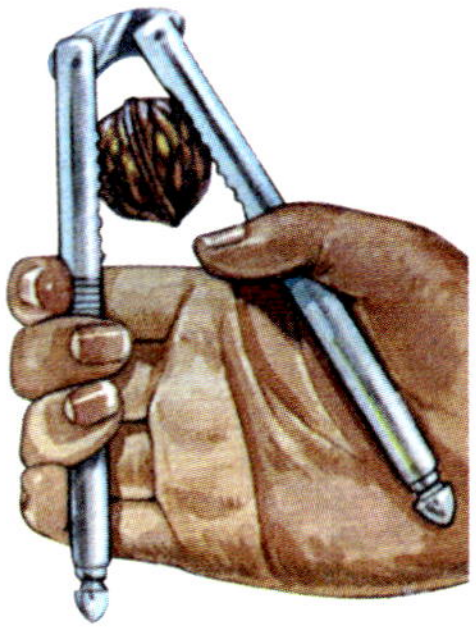
nutcracker

nutmeg (nut′meg) ***noun*** the hard seed of a tropical tree. It is grated for use as a spice.
nut·meg • ***noun,*** *plural* **nutmegs**

nutrient (no͞o′trē ənt *or* nyo͞o′trē ənt) ***noun*** any substance or matter that is needed for the life and growth of plants, animals, or people. Proteins, minerals, and vitamins are nutrients.
nu·tri·ent • ***noun,*** *plural* **nutrients**

nutrition (no͞o trish′ən *or* nyo͞o trish′ən) ***noun*** **1** the process by which an animal or plant takes in food and uses it in living and growing. **2** food; nourishment.
nu·tri·tion • ***noun***

a	cat	ō	go	ʉ	fur	ə = a	*in* ago
ā	ape	ô	law, for	ch	chin	e	*in* agent
ä	cot, car	o͝o	look	sh	she	i	*in* pencil
e	ten	o͞o	tool	th	thin	o	*in* atom
ē	me	oi	oil	*th*	then	u	*in* circus
i	fit	ou	out	zh	measure		
ī	ice	u	up	ŋ	ring		

nutritious (no͞o trish′əs *or* nyo͞o trish′əs) ***adjective*** having value as food [a *nutritious* meal].
nu·tri·tious • ***adjective***

nuts (nuts) [*a slang word*] ***adjective*** crazy; foolish.
—be nuts about [*a slang use*] to like or love very much [She *is nuts about* football.]

nutty (nut′ē) ***adjective*** **1** having nuts in it [a *nutty* candy bar]. **2** that tastes like nuts. **3** [*a slang use*] crazy, silly, or very enthusiastic.
nut·ty • ***adjective*** **nuttier, nuttiest**

nuzzle (nuz′əl) ***verb*** to push against or rub with the nose [The horse *nuzzled* him gently.]
nuz·zle • ***verb*** **nuzzled, nuzzling**

NV *abbreviation for* Nevada.

NW or **N.W.** *abbreviation for* **1** northwest. **2** northwestern.

N.W.T. *abbreviation for* Northwest Territories.

NY or **N.Y.** *abbreviation for* New York.

nylon (nī′län) ***noun*** a very strong, elastic material that is made from chemicals. Nylon is used to make thread, bristles, clothes, fibers, various plastics, and many other things.
ny·lon • ***noun***

nymph (nimf) ***noun*** **1** any of the nature goddesses of old Greek and Roman legends. Nymphs lived in trees, woods, hills, or rivers. They usually were represented as beautiful young women. **2** the form of some insects before they become fully adult.
nymph • ***noun,*** *plural* **nymphs**

N

O o

Oo Oo Oo Oo

The letter **o** *stands for many different vowel sounds. The* **o** *that you hear in the word* **owl** *is just one of these sounds. You hear the long vowel sound of* **o** *in the words* **go** *and* **low**. *The short vowel sound of* **o** *is used in the words* **dot**, **hot**, *and* **not**. *The* **o** *in each of the following words has a different sound:* **come**, **two**, **women**. *Listen to the sound that the combination of* **o** *and another letter forms in these words:* **boil** *and* **boy**, **cloud** *and* **clown**, **could** *and* **cook**. *The double* **o** *is pronounced differently in the words* **food** *and* **foot**.

o or **O** (ō) ***noun*** the fifteenth letter of the English alphabet.
o or **O** • ***noun**, plural* **o's** or **O's**

o' (ə *or* ō) ***preposition*** *a short form of* **of**.

O. *an abbreviation for* Ohio.

oak (ōk) ***noun*** **1** a large tree with hard wood and nuts called acorns. **2** the wood of this tree, used in making furniture and for floors.
oak • ***noun**, plural for sense 1 only* **oaks**

oar (ôr) ***noun*** a long pole with a flat blade at one end. Oars are used to row a boat.
oar • ***noun**, plural* **oars**
• The words **oar, or,** and **ore** sound alike.
The wave knocked the *oar* from my hand.
He is either innocent *or* guilty.
They took iron *ore* from the mine.

oasis (ō ā′sis) ***noun*** a place in a desert where there is water for plants to grow.
o·a·sis • ***noun**, plural* **o·a·ses** (ō ā′sēz)

oat (ōt) ***noun*** **1** *usually* **oats** a widely grown cereal grass. **2** *usually* **oats** the seed, or grain, of this grass, used as food or as animal feed.
oat • ***noun**, plural* **oats**

oath (ōth) ***noun*** **1** a statement in which a person swears that he or she will speak the truth or keep a promise. **2** a curse or swearword.
oath • ***noun**, plural* **oaths** (ō*th*z *or* ōths)

oatmeal (ōt′mēl) ***noun*** **1** meal that is made by grinding or rolling oats. **2** a soft, cooked cereal that is made by boiling such meal.
oat·meal • ***noun***

Obama (ō bä′mə) **Barack** (bə räk′) 1961- ; the forty-fourth president of the U.S., from 2009.
O·bam·a, Ba·rack

obedience (ō bē′dē əns) ***noun*** the act or practice of obeying or a willingness to obey.
o·be·di·ence • ***noun***

obedient (ō bē′dē ənt) ***adjective*** obeying or willing to obey; following orders [Our dog was trained to be *obedient*.]
o·be·di·ent • ***adjective***

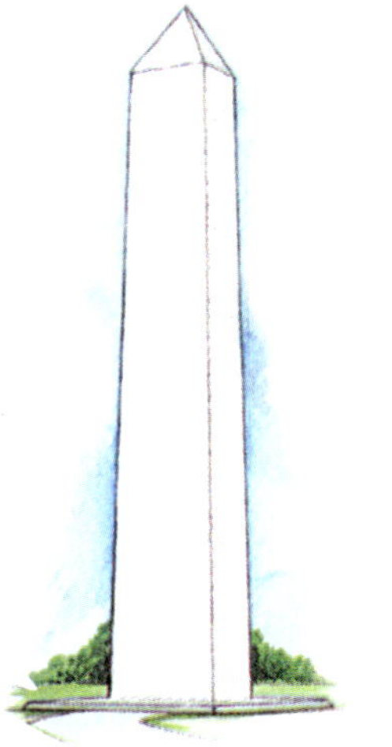

obelisk

obelisk (äb′ə lisk) ***noun*** a tall stone pillar with four sides and a pointed top.
ob·e·lisk • ***noun**, plural* **obelisks**

a	cat	ō	go	ʉ	fur	ə = a *in* ago	
ā	ape	ô	law, for	ch	chin	e *in* agent	
ä	cot, car	oo	look	sh	she	i *in* pencil	
e	ten	ōō	tool	th	thin	o *in* atom	
ē	me	oi	oil	*th*	then	u *in* circus	
i	fit	ou	out	zh	measure		
ī	ice	u	up	ŋ	ring		

obese (ō bēs′) *adjective* very fat [an *obese* person].
o·bese • *adjective*

obey (ō bā′) *verb* **1** to carry out the orders or wishes of [Soldiers must *obey* their officers.] **2** to follow a law, order, or request; do as one is told [*Obey* all traffic laws.]
o·bey • *verb* **obeyed, obeying**

object (äb′jekt *for n.;* əb jekt′ *for v.*) *noun* **1** a thing that can be seen or touched; something that takes up space [That brown *object* is a purse.] **2** a person or thing toward which someone turns his or her thoughts, feelings, or actions [the *object* of his love]. **3** a thing that a person is trying to reach; goal; purpose [Making others happy was her main *object* in life.] **4** *a short form of* **direct object** or **indirect object**. **5** the noun or pronoun that follows a preposition [In "going to the store," "store" is the *object* of the preposition "to."]
verb **1** to dislike or disapprove of something [Bill *objects* to wide neckties.] **2** to tell as a reason for not liking or approving; protest [Jane *objected* that the prices were too high.]
ob·ject • *noun, plural* **objects**
• *verb* **objected, objecting**

objection (äb jek′shən) *noun* **1** a feeling of not liking or not approving [I have no *objection* to the plan.] **2** a reason for not liking or not approving [My *objection* is that it's too cold.]
ob·jec·tion • *noun, plural* **objections**

objective (äb jek′tiv) *adjective* not having or showing a strong opinion for or against something [A judge must remain *objective*.]
noun something that someone tries to reach or achieve; goal; purpose.
ob·jec·tive • *adjective* • *noun, plural* **objectives**

obligate (äb′li gāt′) *verb* to make someone do something by a contract, promise, or sense of duty [I'm *obligated* to finish my chores first.]
ob·li·gate • *verb* **obligated, obligating**

obligation (äb′li gā′shən) *noun* **1** a contract, promise, or feeling of duty that requires a person to do something [As a good citizen, she fulfilled her *obligation* to vote.] **2** the condition of being obligated by duty, a promise, or a contract [His kindness put me under *obligation* to him.]
ob·li·ga·tion • *noun, plural* **obligations**

oblige (ə blīj′) *verb* **1** to make a person do something because a law, promise, or feeling of duty demands it [Some religions *oblige* people to fast on certain days.] **2** to make grateful or thankful for a favor, service, or kindness received [We are much *obliged* for your help.]
o·blige • *verb* **obliged, obliging**

oblique (ō blēk′) *adjective* **1** not level or not straight up and down; slanting. **2** not straight to the point; not direct [an *oblique* remark].
ob·lique • *adjective*

oblong (äb′lôŋ) *adjective* longer than it is wide [an *oblong* box].
ob·long • *adjective*

obnoxious (äb näk′shəs) *adjective* very unpleasant; disgusting [an *obnoxious*, noisy neighbor].
ob·nox·ious • *adjective*

oboe (ō′bō) *noun* a woodwind instrument with a high tone. Its mouthpiece uses two reeds.
o·boe • *noun, plural* **oboes**

oboe

obscure (äb skyoor′) *adjective* **1** not easily understood [an *obscure* answer]. **2** not easily seen or heard [an *obscure* figure in the fog]. **3** not famous or well-known [an *obscure* poet].
verb to make obscure [In an eclipse, the moon *obscures* the sun.]
ob·scure • *adjective* • *verb* **obscured, obscuring**

observation (äb′zər vā′shən) *noun* **1** the act or power of seeing or noticing [It's a good night for *observation* of the stars.] **2** the fact of being seen or noticed [We came in the back way to avoid *observation*.] **3** a remark or comment [the writer's *observations* on life].
ob·ser·va·tion • *noun, plural* **observations**

observatory (äb zurv′ə tôr′ē) *noun* a building with telescopes and other equipment in it for studying the sun, moon, stars, planets, and weather.
ob·serv·a·to·ry • *noun, plural* **observatories**

observe (äb zurv′) *verb* **1** to keep or follow; be guided by [You must *observe* the rules of the game.] **2** to celebrate according to custom [We *observe* Thanksgiving with a turkey dinner.]

O

3 to see, watch, or notice [I *observed* that the child was smiling.] **4** to remark or comment ["It may rain," she observed.]
ob·serve • *verb* **observed, observing**

obsolete (äb sə lēt′) *adjective* no longer in use or fashion; out-of-date [an *obsolete* word; an *obsolete* airplane].
ob·so·lete • *adjective*

obstacle (äb′stə kəl) *noun* anything that gets in the way or blocks progress [Lack of education was the main *obstacle* to his success.]
ob·sta·cle • *noun, plural* **obstacles**

obstinate (äb′sti nət) *adjective* not willing to give in or to change one's mind; stubborn [The *obstinate* child refused to answer.]
ob·sti·nate • *adjective*

obstruct (äb strukt′) *verb* **1** to block or stop up; clog [Grease *obstructed* the sink drain.] **2** to hinder or hold back [A long argument *obstructed* planning for the school picnic.] —Look for the WORD CHOICES box at the entry **hinder**. **3** to be in the way of [The billboards *obstructed* our view.]
ob·struct • *verb* **obstructed, obstructing**

obstruction (äb struk′shən) *noun* **1** anything that obstructs; obstacle [the *obstruction* in the pipe]. **2** an act of obstructing or the condition of being obstructed [the *obstruction* of the road].
ob·struc·tion • *noun, plural* **obstructions**

obtain (äb tān′) *verb* to get through effort [She managed to *obtain* a copy of the book.] —Look for the WORD CHOICES box at the entry **get**.
ob·tain • *verb* **obtained, obtaining**

obvious (äb′vē əs) *adjective* easy to see or understand; plain; clear [an *obvious* danger].
ob·vi·ous • *adjective*

occasion (ō kā′zhən) *noun* **1** a special time or happening; important event [Independence Day is an *occasion* to celebrate.] **2** a particular time [We've met on several *occasions* before now.] **3** a suitable time; opportunity [Did you have *occasion* to visit his relatives?]
oc·ca·sion • *noun, plural* **occasions**

occasional (ō kā′zhə nəl) *adjective* happening only once in a while [an *occasional* trip to town to see a movie].
oc·ca·sion·al • *adjective*

occupant (äk′yoo pənt) *noun* a person or thing that occupies a place or position [a former *occupant* of the White House].
oc·cu·pant • *noun, plural* **occupants**

occupation (äk′yoo pā′shən) *noun* **1** the work that a person does to earn a living; a profession, business, or trade [He left his *occupation* as an actor and became a painter.] **2** the act of occupying or the condition of being occupied [The rebels were in hiding during the army's *occupation* of the city.]
oc·cu·pa·tion • *noun, plural* **occupations**

occupy (äk′yoo pī′) *verb* **1** to take up; fill [The store *occupies* the entire building.] **2** to take possession of a place by capturing it or settling in it [The German army *occupied* the city.] **3** to have and hold [She *occupies* an important position in the government.] **4** to live in [We *occupy* the house next door.] **5** to keep busy; employ [Many activities *occupy* his time.]
oc·cu·py • *verb* **occupied, occupying, occupies**

occur (ə kur′) *verb* **1** to take place; happen [That event *occurred* years ago.] **2** to come into one's mind [The idea never *occurred* to me.] **3** to be found; exist [Fish *occur* in most rivers.]
oc·cur • *verb* **occurred, occurring**

occurrence (ə kur′əns) *noun* **1** the act or fact of occurring [The *occurrence* of rain in the desert is very rare.] **2** something that occurs; an event or happening [tales of strange *occurrences* in the abandoned castle] —Look for the WORD CHOICES box at the entry **event**.
oc·cur·rence • *noun, plural* **occurrences**

ocean (ō′shən) *noun* **1** the whole body of salt water that covers more than two thirds of the earth's surface; the sea. **2** one of the four main parts into which this body of water is divided. The Atlantic, Pacific, Indian, and Arctic are the four oceans.
o·cean • *noun, plural* **oceans**

ocelot (äs′ə lät) *noun* a wildcat that has a yellowish coat spotted with black. Ocelots are found in North and South America.
o·ce·lot • *noun, plural* **ocelots** or **ocelot**

a	cat	ō	go	u̇r	fur	ə =	a *in* ago
ā	ape	ô	law, for	ch	chin		e *in* agent
ä	cot, car	oo	look	sh	she		i *in* pencil
e	ten	o͞o	tool	th	thin		o *in* atom
ē	me	oi	oil	*th*	then		u *in* circus
i	fit	ou	out	zh	measure		
ī	ice	u	up	ŋ	ring		

ocelot

o'clock (ə kläk′ *or* ō kläk′) *adverb* of the clock; according to the clock [12 *o'clock* noon].

Oct. *abbreviation for* October.

octagon (äk′tə gän) *noun* a flat figure that has eight angles and eight sides.
oc·ta·gon • *noun, plural* **octagons**

octave (äk′tiv) *noun* the eight tones that make up a musical scale.
oc·tave • *noun, plural* **octaves**

October (äk tō′bər) *noun* the tenth month of the year. October has 31 days. Abbreviated **Oct.**
Oc·to·ber • *noun*

octopus

octopus (äk′tə po͝os) *noun* a sea animal that has a soft body and eight long arms covered with suckers.
oc·to·pus • *noun, plural* **octopuses**

odd (äd) *adjective* **1** not the usual or regular; strange; peculiar [What an *odd* thing to say!] —Look for the WORD CHOICES box at the entry **strange**. **2** left over from what was once a pair or set [a few *odd* volumes of an encyclopedia]. **3** not regular; occasional [He kept himself busy by doing *odd* jobs.] **4** having a remainder of one when divided by two; not even [7, 15, and 43 are *odd* numbers.]
odd • *adjective* **odder, oddest**

oddity (äd′i tē) *noun* **1** a strange or unusual person or thing [A four-leaf clover is an *oddity*.] **2** the quality or condition of being odd, or strange [the *oddity* of their costumes].
odd·i·ty • *noun, plural* **oddities**

odds (ädz) *plural noun* a difference that favors one side over the other; advantage [a struggle against great *odds*].
—at odds having a quarrel; disagreeing [We were *at odds* over which TV program to watch.]

odds and ends *plural noun* scraps and small bits left over.

odor (ō′dər) *noun* smell; scent [the *odor* of flowers; kitchen *odors*].
o·dor • *noun, plural* **odors**

of (uv *or* äv *or* əv) *preposition* **1** resulting from; caused by [He died *of* a fever.] **2** at a distance from [a mile east *of* town]. **3** written or made by [the novels *of* Dickens]. **4** from the whole that is or the total number that are [part *of* the time; one *of* his sisters]. **5** made from [a sheet *of* paper]. **6** belonging to [the pages *of* a book]. **7** containing [a bag *of* nuts]. **8** that is [a height *of* six feet; the State *of* Iowa]. **9** having as a goal or object [a reader *of* books; the education *of* children]. **10** having as an important quality [a man *of* honor]. **11** about; concerning [Think *of* me when I'm away.] **12** before: this sense is used in telling time [It's ten *of* four.]

off (ôf) *adverb* **1** away; to or at some other place [They moved *off* down the road.] **2** so that it is or they are no longer on or attached [Please take *off* your hat.] **3** at a later time [My birthday is only two weeks *off*.] **4** so that it is or they are no longer working or going on [Turn the radio *off*.] **5** away from work [Let's take the day *off*.]
preposition **1** not on or attached to; away from [There's a car *off* the road.] **2** branching out from [a lane *off* the main road]. **3** free or released from [*off* duty]. **4** below the usual level [20% *off* the usual price].
adjective **1** not on or attached [My shoes are

O

off.] **2** not working or taking place [The radio is *off*. Our trip is *off*.] **3** wrong; in error [Your figures are a little *off*.] **4** below the usual level [Business is *off* a little.]
—off and on now and then.

offend (ə fend′) ***verb*** to hurt the feelings of; make angry or upset; insult.
of·fend • ***verb*** **offended, offending**

WORD CHOICES

Synonyms of **offend**

The words **offend, insult,** and **outrage** share the meaning "to make angry or upset."

Her constant interruptions *offended* me.

I was *insulted* when they called me a liar.

His cruelty to his pets *outraged* me.

offense (ə fens′ *for senses 1 and 2;* ô′fens′ *for sense 3*) ***noun*** **1** the act of doing wrong, or of breaking a rule or law [a traffic *offense*]. **2** something that causes anger or hurt feelings [Those rude remarks would be an *offense* to anyone.] **3** the side that is trying to score in a game [The quarterback leads the *offense*.]
of·fense • ***noun,*** *plural* **offenses**

offensive (ə fen′siv) ***adjective*** **1** unpleasant; disgusting [an *offensive* odor]. **2** causing anger or hurt feelings; insulting [Their *offensive* remarks surprised everybody in the room.] **3** used for attacking [*offensive* weapons].
noun an attack or a position for attacking [The army is ready to take the *offensive*.]
of·fen·sive • ***adjective*** • ***noun,*** *plural* **offensives**

offer (ôf′ər *or* äf′ər) ***verb*** **1** to put forward for someone to take or refuse [She *offered* him a piece of cake.] **2** to present for consideration; propose [He *offered* a few suggestions.]
noun **1** the act of offering [Will you accept our *offer* of help?] **2** something offered [I turned down his *offer* of $50 for the books.]
of·fer • ***verb*** **offered, offering** • ***noun,*** *plural* **offers**

office (ôf′is *or* äf′is) ***noun*** **1** the place where a certain kind of business or work is carried on [a lawyer's *office;* the main *office* of the company]. **2** all the people working in such a place [The *office* gave $100 to the charity.] **3** an important position or duty [the *office* of mayor] —Look for the WORD CHOICES box at the entry **position**.
of·fice • ***noun,*** *plural* **offices**

officer (ôf′i sər *or* äf′i sər) ***noun*** **1** a person who commands others in the armed forces. Generals, admirals, and lieutenants are officers. **2** a person who holds a position of authority in a business, club, or other organization [an *officer* of the local bank]. **3** a member of a police force.
of·fi·cer • ***noun,*** *plural* **officers**

official (ə fish′əl) ***noun*** a person who holds an office, especially in government.
adjective **1** of or having to do with an office [*official* duties]. **2** coming from a person who has authority [an *official* request from the mayor]. **3** fit for an important officer; formal [an *official* welcome to the city]. **4** set by authority [the *official* language of a country].
of·fi·cial • ***noun,*** *plural* **officials** • ***adjective***

offshore (ôf′shôr′) ***adjective*** **1** moving away from the shore [an *offshore* current]. **2** at some distance from shore [an *offshore* island; *offshore* drilling for oil].
off·shore • ***adjective***

offspring (ôf′spriŋ) ***noun*** a child or animal as related to its parent [a mother and her *offspring*].
off·spring • ***noun,*** *plural* **offspring** or **offsprings**

often (ôf′ən *or* ôf′tən) ***adverb*** many times; frequently [She *often* walks into town.]
of·ten • ***adverb***

ogre (ō′gər) ***noun*** **1** a giant who eats people. Ogres appear in legends and fairy tales. **2** a person who is evil or cruel.
o·gre • ***noun,*** *plural* **ogres**

oh (ō) ***interjection*** a word that is used to show surprise, fear, wonder, or other strong feeling.
• The words **oh** and **owe** sound alike.
She cried "*Oh!*" when the door slammed.
We all *owe* you an apology.

a	cat	ō	go	ʉ	fur	ə = a *in* ago	
ā	ape	ô	law, for	ch	chin	e *in* agent	
ä	cot, car	oo	look	sh	she	i *in* pencil	
e	ten	ōō	tool	th	thin	o *in* atom	
ē	me	oi	oil	*th*	then	u *in* circus	
i	fit	ou	out	zh	measure		
ī	ice	u	up	ŋ	ring		

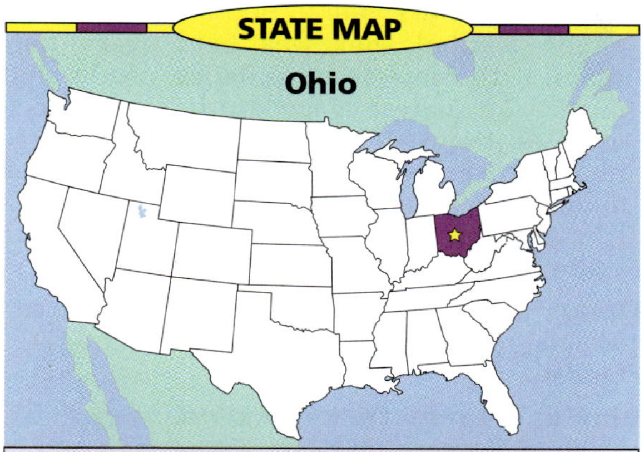

Statehood: 1803, the 17th state • **Capital:** Columbus

Ohio (ō hī′ō) a State in the north central part of the U.S. Its capital is Columbus. Abbreviated **OH** or **O.**
O·hi·o

oil (oil) ***noun*** **1** any one of certain greasy liquids that come from animal, vegetable, or mineral matter. Lard, olive oil, and petroleum are different kinds of oil. **2** a paint made by mixing coloring matter with oil: this kind of paint is also called **oil color** or **oil paint**.
verb to put oil on or in [She *oiled* the hinges.]
oil • ***noun,*** *plural* **oils** • ***verb*** **oiled, oiling**

oil well ***noun*** a well that is drilled through layers of rock or dirt to get petroleum from the earth.
oil well • ***noun,*** *plural* **oil wells**

oily (oi′lē) ***adjective*** **1** of or like oil [an *oily* liquid]. **2** full of or covered with oil; greasy [*oily* hair].
oil·y • ***adjective*** **oilier, oiliest**

ointment (oint′mənt) ***noun*** an oily cream rubbed on the skin to heal it or make it smooth.
oint·ment • ***noun,*** *plural* **ointments**

Ojibwa (ō jib′wā′ *or* ō jib′wä′) ***noun*** **1** a member of a North American Indian people living in Michigan, Wisconsin, Minnesota, and Ontario. **2** the language of this people.
O·jib·wa • ***noun,*** *plural for sense 1 only* **Ojibwas** or **Ojibwa**

OK or **O.K.** (ō′kā′) ***interjection*** all right [*OK* guys, let's go now.]
adjective all right; fine [Your idea is *OK*.]
adverb well; fine [Our team is doing *OK* this year.]
noun approval [You need your teacher's *OK*.]
verb to put an OK on; approve [The board *OK'd* the plans for the new gym.]
OK or **O.K.** • ***interjection*** • ***adjective*** • ***adverb*** • ***noun,*** *plural* **OKs** or **O.K.'s** • ***verb*** **OK'd** or **O.K.'d, OK'ing** or **O.K.'ing**

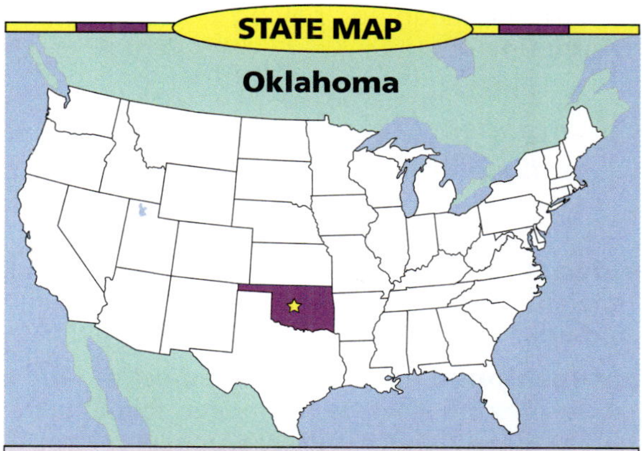

Statehood: 1907, the 46th state • **Capital:** Oklahoma City

Oklahoma (ō klə hō′mə) a State in the south central part of the U.S. Its capital is Oklahoma City. Abbreviated **OK** or **Okla.**
O·kla·ho·ma

Oklahoma City the capital of Oklahoma.

okra (ō′krə) ***noun*** a tall plant with green pods. The pods become soft and sticky when cooked. They are used in soups and stews.
o·kra • ***noun***

WORD HISTORY

okra

We get the English word **okra** from the plant's name in a language of western Africa. The word **okra** is a simplified and changed form of that name.

old (ōld) ***adjective*** **1** having lived or existed for a long time [an *old* man; an *old* building]. **2** in age [a car five years *old*]. **3** made some time ago; not new [*old* books]. **4** worn out by use or age [*old* shoes]. **5** for a long time [*old* friends]. **6** former; at one time [an *old* teacher of mine].
noun time long past; former times [days of *old*].
old • ***adjective*** **older** or **elder, oldest** or **eldest** • ***noun***

WORD CHOICES

Synonyms of **old**

The words **old, ancient,** and **antique** share the meaning "having existed for a long time."

old books

an *ancient* document

antique furniture

olden (ōl′dən) *adjective* of long ago; old; ancient [Chariots were used in *olden* times.]
old·en • *adjective*

old-fashioned (ōld′fash′ənd) *adjective* **1** of a style or kind that is no longer fashionable; out-of-date [an *old-fashioned* dress]. **2** attached to or having the ideas, ways, or tastes of earlier times [an *old-fashioned* family].
old-fash·ioned • *adjective*

Old Glory the flag of the U.S.

Old Testament the first of the two parts of the Christian Bible. It is the Holy Scriptures of Judaism and contains the history of the Hebrews, the laws of Moses, the writing of the prophets, and several other parts.

Old World the Eastern Hemisphere; Europe, Asia, and Africa.

oleomargarine (ō′lē ō mär′jər in) *noun* *another name for* **margarine**.
o·le·o·mar·ga·rine • *noun*

olive (äl′iv) *noun* **1** the small, oval fruit of an evergreen tree that grows in southern Europe, the Middle East, and other warm regions. Olives are eaten or are pressed to make olive oil. **2** the tree that this fruit grows on.
ol·ive • *noun, plural* **olives**

olive oil *noun* a pale yellow oil that is pressed from ripe olives. It is used in cooking and in salads.

Olympia (ō lim′pē ə) the capital of the State of Washington.
O·lym·pi·a

Olympic (ō lim′pik) *adjective* of or having to do with the Olympic games.
noun **Olympics** the Olympic games.
O·lym·pic • *adjective* • *noun, plural* **Olympics**

Olympic games *plural noun* **1** an ancient Greek festival that was held every four years, with contests in athletics, poetry, and music. **2** a contest of modern times in which athletes from all over the world compete in many sports and games. The contest is divided into winter and summer events held two years apart, each occurring every four years.

Oman (ō män′) a country in southeastern Arabia.
O·man

omelet or **omelette** (äm′lət) *noun* eggs beaten up, often with milk or water, and cooked in a frying pan until set.
om·e·let or **om·e·lette** • *noun, plural* **omelets** or **omelettes**

omen (ō′mən) *noun* anything that is supposed to be a sign of something to come [A red sunset is an *omen* of good weather.]
o·men • *noun, plural* **omens**

ominous (äm′i nəs) *adjective* of or like a bad omen; threatening [an *ominous* silence in the room].
om·i·nous • *adjective*

omission (ō mish′ən) *noun* **1** the act of omitting something [the *omission* of her name from the list]. **2** anything omitted.
o·mis·sion • *noun, plural* **omissions**

omit (ō mit′) *verb* to leave out [Don't *omit* any important details from your story.]
o·mit • *verb* **omitted, omitting**

omnipotent (äm nip′ə tənt) *adjective* having power or authority without limit; all-powerful.
om·nip·o·tent • *adjective*

on (än) *preposition* **1** held up by or attached to [a picture *on* the wall]. **2** in contact with; covering [a cloth *on* the table]. **3** in the surface of [a scratch *on* her arm]. **4** near to; by [the seat *on* my right]. **5** having as its location [a house *on* Main Street]. **6** at or during the time of [We got our books *on* the first day of school.] **7** in a condition or state of [*on* sale; *on* vacation]. **8** in the direction of; toward [The light was shining *on* us.] **9** by using; by means of [Most cars run *on* gasoline.] **10** seen

a cat	ō go	ʉ fur	ə = a *in* ago
ā ape	ô law, for	ch chin	e *in* agent
ä cot, car	ʊʊ look	sh she	i *in* pencil
e ten	ōō tool	th thin	o *in* atom
ē me	oi oil	*th* then	u *in* circus
i fit	ou out	zh measure	
ī ice	u up	ŋ ring	

or heard by means of [Have you ever been *on* TV?] **11** having to do with; concerning [a book *on* birds].
adverb **1** in a position of covering, touching, or being held up by something [Put your shoes *on*.] **2** in a forward direction; ahead [Move *on!*] **3** without stopping [The band played *on*.] **4** into operation or action; so that it is working [Turn the light *on*.]
adjective **1** in action; working or acting [The radio is *on*.] **2** planned for [Is the party still *on?*]
—**on and off** stopping and starting; from time to time. —**on and on** without stopping.

ON *abbreviation for* Ontario.

once (wuns) ***adverb*** **1** one time [The magazine comes *once* a week.] **2** at some time in the past; formerly [They were rich *once*.]
conjunction as soon as; whenever [*Once* the horse tires, it will stop.]
noun one time [I'll help you, but just this *once*.]
—**all at once** **1** all at the same time [The phones rang *all at once*.] **2** suddenly [*All at once* I felt better.] —**at once** **1** immediately [Come here *at once!*] **2** at the same time [I can't do two things *at once*.] —**once in a while** now and then; occasionally.

oncoming (än′kum iŋ) ***adjective*** coming nearer; approaching [*oncoming* traffic].
on·com·ing • ***adjective***

one (wun) ***adjective*** **1** being a single thing or unit [*one* vote]. **2** being a certain, but not named, person or thing out of a group [Choose *one* dessert or the other.]
noun **1** the number that names a single thing; the first cardinal number; 1. **2** a single person or thing [That's the best *one*.]
pronoun **1** a certain person or thing [*One* of us must go.] **2** any person or thing; anyone or anything [What can *one* do about it?]
—**one and all** everybody. —**one another** each other [They love *one another*.] —**one by one** one after the other.
● The words **one** and **won** sound alike.
I only need *one* penny.
Our school *won* the State Championship.

oneself (wun self′) ***pronoun*** a person's own self; himself or herself [One must not think only of *oneself*.]
one·self • ***pronoun***

one-sided (wun′sīd′əd) ***adjective*** **1** favoring or showing only one side or point of view; not fair [The article gave a *one-sided* account of the event.] **2** not equal or even [a *one-sided* game between the expert and a beginner].
one-sid·ed • ***adjective***

one-way (wun′wā′) ***adjective*** moving or allowing movement in one direction only [a *one-way* street].

onion (un′yən) ***noun*** **1** a plant with a bulb that has a sharp taste and smell and is eaten as a vegetable. **2** the bulb of this plant.
on·ion • ***noun,*** *plural* **onions**

onion

onlooker (än′lo͝ok ər) ***noun*** a person who watches something without taking part in it; spectator [Several *onlookers* watched the rescue.]
on·look·er • ***noun,*** *plural* **onlookers**

only (ōn′lē) ***adjective*** **1** without any other or others of the same kind [She is their *only* child.] **2** the best [Flying is the *only* way to travel.]
adverb **1** and no other; and no more; just; merely [I have *only* one dollar.] **2** as short a time ago as [I saw him *only* yesterday.]
conjunction [*an informal use*] except that; but [I'd go, *only* it's too late.]
on·ly • ***adjective*** • ***adverb*** • ***conjunction***

onset (än′set) ***noun*** a beginning; start [the *onset* of winter].
on·set • ***noun,*** *plural* **onsets**

Ontario (än ter′ē ō) **1** the smallest of the Great Lakes. It is the lake that is farthest east. **2** a province of south central Canada: abbreviated **ON** or **Ont.**
On·tar·i·o

onto (än′to͞o *or* än′tə) ***preposition*** **1** to a position on [The cat climbed *onto* the roof.] **2** [*a slang use*] aware of [I'm *onto* your tricks this time!]
on·to • ***preposition***

onward (än′wərd) ***adverb*** toward or at a place ahead; forward [They marched *onward*.]
on·ward • ***adverb***

onwards (än′wərdz) ***adverb*** *the same as* **onward**.
on·wards • ***adverb***

O

ooh (o͞o) ***interjection*** a sound made to show a feeling such as surprise, delight, or excitement.

oops (o͝ops *or* o͞ops) ***interjection*** a sound made to show surprise at a mistake, accident, or slip.

ooze (o͞oz) ***verb*** **1** to leak out slowly [Oil *oozed* from the hole in the tank.] **2** to give forth [The maple tree *oozed* sap.]
ooze • ***verb*** **oozed, oozing**

opaque (ō pāk′) ***adjective*** not capable of being seen through; not letting light through [an *opaque* screen].
o·paque • ***adjective***

open (ō′pən) ***adjective*** **1** not closed, shut, covered, or stopped up [an *open* door; an *open* drain]. **2** not closed in, fenced in, or protected [an *open* field]. **3** spread out; unfolded [an *open* book]. **4** having spaces between parts [cloth with an *open* weave]. **5** available to all who wish to enter, take part in, or make use of it [an *open* meeting]. **6** not settled or decided [an *open* question]. **7** not already taken or filled; available [The job is still *open*.] **8** having no prejudice [an *open* mind]. **9** frank; direct [an *open* manner] —Look for the WORD CHOICES box at the entry **frank**.
verb **1** to make or become no longer closed [He *opened* the trunk. The door *opened* slowly.] **2** to spread out; unfold [He *opened* his arms and gave us each a hug.] **3** to begin or start [They *opened* the show with their hit song.] **4** to start operating [She *opened* a new store. School *opens* in September.] **5** to be an opening; lead [This door *opens* onto a porch.]
—open to willing to listen to or consider [I am *open to* suggestions.] **—the open** **1** any open, clear outdoor space [Don't stand in *the open* during a storm.] **2** the condition of being known to all [The secret is now in *the open*.]
o·pen • ***adjective*** • ***verb*** **opened, opening**

opener (ō′pən ər) ***noun*** a person or thing that opens [a bottle *opener*].
o·pen·er • ***noun,*** *plural* **openers**

open-faced (ō′pən fāst) ***adjective*** describing a sandwich without a top slice of bread. This word is also written **open-face**.
o·pen-faced • ***adjective***

opening (ō′pən iŋ) ***noun*** **1** the act of making or becoming open [The *opening* of a flower can be photographed with a special camera.] **2** a hole, clearing, or other open place [an *opening* in the wall]. **3** a beginning [the *opening* of a new store]. **4** a job or other position that is not filled [The company has no *openings* now.]
o·pen·ing • ***noun,*** *plural* **openings**

openly (ō′pən lē) ***adverb*** in an open manner; in a frank, free, or honest way [The candidates should speak *openly* on the issues.]
o·pen·ly • ***adverb***

open-minded (ō′pən mīn′dəd) ***adjective*** willing to consider new ideas; having no prejudice or bias.
o·pen-mind·ed • ***adjective***

opera (äp′ər ə *or* äp′rə) ***noun*** a play in which all or most of the words are sung. An orchestra usually accompanies the singers.
op·er·a • ***noun,*** *plural* **operas**

operate (äp′ər āt) ***verb*** **1** to keep or be in action; run; work [Can you *operate* a sewing machine? The subway does not *operate* at night.] **2** to control or manage [He *operates* a laundry.] **3** to do a surgical operation.
op·er·ate • ***verb*** **operated, operating**

operation (äp′ər ā′shən) ***noun*** **1** the act or way of operating [She explained the *operation* of the computer.] **2** the condition of being in action or use [The factory will be in *operation* soon.] **3** one of a series of actions or movements in some work or plan [Hundreds of *operations* are required to make an automobile.] **4** a treatment by surgery to heal or correct an injury or illness.
op·er·a·tion • ***noun,*** *plural* **operations**

operator (äp′ər āt′ər) ***noun*** a person who operates a machine or device [a telephone *operator*].
op·er·a·tor • ***noun,*** *plural* **operators**

opinion (ō pin′yən) ***noun*** **1** a belief based on what someone thinks to be true or likely [We had different *opinions* about who started the argument.] **2** what someone thinks about how good or valuable a thing is [a low *opinion* of the movie]. **3** a judgment made by an expert [The judge wrote her *opinion* on the case.]
o·pin·ion • ***noun,*** *plural* **opinions**

a	cat	ō	go	ʉ	fur	ə =	a *in* ago
ā	ape	ô	law, for	ch	chin		e *in* agent
ä	cot, car	o͝o	look	sh	she		i *in* pencil
e	ten	o͞o	tool	th	thin		o *in* atom
ē	me	oi	oil	*th*	then		u *in* circus
i	fit	ou	out	zh	measure		
ī	ice	u	up	ŋ	ring		

opossum

opossum (ə päs′əm) *noun* a small animal that lives in trees and moves about mostly at night. The female carries her young in a pouch in her belly. Opossums lie perfectly still, as if dead, when they are in danger.
o·pos·sum • *noun, plural* **opossums** or **opossum**

opponent (ə pō′nənt) *noun* one who opposes or is against another in a fight, contest, or debate.
op·po·nent • *noun, plural* **opponents**

opportunity (äp′ər to͞o′ni tē) *noun* a time or occasion that is right for doing something; good chance [You will have an *opportunity* to ask questions after the speech.]
op·por·tu·ni·ty • *noun, plural* **opportunities**

oppose (ə pōz′) *verb* to act or be against; fight or resist [We *oppose* turning the playground into a place to park cars.]
op·pose • *verb* **opposed, opposing**

WORD CHOICES

Synonyms of **oppose**

The words **oppose, resist,** and **withstand** share the meaning "to speak or act against."

We *oppose* all efforts to restrict free speech.

One can *resist* a law by refusing to obey it.

I *withstood* the pressure from my parents.

opposite (äp′ə zit) *adjective* **1** at the other end or side; directly facing or back to back [the *opposite* end of the table; the *opposite* side of a coin]. **2** different in every way; exactly reverse or in contrast [Black is *opposite* to white.]
noun anything that is opposite [Love is the *opposite* of hate.]
preposition across from; facing [We sat *opposite* each other.]
op·po·site • *adjective* • *noun, plural* **opposites** • *preposition*

opposition (äp′ə zish′ən) *noun* **1** the act of opposing or resisting [*Opposition* to his plan was great.] **2** anything that opposes [Our *opposition* this week has not lost a game.]
op·po·si·tion • *noun*

oppress (ə pres′) *verb* to keep down by the cruel use of power; rule in a very harsh way [The dictator *oppressed* the people.]
op·press • *verb* **oppressed, oppressing**

oppressive (ə pres′iv) *adjective* **1** hard to put up with; being a burden [*oppressive* heat]. **2** cruel and unjust; harsh [an *oppressive* ruler].
op·pres·sive • *adjective*

optical (äp′ti kəl) *adjective* **1** of the sense of sight; visual [an *optical* illusion]. **2** made to give help in seeing [A microscope is an *optical* instrument.]
op·ti·cal • *adjective*

optician (äp tish′ən) *noun* a person who makes or sells eyeglasses and contact lenses.
op·ti·cian • *noun, plural* **opticians**

optimist (äp′tə mist) *noun* a person who is cheerful and hopeful, no matter what happens.
op·ti·mist • *noun, plural* **optimists**

optimistic (äp′tə mis′tik) *adjective* showing optimism [an *optimistic* prediction].
op·ti·mis·tic • *adjective*

option (äp′shən) *noun* **1** the act of choosing; choice [We have the *option* of sitting here or in the balcony.] —Look for the WORD CHOICES box at the entry **choice**. **2** a thing that is or can be chosen [Air conditioning is an *option* on that car.]
op·tion • *noun, plural* **options**

optional (äp′shə nəl) *adjective* allowing one to make a choice; not required [Basketball practice is *optional* this week.]
op·tion·al • *adjective*

optometrist (äp täm′ə trist) *noun* a person who is skilled in optometry.
op·tom·e·trist • *noun, plural* **optometrists**

optometry (äp täm′ə trē) *noun* the science or work of examining people's eyes and fitting them with eyeglasses or contact lenses.
op·tom·e·try • *noun*

O

or (ôr *or* ər) ***conjunction*** *a word that is used before:* **1** the second of two choices or possibilities [Do you want milk *or* cocoa?] **2** the last of a series of choices [Is the light green, yellow, *or* red?] **3** a word or phrase that has the same meaning [biology, *or* the study of life]. **4** the second of two choices when the first comes after *either* or *whether* [Take either this one *or* that one. I don't know whether to laugh *or* cry.]
● The words **or, oar,** and **ore** sound alike.
She will be leaving today *or* tomorrow.
Waves knocked the *oar* from my hand.
They take iron *ore* from the mine.

-or *a suffix meaning* a person or thing that does something [An *inventor* is a person who invents.]

OR *an abbreviation for* Oregon.

oral (ôr′əl) ***adjective*** **1** spoken rather than written [an *oral* report]. **2** of, near, or in the mouth [*oral* surgery].
o·ral • ***adjective***

orally (ôr′ə lē) ***adverb*** **1** by speaking. **2** through the mouth [This medicine is taken *orally*.]
o·ral·ly • ***adverb***

orange

orange (ôr′inj *or* är′inj) ***noun*** **1** a round citrus fruit with a reddish-yellow skin and a sweet, juicy pulp. **2** the evergreen tree that this fruit grows on. **3** reddish yellow.
adjective reddish-yellow.
or·ange • ***noun,*** *plural* **oranges** • ***adjective***

orangutan

orangutan (ō raŋ′ə tan) ***noun*** a large ape with long arms and shaggy, reddish hair. It lives in some tropical jungles of southeast Asia.
o·rang·u·tan • ***noun,*** *plural* **orangutans**

orbit (ôr′bit) ***noun*** **1** the path followed by a planet, moon, or other heavenly body as it travels around another body. The path of the earth around the sun is an orbit. **2** the path or course of a spacecraft or man-made satellite around a planet or other body in space.
verb to move in an orbit around something [Many man-made satellites *orbit* the earth.]
or·bit • ***noun,*** *plural* **orbits** • ***verb*** **orbited, orbiting**

orchard (ôr′chərd) ***noun*** a piece of land where fruit trees or nut trees are grown.
or·chard • ***noun,*** *plural* **orchards**

orchestra
The Cleveland Orchestra

orchestra (ôr′kəs trə) ***noun*** a large group of musicians playing together. An orchestra usually includes most types of instruments.
or·ches·tra • ***noun,*** *plural* **orchestras**

orchid (ôr′kid) ***noun*** **1** a plant with flowers that have three petals. The middle petal is larger than the others and has the shape of a lip. Orchids are of various colors. **2** the flower of such a plant. **3** a pale purple color.
or·chid • ***noun,*** *plural* **orchids**

ordain (ôr dān′) ***verb*** to appoint as a minister, priest, or rabbi.
or·dain • ***verb*** **ordained, ordaining**

ordeal (ôr dēl′) ***noun*** any difficult or painful experience.
or·deal • ***noun,*** *plural* **ordeals**

order (ôr′dər) ***noun*** **1** the way in which things are placed or the way in which things follow one another; arrangement [names in alphabetical *order*]. **2** a condition in which everything is in the right place or is working properly [Let's put this room back in *order*.] **3** a peaceful condition in which people obey the rules or laws [The police were called to restore *order*.] **4** a direction that tells someone what to do; command [an *order* from the general]. **5** a request for something that one wants to buy or receive [He mailed his *order* for the book.]

a cat	ō go	ʉ fur	ə = a *in* ago
ā ape	ô law, for	ch chin	e *in* agent
ä cot, car	oo look	sh she	i *in* pencil
e ten	ōō tool	th thin	o *in* atom
ē me	oi oil	*th* then	u *in* circus
i fit	ou out	zh measure	
ī ice	u up	ŋ ring	

6 the thing requested [The store delivered my *order*.] **7** a single portion of food in a restaurant [an *order* of French fries]. **8** a group of people joined together because they share the same beliefs or interests [an *order* of monks]. **9** a group of related animals or plants that is larger than a family [Whales and dolphins belong to the same *order* of mammals.]
verb **1** to give a command to [I *ordered* them to leave.] **2** to ask for something that one wants to buy or receive [Please *order* the pizza.]
—out of order **1** out of its proper place. **2** not working [My telephone is *out of order*.]
or·der • ***noun,*** *plural* **orders**
• ***verb*** **ordered, ordering**

orderly (ôr′dər lē) ***adjective*** **1** neatly arranged; tidy; in order [an *orderly* desk]. **2** behaving well; obeying the rules [an *orderly* crowd].
noun a person who does general work in a hospital, helping the doctors and nurses.
or·der·ly • ***adjective*** • ***noun,*** *plural* **orderlies**

ordinal number (ôrd′n əl) ***noun*** a number that shows where something comes in a series. First, sixth, and 10th are ordinal numbers.
or·di·nal number • ***noun,*** *plural* **ordinal numbers**

ordinance (ôrd′n əns) ***noun*** a law, especially one made by a city government.
or·di·nance • ***noun,*** *plural* **ordinances**

ordinarily (ôrd′n er′ə lē) ***adverb*** usually; as a rule; generally [I'm *ordinarily* home on Sunday.]
or·di·nar·i·ly • ***adverb***

ordinary (ôrd′n er′ē) ***adjective*** **1** usual, regular, or normal [The *ordinary* price is $10.] **2** not special in any way; common; average [a person of *ordinary* ability]. —Look for the WORD CHOICES box at the entry **common**.
—out of the ordinary not common; unusual.
or·di·nar·y • ***adjective***

ore (ôr) ***noun*** a rock or mineral from which a metal can be obtained [iron *ore*].
ore • ***noun,*** *plural* **ores**
● The words **ore, oar,** and **or** sound alike.
Ore is shipped to the mills by train.
You can steer a boat with an *oar*.
He is either innocent *or* guilty.

Oreg. *an abbreviation for* Oregon.

oregano (ô reg′ə nō) ***noun*** a plant with pleasant-smelling leaves that are used as a seasoning.
o·reg·a·no • ***noun***

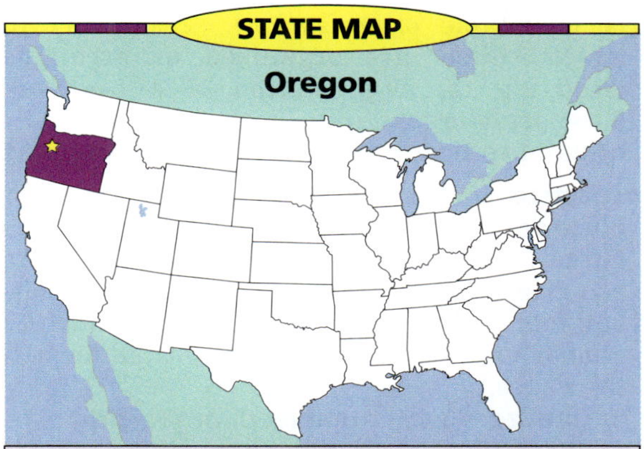

Statehood: 1859, the 33rd state • **Capital:** Salem

Oregon (ôr′ə gən *or* ôr′ə gän′) a State in the northwestern part of the U.S. Its capital is Salem. Abbreviated **OR** or **Oreg.**
Or·e·gon

organ (ôr′gən) ***noun*** **1** a musical instrument that has sets of pipes that make sounds when keys or pedals are pressed to send air through the pipes. **2** an instrument like this, but with reeds or electronic devices instead of pipes. **3** a part of an animal or plant that has some special purpose [The eyes are the *organs* of sight.]
or·gan • ***noun,*** *plural* **organs**

organ

organic (ôr gan′ik) ***adjective*** **1** of, having to do with, or coming from living matter [Coal is an *organic* material formed from decayed plant life.] **2** grown with only animal or vegetable fertilizers and without the use of chemical sprays [*organic* foods].
or·gan·ic • ***adjective***

organism (ôr′gə niz əm) ***noun*** any living thing [Plants, animals, and bacteria are *organisms*.]
or·gan·ism • ***noun,*** *plural* **organisms**

organist (ôr′gə nist) ***noun*** a person who plays the organ.
or·gan·ist • ***noun,*** *plural* **organists**

organization (ôr′gə ni zā′shən) ***noun*** **1** a group of persons organized for some purpose [a charitable *organization*]. **2** the way in which things are organized or arranged [studying the *organization* of a beehive]. **3** the act of organizing.
or·gan·i·za·tion • ***noun,*** *plural* **organizations**

organize (ôr′gə nīz) ***verb*** **1** to arrange or place according to a system [He *organized* the library books according to their subjects.] **2** to bring into being; start [We *organized* a softball team.] **3** to make part of a group, such as a labor union [The workers *organized* for better wages.]
or·gan·ize • ***verb*** **organized, organizing**

Orient (ôr′ē ənt) Asia, especially eastern Asia. China, Korea, and Japan are in the Orient.
O·ri·ent

Oriental (ôr′ē ent′l) ***adjective*** of or having to do with the Orient or its people.
noun a member of any of the peoples whose native country is in the Orient.
O·ri·en·tal • ***adjective*** • ***noun,*** *plural* **Orientals**

orientation (ôr′ē ən tā′shən) ***noun*** the act of making or becoming used to a certain situation [a day for the *orientation* of new students].
o·ri·en·ta·tion • ***noun,*** *plural* **orientations**

origami

origami (ôr′i gä′mē) ***noun*** a Japanese art of folding paper to form flowers or other objects.
o·ri·ga·mi • ***noun***

origin (ôr′i jin *or* är′i jin) ***noun*** **1** the place or point from which something comes [The word "rodeo" has its *origin* in Spanish.] **2** family or ancestors [I am of French *origin*.]
or·i·gin • ***noun,*** *plural* **origins**

WORD CHOICES

Synonyms of **origin**

The words **origin, root,** and **source** share the meaning "a thing or place from which something comes."

What was the *origin* of their conflict?

Selfishness is the *root* of her troubles.

German is the *source* of many English words.

original (ə rij′i nəl) ***adjective*** **1** having to do with an origin; first or earliest [the *original* settlers of North America]. **2** made or thought of for the first time; fresh; new [an *original* idea]. **3** capable of inventing or creating something new [an *original* mind]. **4** being the one from which copies are made [I have the *original* letter and two copies.]
noun something that is original and not a copy, reproduction, or translation [The *original* of the painting is in a museum in Paris.]
o·rig·i·nal • ***adjective*** • ***noun,*** *plural* **originals**

originality (ə rij′i nal′i tē) ***noun*** the condition or quality of being fresh, new, or creative [the *originality* of her ideas].
o·rig·i·nal·i·ty • ***noun***

originally (ə rij′i nəl ē) ***adverb*** at the start; at first [The movie was *originally* five hours long.]
o·rig·i·nal·ly • ***adverb***

originate (ə rij′i nāt′) ***verb*** **1** to bring into being; create; invent [England *originated* the use of government postage stamps.] —Look for the WORD CHOICES box at the entry **create**. **2** to come into being; begin; start [Many TV programs *originate* in Los Angeles.]
o·rig·i·nate • ***verb*** **originated, originating**

oriole (ôr′ē ōl) ***noun*** an American songbird that has orange and black feathers. It builds a hanging nest.
o·ri·ole • ***noun,*** *plural* **orioles**

ornament (ôr′nə mənt) ***noun*** anything added or put on to make something look better; dec-

a	cat	ō	go	ʉ	fur	ə = a *in* ago
ā	ape	ô	law, for	ch	chin	e *in* agent
ä	cot, car	oo	look	sh	she	i *in* pencil
e	ten	ōō	tool	th	thin	o *in* atom
ē	me	oi	oil	*th*	then	u *in* circus
i	fit	ou	out	zh	measure	
ī	ice	u	up	ŋ	ring	

oration [a Christmas tree full of *ornaments*].
or·na·ment • *noun, plural* **ornaments**

ornate (ôr nāt′) *adjective* having much decoration [an *ornate* building].
or·nate • *adjective*

orphan (ôr′fən) *noun* a child whose parents are dead.
verb to cause to become an orphan [Many children were *orphaned* by the war.]
or·phan • *noun, plural* **orphans**
• *verb* **orphaned, orphaning**

orphanage (ôr′fən ij) *noun* a home for taking care of orphans.
or·phan·age • *noun, plural* **orphanages**

orthodontist (ôr′thə dän′tist) *noun* a dentist who works to straighten crooked teeth.
or·tho·don·tist • *noun, plural* **orthodontists**

orthodox (ôr′thə däks) *adjective* keeping to the usual or fixed beliefs and customs; conventional [*orthodox* political views].
or·tho·dox • *adjective*

WORD HISTORY

orthodox

We get **orthodox** from two Greek words that mean "straight" and "opinion." Together, they mean "having the right opinion."

ostrich (äs′trich) *noun* a very large bird of Africa and southwestern Asia, with a long neck and long legs. It cannot fly, but it runs swiftly.
os·trich • *noun, plural* **ostriches**

ostrich

other (u*th*′ər) *adjective* **1** not this one or the one just mentioned, but a different one [Stand on one foot and lift the *other* one. It was not Sue but some *other* girl.] **2** being the one or ones remaining [Bill and the *other* boys went fishing.] **3** additional; extra [I have no *other* hat.]
pronoun **1** the other one [Each loved the *other*.] **2** some other person or thing [That's what *others* say. I want that puppy and no *other*.]
—**the other day** not long ago; recently.
oth·er • *adjective* • *pronoun, plural* **others**

otherwise (u*th*′ər wīz) *adverb* **1** in some other way; differently [He liked the movie, but I felt *otherwise*.] **2** in all other ways [She has a cough, but feels fine *otherwise*.] **3** or else [I'm tired; *otherwise* I would join you.]
oth·er·wise • *adverb*

Ottawa (ät′ə wə) the capital of Canada, in eastern Ontario.
Ot·ta·wa

otter (ät′ər) *noun* a furry animal that is related to the weasel. It has webbed feet for swimming and a long tail.
ot·ter • *noun, plural* **otters**

ouch (ouch) *interjection* a sound made to show sudden or sharp pain.

ought (ôt *or* ät) *verb* (*helping verb*) **1** to be forced by what is right, wise, or necessary [He *ought* to pay his debts.] **2** to be expected or likely [It *ought* to be over soon.]
ought • *verb past tense* **ought**; *he/she/it* **ought**

ounce (ouns) *noun* **1** a unit of weight. An ounce equals $1/16$ pound. **2** a unit of measure for liquids. 32 ounces equal one quart. **3** a small amount.
ounce • *noun, plural* **ounces**

our (our) *adjective* done by us or having to do with us [*our* work; *our* cars].
• The words **our** and **hour** sound alike.
Our mayor was reelected.
It is now five minutes past the *hour*.

ours (ourz) *pronoun* the one or the ones that belong to us [This book is *ours*. Everyone planted flowers, but *ours* haven't bloomed quite yet.]

ourselves (our selvz′) *pronoun* **1** our own selves. This form of **we** is used when the persons who do the action of the verb are the same as the persons who are affected by the action [We introduced *ourselves*.] **2** very much our own selves. This is used to give more force to what is being said [We *ourselves* are telling you this; believe it.]
our·selves • *pronoun*

-ous *a suffix meaning* having, full of, or recognized because of [A *courageous* person is full of courage. A *courageous* act is recognized because of the courage it shows.]

oust (oust) ***verb*** to force out; drive out [The theater usher *ousted* the noisy boys.] —Look for the WORD CHOICES box at the entry **eject**.
oust • ***verb*** **ousted, ousting**

out (out) ***adverb*** **1** away from or beyond a certain position, place, or situation [Open the window and look *out*. Spit it *out*. How will I get *out* of this mess?] **2** away from home, work, or the usual place [We went *out* for dinner.] **3** into being, view, or action [A fire broke *out*. The sun came *out*.] **4** so as to be no longer active or available [The fire died *out*.] **5** completely; thoroughly [I'm tired *out*.] **6** loudly [Call *out* to them.] **7** from among several or many [Pick *out* the one you want.] **8** in a way that makes an out in baseball [He struck *out*.] **9** into an unconscious condition [She passed *out*.]
adjective **1** away from home, school, work, or the usual place [I was *out* when he called. He's *out* with the flu.] **2** not inside [Turn off the lights after everyone is *out*.] **3** known or made public [The story is *out*.] **4** not working or in use [The lights are *out*.] **5** having made an out in baseball [She was *out* at second base.]
preposition through to the outside; out of [She walked *out* the door.]
noun in baseball, a failure to get on base or to the next base safely.
—out of **1** from inside [He went *out of* the room.] **2** through to the outside [thrown *out of* the window]. **3** from the number of [chosen *out of* a crowd]. **4** beyond [*out of* sight]. **5** from; using [made *out of* bricks]. **6** because of [He did it *out of* spite.] **7** not having any [*out of* gas].
out • ***adverb*** • ***adjective*** • ***preposition*** • ***noun, plural*** **outs**

out- *a prefix meaning:* **1** away from; outside [An *outbuilding* is away from a main building.] **2** going away or forth; outward [*Outbound* traffic goes away from the city.] **3** better or more than [You've done better than I can; you've *outdone* me.]

outage (out′ij) ***noun*** a loss of electric power for a time [The heavy storm caused *outages* all over town.]
out·age • ***noun, plural*** **outages**

outboard (out′bôrd) ***adjective*** describing or of a motor, with a propeller attached, that is fixed outside the stern of a boat.
out·board • ***adjective***

outboard

outbound (out′bound) ***adjective*** headed away from a place; outward bound [an *outbound* train].
out·bound • ***adjective***

outbreak (out′brāk) ***noun*** a sudden occurrence, or breaking out, of something unpleasant, such as disease or fighting [the *outbreak* of war].
out·break • ***noun, plural*** **outbreaks**

outbuilding (out′bil diŋ) ***noun*** a barn or other building separate from the main building.
out·build·ing • ***noun, plural*** **outbuildings**

outburst (out′burst) ***noun*** a sudden show of strong feeling or energy [an *outburst* of anger].
out·burst • ***noun, plural*** **outbursts**

outcast (out′kast) ***noun*** a person driven out or rejected by a group [He sometimes felt like an *outcast* in his own family.]
out·cast • ***noun, plural*** **outcasts**

outcome (out′kum) ***noun*** the way something turns out; result [the *outcome* of the election].
out·come • ***noun, plural*** **outcomes**

outcry (out′krī) ***noun*** **1** a scream or shout. **2** a strong protest or objection [The tax caused a public *outcry*.]
out·cry • ***noun, plural*** **outcries**

outdated (out dāt′əd) ***adjective*** behind the times; out-of-date [*outdated* ideas].
out·dat·ed • ***adjective***

outdid (out did′) ***verb*** *past tense of* **outdo**.
out·did • ***verb***

a	cat	ō	go	ʉ	fur	ə = a *in* ago	
ā	ape	ô	law, for	ch	chin	e *in* agent	
ä	cot, car	oo	look	sh	she	i *in* pencil	
e	ten	ōō	tool	th	thin	o *in* atom	
ē	me	oi	oil	*th*	then	u *in* circus	
i	fit	ou	out	zh	measure		
ī	ice	u	up	ŋ	ring		

outdistance (out dis′təns) ***verb*** to get far ahead of [She *outdistanced* the other runners.]
out·dis·tance • ***verb*** **outdistanced, outdistancing**

outdo (out do͞o′) ***verb*** to do better or more than [We worked hard but he *outdid* us.]
—outdo oneself to do one's best or better than expected [I *outdid* myself on that last jump.]
out·do • ***verb*** **outdid, outdone, outdoing**

outdone (out dun′) ***verb*** *past participle of* **outdo**.
out·done • ***verb***

outdoor (out′dôr′) ***adjective*** being, belonging, or done outside a house or other building [an *outdoor* pool; *outdoor* activities].
out·door • ***adjective***

outdoors (out′dôrz′) ***adverb*** in or into the open; outside [Let's play *outdoors*.]
noun the world outside of buildings; the open air.
out·doors • ***adverb*** • ***noun***

outer (out′ər) ***adjective*** on or closer to the outside [the *outer* wall; an *outer* coat].
out·er • ***adjective***

outer space ***noun*** space beyond the earth's atmosphere.

outfield (out′fēld) ***noun*** **1** the part of a baseball field beyond the infield. **2** all of the outfielders.
out·field • ***noun, plural*** **outfields**

outfielder (out′fēld ər) ***noun*** a baseball player whose position is in the outfield.
out·field·er • ***noun, plural*** **outfielders**

outfit (out′fit) ***noun*** **1** the equipment used in some work or activity [Boots and a backpack are part of a hiking *outfit*.] **2** a set of clothes [She was wearing a new *outfit* at church.] **3** a group of people working together.
verb to supply with what is needed [This store *outfits* campers.]
out·fit • ***noun, plural*** **outfits**
• ***verb*** **outfitted, outfitting**

outgoing (out′gō iŋ) ***adjective*** **1** going out; departing [*outgoing* mail]. **2** friendly; agreeable [an *outgoing* person].
out·go·ing • ***adjective***

outgrew (out gro͞o′) ***verb*** *past tense of* **outgrow**.
out·grew • ***verb***

outgrow (out grō′) ***verb*** **1** to grow bigger than [She *outgrew* her older sister.] **2** to grow too big for [I have *outgrown* these clothes.] **3** to lose by growing older [She *outgrew* her interest in dolls.]
out·grow • ***verb*** **outgrew, outgrown, outgrowing**

outgrown (out grōn′) ***verb*** *past participle of* **outgrow**.
out·grown • ***verb***

outgrowth (out′grōth) ***noun*** something that develops from something else; result [Snowboarding is an *outgrowth* of skiing.]
out·growth • ***noun, plural*** **outgrowths**

outhouse (out′hous) ***noun*** an outbuilding used as a toilet. Outhouses were common in the days before houses had indoor plumbing.
out·house • ***noun, plural*** **outhouses**

outing (out′iŋ) ***noun*** a short trip outdoors or away from home, taken for pleasure.
out·ing • ***noun, plural*** **outings**

outlast (out last′) ***verb*** to last longer than [My brown shoes *outlasted* my black ones.] —Look for the WORD CHOICES box at the entry **outlive**.
out·last • ***verb*** **outlasted, outlasting**

outlaw (out′lô *or* out′lä) ***noun*** a criminal who is being hunted by the police.
verb to pass a law against; rule out as not lawful [The city has *outlawed* gambling.]
out·law • ***noun, plural*** **outlaws**
• ***verb*** **outlawed, outlawing**

outlet (out′lət) ***noun*** **1** an opening or passage for letting something out [the *outlet* of a river]. **2** a way of getting rid of something [Tennis is a good *outlet* for his energy.] **3** a place in a wiring system where electric current may be had by putting in a plug. **4** a store, especially a store that sells surplus or defective goods at low prices.
out·let • ***noun, plural*** **outlets**

outline (out′līn) ***noun*** **1** a line around the outer edges of an object, showing its shape [We saw the *outline* of a ship in the fog.] **2** a drawing that shows only the outer lines of a thing. **3** a report or plan that sets out the main points, but not the details [The teacher asked him to do an *outline* of his book report.] —Look for the WORD CHOICES box at the entry **summary**.
verb to make an outline of.
out·line • ***noun, plural*** **outlines**
• ***verb*** **outlined, outlining**

O

outlive (out liv′) ***verb*** to live longer than.
out·live • ***verb*** **outlived, outliving**

WORD CHOICES

Synonyms of **outlive**

The words **outlive, outlast,** and **survive** share the meaning "to exist for a longer time than."

They have *outlived* their enemies.

These shoes have *outlasted* their usefulness.

Two sons *survive* her.

outlook (out′look) ***noun*** **1** one's way of thinking; point of view; attitude [a cheerful *outlook*]. **2** what is likely for the future; prospect [the weather *outlook* for next week].
out·look • ***noun,*** *plural* **outlooks**

outlying (out′lī iŋ) ***adjective*** quite far from the center; remote [the *outlying* suburbs].
out·ly·ing • ***adjective***

outmoded (out mōd′əd) ***adjective*** out-of-date; old-fashioned [an *outmoded* style].
out·mod·ed • ***adjective***

outnumber (out num′bər) ***verb*** to be greater in number than [The girls *outnumber* the boys.]
out·num·ber • ***verb*** **outnumbered, outnumbering**

out-of-date (out əv dāt′) ***adjective*** no longer in style or use; old-fashioned.

out-of-doors (out əv dôrz′) ***adverb, noun*** *the same as* **outdoors**.

outpatient (out′pā shənt) ***noun*** a patient who goes to a hospital for treatment but does not need to stay there overnight.
out·pa·tient • ***noun,*** *plural* **outpatients**

outpost (out′pōst) ***noun*** **1** a small group of soldiers on guard some distance away from the main camp or fort. **2** a place where such soldiers are posted. **3** a village on a frontier.
out·post • ***noun,*** *plural* **outposts**

output (out′poot) ***noun*** **1** the amount made or done [the daily *output* of the factory]. **2** information delivered by a computer. It can be displayed on the screen or printed on paper.
out·put • ***noun,*** *plural* **outputs**

outrage (out′rāj) ***noun*** **1** a cruel or evil act so wicked that it is shocking [Setting fire to the hospital was an *outrage*.] **2** great anger aroused by something that is seen as an insult, injury, or injustice [News of the terrible crime filled the public with *outrage*.]
verb to shock, anger, or hurt deeply by words or actions [The newspaper's attack on the mayor *outraged* many citizens.] —Look for the WORD CHOICES box at the entry **offend**.
out·rage • ***noun,*** *plural* **outrages** • ***verb*** **outraged, outraging**

outrageous (out rā′jəs) ***adjective*** so wrong or bad that it hurts or shocks [an *outrageous* lie].
out·ra·geous • ***adjective***

outrigger

outrigger (out′rig ər) ***noun*** a framework that is built out from the side of a canoe. It prevents the canoe from tipping over.
out·rig·ger • ***noun,*** *plural* **outriggers**

outright (out′rīt) ***adjective*** complete; thorough [an *outright* lie].
adverb at once [She was hired *outright*.]
out·right • ***adjective*** • ***adverb***

outsell (out sel′) ***verb*** to sell in greater amounts than [This brand of tea *outsells* that.]
out·sell • ***verb*** **outsold, outselling**

outset (out′set) ***noun*** the beginning or start [We had problems at the *outset* of our trip.]
out·set • ***noun***

a cat	ō go	ʉ fur	ə = a *in* ago
ā ape	ô law, for	ch chin	e *in* agent
ä cot, car	oo look	sh she	i *in* pencil
e ten	o͞o tool	th thin	o *in* atom
ē me	oi oil	*th* then	u *in* circus
i fit	ou out	zh measure	
ī ice	u up	ŋ ring	

outshine (out shīn′) ***verb*** **1** to shine brighter than. **2** to be better than; surpass [She *outshone* the other players.]
out·shine • ***verb*** **outshone** or **outshined, outshining**

outshone (out shōn′) ***verb*** *a past tense of* **outshine.**
out·shone • ***verb***

outside (out′sīd′) ***noun*** **1** the side or part that faces out; exterior [Wash the *outside* of the window.] **2** any place not inside [The prisoners got little news from the *outside*.]
adjective **1** of or on the outside; outer [the *outside* layer]. **2** from some other person or place [Solve the problems without *outside* help.] **3** small; slight [an *outside* chance].
adverb on or to the outside [Let's play *outside*.]
preposition **1** on, to, or near the outside of [Leave the box *outside* the door.] **2** beyond the limits of [They live *outside* the city.]
out·side • ***noun,*** *plural* **outsides** • ***adjective*** • ***adverb*** • ***preposition***

outsider (out sīd′ər) ***noun*** a person who does not belong to a certain group.
out·sid·er • ***noun,*** *plural* **outsiders**

outskirts (out′skurts) ***plural noun*** the districts or parts far from the center of a town or city.
out·skirts • ***plural noun***

outsmart (out smärt′) ***verb*** to win out over by being more clever or cunning [He *outsmarted* the other team's defense.]
out·smart • ***verb*** **outsmarted, outsmarting**

outsold (out′sōld′) ***verb*** *past tense and past participle of* **outsell.**
out·sold • ***verb***

outspoken (out′spō′kən) ***adjective*** speaking or spoken in a frank, bold, and honest way —Look for the WORD CHOICES box at the entry **frank.**
out·spo·ken • ***adjective***

outstanding (out stan′diŋ) ***adjective*** **1** standing out from others, especially because of being very good or important [an *outstanding* lawyer]. **2** not paid [an *outstanding* debt].
out·stand·ing • ***adjective***

outward (out′wərd) ***adjective*** **1** toward the outside [an *outward* glance]. **2** capable of being noticed [She showed no *outward* sign of fear.]
adverb toward the outside [The door opens *outward*.]
out·ward • ***adjective*** • ***adverb***

outwards (out′wərdz) ***adverb*** *the same as the adverb* **outward.**
out·wards • ***adverb***

outweigh (out wā′) ***verb*** **1** to weigh more than [I *outweigh* my brother.] **2** to be more important than [The good *outweighs* the bad.]
out·weigh • ***verb*** **outweighed, outweighing**

outwit (out wit′) ***verb*** to win out over by being more clever or cunning [He always *outwits* his opponent in chess.]
out·wit • ***verb*** **outwitted, outwitting**

oval (ō′vəl) ***adjective*** shaped like an egg or like an ellipse [The picture was set in an *oval* frame.]
o·val • ***adjective***

ovary (ō′vər ē) ***noun*** **1** the organ in a female in which the eggs are formed. **2** the part of a flowering plant in which the seeds are formed.
o·va·ry • ***noun,*** *plural* **ovaries**

oven (uv′ən) ***noun*** a container or enclosed space that is used for baking or roasting food or for heating or drying things. A kitchen stove usually has an oven.
ov·en • ***noun,*** *plural* **ovens**

over (ō′vər) ***preposition*** **1** in, at, or to a place above; higher than [Hang the picture *over* the fireplace.] **2** so as to cover [Put a blanket *over* my legs.] **3** along [I've driven *over* this road before.] **4** to or on the other side of [Jump *over* the puddle.] **5** across and down from [The car went *over* the cliff.] **6** during; through [*over* the past five years]. **7** more than [It cost *over* $20.] **8** rather than [We chose the brown rug *over* the blue one.] **9** concerning; about [Don't fight *over* it.] **10** by means of [We talked *over* the telephone.]
adverb **1** above or across [A plane flew *over*.] **2** across the brim or edge [The soup boiled *over*.] **3** across a distance or space between two points [Come *over* to my house.] **4** from a standing position; down [The tree fell *over*.] **5** so that the other side is up [Turn the plate *over*.] **6** again [Do the lesson *over*.]
adjective finished; done with [The game is *over*.]
—**over and over** again and again.
o·ver • ***preposition*** • ***adverb*** • ***adjective***

O

over- *a prefix meaning:* **1** above or higher [An *overhead* heater is located above people's heads.] **2** too much [*Overeating* is eating too much.] **3** across or beyond [He shot beyond the target; he *overshot* it.]

WORD MAKER

The prefix over-

Many words contain the prefix **over-** plus a word that you already know. You can understand these words if you add the idea "too" or "too much" to the meaning of the base word.

I. *when added to verbs:*

prefix	*+ base word*	⇨	*new word*
over-	**+ charge**	⇨	**overcharge** *(to ask too much in payment)*
	burden		overburden
	buy		overbuy
	cook		overcook
	crowd		overcrowd
	emphasize		overemphasize
	estimate		overestimate
	exercise		overexercise
	feed		overfeed
	heat		overheat
	pay		overpay
	produce		overproduce
	protect		overprotect
	spend		overspend
	stuff		overstuff

II. *when added to adjectives:*

prefix	*+ base word*	⇨	*new word*
over-	**+ anxious**	⇨	**overanxious** *(too worried about what may happen)*
	active		overactive
	ambitious		overambitious
	careful		overcareful
	cautious		overcautious
	confident		overconfident
	eager		overeager
	emotional		overemotional
	generous		overgenerous
	sensitive		oversensitive

overalls (ō′vər ôlz) ***plural noun*** trousers with a top part that comes up over the chest. They can be worn over other clothes.
o·ver·alls • ***plural noun***

overalls

overate (ō vər āt′) ***verb*** *past tense of* **overeat.**
o·ver·ate • ***verb***

overboard (ō′vər bôrd) ***adverb*** over the side of a ship or boat into the water [He fell *overboard.*]
o·ver·board • ***adverb***

overcame (ō vər kām′) ***verb*** *past tense of* **overcome.**
o·ver·came • ***verb***

overcast (ō′vər kast) ***adjective*** covered with clouds; cloudy; dark [an *overcast* sky].
o·ver·cast • ***adjective***

overcoat (ō′vər kōt) ***noun*** a heavy coat worn outdoors in cold weather.
o·ver·coat • ***noun,*** *plural* **overcoats**

overcome (ō vər kum′) ***verb*** **1** to get the better of; defeat; master [She tried hard to *overcome* her fear of dogs.] **2** to make weak or helpless [We were *overcome* by laughter.]
o·ver·come • ***verb*** **overcame, overcome, overcoming**

overdid (ō vər did′) ***verb*** *past tense of* **overdo.**
o·ver·did • ***verb***

overdo (ō vər do͞o′) ***verb*** **1** to do too much and get tired [Don't *overdo.*] **2** to spoil by exaggerating [Don't *overdo* your praise.] **3** to cook too long [Don't *overdo* the steak.]
o·ver·do • ***verb*** **overdid, overdone, overdoing**

● The words **overdo** and **overdue** sound alike.
Sometimes you *overdo* your criticism.
Because of snow, flights are *overdue.*

overdone (ō vər dun′) ***verb*** *past participle of* **overdo.**
o·ver·done • ***verb***

a cat	ō go	ʉ fur	ə = a *in* ago
ā ape	ô law, for	ch chin	e *in* agent
ä cot, car	o͝o look	sh she	i *in* pencil
e ten	o͞o tool	th thin	o *in* atom
ē me	oi oil	*th* then	u *in* circus
i fit	ou out	zh measure	
ī ice	u up	ŋ ring	

overdose (ō′vər dōs) ***noun*** too large a dose of a drug or medicine.
o·ver·dose • ***noun,*** *plural* **overdoses**

overdress (ō vər dres′) ***verb*** to dress in a way that is too formal or too warm for the occasion.
o·ver·dress • ***verb*** **overdressed, overdressing**

overdue (ō vər do͞o′ *or* ō vər dyo͞o′) ***adjective*** **1** not paid by the time set for payment [an *overdue* bill]. **2** delayed past the arrival time; late [Her plane was three hours *overdue*.]
o·ver·due • ***adjective***
• The words **overdue** and **overdo** sound alike.
Her rent check is two weeks *overdue*.
Be careful not to *overdo* the jogging.

overeat (ō vər ēt′) ***verb*** to eat too much [He *overate* at the party.]
o·ver·eat • ***verb*** **overate, overeaten, overeating**

overeaten (ō vər ēt′n) ***verb*** *past participle of* **overeat**.
o·ver·eat·en • ***verb***

overflow (ō vər flō′) ***verb*** **1** to flow over the usual bounds of something [The river *overflowed* its banks.] **2** to have its contents flowing over [The sink *overflowed*.]
o·ver·flow • ***verb*** **overflowed, overflowing**

overhand (ō′vər hand) ***adjective*** with the hand held higher than the elbow or the arm higher than the shoulder [an *overhand* pitch]. This word can also be used as an adverb [He threw the ball *overhand*.]
o·ver·hand • ***adjective***

overhaul (ō′vər hôl) ***verb*** to check over carefully and make repairs or changes that are needed [The mechanic *overhauled* the truck's engine.]
noun the act of overhauling [I left the car with the mechanic for a complete *overhaul*.]
o·ver·haul • ***verb*** **overhauled, overhauling** • ***noun,*** *plural* **overhauls**

overhead (ō′vər hed *for adj. & n.;* ō vər hed′ *for adv.*) ***adjective*** above one's head [an *overhead* light].
adverb above the head; aloft [We spotted airplanes flying *overhead*.]
noun the regular expenses of running a business. Money spent for taxes, rent, heat, or electricity, for example, is included in the overhead.
o·ver·head • ***adjective*** • ***adverb*** • ***noun,*** *plural* **overheads**

overhear (ō vər hir′) ***verb*** to hear something that one is not meant to hear [We *overheard* a quarrel at the next table.]
o·ver·hear • ***verb*** **overheard, overhearing**

overheard (ō vər hurd′) ***verb*** *past tense and past participle of* **overhear**.
o·ver·heard • ***verb***

overjoyed (ō vər joid′) ***adjective*** very happy; delighted [We were *overjoyed* to hear our team had won.]
o·ver·joyed • ***adjective***

overland (ō′vər land) ***adjective*** by, on, or across land [an *overland* journey to California]. This word can also be used as an adverb [They traveled *overland*.]
o·ver·land • ***adjective***

overlap (ō vər lap′) ***verb*** to rest on top of part of something [The scales of a fish *overlap* one another. The two events *overlapped* in time.]
o·ver·lap • ***verb*** **overlapped, overlapping**

overload (ō vər lōd′) ***verb*** to put too great a load in or on [Don't *overload* the washer.]
o·ver·load • ***verb*** **overloaded, overloading**

overlook (ō vər lo͝ok′) ***verb*** **1** to fail to notice [She *overlooked* the misspelled words.] **2** to pay no attention to; excuse [I can't *overlook* her rudeness.] **3** to give a view of from above; look down on [Your room *overlooks* the sea.]
o·ver·look • ***verb*** **overlooked, overlooking**

overnight (ō vər nīt′ *or* ō′vər nīt) ***adverb*** during or through the night [Plan on staying with us *overnight*.]
adjective **1** lasting for or happening during a night [an *overnight* trip; an *overnight* flight]. **2** staying for the night [an *overnight* guest].
o·ver·night • ***adverb*** • ***adjective***

overpass

overpass (ō′vər pas) ***noun*** a bridge or road that crosses a river, another road, or a railroad.
o·ver·pass • ***noun,*** *plural* **overpasses**

overpower (ō vər pou′ər) ***verb*** **1** to get the better of by greater strength or power [The

O

wrestler *overpowered* his opponent in the match.] **2** to make weak or helpless; overcome [The intense heat *overpowered* the runners.]
o·ver·pow·er • *verb* **overpowered, overpowering**

overran (ō vər ran′) *verb past tense of* **overrun**.
o·ver·ran • *verb*

overrule (ō vər ro͞ol′) *verb* to decide against by higher authority; rule against [The higher court *overruled* the judge's decision.]
o·ver·rule • *verb* **overruled, overruling**

overrun (ō vər run′) *verb* **1** to spread out over so as to cover [Weeds *overran* the garden.] **2** to swarm over [Mice had *overrun* the house.] **3** to go beyond certain limits [He *overran* the base and was tagged out.]
o·ver·run • *verb* **overran, overrun, overrunning**

overseas (ō′vər sēz′) *adverb* over or beyond the sea; abroad [Food was sent *overseas*.]
adjective **1** over or across the sea [an *overseas* flight]. **2** of, from, or to countries across the sea; foreign [an *overseas* visitor].
o·ver·seas • *adverb* • *adjective*

overshoe (ō′vər sho͞o) *noun* a shoe or boot, often of rubber or plastic, worn over the regular shoe in cold or wet weather.
o·ver·shoe • *noun, plural* **overshoes**

oversight (ō′vər sīt) *noun* a mistake that is not made on purpose.
o·ver·sight • *noun, plural* **oversights**

oversize (ō′vər sīz) *adjective* larger than is usual or normal [an *oversize* bed].
o·ver·size • *adjective*

oversleep (ō vər slēp′) *verb* to sleep past the time one meant to get up.
o·ver·sleep • *verb* **overslept, oversleeping**

overslept (ō vər slept′) *verb past tense and past participle of* **oversleep**.
o·ver·slept • *verb*

overtake (ō vər tāk′) *verb* **1** to catch up with and, often, go beyond [The tortoise *overtook* the hare.] **2** to come upon suddenly or by surprise [The storm *overtook* us at the beach.]
o·ver·take • *verb* **overtook, overtaken, overtaking**

overtaken (ō vər tāk′ən) *verb past participle of* **overtake**.
o·ver·tak·en • *verb*

overthrew (ō vər thro͞o′) *verb past tense of* **overthrow**.
o·ver·threw • *verb*

overthrow (ō vər thrō′ *for v.;* ō′vər thrō *for n.*) *verb* to put an end to; cause to fall; defeat [The rebels *overthrew* the government.]
noun the act of causing to fall from power [the *overthrow* of the government].
o·ver·throw • *verb* **overthrew, overthrown, overthrowing** • *noun, plural* **overthrows**

overthrown (ō vər thrōn′) *verb past participle of* **overthrow**.
o·ver·thrown • *verb*

overtime (ō′vər tīm) *noun* time beyond the regular time; extra time [If you work on Saturday, you will be paid for the *overtime*.]
adverb beyond the regular hours [She'll have to work *overtime* to finish the job.]
adjective of or for a period of overtime [*overtime* pay].
o·ver·time • *noun* • *adverb* • *adjective*

overtook (ō vər to͝ok′) *verb past tense of* **overtake**.
o·ver·took • *verb*

overture (ō′vər chər) *noun* **1** the section of music that begins an opera. **2** a proposal [They were making peace *overtures* to their enemy.]
o·ver·ture • *noun, plural* **overtures**

WORD HISTORY

overture

An **overture** has nothing to do with the word *over*, for it is not played when the rest of the work is over, or finished. It actually comes from a French word which comes from a Latin word, both of which mean "an opening." An **overture** is the opening, or beginning, of a larger musical work.

overturn (ō vər turn′) *verb* to turn or throw over; upset [The boat *overturned* in the storm.]
o·ver·turn • *verb* **overturned, overturning**

overweight (ō′vər wāt′) *adjective* weighing more than is normal or proper; too heavy.
o·ver·weight • *adjective*

overwhelm (ō vər hwelm′ *or* ō vər welm′) *verb* **1** to overcome completely; make helpless; crush

a	cat	ō	go	ʉ	fur	ə = a *in* ago	
ā	ape	ô	law, for	ch	chin	e *in* agent	
ä	cot, car	o͝o	look	sh	she	i *in* pencil	
e	ten	o͞o	tool	th	thin	o *in* atom	
ē	me	oi	oil	*th*	then	u *in* circus	
i	fit	ou	out	zh	measure		
ī	ice	u	up	ŋ	ring		

[The pilot's family was *overwhelmed* by the news of the plane crash.] **2** to cover over completely; bury [Flood waters *overwhelmed* the farms.]
o·ver·whelm • *verb* **overwhelmed, overwhelming**

overwork (ō vər wurk′ *for v.;* ō′vər wurk *for n.*) *verb* to work too hard [The cowboys *overworked* the horses.]
noun too much work [illness caused by *overwork*].
o·ver·work • *verb* **overworked, overworking** • *noun*

owe (ō) *verb* **1** to have to pay [I *owe* my sister the $2.00 she lent to me.] **2** to have or feel the need to do or give [She *owes* him an apology.] **3** to be obligated for [She *owes* her life to that doctor.]
owe • *verb* **owed, owing**
● The words **owe** and **oh** sound alike.
How much do I *owe* you for the tickets?
She cried "*Oh!*" when the door slammed.

owl (oul) *noun* a bird that has a large head, large eyes, a short, hooked beak, and sharp claws. Owls hunt their prey mostly at night.
owl • *noun, plural* **owls**

owl

own (ōn) *adjective* belonging to or having to do with oneself or itself [I have my *own* bicycle.]
noun something that belongs to oneself [The car is her *own*.]
verb to have for oneself; possess [We *own* that farm.] —Look for the WORD CHOICES box at the entry **have**.
—of one's own belonging only to oneself [He wants a bicycle *of his own*.] **—on one's own** [*an informal use*] by one's own efforts; without help [Jimmy built a tree house entirely *on his own*.]
own • *adjective* • *noun* • *verb* **owned, owning**

owner (ōn′ər) *noun* a person who owns something.
own·er • *noun, plural* **owners**

ownership (ōn′ər ship) *noun* the condition or fact of being an owner; possession.
own·er·ship • *noun*

ox (äks) *noun* **1** any of a group of animals that chew their cud and have divided hoofs. Farm cattle, buffaloes, and bison are oxen. **2** an adult male of farm cattle that has been operated on so that it cannot father young. An ox is used for pulling loads.
ox • *noun, plural* **oxen**

oxen (äks′ən) *noun plural of* **ox**.
ox·en • *noun*

oxidation (äks′i dā′shən) *noun* the act of oxidizing; act of combining with oxygen.
ox·i·da·tion • *noun*

oxide (äks′īd) *noun* a compound made up of oxygen and some other chemical element. Carbon dioxide and carbon monoxide are oxides.
ox·ide • *noun, plural* **oxides**

oxidize (äks′i dīz′) *verb* to combine with oxygen [When iron *oxidizes*, it forms a compound called rust.]
ox·i·dize • *verb* **oxidized, oxidizing**

oxygen (äks′i jən) *noun* a gas that has no color, taste, or smell and is a chemical element. It makes up almost one fifth of the air around the earth. All living things need oxygen. Oxygen combines easily with almost all other elements and is one of the main ingredients of water.
ox·y·gen • *noun*

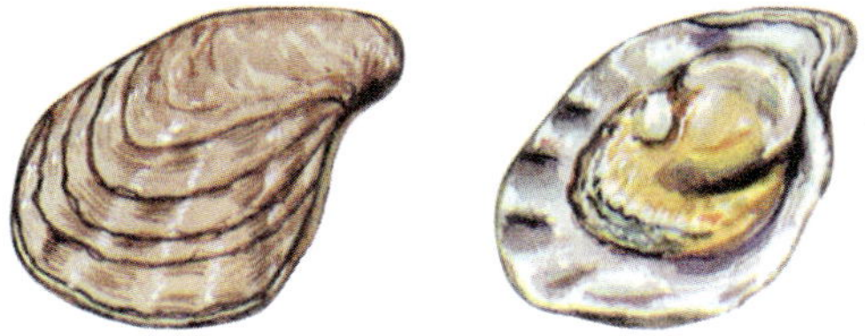
oyster

oyster (ois′tər) *noun* a sea animal that has a soft body enclosed in two rough shells that are hinged together. Some oysters are used as food, while pearls are formed inside others.
oys·ter • *noun, plural* **oysters**

oz. *abbreviation for* ounce.

ozone (ō′zōn) *noun* a pale blue gas with a sharp smell. It is a form of oxygen and is formed when an electric current, such as lightning, passes through air.
o·zone • *noun*

ozone layer *noun* a layer of ozone in the earth's atmosphere. The ozone layer protects the animals and plants on earth from harmful light rays from the sun.

O

P p

Pp Pp Pp Pp

The letter **p** *usually stands for the sound you hear at the beginning of the words* **panda**, **pet**, **pick**, *and* **pull**. *However, you will also see many words that begin with the letter combination* **ph**, *as in* **phone** *and* **phrase**, *where the sound is the sound of* **f**. *In a few words that begin with the letter combinations* **pn** *or* **ps**, *such as* **pneumonia** *and* **psychology**, *the* **p** *is not pronounced at all.*

p or **P** (pē) ***noun*** the sixteenth letter of the English alphabet.
—**mind one's p's and q's** to be careful of what one does and says.
p or **P** • ***noun,*** *plural* **p's** or **P's**

p. *abbreviation for* page.

pa (pä) [*an informal word*] ***noun*** father.
pa • ***noun,*** *plural* **pas**

PA or **Pa.** *abbreviation for* Pennsylvania.

pace (pās) ***noun*** **1** a step in walking or running [three *paces* forward]. **2** the length of a step or stride [The wall measures 20 *paces* from end to end.] **3** the rate of speed at which something moves or develops [The camp counselor set the *pace* on the hike. Science goes forward at a rapid *pace*.]
verb **1** to walk back and forth across [While waiting for the news I *paced* the floor nervously.] **2** to measure by paces [*Pace* off 30 yards.] **3** to set the rate of speed of [He *paces* himself carefully when he runs a long race.]
pace • ***noun,*** *plural* **paces** • ***verb*** **paced, pacing**

Pacific (pə sif′ik) the largest of the oceans. It lies between Asia and the American continents.
adjective of, in, on, or near this ocean [*Pacific* islands].
Pa·cif·ic

WORD HISTORY

Pacific

Ferdinand Magellan, the Portuguese explorer, thought that the ocean to the west of North and South America was very calm and peaceful. He called it the **Pacific** Ocean, using a Latin adjective that comes from a Latin verb meaning "to make peace."

pacifier (pas′i fī′ər) ***noun*** a nipple of rubber or other material that is given to babies to suck on.
pac·i·fi·er • ***noun,*** *plural* **pacifiers**

pacify (pas′i fī′) ***verb*** to make peaceful or calm [An apology can *pacify* an angry neighbor.]
pac·i·fy • ***verb*** **pacified, pacifying, pacifies**

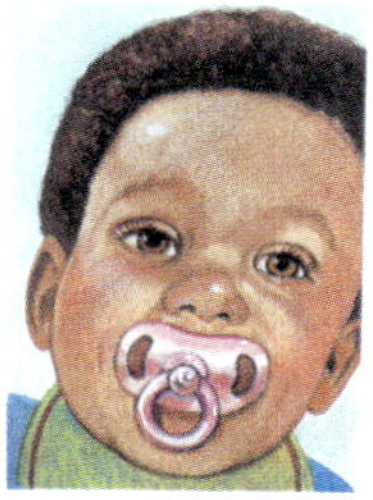

pacifier

a	cat	ō	go	ʉ	fur	ə =	a *in* ago
ā	ape	ô	law, for	ch	chin		e *in* agent
ä	cot, car	oo	look	sh	she		i *in* pencil
e	ten	ōō	tool	th	thin		o *in* atom
ē	me	oi	oil	*th*	then		u *in* circus
i	fit	ou	out	zh	measure		
ī	ice	u	up	ŋ	ring		

pack (pak) ***noun*** **1** a bundle of things wrapped or tied together for carrying. **2** a group or set of persons, animals, or things that are alike [a *pack* of wolves].
verb **1** to put into a box, trunk, or other container for storing or carrying [I *packed* all my records and tapes before the movers arrived.] **2** to fill up with things [*Pack* your suitcase tonight.] **3** to fill as full as possible; crowd or cram [A huge crowd *packed* the stadium.] **4** to press together firmly [The child *packed* sand into the pail.] **5** to cause to go; send [The child was *packed* off to school.]
pack • ***noun, plural*** **packs** • ***verb*** **packed, packing**

package (pak′ij) ***noun*** **1** a thing or group of things wrapped or tied up in a box or in wrapping paper; parcel. **2** a box or wrapping in which something is shipped, stored, delivered, or offered for sale [The *package* lists the ingredients.]
pack·age • ***noun, plural*** **packages**

pact (pakt) ***noun*** an agreement between persons, groups, or nations; treaty.
pact • ***noun, plural*** **pacts**

pad (pad) ***noun*** **1** a soft mass of firmly packed material used for protection or comfort [a football player's shoulder *pads*. The rocking chair has a new seat *pad*.] **2** a number of sheets of paper for writing or drawing that are fastened together along one edge. **3** a small cushion soaked with ink that is used for inking a rubber stamp. **4** the floating leaf of a waterlily. **5** a part that is like a soft, small cushion on the bottom of the foot of an animal such as a dog or lion.
verb **1** to stuff or cover with soft material [They *padded* the seat of the chair.] **2** to make larger or longer by putting in parts not needed [He *padded* his speech with jokes.]
pad • ***noun, plural*** **pads** • ***verb*** **padded, padding**

paddle (pad′əl) ***noun*** **1** a short oar that has a wide blade at one or both ends. It is pulled through the water with both hands to move or steer a canoe or other small boat. **2** a flat, rounded piece of wood with a short handle. It is used to hit the ball in table tennis and other games. **3** a small, flat wooden tool that is used for mixing, stirring, or beating. **4** a board on the edge of a paddle wheel.
verb **1** to row with a paddle [We *paddled* the canoe.] **2** to punish by hitting with a paddle; spank.
pad·dle • ***noun, plural*** **paddles** • ***verb*** **paddled, paddling**

paddle wheel

paddle wheel ***noun*** a wheel with flat boards set around its rim, used to move a steamboat through water.
paddle wheel • ***noun, plural*** **paddle wheels**

paddy (pad′ē) ***noun*** a field where rice is grown. A paddy is usually flooded or heavily irrigated.
pad·dy • ***noun, plural*** **paddies**

padlock (pad′läk) ***noun*** a lock with a U-shaped arm that turns on a hinge at one end. The other end snaps into the body of the lock after the arm is passed through a ring or link.
verb to fasten or keep shut with a padlock.
pad·lock • ***noun, plural*** **padlocks** • ***verb*** **padlocked, padlocking**

pagan (pā′gən) ***noun*** a person who is not a Christian, Muslim, or Jew; heathen.
pa·gan • ***noun, plural*** **pagans**

page[1] (pāj) ***noun*** one side of a leaf of paper in a book, letter, newspaper, or magazine.
page • ***noun, plural*** **pages**

page[2] (pāj) ***noun*** **1** a person who runs errands, carries messages, or acts as a guide in a hotel, office, or legislature. **2** a boy in training to become a knight in the Middle Ages.
verb to try to find by calling out the name of [The secretary *paged* the boss over the factory's loudspeaker.]
page • ***noun, plural*** **pages** • ***verb*** **paged, paging**

pageant (paj′ənt) ***noun*** **1** a large, elaborate public show, parade, or celebration. **2** an

P

elaborate play that is often based on events in history.
pag·eant • *noun, plural* **pageants**

pager (pāj′ər) ***noun*** a device small enough to fit in the pocket of a person's clothing. It makes a sound when a message is sent to it.
pag·er • *noun, plural* **pagers**

pagoda (pə gō′də) ***noun*** a temple in the form of a tower with several stories. There are pagodas in China, Japan, and other countries in Asia.
pa·go·da • *noun, plural* **pagodas**

paid (pād) ***verb*** *past tense and past participle of* **pay**.

pail (pāl) ***noun*** a round, deep container, usually with a handle, for holding and carrying liquids, sand, and other things; bucket.
pail • *noun, plural* **pails**
- The words **pail** and **pale** sound alike.
  The baby dumped sand from her *pail*.
  He turned *pale* with fear.

pain (pān) ***noun*** **1** a feeling of hurting in some part of the body [a sharp *pain* in a tooth]. **2** mental or emotional suffering; sorrow; distress [The news of the accident caused the families a great deal of *pain*.] **3 pains** very careful effort; special care [You must take *pains* to do the work correctly.]
verb to give pain to; cause to suffer; hurt [The wound *pains* me. Their insults *pained* us.]
pain • *noun, plural for senses 1 and 3 only* **pains** • ***verb*** **pained, paining**
- The words **pain** and **pane** sound alike.
  Two aspirins will help relieve the *pain*.
  The baseball broke the window *pane*.

Paine (pān), **Thomas** (täm′əs) 1737-1809; American Revolutionary patriot and writer.
Paine, Thom·as

painful (pān′fəl) ***adjective*** causing or full of pain; hurting [a *painful* wound].
pain·ful • ***adjective***

painless (pān′ləs) ***adjective*** causing no pain; without pain [Getting a haircut is *painless*.]
pain·less • ***adjective***

paint (pānt) ***noun*** a mixture of coloring matter and water, oil, or some other liquid. Paint is used to make a picture or to coat a surface in order to color it or protect it.
verb **1** to make a picture of with paint [The governor was *painted* by a famous artist.] **2** to make pictures with paints [She *paints* as a hobby.] **3** to cover or decorate with paint [*Paint* the walls white. He *painted* the fence.]
paint • *noun, plural* **paints** • ***verb*** **painted, painting**

painter (pānt′ər) ***noun*** **1** a person whose work is painting houses, walls, and other things. **2** an artist who paints pictures.
paint·er • *noun, plural* **painters**

painting (pānt′iŋ) ***noun*** **1** the work or art of using paints. **2** a picture made with paints.
paint·ing • *noun, plural for sense 2 only* **paintings**

pair (per) ***noun*** **1** two things of the same kind that are used together; set of two [a *pair* of skates]. **2** a single thing with two parts that are used together [a *pair* of eyeglasses; a *pair* of pants]. **3** two persons or animals [a *pair* of oxen; a newly married *pair*].
verb to arrange in or form a pair or pairs [He *paired* the socks after washing them. The tennis players *paired* off for the final matches.]
pair • *noun, plural* **pairs** • ***verb*** **paired, pairing**
- The words **pair, pare,** and **pear** sound alike.
  There's a clean *pair* of socks to wear.
  Use a knife to *pare* the peel off fruit.
  A *pear* tree grows in our backyard.

pajamas (pə jä′məz *or* pə jam′əz) ***plural noun*** a loose suit for sleeping. It consists of a jacket and pants.
pa·ja·mas • ***plural noun***

Pakistan (pak′i stan′ *or* pä′ki stän′) a country in southern Asia, west of India.
Pa·ki·stan

pal (pal) [*an informal word*] ***noun*** a close friend; chum.
pal • *noun, plural* **pals**

WORD HISTORY

pal

Our word **pal** comes from a word in the language of the Gypsies of England. To the Gypsies the word means "brother."

a cat	ō go	ʉ fur	ə = a *in* ago
ā ape	ô law, for	ch chin	e *in* agent
ä cot, car	oo look	sh she	i *in* pencil
e ten	ōō tool	th thin	o *in* atom
ē me	oi oil	*th* then	u *in* circus
i fit	ou out	zh measure	
ī ice	u up	ŋ ring	

palace (pal′əs) ***noun*** the official house of a king, queen, or other ruler. A palace is usually a large, grand building.
pal·ace • ***noun, plural*** **palaces**

palate (pal′ət) ***noun*** **1** the roof of the mouth. The bony front part is called the *hard palate*; the fleshy back part is called the *soft palate*. **2** the sense of taste [The food was delicious to our *palates*.]
pal·ate • ***noun, plural*** **palates**
• The words **palate** and **palette** sound alike.
Ice cream feels cold on my *palate*.
The artist mixes paint on a *palette*.

Palau (pä lou′) a country on a group of islands in the western Pacific.
Pa·lau

pale (pāl) ***adjective*** **1** having skin color that is lighter than usual, often because of sickness or sudden emotion [a *pale* complexion. He turned *pale* with fright.] **2** not bright; dim; faint [*pale* blue].
verb to turn pale [Their faces *paled* at the news].
pale • ***adjective*** **paler, palest** • ***verb*** **paled, paling**
• The words **pale** and **pail** sound alike.
His *pale* skin does not tan easily.
Fill the *pail* with water.

Palestine (pal′əs tīn) a region on the eastern coast of the Mediterranean. It was the country of the Jews in Biblical times and is now divided into Arab and Jewish states.
Pal·es·tine

palette (pal′ət) ***noun*** a thin board or other surface on which an artist arranges and mixes paints.
pal·ette • ***noun, plural*** **palettes**
• The words **palette** and **palate** sound alike.
A knife can clean a painter's *palette*.
The hot soup burned my *palate*.

palisade (pal i sād′) ***noun*** **1** a fence made of large, pointed stakes to protect against attack. **2 palisades** a line of steep cliffs, usually along a river.
pal·i·sade • ***noun, plural*** **palisades**

palm[1] (päm) ***noun*** any of a number of trees that grow in warm climates and have a tall trunk with a bunch of large leaves at the top but no branches.
palm • ***noun, plural*** **palms**

palm[2] (päm) ***noun*** the inside part of the hand between the fingers and wrist.
verb to hold or hide in the palm or between the fingers [I'm learning to *palm* coins to perform magic tricks at the school show.]
palm • ***noun, plural*** **palms** • ***verb*** **palmed, palming**

palmetto (pal met′ō) ***noun*** a small palm tree that has leaves shaped like a fan.
pal·met·to • ***noun, plural*** **palmettos** or **palmettoes**

Palm Sunday ***noun*** the Sunday before Easter.

palomino (pal′ə mē′nō) ***noun*** a horse with a golden-tan coat and a whitish mane and tail.
pal·o·mi·no • ***noun, plural*** **palominos**

pamper (pam′pər) ***verb*** to give in easily or too easily to the wishes of; spoil [She *pampered* her only grandson.]
pam·per • ***verb*** **pampered, pampering**

pamphlet (pam′flit) ***noun*** a thin booklet that has a paper cover.
pam·phlet • ***noun, plural*** **pamphlets**

pan (pan) ***noun*** **1** a wide, shallow container that is used for holding liquids and for cooking and baking. Pans are usually made of metal and often do not have a cover. **2** any container that is like a pan. Pans are used for washing out gold from gravel in mining.
verb to wash soil or gravel in a pan to separate the gold in it [The miners *panned* for gold without much success.]
pan • ***noun, plural*** **pans** • ***verb*** **panned, panning**

Panama (pan′ə mä) a country in Central America, on the narrow strip of land (**Isthmus of Panama**) that connects North America and South America.
Pan·a·ma

Panama Canal a ship canal built across Panama, joining the Atlantic and Pacific oceans.

Pan-American (pan′ə mer′i kən) ***adjective*** of or having to do with North, Central, and South America [*Pan-American* relations].
Pan-A·mer·i·can • ***adjective***

pancake (pan′kāk) ***noun*** a thin, flat cake that is made by pouring batter onto a griddle or into a pan and frying it.
pan·cake • ***noun, plural*** **pancakes**

pancreas (pan′krē əs) ***noun*** a large gland behind the stomach. The pancreas gives off juices that help digestion.
pan·cre·as • ***noun, plural*** **pancreases**

panda (pan′də) ***noun*** a white-and-black animal that looks like a bear. It lives in the

P

mountains of China. This animal is also called the **giant panda**.
pan·da • *noun, plural* **pandas**

panda

pane (pān) ***noun*** a single sheet of glass set in a frame in a window or door.
pane • ***noun,*** *plural* **panes**
● The words **pane** and **pain** sound alike.
The baseball broke the window *pane*.
Two aspirins will help relieve the *pain*.

panel (pan′əl) ***noun*** **1** a flat section or part of something that is raised above or sunk below the surfaces around it. A panel may be in a door or a wall or part of a piece of furniture. **2** a board or section containing dials, instruments, and controls for running something [An airplane has a large instrument *panel*.] **3** a group of persons chosen for serving on a jury. **4** a group of persons gathered together to talk about some subject or to take part in a game show, such as one on TV.
verb to cover or decorate with panels [We are *paneling* the library walls with oak.]
pan·el • ***noun,*** *plural* **panels** • ***verb*** **paneled** or **panelled, paneling** or **panelling**

pang (paŋ) ***noun*** a sudden, sharp pain or feeling [hunger *pangs;* guilty *pangs*].
pang • ***noun,*** *plural* **pangs**

panic (pan′ik) ***noun*** a sudden, wild fear that is not controlled.
verb to fill with or show panic [The loud noise *panicked* the birds. The outlaw *panicked* at the sight of the sheriff.]
pan·ic • ***noun,*** *plural* **panics** • ***verb*** **panicked, panicking, panics**

WORD CHOICES

Synonyms of **panic**

Many words share the meaning "a strong or sudden feeling of fear."

alarm	dread	horror
awe	fright	terror

panorama (pan ə ram′ə) ***noun*** an open view in all directions [the *panorama* from a tall building].
pan·o·ra·ma • ***noun,*** *plural* **panoramas**

pansy

pansy (pan′zē) ***noun*** a small plant with flowers that have flat, rounded petals that look like velvet. The flowers are of many colors.
pan·sy • ***noun,*** *plural* **pansies**

pant (pant) ***verb*** **1** to breathe with quick, deep breaths; gasp [The basketball player stood *panting* after scoring a basket.] **2** to speak with quick, heavy breaths [A messenger rushed up and *panted* out the news.]
pant • ***verb*** **panted, panting**

panther (pan′thər) ***noun*** **1** a leopard, especially a black one. **2** *another name for* **cougar**.
pan·ther • ***noun,*** *plural* **panthers** or **panther**

panties (pant′ēz) ***plural noun*** short underpants worn by women or children.
pant·ies • ***plural noun***

pantomime (pan′tə mīm) ***noun*** **1** a play in which actors move and gesture but do not speak. **2** the use of gestures only, without words, to tell something.

a cat	ō go	ʉ fur	ə = a *in* ago
ā ape	ô law, for	ch chin	e *in* agent
ä cot, car	oo look	sh she	i *in* pencil
e ten	ōō tool	th thin	o *in* atom
ē me	oi oil	*th* then	u *in* circus
i fit	ou out	zh measure	
ī ice	u up	ŋ ring	

pan·to·mime • *noun, plural for sense 1 only* **pantomimes**

pantry (pan′trē) ***noun*** a small room near a kitchen, where food, dishes, silverware, and other utensils are kept.
pan·try • ***noun,*** *plural* **pantries**

pants (pants) ***plural noun*** a garment that reaches from the waist to the ankles or the knees and covers each leg separately; trousers.

pantyhose (pan′tē hōz′) ***plural noun*** women's stockings that end in a top part like panties, to form a one-piece garment similar to tights.
pant·y·hose • ***plural noun***

papa (pä′pə) ***noun*** father. This is a word used mainly by children.
pa·pa • ***noun,*** *plural* **papas**

papaya (pə pī′ə) ***noun*** the large, sweet, yellowish-orange fruit of a tropical American tree. The papaya looks like a small melon.
pa·pa·ya • ***noun,*** *plural* **papayas**

paper (pā′pər) ***noun*** **1** thin material in sheets that is used for writing, printing, wrapping, decorating, or covering walls. Paper is made chiefly from wood pulp or rags. **2** a single sheet of this material. **3** a written report, essay, or examination for school [My term *paper* is due tomorrow.] **4** *a short form of* **newspaper**. **5 papers** official documents [Do you have your citizenship *papers* yet?]
verb to cover with wallpaper [We *papered* the living room yesterday.]
pa·per • ***noun,*** *plural for senses 2, 3, 4, and 5 only* **papers** • ***verb*** **papered, papering**

paperback (pā′pər bak) ***noun*** a book that has a thin cardboard cover.
pa·per·back • ***noun,*** *plural* **paperbacks**

paper clip ***noun*** a piece of metal wire that is bent back on itself. It is used to hold loose papers together.
paper clip • ***noun,*** *plural* **paper clips**

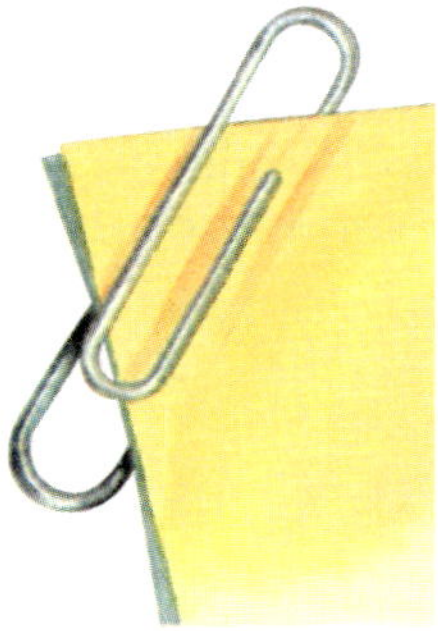
paper clip

papoose (pa po͞os′) ***noun*** a North American Indian baby.
pa·poose • ***noun,*** *plural* **papooses**

Papua New Guinea (pap′ yo͞o ə no͞o′gin′ē) a country that takes up the eastern half of the island of New Guinea.
Pap·u·a New Guin·ea

papyrus (pə pī′rəs) ***noun*** **1** a tall plant that grows in or near water in Egypt and nearby regions. **2** a kind of writing paper made from the inside part of the stems of this plant. The ancient Egyptians, Greeks, and Romans used this kind of paper.
pa·py·rus • ***noun***

par (pär) ***noun*** the average or normal condition or quality [His work is above *par*.]
—on a par equal in quality, rank, or degree [They are *on a par* in ability.]

parachute (per′ə sho͞ot) ***noun*** a large cloth device that opens up like an umbrella. It is used for slowing down a person or thing dropping from an airplane.
verb to jump with or drop by a parachute [The soldiers *parachuted* from the plane. They *parachuted* supplies to their troops.]
par·a·chute • ***noun,*** *plural* **parachutes** • ***verb*** **parachuted, parachuting**

parachute

parade (pə rād′) ***noun*** **1** a large public procession in which people, marching bands, and vehicles pass by spectators. It is usually held in honor of a person or an event. **2** a group of people walking along in a crowd [We watched the Easter *parade*.]
verb **1** to march in a parade [The students *paraded* through downtown.] **2** to show off [They like to *parade* their wealth.]
pa·rade • ***noun,*** *plural* **parades** • ***verb*** **paraded, parading**

paradise (per′ə dīs) ***noun*** **1 Paradise** *another name for* **heaven**. **2** a place or condition of great happiness.
par·a·dise • ***noun***

paradox (per′ə däks) ***noun*** **1** a statement that seems to contradict itself or seems false but may be true in fact. "Water, water, everywhere, and not a drop to drink" is a paradox. **2** a statement that does contradict itself and is therefore false. "The sun was so hot that I froze to death" is a paradox.
par·a·dox • ***noun,*** *plural* **paradoxes**

paraffin (per′ə fin) ***noun*** a white substance like wax that is made from petroleum. It is used for making candles and for sealing jars.
par·af·fin • ***noun***

paragraph (per′ə graf) ***noun*** a separate section of a piece of writing that deals with a specific point and is made up of one or more sentences.
par·a·graph • ***noun,*** *plural* **paragraphs**

Paraguay (per′ə gwā *or* per′ə gwī) a country in central South America.
Par·a·guay

parakeet (per′ə kēt) ***noun*** a small, slender parrot with a long tail. Parakeets are often kept as pets.
par·a·keet • ***noun,*** *plural* **parakeets**

parallel (per′ə lel) ***adjective*** **1** moving or lying in the same direction and always the same distance apart so as never to meet [Writing paper is often marked with *parallel* blue lines.] **2** similar or alike [Their lives followed *parallel* paths.]
noun **1** a parallel line, curve, or plane. **2** a comparison showing how things are alike [The teacher drew a *parallel* between the two books.] **3** any one of the imaginary circles around the earth that are parallel to the equator and that mark degrees of latitude.
verb **1** to be in a parallel line or plane with [The road *parallels* the river.] **2** to be similar to [The story in the film *paralleled* real events.]
par·al·lel • ***adjective*** • ***noun,*** *plural* **parallels** • ***verb*** **paralleled** or **parallelled, paralleling** or **parallelling**

SPELLING TIP

Use this memory aid to spell **parallel**. Write ***all*** the ***l***s in par***all***e***l***.

parallel bars ***plural noun*** two bars parallel to each other that are set on upright posts about 15 inches apart. They are used to perform certain exercises in gymnastics.

parallelogram (per′ə lel′ə gram) ***noun*** a flat figure having four sides, with opposite sides parallel and of equal length.
par·al·lel·o·gram • ***noun,*** *plural* **parallelograms**

parallelogram

paralysis (pə ral′ə sis) ***noun*** a loss of the power to move or feel in a part of the body. It can be caused by an injury to the brain or spinal cord.
pa·ral·y·sis • ***noun***

paralyze (per′ə līz) ***verb*** **1** to cause paralysis in. **2** to make powerless or helpless [Heavy snows *paralyzed* traffic.]
par·a·lyze • ***verb*** **paralyzed, paralyzing**

paramedic (per′ə med′ik) ***noun*** a person who is trained to help doctors and nurses or to give first aid when a doctor or nurse is not present. Paramedics also give first aid in an ambulance on the way to a hospital.
par·a·med·ic • ***noun,*** *plural* **paramedics**

paramount (per′ə mount) ***adjective*** most important; ranking highest [Your problems are of *paramount* concern to us.]
par·a·mount • ***adjective***

parasite (per′ə sīt) ***noun*** **1** a plant or animal that lives on or in another plant or animal and gets food from it. Mistletoe and fleas are parasites. **2** a person who lives at another person's expense without paying that person back in any way.
par·a·site • ***noun,*** *plural* **parasites**

WORD HISTORY

parasite

The word **parasite** comes from a Greek word that means "a person who eats at someone else's table."

parasol (per′ə sôl) ***noun*** a light umbrella that a person carries to provide shade from the sun.
par·a·sol • ***noun,*** *plural* **parasols**

paratrooper (per′ə tro͞op ər) ***noun*** a soldier who has been trained to parachute from an airplane into an area where fighting is going on.
par·a·troop·er • ***noun,*** *plural* **paratroopers**

parcel (pär′səl) ***noun*** **1** a wrapped package; a bundle. **2** a piece of land [a *parcel* of ten acres].
verb to divide into parts for giving away or selling [The land in the new territory was *parceled* out to settlers.]
par·cel • ***noun,*** *plural* **parcels** • ***verb*** **parceled** or **parcelled, parceling** or **parcelling**

a	cat	ō	go	ʉ	fur	ə =	a *in* ago
ā	ape	ô	law, for	ch	chin		e *in* agent
ä	cot, car	o͝o	look	sh	she		i *in* pencil
e	ten	o͞o	tool	th	thin		o *in* atom
ē	me	oi	oil	*th*	then		u *in* circus
i	fit	ou	out	zh	measure		
ī	ice	u	up	ŋ	ring		

parch (pärch) ***verb*** **1** to make or become dry and hot [The sun *parched* the fields.] **2** to make very thirsty.
parch • ***verb*** **parched, parching**

parchment (pärch′mənt) ***noun*** **1** the skin of a sheep or goat that has been prepared so that it can be written on or painted on. **2** a kind of paper that is made to look like parchment.
parch·ment • ***noun***

pardon (pärd′n) ***verb*** **1** to forgive or excuse [*Pardon* me for interrupting.] **2** to free from further punishment [A governor may *pardon* a criminal.]
noun **1** the act of pardoning. **2** an official document that grants a pardon to a person.
par·don • ***verb*** **pardoned, pardoning** • ***noun,*** *plural for sense 2 only* **pardons**

pare (per) ***verb*** **1** to cut or trim away the rind or covering of; to peel [He *pared* the potatoes.] **2** to make less bit by bit [We *pared* down our expenses.]
pare • ***verb*** **pared, paring**
• The words **pare, pair,** and **pear** sound alike.
Use a knife to *pare* the peel off fruit.
There's a new *pair* of shoes to wear.
A *pear* tree grows in our backyard.

parent (per′ənt) ***noun*** **1** a father or mother. **2** an animal or plant as it is related to its offspring.
par·ent • ***noun,*** *plural* **parents**

parental (pə rent′l) ***adjective*** like or having to do with a parent [*parental* advice].
pa·ren·tal • ***adjective***

parenthesis (pə ren′thə sis) ***noun*** either one of two curved lines, (), that are used in writing. Parentheses are used to enclose or set off a word or phrase in a sentence. They are also used to enclose mathematical symbols and numbers.
pa·ren·the·sis • ***noun,*** *plural* **pa·ren·the·ses** (pə ren′thə sēz)

parenting (per′ənt iŋ) ***noun*** the work or skill of a parent in raising a child or children.
par·ent·ing • ***noun***

Paris (per′is) the capital of France.
Par·is

parish (per′ish) ***noun*** **1** a church district in the care of a priest or minister. **2** the people living in this kind of district who go to its church. **3** in Louisiana, a government district that is like a county.
par·ish • ***noun,*** *plural* **parishes**

park (pärk) ***noun*** **1** an area of land in or near a city, with trees, lawns, benches, and other features, where people can come to rest and enjoy themselves. **2** a large area of land set apart by the government to be left in its natural state. **3** a gear arrangement in a motor vehicle in which the clutch is not engaged and the wheels are locked.
verb to leave a car or other vehicle in a certain place for a time [You may not *park* here on weekdays.]
park • ***noun,*** *plural for senses 1 and 2 only* **parks** • ***verb*** **parked, parking**

parka (pär′kə) ***noun*** a heavy winter jacket with a hood. Parkas often have linings of thick, soft material.
par·ka • ***noun,*** *plural* **parkas**

parkway (pärk′wā) ***noun*** a wide road with trees, grass, and bushes planted along its edges or in a center strip that divides the road.
park·way • ***noun,*** *plural* **parkways**

Parliament (pär′lə mənt) ***noun*** the legislature of a country such as Britain or Canada.
Par·lia·ment • ***noun,*** *plural* **Parliaments**

WORD HISTORY

Parliament

Parliament comes from a French verb that means "to speak." The members of **Parliament** or our Congress spend much time talking about proposed laws and other matters before voting on them.

parlor (pär′lər) ***noun*** **1** a living room: this meaning is old-fashioned. **2** a kind of business with special services [a beauty *parlor*].
par·lor • ***noun,*** *plural* **parlors**

parochial (pə rō′kē əl) ***adjective*** in or having to do with a church parish [a *parochial* school].
pa·ro·chi·al • ***adjective***

parole (pə rōl′) ***noun*** the release of a prisoner before his or her whole sentence has been served. The prisoner promises to obey certain rules of good behavior and is supervised by an officer of the court.
verb to free under the rules of parole.
pa·role • ***noun*** • ***verb*** **paroled, paroling**

parrot (per′ət) ***noun*** a tropical bird with a hooked bill and brightly colored feathers. Some parrots can learn to imitate human speech.
verb to repeat or copy without understanding completely [He *parroted* his parents' opinions.]
par·rot • ***noun,*** *plural* **parrots** • ***verb*** **parroted, parroting**

parsley

parsley (pärs′lē) ***noun*** a plant with small, often curly, dark-green leaves that are used to flavor and decorate food.
pars·ley • ***noun***

parson (pär′sən) ***noun*** a minister; pastor.
par·son • ***noun,*** *plural* **parsons**

part (pärt) ***noun*** **1** a section, piece, or portion of a whole [the newer *part* of town; *part* of our class]. **2** a necessary piece that can be replaced [*parts* for cars]. **3** a share of work or duty [You must do your *part.*] **4** a role in a play or movie; character [Who will play the *part* of Cinderella?] **5** a side in an argument or fight [I won't take anyone's *part* in this quarrel.] **6** the dividing line that is formed when hair is combed in different directions.
verb **1** to pull or come apart; to separate [He *parted* the curtains to look out. The rope *parted* in the middle from the strain.] **2** to go away from each other [They *parted* at the crossroads.] **3** to comb so that a part forms [He *parts* his hair in the middle.]
adjective of or having to do with only a part [I am a *part* owner of a small business.]
adverb not completely; partly [The dog is *part* mine.]
—in part not completely; partly. **—part with** to give up; let go [He refused to *part with* his bicycle.] **—take part** to have or take a share in something; participate [We all *took part* in the concert.]
part • ***noun,*** *plural for senses 1, 2, 4, and 6 only* **parts** • ***verb*** **parted, parting** • ***adjective*** • ***adverb***

WORD CHOICES

Synonyms of part

Many words share the meaning "something that goes together with other similar things to form a whole."

component	fragment	section
division	piece	segment
fraction	portion	

Parthenon

Parthenon (pär′thə nän) the ancient Greek temple of Athena on the Acropolis in Athens.
Par·the·non

partial (pär′shəl) ***adjective*** **1** of a part or in only a part; not complete or total [a *partial* eclipse of the sun]. **2** favoring one person or side more than another [A judge should never be *partial.*]
—be partial to to have a special liking for; be fond of.
par·tial • ***adjective***

participate (pär tis′i pāt′) ***verb*** to take part in something with other people; have a share.
par·tic·i·pate • ***verb*** **participated, participating**

participle (pärt′i sip′əl) ***noun*** a form of a verb that can be used as both a verb and an adjec-

a cat	ō go	ʉ fur	ə = a *in* ago
ā ape	ô law, for	ch chin	e *in* agent
ä cot, car	oo look	sh she	i *in* pencil
e ten	ōō tool	th thin	o *in* atom
ē me	oi oil	*th* then	u *in* circus
i fit	ou out	zh measure	
ī ice	u up	ŋ ring	

tive. Present participles end in *-ing*, and past participles usually end in *-ed* or *-en*.
par·ti·ci·ple • *noun, plural* **participles**

particle (pärt′i kəl) *noun* a very small piece.
par·ti·cle • *noun, plural* **particles**

particular (pär tik′yoo lər) *adjective* **1** having to do with only one person, group, part, or thing; individual, not general [What is your *particular* opinion?] **2** apart from any other; specific [Do you have a *particular* color in mind?] **3** more than ordinary; unusual or special [Pay *particular* attention.] **4** hard to please; very careful [We're *particular* about what we eat.]
noun a detail, fact, or item [Give full *particulars* about the accident to the police officer.]
par·tic·u·lar • *adjective* • *noun, plural* **particulars**

partition (pär tish′ən) *noun* a partial wall, a panel, or some other structure that divides or separates space.
verb to divide into parts [We *partitioned* the basement into three rooms.]
par·ti·tion • *noun, plural* **partitions** • *verb* **partitioned, partitioning**

partly (pärt′lē) *adverb* in part; not completely.
part·ly • *adverb*

partner (pärt′nər) *noun* **1** one of the owners of a business who shares in its risks and profits. **2** either one of two players who are on the same side or team. **3** either one of two persons who are dancing together.
part·ner • *noun, plural* **partners**

partnership (pärt′nər ship) *noun* **1** the condition of being a partner. **2** a business firm that is made up of two or more partners.
part·ner·ship • *noun, plural for sense 2 only* **partnerships**

part of speech *noun* any one of the groups or classes in which words are placed according to the way they are used in the structure of a sentence. The usual names for the parts of speech are *noun, verb, pronoun, adjective, adverb, preposition, conjunction,* and *interjection*.
part of speech • *noun, plural* **parts of speech**

partridge (pär′trij) *noun* a wild bird that is hunted as game. Partridges have a plump body and gray, brown, and white feathers.
par·tridge • *noun, plural* **partridges**

part time *adverb* as a part-time employee or student [She works *part time* in a store.]

part-time (pärt′tīm′) *adjective* being an employee or student for periods taking less time than a full, regular schedule [a *part-time* waitress].

party (pär′tē) *noun* **1** a gathering of people to have a good time [a birthday *party*]. **2** a group of people who share the same political ideas. They work together to spread their ideas and to elect certain people to government offices. **3** a group of people who are working or acting together [The scouting *party* found the trail.] **4** [*an informal use*] a person [This *party* insists on talking to you.]
par·ty • *noun, plural* **parties**

pass[1] (pas) *noun* a narrow opening or way through, especially between mountains.
pass • *noun, plural* **passes**

pass[2] (pas) *verb* **1** to go by, beyond, over, or through [I *pass* your house every day. The guards won't let anyone *pass*.] **2** to go; move on [The days *pass* quickly.] —Look for the WORD CHOICES box at the entry **go**. **3** to come up from behind and go beyond [I *passed* everyone else and won the race.] **4** to go or change from one place or condition to another [The liquid *passed* into solid form when it froze.] **5** to come to an end or go away [The fever *passed*.] **6** to get through a test or course of study with success [She *passed* the exam.] **7** to approve or be approved [The city council *passed* the law.] **8** to hand or throw to another person [Please *pass* the bread. He *passed* the ball and ran forward.]
noun **1** a free ticket [We got two *passes* to the movies.] **2** written permission [You can't get into the library without a *pass*.] **3** the act of throwing or hitting a ball or puck to another player.
—**pass away** to die. —**pass out** **1** to give out; distribute [*Pass* the cookies *out* to everyone.] **2** to faint [She *passed out* from the heat.]
pass • *verb* **passed, passing** • *noun, plural* **passes**

passage (pas′ij) *noun* **1** the act of passing [the *passage* of day into night; the *passage* of a bill into law]. **2** permission or right to pass [He was given *passage* through the enemy's lines.] **3** a voyage [Stormy seas made for a difficult *passage* across the Atlantic.] **4** passenger space, especially on a ship [We booked *passage* on a cruise ship.] **5** a way to pass through, such as a road or a hall [a *passage*

P

through the mountains]. **6** a small section of a speech, piece of writing, or piece of music [They read a *passage* from the Bible.]
pas·sage • *noun, plural for senses 3, 5, and 6 only* **passages**

passageway (pas′ij wā′) *noun* a hall, alley, or other narrow passage to go through.
pas·sage·way • *noun, plural* **passageways**

passenger (pas′ən jər) *noun* a person who is traveling in a car, plane, ship, or other form of transportation but not driving or helping to operate it.
pas·sen·ger • *noun, plural* **passengers**

passerby (pas′ər bī′) *noun* a person who is passing by [*Passersby* admired the colorful garden.]
pass·er·by • *noun, plural* **pas·sers·by** (pas′ərz bī′)

passing (pas′iŋ) *adjective* **1** going by or past [a *passing* train]. **2** lasting only a short time; brief [a *passing* fancy]. **3** done or made without careful thought [a *passing* remark]. **4** allowing a person to pass a course or test [a *passing* grade].
noun the act of a person or thing that passes [the *passing* of the old year, the coming of the new].
pass·ing • *adjective* • *noun*

passion (pash′ən) *noun* **1** a very strong feeling such as love, anger, and hatred. **2** strong love between a man and a woman. **3** great liking or enthusiasm [her *passion* for books]. **4** the object of a person's strong liking or great enthusiasm [Golf is my mom's *passion*.]
pas·sion • *noun, plural for senses 1 and 4 only* **passions**

passionate (pash′ən ət) *adjective* having or showing strong feelings [a *passionate* speech].
pas·sion·ate • *adjective*

passive (pas′iv) *adjective* not active, but only acted upon or influenced [*passive* spectators].
pas·sive • *adjective*

Passover (pas′ō vər) *noun* a Jewish holiday in memory of the freeing of the ancient Hebrews from slavery in Egypt.
Pass·o·ver • *noun*

passport (pas′pôrt) *noun* an official paper that is given by a government to a citizen who is traveling in foreign countries. It is used as identification.
pass·port • *noun, plural* **passports**

password (pas′wʉrd) *noun* a secret word or signal that a person must give when a guard or sentry asks for it.
pass·word • *noun, plural* **passwords**

past (past) *adjective* **1** gone by; ended or over [What is *past* is finished.] **2** from the time gone by; before the present time [a *past* president of our club]. **3** just gone by [the *past* week]. **4** showing time that has gone by [the *past* tense of a verb].
noun **1** the time that has gone by [That's all in the *past*.] **2** the history or earlier life of a person, group, or thing [His *past* was filled with exciting adventures.]
preposition **1** later than; beyond [ten minutes *past* two]. **2** farther than; beyond [We drove out *past* the city limits.]
adverb up to and beyond a certain place [The band marched *past*.]
past • *adjective* • *noun, plural for sense 2 only* **pasts** • *preposition* • *adverb*

pasta (päs′tə) *noun* **1** dough made of wheat flour, that is shaped and dried before being cooked. **2** cooked pasta, such as spaghetti or macaroni.
pas·ta • *noun*

paste (pāst) *noun* **1** a mixture of water and a substance such as flour that is used to stick paper or other light things together. **2** a soft, moist, smooth mixture [*toothpaste*, tomato *paste*].
verb to cause to stick with paste [Let's *paste* these pictures in a book.]
paste • *noun* • *verb* **pasted, pasting**

pastel (pas tel′) *noun* **1** a soft, pale shade of some color. **2** a kind of crayon that is made of ground coloring material. **3** a picture that has been drawn with this kind of crayon.
adjective soft and pale [*pastel* blue].
pas·tel • *noun, plural* **pastels** • *adjective*

Pasteur (pas tʉr′), **Louis** (lo͞o′ē) 1822-1895; French scientist who found a way of treating rabies and of killing bacteria in milk.
Pas·teur, Lou·is

pasteurize (pas′chər īz) *verb* to heat a liquid, especially milk, to a certain temperature for a certain length of time. This kills harmful bacteria.
pas·teur·ize • *verb* **pasteurized, pasteurizing**

a cat	ō go	ʉ fur	ə = a *in* ago
ā ape	ô law, for	ch chin	e *in* agent
ä cot, car	o͝o look	sh she	i *in* pencil
e ten	o͞o tool	th thin	o *in* atom
ē me	oi oil	*th* then	u *in* circus
i fit	ou out	zh measure	
ī ice	u up	ŋ ring	

pastime (pas′tīm) ***noun*** a way of spending spare time in a pleasant way; recreation.
pas·time • ***noun,*** *plural* **pastimes**

pastor (pas′tər) ***noun*** a member of the clergy who is in charge of a church; minister or priest.
pas·tor • ***noun,*** *plural* **pastors**

past participle ***noun*** a participle that is used to show time that has gone by or an action that took place in the past. It can also be used as an adjective. In the sentences "We saw a mountain covered with snow" and "She has given me a job," the words "covered" and "given" are past participles.
past participle • ***noun,*** *plural* **past participles**

pastry (pās′trē) ***noun*** **1** pies, tarts, and other baked foods with a crust that is made from flour dough with shortening in it. **2** this kind of dough. **3** a single pie, cake, or other baked food.
pas·try • ***noun,*** *plural for sense 3 only* **pastries**

past tense ***noun*** a form of a verb that shows that the verb's action took place in the past. In the sentence "We talked for hours," the verb "talked" is in the past tense.

pasture (pas′chər) ***noun*** **1** a field or other piece of land where grass and other plants grow and where cattle and sheep can graze. **2** grass and other plants that are eaten by grazing animals.
verb to put into a pasture to graze [We *pasture* our cattle in the field near the brook.]
pas·ture • ***noun,*** *plural for sense 1 only* **pastures** • ***verb*** **pastured, pasturing**

pat (pat) ***noun*** **1** a quick, gentle tap or stroke with the open hand. **2** the sound that this makes. **3** a small lump [a *pat* of butter].
verb to touch or stroke with a pat or pats.
pat • ***noun,*** *plural* **pats** • ***verb*** **patted, patting**

patch (pach) ***noun*** **1** a piece of cloth, metal, or other material that is put on to mend a hole, a tear, or a worn spot. **2** a pad that is worn over an eye that has been hurt. **3** an area or spot [*patches* of blue sky].
verb **1** to put a patch or patches on [We *patched* the worn elbows of the coat.] **2** to make in a hurry, often by putting bits together [He *patched* together a speech.]
—patch up to settle or end [They *patched up* their quarrel.]
patch • ***noun,*** *plural* **patches** • ***verb*** **patched, patching**

patchwork

patchwork (pach′wurk) ***noun*** a design that is sewn from pieces of cloth in various colors and shapes.
patch·work • ***noun***

patent (pat′nt) ***noun*** an official document issued by a government that gives a person or company the right to be the only one to make or sell a certain invention for a certain number of years.
verb to get a patent for [The scientist *patented* his invention.]
pat·ent • ***noun,*** *plural* **patents** • ***verb*** **patented, patenting**

patent leather ***noun*** leather that has a hard, glossy surface. It is usually black.

paternal (pə tur′nəl) ***adjective*** **1** like or having to do with a father [*paternal* advice]. **2** related to a person on the person's father's side [My father's sister is my *paternal* aunt.]
pa·ter·nal • ***adjective***

path (path) ***noun*** **1** a track made by or for walking. **2** a course or route along which something moves [the *path* of the hurricane].
path • ***noun,*** *plural* **paths**

pathetic (pə thet′ik) ***adjective*** causing pity or sorrow [a wounded bird's *pathetic* cries] —Look for the WORD CHOICES box at the entry **moving**.
pa·thet·ic • ***adjective***

pathway (path′wā) ***noun*** *another name for* **path**.
path·way • ***noun,*** *plural* **pathways**

patience (pā′shəns) ***noun*** the quality of being patient [She showed great *patience* in training her dog.]
pa·tience • ***noun***

P

patient (pā′shənt) *adjective* able to put up with pain, trouble, delay, or boredom without complaining [The *patient* children waited in line.]
noun a person who is under the care of a doctor.
pa·tient • *adjective* • *noun, plural* **patients**

patio (pat′ē ō *or* pät′ē ō) *noun* a paved area near a house, with chairs, tables, and other furniture for relaxing and eating outdoors.
pa·ti·o • *noun, plural* **patios**

patriot (pā′trē ət) *noun* a person who shows great love for his or her country and is loyal to it.
pa·tri·ot • *noun, plural* **patriots**

patriotic (pā′trē ät′ik) *adjective* showing great love for one's country and loyalty to it.
pa·tri·ot·ic • *adjective*

patriotism (pā′trē ə tiz′əm) *noun* great love for one's country and loyalty to it.
pa·tri·ot·ism • *noun*

patrol (pə trōl′) *verb* to make regular trips around for the purpose of guarding [The watchman *patrolled* the area all night.]
noun **1** the act of patrolling [They are on *patrol* tonight.] **2** a person or group that patrols [The highway *patrol* uses motorcycles.]
pa·trol • *verb* **patrolled, patrolling** • *noun, plural for sense 2 only* **patrols**

patrolman (pə trōl′mən) *noun* a police officer who patrols a certain area.
pa·trol·man • *noun, plural* **patrolmen**

patron (pā′trən) *noun* **1** a regular customer [a *patron* of a restaurant]. **2** a rich or important person who helps or supports another person, a group, or an institution [the *patrons* of the orchestra; *patrons* of the arts].
pa·tron • *noun, plural* **patrons**

patronage (pā′trən ij *or* pa′trən ij) *noun* **1** the help or support that a patron gives. **2** the regular business or trade of customers. **3** the distribution of political offices or other political favors by a government or a person with political power.
pa·tron·age • *noun*

patronize (pā′trən īz *or* pa′trən īz) *verb* **1** to be a patron to; to support or sponsor. **2** to be a regular customer of [We *patronize* that supermarket.]
pa·tron·ize • *verb* **patronized, patronizing**

patter (pat′ər) *noun* a series of light, quick taps [the *patter* of rain on the window].
verb to make a series of light, quick taps.
pat·ter • *noun* • *verb* **pattered, pattering**

pattern (pat′ərn) *noun* **1** a shaped piece or a plan that is used as a guide for making something [a dress *pattern*] —Look for the WORD CHOICES box at the entry **model**. **2** an arrangement of parts; design [wallpaper with a flower *pattern*].
verb to imitate or model, as if from a pattern [She *patterned* her life on the life of her aunt, who was a doctor.]
pat·tern • *noun, plural* **patterns** • *verb* **patterned, patterning**

patty (pat′ē) *noun* a small, flat cake of ground food.
pat·ty • *noun, plural* **patties**

Paul (pôl) a Christian Apostle who wrote some sections of the New Testament that are in the form of letters to members of various congregations. He is also called *Saint Paul*.

Paul Bunyan (pôl′ bun′yən) a giant lumberjack in American folk tales who did amazing things.
Paul Bun·yan

pauper (pô′pər *or* pä′pər) *noun* a very poor person.
pau·per • *noun, plural* **paupers**

pause (pôz *or* päz) *noun* a short stop in speaking, moving, or acting.
verb to make a pause.
pause • *noun, plural* **pauses** • *verb* **paused, pausing**

pave (pāv) *verb* to cover a surface with asphalt, concrete, bricks, or similar materials.
pave • *verb* **paved, paving**

pavement (pāv′mənt) *noun* a paved surface or covering, especially on a road or driveway.
pave·ment • *noun*

pavilion (pə vil′yən) *noun* **1** a building or part of a building, often with open sides. It is used for exhibits at a fair or for dancing or similar entertainment. **2** a large tent, often with a pointed top.
pa·vil·ion • *noun, plural* **pavilions**

a cat	ō go	ʉ fur	ə = a *in* ago
ā ape	ô law, for	ch chin	e *in* agent
ä cot, car	oo look	sh she	i *in* pencil
e ten	ōō tool	th thin	o *in* atom
ē me	oi oil	*th* then	u *in* circus
i fit	ou out	zh measure	
ī ice	u up	ŋ ring	

pavilion

paw (pô *or* pä) ***noun*** the foot of a four-footed animal that has claws.
verb **1** to touch, dig, or hit with the paws, hoofs, or feet [The horse *pawed* the earth.] **2** to handle in a rough and clumsy way [He *pawed* through the drawer looking for money.]
paw • ***noun,*** *plural* **paws** • ***verb*** **pawed, pawing**

pawn[1] (pôn *or* pän) ***verb*** to leave something with another person in exchange for a loan. When the loan is paid back, the object is returned [She *pawned* her jewelry when she was out of work.]
pawn • ***verb*** **pawned, pawning**

pawn[2] (pôn *or* pän) ***noun*** a chess piece of the lowest value.
pawn • ***noun,*** *plural* **pawns**

Pawnee (pô nē′ *or* pä′nē) ***noun*** **1** a member of a group of North American Indian peoples who used to live in parts of Nebraska. They now live in northern Oklahoma. **2** the language of these peoples.
Paw·nee • ***noun,*** *plural for sense 1 only* **Pawnees** or **Pawnee**

pay (pā) ***verb*** **1** to give money to for products or services [Did you *pay* the cab driver?] **2** to give in exchange [We *paid* ten dollars for our tickets.] **3** to settle or get rid of by giving money [They *paid* the debt.] **4** to give or offer [*Pay* attention.] **5** to make [She *paid* us a visit.] **6** to be worthwhile [It *pays* to follow directions.]
noun money that is paid for work or services [We get our *pay* on Friday.] —Look for the WORD CHOICES box at the entry **wage**.
adjective **1** operated by putting in coins [a *pay* telephone]. **2** describing a service that is paid by subscription or a special fee [*pay* TV].
—pay back to pay in return. **—pay off** **1** to pay all that is owed [We've finally *paid off* the loan.] **2** [*an informal use*] to come to a desired result.
pay • ***verb*** **paid, paying** • ***noun*** • ***adjective***

payable (pā′ə bəl) ***adjective*** due to be paid [This bill is *payable* on the first day of the month.]
pay·a·ble • ***adjective***

paycheck (pā′chek) ***noun*** one of the regular checks that are written to an employee to pay for work that he or she has done.
pay·check • ***noun,*** *plural* **paychecks**

payment (pā′mənt) ***noun*** **1** the act of paying or the fact of being paid [Prompt *payment* is requested.] **2** something that is paid or to be paid [a monthly rent *payment* of $500].
pay·ment • ***noun,*** *plural for sense 2 only* **payments**

payroll (pā′rōl) ***noun*** **1** a list of employees who are to be paid, with the amount that is due to each of them. **2** the total amount of money to be paid to all employees.
pay·roll • ***noun,*** *plural* **payrolls**

PC ***noun*** *the same as* **personal computer**.
PC • ***noun,*** *plural* **PCs**

PE *abbreviation for* Prince Edward Island.

pea

pea (pē) ***noun*** the round green seed of a climbing plant. The seeds grow in pods and are eaten as a vegetable.
pea • ***noun,*** *plural* **peas**

peace (pēs) ***noun*** **1** freedom from war or fighting [a nation living in *peace* with other nations]. **2** public order and safety; law and order [The loud party was disturbing the

P

peace.] **3** a condition of calm or quiet [Living alone in the mountains, he found *peace* of mind.]
● The words **peace** and **piece** sound alike.
He was hoping for some *peace* and quiet.
Would you like a *piece* of cake?

peaceful (pēs′fəl) ***adjective*** **1** free from noise or disorder; quiet or calm [*peaceful* country roads]. **2** fond of peace [*peaceful* people].
peace·ful • ***adjective***

peace pipe

peace pipe ***noun*** a long pipe that some North American Indian peoples formerly smoked as a sign of peace and friendship.
peace pipe • ***noun,*** *plural* **peace pipes**

peach (pēch) ***noun*** **1** a round, orange-yellow fruit with a fuzzy skin, a rough pit, and much juice. **2** the tree that it grows on. **3** an orange-yellow color.
peach • ***noun,*** *plural for senses 1 and 2 only* **peaches**

peach

peacock (pē′käk) ***noun*** a large bird that has long tail feathers of rich blue, green, and other colors. It can spread out these feathers in the shape of a fan.
pea·cock • ***noun,*** *plural* **peacocks**

pea green ***noun*** a light yellowish green.

peak (pēk) ***noun*** **1** the pointed top of a hill or mountain. **2** a hill or mountain with a pointed top. **3** a pointed top or end [the *peak* of a roof]. **4** the highest point or degree [The fireworks were the *peak* of the July 4th celebration.] —Look for the WORD CHOICES box at the entry **climax**.
peak • ***noun,*** *plural* **peaks**
● The words **peak** and **peek** sound alike.
He climbed a ladder to the house's *peak*.
May I take a *peek* at the gifts?

peaked (pēk′id) ***adjective*** looking thin and tired [a *peaked* face].
peak·ed • ***adjective***

peal (pēl) ***noun*** **1** the loud ringing sound of a bell or bells. **2** a loud sound that echoes [*peals* of thunder; *peals* of laughter].
verb to ring out loud and long.
peal • ***noun,*** *plural* **peals** • ***verb*** **pealed, pealing**
● The words **peal** and **peel** sound alike.
Church bells *peal* Sunday mornings.
I threw away the banana *peel*.

peanut (pē′nut) ***noun*** **1** the dry pod of a vine related to the pea plant. The pod contains seeds that are eaten like nuts. **2** one of these seeds.
pea·nut • ***noun,*** *plural* **peanuts**

peanut butter ***noun*** a food paste or spread that is made by grinding peanuts that have been roasted.

pear (per) ***noun*** **1** a soft, juicy fruit that is round at one end and narrows toward the stem. **2** the tree this fruit grows on.
pear • ***noun,*** *plural* **pears**
● The words **pear, pair,** and **pare** sound alike.
A *pear* tree grows in our backyard.
There's a clean *pair* of pants to wear.
Use a knife to *pare* the potatoes.

pear

pearl (purl) ***noun*** a gem that is glossy, creamy white or blue-gray in color, and usually round in shape. It is formed inside the shells of certain kinds of oysters.
pearl • ***noun,*** *plural* **pearls**

peasant (pez′ənt) ***noun*** a member of the class of farm workers and farmers with small farms

a	cat	ō	go	ʉ	fur	ə =	a *in* ago
ā	ape	ô	law, for	ch	chin		e *in* agent
ä	cot, car	oo	look	sh	she		i *in* pencil
e	ten	ōō	tool	th	thin		o *in* atom
ē	me	oi	oil	*th*	then		u *in* circus
i	fit	ou	out	zh	measure		
ī	ice	u	up	ŋ	ring		

in Europe and Asia.
peas·ant • *noun, plural* **peasants**

peat (pēt) ***noun*** a mass of partly rotted plants and grass that is formed in marshes. It is dried and used for fuel.

pebble (peb′əl) ***noun*** a small stone that has been worn down until it is round.
peb·ble • ***noun**, plural* **pebbles**

pecan (pē kän′ *or* pē kan′) ***noun*** **1** an oval nut with a thin, smooth shell. **2** the tree that it grows on, mainly in the southern U.S.
pe·can • ***noun**, plural* **pecans**

peck[1] (pek) ***verb*** **1** to strike or pick up something in the way that a bird does with its beak. **2** to make by doing this [The bird *pecked* a hole in the tree.]
noun **1** a mark or stroke that is made by pecking. **2** [*an informal use*] a quick, light kiss.
peck • ***verb*** **pecked, pecking** • ***noun**, plural* **pecks**

peck[2] (pek) ***noun*** **1** a unit of measure that is used for grain, fruit, vegetables, and other dry things. A peck is equal to eight quarts. **2** [*an informal use*] a large amount [You're in a *peck* of trouble!]
peck • ***noun**, plural for sense 1 only* **pecks**

peculiar (pi kyo͞ol′yər) ***adjective*** **1** odd or strange [We heard a *peculiar* noise and went to investigate.] —Look for the WORD CHOICES box at the entry **strange**. **2** of a particular person, thing, or group; special [Such marks on the wings are *peculiar* to this kind of bird.]
pe·cul·iar • ***adjective***

pedal (ped′əl) ***noun*** a lever that is worked by the foot. The pedals of a bicycle make the back wheel turn.
verb to move or work by pushing on a pedal or pedals [We *pedaled* our bikes home.]
ped·al • ***noun**, plural* **pedals** • ***verb*** **pedaled** or **pedalled, pedaling** or **pedalling**
● The words **pedal** and **peddle** sound alike.
Pedal your bike hard to go uphill.
They *peddle* peanuts outside the stadium.

peddle (ped′əl) ***verb*** to go about from place to place selling things [He *peddles* magazines from house to house.]
ped·dle • ***verb*** **peddled, peddling**
● The words **peddle** and **pedal** sound alike.
Street vendors *peddle* for a living.
He stepped on the brake *pedal* to stop.

pedestal (ped′əs təl) ***noun*** the piece at the bottom of a column, statue, or other thing that supports it or holds it up.
ped·es·tal • ***noun**, plural* **pedestals**

pedestal

pedestrian (pə des′trē ən) ***noun*** a person who is walking [a crosswalk for *pedestrians*].
pe·des·tri·an • ***noun**, plural* **pedestrians**

pediatrician (pē′dē ə trish′ən) ***noun*** a doctor who takes care of babies and children.
pe·di·a·tri·cian • ***noun**, plural* **pediatricians**

pedigree (ped′i grē′) ***noun*** a list or line of ancestors.
ped·i·gree • ***noun**, plural* **pedigrees**

peek (pēk) ***verb*** to take a quick or secret look; to peep [We *peeked* over the fence.]
noun a quick or secret look at something.
peek • ***verb*** **peeked, peeking** • ***noun**, plural* **peeks**
● The words **peek** and **peak** sound alike.
Cover your eyes and don't *peek*.
We climbed to the mountain's *peak*.

peel (pēl) ***verb*** **1** to cut away or pull off the skin or rind of [I *peeled* the potatoes before I boiled them.] **2** to remove or pull off [I can't *peel* this label from the bottle.] **3** to shed a natural covering such as skin or bark [I stayed in the sun too long and I know I'm going to *peel*.] **4** to come off in flakes [The paint on the house is *peeling*.]
noun rind or skin [potato *peels*].
peel • ***verb*** **peeled, peeling** • ***noun**, plural* **peels**
● The words **peel** and **peal** sound alike.
Chimps don't bother to *peel* bananas.
A *peal* of laughter came from the hall.

peep[1] (pēp) ***noun*** **1** the short, high chirp of a young bird. **2** the slightest sound of a voice [I don't want to hear a *peep* from you.]
verb to make the chirp of a young bird.
peep • ***noun**, plural* **peeps** • ***verb*** **peeped, peeping**

peep[2] (pēp) ***verb*** to look quickly or secretly [He *peeped* through the keyhole.]
noun a quick or secret look.
peep • ***verb*** **peeped, peeping** • ***noun**, plural* **peeps**

P

peer[1] (pir) ***noun*** a person or thing of the same rank, skill, or worth; an equal [As a poet she has few *peers*.]
peer • ***noun,*** *plural* **peers**
● The words **peer** and **pier** sound alike.
Everyone in the class is my *peer*.
He walked to the window to *peer* out.
The boat docked at the *pier*.

peer[2] (pir) ***verb*** to squint or look closely in order to see better [We *peered* into the dark room.]
peer • ***verb*** **peered, peering**
● The words **peer** and **pier** sound alike.

peevish (pēv′ish) ***adjective*** cross or easily annoyed [She is *peevish* whenever she has a cold.] —Look for the WORD CHOICES box at the entry **irritable**.
pee·vish • ***adjective***

peg (peg) ***noun*** a thick pin used to hold parts together, plug up an opening, or hang things on [The wooden *pegs* on the wall are for hanging up coats.]
peg • ***noun,*** *plural* **pegs**

P.E.I. *abbreviation for* Prince Edward Island.

Pekingese (pē kə nēz′) ***noun*** a small dog with long hair, short legs, and a flat nose.
Pe·king·ese • ***noun,*** *plural* **Pekingese**

pelican (pel′i kən) ***noun*** a large water bird with webbed feet and with a pouch hanging from its bill. The pouch is used for scooping in fish.
pel·i·can • ***noun,*** *plural* **pelicans**

pellet (pel′ət) ***noun*** **1** a small, round mass of something [*pellets* of cat food]. **2** a bullet or small piece of lead shot.
pel·let • ***noun,*** *plural* **pellets**

pelt[1] (pelt) ***verb*** to strike or beat against again and again [Rain *pelted* the roof. They *pelted* him with snowballs.]
pelt • ***verb*** **pelted, pelting**

pelt[2] (pelt) ***noun*** the skin of an animal with fur [beaver *pelts*].
pelt • ***noun,*** *plural* **pelts**

pen[1] (pen) ***noun*** **1** a small, fenced yard for keeping animals [The pigs are in the *pen*.] **2** any small, enclosed place.
verb to shut up in a pen.
pen • ***noun,*** *plural* **pens** • ***verb*** **penned, penning**

pen[2] (pen) ***noun*** an instrument used for writing or drawing with ink.
pen • ***noun,*** *plural* **pens**

penalize (pē′nəl īz *or* pen′əl īz) ***verb*** to give a penalty to; punish [You will not be *penalized* for giving the wrong answer.]
pe·nal·ize • ***verb*** **penalized, penalizing**

penalty (pen′əl tē) ***noun*** a punishment for breaking a law or rule [A ten-cent fine per day is the *penalty* for returning library books late.]
pen·al·ty • ***noun,*** *plural* **penalties**

pencil (pen′səl) ***noun*** a long, thin stick filled with graphite or crayon and used for writing or drawing.
verb to write, draw, or mark with a pencil [He *penciled* his initials on the note.]
pen·cil • ***noun,*** *plural* **pencils**
• ***verb*** **penciled** or **pencilled, penciling** or **pencilling**

pendant (pen′dənt) ***noun*** a locket, earring, or other ornament that hangs down.
pend·ant • ***noun,*** *plural* **pendants**

WORD HISTORY

pendant

We get **pendant** from a Latin verb that means "to hang." Our word **pendulum** comes from the same source. Both words name something that hangs.

pendulum (pen′jə ləm *or* pen′dyə ləm) ***noun*** a weight hung so that it swings back and forth. It is often used to control a clock's movement.
pen·du·lum • ***noun,*** *plural* **pendulums**

penetrate (pen′ə trāt) ***verb*** to pass into or through; pierce [The car's headlights could not *penetrate* the thick fog.]
pen·e·trate • ***verb*** **penetrated, penetrating**

penguin (peŋ′gwin) ***noun*** a bird mainly of the antarctic region, with webbed feet and flippers for swimming. Penguins cannot fly.
pen·guin • ***noun,*** *plural* **penguins**

penguin

a	cat	ō	go	ʉ	fur	ə =	a *in* ago
ā	ape	ô	law, for	ch	chin		e *in* agent
ä	cot, car	oo	look	sh	she		i *in* pencil
e	ten	ōō	tool	th	thin		o *in* atom
ē	me	oi	oil	*th*	then		u *in* circus
i	fit	ou	out	zh	measure		
ī	ice	u	up	ŋ	ring		

penicillin (pen′i sil′in) ***noun*** a drug used to kill the germs that cause certain diseases. It is produced from a fungus that grows as green mold.
pen·i·cil·lin • ***noun***

peninsula (pə nin′sə lə) ***noun*** a long piece of land almost completely surrounded by water. Italy is a peninsula.
pen·in·su·la • ***noun,*** *plural* **peninsulas**

penknife (pen′nīf) ***noun*** a small pocketknife.
pen·knife • ***noun,*** *plural* **pen·knives**

penmanship (pen′mən ship) ***noun*** the art or skill of writing by hand; handwriting.
pen·man·ship • ***noun***

Penn (pen), **William** (wil′yəm) 1644-1718; English colonist in the U.S. He founded Pennsylvania.
Penn, Wil·liam

Penna. *abbreviation for* Pennsylvania.

pennant (pen′ənt) ***noun*** **1** a long, narrow flag or banner, usually in the shape of a triangle. **2** such a flag that is the symbol of a championship [the National League *pennant*].
pen·nant • ***noun,*** *plural* **pennants**

penniless (pen′ē ləs) ***adjective*** without even a penny; very poor.
pen·ni·less • ***adjective***

STATE MAP

Pennsylvania

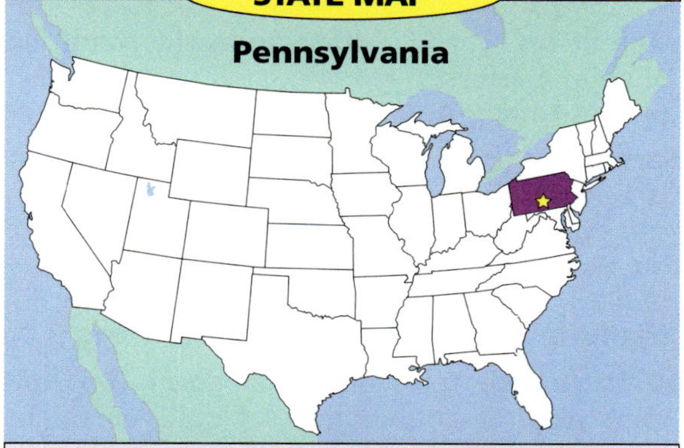

Statehood: 1787, the 2nd state • **Capital:** Harrisburg

Pennsylvania (pen′səl vān′yə) a State in the northeastern part of the U.S. Its capital is Harrisburg. Abbreviated **PA, Pa., Penna.**
Penn·syl·va·ni·a

penny (pen′ē) ***noun*** **1** a U.S. or Canadian cent. **2** a British coin equal to $^1/_{100}$ of a pound.
pen·ny • ***noun,*** *plural* **pennies**

pension (pen′shən) ***noun*** money paid at regular times by a company or government to a person who has retired from work.
pen·sion • ***noun,*** *plural* **pensions**

pentagon (pen′tə gän) ***noun*** **1** a flat figure having five sides and five angles. **2 Pentagon** the five-sided building near Washington, D.C., that contains the main offices of the U.S. armed forces.
pen·ta·gon • ***noun,*** *plural for sense 1 only* **pentagons**

pentagon

penthouse (pent′hous) ***noun*** an apartment built on the roof of a building.
pent·house • ***noun,*** *plural* **penthouses**

peony (pē′ə nē) ***noun*** a plant with large, showy flowers of pink, white, red, or yellow.
pe·o·ny • ***noun,*** *plural* **peonies**

people (pē′pəl) ***plural noun*** **1** human beings; persons. **2** the members of the public generally [The senator claims that he is for the *people*.]
noun all the persons of a particular race, religion, nation, or language [the French *people;* the *peoples* of Asia].
verb to fill with people; populate [The pioneers *peopled* large areas of land.]
peo·ple • ***plural noun*** • ***noun,*** *plural* **peoples** • ***verb*** **peopled, peopling**

pep (pep) [*an informal word*] ***noun*** energy or vigor [I am full of *pep* this morning.]

pepper

pepper (pep′ər) ***noun*** **1** a green or red pod with many seeds. These pods may be sweet or hot. They are eaten as a vegetable or relish. **2** a hot-tasting seasoning made by grinding the dried berries of a tropical plant.
pep·per • ***noun,*** *plural* **peppers**

peppermint (pep′ər mint) ***noun*** **1** a mint plant that produces an oil with a cool, sharp

taste. **2** a candy flavored with this oil.
pep·per·mint • *noun, plural* **peppermints**

pepperoni (pep′ər ō′nē) *noun* a hard, very spicy Italian sausage.
pep·per·o·ni • *noun, plural* **pepperonis** or **pepperoni**

per (pʉr) *preposition* **1** for each; for every [fabric selling at two dollars *per* yard]. **2** during each [a car traveling at 50 miles *per* hour].

perceive (pər sēv′) *verb* **1** to become aware of through one of the senses, especially the sense of sight [Can you *perceive* the difference between these two shades of red?] **2** to take in through the mind [I *perceive* that there are some problems here.]
per·ceive • *verb* **perceived, perceiving**

WORD CHOICES

Synonyms of **perceive**

The words **perceive, see,** and **view** share the meaning "to become aware of through the eyes."

Can you *perceive* the difference between these two shades of red?

You don't *see* many robins in January.

They went outside to *view* the eclipse.

percent (pər sent′) *noun* a hundredth part [Only 10 *percent* of the apples were rotten.] The symbol for percent is %.
per·cent • *noun*

percentage (pər sent′ij) *noun* a certain part or number in every hundred [A large *percentage* of the sugar has been used.]
per·cent·age • *noun, plural* **percentages**

perception (pər sep′shən) *noun* **1** the ability to perceive [My *perception* of color is poor.] **2** knowledge or understanding that comes from perceiving [I don't have a clear *perception* of what you want me to do.]
per·cep·tion • *noun, plural for sense 2 only* **perceptions**

perceptive (pər sep′tiv) *adjective* able to perceive or understand easily [a *perceptive* student] —Look for the WORD CHOICES box at the entry **intelligent**.
per·cep·tive • *adjective*

perch[1] (pʉrch) *noun* **1** a small fish that lives in lakes and streams. It is used for food. **2** a similar fish that lives in salt water.
perch • *noun, plural* **perch**

perch[2] (pʉrch) *noun* **1** a tree branch or other place for a bird to roost. **2** a resting place, especially one that is high up.
verb to rest on a perch [Birds *perched* on the wires.]
perch • *noun, plural* **perches**
• *verb* **perched, perching**

percussion (pər kush′ən) *noun* the hitting of one thing against another; blow.
per·cus·sion • *noun*

percussion instrument *noun* a musical instrument in which the tone is made by striking some part of it. Drums, cymbals, bells, and xylophones are all percussion instruments.
percussion instrument • *noun, plural* **percussion instruments**

perfect (pʉr′fəkt *for adj.;* pər fekt′ *for v.*) *adjective* **1** complete in every way and having no faults or errors [a *perfect* circle; a *perfect* test paper]. **2** being as good as is possible; most excellent [in *perfect* health; a *perfect* evening].
verb to make perfect [Practice will *perfect* your playing.]
per·fect • *adjective* • *verb* **perfected, perfecting**

perfection (pər fek′shən) *noun* the condition of being perfect.
per·fec·tion • *noun*

perform (pər fôrm′) *verb* **1** to do or carry out [I *performed* the task with her help.] **2** to do something requiring skill, especially before an audience [The dancers *performed* a new ballet.]
per·form • *verb* **performed, performing**

performance (pər fôrm′əns) *noun* **1** a concert, play, or other show of skill or talent before an audience [The *performance* starts at 8 o'clock.] **2** the act of performing [The teacher was unhappy with the student's *performance*.]
per·form·ance • *noun, plural for sense 1 only* **performances**

a cat	ō go	ʉ fur	ə = a *in* ago
ā ape	ô law, for	ch chin	e *in* agent
ä cot, car	oo look	sh she	i *in* pencil
e ten	ōō tool	th thin	o *in* atom
ē me	oi oil	*th* then	u *in* circus
i fit	ou out	zh measure	
ī ice	u up	ŋ ring	

performer (pər fôrm′ər) ***noun*** a person who performs for an audience [a circus *performer*].
per·form·er • ***noun,*** *plural* **performers**

perfume (pur′fyo͞om *for n.;* pər fyo͞om′ *for v.*) ***noun*** **1** a sweet smell; pleasing odor [the *perfume* of roses] —Look for the WORD CHOICES box at the entry **scent**. **2** a liquid with a pleasing smell that is put on the body.
verb to give a pleasing smell to [The fresh flowers *perfumed* the entire room.]
per·fume • ***noun,*** *plural for sense 2 only* **perfumes** • ***verb*** **perfumed, perfuming**

perhaps (pər haps′) ***adverb*** possibly; maybe [*Perhaps* it will rain today.]
per·haps • ***adverb***

peril (per′əl) ***noun*** a condition or situation that could result in destruction, injury, or death; danger [the *perils* of travel through the wilderness. The flood put many lives in *peril*.]
per·il • ***noun,*** *plural* **perils**

perimeter (pə rim′ə tər) ***noun*** the boundary or distance around a figure or area [A fence ran along the *perimeter* of his land.]
pe·rim·e·ter • ***noun,*** *plural* **perimeters**

period (pir′ē əd) ***noun*** **1** a portion or interval of time that goes by [the second *period* of a hockey game; a *period* of peace between two wars]. **2** a mark of punctuation (.). It is used at the end of a sentence or after an abbreviation.
pe·ri·od • ***noun,*** *plural* **periods**

WORD CHOICES

Synonyms of **period**

The words **period, age,** and **era** share the meaning "a portion of time."

a *period* of wet weather
the Stone *Age*
an *era* marked by peace and progress

periodic (pir′ē äd′ik) ***adjective*** happening or done at regular times [There will be *periodic* tests to check your progress.]
pe·ri·od·ic • ***adjective***

periodical (pir′ē äd′i kəl) ***noun*** any regular publication, such as a magazine, journal, or newspaper.
pe·ri·od·i·cal • ***noun,*** *plural* **periodicals**

periscope (per′i skōp) ***noun*** an instrument that consists of a long tube with mirrors or prisms inside. It allows a person to see over something or around a corner. Periscopes are used in submarines to see above the surface of the water.
per·i·scope • ***noun,*** *plural* **periscopes**

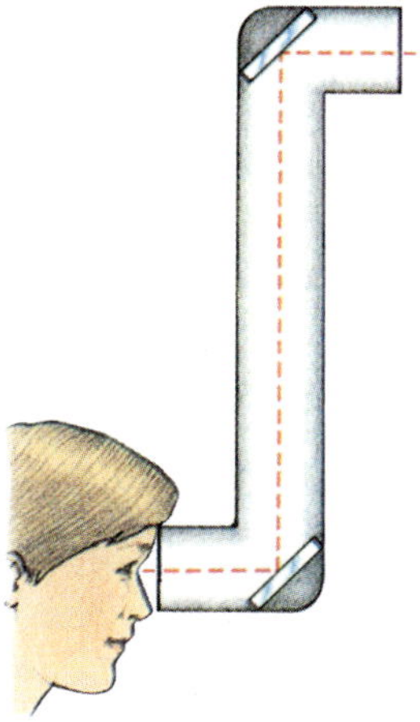
periscope

perish (per′ish) ***verb*** to die, especially in a violent way [Too many people *perish* in auto accidents each year.]
per·ish • ***verb*** **perished, perishing**

perishable (per′ish ə bəl) ***adjective*** likely to decay or spoil [*perishable* fruit].
per·ish·a·ble • ***adjective***

periwinkle (per′i wiŋ′kəl) ***noun*** a small snail with a thick shell that lives in salt water.
per·i·win·kle • ***noun,*** *plural* **periwinkles**

periwinkle

perjury (pur′jər ē) ***noun*** the act of telling a lie after taking an oath to tell the truth.
per·ju·ry • ***noun***

perk (purk) ***verb*** **1** to raise in a quick and lively way [The dog *perked* up its ears.] **2** to make look fresh or lively [The new drapes *perk* up the room.] **3** to become lively or get back one's spirits [We *perked* up on hearing the good news.]
perk • ***verb*** **perked, perking**

perky (pur′kē) ***adjective*** lively or happy [*perky* pups].
perk·y • ***adjective*** **perkier, perkiest**

perm (purm) [*an informal word*] ***noun*** *a short form of* **permanent.**
verb to give a permanent to [He *permed* her hair.]
perm • ***noun,*** *plural* **perms** • ***verb*** **permed, perming**

permafrost (pur′mə frôst) ***noun*** the layer of soil, in some parts of the earth, that is always frozen.
per·ma·frost • ***noun***

permanent (pur′mə nənt) ***adjective*** lasting or meant to last for a very long time [*permanent* teeth].
noun a hair wave put in by means of chemicals and lasting even after the hair is washed.
per·ma·nent • ***adjective*** • ***noun,*** *plural* **permanents**

permission (pər mish′ən) ***noun*** the act of permitting; consent [Did you get *permission* to go?]
per·mis·sion • ***noun***

permit (pər mit′ *for v.;* pur′mit *for n.*) ***verb*** **1** to give consent to; let; allow [The teacher *permitted* me to leave early.] —Look for the WORD CHOICES box at the entry **let**. **2** to give an opportunity [We'll play baseball if the weather *permits*.]
noun a paper or card showing that one has permission; a license [a fishing *permit*].
per·mit • ***verb*** **permitted, permitting** • ***noun,*** *plural* **permits**

perpendicular (pur′pən dik′yoo lər) ***adjective*** **1** at a right angle [The wall is *perpendicular* to the floor.] **2** straight up and down [a *perpendicular* flagpole].
per·pen·dic·u·lar • ***adjective***

perpetrate (pur′pə trāt) ***verb*** to do something bad [He *perpetrated* the crime.]
per·pe·trate • ***verb*** **perpetrated, perpetrating**

perpetual (pər pech′oo əl) ***adjective*** lasting forever or a very long time [*perpetual* happiness].
per·pet·u·al • ***adjective***

Perry (per′ē), **Oliver Hazard** (äl′i vər haz′ərd) 1785-1819; U.S. naval officer. He commanded the fleet that defeated the British on Lake Erie in 1813.
Per·ry, Ol·i·ver Haz·ard

persecute (pur′sə kyoot) ***verb*** to keep on treating in a cruel or harsh way, especially for holding certain beliefs or ideas.
per·se·cute • ***verb*** **persecuted, persecuting**

persecution (pur sə kyoo′shən) ***noun*** the condition of being persecuted [They left the country after many years of *persecution*.]
per·se·cu·tion • ***noun***

Persia (pur′zhə) **1** *old name for* **Iran**. **2** an ancient empire in southwestern Asia (from about 600 B.C. to about 300 B.C.).
Per·sia

Persian (pur′zhən) ***noun*** **1** a person born or living in Persia. **2** the language of Persia. The language spoken nowadays in Iran is a modern form of old Persian.
Per·sian • ***noun,*** *plural for sense 1 only* **Persians**

Persian cat ***noun*** a breed of cat with long, silky fur.
Persian cat • ***noun,*** *plural* **Persian cats**

Persian cat

persist (pər sist′) ***verb*** **1** to refuse to give up; go on in a stubborn way [We will *persist* in our demands.] **2** to last for some time; continue on [The hot weather *persisted* for days.]
per·sist • ***verb*** **persisted, persisting**

persistence (pər sist′əns) ***noun*** the quality of being persistent.
per·sist·ence • ***noun***

persistent (pər sis′tənt) ***adjective*** **1** refusing to give up [a *persistent* salesman]. **2** lasting for some time [*persistent* rain].
per·sist·ent • ***adjective***

WORD HISTORY

person

We get **person** from a Latin word that means "an actor's face mask." In the ancient theater, actors wore masks that told the audience what kind of character or role each was playing. As time passed, the word came to be used, in Latin and in English, for "an individual human being."

person (pur′sən) ***noun*** **1** a human being; man, woman, or child [He shook hands with every *person* in the room.] **2** in grammar, one of the three sets of pronouns that show who or what the subject of a verb is. The *first person* (*I* or *we*)

a	cat	ō	go	u	fur	ə =	a *in* ago
ā	ape	ô	law, for	ch	chin		e *in* agent
ä	cot, car	oo	look	sh	she		i *in* pencil
e	ten	oo	tool	th	thin		o *in* atom
ē	me	oi	oil	*th*	then		u *in* circus
i	fit	ou	out	zh	measure		
ī	ice	u	up	ŋ	ring		

is used for the speaker. The *second person* (*you*) is used for the one that is spoken to. The *third person* (*he, she, it,* or *they*) is used for the one that is spoken about. Most English verbs have a special form for the third person singular.
—**in person** being actually present [You must sign up for the class *in person*. The singer appeared *in person* at the theater.]
per·son • *noun, plural for sense 1 only* **persons**

-person *a suffix meaning* a person, either a man or a woman, who does a certain thing. It is often used in place of **-man** where **-man** may suggest only a male person.

personal (pur′sə nəl) *adjective* **1** of one's own; private or individual [a *personal* opinion]. **2** of the body [*personal* fitness]. **3** describing or having to do with a person's appearance, actions, or character [a *personal* remark]. **4** in grammar, showing person ["I," "you," and "it" are *personal* pronouns.]
per·son·al • *adjective*

personal computer *noun* a very small computer used by one person or a small number of people. It is used in schools, homes, and small businesses.
personal computer • *noun, plural* **personal computers**

personality (pur′sə nal′i tē) *noun* **1** all the special qualities that make a person different from other people [I like her friendly *personality*.] **2** the qualities of a person that attract other people [The qualities of being charming, energetic, or clever are those of a person having *personality*.] **3** a famous or well-known person [a TV *personality*].
per·son·al·i·ty • *noun, plural for senses 1 and 3 only* **personalities**

personally (pur′sə nəl ē) *adverb* **1** by oneself; without the help of others [I mailed the letters *personally*.] **2** speaking for oneself [*Personally*, I think you are right.] **3** as a person [I dislike her *personally*, but I admire her work.]
per·son·al·ly • *adverb*

personnel (pur sə nel′) *noun* persons employed in a certain job or work [office *personnel*].
per·son·nel • *noun*

perspective (pər spek′tiv) *noun* **1** the art of representing objects on a flat surface so that they are shown as they appear to the eye in real life. **2** a certain point of view in understanding or judging things or events [The two leaders had different *perspectives* on solving the hunger problem.]
per·spec·tive • *noun, plural for sense 2 only* **perspectives**

perspiration (pur′spər ā′shən) *noun* **1** the act of perspiring or sweating. **2** sweat [His face was wet with *perspiration*.]
per·spi·ra·tion • *noun*

perspire (pər spīr′) *verb* to sweat.
per·spire • *verb* **perspired, perspiring**

persuade (pər swād′) *verb* to get someone to do or believe something [She *persuaded* him to come along.]
per·suade • *verb* **persuaded, persuading**

persuasion (pər swā′zhən) *noun* **1** the act of persuading. **2** the ability to persuade [A salesperson must have the power of *persuasion*.]
per·sua·sion • *noun*

pertain (pər tān′) *verb* to have to do with; be related [This law *pertains* to civil rights.]
per·tain • *verb* **pertained, pertaining**

pertinent (pur′tə nənt) *adjective* having some connection with the subject that is being considered; relevant [a *pertinent* question].
per·ti·nent • *adjective*

Peru (pə ro͞o′) a country on the western coast of South America.
Pe·ru

perverse (pər vurs′) *adjective* turning aside from what is thought to be right or good; wicked [Cruelty to animals is a *perverse* act.]
per·verse • *adjective*

pesky (pes′kē) [*an informal word*] *adjective* annoying or troublesome [a *pesky* mosquito].
pes·ky • *adjective* **peskier, peskiest**

pessimistic (pes′i mis′tik) *adjective* having or showing a negative attitude about things; expecting things to turn out badly [a *pessimistic* opinion].
pes·si·mis·tic • *adjective*

pest (pest) *noun* **1** an insect or small animal that destroys crops or other things. **2** a person who annoys or causes trouble.
pest • *noun, plural* **pests**

pester (pes′tər) *verb* to keep bothering or annoying [She *pestered* me with silly questions.]
pes·ter • *verb* **pestered, pestering**

pesticide (pes′ti sīd) *noun* any poison used for killing insects, weeds, or other pests.
pes·ti·cide • *noun, plural* **pesticides**

P

pestle (pes′əl *or* pes′təl) ***noun*** a tool used to pound or grind something in a mortar.
pes·tle • ***noun,*** *plural* **pestles**

pet (pet) ***noun*** **1** an animal that is tamed and kept as a companion or treated in a fond way. **2** a person who is liked or treated better than others; favorite [a teacher's *pet*].
adjective **1** kept or treated as a pet [a *pet* hamster]. **2** showing fondness [a *pet* name].
verb to stroke or pat gently [She *petted* the dog.]
pet • ***noun,*** *plural* **pets** • ***adjective*** • ***verb*** **petted, petting**

petal (pet′l) ***noun*** one of the often brightly colored parts that look like leaves and make up the flower of a plant.
pet·al • ***noun,*** *plural* **petals**

petal

Peter (pēt′ər) one of the twelve Apostles of Jesus. He is also called **Saint Peter** or **Simon Peter**.
Pe·ter

petition (pə tish′ən) ***noun*** **1** a prayer or other strong, serious request. **2** a formal, written request to someone in authority.
verb to make a petition to or request for [The citizens *petitioned* the mayor to provide more police protection.]
pe·ti·tion • ***noun,*** *plural* **petitions** • ***verb*** **petitioned, petitioning**

petrify (pe′tri fī′) ***verb*** **1** to change into a substance like stone by replacing normal cells with minerals [Wood *petrifies* over the course of many thousands of years.] **2** to make unable to move or act because of fear.
pet·ri·fy • ***verb*** **petrified, petrifying, petrifies**

petroleum (pə trō′lē əm) ***noun*** an oily liquid found in the earth in certain layers of rock. Gasoline, kerosene, and many other products are made from petroleum.
pe·tro·le·um • ***noun***

petticoat (pet′ē kōt) ***noun*** a kind of skirt worn as an undergarment by women and girls.
pet·ti·coat • ***noun,*** *plural* **petticoats**

petty (pet′ē) ***adjective*** **1** of little importance; small; minor [a *petty* thief] —Look for the WORD CHOICES box at the entry **insignificant**. **2** having or showing a narrow, mean character [*petty* remarks].
pet·ty • ***adjective*** **pettier, pettiest**

petunia (pə to͞on′yə *or* pə tyo͞on′yə) ***noun*** a plant with flowers of various colors, shaped like funnels.
pe·tu·nia • ***noun,*** *plural* **petunias**

pew

pew (pyo͞o) ***noun*** one of the benches with a back that are fixed in rows in a church.
pew • ***noun,*** *plural* **pews**

pewter (pyo͞ot′ər) ***noun*** **1** an alloy consisting mainly of tin. Pewter looks much like silver. **2** dishes or other things made of pewter.
pew·ter • ***noun***

pg. *abbreviation for* page [Turn to *pg.* 2.]

phantom (fan′təm) ***noun*** something that one seems to see although it is not really there; ghost.
phan·tom • ***noun,*** *plural* **phantoms**

Pharaoh (fer′ō) ***noun*** the title of the rulers of ancient Egypt.
Phar·aoh • ***noun,*** *plural* **Pharaohs**

pharmacist (fär′mə sist) ***noun*** a person who is trained to prepare and sell drugs and medicine according to the orders of a doctor.
phar·ma·cist • ***noun,*** *plural* **pharmacists**

pharmacy (fär′mə sē) ***noun*** the place where a pharmacist works.
phar·ma·cy • ***noun,*** *plural* **pharmacies**

a cat	ō go	ʉ fur	ə = a *in* ago
ā ape	ô law, for	ch chin	e *in* agent
ä cot, car	o͝o look	sh she	i *in* pencil
e ten	o͞o tool	th thin	o *in* atom
ē me	oi oil	*th* then	u *in* circus
i fit	ou out	zh measure	
ī ice	u up	ŋ ring	

phase (fāz) ***noun*** **1** any of the ways in which something may be looked at, thought about, or shown; aspect [the many *phases* of a problem]. **2** one of the stages in a series of changes [The moon is full in its third *phase*.]
verb to bring into use or carry out in stages [New textbooks will be *phased* in over the next several years.]
phase • ***noun,*** *plural* **phases** • ***verb*** **phased, phasing**
• The words **phase** and **faze** sound alike.
The baby went through a bashful *phase* earlier this year.
His best pitch didn't *faze* the batter.

Ph.D. *abbreviation for* Doctor of Philosophy: this is a title given to someone who has earned an advanced degree in a university. It is written after a person's name [Anne Wong, *Ph.D.*].

pheasant

pheasant (fez′ənt) ***noun*** a wild bird with a long, sweeping tail and brightly colored feathers. It is hunted as game.
pheas·ant • ***noun,*** *plural* **pheasants** or **pheasant**

phenomenon (fə näm′ə nän) ***noun*** **1** a fact, condition, or happening that can be described and measured in a scientific way. **2** an unusual or remarkable person or thing [A downpour in the desert is a *phenomenon*.]
phe·nom·e·non • ***noun,*** *plural* **phe·nom·en·a** (fə näm′ə nə) *or for sense 2 especially* **phenomenons**

Philadelphia (fil′ə del′fē ə) a city in southeastern Pennsylvania.
Phil·a·del·phi·a

Philippines (fil′i pēnz) a country in the Pacific, north of Indonesia, made up of more than 7,000 islands (**Philippine Islands**).
Phil·ip·pines

philosopher (fi läs′ə fər) ***noun*** a person who studies philosophy.
phi·los·o·pher • ***noun,*** *plural* **philosophers**

philosophic (fil′ə säf′ik) ***adjective*** of or having to do with philosophy [*philosophic* theories].
phil·o·soph·ic • ***adjective***

philosophical (fil′ə säf′i kəl) ***adjective*** *the same as* **philosophic**.
phil·o·soph·i·cal • ***adjective***

philosophy (fi läs′ə fē) ***noun*** **1** the study of the meaning of life, the problems of right and wrong, how we know things, and similar matters. **2** a system of ideas and rules that comes from such study.
phi·los·o·phy • ***noun,*** *plural for sense 2 only* **philosophies**

phobia (fō′bē ə) ***noun*** a very strong fear that is beyond reason [I have a *phobia* about spiders.]
pho·bi·a • ***noun,*** *plural* **phobias**

Phoenicia (fə nish′ə *or* fə nē′shə) an ancient country on the eastern coast of the Mediterranean.
Phoe·ni·cia

Phoenician (fə nish′ən *or* fə nē′shən) ***noun*** **1** a person born or living in Phoenicia. **2** the language of the Phoenicians.
Phoe·ni·cian • ***noun,*** *plural for sense 1 only* **Phoenicians**

Phoenix (fē′niks) the capital of Arizona.
Phoe·nix

phone (fōn) [*an informal word*] ***noun, verb*** *a short form of* **telephone**.
phone • ***noun,*** *plural* **phones** • ***verb*** **phoned, phoning**

phonetics (fə net′iks) ***plural noun*** [*used with a singular verb*] the study of speech sounds and of the ways in which sounds are shown in writing.
pho·net·ics • ***plural noun***

phonics (fän′iks) ***plural noun*** [*used with a singular verb*] the use of a simple system of speech sounds in teaching students how to read words.
phon·ics • ***plural noun***

phono- *a prefix meaning* sound or speech [A *phonograph* reproduces sounds that have been recorded.]

phonograph (fō′nə graf) ***noun*** a device for playing records. Records have grooves on

them in which sounds, especially of music or speech, have been recorded.
pho·no·graph • *noun, plural* **phonographs**

phony (fō′nē) [*an informal word*] *adjective* not real or genuine; fake; false.
noun a person or thing that is not really what it is supposed to be.
pho·ny • *adjective* **phonier, phoniest** • *noun, plural* **phonies**

WORD HISTORY

phony

The word **phony** comes from one of the secret words that British thieves and swindlers used. Their secret word for a gilt ring was *fawney*. They would sell a victim a gilt ring that they said was made of real gold. But the ring was not real or genuine gold, and the word **phony** came to be used in speaking of anything that is fake, especially something meant to deceive.

phosphorus (fäs′fə rəs) *noun* a chemical element that is a white or yellow waxy solid in its pure form. In this form it glows in the dark, starts burning at room temperature, and is very poisonous.
phos·pho·rus • *noun*

photo (fōt′ō) *noun a short form of* **photograph**.
pho·to • *noun, plural* **photos**

photo- *a prefix meaning* of light; produced by light [A *photograph* is an image that is produced on film by light.]

photograph (fōt′ə graf) *noun* a picture made with a camera.
verb to take a photograph or photographs of.
pho·to·graph • *noun, plural* **photographs** • *verb* **photographed, photographing**

photographer (fə täg′rə fər) *noun* a person who takes photographs, especially as a job.
pho·tog·ra·pher • *noun, plural* **photographers**

photographic (fōt′ə graf′ik) *adjective* of, having to do with, or used in photography.
pho·to·graph·ic • *adjective*

photography (fə täg′rə fē) *noun* the art or process of making pictures by means of a camera.
pho·tog·ra·phy • *noun*

photosynthesis (fōt′ō sin′thə sis) *noun* the process in which a green plant uses sunlight to change water and carbon dioxide into food for the plant.
pho·to·syn·the·sis • *noun*

phrase (frāz) *noun* **1** a group of words that is not a complete sentence or a clause, but that gives a single idea. It is usually a separate part of a sentence. "Drinking fresh milk," "with meals," and "to be healthy" are phrases. **2** a short, distinct part of a piece of music or a dance.
phrase • *noun, plural* **phrases**

phys. ed. *abbreviation for* physical education.

physical (fiz′i kəl) *adjective* **1** having to do with the body rather than the mind [Swimming is good *physical* exercise.] **2** having to do with things that can be measured or seen in some way [Length is a *physical* characteristic.]
phys·i·cal • *adjective*

physical education *noun* a course in schools that teaches how to exercise and take proper care of the body.

physician (fi zish′ən) *noun* a doctor of medicine, especially one who is not mainly a surgeon.
phy·si·cian • *noun, plural* **physicians**

physics (fiz′iks) *plural noun* [*used with a singular verb*] the science that deals with energy and matter, and studies the way in which things are moved and work is done. Physics includes the study of light, heat, sound, electricity, and mechanics.
phys·ics • *plural noun*

physique (fi zēk′) *noun* the form or shape of a person's body.
phy·sique • *noun, plural* **physiques**

pianist (pē′ə nist *or* pē an′ist) *noun* a person who plays the piano.
pi·an·ist • *noun, plural* **pianists**

piano (pē an′ō) *noun* a large musical instrument with many wire strings and a keyboard When a key is struck, it makes a small hammer hit a string to produce a tone.
pi·an·o • *noun, plural* **pianos**

a	cat	ō	go	ʉ	fur	ə =	a *in* ago
ā	ape	ô	law, for	ch	chin		e *in* agent
ä	cot, car	oo	look	sh	she		i *in* pencil
e	ten	ōō	tool	th	thin		o *in* atom
ē	me	oi	oil	*th*	then		u *in* circus
i	fit	ou	out	zh	measure		
ī	ice	u	up	ŋ	ring		

piano

piccolo (pik′ə lō) ***noun*** a small flute that sounds notes an octave higher than an ordinary flute does.
pic·co·lo • ***noun,*** *plural* **piccolos**

piccolo

pick[1] (pik) ***noun*** **1** a heavy metal tool with a pointed head, used for breaking up rock and soil. **2** any pointed tool for picking or digging [an ice *pick*]. **3** *another name for* **plectrum**.
pick • ***noun,*** *plural* **picks**

pick[2] (pik) ***verb*** **1** to choose or select [The judges *picked* the winner.] **2** to scratch or dig at with the fingers or with something pointed [She *picked* her teeth with a toothpick.] **3** to pluck or gather with the fingers or hands [He *picked* berries for lunch.] **4** to look for and try to make happen [Don't *pick* a fight.] **5** to open with a wire or other tool instead of a key [The burglar *picked* a lock to get in.] **6** to pluck the strings of.
noun **1** something chosen [She was my *pick* to win the race.] **2** the one most wanted; best [the *pick* of the litter].
—pick on [*an informal use*] to keep criticizing, teasing, or annoying. **—pick out** **1** to choose. **2** to single out; find [Can you *pick* her *out* in the crowd?] **—pick up** **1** to take and lift up. **2** to stop for and take along [We'll *pick* grandmother *up* on the way.] **3** to gain little by little [A plane *picks up* speed as it moves down a runway.]
pick • ***verb*** **picked, picking** • ***noun,*** *plural* **picks**

picket (pik′ət) ***noun*** **1** a pointed stake used in a fence. **2** a soldier or soldiers used to guard troops from surprise attack.
verb to stand or walk outside a place such as a factory or store to protest something that is done by that business or organization [The workers *picketed* for higher wages.]
pick·et • ***noun,*** *plural* **pickets** • ***verb*** **picketed, picketing**

picket fence

picket fence ***noun*** a fence made of pointed stakes.
picket fence • ***noun,*** *plural* **picket fences**

pickle (pik′əl) ***noun*** a cucumber or other vegetable preserved in salt water, vinegar, or a spicy liquid.
verb to preserve in salt water, vinegar, or a spicy liquid.
pick·le • ***noun,*** *plural* **pickles** • ***verb*** **pickled, pickling**

pickup (pik′up) ***noun*** **1** the act of picking up [The shortstop made a good *pickup* of the ball.] **2** the act or power of gaining speed [Our old car still has good *pickup*.] **3** a small, open truck for hauling light loads.
pick·up • ***noun,*** *plural for senses 1 and 3 only* **pickups**

P

picnic (pik′nik) ***noun*** a pleasure trip away from home during which a meal is eaten outdoors.
verb to have or go on a picnic [We *picnicked* out in the country.]
pic·nic • ***noun,** plural* **picnics**
• ***verb*** **picnicked, picnicking, picnics**

picture (pik′chər) ***noun*** **1** a likeness or an image of a person, thing, or scene made by drawing, painting, or photography. **2** any likeness, image, or good example [Joe is the *picture* of health.] **3** a description [Her stories give a clear *picture* of her neighborhood.] **4** an image on a TV screen. **5** a movie; film.
verb **1** to describe or explain [This social studies book *pictures* life in many lands.] **2** to form an idea or picture in the mind; imagine [You can *picture* how pleased I was!]
pic·ture • ***noun,** plural for senses 1, 4, and 5 only* **pictures** • ***verb*** **pictured, picturing**

pie (pī) ***noun*** a dish with a filling usually made of fruit or meat baked in a pastry crust.
pie • ***noun,** plural* **pies**

SPELLING TIP

Use this memory aid to spell **piece**.
Think of a ***pie**ce* of ***pie***.

piece (pēs) ***noun*** **1** a part broken or separated from a whole [The glass broke and I swept up the *pieces*.] **2** a part or section of a whole, thought of as complete by itself [a *piece* of meat; a *piece* of land] —Look for the WORD CHOICES box at the entry **part**. **3** any one of a set or group of things [a set of dishes having 52 *pieces;* a chess *piece*]. **4** a coin [a fifty-cent *piece*]. **5** a single item or example [a *piece* of information]. **6** a work of music, writing, or art [a *piece* for the violin].
verb to join the pieces of [I *pieced* the broken jug together.]
piece • ***noun,** plural* **pieces** • ***verb*** **pieced, piecing**
● The words **piece** and **peace** sound alike.
Would you like a *piece* of cake?
He was hoping for some *peace* and quiet.

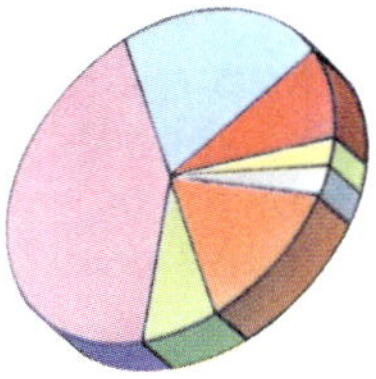

pie chart

pie chart ***noun*** a graph that is in the form of a circle or pie that is divided into sections. Each section stands for an amount or quantity and is in proportion to the size of the amount or quantity represented.
pie chart • ***noun,** plural* **pie charts**

pier

pier (pir) ***noun*** a long, flat surface built out over water on pillars. Piers are used as landing places for boats and ships.
pier • ***noun,** plural* **piers**
● The words **pier** and **peer** sound alike.
We took a romantic walk on the *pier*.
Everyone in the class is my *peer*.
He walked to the window to *peer* out.

WORD CHOICES

Synonyms of **pier**

The words **pier, dock,** and **wharf** share the meaning "a long platform built out over water as a landing place."

fishing from the *pier*
a rowboat tied up at the *dock*
unloading cargo onto the *wharf*

pierce (pirs) ***verb*** **1** to pass into or through; penetrate [The needle *pierced* her finger. A light *pierced* the darkness.] **2** to make a hole through [She *pierced* her ears for earrings.]
pierce • ***verb*** **pierced, piercing**

a	cat	ō	go	ʉ	fur	ə = a *in* ago	
ā	ape	ô	law, for	ch	chin	e *in* agent	
ä	cot, car	oo	look	sh	she	i *in* pencil	
e	ten	ōō	tool	th	thin	o *in* atom	
ē	me	oi	oil	*th*	then	u *in* circus	
i	fit	ou	out	zh	measure		
ī	ice	u	up	ŋ	ring		

Pierce (pirs), **Franklin** (fraŋk′lin) 1804-1869; the fourteenth President of the U.S., from 1853 to 1857.
Pierce, Frank·lin

Pierre (pir) the capital of South Dakota.

pig (pig) ***noun*** an animal with a long, broad snout and a thick, fat body covered with coarse bristles; hog.
pig • ***noun,*** *plural* **pigs**

pigeon (pij′ən) ***noun*** a bird with a small head, plump body, and short legs.
pi·geon • ***noun,*** *plural* **pigeons**

piggyback (pig′ē bak) ***adverb*** on the shoulders or back [I carried my little brother *piggyback.*] This word can also be used as an adjective [Please give me a *piggyback* ride!]
pig·gy·back • ***adverb***

piggy bank (pig′ē) ***noun*** a small bank with a slot for putting coins into. It is often shaped like a pig.
pig·gy bank • ***noun,*** *plural* **piggy banks**

piglet (pig′lət) ***noun*** a little pig.
pig·let • ***noun,*** *plural* **piglets**

pigment (pig′mənt) ***noun*** **1** a colored substance, usually a powder, that is mixed with oil or water to make paints. **2** the substance in cells and tissues that gives color to plants and animals.
pig·ment • ***noun,*** *plural* **pigments**

pigpen (pig′pen) ***noun*** a pen where pigs are kept.
pig·pen • ***noun,*** *plural* **pigpens**

pigsty (pig′stī) ***noun*** *another name for* **pigpen**.
pig·sty • ***noun,*** *plural* **pigsties**

pigtail (pig′tāl) ***noun*** a long braid of hair hanging at the back of the head.
pig·tail • ***noun,*** *plural* **pigtails**

pike (pīk) ***noun*** a slender freshwater fish with a pointed snout and a lower jaw that sticks out.
pike • ***noun,*** *plural* **pike**

pile[1] (pīl) ***noun*** **1** a mass of things put together in a heap [a *pile* of leaves]. **2** [*an informal use*] a large amount [a *pile* of homework].
verb **1** to form or put in a pile [I *piled* the rubbish behind the garage.] **2** to cover or fill with a heap or large amount; to load [We *piled* the cart with hay.]
pile • ***noun,*** *plural* **piles** • ***verb*** **piled, piling**

pile[2] (pīl) ***noun*** the thick, soft, raised surface on a rug or fabric. It is made of loops of yarn that are sometimes cut.

pile[3] (pīl) ***noun*** a long, heavy beam or column, often of concrete, that is driven into the ground to support something. Piles are often placed underwater to support bridges, docks, and piers.
pile • ***noun,*** *plural* **piles**

pilgrim (pil′grəm) ***noun*** **1** a person who travels to a holy place or shrine. **2 Pilgrim** one of the English settlers who started a colony in Plymouth, Massachusetts in 1620.
pil·grim • ***noun,*** *plural* **pilgrims**

pill (pil) ***noun*** a little tablet, ball, or capsule of medicine to be swallowed whole.
pill • ***noun,*** *plural* **pills**

pillar (pil′ər) ***noun*** a long, upright column that is used as a support for a roof, a pier, or some other structure.
pil·lar • ***noun,*** *plural* **pillars**

pillow (pil′ō) ***noun*** a soft pad used to rest the head on in sleeping. It consists of a cloth bag filled with feathers, polyester fiber, or other soft material.
pil·low • ***noun,*** *plural* **pillows**

pilot (pī′lət) ***noun*** **1** a person whose job is steering ships in and out of harbors and through difficult waters. **2** a person who flies an aircraft.
verb to act as a pilot.
pi·lot • ***noun,*** *plural* **pilots** • ***verb*** **piloted, piloting**

pimple (pim′pəl) ***noun*** a small swelling of the skin that is red and sore.
pim·ple • ***noun,*** *plural* **pimples**

pin (pin) ***noun*** **1** a short piece of thin, stiff wire with a pointed end and a flat, round head. It is used for fastening things together. **2** an ornament or badge with a pin or clasp for fastening it to the clothing. **3** a small, thin rod of wood, metal, or other material, used for holding things together or hanging things on; a peg or bolt. **4** any of the wooden clubs at which the ball is rolled in bowling.
verb **1** to fasten with a pin [I *pinned* the hem of the skirt.] **2** to hold firmly in one position [He *pinned* his opponent to the floor.]
pin • ***noun,*** *plural* **pins** • ***verb*** **pinned, pinning**

pinafore (pin′ə fôr) ***noun*** a garment without sleeves, like a kind of apron, worn by little girls over a dress.
pin·a·fore • ***noun,*** *plural* **pinafores**

P

piñata

piñata (pē nyä′tä) ***noun*** a container made from clay or paper and thick glue that is hung from a ceiling. It is filled with treats, and blindfolded children take turns trying to break it open with a stick.
pi·ña·ta • ***noun,*** *plural* **piñatas**

pincers (pin′sərz) ***plural noun*** **1** a tool with two handles and two jaws, used in gripping or for cutting metal. **2** a large claw of a crab, lobster, or similar animal.
pin·cers • ***plural noun***

pinch (pinch) ***verb*** **1** to squeeze between a finger and the thumb or between two surfaces [He gently *pinched* the baby's cheek. She *pinched* her finger in the door.] **2** to press upon in a painful way [These new shoes *pinch* my toes.] **3** to make look thin and worn [The illness had *pinched* her face.]
noun **1** the act of pinching; squeeze; nip [a *pinch* on the arm]. **2** the amount that can be picked up between the finger and the thumb [a *pinch* of salt]. **3** an emergency [You can count on her in a *pinch*.]
pinch • ***verb*** **pinched, pinching** • ***noun,*** *plural for senses 1 and 2 only* **pinches**

pinch-hit (pinch′hit′) ***verb*** in baseball, to bat in place of another player.
pinch-hit • ***verb*** **pinch-hit, pinch-hitting**

pine (pīn) ***noun*** **1** an evergreen tree with cones and clusters of leaves shaped like needles. **2** the wood of this tree, used in building and in making furniture.
pine • ***noun,*** *plural for sense 1 only* **pines**

pineapple (pīn′ap əl) ***noun*** a juicy tropical fruit that looks a little like a large pine cone.
pine·ap·ple • ***noun,*** *plural* **pineapples**

pine cone ***noun*** the cone of a pine tree.
pine cone • ***noun,*** *plural* **pine cones**

ping (piŋ) ***noun*** a sharp sound like that made when a stone strikes something hard.
ping • ***noun,*** *plural* **pings**

pink (piŋk) ***noun*** **1** a plant with white, pink, or red flowers with a spicy smell. **2** pale red.
adjective pale-red.
pink • ***noun,*** *plural* **pinks**
• ***adjective*** **pinker, pinkest**

pinkie (piŋ′kē) ***noun*** the smallest finger.
pink·ie • ***noun,*** *plural* **pinkies**

pinky (piŋ′kē) ***noun*** *another spelling of* **pinkie**.
pink·y • ***noun,*** *plural* **pinkies**

pinpoint (pin′point) ***verb*** to show or find the exact location of [We *pinpointed* the city on a map.]
pin·point • ***verb*** **pinpointed, pinpointing**

pint (pīnt) ***noun*** a unit of volume that is equal to ½ quart.
pint • ***noun,*** *plural* **pints**

pinto (pin′tō) ***adjective*** marked with patches of two or more colors [*pinto* beans].
noun a pinto horse or pony.
pin·to • ***adjective*** • ***noun,*** *plural* **pintos**

pinwheel (pin′hwēl *or* pin′wēl) ***noun*** a small wheel made of pieces of paper or plastic pinned to a stick so that the wheel spins in the wind.
pin·wheel • ***noun,*** *plural* **pinwheels**

pioneer (pī′ə nir′) ***noun*** a person who goes before, opening the way up for others to follow [Daniel Boone was a *pioneer* in Kentucky. Amelia Earhart was a *pioneer* in aviation.]
verb to act as a pioneer; open the way up for others [Dr. Martin Luther King, Jr. *pioneered* in civil rights.]
pi·o·neer • ***noun,*** *plural* **pioneers**
• ***verb*** **pioneered, pioneering**

pip (pip) ***noun*** a small seed of a fruit such as an apple, pear, or orange.
pip • ***noun,*** *plural* **pips**

pipe (pīp) ***noun*** **1** a long tube of metal, concrete, plastic, or other material through which something such as oil, water, or gas can flow. **2** a tube with a small bowl at one end in

a cat	ō go	ʉ fur	ə = a *in* ago
ā ape	ô law, for	ch chin	e *in* agent
ä cot, car	oo look	sh she	i *in* pencil
e ten	ōō tool	th thin	o *in* atom
ē me	oi oil	*th* then	u *in* circus
i fit	ou out	zh measure	
ī ice	u up	ŋ ring	

which tobacco is smoked. **3** a wooden or metal tube through which air is blown for making musical sounds. **4** any of a set of pipes in a musical instrument such as an organ or a bagpipe.
verb **1** to play on a pipe. **2** to speak in a high, shrill voice ["Good morning," *piped* the children.] **3** to move from one place to another by using a pipe or pipes [Oil from Alaska is *piped* to the rest of the United States.]
pipe • ***noun,*** *plural* **pipes** • ***verb*** **piped, piping**

pipeline (pīp′līn) ***noun*** a long line of connected pipes for moving something such as gas or oil.
pipe·line • ***noun,*** *plural* **pipelines**

piper (pīp′ər) ***noun*** a person who plays a pipe, especially a bagpipe.
pip·er • ***noun,*** *plural* **pipers**

piranha (pə rän′ə) ***noun*** a small freshwater fish of South America, having strong jaws and very sharp teeth. In groups, it will attack any animal, including human beings.
pi·ra·nha • ***noun,*** *plural* **piranhas**

pirate (pī′rət) ***noun*** a person who attacks and robs ships on the ocean.
pi·rate • ***noun,*** *plural* **pirates**

pistachio (pi stash′ē ō *or* pi stäsh′ē ō) ***noun*** a sweet, greenish nut.
pis·tach·i·o • ***noun,*** *plural* **pistachios**

pistil (pis′təl) ***noun*** the part of a flower in which the seeds grow.
pis·til • ***noun,*** *plural* **pistils**

- The words **pistil** and **pistol** sound alike.
  Most flowers have a stamen and a *pistil*.
  The sheriff took the outlaw's *pistol*.

pistol (pis′təl) ***noun*** a small gun that can be held with one hand.
pis·tol • ***noun,*** *plural* **pistols**

- The words **pistol** and **pistil** sound alike.

pit[1] (pit) ***noun*** the hard stone in the center of a peach, cherry, olive, or date. The pit holds the seed.
verb to take the pit out of.
pit • ***noun,*** *plural* **pits** • ***verb*** **pitted, pitting**

pit[2] (pit) ***noun*** **1** a hole in the ground, especially a deep one. **2** a small hollow in a surface.
verb **1** to make pits or scars in [Rust *pits* iron.] **2** to set up against; match [Which team is *pitted* against us?]
pit • ***noun,*** *plural* **pits** • ***verb*** **pitted, pitting**

pita (pē′tə) ***noun*** a round, flat bread of the Middle East. It can be split open to form a pocket for a filling of meat or vegetables.
pi·ta • ***noun,*** *plural* **pitas**

pitch[1] (pich) ***noun*** a black, sticky substance formed when petroleum and certain other substances are refined. It is used to cover roofs or pave streets.

pitch[2] (pich) ***verb*** **1** to throw or toss [*Pitch* the newspaper on the porch.] —Look for the WORD CHOICES box at the entry **throw**. **2** in baseball, to throw to the batter [He *pitched* the ball over the plate.] **3** in baseball, to serve as pitcher for [She *pitched* the first three innings.] **4** to set up; make ready for use [We *pitched* a tent.] **5** to be tossed so that the bow rises and falls rapidly [The ship *pitched* badly in the storm.]
noun **1** the act or a way of pitching [a fast *pitch*]. **2** anything pitched or thrown [The wild *pitch* hit the batter.] **3** a certain level, point, or amount [Our excitement was at a high *pitch*.] **4** the high or low quality of a musical sound.
pitch • ***verb*** **pitched, pitching** • ***noun,*** *plural for senses 1, 2, and 4 only* **pitches**

pitch-black (pich′blak′) ***adjective*** very black.

pitcher[1] (pich′ər) ***noun*** • **1** a container for holding and pouring water, milk, and other liquids. It usually has a handle and a lip for pouring. **2** as much as a pitcher will hold [I drank almost a *pitcher* of lemonade.]
pitch·er • ***noun,*** *plural* **pitchers**

pitcher[2] (pich′ər) ***noun*** the baseball player who pitches the ball to the batters.
pitch·er • ***noun,*** *plural* **pitchers**

pitchfork (pich′fôrk) ***noun*** a large fork with a long handle, used for lifting and tossing hay and straw.
pitch·fork • ***noun,*** *plural* **pitchforks**

pith (pith) ***noun*** the soft, spongy tissue in the center of some plant stems.

pitiful (pit′i fəl) ***adjective*** **1** deserving or arousing pity [the *pitiful* sobs of the lost

child]. **2** deserving or arousing contempt or scorn [What a *pitiful* repair job!]
pit·i·ful • *adjective*

Pittsburgh (pits′burg) a city in southwestern Pennsylvania.
Pitts·burgh

pity (pit′ē) *noun* **1** a feeling of sorrow for another's suffering or trouble; sympathy. **2** a cause for sorrow or regret [It's a *pity* that you weren't there.]
verb to feel pity for.
pit·y • *noun* • *verb* **pitied, pitying, pities**

WORD CHOICES

Synonyms of **pity**

The words **pity, compassion,** and **sympathy** share the meaning "sorrow felt for another person's suffering or bad luck."

We felt *pity* for the lost children.

He was moved by *compassion* and paid their bills.

She has no *sympathy* for those who won't look for a job.

pivot (piv′ət) *noun* a point, pin, or rod upon which something such as a swinging door turns.
verb to turn on or as if on a pivot [The dancer *pivoted* on one foot.]
piv·ot • *noun, plural* **pivots** • *verb* **pivoted, pivoting**

pixie or **pixy** (piks′ē) *noun* a fairy or elf, especially one that is full of mischief.
pix·ie or **pix·y** • *noun, plural* **pixies**

pizza (pēt′sə) *noun* an Italian dish made by baking a thin layer of dough that is covered with tomatoes, cheese, and other ingredients.
piz·za • *noun, plural* **pizzas**

pj's [*an informal word*] *plural noun the same as* **pajamas**.

Pkwy. *abbreviation for* Parkway.

pl. *abbreviation for* plural.

Pl. *abbreviation for* Place [124 Acacia *Pl.*].

place (plās) *noun* **1** a space taken up or used by a person or thing [Please take your *places.*] **2** a state, city, town, or village [Topeka is a nice *place* to live.] **3** a house, apartment, or other space where one lives [Visit me at my *place.*] **4** a building or space set aside for a certain purpose [A restaurant is a *place* for eating.] **5** a certain point or area on the body or a surface [a sore *place* on the leg]. **6** rank or position, especially in a series [I finished the race in fifth *place.*] **7** a short city street [I live on Cherry *Place.*] **8** a proper or usual position [Everything is in its *place* now.]
verb **1** to put in a certain place or position [*Place* the pencil on the desk.] **2** to finish in a certain position in a contest [Lynn *placed* sixth in the race.] **3** to recognize by connecting with some time, place, or happening [I can't *place* that person's voice.]
—in place of instead of; rather than. **—take place** to come into being; happen.
place • *noun, plural for all senses except 7* **places** • *verb* **placed, placing**

place kick

place kick *noun* a kick made in football while the ball is held in place on the ground.
place kick • *noun, plural* **place kicks**

placid (plas′id) *adjective* calm and quiet; peaceful [a *placid* brook; a *placid* personality] —Look for the WORD CHOICES box at the entry **calm**.
plac·id • *adjective*

plague (plāg) *noun* a disease that brings death and spreads quickly from person to person.
verb **1** to cause to suffer [As a child she was *plagued* with illness.] **2** to irritate or bother.

a	cat	ō	go	ʉ	fur	ə = a *in* ago	
ā	ape	ô	law, for	ch	chin	e *in* agent	
ä	cot, car	oo	look	sh	she	i *in* pencil	
e	ten	ōō	tool	th	thin	o *in* atom	
ē	me	oi	oil	*th*	then	u *in* circus	
i	fit	ou	out	zh	measure		
ī	ice	u	up	ŋ	ring		

plague • *noun, plural* **plagues** • *verb* **plagued, plaguing**

plaid (plad) *noun* a pattern of checks of different sizes, formed by colored bands and lines that cross each other.
plaid • *noun, plural* **plaids**

plaid

plain (plān) *adjective* **1** open and clear to the eye; not blocked [in *plain* view]. **2** easy to understand; clear to the mind [The meaning is *plain*.] **3** not holding anything back; frank [*plain* talk]. **4** simple; easy [I can do a little *plain* cooking.] **5** not good-looking; homely [a *plain* face]. **6** not fancy; not much decorated [a *plain* necktie]. **7** ordinary [*plain* people].
noun a large stretch of flat land.
plain • *adjective* **plainer, plainest** • *noun, plural* **plains**
● The words **plain** and **plane** sound alike.
Her writing is simple and *plain*.
Oak and *plane* trees line our street.
We took a *plane* to Chicago.
A *plane* is a carpenter's tool.

plan (plan) *noun* **1** a way, thought out ahead of time, of making or doing something. **2** a drawing that shows how the parts of something such as a building are arranged.
verb **1** to think out, ahead of time, a way of making or doing something [They *planned* their escape carefully.] **2** to have in mind; to intend [I *plan* to visit Hawaii soon.]
plan • *noun, plural* **plans** • *verb* **planned, planning**

WORD CHOICES

Synonyms of **plan**

The words **plan, design,** and **scheme** share the meaning "a way of doing something that has been thought out ahead of time."

his *plans* for winning the election
happening by accident, not by *design*
her *scheme* for getting rich quick

plane[1] (plān) *noun* a large tree with bark that comes off in large patches; sycamore.
plane • *noun, plural* **planes**
● The words **plane** and **plain** sound alike.
A *plane* is a tree with broad leaves.
I took a *plane* from Los Angeles.
A *plane* produces wood shavings.
It was a *plain* cake, without icing.

plane[2] (plān) *adjective* of or having to do with flat surfaces or the points and lines on them [A triangle is a *plane* figure.]
noun **1** a flat, level surface [an inclined *plane*]. **2** *a short form of* **airplane**.
plane • *adjective* • *noun, plural* **planes**
● The words **plane** and **plain** sound alike.

plane[3] (plān) *noun* a tool used by carpenters for shaving wood in order to make it smooth or level.
verb to make smooth or level with a plane [She *planed* the edge so that the door would close.]
plane • *noun, plural* **planes** • *verb* **planed, planing**
● The words **plane** and **plain** sound alike.

planet (plan′ət) *noun* any of the large bodies that revolve around the sun. The planets, in their order from the sun, are Mercury, Venus, Earth, Mars, Jupiter, Saturn, Uranus, Neptune, and Pluto.
plan·et • *noun, plural* **planets**

WORD HISTORY

planet

The source of **planet** is the Greek word for "wanderer." At first, *planet* was used to talk about any heavenly body, including the sun and moon, that seemed to move or "wander," compared to the stars that seemed to stay always in the same place for a viewer on the earth.

planetarium (plan′ə ter′ē əm) *noun* a room with a large ceiling shaped like a dome. A special projector casts images of the sky on this ceiling to show the movements of the sun, moon, and planets.
plan·e·tar·i·um • *noun, plural* **planetariums**

plane tree *noun the same as* **plane**[1].
plane tree • *noun, plural* **plane trees**

plank (plaŋk) *noun* a long, wide, thick board.
plank • *noun, plural* **planks**

plankton (plaŋk′tən) ***noun*** the mass of tiny plants and animals found floating in a body of water. It is used as food by fish.
plank·ton • ***noun***

plant (plant) ***noun*** **1** any living thing that cannot move around by itself, has no sense organs, and usually makes its own food by photosynthesis. Trees, cactuses, grass, and mushrooms are all plants. **2** the buildings of a factory [My whole family works at the *plant*.]
verb **1** to put into the ground to grow [We usually *plant* corn.] **2** to place plants in a piece of land [I want to *plant* a garden.] **3** to set firmly in place [*Plant* both feet on the ground.]
plant • ***noun, plural*** **plants** • ***verb*** **planted, planting**

plantain[1] (plan′tin) ***noun*** a common weed with broad leaves and spikes of tiny, green flowers.
plan·tain • ***noun, plural*** **plantains**

plantain[2] (plan′tin) ***noun*** a kind of banana that is cooked and eaten as a vegetable.
plan·tain • ***noun, plural*** **plantains**

plantation (plan tā′shən) ***noun*** a large farm, usually in a warm climate, on which the farm workers live. Plantation crops include tobacco, sugar, cotton, and coffee.
plan·ta·tion • ***noun, plural*** **plantations**

planter (plant′ər) ***noun*** **1** the owner of a plantation. **2** a container in which plants are grown in a house or on a balcony or patio.
plant·er • ***noun, plural*** **planters**

plaque (plak) ***noun*** **1** a thin, flat piece of metal, wood, or other material with decoration or lettering on it. Plaques are usually hung on a wall. **2** a thin film that forms on the teeth. It hardens into tartar if it is not removed.
plaque • ***noun, plural for sense 1 only*** **plaques**

plasma (plaz′mə) ***noun*** the clear liquid part of blood that is left when the blood cells are removed.
plas·ma • ***noun***

plaster (plas′tər) ***noun*** a thick, sticky mixture of lime, sand, and water that becomes hard when it dries. It is used for coating walls, ceilings, and other surfaces.
verb **1** to cover with plaster [You will have to *plaster* the cracked wall.] **2** to cause to stick to a surface [He *plastered* his hair down with a greasy lotion. We *plastered* posters on the wall.]
plas·ter • ***noun*** • ***verb*** **plastered, plastering**

plastic (plas′tik) ***noun*** a substance made from various chemicals that can be molded and hardened into many kinds of products.
adjective made of plastic [a *plastic* comb].
plas·tic • ***noun*** • ***adjective***

plate (plāt) ***noun*** **1** a shallow dish from which food is eaten. **2** the food in a dish [If you finish your *plate*, you may have dessert.] **3** a flat, thin piece of metal or other material. **4** *the same as* **home plate**.
verb **1** to coat with gold, silver, tin, or some other metal. **2** to cover with metal plates for protection.
plate • ***noun, plural*** **plates** • ***verb*** **plated, plating**

plateau (pla tō′) ***noun*** a broad area of high, flat land.
pla·teau • ***noun, plural*** **plateaus**

platform (plat′fôrm) ***noun*** **1** a flat surface or stage higher than the ground or floor around it [a *platform* at a railroad station]. **2** all the plans and goals of a political party.
plat·form • ***noun, plural*** **platforms**

platinum (plat′n əm) ***noun*** a very heavy, silvery-white metal that is a chemical element. Platinum is very valuable and is used in making jewelry.
plat·i·num • ***noun***

platoon (plə to͞on′) ***noun*** a small group of soldiers that is part of a company.
pla·toon • ***noun, plural*** **platoons**

platter (plat′ər) ***noun*** a large, shallow dish used for serving food.
plat·ter • ***noun, plural*** **platters**

platypus

platypus (plat′i pəs) ***noun*** a small animal that lives in lakes and streams in Australia. It

a cat	ō go	ʉ fur	ə = a *in* ago
ā ape	ô law, for	ch chin	e *in* agent
ä cot, car	oo look	sh she	i *in* pencil
e ten	o͞o tool	th thin	o *in* atom
ē me	oi oil	*th* then	u *in* circus
i fit	ou out	zh measure	
ī ice	u up	ŋ ring	

has webbed feet, a tail like a beaver's, and a bill like a duck's. It lays eggs but it is a mammal and feeds its young with milk.
plat·y·pus • *noun, plural* **platypuses**

play (plā) *verb* **1** to have fun; amuse oneself [The children are *playing* in the sand.] **2** to do in fun [Don't *play* a trick on a friend.] **3** to take part in a game or sport [I like to *play* chess.] **4** to take part in a game against [We *play* my sister's team tonight.] **5** to perform music on [He *plays* the flute.] **6** to perform [The orchestra *played* well.] **7** to give out, or cause to give out, music, voices talking, etc. [The radio *played* loudly. We *played* a tape.] **8** to act a part in a drama [Who is *playing* the main role?] **9** to act in a certain way [*Play* fair. Don't *play* dumb.]
noun **1** something done just for fun or to amuse oneself [This job is just *play*, not work.] **2** fun; joking [Jan said it in *play*.] **3** the playing of a game [Rain stopped *play* until tomorrow.] **4** a move or action in a game [It's your *play*. The long forward pass is an exciting *play*.] **5** a story that is acted out on a stage or on radio or television; drama.
play • *verb* **played, playing** • *noun, plural for senses 4 and 5 only* **plays**

player (plā′ər) *noun* **1** a person who plays a game [a football *player*]. **2** a person who plays a musical instrument [a trumpet *player*]. **3** an actor or an actress. **4** a device for playing records, tapes, or compact discs.
play·er • *noun, plural* **players**

playful (plā′fəl) *adjective* **1** fond of play or fun; lively; frisky [a *playful* puppy]. **2** said or done in fun; joking [a *playful* shove].
play·ful • *adjective*

playground (plā′ground) *noun* a place, often near a school, for outdoor games and play.
play·ground • *noun, plural* **playgrounds**

playing cards *plural noun* a set of cards used in playing a number of games. They are divided into four patterns or suits called clubs, diamonds, hearts, and spades. The set used for most card games has 52 cards.

playmate (plā′māt) *noun* a child who joins another child in playing and having fun.
play·mate • *noun, plural* **playmates**

playoff (plā′ôf) *noun* a final game or one of a series of games played to decide who is champion.
play·off • *noun, plural* **playoffs**

playpen (plā′pen) *noun* a small, enclosed space in which a baby can safely be left to crawl and play.
play·pen • *noun, plural* **playpens**

plaything (plā′thiŋ) *noun* a thing to play with; toy.
play·thing • *noun, plural* **playthings**

playwright (plā′rīt) *noun* a person who writes plays.
play·wright • *noun, plural* **playwrights**

plaza (plä′zə *or* plaz′ə) *noun* **1** a public square in a city or town. **2** *another name for* **shopping center**.
pla·za • *noun, plural* **plazas**

plea (plē) *noun* **1** the act of asking for help; an appeal [a *plea* for mercy]. **2** the answer to a charge of having broken the law [a *plea* of not guilty].
plea • *noun, plural* **pleas**

plead (plēd) *verb* **1** to ask in a serious way; beg [I *pleaded* for help.] —Look for the WORD CHOICES box at the entry **appeal**. **2** to make a plea or present a case in a law court.
plead • *verb* **pleaded** or **pled, pleading**

pleasant (plez′ənt) *adjective* **1** giving pleasure or bringing happiness; enjoyable [a *pleasant* day in the park]. **2** having a look or manner that gives pleasure [a *pleasant* person].
pleas·ant • *adjective*

WORD CHOICES

Synonyms of **pleasant**

The words **pleasant, agreeable,** and **pleasing** share the meaning "making one feel happy or satisfied."

a *pleasant* evening at the movies
an *agreeable* odor
a vase with a *pleasing* shape

please (plēz) *verb* **1** to give pleasure to; satisfy [Flowers always *please* my grandmother.] **2** to be kind enough to: this is used to ask in a polite way for something [*Please* shut the door. *Please* tell me what is wrong.] **3** to wish or desire; to like [Do as you *please*.]
please • *verb* **pleased, pleasing**

pleasing (plēz′iŋ) *adjective* giving pleasure; pleasant [a *pleasing* smile] —Look for the WORD CHOICES box at the entry **pleasant**.
pleas·ing • *adjective*

P

pleasure (plezh′ər) *noun* **1** a feeling of delight or satisfaction; enjoyment [Long walks give me great *pleasure*.] **2** something that gives this feeling [Her voice is a *pleasure* to hear.]
pleas·ure • *noun, plural for sense 2 only* **pleasures**

pleat (plēt) *noun* a flat double fold in cloth. It is usually held in place by stitches and is pressed to make the folds sharp and straight.
verb to fold into pleats.
pleat • *noun, plural* **pleats** • *verb* **pleated, pleating**

plectrum (plek′trəm) *noun* a thin piece of plastic, metal, or bone used for plucking the strings of a guitar, banjo, or similar instrument.
plec·trum • *noun, plural* **plectrums**

pled (pled) *verb a past tense and a past participle of* **plead**.

pledge (plej) *noun* **1** a promise or agreement [the *pledge* of allegiance to the flag]. **2** something that is promised, especially money that is to be given to a charity.
verb **1** to promise to give [He *pledged* $100 to the building fund.] **2** to hold by a promise [He is *pledged* to marry her.]
pledge • *noun, plural* **pledges** • *verb* **pledged, pledging**

plentiful (plen′ti fəl) *adjective* great in amount or number; more than enough [a *plentiful* supply of food].
plen·ti·ful • *adjective*

plenty (plen′tē) *noun* a supply that is large enough; all that is needed [We have *plenty* of help.]
plen·ty • *noun*

pliers

pliers (plī′ərz) *plural noun* a tool with two handles and two jaws, for gripping small objects, bending wire, and other jobs.
pli·ers • *plural noun*

plod (pläd) *verb* **1** to walk or move in a heavy way and with effort [An old horse *plodded* along the road.] **2** to work in a slow, steady way [He *plodded* through his homework.]
plod • *verb* **plodded, plodding**

plop (pläp) *noun* a sound like that of something flat falling into water without splashing.
verb to drop with such a sound.
plop • *noun, plural* **plops** • *verb* **plopped, plopping**

plot (plät) *noun* **1** a secret plan, usually to do something that is bad or against the law [a *plot* to rob a bank]. **2** all the events that form the main story in a novel, play, movie or other work [a murder mystery with an exciting *plot*]. **3** a small piece of ground [a garden *plot*].
verb **1** to plan together in secret [They *plotted* against the king.] **2** to make a map, plan, or outline of [The captain *plotted* the path of the ship.]
plot • *noun, plural* **plots** • *verb* **plotted, plotting**

plover (pluv′ər *or* plō′vər) *noun* a shore bird with a short tail and long, pointed wings.
plov·er • *noun, plural* **plovers**

plow (plou) *noun* **1** a farming tool with a blade for cutting into the soil and turning it up. It is usually pulled by a tractor or by animals. **2** a device for clearing away or pushing aside matter such as snow from roads, sidewalks, or railroad tracks.
verb **1** to turn up the soil of with a plow [He *plowed* the field.] **2** to remove matter such as snow with a plow [After the blizzard they *plowed* the city streets.] **3** to move, cut, or start doing in a way that is like plowing [They *plowed* their way through the crowded room.]
plow • *noun, plural* **plows** • *verb* **plowed, plowing**

plowshare (plou′sher) *noun* the cutting blade of a plow.
plow·share • *noun, plural* **plowshares**

ploy (ploi) *noun* a sly or tricky action that is meant to get the better of or confuse another person [When he offered to check the furnace, it was just a *ploy* to get into the house.]
ploy • *noun, plural* **ploys**

pluck (pluk) *verb* **1** to pull out or off; to pick [I *plucked* an apple from the tree.] **2** to grab or tug [He *plucked* at his beard. She *plucked* a burning stick from the fire.] **3** to pull feathers or hair from [The chef *plucked* two chickens. She *plucked* her eyebrows.] **4** to pull and let

a	cat	ō	go	ʉ	fur	ə = a *in* ago	
ā	ape	ô	law, for	ch	chin	e *in* agent	
ä	cot, car	oo	look	sh	she	i *in* pencil	
e	ten	ōō	tool	th	thin	o *in* atom	
ē	me	oi	oil	*th*	then	u *in* circus	
i	fit	ou	out	zh	measure		
ī	ice	u	up	ŋ	ring		

go quickly [You can play a guitar by *plucking* the strings.]
noun **1** the act of pulling; a tug. **2** courage to meet danger or difficulty.
pluck • *verb* **plucked, plucking** • *noun, plural for sense 1 only* **plucks**

plug (plug) *noun* **1** a piece of wood, rubber, or other material that is used to stop up a hole, drain, or other opening. **2** a part with prongs that is fitted into a socket to connect a lamp, TV, or other appliance or tool to an electric circuit.
verb **1** to stop up or close with a plug [We need to *plug* up that hole.] **2** [*an informal use*] to work hard and in a steady way [Just keep *plugging* away at your math problems.]
—plug in to connect to an electric circuit.
plug • *noun, plural* **plugs** • *verb* **plugged, plugging**

plum (plum) *noun* a juicy fruit that has a smooth skin and a smooth pit.
plum • *noun, plural* **plums**
• The words **plum** and **plumb** sound alike.
We have *plum* pudding on holidays.
Submarines *plumb* the ocean's depths.

plum

plumage (plo͞om′ij) *noun* a bird's feathers.
plum·age • *noun*

plumb (plum) *noun* a metal weight that is hung at the end of a line. It is used to find out how deep water is or whether a wall is straight up and down.
verb **1** to test with a plumb. **2** to get to the bottom of; solve [The detective *plumbed* the mystery of her death.]
plumb • *noun, plural* **plumbs** • *verb* **plumbed, plumbing**
• The words **plumb** and **plum** sound alike.

plumber (plum′ər) *noun* a person whose work is putting in and fixing the pipes and other parts of the water and gas systems in a building.
plumb·er • *noun, plural* **plumbers**

plumbing (plum′iŋ) *noun* **1** the work of a plumber. **2** the pipes and other parts of the water and gas systems in a building.
plumb·ing • *noun*

plume (plo͞om) *noun* a large, fluffy feather, especially one used for decoration on a hat or helmet.
plume • *noun, plural* **plumes**

plump[1] (plump) *adjective* full and rounded in form; chubby [a *plump* child].
verb to fill out; puff up [We *plumped* up the pillows before the guests came.]
plump • *adjective* **plumper, plumpest** • *verb* **plumped, plumping**

plump[2] (plump) *verb* to drop in a sudden or heavy way [He *plumped* down on the sofa.]
plump • *verb* **plumped, plumping**

plunder (plun′dər) *verb* to rob or take from by force during a war [They *plundered* the captured cities.]
noun things that have been taken by force; loot.
plun·der • *verb* **plundered, plundering** • *noun*

plunge (plunj) *verb* **1** to thrust or force suddenly [I *plunged* my hand into the freezing water. The action *plunged* the nation into war.] **2** to dive or rush; throw oneself [She *plunged* into the pool.] **3** to move downward rapidly [Last night the temperature *plunged* to -10°F.]
noun a dive or fall.
plunge • *verb* **plunged, plunging** • *noun, plural* **plunges**

plunger (plun′ jər) *noun* a rubber piece shaped like a cup on the end of a long handle. It is used to clear out clogged drains by means of suction.
plung·er • *noun, plural* **plungers**

plural (ploor′əl) *adjective* showing that more than one is meant [The *plural* form of "dog" is "dogs."]
noun the form of a word that shows that more than one is meant. The plurals of most English words are formed with the ending *-s* or *-es* (one *hat*, two *hats*; one *glass*, two *glasses*). Some plurals are formed in other ways (one *foot*, two *feet*; one *child*, two *children*). For some words there is no change in the plural (one *sheep*, two *sheep*).
plu·ral • *adjective* • *noun, plural* **plurals**

plus (plus) *preposition* **1** added to [Two *plus* two equals four.] **2** and in addition [It costs $10 *plus* tax.]
adjective **1** more than zero; positive [a *plus* quantity]. **2** a little higher than [a grade of C *plus*].

P

noun **1** *a short form of* **plus sign**. **2** something extra that is helpful.
plus • *preposition* • *adjective* • *noun, plural* **pluses** or **plusses**

plus sign *noun* a sign (+) in arithmetic put before a number to show that the number is to be added. The plus sign can also show that a number is greater than zero.
plus sign • *noun, plural* **plus signs**

Pluto (plo͞ot′ō) **1** the Greek and Roman god of the dead and of the kingdom of the dead. **2** the smallest planet. It is the ninth in distance away from the sun.
Plu·to

plutonium (plo͞o tō′nē əm) *noun* a radioactive chemical element used in producing nuclear energy.
plu·to·ni·um • *noun*

Plymouth Rock (plim′əth räk) a large rock on the coast of Massachusetts where the Pilgrims are said to have landed.
Plym·outh Rock

plywood

plywood (plī′wo͝od) *noun* a kind of strong board that is made of thin layers of wood that are glued and pressed together.
ply·wood • *noun*

PM or **pm** in the time from noon to midnight. *PM* is the abbreviation of *post meridiem*, a Latin phrase meaning "after noon" [The play starts at 7:30 *PM*.] This abbreviation is also written **P.M.** or **p.m.**

pneumonia (no͞o mōn′yə *or* nyo͞o mōn′yə) *noun* a disease in which the lungs become inflamed and a thin fluid collects in them. It can be caused by bacteria or viruses.
pneu·mo·ni·a • *noun*

P.O. or **PO** *abbreviation for* post office [Write to *P.O.* Box #155.]

poach (pōch) *verb* to cook in water that is just below the boiling point or in a small cup over boiling water.
poach • *verb* **poached, poaching**

Pocahontas (pō kə hän′təs) 1595?-1617; a North American Indian princess who is said to have saved Captain John Smith from being killed.
Po·ca·hon·tas

pocket (päk′ət) *noun* **1** a small part like a bag or pouch that is sewn into a garment for carrying money and small objects. **2** a hollow place, often one that is filled with something [the *pockets* of a pool table; *pockets* of ore in rock]. **3** a small area or group of a certain kind [*pockets* of poor people in a rich country].
adjective meant to be carried in a pocket [a *pocket* watch].
verb to put into a pocket [I *pocketed* my change.]
pock·et • *noun, plural* **pockets** • *adjective* • *verb* **pocketed, pocketing**

pocketbook (päk′ət bo͝ok) *noun* a purse.
pock·et·book • *noun, plural* **pocketbooks**

pocketknife (päk′ət nīf) *noun* a small knife with one or more blades that fold into the handle.
pock·et·knife • *noun, plural* **pocketknives**

pod (päd) *noun* a case or shell that holds the seeds of a plant. Peas and beans grow in pods.
pod • *noun, plural* **pods**

podiatrist (pō dī′ə trist) *noun* a person whose work is treating and preventing disorders of the human foot.
po·di·a·trist • *noun, plural* **podiatrists**

Poe (pō), **Edgar Allan** (ed′gər al′ən) 1809-1849; U.S. poet and writer of short stories.
Poe, Ed·gar Al·lan

poem (pō′əm) *noun* a piece of writing in which the words are chosen and grouped to have a rhythm and often having words that rhyme. Poems are usually written in language that shows more imagination and deep feeling than the language people use every day.
po·em • *noun, plural* **poems**

poet (pō′ət) *noun* a person who writes poems.
po·et • *noun, plural* **poets**

a cat	ō go	ʉ fur	ə = a *in* ago
ā ape	ô law, for	ch chin	e *in* agent
ä cot, car	o͝o look	sh she	i *in* pencil
e ten	o͞o tool	th thin	o *in* atom
ē me	oi oil	*th* then	u *in* circus
i fit	ou out	zh measure	
ī ice	u up	ŋ ring	

poetic (pō et′ik) *adjective* like, having to do with, or suitable for a poet or poetry [*poetic* talent; *poetic* language].
po·et·ic • *adjective*

poetry (pō′ə trē) *noun* poems as a group [I like the *poetry* of Robert Frost.]
po·et·ry • *noun*

pogo stick (pō′gō) *noun* a toy for standing on and bouncing from place to place. It is a pole with a spring at the bottom and supports for the feet.
po·go stick • *noun, plural* **pogo sticks**

pogo stick

poinsettia (poin set′ə *or* poin set′ē ə) *noun* a plant from Mexico and Central America that has tiny yellow flowers and red leaves at the top that look like petals.
poin·set·ti·a • *noun, plural* **poinsettias**

point (point) *noun* **1** a position or place; location [the *point* where the roads meet]. **2** a dot in printing or writing [a decimal *point*]. **3** an exact time or moment [At that *point* the phone rang.] **4** a stage or degree that is reached [the boiling *point* of water]. **5** a unit that is used in measuring or scoring [A touchdown is worth six *points*.] **6** any one of the marks showing direction on a compass. **7** a part or detail; item [Explain the plan *point* by *point*.] **8** a special quality [Courage is one of her strong *points*.] **9** a sharp end [the *point* of a needle]. **10** an important or main idea or fact [the *point* of a joke].
verb **1** to aim [She *pointed* her telescope at Mars.] **2** to aim one's finger [He *pointed* to the book he wanted.] **3** to show or call attention to [I *pointed* out the mistakes.]
—beside the point having nothing to do with the subject that is being talked about. **—make a point of** to make something a strict rule or habit [We *make a point of* watching the evening news.] **—to the point** connected with the subject that is being talked about.
point • *noun, plural* **points** • *verb* **pointed, pointing**

pointed (point′əd) *adjective* having a point or sharp end [shoes with *pointed* toes].
point·ed • *adjective*

pointer (point′ər) *noun* **1** a long, thin rod that is used for pointing to things. **2** a hand or needle on a clock, meter, or other device. **3** a large hunting dog with a smooth coat. It is trained to stand still and face toward game birds. **4** [*an informal use*] a helpful hint or suggestion [The coach gave us some *pointers* on how to hold the bat.]
point·er • *noun, plural* **pointers**

pointless (point′ləs) *adjective* without meaning or purpose [a *pointless* remark].
point·less • *adjective*

point of view *noun* the way in which something is seen; attitude [a limited *point of view*].
point of view • *noun, plural* **points of view**

pointy (point′ē) *adjective* coming to a sharp point.
point·y • *adjective* **pointier, pointiest**

poise (poiz) *noun* a calm and easy manner or way of acting; self-control or self-confidence [I lost my *poise* when the audience laughed at my singing.]
verb to balance or be held in balance [The stork was *poised* on one leg.]
poise • *noun* • *verb* **poised, poising**

poison (poi′zən) *noun* **1** a substance that can make a person ill or cause death when it is taken into the body, even in small amounts. **2** something that harms or destroys [Hatred can be a *poison* to the person who hates.]
verb **1** to harm or kill with poison [They *poisoned* the rats.] **2** to put poison on or into [Enemy soldiers *poisoned* the well.] **3** to harm or destroy [Jealousy can *poison* the mind.]
poi·son • *noun, plural* **poisons** • *verb* **poisoned, poisoning**

poison ivy *noun* **1** a plant with whitish berries and with leaves that grow in groups of three. It can cause a skin rash if it is touched. **2** the rash that this plant causes.

poison oak *noun* **1** *another name for* **poison ivy**. **2** *another name for* **poison sumac**.

poisonous (poi′zə nəs) *adjective* capable of harming or killing by poison [a *poisonous* snake].
poi·son·ous • *adjective*

poison sumac (so͞o′mak) *noun* a plant with leaves that grow in groups of 7 to 13. It is found in swamps and can cause a skin rash if a person touches it.
poison su·mac • *noun*

P

poke (pōk) ***verb*** **1** to push or jab with something such as a finger or stick. **2** to make by pushing or jabbing [I *poked* a hole in the box.] **3** to thrust, stick out, or push forward [Don't *poke* your nose into my business.] **4** to search [I've been *poking* around in the attic.] **5** to move along in a slow or lazy way.
noun the act of poking; a jab or push.
—poke fun at to make jokes about.
poke • ***verb*** **poked, poking** • ***noun,*** *plural* **pokes**

poker[1] (pōk′ər) ***noun*** a card game in which the players bet on the value of the cards they hold.
pok·er • ***noun***

poker[2] (pōk′ər) ***noun*** a metal rod for stirring up a fire.
pok·er • ***noun,*** *plural* **pokers**

poky or **pokey** (pōk′ē) ***adjective*** **1** moving slowly; slow [Don't be so *poky*, or we'll be late.] **2** not lively; dull [a *poky* little town].
pok·y or **pok·ey** • ***adjective*** **pokier, pokiest**

Poland (pō′lənd) a country in central Europe, east of Germany.
Po·land

polar (pō′lər) ***adjective*** near or having to do with the North Pole or the South Pole.
po·lar • ***adjective***

polar bear ***noun*** a large white bear of the arctic coast.
polar bear • ***noun,*** *plural* **polar bears**

pole[1] (pōl) ***noun*** a long, thin piece of wood, metal, or other material [a tent *pole*].
verb to push along with a pole [We *poled* our raft down the river.]
pole • ***noun,*** *plural* **poles** • ***verb*** **poled, poling**

- The words **pole** and **poll** sound alike.
  She won a medal in the *pole* vault.
  Compasses point to the magnetic *pole*.
  They will *poll* every tenth voter.

pole[2] (pōl) ***noun*** **1** either end of the imaginary axis that passes through the center of the earth; the North Pole or the South Pole. **2** either of two opposite forces or parts. A magnet has a positive and a negative pole. The positive and negative terminals on a battery are also called poles.
pole • ***noun,*** *plural* **poles**

- The words **pole** and **poll** sound alike.
  Our plane flew over the South *Pole*.
  The baseball hit the foul *pole*.
  Our candidate did well in the last *poll*.

Pole (pōl) ***noun*** a person born or living in Poland.
Pole • ***noun,*** *plural* **Poles**

pole vault ***noun*** an athletic event in which each contestant leaps as high as possible over a bar, using a long pole to push off the ground.

police (pə lēs′) ***noun*** the department of the government of a city or state that keeps public order, enforces the law, and discovers and prosecutes crimes.
plural noun the members of such a department [The *police* arrest people who break the law.]
verb to keep peaceful and orderly by using police or a similar force [The army is *policing* the streets.]
po·lice • ***noun*** • ***plural noun*** • ***verb*** **policed, policing**

WORD HISTORY

police

The word **police** comes to us through French from a Latin word that means "government of the nation." The source of this Latin word is the ancient Greek word for "city," which is also the source of the English word **politics**.

policeman (pə lēs′mən) ***noun*** a member of the police.
po·lice·man • ***noun,*** *plural* **policemen**

police officer ***noun*** a member of the police.
police officer • ***noun,*** *plural* **police officers**

policewoman (pə lēs′wo͝om ən) ***noun*** a woman who is a member of the police.
po·lice·wom·an • ***noun,*** *plural* **policewomen**

policy[1] (päl′i sē) ***noun*** a plan, rule, or way of acting [It is a good *policy* to be honest. A country's foreign *policy* is its way of dealing with other countries.]
pol·i·cy • ***noun,*** *plural* **policies**

policy[2] (päl′i sē) ***noun*** a written contract between an insurance company and a particular person or group for protection in case of

a	cat	ō	go	ʉ	fur	ə =	a *in* ago
ā	ape	ô	law, for	ch	chin		e *in* agent
ä	cot, car	o͝o	look	sh	she		i *in* pencil
e	ten	o͞o	tool	th	thin		o *in* atom
ē	me	oi	oil	*th*	then		u *in* circus
i	fit	ou	out	zh	measure		
ī	ice	u	up	ŋ	ring		

some emergency like a fire, accident, or theft. It tells how much the company will pay if such an emergency happens, and also how much the person or group has to pay for the protection.
pol·i·cy • *noun, plural* **policies**

polio (pō′lē ō) ***noun*** a disease in which part of the spinal cord becomes infected and sometimes parts of the body are paralyzed. It used to be quite common among children.
po·li·o • ***noun***

polish (päl′ish) ***verb*** **1** to make smooth and bright or shiny, especially by rubbing [We *polished* the car with wax.] **2** to make less rough or crude; improve [You would do well to *polish* your manners.] **3** to finish or perfect [I spent hours *polishing* my speech to the club.]
noun **1** brightness or shine on a surface [a wood floor with a fine *polish*]. **2** a substance used for polishing [fingernail *polish;* shoe *polish*].
—polish off [*an informal use*] to finish or get rid of completely or quickly [They *polished off* their lunch and left.]
pol·ish • ***verb*** **polished, polishing** • ***noun***

Polish (pōl′ish) ***noun*** the language of Poland.
Pol·ish • ***noun***

polite (pə līt′) ***adjective*** having or showing good manners; thoughtful of other people [a *polite* young woman; a *polite* note of thanks] —Look for the WORD CHOICES box at the entry **civil**.
po·lite • ***adjective*** **politer, politest**

political (pə lit′i kəl) ***adjective*** having to do with government, politics, or politicians [a *political* party; a *political* speech].
po·lit·i·cal • ***adjective***

politician (päl′i tish′ən) ***noun*** a person who holds or runs for political office.
pol·i·ti·cian • ***noun,*** *plural* **politicians**

politics (päl′i tiks) ***plural noun*** **1** [*used with a singular verb*] the study of the methods and principles of government. **2** [*used with a singular verb*] the act or work of taking part in political affairs. **3** the opinions and ideas that a person has about political matters [What are his *politics?*]
pol·i·tics • ***plural noun***

Polk (pōk), **James K.** (jāmz) 1795-1849; the eleventh president of the U.S., from 1845 to 1849.

polka (pōl′kə) ***noun*** **1** a fast dance for couples that was first popular in eastern Europe. **2** music for this dance.
pol·ka • ***noun,*** *plural* **polkas**

polka dot (pō′kə *or* pōl′kə) ***noun*** one of the many round dots that are evenly spaced to form a pattern on cloth or other material.
pol·ka dot • ***noun,*** *plural* **polka dots**

poll (pōl) ***noun*** **1** a record of people's opinions or votes on a given subject or a record of their answers to a group of questions. **2 polls** a place where people go to vote in an election.
verb **1** to take or count the votes or opinions of [The president *polled* the committee members.] **2** to get a certain number of votes [Kirby *polled* a majority of the votes cast.]
poll • ***noun,*** *plural* **polls** • ***verb*** **polled, polling**

● The words **poll** and **pole** sound alike.
I was questioned for the *poll.*
A *pole* is used to guide a raft.
Who discovered the North *Pole?*

pollen (päl′ən) ***noun*** the yellow powder that is found on the stamens of flowers. It is made up of male cells that fertilize another flower when the wind or bees carry the pollen to the flower's pistil.
pol·len • ***noun***

pollinate (päl′i nāt′) ***verb*** to place pollen on the pistil of a flower; fertilize.
pol·li·nate • ***verb*** **pollinated, pollinating**

polliwog (päl′ē wôg) ***noun*** *another name for* **tadpole**.
pol·li·wog • ***noun,*** *plural* **polliwogs**

pollutant (pə lo͞ot′nt) ***noun*** something that pollutes, especially a harmful chemical or waste material that gets into the air or water.
pol·lu·tant • ***noun,*** *plural* **pollutants**

pollute (pə lo͞ot′) ***verb*** to make dirty or impure [Smoke from factories *pollutes* the air.] —Look for the WORD CHOICES box at the entry **contaminate**.
pol·lute • ***verb*** **polluted, polluting**

pollution (pə lo͞o′shən) ***noun*** **1** the process of letting out wastes or poisonous substances into the air, water, or land. **2** these wastes and poisons [*Pollution* in the lake killed all the fish.]
pol·lu·tion • ***noun***

polo (pō′lō) ***noun*** a game for players riding horses, with two teams of four players each. The players try to hit a small wooden ball through the other team's goal, using mallets with long handles.
po·lo • ***noun***

P

poltergeist (pōl′tər gīst) *noun* a kind of ghost that some people believe exists. It is thought to make odd or frightening noises.
pol·ter·geist • *noun, plural* **poltergeists**

poly- *a prefix meaning* many or much [A *polysyllable* is a word that has many syllables, usually at least four.]

polyester (päl′ē es′tər) *noun* **1** a man-made fiber that is very strong. **2** thread or fabric that is made from this fiber.
pol·y·es·ter • *noun*

polygon (päl′i gän) *noun* a flat figure that is made up of straight lines, especially one with more than four angles and four sides.
pol·y·gon • *noun, plural* **polygons**

Polynesia (päl ə nē′zhə) a group of many islands in the central and south Pacific. It includes Hawaii.
Pol·y·ne·sia

polyp (päl′ip) *noun* a tiny water animal with a body that is shaped like a tube. It has thin tentacles around a mouth at the top for taking in food. Coral is a collection of the skeletons of one type of polyp.
pol·yp • *noun, plural* **polyps**

pomegranate (päm′gran ət *or* päm′ə gran ət) *noun* a round, red fruit with a hard skin and many seeds. The seeds are covered with a red, juicy pulp that can be eaten.
pome·gran·ate • *noun, plural* **pomegranates**

pomegranate

pompom (päm′päm) *noun* a fluffy ball made of pieces of yarn or strips of paper or cloth. Pompoms are made by attaching the pieces in the center, so that the ends stick out in all directions. A small pompom can be used to decorate a hat.
pom·pom • *noun, plural* **pompoms**

pompous (päm′pəs) *adjective* trying to seem important by acting too dignified.
pom·pous • *adjective*

Ponce de León (pän′sā dā′lā ōn′), **Juan** (hwän) 1460?-1521; a Spanish explorer who was the first European to discover Florida.
Pon·ce de Le·ón, Juan

poncho (pän′chō) *noun* a cloak that is like a blanket with a hole in the center for a person's head. Ponchos were first used in South America.
pon·cho • *noun, plural* **ponchos**

pond (pänd) *noun* a small lake, often one that is man-made rather than natural.
pond • *noun, plural* **ponds**

ponder (pän′dər) *verb* to think about in a deep and careful way [I *pondered* Mrs. Yee's offer of a summer job.]
pon·der • *verb* **pondered, pondering**

pontoon (pän to͞on′) *noun* **1** a floating object that can be linked with others to hold up a temporary bridge. **2** a part of an airplane that can float and that allows it to land on water.
pon·toon • *noun, plural* **pontoons**

pony (pō′nē) *noun* a type of small horse.
po·ny • *noun, plural* **ponies**

pony express *noun* a system of riders on very fast ponies that was once used to carry mail in the western U.S.

ponytail

ponytail (pō′nē tāl) *noun* a hairdo in which the hair is pulled back tightly and fastened high on the back of the head. It hangs down in back like a pony's tail.
po·ny·tail • *noun, plural* **ponytails**

poodle (po͞od′əl) *noun* a breed of dog with very curly hair, like wool.
poo·dle • *noun, plural* **poodles**

a	cat	ō	go	ʉ	fur	ə =	a *in* ago
ā	ape	ô	law, for	ch	chin		e *in* agent
ä	cot, car	o͝o	look	sh	she		i *in* pencil
e	ten	o͞o	tool	th	thin		o *in* atom
ē	me	oi	oil	*th*	then		u *in* circus
i	fit	ou	out	zh	measure		
ī	ice	u	up	ŋ	ring		

pool[1] (po͞ol) ***noun*** **1** a small pond. **2** a puddle [a *pool* of water on the bathroom floor]. **3** *a short form of* **swimming pool**.
pool • ***noun,*** *plural* **pools**

pool[2] (po͞ol) ***noun*** **1** a game that is a kind of billiards and is played on a table that has six pockets into which players knock the balls. **2** an amount of money, a set of things, or a group of skilled people that is shared by a group [This office has a *pool* of people who type letters for any of the officers of the company.]
verb to put together for the use of all of the persons in a group [We *pooled* our money and rented a cottage.]
pool • ***noun,*** *plural for sense 2 only* **pools** • ***verb*** **pooled, pooling**

pooped (po͞opt) [*a slang word*] ***adjective*** tired out.

poor (po͝or) ***adjective*** **1** having little or no money; having hardly enough to live on. **2** not good enough; lacking something [in *poor* health; a *poor* wheat crop]. **3** not having much skill [a *poor* cook]. **4** deserving pity; unfortunate [The *poor* bird had a broken wing.]
—the poor poor people as a group.
poor • ***adjective*** **poorer, poorest**

pop[1] (päp) ***noun*** **1** a sudden, short bursting sound like the sound of a pistol shot. **2** soda water that has been flavored and sweetened.
verb **1** to make a pop or burst with a pop. **2** to cause to burst open [We *popped* a lot of corn and ate it all.] **3** to move or appear in a quick or sudden way [He *popped* out of bed.] **4** to put in a sudden or unexpected way [She *popped* a surprising question.] **5** to hit a baseball high in the air but in the infield.
pop • ***noun,*** *plural for sense 1 only* **pops** • ***verb*** **popped, popping**

pop[2] (päp) [*an informal word*] ***noun*** father.
pop • ***noun,*** *plural* **pops**

pop[3] (päp) ***adjective*** *a short form of* **popular** [*pop* music].

popcorn (päp′kôrn) ***noun*** **1** a kind of corn with hard kernels that pop open into white, puffy masses when they are heated. **2** the popped kernels, often eaten as a snack.
pop·corn • ***noun***

pope (pōp) ***noun*** *usually* **Pope** the bishop who is the head of the Roman Catholic Church.
pope • ***noun,*** *plural* **popes**

popgun (päp′gun) ***noun*** a toy gun that uses air to shoot little pellets or corks with a popping sound.
pop·gun • ***noun,*** *plural* **popguns**

poplar (päp′lər) ***noun*** **1** a tall tree that grows fast and has small leaves. **2** the wood of this tree.
pop·lar • ***noun,*** *plural for sense 1 only* **poplars**

popover (päp′ō vər) ***noun*** a very light kind of muffin that is puffy and hollow.
pop·o·ver • ***noun,*** *plural* **popovers**

poppy

poppy (päp′ē) ***noun*** a plant with flowers of various bright colors and hard seed capsules with many small black seeds.
pop·py • ***noun,*** *plural* **poppies**

popular (päp′yo͞o lər) ***adjective*** **1** having many friends; very well liked [His quiet humor made him very *popular*.] **2** liked by many people [Pizza is a *popular* food.] **3** of, for, or by all the people or most people [election by *popular* vote; a *popular* idea].
pop·u·lar • ***adjective***

populate (päp′yo͞o lāt′) ***verb*** to fill with people [Persons from many countries have *populated* the U.S.]
pop·u·late • ***verb*** **populated, populating**

population (päp′yo͞o lā′shən) ***noun*** **1** all of the people who are living in a particular city, country, or other land area [the *population* of New York]. **2** the total number of these people [a *population* of one million].
pop·u·la·tion • ***noun,*** *plural* **populations**

porcelain (pôr′sə lin) ***noun*** a hard, strong type of clay ware that is made from a fine white clay. It is formed into fine, often very delicate dishes, vases, and figurines.
por·ce·lain • ***noun***

P

porch (pôrch) ***noun*** **1** a covered entrance to a building, usually with a separate roof. **2** a room on the outside of a building, either open or closed in by screens or windows.
porch • ***noun,*** *plural* **porches**

porcupine (pôr′kyo͞o pīn) ***noun*** an animal that has rough hair mixed with long, sharp spines called quills, that it can cause to stand out on its body.
por·cu·pine • ***noun,*** *plural* **porcupines**

WORD HISTORY

porcupine

We get **porcupine** from two Latin words that mean "pig" and "spine." The **porcupine** is really a rodent, but it looks a little like a small pig with long prickly spines on its body.

pore[1] (pôr) ***verb*** to study or read with care [She *pored* over the book.]
pore • ***verb*** **pored, poring**
• The words **pore** and **pour** sound alike.
Sundays they *pore* over the newspaper.
He was sweating from every *pore*.
Please *pour* me a glass of milk.

pore[2] (pôr) ***noun*** a tiny opening in the skin of animals or in the outer covering of a plant leaf. People sweat through pores in the skin.
pore • ***noun,*** *plural* **pores**
• The words **pore** and **pour** sound alike.

porgy (pôr′gē) ***noun*** a saltwater fish that is used for food.
por·gy • ***noun,*** *plural* **porgies**

pork (pôrk) ***noun*** the meat of a pig or hog, especially when used fresh or not cured.

porky (pôrk′ē) ***adjective*** fat in a way that seems to be caused by eating too much.
pork·y • ***adjective*** **porkier, porkiest**

porous (pôr′əs) ***adjective*** full of pores or tiny holes that water, air, or light can pass through. Leather and many kinds of paper are porous.
po·rous • ***adjective***

porpoise (pôr′pəs) ***noun*** a sea animal that is related to the whale but smaller. It is dark above and white below and has a blunt snout.
por·poise • ***noun,*** *plural* **porpoises**

porpoise

porridge (pôr′ij) ***noun*** a soft food that is made of oatmeal or some other cereal grain boiled in water or milk until it is thick.
por·ridge • ***noun***

port[1] (pôrt) ***noun*** **1** a place where boats and ships can dock or anchor safely; harbor. **2** a city with a harbor where ships can load and unload.
port • ***noun,*** *plural* **ports**

port[2] (pôrt) ***noun*** the left-hand side of a ship or airplane as it is seen by a person who is inside and facing forward.

portable (pôrt′ə bəl) ***adjective*** capable of being carried; easy to carry or move [a *portable* TV].
port·a·ble • ***adjective***

porter (pôrt′ər) ***noun*** **1** a person whose work is carrying luggage in a place such as a hotel or an airport. **2** a person who waits on passengers on a train.
por·ter • ***noun,*** *plural* **porters**

porthole (pôrt′hōl) ***noun*** a small opening in a ship's side for letting in light and air.
port·hole • ***noun,*** *plural* **portholes**

portion (pôr′shən) ***noun*** a part that is given to a person or set aside for some use; a share [a large *portion* of salad. I used a *portion* of my free time to visit my aunt.] —Look for the WORD CHOICES box at the entry **part**.
verb to divide into or give out in portions [We *portioned* out the food.]
por·tion • ***noun,*** *plural* **portions**
• ***verb*** **portioned, portioning**

portly (pôrt′lē) ***adjective*** large and heavy in a dignified way [a *portly* judge].
port·ly • ***adjective*** **portlier, portliest**

a cat	ō go	ʉ fur	ə = a *in* ago
ā ape	ô law, for	ch chin	e *in* agent
ä cot, car	o͝o look	sh she	i *in* pencil
e ten	o͞o tool	th thin	o *in* atom
ē me	oi oil	*th* then	u *in* circus
i fit	ou out	zh measure	
ī ice	u up	ŋ ring	

portrait (pôr′trit) ***noun*** **1** a drawing, painting, sculpture, or photograph of a person, especially of the face. **2** a description of a person in a story or play.
por·trait • ***noun,*** *plural* **portraits**

Portugal (pôr′chə gəl) a country in southwestern Europe, west of Spain. It includes some islands in the Atlantic Ocean west of Africa.
Por·tu·gal

Portuguese (pôr′chə gēz) ***noun*** **1** a person born or living in Portugal. **2** the language of Portugal and also of Brazil.
Por·tu·guese • ***noun,*** *plural for sense 1 only* **Portuguese**

pose (pōz) ***verb*** **1** to stay in a certain position for a time, especially in order to have one's portrait taken or painted. **2** to pretend to be what one is not; to act [He *posed* as a police officer and was punished.] **3** to introduce or present [She *posed* an interesting question.]
noun **1** a position of the body that a person holds for an artist or photographer. **2** a way of acting that is meant to fool people [His gruff manner is just a *pose;* he's really very kind.]
pose • ***verb*** **posed, posing** • ***noun,*** *plural* **poses**

position (pə zish′ən) ***noun*** **1** the way that a person or thing is placed or arranged [a sitting *position*]. **2** the place where a person or thing is; location [The ship sent out its *position* by radio.] **3** what a person thinks or believes; the stand that a person takes [What is your *position* on raising taxes for schools?] **4** the usual or proper place; station [The players are in *position* for the start of the game.] **5** a job or office; a post [She has a *position* with the city government.]
verb to put into a particular position [They *positioned* themselves around the house.]
po·si·tion • ***noun,*** *plural* **positions** • ***verb*** **positioned, positioning**

WORD CHOICES

Synonyms of **position**

The words **position, office,** and **post** share the meaning "a job."

a *position* on the hospital staff
the *office* of treasurer
a *post* in the new government

positive (päz′i tiv) ***adjective*** **1** not to be questioned; definitely set and without doubt [Do you have *positive* knowledge that he was there?] **2** completely sure; certain [I'm *positive* I locked the front door.] **3** sure of oneself; confident [a very *positive* person]. **4** saying that something is so; answering "yes" [a *positive* reply]. **5** doing some good or helping in some way [*positive* comments on my acting; a *positive* attitude toward life]. **6** showing that a certain disease or condition is present [She had a *positive* reaction to the allergy test.] **7** describing or having to do with a kind of electrical charge associated with a shortage of electrons. When a piece of silk is rubbed on a glass rod the silk captures electrons and leaves a positive charge on the glass rod. **8** describing an amount or number that is greater than zero.
noun **1** something that is positive. **2** a finished photograph or a film for use in a projector. The positive shows the colors and light and dark areas exactly as they are in the original subject.
pos·i·tive • ***adjective*** • ***noun,*** *plural* **positives**

posse (päs′ē) ***noun*** a group of people called together by a sheriff to help in keeping the peace.
pos·se • ***noun,*** *plural* **posses**

possess (pə zes′) ***verb*** **1** to have or own [She *possesses* great wealth.] —Look for the WORD CHOICES box at the entry **have**. **2** to gain power over; to control [Fear suddenly *possessed* us.]
pos·sess • ***verb*** **possessed, possessing**

possession (pə zesh′ən) ***noun*** **1** the fact of possessing, holding, or owning [We have *possession* of secret facts.] **2** something that a person owns [This bike is my most prized *possession*.]
pos·ses·sion • ***noun,*** *plural for sense 2 only* **possessions**

possessive (pə zes′iv) ***adjective*** **1** having or showing a strong desire for owning things or controlling people [He is very *possessive*.] **2** in grammar, describing a word, form, or phrase that shows possession, ownership, or some similar relationship. These relationships are usually shown by the ending *-'s* (the *dog's* house) or an apostrophe alone after most plurals (the *dogs'* house). Pronouns change their form (This is *my* book. The book is *mine*.)
pos·ses·sive • ***adjective***

P

possibility (päs′i bil′i tē) ***noun*** **1** the fact of being possible; a chance [There is a *possibility* of rain.] **2** something that is possible [Pancakes are one *possibility* for breakfast today.]
pos·si·bil·i·ty • ***noun, plural for sense 2 only*** **possibilities**

possible (päs′i bəl) ***adjective*** **1** capable of existing [The highest *possible* score in bowling is 300. Oxygen in the air makes life on earth *possible*.] **2** capable of happening or being done [It will be colder tomorrow, with *possible* showers in the morning.]
pos·si·ble • ***adjective***

possibly (päs′i blē) ***adverb*** **1** in any possible way [The plan can't *possibly* work.] **2** perhaps; maybe [*Possibly* it's true.]
pos·si·bly • ***adverb***

possum (päs′əm) [*an informal word*] ***noun*** *a short form of* **opossum**.
pos·sum • ***noun, plural*** **possums**

post[1] (pōst) ***noun*** a piece of wood, metal, or other material that is set upright for holding something up [The sign was on a *post* stuck in the ground.]
verb **1** to put up on a wall, fence, or post [He *posted* a sign.] **2** to announce by posting signs [A reward has been *posted* for their capture.]
post • ***noun, plural*** **posts** • ***verb*** **posted, posting**

post[2] (pōst) ***noun*** **1** a place where a soldier or guard is on duty [The sentry walks a *post* just over the hill.] **2** a place where soldiers are stationed [an army *post*]. **3** a position or job to which a person is named [a government *post*] —Look for the WORD CHOICES box at the entry **position**.
verb to place at a post [They *posted* guards at every exit.]
post • ***noun, plural*** **posts** • ***verb*** **posted, posting**

post[3] (pōst) ***noun*** mail or the delivery of mail: this sense is used mainly in Britain [The letter came in this morning's *post*.]
verb **1** to send by mail: this sense is used mainly in Britain [I *posted* the letter yesterday.] **2** to give news to; inform [I will keep you *posted* on my activities.]
post • ***noun*** • ***verb*** **posted, posting**

post- *a prefix meaning* after or following [A *postwar* period is a period after a war.]

postage (pōst′ij) ***noun*** the amount that is charged for delivering a letter or package by mail.
post·age • ***noun***

postage stamp ***noun*** a government stamp that is put on a piece of mail to show that the postage has been paid. The amount of postage in dollars or cents is printed on the stamp.
postage stamp • ***noun, plural*** **postage stamps**

postal (pōs′təl) ***adjective*** having to do with mail or post offices [the *postal* service; a *postal* clerk].
post·al • ***adjective***

postcard (pōst′kärd) ***noun*** **1** a card with a postage stamp printed on it, used for sending a short message by mail without an envelope. **2** a card with a picture on one side and a place for a short message and an address on the other. It can be sent through the mail without an envelope.
post·card • ***noun, plural*** **postcards**

poster (pōs′tər) ***noun*** a large sign or notice put up in a public place [a movie *poster*].
post·er • ***noun, plural*** **posters**

posterity (päs ter′i tē) ***noun*** the people of future times [This music will be played for all *posterity*.]
pos·ter·i·ty • ***noun***

postman (pōst′mən) ***noun*** *another name for* **mail carrier**.
post·man • ***noun, plural*** **postmen**

postmark (pōst′märk) ***noun*** a mark stamped on mail at the post office of the sender. It cancels the postage stamp and shows the place and date.
post·mark • ***noun, plural*** **postmarks**

postmaster (pōst′mas tər) ***noun*** a person in charge of a post office.
post·mas·ter • ***noun, plural*** **postmasters**

post office ***noun*** a building or office where mail is sorted and where postage stamps are sold.
post office • ***noun, plural*** **post offices**

postpone (pōst pōn′) ***verb*** to put off until later; to delay [The game was *postponed* because of rain.]
post·pone • ***verb*** **postponed, postponing**

a	cat	ō	go	ʉ	fur	ə =	a *in* ago
ā	ape	ô	law, for	ch	chin		e *in* agent
ä	cot, car	oo	look	sh	she		i *in* pencil
e	ten	ōō	tool	th	thin		o *in* atom
ē	me	oi	oil	*th*	then		u *in* circus
i	fit	ou	out	zh	measure		
ī	ice	u	up	ŋ	ring		

postscript (pōst′skript) ***noun*** a note added below the signature of a letter.
post·script • ***noun,*** *plural* **postscripts**

posture (päs′chər) ***noun*** the way one holds one's body in sitting or standing.
pos·ture • ***noun***

postwar (pōst′wôr′) ***adjective*** after a war [the *postwar* years].
post·war • ***adjective***

pot (pät) ***noun*** **1** a round container used for cooking or for holding things [a flower*pot*]. **2** the amount that a pot will hold [He made a *pot* of coffee.]
verb to put into a pot [We *potted* the plants.]
—go to pot to become ruined [The old bridge is *going to pot* from lack of repairs.]
pot • ***noun,*** *plural* **pots** • ***verb*** **potted, potting**

potassium (pō tas′ē əm) ***noun*** a soft, silver-white metal that is a chemical element. Potassium is used in fertilizers and to make glass.
po·tas·si·um • ***noun***

potato (pə tāt′ō) ***noun*** a very common vegetable that is part of an underground stem of a plant. It is round or oval, with a thin, red or light-brown skin and white flesh.
po·ta·to • ***noun,*** *plural* **potatoes**

potato

potato chip ***noun*** a very thin slice of potato fried until crisp and usually salted or flavored.
potato chip • ***noun,*** *plural* **potato chips**

potential (pō ten′shəl) ***adjective*** capable of coming into being but not yet actual; possible [Bad wiring is a *potential* cause of fire.]
noun power or skill that may be developed [That team has a lot of *potential*.]
po·ten·tial • ***adjective*** • ***noun***

potion (pō′shən) ***noun*** a drink that is supposed to heal, do magic, or have certain other powers.
po·tion • ***noun,*** *plural* **potions**

potter (pät′ər) ***noun*** a person who makes pottery by shaping clay.
pot·ter • ***noun,*** *plural* **potters**

Potter (pät′ər), **Beatrix** (bē′ə triks) 1866-1943; English writer of children's books, including the stories about Peter Rabbit.
Pot·ter, Be·a·trix

pottery (pät′ər ē) ***noun*** pots, dishes, and other things made of clay that has been hardened by baking.
pot·ter·y • ***noun***

pouch (pouch) ***noun*** **1** a bag or sack [a mail *pouch*]. **2** a loose fold of skin like a pocket on the belly of the female kangaroo and of certain other female animals. It is used for carrying the young. **3** anything shaped like a pouch [the *pouch* of a pelican's bill].
pouch • ***noun,*** *plural* **pouches**

poultry (pōl′trē) ***noun*** chickens, turkeys, ducks, and other fowl raised for food.
poul·try • ***noun***

pounce (pouns) ***verb*** to spring or swoop down in order to attack or seize [The cat *pounced* on the ball of string.]
pounce • ***verb*** **pounced, pouncing**

pound[1] (pound) ***noun*** **1** a unit of weight that is equal to 16 ounces. **2** the basic unit of money of the United Kingdom and certain other countries.
pound • ***noun,*** *plural* **pounds**

pound[2] (pound) ***verb*** **1** to hit with a heavy blow or many heavy blows; hit hard [He *pounded* on the door.] —Look for the WORD CHOICES box at the entry **beat**. **2** to crush into a powder or pulp [He *pounded* the corn into meal.] **3** to beat in a heavy way; throb [Her heart *pounded* from the exercise.]
pound • ***verb*** **pounded, pounding**

pound[3] (pound) ***noun*** a closed-in place where stray animals are kept [a dog *pound*].
pound • ***noun,*** *plural* **pounds**

pour (pôr) ***verb*** **1** to let flow in a steady stream [He *poured* the milk into the glass.] **2** to flow in a steady stream [Wet salt will not *pour*.] **3** to rain heavily [It *poured* all day.]
pour • ***verb*** **poured, pouring**

● The words **pour** and **pore** sound alike.
Please *pour* me a glass of soda.
She will *pore* over her research books.
He was sweating from every *pore*.

pout (pout) ***verb*** to push out the lips to show that one is annoyed or has hurt feelings.
pout • ***verb*** **pouted, pouting**

poverty (päv′ər tē) ***noun*** the condition of being poor; a lack of money.
pov·er·ty • ***noun***

P

powder (pou′dər) ***noun*** a dry substance of fine particles like dust, made by crushing or grinding [baking *powder; gunpowder*].
verb **1** to sprinkle or cover with powder or something like powder [Snow *powdered* the hills.] **2** to make into powder.
pow·der • ***noun,*** *plural* **powders**
• ***verb*** **powdered, powdering**

powder room ***noun*** a restroom for women.
powder room • ***noun,*** *plural* **powder rooms**

powdery (pou′dər ē) ***adjective*** **1** of or like powder [*powdery* snow]. **2** covered with powder.
pow·der·y • ***adjective***

power (pou′ər) ***noun*** **1** ability to do or act [Lobsters have the *power* to grow new claws.] **2** strength or force [the *power* of the boxer's punch]. **3** energy or force that can be put to work [electric *power*]. **4** the ability to control others; authority [the *power* of the law]. **5** a person, nation, or thing that has control or influence over others. **6** the number of times that a certain number is used as a factor in a multiplication. For example, 2 to the fourth power, or 2^4, is equal to 2 x 2 x 2 x 2.
verb to supply with power [The machine is *powered* by a gasoline engine.]
adjective using electricity or another kind of power [a *power* saw].
—in power having control or authority.
pow·er • ***noun,*** *plural for senses 5 and 6 only* **powers** • ***verb*** **powered, powering**
• ***adjective***

WORD CHOICES

Synonyms of **power**

The words **power, authority,** and **control** share the meaning "the right to make decisions and give orders."

a weak leader with little *power*

a general's *authority* over an army

children under the *control* of a guardian

powerful (pou′ər fəl) ***adjective*** having much power; strong [a *powerful* blow].
pow·er·ful • ***adjective***

powerless (pou′ər ləs) ***adjective*** without power; weak or helpless [The small boat was *powerless* against the storm.]
pow·er·less • ***adjective***

power plant

power plant ***noun*** a building where electric power is produced.
power plant • ***noun,*** *plural* **power plants**

pp. *abbreviation for* pages [*pp.* 3-15].

PR or **P.R.** *abbreviation for* Puerto Rico.

practical (prak′ti kəl) ***adjective*** **1** capable of being put to use; useful and sensible [a *practical* idea]. **2** dealing with things in a way that shows good sense [He is not a very *practical* person.]
prac·ti·cal • ***adjective***

practical joke ***noun*** a trick played on someone, especially one that is meant to embarrass the person.
practical joke • ***noun,*** *plural* **practical jokes**

practically (prak′ti kəl ē *or* prak′tik lē) ***adverb*** **1** in a way that is practical, or shows good sense [Let's look at the problem *practically*.] **2** [*an informal use*] almost; nearly [The game was *practically* over before we scored our first run.]
prac·ti·cal·ly • ***adverb***

practice (prak′tis) ***verb*** **1** to do or carry out in a regular way; make a habit of [You should *practice* what you preach.] **2** to do something over and over again in order to become skilled at it [He *practiced* the solo for two hours.] **3** to work at a profession or occupation [She *practiced* medicine for forty years.]

a cat	ō go	ʉ fur	ə = a *in* ago
ā ape	ô law, for	ch chin	e *in* agent
ä cot, car	oo look	sh she	i *in* pencil
e ten	o͞o tool	th thin	o *in* atom
ē me	oi oil	*th* then	u *in* circus
i fit	ou out	zh measure	
ī ice	u up	ŋ ring	

noun **1** a usual action or way of acting; habit or custom [It is his *practice* to sleep late.] **2** the action of doing something over and over again in order to become skilled [batting *practice*]. **3** the skill a person gets by doing something over and over again [I am out of *practice*.] **4** the work of a profession or occupation [the *practice* of law]. **5** the business built up in doing such work [The doctor has a large *practice*.]
prac·tice • ***verb*** **practiced, practicing**
• ***noun,*** *plural for senses 1 and 5 only*
practices

WORD CHOICES

Synonyms of **practice**

The words **practice, drill,** and **exercise** share the meaning "the doing of something over and over in order to improve one's skill."

batting *practice*
a spelling *drill*
a dance *exercise*

prairie (prer′ē) ***noun*** a large area of flat land with much grass and few trees.
prai·rie • ***noun,*** *plural* **prairies**

prairie dog ***noun*** a small North American animal that is a little like a squirrel. Its cry sounds like a bark.
prairie dog • ***noun,*** *plural* **prairie dogs**

prairie schooner ***noun*** a large covered wagon used by pioneers to cross the American prairies.
prairie schooner • ***noun,*** *plural* **prairie schooners**

praise (prāz) ***verb*** to say good things about; give a good opinion of [She *praised* his work.] ***noun*** words that praise or show approval.
praise • ***verb*** **praised, praising** • ***noun,*** *plural* **praises**

prance (prans) ***verb*** to rise up on the hind legs and spring forward [The horses *pranced* around the circus ring.]
prance • ***verb*** **pranced, prancing**

prank (praŋk) ***noun*** a playful or mischievous trick.
prank • ***noun,*** *plural* **pranks**

pray (prā) ***verb*** to say words to God in worship or in asking for something —Look for the WORD CHOICES box at the entry **appeal**.
pray • ***verb*** **prayed, praying**
• The words **pray** and **prey** sound alike.
We were asked to bow our heads and *pray*.
Rodents are often the *prey* of snakes.

prayer (prer) ***noun*** **1** the act of praying. **2** a set of words used in praying.
prayer • ***noun,*** *plural for sense 2 only* **prayers**

praying mantis

praying mantis ***noun*** *another name for* **mantis.**
praying mantis • ***noun,*** *plural* **praying mantises**

pre- *a prefix meaning* before [The casserole was *precooked* so we only had to heat it.]

preach (prēch) ***verb*** **1** to speak to people on a religious subject; give a sermon. **2** to teach or urge by speaking in public [He *preached* peace wherever he went.]
preach • ***verb*** **preached, preaching**

preacher (prēch′ər) ***noun*** a member of the clergy who preaches.
preach·er • ***noun,*** *plural* **preachers**

precaution (prē kô′shən *or* prē kä′shən) ***noun*** care or an action taken ahead of time against danger or failure [She took the *precaution* of locking the door.]
pre·cau·tion • ***noun,*** *plural* **precautions**

precede (prē sēd′) ***verb*** to go or come before [She *preceded* him out the door. May *precedes* June.]
pre·cede • ***verb*** **preceded, preceding**

preceding (prē sēd′iŋ) ***adjective*** going or coming before; previous [Turn back to the

P

preceding page of the book.] —Look for the WORD CHOICES box at the entry **previous**.
pre·ced·ing • *adjective*

precinct (prē′siŋkt) *noun* one of the districts into which a ward or city is divided [a voting *precinct;* a police *precinct*].
pre·cinct • *noun, plural* **precincts**

precious (presh′əs) *adjective* **1** having a high price or value [Freedom is a *precious* right. Diamonds are *precious* stones.] —Look for the WORD CHOICES box at the entry **costly**. **2** much loved; dear [our *precious* baby].
pre·cious • *adjective*

precipice (pres′i pis) *noun* a steep cliff.
prec·i·pice • *noun, plural* **precipices**

precipitation (prē sip′i tā′shən) *noun* **1** rain, snow, or any other moisture that falls from the sky. **2** the amount of moisture that falls [What is the annual *precipitation* in this region?]
pre·cip·i·ta·tion • *noun*

precise (prē sīs′) *adjective* exact in every detail; accurate [She gave them a *precise* report of what had happened.]
pre·cise • *adjective*

precision (prē sizh′ən) *noun* the condition or quality of being exact; accuracy [the *precision* of a fine watch].
pre·ci·sion • *noun*

predator (pred′ə tər) *noun* an animal that lives by killing and eating other animals.
pred·a·tor • *noun, plural* **predators**

predicate (pred′i kət) *noun* the word or group of words in a sentence that says something about the subject of the sentence. A predicate may be a verb or a verb and its object. In the sentence "Boys and girls enjoy sports," the predicate is "enjoy sports."
pred·i·cate • *noun, plural* **predicates**

predict (prē dikt′) *verb* to tell what one thinks will happen in the future [I *predict* that we will win the game tomorrow.] —Look for the WORD CHOICES box at the entry **foretell**.
pre·dict • *verb* **predicted, predicting**

prediction (prē dik′shən) *noun* something predicted [The journalists made their *predictions* for next week's elections.]
pre·dic·tion • *noun, plural* **predictions**

predominant (prē däm′i nənt) *adjective* most frequent or most common; prevailing [Red is the *predominant* color for warning signs.]
pre·dom·i·nant • *adjective*

preface (pref′əs) *noun* statements or remarks made at the beginning of a book or speech.
verb to give or be a preface to [She *prefaced* her talk with a joke.]
pref·ace • *noun, plural* **prefaces**
• *verb* **prefaced, prefacing**

prefer (prē fʉr′) *verb* to like better; choose first [He *prefers* baseball to football.]
pre·fer • *verb* **preferred, preferring**

preference (pref′ər əns) *noun* **1** a greater liking for one thing over others [She has a *preference* for seafood.] **2** a person's choice; something preferred [My *preference* is to go to a movie tonight.]
pref·er·ence • *noun, plural* **preferences**

prefix (prē′fiks) *noun* a syllable or group of syllables that is joined to the beginning of a word to change the word's meaning. Some common prefixes are *pre-, re-, non-,* and *anti-*.
pre·fix • *noun, plural* **prefixes**

pregnancy (preg′nən sē) *noun* the condition or time of being pregnant [In humans, *pregnancy* lasts about nine months.]
preg·nan·cy • *noun, plural* **pregnancies**

pregnant (preg′nənt) *adjective* having an unborn child or offspring growing in the uterus.
preg·nant • *adjective*

prehistoric (prē′his tôr′ik) *adjective* of the time before history was written [Dinosaurs were *prehistoric* creatures.]
pre·his·tor·ic • *adjective*

prejudice (prej′ə dis) *noun* **1** an opinion formed without knowing the facts or by ignoring the facts; unfair or unreasonable opinion. **2** dislike or distrust of people just because they are of another race, religion, or country.
prej·u·dice • *noun, plural for sense 1 only* **prejudices**

preliminary (prē lim′i ner′ē) *adjective* leading up to the main action [There were several *preliminary* races before the featured race.]
pre·lim·i·nar·y • *adjective*

premier (prē mir′) *noun* the chief official of the government in certain countries.
adjective first in importance or position; chief.
pre·mier • *noun, plural* **premiers** • *adjective*

a	cat	ō	go	ʉ	fur	ə = a *in* ago	
ā	ape	ô	law, for	ch	chin	e *in* agent	
ä	cot, car	oo	look	sh	she	i *in* pencil	
e	ten	ōō	tool	th	thin	o *in* atom	
ē	me	oi	oil	*th*	then	u *in* circus	
i	fit	ou	out	zh	measure		
ī	ice	u	up	ŋ	ring		

premise (prem′is) ***noun*** **1** a statement or belief that is accepted as true and is used as the basis for a theory or a philosophy. **2 premises** a building and the land belonging to it [Keep off the *premises*.]
prem·ise • ***noun,*** *plural* **premises**

premium (prē′mē əm) ***noun*** **1** a reward or prize offered to give an added reason to buy or do something [a valuable *premium* of a toy inside the cereal box]. **2** an extra amount added to a regular charge [There is a *premium* for special delivery.] **3** a payment made for an insurance policy. **4** very high value [She puts a *premium* on neat work.]
pre·mi·um • ***noun,*** *plural for senses 1, 2, and 3 only* **premiums**

premolar (prē mō′lər) ***noun*** one of the teeth that is just in front of a molar.
pre·mo·lar • ***noun,*** *plural* **premolars**

prep. *abbreviation for* preposition.

prepaid (prē pād′) ***verb*** *past tense and past participle of* **prepay**.
pre·paid • ***verb***

preparation (prep′ər ā′shən) ***noun*** **1** the act of getting ready or the condition of being ready [*Preparation* is the key to winning in sports.] **2** something done to get ready [His *preparations* before a game include running and stretching.] **3** something such as a medicine that is prepared for a certain purpose [This *preparation* requires a prescription.]
prep·a·ra·tion • ***noun,*** *plural for senses 2 and 3 only* **preparations**

prepare (prē per′) ***verb*** **1** to make or get ready [We *prepared* for the test. She *prepared* the ground for planting.] **2** to make or put together out of parts or materials [Pharmacists *prepare* medicines.]
pre·pare • ***verb*** **prepared, preparing**

prepay (prē pā′) ***verb*** to pay for ahead of time [I had to *prepay* the cost of shipping the crate.]
pre·pay • ***verb*** **prepaid, prepaying**

preposition (prep ə zish′ən) ***noun*** a word that makes a connection between a noun or pronoun and another word in the same sentence. "To," "in," and "for" are prepositions.
prep·o·si·tion • ***noun,*** *plural* **prepositions**

prepositional phrase (prep ə zish′ən əl) ***noun*** a phrase that is made up of a preposition and the noun or pronoun that follows it. For example, in the sentence "Go to the store" the phrase "to the store" is a prepositional phrase.
prepositional phrase • ***noun,*** *plural* **prepositional phrases**

Pres. *abbreviation for* President.

preschool (prē′sko͞ol) ***adjective*** of or for children who are too young for kindergarten [a child of *preschool* age].
noun the same as **nursery school**.
pre·school • ***adjective*** • ***noun,*** *plural* **preschools**

prescribe (prē skrīb′) ***verb*** **1** to set up as a rule or direction to be followed [A fine of $100 is the penalty *prescribed* by law.] **2** to advise to take a certain medicine or treatment [The doctor *prescribed* some pills for my allergy.]
pre·scribe • ***verb*** **prescribed, prescribing**

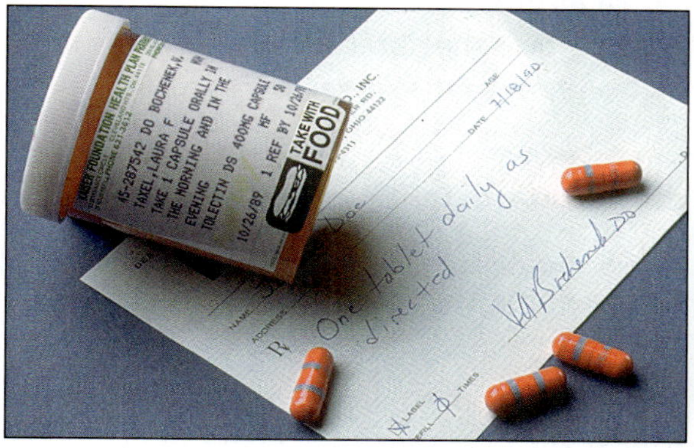

prescription

prescription (prē skrip′shən) ***noun*** **1** a doctor's written instructions telling what medicine is to be prepared and how the patient is to use it. **2** a medicine prepared according to a doctor's instructions.
pre·scrip·tion • ***noun,*** *plural* **prescriptions**

presence (prez′əns) ***noun*** **1** the fact or condition of being present [We need her *presence* at the meeting.] **2** the very place where a certain person is [We came into the king's *presence*.]
pres·ence • ***noun***

present (prez′ənt *for adj. & n.;* prē zent′ *for v.*) ***adjective*** **1** being here or at a certain place; not absent [Is everyone *present* today?] **2** of or at this time; for now [My *present* needs are few.] **3** showing time that is going on right now [the *present* tense of a verb].
noun **1** this time; now [I have no job at *present*.] **2** a gift [a birthday *present*].
verb **1** to make known; introduce [John *presented* his friend to us.] **2** to put on view or

P

place before the public; show [They *presented* a new play last night.] **3** to give as a gift [She *presented* the book to him.] **4** to give to [They *presented* the school with a new piano.] —Look for the WORD CHOICES box at the entry **give**.
pres·ent • *adjective* • *noun, plural for sense 2 only* **presents** • *verb* **pre·sent, presented, presenting**

WORD CHOICES

Synonyms of **present**

The words **present**, **gift**, and **grant** share the meaning "something given to show friendship or support."

a birthday *present*

a *gift* to the library

a *grant* to the research institute

presentation (prez′ən tā′shən *or* prē′zən tā′shən) *noun* **1** the act of presenting [The *presentation* of awards will follow dinner.] **2** something that is presented [His TV show is among the new *presentations* for the fall season.]
pres·en·ta·tion • *noun, plural* **presentations**

presently (prez′ənt lē) *adverb* **1** in a little while; soon [The doctor will see you *presently*.] **2** at this time; now [She is *presently* on vacation.]
pres·ent·ly • *adverb*

present participle *noun* in grammar, a participle that is used to show present time or an action that is still going on. It can also be used as an adjective. Present participles always end in *-ing* (We are *going* right now.)
present participle • *noun, plural* **present participles**

present tense *noun* a form of a verb that shows something that is happening now or that exists now (The plums *are* ripe. She *speaks* French.)

preservation (prez ər vā′shən) *noun* the act of preserving [Airtight cans are used for the *preservation* of food.]
pres·er·va·tion • *noun*

preservative (prē zʉrv′ə tiv) *noun* a substance that is added to food to keep it from spoiling.
pre·serv·a·tive • *noun, plural* **preservatives**

preserve (prē zʉrv′) *verb* **1** to protect from harm or damage [a campaign to *preserve* our national forests]. **2** to prepare food for later use by canning, pickling, or salting it. **3** to keep in a certain condition; maintain [She *preserved* her dignity by staying calm.]
noun **1** *usually* **preserves** fruit preserved by cooking it with sugar and canning it. **2** a place where fish or wild animals are protected or are kept for controlled fishing and hunting.
pre·serve • *verb* **preserved, preserving** • *noun, plural* **preserves**

preside (prē zīd′) *verb* to be in charge of a meeting; to act as chairperson [The Vice President *presides* over the U.S. Senate.]
pre·side • *verb* **presided, presiding**

presidency (prez′i dən sē) *noun* **1** the office of president [The *presidency* was first held by Washington.] **2** the time during which a person holds the office of president [Abraham Lincoln's *presidency* began in 1861.]
pres·i·den·cy • *noun, plural* **presidencies**

president (prez′i dənt) *noun* **1** *often* **President** a person who is head of the government in a republic. The President of the U.S. is elected for a term of four years. **2** the highest officer of a company, college, or club.
pres·i·dent • *noun, plural* **presidents**

presidential (prez′i den′shəl) *adjective* of or having to do with a president or a presidency.
pres·i·den·tial • *adjective*

press (pres) *verb* **1** to act on with steady force or weight; push against, weigh down, or squeeze [She *pressed* the button.] **2** to push closely together; crowd [Thousands *pressed* into the stadium.] **3** to make clothes smooth by ironing; iron. **4** to squeeze out [Oil is *pressed* from olives.] **5** to hold close; hug [She *pressed* the baby to her breast.] **6** to keep on asking or urging [The teacher *pressed* the class to do better work.]
noun **1** the act of pressing [A *press* of the button will start the machine.] **2** a tool or device that presses something [a clothes *press;* a cider *press*]. **3** *a short form of* **printing press**. **4** newspapers and magazines in general [stories of the earthquake in the *press*]. **5** the people who work for or produce newspapers

a cat	ō go	ʉ fur	ə = a *in* ago
ā ape	ô law, for	ch chin	e *in* agent
ä cot, car	oo look	sh she	i *in* pencil
e ten	ōō tool	th thin	o *in* atom
ē me	oi oil	*th* then	u *in* circus
i fit	ou out	zh measure	
ī ice	u up	ŋ ring	

and magazines [The President will speak to the *press* today.]
press • *verb* **pressed, pressing** • *noun, plural for senses 1, 2, and 3 only* **presses**

press conference *noun* an interview granted to a group of journalists by an important or well-known person.
press conference • *noun, plural* **press conferences**

pressing (pres′iŋ) *adjective* needing quick action; urgent [a *pressing* problem].
press·ing • *adjective*

pressure (presh′ər) *noun* **1** the force of pushing or of weight [Put more *pressure* on the brake pedal.] **2** influence or force to make someone do something [They put *pressure* on him to quit.] **3** a condition of trouble, strain, or stress that is hard to bear [They moved to the country to escape the *pressures* of the big city.]
verb to influence or force to do something [They *pressured* me into going with them.]
pres·sure • *noun, plural for sense 3 only* **pressures** • *verb* **pressured, pressuring**

pressure suit *noun* an airtight garment that can be inflated to maintain a more or less normal air pressure inside it. It is worn by a person in space or at a high altitude.
pressure suit • *noun, plural* **pressure suits**

pressure suit

prestige (pres tēzh′) *noun* fame or respect such as that which comes from doing great things or having a good character.
pres·tige • *noun*

prestigious (pres tij′əs *or* pres tē′jəs) *adjective* having or giving prestige [a *prestigious* award].
pres·ti·gious • *adjective*

presume (prē zo͞om′ *or* prē zyo͞om′) *verb* **1** to take for granted; assume [I *presume* you know what you are doing.] **2** to be so bold; dare [I would not *presume* to tell you what to do.]
pre·sume • *verb* **presumed, presuming**

preteen (prē′tēn′) *noun* a person who is nearly a teenager.
pre·teen • *noun, plural* **preteens**

pretend (prē tend′) *verb* **1** to make believe [Let's *pretend* we're cowboys.] **2** to claim or act in a false way [She only *pretended* to be mad.]
pre·tend • *verb* **pretended, pretending**

pretense (pri tens′ *or* prē′tens) *noun* **1** a claim [She made no *pretense* of being rich.] **2** a false claim, excuse, or show [He made a *pretense* of being ill so that he could stay home.]
pre·tense • *noun, plural* **pretenses**

pretentious (prē ten′shəs) *adjective* seeming or pretending to be important or excellent [his *pretentious* manner].
pre·ten·tious • *adjective*

pretty (prit′ē) *adjective* pleasing or attractive in a delicate or graceful way [a *pretty* face; a *pretty* color combination; a *pretty* picture].
adverb somewhat; rather [I'm *pretty* tired.]
pret·ty • *adjective* **prettier, prettiest** • *adverb*

pretzel (pret′səl) *noun* a thin roll of dough, usually twisted in a knot, sprinkled with salt, and baked until it is hard.
pret·zel • *noun, plural* **pretzels**

pretzel

prevail (prē vāl′) *verb* to be successful or win out [The army *prevailed* over the enemy.]
pre·vail • *verb* **prevailed, prevailing**

prevailing (prē vā′liŋ) *adjective* most usual or frequent; predominant [The *prevailing* winds are from the west.]
pre·vail·ing • *adjective*

prevalent (prev′ə lənt) *adjective* existing or happening over a wide area; common; general [Islam is *prevalent* in the Middle East.] —Look for the WORD CHOICES box at the entry **usual**.
prev·a·lent • *adjective*

prevent (prē vent′) *verb* **1** to stop or hinder [A storm *prevented* us from going.] **2** to keep from happening [Careful driving *prevents* accidents.]
pre·vent • *verb* **prevented, preventing**

prevention (prē ven′shən) *noun* the act of preventing [Science has made great progress in the *prevention* of many diseases.]
pre·ven·tion • *noun*

preventive (prē ven′tiv) ***adjective*** having the purpose of preventing something [*preventive* medicine].
pre·ven·tive • ***adjective***

preview (prē′vyo͞o) ***noun*** the act or an instance of showing something such as a movie to a special audience before showing it to the general public.
verb to view or show ahead of time [The movie will be *previewed* in New York before it is shown around the country.]
pre·view • ***noun,*** *plural* **previews**
• ***verb*** **previewed, previewing**

previous (prē′vē əs) ***adjective*** happening or coming before in time or order; earlier [They had moved away the *previous* spring. Turn to the *previous* page.]
—previous to before [Who was the President *previous to* George Bush?]
pre·vi·ous • ***adjective***

WORD CHOICES

Synonyms of **previous**

The words **previous, preceding,** and **prior** share the meaning "coming before something else in time or in order."

during a *previous* meeting
on the *preceding* day
at some *prior* time

prey (prā) ***noun*** **1** an animal hunted and eaten by another animal [Chickens are often the *prey* of hawks.] **2** the action or habit of hunting and eating other animals [The hawk is a bird of *prey*.] **3** a victim of someone or something [The old man became the *prey* of swindlers.]
verb **1** to hunt other animals for food [Eagles *prey* upon small animals.] **2** to take advantage of by cheating or deceiving [Dishonest street vendors *preyed* on the tourists.] **3** to have a harmful influence [His financial troubles *preyed* on his mind.]
prey • ***noun*** • ***verb*** **preyed, preying**
● The words **prey** and **pray** sound alike.
Snakes *prey* upon small rodents.
We were asked to bow our heads and *pray*.

price (prīs) ***noun*** **1** the amount of money asked or paid for something. **2** value or worth [pearls of great *price*]. **3** something that is given up or lost in the process of getting something else [Success came at the *price* of his health.]
verb **1** to set the price of [The rug was *priced* at $100.] **2** [*an informal use*] to find out the price of [I *priced* several cameras before buying this one.]
price • ***noun,*** *plural for sense 1 only* **prices**
• ***verb*** **priced, pricing**

priceless (prīs′ləs) ***adjective*** too valuable to be measured by price [a *priceless* work of art].
price·less • ***adjective***

prick (prik) ***verb*** to make a small hole in with a sharp point [The needle *pricked* my finger. I *pricked* myself with the needle.]
noun **1** a tiny hole made by a sharp point. **2** a sharp pain caused by pricking.
—prick up one's ears **1** to raise the ears [The dog *pricked up its ears* when the phone rang.] **2** to listen closely.
prick • ***verb*** **pricked, pricking** • ***noun,*** *plural* **pricks**

prickle (prik′əl) ***noun*** **1** a small, sharp point. **2** a stinging feeling; tingle.
verb to prick, sting, or tingle [His skin *prickled* from the icy rain.]
prick·le • ***noun,*** *plural* **prickles**
• ***verb*** **prickled, prickling**

prickly (prik′lē) ***adjective*** **1** full of prickles or sharp points. **2** stinging or tingling [a *prickly* sensation].
prick·ly • ***adjective*** **pricklier, prickliest**

prickly pear ***noun*** **1** a cactus that has a flat stem and yellow flowers. **2** its fruit, which is shaped like a pear and can be eaten.
prickly pear • ***noun,*** *plural* **prickly pears**

pride (prīd) ***noun*** **1** an opinion of oneself that is too high; vanity [Her foolish *pride* blinded her to her own faults.] **2** proper respect for oneself; dignity; self-respect [He has too much *pride* to ask his friend for a loan.] **3** pleasure or satisfaction from having or doing something [We take *pride* in our garden.]
verb to be proud of [He *prides* himself on his good grades.]
pride • ***noun*** • ***verb*** **prided, priding**

a	cat	ō	go	ʉ	fur	ə =	a *in* ago
ā	ape	ô	law, for	ch	chin		e *in* agent
ä	cot, car	oo	look	sh	she		i *in* pencil
e	ten	o͞o	tool	th	thin		o *in* atom
ē	me	oi	oil	*th*	then		u *in* circus
i	fit	ou	out	zh	measure		
ī	ice	u	up	ŋ	ring		

priest (prēst) ***noun*** a member of the clergy in certain Christian churches.
priest • ***noun,*** *plural* **priests**

prim (prim) ***adjective*** very proper and precise; somewhat formal in a stiff way [a *prim* reply].
prim • ***adjective*** **primmer, primmest**

primarily (prī mer′i lē) ***adverb*** for the most part; mainly [The audience consisted *primarily* of children.]
pri·mar·i·ly • ***adverb***

primary (prī′mer ē) ***adjective*** **1** first in time or order [the *primary* grades in school]. **2** first in importance; chief [Our *primary* goal is getting the people out safely.]
noun an election for choosing the candidates who will run in the final election.
pri·mar·y • ***adjective*** • ***noun,*** *plural* **primaries**

primary color ***noun*** any of the three basic colors from which all other colors can be made. Red, yellow, and blue are the primary colors in mixing paint.
primary color • ***noun,*** *plural* **primary colors**

primate (prī′māt) ***noun*** any member of the most highly developed order of animals. Human beings, apes, and monkeys are primates.
pri·mate • ***noun,*** *plural* **primates**

prime (prīm) ***adjective*** first in rank, importance, or quality.
noun the best or most active period in a person's life or career [The athlete is in his *prime*.]
verb to make ready by putting something in or on [The plumber *primed* the pump by pouring in water. She *primed* the wall with a coat of white paint.]
prime • ***adjective*** • ***noun*** • ***verb*** **primed, priming**

prime minister ***noun*** in countries with a parliament, the chief official of the government.
prime minister • ***noun,*** *plural* **prime ministers**

prime number ***noun*** a number that can be divided only by itself or by 1 without leaving a fraction. For example, 2, 3, 5, 7, and 11 are prime numbers.
prime number • ***noun,*** *plural* **prime numbers**

primer (prim′ər) ***noun*** **1** a simple book for teaching children to read. **2** a book that gives the first lessons on any subject.
prim·er • ***noun,*** *plural* **primers**

prime time ***noun*** the hours of the evening during which the largest audience is likely to be listening to the radio or watching TV.

primitive (prim′i tiv) ***adjective*** **1** living in or having to do with the earliest times; ancient [Some *primitive* peoples worshiped the sun.] **2** having undergone little development; crude and simple [*primitive* weapons; *primitive* arts].
prim·i·tive • ***adjective***

primp (primp) ***verb*** to spend time in adjusting and fixing one's hair, makeup, or general appearance [She's always *primping* in front of the mirror.]
primp • ***verb*** **primped, primping**

primrose (prim′rōz) ***noun*** a plant that has small, tube-shaped flowers in various colors.
prim·rose • ***noun,*** *plural* **primroses**

prince (prins) ***noun*** **1** a man or boy of a royal family other than the king, especially a son or grandson of a king or queen. **2** a nobleman of very high rank.
prince • ***noun,*** *plural* **princes**

prince consort (kän′sôrt) ***noun*** the husband of a reigning queen or empress.
prince con·sort • ***noun,*** *plural* **princes consort**

Prince Edward Island (prins′ ed′wərd ī′lənd) an island province of eastern Canada, north of Nova Scotia. Abbreviated **PE** or **P.E.I.**

princess (prin′səs) ***noun*** **1** a daughter or granddaughter of a king or queen. **2** the wife of a prince. **3** a noblewoman of very high rank.
prin·cess • ***noun,*** *plural* **princesses**

SPELLING TIP

Use this memory aid to spell **principal**. Isn t the princi***pal*** your ***pal***?

principal (prin′si pəl) ***adjective*** most important; main [Potatoes are our *principal* crop.]
noun **1** a person who is the head of a school. **2** a person in a leading or important position in some activity [the *principals* in a play]. **3** a sum of money that is owed or invested, not counting the interest.

P

prin·ci·pal • *adjective* • *noun, plural for senses 1 and 2 only* **principals**
- The words **principal** and **principle** sound alike.
  Our *principal* spoke to the fifth grade.
  Honesty is a *principle* I live by.

WORD CHOICES

Synonyms of **principal**

The words **principal**, **chief**, and **main** share the meaning "most important."

Iowa's *principal* crop
our *chief* executive
the *main* office of the bank

principally (prin′si pəl ē *or* prin′si plē) *adverb* mainly; most of all.
prin·ci·pal·ly • *adverb*

principle (prin′si pəl) *noun* **1** a rule, truth, or belief that forms the basis of other rules, truths, or beliefs [He taught the basic *principles* of law.] —Look for the WORD CHOICES box at the entry **doctrine**. **2** a rule that is used in deciding how to behave [It is against her *principles* to lie.] **3** a scientific law that explains how a thing works [Living things grow by the *principle* of cell division.]
prin·ci·ple • *noun, plural* **principles**
- The words **principle** and **principal** sound alike.
  Clarity is a *principle* of good writing.
  Filing is my *principal* task at work.

print (print) *noun* **1** a mark that is made on a surface by pressing or stamping [a *footprint*]. **2** cloth that has been stamped with a certain kind of design [She wore a dress in a flower *print*.] **3** letters or words that have been stamped on paper from inked type or plates [a book with small *print*.] **4** a picture or design that is made by pressing an inked engraved or raised surface against paper [a store selling *prints* made by contemporary artists]. **5** a photograph that is made from a negative.
verb **1** to stamp letters, designs, or other marks on a surface with type or plates [We *printed* 500 posters. These designs will not *print* well.] **2** to publish in print [The magazine *printed* her story.] **3** to write in separate letters that look like printed ones [Please *print* your name.] **4** to use a printer to produce on paper information that is in a computer or on a computer screen: often used with *out* [I gave the computer the command to *print* out my answers.]
—in print still for sale by the publisher. **—out of print** no longer for sale by the publisher.
print • *noun, plural except for sense 3* **prints** • *verb* **printed, printing**

printer

printer (print′ər) *noun* **1** a person whose work or business is printing books, newspapers, and other materials. **2** a device connected to a computer that prints the computer's output onto paper.
print·er • *noun, plural* **printers**

printing (print′iŋ) *noun* **1** the art, process, or business of making books, newspapers, magazines, and other printed material. **2** all of the copies of a book that are printed at one time [The first *printing* of her novel was sold almost immediately.] **3** written letters that are shaped like the ones printed in books or printed by a typewriter.
print·ing • *noun, plural for sense 2 only* **printings**

printing press *noun* a machine for printing books, newspapers, and other material from inked type, plates, or rollers.
printing press • *noun, plural* **printing presses**

printout (print′out) *noun* the output of a computer, printed or typewritten by a printer onto sheets of paper.
print·out • *noun, plural* **printouts**

a cat	ō go	ʉ fur	ə = a *in* ago
ā ape	ô law, for	ch chin	e *in* agent
ä cot, car	oo look	sh she	i *in* pencil
e ten	ōō tool	th thin	o *in* atom
ē me	oi oil	*th* then	u *in* circus
i fit	ou out	zh measure	
ī ice	u up	ŋ ring	

prior (prī′ər) ***adjective*** coming before in time, order, or importance [at some *prior* time; a *prior* claim to the land] —Look for the WORD CHOICES box at the entry **previous**.
pri·or • ***adjective***

priority (prī ôr′i tē) ***noun*** **1** the quality or fact of coming before in time, order, or importance [I have *priority* over you in my claim to the land.] **2** something that is thought to be more important than something else [Education is high on our list of *priorities*.]
pri·or·i·ty • ***noun,*** *plural for sense 2 only* **priorities**

prism

prism (priz′əm) ***noun*** **1** a solid figure whose ends are exactly equal and parallel and whose sides are parallelograms. **2** an object of glass or clear plastic that is shaped like this and that has ends that are triangles. It can break up light rays into the colors of the rainbow.
prism • ***noun,*** *plural* **prisms**

prison (priz′ən) ***noun*** a place where people are kept locked up to serve a sentence for breaking the law.
pris·on • ***noun,*** *plural* **prisons**

prisoner (priz′ən ər) ***noun*** **1** a person who is kept locked up in a prison. **2** a person who is held captive by someone else.
pris·on·er • ***noun,*** *plural* **prisoners**

privacy (prī′və sē) ***noun*** **1** the condition of being away from other people or being isolated [She went to her room for *privacy*.] **2** a person's private life [Telling that on TV was an invasion of her *privacy*.]
pri·va·cy • ***noun***

private (prī′vət) ***adjective*** **1** for or having to do with a particular person or group only; not public [*private* property; a person's *private* affairs; a *private* school]. **2** not holding public office [a *private* citizen]. **3** secret; confidential [I hope all our conversations were *private*.] **4** working on one's own, not for an organization [a *private* detective].
noun an enlisted person of the lowest rank in the armed forces.
—in private secretly.
pri·vate • ***adjective*** • ***noun,*** *plural* **privates**

private eye [*a slang word*] ***noun*** a private detective.
private eye • ***noun,*** *plural* **private eyes**

privilege (priv′i ləj) ***noun*** a special right, favor, or advantage that is given to some person or group [The children have the *privilege* of staying up late tonight.]
priv·i·lege • ***noun,*** *plural* **privileges**

prize (prīz) ***noun*** **1** something that is offered or given to a winner of a contest or game [The first *prize* is a bicycle.] **2** something that is worth trying to get [His friendship would be a great *prize*.]
adjective having won a prize or deserving a prize [a *prize* steer at the fair].
verb to think highly of; to value [I *prize* our friendship.] —Look for the WORD CHOICES box at the entry **value**.
prize • ***noun,*** *plural for sense 1 only* **prizes** • ***adjective*** • ***verb*** **prized, prizing**

pro (prō) [*an informal word*] ***noun*** a professional [Her father is a golf *pro*.]
pro • ***noun,*** *plural* **pros**

pro- *a prefix meaning* for; in favor of [A *prolabor* speech is a speech in favor of labor unions.]

probability (präb′ə bil′ə tē) ***noun*** **1** the fact of being probable; good chance [There is some *probability* of rain today.] **2** something that is probable [Their return tonight is thought to be a *probability*.]
prob·a·bil·i·ty • ***noun,*** *plural for sense 2 only* **probabilities**

probable (präb′ə bəl) ***adjective*** likely to happen or turn out to be [He is the *probable* winner of the game.]
prob·a·ble • ***adjective***

probably (präb′ə blē) ***adverb*** almost certainly; without much doubt [It will *probably* rain.]
prob·a·bly • ***adverb***

probation (prō bā′shən) ***noun*** a period of time for testing a person's ability, character, conduct, or qualifications [As a new employee, you will be on *probation* for six months.]
pro·ba·tion • ***noun***

P

probe (prōb) *noun* **1** a slender instrument with a blunt end that a doctor uses in examining the inside of a wound or body opening. **2** a complete investigation [The mayor ordered a *probe* of housing conditions in the neighborhood.] **3** a spacecraft with instruments in it for exploring the upper atmosphere, space, or a planet or moon in order to get information.
verb **1** to examine with a probe [The doctor *probed* the wound.] **2** to examine or investigate with care [He *probed* the secrets of the atom.]
probe • *noun, plural* **probes** • *verb* **probed, probing**

problem (präb′ləm) *noun* **1** a condition, person, or thing that is difficult to deal with or hard to understand [Getting to school in all that snow could be a real *problem*.] **2** a question that must be solved or worked out [an arithmetic *problem;* the *problem* of what to do about reckless drivers].
prob·lem • *noun, plural* **problems**

procedure (prō sē′jər) *noun* a way or method of doing something [Do you know the correct *procedure* to follow during a fire drill?]
pro·ce·dure • *noun, plural* **procedures**

proceed (prō sēd′) *verb* **1** to go on, especially after stopping for a while [After eating, we *proceeded* to the next town.] —Look for the WORD CHOICES box at the entry **go**. **2** to begin and go on doing something [I *proceeded* to build a fire.]
pro·ceed • *verb* **proceeded, proceeding**

process (präs′es) *noun* **1** a method of making or doing something that usually involves a number of steps [the refining *process* used in making gasoline from crude oil]. **2** the act of doing something or the time during which it is done [I was in the *process* of writing a report when you called.]
verb to prepare by a special process.
proc·ess • *noun, plural for sense 1 only* **processes** • *verb* **processed, processing**

procession (prō sesh′ən) *noun* **1** a number of persons or things moving forward in an orderly way [a wedding *procession*]. **2** the act of moving in this way [The students walked in *procession* through the streets.]
pro·ces·sion • *noun, plural for sense 1 only* **processions**

proclaim (prō klām′) *verb* to announce officially; make known to be [They *proclaimed* him a hero.] —Look for the WORD CHOICES box at the entry **say**.
pro·claim • *verb* **proclaimed, proclaiming**

proclamation (präk′lə mā′shən) *noun* a public statement [The king's *proclamation* was read to the people all over the kingdom.]
proc·la·ma·tion • *noun, plural* **proclamations**

procure (prō kyo͝or′) *verb* to get or bring about by trying; obtain [She *procured* a job.]
pro·cure • *verb* **procured, procuring**

prod (präd) *verb* **1** to poke or jab with a stick or other pointed object. **2** to urge or drive into action [They had to *prod* him to do his chores.]
noun **1** a poke or jab. **2** something that is pointed and is used for prodding.
prod • *verb* **prodded, prodding** • *noun, plural* **prods**

prodigal (präd′i gəl) *adjective* wasteful in a reckless way [We have been *prodigal* with our natural resources.]
prod·i·gal • *adjective*

prodigy (präd′i jē) *noun* **1** a person or thing that is good or special enough to cause wonder or awe. **2** a child who has amazing talent or intelligence [a piano *prodigy*].
prod·i·gy • *noun, plural* **prodigies**

produce

produce (prō do͞os′ *or* prō dyo͞os′ *for v.;* prō′ do͞os *for n.*) *verb* **1** to bring forth; to bear or yield [The orchard has many trees that *produce* apples. This is a well that *produces* oil.] **2** to make or manufacture [This company

a	cat	ō	go	ʉ	fur	ə =	a *in* ago		
ā	ape	ô	law, for	ch	chin		e *in* agent		
ä	cot, car	o͝o	look	sh	she		i *in* pencil		
e	ten	o͞o	tool	th	thin		o *in* atom		
ē	me	oi	oil	*th*	then		u *in* circus		
i	fit	ou	out	zh	measure				
ī	ice	u	up	ŋ	ring				

produces bicycles.] **3** to bring out into view; to show [*Produce* your driver's license.] **4** to get ready and bring to the public [They *produced* the new play on a very small budget.]
noun **1** something that is produced. **2** fresh fruits and vegetables.
pro·duce • *verb* **produced, producing**
• *noun*

product (präd′ukt) *noun* **1** something that is produced by nature or made by human beings [Wood is a natural *product*. A wooden desk is a manufactured *product*.] **2** a result [The story is a *product* of her imagination.] **3** a number that is the result of multiplying [4 multiplied by 3 gives a *product* of 12.]
prod·uct • *noun, plural* **products**

production (prō duk′shən) *noun* **1** the act or process of producing [The new car models will go into *production* next week.] **2** the amount that is produced [The new machines increased our *production*.] **3** something that is produced [Her play is a new *production*.]
pro·duc·tion • *noun, plural for sense 3 only* **productions**

profession (prō fesh′ən) *noun* **1** a job or occupation, especially one for which a person must have special education and training [Medicine, law, and teaching are *professions*.] **2** all of the people in this kind of occupation [the medical *profession*].
pro·fes·sion • *noun, plural* **professions**

professional (prō fesh′ə nəl) *adjective* **1** in or having to do with a profession. **2** earning a living from a sport or other activity that is not usually thought of as a job or occupation [a *professional* golfer]. **3** involving professional players [*professional* football].
noun a professional person in a sport or other activity.
pro·fes·sion·al • *adjective* • *noun, plural* **professionals**

professor (prō fes′ər) *noun* a teacher with a high rank in a college or university.
pro·fes·sor • *noun, plural* **professors**

profile (prō′fīl) *noun* **1** a side view of a person's face. **2** a drawing of this. **3** a short biography [The TV station broadcast a *profile* of the new senator.]
pro·file • *noun, plural* **profiles**

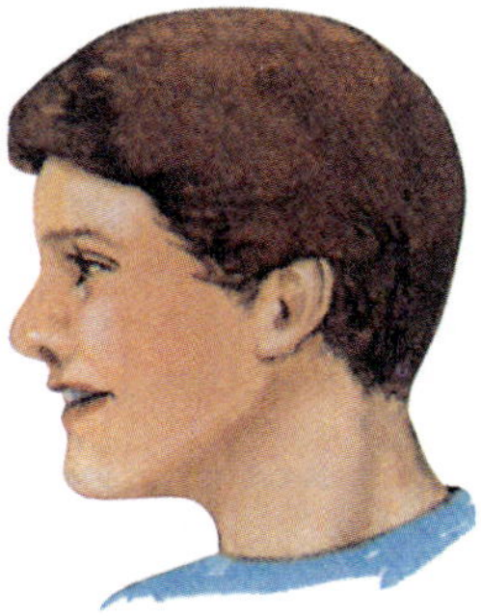

profile

profit (präf′it) *noun* **1** the amount of money that is gained in business after all expenses have been subtracted [They took in $500, of which $120 was *profit*.] **2** gain of any kind; benefit or advantage [There's no *profit* in arguing about this.]
verb **1** to be of advantage to [It will *profit* you to study hard.] **2** to get a benefit; gain [We *profited* by the sale.]
prof·it • *noun, plural for sense 1 only* **profits**
• *verb* **profited, profiting**
• The words **profit** and **prophet** sound alike.
All the sale's *profit* goes to charity.
Elijah is a *prophet* in the Bible.

profitable (präf′it ə bəl) *adjective* bringing profit or benefit [a *profitable* sale; a *profitable* deal].
prof·it·a·ble • *adjective*

profound (prō found′) *adjective* **1** showing great knowledge or thought [the *profound* remarks of the judge]. **2** very deep or strong; intense [*profound* sleep; *profound* grief].
pro·found • *adjective* **profounder, profoundest**

program (prō′gram) *noun* **1** the acts, speeches, musical pieces, and other parts that make up a public ceremony or performance [a graduation *program;* a radio *program*]. **2** a printed list of these items [a *program* for the concert]. **3** a plan for doing something [a government *program* to help farmers]. **4** a series of instructions that tells a computer how to do its work. A program makes the computer able to solve problems and do tasks. Many computers use more than one program.
verb to provide a computer with a program.
pro·gram • *noun, plural* **programs**
• *verb* **programmed, programming**

programmer (prō′gram ər) *noun* a person who programs a computer.
pro·gram·mer • *noun, plural* **programmers**

progress (präg′res *for n.;* prō gres′ *for v.*) *noun* **1** the process of moving forward [the parade's slow *progress* down the street]. **2** the fact or process of developing or improving [She shows *progress* in learning Spanish.]
verb **1** to move forward; go ahead —Look for the WORD CHOICES box at the entry **go**. **2** to develop or improve; to advance.
—in progress going on.

P

prog·ress • *noun* • *verb* **progressed, progressing**

WORD CHOICES

Synonyms of **progress**

The words **progress, advance,** and **improve** share the meaning "to become better."

Science has helped us to *progress.*

His skills *advanced* with practice.

Business has *improved.*

progressive (prō gres′iv) *adjective* **1** moving forward or going ahead step by step [the *progressive* improvement of our city]. **2** working for or in favor of social and political reform [a *progressive* senator].
pro·gres·sive • *adjective*

prohibit (prō hib′it) *verb* to forbid by law or by an order [Smoking is *prohibited* here.] —Look for the WORD CHOICES box at the entry **forbid**.
pro·hib·it • *verb* **prohibited, prohibiting**

project (prä′jekt *for n.;* prō jekt′ *for v.*) *noun* **1** a plan or proposal for doing something [Our next *project* is to build a raft.] **2** an organized job or activity for a certain purpose [The teacher gave us a new science *project*.] **3** a group of houses or apartment buildings that is usually built and operated by a government [a *housing* project].
verb **1** to stick out [The shelf *projects* from the wall.] **2** to cause to be seen on a surface [We *projected* the movie onto a very large screen.] **3** to predict by using facts that are already known [He *projected* sales for the next year.]
proj·ect • *noun, plural* **projects**
• *verb* **pro·ject, projected, projecting**

projectile (prō jek′təl) *noun* an object that is made to be shot with force through the air. A cannon shell and a rocket are projectiles.
pro·jec·tile • *noun, plural* **projectiles**

projection (prō jek′shən) *noun* **1** the act or process of projecting a picture or other image on a screen. **2** something that projects, or sticks out. **3** a prediction that is made by using facts that are already known [He makes financial *projections* for his company.]
pro·jec·tion • *noun, plural for senses 2 and 3 only* **projections**

projector (prō jek′tər) *noun* a machine for projecting pictures or movies onto a screen.
pro·jec·tor • *noun, plural* **projectors**

prologue (prō′lôg) *noun* **1** an introduction to a poem or play. **2** the lines that an actor speaks before the action of a play begins.
pro·logue • *noun, plural* **prologues**

prolong (prō lôŋ′) *verb* to make last longer; stretch out [We *prolonged* our visit by another day.] —Look for the WORD CHOICES box at the entry **extend**.
pro·long • *verb* **prolonged, prolonging**

prom (präm) [*an informal word*] *noun* a ball or dance for a college or high school class.
prom • *noun, plural* **proms**

prominent (präm′i nənt) *adjective* **1** standing out from a surface; projecting [*prominent* eyebrows]. **2** famous; known by a great many people [a *prominent* artist]. **3** sure to be seen; noticeable [The lighthouse was a *prominent* feature on the coast.] —Look for the WORD CHOICES box at the entry **noticeable**.
prom·i·nent • *adjective*

WORD CHOICES

Synonyms of **promise**

The words **promise, swear,** and **vow** share the meaning "to make an agreement to do or not to do something."

He *promised* not to leave before dark.

She *swore* to tell the truth.

The general *vowed* to return.

promise (präm′is) *noun* **1** an agreement to do or not to do something [It is important to keep your *promises*.] **2** a cause for hope [She shows *promise* as a singer.]
verb **1** to make a promise [I *promised* them that I'd arrive at ten. He *promised* his help.] **2** to give reason to expect [Clear skies *promise* good weather.]

a	cat	ō	go	ʉ	fur	ə = a *in* ago	
ā	ape	ô	law, for	ch	chin	e *in* agent	
ä	cot, car	oo	look	sh	she	i *in* pencil	
e	ten	ōō	tool	th	thin	o *in* atom	
ē	me	oi	oil	*th*	then	u *in* circus	
i	fit	ou	out	zh	measure		
ī	ice	u	up	ŋ	ring		

prom·ise • *noun, plural for sense 1 only* **promises** • *verb* **promised, promising**

promising (präm′is iŋ) ***adjective*** likely to be successful [a *promising* piano student].
prom·is·ing • ***adjective***

promote (prō mōt′) ***verb*** **1** to raise to a higher rank, level, or position [She was *promoted* to manager.] **2** to help the growth, success, or development of [The Olympic games *promote* international understanding.] **3** to make more popular or cause to sell faster by advertising [They *promoted* their new gadget on radio and TV.]
pro·mote • ***verb*** **promoted, promoting**

promotion (prō mō′shən) ***noun*** **1** an advance in rank, level, or position [Did he get the *promotion* to supervisor?] **2** the act of helping to make successful [the *promotion* of a new book].
pro·mo·tion • ***noun,*** *plural* **promotions**

prompt (prämpt) ***adjective*** **1** quick in doing what should be done; on time [He is *prompt* in paying his bills.] **2** done, spoken, or given without delay [We would like a *prompt* reply.]
verb **1** to urge or stir to action [Stale food *prompted* the students to complain.] **2** to remind of something that has been forgotten [Her job is to *prompt* the actors when they cannot remember a line.]
prompt • ***adjective*** **prompter, promptest** • ***verb*** **prompted, prompting**

pron. *abbreviation for* pronoun.

prone (prōn) ***adjective*** **1** apt or likely; inclined [This old car is *prone* to breakdowns.] **2** lying face downward.

prong (prôŋ) ***noun*** any one of the pointed ends of an antler or of a fork or other tool.
prong • ***noun,*** *plural* **prongs**

pronghorn (prôŋ′hôrn) ***noun*** an animal that looks like an antelope, found in western North America. It has curved horns, each with one prong. The horns are shed every year.
prong·horn • ***noun,*** *plural* **pronghorns**

pronoun (prō′noun) ***noun*** a word that is used in place of a noun. In the sentence "Who sold it to her yesterday?" the words "who," "it," and "her" are pronouns.
pro·noun • ***noun,*** *plural* **pronouns**

pronounce (prō nouns′) ***verb*** **1** to say or make the particular sounds of [How do you *pronounce* "leisure"?] **2** to declare in an official or serious way ["I now *pronounce* you husband and wife."]
pro·nounce • ***verb*** **pronounced, pronouncing**

pronounced (prō nounst′) ***adjective*** clearly marked; definite [a *pronounced* change].
pro·nounced • ***adjective***

pronunciation (prō nun′sē ā′shən) ***noun*** **1** the act or a way of forming sounds to say words [Your *pronunciation* is clear.] **2** the way that a word is usually pronounced ["Either" has two *pronunciations*.]
pro·nun·ci·a·tion • ***noun,*** *plural for sense 2 only* **pronunciations**

proof (pro͞of) ***noun*** anything that can be used to show that something is true or correct; evidence [Do they have *proof* of his guilt?]

-proof *a suffix meaning* protected against or not allowing [*Waterproof* cloth will not allow water to pass through it.]

proofread (pro͞of′rēd) ***verb*** to read carefully in order to correct mistakes [We *proofread* the school newspaper one last time before we printed it.]
proof·read • ***verb*** **proof·read** (pro͞of′red), **proofreading**

P

prop[1] (präp) ***noun*** a thing that is used to hold something up.
verb **1** to support or hold up with a prop or in a way that is like using a prop [The carpenter *propped* up the sagging roof.] **2** to lean against a support [*Prop* your bike up against the wall.]
prop • ***noun,*** *plural* **props** • ***verb*** **propped, propping**

prop[2] (präp) ***noun*** *a short form of* **propeller**.
prop • ***noun,*** *plural* **props**

propaganda (präp ə gan′də) ***noun*** **1** the process of spreading information or ideas in a way that is meant to make people accept them. **2** the information or ideas that are spread in this way. This word now usually suggests that the ideas are false or misleading.
prop·a·gan·da • ***noun***

propel (prō pel′) ***verb*** to push or drive forward [Some rockets are *propelled* by engines that use liquid fuel.]
pro·pel • ***verb*** **propelled, propelling**

propeller (prō pel′ər) ***noun*** a device that consists of blades mounted on a shaft. An engine

turns the shaft to move the blades so that they make a ship, airplane, or helicopter move.
pro·pel·ler • *noun, plural* **propellers**

propeller

proper (präp′ər) *adjective* **1** right or suitable [the *proper* tool for this job; the *proper* clothes for a party] —Look for the WORD CHOICES box at the entry **fit**[1]. **2** following the rules of good behavior and good taste; correct [*proper* manners] —Look for the WORD CHOICES box at the entry **good**. **3** in a strict or narrow sense; actual [Boston *proper*, not including its suburbs].
prop·er • *adjective*

proper fraction *noun* a fraction in which the numerator is less than the denominator. For example, $^{2}/_{5}$ is a proper fraction.
proper fraction • *noun, plural* **proper fractions**

proper noun *noun* a noun, such as "José" or "Paris," that is the name of a particular person, thing, or place. It begins with a capital letter.
proper noun • *noun, plural* **proper nouns**

property (präp′ər tē) *noun* **1** something that is owned ["This baseball bat is my *property* —don't touch it!" said the boy.] **2** land or real estate that is owned [We have a fence around our *property*.] **3** a special quality that something is known by; a characteristic [One *property* of oxygen is that it has no odor.] **4** any one of the movable articles that are used in a play, except the costumes and scenery.
prop·er·ty • *noun, plural for senses 2, 3, and 4 only* **properties**

prophecy (präf′ə sē) *noun* **1** something that a person says will happen in the future. **2** the act of predicting what will happen in the future.
proph·e·cy • *noun, plural for sense 1 only* **prophecies**

prophet (präf′it) *noun* **1** a religious leader who people believe speaks for God or a god. **2** a person who claims to tell what will happen in the future.
proph·et • *noun, plural* **prophets**
• The words **prophet** and **profit** sound alike.
Elijah is a *prophet* in the Bible.
All the sale's *profit* goes to charity.

proportion (prə pôr′shən) *noun* **1** the relation of one thing to another in size, amount, or another measure [The *proportion* of girls to boys in our class is three to two; that means that there are three girls to every two boys.] **2** a pleasing or proper arrangement or balance of parts [The small desk is not in *proportion* with the large chair.] **3 proportions** length, width, and height; dimensions [a house of large *proportions*].
pro·por·tion • *noun*

proportional (prə pôr′she nəl) *adjective* in proper proportion [The number of U.S. Representatives from a State is *proportional* to the State's population.]
pro·por·tion·al • *adjective*

proposal (prə pōz′əl) *noun* **1** a plan, suggestion, or scheme that is proposed to others [The council approved the mayor's *proposal* for a traffic signal.] **2** an offer of marriage.
pro·pos·al • *noun, plural* **proposals**

propose (prə pōz′) *verb* **1** to suggest for other people to think about, approve, or vote on [We *propose* that the city build a zoo.] **2** to plan or intend [Do you *propose* to leave us?] **3** to make an offer of marriage.
pro·pose • *verb* **proposed, proposing**

proposition (präp ə zish′ən) *noun* something that has been proposed; a proposal or plan.
prop·o·si·tion • *noun, plural* **propositions**

propriety (prə prī′ə tē) *noun* the fact of being proper or correct [I questioned the *propriety* of her suggestion.]
pro·pri·e·ty • *noun*

propulsion (prə pul′shən) *noun* **1** the process of propelling, or driving forward. **2** a force that propels.
pro·pul·sion • *noun*

a	cat	ō	go	ʉ	fur	ə =	a *in* ago
ā	ape	ô	law, for	ch	chin		e *in* agent
ä	cot, car	oo	look	sh	she		i *in* pencil
e	ten	ōō	tool	th	thin		o *in* atom
ē	me	oi	oil	*th*	then		u *in* circus
i	fit	ou	out	zh	measure		
ī	ice	u	up	ŋ	ring		

prose (prōz) ***noun*** speech or writing that is not poetry; ordinary language.

prosecute (präs′ə kyo͞ot) ***verb*** to begin or carry out criminal charges against a person in a court of law.
pros·e·cute • ***verb*** **prosecuted, prosecuting**

prosecution (präs′ə kyo͞o′shən) ***noun*** **1** the act or process of carrying out a case against a person who has been charged with a crime. **2** the prosecutor or prosecutors who carry out a case of this kind [The *prosecution* presented a great deal of evidence to the jury.]
pros·e·cu·tion • ***noun,*** *plural for sense 1 only* **prosecutions**

prosecutor (präs′ə kyo͞ot ər) ***noun*** an attorney who works for the state in prosecuting persons charged with crimes.
pros·e·cu·tor • ***noun,*** *plural* **prosecutors**

prospect (prä′spekt) ***noun*** **1** something that is looked forward to or expected [The happy *prospect* of a party had them excited.] **2** *usually* **prospects** the likely chance of succeeding or of getting something [a team with no *prospects* of winning]. **3** a person who is a likely customer, donor, or candidate. **4** a wide view that can be seen from a high place —Look for the WORD CHOICES box at the entry **view**.
verb to explore or search for something [People *prospected* for gold in California.]
pros·pect • ***noun,*** *plural* **prospects**
• ***verb*** **prospected, prospecting**

prospector (prä′spek tər) ***noun*** a person who searches for deposits of gold or other valuable ores or for oil.
pros·pec·tor • ***noun,*** *plural* **prospectors**

prosper (präs′pər) ***verb*** to succeed, thrive, or grow in a vigorous way [The town *prospered* when oil was discovered nearby.]
pros·per • ***verb*** **prospered, prospering**

prosperity (prä sper′i tē) ***noun*** the condition of being prosperous, wealthy, or successful.
pros·per·i·ty • ***noun***

prosperous (präs′pər əs) ***adjective*** successful, well-to-do, or thriving [a *prosperous* business; a *prosperous* lawyer] —Look for the WORD CHOICES box at the entry **rich**.
pros·per·ous • ***adjective***

protect (prō tekt′) ***verb*** to guard or defend against harm or danger; to shield [You must apply a coat of wax to *protect* the car.]
pro·tect • ***verb*** **protected, protecting**

protection (prō tek′shən) ***noun*** **1** the act of protecting. **2** the fact of being protected [The guard carried a gun for *protection*.] **3** a person or thing that protects [Being careful is your best *protection* against accidents.]
pro·tec·tion • ***noun,*** *plural for sense 3 only* **protections**

protective (prō tek′tiv) ***adjective*** helping to protect or capable of protecting [The *protective* coloring of a bird hides it from its enemies.]
pro·tec·tive • ***adjective***

protein (prō′tēn) ***noun*** a substance that is made up of nitrogen combined with various other elements. Proteins are found in all living things and are a necessary part of an animal's diet. People get protein from such foods as beans, cheese, eggs, and meat.
pro·tein • ***noun,*** *plural* **proteins**

protest (prō test′ *for v.;* prō′test *for n.*) ***verb*** to speak out against; object to [They joined the march to *protest* bad housing conditions.]
noun an objection or complaint.
pro·test • ***verb*** **protested, protesting**
• ***noun,*** *plural* **protests**

Protestant (prät′əs tənt) ***noun*** a member of any of the Christian churches that grew out of the Reformation or have developed since then.
adjective of or having to do with Protestants [*Protestant* churches; *Protestant* doctrine].
Prot·es·tant • ***noun,*** *plural* **Protestants**
• ***adjective***

proton (prō′tän) ***noun*** one of the tiny particles that make up the nucleus of an atom. A proton has a positive electrical charge.
pro·ton • ***noun,*** *plural* **protons**

protoplasm (prōt′ə plaz′əm) ***noun*** the clear, thick liquid substance that is the necessary part of all living animal and plant cells.
pro·to·plasm • ***noun***

protractor (prō′trak′tər) ***noun*** a tool for drawing and measuring angles. It is in the form of a semicircle and is marked with degrees.
pro·trac·tor • ***noun,*** *plural* **protractors**

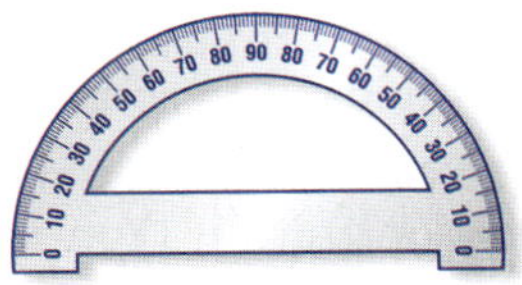

protractor

proud (proud) ***adjective*** **1** thinking too highly of oneself; conceited or haughty [They are too *proud* to say hello to us.] **2** having proper respect for oneself [They are a *proud*, hard-working family.] **3** feeling honored, pleased,

P

or satisfied [*proud* to be chosen for the basketball team. I'm *proud* to know you.]
—proud of very pleased with [Jane was *proud of* her own work.]
proud • *adjective* **prouder, proudest**

WORD CHOICES

Synonyms of **proud**

The words **proud, arrogant,** and **haughty** share the meaning "having or showing too great a sense of one's own importance."

a *proud* unwillingness to admit she had been wrong

an *arrogant* contempt for the feelings of others

the duke's *haughty* stare

prove (pro͞ov) *verb* **1** to show to be true or correct [*Prove* that you can throw that far.] **2** to turn out to be [Your guess *proved* right.]
prove • *verb* **proved, proved** or **proven, proving**

proven (pro͞o′vən) *verb a past participle of* **prove**.
prov·en • *verb*

proverb (präv′ərb) *noun* an old and familiar saying that tells something wise. "A stitch in time saves nine" is a proverb.
prov·erb • *noun, plural* **proverbs**

provide (prō vīd′) *verb* **1** to give what is needed; to supply or furnish [The school *provides* free books.] **2** to furnish the means of support [They both work at two jobs to *provide* for their family.] **3** to get ready ahead of time; prepare [You'd better *provide* for rain by taking umbrellas.] **4** to state as a condition in a contract or other agreement [Our lease *provides* that the rent must be paid monthly.]
pro·vide • *verb* **provided, providing**

provided (prō vīd′əd) *conjunction* on the condition that; if [You may go swimming, *provided* you do your homework first.]
pro·vid·ed • *conjunction*

Providence (präv′i dəns) the capital of Rhode Island.
Prov·i·dence

providing (prō vīd′iŋ) *conjunction* on the condition that; if [You may go to the movie, *providing* your mother agrees.]
pro·vid·ing • *conjunction*

province (präv′ins) *noun* **1** one of the divisions of some countries that are somewhat like the States in the U.S. Canada is made up of ten provinces. **2 provinces** the parts of a country that are away from the large cities. **3** an area of responsibility, activity, or knowledge [Enforcing the law falls within the *province* of the police.]
prov·ince • *noun, plural for senses 1 and 2 only* **provinces**

provincial (prə vin′shəl) *adjective* **1** of or having to do with a province [a *provincial* capital]. **2** of or like country people as apart from city people [*provincial* customs].
pro·vin·cial • *adjective*

provision (prō vizh′ən) *noun* **1** the act of providing or supplying. **2 provisions** a supply or stock of food. **3** a condition or requirement [Her will left him a great deal of money, with the *provision* that he use it for college.]
pro·vi·sion • *noun, plural for senses 2 and 3 only* **provisions**

provoke (prō vōk′) *verb* **1** to annoy or make angry [It *provoked* me to see litter on the lawn.] **2** to arouse or call forth [The clown's tricks *provoked* laughter from the crowd.]
pro·voke • *verb* **provoked, provoking**

prow

prow (prou) *noun* the front part of a ship or boat.
prow • *noun, plural* **prows**

prowl (proul) *verb* to roam around in a quiet, secret way, like an animal looking for prey.

a	cat	ō	go	ʉ	fur	ə =	a *in* ago
ā	ape	ô	law, for	ch	chin		e *in* agent
ä	cot, car	oo	look	sh	she		i *in* pencil
e	ten	o͞o	tool	th	thin		o *in* atom
ē	me	oi	oil	*th*	then		u *in* circus
i	fit	ou	out	zh	measure		
ī	ice	u	up	ŋ	ring		

—**on the prowl** prowling about.
prowl • *verb* **prowled, prowling**

prude (pro͞od) *noun* a person who is very modest, proper, or moral in behavior or speech, in a way that annoys others.
prude • *noun, plural* **prudes**

prudent (pro͞od′nt) *adjective* careful or cautious in a sensible way; wise [a *prudent* driver].
pru·dent • *adjective*

prune[1] (pro͞on) *noun* a plum that has been dried for eating.
prune • *noun, plural* **prunes**

prune[2]

prune[2] (pro͞on) *verb* to trim or cut off branches, twigs, or other parts from [It's time to *prune* the hedges.]
prune • *verb* **pruned, pruning**

pry[1] (prī) *verb* **1** to raise or move with a lever or crowbar [Let's *pry* up the top of the crate.] **2** to get by trying hard [It's hard to *pry* money from a miser.]
pry • *verb* **pried, prying, pries**

pry[2] (prī) *verb* to look or search closely, often to satisfy one's curiosity [Don't *pry* into my business!]
pry • *verb* **pried, prying, pries**

P.S. or **PS** *abbreviation for* postscript.

psalm (säm) *noun* a sacred song, hymn, or poem.
psalm • *noun, plural* **psalms**

psychiatrist (sī kī′ə trist) *noun* a medical doctor who takes care of people who have mental illness.
psy·chi·a·trist • *noun, plural* **psychiatrists**

psychiatry (sī kī′ə trē) *noun* the branch of medicine that deals with mental illness.
psy·chi·a·try • *noun*

psychic (sī′kik) *adjective* having to do with supernatural forces [*psychic* powers].
noun a person who seems to be in touch with supernatural forces.
psy·chic • *adjective* • *noun, plural* **psychics**

psycho- *a prefix meaning* the mind or mental processes [*Psychology* has helped us to understand the human mind.]

psychological (sī′kə läj′i kəl) *adjective* **1** of or using psychology [*psychological* tests]. **2** of the mind; mental [*psychological* development]. **3** using psychology and propaganda to influence or confuse people [*psychological* warfare].
psy·cho·log·i·cal • *adjective*

psychologist (sī käl′ə jist) *noun* a person who specializes in psychology.
psy·chol·o·gist • *noun, plural* **psychologists**

psychology (sī käl′ə jē) *noun* **1** the study of the mind and the reasons for the ways that people think and act. **2** the way that a person or group thinks or acts [the *psychology* of the child; mob *psychology*].
psy·chol·o·gy • *noun*

pt. *abbreviation for* pint.

PTA or **P.T.A.** *abbreviation for* Parent-Teacher Association.

pterodactyl (ter′ə dak′təl) *noun* a flying reptile that lived millions of years ago. It looked like a large lizard with huge wings.
pter·o·dac·tyl • *noun, plural* **pterodactyls**

puberty (pyo͞o′bər tē) *noun* the time of life in which boys and girls start to grow into men and women and become able to have children.
pu·ber·ty • *noun*

public (pub′lik) *adjective* **1** of or having to do with all the people [*public* opinion]. **2** for the use or good of everyone [a *public* park]. **3** known by most people [a *public* figure]. **4** working for the government; serving or acting for all the people [a *public* servant].
noun the people as a whole [The *public* wants better schools.]
—**in public** where all can see or hear; openly.
pub·lic • *adjective* • *noun*

publication (pub′li kā′shən) *noun* **1** the act of publishing [The *publication* of the facts will hurt no one.] **2** a book, magazine, or other thing that is published [This magazine is a weekly *publication*.]
pub·li·ca·tion • *noun, plural for sense 2 only* **publications**

publicity (pub lis′i tē) *noun* **1** information given or things done to bring a person, place, or thing to the attention of the public [The newspaper gave much *publicity* to our play.] **2** the attention of the public [The politician is seeking *publicity*.]
pub·lic·i·ty • *noun*

public opinion *noun* the opinion of most people about some political or social issue [*Public opinion* against smoking is getting stronger.]

public school *noun* an elementary school or high school that is supported by taxes.
public school • *noun, plural* **public schools**

public works *plural noun* highways, dams, or other projects built by a government for public use.

publish (pub′lish) *verb* to prepare and bring out for sale a book, magazine, or newspaper, or other printed material.
pub·lish • *verb* **published, publishing**

publisher (pub′lish ər) *noun* a person or company that publishes.
pub·lish·er • *noun, plural* **publishers**

publishing (pub′lish iŋ) *noun* the work or business of a publisher.
pub·lish·ing • *noun*

puck (puk) *noun* a hard rubber disk that is used in ice hockey.
puck • *noun, plural* **pucks**

pucker (puk′ər) *verb* to draw up into wrinkles or small folds [He *puckered* his lips. The seam *puckered* when she pulled the thread.]
puck·er • *verb* **puckered, puckering**

pudding (pood′iŋ) *noun* a soft, sweet dessert made with eggs, milk, and flavoring.
pud·ding • *noun, plural* **puddings**

puddle (pud′əl) *noun* a small pool of water or water mixed with earth [a mud *puddle*].
pud·dle • *noun, plural* **puddles**

pudgy (puj′ē) *adjective* short and fat [*pudgy* fingers].
pudg·y • *adjective* **pudgier, pudgiest**

pueblo (pweb′lō) *noun* **1** an American Indian village that is made up of stone or adobe buildings built one above the other. Pueblos are found in the southwestern U.S. **2 Pueblo** a member of any of the North American Indian peoples who live in a pueblo.
pueb·lo • *noun, plural* **pueblos**; *for sense 2 only* **Pueblos** or **Pueblo**

pueblo

Puerto Rico (pwer′tə rē′kō) a U.S. island in the West Indies. Puerto Rico is not a State of the U.S. Abbreviated **PR** or **P.R.**
Puer·to Ri·co

puff (puf) *noun* **1** a short, sudden burst of wind, breath, smoke, steam, or something similar. **2** a soft, light shell of pastry filled with a creamy mixture [a cream *puff*]. **3** a soft pad for putting powder on the face or body.
verb **1** to blow in a puff or puffs [She *puffed* out the candle.] **2** to move while giving off puffs [The train *puffed* up the hill.] **3** to breathe hard and fast [She was *puffing* after the race.]
puff • *noun, plural* **puffs** • *verb* **puffed, puffing**

puffin (puf′in) *noun* a bird of northern seas with a body like a duck's. It has a brightly colored beak that is shaped like a triangle.
puf·fin • *noun, plural* **puffins**

puffy (puf′ē) *adjective* puffed up; swollen.
puff·y • *adjective* **puffier, puffiest**

pug (pug) *noun* a small dog with short hair, a curled tail, and a short, turned-up nose.
pug • *noun, plural* **pugs**

pull (pool) *verb* **1** to use force in order to move something, especially to bring it closer [He *pulled* the sled. Please *pull* up your socks.] **2** to draw or pluck out [The dentist *pulled* the tooth.] **3** to tear or rip [The shutter *pulled* loose in the storm.] **4** to stretch to the point of hurting; strain [I *pulled* a muscle in my leg.] **5** to move or go [She *pulled* ahead of the other

a	cat	ō	go	ʉ	fur	ə = a *in* ago	
ā	ape	ô	law, for	ch	chin	e *in* agent	
ä	cot, car	oo	look	sh	she	i *in* pencil	
e	ten	o͞o	tool	th	thin	o *in* atom	
ē	me	oi	oil	*th*	then	u *in* circus	
i	fit	ou	out	zh	measure		
ī	ice	u	up	ŋ	ring		

runners.] **6** [*an informal use*] to perform; do [Don't ever *pull* a stunt like that again!]
noun the act of pulling [Give the door a *pull*.]
—pull for [*an informal use*] to hope for the success of [We're *pulling for* the home team.] **—pull off** [*an informal use*] to manage to do [The thief *pulled off* another robbery.] **—pull oneself together** to gather one's self-control. **—pull over** to drive a car to the curb. **—pull through** [*an informal use*] to get safely through an illness or trouble [In spite of her injuries, she will *pull through*.] **—pull up 1** to bring or come to a stop [She *pulled up* at the red light.] **2** to move ahead [He *pulled up* to the intersection.]
pull • ***verb*** **pulled, pulling** • ***noun,*** *plural* **pulls**

pulley (pool′ē) ***noun*** a small wheel that has a groove in the rim in which a rope or belt moves. A pulley may be used to lift an object fastened to one end of the rope by pulling down on the other end. A pulley is a simple machine.
pul·ley • ***noun,*** *plural* **pulleys**

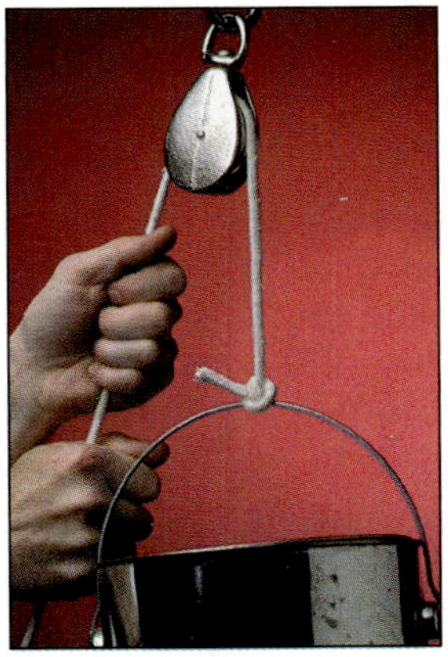
pulley

pullover (pool′ō vər) ***noun*** a shirt or sweater that is put on or taken off by being pulled over the head.
pull·o·ver • ***noun,*** *plural* **pullovers**

pulp (pulp) ***noun*** **1** the soft, juicy part of a fruit. **2** the soft, center part of a tooth. It contains nerves and blood vessels. **3** ground-up wood and other matter, mixed into a soft, wet mass from which paper is made.

pulpit (pool′pit *or* pul′pit) ***noun*** a platform in a church on which a clergyman stands to give a sermon.
pul·pit • ***noun,*** *plural* **pulpits**

pulpy (pul′pē) ***adjective*** of or like pulp [a *pulpy* mass] —Look for the WORD CHOICES box at the entry **soft**.
pulp·y • ***adjective*** **pulpier, pulpiest**

pulsate (pul′sāt) ***verb*** to beat or throb in a regular rhythm [Your heart *pulsates* more slowly when you sleep.]
pul·sate • ***verb*** **pulsated, pulsating**

pulse (puls) ***noun*** **1** the regular beating in the arteries that is caused by the movements of the heart in pumping the blood. **2** any regular beat [the *pulse* of the drums].
pulse • ***noun,*** *plural for sense 1 only* **pulses**

pulverize (pul′vər īz) ***verb*** to crush or grind into a powder [He *pulverized* the stone with a sledgehammer.]
pul·ver·ize • ***verb*** **pulverized, pulverizing**

puma (pyoo′mə *or* poo′mə) ***noun*** *another name for* **cougar**.
pu·ma • ***noun,*** *plural* **pumas**

pump (pump) ***noun*** a device that forces a liquid or gas into or out of something.
verb **1** to raise, move, or force with a pump [She *pumped* water from the well. He *pumped* air into the tire.] **2** to empty with a pump [They *pumped* out the flooded basement.] **3** to fill with a gas [The mechanic *pumped* up the flat tire.] **4** to move with an action like a pump [The heart *pumps* blood.]
pump • ***noun,*** *plural* **pumps** • ***verb*** **pumped, pumping**

pumpernickel (pum′pər nik′əl) ***noun*** a coarse, dark kind of rye bread.
pump·er·nick·el • ***noun***

pumpkin (pum′kin *or* pump′kin) ***noun*** a large, round orange fruit that grows on a vine. The pulp is used as a filling for pies.
pump·kin • ***noun,*** *plural* **pumpkins**

pumpkin

pun (pun) ***noun*** the humorous use of words that have the same sound but have different meanings [The short story title "A Dog's Tale" has a *pun* in it.]
verb to make a pun or puns.
pun • ***noun,*** *plural* **puns** • ***verb*** **punned, punning**

punch[1] (punch) ***noun*** a tool for making holes in something or one for cutting or stamping designs on a surface.
verb to make holes in or designs on with a punch [The train conductor *punched* our tickets.]
punch • ***noun*** • ***verb*** **punched, punching**

punch[2] (punch) ***noun*** a hard blow with the fist.
verb **1** to hit with the fist. **2** to herd or drive cattle.

P

punch • *noun, plural* **punches**
• *verb* **punched, punching**

punch[3] (punch) *noun* a sweet drink made by mixing fruit juices or other liquids. It is often served at parties from a large bowl.

WORD HISTORY

punch

Our word **punch** comes from a word that means "five" in an old language of India. In India, **punch** was first made from five kinds of juice or liquor.

punctuation (puŋk′cho͞o ā′shən) *noun* **1** the use of periods, commas, and other marks in writing to help make the meaning clear [the rules of *punctuation*]. **2** punctuation marks [Do you know what *punctuation* is used to end sentences?]
punc·tu·a·tion • *noun*

punctuation mark *noun* a mark such as a period, comma, question mark, colon or semicolon used in writing or printing to help make the meaning clear.
punctuation mark • *noun, plural* **punctuation marks**

puncture (puŋk′chər) *noun* a hole made by a sharp point.
verb to make a hole in with a sharp point; pierce [He *punctured* the balloon with a pin.]
punc·ture • *noun, plural* **punctures**
• *verb* **punctured, puncturing**

WORD CHOICES

Synonyms of **punish**

The words **punish, correct**, and **discipline** share the meaning "to make someone who has done something wrong suffer for it by paying a penalty."

The court *punished* the speeder by fining her.

Our principal *corrected* the unruly students.

The coach *disciplined* two players for missing practice.

punish (pun′ish) *verb* **1** to cause to suffer pain or loss for doing something wrong [His mother *punished* him for his rude talk to his uncle.] **2** to treat in a harsh or rough way [The rays of the sun are *punishing* my skin.]
pun·ish • *verb* **punished, punishing**

punishment (pun′ish mənt) *noun* **1** the act of punishing [Is *punishment* really needed in this case?] **2** a penalty for doing something wrong [A fifty-dollar fine was the *punishment* for speeding.]
pun·ish·ment • *noun, plural for sense 2 only* **punishments**

punk (puŋk) [*a slang word*] *noun* **1** a young hoodlum. **2** a young person thought of as not having much experience or as being not important. **3** a loud and fast style of rock music.
punk • *noun, plural for senses 1 and 2 only* **punks**

punt (punt) *verb* to kick a football after letting it drop from the hands but before it touches the ground.
noun the kick made by punting.
punt • *verb* **punted, punting** • *noun, plural* **punts**

puny (pyo͞o′nē) *adjective* small or weak; feeble —Look for the WORD CHOICES box at the entry **weak**.
pu·ny • *adjective* **punier, puniest**

pup (pup) *noun* **1** a young dog; puppy. **2** the young of a fox, wolf, seal, whale, or certain other animals.
pup • *noun, plural* **pups**

pupa (pyo͞o′pə) *noun* an insect in the stage of development between a larva and an adult.
pu·pa • *noun, plural* **pu·pae** (pyo͞o′pē) or **pupas**

pupil[1] (pyo͞o′pəl) *noun* a person being taught by a teacher; student.
pu·pil • *noun, plural* **pupils**

pupil[2] (pyo͞o′pəl) *noun* the opening in the center of the eye. It grows larger or smaller to let in more or less light.
pu·pil • *noun, plural* **pupils**

a cat	ō go	ʉ fur	ə = a *in* ago
ā ape	ô law, for	ch chin	e *in* agent
ä cot, car	oo look	sh she	i *in* pencil
e ten	o͞o tool	th thin	o *in* atom
ē me	oi oil	*th* then	u *in* circus
i fit	ou out	zh measure	
ī ice	u up	ŋ ring	

puppet

puppet (pup′ət) ***noun*** a figure like a doll that is moved with the hand or by wires or strings attached to it.
pup·pet • ***noun,*** *plural* **puppets**

puppy (pup′ē) ***noun*** a young dog.
pup·py • ***noun,*** *plural* **puppies**

purchase (pʉr′chəs) ***verb*** to get for money; to buy [She *purchased* a new dress.]
noun **1** anything that is bought [I carried my *purchases* in a bag.] **2** the act of buying [the *purchase* of a house].
pur·chase • ***verb*** **purchased, purchasing** • ***noun,*** *plural for sense 1 only* **purchases**

pure (pyoor) ***adjective*** **1** not mixed with anything else [*pure* maple syrup]. **2** not containing anything dirty or unhealthful; clean [*pure* drinking water]. **3** not bad or evil; virtuous, innocent, or just [a *pure* life; *pure* thoughts]. **4** nothing else but; mere [*pure* luck].
pure • ***adjective*** **purer, purest**

purée (pyoo rā′) ***noun*** a thick paste made of cooked vegetables put through a sieve or whipped in a blender [tomato *purée*].
pu·rée • ***noun,*** *plural* **purées**

purify (pyoor′i fī′) ***verb*** to make pure or clean [The filter *purified* the water.]
pu·ri·fy • ***verb*** **purified, purifying, purifies**

Puritan (pyoor′i tən) ***noun*** a member of an English religious group in the 16th and 17th centuries. The Puritans wanted simpler forms of worship and were very strict about morals. Many Puritans came to New England in the 17th century.
Pu·ri·tan • ***noun,*** *plural* **Puritans**

purity (pyoor′i tē) ***noun*** the condition of being pure.
pu·ri·ty • ***noun***

purple (pʉr′pəl) ***noun*** a color that is a mixture of red and blue.
pur·ple • ***noun,*** *plural* **purples**

purpose (pʉr′pəs) ***noun*** what one plans to get or do; aim or goal [The *purpose* of this meeting is to solve the traffic problem.]
—on purpose in an intentional way; not by accident [You bumped into me *on purpose*.]
pur·pose • ***noun,*** *plural* **purposes**

purr (pʉr) ***noun*** **1** the low, soft rumbling sound that is made by a cat when it seems pleased. **2** a similar sound [the *purr* of the engine].
verb to make this sound [The cat *purred* when she petted it.]
purr • ***noun,*** *plural* **purrs** • ***verb*** **purred, purring**

purse (pʉrs) ***noun*** **1** a small container for carrying money [a coin *purse*]. **2** a bag for carrying things like money, keys, and cosmetics. **3** a sum of money given as a prize [The jockey won the *purse* in the first race.]
verb to draw tightly together; pucker [He *pursed* his lips and began to whistle.]
purse • ***noun,*** *plural* **purses** • ***verb*** **pursed, pursing**

pursue (pər soo′ *or* pər syoo′) ***verb*** **1** to follow in order to catch or catch up to [The rancher *pursued* the runaway horse.] **2** to carry out or follow; go on with [She *pursued* a career in acting.]
pur·sue • ***verb*** **pursued, pursuing**

pursuit (pər soot′ *or* pər syoot′) ***noun*** **1** the act of pursuing [The police are in *pursuit* of the bank robbers.] **2** a job, sport, or other activity to which one gives time and energy [Golf is her favorite *pursuit*.]
pur·suit • ***noun,*** *plural for sense 2 only* **pursuits**

pus (pus) ***noun*** the thick, yellowish matter that forms in a sore.

push (poosh) ***verb*** **1** to press against in order to move; shove [We *pushed* the stalled car.] **2** to move by using force [We *pushed* through the crowd.] **3** to urge or press forward [The boss *pushed* the workers to go faster.] **4** to urge or promote the use, sale, or success of [The company is *pushing* a new line of products.]
noun **1** the act of pushing; a shove or thrust [One hard *push* opened the door.] **2** a strong effort [She made a big *push* to finish her work on time.]

P

push • *verb* **pushed, pushing** • *noun, plural for sense 1 only* **pushes**

> **WORD CHOICES**
>
> Synonyms of **push**
>
> The words **push, shove,** and **thrust** share the meaning "to use force in moving something ahead or aside."
>
> He *pushed* a plate across the table.
>
> They *shoved* me out of their way.
>
> She *thrust* the dirty rag into her pocket.

push button *noun* a small knob or button that is pushed to operate an electrical or electronic device.
push button • *noun, plural* **push buttons**

pushover (po͝osh′ō vər) [*a slang word*] *noun* a person who is very easy to persuade, fool, or defeat.
push·o·ver • *noun, plural* **pushovers**

push-up

push-up or **pushup** (po͝osh′up) *noun* an exercise in which one lies face down and pushes the body up from the floor with the arms.
push-up or **push·up** • *noun, plural* **push-ups** or **pushups**

pushy (po͝osh′ē) [*an informal word*] *adjective* bold or rude in a way that annoys others [We left the store to get away from the *pushy* salesperson.]
push·y • *adjective* **pushier, pushiest**

puss (po͝os) *noun* a cat. This word is used mainly by children.
puss • *noun, plural* **pusses**

pussy willow (po͝os′ē) *noun* a willow with soft, furry, grayish catkins.
pus·sy willow • *noun, plural* **pussy willows**

put (po͝ot) *verb* **1** to cause to be in a certain place or position; place [*Put* soap in the water. *Put* the books side by side.] **2** to cause to be in a certain condition [The sound of the waves *put* me to sleep.] **3** to say or express; to state [Can you *put* the problem in simple words?] **4** to bring about; make happen [That should *put* an end to the problem.] **5** to give or assign; attach [The store *put* a price of $10 on the rug.]
—put aside or **put away** to save for later use. **—put back** to restore [*Put* the book *back* on the shelf.] **—put off** to leave until later; postpone [Don't *put off* until tomorrow what you can do today.] **—put on 1** to dress oneself in [*Put on* a coat before you go out.] **2** to take on; add [I *put on* a few pounds.] **3** to assume or pretend [She *put on* an air of innocence.] **4** to present [We *put on* a play.] **5** [*a slang use*] to fool or trick [You're *putting* me *on*.] **—put out** to stop from burning [*Put out* the fire.] **—put up 1** to offer; to show [The house was *put up* for sale.] **2** to build; erect. **3** to furnish with a place to live [Can you *put* us *up* for two days?] **4** to provide [Who *put up* the money for this project?] **—put up with** to tolerate; to bear [We could not *put up with* the barking dogs.]
put • *verb* **put, putting**

putout (po͝ot′out) *noun* a baseball play in which a player causes the batter or runner to be out [The catcher made the *putout* by tagging the runner.]
put·out • *noun, plural* **putouts**

putt (put) *noun* a light stroke in golf that rolls the ball toward or into the hole.
verb to hit a golf ball with such a stroke.
putt • *noun, plural* **putts** • *verb* **putted, putting**

putter[1] (put′ər) *noun* **1** a short golf club used in putting. **2** a person who putts.
put·ter • *noun, plural* **putters**

putter[2] (put′ər) *verb* to busy oneself in an aimless sort of way [She *puttered* around the house most of the day.]
put·ter • *verb* **puttered, puttering**

a cat	ō go	ʉ fur	ə = a *in* ago
ā ape	ô law, for	ch chin	e *in* agent
ä cot, car	o͝o look	sh she	i *in* pencil
e ten	o͞o tool	th thin	o *in* atom
ē me	oi oil	*th* then	u *in* circus
i fit	ou out	zh measure	
ī ice	u up	ŋ ring	

putty (put′ē) ***noun*** a soft mixture of powdered chalk and linseed oil, used to hold panes of glass in windows or to fill cracks in wood.
verb to hold in place or fill with putty.
put·ty • ***noun*** • ***verb*** **puttied, puttying, putties**

putty knife ***noun*** a tool with a broad, flat blade, used to put on and smooth putty.
putty knife • ***noun,*** *plural* **putty knives**

puzzle (puz′əl) ***noun*** **1** a question or problem that is hard to solve or understand [It's a *puzzle* to me how they got here so quickly.] **2** a toy or problem that tests how clever or skillful a person is [a crossword *puzzle;* a jigsaw *puzzle*].
verb **1** to think hard [He *puzzled* over the difficult math problem.] **2** to confuse [Her answer *puzzled* us.]
puz·zle • ***noun,*** *plural* **puzzles**
• ***verb*** **puzzled, puzzling**

Pvt. *abbreviation for* Private [*Pvt.* Sarah Brown].

Pygmy (pig′mē) ***noun*** a person belonging to one of the African or Asian peoples who are very small.
Pyg·my • ***noun,*** *plural* **Pygmies**

pyramid

pyramid (pir′ə mid) ***noun*** **1** a solid figure whose sloping sides are triangles that come together in a point at the top. **2** something shaped like this, especially any of the huge, four-sided structures built by the ancient Egyptians to be used as royal tombs.
pyr·a·mid • ***noun,*** *plural* **pyramids**

python (pī′thän) ***noun*** a very large snake found in Asia, Africa, and Australia. It kills its prey by twisting around it so tightly that the prey suffocates.
py·thon • ***noun,*** *plural* **pythons**

P

Q q

Qq Qq *Qq* Qq

You will not see the letter **q** *very often because very few words use this letter. It is never used by itself in regular English words—it is always followed by the letter* **u**. *The letter combination* **q+u** *usually stands for the same sound as* **k+w**, *as in the words* **quill** *and* **quiet,** *but it can also represent the sound of* **k** *alone, as in the words* **quay** *and* **unique.**

q or **Q** (kyo͞o) ***noun*** the seventeenth letter of the English alphabet.
q or **Q** • ***noun,*** *plural* **q's** or **Q's**

Qatar (kə tär′) an independent state on the Arabian peninsula.
Qa·tar

QC *abbreviation for* Quebec.

qt. *abbreviation for* **1** quart. **2** quarts.

quack[1] (kwak) ***noun*** the sound a duck makes.
verb to make this sound.
quack • ***noun,*** *plural* **quacks**
• ***verb*** **quacked, quacking**

quack[2] (kwak) ***noun*** a person without proper training or skill who pretends to be a doctor.
quack • ***noun,*** *plural* **quacks**

quadrilateral (kwäd′ri lat′ər əl) ***noun*** a flat figure with four angles and four sides.
quad·ri·lat·er·al • ***noun,*** *plural* **quadrilaterals**

quadruped (kwä′dro͞o ped) ***noun*** an animal with four feet.
quad·ru·ped • ***noun,*** *plural* **quadrupeds**

quadruple (kwä dro͞o′pəl) ***adjective*** four times as much or as many.
verb to make or become four times as much or as many [The population of that region *quadrupled* in the last 20 years.]
quad·ru·ple • ***adjective*** • ***verb*** **quadrupled, quadrupling**

quadruplet (kwä dro͞o′plət) ***noun*** one of four children born at a single birth.
quad·ru·plet • ***noun,*** *plural* **quadruplets**

quahog (kwô′hôg *or* kō′hôg) ***noun*** a clam used for food, found off the east coast of North America. It has a very hard, thick shell.
qua·hog • ***noun,*** *plural* **quahogs**

quail

a	cat	ō	go	ʉ	fur	ə =	a *in* ago
ā	ape	ô	law, for	ch	chin		e *in* agent
ä	cot, car	o͝o	look	sh	she		i *in* pencil
e	ten	o͞o	tool	th	thin		o *in* atom
ē	me	oi	oil	*th*	then		u *in* circus
i	fit	ou	out	zh	measure		
ī	ice	u	up	ŋ	ring		

quail (kwāl) *noun* a small, short-tailed, wild bird that looks like a partridge. It is hunted for sport or for food.
quail • *noun, plural* **quail**

quaint (kwānt) *adjective* unusual or old-fashioned in a pleasing way [a *quaint* cottage].
quaint • *adjective* **quainter, quaintest**

quake (kwāk) *verb* **1** to tremble or shake [The ground *quaked*, causing several buildings to collapse.] **2** to shudder or shiver [We *quaked* at the sight of the monster.]
noun a short form of **earthquake**.
quake • *verb* **quaked, quaking** • *noun, plural* **quakes**

qualification (kwôl′i fi kā′shən *or* kwä′ li fi kā′shən) *noun* **1** any skill, experience, or special training that makes a person fit for a particular task or job. **2** a thing that changes or limits [I can recommend this book without *qualification*.]
qual·i·fi·ca·tion • *noun, plural* **qualifications**

qualified (kwôl′i fīd′ *or* kwä′li fīd′) *adjective* **1** having the qualities that are needed; fit [Is she *qualified* for the job?] **2** having limits; with reservations [*qualified* approval].
qual·i·fied • *adjective*

qualify (kwôl′i fī′ *or* kwä′li fī′) *verb* **1** to make or be fit for some work or activity [Your training *qualifies* you for the job. He *qualified* for the team.] **2** to limit or make less strong [She *qualified* her opinion by saying that she did not know all the facts.] **3** to limit the meaning of; modify [Adjectives *qualify* nouns.]
qual·i·fy • *verb* **qualified, qualifying, qualifies**

quality (kwôl′i tē *or* kwä′li tē) *noun* **1** one of the features that makes a thing what it is [Hardness is a *quality* of diamond.] **2** degree of excellence [That paper is of poor *quality*.]
qual·i·ty • *noun, plural for sense 1 only* **qualities**

qualm (kwäm) *noun* **1** a slight feeling of guilt [The thief had no *qualms* about taking the money.] **2** a sudden uneasy feeling; misgiving [We had *qualms* about sailing in rough water.]
qualm • *noun, plural* **qualms**

quantity (kwän′ti tē) *noun* **1** an amount or portion [A large *quantity* of food was left after the party.] **2** a large amount [The factory makes toys in *quantity*.]
quan·ti·ty • *noun, plural* **quantities**

quarantine (kwôr′ən tēn) *noun* the act of keeping a sick person, animal, or plant away from others so that the disease will not spread.
verb to put in a place away from others so that disease does not spread [The farmer *quarantined* his sick cows.]
quar·an·tine • *noun, plural* **quarantines** • *verb* **quarantined, quarantining**

quarrel (kwôr′əl) *noun* **1** an argument or disagreement; dispute. **2** a reason for arguing [I have no *quarrel* with your methods.]
verb **1** to argue or disagree in an angry way. **2** to find fault; complain [I won't *quarrel* with her decision.]
quar·rel • *noun, plural* **quarrels** • *verb* **quarreled** or **quarrelled, quarreling** or **quarrelling**

WORD HISTORY

quarrel

The word **quarrel** comes from a Latin verb that means "to complain." The Latin word developed from an ancient term that meant "to snort or wheeze." When people **quarrel**, or speak with anger, they may sometimes get very excited and make snorting noises.

WORD CHOICES

Synonyms of **quarrel**

The words **quarrel, bicker,** and **wrangle** share the meaning "to argue or disagree."

We *quarreled* about my religious beliefs.

Even good friends sometimes *bicker* over minor matters.

They *wrangled* over the presidential election.

quarry[1] (kwôr′ē) *noun* an animal that is being chased or hunted down; prey [The hunters closed in on their *quarry*.]
quar·ry • *noun, plural* **quarries**

quarry[2] (kwôr′ē) *noun* a place where stone, marble, or slate is cut or blasted out of the earth.
quar·ry • *noun, plural* **quarries**

Q

quart (kwôrt) ***noun*** a unit of measure for liquids that is equal to two pints, or ¼ gallon. A quart is equal to a little less than a liter.
quart • ***noun,*** *plural* **quarts**

quarter (kwôrt′ər) ***noun*** **1** one of four equal parts of something; fourth [a *quarter* of a mile; the third *quarter* of a football game]. **2** one fourth of a year; three months. **3** the point fifteen minutes before or after any given hour [It's a *quarter* after five.] **4** one fourth of a dollar; 25 cents. **5** a coin of the U.S. or Canada worth 25 cents. **6** a certain section of a city [the French *Quarter* of New Orleans]. **7 quarters** a place to live in, often just for a while. **8** the time in which the moon makes one fourth of its circle around the earth, about seven days.
verb to divide into four equal parts [Mother *quartered* the apple.]
quar·ter • ***noun,*** *plural* **quarters**
• ***verb*** **quartered, quartering**

quarterback (kwôrt′ər bak) ***noun*** the player in football who calls the signals and receives the ball from the center.
quar·ter·back • ***noun,*** *plural* **quarterbacks**

quarterly (kwôrt′ər lē) ***adjective*** happening or appearing four times a year [a *quarterly* magazine].
quar·ter·ly • ***adjective***

quarter note ***noun*** a note in music that is held one fourth as long as a whole note.
quarter note • ***noun,*** *plural* **quarter notes**

quarter note

quartet or **quartette** (kwôr tet′) ***noun*** **1** a group of four people who sing or play music together. **2** any group of four.
quar·tet or **quar·tette** • ***noun,*** *plural* **quartets** or **quartettes**

quartz (kwôrts) ***noun*** a bright mineral, found usually as clear, glassy crystals, but also as colored stones which are used in jewelry.

quay (kē) ***noun*** a wharf, usually of stone or concrete, for loading and unloading ships.
quay • ***noun,*** *plural* **quays**
● The words **quay** and **key** sound alike.
The *quay* was built on the left bank.
I lost the *key* to my car.
We visited a *key* off Florida's coast.

Que. *abbreviation for* Quebec.

queasy (kwē′zē) ***adjective*** feeling as if one might vomit [Sailing made him *queasy*.]
quea·sy • ***adjective*** **queasier, queasiest**

Quebec (kwi bek′) a province of eastern Canada. Abbreviated **QC** or **Que.**
Que·bec

queen (kwēn) ***noun*** **1** a woman who rules a country and whose position is handed down from parent to child. Queens today usually have little power to rule. **2** the wife of a king. **3** a woman who is famous or honored for something [a beauty *queen*]. **4** the female that lays all the eggs for a colony of bees or ants. **5** a playing card with a picture of a queen on it. **6** the most powerful piece in chess.
queen • ***noun,*** *plural* **queens**

queen-size (kwēn′sīz) ***adjective*** larger than usual, but smaller than king-size [a *queen-size* bed].

queer (kwir) ***adjective*** different from what is usual or normal; odd; strange [How *queer* to have snow in June!]

quench (kwench) ***verb*** **1** to put out; extinguish [The water *quenched* the fire.] **2** to satisfy [The lemonade *quenched* my thirst.]
quench • ***verb*** **quenched, quenching**

query (kwir′ē) ***noun*** a question [Did you receive an answer to your *query?*]
verb to ask or ask about; to question [They *queried* my reasons for leaving.]
que·ry • ***noun,*** *plural* **queries**
• ***verb*** **queried, querying, queries**

quest (kwest) ***noun*** **1** a hunt or search [a *quest* for knowledge]. **2** a journey in search of adventure [the *quests* of medieval knights].
quest • ***noun,*** *plural* **quests**

question (kwes′chən) ***noun*** **1** something that is asked in order to learn or know [The doctor answered the patient's *questions*.] **2** doubt [There is no *question* she's honest.] **3** a matter to be considered [It's not a *question* of money.] **4** a matter that is being discussed by a group [The *question* is before the committee.]
verb **1** to ask questions of [The police *questioned* the suspect.] **2** to have doubts about [I

a	cat	ō	go	ʉ	fur	ə =	a *in* ago
ā	ape	ô	law, for	ch	chin		e *in* agent
ä	cot, car	oo	look	sh	she		i *in* pencil
e	ten	o͞o	tool	th	thin		o *in* atom
ē	me	oi	oil	*th*	then		u *in* circus
i	fit	ou	out	zh	measure		
ī	ice	u	up	ŋ	ring		

question his loyalty.] **3** to dispute [The batter *questioned* the umpire's call.]
—beyond question without any doubt. **—out of the question** impossible [Buying such an expensive bike is *out of the question*.]
ques·tion • ***noun,*** *plural* **questions** • ***verb*** **questioned, questioning**

questionable (kwes′chən ə bəl) ***adjective*** doubtful or suspicious [a *questionable* story].
ques·tion·a·ble • ***adjective***

question mark ***noun*** a mark of punctuation (?). It is used after a word or sentence to show that a question is being asked.
question mark • ***noun,*** *plural* **question marks**

questionnaire (kwes chən er′) ***noun*** a printed list of questions used in gathering information from people.
ques·tion·naire • ***noun,*** *plural* **questionnaires**

quick (kwik) ***adjective*** **1** done with speed; rapid; swift [a *quick* throw to second base] —Look for the WORD CHOICES box at the entry **fast**[1]. **2** done at once; prompt [a *quick* reply to my letter]. **3** able to learn or understand easily [a *quick* mind] —Look for the WORD CHOICES box at the entry **intelligent**.
adverb with speed; rapidly [Come *quick!*]
quick • ***adjective*** & • ***adverb*** **quicker, quickest**

quicken (kwik′ən) ***verb*** to move or make move faster; speed up [My pulse *quickened* with fear. The horse *quickened* its pace.]
quick·en • ***verb*** **quickened, quickening**

quickly (kwik′lē) ***adverb*** in a quick way; rapidly or promptly.
quick·ly • ***adverb***

quicksand (kwik′sand) ***noun*** a deep, wet, and loose sand deposit. Quicksand swallows up anything heavy on its surface.
quick·sand • ***noun***

quick-tempered (kwik′tem′pərd) ***adjective*** becoming angry at the slightest thing.
quick-tem·pered • ***adjective***

quiet (kwī′ət) ***adjective*** **1** not noisy [a *quiet* motor]. **2** free from noise [a *quiet* room] —Look for the WORD CHOICES box at the entry **still**. **3** not talking; silent [a *quiet* audience]. **4** not moving; still; calm [a *quiet* pond]. **5** not easily excited [a *quiet* disposition]. **6** peaceful and relaxing [a *quiet* evening at home].
noun the condition of being quiet [We enjoy the peace and *quiet* of the woods.]
verb to make or become quiet [*Quiet* down and go to sleep.]
qui·et • ***adjective*** **quieter, quietest** • ***noun*** • ***verb*** **quieted, quieting**

quill

quill (kwil) ***noun*** **1** a large, stiff feather. **2** a writing pen made from the hollow stem of a feather. **3** one of the sharp, stiff spines that stick out on the body of a porcupine.
quill • ***noun,*** *plural* **quills**

quilt (kwilt) ***noun*** a bed covering that is made of two layers of cloth with down, wool, or other soft material between them. The layers are stitched together in such a way that the stitches form patterns on the cloth.
verb to make a quilt or quilts.
quilt • ***noun,*** *plural* **quilts** • ***verb*** **quilted, quilting**

quince (kwins) ***noun*** a hard, yellow fruit that is shaped like an apple. It is used to make jams and preserves.
quince • ***noun,*** *plural* **quinces**

quintet (kwin tet′) ***noun*** **1** a group of five people who sing or play music together. **2** any group of five.
quin·tet • ***noun,*** *plural* **quintets**

quintuplet (kwin tup′lət *or* kwin to͞o′plət) ***noun*** one of five children born at a single birth.
quin·tu·plet • ***noun,*** *plural* **quintuplets**

quit (kwit) ***verb*** **1** to stop doing something [My father *quit* smoking.] **2** to give up; resign from [She *quit* her job at the bank.]
quit • ***verb*** **quit, quitting**

quite (kwīt) ***adverb*** **1** completely; entirely [I haven't *quite* finished eating.] **2** really; truly [You are *quite* a sports fan.] **3** somewhat; rather [It's *quite* warm outside.]

quitter (kwit′ər) [*an informal word*] ***noun*** a person who quits or gives up too easily.
quit·ter • ***noun,*** *plural* **quitters**

Q

quiver[1] (kwiv′ər) ***verb*** to shake with trembling movements [The leaves *quivered* in the breeze.] —Look for the WORD CHOICES box at the entry **shake**.
noun the act or motion of quivering.
quiv·er • ***verb*** **quivered, quivering** • ***noun,*** *plural* **quivers**

quiver[2] (kwiv′ər) ***noun*** a case for holding arrows.
quiv·er • ***noun,*** *plural* **quivers**

quiz (kwiz) ***noun*** a short or informal test.
verb **1** to ask questions of [Police *quizzed* the suspects.] **2** to give a quiz to [The teacher *quizzed* the class.]
quiz • ***noun,*** *plural* **quizzes** • ***verb*** **quizzed, quizzing**

quiz program or **quiz show** ***noun*** a radio or television program on which people try to win prizes by answering questions correctly.
quiz program or **quiz show** • ***noun,*** *plural* **quiz programs** or **quiz shows**

quizzical (kwiz′i kəl) ***adjective*** showing a puzzled condition [a *quizzical* look on her face].
quiz·zi·cal • ***adjective***

quota (kwōt′ə) ***noun*** the share or part of a total that is required from, or is due to, a person, group, or organization [She sold her *quota* of tickets for the school band concert.]
quo·ta • ***noun,*** *plural* **quotas**

quotation (kwō tā′shən) ***noun*** **1** the act of quoting. **2** the words or sections quoted [The sermon was full of *quotations* from the Bible.]
quo·ta·tion • ***noun,*** *plural for sense 2 only* **quotations**

quotation marks ***plural noun*** a pair of marks (" ") that are used in writing. They are placed before and after words that are quoted ("We won!" yelled Peter.) and before and after the title of a story or song ("Little Red Riding Hood," "This Land Is Your Land").

quote (kwōt) ***verb*** to repeat exactly the words of [The newspaper *quoted* our principal on the subject of busing.]
noun **1** something quoted; a quotation. **2 quotes** [*an informal use*] *the same as* **quotation marks**.
quote • ***verb*** **quoted, quoting** • ***noun,*** *plural* **quotes**

quotient (kwō′shənt) ***noun*** the number that is obtained by dividing one number by another. In the problem 20 ÷ 5 = 4, the number 4 is the quotient.
quo·tient • ***noun,*** *plural* **quotients**

WORD HISTORY

quotient

The word **quotient** comes from a Latin word that means "how often?" or "how many times?", and that word comes from the Latin word for "how many?" The **quotient** in a division problem tells "how many times" the divisor is contained in the dividend.

a	cat	ō	go	ʉ	fur	ə =	a *in* ago
ā	ape	ô	law, for	ch	chin		e *in* agent
ä	cot, car	oo	look	sh	she		i *in* pencil
e	ten	ōō	tool	th	thin		o *in* atom
ē	me	oi	oil	*th*	then		u *in* circus
i	fit	ou	out	zh	measure		
ī	ice	u	up	ŋ	ring		

Rr

Rr Rr Rr Rr

The letter **r** *stands for a single sound—the one you hear at the beginning of the words* **robin** *and* **red.**

r or **R** (är) ***noun*** the eighteenth letter of the English alphabet.
—the three R's reading, writing, and arithmetic, thought of as the basic school subjects. They are called "the three R's" because they are sometimes written in a joking way "reading, 'riting, and 'rithmetic."
r or **R** • ***noun,*** *plural* **r's** or **R's**

rabbi (rab′ī) ***noun*** a teacher of the Jewish law. A rabbi is now usually the leader of a Jewish congregation.
rab·bi • ***noun,*** *plural* **rabbis**

WORD HISTORY

rabbi

The word **rabbi** comes from a Hebrew word that means "my master." The word was used in speaking to a teacher of the Jewish law in order to show great respect for him.

rabbit (rab′it) ***noun*** a burrowing animal that has soft fur, long ears, and a very short tail. Rabbits are related to hares.
rab·bit • ***noun,*** *plural* **rabbits**

rabies (rā′bēz) ***noun*** a disease that can kill dogs and many kinds of wild animals. It causes choking and makes the muscles tighten and twitch. A person can get rabies if bitten by an animal that has the disease.
ra·bies • ***noun***

raccoon

raccoon (ra ko͞on′) ***noun*** a furry animal that has a long tail with black rings. Raccoons have black face markings that look like a mask.
rac·coon • ***noun,*** *plural* **raccoons**

race[1] (rās) ***noun*** **1** a contest to see who can go fastest [a horse *race;* a sailboat *race*]. **2** any contest [two candidates in the *race* for mayor].
verb **1** to take part in a race [How many cars are *racing?*] **2** to go very fast.
race • ***noun,*** *plural* **races** • ***verb*** **raced, racing**

race[2] (rās) ***noun*** a large group of people who have certain physical features in common. The type of blood and the color of hair and skin are some of these features that are

R

passed on from one generation to another.
race • *noun, plural* **races**

racer (rās′ər) *noun* **1** a person, animal, or vehicle that takes part in races. **2** a North American snake that can move very quickly.
rac·er • *noun, plural* **racers**

racetrack (rās′trak) *noun* a course that has been laid out for racing.
race·track • *noun, plural* **racetracks**

racial (rā′shəl) *adjective* of or having to do with a race of people [*racial* prejudice].
ra·cial • *adjective*

racism (rā′siz əm) *noun* unfair treatment of people based only on their race.
rac·ism • *noun*

racist (rā′sist) *adjective* showing racial prejudice.
rac·ist • *adjective*

rack (rak) *noun* a framework for hanging, holding, or displaying things [a magazine *rack*].
rack • *noun, plural* **racks**

racket[1] (rak′ət) *noun* **1** a loud, confused noise; clatter; din [A car without a muffler makes a terrible *racket*.] —Look for the WORD CHOICES box at the entry **noise**. **2** a scheme for getting money in a way that is not honest or legal.
rack·et • *noun, plural* **rackets**

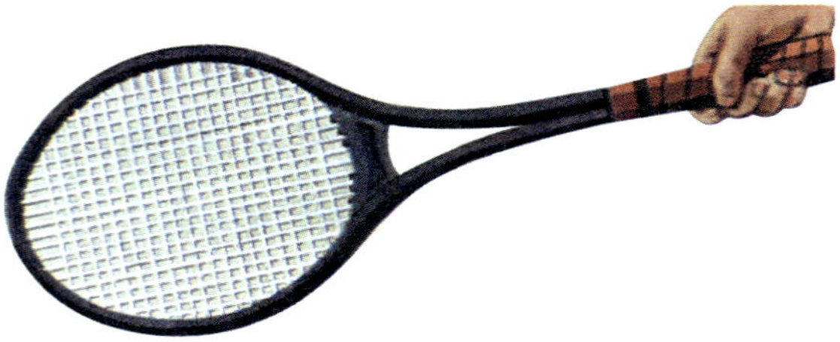

racket

racket[2] (rak′ət) *noun* an object used to strike the ball in tennis and similar games. It consists of a round or oval frame that has a network of tightly laced strings and a handle.
rack·et • *noun, plural* **rackets**

WORD HISTORY

racket

This word **racket** comes from an Arabic word that means "palm of the hand." The first "racket" used in games was certainly the palm of the hand, and it is still used in some games.

racquetball (rak′ət bôl) *noun* a game played by two or four players in an enclosed court with four walls. The players use short-handled rackets to bat a small ball against a wall or walls.
rac·quet·ball • *noun*

radar (rā′där) *noun* a device that sends out radio waves and picks them up again after they strike some object and bounce back. It is used to find out the distance, direction, and speed of storms and of airplanes, ships, and other distant objects.
ra·dar • *noun*

radiant (rā′dē ənt) *adjective* **1** sending out rays of light; shining brightly [the *radiant* sun]. **2** showing very good health, joy, hope, or other positive feeling; glowing [a *radiant* smile]. **3** coming in the form of rays from a source [the *radiant* energy from the sun].
ra·di·ant • *adjective*

radiate (rā′dē āt′) *verb* to send out or be sent out in rays or waves [The stove *radiated* heat. Light *radiates* from the sun.]
ra·di·ate • *verb* **radiated, radiating**

radiation (rā′dē ā′shən) *noun* the energy or rays sent out when certain changes happen in the atoms or molecules of an object or a substance. Light, heat, radio waves, and X-rays are forms of radiation.
ra·di·a·tion • *noun*

radiator (rā′dē āt′ər) *noun* **1** an apparatus that consists of pipes through which hot water or steam moves in order to heat a room. **2** a system of pipes for cooling water that has become hot from passing through an engine. The cooled water is passed back through the engine to keep it from getting too hot.
ra·di·a·tor • *noun, plural* **radiators**

radical (rad′i kəl) *adjective* **1** having to do with the root or source; basic; fundamental [There is a *radical* difference in their views on the matter of school sports.] **2** very great; complete [Moving to the farm made a *radical* change in their lives.] **3** in favor of basic or great changes or reforms [a *radical* political party].
noun a person who favors basic or great changes or reforms.
rad·i·cal • *adjective* • *noun, plural* **radicals**

a	cat	ō	go	ʉ	fur	ə =	a *in* ago
ā	ape	ô	law, for	ch	chin		e *in* agent
ä	cot, car	oo	look	sh	she		i *in* pencil
e	ten	ōō	tool	th	thin		o *in* atom
ē	me	oi	oil	*th*	then		u *in* circus
i	fit	ou	out	zh	measure		
ī	ice	u	up	ŋ	ring		

radii (rā′dē ī) *noun a plural of* **radius**.
ra·di·i • *noun*

radio (rā′dē ō′) *noun* **1** a way of sending sounds through space by changing them into electric waves. These are sent and picked up, without wires, by a device that changes them back to sounds. **2** a device that is used to send or pick up these electric waves.
verb to send a message by radio [The pilot *radioed* for help.]
ra·di·o • *noun, plural for sense 2 only* **radios** • *verb* **radioed, radioing, radioes**

radioactive (rā′dē ō ak′tiv) *adjective* giving off energy in the form of particles or rays when the nuclei of atoms break up [Radium and uranium are naturally *radioactive* substances.]
ra·di·o·ac·tive • *adjective*

radioactivity (rā′dē ō ak tiv′i tē) *noun* the condition of being radioactive [A Geiger counter checks a substance for *radioactivity*.]
ra·di·o·ac·tiv·i·ty • *noun*

radish

radish (rad′ish) *noun* a round or long plant root that has a red or white skin and is eaten raw as a relish or in salads. It has a sharp taste.
rad·ish • *noun, plural* **radishes**

radium (rā′dē əm) *noun* a silvery-white, radioactive metal that is a chemical element. Radium glows in the dark and is used to make some paints that glow in the dark. Radium is also used to treat cancer.
ra·di·um • *noun*

radius (rā′dē əs) *noun* **1** a straight line that goes from the center to the outside of a circle or sphere. **2** a round or almost round area that is measured by its radius [There were no houses within a *radius* of five miles.]
ra·di·us • *noun, plural* **radii** or **radiuses**

radon (rā′dän) *noun* a radioactive gas that has no color, smell, or taste. Radon is a chemical element. Soil and rocks naturally contain very small amounts of radon.
ra·don • *noun*

raft

raft (raft) *noun* **1** a number of logs or boards that are fastened together and used as a floating platform. **2** a tube or a hollow mat made of rubber or plastic that can be used as a boat when it is filled with air or gas.
raft • *noun, plural* **rafts**

rafter (raf′tər) *noun* one of the sloping beams that are used to hold up a roof.
raft·er • *noun, plural* **rafters**

rag (rag) *noun* **1** a piece of cloth that is old, torn, or not needed. **2** any small piece of cloth used for dusting or washing [a dust *rag*]. **3 rags** old, worn clothing [dressed in *rags*].
rag • *noun, plural* **rags**

rage (rāj) *noun* great, uncontrolled anger; fury [In his *rage* he threw the books on the floor.]
verb **1** to show or feel great, uncontrolled anger; act or speak with fury [She *raged* at them for wrecking her bicycle.] **2** to be violent and out of control [The fire *raged* through the barn.]
rage • *noun, plural* **rages** • *verb* **raged, raging**

ragged (rag′əd) *adjective* **1** shabby or torn from being worn a great deal [a *ragged* shirt]. **2** wearing shabby or torn clothes [a *ragged* child]. **3** rough and uneven [the *ragged* edge of a torn sheet of paper].
rag·ged • *adjective*

raggedy (rag′ə dē) *adjective* ragged.
rag·ged·y • *adjective*

ragweed (rag′wēd) ***noun*** a common weed with small greenish flowers. Its pollen can cause hay fever.
rag·weed • ***noun***

raid (rād) ***noun*** a sudden, surprise attack made by a group of people, such as police or soldiers.
verb to make a raid on.
raid • ***noun,*** *plural* **raids** • ***verb*** **raided, raiding**

rail (rāl) ***noun*** **1** a bar of wood or metal that is supported by standing posts in a fence or barrier. **2** either of the metal bars forming the track of a railroad. **3** a railroad [Ship your cartons by *rail*.]
rail • ***noun,*** *plural for senses 1 and 2 only* **rails**

railing (rāl′iŋ) ***noun*** a kind of fence, barrier, or banister that is made of a series of posts and rails [a porch *railing*].
rail·ing • ***noun,*** *plural* **railings**

railroad (rāl′rōd) ***noun*** **1** a road that is a track made up of parallel steel rails along which trains run. **2** a system of transportation that consists of a series of such roads together with the trains, stations, and other property.
rail·road • ***noun,*** *plural* **railroads**

railway (rāl′wā) ***noun*** **1** *another name for* **railroad**. **2** a set of tracks for the wheels of a railroad car.
rail·way • ***noun,*** *plural* **railways**

rain (rān) ***noun*** **1** water that falls to the earth in drops. Rain is formed from the moisture in the air. **2** the falling of such drops; a shower [Sunshine followed the *rain*.]
verb **1** to fall as rain [It is *raining*.] **2** to fall or pour down like rain [Confetti *rained* on the athletes during the parade.]
rain • ***noun,*** *plural for sense 2 only* **rains** • ***verb*** **rained, raining**

● The words **rain, reign,** and **rein** sound alike.
My dry garden needs a good *rain*.
King Henry's *reign* saw many changes.
Pull on the left *rein* to turn left.

rainbow

rainbow (rān′bō) ***noun*** a curved band of many colors across the sky. It is formed when the white light from the sun passes through raindrops and is broken up into light rays of many different colors.
rain·bow • ***noun,*** *plural* **rainbows**

raincoat (rān′kōt) ***noun*** a coat that repels water to protect a person from the rain.
rain·coat • ***noun,*** *plural* **raincoats**

raindrop (rān′dräp) ***noun*** a single drop of rain.
rain·drop • ***noun,*** *plural* **raindrops**

rainfall (rān′fôl) ***noun*** **1** a falling of rain; shower [a gentle *rainfall*]. **2** the amount of rain or other precipitation that falls over a certain area during a certain period of time [What is the annual *rainfall* there?]
rain·fall • ***noun***

rain forest ***noun*** a dense, evergreen forest that has heavy rainfall all year round.
rain forest • ***noun,*** *plural* **rain forests**

rainstorm (rān′stôrm) ***noun*** a storm in which there is much rain.
rain·storm • ***noun,*** *plural* **rainstorms**

rainy (rān′ē) ***adjective*** having much rain [the *rainy* season].
—a rainy day a future time when there may be great need [Save money for *a rainy day*.]
rain·y • ***adjective*** **rainier, rainiest**

raise (rāz) ***verb*** **1** to cause to rise; lift [*Raise* your hand. *Raise* the window.] **2** to make larger, higher, greater, or louder [The store *raised* all its prices. Don't *raise* your voice in the library.] **3** to bring up; take care of [She *raised* five children.] **4** to cause to grow; produce [They *raise* potatoes and cabbages.] **5** to bring up for thinking about [She *raised* the question of the cost of the new books.] **6** to bring together; collect [We *raised* money for the flood victims.]
noun an increase in amount, especially an increase in salary or wages.
raise • ***verb*** **raised, raising** • ***noun,*** *plural* **raises**

● The words **raise** and **raze** sound alike.
My landlord wants to *raise* my rent.
To *raze* a house is to destroy it.

a	cat	ō	go	ʉ	fur	ə =	a *in* ago
ā	ape	ô	law, for	ch	chin		e *in* agent
ä	cot, car	oo	look	sh	she		i *in* pencil
e	ten	ōō	tool	th	thin		o *in* atom
ē	me	oi	oil	*th*	then		u *in* circus
i	fit	ou	out	zh	measure		
ī	ice	u	up	ŋ	ring		

raisin (rā′zən) ***noun*** a sweet grape dried for eating.
rai·sin • ***noun,*** *plural* **raisins**

rake

rake (rāk) ***noun*** a tool that has a long handle with a set of teeth or prongs at one end. It is used for gathering loose grass, leaves, or hay or for smoothing broken ground.
verb to gather together or smooth with a rake [Jim *raked* the leaves. They *raked* the gravel path.]
rake • ***noun,*** *plural* **rakes** • ***verb*** **raked, raking**

Raleigh (rôl′ē *or* rä′lē) the capital of North Carolina.
Ra·leigh

rally (ral′ē) ***verb*** **1** to bring or come together for some purpose [The students *rallied* to cheer the football team.] **2** to come in order to help [He *rallied* to the side of his friend in trouble.] **3** to come or bring back to action or strength; revive [As the fever left her, she began to *rally*.]
noun a large meeting held for a particular purpose [a political *rally*].
ral·ly • ***verb*** **rallied, rallying, rallies** • ***noun,*** *plural* **rallies**

ram (ram) ***noun*** a male sheep.
verb **1** to hit or drive with force [The car *rammed* into the fence.] **2** to force into place by pressing; stuff; cram [He *rammed* more clothes into the packed suitcase.]
ram • ***noun,*** *plural* **rams** • ***verb*** **rammed, ramming**

RAM (ram) ***noun*** a kind of computer memory that lets a person get to information very quickly. *RAM* is taken from the first letters of the words *random-access memory*.

ramble (ram′bəl) ***verb*** **1** to walk or stroll along without any special goal; roam [The children *rambled* through the woods.] **2** to talk and write on and on without sticking to any point or subject [The speaker *rambled* on and never completed the explanation.]
ram·ble • ***verb*** **rambled, rambling**

ramp (ramp) ***noun*** a sloping road, walk, or other surface that goes from a lower to a higher place.
ramp • ***noun,*** *plural* **ramps**

rampart (ram′pärt) ***noun*** a bank of earth, often with a wall along the top, that surrounds a place and serves as a defense.
ram·part • ***noun,*** *plural* **ramparts**

ramrod (ram′räd) ***noun*** **1** a metal rod that is used for ramming ammunition down the muzzle of a gun. **2** a rod that is used to clean the barrel of a rifle.
ram·rod • ***noun,*** *plural* **ramrods**

ran (ran) ***verb*** *past tense of* **run**.

ranch (ranch) ***noun*** a large farm, especially in the western part of the U.S., where cattle, horses, or sheep are raised.
ranch • ***noun,*** *plural* **ranches**

random (ran′dəm) ***adjective*** made or done without planning or purpose; made or done by chance [a *random* choice of three books].
ran·dom • ***adjective***

rang (raŋ) ***verb*** *past tense of* **ring**[1].

range (rānj) ***noun*** **1** the full extent to which something can be seen, heard, felt, or known [The *range* of her knowledge is impressive.] **2** the limits within which something can vary [The shoes come in a wide *range* of sizes. The band played a *range* of songs from ballads to rock.] **3** the greatest distance over which something can travel, extend, or carry [This airplane has a *range* of 1,000 miles without refueling.] **4** a place for practice in shooting. **5** a large, open area of land over which cattle can wander and graze. **6** a large stove with burners and an oven. **7** a row or line of connected mountains [the Appalachian *range*].
verb **1** to be within certain limits [The prices *range* from $5 to $10.] **2** to wander about; roam [Bears *ranged* the forests.] **3** to lie or extend in a certain direction; stretch [Sand dunes *range* along the seashore.]
range • ***noun,*** *plural for all senses except senses 1 and 2* **ranges** • ***verb*** **ranged, ranging**

ranger (rān′jər) ***noun*** **1** a person whose work is looking after or patrolling a forest or park.

R

2 one of a group of special soldiers or police officers who patrol a certain region.
rang·er • *noun, plural* **rangers**

rank[1] (raŋk) *noun* **1** a position or grade [the *rank* of general]. **2** high position in society [The governor, the mayor, and other people of *rank* were invited to the ceremony.] **3** position or standing on a scale of merit or importance [She is a poet of the first *rank*.] **4 ranks** the enlisted members of an army [He rose from the *ranks* to become a captain.]
verb **1** to place in a certain rank [The critics *rank* this movie among the best of the year.] **2** to hold a certain rank [Sarah *ranks* first on our swimming team.]
rank • *noun, plural for senses 1, 3, and 4 only* **ranks** • *verb* **ranked, ranking**

rank[2] (raŋk) *adjective* **1** having a strong, unpleasant taste or smell [*rank* fish]. **2** of the worst or most extreme kind; complete [The coach was accused of *rank* injustice when he fined the football players.]
rank • *adjective* **ranker, rankest**

Rankin (raŋ′kin), **Jeannette** (jə net′) 1880-1973; the first U.S. congresswoman.
Ran·kin, Jean·nette

ransack (ran′sak) *verb* **1** to search through every part of [He *ransacked* his pockets for his house key.] **2** to search through in order to rob; plunder [The pirates *ransacked* the town.]
ran·sack • *verb* **ransacked, ransacking**

ransom (ran′səm) *noun* **1** the price asked or paid for setting free a kidnapped person or other captive. **2** the act of setting free a captive by paying the price demanded.
verb to pay a price in order to set free [The government finally agreed to *ransom* the prisoners of war.]
ran·som • *noun* • *verb* **ransomed, ransoming**

rant (rant) *verb* to talk in a loud, wild way; rave.
rant • *verb* **ranted, ranting**

rap (rap) *verb* to strike or knock sharply [He *rapped* on the door.]
noun **1** a quick, sharp knock [They heard a *rap* on the door.] **2** [*a slang use*] blame; punishment [Why should he take the *rap* for something he didn't do?] **3** a kind of popular music in which verses that rhyme are chanted to the accompaniment of a strong beat that is repeated over and over again.
rap • *verb* **rapped, rapping** • *noun, plural for sense 1 only* **raps**

● The words **rap** and **wrap** sound alike.
She heard a soft *rap* at the door.
I will *wrap* the gift with bright paper.

rapids

rapid (rap′id) *adjective* very swift or quick; fast [the *rapid* growth of the tomato plants] —Look for the WORD CHOICES box at the entry **fast**[1].
noun usually **rapids** a part of a river where the water moves very quickly.
rap·id • *adjective* • *noun, plural* **rapids**

rapture (rap′chər) *noun* a feeling of great joy, love, or delight [The music filled us with *rapture*.]
rap·ture • *noun*

rare[1] (rer) *adjective* **1** not often found or seen; not common [Radium is a *rare* element.] —Look for the WORD CHOICES box at the entry **unusual**. **2** very good; excellent [a *rare* talent for dancing].
rare • *adjective* **rarer, rarest**

rare[2] (rer) *adjective* not completely cooked; partly raw [She likes her steak *rare*.]
rare • *adjective* **rarer, rarest**

rarely (rer′lē) *adverb* not often; seldom [I *rarely* see them these days.]
rare·ly • *adverb*

rascal (ras′kəl) *noun* **1** a bad or dishonest person; scoundrel. **2** a person who is full of mischief.
ras·cal • *noun, plural* **rascals**

a cat	ō go	ʉ fur	ə = a *in* ago
ā ape	ô law, for	ch chin	e *in* agent
ä cot, car	oo look	sh she	i *in* pencil
e ten	o͞o tool	th thin	o *in* atom
ē me	oi oil	*th* then	u *in* circus
i fit	ou out	zh measure	
ī ice	u up	ŋ ring	

rash[1] (rash) ***adjective*** too hasty; reckless [Quitting your job was a *rash* act.]
rash • ***adjective*** **rasher, rashest**

rash[2] (rash) ***noun*** a condition in which red spots break out on the skin.
rash • ***noun,*** *plural* **rashes**

rasp (rasp) ***verb*** to make a rough, grating sound.
noun a rough, grating sound [The sore throat had changed her voice to a *rasp*.]
rasp • ***verb*** **rasped, rasping** • ***noun,*** *plural* **rasps**

raspberry (raz′ber′ē) ***noun*** a small, juicy, red or black fruit that grows on a shrub. Raspberries have many tiny seeds.
rasp·ber·ry • ***noun,*** *plural* **raspberries**

raspberry

rat (rat) ***noun*** a gnawing animal that has a long tail and looks like a mouse but is larger. Rats are destructive pests and carry diseases.
rat • ***noun,*** *plural* **rats**

rate (rāt) ***noun*** **1** an amount, pace, or degree of something expressed in units of a particular kind [The car could go at the *rate* of 150 miles an hour.] **2** the cost or price of something [Postal *rates* went up this year.]
verb **1** to judge or decide how good or valuable something is [He *rated* the book as too difficult for his class.] **2** to put in a certain rank or level [Tim is *rated* among the best cooks.]
rate • ***noun,*** *plural* **rates** • ***verb*** **rated, rating**

rather (ra*th*′ər) ***adverb*** **1** in a more willing way [I would *rather* read than watch TV.] **2** more accurately [We had a bad storm, or *rather*, a hurricane.] **3** to a certain degree; quite [It's *rather* cold out. I *rather* liked him.]
rath·er • ***adverb***

ratify (rat′i fī′) ***verb*** to approve in an official way [The Senate must *ratify* any treaty between the U.S. and another country.]
rat·i·fy • ***verb*** **ratified, ratifying, ratifies**

ratio (rā′shō *or* rā′shē ō) ***noun*** the relation or comparison of number or size between two different things. The ratio means the number of times the second thing can be divided into the first. If there are nine men and three women in a room, the ratio of men to women is three to one.
ra·tio • ***noun,*** *plural* **ratios**

ration (rash′ən *or* rā′shən) ***noun*** a fixed share or portion, especially of food.
verb **1** to give out in rations [The government *rationed* out food to the victims of the earthquake.] —Look for the WORD CHOICES box at the entry **dispense**. **2** to limit the supply of [The government *rationed* oil during the war.]
ra·tion • ***noun,*** *plural* **rations** • ***verb*** **rationed, rationing**

rational (rash′ən əl) ***adjective*** **1** able to reason; thinking clearly [She was too angry to be *rational*.] **2** of or based on reasoning; reasonable; sensible [We must prepare a *rational* plan to deal with the crisis.]
ra·tion·al • ***adjective***

rattle (rat′l) ***verb*** **1** to make or cause to make a series of sharp, short sounds [The shutters *rattled* in the wind. She *rattled* the doorknob.] **2** to say or recite quickly [She *rattled* off a list of names.] **3** to confuse or upset [Boos from the audience *rattled* the speaker.]
noun **1** a baby's toy or other device that is made to rattle when shaken. **2** a series of sharp, short sounds [What caused the *rattle* in your car?] **3** the hard, loosely connected rings at the end of a rattlesnake's tail.
rat·tle • ***verb*** **rattled, rattling** • ***noun,*** *plural* **rattles**

rattler (rat′lər) ***noun*** a rattlesnake.
rat·tler • ***noun,*** *plural* **rattlers**

rattlesnake

rattlesnake (rat′l snāk) ***noun*** a poisonous North American snake that has a series of hard, loosely connected rings at the end of its tail. When the snake is disturbed it shakes

R

its tail, causing the rings to make a buzzing sound.
rat·tle·snake • *noun, plural* **rattlesnakes**

rave (rāv) ***verb*** **1** to talk in a wild way that does not make sense [The fever made him *rave*.] **2** to praise greatly or too greatly [She *raved* about the movie.]
rave • ***verb*** **raved, raving**

ravel (rav′əl) ***verb*** to separate or become separated into threads; fray [The scarf has begun to *ravel* at one end.]
rav·el • ***verb*** **raveled** or **ravelled, raveling** or **ravelling**

raven (rā′vən) ***noun*** a crow of the largest kind. It has shiny black feathers and a sharp beak.
ra·ven • ***noun,*** *plural* **ravens**

ravenous (rav′ə nəs) ***adjective*** very hungry [He's always *ravenous* at the end of the day.]
rav·e·nous • ***adjective***

ravine (rə vēn′) ***noun*** a deep, narrow valley; gorge.
ra·vine • ***noun,*** *plural* **ravines**

ravioli (rav′ē ō′lē) ***plural noun*** little cases of dough filled with ground meat, cheese, or some mixture. Ravioli are boiled and then served in some kind of sauce.
ra·vi·o·li • ***plural noun***

ravishing (rav′ish iŋ) ***adjective*** causing great joy or pleasure; lovely [a *ravishing* voice].
rav·ish·ing • ***adjective***

raw (rô *or* rä) ***adjective*** **1** not cooked [*raw* vegetables]. **2** in its natural condition; not changed by some human process [*raw* silk; *raw* milk]. **3** not yet trained [*raw* recruits]. **4** with the skin rubbed off; sore [Scratching made his back flesh *raw*.] **5** cold and damp [a *raw* wind].

rawboned (rô′bōnd *or* rä′bōnd) ***adjective*** having little fat on the body; very lean [a *rawboned* basketball player].
raw·boned • ***adjective***

rawhide (rô′hīd *or* rä′hīd) ***noun*** a cattle hide that is not tanned.
raw·hide • ***noun***

ray (rā) ***noun*** **1** a line or narrow beam of light or other form of radiant energy [the *rays* of the flashlight; the sun's *rays*]. **2** a tiny amount [a *ray* of hope]. **3** one of a number of straight, thin parts that come out from a center [The petals of a daisy are *rays*.]
ray • ***noun,*** *plural* **rays**
● The words **ray** and **re** sound alike.
A *ray* of sunlight peeked through.
Do, *re*, mi, fa, sol, la, ti, do.

rayon (rā′än) ***noun*** **1** a fiber that is made from cellulose. **2** a fabric woven from such fibers.
ray·on • ***noun***

raze (rāz) ***verb*** to tear down completely; destroy [The city will *raze* the old houses.]
raze • ***verb*** **razed, razing**
● The words **raze** and **raise** sound alike.
Earthquakes may *raze* the ancient wall.
It's not easy to *raise* four children.

razor (rā′zər) ***noun*** a tool with a sharp edge or edges that is used for shaving or cutting hair.
ra·zor • ***noun,*** *plural* **razors**

Rd. *abbreviation for* Road.

re (rā) ***noun*** the second note of a musical scale.
● The words **re** and **ray** sound alike.
Re is the note between do and mi.
The baby was a *ray* of sunshine to us.

re- *a prefix meaning:* **1** again [When the moon *reappears* from behind the clouds, it is appearing again.] **2** back [When you *repay* a loan, you pay it back.]

WORD MAKER

The prefix **re-**

Many words contain the prefix **re-** plus a word that you already know. You can understand these words if you add the idea "again" to the meaning of the base word.

prefix	*+ base word* ⇨	*new word*
re-	**+ sharpen** ⇨	**resharpen** *(to make sharp again)*

reabsorb
reaffirm
reapply
reappoint
rearrest
reassign
reattach
reawaken
rebind
reboil
recheck
rechew
reclassify
reclean
recolor
recombine
reconquer
recook
recopy
redecorate
rededicate
redesign
rediscover
redivide

a cat	ō go	ʉ fur	ə = a *in* ago
ā ape	ô law, for	ch chin	e *in* agent
ä cot, car	oo look	sh she	i *in* pencil
e ten	ōō tool	th thin	o *in* atom
ē me	oi oil	*th* then	u *in* circus
i fit	ou out	zh measure	
ī ice	u up	ŋ ring	

redye	refry	repaint
reedit	rehire	reread
reemphasize	reinflate	resell
reenlist	relearn	restitch
reestablish	reload	restudy
reevaluate	remeasure	retell
reexplain	remelt	retest
refasten	remix	retrain
refocus	remold	rewarm
refold	repack	rewash

reach (rēch) ***verb*** **1** to go as far as; get to [The climbers *reached* the top of the mountain. The news *reached* us this morning.] **2** to stretch out one's hand or arm [He *reached* up and shook the branch.] **3** to touch by stretching out [Can you *reach* the top shelf?] **4** to stretch out; extend [The road *reaches* from one end of the State to the other.] **5** to get in touch with [You can *reach* me at this phone number.]
noun **1** the act or ability of reaching [A long *reach* helps in playing first base.] **2** the distance or extent covered in reaching [We are out of *reach* of danger.]
reach • ***verb*** **reached, reaching** • ***noun***

WORD CHOICES

Synonyms of **reach**

The words **reach, achieve,** and **win** share the meaning "to arrive at some place or goal or point of development."

She has *reached* the age of sixteen.

He *achieves* high scores on tests.

Dickens *won* fame as a writer.

react (rē akt′) ***verb*** to act in response to something [The dog *reacted* to the loud noise by barking.]
re·act • ***verb*** **reacted, reacting**

reaction (rē ak′shən) ***noun*** an action or happening in return for or in response to some other action or happening [The rash was a *reaction* to the medicine.]
re·ac·tion • ***noun**, plural* **reactions**

reactor (rē ak′tər) ***noun*** *a short form of* **nuclear reactor**.
re·ac·tor • ***noun**, plural* **reactors**

read[1] (rēd) ***verb*** **1** to get the meaning of something written or printed by understanding its letters, signs, or numbers [I like to *read* poems aloud. Can you *read* music? Her job is to *read* gas meters.] **2** to speak printed or written words aloud [The teacher *read* the story to the students.] **3** to learn by reading [In our class we *read* about the moon and the tides.] **4** to learn the meaning of [We can *read* the history of a canyon in its rocks.] **5** to measure and show [The thermometer *reads* 18 degrees.]
read • ***verb*** **read, reading**

● The words **read** and **reed** sound alike.
Read the directions carefully.
The saxophone is a *reed* instrument.

read[2] (red) ***verb*** *past tense and past participle of* **read**[1].

● The words **read** and **red** sound alike.
Have you *read* the directions?
Her shoes matched her *red* dress.

reader (rēd′ər) ***noun*** **1** a person who reads. **2** a textbook with lessons for practicing reading.
read·er • ***noun**, plural* **readers**

readily (red′ə lē) ***adverb*** **1** right away and in a willing way [He came *readily* when we called.] **2** without difficulty; easily [She writes in such a way that her meaning is *readily* understood.]
read·i·ly • ***adverb***

reading (rēd′iŋ) ***noun*** **1** the activity of looking at and understanding something that is printed or written [I prefer *reading* to watching TV.] **2** the act of saying out loud something printed or written [Her *reading* of the story was filled with emotion.] **3** the amount measured by a meter or some other instrument [Check the thermometer *readings* every hour.]
read·ing • ***noun**, plural for senses 2 and 3 only* **readings**

ready (red′ē) ***adjective*** **1** prepared to act or to be used at once [Is everyone *ready* to leave? Dinner is *ready*.] **2** willing [She is always *ready* to help.] **3** about to; likely or liable [I was so upset, I was *ready* to cry.] **4** quick or prompt [She always has a *ready* answer.] **5** easy to get at and use [Keep some *ready* cash at home for an emergency.]
verb to prepare [We must *ready* the house for our guests.]
read·y • ***adjective*** **readier, readiest** • ***verb*** **readied, readying, readies**

ready-made (red′ē mād′) ***adjective*** made so as to be ready for use or sale at once [He bought a *ready-made* suit.]
read·y-made • ***adjective***

R

Reagan (rā′gən), **Ronald** (rän′əld) 1911-2004; the fortieth president of the U.S., from 1981-1989.
Rea·gan, Ron·ald

real (rēl) ***adjective*** **1** not imagined; actual; true [He could hardly believe that his good luck was *real*.] **2** not imitation; genuine [Are these *real* pearls?]
● The words **real** and **reel** sound alike.
She wore a necklace with *real* diamonds.
I began to *reel* after being hit.
We danced a *reel* at the wedding.
Her fishing line tangled in the *reel*.

real estate ***noun*** land and anything on it, including buildings, trees, and water.

realism (rē′ə liz əm) ***noun*** the ability to see things as they really are, not as one might wish them to be [With her usual *realism*, she recognized that she would never be a movie star.]
re·al·ism • ***noun***

realistic (rē′ə lis′tik) ***adjective*** **1** tending to see things as they really are; facing facts with realism; practical [A *realistic* athlete does not always expect to win in a contest.] **2** showing people and things as they are in real life or nature [A *realistic* painting can look like a photograph.]
re·al·is·tic • ***adjective***

reality (rē al′i tē) ***noun*** **1** the condition of being real [She doubted the *reality* of UFOs.] **2** a person or thing that is real [His dream of fame became a *reality*.]
re·al·i·ty • ***noun,*** *plural for sense 2 only* **realities**

realize (rē′ə līz) ***verb*** **1** to understand fully [I *realize* that good grades depend upon study.] **2** to make real; achieve [He worked hard to *realize* his ambition.]
re·al·ize • ***verb*** **realized, realizing**

really (rēl′ē) ***adverb*** **1** in fact; actually [I am not *really* angry; I was just teasing.] **2** truly; very [It's a *really* hot day.]
real·ly • ***adverb***

WORD CHOICES

Synonyms of **really**

The words **really, actually,** and **truly** share the meaning "in fact."

He didn't *really* mean to say that.
Actually, we have no money.
Are you *truly* sorry?

realm (relm) ***noun*** **1** a kingdom [The king lost his *realm* to the invaders.] **2** the special area or field of something [The *realm* of the imagination has no boundaries.]
realm • ***noun,*** *plural* **realms**

reap (rēp) ***verb*** **1** to cut down grain when it is ripe. **2** to gather in after cutting [The farmers were busy this season *reaping* their crops.] **3** to get in return for work or effort [His attention to his work *reaped* high praise from his teacher.]
reap • ***verb*** **reaped, reaping**

reaper (rē′pər) ***noun*** **1** a person who reaps. **2** a machine for reaping grain.
reap·er • ***noun,*** *plural* **reapers**

reappear (rē ə pir′) ***verb*** to appear again.
re·ap·pear • ***verb*** **reappeared, reappearing**

rear[1] (rir) ***noun*** the part of something or the place that is behind or opposite the front [the *rear* of the house].
adjective at or in the rear [a *rear* entrance; the left *rear* wheel].
—bring up the rear to come at the end [A caboose *brings up the rear* of a train.]

rear[2] (rir) ***verb*** **1** to help grow up; bring up [They have *reared* many children.] **2** to rise up on the hind legs [The frightened horse *reared*.]
rear • ***verb*** **reared, rearing**

rear admiral ***noun*** an officer of high rank in the navy.
rear admiral • ***noun,*** *plural* **rear admirals**

rearrange (rē ə rānj′) ***verb*** to arrange again or in a different way.
re·ar·range • ***verb*** **rearranged, rearranging**

reason (rē′zən) ***noun*** **1** something said or written to explain or try to explain an act, idea, or event [Write the *reasons* for your answer.] **2** a cause or motive for some action or feeling [What was your *reason* for moving?] **3** the power to think, get ideas, and decide things [Human beings are the only creatures that truly have *reason*.]
verb **1** to think in a sensible way; come to a conclusion by considering facts [She *reasoned* that her money would be best spent on books.] **2** to argue or persuade in a careful,

a cat	ō go	ʉ fur	ə = a *in* ago
ā ape	ô law, for	ch chin	e *in* agent
ä cot, car	oo look	sh she	i *in* pencil
e ten	ōō tool	th thin	o *in* atom
ē me	oi oil	*th* then	u *in* circus
i fit	ou out	zh measure	
ī ice	u up	ŋ ring	

sensible way [You must *reason* with a child who is afraid of the dark.]
rea·son • ***noun,*** *plural for senses 1 and 2 only* **reasons** • ***verb*** **reasoned, reasoning**

reasonable (rē′zən ə bəl) ***adjective*** **1** using or showing reason; sensible [a *reasonable* decision]. **2** not too much or too great [a *reasonable* price].
rea·son·a·ble • ***adjective***

reasoning (rē′zən iŋ) ***noun*** **1** the act of coming to a conclusion based on facts [Careful *reasoning* is needed to solve complicated problems.] **2** reasons or arguments [I didn't agree with his *reasoning*.]
rea·son·ing • ***noun***

reassemble (rē′ə sem′bəl) ***verb*** to come or put together again [The team *reassembles* after each play to plan the next one.]
re·as·sem·ble • ***verb*** **reassembled, reassembling**

reassure (rē ə shoor′) ***verb*** to remove someone's doubts and fears; make someone feel secure again.
re·as·sure • ***verb*** **reassured, reassuring**

rebate (rē′bāt) ***noun*** a part given back from an amount paid [The company is giving a $500 *rebate* to people who buy its cars.]
re·bate • ***noun,*** *plural* **rebates**

rebel (reb′əl *for n.;* rē bel′ *for v.*) ***noun*** **1** a person who fights against any kind of control or authority. **2 Rebel** a soldier who fought for the Confederacy in the Civil War.
verb to fight or struggle against any kind of control [The peasants *rebelled* against the king.]
reb·el • ***noun,*** *plural* **rebels** • ***verb*** **re·bel, rebelled, rebelling**

rebellion (rē bel′yən) ***noun*** **1** an armed fight against the government of one's country. **2** a fight or struggle against any kind of authority or control.
re·bel·lion • ***noun,*** *plural* **rebellions**

rebound (rē bound′ *for v.;* rē′bound *for n.*) ***verb*** **1** to bounce back after hitting something [Catch the ball as it *rebounds* from the fence.] **2** to seize a basketball that has bounced off the backboard or rim of the basket.
noun the act of rebounding a basketball.
re·bound • ***verb*** **rebounded, rebounding** • ***noun,*** *plural* **rebounds**

rebus (rē′bəs) ***noun*** a puzzle in which words or phrases are shown by means of pictures, signs, and letters.
re·bus • ***noun,*** *plural* **rebuses**

rebus

recall (rē kôl′ *for v.;* rē′kôl *for n.*) ***verb*** **1** to bring back to mind; remember [I don't *recall* meeting him.] —Look for the WORD CHOICES box at the entry **remember**. **2** to call back; order to return [The company *recalled* all the defective cars.]
noun **1** the act of remembering or the ability to remember [He has no *recall* of the accident.] **2** the act of calling back [The company issued a *recall* of the new toasters.]
re·call • ***verb*** **recalled, recalling** • ***noun,*** *plural for sense 2 only* **recalls**

recede (rē sēd′) ***verb*** to go or move backward [The flood waters *receded*.]
re·cede • ***verb*** **receded, receding**

receipt (rē sēt′) ***noun*** **1** the act of receiving [Upon *receipt* of the gift, she thanked him.] **2** a written or printed piece of paper that shows that something has been received [The clerk gave me a *receipt* when I bought the notebook.] **3 receipts** the amount of money that has been received [The theater's weekend *receipts* were over $2,000.]
re·ceipt • ***noun,*** *plural for sense 2* **receipts**

receive (rē sēv′) ***verb*** **1** to take or get what has been given or sent [She *received* a letter.] **2** to greet guests and let them in [Our hostess *received* us at the door.]
re·ceive • ***verb*** **received, receiving**

receiver (rē sē′vər) ***noun*** **1** a person who receives something. **2** a device that receives electric waves or signals and changes them into sound or light [a TV *receiver;* a telephone *receiver*]. **3** a football player who receives forward passes.
re·ceiv·er • ***noun,*** *plural* **receivers**

recent (rē′sənt) ***adjective*** **1** done or made just before the present time; modern [a *recent* addition built onto the school]. **2** having to do

R

with a time just before the present [the *recent* past; a *recent* storm].
re·cent • *adjective*

reception (rē sep′shən) ***noun*** **1** the act of receiving or greeting [The crowd gave the visiting team a friendly *reception*.] **2** a party or gathering at which guests are received [a wedding *reception*]. **3** the quality of electric waves or signals received by a radio or TV set [poor *reception*].
re·cep·tion • ***noun**, plural for sense 2 only* **receptions**

receptionist (rē sep′shən ist) ***noun*** an employee in an office who receives or greets visitors, gives information, and performs various other duties.
re·cep·tion·ist • ***noun**, plural* **receptionists**

recess (rē′ses *or* rē ses′) ***noun*** **1** the act of stopping work or play for a short time, to relax. **2** a hollow place in a wall or other surface.
re·cess • ***noun**, plural* **recesses**

recharge (rē chärj′) ***verb*** to charge again [You must *recharge* the battery.]
re·charge • ***verb*** **recharged, recharging**

recipe (res′i pē) ***noun*** a list of ingredients and directions for making something to eat or drink [a *recipe* for cookies].
rec·i·pe • ***noun**, plural* **recipes**

recital (rē sīt′l) ***noun*** a program of music or dances performed by one person or a small group.
re·cit·al • ***noun**, plural* **recitals**

recite (rē sīt′) ***verb*** **1** to say aloud from memory, especially before an audience [He *recited* a poem.] **2** to tell in detail; give an account of [He *recited* his adventures in the Amazon.]
re·cite • ***verb*** **recited, reciting**

reckless (rek′ləs) ***adjective*** not careful or responsible; taking chances [a *reckless* driver].
reck·less • *adjective*

reckon (rek′ən) ***verb*** to count; figure up [We must *reckon* our hotel bill.]
—**reckon with** to think about; consider [We have to *reckon with* the possible danger.]
reck·on • ***verb*** **reckoned, reckoning**

recline (rē klīn′) ***verb*** to lie down or lean back.
re·cline • ***verb*** **reclined, reclining**

recluse (rek′lo͞os *or* rē klo͞os′) ***noun*** a person who lives alone, away from others.
rec·luse • ***noun**, plural* **recluses**

recognition (rek əg nish′ən) ***noun*** **1** the act of showing that one recognizes or knows a person or thing [She passed me without a sign of *recognition*.] **2** attention; notice; approval [an award in *recognition* of a job well done].
rec·og·ni·tion • *noun*

recognizable (rek′əg nī′zə bəl) ***adjective*** capable of being recognized [They were no longer *recognizable* after they put on their clown makeup.]
rec·og·niz·a·ble • *adjective*

recognize (rek′əg nīz) ***verb*** **1** to realize or notice that one has seen, heard, or known something or someone before [I *recognized* her old house. Do you *recognize* this tune?] **2** to know by a certain feature; identify [We can *recognize* a giraffe by its long neck.] **3** to admit as true; accept [The team had to *recognize* defeat.]
rec·og·nize • ***verb*** **recognized, recognizing**

recollect (rek ə lekt′) ***verb*** to remember; bring back to mind [He tried to *recollect* the words to the old song.] —Look for the WORD CHOICES box at the entry **remember**.
rec·ol·lect • ***verb*** **recollected, recollecting**

recommend (rek ə mend′) ***verb*** **1** to speak of someone or something as being good for a certain use, job, or purpose [Can you *recommend* a good plumber?] **2** to give advice; advise [I *recommend* that you study harder.]
rec·om·mend • ***verb*** **recommended, recommending**

recommendation (rek ə mən dā′shən) ***noun*** **1** the act of recommending [His *recommendation* is important to me.] **2** a letter or something else that recommends a person or thing. **3** advice; suggestion [You should follow your parents' *recommendations*.]
rec·om·men·da·tion • ***noun**, plural for senses 2 and 3 only* **recommendations**

record (rē kôrd′ *for v.;* rek′ərd *for n.*) ***verb*** **1** to write down for future use; keep an account of [She *recorded* the events of the day in her diary.] **2** to show or register [We use a thermometer to *record* temperatures.] **3** to store sound or visual images in some permanent form for future listening or viewing.
noun **1** anything written down and saved for future use [We kept a *record* of how much we spent on gas.] **2** something written down and

a cat	ō go	ʉ fur	ə = a *in* ago
ā ape	ô law, for	ch chin	e *in* agent
ä cot, car	oo look	sh she	i *in* pencil
e ten	o͞o tool	th thin	o *in* atom
ē me	oi oil	*th* then	u *in* circus
i fit	ou out	zh measure	
ī ice	u up	ŋ ring	

kept as evidence or history [official government *records*]. **3** the known facts about something or someone [her fine *record* as mayor]. **4** a thin, flat, usually black disc with grooves on which sound has been recorded. It is played on a phonograph. **5** the best that has yet been done [the *record* for the high jump].
re·cord • *verb* **recorded, recording** • *noun*
rec·ord, *plural for all senses except 3* **records**

recorder (rē kôrd′ər) *noun* **1** a person appointed or elected to keep official records. **2** *a short form of* **tape recorder**. **3** a wind instrument that is a wooden or plastic tube with a mouthpiece like a whistle at one end.
re·cord·er • *noun, plural* **recorders**

recorder

recording (rē kôrd′iŋ) *noun* **1** something that is recorded. A recording may be made on a phonograph record, magnetic tape, compact disc, or other medium. **2** the record, tape, disc, or other medium on which sound or images are recorded.
re·cord·ing • *noun, plural* **recordings**

record player *noun* a machine on which phonograph records may be played.
record player • *noun, plural* **record players**

recount[1] (rē kount′) *verb* to tell about in detail [She *recounted* her adventures.]
re·count • *verb* **recounted, recounting**

recount[2] (rē kount′ *for v.;* rē′kount *for n.*) *verb* to count again.
noun a second count, especially of votes [The losing candidate demanded a *recount*.]
re·count • *verb* **recounted, recounting** • *noun, plural* **recounts**

WORD CHOICES

Synonyms of **recover**

The words **recover, regain,** and **retrieve** share the meaning "to get back something that was lost or taken."

She *recovered* her lost dog.
The team *regained* the championship.
They *retrieved* the kite from the tree.

recover (rē kuv′ər) *verb* **1** to get well again [Have you *recovered* from your cold?] **2** to get back something lost; regain [He *recovered* their stolen car.]
re·cov·er • *verb* **recovered, recovering**

recovery (rē kuv′ər ē) *noun* **1** a return to good health or a normal condition [He has a good chance for a complete *recovery*.] **2** the act of getting back something that was lost or stolen [The detective was responsible for the *recovery* of the stolen items.]
re·cov·er·y • *noun, plural for sense 1 only* **recoveries**

recreation (rek′rē ā′shən) *noun* **1** the act of refreshing one's body or mind after working [He plays chess for *recreation*.] **2** any sport, exercise, hobby, or amusement by which one does this [Hiking is my favorite kind of *recreation*.]
rec·re·a·tion • *noun, plural for sense 2 only* **recreations**

recruit (rē kro͞ot′) *noun* a person who has recently joined an organization or group, especially the armed forces.
verb to get to join [Our club *recruited* six new members.]
re·cruit • *noun, plural* **recruits** • *verb* **recruited, recruiting**

rectangle (rek′taŋ gəl) *noun* a flat figure with four sides and four right angles, especially one that is not a square.
rec·tan·gle • *noun, plural* **rectangles**

rectangular (rek taŋ′gyo͞o lər) *adjective* shaped like a rectangle [a *rectangular* garden plot].
rec·tan·gu·lar • *adjective*

recuperate (rē ko͞o′pər āt′) *verb* to get well again; recover [Aaron is *recuperating* from the flu.]
re·cup·er·ate • *verb* **recuperated, recuperating**

recycle (rē sī′kəl) *verb* to put something through a special process so that it can be used again [The city *recycles* aluminum cans, bottles, and paper.]
re·cy·cle • *verb* **recycled, recycling**

red (red) *adjective* having the color of blood or of a ripe cherry.
noun the color of blood or of a ripe cherry.
red • *adjective* **redder, reddest** • *noun, plural* **reds**
• The words **red** and **read** sound alike.
Her shoes matched her *red* dress.
Have you *read* the directions?

R

red blood cell ***noun*** a very small red-colored blood cell. It carries oxygen from the lungs to the cells in the rest of the body and carbon dioxide from the cells back to the lungs.
red blood cell • ***noun,*** *plural* **red blood cells**

redcoat (red′kōt) ***noun*** a British soldier, especially during the American Revolution. British soldiers wore uniforms with red coats.
red·coat • ***noun,*** *plural* **redcoats**

red corpuscle ***noun*** *the same as* **red blood cell**.
red corpuscle • ***noun,*** *plural* **red corpuscles**

reddish (red′ish) ***adjective*** somewhat red.
red·dish • ***adjective***

redeem (rē dēm′) ***verb*** **1** to turn in for a prize or for a lower price [He *redeemed* the coupon for a free bar of soap.] **2** to make up for [Her brave act *redeemed* her faults.]
re·deem • ***verb*** **redeemed, redeeming**

red-handed (red′han′dəd) ***adverb*** while committing a crime or doing something wrong [The thief was caught *red-handed*.]
red-hand·ed • ***adverb***

redhead (red′hed) ***noun*** a person who has red hair.
red·head • ***noun,*** *plural* **redheads**

Red Sea a sea between Arabia and Africa. The Suez Canal connects it with the Mediterranean Sea.

reduce (rē do͞os′ *or* rē dyo͞os′) ***verb*** **1** to make less, fewer, or smaller; decrease [The store *reduced* prices during the sale. We must *reduce* pollution.] **2** to lose weight by dieting. **3** to bring something or someone to a particular or a different form or condition [The earthquake *reduced* the city to rubble. The grinding machine *reduces* peanuts to a paste. The story *reduced* him to tears.]
re·duce • ***verb*** **reduced, reducing**

reduction (rē duk′shən) ***noun*** **1** the act of reducing [Buses, trolleys, and subways help in traffic *reduction*.] **2** the amount by which a thing is reduced [a 50% *reduction* in price].
re·duc·tion • ***noun,*** *plural* **reductions**

redwood (red′wood) ***noun*** **1** a giant evergreen tree of California and Oregon; sequoia. **2** the reddish wood of this tree.
red·wood • ***noun,*** *plural for sense 1 only* **redwoods**

reed (rēd) ***noun*** **1** a kind of tall, slender grass that grows along the edges of lakes, streams, and marshes. **2** a thin strip of wood, plastic, or metal that is used with the mouthpiece of musical instruments such as the clarinet, oboe, and saxophone. It vibrates when air is blown against it and produces a tone.
reed • ***noun,*** *plural* **reeds**
● The words **reed** and **read** sound alike.
The saxophone is a *reed* instrument.
Read the directions carefully.

reef (rēf) ***noun*** a ridge of rock, coral, or sand that lies very near the surface of the water.
reef • ***noun,*** *plural* **reefs**

reek (rēk) ***verb*** to have a strong, bad smell; stink.
noun a strong, bad smell; stench.
reek • ***verb*** **reeked, reeking**
• ***noun,*** *plural* **reeks**
● The words **reek** and **wreak** sound alike.
The dump's *reek* made me cover my nose.
Tornadoes *wreak* destruction.

reel[1] (rēl) ***verb*** **1** to move or stand in an unsteady way; stagger [He *reeled* from the blow.] —Look for the WORD CHOICES box at the entry **stagger**. **2** to spin or whirl [I was so dizzy that the room *reeled*.]
reel • ***verb*** **reeled, reeling**
● The words **reel** and **real** sound alike.
I began to *reel* after being hit.
We danced a *reel* at the wedding.
Her fishing line tangled in the *reel*.
She wore a necklace with *real* diamonds.

reel[2] (rēl) ***noun*** a lively folk dance or the music for it.
reel • ***noun,*** *plural* **reels**
● The words **reel** and **real** sound alike.

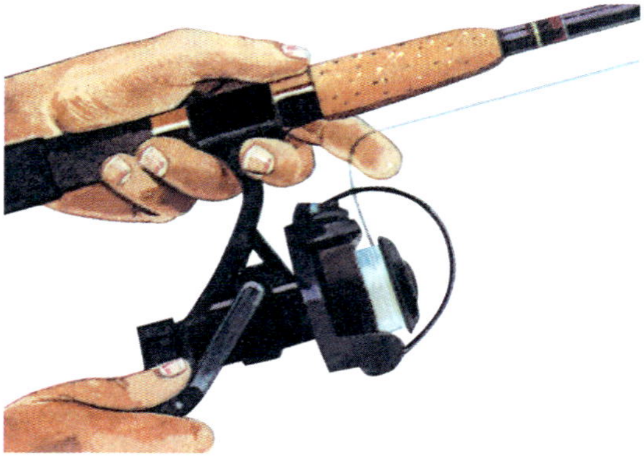

reel

a	cat	ō	go	ʉ	fur	ə =	a *in* ago
ā	ape	ô	law, for	ch	chin		e *in* agent
ä	cot, car	o͝o	look	sh	she		i *in* pencil
e	ten	o͞o	tool	th	thin		o *in* atom
ē	me	oi	oil	*th*	then		u *in* circus
i	fit	ou	out	zh	measure		
ī	ice	u	up	ŋ	ring		

reel[3] (rēl) ***noun*** **1** a frame or spool on which film, fishing line, wire, or some other material is wound. **2** the amount of movie film, wire, or other material that a reel usually holds [She used a whole *reel* of film on the birthday party.]
verb to wind on a reel.
—reel in to pull in by winding a line on a reel [He *reeled in* a ten-pound salmon.] **—reel off** to say or write easily or quickly [She *reeled off* a long list of names.]
reel • ***noun,*** *plural* **reels** • ***verb*** **reeled, reeling**
● The words **reel** and **real** sound alike.

reelect (rē′i lekt′) ***verb*** to elect again [He was *reelected* for another two years.]
re·e·lect • ***verb*** **reelected, reelecting**

reentry or **re-entry** (rē en′trē) ***noun*** the act of coming back into the earth's atmosphere [The spacecraft's *reentry* was right on schedule.]
re·en·try or **re-entry** • ***noun,*** *plural* **reentries** or **re-entries**

ref (ref) ***noun*** *a short form of* **referee**.
ref • ***noun,*** *plural* **refs**

refer (rē fur′) ***verb*** **1** to speak of or call attention to; mention [You seldom *refer* to your injury.] **2** to go to for facts or help [We had to *refer* to the map several times.] **3** to tell to go to a certain person or place for help, service, or information [Our neighbor *referred* me to a good doctor.]
re·fer • ***verb*** **referred, referring**

referee (ref ə rē′) ***noun*** a person who makes sure that the rules are followed in certain sports and games.
verb to act as a referee for [How many people *referee* a football game?]
ref·er·ee • ***noun,*** *plural* **referees** • ***verb*** **refereed, refereeing**

reference (ref′ər əns *or* ref′rəns) ***noun*** **1** the act or fact of referring; a mention [They made no *reference* to the accident.] **2** the fact of having to do with; relation; connection [I am writing in *reference* to your letter.] **3** a reference book or other source that gives information [Look in the encyclopedia and other *references*.] **4** a person who can tell about another person's character or ability to do a job or give some other information.
ref·er·ence • ***noun,*** *plural for senses 1, 3, and 4 only* **references**

reference book ***noun*** a book that contains organized information or useful facts about a particular subject. Dictionaries and encyclopedias are reference books.
reference book • ***noun,*** *plural* **reference books**

refill (rē fil′ *for v.;* rē′fil *for n.*) ***verb*** to fill again.
noun an amount or part of something that replaces an amount or part that has been used up [a free *refill* of a soft drink].
re·fill • ***verb*** **refilled, refilling** • ***noun,*** *plural* **refills**

refine (rē fīn′) ***verb*** to remove dirt or other matter that is not wanted; make pure [Special equipment is used to *refine* crude oil.]
re·fine • ***verb*** **refined, refining**

refinery (rē fīn′ər ē) ***noun*** a place where some raw material, such as oil or sugar cane, is refined or purified.
re·fin·er·y • ***noun,*** *plural* **refineries**

reflect (rē flekt′) ***verb*** **1** to throw back light, heat, or sound [A polished metal surface *reflects* both light and heat.] **2** to give back an image of [The calm lake *reflected* the trees on the shore.] **3** to bring blame or doubt: used with *on* [Not paying the money back will *reflect* on your honesty.] **4** to think seriously: used with *on* [You should *reflect* on your past mistakes.] —Look for the WORD CHOICES box at the entry **consider**.
re·flect • ***verb*** **reflected, reflecting**

reflection (rē flek′shən) ***noun*** **1** the fact of heat, light, or sound being reflected [An echo is caused by the *reflection* of sound off some surface.] **2** something that is reflected from a surface such as a mirror; image [I saw my *reflection* in a mirror.] **3** serious thought or careful study [After much *reflection*, she began to write.] **4** a remark or an action that brings blame or doubt [That joke was not meant as a *reflection* on your skill.]
re·flec·tion • ***noun,*** *plural for senses 1, 2, and 4 only* **reflections**

reflector (rē flek′tər) ***noun*** an object or surface that reflects light, heat, or sound. A piece of polished metal is a good reflector of light and heat.
re·flec·tor • ***noun,*** *plural* **reflectors**

reflex (rē′fleks) ***noun*** an action of the muscles or glands that is not controlled by thinking. It happens automatically when a message is sent by the brain through the nerves.
re·flex • ***noun,*** *plural* **reflexes**

reform (rē fôrm′) ***verb*** **1** to make better by getting rid of faults or defects; correct [The

union officials promised to *reform* working conditions in the factory.] **2** to become better; give up one's bad ways [The outlaw *reformed* and became a useful citizen.]
noun correction of faults or evils [Each candidate promised *reforms* in the government.]
re·form • ***verb*** **reformed, reforming** • ***noun,*** *plural* **reforms**

reformation (ref′ər mā′shən) ***noun*** **1** the act of reforming. **2 Reformation** the sixteenth-century religious movement that aimed at reforming the Roman Catholic Church. It led to the formation of the Protestant churches.
ref·or·ma·tion • ***noun***

refrain (rē frān′) ***noun*** a phrase or verse that is repeated regularly in a song or poem.
re·frain • ***noun,*** *plural* **refrains**

refresh (rē fresh′) ***verb*** to make fresh again; bring back into good condition [She *refreshed* herself with a short nap. *Refresh* my memory by reading the paragraph again.] —Look for the WORD CHOICES box at the entry **renew**.
re·fresh • ***verb*** **refreshed, refreshing**

refreshments (rē fresh′mənts) ***plural noun*** food or drink or both, especially when not a full meal.
re·fresh·ments • ***plural noun***

refrigerate (rē frij′ər āt′) ***verb*** to make or keep cold [Milk will sour quickly if it is not *refrigerated*.]
re·frig·er·ate • ***verb*** **refrigerated, refrigerating**

refrigerator (rē frij′ər āt′ər) ***noun*** an appliance or room in which the air is kept very cool to keep food from spoiling.
re·frig·er·a·tor • ***noun,*** *plural* **refrigerators**

refuge (ref′yo͞oj) ***noun*** **1** shelter or protection from trouble or danger [Higher ground gave us *refuge* from the flood waters.] **2** a safe or protected place to stay [a wildlife *refuge*] —Look for the WORD CHOICES box at the entry **shelter**.
ref·uge • ***noun,*** *plural for sense 2 only* **refuges**

refugee (ref′yo͞o jē) ***noun*** a person who flees from his or her home or country to seek refuge, or a safe place to stay.
ref·u·gee • ***noun,*** *plural* **refugees**

refund (rē fund′ *for v.;* rē′fund *for n.*) ***verb*** to give back an amount paid; repay [We will *refund* the full price if you are not satisfied.]
noun **1** the act of refunding [The *refund* was taken care of right away.] **2** the amount refunded [a $20 *refund*].
re·fund • ***verb*** **refunded, refunding** • ***noun,*** *plural* **refunds**

refuse[1] (rē fyo͞oz′) ***verb*** **1** to say that one will not take something that is offered; reject [She *refused* the gift.] **2** to say that one will not give, do, or agree to something; turn down [The teacher *refused* his request to be excused. I *refuse* to go to the beach.] —Look for the WORD CHOICES box at the entry **decline**.
re·fuse • ***verb*** **refused, refusing**

refuse[2] (ref′yo͞os *or* ref′yo͞oz) ***noun*** waste; trash.
ref·use • ***noun***

regain (rē gān′) ***verb*** to get back again; recover [He *regained* his health slowly. The red car *regained* the lead in the race.] —Look for the WORD CHOICES box at the entry **recover**.
re·gain • ***verb*** **regained, regaining**

regal (rē′gəl) ***adjective*** of, like, or fit for a king or queen; royal; splendid.
re·gal • ***adjective***

regard (rē gärd′) ***verb*** **1** to think of in a certain way; consider [I *regard* them as friends.] **2** to pay attention to; show respect for [Please *regard* the feelings of others.] **3** to look carefully at; gaze upon; observe [The man *regarded* the stranger with suspicion.]
noun **1** respect and liking [She has a high *regard* for her teachers.] **2** concern; attention [She has no *regard* for their safety.] **3 regards** good wishes; greetings [Give my *regards* to your parents.]
re·gard • ***verb*** **regarded, regarding** • ***noun,*** *plural for sense 3 only* **regards**

regarding (rē gärd′iŋ) ***preposition*** having to do with; about [I wrote to them *regarding* my membership.]
re·gard·ing • ***preposition***

regardless (rē gärd′ləs) ***adverb*** anyway [We objected but they went *regardless*.]
—regardless of in spite of [*Regardless of* the cost, I'll buy it.]
re·gard·less • ***adverb***

regime or **régime** (rā zhēm′) ***noun*** a system or form of government.

a	cat	ō	go	ʉ	fur	ə = a *in* ago	
ā	ape	ô	law, for	ch	chin	e *in* agent	
ä	cot, car	o͝o	look	sh	she	i *in* pencil	
e	ten	o͞o	tool	th	thin	o *in* atom	
ē	me	oi	oil	*th*	then	u *in* circus	
i	fit	ou	out	zh	measure		
ī	ice	u	up	ŋ	ring		

re·gime or **ré·gime** • *noun, plural* **regimes** or **régimes**

regiment (rej′i mənt) *noun* a unit of soldiers, made up of two or more battalions.
reg·i·ment • *noun, plural* **regiments**

region (rē′jən) *noun* **1** a large stretch of land; an area [a mining *region* in Idaho]. **2** any area, place, or space [the lower *regions* of the sea. I have a pain in the *region* of my back.]
re·gion • *noun, plural* **regions**

register (rej′is tər) *noun* **1** a book in which a record or list of names, events, or things is kept [a hotel *register*]. **2** a device for counting and keeping a record of money and purchases [a cash *register*]. **3** an opening that can be closed to control a flow of air in a heating or cooling system.
verb **1** to keep a record of in a register [The clerk *registered* the birth of their son.] **2** to put one's name in a register [Did you *register* to vote?] **3** to show on a gauge, scale, or other device [The thermometer *registers* 32°F.] **4** to show by the face or body [He *registered* surprise at the news.]
reg·is·ter • *noun, plural* **registers** • *verb* **registered, registering**

registered nurse *noun* a nurse who has completed a required number of classes and passed an examination given by a State government.
registered nurse • *noun, plural* **registered nurses**

registration (rej′i strā′shən) *noun* the act or process of recording information in a register or record [School *registration* takes place next week.]
reg·is·tra·tion • *noun, plural* **registrations**

regret (rē gret′) *verb* to feel sorry about [I *regret* having given you the wrong information.]
noun **1** a troubled or guilty feeling about something that a person has done or not done [I have no *regrets* about sharing my last piece of pizza.] **2 regrets** a polite way of turning down an invitation [She sent her *regrets*.]
re·gret • *verb* **regretted, regretting** • *noun, plural* **regrets**

regular (reg′yoo lər) *adjective* **1** formed or arranged in an orderly way; balanced [a *regular* pattern in a fabric; a face with *regular* features]. **2** according to some rule or habit; usual [a *regular* customer. Sit in your *regular* place.] —Look for the WORD CHOICES box at the entry **usual**. **3** steady and even; not changing [A band marches to a *regular* beat.] **4** describing a verb that changes its forms in the usual way. "Walk" is a regular verb. Its forms are "walks," "walked," and "walking."
reg·u·lar • *adjective*

regulate (reg′yoo lāt′) *verb* **1** to control according to rules or a system [Laws that *regulate* traffic help to prevent accidents and traffic jams.] **2** to adjust to a particular speed, amount, or some other standard [This valve will *regulate* the heat in the furnace.]
reg·u·late • *verb* **regulated, regulating**

regulation (reg′yoo lā′shən) *noun* **1** the act of regulating something [the *regulation* of the sale of harmful toys]. **2** a rule or law that regulates, or controls [traffic *regulations*].
reg·u·la·tion • *noun, plural for sense 2 only* **regulations**

rehearsal (rē hur′səl) *noun* a performance of a play, concert, or some similar activity for practice. It prepares the players for a public performance.
re·hears·al • *noun, plural* **rehearsals**

rehearse (rē hurs′) *verb* to go through a play, speech, piece of music, or other performance before giving it in public.
re·hearse • *verb* **rehearsed, rehearsing**

reheat (rē hēt′) *verb* to heat again [Mary *reheated* the leftovers for supper.]
re·heat • *verb* **reheated, reheating**

reign (rān) *noun* a period of rule or government by a monarch [the long *reign* of the last king].
verb **1** to rule as a monarch [King Arthur *reigned* in England according to legend.] **2** to be common; be widespread [Peace *reigned* for many years.]
reign • *noun, plural* **reigns** • *verb* **reigned, reigning**

● The words **reign, rain,** and **rein** sound alike.
Not all monarchs *reign* with goodwill.
My dry garden needs a good *rain*.
The driver pulled on the left *rein*.

rein (rān) *noun* **1** a narrow strap of leather attached to each end of a horse's bit. Reins are held by the driver or rider for guiding and controlling the horse. **2 reins** a means of guiding or controlling [the *reins* of leadership].
verb to guide, control, or stop with the reins.

R

rein • *noun, plural* **reins** • *verb* **reined, reining**
● The words **rein, rain,** and **reign** sound alike.

rein

reindeer (rān′dir) *noun* a large deer found in northern regions. In some places it is tamed and used for work and as food. Both the male and the female have antlers.
rein·deer • *noun, plural* **reindeer**

reindeer

reinforce (rē′in fôrs′) *verb* to make stronger by adding something [This strong wall is made of concrete that is *reinforced* with steel bars.]
re·in·force • *verb* **reinforced, reinforcing**

reject (rē jekt′ *for v.;* rē′jekt *for n.*) *verb* to refuse to take, agree to, use, or believe [He *rejected* his parents' advice.] —Look for the WORD CHOICES box at the entry **decline**.
noun something that has been rejected.
re·ject • *verb* **rejected, rejecting** • *noun, plural* **rejects**

rejoice (rē jois′) *verb* to be or make glad or happy [We *rejoiced* at their good fortune.]
re·joice • *verb* **rejoiced, rejoicing**

relapse (rē laps′ *or* rē′laps) *noun* the act of falling back into an earlier condition, especially into illness after seeming to get better [If you don't take care of yourself, you'll have a *relapse*.]
re·lapse • *noun, plural* **relapses**

relate (rē lāt′) *verb* **1** to tell the story of [*Relate* to us what you did.] **2** to have a connection or relationship to [Proper diet *relates* to good health.]
re·late • *verb* **related, relating**

related (rē lāt′əd) *adjective* of the same family or kind [He is *related* to my mother. The horse is *related* to the zebra.]
re·lat·ed • *adjective*

relation (rē lā′shən) *noun* **1** a connection between two or more things [There is a close *relation* between a proper diet and good health.] **2** a member of the same family; relative [He is a close *relation*.] **3 relations** the dealings between people, countries, or other groups [We have good *relations* with our neighbors.]
re·la·tion • *noun, plural* **relations**

relationship (rē lā′shən ship′) *noun* **1** the condition of being related; connection [There is no *relationship* between the two events.] **2** a particular example of being related or connected [The teacher has a good *relationship* with his students.]
re·la·tion·ship • *noun, plural* **relationships**

relative (rel′ə tiv) *noun* a person of the same family by blood or by marriage.
rel·a·tive • *noun, plural* **relatives**

relax (rē laks′) *verb* **1** to make or become less firm or tense; loosen up [The body *relaxes* in sleep.] **2** to rest from work or effort [She *relaxes* by going fishing.] **3** to make or become less strict or severe [They *relaxed* the rules and let us stay up late that night.]
re·lax • *verb* **relaxed, relaxing**

a	cat	ō	go	ʉ	fur	ə = a *in* ago
ā	ape	ô	law, for	ch	chin	e *in* agent
ä	cot, car	oo	look	sh	she	i *in* pencil
e	ten	ōō	tool	th	thin	o *in* atom
ē	me	oi	oil	*th*	then	u *in* circus
i	fit	ou	out	zh	measure	
ī	ice	u	up	ŋ	ring	

relay (rē′lā *for n.;* rē′lā *or* rē lā′ *for v.*) ***noun*** a race in which each member of a team runs only a certain part of the whole distance. This race is also called **relay race**.
verb to get and pass on [He *relayed* the message to her parents.]
re·lay • ***noun,*** *plural* **relays** • ***verb*** **relayed, relaying**

release (rē lēs′) ***verb*** **1** to set free [*Release* the bird from the cage.] **2** to allow to be shown, published, or broadcast [When will you *release* the information to the reporters?]
noun the act of setting someone or something free [the *release* of animals back into the wild].
re·lease • ***verb*** **released, releasing** • ***noun,*** *plural* **releases**

relevant (rel′ə vənt) ***adjective*** having to do with the subject that is being discussed or the situation at hand; to the point [a *relevant* comment].
rel·e·vant • ***adjective***

reliable (rē lī′ə bəl) ***adjective*** capable of being trusted or depended on [an old but *reliable* car].
re·li·a·ble • ***adjective***

relic (rel′ik) ***noun*** a thing or part that remains from the past [This cannon is a *relic* of the Civil War.]
rel·ic • ***noun,*** *plural* **relics**

relief (rē lēf′) ***noun*** **1** the lessening of pain, discomfort, or worry [This salve will give *relief* from itching.] **2** something that lessens pain or worry or that gives a pleasing change [It's a *relief* to know that you're safe.] **3** help that is given to poor people or to victims of a flood or other disaster. **4** a person who takes over work or duty so that someone else can rest [When will my *relief* arrive?]
—in relief carved so as to stand out from a surface.
re·lief • ***noun***

relief map ***noun*** a map that shows the differences in height or depth of hills, valleys, and other features in an area.
relief map • ***noun,*** *plural* **relief maps**

relieve (rē lēv′) ***verb*** **1** to make less or easier [This medicine *relieves* pain and swelling. Our long talk *relieved* their fears.] **2** to free from pain, worry, or other difficulty [We were *relieved* by the improvement in our son's condition.] **3** to set free from duty or work by replacing [The guard is *relieved* every four hours.]
re·lieve • ***verb*** **relieved, relieving**

religion (rē lij′ən) ***noun*** **1** belief in, or the worship of, God or a group of gods. **2** a particular system of belief or worship that is built around God and usually including moral ideas and a philosophy of life [the Jewish *religion*].
re·li·gion • ***noun,*** *plural for sense 2 only* **religions**

religious (rē lij′əs) ***adjective*** **1** having strong belief in a religion [a *religious* person]. **2** having to do with religion [a *religious* service].
re·li·gious • ***adjective***

relish (rel′ish) ***noun*** **1** enjoyment [He ate the pear with great *relish*.] **2** *often* **relishes** pickles, olives, and similar additions to a meal to add flavor. **3** a mixture of chopped pickle and other ingredients that is served on hot dogs and hamburgers.
verb to like or enjoy [She *relished* every bite of the stew. He *relishes* a good joke.]
rel·ish • ***noun,*** *plural for senses 2 and 3 only* **relishes** • ***verb*** **relished, relishing**

relocate (rē lō′kāt) ***verb*** to move to a new location [They have *relocated* to Delaware.]
re·lo·cate • ***verb*** **relocated, relocating**

reluctant (rē luk′tənt) ***adjective*** not wanting to do something; unwilling [*reluctant* to leave].
re·luc·tant • ***adjective***

rely (rē lī′) ***verb*** to depend: used with *on* [You can *rely* on me to pick you up.]
re·ly • ***verb*** **relied, relying, relies**

WORD CHOICES

Synonyms of **rely**

The words **rely, count,** and **depend** share the meaning "to put one's trust in."

You can *rely* on Ted to be on time.
Count on me to help.
I *depend* on him for support.

remade (rē mād′) ***verb*** *past tense and past participle of* **remake**.
re·made • ***verb***

remain (rē mān′) ***verb*** **1** to stay while others go [We *remained* at home while they went to a

movie.] —Look for the WORD CHOICES box at the entry **stay**. **2** to be left [Only the walls of the old barn *remain*.] **3** to go on being; continue [She *remained* loyal to her friends.]
re·main • *verb* **remained, remaining**

remainder (rē mān′dər) ***noun*** **1** a part that is left over [I ate half of the candy and shared the *remainder*.] **2** the amount that is left over when one number is divided by another. In 20 ÷ 6 = 3, the remainder is 2. **3** the amount that is left over when one number is subtracted from another. In 3 - 2 = 1, the remainder is 1.
re·main·der • *noun, plural* **remainders**

remake (rē māk′) ***verb*** to make again or in a new way [We *remade* my coat into a jacket.]
re·make • *verb* **remade, remaking**

remark (rē märk′) ***verb*** to say or comment; to mention [He *remarked* that he was tired.]
noun something that is said briefly; a comment.
re·mark • *verb* **remarked, remarking**
• *noun, plural* **remarks**

remarkable (rē märk′ə bəl) ***adjective*** worth noticing because it is very unusual [the *remarkable* beauty of this evening's sunset]. —Look for the WORD CHOICES box at the entry **noticeable**.
re·mark·a·ble • *adjective*

remedy (rem′ə dē) ***noun*** a medicine or treatment that cures, heals, or relieves.
verb to cure, correct, or make better [A joke would *remedy* the tense situation.]
rem·e·dy • *noun, plural* **remedies**
• *verb* **remedied, remedying, remedies**

WORD CHOICES

Synonyms of **remember**

The words **remember, recall,** and **recollect** share the meaning "to bring back to mind."

I'll always *remember* her face.

Can you *recall* his name?

Do you *recollect* those happy times?

remember (rē mem′bər) ***verb*** **1** to think of again [I suddenly *remembered* I was supposed to mow the lawn.] **2** to bring back to mind by trying; recall [I just can't *remember* your name.] **3** to be careful not to forget [*Remember* to buy some milk.] **4** to mention as someone sending greetings [*Remember* me to your family.] **5** to keep in mind in giving something [Grandma *remembered* me in her will.]
re·mem·ber • *verb* **remembered, remembering**

remind (rē mīnd′) ***verb*** to cause to remember or think of [*Remind* me to go to soccer practice.]
re·mind • *verb* **reminded, reminding**

reminder (rē mīn′dər) ***noun*** a thing that helps a person remember something [The pictures were a *reminder* of their wonderful trip.]
re·mind·er • *noun, plural* **reminders**

remodel (rē mäd′əl) ***verb*** to make a room or building new or different by changing or adding parts [They *remodeled* their kitchen.]
re·mod·el • *verb* **remodeled** or **remodelled, remodeling** or **remodelling**

remorse (rē môrs′) ***noun*** a deep feeling of sorrow and guilt that a person has after doing something wrong.
re·morse • *noun*

remote (rē mōt′) ***adjective*** **1** far off or far away from a particular place [a *remote* cabin in the woods]. **2** far off or far away in time [a *remote* ancestor]. **3** slight [only a *remote* chance of winning].
re·mote • *adjective* **remoter, remotest**

remote control ***noun*** a device that can be held in the hand and is used to operate something, such as a TV set, from a distance.
remote control • *noun, plural* **remote controls**

removal (rē mo͞ov′əl) ***noun*** the act of removing or the fact of being removed [Thursday is the day for *removal* of trash on our street.]
re·mov·al • *noun*

remove (rē mo͞ov′) ***verb*** **1** to move to another place; to take away or take off [*Remove* the rugs so we can dance. He *removed* his coat.] **2** to put out from an office or position; dismiss [The treasurer was *removed* for stealing.] **3** to get rid of [The bleach *removed* the stain.]
re·move • *verb* **removed, removing**

a	cat	ō	go	ʉ	fur	ə = a *in* ago	
ā	ape	ô	law, for	ch	chin	e *in* agent	
ä	cot, car	o͝o	look	sh	she	i *in* pencil	
e	ten	o͞o	tool	th	thin	o *in* atom	
ē	me	oi	oil	*th*	then	u *in* circus	
i	fit	ou	out	zh	measure		
ī	ice	u	up	ŋ	ring		

Renaissance (ren′ə säns) the great renewal of art, literature, and learning in Europe in the 14th, 15th, and 16th centuries.
Ren·ais·sance

rename (rē nām′) ***verb*** to give a new or different name to [Ceylon was *renamed* Sri Lanka.]
re·name • ***verb*** **renamed, renaming**

render (ren′dər) ***verb*** **1** to give or present; deliver [The doctor *rendered* a bill on the first day of the month.] **2** to cause to be; make [The illness *rendered* her helpless.]
ren·der • ***verb*** **rendered, rendering**

renew (rē no͞o′ *or* rē nyo͞o′) ***verb*** **1** to make new or fresh again; restore [You can *renew* that dress by dyeing it.] **2** to begin again; start again after a break [The enemy *renewed* its attack.] **3** to give or get again for a new period of time [It is time to *renew* your subscription to the magazine.]
re·new • ***verb*** **renewed, renewing**

WORD CHOICES

Synonyms of **renew**

The words **renew, refresh,** and **restore** share the meaning "to make new or fresh again."

Renew your old car by painting it.

A short nap will *refresh* you.

They have *restored* the old house.

renewal (rē no͞o′əl *or* rē nyo͞o′əl) ***noun*** the act of renewing or something renewed [a subscription *renewal*].
re·new·al • ***noun,*** *plural* **renewals**

renovate (ren′ə vāt) ***verb*** to make new or make like new; restore [We *renovated* an old house.]
ren·o·vate • ***verb*** **renovated, renovating**

rent (rent) ***noun*** money that is paid at regular times for the use of a house, an office, or other property.
verb **1** to get the use of in exchange for the payment of money at regular times [We *rented* a car when we were on vacation.] **2** to allow the use of for the regular payment of money [She *rented* us the apartment.] **3** to be for rent [This bicycle *rents* for $5 an hour.]
—for rent available to be rented [Is your house *for rent?*]
rent • ***noun,*** *plural* **rents** • ***verb*** **rented, renting**

reopen (rē ō′pən) ***verb*** **1** to open again. **2** to begin again [They *reopened* their discussion.]
re·o·pen • ***verb*** **reopened, reopening**

Rep. *abbreviation for* Republican.

repaid (rē pād′) ***verb*** *past tense and past participle of* **repay**.
re·paid • ***verb***

repair (rē per′) ***verb*** to put into good condition again; fix or mend [He *repaired* the broken toy.]
noun **1** the act of repairing [This TV set is in need of *repair*.] **2** *usually* **repairs** work that is done in fixing something [We made *repairs* on the house.] **3** the condition that something is in [an old house in bad *repair*].
re·pair • ***verb*** **repaired, repairing** • ***noun,*** *plural for sense 2 only* **repairs**

repairman (rē per′mən) ***noun*** a person whose work is fixing things.
re·pair·man • ***noun,*** *plural* **repairmen**

repay (rē pā′) ***verb*** **1** to pay back [We *repaid* the loan.] **2** to do or give something in return [How can I every *repay* your kindness?]
re·pay • ***verb*** **repaid, repaying**

repeal (rē pēl′) ***verb*** to do away with; cancel [They *repealed* the old law.]
re·peal • ***verb*** **repealed, repealing**

repeat (rē pēt′) ***verb*** **1** to say again [Will you *repeat* that question?] **2** to say over; recite [I *repeated* the poem for my teacher.] **3** to tell to others [Don't *repeat* this secret!] **4** to do or perform again [*Repeat* the exercise.]
noun something that is repeated [The team's win was a *repeat* of last year's success.]
re·peat • ***verb*** **repeated, repeating** • ***noun,*** *plural* **repeats**

repel (rē pel′) ***verb*** **1** to drive back or away [The troops *repelled* the attack.] **2** to make feel disgusted [The odor *repelled* us.] **3** to keep out; resist [This coating of enamel *repels* water.]
re·pel • ***verb*** **repelled, repelling**

repellent (rē pel′ənt) ***adjective*** repelling in some way [a *water-repellent* jacket].
noun something that repels [an insect *repellent*].
re·pel·lent • ***adjective*** • ***noun,*** *plural* **repellents**

R

repent (rē pent′) *verb* to feel sorry for having done something wrong or for failing to do something [He *repented* his harsh words.]
re·pent • *verb* **repented, repenting**

repetition (rep ə tish′ən) *noun* the act of repeating; saying or doing something again [Avoid unnecessary *repetition* in your writing.]
rep·e·ti·tion • *noun, plural* **repetitions**

replace (rē plās′) *verb* **1** to put back in the right place [*Replace* the tools in the cabinet when you are through with them.] **2** to take the place of [Computers have *replaced* many typewriters.] **3** to put another one in the place of [I *replaced* the book that I lost.]
re·place • *verb* **replaced, replacing**

replacement (rē plās′mənt) *noun* **1** the act of replacing or the fact of being replaced. **2** a person or thing that takes the place of another [The school board hired a *replacement* when our teacher moved away.]
re·place·ment • *noun, plural for sense 2 only* **replacements**

replay (rē′plā *or* rē plā′ *for v.;* rē′plā *for n.*) *verb* **1** to play again. **2** to show an instant replay [They *replayed* the touchdown in slow motion.]
noun the same as **instant replay**.
re·play • *verb* **replayed, replaying** • *noun, plural* **replays**

replica (rep′li kə) *noun* an exact copy [a *replica* of the famous statue].
rep·li·ca • *noun, plural* **replicas**

reply (rē plī′) *verb* to answer [Did he *reply* to your letter?]
noun an answer [a *reply* to an invitation].
re·ply • *verb* **replied, replying, replies** • *noun, plural* **replies**

report (rē pôrt′) *verb* **1** to tell about something; give an account [We *reported* the theft as soon as we got home.] —Look for the WORD CHOICES box at the entry **say**. **2** to tell about something in a formal way; make an announcement [The committee *reported* on plans for the dance.] **3** to be present at a certain place; appear [*Report* for work at eight o'clock.]
noun an account of something, often one in written or printed form [a financial *report*].
re·port • *verb* **reported, reporting** • *noun, plural* **reports**

report card *noun* a written report of a student's grades that is sent to his or her parents or guardians at regular times.
report card • *noun, plural* **report cards**

reporter (rē pôrt′ər) *noun* a person who gathers news and writes about it for a newspaper, a magazine, radio, or TV.
re·port·er • *noun, plural* **reporters**

represent (rep′rē zent′) *verb* **1** to stand for; be a symbol of ["X" *represents* the number "ten" in Roman numerals.] **2** to show or picture [The artist *represented* America as a woman holding a torch.] **3** to act or speak for [She *represents* us in Congress.]
rep·re·sent • *verb* **represented, representing**

representative (rep′rē zen′tə tiv) *adjective* **1** being an example of a kind of thing; typical [This building is *representative* of modern architecture.] **2** based on or made up of elected officials [*representative* government].
noun **1** a typical example [The automobile is a good *representative* of modern technology.] **2** a person who is chosen to act or speak for others [She is our *representative* on the committee.] **3** *also* **Representative** a member of the lower house in Congress or in a State legislature.
rep·re·sent·a·tive • *adjective* • *noun, plural* **representatives**

reproduce (rē prə do͞os′ *or* rē prə dyo͞os′) *verb* **1** to have offspring [Most animals *reproduce* by fertilizing eggs.] **2** to make a copy or imitation of [Tape recorders *reproduce* sound.]
re·pro·duce • *verb* **reproduced, reproducing**

reproduction (rē′prə duk′shən) *noun* **1** the process of reproducing or being reproduced [the *reproduction* of sound by a tape recorder]. **2** a copy or imitation [a *reproduction* of a famous statue]. **3** the process by which animals and plants produce new individuals like themselves.
re·pro·duc·tion • *noun, plural for sense 2 only* **reproductions**

reptile (rep′təl *or* rep′tīl) *noun* a coldblooded animal that has a backbone and scales, and crawls on its belly or creeps on short legs. Snakes, lizards, alligators, and turtles are reptiles. The dinosaurs also were reptiles.
rep·tile • *noun, plural* **reptiles**

republic (rē pub′lik) *noun* a nation in which the citizens elect the officials who make the laws and run the government.
re·pub·lic • *noun, plural* **republics**

a cat	ō go	ʉ fur	ə = a *in* ago
ā ape	ô law, for	ch chin	e *in* agent
ä cot, car	oo look	sh she	i *in* pencil
e ten	o͞o tool	th thin	o *in* atom
ē me	oi oil	*th* then	u *in* circus
i fit	ou out	zh measure	
ī ice	u up	ŋ ring	

republican (rē pub′li kən) ***adjective*** **1** of or having to do with a republic [a *republican* form of government]. **2 Republican** belonging to or having to do with the Republican Party [a *Republican* candidate].
noun **1** a person who believes in and supports a republic. **2 Republican** a member of the Republican Party.
re·pub·li·can • ***adjective*** • ***noun,*** *plural* **republicans**

Republican Party one of the two major political parties in the U.S.

repulsive (rē pul′siv) ***adjective*** causing strong dislike or disgust; disgusting [a *repulsive* bug].
re·pul·sive • ***adjective***

reputation (rep′yo͞o tā′shən) ***noun*** what people in general think about the character of a person or thing [a *reputation* for being a good doctor].
rep·u·ta·tion • ***noun,*** *plural* **reputations**

request (rē kwest′) ***verb*** to ask or ask for [She *requested* that he shut the door. I *requested* a new desk.]
noun **1** the act of requesting [a *request* for help]. **2** something that is asked for [Will you grant our *request?*]
re·quest • ***verb*** **requested, requesting** • ***noun,*** *plural* **requests**

require (rē kwīr′) ***verb*** **1** to need [Most plants *require* the light of the sun.] —Look for the WORD CHOICES box at the entry **demand**. **2** to order, command, or insist upon [Traffic laws *require* drivers to stop at a red light.]
re·quire • ***verb*** **required, requiring**

requirement (rē kwīr′mənt) ***noun*** something that is needed or demanded [Vitamins are a *requirement* for a healthful diet. Does she meet the *requirements* for the job?]
re·quire·ment • ***noun,*** *plural* **requirements**

rerun (rē run′ *for v.;* rē′run *for n.*) ***verb*** to run again [We *reran* the tape to try to learn all the words to the song.]
noun **1** a showing again of a movie, TV show, or other program. **2** the movie or program that is shown again.
re·run • ***verb*** **re·ran** (rē ran′), **rerunning** • ***noun,*** *plural* **reruns**

rescue (res′kyo͞o) ***verb*** to free or save from danger, harm, or anything bad [He *rescued* three persons from the burning building.]
noun the act of rescuing.
res·cue • ***verb*** **rescued, rescuing** • ***noun,*** *plural* **rescues**

research (rē′ sʉrch *or* rē sʉrch′) ***noun*** careful, patient study in order to find out facts and principles about a subject [The clinic is conducting *research* into the causes of cancer.]
verb to do research.
re·search • ***noun*** • ***verb*** **researched, researching**

resemblance (rē zem′bləns) ***noun*** the condition or fact of being or looking alike [There is no *resemblance* between John and his brother.]
re·sem·blance • ***noun,*** *plural* **resemblances**

WORD CHOICES

Synonyms of **resemblance**

The words **resemblance, likeness,** and **similarity** share the meaning "a being or looking alike."

the *resemblance* between a diamond and a piece of crystal

his remarkable *likeness* to his brother

the strong *similarity* of her tastes to mine

resemble (rē zem′bəl) ***verb*** to be like or look like [He *resembles* his father in the way he looks and the way he thinks.]
re·sem·ble • ***verb*** **resembled, resembling**

resent (rē zent′) ***verb*** to feel bitter hurt and anger about [He *resented* my opinion of his new suit.]
re·sent • ***verb*** **resented, resenting**

resentment (rē zent′mənt) ***noun*** a feeling of bitter hurt and anger.
re·sent·ment • ***noun***

reservation (rez′ər vā′shən) ***noun*** **1** an arrangement for setting aside something such as a hotel room or plane ticket until the buyer calls for it. **2** something that is set aside in this way [I have a *reservation* for this flight to New York.] **3** public land that has been set aside for some special use [an Indian *reservation*]. **4** a lack of complete agreement; a limiting condition [He had some *reservations* about the pledge, but he signed it.]
res·er·va·tion • ***noun,*** *plural* **reservations**

reserve (rē zʉrv′) ***verb*** **1** to set apart for a special use or for a later time [It is good to

reserve part of your allowance for emergencies.] **2** to have set aside for oneself [Call the theater and *reserve* two seats.]
noun **1** something that is kept back or stored up, often for use at a later time [a bank's *reserve* of cash]. **2** the habit of keeping one's thoughts to oneself; silent manner. **3 reserves** units in the armed forces with members in civilian life who can be called up for active duty when they are needed.
—**in reserve** reserved for use at a later time.
re·serve • ***verb*** **reserved, reserving** • ***noun,*** *plural for senses 1 and 3 only* **reserves**

reserved (rē zurvd′) ***adjective*** **1** set apart for a certain person or purpose [*reserved* seats for the baseball game]. **2** keeping one's thoughts to oneself [a quiet, *reserved* person].
re·served • ***adjective***

reservoir (rez′ər vwär *or* rez′ə vôr) ***noun*** a place where water is collected and stored for use.
res·er·voir • ***noun,*** *plural* **reservoirs**

reset (rē set′) ***verb*** to set again [The doctor *reset* the broken bone. Please *reset* the clock with the correct time.]
re·set • ***verb*** **reset, resetting**

reside (rē zīd′) ***verb*** to make one's home; live [Her family *resides* in Florida.]
re·side • ***verb*** **resided, residing**

residence (rez′i dəns) ***noun*** the place where a person lives; home.
res·i·dence • ***noun,*** *plural* **residences**

resident (rez′i dənt) ***noun*** a person who lives in a place and is not just a visitor.
res·i·dent • ***noun,*** *plural* **residents**

resign (rē zīn′) ***verb*** to give up a job, membership, or other position in a group [He *resigned* as principal of the school.]
—**resign oneself** to accept something without complaining [I *resigned myself* to doing a lot of hard work on my science project.]
re·sign • ***verb*** **resigned, resigning**

resignation (rez′ig nā′shən) ***noun*** **1** the act of resigning [The students were surprised by the principal's *resignation*.] **2** a written statement that a person is resigning [She handed her *resignation* to her boss.] **3** the fact or condition of accepting something in a calm or patient way, without complaining.
res·ig·na·tion • ***noun,*** *plural for senses 1 and 2 only* **resignations**

resin (rez′in) ***noun*** a sticky substance that comes out of pine and certain other trees and plants. Natural resins are used in medicines, varnishes, and other products.
res·in • ***noun,*** *plural* **resins**

resist (rē zist′) ***verb*** **1** to fight or work against; oppose [The thief *resisted* arrest.] —Look for the WORD CHOICES box at the entry **oppose**. **2** to hold off; withstand [Gold *resists* rust.] **3** to refuse to give in to [He *resisted* the temptation of a fudge sundae.]
re·sist • ***verb*** **resisted, resisting**

resistance (rē zis′təns) ***noun*** **1** the act of resisting [They offered no *resistance* to the suggestion.] **2** the power to resist or withstand [My *resistance* to colds has been low.]
re·sist·ance • ***noun***

resistant (rē zis′tənt) ***adjective*** resisting; capable of withstanding or opposing [*fire-resistant* paint].
re·sist·ant • ***adjective***

resolution (rez ə lo͞o′shən) ***noun*** **1** something that has been decided upon [a New Year's *resolution* to work harder]. **2** the quality of being very determined or of having a fixed purpose [Don't hesitate—act with *resolution*.]
res·o·lu·tion • ***noun,*** *plural for sense 1 only* **resolutions**

resolve (rē zälv′ *or* rē zôlv′) ***verb*** **1** to decide; make up one's mind [I *resolved* to help them.] **2** to make clear; solve or explain [He is having trouble *resolving* the problem.]
noun firm purpose or determination [Her *resolve* to become a dancer has not changed.]
re·solve • ***verb*** **resolved, resolving** • ***noun***

resort (rē zôrt′) ***verb*** to turn for help [He *resorted* to threats in order to get his way.]
noun **1** a place where many people go for fun or a vacation [a winter *resort* for skiing]. **2** a person or thing that one turns to for help [He is our last *resort* for a loan.]
re·sort • ***verb*** **resorted, resorting** • ***noun,*** *plural* **resorts**

resound (rē zound′) ***verb*** **1** to echo or be filled with sound [The auditorium *resounded* with music.] **2** to make a loud, echoing sound [His laughter *resounded* through the room.]
re·sound • ***verb*** **resounded, resounding**

a cat	ō go	u fur	ə = a *in* ago
ā ape	ô law, for	ch chin	e *in* agent
ä cot, car	o͝o look	sh she	i *in* pencil
e ten	o͞o tool	th thin	o *in* atom
ē me	oi oil	*th* then	u *in* circus
i fit	ou out	zh measure	
ī ice	u up	ŋ ring	

resource (rē′sôrs *or* rē sôrs′) ***noun*** something that is available to take care of a need [Oil is an important natural *resource*.]
re·source • ***noun,*** *plural* **resources**

resourceful (rē sôrs′fəl) ***adjective*** skillful at solving problems or getting out of trouble [Jane is a *resourceful* girl.]
re·source·ful • ***adjective***

respect (rē spekt′) ***verb*** **1** to have a high opinion of or show that one has a high opinion of [We *respect* wise and good people.] **2** to be thoughtful about or careful with; have regard for [Be sure to *respect* other people's rights.] ***noun*** **1** a feeling of honor or polite regard [We have great *respect* for our grandmother.] **2** concern or care [She had *respect* for our feelings.] **3 respects** a polite show of respect [Let's pay our *respects* to our hostess before we leave.] **4** a particular point or detail [In that *respect* he's wrong.] **5** relation or reference [With *respect* to this problem, there is nothing I can do.]
re·spect • ***verb*** **respected, respecting** • ***noun, plural for senses 3 and 4 only*** **respects**

respectable (rē spek′tə bəl) ***adjective*** **1** having a good reputation; decent, proper, or correct —Look for the WORD CHOICES box at the entry **good**. **2** fairly good in quality, size, or amount; good enough [a *respectable* score for an amateur player].
re·spect·a·ble • ***adjective***

respectful (rē spekt′fəl) ***adjective*** feeling or showing respect; polite.
re·spect·ful • ***adjective***

respective (rē spek′tiv) ***adjective*** of or for each one separately [They went their *respective* ways.]
re·spec·tive • ***adjective***

respectively (rē spek′tiv lē) ***adverb*** in regard to each one in the order in which they are named [The first and second prizes went to Alicia and Carl, *respectively*.]
re·spec·tive·ly • ***adverb***

respell (rē spel′) ***verb*** to spell a word in a different way, using special symbols to show how it is pronounced [In this dictionary the word "eat" is *respelled* "(ēt)."]
re·spell • ***verb*** **respelled, respelling**

respiration (res′pər ā′shən) ***noun*** the act or process of breathing.
res·pi·ra·tion • ***noun***

respiratory (res′pər ə tôr′ē) ***adjective*** having to do with breathing or with the organs of the body that are used in breathing.
res·pi·ra·to·ry • ***adjective***

respiratory system ***noun*** the system of organs that is involved in breathing. In human beings this system extends from the air passages in the nose down to the lungs.
respiratory system • ***noun,*** *plural* **respiratory systems**

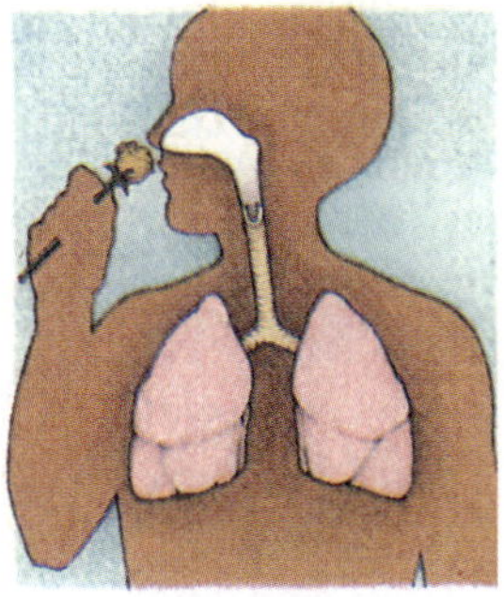

respiratory system

respond (rē spänd′) ***verb*** **1** to answer; to reply [You didn't *respond* to my question.] **2** to have a good reaction [His infection is *responding* to treatment.]
re·spond • ***verb*** **responded, responding**

response (rē späns′) ***noun*** something that is said or done in answer; a reply [I wrote them a letter but got no *response*.]
re·sponse • ***noun,*** *plural* **responses**

responsibility (rē spän′si bil′i tē) ***noun*** **1** the condition of being responsible [He took *responsibility* for the mistake.] **2** a thing or person to be taken care of or looked after [The care of our dog is my *responsibility*.]
re·spon·si·bil·i·ty • ***noun, plural for sense 2 only*** **responsibilities**

responsible (rē spän′si bəl) ***adjective*** **1** expected to take care of something or do something [I am *responsible* for mowing the lawn.] **2** deserving the credit or blame [All of us are *responsible* for our own actions.] **3** having to do with important duties [a *responsible* job]. **4** able to be trusted or depended upon [a *responsible* person].
re·spon·si·ble • ***adjective***

rest
Musical rests

rest[1] (rest) ***noun*** **1** the act or a period of not using any energy but just being quiet and at ease, especially after working or being active

[The workers stopped for a brief *rest.*] **2** freedom from worry, trouble, or pain; quiet; peace of mind [The patient needs plenty of *rest.*] **3** the condition of being still, or not moving [Her golf ball came to *rest* near the hole.] **4** a thing or device for holding something up; a support [a *headrest*]. **5** a pause between musical notes that is written into the music.
verb **1** to stop work or other activity in order to refresh oneself, by sleeping or relaxing [He likes to *rest* after a tennis game.] **2** to give rest to; refresh with rest [He *rested* his horse.] **3** to support or be supported; to lay or lie [*Rest* your head on the pillow. The hoe *rested* against the fence.] **4** to stay or be fixed [His eyes *rested* on the picture.]
rest • ***noun,*** *plural for senses 1, 4, and 5 only* **rests** • ***verb*** **rested, resting**
● The words **rest** and **wrest** sound alike.
Let the horse *rest* awhile.
She gave me the *rest* of the ice cream.
She tried to *wrest* the toy from him.

rest[2] (rest) ***noun*** **1** the part that is left over; remainder [Eat what you want and save the *rest* for later.] **2** [*used with a plural verb*] those that are left; the others [We are going, but the *rest* are staying.]
verb to go on being; remain [*Rest* assured that I'll be here.]
rest • ***noun*** • ***verb*** **rested, resting**
● The words **rest** and **wrest** sound alike.

restaurant (res′tər änt) ***noun*** a place where meals can be bought and eaten.
res·tau·rant • ***noun,*** *plural* **restaurants**

restful (rest′fəl) ***adjective*** **1** full of rest or letting a person rest [a *restful* vacation]. **2** quiet; peaceful [*restful* music].
rest·ful • ***adjective***

restless (rest′ləs) ***adjective*** **1** without rest or not giving rest [I spent a *restless* night worrying.] **2** unable to rest; moving about in an uneasy way [The animals are *restless* in the barn because of the thunderstorm.]
rest·less • ***adjective***

restore (rē stôr′) ***verb*** **1** to bring back to an earlier or normal condition [Rest and good medical care *restored* her health.] —Look for the WORD CHOICES box at the entry **renew**. **2** to put back into a place, position, or rank [They *restored* the king to power.]
re·store • ***verb*** **restored, restoring**

restrain (rē strān′) ***verb*** to hold back; keep under control [You can *restrain* that dog by using a leash.]
re·strain • ***verb*** **restrained, restraining**

restrict (rē strikt′) ***verb*** to keep within certain limits; confine or limit [We should *restrict* the amount of fat in the foods we eat.]
re·strict • ***verb*** **restricted, restricting**

restriction (rē strik′shən) ***noun*** a rule, condition, or other thing that restricts or limits [Certain *restrictions* apply to weekend travel.]
re·stric·tion • ***noun,*** *plural* **restrictions**

restroom (rest′ro͞om) ***noun*** a room in a public building that has toilets and sinks.
rest·room • ***noun,*** *plural* **restrooms**

result (rē zult′) ***noun*** anything that is caused by something else; an effect or outcome [The juggler's skill is the *result* of practice.]
verb **1** to happen because of something else [Floods may *result* from heavy rains.] **2** to end as a result [The argument *resulted* in a fight.]
re·sult • ***noun,*** *plural* **results**
• ***verb*** **resulted, resulting**

resume (rē zo͞om′ *or* rē zyo͞om′) ***verb*** **1** to take or occupy again [We *resumed* our seats after the intermission.] **2** to begin again; continue [The baseball game will *resume* when the rain stops.]
re·sume • ***verb*** **resumed, resuming**

WORD HISTORY

retail

We get **retail** from a 600-year-old English word that comes from a French word that means "to cut up in parts." The person in a **retail** business buys a large portion of goods from a person in a wholesale business, who sells the "whole" amount. Then the person in the **retail** business divides, or "cuts," that large amount into units to sell to individual customers.

retail (rē′tāl) ***noun*** the sale of goods or products in small amounts to the people who will actually use them, not to people who will sell

a cat	ō go	ʉ fur	ə = a *in* ago
ā ape	ô law, for	ch chin	e *in* agent
ä cot, car	o͝o look	sh she	i *in* pencil
e ten	o͞o tool	th thin	o *in* atom
ē me	oi oil	*th* then	u *in* circus
i fit	ou out	zh measure	
ī ice	u up	ŋ ring	

them again at a profit.
re·tail • *noun*

retain (rē tān′) *verb* **1** to keep or hold [He *retained* a firm grip on the rope. This oven *retains* heat well.] **2** to keep in mind; remember [She *retains* what she reads.]
re·tain • *verb* **retained, retaining**

retainer (rē tān′ər) *noun* a device that holds teeth in place after they have been straightened by braces.
re·tain·er • *noun, plural* **retainers**

retina (ret′n ə) *noun* the inner layer of the lining of the eyeball. It is made up of special cells that react to light. The image that is picked up by the lens of the eye is formed on the retina.
ret·i·na • *noun, plural* **retinas**

retire (rē tīr′) *verb* **1** to give up a job, business, or career, especially because of getting older [Dr. Miller is 84, but he refuses to *retire*.] **2** to go to bed [He *retired* very early tonight.] **3** to end the batting turn of [Our pitcher *retired* three batters in a row and *retired* the other side.]
re·tire • *verb* **retired, retiring**

retouch (rē tuch′) *verb* to change some of the details of something, in order to make it look better [They *retouched* the actor's photograph.]
re·touch • *verb* **retouched, retouching**

retreat (rē trēt′) *noun* **1** the act of going back or backward during an attack [The enemy was in full *retreat*.] **2** a signal for a retreat [The bugle sounded the *retreat*.] **3** a safe, quiet place [The cabin was our *retreat* in the woods.]
verb to go back; withdraw [The bear *retreated* from the camp when it saw the dog.]
re·treat • *noun, plural* **retreats**
• *verb* **retreated, retreating**

retrieve (rē trēv′) *verb* **1** to find and bring back [The dog *retrieved* the ball.] **2** to get back; recover [He *retrieved* the kite from the tree.] —Look for the WORD CHOICES box at the entry **recover**. **3** to get back information that is stored in a computer's files.
re·trieve • *verb* **retrieved, retrieving**

retriever (rē trēv′ər) *noun* a dog that is trained to retrieve game in hunting.
re·triev·er • *noun, plural* **retrievers**

retrorocket or **retro-rocket** (re′trō räk′ət) *noun* a small rocket on a spacecraft, used to help the spacecraft reduce speed. It fires in a direction opposite to the direction in which the spacecraft is flying.
ret·ro·rock·et or **ret·ro-rock·et** • *noun, plural* **retrorockets** or **retro-rockets**

return (rē turn′) *verb* **1** to go back or come back [When did you *return* from your trip?] **2** to bring, send, carry, or put back [Our neighbor *returned* the ladder.] **3** to pay back by doing the same [We *returned* their favor.] **4** to report back [The jury *returned* a verdict of "not guilty."]
noun **1** the act of coming back or going back [the *return* of summer]. **2** the act of bringing, sending, putting, or paying back. **3** something returned [There were a lot of *returns* on this merchandise.] **4** *often* **returns** an amount that is received as profit. **5** an official report [an income tax *return;* election *returns* from all counties].
—**in return** in exchange; as a return.
re·turn • *verb* **returned, returning** • *noun, plural for senses 3, 4, and 5 only* **returns**

returnable (rē tur′nə bəl) *adjective* capable of being returned [*returnable* pop bottles].
noun a glass bottle or other container for which the buyer pays a small extra amount. This money is given back when the buyer returns the empty container so that it can be used again.
re·turn·a·ble • *adjective* • *noun, plural* **returnables**

reunion (rē yo͞on′yən) *noun* a gathering of persons who have been apart [a *reunion* of the class that graduated in 1985].
re·un·ion • *noun, plural* **reunions**

reunite (rē′yo͞o nīt′) *verb* to bring or come together again [The States were *reunited* after the Civil War.]
re·u·nite • *verb* **reunited, reuniting**

reusable (rē yo͞o′zə bəl) *adjective* capable of being used again [These plastic cups are *reusable*.]
re·us·a·ble • *adjective*

reuse (rē yo͞oz′) *verb* to use again or in a different way [You can *reuse* that plastic glass by starting flower seeds in it.]
re·use • *verb* **reused, reusing**

reveal (rē vēl′) *verb* **1** to make known [The map *revealed* the secret location of the buried treasure.] **2** to show [She took off her hat, *revealing* her red hair.]
re·veal • *verb* **revealed, revealing**

revelation (rev ə lā′shən) *noun* something that is revealed or made known [His bad man-

R

ners were a great *revelation* to her.]
rev·e·la·tion • *noun, plural* **revelations**

revenge (rē venj′) *noun* **1** the act of doing harm or evil in return for harm or evil that has been done. **2** a wish to do this. **3** what is done in the act of revenge.
re·venge • *noun*

revenue (rev′ə no͞o *or* rev′ə nyo͞o) *noun* **1** money that is taken in by a business or company. **2** the income of a government, mainly in the form of taxes.
rev·e·nue • *noun, plural* **revenues**

Revere (rē vir′), **Paul** (pôl) 1735-1818; American silversmith and patriot who rode at night to tell the colonists that British troops were coming.
Re·vere, Paul

reverence (rev′ər əns *or* rev′rəns) *noun* great love and respect for something holy or for a great person.
rev·er·ence • *noun*

reverse (rē vurs′) *adjective* **1** turned backward or upside down; opposite in position or direction [the *reverse* side of a piece of cloth; in *reverse* order]. **2** causing a car or other vehicle to move backward [a *reverse* gear].
noun **1** the opposite [He said "Yes," but he meant just the *reverse*.] **2** the back side [the *reverse* of the rare coin]. **3** a reverse gear [Shift into *reverse*.]
verb **1** to turn backward, upside down, or inside out [*Reverse* the vest and wear the other side out.] **2** to change to the opposite, or to something completely different [I *reversed* my opinion on hearing his side of the story.] **3** to go or cause to go in an opposite direction.
re·verse • *adjective* • *noun, plural for sense 2 only* **reverses** • *verb* **reversed, reversing**

review (rē vyo͞o′) *verb* **1** to go over or study again [I *reviewed* my math before the test.] **2** to think back on [He *reviewed* the events that led to their fight.] **3** to inspect or examine in an official way [The general *reviewed* his troops.] **4** to write or give a critical account of something such as a book, play, or concert [She *reviews* movies for our local newspaper.]
noun **1** the act of reviewing [a *review* of the week's events]. **2** a critical report of a book, play, or other work or performance [The *review* of the play was good.] **3** an official inspection of soldiers or ships.
re·view • *verb* **reviewed, reviewing** • *noun, plural* **reviews**

revise (rē vīz′) *verb* **1** to read with care and make needed changes in order to make better or bring up to date [They *revised* the history book.] **2** to think about and change [I *revised* my opinion of the new teacher.]
re·vise • *verb* **revised, revising**

revision (rē vizh′ən) *noun* **1** the act or work of revising [A chapter was added in the *revision* of the book.] **2** something that has been revised [This *revision* of the geography book has more pictures.]
re·vi·sion • *noun, plural* **revisions**

revive (rē vīv′) *verb* **1** to bring back or come back to life or to a conscious condition [The doctor *revived* the patient who had stopped breathing.] **2** to bring back or come back to a healthy, active condition [A cool shower *revives* me after a hot day.] **3** to bring back or show again, or to make popular again [That radio station is trying to *revive* old songs from the 1950's.]
re·vive • *verb* **revived, reviving**

revolt (rē vōlt′) *noun* the act of rising up against the government or other authority; rebellion.
verb **1** to rise up against the government or other authority; rebel. **2** to fill with disgust [The sight *revolted* her.]
re·volt • *noun, plural* **revolts**
• *verb* **revolted, revolting**

revolution (rev ə lo͞o′shən) *noun* **1** the overthrow of a government, with another government taking its place [The American *Revolution* put an end to British rule.] **2** a complete change of any kind [The telephone caused a *revolution* in communication.] **3** the act of revolving; movement in an orbit [the *revolution* of the moon around the earth]. **4** a turning motion of an object on a center or axis; rotation. **5** one complete turn [The record turntable makes 45 *revolutions* per minute.]
rev·o·lu·tion • *noun, plural for senses 1, 2, and 5 only* **revolutions**

revolutionary (rev′ə lo͞o′shən er′ē) *adjective* **1** of, causing, or carrying on a revolution against a government [a *revolutionary* army]. **2** bringing about very great change [The automobile was a *revolutionary* invention.]
rev·o·lu·tion·ar·y • *adjective*

a	cat	ō	go	ʉ	fur	ə = a *in* ago	
ā	ape	ô	law, for	ch	chin	e *in* agent	
ä	cot, car	oo	look	sh	she	i *in* pencil	
e	ten	o͞o	tool	th	thin	o *in* atom	
ē	me	oi	oil	*th*	then	u *in* circus	
i	fit	ou	out	zh	measure		
ī	ice	u	up	ŋ	ring		

Revolutionary War the war in which the American colonies won their independence from England. It lasted from 1775 to 1783.

revolve (rē välv′ *or* rē vôlv′) ***verb*** **1** to move in a circle or orbit around something [The earth *revolves* around the sun.] —Look for the WORD CHOICES box at the entry **turn**. **2** to turn around, in the way that a wheel does on its axle; rotate.
re·volve • ***verb*** **revolved, revolving**

revolver (rē väl′vər *or* rē vôl′vər) ***noun*** a pistol with a revolving section that holds several bullets. The gun can fire the bullets one at a time without being loaded after each shot.
re·volv·er • ***noun, plural*** **revolvers**

revolving door ***noun*** a door that has three to five panels set upright around a center pole. A person who is using the door turns it around by pushing on one of the panels.
revolving door • ***noun, plural*** **revolving doors**

reward (rē wôrd′) ***noun*** **1** something that is given in return, especially for good work or a good deed [a *reward* for her honesty]. **2** money that is offered for some kind of help [I'm offering a *reward* for the return of my wallet.]
verb to give a reward to.
re·ward • ***noun, plural*** **rewards**
• ***verb*** **rewarded, rewarding**

reword (rē wurd′) ***verb*** to put into other words [You must *reword* that sentence to make it clearer.]
re·word • ***verb*** **reworded, rewording**

rhinestone (rīn′stōn) ***noun*** an artificial gem that is made of glass and shaped to look like a diamond.
rhine·stone • ***noun, plural*** **rhinestones**

rhino (rī′nō) ***noun*** *a short form of* **rhinoceros**.
rhi·no • ***noun, plural*** **rhinos**

rhinoceros

rhinoceros (rī näs′ər əs) ***noun*** a large animal with a thick skin and one or two horns on its snout. Rhinoceroses are found in Africa and Asia.
rhi·noc·er·os • ***noun, plural*** **rhinoceroses**

STATE MAP

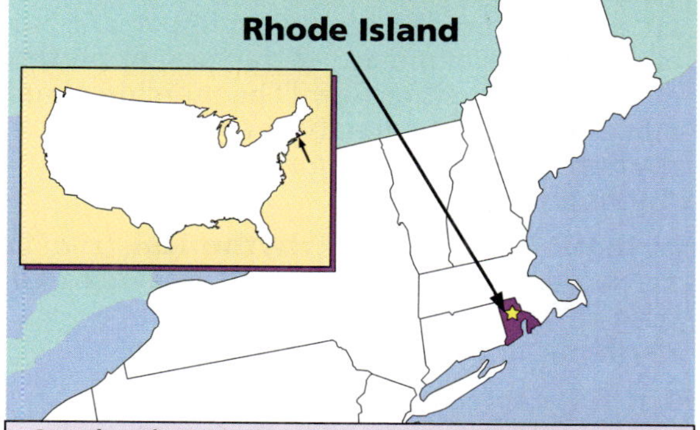

Statehood: 1790, the 13th state • **Capital:** Providence

Rhode Island (rōd ī′lənd) a New England State of the U.S. Its capital is Providence. Abbreviated **RI** or **R.I.**

rhododendron (rō də den′drən) ***noun*** an evergreen shrub or small tree that bears clusters of pink, white, or purple flowers.
rho·do·den·dron • ***noun, plural*** **rhododendrons**

rhododendron

rhombus (räm′bəs) ***noun*** a flat figure that has four equal sides and, usually, no right angles.
rhom·bus • ***noun, plural*** **rhombuses**

rhubarb (ro͞o′bärb) ***noun*** the long, reddish or green stalks of a low-growing plant with very large leaves. The stalks are eaten cooked in desserts, but the leaves are poisonous.
rhu·barb • ***noun***

rhyme (rīm) ***noun*** **1** the sameness in sound of the ends of words. Rhyme is often used at the ends of lines of poetry. **2** a word that has the same end sound as another. "Glassy" is a rhyme for "sassy." **3** a poem that uses end sounds like this.
verb **1** to have the same end sound; form a

rhyme ["Mild" *rhymes* with "wild."] **2** to have rhymes [Some poems do not *rhyme*.]
rhyme • *noun, plural for senses 2 and 3 only* **rhymes** • *verb* **rhymed, rhyming**

rhythm (ri*th*′əm) *noun* **1** movement or flow in which the features or parts such as sounds follow a regular pattern, with accents or beats coming at certain fixed times [The heart has an even *rhythm*. *Rhythm* is an important part of most kinds of music.] **2** the form or pattern of this movement or flow [The marching band moves to a strong, steady *rhythm*.]
rhythm • *noun, plural for sense 2 only* **rhythms**

rhythmic (ri*th*′mik) or **rhythmical** (ri*th*′mi kəl) *adjective* having rhythm or having to do with rhythm.
rhyth·mic or **rhyth·mi·cal** • *adjective*

RI or **R.I.** *abbreviation for* Rhode Island.

rib (rib) *noun* **1** any one of the curved bones that are attached to the backbone and reach around to form the chest. The human body has twelve pairs of these bones. **2** a raised ridge in cloth or knitted material. **3** a long piece like a rib that is used to form a frame of some kind [the *ribs* of an umbrella].
rib • *noun, plural* **ribs**

ribbon (rib′ən) *noun* **1** a narrow strip of velvet or other material, for tying things or for decoration. **2** a strip of something that is like a ribbon in some way [a typewriter *ribbon*].
rib·bon • *noun, plural* **ribbons**

rice (rīs) *noun* the seeds, or grains, of a kind of grass that is grown in warm climates. Rice is eaten cooked. It is a very important food.

WORD CHOICES

Synonyms of rich

Many words share the meaning "having much money."

opulent	wealthy	well-to-do
prosperous	well-off	

rich (rich) *adjective* **1** having wealth; owning much money or property. **2** having much of something; well supplied [Tomatoes are *rich* in vitamin C.] **3** full of fats, or full of fats and sugar [*rich* foods]. **4** full, deep, and brilliant [a *rich* voice; a *rich* blue color]. **5** capable of producing much; fertile [*rich* soil].
—**the rich** wealthy people as a group.
rich • *adjective* **richer, richest**

riches (rich′əz) *plural noun* much money or property; wealth [The emperor possessed great *riches*.]
rich·es • *plural noun*

Richmond (rich′mənd) the capital of Virginia.
Rich·mond

Richter scale (rik′tər) *noun* a scale for measuring how strong an earthquake is. The scale has graded steps beginning with 1. An earthquake measuring 3 is about 10 times stronger than one measuring 2. The strongest earthquakes ever recorded measured 8.9.
Rich·ter scale • *noun*

rickety (rik′ət ē) *adjective* weak and shaky; not firm [a *rickety* old barn].
rick·e·ty • *adjective*

rickshaw (rik′shô *or* rik′shä) *noun* a small carriage with two wheels that is pulled by one or two people. It once was used a great deal in some countries of Asia.
rick·shaw • *noun, plural* **rickshaws**

rid (rid) *verb* to clear or free of something that is not wanted [*Rid* your room of all this clutter.]
—**get rid of** to do away with.
rid • *verb* **rid** or **ridded, ridding**

riddance (rid′ns) *noun used mainly in the phrase* **good riddance!,** I am glad to be rid of this!
rid·dance • *noun*

ridden (rid′n) *verb past participle of* **ride**.
rid·den • *verb*

riddle[1] (rid′əl) *noun* a puzzle in the form of a question or statement with a tricky meaning or answer that is hard to guess. For example: "What has four wheels and flies?" "A garbage truck."
rid·dle • *noun, plural* **riddles**

riddle[2] (rid′əl) *verb* to make full of holes [The apples were *riddled* with worm holes.]
rid·dle • *verb* **riddled, riddling**

ride (rīd) *verb* **1** to sit on and make move along [We *rode* horses on the farm. I *ride* my

a cat	ō go	ʉ fur	ə = a *in* ago
ā ape	ô law, for	ch chin	e *in* agent
ä cot, car	oo look	sh she	i *in* pencil
e ten	ōō tool	th thin	o *in* atom
ē me	oi oil	*th* then	u *in* circus
i fit	ou out	zh measure	
ī ice	u up	ŋ ring	

bike to school.] **2** to move along in or on [We *ride* the bus to school.] **3** to move along in or on something [Let's *ride* today instead of walking.] **4** to be carried along on or by [The ship *rode* the waves.]
noun **1** a trip by horse, car, train, or other means [Let's go for a *ride* around the block.] **2** any of various kinds of large machine with seats, in which people can ride for fun at an amusement park or carnival [The roller coaster is a popular *ride* at the park.]
ride • *verb* **rode, ridden, riding** • *noun, plural* **rides**

Ride (rīd), **Sally** (sal′ē) 1951- ; U.S. astronaut. She was the first U.S. woman in space (1983).
Ride, Sal·ly

rider (rīd′ər) *noun* a person who rides on or in something.
rid·er • *noun, plural* **riders**

ridge (rij) *noun* **1** a top or high part that is long and narrow; a crest [the *ridge* of a roof]. **2** a range of hills or mountains. **3** a narrow, raised strip [tiny *ridges* in the sand].
ridge • *noun, plural* **ridges**

ridicule (rid′i kyo͞ol′) *noun* **1** the act of making a person or thing seem foolish by mocking, making fun, or some other means. **2** words or actions that are used to do this.
verb to make fun of or make others laugh at.
rid·i·cule • *noun* • *verb* **ridiculed, ridiculing**

ridiculous (ri dik′yə ləs) *adjective* deserving ridicule; foolish or absurd.
ri·dic·u·lous • *adjective*

rifle (rī′fəl) *noun* a gun with a long barrel. A rifle is meant to be fired from the shoulder.
ri·fle • *noun, plural* **rifles**

rig (rig) *verb* **1** to put the sails, braces, ropes, and other parts of a ship or boat into place [*Rig* the ship for sailing.] **2** to supply or equip [He *rigged* his truck with a box to carry his tools.] **3** to put together quickly [We *rigged* up a table from boards and boxes.] **4** to arrange in a way that is not honest [They *rigged* the election.]
noun **1** the way the sails and masts are arranged on a boat or ship. **2** equipment or gear [fishing *rig*]. **3** a tractor-trailer.
rig • *verb* **rigged, rigging** • *noun, plural for sense 3 only* **rigs**

rigging (rig′iŋ) *noun* the chains and ropes that are used to hold up and work the masts, sails, and other parts of a boat or ship.
rig·ging • *noun*

right

right (rīt) *adjective* **1** agreeing with what is demanded by law, justice, or conscience; just and good [Telling lies is not *right*.] **2** agreeing with the facts; correct or true [the *right* answer; the *right* time] —Look for the WORD CHOICES box at the entry **true**. **3** proper or suitable [the *right* dress for the dance]. **4** having a finished surface and meant to be seen [the *right* side of a piece of cloth]. **5** healthy, normal, or well [He doesn't look *right*.] **6** on or to the side that is toward the east when a person faces north [the *right* hand; a *right* turn].
noun **1** something that is just, lawful, proper, or correct [He knows *right* from wrong.] **2** something to which a person has a just claim under the law or by nature [All citizens have the *right* to vote.] **3** the right side [Enter the first door on the *right*.] **4** a turn toward the right side [Take a *right* at the next corner.]
adverb **1** in a straight line; directly [Go *right* home.] **2** in a correct, proper, or fair way; well [Do it *right*.] **3** exactly [*right* here; *right* now]. **4** immediately; at once [I'll come *right* over.] **5** on or toward the right hand or side [Turn *right* at the next light.]
verb **1** to put back in a proper or upright position [We *righted* the boat.] **2** to make right; to correct [He *righted* many wrongs.]
—right away at once; immediately. **—right off** at once; immediately. **—right on!** [*a slang use*] a phrase used to show approval or support.
right • *adjective* • *noun, plural for senses 2 and 4 only* **rights** • *adverb* • *verb* **righted, righting**

● The words **right, rite,** and **write** sound alike.
Turn *right* at the stop sign.
The people had their own funeral *rite*.
Write to me when you get there.

R

right angle *noun* an angle of 90 degrees. It is formed by two lines that are perpendicular to each other.
right angle • *noun, plural* **right angles**

righteous (rī′chəs) *adjective* **1** doing what is right [a *righteous* person]. **2** fair and just; right [a *righteous* action].
right·eous • *adjective*

rightful (rīt′fəl) *adjective* having or based on a just claim or lawful right [the *rightful* owner; his *rightful* share of the property].
right·ful • *adjective*

right-hand (rīt′hand′) *adjective* **1** on or to the right [Make a *right-hand* turn at the next corner.] **2** for, with, or having to do with the right hand [a *right-hand* glove]. **3** most helpful [the president's *right-hand* man].

right-handed (rīt′han′dəd) *adjective* **1** using the right hand more easily than the left [a *right-handed* person]. **2** done with the right hand [a *right-handed* throw]. **3** made for people who are right-handed [*right-handed* scissors].
right-hand·ed • *adjective*

right triangle *noun* a triangle with a right angle.
right triangle • *noun, plural* **right triangles**

right triangle

rigid (rij′id) *adjective* **1** not bending or moving; stiff and firm [a *rigid* steel bar]. **2** strict; not changing [a *rigid* rule].
rig·id • *adjective*

rile (rīl) [*an informal word*] *verb* to make angry.
rile • *verb* **riled, riling**

rim (rim) *noun* **1** an edge or border, especially the edge of something round [the *rim* of a bowl] —Look for the WORD CHOICES box at the entry **border**. **2** the metal hoop of a basketball net.
rim • *noun, plural* **rims**

rind (rīnd) *noun* a hard or firm outer layer or coating [an orange *rind;* the *rind* of a cheese].
rind • *noun, plural* **rinds**

ring[1] (riŋ) *verb* **1** to make a clear, full sound when it is hit or moved in a certain way [The bell *rang* loudly.] **2** to cause a bell to sound [*Ring* the doorbell.] **3** to make a sound something like a bell [The phone *rang*.] **4** to call for someone or announce something by ringing a bell, or in a way that is like using a bell [*Ring* for the steward. *Ring* in the new year.] **5** to seem to be full of the sound of bells [The blow to his head made his ears *ring*.] **6** to call by telephone [He *rang* her after the meeting.]
noun **1** the sound of a bell. **2** a sound that is like this, especially when it is loud and long [The actor loved the *ring* of applause.] **3** a telephone call [Give me a *ring* soon.]
—ring a bell to sound familiar [Your name *rings a bell*. Have we met before?] **—ring up 1** to record on a cash register [The clerk *rang up* the sale.] **2** to call by telephone.
ring • *verb* **rang** (raŋ), **rung** (ruŋ), **ringing** • *noun, plural for sense 1 only* **rings**
● The words **ring** and **wring** sound alike.
I thought I heard the telephone *ring*.
She wears a *ring* on her finger.
Wring out the wet dish towel.

ring[2] (riŋ) *noun* **1** a thin band of metal, plastic, or other material that is shaped like a circle and worn on the finger [a wedding *ring*]. **2** a band like this that is used to hold or fasten things [a curtain *ring*]. **3** something that is shaped like a circle [Ice crystals form the *rings* of Saturn.] **4** an enclosed space for contests, shows, or other events [a circus *ring*].
verb to make a circle around or form in a ring [Gardens *ringed* the palace.]
ring • *noun, plural* **rings** • *verb* **ringed, ringing**
● The words **ring** and **wring** sound alike.

rink (riŋk) *noun* **1** a smooth area of ice for skating or playing hockey. **2** a smooth wooden floor for roller-skating. **3** a building that has an area for skating.
rink • *noun, plural* **rinks**

rinse (rins) *verb* **1** to wash lightly by running water over or into [I *rinsed* the dishes. *Rinse* out your mouth.] **2** to remove soap or another substance from by washing in clear water [*Rinse* the clothes after washing them.]
noun the act of rinsing [Give the dishes a good *rinse*.]
rinse • *verb* **rinsed, rinsing** • *noun, plural* **rinses**

riot (rī′ət) *noun* **1** an outburst of great disorder, confusion, or violence by a crowd of people. **2** a very bright show or display [The

a cat	ō go	ʉ fur	ə = a *in* ago
ā ape	ô law, for	ch chin	e *in* agent
ä cot, car	ꝏ look	sh she	i *in* pencil
e ten	ꝏ̄ tool	th thin	o *in* atom
ē me	oi oil	*th* then	u *in* circus
i fit	ou out	zh measure	
ī ice	u up	ŋ ring	

spring flowers are a *riot* of color.] **3** [*an informal use*] a very amusing person or thing.
verb to take part in a riot [The crowd *rioted* when the game was over.]
ri·ot • ***noun,*** *plural for sense 1 only* **riots** • ***verb*** **rioted, rioting**

riotous (rī′ət əs) ***adjective*** like or having to do with a riot; wild [a *riotous* celebration].
ri·ot·ous • ***adjective***

rip (rip) ***verb*** to tear or pull apart [I *ripped* the hem of my new skirt. My sleeve *ripped* on the nail.]
noun a ripped or torn place or part.
—rip off [*a slang use*] to steal from, rob, or cheat.
rip • ***verb*** **ripped, ripping** • ***noun,*** *plural* **rips**

ripe (rīp) ***adjective*** **1** fully mature and ready to be gathered and used for food [*ripe* fruit; *ripe* grain]. **2** ready to be used [*ripe* cheese].
ripe • ***adjective*** **riper, ripest**

ripen (rī′pən) ***verb*** to get ripe; to mature [The fruit has *ripened* on the vine.]
rip·en • ***verb*** **ripened, ripening**

rip-off (rip′ôf) [*a slang word*] ***noun*** **1** an act of stealing, robbing, or cheating. **2** something that is cheap or of poor quality.
rip-off • ***noun,*** *plural* **rip-offs**

ripple (rip′əl) ***verb*** to form little waves on the surface, in the way that water does when it is stirred by a breeze.
noun **1** a little wave. **2** a movement like a little wave [*ripples* in a field of wheat]. **3** a sound like the sound of water rippling [a *ripple* of applause].
rip·ple • ***verb*** **rippled, rippling** • ***noun,*** *plural* **ripples**

Rip van Winkle (rip′ van wiŋ′kəl) a character in a story with the same name, written by Washington Irving. Rip wakens after sleeping for 20 years and finds everything changed.
Rip van Win·kle

rise (rīz) ***verb*** **1** to get up from a lying or sitting position. **2** to get up after sleeping [We usually *rise* at dawn.] **3** to move toward or reach a higher place or position [The sun is *rising*. She *rose* to be president of the company. The river *rose* above its banks.] **4** to slope or extend upward [The cliffs *rise* sharply above the river.] **5** to become greater, higher, or stronger [The temperature *rose* in the afternoon. Prices are *rising*. Her voice *rose* in anger.] **6** to puff up and become larger [The dough *rose* quickly on the warm stove.]
noun **1** the act of moving to a higher place or position; a climb [Lincoln's *rise* to the presidency was inspiring. We feared the *rise* of the flood waters.] **2** a piece of ground that is higher than the land around it [There's a good view from the top of this *rise*.] **3** the fact of becoming greater, bigger, or higher; an increase [a *rise* in prices].
—give rise to to bring about; cause.
rise • ***verb*** **rose, risen, rising** • ***noun,*** *plural for sense 3 only* **rises**

risk (risk) ***noun*** the chance of losing, failing, or getting hurt; danger [He ran into the burning house at the *risk* of his own life.]
verb **1** to lay open to risk; put in danger [You are *risking* your health by smoking.] **2** to take the chance of [Are you willing to *risk* failure?]
—at risk in danger of losing, failing, or getting hurt.
risk • ***noun,*** *plural* **risks** • ***verb*** **risked, risking**

risky (ris′kē) ***adjective*** full of risk; dangerous.
risk·y • ***adjective*** **riskier, riskiest**

rite (rīt) ***noun*** a formal act or ceremony that is carried out according to fixed rules [marriage *rites*] —Look for the WORD CHOICES box at the entry **ceremony**.
rite • ***noun,*** *plural* **rites**

• The words **rite, right,** and **write** sound alike.
They had their own funeral *rite*.
Turn *right* at the stop sign.
Write to me when you get there.

ritual (rich′o͞o əl) ***noun*** a set form or system of rites, especially in a religion.
rit·u·al • ***noun,*** *plural* **rituals**

WORD HISTORY

rival

The word **rival** comes from a Latin word for "river" or "brook." Persons living along the same river or stream would compete with each other, or be **rivals,** in using the water.

rival (rī′vəl) ***noun*** a person who tries to get the same thing as another, or a person who tries to do something better than another; competitor [They were *rivals* for the top prize.]
adjective acting as a rival or rivals; competing [*rival* businesses].

R

verb to equal or be as good as [Her paintings soon *rivaled* her teacher's.]
ri·val • *noun, plural* **rivals** • *adjective* • *verb* **rivaled** or **rivalled, rivaling** or **rivalling**

rivalry (rī′vəl rē) *noun* **1** the act of rivaling. **2** the fact of being rivals.
ri·val·ry • *noun, plural* **rivalries**

river (riv′ər) *noun* **1** a large, natural stream of water flowing into an ocean, a lake, or another large stream. **2** a large, flowing stream like a river [a *river* of lava].
riv·er • *noun, plural* **rivers**

rivet (riv′ət) *noun* a metal bolt with a head on one end that is used for fastening metal beams or plates together. The rivet is put through holes in the parts, and then the plain end is hammered into a head so it will not pull out.
verb **1** to fasten together with rivets. **2** to fix or hold in place [He was *riveted* to the spot with fear.]
riv·et • *noun, plural* **rivets** • *verb* **riveted, riveting**

rivulet (riv′yo͞o lət) *noun* a little stream; brook.
riv·u·let • *noun, plural* **rivulets**

RN or **R.N.** *abbreviation for* Registered Nurse.

roach (rōch) *noun a short form of* **cockroach**.
roach • *noun, plural* **roaches**

road (rōd) *noun* **1** a surface or way for cars and other vehicles to travel on from place to place. **2** a way or course [the *road* to success].
—**on the road** traveling [The salesman was *on the road* again.]
road • *noun, plural* **roads**
● The words **road** and **rode** sound alike.
Our baseball team is now on the *road*.
My sisters *rode* the bus for years.

roadblock (rōd′bläk) *noun* a blockade that is set up in a road to keep vehicles from going on.
road·block • *noun, plural* **roadblocks**

roadside (rōd′sīd) *noun* the side of a road.
road·side • *noun, plural* **roadsides**

roadway (rōd′wā) *noun* a road, especially the part of the surface where the vehicles travel.
road·way • *noun, plural* **roadways**

roam (rōm) *verb* to travel about with no special plan or purpose; wander [We *roamed* about the countryside. They *roamed* the streets.]
roam • *verb* **roamed, roaming**

roar (rôr) *verb* **1** to make a loud, deep, rumbling sound [A lion *roars*.] **2** to talk or laugh in a loud, noisy way [The clown made us *roar* with laughter.]
noun a loud, deep, rumbling sound [the *roar* of a jet engine].
roar • *verb* **roared, roaring** • *noun, plural* **roars**

roast (rōst) *verb* **1** to cook or be cooked with little or no liquid, in an oven or over an open fire [A chicken is *roasting* in the oven. We *roasted* hot dogs over the fire.] **2** to dry or brown with great heat [We *roasted* the peanuts and ate them.] **3** to make or become very hot [We were *roasting* under the hot sun.]
noun **1** a piece of roasted meat. **2** a piece of meat for roasting [The pork *roasts* were on sale.] **3** a picnic or other gathering where food is roasted and eaten [a steer *roast;* a corn *roast*].
adjective roasted [*roast* beef].
roast • *verb* **roasted, roasting** • *noun, plural* **roasts** • *adjective*

rob (räb) *verb* to steal from by using force or threats [They *robbed* a bank.]
rob • *verb* **robbed, robbing**

robber (räb′ər) *noun* a person who robs or steals [a bank *robber*].
rob·ber • *noun, plural* **robbers**

robbery (räb′ər ē) *noun* the act of robbing; theft.
rob·ber·y • *noun, plural* **robberies**

robe (rōb) *noun* **1** a long, loose outer garment [a *bathrobe*]. **2** a loose garment like this that a person wears as a sign of rank or office [a judge's *robe*].
robe • *noun, plural* **robes**

robin

a	cat	ō	go	ʉ	fur	ə = a *in* ago		
ā	ape	ô	law, for	ch	chin	e *in* agent		
ä	cot, car	o͝o	look	sh	she	i *in* pencil		
e	ten	o͞o	tool	th	thin	o *in* atom		
ē	me	oi	oil	*th*	then	u *in* circus		
i	fit	ou	out	zh	measure			
ī	ice	u	up	ŋ	ring			

robin (räb′in) *noun* a large songbird of North America. The male is brownish with a dull-red breast.
rob·in • *noun, plural* **robins**

Robin Hood (räb′in hood′) an outlaw in English legend who robbed the rich in order to help the poor.
Rob·in Hood

Robinson (räb′in sən), **Jackie** (jak′ē) 1919-1972; U.S. baseball player. His full name was *Jack Roosevelt Robinson.*
Rob·in·son, Jack·ie

Robinson Crusoe (räb′in sən kro͞o′sō) *see* **Crusoe**, Robinson
Rob·in·son Cru·soe

robot (rō′bät) *noun* **1** a machine that is made to look and work like a human being. **2** an automatic mechanical device for performing a certain job again and again.
ro·bot • *noun, plural* **robots**

robust (rō bust′ *or* rō′bust) *adjective* strong and healthy [a *robust* farmer].
ro·bust • *adjective*

rock[1] (räk) *noun* **1** a large mass of stone such as a cliff or peak. **2** mineral matter that is formed naturally and is part of the earth's crust. Slate and granite are kinds of rock. **3** a piece of rock or a stone, especially a large one.
rock • *noun, plural for sense 3 only* **rocks**

rock[2] (räk) *verb* **1** to move or swing back and forth or from side to side [The father *rocked* the baby's cradle. The cradle *rocked* slowly.] **2** to move or sway strongly; shake [The explosion *rocked* the nearby buildings.]
noun **1** a rocking movement. **2** *a short form of* **rock-and-roll**. **3** a form of loud popular music that developed from rock-and-roll.
rock • *verb* **rocked, rocking** • *noun*

rock-and-roll (räk′ən rōl′) *noun* a form of popular music with a strong rhythm. It developed from jazz and the blues.

rocker (räk′ər) *noun* **1** a curved piece on the bottom of a cradle or rocking chair. **2** *another name for* **rocking chair**.
rock·er • *noun, plural* **rockers**

rocket (räk′ət) *noun* a long, narrow, jet-propelled device or vehicle that is used as a signal or weapon or for fireworks, or to provide the power for spacecraft.
verb **1** to shoot ahead like a rocket. **2** to rise fast [Prices *rocketed* in July.]
rock·et • *noun, plural* **rockets**
• *verb* **rocketed, rocketing**

rocking chair *noun* a chair that is set on curved pieces of wood or on springs so that it can move back and forth.
rocking chair • *noun, plural* **rocking chairs**

rocking horse *noun* a toy horse on curved pieces of wood or on springs for a child to ride.
rocking horse • *noun, plural* **rocking horses**

rocky (räk′ē) *adjective* full of rocks [*rocky* soil].
rock·y • *adjective* **rockier, rockiest**

Rocky Mountains a mountain system in western North America. It stretches from New Mexico to Alaska. This mountain system is also called **the Rockies**.

rod (räd) *noun* **1** a straight, thin bar of wood, metal, or other strong material [a curtain *rod;* a fishing *rod*]. **2** a stick for beating someone as a punishment.
rod • *noun, plural* **rods**

rode (rōd) *verb past tense of* **ride**.
● The words **rode** and **road** sound alike.
I *rode* a horse last summer.
We pulled over to the side of the *road.*

rodent (rōd′nt) *noun* an animal that has sharp front teeth for gnawing. Rats, mice, squirrels, porcupines, and beavers are rodents.
ro·dent • *noun, plural* **rodents**

rodeo (rō′dē ō) *noun* a contest or show in which cowboys compete in tests of skill in riding horses, roping cattle, and performing other ranching tasks.
ro·de·o • *noun, plural* **rodeos**

roe (rō) *noun* fish eggs.
● The words **roe** and **row** sound alike.
Some people eat *roe.*
A *row* of elms lines our street.
He'll *row* you to shore for a fee.

rogue (rōg) *noun* **1** a tricky or dishonest person. **2** a person who likes to have fun and play tricks on other people.
rogue • *noun, plural* **rogues**

role (rōl) *noun* **1** the part that an actor takes in a play [Tonya had the queen's *role.*] **2** a function or duty that a person has [That company supplies uniforms in its *role* as team sponsor.]
role • *noun, plural* **roles**
● The words **role** and **roll** sound alike.
I'm uncomfortable with a leader's *role.*
I had a *roll* and a glass of milk.

roll (rōl) ***verb*** **1** to move by turning over and over [The dog *rolled* on the grass. They *rolled* the logs to the river.] **2** to travel or move on wheels or rollers [The car *rolled* smoothly along. *Roll* the cart over here.] **3** to move or pass in a smooth way, one after another [Waves *rolled* to the shore. The weeks *rolled* by.] **4** to wrap up or wind into a ball or tube [*Roll* up the rug.] **5** to move back and forth or from side to side [The ship *rolled* in heavy seas. Rose *rolled* her eyes.] **6** to say with a trill [*Roll* your r's when you pronounce Spanish words.] **7** to make flat or spread out by or as if by using a roller or rolling pin [*Roll* the dough for the cookies.]
noun **1** a list of names for checking who is present. **2** something that is rolled up into a ball or tube [a *roll* of stamps; a *roll* of wallpaper]. **3** bread that has been baked in a small, shaped piece. **4** a rolling motion [the *roll* of a ship on the waves]. **5** a loud, echoing sound [a *roll* of thunder]. **6** a series of light, rapid blows on a drum.
—**roll out** to spread out by unrolling [*Roll out* the rug so we can see it.]
roll • ***verb*** **rolled, rolling** • ***noun,*** *plural except for sense 4* **rolls**

● The words **roll** and **role** sound alike.
We will *roll* out the red carpet for her.
He played the *role* of Hamlet's uncle.

rollaway (rōl′ə wā) ***adjective*** having wheels underneath for easy moving and storage [a *rollaway* bed].
roll·a·way • ***adjective***

roll call ***noun*** the act or time of reading a list of names out loud to find out who is present and who is absent.
roll call • ***noun,*** *plural* **roll calls**

roller (rōl′ər) ***noun*** **1** a tube or cylinder on which something is rolled up [the *roller* of a window shade; a hair *roller*]. **2** a small wheel that is placed under something heavy to help move it more easily. **3** a heavy cylinder that is used to roll over something in order to crush, smooth, or spread it. **4** a cylinder that is covered with a fuzzy fabric, for painting walls. **5** a long, heavy wave that breaks on the shoreline.
roll·er • ***noun,*** *plural* **rollers**

Rollerblade (rōl′ər blād) ***trademark*** a kind of in-line skate.
Rol·ler·blade • ***trademark,*** *plural* **Rollerblades**

roller coaster

roller coaster ***noun*** a ride in an amusement park that has open cars moving on tracks that rise, curve, and go down in a sudden way.
roller coaster • ***noun,*** *plural* **roller coasters**

roller skates

roller skate ***noun*** a skate that has wheels on the bottom, for skating on floors and sidewalks.
roller skate • ***noun,*** *plural* **roller skates**

roller-skate (rōl′ər skāt) ***verb*** to move on roller skates.
roll·er-skate • ***verb*** **roller-skated, roller-skating**

rolling pin ***noun*** a heavy, smooth cylinder of wood or other material that is used to roll out a lump of dough and make it flat.
rolling pin • ***noun,*** *plural* **rolling pins**

roly-poly (rō′lē pō′lē) ***adjective*** short and plump; pudgy [a *roly-poly* baby].
ro·ly-po·ly • ***adjective***

a cat	ō go	ʉ fur	ə = a *in* ago
ā ape	ô law, for	ch chin	e *in* agent
ä cot, car	oo look	sh she	i *in* pencil
e ten	ōō tool	th thin	o *in* atom
ē me	oi oil	*th* then	u *in* circus
i fit	ou out	zh measure	
ī ice	u up	ŋ ring	

ROM (räm) ***noun*** a kind of computer memory that holds information that cannot be changed or erased. *ROM* is taken from the first letters of the words *read-only memory*.

Roman (rō′mən) ***adjective*** **1** of or having to do with ancient Rome, its people, or its culture [*Roman* ruins]. **2** *usually* **roman** describing the common style of printing type, in which the letters do not slant. This is roman type.
noun **1** a person born or living in ancient Rome. **2** *usually* **roman** roman type.
Ro·man • ***adjective*** • ***noun,*** *plural for sense 1 only* **Romans**

Roman Catholic ***adjective*** of or belonging to the Christian church that has the pope as its head.
noun a member of this church.
Roman Catholic • ***adjective*** • ***noun,*** *plural* **Roman Catholics**

romance (rō mans′ *or* rō′mans) ***noun*** **1** a story of love and adventure. **2** a story or poem like this from the past, with knights as the heroes. **3** love, adventure, or excitement of the kind that is found in these stories [She wishes there were more *romance* in her life.]
ro·mance • ***noun,*** *plural for senses 1 and 2 only* **romances**

Romance (rō mans′ *or* rō′mans) ***adjective*** describing any of the languages that grew out of Latin [French, Spanish, and Italian are three of the *Romance* languages.]
Ro·mance • ***adjective***

Roman Empire the empire of ancient Rome. At its peak it included western and southern Europe, Britain, and all the lands bordering the Mediterranean Sea.

Romania (rō mā′nē ə) a country in south central Europe, on the Black Sea.
Ro·ma·ni·a

Roman numerals ***plural noun*** letters of the Roman alphabet that are used as numerals. In this system, I = 1, V = 5, X = 10, L = 50, C = 100, D = 500, and M = 1000. These were the only numerals that were used in Europe until the tenth century A.D.

romantic (rō man′tik) ***adjective*** filled or having to do with romance, or love and adventure.
ro·man·tic • ***adjective***

Rome (rōm) the capital of Italy. In ancient times it was the capital of the Roman Empire.

romp (rämp) ***verb*** to play in a lively, somewhat rough way; to frolic.
noun rough, lively play.
romp • ***verb*** **romped, romping** • ***noun,*** *plural* **romps**

roof (ro͞of *or* ro͝of) ***noun*** **1** the outside top covering of a building. **2** the upper inside surface of the mouth. **3** something that is like a roof [the *roof* of a car].
roof • ***noun,*** *plural* **roofs**

roofing (ro͞of′iŋ *or* ro͝of′iŋ) ***noun*** material used for roofs.
roof·ing • ***noun***

rook (ro͝ok) ***noun*** a chess piece that can move straight ahead or to either side across any number of empty squares.
rook • ***noun,*** *plural* **rooks**

rookie (ro͝ok′ē) ***noun*** **1** a new player in a professional sport. **2** [*an informal use*] a person who is new to any job or activity.
rook·ie • ***noun,*** *plural* **rookies**

room (ro͞om) ***noun*** **1** a space inside a building that is separated by walls and doors from other spaces. **2** enough space [Is there *room* for me at the table?] **3** all of the people in a room [The whole *room* grew silent when he walked in.] **4** a chance or opportunity [There's *room* for improvement in your homework.]
verb to live in a room or rooms; to lodge [I'm *rooming* with friends.]
room • ***noun,*** *plural for senses 1 and 3 only* **rooms** • ***verb*** **roomed, rooming**

rooming house ***noun*** a house where a person can rent a room with furniture and live in it.
rooming house • ***noun,*** *plural* **rooming houses**

roommate (ro͞om′māt) ***noun*** a person with whom one shares a room or rooms.
room·mate • ***noun,*** *plural* **roommates**

roomy (ro͞om′ē) ***adjective*** having plenty of room or space [a *roomy* car].
room·y • ***adjective*** **roomier, roomiest**

Roosevelt (rō′zə velt), **Franklin D.** (fraŋk′lin) 1882-1945; the thirty-second president of the U.S., from 1933 to 1945.
Roo·se·velt, Frank·lin D.

Roosevelt (rō′zə velt), **Theodore** (thē′ə dôr) 1858-1919; the twenty-sixth president of the U.S., from 1901 to 1909.
Roo·se·velt, The·o·dore

roost (ro͞ost) ***noun*** a pole or shelf where a bird can rest or sleep; a perch.

R

verb to rest or sleep on a roost.
roost • *noun, plural* **roosts** • *verb* **roosted, roosting**

rooster (ro͞os′tər) *noun* a fully grown male chicken.
roost·er • *noun, plural* **roosters**

root[1] (ro͞ot *or* ro͝ot) *noun* **1** the part of a plant that grows into the ground. It holds the plant in place and takes water and food from the soil. **2** the part of a tooth or hair that is attached to the body. **3** a source or cause [This mistake is the *root* of our trouble.] —Look for the WORD CHOICES box at the entry **origin**. **4** a word or part of a word that is used as a base for making other words. The word "easy" is the root for the words "easily" and "uneasy."
verb **1** to start to grow by putting out roots. **2** to put firmly in place; settle [Her love of adventure was *rooted* deep in her mind.]
root • *noun, plural* **roots** • *verb* **rooted, rooting**

- The words **root** and **route** sometimes sound alike.
  Love of money is the *root* of all evil.
  Pigs *root* around for food.
  Which State *route* will get me there?

root[2] (ro͞ot *or* ro͝ot) *verb* **1** to dig up with the snout [The wild pigs *rooted* up acorns in the forest.] **2** to search by moving things about; rummage [I *rooted* through the desk drawer looking for a paper clip.] **3** [*an informal use*] to support a team or player by cheering.
root • *verb* **rooted, rooting**

- The words **root** and **route** sometimes sound alike.

root beer *noun* a sweet drink that is made of soda water and flavored with juices from the roots and bark of certain plants.

rope (rōp) *noun* **1** a thick, strong cord that is made by twisting fibers or wires together. **2** a number of things that have been strung together on a line or thread [a *rope* of pearls].
verb **1** to fasten or tie together with a rope. **2** to set off or keep apart with a rope [*Rope* off the hole in the ice.] **3** to catch with a lasso [The cowboy *roped* the steer.]
—know the ropes [*an informal use*] to know the details of a particular job. **—the end of one's rope** the end of one's strength, courage, energy, or patience [Mother was at *the end of her rope* long before vacation ended.]
rope • *noun, plural* **ropes** • *verb* **roped, roping**

rosary (rō′zər ē) *noun* a string of beads that Roman Catholics use to keep count when they say a certain series of prayers.
ro·sa·ry • *noun, plural* **rosaries**

rose[1] (rōz) *noun* **1** the sweet-smelling flower of a bush or shrub that has stems with thorns on them. The flowers usually have many petals and come in many different colors. **2** a dark pink color.
rose • *noun, plural* **roses**

rose

rose[2] (rōz) *verb past tense of* **rise**.

rosebud (rōz′bud) *noun* the bud of a rose.
rose·bud • *noun, plural* **rosebuds**

rosebush (rōz′bo͝osh) *noun* a shrub that bears roses.
rose·bush • *noun, plural* **rosebushes**

Rosh Hashana (rōsh′ hə shô′nə *or* rōsh′ hə shä′nə) *noun* the Jewish New Year. It comes in the fall.
Rosh Ha·sha·na • *noun*

rosin (räz′in) *noun* a hard, pale yellow to dark brown resin that is made from pine trees. It is rubbed on violin bows so that the hairs grip the strings better and on the hands of gymnasts to keep them from slipping. Rosin is also used to make varnish.
ros·in • *noun*

Ross (rôs), **Betsy** (bet′sē) 1752-1836; American woman who, according to tradition, made the first American flag.
Ross, Bet·sy

rosy (rō′zē) *adjective* **1** like a rose in color; red or pink [*rosy* cheeks]. **2** bright, hopeful, or cheerful [a *rosy* outlook; a *rosy* future].
ros·y • *adjective* **rosier, rosiest**

rot (rät) *verb* **1** to fall apart or spoil, because of the action of bacteria, fungi, or dampness; to decay [A dead tree will *rot*.] **2** to cause this to happen [Too much water *rots* plants.]
noun **1** the process of rotting. **2** the result of

a	cat	ō	go	ʉ	fur	ə =	a *in* ago
ā	ape	ô	law, for	ch	chin		e *in* agent
ä	cot, car	o͝o	look	sh	she		i *in* pencil
e	ten	o͞o	tool	th	thin		o *in* atom
ē	me	oi	oil	*th*	then		u *in* circus
i	fit	ou	out	zh	measure		
ī	ice	u	up	ŋ	ring		

rotting. **3** any one of the diseases that cause plants or animals to rot.
rot • *verb* **rotted, rotting** • *noun, plural for sense 3 only* **rots**

WORD CHOICES

Synonyms of **rot**

The words **rot, decay,** and **spoil** share the meaning "to change for the worse from a normal condition."

Apples were *rotting* on the ground.
Our dog's teeth began to *decay*.
Fish *spoils* quickly on hot days.

rotary (rōt′ər ē) *adjective* **1** turning around a point or axis in the middle; rotating [the *rotary* motion of a wheel]. **2** having a part or parts that rotate [a *rotary* printing press].
ro·ta·ry • *adjective*

rotate (rō′tāt) *verb* **1** to turn around a center point or axis in the way that a wheel does [The earth *rotates* on its axis.] —Look for the WORD CHOICES box at the entry **turn**. **2** to change by turns in regular order [Farmers *rotate* crops to keep the soil rich.]
ro·tate • *verb* **rotated, rotating**

rotation (rō tā′shən) *noun* **1** the act of rotating; movement around a center or axis [the *rotation* of a wheel on its axle]. **2** a series of changes in regular order [*rotation* of crops on a farm; *rotation* of duties on a ship's crew].
ro·ta·tion • *noun*

rote (rōt) *noun* a fixed or set way of doing something; routine.
—by rote by memory alone, without thought or understanding [He repeated the rules *by rote*.]
● The words **rote** and **wrote** sound alike.
Learn the multiplication tables by *rote*.
I *wrote* her a long letter.

rotor (rōt′ər) *noun* **1** the part of a motor or other machine that turns or rotates. **2** a set of large, rotating blades that lifts and moves a helicopter.
ro·tor • *noun, plural* **rotors**

rotten (rät′n) *adjective* **1** having rotted; decayed or spoiled [*rotten* apples; a *rotten* floor]. **2** wicked; not honest [*rotten* politics]. **3** [*a slang use*] very bad [a *rotten* movie].
rot·ten • *adjective* **rottener, rottenest**

rough (ruf) *adjective* **1** not smooth or level; not even [a *rough* road; *rough* fur or cloth]. **2** wild in motion or force [a *rough* sea]. **3** full of storms [*rough* weather]. **4** not quiet, mild, or gentle [*rough* play during recess; *rough* language; a *rough* temper]. **5** not having much comfort or luxury [the *rough* life of a pioneer]. **6** not finished; not worked out in detail [a *rough* sketch of the house; a *rough* estimate of the price]. **7** [*an informal use*] unpleasant or difficult [We had a *rough* time when my Dad was out of work.]
verb **1** to treat in a rough or violent way [The gangsters *roughed* up their victim.] **2** to make or shape in a rough way [He *roughed* in the windows on the sketch of the house.]
—rough it to live without comforts [We decided to *rough it* and go on a camping trip in the mountains.]
rough • *adjective* **rougher, roughest**
• *verb* **roughed, roughing**
● The words **rough** and **ruff** sound alike.
His hands are *rough* from outdoor work.
A *ruff* is a kind of high, stiff collar.

roughage (ruf′ij) *noun* coarse food or fodder that can be only partly digested but helps to move waste products through the intestines. Bran and straw are roughage.
rough·age • *noun*

roughen (ruf′ən) *verb* to make or become rough.
rough·en • *verb* **roughened, roughening**

roughly (ruf′lē) *adverb* **1** in a rough way. **2** more or less; about [*Roughly* 50 people came to the party.]
rough·ly • *adverb*

round (round) *adjective* **1** shaped like a ball, a circle, or a tube; having an outline that forms a circle or curve [The earth is *round*. Wheels are *round*. The ship has a *round* smokestack.] **2** plump; chubby [his *round* cheeks]. **3** given as a number that is not exact. For example, 20 can be a round number for 18 or 21.
noun **1** *often* **rounds** a route or course that is taken on a regular schedule [Has the guard made the *rounds* yet? Doctors in this hospital make their *rounds* early.] **2** a series of actions or events [We attended a *round* of parties in honor of our friends.] **3** a single serving of something to each person in a group [Let's have another *round* of sodas.] **4** a single shot from a gun, or from several guns that are fired together. **5** bullets or

shells for a single shot [They passed out one *round* of ammunition.] **6** a single outburst [He was greeted by a *round* of applause.] **7** a single period of action or one complete game [a *round* of golf]. **8** one of the timed periods in boxing [The champion was knocked out in the third *round*.] **9** a short song for two or more persons or groups in which each person or group begins the song at a different time.
verb **1** to make or become round [*Round* off the corners of the board.] **2** to complete; to finish: used with *out* or *off* [We *rounded* out the day with some singing at the campfire.] **3** to go around or pass by [The car *rounded* the corner.]
adverb *the same as* **around**.
preposition *the same as* **around**. In Britain, the word *round* is usually used for the meanings of *around* as an adverb and preposition.
—round about **1** in or to the opposite direction [She turned *round about*.] **2** in every direction around [There aren't many trees *round about*.] **—round up** to drive together into a group or herd [The cowboys *rounded up* the cattle.]
round • ***adjective*** **rounder, roundest** • ***noun,*** *plural* **rounds** • ***verb*** **rounded, rounding** • ***adverb*** • ***preposition***

roundabout (round′ə bout) ***adjective*** not straight or direct [a *roundabout* trip; *roundabout* answers] —Look for the WORD CHOICES box at the entry **subtle**.
round·a·bout • ***adjective***

roundhouse (round′hous) ***noun*** a building for storing and repairing locomotives. It is usually round, with a turning platform in the center.
round·house • ***noun,*** *plural* **roundhouses**

Round Table the table around which King Arthur and his knights sat.

round trip ***noun*** a trip to a place and back to the starting point.
round trip • ***noun,*** *plural* **round trips**

roundup (round′up) ***noun*** **1** the act of driving cattle together into a group, for branding or shipping. **2** the act of collecting a group of any kind. **3** a summary [a *roundup* of the local news].
round·up • ***noun,*** *plural* **roundups**

rouse (rouz) ***verb*** **1** to wake; come or bring out of sleep. **2** to stir up; excite [The bad news *roused* her anger.]
rouse • ***verb*** **roused, rousing**

rout (rout) ***noun*** **1** a confused retreat [The enemy's army was put to *rout*.] **2** a complete, crushing defeat.
verb **1** to cause to retreat in a confused way [The army *routed* the enemy's troops.] **2** to defeat completely.
rout • ***noun,*** *plural* **routs** • ***verb*** **routed, routing**

● The words **rout** and **route** sometimes sound alike.
Our loss in the big game was a *rout*.
My newspaper *route* covers four blocks.

route (ro͞ot *or* rout) ***noun*** **1** a road or course that is or has been traveled or is to be traveled [We took the scenic *route* west.] **2** a set of customers to whom a person delivers something at regular times [the mail carrier's *route*].
verb to send by a certain route [They *routed* my luggage through a city that I was not going to.]
route • ***noun,*** *plural* **routes** • ***verb*** **routed, routing**

● The words **route** and **root** sometimes sound alike.
They'll *route* traffic around the bridge.
The shovel cut into a tree *root*.
Hogs *root* around for food.

● The word **route** is also sometimes pronounced like **rout**.

routine (ro͞o tēn′) ***noun*** **1** a regular way of doing something, fixed by habit, rules, or some other cause [The *routine* of fixing breakfast can be boring.] **2** a series of steps for a dance.
adjective using or done by routine [a *routine* task].
rou·tine • ***noun,*** *plural* **routines** • ***adjective***

rove (rōv) ***verb*** to wander about; roam [We *roved* the woods.]
rove • ***verb*** **roved, roving**

row[1] (rō) ***noun*** a number of people or things that are placed in a line [a *row* of oaks; *rows* of seats].
row • ***noun,*** *plural* **rows**

● The words **row** and **roe** sound alike.
We sat in the front *row* by the stage.
He'll *row* you to shore for a fee.
Some people eat *roe*.

a	cat	ō	go	ʉ	fur	ə =	a *in* ago
ā	ape	ô	law, for	ch	chin		e *in* agent
ä	cot, car	oo	look	sh	she		i *in* pencil
e	ten	o͞o	tool	th	thin		o *in* atom
ē	me	oi	oil	*th*	then		u *in* circus
i	fit	ou	out	zh	measure		
ī	ice	u	up	ŋ	ring		

WORD CHOICES

Synonyms of **row**

The words **row, line,** and **string** share the meaning "a number of people or things positioned one after another."

a *row* of corn

a *line* of customers waiting to enter

a *string* of lights

row[2] (rō) ***verb*** **1** to move or cause to move on water by using oars [Let's *row* to shore. Let's *row* the boat all the way to that island.] **2** to carry in a rowboat [I'll *row* you across the lake.]
noun a trip in a rowboat [We are going for a *row* on the lake.]
row • ***verb*** **rowed, rowing** • ***noun***
● The words **row** and **roe** sound alike.

row[3] (rou) ***noun*** a noisy quarrel or fight; uproar or commotion.
row • ***noun, plural*** **rows**

rowboat (rō′bōt) ***noun*** a boat that is made to be moved by rowing with oars.
row·boat • ***noun, plural*** **rowboats**

rowdy (rou′dē) ***noun*** a rough, noisy person who starts fights.
adjective rough and noisy [a *rowdy* party].
row·dy • ***noun, plural*** **rowdies**
• ***adjective*** **rowdier, rowdiest**

royal (roi′əl) ***adjective*** **1** by or having to do with a king or queen [a *royal* decree; *royal* power]. **2** having to do with a kingdom or its government [the *royal* navy]. **3** like or fit for a king or queen; splendid or magnificent [a *royal* meal].
roy·al • ***adjective***

royalty (roi′əl tē) ***noun*** **1** royal persons as a group [She is a member of British *royalty*.] **2** an amount of money that is paid to someone such as an inventor, author, or composer who has allowed his or her work to be made, used, or published.
roy·al·ty • ***noun, plural for sense 2 only*** **royalties**

rpm or **r.p.m.** *abbreviation for* revolutions per minute.

RR or **R.R.** **1** railroad. **2** Rural Route.

R.S.V.P. or **r.s.v.p.** *abbreviation for* a French phrase that means "Please reply." R.S.V.P. is written in invitations when the host of a party needs to know who will be attending.

rub (rub) ***verb*** **1** to move a hand, cloth, or other thing back and forth over [*Rub* hard to make the wood shine. *Rub* the wood to make it shine.] **2** to move back and forth over something [I *rubbed* the washcloth over my face to take off the clown makeup.] **3** to move with pressure and friction [The chair *rubbed* against the wall.] **4** to spread by rubbing [*Rub* the wax on the car.] **5** to remove by rubbing [*Rub* out that mark with an eraser.]
noun the act of rubbing.
—rub down to massage. **—rub it in** [*a slang use*] to keep mentioning a mistake that someone has made.
rub • ***verb*** **rubbed, rubbing** • ***noun, plural*** **rubs**

rubber (rub′ər) ***noun*** **1** a springy substance that is made from the sap of certain tropical plants or from chemicals. It is used in making erasers, tires, waterproof material, and many other things. **2** a kind of low shoe that is made of rubber and protects regular shoes from water.
rub·ber • ***noun, plural for sense 2 only*** **rubbers**

rubber band ***noun*** a narrow band or loop of rubber that can be used to hold small objects together.
rubber band • ***noun, plural*** **rubber bands**

rubber stamp ***noun*** a device that is made of rubber with raised printing or designs on it. It is pressed onto a pad containing ink and then pressed onto paper to print dates, words, or designs.
rubber stamp • ***noun, plural*** **rubber stamps**

rubbish (rub′ish) ***noun*** something that is thrown away because it has no value or use; trash. **2** nonsense; foolish ideas or talk.
rub·bish • ***noun***

rubble (rub′əl) ***noun*** rough, broken pieces of stone, brick, or other material [the *rubble* of a demolished building].
rub·ble • ***noun***

rubdown (rub′doun) ***noun*** a massage.
rub·down • ***noun, plural*** **rubdowns**

ruby (ro͞o′bē) ***noun*** a very valuable stone that is used in jewelry. It is deep red in color.
ru·by • ***noun, plural*** **rubies**

R

rudder

rudder (rud′ər) *noun* **1** a broad, flat piece of wood or metal that is attached by hinges to the back of a boat or ship. It is used for steering. **2** a piece like this on an airplane.
rud·der • *noun, plural* **rudders**

ruddy (rud′ē) *adjective* **1** having a healthy red color [He had a *ruddy* face.] **2** red or somewhat red [the *ruddy* glow of the fire].
rud·dy • *adjective* **ruddier, ruddiest**

rude (ro͞od) *adjective* **1** without respect for others; not polite [It was *rude* of them not to thank you.] **2** rough or crude [a *rude* hut in the woods].
rude • *adjective* **ruder, rudest**

rue (ro͞o) *verb* to feel sorry because of; to regret [He *rued* his angry words.]
rue • *verb* **rued, ruing**

ruff
Left: Collar *Right: Bird's ruff*

ruff (ruf) *noun* **1** a stiff collar with tight ruffles that was worn by men and women 300 or 400 years ago. **2** a ring of feathers or fur standing out around the neck of a bird or animal.
ruff • *noun, plural* **ruffs**
● The words **ruff** and **rough** sound alike.
Shakespeare is pictured wearing a *ruff*.
Some *rough* weather is heading this way.

ruffle (ruf′əl) *noun* a strip of cloth or lace that is gathered in pleats or puckers along one edge and is used to decorate clothing.
verb **1** to fold into ruffles. **2** to disturb the smooth surface or condition of [Wind *ruffled* the pond. The bird *ruffled* its feathers.]
ruf·fle • *noun, plural* **ruffles** • *verb* **ruffled, ruffling**

rug (rug) *noun* a piece of thick, heavy fabric or an animal skin that is used to cover a floor.
rug • *noun, plural* **rugs**

rugged (rug′əd) *adjective* **1** having a surface that is not smooth or even; rough [*rugged* ground]. **2** heavy and not regular [the *rugged* features of his face]. **3** very strong or tough; sturdy [a *rugged* truck]. **4** stormy or difficult; harsh [*rugged* weather; a *rugged* life].
rug·ged • *adjective*

ruin (ro͞o′in) *noun* **1 ruins** a building, city, or area that has decayed or has been destroyed [We saw the *ruins* of the old castle.] **2** the condition of being destroyed, decayed, or rundown [The barn that was not used fell into *ruin*.] **3** great damage or destruction [It meant the *ruin* of our hopes.] **4** complete loss of money or social position [The banker faced *ruin* with courage.] **5** something that causes great damage, destruction, or loss [Gambling was the *ruin* of them.]
verb **1** to destroy or damage beyond repair [The mud will *ruin* your shoes.] **2** to cause complete loss of money or social position [Three years with little rain *ruined* the farmer. The senator was *ruined* by the scandal.]
ru·in • *noun, plural for sense 1 only* **ruins** • *verb* **ruined, ruining**

rule (ro͞ol) *noun* **1** a statement or law that is meant to guide or control the way a person acts or does something [the *rules* of grammar; baseball *rules*]. **2** a usual way of doing something or behaving [I make it a *rule* never to eat between meals.] **3** the usual or expected thing [Cold winters are the *rule* in North Dakota.]
verb **1** to have power or control over; govern

a cat	ō go	ʉ fur	ə = a *in* ago
ā ape	ô law, for	ch chin	e *in* agent
ä cot, car	oo look	sh she	i *in* pencil
e ten	o͞o tool	th thin	o *in* atom
ē me	oi oil	*th* then	u *in* circus
i fit	ou out	zh measure	
ī ice	u up	ŋ ring	

or manage [He *ruled* the kingdom for many years.] —Look for the WORD CHOICES box at the entry **govern**. **2** to decide in an official way [The judge *ruled* that we had to pay a fine.] **3** to mark straight lines on with a ruler [This paper has been *ruled* with lines.]
—**as a rule** usually. —**rule out** to decide to leave out or ignore.
rule • ***noun,*** *plural for senses 1 and 2 only* **rules** • ***verb*** **ruled, ruling**

ruler (ro͞ol′ər) ***noun*** **1** a person who rules or governs, especially a king or queen. **2** a straight, thin strip of wood or other material that is used in measuring and drawing. It is marked in inches or other measuring units.
rul·er • ***noun,*** *plural* **rulers**

rum (rum) ***noun*** a strong liquor that is made from molasses or sugar cane.

Rumania (ro͞o mā′nē ə) *another spelling of* **Romania**.
Ru·ma·ni·a

rumble (rum′bəl) ***verb*** **1** to make a deep, heavy, rolling sound [Thunder *rumbled* in the distance.] **2** to move with this kind of sound [Trucks *rumble* through the town day and night.]
noun a deep, heavy, rolling sound.
rum·ble • ***verb*** **rumbled, rumbling** • ***noun,*** *plural* **rumbles**

ruminant (ro͞o′mi nənt) ***noun*** an animal that has a stomach with three or four chambers. Food that has been quickly swallowed into the first chamber is brought back to the mouth as cud to be chewed completely. Cows, sheep, goats, deer, and camels are ruminants.
ru·mi·nant • ***noun,*** *plural* **ruminants**

rummage (rum′ij) ***verb*** to search by looking through a place in a thorough way and moving things around [I *rummaged* in the closet, trying to find my boots.]
rum·mage • ***verb*** **rummaged, rummaging**

rummage sale ***noun*** a sale of a mixture of articles or odds and ends that have been donated. The purpose of such a sale is to raise money for charity or for some organization.
rummage sale • ***noun,*** *plural* **rummage sales**

rumor (ro͞o′mər) ***noun*** a story that is told as news, which may or may not be true and which is passed on from person to person [I heard a *rumor* that we all failed the exam.]
verb to tell as a rumor [It has been *rumored* that you are moving away. Is it true?]
ru·mor • ***noun,*** *plural* **rumors** • ***verb*** **rumored, rumoring**

rump (rump) ***noun*** **1** the hind part of an animal, where the legs and back join. **2** a cut of beef from this part.
rump • ***noun,*** *plural* **rumps**

rumple (rum′pəl) ***verb*** **1** to make wrinkles in; crumple. **2** to make untidy [His hair was *rumpled* by the wind.]
rum·ple • ***verb*** **rumpled, rumpling**

run (run) ***verb*** **1** to go by moving the legs faster than in walking. When a person runs, both feet are off the ground at the same time for a moment with each step. **2** to move or go in a swift, easy, or free way [He *ran* his eyes down the page quickly.] **3** to make a quick trip [Let's *run* down to the seashore for the weekend.] **4** to go away quickly; flee [*Run* for your life!] **5** to take part in a race or contest [Lou *ran* in the 100-yard dash. Shannon *ran* for mayor.] **6** to go or travel in a regular way [Buses *run* between Detroit and Pittsburgh.] **7** to keep on going; continue or extend [The play *ran* for a year. This path *runs* through the woods.] **8** to pass [The years *ran* by so quickly.] **9** to operate; to work [*Run* the electric saw with care. This car *runs* well.] **10** to flow or cause to flow [*Run* the water until it gets hot.] **11** to be in charge of; manage [We *run* the household very well.] **12** to perform or do by running or in a way that is like running [He *ran* the mile very fast. I have many errands to *run*.] **13** to bring, pass, or force into a certain condition or position [He *ran* the business into debt. You're going to *run* into trouble.] **14** to spread into other parts [The colors *ran* when the plaid shirt was washed.] **15** to give out liquid [My nose is *running*.] **16** to come apart or ravel [Her stocking *ran*.] **17** to get past or through [The ship *ran* the enemy's blockade.] **18** to cost [Such boots can *run* as much as $150 a pair.] **19** to be affected by; undergo [She was *running* a fever.] **20** to publish [She *ran* an ad in the newspaper.]
noun **1** the act of running [Let's take a *run* around the block.] **2** a running pace or speed [The horses broke into a *run*.] **3** a trip; a journey [a plane on the regular *run* to Boston]. **4** the distance that is covered or the time that is spent in running [a four-mile *run;* a thirty-minute *run*]. **5** a series of happenings or performances that goes on without a change or break [I had a *run* of good luck. The play had a long *run*.] **6** a sloping path or course [a ski *run*]. **7** freedom to move about as one pleases

R

[We had the *run* of the house.] **8** a place in knitted material where the threads have come apart [a *run* in a stocking]. **9** a point that a baseball player scores by touching all the bases in order.
—in the long run in the end; finally. **—on the run** **1** running. **2** running away. **—run across** to come upon or find by chance. **—run along** to leave or depart. **—run away** **1** to leave in a hurry; flee. **2** to go away from one's home or family when one should not leave [He *ran away* from home when he was 14.] **—run into** **1** to meet or come up against by chance; run across [We *ran into* her parents at the theater.] **2** to bump or crash into. **—run out** to come to an end; become used up. **—run out of** to use up. **—run over** **1** to drive over with a car or other vehicle. **2** to overflow. **3** to go beyond a limit.
run • ***verb*** **ran, run, running** • ***noun,*** *plural except for senses 2 and 7* **runs**

runaway (run′ə wā) ***noun*** a person or animal that runs away.
run·a·way • ***noun,*** *plural* **runaways**

rundown (run′doun) ***noun*** a brief report [Give us a *rundown* on the baseball game.]
run·down • ***noun,*** *plural* **rundowns**

run-down (run′doun′) ***adjective*** **1** in poor health, from working too hard or not taking care of oneself. **2** in need of repair; falling apart [a *run-down* house].

rung[1] (ruŋ) ***noun*** a strong stick or bar that forms a step of a ladder or connects two legs of a chair.
rung • ***noun,*** *plural* **rungs**
● The words **rung** and **wrung** sound alike.
One ladder *rung* was broken.
Have the church bells *rung?*
The towel was *wrung* dry.

rung[2] (ruŋ) ***verb*** *past participle of* **ring**[1].
● The words **rung** and **wrung** sound alike.

run-in (run′in) [*an informal word*] ***noun*** a quarrel or fight.
run-in • ***noun,*** *plural* **run-ins**

runner (run′ər) ***noun*** **1** a person or animal that runs [This horse is a good *runner* and has won many races.] **2** a person who does errands or carries messages. **3** a long, narrow cloth or rug [an embroidered *runner* on top of the chest of drawers]. **4** a long, trailing stem that puts out roots along the ground to make new plants. **5** the blade of an ice skate. **6** either one of the long, narrow pieces on which a sled or sleigh slides.
run·ner • ***noun,*** *plural* **runners**

runner-up (run′ər up′) ***noun*** a person or team that finishes second in a race or contest.
run·ner-up • ***noun,*** *plural* **runners-up**

running (run′iŋ) ***noun*** the act of a person or thing that runs [*Running* is a popular form of exercise.]
adjective **1** going at a run or moving fast. **2** flowing [*running* water]. **3** letting out a liquid such as pus or mucus [a *running* sore]. **4** in operation; working [Do not touch a *running* engine.] **5** done by starting with a run [a *running* jump]. **6** going on without a break; continuous [his *running* commentary during the movie]. **7** having to do with the run of a train or bus [The *running* time is two hours.]
adverb one after another [It has snowed for five days *running*.]
—in the running having a chance to win. **—out of the running** having no chance to win.
run·ning • ***noun*** • ***adjective*** • ***adverb***

running mate ***noun*** a candidate who runs for the less important of two offices that are closely associated. The candidate for Vice President is the running mate of the candidate for President.
running mate • ***noun,*** *plural* **running mates**

runny (run′ē) ***adjective*** **1** soft and liquid and flowing [My ice cream became *runny* before I could eat it.] **2** continuing to let out mucus [a *runny* nose].
run·ny • ***adjective*** **runnier, runniest**

runoff (run′ôf) ***noun*** a final election or contest that is held to decide who wins in case of a tie.
run·off • ***noun,*** *plural* **runoffs**

runt (runt) ***noun*** an animal or plant that is much smaller than others of the same kind. This word is usually used to show scorn.
runt • ***noun,*** *plural* **runts**

runway (run′wā) ***noun*** a track or path on which something moves. The paved strip at an airport that airplanes use for taking off or landing is a runway.
run·way • ***noun,*** *plural* **runways**

a	cat	ō	go	ʉ	fur	ə =	a *in* ago
ā	ape	ô	law, for	ch	chin		e *in* agent
ä	cot, car	oo	look	sh	she		i *in* pencil
e	ten	ōō	tool	th	thin		o *in* atom
ē	me	oi	oil	*th*	then		u *in* circus
i	fit	ou	out	zh	measure		
ī	ice	u	up	ŋ	ring		

rupture (rup′chər) ***noun*** **1** the act or fact of breaking apart or bursting [The *rupture* of a blood vessel can be very dangerous.] **2** the condition of being broken apart or burst [a *rupture* in a gas line].
verb to break or burst [His appendix *ruptured.*]
rup·ture • ***noun,*** *plural* **ruptures** • ***verb*** **ruptured, rupturing**

rural (roor′əl *or* rur′əl) ***adjective*** **1** having to do with the countryside or with people who live there. **2** having to do with farms.
ru·ral • ***adjective***

WORD CHOICES

Synonyms of **rural**

The words **rural, country,** and **rustic** share the meaning "having to do with life on farms or in the country."

rural schools
country music
rustic furniture

rush[1] (rush) ***verb*** **1** to move, send, or take with great speed [I *rushed* from the room. We *rushed* him to a hospital.] **2** to act in haste, without taking care to think things through [Don't *rush* into an important decision.] **3** to do or make with great haste; to hurry [If you *rush* the job, you'll make mistakes.]
noun **1** the act or fact of rushing [the *rush* of the crowd from the stadium; the *rush* of the wind]. **2** an eager movement of many people to get to a place [the *rush* to California for gold in 1849]. **3** haste or hurry [In the *rush* to finish the scenery for the play, we made some mistakes.]
adjective needing to be done or sent in a hurry [a *rush* job; a *rush* order for parts].
rush • ***verb*** **rushed, rushing** • ***noun,*** *plural for sense 2 only* **rushes** • ***adjective***

rush[2] (rush) ***noun*** a plant that is a type of grass and grows in wet places. The hollow, pliable stems of rushes are woven to make baskets, mats, and furniture.
rush • ***noun,*** *plural* **rushes**

rush hour ***noun*** a time of day when traffic is very heavy. On weekdays, the rush hour is the time when people are traveling to or from work.
rush hour • ***noun,*** *plural* **rush hours**

Russia (rush′ə) **1** a former empire in eastern Europe and northern Asia, ruled by the czars. **2** a country in eastern Europe and northern Asia. It was formerly a part of the Soviet Union.
Rus·sia

Russian (rush′ən) ***noun*** **1** a person born or living in Russia. **2** the chief language of Russia and the former Soviet Union.
Rus·sian • ***noun,*** *plural for sense 1 only* **Russians**

rust (rust) ***noun*** **1** the reddish-brown coating that can form on iron, steel, and other metals that contain iron. Rust is a compound that is formed when oxygen in air or water combines with iron. **2** reddish brown. **3** a disease of plants that makes brown spots on stems and leaves.
verb to make or become coated with rust [Our car has *rusted* badly underneath.]
rust • ***noun*** • ***verb*** **rusted, rusting**

rustic (rus′tik) ***adjective*** **1** having to do with the countryside —Look for the WORD CHOICES box at the entry **rural**. **2** like country people; plain, simple, or natural [*rustic* manners].
rus·tic • ***adjective***

rustle (rus′əl) ***verb*** to make or move with soft, rubbing sounds [A breeze *rustled* the leaves. The leaves *rustled* in the breeze.]
noun a soft, rubbing sound [the *rustle* of papers].
rus·tle • ***verb*** **rustled, rustling** • ***noun,*** *plural* **rustles**

rustproof (rust′proof) ***adjective*** able to withstand rust; not allowing rust to form [a *rustproof* snow shovel].
rust·proof • ***adjective***

rusty (rus′tē) ***adjective*** **1** rusted [a *rusty* knife; a *rusty* lock]. **2** not so good, strong, or skillful as before, because of a lack of practice or use [My piano playing is a little *rusty*.] —Look for the WORD CHOICES box at the entry **awkward**.
rust·y • ***adjective*** **rustier, rustiest**

rut (rut) ***noun*** **1** a groove that is made in the ground by the wheels of cars, wagons, or other vehicles. **2** a way of doing something, thinking, or acting that is always exactly the same [I'm stuck in a *rut* and afraid to change.]
verb to make ruts in [Heavy rain and too much traffic had *rutted* the dirt road.]

R

rut • *noun, plural* **ruts** • *verb* **rutted, rutting**

Ruth (ro͞oth), **Babe** (bāb) 1895-1948; U.S. baseball player. His real name was *George Herman Ruth.*

ruthless (ro͞oth′ləs) *adjective* without pity or kindness; cruel [a *ruthless* pirate].
ruth·less • *adjective*

RV

RV *noun* a vehicle that is furnished as a place for people to live in on a camping trip or vacation.
RV • *noun, plural* **RVs**

Rwanda (ro͞o än′də) a country in east central Africa.
Rwan·da

Rx *the symbol for* prescription. It is used on the labels of medicines that are prescribed by doctors.

rye (rī) *noun* **1** a kind of grass that farmers grow for its seeds, which are used for food. **2** the seeds of this grass, which are made into flour and cattle feed.

rye

rye bread *noun* bread made from rye flour.

a	cat	ō	go	ʉ	fur	ə =	a *in* ago
ā	ape	ô	law, for	ch	chin		e *in* agent
ä	cot, car	ʊo	look	sh	she		i *in* pencil
e	ten	o͞o	tool	th	thin		o *in* atom
ē	me	ʊi	oil	*th*	then		u *in* circus
i	fit	ʊu	out	zh	measure		
ī	ice	u	up	ŋ	ring		

S s

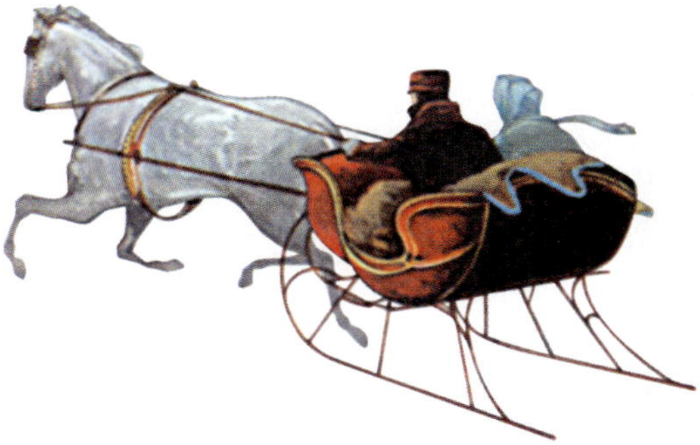

Ss Ss *Ss* **Ss**

The letter **s** *usually stands for the sound you hear at the beginning of the words* **say** *and* **sleigh.** *In some words, like* **busy,** *it stands for the same sound as the letter* **z.** **S** *can also combine with the letter* **h** *to represent the sound you hear at the beginning of the words* **shirt** *and* **shelf**; *sometimes an* **s** *alone will produce this sound, as in* **sure** *and* **sugar.** *In a very few words, such as* **island,** *the* **s** *is not pronounced at all.*

s or **S** (es) ***noun*** **1** the nineteenth letter of the English alphabet. **2** something shaped like an S.
s or **S** • ***noun,*** *plural* **s's** or **S's**

-'s *a suffix used to make:* **1** the possessive form of singular nouns [that *child's* toy]. **2** the possessive form of plural nouns that do not end in *s* [the *children's* toys]. **3** the possessive form of some pronouns [*someone's* toy].

S or **S.** *abbreviation for* **1** south. **2** southern.

Sabbath (sab′əth) ***noun*** the day of the week that is devoted to worship and rest. Sunday is the Sabbath for most Christians. Saturday is the Sabbath for Jews.
Sab·bath • ***noun,*** *plural* **Sabbaths**

saber (sā′bər) ***noun*** a heavy sword that has a single-edged blade with a slight curve in it.
sa·ber • ***noun,*** *plural* **sabers**

sabotage (sab′ə täzh) ***noun*** the destroying of buildings, factories, roads, or other property, especially by enemy agents or by workers during labor disputes.
verb to damage or destroy by sabotage [The workers *sabotaged* the machinery at the plant.]
sab·o·tage • ***noun*** • ***verb*** **sabotaged, sabotaging**

sac (sak) ***noun*** a part of a plant or animal that is somewhat like a bag. It is often full of some kind of liquid.
sac • ***noun,*** *plural* **sacs**
• The words **sac** and **sack** sound alike.

sack[1] (sak) ***noun*** a large strong bag for holding grain or other things [a *sack* of potatoes].
sack • ***noun,*** *plural* **sacks**
• The words **sack** and **sac** sound alike.
Coffee beans were sold by the *sack*.
Barbarians were known to *sack* cities.
A *sac* surrounds an egg yolk.

sack[2] (sak) ***noun*** the act of robbing a city or town that has been captured by an army [We are reading about the *sack* of ancient Rome.]
verb to rob a city or town.
sack • ***noun*** • ***verb*** **sacked, sacking**
• The words **sack** and **sac** sound alike.

sacrament (sak′rə mənt) ***noun*** a very sacred ceremony in Christian churches. Baptism and Communion are sacraments.
sac·ra·ment • ***noun,*** *plural* **sacraments**

Sacramento (sak′rə men′tō) the capital of California.
Sac·ra·men·to

sacred (sā′krəd) ***adjective*** **1** having to do with religion; holy [a *sacred* song]. **2** given or deserving the greatest respect [a place *sacred* to the memory of the Pilgrims].
sa·cred • ***adjective***

sacrifice (sak′ri fīs) ***noun*** **1** the act of offering something to God or a god [The *sacrifice* of animals was common in some ancient

religions.] **2** the thing offered. **3** the act of giving up one thing for the sake of something else [Parents often make *sacrifices* in order to send their children to college.]
verb **1** to offer as a sacrifice [The priests *sacrificed* a lamb to the gods.] **2** to give up something for the sake of something more important.
sac·ri·fice • ***noun,*** *plural for senses 2 and 3 only* **sacrifices** • ***verb*** **sacrificed, sacrificing**

sad (sad) ***adjective*** **1** feeling unhappy [Tom was *sad* when his puppy ran away.] **2** causing a gloomy or unhappy feeling [a *sad* song].
sad • ***adjective*** **sadder, saddest**

WORD CHOICES

Synonyms of **sad**

Many words share the meaning "feeling or showing sorrow or grief."

dejected	melancholy	unhappy
downcast	miserable	wretched
gloomy	sorrowful	

sadden (sad′n) ***verb*** to make or become sad [The rainy weather *saddened* the baseball players and the fans.]
sad·den • ***verb*** **saddened, saddening**

saddle

saddle (sad′əl) ***noun*** a seat for a rider on a horse or bicycle.
verb **1** to put a saddle on [I *saddled* my horse.] **2** to weigh down; burden [The manager *saddled* her with all the difficult work.]
sad·dle • ***noun,*** *plural* **saddles**
• ***verb*** **saddled, saddling**

saddle shoes ***plural noun*** shoes with flat heels and a band of different-colored leather across the top.

safari (sə fär′ē) ***noun*** a journey or hunting trip, especially in Africa.
sa·fa·ri • ***noun,*** *plural* **safaris**

WORD HISTORY

safari

The word **safari** comes to us, through a language of eastern Africa, from an Arabic verb that means "to make a journey."

safe (sāf) ***adjective*** **1** free from harm or danger [*safe* at home]. **2** giving protection from harm or danger [a *safe* hiding place]. **3** not dangerous [a *safe* bike; a *safe* journey]. **4** taking no risks; careful [a *safe* driver]. **5** having reached a base without being put out [Jim was *safe* at first base.]
noun a strong metal box with a lock. It is used for keeping money or other valuable things.
safe • ***adjective*** **safer, safest** • ***noun,*** *plural* **safes**

safeguard (sāf′gärd) ***noun*** something that protects; protection [Wear gloves as a *safeguard* against frostbite.]
verb to protect or guard [The new alarm will *safeguard* the house against burglars.]
safe·guard • ***noun,*** *plural* **safeguards**
• ***verb*** **safeguarded, safeguarding**

safety (sāf′tē) ***noun*** freedom from danger or harm [Lifeboats carried the passengers to *safety*.]
safe·ty • ***noun***

safety pin ***noun*** a pin that is bent back on itself so as to form a spring. A guard for the point at one end keeps the pin from springing free.
safety pin • ***noun,*** *plural* **safety pins**

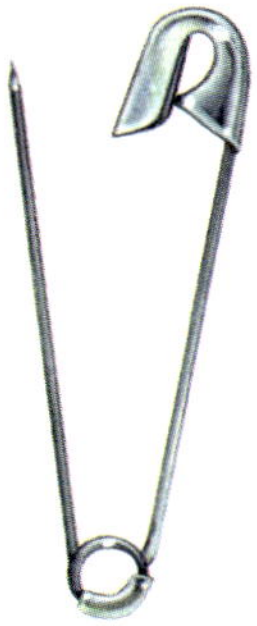

safety pin

a cat	ō go	ʉ fur	ə = a *in* ago
ā ape	ô law, for	ch chin	e *in* agent
ä cot, car	oo look	sh she	i *in* pencil
e ten	ōō tool	th thin	o *in* atom
ē me	oi oil	*th* then	u *in* circus
i fit	ou out	zh measure	
ī ice	u up	ŋ ring	

sag (sag) ***verb*** **1** to bend or sink, especially in the middle [The heavy books made the shelves *sag*.] **2** to lose strength; weaken [Car sales have begun to *sag*.]
sag • ***verb*** **sagged, sagging**

saga (sä′gə) ***noun*** a long story of adventures or brave deeds or one telling about several generations of a family.
sa·ga • ***noun,*** *plural* **sagas**

sage (sāj) ***adjective*** showing good judgment; wise [a *sage* teacher].
noun a very wise person.
sage • ***adjective*** **sager, sagest** • ***noun,*** *plural* **sages**

sagebrush (sāj′brush) ***noun*** a shrub that has tiny white or yellow flowers. It grows on the plains of western North America.
sage·brush • ***noun***

Sahara (sə her′ə) a very large desert covering much of northern Africa.
Sa·ha·ra

said (sed) ***verb*** *past tense and past participle of* **say**.

sail (sāl) ***noun*** a sheet of canvas or other strong material that is attached to a ship or boat. It is used to catch the wind and move the ship or boat forward.
verb **1** to travel on or across water in a boat or ship [We *sailed* to Hawaii on a large ship. The priates *sailed* the seven seas.] **2** to begin a trip by water [We *sail* on Monday for Europe.] **3** to guide or operate a ship or boat, especially a sailboat [She is learning how to *sail* at the yacht club.] **4** to move in a smooth and easy way [The hawk *sailed* across the sky.]
sail • ***noun,*** *plural* **sails** • ***verb*** **sailed, sailing**
● The words **sail** and **sale** sound alike.
I am able to *sail* a small yacht.
The cash register rang up our *sale*.

sailboat (sāl′bōt) ***noun*** a boat with a sail or sails.
sail·boat • ***noun,*** *plural* **sailboats**

sailboat

sailor (sāl′ər) ***noun*** **1** a person who makes a living by sailing or working on a boat. **2** an enlisted person in the navy.
sail·or • ***noun,*** *plural* **sailors**

saint (sānt) ***noun*** **1** a very holy person. Some churches honor such holy people after they have died. **2** a very kind and patient person.
saint • ***noun,*** *plural* **saints**

Saint Bernard (bər närd′) ***noun*** a large brown and white dog, at one time used in the Swiss Alps to rescue people lost in the snow.
Saint Ber·nard • ***noun,*** *plural* **Saint Bernards**

sake (sāk) ***noun*** **1** purpose or reason [The child has the habit of crying for the *sake* of getting attention.] **2** advantage or benefit; good [You must eat spinach for your own *sake*.]
sake • ***noun,*** *plural for sense 2 only* **sakes**

salad (sal′əd) ***noun*** a mixture of vegetables, fruit, or other foods. Usually it is served cold and includes lettuce and some kind of dressing.
sal·ad • ***noun,*** *plural* **salads**

salamander (sal′ə man dər) ***noun*** a small animal that looks like a lizard. It has soft, wet skin like a frog's. It is an amphibian.
sal·a·man·der • ***noun,*** *plural* **salamanders**

salami (sə lä′mē) ***noun*** a spicy sausage made of pork and beef or of beef alone.
sa·la·mi • ***noun,*** *plural* **salamis**

salary (sal′ər ē) ***noun*** a fixed amount of money paid to a worker at regular times —Look for the WORD CHOICES box at the entry **wage**.
sal·a·ry • ***noun,*** *plural* **salaries**

sale (sāl) ***noun*** **1** the act of selling something for money [The clerk made ten *sales* today.] **2** a special selling of something at a price that is lower than normal [a *sale* on toys].
—for sale available to be sold. **—on sale** to be sold, especially at a price lower than usual.
sale • ***noun,*** *plural* **sales**
● The words **sale** and **sail** sound alike.
Plastic watches are now on *sale*.
The wind tore a *sail* on our boat.

Salem (sā′ləm) the capital of Oregon.
Sa·lem

salesman (sālz′mən) ***noun*** a man who sells goods or services.
sales·man • ***noun,*** *plural* **salesmen**

salesperson (sālz′pur sən) ***noun*** a salesman or saleswoman.
sales·per·son • ***noun,*** *plural* **salespersons**

sales tax ***noun*** a tax on an item, paid by the buyer at the time of the sale.
sales tax • ***noun,*** *plural* **sales taxes**

saleswoman (sālz′woom ən) ***noun*** a woman who sells goods or services.
sales·wom·an • ***noun,*** *plural* **saleswomen**

S

saline (sā′līn *or* sā′lēn) ***adjective*** of, like, or containing common salt; salty [a *saline* solution].
sa·line • ***adjective***

saliva (sə lī′və) ***noun*** the watery liquid produced in the mouth; spit. It helps to digest food.
sa·li·va • ***noun***

Salk (sôlk), **Jonas** (jō′nəs) 1914-1995; U.S. physician. He developed a polio vaccine.
Salk, Jo·nas

salmon (sam′ən) ***noun*** a large fish with silver scales. Its flesh is orange-pink when cooked. Salmon live in the ocean but swim up rivers to lay their eggs.
salm·on • ***noun,*** *plural* **salmon**

salt (sôlt) ***noun*** **1** a white substance made up of crystals and used to flavor and preserve foods. **2** a chemical compound that is formed by the reaction of an acid with a base.
adjective containing or preserved with salt [*salt* water; *salt* pork].
verb to add salt to for seasoning, preserving, or melting [The cook *salted* the food.]
salt • ***noun*** • ***adjective*** • ***verb*** **salted, salting**

Salt Lake City the capital of Utah.

saltwater (sôlt′wôt ər) ***adjective*** of or living in the sea or salty water [a *saltwater* fish].
salt·wa·ter • ***adjective***

salty (sôl′tē) ***adjective*** **1** having the taste of salt or containing salt. **2** having the smell of the sea.
salt·y • ***adjective*** **saltier, saltiest**

salute (sə lo͞ot′) ***verb*** to show honor and respect for by raising the right hand held straight to the forehead or by firing shots from a gun.
noun an act of saluting [my *salute* to the flag].
sa·lute • ***verb*** **saluted, saluting** • ***noun,*** *plural* **salutes**

salvage (sal′vij) ***noun*** material or goods saved from damage, destruction, or going to waste.
verb to use what can be saved from something damaged or destroyed [They *salvaged* the tires from the old wreck.]
sal·vage • ***noun*** • ***verb*** **salvaged, salvaging**

salvation (sal vā′shən) ***noun*** **1** a person or thing that saves [The cellar was our *salvation* in the tornado.] **2** in religion, the saving of the soul from evil and death.
sal·va·tion • ***noun***

salve (sav) ***noun*** a greasy medicine put on wounds, burns, or sores to soothe or heal them.
salve • ***noun,*** *plural* **salves**

same (sām) ***adjective*** **1** being the very one [She is the *same* girl who runs on this track every day.] **2** alike in some way; similar [He has the *same* bike as Martin.] **3** without any change; not different [She is the *same* happy person today.]
pronoun the same person or thing [Marie wants a lemonade and I'll have the *same*.]
adverb in the same way [Treat us all the *same;* that's all we ask.]

WORD CHOICES

Synonyms of **same**

The words **same, identical,** and **very** share the meaning "being the exact one and not another."

> That is the *same* man who called last night.
>
> This is the *identical* bed Lincoln slept in.
>
> He bought the *very* house we once lived in.

Samoa (sə mō′ə) a country on a group of islands in the southern Pacific Ocean.
Sa·mo·a

sample (sam′pəl) ***noun*** a part that shows what the whole thing is like; example [Little pieces of carpet were used for *samples*. He gave me a *sample* of his typing.]
verb to test something by trying a sample [Roberta *sampled* the basket of grapes.]
sam·ple • ***noun,*** *plural* **samples** • ***verb*** **sampled, sampling**

sanction (saŋk′shən) ***noun*** **1** approval or permission given by someone in authority. **2** often **sanctions** a blockade of shipping or other action taken by several countries together to make another country do something or stop doing something.
verb to approve or permit [The principal *sanctioned* our class trip again this year.]
sanc·tion • ***noun,*** *plural* **sanctions** • ***verb*** **sanctioned, sanctioning**

a cat	ō go	ʉ fur	ə = a *in* ago
ā ape	ô law, for	ch chin	e *in* agent
ä cot, car	o͝o look	sh she	i *in* pencil
e ten	o͞o tool	th thin	o *in* atom
ē me	oi oil	*th* then	u *in* circus
i fit	ou out	zh measure	
ī ice	u up	ŋ ring	

sanctuary (saŋk′cho͞o er′ē) ***noun*** **1** a place set aside for religious worship. **2** a place where someone can find safety or shelter. **3** a place where birds and animals are kept to protect them from hunters.
sanc·tu·ar·y • ***noun,*** *plural* **sanctuaries**

sand (sand) ***noun*** tiny, loose grains worn away from rock by the weather. They form the ground of beaches or deserts.
verb to make smooth by using sand or sandpaper [We *sanded* the old floor before we painted it.]
sand • ***noun*** • ***verb*** **sanded, sanding**

sandal (san′dəl) ***noun*** a kind of shoe with a top that is made up of straps so that much of the foot is left uncovered.
san·dal • ***noun,*** *plural* **sandals**

sandbar (sand′bär) ***noun*** a ridge of sand formed in a river or along a shore. It is shaped by the current or by the tides. This word is also written **sand bar.**
sand·bar • ***noun,*** *plural* **sandbars**

sandblast (sand′blast) ***verb*** to clean with sand propelled by a strong stream of air [The workers carefully *sandblasted* the monument.]
sand·blast • ***verb*** **sandblasted, sandblasting**

sandbox (sand′bäks) ***noun*** a large box or enclosed area filled with sand for children to play in.
sand·box • ***noun,*** *plural* **sandboxes**

San Diego (san′ dē ā′gō) a seaport in southern California.
San Di·e·go

sandpaper (sand′pā pər) ***noun*** strong paper coated with sand on one side. It is used to smooth and polish wood and other materials.
verb to rub with sandpaper.
sand·pa·per • ***noun*** • ***verb*** **sandpapered, sandpapering**

sandstone (sand′stōn) ***noun*** a type of rock formed from sand held together by lime and other substances.
sand·stone • ***noun***

sandwich (san′dwich *or* san′wich) ***noun*** two or more slices of bread with meat, cheese, or other foods in between.
verb to squeeze in [The shed was *sandwiched* between two houses.]
sand·wich • ***noun,*** *plural* **sandwiches** • ***verb*** **sandwiched, sandwiching**

WORD HISTORY

sandwich

The **sandwich** was named after the Fourth Earl of *Sandwich*, an English nobleman who lived in the eighteenth century. It is said that he ate his bread and meat together in this way so that he would not have to leave the table in the middle of a card game in order to eat a regular meal.

sandy (san′dē) ***adjective*** **1** full of sand or covered with sand [a *sandy* shore. My shoes were *sandy* from walking on the beach.] **2** of the color of sand; reddish-yellow [*sandy* hair].
sand·y • ***adjective*** **sandier, sandiest**

sane (sān) ***adjective*** **1** having a sound, healthy mind [a *sane* citizen]. **2** showing good sense; reasonable [a *sane* plan].
sane • ***adjective*** **saner, sanest**

San Francisco (san′ fran sis′kō) a city on the coast of central California.
San Fran·cis·co

sang (saŋ) ***verb*** *past tense of* **sing.**

sanitary (san′i ter′ē) ***adjective*** free from dirt and germs; clean [a *sanitary* kitchen].
san·i·tar·y • ***adjective***

sanitation (san′i tā′shən) ***noun*** the practice of keeping clean and healthy conditions by disposing of sewage and garbage.
san·i·ta·tion • ***noun***

sanity (san′i tē) ***noun*** **1** the condition of being sane; mental health. **2** the condition of having sound judgment; good sense.
san·i·ty • ***noun***

San Juan (san hwän′) the capital of Puerto Rico.

sank (saŋk) ***verb*** *past tense of* **sink.**

San Marino (san′ mə rē′nō) a tiny country within eastern Italy.
San Ma·ri·no

Santa (san′tə) *the same as* **Santa Claus.**
San·ta

Santa Claus (san′tə klôz *or* san′tə kläz) a fat, jolly old man in popular legends, with a white beard and a red suit, who hands out gifts at Christmastime.
San·ta Claus

S

Santa Fe (san′tə fā′) the capital of New Mexico.
San·ta Fe

São Tomé and Príncipe (sou tə mā′ and prin′si pē′) a country made up of two islands (*São Tomé* and *Príncipe*) off the western coast of Africa.
São To·mé and Prín·ci·pe

sap[1] (sap) ***noun*** the juice that flows through a plant. It carries food and water to all parts of the plant.

sap[2] (sap) ***verb*** to weaken or wear away slowly [Hours of work *sapped* his energy.]
sap • ***verb*** **sapped, sapping**

sapling (sap′liŋ) ***noun*** a young tree.
sap·ling • ***noun,*** *plural* **saplings**

sapphire (saf′īr) ***noun*** a clear, usually deep-blue, precious stone.
sap·phire • ***noun,*** *plural* **sapphires**

sarcastic (sär kas′tik) ***adjective*** using mocking or cruel remarks to be funny or to hurt someone's feelings [a *sarcastic* reply].
sar·cas·tic • ***adjective***

sarcophagus

sarcophagus (sär käf′ə gəs) ***noun*** a stone coffin with carvings on it that has been set in a tomb.
sar·coph·a·gus • ***noun,*** *plural* **sar·coph·a·gi** (sär käf′ə jī) or **sarcophaguses**

sardine (sär dēn′) ***noun*** a small ocean fish that has been preserved in oil and tightly packed into flat cans.
sar·dine • ***noun,*** *plural* **sardines**

sari (sä′rē) ***noun*** an outer garment worn by women in places such as India and Pakistan. It is one long piece of cloth with one end wrapped around the waist to form a long skirt and the other end draped over the shoulder or over the head.
sa·ri • ***noun,*** *plural* **saris**

sari

sash[1] (sash) ***noun*** a band, ribbon, or scarf worn around the waist or over the shoulder.
sash • ***noun,*** *plural* **sashes**

sash[2] (sash) ***noun*** a frame that holds the glass pane or panes of a window or door.
sash • ***noun,*** *plural* **sashes**

Saskatchewan (sas kach′ə wän) a province of western Canada. Abbreviated **SK** or **Sask.**
Sas·katch·e·wan

sassy (sas′ē) [*an informal word*] ***adjective*** not showing proper manners or respect; saucy [a *sassy* answer].
sass·y • ***adjective*** **sassier, sassiest**

sat (sat) ***verb*** *past tense and past participle of* **sit.**

Sat. *abbreviation for* Saturday.

Satan (sāt′n) *another name for* **the Devil**.
Sa·tan

satchel (sach′əl) ***noun*** a small bag for carrying clothing, books, or other items. It sometimes has a shoulder strap.
satch·el • ***noun,*** *plural* **satchels**

satellite (sat′l īt) ***noun*** **1** a natural moon that revolves around a planet. **2** a man-made object that has been put into orbit around the earth, moon, or other heavenly body.
sat·el·lite • ***noun,*** *plural* **satellites**

satin (sat′n) ***noun*** a cloth with a very smooth, glossy, slippery surface on one side. It is usually made of polyester, rayon, or silk.
sat·in • ***noun***

satisfaction (sat′is fak′shən) ***noun*** the condition of being satisfied [Knowing she had done a good job brought Alana *satisfaction*.]
sat·is·fac·tion • ***noun***

satisfactory (sat′is fak′tər ē) ***adjective*** good enough to satisfy [a *satisfactory* report card].
sat·is·fac·to·ry • ***adjective***

satisfy (sat′is fī′) ***verb*** **1** to meet the needs or wishes of; please [Only first place will *satisfy* the runner.] **2** to make feel sure; convince someone [His mother was *satisfied* that he had told her the truth.]
sat·is·fy • ***verb*** **satisfied, satisfying, satisfies**

a cat	ō go	ʉ fur	ə = a *in* ago
ā ape	ô law, for	ch chin	e *in* agent
ä cot, car	oo look	sh she	i *in* pencil
e ten	ōō tool	th thin	o *in* atom
ē me	oi oil	*th* then	u *in* circus
i fit	ou out	zh measure	
ī ice	u up	ŋ ring	

WORD CHOICES

Synonyms of **satisfy**

The words **satisfy, fulfill,** and **meet** share the meaning "to be what is wanted or required by."

That player should *satisfy* the team's needs.

Her success *fulfills* her parents' hopes.

The new car is designed to *meet* customer needs.

saturate (sach′ər āt) ***verb*** to soak completely through [His tennis shoes were *saturated* with rain water.] —Look for the WORD CHOICES box at the entry **soak**.
sat·u·rate • ***verb*** **saturated, saturating**

Saturday (sat′ər dā) ***noun*** the seventh and last day of the week. Abbreviated **Sat.**
Sat·ur·day • ***noun,*** *plural* **Saturdays**

WORD HISTORY

Saturday

Saturday comes from a thousand-year-old English word that means "the day of the planet *Saturn*." The English name was a translation of part of this day's name in Latin. The planet *Saturn* itself gets its name from the Roman god *Saturn*, who was believed to watch over agriculture.

Saturn (sat′ərn) the second largest planet and sixth in distance away from the sun. It is known for the rings that can be seen around it.
Sat·urn

sauce (sôs *or* säs) ***noun*** a liquid or soft mixture served with food to make it taste better.
sauce • ***noun,*** *plural* **sauces**

saucepan (sôs′pan *or* säs′pan) ***noun*** a small metal pot with a long handle, used for cooking.
sauce·pan • ***noun,*** *plural* **saucepans**

saucer (sô′sər *or* sä′sər) ***noun*** a small, shallow dish, especially one that is meant to hold a cup.
sau·cer • ***noun,*** *plural* **saucers**

saucy (sô′sē *or* sä′sē) ***adjective*** too bold; not showing proper manners or respect [a *saucy* child].
sau·cy • ***adjective*** **saucier, sauciest**

Saudi Arabia (sou′dē ə rā′bē ə *or* sô′dē ə rā′bē ə) a kingdom that occupies most of Arabia.
Sa·u·di A·ra·bi·a

sauna (sô′nə *or* sä′nə) ***noun*** a room equipped with a device to produce very dry, hot air to cause perspiration. People stay in such a room for a short while to cleanse or refresh themselves.
sau·na • ***noun,*** *plural* **saunas**

sausage (sô′sij *or* sä′sij) ***noun*** pork or other meat that is chopped up and seasoned. It is usually stuffed into a long tube of thin skin.
sau·sage • ***noun,*** *plural* **sausages**

savage (sav′ij) ***adjective*** **1** not civilized; primitive [a *savage* tribe]. **2** not tamed; wild [a *savage* tiger]. **3** very cruel; brutal [*savage* fighting]. ***noun*** **1** a person who lives in a way that is not civilized. **2** a cruel, brutal person.
sav·age • ***adjective*** • ***noun,*** *plural* **savages**

savanna or **savannah** (sə van′ə) ***noun*** a flat, open region without trees; a plain.
sa·van·na or **sa·van·nah** • ***noun,*** *plural* **savannas** or **savannahs**

save (sāv) ***verb*** **1** to rescue or keep from harm or danger [The lifeguard *saved* the child.] **2** to keep or store for future use [Juan *saved* his allowance for a new bat.] **3** to keep from being lost or wasted [They *saved* time by taking the bus.] **4** to avoid expense, loss, or waste [Mollie used coupons to *save* on the cost of food.]
save • ***verb*** **saved, saving**

saving (sā′viŋ) ***noun*** *often* **savings** something that is saved, especially money.
sav·ing • ***noun,*** *plural* **savings**

savior (sāv′yər) ***noun*** a person who rescues. —**the Savior** Jesus Christ.
sav·ior • ***noun,*** *plural* **saviors**

saw

saw[1] (sô *or* sä) ***noun*** a cutting tool that has a thin metal blade with sharp teeth along the edge.

S

verb to cut with a saw [He *sawed* the board into two pieces.]
saw • *noun, plural* **saws** • *verb* **sawed, sawing**

saw[2] (sô *or* sä) *verb past tense of* **see**.

sawdust (sô′dust *or* sä′dust) *noun* tiny bits of wood that are produced as a saw cuts through wood.
saw·dust • *noun*

sawmill (sô′mil *or* sä′mil) *noun* a place where logs are sawed into boards.
saw·mill • *noun, plural* **sawmills**

sax (saks) [*an informal word*] *noun a short form of* **saxophone**.
sax • *noun, plural* **saxes**

Saxon (sak′sən) *noun* a member of a people who lived in northern Germany long ago. Saxons invaded England in the fifth and sixth centuries A.D. and then settled there.
Sax·on • *noun, plural* **Saxons**

saxophone (sak′sə fōn) *noun* a woodwind musical instrument with a curved metal body. Its mouthpiece has a single reed.
sax·o·phone • *noun, plural* **saxophones**

saxophone

say (sā) *verb* **1** to speak or to pronounce [Don't *say* that.] **2** to put into words; tell [The paper *said* that it is going to rain.] **3** to recite or repeat [We *said* the pledge of allegiance to the flag.] **4** to show or indicate [The watch *says* it is 11:30.]
noun **1** a chance to speak [Has the whole class had its *say*?] **2** the power to decide [Mom has the final *say*.]
say • *verb* **said, saying** • *noun*

WORD CHOICES

Synonyms of **say**

Many words share the meaning "to express or make known in words."

announce	proclaim	state
assert	report	tell
declare		

saying (sā′iŋ) *noun* something said, especially a proverb, such as "Waste not, want not."
say·ing • *noun, plural* **sayings**

says (sez) *verb* the form of the verb **say** that is used to show the present time with *he, she,* or *it*. This form is also used with singular nouns.

SC or **S.C.** *abbreviation for* South Carolina.

scab (skab) *noun* a crust that forms over a cut or sore as it is healing.
verb to become covered with a scab [The cut on her arm *scabbed* quickly.]
scab • *noun, plural* **scabs** • *verb* **scabbed, scabbing**

scaffold (skaf′əld) *noun* a framework put up to support workers while they are building, repairing, or painting something high off the ground.
scaf·fold • *noun, plural* **scaffolds**

scald (skôld) *verb* to burn with hot liquid or steam [The hot bath *scalded* me.]
scald • *verb* **scalded, scalding**

scale[1] (skāl) *noun* **1** a series of marks along a line, with regular spaces in between. It is used for measuring [That thermometer has a basic *scale* of 100 degrees.] **2** the way that the size of a map, drawing, or model compares with the size of the thing that it stands for [a *scale* of one inch to a mile]. **3** a series of musical notes arranged in order from the lowest to the highest in pitch or from the highest to the lowest.
verb to climb up [Anita *scaled* the mountain.]
scale • *noun, plural* **scales** • *verb* **scaled, scaling**

scale[2] (skāl) *noun* **1** any of the thin, flat, hard plates that cover and protect certain fish and reptiles. **2** a thin piece or layer; flake [The rust on the car is coming off in *scales*.]
verb to scrape scales from [He *scaled* the fish.]
scale • *noun, plural* **scales** • *verb* **scaled, scaling**

scale[3] (skāl) *noun often* **scales** any device or machine used for weighing something.
scale • *noun, plural* **scales**

scallion (skal′yən) *noun* a kind of onion, especially a young green onion.
scal·lion • *noun, plural* **scallions**

a	cat	ō	go	u̶	fur	ə = a *in* ago	
ā	ape	ô	law, for	ch	chin	e *in* agent	
ä	cot, car	oo	look	sh	she	i *in* pencil	
e	ten	o͞o	tool	th	thin	o *in* atom	
ē	me	oi	oil	*th*	then	u *in* circus	
i	fit	ou	out	zh	measure		
ī	ice	u	up	ŋ	ring		

scallop (skäl′əp *or* skal′əp) *noun* a water animal with a soft body inside two hard shells that are hinged together. It swims by snapping its shells together. It has a large muscle that is used as food.
scal·lop • *noun, plural* **scallops**

scalp (skalp) *noun* **1** the skin on the top and back of the head, usually covered with hair. **2** a piece of skin and hair that is cut from the head of an enemy. In earlier times, some North American Indians and frontier people kept scalps as trophies.
verb to cut the scalp from someone.
scalp • *noun, plural* **scalps** • *verb* **scalped, scalping**

scalpel (skal′pəl) *noun* a small, very sharp knife, used by surgeons in operations.
scal·pel • *noun, plural* **scalpels**

scaly (skā′lē) *adjective* covered with scales [a *scaly* lizard].
scal·y • *adjective* **scalier, scaliest**

scamper (skam′pər) *verb* to move quickly or in a hurry [The squirrels *scampered* up the tree.]
noun a quick run or dash.
scam·per • *verb* **scampered, scampering** • *noun, plural* **scampers**

scan (skan) *verb* **1** to look at very carefully; examine [The explorer *scanned* the horizon for land.] **2** to glance at or look over quickly [I *scanned* the list of names to find yours.]
scan • *verb* **scanned, scanning**

scandal (skan′dəl) *noun* **1** someone or something that shocks people and causes shame or disgrace [Years ago, it was a *scandal* for women to wear short dresses.] **2** the shame or disgrace caused by this. **3** talk that ruins a person's good name.
scan·dal • *noun, plural* **scandals**

Scandinavia (skan′di nā′vē ə) **1** a large peninsula of northern Europe, on which Norway and Sweden are located. **2** the countries of Norway, Sweden, Denmark, and Iceland.
Scan·di·na·vi·a

Scandinavian (skan′di nā′vē ən) *adjective* of or having to do with Scandinavia, its peoples, or its languages.
Scan·di·na·vi·an • *adjective*

scant (skant) *adjective* **1** not as much as is needed; not enough [a *scant* supply of food]. **2** not quite full [Add a *scant* teaspoon of salt.]
scant • *adjective* **scanter, scantest**

scanty (skan′tē) *adjective* not enough or just barely enough [a *scanty* helping of food] —Look for the WORD CHOICES box at the entry **meager**.
scant·y • *adjective* **scantier, scantiest**

scapegoat (skāp′gōt) *noun* a person, group, or thing that is forced to take the blame for the mistakes or crimes of others.
scape·goat • *noun, plural* **scapegoats**

scar (skär) *noun* **1** a mark left on the skin after a cut, burn, or wound has healed. **2** any mark that is like a scar.
verb to mark with or form a scar [The cat *scarred* the top of the table with its claws. The baby's hand *scarred* after she burned it.]
scar • *noun, plural* **scars** • *verb* **scarred, scarring**

scarce (skers) *adjective* **1** not common; not often seen [Snow is *scarce* in Georgia.] —Look for the WORD CHOICES box at the entry **unusual**. **2** not great in amount or number; hard to get [Good food was *scarce*.]
scarce • *adjective* **scarcer, scarcest**

scarcely (skers′lē) *adverb* **1** only just; barely; hardly [We *scarcely* made it home in time.] **2** certainly not [You can *scarcely* expect us to believe that.]
scarce·ly • *adverb*

scare (sker) *verb* to make or become afraid; frighten [The loud noise *scared* the animals. He doesn't *scare* easily.] —Look for the WORD CHOICES box at the entry **frighten**.
noun a sudden fear [We had a terrible *scare* when my brother fell off the ladder.]
—scare away or **scare off** to drive away or drive off by frightening.
scare • *verb* **scared, scaring** • *noun, plural* **scares**

scarecrow (sker′krō) *noun* a figure of a person made with sticks and old clothes and set up in a field to scare birds away from crops.
scare·crow • *noun, plural* **scarecrows**

scarecrow

scarf (skärf) *noun* a piece of cloth worn around the head, neck, or shoulders. It is worn for decoration or for warmth.
scarf • *noun, plural* **scarves**

S

scarlet (skär′lət) ***noun*** a very bright red with an orange tinge.
scar·let • ***noun***

scary (sker′ē) [*an informal word*] ***adjective*** causing fear; frightening [a *scary* experience].
scar·y • ***adjective*** **scarier, scariest**

scatter (skat′ər) ***verb*** **1** to throw here and there; sprinkle [*Scatter* the grass seed over the lawn.] **2** to separate and send or go in many directions; spread about [The wind *scattered* the leaves. The crowd *scattered* after the game.] —Look for the WORD CHOICES box at the entry **sprinkle**.
scat·ter • ***verb*** **scattered, scattering**

scavenger (skav′ən jər) ***noun*** **1** an animal that feeds on rotting meat and garbage. **2** a person who gathers things that other people have thrown away.
scav·eng·er • ***noun,*** *plural* **scavengers**

scene (sēn) ***noun*** **1** a place where something has happened [the *scene* of an accident]. **2** the place in which the action of a story, play, or movie occurs. **3** a division of a play. It is usually a separate part of an act. **4** a particular event in a story or movie [The best *scene* was the boat chase.] **5** a view of nature [a picture of a winter *scene*] —Look for the WORD CHOICES box at the entry **view**. **6** a show of anger or bad temper in front of others.
scene • ***noun,*** *plural* **scenes**
● The words **scene** and **seen** sound alike.
Which *scene* of the play was the best?
Have you *seen* her latest movie?

scenery (sēn′ər ē) ***noun*** **1** the way a certain area looks [the *scenery* along the river]. **2** painted screens used on a stage to show where the action in a play or movie is taking place.
sce·ner·y • ***noun***

scenic (sēn′ik) ***adjective*** **1** having to do with scenery [a *scenic* view]. **2** having beautiful scenery [a very *scenic* road].
sce·nic • ***adjective***

scent (sent) ***noun*** **1** a smell; odor [the *scent* of hot peanuts]. **2** the sense of smell [Lions hunt partly by *scent*.] **3** a smell left by an animal [The dogs lost the fox's *scent* at the river.] **4** a liquid with a pleasing smell; perfume.
verb to smell [The dog quickly *scented* the cat.]
scent • ***noun,*** *plural for senses 1, 3, and 4 only* **scents** • ***verb*** **scented, scenting**
● The words **scent, cent,** and **sent** sound alike.
The perfume has a lovely *scent*.
A penny is worth one *cent*.
We *sent* her a birthday card.

WORD CHOICES

Synonyms of **scent**

The words **scent, fragrance,** and **perfume** share the meaning "a smell."

the *scent* of freshly cut hay
the *fragrance* of just-baked bread
the *perfume* of gardenias

schedule (ske′jo͞ol *or* ske′jo͞o əl) ***noun*** **1** a list of the times at which certain things are supposed to happen. **2** the time at which something is supposed to happen [The work is ahead of *schedule*.]
verb **1** to make a schedule of [She *scheduled* her hours of work.] **2** to plan for a certain time [Adam *scheduled* an appointment for noon.]
sched·ule • ***noun,*** *plural* **schedules** • ***verb*** **scheduled, scheduling**

scheme (skēm) ***noun*** **1** a plan or system in which things are put together with care [the color *scheme* of a painting] —Look for the WORD CHOICES box at the entry **plan**. **2** a secret or dishonest plan or program [a *scheme* for getting rich quickly].
verb to make secret or dishonest plans; plot [He is always *scheming* to get out of work.]
scheme • ***noun,*** *plural* **schemes** • ***verb*** **schemed, scheming**

scholar (skäl′ər) ***noun*** a person who has learned much through study.
schol·ar • ***noun,*** *plural* **scholars**

scholarship (skäl′ər ship) ***noun*** **1** the knowledge of a person who has learned much; great learning. **2** the kind of knowledge that a student shows [Her paper shows good *scholarship*.] **3** a gift of money to help a student pay for instruction.
schol·ar·ship • ***noun,*** *plural for sense 3 only* **scholarships**

a	cat	ō	go	ʉ	fur	ə =	a *in* ago
ā	ape	ô	law, for	ch	chin		e *in* agent
ä	cot, car	o͝o	look	sh	she		i *in* pencil
e	ten	o͞o	tool	th	thin		o *in* atom
ē	me	oi	oil	*th*	then		u *in* circus
i	fit	ou	out	zh	measure		
ī	ice	u	up	ŋ	ring		

school[1] (sko͞ol) ***noun*** **1** a place, usually a special building, for teaching and learning. **2** the students and teachers of a school [The whole *school* was at the play.] **3** the time during which students attend school [*School* usually begins in September.]
verb to teach or train; educate [She is *schooled* in house repair.]
school • ***noun,*** *plural for senses 1 and 2 only* **schools** • ***verb*** **schooled, schooling**

school[2] (sko͞ol) ***noun*** a large group of fish or water animals of the same kind swimming together [a *school* of sharks].
school • ***noun,*** *plural* **schools**

school board ***noun*** a group of people chosen to be in charge of local public schools.
school board • ***noun,*** *plural* **school boards**

schoolbook (sko͞ol′bo͝ok) ***noun*** a book used for study in schools; textbook.
school·book • ***noun,*** *plural* **schoolbooks**

schoolboy (sko͞ol′boi) ***noun*** a boy who goes to school.
school·boy • ***noun,*** *plural* **schoolboys**

school bus

school bus ***noun*** a bus for taking children to or from school. School buses may be used on other trips having to do with school.
school bus • ***noun,*** *plural* **school buses** or **school busses**

schoolchild (sko͞ol′chīld) ***noun*** a child who goes to school.
school·child • ***noun,*** *plural* **schoolchildren**

schoolgirl (sko͞ol′gʉrl) ***noun*** a girl who goes to school.
school·girl • ***noun,*** *plural* **schoolgirls**

schoolhouse (sko͞ol′hous) ***noun*** a building used as a school.
school·house • ***noun,*** *plural* **schoolhouses**

schooling (sko͞ol′iŋ) ***noun*** the teaching or training a person gets at school; education.
school·ing • ***noun***

schoolmate (sko͞ol′māt) ***noun*** a person going to the same school at the same time as someone else.
school·mate • ***noun,*** *plural* **schoolmates**

schoolroom (sko͞ol′ro͞om) ***noun*** a room in a school, in which pupils are taught.
school·room • ***noun,*** *plural* **schoolrooms**

schoolteacher (sko͞ol′tē chər) ***noun*** a person whose work is teaching in a school.
school·teach·er • ***noun,*** *plural* **schoolteachers**

schoolwork (sko͞ol′wʉrk) ***noun*** the lessons worked on in school or done as homework.
school·work • ***noun***

schoolyard (sko͞ol′yärd) ***noun*** the ground around a school. It is often used as a playground.
school·yard • ***noun,*** *plural* **schoolyards**

school year ***noun*** the part of the year during which school is held. It is usually from September to June.
school year • ***noun,*** *plural* **school years**

schooner (sko͞on′ər) ***noun*** a sailing ship with two or more masts and with sails that are set lengthwise rather than across the width of the ship.
schoon·er • ***noun,*** *plural* **schooners**

schwa (shwä) ***noun*** **1** the usual sound of the vowel in a syllable that is not accented. This is the sound that is spelled by the letter *a* in "ago," *e* in "baker," or *o* in "terror," for example. **2** the symbol (ə) that is used to show this sound. An example is (ə gō′) for "ago."
schwa • ***noun,*** *plural* **schwas**

science (sī′əns) ***noun*** **1** a system of knowledge about the nature of things in the world. It is the result of observing, studying what is observed, and experimenting to test one's ideas about what is observed. **2** a particular branch of this knowledge [the *science* of astronomy].
sci·ence • ***noun,*** *plural for sense 2 only* **sciences**

science fiction ***noun*** movies, stories, and books that are fantastic and that make use of scientific devices, space travel, robots, and other things that are real or imagined.

scientific (sī′ən tif′ik) ***adjective*** **1** having to do with science [a *scientific* study]. **2** used in science [*scientific* equipment; *scientific* methods].
sci·en·tif·ic • ***adjective***

S

scientist (sī′ən tist) ***noun*** an expert in science.
sci·en·tist • ***noun,*** *plural* **scientists**

scissors (siz′ərz) ***plural noun*** [*also used with a singular verb*] a tool for cutting that has two blades that are joined together in the middle. The blades slide over each other when their handles are moved.
scis·sors • ***plural noun***

scold (skōld) ***verb*** to find fault with someone in an angry way [I *scolded* him for being late.]
scold • ***verb*** **scolded, scolding**

scoop (sko͞op) ***noun*** **1** a kitchen tool like a small shovel, used to take up foods such as sugar or flour. **2** a similar tool with a small round bowl that is used for taking up soft foods such as ice cream or mashed potatoes. **3** the amount taken up at one time by a scoop [three *scoops* of ice cream]. **4** the part of a large machine that takes up sand, dirt, rocks, or other material from the ground.
verb **1** to take up using a scoop or something like a scoop [We *scooped* up water with our hands.] **2** to make a hole by digging [The machine *scooped* out a hole for the swimming pool.]
scoop • ***noun,*** *plural* **scoops**
• ***verb*** **scooped, scooping**

scoot (sko͞ot) [*an informal word*] ***verb*** to go quickly; to scamper [The chipmunk *scooted* into the leaves to hide.]
scoot • ***verb*** **scooted, scooting**

scooter (sko͞ot′ər) ***noun*** a child's toy for riding on. It has a low board for the foot, with a wheel at each end, and a handlebar for steering. It is moved by pushing against the ground with the other foot.
scoot·er • ***noun,*** *plural* **scooters**

scope (skōp) ***noun*** **1** the amount that a person can understand; the range of a person's mind [This problem is beyond my *scope*.] **2** the amount or kind of material that is covered or included [the *scope* of a school dictionary].

-scope *a suffix meaning* a device for seeing or looking [A *microscope* is an instrument for seeing very small things.]

scorch (skôrch) ***verb*** **1** to burn slightly [He *scorched* his new shirt with the iron.] —Look for the WORD CHOICES box at the entry **burn**. **2** to dry up with heat [The sun *scorched* the grass until it died.]
scorch • ***verb*** **scorched, scorching**

score (skôr) ***noun*** **1** the number of points made in a contest [The *score* is two to one.] **2** a grade or rating [a test *score* of 98%]. **3** a set or group of 20 people or things [a *score* of birds]. **4** a piece of music showing all the parts for the instruments or voices [the *score* of an opera].
verb **1** to make points in a game [The team *scored* immediately.] **2** to keep the score of a game [My dad *scored* for us.] **3** to give a grade to [The teacher *scored* the math test.] **4** to win or achieve [They *scored* a great success with their new album.]
score • ***noun,*** *plural* **scores** • ***verb*** **scored, scoring**

scorn (skôrn) ***noun*** a feeling that a person or thing is weak, mean, or worthless and not deserving of sympathy or pity [She felt no pity, but only *scorn* for the friend who had stolen from her.]
verb **1** to think of and treat someone or something with scorn [She *scorned* teammates who skipped practice.] **2** to refuse to do something thought of as wrong [They *scorned* the idea of cutting funds for the new library.]
scorn • ***noun*** • ***verb*** **scorned, scorning**

scornful (skôrn′fəl) ***adjective*** full of scorn or contempt.
scorn·ful • ***adjective***

scorpion (skôr′pē ən) ***noun*** a small crawling animal with eight legs. It has two large pincers and a long tail with a poisonous stinger on the end.
scor·pi·on • ***noun,*** *plural* **scorpions**

scorpion

Scot (skät) ***noun*** a person born or living in Scotland.
Scot • ***noun,*** *plural* **Scots**

Scotch (skäch) ***adjective, noun*** *another word for* **Scottish**. *See note at* **Scottish**.

Scotchman (skäch′mən) ***noun*** *another name for* **Scotsman**. *See note at* **Scottish**.
Scotch·man • ***noun,*** *plural* **Scotchmen**

a	cat	ō	go	ʉ	fur	ə =	a *in* ago
ā	ape	ô	law, for	ch	chin		e *in* agent
ä	cot, car	oo	look	sh	she		i *in* pencil
e	ten	o͞o	tool	th	thin		o *in* atom
ē	me	oi	oil	*th*	then		u *in* circus
i	fit	ou	out	zh	measure		
ī	ice	u	up	ŋ	ring		

Scotland (skät′lənd) a part of Great Britain, north of England.
Scot·land

Scotsman (skäts′mən) ***noun*** a person, especially a man, born or living in Scotland.
Scots·man • ***noun,*** *plural* **Scotsmen**

Scotswoman (skäts′woom ən) ***noun*** a woman born or living in Scotland.
Scots·wom·an • ***noun,*** *plural* **Scotswomen**

Scottish (skät′ish) ***adjective*** of or having to do with Scotland or its people [*Scottish* dances].
noun the dialect of English that is spoken by the people of Scotland.
—the Scottish the people of Scotland.
Scot·tish • ***adjective*** • ***noun***
■ **Scottish** is more common than **Scotch** in formal use when speaking of the people of Scotland, their language, or their culture.

scoundrel (skoun′drəl) ***noun*** a bad or dishonest person; villain.
scoun·drel • ***noun,*** *plural* **scoundrels**

scour[1] (skour) ***verb*** to clean by rubbing hard with something rough [*Scour* the dirty pots.]
scour • ***verb*** **scoured, scouring**

scour[2] (skour) ***verb*** to search about in a quick but complete way [The police *scoured* the woods looking for the lost child.]
scour • ***verb*** **scoured, scouring**

scout (skout) ***noun*** **1** a soldier, ship, or plane sent out to spy on the enemy and report back information. **2 Scout** a member of the Boy Scouts or Girl Scouts. **3** a person sent out to find something [a talent *scout*].
verb **1** to go out looking for information [The helicopter *scouted* the valley looking for the enemy's camp.] **2** to go looking for something or someone [He *scouted* around for berries.]
scout • ***noun,*** *plural* **scouts** • ***verb*** **scouted, scouting**

scoutmaster (skout′mas tər) ***noun*** the adult leader of a troop of Boy Scouts.
scout·mas·ter • ***noun,*** *plural* **scoutmasters**

scow (skou) ***noun*** a large boat for carrying heavy loads. It has a flat bottom and square ends.
scow • ***noun,*** *plural* **scows**

scowl (skoul) ***noun*** an angry or mean look made by lowering the eyebrows and the corners of the mouth.
verb to make a scowl.
scowl • ***noun,*** *plural* **scowls** • ***verb*** **scowled, scowling**

scraggly (skrag′lē) ***adjective*** uneven, ragged, or irregular [a *scraggly* beard].
scrag·gly • ***adjective*** **scragglier, scraggliest**

scram (skram) [*a slang word*] ***verb*** to get out or go away in a hurry [The guard told us to *scram*.]
scram • ***verb*** **scrammed, scramming**

scramble (skram′bəl) ***verb*** **1** to climb or crawl in a quick, rough way [They *scrambled* up the hill.] **2** to struggle or fight for something [The dogs *scrambled* for the piece of meat.] **3** to cook eggs while stirring together the yolks and whites. **4** to mix up a message or signal so that it cannot be understood [The spies *scrambled* the radio signal.]
noun an act of scrambling [a *scramble* up the hill; a *scramble* for a loose football].
scram·ble • ***verb*** **scrambled, scrambling** • ***noun,*** *plural* **scrambles**

scrap[1] (skrap) ***noun*** **1** a small piece; bit [a *scrap* of paper]. **2** something that has been thrown away because it is useless. **3 scraps** bits of leftover food [We gave the *scraps* to the dog.]
adjective in the form of broken bits and pieces or of odds and ends [*scrap* metal; *scrap* paper].
verb **1** to break up into scraps. **2** to get rid of as worthless; discard [We *scrapped* our plans when it started to rain.]
scrap • ***noun,*** *plural* **scraps** • ***adjective*** • ***verb*** **scrapped, scrapping**

scrap[2] (skrap) [*an informal word*] ***noun*** a fight or quarrel.
verb to fight or quarrel.
scrap • ***noun,*** *plural* **scraps** • ***verb*** **scrapped, scrapping**

scrapbook (skrap′book) ***noun*** a book of blank pages for mounting pictures or clippings.
scrap·book • ***noun,*** *plural* **scrapbooks**

scrape (skrāp) ***verb*** **1** to make something smooth or clean by rubbing with a tool or with something rough [He *scraped* his muddy shoes on the mat.] **2** to remove something in this way [He *scraped* the mud off his shoes.] **3** to scratch or rub off the skin from [She fell and *scraped* her knees.] **4** to rub with a harsh or grating sound [The shovel *scraped* across the sidewalk.] **5** to get together bit by bit, with some effort [He *scraped* up enough money to buy a new bike.]
noun **1** the act of scraping. **2** a scraped place

[a *scrape* on the arm]. **3** a harsh, grating sound caused by rubbing or scratching. **4** an unpleasant situation that is hard to get out of [She got into a *scrape* by lying.] **5** a fight or conflict [He got into a *scrape* and received a black eye.]
scrape • *verb* **scraped, scraping** • *noun, plural* **scrapes**

scratch (skrach) *verb* **1** to mark or cut the surface of slightly with something sharp [The thorns *scratched* her legs.] **2** to rub or scrape with the fingernails to relieve itching. **3** to rub or scrape with a harsh, grating noise [The branches *scratched* against the window.] **4** to cross out by drawing lines through [She *scratched* out the wrong answer.]
noun **1** a mark or cut made in a surface by something sharp. **2** a slight wound. **3** a harsh, grating sound made by rubbing or scraping [The *scratch* of the chalk on the blackboard made me shiver.]
adjective used for figuring or for notes taken in a hurry [*scratch* paper].
—from scratch **1** from little or nothing [She built up the business *from scratch*.] **2** from the beginning, using basic materials or elements [He baked the cake *from scratch*.]
scratch • *verb* **scratched, scratching** • *noun, plural* **scratches** • *adjective*

scratchy (skrach′ē) *adjective* rough or sharp so as to scratch, scrape, or itch [a *scratchy* sweater].
scratch·y • *adjective* **scratchier, scratchiest**

scrawl (skrôl) *verb* to write or draw in a quick, careless way [He *scrawled* his name on the letter.]
scrawl • *verb* **scrawled, scrawling**

scrawny (skrô′nē *or* skrä′nē) *adjective* very thin; skinny [a *scrawny* neck].
scraw·ny • *adjective* **scrawnier, scrawniest**

scream (skrēm) *verb* **1** to give a loud, shrill cry in fright or pain [They *screamed* as the roller coaster hurtled downward.] **2** to make a noise like this [The sirens *screamed*.]
noun a loud, shrill cry or sound; shriek.
scream • *verb* **screamed, screaming** • *noun, plural* **screams**

screech (skrēch) *verb* to give a harsh, high shriek [The tires *screeched* when he slammed on the brakes.]
noun a harsh, high shriek.
screech • *verb* **screeched, screeching** • *noun, plural* **screeches**

screen (skrēn) *noun* **1** a mesh of wires woven so that there are small openings between them. Screens are used in windows and doors to keep insects out. **2** anything that hides, separates, or protects [A *screen* of trees protected the house from the strong winds.] **3** a surface on which movies or slides are shown with a projector. **4** a surface on a TV, computer, or radar for showing pictures or information.
verb **1** to hide, separate, or protect with a screen [They *screened* in the patio. The fog *screened* his movements.] **2** to test and question in order to separate according to skills or other qualities [This department *screens* people who apply for jobs.]
screen • *noun, plural* **screens** • *verb* **screened, screening**

screw (skrōō) *noun* **1** a piece of metal used to fasten things together. It is like a nail but with a groove winding around it in a spiral and a slot across its head. **2** anything that looks or turns like a screw. **3** a propeller on a ship or plane.
verb **1** to fasten or be fastened with screws [He *screwed* the shelf to the wall. This hinge *screws* to the door.] **2** to turn or twist like a screw [*Screw* the lid on tight.]
screw • *noun, plural* **screws** • *verb* **screwed, screwing**

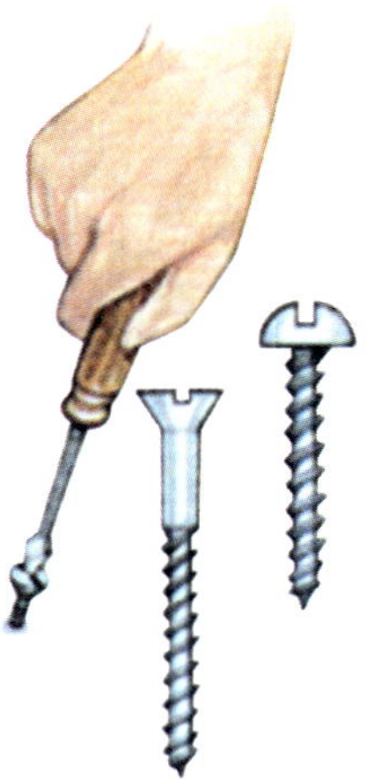
screw
2 kinds of screws

screwball (skrōō′bôl) *noun* **1** a pitched baseball that curves before it reaches the plate. It curves to the left when thrown by a left-handed pitcher and to the right when thrown by a right-handed pitcher. **2** [*a slang use*] an odd person.
screw·ball • *noun, plural* **screwballs**

screwdriver (skrōō′drī vər) *noun* a tool used for turning screws. It has an end that fits into the slot in the head of the screw.
screw·driv·er • *noun, plural* **screwdrivers**

a	cat	ō	go	ʉ	fur	ə =	a *in* ago
ā	ape	ô	law, for	ch	chin		e *in* agent
ä	cot, car	oo	look	sh	she		i *in* pencil
e	ten	ōō	tool	th	thin		o *in* atom
ē	me	oi	oil	*th*	then		u *in* circus
i	fit	ou	out	zh	measure		
ī	ice	u	up	ŋ	ring		

scribble (skrib′əl) ***verb*** **1** to write in a quick or careless way. **2** to make marks that have no meaning [The baby *scribbled* on the wall.]
noun writing or marks that are scribbled.
scrib·ble • ***verb*** **scribbled, scribbling** • ***noun,*** *plural* **scribbles**

scribe (skrīb) ***noun*** **1** a person who wrote out copies of books before the invention of printing. **2** a writer or author.
scribe • ***noun,*** *plural* **scribes**

scrimmage (skrim′ij) ***noun*** the entire play that follows the pass from center in a football game.
—line of scrimmage the imaginary line along which football teams line up to play.
scrim·mage • ***noun,*** *plural* **scrimmages**

scrimp (skrimp) ***verb*** to spend or use as little as possible [We *scrimped* all winter to save money for our vacation.]
scrimp • ***verb*** **scrimped, scrimping**

script (skript) ***noun*** **1** handwriting. **2** a printing type that looks like handwriting. **3** a copy of a play, TV show, or movie, used by the people who are putting it on.
script • ***noun,*** *plural* **scripts**

scripture (skrip′chər) ***noun*** **1** *often* **Scriptures** the Bible. **2** any sacred writing [The Koran is Muslim *scripture*.]
scrip·ture • ***noun,*** *plural* **scriptures**

scrod (skräd) ***noun*** a young haddock or cod prepared for cooking.

scroll (skrōl) ***noun*** a roll of parchment or paper, usually with writing on it.
scroll • ***noun,*** *plural* **scrolls**

Scrooge (skrōōj) the mean and stingy old man in Charles Dickens' story *A Christmas Carol*.

scrub (skrub) ***verb*** **1** to clean or wash by rubbing hard [We *scrubbed* the floors.] **2** [*an informal use*] to call off or cancel [They *scrubbed* the space mission during the final countdown.]
noun the act of scrubbing [Give the bathtub a good *scrub*.]
scrub • ***verb*** **scrubbed, scrubbing** • ***noun,*** *plural* **scrubs**

scruff (skruf) ***noun*** the back of the neck or the loose skin there.
scruff • ***noun,*** *plural* **scruffs**

scruffy (skruf′ē) ***adjective*** not tidy, neat, or clean; grubby [*scruffy* clothes].
scruff·y • ***adjective*** **scruffier, scruffiest**

scrumptious (skrump′shəs) [*an informal word*] ***adjective*** very pleasing to the taste; delicious [a *scrumptious* meal].
scrump·tious • ***adjective***

scrunch (skrunch) ***verb*** **1** to crunch, crush, or crumple [She *scrunched* the fender of the car.] **2** to hunch, huddle, or squeeze [He *scrunched* down in his seat.]
scrunch • ***verb*** **scrunched, scrunching**

scruple (skrōō′pəl) ***noun*** a feeling of doubt about doing something that a person thinks may be wrong [His *scruples* did not allow him to accept the reward money for turning in the thief.]
scru·ple • ***noun,*** *plural* **scruples**

scrutinize (skrōōt′n īz) ***verb*** to look at very carefully; examine closely [The doctor *scrutinized* the X-ray.]
scru·ti·nize • ***verb*** **scrutinized, scrutinizing**

scrutiny (skrōōt′n ē) ***noun*** a long, careful look; close examination.
scru·ti·ny • ***noun***

scuba

scuba (skōō′bə) ***noun*** air tanks and other equipment used by divers for breathing under water.
scu·ba • ***noun***

scuff (skuf) ***verb*** to wear a rough place on the surface of [I *scuffed* my shoes when I fell.]
noun a worn or rough spot.
scuff • ***verb*** **scuffed, scuffing** • ***noun,*** *plural* **scuffs**

scuffle (skuf′əl) ***verb*** to fight or struggle in a rough, confused way.
noun a rough, confused fight.
scuf·fle • ***verb*** **scuffled, scuffling** • ***noun,*** *plural* **scuffles**

scull (skul) ***noun*** **1** a short, light oar used in rowing. **2** a light, narrow rowboat used in racing.

S

verb to row with a scull or sculls.
scull • ***noun,*** *plural* **sculls** • ***verb*** **sculled, sculling**

● The words **scull** and **skull** sound alike.
It's hard work to *scull* across the lake.
The pirate flag depicts a human *skull*.

sculpt (skulpt) ***verb*** to shape or give form to [She *sculpted* the clay.]
sculpt • ***verb*** **sculpted, sculpting**

sculptor (skulp′tər) ***noun*** an artist who makes sculptures.
sculp·tor • ***noun,*** *plural* **sculptors**

sculpture (skulp′chər) ***noun*** **1** the art of carving wood, chiseling stone, casting or welding metal, or modeling clay or wax into statues or other objects. **2** a statue or other object made in this way.
verb to carve, chisel, cast, weld, or model into statues or other sculptures.
sculp·ture • ***noun,*** *plural for sense 2 only* **sculptures** • ***verb*** **sculptured, sculpturing**

sculpture

scum (skum) ***noun*** a thin layer of dirt or waste matter that forms on the top of a liquid.

scummy (skum′ē) ***adjective*** covered with scum [a *scummy* pond].
scum·my • ***adjective*** **scummier, scummiest**

scurry (skʉr′ē) ***verb*** to run quickly; scamper [A mouse *scurried* across the floor.]
scur·ry • ***verb*** **scurried, scurrying, scurries**

scuttle[1] (skut′l) ***noun*** a bucket for carrying coal.
scut·tle • ***noun,*** *plural* **scuttles**

scuttle[2] (skut′l) ***verb*** to run quickly from danger [He *scuttled* out of the path of the car.]
scut·tle • ***verb*** **scuttled, scuttling**

scythe (sīth) ***noun*** a tool with a long blade at the end of a long, curved handle. It is used for cutting grain or long grass.
scythe • ***noun,*** *plural* **scythes**

scythe

SD, S.D., or **S.Dak.** *abbreviation for* South Dakota.

SE or **S.E.** *abbreviation for* **1** southeastern. **2** southeast.

sea (sē) ***noun*** **1** the whole body of salt water that covers much of the earth; ocean. **2** a large body of salt water more or less enclosed by land [the Mediterranean *Sea*]. **3** a great amount or number [The stage actor looked out at the *sea* of faces in the audience.]
—at sea 1 sailing on the sea [He was *at sea* for three months.] **2** not knowing what to do or what is going on [She was completely *at sea* in her new surroundings.] **—go to sea** to become a sailor [He will *go to sea* after high school.] **—put to sea** to sail away [The ship *put to sea* in the middle of the night.]
sea • ***noun,*** *plural for sense 2 only* **seas**

● The words **sea** and **see** sound alike.
A storm threatened the ship at *sea*.
Can you *see* the bus from here?

seaboard (sē′bôrd) ***noun*** land along the sea; seacoast [Virginia is on the Atlantic *seaboard*.]
sea·board • ***noun,*** *plural* **seaboards**

seacoast (sē′kōst) ***noun*** land along the sea.
sea·coast • ***noun,*** *plural* **seacoasts**

seafarer (sē′fer ər) ***noun*** a sailor.
sea·far·er • ***noun,*** *plural* **seafarers**

seafood (sē′fo͞od) ***noun*** saltwater fish or shellfish used as food.
sea·food • ***noun***

seagoing (sē′gō iŋ) ***adjective*** made for use on the sea [a *seagoing* ship].
sea·go·ing • ***adjective***

sea gull ***noun*** a gull living along a seacoast.
sea gull • ***noun,*** *plural* **sea gulls**

sea horse ***noun*** a small fish with a slender tail and a head a little like that of a horse.
sea horse • ***noun,*** *plural* **sea horses**

sea horse

seal[1] (sēl) ***noun*** **1** a design placed on an official document to show that it is

a	cat	ō	go	ʉ	fur	ə = a *in* ago		
ā	ape	ô	law, for	ch	chin	e *in* agent		
ä	cot, car	oo	look	sh	she	i *in* pencil		
e	ten	o͞o	tool	th	thin	o *in* atom		
ē	me	oi	oil	*th*	then	u *in* circus		
i	fit	ou	out	zh	measure			
ī	ice	u	up	ŋ	ring			

genuine. The seal is usually pressed into a piece of paper or into wax. Wax seals were once also used to close letters. **2** a stamp or ring that presses such designs. **3** something that closes or fastens tightly [She could not remove the plastic *seal* that covered the bottle of medicine.] **4** a paper stamp used for decoration [Christmas *seals*]. **5** a sign or token [Their handshake was a *seal* of friendship.]
verb **1** to close or fasten tight [He *sealed* the cracks with putty. She *sealed* the letter.] **2** to settle in a definite way [They *sealed* the agreement by signing the contract.]
—seal off to enclose or surround with barriers or guards [The fire department *sealed off* the area where gas was leaking.]
seal • ***noun,*** *plural for all senses except 5* **seals** • ***verb*** **sealed, sealing**

seal[2] (sēl) ***noun*** a sea animal with a head more or less like a dog's and four flippers. It lives in cold waters and eats fish.
seal • ***noun,*** *plural* **seals**

sea level ***noun*** the level of the surface of the sea, halfway between high and low tide. It is used as a starting point in measuring heights and depths [Denver is often called the "Mile High City" because it is a mile above *sea level.*]

sea lion ***noun*** a large seal of the North Pacific.
sea lion • ***noun,*** *plural* **sea lions**

sea lion

seam (sēm) ***noun*** the line formed by sewing or joining together two pieces of material.
seam • ***noun,*** *plural* **seams**
• The words **seam** and **seem** sound alike.
A *seam* on the coat was coming apart.
Some players *seem* nervous before a game.

seaman (sē′mən) ***noun*** **1** a sailor. **2** a person in the navy who is not an officer.
sea·man • ***noun,*** *plural* **seamen**

seamstress (sēm′strəs) ***noun*** a woman who sews well or makes her living by sewing.
seam·stress • ***noun,*** *plural* **seamstresses**

sea otter ***noun*** a dark-brown otter found along the northern Pacific coast.
sea otter • ***noun,*** *plural* **sea otters**

seaplane (sē′plān) ***noun*** a plane that can land on water or take off from water.
sea·plane • ***noun,*** *plural* **seaplanes**

seaport (sē′pôrt) ***noun*** **1** a port or harbor for ocean ships. **2** a city or town with such a port [Boston is a major *seaport.*]
sea·port • ***noun,*** *plural* **seaports**

sear (sir) ***verb*** **1** to dry up; wither [The hot sun *seared* the crops.] **2** to burn or scorch the surface of [Hot grease *seared* his arm.]
sear • ***verb*** **seared, searing**

search (surch) ***verb*** **1** to look over or through in order to find something [We *searched* the house for the missing keys. We *searched* the sky but we could not see the plane.] —Look for the WORD CHOICES box at the entry **seek**. **2** to try to find [She *searched* for an answer.]
noun an act of searching [The police organized a *search* for the missing child.]
—in search of trying to find [The miners traveled west *in search of* gold.]
search • ***verb*** **searched, searching** • ***noun,*** *plural* **searches**

searchlight (surch′līt) ***noun*** **1** a device that can throw a strong, far-reaching beam of light. **2** the beam of light from such a device.
search·light • ***noun,*** *plural* **searchlights**

seascape (sē′skāp) ***noun*** **1** a view of the sea. **2** a picture of such a view [She paints mostly landscapes and *seascapes.*]
sea·scape • ***noun,*** *plural* **seascapes**

seashell (sē′shel) ***noun*** the shell of an oyster, clam, or other mollusk that lives in the sea.
sea·shell • ***noun,*** *plural* **seashells**

seashore (sē′shôr) ***noun*** land by the sea.
sea·shore • ***noun,*** *plural* **seashores**

seasick (sē′sik) ***adjective*** made sick in the stomach and dizzy by the rolling motion of a ship at sea.
sea·sick • ***adjective***

seaside (sē′sīd) ***noun*** land along the sea.
sea·side • ***noun,*** *plural* **seasides**

season (sē′zən) ***noun*** **1** one of the four parts into which the year is divided; winter, spring, summer, or fall. **2** a special time of the year [hunting *season*]. **3** a period of time [This is the busy *season* at work.]
verb **1** to add to or change the flavor of [He *seasoned* the meat with herbs.] **2** to make more fit for use by aging or drying [The timber was *seasoned* before it was used.]
—in season **1** possible to get fresh for eating

S

[Corn is *in season* in late summer.] **2** allowed to be hunted [Ducks are *in season* now.] **—out of season** not in season.
sea·son • *noun, plural* **seasons**
• *verb* **seasoned, seasoning**

seasonal (sē′zən əl) *adjective* of or having to do with a season or seasons [The *seasonal* rains begin in March. Picking crops is *seasonal* work.]
sea·son·al • *adjective*

seasoning (sē′zən iŋ) *noun* flavoring added to food.
sea·son·ing • *noun, plural* **seasonings**

seat (sēt) *noun* **1** a chair, bench, or other thing to sit on. **2** a place to sit or the right to such a place [We bought two *seats* for the game. She won a *seat* in the Senate.] **3** the part of something on which a person sits [The chair has a broken *seat*.] **4** the buttocks or the part of a piece of clothing that covers the buttocks [He got wet paint on the *seat* of his pants.]
verb **1** to cause to sit; put in or on a seat [*Seat* yourself quickly.] **2** to have seats for [This car *seats* six people.]
—be seated to sit down. **—take a seat** to sit down.
seat • *noun, plural* **seats** • *verb* **seated, seating**

seat belt *noun* a safety device like a belt across the hips and, often, over one shoulder. It is used especially in cars and airplanes to keep a person in the seat in case of an accident, to prevent injury.
seat belt • *noun, plural* **seat belts**

Seattle (sē at′l) a city in the State of Washington.
Se·at·tle

sea urchin (ʉr′chin) *noun* a small sea animal with a round body in a shell covered with sharp spines.
sea ur·chin • *noun, plural* **sea urchins**

sea urchin

seaward (sē′wərd) *adjective* **1** toward the sea [a *seaward* view]. **2** from the sea [a *seaward* breeze].
adverb toward the sea [marching *seaward*].
sea·ward • *adjective* • *adverb*

seawards (sē′wərdz) *adverb the same as the adverb* **seaward**.
sea·wards • *adverb*

seaway (sē′wā) *noun* **1** an inland waterway to the sea, used by large ships. **2** a route for ships to travel on the sea.
sea·way • *noun, plural* **seaways**

seaweed (sē′wēd) *noun* a plant or plants that grow in the sea.
sea·weed • *noun*

sec. *abbreviation for* **1** second. **2** seconds.

secede (sə sēd′) *verb* **1** to stop being a member of some group. **2** to leave a political union [The Confederacy was made up of the States that *seceded* from the U.S.]
se·cede • *verb* **seceded, seceding**

secluded (sə klo͞od′əd) *adjective* **1** kept away from others [a *secluded* patient]. **2** cut off from public view; hidden [a *secluded* cabin].
se·clud·ed • *adjective*

second[1] (sek′ənd) *adjective* **1** coming next after the first in a series; 2nd in order [*second* prize. You're the *second* person to ask me that.] **2** playing or singing the lower part [*second* violin].
noun **1** the number, person, or thing that is second [She was the *second* to arrive.] **2 seconds** a second helping of food.
sec·ond • *adjective* • *noun, plural* **seconds**

second[2] (sek′ənd) *noun* one of the 60 equal parts of a minute.
sec·ond • *noun, plural* **seconds**

secondary (sek′ən der′ē) *adjective* **1** next after the first in time or order [A high school is a *secondary* school.] **2** less important; minor [He loves football, but baseball is of *secondary* interest to him.]
sec·ond·ar·y • *adjective*

secondary color *noun* a color that is made by mixing two primary colors. Green, orange, and purple are some of the secondary colors.
secondary color • *noun, plural* **secondary colors**

secondary school *noun another name for* **high school**.
secondary school • *noun, plural* **secondary schools**

second-class (sek′ənd klas′) *adjective* next

a	cat	ō	go	ʉ	fur	ə = a *in* ago	
ā	ape	ô	law, for	ch	chin	e *in* agent	
ä	cot, car	oo	look	sh	she	i *in* pencil	
e	ten	o͞o	tool	th	thin	o *in* atom	
ē	me	oi	oil	*th*	then	u *in* circus	
i	fit	ou	out	zh	measure		
ī	ice	u	up	ŋ	ring		

below the highest or best [a *second-class* hotel].
sec·ond-class • ***adjective***

second cousin ***noun*** the child of a first cousin of a person's parent.
second cousin • ***noun,*** *plural* **second cousins**

secondhand (sek′ənd hand′) ***adjective*** **1** used first by another; not new [*secondhand* clothes]. **2** not straight from the source [*secondhand* news].
sec·ond·hand • ***adjective***

second person ***noun*** **1** the form of a pronoun that refers to the person who is being spoken to or the persons who are being spoken to. *You* is the pronoun for the second person. **2** the form of a verb that belongs with this kind of pronoun. *Are* in "You are" and *do* in "You do" are in the second person.

second-rate (sek′ənd rāt′) ***adjective*** second in quality; not among the best [a *second-rate* actor].
sec·ond-rate • ***adjective***

secrecy (sē′krə sē) ***noun*** the condition of being secret [He worked on his book in *secrecy*.]
se·cre·cy • ***noun***

secret (sē′krət) ***adjective*** **1** kept from being known or seen by others; hidden [a *secret* formula; a *secret* entrance]. **2** acting without others knowing [a *secret* agent].
noun **1** something hidden or to be kept hidden from the knowledge of others. **2** something that is not known or understood [Scientists try to learn the *secrets* of nature.]
—in secret without others knowing [They worked *in secret* on their invention.]
se·cret • ***adjective*** • ***noun,*** *plural* **secrets**

secretary (sek′rə ter′ē) ***noun*** **1** a person whose work is keeping records and writing letters for a person, company, or group. **2** the head of a department of government [the *Secretary* of State].
sec·re·tar·y • ***noun,*** *plural* **secretaries**

secrete (sə krēt′) ***verb*** to make and give off into or out of the body [Glands in the skin *secrete* oil.]
se·crete • ***verb*** **secreted, secreting**

secretion (sə krē′shən) ***noun*** **1** the act of secreting. **2** something that is secreted [Saliva is a *secretion* that helps us digest food.]
se·cre·tion • ***noun,*** *plural for sense 2 only* **secretions**

secretly (sē′krət lē) ***adverb*** in a secret way [He watched *secretly* from behind the curtains.]
se·cret·ly • ***adverb***

secret service ***noun*** an agency of the Federal government that does special detective work such as investigating counterfeiters and also guards the President.

sect (sekt) ***noun*** a group of people having the same leader or beliefs. A sect is usually a small group that once was part of a larger group and chose to separate from it.
sect • ***noun,*** *plural* **sects**

section (sek′shən) ***noun*** **1** a part cut off; separate part; division [a *section* of an orange] —Look for the WORD CHOICES box at the entry **part**. **2** a part of an area, city, or country [the business *section* of a city].
sec·tion • ***noun,*** *plural* **sections**

secular (sek′yə lər) ***adjective*** not connected with religion or a church; not sacred or religious [*secular* music; *secular* schools].
sec·u·lar • ***adjective***

secure (si kyoor′) ***adjective*** **1** free from fear, care, or worry [I feel *secure* about the future.] **2** safe from harm or loss [a *secure* hiding place]. **3** fastened or fixed in a firm way [He tied a *secure* knot.]
verb **1** to make safe; guard or protect [A high stone wall *secured* the property from trespassers.] **2** to tie or fasten in a firm way [We *secured* the boat to the dock.] **3** to get; obtain [He *secured* a job at the factory.]
se·cure ***adjective*** • ***verb*** **secured, securing**

securely (si kyoor′lē) ***adverb*** tightly or firmly [Close the gate *securely*.]
se·cure·ly • ***adverb***

security (si kyoor′i tē) ***noun*** the condition or feeling of being safe or sure; freedom from danger, fear, or doubt.
se·cu·ri·ty • ***noun***

sedan (sə dan′) ***noun*** a closed automobile with front and rear seats and two or four doors.
se·dan • ***noun,*** *plural* **sedans**

sedative (sed′ə tiv) ***noun*** a medicine that calms a person who is very nervous or excited.
sed·a·tive • ***noun,*** *plural* **sedatives**

sediment (sed′i mənt) ***noun*** **1** matter that settles to the bottom of a liquid. **2** sand or other matter set down by wind or water.
sed·i·ment • ***noun***

S

sedimentary (sed′i men**′**tər ē) ***adjective*** formed from sediment [*sedimentary* rock].
sed·i·men·ta·ry • ***adjective***

see (sē) ***verb*** **1** to be aware of through the eyes; have or use the sense of sight [We *saw* two robins. I don't *see* so well.] —Look for the WORD CHOICES box at the entry **perceive**. **2** to get the meaning of; understand [I don't *see* the point of his story.] **3** to find out; learn [*See* what they want.] **4** to make sure [*See* that the door is locked.] **5** to undergo or live through; to experience [He has *seen* some hard times.] **6** to go along with; accompany [I'll *see* you to the door.] **7** to visit with [We stopped to *see* our friend.] **8** to go to for information or advice; consult [You should *see* a doctor about your cough.]
—**see off** to go with to a place of departure to say goodbye [We *saw* them *off* at the airport.]
—**see to** to take care of; look after [*See to* the baby while I answer the phone.]
see • ***verb*** **saw, seen, seeing**
• The words **see** and **sea** sound alike.
Can you *see* the bus from here?
A storm threatened the ship at *sea*.

seed (sēd) ***noun*** **1** the part of a flowering plant that is able to grow into a new plant. **2** seeds as a group [We scattered the grass *seed* by hand.]
verb to plant with seeds [We *seeded* the lawn.]
seed • ***noun**, plural for sense 1 only* **seeds**
• ***verb*** **seeded, seeding**

seedling

seedling (sēd**′**liŋ) ***noun*** a young plant grown from a seed, not from a cutting.
seed·ling • ***noun**, plural* **seedlings**

seedy (sēd**′**ē) ***adjective*** shabby; run-down [a *seedy* coat].
seed·y • ***adjective*** **seedier, seediest**

seek (sēk) ***verb*** **1** to try to find; search for [The children are *seeking* their lost dog.] **2** to try to get; aim for [He is *seeking* a promotion.]
seek • ***verb*** **sought, seeking**

WORD CHOICES

Synonyms of **seek**

The words **seek**, **hunt**, and **search** share the meaning "to try to find."

Philosophers *seek* the truth.

They spent hours *hunting* for the missing piece.

The detectives were *searching* for clues.

seem (sēm) ***verb*** **1** to have the look of being; appear to be [She *seems* happy. The house *seems* empty.] **2** to appear to one's own mind [The ten-minute wait *seemed* like an hour.] **3** to appear to be true [It *seems* that you are right.]
seem • ***verb*** **seemed, seeming**
• The words **seem** and **seam** sound alike.
Some players *seem* nervous before a game.
A *seam* on the coat was coming apart.

seen (sēn) ***verb*** *past participle of* **see**.
• The words **seen** and **scene** sound alike.
Have you *seen* her latest movie?
A lake by the woods made a pretty *scene*.

seep (sēp) ***verb*** to leak through small openings; ooze [Rain *seeped* through cracks in the roof.]
seep • ***verb*** **seeped, seeping**

seersucker (sir**′**suk′ər) ***noun*** a light, crinkled cloth of cotton or linen, usually with a striped pattern.
seer·suck·er • ***noun***

seesaw (sē**′**sô *or* sē**′**sä) ***noun*** **1** a board balanced on a support at the middle and used by children at play. The children ride the ends so that when one person goes up the other comes down. **2** any movement or change up and down or back and forth.

a	cat	ō	go	ʉ	fur	ə =	a *in* ago
ā	ape	ô	law, for	ch	chin		e *in* agent
ä	cot, car	oo	look	sh	she		i *in* pencil
e	ten	ōō	tool	th	thin		o *in* atom
ē	me	oi	oil	*th*	then		u *in* circus
i	fit	ou	out	zh	measure		
ī	ice	u	up	ŋ	ring		

verb to move up and down on a seesaw or as if on a seesaw.
see·saw • ***noun**, plural* **seesaws**
• ***verb*** **seesawed, seesawing**

seesaw

seethe (sēth) ***verb*** to be very disturbed or upset [He was *seething* with anger.]
seethe • ***verb*** **seethed, seething**

segment (seg′mənt) ***noun*** one of the parts into which something is divided; section [The body of an insect has three main *segments*.] —Look for the WORD CHOICES box at the entry **part**.
seg·ment • ***noun**, plural* **segments**

segregate (seg′rə gāt) ***verb*** **1** to set apart from others [The people who smoked were *segregated* from those who did not.] **2** to keep people of different racial groups apart.
seg·re·gate • ***verb*** **segregated, segregating**

segregation (seg′rə gā′shən) ***noun*** the practice of forcing people of different racial groups to live apart from each other or to go to separate schools.
seg·re·ga·tion • ***noun***

seismograph (sīz′mə graf) ***noun*** an instrument that measures the strength of earthquakes or explosions.
seis·mo·graph • ***noun**, plural* **seismographs**

seize (sēz) ***verb*** **1** to take hold of in a sudden, strong, or eager way; grasp [He *seized* his weapon and began to fight.] —Look for the WORD CHOICES box at the entry **grasp**. **2** to capture or arrest [The police *seized* the criminal.] **3** to take over by force [The troops *seized* the fort.]
seize • ***verb*** **seized, seizing**

seldom (sel′dəm) ***adverb*** not often; rarely [I *seldom* see my old friends since I've moved.]
sel·dom • ***adverb***

select (sə lekt′) ***verb*** to choose or pick out [He *selected* a red tie to go with his gray suit.]
adjective chosen with care; picked as being best [The butcher sells only *select* cuts of meat.]
se·lect • ***verb*** **selected, selecting** • ***adjective***

selection (sə lek′shən) ***noun*** **1** the act of selecting; choice [The *selection* of candidates is up to the committee.] **2** a person, thing, or group chosen [Her *selection* for dessert was lemon pie.] **3** things to choose from [a wide *selection* of colors].
se·lec·tion • ***noun**, plural for senses 2 and 3 only* **selections**

selective (sə lek′tiv) ***adjective*** tending to select carefully [He is very *selective* about what he reads.]
se·lec·tive • ***adjective***

self (self) ***noun*** one's own person or being when it is thought of as being separate from all others.
self • ***noun**, plural* **selves**

self- *a prefix meaning:* **1** of oneself or itself [*Self*-control is control of oneself.] **2** by oneself or itself [A *self*-taught violinist has been taught by himself.] **3** to oneself [A *self*-addressed envelope is addressed to oneself.] **4** in oneself or itself [Being *self*-confident is being confident in oneself.] **5** for oneself [*Self*-pity is pity for oneself.]

self-appointed (self′ə point′əd) ***adjective*** acting on one's own, but behaving as though chosen by others [a *self-appointed* leader].
self-ap·point·ed • ***adjective***

self-assurance (self′ə shoor′əns) ***noun*** confidence in oneself and in one's own abilities.
self-as·sur·ance • ***noun***

self-centered (self′sent′ərd) ***adjective*** thinking mostly of oneself or one's own affairs; selfish.
self-cen·tered • ***adjective***

self-confidence (self′kän′fi dəns) ***noun*** confidence in oneself and in one's own abilities.
self-con·fi·dence • ***noun***

self-confident (self′kän′fi dənt) ***adjective*** sure of oneself; confident of one's own ability.
self-con·fi·dent • ***adjective***

self-conscious (self′kän′shəs) ***adjective*** **1** too conscious of oneself so that one feels embarrassed when one is with others. **2** showing that one is embarrassed [a *self-conscious* giggle].
self-con·scious • ***adjective***

self-control (self′kən trōl′) ***noun*** control of one's own feelings and actions.
self-con·trol • ***noun***

self-defense (self′dē fens′) *noun* defense of oneself or one's own property or rights [Judo is a method of *self-defense*.]
self-de·fense • *noun*

self-employed (self′em ploid′) *adjective* working for oneself, not for another person or company; having one's own business.
self-em·ployed • *adjective*

self-explanatory (self′ek splan′ə tôr′ē) *adjective* able to be understood without being explained [The instructions should be *self-explanatory*, but call me if you have any questions.]
self-ex·plan·a·to·ry • *adjective*

selfish (sel′fish) *adjective* caring too much about oneself and little about others [a *selfish* person].
self·ish • *adjective*

self-made (self′mād′) *adjective* successful through one's own efforts [a *self-made* millionaire].

self-pity (self′pit′ē) *noun* too much pity for oneself.
self-pit·y • *noun*

self-preservation (self′prez ər vā′shən) *noun* the act or instinct of keeping oneself safe.
self-pres·er·va·tion • *noun*

self-respect (self′rē spekt′) *noun* a proper regard for oneself; a sense of one's own worth.
self-re·spect • *noun*

self-sacrifice (self′sak′ri fis) *noun* sacrifice of oneself or one's own interests for the benefit of others.
self-sac·ri·fice • *noun*

self-service (self′sur′vis) *adjective* set up so that customers serve themselves [a *self-service* gas station].
self-serv·ice • *adjective*

self-sufficient (self′sə fish′ənt) *adjective* able to get along without help from others; independent.
self-suf·fi·cient • *adjective*

sell (sel) *verb* **1** to give in return for money [Will you *sell* me your skates for $10?] **2** to offer for sale; deal in [This store *sells* shoes.] **3** to be for sale [These jeans *sell* for $20.] **4** to help the sale of [TV *sells* many products.] **5** to be a popular item on the market; attract buyers [These shirts are *selling* very well.] **6** [*an informal use*] to win approval for or from [We *sold* him on the idea.]
sell • *verb* **sold, selling**
● The words **sell** and **cell** sound alike.
A salesman's job is to *sell* things.
The prison *cell* was without windows.

WORD CHOICES

Synonyms of sell

The words **sell, barter,** and **trade** share the meaning "to give something to someone in return for something else."

The Greens *sold* their house for $80,000.

The farmer *bartered* a bushel of potatoes for a pair of shoes.

He *traded* his old bicycle to me for my sled.

seller (sel′ər) *noun* **1** a person who sells something. **2** a thing sold, according to how well it has sold [This car is our biggest *seller*.]
sell·er • *noun, plural* **sellers**
● The words **seller** and **cellar** sound alike.
That ticket *seller* is always friendly.
Go into the *cellar* if there's a storm.

seltzer (selt′sər) *noun* **1** *also* **Seltzer** natural mineral water that has bubbles. **2** any carbonated water, especially a kind that is flavored with fruit juice.
selt·zer • *noun, plural* **seltzers**

selves (selvz) *noun plural of* **self**.

semaphore

a	cat	ō	go	ʉ	fur	ə = a	*in* ago
ā	ape	ô	law, for	ch	chin	e	*in* agent
ä	cot, car	oo	look	sh	she	i	*in* pencil
e	ten	ōō	tool	th	thin	o	*in* atom
ē	me	oi	oil	*th*	then	u	*in* circus
i	fit	ou	out	zh	measure		
ī	ice	u	up	ŋ	ring		

semaphore (sem′ə fôr) ***noun*** a system of signaling by the use of two flags, one held in each hand. The arms are moved to a different position for each letter of the alphabet.
sem·a·phore • ***noun***

semester (sə mes′tər) ***noun*** one of the two terms that usually make up a school year.
se·mes·ter • ***noun,*** *plural* **semesters**

semi (sem′ī) [*an informal word*] ***noun*** a large vehicle that is made up of a truck tractor and a trailer.
sem·i • ***noun,*** *plural* **semis**

semi- *a prefix meaning:* **1** half [A *semicircle* is a half circle.] **2** partly [A *semiprivate* room in a hospital is not completely private because it has at least two beds.] **3** twice in a certain length of time [A *semiannual* meeting takes place twice a year.]

semicircle (sem′i sur′kəl) ***noun*** a half circle.
sem·i·cir·cle • ***noun,*** *plural* **semicircles**

semicolon (sem′i kō′lən) ***noun*** a mark of punctuation (;). It is used to show a pause that is shorter than the pause at the end of a sentence, but longer than the pause that a comma marks.
sem·i·co·lon • ***noun,*** *plural* **semicolons**

semifinal (sem′i fī′nəl) ***noun*** a game, round, or match that comes just before the final one in a contest or tournament.
sem·i·fi·nal • ***noun,*** *plural* **semifinals**

seminary (sem′i ner′ē) ***noun*** a school or college where priests, ministers, or rabbis are trained.
sem·i·nar·y • ***noun,*** *plural* **seminaries**

Seminole (sem′i nōl) ***noun*** a member of any of the North American Indian peoples who settled in Florida. They now also live in Oklahoma.
Sem·i·nole • ***noun,*** *plural* **Seminoles** or **Seminole**

semiprecious (sem′i presh′əs) ***adjective*** describing stones that are of less value than precious stones [The garnet is a *semiprecious* stone.]
sem·i·pre·cious • ***adjective***

senate (sen′ət) ***noun*** **1** an assembly or council. **2 Senate** the upper house of the U.S. Congress, made up of two senators from each State. Senators are elected to terms of six years. **3 Senate** the upper house of most State legislatures.
sen·ate • ***noun,*** *plural for senses 1 and 3 only* **senates**

WORD HISTORY

senate

We get **senate** from a Latin word that means "old." The **senate** of ancient Rome was a council of older men who were thought to be wiser and more experienced than younger people in ruling a country.

senator (sen′ə tər) ***noun*** *also* **Senator** a member of a senate or the Senate.
sen·a·tor • ***noun,*** *plural* **senators**

send (send) ***verb*** **1** to cause to be carried or delivered [She *sent* a letter. He *sent* her flowers.] **2** to cause or force to go [The teacher *sent* her home. He *sent* the ball over the fence.] **3** to put into some condition [The news *sent* him into a rage.]
—send for **1** to call to come; summon [*Send for* the doctor.] **2** to place an order for [I *sent for* the tickets.] **—send out** to mail, issue, or distribute from a central point [The new video will be *sent out* to the stores next week.]
send • ***verb*** **sent, sending**

Senegal (sen′ə gôl′) a country in western Africa, on the Atlantic Ocean.
Sen·e·gal

senile (sē′nīl) ***adjective*** showing confusion, great loss of memory, or other weakness of the mind that sometimes comes with old age.
se·nile • ***adjective***

senior (sēn′yər) ***adjective*** **1** the older of two: this word is written after the name of a father whose son has exactly the same name. **2** of higher rank or longer service [the *senior* partner]. **3** of seniors in a high school or college [the *senior* class].
noun **1** a person who is older or has a higher rank than another [She is his *senior* by ten years.] **2** a student in the last year of high school or college.
sen·ior • ***adjective*** • ***noun,*** *plural* **seniors**

senior citizen ***noun*** an elderly person, especially one who is retired.
senior citizen • ***noun,*** *plural* **senior citizens**

senior high school ***noun*** a high school following junior high school. It usually has the tenth, eleventh, and twelfth grades.

senior high school • *noun, plural* **senior high schools**

seniority (sēn yôr′i tē) *noun* the condition or fact of being older, higher in rank, or longer in service [The workers with *seniority* receive higher wages and longer vacations.]
sen·ior·i·ty • *noun*

señor (se nyôr′) *noun* a Spanish word used, like "Mr.," as a title for a man.
se·ñor • *noun, plural* **se·ño·res** (se nyô′res)

señora (se nyô′rä) *noun* a Spanish word used, like "Mrs.," as a title for a married woman.
se·ño·ra • *noun, plural* **se·ño·ras** (se nyô′räs)

señorita (se′nyô rē′tä) *noun* a Spanish word used, like "Miss," as a title for an unmarried woman.
se·ño·ri·ta • *noun, plural* **se·ño·ri·tas** (se nyô rē′täs)

sensation (sen sā′shən) *noun* **1** a feeling that comes from the senses or the mind [a warm *sensation*; a dizzy *sensation*]. **2** a feeling of great excitement [The news of her wedding caused a *sensation* back home.] **3** something that stirs up great excitement [Her new book will be a *sensation*.]
sen·sa·tion • *noun, plural* **sensations**

sensational (sen sā′shə nəl) *adjective* **1** stirring up great excitement [a *sensational* new product]. **2** [*an informal use*] very good [Her grades are *sensational!*]
sen·sa·tion·al • *adjective*

sense (sens) *noun* **1** one of the special powers of the body and mind that let a person or animal see, hear, feel, taste, or smell. The five senses are sight, hearing, touch, taste, and smell. **2** a feeling or sensation [a *sense* of warmth; a *sense* of guilt]. **3** a special understanding [a *sense* of honor; a *sense* of beauty; a *sense* of rhythm; a *sense* of humor]. **4** judgment; good thinking [She showed good *sense* in her decision. There's no *sense* in going there late.] **5** a meaning of a word [This dictionary has definitions for several *senses* for the word "sensitive."]
verb to be or become aware of; feel [I *sensed* something wrong as soon as I saw them.]
—make sense to have a meaning that can be understood; be reasonable or logical [His excuse *makes sense* to me.]
sense • *noun, plural for senses 1 and 5 only* **senses** • *verb* **sensed, sensing**

senseless (sens′ləs) *adjective* **1** not able to feel and think [He was knocked *senseless* by the punch.] **2** having no meaning; stupid or foolish [a *senseless* act of violence].
sense·less • *adjective*

sensible (sen′si bəl) *adjective* having or showing good sense; reasonable; wise [a *sensible* person; *sensible* advice].
sen·si·ble • *adjective*

sensitive (sen′si tiv) *adjective* **1** quick to feel or notice [A dog's nose is *sensitive* to smells.] **2** able to understand [Artists are *sensitive* to beauty.] **3** quick to change or react when acted on by something [Camera film is *sensitive* to light.] **4** easily hurt or irritated [Don't be so *sensitive* about being teased.] **5** sore or tender [a *sensitive* bruise].
sen·si·tive • *adjective*

sensory (sen′sər ē) *adjective* having to do with the senses [*sensory* impressions].
sen·so·ry • *adjective*

sent (sent) *verb past tense and past participle of* **send**.
• The words **sent, cent,** and **scent** soun alike.
We *sent* her a birthday card.
A penny is worth one *cent*.
The perfume has a lovely *scent*.

sentence (sen′təns) *noun* **1** a group of words that is used to tell, ask, command, or exclaim something. It usually has a subject and a verb. A sentence begins with a capital letter and ends with a period, question mark, or exclamation mark. These are sentences: I am angry. Do you like spaghetti? Come here, please. Wow, we won! **2** the judgment of a court on the punishment to be given to a person who has been found guilty. **3** the punishment itself [He served his *sentence* at the State prison.]
verb to pass sentence on [The judge *sentenced* him to ten years in prison.]
sen·tence • *noun, plural* **sentences** • *verb* **sentenced, sentencing**

sentiment (sen′ti mənt) *noun* **1** a feeling about something [Loyalty is a noble *sentiment*.] **2** gentle or tender feeling [The love story was full of *sentiment*.]
sen·ti·ment • *noun, plural for sense 1 only* **sentiments**

sentimental (sen′ti ment′l) *adjective* showing or causing tender, gentle feelings [I always

a cat	ō go	ʉ fur	ə = a *in* ago
ā ape	ô law, for	ch chin	e *in* agent
ä cot, car	oo look	sh she	i *in* pencil
e ten	ōō tool	th thin	o *in* atom
ē me	oi oil	*th* then	u *in* circus
i fit	ou out	zh measure	
ī ice	u up	ŋ ring	

cry when I watch *sentimental* movies.]
sen·ti·men·tal • *adjective*

sentry (sen′trē) ***noun*** a soldier or other person who guards or keeps watch over a group.
sen·try • ***noun,*** *plural* **sentries**

sepal (sē′pəl) ***noun*** one of the leaves that grow in a ring around the base of a flower.
se·pal • ***noun,*** *plural* **sepals**

separate (sep′ə rāt *for v.;* sep′ə rət *or* sep′rət *for adj.*) ***verb*** **1** to set apart or divide into groups [*Separate* the good apples from the bad ones.] **2** to keep things apart by being between them or by putting something between them [The fence *separates* the two back yards.] **3** to go apart or in different directions [The friends *separated* at the street corner.]
adjective **1** not connected to something else [The garage is *separate* from the house.] **2** set apart or kept apart [His toys are kept *separate* from mine.] **3** single or individual [Name the *separate* parts of an insect's body.]
sep·a·rate • ***verb*** **separated, separating** • ***adjective***

SPELLING TIP

Use this memory aid to spell **separate**. There is ***a rat*** in sep***arat***e.

separation (sep′ə rā′shən) ***noun*** **1** the act of separating or the condition of being separated [Recycling requires the *separation* of metal from paper.] **2** a gap or other space that separates.
sep·a·ra·tion • ***noun,*** *plural* **separations**

September (sep tem′bər) ***noun*** the ninth month of the year. September has 30 days. Abbreviated **Sept.**
Sep·tem·ber • ***noun***

WORD HISTORY

September

The name of this month comes from the Latin word for "seven." **September** was the seventh month of the ancient Roman year, which began with March, not January.

septic tank (sep′tik) ***noun*** a large tank that is buried in the ground. The waste and water from the drains of a house flow into it. Bacteria in the tank help the waste to change into less dangerous materials.
sep·tic tank • ***noun,*** *plural* **septic tanks**

sequence (sē′kwens) ***noun*** **1** the order in which things follow one another [Line them up in *sequence* from shortest to tallest.] **2** a series of things, in order [He was asked to memorize a *sequence* of numbers.] —Look for the WORD CHOICES box at the entry **series**.
se·quence • ***noun,*** *plural for sense 2 only* **sequences**

sequin (sē′kwin) ***noun*** a very small, round, shiny piece of metal or plastic. Sequins are sewn in clusters onto clothing as decoration.
se·quin • ***noun,*** *plural* **sequins**

sequoia (si kwoi′ə) ***noun*** a giant evergreen tree of California. The bark of the tree resists fire.
se·quoi·a • ***noun,*** *plural* **sequoias**

sequoia

Serbia (sur′bē ə) a country in southeastern Europe. It was part of Yugoslavia.
Ser·bi·a

serenade (ser ə nād′) ***verb*** to perform music outdoors at night for someone [He *serenaded* his sweetheart beneath her window.]
noun the outdoor performance of music for someone.
ser·e·nade • ***verb*** **serenaded, serenading** • ***noun,*** *plural* **serenades**

serene (sə rēn′) ***adjective*** calm or peaceful.
se·rene • ***adjective***

serf (surf) ***noun*** in past times in Europe, a kind of slave who lived and worked on a particular farm.
serf • ***noun,*** *plural* **serfs**
• The words **serf** and **surf** sound alike.
A *serf* and his family harvested crops.
We watched the *surf* break on the shore.

sergeant (sär′jənt) ***noun*** a noncommissioned officer in the armed forces.
ser·geant • ***noun,*** *plural* **sergeants**

serial (sir′ē əl) ***adjective*** having to do with a series, or in a series [a *serial* number].

S

se·ri·al • *adjective*

• The words **serial** and **cereal** sound alike.
Write down your car's *serial* number.
I eat cold *cereal* in the morning.

serial number *noun* a number given to each thing in a series. Cars, refrigerators, watches, and certain other items can have serial numbers, which are used to identify them [Dollar bills have *serial numbers* printed on them.]
serial number • *noun, plural* **serial numbers**

series (sir′ēz) *noun* **1** a set of similar things, in order or in a row [The band scheduled a *series* of concerts across the country. She collects books in a *series* on home repair.] **2** something, such as a TV show or set of novels, that is produced as a group and has a regular set of characters or related episodes.
se·ries • *noun, plural* **series**

WORD CHOICES

Synonyms of series

The words **series, sequence,** and **succession** share the meaning "a number of things coming one after another."

a *series* of concerts

the *sequence* of happenings which forms the plot of a novel

a puzzling *succession* of minor accidents

serious (sir′ē əs) *adjective* **1** having or showing deep or careful thought; thoughtful [a *serious* student; a *serious* discussion]. **2** sincere; not joking [Is he *serious* about wanting to help?] **3** important or complicated; needing careful thought [Poverty is a *serious* problem.] **4** causing worry; dangerous [We hoped the injury wasn't too *serious*.]
se·ri·ous • *adjective*

sermon (sʉr′mən) *noun* **1** a speech by a minister or priest given during a religious service [Sunday's *sermon* was about the love of God.] **2** any serious talk about how a person should act or think, especially a talk that is boring or not wanted [Her uncle gave us a long *sermon* about avoiding snacks between meals.]
ser·mon • *noun, plural* **sermons**

serpent (sʉr′pənt) *noun* a snake, especially a large or poisonous one.
ser·pent • *noun, plural* **serpents**

servant (sʉr′vənt) *noun* **1** a person who is hired to work in someone's home as a maid, cook, or other household help. **2** a person who works for the government [a civil *servant*].
serv·ant • *noun, plural* **servants**

serve (sʉrv) *verb* **1** to work as a servant [He *served* as butler in our home for 20 years.] **2** to perform services for; be of use to; help [She *served* her country well. One hospital *serves* the entire area.] **3** to be useful for [A wrench is a tool that *serves* many purposes.] **4** to wait on [The waiter *served* our table first.] **5** to offer or pass food or drink [The waitress *served* the dessert.] **6** to hold a certain office [She *served* as mayor for two terms.] **7** to be in the military [He *served* in the navy.] **8** to spend time as a prisoner in a prison [They will each be *serving* six years for the robbery.] **9** to be enough for [This recipe *serves* four.] **10** in tennis and other games, to hit the ball first to start it going back and forth between players [I'll *serve* first, and then it will be your turn.]
noun **1** the act of serving the ball in tennis and some other games, or a way of doing this [She has a *serve* that curves sharply.] **2** a person's turn to do this [It's your *serve*.]
serve • *verb* **served, serving** • *noun, plural* **serves**

service (sʉr′vis) *noun* **1** work done or duty performed for others [We gave her a special dinner for her years of *service* to the community. Our janitor performs many *services* each day.] **2 services** helpful acts, especially when done as the work of a professional person [Do you know the fee for the doctor's *services?*] **3** the condition or work of being in the employment of someone [The cook has been in their *service* for 20 years.] **4** work for the government, or the people who do it [a clerk in the civil *service*]. **5** the act or manner of serving food [The new restaurant has very poor *service*.] **6** a system or method of providing people with something [We have good telephone *service* in town.] **7** the armed forces, or a branch of the armed forces [She went into the *service* right after college.] **8** a religious ceremony [Sunday morning *service*]. **9** a set of articles used in serving food [They were given a silver tea *service* as a wedding present.]

a	cat	ō	go	ʉ	fur	ə =	a *in* ago
ā	ape	ô	law, for	ch	chin		e *in* agent
ä	cot, car	oo	look	sh	she		i *in* pencil
e	ten	ōō	tool	th	thin		o *in* atom
ē	me	oi	oil	*th*	then		u *in* circus
i	fit	ou	out	zh	measure		
ī	ice	u	up	ŋ	ring		

10 maintenance or repair of a car or other piece of equipment.
adjective **1** of or for service [Bring the TV set to a *service* center when it needs repairs.] **2** for servants or workers [All deliveries are taken to the *service* entrance at the back of the store.]
verb **1** to repair or adjust [They *service* radios and tape players.] **2** to perform a service for; serve [One gas company *services* the whole county.]
—of service helpful; useful [The salesman asked if he could be *of service* to us.]
serv·ice • ***noun,*** *plural for senses 1, 2, 7, 8, and 9 only* **services** • ***adjective***
• ***verb*** **serviced, servicing**

serviceman (sʉr′vis man′) ***noun*** a member of the military; soldier or sailor.
serv·ice·man • ***noun,*** *plural* **servicemen**

service station

service station ***noun*** a place where gasoline for motor vehicles is sold and where repairs are made.
service station • ***noun,*** *plural* **service stations**

serving (sʉr′viŋ) ***noun*** a single helping of food.
serv·ing • ***noun,*** *plural* **servings**

sesame seed (ses′ə mē) ***noun*** the flat seed of a plant, used as a seasoning and on bread and rolls.
ses·a·me seed • ***noun,*** *plural* **sesame seeds**

session (sesh′ən) ***noun*** **1** the meeting of a court, legislature, class, or other group to do its work [The committee holds three *sessions* a week.] **2** a series of these meetings [School is now in its summer *session*.] **3** the period of time a meeting or series of meetings goes on [Our State legislature has *sessions* that last from two to four months.]
—in session meeting [Court is now *in session!*]
ses·sion • ***noun,*** *plural* **sessions**

set (set) ***verb*** **1** to put in a certain place or position [*Set* the book on the table.] **2** to cause to be in a certain condition [Who *set* the house on fire?] **3** to put in order or adjust; arrange; fix [The hunter *set* a trap for the bear. Johnny *set* the table for supper. The doctor *set* her broken leg.] **4** to adjust so as to be in the right position for use [I *set* the alarm for 6 A.M.] **5** to cause to be directed toward or aimed at [If you *set* your mind to it, you can pass the course. His heart is *set* on winning the championship.] **6** to make or become firm, rigid, or fixed [Has the cement *set* yet? She *set* her jaw stubbornly.] **7** to establish or fix a price, time, rule, or limit [She *set* the chair's price at $100. The league *sets* the rules we play by.] **8** to compose a melody to fit words [She *set* the poem to music.] **9** to sink below the horizon [The sun *sets* in the west.]
adjective **1** fixed, established, firm, or rigid [a *set* time for the party; *set* in her ways]. **2** ready [We were all *set* to board the plane.]
noun **1** the special scenery, walls, furniture, and props for a scene in a play, movie, or TV show [The movie *set* looked like a room in a castle.] **2** a group of persons or things that go together [He is not in her social *set*. I bought a *set* of tools.] **3** a television or radio in its own cabinet [A large TV *set* was in front of the sofa.] **4** in mathematics, a collection of numbers, points, or other units [2, 4, 6, and 8 make up the *set* of even numbers between 0 and 10.] **5** one of a group of six or more games in tennis.
—all set [*an informal use*] ready; prepared [They were *all set* to leave.] **—set aside** to separate and keep for some special purpose [Her parents *set aside* money every year for her college education.] **—set in** to begin [Winter *set in* early this year.] **—set off** **1** to start out [The hikers *set off* for the lake right after breakfast.] **2** to show off as being different or by contrast [The blue scarf *set off* her eyes.] **—set out** **1** to start out [She *set out* for Boston on Friday.] **2** to plan or intend [The scientist *set out* to prove that the new theory was wrong.] **—set straight** to give the correct facts to [I *set* him *straight* about the coach's remarks.] **—set up** to make something ready [They were *setting up* the display when we got there.]

S

set • *verb* **set, setting** • *adjective* • *noun, plural* **sets**

Seton (sēt′n), Saint **Elizabeth Ann** (ē liz′ə bəth an′) 1774-1821; the first American-born woman to be named a saint (1975).
Se·ton, Saint **E·liz·a·beth Ann**

setter (set′ər) *noun* a hunting dog with long hair. Setters are trained to find birds and point them out by standing in a stiff position.
set·ter • *noun, plural* **setters**

settle (set′l) *verb* **1** to bring or come to an agreement or decision; decide [We *settled* the argument by splitting the cost of the ticket.] **2** to set in place in a firm or comfortable way [He *settled* himself in the chair to read.] **3** to calm or quiet [This medicine will *settle* your stomach.] **4** to come to rest [The bird *settled* on the branch.] **5** to make a home for or go to live in [Mr. Gomez *settled* his family in the country. The Dutch *settled* New York.] **6** to move downward; sink or make something sink [The car *settled* into the mud. Rain *settled* the dust.] **7** to pay a bill or debt [Hotel policy requires that you *settle* your bill before checking out.]
—settle down **1** to lead a more stable or routine life [After marriage, they *settled down* and raised a family.] **2** to become calmer [Everyone *settled down* when the fight broke up.] **—settle for** to accept something in place of what was asked for or wanted [He *settled for* a ticket to the bleachers when he heard the better seats were sold.]
set·tle • *verb* **settled, settling**

settlement (set′l mənt) *noun* **1** the settling of people in a new land or in a frontier [We learned about the *settlement* of Europeans throughout America.] **2** a place where people have gone to settle; colony [There were many early Spanish *settlements* in the Southwest.] **3** a small village [A *settlement* grew up where the rivers met.] **4** an agreement [The owners reached a *settlement* with the union.]
set·tle·ment • *noun, plural for senses 2, 3, and 4 only* **settlements**

settler (set′lər) *noun* a person who goes to live in a new country, colony, or region [The railroad brought new *settlers* to the area.]
set·tler • *noun, plural* **settlers**

setup (set′up) *noun* the way something is set up; its plan, arrangement, or details.
set·up • *noun, plural* **setups**

Seuss (so͞os), **Dr.** 1904-1991; U.S. writer and artist. He wrote books mainly for children. His real name was *Theodor Seuss Geisel*.

seven (sev′ən) *noun* the cardinal number between six and eight; 7.
adjective being one more than six [*seven* days in a week].
sev·en • *noun, plural* **sevens** • *adjective*

seven seas *plural noun* all the oceans of the world.

seventeen (sev′ən tēn′) *noun* the cardinal number between sixteen and eighteen; 17.
adjective being one more than sixteen [*seventeen* years].
sev·en·teen • *noun, plural* **seventeens** • *adjective*

seventeenth (sev′ən tēnth′) *adjective* coming next after sixteen others in a series; 17th in order.
noun **1** the number, person, or thing that is seventeenth. **2** one of seventeen equal parts of something; $^{1}/_{17}$.
sev·en·teenth • *adjective* • *noun, plural* **seventeenths**

seventh (sev′ənth) *adjective* coming next after six others in a series; 7th in order.
noun **1** the number, person, or thing that is seventh. **2** one of seven equal parts of something; $^{1}/_{7}$.
sev·enth • *adjective* • *noun, plural* **sevenths**

seventieth (sev′ən tē əth) *adjective* being ten more than sixty others in a series; 70th in order.
noun **1** the number, person, or thing that is seventieth. **2** one of seventy equal parts of something; $^{1}/_{70}$.
sev·en·ti·eth • *adjective* • *noun, plural* **seventieths**

seventy (sev′ən tē) *noun* the cardinal number that is equal to seven times ten; 70.
adjective being seven times ten [*seventy* miles].
sev·en·ty • *noun, plural* **seventies** • *adjective*

several (sev′ər əl *or* sev′rəl) *adjective* more than two but not many [*Several* people called

a	cat	ō	go	ʉ	fur	ə =	a *in* ago
ā	ape	ô	law, for	ch	chin		e *in* agent
ä	cot, car	o͝o	look	sh	she		i *in* pencil
e	ten	o͞o	tool	th	thin		o *in* atom
ē	me	oi	oil	*th*	then		u *in* circus
i	fit	ou	out	zh	measure		
ī	ice	u	up	ŋ	ring		

while you were out.]
pronoun, noun [*used with a plural verb*] a small number; some [Most of them left, but *several* stayed. *Several* of the windows were broken.]
sev·er·al • ***adjective*** • ***pronoun*** • ***noun***

severe (sə vir′) ***adjective*** **1** strict or harsh; stern; not gentle or kind [*severe* punishment]. **2** causing great damage or pain [a *severe* headache; a *severe* winter storm].
se·vere • ***adjective*** **severer, severest**

WORD CHOICES

Synonyms of **severe**

The words **severe, harsh,** and **stern** share the meaning "not gentle or kind."

a *severe* scolding
harsh punishment
a *stern* look

sew (sō) ***verb*** to work, mend, or fasten with a needle and thread, or with a sewing machine [Can you *sew*? Please *sew* the torn sleeve. I can *sew* buttons on the coat myself.]
sew • ***verb*** **sewed, sewn** or **sewed, sewing**
• The words **sew, so,** and **sow** sound alike.
It's easy to *sew* on buttons.
How can you be *so* mean?
Sow flower seeds in the spring.

sewage (so͞o′ij *or* syo͞o′ij) ***noun*** the waste matter carried off by sewers.
sew·age • ***noun***

sewer (so͞o′ər *or* syo͞o′ər) ***noun*** an underground pipe or drain for carrying off water and waste matter.
sew·er • ***noun,*** *plural* **sewers**

sewing machine ***noun*** a machine with a motor that moves a needle and thread through fabric to make stitches.
sewing machine • ***noun,*** *plural* **sewing machines**

sewn (sōn) ***verb*** *a past participle of* **sew.**

sex (seks) ***noun*** **1** either of two groups, male or female, into which persons, animals, and plants are divided [A driver's license identifies a person's *sex*.] **2** the fact or condition of being male or female [Unfair treatment of people based on *sex*, age, or race is against the law.] **3** sexual reproduction and sexual matters in general.
sex • ***noun,*** *plural for sense 1 only* **sexes**

sexism (seks′iz əm) ***noun*** unfair treatment of people based only on whether they are male or female.
sex·ism • ***noun***

sexist (seks′ist) ***adjective*** being unfair to people or showing prejudice toward them merely because of their sex.
sex·ist • ***adjective***

sexual (sek′sho͞o əl) ***adjective*** having to do with sex.
sex·u·al • ***adjective***

Seychelles (sā shel′ *or* sā shelz′) a country on a group of islands in the Indian Ocean, northeast of Madagascar.
Sey·chelles

Sgt. *abbreviation for* Sergeant.

sh (sh) ***interjection*** a word that is used when asking for quiet.

shabby (shab′ē) ***adjective*** **1** old and worn out [a *shabby* suit]. **2** run-down; falling apart [a *shabby* neighborhood]. **3** not proper; mean [a *shabby* way to treat guests].
shab·by • ***adjective*** **shabbier, shabbiest**

shack (shak) ***noun*** a small, crude hut.
shack • ***noun,*** *plural* **shacks**

shad (shad) ***noun*** a food fish related to the herring. Shad live in the ocean but swim up rivers to lay their eggs.
shad • ***noun,*** *plural* **shad**

shade (shād) ***noun*** **1** darkness caused by something blocking the sun's rays [Some flowers do better in *shade* than in direct sunlight.] **2** a shady area [We sat in the *shade* of an oak tree.] **3** any device for screening or directing light [a window *shade;* a *shade* for a lamp]. **4** a degree of darkness of a color [He chose a lighter *shade* of green for the carpet.] **5** a small amount, degree, or variation [There's a *shade* of anger in her voice.]
verb **1** to protect or screen from light and heat [Trees *shade* the house.] **2** to change little by little [The carpet *shades* from blue to green.] **3** to use lines or dark colors in a picture to show shade or shadow.
shade • ***noun,*** *plural for senses 3, 4, and 5 only* **shades** • ***verb*** **shaded, shading**

shadow (shad′ō) ***noun*** **1** the darkness or the dark shape cast upon a surface by something blocking light [We cast *shadows* on the side-

S

walk.] **2** a small amount; trace or remainder [The *shadow* of a smile crossed his face.]
shad·ow • *noun, plural* **shadows**

shadow

shady (shā′dē) ***adjective*** **1** giving shade [a *shady* tree]. **2** shaded from the sun [a *shady* path]. **3** [*an informal use*] not clearly honest or proper; suspicious [a *shady* business deal].
shad·y • ***adjective*** **shadier, shadiest**

shaft (shaft) ***noun*** **1** a long, slender stem or handle [the *shaft* of an arrow; the *shaft* of a golf club]. **2** a ray or beam [*shafts* of light]. **3** a long, narrow opening dug down into the earth [a mine *shaft*]. **4** a long passage going up through a building [an elevator *shaft*].
shaft • *noun, plural* **shafts**

shaggy (shag′ē) ***adjective*** having long, thick hair, wool, or nap [a *shaggy* dog; a *shaggy* carpet].
shag·gy • ***adjective*** **shaggier, shaggiest**

WORD CHOICES

Synonyms of **shake**

The words **shake, quiver,** and **tremble** share the meaning "to move up and down or back and forth with short, quick motions."

The sails *shook* in the breeze.

Her lips *quivered* with emotion.

The old man's hand *trembled.*

shake (shāk) ***verb*** **1** to move something quickly up and down or back and forth [She *shook* the can to see if it was empty.] **2** to bring, throw, remove, mix, or rearrange something by short, quick movements [*Shake* the medicine well before you take it. He *shook* salt on the popcorn.] **3** to clasp someone's hand in greeting [They *shook* hands when they met.] **4** to tremble or make something tremble [His voice *shook* with fear.] **5** to shock or upset [He was *shaken* by the news.]
noun **1** a shaking or trembling movement [a *shake* of the fist]. **2** *a short form of* **milkshake.**
—**shake up** **1** to mix something by shaking it. **2** to jar or disturb something. **3** to shock or excite someone [The news of the team's defeat *shook* them *up*.]
shake • ***verb*** **shook, shaken, shaking** • *noun, plural* **shakes**

shaken (shāk′ən) ***verb*** *past participle of* **shake.**
shak·en • ***verb***

Shakespeare (shāk′spir), **William** (wil′yəm) 1564-1616; English poet and writer of plays.
Shake·speare, Wil·liam

shaky (shā′kē) ***adjective*** **1** not firm or steady; weak [a *shaky* bridge]. **2** shaking or trembling [a *shaky* hand].
shak·y • ***adjective*** **shakier, shakiest**

shale (shāl) ***noun*** a rock formed of hardened clay. It splits into thin layers when broken.

shall (shal) ***verb*** (*helping verb*) *Shall* is used with other verbs to show future time. The word "to" is not used between *shall* and the verb that follows it [I *shall* leave tomorrow. *Shall* we eat?]
shall • ***verb*** *past tense* **should;** *he / she / it* **shall**

shallow (shal′ō) ***adjective*** not deep [a *shallow* lake].
shal·low • ***adjective*** **shallower, shallowest**

sham (sham) ***noun*** something false or fake [His act of sympathy was a *sham*.]
sham • *noun, plural* **shams**

shambles (sham′bəlz) ***plural noun*** [*used with a singular verb*] a place where there is great disorder and confusion [The children left the room a *shambles*.]
sham·bles • ***plural noun***

shame (shām) ***noun*** **1** a painful feeling of los-

a cat	ō go	ʉ fur	ə = a *in* ago
ā ape	ô law, for	ch chin	e *in* agent
ä cot, car	oo look	sh she	i *in* pencil
e ten	ōō tool	th thin	o *in* atom
ē me	oi oil	*th* then	u *in* circus
i fit	ou out	zh measure	
ī ice	u up	ŋ ring	

ing the respect of others because of having done something wrong [I felt *shame* after I yelled at my little sister.] **2** loss of honor; disgrace [The thief brought *shame* to her family.] **3** something to regret or feel sorry about [It's a *shame* you missed the party.]
verb **1** to bring shame or disgrace to someone [The actions of a few *shamed* the whole school.] **2** to force someone into doing something by making that person ashamed [Nadira's hurt look *shamed* Sonia into apologizing.]
shame • ***noun*** • ***verb*** **shamed, shaming**

shameful (shām′fəl) ***adjective*** bringing shame or disgrace [*shameful* behavior].
shame·ful • ***adjective***

shameless (shām′ləs) ***adjective*** feeling or showing no shame or decency [a *shameless* liar].
shame·less • ***adjective***

shampoo (sham po͞o′) ***verb*** to wash something, such as the hair or a rug, with a special soap.
noun **1** the act of shampooing [Give her a *shampoo* before cutting her hair.] **2** a special soap that makes suds for washing something such as the hair or a rug.
sham·poo • ***verb*** **shampooed, shampooing** • ***noun,*** *plural* **shampoos**

shamrock (sham′räk) ***noun*** a kind of clover with leaves in three parts. It is the emblem of Ireland.
sham·rock • ***noun,*** *plural* **shamrocks**

shamrock

shank (shaŋk) ***noun*** a cut of meat from the leg of an animal.
shank • ***noun,*** *plural* **shanks**

shan't (shant) shall not.

shanty (shan′tē) ***noun*** a small, shabby hut; shack.
shan·ty • ***noun,*** *plural* **shanties**

shape (shāp) ***noun*** **1** the way a thing looks because of its outline; outer form; figure [The cloud had the *shape* of a lamb.] **2** definite or regular form [Our class is getting the play into *shape*.] **3** [*an informal use*] condition [The house was in very bad *shape*.] **4** [*an informal use*] good physical condition [You should exercise to keep in *shape*.]
verb to give a certain shape to [The potter *shaped* the clay into a bowl.]
—shape up [*an informal use*] **1** to develop in a definite or favorable way [The picnic is *shaping up* well.] **2** to do what is expected; behave oneself [If you don't *shape up*, you won't be allowed to go with us.] **—take shape** to develop or show a definite form [Plans for the party are beginning to *take shape*.]
shape • ***noun,*** *plural for sense 1 only* **shapes** • ***verb*** **shaped, shaping**

shapeless (shāp′ləs) ***adjective*** without a definite or well-formed shape.
shape·less • ***adjective***

share (sher) ***noun*** **1** a portion of something that each one of a group gets or has [your *share* of the cake; my *share* of the blame]. **2** one of the equal parts into which ownership of a company is divided [He inherited 20 *shares* of stock.]
verb **1** to divide something and give it out in portions [I *shared* my lunch with the new student.] **2** to have or use together [The three of you will *share* the back seat.] **3** to take part; have a share [We all *shared* in the cooking.]
share • ***noun,*** *plural* **shares** • ***verb*** **shared, sharing**

shark

shark (shärk) ***noun*** a large ocean fish that eats other fish and sometimes attacks people.
shark • ***noun,*** *plural* **sharks**

sharp (shärp) ***adjective*** **1** having a thin edge for cutting or a fine point for piercing [a *sharp* knife; a *sharp* needle]. **2** having an edge or point; not round or blunt [a *sharp* ridge; a *sharp* nose]. **3** not gradual; sudden [a *sharp* turn]. **4** easily seen; clear [a *sharp* picture]. **5** very clever or shrewd [a *sharp* mind] —Look for the WORD CHOICES box at the entry **intelligent**. **6** alert [*sharp* eyes]. **7** harsh or severe [a *sharp* reply]. **8** sudden or forceful [a *sharp* blow]. **9** very strong or intense [a *sharp* pain]. **10** strong in odor or taste [*sharp* cheese].
adverb **1** exactly or promptly [She will arrive

S

at 6:30 *sharp*.] **2** in a watchful or alert way [Look *sharp* before crossing the street.]
noun **1** a musical note one half step above another. **2** the sign (♯) used to mark such a note.
sharp • ***adjective*** & • ***adverb*** **sharper, sharpest** • ***noun,*** *plural* **sharps**

sharpen (shär′pən) ***verb*** to make or become sharp or sharper.
sharp·en • ***verb*** **sharpened, sharpening**

sharpener (shär′pən ər) ***noun*** a device that sharpens something [a pencil *sharpener*].
sharp·en·er • ***noun,*** *plural* **sharpeners**

shatter (shat′ər) ***verb*** **1** to break into many pieces; to smash [Our baseball *shattered* the window.] —Look for the WORD CHOICES box at the entry **break**. **2** to ruin or destroy [The loss of their savings *shattered* their dream of owning their own home.]
shat·ter • ***verb*** **shattered, shattering**

shave (shāv) ***verb*** **1** to cut off hair with a razor, close to the skin [My father *shaves* every morning. He *shaved* off his mustache.] **2** to cut or scrape away a thin slice from [I *shaved* the ham with an electric knife.]
noun the act of cutting off hair from the face with a razor [The barber can give you a *shave*.]
shave • ***verb*** **shaved, shaving** • ***noun,*** *plural* **shaves**

shaver (shā′vər) ***noun*** an electric device that shaves hair.
shav·er • ***noun,*** *plural* **shavers**

shaving (shā′viŋ) ***noun*** **1** the act of one who shaves [*Shaving* with an electric razor won't cut you.] **2** a thin piece of wood or metal shaved off a large piece [There were wood *shavings* all over the carpenter's floor.]
shav·ing • ***noun,*** *plural for sense 2 only* **shavings**

shawl (shôl *or* shäl) ***noun*** a large piece of cloth worn especially by women over the shoulders or head.
shawl • ***noun,*** *plural* **shawls**

she (shē) ***pronoun*** the woman, girl, or female animal that is being talked about [Annette thought *she* heard a noise.]
noun a woman, girl, or female animal [This dog is a *she*.]
she • ***pronoun,*** *plural* **they** • ***noun,*** *plural* **shes**

sheaf (shēf) ***noun*** **1** cut stalks of wheat, straw, or something similar, tied up together in a bundle. **2** a bundle of things gathered together [a *sheaf* of papers].
sheaf • ***noun,*** *plural* **sheaves**

shear (shir) ***verb*** **1** to cut, slice, or tear off [The machine *shears* off bark from the wood.] **2** to clip off hair or wool [It was time to *shear* the sheep.]
shear • ***verb*** **sheared, sheared** or **shorn, shearing**
● The words **shear** and **sheer** sound alike.
The saw can *shear* and trim metal sheets.
The roof was high and *sheer*.

shears (shirz) ***plural noun*** any tool that is like large scissors, used to cut cloth or metal or to prune plants.

sheath (shēth) ***noun*** a case for the blade of a knife or a sword or similar weapon.
sheath • ***noun,*** *plural* **sheaths** (shē*th*z *or* shēths)

sheathe (shē*th*) ***verb*** to put into a sheath [The knight *sheathed* his sword.]
sheathe • ***verb*** **sheathed, sheathing**

sheaves (shēvz) ***noun*** *plural of* **sheaf**.

shed[1] (shed) ***noun*** a small, rough building for storing things.
shed • ***noun,*** *plural* **sheds**

shed[2] (shed) ***verb*** **1** to let something flow or fall; pour out [The country *shed* many tears when Lincoln died.] **2** to let something roll off or flow off without penetrating [Raincoats *shed* water.] **3** to lose or drop [Some dogs *shed* fur. Our cat *sheds* too.] **4** to get rid of [Uncle Harry *shed* a few pounds.] **5** to send out [That lamp *sheds* very little light.]
shed • ***verb*** **shed, shedding**

she'd (shēd) **1** she had. **2** she would.

sheen (shēn) ***noun*** gloss; luster [His straight black hair has a *sheen*.]

sheep (shēp) ***noun*** an animal that chews its cud and is related to the goat. Its body is covered with wool.
sheep • ***noun,*** *plural* **sheep**

sheep dog ***noun*** a dog trained to help herd sheep.
sheep dog • ***noun,*** *plural* **sheep dogs**

a cat	ō go	ʉ fur	ə = a *in* ago
ā ape	ô law, for	ch chin	e *in* agent
ä cot, car	oo look	sh she	i *in* pencil
e ten	ōō tool	th thin	o *in* atom
ē me	oi oil	*th* then	u *in* circus
i fit	ou out	zh measure	
ī ice	u up	ŋ ring	

sheepish (shēp′ish) ***adjective*** shy or embarrassed in an awkward way [The little boy gave us a *sheepish* grin.]
sheep·ish • ***adjective***

sheer (shir) ***adjective*** **1** thin enough to be seen through [*sheer* stockings]. **2** absolute; downright [His speech was *sheer* nonsense.] **3** straight up and down, or almost so; very steep [the *sheer* face of a cliff].
● The words **sheer** and **shear** sound alike.
He put up *sheer* curtains in his room.
Next year she'll help *shear* the sheep.

sheet (shēt) ***noun*** **1** a large piece of cloth used on a bed. **2** a single piece of paper. **3** a surface or piece that is broad and thin [a *sheet* of ice; a *sheet* of glass].
sheet • ***noun, plural*** **sheets**

sheik or **sheikh** (shēk *or* shāk) ***noun*** the chief or leader of an Arab family, tribe, or village.
sheik or **sheikh** • ***noun, plural*** **sheiks** or **sheikhs**
● The words **sheik** and **chic** sound alike.
The *sheik* led them to the oasis.
Her clothes are always very *chic*.

shelf (shelf) ***noun*** **1** a thin, flat piece of a material, such as wood or metal, that is fastened against a wall or built into a frame so as to hold things [Put the vase on the top *shelf* in the closet.] **2** something, such as a ledge of rock, like a shelf.
shelf • ***noun, plural*** **shelves**

shell (shel) ***noun*** **1** a hard outer covering [Eggs, nuts, turtles, clams, and snails all have *shells*.] **2** something like a shell in being hollow, or in being an outer covering or layer [a pie *shell*]. **3** a cartridge for holding the gunpowder, a bullet, or shot to be fired from a gun.
verb **1** to remove the shell from [We *shelled* peas before dinner.] **2** to fire shells at from a large gun [Their troops *shelled* the bridge all night.]
shell • ***noun, plural*** **shells** • ***verb*** **shelled, shelling**

she'll (shēl) she will.

shellac (shə lak′) ***noun*** a kind of thin varnish.
verb **1** to cover or varnish with shellac. **2** [*a slang use*] to defeat; to beat.
shel·lac • ***noun*** • ***verb*** **shellacked, shellacking**

Shelley (shel′ē), **Percy Bysshe** (pur′sē bish) 1792-1822; English poet.
Shel·ley, Per·cy Bysshe

shellfish (shel′fish) ***noun*** an animal that lives in water and has a shell. Lobsters, clams, and certain other shellfish can be eaten.
shell·fish • ***noun, plural*** **shellfish**

shelter (shel′tər) ***noun*** **1** a place or thing that protects someone from weather or danger. **2** protection [Give us *shelter*.]
verb to protect or give shelter to [This barn will *shelter* us from the rain.]
shel·ter • ***noun, plural for sense 1 only*** **shelters** • ***verb*** **sheltered, sheltering**

WORD CHOICES

Synonyms of **shelter**

The words **shelter, haven,** and **refuge** share the meaning "a place or thing that covers or protects."

They built a *shelter* for the cows.

The Smiths' front porch was our *haven* during the storm.

National parks serve as wildlife *refuges*.

shelve (shelv) ***verb*** to place on shelves [The librarian *shelved* the books.]
shelve • ***verb*** **shelved, shelving**

shelves (shelvz) ***noun plural of*** **shelf**.

shenanigans (shi nan′i gənz) [*an informal word*] ***plural noun*** tricks or mischief.
she·nan·i·gans • ***plural noun***

shepherd (shep′ərd) ***noun*** a person who herds and takes care of sheep.
verb to herd or lead like a shepherd.
shep·herd • ***noun, plural*** **shepherds** • ***verb*** **shepherded, shepherding**

shepherdess (shep′ərd əs) ***noun*** a girl or woman who herds and takes care of sheep.
shep·herd·ess • ***noun, plural*** **shepherdesses**

sherbet (shur′bət) ***noun*** a frozen dessert of fruit juice, sugar, and milk.
sher·bet • ***noun, plural*** **sherbets**

sheriff (sher′if) ***noun*** the chief law officer of a county.
sher·iff • ***noun, plural*** **sheriffs**

Sherlock Holmes (shur′läk hōmz′) a British detective in many stories by A. Conan Doyle. His great powers of reasoning help him solve the mysteries in the stories.
Sher·lock Holmes

she's (shēz) **1** she is. **2** she has.

S

Shetland pony (shet′lənd) ***noun*** a sturdy pony that has a shaggy coat and a long, thick tail and mane.
Shet·land pony • ***noun,*** *plural* **Shetland ponies**

shield (shēld) ***noun*** **1** a piece of armor that is carried on the arm to ward off blows or flying objects during battle. **2** something that is a barrier to dirt or flying objects, or that serves as a guard or screen. **3** something shaped like a shield. A coat of arms or a police officer's badge is called a shield.
verb to guard or protect [Trees *shield* our house from winter winds.]
shield • ***noun,*** *plural* **shields** • ***verb*** **shielded, shielding**

shift (shift) ***verb*** **1** to move or change from one person, place, position, or direction to another [He *shifted* his feet. Don't try to *shift* the blame. The wind is *shifting*.] **2** to change from one gear arrangement to another in a car or similar vehicle [She *shifted* from neutral into reverse.]
noun **1** the act of shifting; a change [a *shift* of public opinion; a *shift* in the wind]. **2** a group of workers taking turns with other groups at the same jobs [The night *shift* will take over soon.] **3** the regular work period of a shift [I work the night *shift*.]
shift • ***verb*** **shifted, shifting** • ***noun,*** *plural* **shifts**

shimmer (shim′ər) ***verb*** to shine with an unsteady light.
shim·mer • ***verb*** **shimmered, shimmering**

shimmy (shim′ē) ***verb*** to shake or wobble.
shim·my • ***verb*** **shimmied, shimmying, shimmies**

shin (shin) ***noun*** the front part of the leg between the knee and ankle.
verb to climb by gripping with the hands and legs.
shin • ***noun,*** *plural* **shins** • ***verb*** **shinned, shinning**

shine (shīn) ***verb*** **1** to give off light or reflect light; be bright [The sun *shines*. Her hair *shone*.] **2** to make something give off light [*Shine* the flashlight into that corner.] **3** to do especially well [She *shines* in arithmetic.] **4** to make bright by polishing [I'll *shine* my shoes before we leave.]
noun **1** the condition of being shiny [The car had a glossy *shine*.] **2** the act of polishing [I gave my shoes a *shine* before I left.]
shine • ***verb*** **shone** or **shined** (*for senses 1, 2, and 3*), **shined** (*for sense 4*), **shining** • ***noun***

shingle (shiŋ′gəl) ***noun*** a thin, flat piece of wood or other material that is laid with others as a covering on a roof or the side of a house.
verb to cover with shingles.
shin·gle • ***noun,*** *plural* **shingles** • ***verb*** **shingled, shingling**

shiny (shī′nē) ***adjective*** **1** bright; shining [a clean, *shiny* face]. **2** highly polished [a *shiny* dime].
shin·y • ***adjective*** **shinier, shiniest**

ship (ship) ***noun*** **1** a vessel, larger than a boat, for traveling on deep water. **2** an aircraft or spaceship.
verb **1** to put, take, go, or send in a ship or boat [The cargo was *shipped* from New York.] **2** to send by some other means; transport [They will *ship* coal by rail.]
ship • ***noun,*** *plural* **ships** • ***verb*** **shipped, shipping**

WORD HISTORY

ship

The basic meaning of the thousand-year-old English word from which **ship** comes is "a hollowed-out tree trunk." The first **ships** were made by splitting tree trunks and hollowing out the inside.

-ship *a suffix meaning:* **1** the quality or condition of [*Friendship* is the condition of being friends.] **2** the rank or office of [A *professorship* is the rank or office of a professor.] **3** skill as [*Leadership* is a person's skill as a leader.]

shipment (ship′mənt) ***noun*** **1** the act of shipping or transporting goods by any means [The *shipment* of small packages is this company's business.] **2** the goods shipped [The damaged *shipment* will be returned tomorrow.]
ship·ment • ***noun,*** *plural for sense 2 only* **shipments**

shipping (ship′iŋ) ***noun*** **1** the act or business of sending or carrying goods from place to

a	cat	ō	go	ʉ	fur	ə = a *in* ago	
ā	ape	ô	law, for	ch	chin	e *in* agent	
ä	cot, car	oo	look	sh	she	i *in* pencil	
e	ten	ōō	tool	th	thin	o *in* atom	
ē	me	oi	oil	*th*	then	u *in* circus	
i	fit	ou	out	zh	measure		
ī	ice	u	up	ŋ	ring		

place [*Shipping* is usually an important industry.] **2** all the ships belonging to a country or port [New York is a port open to the world's *shipping*.]
ship·ping • *noun*

shipshape (ship′shāp) ***adjective*** having everything neatly in place; trim [The house was *shipshape* by the time of the party.]
ship·shape • ***adjective***

shipwreck (ship′rek) ***noun*** **1** the remains of a wrecked ship [The *shipwreck* lay half buried in the sand.] **2** the loss or ruin of a ship in a storm or crash [All the cargo was lost in the *shipwreck*.]
verb to cause to suffer a shipwreck [They were *shipwrecked* in the storm.]
ship·wreck • ***noun,*** *plural* **shipwrecks** • ***verb*** **shipwrecked, shipwrecking**

shipyard (ship′yärd) ***noun*** a place where ships are built and repaired.
ship·yard • ***noun,*** *plural* **shipyards**

shirk (shurk) ***verb*** to get out of doing or to leave undone something that should be done [She *shirked* her homework to go swimming.]
shirk • ***verb*** **shirked, shirking**

shirt (shurt) ***noun*** **1** the common piece of clothing worn by a boy or man on the upper part of the body. It usually has a collar and a buttoned opening down the front. A shirt is often worn with a necktie. **2** a similar piece of clothing for a girl or woman.
shirt • ***noun,*** *plural* **shirts**

shirttail (shurt′tāl) ***noun*** the part of a shirt below the waist.
shirt·tail • ***noun,*** *plural* **shirttails**

shish kebab (shish′ kə bäb) ***noun*** a dish made up of small pieces of meat stuck on a skewer along with pieces of onion, tomato, green pepper, and other vegetables. It is broiled or roasted.
shish ke·bab • ***noun,*** *plural* **shish kebabs**

shiver (shiv′ər) ***verb*** to shake or tremble from fear or cold.
noun the act or an instance of shaking or trembling.
shiv·er • ***verb*** **shivered, shivering** • ***noun,*** *plural* **shivers**

shoal (shōl) ***noun*** a shallow place in a river, sea, or other body of water.
shoal • ***noun,*** *plural* **shoals**

shock[1] (shäk) ***noun*** **1** a sudden, powerful blow, shake, or jar [the *shock* of an earthquake]. **2** a sudden and strong upsetting of the mind or feelings [Their faces showed *shock* and disbelief.] **3** the event that causes this [Her accident was a *shock* to us.] **4** the feeling or effect caused by an electric current passing through the body. **5** a dangerous condition of the body that happens when the blood does not flow properly through the body. It can be caused by serious injury, disease, or emotional upset [The accident victim went into *shock*.]
verb **1** to upset the mind or feelings of someone with sudden force; to astonish, horrify, or disgust [His crime *shocked* us.] **2** to give an electrical shock to [Never pick up fallen electrical wires because they can *shock* you.]
shock • ***noun,*** *plural for senses 1, 2, and 3 only* **shocks** • ***verb*** **shocked, shocking**

WORD CHOICES

Synonyms of **shock**

The words **shock, startle,** and **stun** share the meaning "to have a sudden disturbing effect on the mind or feelings of."

His display of temper *shocked* us.

The lightning flash *startled* her.

We were *stunned* by the news of the bombing.

shock

shock[2] (shäk) ***noun*** bundles of grain stacked in a pile to dry.
shock • ***noun,*** *plural* **shocks**

shock[3] (shäk) ***noun*** a thick, bushy mass [a *shock* of hair].
shock • ***noun,*** *plural* **shocks**

S

shocking (shäk′iŋ) ***adjective*** causing great surprise, horror, disgust, or some other strong negative emotion [*shocking* news of a disaster].
shock·ing • ***adjective***

shod (shäd) ***verb*** *a past tense and past participle of* **shoe**.

shoddy (shäd′ē) ***adjective*** **1** made of cheap, poor material [a *shoddy* building]. **2** low or mean [a *shoddy* trick].
shod·dy • ***adjective*** **shoddier, shoddiest**

shoe (sho͞o) ***noun*** **1** an outer covering for the foot, often made of leather. **2** *a short form of* **horseshoe**.
verb to supply with shoes; put shoes on [The farmer learned to *shoe* horses.]
shoe • ***noun,*** *plural* **shoes** • ***verb*** **shod** or **shoed, shoeing**
● The words **shoe** and **shoo** sound alike.
One *shoe* came off when he ran.
I *shoo* flies away by waving.

shoehorn (sho͞o′hôrn) ***noun*** a small, curved piece of metal, plastic, or other material for helping to slip one's heel into a shoe.
shoe·horn • ***noun,*** *plural* **shoehorns**

shoelace (sho͞o′lās) ***noun*** a length of cord, leather, or other material used for fastening a shoe.
shoe·lace • ***noun,*** *plural* **shoelaces**

shoemaker (sho͞o′māk ər) ***noun*** a person whose work is making or repairing shoes.
shoe·mak·er • ***noun,*** *plural* **shoemakers**

shoeshine (sho͞o′shīn) ***noun*** the act of cleaning and polishing a pair of shoes.
shoe·shine • ***noun,*** *plural* **shoeshines**

shoestring (sho͞o′striŋ) ***noun*** **1** *the same as* **shoelace**. **2** very little money [They started the business on a *shoestring*.]
adjective at or near the ankles [The fielder made a *shoestring* catch of the baseball.]
shoe·string • ***noun,*** *plural for sense 1 only* **shoestrings** • ***adjective***

shone (shōn) ***verb*** *a past tense and a past participle of* **shine**.

shoo (sho͞o) ***interjection*** a word used to drive away chickens and other animals.
verb to drive away by crying "shoo" or by waving the hands [She *shooed* the chickens away.]
shoo • ***interjection*** • ***verb*** **shooed, shooing**
● The words **shoo** and **shoe** sound alike.
She said "*Shoo!*" to the friendly dog.
The lace on her right *shoe* snapped.

shook (sho͝ok) ***verb*** *past tense of* **shake**.

shoot (sho͞ot) ***verb*** **1** to send out with force from a gun, bow, or other weapon [He *shot* an arrow at the knight.] **2** to cause a bullet, arrow, or other missile to be sent out from a weapon [The soldier *shot* his gun.] **3** to discharge, or give out, bullets or other missiles [This gun won't *shoot* straight.] **4** to hit, wound, or kill with a bullet or other missile [The hunters *shot* ducks and other birds.] **5** to send out or throw swiftly and with force [The volcano *shot* molten rock into the air.] **6** to move out, by, over, across, or in some other direction swiftly and with force [The horses *shot* out of the barn. Lightning *shot* across the sky.] **7** to take a picture or film a movie of with a camera [It usually takes about ten weeks to *shoot* a movie.] **8** to push forth; sprout [The plants are *shooting* out their new leaves.] **9** to score a goal or points in certain games.
noun **1** a shooting trip or contest [a turkey *shoot*]. **2** a new, growing thing or part [Bamboo *shoots* are eaten as a vegetable.]
shoot • ***verb*** **shot, shooting** • ***noun,*** *plural* **shoots**
● The words **shoot** and **chute** sound alike.
The hunter will *shoot* only at birds.
Dirty laundry goes down the *chute*.

shooting star ***noun*** *another name for* **meteor**.
shooting star • ***noun,*** *plural* **shooting stars**

shop (shäp) ***noun*** **1** a place where things are sold; store [a book *shop*]. **2** a place where a certain kind of work is done [a machine *shop*].
verb to go to shops to look over and buy things.
shop • ***noun,*** *plural* **shops** • ***verb*** **shopped, shopping**

shopkeeper (shäp′kēp ər) ***noun*** a person who owns or runs a shop, or small store.
shop·keep·er • ***noun,*** *plural* **shopkeepers**

shoplifter (shäp′lif tər) ***noun*** a person who steals things from stores during the time in which the stores are open.
shop·lift·er • ***noun,*** *plural* **shoplifters**

shopper (shäp′ər) ***noun*** a person who shops.
shop·per • ***noun,*** *plural* **shoppers**

shopping center ***noun*** a group of stores,

a	cat	ō	go	ʉ	fur	ə =	a *in* ago
ā	ape	ô	law, for	ch	chin		e *in* agent
ä	cot, car	o͝o	look	sh	she		i *in* pencil
e	ten	o͞o	tool	th	thin		o *in* atom
ē	me	oi	oil	*th*	then		u *in* circus
i	fit	ou	out	zh	measure		
ī	ice	u	up	ŋ	ring		

restaurants, and other businesses with one large parking lot for all.
shopping center • *noun, plural* **shopping centers**

shore (shôr) ***noun*** land at the edge of a sea or lake.
shore • ***noun**, plural* **shores**

shoreline (shôr′līn) ***noun*** the edge of a body of water.
shore·line • ***noun**, plural* **shorelines**

shorn (shôrn) ***verb*** *a past participle of* **shear**.

short (shôrt) ***adjective*** **1** not measuring much from end to end; not long or not long enough [a *short* stick. These pants are too *short*.] **2** not long from beginning to end [a *short* book; a *short* trip; a *short* wait]. **3** not tall; low [a *short* tree]. **4** brief and rude [a *short* answer]. **5** less or having less than what is enough or correct [Our supply of food is *short*. We are *short* ten dollars.] **6** describing a vowel sound that takes a shorter time to say than sounds that are diphthongs. Short sounds in English include (a) in *bat*, (e) in *bet*, and (i) in *bit*.
noun **1 shorts** short trousers that do not reach down to the knee. **2 shorts** a piece of clothing like this that is worn by men and boys as underwear. **3** *a short form of* **short circuit**.
adverb suddenly [The car stopped *short*.]
—short for being a shorter form of ["Gym" is *short for* "gymnasium."]
short • ***adjective*** **shorter, shortest** • ***noun**, plural* **shorts** • ***adverb***

shortage (shôrt′ij) ***noun*** a lack in the amount that is needed or expected [a *shortage* of food].
short·age • ***noun**, plural* **shortages**

shortbread (shôrt′bred) ***noun*** a rich, crumbly cake or cookie made with much shortening.
short·bread • ***noun***

shortcake (shôrt′kāk) ***noun*** a dessert made with a light biscuit or sweet cake covered with fruit and whipped cream [strawberry *shortcake*].
short·cake • ***noun**, plural* **shortcakes**

short circuit ***noun*** an electric circuit that allows too much current to flow through it. It is most often accidental and can cause a fire or blow a fuse.
short circuit • ***noun**, plural* **short circuits**

shortcoming (shôrt′kum iŋ) ***noun*** a fault or weakness [Lying is a serious *shortcoming*.]
short·com·ing • ***noun**, plural* **shortcomings**

shortcut (shôrt′kut) ***noun*** **1** a shorter way of getting to a place. **2** any way of saving time, money, or some other thing [There are no *shortcuts* to doing a good job.]
short·cut • ***noun**, plural* **shortcuts**

shorten (shôrt′n) ***verb*** to make or become short or shorter [The tailor *shortened* the sleeves of the coat.]
short·en • ***verb*** **shortened, shortening**

shortening (shôrt′n iŋ) ***noun*** butter, lard, or other fat that is used in pastry to make it flaky.
short·en·ing • ***noun***

shortly (shôrt′lē) ***adverb*** in a short time; soon [I'll leave *shortly*.]
short·ly • ***adverb***

shortsighted (shôrt′sīt əd) ***adjective*** **1** *the same as* **nearsighted**. **2** not looking ahead or planning for the future.
short·sight·ed • ***adjective***

shortstop (shôrt′stäp) ***noun*** a baseball player whose position is between second and third base.
short·stop • ***noun**, plural* **shortstops**

shot[1] (shät) ***noun*** **1** the act or sound of shooting a gun or cannon [I heard a *shot*.] **2** something to be fired from a gun or cannon [Fill the cannon with *shot*.] **3** an attempt to hit something with a bullet, rocket, or other missile [The first *shot* missed.] **4** any attempt or try [I gave it my best *shot*.] **5** a guess [Take a *shot* at answering the riddle.] **6** a person who shoots [She's a good *shot*.] **7** a single photograph [Get a *shot* of us by the statue.] **8** an injection of a vaccine or other medicine. **9** a throw or other attempt to score in certain games [He missed an easy *shot* at the basket.]
—like a shot quickly or suddenly.
shot • ***noun**, plural except for sense 2* **shots**

shot[2] (shät) ***verb*** *past tense and past participle of* **shoot**.

shotgun (shät′gun) ***noun*** a gun for firing cartridges or shells filled with shot, or little metal balls.
shot·gun • ***noun**, plural* **shotguns**

should (shood) ***verb*** (*helping verb*) **I.** *past tense of* **shall** [I thought I *should* never see her again.] **II.** *Should* as a helping verb is used: **1** to talk about something that might happen or is likely to happen [If I *should* go, would you care?] **2** to talk about something that one ought to do [We *should* obey the law.] The

S

word "to" is not used between *should* and the verb that follows it.

shoulder (shōl′dər) ***noun*** **1** the part of the body to which an arm or foreleg is connected. **2 shoulders** the two shoulders and the part of the back between them [He has rounded *shoulders*.] **3** the part of a piece of clothing that covers the shoulder. **4** the edge of a road [A sign warned drivers of the soft *shoulder*.]
verb to push with the shoulder or shoulders [I had to *shoulder* my way through the crowd.]
shoul·der • ***noun,*** *plural* **shoulders** • ***verb*** **shouldered, shouldering**

shoulder blade ***noun*** either of two flat bones in the upper back.
shoulder blade • ***noun,*** *plural* **shoulder blades**

shouldn't (shood′nt) should not.
should·n't

shout (shout) ***noun*** a sudden, loud cry or call.
verb to say or cry out in a loud voice.
shout • ***noun,*** *plural* **shouts** • ***verb*** **shouted, shouting**

shove (shuv) ***verb*** **1** to push along a surface [*Shove* that chair across the room.] **2** to push in a rough or hurried way [In their haste, they *shoved* everyone aside.] —Look for the WORD CHOICES box at the entry **push**.
noun a push or thrust.
shove • ***verb*** **shoved, shoving** • ***noun,*** *plural* **shoves**

shovel (shuv′əl) ***noun*** **1** a tool with a broad scoop and a handle. It is used for lifting and moving loose material. **2** a machine with a part like a shovel. It is used for digging or moving large amounts of loose material.
verb **1** to lift and move with a shovel [He *shoveled* sand into the bucket.] **2** to dig out with a shovel [When the snowstorm stopped, we *shoveled* our walks.] **3** to put in large amounts [Try not to *shovel* food into your mouth.]
shov·el • ***noun,*** *plural* **shovels** • ***verb*** **shoveled** or **shovelled, shoveling** or **shovelling**

show (shō) ***verb*** **1** to bring into sight; allow to be seen; reveal [His red face *showed* his embarrassment. *Show* us the new puppies.] **2** to be or become seen; appear [Daylight began to *show* in the sky.] **3** to guide or lead [*Show* the new girl to her classroom.] **4** to point out [We *showed* them the sights of the city. A thermometer *shows* the temperature.] **5** to be easily noticed [The stain won't *show*.] **6** to make clear; explain, prove, or teach [He *showed* how it could be done.]
noun **1** the act of showing [a *show* of anger; a *show* of hands]. **2** a collection of things that are shown in public; a display [an art *show*]. **3** a performance of something, such as a play or movie, or a radio or TV program. **4** something false or pretended [She made a big *show* of being happy.] **5** something meant to attract attention [a great *show* of wealth].
—for show in order to attract attention.
—show off **1** to put or spread something out so that it may be seen [They proudly *showed off* their new team jackets.] **2** to do something that is meant to attract attention [He likes to *show off* by doing tricks on his skateboard.]
—show up **1** to be clearly seen; stand out [The small spot in your dress will not *show up* in the photograph.] **2** to come or arrive [It's about time they *showed up*.]
show • ***verb*** **showed, shown** or **showed, showing** • ***noun,*** *plural for senses 2 and 3 only* **shows**

WORD CHOICES

Synonyms of show

The words **show, display,** and **exhibit** share the meaning "to allow to be seen."

Please *show* us the garden.

Don't *display* your feelings so openly.

This is the room where they *exhibit* the French paintings.

show business ***noun*** the theater, movies, television, and similar kinds of entertainment thought of as a business or industry.

showcase (shō′kās) ***noun*** a glass case for displaying things. Many stores have showcases.
show·case • ***noun,*** *plural* **showcases**

shower (shou′ər) ***noun*** **1** a short fall of rain or hail. **2** a sudden fall or flow [a *shower* of sparks from the fireworks]. **3** a bath in which the body is sprayed with fine streams of

a	cat	ō	go	ʉ	fur	ə =	a *in* ago
ā	ape	ô	law, for	ch	chin		e *in* agent
ä	cot, car	oo	look	sh	she		i *in* pencil
e	ten	ōō	tool	th	thin		o *in* atom
ē	me	oi	oil	*th*	then		u *in* circus
i	fit	ou	out	zh	measure		
ī	ice	u	up	ŋ	ring		

water. **4** a device that sprays water for such a bath. It has a nozzle with holes in it. **5** a room or enclosed place where a person can take a shower. **6** a party where gifts are given to a special guest [a *shower* for the bride].
verb **1** to fall or come in a shower [It *showered* all morning. They *showered* the bride and groom with rice after their wedding.] **2** to spray or sprinkle with water [The enormous splash *showered* us with water.] **3** to bathe under a shower [I *shower* every morning.] **4** to give much or many of [They *showered* praise upon her.]
show·er • *noun, plural* **showers**
• *verb* **showered, showering**

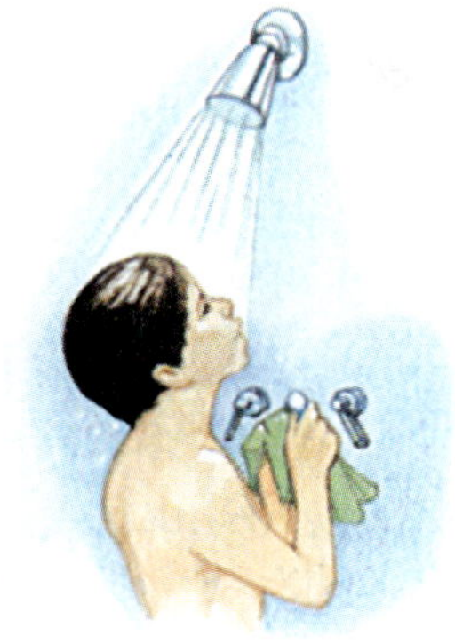

shower

shown (shōn) *verb a past participle of* **show**.

showoff (shō′ôf) *noun* a person who shows off, or does things to attract attention.
show·off • *noun, plural* **showoffs**

showy (shō′ē) *adjective* **1** bright or colorful in an attractive way [a *showy* flower]. **2** too bright or flashy; gaudy [a *showy* suit].
show·y • *adjective* **showier, showiest**

shrank (shraŋk) *verb a past tense of* **shrink**.

shred (shred) *noun* **1** a long, narrow strip or piece cut or torn off [My shirt was torn to *shreds*.] **2** a tiny piece or amount; fragment [a story without a *shred* of truth].
verb to cut or tear into shreds [*Shred* the coconut before adding it to the batter.]
shred • *noun, plural* **shreds**
• *verb* **shredded** or **shred, shredding**

shrew (shro͞o) *noun* a tiny animal like a small mouse. It has soft brown fur and a long snout.
shrew • *noun, plural* **shrews**

shrewd (shro͞od) *adjective* clever or sharp in practical matters [A *shrewd* customer is always looking for bargains.]
shrewd • *adjective* **shrewder, shrewdest**

shriek (shrēk) *noun* a loud, shrill cry; a screech; a scream.
verb to cry out with a shriek [Everyone *shrieked* when the ghost appeared on stage.]
shriek • *noun, plural* **shrieks**
• *verb* **shrieked, shrieking**

shrill (shril) *adjective* having or making a sharp, high sound [a *shrill* voice; a *shrill* whistle].

shrimp

shrimp (shrimp) *noun* a small shellfish with a long tail. It is eaten as food.
shrimp • *noun, plural* **shrimp**

shrine (shrīn) *noun* **1** a building or place for religious worship. It usually has a sacred scene or object as its center. **2** a place or thing that is honored because of someone or something important connected with it [George Washington's house is a national *shrine*.]
shrine • *noun, plural* **shrines**

shrink (shriŋk) *verb* **1** to make or become smaller and more compact or dense by drawing the parts together [Wool often *shrinks* when it is washed.] **2** to become fewer or less [Club membership *shrank* from ten people to two.] **3** to draw back or turn away [He *shrank* in fear.]
shrink • *verb* **shrank** or **shrunk, shrunk** or **shrunken, shrinking**

shrivel (shriv′əl) *verb* to curl up and shrink or wither [Without water, the flowers *shriveled* and died.]
shriv·el • *verb* **shriveled** or **shrivelled, shriveling** or **shrivelling**

shroud (shroud) *noun* something that covers or hides; a veil.
verb to hide from view; to cover; to screen [Darkness *shrouded* the village.]
shroud • *noun, plural* **shrouds**
• *verb* **shrouded, shrouding**

shrub (shrub) *noun* a woody plant that is smaller than a tree and has a number of stems instead of one trunk; bush.
shrub • *noun, plural* **shrubs**

shrug (shrug) *verb* to draw up the shoulders to show that one does not care or that one does not know.

noun the act of shrugging [She answered with only a *shrug*.]
shrug • *verb* **shrugged, shrugging** • *noun, plural* **shrugs**

shrunk (shruŋk) *verb a past tense and a past participle of* **shrink**.

shrunken (shruŋ′kən) *verb a past participle of* **shrink**.
shrunk·en • *verb*

shuck (shuk) *noun* a shell, pod, or husk.
verb to remove the shucks of [We *shucked* the corn before cooking it.]
shuck • *noun, plural* **shucks** • *verb* **shucked, shucking**

shudder (shud′ər) *verb* to tremble in a sudden, violent way [I *shuddered* with fear.]
noun the act of shuddering; a sudden, strong trembling.
shud·der • *verb* **shuddered, shuddering** • *noun, plural* **shudders**

shuffle (shuf′əl) *verb* **1** to move the feet with a dragging motion in walking or dancing [She got out of bed and *shuffled* off to take a shower.] **2** to mix playing cards to change their order. **3** to keep shifting from one place to another [She *shuffled* the papers about on her desk.]
noun the act of shuffling [a *shuffle* of the cards. He walks with a *shuffle*.]
shuf·fle • *verb* **shuffled, shuffling** • *noun, plural* **shuffles**

shun (shun) *verb* to keep away from; avoid [A hermit *shuns* other people.]
shun • *verb* **shunned, shunning**

shush (shush) *interjection* a word used to tell someone to be quiet.
verb to tell to be quiet by saying "shush!"
shush • *interjection* • *verb* **shushed, shushing**

shut (shut) *verb* **1** to move something in order to close an opening [Please *shut* the door.] **2** to become closed [The door *shut* with a bang.] **3** to close by bringing together or folding the parts of [The teacher told the students to *shut* their books.] **4** to confine; enclose [She *shut* the cat inside the house.]
adjective fastened, locked up, or closed in some other way [Keep the lid *shut*.]
—shut down to stop work in, usually just for a time [The factory was *shut down* for two weeks.] **—shut in** to surround or enclose; keep inside [The fog *shut* everyone *in* for the night.] **—shut off** to keep from flowing, running, or moving in some other way [*Shut off* the water before you leave.] **—shut out** **1** to keep out [The curtains *shut out* the light.] **2** to keep from scoring even once in a game. **—shut up** **1** to lock up or enclose in a prison or elsewhere. **2** [*an informal use*] to stop talking or make stop talking.
shut • *verb* **shut, shutting** • *adjective*

shutter (shut′ər) *noun* **1** a cover for a window. It usually swings on hinges. **2** a part on a camera that opens and closes to control the amount of light that enters the camera.
shut·ter • *noun, plural* **shutters**

shuttle (shut′l) *noun* **1** a device in weaving that carries a thread back and forth between the threads that go up and down. **2** a bus, train, or airplane that makes frequent trips back and forth over a short route.
verb to move back and forth rapidly [The teacher *shuttled* between her own class and the class of a teacher who was absent.]
shut·tle • *noun, plural* **shuttles** • *verb* **shuttled, shuttling**

WORD HISTORY

shuttle

We get **shuttle** from a thousand-year-old English word that means "to shoot." The **shuttle** in weaving got its name because it is "shot" back and forth between the threads that are stretched up and down on a frame. Today, the idea "back and forth" is more common than the idea of shooting. A bus that travels back and forth over a short route between two places is called a **shuttle**. The space **shuttle** is designed to travel into space and return to earth.

shy (shī) *adjective* **1** easily frightened; timid [a *shy* animal]. **2** not at ease with other people; bashful [a *shy* child].
verb to move or pull back suddenly; start [The horse *shied* when the gun went off.]
shy • *adjective* **shier** or **shyer, shiest** or **shyest** • *verb* **shied, shying, shies**

a	cat	ō	go	ʉ	fur	ə =	a *in* ago		
ā	ape	ô	law, for	ch	chin		e *in* agent		
ä	cot, car	o͝o	look	sh	she		i *in* pencil		
e	ten	o͞o	tool	th	thin		o *in* atom		
ē	me	oi	oil	*th*	then		u *in* circus		
i	fit	ou	out	zh	measure				
ī	ice	u	up	ŋ	ring				

Siamese cat (sī ə mēz′) ***noun*** a cat with blue eyes and light-colored, short hair.
Si·a·mese cat • ***noun,*** *plural* **Siamese cats**

Siamese cat

sibling (sib′liŋ) ***noun*** a sister or brother.
sib·ling • ***noun,*** *plural* **siblings**

sic (sik) ***verb*** to encourage to attack [He *sicked* his dog on the burglar.]
sic • ***verb*** **sicked, sicking, sics**
● The words **sic** and **sick** sound alike.
He would never *sic* his dog on anyone.
They were *sick* of waiting in line.

sick (sik) ***adjective*** **1** suffering from disease or illness; not well; ill [a *sick* baby; *sick* with the flu]. **2** having a feeling that makes one vomit or want to vomit. **3** very upset or disturbed [She was *sick* over the loss of her dog.] **4** disgusted by too much of something; tired: usually used with *of* [I'm *sick* of your foolish excuses.] **5** [*an informal use*] unpleasant, disgusting, or cruel [a *sick* joke].
sick • ***adjective*** **sicker, sickest**
● The words **sick** and **sic** sound alike.

sicken (sik′ən) ***verb*** to make or become sick or ill.
sick·en • ***verb*** **sickened, sickening**

sickening (sik′ən iŋ) ***adjective*** **1** causing sickness or nausea [a *sickening* smell]. **2** causing disgust or revulsion.
sick·en·ing • ***adjective***

sickle (sik′əl) ***noun*** a tool with a curved blade and a short handle. It is used for cutting tall grass and weeds and sometimes for harvesting crops.
sick·le • ***noun,*** *plural* **sickles**

sickly (sik′lē) ***adjective*** **1** sick much of the time; in poor health [a *sickly* child]. **2** of or caused by sickness [a face with a pale, *sickly* color].
sick·ly • ***adjective*** **sicklier, sickliest**

sickness (sik′nəs) ***noun*** the condition of being sick; illness.
sick·ness • ***noun,*** *plural* **sicknesses**

side (sīd) ***noun*** **1** the right or left half of a human or animal body, especially either half of the trunk [I have pain in my *side*.] **2** a position or space beside someone or something [She never left my *side*.] **3** one of the lines or surfaces that mark the boundaries of something [A triangle has three *sides*.] **4** a surface of an object that is not the back or front, nor the top or bottom [a door at the *side* of a house]. **5** either of the two surfaces of a piece of paper or some other flat object [You may write on both *sides* of the sheet.] **6** the position that a place or direction has as it relates to the position of the person speaking [this *side* of the street; the other *side* of the lake]. **7** the position that an area or place has as it relates to the position of a central line [the east *side* of town]. **8** a particular quality of a person or thing in contrast with another or other qualities [He has a cruel *side*. Look on the bright *side* of life.] **9** one of the groups that are against each other in a fight, argument, contest, or game [Our *side* scored enough runs in the last inning to win.] **10** the ideas, opinions, or points of view of one person or group that are against or different from the ideas of another person or group [Don't you want to hear my *side* of the argument?] **11** all the relatives of either one's mother or one's father [an uncle on my mother's *side*].
adjective **1** of, at, or on a side or sides [a *side* door]. **2** to or from one side [a *side* glance]. **3** done or happening as something extra [a *side* effect]. **4** ordered separately, along with the main dish [a *side* order of cole slaw].
verb to take the side or position of a person or group that is against another person or group [The town council *sided* with the mayor.]
—on the side in addition to the main thing, part, or course [I'd like some fries *on the side*.] **—side by side** beside one another; together [working *side by side*]. **—take sides** to give help or support to one person or group in a fight or argument.
side • ***noun,*** *plural* **sides** • ***adjective*** • ***verb*** **sided, siding**

sidearm (sīd′ärm) ***adjective*** with the arm sweeping forward from the side of the body [a *sidearm* pitch]. This word can also be used as an adverb [He pitches *sidearm*.]
side·arm • ***adjective***

S

sideburns (sīd′bʉrnz) ***plural noun*** the hair on the side of a man's face, just in front of the ears.
side·burns • ***plural noun***

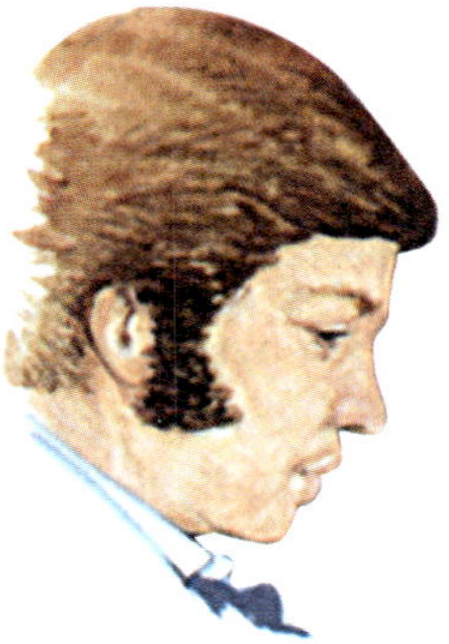

sideburns

sideline (sīd′līn) ***noun*** **1** either of the lines that mark the side limits of a football field or other playing area. **2 side-lines** the area just outside these lines [The coach paced back and forth on the *sidelines*.] **3** an activity or work in addition to a regular job [His father raises German shepherds as a *sideline*.]
side·line • ***noun,*** *plural* **sidelines**

sideshow (sīd′shō) ***noun*** a small, separate show connected with the main show of a circus.
side·show • ***noun,*** *plural* **sideshows**

sidestep (sīd′step) ***verb*** **1** to keep away from by stepping aside. **2** to avoid; dodge [The President *sidestepped* the reporter's question.]
side·step • ***verb*** **sidestepped, sidestepping**

sidetrack (sīd′trak) ***verb*** to turn away from the main subject [I got *sidetracked* by all that talk about food.]
side·track • ***verb*** **sidetracked, sidetracking**

sidewalk (sīd′wôk) ***noun*** a path for walking along the side of a street. It is usually paved.
side·walk • ***noun,*** *plural* **sidewalks**

sideways (sīd′wāz) ***adverb*** **1** from the side [Seen *sideways*, it looks quite thin.] **2** with one side toward the front [He turned his head *sideways* to show his profile.] **3** toward one side [The car skidded *sideways* on the ice.]
adjective toward one side [a *sideways* glance].
side·ways • ***adverb*** • ***adjective***

siding (sīd′iŋ) ***noun*** a covering for an outside wall. Siding on houses can be made of shingles, boards, or aluminum panels.
sid·ing • ***noun***

siege (sēj) ***noun*** the act of surrounding a city or fort by an enemy army that is trying to capture it.
siege • ***noun,*** *plural* **sieges**

sierra (sē er′ə) ***noun*** a chain of mountains whose peaks from a distance look like the edge of a saw.
si·er·ra • ***noun,*** *plural* **sierras**

Sierra Leone (sē er′ə lē ōn′) a country on the western coast of Africa.
Si·er·ra Le·one

siesta (sē es′tə) ***noun*** a short nap or rest that is taken after the noon meal. This is a custom in some countries, such as Spain or Mexico.
si·es·ta • ***noun,*** *plural* **siestas**

sieve (siv) ***noun*** a strainer used to separate liquids from solids or tiny pieces from large ones.
sieve • ***noun,*** *plural* **sieves**

sift (sift) ***verb*** to pass something through a sieve in order to separate the large pieces from the tiny ones or to break up the lumps [We *sifted* the sand to remove the pebbles.]
sift • ***verb*** **sifted, sifting**

sigh (sī) ***verb*** to let out a long, deep breath along with a soft sound, especially when one is sad, tired, or relieved [He *sighed* when he saw the job was only half finished.]
noun the act or sound of sighing [She breathed a *sigh* of relief.]
sigh • ***verb*** **sighed, sighing** • ***noun,*** *plural* **sighs**

sight (sīt) ***noun*** **1** something that is seen; a view [a familiar *sight*]. **2** something worth seeing [The book described the *sights* of the city.] **3** the act of seeing [It was our first *sight* of the city.] **4** the ability to see; vision; eyesight [He lost his *sight* in the war.] **5** the distance over which a person can see [The airplane passed out of *sight*.] **6** something that looks very strange, funny, or unpleasant [She was quite a *sight* in her mermaid costume.] **7** a device on a gun or telescope that helps one aim it.
verb to catch sight of; see [The sailor *sighted* land.]
sight • ***noun,*** *plural for senses 1, 2, and 7 only* **sights** • ***verb*** **sighted, sighting**

● The words **sight** and **site** sound alike.
The newborn baby was a beautiful *sight*.
He showed me the *site* for his new house.

sightless (sīt′ləs) ***adjective*** blind; not able to see.
sight·less • ***adjective***

a	cat	ō	go	ʉ	fur	ə =	a *in* ago
ā	ape	ô	law, for	ch	chin		e *in* agent
ä	cot, car	oo	look	sh	she		i *in* pencil
e	ten	o͞o	tool	th	thin		o *in* atom
ē	me	oi	oil	*th*	then		u *in* circus
i	fit	ou	out	zh	measure		
ī	ice	u	up	ŋ	ring		

sightseeing (sīt′sē iŋ) ***noun*** the act of going about to see interesting places and things.
sight·see·ing • ***noun***

sign (sīn) ***noun*** **1** a board or card with writing or pictures on it that is put up where it is easy for people to see. It gives the name of a store or business, a warning about traffic, or some other kind of information. **2** a mark that stands for something else; symbol [The *sign* ¢ means "cent."] **3** a movement or gesture that gives a command, a warning, or other information [Nodding is a *sign* that shows agreement.] **4** something that indicates a fact, quality, or condition [Black is worn as a *sign* of grief. All *signs* point to her as the thief.] **5** something that shows that something else exists or is coming [Dark clouds are a *sign* of a coming storm.]
verb **1** to write one's name on something [You must *sign* your name in order to get a library card.] **2** to communicate by using sign language [She knows how to *sign* as well as how to lip-read.]
—sign off to stop broadcasting a radio or TV signal, especially for the night. **—sign up** to put one's name on a list [Stand in this line if you want to *sign up* for the field trip.]
sign • ***noun,*** *plural* **signs** • ***verb*** **signed, signing**

SPELLING TIP

Use this memory aid to spell **sign**.
When you spell ***sign***, think of the ***g*** in si**g**nal.

signal (sig′nəl) ***noun*** **1** something that tells when some action is to start or end [A loud bell is the *signal* for a fire drill.] **2** something that is used as a warning or a direction [The traffic *signal* is green, telling us to go.] **3** the electrical waves that are sent out or received as sounds or pictures in radio and TV.
verb **1** to make a signal or signals to [The driver *signaled* that she was turning left.] **2** to give or send information by means of signals [The ship *signaled* that it was sinking.]
sig·nal • ***noun,*** *plural* **signals** • ***verb*** **signaled** or **signalled, signaling** or **signalling**

signature (sig′nə chər) ***noun*** a person's name written by that person.
sig·na·ture • ***noun,*** *plural* **signatures**

significance (sig nif′i kəns) ***noun*** **1** meaning or sense [I don't understand the *significance* of her remark.] **2** importance [What a person looks like is of little *significance*.]
sig·nif·i·cance • ***noun***

significant (sig nif′i kənt) ***adjective*** very important [The President gave a *significant* speech.]
sig·nif·i·cant • ***adjective***

sign language ***noun*** a system for the communication of ideas and thoughts by means of gestures with the fingers, hands, and arms instead of speech.
sign language • ***noun,*** *plural* **sign languages**

silence (sī′ləns) ***noun*** **1** the act of keeping still and not speaking or making any noise [His *silence* meant he agreed.] **2** a lack of any sound or noise [Deep in the forest there was complete *silence*.]
verb to make silent [The teacher *silenced* the class by clapping his hands.]
si·lence • ***noun,*** *plural for sense 1 only* **silences** • ***verb*** **silenced, silencing**

silent (sī′lənt) ***adjective*** **1** making no sound with the voice; not speaking [A sentry must be alert and *silent*.] **2** saying little; not talking much [She's the *silent* type.] **3** with no sound or noise [Find a *silent* place to study. We rented an old *silent* movie.] —Look for the WORD CHOICES box at the entry **still**. **4** included in a word's spelling but not expressed out loud or spoken [*silent b* in "debt"; *silent gh* in "thought"].
si·lent • ***adjective***

silhouette

silhouette (sil′o͞o et′) ***noun*** **1** an outline of a figure, especially a person's profile, that is usually cut from black paper and is set

S

against a light background. **2** any dark shape seen against a light background [the *silhouette* of a bird against the sky].
verb to show as a silhouette [The flock of birds was *silhouetted* against the sky.]
sil·hou·ette • ***noun,*** *plural* **silhouettes**
• ***verb*** **silhouetted, silhouetting**

silicon (sil′i kän) ***noun*** a hard, dark-gray chemical element. Silicon is, after oxygen, the most common element in the earth's crust. It is used in making concrete, bricks, glass, and china. Silicon is also used in electronics.
sil·i·con • ***noun***

silk (silk) ***noun*** **1** the fine, soft fiber that is spun by silkworms to form their cocoons. **2** thread or cloth that is made from this fiber. **3** any slender thread or fiber that is soft and shiny like silk [The fine fibers at the end of an ear of corn are called corn *silk*.]

silken (sil′kən) ***adjective*** **1** made of silk [a *silken* gown]. **2** like silk; shiny, soft, and smooth [*silken* hair].
silk·en • ***adjective***

silkworm (silk′wʉrm) ***noun*** a kind of caterpillar that spins silk fiber for its cocoon.
silk·worm • ***noun,*** *plural* **silkworms**

silky (sil′kē) ***adjective*** of or like silk; soft, smooth, and shiny [*silky* fur].
silk·y • ***adjective*** **silkier, silkiest**

sill (sil) ***noun*** a board or slab of stone that forms the bottom of the frame in a door or window.
sill • ***noun,*** *plural* **sills**

silly (sil′ē) ***adjective*** not showing or having good sense; foolish; not wise [a *silly* idea].
sil·ly • ***adjective*** **sillier, silliest**

silo (sī′lō) ***noun*** **1** an airtight tower for storing green stalks of corn and grasses that are used as food for cattle. **2** a large, underground facility for the storage, launching, and control of a missile.
si·lo • ***noun,*** *plural* **silos**

silt (silt) ***noun*** tiny particles of sand or soil that are carried by flowing water and eventually settle to the bottom of rivers or lakes.

silver (sil′vər) ***noun*** **1** a white metal that is a chemical element. Silver is soft and easy to mold and polish. It is used to make coins, jewelry, and decorations and is thought of as very valuable. **2** knives, forks, spoons, and other table utensils that are made of silver. **3** coins made of silver; change [two dollars in *silver*]. **4** the grayish-white color of silver.
adjective **1** made of, coated with, or containing silver [a *silver* tray; *silver* thread]. **2** having the color of silver [*silver* hair].
sil·ver • ***noun*** • ***adjective***

silversmith (sil′vər smith) ***noun*** a skilled worker who makes or repairs silver objects.
sil·ver·smith • ***noun,*** *plural* **silversmiths**

silverware (sil′vər wer) ***noun*** **1** table utensils made of or coated with silver. **2** table utensils made of some silvery metal.
sil·ver·ware • ***noun***

silvery (sil′vər ē) ***adjective*** having the color of or shining like silver [the *silvery* moon].
sil·ver·y • ***adjective***

similar (sim′i lər) ***adjective*** almost but not exactly the same; alike [Your ideas are *similar* to mine.]
sim·i·lar • ***adjective***

similarity (sim′i ler′i tē) ***noun*** **1** the condition of being similar [the *similarity* between lions and pet cats] —Look for the WORD CHOICES box at the entry **resemblance**. **2** a similar point or quality [These two cars are red, and they have other *similarities* too.]
sim·i·lar·i·ty • ***noun,*** *plural for sense 2 only* **similarities**

simmer (sim′ər) ***verb*** to keep at or just below the boiling point, usually forming tiny bubbles with a murmuring sound [*Simmer* the stew about two hours.]
sim·mer • ***verb*** **simmered, simmering**

simple (sim′pəl) ***adjective*** **1** having only one or a few parts; not complicated [The amoeba is a *simple* animal.] **2** easy to do or understand [a *simple* task; *simple* directions]. **3** without anything added; plain [the *simple* facts]. **4** not fancy [a *simple* dress].
sim·ple • ***adjective*** **simpler, simplest**

simple machine ***noun*** a basic device that makes doing some kind of work easier. The lever, pulley, wedge, screw, wheel and axle, and inclined plane are the six simple machines.
simple machine • ***noun,*** *plural* **simple machines**

a	cat	ō	go	ʉ	fur	ə =	a *in* ago
ā	ape	ô	law, for	ch	chin		e *in* agent
ä	cot, car	oo	look	sh	she		i *in* pencil
e	ten	ōō	tool	th	thin		o *in* atom
ē	me	oi	oil	*th*	then		u *in* circus
i	fit	ou	out	zh	measure		
ī	ice	u	up	ŋ	ring		

simplicity (sim plis′i tē) ***noun*** **1** the condition or fact of being simple, not complicated, or not difficult. **2** the condition of being plain or not fancy [the *simplicity* of a pioneer's cabin].
sim·plic·i·ty • ***noun***

simplify (sim′pli fī′) ***verb*** to make something easier or simpler [Putting a number of things in a box *simplifies* the task of carrying them.]
sim·pli·fy • ***verb*** **simplified, simplifying, simplifies**

simply (sim′plē) ***adverb*** **1** in a simple or plain way [He spoke *simply* and honestly about his troubles.] **2** only; just [I'm *simply* trying to help.] **3** completely; absolutely [I'm *simply* delighted to hear that.]
sim·ply • ***adverb***

simulcast (sī′məl kast) ***verb*** to broadcast a program or event at the same time on both radio and TV.
noun a program or event that is simulcast.
si·mul·cast • ***verb*** **simulcast** or **simulcasted, simulcasting** • ***noun,*** *plural* **simulcasts**

simultaneous (sī′məl tā′nē əs) ***adjective*** done, happening, or existing at the same time [two *simultaneous* acts].
si·mul·ta·ne·ous • ***adjective***

sin (sin) ***noun*** **1** the act of breaking a religious law. **2** a wrong or fault [It's a *sin* to waste good food.]
verb to commit a sin.
sin • ***noun,*** *plural* **sins** • ***verb*** **sinned, sinning**

Sinbad the Sailor (sin′bad *thə* sāl′ər) a merchant in *The Arabian Nights* who made seven voyages.
Sin·bad the Sailor

since (sins) ***adverb*** **1** from then until now [Lynn came Monday and has been here ever *since*.] **2** at a time between then and now [He was ill last week but has *since* recovered.]
preposition from or during the time that has been mentioned [I've been up *since* dawn.]
conjunction **1** after the time that [It's been two years *since* I saw you.] **2** because [*Since* it's such a hot day, I'll buy ice cream for all of you.]

sincere (sin sir′) ***adjective*** **1** not pretending or fooling; honest; truthful [Are you *sincere* in wanting to help?] **2** real; not pretended [The sorrow he showed was quite *sincere*.]
sin·cere • ***adjective*** **sincerer, sincerest**

sinew (sin′yo͞o) ***noun*** a tendon.
sin·ew • ***noun,*** *plural* **sinews**

sing (siŋ) ***verb*** **1** to make musical sounds with the voice [She *sings* well.] **2** to perform by singing [He *sang* a song at the party.] **3** to make musical sounds [I like to hear the birds *singing* in the spring.] **4** to hum, buzz, whistle, or make some similar sound [The kettle *sings* when the water boils.]
sing • ***verb*** **sang, sung, singing**

Singapore (siŋ′ə pôr) **1** a country on an island, south of Malaysia. **2** its capital city.
Sin·ga·pore

singe (sinj) ***verb*** to burn a little bit, on the surface or at the ends [If you stand too near the fire, you might *singe* your clothing.] —Look for the WORD CHOICES box at the entry **burn**.
singe • ***verb*** **singed, singeing**

singer (siŋ′ər) ***noun*** a person or bird that sings.
sing·er • ***noun,*** *plural* **singers**

single (siŋ′gəl) ***adjective*** **1** only one [a *single* piece of candy]. **2** of or for one person or family [a *single* bed; a *single* house]. **3** not married [a *single* woman].
verb **1** to select one from many [The track coach *singled* out Jesse as our best sprinter.] **2** to hit a single in baseball [Our worst batter *singled* sharply.]
noun **1** a single person or thing. **2** a hit in baseball by which the batter reaches first base and stops there.
sin·gle • ***adjective*** • ***verb*** **singled, singling** • ***noun,*** *plural* **singles**

single file ***noun*** a single line of persons or things, one behind another.
single file • ***noun,*** *plural* **single files**

single-handed (siŋ′gəl han′dəd) ***adjective*** without help [The lifeguard was praised for his *single-handed* effort to rescue the swimmers.]
sin·gle-hand·ed • ***adjective***

single-minded (siŋ′gəl mīn′dəd) ***adjective*** sticking to one purpose [The *single-minded* mother insisted that her son learn how to play the piano.]
sin·gle-mind·ed • ***adjective***

singular (siŋ′gyə lər) ***adjective*** showing that only one is meant [The *singular* form of "dogs" is "dog."]
noun the form of a word that shows that only one is meant.
sin·gu·lar • ***adjective*** • ***noun,*** *plural* **singulars**

S

sinister (sin′is tər) *adjective* threatening or suggesting harm or evil [*sinister* storm clouds].
sin·is·ter • *adjective*

sink (siŋk) *verb* **1** to go or put down below the surface [The heavy storm *sank* the ships. He *sank* the spade into the ground.] **2** to go down slowly; fall [The balloon *sank* to the earth.] **3** to seem to come down [The sun is *sinking* in the sky.] **4** to make or become lower in level, value, amount, or force [Her voice *sank* to a whisper. The price of gas *sank* to a new low.] **5** to go gradually into a certain condition [Joyce *sank* into a restless sleep.] **6** to go into deeply [The song *sank* into her mind.] **7** to make by digging [They *sank* a new well nearby.]
noun a basin with water faucets and a drain.
sink • *verb* **sank** or **sunk, sunk, sinking** • *noun, plural* **sinks**

sinus (sī′nəs) *noun* any of the cavities in the bones of the skull that open into the nose.
si·nus • *noun, plural* **sinuses**

Sioux (so͞o) *noun another name for* **Dakota** (sense 1).
Sioux • *noun, plural* **Sioux**

sip (sip) *verb* to drink a little at a time.
noun **1** a small amount sipped [Can I have a *sip* of lemonade?] **2** the act of sipping [One *sip* and I knew the milk was bad.]
sip • *verb* **sipped, sipping** • *noun, plural* **sips**

siphon (sī′fən) *noun* a U-shaped or a flexible tube that is used to move fluids over an edge from one container into a lower container. The tube is placed in the liquid, and suction is used to pull out the liquid. The liquid continues to flow by the action of air pressure.
verb to draw off through a siphon [The man *siphoned* the water out of the container.]
si·phon • *noun, plural* **siphons** • *verb* **siphoned, siphoning**

sir (sʉr) *noun* **1** a word used to show respect in talking to a man. **2 Sir** a title used before the name of a knight [*Sir* Francis Drake].
sir • *noun, plural* **sirs**

sire (sīr) *noun* a title of respect used in talking to a king.
sire • *noun, plural* **sires**

siren (sī′rən) *noun* a device that makes a loud steady sound. It is used as a warning signal.
si·ren • *noun, plural* **sirens**

sis (sis) [*an informal word*] *noun a short form of* **sister**.

sissy (sis′ē) [*an informal word*] *noun* a timid, shy, or cowardly person.
sis·sy • *noun, plural* **sissies**

sister (sis′tər) *noun* a girl or woman as she is related to the other children of her parents.
sis·ter • *noun, plural* **sisters**

sisterhood (sis′tər ho͝od) *noun* **1** the tie between sisters or between women who feel they all belong to one big family. **2** a group of women joined together in the same interest, work, or belief.
sis·ter·hood • *noun, plural for sense 2 only* **sisterhoods**

sister-in-law (sis′tər in lô′ *or* sis′tər in lä′) *noun* **1** the sister of one's husband or wife. **2** the wife of one's brother.
sis·ter-in-law • *noun, plural* **sisters-in-law**

sit (sit) *verb* **1** to rest the weight of the body upon the lower back part and not the feet [He *sat* on a bench. The dog *sat* still.] **2** to make sit; seat [*Sit* yourself down.] **3** to perch, rest, or lie [A bird *sat* on the fence.] **4** to be located [His house *sits* up on the hill.] **5** to pose [When are you *sitting* for the photographer?] **6** to have a seat; be a member of [Mrs. Colavito *sits* in the State Senate.] **7** to hold a session or meeting [This court will *sit* again next Monday.] **8** to baby-sit [Can you *sit* for us tonight?]
—sit down to take a seat. **—sit up** **1** to rise to a sitting position. **2** to sit with the back straight. **3** to stay up late at night.
sit • *verb* **sat, sitting**

site (sīt) *noun* **1** a piece of land to be used for a special purpose [This is a good *site* for a new stadium.] **2** the place where something is or was [We visited the *site* of an important Civil War battle.]
site • *noun, plural* **sites**
● The words **site** and **sight** sound alike.
He showed me the *site* for his new house.
The newborn baby was a beautiful *sight*.

sitter (sit′ər) *noun a short form of* **baby sitter**.
sit·ter • *noun, plural* **sitters**

sitting (sit′iŋ) *noun* **1** the act or position of one that sits posing for a picture [Your *sitting* with the photographer is scheduled for

a cat	ō go	ʉ fur	ə = a *in* ago
ā ape	ô law, for	ch chin	e *in* agent
ä cot, car	o͝o look	sh she	i *in* pencil
e ten	o͞o tool	th thin	o *in* atom
ē me	oi oil	*th* then	u *in* circus
i fit	ou out	zh measure	
ī ice	u up	ŋ ring	

today.] **2** a period of being seated [Archie read the book in one *sitting.*] **3** a meeting of a council, court, or other group.
sit·ting • *noun, plural* **sittings**

Sitting Bull (sit′iŋ bo͝ol′) 1834?-1890; a Dakota Indian chief.
Sit·ting Bull

situate (sich′o͞o āt′) *verb* to put or place; locate [The cabin is *situated* in the woods near the ski trails.]
sit·u·ate • *verb* **situated, situating**

situation (sich′o͞o ā′shən) *noun* a state or condition in relation to things that have happened [The argument created a tense *situation* between the two families.]
sit·u·a·tion • *noun, plural* **situations**

sit-up or **situp** (sit′up) *noun* an exercise in which a person lying flat on the back rises to a sitting position without using the hands.
sit·up or **sit·up** • *noun, plural* **sit-ups** or **situps**

six (siks) *noun* the cardinal number between five and seven; 6.
adjective being one more than five [*six* sisters].
six • *noun, plural* **sixes** • *adjective*

sixteen (siks′tēn′) *noun* the cardinal number between fifteen and seventeen; 16.
adjective being one more than fifteen [*sixteen* miles].
six·teen • *noun, plural* **sixteens** • *adjective*

sixteenth (siks′tēnth′) *adjective* coming next after fifteen others in a series; 16th in order.
noun **1** the number, person, or thing that is sixteenth. **2** one of sixteen equal parts of something; $\frac{1}{16}$.
six·teenth • *adjective* • *noun, plural* **sixteenths**

sixteenth note *noun* a note in music that is held one sixteenth as long as a whole note.
six·teenth note • *noun, plural* **sixteenth notes**

sixth (siksth) *adjective* coming next after five others in a series; 6th in order.
noun **1** the number, person, or thing that is sixth. **2** one of six equal parts of something; $\frac{1}{6}$.
sixth • *adjective* • *noun, plural* **sixths**

sixtieth (siks′tē əth) *adjective* being ten more than fifty others in a series; 60th in order.
noun **1** the number, person, or thing that is sixtieth. **2** one of sixty equal parts of something; $\frac{1}{60}$.
six·ti·eth • *adjective* • *noun, plural* **sixtieths**

sixty (siks′tē) *noun* the cardinal number that is equal to six times ten; 60.
adjective being six times ten [*sixty* degrees].
six·ty • *noun, plural* **sixties** • *adjective*

sizable or **sizeable** (sī′zə bəl) *adjective* fairly large [a *sizable* lead in the game].
siz·a·ble or **size·a·ble** • *adjective*

size (sīz) *noun* **1** the amount of space taken up by a thing; how large or how small a thing is [Tell me the *size* of your room. He is strong for his *size*.] **2** one of a series of numbers that are used to show measurement [She wears a *size* 12 dress.] **3** extent or amount [Attendance at the games has increased in *size* this season.]
size • *noun, plural for senses 1 and 2 only* **sizes**

sizzle (siz′əl) *verb* to make a hissing sound [The oil *sizzled* in the frying pan.]
siz·zle • *verb* **sizzled, sizzling**

WORD HISTORY

sizzle

The word **sizzle** was made up to sound like the hissing of hot grease in a frying pan or of drops of water when they hit hot metal. Another word of this kind is **hiss**. There are many words like **sizzle** and **hiss** that were made up to sound like what the word describes; two more are **buzz** and **whiz**.

SK *abbreviation for* Saskatchewan.

skate[1] (skāt) *noun* **1** *a short form of* **ice skate**. **2** *a short form of* **roller skate**.
verb to move along on skates.
skate • *noun, plural* **skates** • *verb* **skated, skating**

skate[2] (skāt) *noun* an ocean fish with a wide, flat body and a long, slender tail.
skate • *noun, plural* **skates**

skateboard (skāt′bôrd) *noun* a short board with a pair of wheels at each end. A person stands on the board, pushes off, and rides or coasts on it.
verb to ride or coast on a skateboard.

S

skate·board • *noun, plural* **skateboards** • *verb* **skateboarded, skateboarding**

skateboard

skeleton (skel′ə tən) *noun* **1** the framework of bones of an animal's body. **2** anything like an animal's skeleton, such as a very thin person or the framework of a building.
skel·e·ton • *noun, plural* **skeletons**

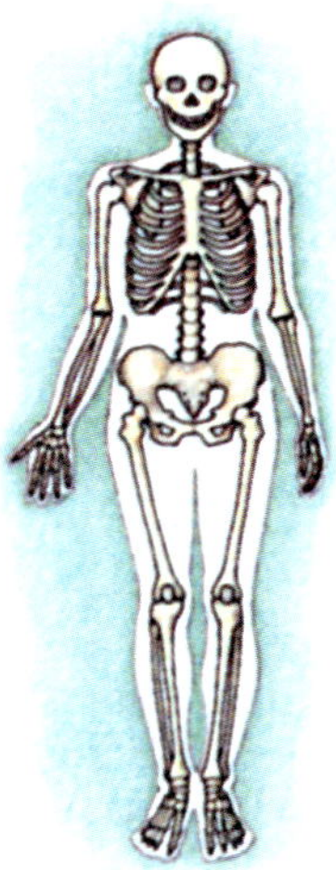

skeleton

skeptical (skep′ti kəl) *adjective* having or showing doubt; not believing easily [After Jake lied twice to us, we were *skeptical* about any story he told us.]
skep·ti·cal • *adjective*

sketch (skech) *noun* **1** a quick, rough drawing. **2** a short outline, giving the main ideas. **3** a short, light story.
verb to make a sketch or sketches [Andy *sketched* the pine tree. She is learning how to *sketch*.]
sketch • *noun, plural* **sketches** • *verb* **sketched, sketching**

sketchy (skech′ē) *adjective* not very detailed; not complete [a *sketchy* report].
sketch·y • *adjective* **sketchier, sketchiest**

skewer (skyo͞o′ər) *noun* a long pin used to hold chunks of meat and vegetables for broiling.
skew·er • *noun, plural* **skewers**

ski (skē) *noun* one of a pair of long runners, curved slighty upward at the tip, that are fastened to boots and are used for gliding over snow.
verb to glide on skis [The patrol *skied* down from the top of the mountain.]
ski • *noun, plural* **skis** • *verb* **skied, skiing, skis**

skid (skid) *verb* to slide out of control or sideways [The car *skidded* on the icy road.]
noun the act of skidding [The *skid* nearly caused an accident.]
skid • *verb* **skidded, skidding** • *noun, plural* **skids**

skies (skīz) *noun plural of* **sky**.

skill (skil) *noun* **1** ability that comes from training and practice [He teaches children with poor reading *skills*. He plays the violin with *skill*.] **2** a special art, craft, or science that usually involves the hands [Weaving is a *skill* often taught to the blind.] —Look for the WORD CHOICES box at the entry **art**.
skill • *noun, plural* **skills**

skillet (skil′ət) *noun* a shallow pan with a handle; frying pan.
skil·let • *noun, plural* **skillets**

skillful (skil′fəl) *adjective* having or showing skill [a *skillful* cook; a *skillful* piano player].
skill·ful • *adjective*

skim (skim) *verb* **1** to take off floating matter from the top of a liquid [She *skimmed* the fat from the gravy.] **2** to look through or read quickly [Marcy *skimmed* over the newspaper.] **3** to glide lightly over [The dragonfly *skimmed* over the pond.]
skim • *verb* **skimmed, skimming**

skim milk *noun* milk from which cream has been removed. This is also called **skimmed milk**.

skin (skin) *noun* **1** the tissue that covers the body of a person or animal. **2** the hide or pelt of certain animals [Early settlers made coats from beaver *skins*.] **3** the outer covering of some fruits and vegetables.
verb to remove the skin from [Sandy *skinned* her elbow when she fell from her bicycle.]
—by the skin of one's teeth by the smallest possible margin; barely [He won the race *by the skin of his teeth*.]
skin • *noun, plural* **skins** • *verb* **skinned, skinning**

a	cat	ō	go	ʉ	fur	ə =	a *in* ago
ā	ape	ô	law, for	ch	chin		e *in* agent
ä	cot, car	o͝o	look	sh	she		i *in* pencil
e	ten	o͞o	tool	th	thin		o *in* atom
ē	me	oi	oil	*th*	then		u *in* circus
i	fit	ou	out	zh	measure		
ī	ice	u	up	ŋ	ring		

skin diving ***noun*** the act or sport of swimming underwater while breathing from an air tank fastened to the body. A face mask and flippers are also worn.

skinny (skin′ē) ***adjective*** very thin or lean [a *skinny* child].
skin·ny • ***adjective*** **skinnier, skinniest**

skip (skip) ***verb*** **1** to move along by hopping lightly on one foot and then on the other. **2** to pass over; omit [We *skipped* the hard part of the song.] **3** to jump lightly over [Joyce *skipped* over the puddle. Can you *skip* rope?] **4** to bounce or make bounce across a surface [We *skipped* flat stones across the pond.] **5** to be promoted in school beyond the next regular grade [Karim *skipped* fourth grade.]
noun a light leap or jump.
skip • ***verb*** **skipped, skipping** • ***noun, plural*** **skips**

skipper (skip′ər) ***noun*** the captain of a ship.
skip·per • ***noun, plural*** **skippers**

skirt (skurt) ***noun*** **1** the part of a dress or other similar piece of clothing that hangs below the waist. **2** a woman's or girl's garment that hangs from the waist. It is worn with a blouse, sweater, or other kind of garment on top.
verb to go along the edge of; pass around rather than through [We *skirted* the airport area because of the heavy traffic.]
skirt • ***noun, plural*** **skirts** • ***verb*** **skirted, skirting**

skit (skit) ***noun*** a short, usually funny play [The girls did a nice *skit* in front of the class.]
skit • ***noun, plural*** **skits**

skull (skul) ***noun*** the bony covering of the head, that encloses and protects the brain.
skull • ***noun, plural*** **skulls**
● The words **skull** and **scull** sound alike.
The pirate flag depicts a human *skull.*
It's hard work to *scull* across the lake.

skunk (skuŋk) ***noun*** an animal that has a bushy tail and black fur with white stripes down its back. It sprays out a very bad-smelling liquid when it is attacked or frightened.
skunk • ***noun, plural*** **skunks**

sky (skī) ***noun*** **1** *often* **skies** the upper part of the air around the earth, especially when referring to its appearance [a cloudy *sky;* blue *skies*]. **2** the dome that seems to cover the earth.
sky • ***noun, plural for sense 1 only*** **skies**

sky diving ***noun*** the act or sport of jumping from an airplane and falling freely for some time before opening a parachute.

sky diving

skylark (skī′ lärk) ***noun*** a European bird that is known for its singing.
sky·lark • ***noun, plural*** **skylarks**

skylight (skī′līt) ***noun*** a window in a roof or ceiling.
sky·light • ***noun, plural*** **skylights**

skyline (skī′līn) ***noun*** **1** a line where the sky seems to touch the earth; horizon. **2** the outline of something, such as the buildings of a city, seen against the sky [the *skyline* of New York City at night].
sky·line • ***noun, plural*** **skylines**

skyrocket (skī′räk ət) ***noun*** a firework that explodes high in the air in a shower of colored sparks.
verb to rise rapidly [The cost of a new car has *skyrocketed.*]
sky·rock·et • ***noun, plural*** **skyrockets** • ***verb*** **skyrocketed, skyrocketing**

skyscraper (skī′skrā pər) ***noun*** a very tall building.
sky·scrap·er • ***noun, plural*** **skyscrapers**

slab (slab) ***noun*** a piece of something that is flat, broad, and fairly thick [a *slab* of concrete].
slab • ***noun, plural*** **slabs**

slack (slak) ***adjective*** **1** not tight; loose [a *slack* tennis net]. **2** careless or lazy [a *slack* helper]. **3** without energy or force; slow [a *slack* pace].
noun **1** a part of something that is hanging loose [The *slack* in the wire was dangerous.] **2 slacks** pants that are not part of a suit.
slack • ***adjective*** • ***noun, plural for sense 2 only*** **slacks**

slain (slān) ***verb past participle of*** **slay**.

slam (slam) ***verb*** **1** to shut with force and noise [He *slammed* the door as he left.] **2** to put, hit, or throw with force and noise [Please don't *slam* the phone down.]
noun the act or sound of slamming.
slam • ***verb*** **slammed, slamming** • ***noun***

S

slang (slaŋ) ***noun*** words and phrases that are used in everyday talk but are out of place in fine or serious writing or speech. Slang often uses special words and new and different meanings for standard words.

slant (slant) ***verb*** to turn or lie in a direction that is not straight up and down or straight across [The picture on the wall *slants* to the left.]
noun a surface or line that slants; slope [The ramp goes up at a *slant*.]
slant • ***verb*** **slanted, slanting** • ***noun,*** *plural* **slants**

slap (slap) ***noun*** a blow with something flat, such as the palm of the hand [She gave him a *slap* on the back.]
verb **1** to hit with something flat. **2** to put or throw carelessly or with force [We *slapped* a fresh coat of paint on the fence.]
slap • ***noun,*** *plural* **slaps** • ***verb*** **slapped, slapping**

slash (slash) ***verb*** **1** to cut by striking with something sharp [The knife slipped and I *slashed* my finger.] **2** to make much less or much lower [The store *slashed* prices.]
noun **1** a sweeping blow or stroke [He ducked when he heard the *slash* of the sword.] **2** a long cut or wound; a gash. **3** a big decrease or reduction [The store manager announced a *slash* in prices.]
slash • ***verb*** **slashed, slashing** • ***noun,*** *plural* **slashes**

slat (slat) ***noun*** a thin, narrow strip of wood or other material [He cleaned the *slats* of the Venetian blind.]
slat • ***noun,*** *plural* **slats**

slate (slāt) ***noun*** **1** a hard rock that splits easily into thin layers. **2** the bluish-gray color of this rock. **3** a thin piece of slate that is used to cover a roof or is used as a chalkboard.
slate • ***noun,*** *plural for sense 3 only* **slates**

slaughter (slôt′ər *or* slät′ər) ***noun*** **1** the killing of animals for food. **2** the killing of large numbers of people or animals in a cruel and violent way.
verb **1** to kill for food. **2** to kill in a cruel way or in large numbers.
slaugh·ter • ***noun,*** *plural* **slaughters** • ***verb*** **slaughtered, slaughtering**

slave (slāv) ***noun*** **1** a person who is owned by another person and has no freedom at all. **2** a person who is completely controlled by a habit or influence [She is a *slave* to soap operas.] **3** a person who works very hard at something.
verb to work hard; toil [Colleen *slaved* in the garden all day.]
slave • ***noun,*** *plural* **slaves** • ***verb*** **slaved, slaving**

slavery (slā′vər ē) ***noun*** **1** the practice of owning slaves. **2** the condition of being a slave; bondage. **3** hard work.
slav·er·y • ***noun***

slay (slā) ***verb*** to kill in a violent way [A dozen knights were *slain* during the battle.]
slay • ***verb*** **slew, slain, slaying**

● The words **slay** and **sleigh** sound alike.
Soldiers try to *slay* one another in war.
Santa's *sleigh* is pulled by reindeer.

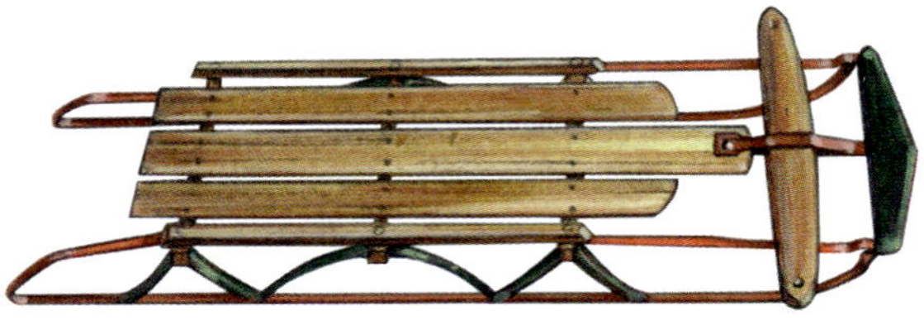

sled

sled (sled) ***noun*** a low platform on runners that is used for riding or for carrying things over ice or snow.
verb to ride, carry, or coast on a sled [We *sledded* to town after the blizzard.]
sled • ***noun,*** *plural* **sleds** • ***verb*** **sledded, sledding**

sleek (slēk) ***adjective*** **1** smooth and shiny; glossy [the *sleek* fur of a seal]. **2** looking healthy and well-groomed [*sleek* horses].
sleek • ***adjective*** **sleeker, sleekest**

sleep (slēp) ***noun*** **1** a condition of rest for the body and mind in which the eyes stay closed. It occurs naturally and regularly. During sleep the mind does not control the body but may dream. **2** any condition like sleep, such as death or a hibernating state [The bear's *sleep* lasted six months.]
verb to be in the condition of sleep [She needs to *sleep* eight hours every night.]
sleep • ***noun*** • ***verb*** **slept, sleeping**

a	cat	ō	go	ʉ	fur	ə =	a *in* ago
ā	ape	ô	law, for	ch	chin		e *in* agent
ä	cot, car	oo	look	sh	she		i *in* pencil
e	ten	ōō	tool	th	thin		o *in* atom
ē	me	oi	oil	*th*	then		u *in* circus
i	fit	ou	out	zh	measure		
ī	ice	u	up	ŋ	ring		

sleeping bag ***noun*** a large, soft bag that is used by campers for sleeping outdoors. It is usually padded and has a warm lining.
sleeping bag • ***noun,*** *plural* **sleeping bags**

sleepless (slēp′ləs) ***adjective*** with little or no sleep [a *sleepless* night].
sleep·less • ***adjective***

sleepy (slēp′ē) ***adjective*** **1** ready to fall asleep; drowsy [a *sleepy* child]. **2** not very active; quiet [a *sleepy* little town].
sleep·y • ***adjective*** **sleepier, sleepiest**

sleet (slēt) ***noun*** rain that is partly frozen or mixed with snow.
verb to shower in the form of sleet.
sleet • ***noun*** • ***verb*** **sleeted, sleeting**

sleeve (slēv) ***noun*** the part of a garment that covers all or part of an arm.
sleeve • ***noun,*** *plural* **sleeves**

sleigh

sleigh (slā) ***noun*** a carriage with runners instead of wheels. It is used to travel over snow or ice.
verb to travel in a sleigh.
sleigh • ***noun,*** *plural* **sleighs**
• ***verb*** **sleighed, sleighing**
● The words **sleigh** and **slay** sound alike.
It takes two horses to pull the *sleigh*.
The Black Knight attempted to *slay* him.

slender (slen′dər) ***adjective*** **1** long and thin [a *slender* basketball player] —Look for the WORD CHOICES box at the entry **thin**. **2** small in amount or size [He has only a *slender* chance to win the race.]
slen·der • ***adjective***

slept (slept) ***verb*** *past tense and past participle of* **sleep**.

slew[1] (slo͞o) ***verb*** *past tense of* **slay**.

slew[2] (slo͞o) [*an informal word*] ***noun*** a large number [A *slew* of pigeons were in the park.]
slew • ***noun,*** *plural* **slews**

slice (slīs) ***noun*** a thin, flat piece cut from something [a *slice* of cheese; a *slice* of bread].
verb **1** to cut into slices [Anne *sliced* the cake.] **2** to cut or move through like a sharp knife [The boat *sliced* the waters of the lake. The karate player's hands *sliced* through the air.]
slice • ***noun,*** *plural* **slices** • ***verb*** **sliced, slicing**

slick (slik) ***adjective*** **1** smooth and shiny [Her hair was wet and *slick*.] **2** slippery [a *slick* sidewalk].
verb to make smooth and shiny [She *slicked* her hair back.]
noun a smooth or slippery area on water, pavement, or some other surface [Oil *slicks* on the ocean are polluting the environment.]
slick • ***adjective*** **slicker, slickest**
• ***verb*** **slicked, slicking** • ***noun,*** *plural* **slicks**

slid (slid) ***verb*** *past tense and past participle of* **slide**.

slide (slīd) ***verb*** **1** to move easily and smoothly along a surface; to glide [Children run and *slide* on the ice. *Slide* the note under the door.] **2** to fall or shift suddenly from a position; to slip [The wet glass *slid* from my hand and fell on the kitchen counter.] **3** to pass or move slowly or without being noticed [The cat *slid* past the noisy dog.]
noun **1** an act of sliding. **2** a smooth surface down which a person or thing slides [a playground *slide*]. **3** the fall of a mass of rock, mud, or soil down a hill or cliff. **4** a small photographic image on film. It can be projected on a screen to show the picture. **5** a small, clear piece of glass on which things are placed for study under a microscope.
slide • ***verb*** **slid, sliding** • ***noun,*** *plural* **slides**

slight (slīt) ***adjective*** **1** small in amount or degree; not great, strong, or important [a *slight* change in temperature; a *slight* chance]. **2** light in build; slender [Some runners are short and *slight*.] —Look for the WORD CHOICES box at the entry **thin**.
verb **1** to pay little or no attention to; neglect [You shouldn't *slight* your homework.] **2** to treat as not important or with lack of respect [He *slighted* her when he did not return her call.]

noun the act of slighting someone [I will not excuse their *slights* anymore.]
slight • *adjective* **slighter, slightest** • *verb* **slighted, slighting** • *noun, plural* **slights**

slim (slim) *adjective* **1** slender or thin [a *slim* dancer]. **2** small or little [The team had a *slim* lead at the end of the first half.]
verb to make or become slim [Diet and exercise help a person to *slim* down.]
slim • *adjective* **slimmer, slimmest** • *verb* **slimmed, slimming**

slime (slīm) *noun* any soft, moist, slippery matter. It is often thought of as filthy or disgusting.

slimy (slīm′ē) *adjective* of, like, or covered with slime [a *slimy* pond].
slim·y • *adjective* **slimier, slimiest**

sling (sliŋ) *noun* **1** a weapon of ancient times used to hurl small stones. It was made of a piece of leather tied to cords. **2** a strap or rope used for holding or lifting a heavy object [The soldier placed his rifle in its *sling*.] **3** a loop of cloth hanging down from the neck. It is used to hold an injured arm.
verb **1** to throw or fling [The campers *slung* their packs over their backs.] **2** to carry, hold, or hang so as to swing freely [They *slung* the hammock between two trees.]
sling • *noun, plural* **slings** • *verb* **slung, slinging**

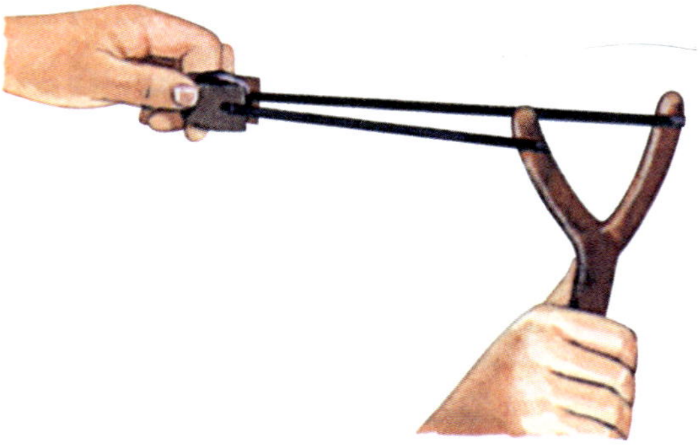

slingshot

slingshot (sliŋ′shät) *noun* a stick that is shaped like a Y and has a rubber band tied to the upper tips. It is used for shooting stones.
sling·shot • *noun, plural* **slingshots**

slink (sliŋk) *verb* to move in a fearful or sneaky way, or as if ashamed [He tried to *slink* behind his desk because he was late.]
slink • *verb* **slunk, slinking**

slip[1] (slip) *verb* **1** to move or go quietly or without being noticed [We *slipped* out the door. Time *slipped* by.] **2** to fail to be remembered [His name always *slips* my mind.] **3** to pass slowly into a certain state [The children *slipped* into bad habits.] **4** to move suddenly or by accident into or away from a position or out of control [The glass *slipped* from my hand.] **5** to slide by accident [He *slipped* on the sidewalk.] **6** to make a mistake [Selena *slipped* when she told my secret to her friends.] **7** to put or move smoothly, easily, or quickly [She *slipped* her shoes off.] **8** to become weaker, lower, or less [Your memory is *slipping*. Prices have *slipped*.]
noun **1** an undergarment worn by girls and women, about the length of a dress or skirt. **2** the act of slipping [Tom's *slip* gave him a broken wrist.] **3** a mistake or accident [His little *slip* on the test cost him a perfect score.]
slip • *verb* **slipped, slipping** • *noun, plural* **slips**

slip[2] (slip) *noun* a small piece of paper that is used for making notes or for records [Save the sales *slip* in case you need to return your purchase.]
slip • *noun, plural* **slips**

slipper (slip′ər) *noun* a light shoe that is usually worn while a person is relaxing at home. It slips on and off easily.
slip·per • *noun, plural* **slippers**

slippery (slip′ər ē *or* slip′rē) *adjective* **1** able to cause slipping [a *slippery* floor]. **2** likely to slip [a *slippery* dish].
slip·per·y • *adjective* **slipperier, slipperiest**

slit (slit) *verb* to cut or split open [Bruce *slit* open the juicy watermelon.]
noun a long, narrow cut or opening.
slit • *verb* **slit, slitting** • *noun, plural* **slits**

slither (sli*th*′ər) *verb* to slide along on the ground [The snake *slithered* across the patio.]
slith·er • *verb* **slithered, slithering**

sliver (sliv′ər) *noun* a thin, sharp piece that has been cut or split off; a splinter [A *sliver* of glass stuck to her finger.]
sliv·er • *noun, plural* **slivers**

slob (släb) [*an informal word*] *noun* a person who is not neat or careful, or one who has bad manners and poor taste.
slob • *noun, plural* **slobs**

a	cat	ō	go	ʉ	fur	ə = a *in* ago	
ā	ape	ô	law, for	ch	chin	e *in* agent	
ä	cot, car	oo	look	sh	she	i *in* pencil	
e	ten	ōō	tool	th	thin	o *in* atom	
ē	me	oi	oil	*th*	then	u *in* circus	
i	fit	ou	out	zh	measure		
ī	ice	u	up	ŋ	ring		

WORD HISTORY

slob

We get **slob** from an Irish word for "mud." The meaning developed through the idea of "muddy land" to "a mess," and finally the word came to be an unkind name for a messy or sloppy person.

slobber (släb′ər) *verb* to let saliva drool from the mouth [The baby *slobbered* on her new toy.]
slob·ber • *verb* **slobbered, slobbering**

slogan (slō′gən) *noun* a word or phrase that is used by a business, team, school, or other group to get attention or to advertise some product or idea.
slo·gan • *noun, plural* **slogans**

slop (släp) *noun* **1** wet snow, slush, or mud. **2** watery food that tastes bad.
verb to spill or splash [She *slopped* her breakfast all over the table.]
slop • *noun* • *verb* **slopped, slopping**

slope (slōp) *noun* **1** land that is not flat and level [a snow-covered *slope*]. **2** a surface, line, or direction that slants or the amount of this slant [The roof has a steep *slope*.]
verb to have a slope; slant up or down [The roof *slopes* down.]
slope • *noun, plural* **slopes** • *verb* **sloped, sloping**

sloppy (släp′ē) *adjective* **1** wet, muddy, or full of slush. **2** not neat or careful; messy.
slop·py • *adjective* **sloppier, sloppiest**

slot (slät) *noun* a narrow, straight opening [Drop the letter in the *slot*.]
slot • *noun, plural* **slots**

sloth (slôth *or* släth) *noun* **1** the condition of being lazy. **2** an animal of South America that moves slowly and lives in trees. It often hangs upside down from the branches.
sloth • *noun, plural for sense 2 only* **sloths**

slouch (slouch) *verb* to sit, stand, or walk with the head drooping and the shoulders slumping.
noun the act or position of slouching [She walks with a *slouch*.]
slouch • *verb* **slouched, slouching** • *noun*

Slovakia (slō vä′kē ə) a country in central Europe. It was the eastern part of Czechoslovakia.
Slo·va·ki·a

Slovenia (slō vē′nē ə) a country in southeastern Europe. It was a part of Yugoslavia.
Slo·ve·ni·a

slow (slō) *adjective* **1** not fast or quick in moving, working, or acting in any way [a *slow* runner]. **2** taking a longer time than is usual [He was *slow* to answer my question.] **3** showing a time that is behind the real time [Your watch is *slow*.] **4** not lively, active, or interesting; dull [This book has a *slow* plot. Business is *slow* today.] **5** not quick in understanding [He is a *slow* learner.]
adverb in a slow way [Please go *slow*.]
verb to make or become slow or slower.
slow • *adjective* & • *adverb* **slower, slowest** • *verb* **slowed, slowing**

slowly (slō′lē) *adverb* in a slow way.
slow·ly • *adverb*

slow-motion (slō′mō′shən) *adjective* describing a movie or videotape in which the action is made to seem much slower than the real action.
slow-mo·tion • *adjective*

sludge (sluj) *noun* **1** soft mud. **2** any heavy, slimy waste material, such as thick, dirty oil.
sludge • *noun, plural for sense 2 only* **sludges**

slug[1] (slug) *noun* a small, slow-moving animal like a snail. It has no outer shell. Slugs live in damp places and feed on plants.
slug • *noun, plural* **slugs**

slug[2] (slug) *noun* **1** a small, round piece of metal that is used, especially illegally, in place of a coin in coin-operated machines. **2** a bullet.
slug • *noun, plural* **slugs**

slug[3] (slug) [*an informal word*] *verb* to hit very hard [He *slugged* the ball over the fence.]
noun a hard blow.
slug • *verb* **slugged, slugging** • *noun, plural* **slugs**

sluggish (slug′ish) *adjective* not having much energy or vigor; not active; lazy.
slug·gish • *adjective*

slum (slum) *noun* a very poor, crowded area in a town or city.
slum • *noun, plural* **slums**

S

slumber (slum′bər) *verb* **1** to sleep. **2** to be very quiet or calm [The volcano had been *slumbering* for hundreds of years.]
noun sleep.
slum·ber • *verb* **slumbered, slumbering** • *noun*

slump (slump) *verb* to fall or drop in a sudden way [She *slumped* to the floor. Sales have *slumped*.]
noun **1** a sudden fall or drop [a *slump* in sales]. **2** a period when business is slow or the way a person performs is not as good as usual [The team was in a *slump*.]
slump • *verb* **slumped, slumping** • *noun, plural* **slumps**

slung (sluŋ) *verb past tense and past participle of* **sling**.

slunk (sluŋk) *verb past tense and past participle of* **slink**.

slurp (slʉrp) [*a slang word*] *verb* to eat or drink in a noisy way.
noun a loud sipping or sucking sound.
slurp • *verb* **slurped, slurping** • *noun, plural* **slurps**

slush (slush) *noun* **1** snow that is partly melted. **2** shaved or crushed ice with a fruit-flavored syrup poured over it.

sly (slī) *adjective* **1** able to fool or trick others; cunning [In fables, the fox is often a *sly* animal.] —Look for the WORD CHOICES box at the entry **wily**. **2** teasing in a playful way [a *sly* remark].
sly • *adjective* **slier** or **slyer, sliest** or **slyest**

smack (smak) *noun* **1** a sudden noise produced by closing and opening the lips quickly. **2** a loud kiss. **3** a harsh slap [The cat got a *smack* for clawing the rug.]
verb **1** to make a smack with [He *smacked* his lips after eating the ice cream.] **2** to kiss with a loud noise. **3** to strike something in a harsh and loud way [He *smacked* into the desk.]
adverb sharply or violently [The car ran *smack* into the tree.]
smack • *noun, plural* **smacks** • *verb* **smacked, smacking** • *adverb*

small (smôl) *adjective* **1** little in size; not large or big [a *small* hand; a *small* town]. **2** soft and weak [a *small* voice]. **3** not very important [a *small* problem; *small* talk]. **4** young [Do you have any *small* children?] **5** carrying on some activity on a limited scale [a *small* business in town].
noun the small or narrow part of something [The ball hit him in the *small* of the back.]
small • *adjective* **smaller, smallest** • *noun*

WORD CHOICES

Synonyms of **small**

The words **small**, **little**, and **tiny** share the meaning "not large or big."

a *small* piece of pie
of *little* interest to a nonreader
needing only a *tiny* dose of medicine

small intestine *noun* the narrow section of the intestine. It is between the stomach and the large intestine.
small intestine • *noun, plural* **small intestines**

small letter *noun* the form of a letter that is used most of the time in writing. Small letters are not used at the beginning of a name or a sentence.
small letter • *noun, plural* **small letters**

smallpox (smôl′päks) *noun* a disease that causes a high fever and sores on the skin that often leave scars. It is very contagious but use of vaccine has made it rare.
small·pox • *noun*

smart (smärt) *adjective* **1** intelligent or clever [a *smart* student] —Look for the WORD CHOICES box at the entry **intelligent**. **2** of the newest fashion; stylish [a *smart* new dress]. **3** sharp or intense [a *smart* pain]. **4** quick or lively [We jogged at a *smart* pace.] **5** [*an informal use*] talking back in a way that is not respectful [Don't get *smart* with me.]
verb **1** to cause a sharp, stinging pain [A bee sting *smarts*.] **2** to feel hurt or to be in sharp pain [The scolding left him *smarting*. My eyes *smart* from the smoke.]
smart • *adjective* **smarter, smartest** • *verb* **smarted, smarting**

smash (smash) *verb* **1** to break into many pieces with noise or force [The baby *smashed* the toy. The plate *smashed* as it hit the floor.] —Look for the WORD CHOICES box at the entry **break**. **2** to move, throw, or strike with much force [A car *smashed* into the pole.] **3** to

a	cat	ō	go	ʉ	fur	ə =	a *in* ago
ā	ape	ô	law, for	ch	chin		e *in* agent
ä	cot, car	oo	look	sh	she		i *in* pencil
e	ten	ōō	tool	th	thin		o *in* atom
ē	me	oi	oil	*th*	then		u *in* circus
i	fit	ou	out	zh	measure		
ī	ice	u	up	ŋ	ring		

destroy completely [Our hopes were *smashed* when they won the game.]
noun **1** the act or sound of smashing. **2** a violent collision [The cars were completely ruined in the *smash*.]
adjective [*an informal use*] very successful [The movie was a *smash* hit.]
smash • ***verb*** **smashed, smashing** • ***noun,*** *plural* **smashes** • ***adjective***

smear (smir) ***verb*** **1** to cover with something greasy or sticky [We *smeared* ourselves with lotion to protect us against sunburn.] **2** to rub or spread [*Smear* some grease on the wheel.] **3** to become blurred or messy [This paint *smears* easily.]
noun a mark or streak made by smearing.
smear • ***verb*** **smeared, smearing** • ***noun,*** *plural* **smears**

smell (smel) ***verb*** **1** to notice the odor of through a special sense in the nose [I *smell* something burning.] **2** to give off a certain scent [This perfume *smells* of roses.] **3** to give off an unpleasant odor [The fish began to rot and *smell*.] **4** to become aware of [The detective *smelled* trouble.]
noun **1** the sense in the nose that detects odors. **2** the odor or scent that is detected by the nose. **3** the act of smelling [One *smell* told me he was baking bread.]
smell • ***verb*** **smelled** or **smelt, smelling** • ***noun,*** *plural for senses 2 and 3 only* **smells**

smelly (smel′ē) ***adjective*** having a bad smell.
smell·y • ***adjective*** **smellier, smelliest**

smelt (smelt) ***verb*** *a past tense and a past participle of* **smell**.

smile (smīl) ***noun*** an expression of the face that is made by making the corners of the mouth turn up. A smile can show that a person is pleased, happy, or friendly or that a person is being sarcastic or is full of scorn.
verb **1** to have or give a smile. **2** to show with or express by a smile [He *smiled* his approval.]
smile • ***noun,*** *plural* **smiles** • ***verb*** **smiled, smiling**

smirk (smurk) ***verb*** to smile in a silly or conceited way.
noun a silly or conceited smile.
smirk • ***verb*** **smirked, smirking** • ***noun,*** *plural* **smirks**

smith (smith) ***noun*** a person who makes or repairs metal objects [a *silversmith*].
smith • ***noun,*** *plural* **smiths**

Smith (smith), Captain **John** (jän) 1580?-1631; English explorer who settled a colony in Virginia.

smock (smäk) ***noun*** a loose outer garment like a long shirt. It is worn over other clothes to protect them from stains or dirt.
smock • ***noun,*** *plural* **smocks**

smog (smôg) ***noun*** a mixture of smoke and fog.

smoke (smōk) ***noun*** **1** the gas with bits of carbon in it that rises from something that is burning [*smoke* from a campfire]. **2** a cloud or mist that looks like this substance.
verb **1** to give off smoke [The volcano *smoked* for days.] **2** to breathe smoke from something such as a cigarette or pipe into the mouth and blow it out again. **3** to treat with smoke in order to flavor and keep from spoiling [That company *smokes* millions of hams every year.]
smoke • ***noun*** • ***verb*** **smoked, smoking**

smoke detector ***noun*** a device that sets off a loud signal to show that there is smoke from a fire in the area.
smoke detector • ***noun,*** *plural* **smoke detectors**

smoker (smōk′ər) ***noun*** a person who smokes tobacco.
smok·er • ***noun,*** *plural* **smokers**

smokestack (smōk′stak) ***noun*** a tall chimney or pipe for carrying away smoke from a ship or a factory.
smoke·stack • ***noun,*** *plural* **smokestacks**

smoky (smō′kē) ***adjective*** **1** giving off smoke, especially too much smoke [a *smoky* fireplace]. **2** like smoke or having the color or taste of smoke [a *smoky* blue haze; *smoky* cheese]. **3** filled with smoke [a *smoky* room].
smok·y • ***adjective*** **smokier, smokiest**

smolder (smōl′dər) ***verb*** **1** to burn and smoke without a flame. **2** to be present but be kept under control [A wish for revenge *smoldered* within him.]
smol·der • ***verb*** **smoldered, smoldering**

smooth (sm*ōō*th) ***adjective*** **1** having an even surface, with no bumps or rough spots [as *smooth* as marble; *smooth* water on the lake]. **2** without lumps [a *smooth* paste]. **3** even or gentle in movement; not rough [a *smooth* airplane flight]. **4** with no trouble or difficulty [My trumpet teacher says I'm making *smooth* progress.] **5** speaking or spoken in an easy and polite way, often in a way that does not seem sincere [a *smooth* talker; *smooth* words].
adverb in a smooth way [The engine is running *smooth* now.]
verb **1** to make level or even [*Smooth* the board with sandpaper.] **2** to make easy by tak-

S

ing away troubles or difficulties [She *smoothed* our way by introducing us to the other guests.]
smooth • *adjective* & • *adverb* **smoother, smoothest** *verb* **smoothed, smoothing**

smother (smu*th*′ər) *verb* **1** to keep from getting enough air to breathe. **2** to kill in this way [The murderer *smothered* her victim with a pillow.] **3** to be kept from getting enough air to breathe [I almost *smothered* in the hot room.] **4** to keep air from in order to stop burning [We *smothered* the fire with sand.] **5** to cover with a thick layer [The liver was *smothered* in onions.] **6** to hold back or hide [He *smothered* a yawn.]
smoth·er • *verb* **smothered, smothering**

smudge (smuj) *noun* a dirty spot; a smear.
verb to streak with dirt; to smear [They came up from the mine *smudged* with coal dust.]
smudge • *noun, plural* **smudges**
• *verb* **smudged, smudging**

smug (smug) *adjective* too pleased or satisfied with oneself [He was *smug* about his test grade.]
smug • *adjective* **smugger, smuggest**

smuggle (smug′əl) *verb* **1** to bring into a country or take out of a country in a way that is secret and against the law [They were arrested because they were *smuggling* drugs into the country.] **2** to bring or take in a secret way [His sister *smuggled* dessert to him when he was being punished.]
smug·gle • *verb* **smuggled, smuggling**

snack (snak) *noun* **1** a small amount of food. **2** a light meal that is eaten between regular meals.
verb to eat a snack or snacks [The children often *snack* on cookies and milk.]
snack • *noun,* plural **snacks** • *verb* **snacked, snacking**

snag (snag) *noun* **1** a tear in cloth that is made by a sharp object [The nail made a *snag* in my sweater.] **2** something that is hidden or not expected but gets in the way [Our plans hit a *snag* when I got sick.]
verb to tear or catch on a snag [I *snagged* my sleeve on a thorn.]
snag • *noun, plural* **snags** • *verb* **snagged, snagging**

snail (snāl) *noun* a slow-moving animal with a soft body and a spiral shell into which it can draw back for protection. Snails live on land or in the water.
snail • *noun, plural* **snails**

snake (snāk) *noun* a crawling reptile that has a long, thin body and no legs. Its body is covered with scales. Certain kinds of snakes can poison other animals by biting them.
verb to move, twist, or turn like a snake [The road *snaked* around the mountains.]
snake • *noun, plural* **snakes** • *verb* **snaked, snaking**

snap (snap) *verb* **1** to bite or grasp suddenly [The frog *snapped* at the fly. We *snapped* up her offer at once.] **2** to say or speak in a short, sharp way [The boss *snapped* out his orders. She was so angry she *snapped* at me.] **3** to break suddenly with a sharp, cracking sound [The stick *snapped* in two when I stepped on it. I *snapped* the cracker in half.] **4** to give way suddenly [His nerves *snapped* under the strain.] **5** to make or cause to make a short, cracking sound [Lightning *snapped* and crackled around the tree. She *snapped* her fingers.] **6** to close, fasten, or let go with a sound like this [The lock *snapped* shut.]
noun **1** a sudden bite or grasp. **2** a sharp cracking or clicking sound [The purse closed with a *snap*.] **3** a device for fastening that closes with this kind of sound. **4** a short period of cold weather. **5** a hard, thin cookie. **6** [*a slang use*] an easy job or problem [The math test was a *snap*.]
adjective **1** made or done quickly without much thought [a *snap* decision]. **2** [*a slang use*] easy; simple [Chemistry is not a *snap* course.]
—snap out of it to get back to having one's normal feelings and acting in a normal way [I was groggy all morning and could not *snap out of it*.]
snap • *verb* **snapped, snapping** • *noun, plural for all senses except 6* **snaps**
• *adjective*

snapdragon (snap′drag ən) *noun* a plant that has spikes of red, white, yellow, or purple flowers.
snap·drag·on • *noun, plural* **snapdragons**

snapdragon

a cat	ō go	ʉ fur	ə = a *in* ago
ā ape	ô law, for	ch chin	e *in* agent
ä cot, car	oo look	sh she	i *in* pencil
e ten	ōō tool	th thin	o *in* atom
ē me	oi oil	*th* then	u *in* circus
i fit	ou out	zh measure	
ī ice	u up	ŋ ring	

WORD HISTORY

snapdragon

The **snapdragon** gets its name from the shape of its flowers. They look a little like mouths; some people think they look like animals' heads. If you pinch one of these flowers at its closed end, the two "lips" of the "mouth" will open. When you stop pinching, the flower will *snap* shut.

snapping turtle *noun* a large turtle of North America that lives in ponds and rivers. It has powerful jaws that snap shut with great force.
snapping turtle • *noun, plural* **snapping turtles**

snapshot (snap′shät) *noun* a simple, informal picture that is taken quickly with a small hand camera.
snap·shot • *noun, plural* **snapshots**

snare (sner) *noun* a trap for catching animals. It is usually made with a noose that jerks tight around the animal's body.
verb to catch in a snare; to trap.
snare • *noun, plural* **snares** • *verb* **snared, snaring**

snare drum

snare drum *noun* a small drum with strings of wire or gut stretched across the bottom. When the drum is struck, these strings vibrate and give the drum a rattling sound.
snare drum • *noun, plural* **snare drums**

snarl[1] (snärl) *verb* **1** to growl in a fierce way, showing the teeth [The dog *snarled* as we came near.] **2** to speak or say in a harsh or angry tone ["Go away!" she *snarled*.]
noun **1** the act of snarling. **2** the sound of snarling.
snarl • *verb* **snarled, snarling** • *noun, plural* **snarls**

snarl[2] (snärl) *verb* to make or become tangled or confused [I *snarled* the fishing line while reeling it in. Traffic is *snarled* on the freeway.]
noun **1** a tangle or knot [hair full of *snarls*]. **2** a confused condition [These files are in a *snarl*.]
snarl • *verb* **snarled, snarling** • *noun, plural* **snarls**

snatch (snach) *verb* to reach for or seize in a sudden way; to grab or grasp [The thief *snatched* the purse and ran.] —Look for the WORD CHOICES box at the entry **grasp**.
noun **1** the act of snatching; a grab. **2** a small amount; a bit [I remember a *snatch* of the tune.]
snatch • *verb* **snatched, snatching** • *noun, plural* **snatches**

sneak (snēk) *verb* **1** to move or act in a quiet or secret way to keep from being noticed [They *sneaked* out of the room while we were talking.] **2** to give, put, carry, or take in this way [Try to *sneak* the presents into the closet, and hide them well.]
noun a dishonest, cheating person.
adjective done without warning [a *sneak* attack].
sneak • *verb* **sneaked** or **snuck, sneaking** • *noun, plural* **sneaks** • *adjective*

sneaker (snē′kər) *noun* a cloth shoe with a flat sole that is made of rubber. Sneakers are worn for play and for sports.
sneak·er • *noun, plural* **sneakers**

sneaky (snē′kē) *adjective* like or having to do with a person who sneaks; dishonest or cheating.
sneak·y • *adjective* **sneakier, sneakiest**

sneer (snir) *verb* **1** to look scornful or sarcastic, by curling the upper lip. **2** to show scorn or be sarcastic in speaking or writing [Many people *sneered* at the new invention.]
noun a sneering look or remark.
sneer • *verb* **sneered, sneering** • *noun, plural* **sneers**

sneeze (snēz) *verb* to blow out breath from the mouth and nose in a sudden way that cannot be controlled.
noun an act of sneezing.

S

sneeze • *verb* **sneezed, sneezing** • *noun, plural* **sneezes**

snicker (snik′ər) *verb* to give a sly or silly laugh that is partly held back and that shows scorn or ridicule —Look for the WORD CHOICES box at the entry **laugh**.
noun this kind of laugh.
snick·er • *verb* **snickered, snickering** • *noun, plural* **snickers**

snide (snīd) *adjective* done to hurt someone in a sly way; mean [a *snide* remark].
snide • *adjective* **snider, snidest**

sniff (snif) *verb* **1** to make a noise in drawing air in through the nose when trying to smell something. **2** to smell in this way [I *sniffed* the milk to see if it was fresh.]
noun the act or sound of sniffing.
sniff • *verb* **sniffed, sniffing** • *noun, plural* **sniffs**

sniffle (snif′əl) *verb* to sniff again and again, in the way that a person does when suffering from a head cold.
noun the act or sound of sniffling.
—**the sniffles** [*an informal use*] a runny nose caused by a cold.
snif·fle • *verb* **sniffled, sniffling** • *noun, plural* **sniffles**

snip (snip) *verb* to cut or cut off, using scissors or shears, with a short, quick stroke [*Snip* off the ends of the threads.]
noun **1** a small cut that is made with scissors or shears. **2** a small piece that has been cut off by snipping.
snip • *verb* **snipped, snipping** • *noun, plural* **snips**

snipe (snīp) *noun* a wading bird with a long bill. It lives mainly in marshes.
verb to shoot from a hidden place at people, one at a time.
snipe • *noun, plural* **snipes** or **snipe** • *verb* **sniped, sniping**

sniper (snī′pər) *noun* a soldier or other person who shoots from a hidden place.
snip·er • *noun, plural* **snipers**

snitch (snich) [*a slang word*] *verb* **1** to steal something of little value [They *snitched* some cookies from the kitchen.] **2** to tell the secrets of others; be a tattletale [He *snitched* on his friends.]
noun a tattletale.
snitch • *verb* **snitched, snitching** • *noun, plural* **snitches**

snob (snäb) *noun* **1** a person who thinks that people who have money and a high social position are very important. A snob may also be someone who ignores or looks down on people who he or she thinks are not important. **2** a person who feels he or she is better than others.
snob • *noun, plural* **snobs**

snoop (sno͞op) [*an informal word*] *verb* to look about or search in a sneaking way; to spy.
noun a person who snoops.
snoop • *verb* **snooped, snooping** • *noun, plural* **snoops**

snooze (sno͞oz) [*an informal word*] *noun* a short sleep; a nap.
verb to take a nap.
snooze • *noun, plural* **snoozes** • *verb* **snoozed, snoozing**

snore (snôr) *verb* to breathe with noisy, rough sounds while one sleeps.
noun the act or sound of snoring.
snore • *verb* **snored, snoring** • *noun, plural* **snores**

snorkel (snôr′kəl) *noun* a short tube with curved ends that a swimmer holds in the mouth for breathing under the surface of the water.
verb to swim using a snorkel.
snor·kel • *noun, plural* **snorkels** • *verb* **snorkeled, snorkeling**

snort (snôrt) *verb* **1** to force breath from the nose in a sudden and noisy way, as a horse does. **2** to make a noise like a snort.
noun the act or sound of snorting.
snort • *verb* **snorted, snorting** • *noun, plural* **snorts**

snout (snout) *noun* the part including the nose and jaws that sticks out from the face of pigs, dogs, and certain other animals.
snout • *noun, plural* **snouts**

snow (snō) *noun* **1** soft, white flakes that form from tiny drops of water that freeze in the upper air and fall to earth. **2** a fall of snow [We are expecting heavy *snow* tonight.]
verb **1** to shower down snow [It is *snowing*.] **2** to cover or shut in with snow [The town was *snowed* in by the last storm.]
snow • *noun, plural for sense 2 only* **snows** • *verb* **snowed, snowing**

a	cat	ō	go	ʉ	fur	ə =	a *in* ago
ā	ape	ô	law, for	ch	chin		e *in* agent
ä	cot, car	oo	look	sh	she		i *in* pencil
e	ten	o͞o	tool	th	thin		o *in* atom
ē	me	oi	oil	*th*	then		u *in* circus
i	fit	ou	out	zh	measure		
ī	ice	u	up	ŋ	ring		

snowball (snō′bôl) ***noun*** a mass of snow that has been packed into a firm ball.
verb to grow larger very quickly like a ball of snow rolling down a hill [Her problems began to *snowball*.]
snow·ball • ***noun,*** *plural* **snowballs** • ***verb*** **snowballed, snowballing**

snowbank (snō′baŋk) ***noun*** a large mound of snow.
snow·bank • ***noun,*** *plural* **snowbanks**

snow blower (blō′ər) ***noun*** a machine that is powered by a motor and is used for removing snow from walks and driveways.
snow blow·er • ***noun,*** *plural* **snow blowers**

snowboard (snō′bôrd) ***noun*** a board on which a person stands to slide down a snowy hill.
verb to slide down snowy hills on a snowboard [There is enough snow now to *snowboard* down the slope.]
snow·board • ***noun,*** *plural* **snowboards** • ***verb*** **snowboarded, snowboarding**

snowboard

snowdrift (snō′drift) ***noun*** a bank or pile of snow that has been pushed into a heap by the wind.
snow·drift • ***noun,*** *plural* **snowdrifts**

snowdrop (snō′dräp) ***noun*** a small plant with a drooping white flower that blooms in early spring.
snow·drop • ***noun,*** *plural* **snowdrops**

snowfall (snō′fôl) ***noun*** **1** a fall of snow. **2** the amount of snow that falls over a certain area during a certain time [We had a 12-inch *snowfall* on February 20.]
snow·fall • ***noun,*** *plural* **snowfalls**

snowflake (snō′flāk) ***noun*** a flake of snow. Snowflakes are crystals.
snow·flake • ***noun,*** *plural* **snowflakes**

snowman (snō′man) ***noun*** a figure that is made of snow packed together and is meant to look somewhat like a person.
snow·man • ***noun,*** *plural* **snowmen**

snowman

snowmobile (snō′mō bēl′) ***noun*** a motor vehicle for traveling on snow. It has runners in front that move so that it can be steered.
snow·mo·bile • ***noun,*** *plural* **snowmobiles**

snowplow

snowplow (snō′plou) ***noun*** a machine or vehicle that is used to clear snow from a road, driveway, or other surface.
snow·plow • ***noun,*** *plural* **snowplows**

snowshoe (snō′sho͞o) ***noun*** a wooden frame that is strung with strips of leather. A person wears one of these frames on each foot attached to the shoe or boot to keep from sinking while walking in deep snow.
snow·shoe • ***noun,*** *plural* **snowshoes**

snowstorm (snō′stôrm) ***noun*** a storm with a heavy snowfall.
snow·storm • ***noun,*** *plural* **snowstorms**

snowy (snō′ē) ***adjective*** **1** having snow [a *snowy* day]. **2** covered with snow [a *snowy* playground]. **3** white like snow [*snowy* hair].
snow·y • ***adjective*** **snowier, snowiest**

snub (snub) ***verb*** to act toward in an unfriendly or scornful way; to slight [He *snubbed* me by saying hello to everyone in the room except me.]
noun a scornful or unfriendly way of dealing with someone.
snub • ***verb*** **snubbed, snubbing** • ***noun,*** *plural* **snubs**

snuck (snuk) ***verb*** *a past tense and a past participle of* **sneak**.

snuff (snuf) ***verb*** to put out the flame of [*Snuff* the candle when you go to bed.]
snuff • ***verb*** **snuffed, snuffing**

snuffle (snuf′əl) ***verb*** to breathe with much noise, in the way that a person does when the nose is stopped up with a cold.

noun the act or sound of snuffling.
snuf·fle • *verb* **snuffled, snuffling** • *noun, plural* **snuffles**

snug (snug) *adjective* **1** warm and comfortable; cozy [We were *snug* in our beds.] **2** fitting in a tight way [a *snug* vest].
snug • *adjective* **snugger, snuggest**

snuggle (snug′əl) *verb* to lie close or hold close in a cozy way; cuddle [The kittens *snuggled* together. He *snuggled* the baby in his arms.]
snug·gle • *verb* **snuggled, snuggling**

so (sō) *adverb* **1** to the degree or amount that has been expressed [She is not *so* tall as I am. Why are you *so* late?] **2** as a result; therefore [He couldn't swim and *so* was drowned.] **3** very [They are *so* happy.] **4** also; in the same way [I am hungry and *so* is she.] **5** more or less; just about [I spent a dollar or *so* on candy.] **6** after all; then [*So* you really don't care.] **7** as it has been shown or told; in this or that way [Hold your pencil just *so*.]
conjunction **1** for the reason that; in order that [Talk louder *so* that I can hear you.] **2** [*an informal use*] with the result that [She didn't study, *so* she failed the test.]
pronoun the same [I am his friend and will remain *so*.]
interjection a word that is used to show surprise, dislike, or doubt [*So!* I caught you!]
adjective **1** being a fact; true [I guess it's really *so*.] **2** in proper order [Everything for his boss must be just *so*.]
—and so forth and the rest; and others. **—and so on** and the rest; and others. **—so as** in order; for the purpose [She left early *so as* to be on time.]

• The words **so, sew,** and **sow** sound alike.
How can you be *so* mean?
It's easy to *sew* on buttons.
Sow flower seeds in the spring.

WORD CHOICES

Synonyms of soak

The words **soak, drench,** and **saturate** share the meaning "to make very wet."

The ocean spray *soaked* her clothes.

Tropical rains *drenched* the jungle.

Saturate the sponge with liquid cleanser.

soak (sōk) *verb* **1** to make or become wet all the way through by keeping or staying in a liquid [*Soak* your sore hand in hot water. Let the beans *soak* all night to soften them.] **2** to absorb or suck up [Use a sponge to *soak* up that water.]
noun the act or process of soaking.
soak • *verb* **soaked, soaking** • *noun, plural* **soaks**

so-and-so (sō′ən sō) [*an informal word*] *noun* a certain person whose name is not mentioned or remembered.
so-and-so • *noun, plural* **so-and-sos**

soap (sōp) *noun* a substance that is used with water to make suds for washing things. It is made from lye and fats and in the form of bars, powders, and liquids.
verb to rub or wash with soap [He *soaped* his whole body in the shower.]
soap • *noun, plural* **soaps** • *verb* **soaped, soaping**

soap opera *noun* a TV or radio drama program that is presented at the same time each day. The story goes on from one day to the next and is told in a sentimental way.
soap opera • *noun, plural* **soap operas**

WORD HISTORY

soap opera

This sort of drama came to be called a **soap opera** because many of the original sponsors of programs of this kind were soap companies.

soapsuds (sōp′sudz) *plural noun* water with soap stirred in until it makes foam.
soap·suds • *plural noun*

soapy (sō′pē) *adjective* **1** covered with soapsuds or full of soap [*soapy* water]. **2** like or having to do with soap or soapsuds [*soapy* foam on ocean waves].
soap·y • *adjective* **soapier, soapiest**

soar (sôr) *verb* **1** to rise or fly high in the air [The plane *soared* out of sight.] **2** to rise above the usual level or limit [Her grades *soared* after she started spending more time studying.]

soar • *verb* **soared, soaring**
● The words **soar** and **sore** sound alike.
We watched the gulls *soar* in the air.
The runner was *sore* after the race.

sob (säb) ***verb*** to cry or weep with a break in the voice and short gasps —Look for the WORD CHOICES box at the entry **cry**.
noun the act or sound of sobbing.
sob • ***verb*** **sobbed, sobbing** • ***noun,*** *plural* **sobs**

sober (sō′bər) ***adjective*** **1** not drunk. **2** serious, quiet, or plain [a *sober* look on her face].
verb to make or become sober [The sad news *sobered* us up.]
so·ber • ***adjective*** • ***verb*** **sobered, sobering**

so-called (sō′kôld′) ***adjective*** called by this name, but usually not really so [Your *so-called* friends lied to you.]

soccer (sä′kər) ***noun*** a kind of football game that is played with a round ball. Players move the ball by kicking or by using any part of the body except the hands and arms.
soc·cer • ***noun***

social (sō′shəl) ***adjective*** **1** having to do with human beings as they live together in a group or groups [*social* problems; *social* trends]. **2** living in groups or colonies [Ants and bees are *social* insects.] **3** liking to be with other people [A hermit is not a *social* person.] **4** having to do with the upper classes or levels of society [That party was the *social* event of the year.]
noun a friendly gathering; a party [a church *social*].
so·cial • ***adjective*** • ***noun,*** *plural* **socials**

socialism (sō′shəl iz əm) ***noun*** any system in which the means of producing goods are owned by the public or the government.
so·cial·ism • ***noun***

socialist (sō′shəl ist) ***noun*** a person who is in favor of socialism.
so·cial·ist • ***noun,*** *plural* **socialists**

social security ***noun*** an insurance system in which the government makes payments to people who are retired or unable to work.

social work ***noun*** a service or activity that is designed to improve the living conditions of people in a community. These services may include health clinics, recreation programs, and care for people who are poor or elderly.

society (sə sī′ə tē) ***noun*** **1** people living together as a group, or forming a group, with the same way of life [a primitive *society*]. **2** the way of life of this kind of group [urban *society*]. **3** all people [This law is for the good of *society*.] **4** a group of people who have joined together for some goal, interest, or activity [a medical *society*]. **5** the wealthy upper class.
so·ci·e·ty • ***noun,*** *plural for senses 1 and 4 only* **societies**

sock[1] (säk) ***noun*** a short stocking that usually covers the leg only part of the way to the knee.
sock • ***noun,*** *plural* **socks** or **sox**

sock[2] (säk) [*a slang word*] ***verb*** to hit hard with the fist.
noun a hard blow or hit.
sock • ***verb*** **socked, socking** • ***noun,*** *plural* **socks**

socket (säk′ət) ***noun*** a hollow part into which something fits [the eye *socket;* a *socket* for a light bulb].
sock·et • ***noun,*** *plural* **sockets**

sod (säd) ***noun*** the top layer of earth containing grass with its roots; turf.

soda (sō′də) ***noun*** **1** any one of certain substances that contain sodium. **2** *a short form of* **baking soda**. **3** *a short form of* **soda water**. **4** a drink that is made of soda water, syrup, and ice cream.
so·da • ***noun,*** *plural for sense 4 only* **sodas**

soda fountain ***noun*** a counter where sodas, sundaes, and other drinks and desserts with ice cream are made and served.
soda fountain • ***noun,*** *plural* **soda fountains**

soda water ***noun*** water that is filled with carbon dioxide gas to make it bubble.

sodium (sō′dē əm) ***noun*** a soft, silver-white metal that is a chemical element. It is found in nature only combined with other elements. Salt, baking soda, and lye all contain sodium.
so·di·um • ***noun***

sofa (sō′fə) ***noun*** an upholstered couch with a back and arms.
so·fa • ***noun,*** *plural* **sofas**

soft (sôft) ***adjective*** **1** not hard or firm; easy to bend, crush, or cut [This pillow is *soft*. Lead is a *soft* metal.] **2** smooth to the touch; not rough [*soft* skin]. **3** not bright or sharp [*soft* gray; a *soft* light]. **4** weak; not strong or powerful [*soft* muscles; a *soft* wind]. **5** not harsh [*soft* words; a *soft* life] —Look for the WORD CHOICES box at the entry **gentle**. **6** weak or low in sound [a *soft* chime].
soft • ***adjective*** **softer, softest**

solar system

WORD CHOICES

Synonyms of **soft**

Many words share the meaning "not hard or firm."

downy	mushy	spongy
fluffy	pulpy	

softball (sôft′bôl) *noun* **1** a game that is like baseball but is played on a smaller diamond. **2** the ball that is used in this game. It is larger and softer than an ordinary baseball.
soft·ball • *noun, plural for sense 2 only* **softballs**

soft-boiled (sôft′boild) *adjective* cooked in hot water only a short time so that the yolk is still soft [a *soft-boiled* egg].

soft drink *noun* a drink that does not contain alcohol and usually is carbonated.
soft drink • *noun, plural* **soft drinks**

soften (sôf′ən) *verb* to make or become soft or softer.
sof·ten • *verb* **softened, softening**

software (sôft′wer) *noun* all of the programs that make a computer operate.
soft·ware • *noun*

soggy (säg′ē *or* sôg′ē) *adjective* very wet and heavy; soaked.
sog·gy • *adjective* **soggier, soggiest**

soil[1] (soil) *noun* **1** the top layer of earth, in which plants grow. **2** country [I've lived my whole life on my native *soil*.]

soil[2] (soil) *verb* **1** to make or become dirty; to stain or spot [She *soiled* her clothes playing in the mud. This shirt *soils* easily.] **2** to disgrace [You've *soiled* your good name with your evil deeds.]
soil • *verb* **soiled, soiling**

sol (sōl) *noun* the fifth note of a musical scale.
• The words **sol, sole,** and **soul** sound alike.
Sol is the note between fa and la.
The *sole* of my right shoe is worn out.
She was the *sole* survivor of the flood.
We ate fillet of *sole* for dinner.
The beautiful music touched my *soul*.

solar (sō′lər) *adjective* **1** having to do with the sun [a *solar* eclipse; *solar* energy]. **2** depending on light or energy from the sun [*solar* heating].
so·lar • *adjective*

solar system *noun* the sun and all the planets, moons, comets, and asteroids that move around the sun.

sold (sōld) *verb past tense and past participle of* **sell**.

solder (säd′ər) *noun* a mixture of metals that is melted and used to join or patch metal parts.
verb to join or patch with solder.
sol·der • *noun* • *verb* **soldered, soldering**

soldier (sōl′jər) *noun* **1** a person who serves in an army. **2** a person in an army who is not an officer.
sol·dier • *noun, plural* **soldiers**

sole[1] (sōl) *noun* **1** the bottom surface of the foot. **2** the bottom surface of a shoe, sock, or other covering for the foot.
verb to fasten a sole to [The old pair of boots were *soled* to make them last longer.]
sole • *noun, plural* **soles** • *verb* **soled, soling**
• The words **sole, sol,** and **soul** sound alike.
A nail was stuck in the boot's *sole*.

a cat	ō go	ʉ fur	ə = a *in* ago
ā ape	ô law, for	ch chin	e *in* agent
ä cot, car	oo look	sh she	i *in* pencil
e ten	ōō tool	th thin	o *in* atom
ē me	oi oil	*th* then	u *in* circus
i fit	ou out	zh measure	
ī ice	u up	ŋ ring	

My *sole* task today is mowing the lawn.
She and I fished for flounder and *sole*.
Do, re, mi, fa, *sol*, la, ti, do.
Her piano playing has no *soul*.

sole[2] (sōl) ***adjective*** without others; one and only [He is the *sole* owner of the store.]
● The words **sole, sol,** and **soul** sound alike.

sole[3] (sōl) ***noun*** a kind of flatfish that is used as food.
sole • ***noun,*** *plural* **sole**
● The words **sole, sol,** and **soul** sound alike.

solely (sōl′lē) ***adverb*** **1** alone; without others [We are *solely* to blame.] **2** only; merely [I read *solely* for fun.]
sole·ly • ***adverb***

solemn (säl′əm) ***adjective*** serious or grave; very sincere [a *solemn* face; a *solemn* oath].
sol·emn • ***adjective***

solid (säl′id) ***adjective*** **1** keeping its shape instead of spreading out like a liquid or gas; quite firm or hard [Ice is water in a *solid* form.] —Look for the WORD CHOICES box at the entry **firm**[1]. **2** filled with matter all the way through; not hollow [a *solid* block of wood]. **3** having length, width, and thickness [A square is a flat figure, while a cube is a *solid* figure.] **4** strong, firm, or sound [*solid* thinking; a *solid* building]. **5** with no breaks, stops, or rests; continuous [They built a *solid* wall around the castle. We still have two *solid* hours of work.] **6** of one color or material all the way through [a tray of *solid* silver].
noun **1** something that is solid, not a liquid or gas [Iron and glass are *solids*.] **2** anything that has length, width, and thickness [A sphere is a *solid*.]
sol·id • ***adjective*** • ***noun,*** *plural* **solids**

solidify (sə lid′i fī′) ***verb*** to make or become solid or firm [Butter *solidifies* as it cools.]
so·lid·i·fy • ***verb*** **solidified, solidifying, solidifies**

solitary (säl′i ter′ē) ***adjective*** **1** living or being alone; lonely [a *solitary* traveler; a *solitary* lighthouse] —Look for the WORD CHOICES box at the entry **alone**. **2** single; only [a *solitary* example].
sol·i·tar·y • ***adjective***

solitude (säl′i to͞od *or* säl′i tyo͞od) ***noun*** the condition of being solitary, or alone.
sol·i·tude • ***noun***

solo (sō′lō) ***noun*** **1** a piece of music that is sung or played by one person. **2** a performance by one person alone.
adjective **1** for or by one singer or instrument [a *solo* performance]. **2** made or done by one person [a *solo* flight in an airplane].
adverb without anyone else [She flew *solo*.]
verb **1** to fly an airplane alone. **2** to play or sing a musical solo [She *soloed* on drums.]
so·lo • ***noun,*** *plural* **solos** • ***adjective*** • ***adverb*** • ***verb*** **soloed, soloing, solos**

Solomon (säl′ə mən) a wise king of Israel in the tenth century B.C.
Sol·o·mon

Solomon Islands a country on a group of islands in the southwestern Pacific, east of New Guinea.

solution (sə lo͞o′shən) ***noun*** **1** the act or process of solving a problem. **2** an answer or explanation [We found the *solution* to the mystery of the disappearing books.] **3** a mixture that is formed by dissolving something in a liquid [If you have a sore throat, gargle with a *solution* of salt and water.]
so·lu·tion • ***noun,*** *plural for senses 2 and 3 only* **solutions**

solve (sôlv *or* sälv) ***verb*** to find the answer to; explain [*Solve* this math problem for the class.]
solve • ***verb*** **solved, solving**

Somalia (sō mä′lē ə) a country on the eastern coast of Africa.
So·ma·li·a

somber (säm′bər) ***adjective*** **1** dark and gloomy or dull [*somber* colors] —Look for the WORD CHOICES box at the entry **dark**. **2** sad or serious [*somber* thoughts on a rainy day].
som·ber • ***adjective***

sombrero

sombrero (säm brer′ō) ***noun*** a large hat with a wide brim. It is worn in Mexico and the southwestern U.S.
som·bre·ro • ***noun,*** *plural* **sombreros**

some (sum) ***adjective*** **1** being a certain person or thing that is not named or not known [We will leave *some* day next week.] **2** being a certain group of persons or things that are not named or not known [*Some* people were playing ball.] **3** being of a certain, but not definite, number or amount [Have *some* candy.] **4** [*an informal use*] outstanding or remarkable [That was *some* party!]
pronoun **1** a certain person, thing, or group that is not named or not known [*Some* agree.] **2** a certain number or amount, but not all [Take *some*.]
adverb **1** about [*Some* ten people were hired.] **2** [*an informal use*] to some degree or limit [I slept *some*.] **3** [*an informal use*] to a great degree [You must run *some* to catch up.]
● The words **some** and **sum** sound alike.
Some people never learn.
The *sum* of 20 and 30 is 50.

-some[1] *a suffix meaning:* **1** tending to [A *tiresome* story tends to tire the person who is listening.] **2** tending to be [A *burdensome* problem tends to be a burden.]

-some[2] *a suffix meaning* group of [A *threesome* is a group of three.]

somebody (sum′bud′ē *or* sum′bäd′ē) ***pronoun*** a certain person who is not known or named; someone [*Somebody* left the door open.]
noun a person who is important [I want to be *somebody* when I grow up.]
some·bod·y • ***pronoun*** • ***noun,*** *plural* **somebodies**

someday (sum′dā) ***adverb*** at some time in the future.
some·day • ***adverb***

somehow (sum′hou) ***adverb*** in a way that is not known or explained; by some means or method [*Somehow* the pilot managed to land.]
some·how • ***adverb***

someone (sum′wun) ***pronoun*** *the same as* **somebody**.
some·one • ***pronoun***

someplace (sum′plās) [*an informal word*] ***adverb*** *the same as* **somewhere**.
some·place • ***adverb***

somersault (sum′ər sôlt) ***noun*** a movement in which a person turns the body completely over forward or backward, heels over head.
verb to do a somersault.
som·er·sault • ***noun,*** *plural* **somersaults** • ***verb*** **somersaulted, somersaulting**

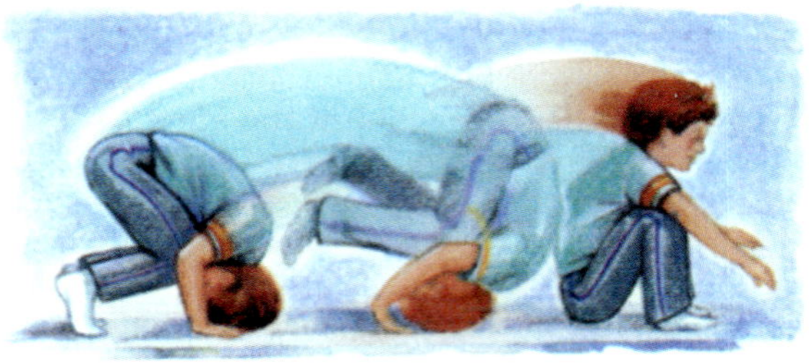

somersault

something (sum′thiŋ) ***noun*** **1** a certain thing that is not named or known [I have *something* to tell you. I'd like *something* to eat.] **2** a thing that is not known for sure or not understood [*Something* is wrong with my car.]
adverb somewhat; a little [You look *something* like your cousin.]
some·thing • ***noun*** • ***adverb***

sometime (sum′tīm) ***adverb*** **1** at some time in the future [Come see us *sometime* soon.] **2** at some time that is not known or named [I saw them *sometime* last week.]
some·time • ***adverb***

sometimes (sum′tīmz) ***adverb*** once in a while; now and then [*Sometimes* we go swimming.]
some·times • ***adverb***

somewhat (sum′hwut *or* sum′wut) ***adverb*** to some degree; a little [They are *somewhat* late.]
noun a certain part, amount, or degree [You are being *somewhat* of a fool.]
some·what • ***adverb*** • ***noun***

somewhere (sum′hwer *or* sum′wer) ***adverb*** **1** in, to, or at some place that is not known or named [They live *somewhere* near here.] **2** at some time, degree, or number [Be there *somewhere* around ten o'clock.]
some·where • ***adverb***

son (sun) ***noun*** a boy or man as he is related to a parent or to both parents.
son • ***noun,*** *plural* **sons**
● The words **son** and **sun** sound alike.

a	cat	ō	go	ʉ	fur	ə = a *in* ago	
ā	ape	ô	law, for	ch	chin	e *in* agent	
ä	cot, car	oo	look	sh	she	i *in* pencil	
e	ten	ōō	tool	th	thin	o *in* atom	
ē	me	oi	oil	*th*	then	u *in* circus	
i	fit	ou	out	zh	measure		
ī	ice	u	up	ŋ	ring		

My parents have two daughters and a *son*.
The window lets in plenty of *sun*.

sonar (sō′när) ***noun*** a device that sends sound waves through water and picks them up after they strike some object and bounce back. It is used to find submarines and to locate the bottoms of very deep bodies of water.
so·nar • ***noun***

song (sôŋ) ***noun*** **1** a piece of music for singing [a popular *song*]. **2** the act of singing [They broke into *song*.] **3** a musical sound that is like singing [the *song* of a canary].
song • ***noun, plural for senses 1 and 3 only*** **songs**

songbird (sôŋ′burd) ***noun*** a bird that makes sounds that are like music.
song·bird • ***noun, plural*** **songbirds**

son-in-law (sun′in lô′ *or* sun′in lä′) ***noun*** the husband of one's daughter.
son-in-law • ***noun, plural*** **sons-in-law**

sonnet (sän′ət) ***noun*** a poem that has 14 lines that rhyme in certain patterns.
son·net • ***noun, plural*** **sonnets**

soon (sōōn) ***adverb*** **1** in a short time; before much time has passed [Spring will *soon* be here.] **2** fast or quickly [as *soon* as possible]. **3** ahead of time; early [She left too *soon*.]
—sooner or later in the end; finally.
soon • ***adverb*** **sooner, soonest**

soot (soot) ***noun*** a black powder that is formed when certain things burn. Most of it is made up of carbon. It makes smoke gray or black.

soothe (sōō*th*) ***verb*** **1** to make quiet or calm by being gentle or friendly [The clerk *soothed* the angry customer with helpful answers.] —Look for the WORD CHOICES box at the entry **comfort**. **2** to take away some of the pain or sorrow of; to ease [This lotion will *soothe* your sunburn.]
soothe • ***verb*** **soothed, soothing**

sop (säp) ***verb*** **1** to suck up or absorb [I used the bread to *sop* up the gravy.] **2** to make very wet; to soak [Our clothes were *sopped*.]
sop • ***verb*** **sopped, sopping**

sophisticated (sə fis′ti kāt′əd) ***adjective*** **1** not simple, natural, or innocent; wise in the ways of the world. **2** very complicated and based on the latest ideas, techniques, or devices [*sophisticated* electronic equipment].
so·phis·ti·cat·ed • ***adjective***

sophomore (säf′ə môr *or* sôf′môr) ***noun*** a student in the tenth grade or in the second year of college.
soph·o·more • ***noun, plural*** **sophomores**

soprano (sə pran′ō *or* sə prä′nō) ***noun*** **1** the highest kind of singing voice of women, girls, or young boys. **2** a singer with this kind of voice.
so·pra·no • ***noun, plural*** **sopranos**

sorcerer (sôr′sər ər) ***noun*** a person who works magic or sorcery in fairy tales; a magician or wizard.
sor·cer·er • ***noun, plural*** **sorcerers**

sorceress (sôr′sər əs) ***noun*** a woman who works magic or sorcery in fairy tales; a witch.
sor·cer·ess • ***noun, plural*** **sorceresses**

sorcery (sôr′sər ē) ***noun*** the supposed practice of using spells and charms to gain magic power for bad or harmful purposes.
sor·cer·y • ***noun***

sore (sôr) ***adjective*** **1** giving pain; aching or painful [a *sore* toe]. **2** feeling pain, from a bruise or some other cause [I am *sore* all over.] **3** making a person angry or irritated [Losing the game was a *sore* point for them.] **4** [*an informal use*] angry or irritated.
noun a place on the body where tissue is injured.
sore • ***adjective*** **sorer, sorest** • ***noun, plural*** **sores**

● The words **sore** and **soar** sound alike.
The runner was *sore* after her race.
We watched the gulls *soar* in the air.

sorrow (sär′ō) ***noun*** **1** a sad or troubled feeling; grief. **2** a loss, death, or trouble that causes this kind of feeling [Grandma's illness is a great *sorrow* to us.]
sor·row • ***noun, plural for sense 2 only*** **sorrows**

sorrowful (sär′ə fəl) ***adjective*** **1** feeling or showing sorrow; sad [a *sorrowful* face] —Look for the WORD CHOICES box at the entry **sad**. **2** causing sorrow [a *sorrowful* duty].
sor·row·ful • ***adjective***

sorry (sär′ē) ***adjective*** **1** full of sorrow or pity [I was *sorry* to hear that their dog had died.] **2** feeling mild regret [I'm *sorry* to have to leave now.] **3** low in value or quality; poor [The actor gave a *sorry* performance.] **4** causing suffering; deserving pity [a *sorry* sight].
sor·ry • ***adjective*** **sorrier, sorriest**

sort (sôrt) ***noun*** a group of things that are alike in some way; a kind or class [all *sorts* of toys] —Look for the WORD CHOICES box at the entry **type**.
verb to separate or arrange according to kind or class [*Sort* out the clothes that need to be mended.]
—**out of sorts** [*an informal use*] not in a good mood or not feeling well. —**sort of** [*an informal use*] somewhat; a little.
sort • ***noun,*** *plural* **sorts** • ***verb*** **sorted, sorting**

SOS ***noun*** a signal calling for help [The ship sent an *SOS* when fire broke out.]

so-so (sō′sō) ***adjective*** neither too good nor too bad.
adverb neither too well nor too badly; fairly well.

sought (sôt *or* sät) ***verb*** *past tense and past participle of* **seek**.

soul (sōl) ***noun*** **1** the part of a person that is thought of as the center of feeling, thinking, and deciding how to act. It is thought of as being separate from the body. **2** warmth and strength of feeling or spirit [That painting has no *soul*.] **3** a person [Not a *soul* left the room.]
soul • ***noun,*** *plural for senses 1 and 3 only* **souls**

● The words **soul, sol,** and **sole** sound alike.
His music has no *soul*.
Do, re, mi, fa, *sol*, la, ti, do.
The *sole* of my right shoe is worn out.
He was the *sole* survivor of the flood.
We ate fillet of *sole* for dinner.

sound[1] (sound) ***noun*** **1** the form of energy that acts on the ears so that a person can hear. Sound is made up of waves of vibrations that pass through air and water [In the air, *sound* travels at a speed of about 1,088 feet per second.] **2** something that can be heard; a noise or tone [the *sound* of bells]. **3** any one of the noises that are made in speaking [a vowel *sound*]. **4** the distance within which something can be heard [within *sound* of her voice].
verb **1** to make a sound [Your voice *sounds* hoarse.] **2** to cause to make a sound [*Sound* your horn.] **3** to seem; appear [The plan *sounds* all right.] **4** to say in a clear way [He doesn't *sound* his r's.]
sound • ***noun,*** *plural for senses 2 and 3 only* **sounds** • ***verb*** **sounded, sounding**

sound[2] (sound) ***adjective*** **1** in good condition; not damaged or rotted [*sound* timber]. **2** normal and healthy [a *sound* mind in a *sound* body]. **3** firm, safe, or secure [Put your money in a *sound* bank.] **4** full of good sense; wise [a *sound* plan]. **5** deep and not disturbed [a *sound* sleep]. **6** thorough; complete [a *sound* defeat on the football field].
adverb in a sound or deep way; completely [They are *sound* asleep.]
sound • ***adjective*** & • ***adverb*** **sounder, soundest**

sound[3] (sound) ***noun*** **1** a channel of water that connects two large bodies of water or separates an island from the mainland. **2** a long inlet or arm of the sea.
sound • ***noun,*** *plural* **sounds**

sound[4] (sound) ***verb*** to measure the depth of water, often by lowering a weight that is fastened to a line [They are *sounding* the channel to find out if large boats can go through it.]
sound • ***verb*** **sounded, sounding**

soundless (sound′ləs) ***adjective*** without sound; quiet or silent —Look for the WORD CHOICES box at the entry **still**.
sound·less • ***adjective***

soundproof (sound′pro͞of) ***adjective*** capable of keeping sound from coming through [*soundproof* walls].
verb to make soundproof.
sound·proof • ***adjective***
• ***verb*** **soundproofed, soundproofing**

sound wave ***noun*** a vibration in air or water that is caused by a moving object. This vibration causes the air or water around it to vibrate also, creating a disturbance that the human ear can hear.
sound wave • ***noun,*** *plural* **sound waves**

soup (so͞op) ***noun*** a liquid food that is made by cooking meat, fish, or vegetables, or a combination of these in water or milk.
soup • ***noun,*** *plural* **soups**

sour (sour) ***adjective*** **1** having the sharp, acid taste of lemon juice or vinegar. **2** made acid or spoiled by fermenting [*sour* milk]. **3** cross; bad-tempered [He is in a *sour* mood.] **4** below normal; bad [His batting has gone *sour*.]

a	cat	ō	go	ʉ	fur	ə = a *in* ago	
ā	ape	ô	law, for	ch	chin	e *in* agent	
ä	cot, car	o͝o	look	sh	she	i *in* pencil	
e	ten	o͞o	tool	th	thin	o *in* atom	
ē	me	oi	oil	*th*	then	u *in* circus	
i	fit	ou	out	zh	measure		
ī	ice	u	up	ŋ	ring		

5 sounding wrong; not having the right pitch [a *sour* note].
verb to make or become sour [The hot weather *soured* the milk quickly.]
sour • ***adjective*** **sourer, sourest**
• ***verb*** **soured, souring**

WORD CHOICES

Synonyms of **sour**

The words **sour, acid,** and **tart** share the meaning "sharp in taste."

I like very *sour* dill pickles.

A lemon is an *acid* fruit.

A cherry pie should be slightly *tart*.

sourball (sour′bôl) ***noun*** a small ball of sour, hard candy.
sour·ball • ***noun,*** *plural* **sourballs**

source (sôrs) ***noun*** **1** a spring or fountain that is the starting point of a stream. **2** a thing or place from which something comes or is gotten [The sun is our *source* of energy. This book is the *source* of my information.] —Look for the WORD CHOICES box at the entry **origin**.
source • ***noun,*** *plural* **sources**

Sousa (so͞o′zə), **John Philip** (jän fil′ip) 1854-1932; U.S. band conductor and composer of marches.
Sou·sa, John Phil·ip

south (south) ***noun*** **1** the direction to the left of a person facing the sunset [Look to the *south*.] **2** a place or region in this direction [They live in the *south*.]
adjective **1** in, of, or to the south [driving to the *south* side of town]. **2** from the south [a *south* wind].
adverb in the direction of the south; to the south [Go *south* ten miles.]
—the South **1** the southern part of the U.S. **2** the southern part of the U.S. that formed the Confederacy in the Civil War.

South Africa a country in southern Africa.

South America the southern continent in the Western Hemisphere.

South Carolina (south′ker′ə lī′nə) a State in the southeastern part of the U.S. Its capital is Columbia. Abbreviated **SC** or **S.C.**
South Car·o·li·na

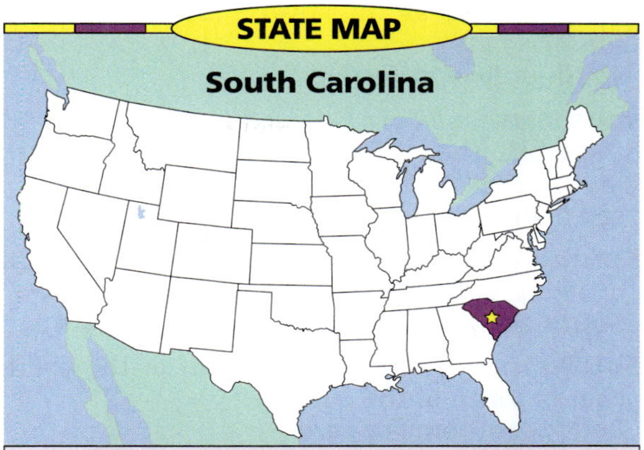

Statehood: 1788, the 8th state • **Capital:** Columbia

South Dakota a State in the north central part of the U.S. Its capital is Pierre. Abbreviated **SD, S.D.,** or **S.Dak.**

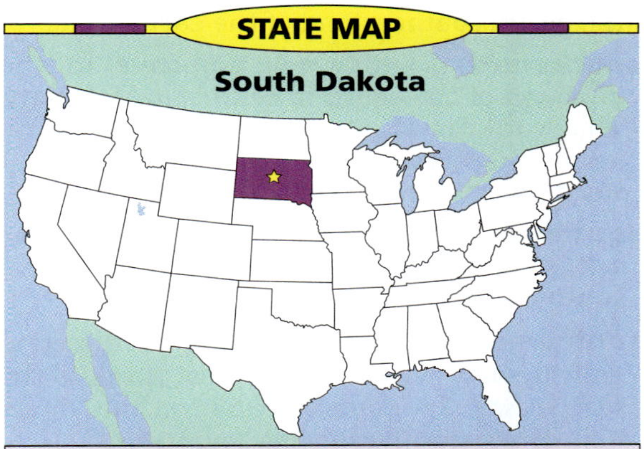

Statehood: 1889, the 40th state • **Capital:** Pierre

southeast (south ēst′) ***noun*** **1** the direction halfway between south and east [Look to the *southeast*.] **2** a place or region in this direction [My sister lives in the *southeast*.]
adjective **1** in, of, or to the southeast [the *southeast* part of the country; a *southeast* route]. **2** from the southeast [*southeast* winds].
adverb in the direction of the southeast; to the southeast [We sailed *southeast*.]
south·east • ***noun*** • ***adjective*** • ***adverb***

southeastern (south ēs′tərn) ***adjective*** **1** in, of, or to the southeast [a *southeastern* city; a *southeastern* view]. **2** from the southeast [*southeastern* winds].
south·east·ern • ***adjective***

southerly (su*th*′ər lē) ***adjective*** **1** in or toward the south [a *southerly* route to work]. **2** from the south [*southerly* winds]. This word can

S

also be used as an adverb [The wind blew *southerly.*]
south·er·ly • *adjective*

southern (su*th*ʹərn) ***adjective*** **1** in, of, or to the south [the *southern* sky]. **2** from the south [a *southern* wind].
south·ern • *adjective*

Southerner (su*th*ʹər nər) ***noun*** a person born or living in the South.
South·ern·er • ***noun,*** *plural* **Southerners**

Southern Hemisphere the half of the earth that is south of the equator.
South·ern Hem·i·sphere

southpaw (sou̇thʹpô *or* sou̇thʹpä) [*a slang word*] ***noun*** **1** a person who is left-handed. **2** a baseball pitcher who is left-handed.
south·paw • ***noun,*** *plural* **southpaws**

South Pole the spot that is farthest south on the earth; southern end of the earth's axis.

southward (sou̇thʹwərd) ***adjective*** in the direction of the south [a *southward* journey]. This word can also be used as an adverb [We journeyed *southward.*]
south·ward • *adjective*

southwards (sou̇thʹwərdz) ***adverb*** *the same as the adverb* **southward**.
south·wards • *adverb*

southwest (sou̇th westʹ) ***noun*** **1** the direction halfway between south and west [Look to the *southwest.*] **2** a place or region in this direction [His sister lives in the *southwest.*]
adjective **1** in, of, or to the southwest [the *southwest* part of the country; a *southwest* route]. **2** from the southwest [*southwest* winds].
adverb in the direction of the southwest; to the southwest [They moved *southwest.*]
south·west • *noun* • *adjective* • *adverb*

South West Africa *old name of* **Namibia**. This country was administered by South Africa.

southwester (sou̇ wesʹtər) ***noun*** a sailor's waterproof hat. It has a broad brim in the back to cover the neck.
south·west·er • ***noun,*** *plural* **southwesters**

southwestern (sou̇th wesʹtərn) ***adjective*** **1** in, of, or to the southwest [*southwestern* migration; a *southwestern* view]. **2** from the southwest [*southwestern* winds].
south·west·ern • *adjective*

souvenir (so͞o və nirʹ) ***noun*** an object kept as a reminder of something [He has pennants, programs, and other *souvenirs* from the baseball games that he's seen.]
sou·ve·nir • ***noun,*** *plural* **souvenirs**

sovereign (sävʹrən *or* sävʹər in) ***adjective*** **1** highest in power or rank; supreme [a *sovereign* prince]. **2** not controlled by others; independent [a *sovereign* country].
noun a ruler such as a king, queen, or emperor.
sov·er·eign • *adjective* • ***noun,*** *plural* **sovereigns**

Soviet Union (sōʹvē et yo͞onʹyən) *a short form of* **Union of Soviet Socialist Republics**.
So·vi·et Un·ion

sow[1] (sou̇) ***noun*** a full-grown, female pig.
sow • ***noun,*** *plural* **sows**

sow[2] (sō) ***verb*** to scatter or plant seed for growing [The farmer *sowed* wheat.]
sow • ***verb*** **sowed, sown** or **sowed, sowing**
● The words **sow, sew,** and **so** sound alike.
Sow flower seeds in the spring.
It's easy to *sew* on buttons.
How can you be *so* mean?

sown (sōn) ***verb*** *a past participle of* **sow**[2].

sox (säks) ***noun*** *a plural of* **sock**[1].

soybean (soiʹbēn) ***noun*** the seed, or bean, of a plant that is grown for food. Oil from the soybean is also used as food.
soy·bean • ***noun,*** *plural* **soybeans**

soy sauce (soi) ***noun*** a dark, salty sauce made from soybeans, used especially as a flavoring in Chinese and Japanese dishes.

spa (spä) ***noun*** **1** a place with a spring of mineral water, to which people go for their health. **2** a health club or resort with facilities such as exercise rooms and sauna baths.
spa • ***noun,*** *plural* **spas**

space (spās) ***noun*** **1** the area that stretches in all directions, has no limits, and contains all things in the universe. **2** the distance or area between things [There was very little *space* between the buildings.] **3** the distance or area inside of something [There is much *space* in the hall closet.] **4** an area used for some purpose [a parking *space*]. **5** *a short form of* **outer space**.

a cat	ō go	ʉ fur	ə = a *in* ago
ā ape	ô law, for	ch chin	e *in* agent
ä cot, car	o͝o look	sh she	i *in* pencil
e ten	o͞o tool	th thin	o *in* atom
ē me	oi oil	*th* then	u *in* circus
i fit	ou out	zh measure	
ī ice	u up	ŋ ring	

verb to arrange with spaces in between [The gardener *spaced* the plants evenly.]
space • *noun, plural for sense 4 only* **spaces** • *verb* **spaced, spacing**

spacecraft (spās′kraft) *noun* any vehicle designed for use in outer space.
space·craft • *noun, plural* **spacecraft**

spaceship (spās′ship) *noun* a spacecraft that has people inside operating it.
space·ship • *noun, plural* **spaceships**

space shuttle

space shuttle *noun* a spacecraft designed to carry people and equipment back and forth between earth and space.
space shuttle • *noun, plural* **space shuttles**

space station *noun* a spacecraft designed to remain in space for long periods of time. It can be used as a base for making scientific studies or for launching other spacecraft.
space station • *noun, plural* **space stations**

spacesuit (spās′so͞ot) *noun* a special suit worn by an astronaut. Air pressure inside the suit is kept at a level that lets the astronaut breathe in a normal way while in outer space.
space·suit • *noun, plural* **spacesuits**

spacious (spā′shəs) *adjective* having much space, or room; very large; vast [She lives in a *spacious* house.]
spa·cious • *adjective*

spade[1] (spād) *noun* a tool with a heavy, flat blade and a handle, used for digging.
spade • *noun, plural* **spades**

spade[2] (spād) *noun* **1** the mark ♠, used on a black suit of playing cards. **2** a card of this suit.
spade • *noun, plural* **spades**

spaghetti (spə get′ē) *noun* long, thin strings of pasta, cooked by boiling or steaming and served with a sauce.
spa·ghet·ti • *noun*

Spain (spān) a country on a large peninsula in southwestern Europe.

span (span) *noun* **1** the distance between the tip of the thumb and the tip of the little finger when the hand is fully spread. **2** the distance between two ends or two supports [The *span* of the bridge is one mile.] **3** the part between two ends or two supports [Thousands of cars travel the *span* of the bridge each day.] **4** a certain period of time [He has a short *span* of attention.]
verb to stretch or reach across [The bridge *spans* the river.]
span • *noun, plural* **spans** • *verb* **spanned, spanning**

spangle (spaŋ′gəl) *noun* one of the small, shiny pieces of metal sewn on some clothing as a decoration.
span·gle • *noun, plural* **spangles**

spangled (spaŋ′gəld) *adjective* covered or decorated with spangles or other bright objects [the Star-*Spangled* Banner].
span·gled • *adjective*

Spaniard (span′yərd) *noun* a person born or living in Spain.
Span·iard • *noun, plural* **Spaniards**

spaniel (span′yəl) *noun* a dog with long silky hair, large drooping ears, and short legs.
span·iel • *noun, plural* **spaniels**

Spanish (span′ish) *noun* the language of Spain, Mexico, Central America, and parts of South America.
—the Spanish the people of Spain.
Span·ish • *noun*

Spanish moss *noun* a plant that has no roots. It grows in long, graceful strands from the branches of trees in the southeastern U.S.

spank (spaŋk) *verb* to slap on the buttocks as a way of punishing.
spank • *verb* **spanked, spanking**

spar (spär) *noun* a strong, heavy pole for holding up the sails on a ship. Masts, yards, and booms are spars.
spar • *noun, plural* **spars**

spare (sper) *verb* **1** to hold back from hurting or killing [She *spared* his feelings.] **2** to save or free from something [*Spare* us from having to hear that same story for the fifth time.] **3** to get along without; give up [I can't *spare* the money for a vacation this year.] **4** to keep from using [The police *spared* no effort to find the missing child.]

S

adjective **1** kept for use when needed [a *spare* tire]. **2** not taken up by work or duty; free [*spare* time]. **3** small in amount; meager; scanty [The poor family lives on a *spare* budget.] **4** lean and thin [The man is tall and *spare*.]
noun **1** an extra part or thing. **2** in bowling, the act of knocking down all ten pins with two rolls of the ball.
spare • *verb* **spared, sparing** • *adjective* **sparer, sparest** • *noun, plural* **spares**

spareribs (sper′ribz) *plural noun* a cut of meat, especially pork, that is the thin end of the ribs with most of the meat cut away.
spare·ribs • *plural noun*

spark (spärk) *noun* **1** a small bit of burning matter thrown off by a fire. **2** any flash of light that is like this. **3** a bit or trace [a *spark* of enthusiasm].
verb **1** to make or give off sparks. **2** to stir up; excite [This book *sparked* my interest in reptiles.]
spark • *noun, plural* **sparks** • *verb* **sparked, sparking**

sparkle (spär′kəl) *verb* **1** to give off sparks or flashes of light; glitter; glisten [The lake *sparkles* in the sunlight.] **2** to bubble [The ginger ale *sparkled* in the glass.]
noun **1** a spark of light. **2** glitter [the *sparkle* of a diamond].
spar·kle • *verb* **sparkled, sparkling** • *noun, plural for sense 1 only* **sparkles**

sparkler (spär′klər) *noun* a thin wire covered with a substance that burns with bright sparks.
spar·kler • *noun, plural* **sparklers**

spark plug *noun* an electrical device put into the cylinder of a gasoline engine. It makes sparks that cause the fuel mixture in the cylinder to burn.
spark plug • *noun, plural* **spark plugs**

sparrow (sper′ō) *noun* a common, small gray and brown songbird with a short beak.
spar·row • *noun, plural* **sparrows**

sparse (spärs) *adjective* not thick or crowded; spread or scattered in small amounts [a *sparse* crowd; *sparse* hair] —Look for the WORD CHOICES box at the entry **meager**.
sparse • *adjective* **sparser, sparsest**

spasm (spaz′əm) *noun* a sudden tightening of a muscle that cannot be controlled [a back *spasm*].
spasm • *noun, plural* **spasms**

spat[1] (spat) [*an informal word*] *noun* a small quarrel or argument.
spat • *noun, plural* **spats**

spat[2] (spat) *verb a past tense and a past participle of* **spit**[2].

spatter (spat′ər) *verb* **1** to spot or splash with small drops [The hot fat *spattered* the stove.] **2** to fall or strike in drops or in a shower.
noun the act or sound of spattering.
spat·ter • *verb* **spattered, spattering** • *noun, plural* **spatters**

spatula (spach′ə lə) *noun* a tool with a broad, flat blade that bends easily. It is used to spread or mix food, paint, or another substance.
spat·u·la • *noun, plural* **spatulas**

spawn (spôn *or* spän) *noun* the eggs or newly hatched young of fish, lobsters, frogs, or some other water animals.
verb to produce eggs in large numbers [Salmon *spawn* in freshwater streams.]
spawn • *noun* • *verb* **spawned, spawning**

SPCA or **S.P.C.A.** *abbreviation for* Society for the Prevention of Cruelty to Animals.

WORD CHOICES

Synonyms of **speak**

The words **speak, converse,** and **talk** share the meaning "to have a conversation."

I haven't *spoken* with them for weeks.

They work together but seldom *converse*.

We were *talking* about politics.

speak (spēk) *verb* **1** to say something with the voice; talk [They *spoke* to each other on the phone.] **2** to tell or make known one's ideas, opinions, or feelings [*Speak* your mind freely.] **3** to make a speech [He will *speak* at the meeting.] **4** to be able to talk in a certain language [Our friend *speaks* French.]
—speak out or **speak up 1** to speak loudly.

a cat	ō go	ʉ fur	ə = a *in* ago	
ā ape	ô law, for	ch chin	e *in* agent	
ä cot, car	oo look	sh she	i *in* pencil	
e ten	ōō tool	th thin	o *in* atom	
ē me	oi oil	*th* then	u *in* circus	
i fit	ou out	zh measure		
ī ice	u up	ŋ ring		

2 to speak in an open or free way [He *spoke out* against crime.]
speak • *verb* **spoke, spoken, speaking**

speaker (spē′kər) *noun* **1** a person who speaks. **2 Speaker** the chairman of the U.S. House of Representatives: the full name for this person is *Speaker of the House*. **3** a device that changes electric current into sound waves [stereo *speakers*].
speak·er • *noun, plural* **speakers**

spear (spir) *noun* **1** a weapon made up of a long shaft with a sharp head. It is thrust or thrown by hand. **2** a long blade, shoot, or stalk of a plant [asparagus *spears*].
verb to pass through or stab with a spear or other sharp object [*Spear* the pickle with a fork.]
spear • *noun, plural* **spears** • *verb* **speared, spearing**

spearmint (spir′mint) *noun* a common type of mint plant, used for flavoring.
spear·mint • *noun*

special (spesh′əl) *adjective* **1** not like others; different [The cook has a *special* recipe for tacos.] **2** not ordinary; unusual [a *special* request]. **3** more than others; chief; main [a *special* friend]. **4** of or for a certain purpose, use, or occasion [a *special* meeting to elect officers; a *special* tool to fix a machine].
noun **1** something featured on sale or on a menu [Today's *special* is fish.] **2** a TV program that is not part of a regular series.
spe·cial • *adjective* • *noun, plural* **specials**

specialist (spesh′əl ist) *noun* a person who has special knowledge or skills in some subject or profession [a *specialist* in bone diseases].
spe·cial·ist • *noun, plural* **specialists**

specialize (spesh′əl īz) *verb* to make a special study of something or work in a special branch of some profession [The lawyer *specializes* in criminal cases.]
spe·cial·ize • *verb* **specialized, specializing**

specially (spesh′əl ē) *adverb* in a special way [a frame made *specially* to fit the picture].
spe·cial·ly • *adverb*

specialty (spesh′əl tē) *noun* **1** a special interest, skill, study, or work [The artist's *specialty* is painting portraits.] **2** a special product [Steak is the *specialty* at that restaurant.]
spe·cial·ty • *noun, plural* **specialties**

species (spē′shēz *or* spē′sēz) *noun* a group of plants or animals that are alike in certain ways [The lion and tiger are two different *species* of cat.]
spe·cies • *noun, plural* **species**

specific (spə sif′ik) *adjective* definite; exact [We have no *specific* plans.]
spe·cif·ic • *adjective*

specify (spes′i fī′) *verb* to state or call for in detail or in a definite way [She *specified* the time and place of the meeting.]
spec·i·fy • *verb* **specified, specifying, specifies**

specimen (spes′i mən) *noun* **1** a part of a whole, or one thing of a group, used as a sample of the rest [He compared the letter with a *specimen* of her writing.] **2** a small amount of something such as blood or urine used for medical tests.
spec·i·men • *noun, plural* **specimens**

speck (spek) *noun* **1** a small spot or mark [A few *specks* of paint got on the rug.] **2** a very small bit; particle.
verb to mark with specks; to spot [The windshield was *specked* with dead insects.]
speck • *noun, plural* **specks** • *verb* **specked, specking**

speckle (spek′əl) *noun* a small mark; speck.
verb to mark with speckles [The white walls are *speckled* with green.]
speck·le • *noun, plural* **speckles** • *verb* **speckled, speckling**

spectacle (spek′tə kəl) *noun* **1** an unusual sight or a grand public show [The fireworks display was a *spectacle*.] **2 spectacles** a pair of eyeglasses: this is an old-fashioned word.
—make a spectacle of oneself to behave in public in a foolish or improper way.
spec·ta·cle • *noun, plural* **spectacles**

spectacular (spek tak′yə lər) *adjective* of or like a spectacle; showy; striking [Her garden is a *spectacular* display of flowers.]
spec·tac·u·lar • *adjective*

spectator (spek′tāt ər) *noun* a person who watches something without taking part.
spec·ta·tor • *noun, plural* **spectators**

spectrum (spek′trəm) *noun* a series of colored bands that are formed when light is broken up by being passed through a prism or in some other way. The light spectrum is made up of six main colors: red, orange, yellow, green, blue, and violet.
spec·trum • *noun, plural* **spectrums**

S

speculate (spek′yoo͞ lāt′) ***verb*** to think about or make guesses; ponder [Scientists *speculate* about the size of the universe.]
spec·u·late • ***verb*** **speculated, speculating**

sped (sped) ***verb*** *a past tense and a past participle of* **speed**.

speech (spēch) ***noun*** **1** the act or way of speaking [We knew from their *speech* that they were from the South.] **2** the power to speak [She lost her *speech* from a stroke.] **3** a talk given in public [We watched her *speech* on TV.]
speech • ***noun,*** *plural for sense 3 only* **speeches**

speechless (spēch′ləs) ***adjective*** not able to speak [He was *speechless* with rage.]
speech·less • ***adjective***

speed (spēd) ***noun*** **1** fast motion; swiftness. **2** rate of motion; velocity [Our *speed* is 30 miles per hour.] **3** rate of doing any action [I am trying to increase my reading *speed*.] **4** an arrangement of gears for driving an engine [Our car has five forward *speeds*.]
verb **1** to go or move fast [The arrow *sped* to its mark.] **2** to go or move too fast [He was *speeding* when the police officer spotted him.]
—speed up to go or make go faster [She *sped up* to pass the slow car.]
speed • ***noun,*** *plural for all senses expect 1* **speeds** • ***verb*** **sped** or **speeded, speeding**

speedboat

speedboat (spēd′bōt) ***noun*** a fast motorboat.
speed·boat • ***noun,*** *plural* **speedboats**

speedometer (spi däm′ət ər) ***noun*** a device that shows the speed of a moving vehicle.
speed·om·e·ter • ***noun,*** *plural* **speedometers**

speedy (spēd′ē) ***adjective*** **1** very fast; swift [*speedy* runners] —Look for the WORD CHOICES box at the entry **fast**[1]. **2** without delay; prompt [a *speedy* reply].
speed·y • ***adjective*** **speedier, speediest**

spell[1] (spel) ***noun*** **1** a word or group of words supposed to have some magic power. **2** power or control that seems magical [Her acting cast a *spell* over the audience.]
spell • ***noun,*** *plural* **spells**

spell[2] (spel) ***verb*** **1** to say or write in order the letters that make up a word or words [*Spell* your last name. She *spells* poorly.] **2** to make up; form [What word do these letters *spell?*] **3** to be a sign of; mean [Her visit *spells* trouble to us.]
—spell out to explain in an exact way or in detail [*Spell out* the details of your plan for the party.]
spell • ***verb*** **spelled** or **spelt, spelling**

spell[3] (spel) ***verb*** to do something in place of another for a time; relieve [I'll *spell* you at mowing the lawn.]
noun a period of time during which something is done or happens [a *spell* of hot weather].
spell • ***verb*** **spelled, spelling** • ***noun,*** *plural* **spells**

spellbound (spel′bound) ***adjective*** held fast as if by a spell; fascinated; enchanted [The audience was *spellbound* by his performance.]
spell·bound • ***adjective***

speller (spel′ər) ***noun*** **1** a person who spells [a poor *speller*]. **2** a book used to teach spelling.
spell·er • ***noun,*** *plural* **spellers**

spelling (spel′iŋ) ***noun*** **1** the act of telling or writing the letters of a word in proper order. **2** the way in which a word is spelled.
spell·ing • ***noun,*** *plural for sense 2 only* **spellings**

spelling bee ***noun*** a spelling contest. A person who spells a word wrong must leave the contest. The last person left is the winner.
spelling bee • ***noun,*** *plural* **spelling bees**

spelt (spelt) ***verb*** *a past tense and a past participle of* **spell**[2].

spend (spend) ***verb*** **1** to pay out [I *spent* three dollars on lunch.] **2** to pay out money [He *spent* too much for his new car.] **3** to use up [She *spent* a lot of time trying to fix her bicycle.] **4** to pass [We *spent* the summer at grandfather's farm.]
spend • ***verb*** **spent, spending**

a	cat	ō	go	ʉ	fur	ə =	a *in* ago
ā	ape	ô	law, for	ch	chin		e *in* agent
ä	cot, car	oo	look	sh	she		i *in* pencil
e	ten	o͞o	tool	th	thin		o *in* atom
ē	me	oi	oil	*th*	then		u *in* circus
i	fit	ou	out	zh	measure		
ī	ice	u	up	ŋ	ring		

spent (spent) *verb past tense and past participle of* **spend**.

sperm (spurm) *noun* a cell from the male that fertilizes the egg of the female in reproduction.
sperm • *noun, plural* **sperm**

sperm whale *noun* a large whale that is found in warm seas. It is valuable for its oil.
sperm whale • *noun, plural* **sperm whales**

spew (spyo͞o) *verb* **1** to throw or force out [He *spewed* out soup that was too hot. She *spewed* out words of scorn.] **2** to gush forth [The volcano *spewed* lava.]
spew • *verb* **spewed, spewing**

sphere (sfir) *noun* any round object that has a surface that is the same distance from its center at all points; ball; globe.
sphere • *noun, plural* **spheres**

spherical (sfer′i kəl *or* sfir′i kəl) *adjective* of or shaped like a sphere [*spherical* objects].
spher·i·cal • *adjective*

sphinx
The Great Sphinx in Egypt

sphinx (sfiŋks) *noun* any ancient Egyptian statue that has a lion's body and the head of a man, ram, or hawk.
sphinx • *noun, plural* **sphinxes**

spice (spīs) *noun* **1** a vegetable substance used to give a special flavor or smell to food. Cinnamon, nutmeg, and pepper are kinds of spice. **2** an interesting touch or detail [Humor added *spice* to her talk.]
verb **1** to season or flavor with spice [He *spiced* the sauce with pepper.] **2** to add interest to [She *spiced* her talk with humor.]
spice • *noun, plural for sense 1 only* **spices** • *verb* **spiced, spicing**

spick-and-span (spik′ən span′) *adjective* neat and clean.

spicy (spī′sē) *adjective* **1** seasoned with spices [a *spicy* dish]. **2** interesting; lively [*spicy* gossip].
spic·y • *adjective* **spicier, spiciest**

spider (spī′dər) *noun* a small animal with eight legs and a body made up of two parts. The back part of the body has organs that spin silk threads into webs to trap insects.
spi·der • *noun, plural* **spiders**

spies (spīz) *noun plural of* **spy**.

spigot (spig′ət) *noun another name for* **faucet**.
spig·ot • *noun, plural* **spigots**

spike[1] (spīk) *noun* **1** a pointed piece of metal or other material [*spikes* along the top of an iron gate; football shoes with *spikes*]. **2** a large, strong nail [a railroad *spike*].
verb **1** to pierce, cut, or fasten with a spike or spikes [The catcher was *spiked* by the sliding runner.] **2** to jump at a volleyball net and hit the ball over it with great force.
spike • *noun, plural* **spikes** • *verb* **spiked, spiking**

spike[2] (spīk) *noun* **1** a long cluster of flowers attached right to the stalk. **2** an ear of grain.
spike • *noun, plural* **spikes**

spill (spil) *verb* **1** to let flow over or run out [Who *spilled* water on the floor? Try not to *spill* any sugar.] **2** to flow over or run out [Tears *spilled* from her eyes.]
noun **1** something spilled [an oil *spill*]. **2** a fall or tumble [She took a *spill* while riding her horse.]
spill • *verb* **spilled** or **spilt, spilling** • *noun, plural* **spills**

spilt (spilt) *verb a past tense and a past participle of* **spill**.

spin (spin) *verb* **1** to draw out and twist the fibers of [The workers *spin* cotton and wool.] **2** to make by drawing out and twisting fibers [The machine *spins* thread from cotton. They *spin* yarn from wool.] **3** to make from a thread given out by the body [Spiders *spin* webs.] **4** to tell slowly, with many details [He *spun* an exciting story.] **5** to whirl around or cause to whirl around [The earth *spins*. *Spin* the wheel.] **6** to seem to be whirling [My head is *spinning*.] **7** to turn freely without holding or sticking [The wheels of the car *spun* on the ice.]
noun **1** a whirling movement [Give the wheel

S

a *spin*.] **2** a fast ride or drive [a *spin* around the block].
spin • *verb* **spun, spinning** • *noun, plural* **spins**

spinach (spin′əch) *noun* a vegetable with large, dark-green leaves that are eaten raw or cooked.
spin·ach • *noun*

spinach

spinal (spī′nəl) *adjective* of the spine or spinal cord.
spi·nal • *adjective*

spinal column *noun* the long row of connected bones that forms the backbone; spine.
spinal column • *noun, plural* **spinal columns**

spinal cord *noun* the thick cord of nerve tissue inside the spinal column.
spinal cord • *noun, plural* **spinal cords**

spindle (spin′dəl) *noun* a slender rod used to twist and hold thread in spinning.
spin·dle • *noun, plural* **spindles**

spindly (spind′lē) *adjective* long and thin and, often, weak [*spindly* legs of the table].
spin·dly • *adjective* **spindlier, spindliest**

spine (spīn) *noun* **1** a thin, sharp, stiff part that sticks out on certain plants and animals; thorn or quill [the *spines* of a cactus or porcupine]. **2** the backbone; spinal column. **3** the back part of a book. It is the part that faces out when the book is placed upright on a shelf.
spine • *noun, plural* **spines**

spineless (spīn′ləs) *adjective* **1** having no backbone. **2** having no courage or strength of will [a *spineless* coward].
spine·less • *adjective*

spinning wheel *noun* a spinning machine with one spindle that is turned by a large wheel.
spinning wheel • *noun, plural* **spinning wheels**

spinster (spin′stər) *noun* an older woman who has never married.
spin·ster • *noun, plural* **spinsters**

spiny (spī′nē) *adjective* covered with spines [a *spiny* plant].
spin·y • *adjective* **spinier, spiniest**

spiral (spī′rəl) *adjective* circling around a center in a curve that rises or keeps growing larger [the *spiral* thread of a screw].
noun a spiral curve or coil.
verb to move in a spiral or form into a spiral [The road *spiraled* up the mountain.]
spi·ral • *adjective* • *noun, plural* **spirals** • *verb* **spiraled** or **spiralled, spiraling** or **spiralling**

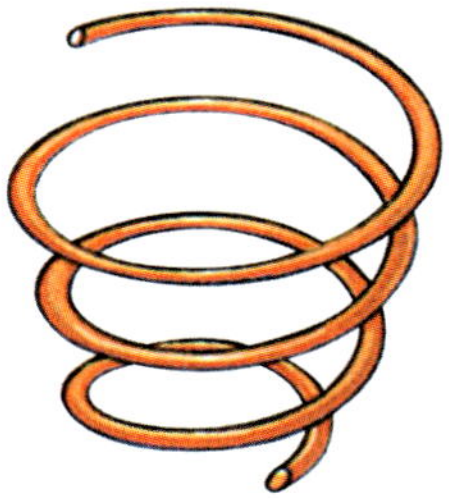
spiral

spire (spīr) *noun* something that tapers to a point at its top [the *spire* on a church steeple].
spire • *noun, plural* **spires**

spire

spirit (spir′it) *noun* **1** the soul. **2** a ghost, angel, fairy, or other being that is not of this world. **3** *often* **spirits** state of mind; mood [The patient is in good *spirits*.] **4** enthusiasm and loyalty [school *spirit*]. **5** the true meaning [The *spirit* of the law is more than just the exact words that are written down.]
verb to carry away secretly and swiftly [The fox *spirited* off a chicken.]
spir·it • *noun, plural for sense 1, 2, and 3 only* **spirits** • *verb* **spirited, spiriting**

spirited (spir′it əd) *adjective* **1** having a certain spirit, or mood [The team was low-*spirited* after losing the game.] **2** lively; vigorous [a *spirited* discussion; a *spirited* horse].
spir·it·ed • *adjective*

spiritual (spir′i chōō əl) *adjective* **1** of the spirit or soul as apart from the body or the material world [She prayed for *spiritual* strength.] **2** having to do with religion or the church; sacred [*spiritual* music].

a cat	ō go	ʉ fur	ə = a *in* ago	
ā ape	ô law, for	ch chin	e *in* agent	
ä cot, car	oo look	sh she	i *in* pencil	
e ten	ōō tool	th thin	o *in* atom	
ē me	oi oil	*th* then	u *in* circus	
i fit	ou out	zh measure		
ī ice	u up	ŋ ring		

noun a folk hymn of the kind sung by blacks in the South in the nineteenth century.
spir·it·u·al • *adjective* • *noun, plural* **spirituals**

spit[1] (spit) *noun* a thin, pointed rod on which meat is fixed for roasting over a fire.
spit • *noun, plural* **spits**

spit[2] (spit) *verb* to force out saliva or other matter from the mouth [She *spit* into the bowl in the dentist's office. He *spit* his gum into the wastebasket.]
noun another name for **saliva**.
spit • *verb* **spit** or **spat, spitting** • *noun*

spite (spīt) *noun* a mean feeling toward another that makes one want to hurt or annoy that person; ill will; malice.
verb to show one's spite for by hurting or annoying [She played the radio loud to *spite* them.]
—**in spite of** not giving attention to; regardless of [They went out *in spite of* the storm.]
spite • *noun* • *verb* **spited, spiting**

spiteful (spīt′fəl) *adjective* showing or full of spite [a *spiteful* act].
spite·ful • *adjective*

spittle (spit′l) *noun* spit; saliva.
spit·tle • *noun*

splash (splash) *verb* **1** to make a liquid scatter and fall in drops [He *splashed* water on us.] **2** to wet or soil by dashing a liquid on [The car *splashed* my coat with mud.] **3** to move or fall with a splash [I *splashed* through the swamp.]
noun **1** the act or sound of splashing. **2** a mass of splashed water, mud, or other liquid. **3** a spot or mark made by liquid that is splashed.
—**make a splash** [*an informal use*] to get much attention.
splash • *verb* **splashed, splashing** • *noun, plural* **splashes**

splatter (splat′ər) *noun* a spatter or splash.
verb to spatter or splash.
splat·ter • *noun, plural* **splatters** • *verb* **splattered, splattering**

spleen (splēn) *noun* an organ of the body, near the stomach. It performs various functions related to the way the blood is made up.
spleen • *noun, plural* **spleens**

splendid (splen′did) *adjective* **1** magnificent or glorious [a *splendid* gown; a *splendid* act of courage]. **2** [*an informal use*] very good; excellent [a *splendid* trip].
splen·did • *adjective*

splendor (splen′dər) *noun* great beauty or magnificence [the *splendor* of the royal palace].
splen·dor • *noun, plural* **splendors**

splice (splīs) *verb* **1** to join ropes or cables by weaving together strands at the ends. **2** to fasten together ends of something such as movie film or sound tape.
splice • *verb* **spliced, splicing**

splint (splint) *noun* a thin, stiff piece of wood, metal, or plastic. It keeps a person from bending or moving a part of the body where a broken bone is healing.
splint • *noun, plural* **splints**

splinter (splin′tər) *verb* to break or split into thin, sharp pieces [Pine wood *splinters* easily.]
noun a thin, sharp piece broken off.
splin·ter • *verb* **splintered, splintering** • *noun, plural* **splinters**

split (split) *verb* **1** to separate or divide along the length into two or more parts [I *split* the log with an ax.] **2** to break apart by force; burst [The seam *split* when I sat down.] **3** to divide into parts or shares [We *split* the cost of our trip.]
noun **1** the act of splitting. **2** a break, crack, or tear [a *split* in a seam]. **3** a division in a group [The argument caused a *split* in our club.] **4** an arrangement of bowling pins left standing after the ball is rolled the first time. The pins are very widely separated.
split • *verb* **split, splitting** • *noun, plural* **splits**

split-level (split′lev′əl) *adjective* describing a house with rooms on two or more levels that are joined by short flights of stairs.
split-lev·el • *adjective*

splitting (split′iŋ) *adjective* very painful [a *splitting* headache].
split·ting • *adjective*

splotch (spläch) *noun* a spot or stain.
splotch • *noun, plural* **splotches**

splurge (splurj) [*an informal word*] *verb* to spend a great deal of money or effort on something [Her parents *splurged* on a big wedding.]
noun the act of splurging.
splurge • *verb* **splurged, splurging** • *noun, plural* **splurges**

splutter (splut′ər) *verb* **1** to make hissing or spitting sounds [The kettle *spluttered* on the stove.] **2** to say in a fast, confused way when

S

embarrassed or angry [She *spluttered* an excuse for arriving so late.]
noun the act of spluttering.
splut·ter • *verb* **spluttered, spluttering** • *noun*

spoil (spoil) *verb* **1** to make or become useless, worthless, or rotten; to damage; to ruin [Illness *spoiled* my attendance record. Meat *spoils* fast in warm weather.] —Look for the WORD CHOICES box at the entry **rot**. **2** to cause a person to expect too much by giving in to all of that person's wishes [Don't *spoil* the child.]
noun usually **spoils** goods taken by force in war; loot; booty.
spoil • *verb* **spoiled** or **spoilt, spoiling** • *noun, plural* **spoils**

spoilt (spoilt) *verb a past tense and a past participle of* **spoil**.

spoke[1] (spōk) *noun* one of the braces that reach from the hub of a wheel to the rim.
spoke • *noun, plural* **spokes**

spoke[2] (spōk) *verb past tense of* **speak**.

spoken (spō′kən) *verb past participle of* **speak**.
adjective **1** said aloud; oral [a *spoken* order]. **2** speaking or said in a certain kind of voice [a soft-*spoken* person].
spo·ken • *verb* • *adjective*

spokesman (spōks′mən) *noun* a person who speaks for another or for a group.
spokes·man • *noun, plural* **spokesmen**

spokesperson (spōks′pur sən) *noun another name for* **spokesman**. Many people prefer this word.
spokes·per·son • *noun, plural* **spokespersons**

sponge (spunj) *noun* **1** a sea animal that is like a plant and grows fixed to surfaces under water. **2** the light, elastic skeleton of such an animal. It is full of holes and can soak up much water. Sponges are used for washing, bathing, and cleaning. **3** a piece of plastic or other artificial substance that can soak up water and be used in the same way as natural sponge.
verb to wipe, clean, make wet, or soak up with a sponge or something like a sponge [She *sponged* up the spilled milk.]
sponge • *noun, plural* **sponges** • *verb* **sponged, sponging**

spongecake (spunj′kāk) *noun* a light, spongy cake made without shortening. This word is also written **sponge cake**.
sponge·cake • *noun, plural* **spongecakes**

spongy (spun′jē) *adjective* **1** like a sponge; light, elastic, or full of holes [Her running shoes have a *spongy* lining.] **2** soft and mushy [*spongy* ground] —Look for the WORD CHOICES box at the entry **soft**.
spon·gy • *adjective* **spongier, spongiest**

sponsor (spän′sər) *noun* **1** a person who agrees to pay expenses or give other support to another person or to a group [Our softball team needs a *sponsor*.] **2** a person or business that pays the cost of a radio or TV program. The sponsor is then able to show commercials during the program. **3** *another name for* **godparent**.
verb to be a sponsor for.
spon·sor • *noun, plural* **sponsors** • *verb* **sponsored, sponsoring**

spontaneous (spän tā′nē əs) *adjective* **1** done in a free, natural way, without effort or much thought [We broke into *spontaneous* song.] **2** seeming to happen by itself, with no outside help [There was a *spontaneous* explosion when the chemical was exposed to fire.]
spon·ta·ne·ous • *adjective*

spook (spo͞ok) [*an informal word*] *noun* a ghost.
verb to frighten or startle [The loud noise *spooked* the horses.]
spook • *noun, plural* **spooks** • *verb* **spooked, spooking**

spooky (spo͞o′kē) [*an informal word*] *adjective* of or having to do with ghosts; weird; eerie [a *spooky*, old house].
spook·y • *adjective* **spookier, spookiest**

spool (spo͞ol) *noun* a small roller with a rim at each end. Thread, wire, and yarn are wound around spools.
spool • *noun, plural* **spools**

spoon (spo͞on) *noun* a tool made up of a shallow bowl with a handle. It is used for eating and stirring food and drink.
verb to take up with a spoon and usually move from one place to another [She *spooned* some gravy onto her potatoes.]
spoon • *noun, plural* **spoons** • *verb* **spooned, spooning**

spoonful (spo͞on′fo͝ol) *noun* the amount that a spoon will hold.
spoon·ful • *noun, plural* **spoonfuls**

a	cat	ō	go	ʉ	fur	ə =	a *in* ago
ā	ape	ô	law, for	ch	chin		e *in* agent
ä	cot, car	o͝o	look	sh	she		i *in* pencil
e	ten	o͞o	tool	th	thin		o *in* atom
ē	me	oi	oil	*th*	then		u *in* circus
i	fit	ou	out	zh	measure		
ī	ice	u	up	ŋ	ring		

spore (spôr) ***noun*** a tiny cell produced by certain plants and animals that can grow into a new plant or animal. Mosses and ferns produce spores.
spore • ***noun,*** *plural* **spores**

sport (spôrt) ***noun*** **1** a game or some kind of active play done for exercise or pleasure. It is sometimes done as a profession. Football, golf, bowling, and swimming are sports. **2** [*an informal use*] a person judged by the way he or she takes loss, defeat, or teasing [Be a good *sport* if you lose.]
adjective **1** suitable for informal or casual wear [a *sport* coat]. **2** of or having to do with sports or athletic games.
sport • ***noun,*** *plural* **sports** • ***adjective***

sporting (spôrt′iŋ) ***adjective*** having to do with sports [*sporting* goods].
sport·ing • ***adjective***

sports (spôrts) ***adjective*** *the same as the adjective* **sport**.

sports car ***noun*** a small, low, and fast automobile that usually seats only two people.
sports car • ***noun,*** *plural* **sports cars**

sportscast (spôrts′kast) ***noun*** a broadcast of sports news on radio or TV.
sports·cast • ***noun,*** *plural* **sportscasts**

sportsman (spôrts′mən) ***noun*** **1** a man who takes part in or is interested in sports, especially hunting or fishing. **2** a person who plays fair and does not complain about losing or boast about winning.
sports·man • ***noun,*** *plural* **sportsmen**

sportsmanlike (spôrts′mən līk) ***adjective*** like a sportsman; fair.
sports·man·like • ***adjective***

sportsmanship (spôrts′mən ship) ***noun*** the qualities and behavior that a person should have and show when taking part in a sport.
sports·man·ship • ***noun***

sportswear (spôrts′wer) ***noun*** clothes worn while taking part in sports or when relaxing.
sports·wear • ***noun***

sportswoman (spôrts′woom ən) ***noun*** a woman who takes part in sports or is interested in sports.
sports·wom·an • ***noun,*** *plural* **sportswomen**

sportswriter (spôrts′rīt ər) ***noun*** a reporter who writes about sports or sports events.
sports·writ·er • ***noun,*** *plural* **sportswriters**

spot (spät) ***noun*** **1** a small part that is different from the parts around it [a leopard's *spots;* a sore *spot*]. **2** a stain or mark [an ink *spot*]. **3** a place [a quiet *spot* in the country].
verb **1** to mark or become marked with spots [Drops of paint *spotted* the floor. This fabric *spots* easily.] **2** to see or recognize [I can *spot* our house from here.]
spot • ***noun,*** *plural* **spots** • ***verb*** **spotted, spotting**

spotless (spät′ləs) ***adjective*** **1** perfectly clean [a *spotless* house]. **2** having no faults or weak parts [a *spotless* reputation].
spot·less • ***adjective***

spotlight (spät′līt) ***noun*** **1** a lamp that shines a strong beam of light on a person or thing. **2** the strong beam from such a lamp [The stage actor stood in the *spotlight*.] **3** the attention or notice of the public [The President is always in the *spotlight*.]
spot·light • ***noun,*** *plural for senses 1 and 2 only* **spotlights**

spotty (spät′ē) ***adjective*** **1** marked with spots. **2** not regular, even, or steady [Attendance at our meetings has been *spotty*.]
spot·ty • ***adjective*** **spottier, spottiest**

spouse (spous) ***noun*** a husband or a wife.
spouse • ***noun,*** *plural* **spouses**

spout (spout) ***noun*** a pipe, tube, or lip by which a liquid pours from a container.
verb to shoot out with force [The well *spouted* oil.]
spout • ***noun,*** *plural* **spouts** ***verb*** **spouted, spouting**

sprain (sprān) ***verb*** to twist a muscle or ligament without putting the bones out of place [I *sprained* my wrist.]
noun an injury caused by this.
sprain • ***verb*** **sprained, spraining** • ***noun,*** *plural* **sprains**

sprang (spraŋ) ***verb*** *a past tense of* **spring**.

sprawl (sprôl *or* spräl) ***verb*** **1** to sit or lie with the arms and legs spread out in a relaxed or awkward way [He *sprawled* on the grass.] **2** to spread out in an awkward or uneven way [Her handwriting *sprawls* across the page.]
sprawl • ***verb*** **sprawled, sprawling**

spray (sprā) ***noun*** **1** a mist of tiny drops of water or other liquid [A cold *spray* rose from the waterfall.] **2** a device that forces out a mist of tiny drops. **3** a mist of tiny drops from such a device. **4** something that is like a spray [a *spray* of bullets].

verb to put something on in the form of spray [He *sprayed* the car with paint. She *sprayed* perfume on herself.]
spray • ***noun,*** *plural for all senses except sense 1* **sprays** • ***verb*** **sprayed, spraying**

spread (spred) ***verb*** **1** to open out or stretch out [*Spread* the tablecloth. The eagle *spread* its wings. Our trip *spread* out over two weeks.] **2** to lay out in order to show [*Spread* the cards on the table.] **3** to put on or cover [*Spread* newspapers on the floor before you paint the walls. She *spread* jelly on the bread.] **4** to lie or extend [The valley *spread* out before us.] **5** to make or become widely known [*Spread* the news. The rumor *spread* quickly.] **6** to pass on; transmit [Flies can *spread* disease.]
noun **1** the act of spreading. **2** the amount or distance that something can be spread [The bird's wings have a *spread* of 6 feet.] **3** a cloth cover for a table or bed. **4** jam, butter, or some other soft substance that can be spread.
spread • ***verb*** **spread, spreading** • ***noun,*** *plural for senses 3 and 4 only* **spreads**

sprig (sprig) ***noun*** a little branch with leaves or flowers on it.
sprig • ***noun,*** *plural* **sprigs**

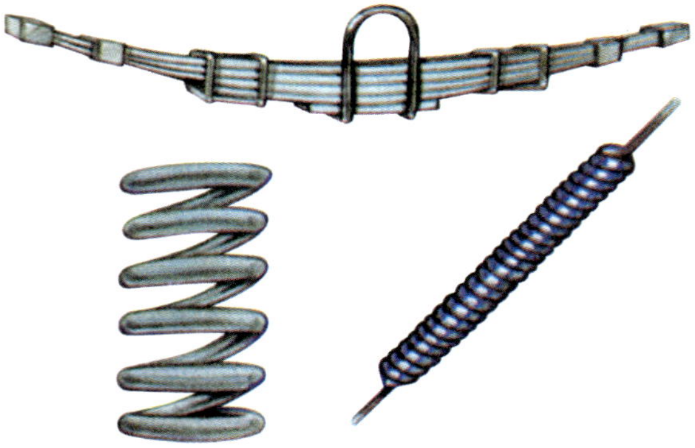

spring
Three kinds of springs

spring (spriŋ) ***verb*** **1** to move forward and upward quickly; leap [I *sprang* to my feet.] **2** to move in a sudden and quick way [The door *sprang* shut behind her.] **3** to come into being or appear quickly [New towns were *springing* up all along the river. Weeds have *sprung* up in the lawn.] **4** to make known in a sudden way [He is always *springing* surprises on us.]
noun **1** the act of springing; a jump or leap. **2** a coil of wire or other device that goes back to its original form after being forced out of shape. Springs are used in many things such as automobiles, beds, and clocks. **3** the ability to snap back into position or shape [This elastic has lost its *spring*.] **4** a place where water flows up from the ground. **5** the season between winter and summer, when plants begin to grow.
spring • ***verb*** **sprang** or **sprung, sprung, springing** • ***noun,*** *plural for senses 1, 2, 4, and 5 only* **springs**

Springfield (spriŋ′fēld) the capital of Illinois.
Spring·field

springtime (spriŋ′tīm) ***noun*** the season of spring.
spring·time • ***noun,*** *plural* **springtimes**

springy (spriŋ′ē) ***adjective*** full of spring or bounce [a *springy* mattress].
spring·y • ***adjective*** **springier, springiest**

sprinkle (spriŋ′kəl) ***verb*** **1** to scatter in bits or drops [She *sprinkled* salt on the eggs.] **2** to scatter drops or bits on [He *sprinkled* the lawn with water.] **3** to rain in a small amount.
noun **1** a small amount; sprinkling [a *sprinkle* of salt]. **2** a light rain. **3 sprinkles** tiny bits of candy, used on pastry or ice cream.
sprin·kle • ***verb*** **sprinkled, sprinkling** • ***noun,*** *plural* **sprinkles**

WORD CHOICES

Synonyms of **sprinkle**

The words **sprinkle, broadcast,** and **scatter** share the meaning "to spread here and there."

Try *sprinkling* sugar on the berries.

We *broadcast* wildflower seeds in the yard.

The breeze *scattered* the papers.

sprinkler (spriŋ′klər) ***noun*** a device that is used to water lawns or plants.
sprin·kler • ***noun,*** *plural* **sprinklers**

a cat	ō go	ʉ fur	ə = a *in* ago	
ā ape	ô law, for	ch chin	e *in* agent	
ä cot, car	oo look	sh she	i *in* pencil	
e ten	ōō tool	th thin	o *in* atom	
ē me	oi oil	*th* then	u *in* circus	
i fit	ou out	zh measure		
ī ice	u up	ŋ ring		

sprint (sprint) ***verb*** to run or move very fast [The horse *sprinted* across the field.]
noun a short run or race at full speed.
sprint • ***verb*** **sprinted, sprinting** • ***noun,*** *plural* **sprints**

sprite (sprīt) ***noun*** an elf, fairy, or other imaginary being in certain tales.
sprite • ***noun,*** *plural* **sprites**

sprout (sprout) ***verb*** **1** to begin to grow [Buds *sprouted* on the rose bushes.] **2** to grow or develop very fast [The young child began to *sprout* up this summer.]
noun a young, new growth from a plant, bud, or seed.
sprout • ***verb*** **sprouted, sprouting** • ***noun,*** *plural* **sprouts**

spruce[1] (sprōōs) ***noun*** **1** an evergreen tree with thin needles. **2** the soft wood of this tree.
spruce • ***noun,*** *plural for sense 1 only* **spruces**

spruce[2] (sprōōs) ***verb*** to make or become neat and trim [New drapes will *spruce* up this room.]
spruce • ***verb*** **spruced, sprucing**

sprung (spruŋ) ***verb*** *a past tense and the past participle of* **spring**.

spry (sprī) ***adjective*** moving in a quick and easy way; lively [a *spry* colt] —Look for the WORD CHOICES box at the entry **nimble**.
spry • ***adjective*** **sprier** or **spryer, spriest** or **spryest**

spud (spud) [*an informal word*] ***noun*** a potato.
spud • ***noun,*** *plural* **spuds**

spun (spun) ***verb*** *past tense and past participle of* **spin**.

spunk (spuŋk) [*an informal word*] ***noun*** courage or a brave spirit.

spunky (spuŋ′kē) [*an informal word*] ***adjective*** having courage; brave.
spunk·y • ***adjective*** **spunkier, spunkiest**

spur (spʉr) ***noun*** **1** a metal piece with sharp points, worn on the heel of a riding boot. It is used to poke a horse to make it move forward. **2** anything that urges a person on [The desire to finish first was the *spur* that kept us going.]
verb **1** to poke with a spur or spurs [The cowboy *spurred* his horse.] **2** to urge someone on [The crowd *spurred* the runner on with shouts and cheers.]
—on the spur of the moment in a quick way, without thinking ahead.
spur • ***noun,*** *plural* **spurs** • ***verb*** **spurred, spurring**

spurt (spʉrt) ***verb*** **1** to shoot out suddenly in a stream [Juice *spurted* from the grapefruit.] **2** to show a sudden, short burst of energy [The runner *spurted* ahead near the turn.]
noun **1** a sudden, short stream of fluid. **2** a sudden, short burst of energy or activity [She worked in *spurts*.]
spurt • ***verb*** **spurted, spurting** • ***noun,*** *plural* **spurts**

sputter (sput′ər) ***verb*** **1** to talk in a fast, confused manner [The man *sputtered* angrily about the accident.] **2** to make hissing or spitting sounds [Meat *sputters* on a grill.] **3** to spit out saliva or bits of food when speaking in an excited way or too fast [The baby *sputtered* and coughed.]
noun the act or sound of sputtering.
sput·ter • ***verb*** **sputtered, sputtering** • ***noun,*** *plural* **sputters**

spy (spī) ***noun*** **1** a person who watches in secret the activities of other people. **2** a person who works for a government in secret, to watch activities in another country.
verb **1** to act as a spy [She *spied* for the enemy.] **2** to catch sight of; see [Can you *spy* the ship yet?]
spy • ***noun,*** *plural* **spies** • ***verb*** **spied, spying, spies**

sq. *abbreviation for* square.

squabble (skwäb′əl) ***verb*** to quarrel in a noisy way about something not important.
noun a noisy quarrel about something not important.
squab·ble • ***verb*** **squabbled, squabbling** • ***noun,*** *plural* **squabbles**

squad (skwäd) ***noun*** **1** a small group of soldiers. **2** a small group of people who are working together [a police *squad;* a football *squad*].
squad • ***noun,*** *plural* **squads**

square (skwer) ***noun*** **1** a flat figure having four equal sides and four right angles. **2** anything shaped like this [Arrange the chairs in a *square*.] **3** an area in a city, with streets on four sides, often used as a public park. **4** the result of multiplying a number by itself [The *square* of three is 9 (3 x 3 = 9).]
adjective **1** having the shape of a square. **2** forming a right angle [a *square* corner]. **3** fair; honest [a *square* deal]. **4** describing a unit of measure that is a square of a particular size [A *square* foot is the area of a square that measures one foot on each side.] **5** [*an*

S

informal use] capable of satisfying [a *square* meal].
verb **1** to make straight, level, or even [The carpenter *squared* the door frame. *Square* your shoulders.] **2** to multiply some number by itself [5 *squared* is 25.] **3** to agree or fit [His story *squares* with mine.]
square • *noun, plural* **squares** • *adjective* **squarer, squarest** • *verb* **squared, squaring**

squash[1] (skwôsh *or* skwäsh) *verb* **1** to crush something into a flat mass [She *squashed* the bug by accident.] **2** to stop something from happening [The army *squashed* the revolution.] **3** to crowd or squeeze [We were *squashed* in the little car.]
noun the act or sound of squashing.
squash • *verb* **squashed, squashing** • *noun*

squash[2] (skwôsh *or* skwäsh) *noun* a fruit that grows on a vine in many shapes, sizes, and colors. It is eaten as a cooked vegetable.
squash • *noun, plural* **squashes**

squash

squat (skwät) *verb* to sit on the heels with the knees bent.
adjective short and heavy or thick [a *squat* football player].
squat • *verb* **squatted, squatting** • *adjective* **squatter, squattest**

squawk (skwôk *or* skwäk) *noun* a loud, harsh cry [The *squawk* of the parrot bothered us.]
verb to let out a squawk.
squawk • *noun, plural* **squawks** • *verb* **squawked, squawking**

squeak (skwēk) *noun* a short, high cry or sound [the *squeak* of a mouse].
verb to make a squeak [His new shoes *squeaked*.]
squeak • *noun, plural* **squeaks** • *verb* **squeaked, squeaking**

squeal (skwēl) *noun* a long, high cry or sound.
verb to make a squeal [The tires *squealed* going around the corner.]
squeal • *noun, plural* **squeals** • *verb* **squealed, squealing**

squeeze (skwēz) *verb* **1** to press hard; put pressure on, especially from both sides or all around [*Squeeze* the sponge to get rid of the water.] **2** to get by pressing or by force [He *squeezed* the juice from the orange.] **3** to hug someone [Mom *squeezed* Terri and kissed her.] **4** to force by pushing or shoving [He *squeezed* his hand into the jar.]
noun the act of squeezing; a hard press [She gave my hand a *squeeze*.]
squeeze • *verb* **squeezed, squeezing** • *noun, plural* **squeezes**

squid (skwid) *noun* a long, slender sea animal that is similar to an octopus. It has eight arms and two long tentacles.
squid • *noun, plural* **squid** or **squids**

squiggle (skwig′əl) *noun* a short curved or wavy line.
squig·gle • *noun, plural* **squiggles**

WORD HISTORY

squiggle

This noun is made up of parts of two other words, the verbs *squirm* and *wiggle*. A **squiggle** looks somewhat like a worm squirming and wiggling across a piece of paper.

squint (skwint) *verb* to look with the eyes partly closed [He *squinted* in the glare.]
noun the act of squinting at something.
squint • *verb* **squinted, squinting** • *noun, plural* **squints**

squire (skwīr) *noun* **1** a country gentleman who owns much land in England. **2** in earlier times, a young man who helped a knight.
squire • *noun, plural* **squires**

squirm (skwʉrm) *verb* **1** to twist and turn the body as a snake does; wiggle [The rabbit *squirmed* out of the trap.] **2** to feel ashamed or embarrassed [He *squirmed* when the teacher read his report.]
squirm • *verb* **squirmed, squirming**

squirrel (skwʉr′əl) *noun* a small animal that lives in trees. It usually has a long, bushy tail.
squir·rel • *noun, plural* **squirrels**

a	cat	ō	go	ʉ	fur	ə =	a *in* ago
ā	ape	ô	law, for	ch	chin		e *in* agent
ä	cot, car	oo	look	sh	she		i *in* pencil
e	ten	o͞o	tool	th	thin		o *in* atom
ē	me	oi	oil	*th*	then		u *in* circus
i	fit	ou	out	zh	measure		
ī	ice	u	up	ŋ	ring		

squirrel

WORD HISTORY

squirrel

Our word **squirrel** comes from a combination of the Greek words for "shadow" and "tail." The bushy tail of the **squirrel** looks like the shadow of its body.

squirt (skwurt) *verb* **1** to shoot out in a thin stream; spurt. **2** to wet with liquid shot out in a thin stream [Did you *squirt* the dog with the hose?]
noun **1** the act of squirting. **2** a small, thin stream of liquid.
squirt • *verb* **squirted, squirting** • *noun, plural* **squirts**

squirt gun *noun* a toy gun that shoots a stream of water.
squirt gun • *noun, plural* **squirt guns**

squish (skwish) *verb* to make a soft, splashing sound when stepped on or squeezed [The wet carpet *squished* under our feet.]
squish • *verb* **squished, squishing**

Sr. *abbreviation for* senior [Luis Montero, *Sr.*]

Sri Lanka (srē läŋ′kə) a country on an island south of India. It was formerly called *Ceylon.*
Sri Lan·ka

St. *abbreviation for* **1** Saint [*St.* Paul, Minnesota]. **2** Street [42nd *St.*]

stab (stab) *verb* **1** to pierce or wound with a knife or other pointed object [She *stabbed* herself with a pencil.] **2** to stick or drive a pointed object into something [The farmer *stabbed* the pitchfork into the hay.]
noun a thrust or a wound made with a pointed object.
—make a stab at or **take a stab at** to make an attempt at; to try [Let's *make a stab at* fixing her bicycle.]
stab • *verb* **stabbed, stabbing** • *noun, plural* **stabs**

stability (stə bil′i tē) *noun* the condition of being stable or firm [The *stability* of the government was threatened by the war.]
sta·bil·i·ty • *noun*

stable[1] (stā′bəl) *adjective* **1** not likely to fall over or give way; firm and steady [a *stable* chair]. **2** not likely to change [a *stable* business].
sta·ble • *adjective* **stabler, stablest**

stable[2] (stā′bəl) *noun* a building in which horses and other animals are kept.
verb to put or keep in a stable or similar place [Can we *stable* our horses in your barn tonight?]
sta·ble • *noun, plural* **stables** • *verb* **stabled, stabling**

stack (stak) *noun* **1** a large, neat pile of something such as straw or hay stored outdoors [a *haystack*]. **2** a neat pile of something arranged in layers [a *stack* of magazines]. **3** a chimney or smokestack.
verb to pile or arrange in a stack [*Stack* your books.]
stack • *noun, plural* **stacks** • *verb* **stacked, stacking**

stadium (stā′dē əm) *noun* a place that is used for outdoor athletic events and other activities. It usually has rising rows of seats around an open playing field.
sta·di·um • *noun, plural* **stadiums**

staff (staf) *noun* **1** a stick or pole that is used as a support in walking or as a weapon [a shepherd's *staff*]. **2** a pole for supporting a flag or banner. **3** a group of people who work for a company, person, or institution [a newspaper *staff*]. **4** the set of five parallel lines and the four spaces between them on which music is written.
verb to supply with a staff of workers [Summer camp is *staffed* with students.]
staff • *noun, plural* **staffs** *or sometimes for senses 1 and 4 only* **staves** • *verb* **staffed, staffing**

stag (stag) *noun* a full-grown male deer.
stag • *noun, plural* **stags**

S

stage (stāj) *noun* **1** a raised platform that is used for plays, speeches, or other public activities. **2** the profession of acting [He left the *stage* to write.] **3** a period or step in growth or development [She has reached a new *stage* in her career.] **4** any of the separate jet propulsion systems that work one after another in getting a rocket into outer space. **5** *a short form of* **stagecoach**.
verb **1** to present on a stage [The fifth grade will *stage* a show on Friday afternoon.] **2** to plan and carry out [The soldiers *staged* an attack on the enemy camp.]
stage • *noun, plural for all senses except 2* **stages** • *verb* **staged, staging**

stagecoach (stāj′kōch) *noun* a horse-drawn coach that traveled a regular route. It was used to deliver mail or carry passengers.
stage·coach • *noun, plural* **stagecoaches**

stagecraft (stāj′kraft) *noun* skill in, or the art of, writing or staging plays.
stage·craft • *noun*

stage door *noun* an outside door leading to the area behind the stage in a theater. It is used by actors and other theater people.
stage door • *noun, plural* **stage doors**

stagger (stag′ər) *verb* **1** to walk in an unsteady way, as if about to fall [The tired runner *staggered* across the finish line.] **2** to make stagger [The blow to his head *staggered* him.] **3** to shock, amaze, or stun [They were *staggered* by the news.]
noun the act of staggering; an unsteady or swaying motion.
stag·ger • *verb* **staggered, staggering** • *noun*

WORD CHOICES

Synonyms of **stagger**

The words **stagger, reel,** and **totter** share the meaning "to walk in an unsteady way."

The burro *staggered* along under its load.

She spun around four times, then *reeled* down the hall.

A feeble old man *tottered* toward the exit.

stagnant (stag′nənt) *adjective* **1** not flowing and therefore stale and dirty [*stagnant* water in the pond]. **2** not active [a *stagnant* economy].
stag·nant • *adjective*

stain (stān) *verb* **1** to spoil with spots of dirt, food, or other colored matter [Wine *stained* the rug.] **2** to change the color of; dye [I *stained* the wood to look like oak.]
noun **1** a dirty or colored spot [a grass *stain*]. **2** a dye used to color something such as wood.
stain • *verb* **stained, staining** • *noun, plural* **stains**

stair (ster) *noun* **1** one of a series of steps that go up or down. **2** *usually* **stairs** *the same as* **stairway** *or* **staircase**.
stair • *noun, plural* **stairs**
● The words **stair** and **stare** sound alike.
She tripped on the broken *stair*.
I tried not to *stare* at his loud tie.

staircase (ster′kās) *noun* a stairway, especially one with a banister, that is built for going from one floor to another inside a building.
stair·case • *noun, plural* **staircases**

stairway (ster′wā) *noun* a series of stairs for going from one level to another [There is a *stairway* leading down to the beach.]
stair·way • *noun, plural* **stairways**

stake (stāk) *noun* **1** a pointed stick or rod that is driven into the ground. It can be used to mark a place or to hold something. **2** *often* **stakes** the money bet in a game. **3** a share or interest in something [She has a *stake* in the family's business.]
verb **1** to mark the boundary of with or as if with stakes [The prospectors *staked* out their claims.] **2** to hold up with a stake [*Stake* up the tomato plants.]
stake • *noun, plural* **stakes** • *verb* **staked, staking**
● The words **stake** and **steak** sound alike.
We need a *stake* for the rosebush.
My father likes *steak* and eggs.

stalactite (stə lak′tīt) *noun* a rock formation that is shaped like an icicle and hangs from the roof of a cave. It slowly grows in size as water drips down to the tip and evaporates.
sta·lac·tite • *noun, plural* **stalactites**

a	cat	ō	go	ʉ	fur	ə =	a *in* ago
ā	ape	ô	law, for	ch	chin		e *in* agent
ä	cot, car	oo	look	sh	she		i *in* pencil
e	ten	ōō	tool	th	thin		o *in* atom
ē	me	oi	oil	*th*	then		u *in* circus
i	fit	ou	out	zh	measure		
ī	ice	u	up	ŋ	ring		

stalactite

WORD HISTORY

stalactite

Both **stalactite** and **stalagmite** come from an ancient Greek verb that means "to drop or drip."

stalagmite (stə lag′mīt) *noun* a rock formation that is shaped like an upside-down icicle, that builds up on the floor of a cave. It slowly grows in size as water drips down on it from above.
sta·lag·mite • *noun, plural* **stalagmites**

stalagmite

stale (stāl) *adjective* **1** no longer fresh; made bad or dry from being kept too long [*stale* bread; *stale* air]. **2** no longer new or interesting [a *stale* joke; *stale* news].
stale • *adjective* **staler, stalest**

stalk[1] (stôk) *verb* **1** to hunt or track a person or animal in a quiet, secret way. **2** to walk in a stiff, deliberate way [We knew he was angry by the way he *stalked* out of the room.]
stalk • *verb* **stalked, stalking**

stalk[2] (stôk) *noun* the stem of a plant.
stalk • *noun, plural* **stalks**

stall[1] (stôl) *noun* **1** an area in a barn or stable for one animal. **2** a stand or booth for displaying and selling things. **3** an enclosed space for taking a shower.
verb to bring or come to a stop without meaning to [The motor *stalled* when it got wet.]
stall • *noun, plural* **stalls** • *verb* **stalled, stalling**

stall[2] (stôl) *verb* **1** to hold off by sly or clever means [We *stalled* him before his surprise party.] **2** to delay some activity on purpose [Our team *stalled* to prevent the other team from scoring.]
stall • *verb* **stalled, stalling**

stallion (stal′yən) *noun* a full-grown male horse that can be used for breeding.
stal·lion • *noun, plural* **stallions**

stamen (stā′mən) *noun* the part of a flower in which the pollen grows.
sta·men • *noun, plural* **stamens**

stamina (stam′i nə) *noun* the strength to carry on or to last [You need *stamina* for this job.]
stam·i·na • *noun*

stammer (stam′ər) *verb* to speak in an unsure way, often stopping or repeating certain sounds. People stammer when they are excited or embarrassed.
noun the act of stammering.
stam·mer • *verb* **stammered, stammering** • *noun*

stamp (stamp) *verb* **1** to bring one's foot down with force ["No!" she cried, *stamping* on the floor.] **2** to beat down, crush, or press [We *stamped* out the fire before leaving.] **3** to press or print marks, letters, or other designs on something [He *stamped* his initials on all his books.] **4** to put a postage stamp or seal on an envelope or document [She *stamped* her letters at the post office.]
noun **1** a postage stamp. **2** any similar piece of paper that is issued by a business and given to customers [trading *stamps*]. **3** a machine

S

or tool that is used for pressing or printing marks, letters, or designs on something.
stamp • *verb* **stamped, stamping** • *noun, plural* **stamps**

stampede (stam pēd′) *noun* a sudden rush of animals or people in one direction.
verb to move in or cause a stampede [The crowd *stampeded* when someone smelled smoke.]
stam·pede • *noun, plural* **stampedes**
• *verb* **stampeded, stampeding**

stand (stand) *verb* **1** to be in or get into an upright position on one's feet [*Stand* by your desk.] **2** to be or place in an upright position or on its base or bottom [Our trophy *stands* on the shelf. *Stand* the broom in the corner.] **3** to hold a certain opinion or attitude [I *stand* with you in this matter.] **4** to be in a certain rank or level [Where do you *stand* in your class?] **5** to be placed or located [Our house *stands* on a hill.] **6** to put up with; tolerate; endure [I can't *stand* rude people.] **7** to be not affected by; to resist or tolerate [Can you *stand* the pain? This sofa will *stand* a lot of abuse.] **8** to stay without change [My orders *stand* until I cancel them.] **9** to be forced to go through [She is charged with theft and must *stand* trial.]
noun **1** a stop or halt for defense [The soldiers made their last *stand* near the hill.] **2** an opinion or position [What is your *stand* on longer school hours?] **3** a place where someone is supposed to stand or sit [Please take the witness *stand*.] **4** *often* **stands** the benches or seats in rising rows in a stadium or at a playing field. **5** a booth or counter where items are sold [a candy *stand*]. **6** a rack for holding something [a music *stand*].
—stand by **1** to be near and ready if needed. **2** to help, support, or defend [We *stood by* him when he was accused of cheating on his test.] **—stand for** **1** to be a sign for; represent [The mark "&" *stands for* the word "and."] **2** [*an informal use*] to put up with; tolerate [We won't *stand for* this lack of respect.] **—stand in for** to take the place of; act for. **—stand out** to be easily noticed; be easy to see [His red shirt makes him *stand out* in the picture.]
stand • *verb* **stood, standing** • *noun, plural for all senses except 1* **stands**

standard (stan′dərd) *noun* **1** something set up as a rule or model with which other things like it are to be compared [The government sets the *standards* for pure air to keep air pollution down.] **2** a flag or banner of a nation or military group.
adjective **1** used or accepted as a standard, rule, or model [A meter is a *standard* unit of length in the metric system.] **2** not special or extra; ordinary [Headlights are *standard* equipment on all cars.] **3** accepted as good or proper [Both "catalog" and "catalogue" are *standard* spellings.]
stand·ard • *noun, plural* **standards**
• *adjective*

standard time *noun* the official time for any of the twenty-four time zones in which the world is divided. The first time zone is in England. The four time zones of the mainland U.S. are Eastern, Central, Mountain, and Pacific.

standing (stan′diŋ) *adjective* **1** done from a standing position [a *standing* long jump]. **2** not moving or flowing [*standing* water]. **3** going on in a regular way without change [a *standing* order for coffee].
noun **1** position, rank, or reputation [Her father is a lawyer of high *standing*.] **2** the time that something lasts [a belief of long *standing*].
stand·ing • *adjective* • *noun, plural for sense 1 only* **standings**

Standish (stan′dish), Captain **Miles** (mīlz) 1584?-1656; the English military leader of the Pilgrims at Massachusetts.
Stan·dish, Captain **Miles**

standpoint (stand′point) *noun* the position from which something is seen or understood; point of view.
stand·point • *noun, plural* **standpoints**

standstill (stand′stil) *noun* a stop or halt [Traffic came to a *standstill*.]
stand·still • *noun*

stank (staŋk) *verb a past tense of* **stink**.

Stanton (stan′tən), **Elizabeth Cady** (ē liz′ə bəth kā′dē) 1815-1902; U.S. worker for women's right to vote.
Stan·ton, E·liz·a·beth Ca·dy

stanza (stan′zə) *noun* a group of lines forming one of the sections of a poem or song; verse.
stan·za • *noun, plural* **stanzas**

a	cat	ō	go	ʉ	fur	ə =	a *in* ago
ā	ape	ô	law, for	ch	chin		e *in* agent
ä	cot, car	oo	look	sh	she		i *in* pencil
e	ten	ōō	tool	th	thin		o *in* atom
ē	me	oi	oil	*th*	then		u *in* circus
i	fit	ou	out	zh	measure		
ī	ice	u	up	ŋ	ring		

staple[1] (stā′pəl) ***noun*** **1** any article of food or other common item that is used regularly and is kept in large amounts [Flour, sugar, and salt are *staples*.] **2** the main product that is grown or produced in a region [Coffee is a *staple* of Brazil.]
sta·ple • ***noun,*** *plural* **staples**

staple[2] (stā′pəl) ***noun*** **1** a small, thin piece of metal with sharp ends that is shaped like an E without the middle stroke. When the staple is driven through something, such as pieces of paper, the ends bend over to hold the pieces together. **2** a similar heavier, thicker piece of metal. It is driven into a surface to hold something such as a wire or hook in place.
verb to fasten with a staple or staples [He *stapled* the poster to the wall.]
sta·ple • ***noun,*** *plural* **staples** • ***verb*** **stapled, stapling**

stapler (stā′plər) ***noun*** a tool that is used to staple things together.
sta·pler • ***noun,*** *plural* **staplers**

star (stär) ***noun*** **1** a heavenly body that shines by its own light and is usually seen as a point of light in the night sky. The sun is the nearest star to the earth. **2** a flat figure with four or more points. It is used to decorate or mark something. **3** a person who is outstanding in a sport, in acting, or in some other activity.
verb **1** to play a leading role in a play, movie, or TV show [She is *starring* in the new TV series.] **2** to decorate or mark something with stars [The teacher *starred* the best reports in the class.]
star • ***noun,*** *plural* **stars** • ***verb*** **starred, starring**

starboard (stär′bərd) ***noun*** the right-hand side of a ship or aircraft as a person inside faces forward.
star·board • ***noun***

starch (stärch) ***noun*** **1** a white substance that is found in potatoes, grains, and many other vegetables. **2** a powder that is made from starch. It is mixed with water and used to make cloth stiff.
verb to make stiff with starch.
starch • ***noun*** • ***verb*** **starched, starching**

stare (ster) ***verb*** to look at in a steady way with the eyes wide open —Look for the WORD CHOICES box at the entry **look**.
noun a long, steady look.
stare • ***verb*** **stared, staring** • ***noun,*** *plural* **stares**
● The words **stare** and **stair** sound alike.
I tried not to *stare* at his loud tie.
She tripped on the broken *stair*.

starfish (stär′fish) ***noun*** a small sea animal that has a hard covering and five or more arms arranged like the points of a star.
star·fish • ***noun,*** *plural* **starfish**

starfish

Stars and Stripes the red, white, and blue flag of the U.S. It has 13 stripes (for the 13 original colonies) and 50 stars (for the 50 States).

Star-Spangled Banner (stär′spaŋ′gəld) **1** the U.S. flag. **2** the national anthem of the U.S. The words were written by Francis Scott Key in 1814.
Star-Span·gled Banner

start (stärt) ***verb*** **1** to begin to go, do, or act [If you are ready, we can *start*. The show *starts* at 8:30.] **2** to cause to begin [*Start* the car. Who *started* the fight?] **3** to move or jump in a sudden way when surprised [The noise made the baby *start*.]
noun **1** the act of starting [We got a late *start* yesterday.] **2** a sudden jump in surprise or fear [The dream caused her to wake with a *start*.] **3** the time or place at which something begins [She was ahead from the *start*.]
start • ***verb*** **started, starting** • ***noun,*** *plural* **starts**

startle (stärt′l) ***verb*** to cause to move suddenly in surprise or fear [The ring of the telephone *startled* me.] —Look for the WORD CHOICES box at the entry **shock**[1].
star·tle • ***verb*** **startled, startling**

starvation (stär vā′shən) ***noun*** the condition of not having enough food to eat.
star·va·tion • ***noun***

starve (stärv) ***verb*** **1** to suffer or die from lack of food [The refugees were *starving*.] **2** [*an informal use*] to be very hungry [We were *starving* after school.]
starve • ***verb*** **starved, starving**

state (stāt) ***noun*** **1** the condition in which a person or thing is [Things are in a *state* of change.] **2** a group of people united under one government; nation. **3** *usually* **State** any of the political units that make up a country such as the U.S.
verb to express in words; tell or explain [The

S

coach *stated* the rules.] —Look for the WORD CHOICES box at the entry **say**.
state • *noun, plural* **states** • *verb* **stated, stating**

stately (stāt′lē) *adjective* grand or having great dignity in appearance or manner [a *stately* march; a *stately* mansion] —Look for the WORD CHOICES box at the entry **grand**.
state·ly • *adjective* **statelier, stateliest**

statement (stāt′mənt) *noun* **1** something that is expressed in words [The mayor gave a *statement* to the press.] **2** a report or record of some business matter [Did you get your bank *statement* this month?]
state·ment • *noun, plural* **statements**

statesman (stāts′mən) *noun* a person who is wise and skillful in government.
states·man • *noun, plural* **statesmen**

static (stat′ik) *adjective* **1** not active, moving, or changing [a *static* situation]. **2** having to do with electrical charges that are produced by friction [*static* electricity].
noun any of the electrical disturbances in the air that interfere with radio or TV reception.
stat·ic • *adjective* • *noun*

station (stā′shən) *noun* **1** a place where a person or thing stands or is supposed to stand [The guards were not allowed to leave their *station*.] **2** a building or place used by a business or other organization [a gas *station*; a fire *station*]. **3** a regular stopping place along a route, especially a building at such a place [I will meet you at the train *station*.] **4** a place with electronic equipment that is used to send out radio or TV programs.
verb to place someone at a particular location [The soldier was *stationed* in New Mexico.]
sta·tion • *noun, plural* **stations**
• *verb* **stationed, stationing**

stationary (stā′shə ner′ē) *adjective* **1** not moving or not capable of being moved [a *stationary* desk]. **2** not changing in any way [*stationary* prices].
sta·tion·ar·y • *adjective*
● The words **stationary** and **stationery** sound alike.
I pedal a *stationary* bike in my room.
I write letters on special *stationery*.

stationery (stā′shə ner′ē) *noun* paper and envelopes that are used for writing letters.
sta·tion·er·y • *noun*
● The words **stationery** and **stationary** sound alike.

SPELLING TIP

Use this memory aid to spell **stationery**. Station*e*ry is pap*er*.

station wagon *noun* an automobile with rear seats that can be folded down and a back end that opens for easy loading and unloading.
station wagon • *noun, plural* **station wagons**

statistics (stə tis′tiks) *plural noun* facts about a particular subject that are collected in the form of numbers [*Statistics* show that people in general live longer these days.]
sta·tis·tics • *plural noun*

statue (stach′o͞o) *noun* a form or likeness of a person or animal made by an artist out of bronze, marble, clay, or some other solid material.
stat·ue • *noun, plural* **statues**

Statue of Liberty a huge copper statue of a woman wearing a crown and holding a torch high. It represents liberty and stands on an island in the harbor of New York City. It was a gift to the U.S. from France.

stature (stach′ər) *noun* the height of a person [She is of short *stature*.]
stat·ure • *noun*

status (stat′əs *or* stāt′əs) *noun* **1** a person's professional or social position or rank [Doctors usually have high *status* in our society.] **2** a legal state or condition [Do you have the *status* of being a full citizen?]
sta·tus • *noun*

statute (stach′o͞ot) *noun* a rule or law.
stat·ute • *noun, plural* **statutes**

stave (stāv) *noun* one of the long, curved strips of wood that form the sides of a barrel or cask.
stave • *noun, plural* **staves**

staves (stāvz) *noun a plural of* **staff**.

stay (stā) *verb* **1** to keep on being in some place or condition; remain [*Stay* at home. The weather *stayed* bad all day.] **2** to live for a time; dwell [The boy *stayed* with his aunt.]

a	cat	ō	go	ʉ	fur	ə =	a *in* ago
ā	ape	ô	law, for	ch	chin		e *in* agent
ä	cot, car	oo	look	sh	she		i *in* pencil
e	ten	o͞o	tool	th	thin		o *in* atom
ē	me	oi	oil	*th*	then		u *in* circus
i	fit	ou	out	zh	measure		
ī	ice	u	up	ŋ	ring		

noun the time spent somewhere [a long *stay* in the hospital].
stay • ***verb*** **stayed, staying** • ***noun,*** *plural* **stays**

WORD CHOICES

Synonyms of **stay**

The words **stay, linger,** and **remain** share the meaning "to go on being in some place."

Stay in your seat until recess.

I *lingered* awhile in the beautiful old church.

We *remained* after everyone else had left.

Ste. *abbreviation for* Sainte. *Sainte* is the French word for a woman saint.

steadfast (sted′fast) ***adjective*** firm or fixed; not changing [a *steadfast* friendship] —Look for the WORD CHOICES box at the entry **faithful**.
stead·fast • ***adjective***

steady (sted′ē) ***adjective*** **1** firm or stable; not shaky [a *steady* chair]. **2** not changing or letting up [a *steady* rain; a *steady* rhythm]. **3** not easily excited; calm [*steady* nerves]. **4** serious and sensible; reliable [a *steady* worker]. **5** appearing again and again; regular [a *steady* customer].
verb to make or become steady [We *steadied* the old ladder.]
stead·y • ***adjective*** **steadier, steadiest** • ***verb*** **steadied, steadying, steadies**

WORD HISTORY

steak

The source of **steak** is a 600-year-old English word that comes from an earlier Scandinavian word that means "to roast on a spit." That is how this cut of meat was usually cooked in those times.

steak (stāk) ***noun*** a slice of meat or fish, especially a slice of beef. It is cut thick for broiling or frying.
steak • ***noun,*** *plural* **steaks**
● The words **steak** and **stake** sound alike.
My uncle likes *steak* and eggs.
We need a *stake* for the rosebush.

steal (stēl) ***verb*** **1** to take away, in a secret way and without permission, something that belongs to another [She *stole* candy from my drawer.] **2** to do something in a secret way [I wanted to *steal* a look out the window.] **3** in baseball, to get to the next base safely without the help of a hit or error [The runner *stole* second base.]
noun [*an informal use*] something that can be bought for a very low price.
steal • ***verb*** **stole, stolen, stealing** • ***noun,*** *plural* **steals**
● The words **steal** and **steel** sound alike.
The thief tried to *steal* my purse.
Some buildings are made of concrete and *steel*.

steam (stēm) ***noun*** **1** water that has been changed into a vapor or gas. Water turns to steam when it is heated to the boiling point. **2** a mist formed when water vapor cools. **3** [*an informal use*] energy and strength [I ran out of *steam* by noon.]
verb **1** to give off steam [The pan of boiling water is *steaming*.] **2** to become covered with mist [His glasses *steamed* up.] **3** to move by the power of steam under pressure [The ship *steamed* out of the port.] **4** to cook, soften, or remove with steam [The cook *steamed* the rice. Let's *steam* the wallpaper off the bathroom walls.]
steam • ***noun*** • ***verb*** **steamed, steaming**

steamboat (stēm′bōt) ***noun*** a boat that is powered by steam.
steam·boat • ***noun,*** *plural* **steamboats**

steam engine ***noun*** an engine that produces power by boiling water under pressure. The escaping steam is used to drive mechanical parts.
steam engine • ***noun,*** *plural* **steam engines**

steamship (stēm′ship) ***noun*** a ship that is powered by steam.
steam·ship • ***noun,*** *plural* **steamships**

steamy (stē′mē) ***adjective*** filled or covered with steam or mist [a *steamy* bathroom].
steam·y • ***adjective*** **steamier, steamiest**

steel (stēl) ***noun*** **1** a hard, tough metal that is made from iron mixed with a little carbon. **2** great hardness or strength [muscles of *steel*].
● The words **steel** and **steal** sound alike.
Water causes *steel* tools to rust.
She tried to *steal* second base.

steep (stēp) ***adjective*** **1** having a sharp slant up or down [a *steep* hill]. **2** [*an informal use*] too high [a *steep* price].
steep • ***adjective*** **steeper, steepest**

steeple (stē′pəl) ***noun*** a high tower on a church or other building. It usually has a spire on top.
stee·ple • ***noun,*** *plural* **steeples**

steeple

steer[1] (stir) ***verb*** **1** to guide or control a moving car, boat, or other vehicle by means of a wheel or rudder [She *steered* the car into the garage.] **2** to be guided [This car *steers* easily.] **3** to direct or guide [The coach *steered* his team to victory.]
steer • ***verb*** **steered, steering**

steer[2] (stir) ***noun*** a young male of domestic cattle that is raised for its beef.
steer • ***noun,*** *plural* **steers**

stegosaurus

stegosaurus (steg ə sôr′əs *or* steg ə sär′əs) ***noun*** a large dinosaur with a small head. It had two rows of large bony plates that stuck up from its back.
steg·o·sau·rus • ***noun,*** *plural* **steg·o·sau·ri** (steg ə sôr′ī *or* steg ə sär′ī)

stem[1] (stem) ***noun*** **1** the main part of a plant or tree that grows up from the ground and bears leaves or flowers. **2** any of the parts of a plant or tree that branch out from the main stem and end in one or more flowers or leaves.
verb to come from [The problem *stems* from lack of understanding.]
stem • ***noun,*** *plural* **stems** • ***verb*** **stemmed, stemming**

stem[2] (stem) ***verb*** to stop or check [We must *stem* the bleeding quickly.]
stem • ***verb*** **stemmed, stemming**

stench (stench) ***noun*** a very bad smell.
stench • ***noun,*** *plural* **stenches**

stencil

stencil (sten′səl) ***noun*** **1** a thin sheet of paper, plastic, metal, or other material with holes cut through in the shape of letters or designs. When ink or paint is spread over the stencil, the letters or designs are marked on the surface beneath. **2** a design or letter marked in this way.
verb to mark with a stencil [We will *stencil* your name on the box later.]
sten·cil • ***noun,*** *plural* **stencils**
• ***verb*** **stenciled** or **stencilled, stenciling** or **stencilling**

step (step) ***noun*** **1** the act of moving and placing the foot forward, backward, sideways, up, or down in walking, dancing, or climbing. **2** the distance covered by such a movement [He was only two *steps* away.] **3** the sound of a step [I hear *steps* outside.] **4** a way of walking [light, skipping *steps*]. **5** a place to put one's foot in going up or down on stairs or a ladder. **6 steps** a flight of stairs. **7** an act or stage in a series [After giving first aid, the next *step* is to call a doctor.]

a	cat	ō	go	u̵	fur	ə =	a *in* ago
ā	ape	ô	law, for	ch	chin		e *in* agent
ä	cot, car	oo	look	sh	she		i *in* pencil
e	ten	o͞o	tool	th	thin		o *in* atom
ē	me	oi	oil	*th*	then		u *in* circus
i	fit	ou	out	zh	measure		
ī	ice	u	up	ŋ	ring		

verb **1** to move by taking steps [We *stepped* out of the elevator.] **2** to press the foot down [I *stepped* on the brake.]
—in step marching, dancing, or walking with the rhythm of others or of music [Keep *in step* with the band.] **—out of step** not in step. **—step by step** in a gradual and steady way. **—step up** to increase or accelerate [We must *step up* production this month.]
step • *noun, plural* **steps** • *verb* **stepped, stepping**
● The words **step** and **steppe** sound alike.
He took a *step* backwards.
Snow covered the barren *steppe*.

stepfather (step′fä *th*ər) *noun* the man who has married a person's mother after the death or divorce of that person's father.
step·fa·ther • *noun, plural* **stepfathers**

stepmother (step′mu*th* ər) *noun* the woman who has married a person's father after the death or divorce of that person's mother.
step·moth·er • *noun, plural* **stepmothers**

stepparent (step′per ənt) *noun* a person's stepfather or stepmother.
step·par·ent • *noun, plural* **stepparents**

steppe (step) *noun* a large area of southeastern Europe and Asia where the land is flat and there are few trees.
steppe • *noun, plural* **steppes**
● The words **steppe** and **step** sound alike.
Wolves roamed the *steppe*.
The baby took just a *step* before falling.

stereo (ster′ē ō) *noun* a stereophonic record player, radio, or other sound system.
ster·e·o • *noun, plural* **stereos**

stereophonic (ster′ē ō fän′ik) *adjective* describing or having to do with a way of recording or broadcasting so that a listener hears sounds in a natural way. Stereophonic systems use two or more speakers.
ster·e·o·phon·ic • *adjective*

sterile (ster′əl) *adjective* **1** not able to produce children, fruit, or plants; not fertile [a *sterile* animal; *sterile* soil]. **2** free from living germs [Medical tools must be kept *sterile*.]
ster·ile • *adjective*

sterilize (ster′ə līz) *verb* to make sterile [I *sterilized* the baby bottles in boiling water.]
ster·i·lize • *verb* **sterilized, sterilizing**

sterling (stur′liŋ) *adjective* **1** made of silver that is at least 92.5% pure [*sterling* candlesticks]. **2** very fine; excellent [a person of *sterling* character].
ster·ling • *adjective*

stern[1] (sturn) *adjective* strict or harsh; not gentle, tender, or easy [a *stern* teacher; *stern* punishment] —Look for the WORD CHOICES box at the entry **severe**.
stern • *adjective* **sterner, sternest**

stern[2] (sturn) *noun* the back end of a ship or boat.
stern • *noun, plural* **sterns**

stethoscope (steth′ə skōp) *noun* a medical instrument used by doctors for listening to sounds from the heart and lungs.
steth·o·scope • *noun, plural* **stethoscopes**

Stevenson (stē′vən sən), **Robert Louis** (räb′ ərt lo͞o′is) 1850-1894; Scottish poet and writer of novels.
Ste·ven·son, Rob·ert Lou·is

stew (sto͞o *or* styo͞o) *noun* a dish of meat and vegetables cooked by slow boiling.
verb to cook by boiling slowly, usually for a long time.
stew • *noun, plural* **stews** • *verb* **stewed, stewing**

steward (sto͞o′ərd *or* styo͞o′ərd) *noun* a person whose work is to serve food and drink and otherwise look after the comfort of customers in a club or restaurant or passengers on a ship or airplane.
stew·ard • *noun, plural* **stewards**

stewardess (sto͞o′ər dəs *or* styo͞o′ər dəs) *noun* a female flight attendant.
stew·ard·ess • *noun, plural* **stewardesses**

stick (stik) *noun* **1** a twig or branch that is broken or cut off. **2** any long, thin piece of wood, such as a cane or club, with a special shape [a walking *stick*]. **3** a long, thin piece [a *stick* of chewing gum; carrot *sticks*].
verb **1** to press a sharp point into; to stab [He *stuck* his finger with a needle.] **2** to fasten or be fastened by pinning or gluing [I *stuck* my name tag on my coat. The stamp *sticks* to the paper.] **3** to thrust or push [*Stick* your hands in your pockets. My ears *stick* out.] **4** to become caught and unable to move [The rear wheels *stuck* in the mud.] **5** to keep close or hold fast [*Stick* to your job until you finish. Friends *stick* together.]
—stick by or **stick to** to stay loyal to [She *stuck by* her decision even though it was not popular.] **—stick up for** [*an informal use*] to defend

or support [I *stuck up for* him because I thought he was right.]
stick • *noun, plural* **sticks** • *verb* **stuck, sticking**

sticker (stik′ər) *noun* a label with glue on the back.
stick·er • *noun, plural* **stickers**

sticky (stik′ē) *adjective* **1** tending to hold on to anything that is touched [His fingers were *sticky* with candy.] **2** [*an informal use*] hot and damp; humid [a *sticky* August day].
stick·y • *adjective* **stickier, stickiest**

stiff (stif) *adjective* **1** hard to bend or stretch; rigid [*stiff* cardboard]. **2** not able to move easily [*stiff* muscles]. **3** not flowing easily; thick [Beat the egg whites until they are *stiff*.] **4** strong; powerful [a *stiff* breeze]. **5** not easy; difficult [*stiff* punishment].
stiff • *adjective* **stiffer, stiffest**

stiffen (stif′ən) *verb* to make or become stiff or stiffer [The cat *stiffened* at the sight of the dog. He *stiffened* the paper with cardboard.]
stiff·en • *verb* **stiffened, stiffening**

stifle (stī′fəl) *verb* **1** to suffer from a lack of fresh, cool air [I'm *stifling* in this room.] **2** to hold back or stop [He *stifled* a yawn.]
sti·fle • *verb* **stifled, stifling**

still (stil) *adjective* **1** without sound; quiet; silent [The empty house is *still*.] **2** calm; peaceful; serene [the *still* water of the lake].
noun silence; quiet [in the *still* of the night].
adverb **1** until then or now [Is she *still* talking?] **2** even; yet [It became *still* colder.] **3** in spite of that; nevertheless [She's rich, but *still* unhappy.]
conjunction nevertheless; yet [I admire her bravery; *still* I think it was foolish.]
verb to make or become still, quiet, or calm [The audience *stilled* as the play began. She *stilled* the crying baby with a lullaby.]
still • *adjective* • *noun* • *adverb* • *conjunction* • *verb* **stilled, stilling**

WORD CHOICES

Synonyms of still

Many words share the meaning "with little or no sound."

mute	silent
quiet	soundless

stilt (stilt) *noun* **1** a long pole with a support for the foot part way up it. A person can walk high above the ground on a pair of stilts. **2** any tall pole used as a support for a building, dock, or other structure [In the bayou, houses are built on *stilts*.]
stilt • *noun, plural* **stilts**

stimulate (stim′yo͞o lāt′) *verb* to make more active; excite [Smells of cooking *stimulate* my appetite.]
stim·u·late • *verb* **stimulated, stimulating**

stimulus (stim′yo͞o ləs) *noun* anything that causes some action or activity [Wanting a new car is a *stimulus* to work.]
stim·u·lus • *noun, plural* **stim·u·li** (stim′yo͞o lī)

sting (stiŋ) *verb* **1** to hurt by pricking [Wasps can *sting* you.] **2** to cause or feel sharp pain [The cold wind *stung* her cheeks.]
noun **1** the act or power of stinging [The *sting* of a bee may be dangerous.] **2** a pain or wound caused by stinging [I saw the bee *sting* on her arm.] **3** a sharp, pointed part of an insect or animal that can be used to sting; stinger [The *sting* of a bee is at the end of its abdomen.]
sting • *verb* **stung, stinging** • *noun, plural* **stings**

stinger (stiŋ′ər) *noun* a sharp, pointed part of an insect or animal that can be used to sting.
sting·er • *noun, plural* **stingers**

stingray

stingray (stiŋ′rā) *noun* a large, flat fish with a long, thin tail. The tail has one or more spines that can cause serious wounds.
sting·ray • *noun, plural* **stingrays**

a	cat	ō	go	ʉ	fur	ə =	a *in* ago
ā	ape	ô	law, for	ch	chin		e *in* agent
ä	cot, car	o͝o	look	sh	she		i *in* pencil
e	ten	o͞o	tool	th	thin		o *in* atom
ē	me	oi	oil	*th*	then		u *in* circus
i	fit	ou	out	zh	measure		
ī	ice	u	up	ŋ	ring		

stingy (stin′jē) ***adjective*** not willing to give or spend money; not generous.
stin·gy • ***adjective*** **stingier, stingiest**

stink (stiŋk) ***verb*** **1** to give off a strong, bad smell. **2** [*a slang use*] to be no good, or worth nothing [This cheap radio *stinks*.]
noun a strong, bad smell.
stink • ***verb*** **stank** or **stunk, stunk, stinking** • ***noun,*** *plural* **stinks**

stir (stʉr) ***verb*** **1** to move or shake slightly [Not a leaf *stirred* in the quiet air.] **2** to move around or be active [It was early and no one was *stirring*.] **3** to mix something by moving it around with a spoon, fork, stick, or similar object [*Stir* the paint well.] **4** to cause strong feelings in; excite [Her speech *stirred* the crowd.]
noun **1** the act of stirring [Give the fire a *stir*.] **2** the condition of being excited; commotion [The news caused quite a *stir*.]
stir • ***verb*** **stirred, stirring** • ***noun,*** *plural for sense 1 only* **stirs**

stirrup (stʉr′əp *or* stir′əp) ***noun*** either one of two rings with flat bottoms that hang by straps from the sides of a saddle and hold a rider's foot.
stir·rup • ***noun,*** *plural* **stirrups**

stitch (stich) ***noun*** **1** one complete movement of a needle and thread into and out of the material in sewing. **2** one complete movement done in various ways in knitting, crocheting, and other needlework. **3** one of the loops of thread or yarn made in sewing and other needlework.
verb to sew or fasten with stitches [Can you show me how to *stitch* a seam?]
stitch • ***noun,*** *plural* **stitches** • ***verb*** **stitched, stitching**

St. Kitts and Nevis (sānt kits and nē′vis) a country made up of two islands in the West Indies.
St. Kitts and Ne·vis

St. Lawrence (sānt′ lôr′əns *or* sānt′ lär′əns) a river that flows from Lake Ontario into the Atlantic Ocean.
St. Law·rence

St. Louis (sānt′ lo͞o′is *or* sānt′ lo͞o′ē) a city in eastern Missouri, on the Mississippi River.
St. Lou·is

St. Lucia (sānt lo͞o′shē ə) a country on an island in the West Indies.
St. Lu·ci·a

stock (stäk) ***noun*** **1** a supply of something for use when needed [Our *stock* of food is low.] **2** livestock; cattle, horses, sheep, pigs, and other farm animals. **3** family or ancestors [We come from Polish *stock*.] **4** shares of ownership in a company [Each of his children had *stock* in the family business.] **5** the part that serves as a handle or body for the working parts of something [The *stock* of a rifle holds the barrel in place.] **6** a liquid in which meat, fish, or poultry has been boiled. **7 stocks** a wooden frame with holes in it for locking around a person's ankles and, sometimes, wrists. The stocks were used in earlier times as a punishment.
verb **1** to provide with a stock or a supply [We *stocked* our farm with cattle. They *stocked* the store with new items.] **2** to put in or keep a supply of [We *stocked* up on food for the winter. This shop *stocks* many shirts.]
—in stock on hand for sale or use. **—out of stock** not on hand for sale or use.
stock • ***noun,*** *plural for all senses except 2 and 3* **stocks** • ***verb*** **stocked, stocking**

stockade (stä kād′) ***noun*** **1** a wall of tall stakes built around a place for defense. **2** the area enclosed by a stockade.
stock·ade • ***noun,*** *plural* **stockades**

stocking (stäk′iŋ) ***noun*** a knitted covering for the foot and, usually, most of the leg.
stock·ing • ***noun,*** *plural* **stockings**

stocky (stäk′ē) ***adjective*** having a short, heavy build.
stock·y • ***adjective*** **stockier, stockiest**

stoke (stōk) ***verb*** to stir up and add fuel to [They *stoked* the fire in the furnace.]
stoke • ***verb*** **stoked, stoking**

stole[1] (stōl) ***noun*** a woman's long scarf of cloth or fur worn with the ends hanging down in front.
stole • ***noun,*** *plural* **stoles**

stole[2] (stōl) ***verb*** *past tense of* **steal**.

stolen (stō′lən) ***verb*** *past participle of* **steal**.
stol·en • ***verb***

stomach (stum′ək) ***noun*** **1** the large, hollow organ into which food goes after it is swallowed. Food is partly digested in the stomach. **2** the belly, or abdomen [This shirt won't button over my *stomach*.]
verb to bear or put up with [We could not *stomach* such rude behavior.]
stom·ach • ***noun,*** *plural* **stomachs** • ***verb*** **stomached, stomaching**

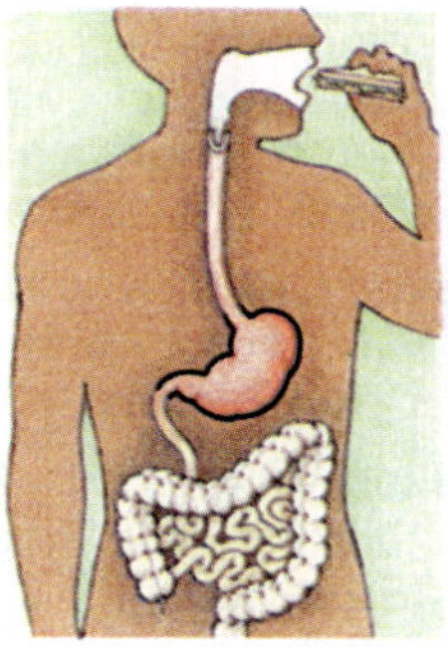
stomach

S

stomp (stämp) ***verb*** to hurt or kill by stamping on.
stomp • ***verb*** **stomped, stomping**

stone (stōn) ***noun*** **1** hard mineral matter that is found in the earth but is not metal; rock [Granite, quartz, and limestone are kinds of *stone*.] **2** a small piece of this [Don't throw *stones*.] **3** a rare mineral or other hard substance that has a beautiful color or brightness and that is cut and polished for use in jewelry [Rubies are precious *stones*.] **4** the hard seed of certain fruits [the *stone* of a peach].
verb to throw stones at or kill with stones.
—leave no stone unturned to do everything possible.
stone • ***noun,*** *plural for senses 2, 3, and 4 only* **stones** • ***verb*** **stoned, stoning**

Stone (stōn), **Lucy** (lo͞o′sē) 1818-1893; U.S. worker for women's right to vote and the right of a married woman to keep her own name.
Stone, Lu·cy

stony (stōn′ē) ***adjective*** **1** covered with stones [a *stony* road]. **2** like stone in appearance, texture, or hardness [a *stony* building material; a *stony* heart].
ston·y • ***adjective*** **stonier, stoniest**

stood (stood) ***verb*** *past tense and past participle of* **stand**.

stool (sto͞ol) ***noun*** **1** a single seat that has three or four legs and no back or arms. **2** *a short form of* **footstool**. **3** waste matter from the bowels.
stool • ***noun,*** *plural* **stools**

stoop[1] (sto͞op) ***verb*** **1** to bend the body forward or in a crouch [He *stooped* to tie his shoes.] **2** to stand or walk with the head and shoulders bent forward [Stand up straight and don't *stoop*.] **3** to make oneself lower in moral character or dignity [Would you *stoop* to taking a bribe?]
noun the act or position of stooping the body [Some people walk with a *stoop*.]
stoop • ***verb*** **stooped, stooping** • ***noun***

stoop[2] (sto͞op) ***noun*** a small porch or platform with steps, at an entrance of a house.
stoop • ***noun,*** *plural* **stoops**

stop (stäp) ***verb*** **1** to keep from going on, continuing some activity, or moving in some way [*Stop* the car.] **2** to come to an end; halt [My watch *stopped*. The noise finally *stopped*.] **3** to keep from beginning, happening, or doing; prevent [They *stopped* us from talking. The leash *stopped* the dog from chasing cars.] **4** to close by filling, shutting off, or covering [*Stop* the cracks with putty.] **5** to clog or block: often with *up* [Hair has *stopped* up the drain.]
noun **1** the act or fact of stopping; a finish; an end [Let's put a *stop* to this argument.] **2** a place where a stop is made [a *stop* on a bus route. The drugstore is my last *stop*.] **3** a brief stay or visit [We planned a *stop* of several days at my aunt's.]
—stop in or **stop by** to visit for a while. **—stop off** to stop for a short visit on the way to another place. **—stop over** **1** to visit for a while [I thought I'd *stop over*.] **2** to halt a journey for a time [We *stopped over* for a day in Phoenix.]
stop • ***verb*** **stopped, stopping** • ***noun,*** *plural* **stops**

stopover (stäp′ō vər) ***noun*** a short stay at a place in the course of a journey [We made a *stopover* in Des Moines.]
stop·o·ver • ***noun,*** *plural* **stopovers**

stopper (stäp′ər) ***noun*** something put into an opening to close it [a cork bottle *stopper*].
stop·per • ***noun,*** *plural* **stoppers**

stopwatch (stäp′wäch) ***noun*** a watch that can be started and stopped to measure exactly the time taken for a race or other event.
stop·watch • ***noun,*** *plural* **stopwatches**

storage (stôr′ij) ***noun*** **1** the act of storing something [A silo is for the *storage* of food for farm animals.] **2** the condition of being stored [Our furniture is in *storage*.]
stor·age • ***noun***

store (stôr) ***noun*** **1** a place of business where things are sold [a candy *store;* a department *store*]. **2** a supply or stock of something for use when needed [a *store* of coal]. **3** a great amount [a *store* of knowledge].
verb **1** to put aside or collect something until it is needed [We'll *store* the extra chairs in the attic.] **2** to fill with a supply or store [The cabin has been *stored* with plenty of food.] **3** to put or keep information in the memory of a computer [Many files can be *stored* in one computer.]
—in store waiting to be used or to happen [Guess what we have *in store* for you!]
store • ***noun,*** *plural* **stores** • ***verb*** **stored, storing**

a	cat	ō	go	ʉ	fur	ə =	a *in* ago
ā	ape	ô	law, for	ch	chin		e *in* agent
ä	cot, car	oo	look	sh	she		i *in* pencil
e	ten	o͞o	tool	th	thin		o *in* atom
ē	me	oi	oil	*th*	then		u *in* circus
i	fit	ou	out	zh	measure		
ī	ice	u	up	ŋ	ring		

storehouse (stôr′hous) *noun* a place where things are stored; warehouse.
store·house • *noun, plural* **storehouses**

storekeeper (stôr′kēp ər) *noun* a person who owns or runs a store where things are sold to the public.
store·keep·er • *noun, plural* **storekeepers**

storeroom (stôr′ro͞om) *noun* a room where things are stored.
store·room • *noun, plural* **storerooms**

stork (stôrk) *noun* a large bird with long legs and a long neck and bill. It is often found wading in shallow water. The white stork of Europe often nests on rooftops and has long been associated with good luck and the birth of babies.
stork • *noun, plural* **storks**

stork

storm (stôrm) *noun* **1** a strong wind along with heavy rain, snow, sleet, or hail. A storm often includes thunder and lightning. **2** a heavy fall of rain, snow, or hail. **3** a heavy shower of objects [a *storm* of arrows]. **4** a strong outburst [a *storm* of applause].
verb **1** to blow with very strong winds and rain, snow, sleet, or hail [It *stormed* for hours.] **2** to rush with violence and anger [They *stormed* out of the house.] **3** to attack with great force [The soldiers *stormed* the fort.]
storm • *noun, plural* **storms**
• *verb* **stormed, storming**

stormy (stôr′mē) *adjective* **1** of or having storms [*stormy* weather; a *stormy* day]. **2** wild, rough, or angry [a *stormy* argument].
storm·y • *adjective* **stormier, stormiest**

story[1] (stôr′ē) *noun* **1** an account of some happening, whether true or made up [Let me tell you the *story* of the first Thanksgiving.] **2** a made-up tale that is written down. It is shorter than a novel [the *stories* of Aesop]. **3** [*an informal use*] a lie [Stop telling *stories*.]
sto·ry • *noun, plural* **stories**

story[2] (stôr′ē) *noun* the space or rooms making up one level of a building, from a floor to the ceiling above it [a building with ten *stories*].
sto·ry • *noun, plural* **stories**

stout (stout) *adjective* **1** having a fat body [a *stout* pony] —Look for the WORD CHOICES box at the entry **heavy**. **2** strong and firm; sturdy [a *stout* wall]. **3** brave; full of courage [She has a *stout* heart.]
stout • *adjective* **stouter, stoutest**

stove (stōv) *noun* a device for cooking or heating that uses gas, oil, electricity, or some other form of energy.
stove • *noun, plural* **stoves**

stow (stō) *verb* to pack or store away [We *stowed* the luggage in the trunk of the car.]
—stow away **1** to store or hide away [*Stow away* those books.] **2** to be a stowaway [They *stowed away* in the baggage compartment.]
stow • *verb* **stowed, stowing**

stowaway (stō′ə wā) *noun* a person who hides aboard a ship, plane, or other vehicle for a free or secret ride.
stow·a·way • *noun, plural* **stowaways**

Stowe (stō), **Harriet Beecher** (her′ē ət bē′chər) 1811-1896; U.S. author. She wrote *Uncle Tom's Cabin*.
Stowe, Har·ri·et Bee·cher

St. Paul (sānt′ pôl′) the capital of Minnesota, on the Mississippi River.

straddle (strad′əl) *verb* to stand or sit with one leg on either side of something [He stood *straddling* the row of beans in the garden.]
strad·dle • *verb* **straddled, straddling**

straggle (strag′əl) *verb* to leave, arrive, or happen with uneven distances or periods of time between [The last runners *straggled* across the finish line.]
strag·gle • *verb* **straggled, straggling**

straight (strāt) *adjective* **1** having the same direction all the way; not curved [a *straight* line]. **2** not crooked, bent, wavy, or curly [*straight* hair]. **3** not bending or leaning [*straight* posture]. **4** level or even [a *straight* hem]. **5** not turning aside; direct [a *straight* course of action]. **6** honest and sincere [a *straight* answer].
adverb **1** in a straight line or direction [The road runs *straight* for a few miles.] **2** upright; erect [Stand up *straight*.] **3** without turning aside or putting off [Go *straight* home.]
straight • *adjective* & • *adverb* **straighter, straightest**

• The words **straight** and **strait** sound alike.
A ruler is used to draw *straight* lines.
A *strait* connects the two seas.

S

straighten (strāt′n) ***verb*** **1** to make or become straight [He *straightened* his tie.] **2** to put in order [*Straighten* your room.]
straight·en • ***verb*** **straightened, straightening**

straightforward (strāt fôr′wərd) ***adjective*** honest; frank [She gave a *straightforward* answer.]
straight·for·ward • ***adjective***

strain[1] (strān) ***verb*** **1** to draw or stretch tight [The heavy weight *strained* the ropes until they broke.] **2** to hurt or weaken by too much force or effort [She *strained* a muscle.] **3** to try very hard [She *strained* to hear him.] **4** to pull with force [The horse *strained* at the harness.] **5** to put or pass through a screen, sieve, or filter [He *strained* the soup to get a clear broth.]
noun **1** hard, tiring effort of the body or mind [The week of tests was quite a *strain* for her.] **2** great force or pressure [The *strain* of the weight on the bridge made it collapse.] **3** an injury to part of the body as a result of too much effort [muscle *strain*].
strain • ***verb*** **strained, straining** • ***noun,*** *plural* **strains**

strain[2] (strān) ***noun*** a group of animals or plants that have developed from a common ancestor; stock, breed, or variety [This *strain* of flowers grows well in dry soil.]
strain • ***noun,*** *plural* **strains**

strained (strānd) ***adjective*** not natural or relaxed; forced [a *strained* laugh].

strainer (strān′ər) ***noun*** a sieve, filter, or other device used for straining.
strain·er • ***noun,*** *plural* **strainers**

strait (strāt) ***noun*** **1** a narrow body of water that joins two larger ones. **2** *usually* **straits** trouble or need [Due to the earthquake, the country is in desperate *straits*.]
strait • ***noun,*** *plural* **straits**
• The words **strait** and **straight** sound alike.
The explorer crossed the *strait* by boat.
She has *straight*, not curly, hair.

strand[1] (strand) ***verb*** **1** to run or drive into shallow water at the shore, or onto a reef or shoal [The storm *stranded* the ship on a sandbar.] **2** to leave in or be put into a difficult, helpless situation [We were *stranded* in a strange city with no money.]
strand • ***verb*** **stranded, stranding**

strand[2] (strand) ***noun*** **1** any of the threads, fibers, or wires that are twisted together to make string, rope, or cable. **2** anything like a string or rope [a *strand* of hair].
strand • ***noun,*** *plural* **strands**

strange (strānj) ***adjective*** **1** not known, seen, or heard before; not familiar [I saw a *strange* person at the door.] **2** different from what is usual; odd; peculiar [a *strange* costume].
adverb in a strange way [You have been acting very *strange* lately.]
strange • ***adjective*** & • ***adverb*** **stranger, strangest**

WORD CHOICES

Synonyms of **strange**

The words **strange, odd,** and **peculiar** share the meaning "unusual or unfamiliar."

strange customs
an *odd* way of speaking
a *peculiar* smell

stranger (strān′jər) ***noun*** **1** a person who is new to a place; outsider or foreigner [a *stranger* in town]. **2** a person not known to one [Don't speak to *strangers*.]
stran·ger • ***noun,*** *plural* **strangers**

strangle (straŋ′gəl) ***verb*** **1** to kill by squeezing the throat so as to stop the breathing. **2** to choke or suffocate in any way [We were *strangling* in the smoky air.]
stran·gle • ***verb*** **strangled, strangling**

strap (strap) ***noun*** **1** a narrow strip of leather, canvas, or other material for tying or holding things together. It often has a buckle. **2** any narrow strip like a strap [a shoulder *strap*].
verb to fasten with a strap [*Strap* the boxes together.]
strap • ***noun,*** *plural* **straps** • ***verb*** **strapped, strapping**

strategy (strat′ə jē) ***noun*** **1** the science of planning and directing military movements and operations. **2** skill in managing any mat-

a	cat	ō	go	ʉ	fur	ə =	a *in* ago
ā	ape	ô	law, for	ch	chin		e *in* agent
ä	cot, car	oo	look	sh	she		i *in* pencil
e	ten	ōō	tool	th	thin		o *in* atom
ē	me	oi	oil	*th*	then		u *in* circus
i	fit	ou	out	zh	measure		
ī	ice	u	up	ŋ	ring		

ter, especially by using tricks and schemes [It took *strategy* to get them to come with us.] **3** a clever plan or system.
strat·e·gy • *noun, plural for sense 3 only* **strategies**

stratosphere (strat′ə sfir) ***noun*** the part of the earth's atmosphere from about 12 miles to about 31 miles above the surface of the earth.
strat·o·sphere • ***noun***

straw (strô *or* strä) ***noun*** **1** the hollow stalks of wheat, rye, or other cereal plants that are left after the grain is removed. Straw is used as stuffing or can be woven into things such as hats or baskets. **2** a single one of such stalks [I picked the *straws* out of my hair.] **3** a slender tube of paper or plastic used for sucking a drink.
straw • *noun, plural for senses 2 and 3 only* **straws**

strawberry

strawberry (strô′ber′ē *or* strä′ber′ē) ***noun*** the small, red, juicy fruit of a low plant of the rose family.
straw·ber·ry • *noun, plural* **strawberries**

stray (strā) ***verb*** to wander from a certain place or path; roam [Don't *stray* from the camp. My thoughts *strayed* from the test.]
noun a lost or wandering person or animal.
stray • ***verb*** **strayed, straying** • *noun, plural* **strays**

streak (strēk) ***noun*** **1** a long, thin mark, stripe, or smear [a *streak* of dirt; gray *streaks* in his hair]. **2** a certain amount of some quality [He has a mean *streak*.] **3** a period or spell [a *streak* of bad luck].
verb **1** to mark with streaks [The sunset *streaked* the sky with many colors.] **2** to form streaks [Lightning *streaked* across the sky.] **3** to go fast; hurry [The car *streaked* away.]
streak • *noun, plural* **streaks**
• ***verb*** **streaked, streaking**

stream (strēm) ***noun*** **1** a body of flowing water; a brook or small river. **2** a steady flow of anything [a *stream* of cold air; a *stream* of light; a *stream* of cars].
verb **1** to flow in a stream [Rain *streamed* down the roof.] **2** to pour out or flow [Their eyes *streamed* with tears.] **3** to move without stopping or letting up [The crowd *streamed* out of the stadium.] **4** to float or fly [The flag *streamed* in the breeze.]
stream • *noun, plural* **streams**
• ***verb*** **streamed, streaming**

streamer (strēm′ər) ***noun*** a long, narrow strip of cloth, paper, or other material that hangs loose at one end.
stream·er • *noun, plural* **streamers**

streamline (strēm′līn) ***verb*** to make streamlined.
stream·line • ***verb*** **streamlined, streamlining**

streamlined (strēm′līnd) ***adjective*** **1** having a shape that allows smooth, easy movement through water or air [a *streamlined* boat, plane, or car]. **2** arranged so that it needs less time and effort [a *streamlined* system to manage the town's affairs].
stream·lined • ***adjective***

street (strēt) ***noun*** **1** a road in a city or town, often with the sidewalks and buildings along the sides [Let's take a stroll down Main *Street*.] **2** the people who live or work on a certain street [Our whole *street* gave money to the charity.]
street • *noun, plural* **streets**

streetcar (strēt′kär) ***noun*** a large vehicle on rails for carrying people along the streets.
street·car • *noun, plural* **streetcars**

strength (streŋkth *or* streŋth) ***noun*** **1** the quality of being strong; force; power [I have no *strength* in my arms.] **2** the power to hold off strain or stress; the condition of being able to last [the *strength* of a steel beam]. **3** the quality of having an effect on the senses in a strong way [the *strength* of a color, smell, or sound].

strengthen (streŋkth′ən *or* streŋth′ən) ***verb*** to make or become stronger [Exercise *strengthens* muscles.]
strength·en • ***verb*** **strengthened, strengthening**

strenuous (stren′yo͞o əs) ***adjective*** **1** needing much energy or effort [a *strenuous* task]. **2** very active or vigorous [There was *strenuous* opposition to his plan to build a parking lot.]
stren·u·ous • ***adjective***

S

strep throat (strep) [*an informal use*] *noun* a sore throat with a fever, caused by certain bacteria.

stress (stres) *noun* **1** strain or pressure [Too much *stress* on the feet can cause pain. Leaving things to the last minute can put you under a lot of *stress*.] **2** special attention; importance [Our doctor puts *stress* on good health habits.] **3** the special force that is given to a syllable or word in speaking; accent. In the word "stranger," the stress is on the first syllable.
verb to give special attention or importance to something; emphasize [My parents *stress* the importance of a good night's sleep.]
stress • *noun, plural for sense 3 only* **stresses** • *verb* **stressed, stressing**

stress mark *noun* a mark that is used to show the stress in a syllable or word. In this dictionary, the mark (**ʹ**) shows the strongest or heaviest stress, and the mark (ʹ) shows a stress that is weaker.
stress mark • *noun, plural* **stress marks**

stretch (strech) *verb* **1** to reach out or hold out [He *stretched* out a helping hand.] **2** to draw out the body, arms, or legs to full length [She *stretched* out on the sofa. He *stretched* his arms and yawned.] **3** to pull or spread something out to its full size or to a greater size [*Stretch* the rope between two trees. Knitted materials will *stretch*.] **4** to extend or continue over a certain distance or period of time [This road *stretches* for miles.]
noun **1** an act of stretching or the condition of being stretched [a *stretch* of the arms]. **2** the ability to be stretched [The elastic at the waist of my skirt has lost its *stretch*.] **3** an unbroken space of time [a *stretch* of ten days]. **4** an unbroken length or distance [a long *stretch* of beach].
stretch • *verb* **stretched, stretching** • *noun, plural for senses 1, 3, and 4 only* **stretches**

stretcher (strechʹər) *noun* a light frame covered with canvas or some other material. It is used for carrying people who are sick or hurt.
stretch·er • *noun, plural* **stretchers**

stricken (strikʹən) *verb a past participle of* **strike**.
adjective suffering from pain or trouble [a grief-*stricken* friend].
strick·en • *verb* • *adjective*

strict (strikt) *adjective* **1** keeping to rules in a careful, exact way [*strict* parents]. **2** never changing; rigid [a *strict* rule].
strict • *adjective* **stricter, strictest**

stridden (stridʹn) *verb past participle of* **stride**.
strid·den • *verb*

stride (strīd) *verb* to walk with long steps [He *strode* down the street.]
noun a long step in walking or running.
stride • *verb* **strode, stridden, striding** • *noun, plural* **strides**

strike (strīk) *verb* **1** to hit by giving a blow [Pat *struck* him in anger.] **2** to come against with force [The car *struck* the curb. I *struck* my head on the beam.] **3** to tell the time by making a sound [The clock *struck* midnight.] **4** to set on fire by rubbing [*Strike* a match.] **5** to attack [A rattlesnake makes noise before it *strikes*.] **6** to come upon; find [They drilled and *struck* oil.] **7** to hit one's mind or feelings [The idea just *struck* me. It *strikes* me as silly.] **8** to stop working in order to get an employer to improve the pay, the working conditions, or something else [The workers are *striking* for shorter hours.]
noun **1** the act of striking; a blow [One *strike* of the hammer drove the tack in.] **2** the act of stopping work in order to get higher pay or some other improvement [The *strike* lasted three months.] **3** in baseball, a good pitch over home plate that is not hit into fair territory by the batter. Three strikes put the batter out. **4** in bowling, the act of knocking down all ten pins with the first roll of the ball.
—strike out 1 in baseball, to put out by pitching three strikes [The pitcher *struck out* our best hitter.] **2** to be put out by three strikes [The batter *struck out*.] **—strike up** to begin [We *struck up* a friendship right away.]
strike • *verb* **struck, struck** or **stricken, striking** • *noun, plural* **strikes**

striking (strīʹkiŋ) *adjective* getting attention because of an unusual or outstanding quality [a *striking* dress].
strik·ing • *adjective*

string (striŋ) *noun* **1** a thin line of twisted fiber that is used for tying, pulling, or fastening; a thin cord or thick thread. **2** a narrow

a	cat	ō	go	ʉ	fur	ə =	a *in* ago
ā	ape	ô	law, for	ch	chin		e *in* agent
ä	cot, car	oo	look	sh	she		i *in* pencil
e	ten	ōō	tool	th	thin		o *in* atom
ē	me	oi	oil	*th*	then		u *in* circus
i	fit	ou	out	zh	measure		
ī	ice	u	up	ŋ	ring		

strip of fabric or leather that is used for fastening shoes or clothing; lace [apron *strings*]. **3** a number of objects on a string [a *string* of pearls]. **4** a number of things in a row [a *string* of houses] —Look for the WORD CHOICES box at the entry **row**[1]. **5** a thin cord of wire, gut, nylon, or other material that is plucked, struck, or played with a bow in order to make a musical sound. **6 strings** the stringed instruments in an orchestra or other musical group that are played with a bow.
verb **1** to put strings on [I learned how to *string* my tennis racket myself.] **2** to put on a string [They were *stringing* many different kinds of beads.] **3** to arrange in a series, as if on a string [We *strung* lights along the front of the house.] **4** to stretch like a string; extend [They *strung* a cable across the lake.]
string • ***noun,*** *plural* **strings** • ***verb*** **strung, stringing**

string bean ***noun*** a long, narrow green or yellow bean pod that is eaten as a vegetable.
string bean • ***noun,*** *plural* **string beans**

string bean

stringed instrument (striŋd) ***noun*** any of a group of musical instruments that have strings that vibrate to make the musical sounds. Stringed instruments are usually made of wood. Violins, guitars, harps, and zithers are all stringed instruments.
stringed instrument • ***noun,*** *plural* **stringed instruments**

stringy (striŋ′ē) ***adjective*** **1** like a string; long and thin [*stringy* muscles]. **2** having tough fibers [Celery is a very *stringy* vegetable.]
string·y • ***adjective*** **stringier, stringiest**

strip[1] (strip) ***verb*** **1** to take off one's clothes; undress [I *stripped* down to my underwear and dove in.] **2** to pull, tear, or take off [*Strip* the husks from the corn.] **3** to make bare or clear by taking things away [We *stripped* the room of furniture before painting.]
strip • ***verb*** **stripped, stripping**

strip[2] (strip) ***noun*** a long, narrow piece of something [a *strip* of land; a decorative *strip* of wood along the wall].
strip • ***noun,*** *plural* **strips**

stripe (strīp) ***noun*** a narrow band of a different color or material from the part around it [The American flag has red and white *stripes*.]
verb to mark with a stripe or stripes [The road was *striped* with a yellow line.]
stripe • ***noun,*** *plural* **stripes**
• ***verb*** **striped, striping**

strive (strīv) ***verb*** to try very hard [We must *strive* to do well.] —Look for the WORD CHOICES box at the entry **try**.
strive • ***verb*** **strove, striven, striving**

striven (striv′ən) ***verb*** *past participle of* **strive**.
striv·en • ***verb***

strode (strōd) ***verb*** *past tense of* **stride**.

stroke (strōk) ***noun*** **1** the act of striking; a blow [Three *strokes* of the hammer drove the nail in.] **2** a sudden action or event that has a powerful effect [a *stroke* of lightning; a *stroke* of luck]. **3** a sudden illness caused by the blocking or breaking of a blood vessel in the brain. **4** a mark made in writing, drawing, or painting [He outlined the tree with a few quick *strokes*.] **5** a combination of arm and leg movements that is repeated often [She swam with powerful *strokes*.]
verb to rub in a gentle way with one's hand or a brush [He *stroked* the cat's soft fur.]
stroke • ***noun,*** *plural* **strokes**
• ***verb*** **stroked, stroking**

stroll (strōl) ***verb*** to walk in a slow, easy way [They were *strolling* down the beach.]
noun a slow, easy walk [an afternoon *stroll*].
stroll • ***verb*** **strolled, strolling** • ***noun,*** *plural* **strolls**

stroller (strōl′ər) ***noun*** a light baby carriage that is like a chair.
stroll·er • ***noun,*** *plural* **strollers**

WORD CHOICES

Synonyms of **strong**

The words **strong, sturdy,** and **tough** share the meaning "solidly made and hard to break or destroy."

a *strong* wall
sturdy oaks
a *tough* fabric

strong (strôŋ) ***adjective*** **1** having great force or power; not weak; powerful [a *strong* person;

S

strong winds]. **2** able to last; durable; tough [a *strong* wall; a *strong* rope]. **3** having a powerful effect on the senses or mind; not mild [a *strong* taste; a *strong* smell].
strong • ***adjective*** **stronger, strongest**

stronghold (strôŋ′hōld) ***noun*** a place that is made strong against attack.
strong·hold • ***noun**, plural* **strongholds**

strove (strōv) ***verb*** *past tense of* **strive**.

struck (struk) ***verb*** *past tense and a past participle of* **strike**.

structure (struk′chər) ***noun*** **1** something that has been built [Buildings and dams are *structures*.] **2** the way in which something is put together; an arrangement, plan, or design [Plant cells have a different *structure* from animal cells.]
struc·ture • ***noun**, plural* **structures**

strudel (strōō͞d′əl) ***noun*** a kind of pastry made by rolling slices of fruit or cheese up in a thin sheet of dough and baking it.
stru·del • ***noun**, plural* **strudels**

struggle (strug′əl) ***verb*** **1** to fight hard [The wrestlers *struggled* with one another.] **2** to try very hard; strive [She *struggled* to learn French.] **3** to make one's way through something with great effort [He *struggled* through the tall reeds to get to the water's edge.]
noun **1** a great effort [It was a *struggle* just to stay awake.] **2** a fight or conflict.
strug·gle • ***verb*** **struggled, struggling** • ***noun**, plural* **struggles**

strum (strum) ***verb*** to play with long strokes across the strings [She *strummed* the banjo.]
noun the act or sound of strumming [We could hear the *strum* of a guitar.]
strum • ***verb*** **strummed, strumming** • ***noun**, plural* **strums**

strung (struŋ) ***verb*** *past tense and past participle of* **string**.

strut (strut) ***verb*** to walk in a self-confident way, especially in trying to attract attention [The singer *strutted* across the stage.]
noun a strutting walk.
strut • ***verb*** **strutted, strutting** • ***noun***

stub (stub) ***noun*** **1** a short piece that is left after the main part has been used up or cut off [a pencil *stub*]. **2** any part or thing that is short and blunt [a mere *stub* of a tail].
verb to strike against something [He *stubbed* his toe on the rock.]
stub • ***noun**, plural* **stubs** • ***verb*** **stubbed, stubbing**

stubble (stub′əl) ***noun*** **1** the short stumps of grain that are left standing after the harvest. **2** any short, uneven growth [a *stubble* of beard].
stub·ble • ***noun***

stubborn (stub′ərn) ***adjective*** **1** set on having one's way; not willing to give in [a *stubborn* person; a *stubborn* mule]. **2** hard to treat or deal with [a *stubborn* cold].
stub·born • ***adjective*** **stubborner, stubbornest**

stubby (stub′ē) ***adjective*** **1** short and thick [*stubby* fingers]. **2** short and dense [a *stubby* beard].
stub·by • ***adjective*** **stubbier, stubbiest**

stucco (stuk′ō) ***noun*** plaster used for coating inside or outside walls. It often has a rough or wavy finish.
stuc·co • ***noun***

stuck (stuk) ***verb*** *past tense and past participle of* **stick**.

stuck-up (stuk′up) [*an informal word*] ***adjective*** having too high an opinion of oneself; conceited.

stud (stud) ***noun*** a small knob or nail with a round head. It is used to decorate leather and other materials.
verb to decorate with studs or objects like studs [Rubies *studded* the crown.]
stud • ***noun**, plural* **studs** • ***verb*** **studded, studding**

student (stōō͞d′nt *or* styōō͞d′nt) ***noun*** a person who studies at a school or college.
stu·dent • ***noun**, plural* **students**

studio (stōō′dē ō *or* styōō′dē ō) ***noun*** **1** a room or building where an artist or photographer works. **2** a place where movies are made. **3** a place from which radio or TV programs are broadcast or where recordings are made.
stu·di·o • ***noun**, plural* **studios**

study (stud′ē) ***verb*** **1** to try to learn by reading and thinking [She *studies* history as a hobby.] **2** to read in order to understand and remember [He *studied* the poem and memorized it.]

a cat	ō go	ʉ fur	ə = a *in* ago
ā ape	ô law, for	ch chin	e *in* agent
ä cot, car	oo look	sh she	i *in* pencil
e ten	ōō tool	th thin	o *in* atom
ē me	oi oil	*th* then	u *in* circus
i fit	ou out	zh measure	
ī ice	u up	ŋ ring	

3 to take a class or course in [My mother is *studying* science at college.] **4** to look at or into in a careful way; examine or investigate [They are *studying* the problem of pollution.]
noun **1** the act of reading or thinking in order to learn something [It takes years of *study* and practice to be a fine musician.] **2** careful and serious examination [a *study* of traffic problems]. **3 studies** education; schooling [I continued my *studies* at college.] **4** a room used for studying or reading.
stud·y • *verb* **studied, studying, studies** • *noun, plural for senses 2, 3, and 4 only* **studies**

stuff (stuf) *noun* **1** what anything is made of; material. **2** a collection of belongings or other objects [I emptied the *stuff* from my bag.]
verb **1** to fill or pack the inside of something [My pockets were *stuffed* with candy.] **2** to force or push [I *stuffed* the money into my wallet.] **3** to fill with seasoning, bread crumbs, and other foods before roasting [The cook *stuffed* the turkey.] **4** to eat too much or too quickly [Stop *stuffing* yourself.]
stuff • *noun* • *verb* **stuffed, stuffing**

stuffing (stuf′iŋ) *noun* **1** the soft, springy material used to stuff pillows, cushions, and other articles. **2** a mixture of seasoning, bread crumbs, and various other foods that is put into a turkey or other food.
stuff·ing • *noun*

stuffy (stuf′ē) *adjective* **1** having little fresh air; close [a *stuffy* room]. **2** having the nose stopped up from a cold or allergies [My head feels *stuffy*.] **3** [*an informal use*] dull, old-fashioned, or pompous [a *stuffy* person].
stuff·y • *adjective* **stuffier, stuffiest**

stumble (stum′bəl) *verb* **1** to trip or almost fall in walking or running [I *stumbled* a couple of times in the dark.] **2** to walk in an unsteady way [The tired boy *stumbled* off to bed.] **3** to find or come upon by chance or luck [We *stumbled* upon a clue to the mystery.] **4** to speak or act in a confused way [She forgot her speech and began to *stumble*.]
stum·ble • *verb* **stumbled, stumbling**

stump (stump) *noun* **1** the lower part of a tree or plant left in the ground after most of the trunk or stem has been cut down. **2** the part of anything that is left after the rest has been removed.
verb [*an informal use*] to puzzle; to make someone unable to answer [Her question *stumped* the expert.]
stump • *noun, plural* **stumps** • *verb* **stumped, stumping**

stun (stun) *verb* **1** to make someone unable to feel or think [The blow *stunned* him, and he fell.] **2** to shock in a great or deep way [The news of his death *stunned* us.] —Look for the WORD CHOICES box at the entry **shock**[1].
stun • *verb* **stunned, stunning**

stung (stuŋ) *verb past tense and past participle of* **sting**.

stunk (stuŋk) *verb a past tense and the past participle of* **stink**.

stunning (stun′iŋ) *adjective* **1** having the power to stun [a *stunning* blow]. **2** [*an informal use*] very attractive, excellent, or remarkable [a *stunning* victory].
stun·ning • *adjective*

stunt[1] (stunt) *verb* to keep from growing or developing [Poor soil *stunted* the plants.]
stunt • *verb* **stunted, stunting**

stunt[2] (stunt) *noun* something that is done for a thrill, to show off a person's skill, or to get attention [a dangerous *stunt*].
stunt • *noun, plural* **stunts**

stupid (sto͞o′pid *or* styo͞o′pid) *adjective* **1** slow to learn or understand; not intelligent. **2** foolish or silly [a *stupid* idea].
stu·pid • *adjective* **stupider, stupidest**

stupidity (sto͞o pid′i tē *or* styo͞o pid′i tē) *noun* the condition of being stupid [His poor grades are due to laziness, not *stupidity*.]
stu·pid·i·ty • *noun*

sturdy (stʉr′dē) *adjective* **1** strong; hardy [*sturdy* arms; a *sturdy* worker]. **2** built or made so that it is strong and able to last [a *sturdy* table] —Look for the WORD CHOICES box at the entry **strong**.
stur·dy • *adjective* **sturdier, sturdiest**

sturgeon

sturgeon (stʉr′jən) *noun* a large food fish with a long snout and rows of hard plates on the skin. Fine caviar comes from sturgeons.
stur·geon • *noun, plural* **sturgeons** or **sturgeon**

S

stutter (stut′ər) *verb* to speak with short stops that one cannot control, often repeating certain sounds.
noun the act or habit of stuttering.
stut·ter • *verb* **stuttered, stuttering** • *noun*

St. Vincent and the Grenadines (sānt vin′ sənt and *th*ə gren′ə dēnz) a country on an island in the West Indies. It includes some small nearby islands.
St. Vin·cent and the Gren·a·dines

sty[1] (stī) *noun* a pen for pigs.
sty • *noun, plural* **sties**

sty[2] (stī) *noun* a swollen, sore gland on the rim of the eyelid.
sty • *noun, plural* **sties**

style (stīl) *noun* **1** the way in which anything is written, spoken, made, or done [I don't like this painter's *style*.] **2** the way in which most people dress and act in any particular period; fashion [*Styles* in clothes keep changing.] **3** sort; kind; type [a *style* of skate for racing].
verb to design, make, or arrange in a particular way [I like the way he *styles* my hair.]
style • *noun, plural* **styles** • *verb* **styled, styling**

stylish (stīl′ish) *adjective* in keeping with the latest style; fashionable [a *stylish* coat].
styl·ish • *adjective*

stylus (stī′ləs) *noun* **1** a sharp, pointed device that moves in the groove of a phonograph record; phonograph needle. **2** a pointed tool used for writing in wax or some other soft material.
sty·lus • *noun, plural* **styluses**

Styrofoam (stī′rə fōm) *trademark* a kind of lightweight, plastic material that has many uses.
Sty·ro·foam • *trademark*

sub (sub) *noun* **1** *a short form of* **submarine**. **2** *a short form of* **substitute**.
verb [*an informal use*] to be a substitute for another person [She *subbed* for me again.]
sub • *noun, plural* **subs** • *verb* **subbed, subbing**

sub- *a prefix meaning:* **1** under or below [*Subsoil* is soil under the topsoil.] **2** not quite; somewhat [A *subtropical* region is somewhat tropical in climate.] **3** forming or being a division [A *subcommittee* is a division of a committee.]

subdue (səb do͞o′ *or* səb dyo͞o′) *verb* to get control over someone or something; to overcome [They *subdued* the angry bear.]
sub·due • *verb* **subdued, subduing**

subdued (səb do͞od′ *or* səb dyo͞od′) *adjective* **1** not strong or harsh [*subdued* lighting]. **2** more quiet than is usual for a particular person [He was very *subdued* after the quarrel.]
sub·dued • *adjective*

subj. *abbreviation for* subject.

subject (sub′jekt *for adj. and n.;* səb jekt′ *for v.*) *adjective* **1** likely to have [She is *subject* to fits of anger.] **2** depending on some action or condition [Our plans are *subject* to the weather.]
noun **1** a person who owes allegiance to a ruler. British citizens are subjects of Queen Elizabeth II. **2** a person or thing being discussed or examined [Presidents have been the *subject* of many books. Rats are used as the *subjects* of experiments.] —Look for the WORD CHOICES box at the entry **theme**. **3** the word or group of words in a sentence about which something is said. In the sentence "Boys and girls enjoy sports," the subject is "boys and girls." **4** a course of study in school.
verb **1** to make undergo [The suspect was *subjected* to much questioning by the police.] **2** to make liable [Her poor diet *subjected* her to serious illness.]
sub·ject • *adjective* • *noun, plural* **subjects** • *verb* **subjected, subjecting**

subjective (səb jek′tiv) *adjective* resulting from a person's own feelings or thinking rather than from the facts.
sub·jec·tive • *adjective*

submarine (sub′mə rēn) *noun* a type of ship that can travel underwater.
sub·ma·rine • *noun, plural* **submarines**

submerge (sub mʉrj′) *verb* to put, go, or stay underwater.
sub·merge • *verb* **submerged, submerging**

submit (sub mit′) *verb* **1** to give or offer to others for them to look over or decide about [A proposal for a new parking lot was *submitted* to the club members.] **2** to give in to the power or control of another; surrender [We will never *submit* to the enemy.]
sub·mit • *verb* **submitted, submitting**

a	cat	ō	go	ʉ	fur	ə = a *in* ago
ā	ape	ô	law, for	ch	chin	e *in* agent
ä	cot, car	oo	look	sh	she	i *in* pencil
e	ten	o͞o	tool	th	thin	o *in* atom
ē	me	oi	oil	*th*	then	u *in* circus
i	fit	ou	out	zh	measure	
ī	ice	u	up	ŋ	ring	

subordinate (sə bôrd′n ət) *adjective* **1** low or lower in rank; less important [a *subordinate* position]. **2** under the power or control of another [The team members are *subordinate* to the captain.]
noun a subordinate person.
sub·or·di·nate • *adjective* • *noun, plural* **subordinates**

subordinate clause *noun* a clause that cannot stand alone as a complete sentence. In the sentence "They will visit us if they can," the words "if they can" form a subordinate clause.
subordinate clause • *noun, plural* **subordinate clauses**

subscribe (səb skrīb′) *verb* to agree to take and pay for [We used to *subscribe* to this magazine.]
sub·scribe • *verb* **subscribed, subscribing**

subscription (səb skrip′shen) *noun* an agreement to take and pay for a magazine, theater tickets, or something else for a particular period of time.
sub·scrip·tion • *noun, plural* **subscriptions**

subside (səb sīd′) *verb* **1** to sink to a lower level [The water in the tank *subsided.*] **2** to become less intense or active [The crowd's enthusiasm *subsided* as the home team played badly.]
sub·side • *verb* **subsided, subsiding**

subsistence (səb sis′təns) *noun* a means of staying alive, especially just enough food, clothing, and shelter and no more [The job paid only enough for our *subsistence.*]
sub·sist·ence • *noun*

substance (sub′stəns) *noun* **1** the material of which something is made. **2** the basic part of something; meaning [The *substance* of the letter was that they wanted to come home.]
sub·stance • *noun, plural* **substances**

substantial (səb stan′shəl) *adjective* **1** of or having substance; real or true [Your fears turned out not to be *substantial.*] **2** strong; solid; firm [This bridge does not look very *substantial.*] **3** more than usual; large [A *substantial* number of children forgot to bring in their money.]
sub·stan·tial • *adjective*

substitute (sub′sti to͞ot′ *or* sub′sti tyo͞ot′) *noun* a person or thing that takes the place of another.
verb **1** to use something or someone as a substitute [We *substituted* milk for cream.] **2** to be a substitute [I *substituted* for the star player.]
sub·sti·tute • *noun, plural* **substitutes** • *verb* **substituted, substituting**

subtle (sut′l) *adjective* **1** not obvious, sharp, or strong; faint and delicate [a *subtle* smell]. **2** not open or direct; clever [a *subtle* hint].
sub·tle • *adjective* **subtler, subtlest**

WORD CHOICES

Synonyms of **subtle**

The words **subtle, indirect,** and **roundabout** share the meaning "not open or direct."

a *subtle* hint
an *indirect* request for help
a *roundabout* reply to my question

subtract (səb trakt′) *verb* to take away a part from a whole or one number from another [If 3 is *subtracted* from 5, then 2 remains.]
sub·tract • *verb* **subtracted, subtracting**

subtraction (səb trak′shən) *noun* the act of subtracting one part or number from another.
sub·trac·tion • *noun*

subtrahend (sub′trə hend) *noun* a number to be subtracted from another number [In the problem 5 - 3 = 2, the *subtrahend* is 3.]
sub·tra·hend • *noun, plural* **subtrahends**

subtropical (sub′träp′i kəl) *adjective* nearly tropical in climate [a *subtropical* region].
sub·trop·i·cal • *adjective*

suburb (sub′ərb) *noun* a district that is on or near the outskirts of a city. Some suburbs are towns or cities themselves. Most suburbs have mainly homes, with few businesses.
sub·urb • *noun, plural* **suburbs**

suburban (sə bur′bən) *adjective* of or like a suburb or the people who live in a suburb [a *suburban* style of living].
sub·ur·ban • *adjective*

subway (sub′wā) *noun* an underground public transportation system in a city. It uses cars that run on rails and are powered by electricity.
sub·way • *noun, plural* **subways**

succeed (sək sēd′) *verb* **1** to manage to do what was planned [I *succeeded* in getting them to come with us.] **2** to come next after;

to follow someone or something [Bill Clinton *succeeded* George Bush as president.]
suc·ceed • *verb* **succeeded, succeeding**

success (sək ses′) *noun* **1** the result that was hoped for [Did you have *success* in training your dog?] **2** the fact of becoming rich, famous, or important [Her *success* did not change her.] **3** a successful person or thing [Our report was a complete *success*.]
suc·cess • *noun, plural for senses 1 and 3 only* **successes**

successful (sək ses′fəl) *adjective* **1** having success; turning out well [a *successful* meeting]. **2** having become rich, famous, or important [a *successful* lawyer].
suc·cess·ful • *adjective*

succession (sək sesh′ən) *noun* **1** a number of persons or things coming one after another [A *succession* of warm days is always welcome.] —Look for the WORD CHOICES box at the entry **series**. **2** the act of coming after some other person or thing [The explosions came in quick *succession*.]
suc·ces·sion • *noun, plural for sense 1 only* **successions**

successive (sək ses′iv) *adjective* coming in regular order without a break [I won six *successive* games.]
suc·ces·sive • *adjective*

successor (sək ses′ər) *noun* a person who follows another to a job or position.
suc·ces·sor • *noun, plural* **successors**

such (such) *adjective* **1** of this or that kind [*Such* rugs are expensive.] **2** like those mentioned or meant [It was on just *such* a night that he was born.] **3** so much or so great [We had *such* fun that nobody left.]
pronoun a person or thing of that kind [We have fruit juices and soft drinks and *such*.]
—**such as** for example [She speaks several foreign languages, *such as* French and German.]

suck (suk) *verb* **1** to draw a liquid into the mouth by using the tongue, cheeks, and lips to create a vacuum inside the mouth [He *sucked* the chocolate milk through a straw.] **2** to draw in or inhale [They *sucked* in enough smoke to cause choking.] **3** to hold in the mouth and lick with the tongue [I *sucked* a piece of candy.]
suck • *verb* **sucked, sucking**

sucker (suk′ər) *noun* **1** a part of the body of certain animals, such as a leech or octopus, that is used to hold tight to something. **2** a piece of hard candy on the end of a short stick. **3** [*a slang use*] a person who is easily fooled or cheated.
suck·er • *noun, plural* **suckers**

suction (suk′shən) *noun* the act of drawing air out of a space to make a vacuum. This causes the surrounding air, water, or other substance to move into the empty space [*Suction* is created when you drink through a straw.]
suc·tion • *noun*

Sudan (so͞o dan′) a country in northeastern Africa, south of Egypt.
Su·dan

sudden (sud′n) *adjective* **1** happening or appearing without warning; not expected [a *sudden* storm]. **2** done or taking place in a quick or abrupt way [a *sudden* change in direction].
sud·den • *adjective*

suds (sudz) *plural noun* the foam on the surface of soapy water.

sue (so͞o) *verb* to begin a lawsuit in court against someone [My parents *sued* the reckless driver.]
sue • *verb* **sued, suing**

suede (swād) *noun* tanned leather with the flesh side rubbed until it is soft like velvet.

Suez Canal (so͞o ez′ kə nal′) a ship canal in Egypt that joins the Mediterranean and Red seas.
Su·ez Ca·nal

suffer (suf′ər) *verb* **1** to feel or have pain or discomfort [I *suffered* from a headache.] **2** to experience or undergo something [The team *suffered* a loss when the best player was hurt.] **3** to become worse or go from good to bad [Her grades *suffered* when she didn't study.]
suf·fer • *verb* **suffered, suffering**

suffering (suf′ər iŋ *or* suf′riŋ) *noun* pain, sorrow, or loss [War causes great *suffering*.] —Look for the WORD CHOICES box at the entry **distress**.
suf·fer·ing • *noun, plural* **sufferings**

a cat	ō go	ʉ fur	ə = a *in* ago
ā ape	ô law, for	ch chin	e *in* agent
ä cot, car	o͝o look	sh she	i *in* pencil
e ten	o͞o tool	th thin	o *in* atom
ē me	oi oil	*th* then	u *in* circus
i fit	ou out	zh measure	
ī ice	u up	ŋ ring	

sufficient (sə fish′ənt) *adjective* as much as is needed; enough [a *sufficient* supply].
suf·fi·cient • *adjective*

suffix (suf′iks) *noun* a syllable or group of syllables, joined to the end of a word to change its meaning. Some common suffixes are *-able*, *-ed*, *-ly*, and *-ness*.
suf·fix • *noun, plural* **suffixes**

suffocate (suf′ə kāt) *verb* **1** to kill by cutting off the supply of air or oxygen. **2** to die from this cause. **3** to keep from breathing easily. **4** to have trouble breathing [I am *suffocating* from the heat in this room.]
suf·fo·cate • *verb* **suffocated, suffocating**

sugar (shoog′ər) *noun* a sweet food substance. It is a crystal that dissolves in water.
sug·ar • *noun*

sugar cane *noun* a tall grass that is grown in hot climates. Most sugar used for food comes from sugar cane.

sugar cane

sugarless (shoog′ər ləs) *adjective* having no sugar [*sugarless* gum]. This word is used especially to describe food sweetened by an artificial substance.
sug·ar·less • *adjective*

suggest (səg jest′) *verb* **1** to mention as something to think over or act on [I *suggest* we meet at the theater.] **2** to bring to mind as something similar or in some way connected [The white sand *suggests* snow.]
sug·gest • *verb* **suggested, suggesting**

suggestion (səg jes′chən) *noun* **1** the act of suggesting [It was done at your *suggestion*.] **2** something suggested [Give me a *suggestion* for solving this problem.]
sug·ges·tion • *noun, plural for sense 2 only* **suggestions**

suicide (so͞o′i sīd′) *noun* the act of killing oneself on purpose.
su·i·cide • *noun, plural* **suicides**

suit (so͞ot) *noun* **1** a set of clothes that match. Usually the jacket and pants or skirt are of the same fabric. **2** *a short form of* **lawsuit**. **3** any of the four matching sets of cards that are used in card games. Diamonds, hearts, clubs, and spades are the four suits.
verb **1** to meet the needs of; be right for [This hat *suits* me fine.] **2** to make something fit [The dance was *suited* to the music.]
suit • *noun, plural* **suits** • *verb* **suited, suiting**

suitable (so͞ot′ə bəl) *adjective* right for the purpose; proper [a *suitable* gift] —Look for the WORD CHOICES box at the entry **fit**[1].
suit·a·ble • *adjective*

suitcase (so͞ot′kās) *noun* a case for carrying clothing and other items when traveling. It has a handle and is usually small enough to be carried by one person.
suit·case • *noun, plural* **suitcases**

suite (swēt) *noun* **1** a group of connected rooms that are used together [a hotel *suite*]. **2** a piece of music made up of several parts.
suite • *noun, plural* **suites**
● The words **suite** and **sweet** sound alike.
We reserved a *suite* at the hotel.
The icing on the cake is too *sweet*.

suitor (so͞ot′ər) *noun* a man who is courting a woman.
suit·or • *noun, plural* **suitors**

sulfur (sul′fər) *noun* a pale-yellow solid substance that is a chemical element. It burns with a blue flame and gives off choking fumes. Sulfur is used in gunpowder and fertilizer.
sul·fur • *noun*

sulk (sulk) *verb* to be sulky.
sulk • *verb* **sulked, sulking**

sulky (sul′kē) *adjective* showing that one is unhappy, dissatisfied, or angry by keeping to oneself.
sulk·y • *adjective* **sulkier, sulkiest**

sullen (sul′ən) *adjective* silent and keeping to oneself because one feels angry, bitter, or hurt [They've had a *sullen* attitude since they lost the game.]
sul·len • *adjective*

sultan (sult′n) *noun* a ruler in certain Muslim countries.
sul·tan • *noun, plural* **sultans**

sultry (sul′trē) *adjective* hot and damp, without a breeze [a *sultry* summer day].
sul·try • *adjective* **sultrier, sultriest**

sum (sum) *noun* **1** a result or total gotten by adding things together. **2** an amount of money [The *sum* paid was $100.]
sum • *noun, plural* **sums**
● The words **sum** and **some** sound alike.
The *sum* of 20 and 40 is 60.
Some people never learn.

S

summarize (sum′ər īz) ***verb*** to tell in a few words [Please *summarize* the plot of the movie.]
sum·ma·rize • ***verb*** **summarized, summarizing**

summary (sum′ər ē) ***noun*** a brief report that tells the main ideas or points in a few words.
sum·ma·ry • ***noun,*** *plural* **summaries**

WORD CHOICES

Synonyms of **summary**

The words **summary, digest,** and **outline** share the meaning "a brief report that tells only the main points."

a *summary* of the novel's plot
a *digest* of recent law cases
an *outline* of English history

summer (sum′ər) ***noun*** the warmest season of the year, following spring.
verb to spend the summer somewhere [We *summered* in Maine.]
sum·mer • ***noun,*** *plural* **summers**
• ***verb*** **summered, summering**

summertime (sum′ər tīm) ***noun*** the season of summer.
sum·mer·time • ***noun,*** *plural* **summertimes**

summit (sum′it) ***noun*** the highest point; top [the *summit* of the hill] —Look for the WORD CHOICES box at the entry **climax**.
sum·mit • ***noun,*** *plural* **summits**

summon (sum′ən) ***verb*** to call together; call or send for [The team was *summoned* to the gymnasium.]
sum·mon • ***verb*** **summoned, summoning**

summons (sum′ənz) ***noun*** an order to appear somewhere or to do something [He received a *summons* to appear in court.]
sum·mons • ***noun,*** *plural* **summonses**

sun (sun) ***noun*** **1** the very hot, bright star that is the center of the solar system. The earth revolves around it and receives heat and light from it. **2** the heat or light of the sun [The *sun* is in my eyes.]
verb to stay in the heat and light of the sun [We *sunned* ourselves by the pool.]
sun • ***noun*** • ***verb*** **sunned, sunning**
• The words **sun** and **son** sound alike.
The window let in enough *sun* for warmth.
They have two daughters and a *son*.

Sun. *abbreviation for* Sunday.

sunbathe (sun′bā*th*) ***verb*** to expose the body to sunshine or to a sunlamp.
sun·bathe • ***verb*** **sunbathed, sunbathing**

sunbeam (sun′bēm) ***noun*** a beam of sunlight.
sun·beam • ***noun,*** *plural* **sunbeams**

sunblock (sun′bläk) ***noun*** a lotion or cream which helps prevent sunburn by blocking some of the harmful rays of the sun.
sun·block • ***noun***

sunburn (sun′burn) ***noun*** a condition in which the skin is red and sore from being in the sun or under a sunlamp too long.
verb to get a sunburn [I *sunburn* easily.]
sun·burn • ***noun,*** *plural* **sunburns**
• ***verb*** **sunburned** or **sunburnt, sunburning**

sunburnt (sun′burnt) ***verb*** *a past tense and a past participle of* **sunburn**.
sun·burnt • ***verb***

sundae (sun′dā) ***noun*** a serving of ice cream that is covered with syrup, nuts, and other foods.
sun·dae • ***noun,*** *plural* **sundaes**

Sunday (sun′dā) ***noun*** the first day of the week. Abbreviated **Sun.**
Sun·day • ***noun,*** *plural* **Sundays**

WORD HISTORY

Sunday

Sunday comes from a thousand-year-old English word that means "sun's day." The English name was a translation of this day's name in Latin.

Sunday school ***noun*** a school which holds classes on Sunday for the teaching of religion.

sundown (sun′doun) ***noun*** *another name for* **sunset**.
sun·down • ***noun***

a cat	ō go	u fur	ə = a *in* ago
ā ape	ô law, for	ch chin	e *in* agent
ä cot, car	oo look	sh she	i *in* pencil
e ten	ōō tool	th thin	o *in* atom
ē me	oi oil	*th* then	u *in* circus
i fit	ou out	zh measure	
ī ice	u up	ŋ ring	

sunflower (sun′flou ər) ***noun*** a tall plant with large, yellow flowers like daisies. The seeds can be eaten or used to make an oil.
sun·flow·er • ***noun,*** *plural* **sunflowers**

sunflower

sung (suŋ) ***verb*** *past participle of* **sing.**

sunglasses (sun′glas əs) ***plural noun*** eyeglasses that have dark lenses to shade the eyes from the sun.
sun·glass·es • ***plural noun***

sunk (suŋk) ***verb*** *a past tense and the past participle of* **sink.**

sunken (suŋk′ən) ***adjective*** **1** sunk in water or other liquid [a *sunken* boat]. **2** in or forming a hollow [*sunken* eyes].
sunk·en • ***adjective***

sunlamp (sun′lamp) ***noun*** an electric lamp that gives off ultraviolet rays like those of sunlight. It is used for indoor tanning without the sun.
sun·lamp • ***noun,*** *plural* **sunlamps**

sunlight (sun′līt) ***noun*** the light from the sun.
sun·light • ***noun***

sunny (sun′ē) ***adjective*** **1** full of or bright with sunlight [a *sunny* day; a *sunny* room]. **2** cheerful, bright, or happy [a *sunny* person].
sun·ny • ***adjective*** **sunnier, sunniest**

sunrise (sun′rīz) ***noun*** **1** the rising of the sun each day in the eastern sky. **2** the time when the sun rises [We will leave at *sunrise*.]
sun·rise • ***noun,*** *plural* **sunrises**

sunset (sun′set) ***noun*** **1** the setting of the sun each day in the western sky. **2** the time when the sun sets [We stopped at *sunset*.]
sun·set • ***noun,*** *plural* **sunsets**

sunshine (sun′shīn) ***noun*** the light and heat from the sun.
sun·shine • ***noun***

sunstroke (sun′strōk) ***noun*** an illness caused by being out in the hot sun too long.
sun·stroke • ***noun***

sunup (sun′up) ***noun*** *another name for* **sunrise.**
sun·up • ***noun***

sup (sup) ***verb*** to have dinner.
sup • ***verb*** **supped, supping**

super (so͞o′pər) [*an informal word*] ***adjective*** excellent or outstanding [a *super* team].
su·per • ***adjective***

super- *a prefix meaning:* **1** over or above; on top of [A *superstructure* is a structure built on top of another.] **2** very or very much; more than normal [A *supersensitive* person is one who is more sensitive than a normal person.] **3** greater than others of its kind [A *supermarket* is bigger than other markets.]

superb (sə purb′) ***adjective*** excellent or outstanding [a *superb* meal].
su·perb • ***adjective***

superficial (so͞o′pər fish′əl) ***adjective*** on the surface only; not deep [a *superficial* cut].
su·per·fi·cial • ***adjective***

superhuman (so͞o′pər hyo͞o′mən) ***adjective*** greater than that of a normal person [*superhuman* strength].
su·per·hu·man • ***adjective***

superintendent (so͞o′pər in ten′dənt) ***noun*** **1** a person in charge of a school system or some other type of large organization. **2** a person who manages an apartment building or some other type of building.
su·per·in·tend·ent • ***noun,*** *plural* **superintendents**

superior (sə pir′ē ər) ***adjective*** **1** higher in rank or position [a *superior* officer in the army]. **2** above average quality, value, or skill; excellent [*superior* jumping ability]. **3** showing or having a feeling of being better than others [a *superior* attitude].
noun a person who is of higher rank or has greater skills.
su·pe·ri·or • ***adjective*** • ***noun,*** *plural* **superiors**

Superior (sə pir′ē ər), **Lake** the largest of the Great Lakes. It is the one farthest west.
Su·pe·ri·or, Lake

superlative (sə pur′lə tiv) ***adjective*** **1** of the highest sort; being the very best [a *superlative* performance]. **2** designating the form of an adjective or adverb that shows the greatest degree in meaning. The superlative degree is usually made with the suffix *-est* or the word *most.* For example: *warmest,* from *warm; most beautiful,* from *beautiful;* and *best,* from *good* and *well.*
noun the superlative degree or the superlative form of a word [The *superlative* of "good" is "best."]

su·per·la·tive • *adjective* • *noun, plural* **superlatives**

superman (so͞o′pər man) *noun* a man who seems to have greater powers and ability than a normal person.
su·per·man • *noun, plural* **supermen**

supermarket (so͞o′pər mär′kət) *noun* a large food store in which buyers pick out their food from open shelves and pay for it near the exit.
su·per·mar·ket • *noun, plural* **supermarkets**

supernatural (so͞o′pər nach′ər əl) *adjective* outside or beyond the known forces of nature; especially, describing or involving God or a god [a *supernatural* event].
su·per·nat·u·ral • *adjective*

supersonic (so͞o′pər sän′ik) *adjective* of or moving at a speed greater than the speed of sound [a *supersonic* jet plane].
su·per·son·ic • *adjective*

superstar (so͞o′pər stär) *noun* a very famous athlete or entertainer who is considered to be more talented than most others.
su·per·star • *noun, plural* **superstars**

superstition (so͞o′pər stish′ən) *noun* a belief or practice that comes from fear and ignorance and that is against the laws of science or against what is generally thought of as true and rational. A common superstition is that if a black cat crosses your path you will have bad luck.
su·per·sti·tion • *noun, plural* **superstitions**

superstitious (so͞o′pər stish′əs) *adjective* caused by or believing in superstitions.
su·per·sti·tious • *adjective*

supervise (so͞o′pər vīz) *verb* to direct or manage a group of people; be in charge of.
su·per·vise • *verb* **supervised, supervising**

supervision (so͞o′pər vizh′ən) *noun* the direction or management of people and their activities.
su·per·vi·sion • *noun*

supervisor (so͞o′pər vī′zər) *noun* a person who manages other people; director.
su·per·vi·sor • *noun, plural* **supervisors**

supper (sup′ər) *noun* **1** the last meal of the day. It is eaten in the evening. **2** a party or event in the evening at which food is served [a church *supper*].
sup·per • *noun, plural* **suppers**

supplement (sup′lə mənt *for n.;* sup′lə ment *for v.*) *noun* something added to complete another thing or to make up for what was missing [Vitamin pills are a *supplement* to a poor diet.]
verb to add as a supplement.
sup·ple·ment • *noun, plural* **supplements** • *verb* **supplemented, supplementing**

supply (sə plī′) *verb* **1** to give what is needed [This cereal does *supply* several of the necessary vitamins.] **2** to take care of the needs of [We will *supply* the workers with tools.]
noun **1** the amount that one has available for use [The birds have a large *supply* of seeds stored away.] **2** **supplies** materials that are needed to do something [We need new school *supplies*.]
sup·ply • *verb* **supplied, supplying, supplies** • *noun, plural* **supplies**

support (sə pôrt′) *verb* **1** to hold up [The ladder is too weak to *support* you.] **2** to earn a living for; provide for [The parents work to *support* their family.] **3** to help prove; show to be true [Use examples to *support* your idea.]
noun **1** the act of supporting or the condition of being supported [This wall needs *support*.] **2** a person or thing that supports.
sup·port • *verb* **supported, supporting** • *noun, plural for sense 2 only* **supports**

WORD CHOICES

Synonyms of **support**

The words **support**, **back**, and **uphold** share the meaning "to give help or one's approval to."

She *supported* the candidate who won.

He needs patrons to *back* his project.

I will *uphold* your right to speak at the meeting.

suppose (sə pōz′) *verb* **1** to assume that something is true or possible [Let's *suppose* we win the game.] **2** to believe or guess; think [I *suppose* you are right.] **3** to expect [It is *supposed* to rain today.]
sup·pose • *verb* **supposed, supposing**

a	cat	ō	go	ʉ	fur	ə = a	*in* ago
ā	ape	ô	law, for	ch	chin	e	*in* agent
ä	cot, car	o͝o	look	sh	she	i	*in* pencil
e	ten	o͞o	tool	th	thin	o	*in* atom
ē	me	oi	oil	*th*	then	u	*in* circus
i	fit	ou	out	zh	measure		
ī	ice	u	up	ŋ	ring		

supreme (sə prēm′) *adjective* highest in power, rank, quality, degree, or authority [succeeding by a *supreme* effort].
su·preme • *adjective*

Supreme Being *another name for* **God**.

Supreme Court *noun* **1** the highest court in the U.S. It has nine judges. **2** the highest court in most States.

sure (shoor) *adjective* **1** not capable of failing; safe or certain [a *sure* cure; a *sure* friend]. **2** firm or steady [*sure* footing on the steps]. **3** without doubt; true or certain [I am *sure* we can go.] **4** not possible to avoid [a *sure* defeat].
adverb [*an informal use*] without a doubt; indeed [*Sure*, I'll go.]
sure • *adjective* **surer, surest** • *adverb*

surely (shoor′lē) *adverb* in a sure way; without a doubt [*Surely* you care about your pet.]
sure·ly • *adverb*

surf

surf (surf) *noun* the waves of the sea as they break against the shore.
verb **1** to balance oneself on a board while riding on these waves. **2** [*an informal use*] to browse quickly through television channels, computer files, or sources of information on the Internet.
surf • *noun* • *verb* **surfed, surfing**
• The words **surf** and **serf** sound alike.
We watched the *surf* break on the shore.
A *serf* and his family harvested crops.

surface (sur′fəs) *noun* **1** the outside of something. **2** any side of a thing that has several sides. **3** outward appearance [On the *surface* he seemed friendly.]
verb to rise up to the surface [The submarine *surfaced* quickly.]
sur·face • *noun, plural for senses 1 and 2 only* **surfaces** • *verb* **surfaced, surfacing**

surge (surj) *noun* a sudden, strong rush [A *surge* of people pushed through the gate.]
verb to move in a surge [The water *surged* through the pipe.]
surge • *noun, plural* **surges** • *verb* **surged, surging**

surgeon (sur′jən) *noun* a doctor whose work is doing surgery.
sur·geon • *noun, plural* **surgeons**

surgery (sur′jər ē) *noun* **1** the treating of disease or injury by cutting into and removing or repairing parts of the body. **2** an operation of this kind performed by a surgeon.
sur·ger·y • *noun*

surgical (sur′ji kəl) *adjective* having to do with surgery [*surgical* tools].
sur·gi·cal • *adjective*

Suriname (soor′i näm′) a country in northeastern South America.
Su·ri·name

surname (sur′nām) *noun* a family name, or last name.
sur·name • *noun, plural* **surnames**

surpass (sər pas′) *verb* to be better or greater than another person or thing [The performance of this car *surpasses* the performance of all the others.]
sur·pass • *verb* **surpassed, surpassing**

surplus (sur′plus) *noun* an amount more than what is needed; that which is left over; excess [There was a *surplus* of grain last year.]
sur·plus • *noun, plural* **surpluses**

surprise (sər prīz′) *verb* **1** to cause to feel wonder by being unexpected [Her sudden anger *surprised* us.] **2** to come upon in a sudden or unexpected way [I *surprised* him in the act of stealing a watch.]
noun **1** the act of surprising [The news took them by *surprise*.] **2** the condition of being surprised [Much to our *surprise* it began to snow.] **3** something that causes wonder because it is not expected [Your answer was quite a *surprise*.]
sur·prise • *verb* **surprised, surprising** • *noun, plural for sense 3 only* **surprises**

surrender (sər ren′dər) *verb* to give oneself up as a prisoner [The bank robber *surrendered*.]
noun the act of surrendering.
sur·ren·der • *verb* **surrendered, surrendering** • *noun, plural* **surrenders**

surround (sər round′) *verb* to form or put around on all sides; enclose [Trees *surround* the house.]
sur·round • *verb* **surrounded, surrounding**

surroundings (sər roun′diŋz) ***plural noun*** the things or conditions around a person or place [They work in fine *surroundings.*]
sur·round·ings • ***plural noun***

survey (sər vā′ *for v.;* sʉr′vā *for n.*) ***verb*** **1** to look over something in a careful way [The lookout *surveyed* the horizon. We *surveyed* the problem.] **2** to measure the size and shape of a piece of land with special instruments [The men *surveyed* the region to prepare a new map.]
noun **1** a detailed study or inspection, made by gathering information and analyzing it [a *survey* of voters on the need for a new school]. **2** a general study that covers the main facts [a *survey* of Italian art]. **3** the process of surveying a piece of land [The *survey* of our town was finally finished.]
sur·vey • ***verb*** **surveyed, surveying** • ***noun,*** *plural* **surveys**

survival (sər vī′vəl) ***noun*** the act or fact of continuing to exist in spite of difficulties or danger [Nuclear war is a danger to the *survival* of the whole world.]
sur·viv·al • ***noun***

survive (sər vīv′) ***verb*** **1** to continue to live or exist [Many old customs *survive* even now.] **2** to continue to live or exist in spite of [We *survived* the bitter winter.] —Look for the WORD CHOICES box at the entry **outlive**.
sur·vive • ***verb*** **survived, surviving**

survivor (sər vīv′ər) ***noun*** a person or thing that survives [*survivors* of an airplane crash].
sur·vi·vor • ***noun,*** *plural* **survivors**

suspect (sə spekt′ *for v.;* sus′pekt *for n.*) ***verb*** **1** to think of someone as probably guilty of some wrong action although there is little proof [She was sure the detective *suspected* her.] **2** to guess or suppose [I *suspect* that they may not want to come.]
noun a person suspected of doing something wrong [a *suspect* in the robbery].
sus·pect • ***verb*** **suspected, suspecting** • ***noun,*** *plural* **suspects**

suspend (sə spend′) ***verb*** **1** to hang by a support from above [The basket was *suspended* from the ceiling.] **2** to stay in place as if hung from above [The helicopter was *suspended* over the highway.] **3** to keep out for a while as a punishment [The student was *suspended* from school for not behaving.] **4** to stop from operating for a time [The city *suspended* bus service.] **5** to hold back or put off [The judge *suspended* her sentence.]
sus·pend • ***verb*** **suspended, suspending**

suspenders (sə spen′dərz) ***plural noun*** a pair of elastic straps that extend over the shoulders to hold up pants.
sus·pend·ers • ***plural noun***

suspenders

suspense (sə spens′) ***noun*** **1** the condition of not being certain or at ease [We waited in *suspense* for the announcement.] **2** the growing excitement felt as a story or play builds to a high point [a movie full of *suspense*].
sus·pense • ***noun***

suspension (sə spen′shən) ***noun*** the act of suspending someone or something [The *suspension* of several players hurt the team's chances of winning the tournament.]
sus·pen·sion • ***noun,*** *plural* **suspensions**

suspension bridge
Mackinac Bridge, Michigan

suspension bridge ***noun*** a bridge that is held up by large cables that run between a series of towers.
suspension bridge • ***noun,*** *plural* **suspension bridges**

suspicion (sə spish′ən) ***noun*** **1** the act of suspecting guilt or wrongdoing with little or no

a	cat	ō	go	ʉ	fur	ə =	a *in* ago
ā	ape	ô	law, for	ch	chin		e *in* agent
ä	cot, car	oo	look	sh	she		i *in* pencil
e	ten	ōō	tool	th	thin		o *in* atom
ē	me	oi	oil	*th*	then		u *in* circus
i	fit	ou	out	zh	measure		
ī	ice	u	up	ŋ	ring		

proof [No one here is above *suspicion.*] **2** the feeling of one who suspects [I have a *suspicion* that you are right.]
sus·pi·cion • *noun, plural for sense 2 only* **suspicions**

suspicious (sə spish′əs) *adjective* **1** causing suspicion [*suspicious* behavior]. **2** feeling or showing suspicion [She gave the stranger a *suspicious* look.]
sus·pi·cious • *adjective*

sustain (sə stān′) *verb* **1** to give courage or strength to [Hope of rescue *sustained* the trapped miners.] **2** to undergo or suffer [Did you *sustain* any serious injuries in the car accident?]
sus·tain • *verb* **sustained, sustaining**

SW or **S.W.** *abbreviation for* **1** southwest. **2** southwestern.

swab (swäb) *noun* **1** a small piece of cotton, cloth, or sponge, often fixed to a small stick. It can be used to clean a wound or put medicine on. **2** a mop used with water to clean floors or decks.
verb to clean or mop with a swab [She *swabbed* the cut on his hand. The sailor *swabbed* the deck.]
swab • *noun, plural* **swabs**
• *verb* **swabbed, swabbing**

swagger (swag′ər) *verb* to walk in a showy, strutting way [He *swaggered* in and started to brag.]
swag·ger • *verb* **swaggered, swaggering**

swallow[1] (swä′lō) *noun* a small, swift bird with pointed wings and a forked tail.
swal·low • *noun, plural* **swallows**

swallow[2] (swä′lō) *verb* **1** to let something such as food or drink go through the throat into the stomach. **2** to cause to disappear; take in and cover [The raging sea *swallowed* the ship.] **3** to keep from showing; hold back [He *swallowed* his pride.] **4** [*an informal use*] to believe without questioning [She didn't *swallow* his wild story.]
noun **1** the act of swallowing. **2** the amount swallowed at one time [a *swallow* of water].
swal·low • *verb* **swallowed, swallowing**
• *noun, plural* **swallows**

swam (swam) *verb past tense of* **swim.**

swamp (swämp) *noun* a piece of wet, spongy land; marsh; bog.
verb **1** to flood or to sink by flooding [The rainstorm *swamped* the streets. High waves *swamped* the boat.] **2** to weigh down; burden; overwhelm [The family was *swamped* by medical bills.]
swamp • *noun, plural* **swamps**
• *verb* **swamped, swamping**

swampy (swäm′pē) *adjective* of or like a swamp; wet and spongy [a *swampy* golf course].
swamp·y • *adjective* **swampier, swampiest**

swan

swan (swän) *noun* a large water bird with webbed feet and a long, graceful neck. Swans usually have white feathers.
swan • *noun, plural* **swans**

swap (swäp) [*an informal word*] *noun* a trade or exchange [We made a *swap* for a catcher.]
verb to trade or exchange [We *swapped* phone numbers.]
swap • *noun, plural* **swaps**
• *verb* **swapped, swapping**

WORD HISTORY

swap

Our word **swap** comes from a 600-year-old English word that means "to strike or hit." Today's meaning of **swap** is connected with the ancient custom of striking hands together to complete a bargain.

swarm (swôrm) *noun* **1** a large number of bees, led by a queen, leaving a hive to start a new colony. **2** a colony of bees in a hive. **3** any large, moving crowd [a *swarm* of visitors].
verb **1** to fly off in a swarm to start a new colony [The bees *swarmed* from their hive.]

S

2 to move or gather in large numbers [Shoppers *swarmed* into the stores.] **3** to be filled with a crowd [On Sundays the beach is always *swarming* with people.]
swarm • *noun, plural* **swarms**
• *verb* **swarmed, swarming**

swashbuckler (swäsh′buk lər) *noun* a fighting man who brags and swaggers.
swash·buck·ler • *noun, plural* **swashbucklers**

swat (swät) *verb* to hit or strike with a quick, sharp blow [He *swatted* the fly with a newspaper.]
noun a quick, sharp blow.
swat • *verb* **swatted, swatting** • *noun, plural* **swats**

swatch (swäch) *noun* a small piece of cloth or other material used as a sample.
swatch • *noun, plural* **swatches**

sway (swā) *verb* **1** to swing or bend back and forth or from side to side [The flowers *swayed* in the breeze.] **2** to change the thinking or actions of; to influence [He had made up his mind and nothing could *sway* him.]
sway • *verb* **swayed, swaying**

WORD CHOICES

Synonyms of **sway**

The words **sway**, **bias**, and **influence** share the meaning "to have an indirect or emotional effect on."

We were not *swayed* by the candidate's promises.

Reading that book *biased* him against politicians.

Her advice *influenced* my decision.

Swaziland (swä′zē land) a country in southeastern Africa. It is almost surrounded by South Africa.
Swa·zi·land

swear (swer) *verb* **1** to say or promise in a serious or solemn way; to vow [I *swear* that I am telling the truth.] —Look for the WORD CHOICES box at the entry **promise**. **2** to curse or use bad language.
—swear in to make take an oath [The Chief Justice *swears in* the new President.] **—swear off** to promise to give up [He *swore off* smoking.]
swear • *verb* **swore, sworn, swearing**

swearword (swer′wurd) *noun* a word used in swearing, or cursing.
swear·word • *noun, plural* **swearwords**

sweat (swet) *verb* **1** to give out a salty liquid through the pores of the skin; perspire [Running makes me *sweat*.] **2** to form little drops of water on its surface [A glass full of iced tea will *sweat* in a warm room.]
noun **1** the salty liquid given out through the pores of the skin. **2** the little drops of water that form on a cold surface. **3** the condition of sweating [The horse worked up a *sweat* in the corral.]
sweat • *verb* **sweat** or **sweated, sweating**
• *noun, plural* **sweats**

sweater (swet′ər) *noun* a knitted outer garment for the upper part of the body.
sweat·er • *noun, plural* **sweaters**

sweaty (swet′ē) *adjective* **1** wet with sweat; sweating [*sweaty* athletes]. **2** having or containing sweat [a *sweaty* odor]. **3** causing sweat [*sweaty* work].
sweat·y • *adjective* **sweatier, sweatiest**

Swede (swēd) *noun* a person born or living in Sweden.
Swede • *noun, plural* **Swedes**

Sweden (swēd′n) a country in northern Europe, east of Norway.
Swe·den

Swedish (swēd′ish) *noun* the language of the Swedes.
Swed·ish • *noun*

sweep (swēp) *verb* **1** to clean by brushing with a broom [*Sweep* the floor.] **2** to clear away with a broom [*Sweep* the dirt from the porch.] **3** to carry away or destroy with a quick, strong motion [The flood *swept* away their barn.] **4** to move in a quick, steady, important way [She *swept* down the aisle to the stage.]
noun **1** the act of sweeping [Give the room a good *sweep*.] **2** a steady, sweeping movement [the *sweep* of the oars]. **3** an unbroken stretch

a	cat	ō	go	ʉ	fur	ə =	a *in* ago
ā	ape	ô	law, for	ch	chin		e *in* agent
ä	cot, car	oo	look	sh	she		i *in* pencil
e	ten	ōō	tool	th	thin		o *in* atom
ē	me	oi	oil	*th*	then		u *in* circus
i	fit	ou	out	zh	measure		
ī	ice	u	up	ŋ	ring		

[a *sweep* of flat country]. **4** a line or curve [the graceful *sweep* of her dress].
sweep • *verb* **swept, sweeping** • *noun, plural* **sweeps**

sweeping (swēp′iŋ) *adjective* **1** reaching over a wide area [a *sweeping* look]. **2** including a great deal; very broad [The new boss made *sweeping* changes.]
sweep·ing • *adjective*

sweet (swēt) *adjective* **1** containing sugar or having the taste of sugar [a *sweet* apple]. **2** pleasant in taste, smell, sound, or manner [*sweet* music; a *sweet* child].
noun a piece of candy or other sweet thing.
sweet • *adjective* **sweeter, sweetest** • *noun, plural* **sweets**
● The words **sweet** and **suite** sound alike.
The icing on the cake is too *sweet*.
We reserved a *suite* at the hotel.

sweeten (swēt′n) *verb* to make or become sweet [Don't *sweeten* the iced tea too much. Grapes *sweeten* on the vine.]
sweet·en • *verb* **sweetened, sweetening**

sweetener (swēt′n ər) *noun* something used to make food sweeter. Sweeteners are usually artificial substances rather than sugar or honey.
sweet·en·er • *noun, plural* **sweeteners**

sweetheart (swēt′härt) *noun* a person with whom one is in love.
sweet·heart • *noun, plural* **sweethearts**

sweetly (swēt′lē) *adverb* in a pleasant manner [She smiled *sweetly* at us.]
sweet·ly • *adverb*

sweet pea *noun* a climbing plant with sweet-smelling flowers of many colors.
sweet pea • *noun, plural* **sweet peas**

sweet potato

sweet potato *noun* the sweet, yellow, thick root of a tropical vine that is cooked and eaten as a vegetable.
sweet potato • *noun, plural* **sweet potatoes**

swell (swel) *verb* **1** to make or become larger, greater, or stronger [Buds *swell* in the spring. The crowd *swelled* outside the gates of the stadium.] —Look for the WORD CHOICES box at the entry **expand**. **2** to bulge or cause to bulge; to curve out [Wind *swelled* the sails. The sails *swelled*.]
noun a large, rolling wave or a rounded hill or slope.
adjective [*a slang use*] fine; excellent [It was a *swell* vacation.]
swell • *verb* **swelled, swelled** or **swollen, swelling** • *noun, plural* **swells** • *adjective*

swelling (swel′iŋ) *noun* a swollen place on the body [The insect bite caused a small *swelling* on her wrist.]
swell·ing • *noun, plural* **swellings**

swept (swept) *verb past tense and past participle of* **sweep**.

swerve (swurv) *verb* to turn aside from a straight line or path [She *swerved* the car to avoid hitting the dog.]
swerve • *verb* **swerved, swerving**

swift (swift) *adjective* **1** moving or able to move very fast [a *swift* runner] —Look for the WORD CHOICES box at the entry **fast**[1]. **2** coming, happening, or done quickly [a *swift* reply].
noun a brown bird that looks like the swallow. It flies very fast.
swift • *adjective* **swifter, swiftest** • *noun, plural* **swifts**

swiftly (swift′lē) *adverb* with great speed; quickly [He ran *swiftly*.]
swift·ly • *adverb*

swig (swig) [*an informal word*] *verb* to drink in large gulps [He *swigged* milk right from the carton.]
noun a large gulp of liquid [Give me a *swig* of your soda.]
swig • *verb* **swigged, swigging** • *noun, plural* **swigs**

swim (swim) *verb* **1** to move through water by moving the arms and legs or the fins, flippers, or tail. **2** to move in or across by swimming [We could not *swim* the river.] **3** to float on or be covered by a liquid [The potatoes were *swimming* in gravy.]
noun **1** an act of swimming [Let's go for a *swim*.] **2** the time or distance that one swims [a short *swim*].
swim • *verb* **swam, swum, swimming** • *noun*

swimmer (swim′ər) *noun* **1** a person who swims. **2** a person or animal that swims in a

S

certain way [Beavers are good *swimmers*.]
swim·mer • *noun, plural* **swimmers**

swimming (swim′iŋ) ***noun*** the act or sport of a person who swims.
swim·ming • ***noun***

swimming pool ***noun*** a pool or tank of water for swimming. It may be either indoors or outdoors.
swimming pool • *noun, plural* **swimming pools**

swindle (swin′dəl) ***verb*** to cheat or trick out of money or property [He told the police that he had been *swindled* out of all his savings.] —Look for the WORD CHOICES box at the entry **cheat**.
noun an act of swindling [Many people were victims of that *swindle*.]
swin·dle • *verb* **swindled, swindling** • *noun, plural* **swindles**

swindler (swind′lər) ***noun*** a person who swindles another person.
swin·dler • *noun, plural* **swindlers**

swine (swīn) ***noun*** a pig or hog [a herd of *swine*]. This word is usually used in the plural.
swine • *noun, plural* **swine**

swing

swing (swiŋ) ***verb*** **1** to move or sway back and forth [A pendulum *swings*.] **2** to turn on a hinge or a pivot [The door *swung* open. He *swung* his chair around to face us.] **3** to move with a sweeping motion [The batter *swung* at the pitch. He *swung* the sack over his shoulder.]
noun **1** the act of swinging. **2** the curved path of something that swings [the wide *swing* of the pendulum]. **3** a sweeping blow or stroke [He took a *swing* at my jaw.] **4** a seat hanging from ropes or chains on which one can swing.
swing • *verb* **swung, swinging** • *noun, plural* **swings**

swipe (swīp) ***noun*** [*an informal use*] a hard, sweeping blow [He took a *swipe* at me.]
verb **1** [*an informal use*] to hit with a hard, sweeping blow. **2** [*a slang use*] to steal [Someone *swiped* my pen.]
swipe • *noun, plural* **swipes** • *verb* **swiped, swiping**

swirl (swurl) ***verb*** to move with a twisting or curving motion; whirl [I unplugged the sink and the water *swirled* down the drain.]
noun **1** a swirling motion [a *swirl* of water down the drain]. **2** a twist or curl.
swirl • *verb* **swirled, swirling** • *noun, plural* **swirls**

swish (swish) ***verb*** **1** to move with a sharp, hissing sound [He *swished* his sword through the air.] **2** to move with soft, rubbing sounds [Her skirt *swished* as she walked.]
noun **1** a hissing or soft, rubbing sound. **2** a movement that makes a hissing or soft, rubbing sound.
swish • *verb* **swished, swishing** • *noun, plural* **swishes**

Swiss (swis) ***noun*** a person born or living in Switzerland.
Swiss • *noun, plural* **Swiss**

Swiss cheese ***noun*** a pale-yellow, hard cheese with many large holes. It was first made in Switzerland.

switch (swich) ***noun*** **1** a thin stick that is used like a whip. **2** a sharp stroke with such a stick or with a whip. **3** a device which opens or closes an electric circuit. **4** a section of railroad track that can be moved to shift a train from one track to another. **5** a change or shift [There was a sudden *switch* in the conversation.]
verb **1** to whip [The jockey *switched* his horse in the final stretch.] **2** to jerk or swing sharply [The horse *switched* its tail.] **3** to change or exchange [Can we *switch* the committee meeting to a later date? The dancers

a	cat	ō	go	ʉ	fur	ə =	a *in* ago
ā	ape	ô	law, for	ch	chin		e *in* agent
ä	cot, car	oo	look	sh	she		i *in* pencil
e	ten	ōō	tool	th	thin		o *in* atom
ē	me	oi	oil	*th*	then		u *in* circus
i	fit	ou	out	zh	measure		
ī	ice	u	up	ŋ	ring		

switched partners.] **4** to turn a light or other electric device on or off.
switch • *noun, plural* **switches**
• *verb* **switched, switching**

switchboard (swich′bôrd) *noun* a board or panel that has switches or other devices for controlling a number of electric circuits [a telephone *switchboard*].
switch·board • *noun, plural* **switchboards**

Switzerland (swit′sər lənd) a country in western Europe, in the Alps.
Swit·zer·land

swivel (swiv′əl) *verb* to turn or rotate freely at a point where two parts are joined together [The seat of this chair *swivels* on its base.]
swiv·el • *verb* **swiveled** or **swivelled, swiveling** or **swivelling**

swollen (swō′lən) *verb a past participle of* **swell.**
swol·len • *verb*

swoop (swo͞op) *verb* to sweep down or pounce upon suddenly [The hawk *swooped* down on its prey.]
noun the act of swooping.
swoop • *verb* **swooped, swooping** • *noun, plural* **swoops**

sword (sôrd) *noun* a weapon that has a long, sharp blade with a hilt, or handle, at one end.
sword • *noun, plural* **swords**

swordfish (sôrd′fish) *noun* a large ocean fish with an upper jaw that ends in a long point, like a sword.
sword·fish • *noun, plural* **swordfish**

swordsman (sôrdz′mən) *noun* a person who has great skill in using a sword.
swords·man • *noun, plural* **swordsmen**

swore (swôr) *verb past tense of* **swear.**

sworn (swôrn) *verb past participle of* **swear.**

swum (swum) *verb past participle of* **swim.**

swung (swuŋ) *verb past tense and past participle of* **swing.**

sycamore (sik′ə môr) *noun* a shade tree that has large leaves and smooth bark that flakes off in large pieces.
syc·a·more • *noun, plural* **sycamores**

syllabify (si lab′i fī′) *verb* to divide into syllables [The teacher asked her to *syllabify* those words.]
syl·lab·i·fy • *verb* **syllabified, syllabifying, syllabifies**

syllable (sil′ə bəl) *noun* a word or part of a word in which the voice sounds only once. "Moon" is a word of one syllable. "Moonlight" is a word of two syllables. A syllable always has a vowel sound and usually also has one or more consonant sounds.
syl·la·ble • *noun, plural* **syllables**

WORD HISTORY

syllable

The word **syllable** comes from a Greek prefix that means "together" and a Greek verb that means "to put or hold." We put **syllables** together to form words.

symbol (sim′bəl) *noun* an object, mark, or sign that stands for something else such as another object, or for an idea or quality [The dove is the *symbol* of peace. The mark $ is the *symbol* for dollars.]
sym·bol • *noun, plural* **symbols**
• The words **symbol** and **cymbal** sound alike.
The lion is a *symbol* of royalty.
The *cymbal* is common in school bands.

symbolize (sim′bəl īz) *verb* to be a symbol of; to stand for [A heart *symbolizes* love.]
sym·bol·ize • *verb* **symbolized, symbolizing**

symmetrical (si me′tri kəl) *adjective* having matching parts or shapes on both sides of the center line; balanced [a *symmetrical* design].
sym·met·ri·cal • *adjective*

symmetry (sim′ə trē) *noun* a symmetrical shape or arrangement of parts [The human body has *symmetry*.]
sym·me·try • *noun*

sympathetic (sim′pə thet′ik) *adjective* **1** feeling or showing sympathy [He spoke *sympathetic* words to her.] **2** showing favor or support [He is *sympathetic* to our plans.]
sym·pa·thet·ic • *adjective*

sympathize (sim′pə thīz) *verb* to share the feelings or ideas of another; feel or show sympathy [I *sympathize* with your sadness.]
sym·pa·thize • *verb* **sympathized, sympathizing**

sympathy (sim′pə thē) *noun* **1** the quality of feeling sorry for another's suffering or of sharing another's feelings in some way [He showed

S

his *sympathy* by giving her a hug.] —Look for the WORD CHOICES box at the entry **pity**. **2** a feeling of favor or support [She has *sympathy* for the strikers' cause.]
sym·pa·thy • ***noun***

symphony (sim′fə nē) ***noun*** a long piece of music for a full orchestra. It is usually divided into four movements, or sections.
sym·pho·ny • ***noun,*** *plural* **symphonies**

symptom (simp′təm) ***noun*** something that shows that a disease or some other thing is present [Fever is a *symptom* of the flu.]
symp·tom • ***noun,*** *plural* **symptoms**

synagogue (sin′ə gäg *or* sin′ə gôg) ***noun*** a building where Jews gather for worship and religious study.
syn·a·gogue • ***noun,*** *plural* **synagogues**

synchronize (siŋ′krə nīz) ***verb*** to cause to move or happen at the same time or speed; make agree [Let's *synchronize* our watches.]
syn·chro·nize • ***verb*** **synchronized, synchronizing**

syndrome (sin′drōm) ***noun*** a number of symptoms that occur together and make up a particular disease or condition.
syn·drome • ***noun,*** *plural* **syndromes**

synonym (sin′ə nim) ***noun*** a word that means the same or almost the same as another word. "Big" is a synonym of "large."
syn·o·nym • ***noun,*** *plural* **synonyms**

syntax (sin′taks) ***noun*** the way words are put together and related to one another in a sentence.
syn·tax • ***noun***

synthetic (sin thet′ik) ***adjective*** made by putting together chemicals rather than by using natural products [*synthetic* rubber].
noun something that is synthetic [Nylon is a *synthetic*.]
syn·thet·ic • ***adjective*** • ***noun,*** *plural* **synthetics**

Syria (sir′ē ə) a country at the eastern end of the Mediterranean, south of Turkey.
Syr·i·a

syringe (sə rinj′) ***noun*** a device made up of a narrow tube with a rubber bulb or a plunger at one end. Liquid can be drawn into the tube and then pushed out in a stream. Syringes are used for many purposes such as to inject medicine into the body or to wash out wounds.
sy·ringe • ***noun,*** *plural* **syringes**

syrup (sʉr′əp *or* sir′əp) ***noun*** **1** a sweet, thick liquid made by boiling sugar with water, usually with some flavoring [chocolate *syrup*]. **2** a sweet, thick liquid made by boiling the juice of certain plants [maple *syrup*]. **3** a sweet, thick liquid that contains medicine [cough *syrup*].
syr·up • ***noun,*** *plural* **syrups**

system (sis′təm) ***noun*** **1** a group of things or parts working together or connected in some way so as to form a whole [a school *system;* the solar *system;* the nervous *system*]. **2** a set of facts, rules, or ideas that make up an orderly plan [a democratic *system* of government]. **3** an orderly way of doing something; method [a *system* for losing weight]. **4** the body as a whole [She had poison in her *system*.]
sys·tem • ***noun,*** *plural* **systems**

a cat	ō go	ʉ fur	ə = a *in* ago
ā ape	ô law, for	ch chin	e *in* agent
ä cot, car	ꝏ look	sh she	i *in* pencil
e ten	ō͞o tool	th thin	o *in* atom
ē me	oi oil	*th* then	u *in* circus
i fit	ou out	zh measure	
ī ice	u up	ŋ ring	

T t

Tt Tt Tt Tt

When used by itself, the letter **t** *usually stands for the sound you hear at the beginning of the words* **tiger** *and* **trap.** **T** *can also combine with the letter* **h** *to represent the two different sounds you hear at the beginning of the words* **thought** *and* **this.** *When* **t** *is followed by* **i** *in the middle of a word, it can have the sound of* **sh,** *as in the word* **attention.**

t or **T** (tē) ***noun*** **1** the twentieth letter of the English alphabet. **2** something shaped like T.
—to a T in a perfect or exact way [That dress suits you *to a T*.]
t or **T** • ***noun,*** *plural* **t's** or **T's**

t or **t.** *abbreviation for* **1** teaspoon. **2** teaspoons.

T or **T.** *abbreviation for* **1** tablespoon. **2** tablespoons.

tab[1] (tab) ***noun*** a small loop or tag fastened to something [The folders in the file have *tabs* lettered A to Z.]
tab • ***noun,*** *plural* **tabs**

tab[2] (tab) [*an informal word*] ***noun*** a record of money owed; bill [His dinner *tab* is $12.]
—keep tabs on or **keep a tab on** [*an informal use*] to follow or watch every move of [The police are *keeping tabs on* them.]
tab • ***noun,*** *plural* **tabs**

tabby (tab′ē) ***noun*** **1** a gray or brown cat with dark stripes. **2** any pet cat, especially a female one.
tab·by • ***noun,*** *plural* **tabbies**

table (tā′bəl) ***noun*** **1** a piece of furniture made up of a flat top set on legs. **2** a list in some kind of order [a *table* of contents]. **3** an arrangement of facts or figures, usually in columns [the multiplication *table*].
verb to put off talking about; set aside [The Congress *tabled* the bill.]
—turn the tables to make a situation just the opposite of what it was. **—under the table** [*an informal use*] in a secret, and often illegal, way [The mayor was taking money *under the table*.]
ta·ble • ***noun,*** *plural* **tables** • ***verb*** **tabled, tabling**

tablecloth (tā′bəl klôth) ***noun*** a cloth placed over a table, especially at meals.
ta·ble·cloth • ***noun,*** *plural* **tablecloths**

tablespoon (tā′bəl spo͞on) ***noun*** **1** a large spoon for serving food, for eating soup, or for measuring things in cooking. **2** a measuring unit used in cooking. It is usually equal to ½ fluid ounce.
ta·ble·spoon • ***noun,*** *plural* **tablespoons**

tablet (tab′lət) ***noun*** **1** a number of sheets of writing paper fastened together at one end. **2** a small, flat, hard cake of medicine or other substance [an aspirin *tablet*]. **3** a flat, thin piece of metal or stone with words or pictures on it [A *tablet* on the museum wall lists the names of the founders.]
tab·let • ***noun,*** *plural* **tablets**

table tennis ***noun*** a game like tennis, played on a table with a small, hollow ball and paddles.

taboo (ta bo͞o′ *or* tə bo͞o′) ***noun*** a rule or custom that forbids doing certain things [a *taboo* against using certain words on the radio].
ta·boo • ***noun,*** *plural* **taboos**

tack (tak) *noun* **1** a short nail with a large, flat head. **2** the direction in which a boat is moving in relation to the position of the sails.
verb **1** to fasten with tacks [We *tacked* the carpet to the floor.] **2** to add something extra or different [She *tacked* on a new ending to her story.]
tack • *noun, plural* **tacks** • *verb* **tacked, tacking**

tackle (tak′əl) *noun* **1** the tools or equipment needed for doing something; gear [fishing *tackle*]. **2** the act of throwing to the ground the football player carrying the ball. **3** a football player whose position is next to an end on the line.
verb **1** to try to do or solve; take on [He *tackled* the hard math problems.] **2** to seize and throw to the ground [The police officer *tackled* the fleeing robber.]
tack·le • *noun, plural for senses 2 and 3 only* **tackles** • *verb* **tackled, tackling**

tacky[1] (tak′ē) *adjective* sticky because not yet dry [The fresh coat of paint is still *tacky*.]
tack·y • *adjective* **tackier, tackiest**

tacky[2] (tak′ē) [*an informal word*] *adjective* **1** worn-out or out of style [*tacky* clothes]. **2** not proper; in bad taste [*tacky* remarks].
tack·y • *adjective* **tackier, tackiest**

taco (tä′kō) *noun* a Mexican food made of a tortilla that is folded over chopped meat and vegetables.
ta·co • *noun, plural* **tacos**

tact (takt) *noun* a sense of what is the right thing to do or say without causing anger or hurt feelings; skill in dealing with people.

tactics (tak′tiks) *plural noun* skillful methods used to bring something about [The coach explained the *tactics* the team should use to win the game.]
tac·tics • *plural noun*

tadpole (tad′pōl) *noun* a young toad or frog. It has a tail but no legs, and lives only in water.
tad·pole • *noun, plural* **tadpoles**

taffy (taf′ē) *noun* a chewy candy made of sugar or molasses that is boiled down and stretched back and forth.
taf·fy • *noun*

Taft (taft), **William Howard** (wil′yəm hou′ərd) 1857-1930; the twenty-seventh president of the U.S., from 1909 to 1913.
Taft, Wil·liam How·ard

tag (tag) *noun* **1** something, such as a card or slip of paper, attached to something else as a label [a price *tag;* a name *tag*]. **2** a children's game. One player is called "it." He or she chases the others until touching one of them. The player touched then becomes "it."
verb **1** to put a tag, or label, on [The clerk *tagged* the goods and put them in the shop.] **2** to touch in the game of tag. **3** [*an informal use*] to follow close behind [Wherever we go, our dog *tags* along.]
tag • *noun, plural for sense 1 only* **tags** • *verb* **tagged, tagging**

tail (tāl) *noun* **1** the part at the rear of an animal's body that sticks out beyond the backbone. **2** any part or thing like an animal's tail, either in shape or position [the *tail* of a shirt]. **3** *often* **tails** the side of a coin opposite the head, or main side.
verb [*an informal use*] to follow close behind [My kid brother *tailed* after us.]
adjective at or from the rear [a *tail* wind].
tail • *noun, plural* **tails** • *verb* **tailed, tailing** • *adjective*

● The words **tail** and **tale** sound alike.
The baby pulled on the dog's *tail*.
I read him a fairy *tale* at bedtime.

tailgate

tailgate (tāl′gāt) *noun* a rectangular section at the rear of a station wagon or truck. It can be folded down or taken off when loading or unloading the vehicle.
verb to follow another vehicle with not enough space between.
tail·gate • *noun, plural* **tailgates** • *verb* **tailgated, tailgating**

a cat	ō go	ʉ fur	ə = a *in* ago
ā ape	ô law, for	ch chin	e *in* agent
ä cot, car	oo look	sh she	i *in* pencil
e ten	ōō tool	th thin	o *in* atom
ē me	oi oil	*th* then	u *in* circus
i fit	ou out	zh measure	
ī ice	u up	ŋ ring	

taillight (tāl′līt) ***noun*** a red light at the rear of a vehicle.
tail·light • ***noun,*** *plural* **taillights**

tailor (tā′lər) ***noun*** a person who makes or repairs suits, coats, and other clothing.
verb to make or change so as to fit a certain need [They *tailored* the movie for children.]
tai·lor • ***noun,*** *plural* **tailors** • ***verb*** **tailored, tailoring**

tailpipe (tāl′pīp) ***noun*** an exhaust pipe at the rear of a car or truck.
tail·pipe • ***noun,*** *plural* **tailpipes**

tailspin (tāl′spin) ***noun*** a downward fall of an airplane out of control, with the tail up and spinning in circles.
tail·spin • ***noun,*** *plural* **tailspins**

Taiwan (tī wän′) an island off the southeastern coast of China. On this island is a country that is called the *Republic of China.*
Tai·wan

Tajikistan (tä jik′i stan′) a country in southwestern Asia. It was a part of the Soviet Union.
Ta·jik·i·stan

take (tāk) ***verb*** **1** to get hold of; grasp [*Take* my hand as we cross the street.] **2** to get by force or skill; capture; seize; win [Our team *took* the first game. The soldiers *took* the town.] **3** to get as one's own [She *took* the job. When does the senator *take* office?] **4** to buy, rent, or subscribe to [We *take* the daily newspaper.] **5** to be used with [This bolt *takes* a larger nut. The verb "hit" *takes* an object.] **6** to travel by or on [We *took* the bus. I *took* a short cut.] **7** to call for; require; need [It *took* courage to do that.] **8** to study [We *take* geography next year.] **9** to write down [We *take* notes in class.] **10** to receive or accept [He *took* her advice.] **11** to have or feel [*Take* pity on me.] **12** to do, make, or use [*Take* care. *Take* a look at this. She *took* a picture.] **13** to remove or steal [Someone *took* my coat.] **14** to carry [*Take* your skis with you.] **15** to bring or lead [I *took* her to a movie.]
—take after to be, act, or look like [He *takes after* his father.] **—take down** to write down [The police officer *took down* my name and address.] **—take in** **1** to make smaller [The tailor *took in* the pants at the waist.] **2** to visit [We *took in* all the sights.] **—take off** **1** to rise from the earth [The jet *took off.*] **2** to remove [*Take off* your muddy shoes.] **3** to go away; leave [They *took off* about an hour ago.] **—take one's time** to be in no hurry. **—take over** to begin managing [She will *take over* the family business.] **—take up** **1** to become interested in [I *took up* golf this summer.] **2** to fill [This job *takes up* all my time.]
take • ***verb*** **took, taken, taking**

taken (tāk′ən) ***verb*** *past participle of* **take.**
tak·en • ***verb***

takeoff (tāk′ôf) ***noun*** the act of rising from the ground [during the airplane's *takeoff*].
take·off • ***noun,*** *plural* **takeoffs**

talc (talk) ***noun*** a soft mineral that is ground up to make talcum powder.

talcum powder (tal′kəm) ***noun*** a powder made of talc. It is put on the face and body.
tal·cum powder • ***noun***

tale (tāl) ***noun*** a story about things that are made up or imagined [a fairy *tale*].
tale • ***noun,*** *plural* **tales**
● The words **tale** and **tail** sound alike.
A Paul Bunyan story is a "tall *tale.*"
The caboose is at the *tail* end of a train.

talent (tal′ənt) ***noun*** **1** a natural skill that is unusual [She has *talent* as an artist.] **2** a person or people with talent [The music teacher develops young *talent.*]
tal·ent • ***noun,*** *plural* **talents**

WORD CHOICES

Synonyms of **talent**

The words **talent, aptitude,** and **gift** share the meaning "a natural ability to do a certain thing."

a *talent* for drawing
having little *aptitude* for cooking
a *gift* for making plants grow

talented (tal′ən təd) ***adjective*** having an unusual amount of natural skill; gifted.
tal·ent·ed • ***adjective***

talisman (tal′is mən) ***noun*** an object thought to have magic power or to bring good luck.
tal·is·man • ***noun,*** *plural* **talismans**

talk (tôk) ***verb*** **1** to say words or put ideas in words; speak [The baby is learning to *talk.*] —Look for the WORD CHOICES box at the entry

speak. **2** to make or bring about by talking [He *talked* himself hoarse. We *talked* her into going.] **3** to speak about [Let's *talk* business.]
noun **1** the act of talking; conversation. **2** a speech [He gave a *talk* to the members of the club.] **3** a formal discussion; conference [There were *talks* between the company and the union.] **4** a rumor or gossip [There is *talk* that they are getting engaged.] **5** a person or thing that is being talked about [Her new play is the *talk* of the town.]
—talk back to answer without showing respect [Don't *talk back* to your parents.]
—talk over to have a talk about; discuss [We *talked over* the problem.]
talk • ***verb*** **talked, talking** • ***noun,*** *plural for senses 1, 2, and 3 only* **talks**

talkative (tôk′ə tiv) ***adjective*** fond of talking or talking a great deal [a *talkative* salesman].
talk·a·tive • ***adjective***

tall (tôl) ***adjective*** **1** reaching a long way up; not low or short [a *tall* building]. **2** having a certain height [The man is six feet *tall*.] **3** [*an informal use*] hard to believe [a *tall* tale].
tall • ***adjective*** **taller, tallest**

Tallahassee (tal′ə has′ē) the capital of Florida.
Tal·la·has·see

tallow (tal′ō) ***noun*** hard fat that is melted and used in making such products as candles or soap. It comes from animals such as cows and sheep.
tal·low • ***noun***

tally (tal′ē) ***noun*** an account, record, or score [Keep a *tally* of the money you spend.]
verb to count; add [He *tallied* up his score.]
tal·ly • ***noun,*** *plural* **tallies** • ***verb*** **tallied, tallying, tallies**

Talmud (täl′mood *or* tal′mood) the collection of writings that make up the Jewish civil and religious law.
Tal·mud

talon (tal′ən) ***noun*** the claw of an eagle or other bird that kills other animals for food.
tal·on • ***noun,*** *plural* **talons**

tamale (tə mä′lē) ***noun*** a Mexican food of chopped meat and red peppers, rolled in cornmeal. The mixture is wrapped in corn husks and cooked.
ta·ma·le • ***noun,*** *plural* **tamales**

tambourine (tam bə rēn′) ***noun*** a small, shallow drum with only one head and jingling metal disks in the rim. It is played by shaking it or striking it with the hand.
tam·bou·rine • ***noun,*** *plural* **tambourines**

tame (tām) ***adjective*** **1** no longer wild, but trained for use by people or as a pet [a *tame* elephant]. **2** gentle, easy to control, and not afraid of people [The bronco soon became *tame*.] **3** without force or energy; dull [a *tame* debate].
verb **1** to make tame, or train to obey [She *tames* elephants for the circus.] **2** to make more gentle or easier to manage; subdue [She *tamed* his anger with a few kind words.]
tame • ***adjective*** **tamer, tamest**
• ***verb*** **tamed, taming**

tamer (tām′ər) ***noun*** a person who tames wild animals [a lion *tamer*].
tam·er • ***noun,*** *plural* **tamers**

tamp (tamp) ***verb*** to pack or pound down with taps or blows [She *tamped* down the soil around the base of the plant.]
tamp • ***verb*** **tamped, tamping**

tamper (tam′pər) ***verb*** to meddle or interfere in a way that is wrong or that causes damage [He *tampered* with the clock and now it's slow.]
tam·per • ***verb*** **tampered, tampering**

tan (tan) ***noun*** **1** a somewhat yellow brown. **2** the brown color that fair skin gets from being much in the sun.
adjective yellow-brown [a *tan* carpet].
verb **1** to make into leather by soaking in an acid that comes from the bark of certain trees [They *tanned* the cowhides.] **2** to make or become brown, as from being much in the sun.
tan • ***noun*** • ***adjective*** **tanner, tannest**
• ***verb*** **tanned, tanning**

tanager (tan′ə jər) ***noun*** a small American songbird. The male often has bright colors.
tan·a·ger • ***noun,*** *plural* **tanagers**

tang (taŋ) ***noun*** a sharp, strong taste or smell [This tea has a spicy *tang*.]

tangerine (tan jə rēn′) ***noun*** a small orange with a loose skin and sections that come apart easily.
tan·ge·rine • ***noun,*** *plural* **tangerines**

tangle (taŋ′gəl) ***verb*** **1** to make or become knotted or mixed up [Our fishing lines are *tangled*.] **2** to catch or hold back [His feet

a cat	ō go	ʉ fur	ə = a *in* ago
ā ape	ô law, for	ch chin	e *in* agent
ä cot, car	oo look	sh she	i *in* pencil
e ten	ōō tool	th thin	o *in* atom
ē me	oi oil	*th* then	u *in* circus
i fit	ou out	zh measure	
ī ice	u up	ŋ ring	

became *tangled* in the garden hose.]
noun **1** a twisted or knotted mass of something such as thread or hair [a *tangle* of vines]. **2** a confused or mixed-up condition; muddle [Her affairs are in a *tangle*.]
tan·gle • *verb* **tangled, tangling** • *noun, plural* **tangles**

tangy (taŋ′ē) *adjective* having a sharp, strong taste or smell [a *tangy* orange].
tang·y • *adjective* **tangier, tangiest**

tank (taŋk) *noun* **1** any large container for liquid or gas [a fuel *tank*]. **2** a military vehicle covered with armor and carrying heavy guns. It moves on metal belts that let it travel over rough ground.
tank • *noun, plural* **tanks**

WORD HISTORY

tank

The army **tank** got its name because tanks were a secret when they were first being made. When workers put parts for these vehicles into large boxes to ship somewhere else, they stamped "tank" or "tanks" on the boxes so that anyone who saw these words would think that the boxes held containers of some kind. By the time the secret got out, the secret name for the vehicle had become its real name, **tank**.

tanker (taŋk′ər) *noun* a ship with large tanks in its hull for carrying liquids [an oil *tanker*].
tank·er • *noun, plural* **tankers**

tantrum (tan′trəm) *noun* a fit of bad temper.
tan·trum • *noun, plural* **tantrums**

Tanzania (tan zə nē′ə) a country on the eastern coast of Africa and on Zanzibar.
Tan·za·ni·a

tap[1] (tap) *verb* **1** to hit lightly [She *tapped* my shoulder.] **2** to strike light blows with [She *tapped* the chalk against the blackboard.] **3** to make or do by tapping [He *tapped* out a rhythm with his fingers.]
noun **1** a light blow. **2** the sound made by a light blow [I heard a *tap* on the window.]
tap • *verb* **tapped, tapping** • *noun, plural* **taps**

tap[2] (tap) *noun* a device for turning the flow of liquid from a pipe on or off; faucet.
verb **1** to make or open a hole in, in order to draw off liquid [We *tapped* the maple tree for its sap.] **2** to make a connection with [The police *tapped* their telephone line.]
tap • *noun, plural* **taps** • *verb* **tapped, tapping**

tap dance *noun* a dance that is done by making sharp, loud taps with the foot, heel, or toe at each step.

tape (tāp) *noun* **1** a strong, narrow strip of cloth, paper, or plastic that is used to hold things together [adhesive *tape*]. **2** a narrow strip of material for some purpose [a measuring *tape*]. **3** *a short form of* **magnetic tape**.
verb **1** to bind or tie with tape [Please *tape* the bow to the birthday present.] **2** to record on a tape [We *taped* the children's song during the school recital.]
tape • *noun, plural* **tapes** • *verb* **taped, taping**

tape measure *noun* a tape that is marked off in units for measuring length or distance.
tape measure • *noun, plural* **tape measures**

taper (tā′pər) *verb* **1** to make or become less wide or less thick a little at a time [A sword *tapers* to a point.] **2** to make or become less a little at a time [The noise *tapered* off.]
noun a slender candle.
ta·per • *verb* **tapered, tapering** • *noun, plural* **tapers**

tape recorder *noun* a device for recording on magnetic tape and playing it back after it has been recorded.
tape recorder • *noun, plural* **tape recorders**

tapestry (tap′əs trē) *noun* a heavy cloth with designs and pictures woven into it. It can be hung on a wall or used to cover furniture.
tap·es·try • *noun, plural* **tapestries**

tapioca (tap′ē ō′kə) *noun* a substance used in puddings. It contains starch from a tropical plant.
tap·i·o·ca • *noun*

tar (tär) *noun* a thick, sticky, dark liquid that is made from wood or coal.

tarantula (tə ran′chə lə) *noun* a large, hairy spider. Its bite is slightly poisonous.
ta·ran·tu·la • *noun, plural* **tarantulas**

tardy (tär′dē) *adjective* not on time; late [I was *tardy* for yesterday morning's classes.]
tar·dy • *adjective* **tardier, tardiest**

target (tär′gət) *noun* **1** a thing that is aimed at in shooting practice, often a board with cir-

T

cles on it, one inside the other. **2** a goal or objective [The *target* of the charity drive is $50,000.]
tar·get • *noun, plural* **targets**

tariff (ter′if) *noun* a tax that is placed on goods that are brought into one country from another or, sometimes, on goods that are sent out of a country.
tar·iff • *noun, plural* **tariffs**

tarnish (tär′nish) *verb* **1** to become dull or stained [Silver *tarnishes* easily.] **2** to cause to be dull or stained [Exposure to the air *tarnishes* metals.]
tar·nish • *verb* **tarnished, tarnishing**

tart[1] (tärt) *adjective* sharp in taste; sour [a *tart* apple] —Look for the WORD CHOICES box at the entry **sour**.

tart[2] (tärt) *noun* a small pie with a filling of fruit, jam, or custard [strawberry *tarts*].
tart • *noun, plural* **tarts**

tartar (tär′tər) *noun* a hard substance that forms on the teeth.
tar·tar • *noun*

task (task) *noun* a piece of work that a person must do [Each of us was given a small *task*.]
task • *noun, plural* **tasks**

WORD CHOICES

Synonyms of **task**

The words **task, chore,** and **job** share the meaning "a piece of work that someone must do."

She has the *task* of answering letters.
His *chore* is washing the dishes.
It's my *job* to paint the barn.

tassel (tas′əl) *noun* **1** a bunch of cords or threads hanging from a knot. **2** something like this [the *tassel* of silk on an ear of corn].
tas·sel • *noun, plural* **tassels**

tassel

taste (tāst) *verb* **1** to be aware of by a special sense in the mouth; notice the flavor of [I *tasted* salt in the water.] **2** to test the flavor of by putting some into the mouth [*Taste* this sauce for me.] **3** to have a certain flavor [The milk *tastes* sour.]
noun **1** the power to taste something; the sense in the taste buds of the tongue that allows a person to know the flavors of things. **2** the quality of a thing that is noticed by the tongue; flavor [Lemons have a sour *taste*.] **3** a small sample of something [a *taste* of the cake; a *taste* of fame]. **4** the ability to know and judge what is good, beautiful, or proper [She has good *taste* in clothes.]
taste • *verb* **tasted, tasting** • *noun, plural for senses 2 and 3 only* **tastes**

taste bud *noun* any one of the cells in the tongue that tell whether something is sweet, sour, salty, or bitter.
taste bud • *noun, plural* **taste buds**

tasty (tās′tē) *adjective* tasting good; full of flavor [a *tasty* meal].
tast·y • *adjective* **tastier, tastiest**

tatter (tat′ər) *noun* **1** a torn and hanging piece of cloth [That towel is in *tatters*.] **2 tatters** torn, ragged clothes [dressed in *tatters*].
tat·ter • *noun, plural* **tatters**

tattered (tat′ərd) *adjective* torn and ragged [*tattered* clothes].
tat·tered • *adjective*

tattle (tat′l) *verb* to tell other people's secrets [You *tattled* to the teacher.]
tat·tle • *verb* **tattled, tattling**

tattletale (tat′l tāl) *noun* a person who tells other people's secrets.
tat·tle·tale • *noun, plural* **tattletales**

tattoo (ta to͞o′) *verb* to make marks or designs on the skin by pricking it with needles and putting colors in.
noun a mark or design made in this way.
tat·too • *verb* **tattooed, tattooing** • *noun, plural* **tattoos**

taught (tôt *or* tät) *verb past tense and past participle of* **teach**.
● The words **taught** and **taut** sound alike.
He *taught* me how to fish.
The trout pulled my fishing line *taut*.

taunt (tônt *or* tänt) *verb* to tease or make fun of in a rude or mean way; to jeer at [The big

a	cat	ō	go	ʉ	fur	ə = a *in* ago	
ā	ape	ô	law, for	ch	chin	e *in* agent	
ä	cot, car	oo	look	sh	she	i *in* pencil	
e	ten	o͞o	tool	th	thin	o *in* atom	
ē	me	oi	oil	*th*	then	u *in* circus	
i	fit	ou	out	zh	measure		
ī	ice	u	up	ŋ	ring		

kids *taunted* the little girl.]
noun a scornful or jeering remark.
taunt • *verb* **taunted, taunting** • *noun, plural* **taunts**

taut (tôt *or* tät) *adjective* stretched tight [a *taut* rope between the poles].
taut • *adjective* **tauter, tautest**
● The words **taut** and **taught** sound alike.

tavern (tav′ərn) *noun* a place where alcoholic drinks such as beer and whiskey are sold and drunk; a bar.
tav·ern • *noun, plural* **taverns**

tawny (tô′nē *or* tä′nē) *adjective* brownish-yellow; tan [A lion has a *tawny* coat.]
taw·ny • *adjective* **tawnier, tawniest**

tax (taks) *noun* money that citizens pay to help support a government. It is usually a percentage of what a person earns or of the value of something that a person buys or owns.
verb **1** to put a tax on [Do they *tax* gasoline?] **2** to make pay a tax [Congress has the power to *tax* the people.] **3** to put a heavy load or strain on [Your pranks *tax* my patience.]
tax • *noun, plural* **taxes** • *verb* **taxed, taxing**

taxation (taks ā′shən) *noun* the act or system of taxing.
tax·a·tion • *noun*

taxi (tak′sē) *noun a short form of* **taxicab**.
verb to move slowly along the ground or water before taking off or after landing [The plane *taxied* to the main runway.]
tax·i • *noun, plural* **taxis** • *verb* **taxied, taxiing** or **taxying**

taxicab (tak′sē kab′) *noun* an automobile that carries passengers for a fee. It usually has a meter to show the amount that is owed.
tax·i·cab • *noun, plural* **taxicabs**

Taylor (tā′lər), **Zachary** (zak′ər ē) 1784-1850; the twelfth president of the U.S., from 1849 to 1850.
Tay·lor, Zach·a·ry

tbs. or **tbsp.** *abbreviation for* **1** tablespoon. **2** tablespoons.

tea (tē) *noun* **1** a plant that is grown in Asia. Its leaves are dried and used to make a drink that is served hot or cold. **2** the dried leaves of this plant. **3** the drink that is made by soaking these leaves in very hot water. **4** a meal in the late afternoon at which tea is usually served. **5** a drink that is made in the same way as tea, but from some other plant or from meat.
tea • *noun, plural for sense 4 only* **teas**
● The words **tea, tee,** and **ti** sound alike.
We drink iced *tea* in the summer.
She placed a golf ball on the *tee*.
Do, re, mi, fa, sol, la, *ti*, do.

tea bag *noun* a small bag of cloth or paper that contains dried tea leaves. It is put into hot water to make tea.
tea bag • *noun, plural* **tea bags**

teach (tēch) *verb* **1** to show or help to learn how to do something; to train [She *taught* us to skate.] **2** to give lessons to [Who *teaches* your class?] **3** to give lessons in [He *teaches* French.] **4** to be a teacher [I plan to *teach* after I graduate.]
teach • *verb* **taught, teaching**

teacher (tēch′ər) *noun* a person who teaches in a school or college.
teach·er • *noun, plural* **teachers**

teaching (tēch′iŋ) *noun* **1** the work or job of a teacher. **2** *usually* **teachings** something taught [the *teachings* of a religion].
teach·ing • *noun, plural for sense 2 only* **teachings**

teakettle (tē′ket′l) *noun* a kettle with a spout, used to boil water.
tea·ket·tle • *noun, plural* **teakettles**

team (tēm) *noun* **1** two or more horses or oxen that are harnessed together for pulling a plow or wagon. **2** a group of people working together [a *team* of doctors; a soccer *team*].
verb to join together in a team [Let's *team* up with them.]
team • *noun, plural* **teams** • *verb* **teamed, teaming**
● The words **team** and **teem** sound alike.
Our city's baseball *team* won the series.
The local creeks *teem* with catfish.

teammate (tēm′māt) *noun* a fellow member of a team.
team·mate • *noun, plural* **teammates**

teamwork (tēm′wurk) *noun* the effort or action of people working together as a group.
team·work • *noun*

teapot (tē′pät) *noun* a pot with a spout, handle, and lid. It is used for making and pouring tea.
tea·pot • *noun, plural* **teapots**

tear[1] (ter) *verb* **1** to pull apart by force; to rip [*Tear* the cloth into strips.] **2** to be pulled apart in this way [Paper *tears* easily.] **3** to make by tearing [The nail *tore* a hole in her

T

coat.] **4** to pull up, down, out, at, away, or off [The wind *tore* up trees by their roots.] **5** to divide by struggle or fighting [The country was *torn* by civil war.] **6** to move with speed.
noun a torn place; a rip.
tear • ***verb*** **tore, torn, tearing** • ***noun,*** *plural* **tears**

tear[2] (tir) ***noun*** a drop of the salty liquid that flows in the eyes.
tear • ***noun,*** *plural* **tears**
● The words **tear** and **tier** sound alike.
A *tear* rolled down the crying boy's cheek.
The third *tier* of the cake is chocolate.

teardrop (tir′dräp) ***noun*** *the same as* **tear**[2].
tear·drop • ***noun,*** *plural* **teardrops**

tearful (tir′fəl) ***adjective*** **1** weeping. **2** causing tears; sad [a *tearful* story].
tear·ful • ***adjective***

tear gas (tir) ***noun*** a gas that makes the eyes hurt and blinds them with tears.

tease (tēz) ***verb*** to bother or annoy with joking or playful fooling [I *teased* him about his necktie.]
noun a person who teases.
tease • ***verb*** **teased, teasing** • ***noun,*** *plural* **teases**

teaspoon (tē′spo͞on) ***noun*** **1** a spoon that is used for stirring tea or coffee and for eating some soft foods. **2** a measuring unit used in cooking. It is equal to one-third of a tablespoon.
tea·spoon • ***noun,*** *plural* **teaspoons**

technical (tek′ni kəl) ***adjective*** **1** having to do with the skills that are used in building and fixing things [a *technical* school]. **2** having to do with a particular art, science, or profession [a *technical* vocabulary].
tech·ni·cal • ***adjective***

technician (tek nish′ən) ***noun*** a person who has skill in the techniques of some art or science [a laboratory *technician*].
tech·ni·cian • ***noun,*** *plural* **technicians**

technique (tek nēk′) ***noun*** a way of using tools, instruments, or materials and following rules in doing something artistic or carrying out a scientific experiment [a violinist with good bowing *technique*].
tech·nique • ***noun,*** *plural* **techniques**

technology (tek näl′ə jē) ***noun*** science as it is put to use in the work of everyday life [medical *technology*].
tech·nol·o·gy • ***noun***

teddy bear (ted′ē ber′) ***noun*** a stuffed toy that looks like a bear cub.
ted·dy bear • ***noun,*** *plural* **teddy bears**

tee (tē) ***noun*** **1** a small holder on which a golf player sometimes places the ball before hitting it. **2** the place from which a golf player makes the first shot toward a hole.
tee • ***noun,*** *plural* **tees**
● The words **tee, tea,** and **ti** sound alike.
She placed a golf ball on the *tee*.
We drink iced *tea* in the summer.
Do, re, mi, fa, sol, la, *ti*, do.

teem (tēm) ***verb*** to be very full [The lake *teemed* with fish.]
teem • ***verb*** **teemed, teeming**
● The words **teem** and **team** sound alike.
The woods *teem* with living things.
We worked as a *team* to finish the dishes.

teen (tēn) ***noun*** **1** *a short form of* **teenager**. **2 teens** the years from 13 to 19.
teen • ***noun,*** *plural* **teens**

teenager (tēn′āj ər) ***noun*** a person who is 13 through 19 years of age.
teen·ag·er • ***noun,*** *plural* **teenagers**

teeny (tē′nē) [*an informal word*] ***adjective*** *the same as* **tiny**.
tee·ny • ***adjective*** **teenier, teeniest**

teepee (tē′pē) ***noun*** *another spelling of* **tepee**.
tee·pee • ***noun,*** *plural* **teepees**

teeter (tēt′ər) ***verb*** to move in an unsteady way; to wobble [The ladder *teetered* and fell.]
tee·ter • ***verb*** **teetered, teetering**

teeter-totter (tēt′ər tät′ər) ***noun*** *another name for* **seesaw**.
tee·ter-tot·ter • ***noun,*** *plural* **teeter-totters**

teeth (tēth) ***noun*** *plural of* **tooth**.

teethe (tē*th*) ***verb*** to grow teeth [The baby cried because she is *teething* and her gums hurt.]
teethe • ***verb*** **teethed, teething**

telecast (tel′ə kast) ***noun*** a television broadcast.
tel·e·cast • ***noun,*** *plural* **telecasts**

telegram (tel′ə gram) ***noun*** a message that is sent by telegraph.
tel·e·gram • ***noun,*** *plural* **telegrams**

a	cat	ō	go	ʉ	fur	ə = a *in* ago	
ā	ape	ô	law, for	ch	chin	e *in* agent	
ä	cot, car	o͝o	look	sh	she	i *in* pencil	
e	ten	o͞o	tool	th	thin	o *in* atom	
ē	me	oi	oil	*th*	then	u *in* circus	
i	fit	ou	out	zh	measure		
ī	ice	u	up	ŋ	ring		

telegraph (tel′ə graf) *noun* a device or system for sending messages. It uses a code of electrical signals sent through a wire or by radio.
verb **1** to send by telegraph [They *telegraphed* the message to China.] **2** to send a telegram to [*Telegraph* them at once.]
tel·e·graph • *noun, plural* **telegraphs** • *verb* **telegraphed, telegraphing**

telephone (tel′ə fōn) *noun* **1** a system for sending sounds over distances by changing them into electrical signals which are sent through a wire or by radio and then changed back into sounds. **2** a device for sending and receiving sounds in this way.
verb **1** to talk over a telephone [He *telephones* every week.] **2** to send by telephone [We *telephoned* the good news right away.] **3** to speak to by telephone [*Telephone* Grandmother on her birthday.]
tel·e·phone • *noun, plural for sense 2 only* **telephones** • *verb* **telephoned, telephoning**

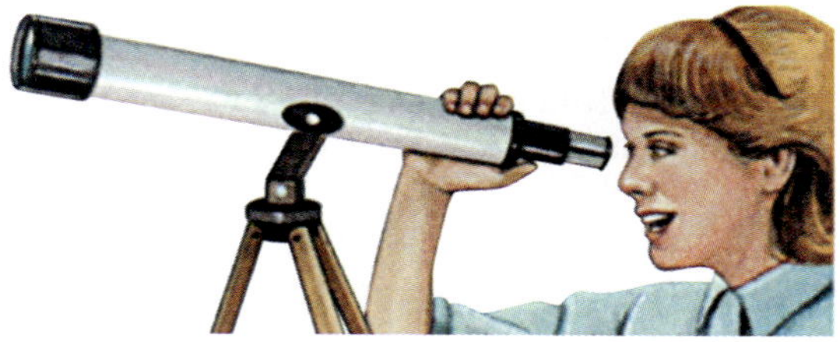

telescope

telescope (tel′ə skōp) *noun* a device to look through that makes far-off objects seem closer and larger. It is made up of one or more tubes containing lenses and, often, mirrors.
tel·e·scope • *noun, plural* **telescopes**

televise (tel′ə vīz) *verb* to send pictures of by television [The football game was *televised*.]
tel·e·vise • *verb* **televised, televising**

television (tel′ə vizh ən) *noun* **1** a system for sending pictures through space. The light rays are changed to electrical waves that are picked up by a receiver that changes them back to light rays and shows them on a screen. The sound that goes with the picture is sent by radio at the same time. **2** such a receiver.
tel·e·vi·sion • *noun, plural for sense 2 only* **televisions**

tell (tel) *verb* **1** to put into words; say [*Tell* the truth.] —Look for the WORD CHOICES box at the entry **say**. **2** to give the story; to report [The book *tells* of their adventures.] **3** to be a sign of something [Her smile *told* of her joy.] **4** to let know; inform [*Tell* me about the game.] **5** to know by seeing or hearing; recognize [I can *tell* the difference between them.] **6** to order or command [She *told* us to leave.] **7** to have a result [The strain is beginning to *tell*.] **—tell off** [*an informal use*] to scold or criticize in a harsh way. **—tell on** [*an informal use*] to tell secrets about; to tattle.
tell • *verb* **told, telling**

teller (tel′ər) *noun* a worker in a bank who receives and pays out money.
tell·er • *noun, plural* **tellers**

temp. *abbreviation for* temperature.

temper (tem′pər) *noun* **1** a mood or state of mind [Is she in a good *temper* today?] **2** a calm state of mind; self-control [Keep your *temper*. He lost his *temper*.] **3** a tendency to get angry [What a *temper* he has!]
tem·per • *noun, plural* **tempers**

temperate (tem′pər ət) *adjective* neither very hot nor very cold [a *temperate* climate].
tem·per·ate • *adjective*

temperature (tem′prə chər *or* tem′pər ə chər) *noun* **1** the degree of heat or cold in something. It is measured by a thermometer. **2** body heat that is above normal; a fever [She has a *temperature* again.]
tem·per·a·ture • *noun, plural* **temperatures**

temple[1] (tem′pəl) *noun* **1** a building for the worship of God or a god. **2** *another name for* **synagogue**.
tem·ple • *noun, plural* **temples**

temple[2] (tem′pəl) *noun* the flat area at either side of the forehead, above and behind the eye.
tem·ple • *noun, plural* **temples**

tempo (tem′pō) *noun* the rate of speed for playing a certain piece of music [Play the march at a slow *tempo*.]
tem·po • *noun, plural* **tempos**

temporary (tem′pər er′ē) *adjective* lasting only for a short time; not permanent [He took a *temporary* job.]
tem·po·rar·y • *adjective*

tempt (tempt) *verb* **1** to try to get a person to do or want something that is wrong or is not allowed [He *tempted* me to eat all the cake.] **2** to be attractive to [The bowl of goldfish *tempted* the cat.]
tempt • *verb* **tempted, tempting**

temptation (temp tā′shən) *noun* **1** something that tempts [The fresh cookies were a *temptation* to all of us.] **2** the act of tempting.
temp·ta·tion • *noun, plural* **temptations**

T

ten (ten) ***noun*** the cardinal number between nine and eleven; 10.
adjective being one more than nine [*ten* fingers].
ten • ***noun,*** *plural* **tens** • ***adjective***

tenant (ten′ənt) ***noun*** a person who pays rent to use land or to live in a building or apartment.
ten·ant • ***noun,*** *plural* **tenants**

Ten Commandments in the Bible, the ten laws that God gave to Moses.

tend[1] (tend) ***verb*** to take care of; watch over [Shepherds *tend* sheep. I'll *tend* the store.]
tend • ***verb*** **tended, tending**

tend[2] (tend) ***verb*** to be likely [Those children *tend* to stay up too late.]
tend • ***verb*** **tended, tending**

tendency (ten′dən sē) ***noun*** the fact of being likely to move or act in a certain way [She has a *tendency* to complain.]
tend·en·cy • ***noun,*** *plural* **tendencies**

tender (ten′dər) ***adjective*** **1** soft or delicate and easy to chew or cut [*tender* meat]. **2** hurting or feeling pain easily; sensitive [*tender* skin]. **3** warm; loving [a *tender* smile].
ten·der • ***adjective***

tendon (ten′dən) ***noun*** the cord of tough fiber that fastens a muscle to a bone or other body part.
ten·don • ***noun,*** *plural* **tendons**

tendril (ten′drəl) ***noun*** any one of the small, curling stems that hold up a climbing plant by coiling around something.
ten·dril • ***noun,*** *plural* **tendrils**

tenement (ten′ə mənt) ***noun*** an old, crowded apartment house in the poor part of a city.
ten·e·ment • ***noun,*** *plural* **tenements**

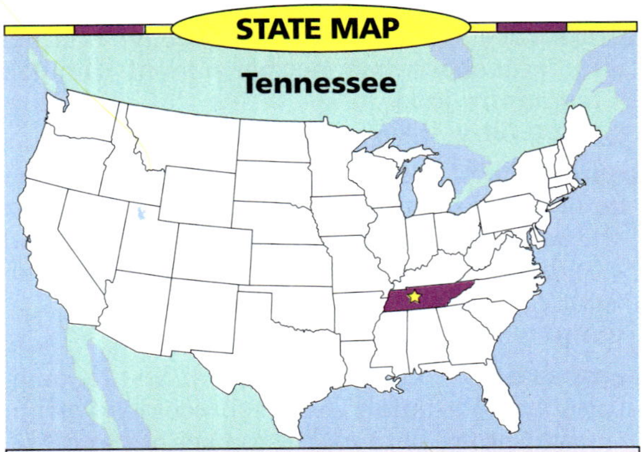

Statehood: 1796, the 16th state • **Capital:** Nashville

Tennessee (ten ə sē′) a State in the east central part of the U.S. Its capital is Nashville. Abbreviated **TN** or **Tenn.**
Ten·nes·see

tennis (ten′is) ***noun*** a game that is played on a court divided by a net. Players hit a ball back and forth over the net with rackets.
ten·nis • ***noun***

tenor (ten′ər) ***noun*** **1** the highest kind of man's singing voice. **2** a singer with such a voice.
ten·or • ***noun,*** *plural* **tenors**

tense[1] (tens) ***adjective*** **1** stretched tight [*tense* muscles]. **2** feeling or showing nervous strain; anxious [a *tense* silence]. **3** causing a nervous feeling [a *tense* situation].
verb to make or become tense; tighten [His muscles *tensed* before the race.]
tense • ***adjective*** **tenser, tensest**
• ***verb*** **tensed, tensing**

tense[2] (tens) ***noun*** any one of the forms of a verb that show whether the action took place in the past, takes place at the present time, or will take place in the future [The past *tense* of "go" is "went."]
tense • ***noun,*** *plural* **tenses**

tension (ten′shən) ***noun*** **1** the fact or condition of stretching or being stretched [The great *tension* in the wire made it snap.] **2** nervous strain; an anxious feeling [The surprise quiz created *tension* in the classroom.]
ten·sion • ***noun***

tents

a	cat	ō	go	ʉ	fur	ə =	a *in* ago
ā	ape	ô	law, for	ch	chin		e *in* agent
ä	cot, car	oo	look	sh	she		i *in* pencil
e	ten	ōō	tool	th	thin		o *in* atom
ē	me	oi	oil	*th*	then		u *in* circus
i	fit	ou	out	zh	measure		
ī	ice	u	up	ŋ	ring		

tent (tent) ***noun*** a shelter of canvas or other material that is stretched over poles and attached to stakes.
tent • ***noun,*** *plural* **tents**

tentacle (ten′tə kəl) ***noun*** a long, slender part growing around the head or mouth of some animals. Tentacles are used for feeling, gripping, or moving.
ten·ta·cle • ***noun,*** *plural* **tentacles**

tenth (tenth) ***adjective*** coming after nine others in a series; 10th in order.
noun **1** the number, person, or thing that is tenth. **2** one of ten equal parts of something; 1/10.
tenth • ***adjective*** • ***noun,*** *plural* **tenths**

tepee

tepee (tē′pē) ***noun*** a tent made of animal skins or other material and shaped like a cone. Some Native American peoples used tepees.
te·pee • ***noun,*** *plural* **tepees**

WORD HISTORY

tepee

The word **tepee** comes from a word that means "a place to live," in the language of a Native American people of the northern plains of the U.S.

tepid (tep′id) ***adjective*** slightly warm; lukewarm.
tep·id • ***adjective***

term (tʉrm) ***noun*** **1** the time during which something lasts; the time that is set by law or agreement [a *term* of office]. **2** a division of a school year [spring *term*]. **3 terms** the conditions of a contract, agreement, will, or sale. **4 terms** relations between persons [We are still on good *terms*.] **5** a word or phrase with a special meaning in some science or art [a computer *term;* a musical *term*].
term • ***noun,*** *plural* **terms**

terminal (tʉr′mi nəl) ***adjective*** **1** at or forming the end of something [a *terminal* bud on a branch]. **2** describing the last stages of a disease that will soon cause death [*terminal* cancer].
noun **1** either end of an electrical circuit. **2** a main station for trains, airplanes, or buses. **3** an electronic device with a typewriter keyboard and a video screen. It allows the user to communicate directly with a computer.
ter·mi·nal • ***adjective*** • ***noun,*** *plural* **terminals**

terminate (tʉr′mi nāt′) ***verb*** to bring or come to an end; to stop or end [They *terminated* their contract.]
ter·mi·nate • ***verb*** **terminated, terminating**

termite (tʉr′mīt) ***noun*** a small insect somewhat like an ant. It eats wood, lives in large colonies, and damages wooden buildings.
ter·mite • ***noun,*** *plural* **termites**

tern (tʉrn) ***noun*** a sea bird that is like a small gull. It has webbed feet, a slender body, a straight bill, and a forked tail.
tern • ***noun,*** *plural* **terns**
● The words **tern** and **turn** sound alike.
A gull and a *tern* flew over the beach.
It's my *turn* to walk the dog.

terrace (ter′əs) ***noun*** **1** a flat platform of earth with sloping sides. **2** any one of a series of such platforms, rising one above another. **3** a paved area next to a house; a patio.
ter·race • ***noun,*** *plural* **terraces**

terrapin (ter′ə pin) ***noun*** a North American turtle that lives in or near fresh water or along seacoasts.
ter·ra·pin • ***noun,*** *plural* **terrapins**

terrarium (tə rer′ē əm) ***noun*** a glass container holding a garden of small plants, or one used for raising small land animals.
ter·rar·i·um • ***noun,*** *plural* **terrariums**

terrestrial (tər es′trē əl) ***adjective*** living on land, not in water [a *terrestrial* animal].
ter·res·tri·al • ***adjective***

terrible (ter′i bəl) ***adjective*** **1** causing great fear or terror [a *terrible* flood]. **2** very great

T

[*terrible* suffering]. **3** [*an informal use*] very bad; unpleasant [a *terrible* movie].
ter·ri·ble • *adjective*

terrier (ter′ē ər) *noun* any one of several kinds of small, active dog.
ter·ri·er • *noun, plural* **terriers**

terrific (tər if′ik) *adjective* **1** causing great fear [a *terrific* hurricane]. **2** [*an informal use*] very great or unusual [We saw a *terrific* movie.]
ter·rif·ic • *adjective*

terrify (ter′i fī′) *verb* to fill with terror; frighten very badly [The mean dog *terrified* the little girl.] —Look for the WORD CHOICES box at the entry **frighten**.
ter·ri·fy • *verb* **terrified, terrifying, terrifies**

territory (ter′i tôr′ē) *noun* **1** the land ruled by a nation or state. **2** any large area of land; region. **3 Territory** a large division of a country, that does not have the full rights of a province or state.
ter·ri·to·ry • *noun, plural* **territories**

terror (ter′ər) *noun* **1** great fear —Look for the WORD CHOICES box at the entry **panic**. **2** a person or thing that causes great fear.
ter·ror • *noun, plural for sense 2 only* **terrors**

terrorism (ter′ər iz əm) *noun* the use of force and threats to frighten people into obeying.
ter·ror·ism • *noun*

terrorize (ter′ər īz) *verb* **1** to fill with terror [The tiger *terrorized* the village.] **2** to keep power over by force or threats [The enemy army *terrorized* the people it captured.]
ter·ror·ize • *verb* **terrorized, terrorizing**

terry (ter′ē) *noun* a kind of cotton cloth that is covered with tiny loops of thread that have not been cut. It is made into towels and bathrobes. This fabric is also called **terry cloth**.
ter·ry • *noun*

test (test) *noun* **1** an examination or trial to find out what something is like, what it contains, or how good it is [an eye *test;* a *test* of courage]. **2** a set of questions or problems for finding out how much someone knows or how much skill someone has [a driver's *test*].
verb to give a test to [Mrs. Jones *tested* the class yesterday.]
test • *noun, plural* **tests** • *verb* **tested, testing**

Testament (tes′tə mənt) *noun* either of the two parts of the Christian Bible, the **Old Testament** and the **New Testament**.
Tes·ta·ment • *noun, plural* **Testaments**

testify (tes′ti fī′) *verb* **1** to tell or give as proof in a court [Mr. Johnson *testified* that we had stolen his lawnmower.] **2** to be or give a sign of [Her look *testified* to her impatience.]
tes·ti·fy • *verb* **testified, testifying, testifies**

testimony (tes′ti mō′nē) *noun* a statement made by a person who testifies in a court.
tes·ti·mo·ny • *noun*

test tube *noun* a glass tube that is closed at one end. It is used in chemical experiments.
test tube • *noun, plural* **test tubes**

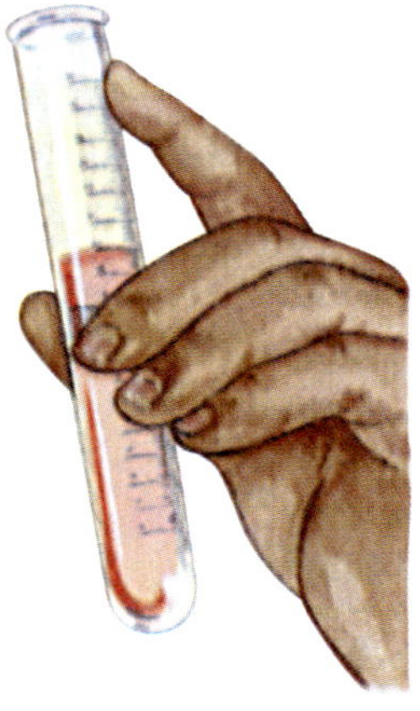
test tube

tetanus (tet′n əs) *noun* a disease that causes muscles, especially in the jaw, to become stiff or tight and that often causes death. It is caused by germs that get into the blood through a deep cut or wound.
tet·a·nus • *noun*

tether (te*th*′ər) *noun* a rope or chain that is tied to an animal to keep it from roaming.
verb to tie to a place with a tether [The horse was *tethered* to the fence post.]
teth·er • *noun, plural* **tethers**
• *verb* **tethered, tethering**

STATE MAP

Texas

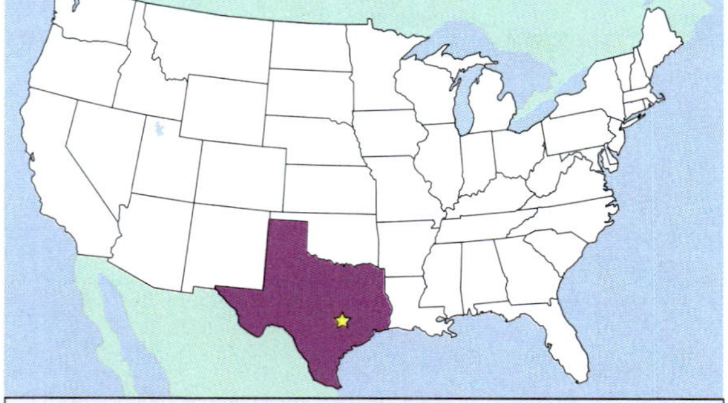

Statehood: 1845, the 28th state • **Capital:** Austin

a cat	ō go	ʉ fur	ə = a *in* ago
ā ape	ô law, for	ch chin	e *in* agent
ä cot, car	oo look	sh she	i *in* pencil
e ten	ōō tool	th thin	o *in* atom
ē me	oi oil	*th* then	u *in* circus
i fit	ou out	zh measure	
ī ice	u up	ŋ ring	

Texas (teks′əs) a State in the south central part of the U.S. Its capital is Austin. Abbreviated **TX** or **Tex.**
Tex·as

text (tekst) ***noun*** **1** the main part of the printed material on a page, not including notes or pictures. **2** the exact words that are used in a book or speech. **3** *a short form of* **textbook**.
text • ***noun, plural for senses 2 and 3 only*** **texts**

textbook (tekst′bo͝ok) ***noun*** a book that is used in teaching and studying a subject in a school or college.
text·book • ***noun, plural*** **textbooks**

textile (teks′tīl *or* teks′təl) ***noun*** a fabric that is made by weaving or knitting; cloth.
adjective having to do with weaving or woven fabrics [the *textile* industry].
tex·tile • ***noun, plural*** **textiles** • ***adjective***

texture (teks′chər) ***noun*** the look and feel of a fabric or of any other kind of material [Bricks may have a rough *texture*.]
tex·ture • ***noun, plural*** **textures**

Thai (tī) ***noun*** **1** a person born or living in Thailand. **2** the language of Thailand.
Thai • ***noun, plural for sense 1 only*** **Thais** or **Thai**

Thailand (tī′land) a country in southeastern Asia. Its older name is **Siam**.
Thai·land

than (*th*an *or th*ən) ***conjunction*** **1** compared to. This word is used before the second part of a comparison [I am taller *than* you.] **2** besides; except [What could I do other *than* stop?]

thank (thaŋk) ***verb*** **1** to say that one is grateful to another person for something good or useful [We *thanked* her for helping us.] **2** to blame [We have him to *thank* for this mess.]
thank • ***verb*** **thanked, thanking**

thankful (thaŋk′fəl) ***adjective*** feeling or showing thanks; grateful [I'm *thankful* for your help with the party.]
thank·ful • ***adjective***

thankless (thaŋk′ləs) ***adjective*** not likely to bring thanks; not appreciated [a *thankless* task].
thank·less • ***adjective***

thanks (thaŋks) ***plural noun*** the act or fact of thanking someone [I owe you *thanks*.]
interjection I thank you [*Thanks!* I really needed your help.]

thanksgiving (thaŋks′giv′iŋ) ***noun*** **1** the act of giving thanks [He said a few words of *thanksgiving* for my safe return.] **2 Thanksgiving** *a short form of* **Thanksgiving Day**.
thanks·giv·ing • ***noun***

Thanksgiving Day ***noun*** **1** a U.S. holiday for feasting and giving thanks. It honors the Pilgrims' celebration of the good harvest in 1621. It is held on the fourth Thursday in November. **2** a similar Canadian holiday held on the second Monday of October.

that (*th*at *or th*ət) ***pronoun*** **1** the person or thing that is being talked about [*That* is José.] **2** the thing farther away or different in some way [This is smaller than *that*.] **3** who, whom, or which [She's the one *that* we will vote for. Here's the book *that* I borrowed.] **4** when [It snowed on the day *that* we left.]
adjective **1** being the person or thing talked about [*That* girl is Sue.] **2** being the person or thing farther away or different in some way [This bicycle cost more than *that* one.]
conjunction *that* is used before: **1** a noun clause that states a fact [It's clear *that* you are wrong.] **2** a clause showing a purpose [They died *that* we might live.] **3** a clause showing a result [I ate so much *that* I was sick.] **4** a clause showing the cause of something [I'm sorry *that* you fell.] **5** an incomplete sentence showing a wish or feeling [Oh, *that* it could be spring!]
adverb to the degree or extent being expressed; so [I can't see *that* far.]
—that's that! that is decided! that is finished!
that • ***pronoun, plural*** **those** • ***adjective, plural*** **those** • ***conjunction*** • ***adverb***

thatch (thach) ***noun*** material for covering a roof, such as straw, rushes, or palm leaves.
verb to cover with thatch.
thatch • ***noun*** • ***verb*** **thatched, thatching**

thaw (thô *or* thä) ***verb*** **1** to melt [The snow *thawed*.] —Look for the WORD CHOICES box at the entry **melt**. **2** to pass out of a frozen condition [We let the frozen steaks *thaw*.]
noun weather that is warm enough to melt snow and ice [The spring *thaw* came early.]
thaw • ***verb*** **thawed, thawing** • ***noun, plural*** **thaws**

the (*th*ə *or th*ē) ***definite article*** **1** that one which is here or which has been mentioned [*The* day is hot. *The* story ended.] **2** one and only [*the* universe]. **3** that one of a number or group [Open *the* front door. Take *the* one on top.] **4** that one which is thought of as best or

outstanding [*the* football player of the year]. **5** any one of a certain kind [*The* goat is a mammal.]
adverb **1** that much; to that degree [*the* better to see you with]. **2** by that much [*the* sooner *the* better].

theater or **theatre** (thē′ə tər) *noun* **1** a place where plays or movies are shown. **2** the art or business of acting or of producing plays.
the·a·ter or **the·a·tre** • *noun, plural for sense 1 only* **theaters** or **theatres**

theft (theft) *noun* the act of stealing.
theft • *noun, plural* **thefts**

their (*th*er) *adjective* done by them or having to do with them [*their* work; *their* shoes].
- The words **their, there,** and **they're** sound alike.
  Their house has green shutters.
  There is no place like home.
  They're going, aren't they?

theirs (*th*erz) *pronoun* the one or the ones that belong to them [This book is *theirs*. *Theirs* are nicer than ours.]

them (*th*em) *pronoun* the form of **they** that is used: **1** after certain verbs [Their parents drove *them* to school. I saw *them*.] **2** after prepositions [Give it to *them*.]

theme (thēm) *noun* **1** a topic or subject [What is the *theme* of your report?] **2** a short essay or piece of writing on a single subject that is written for a class in school. **3** the main tune or song from a movie, play, or TV program.
theme • *noun, plural* **themes**

WORD CHOICES

Synonyms of **theme**

The words **theme, subject,** and **topic** share the meaning "the chief matter being talked about or written about."

Charity was the *theme* of the sermon.
War is the *subject* of her new book.
What was the *topic* of the debate?

themselves (*th*em selvz′) *pronoun* **1** their own selves. This form of **they** is used when the persons who do the action of the verb are the same as the persons who have the action done to them [They hurt *themselves*.] **2** their usual or true selves [They're not *themselves* today.] This word is also used to give more force to what is being said [They *themselves* told me.]
them·selves • *pronoun*

then (*th*en) *adverb* **1** at that time [We were young *then*.] **2** soon afterward; next in time [The party ended, and *then* we left.] **3** next in order [Our house is on the corner and *then* comes the neighbor's house.] **4** in that case; therefore [If you read it, *then* you'll know.]
noun that time [They were gone by *then*.]
—then and there at once.

theology (thē äl′ə jē) *noun* **1** the study of God and of religious beliefs. **2** a system of religious beliefs [Catholic *theology;* Jewish *theology*].
the·ol·o·gy • *noun, plural for sense 2 only* **theologies**

theoretical (thē′ə ret′i kəl) *adjective* based on or having to do with a theory [a *theoretical* plan].
the·o·ret·i·cal • *adjective*

theory (thē′ə rē *or* thir′ē) *noun* **1** an explanation of how or why something happens. **2** the basic principles of a science or art [music *theory*]. **3** an opinion or idea about something [My *theory* is that the witness lied.]
the·o·ry • *noun, plural for senses 1 and 3 only* **theories**

therapy (ther′ə pē) *noun* any method of treating disease or injury [heat *therapy*].
ther·a·py • *noun, plural* **therapies**

there (*th*er) *adverb* **1** at or in that place [Who lives *there?*] **2** to, toward, or into that place [Let's go *there*.] **3** at that point; then [I read to page 51 and stopped *there*.] **4** in that matter [*There* you are wrong.] **5** right now [*There* goes the bell.]
noun that place [We left from *there*.]
- The words **there, their,** and **they're** sound alike.
  There is no place like home.
  Sometimes, they eat *their* lunch outside.
  I don't know how *they're* doing.

thereabouts (*th*er′ə bouts) or **thereabout** (*th*er′ə bout) *adverb* **1** near that time [I'll

a cat	ō go	ʉ fur	ə = a *in* ago
ā ape	ô law, for	ch chin	e *in* agent
ä cot, car	oo look	sh she	i *in* pencil
e ten	ōō tool	th thin	o *in* atom
ē me	oi oil	*th* then	u *in* circus
i fit	ou out	zh measure	
ī ice	u up	ŋ ring	

meet you at 6 o'clock or *thereabouts*.] **2** near that place. **3** near that number or amount.
there·a·bouts or **there·a·bout** • *adverb*

thereafter (*th*er af′tər) *adverb* after that [She left the city and lived on a farm *thereafter*.]
there·af·ter • *adverb*

thereby (*th*er bī′) *adverb* **1** by that means. **2** connected with that [*Thereby* hangs a tale.]
there·by • *adverb*

therefore (*th*er′fôr) *adverb* for this or that reason; as a result of this or that; hence [I missed the bus and *therefore* was late.]
there·fore • *adverb*

there's (*th*erz) there is.

thermal (thʉr′məl) *adjective* **1** having to do with heat. **2** made with air spaces that hold in the warmth of the body [*thermal* underwear].
ther·mal • *adjective*

thermometer

thermometer (thər mäm′ə tər) *noun* a device for measuring the temperature. An ordinary thermometer is a glass tube with a scale showing degrees. It contains a small amount of mercury that rises or falls in the tube as the temperature changes.
ther·mom·e·ter • *noun, plural* **thermometers**

thermos (thʉr′məs) *noun* a container for keeping liquids at almost the same temperature for several hours [a *thermos* of soup]. This container is also called a **thermos bottle**.
ther·mos • *noun, plural* **thermoses**

thermostat (thʉr′mə stat) *noun* a device that keeps the temperature even. It is connected to a heating or cooling device, such as a furnace or air conditioner, which it turns on when the temperature changes and turns off when the proper temperature has been reached.
ther·mo·stat • *noun, plural* **thermostats**

thesaurus (thi sôr′əs *or* thi sär′əs) *noun* a book that contains lists of synonyms and antonyms.
the·sau·rus • *noun, plural* **thesauri** (thi sôr′ī) or **thesauruses**

these (*th*ēz) *pronoun, adjective plural of* **this**.

they (*th*ā) *pronoun* **1** the persons, animals, or things that are being talked about [The players knew *they* had won the game. Put the keys back where *they* were.] **2** people in general [*They* say it will be a very cold winter.]
they • *pronoun, singular* **he, she,** or **it**

they'd (*th*ād) **1** they had. **2** they would.

they'll (*th*āl) they will.

they're (*th*er *or* *th*ā′ər) they are.

- The words **they're, their,** and **there** sound alike.
  They're going, aren't they?
  Their house has green shutters.
  He stood *there*, by the big tree.

they've (*th*āv) they have.

thick (thik) *adjective* **1** great in width or depth; not thin [a *thick* board]. **2** as measured from one side to the other [a wall ten inches *thick*]. **3** growing or put close together; dense; heavy [*thick* hair; *thick* smoke; a *thick* crowd]. **4** flowing or pouring slowly [*thick* soup].
adverb in a thick way [Trees grew *thick* in the forest.]
noun the most active part [the *thick* of the fight].
thick • *adjective* **thicker, thickest** • *adverb* • *noun*

thicken (thik′ən) *verb* to make or become thicker [She *thickened* the gravy with flour.]
thick·en • *verb* **thickened, thickening**

thicket (thik′ət) *noun* a place where shrubs or small trees grow close together.
thick·et • *noun, plural* **thickets**

thickness (thik′nəs) *noun* **1** the fact or condition of being thick. **2** the distance from one side through to the other [a *thickness* of four inches]. **3** a layer [three *thicknesses* of cloth].
thick·ness • *noun, plural for senses 2 and 3 only* **thicknesses**

thief (thēf) *noun* a person who steals in a secret way.
thief • *noun, plural* **thieves** (thēvz)

thigh (thī) *noun* the part of the leg between the knee and the hip.
thigh • *noun, plural* **thighs**

T

thighbone (thī′bōn) ***noun*** the bone in the thigh which goes from the hip to the knee; femur. It is the largest and longest bone in the body.
thigh·bone • ***noun,*** *plural* **thighbones**

thimble (thim′bəl) ***noun*** a small, metal or plastic cap used in sewing. It is worn over the tip of the finger that pushes the needle.
thim·ble • ***noun,*** *plural* **thimbles**

thin (thin) ***adjective*** **1** small in width or depth; not thick [a *thin* board]. **2** having little fat or flesh; lean; slender [a *thin* man]. **3** not being close together; not dense; sparse [*thin* hair; a *thin* crowd]. **4** flowing or pouring quickly [*thin* soup]. **5** not deep and strong; weak [a *thin* voice]. **6** seen through easily; flimsy [a *thin* veil; a *thin* excuse].
adverb in a thin way [Spread it *thin*.]
verb to make or become thin [He *thinned* the soup by adding water.]
thin • ***adjective*** **thinner, thinnest** • ***adverb*** • ***verb*** **thinned, thinning**

WORD CHOICES

Synonyms of **thin**

The words **thin, slender,** and **slight** share the meaning "having little fat or flesh."

too *thin* after his recent illness
slender again because of exercise
as short and *slight* as a jockey

thing (thiŋ) ***noun*** **1** a real object or substance that can be seen or felt. **2** any matter or affair [How are *things* with you?] **3 things** clothing or other personal belongings.
thing • ***noun,*** *plural* **things**

think (thiŋk) ***verb*** **1** to use the mind [*Think* before you act.] **2** to form or have in the mind [She *thinks* happy thoughts.] **3** to consider or judge [I *thought* the movie was great.] **4** to believe, expect, or imagine [I *think* I heard the phone ring.] **5** to remember [He *thinks* about the old days.] **6** to give thought [He *thinks* about the future.] **7** to be thoughtful [She *thinks* of the needs of others.]
—think nothing of to think of as easy or not important [She *thinks nothing of* running five miles.] **—think over** to give thought to; consider [He *thought over* the question before answering.] **—think up** to invent or plan by thinking [He *thinks up* new songs every day.]
think • ***verb*** **thought, thinking**

third (thurd) ***adjective*** coming after two others in a series; 3rd in order.
noun **1** the number, person, or thing that is third. **2** one of three equal parts of something; ⅓.
third • ***adjective*** • ***noun,*** *plural for sense 2 only* **thirds**

third person ***noun*** **1** the form of a pronoun that refers to the person or thing that is being talked about, or the persons or things that are being talked about. *He, him, she, her, it, they,* and *them* are in the third person. **2** the form of a verb that belongs with this kind of pronoun. *Does* in "She does" and *is* in "It is" are in the third person.

thirst (thurst) ***noun*** **1** the dry and uncomfortable feeling caused by a need for water; strong desire to drink. **2** any strong desire [a *thirst* for fame].
verb **1** to have a strong desire to drink. **2** to have a strong desire [I *thirst* for power.]
thirst • ***noun*** • ***verb*** **thirsted, thirsting**

thirsty (thurs′tē) ***adjective*** **1** wanting to drink. **2** having a strong desire [*thirsty* for power].
thirst·y • ***adjective*** **thirstier, thirstiest**

thirteen (thur′tēn′) ***noun*** the cardinal number between twelve and fourteen; 13.
adjective being one more than twelve [*thirteen* apples].
thir·teen • ***noun,*** *plural* **thirteens** • ***adjective***

thirteenth (thur′tēnth′) ***adjective*** coming after twelve others in a series; 13th in order.
noun **1** the number, person, or thing that is thirteenth. **2** one of thirteen equal parts of something; $\frac{1}{13}$.
thir·teenth • ***adjective*** • ***noun,*** *plural* **thirteenths**

thirtieth (thur′tē əth) ***adjective*** being ten more than twenty others in a series; 30th in order.
noun **1** the number, person, or thing that is

a	cat	ō	go	ʉ	fur	ə =	a *in* ago
ā	ape	ô	law, for	ch	chin		e *in* agent
ä	cot, car	oo	look	sh	she		i *in* pencil
e	ten	o͞o	tool	th	thin		o *in* atom
ē	me	oi	oil	*th*	then		u *in* circus
i	fit	ou	out	zh	measure		
ī	ice	u	up	ŋ	ring		

thirtieth. **2** one of thirty equal parts of something; 1/30.
thir·ti·eth • *adjective* • *noun, plural* **thirtieths**

thirty (thurt′ē) *noun* the cardinal number that is equal to three times ten; 30.
adjective being three times ten [*thirty* days in March].
thir·ty • *noun, plural* **thirties** • *adjective*

this (*th*is) *pronoun* **1** the person or thing that is being talked about or that is understood [*This* is Juan. What is the meaning of *this?*] **2** the thing that is present or nearer [*This* is prettier than that.] **3** the fact or idea that is about to be told [Listen to *this*.]
adjective **1** being the person or thing that is being talked about or that is understood [Copy down *this* rule.] **2** being the person or thing that is present or nearer [*This* house is newer than that one.]
adverb to the degree that is being pointed out; so [It was *this* big.]
this *pronoun, plural* **these** • *adjective* • *adverb*

thistle (this′əl) *noun* a plant with prickly leaves and flower heads of purple, white, pink, or yellow.
this·tle • *noun, plural* **thistles**

thong (thôŋ) *noun* **1** a narrow strip of leather, used as a lace or strap. **2** a kind of sandal with a flat sole. It is held on the foot by a strap between the big toe and the next toe.
thong • *noun, plural* **thongs**

Thoreau (thôr′ō *or* thə rō′), **Henry David** (hen′rē dā′vid) 1817-1862; U.S. writer of essays and books about nature.
Thor·eau, Hen·ry Da·vid

thorn (thôrn) *noun* a short, sharp point growing out of a plant stem.
thorn • *noun, plural* **thorns**

thorny (thôrn′ē) *adjective* **1** full of thorns [a *thorny* bush]. **2** difficult or painful [a *thorny* problem].
thorn·y • *adjective* **thornier, thorniest**

thorough (thur′ō) *adjective* **1** complete in every way; with nothing left out [a *thorough* search]. **2** very careful and exact [a *thorough* worker].
thor·ough • *adjective*

thoroughbred (thur′ō bred) *adjective* of pure breed [a *thoroughbred* cocker spaniel].
noun **1** any animal of pure breed. **2 Thoroughbred** a breed of horse used mainly for racing.
thor·ough·bred • *adjective* • *noun, plural* **thoroughbreds** or **Thoroughbreds**

thoroughfare (thur′ō fer) *noun* a main road.
thor·ough·fare • *noun, plural* **thoroughfares**

thoroughly (thur′ə lē) *adverb* in a thorough way [We searched the house *thoroughly*.]
thor·ough·ly • *adverb*

Thorpe (thôrp), **Jim** (jim) 1888-1953; U.S. athlete. His full name was *James Francis Thorpe*.

those (*th*ōz) *pronoun, adjective plural of* **that**.

though (*th*ō) *conjunction* **1** in spite of the fact that; although [*Though* it rained, we went.] **2** and yet; however [They will probably win, *though* no one thinks so.] **3** even if [*Though* you may fail, you will have tried.]
adverb however [I must leave; I'll be back, *though*.]

thought[1] (thôt *or* thät) *noun* **1** the act or process of thinking [She is deep in *thought*.] **2** what one thinks; an idea or opinion [a penny for your *thoughts*] —Look for the WORD CHOICES box at the entry **idea**. **3** attention or care [Give this matter some *thought*.]
thought • *noun, plural for sense 2 only* **thoughts**

thought[2] (thôt *or* thät) *verb past tense and past participle of* **think**.

thoughtful (thôt′fəl *or* thät′fəl) *adjective* **1** full of thought or showing thought; serious [a *thoughtful* book]. **2** showing care or paying attention to others; considerate [It was *thoughtful* of you to remember her birthday.]
thought·ful • *adjective*

thoughtless (thôt′ləs *or* thät′ləs) *adjective* showing little care for others; not considerate [Our *thoughtless* neighbors are very noisy.]
thought·less • *adjective*

thousand (thou′zənd) *noun* the cardinal number that is equal to ten times one hundred; 1,000.
adjective being ten times one hundred [a *thousand* miles].
thou·sand • *noun, plural* **thousands** • *adjective*

thousandth (thou′zəndth) *adjective* coming last in a series of a thousand; 1,000th.
noun **1** the thousandth one. **2** one of a thousand equal parts of something; 1/1000.

T

thou·sandth • *adjective* • *noun, plural* **thousandths**

thrash (thrash) *verb* **1** to give a severe beating to [She *thrashed* him with her cane.] —Look for the WORD CHOICES box at the entry **beat**. **2** to move about in a violent or jerky way [The hurt bird *thrashed* its wings.]
thrash • *verb* **thrashed, thrashing**

thread (thred) *noun* **1** a very thin cord used in sewing. It is made of strands of material such as spun cotton or silk. **2** anything long and slender like sewing thread. **3** the way that a number of ideas or events are joined together [I can't follow the *thread* of this story.] **4** the ridge that winds in a sloping way around a screw or inside a nut.
verb **1** to put a thread through the eye of [She *threaded* the needle.] **2** to get through by following a winding course [We *threaded* our way through the crowd.]
thread • *noun, plural* **threads** • *verb* **threaded, threading**

thread

threat (thret) *noun* **1** a warning that one plans to harm another if a certain thing is done or not done [The bully made *threats* to beat us up if we didn't give him some money.] **2** a sign of something dangerous, harmful, or unpleasant that is about to happen [There is a *threat* of rain in those clouds.]
threat • *noun, plural* **threats**

threaten (thret′n) *verb* **1** to make a threat; say that one plans to harm or punish [The umpire *threatened* to throw him out of the game.] **2** to be a possible danger to [The forest fire *threatened* the cabin.]
threat·en • *verb* **threatened, threatening**

three (thrē) *noun* the cardinal number between two and four; 3.
adjective being one more than two [*three* strikes].
three • *noun, plural* **threes** • *adjective*

thresh (thresh) *verb* to separate the seed, or grain, from by beating [Workers *threshed* the wheat.]
thresh • *verb* **threshed, threshing**

thresher (thresh′ər) *noun* a large machine used on farms for threshing grain. This machine is also called a **threshing machine**.
thresh·er • *noun, plural* **threshers**

threshold (thresh′ōld *or* thresh′hōld) *noun* **1** the sill of a door. **2** the point where something begins [at the *threshold* of a new career].
thresh·old • *noun, plural* **thresholds**

threw (thro͞o) *verb past tense of* **throw**.
● The words **threw** and **through** sound alike.
She *threw* three strikes past the batter.
The street runs *through* downtown.

thrift (thrift) *noun* care in the use of money so that there is no waste [By practicing *thrift*, he could live on his small income.]

thrifty (thrif′tē) *adjective* practicing or showing thrift [a *thrifty* buyer].
thrift·y • *adjective* **thriftier, thriftiest**

thrill (thril) *verb* to feel or make very excited [She *thrilled* at the praise. His playing *thrilled* us.]
noun **1** a strong feeling of excitement [Skiing gives me a *thrill*.] **2** something that causes such a feeling [My first airplane ride was a real *thrill*.]
thrill • *verb* **thrilled, thrilling** • *noun, plural* **thrills**

thriller (thril′ər) *noun* something that thrills people, especially a book, play, or film that is filled with suspense.
thrill·er • *noun, plural* **thrillers**

thrive (thrīv) *verb* **1** to succeed or prosper [Our business is *thriving*.] **2** to grow in a strong and healthy way [Plants *thrive* in good soil.]
thrive • *verb* **thrived** or **throve, thrived** or **thriv·en** (thriv′ən), **thriving**

throat (thrōt) *noun* **1** the front part of the neck. **2** the passage through the neck, leading to the stomach and lungs [I have a sore *throat*.]
throat • *noun, plural* **throats**

throb (thräb) *verb* to beat hard or fast [His heart *throbbed* with excitement.]
noun the act of throbbing; a strong beat [the *throb* of the music].
throb • *verb* **throbbed, throbbing** • *noun*

a	cat	ō	go	ʉ	fur	ə =	a *in* ago
ā	ape	ô	law, for	ch	chin		e *in* agent
ä	cot, car	o͝o	look	sh	she		i *in* pencil
e	ten	o͞o	tool	th	thin		o *in* atom
ē	me	oi	oil	*th*	then		u *in* circus
i	fit	ou	out	zh	measure		
ī	ice	u	up	ŋ	ring		

throne (thrōn) ***noun*** **1** the raised chair used during ceremonies by an official such as a queen or bishop. **2** the power or rank of a monarch [The king lost his *throne* in the revolution.]
throne • ***noun,*** *plural* **thrones**

throttle (thrät′l) ***noun*** **1** a valve that controls the flow of fuel into an engine. **2** a handle or pedal that works this valve.
verb to choke or strangle.
throt·tle • ***noun,*** *plural* **throttles**
• ***verb*** **throttled, throttling**

through (thro͞o) ***preposition*** **1** in one side and out the other side of; from end to end of [The nail went *through* the board. We drove *through* the tunnel.] **2** from one part of to another [Birds fly *through* the air.] **3** by way of [a route to Boston *through* New York]. **4** to many places in; around [We toured *through* Utah.] **5** from the beginning to the end of [We stayed in Maine *through* the summer.] **6** up to and including [This sale is on *through* Friday.] **7** by means of [We heard the news *through* friends.] **8** as a result of; because of [He won out *through* great courage.] **9** without making a stop for [He went *through* a red light.]
adverb **1** in one side and out the other [The target was pierced *through* by the arrow.] **2** from the beginning to the end [He saw the job *through*.] **3** in a complete and thorough way [We were soaked *through* by the rain.]
adjective **1** leading from one place to another; open [a *through* street]. **2** going on to the end without a stop or change [a *through* train to Boston]. **3** finished [I'm *through* with my work.]
● The words **through** and **threw** sound alike.
Are you *through* with your homework?
She *threw* out yesterday's newspaper.

throughout (thro͞o out′) ***preposition*** all the way through; in every part of [Fire spread *throughout* the town. It rained *throughout* the day.]
adverb **1** in every part; everywhere [The walls were painted white *throughout*.] **2** from start to finish [They stayed hopeful *throughout*.]
through·out • ***preposition*** • ***adverb***

throve (thrōv) ***verb*** *a past tense of* **thrive**.

throw (thrō) ***verb*** **1** to send through the air by a fast motion of the arm; to hurl or toss [She *threw* the ball.] **2** to send or cast in a certain direction [The trees *threw* shadows on the ground.] **3** to put into a certain condition or place [We were *thrown* into confusion. The judge *threw* her into jail.] **4** [*an informal use*] to lose on purpose [The boxer *threw* the fight.]
noun **1** the act of throwing. **2** the distance that something is or can be thrown [It's a stone's *throw* from here.]
—throw away **1** to get rid of; discard [*Throw away* the old newspapers.] **2** to fail to make use of; to waste [He *threw away* his chances by quitting school.] **—throw in** to add extra or free [I'll buy your camera if you *throw in* some film.] **—throw out** **1** to get rid of. **2** in baseball, to put out by throwing the ball to a base [The runner was *thrown out* at third.] **—throw up** *the same as the verb* **vomit**.
throw • ***verb*** **threw, thrown, throwing**
• ***noun,*** *plural for sense 1 only* **throws**

WORD CHOICES

Synonyms of **throw**

Many words share the meaning "to make something go through the air by a quick movement of the arm."

fire	hurl	toss
fling	pitch	

throwaway (thrō′ə wā) ***adjective*** made to be thrown away after being used [The soda comes in *throwaway* bottles.]
throw·a·way • ***adjective***

thrown (thrōn) ***verb*** *past participle of* **throw**.

thru (thro͞o) [*an informal word*] ***preposition, adverb, adjective*** *another spelling of* **through**.

thrush (thrush) ***noun*** one of a large group of songbirds. Some are plain in color, but others have a spotted or bright breast. The robin and bluebird are two kinds of thrush.
thrush • ***noun,*** *plural* **thrushes**

thrust (thrust) ***verb*** to push with sudden force [She *thrust* the money into his hand.] —Look for the WORD CHOICES box at the entry **push**.
noun **1** a sudden push or shove. **2** a lunge with a pointed weapon. **3** the forward force produced by the engines of a plane or rocket.
thrust • ***verb*** **thrust, thrusting** • ***noun,*** *plural for senses 1 and 2 only* **thrusts**

thruway (thro͞o′wā) ***noun*** *the same as* **expressway**.
thru·way • ***noun,*** *plural* **thruways**

T

thud (thud) ***noun*** the dull sound made when something heavy drops to the ground.
verb to hit with a thud [The boulder *thudded* at the base of the cliff.]
thud • ***noun,*** *plural* **thuds** • ***verb*** **thudded, thudding**

thug (thug) ***noun*** a rough, violent criminal.
thug • ***noun,*** *plural* **thugs**

thumb (thum) ***noun*** **1** the short, thick finger nearest the wrist. **2** the part of a glove that covers the thumb.
verb to handle or turn with the thumb [She *thumbed* the pages of the book.]
—all thumbs clumsy; awkward.
thumb • ***noun,*** *plural* **thumbs** • ***verb*** **thumbed, thumbing**

thumbnail (thum′nāl) ***noun*** the nail of the thumb.
adjective very small or brief [a *thumbnail* sketch].
thumb·nail • ***noun,*** *plural* **thumbnails** • ***adjective***

thumbtack (thum′tak) ***noun*** a tack with a wide, flat head, that can be pressed into something with the thumb.
thumb·tack • ***noun,*** *plural* **thumbtacks**

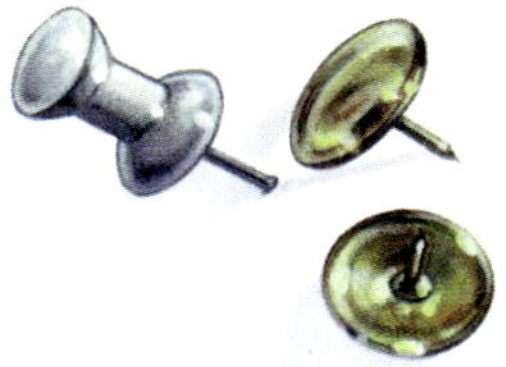
thumbtack

thump (thump) ***noun*** **1** a blow with something heavy and blunt. **2** the dull sound made by such a blow.
verb to hit, fall, or pound with a thump [My heart *thumped* after the race.]
thump • ***noun,*** *plural* **thumps** • ***verb*** **thumped, thumping**

thunder (thun′dər) ***noun*** **1** the loud noise that comes after a flash of lightning. It is caused by the sudden, violent movement of air which the flash produces. **2** any loud, rumbling noise that is like thunder [the *thunder* of applause].
verb **1** to produce thunder [It rained and *thundered* all night.] **2** to make, or move with, a sound like thunder [The crowd *thundered* down the steps.]
thun·der • ***noun*** • ***verb*** **thundered, thundering**

thunderbolt (thun′dər bōlt) ***noun*** a flash of lightning with the thunder that comes after it.
thun·der·bolt • ***noun,*** *plural* **thunderbolts**

thunderclap (thun′dər klap) ***noun*** a loud crash of thunder.
thun·der·clap • ***noun,*** *plural* **thunderclaps**

thunderous (thun′dər əs) ***adjective*** making a loud, rumbling noise like thunder.
thun·der·ous • ***adjective***

thundershower (thun′dər shou ər) ***noun*** a rain shower with thunder and lightning.
thun·der·show·er • ***noun,*** *plural* **thundershowers**

thunderstorm (thun′dər stôrm) ***noun*** a storm that has thunder and lightning.
thun·der·storm • ***noun,*** *plural* **thunderstorms**

Thursday (thurz′dā) ***noun*** the fifth day of the week. Abbreviated **Thurs.**
Thurs·day • ***noun,*** *plural* **Thursdays**

WORD HISTORY

Thursday

Thursday comes from a very old English word that means "Thor's day." *Thor* was the god of war, thunder, and strength in the ancient Scandinavian myths.

thus (*th*us) ***adverb*** **1** in this or that way [Do it *thus*.] **2** to this or that amount or degree; so [*Thus* far he has done well.] **3** as a result; therefore [She is ill and *thus* absent.]

thwart (thwôrt) ***verb*** to keep from doing; block [The guards *thwarted* his attempt to escape from the prison.]
thwart • ***verb*** **thwarted, thwarting**

thyroid (thī′roid) ***noun*** a gland near the windpipe. It makes a substance which controls the growth of the body.
thy·roid • ***noun,*** *plural* **thyroids**

ti (tē) ***noun*** the seventh note of a musical scale.
● The words **ti, tea,** and **tee** sound alike.
Do, re, mi, fa, sol, la, *ti*, do.
We drink iced *tea* in the summer.
She placed a golf ball on the *tee*.

a	cat	ō	go	ʉ	fur	ə =	a *in* ago
ā	ape	ô	law, for	ch	chin		e *in* agent
ä	cot, car	oo	look	sh	she		i *in* pencil
e	ten	ōō	tool	th	thin		o *in* atom
ē	me	oi	oil	*th*	then		u *in* circus
i	fit	ou	out	zh	measure		
ī	ice	u	up	ŋ	ring		

tiara (tē er′ə *or* tē är′ə) ***noun*** a small crown decorated with things such as jewels or flowers and worn by a woman.
ti·ar·a • ***noun,*** *plural* **tiaras**

Tibet (ti bet′) a region of China.
Ti·bet

tic (tik) ***noun*** a twitch of a muscle, especially of the face, that cannot be controlled.
tic • ***noun,*** *plural* **tics**
● The words **tic** and **tick** sound alike.

tick[1] (tik) ***noun*** **1** a light clicking sound [the *tick* of the clock]. **2** a mark (✓) made in checking off things.
verb **1** to make a tick or ticks [The watch *ticked* quietly.] **2** to count by ticks [The clock *ticked* away the seconds.]
tick • ***noun,*** *plural* **ticks** • ***verb*** **ticked, ticking**
● The words **tick** and **tic** sound alike.
I could hear the old clock *tick*.
My dog has a flea and *tick* problem.
He twitches from a nervous *tic*.

tick[2] (tik) ***noun*** one of a group of insects that suck the blood of people or animals.
tick • ***noun,*** *plural* **ticks**
● The words **tick** and **tic** sound alike.

ticket (tik′ət) ***noun*** **1** a printed card or piece of paper that one buys to get a certain right, such as the right to a seat in a theater or on a train. **2** the list of candidates of a political party in an election [the Republican *ticket*]. **3** [*an informal use*] a written order to appear in court for breaking a traffic law [a traffic *ticket*].
verb [*an informal use*] to give a traffic ticket to.
tick·et • ***noun,*** *plural* **tickets** • ***verb*** **ticketed, ticketing**

tickle (tik′əl) ***verb*** **1** to touch or stroke lightly in a way that causes laughter, twitching, or squirming [She *tickled* me with a feather.] **2** to have a scratching or twitching feeling [My nose *tickled* because of the dust.] **3** to give pleasure to; delight; amuse [The joke really *tickled* her.]
noun **1** an act of tickling. **2** a scratching or twitching feeling [a *tickle* in the throat].
tick·le • ***verb*** **tickled, tickling** • ***noun,*** *plural* **tickles**

ticklish (tik′lish) ***adjective*** **1** easy to make laugh or squirm by tickling [She is *ticklish* under her arms.] **2** needing careful handling; delicate [a *ticklish* situation].
tick·lish • ***adjective***

tick-tack-toe or **tic-tac-toe** (tik′tak tō′) ***noun*** a game in which two players take turns marking either X's or O's in a block of nine squares. Each player tries to get three of the same marks in a line.

tick-tack-toe

tidal (tīd′əl) ***adjective*** having to do with or caused by a tide or tides [*tidal* currents].
tid·al • ***adjective***

tidal wave ***noun*** a very large wave that can cause much damage. It is caused by an earthquake or a very strong wind.
tidal wave • ***noun,*** *plural* **tidal waves**

tidbit (tid′bit) ***noun*** a pleasing bit of food or information [*tidbits* of gossip].
tid·bit • ***noun,*** *plural* **tidbits**

tide (tīd) ***noun*** the regular rise and fall of the ocean's surface about every 12 hours.
tide • ***noun,*** *plural* **tides**

tidings (tīd′iŋz) ***plural noun*** news; information [I bring good *tidings*.]
ti·dings • ***plural noun***

tidy (tī′dē) ***adjective*** neat and orderly [a *tidy* desk] —Look for the WORD CHOICES box at the entry **neat**.
verb to make neat and orderly [Please *tidy* up your room.]
ti·dy • ***adjective*** **tidier, tidiest** • ***verb*** **tidied, tidying, tidies**

tie (tī) ***verb*** **1** to bind together or fasten with something such as string or rope [*Tie* the boat to the pier.] —Look for the WORD CHOICES box at the entry **bind**. **2** to tighten and knot the laces of [*Tie* your shoes.] **3** to make a knot or bow [Sailors learn to *tie* knots.] **4** to make a knot or bow in [*Tie* your necktie.] **5** to equal in some way, such as by getting the same score [Our team *tied* theirs in the ninth inning.]
noun **1** something that joins or holds tight [strong family *ties*]. **2** *a short form of* **necktie**. **3** one of the wood beams that hold railroad tracks in place. **4** the fact of being equal in such matters as the scores made or the votes received [The game ended in a *tie*.] **5** a contest in which the scores are equal [The team has three wins, two losses, and a *tie*.]

T

—tie up **1** to stop or get in the way of [The accident *tied up* traffic for hours.] **2** to cause to be busy or in use [Stop *tying up* the telephone!]
tie • *verb* **tied, tying** • *noun, plural* **ties**

tier (tir) *noun* one of a series of rows or layers set one above the other [We sat in the upper *tier* at the stadium.]
tier • *noun, plural* **tiers**
● The words **tier** and **tear** sound alike.
The third *tier* of the cake is chocolate.
A *tear* rolled down the crying boy's cheek.

tiger

tiger (tī′gər) *noun* a large, fierce Asian cat that has a tan coat with black stripes.
ti·ger • *noun, plural* **tigers**

tight (tīt) *adjective* **1** made so that liquids or gases cannot pass through [a container with a *tight* seal]. **2** put together or holding on in a close or firm way [a *tight* knot; a *tight* grip]. **3** fitting in a way that is too close [*tight* shoes]. **4** stretched as much as possible; not loose or slack [a *tight* wire]. **5** difficult or dangerous [a *tight* situation]. **6** almost even; close in score [a *tight* game]. **7** [*an informal use*] not willing to spend or give money; stingy.
adverb in a tight way [Hold *tight* to the rail.]
—sit tight to keep one's place and not move [Let's *sit tight* until this storm passes.]
tight • *adjective* **tighter, tightest** • *adverb*

tighten (tīt′n) *verb* to make or become tight or tighter [She *tightened* the nuts on the wheel. His muscles *tightened*.]
tight·en • *verb* **tightened, tightening**

tightrope (tīt′rōp) *noun* a rope stretched tight above the ground. It is used by acrobats to do balancing tricks.
tight·rope • *noun, plural* **tightropes**

tightrope

tights (tīts) *plural noun* a garment that fits very close over the lower half of the body. Tights are worn by dancers and acrobats.

tigress (tī′grəs) *noun* a female tiger.
ti·gress • *noun, plural* **tigresses**

tike (tīk) *noun another spelling of* **tyke**.
tike • *noun, plural* **tikes**

tile (tīl) *noun* **1** a thin piece of stone, baked clay, or plastic. Tiles are used to cover roofs, floors, or walls. **2** a pipe made of baked clay, used for a drain.
verb to cover with tiles [We *tiled* the floor.]
tile • *noun, plural* **tiles** • *verb* **tiled, tiling**

till[1] (til) *preposition, conjunction the same as* **until**.

till[2] (til) *verb* to prepare and use for growing crops [Peasants *tilled* the soil by hand.]
till • *verb* **tilled, tilling**

tiller (til′ər) *noun* a bar or handle for turning the rudder on a boat.
till·er • *noun, plural* **tillers**

tilt (tilt) *verb* to slope or tip [The deck *tilted* suddenly. He *tilted* his head to one side.]
noun the condition of tilting, or sloping; a slant [the *tilt* of the table].
—at full tilt at full speed; with full force [He charged *at full tilt*.]
tilt • *verb* **tilted, tilting** • *noun*

timber (tim′bər) *noun* **1** wood used for building such things as houses and boats. **2** a

a	cat	ō	go	ʉ	fur	ə =	a *in* ago
ā	ape	ô	law, for	ch	chin		e *in* agent
ä	cot, car	oo	look	sh	she		i *in* pencil
e	ten	o͞o	tool	th	thin		o *in* atom
ē	me	oi	oil	*th*	then		u *in* circus
i	fit	ou	out	zh	measure		
ī	ice	u	up	ŋ	ring		

large, thick piece of such wood; beam. **3** trees or forests.
interjection a word shouted by a logger to warn others that a cut tree is about to fall.
tim·ber • *noun, plural for sense 2 only* **timbers** • *interjection*

timberland (tim′bər land) *noun* land that has trees on it fit for timber; wooded land.
tim·ber·land • *noun, plural* **timberlands**

time (tīm) *noun* **1** the past, present, and future; every moment that has ever been or ever will be. **2** a system of measuring the passing of hours [standard *time*]. **3** the period between two events or the period during which something happens [an hour's *time;* a *time* of peace]. **4** *usually* **times** a period of history; age; era [ancient *times*]. **5** the exact or proper instant, hour, day, or year [The *time* is 2:17 PM. It's *time* for lunch.] **6** any one of a series of moments in which the same thing happens or is done [I read this book four *times*.] **7** a period of work [We put in extra *time* during the busy season.] **8** the pay for a period of work [We get double *time* for working on a holiday.] **9** the rate of speed for marching or playing a piece of music; tempo; rhythm [march *time;* waltz *time*].
verb **1** to arrange or choose a proper time for something [We *timed* our visit so as to find her at home.] **2** to measure the speed of [The coach *timed* each runner.]
adjective **1** having to do with time. **2** set to work at a certain time [a *time* bomb].
—ahead of time early [I finished *ahead of time*.] **—at one time 1** together [You can't all talk *at one time*.] **2** earlier; formerly [There were farms in this area *at one time*.] **—at times** sometimes [*At times* I wish I lived in the South.] **—behind the times** out-of-date; old-fashioned [Their methods are *behind the times*.] **—for the time being** for the present time [Sit at this desk *for the time being*.] **—from time to time** now and then [I go bowling *from time to time*.] **—in no time** within a very short period of time [The ambulance arrived *in no time*.] **—in time** before it is too late [The police showed up just *in time*.] **—on time** at the set time; not late [The letter arrived *on time*.] **—time after time** or **time and again** again and again [I've told you *time after time* not to run in the halls.]
time • *noun, plural for senses 3, 4, 5, and 6 only* **times** • *verb* **timed, timing** • *adjective*

timekeeper (tīm′kē pər) *noun* a person who keeps track of the time in a contest.
time·keep·er • *noun, plural* **timekeepers**

timely (tīm′lē) *adjective* coming at the right time [a *timely* remark].
time·ly • *adjective* **timelier, timeliest**

timepiece (tīm′pēs) *noun* a clock or watch.
time·piece • *noun, plural* **timepieces**

timer (tīm′ər) *noun* **1** any device that can be set to start or stop the operation of some mechanism [She set the *timer* on the microwave oven.] **2** a device for measuring how much time has passed since the beginning of some activity.
tim·er • *noun, plural* **timers**

times (tīmz) *preposition* multiplied by [Two *times* ten is twenty.] The symbol for this term is x [2 x 10 = 20].

timetable (tīm′tā bəl) *noun* a schedule that shows the times when vehicles that provide public transportation, such as buses or trains, arrive and leave.
time·ta·ble • *noun, plural* **timetables**

timid (tim′id) *adjective* feeling or showing fear or shyness [a *timid* reply].
tim·id • *adjective*

timing (tīm′iŋ) *noun* the act of setting the speed or time of doing something in order to get the best results [A batter needs good *timing* to hit a home run.]
tim·ing • *noun*

timpani (tim′pə nē) *plural noun* a set of kettledrums played by one musician in an orchestra.
tim·pa·ni • *plural noun*

tin (tin) *noun* a soft, silver-white metal that is a chemical element. It is easy to bend and shape. Tin is mixed with other metals to make pewter and bronze.

tinder (tin′dər) *noun* any dry material that burns easily.
tin·der • *noun*

tine (tīn) *noun* a thin, pointed part that sticks out; prong [This fork has four *tines*.]
tine • *noun, plural* **tines**

tinfoil (tin′foil) *noun* a thin sheet or sheets of aluminum, used for wrapping food.
tin·foil • *noun*

tinge (tinj) *verb* **1** to color in a slight way [The sunset *tinged* the sky.] **2** to give a slight trace to [Our joy was *tinged* with sad feelings.]

noun **1** a slight coloring; a tint [There is a *tinge* of yellow in his tie.] **2** a slight trace [There was a *tinge* of sadness in her voice.]
tinge • *verb* **tinged, tingeing** or **tinging** • *noun, plural* **tinges**

tingle (tiŋʹgəl) *verb* to have or cause a prickling or stinging feeling [Her cheek *tingled* from the slap. The icy water *tingled*.]
noun such a feeling.
tin·gle • *verb* **tingled, tingling** • *noun, plural* **tingles**

tinker (tiŋkʹər) *noun* a person of earlier times who mended pots and pans. Tinkers often traveled about from place to place.
verb to make clumsy attempts to repair something [He *tinkered* with the motor all day.]
tin·ker • *noun, plural* **tinkers** • *verb* **tinkered, tinkering**

tinkle (tiŋkʹəl) *verb* **1** to make a series of light, ringing sounds [The bell *tinkled*.] **2** to cause to make such sounds [She *tinkled* the bell.]
noun the act or sound of tinkling [Give the bell a *tinkle*. I hear the *tinkle* of a bell.]
tin·kle • *verb* **tinkled, tinkling** • *noun*

tinny (tinʹē) *adjective* high-pitched and thin; not having a full, deep sound [*tinny* music].
tin·ny • *adjective* **tinnier, tinniest**

tinsel (tinʹsəl) *noun* thin, shiny strips of tin or metal foil, used for decoration.
tin·sel • *noun*

tint (tint) *noun* **1** a light or pale color; tinge. **2** a shade of a color [several *tints* of green].
verb to give a tint to [She *tints* her hair.]
tint • *noun, plural* **tints** • *verb* **tinted, tinting**

tiny (tīʹnē) *adjective* very small; minute [a *tiny* insect] —Look for the WORD CHOICES box at the entry **small**.
ti·ny • *adjective* **tinier, tiniest**

tip[1] (tip) *noun* **1** the rounded or pointed end of something [the *tip* of the nose; the *tip* of a spear]. **2** something attached to the end [The cane had a rubber *tip*.]
verb to make or put a tip on [The pencils were *tipped* with erasers.]
tip • *noun, plural* **tips** • *verb* **tipped, tipping**

tip[2] (tip) *verb* **1** to hit in a light, sharp way; to tap [She *tipped* the basketball into the net.] **2** to give a small gift of money to for some service [We *tipped* the waiter.] **3** [*an informal use*] to give secret information to [Someone *tipped* the police about the robbery.]
noun **1** a light, sharp blow; a tap. **2** a piece of secret information. **3** a warning, hint, or some words of advice [The coach gave us some *tips* on hitting the ball.] **4** a small gift of money given for some service [We left a *tip* for our waitress.]
tip • *verb* **tipped, tipping** • *noun, plural* **tips**

tip[3] (tip) *verb* **1** to turn over; upset [He *tipped* over the glass with his elbow.] **2** to tilt or slant [She *tipped* the bowl toward herself.] **3** to raise a small amount in greeting [He *tipped* his hat.]
noun an act of tipping [a *tip* of the hat].
tip • *verb* **tipped, tipping** • *noun*

tiptoe (tipʹtō) *noun* the tip of a toe.
verb to walk on one's tiptoes in a quiet or careful way [We *tiptoed* past the sleeping baby.]
—on tiptoe **1** on the tips of one's toes [She danced *on tiptoe*.] **2** in a quiet or careful way [We sneaked out of the house *on tiptoe*.]
tip·toe • *noun, plural* **tiptoes** • *verb* **tiptoed, tiptoeing**

tire[1] (tīr) *verb* **1** to make or become unable to go on because of a need for rest; to exhaust [Climbing stairs *tires* me. I *tire* easily when I have a cold.] **2** to make or become bored [I'm *tired* of watching TV.]
tire • *verb* **tired, tiring**

tire[2] (tīr) *noun* a solid rubber hoop or a rubber tube filled with air. It is fixed around the rim of a wheel.
tire • *noun, plural* **tires**

tired (tīrd) *adjective* worn-out; weary.

WORD CHOICES

Synonyms of **tired**

The words **tired, weary,** and **worn-out** share the meaning "in need of rest."

tired from hiking
weary after the long climb
a *worn-out* traveler, unable to sleep

a cat	ō go	ʉ fur	ə = a *in* ago
ā ape	ô law, for	ch chin	e *in* agent
ä cot, car	oo look	sh she	i *in* pencil
e ten	ōō tool	th thin	o *in* atom
ē me	oi oil	*th* then	u *in* circus
i fit	ou out	zh measure	
ī ice	u up	ŋ ring	

tireless (tīr′ləs) ***adjective*** not becoming tired [a *tireless* worker].
tire·less • ***adjective***

tiresome (tīr′səm) ***adjective*** **1** tiring; boring [a *tiresome* story]. **2** annoying [*tiresome* nagging].
tire·some • ***adjective***

'tis (tiz) it is [*'Tis* the season to be jolly.]

tissue (tish′o͞o *or* tish′yo͞o) ***noun*** **1** any material that forms some part of a plant or animal. Tissue is made up of cells [muscle *tissue;* nerve *tissue*]. **2** a network; mesh [a *tissue* of lies]. **3** a thin, soft paper, formed into pieces or rolls. Paper tissues are used as handkerchiefs or toilet paper. **4** a thin, crisp paper that can almost be seen through, used to wrap things: this paper is also called **tissue paper**.
tis·sue • ***noun, plural for senses 1 and 3 only*** **tissues**

tithe (tīth) ***noun*** one tenth of a person's income, paid to support a church.
verb to pay a tithe.
tithe • ***noun, plural*** **tithes** • ***verb*** **tithed, tithing**

title (tīt′l) ***noun*** **1** the name of something such as a book, poem, picture, or piece of music. **2** a word showing the rank, profession, or occupation of a person. "Baron," "Ms.," and "Dr." are titles. **3** a legal right to own something, such as land, or proof of such a right. **4** a championship [Our team won the *title* last year.]
verb to give a title to [What did you *title* your book?]
ti·tle • ***noun, plural for senses 1, 2, and 4 only*** **titles** • ***verb*** **titled, titling**

titmouse (tit′mous) ***noun*** a small bird found in most parts of the world.
tit·mouse • ***noun, plural*** **titmice**

titter (tit′ər) ***verb*** to laugh in a silly or nervous way, as if trying to hold back the sound; to giggle [The children *tittered* at the sight of his strange hat.] —Look for the WORD CHOICES box at the entry **laugh**.
noun a nervous laugh; a giggle.
tit·ter • ***verb*** **tittered, tittering** • ***noun, plural*** **titters**

TLC or **T.L.C.** *abbreviation for* tender, loving care.

TN *abbreviation for* Tennessee.

TNT (tē′en′tē′) ***noun*** a powerful substance used to blow things up and destroy them.

to (to͞o *or* too *or* tə) ***preposition*** **1** in the direction of [Turn *to* the right.] **2** as far as [when we got *to* Boston; wet *to* the skin]. **3** until [from dawn *to* dusk]. **4** before [The time is ten *to* nine.] **5** on, onto, against, or at [Put your hand *to* your mouth. Apply the lotion *to* the skin.] **6** for the purpose of [Come *to* lunch.] **7** having to do with; involving [That's all there is *to* it.] **8** causing or resulting in [torn *to* pieces; *to* my surprise]. **9** with; along with [Add this *to* the others.] **10** belonging with [Here's the coat *to* that suit.] **11** compared with [The score was 8 *to* 0.] **12** in agreement with [That's not *to* my taste.] **13** in or for each [two pints *to* a quart].
—**to and fro** back and forth; from side to side.

■ *To* is also used as a sign of the infinitive form of verbs [That was easy *to* read.]

● The words **to, too,** and **two** sound alike.
Does this bus go *to* Cleveland?
Are you a freshman, *too?*
I took *two* sandwiches for lunch.

toad

toad (tōd) ***noun*** a small animal that is much like a frog. It usually lives on land after an early time of growth in the water.
toad • ***noun, plural*** **toads**

toadstool (tōd′sto͞ol) ***noun*** any mushroom that is poisonous.
toad·stool • ***noun, plural*** **toadstools**

toast[1] (tōst) ***verb*** to brown the surface of bread, cheese, or other food by heating.
noun toasted bread [a slice of *toast*.]
toast • ***verb*** **toasted, toasting** • ***noun***

toast[2] (tōst) ***noun*** **1** the act of honoring a person or thing by holding up one's glass and drinking. **2** the brief statement of praise or good wishes made before drinking in this way.
verb to take part in a toast to [We *toasted* the bride and groom.]
toast • ***noun, plural*** **toasts** • ***verb*** **toasted, toasting**

toaster (tōs′tər) ***noun*** a device that is used for toasting bread.
toast·er • ***noun, plural*** **toasters**

T

tobacco (tə bak′ō) ***noun*** **1** a plant grown for its large leaves. **2** the dried leaves of this plant, used for smoking or chewing.
to·bac·co • ***noun***

toboggan

toboggan (tə bäg′ən) ***noun*** a long, flat sled without runners. Toboggans are used to coast down hills.
verb to coast downhill in a toboggan.
to·bog·gan • ***noun, plural*** **toboggans** • ***verb*** **tobogganed, tobogganing**

today (to͞o dā′) ***adverb*** **1** on or during this day [She will arrive *today*.] **2** in these times; nowadays [There are great strides being made in medicine *today*.]
noun **1** this day [*today's* game]. **2** the present time or period [the fashions of *today*].
to·day • ***adverb*** • ***noun***

toddle (täd′əl) ***verb*** to walk with short, unsteady steps [The baby *toddled* across the room to his mother.]
tod·dle • ***verb*** **toddled, toddling**

toddler (täd′lər) ***noun*** a young child just learning to walk.
tod·dler • ***noun, plural*** **toddlers**

to-do (tə do͞o′) [*an informal word*] ***noun*** a stir; fuss [Don't make a big *to-do* about the broken window.]
to-do • ***noun, plural*** **to-dos**

toe (tō) ***noun*** **1** one of the five parts at the end of the foot. **2** the part of a shoe or stocking that covers the toes.
—on one's toes [*an informal use*] alert; ready.
toe • ***noun, plural*** **toes**
● The words **toe** and **tow** sound alike.
I stubbed my big *toe* in the dark.
They offered to *tow* our boat to shore.

toenail (tō′nāl) ***noun*** the hard, tough cover on the top of the end of the toe.
toe·nail • ***noun, plural*** **toenails**

toffee or **toffy** (tôf′ē) ***noun*** a hard, chewy candy that is made with brown sugar or molasses and butter. It is a kind of taffy.
tof·fee or **tof·fy** • ***noun***

together (to͞o geth′ər) ***adverb*** **1** in or into one gathering, group, or place [The reunion brought the whole family *together*.] **2** with one another [They arrived *together*.] **3** in such a way as to hit, be joined, or touch [The cars skidded *together*.] **4** at the same time [The shots were fired *together*.] **5** in or into a unit or whole [She glued the parts back *together*.] **6** in or into agreement [They got *together* on a deal.]
to·geth·er • ***adverb***

Togo (tō′gō) a country on the western coast of Africa.
To·go

toil (toil) ***verb*** **1** to work hard; to labor [Farmers *toiled* in their fields.] **2** to go slowly with pain or effort [The climbers *toiled* up the cliff.]
noun hard work —Look for the WORD CHOICES box at the entry **work**.
toil • ***verb*** **toiled, toiling** • ***noun***

toilet (toi′lət) ***noun*** **1** a bowl-shaped device with a drain. It is used to get rid of waste from the body. **2** a room with such a device; bathroom.
toi·let • ***noun, plural*** **toilets**

token (tō′kən) ***noun*** **1** a sign or symbol [This is a *token* of my love.] **2** a piece of stamped metal that is used in place of money for paying the fare on a bus or subway.
to·ken • ***noun, plural*** **tokens**

Tokyo (tō′kē ō) the capital of Japan.
To·ky·o

told (tōld) ***verb past tense and past participle of*** **tell**.

tolerance (täl′ər əns) ***noun*** the condition of being willing to let others have their own beliefs and ways of behaving, even though these are not like one's own.
tol·er·ance • ***noun***

a cat	ō go	ʉ fur	ə = a *in* ago
ā ape	ô law, for	ch chin	e *in* agent
ä cot, car	oo look	sh she	i *in* pencil
e ten	o͞o tool	th thin	o *in* atom
ē me	oi oil	*th* then	u *in* circus
i fit	ou out	zh measure	
ī ice	u up	ŋ ring	

tolerant (täl′ər ənt) ***adjective*** having or showing tolerance; willing to let others have their own beliefs and customs [*tolerant* of others' ways].
tol·er·ant • ***adjective***

tolerate (täl′ər āt) ***verb*** **1** to let something be done or go on without trying to stop it [I won't *tolerate* such talk.] **2** to recognize and respect the beliefs and practices of others without sharing them [We can't live together unless we *tolerate* each other's differences.] **3** to put up with; to bear [I can't *tolerate* loud noises.]
tol·er·ate • ***verb*** **tolerated, tolerating**

toll[1] (tōl) ***noun*** **1** a tax or charge paid for the use of a bridge or highway. **2** a charge made for a long-distance telephone call. **3** the number lost or taken [The storm took a heavy *toll* of lives.]
toll • ***noun,*** *plural for senses 1 and 2 only* **tolls**

toll[2] (tōl) ***verb*** **1** to ring a bell with slow, regular strokes, especially when someone dies. **2** to announce by ringing a bell in this way.
toll • ***verb*** **tolled, tolling**

tollgate (tōl′gāt) ***noun*** a gate on a highway or bridge. It cannot be passed until a toll is paid.
toll·gate • ***noun,*** *plural* **tollgates**

tomahawk (täm′ə hôk *or* täm′ə häk) ***noun*** a light ax used by North American Indians as a tool and a weapon.
tom·a·hawk • ***noun,*** *plural* **tomahawks**

tomato

tomato (tə māt′ō *or* tə mät′ō) ***noun*** a red or yellow, round fruit with a juicy pulp, that grows on an annual plant. It is used as a vegetable and is eaten raw or cooked.
to·ma·to • ***noun,*** *plural* **tomatoes**

tomb (to͞om) ***noun*** a grave or special room or building for the dead.
tomb • ***noun,*** *plural* **tombs**

tomboy (täm′boi) ***noun*** a girl who behaves or plays like an active boy; bold, active girl.
tom·boy • ***noun,*** *plural* **tomboys**

tombstone (to͞om′stōn) ***noun*** a stone put on a tomb or grave. It tells who is buried there.
tomb·stone • ***noun,*** *plural* **tombstones**

tomcat (täm′kat) ***noun*** a male cat.
tom·cat • ***noun,*** *plural* **tomcats**

tomorrow (to͞o mär′ō) ***adverb*** on the day after today [We can go *tomorrow*.]
noun the day after today [*Tomorrow* is Sunday.]
to·mor·row • ***adverb*** • ***noun,*** *plural* **tomorrows**

tom-tom (täm′täm) ***noun*** a simple kind of drum that is usually beaten with the hands.
tom-tom • ***noun,*** *plural* **tom-toms**

ton (tun) ***noun*** **1** a measure of weight that is equal to 2,000 pounds in the U.S. and Canada and 2,240 pounds in Great Britain. **2** a unit of weight in the metric system that is equal to 1,000 kilograms.
ton • ***noun,*** *plural* **tons**

tone (tōn) ***noun*** **1** a sound, especially one that is pleasing or musical [the clear *tones* of an oboe]. **2** one of a series of such sounds arranged in a musical scale; note [The scale of C begins and ends with the *tone* of C.] **3** a way of speaking or writing that shows a certain feeling [Her letter had a friendly *tone*.] **4** a color, shade, or tint [His suit has several *tones* of brown.] **5** the normal, healthy condition of an organ or muscle [Exercise improves your muscle *tone*.]
verb to give a certain tone of color or sound to.
—tone down to make or become less bright or loud; soften [*Tone down* that music, please.]
tone • ***noun,*** *plural except for sense 5* **tones** • ***verb*** **toned, toning**

Tonga (täŋ′gə) a country on a group of islands in the southwestern Pacific.
Ton·ga

tongs (tôŋz) ***plural noun*** a tool for seizing or lifting things. Tongs are usually made with two long arms that are hinged together.

tongue (tuŋ) ***noun*** **1** the movable muscle attached to the floor of the mouth. It is used in tasting, eating, and speaking. **2** an animal's tongue used as food. **3** the act or power of speaking [Have you lost your *tongue?*] **4** a way of speaking [He has a sharp *tongue*.] **5** a language [the French *tongue*]. **6** the flap

T

under the laces or strap of a shoe.
—**hold one's tongue** to keep quiet [*Hold your tongue!*]
tongue • *noun, plural* **tongues**

tongue-tied (tuŋ′tīd) ***adjective*** not able to speak because one is amazed or embarrassed.

tonic (tän′ik) ***noun*** **1** a medicine, liquid, or cream that gives or is said to give strength or energy. **2** a lotion for the scalp or hair.
ton·ic • *noun, plural* **tonics**

tonight (to͞o nīt′) ***adverb*** on or during this night or the night of today [It's chilly *tonight*.]
noun this night or the night of today.
to·night • ***adverb*** • ***noun***

tonsil (tän′səl) ***noun*** either one of the two soft, oval masses of tissue at the back of the mouth.
ton·sil • *noun, plural* **tonsils**

tonsillitis (tän səl īt′is) ***noun*** a condition in which a person's tonsils become swollen and sore.
ton·sil·li·tis • ***noun***

too (to͞o) ***adverb*** **1** in addition; also [He came *too*.] **2** more than enough [This hat is *too* big.] **3** very [You are *too* kind.] This word can also be used as an adjective with *much* or *many* [We have *too* much to do.]
● The words **too, to,** and **two** sound alike.
Are you a freshman, *too?*
Does this bus go *to* Cleveland?
I took *two* sandwiches for lunch.

took (to͝ok) ***verb*** *past tense of* **take**.

tool (to͞ol) ***noun*** **1** any instrument that is held in the hand and is used to do some kind of work. Some tools get their power from motors. **2** any person or thing that is used as a way to get something done [Books are *tools* that are used in learning.]
tool • *noun, plural* **tools**

toot (to͞ot) ***noun*** a short blast from a horn, whistle, or similar device.
verb to sound in short blasts [She *tooted* the horn as she drove off.]
toot • *noun, plural* **toots** • ***verb*** **tooted, tooting**

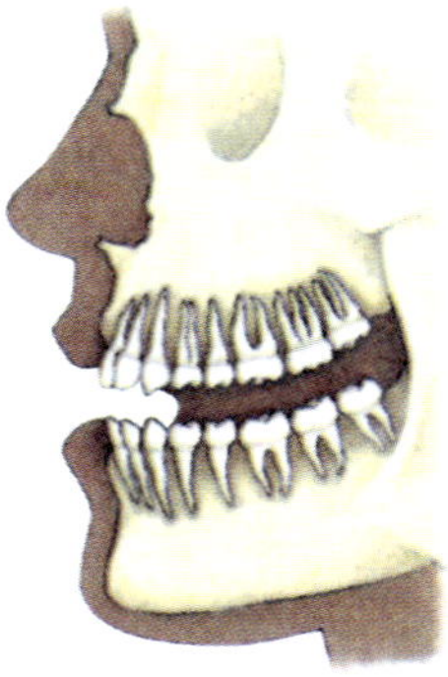

tooth

tooth (to͞oth) ***noun*** **1** any of the white, bony parts that grow from the jaws and are used for biting and chewing. **2** any part of something that is more or less like a tooth [Saws, combs, and gearwheels all have *teeth*.]
tooth • *noun, plural* **teeth**

toothache (to͞oth′āk) ***noun*** a pain in or near a tooth.
tooth·ache • *noun, plural* **toothaches**

toothbrush (to͞oth′brush) ***noun*** a small brush that is used for cleaning the teeth.
tooth·brush • *noun, plural* **toothbrushes**

toothpaste (to͞oth′pāst) ***noun*** a paste used in cleaning the teeth with a toothbrush.
tooth·paste • *noun, plural* **toothpastes**

toothpick (to͞oth′pik) ***noun*** a small, pointed stick that is used to get bits of food free from between the teeth.
tooth·pick • *noun, plural* **toothpicks**

top[1] (täp) ***noun*** **1** the highest part or point [the *top* of the hill; the *top* of the page]. **2** the part of a plant growing above the ground [carrot *tops*]. **3** the head or the crown of a head [My hair is cut short on *top*.] **4** a lid or cover [a box *top*]. **5** the highest degree or pitch [He shouted at the *top* of his voice.] **6** the highest rank or position [at the *top* of her class]. **7** the best part; the pick [This car is the *top* of the line.] **8** the upper part of a two-piece garment [Where is the *top* of my pajamas?]
adjective of or at the top; highest [a *top* student].
verb **1** to put a top on [We'll *top* the cake with icing.] **2** to cut off the top of [They *topped* the old pine tree.] **3** to be at the top of [Snow *topped* the mountain. Jim *topped* our class.] **4** to be more than [The fish *topped* 15 pounds.]
—**on top of** **1** resting upon [bananas *on top of* the refrigerator]. **2** in addition to; besides [*On top of* everything else, the cat got sick.] —**top off** to finish by adding a final touch [He *topped off* the sundae with a cherry.]
top • *noun, plural for senses 1, 2, 3, 4, and 8 only* **tops** • ***adjective*** • ***verb*** **topped, topping**

top[2] (täp) ***noun*** a child's toy that is shaped like a cone. It is spun on its pointed end.
top • *noun, plural* **tops**

topaz (tō′paz) ***noun*** a clear, crystal stone used as a gem. It is usually yellow.
to·paz • *noun, plural* **topazes**

a cat	ō go	ʉ fur	ə = a *in* ago
ā ape	ô law, for	ch chin	e *in* agent
ä cot, car	o͝o look	sh she	i *in* pencil
e ten	o͞o tool	th thin	o *in* atom
ē me	oi oil	*th* then	u *in* circus
i fit	ou out	zh measure	
ī ice	u up	ŋ ring	

Topeka (tə pē′kə) the capital of Kansas.
To·pe·ka

topic (täp′ik) ***noun*** the subject of a piece of writing or of a speech, talk, or debate [What is the main *topic* in this paragraph?] —Look for the WORD CHOICES box at the entry **theme**.
top·ic • ***noun,*** *plural* **topics**

topmost (täp′mōst) ***adjective*** at the very top; highest [the *topmost* branch].
top·most • ***adjective***

topping (täp′iŋ) ***noun*** something that is put on top of something else [What *toppings* would you like on your pizza?]
top·ping • ***noun,*** *plural* **toppings**

topple (täp′əl) ***verb*** to fall over or cause to fall over [The tall pile of books *toppled*. Strong winds *toppled* several trees.]
top·ple • ***verb*** **toppled, toppling**

topsoil (täp′soil) ***noun*** the top layer of soil. It is usually richer than the soil underneath.
top·soil • ***noun***

topsy-turvy (täp′sē tur′vē) ***adverb*** upside down, or in confusion or disorder [The tornado left many houses *topsy-turvy*.]
top·sy-tur·vy • ***adverb***

Torah or **Tora** (tôr′ə *or* tō rä′) in Judaism, the first five books of the Bible.
To·rah or **To·ra**

torch (tôrch) ***noun*** **1** a flaming light that can be carried in the hand. **2** any device that makes a very hot flame, such as a blowtorch.
torch • ***noun,*** *plural* **torches**

torch

tore (tôr) ***verb*** *past tense of* **tear**[1].

torment (tôr′ment *for n.;* tôr ment′ *for v.*) ***noun*** great pain or suffering of the body or mind.
verb **1** to make suffer in body or mind [Guilt *tormented* her.] **2** to annoy or worry [Stop *tormenting* your little brother.]
tor·ment • ***noun,*** *plural* **torments**
• ***verb*** **tormented, tormenting**

> **WORD CHOICES**
>
> Synonyms of **torment**
>
> The words **torment, agony,** and **torture** share the meaning "great pain or suffering."
>
> the mental *torment* of those without hope
>
> in *agony* after twisting my knee
>
> the *torture* of a broken heart

torn (tôrn) ***verb*** *past participle of* **tear**[1].

tornado (tôr nā′dō) ***noun*** a column of air that is whirling very fast. It is usually seen as a slender cloud that is shaped like a funnel. It usually destroys everything in its narrow path.
tor·na·do • ***noun,*** *plural* **tornadoes** or **tornados**

Toronto (tə rän′tō) the capital of Ontario, Canada.
To·ron·to

torpedo (tôr pē′dō) ***noun*** a large, exploding missile that is shaped like a cigar. It is fired under water, where it moves under its own power to blow up enemy ships.
tor·pe·do • ***noun,*** *plural* **torpedoes**

torrent (tôr′ənt) ***noun*** **1** a swift, rushing stream of water. **2** a heavy fall of rain.
tor·rent • ***noun,*** *plural* **torrents**

torrid (tôr′id) ***adjective*** very hot and dry [a *torrid* desert].
tor·rid • ***adjective***

torso (tôr′sō) ***noun*** the human body, not including the head, arms, and legs; trunk.
tor·so • ***noun,*** *plural* **torsos**

tortilla (tôr tē′ə) ***noun*** a kind of very thin pancake made of cornmeal or flour.
tor·til·la • ***noun,*** *plural* **tortillas**

tortoise (tôr′təs) ***noun*** a turtle, especially one that lives on land.
tor·toise • ***noun,*** *plural* **tortoises**

torture (tôr′chər) ***noun*** **1** the act of hurting someone very much and on purpose as a punishment or to cause the person to confess something. **2** any great pain [the *torture* of a toothache] —Look for the WORD CHOICES box at the entry **torment**.

T

verb **1** to use torture on. **2** to cause great pain to someone [I was *tortured* by doubts.]
tor·ture • *noun* • *verb* **tortured, torturing**

Tory (tôr′ē) *noun* any American colonist who favored Great Britain during the American Revolution.
To·ry • *noun, plural* **Tories**

toss (tôs) *verb* **1** to throw from the hand in a light, easy way [She *tossed* the newspaper onto the porch.] —Look for the WORD CHOICES box at the entry **throw**. **2** to fling or be flung here and there [The waves *tossed* the boat. The kite *tossed* in the wind.] **3** to jerk upward [The horse *tossed* its head.] **4** to flip a coin into the air in order to decide something according to which side lands up.
noun the act of tossing [a *toss* of a ball].
toss • *verb* **tossed, tossing** • *noun, plural* **tosses**

tot (tät) *noun* a young child.
tot • *noun, plural* **tots**

total (tōt′l) *noun* the whole amount; sum.
adjective **1** making up the whole amount; entire [The *total* amount of your bill is $10.50.] **2** complete [a *total* eclipse of the moon].
verb to find the sum or total of; add [*Total* the first column of figures.]
to·tal • *noun, plural* **totals** • *adjective* • *verb* **totaled** or **totalled, totaling** or **totalling**

totally (tōt′l ē) *adverb* in a complete way; altogether [You're *totally* wrong about them.]
to·tal·ly • *adverb*

tote (tōt) [*an informal word*] *verb* to carry or haul in the arms or on the back.
tote • *verb* **toted, toting**

tote bag *noun* a large handbag made of cloth, straw, or other material. It is used to carry shoes, small packages, or other items.
tote bag • *noun, plural* **tote bags**

totem pole (tōt′əm) *noun* a post carved and painted with animals and other natural objects. Totem poles are often placed in front of the homes of certain North American Indians.
to·tem pole • *noun, plural* **totem poles**

totter (tät′ər) *verb* **1** to rock and sway back and forth as if about to fall [Buildings *tottered* during the earthquake.] **2** to walk in an unsteady way; to stagger [A baby *totters* when it first learns to walk.] —Look for the WORD CHOICES box at the entry **stagger**.
tot·ter • *verb* **tottered, tottering**

toucan

toucan (to͞o′kan) *noun* a brightly colored bird of tropical America. It has a very large beak that curves downward.
tou·can • *noun, plural* **toucans**

touch (tuch) *verb* **1** to put the hand, finger, or some other part of the body on something in order to feel it [He *touched* the fence to see if the paint was wet.] **2** to handle, use, or disturb [Don't *touch* the papers on my desk.] **3** to bring or come into contact with something else, often in a light or gentle way [She *touched* a match to the candle. The bumpers of the cars *touched*.] **4** to eat or drink [He won't *touch* carrots.] **5** to cause to have warm feelings [Your kindness *touched* me.]
noun **1** the act of touching or the condition of being touched; a light tap or stroke [I felt the *touch* of a hand on my arm.] **2** the sense in the skin, especially of the fingers, by which one becomes aware of the size, shape, hardness, and smoothness of a thing; power to feel. **3** a very small amount or degree [Add a *touch* of salt.] **4** contact or communication [I try to keep in *touch* with friends.]
—**touch up** to improve by making small changes in something [Instead of buying a new dresser we *touched up* the old one.]
touch • *verb* **touched, touching** • *noun, plural for senses 1 and 3 only* **touches**

touchdown (tuch′doun) *noun* **1** a goal scored in football by putting the ball across the opponent's goal line. **2** a score of six points made in this way [They won by a *touchdown*.]
touch·down • *noun, plural* **touchdowns**

touching (tuch′iŋ) *adjective* making one feel pity, sympathy, or other warm feelings [The

a	cat	ō	go	ʉ	fur	ə =	a *in* ago
ā	ape	ô	law, for	ch	chin		e *in* agent
ä	cot, car	oo	look	sh	she		i *in* pencil
e	ten	o͞o	tool	th	thin		o *in* atom
ē	me	oi	oil	*th*	then		u *in* circus
i	fit	ou	out	zh	measure		
ī	ice	u	up	ŋ	ring		

sleeping kittens were a *touching* sight.] —Look for the WORD CHOICES box at the entry **moving**.
touch·ing • *adjective*

touchy (tuch′ē) *adjective* easily hurt, annoyed, or made angry [He's *touchy* today, so don't bother him.] —Look for the WORD CHOICES box at the entry **irritable**.
touch·y • *adjective* **touchier, touchiest**

tough (tuf) *adjective* **1** able to bend or twist without tearing or breaking [*tough* rubber] —Look for the WORD CHOICES box at the entry **strong**. **2** not able to be cut or chewed easily [*tough* meat]. **3** very difficult or hard [a *tough* job]. **4** rough or violent [Don't get *tough* with me.] **5** [*an informal use*] not lucky or helpful; bad [They've had too many *tough* breaks.]
tough • *adjective* **tougher, toughest**

toughen (tuf′ən) *verb* to make or become tough or tougher.
tough·en • *verb* **toughened, toughening**

toupee (to͞o pā′) *noun* a man's wig for covering a bald spot on the head.
tou·pee • *noun, plural* **toupees**

tour (to͝or) *noun* **1** a long trip for pleasure and sightseeing [Our *tour* included England, France, and Germany.] **2** any trip for inspecting something [We took a *tour* of their new house.] **3** a round trip by a group of performers who travel from city to city [Many musical groups go on *tour* during the summer.]
verb **1** to go on a tour [The acting company will *tour* with the play starting next month.] **2** to take a tour through [We're going to *tour* New England next summer.]
tour • *noun, plural* **tours** • *verb* **toured, touring**

tourist (to͝or′ist) *noun* a person who tours or travels for pleasure.
tour·ist • *noun, plural* **tourists**

tournament (to͝or′nə mənt *or* tur′nə mənt) *noun* **1** a contest in which knights on horseback tried to knock each other off the horses with lances. **2** a series of contests in some sport or game. In a tournament, a number of people or teams take part, trying to win the championship.
tour·na·ment • *noun, plural* **tournaments**

tousle (tou′zəl) *verb* to make untidy, or muss up; rumple [The wind *tousled* her hair.]
tou·sle • *verb* **tousled, tousling**

tow (tō) *verb* to pull by a rope or chain [A horse *towed* the canal boat.] —Look for the WORD CHOICES box at the entry **drag**.
noun the act of towing [That garage charges $20 for a *tow*.]
—in tow in a person's company [He arrived with several friends *in tow*.]
tow • *verb* **towed, towing** • *noun, plural* **tows**

• The words **tow** and **toe** sound alike.
They offered to *tow* our boat to shore.
I stubbed my big *toe* in the dark.

toward (tôrd *or* twôrd) *preposition* **1** in the direction of [The house faces *toward* the park.] **2** leading to [The nations took steps *toward* peace.] **3** having to do with; about [What is your feeling *toward* the new neighbors?] **4** just before; near [It became cold *toward* morning.] **5** for [He's saving money *toward* a new bike.]

towards (tôrdz *or* twôrdz) *preposition the same as* **toward**.

towel (tou′əl) *noun* a piece of soft paper or cloth that is used for drying things by wiping.
tow·el • *noun, plural* **towels**

tower (tou′ər) *noun* a building or structure that is much higher than it is wide, either standing alone or as part of another building [a water *tower;* the bell *tower* of a church; an office *tower*].
verb to stand or rise above the others [The giraffe *towers* over other animals.]
tow·er • *noun, plural* **towers** • *verb* **towered, towering**

tower

towering (tou′ər iŋ) *adjective* **1** very tall [*towering* cliffs]. **2** very great [a *towering* rage].
tow·er·ing • *adjective*

towhead (tō′hed) *noun* a person having very light yellow hair.
tow·head • *noun, plural* **towheads**

town (toun) *noun* **1** a place with houses, stores, and other buildings. It is larger than a village but smaller than a city. **2** the business center of a city or town [She went into *town* to shop.] **3** the people of a town [a friendly *town*].
town • *noun, plural for senses 1 and 3 only* **towns**

T

town hall *noun* a building in which the offices of a town government are located.
town hall • *noun, plural* **town halls**

township (toun′ship) *noun* a part of a county that has its own government with control over its schools, roads, and other local matters.
town·ship • *noun, plural* **townships**

townspeople (tounz′pē pəl) *plural noun* the people of a town.
towns·peo·ple • *plural noun*

tow truck *noun* a truck with equipment for towing away cars and other vehicles that are not able to operate or are not parked legally.
tow truck • *noun, plural* **tow trucks**

toxic (täks′ik) *adjective* having to do with or caused by a poison [Toadstools have a *toxic* effect.]
tox·ic • *adjective*

toy (toi) *noun* **1** a thing for children to play with. **2** anything to play with [This rubber band is the cat's favorite *toy*.]
adjective **1** like a toy in size or use [A *toy* poodle is a very small dog.] **2** made for use as a toy [a *toy* stove or train].
verb to play [The child *toyed* with the food instead of eating.]
toy • *noun, plural* **toys** • *adjective* • *verb* **toyed, toying**

trace (trās) *noun* **1** a mark, track, or sign left by someone or something [There was no *trace* of human beings on the island.] **2** a very small amount [I could taste a *trace* of garlic in the dressing.]
verb **1** to follow the trail or footprints of someone or something; to track [The police *traced* the thieves to their hiding place.] **2** to follow or study the path or development of something [We *traced* the history of Plymouth back to the Mayflower.] **3** to copy a picture or drawing by following its lines on a piece of thin paper that is placed over it.
trace • *noun, plural* **traces** • *verb* **traced, tracing**

track (trak) *noun* **1** a mark that is left when someone or something has passed. Footprints and wheel ruts are both tracks. **2** a path or trail [This *track* leads to the river.] **3** steel rails that are usually laid on the ground in pairs. The wheels of trains, trolleys, and similar vehicles run on tracks. **4** a path or course, often in an oval, laid out for racing. **5** contests, such as running and hurdling, held on such a track. **6** a way of doing something [You're on the right *track* to solve the problem.]
verb **1** to follow the tracks of someone or something [We *tracked* the fox to its den.] **2** to make tracks or dirty marks [The children *tracked* up the clean floor.] **3** to make tracks with [The dog *tracked* snow into the house.]
—**keep track of** to go on knowing about [We've *kept track of* them since they moved away.]
—**lose track of** to stop knowing about [I've *lost track of* how many people have left.]
track • *noun, plural for senses 1, 2, 3, and 4 only* **tracks** • *verb* **tracked, tracking**

tract (trakt) *noun* a large stretch of land [America was once covered with great *tracts* of forest.]
tract • *noun, plural* **tracts**

traction (trak′shən) *noun* the power to grip or hold to a surface while moving, without slipping [The tires lost *traction* on the icy hill.]
trac·tion • *noun*

tractor

tractor (trak′tər) *noun* **1** a powerful motor vehicle for pulling farm machinery and heavy loads. **2** a kind of truck that has a cab for the driver but no body. It is used to haul large trailers.
trac·tor • *noun, plural* **tractors**

tractor-trailer (trak′tər trā′lər) *noun* a combination of a tractor and a trailer that is used for hauling goods.
trac·tor-trail·er • *noun, plural* **tractor-trailers**

trade (trād) *noun* **1** the act of giving one thing for another; an exchange [My baseball bat for

a cat	ō go	ʉ fur	ə = a *in* ago
ā ape	ô law, for	ch chin	e *in* agent
ä cot, car	oo look	sh she	i *in* pencil
e ten	o͞o tool	th thin	o *in* atom
ē me	oi oil	*th* then	u *in* circus
i fit	ou out	zh measure	
ī ice	u up	ŋ ring	

your football is an even *trade*.] **2** any work done with the hands that needs special training [learning the carpentry *trade*]. **3** buying and selling; commerce [*trade* between nations].
verb **1** to exchange [I *traded* my stamp collection for a camera.] —Look for the WORD CHOICES box at the entry **sell**. **2** to carry on a business; buy and sell [This company *trades* in tea. Our country *trades* with other countries.]
trade • *noun, plural for senses 1 and 2 only* **trades** • *verb* **traded, trading**

trademark (trād′märk) *noun* a special picture, mark, or word placed on a product to show who its maker or dealer is. The law protects most trademarks.
trade·mark • *noun, plural* **trademarks**

trader (trād′ər) *noun* a person who buys and sells goods; merchant.
trad·er • *noun, plural* **traders**

trading post (trād′iŋ) *noun* a store in a frontier town or other place far away from other towns, where things are bought and sold.
trading post • *noun, plural* **trading posts**

tradition (trə dish′ən) *noun* **1** the handing down of customs and beliefs from generation to generation. Tradition is passed on by talking rather than in written records. **2** a custom or belief that is handed down in this way [It's a *tradition* to eat turkey on Thanksgiving.]
tra·di·tion • *noun, plural for sense 2 only* **traditions**

traditional (trə dish′ə nəl) *adjective* having to do with or handed down by tradition [a *traditional* costume].
tra·di·tion·al • *adjective*

traffic (traf′ik) *noun* **1** the movement or number of persons or things moving along a road or other route of travel [Automobile *traffic* on this road is heavier on weekends.] **2** buying and selling; trade [illegal drug *traffic*].
adjective for or controlling traffic [a *traffic* light].
verb to carry on traffic, or trade, especially illegal trade [The criminals *traffic* in drugs.]
traf·fic • *noun* • *adjective* • *verb* **trafficked, trafficking**

traffic light or **traffic signal** *noun* a set of three lights that is used as a traffic signal, usually where streets meet. The green light tells the cars or walkers to go, the yellow light tells them to get ready to stop, and the red light tells them to stop.
traffic light or **traffic signal** • *noun, plural* **traffic lights** or **traffic signals**

tragedy (traj′ə dē) *noun* **1** a serious play with a sad ending. **2** a very sad or tragic happening [The death of their leader was a *tragedy*.]
trag·e·dy • *noun, plural* **tragedies**

tragic (traj′ik) *adjective* **1** like or having to do with a tragedy [a *tragic* tale]. **2** bringing great harm or suffering; dreadful [a *tragic* accident].
trag·ic • *adjective*

trail (trāl) *verb* **1** to drag or bring along behind [The bride's veil *trailed* on the floor. He *trailed* dirt through the house.] **2** to flow or drift behind in a long, thin stream or wisp [Smoke *trailed* from the chimney.] **3** to follow or lag behind [The children *trailed* along after us. She is *trailing* in the race.] **4** to follow the tracks of something; to track [They *trailed* the animal to the river.] **5** to become weaker or less [Her voice *trailed* off into a whisper.]
noun **1** something that trails behind [a *trail* of dust]. **2** a mark, scent, footprint, or other sign that is left behind [The dogs followed the fresh *trail*.] **3** a path that is formed when people or animals pass; track.
trail • *verb* **trailed, trailing** • *noun, plural* **trails**

trailer (trā′lər) *noun* a wagon or cart that is made to be pulled by an automobile, truck, or tractor. Some trailers have beds, tables, and cabinets and can be lived in.
trail·er • *noun, plural* **trailers**

train (trān) *noun* **1** a line of connected railroad cars that is pulled by a locomotive. **2** a group of persons or vehicles moving in a line; caravan [The wagon *train* was heading West.] **3** a series of connected things [I lost my *train* of thought.] **4** something that drags along behind [the *train* of a gown].
verb **1** to develop the mind and character of; to rear [They *trained* their children to be kind.] **2** to teach, or give practice in, some skill [This school *trains* airplane pilots. I *trained* my pets to do some tricks.] **3** to make ready or become fit for some contest or sport [The football players *trained* by lifting weights and practicing plays.] **4** to make grow in a certain direction [He *trained* the roses along a trellis.] **5** to aim [The scientists *trained* the telescope on a very distant star.]
train • *noun, plural* **trains** • *verb* **trained, training**

trainer (trān′ər) *noun* **1** a person who trains animals. **2** a person who helps athletes train for a contest or sport.
train·er • *noun, plural* **trainers**

training (trān′iŋ) *noun* **1** the practice or drills given by a person who trains or received by a person or animal that is being trained [That exercise is part of our regular *training*.] **2** the process of getting ready or becoming fit for some contest or sport by exercise and practice [The boxers are in *training* for their fight next month.]
train·ing • *noun*

trait (trāt) *noun* a special quality or characteristic [A sense of humor is her finest *trait*.]
trait • *noun, plural* **traits**

traitor (trāt′ər) *noun* a person who helps the enemy of his or her country, friends, or cause.
trai·tor • *noun, plural* **traitors**

tramp (tramp) *verb* **1** to walk with heavy steps [They *tramped* through the house in their heavy boots.] **2** to step down on something in a firm, heavy way; stamp [The horse *tramped* on my foot.] **3** to walk; roam about on foot [We *tramped* through the fields.]
noun **1** a person who wanders from place to place, doing odd jobs or begging. **2** a journey on foot; hike [a *tramp* through the woods]. **3** the sound of heavy steps [We could hear the *tramp* of the marching soldiers.]
tramp • *verb* **tramped, tramping** • *noun, plural for senses 1 and 2 only* **tramps**

trample (tram′pəl) *verb* to crush or hurt by stepping hard on [When I ran for the ball, I accidentally *trampled* some flowers.]
tram·ple • *verb* **trampled, trampling**

trampoline (tram′pə lēn *or* tram pə lēn′) *noun* a strong piece of canvas stretched tightly on a frame. It is used to bounce on and do tumbling tricks.
tram·po·line • *noun, plural* **trampolines**

trance (trans) *noun* a condition that is like sleep. It is brought on by such factors as shock or hypnosis. The person in this condition seems to know what is going on, but is not able to move or act.
trance • *noun, plural* **trances**

tranquil (traŋ′kwəl) *adjective* **1** calm or peaceful [a *tranquil* evening at home] —Look for the WORD CHOICES box at the entry **calm**. **2** quiet or not moving [the *tranquil* water of a pond].
tran·quil • *adjective*

trans- *a prefix meaning* over, across, or beyond [A *transatlantic* cable is a cable that goes across the Atlantic Ocean.]

transatlantic (trans′at lan′tik *or* tranz′at lan′tik) *adjective* crossing the Atlantic [a *transatlantic* flight].
trans·at·lan·tic • *adjective*

transcontinental (trans′kän ti nent′l *or* tranz′kän ti nent′l) *adjective* going from one side of a continent to the other [a *transcontinental* train trip].
trans·con·ti·nen·tal • *adjective*

transfer (trans fʉr′ *or* trans′fər *for v.;* trans′fər *for n.*) *verb* **1** to move, carry, send, or change from one person or place to another [He *transferred* his notes to another notebook. She has *transferred* to another school.] **2** to change from one bus, train, or trolley to another [I have to *transfer* twice on my way to work.]
noun **1** the act of transferring [I got a *transfer* to another school.] **2** a thing or person that is transferred [They are *transfers* from another school.] **3** a ticket that allows one to change from one bus, train, or trolley to another.
trans·fer • *verb* **transferred, transferring** • *noun, plural* **transfers**

transform (trans fôrm′) *verb* **1** to change the form or looks of something [A vase of roses *transformed* the drab room.] **2** to change the nature or condition of something [The barn was *transformed* into a house.]
trans·form • *verb* **transformed, transforming**

WORD CHOICES

Synonyms of **transform**

The words **transform, alter,** and **convert** share the meaning "to make different in form or use."

Can matter be *transformed* into energy?

They *altered* the coat to fit my son.

Architects *converted* the barn into a restaurant.

a	cat	ō	go	ʉ	fur	ə =	a *in* ago
ā	ape	ô	law, for	ch	chin		e *in* agent
ä	cot, car	oo	look	sh	she		i *in* pencil
e	ten	o͞o	tool	th	thin		o *in* atom
ē	me	oi	oil	*th*	then		u *in* circus
i	fit	ou	out	zh	measure		
ī	ice	u	up	ŋ	ring		

transformer (trans fôr′mər) ***noun*** a device that changes the voltage of an electric current.
trans·form·er • ***noun,*** *plural* **transformers**

transfusion (trans fyo͞o′zhən) ***noun*** the act of passing blood or plasma that has been taken from one person into a vein of another.
trans·fu·sion • ***noun,*** *plural* **transfusions**

transistor (tran zis′tər *or* tran sis′tər) ***noun*** an electronic device that controls the flow of an electric current. It is often made of silicon. Transistors are small and last a long time.
tran·sis·tor • ***noun,*** *plural* **transistors**

transit (tran′sit *or* tran′zit) ***noun*** a system of public transportation in a city [urban *transit*].
trans·it • ***noun***

transition (tran zish′ən *or* tran sish′ən) ***noun*** the act or process of passing from one condition or form to another [a caterpillar's *transition* into a moth or butterfly].
tran·si·tion • ***noun,*** *plural* **transitions**

transitive (tran′si tiv *or* tran′zi tiv) ***adjective*** describing a verb that takes a direct object. Some verbs can be either transitive or intransitive, depending on the way they are used. In the sentence "I understand the question," "understand" is a transitive verb, whereas "understand" in the sentence "I understand" is intransitive.
tran·si·tive • ***adjective***

translate (trans lāt′ *or* tranz lāt′) ***verb*** to put into words of a different language [She *translated* a German poem into English.]
trans·late • ***verb*** **translated, translating**

translation (trans lā′shən *or* tranz lā′shən) ***noun*** **1** the act of translating [He is good at *translation*.] **2** writing or speech translated into a different language [the many *translations* of the Bible].
trans·la·tion • ***noun,*** *plural for sense 2 only* **translations**

translator (trans lāt′ər *or* tranz lāt′ər) ***noun*** a person who translates from one language into another.
trans·la·tor • ***noun,*** *plural* **translators**

transmission (trans mish′ən *or* tranz mish′ən) ***noun*** **1** the act of transmitting or passing something along [the *transmission* of messages by telegraph]. **2** something transmitted [a *transmission* from a spacecraft]. **3** the part of a car that transmits power from the engine to the wheels.
trans·mis·sion • ***noun,*** *plural* **transmissions**

transmit (trans mit′ *or* tranz mit′) ***verb*** **1** to send from one person or place to another; pass on; transfer [Some insects *transmit* disease to human beings.] **2** to allow the passage of such things as light, sound, or motion; conduct [Water *transmits* sound.] **3** to cause to pass through air or some other substance [The sun *transmits* energy.] **4** to send out radio or TV signals.
trans·mit • ***verb*** **transmitted, transmitting**

transmitter (trans mit′ər *or* tranz mit′ər) ***noun*** **1** the part of a telegraph or telephone that sends out sounds or signals. **2** the equipment for sending out electric waves in radio or TV.
trans·mit·ter • ***noun,*** *plural* **transmitters**

transom (tran′səm) ***noun*** a small window just above a door or other window. It is usually hinged to a bar below it.
tran·som • ***noun,*** *plural* **transoms**

transom

transparent (trans per′ənt) ***adjective*** so clear or so fine that a person can see objects on the other side very easily [*transparent* glass; a *transparent* veil].
trans·par·ent • ***adjective***

transplant (trans plant′ *for v.;* trans′plant *for n.*) ***verb*** **1** to dig up from one place and plant in another [He *transplanted* the daffodils to the front yard.] **2** to move tissue or an organ by surgery from one person or part of the body to another [The doctors *transplanted* a new heart into the little girl so that she could live longer.]
noun **1** the act of transplanting [a heart *transplant*]. **2** something transplanted.
trans·plant • ***verb*** **transplanted, transplanting** • ***noun,*** *plural* **transplants**

transport (trans pôrt′ *for v;* trans′pôrt *for n.*) ***verb*** to carry from one place to another [It is cheaper to *transport* goods by train than by truck.] —Look for the WORD CHOICES box at the entry **carry**.
noun a ship, plane, or other vehicle that is used for transporting goods or soldiers.
trans·port • ***verb*** **transported, transporting** • ***noun,*** *plural* **transports**

T

transportation (trans pər tā′shən) *noun* the act of transporting something [The table was free, but we had to pay for *transportation*.]
trans·por·ta·tion • *noun*

trap (trap) *noun* **1** any device for catching animals. One kind of trap snaps shut when it is stepped on. **2** a trick used to fool or catch someone [That question was a *trap* to make the witness tell the truth.]
verb **1** to catch in a trap. **2** to set traps to catch animals [Some early settlers *trapped* for a living.]
trap • *noun, plural* **traps** • *verb* **trapped, trapping**

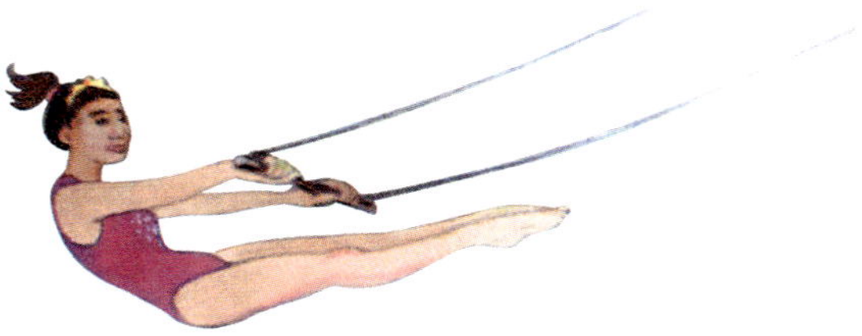

trapeze

trapeze (tra pēz′) *noun* a kind of swing that has a short bar that is held by two ropes. Acrobats do stunts on trapezes.
tra·peze • *noun, plural* **trapezes**

trapezoid (trap′ə zoid) *noun* a flat figure with four sides. Two of the sides are parallel.
trap·e·zoid • *noun, plural* **trapezoids**

trapper (trap′ər) *noun* a person who traps wild animals for their furs.
trap·per • *noun, plural* **trappers**

trash (trash) *noun* **1** anything thrown away as worthless; rubbish [Please take out the *trash*.] **2** something worthless or disgusting [That movie is nothing but *trash*.]

travel (trav′əl) *verb* **1** to go from one place to another [He *traveled* around the world.] —Look for the WORD CHOICES box at the entry **go**. **2** to make a journey over or through [We *travel* this road every day.] **3** to move or pass [Light *travels* faster than sound.]
noun **travels** trips or journeys [I've visited many countries in my *travels*.]
trav·el • *verb* **traveled** or **travelled, traveling** or **travelling** • *noun, plural* **travels**

traveler or **traveller** (trav′ə lər *or* trav′lər) *noun* a person or thing that travels.
trav·el·er or **trav·el·ler** • *noun, plural* **travelers** or **travellers**

trawl (trôl) *noun* a large fishing net that is dragged by a boat along the bottom of a shallow part of the sea.
verb to fish with a trawl [The fishermen *trawled* for lobster.]
trawl • *noun, plural* **trawls** • *verb* **trawled, trawling**

trawler (trô′lər) *noun* a boat used in trawling.
trawl·er • *noun, plural* **trawlers**

tray (trā) *noun* a flat piece of wood, metal, plastic, or other material for carrying food or other things. It often has a low rim.
tray • *noun, plural* **trays**

tread (tred) *verb* **1** to walk on, in, along, or over [We were *treading* the path toward home.] **2** to beat or press with the feet; trample [People used to *tread* grapes when making wine.]
noun **1** a way of treading or the sound of treading [walking with a heavy *tread*]. **2** something on which a person or thing treads or moves. The surface of a stairway step, and the belt that moves around the wheels of a tractor or tank, are treads. **3** the outer layer of an automobile tire.
—tread water to keep the body upright and the head above water by moving the legs.
tread • *verb* **trod, trodden** or **trod, treading, treaded** (*for the phrase* **tread water** *only*) • *noun, plural for sense 2 only* **treads**

treadmill (tred′mil) *noun* a device that is worked by persons or animals who walk on a continuous belt or on the inside of a wheel. Some treadmills are used for exercising.
tread·mill • *noun, plural* **treadmills**

treason (trē′zən) *noun* the act of betraying one's country, especially by helping the enemy during a war.
trea·son • *noun*

treasure (trezh′ər) *noun* **1** money, jewels, or other valuable things that are collected and stored up [buried *treasure*]. **2** a person or thing that is loved or held dear [My children are my greatest *treasures*.]
verb to love or hold dear; cherish [I *treasure* our friendship.]
treas·ure • *noun, plural for sense 2 only* **treasures** • *verb* **treasured, treasuring**

a	cat	ō	go	ʉ	fur	ə =	a *in* ago
ā	ape	ô	law, for	ch	chin		e *in* agent
ä	cot, car	oo	look	sh	she		i *in* pencil
e	ten	ōō	tool	th	thin		o *in* atom
ē	me	oi	oil	*th*	then		u *in* circus
i	fit	ou	out	zh	measure		
ī	ice	u	up	ŋ	ring		

treasurer (trezh′ər ər) *noun* a person in charge of the money of a government, company, or club.
treas·ur·er • *noun, plural* **treasurers**

treasury (trezh′ər ē) *noun* **1** the funds of a government, company, or club. **2 Treasury** the department of a government in charge of money and taxes. **3** a place where money is kept.
treas·ur·y • *noun, plural for senses 1 and 3 only* **treasuries**

treat (trēt) *verb* **1** to deal with or act toward someone or something in a certain way [We were *treated* with respect. *Treat* this matter in a serious way.] **2** to try to cure or heal with medicine [The doctor *treated* my cuts.] **3** to act upon by adding something [The water is *treated* with chlorine.] **4** to pay for the food or entertainment of [Our aunt and uncle *treated* us to the movies.]
noun **1** the act of treating another to food or entertainment [You paid last time, so this is my *treat*.] **2** the food or entertainment paid for by another [There were special games and *treats* for the children.] **3** anything that gives pleasure [It was a *treat* to hear them sing.]
treat • *verb* **treated, treating** • *noun, plural* **treats**

treatment (trēt′mənt) *noun* **1** act or way of dealing with a person or thing [The children needed gentle *treatment* every day.] **2** the use of medical methods to try to cure or heal.
treat·ment • *noun, plural for sense 2 only* **treatments**

treaty (trēt′ē) *noun* an agreement between two or more nations that has to do with trade or cooperation [a peace *treaty*].
trea·ty • *noun, plural* **treaties**

tree (trē) *noun* **1** a large, woody plant with a long trunk and many branches in the upper part. **2** anything that is like a tree in some way [A family *tree* is a diagram with many branching lines. Hang your jacket on the clothes *tree*.]
verb to chase up a tree [The dogs *treed* the cat.]
tree • *noun, plural* **trees** • *verb* **treed, treeing**

trek (trek) *verb* to travel slowly or with difficulty [The pioneers *trekked* across the desert.]
noun a long, slow journey.
trek • *verb* **trekked, trekking** • *noun, plural* **treks**

trellis (trel′is) *noun* a frame of crossed strips of wood on which vines are trained to grow.
trel·lis • *noun, plural* **trellises**

tremble (trem′bəl) *verb* **1** to shake from cold, fear, excitement, or other causes [Your hand is *trembling*.] —Look for the WORD CHOICES box at the entry **shake**. **2** to quiver or quake [The earth *trembled* from the shock wave.]
noun the act of trembling.
trem·ble • *verb* **trembled, trembling** • *noun*

tremendous (tri men′dəs) *adjective* **1** very large or great; enormous [a *tremendous* mountain]. **2** [*an informal use*] wonderful, very fine, or amazing [a *tremendous* opportunity].
tre·men·dous • *adjective*

WORD HISTORY

tremendous

This word comes from a Latin verb that means "to tremble." An earlier meaning of **tremendous** was "great or terrible enough to make a person tremble." The idea of trembling was lost, but the idea of great size has stayed.

tremor (trem′ər) *noun* an act of shaking or trembling [an earth *tremor*].
trem·or • *noun, plural* **tremors**

trench (trench) *noun* **1** a ditch; a deep furrow. **2** a long ditch with earth piled in front that is used to protect soldiers in battle.
trench • *noun, plural* **trenches**

trend (trend) *noun* the general direction or course that something takes [The current *trend* is to make smaller cars.]
trend • *noun, plural* **trends**

Trenton (trent′n) the capital of New Jersey.
Tren·ton

trespass (tres′pas) *verb* to go on another person's property without permission ["No *trespassing*" means "Keep out."]
noun the act of trespassing.
tres·pass • *verb* **trespassed, trespassing** • *noun, plural* **trespasses**

tress (tres) *noun* **1** a lock of hair. **2 tresses** a woman's or girl's hair when it is long and hanging loosely.
tress • *noun, plural* **tresses**

tri- *a prefix meaning* three [A *triangle* is a figure having three angles.]

trial (trī′əl) *noun* **1** the act of hearing a case in court to decide whether a claim or charge is

T

true [The *trial* proved that he was guilty.] **2** the act of testing or trying; a test [the *trial* of a new engine].
adjective **1** of or for a trial or test [a *trial* run; a *trial* sample of toothpaste]. **2** having to do with a law court [a *trial* lawyer].
tri·al • *noun, plural* **trials** • *adjective*

triangle (trī′aŋ gəl) *noun* **1** a flat figure with three angles and three sides. **2** anything shaped like this. **3** a kind of musical instrument that is a steel rod bent into a triangle. It is struck with a metal rod to produce a high, tinkling sound.
tri·an·gle • *noun, plural* **triangles**

triangle

triangular (trī aŋ′gyo͞o lər) *adjective* having to do with or shaped like a triangle; having three corners [a *triangular* pennant].
tri·an·gu·lar • *adjective*

tribe (trīb) *noun* a group of people or families living together under a leader or chief [a Native American *tribe*].
tribe • *noun, plural* **tribes**

tributary (trib′yo͞o ter′ē) *noun* a stream or river that flows into a larger one.
trib·u·tar·y • *noun, plural* **tributaries**

tribute (trib′yo͞ot) *noun* **1** something that is given, done, or said to show thanks or respect [The city put up a statue as a *tribute* to the hero.] **2** money that one nation is forced to pay to another nation that is more powerful.
trib·ute • *noun, plural for sense 1 only* **tributes**

trick (trik) *noun* **1** something that is done to fool or cheat someone [Those tears were just a *trick* to get our sympathy.] **2** a piece of playful mischief; a prank. **3** a clever or skillful act [a card *trick*].
verb to work a trick on; to fool or cheat [They *tricked* me into giving up my money.] —Look for the WORD CHOICES box at the entry **cheat**.
adjective **1** done by a trick [*trick* photography]. **2** capable of tricking [a *trick* question].
trick • *noun, plural* **tricks** • *verb* **tricked, tricking** • *adjective*

trickle (trik′əl) *verb* **1** to flow slowly in a thin stream or fall in drops [Rain *trickled* down the window.] **2** to move little by little [The crowd *trickled* away.]
noun a thin flow or drip.
trick·le • *verb* **trickled, trickling** • *noun, plural* **trickles**

tricky (trik′ē) *adjective* **1** using tricks [a *tricky* plan]. **2** hard or difficult [a *tricky* problem].
trick·y • *adjective* **trickier, trickiest**

tricycle (trī′si kəl) *noun* a vehicle for children that has three wheels, one in front and two in back. It has foot pedals and a handlebar.
tri·cy·cle • *noun, plural* **tricycles**

tricycle

trifle (trī′fəl) *noun* **1** something that has little value or importance. **2** a small amount; a bit.
tri·fle • *noun, plural* **trifles**

trigger (trig′ər) *noun* a lever that causes a gun to fire when it is pressed by the finger.
verb to start; set off [The fight *triggered* a riot.]
trig·ger • *noun, plural* **triggers** • *verb* **triggered, triggering**

trill (tril) *noun* **1** a wavering or trembling sound made when playing a musical instrument or singing. **2** a sound like this made by a bird.
verb to sing or play with a trill.
trill • *noun, plural* **trills** • *verb* **trilled, trilling**

trillion (tril′yən) *noun* a thousand billions (1,000,000,000,000).
adjective adding up to a trillion.
tril·lion • *noun, plural* **trillions** • *adjective*

trim (trim) *verb* **1** to make neat or tidy by cutting or clipping [Becky *trimmed* her hair last night.] **2** to cut or clip [I need to *trim* dead branches from the bush.] **3** to decorate [I *trimmed* the Christmas tree.]

a	cat	ō	go	ʉ	fur	ə =	a *in* ago
ā	ape	ô	law, for	ch	chin		e *in* agent
ä	cot, car	oo	look	sh	she		i *in* pencil
e	ten	o͞o	tool	th	thin		o *in* atom
ē	me	oi	oil	*th*	then		u *in* circus
i	fit	ou	out	zh	measure		
ī	ice	u	up	ŋ	ring		

noun the act of trimming [Give my hair a *trim*.]
adjective neat, tidy, or in good condition [a *trim* little house] —Look for the WORD CHOICES box at the entry **neat**.
trim • *verb* **trimmed, trimming** • *noun, plural* **trims** • *adjective* **trimmer, trimmest**

trimming (trim′iŋ) *noun* **1** something that is used to decorate something else. **2 trimmings** the side dishes of a meal [We ordered turkey and all the *trimmings*.] **3 trimmings** parts that have been trimmed off something.
trim·ming • *noun, plural* **trimmings**

Trinidad and Tobago (trin′i dad ən tō bā′gō) a country on islands in the West Indies.
Trin·i·dad and To·ba·go

trinket (triŋ′kət) *noun* a small ornament or piece of jewelry of little value.
trin·ket • *noun, plural* **trinkets**

trio (trē′ō) *noun* **1** a group of three people who sing or play music together. **2** any group of three.
tri·o • *noun, plural* **trios**

trip (trip) *verb* to stumble or cause to stumble [He *tripped* on the stick. She put out her foot and *tripped* me.]
noun the act of traveling; a journey.
trip • *verb* **tripped, tripping** • *noun, plural* **trips**

WORD CHOICES

Synonyms of **trip**

The words **trip**, **journey**, and **voyage** share the meaning "the act of traveling from one place to another."

a short vacation *trip*

a *journey* through India and China

a *voyage* across the Pacific

triple (trip′əl) *adjective* **1** three times as much or as many [a *triple* order of fries]. **2** made up of three [A *triple* cone has three scoops of ice cream.]
noun **1** an amount that is three times as much or as many. **2** a hit in baseball on which the batter gets to third base.
verb **1** to make or become three times as much or as many [He *tripled* his collection of cards in one day.] **2** to hit a triple in baseball.
tri·ple • *adjective* • *noun, plural* **triples** • *verb* **tripled, tripling**

triplet (trip′lət) *noun* any one of three children born at the same time to the same mother.
tri·plet • *noun, plural* **triplets**

tripod (trī′päd) *noun* a stand or frame with three legs. It can be used to hold a camera.
tri·pod • *noun, plural* **tripods**

tripod

trite (trīt) *adjective* used so much that it is no longer fresh or new; stale [a *trite* expression].
trite • *adjective* **triter, tritest**

triumph (trī′əmf) *noun* a victory; success [a *triumph* over illness; a *triumph* in battle].
verb to be the winner; be successful [The nation *triumphed* over hunger.]
tri·umph • *noun, plural* **triumphs** • *verb* **triumphed, triumphing**

trivia (triv′ē ə) *plural noun* [*often used with a singular verb*] small, unimportant matters [Don't waste your time with such *trivia*.]
triv·i·a • *plural noun*

trivial (triv′ē əl) *adjective* not important [a *trivial* question] —Look for the WORD CHOICES box at the entry **insignificant**.
triv·i·al • *adjective*

trod (träd) *verb* **1** *past tense of* **tread**. **2** *a past participle of* **tread**.

trodden (träd′n) *verb a past participle of* **tread**.
trod·den • *verb*

troll (trōl) *noun* in fairy stories, a giant or dwarf that lives in a cave or underground.
troll • *noun, plural* **trolls**

trolley (trä′lē) *noun* an electric streetcar that runs on tracks.
trol·ley • *noun, plural* **trolleys**

trombone (träm bōn′ *or* träm′bōn) *noun* a large brass musical instrument with a long,

bent tube that slides in and out to change the tones.
trom·bone • *noun, plural* **trombones**

trombone

troop (tro͞op) ***noun*** **1 troops** soldiers. **2** a group of Boy Scouts or Girl Scouts under an adult leader.
verb to gather or move in a group [The workers *trooped* into the cafeteria.]
troop • ***noun,*** *plural* **troops** • ***verb*** **trooped, trooping**
- The words **troop** and **troupe** sound alike.
  A *troop* of Scouts camped in the park.
  A *troupe* of actors performed.

trooper (tro͞o′pər) ***noun*** **1** a soldier or policeman who rides a horse. **2** a member of a State police force.
troop·er • ***noun,*** *plural* **troopers**

trophy (trō′fē) ***noun*** something that is kept as a reminder of some victory or success, such as a silver cup from a sports contest.
tro·phy • ***noun,*** *plural* **trophies**

tropic (träp′ik) ***noun*** **1** either of the two imaginary circles around the earth that are parallel to the equator and about 23½ degrees from it. The one to the north is called the **Tropic of Cancer**. The one to the south is called the **Tropic of Capricorn**. **2 tropics** or **Tropics** the region of the earth that is between these two lines. This region has a very hot climate.
trop·ic • ***noun,*** *plural* **tropics** or **Tropics**

tropical (träp′i kəl) ***adjective*** in or having to do with the tropics [a *tropical* storm].
trop·i·cal • ***adjective***

trot (trät) ***verb*** **1** to step along, in the way that a horse sometimes does, by moving a front leg and the opposite hind leg at the same time. **2** to run slowly, with a loose, easy motion [The boys *trotted* to school.]
noun **1** the movement of a trotting horse. **2** a slow run.
trot • ***verb*** **trotted, trotting** • ***noun***

trouble (trub′əl) ***noun*** **1** worry, care, or suffering [My mind is free of *trouble*.] **2** a difficult or unhappy situation [getting into *trouble*]. **3** great care; an effort [She took the *trouble* to call.] **4** a sick condition; an illness [heart *trouble*]. **5** a person or thing that causes worry, difficulty, or unhappiness.
verb **1** to give trouble to; to worry, annoy, or disturb [Alex was *troubled* by the test results.] **2** to put or go to extra work; to bother [May I *trouble* you for a drink of water? Don't *trouble* to return the pencil.]
trou·ble • ***noun,*** *plural except for sense 3,* **troubles** • ***verb*** **troubled, troubling**

troublesome (trub′əl səm) ***adjective*** giving trouble; disturbing [a *troublesome* cough].
trou·ble·some • ***adjective***

trough (trôf *or* träf) ***noun*** a long, narrow, open container from which animals eat or drink.
trough • ***noun,*** *plural* **troughs**

troupe (tro͞op) ***noun*** a group of actors, singers, or other performers.
troupe • ***noun,*** *plural* **troupes**
- The words **troupe** and **troop** sound alike.
  He performs with a *troupe* of acrobats.
  The tourists *troop* through town.

trousers (trou′zərz) ***plural noun*** *another name for* **pants**.
trou·sers • ***plural noun***

trout (trout) ***noun*** a small fish that is used for food. It is related to the salmon and is usually found in lakes, streams, and rivers.
trout • ***noun,*** *plural* **trout**

trowel

trowel (trou′əl) ***noun*** **1** a tool with a flat blade for making plaster smooth or for spreading mortar on bricks. **2** a tool with a pointed scoop that is used for digging in a garden.
trow·el • ***noun,*** *plural* **trowels**

a cat	ō go	ʉ fur	ə = a *in* ago
ā ape	ô law, for	ch chin	e *in* agent
ä cot, car	oo look	sh she	i *in* pencil
e ten	o͞o tool	th thin	o *in* atom
ē me	oi oil	*th* then	u *in* circus
i fit	ou out	zh measure	
ī ice	u up	ŋ ring	

truant (tro͞o′ənt) ***noun*** a pupil who stays away from school without permission.
tru·ant • ***noun,*** *plural* **truants**

truce (tro͞os) ***noun*** a stop in war or fighting for a time, when both sides agree to stop fighting.
truce • ***noun,*** *plural* **truces**

truck (truk) ***noun*** a large motor vehicle for carrying heavy loads on highways and streets.
verb to carry in a truck [They *trucked* vegetables to markets in the nearby city.]
truck • ***noun,*** *plural* **trucks** • ***verb*** **trucked, trucking**

trudge (truj) ***verb*** to walk in a tired way or with effort [We *trudged* through the muddy field.]
trudge • ***verb*** **trudged, trudging**

true (tro͞o) ***adjective*** **1** agreeing with the facts; not false [a *true* story]. **2** as it should be; real or genuine [*true* love]. **3** capable of being trusted; faithful or loyal [a *true* friend]. **4** exact or accurate [a *true* copy]. **5** according to law [the *true* owner].
adverb truly; exactly [The arrow sped straight and *true* toward the target.]
noun what is true [Can you tell *true* from false?]
—come true to happen as expected or hoped for.
true • ***adjective*** & • ***adverb*** **truer, truest** • ***noun***

WORD CHOICES

Synonyms of **true**

The words **true, correct,** and **right** share the meaning "in agreement with the facts."

a *true* story
the *correct* answer
the *right* time

truly (tro͞o′lē) ***adverb*** **1** in a true way; honestly [I love you *truly*.] **2** in fact; really [Are you *truly* sorry?] —Look for the WORD CHOICES box at the entry **really**.
tru·ly • ***adverb***

Truman (tro͞o′mən), **Harry S** (her′ē) 1884-1972; the thirty-third president of the U.S., from 1945 to 1953.
Tru·man, Har·ry S

trumpet

trumpet (trum′pət) ***noun*** a small brass musical instrument that is made of a long, looped metal tube that widens out like a funnel at the end. It makes a loud, blaring sound.
verb to make a sound like a trumpet.
trum·pet • ***noun,*** *plural* **trumpets** • ***verb*** **trumpeted, trumpeting**

trunk (truŋk) ***noun*** **1** the main stem of a tree. **2** the body of a human being or animal, not including the head, arms, or legs. **3** a long snout [an elephant's *trunk*]. **4** a large, strong box for storing things or for holding clothes while traveling. **5** the part of a car, usually at the rear, that is used for carrying luggage and a spare tire. **6 trunks** very short pants worn by men for sports such as swimming or boxing.
trunk • ***noun,*** *plural* **trunks**

trust (trust) ***noun*** **1** a strong belief that some person or thing is honest or can be depended on [You can put your *trust* in that bank.] —Look for the WORD CHOICES box at the entry **belief**. **2** property that is held and managed by a person or bank for the benefit of another.
verb **1** to have or put trust in; depend or rely on [I *trust* my boss. Don't *trust* that old ladder.] **2** to put something in the care of [We *trusted* her with our car.]
trust • ***noun,*** *plural for sense 1 only* **trusts** • ***verb*** **trusted, trusting**

trustee (trus tē′) ***noun*** **1** a person who is put in charge of the property or affairs of another person. **2** any one of a group of people that manages the business of an organization such as a college or hospital.
trus·tee • ***noun,*** *plural* **trustees**

trustworthy (trust′wʉr′*th*ē) ***adjective*** deserving to be trusted; reliable [a *trustworthy* leader].
trust·wor·thy • ***adjective***

trusty (trus′tē) ***adjective*** capable of being trusted; reliable [my *trusty* old car].
trust·y • ***adjective*** **trustier, trustiest**

truth (tro͞oth) ***noun*** **1** the fact or quality of being true, real, honest, or accurate. **2** what is true; the facts [Did the newspaper print the *truth* about you?] **3** a fact or principle that has been proved [a scientific *truth*].
truth • ***noun,*** *plural for sense 3 only* **truths** (tro͞o*th*z *or* tro͞oths)

truthful (tro͞oth′fəl) ***adjective*** **1** telling the truth; honest [a *truthful* person]. **2** being the truth; accurate [a *truthful* report].
truth·ful • ***adjective***

try (trī) ***verb*** **1** to make an effort; attempt [*Try* to remember the name.] **2** to seek to find out about; to test [Please *try* my idea. *Try* the window to see if it is locked.] **3** to carry on the trial of in a law court [They *tried* him and found him guilty.] **4** to put to a hard test [Your nonsense is *trying* my patience!]
noun an effort or attempt [She passed the test on her first *try*.]
—try on to put on to see how it fits and looks [I'd like to *try on* that sweater.] **—try out** **1** to test by putting into use [*Try out* your new bike in the driveway.] **2** to test one's fitness for something, such as a place on a team or a part in a play [I *tried out* for the band.]
try • ***verb*** **tried, trying, tries** • ***noun,*** *plural* **tries**

WORD CHOICES

Synonyms of try

The words **try, attempt,** and **strive** share the meaning "to make an attempt to do something."

Try to keep your room neat.

She *attempted* to scale the cliff.

He has been *striving* to understand mathematics.

trying (trī′iŋ) ***adjective*** hard to bear; annoying [a *trying* day at the office].
try·ing • ***adjective***

tryout (trī′out) [*an informal word*] ***noun*** a test to decide which persons are able or fit to do something [They held a *tryout* for the play.]
try·out • ***noun,*** *plural* **tryouts**

T-shirt (tē′shʉrt) ***noun*** a knitted shirt or undershirt with short sleeves and no collar. It is pulled on over the head.
T-shirt • ***noun,*** *plural* **T-shirts**

WORD HISTORY

T-shirt

The **T-shirt** got its name from its shape. If the shirt lies flat, it looks like a **T**. The long part forms the upright part of the letter, and the arms form the bar that crosses the **T**.

tsp. *abbreviation for* **1** teaspoon. **2** teaspoons.

tub (tub) ***noun*** **1** a round, open, wooden container like a large bucket. **2** any large, open container [a *tub* for washing clothes]. **3** the amount a tub will hold [a *tub* of warm water]. **4** *a short form of* **bathtub**.
tub • ***noun,*** *plural* **tubs**

tuba (to͞o′bə *or* tyo͞o′bə) ***noun*** a large brass musical instrument with a wide bell. It has three valves and a full, deep tone.
tu·ba • ***noun,*** *plural* **tubas**

tuba

tubby (tub′ē) ***adjective*** short and fat [a *tubby* little doll].
tub·by • ***adjective*** **tubbier, tubbiest**

tube (to͞ob *or* tyo͞ob) ***noun*** **1** a long, slender, hollow piece of material in which liquids or gases can flow or be kept [a test *tube*]. **2** a long, narrow container made of soft metal or plastic with a cap at one end [a toothpaste *tube*]. **3** an electronic device in the shape of a tube. **4** a hollow ring of thin rubber that is put inside some bicycle tires and filled with air. **5** a video screen in a TV receiver.
tube • ***noun,*** *plural* **tubes**

a cat	ō go	ʉ fur	ə = a *in* ago
ā ape	ô law, for	ch chin	e *in* agent
ä cot, car	o͝o look	sh she	i *in* pencil
e ten	o͞o tool	th thin	o *in* atom
ē me	oi oil	*th* then	u *in* circus
i fit	ou out	zh measure	
ī ice	u up	ŋ ring	

tuber (to͞o′bər *or* tyo͞o′bər) ***noun*** a short, thick part of an underground stem of a plant. Potatoes are tubers.
tu·ber • ***noun,*** *plural* **tubers**

tuberculosis (to͞o bur′kyo͞o lō′sis *or* tyo͞o bur′ kyo͞o lō′sis) ***noun*** a disease that is caused by a germ. Hard, swollen masses form in the lungs, and tissues are destroyed.
tu·ber·cu·lo·sis • ***noun***

Tubman (tub′mən), **Harriet** (her′ē ət) 1820?-1913; a black woman who was one of the leaders in the fight against slavery in the U.S.
Tub·man, Har·ri·et

tuck (tuk) ***verb*** **1** to gather in folds in order to make shorter [She *tucked* up her dress to wade in the stream.] **2** to push the edges of something in or under [*Tuck* in the sheets when making the bed.] **3** to cover or wrap in a snug way [Mom *tucked* the baby in every night.]
tuck • ***verb*** **tucked, tucking**

Tuesday (to͞oz′dā *or* tyo͞oz′dā) ***noun*** the third day of the week. Abbreviated **Tues.**
Tues·day • ***noun,*** *plural* **Tuesdays**

tuft (tuft) ***noun*** a bunch of hairs, feathers, grass, threads, or other similar material that is tied close together.
tuft • ***noun,*** *plural* **tufts**

tug (tug) ***verb*** to pull with force or effort; drag [She *tugged* the trunk out of the closet.] ***noun*** **1** a hard pull [One good *tug* will open the broken door.] **2** *a short form of* **tugboat.**
tug • ***verb*** **tugged, tugging** • ***noun,*** *plural* **tugs**

tugboat

tugboat (tug′bōt) ***noun*** a small, powerful boat that tows or pushes ships and barges.
tug·boat • ***noun,*** *plural* **tugboats**

tug of war ***noun*** a contest in which two teams pull at opposite ends of a rope. Each team tries to drag the other across a center line.

tuition (to͞o ish′ən *or* tyo͞o ish′ən) ***noun*** money that a person pays for being taught in a college or private school.
tu·i·tion • ***noun***

tulip (to͞o′lip *or* tyo͞o′lip) ***noun*** a plant with long, pointed leaves and a large flower shaped like a cup. It grows from a bulb.
tu·lip • ***noun,*** *plural* **tulips**

WORD HISTORY

tulip

The word **tulip** comes from a Turkish word that means "turban." The flower of this plant looks a little like a turban.

tumble (tum′bəl) ***verb*** **1** to do somersaults, handsprings, or other tricks of an acrobat. **2** to fall in a sudden or clumsy way [He slipped and *tumbled* down the steps.] **3** to toss or roll about [The dryer *tumbles* the clothes.] **4** to move in a quick, disorderly way [The children *tumbled* out of the house and into the yard.] ***noun*** a fall [The horse and rider took a nasty *tumble*.]
tum·ble • ***verb*** **tumbled, tumbling** • ***noun,*** *plural* **tumbles**

tumbler (tum′blər) ***noun*** **1** an ordinary drinking glass, without a stem. **2** an acrobat who does tricks such as somersaults and handsprings. **3** any of the parts inside a lock that must be moved by a key or dial in order to open the lock.
tum·bler • ***noun,*** *plural* **tumblers**

tumbleweed (tum′bəl wēd) ***noun*** a plant that breaks off near the ground in autumn and is blown about by the wind.
tum·ble·weed • ***noun,*** *plural* **tumbleweeds**

tummy (tum′ē) [*an informal word*] ***noun*** the stomach or abdomen.
tum·my • ***noun,*** *plural* **tummies**

tumor (to͞o′mər *or* tyo͞o′mər) ***noun*** a growth of extra tissue in some part of the body. Tumors have no useful purpose and are sometimes harmful.
tu·mor • ***noun,*** *plural* **tumors**

tuna (to͞o′nə *or* tyo͞o′nə) ***noun*** **1** one of various large ocean fishes. **2** the oily flesh of the tuna, often canned as food: this food is also called **tuna fish.**
tu·na • ***noun,*** *plural* **tuna**

T

tundra (tun′drə *or* to͞on′drə) ***noun*** a large, flat plain without trees in the arctic regions.
tun·dra • ***noun***

tune (to͞on *or* tyo͞on) ***noun*** **1** a series of musical tones with a regular rhythm; melody [The music of "America" is a very old *tune*.] **2** the condition of having correct musical pitch [Every instrument was in *tune*.] **3** harmony; agreement [in *tune* with the times].
verb to put in the condition of correct musical pitch [He *tuned* the guitar before playing.]
—tune in to set a radio or TV to receive a certain station or program. **—tune up** to put into good working condition by adjusting the parts [A mechanic *tuned up* the engine.]
tune • ***noun,*** *plural for sense 1 only* **tunes** • ***verb*** **tuned, tuning**

tungsten (tuŋ′stən) ***noun*** a hard, heavy metal that is a chemical element. It is mixed with other metals to make them hard and tough. Tungsten is also used to make the wire that lights up inside a light bulb.
tung·sten • ***noun***

tunic (to͞o′nik *or* tyo͞o′nik) ***noun*** **1** a garment that is like a loose gown. It was worn by men and women in ancient Greece and Rome. **2** a blouse or jacket that reaches to the hips. It is often worn with a belt.
tu·nic • ***noun,*** *plural* **tunics**

Tunisia (to͞o nē′zhə *or* tyo͞o nē′zhə) a country in northern Africa, on the Mediterranean Sea.
Tu·ni·sia

tunnel (tun′əl) ***noun*** **1** a passage under the ground for use by cars, trains, or other vehicles. **2** any passage or place in the ground like this. An animal's burrow is a kind of tunnel.
verb to make a tunnel [Moles *tunneled* under the garden.]
tun·nel • ***noun,*** *plural* **tunnels** • ***verb*** **tunneled** or **tunnelled, tunneling** or **tunnelling**

turban (tʉr′bən) ***noun*** **1** a long scarf wound around and around the head. It is worn by men in the Middle East and Asia. **2** any head covering or hat like this.
tur·ban • ***noun,*** *plural* **turbans**

turbine (tʉr′bin *or* tʉr′bīn) ***noun*** an engine in which a wheel of curved vanes is attached to the driving shaft. The pressure of steam, water, or air against the vanes causes the shaft to turn.
tur·bine • ***noun,*** *plural* **turbines**

turbojet (tʉr′bō jet′) ***noun*** a jet airplane engine that has a turbine which compresses the air before it is mixed with the fuel.
tur·bo·jet • ***noun,*** *plural* **turbojets**

turboprop (tʉr′bō präp′) ***noun*** a turbojet with a shaft that drives a propeller.
tur·bo·prop • ***noun,*** *plural* **turboprops**

turbulent (tʉr′byo͞o lənt) ***adjective*** **1** very excited or upset; wild or unruly [a *turbulent* crowd]. **2** full of violent motion [*turbulent* rapids].
tur·bu·lent • ***adjective***

tureen (to͝o rēn′) ***noun*** a large, deep dish with a lid, used to serve soups or stews.
tu·reen • ***noun,*** *plural* **tureens**

turf (tʉrf) ***noun*** a top layer of earth containing grass with its roots; sod.

Turk (tʉrk) ***noun*** a person born or living in Turkey.
Turk • ***noun,*** *plural* **Turks**

turkey (tʉr′kē) ***noun*** **1** a large bird of North America with a small head and spreading tail. **2** the meat of this bird, used as food. **3** [*a slang use*] something that has failed [That movie was a *turkey*.]
tur·key • ***noun,*** *plural for senses 1 and 3 only* **turkeys**

turkey

Turkey (tʉr′kē) a country mostly in western Asia, but partly in southeastern Europe.
Tur·key

turkey vulture ***noun*** a dark-colored vulture. Its head is somewhat red and without feathers.
turkey vulture • ***noun,*** *plural* **turkey vultures**

Turkish (tʉr′kish) ***noun*** the language of Turkey.
Turk·ish • ***noun***

Turkmenistan (tərk men′i stan′) a country in southwestern Asia. It was a part of the Soviet Union.
Turk·men·i·stan

a	cat	ō	go	ʉr	fur	ə =	a *in* ago
ā	ape	ô	law, for	ch	chin		e *in* agent
ä	cot, car	o͝o	look	sh	she		i *in* pencil
e	ten	o͞o	tool	th	thin		o *in* atom
ē	me	oi	oil	*th*	then		u *in* circus
i	fit	ou	out	zh	measure		
ī	ice	u	up	ŋ	ring		

turmoil (tʉr′moil) ***noun*** a noisy or confused condition [The city was in *turmoil* after the flood.]
tur·moil • ***noun***

turn (tʉrn) ***verb*** **1** to move around a center point; revolve; rotate [The wheels *turned*. *Turn* the key.] **2** to do by moving in a circle [She *turned* a somersault.] **3** to change in position or direction [*Turn* your chair around. *Turn* to the left.] **4** to change so that the part that was on the bottom is on the top [*Turn* the page. The farmer *turned* over the soil.] **5** to change in feelings or attitudes [His crime *turned* his family against him.] **6** to shift one's attention [He *turned* to music for relaxing.] **7** to change from one form or condition to another [Leaves *turn* color in the fall. The milk *turned* sour.] **8** to drive, set, or let go in some way [The cat was *turned* loose.] **9** to go to for help [He *turned* to her for help.] **10** to upset or unsettle [The smell *turned* my stomach.] **11** to reach or pass [She *turns* 21 today.] ***noun*** **1** the act of turning around [He gave the wheel a *turn*.] **2** a change in direction or position [a *turn* to the right]. **3** a short walk or ride [We took a *turn* around the block.] **4** a place where there is a change in direction [a sharp *turn* in the road]. **5** a right, duty, or chance to do something in regular order [It's your *turn* to wash dishes.] **6** an action or deed [One good *turn* deserves another.] **7** a change in condition [The sick man took a *turn* for the worse.]
—in turn in the proper order. **—out of turn** **1** not in the proper order [She batted *out of turn*.] **2** at the wrong time [He spoke *out of turn*.] **—take turns** to say or do something one after the other in a regular order. **—turn down** to refuse or reject [He *turned down* our offer.] **—turn in** **1** to make a turn into; enter [*Turn in* that driveway.] **2** to hand over; deliver [*Turn in* your homework.] **3** [*an informal use*] to go to bed [I *turned in* at 9 o'clock.] **—turn off** **1** to leave [*Turn off* this road at the next light.] **2** to shut off [*Turn off* the water.] **—turn on** to cause to operate; start [*Turn on* the radio.] **—turn out** **1** to shut off or put out [*Turn out* the lights.] **2** to come or gather [Many people *turned out* for the picnic.] **3** to result or become [Everything *turned out* fine.] **—turn over** to hand over; give [She *turned over* the information to her boss.] **—turn up** to happen or arrive [The guests *turned up* late.]
turn • ***verb*** **turned, turning** • ***noun,*** *plural* **turns**

● The words **turn** and **tern** sound alike.
It's my *turn* to walk the dog.
A gull and a *tern* flew over the beach.

WORD CHOICES

Synonyms of **turn**

The words **turn, revolve,** and **rotate** share the meaning "to move around a center."

The wheel *turned* slowly.
The earth *revolves* around the sun.
The earth *rotates* on its axis.

turncoat (tʉrn′kōt) ***noun*** a person who goes over to the opposite side or party; a traitor.
turn·coat • ***noun,*** *plural* **turncoats**

Turner (tʉr′nər), **Nat** (nat) 1800-1831; a U.S. black slave who led a revolt in 1831.
Tur·ner, Nat

turnip (tʉr′nip) ***noun*** a plant with a round, white or yellow root that is eaten as a vegetable.
tur·nip • ***noun,*** *plural* **turnips**

turnout (tʉrn′out) ***noun*** a group or gathering of people [a large *turnout* at the picnic].
turn·out • ***noun***

turnover (tʉrn′ō vər) ***noun*** a small pie with one half of the crust turned over the other half, with a filling between.
turn·o·ver • ***noun,*** *plural* **turnovers**

turnpike (tʉrn′pīk) ***noun*** a highway or expressway on which drivers are charged a toll.
turn·pike • ***noun,*** *plural* **turnpikes**

turnstile

turnstile (tʉrn′stīl) ***noun*** a device in an entrance or exit that turns to let through only one person at a time.
turn·stile • ***noun,*** *plural* **turnstiles**

T

turntable (tʉrn′tā bəl) *noun* a round platform that turns, used to play a phonograph record.
turn·ta·ble • *noun, plural* **turntables**

turpentine (tʉr′pən tīn) *noun* a clear liquid made from the sap of pines and certain other trees. It is used in paints and varnishes.
tur·pen·tine • *noun*

turquoise (tʉr′kwoiz *or* tʉr′koiz) *noun* **1** a greenish-blue stone, used in jewelry. **2** a greenish blue.
adjective greenish-blue.
tur·quoise • *noun, plural for sense 1 only* **turquoises** • *adjective*

turquoise

WORD HISTORY

turquoise

The word **turquoise** is an old English word which comes from a French word that means "Turkish." The first **turquoise** stones in western Europe came by way of Turkey, so people thought the stones were Turkish.

turret (tʉr′ət) *noun* **1** a small tower that sticks out from the walls of a building, usually at a corner [Castles often have *turrets*.] **2** a low dome on a ship, tank, or airplane, that houses a gun. The turret often revolves so that the gun can be fired in different directions.
tur·ret • *noun, plural* **turrets**

turtle (tʉrt′l) *noun* an animal with a soft body covered by a hard shell. It can pull its head, tail, and legs into its shell to protect itself. Turtles live on land and in the water.
tur·tle • *noun, plural* **turtles**

turtledove (tʉrt′l duv) *noun* a wild dove known for its sad cooing and the love that the mates seem to show for each other.
tur·tle·dove • *noun, plural* **turtledoves**

turtleneck (tʉrt′l nek) *noun* **1** a high collar that turns down and fits close around the neck. **2** a sweater or shirt with such a collar.
tur·tle·neck • *noun, plural* **turtlenecks**

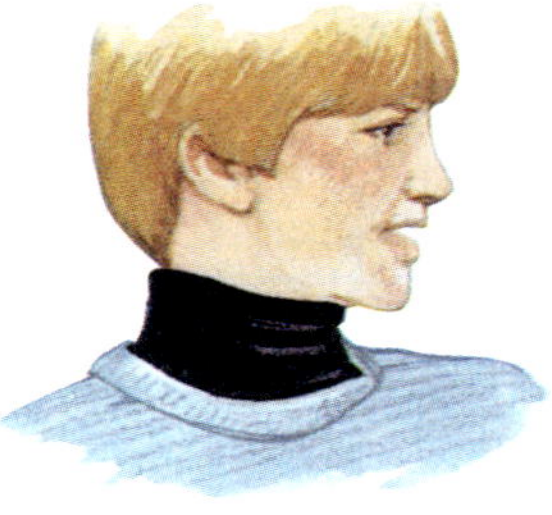

turtleneck

tusk (tusk) *noun* a very long and pointed tooth, usually one of a pair, that sticks out of the mouth. Elephants and walruses have tusks.
tusk • *noun, plural* **tusks**

tussle (tus′əl) *verb* to struggle or wrestle; scuffle [Two boys *tussled* in the hall.]
noun a short, rough struggle or fight [A teacher broke up the *tussle* on the playground.]
tus·sle • *verb* **tussled, tussling** • *noun, plural* **tussles**

tut (tut) *interjection* a word that is used to show that one is impatient, annoyed, or angry.

tutor (to͞ot′ər *or* tyo͞ot′ər) *noun* a teacher who teaches one student at a time; private teacher.
verb to act as a tutor to [She *tutored* him in spelling.]
tu·tor • *noun, plural* **tutors** • *verb* **tutored, tutoring**

tutu (to͞o′to͞o) *noun* a short, full skirt worn by a ballerina.
tu·tu • *noun, plural* **tutus**

tutu

Tuvalu (to͞o′və lo͞o′) a country consisting of a group of nine islands in the west central Pacific.
Tu·va·lu

tuxedo (tuk sē′dō) *noun* **1** a man's jacket worn at formal events and parties. It is black or colored, with satin lapels and no tails. **2** a suit with such a jacket, worn with a dark necktie that is tied in a bow.
tux·e·do • *noun, plural* **tuxedos**

TV *noun* television or a television receiver.
TV • *noun, plural* **TVs**

Twain (twān), **Mark** (märk) 1835-1910; U.S. writer. His real name was *Samuel Langhorne Clemens*.

twang (twaŋ) *noun* **1** a sharp, vibrating sound [the *twang* of the banjo]. **2** a way of making speech sounds by letting some air pass through the nose to produce nasal sounds.
verb **1** to make or cause to make a twang

a	cat	ō	go	ʉ	fur	ə =	a *in* ago
ā	ape	ô	law, for	ch	chin		e *in* agent
ä	cot, car	o͝o	look	sh	she		i *in* pencil
e	ten	o͞o	tool	th	thin		o *in* atom
ē	me	oi	oil	*th*	then		u *in* circus
i	fit	ou	out	zh	measure		
ī	ice	u	up	ŋ	ring		

[The guitar *twanged*. She *twanged* the guitar.] **2** to speak with a twang.
twang • *noun, plural* **twangs**
• *verb* **twanged, twanging**

'twas (twuz *or* twäz) it was [*'Twas* a dark and stormy night.]

tweak (twēk) *verb* to give a sudden, twisting pinch to [She *tweaked* his cheek.]
noun a sudden, twisting pinch.
tweak • *verb* **tweaked, tweaking** • *noun, plural* **tweaks**

tweed (twēd) *noun* **1** a rough wool cloth in a weave of two or more colors. **2 tweeds** clothes of tweed.
tweed • *noun, plural* **tweeds**

tweet (twēt) *noun* the high, chirping sound of a small bird.
verb to make this sound.
tweet • *noun* • *verb* **tweeted, tweeting**

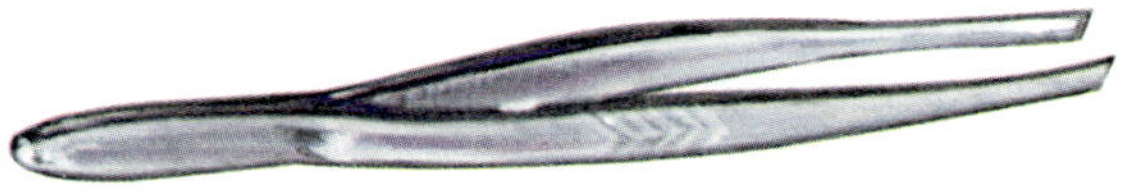

tweezers

tweezers (twē′zərz) *plural noun* small pincers for plucking out hairs or handling small things.
tweez·ers • *plural noun*

twelfth (twelfth) *adjective* coming after eleven others in a series; 12th in order.
noun **1** the number, person, or thing that is twelfth. **2** one of twelve equal parts of something; $\frac{1}{12}$.
twelfth • *adjective* • *noun, plural* **twelfths**

twelve (twelv) *noun* the cardinal number between eleven and thirteen; 12.
adjective being one more than eleven [*twelve* eggs].
twelve • *noun, plural* **twelves** • *adjective*

twentieth (twen′tē əth) *adjective* coming after nineteen others in a series; 20th in order.
noun **1** the number, person, or thing that is twentieth. **2** one of twenty equal parts of something; $\frac{1}{20}$.
twen·ti·eth • *adjective* • *noun, plural* **twentieths**

twenty (twen′tē) *noun* the cardinal number that is equal to two times ten; 20.
adjective being two times ten [*twenty* days].
twen·ty • *noun, plural* **twenties** • *adjective*

twice (twīs) *adverb* **1** two times [Don't make me ask you *twice*.] **2** two times as much or as many [You have *twice* the energy that I do when we play tennis.]

twiddle (twid′əl) *verb used mainly in the phrase* **twiddle one's thumbs, 1** to twirl one's thumbs around each other in an idle way. **2** to be idle [Don't just sit there *twiddling your thumbs!*]
twid·dle • *verb* **twiddled, twiddling**

twig (twig) *noun* a small branch or shoot of a tree or shrub.
twig • *noun, plural* **twigs**

twilight (twī′līt) *noun* **1** the dim light just after sunset [Everything looks gray in *twilight*.] **2** the time between sunset and dark [We have to be home by *twilight*.]
twi·light • *noun*

twin (twin) *noun* **1** either of two children born at the same time to the same mother [*Twins* run in families.] **2** either of two persons or things very much alike or forming a pair [It is the *twin* of a chair I bought yesterday.]
adjective being a twin or twins [*twin* sisters].
twin • *noun, plural* **twins** • *adjective*

twine (twīn) *noun* a strong string or cord made of two or more strands twisted together.
verb to wind or grow in a winding way [The ivy *twined* around the post.]
twine • *noun* • *verb* **twined, twining**

twinkle (twiŋk′əl) *verb* **1** to shine with quick flashes of light; sparkle [The stars *twinkled* in the night sky.] **2** to light up with pleasure or amusement [His eyes *twinkled*.]
noun **1** a quick flash of light; sparkle [the *twinkle* of the lights in the valley]. **2** a quick look of pleasure or amusement [a *twinkle* in her eye].
twin·kle • *verb* **twinkled, twinkling** • *noun*

twirl (twurl) *verb* **1** to turn in a very quick way; spin [The ballerina *twirled* on her toes.] **2** to whirl in a circle [She *twirled* the baton.] **3** to twist or coil [He *twirled* his mustache.]
noun the act of twirling.
twirl • *verb* **twirled, twirling** • *noun, plural* **twirls**

twist (twist) *verb* **1** to wind or twine together or around something [Wool fibers are *twisted* into yarn.] **2** to move or turn in a spiral or in curves [Dough is *twisted* to make pretzels. The road *twists* up the hill.] **3** to turn around [*Twist* the lid to take it off.] **4** to break off by turning the end [I *twisted* the stem from the apple.] **5** to force out of its usual shape or position; to sprain [I tripped and *twisted* my

T

ankle.] **6** to give the wrong meaning to something on purpose [He *twisted* my compliment into an insult.]
noun **1** the act of twisting [I gave the cap a light *twist* and it came right off.] **2** a place where something twists or turns [a *twist* in the road]. **3** a special meaning or way of looking at things [He gave a new *twist* to the old joke.]
twist • ***verb*** **twisted, twisting** • ***noun,*** *plural* **twists**

twister (twis′tər) [*an informal word*] ***noun*** a tornado or cyclone.
twist·er • ***noun,*** *plural* **twisters**

twitch (twich) ***verb*** to move with a sudden jerk [A rabbit's nose *twitches.*]
noun a sudden, quick motion, often one that cannot be controlled [a *twitch* near one eye].
twitch • ***verb*** **twitched, twitching** • ***noun,*** *plural* **twitches**

twitter (twit′ər) ***verb*** to make a series of chirping sounds [Birds were *twittering* in the bushes.]
noun the act or sound of twittering.
twit·ter • ***verb*** **twittered, twittering** • ***noun***

two (to͞o) ***noun*** the cardinal number between one and three; 2.
adjective being one more than one [*two* apples].
—in two in two parts [It was cut *in two.*]
two • ***noun,*** *plural* **twos** • ***adjective***
● The words **two, to,** and **too** sound alike.
I took *two* sandwiches for lunch.
Does this bus go *to* Boston?
Are you a sophomore, *too?*

twofold (to͞o′fōld) ***adjective*** **1** having two parts [A parent's duties are *twofold.*] **2** being two times as much or as many [a *twofold* increase].
adverb two times as much or as many [I sold my car and got my money back *twofold.*]
two·fold • ***adjective*** • ***adverb***

two-way (to͞o′wā′) ***adjective*** **1** moving or letting one move in either direction [*two-way* traffic; a *two-way* street]. **2** used for both sending and receiving [a *two-way* radio].

Twp. *abbreviation for* Township.

TX *an abbreviation for* Texas.

tycoon (tī ko͞on′) ***noun*** a businessman with much money and power.
ty·coon • ***noun,*** *plural* **tycoons**

tying (tī′iŋ) ***verb*** *present participle of* **tie**.
ty·ing • ***verb***

tyke (tīk) [*an informal word*] ***noun*** a small child.
tyke • ***noun,*** *plural* **tykes**

Tyler (tī′lər), **John** (jän) 1790-1862; the tenth president of the U.S., from 1841 to 1845.
Ty·ler, John

type (tīp) ***noun*** **1** a group or class of people or things that are alike in some way; kind; sort [people of the bravest *type*]. **2** the general form, features, or style of a particular kind or class of things [That's not the *type* of shoe I wanted.] **3** a piece of metal with a raised letter or mark on its top. It is used in printing. **4** the letters printed from such pieces [The *type* in that book is small and hard to read.] **5** similar letters that are produced by a computer printer.
verb to write with a typewriter [I *typed* a letter to my friend in California.]
type • ***noun,*** *plural for senses 1 and 2 only* **types** • ***verb*** **typed, typing**

WORD CHOICES

Synonyms of type

The words **type**, **kind**, and **sort** share the meaning "a group of things or people that are alike in some way."

a new *type* of citrus fruit
games of every *kind*
just the *sort* of person they like best

typewrite (tīp′rīt) ***verb*** to write with a typewriter. This word is now usually shortened to *type.*
type·write • ***verb*** **typewrote, typewritten, typewriting**

typewriter (tīp′rīt ər) ***noun*** a machine with a keyboard for making printed letters on paper.
type·writ·er • ***noun,*** *plural* **typewriters**

typhoid (tī′foid) ***noun*** a serious disease that is spread by infected food and drinking water. It causes fever and sores in the intestines. The full name is **typhoid fever**.
ty·phoid • ***noun***

a	cat	ō	go	ʉ	fur	ə =	a *in* ago
ā	ape	ô	law, for	ch	chin		e *in* agent
ä	cot, car	o͝o	look	sh	she		i *in* pencil
e	ten	o͞o	tool	th	thin		o *in* atom
ē	me	oi	oil	*th*	then		u *in* circus
i	fit	ou	out	zh	measure		
ī	ice	u	up	ŋ	ring		

typhoon (tī fo͞on′) ***noun*** any violent tropical cyclone that starts in the western Pacific.
ty·phoon • ***noun,*** *plural* **typhoons**

typical (tip′i kəl) ***adjective*** **1** being a good example of its kind [The tulip is a *typical* garden flower.] **2** of or belonging to a type; helping to make up the special character of a person or thing [Long ears are *typical* of hares.]
typ·i·cal • ***adjective***

typist (tīp′ist) ***noun*** **1** a person who uses a typewriter. **2** a person whose work is typing.
typ·ist • ***noun,*** *plural* **typists**

tyrannosaur (tə ran′ə sôr *or* tī ran′ə sôr) ***noun*** a huge meat-eating dinosaur that walked upright on its hind legs.
ty·ran·no·saur • ***noun,*** *plural* **tyrannosaurs**

tyranny (tir′ə nē) ***noun*** very cruel and unfair use of power [the *tyranny* of a dictator].
tyr·an·ny • ***noun***

tyrant (tī′rənt) ***noun*** **1** a ruler who is cruel and unfair. **2** a person who uses power in a cruel or unfair way [Their coach is a *tyrant*.]
ty·rant • ***noun,*** *plural* **tyrants**

U u

Uu Uu *Uu* **Uu**

The letter **u** *can stand for a long vowel sound, as in the word* **rude,** *or a short vowel sound, as in the word* **cut.** *Sometimes a* **u** *can stand for the combination sound of* **y+u,** *as in the words* **unique** *and* **ukulele.**

u or **U** (yo͞o) ***noun*** the twenty-first letter of the English alphabet.
u or **U** • ***noun,*** *plural* **u's** or **U's**

udder (ud′ər) ***noun*** an organ that looks like a bag, in cows, goats, and certain other female animals. It makes and gives out milk.
ud·der • ***noun,*** *plural* **udders**

UFO ***noun*** any one of a number of strange flying objects that people say they have seen. According to one idea, they are spacecraft from another planet.
UFO • ***noun,*** *plural* **UFOs**

WORD HISTORY

UFO

The name **UFO** comes from the first letter of each of the three words *unidentified flying object.*

Uganda (yo͞o gan′də *or* o͞o gän′dä) a country in east central Africa.
U·gan·da

ugh (ug) ***interjection*** a sound made in the throat to show disgust or horror.

ugly (ug′lē) ***adjective*** **1** not pleasing to look at [an *ugly* house]. **2** bad, unpleasant, or disgusting [an *ugly* lie; an *ugly* habit].
ug·ly • ***adjective*** **uglier, ugliest**

uh (u) ***interjection*** **1** *the same as* **huh**. **2** a long sound that is sometimes made between words or sentences when a person is talking. It usually shows that the person is looking for a word or taking time to think.

uh-huh (u hu′) ***interjection*** a sound made in the throat that shows that a person is answering "yes" or that a person is listening.

uh-uh (u′u′) ***interjection*** a sound made in the throat that shows that a person is answering "no."

Ukraine (yo͞o krān′) a country in southeastern Europe. It was a part of the Soviet Union.
U·kraine

Ukrainian (yo͞o krā′nē ən) ***noun*** **1** a person born or living in Ukraine. **2** the language of Ukraine.
U·krain·i·an • ***noun,*** *plural for sense 1 only* **Ukrainians**

ukulele (yo͞o′kə lā′lē) ***noun*** a musical instrument with four strings. It is played like a guitar.
u·ku·le·le • ***noun,*** *plural* **ukuleles**

a cat	ō go	ʉ fur	ə = a *in* ago
ā ape	ô law, for	ch chin	e *in* agent
ä cot, car	o͝o look	sh she	i *in* pencil
e ten	o͞o tool	th thin	o *in* atom
ē me	oi oil	*th* then	u *in* circus
i fit	ou out	zh measure	
ī ice	u up	ŋ ring	

ulcer (ul′sər) ***noun*** an open sore with pus on the skin or the lining of the stomach.
ul·cer • ***noun,*** *plural* **ulcers**

ultimate (ul′ti mət) ***adjective*** **1** final; last [Her *ultimate* decision was fair to everyone.] **2** most basic; primary [I believe in the *ultimate* goodness of people.]
ul·ti·mate • ***adjective***

ultra- *a prefix meaning:* **1** beyond [*Ultraviolet* rays lie beyond the violet end of the spectrum.] **2** beyond what is usual; very [An *ultramodern* house is a very modern house.]

ultrasonic (ul′trə sän′ik) ***adjective*** describing or having to do with sounds that are too high for human beings to hear.
ul·tra·son·ic • ***adjective***

ultraviolet (ul′trə vī′ə lət) ***adjective*** lying just beyond the violet end of the light spectrum. Ultraviolet light is invisible.
ul·tra·vi·o·let • ***adjective***

umbilical cord (um bil′i kəl) ***noun*** the cord that connects an unborn baby with its mother. The baby gets nourishment through it until it is born.
um·bil·i·cal cord • ***noun,*** *plural* **umbilical cords**

umbrella (um brel′ə) ***noun*** a screen that is made of cloth or plastic that is stretched over a folding frame and held up by a stick. It is used to protect a person from rain or the sun.
um·brel·la • ***noun,*** *plural* **umbrellas**

umpire (um′pīr) ***noun*** a person who rules on the plays of a game.
verb to be an umpire in a game [My uncle *umpired* our baseball game.]
um·pire • ***noun,*** *plural* **umpires**
• ***verb*** **umpired, umpiring**

un- *a prefix meaning:* **1** not; the opposite of [An *unhappy* person is one who is not happy, but sad.] **2** to change the action of something to the opposite or to do away with it [*Untying* a shoe means doing the opposite of tying it.]

WORD MAKER

The prefix **un-**

Many words contain the prefix **un-** plus a word that you already know. You can understand these words if you add the idea "not" or "to do the opposite of" to the meaning of the base word.

I. *when added to adjectives:*

prefix	*+ base word*	⇨	*new word*
un-	**+ afraid**	⇨	**unafraid** *(not feeling fear; not frightened)*

Below is a list of words that contain the prefix **un-**

unacceptable	unneighborly
unambitious	unnoticeable
unashamed	unofficial
uncivil	unoriginal
undesirable	unpatriotic
unemotional	unsafe
unexciting	unskillful
unfavorable	unsophisticated
unfunny	unsuccessful
ungrateful	unsuitable
unhealthful	unsure
unimaginative	unthoughtful
unintelligent	unusable *or*
unintentional	unuseable
unmerciful	unwelcome

II. *when added to verbs:*

prefix	*+ base word*	⇨	*new word*
un-	**+ bind**	⇨	**unbind** *(to do the opposite of tying together; to untie)*

unbend	unclog	unpin
unbolt	uncoil	unseal
unbraid	uncurl	unstick
unchain	unfreeze	untwist
unclasp	unmask	unyoke

unable (un ā′bəl) ***adjective*** not able; not having the means or power to do something [I'm *unable* to come on Saturday.]
un·a·ble • ***adjective***

WORD HISTORY

unanimous

The word **unanimous** comes from two Latin words that mean "one" and "the mind." When a vote or decision is **unanimous,** it means that everyone is "of one mind," or everyone agrees.

U

unanimous (yoo nan′i məs) ***adjective*** showing complete agreement; with no one opposed [She was elected by a *unanimous* vote.]
u·nan·i·mous • ***adjective***

unattractive (un′ə trak′tiv) ***adjective*** not attractive; homely, bad, or offensive [an *unattractive* room; *unattractive* behavior].
un·at·trac·tive • ***adjective***

unavailable (un′ə vāl′ə bəl) ***adjective*** not able to be gotten, used, or reached [This book is now *unavailable*.]
un·a·vail·a·ble • ***adjective***

unavoidable (un′ə void′ə bəl) ***adjective*** not able to be avoided or escaped [The street was so icy that the accident was *unavoidable*.]
un·a·void·a·ble • ***adjective***

unaware (un ə wer′) ***adjective*** not aware; not knowing or noticing [We were *unaware* that the steps were dangerous.]
adverb *the same as* **unawares**.
un·a·ware • ***adjective*** • ***adverb***

unawares (un ə werz′) ***adverb*** by surprise; in a way that is not expected [We sneaked up on them *unawares*.]
un·a·wares • ***adverb***

unbearable (un ber′ə bəl) ***adjective*** not capable of being endured [The pain was *unbearable*.]
un·bear·a·ble • ***adjective***

unbeatable (un bēt′ə bəl) ***adjective*** **1** so good that defeat is impossible [Our team is *unbeatable* this year.] **2** so good that no improvement can be imagined [an *unbeatable* deal on a car].
un·beat·a·ble • ***adjective***

unbeaten (un bēt′n) ***adjective*** not defeated or improved upon [an *unbeaten* team].
un·beat·en • ***adjective***

unbecoming (un′bē kum′iŋ) ***adjective*** not becoming; not attractive or not proper [an *unbecoming* dress; *unbecoming* behavior].
un·be·com·ing • ***adjective***

unbending (un ben′diŋ) ***adjective*** not bending; stiff, firm, or severe [an *unbending* attitude].
un·bend·ing • ***adjective***

unborn (un bôrn′) ***adjective*** not yet born [an *unborn* baby; *unborn* generations].
un·born • ***adjective***

unbreakable (un brāk′ə bəl) ***adjective*** not able to be broken or not likely to be broken.
un·break·a·ble • ***adjective***

unbroken (un brō′kən) ***adjective*** **1** not broken; all in one piece; whole [Only one glass was left *unbroken*.] **2** without any interruption; going on without a stop or break [an *unbroken* silence]. **3** not bettered or gone beyond [an *unbroken* record in sports].
un·bro·ken • ***adjective***

unbuckle (un buk′əl) ***verb*** to unfasten the buckle or buckles of [*Unbuckle* your seat belt.]
un·buck·le • ***verb*** **unbuckled, unbuckling**

unbutton (un but′n) ***verb*** to unfasten the button or buttons of.
un·but·ton • ***verb*** **unbuttoned, unbuttoning**

uncalled-for (un kôld′fôr′) ***adjective*** not needed or asked for; out of place [an *uncalled-for* remark].
un·called-for • ***adjective***

uncanny (un kan′ē) ***adjective*** **1** mysterious and unnatural; weird [The empty house had an *uncanny* look.] **2** so good as to seem not natural [an *uncanny* sense of hearing].
un·can·ny • ***adjective***

WORD CHOICES

Synonyms of **uncanny**

The words **uncanny, eerie,** and **weird** share the meaning "strange or mysterious."

the *uncanny* look of the dark, deserted house

an *eerie*, wailing cry from overhead

weird, distorted figures emerging from the cave

uncertain (un surt′n) ***adjective*** **1** not certain or sure; full of doubt [He looked *uncertain* about what to do.] **2** not definite; vague [an *uncertain* number of people]. **3** not steady or constant; likely to change [*uncertain* weather].
un·cer·tain • ***adjective***

uncle (uŋ′kəl) ***noun*** **1** the brother of one's father or mother. **2** the husband of one's aunt.
un·cle • ***noun, plural*** **uncles**

unclean (un klēn′) ***adjective*** dirty; filthy [*unclean* hands] —Look for the WORD CHOICES

a	cat	ō	go	ʉ	fur	ə = a *in* ago	
ā	ape	ô	law, for	ch	chin	e *in* agent	
ä	cot, car	oo	look	sh	she	i *in* pencil	
e	ten	ōō	tool	th	thin	o *in* atom	
ē	me	oi	oil	*th*	then	u *in* circus	
i	fit	ou	out	zh	measure		
ī	ice	u	up	ŋ	ring		

box at the entry **dirty**.
un·clean • *adjective*

unclear (un klir′) ***adjective*** not clear; hard to see or understand [He saw only an *unclear* outline.]
un·clear • *adjective*

Uncle Sam the U.S. government or people, represented as a tall, thin man with chin whiskers, dressed in a red, white, and blue suit.

uncomfortable (un kum′fər tə bəl *or* un kumf′tər bəl) ***adjective*** **1** not comfortable; not able to relax or be at ease [I'm very *uncomfortable* in this chair. He's *uncomfortable* around strangers.] **2** not pleasant or agreeable; giving an unpleasant feeling [*uncomfortable* new shoes; an *uncomfortable* silence].
un·com·fort·a·ble • *adjective*

uncommon (un käm′ən) ***adjective*** not common or usual; unusual [It is *uncommon* to see a robin so late in the fall.]
un·com·mon • *adjective*

unconcerned (un kən surnd′) ***adjective*** not concerned, interested, or worried [They seemed *unconcerned* about being late.]
un·con·cerned • *adjective*

unconscious (un kän′shəs) ***adjective*** **1** not conscious; not able to feel and think [He is *unconscious* from a blow to the head.] **2** not aware [She is *unconscious* of her mistake.] **3** not done on purpose [an *unconscious* habit].
un·con·scious • *adjective*

unconventional (un kən ven′shə nəl) ***adjective*** not agreeing with the way things are usually done or with the usual rules.
un·con·ven·tion·al • *adjective*

uncooperative (un′kō äp′ər ə tiv *or* un′kō äp′rə tiv) ***adjective*** not willing to cooperate.
un·co·op·er·a·tive • *adjective*

uncover (un kuv′ər) ***verb*** **1** to remove the cover or covering from [Don't *uncover* the snacks until we are ready to serve them.] **2** to make something known [The detective *uncovered* the most important clue in the case.]
un·cov·er • *verb* **uncovered, uncovering**

undecided (un′dē sīd′əd) ***adjective*** **1** not having made up one's mind [We are *undecided* whether to go or stay.] **2** not having been decided [The date for the party is *undecided*.]
un·de·cid·ed • *adjective*

under (un′dər) ***preposition*** **1** in or to a place, position, amount, or value that is lower than [It rolled *under* the table. It weighs *under* a pound.] **2** below and to the other side of [We drove *under* the bridge.] **3** beneath the surface of [There are oil wells *under* the sea.] **4** covered or hidden by [I wore a sweater *under* my coat. She writes *under* a different name.] **5** controlled, led, or bound by [*under* orders from the President; *under* oath]. **6** receiving the effect of [working *under* a strain; a bridge *under* repair]. **7** being the subject of [the question *under* discussion]. **8** because of [*under* the circumstances].
adverb **1** in or to a lower position or condition [We passed *under*.] **2** so that it is covered or hidden [The car was snowed *under*.] **3** less in amount [It will cost two dollars or *under*.]
adjective lower in position, rank, or amount [the *under* part of the car].
un·der • *preposition* • *adverb* • *adjective*

under- *a prefix meaning:* **1** lower than; below or beneath [*Underclothes* are worn beneath a dress, shirt and pants, or other outfit.] **2** too little; less than is usual or right [An *underpaid* worker is paid too little.]

underarm (un′dər ärm) ***adjective*** having to do with or used on the area under the arm, or the armpit [*underarm* deodorant].
un·der·arm • *adjective*

underbrush (un′dər brush) ***noun*** bushes and other plants under the large trees in a forest.
un·der·brush • *noun*

underclothes (un′dər klōz *or* un′dər klōthz) ***plural noun*** *another name for* **underwear**.
un·der·clothes • *plural noun*

underclothing (un′dər klōth′iŋ) ***noun*** *another name for* **underwear**.
un·der·cloth·ing • *noun*

undercover (un dər kuv′ər) ***adjective*** acting or done in secret [an *undercover* police investigation].
un·der·cov·er • *adjective*

underdog (un′dər dôg) ***noun*** a person, team, or side that is expected to lose a game, race, election, or other contest.
un·der·dog • *noun, plural* **underdogs**

underdone (un dər dun′) ***adjective*** not cooked enough [This meat is so *underdone* that it's almost raw.]
un·der·done • *adjective*

underfoot (un dər foot′) ***adverb*** **1** under one's foot or feet [They trampled the flowers *underfoot*.] **2** in the way [That cat is always getting *underfoot*.]
un·der·foot • *adverb*

U

undergarment (un′dər gär mənt) ***noun*** a piece of underwear.
un·der·gar·ment • ***noun,*** *plural* **undergarments**

undergo (un dər gō′) ***verb*** to go through; have happen to a person [She needs to *undergo* a series of operations.]
un·der·go • ***verb*** **underwent, undergone, undergoing**

undergone (un dər gôn′) ***verb*** *past participle of* **undergo**.
un·der·gone • ***verb***

underground (un′dər ground) ***adjective*** **1** beneath the surface of the earth [an *underground* lake]. **2** done in secret; undercover [an *underground* revolution].
adverb **1** beneath the surface of the earth [Moles burrow *underground*.] **2** into hiding [The escaped criminal went *underground*.]
noun **1** the whole region beneath the surface of the earth. **2** a group of people working in a secret way against the government or against an enemy that is occupying and controlling their country.
un·der·ground • ***adjective*** • ***adverb*** • ***noun,*** *plural for sense 2 only* **undergrounds**

undergrowth (un′dər grōth) ***noun*** *another name for* **underbrush**.
un·der·growth • ***noun***

underhand (un′dər hand) ***adjective*** **1** done with the hand kept lower than the elbow or shoulder [an *underhand* pitch in softball]. **2** *the same as* **underhanded**.
adverb with an underhand motion [Toss the ball *underhand*.]
un·der·hand • ***adjective*** • ***adverb***

underhanded (un′dər han′dəd) ***adjective*** not honest or fair; sly and deceitful [They won the game because they used *underhanded* tricks.]
un·der·hand·ed • ***adjective***

underlain (un dər lān′) ***verb*** *past participle of* **underlie**.
un·der·lain • ***verb***

underlay (un dər lā′) ***verb*** *past tense of* **underlie**.
un·der·lay • ***verb***

underlie (un dər lī′) ***verb*** **1** to lie beneath [Solid rock *underlies* this topsoil.] **2** to be the basis of something [Hard work *underlies* their success.]
un·der·lie • ***verb*** **underlay, underlain, underlying**

underline (un′dər līn) ***verb*** **1** to draw a line under [He *underlined* the word "now."] **2** to emphasize [The speaker *underlined* her main points by repeating them.]
un·der·line • ***verb*** **underlined, underlining**

undermine (un′dər mīn′) ***verb*** **1** to wear away or weaken the supports of something [Erosion is *undermining* the wall.] **2** to injure or weaken in a slow or sneaky way [False rumors had *undermined* their confidence in us.]
un·der·mine • ***verb*** **undermined, undermining**

underneath (un dər nēth′) ***adverb*** beneath; under [Does your car have rust *underneath?*]
preposition beneath; under [We swam in the stream *underneath* the bridge.]
un·der·neath • ***adverb*** • ***preposition***

underpants (un′dər pants) ***plural noun*** short or long pants worn as a piece of underwear.
un·der·pants • ***plural noun***

underpass

underpass (un′dər pas) ***noun*** a passageway or road under a railroad or highway.
un·der·pass • ***noun,*** *plural* **underpasses**

undersea (un dər sē′) ***adjective*** beneath the surface of the sea [*undersea* exploration].
un·der·sea • ***adjective***

undershirt (un′dər shʉrt) ***noun*** a shirt without a collar and often without sleeves, worn as a piece of underwear.
un·der·shirt • ***noun,*** *plural* **undershirts**

undershorts (un′dər shôrts) ***plural noun*** short underpants that are worn by men and boys.
un·der·shorts • ***plural noun***

a	cat	ō	go	ʉ	fur	ə =	a *in* ago
ā	ape	ô	law, for	ch	chin		e *in* agent
ä	cot, car	oo	look	sh	she		i *in* pencil
e	ten	o͞o	tool	th	thin		o *in* atom
ē	me	oi	oil	*th*	then		u *in* circus
i	fit	ou	out	zh	measure		
ī	ice	u	up	ŋ	ring		

underside (un′dər sīd) *noun* the side underneath.
un·der·side • *noun, plural* **undersides**

understand (un dər stand′) *verb* **1** to get the meaning of; know what is meant by something or someone [Do you *understand* my question?] **2** to get an idea or notion from what is heard, seen, read, or known in some other way [I *understand* that you like to fish.] **3** to take for granted; take as a fact [It is *understood* that no one is to leave.] **4** to have knowledge of [Do you *understand* French?] **5** to know the feelings of and have sympathy for someone [She felt that no one *understood* her.]
un·der·stand • *verb* **understood, understanding**

understanding (un dər stan′diŋ) *noun* **1** the fact of knowing what is meant; knowledge [a full *understanding* of the subject]. **2** a meaning or explanation [What is your *understanding* of this poem?] **3** an agreement, especially one that settles a quarrel [The feuding families have reached an *understanding*.]
adjective able to understand; having sympathy and good sense [an *understanding* friend].
un·der·stand·ing • *noun, plural for sense 3 only* **understandings** • *adjective*

understood (un dər stood′) *verb past tense and past participle of* **understand**.
un·der·stood • *verb*

undertake (un dər tāk′) *verb* to agree to do; to take upon oneself [I *undertook* a difficult job in order to test myself.]
un·der·take • *verb* **undertook, undertaken, undertaking**

undertaken (un dər tā′kən) *verb past participle of* **undertake**.
un·der·tak·en • *verb*

undertaking (un′dər tā′kiŋ) *noun* something undertaken; a task [Climbing a tall mountain is a dangerous *undertaking*.]
un·der·tak·ing • *noun, plural* **undertakings**

undertook (un dər took′) *verb past tense of* **undertake**.
un·der·took • *verb*

underwater (un′dər wôt′ər) *adjective* **1** under the surface of the water [We explored the *underwater* caves.] **2** used or for use under water [*Underwater* equipment is waterproof.]
adverb under the surface of the water [I dived *underwater*.]
un·der·wa·ter • *adjective* • *adverb*

underwear (un′dər wer) *noun* clothing that is worn under a person's outer clothes. Undershirts, underpants, and slips are underwear.
un·der·wear • *noun*

underweight (un′dər wāt′) *adjective* not weighing enough; less than normal in weight.
un·der·weight • *adjective*

underwent (un dər went′) *verb past tense of* **undergo**.
un·der·went • *verb*

undid (un did′) *verb past tense of* **undo**.
un·did • *verb*

undivided (un′di vīd′əd) *adjective* not divided; whole; complete [Give me your *undivided* attention.]
un·di·vid·ed • *adjective*

undo (un do͞o′) *verb* **1** to untie or unfasten [Can you *undo* this knot?] **2** to open a door, parcel, or something else by untying or unfastening [I *undid* the package.] **3** to get rid of the effect of something; reverse [You cannot *undo* the damage of your unkind remark.]
un·do • *verb* **undid, undone, undoing**
● The words **undo** and **undue** sound alike.
You cannot *undo* the destruction of war.
Flattery is *undue* praise.

undone (un dun′) *verb past participle of* **undo**.
adjective not done; not finished [We left no work *undone*.]
un·done • *verb* • *adjective*

undress (un dres′) *verb* to take the clothes off.
un·dress • *verb* **undressed, undressing**

undue (un do͞o′ *or* un dyo͞o′) *adjective* more than is proper or right; too much [Don't give *undue* attention to the way you look.]
un·due • *adjective*
● The words **undue** and **undo** sound alike.
The team felt *undue* pressure to win.
I helped the child *undo* her shoelace.

undying (un dī′iŋ) *adjective* not dying or ending; lasting forever [*undying* devotion to a cause].
un·dy·ing • *adjective*

unearned (un urnd′) *adjective* not deserved [*unearned* praise].
un·earned • *adjective*

unearth (un urth′) *verb* **1** to dig up from the earth [The expedition *unearthed* dinosaur fossils.] **2** to discover or find [She *unearthed* some old books in the attic.]
un·earth • *verb* **unearthed, unearthing**

unearthly (un ʉrth′lē) *adjective* **1** not of this world; supernatural. **2** mysterious; weird [an *unearthly* scream].
un·earth·ly • *adjective*

uneasy (un ē′zē) *adjective* **1** having or giving no ease; not comfortable [an *uneasy* conscience; an *uneasy* position]. **2** not natural; awkward [an *uneasy* smile]. **3** worried; anxious [Dad felt *uneasy* when Bud was late with the car.]
un·eas·y • *adjective* **uneasier, uneasiest**

unemployed (un′em ploid′) *adjective* having no job or work.
—the unemployed people who are out of work.
un·em·ployed • *adjective*

unemployment (un′em ploi′mənt) *noun* **1** the condition of being unemployed, or out of work. **2** the number of people out of work [*Unemployment* figures are expected to decrease.]
un·em·ploy·ment • *noun*

unequal (un ē′kwəl) *adjective* not equal in amount, size, strength, value, or degree [We received *unequal* shares.]
un·e·qual • *adjective*

uneven (un ē′vən) *adjective* **1** not even, level, or smooth; rough; irregular [*uneven* ground]. **2** not equal in size or amount [pencils of *uneven* length]. **3** not straight or parallel [*uneven* lines]. **4** leaving a remainder when divided by two; odd [Five is an *uneven* number.]
un·e·ven • *adjective*

uneventful (un′ē vent′fəl) *adjective* with no unusual or important happenings [an *uneventful* trip].
un·e·vent·ful • *adjective*

unexpected (un′ek spek′təd) *adjective* not expected; surprising; sudden [*unexpected* visitors].
un·ex·pect·ed • *adjective*

unfair (un fer′) *adjective* not fair or just [The referee made an *unfair* decision.]
un·fair • *adjective*

unfaithful (un fāth′fəl) *adjective* not loyal or trustworthy [an *unfaithful* friend].
un·faith·ful • *adjective*

unfamiliar (un fə mil′yər) *adjective* **1** not familiar or well-known; strange [an *unfamiliar* place]. **2** not knowing about or acquainted with [I'm *unfamiliar* with these books.]
un·fa·mil·iar • *adjective*

unfasten (un fas′ən) *verb* to open or make loose; untie, unlock, or open in some other way [She *unfastened* the necklace and put it away.]
un·fas·ten • *verb* **unfastened, unfastening**

unfinished (un fin′isht) *adjective* **1** not finished or completed [an *unfinished* painting]. **2** having no finish, or final coat or coating [We will paint the *unfinished* furniture we bought.]
un·fin·ished • *adjective*

unfit (un fit′) *adjective* not fit or proper [This food is *unfit* to eat.]
un·fit • *adjective*

unfold (un fōld′) *verb* to open and spread out something that has been folded [*Unfold* the map.]
un·fold • *verb* **unfolded, unfolding**

unforgettable (un fər get′ə bəl) *adjective* so important, beautiful, shocking, or remarkable as never to be forgotten.
un·for·get·ta·ble • *adjective*

unfortunate (un fôr′chə nət) *adjective* **1** not fortunate; having bad luck; unlucky [What else can happen to that *unfortunate* family?] **2** bringing misfortune or bad luck [Things have gone wrong ever since that *unfortunate* day.] **3** not wise, proper, or as a person would have wanted [It turned out to be an *unfortunate* choice.]
un·for·tu·nate • *adjective*

unfriendly (un frend′lē) *adjective* not friendly.
un·friend·ly • *adjective* **unfriendlier, unfriendliest**

unfurnished (un fʉr′nisht) *adjective* without furniture [an *unfurnished* apartment].
un·fur·nished • *adjective*

unhappy (un hap′ē) *adjective* **1** full of sorrow; sad [an *unhappy* face] —Look for the WORD CHOICES box at the entry **sad**. **2** not lucky or fortunate [an *unhappy* result].
un·hap·py • *adjective* **unhappier, unhappiest**

unhealthy (un hel′thē) *adjective* **1** having or showing poor health; not well [He has an

a cat	ō go	ʉ fur	ə = a *in* ago
ā ape	ô law, for	ch chin	e *in* agent
ä cot, car	oo look	sh she	i *in* pencil
e ten	o͞o tool	th thin	o *in* atom
ē me	oi oil	*th* then	u *in* circus
i fit	ou out	zh measure	
ī ice	u up	ŋ ring	

unhealthy color to his skin.] **2** bad for a person's health [an *unhealthy* habit].
un·health·y • *adjective* **unhealthier, unhealthiest**

unheard-of (un hʉrd′uv) ***adjective*** not heard of before; never known or done before [an *unheard-of* experiment; *unheard-of* behavior].
un·heard-of • ***adjective***

unhitch (un hich′) ***verb*** to free something from being hitched; unfasten [We parked and *unhitched* the trailer.]
un·hitch • ***verb*** **unhitched, unhitching**

unhook (un ho͝ok′) ***verb*** **1** to set loose from a hook [She *unhooked* the fish.] **2** to unfasten the hook or hooks of [He *unhooked* the gate and passed through.]
un·hook • ***verb*** **unhooked, unhooking**

unhurried (un hʉr′ēd) ***adjective*** done or acting without haste [a relaxed, *unhurried* lunch].
un·hur·ried • ***adjective***

uni- *a prefix meaning* one [A *unicycle* has only one wheel.]

unicorn (yo͞o′ni kôrn) ***noun*** an imaginary animal something like a horse with one long horn in the center of its forehead.
u·ni·corn • ***noun,*** *plural* **unicorns**

unicycle (yo͞o′ni sī′kəl) ***noun*** a riding device that has pedals like a bicycle but only one wheel. It is used for trick riding.
u·ni·cy·cle • ***noun,*** *plural* **unicycles**

unidentified (un′ī den′ti fīd) ***adjective*** not identified; not known or recognized [an *unidentified* flying object; an *unidentified* visitor].
un·i·den·ti·fied • ***adjective***

uniform (yo͞o′ni fôrm) ***adjective*** **1** always the same; never changing [Driving at a *uniform* speed saves gas.] **2** all alike; not different from one another [a row of *uniform* houses].
noun the special clothes worn by the members of a certain group [a nurse's *uniform*].
u·ni·form • ***adjective*** • ***noun,*** *plural* **uniforms**

uniform

unify (yo͞o′ni fī′) ***verb*** to make into one; unite [After many years as separate nations, the two countries were *unified* once again.]
u·ni·fy • ***verb*** **unified, unifying, unifies**

unimportant (un′im pôrt′nt) ***adjective*** not important; minor [an *unimportant* remark].
un·im·por·tant • ***adjective***

uninhabited (un′in hab′it əd) ***adjective*** not inhabited; not lived in [an *uninhabited* desert].
un·in·hab·it·ed • ***adjective***

uninterested (un in′trist əd *or* un in′tər est əd) ***adjective*** not interested [He seemed *uninterested* in learning the rules of the game.]
un·in·ter·est·ed • ***adjective***

uninteresting (un in′trist iŋ *or* un in′tər est iŋ) ***adjective*** not interesting; dull.
un·in·ter·est·ing • ***adjective***

uninvited (un′in vīt′əd) ***adjective*** not invited; having no invitation [*uninvited* party guests].
un·in·vit·ed • ***adjective***

union (yo͞on′yən) ***noun*** **1** the act of uniting; combination [a corporation formed by the *union* of four companies]. **2** a number of nations, people, or other groups joined together in a larger unit **3** a group of workers joined together to promote and protect their interests. **4** marriage [a happy *union*].
—the Union **1** the United States of America. **2** the North in the Civil War.
un·ion • ***noun,*** *plural for all senses except 1* **unions**

Union of Soviet Socialist Republics a country, from 1922 to 1991, in eastern Europe and northern Asia.

unique (yo͞o nēk′) ***adjective*** **1** being the only one; having nothing like it [Mercury is a *unique* metal because it is a liquid at room temperature.] **2** unusual; remarkable.
u·nique • ***adjective***

unison (yo͞o′ni sən) ***noun*** *used mainly in the phrase* **in unison, 1** singing or playing the same notes at the same time [The choir sang the second verse *in unison*.] **2** saying the same word or words at the same time [The whole class answered "Yes!" *in unison*.]
u·ni·son • ***noun***

unit (yo͞o′nit) ***noun*** **1** a single person or group, especially when thought of as part of a whole [an army *unit*]. **2** a single part with some special use [the lens *unit* of a camera]. **3** a fixed amount or measure used as a standard [The

U

ounce is a *unit* of weight.]
u·nit • *noun, plural* **units**

unite (yoo͞ nīt′) *verb* **1** to put or join together in order to make one; combine [The two schools *united* to form a new school.] —Look for the WORD CHOICES box at the entry **join**. **2** to bring or join together in doing something [Let us *unite* in the search for peace.]
u·nite • *verb* **united, uniting**

united (yoo͞ nīt′əd) *adjective* **1** joined together in one; combined [the *united* efforts of many people]. **2** in agreement [They were *united* in wanting to stay.]
u·nit·ed • *adjective*

United Arab Emirates (em′ər əts) a country in eastern Arabia, on the Persian Gulf.
United Arab E·mir·ates

United Kingdom a country made up of Great Britain and Northern Ireland.

United Nations an organization set up in 1945 to work for world peace and security. Most of the nations of the world belong to it. Its headquarters are in New York City.

United States of America a country, mostly in North America, made up of 50 States and the District of Columbia.

unity (yoo͞′ni tē) *noun* the condition of being united or combined ["In *unity* there is strength" was the coach's motto.]
u·ni·ty • *noun*

universal (yoo͞′ni vur′səl) *adjective* **1** of, for, or by all people; concerning everyone [a *universal* human need]. **2** present everywhere [a *universal* custom].
u·ni·ver·sal • *adjective*

universe (yoo͞′ni vurs′) *noun* all space and everything in it; earth, the sun, stars, and all things that exist.
u·ni·verse • *noun*

university (yoo͞′ni vur′si tē) *noun* a school for the highest level of education, that a person can go to after high school. A university is made up of colleges.
u·ni·ver·si·ty • *noun, plural* **universities**

unjust (un just′) *adjective* not just or right; unfair [an *unjust* rule] —Look for the WORD CHOICES box at the entry **bad**.
un·just • *adjective*

unkempt (un kempt′) *adjective* not tidy; messy [an *unkempt* house].
un·kempt • *adjective*

unkind (un kīnd′) *adjective* not kind; hurting the feelings of others [*unkind* words].
un·kind • *adjective* **unkinder, unkindest**

unknown (un nōn′) *adjective* **1** not seen or heard before [That song is *unknown* to me.] **2** not discovered, explored, or identified [an *unknown* substance].
noun someone or something that is not known [There are many *unknowns* in science.]
un·known • *adjective* • *noun, plural* **unknowns**

unlace (un lās′) *verb* to untie the laces of [He *unlaced* his boots.]
un·lace • *verb* **unlaced, unlacing**

unlawful (un lô′fəl *or* un lä′fəl) *adjective* against the law; illegal [an *unlawful* act].
un·law·ful • *adjective*

unleaded (un led′əd) *adjective* describing gasoline that does not have lead added to it.
un·lead·ed • *adjective*

unleash (un lēsh′) *verb* to release or let loose [She *unleashed* the dog.]
un·leash • *verb* **unleashed, unleashing**

unless (un les′) *conjunction* in any case other than; except if [I won't go *unless* you do.]
un·less • *conjunction*

unlike (un līk′) *adjective* not alike; different [The twins are *unlike* in their interests.]
preposition **1** not like; different from [an adventure *unlike* any other]. **2** not typical of [It's *unlike* her to give up.]
un·like • *adjective* • *preposition*

unlikely (un līk′lē) *adjective* **1** not likely to happen [A storm is *unlikely* today.] **2** not likely to be true [That's an *unlikely* story.] **3** not likely to be right or successful [This is an *unlikely* place to dig for gold.]
un·like·ly • *adjective*

unlimited (un lim′it əd) *adjective* without limits or bounds [*unlimited* patience].
un·lim·it·ed • *adjective*

unlisted (un lis′təd) *adjective* not entered on a list or not made known to the public [an *unlisted* phone number].
un·list·ed • *adjective*

a	cat	ō	go	ʉ	fur	ə =	a *in* ago
ā	ape	ô	law, for	ch	chin		e *in* agent
ä	cot, car	oo	look	sh	she		i *in* pencil
e	ten	oo͞	tool	th	thin		o *in* atom
ē	me	oi	oil	*th*	then		u *in* circus
i	fit	ou	out	zh	measure		
ī	ice	u	up	ŋ	ring		

unload (un lōd′) *verb* **1** to take a load from [I *unloaded* the truck.] **2** to take the charge or film from [She *unloaded* the gun. He *unloaded* the camera.] **3** to get rid of [The store *unloaded* its stock by having a big sale.]
un·load • *verb* **unloaded, unloading**

unlock (un läk′) *verb* **1** to open by undoing a lock [Please *unlock* the door.] **2** to become unlocked [The door *unlocks* with this key.]
un·lock • *verb* **unlocked, unlocking**

unlucky (un luk′ē) *adjective* having or bringing bad luck; not lucky [an *unlucky* person].
un·luck·y • *adjective* **unluckier, unluckiest**

unmanned (un mand′) *adjective* not having people on board and operating by automatic or remote control [an *unmanned* spacecraft].
un·manned • *adjective*

unmoved (un mo͞ovd′) *adjective* not feeling pity or sympathy [He was *unmoved* by their suffering.]
un·moved • *adjective*

unnatural (un nach′ər əl) *adjective* **1** not natural or normal; abnormal [an *unnatural* craving for sweets]. **2** artificial or put on; not sincere [an *unnatural* smile].
un·nat·u·ral • *adjective*

unnecessary (un nes′ə ser′ē) *adjective* not necessary; not needed [Don't take *unnecessary* items with you on your trip.]
un·nec·es·sar·y • *adjective*

unoccupied (un äk′yo͞o pīd′) *adjective* having no occupant; vacant [an *unoccupied* house].
un·oc·cu·pied • *adjective*

unorganized (un ôr′gə nīzd′) *adjective* not having or following any regular order or plan [The hike was completely *unorganized*, so people simply started out when they were ready.]
un·or·gan·ized • *adjective*

unpack

unpack (un pak′) *verb* **1** to open and empty out [I'll *unpack* the suitcase.] **2** to take from a box, crate, or other container [She *unpacked* the books.]
un·pack • *verb* **unpacked, unpacking**

unpaid (un pād′) *adjective* **1** not receiving pay [an *unpaid* helper]. **2** not yet paid [an *unpaid* bill].
un·paid • *adjective*

unpleasant (un plez′ənt) *adjective* disagreeable or offensive [an *unpleasant* taste].
un·pleas·ant • *adjective*

unplug (un plug′) *verb* **1** to take out the plug of from an electric socket [I *unplugged* the TV.] **2** to open by taking out a plug or by clearing away something that blocks up [I *unplugged* the drain.]
un·plug • *verb* **unplugged, unplugging**

unpopular (un päp′yo͞o lər) *adjective* not liked by most people or by the public; not popular [an *unpopular* rule].
un·pop·u·lar • *adjective*

unprepared (un′prē perd′) *adjective* not prepared or ready [She was *unprepared* for the test.]
un·pre·pared • *adjective*

unprofitable (un präf′it ə bəl) *adjective* **1** not making a profit [an *unprofitable* business]. **2** not worthwhile [an *unprofitable* discussion].
un·prof·it·a·ble • *adjective*

unpromising (un präm′i siŋ) *adjective* not likely to be good or successful [The rain was an *unpromising* beginning to our trip.]
un·prom·is·ing • *adjective*

unprotected (un prō tekt′əd) *adjective* not protected; open to danger or harm.
un·pro·tect·ed • *adjective*

unqualified (un kwôl′i fīd′ *or* un kwä′li fīd′) *adjective* **1** not having the knowledge or skills that are needed [He is *unqualified* for this job.] **2** complete [an *unqualified* success].
un·qual·i·fied • *adjective*

unquestionable (un kwes′chən ə bəl) *adjective* not to be questioned or doubted; certain [She is a person of *unquestionable* honesty.]
un·ques·tion·a·ble • *adjective*

unravel (un rav′əl) *verb* to separate or undo the threads of something woven, knitted, or tangled [She *unraveled* the ball of yarn.]
un·rav·el • *verb* **unraveled** or **unravelled, unraveling** or **unravelling**

unread (un red′) *adjective* not read [The Sunday paper is still lying there *unread*.]
un·read • *adjective*

U

unreadable (un rēd′ə bəl) *adjective* **1** unable to be read because badly written or printed [an *unreadable* signature]. **2** too difficult or boring to read [an *unreadable* book].
un·read·a·ble • *adjective*

unready (un red′ē) *adjective* not ready [We were still *unready* when the taxi arrived.]
un·read·y • *adjective*

unreasonable (un rē′zən ə bəl) *adjective* **1** not showing reason or good sense [an *unreasonable* mood. Don't be so *unreasonable*.] **2** beyond the limits of what is reasonable [an *unreasonable* price].
un·rea·son·a·ble • *adjective*

unrest (un rest′) *noun* a troubled or disturbed condition [political *unrest*].
un·rest • *noun*

unripe (un rīp′) *adjective* not ripe or mature; green [*unripe* fruit].
un·ripe • *adjective*

unroll (un rōl′) *verb* to open or spread out something rolled up [We *unrolled* our sleeping bags.]
un·roll • *verb* **unrolled, unrolling**

unruly (un ro͞o′lē) *adjective* hard to control or keep in order [an *unruly* horse; *unruly* hair].
un·rul·y • *adjective* **unrulier, unruliest**

unsaid (un sed′) *adjective* not said or expressed [Some things are better left *unsaid*.]
un·said • *adjective*

unsatisfactory (un′sat is fak′tər ē) *adjective* not good enough to satisfy [an *unsatisfactory* report card].
un·sat·is·fac·to·ry • *adjective*

unscramble (un skram′bəl) *verb* to make no longer mixed up; put back in order [She *unscrambled* the letters and formed a word.]
un·scram·ble • *verb* **unscrambled, unscrambling**

unscrew (un skro͞o′) *verb* **1** to unfasten or loosen by taking out screws [The worker *unscrewed* the hinges on the door.] **2** to take out, take off, or loosen by turning [He *unscrewed* the lid of the jar. She *unscrewed* the light bulb.] **3** to become unscrewed [This bolt won't *unscrew*.]
un·screw • *verb* **unscrewed, unscrewing**

unseemly (un sēm′lē) *adjective* not proper, fitting, or decent [*unseemly* behavior].
un·seem·ly • *adjective* **unseemlier, unseemliest**

unseen (un sēn′) *adjective* not seen [We remained *unseen* in the bushes.]
un·seen • *adjective*

unselfish (un sel′fish) *adjective* not selfish; putting the good of others before a person's own interest [an *unselfish* act; an *unselfish* person].
un·sel·fish • *adjective*

unsettle (un set′l) *verb* to make shaky, troubled, or upset [The news *unsettled* us.]
un·set·tle • *verb* **unsettled, unsettling**

unsightly (un sīt′lē) *adjective* not pleasant to look at; ugly [an *unsightly* garbage dump].
un·sight·ly • *adjective*

unskilled (un skild′) *adjective* **1** not having or needing a special skill or training [Digging ditches is *unskilled* work.] **2** showing a lack of skill [an *unskilled* effort] —Look for the WORD CHOICES box at the entry **awkward**.
un·skilled • *adjective*

unsound (un sound′) *adjective* **1** not normal and healthy [an *unsound* mind]. **2** not safe and secure [an *unsound* boat]. **3** not showing good sense [an *unsound* theory].
un·sound • *adjective*

unspeakable (un spēk′ə bəl) *adjective* hard to describe or speak about because so wonderful or marvelous or so bad or evil [*unspeakable* joy; *unspeakable* pain].
un·speak·a·ble • *adjective*

unstable (un stā′bəl) *adjective* **1** not firm and steady [an *unstable* ladder]. **2** likely to change [*unstable* weather conditions].
un·sta·ble • *adjective*

unsteady (un sted′ē) *adjective* not steady or firm; shaky [The baby walked with *unsteady* steps.]
un·stead·y • *adjective*

unsung (un suŋ′) *adjective* not honored or praised [an *unsung* hero].
un·sung • *adjective*

untangle (un taŋ′gəl) *verb* **1** to remove the knots or tangles from [The fishermen *untangled* their lines.] **2** to free from confusion; straighten out [The lawyer *untangled* our legal problems.]
un·tan·gle • *verb* **untangled, untangling**

a cat	ō go	ʉ fur	ə = a *in* ago
ā ape	ô law, for	ch chin	e *in* agent
ä cot, car	oo look	sh she	i *in* pencil
e ten	o͞o tool	th thin	o *in* atom
ē me	oi oil	*th* then	u *in* circus
i fit	ou out	zh measure	
ī ice	u up	ŋ ring	

untidy (un tī′dē) ***adjective*** not tidy or neat; messy [an *untidy* room].
un·ti·dy • ***adjective*** **untidier, untidiest**

untie (un tī′) ***verb*** to loosen or unfasten something that is tied or knotted [He *untied* his shoes. She *untied* the boat.]
un·tie • ***verb*** **untied, untying**

until (un til′) ***preposition*** **1** up to the time of; till [Wait *until* noon.] **2** before [Don't tell her *until* tomorrow.]
conjunction **1** up to the time when [We were enjoying ourselves *until* it began to rain.] **2** to the point, degree, or place that [She ate *until* she was full.] **3** before [Don't start *until* he tells you.]
un·til • ***preposition*** • ***conjunction***

untimely (un tīm′lē) ***adjective*** **1** coming too soon [her *untimely* death]. **2** coming at the wrong time [an *untimely* remark].
un·time·ly • ***adjective***

untold (un tōld′) ***adjective*** **1** not told or made known [a story left *untold*]. **2** too much to be counted; very great [*untold* wealth].
un·told • ***adjective***

untrue (un tro͞o′) ***adjective*** **1** not correct; false [an *untrue* statement]. **2** not faithful or loyal [Don't be *untrue* to your school.]
un·true • ***adjective***

untruth (un tro͞oth′) ***noun*** a statement that is not true; a lie.
un·truth • ***noun**, plural* **untruths**

unused (un yo͞ozd′) ***adjective*** **1** not in use [*unused* space]. **2** never having been used [*unused* clothing]. **3** not accustomed; not familiar with: used with *to* [I am *unused* to traveling by train.]
un·used • ***adjective***

unusual (un yo͞o′zho͞o əl) ***adjective*** not usual or common; rare; remarkable [an *unusual* sight].
un·u·su·al • ***adjective***

WORD CHOICES

Synonyms of **unusual**

The words **unusual, rare,** and **scarce** share the meaning "not usual or common."

Such hot days are *unusual* in April.

We sighted a *rare* kind of wren.

Wild turkeys are *scarce* in Ohio.

unusually (un yo͞o′zho͞o ə lē) ***adverb*** in an exceptional or remarkable way [an *unusually* bright person].
un·u·su·al·ly • ***adverb***

unveil (un vāl′) ***verb*** to show or reveal by removing a veil or covering from [They *unveiled* the statue.]
un·veil • ***verb*** **unveiled, unveiling**

unwary (un wer′ē) ***adjective*** not watchful; not on guard [an *unwary* victim of crime].
un·war·y • ***adjective***

unwell (un wel′) ***adjective*** not well; ill; sick [I feel *unwell*.]
un·well • ***adjective***

unwilling (un wil′iŋ) ***adjective*** not willing or ready [He was *unwilling* to take the blame.]
un·will·ing • ***adjective***

unwind (un wīnd′) ***verb*** **1** to undo something that is wound up by turning or rolling in the opposite direction [*Unwind* some thread from the spool.] **2** to relax or become relaxed [I *unwind* by going fishing.]
un·wind • ***verb*** **unwound, unwinding**

unwise (un wīz′) ***adjective*** not wise; not showing good sense; foolish [an *unwise* choice].
un·wise • ***adjective***

unworthy (un wʉr′*th*ē) ***adjective*** **1** not worthy or deserving [He felt he was *unworthy* of such gifts.] **2** not fitting or proper [That remark is *unworthy* of such a fine person.]
un·wor·thy • ***adjective*** **unworthier, unworthiest**

unwound (un wound′) ***verb*** *past tense and past participle of* **unwind**.
un·wound • ***verb***

unwrap (un rap′) ***verb*** to open by taking off the wrapping [She *unwrapped* the gift.]
un·wrap • ***verb*** **unwrapped, unwrapping**

unwritten (un rit′n) ***adjective*** accepted or observed without being written down [an *unwritten* agreement; an *unwritten* law].
un·writ·ten • ***adjective***

unzip (un zip′) ***verb*** to undo the zipper of [He *unzipped* his sleeping bag.]
un·zip • ***verb*** **unzipped, unzipping**

up (up) ***adverb*** **1** to, in, or on a higher place or position [She climbed *up*. The sun comes *up* at dawn.] **2** to a larger amount or size; to a greater degree [Gas went *up* in price. My ankle swelled *up*.] **3** in or into an upright position [Please stand *up*. I got *up* from the

floor.] **4** into action, discussion, or view [You bring *up* a good point. Let's put *up* a sign.] **5** in order to be even with [He ran to keep *up* with her.] **6** in a complete way [He ate *up* all the food.] **7** apiece; each [The score is six *up*.]
preposition **1** to or at a higher place in or on [We climbed *up* the ladder.] **2** to or at the higher or farther part of [They bicycled *up* the hill.]
adjective **1** put, brought, going, or gone up [Her hand is *up*. The sun is *up*. Prices are *up*.] **2** out of bed [Aren't you *up* yet?] **3** above the ground [The new grass is *up*.] **4** at an end; over [Time's *up*.] **5** at bat in baseball [You're *up* next.] **6** working and available for use [After some quick repairs, the computer was back *up* again.] **7** [*an informal use*] going on; happening [What's *up?*]
noun a turn for the better or a piece of good luck [Life has its *ups* and downs.]
—up to [*an informal use*] **1** doing or getting ready to do [He is *up to* some mischief.] **2** as many as [*Up to* four can play.] **3** as far as [My land runs *up to* those trees.] **4** to be decided by [It's *up to* you.]
up • ***adverb*** • ***preposition*** • ***adjective*** • ***noun,*** *plural* **ups**

upbringing (up′briŋ′iŋ) ***noun*** the care and training a person gets while growing up.
up·bring·ing • ***noun***

upcoming (up′kum′iŋ) ***adjective*** coming soon [an *upcoming* event].
up·com·ing • ***adjective***

update (up dāt′ *or* up′dāt *for v.;* up′dāt *for n.*) ***verb*** to bring up to date with the latest knowledge or information [He used the new facts to *update* his report.]
noun something that has been updated [the latest *update* on the weather].
up·date • ***verb*** **updated, updating** • ***noun,*** *plural* **updates**

upend (up end′) ***verb*** **1** to set or stand on end [The movers *upended* the sofa.] **2** to upset or topple [I *upended* the vase as I walked by.]
up·end • ***verb*** **upended, upending**

upheaval (up hē′vəl) ***noun*** **1** a forceful lifting up from beneath [The earthquake caused an *upheaval* of the ground.] **2** a sudden, violent change [the *upheaval* begun by the revolution].
up·heav·al • ***noun,*** *plural* **upheavals**

upheld (up held′) ***verb*** *past tense and past participle of* **uphold**.
up·held • ***verb***

uphill (up′hil′) ***adjective*** needing much effort; difficult [an *uphill* battle against illness].
adverb toward the top of a hill [We ran *uphill*.]
up·hill • ***adjective*** • ***adverb***

uphold (up hōld′) ***verb*** to agree with and support against attack by others [The Constitution *upholds* the right to vote.] —Look for the WORD CHOICES box at the entry **support**.
up·hold • ***verb*** **upheld, upholding**

upholster (up hōl′stər) ***verb*** to put springs and padding in, and cover with material [She *upholstered* the chair.]
up·hol·ster • ***verb*** **upholstered, upholstering**

upholstery (up hōl′stər ē) ***noun*** **1** the work of upholstering. **2** the materials used in upholstering.
up·hol·ster·y • ***noun***

upon (ə pän′) ***preposition*** on or up and on [He put the box *upon* the table.]
up·on • ***preposition***

upper (up′ər) ***adjective*** **1** above another [the *upper* lip; an *upper* floor]. **2** of more importance or higher rank [the *upper* house of a legislature].
noun the part of a shoe or boot above the sole.
up·per • ***adjective*** • ***noun,*** *plural* **uppers**

upper hand ***noun*** a position of advantage or control [Our enemy has the *upper hand*.]

uppermost (up′ər mōst) ***adjective*** highest in place or importance [Safety is *uppermost* in my mind.]
up·per·most • ***adjective***

uppity (up′i tē) [*an informal word*] ***adjective*** tending to think of oneself as better than others.
up·pi·ty • ***adjective***

upright (up′rīt) ***adjective*** **1** standing or pointing straight up; erect [*upright* fence posts]. **2** honest and just [an *upright* judge]. **3** describing a piano in which the strings run up and down.
adverb in an upright position [The dog stood *upright* on its hind legs.]
noun an upright pole or beam [The *uprights* for the fence were set five feet apart.]

a	cat	ō	go	ʉ	fur	ə =	a *in* ago
ā	ape	ô	law, for	ch	chin		e *in* agent
ä	cot, car	oo	look	sh	she		i *in* pencil
e	ten	ōō	tool	th	thin		o *in* atom
ē	me	oi	oil	*th*	then		u *in* circus
i	fit	ou	out	zh	measure		
ī	ice	u	up	ŋ	ring		

up·right • *adjective* • *adverb* • *noun, plural* **uprights**

uprising (up′rīz′iŋ) *noun* a rebellion or revolt.
up·ris·ing • *noun, plural* **uprisings**

uproar (up′rôr) *noun* **1** a noisy, confused condition [Her remark threw the meeting into an *uproar*.] **2** a loud, confused noise [I couldn't hear you because of the *uproar*.] —Look for the WORD CHOICES box at the entry **noise**.
up·roar • *noun, plural for sense 1 only* **uproars**

uproarious (up rôr′ē əs) *adjective* making or causing an uproar [an *uproarious* comedy].
up·roar·i·ous • *adjective*

uproot

uproot (up ro͞ot′) *verb* **1** to pull out by the roots [The storm *uprooted* some small trees.] **2** to get rid of in a complete way [The police chief promised to *uproot* crime from the city.]
up·root • *verb* **uprooted, uprooting**

upset (up set′ *for v.;* up′set *for n. and adj.*) *verb* **1** to turn or tip over [The frightened horse *upset* the wagon.] **2** to disturb the order or working of [A flat tire *upset* our plans.] **3** to defeat a person or group that almost everyone expects will win [Our team *upset* the champions.] **4** to make nervous or troubled [The news *upset* our parents.]
noun **1** the act of upsetting. **2** the act or fact of defeating a person or group that almost everyone expects will win [Sunday's *upset* of our football team].
adjective **1** turned or tipped over [An *upset* garbage can rolled into the street.] **2** disturbed; out of order [I have an *upset* stomach.]
up·set • *verb* **upset, upsetting** • *noun, plural* **upsets** • *adjective*

upside down (up′sīd) *adverb* with the top side on the bottom or facing down [The stunt plane flew *upside down*.]
up·side down • *adverb*

upside-down (up′sīd doun′) *adjective* having the top side on the bottom or facing down; turned over [The sloth hangs from branches in an *upside-down* position.]
up·side-down • *adjective*

upstairs (up′sterz′) *adverb* **1** up the stairs [He walked *upstairs* instead of taking the elevator.] **2** to or on an upper floor [My grandparents live *upstairs*.]
adjective on an upper floor [an *upstairs* bedroom].
noun [*used with a singular verb*] an upper floor or floors [The *upstairs* gets hot in the summer.]
up·stairs • *adverb* • *adjective* • *noun*

upstanding (up′stan′diŋ) *adjective* honest; honorable [an *upstanding* citizen].
up·stand·ing • *adjective*

upstart (up′stärt) *noun* a person who has just become rich or important and who is bold and pushy in a way that bothers others.
up·start • *noun, plural* **upstarts**

upstream (up′strēm′) *adverb* in the direction against the current or flow of a stream [The current was too strong for us to swim *upstream*.] This word can also be used as an adjective [in an *upstream* direction].
up·stream • *adverb*

up-to-date (up′tə dāt′) *adjective* **1** including the latest information [an *up-to-date* report]. **2** keeping up with the latest information or newest styles.

uptown (up′toun′) *adjective* in or toward the part of a city, especially New York, away from the main business section [an *uptown* bus; an *uptown* restaurant]. This word can also be used as an adverb [Let's drive *uptown*.]
up·town • *adjective*

upward (up′wərd) *adverb* from a lower to a higher place or position [The jet climbed *upward* through the clouds.] This word can also be used as an adjective [an *upward* motion].
up·ward • *adverb*

upwards (up′wərdz) *adverb the same as the adverb* **upward**.
up·wards • *adverb*

uranium (yo͞o rā′nē əm) *noun* a very hard, heavy, silvery-white metal that is a chemical element. It is radioactive. Uranium is used in producing atomic energy.
u·ra·ni·um • *noun*

U

Uranus (yoor′ə nəs *or* yoo rā′nəs) the third largest planet. It is the seventh in distance from the sun.
U·ra·nus

urban (ur′bən) *adjective* of or having to do with cities or towns [a crowded *urban* area].
ur·ban • *adjective*

urbane (ur bān′) *adjective* polite and courteous in a smooth way [an *urbane* gentleman].
ur·bane • *adjective*

Urdu (oor′dōō) *noun* a language of Pakistan and northern India.
Ur·du • *noun*

urge (urj) *verb* **1** to plead with or encourage in a strong way to do something [Her parents *urged* her to finish college.] **2** to speak in favor of; recommend [He *urged* caution in swimming here.]
noun a sudden feeling that makes one want to do something; impulse [an *urge* to sneeze; an *urge* to buy something].
urge • *verb* **urged, urging** • *noun, plural* **urges**

urgent (ur′jənt) *adjective* **1** needing quick action [an *urgent* situation]. **2** asking for in a strong and serious way [an *urgent* call for help].
ur·gent • *adjective*

urinate (yoor′i nāt′) *verb* to get rid of urine from the body.
u·ri·nate • *verb* **urinated, urinating**

urine (yoor′in) *noun* the liquid waste product of the body. It is passed from the kidneys to the bladder and then out of the body.
u·rine • *noun*

urn (urn) *noun* **1** a vase with a foot or pedestal. **2** a metal container with a faucet, for making and serving coffee or tea.
urn • *noun, plural* **urns**

● The words **urn** and **earn** sound alike.
The museum has a Greek *urn* collection.
He will *earn* more money next year.

Uruguay (yoor′ə gwā *or* oor′ə gwā) a country in southeastern South America.
U·ru·guay

us (us) *pronoun* the form of **we** that is used: **1** after certain verbs [The dog bit *us*. He saw *us*. Tell *us* the truth.] **2** after prepositions [Tell the story to *us*. The song was written by *us*.]

U.S. or **US** *abbreviation for* United States.

U.S.A. or **USA** *abbreviation for* United States of America.

usable or **useable** (yōō′zə bəl) *adjective* able or fit to be used [The old tools were still *usable*.]
us·a·ble or **use·a·ble** • *adjective*

usage (yōō′sij) *noun* the act or way of using something [Work shoes will stand up to rough *usage*.]
us·age • *noun*

use (yōōz *for v.;* yōōs *for n.*) *verb* **1** to put or bring into service or action [*Use* the vacuum cleaner on the rugs. What kind of toothpaste do you *use*?] **2** to do away with by using; consume [She *used* up the soap.]
noun **1** the act of using [The *use* of power tools requires great care.] **2** the condition of being used [The old bus is still in *use*.] **3** the ability or the right or permission to use [He lost the *use* of his left hand. May I have the *use* of your car?] **4** the quality that makes something helpful or suitable for a purpose [This gadget has many *uses*.] **5** benefit or advantage [There's no *use* in arguing about it.]
—used to **1** did at one time [I *used to* live in Iowa.] **2** accustomed to; familiar with [She's *used to* hard work.]
use • *verb* **used, using** • *noun, plural for sense 4 only* **uses**

used (yōōzd) *adjective* **1** having been used; not new or clean [a *used* towel]. **2** having belonged to someone else; secondhand [a *used* car].

useful (yōōs′fəl) *adjective* able to be put to good use; helpful [*useful* advice].
use·ful • *adjective*

useless (yōōs′ləs) *adjective* having no use; worthless [The candle is *useless* without a match.]
use·less • *adjective*

usher (ush′ər) *noun* a person who shows people to their seats in a church or theater.
verb to show the way or bring in [He *ushered* us to our seats. That scientist helped *usher* in the Space Age.]
ush·er • *noun, plural* **ushers**
• *verb* **ushered, ushering**

U.S.S.R. or **USSR** *abbreviation for* Union of Soviet Socialist Republics.

usual (yōō′zhōō əl) *adjective* such as is most often seen, heard, or used; ordinary; normal

a	cat	ō	go	ʉ	fur	ə =	a *in* ago
ā	ape	ô	law, for	ch	chin		e *in* agent
ä	cot, car	oo	look	sh	she		i *in* pencil
e	ten	ōō	tool	th	thin		o *in* atom
ē	me	oi	oil	*th*	then		u *in* circus
i	fit	ou	out	zh	measure		
ī	ice	u	up	ŋ	ring		

[The car was parked in its *usual* place.] **—as usual** in the usual way [She was late, *as usual*.]
u·su·al • ***adjective***

WORD CHOICES

Synonyms of usual

Many words share the meaning "happening or used or done regularly."

customary	habitual	prevalent
everyday	normal	regular

usually (yo͞o′zho͞o ə lē) ***adverb*** in the usual way; as usual [It is *usually* cold during January.]
u·su·al·ly • ***adverb***

STATE MAP

Utah

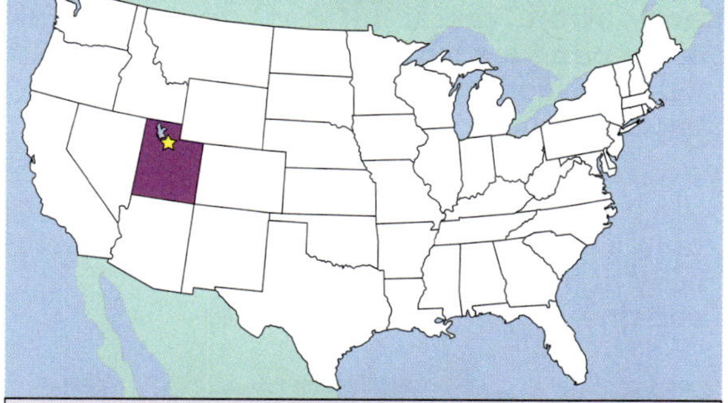

Statehood: 1896, the 45th state • **Capital:** Salt Lake City

Utah (yo͞o′tô *or* yo͞o′tä) a State in the southwestern part of the U.S. Its capital is Salt Lake City. Abbreviated **UT** or **Ut.**
U·tah

utensil (yo͞o ten′səl) ***noun*** a tool or other thing having a special purpose [A can opener is a kitchen *utensil*.]
u·ten·sil • ***noun,*** *plural* **utensils**

uterus (yo͞ot′ər əs) ***noun*** a hollow organ of female mammals in which the young grow before birth; womb.
u·ter·us • ***noun,*** *plural* **u·ter·i** (yo͞ot′ər ī)

utility (yo͞o til′i tē) ***noun*** a company that provides water, gas, electricity, or telephone service to the public.
adjective useful or used in a number of ways [We have a *utility* room beside the kitchen for hanging coats and for storage and laundry.]
u·til·i·ty • ***noun,*** *plural* **utilities** • ***adjective***

utilize (yo͞ot′l īz) ***verb*** to put to use; make use of [He *utilizes* all his talents in his new job.]
u·ti·lize • ***verb*** **utilized, utilizing**

utmost (ut′mōst) ***adjective*** greatest or highest [This meeting is of the *utmost* importance.]
noun the most that is possible [He strained his muscles to the *utmost*.]
ut·most • ***adjective*** • ***noun***

WORD HISTORY

utmost

The word **utmost** comes from a very old English word that was the superlative form of the word *out*. It means "the farthest out." The word was first used to speak only of a place that was far away. Now it also means "greatest."

utter[1] (ut′ər) ***adjective*** complete; total [The experiment was an *utter* failure.]
ut·ter • ***adjective***

utter[2] (ut′ər) ***verb*** to make or express with the voice [He *uttered* a cry of pain.]
ut·ter • ***verb*** **uttered, uttering**

U-turn (yo͞o′turn′) ***noun*** a turn of a vehicle in the street so that it is heading in the opposite direction [It is illegal to make a *U-turn* here.]
U-turn • ***noun,*** *plural* **U-turns**

uvula (yo͞o′vyo͞o lə) ***noun*** the small, soft piece of flesh that hangs down at the rear of the mouth.
u·vu·la • ***noun,*** *plural* **uvulas**

Uzbekistan (o͞oz bek′i stan′) a country in central Asia. It was a part of the Soviet Union.
Uz·bek·i·stan

U

V v

Vv Vv Vv Vv

The letter **v** *stands for a single sound—the sound you hear at the beginning of the words* **visit, very,** *and* **volcano.** *Be sure that you write this letter very carefully; if you forget to do so, it could look like the letter* **u.**

v or **V** (vē) ***noun*** **1** the twenty-second letter of the English alphabet. **2** something shaped like a V.
v or **V** • ***noun,*** *plural* **v's** or **V's**

V (vē) ***noun*** the Roman numeral for five.

v. *abbreviation for* verb.

VA or **Va.** *abbreviation for* Virginia.

vacancy (vā′kən sē) ***noun*** **1** a job or position that is unfilled, or not occupied. **2** a place such as a motel room or apartment that is not occupied [It will be hard to find a motel with a *vacancy*.]
va·can·cy • ***noun,*** *plural* **vacancies**

vacant (vā′kənt) ***adjective*** having nothing or no one in it; empty [a *vacant* lot; a *vacant* seat; a *vacant* house].
va·cant • ***adjective***

vacate (vā′kāt) ***verb*** to make a place empty; to leave [Please *vacate* your hotel room by noon.]
va·cate • ***verb*** **vacated, vacating**

vacation (vā kā′shən *or* və kā′shən) ***noun*** a period of time when one stops working or going to school, in order to rest and have recreation.
verb to take one's vacation [We *vacation* in Maine each summer.]
va·ca·tion • ***noun,*** *plural* **vacations**
• ***verb*** **vacationed, vacationing**

vaccinate (vak′si nāt′) ***verb*** to inject a vaccine into, in order to keep from getting a certain disease [We were *vaccinated* for polio.]
vac·ci·nate • ***verb*** **vaccinated, vaccinating**

vaccination (vak′si nā′shən) ***noun*** **1** the act of injecting a vaccine. **2** the scar on the skin where a vaccine has been injected.
vac·ci·na·tion • ***noun,*** *plural* **vaccinations**

vaccine (vak sēn′) ***noun*** a substance put into the body to help fight off a disease. It is made up of dead or weakened germs that cause the body to produce antibodies.
vac·cine • ***noun,*** *plural* **vaccines**

WORD HISTORY

vaccine

The source of the word **vaccine** is the Latin word for "cow." At first, *vaccine* was used to mean only the substance that was used to prevent smallpox. It was made from a mild virus of a disease of cows. Now the word is used for any substance that works in this way.

vacuum (vak′yo͞om *or* vak′yo͞o əm) ***noun*** **1** a space that has nothing at all in it; empty space

a	cat	ō	go	ʉ	fur	ə =	a *in* ago
ā	ape	ô	law, for	ch	chin		e *in* agent
ä	cot, car	o͝o	look	sh	she		i *in* pencil
e	ten	o͞o	tool	th	thin		o *in* atom
ē	me	oi	oil	*th*	then		u *in* circus
i	fit	ou	out	zh	measure		
ī	ice	u	up	ŋ	ring		

[Astronauts need special suits so that they can breathe in the *vacuum* of space.] **2** an enclosed space from which most of the air or gas has been taken [A container that has double walls with a *vacuum* between them will keep food hot or cold.] **3** *a short form of* **vacuum cleaner**.
verb to clean with a vacuum cleaner [He *vacuumed* the carpet.]
vac·u·um • *noun, plural* **vacuums** • *verb* **vacuumed, vacuuming**

vacuum cleaner *noun* a machine that cleans floors and furniture by sucking up the dirt.
vacuum cleaner • *noun, plural* **vacuum cleaners**

vagrant (vā′grənt) *noun* a person who wanders from place to place, doing odd jobs or begging.
va·grant • *noun, plural* **vagrants**

vague (vāg) *adjective* not clear or definite in form, meaning, or purpose [a *vague* figure in the fog; a *vague* answer].
vague • *adjective* **vaguer, vaguest**

vain (vān) *adjective* **1** having too high an opinion of oneself; conceited [He is *vain* about his looks.] **2** with little or no result; not successful [a *vain* attempt to put out the fire].
—in vain **1** without success [I pleaded *in vain* for help.] **2** without the proper respect [Do not use the name of God *in vain*.]
vain • *adjective* **vainer, vainest**
- The words **vain, vane,** and **vein** sound alike.
  Some people are *vain* about their hair.
  A weather *vane* points toward the wind.
  I know every major *vein* in the body.

valentine (val′ən tīn) *noun* a card or gift sent as a greeting on Valentine's Day.
val·en·tine • *noun, plural* **valentines**

valentine

Valentine's Day *noun* February 14. It is named in honor of Saint Valentine, an early Christian saint. It is the custom to send valentines on this day. This holiday is also called **Saint Valentine's Day**.

valet (val′ət *or* va lā′) *noun* a man who works as a servant to another man, taking care of his clothes and helping him dress.
adjective describing a service for cleaning and pressing clothes [The hotel has a *valet* service.]
val·et • *noun, plural* **valets** • *adjective*

valiant (val′yənt) *adjective* full of courage; brave [a *valiant* struggle].
val·iant • *adjective*

valid (val′id) *adjective* **1** based on facts or good reasoning; true or sound [a *valid* argument]. **2** acceptable under the law or rules; having legal force [a *valid* contract].
val·id • *adjective*

valley (val′ē) *noun* **1** low land lying between hills or mountains. **2** the land that is drained or watered by a large river and its branches [the Mississippi *valley*].
val·ley • *noun, plural* **valleys**

valor (val′ər) *noun* courage or bravery [The soldiers showed their *valor* in battle.]
val·or • *noun*

valuable (val′yōō ə bəl *or* val′yə bəl) *adjective* **1** having value or worth [a *valuable* ring]. **2** thought of as precious, useful, or worthy [This book contains *valuable* information. He's our most *valuable* player.]
noun a piece of jewelry or other thing of value [She locked her *valuables* in the safe.]
val·u·a·ble • *adjective* • *noun, plural* **valuables**

value (val′yōō) *noun* **1** the quality of a thing that makes it wanted or desirable; worth [What is the *value* of true friendship?] **2** the worth of a thing in money or in other goods [The *value* of our house has gone up.] **3 values** beliefs or ideals [She has strong moral *values*.]
verb **1** to set the value of [The property was *valued* at $50,000.] **2** to think very much of [I *value* your friendship.]
val·ue • *noun, plural for senses 2 and 3 only* **values** • *verb* **valued, valuing**

WORD CHOICES

Synonyms of **value**

The words **value, appreciate,** and **prize** share the meaning "to find goodness and pleasure in."

You don't *value* your health enough.
I'm learning to *appreciate* ballet.
He *prizes* her friendship.

valve (valv) *noun* **1** a device in a pipe or tube that controls the flow of a gas or liquid. This device has a flap, lid, or plug that moves to open or close the pipe or tube. **2** a membrane

V

in the heart or other part of the body that controls the flow of blood or other fluid. **3** a device for changing the pitch of certain brass instruments such as a trumpet or tuba.
valve • *noun, plural* **valves**

vampire (vam′pīr) *noun* **1** in folk tales, a dead body that moves about at night and sucks the blood of sleeping persons. **2** a tropical American bat that lives on the blood of other animals, especially livestock: the full name of this animal is **vampire bat**.
vam·pire • *noun, plural* **vampires**

van (van) *noun* a closed truck for moving furniture, carrying people, or making deliveries to customers.
van • *noun, plural* **vans**

Van Buren (van byoor′ən), **Martin** (märt′n) 1782-1862; the eighth president of the U.S., from 1837 to 1841.
Van Bu·ren, Mar·tin

vandal (van′dəl) *noun* a person who damages or destroys things on purpose.
van·dal • *noun, plural* **vandals**

vandalism (van′dəl iz əm) *noun* the act of vandalizing; destruction of property.
van·dal·ism • *noun*

vandalize (van′dəl īz) *verb* to destroy or damage property out of a desire to do harm or mischief [Someone *vandalized* his car.]
van·dal·ize • *verb* **vandalized, vandalizing**

vane (vān) *noun* one of the blades of a windmill, electric fan, or propeller.
vane • *noun, plural* **vanes**

● The words **vane, vain,** and **vein** sound alike.
A windmill *vane* is turned by the wind.
Some people are *vain* about their hair.
I know every major *vein* in the body.

vanilla (və nil′ə) *noun* a flavoring made from the pods of an orchid that twines around trees.
va·nil·la • *noun*

WORD CHOICES

Synonyms of vanish

The words **vanish, disappear,** and **fade** share the meaning "to pass out of sight or existence."

My pen *vanished* from my desk.
Most old slang words just *disappear*.
Our memories of the place have *faded*.

vanish (van′ish) *verb* **1** to go suddenly out of sight; disappear [The sun *vanished* below the horizon.] **2** to stop existing; come to an end [The dodo is a bird that *vanished* about 200 years ago.]
van·ish • *verb* **vanished, vanishing**

vanity (van′i tē) *noun* the quality of being vain or conceited.
van·i·ty • *noun*

vantage (van′tij) *noun* a position that allows a clear and wide view. Such a position is also called **vantage point** [From his *vantage* in the tower, the forest ranger could watch for fires.]
van·tage • *noun*

Vanuatu (vän′wä to͞o′) a country on a group of islands in the southwestern Pacific.
Va·nua·tu

vapor (vā′pər) *noun* **1** fog, steam, or some other mass of tiny water drops floating in the air. **2** the gas formed when certain solid or liquid substances are heated [Mercury *vapor* is used in some lamps.]
va·por • *noun, plural* **vapors**

vaporize (vā′pər īz) *verb* to change into vapor [The water *vaporized* in the sun.]
va·por·ize • *verb* **vaporized, vaporizing**

variable (ver′ē ə bəl) *adjective* **1** likely to change or vary [*variable* winds; his *variable* moods]. **2** able to be changed [a *variable* price].
var·i·a·ble • *adjective*

variation (ver′ē ā′shən) *noun* **1** the act or process of changing from a former state or from a standard [a story told again without *variation*]. **2** the amount of change [a *variation* of ten feet].
var·i·a·tion • *noun, plural* **variations**

varied (ver′ēd) *adjective* of different kinds [a program of *varied* entertainment].
var·ied • *adjective*

variety (və rī′ə tē) *noun* **1** change; difference [I like *variety* in my meals.] **2** any of the different forms of something [many *varieties* of cloth; a cat of the striped *variety*]. **3** a number of different kinds [There is a *variety* of fruits at the market.]
va·ri·e·ty • *noun, plural for sense 2 only* **varieties**

a	cat	ō	go	ʉ	fur	ə =	a *in* ago
ā	ape	ô	law, for	ch	chin		e *in* agent
ä	cot, car	o͝o	look	sh	she		i *in* pencil
e	ten	o͞o	tool	th	thin		o *in* atom
ē	me	oi	oil	*th*	then		u *in* circus
i	fit	ou	out	zh	measure		
ī	ice	u	up	ŋ	ring		

various (ver′ē əs) *adjective* **1** of several different kinds [We planted *various* seeds.] **2** several or many [*Various* people have said so.]
var·i·ous • *adjective*

varnish (vär′nish) *noun* a liquid made of resins mixed in oil, alcohol, or turpentine. It is spread over a surface to give it a hard and glossy coat.
verb to cover with varnish.
var·nish • *noun, plural* **varnishes** • *verb* **varnished, varnishing**

varsity (vär′si tē) *noun* the team that represents a college or school in games against others.
var·si·ty • *noun, plural* **varsities**

vary (ver′ē) *verb* **1** to make or become different; change [She *varies* her hairstyle. Her schedule *varied* from week to week.] **2** to be different; differ [Opinions *vary* on this matter.] **3** to give variety to [*Vary* your reading.]
var·y • *verb* **varied, varying, varies**

vascular (vas′kyə lər) *adjective* having to do with vessels for carrying blood or other body fluids, or sap [a *vascular* system; *vascular* disease].
vas·cu·lar • *adjective*

vase (vās *or* vāz) *noun* an open container used for decoration or for holding flowers.
vase • *noun, plural* **vases**

Vaseline (vas′ə lēn) *trademark* a white or yellow jelly made from petroleum. It is used as a salve or ointment.
Vas·e·line • *trademark*

vast (vast) *adjective* very great or very large [a *vast* desert; *vast* knowledge] —Look for the WORD CHOICES box at the entry **enormous**.
vast • *adjective* **vaster, vastest**

vat (vat) *noun* a large tank, tub, or cask for holding liquids.
vat • *noun, plural* **vats**

Vatican City (vat′i kən si′tē) a country inside the city of Rome, with the Pope as its head.
Vat·i·can Ci·ty

vault[1] (vôlt) *noun* **1** a room or space with an arched ceiling, especially one that is underground. **2** a room for keeping money or valuables safe in a bank.
vault • *noun, plural* **vaults**

vault[2] (vôlt) *verb* **1** to jump or leap over by resting one's hands on the thing being jumped over [We *vaulted* the fence.] **2** to jump over by using a long pole to push off from the ground.
vault • *verb* **vaulted, vaulting**

vault

VCR *noun the same as* **videocassette recorder**.
VCR • *noun, plural* **VCRs**

veal (vēl) *noun* the flesh of a calf, used as meat.

veer (vir) *verb* to change direction; shift; turn [He *veered* to the left to avoid the hole in the road.]
veer • *verb* **veered, veering**

vegetable (vej′tə bəl *or* vej′ə tə bəl) *noun* **1** a plant, or part of a plant, that is used as food. Some vegetables can be eaten raw. Others are always cooked and usually served with meat or other foods. **2** any plant [Is coral animal, *vegetable*, or mineral?]
adjective **1** having to do with or made from vegetables [*vegetable* oil]. **2** having to do with plants in general [the *vegetable* kingdom].
veg·e·ta·ble • *noun, plural* **vegetables** • *adjective*

vegetarian (vej′ə ter′ē ən) *noun* a person who chooses to eat no meat and eats mainly vegetables, grains, and fruits.
adjective **1** having to do with vegetarians or their way of eating [a *vegetarian* cookbook]. **2** made up only of vegetables [a *vegetarian* dish].
veg·e·tar·i·an • *noun, plural* **vegetarians** • *adjective*

vegetation (vej′ə tā′shən) *noun* things growing from the ground; plant life [There is thick *vegetation* in the jungle.]
veg·e·ta·tion • *noun*

vehicle (vē′i kəl *or* vē′hi kəl) *noun* something used for carrying persons or things over land or in space. Automobiles, bicycles, and spacecraft are vehicles.
ve·hi·cle • *noun, plural* **vehicles**

veil (vāl) *noun* a piece of thin cloth that is worn especially by women over the face or the head. It is used to hide the face, as a decoration, or as part of a uniform.
verb to cover or hide in the way a veil does [The clouds *veiled* the moon from our sight.]
veil • *noun, plural* **veils** • *verb* **veiled, veiling**

vein (vān) *noun* **1** any blood vessel that carries blood back to the heart from some part of the body. **2** any one of the fine lines or ribs in a leaf or in an insect's wing. **3** a layer of mineral or rock that forms in a crack of some different kind of rock [a *vein* of coal].
vein • *noun, plural* **veins**
● The words **vein, vain,** and **vane** sound alike.
I know every major *vein* in the body.
Some people are *vain* about their hair.
A windmill *vane* is turned by the wind.

veined (vānd) *adjective* having veins or markings like veins [the old man's blue-*veined* hands].

velocity (və läs′i tē) *noun* rate of motion; speed [a wind *velocity* of 15 miles per hour].
ve·loc·i·ty • *noun, plural* **velocities**

velour or **velours** (və lo͝or′) *noun* a cloth with a soft nap like velvet. It is used for clothing.
ve·lour or **ve·lours** • *noun*

velvet (vel′vət) *noun* a cloth with a soft surface made of short, raised loops or ends of yarn on one side. It is usually made of cotton, rayon, or nylon and is used for clothing, drapes, and other things.
adjective **1** made of velvet [a *velvet* dress]. **2** soft or smooth like velvet [a cat's *velvet* paws].
vel·vet • *noun* • *adjective*

vending machines

vending machine (ven′diŋ) *noun* a machine for selling small packages of items such as candy, snacks, or stamps. It is worked by putting coins in a slot.
vend·ing machine • *noun, plural* **vending machines**

vendor (ven′dər) *noun* a person who sells; seller.
ven·dor • *noun, plural* **vendors**

veneer (və nir′) *noun* **1** a thin layer of fine wood or costly material put over an inexpensive material [a walnut *veneer* on a pine chest]. **2** an outward look that hides what is below [a nasty person with a *veneer* of kindness].
ve·neer • *noun, plural* **veneers**

Venetian blind (və nē′shən) *noun* a window blind made of a number of thin slats that can be set at any angle, by pulling cords. Venetian blinds control the amount of light or air passing through.
Ve·ne·tian blind • *noun, plural* **Venetian blinds**

Venezuela (ven′i zwā′lə) a country in northern South America.
Ven·e·zue·la

vengeance (ven′jəns) *noun* the act of getting even for a wrong or injury; punishment in return for harm done; revenge.
—with a vengeance with great force or fury [The storm hit the town *with a vengeance*.]
venge·ance • *noun*

venom (ven′əm) *noun* the poison of snakes, spiders, scorpions, and other animals.
ven·om • *noun*

venomous (ven′əm əs) *adjective* full of venom; poisonous [a *venomous* snake].
ven·om·ous • *adjective*

vent (vent) *noun* an opening or passage for air, steam, or other gas to pass through or escape.
vent • *noun, plural* **vents**

ventilate (vent′l āt) *verb* to get fresh air to move into or through [Open the windows to *ventilate* the room.]
ven·ti·late • *verb* **ventilated, ventilating**

ventriloquism (ven tril′ə kwiz əm) *noun* the art or act of speaking without moving the lips much, so that the voice seems to come from another point. Many ventriloquists use puppets or dummies.
ven·tril·o·quism • *noun*

a	cat	ō	go	ʉ	fur	ə =	a *in* ago
ā	ape	ô	law, for	ch	chin		e *in* agent
ä	cot, car	o͝o	look	sh	she		i *in* pencil
e	ten	o͞o	tool	th	thin		o *in* atom
ē	me	oi	oil	*th*	then		u *in* circus
i	fit	ou	out	zh	measure		
ī	ice	u	up	ŋ	ring		

ventriloquist (ven tril′ə kwist) ***noun*** an expert in ventriloquism.
ven·tril·o·quist • ***noun,*** *plural* **ventriloquists**

venture (ven′chər) ***noun*** an activity or undertaking in which there is a risk of losing something [a business *venture*].
verb to go in spite of some risk [They *ventured* out on the ice.]
ven·ture • ***noun,*** *plural* **ventures** • ***verb*** **ventured, venturing**

Venus (vē′nəs) **1** the Roman goddess of love and beauty. **2** the sixth largest planet. It is the brightest planet and the second in distance away from the sun.
Ve·nus

veranda or **verandah** (vər an′də) ***noun*** an open porch, usually with a roof, along the side of a building.
ve·ran·da or **ve·ran·dah** • ***noun,*** *plural* **verandas** or **verandahs**

verb (vurb) ***noun*** a word that expresses action [I *walked*. You *slept*. Jane *makes* good cookies.] It also tells the condition, or state, of someone or something [We *are* here. They *became* rich. It *happened*.] It can also help another verb show special features [He *will* walk. Joe *did* see it. They *have* gone.]
verb • ***noun,*** *plural* **verbs**

verbal (vur′bəl) ***adjective*** **1** of, in, or by means of words [This author has great *verbal* skill.] **2** spoken, not written; oral [a *verbal* agreement].
ver·bal • ***adjective***

verdict (vur′dikt) ***noun*** the decision of a judge or jury in a law case [a *verdict* of "not guilty"].
ver·dict • ***noun,*** *plural* **verdicts**

verge (vurj) ***noun*** **1** the edge or border [the *verge* of the forest]. **2** the point at which something begins [on the *verge* of tears].
verb to come close to the edge or border [It is a comedy that *verges* on sadness.]
verge • ***noun*** • ***verb*** **verged, verging**

verify (ver′i fī′) ***verb*** **1** to prove to be true; confirm [New research has *verified* that idea.] **2** to make sure of [Will you please *verify* these numbers?]
ver·i·fy • ***verb*** **verified, verifying, verifies**

vermin (vur′min) ***plural noun*** small animals or insects, such as rats or flies, that cause harm or are troublesome to people.
ver·min • ***plural noun***

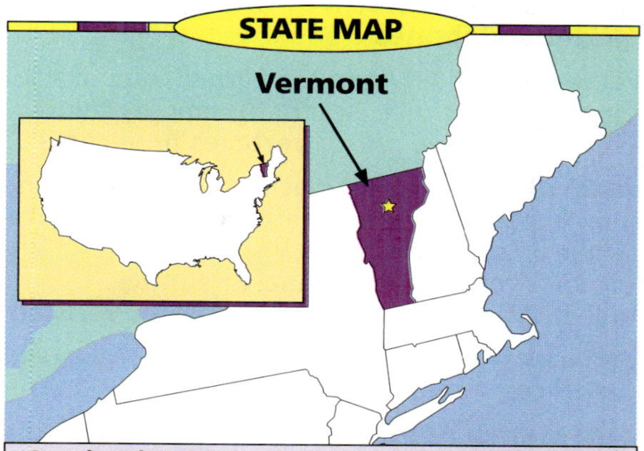

Statehood: 1791, the 14th state • **Capital:** Montpelier

Vermont (vər mänt′) a New England State of the U.S. Its capital is Montpelier. Abbreviated **VT** or **Vt.**
Ver·mont

Verne (vurn), **Jules** (jo͞olz) 1828-1905; French novelist.

versatile (vur′sə təl) ***adjective*** **1** able to do a number of things well [She is a *versatile* musician who can play five instruments.] **2** able to be used in a number of ways [This table is a *versatile* piece of furniture.]
ver·sa·tile • ***adjective***

verse (vurs) ***noun*** **1** a group of lines forming one of the sections of a song or poem; stanza. **2** poems or the form of writing found in poems [a book of *verse*].
verse • ***noun,*** *plural for sense 1 only* **verses**

version (vur′zhən) ***noun*** **1** a report or description from one person's point of view [Give us your *version* of the accident.] **2** a particular form of something [the movie *version* of a play.]
ver·sion • ***noun,*** *plural* **versions**

versus (vur′səs) ***preposition*** **1** in a contest against [a game of the students *versus* the teachers]. **2** as contrasted with [peace *versus* war].
ver·sus • ***preposition***

vertebra (vur′tə brə) ***noun*** any of the bones that make up the spinal column, or backbone.
ver·te·bra • ***noun,*** *plural* **ver·te·brae** (vur′tə brā *or* vur′tə brē)

vertebrate (vur′tə brət *or* vur′tə brāt) ***adjective*** having a backbone [a *vertebrate* animal].
noun an animal that has a backbone [Mammals, birds, reptiles, and fishes are *vertebrates*.]

V

ver·te·brate • *adjective* • *noun,* *plural* **vertebrates**

vertex (vʉr′teks) *noun* any corner point of a triangle, square, cube, or other geometric figure.
ver·tex • *noun, plural* **vertexes** or **vertices**

vertical (vʉr′ti kəl) *adjective* straight up and down; perpendicular to a horizontal line [The walls of a house are *vertical*.]
noun a vertical line, plane, or surface.
ver·ti·cal • *adjective* • *noun, plural* **verticals**

vertices (vʉr′tə sēz) *noun a plural of* **vertex**.
ver·ti·ces • *noun*

very (ver′ē) *adverb* **1** in a high degree; to a great extent [*very* cold; *very* funny; *very* sad]. **2** truly; really [This is the *very* same place.]
adjective **1** in the fullest sense; complete [This is the *very* opposite of what I wanted.] **2** same; identical [She is the *very* person I talked with.] —Look for the WORD CHOICES box at the entry **same**.
ver·y • *adverb* • *adjective*

vessel (ves′əl) *noun* **1** anything hollow for holding something [a cooking *vessel*]. **2** a large boat or ship. **3** any of the tubes in the body that carry fluids [a blood *vessel*].
ves·sel • *noun, plural* **vessels**

vest (vest) *noun* **1** a short garment without sleeves that is worn by men under a suit coat. **2** a similar garment worn by women.
verb to give some power or right to [The power to raise taxes is *vested* in Congress.]
vest • *noun,* *plural* **vests** • *verb* **vested, vesting**

vest

vestibule (ves′ti byo͞ol) *noun* a small hall through which a person enters a building or room.
ves·ti·bule • *noun,* *plural* **vestibules**

vet[1] (vet) *noun a short form of* **veterinarian**.
vet • *noun, plural* **vets**

vet[2] (vet) *noun a short form of* **veteran**.
vet • *noun, plural* **vets**

veteran (vet′ər ən *or* ve′trən) *noun* **1** a person who has served in the armed forces [a World War II *veteran*]. **2** a person who has had long experience in some work or position [She is a *veteran*, with 20 years' experience on the city council.]
vet·er·an • *noun, plural* **veterans**

veterinarian (vet′ər i ner′ē ən) *noun* a doctor who treats the diseases and injuries of animals.
vet·er·i·nar·i·an • *noun, plural* **veterinarians**

veto (vē′tō) *noun* **1** the power to keep a bill passed by a legislature from becoming a law. The President of the U.S. or the governor of a State has this power. **2** the act of keeping a bill from becoming law.
verb to use the power of veto on [The President *vetoed* the bill.]
ve·to • *noun, plural* **vetoes** • *verb* **vetoed, vetoing, vetoes**

vex (veks) *verb* to disturb, annoy, or trouble, often in little ways [I shall be *vexed* if you are late.]
vex • *verb* **vexed, vexing**

via (vī′ə *or* vē′ə) *preposition* **1** by way of or passing through [from Portland to Anchorage *via* Seattle]. **2** by means of [Send the package to the office *via* airmail.]
vi·a • *preposition*

vial (vī′əl) *noun* a small bottle, usually of glass, for holding medicine or some other liquid.
vi·al • *noun, plural* **vials**

vibrate (vī′brāt) *verb* to move in a rapid way back and forth; quiver [A guitar string *vibrates* when plucked.]
vi·brate • *verb* **vibrated, vibrating**

vibration (vī brā′shən) *noun* rapid motion back and forth [The *vibration* of the motor shook the bolts loose.]
vi·bra·tion • *noun*

vice (vīs) *noun* **1** bad or evil behavior; wickedness [They led a life of *vice*.] **2** a bad or evil habit [Greed is her worst *vice*.]
vice • *noun, plural for sense 2 only* **vices**

vice- *a prefix meaning* a person who acts in the place of; substitute. It is usually written with a hyphen [The *vice*-consul signed the documents because the consul was out of town.]

vice-presidency (vīs′prez′i dən sē) *noun* **1** the office of a vice-president. **2** the time

a	cat	ō	go	ʉ	fur	ə =	a *in* ago
ā	ape	ô	law, for	ch	chin		e *in* agent
ä	cot, car	o͝o	look	sh	she		i *in* pencil
e	ten	o͞o	tool	th	thin		o *in* atom
ē	me	oi	oil	*th*	then		u *in* circus
i	fit	ou	out	zh	measure		
ī	ice	u	up	ŋ	ring		

during which a person holds this office.
vice-pres·i·den·cy • *noun, plural* **vice-presidencies**

vice-president (vīs′prez′i dənt) ***noun*** **1** an officer next in rank to a president. The vice-president takes the place of the president if the president should die or be absent. **2 Vice President** such an officer in the U.S. government.
vice-pres·i·dent • ***noun,*** *plural* **vice-presidents**

viceroy (vīs′roi) ***noun*** a person who rules a colony or territory for a king or queen.
vice·roy • ***noun,*** *plural* **viceroys**

vice versa (vīs′ vur′sə) ***adverb*** the other way around; turning the order around [We like them and *vice versa*—that is, they like us.]
vi·ce ver·sa • ***adverb***

vicinity (vi sin′i tē) ***noun*** a nearby or surrounding area; neighborhood [Our house is in the *vicinity* of the public library.]
vi·cin·i·ty • ***noun,*** *plural* **vicinities**

vicious (vish′əs) ***adjective*** **1** likely to attack or bite someone or something [a *vicious* dog]. **2** meant to harm; cruel [a *vicious* rumor].
vi·cious • ***adjective***

victim (vik′tim) ***noun*** **1** someone or something killed, destroyed, or hurt [a *victim* of the storm; the *victims* of hate]. **2** a person who is cheated or tricked [a *victim* of swindlers].
vic·tim • ***noun,*** *plural* **victims**

victor (vik′tər) ***noun*** the winner in a battle, struggle, or contest [The *victors* received a trophy.]
vic·tor • ***noun,*** *plural* **victors**

victorious (vik tôr′ē əs) ***adjective*** having won a victory [the *victorious* team].
vic·to·ri·ous • ***adjective***

victory (vik′tər ē) ***noun*** the winning of a battle, struggle, or contest; success in defeating an enemy or an opponent.
vic·to·ry • ***noun,*** *plural* **victories**

victuals (vit′lz) [*an informal word*] ***plural noun*** food. This is mainly a dialect word.
vic·tuals • ***plural noun***

video (vid′ē ō′) ***adjective*** **1** having to do with television. **2** having to do with the picture portion of a television broadcast [the *video* image]. **3** having to do with the way information is shown on a computer screen [a *video* display].
noun **1** *a short form of* **videocassette**. **2** *a short form of* **videotape**. **3** a program that is recorded on film or videotape. It can be watched on television or videocassette [music *videos*]. **4** television.
vid·e·o • ***adjective*** • ***noun,*** *plural for all senses except 4* **videos**

videocassette (vid′ē ō′kə set′) ***noun*** a cassette with videotape in it. It is used to record and play back sounds and pictures.
vid·e·o·cas·sette • ***noun,*** *plural* **videocassettes**

videocassette recorder ***noun*** a device for recording on, and playing back, videocassettes. It is also called a **video recorder**.
videocassette recorder • ***noun,*** *plural* **videocassette recorders**

video game ***noun*** a game that is played using some kind of electronic screen. The images on the screen are controlled by the player or players.
video game • ***noun,*** *plural* **video games**

videotape (vid′ē ō tāp′) ***noun*** a thin, plastic ribbon with a special magnetic coating, used to record, and play back, sounds and pictures.
verb to record on videotape [Many TV programs are *videotaped* in advance.]
vid·e·o·tape • ***noun,*** *plural* **videotapes** • ***verb*** **videotaped, videotaping**

Vietnam (vē′ət näm′) a country in southeastern Asia.
Vi·et·nam

Vietnamese (vē et nə mēz′) ***noun*** **1** a person born or living in Vietnam. **2** the language of Vietnam.
Vi·et·nam·ese • ***noun,*** *plural for sense 1 only* **Vietnamese**

view (vyōō) ***noun*** **1** the act of seeing or looking; examination [On closer *view*, I saw that the bird was a robin.] **2** the distance over which a person can see; sight [The parade marched out of *view*.] **3** that which is seen; scene [We admired the *view* from the bridge.] **4** a way of thinking about something; opinion [What are your *views* on this matter?]
verb **1** to look at with great care; inspect [The landlord *viewed* the damage.] **2** to see [A crowd gathered to *view* the fireworks.] **3** to think about; consider [Her plan was *viewed* with scorn.] —Look for the WORD CHOICES box at the entry **perceive**.
—in view in sight [Around the bend in the road the house comes *in view*.] **—on view** placed where the public can see [A special exhibit is *on view* at the museum.]

V

view • *noun, plural for senses 3 and 4 only* **views** • *verb* **viewed, viewing**

WORD CHOICES

Synonyms of **view**

The words **view, prospect,** and **scene** share the meaning "that which is seen."

with the *view* cut off by the next building

admiring the *prospect* from the hilltop

a peaceful country *scene*

viewer (vyo͞o′ər) *noun* **1** a person who views something such as a scene or a TV show. **2** a device that lets one person look at photographic slides, filmstrips, and similar items.
view·er • *noun, plural* **viewers**

viewpoint (vyo͞o′point) *noun* a way of thinking about something; attitude; point of view.
view·point • *noun, plural* **viewpoints**

vigil (vij′əl) *noun* the act or a time of staying awake during the usual hours of sleep [The nurse kept a *vigil* by the patient's bed.]
vig·il • *noun, plural* **vigils**

vigor (vig′ər) *noun* **1** strength and energy of the body or mind [He walked with *vigor*.] **2** great strength or force [The two debate teams argued with intelligence and *vigor*.]
vig·or • *noun*

vigorous (vig′ər əs) *adjective* **1** full of vigor; living or growing with full strength [a healthy, *vigorous* plant; a *vigorous* young dancer] —Look for the WORD CHOICES box at the entry **active**. **2** having to do with or needing vigor or energy [*vigorous* exercise].
vig·or·ous • *adjective*

viking or **Viking** (vī′kiŋ) *noun* any one of the pirates of Scandinavia who raided the coasts of Europe during the eighth, ninth, and tenth centuries.
vik·ing or **Viking** • *noun, plural* **vikings** or **Vikings**

vile (vīl) *adjective* **1** very evil or wicked [*vile* crimes]. **2** very unpleasant or disgusting [*vile* language].
vile • *adjective* **viler, vilest**

villa (vil′ə) *noun* a large, luxurious country house.
vil·la • *noun, plural* **villas**

village (vil′ij) *noun* **1** a group of houses in the country, smaller than a town. **2** the people of a village [The *village* had a dance Saturday.]
vil·lage • *noun, plural* **villages**

villager (vil′ij ər) *noun* a person who lives in a village.
vil·lag·er • *noun, plural* **villagers**

villain (vil′ən) *noun* **1** an evil or wicked person. **2** such a person as a character in a play, novel, or story.
vil·lain • *noun, plural* **villains**

WORD HISTORY

villain

The word **villain** comes from a Latin word that means "farm." In English it first meant "a farm worker," then "a rough, ignorant person," and finally "a wicked person."

vine (vīn) *noun* any plant with a long, thin stem that grows along the ground or climbs walls, trees, or other surfaces by fastening itself to them [Pumpkins, melons, and grapes grow on *vines*.]
vine • *noun, plural* **vines**

vinegar (vin′ə gər) *noun* a sour liquid that is made when cider, wine, or certain other liquids ferment. Vinegar is used to flavor or pickle foods.
vin·e·gar • *noun*

vineyard (vin′yərd) *noun* a piece of land where grapevines are grown.
vine·yard • *noun, plural* **vineyards**

vinyl (vī′nəl) *noun* a kind of plastic used for making such things as phonograph records, water pipes, floor tiles, and clothing.
vi·nyl • *noun*

viola (vē ō′lə) *noun* a stringed instrument like the violin, but a little larger and lower in pitch.
vi·o·la • *noun, plural* **violas**

a	cat	ō	go	ʉ	fur	ə =	a *in* ago
ā	ape	ô	law, for	ch	chin		e *in* agent
ä	cot, car	o͝o	look	sh	she		i *in* pencil
e	ten	o͞o	tool	th	thin		o *in* atom
ē	me	oi	oil	*th*	then		u *in* circus
i	fit	ou	out	zh	measure		
ī	ice	u	up	ŋ	ring		

viola

violin

violate (vī′ə lāt) ***verb*** **1** to break or fail to keep a law, rule, or promise [He got a ticket because he *violated* the speed limit.] **2** to break in upon; disturb [They *violated* my privacy.]
vi·o·late • ***verb*** **violated, violating**

violation (vī′ə lā′shən) ***noun*** the act of violating or an instance of being violated [the *violation* of someone's privacy; a traffic *violation*].
vi·o·la·tion • ***noun,*** *plural* **violations**

violence (vī′ə ləns) ***noun*** **1** force that is used to cause harm or damage [The prisoners attacked their guards with *violence*.] **2** great strength or force [the *violence* of the tornado].
vi·o·lence • ***noun***

violent (vī′ə lənt) ***adjective*** **1** showing or acting with great force that causes damage or injury [*violent* blows of the fist; *violent* winds]. **2** caused by such a force [a *violent* death]. **3** very strong; severe [a *violent* sneeze].
vi·o·lent • ***adjective***

violet (vī′ə lət) ***noun*** **1** a small plant with white, blue, purple, or yellow flowers. **2** bluish purple. ***adjective*** bluish-purple.
vi·o·let • ***noun,*** *plural for sense 1 only* **violets** • ***adjective***

violet

violin (vī ə lin′) ***noun*** the smallest of a group of musical instruments made of wood. It has four strings that are played with a bow. The viola, cello, and double bass belong to the same group.
vi·o·lin • ***noun,*** *plural* **violins**

violinist (vī ə lin′ist) ***noun*** a violin player.
vi·o·lin·ist • ***noun,*** *plural* **violinists**

VIP ***noun*** an important guest or official who receives special treatment. VIP stands for *very important person*.
VIP • ***noun,*** *plural* **VIPs**

viper (vī′pər) ***noun*** a kind of poisonous snake.
vi·per • ***noun,*** *plural* **vipers**

Virgil (vʉr′jəl) 70-19 B.C.; Roman poet.
Vir·gil

virgin (vʉr′jin) ***adjective*** pure and fresh; not touched or used [*virgin* snow; a *virgin* forest]. —**the Virgin** Mary, the mother of Jesus.
vir·gin • ***adjective***

STATE MAP

Virginia

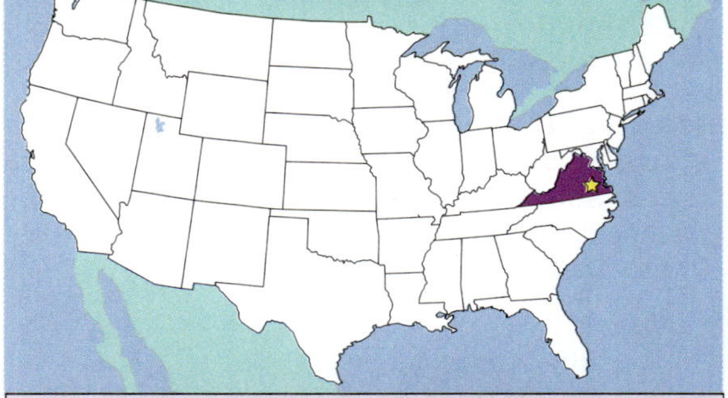

Statehood: 1788, the 10th state • **Capital:** Richmond

Virginia (vər jin′yə) a State on the eastern coast of the U.S. Its capital is Richmond. Abbreviated **VA** or **Va.**
Vir·gin·ia

virtual (vʉr′cho͞o əl) ***adjective*** being almost so, although not in actual fact or name [Although we have met, they are *virtual* strangers to me.]
vir·tu·al • ***adjective***

virtually (vʉr′cho͞o ə lē) ***adverb*** really; practically; nearly [These purses are *virtually* identical.]
vir·tu·al·ly • ***adverb***

virtue (vʉr′cho͞o *or* vʉr′chyo͞o) ***noun*** **1** goodness; right action and thinking [*Virtue* is its own reward.] **2** a particular moral quality thought of as good [Courage is his greatest *virtue*.] **3** a good quality or good qualities; merit [Your plan has certain *virtues*.]
vir·tue • ***noun,*** *plural for senses 2 and 3 only* **virtues**

virtuous (vʉr′cho͞o əs *or* vʉr′chyo͞o əs) ***adjective*** having virtue; good, moral, or pure —Look for the WORD CHOICES box at the entry **moral**.
vir·tu·ous • ***adjective***

virus (vī′rəs) ***noun*** a form of matter smaller than any of the bacteria. It grows in the cells of other living things and causes disease in animals and plants. Smallpox, measles, and the flu are caused by viruses.
vi·rus • ***noun,*** *plural* **viruses**

WORD HISTORY

virus

The word **virus** comes from a Latin word that means "poison." *Virus* was used long ago in English to mean "venom," the poison of snakes. Later it came to mean the small forms of matter which, like snake venom, could sometimes bring death.

visa (vē′zə) ***noun*** something written or stamped on a passport by an official of a country. It shows that the person who holds the passport has permission to enter that country.
vi·sa • ***noun,*** *plural* **visas**

vise

vise (vīs) ***noun*** a device that has two jaws that are opened and closed by a screw. A vise is used for holding an object in a firm way while it is being worked on.
vise • ***noun,*** *plural* **vises**

visibility (viz′i bil′i tē) ***noun*** the distance within which things are visible [Fog reduced the *visibility* to 500 feet.]
vis·i·bil·i·ty • ***noun***

visible (viz′i bəl) ***adjective*** able to be seen or noticed [a *visible* scar; a *visible* rise in crime].
vis·i·ble • ***adjective***

vision (vizh′ən) ***noun*** **1** the act or power of seeing; sight [She wears glasses to improve her *vision*.] **2** something seen in the mind, or in a dream or trance [a *vision* of the future].
vi·sion • ***noun,*** *plural for sense 2 only* **visions**

visit (viz′it) ***verb*** **1** to go or come to see someone out of friendship or for business reasons [We *visit* our cousins every year. The doctor *visited* his patient in the hospital.] **2** to stay with as a guest [They *visited* us for two days.] **3** to go or come to a place for a time [I *visited* the museum on Sunday.]
noun an act of visiting [a short *visit* at a friend's house; a *visit* to the doctor's office].
vis·it • ***verb*** **visited, visiting** • ***noun,*** *plural* **visits**

visitor (viz′it ər) ***noun*** a person making a visit; caller or guest.
vis·i·tor • ***noun,*** *plural* **visitors**

visor
Three kinds of visors

visor (vī′zər) ***noun*** **1** a part of a helmet that can be pulled down to cover the face. **2** the brim of a cap, sticking out in front to shade the eyes. **3** any device for shading the eyes [the *visor* above the windshield of a car].
vi·sor • ***noun,*** *plural* **visors**

a	cat	ō	go	ʉ	fur	ə =	a *in* ago
ā	ape	ô	law, for	ch	chin		e *in* agent
ä	cot, car	oo	look	sh	she		i *in* pencil
e	ten	o͞o	tool	th	thin		o *in* atom
ē	me	oi	oil	*th*	then		u *in* circus
i	fit	ou	out	zh	measure		
ī	ice	u	up	ŋ	ring		

visual (vizh′o͞o əl) ***adjective*** having to do with sight or used in seeing [*visual* aids].
vis·u·al • ***adjective***

visual aids ***plural noun*** movies, slides, charts, and other items, but not books, that are used in teaching, lectures, and elsewhere.

visualize (vizh′o͞o əl īz′) ***verb*** to form a picture of in the mind; imagine [Try to *visualize* her with longer hair.]
vis·u·al·ize • ***verb*** **visualized, visualizing**

vital (vīt′l) ***adjective*** **1** necessary to life [The heart is a *vital* organ.] **2** very important [Her help is *vital* to the success of our plan.]
vi·tal • ***adjective***

vitality (vī tal′ə tē) ***noun*** energy or strength of mind or body; vigor.
vi·tal·i·ty • ***noun***

vitamin (vīt′ə min) ***noun*** any one of certain substances needed by the body to keep healthy. They are found in most kinds of food. A lack of vitamins can cause certain diseases.
vi·ta·min • ***noun,*** *plural* **vitamins**

vivid (viv′id) ***adjective*** **1** bright and strong [*vivid* colors]. **2** forming or giving a clear picture in the mind [a *vivid* description].
viv·id • ***adjective***

vixen (vik′sən) ***noun*** a female fox.
vix·en • ***noun,*** *plural* **vixens**

vocabulary (vō kab′yo͞o ler′ē) ***noun*** **1** all the words of a language [the English *vocabulary*]. **2** all the words used by a certain person or group [Her *vocabulary* is large. The word "fracture" is part of the medical *vocabulary*.] **3** a list of words, usually in alphabetical order with their meanings.
vo·cab·u·lar·y • ***noun,*** *plural* **vocabularies**

vocal (vō′kəl) ***adjective*** **1** made by the voice [*vocal* sounds]. **2** having to do with the voice [the *vocal* cords]. **3** for singing [*vocal* music]. **4** speaking in a strong or open way [She was very *vocal* at the meeting of the town council.]
vo·cal • ***adjective***

vocal cords ***plural noun*** the folds or cords at the upper end of the windpipe. They vibrate and make voice sounds when air from the lungs passes through.

vocalist (vō′kəl ist) ***noun*** a person who sings; singer.
vo·cal·ist • ***noun,*** *plural* **vocalists**

vocation (vō kā′shən) ***noun*** a person's profession, occupation, trade, or career.
vo·ca·tion • ***noun,*** *plural* **vocations**

vodka (väd′kə) ***noun*** an alcoholic liquor made from grain. It has no color.
vod·ka • ***noun***

vogue (vōg) ***noun*** the general fashion or style [Powdered wigs were in *vogue* in the eighteenth century.]

voice (vois) ***noun*** **1** sound made through the mouth, especially by human beings in talking or singing [a man's deep *voice*]. **2** the ability to make such sounds [She lost her *voice* in terror.] **3** the quality of the sounds made in speaking or singing [a fine *voice* for radio]. ***verb*** to put an idea or feeling into words; utter [He *voiced* his doubts.]
voice • ***noun,*** *plural* **voices** • ***verb*** **voiced, voicing**

voice mail ***noun*** an electronic system for recording telephone messages.

void (void) ***noun*** **1** an empty space [Most of outer space is a huge *void*.] **2** a feeling of having lost someone or something; an empty feeling [Bill's death left a *void* in our group.] ***adjective*** **1** being without; lacking [The moon is *void* of living things.] **2** having no legal force; not valid [The contract is *void*.]
void • ***noun,*** *plural for sense 1 only* **voids** • ***adjective***

vol. *abbreviation for* volume.

volcanic (vôl kan′ik *or* väl kan′ik) ***adjective*** having to do with or produced by a volcano [*volcanic* rock].
vol·can·ic • ***adjective***

volcano

volcano (vôl kā′nō *or* väl kā′nō) ***noun*** **1** an opening in the earth's surface that forms when melted rock from deep inside the earth is thrown up. **2** a hill or mountain of ash and melted rock that builds up around such an opening.
vol·ca·no • ***noun,*** *plural* **volcanoes** or **volcanos**

V

volley (väl′ē) *noun* **1** in certain sports, the flight or return of the ball before it touches the ground. **2** in certain sports, a series of shots back and forth between the opposing players.
verb **1** to return the ball as a volley. **2** to exchange shots in a volley [The tennis players *volleyed* for the serve.]
vol·ley • *noun, plural* **volleys**
• *verb* **volleyed, volleying**

volleyball (väl′ē bôl′) *noun* **1** a game played by two teams who hit a large, light ball back and forth over a high net with their hands. **2** the ball used in this game.
vol·ley·ball • *noun, plural for sense 2 only* **volleyballs**

volt (vōlt) *noun* a unit for measuring the force of an electric current.
volt • *noun, plural* **volts**

voltage (vōl′tij) *noun* the force that causes an electric current to flow through a circuit. It is measured in volts.
volt·age • *noun, plural* **voltages**

volume (väl′yoom) *noun* **1** a book [His collected poems made up a small *volume.*] **2** one of the books of a set [*volume* III of the encyclopedia]. **3** loudness of sound [Lower the *volume* of your radio.] **4** the amount of space inside something that has a length, a width, and a height. Volume is measured in cubic inches, cubic feet, or other cubic units. A figure that is three feet long, three feet wide, and three feet high has a volume of 27 cubic feet. **5** an amount, bulk, or mass [a large *volume* of sales].
vol·ume • *noun, plural for senses 1, 2, and 5 only* **volumes**

voluntary (väl′ən ter′ē) *adjective* **1** acting, done, or given by a person's own choice [a *voluntary* gift to a charity]. **2** controlled by a person's mind or will [*voluntary* muscles].
vol·un·tar·y • *adjective*

volunteer (väl ən tir′) *noun* a person who offers to do something by his or her own choice.
verb **1** to do or give by a person's own choice [He *volunteered* some information. Sarah *volunteered* to write the letter.] **2** to enter into a service by a person's own choice [They *volunteered* to serve in the Navy.]
vol·un·teer • *noun, plural* **volunteers**
• *verb* **volunteered, volunteering**

vomit (väm′it) *verb* to be sick and have matter from the stomach come back up through the mouth; to throw up.
noun matter that is thrown up from the stomach.
vom·it • *verb* **vomited, vomiting** • *noun*

vote (vōt) *noun* **1** a person's decision on some plan or idea. **2** a person's choice among people running for office. **3** a ballot, a raised hand, or another way by which someone shows the decision or choice [They counted the *votes.*] **4** all the votes together [a heavy *vote*]. **5** the act of choosing by a vote [I call for a *vote.*] **6** the right to take part in a vote [The 19th Amendment gave the *vote* to women.]
verb **1** to give or make a vote [For whom did you *vote?*] **2** to decide, elect, or bring about by vote [We *voted* her into office.]
vote • *noun, plural for all senses except 4 and 6* **votes** • *verb* **voted, voting**

voter (vōt′ər) *noun* a person who votes or has the power to vote •
vot·er • *noun, plural* **voters**

voting machine *noun* a machine on which the votes in an election are made and recorded.
voting machine • *noun, plural* **voting machines**

vouch (vouch) *verb* to give a guarantee [Her friends can *vouch* for her honesty.]
vouch • *verb* **vouched, vouching**

voucher (vou′chər) *noun* a document or piece of paper that serves as proof that a payment was made.
vouch·er • *noun, plural* **vouchers**

vow (vou) *noun* a serious promise or pledge [marriage *vows*].
verb **1** to make a vow or serious promise [She *vowed* to take care of her little brothers.] —Look for the WORD CHOICES box at the entry **promise**. **2** to say in a forceful or earnest way [He *vowed* that he had never heard such a noise.]
vow • *noun, plural* **vows** • *verb* **vowed, vowing**

vowel (vou′əl) *noun* **1** a speech sound that is made by using the voice without stopping the breath with the tongue, teeth, or lips. Some English vowels are (a), (ā), (ä), (e), and (ō). **2** a letter that represents a sound like this. The English vowels are *a, e, i, o, u,* and sometimes *y.*

a	cat	ō	go	u	fur	ə = a *in* ago	
ā	ape	ô	law, for	ch	chin	e *in* agent	
ä	cot, car	oo	look	sh	she	i *in* pencil	
e	ten	ōō	tool	th	thin	o *in* atom	
ē	me	oi	oil	*th*	then	u *in* circus	
i	fit	ou	out	zh	measure		
ī	ice	u	up	ŋ	ring		

vow·el • *noun, plural* **vowels**

voyage (voi′ij) ***noun*** **1** a journey by water [an ocean *voyage*]. **2** a journey through the air or outer space [a *voyage* by rocket] —Look for the WORD CHOICES box at the entry **trip**.
voy·age • ***noun,*** *plural* **voyages**

V.P. *abbreviation for* vice-president.

vs. *abbreviation for* versus [the Red Team *vs.* the Blue Team].

VT or **Vt.** *abbreviation for* Vermont.

vulgar (vul′gər) ***adjective*** showing bad taste or bad manners; crude; coarse [a *vulgar* joke] —Look for the WORD CHOICES box at the entry **coarse**.
vul·gar • ***adjective***

vulnerable (vul′nər ə bəl) ***adjective*** **1** able to be hurt in the body [Old and sick animals are *vulnerable* to predators.] **2** able to be destroyed or attacked [The town was *vulnerable* because there was no fort nearby.]
vul·ner·a·ble • ***adjective***

vulture (vul′chər) ***noun*** a large bird that is related to eagles and hawks. It eats carcasses.
vul·ture • ***noun,*** *plural* **vultures**

V

W w

Ww Ww *Ww* **Ww**

In most words, the letter **w** *stands for the sound you hear at the beginning of the words* **wild, world,** *and* **wolf.** *Some people pronounce the letter combination* **w+h** *differently from the way they pronounce a simple* **w**; *this will make a difference in the beginning sounds of* **witch** *and* **which.**

w or **W** (dub′əl yo͞o) ***noun*** the twenty-third letter of the English alphabet.
w or **W** • ***noun,*** *plural* **w's** or **W's**

W or **W.** *abbreviation for* west.

WA *an abbreviation for* Washington (State).

wad (wäd) ***noun*** a small ball or piece of something [a *wad* of cotton; a *wad* of chewing gum]. ***verb*** to roll up into a tight wad [I *wadded* the paper into a ball.]
wad • ***noun,*** *plural* **wads** • ***verb*** **wadded, wadding**

waddle (wäd′əl) ***verb*** to walk with short steps, swaying from side to side, as a duck does. ***noun*** the act of waddling.
wad·dle • ***verb*** **waddled, waddling** • ***noun***

wade (wād) ***verb*** **1** to walk through something soft or liquid, such as mud or water, that slows a person down. **2** to get through with difficulty [She had to *wade* through a long, dull report.]
wade • ***verb*** **waded, wading**

wafer (wā′fər) ***noun*** **1** a thin, flat, crisp cracker or cookie. **2** a thin, flat piece of candy.
wa·fer • ***noun,*** *plural* **wafers**

waffle (wäf′əl) ***noun*** a crisp cake with small, square hollows. It is baked in a waffle iron.
waf·fle • ***noun,*** *plural* **waffles**

waffle iron ***noun*** a device for baking waffles by pressing batter between its two heated plates.
waffle iron • ***noun,*** *plural* **waffle irons**

wag (wag) ***verb*** to move rapidly back and forth or up and down [The dog *wagged* its tail.] ***noun*** the act of wagging [The puppy gave a *wag* of its tail.]
wag • ***verb*** **wagged, wagging** • ***noun,*** *plural* **wags**

wage (wāj) ***verb*** to take part in; carry on [The two countries *waged* war against each other.] ***noun often*** **wages** money paid to an employee for work done.
wage • ***verb*** **waged, waging** • ***noun,*** *plural* **wages**

WORD CHOICES

Synonyms of **wage**

The words **wage, pay,** and **salary** share the meaning "money paid to an employee for work done."

the weekly *wage* for a salesperson
his *pay* for mowing the grass
a teacher's monthly *salary*

a	cat	ō	go	ʉ	fur	ə =	a *in* ago
ā	ape	ô	law, for	ch	chin		e *in* agent
ä	cot, car	oo	look	sh	she		i *in* pencil
e	ten	o͞o	tool	th	thin		o *in* atom
ē	me	oi	oil	*th*	then		u *in* circus
i	fit	ou	out	zh	measure		
ī	ice	u	up	ŋ	ring		

wagon (wag′ən) ***noun*** **1** a vehicle with four wheels that is pulled by a horse or horses and is used to carry heavy loads. **2** a small cart that is pulled or steered by a long handle.
wag·on • ***noun,*** *plural* **wagons**

waif (wāf) ***noun*** a person without a home or friends, especially a lost or deserted child.
waif • ***noun,*** *plural* **waifs**

wail (wāl) ***verb*** **1** to show that one is sad or hurt by making long, loud cries [The hungry baby *wailed.*] —Look for the WORD CHOICES box at the entry **cry**. **2** to make a sad, crying sound [The wind *wailed* in the trees.]
noun **1** a long cry of sadness or pain. **2** a sound like this [the *wail* of a siren].
wail • ***verb*** **wailed, wailing** • ***noun,*** *plural* **wails**

waist (wāst) ***noun*** **1** the part of the body between the ribs and the hips [a narrow *waist*]. **2** the part of the body from the shoulders to the top of the hips [I have a long *waist.*]
waist • ***noun,*** *plural* **waists**
● The words **waist** and **waste** sound alike.
The swimmer has a narrow *waist.*
That TV show is a *waste* of time.

waistline (wāst′līn) ***noun*** **1** the part of the body between the ribs and the hips. **2** the part of a garment where the top joins the skirt or pants.
waist·line • ***noun,*** *plural* **waistlines**

wait (wāt) ***verb*** **1** to stay in a place or to do nothing while expecting a certain thing to happen [*Wait* for the signal. I *waited* until six o'clock, but they never arrived.] **2** to remain undone for a time [Let it *wait* until next week.]
noun a period of waiting [We had an hour's *wait* for the train.]
—lie in wait to keep hidden in order to make a surprise attack. **—wait on** **1** to act as a servant to [The butler *waited on* the guests.] **2** to work as a clerk, waiter, or waitress in a store or restaurant [Be courteous when you *wait on* customers.]
wait • ***verb*** **waited, waiting** • ***noun,*** *plural* **waits**
● The words **wait** and **weight** sound alike.
At least *wait* until the game is over.
Write down your height and *weight.*

waiter (wāt′ər) ***noun*** a man who waits on patrons in a restaurant.
wait·er • ***noun,*** *plural* **waiters**

waiting room ***noun*** a room in a place such as a doctor's office, for people who are waiting.
waiting room • ***noun,*** *plural* **waiting rooms**

waitress (wā′trəs) ***noun*** a woman who waits on patrons in a restaurant.
wait·ress • ***noun,*** *plural* **waitresses**

wake[1] (wāk) ***verb*** to come or bring out of sleep; awake [*Wake* up! Don't *wake* the baby!]
noun a watch over or the act of viewing a dead body before the funeral.
wake • ***verb*** **woke** or **waked, waked** or **woken, waking** • ***noun,*** *plural* **wakes**

wake[2] (wāk) ***noun*** **1** the trail left in water by a moving boat or ship. **2** any track left behind [The storm left much wreckage in its *wake.*]

waken (wā′kən) ***verb*** **1** to become awake [I *wakened* before the alarm went off.] **2** to cause to wake; awake [The birds *wakened* me at dawn.]
wak·en • ***verb*** **wakened, wakening**

Wales (wālz) a part of Great Britain, west of England.

walk (wôk) ***verb*** **1** to move along on foot at a normal speed [*Walk* calmly to the nearest exit.] **2** to go through, over, or along by walking [I *walk* this path twice a day.] **3** to cause a dog, horse, or other animal to walk [It's time to *walk* the dog.] **4** to go along with on foot [I'll *walk* you home.] **5** in baseball, to move to first base as a result of four pitched balls [The pitcher *walked* the batter. I *walked* on my first time at bat.]
noun **1** the act of walking, often for pleasure or exercise; stroll or hike [an afternoon *walk;* a *walk* by the seashore]. **2** a way of walking [We knew her by her *walk.*] **3** a sidewalk or path for walking on [The park has gravel *walks.*] **4** a distance walked, often measured in time [a two-mile *walk;* an hour's *walk*]. **5** in baseball, the act of walking a batter or of being walked. **6** a way of living, a kind of work, or a position in society [Our group is made up of people from all *walks* of life.]
—walk away with **1** to steal [Someone *walked away with* my radio!] **2** to win easily [She *walked away with* the first prize.]
walk • ***verb*** **walked, walking** • ***noun,*** *plural* **walks**

walker (wôk′ər) ***noun*** **1** a person who walks [I'm a good *walker.*] **2** a frame with wheels that is used by babies when they are learning how to walk. **3** a frame without wheels that is

W

used by people who have trouble walking because they are sick or hurt.
walk·er • *noun, plural* **walkers**

walkie-talkie (wôk′ē tôk′ē) *noun* a radio set for sending and receiving messages. It is small enough to be carried by one person.
walk·ie-talk·ie • *noun, plural* **walkie-talkies**

wall (wôl) *noun* **1** a structure of wood, brick, plaster, or other material that forms the side of a building or shuts off a space [a stone *wall* around the town; a picture on the bedroom *wall*]. **2** anything like a wall because it shuts something in or divides one thing from another [a *wall* of secrecy].
verb **1** to close in, divide, or provide with a wall [They *walled* in the garden for privacy.] **2** to close up with a wall [We *walled* up that window to keep out the cold.]
wall • *noun, plural* **walls** • *verb* **walled, walling**

wallet (wôl′ət *or* wäl′ət) *noun* a thin, flat case for carrying money or cards in a pocket or purse.
wal·let • *noun, plural* **wallets**

walleye (wôl′ī) *noun* a freshwater fish of North America that has large, glossy eyes.
wall·eye • *noun, plural* **walleyes** or **walleye**

wallop (wôl′əp *or* wäl′əp) [*an informal word*] *verb* **1** to hit with a very hard blow [He *walloped* the ball out of the ballpark.] **2** to defeat in a complete way [Their team *walloped* ours.]
noun a hard blow.
wal·lop • *verb* **walloped, walloping** • *noun, plural* **wallops**

wallow (wôl′ō *or* wäl′ō) *verb* to roll about or lie in mud or dust in the way that some animals do [The pigs *wallowed* in the cool mud.]
wal·low • *verb* **wallowed, wallowing**

wallpaper (wôl′pā pər) *noun* a kind of paper, often printed with colored patterns, for covering the walls or ceiling of a room.
verb to put wallpaper on.
wall·pa·per • *noun* • *verb* **wallpapered, wallpapering**

walnut (wôl′nut) *noun* **1** a round nut with a hard, wrinkled shell and a seed that is eaten. **2** the tree it grows on. **3** the wood of this tree.
wal·nut • *noun, plural for senses 1 and 2 only* **walnuts**

walrus (wôl′rəs) *noun* a large sea animal like the seal, found in northern oceans. It has two tusks and a thick layer of blubber.
wal·rus • *noun, plural* **walruses**

walrus

waltz (wôlts) *noun* **1** a dance for couples, with three beats to the measure. **2** music for this dance.
verb to dance a waltz.
waltz • *noun, plural* **waltzes** • *verb* **waltzed, waltzing**

wampum (wäm′pəm) *noun* small beads made of shells that were once used by eastern North American Indian peoples as money or as decoration.
wam·pum • *noun*

wan (wän) *adjective* **1** having a pale, sickly color [a *wan* complexion]. **2** with little strength or spirit; weak [a *wan* smile].
wan • *adjective* **wanner, wannest**

wand (wänd) *noun* a slender rod thought of as having magic powers [a magician's *wand*].
wand • *noun, plural* **wands**

wander (wän′dər) *verb* **1** to go from place to place in an aimless way; ramble; roam [We *wandered* about the city.] **2** to go away from a path or course [The ship *wandered* off course.]
wan·der • *verb* **wandered, wandering**

WORD CHOICES

Synonyms of **wane**

Many words share the meaning "to become less or weaker."

abate	decrease	dwindle
decline	diminish	ebb

a	cat	ō	go	ʉ	fur	ə = a *in* ago	
ā	ape	ô	law, for	ch	chin	e *in* agent	
ä	cot, car	ꝏ	look	sh	she	i *in* pencil	
e	ten	ꝏ̄	tool	th	thin	o *in* atom	
ē	me	oi	oil	*th*	then	u *in* circus	
i	fit	ou	out	zh	measure		
ī	ice	u	up	ŋ	ring		

wane (wān) ***verb*** **1** to become less in size or strength [The moon *wanes* after the full moon. My interest in sports has *waned*.] **2** to draw near to the end [The day is *waning*.]
wane • ***verb*** **waned, waning**

want (wänt) ***verb*** **1** to feel that one would like to have, do, or get; wish or long for; desire [Do you *want* to eat dessert? I *want* to visit Tokyo.] —Look for the WORD CHOICES box at the entry **desire**. **2** to wish to see or speak to [Your mother *wants* you.] **3** to wish to capture for arrest or questioning [That man is *wanted* by the police.]
noun **1** a lack or need [His *wants* are few. The refugees were starving for *want* of food.] **2** the condition of being very poor or needy [a family in *want*].
want • ***verb*** **wanted, wanting** • ***noun,*** *plural for sense 1 only* **wants**

war (wôr) ***noun*** **1** a state or time of combat or fighting between countries or parts of a country. **2** any fight or struggle [the *war* against disease and poverty].
verb to carry on a war [Each tribe *warred* against neighboring tribes.]
war • ***noun,*** *plural* **wars** • ***verb*** **warred, warring**

warble (wôr′bəl) ***verb*** to sing in a pleasant way with a melody as some birds do [The birds *warbled* a sweet spring song.]
noun the act or sound of warbling.
war·ble • ***verb*** **warbled, warbling** • ***noun***

warbler (wôr′blər) ***noun*** a small songbird that eats insects. Some warblers are brightly colored.
war·bler • ***noun,*** *plural* **warblers**

ward (wôrd) ***noun*** **1** a person under the care of a guardian or law court. **2** a division of a hospital [the children's *ward*]. **3** a district of a city or town for voting.
verb to turn aside or keep off [You can *ward* off tooth decay with proper care of your teeth.]
ward • ***noun,*** *plural* **wards** • ***verb*** **warded, warding**

-ward *a suffix meaning* in the direction of; toward [*Inward* means toward the inside.]

warden (wôrd′n) ***noun*** **1** a person who guards or takes care of something [a game *warden*]. **2** the chief official in a prison.
war·den • ***noun,*** *plural* **wardens**

wardrobe (wôr′drōb) ***noun*** **1** a closet or cabinet in which clothes are hung. **2** a person's supply of clothes [a spring *wardrobe*].
ward·robe • ***noun,*** *plural* **wardrobes**

-wards *a suffix the same as* **-ward**.

ware (wer) ***noun*** **1** a thing or things for sale. **2** things that are of the same general kind and are for sale [*hardware; earthenware*].
ware • ***noun,*** *plural for sense 1 only* **wares**
● The words **ware** and **wear** sound alike.
Merchants sold their *wares* at the fair.
He *wears* his best suit on Sundays.

warehouse (wer′hous) ***noun*** a building where wares or goods are stored; storehouse.
ware·house • ***noun,*** *plural* **warehouses**

warfare (wôr′fer) ***noun*** war or any conflict.
war·fare • ***noun***

warhead (wôr′hed) ***noun*** the front part of a torpedo or missile. It carries the explosive.
war·head • ***noun,*** *plural* **warheads**

warlike (wôr′līk) ***adjective*** **1** liking to make war; ready to start a fight [a *warlike* general]. **2** having to do with war [*warlike* preparations]. **3** threatening war [a *warlike* speech].
war·like • ***adjective***

warm (wôrm) ***adjective*** **1** having or giving off a little heat; not cool but not hot [*warm* weather. The radiator is *warm*.] **2** giving off pleasant heat [a *warm* fire]. **3** heated from exercise or hard work [I was *warm* from chopping wood.] **4** keeping the body heat in [a *warm* coat]. **5** full of love or kindness [*warm* friends; a *warm* heart]. **6** showing strong, positive feeling; lively or enthusiastic [a *warm* welcome; *warm* applause]. **7** [*an informal use*] close to discovering something or finding something out [Your guesses are getting very *warm*.]
verb **1** to make or become warm [I *warmed* myself by the fire. The rocks *warmed* in the sun.] **2** to fill with pleasant emotions [Your kind words *warmed* my heart.] **3** to make or become more interested, pleased, or friendly [They *warmed* to him after a while.]
—warm up **1** to make or become warm [The hot chocolate helped *warm* me *up*. I'll *warm up* the leftovers.] **2** to practice or exercise before doing something [Athletes should *warm up* before a game.]
warm • ***adjective*** **warmer, warmest** • ***verb*** **warmed, warming**

warmblooded (wôrm′blud əd) ***adjective*** having a body heat that stays the same and is usually warmer than the temperature of the surroundings [Mammals and birds are *warm-blooded* animals; fish are not.]
warm·blood·ed • ***adjective***

W

warmth (wôrmth) ***noun*** **1** the condition of being warm [the sun's *warmth*]. **2** love, enthusiasm, or some other strong feeling.

warm-up (wôrm′up) ***noun*** the act of practicing or exercising before playing in a game or giving a performance.
warm-up • ***noun,*** *plural* **warm-ups**

warn (wôrn) ***verb*** **1** to tell of a danger; tell to be careful [I *warned* him not to play with matches.] **2** to let know in advance [The driver's signal *warned* us that she was going to turn left.]
warn • ***verb*** **warned, warning**
● The words **warn** and **worn** sound alike.
The signs *warn* us about the detour.
The soles of my shoes are *worn* out.

warning (wôrn′iŋ) ***noun*** something that warns [Pain in the body is a *warning* of trouble.]
warn·ing • ***noun,*** *plural* **warnings**

warp (wôrp) ***verb*** to bend or twist out of shape [Rain and heat had *warped* the boards.]
warp • ***verb*** **warped, warping**

warrant (wôr′ənt) ***noun*** an official paper that gives the legal power to do something [The police must have a *warrant* to search a house.]
verb **1** to be a good reason for [Her good work *warrants* our praise.] **2** to give a warranty for [This appliance is *warranted* for a year.]
war·rant • ***noun,*** *plural* **warrants**
• ***verb*** **warranted, warranting**

warranty (wôr′ən tē) ***noun*** a promise made by a seller to repair or replace the thing sold if it is not as good as it is supposed to be or if something goes wrong within a certain time.
war·ran·ty • ***noun,*** *plural* **warranties**

warrior (wôr′ē ər) ***noun*** a person who fights or is experienced in war or fighting.
war·ri·or • ***noun,*** *plural* **warriors**

warship (wôr′ship) ***noun*** any ship for use in war. Cruisers and destroyers are warships.
war·ship • ***noun,*** *plural* **warships**

wart (wôrt) ***noun*** a small, hard growth on the skin.
wart • ***noun,*** *plural* **warts**

wary (wer′ē) ***adjective*** **1** on one's guard; cautious [Be *wary* with strangers.] **2** showing caution or suspicion [a *wary* look].
—wary of careful of [People should be *wary of* free offers that seem too good to be true.]
war·y • ***adjective*** **warier, wariest**

was (wuz *or* wäz) ***verb*** the form of the verb **be** that is used to show past time with *I, he, she,* and *it*. This form is also used with singular nouns [*Was* I late? She *was* so kind. This tree *was* beautiful last fall.]

wash (wôsh) ***verb*** **1** to clean with water or some other liquid, often using soap [*Wash* your face.] **2** to wash clothes; do the laundry. **3** to carry away by the action of water [*Wash* the dirt off your hands. The bridge was *washed* out.] **4** to wear away by flowing over [The flood *washed* out the road.]
noun **1** the act of washing [Your car needs a *wash*.] **2** a load of clothes or other items that has been washed or is to be washed [I'll hang out the *wash*.]
wash • ***verb*** **washed, washing** • ***noun,*** *plural for sense 1 only* **washes**

Wash. *an abbreviation for* Washington (State).

washable (wôsh′ə bəl) ***adjective*** able to be washed without being damaged.
wash·a·ble • ***adjective***

washcloth (wôsh′klôth *or* wôsh′kläth) ***noun*** a small cloth used in washing the face or body.
wash·cloth • ***noun,*** *plural* **washcloths**

washer (wôsh′ər) ***noun*** **1** a machine for washing [an automatic clothes *washer*]. **2** a disk or flat ring of metal, rubber, or other material. It is used to help bolts and faucet valves fit in a tight way. **3** a person whose work is washing things [a window *washer*].
wash·er • ***noun,*** *plural* **washers**

washing (wôsh′iŋ) ***noun*** **1** the act of a person or thing that washes. **2** clothes or other things that have been washed or are to be washed.
wash·ing • ***noun,*** *plural for sense 1 only* **washings**

washing machine ***noun*** a machine for washing clothes, linens, and similar things.
washing machine • ***noun,*** *plural* **washing machines**

Washington (wôsh′iŋ tən), **Booker T.** (book′ər) 1856-1915; U.S. educator and author.
Wash·ing·ton, Book·er T.

Washington (wôsh′iŋ tən), **George** (jôrj) 1732-1799; the first president of the U.S., from

a	cat	ō	go	ʉ	fur	ə =	a *in* ago
ā	ape	ô	law, for	ch	chin		e *in* agent
ä	cot, car	oo	look	sh	she		i *in* pencil
e	ten	ōō	tool	th	thin		o *in* atom
ē	me	oi	oil	*th*	then		u *in* circus
i	fit	ou	out	zh	measure		
ī	ice	u	up	ŋ	ring		

1789 to 1797. He was commander in chief of the American army in the Revolutionary War.
Wash·ing·ton, George

STATE MAP

Statehood: 1889, the 42nd state • **Capital:** Olympia

Washington (wôsh′iŋ tən) **1** a State in the northwestern part of the U.S. Its capital is Olympia. Abbreviated **WA** or **Wash.** **2** the capital of the U.S., in the District of Columbia.
Wash·ing·ton

washroom (wôsh′ro͞om) ***noun*** *another name for* **restroom.**
wash·room • ***noun,*** *plural* **washrooms**

wasn't (wuz′ənt *or* wäz′ənt) was not.
was·n't

wasp (wäsp) ***noun*** a flying insect with a slender body. Some wasps have a sharp sting.
wasp • ***noun,*** *plural* **wasps**

waste (wāst) ***verb*** **1** to use up or spend without real need or purpose; make bad use of [Please do not *waste* paper.] **2** to fail to take advantage of [They *wasted* a chance to win the game.] **3** to lose or cause to lose strength [In his old age, he *wasted* away.]
noun **1** the act of wasting or loss by wasting [Prevent *waste* at home.] **2** useless material or scraps [Sewers carry away *waste*.] **3** liquids and solids given off by the body.
adjective **1** left over or thrown out as useless [*waste* materials]. **2** used to carry off or hold waste [a *waste* container].
waste • ***verb*** **wasted, wasting** • ***noun,*** *plural for sense 3 only* **wastes** • ***adjective***
● The words **waste** and **waist** sound alike.
That TV show is a *waste* of time.
The swimmer has a narrow *waist*.

wastebasket (wāst′bas kət) ***noun*** a container that is used for wastepaper or bits of trash.
waste·bas·ket • ***noun,*** *plural* **wastebaskets**

wasteful (wāst′fəl) ***adjective*** using or spending more than is needed [a *wasteful* person].
waste·ful • ***adjective***

wasteland (wāst′land) ***noun*** land that is barren, empty, or ruined.
waste·land • ***noun,*** *plural* **wastelands**

wastepaper (wāst′pā pər) ***noun*** paper that is thrown away.
waste·pa·per • ***noun***

watch (wäch *or* wôch) ***verb*** **1** to look at [We *watched* the parade.] **2** to pay attention to; observe [We *watched* the school get larger each year.] **3** to guard or take care of [Please *watch* the baby now.] **4** to be looking or waiting [*Watch* for the signal.] **5** to be alert or on guard [*Watch* that you don't drop the plate.]
noun **1** the act of watching or guarding [The dog keeps *watch* over the house.] **2** a person or group that guards [The night *watch* fell asleep.] **3** the time that a guard is on duty [His *watch* ends at dawn.] **4** a device for keeping time that is like a small clock and is usually worn on the wrist.
watch • ***verb*** **watched, watching** • ***noun,*** *plural for all senses except 1* **watches**

watchdog (wäch′dôg *or* wôch′dôg) ***noun*** a dog that is kept to guard a building or other place.
watch·dog • ***noun,*** *plural* **watchdogs**

watchful (wäch′fəl *or* wôch′fəl) ***adjective*** watching in a careful way; alert [a *watchful* guard].
watch·ful • ***adjective***

watchman (wäch′mən *or* wôch′mən) ***noun*** a person hired to guard a building at night.
watch·man • ***noun,*** *plural* **watchmen**

water (wôt′ər) ***noun*** **1** a liquid that has no color and is made up of hydrogen and oxygen. It falls as rain and fills the oceans, rivers, and lakes. Water forms a large part of the cells of all living things. **2 waters** the water in a stream, river, lake, or ocean. **3** a liquid that is similar to water [soda *water*].
verb **1** to give water to [Did you *water* the horses?] **2** to put water on or in [Please *water* my plants while I'm away.] **3** to fill with tears [The gas fumes made her eyes *water*.] **4** to fill with saliva [The smell of hot dogs made my mouth *water*.]
wa·ter • ***noun,*** *plural for sense 2 only* **waters** • ***verb*** **watered, watering**

water buffalo ***noun*** a slow, strong buffalo that is found in southern Asia. It is used to pull loads.

water buffalo • *noun, plural* **water buffaloes** or **water buffalo** or **water buffalos**

watercolor (wôt′ər kul ər) ***noun*** **1** paint that is made by mixing coloring matter with water instead of oil. **2** a picture that is painted with watercolors.
wa·ter·col·or • ***noun,*** *plural* **watercolors**

waterfall (wôt′ər fôl) ***noun*** a place in a river or stream where water drops a long way down a steep cliff.
wa·ter·fall • ***noun,*** *plural* **waterfalls**

waterfall

waterfront (wôt′ər frunt) ***noun*** **1** land at the edge of a river, lake, or other body of water. **2** an area of such land in a city, often with docks and warehouses.
wa·ter·front • ***noun,*** *plural* **waterfronts**

waterlily (wôt′ər lil′ē) ***noun*** a water plant with large, flat, floating leaves and colorful flowers.
wa·ter·lil·y • ***noun,*** *plural* **waterlilies**

waterlily

water main ***noun*** a main pipe in a system of pipes that carry water.
water main • ***noun,*** *plural* **water mains**

watermelon

watermelon (wôt′ər mel′ən) ***noun*** a large melon with a green rind. It has juicy, sweet red pulp with many seeds.
wa·ter·mel·on • ***noun,*** *plural* **watermelons**

waterproof (wôt′ər pro͞of) ***adjective*** treated with rubber, plastic, or some other substance so that water cannot come through [a *waterproof* raincoat].
verb to make waterproof [We should *waterproof* our basement.]
wa·ter·proof • ***adjective*** • ***verb*** **waterproofed, waterproofing**

water-ski (wôt′ər skē) ***verb*** to be towed over water on boards that are like skis while holding on to a line attached to a speedboat.
wa·ter-ski • ***verb*** **water-skied, water-skiing**

watertight (wôt′ər tīt) ***adjective*** so tight that no water can get through [a *watertight* jar].
wa·ter·tight • ***adjective***

water wheel ***noun*** a wheel turned by flowing or falling water. It gives power to run machines.
water wheel • ***noun,*** *plural* **water wheels**

watery (wôt′ər ē) ***adjective*** **1** having to do with or full of water [*watery* soil]. **2** having too much water in it [*watery* soup].
wa·ter·y • ***adjective*** **waterier, wateriest**

watt (wät) ***noun*** a unit for measuring electrical power.
watt • ***noun,*** *plural* **watts**

wattle (wät′l) ***noun*** the loose flap of skin that hangs at the throat of a chicken or turkey.
wat·tle • ***noun,*** *plural* **wattles**

wave (wāv) ***verb*** **1** to move up and down or back and forth in a curving motion; to flap or sway [The flag *waved* in the wind.] **2** to wave the hand or a handkerchief [The crowd *waved* as we passed.] **3** to signal by waving [I *waved* goodbye.]
noun **1** a curving ridge of water that moves along the surface of an ocean or lake. **2** something that travels through air or space with a motion like a wave [a light *wave;* sound *waves*]. **3** a curve or pattern of curves [hair with a natural *wave*]. **4** a motion of the hand as a signal. **5** a sudden increase or rise that builds up, then goes down [a heat *wave;* a *wave* of visitors].
wave • ***verb*** **waved, waving** • ***noun,*** *plural* **waves**

waver (wā′vər) ***verb*** **1** to show doubt or be uncertain [He *wavered* in his promise to study harder.] **2** to flicker, quiver, or tremble [My voice *wavered*.]
wa·ver • ***verb*** **wavered, wavering**

a	cat	ō	go	ʉ	fur	ə =	a *in* ago
ā	ape	ô	law, for	ch	chin		e *in* agent
ä	cot, car	oo	look	sh	she		i *in* pencil
e	ten	o͞o	tool	th	thin		o *in* atom
ē	me	oi	oil	*th*	then		u *in* circus
i	fit	ou	out	zh	measure		
ī	ice	u	up	ŋ	ring		

wavy (wā′vē) ***adjective*** having or moving in waves [*wavy* hair; the *wavy* surface of the lake].
wav·y • ***adjective*** **wavier, waviest**

wax[1] (waks) ***noun*** **1** a yellow substance that bees make and use for building honeycombs. **2** any substance like this, such as paraffin. Candles and polishes are made from wax.
verb to put wax or polish on.
wax • ***noun,*** *plural for sense 2 only* **waxes** • ***verb*** **waxed, waxing**

wax[2] (waks) ***verb*** to become larger, stronger, or fuller [The moon *waxes* and wanes.]
wax • ***verb*** **waxed, waxing**

waxy (waks′ē) ***adjective*** having the look or feel of wax [Some plants have *waxy* leaves.]
wax·y • ***adjective*** **waxier, waxiest**

way (wā) ***noun*** **1** room to pass through [Make *way* for the police car.] **2** a route from one place to another [Take the long *way* home.] **3** distance [He ran a long *way*.] **4** direction [Go that *way*.] **5** a method of doing something [Do this the fastest *way*.] **6** manner or style [She smiled in a friendly *way*.] **7** a usual or typical manner of acting or living [He's studying the *ways* of ants.] **8** what a person wishes; a desire [Did George get his *way* again?] **9** a point or detail [It's a bad idea in some *ways*.]
adverb [*an informal use*] to a great degree; far [Roberto was *way* ahead of the other runners.]
—by the way as a new but related idea or point [*By the way*, is it raining now?] **—in the way** in a position that keeps something or someone from passing or going on [That chair is *in the way*.] **—out of the way** in or into a position so as not to hinder [I moved the chair *out of the way*.] **—under way** moving ahead; going on [The program has been *under way* for half an hour.]
way • ***noun,*** *plural for all senses except 1, 3, and 8* **ways** • ***adverb***
● The words **way** and **weigh** sound alike.
Do you know the *way* to the stadium?
What did the baby *weigh* at birth?

wayside (wā′sīd) ***noun*** the land along the side of a road.
way·side • ***noun,*** *plural* **waysides**

we (wē) ***pronoun*** the persons speaking or writing [*We* like candy. Are *we* still friends?]

weak (wēk) ***adjective*** **1** having little strength, force, or power; not strong or firm [*weak* from illness; a *weak* team; a *weak* argument]. **2** not able to last under use or strain [a *weak* chair]. **3** not having the normal strength or power [*weak* eyes]. **4** not having the needed skill [I am *weak* in reading.]
weak • ***adjective*** **weaker, weakest**
● The words **weak** and **week** sound alike.
She felt *weak* after her surgery.
Classes began last *week*.

WORD CHOICES

Synonyms of **weak**

The words **weak, feeble,** and **puny** share the meaning "having little strength or power."

a *weak* muscle
a *feeble* old woman
a *puny* effort that was sure to fail

weaken (wē′kən) ***verb*** to make or become weak or weaker [The fever had *weakened* him.]
weak·en • ***verb*** **weakened, weakening**

weakling (wēk′liŋ) ***noun*** a person who is weak in some way. This word is used to speak unkindly of someone.
weak·ling • ***noun,*** *plural* **weaklings**

weakness (wēk′nəs) ***noun*** **1** a lack of strength, force, or power. **2** a weak point; a fault [His biggest *weakness* is his habit of being late.] **3** a special liking that is hard to control [a *weakness* for ice cream].
weak·ness • ***noun,*** *plural* **weaknesses**

wealth (welth) ***noun*** **1** a great deal of money or property; riches. **2** a large amount [A *wealth* of information can be found at the library.]

wealthy (wel′thē) ***adjective*** having wealth; rich [a *wealthy* family; a *wealthy* nation] —Look for the WORD CHOICES box at the entry **rich**.
wealth·y • ***adjective*** **wealthier, wealthiest**

weapon (wep′ən) ***noun*** **1** a sword, club, gun, bomb, or other thing that is used for fighting. **2** anything that can be used to attack or defend [Her best *weapon* was silence.]
weap·on • ***noun,*** *plural* **weapons**

wear (wer) ***verb*** **1** to have or carry on the body [He was *wearing* a gray suit and black shoes. Do you *wear* glasses?] **2** to have or show as part of one's expression or appearance [He

wore a smile.] **3** to make or become damaged or used up, by friction or much use [The river *wore* away the rocks along its bank.] **4** to make by use or friction [I *wore* a hole in my sock.] **5** to last or stay strong after much use [These shoes *wear* very well.] **6** to pass little by little [The year *wears* on day by day.]
noun **1** the act of wearing or the condition of being worn [This shirt is for holiday *wear*.] **2** clothes; clothing [Men's *wear* is sold on the third floor.] **3** damage or loss from use [These shoes show a little *wear*.]
—wear off to pass away a little at a time [The effects of the medicine *wore off*.] **—wear out** **1** to make or become useless from friction or much use. **2** to tire out; to exhaust.
wear • *verb* **wore, worn, wearing** • *noun*
● The words **wear** and **ware** sound alike.
He *wears* a suit to work.
Merchants sold their *wares* at the fair.

weary (wir′ē) *adjective* **1** tired [*weary* after a day's work] —Look for the WORD CHOICES box at the entry **tired**. **2** having little or no patience or interest left; bored.
wea·ry • *adjective* **wearier, weariest**

weasel (wē′zəl) *noun* a small animal with a long body, a long tail, and short legs. It eats rats, mice, and birds.
wea·sel • *noun, plural* **weasels**

weather (weth′ər) *noun* the conditions outside at any particular time and place. Weather conditions include temperature, air pressure, rainfall, and sunshine.
verb **1** to pass through without harm [The ship *weathered* the storm.] **2** to bleach, dry, season, or harden by being exposed to the weather [The shingles of the beach house *weathered* to a soft gray.]
weath·er • *noun* • *verb* **weathered, weathering**

SPELLING TIP

Use this memory aid to spell **weather**.
We ***eat*** in all kinds of w**eat**her.

weather vane *noun* a device that swings in the wind to show the direction from which the wind is blowing.
weather vane • *noun, plural* **weather vanes**

weave (wēv) *verb* **1** to make by passing threads or strips over and under one another, usually on a loom [The yarn was *woven* into cloth. Can you *weave* a straw mat?] **2** to twist into or through [She *wove* flowers into her hair.] **3** to put together [We *wove* the facts into a story.] **4** to spin [The spider *wove* a huge web.] **5** to move from side to side or in and out [a car *weaving* through traffic].
noun a method or pattern of weaving [That cloth has a coarse *weave*.]
weave • *verb* **wove** or **weaved** (*for sense 5*), **woven** or **wove** or **weaved** (*for sense 5*), **weaving** • *noun, plural* **weaves**
● The words **weave** and **we've** sound alike.
I learned to *weave* rugs by hand.
We've never taken an airplane before.

web (web) *noun* **1** the network of threads that is spun by a spider or other insect. **2** anything put together in a careful or complicated way [a *web* of lies]. **3** the skin joining the toes of a duck, frog, or other swimming animal.
web • *noun, plural* **webs**

web

webbed (webd) *adjective* **1** having the toes joined by a piece of skin [the *webbed* feet of a duck]. **2** made like a web [*webbed* material].

website (web′sīt) *noun* a place on the Internet where a person can look at pictures, hear sounds, and read words. Websites as a group make up the World Wide Web.
web·site • *noun, plural* **websites**

wed (wed) *verb* to marry [In fairy tales, the prince usually *weds* the princess in the end.]
wed • *verb* **wedded, wedded** or **wed, wedding**

we'd (wēd) **1** we had. **2** we would.
● The words **we'd** and **weed** sound alike.
We'd often go fishing in the summer.
My job was to *weed* the garden.

Wed. *abbreviation for* Wednesday.

wedding (wed′iŋ) *noun* a marriage ceremony.
wed·ding • *noun, plural* **weddings**

a cat	ō go	ʉ fur	ə = a *in* ago
ā ape	ô law, for	ch chin	e *in* agent
ä cot, car	ꝏ look	sh she	i *in* pencil
e ten	ꝏ̄ tool	th thin	o *in* atom
ē me	oi oil	*th* then	u *in* circus
i fit	ou out	zh measure	
ī ice	u up	ŋ ring	

wedge (wej) ***noun*** **1** a piece of hard material, such as wood or metal, with two flat sides that taper to a thin edge. It is a simple machine. It can be driven into a log to split it. **2** anything that is shaped like this [a *wedge* of pie].
verb **1** to split, force, or hold open or apart with a wedge [We *wedged* the door open.] **2** to pack very close together [We *wedged* four people into the back seat of the car.]
wedge • ***noun,*** *plural* **wedges**
• ***verb*** **wedged, wedging**

wedlock (wed′läk) ***noun*** the condition of being married; marriage.
wed·lock • ***noun***

Wednesday (wenz′dā) ***noun*** the fourth day of the week. Abbreviated **Wed.**
Wednes·day • ***noun,*** *plural* **Wednesdays**

WORD HISTORY

Wednesday

Wednesday comes from two very old English words that were put together to mean "the day of Woden, or Odin." *Odin* was the chief god in the myths of Scandinavia.

weed (wēd) ***noun*** a plant that grows where it is not wanted, especially a wild plant that grows in large numbers and is hard to get rid of.
verb **1** to remove weeds from [Sam *weeded* the garden yesterday.] **2** to pick out and remove something because it is useless or harmful [The coach *weeded* out the slow runners.]
weed • ***noun,*** *plural* **weeds** • ***verb*** **weeded, weeding**
• The words **weed** and **we'd** sound alike.
Many call the dandelion a *weed.*
We'd never eaten squid before.

week (wēk) ***noun*** **1** a period of seven days. **2** the period from Sunday through the next Saturday [I was sick last *week.*] **3** the hours or days that a person works each week [a 35-hour *week*].
week • ***noun,*** *plural* **weeks**
• The words **week** and **weak** sound alike.
I have a day off next *week.*
The bridge was made *weak* by the quake.

weekday (wēk′dā) ***noun*** any day of the week except Sunday and sometimes Saturday.
week·day • ***noun,*** *plural* **weekdays**

weekend (wēk′end) ***noun*** the period from Friday night or Saturday morning to Monday morning, as a time for resting from work or school.
week·end • ***noun,*** *plural* **weekends**

weekly (wēk′lē) ***adjective*** done, happening, or appearing once a week or every week [a *weekly* visit; a *weekly* magazine].
adverb once a week; every week [They shop *weekly.*]
noun a newspaper or other publication that comes out once a week.
week·ly • ***adjective*** • ***adverb*** • ***noun,*** *plural* **weeklies**

weep (wēp) ***verb*** to shed tears; to cry.
weep • ***verb*** **wept, weeping**

weevil (wē′vəl) ***noun*** a small beetle whose larvae destroy crops such as grain, cotton, or fruit.
wee·vil • ***noun,*** *plural* **weevils**

weigh (wā) ***verb*** **1** to find out the weight of by using a scale [The clerk *weighed* the fruit.] **2** to have a weight of [The car *weighs* over 3,000 pounds.] **3** to think about with care before choosing [We must *weigh* the good against the bad.] —Look for the WORD CHOICES box at the entry **consider**.
weigh • ***verb*** **weighed, weighing**
• The words **weigh** and **way** sound alike.
What did the baby *weigh* at birth?
Do you know the *way* to the stadium?

weight (wāt) ***noun*** **1** the quality or condition of being heavy. **2** the measure of how heavy a thing is [What is your *weight?*] **3** a piece of metal that is used in weighing [Put the two-ounce *weight* on the balance.] **4** any solid mass that is used because it is heavy [lifting *weights* for exercise; a *paperweight*]. **5** a unit, such as the pound or kilogram, that is used for measuring how heavy something is.
weight • ***noun,*** *plural for all senses except 1* **weights**
• The words **weight** and **wait** sound alike.
Write your height and *weight* on the form.
At least *wait* until the game is over.

weightless (wāt′ləs) ***adjective*** having little or no weight, especially because of being beyond the pull of gravity [Astronauts are *weightless* in space.]
weight·less • ***adjective***

weird (wird) ***adjective*** **1** strange or mysterious in a ghostly way [*Weird* sounds came from

the cave.] —Look for the WORD CHOICES box at the entry **uncanny**. **2** very odd or strange [What a *weird* hat! I thought his behavior was *weird*.]
weird • *adjective* **weirder, weirdest**

weirdo (wir′dō) [*a slang word*] *noun* a person or thing that is weird, or very odd.
weird·o • *noun, plural* **weirdos**

welcome (wel′kəm) *adjective* **1** received with pleasure [a *welcome* guest; *welcome* news]. **2** gladly allowed or invited [You are *welcome* to use my paints.] **3** *used in the phrase* **You're welcome**, a polite answer to someone who has thanked you.
noun words or actions that are used in greeting [We'll give them a warm *welcome*.]
verb to greet or receive with pleasure [I *welcome* your advice. We *welcomed* the guests.]
interjection a word used to express that a person is glad that someone has come.
wel·come • *adjective* • *noun, plural* **welcomes** • *verb* **welcomed, welcoming** • *interjection*

weld (weld) *verb* **1** to join pieces of metal or plastic by heating until they melt together or can be hammered or pressed together. **2** to join together; unite [The players have been *welded* into a solid team.]
weld • *verb* **welded, welding**

welfare (wel′fer) *noun* **1** health or happiness; well-being. **2** aid that a government agency gives to people, such as those who are poor or out of work.
—on welfare receiving help from the government because of being poor or out of work.
wel·fare • *noun*

well[1] (wel) *noun* **1** a deep hole or shaft that is dug in the earth to get water, gas, or oil. **2** a supply or store [That book is a *well* of information.] **3** a shaft in a building [a *stairwell*].
verb to flow or gush [Pity *welled* up in her heart.]
well • *noun, plural for senses 1 and 3 only* **wells** • *verb* **welled, welling**

well[2] (wel) *adverb* **1** in a way that is pleasing, wanted, good, or right [The work is going *well*. Treat him *well*.] **2** in comfort and plenty [They live *well*.] **3** with good reason [You may *well* ask for a bigger allowance.] **4** to a large degree; much [The campers are *well* supplied with food and water.] **5** with certainty [You know very *well* why I did it.] **6** in a thorough or complete way [Stir the soup *well*.] **7** in a familiar or close way [I know him *well*.]
adjective **1** in good health; not ill [She is *well* again after the measles.] **2** comfortable or satisfactory [Things are *well* with us.]
interjection a word that is used to show surprise, relief, or agreement, or to begin or continue what is being said.
—as well 1 besides. **2** in an equal way [You could *as well* stay home.] **—as well as** in addition to [for fun *as well as* profit].
well • *adverb* & • *adjective* **better, best** • *interjection*

we'll (wēl *or* wil) **1** we shall. **2** we will.

well-being (wel′bē′iŋ) *noun* the condition of being well, happy, or wealthy.
well-be·ing • *noun*

well-done (wel′dun′) *adjective* **1** done with skill [a job *well-done*]. **2** cooked all the way through [I want my steak to be *well-done*.]

well-fed (wel′fed′) *adjective* showing the results of eating much good food; plump.

well-known (wel′nōn′) *adjective* known by many people or over a wide area; famous.

well-off (wel′ôf′) *adjective* **1** in a good or fortunate condition. **2** wealthy; well-to-do —Look for the WORD CHOICES box at the entry **rich**.

well-read (wel′red′) *adjective* having read much.

well-rounded (wel′roun′dəd) *adjective* **1** well planned for the right balance of parts [a *well-rounded* program of studies]. **2** showing interest or ability in many fields [a *well-rounded* student].
well-round·ed • *adjective*

Wells (welz), **H. G.** 1866-1946; English writer. His full name was *Herbert George Wells*.

well-to-do (wel′tə do͞o′) *adjective* wealthy; well-off —Look for the WORD CHOICES box at the entry **rich**.

well-wisher (wel′wish ər) *noun* a person who gives good wishes to another or to a cause.
well-wish·er • *noun, plural* **well-wishers**

a	cat	ō	go	ʉ	fur	ə =	a *in* ago
ā	ape	ô	law, for	ch	chin		e *in* agent
ä	cot, car	o͝o	look	sh	she		i *in* pencil
e	ten	o͞o	tool	th	thin		o *in* atom
ē	me	oi	oil	*th*	then		u *in* circus
i	fit	ou	out	zh	measure		
ī	ice	u	up	ŋ	ring		

Welsh (welsh) ***noun*** the Celtic language that is spoken by some of the people in Wales.
—the Welsh the people of Wales.

went (went) ***verb*** *past tense of* **go**.

wept (wept) ***verb*** *past tense and past participle of* **weep**.

were (wʉr) ***verb*** the form of the verb **be** that is used to show past time with *you, we,* and *they*. This form is also used with plural nouns [*Were* we late? You *were* so kind. These trees *were* beautiful last fall.]

we're (wir) we are.

weren't (wʉrnt) were not.

werewolf (wir′wo͝olf *or* wer′wo͝olf) ***noun*** in folk tales, a person who has been changed into a wolf or can change into a wolf at any time.
were·wolf • ***noun,*** *plural* **werewolves**

west (west) ***noun*** **1** the direction a person faces to see the sun set [Look to the *west*.] **2** a place or region in this direction [She lives in the *west*.]
adjective **1** in, of, or to the west [the *west* side of town]. **2** from the west [a *west* wind].
adverb in the direction of the west; to the west [Go *west* two miles.]
—the West the western part of the U.S., especially the part west of the Mississippi River.

westerly (wes′tər lē) ***adjective*** **1** in or toward the west [a *westerly* migration]. **2** from the west [a *westerly* wind]. This word can also be used as an adverb [The pioneers migrated *westerly* across the continent.]
west·er·ly • ***adjective***

western (wes′tərn) ***adjective*** **1** in, of, or to the west [the *western* sky]. **2** from the west [a *western* breeze].
noun a story or film about cowboys or pioneers in the western U.S.
west·ern • ***adjective*** • ***noun,*** *plural* **westerns**

Western Hemisphere the half of the earth that includes the continents of North America and South America.

West Germany the name of a former country consisting of the western part of Germany. It existed from 1949 to 1990.

West Indies a large group of islands in the Atlantic Ocean between North and South America.

STATE MAP

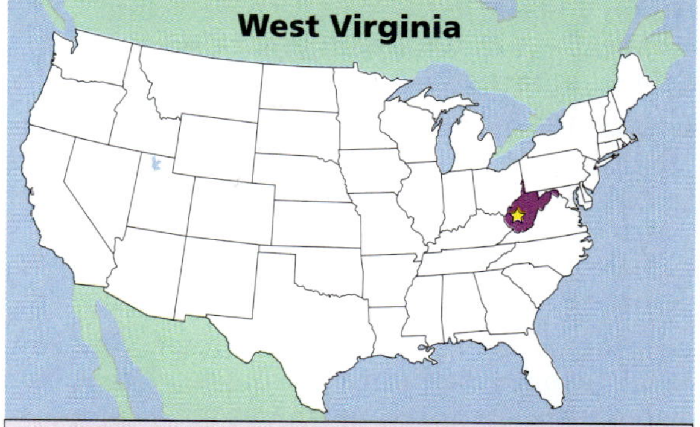

Statehood: 1863, the 35th state • **Capital:** Charleston

West Virginia a State in the northeastern part of the U.S. Its capital is Charleston. Abbreviated **WV** or **W.Va.**

westward (west′wərd) ***adjective*** in the direction of the west [our *westward* trip]. This word can also be used as an adverb [We traveled *westward*.]
west·ward • ***adjective***

westwards (west′wərdz) ***adverb*** *the same as the adverb* **westward**.
west·wards • ***adverb***

wet (wet) ***adjective*** **1** covered or soaked with water or some other liquid [Wipe the counter with a *wet* cloth.] **2** rainy [a *wet* day]. **3** not dry yet [Don't sit in the *wet* paint on the bench.]
noun **1** water or other liquid; moisture. **2** rain or rainy weather [Come in out of the *wet*.]
verb to make or become wet.
wet • ***adjective*** **wetter, wettest** • ***noun*** • ***verb*** **wet** or **wetted, wetting**

WORD CHOICES

Synonyms of wet

The words **wet, damp,** and **moist** share the meaning "having water or some other liquid in or on it."

a *wet* surface
a *damp* basement
moist air

we've (wēv) we have.
• The words **we've** and **weave** sound alike.
We've never taken an airplane before.
I learned to *weave* rugs by hand.

whack (hwak *or* wak) [*an informal word*] ***verb*** to hit or slap with a sharp sound.
noun a blow that makes a sharp sound.
whack • ***verb*** **whacked, whacking** • ***noun,*** *plural* **whacks**

whale (hwāl *or* wāl) ***noun*** a very large animal that lives in the sea and looks somewhat like a fish. Whales are mammals that breathe air.
verb to hunt for whales.
whale • ***noun,*** *plural* **whales** • ***verb*** **whaled, whaling**

whaler (hwāl′ər *or* wāl′ər) ***noun*** **1** a ship that is used in hunting whales. **2** a person whose work is hunting whales.
whal·er • ***noun,*** *plural* **whalers**

wham (hwam *or* wam) ***noun*** the sound of a heavy blow or an explosion.

wharf (hwôrf *or* wôrf) ***noun*** a long platform that is built out over water so that ships can dock beside it to load and unload —Look for the WORD CHOICES box at the entry **pier**.
wharf • ***noun,*** *plural* **wharves** or **wharfs**

wharves (hwôrvz *or* wôrvz) ***noun*** *a plural of* **wharf**.

what (hwut *or* wut) ***pronoun*** **1** which thing, happening, or condition? [*What* is that thing? *What* did he ask? *What* is your name?] **2** that which or those which [I heard *what* she said.]
adjective **1** which or which kind of [*What* dog is your favorite? I know *what* cookies you like.] **2** as much as or as many as [Borrow *what* books you need.] **3** how great! so much! [*What* nonsense he's talking!]
adverb **1** in what way? how? [*What* does it help to complain?] **2** in some way [*What* with all our joking, the time passed quickly.]
interjection a word that is used to express surprise or anger ["*What!* Late again?"]
—what for? for what reason? why? **—what if** what would happen if; suppose.

whatever (hwət ev′ər *or* wət ev′ər) ***pronoun*** **1** anything that [Tell her *whatever* you wish.] **2** no matter what [*Whatever* you do, don't be late.] **3** [*an informal use*] anything at all [She reads novels, biographies, or *whatever*.]
adjective **1** of any type or kind [I have no plans *whatever*.] **2** no matter what [*Whatever* game I play, I try hard to win.]
what·ev·er • ***pronoun*** • ***adjective***

what's (hwuts *or* wuts) **1** what is. **2** what has.

wheat (hwēt *or* wēt) ***noun*** **1** a kind of grass that is grown for its seeds. **2** these seeds, which are used as food in the form of flour.

wheat germ ***noun*** a substance that comes from wheat seeds. It has vitamins and can be added to other foods.

Wheatley (hwēt′lē *or* wēt′lē), **Phillis** (fil′is) 1753?-1784; American poet. She was born in Africa and was brought to America as a slave.
Wheat·ley, Phil·lis

wheel (hwēl *or* wēl) ***noun*** **1** a round disk or frame that turns on an axle that is fixed at its center [a wagon *wheel*]. **2** anything that is like a wheel or has a wheel as its main part [the steering *wheel* of a car; a spinning *wheel*]. **3** *usually* **wheels** the forces or machines that move or control something [the *wheels* of progress]. **4 wheels** [*a slang use*] an automobile; car.
verb **1** to move on wheels or in a vehicle with wheels [I *wheeled* the grocery cart down the aisle.] **2** to turn around; revolve, rotate, or pivot [The deer *wheeled* to face the dogs.]
—at the wheel steering or driving.
wheel • ***noun,*** *plural* **wheels**
• ***verb*** **wheeled, wheeling**

wheelbarrow

wheelbarrow (hwēl′ber′ō *or* wēl′ber′ō) ***noun*** a type of small cart that has a single wheel at the front and is pushed or pulled by hand.
wheel·bar·row • ***noun,*** *plural* **wheelbarrows**

a cat	ō go	ʉ fur	ə = a *in* ago
ā ape	ô law, for	ch chin	e *in* agent
ä cot, car	oo look	sh she	i *in* pencil
e ten	o͞o tool	th thin	o *in* atom
ē me	oi oil	*th* then	u *in* circus
i fit	ou out	zh measure	
ī ice	u up	ŋ ring	

wheelchair (hwēl′cher *or* wēl′cher) ***noun*** a chair on wheels that a sick or injured person uses in moving around.
wheel·chair • ***noun, plural*** **wheelchairs**

wheeze (hwēz *or* wēz) ***verb*** to breathe hard with a whistling or rough sound [A person who has asthma sometimes *wheezes*.]
noun the act or sound of wheezing.
wheeze • ***verb*** **wheezed, wheezing** • ***noun, plural*** **wheezes**

whelk (hwelk *or* welk) ***noun*** a large sea snail with a spiral shell. Some kinds are used for food.
whelk • ***noun, plural*** **whelks**

when (hwen *or* wen) ***adverb*** at what time? [*When* did they leave?]
conjunction **1** at what time [They told us *when* to come.] **2** at which time [The rooster crowed at six, *when* the sun rose.] **3** at or during the time that [*When* I was your age, I couldn't swim.] **4** although [She's reading *when* she could be playing.] **5** if [How can we finish, *when* you don't help?]
pronoun what time or which time [Until *when* will you be here?]

whenever (hwen ev′ər *or* wen ev′ər) ***conjunction*** at whatever time; at any time that [Visit us *whenever* you can.]
when·ev·er • ***conjunction***

where (hwer *or* wer) ***adverb*** **1** in or at what place? [*Where* is the car?] **2** to what place? [*Where* did he go next?] **3** in what way? how? [*Where* is she at fault?] **4** from what place, person, or source? [*Where* did you find out?]
conjunction **1** in or at what place [I know *where* it is.] **2** in or at the place in which [Stay home *where* you belong. Moss grows *where* there is shade.] **3** to the place to which [We'll go *where* you go.] **4** in or at which place [We came home, *where* we had dinner.]
pronoun **1** what place? [*Where* are you from?] **2** the place at which [It is a mile to *where* I live.]

whereabouts (hwer′ə bouts *or* wer′ə bouts) ***noun*** the place where a person or thing is [The police know the *whereabouts* of the robber.]
adverb at what place? where? [*Whereabouts* are we?]
where·a·bouts • ***noun*** • ***adverb***

whereas (hwer az′ *or* wer az′) ***conjunction*** **1** because; since [*Whereas* the club needs more money, we shall raise the dues.] **2** while on the other hand [We succeeded, *whereas* they failed.]
where·as • ***conjunction***

where's (hwerz *or* werz) **1** where is. **2** where has.

wherever (hwer ev′ər *or* wer ev′ər) ***conjunction*** in, at, or to whatever place [I'll go *wherever* you say.]
wher·ev·er • ***conjunction***

wherewithal (hwer′with ôl′ *or* wer′with ôl′) ***noun*** what is needed in order to get something done, especially money [Do you have the *wherewithal* to travel?]
where·with·al • ***noun***

whet (hwet *or* wet) ***verb*** **1** to make sharp by grinding or rubbing [*Whet* the edge of the ax.] **2** to make stronger [The sight of that stew *whets* my appetite.]
whet • ***verb*** **whetted, whetting**

whether (hweth′ər *or* weth′ər) ***conjunction*** **1** if it is true or likely that [I don't know *whether* I can go.] **2** in either case that [It makes no difference *whether* he comes or not.]
wheth·er • ***conjunction***

whew (hwyo͞o *or* hyo͞o) ***interjection*** a word or sharp breathing sound that can show a strong feeling of surprise, relief, or disgust.

whey (hwā *or* wā) ***noun*** the thin, watery part of milk, that separates from the curds when cheese is made.

which (hwich *or* wich) ***pronoun*** **1** what one or what ones out of those that are being talked about or suggested? [*Which* will you choose?] **2** the one or the ones that [I know *which* I like best.] **3** that [The story *which* we all believed turned out to be a lie.]
adjective what one or ones [*Which* apples are best for baking?]

whichever (hwich ev′ər *or* wich ev′ər) ***pronoun*** **1** any one [Take *whichever* you like.] **2** no matter which [*Whichever* you take, you'll like it.]
adjective **1** any [Choose *whichever* desk you like.] **2** no matter which [*Whichever* desk you choose, you'll be comfortable.]
which·ev·er • ***pronoun*** • ***adjective***

whiff (hwif *or* wif) ***noun*** **1** a light puff of air or wind. **2** a faint smell [a *whiff* of garlic].
whiff • ***noun, plural*** **whiffs**

Whig (hwig *or* wig) ***noun*** **1** any American colonist who supported the Revolution against England. **2** a member of an earlier political party in the U.S., that opposed the Democratic Party.
Whig • ***noun, plural*** **Whigs**

while (hwīl *or* wīl) ***noun*** a period of time [I waited a short *while*.]
conjunction **1** during the time that [I read a book *while* I waited.] **2** in spite of the fact that; although [*While* the car isn't large, it will hold five persons.] **3** and on the other hand [She likes chocolate ice cream, *while* I like strawberry.]
verb to spend or pass in a pleasant way [We *whiled* away a few hours.]
—worth someone's while worth the time that it takes someone.
while • ***noun*** • ***conjunction*** • ***verb*** **whiled, whiling**

whim (hwim *or* wim) ***noun*** a sudden thought or wish to do something, without any particular reason [On a *whim*, he climbed aboard the bus.]
whim • ***noun, plural*** **whims**

whimper (hwim′pər *or* wim′pər) ***verb*** to make low, broken crying sounds [The dog *whimpered* in fear of the bear.] —Look for the WORD CHOICES box at the entry **cry**.
noun the act or sound of whimpering.
whim·per • ***verb*** **whimpered, whimpering** • ***noun***

whine (hwīn *or* wīn) ***verb*** **1** to make a long, high, weak sound or cry, in the way that a person may do in complaining [a child who *whines* all the time]. **2** to say or beg in a whining way [Please stop *whining* about your troubles.]
noun the act or sound of whining.
whine • ***verb*** **whined, whining** • ***noun***

whinny (hwin′ē *or* win′ē) ***noun*** the low neighing sound that a horse makes when it is comfortable.
verb to make this sound.
whin·ny • ***noun*** • ***verb*** **whinnied, whinnying, whinnies**

whip (hwip *or* wip) ***noun*** a thing for striking or beating a person or animal. Usually it is a rod with a lash at one end.
verb **1** to strike with a whip or strap; to beat or lash. **2** to move, pull, or throw suddenly [He *whipped* off his hat.] **3** to beat into a froth [*Whip* the cream.] **4** [*an informal use*] to defeat [Their team *whipped* us again.]
whip • ***noun, plural*** **whips** • ***verb*** **whipped, whipping**

whippersnapper (hwip′ər snap′ər *or* wip′ər snap′ər) ***noun*** a young person who is thought to show lack of respect for those who are older or in a higher position.
whip·per·snap·per • ***noun, plural*** **whippersnappers**

whipping cream ***noun*** cream with a large amount of fat. It can be whipped until stiff.

whippoorwill (hwip′ər wil *or* wip′ər wil) ***noun*** a gray bird of North America with a call that sounds a little like its name. It is active only at night.
whip·poor·will • ***noun, plural*** **whippoorwills**

whir or **whirr** (hwʉr *or* wʉr) ***verb*** to move quickly with a whizzing or buzzing sound.
noun a sound like this [the *whir* of a propeller].
whir or **whirr** • ***verb*** **whirred, whirring** • ***noun***

whirl (hwʉrl *or* wʉrl) ***verb*** **1** to turn rapidly around and around; spin fast [The dancers *whirled* around the room.] **2** to seem to be spinning [My head is *whirling*.]
noun **1** the act of whirling [dancers in a *whirl*]. **2** a whirling motion [the *whirl* of the spinning top]. **3** a dizzy or confused condition [My head's in a *whirl*.]
whirl • ***verb*** **whirled, whirling** • ***noun***

whirlpool (hwʉrl′po͞ol *or* wʉrl′po͞ol) ***noun*** water whirling rapidly around and around. A whirlpool sucks floating things in toward its center.
whirl·pool • ***noun, plural*** **whirlpools**

whirlwind (hwʉrl′wind *or* wʉrl′wind) ***noun*** a current of air whirling around and around with great force. It moves forward, causing a storm.
whirl·wind • ***noun, plural*** **whirlwinds**

whisk (hwisk *or* wisk) ***verb*** **1** to move, brush, or remove with a quick, sweeping motion [He *whisked* the lint from his coat with a brush.] **2** to move or carry quickly [He *whisked* the cat out the door.]
noun the act or motion of whisking.
whisk • ***verb*** **whisked, whisking** • ***noun, plural*** **whisks**

whisker (hwis′kər *or* wis′kər) ***noun*** **1 whiskers** the hair growing on a man's face, especially the beard on the cheeks. **2** a single hair of a man's

a cat	ō go	ʉ fur	ə = a *in* ago
ā ape	ô law, for	ch chin	e *in* agent
ä cot, car	oo look	sh she	i *in* pencil
e ten	o͞o tool	th thin	o *in* atom
ē me	oi oil	*th* then	u *in* circus
i fit	ou out	zh measure	
ī ice	u up	ŋ ring	

beard. **3** any one of the long, stiff hairs near the mouth of certain animals, such as the cat.
whisk·er • ***noun,*** *plural* **whiskers**

whisker
Left: Of cat *Right: Of man*

whiskey (hwis′kē *or* wis′kē) ***noun*** a strong liquor that is made from certain kinds of grain. It may be made from rye, corn, barley, or wheat.
whis·key • ***noun,*** *plural* **whiskeys** or **whiskies**

whisper (hwis′pər *or* wis′pər) ***verb*** to speak or say in a low, soft voice.
noun **1** a soft, low tone of voice [She spoke in a *whisper*.] **2** a soft, rustling sound [the *whisper* of the wind in the trees].
whis·per • ***verb*** **whispered, whispering** • ***noun,*** *plural* **whispers**

whistle (hwis′əl *or* wis′əl) ***verb*** **1** to make a high, shrill sound by forcing breath through puckered lips. **2** to make this sound by sending steam through a small opening [Our kettle *whistles*.] **3** to move with a high, shrill sound [The arrow *whistled* past her ear.] **4** to blow a device that whistles. **5** to produce by whistling [*Whistle* a tune for me.]

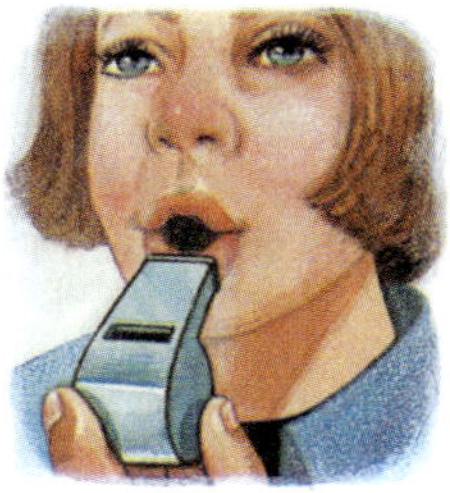

whistle

noun **1** a device for making high, shrill sounds. **2** the act or sound of whistling.
whis·tle • ***verb*** **whistled, whistling** • ***noun,*** *plural* **whistles**

white (hwīt *or* wīt) ***adjective*** **1** having the color of snow or milk. Although we speak of white as a color, it is really the blending of all colors. A surface is white only when it reflects all the light rays that make color. **2** of a light or pale color [*white* meat of the turkey]. **3** pale or wan [He turned *white* with fear.] **4** having a light-colored skin [*white* people].
noun **1** white color, white paint, or white dye. **2** a person with light-colored skin. **3** a white or light-colored part or thing [the *white* of an egg; the *whites* of the eyes].
white • ***adjective*** **whiter, whitest** • ***noun,*** *plural for senses 2 and 3 only* **whites**

white blood cell ***noun*** any one of several kinds of small blood cells with no color. They help the body defend itself against infections.
white blood cell • ***noun,*** *plural* **white blood cells**

white-hot (hwīt′hät′ *or* wīt′hät′) ***adjective*** glowing white with heat; extremely hot.

White House, the the large white mansion in Washington, D.C., where the President of the U.S. lives.

whiten (hwīt′n *or* wīt′n) ***verb*** to make or become white or whiter.
whit·en • ***verb*** **whitened, whitening**

whitewash (hwīt′wôsh *or* wīt′wôsh) ***noun*** **1** a white liquid that is made of lime, powdered chalk, and water. It is used to whiten walls. **2** the act of covering up someone's faults or mistakes so that the person will not be blamed.
verb **1** to cover with whitewash. **2** to cover up the faults or mistakes of someone.
white·wash • ***noun,*** *plural for sense 2 only* **whitewashes** • ***verb*** **whitewashed, whitewashing**

Whitman (hwit′mən *or* wit′mən), **Walt** (wôlt) 1819-1892; U.S. poet.
Whit·man, Walt

Whitney (hwit′nē *or* wit′nē), **Eli** (ē′lī) 1765-1825; U.S. inventor of the cotton gin.
Whit·ney, E·li

whittle (hwit′l *or* wit′l) ***verb*** **1** to cut or shave thin bits from wood with a knife. **2** to carve by doing this [Grandpa *whittled* a doll's head for me.] **3** to make less bit by bit [Let's try to *whittle* down the costs of the project.]
whit·tle • ***verb*** **whittled, whittling**

whiz (hwiz *or* wiz) ***verb*** **1** to make the buzzing or hissing sound of something that is moving rapidly through the air. **2** to rush with this sound [The bus *whizzed* by us.]
noun a whizzing sound.
whiz • ***verb*** **whizzed, whizzing** • ***noun***

whiz kid ***noun*** a young and unusually bright, skilled, or successful person [the *whiz kid* of the spelling bee].
whiz kid • ***noun,*** *plural* **whiz kids**

W

who (ho͞o) ***pronoun*** **1** what or which person or persons? [*Who* helped you? I know *who* she is.] **2** that [the girl *who* lives next door].

whoa (hwō *or* wō) ***interjection*** a word that is spoken to a horse, meaning "Stop!"

who'd (ho͞od) **1** who would. **2** who had.

whoever (ho͞o ev′ər) ***pronoun*** **1** any person that [*Whoever* wins gets a prize.] **2** no matter what person [*Whoever* told you that, it isn't true.]
who·ev·er • ***pronoun***

whole (hōl) ***adjective*** **1** not divided or cut up; in one piece [Put *whole* carrots in the stew.] **2** having all its parts; complete [The *whole* opera is on two CD's.] **3** being the entire amount of; all of [We spent the *whole* five dollars.]
noun **1** the total amount [He saved the *whole* of his allowance.] **2** something that is complete in itself [The different flowers in the vase combined to form a pleasing *whole*.]
—on the whole considering everything; in general.
whole • ***adjective*** • ***noun,*** *plural for sense 2 only* **wholes**
• The words **whole** and **hole** sound alike.
They ate the *whole* pizza in one night.
That *hole* was dug by a chipmunk.

wholehearted (hōl′härt əd) ***adjective*** with all of a person's energy or interest [I give you my *wholehearted* support in the election.]
whole·heart·ed • ***adjective***

whole note ***noun*** a note in music held four times as long as a quarter note.
whole note • ***noun,*** *plural* **whole notes**

whole number ***noun*** any number that is not a fraction; integer. For example, 7 and 12 are whole numbers; $4^3/_4$ is not.
whole number • ***noun,*** *plural* **whole numbers**

wholesale (hōl′sāl) ***noun*** the sale of goods in large amounts, especially to retail stores that then sell them to consumers.
whole·sale • ***noun***

wholesome (hōl′səm) ***adjective*** **1** good for people's health; healthful [a *wholesome* climate]. **2** suggesting good health of body and mind; healthy [She has a *wholesome* look about her.]
whole·some • ***adjective***

whole-wheat (hōl′hwēt′ *or* hōl′wēt′) ***adjective*** made from the whole kernels, or seeds, of wheat [*whole-wheat* flour or bread].

who'll (ho͞ol) who will.

wholly (hō′lē) ***adverb*** to the whole amount or degree; in a complete way [The house has been *wholly* remodeled.]
whol·ly • ***adverb***
• The words **wholly** and **holy** sound alike.
The mistake is *wholly* my fault.
For many, Sunday is a *holy* day.

whom (ho͞om) ***pronoun*** **1** what or which person or persons [*Whom* did the dog bite? I don't know *whom* to ask.] **2** the form of **who** that is used after prepositions [For *whom* are they giving the party? Here is the person from *whom* she heard the news.]

whoop (hwo͞op *or* wo͞op) ***noun*** a loud shout or cry, especially a shout of joy.
verb to shout with whoops.
whoop • ***noun,*** *plural* **whoops**
• ***verb*** **whooped, whooping**

whoopee (hwo͞o′pē *or* wo͞o′pē) ***interjection*** a loud shout or cry of great joy or triumph.
whoop·ee • ***interjection***

whooping cough (hwo͞o′piŋ *or* ho͞o′piŋ) ***noun*** a disease in which there are fits of coughing that end in a long, loud, gasping breath.
whoop·ing cough • ***noun***

whoops (hwoops *or* woops) ***interjection*** a word that a person may say after stumbling or after saying something embarrassing.

whoosh (hwoosh *or* woosh) ***verb*** **1** to make the quick hissing or rushing sound of something that is moving rapidly through the air. **2** to move rapidly with this sound [The police car *whooshed* by with its lights flashing.]
noun this sound or movement.
whoosh • ***verb*** **whooshed, whooshing**
• ***noun,*** *plural* **whooshes**

whopper (hwäp′ər *or* wäp′ər) [*an informal word*] ***noun*** **1** something that is very large. **2** a very big lie.
whop·per • ***noun,*** *plural* **whoppers**

who's (ho͞oz) **1** who is. **2** who has.
• The words **who's** and **whose** sound alike.
He's the one *who's* selling tickets.
He's the one *whose* bike is on the lawn.

whose (ho͞oz) ***pronoun*** the one or the ones that belong to whom [*Whose* are these books?]

a cat	ō go	ʉ fur	ə = a *in* ago
ā ape	ô law, for	ch chin	e *in* agent
ä cot, car	oo look	sh she	i *in* pencil
e ten	o͞o tool	th thin	o *in* atom
ē me	oi oil	*th* then	u *in* circus
i fit	ou out	zh measure	
ī ice	u up	ŋ ring	

adjective done by whom or which, or having to do with whom or which [*Whose* work is this? This is the person *whose* words inspired me.]
● The words **whose** and **who's** sound alike.
Whose bicycle is in the driveway?
Who's never eaten a taco?

why (hwī *or* wī) ***adverb*** for what reason, cause, or purpose? [*Why* did he go?]
conjunction **1** because of which [There is no reason *why* you shouldn't go.] **2** the reason for which [That is *why* we went.]
noun the reason, cause, or purpose [Never mind the *why* of it.]
interjection a word that is used to express surprise or annoyance or to show that a person is pausing to think [*Why*, I didn't know it was so late!]
why • ***adverb*** • ***conjunction*** • ***noun,*** *plural* **whys** • ***interjection***

WI *an abbreviation for* Wisconsin.

wick (wik) ***noun*** a piece of cord or a bundle of threads in a candle or oil lamp. It soaks up the fuel and burns with a steady flame when it is lighted.
wick • ***noun,*** *plural* **wicks**

wicked (wik′əd) ***adjective*** **1** bad or harmful on purpose; evil [a *wicked* scheme] —Look for the WORD CHOICES box at the entry **bad**. **2** causing pain or trouble [a *wicked* blow on the head]. **3** naughty or full of mischief.
wick·ed • ***adjective*** **wickeder, wickedest**

wicker (wik′ər) ***noun*** **1** thin twigs or long, woody strips that bend easily and are woven together to make baskets or furniture. **2** articles that are made in this way.
wick·er • ***noun***

wicket (wik′ət) ***noun*** any one of the small arches through which the balls are hit in croquet.
wick·et • ***noun,*** *plural* **wickets**

wide (wīd) ***adjective*** **1** measuring much from side to side; broad [a *wide* street]. **2** reaching over a particular distance from side to side [four feet *wide*]. **3** large or not limited in number or amount [a *wide* variety of foods]. **4** opened as far as possible [eyes *wide* with surprise]. **5** far from the point or goal aimed at [an arrow *wide* of the mark].
adverb **1** over a large area [The news spread far and *wide*.] **2** in order to be wide in some way [Open your mouth *wide*.]
wide • ***adjective*** & • ***adverb*** **wider, widest**

-wide *a suffix meaning* existing or reaching all the way through [A *nationwide* rebellion is one that reaches throughout the whole nation.]

wide-awake (wīd′ə wāk′) ***adjective*** **1** completely awake. **2** watching carefully and ready; alert.
wide-a·wake • ***adjective***

wide-eyed (wīd′īd) ***adjective*** with the eyes wide open [The children were *wide-eyed* with wonder.]

widen (wīd′n) ***verb*** to make or become wide or wider.
wid·en • ***verb*** **widened, widening**

widespread (wīd′spred′) ***adjective*** spread, scattered, or happening over a large area [The fire caused *widespread* damage.]
wide·spread • ***adjective***

widow (wid′ō) ***noun*** a woman whose husband has died and who has not married again.
verb to make a widow or a widower of [My grandmother was *widowed* late in life.]
wid·ow • ***noun,*** *plural* **widows**
• ***verb*** **widowed, widowing**

widower (wid′ō ər) ***noun*** a man whose wife has died and who has not married again.
wid·ow·er • ***noun,*** *plural* **widowers**

width (width) ***noun*** the measure of how wide a thing is; distance from side to side [a river 500 yards in *width*].
width • ***noun,*** *plural* **widths**

wiener (wē′nər) ***noun*** a smoked sausage of beef or of beef and pork; frankfurter.
wie·ner • ***noun,*** *plural* **wieners**

WORD HISTORY

wiener

The word **wiener** is short for *wienerwurst*, which comes from two German words that are used together to mean "Vienna sausage." One type of small sausage that was brought to the U.S. was made in Vienna, Austria.

wife (wīf) ***noun*** the woman to whom a man is married.
wife • ***noun,*** *plural* **wives**

wig (wig) ***noun*** a false covering of hair for the head. A wig is sometimes worn as part of a costume.
wig • ***noun,*** *plural* **wigs**

Wiggin (wig′in), **Kate Douglas** (kāt dug′ləs) 1856-1923; U.S. teacher and author of children's books.
Wig·gin, Kate Doug·las

wiggle (wig′əl) *verb* to twist and turn from side to side [The tadpole moves by *wiggling* its tail.] *noun* a wiggling movement.
wig·gle • *verb* **wiggled, wiggling** • *noun, plural* **wiggles**

wiggly (wig′lē) *adjective* **1** wiggling a great deal [a *wiggly* worm]. **2** having a shape or form that suggests wiggling [a *wiggly* line].
wig·gly • *adjective* **wigglier, wiggliest**

wigwam (wig′wäm) *noun* a kind of hut that was used by some American Indian peoples in the eastern U.S. It has a dome-shaped framework of poles that is covered with bark or with rushes.
wig·wam • *noun, plural* **wigwams**

wild (wīld) *adjective* **1** living or growing in nature; not tamed or cultivated by human beings [*wild* animals; *wild* grapes]. **2** not controlled; unruly, rough, or noisy [*wild* children]. **3** very excited or showing great interest [*wild* with delight; *wild* about video games]. **4** reckless, fantastic, or crazy [a *wild* plan to get rich].
adverb in a wild way; without aim or control [running *wild*].
noun usually **wilds** a wilderness or wasteland.
wild • *adjective* & • *adverb* **wilder, wildest** • *noun, plural* **wilds**

wild boar *noun* a wild animal like a pig. Domestic pigs are descended from the wild boar.

wildcat (wīld′kat) *noun* a wild animal of the cat family, such as the lynx or ocelot.
wild·cat • *noun, plural* **wildcats**

Wilder (wīl′dər), **Laura Ingalls** (lôr′ə iŋ′gəlz) 1867-1957; U.S. author of children's books.
Wil·der, Lau·ra In·galls

wilderness (wil′dər nəs) *noun* a wild area; land that has no settlers and is covered with wild plants and trees.
wil·der·ness • *noun, plural* **wildernesses**

wildflower (wīld′flou ər) *noun* a plant that has flowers and that grows wild.
wild·flow·er • *noun, plural* **wildflowers**

wildlife (wīld′līf) *noun* wild animals as a group.
wild·life • *noun*

will[1] (wil) *noun* **1** the power that the mind has to choose, debate, or control a person's own actions [He has a weak *will* when there's chocolate around.] **2** something that is wished or ordered; a wish or desire [What is your *will*?] **3** strong and firm purpose; the quality of being determined to do something ["Where there's a *will*, there's a way."] **4** a legal paper in which a person tells what should be done with his or her money and property after the person's death.
verb **1** to decide or choose [Let her do as she *wills*.] **2** to leave to someone by a will [Mother *willed* the house to me.]
will • *noun, plural for sense 4 only* **wills** • *verb* **willed, willing**

will[2] (wil) *verb* (*helping verb*) *Will* is used with other verbs to show future time. The word "to" is not used between *will* and the verb that follows it [We *will* leave next week. *Will* you please save some dessert for me?]
will • *verb past tense* **would**; *he / she / it* **will**

willful (wil′fəl) *adjective* always wanting one's own way; stubborn [his *willful* daughter].
will·ful • *adjective*

willing (wil′iŋ) *adjective* **1** ready or agreeing to do something [Are you *willing* to try?] **2** doing or giving easily or gladly [a *willing* helper].
will·ing • *adjective*

willow (wil′ō) *noun* a shrub that has narrow leaves and long, slender twigs that bend easily.
wil·low • *noun, plural* **willows**

willpower (wil′pou ər) *noun* strength of will, mind, or purpose; self-control.
will·pow·er • *noun*

Wilson (wil′sən), **Woodrow** (wood′rō) 1856-1924; the twenty-eighth president of the U.S., from 1913 to 1921.
Wil·son, Wood·row

wilt (wilt) *verb* to become limp; wither or droop [Water the flowers so that they won't *wilt*.]
wilt • *verb* **wilted, wilting**

wily (wī′lē) *adjective* full of sly tricks; cunning or crafty [a *wily* enemy].
wil·y • *adjective* **wilier, wiliest**

a	cat	ō	go	ʉ	fur	ə =	a *in* ago
ā	ape	ô	law, for	ch	chin		e *in* agent
ä	cot, car	oo	look	sh	she		i *in* pencil
e	ten	ōō	tool	th	thin		o *in* atom
ē	me	oi	oil	*th*	then		u *in* circus
i	fit	ou	out	zh	measure		
ī	ice	u	up	ŋ	ring		

WORD CHOICES

Synonyms of **wily**

The words **wily**, **crafty**, and **sly** share the meaning "clever in tricking or cheating others."

a *wily* villain

a *crafty* politician

the *sly* old fox

win (win) ***verb*** **1** to get by work, struggle, or skill [I *won* the prize for the best essay. The actor *won* the audience's applause.] **2** to get the victory in a contest, game, or debate [Our team *won*. You *win* the argument.] **3** to get the approval or favor of; persuade [I *won* them over to our side. She *won* new friends.]
noun [*an informal use*] an act of winning.
win • ***verb*** **won, winning** • ***noun,*** *plural* **wins**

wince (wins) ***verb*** to draw back a little and twist the face, because of pain or disgust.
wince • ***verb*** **winced, wincing**

winch

winch (winch) ***noun*** a machine for lifting or pulling a load. It has a drum that is turned by a crank or by a motor. A rope or chain that is tied to the load is wound on this drum.
winch • ***noun,*** *plural* **winches**

wind[1] (wīnd) ***verb*** **1** to turn something around itself or around something else [He *wound* yarn in a ball. She asked him to *wind* the bandage around her hand.] **2** to grow or pass by turning [The grapevine *wound* around the tree.] **3** to cover by circling with something [*Wind* the spool with thread.] **4** to tighten the spring of by turning a knob [Did you *wind* up the music box?] **5** to move or go in a twisting or curving course [The river *winds* through the valley.]
—**wind up** **1** to bring or come to an end; to finish [Let's *wind up* this day's work and go home.] **2** to swing the arm before pitching a baseball.
wind • ***verb*** **wound, winding**

wind[2] (wind) ***noun*** **1** air that is moving [Some seeds are carried by the *wind*.] **2** a strong current of air; gale or storm [A big *wind* blew the tree down.] **3** breath or the power of breathing [The fall knocked the *wind* out of me.]
verb to cause to be out of breath [We were *winded* by the long climb.]
wind • ***noun,*** *plural for senses 1 and 2 only* **winds** • ***verb*** **winded, winding**

windchill factor (wind′chil) ***noun*** the effect that wind has in making a temperature feel colder than it really is.
wind·chill factor • ***noun***

windfall (wind′fôl) ***noun*** money that a person gets when not expecting it.
wind·fall • ***noun,*** *plural* **windfalls**

wind instrument (wind) ***noun*** a musical instrument that is played by blowing air, especially one's breath, through it. Trombones, tubas, flutes, and oboes are all wind instruments.
wind instrument • ***noun,*** *plural* **wind instruments**

windmill (wind′mil) ***noun*** a machine that gets its power from the movement of the wind. The wind pushes against, and turns, a wheel that has large, flat blades on it. The turning motion provides power to grind grain, pump water, or produce electricity.
wind·mill • ***noun,*** *plural* **windmills**

windmill

window (win′dō) ***noun*** **1** an opening in a building, car, or other thing, for letting in light and air. **2** a frame with one or more panes of glass in it that is set in this kind of opening.
win·dow • ***noun,*** *plural* **windows**

W

WORD HISTORY

window

The word **window** comes from a word in the old Scandinavian language made up of two words meaning "wind" and "eye." Many centuries ago, windows were only small holes like eyes in the wall of a house. The wind could come right in, unless the shutters were closed.

windowpane (win′dō pān′) *noun* a pane, or sheet, of glass in a window.
win·dow·pane • *noun, plural* **windowpanes**

windowsill (win′dō sil′) *noun* the horizontal piece of wood, stone, or metal that forms the bottom section of a window frame.
win·dow·sill • *noun, plural* **windowsills**

windpipe (wind′pīp) *noun* the tube or passage from the back of the mouth to the lungs, through which the air passes in breathing.
wind·pipe • *noun, plural* **windpipes**

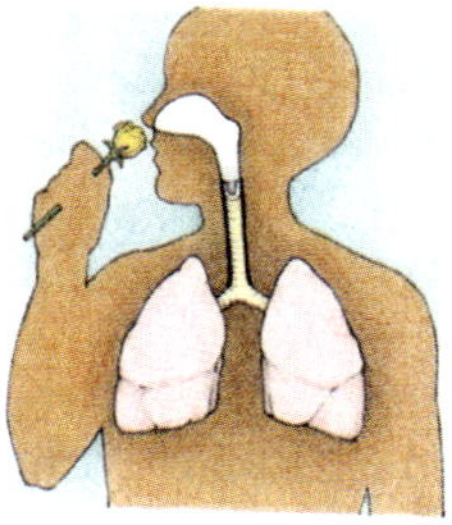

windpipe

windshield (wind′shēld) *noun* a sheet of glass located in the front of a car, motorcycle, or motorboat to protect against the wind.
wind·shield • *noun, plural* **windshields**

windstorm (wind′stôrm) *noun* a storm with a strong wind but little or no rain.
wind·storm • *noun, plural* **windstorms**

windsurfing (wind′surf iŋ) *noun* the sport of sailing while one stands on a special board that has a sail. The sail can be turned to control the board's movement.
wind·surf·ing • *noun*

windsurfing

windy (win′dē) *adjective* with much wind [a *windy* day in March; a *windy* city].
wind·y • *adjective* **windier, windiest**

wine (wīn) *noun* the juice of grapes that has been fermented and contains alcohol.
wine • *noun, plural* **wines**

wing (wiŋ) *noun* **1** one of a pair of parts covered with feathers that a bird spreads out from its sides in flying. **2** one of a pair of parts that other creatures use like this for flying [Bats' *wings* are formed of thin skin. Most insects have two pairs of *wings*.] **3** something that is like a wing in shape or use [the *wings* of an airplane]. **4** a part that sticks out from a main part [The *wing* of a building is often a part that is added on later.]
verb to make by flying [The bird *winged* its way across the lake.]
—**on the wing** in flight. —**take wing** to fly away. —**under someone's wing** under someone's protection.
wing • *noun, plural* **wings** • *verb* **winged, winging**

winged (wiŋd) *adjective* having wings.

wink (wiŋk) *verb* to close and open one eye quickly, as a signal [He *winked* to show that he was joking.]
noun **1** the act of winking. **2** a very short time; an instant [I'll be there in a *wink*.]
—**wink at** to pretend not to see [The bad judge *winked at* the crimes of his friends.]
wink • *verb* **winked, winking** • *noun, plural* **winks**

winner (win′ər) *noun* **1** a person or thing that wins. **2** [*an informal use*] a person who seems very likely to win or be successful.
win·ner • *noun, plural* **winners**

winning (win′iŋ) *adjective* **1** being the one that wins [the *winning* team]. **2** attractive; charming [a *winning* smile].
noun **winnings** something that is won, especially money won at gambling.
win·ning • *adjective* • *noun, plural* **winnings**

winnow (win′ō) *verb* to blow away the chaff from grain [Farmers *winnow* barley after it is threshed.]
win·now • *verb* **winnowed, winnowing**

winter (win′tər) *noun* the coldest season of the year, coming after autumn.
verb to spend or cause to spend the winter [We *winter* in Florida.]

a	cat	ō	go	ʉ	fur	ə =	a *in* ago
ā	ape	ô	law, for	ch	chin		e *in* agent
ä	cot, car	oo	look	sh	she		i *in* pencil
e	ten	ōō	tool	th	thin		o *in* atom
ē	me	oi	oil	*th*	then		u *in* circus
i	fit	ou	out	zh	measure		
ī	ice	u	up	ŋ	ring		

win·ter • ***noun,*** *plural* **winters**
• ***verb*** **wintered, wintering**

wintertime (win′tər tīm) ***noun*** the season of winter.
win·ter·time • ***noun,*** *plural* **wintertimes**

wintry (win′trē) ***adjective*** like or having to do with winter; cold or snowy [a *wintry* day].
win·try • ***adjective*** **wintrier, wintriest**

wipe (wīp) ***verb*** **1** to clean or dry by rubbing [*Wipe* the dishes with this cloth. Please *wipe* your shoes on the mat.] **2** to remove by rubbing [*Wipe* the dust from this table.]
noun the act of wiping.
—wipe out **1** to remove; erase. **2** to kill or destroy.
wipe • ***verb*** **wiped, wiping** • ***noun,*** *plural* **wipes**

wire (wīr) ***noun*** **1** metal that has been pulled into a very long, thin thread [a coil of copper *wire;* hay bales tied with *wire;* barbed *wire*]. **2** a piece of this, used for a special purpose [Telephone *wires* run from the pole to our house.]
verb **1** to fasten with wire [*Wire* the vine to this stake.] **2** to provide something with wiring [These old log cabins are not *wired* for electricity.]
wire • ***noun,*** *plural for sense 2 only* **wires**
• ***verb*** **wired, wiring**

wiring (wīr′iŋ) ***noun*** a system of wires for carrying electric current.
wir·ing • ***noun***

wiry (wīr′ē) ***adjective*** **1** like wire; stiff [a dog with *wiry* hair]. **2** slender and strong [a *wiry* boy].
wir·y • ***adjective*** **wirier, wiriest**

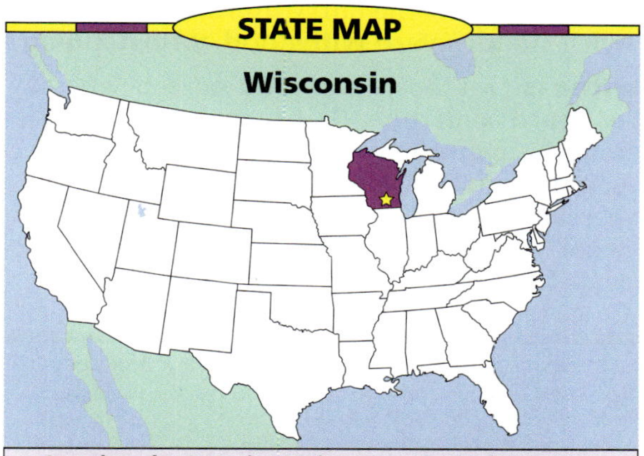

Statehood: 1848, the 30th state • **Capital:** Madison

Wisconsin (wis kän′sən) a State in the north central part of the U.S. Its capital is Madison. Abbreviated **WI, Wis.,** or **Wisc.**
Wis·con·sin

wisdom (wiz′dəm) ***noun*** **1** the quality of being wise; good judgment, which comes from knowledge and experience in life [She had the *wisdom* to save money for her later years.] **2** learning; knowledge [a book that is filled with the *wisdom* of the ages].
wis·dom • ***noun***

wisdom tooth ***noun*** the tooth that is farthest back on each side of each jaw. The wisdom teeth do not usually appear until a person is fully grown.
wisdom tooth • ***noun,*** *plural* **wisdom teeth**

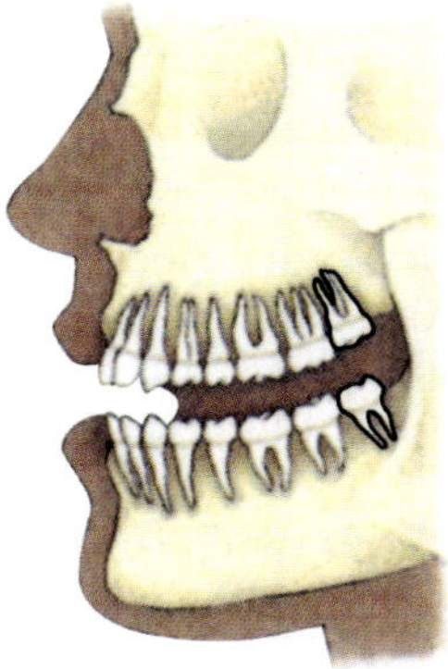
wisdom tooth

wise (wīz) ***adjective*** having or showing good judgment [a *wise* judge; a *wise* decision].
wise • ***adjective*** **wiser, wisest**

-wise *a suffix meaning:* **1** in a certain way, position, or direction [*Lengthwise* means along the length of an object.] **2** in the same way or direction as [Something moving *clockwise* goes in the same direction as the hands of a clock.]

wisecrack (wīz′krak) [*a slang word*] ***noun*** a joke or clever remark, often one that shows a lack of respect.
wise·crack • ***noun,*** *plural* **wisecracks**

wish (wish) ***verb*** **1** to have a longing for; want; desire [You may have whatever you *wish.*] **2** to have or express a desire for [I *wish* you were here. We *wished* her good luck.]
noun **1** a desire or longing for something [Her *wish* was to be a nurse.] **2** something wanted or hoped for [He got his *wish.*] **3** a request or order [We must obey her *wishes.*] **4 wishes** a desire for another to have health and happiness [I send you my best *wishes.*]
wish • ***verb*** **wished, wishing** • ***noun,*** *plural* **wishes**

wishbone (wish′bōn) ***noun*** the bone in front of the breastbone of most birds. It has the shape of the letter Y.
wish·bone • ***noun,*** *plural* **wishbones**

wishful (wish′fəl) ***adjective*** having or showing a wish; longing or hopeful [a *wishful* look].
wish·ful • ***adjective***

wisp (wisp) ***noun*** **1** a small bunch or tuft [a *wisp* of hair]. **2** a thin, hazy bit or puff [a *wisp* of smoke].
wisp • ***noun, plural*** **wisps**

wisteria (wis tir′ē ə) ***noun*** a shrub that grows as a vine with groups of blue, white, or purple flowers.
wis·te·ri·a • ***noun***

wistful (wist′fəl) ***adjective*** showing a wish or longing [The memory of her past vacation brought a *wistful* smile to her face.]
wist·ful • ***adjective***

wit (wit) ***noun*** **1** the ability to say clever things in a sharp, amusing way. **2 wits** the power to think or reason [The snake frightened him out of his *wits*.]
wit • ***noun, plural for sense 2 only*** **wits**

witch (wich) ***noun*** a person who is thought to have magic power with the help of the devil.
witch • ***noun, plural*** **witches**

witchcraft (wich′kraft) ***noun*** the magic power of a witch.
witch·craft • ***noun***

with (wi*th* *or* with) ***preposition*** **1** in the company of [Come *with* me.] **2** in the care of [Leave the baby *with* Aunt Jane.] **3** as part of; into [Mix blue *with* yellow to get green.] **4** as a member of [She sings *with* the choir.] **5** having the same opinions or beliefs as; on the side of [I'm *with* you.] **6** against [Don't argue *with* them.] **7** in regard to [Deal *with* that problem by yourself.] **8** in the opinion of [It's all right *with* me.] **9** as a result of [He was pale *with* fear.] **10** by means of [Paint *with* a large brush.] **11** by [a pail filled *with* sand]. **12** having received [*With* their help we finished on time.] **13** having or showing [She has a dress *with* red buttons. He greeted her *with* a big smile.] **14** in spite of [*With* all his faults, I still love him.] **15** at the same time as [*With* the coming of spring, the birds returned.] **16** to or onto [Join this end of the pipe *with* that one.] **17** as well as [She can run *with* the best of them.] **18** from [I parted *with* him in July.] **19** after [*With* that remark, I left.]

withdraw (wi*th* drô′ *or* with drô′) ***verb*** **1** to take back; pull out; remove [He *withdrew* his hand from his pocket.] **2** to move back; go away; retreat [The troops *withdrew* from the city.]
with·draw • ***verb*** **withdrew, withdrawn, withdrawing**

withdrawn (wi*th* drôn′ *or* with drôn′) ***verb*** *past participle of* **withdraw**.
adjective very shy or thinking quietly.
with·drawn • ***verb*** • ***adjective***

withdrew (wi*th* drōō′ *or* with drōō′) ***verb*** *past tense of* **withdraw**.
with·drew • ***verb***

wither (wi*th*′ər) ***verb*** to dry up or cause to dry up; shrivel [The hot sun *withered* the grass.]
with·er • ***verb*** **withered, withering**

withheld (with held′) ***verb*** *past tense and past participle of* **withhold**.
with·held • ***verb***

withhold (with hōld′) ***verb*** **1** to keep from giving or granting; refuse [She *withheld* her approval of the plan.] **2** to hold back; keep back; check [He *withheld* his anger.]
with·hold • ***verb*** **withheld, withholding**

within (wi*th* in′ *or* with in′) ***preposition*** **1** in the inner part of; inside [Stay *within* the house.] **2** not more than; not beyond [They live *within* a mile of us.] **3** inside the limits of [Stay *within* the law.]
adverb in or to the inside [It is cold outside but warm *within*.]
with·in • ***preposition*** • ***adverb***

without (wi*th* out′ *or* with out′) ***preposition*** **1** free from; not having [a person *without* a worry; a cup *without* a saucer]. **2** in a way that avoids [We pass by each other *without* speaking.]
with·out • ***preposition***

withstand (with stand′) ***verb*** to stand strongly against; resist or survive [These trees can *withstand* cold winters.] —Look for the WORD CHOICES box at the entry **oppose**.
with·stand • ***verb*** **withstood, withstanding**

witness (wit′nəs) ***noun*** **1** a person who saw or heard something that happened [A *witness* told the police how the fire started.] **2** a person who gives evidence in a court of law. **3** a person who watches a contract, will, or other legal paper being signed and then, as proof that this was done, signs it as well.

a	cat	ō	go	ʉ	fur	ə =	a *in* ago
ā	ape	ô	law, for	ch	chin		e *in* agent
ä	cot, car	oo	look	sh	she		i *in* pencil
e	ten	ōō	tool	th	thin		o *in* atom
ē	me	oi	oil	*th*	then		u *in* circus
i	fit	ou	out	zh	measure		
ī	ice	u	up	ŋ	ring		

verb **1** to be present at; see [He *witnessed* the accident on the highway.] **2** to act as a witness of a contract, will, or other legal paper.
wit·ness • *noun, plural* **witnesses**
• *verb* **witnessed, witnessing**

witty (wit′ē) *adjective* showing wit; clever in an amusing way [a *witty* person; a *witty* remark].
wit·ty • *adjective* **wittier, wittiest**

wives (wīvz) *noun plural of* **wife**.

wizard (wiz′ərd) *noun* **1** a magician or sorcerer. **2** [*an informal use*] a person who is very clever or gifted at a particular activity [He is a *wizard* at math.]
wiz·ard • *noun, plural* **wizards**

wk. *abbreviation for* week.

wobble (wäb′əl) *verb* to move from side to side in an unsteady way [This chair *wobbles*.]
wob·ble • *verb* **wobbled, wobbling**

woke (wōk) *verb a past tense of* **wake**[1].

woken (wō′kən) *verb a past participle of* **wake**[1].
wo·ken • *verb*

wolf

wolf (woolf) *noun* a wild animal that looks like a dog. It kills other animals for food.
verb to eat in a greedy, quick way [He *wolfed* down his dinner and left the room.]
—cry wolf to give a false alarm.
wolf • *noun, plural* **wolves** • *verb* **wolfed, wolfing**

wolfhound (woolf′hound) *noun* a large dog of a breed that was once used for hunting wolves.
wolf·hound • *noun, plural* **wolfhounds**

wolverine (wool vər ēn′) *noun* an animal that has a thick body, thick, dark fur, and a bushy tail. It kills other animals for food. Wolverines are found in northern regions.
wol·ver·ine • *noun, plural* **wolverines**

wolverine

wolves (woolvz) *noun plural of* **wolf**.

woman (woom′ən) *noun* **1** an adult female human being. **2** women as a group.
wom·an • *noun, plural for sense 1 only* **women**

WORD HISTORY

woman

Our word **woman** comes from an old English word that combines the words for "female" and "human being." The part of the old word that looks like today's *man* really means "human being."

womanhood (woom′ən hood) *noun* **1** the time or condition of being a woman. **2** the characteristics of a woman. **3** women as a group.
wom·an·hood • *noun*

womankind (woom′ən kīnd) *noun* all women; women in general.
wom·an·kind • *noun*

womanly (woom′ən lē) *adjective* like or fit for a woman [a *womanly* figure].
wom·an·ly • *adjective*

womb (wōōm) *noun* a hollow organ of female mammals in which the young grow before birth; uterus.
womb • *noun, plural* **wombs**

women (wim′ən) *noun plural of* **woman**.
wom·en • *noun*

won (wun) *verb past tense and past participle of* **win**.
- The words **won** and **one** sound alike.
  Our school *won* the State Championship.
  You still owe *one* more penny.

W

wonder (wun′dər) ***noun*** **1** something so unusual that it causes surprise or amazement; marvel [The Grand Canyon is one of the *wonders* of nature.] **2** the feeling caused by something strange and remarkable; awe [We gazed in *wonder* at the shower of meteors.]
verb **1** to feel wonder or surprise; to marvel [I *wonder* that you were able to climb that mountain.] **2** to have doubt and curiosity about; want to know [I *wonder* why they came.]
won·der • ***noun,*** *plural for sense 1 only* **wonders** • ***verb*** **wondered, wondering**

WORD CHOICES

Synonyms of **wonder**

The words **wonder, amazement,** and **awe** share the meaning "the feeling caused by something strange and remarkable."

staring in *wonder* at the comet

children watching the dancing bears with *amazement*

our *awe* in the presence of the great singer

wonderful (wun′dər fəl) ***adjective*** **1** capable of causing wonder; marvelous; amazing [the *wonderful* world of magic]. **2** [*an informal use*] very good; excellent [We saw a *wonderful* movie on TV.]
won·der·ful • ***adjective***

won't (wōnt) will not.

woo (wo͞o) ***verb*** to try to get the love of in order to marry; to court [The prince was *wooing* a young lady of noble birth.]
woo • ***verb*** **wooed, wooing**

wood (wo͝od) ***noun*** **1** the hard material beneath the bark of trees and shrubs. **2** *usually* **woods** a thick growth of trees; forest or grove.
wood • ***noun,*** *plural for sense 2 only* **woods**
• The words **wood** and **would** sound alike.
He carved a duck from a block of *wood*.
Would you go to the movies with me?

woodchuck (wo͝od′chuk) ***noun*** a North American animal that has a thick body and coarse, brown fur; groundhog. It burrows in the ground and sleeps all winter.
wood·chuck • ***noun,*** *plural* **woodchucks**

wooded (wo͝od′əd) ***adjective*** covered with trees or woods.
wood·ed • ***adjective***

wooden (wo͝od′ən) ***adjective*** **1** made of wood. **2** stiff, clumsy, or without life [He had a *wooden* expression on his face.]
wood·en • ***adjective***

woodland (wo͝od′land *or* wo͝od′lənd) ***noun*** land covered with trees; forest.
wood·land • ***noun,*** *plural* **woodlands**

woodpecker (wo͝od′pek ər) ***noun*** a bird that has a long, strong, pointed bill. The woodpecker drills holes into the bark of trees to get insects.
wood·peck·er • ***noun,*** *plural* **woodpeckers**

woodpecker

woodshed (wo͝od′shed) ***noun*** a shed for storing firewood.
wood·shed • ***noun,*** *plural* **woodsheds**

woodsman (wo͝odz′mən) ***noun*** a person who lives or works in the woods.
woods·man • ***noun,*** *plural* **woodsmen**

woodwind instrument (wo͝od′wind) ***noun*** a musical instrument that was once made of wood but is now often made of metal. It has a mouthpiece into which the player blows to produce the tones. The clarinet, flute, oboe, and bassoon are woodwind instruments.
wood·wind instrument • ***noun,*** *plural* **woodwind instruments**

woodwork (wo͝od′wurk) ***noun*** things that are made of wood, especially the moldings, doors, stairs, and other parts inside a house.
wood·work • ***noun***

woody (wo͝od′ē) ***adjective*** **1** covered with trees; wooded [a *woody* hillside]. **2** made up of wood [the *woody* stem of a shrub].
wood·y • ***adjective*** **woodier, woodiest**

woof (wo͝of *or* wo͞of) ***noun*** a harsh barking sound that a dog makes.
verb to make such a sound.

a	cat	ō	go	ʉ	fur	ə = a *in* ago	
ā	ape	ô	law, for	ch	chin	e *in* agent	
ä	cot, car	o͝o	look	sh	she	i *in* pencil	
e	ten	o͞o	tool	th	thin	o *in* atom	
ē	me	oi	oil	*th*	then	u *in* circus	
i	fit	ou	out	zh	measure		
ī	ice	u	up	ŋ	ring		

woof • *noun, plural* **woofs** • *verb* **woofed, woofing**

wool (wool) *noun* **1** the soft, curly hair of sheep, or the hair of some other animals, such as the goat or llama. **2** yarn, cloth, or clothing made of wool.

woolen (wool′ən) *adjective* made of wool.
wool·en • *adjective*

woolly (wool′ē) *adjective* **1** of, like, or covered with wool. **2** crude, rough, and not civilized [the wild and *woolly* West].
noun **woollies** long underwear made of wool.
wool·ly • *adjective* **woollier, woolliest** • *noun, plural* **woollies**

word (wurd) *noun* **1** a spoken sound or group of sounds that has meaning and is used as a single unit of speech. **2** a letter or a group of letters that stand for a spoken word. **3** a brief statement; a remark [a *word* of advice]. **4** news; information [Send *word* of your progress.] **5** a promise [Give me your *word*.] **6** a signal or order [We got the *word* to go ahead.]
verb to put into words [How shall I *word* this request?]
—have a word with to have a short talk with [May I *have a word with* you?] **—word for word** in exactly the same words.
word • *noun, plural for senses 1, 2, and 3 only* **words** • *verb* **worded, wording**

wording (wurd′iŋ) *noun* the way something is put into words; choice and arrangement of words.
word·ing • *noun*

word of mouth *noun* speech or conversation between persons, not writing [News of her arrival spread by *word of mouth*.]

word processing *noun* a system for preparing, editing, storing, and copying material such as letters and records for a business. This work is usually done on a computer.

Wordsworth (wurdz′wərth), **William** (wil′ yəm) 1770-1850; English poet.
Words·worth, Wil·liam

wordy (wur′dē) *adjective* having or using too many words [a *wordy* statement; a *wordy* letter].
word·y • *adjective* **wordier, wordiest**

wore (wôr) *verb past tense of* **wear**.

work (wurk) *noun* **1** the use of energy or skill in doing or making something; labor [Chopping wood is hard *work*.] **2** something that a person does to earn a living; occupation, trade, or profession [His *work* is teaching.] **3** something to be done; a task [She had to bring some *work* home from the office.] **4** an act or deed [good *works*]. **5 works** [*used with a singular verb*] a place where work is done; factory; plant [The steel *works* is shut down.]
verb **1** to use effort or energy to do or make something; to labor or toil [She *works* hard to support her family.] **2** to have a job for pay; be employed [He *works* in an office.] **3** to cause to work [He *works* himself too hard.] **4** to perform as it should; operate [My watch doesn't *work*.] **5** to cause to operate; manage [Can you *work* this computer?] **6** to bring about; to cause [Her plan *worked* wonders.] **7** to make or shape [*Work* the clay into a ball.]
—the works 1 the working parts of a clock, watch, or other piece of machinery. **2** [*an informal use*] everything that can be included [I want mustard, relish, onions, ketchup — *the works!*] **—work out 1** to develop or come to some end [We *worked out* a plan to leave school early; however, it didn't *work out* too well.] **2** to have a workout [I *work out* every morning.] **3** to solve [She *worked out* the math problem.]
work • *noun, plural for senses 4 and 5 only* **works** • *verb* **worked, working**

WORD CHOICES

Synonyms of work

The words **work, labor,** and **toil** share the meaning "the effort used to do or make something."

> the *work* involved in training a horse
> a hard job calling for hard *labor*
> years of *toil* in a factory

workable (wurk′ə bəl) *adjective* capable of being done [a *workable* plan].
work·a·ble • *adjective*

workbench (wurk′bench) *noun* a table at which work is done by a carpenter or technician.
work·bench • *noun, plural* **workbenches**

workbook (wurk′book) *noun* a book that has questions and exercises to be worked out by students.
work·book • *noun, plural* **workbooks**

workday (wurk′dā) *noun* **1** a day on which work is done. A workday is usually a weekday.

W

2 the part of a day during which work is done [a 7-hour *workday*].
work·day • *noun, plural* **workdays**

worker (wʉrk′ər) *noun* **1** person who works for a living. **2** any of the ants, bees, termites, and other insects that do the work for the colony.
work·er • *noun, plural* **workers**

workman (wʉrk′mən) *noun* a person who works with the hands; laborer.
work·man • *noun, plural* **workmen**

workmanship (wʉrk′mən ship) *noun* skill as a workman or the quality of work shown.
work·man·ship • *noun*

workout (wʉrk′out) *noun* exercise or practice to develop one's body or improve one's skill in a sport or other activity.
work·out • *noun, plural* **workouts**

world (wʉrld) *noun* **1** the earth [a cruise around the *world*]. **2** the universe. **3** any planet or place thought of as like the earth [Are there other *worlds* in space?] **4** all people [He thinks the *world* is against him.] **5** some part of the world [the Old *World*]. **6** a field of activity [the business *world*]. **7** some special group of things [the animal *world*]. **8** *often* **worlds** a large amount; a great deal [Your visit did me a *world* of good.]
world • *noun, plural for all senses except 1, 2, and 4* **worlds**

world-class (wʉrld′klas′) *adjective* of the highest class; superior [a *world-class* hotel].

worldly (wʉrld′lē) *adjective* **1** of this world; not heavenly or spiritual [our *worldly* cares]. **2** wise in the ways of the world; not simple, natural, or innocent [a *worldly* old gentleman].
world·ly • *adjective*

World War I a war from 1914 to 1918, between Great Britain, France, Russia, the U.S., and their allies on one side and Germany and its allies on the other.

World War II a war from 1939 to 1945, between Great Britain, France, the U.S.S.R., the U.S., and their allies on one side and Germany, Japan, and their allies on the other.

worldwide (wʉrld′wīd′) *adjective* throughout the world [a *worldwide* reputation for good food].
world·wide • *adjective*

World Wide Web the part of the Internet that lets a person see pictures and hear sounds as well as read words.

worm (wʉrm) *noun* a small, creeping animal that has a soft, slender body and no legs. Worms have no backbone.
verb to move like a worm, in a winding or creeping way [The hunter *wormed* his way through the thick grass.]
worm • *noun, plural* **worms**
• *verb* **wormed, worming**

wormy (wʉr′mē) *adjective* having a worm or worms; eaten into by worms [*wormy* apples].
worm·y • *adjective* **wormier, wormiest**

worn (wôrn) *verb past participle of* **wear**.
● The words **worn** and **warn** sound alike.
The soles of my shoes are *worn* out.
The signs *warn* us about the detour.

worn-out (wôrn′out′) *adjective* **1** used until no longer useful; not in good condition anymore [a *worn-out* tire]. **2** very tired; exhausted [*worn-out* football players] —Look for the WORD CHOICES box at the entry **tired**.

worry (wʉr′ē) *verb* to feel or make uneasy or anxious [Don't *worry;* she will come. Her absence *worried* him.]
noun **1** a troubled feeling; anxiety; care [She was sick with *worry*.] **2** a cause of this [He has many financial *worries*.]
wor·ry • *verb* **worried, worrying, worries**
• *noun, plural for sense 2 only* **worries**

worse (wʉrs) *adjective* **1** *comparative of* **bad** and **ill**. **2** more evil, harmful, bad, or unpleasant; less good [He committed an even *worse* crime.] **3** of poorer quality or condition [cheaper but *worse* equipment]. **4** in poorer health; more ill [The patient is *worse* today.]
adverb **1** *comparative of* **badly** and **ill**. **2** in a worse way [He acted *worse* than ever.]
noun a person or thing that is worse [I have *worse* to tell you.]

worship (wʉr′ship) *noun* **1** very great love or admiration [our *worship* of heroes]. **2** the act of showing honor and respect for God or a god [The family attends *worship* every Sunday.]
verb **1** to show great love and respect for in a religious way [We *worship* God.] **2** to have very great love or admiration for [They *worship* their parents.] **3** to take part in a religious service [Where do you *worship?*]

a cat	ō go	ʉ fur	ə = a *in* ago
ā ape	ô law, for	ch chin	e *in* agent
ä cot, car	oo look	sh she	i *in* pencil
e ten	ōō tool	th thin	o *in* atom
ē me	oi oil	*th* then	u *in* circus
i fit	ou out	zh measure	
ī ice	u up	ŋ ring	

wor·ship • *noun* • *verb* **worshiped** or **worshipped, worshiping** or **worshipping**

worst (wurst) *adjective* **1** *superlative of* **bad** and **ill**. **2** most evil, harmful, bad, or unpleasant; least good [the *worst* cold I've ever had.]
adverb **1** *superlative of* **badly** and **ill**. **2** in the worst way; to the worst degree [Of the three, he played *worst*.]
noun a person or thing that is worst [The *worst* of it is that she never told me.]
—if worst comes to worst if the worst possible thing happens. **—in the worst way** [*a slang use*] very much [He wants to buy a new bicycle *in the worst way*.]

worth (wurth) *noun* **1** the quality of a thing that makes it have value; merit [I know his *worth* as a friend.] **2** the value of a thing in money or in other goods [What is this chair's *worth* to you?] **3** the amount to be had for a certain sum of money [Get me a quarter's *worth* of candy, please.]
adjective **1** equal in value to [This magazine is not *worth* $10.] **2** deserving or worthy of [a movie *worth* seeing]. **3** having wealth amounting to [She's *worth* a million dollars.]

worthless (wurth′ləs) *adjective* having no worth, use, or value [That chair is a *worthless* piece of furniture.]
worth·less • *adjective*

worthwhile (wurth′hwīl′ *or* wurth′wīl′) *adjective* worth the time or effort needed for it [a *worthwhile* activity; a *worthwhile* book].
worth·while • *adjective*

worthy (wur′*thē*) *adjective* **1** having worth or merit [a *worthy* cause]. **2** good enough for; deserving [He's not *worthy* of her love.]
wor·thy • *adjective* **worthier, worthiest**

would (wood) *verb* (*helping verb*) **I.** *Past tense of* **will**[2] [They thought they *would* enjoy the circus, but they didn't like it.] **II.** *Would* as a helping verb is used: **1** to talk about something that depends on something else [I *would* have helped if you had asked me.] **2** to ask something in a polite way [*Would* you please leave?] The word "to" is not used between *would* and the verb that follows it.
would • *verb he/she/it* **would**
• The words **would** and **wood** sound alike.
Would you go to the movies with me?
He carved a duck from a block of *wood*.

wouldn't (wood′nt) would not.
would·n't

wound[1] (wōōnd) *noun* an injury in which some part of the body is cut, torn, or broken.
verb **1** to give a wound to; injure [The knight *wounded* his enemy.] **2** to hurt the feelings of [Your cruel words *wounded* me.]
wound • *noun, plural* **wounds** • *verb* **wounded, wounding**

wound[2] (wound) *verb past tense and past participle of* **wind**[1].

wove (wōv) *verb a past tense and a past participle of* **weave**.

woven (wō′vən) *verb a past participle of* **weave**.
wo·ven • *verb*

wow (wou) *interjection* a word that expresses surprise, pain, delight, or other strong emotion.

wrangle (raŋ′gəl) *verb* to argue in an angry, noisy way [They were talking but soon turned to *wrangling* about the game.] —Look for the WORD CHOICES box at the entry **quarrel**.
wran·gle • *verb* **wrangled, wrangling**

wrap (rap) *verb* **1** to wind or fold around something [She *wrapped* a scarf around her head.] **2** to cover in this way [They *wrapped* the baby in a blanket.] **3** to cover with paper or other material [He *wrapped* the present.]
noun an outer covering or an outer garment [She placed her *wrap* in the closet.]
wrap • *verb* **wrapped, wrapping** • *noun, plural* **wraps**
• The words **wrap** and **rap** sound alike.
I will *wrap* the gift with bright paper.
She heard a soft *rap* at the door.

wrapper (rap′ər) *noun* **1** a person or thing that wraps. **2** a covering or cover [Mail the newspaper in a paper *wrapper*.]
wrap·per • *noun, plural* **wrappers**

wrapping (rap′iŋ) *noun often* **wrappings** the paper or other material in which something is wrapped.
wrap·ping • *noun, plural* **wrappings**

wrath (rath) *noun* great anger; rage; fury.

wreak (rēk) *verb* **1** to let out in words or acts [He *wreaked* his fury on me.] **2** to put into effect; to cause.
wreak • *verb* **wreaked, wreaking**
• The words **wreak** and **reek** sound alike.
Tornadoes *wreak* destruction.
The dump's *reek* made me gag.

W

wreath

wreath (rēth) *noun* a ring of flowers, leaves, or branches that are twisted together.
wreath • *noun, plural* **wreaths** (rē*th*z *or* rēths)

wreathe (rē*th*) *verb* to decorate with or as if with a wreath [Her face was *wreathed* in smiles.]
wreathe • *verb* **wreathed, wreathing**

wreck (rek) *verb* **1** to destroy or damage badly [He *wrecked* the car in an accident.] **2** to tear down [The workmen *wrecked* the house.]
noun **1** the act of destroying or ruining; destruction [the *wreck* of all our hopes]. **2** the remains of something that has been destroyed or badly damaged [an old *wreck* aground on the reef].
wreck • *verb* **wrecked, wrecking** • *noun, plural for sense 2 only* **wrecks**

wreckage (rek′ij) *noun* **1** the act of wrecking. **2** the remains of something that has been wrecked [Call the highway patrol to remove the *wreckage* from the road.]
wreck·age • *noun*

wren (ren) *noun* a small songbird that has a long bill and a short tail that tilts up.
wren • *noun, plural* **wrens**

wrench (rench) *noun* **1** a sudden, sharp twist or pull [With one *wrench*, he loosened the lid.] **2** a tool for holding and turning nuts, bolts, or pieces of pipe.
verb **1** to twist or pull with sudden force [She *wrenched* the keys from my hand.] **2** to injure by twisting or straining [He *wrenched* his knee when he fell.]
wrench • *noun, plural* **wrenches** • *verb* **wrenched, wrenching**

wrest (rest) *verb* **1** to pull away with a sharp twist [He *wrested* the ball from the quarterback.] **2** to take by force [Rebels *wrested* control of the government.]
wrest • *verb* **wrested, wresting**
• The words **wrest** and **rest** sound alike.
Jane tried to *wrest* the toy from him.
He took a *rest* after working outdoors.
She gave me the *rest* of the cake.

wrestle (res′əl) *verb* **1** to struggle with, trying to throw or force to the ground without striking blows with the fists. **2** to struggle hard; contend [He *wrestled* with the math problem.]
wres·tle • *verb* **wrestled, wrestling**

WORD HISTORY

wrestle

The word **wrestle** comes from a thousand-year-old English word that means "to twist with great force." When two people **wrestle**, they twist and turn, trying to force each other to the ground.

wrestler (res′lər) *noun* a person who practices the sport of wrestling.
wres·tler • *noun, plural* **wrestlers**

wrestling (res′liŋ) *noun* a sport in which two people wrestle with each other.
wres·tling • *noun*

wretched (rech′əd) *adjective* **1** very unhappy or troubled; miserable —Look for the WORD CHOICES box at the entry **sad**. **2** bad in quality; very poor [a *wretched* meal].
wretch·ed • *adjective*

wriggle (rig′əl) *verb* to twist and turn from side to side; squirm [The boy *wriggled* in his seat.]
wrig·gle • *verb* **wriggled, wriggling**

Wright (rīt), **Orville** (ôr′vəl) 1871-1948; U.S. inventor who, with his brother **Wilbur Wright** (wil′bər) (1867-1912), built the first airplane to have a successful flight.
Wright, Or·ville

wring (riŋ) *verb* **1** to squeeze and twist with force [He *wrung* out the wet clothes.] **2** to force out by squeezing and twisting [*Wring* the water from the wet towel and put it in the dryer.] **3** to get by force, threats, or other such

a	cat	ō	go	ʉ	fur	ə = a *in* ago	
ā	ape	ô	law, for	ch	chin	e *in* agent	
ä	cot, car	oo	look	sh	she	i *in* pencil	
e	ten	ōō	tool	th	thin	o *in* atom	
ē	me	oi	oil	*th*	then	u *in* circus	
i	fit	ou	out	zh	measure		
ī	ice	u	up	ŋ	ring		

means [The police officer *wrung* a confession from the thief.]
wring • *verb* **wrung, wringing**
● The words **wring** and **ring** sound alike.
Wring out the wet dish towel.
I thought I heard the telephone *ring*.
She wears a *ring* on her finger.

wrinkle (riŋ′kəl) ***noun*** a small or uneven crease or fold [Her dress was full of *wrinkles*. He has no *wrinkles* on his face.]
verb **1** to make wrinkles in [Too many worries had *wrinkled* his face.] **2** to form wrinkles [This fabric *wrinkles* easily.]
win·kle • *noun, plural* **wrinkles**
• *verb* **wrinkled, wrinkling**

wrist (rist) ***noun*** the joint or part of the arm that is between the hand and forearm.
wrist • *noun, plural* **wrists**

wristwatch (rist′wäch *or* rist′wôch) ***noun*** a watch that is worn on a strap or band that fits around the wrist.
wrist·watch • *noun, plural* **wristwatches**

write (rīt) ***verb*** **1** to form letters or words on a surface with something such as a pen or pencil [*Write* on the paper.] **2** to form the words or letters of [*Write* your address here.] **3** to send a message in writing; send a letter to [*Write* me every week. He *wrote* that he was ill.] **4** to fill in or cover with writing [She *wrote* a check.] **5** to be the author or composer of [Laura Ingalls Wilder *wrote* children's books. Mozart *wrote* symphonies.]
write • *verb* **wrote, written, writing**
● The words **write, right,** and **rite** sound alike.
Write to me when you get there.
Turn *right* at the stop sign.
The people had a different funeral *rite*.

writer (rīt′ər) ***noun*** a person who writes, especially one whose work is writing books, articles, or other materials; author.
writ·er • *noun, plural* **writers**

writhe (rīth) ***verb*** to twist and turn in pain or other similar feeling.
writhe • *verb* **writhed, writhing**

writing (rīt′iŋ) ***noun*** **1** the act of one who writes. **2** something, such as a letter, article, or book, that is written [the *writings* of Thomas Jefferson]. **3** written form [Please put your request in *writing*.] **4** handwriting [Can you read her *writing*?]
writ·ing • *noun, plural for sense 2 only* **writings**

written (rit′n) ***verb*** *past participle of* **write**.
writ·ten • *verb*

wrong (rôŋ) ***adjective*** **1** not the one that is true, correct, or wanted [the *wrong* answer]. **2** not right, just, or good; unlawful or wicked [It is *wrong* to steal.] **3** not proper or suitable [Purple is the *wrong* color for her.] **4** in error; mistaken [He's not *wrong*.] **5** not working properly [What's *wrong* with the TV?]
noun something that is wrong, especially an act that is not right or fair [Does she know right from *wrong*?]
adverb in a wrong way; incorrectly [You did it *wrong*.]
verb to treat in a way that is not right or fair [They *wronged* her by telling lies.]
—go wrong **1** to turn out badly. **2** to change from being good to being bad.
wrong • *adjective* • *noun, plural* **wrongs**
• *adverb* • *verb* **wronged, wronging**

wrongdoing (rôŋ′do͞o iŋ) ***noun*** any act or behavior that is wrong, wicked, or unlawful.
wrong·do·ing • *noun*

wrote (rōt) ***verb*** *past tense of* **write**.
● The words **wrote** and **rote** sound alike.
I *wrote* her a long letter.
Learn the multiplication tables by *rote*.

wrung (ruŋ) ***verb*** *past tense and past participle of* **wring**.
● The words **wrung** and **rung** sound alike.
The towel was *wrung* dry.
One ladder *rung* was broken.
The doorbell was *rung* over and over.

wt. *abbreviation for* weight.

WV or **W.Va.** *abbreviation for* West Virginia.

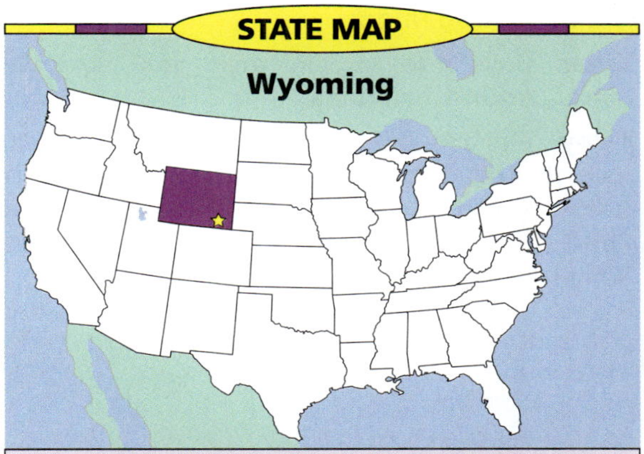

Statehood: 1890, the 44th state • **Capital:** Cheyenne

Wyoming (wī ō′miŋ) a State in the northwestern part of the U.S. Its capital is Cheyenne. Abbreviated **WY** *or* **Wyo.**
Wy·o·ming

X x

Xx Xx Xx Xx

The letter **x** *can stand for many sounds, and these sounds can all be made by different letter combinations.* **X** *can stand for the sounds of* **ks,** *as in the word* **six,** *the sounds of* **gz,** *as in the word* **examine,** *and even the sound of* **z,** *as in the word* **xylophone.**

x or **X** (eks) ***noun*** the twenty-fourth letter of the English alphabet.
x or **X** • ***noun,*** *plural* **x's** or **X's**

X (eks) ***noun*** **1** the Roman numeral for ten. **2** a mark shaped like an X, used to show a place on something such as a map or to stand for a kiss in letters. **3** a person or thing that is not known.
X • ***noun,*** *plural* **X's**

Xerox (zir′äks) ***trademark*** a machine that makes photographic copies of printed or written material.
Xe·rox • ***trademark***

Xmas (kris′məs *or* eks′məs) [*an informal word*] ***noun*** Christmas.

X-ray (eks′rā) ***noun*** **1** an invisible ray that can go through solid substances. X-rays are used to study the bones and organs inside the body and to treat certain diseases. **2** a photograph made by means of X-rays. ***verb*** to examine, treat, or photograph with X-rays.
X-ray • ***noun,*** *plural* **X-rays** • ***verb*** **X-rayed, X-raying**

xylophone (zī′lə fōn) ***noun*** a musical instrument that is made up of a row of wooden bars of different sizes. These bars are struck with wooden hammers to produce sounds.
xy·lo·phone • ***noun,*** *plural* **xylophones**

WORD HISTORY

xylophone

The name of the **xylophone** comes from two Greek words that mean "wood" and "sound." A wooden bar is struck to make a sound.

a	cat	ō	go	ʉ	fur	ə =	a *in* ago
ā	ape	ô	law, for	ch	chin		e *in* agent
ä	cot, car	oo	look	sh	she		i *in* pencil
e	ten	ōō	tool	th	thin		o *in* atom
ē	me	oi	oil	*th*	then		u *in* circus
i	fit	ou	out	zh	measure		
ī	ice	u	up	ŋ	ring		

Y y

Yy Yy Yy Yy

The letter **y** *can stand for a consonant sound or a vowel sound. As a consonant, it stands for the sound you hear at the beginning of the words* **yellow** *and* **yo-yo.** *As a vowel,* **y** *can stand for several different sounds, as in the words* **my, baby,** *and* **lyrics.**

y or **Y** (wī) ***noun*** the twenty-fifth letter of the English alphabet.
y or **Y** • ***noun,*** *plural* **y's** or **Y's**

-y[1] *a suffix meaning* little or dear [A *dolly* is a little doll.]

-y[2] *a suffix meaning*: **1** having; full of or covered with [*Dirty* hands are covered with dirt.] **2** somewhat; a little [A *chilly* room is somewhat chilled.] **3** apt to [*Sticky* fingers are apt to stick to things.] **4** somewhat like [*Wavy* hair looks somewhat like waves.]

yacht (yät) ***noun*** a large boat or small ship for racing or taking pleasure cruises.
yacht • ***noun,*** *plural* **yachts**

yak (yak) ***noun*** an ox with long hair that is found wild or is raised in the mountains of central Asia.
yak • ***noun,*** *plural* **yaks**

yam (yam) ***noun*** **1** the root of a climbing plant that grows in tropical countries. It is used as food. **2** a kind of sweet potato: this name is used mainly in the southern U.S.
yam • ***noun,*** *plural* **yams**

yank (yaŋk) [*an informal word*] ***noun*** a sudden, strong pull; jerk.
verb to give a sudden, strong pull; to jerk [He *yanked* the rope to ring the bell.]
yank • ***noun,*** *plural* **yanks** • ***verb*** **yanked, yanking**

Yankee (yaŋ′kē) ***noun*** **1** a person born or living in the U.S. **2** a person born or living in one of the Northern States, especially in New England.
Yan·kee • ***noun,*** *plural* **Yankees**

yap (yap) ***noun*** a short, sharp bark like that of a small dog.
verb **1** to bark with yaps. **2** [*a slang use*] to talk in a noisy or stupid way.
yap • ***noun,*** *plural* **yaps** • ***verb*** **yapped, yapping**

yard[1] (yärd) ***noun*** **1** a unit of length that is equal to three feet, or 36 inches. One yard equals .9144 meter. **2** a long pole that is fastened across a mast to support a sail.
yard • ***noun,*** *plural* **yards**

yard[2] (yärd) ***noun*** **1** a piece of ground around or next to a house or other building [We have a tree in our front *yard.*] **2** an open area that is used for a special purpose or for some work or business [a *lumberyard;* a navy *yard*]. **3** a railroad center where trains are made up, stored, or repaired.
yard • ***noun,*** *plural* **yards**

yardstick (yärd′stik) ***noun*** a measuring stick that is one yard long.
yard·stick • ***noun,*** *plural* **yardsticks**

yarn (yärn) ***noun*** **1** fibers of wool, silk, nylon, cotton, or other material that are spun into

strands for use especially in knitting. **2** [*an informal use*] a long tale or story.
yarn • *noun, plural for sense 2 only* **yarns**

yawn (yôn *or* yän) *verb* to open the mouth wide and breathe in deeply in a way that is not controlled. This happens when a person is sleepy, tired, or bored.
noun the act of yawning.
yawn • *verb* **yawned, yawning** • *noun, plural* **yawns**

yd. *abbreviation for* yard.

yea (yā) *adverb* yes.
noun a vote of "yes."
yea • *adverb* • *noun, plural* **yeas**

yeah (ya *or* ye) [*an informal word*] *adverb* yes.

year (yir) *noun* **1** a period of 365 days (in leap year, 366 days) divided into 12 months [It took her two *years* to write the novel.] **2** the period from January through the next December [His salary is higher this *year*.] **3** the period of time taken by the earth to go completely around the sun, about 365 days and 6 hours. **4** a part of a year during which certain things take place [the school *year*].
year • *noun, plural* **years**

yearbook (yir′bo͝ok) *noun* a book that is published each year, with information about the year just ended.
year·book • *noun, plural* **yearbooks**

yearling (yir′liŋ) *noun* an animal that is one year old or one that is in its second year.
year·ling • *noun, plural* **yearlings**

yearly (yir′lē) *adjective* **1** happening or done once a year, or every year [They spent their *yearly* vacation in California.] **2** of, for, or during a single year [her *yearly* income].
adverb once a year; every year [We have returned *yearly* to the same place for our vacation.]
year·ly • *adjective* • *adverb*

yearn (yʉrn) *verb* to be filled with longing or desire [She *yearns* to travel.]
yearn • *verb* **yearned, yearning**

yeast (yēst) *noun* **1** a yellow substance in the form of froth or foam. It is made up of tiny fungi. It is used in baking to make dough rise. **2** this substance dried in flakes or tiny grains, or made up in small cakes.

yell (yel) *verb* to cry out loudly; to scream.
noun a loud shout; a scream.
yell • *verb* **yelled, yelling** • *noun, plural* **yells**

yellow (yel′ō) *adjective* having the color of ripe lemons, or of an egg yolk.
noun **1** a yellow color. **2** something that has this color, especially the yolk of an egg.
verb to make or become yellow or yellowish [The pages of the book *yellowed* with age.]
yel·low • *adjective* **yellower, yellowest** • *noun, plural for sense 2 only* **yellows** • *verb* **yellowed, yellowing**

yellow fever *noun* a tropical disease that causes fever and yellowing of the skin. Its virus is carried to man by certain mosquitoes.

yellowish (yel′ō ish) *adjective* somewhat yellow.
yel·low·ish • *adjective*

yellow jacket *noun* a wasp or hornet that has bright-yellow markings.
yellow jacket • *noun, plural* **yellow jackets**

yelp (yelp) *noun* a short, sharp cry, such as the one given by a dog in pain.
verb to give such a cry or cries.
yelp • *noun, plural* **yelps** • *verb* **yelped, yelping**

Yemen (yem′ən) a country in southern Arabia, on the Red Sea.
Yem·en

yen[1] (yen) *noun* the basic unit of money in Japan.
yen • *noun, plural* **yen**

yen[2] (yen) [*an informal word*] *noun* a deep longing or desire.

yes (yes) *adverb* it is so. *Yes* is the opposite of *no* and can mean "I will," "I can," "I agree," "I allow," or "it is."
noun **1** the act of saying "yes"; agreement or consent. **2** a vote in favor of something.
yes • *adverb* • *noun, plural* **yeses**

yesterday (yes′tər dā) *adverb* on the day before today [I talked to her *yesterday*.]
noun **1** the day before today [*Yesterday* was a busy day.] **2** some time in the past [fashions of *yesterday*].
yes·ter·day • *adverb* • *noun, plural for sense 1 only* **yesterdays**

yet (yet) *adverb* **1** up to now; so far [He has not gone *yet*.] **2** at the present time; now [We

a cat	ō go	ʉ fur	ə = a *in* ago
ā ape	ô law, for	ch chin	e *in* agent
ä cot, car	o͝o look	sh she	i *in* pencil
e ten	o͞o tool	th thin	o *in* atom
ē me	oi oil	*th* then	u *in* circus
i fit	ou out	zh measure	
ī ice	u up	ŋ ring	

can't leave just *yet*.] **3** even now; still [There's *yet* some hope.] **4** at some time to come [We'll get there *yet*.] **5** in addition; even [She had *yet* another reason to refuse.] **6** now, after a long time [Haven't you finished *yet?*] **7** but; nevertheless [He is comfortable, *yet* lonely.]
conjunction nevertheless; however [She seems happy, *yet* she is worried.]

yew (yo͞o) ***noun*** **1** an evergreen tree or shrub. **2** the wood of this tree.
yew • ***noun,*** *plural for sense 1 only* **yews**
● The words **yew, ewe,** and **you** sound alike.
A row of *yew* trees lines the driveway.
He made pets of the *ewe* and her lamb.
Where are *you* going?

Yiddish (yid′ish) ***noun*** a language spoken by many Jews in Europe and elsewhere. It developed from an old form of German but has many words taken from Hebrew and other languages. It is written with the Hebrew alphabet.
Yid·dish • ***noun***

yield (yēld) ***verb*** **1** to bring forth or bring about; produce; give [The orchard *yielded* a good crop of apples.] **2** to give up; surrender [They *yielded* to his demands. The army *yielded* the city to the enemy.] **3** to give way to pressure or force [The castle gate would not *yield*.]
noun the amount produced [The farmer hoped to increase his *yield* of apples.]
yield • ***verb*** **yielded, yielding** • ***noun,*** *plural* **yields**

yipe (yīp) ***interjection*** a word that is used to express sudden pain or fear.

yippee (yip′ē) ***interjection*** a word that is used to express delight or joy.
yip·pee • ***interjection***

YMCA *abbreviation for* Young Men's Christian Association.

YMHA *abbreviation for* Young Men's Hebrew Association.

yodel (yō′dəl) ***verb*** to sing so that the voice changes back and forth between its usual range and a much higher range.
noun the act or sound of yodeling.
yo·del • ***verb*** **yodeled** or **yodelled, yodeling** or **yodelling** • ***noun,*** *plural* **yodels**

yogurt (yō′gərt) ***noun*** a thick, soft food that is made from fermented milk.
yo·gurt • ***noun,*** *plural* **yogurts**

yoke

yoke (yōk) ***noun*** a wooden frame that fits around the necks of a pair of oxen or other work animals. The yoke joins them together.
verb **1** to put a yoke on [The farmer *yoked* the oxen.] **2** to harness an animal to something [The farmer *yoked* the oxen to a plow.]
yoke • ***noun,*** *plural* **yokes** • ***verb*** **yoked, yoking**
● The words **yoke** and **yolk** sound alike.
The oxen were fitted with a *yoke*.
Beat the egg white and *yolk* together.

yolk (yōk) ***noun*** the yellow part of an egg.
yolk • ***noun,*** *plural* **yolks**
● The words **yolk** and **yoke** sound alike.

WORD HISTORY

yolk

The source of **yolk** is a thousand-year-old English word that means "the yellow part." Our word **yellow** is related to this word.

Yom Kippur (yäm kip′ər) ***noun*** the holiest Jewish holiday and a day of fasting.
Yom Kip·pur • ***noun***

yonder (yän′dər) ***adjective*** at a distance but able to be seen [Go to *yonder* village.]
adverb at or in that place; over there [The castle lies *yonder* in the forest.]
yon·der • ***adjective*** • ***adverb***

you (yo͞o) ***pronoun*** **1** the person or persons that are being spoken to. *You* is used as the subject of a verb and also as the object of a verb or preposition. *You* is both singular and plural [*You* are a good friend. I saw *you* both. There's room for three of *you* in the car.] **2** a person; one [*You* seldom see a horse and buggy now.]
you • ***pronoun,*** *plural* **you**
● The words **you, ewe,** and **yew** sound alike.
Will *you* and I be going to the movies?

Y

The *ewe* strayed from the other sheep.
We planted maple and *yew* trees.

you'd (yo͞od) **1** you had. **2** you would.

you'll (yo͞ol) you will.
● The words **you'll** and **yule** sound alike.
You'll laugh when you see my costume.
We visit our relatives at the *yule* season.

young (yuŋ) ***adjective*** **1** being in an early part of life or growth; not old [a *young* actor; a *young* tree]. **2** of or like a young person; fresh; vigorous [She is *young* for her age.]
noun young offspring [The bear defended its *young*.]
young • ***adjective*** **younger, youngest**
• ***noun***

youngster (yuŋ′stər) ***noun*** a child or youth.
young·ster • ***noun, plural*** **youngsters**

your (yo͝or) ***adjective*** done by you or having to do with you [*your* work; *your* shoes].
● The words **your** and **you're** sound alike.
Your name is unusual.
You're not going anywhere.

you're (yo͝or *or* yo͞or) you are.
● The words **you're** and **your** sound alike.

yours (yo͝orz) ***pronoun*** the one or the ones that belong to you [I know that this book is *yours*. *Yours* costs more than ours.]

yourself (yo͝or self′) ***pronoun*** **1** your own self. This form of *you* is used when the person who does the action of the verb is the same as the person who receives the action [Did you cut *yourself*?] **2** your usual or true self [You are not *yourself* today.] This word is also used to give more force to what is being said [But you *yourself* told me it was true.]
your·self • ***pronoun, plural*** **yourselves**

yourselves (yo͝or selvz′) ***pronoun plural of*** **yourself**.
your·selves • ***pronoun***

youth (yo͞oth) ***noun*** **1** the time when a person is no longer a child but not yet an adult. **2** the quality of being young or fresh [The long vacation seemed to restore her *youth*.] **3** a young person, especially a boy or young man. **4** young people [a club for the *youth* of our city].
youth • ***noun, plural for sense 3 only*** **youths**

youthful (yo͞oth′fəl) ***adjective*** **1** not yet old; young [a *youthful* widow]. **2** having to do with, like, or fit for a young person [a *youthful* style]. **3** fresh; vigorous; active [still *youthful* at eighty].
youth·ful • ***adjective***

you've (yo͞ov) you have.

yo-yo (yō′yō) ***noun*** a toy that looks like a spool fastened to one end of a string. The yo-yo can be made to spin up and down on the string.
yo-yo • ***noun, plural*** **yo-yos**

yr. *abbreviation for* **1** year. **2** years.

YT or **Y.T.** *abbreviation for* Yukon (Territory).

yucca (yuk′ə) ***noun*** a tall plant that has long, stiff, pointed leaves. It bears a cluster of large, white flowers.
yuc·ca • ***noun, plural*** **yuccas**

yucca

yuck (yuk) [*a slang word*] ***interjection*** a word that is used to express strong dislike or disgust.

Yugoslavia (yo͞o′gō slä′vē ə) a former country in southeastern Europe.
Yu·go·sla·vi·a

Yukon (yo͞o′kän) a territory of northwestern Canada. Its full name is *Yukon Territory*. Abbreviated **YT** or **Y.T.**
Yu·kon

yule (yo͞ol) ***noun*** Christmas or Christmastime.
yule • ***noun, plural*** **yules**
● The words **yule** and **you'll** sound alike.
We visit our relatives at the *yule* season.
You'll laugh when you see my costume.

yuletide (yo͞ol′tīd) ***noun*** Christmastime.
yule·tide • ***noun, plural*** **yuletides**

yum (yum) [*an informal word*] ***interjection*** a word that is used to show pleasure or enjoyment or to show that something tastes good.

yummy (yum′ē) [*an informal word*] ***adjective*** very tasty; delicious [a *yummy* cake].
yum·my • ***adjective*** **yummier, yummiest**

YWCA *abbreviation for* Young Women's Christian Association.

YWHA *abbreviation for* Young Women's Hebrew Association.

a	cat	ō	go	ʉ	fur	ə =	a *in* ago
ā	ape	ô	law, for	ch	chin		e *in* agent
ä	cot, car	o͝o	look	sh	she		i *in* pencil
e	ten	o͞o	tool	th	thin		o *in* atom
ē	me	oi	oil	*th*	then		u *in* circus
i	fit	ou	out	zh	measure		
ī	ice	u	up	ŋ	ring		

Zz

Zz Zz Zz Zz

The last letter of the alphabet, **z** *is also the letter used least often in English. It can stand for two different sounds: the sound at the beginning of the words* **zero** *and* **zither,** *and the sound in the middle of the words* **seizure** *and* **azure.**

z or **Z** (zē) ***noun*** the twenty-sixth and last letter of the English alphabet.
z or **Z** • ***noun,*** *plural* **z's** or **Z's**

Zaire or **Zaïre** (zä ir′) *old name for* Democratic Republic of the Congo (see **Congo**).
Za·ire or **Za·ïre**

Zambia (zam′bē ə) a country in southern Africa.
Zam·bi·a

zap (zap) [*a slang word*] ***verb*** to move, strike, stun, defeat, or kill with sudden speed and force.
zap • ***verb*** **zapped, zapping**

zeal (zēl) ***noun*** a strong, eager feeling; great enthusiasm [their *zeal* in supporting the school team].

zebra

zebra (zē′brə) ***noun*** a wild animal of Africa that is related to the horse. It has dark stripes on a white or tan body.
ze·bra • ***noun,*** *plural* **zebras**

zebra mussel ***noun*** a kind of mussel that tends to gather in large numbers on surfaces. If too many of these mussels gather in one place, they can block water pipes.
zebra mussel • ***noun,*** *plural* **zebra mussels**

zebra mussel

zenith (zē′nith) ***noun*** **1** the point in the sky that is directly overhead. **2** the highest point; peak [the *zenith* of her career].
ze·nith • ***noun***

zero (zir′ō *or* zē′rō) ***noun*** **1** the number or symbol 0. **2** a point marked 0, from which something is measured in degrees [a temperature of ten below *zero*]. **3** nothing [All their efforts added up to *zero*.]
ze·ro • ***noun,*** *plural for senses 1 and 2 only* **zeros** or **zeroes**

zest (zest) ***noun*** exciting or interesting quality; relish [Danger adds *zest* to an acrobat's work.]

WORD HISTORY

zest

The word **zest** comes from a French word for "a piece of orange peel used to give flavor to a food." In English, **zest** came to be used in speaking of anything that might add flavor or excitement.

Zeus (zo͞os) the chief Greek god, ruling over all other gods. The Romans called this god *Jupiter*.

zigzag (zig′zag) *noun* **1** a series of short slanting lines, connected by sharp turns or angles. **2** a design or course that is like this [The lightning made a *zigzag* in the sky.]
verb to form or move in a zigzag [The bicycle *zigzagged* around the holes in the street.]
zig·zag • *noun, plural* **zigzags**
• *verb* **zigzagged, zigzagging**

zillion (zil′yən) [*an informal word*] *noun* a very large number that is not known [A *zillion* cars jammed the highways.]
zil·lion • *noun, plural* **zillions**

WORD HISTORY

zillion

This is a humorous or informal word that was made up to suggest a number so large that a person could hardly imagine it. It was based on the word *million*.

Zimbabwe (zim bä′bwā′) a country in southern Africa.
Zim·ba·bwe

zinc (ziŋk) *noun* a bluish-white metal that is a chemical element. Zinc does not rust easily and is used to coat iron and steel.

zinnia (zin′ē ə) *noun* a garden plant that has brightly colored flowers with many petals.
zin·ni·a • *noun, plural* **zinnias**

zinnia

zip (zip) *verb* **1** to make a short, sharp, hissing sound [A bullet *zipped* past.] **2** [*an informal use*] to move fast [We *zipped* through our work.] **3** to fasten with a zipper [*Zip* up your jacket.]
noun **1** [*an informal use*] force or energy. **2** [*a slang use*] nothing.
zip • *verb* **zipped, zipping** • *noun*

ZIP Code (zip) *trademark* a system of special code numbers given by the post office to each area and place in the U.S. They are used as part of the mailing address.

zipper (zip′ər) *noun* a device that is used to fasten and unfasten two edges of material. It consists of two rows of teeth on separate edges that are locked together and separated by a part that slides up and down.
zip·per • *noun, plural* **zippers**

zit (zit) [*a slang word*] *noun* a pimple, especially one on the face.
zit • *noun, plural* **zits**

zither

zither (zith′ər *or* zi*th*′ər) *noun* a musical instrument that is made up of a flat, hollow board with 30 to 40 strings stretched across it. It is played by plucking the strings.
zith·er • *noun, plural* **zithers**

zodiac (zō′dē ak′) *noun* an imaginary belt across the sky that contains the path that the sun seems to travel. It is divided into twelve parts, each of which is named after a different constellation.
zo·di·ac • *noun*

a	cat	ō	go	ʉ	fur	ə =	a *in* ago
ā	ape	ô	law, for	ch	chin		e *in* agent
ä	cot, car	o͝o	look	sh	she		i *in* pencil
e	ten	o͞o	tool	th	thin		o *in* atom
ē	me	oi	oil	*th*	then		u *in* circus
i	fit	ou	out	zh	measure		
ī	ice	u	up	ŋ	ring		

zone (zōn) ***noun*** **1** an area or region that is set apart in some special way [a "No Parking" *zone*]. **2** any of the five areas into which the earth's surface is divided by imaginary lines. They are named according to their general climate. There are two frigid zones, two temperate zones, and one torrid zone.
verb to mark off or divide into zones [This section of the city is *zoned* for industry.]
zone • ***noun, plural*** **zones** • ***verb*** **zoned, zoning**

zoo (zo͞o) ***noun*** a place where wild animals are kept for the public to see.
zoo • ***noun, plural*** **zoos**

zoo- *a prefix meaning* an animal or animals [*Zoology* is the study of animals.]

zoological (zō′ə läj′i kəl) ***adjective*** having to do with zoology or with animals.
zo·o·log·i·cal • ***adjective***

zoology (zō äl′ə jē) ***noun*** the science that studies animals and animal life.
zo·ol·o·gy • ***noun***

zoom (zo͞om) ***verb*** **1** to move with a loud, humming sound [The car *zoomed* past.] **2** to climb or rise rapidly [Prices *zoomed* last month.]
zoom • ***verb*** **zoomed, zooming**

zucchini

zucchini (zo͞o kē′nē) ***noun*** a long, narrow squash that has a green skin.
zuc·chi·ni • ***noun, plural*** **zucchini**

Acknowledgments

We wish to thank the following for special assistance on this project:

Robert P. Davis, *Associate Professor Emeritus, Developmental Biology, Case Western Reserve University*, for checking the accuracy of many plant and animal illustrations.

Joseph P. Frolkis, MD, Ph.D., for checking anatomical illustrations.

Eleanor Holt, *Director of Preparatory and Continuing Education, Cleveland Institute of Music*, for making arrangements for photographing musical instruments and supplying instruments and models.

Kurt Kaptur, *Kaptur Design*, for creating maps of the states.

We also thank Silver Burdett & Ginn, educational publisher, for permission to use the graded vocabulary lists of approximately 14,000 children's compositions, from *A Study of Students' Writing, Grades 1–8: Word Frequency Report and Misspelling Analysis* by Richard E. Hodges, © 1990 by Silver Burdett & Ginn.

Photo Credits

aqueduct — The Purcell Team/WORDS AND PICTURES; **astronaut** — National Aeronautics and Space Administration; **automobile** — © 1999 Comstock, Inc.; **backpack** — © 2005 PhotoSpin Inc.; **bison** — © 2004 Comstock Klips; **blastoff** — National Aeronautics and Space Administration; **bobsled** — Richard Dean/The Image Works, Inc.; **brim** — © 1999 PhotoDisc, Inc.; **brush** — © 1999 PhotoDisc, Inc.; **canal** — Dennie Cody/FPG International LLC; **Capitol** — Architect of the Capitol; **caribou** — PC Paintbrush®/PhotoLibrary™; **cash register** — © 1999 Comstock, Inc.; **cheetah** — © 1999 Corel Corp.; **corsage** — © 2005 PhotoSpin Inc.; **clipper** — PC Paintbrush®/PhotoLibrary™; **colonnade** — © 1990 Allan A. Philiba; **coral** — © 1999 Comstock, Inc.; **crater** — © 1990 Wolfgang Kaehler Photography; **cucumber** — © 2005 PhotoSpin Inc.; **dam** — Bureau of Reclamation; **destroyer** — U.S. Navy Photo by Bath Iron Works Shipbuilding, Inc.; **fiord** — © Ken Ehlers/International Stock; **flag** — © 1999 PhotoDisc, Inc.; **geyser** — © Roger Markham-Smith/International Stock; **guitar** (p. 300) — © 1999 PhotoDisc, Inc.; **halo** — Robert Campin (Master of the Flémalle), Netherlandish, c. 1375-1444. John the Baptist, early 1410s. Oil (with tempera?) and gold on wood, 17.3 x 11.6 cm. © The Cleveland Museum of Art, 1998, Gift of the John Huntington Art and Polytechnic Trust, 1966.238; **iceberg** (p. 366) — The Purcell Team/WORDS AND PICTURES; **in-line skate** — © 2005 PhotoSpin Inc.; **instrument** — © 2005 PhotoSpin Inc.; **intersection** — © 1999 PhotoDisc, Inc.; **irrigation** — © Mark E. Gibson/The Image Finders; **kayak** — © 2005 PhotoSpin Inc.; **keys** (p. 403) — © 1999 PhotoDisc, Inc.; **laptop** — © 1999 PhotoDisc, Inc.; **liftoff** — National Aeronautics and Space Administration; **lighthouse** — © 1990 Wolfgang Kaehler Photography; **merry-go-round** — PC Paintbrush®/PhotoLibrary™; **microscope** — © 1999 PhotoDisc, Inc.; **nozzle** — © 2005 PhotoSpin Inc.; **orchestra** — © 1999 Roger Mastroianni & Co., Inc.; **parachute** — PC Paintbrush®/PhotoLibrary™; **Parthenon** — © Guy Marche/International Stock; **pedestal** — © 1999 Corel Corp.; **piano** — EyeWire Images, © EyeWire, Inc.; **pressure suit** — National Aeronautics and Space Administration; **propeller** — © Jeffrey Sylvester/FPG International LLC; **pueblo** — © Farrell Grehan/FPG International LLC; **pyramid** — © Peter Krinninger/International Stock; **rapid** — © Todd Williams/The Image Finders; **scuba** — © 1999 PhotoDisc, Inc.; **sequoia** — © Michael Paras/International Stock; **sky diving** — © 1999 PhotoDisc, Inc.; **snowboard** — © 1999 Doug Wolfe/Flashback Photography; **space shuttle** — National Aeronautics and Space Administration; **sphinx** — © Robert Tulin/International Stock; **stalactite** — © James R. Goodbar/Bat Wing Publications; **stalagmite** — © James R. Goodbar/Bat Wing Publications; **sugar cane** — © 1999 Comstock, Inc.; **surf** — © 1990 Jeff Divine/FPG International LLC; **thermometer** — © 2005 PhotoSpin Inc.; **volcano** (and p. 832) — © Weatherstock, Inc./International Stock; **windmill** — © Mike Howell/International Stock; **windsurfing** — © 1999 Comstock, Inc.; **yo-yo** (p. 877) — © 1999 Doug Wolfe/Flashback Photography; **zither** (p. 881) — EyeWire Images, © EyeWire, Inc.

All other photos by Barney Taxel, Cleveland, OH, especially commissioned for this book.

Introduction to the Thesaurus

It is useful to be able to express ideas and thoughts in more than one way. Your writing will be interesting and colorful if you don't use the same words all the time. One way to give variety to your writing is to substitute a *synonym*—a word that has the same or almost the same meaning as another word—for a word you have already used. In this way you can make your writing more or less formal, more or less like your conversation when you talk with friends, or more or less like the writing in the books you read.

This thesaurus section of your dictionary will help you improve your writing skills and develop your vocabulary. Like the dictionary, it contains main entries in alphabetical order. Each entry word has a label to show the part of speech. Following the label you will find a list of synonyms for the entry word; the synonyms are printed in boldface type and are also in alphabetical order. The meaning shared by the entry word and its synonyms is given. The sample sentence for each synonym will help you see how the synonym can be used.

Some of the entry words have *antonyms*. An antonym is a word that is opposite or almost opposite in meaning to another word. Antonyms are included at the very end of an entry.

A few entries have more than one sense. The different senses are numbered. Each boldface number is followed by the synonyms for that sense, and the meaning shared by the entry word and the synonyms is given for each sense. If a sense has an antonym, the antonym is included at the sense to which it applies.

We hope you will use your thesaurus often and that it will be a useful tool for you when you write.

Thesaurus

absorbed *adjective* **engrossed, immersed, intent, preoccupied**
These words share the meaning "having the mind completely occupied."
- The musician was *absorbed* in practicing.
- The child was *engrossed* in reading.
- I was *immersed* in thought.
- *Intent* on their chess game, the boys didn't hear the doorbell.
- My friend was so *preoccupied* with the news that she forgot to call me.

antonym: distracted

abuse *verb* **1 maltreat, mistreat**
These words share the meaning "to hurt by treating in a wrong or bad way."
- She *abused* her health by smoking.
- If you pull your dog's ears, you are *maltreating* him.
- My friend will protect me if someone tries to *mistreat* me.

2 exploit, impose on
These words share the meaning "to make use of in a way that is not fair or proper."
- He *abused* my trust by telling my secret.
- The king *exploited* the farmers by not paying them.
- Guests should not *impose on* hosts by staying too late in the evening.

active *adjective* **brisk, dynamic, energetic, lively, vigorous**
These words share the meaning "full of energy or activity."
- Her aunt is an *active* horsewoman.
- I take a *brisk* walk every morning.
- The president of the company began his career as a *dynamic* salesman.
- The actress owes much of her success to her *energetic* manager.
- We had a *lively* discussion about politics.
- The police took *vigorous* action to prevent further vandalism in the neighborhood.

antonym: inactive

admit *verb* **acknowledge, concede**
These words share the meaning "to say or accept that something is true."
- Why won't you *admit* that you had fun?
- I *acknowledge* that I made a mistake.
- Dad *conceded* that Mom was probably right.

antonym: deny

affect *verb* **impress, influence, move, touch**
These words share the meaning "to have a strong effect on the feelings, thoughts, or behavior of."
- Her father's illness *affected* her deeply.
- The musician's skill *impressed* the critic.
- Public opinion can *influence* the actions of legislators.
- The movie's sad ending *moved* us.
- The teacher was *touched* by the affection of her students.

angry *adjective* **enraged, furious, mad**
These words share the meaning "feeling or showing anger."
- My mother was *angry* with me when I didn't clean up my room.
- Many countries were *enraged* by the tyrant's cruel actions.
- It makes me *furious* that I'm so forgetful.
- Don't get *mad*—I'm only joking.

annoy *verb* **bother, pester, plague, vex**
These words share the meaning "to upset or disturb in little ways."
- It *annoys* my mother when I play my radio too loud.
- Your constant complaints really *bother* me.
- The child *pestered* her parents to buy her the toy.
- The speaker was *plagued* by silly questions from the audience.
- Being stuck in the traffic jam *vexed* the truck driver.

antonym: soothe

answer *verb* **reply, respond**
These words share the meaning "to speak, write, act, or react in response."
- You must *answer* every question on the test.
- She told her joke, and I *replied* with my own.
- The patient *responded* well to the treatment.

appear *verb* **look, seem**
These words share the meaning "to have the outward appearance of being."
- My aunt *appears* calm, but she is really worried.
- His face *looked* pink and healthy.
- Your term paper *seems* thorough, but you forgot to check your spelling.

arrange *verb* **classify, group, sort**
These words share the meaning "to put in place or order."
- I *arranged* the flowers in a silver bowl.
- Fossils can be *classified* according to their age.
- The shoes in the shop are *grouped* by size.
- The workers *sorted* the trash and set aside what could be recycled.

attack *verb* **assail, assault, beset, storm**
These words share the meaning "to strike at in some way."

- The rebels *attacked* the government forces at dawn.
- Critics *assailed* the president's speech.
- The robber *assaulted* the pedestrian and knocked him down.
- The project was *beset* by problems from the very beginning.
- Enemy troops *stormed* the palace gates.

antonym: defend

attract *verb* **charm, enchant, fascinate**
These words share the meaning "to draw by means of a special quality or appeal."

- The boy's excellent coordination *attracted* the coach's attention.
- She *charmed* the guests with her wit and intelligence.
- The children were *enchanted* by the wildlife film.
- Learning about outer space *fascinates* many students.

antonym: repel

avoid *verb* **dodge, duck, elude, escape, evade, shun**
These words share the meaning "to move or keep away from."

- We left early to *avoid* heavy traffic.
- Don't try to *dodge* responsibility.
- The senator *ducked* the reporter's question.
- The fugitive *eluded* capture.
- The child somehow *escaped* catching chicken pox.
- Never *evade* your responsibilities.
- Some famous people *shun* photographers.

antonym: face

awkward *adjective* **clumsy, unskilled**
These words share the meaning "lacking grace or skill."

- He may be too *awkward* to become a top gymnast.
- I felt *clumsy* with a cast on my foot.
- She is an *unskilled* piano player.

antonyms: graceful; skilled

beam *verb* **blaze, burn, shine**
These words share the meaning "to give off a bright light."

- The beacon *beamed* in the dark night.
- The hot sun *blazed* overhead.
- Floodlights *burn* down on the football field.
- The full moon is *shining* in through the window.

beat *verb* **batter, hammer, pound**
These words share the meaning "to strike again and again."

- The band *beat* a dance rhythm on steel drums.
- Firemen *battered* open the door.
- The worker *hammered* the silver into a bowl.
- Waves are *pounding* on the shore.

begin *verb* **commence, initiate, start**
These words share the meaning "to become or make active."

- School will *begin* at 8:30.
- The party *commenced* when I entered the room and everybody yelled "Surprise!"
- The state will *initiate* a new health program.
- Don't *start* crying.

antonym: end

bit *noun* **dab, dash, particle, speck**
These words share the meaning "a very small amount."

- You haven't changed a *bit* over the past two years.
- I put a *dab* of whipped cream on my pudding.
- The material is white with a *dash* of blue.
- There isn't a *particle* of truth in the report.
- If you have even a *speck* of doubt, speak up.

blame *noun* **fault**
These words share the meaning "responsibility for a mistake, an offense, or wrong."

- Those who failed to vote must share the *blame* for the problem.
- It isn't the waiter's *fault* that the food is poor.

bold *adjective* **audacious, daring, fearless**
These words share the meaning "having or showing courage or lacking fear."

- *Bold* explorers traveled to the South Pole.
- The senator offered an *audacious* plan to cut taxes.
- A *daring* engineer designed the new sports car.
- *Fearless* pioneers lived on the frontier.

antonym: timid

border *noun* **boundary, brink, edge, margin**
These words share the meaning "a line or part where something begins or ends."
- We live on the *border* of a state forest.
- Don't cross the *boundary* of your neighbor's property.
- The crisis brought the nation to the *brink* of war.
- There is a dock on the *edge* of the lake.
- The hunters came to the *margin* of a small clearing.

branch *verb* **divide, fork**
These words share the meaning "to separate into parts like the branches of a tree."
- Large streets *branch* away from the airport.
- The river *divides* to form a delta near the seacoast.
- The road *forks* just past the post office.

broad *adjective* **ample, extensive, wide**
These words share the meaning "of great size, amount, range, extent, or scope."
- Her mother is an educated woman of *broad* interests.
- My allowance is more than *ample* for a student my age.
- I did *extensive* reading before I began my term paper.
- The restaurant offers a *wide* choice on its menu.

antonym: narrow

build *verb* **construct, erect, raise**
These words share the meaning "to make or form by putting together materials and parts."
- The gardener *built* a shed where he could store tools.
- Many workers are needed to *construct* a highway.
- The bank will *erect* a new skyscraper next year.
- Neighbors helped the farmer *raise* a new barn.

burst *verb* **blow up, explode, pop**
These words share the meaning "to come or cause to come apart suddenly and violently, usually because of internal pressure."
- Steam built up and the boiler *burst*.
- Wreckers used dynamite to *blow up* the old factory.
- The rocket *exploded* just after it was launched.
- We could hear the corn *pop* in the microwave oven.

call *verb* **designate, term**
These words share the meaning "to describe by using a name, term, or word."
- Don't *call* me a loser—I always try my best.
- The Middle Ages are sometimes *designated* the Dark Ages.
- The car has a shape that can be *termed* streamlined.

capture *verb* **get, take, win**
These words share the meaning "to gain control or possession of."
- The knights *captured* the ancient fortress.
- She worked hard to *get* what she wanted.
- My brother's model airplane could *take* first prize at the fair.
- The student tried to *win* his teacher's affection.

careful *adjective* **cautious, prudent, wary**
These words share the meaning "taking or showing care to avoid danger, risk, or offense."
- Be *careful* to look both ways before you cross the street.
- *Cautious* drivers slow down at intersections.
- It seemed *prudent* to check the safety of the playground.
- The *wary* diplomat said she had no comment.

antonym: careless

careless *adjective* **heedless, inattentive, thoughtless**
These words share the meaning "having or showing a lack of care."
- Take your time and avoid *careless* errors.
- *Heedless* of the effect on workers, the company raised the cost of health insurance.
- If you are *inattentive* at school, you may not get good grades.
- It was *thoughtless* of me to keep you waiting.

antonym: careful

cause *noun* **reason**
These words share the meaning "something that produces an effect or result."
- Firefighters are trying to find the *cause* of the explosion.
- What are the *reasons* for this artist's success?

antonym: effect

celebrate *verb* **commemorate, observe**
These words share the meaning "to mark an occasion with festivity or ceremony."
- We *celebrated* his birthday with a party.
- My parents *commemorated* their anniversary with a trip to Europe.
- We *observe* Memorial Day in May.

center *noun* **focus, heart, hub**
These words share the meaning "a place or point where many activities are carried on, from which influences flow, or to which many people are attracted."
- Chicago is a railway *center*.
- Washington, D.C., is the *focus* of political lobbies.
- We live in the *heart* of the city.
- Boston was once called "the *hub* of the universe."

change *verb* **alter, modify, vary**
These words share the meaning "to make or become different."
- We *changed* our plans at the last minute.
- Don't *alter* a single word of this article.
- She was polite to us, and we *modified* our opinion of her.
- The humidity in the air will *vary* from day to day.

chatter *verb* **babble, jabber**
These words share the meaning "to talk on and on about things that are not serious or important."
- All evening long he *chattered* about his vacation.
- My friends *babbled* for a long time about the actor's good looks.
- Even though it was time to go, they would not stop *jabbering*.

cheerful *adjective* **cheery, lighthearted, sunny**
These words share the meaning "feeling or showing lively good spirits."
- The mailman called out a *cheerful* greeting.
- You look *cheery* this morning.
- He began to joke in a *lighthearted* way.
- A child with a sweet and *sunny* expression stopped to pat my dog.

antonym: gloomy

choose *verb* **elect, pick, select, single out**
These words share the meaning "to take as a choice from what is available."
- Let me *choose* the suit I want.
- The boy *elected* to return home.
- Try to *pick* the correct answer from these four possibilities.
- She *selected* the most expensive dish on the menu.
- The critic *singled out* one painting for particular praise.

antonym: reject

clean *adjective* **immaculate, spotless**
These words share the meaning "free from dirt or stains."
- Put on a *clean* shirt for the party.
- She wore *immaculate* white gloves.
- Our kitchen is *spotless*.

antonym: dirty

color *noun* **hue, shade, tone**
These words share the meaning "the property of reflecting light rays in a distinctive way that can be seen."
- Pink is not a primary *color*.
- Flowers of every *hue* grew in the greenhouse.
- The artist used many *shades* of blue in the watercolor.
- She bought a dress in a light *tone* of green.

command *verb* **direct, instruct, order**
These words share the meaning "to give an order or orders to."
- The captain *commanded* the soldiers to retreat.
- The judge *directed* the lawyer to ask the question in different words.
- Students are *instructed* to type their essays.
- Mother *ordered* me to hang up my coat.

compete *verb* **contend, contest**
These words share the meaning "to try to equal or do better than another or others."
- The best athletes of every country *compete* for medals in the Olympics.
- Two huge men will *contend* for the wrestling championship.
- Our team will *contest* with one from another school in a debate.

complain *verb* **grumble, whine**
These words share the meaning "to express feelings of displeasure or discontent."
- The students *complain* that they have too much homework.
- My parents *grumbled* about the bad service at the restaurant.
- Don't *whine* because you lost.

confidence *noun* **assurance, self-confidence**
These words share the meaning "belief in one's own abilities."
- She speaks in public with ease and *confidence*.
- The pupil took the test in the complete

assurance that he would pass.
- *Self-confidence* is the most important requirement for success.

confuse *verb* **bewilder, fluster**
These words share the meaning "to cause to be unclear in the mind."
- Your directions *confused* me and I got lost.
- The number of choices available *bewildered* him.
- The candidate was *flustered* by the reporter's questions.

contest *noun* **competition, meet**
These words share the meaning "a struggle with another or others for victory or a prize."
- Our class won the spelling *contest*.
- My brother finished second in an archery *competition*.
- The city holds a swimming *meet* every year.

conversation *noun* **chat, dialogue, talk**
These words share the meaning "spoken exchange of ideas and opinions."
- I sat in silence and listened to their *conversation*.
- Call me up and we'll have a long *chat*.
- The diplomats had a useful *dialogue*.
- I had a *talk* with the principal about my future.

correct *verb* **amend, remedy**
These words share the meaning "to make right something that is wrong."
- The teacher *corrects* our homework every night.
- It was necessary to *amend* the text to remove the errors.
- Many problems can be *remedied* by hard work.

crack *verb* **pop, snap**
These words share the meaning "to make a sudden sharp noise like that of something breaking."
- Thunder was *cracking* and booming in the distance.
- The cork *popped* when we removed it from the bottle.
- Dry wood *snapped* as the fire roared through the building.

crowd *noun* **drove, flock, mob, swarm**
These words share the meaning "a very large number."
- A *crowd* waited outside the stadium.
- *Droves* of tourists are visiting the city.
- *Flocks* of sports fans came to the game.
- Police were barely able to control the *mob* of angry protesters.
- *Swarms* of insects ruined the picnic.

cruel *adjective* **ferocious, fierce, savage, vicious**
These words share the meaning "causing or likely to cause great pain, hardship, or distress."
- *Cruel* arctic winds swept down over the area.
- The tiger is a *ferocious* animal.
- A *fierce* fire broke out in the building.
- My brother finally learned to control his *savage* temper.
- The enemy launched a *vicious* attack.

antonym: mild

crush *verb* **mash, squash**
These words share the meaning "to press or squeeze with force."
- The wall of the store collapsed and *crushed* a car parked at the curb.
- Will you *mash* the potatoes while I prepare the corn?
- I stepped on the tomato and *squashed* it.

cry *verb* **bawl, howl, sob, wail, weep**
These words share the meaning "to make sounds of sorrow, pain, or distress, usually while shedding tears."
- Don't *cry* if you aren't hurt.
- I was so disappointed that I sat down and *bawled*.
- The child fell down and *howled* in pain.
- Family members *sobbed* during the entire funeral.
- The hungry baby *wailed* for his mother.
- Susan went up to her room and *wept* alone.

dark *adjective* **dim, gloomy, murky, somber**
These words share the meaning "having little or no light."
- The family is away, and the house is *dark*.
- The light coming through the dirty window was *dim* and gray.
- Thousands of bats flew around in the *gloomy* cave.
- The cabin stands next to a *murky* pond.
- Their living room is *somber* and depressing.

antonym: bright

decide *verb* **conclude, determine, resolve, settle**
These words share the meaning "to make up one's mind."
- I can't *decide* whether or not to buy a new car.
- She *concluded* that she had been mistaken.
- The judge *determined* that the witness was lying.

- He *resolved* that he had to find work.
- We have to *settle* on a plan of action.

defend *verb* **guard, protect, safeguard, shield**
These words share the meaning "to keep safe from hardship, danger, injury, or attack."
- Marines were assigned to *defend* the embassy.
- We bought a dog to *guard* the house.
- Always wear a helmet to *protect* your head when you ride your bicycle.
- The first ten amendments to the Constitution *safeguard* the rights of all citizens.
- I used my hand to *shield* my eyes from the sun's glare.

antonym: attack

delay *verb* **detain, hold up**
These words share the meaning "to cause to be late."
- I was *delayed* by heavy traffic.
- I will not *detain* you—go right in.
- A strike could *hold up* delivery of the mail.

antonym: expedite

describe *verb* **narrate, recite, recount, relate, report**
These words share the meaning "to tell or write about in detail."
- I can't *describe* my symptoms; I just know that I am sick.
- It would take hours to *narrate* all the events of the day.
- Grandfather loves to *recite* his adventures.
- She *recounted* everything that had happened.
- Please *relate* the good news to his wife.
- You should *report* the crime to police.

despise *verb* **disdain, scorn**
These words share the meaning "to look down on with contempt."
- I *despise* sloppy writing.
- He always *disdains* expensive gifts.
- Never *scorn* someone's honest attempts to do what is right.

antonym: respect

destroy *verb* **demolish, level**
These words share the meaning "to wreck or ruin completely."
- Fire *destroyed* the building.
- The church was *demolished* in an air raid.
- They will *level* the old buildings to make room for a new housing project.

difficult *adjective* **hard, knotty, tough**
These words share the meaning "not easy to do, make, manage, or understand."
- Dictionaries explain the meanings of *difficult* words.
- He finds it *hard* to concentrate on his work.
- There were some *knotty* problems on the math test.
- Digging ditches is *tough* work.

antonym: simple

dirty *adjective* **filthy, grimy, soiled, unclean**
These words share the meaning "covered, filled, or stained with dirt."
- Go wash your *dirty* hands.
- The apartment is so *filthy* that it's impossible to rent out.
- I used bleach on the *grimy* sheets.
- We sent the *soiled* tablecloth to the laundry.
- Don't put *unclean* handkerchiefs on the table.

antonym: clean

disgust *verb* **repel, revolt, sicken**
These words share the meaning "to cause to feel offended or be filled with distaste."
- Cockroaches *disgust* me.
- We were *repelled* by such cruelty.
- The smell of rotten fish would *revolt* anyone.
- I'm *sickened* by any abuse of animals.

earn *verb* **deserve, merit, win**
These words share the meaning "to gain as a result of something one has done."
- The only way to get respect is to *earn* it.
- Hard workers *deserve* praise.
- Do you think you *merit* a good mark?
- He *won* first prize in a writing contest.

effect *noun* **consequence, outcome, result**
These words share the meaning "something that is produced by a cause."
- The *effect* of overeating is often an upset stomach.
- She didn't pay attention in school and as a *consequence* received poor marks.

- The polls are still open, so the *outcome* of the election isn't yet certain.
- The scar on his leg is the *result* of a bad fall.

antonym: cause

effort *noun* **exertion, pains, struggle**
These words share the meaning "the use of energy to get something done."
- Only a big *effort* on the part of the community saved the hospital from being closed.
- Moving the heavy couch required a lot of *exertion*.
- She spared no *pains* on party preparations.
- It will be a *struggle* to succeed, but I know you'll keep trying.

embrace *verb* **clasp, hug**
These words share the meaning "to take in one's arms."
- Grandmother *embraced* the children and then greeted the grown-ups.
- We sat in front of the fire, *clasping* our knees.
- The girl threw her arms around her friend and *hugged* him tight.

encourage *verb* **cheer, hearten**
These words share the meaning "to give courage, hope, or confidence to."
- I *encouraged* him to take flying lessons.
- I was *cheered* by your visit while I was in the hospital.
- The doctor said the girl would soon feel better, which *heartened* her mother.

antonym: discourage

end *verb* **cease, close, complete, conclude, finish, wind up**
These words share the meaning "to bring or come to an end."
- He will *end* his speech with an appeal for money.
- The dreadful noise finally *ceased*.
- She *closed* her letter with an affectionate message for her sister.
- Did you *complete* your homework?
- The war *concluded*, but the hatred continued on both sides.
- After you *finish* mowing the lawn, take a rest.
- The meeting is expected to *wind up* early.

antonym: begin

enormous *adjective* **colossal, gigantic, huge, immense, mammoth, massive, vast**
These words share the meaning "extremely large."
- Elephants have *enormous* ears.
- We saw a *colossal* statue of Christopher Columbus.
- We ate a *gigantic* dinner.
- Great Danes are *huge* dogs.
- The library is an *immense* room.
- New York is a *mammoth* city.
- *Massive* steel beams support the skyscraper.
- We saw *vast* icebergs from the ship.

antonym: tiny

examine *verb* **check, inspect, study**
These words share the meaning "to look at or into carefully and in detail."
- The dealer *examined* the coin to see if it was genuine.
- He always *checks* his bank statement to be sure there are no mistakes.
- We walked through the garden, stopping often to *inspect* the flowers.
- She put the slide under the microscope to *study* the structure of the cells.

exhaust *verb* **consume, drain**
These words share the meaning "to use up completely."
- Buying a house would *exhaust* our savings.
- Our heating system *consumes* gallons of oil.
- Running the marathon *drained* the athlete's strength.

expect *verb* **anticipate, await, hope**
These words share the meaning "to look for as likely to occur or appear."
- I *expected* you to come sooner.
- Do you *anticipate* any trouble?
- I *await* your answer.

- The teacher *hopes* for great things from the gifted student.

expression *noun* **gesture, indication, sign, token**
These words share the meaning "a way of expressing feelings and thoughts without using words."
- I touched her shoulder as an *expression* of sympathy.
- He will give the nurse a box of chocolates as a *gesture* of thanks.
- Her raised eyebrows were the only *indication* that she was surprised.
- The teacher shook her finger as a warning *sign*.
- We shook hands as a *token* of agreement.

fair *adjective* **clear, cloudless, sunny**
These words share the meaning "free from rain, snow, or clouds."
- We waited for *fair* weather to go sailing.
- On a *clear* day you can see for miles.
- It was a *cloudless* night, and the stars sparkled in the sky.
- That year October was *sunny*, and the autumn colors were magnificent.

fall *verb* **drop, pitch, topple, tumble**
These words share the meaning "to come down suddenly from a standing or sitting position."
- The man slipped and *fell* on the icy sidewalk.
- She's so tired that she's afraid she'll *drop*.
- The mailman lost his balance and *pitched* down the front steps.
- The statue *toppled* to the ground during the earthquake.
- The worker *tumbled* off the roof.

famous *adjective* **eminent, noted, popular, prominent, well-known**
These words share the meaning "widely known and talked about."
- My friend's mother is a *famous* scientist.
- An *eminent* professor is going to address our class.
- A *noted* artist donated a painting to charity.
- A *popular* rock group will perform in our town this weekend.
- Many *prominent* politicians attended the presidential inauguration.
- He comes from a *well-known* family.

antonym: obscure

fast *adjective* **fleet, quick, rapid, speedy, swift**
These words share the meaning "moving with, acting at, or marked by high speed."
- His brother bought a *fast* new convertible.
- The cheetah is a *fleet* animal.
- Take a *quick* walk to the store, please, and buy me a dozen eggs.
- It's fine to be a *rapid* worker, but don't be careless.
- The student made *speedy* progress in reading.
- A *swift* wipe with a sponge was all that was needed to clean the table.

antonym: slow

feel *verb* **experience, know**
These words share the meaning "to be aware of as an emotional reaction."
- The boy *felt* regret at having to move away.
- Have you *experienced* the joys of an amusement park?
- Many children *know* the fun of having a pet.

find *verb* **locate, pinpoint, spot**
These words share the meaning "to discover by making an effort or a search."
- I can't *find* my pen.
- The worker tried to *locate* the leak in the roof.
- The doctor can't *pinpoint* the cause of the patient's illness.
- She *spotted* an old friend in the audience.

antonym: lose

flexible *adjective* **elastic, resilient, supple**
These words share the meaning "capable of being bent, compressed, or stretched without breaking."
- The willow tree has slender, *flexible* branches.
- Rubber bands are *elastic*.
- Tennis balls are *resilient*.
- The horseman wore beautiful boots of *supple* leather.

antonym: inflexible

forgive *verb* **excuse, pardon**
These words share the meaning "to stop being angry with."
- *Forgive* me for hurting your feelings.
- Please *excuse* him for interrupting; he didn't realize you were busy.
- *Pardon* me for being so rude.

form *noun* **figure, shape**
These words share the meaning "the outline of something."
- He had a swimming pool built in the *form* of a grand piano.
- A circle is a geometric *figure*.
- We molded the clay into the *shape* of a pear.

free *verb* **discharge, emancipate, liberate, release**
These words share the meaning "to set at liberty."

- The hostages were finally *freed*.
- The doctor will *discharge* the patient from the hospital tomorrow.
- Abraham Lincoln *emancipated* the slaves.
- Vacation *liberated* her from her worries.
- The prisoner was *released* early for good behavior.

funny *adjective* **amusing, comical, hilarious, humorous, laughable**
These words share the meaning "causing or intended to cause laughter or amusement."
- They sat around and swapped *funny* stories.
- Her joke was very *amusing*.
- I wore a *comical* costume to the Halloween party.
- The situation is more than funny, it's *hilarious*!
- Life is awfully dull when you can't see the *humorous* side of it.
- What have I done that's so *laughable*?

antonym: unfunny

genuine *adjective* **authentic, real, true**
These words share the meaning "not counterfeit or artificial."
- The ring is solid gold with a *genuine* diamond.
- The museum has many *authentic* paintings by the old masters.
- I bought a new purse made of *real* leather.
- The president's record shows he is a *true* statesman.

antonym: sham

gesture *verb* **motion, signal**
These words share the meaning "to make a movement of the body to express an idea or emotion."
- The policeman *gestured* to us to stop.
- The teacher *motioned* to them to be quiet.
- Officers *signaled* the troops to attack.

gloomy *adjective* **bleak, dismal, dreary, somber**
These words share the meaning "dark and lacking cheer."
- On a *gloomy* day I like to curl up with a good book.
- Six workers shared one *bleak* room.
- Heavy fog rolled in off the ocean, making the city seem *dismal* and depressing.
- The *dreary* winter twilight fell over the deserted cabin.
- The family members wore *somber* clothes to the funeral.

antonym: bright

go *verb* **journey, pass, proceed, travel**
These words share the meaning "to move from one place to another."
- Let's *go* home.
- They plan to *journey* north toward ski country.
- Many tourists *pass* this way every day.
- With our teacher escorting us, we *proceeded* to the museum.
- Do you intend to *travel* to Europe next summer?

antonym: stop

graceful *adjective* **adroit, agile, deft, nimble**
These words share the meaning "having or showing skill, quickness, and ease in movement or action."
- My sister is a *graceful* dancer.
- He gave an *adroit* answer that offended nobody.
- An *agile* gymnast practiced on the trampoline.
- The painter had a *deft* touch with a brush.
- Pianists need *nimble* fingers.

antonym: awkward

grasp *verb* **clutch, grab, grip, seize**
These words share the meaning "to take firm hold of with the hand."
- The old man *grasped* his cane in his right hand.
- The child *clutched* her mother's arm.
- I *grabbed* a piece of paper and quickly began to write.
- The boy *gripped* his fishing rod and waited.
- You should never *seize* a dog by the tail.

grow *verb* **breed, cultivate, raise**
These words share the meaning "to bring about the development of something living."
- We *grow* carnations in our greenhouse.
- My friend *breeds* prize cattle.
- Local farmers *cultivate* corn, squash, and apples.
- I *raised* tomatoes in my garden.

gruff *adjective* **abrupt, blunt, curt, short**
These words share the meaning "rough and brief to the point of rudeness in manner or speech."
- Don't be afraid; he's *gruff*, but he has a kind heart.
- She gave an *abrupt* answer and walked away.
- My friend offered some *blunt* criticism that hurt my feelings.
- We are surprised by your *curt* refusal of our invitation.
- She is often *short* with her sister.

guarantee *verb* **assure, ensure, secure**
These words share the meaning "to make sure or certain."
- Long hours of practice do not *guarantee* success.
- I work two jobs to *assure* myself a more comfortable life.
- Regular exercise helps *ensure* physical fitness.
- My parents opened a savings account to *secure* my education.

harm *noun* **damage, hurt, injury**
These words share the meaning "an act or the result of causing pain or loss."
- Seat belts help prevent *harm* to passengers.
- The fire caused severe *damage* to the house.
- The only *hurt* was to his pride.
- The doctor treated my *injuries*.

antonym: benefit

harmony *noun* **accord, unity**
These words share the meaning "agreement among persons in feeling, ideas, actions, and interests."
- Few families live in perfect *harmony*.
- Congress is trying to reach *accord* on the budget.
- *Unity* of purpose creates strong alliances.

antonym: discord

healthy *adjective* **fit, hale, hearty, sound, well**
These words share the meaning "having or showing good health."
- *Healthy* children eat well and sleep soundly.
- A wholesome diet and exercise will keep you *fit*.
- Even as an old man he was *hale* and strong.
- A *hearty* young sailor strolled down the street.
- Her heart and lungs are *sound*.
- My elderly uncle is not a *well* man.

antonym: sick

heap *verb* **drift, pile, stack**
These words share the meaning "to come or bring together in a jumbled pile."
- I *heaped* the books on the table.
- High winds *drifted* the sand around the window and door frames.
- Packages were *piled* on the counter.
- Please *stack* the logs near the fireplace.

hinder *verb* **bar, block, hamper, obstruct**
These words share the meaning "to get in the way of, slow down, or hold back."
- Talking on the telephone can *hinder* you from studying effectively.
- Nothing *bars* a merchant from charging high prices.
- An accident on the highway *blocked* traffic.
- Lack of money *hampered* her in redecorating her apartment.
- Bystanders must never *obstruct* police officers in doing their duty.

antonym: further

hoarse *adjective* **croaking, husky**
These words share the meaning "rough and harsh in sound."
- He's back at work now, but his voice is still *hoarse*.
- Every evening *croaking* frogs fill the air with noise.
- Her voice was *husky* with emotion.

hole *noun* **cavity, hollow**
These words share the meaning "an opening or break in something solid."
- Swiss cheese is full of *holes*.
- Brush your teeth often to prevent *cavities*.
- We hid the message in the *hollow* of an oak tree.

home *noun* **abode, dwelling, house, residence**
These words share the meaning "the place where one lives."
- We're buying a new *home*.
- Their humble *abode* stood in a quiet valley.
- The dormitory is the student's *dwelling*.
- Come to our *house* for dinner.
- The governor's *residence* is a mansion.

hopeful *adjective* **encouraging, likely, promising, rosy**
These words share the meaning "inspiring or giving hope."
- It's a *hopeful* sign that you don't have a fever today.
- The boy received an *encouraging* letter from his teacher.
- The party is looking for *likely* candidates for the next election.
- Being late for an interview isn't a *promising*

beginning.
- The student has a *rosy* future.

antonym: hopeless

hum *verb* **buzz, drone, whir**
These words share the meaning "to make a continuous sound like that of an insect or a motor."
- I tried to sleep, but it wasn't easy with a mosquito *humming* in my ear.
- Flies *buzzed* around the open jar of jam.
- A plane *droned* overhead.
- The sewing machine *whirred* on in the next room.

idea *noun* **concept, conception, impression, notion, thought**
These words share the meaning "something that one thinks, knows, plans, or imagines."
- She has a very clear *idea* of what her duty is.
- Time is an abstract *concept*.
- I had no *conception* of the immense size of the Grand Canyon.
- Do you have the *impression* that we've talked about this before?
- The *notion* of his becoming a doctor is very ambitious.
- Her first *thought* was that there must be some mistake.

intelligent *adjective* **bright, brilliant, clever, smart**
These words share the meaning "having or showing a keen mind."
- An *intelligent* reader could easily guess who the spy was.
- The *brightest* student in the class won the mathematics prize.
- A *brilliant* scientist found a way to split the atom.
- The play has a very *clever* plot.
- A *smart* businesswoman marketed a sauce made from her mother's special recipe.

introduce *verb* **acquaint, present**
These words share the meaning "to make one person known to another."
- He *introduced* his guest to his parents.
- Are you *acquainted* with my friend?
- The new employee was *presented* to the head of the company.

inventive *adjective* **creative, ingenious, original**
These words share the meaning "having or showing cleverness and skill in producing new ideas and new things."
- The zipper is an *inventive* substitute for buttons.
- Many *creative* composers are experimenting with the use of electronic instruments.
- The microwave oven is an *ingenious* piece of kitchen equipment.
- Albert Einstein was a great *original* genius.

jump *verb* **bounce, bound, leap, spring, vault**
These words share the meaning "to move suddenly by using the leg muscles."
- I *jumped* up from my chair.
- The happy student *bounced* into the room.
- As soon as we detached his leash, the dog *bounded* across the lawn.
- The audience *leaped* to its feet and loudly applauded.
- Mother *sprang* up from the couch to answer the doorbell.
- The rider *vaulted* into the saddle.

know *verb* **1 comprehend, fathom, grasp, understand**
These words share the meaning "to have a firm mental hold of."
- His father *knows* Spanish and Italian.
- I don't *comprehend* the need for these exercises.
- His refusal to cooperate isn't easy to *fathom*.
- Do you *grasp* the basic principles of grammar?
- She feels she'll never *understand* the techniques of cooking.

2 differentiate, discriminate, distinguish, separate
These words share the meaning "to recognize the difference between."
- It's not always easy to *know* truth from lies.
- Medical students must learn to *differentiate* viruses from bacteria.
- You must *discriminate* between good and bad behavior.
- How do you *distinguish* right from wrong?
- It's not difficult to *separate* airplanes from helicopters.

laugh *verb* **chortle, chuckle, giggle, snicker, titter**
These words share the meaning "to smile and make sounds showing that one is happy or amused."
- No one ever *laughs* at my jokes.
- The speaker *chortled* over her mistake.
- We all *chuckled* over the story.
- *Giggling* children ran all over the house.
- We *snickered* when their team lost.
- People in the audience *tittered* when the actor forgot his lines.

leader *noun* **boss, chief, director, head**
These words share the meaning "a person who

is highest in authority or rank."
- Governors, mayors, and many other political *leaders* will attend the conference.
- A former worker is now the *boss* of the construction crew.
- The fire *chief* asked people to conserve water during the drought.
- Our classmate's father was appointed *director* of athletics at the high school.
- She is the *head* of the English department.

lift *verb* **boost, elevate, hoist, raise**
These words share the meaning "to move to a higher position or level."

- Don't try to *lift* the piano by yourself.
- He *boosted* the child onto his shoulder so he could see the parade.
- The good news *elevated* our spirits.
- A crane was needed to *hoist* the beam into place.
- She *raised* her eyes from her book.

antonym: lower

limit *noun* **bounds, confines, end**
These words share the meaning "a point or line where something ends or must end."
- Their joy had no *limit*.
- Your request is beyond the *bounds* of reason.
- We kept the dog within the *confines* of the yard.
- There is no *end* to the benefits of a good education.

long *adjective* **drawn-out, lengthy, overlong, prolonged, protracted**
These words share the meaning "of greater length than is usual or desirable."
- The book is *long* and tedious.
- Keep it short; I hate *drawn-out* explanations.
- The *lengthy* speech bored the audience.
- The teacher thought the student's essay was *overlong*.
- Our friends came for a *prolonged* visit.
- The country was left in ruins after a *protracted* war.

antonym: short

lose *verb* **mislay, misplace**
These words share the meaning "to be unable to find."
- She might *lose* her gloves.
- Be careful not to *mislay* library books.
- The teacher *misplaced* her glasses.

antonym: find

lucky *adjective* **fortunate, happy**
These words share the meaning "having, bringing, or marked by good luck."
- My friend is *lucky* that his roommate is a pleasant fellow.
- She considers herself *fortunate* to have gotten the scholarship.
- Their old aunt has the *happy* ability to make friends among younger people.

antonym: unlucky

maintain *verb* **keep up, preserve, sustain**
These words share the meaning "to keep in a condition of good repair or efficiency."
- The town set aside funds to *maintain* roads and bridges.
- Our neighbors don't *keep up* their lawn and garden.
- We take special care to *preserve* our old family photographs.
- Eat properly to *sustain* good health.

mature *adjective* **adult, grown, grown-up**
These words share the meaning "fully grown or developed."
- Pick and eat the strawberries when they're *mature*.
- *Adult* citizens have the right to vote.
- He's not a boy any longer; he's a *grown* man.
- She has four *grown-up* daughters.

antonym: immature

meddle *verb* **interfere, tamper**
These words share the meaning "to concern oneself with something without having the right or without being asked or needed."
- Parents shouldn't *meddle* in the lives of their grown-up children.
- I asked you not to *interfere* with my work.
- Never *tamper* with another person's computer.

meet *verb* **confront, encounter, face**
These words share the meaning "to come face to face with."
- I crossed the street so as not to *meet* her.
- He was *confronted* by a guard, who asked him for identification.
- The students *encountered* their teacher at the museum.
- The senator *faced* his critics at a news conference.

antonym: avoid

memory *noun* **recall, recollection, remembrance**
These words share the meaning "the ability to remember or an act of remembering."
- He has no *memory* for faces.
- She had an almost perfect *recall* of that evening's events.
- She told, to the best of her *recollection*, what had happened the night of the accident.
- The *remembrance* of our trip always gives us pleasure.

misery *noun* **suffering, unhappiness**
These words share the meaning "a condition of great distress caused by poverty or misfortune."
- The family lived in *misery* in a dingy and overcrowded tenement.
- The homeless undergo great *suffering*.
- You can imagine the children's *unhappiness* when their dog ran away.

mixture *noun* **blend, compound, mix**
These words share the meaning "something made by mixing."
- This book is a *mixture* of fact and fiction.
- The fabric is a *blend* of cotton and nylon.
- Aspirin is a *compound*.
- We made brownies from a *mix*.

motion *noun* **move, movement, stir**
These words share the meaning "the act or process of moving."
- The conductor made a *motion* with his hand.
- Sit still; don't make a *move*.
- She slid the letter across the table in a quick *movement*.
- The wind blew, and there was a sudden *stir* of leaves.

move *noun* **measure, procedure, step, tactic**
These words share the meaning "an action taken to accomplish a goal."
- Going to college is an excellent *move*.
- What *measures* have been taken to prevent forest fires?
- The cook's first *procedure* was to read the recipe.
- After the lawn is mowed, the next *step* is to clear away the cut grass.
- Lying was a *tactic* that got us in trouble.

muffle *verb* **deaden, mute**
These words share the meaning "to soften or dull the sound of."
- The thick, soft slippers *muffled* her footsteps.
- Special tiles on the ceiling and walls *deaden* the whine of the machines.
- The composer indicated that the strings should be *muted* in the slow movement.

mystery *noun* **puzzle, riddle**
These words share the meaning "something that is puzzling or excites curiosity."
- The cause of his sickness remains a *mystery*.
- How he got my telephone number is a *puzzle*.
- Her older brother enjoyed solving *riddles*.

neglect *verb* **disregard, shirk**
These words share the meaning "to fail to carry out or give proper attention to."
- Never *neglect* your health.
- She *disregarded* the teacher's warning.
- The soldier was punished for *shirking* his duty.

neighborhood *noun* **area, district, quarter**
These words share the meaning "a part or region of a city or town."
- Houses are usually built in residential *neighborhoods*.
- There are three drugstores in the shopping *area*.
- We went down to the theater *district* to buy tickets.
- The students' *quarter* of Paris is a lively place.

news *noun* **information, intelligence, word**
These words share the meaning "a report of recent happenings previously not known."
- Have you heard the *news* of the crash?
- The hospital gave me the latest *information* about my friend's condition.
- Don't trust anonymous sources of *intelligence*.
- *Word* came that the war had ended.

noise *noun* **clamor, clatter, din, racket, uproar**
These words share the meaning "a loud or confused sound."
- Traffic *noise* disturbed his sleep.

- The village celebrated the wedding with the *clamor* of church bells.
- We couldn't talk above the *clatter* of pots and pans in the kitchen.
- The air was filled with the *din* of car horns.
- Workers wear devices to protect their ears from the *racket* of loud drills.
- The crowd made a tremendous *uproar* when the decision was announced.

notice *verb* **note, observe, see**
These words share the meaning "to become aware of and pay attention to."
- He *noticed* that the dog had gotten loose.
- Please *note* that you have a doctor's appointment this afternoon.
- She *observed* several new photographs on the wall.
- I *see* that you don't agree with me.

obedient *adjective* **compliant, submissive**
These words share the meaning "carrying or willing to carry out the instructions or orders of others."
- *Obedient* children aren't likely to get into trouble.
- The salesman was *compliant* and eager to please.
- Some dogs quickly learn to be *submissive* to the commands of their owner.

antonym: disobedient

offer *verb* **extend, present, volunteer**
These words share the meaning "to hold out to another for acceptance or refusal."
- Her friend *offered* her an apple.
- Please *extend* my sympathy to your cousin.
- He *presented* his ideas to the class.
- The students *volunteered* their help.

operate *verb* **handle, run, use, work**
These words share the meaning "to put or keep in action or in operation."
- Can you *operate* a sewing machine?
- She was taught to *handle* an electric drill.
- We *ran* the copying machine too long, and it overheated.
- Students are learning to *use* the computer.
- His father taught him how to *work* a sanding machine.

opportunity *noun* **chance, occasion, shot**
These words share the meaning "a time or situation favorable to some purpose."
- She was given an *opportunity* to go to college.
- I saw a *chance* to make some money.
- He took the *occasion* to say thank you.
- The director gave the young actor a *shot* at the part.

outburst *noun* **burst, explosion, fit, outbreak**
These words share the meaning "a sudden violent release of something such as emotion or energy."
- She regrets her *outburst* of anger.
- The comedian was rewarded with a *burst* of laughter.
- An *explosion* of violence in the streets shattered the calm in the neighborhood.
- The play was funny enough to give us *fits* of laughter.
- There was an *outbreak* of flu.

overwhelm *verb* **engulf, overcome, overpower**
These words share the meaning "to make helpless with something such as deep emotion."
- They were *overwhelmed* with sorrow.
- He was *engulfed* by stage fright.
- What a beautiful gift! I am *overcome* with gratitude.
- She was *overpowered* by the need to sleep.

pain *noun* **ache, twinge**
These words share the meaning "hurt caused by injury or disease."
- He felt a deep *pain* in his chest.
- I felt an *ache* from the injured muscle.
- She had a sharp *twinge* from her sprained ankle.

pause *noun* **break, intermission, interval**
These words share the meaning "a temporary interruption in activity."
- His speech was filled with *pauses*.
- Let's take a *break* for lunch.
- There's a 10-minute *intermission* between the acts.
- There was only a brief *interval* between the question and the answer.

perfect *adjective* **faultless, flawless**
These words share the meaning "having no defects or being of the highest quality."
- The pianist gave a *perfect* performance.
- Her reading of the poem was *faultless*.
- The brilliant diamond was *flawless*.

antonym: imperfect

perform *verb* **achieve, do, execute**
These words share the meaning "to carry out to completion."
- The surgeon *performed* a delicate operation.
- You'll have to work hard to *achieve* your goal.
- Why do I always have to *do* the hardest work?

- The skating champion *executed* a beautiful triple jump.

persuade *verb* **convince, get, prevail on**
These words share the meaning "to cause another person to do or believe something."
- Try to *persuade* him to join the team.
- She *convinced* them that she was right.
- We *got* the teacher to say yes.
- He *prevailed on* his father to let him take flying lessons.

antonym: dissuade

play *noun* **diversion, fun, recreation**
These words share the meaning "activity engaged in for amusement and pleasure."
- Don't just work; leave time for *play*, too.
- Skiing is their favorite *diversion*.
- She sews for *fun*.
- Gardening is his chief *recreation*.

antonym: work

please *verb* **delight, gladden, gratify, tickle**
These words share the meaning "to give pleasure to."
- His English composition will *please* the teacher.
- We were *delighted* at the good news.
- Spring flowers *gladden* the eye and the spirit.
- Her son's success will *gratify* her.
- The progress you're making really *tickles* me.

antonym: displease

plot *noun* **conspiracy, intrigue, scheme**
These words share the meaning "a secret plan to do something, usually something evil."
- There was a *plot* to assassinate the dictator.
- A *conspiracy* was formed to overthrow the government.
- He doesn't take part in office *intrigues*.
- Criminals hatched a *scheme* to rob the bank.

poisonous *adjective* **poison, toxic, venomous**
These words share the meaning "being, containing, or having the effect of a poison."
- This mushroom is known to be *poisonous*.
- The use of *poison* gas is a violation of international law.
- How to dispose of *toxic* waste is a major problem.
- He was bitten by a *venomous* snake.

popular *adjective* **1 general, public**
These words share the meaning "of, for, or held by most of the people."
- It was once a *popular* belief that the sun revolved around the earth.
- Dishonest officials are viewed with *general* contempt.
- *Public* opinion forced the governor to change his mind.

2 favored, favorite
These words share the meaning "liked by very many or most people."
- That radio station broadcasts *popular* music.
- The beach is our *favored* vacation spot.
- Audiences always demand that she play their *favorite* piece as an encore.

antonym: unpopular

posture *noun* **attitude, carriage**
These words share the meaning "the bearing or position of the body."
- Soldiers are trained to have erect *posture*.
- The lifeguard stood by his boat in an *attitude* of readiness.
- She has the *carriage* of a confident person.

practical *adjective* **handy, useful**
These words share the meaning "capable of being applied or put to use."
- This book is a *practical* guide for people who want to learn carpentry.
- A flashlight is a *handy* gadget to keep in the car.
- The gloves you sent are a *useful* gift.

antonym: impractical

practice *verb* **drill, exercise, rehearse**
These words share the meaning "to do or cause to do something over and over in order to develop skill or strength."
- The boy *practices* the piano daily.
- The teacher *drilled* us in the multiplication tables.
- She *exercises* in the gym twice a week.
- My father *rehearsed* his speech until he knew it by heart.

praise *verb* **acclaim, applaud, commend, compliment**
These words share the meaning "to express approval or admiration of."
- The mayor *praised* the police officer for her courage.
- The painting is a masterpiece, widely *acclaimed* by experts.
- The public *applauded* the president's decision.
- I *commend* you for your hard work and persistence.
- Guests *complimented* the chef on the wonderful meal.

antonym: criticize

program *noun* **calendar, schedule**
These words share the meaning "a list of activities or events, especially in the order in which they are to be done or to happen."

- My *program* today includes shopping and a trip to the library.
- There are several parties on our *calendar* this week.
- He has a full *schedule* today.

project *noun* **enterprise, venture**
These words share the meaning "something that a person undertakes to do, especially something involving planning or risk."

- Restoring an old house is an ambitious *project*.
- Her latest *enterprise*, an expensive dress shop, is a great success.
- An investor supplied the money for their business *venture*.

public *adjective* **civic, civil**
These words share the meaning "of, for, or by the community as a whole."
- Air pollution is a threat to the *public* health.
- The new town hall is a source of *civic* pride.
- Courts of law are *civil* institutions.

antonym: private

pure *adjective* **absolute, perfect, sheer, simple**
These words share the meaning "being nothing less than."
- It's *pure* luck that he found his wallet.
- That's an *absolute* tragedy.
- There was *perfect* silence in the room.
- *Sheer* stubbornness made her act that way.
- Just tell me the *simple* truth.

quality *noun* **1 attribute, characteristic, feature, mark, property, trait**
These words share the meaning "one of the distinctive elements that make something what it is."
- Hardness is the most important *quality* of steel.
- Her best *attribute* is her honesty.
- A pleasing scent is the most important *characteristic* of a perfume.
- Fireworks are an enjoyable *feature* of the Fourth of July.
- Good manners are the *mark* of a mature person.
- Heat is a *property* of fire.
- Deceitfulness is a bad character *trait*.

2 class, grade
These words share the meaning "the degree of excellence that a thing has."
- The restaurant serves food of poor *quality*.
- I bought silk of the finest *class*.
- Diamonds of such low *grade* can't be used for jewelry.

rash *adjective* **hasty, reckless**
These words share the meaning "showing too great haste and too little thought."
- Don't make *rash* promises that you can't keep.
- His decision to drop out of school was *hasty* and very unwise.
- She regretted her *reckless* purchase.

antonym: deliberate

ready *adjective* **prepared, set**
These words share the meaning "in proper condition for use or action."
- Dinner is *ready*.
- Are you *prepared* for the test?
- He was all *set* to leave for work.

antonym: unready

recede *verb* **ebb, retreat**
These words share the meaning "to go or move backward."
- We watched from the ship as the shoreline *receded* from view.
- Her energy *ebbed* away.
- I *retreated* from the window.

antonym: advance

relieve *verb* **ease, lessen, lighten**
These words share the meaning "to make more bearable or less intense."
- An aspirin will *relieve* your headache.
- Nothing could *ease* their sorrow.
- Taking a minute to relax will *lessen* the pressure you're feeling.
- Two friends helped him, which *lightened* his work.

antonym: intensify

rescue *verb* **deliver, save**
These words share the meaning "to free from something such as danger, harm, or captivity."
- The lifeguard *rescued* the exhausted swimmer.
- After the war thousands were *delivered* from captivity.
- Firefighters *saved* the lives of everyone in the building.

rest *noun* **ease, leisure, relaxation**
These words share the meaning "freedom or relief from work or stress."
- The farmer is at *rest* in the shade.
- They left the dinner dishes in the sink and

took their *ease*.
- He led a life of *leisure* after he retired.
- She finds *relaxation* in listening to music.

reveal *verb* **betray, disclose, expose, tell, uncover**
These words share the meaning "to make known something that has been or ought to be kept secret."

- He *revealed* the plans I had confided to him.
- The expression on her face *betrayed* her real feelings.
- An anonymous source *disclosed* that an agreement had been reached.
- The morning newspaper *exposed* the scandal.
- I won't *tell* if you'd rather I didn't.
- A reporter *uncovered* evidence of a hidden crime.

antonym: conceal

reward *noun* **award, prize**
These words share the meaning "something given in return for service, merit, or achievement."
- The best *reward* for winning was the respect of the other competitors.
- The reporter won an *award* for the best news article of the year.
- The student hopes to win a *prize* in the writing contest.

rough *adjective* **coarse, harsh, jagged, ragged, rugged, uneven**
These words share the meaning "not smooth or level."
- The floor is made of *rough* stone.
- Sandpaper has a *coarse* surface.
- The *harsh* wool sweater irritated his skin.
- The glass broke, leaving a *jagged* edge.
- The old man had a *ragged* beard.
- After the harvest the corn fields are filled with *rugged* stubble.
- The shack was built of *uneven* boards.

antonym: smooth

ruddy *adjective* **flushed, glowing, rosy**
These words share the meaning "having a healthy red color."
- He has the *ruddy* face of someone who works outdoors.
- The boy's cheeks were *flushed* with excitement.
- The child had a *glowing* complexion.
- She has *rosy* lips and needs no lipstick.

antonym: pale

rude *adjective* **discourteous, disrespectful, impertinent, impolite**
These words share the meaning "lacking good manners."
- It's *rude* to stare.
- He was scolded for his *discourteous* behavior.
- Never be *disrespectful* to your teachers.
- What an *impertinent* question!
- She was sorry for her *impolite* comment.

antonyms: civil; polite

save *verb* **conserve, preserve**
These words share the meaning "to keep from being damaged or ruined."
- Gentle washing helps *save* old lace.
- It is important to *conserve* the tropical forests.
- Furniture polish *preserves* wood.

scatter *verb* **disperse, dissipate**
These words share the meaning "to separate and drive in different directions."
- The farmer *scattered* the seeds over the plowed ground.
- The soldiers used tear gas to *disperse* the mob.
- Wind quickly *dissipated* the fog.

antonym: gather

scrape *verb* **scour, scrub**
These words share the meaning "to remove or clean by rubbing."
- I *scraped* the paint off the table.
- She *scoured* the kitchen sink until it glistened.
- Go *scrub* your hands.

send *verb* **dispatch, ship, transmit**
These words share the meaning "to cause to go or be carried."
- He *sent* a Christmas present to his friend.
- The store *dispatched* a clerk to deliver the flowers.
- The computer will have to be *shipped* by plane.
- Please *transmit* this message to your supervisor.

antonym: receive

separate *verb* **divide, part, split**
These words share the meaning "to put or come apart."
- She *separated* the tangled strands of yarn.
- The officer *divided* his men into three squads.
- The drapes *parted*, and a face peered out.

- The guests *split* into couples when the dance began.

antonym: combine

serious *adjective* **earnest, grave, solemn**
These words share the meaning "not carefree, joking, or playful."
- The doctor looked *serious* when she gave us her diagnosis.
- The president expressed an *earnest* desire for peace.
- The judge pronounced sentence in a *grave* tone.
- Our teacher isn't often in such a *solemn* mood.

antonym: frivolous

serve *verb* **do, suit**
These words share the meaning "to be used or capable of being used for a particular purpose."
- An orange crate can *serve* as a chair.
- I need a big hammer, so this small one just won't *do*.
- She was interviewed for the job but was told she didn't *suit* the requirements.

set *verb* **lay, place, put, stick**
These words share the meaning "to cause to be in a particular position or place."
- *Set* the flowers on the table.
- My father *laid* his arm on my shoulder.
- The suspect *placed* his hands on his head.
- *Put* the chair next to the desk.
- She *stuck* the letters in a drawer.

shoot *verb* **fire, launch, loose**
These words share the meaning "to come or send forth with great speed or sudden force."
- The arrow *shot* through the air.
- A police officer *fired* two bullets.
- A satellite will be *launched* to study the planet Venus.
- The destroyer *loosed* a torpedo at the submarine.

short *adjective* **brief**
These words share the meaning "not long in time or space."
- She has *short* fingers.
- We had a *brief* chat.

antonym: long

shout *verb* **bawl, cry, whoop, yell**
These words share the meaning "to utter or express with a loud cry or call."
- The frightened child *shouted* for help.
- The coach *bawled* instructions to the players.
- The crowd *cried*, "There she is!"
- Children ran *whooping* across the playground.
- There's no need to *yell*; I can hear you.

antonym: whisper

sickness *noun* **disorder, illness**
These words share the meaning "the condition of being sick."
- Many of the villagers suffered from the same mysterious *sickness*.
- Her father has a rare blood *disorder*.
- *Illness* kept him home from school.

antonym: health

silence *noun* **hush, quiet, still, stillness**
These words share the meaning "absence of sound or noise."
- The teacher asked for *silence*.
- There was a sudden *hush* in the auditorium.
- Nothing should disturb the *quiet* of the library.
- Stars twinkled in the *still* of the night.
- We were struck by the *stillness* of the church.

antonyms: sound; noise

simple *adjective* **easy, effortless, light**
These words share the meaning "not hard to do, make, manage, or understand."
- Put the table together by following these *simple* instructions.
- Solving math problems is *easy* for some students.
- The pianist's playing seemed *effortless*.
- I did a little *light* reading to pass the time.

antonym: difficult

size *noun* **extent, magnitude, measure, proportions**
These words share the meaning "the amount of space occupied by something."
- The house next door is the same *size* as ours.
- The farm is four acres in *extent*.
- Viruses are of such small *magnitude* that they cannot be seen under an ordinary microscope.
- I cannot express the full *measure* of my disappointment at what happened.
- A new skyscraper of gigantic *proportions* has been built in the business district.

slide *verb* **glide, slip, slither**
These words share the meaning "to move smoothly, quietly, and easily."
- The train *slid* into the station.
- We saw an eagle *gliding* through the air.
- He's trying to *slip* in through the back door.
- A rattlesnake *slithered* across the road.

slow *adjective* **deliberate, unhurried**
These words share the meaning "taking or needing a longer time than is expected or usual."

- She is a *slow* but careful worker.
- Our teacher is *deliberate* in speech.
- On Sundays we eat an *unhurried* breakfast.

antonym: fast

smell *verb* **scent, sniff**
These words share the meaning "to use the nose to detect an odor."
- *Smell* the flowers.
- The tiger *scented* its prey.
- The dog *sniffed* the breeze.

snoop *verb* **nose, poke, pry**
These words share the meaning "to look around or try to get information in a nosy or impudent way."
- His sister reads his mail so she can *snoop* into what's going on in his life.
- Reporters were *nosing* around trying to uncover a scandal.
- Fans were *poking* into the star's private concerns.
- My brother is always *prying* into my secrets.

speech *noun* **address, lecture, talk**
These words share the meaning "a formal spoken communication of thoughts, ideas, and facts to an audience."
- The guest of honor made a *speech* of thanks.
- The president's *address* will be broadcast.
- A painter gave a series of *lectures* at the museum.
- The principal will give a *talk* on democracy at this morning's assembly.

spin *verb* **swirl, twirl, whirl**
These words share the meaning "to turn or cause to turn swiftly in a circular path."
- *Spin* a coin on the desk and watch it come to rest.
- The wind blew, and dust *swirled* on the sidewalks.
- The drum majorette *twirled* her baton.
- He *whirled* around to see who had shouted.

spread *verb* **expand, extend, open, unfold**
These words share the meaning "to stretch out, especially to the fullest extent."
- I *spread* the map on the table.
- The wind *expanded* the sail.
- The eagle *extended* its wings.
- *Open* your umbrella at the first sign of rain.
- The daffodil *unfolded* its petals.

antonym: close

stop *verb* **cease, halt, quit**
These words share the meaning "to suspend action, motion, or operation."
- My watch *stopped*.
- I wish the rain would *cease*.
- The sergeant ordered the squad to *halt*.
- The engine *quit* just a few miles from our destination.

antonym: start

strength *noun* **might, power, vigor**
These words share the meaning "the condition or quality of being physically strong."
- She doesn't have the *strength* to move the washing machine.
- I pulled on the rope with all my *might*.
- The wrestler with the greatest *power* won.
- As he got better, he could feel the return of his former *vigor*.

antonym: weakness

surprise *verb* **amaze, astonish, astound**
These words share the meaning "to cause to feel astonishment by being unusual, unexpected, or startling."
- I am *surprised* at how angry you are.
- The sight of human beings walking on the surface of the moon *amazed* the world.
- She doesn't spend much time studying, so getting a good mark *astonished* her.
- The size of the elephant *astounded* the children.

surround *verb* **circle, encircle, ring**
These words share the meaning "to enclose on all or nearly all sides."
- Fields and orchards *surround* the farmhouse.
- The racetrack is *circled* by a high fence.
- A leather belt *encircled* his waist.
- Dark fur *rings* the eyes of the panda.

swamp *noun* **bog, marsh**
These words share the meaning "an area of soft ground that is soaked with water and in which water collects."
- The town sprayed the *swamp* to keep mosquitoes from multiplying.

- In the Irish countryside, peat from *bogs* is often used as fuel for fires.
- When the water level dropped, the pond became little more than a *marsh*.

symbol *noun* **emblem**
These words share the meaning "something that stands for or represents something else."
- The olive branch is a *symbol* of peace.
- The maple leaf is the national *emblem* of Canada.

take *verb* **accept, admit**
These words share the meaning "to allow to join or take part in a particular function, position, or association."
- The club isn't *taking* new members this year.
- Her mother's law firm *accepted* two new partners.
- He hopes to be *admitted* to college.

antonym: refuse

taste *noun* **1 flavor, savor, tang**
These words share the meaning "the quality of a substance that is perceived when it is taken into the mouth."
- Do you like the *taste* of liver?
- Water has no *flavor*.
- The cook described the *savor* of the stew as being neither too spicy nor too bland.
- The dessert is a custard with the *tang* of lemon.

2 appetite, fondness, inclination, weakness
These words share the meaning "a preference or liking for something."
- We get along because we have similar *tastes*.
- They have an *appetite* for gossip.
- A *fondness* for books keeps me from being lonely.
- The boy shows a strong *inclination* toward music.
- She has a *weakness* for pizza.

antonym: distaste

teem *verb* **abound, crawl, swarm**
These words share the meaning "to be full or plentiful."
- Tropical forests *teem* with wildlife.
- The plain *abounds* in grain.
- During the summer the city was *crawling* with tourists.
- The skies *swarmed* with planes.

antonym: lack

temper *noun* **fit, huff, tantrum**
These words share the meaning "an outburst of rage, resentment, or annoyance."
- He was scolded for his display of *temper*.
- The principal will have a *fit* when he sees the broken window.
- We had an argument, and she left in a *huff*.
- Only spoiled children have *tantrums*.

tend *verb* **attend, care for, look after, mind, watch**
These words share the meaning "to supervise someone or something."
- Please *tend* my plants while I'm away.
- Nurses *attend* the patients.
- The librarian knows how to *care for* books.
- Babies can't *look after* themselves.
- The janitor *minds* the boiler.
- She *watched* her little brother while her parents were out.

antonym: neglect

tense *adjective* **nervous, uneasy**
These words share the meaning "feeling, showing, or causing mental strain."
- The athlete was *tense* with excitement just before the race began.
- She's developed a severe *nervous* twitch.
- Her parents had some *uneasy* moments before they were told she was all right.

antonym: relaxed

thorough *adjective* **complete, exhaustive, intensive**
These words share the meaning "covering every possible detail and leaving nothing out."
- The police made a *thorough* search of the house but found no evidence.
- You should have a *complete* dental checkup at least once a year.
- This book is an introduction to American history, not an *exhaustive* survey.
- The class made an *intensive* study of English grammar.

antonym: superficial

throw *verb* **fling, heave, hurl, pitch, toss**
These words share the meaning "to send through the air by hand."
- A fan *threw* a flower to the dancer.
- The baby *flung* her bottle on the floor.
- Don't *heave* your coat on the chair.
- The delivery boy *hurled* the newspaper on the porch.
- I *pitched* the letter in the wastebasket.
- Just *toss* the trash in the incinerator.

tight *adjective* **snug, taut, tense**
These words share the meaning "drawn, stretched, or fitting closely."
- The dress is too *tight*.
- She feels warm in her *snug* new parka.

- The string of the bow must be *taut*.
- *Tense* neck muscles can lead to a headache.

antonym: loose

tiny *adjective* **diminutive, miniature, minute**
These words share the meaning "extremely small."
- The baby has *tiny* hands.
- She is *diminutive* in stature.
- He has a collection of *miniature* cars on his shelf.
- The gnat is a *minute* insect.

antonym: enormous

transportation *noun* **conveyance, transit, transport**
These words share the meaning "the means or process of carrying something from one place to another."
- The *transportation* of fresh fruits and vegetables is a big business.
- Trucks and trains are often used for the *conveyance* of heavy loads.
- Use the subway instead of your car as a means of *transit* in town.
- Supermarket prices have to be high enough to cover the cost of *transport*.

treat *verb* **deal, handle**
These words share the meaning "to act or behave toward someone or something in a particular way."
- Parents should *treat* their children with love.
- The judge *dealt* fairly with everyone in her courtroom.
- The teacher *handles* the pupils' feelings with care.

turn *noun* **shift, spell**
These words share the meaning "a period of work, duty, or play."
- I took a *turn* at the computer.
- Firefighters work in *shifts*.
- Come in and sit for a *spell*.

universal *adjective* **global, worldwide**
These words share the meaning "present or happening everywhere."
- There's no such thing as *universal* happiness.
- The practice could contribute to *global* warming.
- She has a *worldwide* reputation as a scientist.

antonym: local

unlucky *adjective* **luckless, unfortunate**
These words share the meaning "having, bringing, or marked by bad luck."
- He was *unlucky* enough to lose his wallet.
- The *luckless* job applicant left immediately after her interview.
- The *unfortunate* accident took the lives of two passengers.

antonym: lucky

unpleasant *adjective* **bad, disagreeable, displeasing, offensive**
These words share the meaning "not pleasant."
- *Unpleasant* news is never welcome.
- My brother is in a *bad* mood.
- She is a very *disagreeable* person.
- Your behavior is *displeasing* to the teacher.
- Garbage has an *offensive* odor.

antonym: pleasant

urge *verb* **goad, prod, prompt, spur**
These words share the meaning "to stir or drive to action."
- *Urged* by her mother, she studied harder.
- Her impertinence *goaded* her uncle to fury.
- He has to be *prodded* to write to his grandmother.
- A desire to help others *prompted* us to collect food for the homeless.
- Fear of failure *spurs* some to work hard.

victim *noun* **casualty, prey**
These words share the meaning "one who has been harmed by or suffers from an action, condition, or circumstance."
- The plane accident claimed many *victims*.
- Unemployed workers are the *casualties* of unsuccessful businesses.
- Don't fall *prey* to jealousy.

victory *noun* **conquest, triumph, win**
These words share the meaning "success in overcoming an opponent."
- Her *victory* over her handicap is inspiring.
- Vaccines brought about the *conquest* of polio.
- His getting the job is a *triumph* over many obstacles.
- Our football team had enough *wins* to become state champion.

antonym: defeat

vision *noun* **1 eye, eyesight, sight**
These words share the meaning "the power of seeing with the eyes."
- If you have good *vision*, you don't need glasses.
- He has the *eye* of a true painter.

- Use proper lighting to save your *eyesight* when you read.
- Her *sight* is sharp and clear.

2 foresight
These words share the meaning "unusual power to anticipate and plan for the future."
- Political leaders need *vision* to deal with international affairs.
- Mother had the *foresight* to order a supply of candles in case of a power failure.

walk *noun* **promenade, ramble, stroll**
These words share the meaning "the act of going along on foot for exercise, recreation, or pleasure."
- Take a *walk* after breakfast; it'll do you good.
- The beach was a fine place for an afternoon *promenade*.
- During our *ramble* we met our neighbor.
- This is where we take our regular evening *stroll*.

warn *verb* **alert, caution**
These words share the meaning "to let a person know of possible danger or trouble."
- I *warned* the guests about the icy sidewalk.
- The police car's flashing lights first *alerted* us to the danger.
- You don't need to *caution* her about speeding.

welfare *noun* **advantage, benefit, good, interest, well-being**
These words share the meaning "a condition of being or doing well."
- The *welfare* of their children comes first with good parents.
- Reading lots of books is to your *advantage*.
- His mother opened a savings account for his *benefit*.
- The company donated money for the *good* of the community.
- Being honest is in your best *interest*.
- Crime is a threat to the *well-being* of our society.

whole *adjective* **all, complete, entire, total**
These words share the meaning "including every element or part."
- The *whole* class laughed.
- *All* homework must be done by nine o'clock.
- He's trying to get a *complete* set of baseball cards.
- She stayed away an *entire* week.
- What's our *total* bill?

antonym: partial

willing *adjective* **agreeable, game, ready**
These words share the meaning "not opposed to doing, or glad to do, what is requested or required."
- Are you *willing* to help me?
- We're *agreeable* to your suggestion.
- He's *game* to join our group.

antonym: unwilling

worry *verb* **concern, distress, trouble, upset**
These words share the meaning "to feel or cause to feel uneasy or anxious."
- I *worry* about you when you're out late.
- Her parents are *concerned* about her low marks.
- Rumors that war might break out *distressed* the whole country.
- The doctor was *troubled* by my persistent cough.
- We could see that the mysterious telephone call had *upset* her.

yield *noun* **output, production**
These words share the meaning "the total amount of something that is produced."
- They live on the *yield* of their orchards and their dairy.
- The mine's *output* of coal has fallen off.
- Wheat *production* in Kansas is enormous.

Atlas

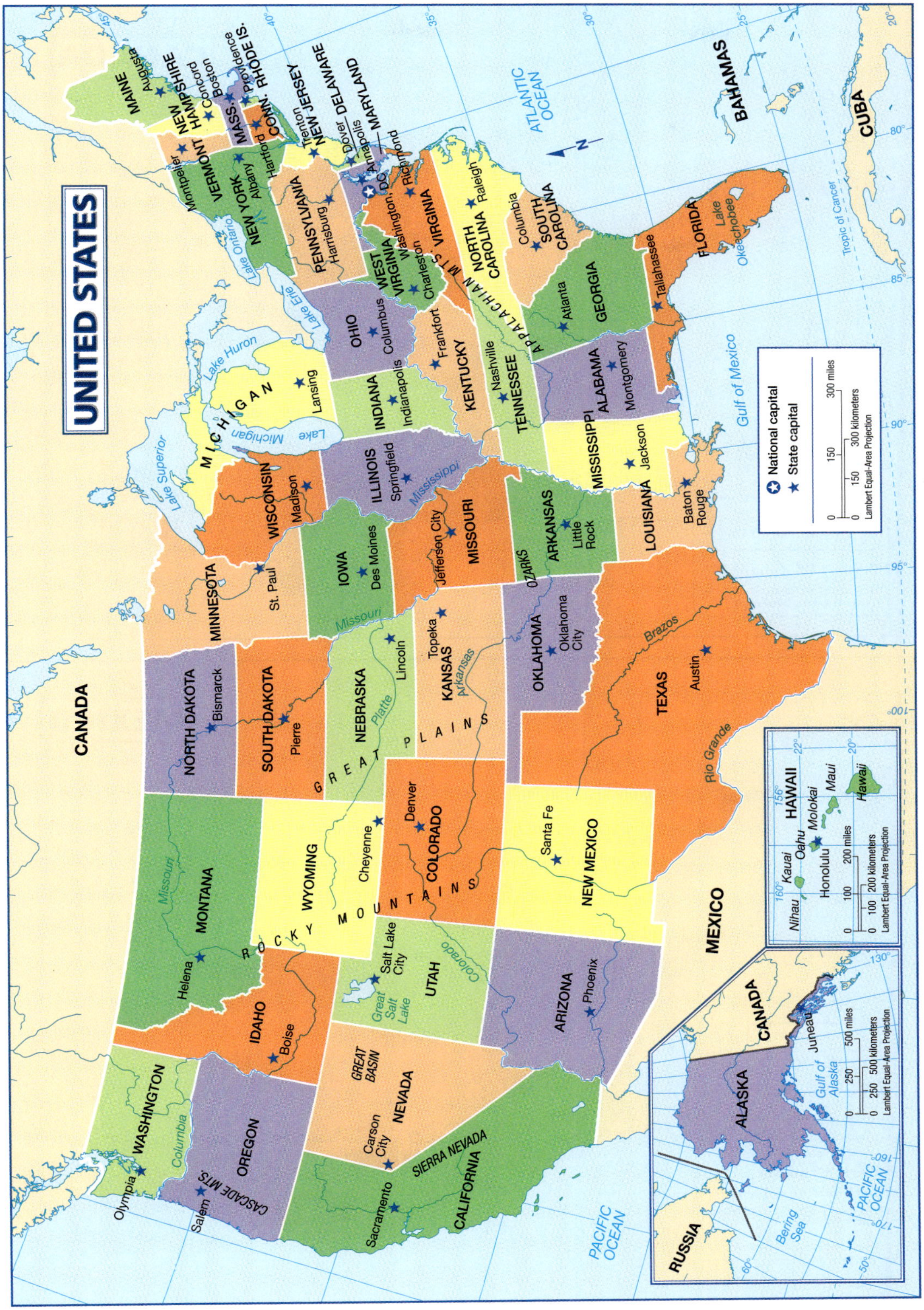
UNITED STATES
CANADA
MEXICO
BAHAMAS
CUBA
RUSSIA
ATLANTIC OCEAN
PACIFIC OCEAN
Gulf of Mexico
Tropic of Cancer
Lake Superior
Lake Michigan
Lake Huron
Lake Erie
Lake Ontario
Lake Okeechobee
Great Salt Lake
GREAT PLAINS
ROCKY MOUNTAINS
APPALACHIAN MTS.
CASCADE MTS.
SIERRA NEVADA
GREAT BASIN
OZARKS
Mississippi
Missouri
Platte
Arkansas
Colorado
Columbia
Brazos
Rio Grande
MAINE
Augusta
NEW HAMPSHIRE
Concord
VERMONT
Montpelier
MASS.
Boston
RHODE IS.
Providence
CONN.
Hartford
NEW YORK
Albany
NEW JERSEY
Trenton
DELAWARE
Dover
MARYLAND
Annapolis
Washington, D.C.
PENNSYLVANIA
Harrisburg
VIRGINIA
Richmond
WEST VIRGINIA
Charleston
NORTH CAROLINA
Raleigh
SOUTH CAROLINA
Columbia
GEORGIA
Atlanta
FLORIDA
Tallahassee
ALABAMA
Montgomery
MISSISSIPPI
Jackson
TENNESSEE
Nashville
KENTUCKY
Frankfort
OHIO
Columbus
MICHIGAN
Lansing
INDIANA
Indianapolis
ILLINOIS
Springfield
WISCONSIN
Madison
MINNESOTA
St. Paul
IOWA
Des Moines
MISSOURI
Jefferson City
ARKANSAS
Little Rock
LOUISIANA
Baton Rouge
TEXAS
Austin
OKLAHOMA
Oklahoma City
KANSAS
Topeka
NEBRASKA
Lincoln
SOUTH DAKOTA
Pierre
NORTH DAKOTA
Bismarck
MONTANA
Helena
WYOMING
Cheyenne
COLORADO
Denver
NEW MEXICO
Santa Fe
ARIZONA
Phoenix
UTAH
Salt Lake City
NEVADA
Carson City
IDAHO
Boise
WASHINGTON
Olympia
OREGON
Salem
CALIFORNIA
Sacramento
National capital
State capital
0 150 300 miles
0 150 300 kilometers
Lambert Equal-Area Projection
HAWAII
Niihau
Kauai
Oahu
Honolulu
Molokai
Maui
Hawaii
0 100 200 miles
0 100 200 kilometers
Lambert Equal-Area Projection
ALASKA
Juneau
Gulf of Alaska
Bering Sea
0 250 500 miles
0 250 500 kilometers
Lambert Equal-Area Projection

Atlas

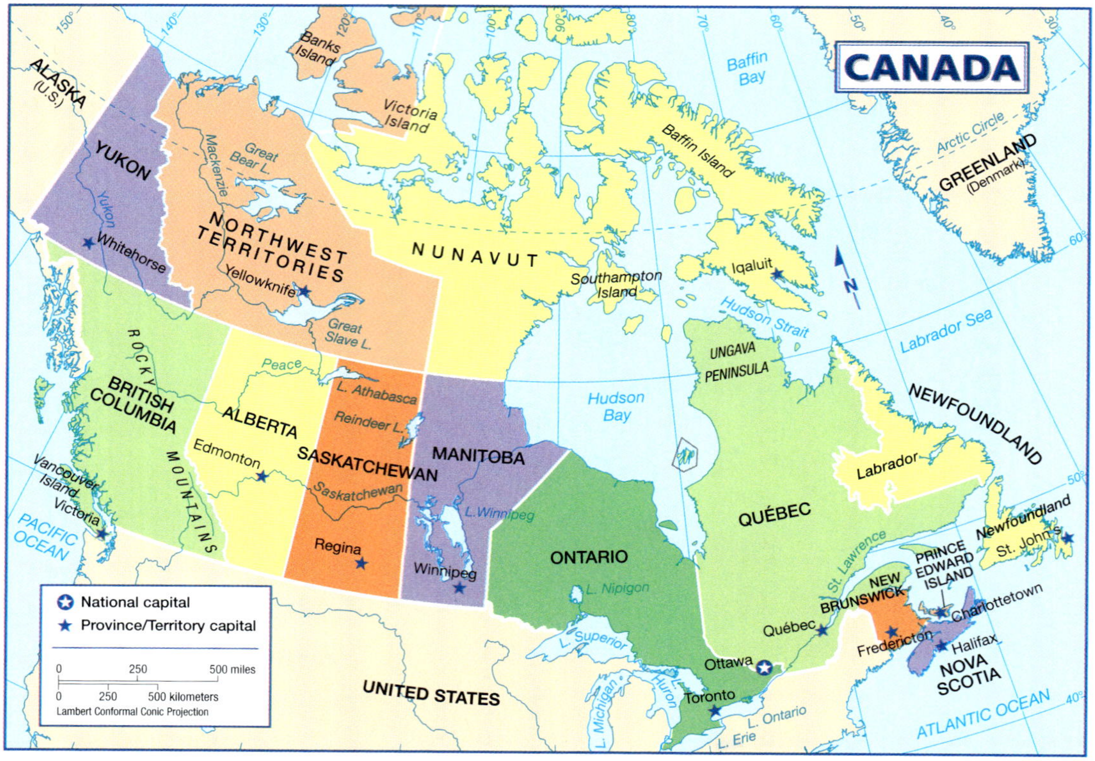
CANADA
ALASKA (U.S.)
YUKON
Yukon
Whitehorse
NORTHWEST TERRITORIES
Mackenzie
Great Bear L.
Yellowknife
Great Slave L.
Banks Island
Victoria Island
NUNAVUT
Baffin Bay
Baffin Island
Iqaluit
Southampton Island
Hudson Strait
Hudson Bay
UNGAVA PENINSULA
Labrador Sea
Arctic Circle
GREENLAND (Denmark)
NEWFOUNDLAND
Labrador
Newfoundland
St. John's
QUÉBEC
St. Lawrence
Québec
BRITISH COLUMBIA
ROCKY MOUNTAINS
Vancouver Island
Victoria
PACIFIC OCEAN
ALBERTA
Peace
Edmonton
SASKATCHEWAN
L. Athabasca
Reindeer L.
Saskatchewan
Regina
MANITOBA
L. Winnipeg
Winnipeg
ONTARIO
L. Nipigon
L. Superior
Ottawa
Toronto
L. Michigan
L. Huron
L. Ontario
L. Erie
NEW BRUNSWICK
Fredericton
PRINCE EDWARD ISLAND
Charlottetown
NOVA SCOTIA
Halifax
ATLANTIC OCEAN
UNITED STATES
N
National capital
Province/Territory capital
0 250 500 miles
0 250 500 kilometers
Lambert Conformal Conic Projection

MEXICO
UNITED STATES
Mexicali
BAJA CALIFORNIA
SONORA
Hermosillo
Gulf of California
BAJA CALIFORNIA SUR
La Paz
CHIHUAHUA
Chihuahua
Rio Grande
SIERRA MADRE OCCIDENTAL
SINALOA
Culiacán
DURANGO
Durango
COAHUILA
Saltillo
SIERRA MADRE ORIENTAL
NUEVO LEÓN
Monterrey
TAMAULIPAS
Ciudad Victoria
GULF OF MEXICO
Tropic of Cancer
ZACATECAS
Zacatecas
SAN LUIS POTOSÍ
San Luis Potosí
NAYARIT
Tepic
Aguascalientes
Guadalajara
JALISCO
Guanajuato
Querétaro
HIDALGO
Pachuca
VERACRUZ
Jalapa
Tlaxcala
Mexico City
Toluca
Morelia
MICHOACÁN
Colima
COLIMA
Cuernavaca
PUEBLA
Puebla
GUERRERO
Chilpancingo
OAXACA
Oaxaca
TABASCO
Villahermosa
CHIAPAS
Tuxtla Gutiérrez
Mérida
YUCATÁN
YUCATÁN PENINSULA
Campeche
CAMPECHE
QUINTANA ROO
Chetumal
BELIZE
GUATEMALA
PACIFIC OCEAN
N
1. AGUASCALIENTES
2. GUANAJUATO
3. QUERÉTARO
4. MÉXICO
5. MORELOS
6. DISTRITO FEDERAL
7. TLAXCALA
National capital
State capital
0 150 300 miles
0 150 300 kilometers
Lambert Azimuthal Equal-Area Projection

CENTRAL AMERICA AND THE CARIBBEAN
Gulf of Mexico
Tropic of Cancer
ATLANTIC OCEAN
PACIFIC OCEAN
Caribbean Sea
UNITED STATES
MEXICO
BAHAMAS
Nassau
CUBA
Havana
Turks & Caicos Islands (U.K.)
Cayman Islands (U.K.)
JAMAICA
Kingston
HAITI
Port-au-Prince
Hispaniola
DOMINICAN REPUBLIC
Santo Domingo
Puerto Rico (U.S.)
Virgin Islands (U.S.)
Virgin Islands (U.K.)
ST. KITTS AND NEVIS
Montserrat (U.K.)
ANTIGUA AND BARBUDA
Guadeloupe (France)
DOMINICA
Martinique (France)
ST. LUCIA
BARBADOS
ST. VINCENT AND THE GRENADINES
GRENADA
TRINIDAD AND TOBAGO
LESSER ANTILLES
GREATER ANTILLES
NETHERLANDS ANTILLES
SOUTH AMERICA
BELIZE
Belmopan
GUATEMALA
Guatemala City
EL SALVADOR
San Salvador
HONDURAS
Tegucigalpa
NICARAGUA
Managua
COSTA RICA
San José
PANAMA
Panama City
Panama Canal
N
National capital
0 125 250 miles
0 125 250 kilometers
Lambert Equal-Area Projection
25°
20°
15°
10°
90°
85°
80°
75°
70°
65°
60°

Atlas

SOUTH AMERICA
CARIBBEAN SEA
ATLANTIC OCEAN
SOUTH PACIFIC OCEAN
SOUTH ATLANTIC OCEAN
Caracas
VENEZUELA
Georgetown
Paramaribo
GUYANA
SURINAME
French Guiana (France)
GUIANA HIGHLANDS
Bogotá
COLOMBIA
Quito
ECUADOR
Equator
AMAZON BASIN
Amazon
Negro
Madeira
Tapajós
Xingu
Tocantins
São Francisco
PERU
Lima
ANDES
Lake Titicaca
La Paz
BOLIVIA
Sucre
BRAZIL
MATO GROSSO PLATEAU
Brasília
BRAZILIAN HIGHLANDS
GRAN CHACO
PARAGUAY
Asunción
Tropic of Capricorn
CHILE
MOUNTAINS
URUGUAY
Montevideo
Santiago
Buenos Aires
ARGENTINA
PAMPAS
PATAGONIA
Strait of Magellan
Tierra del Fuego
Cape Horn
Falkland Islands (U.K.)
South Georgia Island (U.K.)
N
National capital
0 250 500 miles
0 250 500 kilometers
Lambert Equal-Area Projection
20° 10° 0° 10° 20° 30° 40° 50°
100° 90° 80° 70° 60° 50° 40° 30° 20°

Atlas

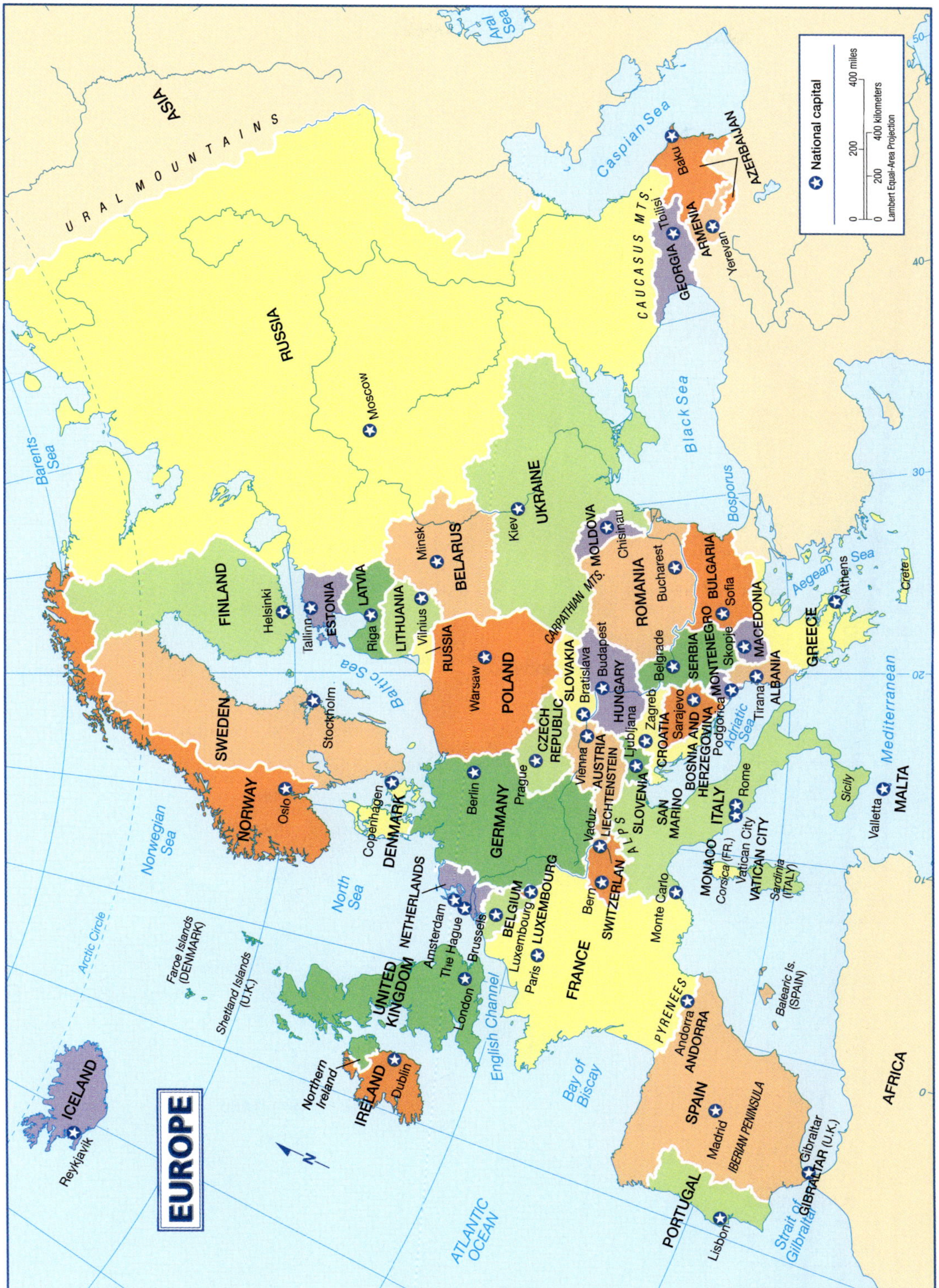
EUROPE
National capital
0 200 400 miles
0 200 400 kilometers
Lambert Equal-Area Projection
ASIA
URAL MOUNTAINS
Aral Sea
Caspian Sea
CAUCASUS MTS.
AZERBAIJAN
Baku
ARMENIA
Yerevan
GEORGIA
Tbilisi
RUSSIA
Moscow
Barents Sea
Black Sea
Bosporus
UKRAINE
Kiev
MOLDOVA
Chisinau
BELARUS
Minsk
CARPATHIAN MTS.
ROMANIA
Bucharest
BULGARIA
Sofia
MACEDONIA
Skopje
Aegean Sea
Athens
Crete
GREECE
ALBANIA
Tirana
MONTENEGRO
Podgorica
SERBIA
Belgrade
BOSNIA AND HERZEGOVINA
Sarajevo
CROATIA
Zagreb
SLOVENIA
Ljubljana
HUNGARY
Budapest
SLOVAKIA
Bratislava
AUSTRIA
Vienna
CZECH REPUBLIC
Prague
POLAND
Warsaw
RUSSIA
LITHUANIA
Vilnius
LATVIA
Riga
ESTONIA
Tallinn
FINLAND
Helsinki
Baltic Sea
SWEDEN
Stockholm
NORWAY
Oslo
Norwegian Sea
DENMARK
Copenhagen
GERMANY
Berlin
NETHERLANDS
Amsterdam
The Hague
BELGIUM
Brussels
LUXEMBOURG
Luxembourg
LIECHTENSTEIN
Vaduz
ALPS
SWITZERLAND
Bern
FRANCE
Paris
MONACO
Monte Carlo
SAN MARINO
ITALY
Rome
VATICAN CITY
Vatican City
Corsica (FR.)
Sardinia (ITALY)
Sicily
Adriatic Sea
Mediterranean Sea
MALTA
Valletta
North Sea
Faroe Islands (DENMARK)
Shetland Islands (U.K.)
Arctic Circle
UNITED KINGDOM
London
English Channel
Northern Ireland
IRELAND
Dublin
ICELAND
Reykjavik
ATLANTIC OCEAN
Bay of Biscay
PYRENEES
ANDORRA
Andorra
Balearic Is. (SPAIN)
SPAIN
Madrid
IBERIAN PENINSULA
PORTUGAL
Lisbon
GIBRALTAR (U.K.)
Gibraltar
Strait of Gibraltar
AFRICA
N

Atlas

AFRICA
EUROPE
ASIA
NORTH ATLANTIC OCEAN
North Sea
Baltic Sea
Black Sea
Caspian Sea
Aral Sea
Strait of Gibraltar
Mediterranean Sea
Suez Canal
Persian Gulf
Red Sea
Gulf of Aden
Nile
Blue Nile
White Nile
Niger
Congo
Zambezi
Orange
L. Chad
L. Turkana
L. Victoria
L. Tanganyika
L. Nyasa
Tropic of Cancer
Equator
Tropic of Capricorn
INDIAN OCEAN
SOUTH ATLANTIC OCEAN
ATLAS MTS.
S A H A R A
TIBESTI MTS.
KALAHARI DESERT
MOROCCO
Rabat
ALGERIA
Algiers
TUNISIA
Tunis
LIBYA
Tripoli
EGYPT
Cairo
WESTERN SAHARA
MAURITANIA
Nouakchott
MALI
Bamako
NIGER
Niamey
CHAD
N'Djamena
SUDAN
Khartoum
ERITREA
Asmara
DJIBOUTI
Djibouti
ETHIOPIA
Addis Ababa
SOMALIA
Mogadishu
SENEGAL
Dakar
GAMBIA
Banjul
GUINEA-BISSAU
Bissau
GUINEA
Conakry
SIERRA LEONE
Freetown
LIBERIA
Monrovia
IVORY COAST
Yamoussoukro
BURKINA FASO
Ouagadougou
GHANA
Accra
TOGO
Lomé
BENIN
Porto Novo
NIGERIA
Abuja
CAMEROON
Yaoundé
CENTRAL AFRICAN REPUBLIC
Bangui
EQUATORIAL GUINEA
Malabo
SÃO TOMÉ AND PRÍNCIPE
São Tomé
GABON
Libreville
REP. CONGO
Brazzaville
DEMOCRATIC REPUBLIC OF THE CONGO
Kinshasa
CABINDA (ANGOLA)
UGANDA
Kampala
KENYA
Nairobi
RWANDA
Kigali
BURUNDI
Bujumbura
TANZANIA
Dodoma
SEYCHELLES
Victoria
ANGOLA
Luanda
ZAMBIA
Lusaka
MALAWI
Lilongwe
COMOROS
Moroni
MOZAMBIQUE
Maputo
ZIMBABWE
Harare
MADAGASCAR
Antananarivo
MAURITIUS
Port Louis
Réunion (Fr.)
NAMIBIA
Windhoek
BOTSWANA
Gaborone
SOUTH AFRICA
Pretoria
Cape Town
SWAZILAND
Mbabane
LESOTHO
Maseru
CAPE VERDE
Praia
N
National capital
0 350 700 miles
0 350 700 kilometers
Lambert Equal-Area Projection

ASIA
NORTH PACIFIC OCEAN
PACIFIC OCEAN
Tropic of Cancer
Equator
ARCTIC OCEAN
Arctic Circle
Bering Sea
KAMCHATKA PENINSULA
Sea of Okhotsk
Sakhalin
East Siberian Sea
Laptev Sea
Kara Sea
Barents Sea
Norwegian Sea
North Sea
Baltic Sea
RUSSIA
S I B E R I A
Lake Baikal
URAL MOUNTAINS
Moscow
EUROPE
AFRICA
Mediterranean Sea
Black Sea
Caspian Sea
Aral Sea
Red Sea
Persian Gulf
Arabian Sea
Bay of Bengal
INDIAN OCEAN
South China Sea
East China Sea
Sea of Japan
Java Sea
Banda Sea
Arafura Sea
Timor Sea
JAPAN
Tokyo
N. KOREA
Pyongyang
S. KOREA
Seoul
TAIWAN
Taipei
MACAO
PHILIPPINES
Manila
MONGOLIA
Ulan Bator
GOBI DESERT
CHINA
Beijing
Huang
Chang
TIEN SHAN
KUNLUN SHAN
H I M A L A Y A S
KAZAKHSTAN
Astana
KYRGYZSTAN
Bishkek
TAJIKISTAN
Dushanbe
UZBEKISTAN
Tashkent
TURKMENISTAN
Ashgabat
AFGHANISTAN
Kabul
PAKISTAN
Islamabad
INDIA
New Delhi
DECCAN PLATEAU
NEPAL
Katmandu
BHUTAN
Thimphu
BANGLADESH
Dhaka
SRI LANKA
Colombo
MALDIVES
Malé
MYANMAR (BURMA)
Yangon
THAILAND
Bangkok
LAOS
Vientiane
VIETNAM
Hanoi
CAMBODIA
Phnom Penh
MALAYSIA
Kuala Lumpur
SINGAPORE
Singapore
BRUNEI
Bandar Seri Begawan
INDONESIA
Jakarta
Sumatra
Java
Borneo
Sulawesi
New Guinea
EAST TIMOR
AUSTRALIA
IRAN
Tehran
IRAQ
Baghdad
TURKEY
Ankara
SYRIA
Damascus
CYPRUS
Nicosia
LEBANON
Beirut
ISRAEL
Jerusalem
JORDAN
Amman
KUWAIT
Kuwait
BAHRAIN
Manama
QATAR
Doha
U.A.E.
Abu Dhabi
OMAN
Muscat
SAUDI ARABIA
Riyadh
ARABIAN PENINSULA
YEMEN
Sana
National capital
0 500 1000 miles
0 500 1000 kilometers
Lambert Conformal Conic Projection

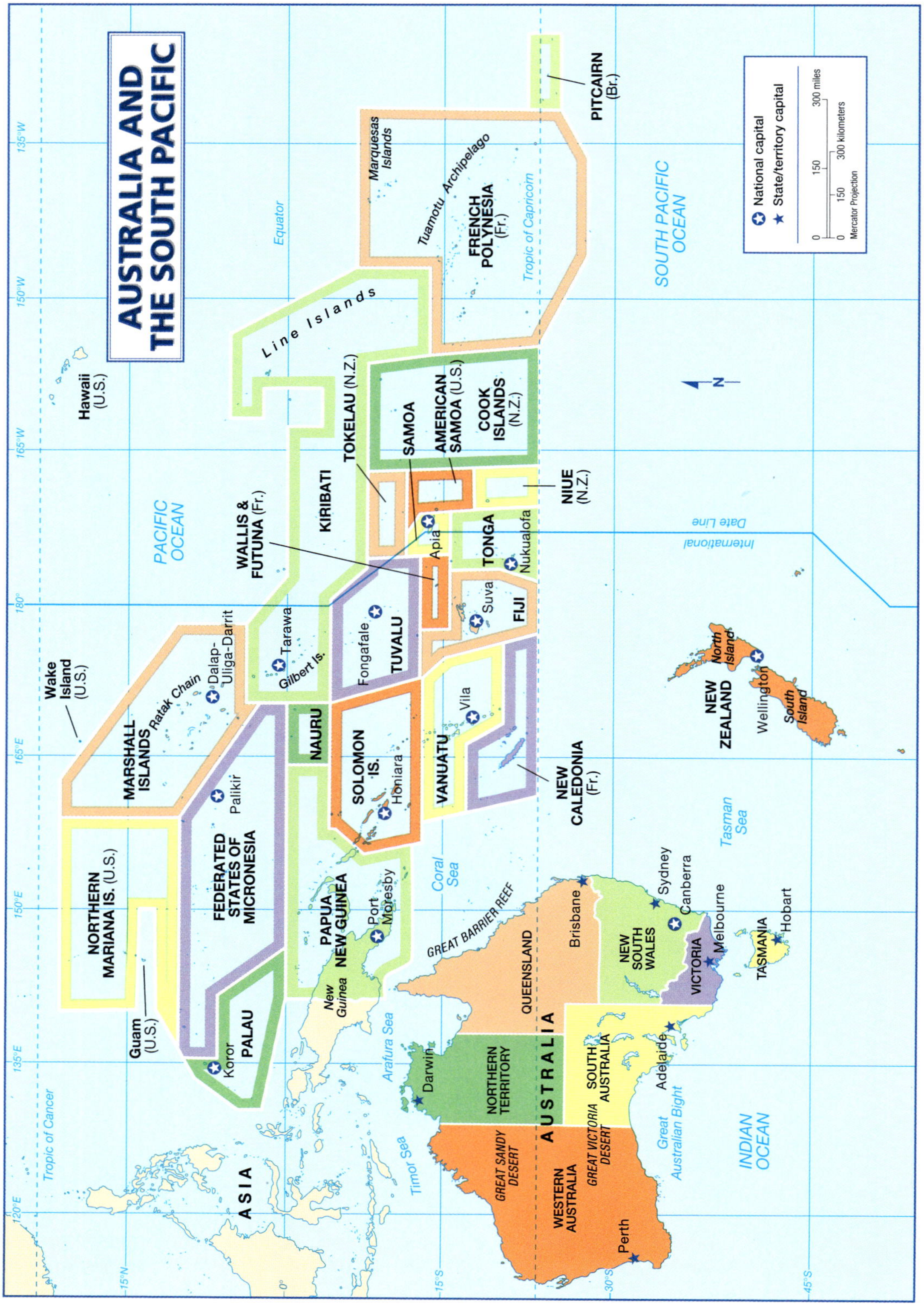
AUSTRALIA AND THE SOUTH PACIFIC
National capital
State/territory capital
0 150 300 miles
0 150 300 kilometers
Mercator Projection
PACIFIC OCEAN
SOUTH PACIFIC OCEAN
INDIAN OCEAN
Tasman Sea
Coral Sea
Arafura Sea
Timor Sea
Great Australian Bight
GREAT BARRIER REEF
Equator
Tropic of Cancer
Tropic of Capricorn
International Date Line
ASIA
AUSTRALIA
WESTERN AUSTRALIA
NORTHERN TERRITORY
SOUTH AUSTRALIA
QUEENSLAND
NEW SOUTH WALES
VICTORIA
TASMANIA
GREAT SANDY DESERT
GREAT VICTORIA DESERT
Perth
Darwin
Adelaide
Brisbane
Sydney
Canberra
Melbourne
Hobart
NEW ZEALAND
North Island
South Island
Wellington
PAPUA NEW GUINEA
New Guinea
Port Moresby
PALAU
Koror
Guam (U.S.)
NORTHERN MARIANA IS. (U.S.)
FEDERATED STATES OF MICRONESIA
Palikir
MARSHALL ISLANDS
Ratak Chain
Dalap-Uliga-Darrit
Wake Island (U.S.)
Hawaii (U.S.)
NAURU
SOLOMON IS.
Honiara
VANUATU
Vila
NEW CALEDONIA (Fr.)
TUVALU
Fongafale
KIRIBATI
Gilbert Is.
Tarawa
Line Islands
WALLIS & FUTUNA (Fr.)
FIJI
Suva
TONGA
Nukualofa
TOKELAU (N.Z.)
SAMOA
Apia
AMERICAN SAMOA (U.S.)
COOK ISLANDS (N.Z.)
NIUE (N.Z.)
FRENCH POLYNESIA (Fr.)
Marquesas Islands
Tuamotu Archipelago
PITCAIRN (Br.)
N

Weights and Measures

Length

Metric

1 centimeter = 10 millimeters
1 meter = 100 centimeters
1 meter = 1,000 millimeters
1 kilometer = 1,000 meters

U.S. System

1 foot = 12 inches
1 yard = 36 inches or 3 feet
1 mile = 5,280 feet or 1,760 yards

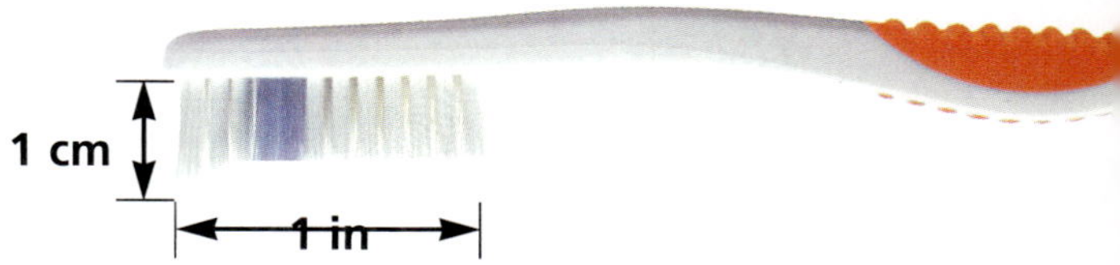

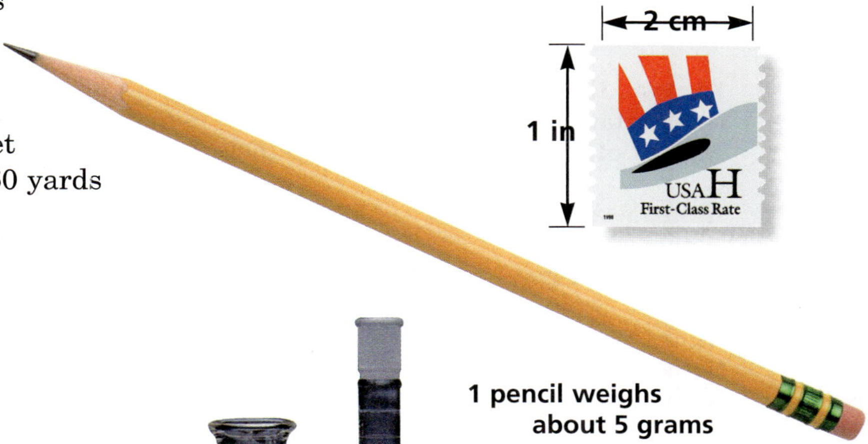

1 pencil weighs about 5 grams

Mass or Weight

Metric

1 gram = 1,000 milligrams
1 kilogram = 1,000 grams

U.S. System

1 pound = 16 ounces
1 ton = 2,000 pounds

Volume

Metric

1 liter = 1,000 milliliters
1 liter = 1,000 cubic centimeters

U.S. System

1 pint = 2 cups
1 quart = 2 pints
1 gallon = 4 quarts
1 gallon = 231 cubic inches

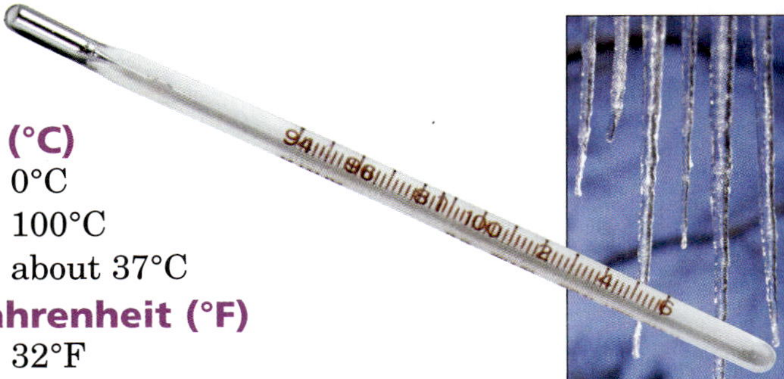

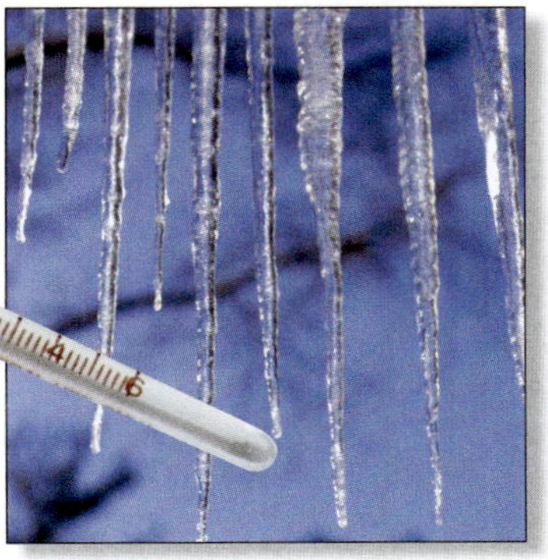

Temperature

Metric—Degrees Celsius (°C)

Freezing point of water = 0°C
Boiling point of water = 100°C
Normal body temperature = about 37°C

U.S. System—Degrees Fahrenheit (°F)

Freezing point of water = 32°F
Boiling point of water = 212°F
Normal body temperature = about 98.6°F

Presidents of the U.S.

1 **George Washington** **1732-1799**
Native state: Virginia
Term of office: 1789 to 1797

2 **John Adams** **1735-1826**
Native state: Massachusetts
Term of office: 1797 to 1801

3 **Thomas Jefferson** **1743-1826**
Native state: Virginia
Term of office: 1801 to 1809

4 **James Madison** **1751-1836**
Native state: Virginia
Term of office: 1809 to 1817

5 **James Monroe** **1758-1831**
Native state: Virginia
Term of office: 1817 to 1825

6 **John Quincy Adams** **1767-1848**
Native state: Massachusetts
Term of office: 1825 to 1829

7 **Andrew Jackson** **1767-1845**
Native state: South Carolina
Term of office: 1829 to 1837

8 **Martin Van Buren** **1782-1862**
Native state: New York
Term of office: 1837 to 1841

9 **William Henry Harrison** **1773-1841**
Native state: Virginia
Term of office: 1841

10 **John Tyler** **1790-1862**
Native state: Virginia
Term of office: 1841 to 1845

11 **James K. Polk** **1795-1849**
Native state: North Carolina
Term of office: 1845 to 1849

12 **Zachary Taylor** **1784-1850**
Native state: Virginia
Term of office: 1849 to 1850

13 **Millard Fillmore** **1800-1874**
Native state: New York
Term of office: 1850 to 1853

14 **Franklin Pierce** **1804-1869**
Native state: New Hampshire
Term of office: 1853 to 1857

15 **James Buchanan** **1791-1868**
Native state: Pennsylvania
Term of office: 1857 to 1861

16 **Abraham Lincoln** **1809-1865**
Native state: Kentucky
Term of office: 1861 to 1865

17 **Andrew Johnson** **1808-1875**
Native state: North Carolina
Term of office: 1865 to 1869

18 **Ulysses S. Grant** **1822-1885**
Native state: Ohio
Term of office: 1869 to 1877

19 **Rutherford B. Hayes** **1822-1893**
Native state: Ohio
Term of office: 1877 to 1881

20 **James A. Garfield** **1831-1881**
Native state: Ohio
Term of office: 1881

21 **Chester Alan Arthur** **1829-1886**
Native state: Vermont
Term of office: 1881 to 1885

22 **Grover Cleveland** **1837-1908**
Native state: New Jersey
Term of office: 1885 to 1889

23 **Benjamin Harrison** **1833-1901**
Native state: Ohio
Term of office: 1889 to 1893

24 **Grover Cleveland** **1837-1908**
Native state: New Jersey
Term of office: 1893 to 1897

Presidents of the U.S.

25	**William McKinley**	**1843-1901**
	Native state:	Ohio
	Term of office:	1897 to 1901
26	**Theodore Roosevelt**	**1858-1919**
	Native state:	New York
	Term office:	1901 to 1909
27	**William Howard Taft**	**1857-1930**
	Native state:	Ohio
	Term of office:	1909 to 1913
28	**Woodrow Wilson**	**1856-1924**
	Native state:	Virginia
	Term of office:	1913 to 1921
29	**Warren G. Harding**	**1865-1923**
	Native state:	Ohio
	Term of office:	1921 to 1923
30	**Calvin Coolidge**	**1872-1933**
	Native state:	Vermont
	Term of office:	1923 to 1929
31	**Herbert Hoover**	**1874-1964**
	Native state:	Iowa
	Term of office:	1929 to 1933
32	**Franklin D. Roosevelt**	**1882-1945**
	Native state:	New York
	Term of office:	1933 to 1945
33	**Harry S Truman**	**1884-1972**
	Native state:	Missouri
	Term of office:	1945 to 1953
34	**Dwight D. Eisenhower**	**1890-1969**
	Native state:	Texas
	Term of office:	1953 to 1961
35	**John F. Kennedy**	**1917-1963**
	Native state:	Massachusetts
	Term of office:	1961 to 1963
36	**Lyndon B. Johnson**	**1908-1973**
	Native state:	Texas
	Term of office:	1963 to 1969
37	**Richard M. Nixon**	**1913-1994**
	Native state:	California
	Term of office:	1969 to 1974
38	**Gerald R. Ford**	**1913-2006**
	Native state:	Nebraska
	Term of office:	1974 to 1977
39	**Jimmy Carter**	**1924-**
	Native state:	Georgia
	Term of office:	1977 to 1981
40	**Ronald Reagan**	**1911-2004**
	Native state:	Illinois
	Term of office:	1981 to 1989
41	**George Bush**	**1924-**
	Native state:	Massachusetts
	Term of office:	1989 to 1993
42	**William J. Clinton**	**1946-**
	Native state:	Arkansas
	Term of office:	1993 to 2001
43	**George W. Bush**	**1946-**
	Native state:	Connecticut
	Term of office:	2001 to 2009
44	**Barack Obama**	**1961-**
	Native state:	Hawaii
	Term of office:	2009 to —

To run for the office of President of the United States, a person must be at least 35 years old. He or she must be a natural-born citizen and must have lived in the United States for 14 years. The President is elected for a term of 4 years. According to the 22nd Amendment to the Constitution, passed in 1951, no person can be elected to the office of the President more than twice.

Album of the States

Alabama

Alabama (AL)

Capital Montgomery
Statehood 1819, the 22nd state
Area 50,744 square miles
Population 4,447,000

State flag

Camellia

Yellowhammer (Yellow-shafted flicker)

Alaska

Alaska (AK)

Capital Juneau
Statehood 1959, the 49th state
Area 571,951 square miles
Population 627,000

State flag

Forget-me-not

Willow ptarmigan

Arizona

Arizona (AZ)

Capital Phoenix
Statehood 1912, the 48th state
Area 113,635 square miles
Population 5,131,000

State flag

Saguaro blossom

Cactus wren

Arkansas

Arkansas (AR)

Capital Little Rock
Statehood 1836, the 25th state
Area 52,068 square miles
Population 2,673,000

State flag

Apple blossom

Mockingbird

California

California (CA)

Capital Sacramento
Statehood 1850, the 31st state
Area 155,959 square miles
Population 33,872,000

State flag

California poppy

California valley quail

Colorado

Colorado (CO)

Capital	Denver
Statehood	1876, the 38th state
Area	103,718 square miles
Population	4,301,000

State flag

Rocky Mountain columbine

Lark bunting

Connecticut

Connecticut (CT)

Capital	Hartford
Statehood	1788, the 5th state
Area	4,845 square miles
Population	3,406,000

State flag

Mountain laurel

American robin

Delaware

Delaware (DE)

Capital	Dover
Statehood	1787, the 1st state
Area	1,954 square miles
Population	784,000

State flag

Peach blossom

Blue hen chicken

Florida

Florida (FL)

Capital	Tallahassee
Statehood	1845, the 27th state
Area	53,927 square miles
Population	15,982,000

State flag

Orange blossom

Mockingbird

Georgia

Georgia (GA)

Capital	Atlanta
Statehood	1788, the 4th state
Area	57,906 square miles
Population	8,186,000

State flag

Cherokee rose

Brown thrasher

Album of the States

Hawaii

Hawaii (HI)

Capital	Honolulu
Statehood	1959, the 50th state
Area	6,423 square miles
Population	1,212,000

State flag

Yellow hibiscus

Nene (Hawaiian goose)

Idaho

Idaho (ID)

Capital	Boise
Statehood	1890, the 43rd state
Area	82,747 square miles
Population	1,294,000

State flag

Syringa mock orange

Mountain bluebird

Illinois

Illinois (IL)

Capital	Springfield
Statehood	1818, the 21st state
Area	55,584 square miles
Population	12,419,000

State flag

Violet

Cardinal

Indiana

Indiana (IN)

Capital	Indianapolis
Statehood	1816, the 19th state
Area	35,867 square miles
Population	6,080,000

State flag

Peony

Cardinal

Iowa

Iowa (IA)

Capital	Des Moines
Statehood	1846, the 29th state
Area	55,869 square miles
Population	2,926,000

State flag

Wild rose

Eastern goldfinch

with state flags, birds, and flowers

Kansas

Kansas (KS)

Capital Topeka
Statehood 1861, the 34th state
Area 81,815 square miles
Population 2,688,000

State flag

Sunflower

Western meadowlark

Kentucky

Kentucky (KY)

Capital Frankfort
Statehood 1792, the 15th state
Area 39,728 square miles
Population 4,042,000

State flag

Goldenrod

Kentucky cardinal

Louisiana

Louisiana (LA)

Capital Baton Rouge
Statehood 1812, the 18th state
Area 43,562 square miles
Population 4,469,000

State flag

Magnolia

Brown pelican

Maine

Maine (ME)

Capital Augusta
Statehood 1820, the 23rd state
Area 30,862 square miles
Population 1,275,000

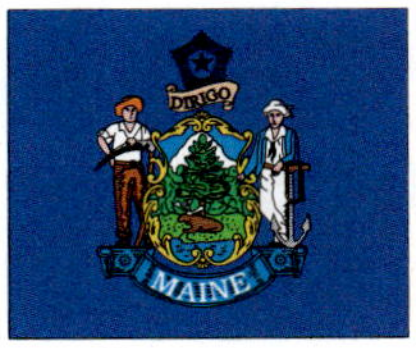

State flag

White pine cone and tassel

Chickadee

Maryland

Maryland (MD)

Capital Annapolis
Statehood 1788, the 7th state
Area 9,774 square miles
Population 5,296,000

State flag

Black-eyed Susan

Baltimore oriole

Album of the States

Massachusetts

Massachusetts (MA)

Capital	Boston
Statehood	1788, the 6th state
Area	7,840 square miles
Population	6,349,000

State flag

Mayflower

Black-capped chickadee

Michigan

Michigan (MI)

Capital	Lansing
Statehood	1837, the 26th state
Area	56,804 square miles
Population	9,938,000

State flag

Apple blossom

Robin

Minnesota

Minnesota (MN)

Capital	St. Paul
Statehood	1858, the 32nd state
Area	79,610 square miles
Population	4,919,000

State flag

Showy lady-slipper

Common loon

Mississippi

Mississippi (MS)

Capital	Jackson
Statehood	1817, the 20th state
Area	46,907 square miles
Population	2,845,000

State flag

Magnolia

Mockingbird

Missouri

Missouri (MO)

Capital	Jefferson City
Statehood	1821, the 24th state
Area	68,886 square miles
Population	5,595,000

State flag

Hawthorn

Bluebird

with state flags, birds, and flowers

Montana

Montana (MT)

Capital Helena
Statehood 1889, the 41st state
Area 145,552 square miles
Population 902,000

State flag

Bitterroot

Western meadowlark

Nebraska

Nebraska (NE)

Capital Lincoln
Statehood 1867, the 37th state
Area 76,872 square miles
Population 1,711,000

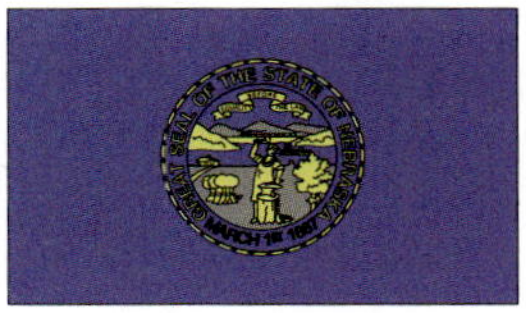

State flag

Goldenrod

Western meadowlark

Nevada

Nevada (NV)

Capital Carson City
Statehood 1864, the 36th state
Area 109,826 square miles
Population 1,998,000

State flag

Sagebrush

Mountain bluebird

New Hampshire

New Hampshire (NH)

Capital Concord
Statehood 1788, the 9th state
Area 8,968 square miles
Population 1,236,000

State flag

Purple lilac

Purple finch

New Jersey

New Jersey (NJ)

Capital Trenton
Statehood 1787, the 3rd state
Area 7,417 square miles
Population 8,414,000

State flag

Violet

Eastern goldfinch

Album of the States

New Mexico

New Mexico (NM)

Capital	Santa Fe
Statehood	1912, the 47th state
Area	121,356 square miles
Population	1,819,000

State flag

Yucca flower

Roadrunner

New York

New York (NY)

Capital	Albany
Statehood	1788, the 11th state
Area	47,214 square miles
Population	18,976,000

State flag

Rose

Bluebird

North Carolina

North Carolina (NC)

Capital	Raleigh
Statehood	1789, the 12th state
Area	48,711 square miles
Population	8,049,000

State flag

Dogwood

Cardinal

North Dakota

North Dakota (ND)

Capital	Bismarck
Statehood	1889, the 39th state
Area	68,976 square miles
Population	642,000

State flag

Wild prairie rose

Western meadowlark

Ohio

Ohio (OH)

Capital	Columbus
Statehood	1803, the 17th state
Area	40,948 square miles
Population	11,353,000

State flag

Scarlet carnation

Cardinal

Oklahoma

Oklahoma (OK)

Capital	Oklahoma City
Statehood	1907, the 46th state
Area	68,667 square miles
Population	3,451,000

State flag

Mistletoe

Scissor-tailed flycatcher

Oregon

Oregon (OR)

Capital	Salem
Statehood	1859, the 33rd state
Area	95,997 square miles
Population	3,421,000

State flag

Oregon grape

Western meadowlark

Pennsylvania

Pennsylvania (PA)

Capital	Harrisburg
Statehood	1787, the 2nd state
Area	44,817 square miles
Population	12,281,000

State flag

Mountain laurel

Ruffed grouse

Rhode Island

Rhode Island (RI)

Capital	Providence
Statehood	1790, the 13th state
Area	1,045 square miles
Population	1,048,000

State flag

Violet

Rhode Island Red

South Carolina

South Carolina (SC)

Capital	Columbia
Statehood	1788, the 8th state
Area	30,109 square miles
Population	4,012,000

State flag

Yellow jessamine

Carolina wren

Album of the States

South Dakota

South Dakota (SD)

Capital Pierre

Statehood 1889, the 40th state

Area 75,885 square miles

Population 755,000

State flag

Pasque

Chinese ring-necked pheasant

Tennessee

Tennessee (TN)

Capital Nashville

Statehood 1796, the 16th state

Area 41,217 square miles

Population 5,689,000

State flag

Iris

Mockingbird

Texas

Texas (TX)

Capital Austin

Statehood 1845, the 28th state

Area 261,797 square miles

Population 20,852,000

State flag

Bluebonnet

Mockingbird

Utah

Utah (UT)

Capital Salt Lake City

Statehood 1896, the 45th state

Area 82,144 square miles

Population 2,233,000

State flag

Sego lily

Seagull

Vermont

Vermont (VT)

Capital Montpelier

Statehood 1791, the 14th state

Area 9,250 square miles

Population 609,000

State flag

Red clover

Hermit thrush

Virginia

Virginia (VA)

Capital	Richmond
Statehood	1788, the 10th state
Area	39,594 square miles
Population	7,079,000

State flag

Dogwood

Cardinal

Washington

Washington (WA)

Capital	Olympia
Statehood	1889, the 42nd state
Area	66,544 square miles
Population	5,894,000

State flag

Coast rhododendron

Willow goldfinch

West Virginia

West Virginia (WV)

Capital	Charleston
Statehood	1863, the 35th state
Area	24,078 square miles
Population	1,808,000

State flag

Rhododendron

Cardinal

Wisconsin

Wisconsin (WI)

Capital	Madison
Statehood	1848, the 30th state
Area	54,310 square miles
Population	5,364,000

State flag

Wood violet

Robin

Wyoming

Wyoming (WY)

Capital	Cheyenne
Statehood	1890, the 44th state
Area	97,100 square miles
Population	494,000

State flag

Indian paintbrush

Meadowlark

Washington, D.C.

Washington, D.C.

Area 61 square miles

Population 572,000

Washington, D.C., *is the capital city of the United States. It covers the entire area of the District of Columbia.*

Capital flag

White House

Capitol

Credits

Credits, pp. 884-928:

Photos, pp. 884-906: EyeWire Images, © EyeWire, Inc.

Atlas Maps, pp. 907-914: Gary Antonetti/Ortelius Design

Photos, p. 915: **stamp, toothbrush**—Doug Wolfe/Flashback Photography; **icicle**—Jim Baron/The Image Finders; **beakers, pencil, thermometer**—© 1999 PhotoDisc, Inc.

Album of the States, pp. 918-928:

State Birds, State Flowers: Kathy Hendrickson; Rebecca Merrilees; Herman Vestal

State Flags: EyeWire Images, © EyeWire, Inc.

Capitol, p. 928: (upper right) © 1999 PhotoDisc, Inc.; **White House,** p. 928: (lower left) © 2005 PhotoSpin Inc.

Word Finder Table

Consonant Sounds

If the sound is like the sound described below,	*try spelling it with the letters in this column,*	*as in the sample words in this column.*
b as in *bed*	b, bb	ru**b**, ru**bb**er
ch as in *chin*	ch, tch, t, ti, te, cz	**ch**air, ca**tch**, na**t**ure, ques**ti**on, righ**te**ous, **Cz**ech
d as in *dog*	d, dd, ed	no**d**, ri**dd**le, endanger**ed**
f as in *fall*	f, ff, gh, ph, lf	**f**ix, di**ff**erent, lau**gh**, **ph**one, ca**lf**
g as in *get*	g, gg, gh, gu, gue	**g**ive, e**gg**, **gh**ost, **gu**ard, catalo**gue**
h as in *help*	h, wh	**h**er, **wh**o
j as in *jump*	j, g, gg, d, di, dg, dj	**j**am, **g**em, exa**gg**erate, gra**d**uate, sol**di**er, ju**dg**ment, a**dj**ective
k as in *kiss*	k, lk, c, cc, ch, kh, ck, cqu, cu, qu, q, que	**k**ite, wa**lk**, **c**an, a**cc**ount, an**ch**or, **kh**aki, lu**ck**, la**cqu**er, bis**cu**it, li**qu**or, li**q**uid, uni**que**
l as in *leg*	l, ll, sl, ln	**l**eave, ca**ll**, i**sl**and, ki**ln**
m as in *meat*	m, mm, mb, mn, lm, gm	dru**m**, ha**mm**er, cli**mb**, hy**mn**, ca**lm**, diaphra**gm**
n as in *nose*	n, nn, gn, kn, pn	**n**ear, di**nn**er, **gn**ome, **kn**eel, **pn**eumonia
ng as in *ring*	ng, nk, ngue	lo**ng**, thi**nk**, to**ngue**
p as in *put*	p, pp, ph	ho**p**, di**pp**er, she**ph**erd
r as in *red*	r, rr, rh, wr	**r**iver, be**rr**y, **rh**yme, **wr**ong
s as in *see*	s, ss, sc, c, ps	**s**it, mi**ss**, **sc**ience, **c**ent, **ps**ychology
s as in *pleasure*	z, ge, s, si	a**z**ure, gara**ge**, lei**s**ure, confu**si**on
sh as in *she*	sh, s, ss, sch, sci, si, ssi, ce, ch, ci, ti	**sh**are, **s**ure, i**ss**ue, **sch**wa, con**sci**ence, man**si**on, mi**ssi**on, o**ce**an, ma**ch**ine, spe**ci**al, na**ti**on
t as in *top*	t, th, tt, ght, ed	**t**eam, **Th**omas, be**tt**er, bou**ght**, hook**ed**
v as in *vat*	v, lv, f	lo**v**e, sa**lv**e, o**f**
w as in *wish*	w, wh, o, u	**w**ait, **wh**ile, ch**o**ir, q**u**iet
y as in *yard*	y, i, j	**y**ellow, on**i**on, hallelu**j**ah
z as in *zebra*	z, zz, s, ss, x, cz	**z**one, bu**zz**ard, bu**s**y, sci**ss**ors, **x**ylophone, **cz**ar